A SHAKESPEAREAN GENEALOGY

This chart reflects Shakespeare's history plays and is thus not historically accurate. Many descendants of Henry II and Edward III are omitted. On occasion, Shakespeare combined or simply invented historical figures. These deviations from fact are explained in the notes.

In the chart, the names of Kings and Queens are printed in capitals, and the dates of their reigns are printed in bold. The names of characters appearing in the plays are underlined.

Henry
d. 1183

Edward, Prince of
Wales 1330–1376

RICHARD II
1367–1400
(**1377–99**)

William of
Hatfield

Lionel, Duke of
Clarence 1338–1368

Philippa
m. Edmund
Mortimer, Earl
of March

RICHARD I
1157–1199
(**1189–99**)

Philip Faulconbridge*
(Richard Plantagenet)

John of Gaunt,
Duke of Lancaster
1340–1399
m. Blanche of
Lancaster
m. Constance of
Castile
m. Katherine
Swynford

HENRY IV
1367–1413
(**1399–1413**)

Thomas Beaufort,
Duke of Exeter
1377–1427

Henry Beaufort,
Bishop of Winchester
1375–1447

John Beaufort,
Earl of Somerset
1372–1409

Joan Beaufort
m. Ralph Neville,
Earl of
Westmoreland

HENRY II
1133–1189
(**1154–89**)
m. Eleanor
of Aquitaine
d. 1204

Geoffrey, d. 1186
m. Constance
of Brittany

Arthur
1187–1203

JOHN 1167–1216
(**1199–1216**)

HENRY III
1207–1272
(**1216–72**)

EDWARD I
1239–1307
(**1272–1307**)

EDWARD II
1284–1327
(**1307–27**)

Edmund of Langley,
Duke of York
1341–1402

Edward, Duke of
Aumerle d. 1415

Richard, Earl
of Cambridge
d. 1415 m. Anne
Mortimer (above)

EDWARD III
1312–1377
(**1327–77**)
m. Philippa of
Hainault

Thomas of
Woodstock, Duke of
Gloucester 1355–1397

Anne

Eleanor
m. Alfonso VIII,
King of Castile

Blanche, d. 1252
m. Louis VIII
of France

William of
Windsor

*Philip Faulconbridge, the bastard son of Richard I, had no historical existence. Such a character appears in the play *The Life and Death of King John* and is referred to in passing in Holinshed's *Chronicles*.

† In the character of Edmund Mortimer, Shakespeare combines two historical figures. The Edmund Mortimer who married Catrin, daughter of Owain Glyndŵr, was the grandson of Lionel, Duke of Clarence, and the younger brother of Roger, Earl of March. He died in 1409. Shakespeare combines him with his nephew, the Edmund Mortimer recognized by Richard II as his heir (d. 1424). This second Edmund was the brother of Anne Mortimer and the uncle of Richard Plantagenet.

‡ The character of the Duke of Somerset combines Henry Beaufort with his younger brother Edmund (d. 1471), who succeeded him as Duke.

Elizabeth Mortimer
("Kate")
m. Henry Percy
("Hotspur")
1364–1403

Henry, Earl of
Northumberland
1394–1455

EDWARD IV
1442–1483 (1461–83)
m. Elizabeth
Woodville d. 1492

EDWARD V
1470–1483 (1483)

Richard, Duke
of York 1472–1483

Elizabeth of York
1465–1503
m. HENRY VII
(below)

Edmund, Earl of
Rutland 1443–1460

Edmund Mortimer†

George, Duke of
Clarence 1449–1478
m. Isabel Neville
(below)

Anne Mortimer
m. Richard, Earl of
Cambridge (below)

Richard Plantagenet,
Duke of York
1411–1460
m. Cicely Neville
(below)

RICHARD III
1452–1485 (1483–85)
m. Anne Neville
(below)

Edward, Prince of Wales

HENRY V 1387–1422
(1413–22)
m. Catherine
1401–1437

HENRY VI 1421–1471
(1422–61)
m. Margaret of Anjou
d. 1482

Edward, Prince of
Wales 1453–1471
m. Anne Neville
(below)

Arthur
m. Catherine of
Aragon (below)

Thomas, Duke of
Clarence d. 1421

Margaret
m. James IV
of Scotland

James V
of Scotland

John of Lancaster,
Duke of Bedford
1389–1435

Mary, Queen of
Scots

Humphrey, Duke of
Gloucester 1391–1447
m. Eleanor Cobham
d. 1454

JAMES I
1566–1625
(1603–25)

John Beaufort, Duke
of Somerset
1403–1444

Margaret Beaufort
m. Edmund Tudor,
Earl of Richmond

HENRY VII 1457–1509
(1485–1509)
m. Elizabeth of York
(above)

HENRY VIII
1491–1547
(1509–47)
m. Catherine of
Aragon

MARY I 1516–1558
(1553–58)
m. Philip of Spain

Edmund Beaufort,
Duke of Somerset
1406–1455

Henry Beaufort,
Duke of Somerset
1436–1464‡

m. Anne Boleyn

ELIZABETH I
1533–1603
(1558–1603)

m. Jane Seymour

EDWARD VI
1537–1553
(1547–53)

Isabel Neville
d. 1476
m. George, Duke
of Clarence
(above)

Richard Neville,
Earl of Warwick
1428–1471

Richard Neville,
Earl of Salisbury
1400–1460

m. Anne of Cleves

m. Katherine Howard

John Neville,
Marquess of
Montague d. 1471

Anne Neville
d. 1485
m. Edward, Prince
of Wales (above)

m. RICHARD III
(above)

m. Katherine Parr

Cicely Neville
m. Richard
Plantagenet,
Duke of York (above)

Mary
m. Charles Brandon

Frances

Jane Grey
1537–1554

Humphrey, Duke of
Buckingham
1402–1460

Humphrey Stafford
d. 1455

Henry, Duke of
Buckingham
1454?–1483

Edward, Duke of
Buckingham
1478–1521

1377–1625

RICHARD II, 1377–99 RICHARD was the eldest son of EDWARD THE BLACK PRINCE, himself the eldest son of KING EDWARD III, who ruled England from 1327 to 1377. When the BLACK PRINCE died in battle in France in 1376, RICHARD became the legitimate heir to the throne. He ruled from EDWARD's death in 1377 until he was deposed in 1399 by HENRY BOLINGBROKE, the eldest son of JOHN OF GAUNT, DUKE OF LANCASTER. Because he was the fourth son of EDWARD III, GAUNT and his Lancastrian descendants had weaker hereditary claims to the throne than did RICHARD. When deposed, RICHARD had no children to succeed him, but he recognized EDMUND MORTIMER, FIFTH EARL OF MARCH, as his heir presumptive. This MORTIMER was descended from LIONEL, DUKE OF CLARENCE, the third son of EDWARD III, and therefore also had stronger hereditary claims to the throne than did BOLINGBROKE. SHAKESPEARE combined this MORTIMER with his uncle EDMUND MORTIMER, who married OWAIN GLYNDŴR'S DAUGHTER.

HENRY IV, 1399–1413 HENRY BOLINGBROKE, eldest son of JOHN OF GAUNT, seized the throne from RICHARD II in 1399. When HENRY died in 1413, he was succeeded by his eldest son, PRINCE HAL, who became HENRY V.

HENRY V, 1413–22 HENRY V became king in 1413 and reigned until his death in 1422. He was succeeded by his son, HENRY VI.

HENRY VI, 1422–61 HENRY VI was less than one year old when he succeeded his father, HENRY V. In the young king's minority, his uncle HUMPHREY, DUKE OF GLOUCESTER, was named Lord Protector, and the kingdom was ruled by an aristocratic council. HENRY VI assumed personal authority in 1437. He was deposed in 1461 by his third cousin, who was crowned EDWARD IV. HENRY was murdered in 1471.

EDWARD IV, 1461–83 EDWARD, the eldest son of RICHARD, DUKE OF YORK, seized the throne from HENRY VI in 1461. His Yorkist claim to the throne derived from his grandmother, ANNE MORTIMER, who was descended from LIONEL, third son of EDWARD III, and was sister to that EDMUND MORTIMER recognized by RICHARD II as his heir presumptive; EDWARD IV's grandfather, RICHARD, EARL OF CAMBRIDGE, was the son of EDMUND OF LANGLEY, fifth son of EDWARD III. EDWARD IV reigned until his death in 1483. His heir was his eldest son (EDWARD), but the throne was usurped by his brother RICHARD, DUKE OF GLOUCESTER.

RICHARD III, 1483–85 RICHARD III was the youngeer brother of EDWARD IV. After the death of EDWARD IV in 1483, RICHARD prevented the coronation of EDWARD V with a claim of illegitimacy and succeeded to the throne himself. EDWARD and his younger brother, RICHARD, DUKE OF YORK, were murdered in the Tower of London. RICHARD III was killed at the Battle of Bosworth Field in 1485, and the kingdom fell to the victor, HENRY TUDOR, EARL OF RICHMOND.

HENRY VII, 1485–1509 HENRY TUDOR seized the throne from RICHARD III in 1485. He was descended from JOHN OF GAUNT by JOHN's third marriage, with CATHERINE SWYNFORD. He married ELIZABETH, daughter of EDWARD IV, uniting the houses of Lancaster and York. He died in 1509 and was succeeded by his son, HENRY VIII.

HENRY VIII, 1509–47 HENRY was the second son of HENRY VII. His older brother, ARTHUR, died in 1502. HENRY VIII's first wife was CATHERINE OF ARAGON, who bore his daughter MARY. His second wife, ANNE BOLEYN, was the mother of ELIZABETH. His third wife, JANE SEYMOUR, bore him a son, who succeeded to the throne as EDWARD VI after HENRY VIII died in 1547.

EDWARD VI, 1547–53 EDWARD VI was nine years old when he became king. From 1547 to 1549, the realm was governed by a Lord Protector, the DUKE OF SOMERSET; power then passed to JOHN DUDLEY, DUKE OF NORTHUMBERLAND. When EDWARD VI died in 1553, NORTHUMBERLAND attempted unsuccessfully to prevent the succession of MARY TUDOR by installing as queen his daughter-in-law, LADY JANE GREY, a great-granddaughter of HENRY VII.

MARY I, 1553–58 MARY, daughter of HENRY VIII and his first wife, CATHERINE OF ARAGON, came to the throne in 1553. She married KING PHILIP OF SPAIN but died childless. She was succeeded by her half sister, ELIZABETH.

ELIZABETH I, 1558–1603 ELIZABETH, the daughter of HENRY VIII and his second wife, ANNE BOLEYN, became queen after the death of her half sister, MARY, in 1558. She ruled until her death in 1603. She was succeeded by her cousin JAMES.

JAMES I, 1603–1625 JAMES VI OF SCOTLAND became JAMES I OF ENGLAND in 1603. His claim to the throne of England derived from his great-grandmother, MARGARET TUDOR, a daughter of HENRY VII who married JAMES IV OF SCOTLAND. JAMES ruled England and Scotland until his death in 1625; he was succeeded by his son, CHARLES I.

THE NORTON
SHAKESPEARE

THIRD EDITION

Volume II
Later Plays and Poems

TEXTUAL EDITORS

DAVID M. BERGERON, University of Kansas, *The Winter's Tale*

THOMAS CARTELLI, Muhlenberg College, *Richard III*

DERMOT CAVANAGH, University of Edinburgh, *King John*

PATRICK CHENEY, Pennsylvania State University, *Venus and Adonis*, *The Rape of Lucrece*,
  The Passionate Pilgrim, *The Phoenix and Turtle*, and *Attributed Poems*

LINE COTTEGNIES, Université Sorbonne Nouvelle–Paris 3, *2 Henry IV*

HANNAH CRAWFORTH, King's College London, *The Two Noble Kinsmen*

TRUDI L. DARBY, King's College London, *Much Ado About Nothing*

ANTHONY B. DAWSON, University of British Columbia, *Hamlet*

MATTHEW DIMMOCK, University of Sussex, *2 Henry VI*

PASCALE DROUET, University of Poitiers, *Henry VIII*

LUKAS ERNE, University of Geneva, *A Midsummer Night's Dream*

JENNIFER FORSYTH, Kutztown University, *1 Henry VI*

EUGENE GIDDENS, Anglia Ruskin University, *Timon of Athens*

SUZANNE GOSSETT, Loyola University Chicago, *All's Well That Ends Well*

GRACE IOPPOLO, University of Reading, *King Lear*

JANE KINGSLEY-SMITH, University of Roehampton, *Love's Labor's Lost*

JAMES A. KNAPP, Loyola University Chicago, *The Comedy of Errors*

JESSE M. LANDER, University of Notre Dame, *1 Henry IV*

LYNNE MAGNUSSON, University of Toronto, *The Sonnets* and *A Lover's Complaint*

HOWARD MARCHITELLO, Rutgers University–Camden, *Henry V*

LEAH S. MARCUS, Vanderbilt University, *As You Like It* and *The Merchant of Venice*

CLARE McMANUS, University of Roehampton, *Othello*

GORDON McMULLAN, King's College London, *Romeo and Juliet*

GRETCHEN E. MINTON, Montana State University, *Troilus and Cressida*

ROBERT S. MIOLA, Loyola University Maryland, *Macbeth*

HELEN OSTOVICH, McMaster University, *The Merry Wives of Windsor*

GAIL KERN PASTER, Folger Shakespeare Library, *Twelfth Night*

LOIS POTTER, University of Delaware, *Pericles*

NATHALIE RIVÈRE DE CARLES, University of Toulouse–Jean Jaurès,
  The Two Gentlemen of Verona

WILLIAM H. SHERMAN, University of York, *The Tempest*

CATHY SHRANK, University of Sheffield, *Coriolanus*

JAMES R. SIEMON, Boston University, *Julius Caesar*

CATHERINE SILVERSTONE, Queen Mary University of London, *Titus Andronicus*

MATTHEW STEGGLE, Sheffield Hallam University, *Measure for Measure*

ALAN STEWART, Columbia University, *Richard II*

HOLGER SCHOTT SYME, University of Toronto, *Edward III* and *Sir Thomas More*

NEIL TAYLOR, University of Roehampton, *3 Henry VI*

ANN THOMPSON, King's College London, *Cymbeline*

VIRGINIA MASON VAUGHAN, Clark University, *Antony and Cleopatra*

SARAH WERNER, Folger Shakespeare Library, *The Taming of the Shrew*

The Theater of Shakespeare's Time, HOLGER SCHOTT SYME, University of Toronto
Performance Notes, BRETT GAMBOA, Dartmouth College

THE NORTON
SHAKESPEARE

THIRD EDITION

Volume II
Later Plays and Poems

Stephen Greenblatt, *General Editor*
HARVARD UNIVERSITY

Walter Cohen
UNIVERSITY OF MICHIGAN

Suzanne Gossett, *General Textual Editor*
LOYOLA UNIVERSITY CHICAGO (EMERITA)

Jean E. Howard
COLUMBIA UNIVERSITY

Katharine Eisaman Maus
UNIVERSITY OF VIRGINIA

Gordon McMullan, *General Textual Editor*
KING'S COLLEGE LONDON

W · W · NORTON & COMPANY · NEW YORK · LONDON

W. W. Norton & Company has been independent since its founding in 1923, when William Warder Norton and Mary D. Herter Norton first published lectures delivered at the People's Institute, the adult education division of New York City's Cooper Union. The firm soon expanded its program beyond the Institute, publishing books by celebrated academics from America and abroad. By mid-century, the two major pillars of Norton's publishing program—trade books and college texts—were firmly established. In the 1950s, the Norton family transferred control of the company to its employees, and today—with a staff of 400 and a comparable number of trade, college, and professional titles published each year—W. W. Norton & Company stands as the largest and oldest publishing house owned wholly by its employees.

Editor: Julia Reidhead
Managing Editor, College: Marian Johnson
Associate Editor: Emily Stuart
Manuscript Editors: Harry Haskell, Alice Vigliani
Media Editor: Carly Fraser Doria
Media Project Editor: Kristin Sheerin
Production Manager: Eric Pier-Hocking
Digital Production: Mateus Texeira, Colleen Caffrey
Marketing Manager, Literature: Kim Bowers
Photo Editor: Trish Marx
Composition: Westchester Book Company
Manufacturing: LSC Communications

The Library of Congress has catalogued the full edition as follows:
Shakespeare, William, 1564–1616.
The Norton Shakespeare / Stephen Greenblatt, General Editor, Harvard
University; Walter Cohen, University of Michigan; Suzanne Gossett, General
Textual Editor, Loyola University Chicago (Emerita); Jean E. Howard, Columbia
University; Katharine Eisaman Maus, University of Virginia; Gordon McMullan,
General Textual Editor, King's College London.—Third edition.
pages cm
Includes bibliographical references and index.
      ISBN 978-0-393-93499-1 (hardcover)
I. Greenblatt, Stephen, 1943– editor. II. Cohen, Walter, 1949– editor.
III. Gossett, Suzanne, editor. IV. Howard, Jean E. (Jean Elizabeth), 1948– editor.
V. Maus, Katharine Eisaman, 1955– editor. VI. McMullan, Gordon,
1962– editor. VII. Title.
PR2754.G74 2015
822.3'3—dc23
                              2015018869

This edition: ISBN 978-0-393-93858-6

W. W. Norton & Company, Inc., 500 Fifth Avenue, New York, NY 10110-0017
wwnorton.com

W. W. Norton & Company Ltd., Castle House, 75/76 Wells Street, London W1T 3QT

2 3 4 5 6 7 8 9 0

Contents

Additional works, media, contextual materials, and bibliographies
are available in the Digital Edition

LATER PLAYS AND POEMS

Appendices

An Act to Restrain Abuses of Players (May 27, 1606)
Elegy on Richard Burbage (1619?)

GENEALOGIES
    A Shakespearean Genealogy
    The Kings and Queens of England, 1377–1625
    The House of Lancaster
    The House of York
    The Houses of Tudor and Stuart

COMPARATIVE SCENES AND POEMS *digital-only*
    Othello 4.3 (Quarto and Folio)
    Richard III 4.2 (Quarto and Folio)
    Henry V opening (Folio and Quarto)
    Romeo and Juliet 2.1 (Second Quarto and First Quarto)
    A Midsummer Night's Dream 5.1 (Quarto and Folio)
    Hamlet 3.1 (Second Quarto and First Quarto)
    Sonnet 138 (with *Passionate Pilgrim* 1)
    Sonnet 144 (with *Passionate Pilgrim* 2)

Contents by Genre

Comedies

Histories

Tragedies

Romances

Poems

Lost Plays

Contents by Date of First Publication

Most of the composition dates of Shakespeare's plays and poems are conjectural. The dates of first known publication are given here. However, since the first quarto of *Hamlet* was only discovered in 1823, and only one copy of the first quarto of *Titus Andronicus* survives, it may well be that early editions of which we are unaware did in fact exist, and some may even turn up yet. At first many of Shakespeare's plays were published anonymously; once he was famous and successful, quite a few plays and some poems whose authorship is either rejected or currently under dispute were advertised with his name (or the initials W.S.). Other plays published anonymously are believed by some scholars to be all or in part by Shakespeare. The earliest published text of a given play is not necessarily the fullest or most authoritative, so while *The Norton Shakespeare* includes editions of all such texts in the Digital Edition, the earliest publication is not always chosen to represent the play in the print edition. The following list includes those plays and poems found in *The Norton Shakespeare*.

Illustrations

Preface

This Third Edition of *The Norton Shakespeare* is both a continuation and a new beginning. Readers who have already found the format of the printed book and its editorial apparatus to their liking will get what they are looking for. The emphasis continues to be on the pleasure of reading, with a particular attention to undergraduates who may be encountering Shakespeare for the first time. "If then you do not like him," wrote Shakespeare's first editors almost four hundred years ago, "surely you are in some manifest danger not to understand him." We have from the start made every effort, through the glosses, notes, introductions, and other materials, to facilitate understanding and hence to enhance liking. We are careful not to overburden Shakespeare's words with explication or to crowd the page with distracting commentary. The clear, uncluttered, single-column format is designed to encourage absorption. But we try to offer enough help to allow the beauty and the luminous intelligence of these stupendous works to shine.

We have in this edition carefully revised each of our introductions (including the long General Introduction) and reviewed every one of our notes and glosses, altering and adding where appropriate. Our goal has been to hold onto what our readers have told us works well, but also to update the introductions, bibliographies, filmographies, and other materials to reflect current scholarship, shifting emphases, and newly released films. An entirely new feature of this edition is an illuminating Performance Note, by Brett Gamboa (Dartmouth College), that accompanies each of the plays. These notes describe the particular and recurrent theatrical challenges with which actors and directors have grappled in mounting any given work. The strategies devised over the centuries in response to these challenges are a fascinating point of entry into critical issues of interpretation. The notes are also an invaluable guide to what audiences should look for when they attend a new production.

From its inception, *The Norton Shakespeare* has paid exceptionally close attention to the accuracy as well as the accessibility of the texts and, in particular, to the challenge posed by those plays that exist in multiple substantive versions. For the Third Edition, all of Shakespeare's plays and poems have been newly edited, from scratch, by an international team of leading textual scholars. This hugely ambitious and complex undertaking has been based on the principle of single-text editing—that is, where more than one early authoritative text of a given play has survived, rather than merging them into one (as has been traditionally done), we have edited each text in its own right. We thereby offer the reader texts as close as possible to the original versions as read by Shakespeare's contemporaries. A lively and accessible new General Textual Introduction fully articulates this principle, explores the nature of the documents that have come down to us from Shakespeare's own time, and explains in detail the editorial practices on which this new text of the complete works is meticulously based.

Approximately half of Shakespeare's plays appeared both in small-format versions (quartos), printed in the playwright's own lifetime, and in the large-format First Folio (1623), published seven years after his death. As early as the eighteenth century, careful readers began to notice that there were differences, sometimes minor and sometimes quite significant, between these printings of the same plays. Starting with the landmark Shakespeare editions of Alexander Pope (1723) and Lewis Theobald (1733), editors initiated the practice of blending the different versions together, picking and choosing as their taste dictated or as they imagined that Shakespeare would have done, had he himself produced a definitive text. Hence, for example, the two distinct texts of *King Lear* were routinely fashioned into a single text, with editors combining lines that appear only in one or the other early version and choosing among hundreds of variant readings.

From its inception, *The Norton Shakespeare* rejected this editorial method (known as "conflation"). We have continued in the current print edition our hallmark practice of offering, on facing pages, the 1608 Quarto text of *King Lear* and the substantial revision of the play as printed in the First Folio (1623). While each version may be read independently—we have provided glosses and footnotes for each—the significant points of difference between the two are immediately apparent and available for comparison. It is thus possible to watch in extraordinarily sharp focus changes in the early modern text of one of Shakespeare's greatest plays. We recognize at the same time that a combined text, in one form or another, has long served as the *King Lear* upon which innumerable performances of the play have been based and on which a huge body of literary criticism has been written. Hence in addition to providing the Quarto and Folio texts, we wanted to offer readers a version of this great tragedy that combines the two without entirely erasing their differences. The solution that we provide in these pages is what in the first two editions of *The Norton Shakespeare* we used in the comparable case of *Hamlet*. We print the Folio text of *King Lear*, but we have moved the lines that are solely in the Quarto into the body of the play. In doing so, however, we did not want simply to produce a conflated version. We have therefore indented the Q-only passages, printed them in a slightly different typeface, and numbered them in such a way as to make clear their provenance. We call this a "scars-and-stitches" solution, since, though still eminently readable and enjoyable, it clearly marks the points of insertion and difference.

The Norton Shakespeare, then, includes three separate texts of *King Lear*. The reader can compare them, analyze the role of editors in constructing the texts we now call Shakespeare's, explore in detail the kinds of decisions that playwrights, editors, and printers make and remake, witness firsthand the historical transformation of what might at first glance seem fixed and unchanging. We offer extraordinary access to this supremely brilliant, difficult, compelling play.

Hamlet, the other great tragedy at the very center of Shakespeare's achievement, similarly exists in multiple versions: the 1604 Second Quarto (Q2), the longest of the early editions; the 1623 Folio text (F), which lacks some 200 lines found in Q2 but includes more than 70 lines not found there; and, casting a fascinating light on the more familiar version of the tragedy, the drastically different First Quarto (Q1, the so-called Bad Quarto). As in the case of *Lear*, editors for centuries have routinely conflated the Q2 and F *Hamlets*.

The realities of bookbinding—not to mention our recognition of the limited time in the typical undergraduate syllabus—preclude our offering in the print edition four *Hamlets* (Q1, Q2, F, and combined) to parallel the three *Lears*. What we have provided in these pages instead is a new incarnation of the solution we came up with in the first two editions of *The Norton Shakespeare*. While basing our *Hamlet* on the Q2 text, we have moved the Folio passages, among which are some of the tragedy's most famous lines, into the body of the play. But, as with the "scars-and-stitches" *Lear*, we have made it possible for readers who are interested to see what has been added.

The growing interest in the possibility of teaching the First Quarto of *Hamlet* has also led us to add that strange text, in fully glossed and annotated form, alongside the more familiar version of Shakespeare's most famous tragedy. Readers can wonder at a *Hamlet* in which the hero muses "To be, or not to be—ay, there's the point," and they can see how drastically one theater troupe in Shakespeare's own time probably cut the play for performance.

These and other changes all serve to keep *The Norton Shakespeare* fresh and current. But this Third Edition, as I have already suggested, is much more than a careful revision and updating. It is a thoroughgoing rethinking both of the entire Shakespeare corpus and of the whole way in which Shakespeare is experienced by contemporary readers. For the purposes of this preface, a single feature of the newly edited text should be emphasized: it was created not only for the print edition, but also for a new and exciting Digital Edition. From its inception the print edition featured both the Quarto and the Folio texts of *King Lear,* and we have now added the First Quarto of *Hamlet.* Our Digital Edition makes available fully glossed and annotated Quarto and Folio versions of the plays—fifteen in all—for which more than one early authoritative text exists, thereby offering the reader access to these plays as they were first experienced by Shakespeare's contemporaries. This means not only the two versions of *Lear,* which can be viewed in side-by-side scrolling format for comparison as well as individually, and not only the three versions of *Hamlet.* It also means multiple versions, with fascinating variants, of such beloved, centrally important plays as *Romeo and Juliet, Othello, Richard II, Richard III, Henry V, Love's Labor's Lost,* and *A Midsummer Night's Dream.* There are Quarto and Folio versions as well of *2* and *3 Henry VI, Titus Andronicus, 2 Henry IV, The Merry Wives of Windsor,* and *Troilus and Cressida.* The Digital Edition also offers an appendix of selected scenes from a number of multiple-version plays, presented side-by-side so that they can easily be compared for teaching purposes. For anyone interested in Shakespeare's practices of composition and revision and in the fascinating process through which his plays, passing through the printing house, have managed to reach us, the digital *Norton Shakespeare* is an unprecedented resource.

Links to the widely respected *Norton Facsimile of the First Folio of Shakespeare,* edited by Charlton Hinman, and to quarto facsimile pages make it possible for readers to see for themselves the original materials with which the editors have been working to create this new text of the complete works.

In the digital *Norton Shakespeare* we also include for the first time an edition of the full text of *Sir Thomas More,* a multi-authored play, unpublished in the period, whose manuscript includes a section in Shakespeare's own hand, the only surviving one of its kind. We also include an edition of *Edward III,* another play of which Shakespeare appears to have been part-author. Both texts are interesting as examples of the collaborative nature of much Elizabethan and Jacobean theater, a collaboration reflected as well in the late plays *Pericles, Henry VIII, The Two Noble Kinsmen,* the lost *Cardenio,* and—more debatably—such works as *1 Henry VI, Titus Andronicus,* and *Timon of Athens.*

This extraordinary wealth of texts, all complete with introductions, notes, and glosses, has been made possible by the vastness of the digital space. That space has allowed us to supplement the useful aids in the print edition—including maps, genealogies, a glossary, a short bibliography, a timeline, and a selection of key documents—with further resources. For the Digital Edition, the volume editors have created expanded bibliographies for the study of Shakespeare's works, and Misha Teramura (Harvard University), who edited and glossed the documents in the print text, has assembled and edited a larger archive of Tudor and Stuart documents relevant to Shakespeare and his theater world.

The remarkable expansion of texts is only the beginning. The resources of the Digital Edition have made possible innovations that were, until very recently, only a teacher's idle daydreams. Shakespeare scholars have long understood that the decisions editors make—for example, choosing one variant over another, or adding stage directions, or making consistent the multiple speech prefixes often used for a single character—can affect the meaning of the plays. But on the printed page it has been difficult to call attention to the significance of these decisions without interrupting the flow of the reading experience, while the long lists of textual variants printed at the ends of plays are so much raw data, rarely consulted or understood by anyone but experts. Now, by clicking a marginal icon, readers can summon illuminating Textual Comments for each play, written by the textual editor, that focus on textual-editing decision points influencing interpretation. It is possible for all interested readers now to understand textual cruxes and to see—and, for that matter, to call into question—key editorial choices.

Similarly, a crucially important dimension of Shakespeare's texts, as everyone grasps, is that they were originally intended for performance. Hence the brief discussion in the General Introduction of the theatrical scene Shakespeare encountered and helped to transform is now greatly enriched in "The Theater of Shakespeare's Time," a lively and original essay by Holger Schott Syme (University of Toronto). Syme conjures up a fiercely competitive world of multiple theater companies and rival venues, all scrambling for plays that will survive the attention of the government censor and lure crowds of spectators to part with their pennies.

Performance is obviously not only a matter of historical interest. It remains, for most of us and certainly for our students, central to the full experience of the plays. But, without overfreighting the page, it has been difficult to highlight this dimension in the printed book. Descriptions of famous performances, from Garrick to the present, rarely capture the significance of key interpretive choices by actors or directors. Now clicking on marginal icons keyed to particular moments in the texts allows one to read incisive and insightful Performance Comments that supplement the Performance Note preceding each play. These comments, by Brett Gamboa, highlight passages that are particularly famous challenges in performance and explore how a director or actor's interpretive choices affect meaning. Taken individually, the Performance Comments call attention to specific decisions that must be made in the realization of a play; taken together, they constitute a brilliant exploration of the performative dimensions of Shakespeare's art.

The performative dimension is enhanced by two further features of the Digital Edition. First, there are recordings of all of the songs—66 of them—in the plays, from the award-winning *Shakespeare's Songbook* audio companion by Ross Duffin. It is now possible for readers to take in fully the pervasive presence of music in Shakespeare's plays, something that the printed stage direction *"Music"* cannot hope to do. Second, there are over eight hours of spoken-word audio of key passages and scenes and those that pose particular challenges to readers. These have been specially recorded for the Digital Edition by the highly regarded company, Actors from the London Stage. With a simple click it is now possible for readers to hear the words on the page come alive in the voices of gifted actors.

The digital *Norton Shakespeare* brings together in one place an unparalleled array of resources for understanding and enjoying Shakespeare. These resources are not the primitive accumulation of materials, of dubious utility or reliability, which often makes the web an untrustworthy guide. Rather, each of the texts and other material has received the same careful scholarly and pedagogical attention that has made the print edition a success. But we are aware that different readers will have different interests and needs, often varying from time to time. The reading experience of the Digital Edition, including the visibility of icons, line numbers, glosses, and notes, can be easily customized, so that with a click readers can either "quiet" the page or access Norton's abundant reading help. The Digital Edition platform provides customizable highlighting, annotating, and comment-sharing tools that facilitate active reading.

The publisher also provides instructors with a wealth of free resources beyond the Digital Edition. An Instructor Resource Disc created for the new edition features the more than eight hours of spoken-word audio recorded by Actors from the London Stage, 150 songs, and over 100 images from the book in both JPEG and PowerPoint for easy classroom presentation. The images are available for download on the publisher's instructor resource page, wwnorton.com/instructors. In addition, the Norton Shakespeare YouTube channel brings together a carefully curated and regularly updated collection of the best of the web's Shakespeare video resources, allowing instructors to easily show clips from stage and film in class.

The extraordinary labor of love that has led to this new and revised edition of *The Norton Shakespeare* has involved a large number of collaborators. The volume editors owe a substantial debt of thanks to the readers of the earlier editions. Our readers have formed a large, engaged community, and their endorsements, observations, and suggestions for revision and expansion have proved invaluable. We have also profited from the highly detailed reviews of each individual feature of the edition commissioned by the publisher and performed with exemplary seriousness by many of our most esteemed professional colleagues.

At the very center of the Third Edition is the newly edited text of the Complete Works, an enormous, exhaustive, and exhausting enterprise. We wish to acknowledge with deepest gratitude the extraordinary labors of our gifted team of textual editors, listed on the title-page spread, led with an exemplary blend of discipline, patience, intellectual seriousness, and scholarly rigor by Gordon McMullan and Suzanne Gossett.

The *Norton Shakespeare* editors have had the valuable—indeed, indispensable—support of our publisher and a host of undergraduate and graduate research assistants, colleagues, friends, and family, whose names we gratefully note in the Acknowledgments that follow. All of these companions have helped us find in this long collective enterprise what the "Dedicatorie Epistle" to the First Folio promises to its readers: delight. We make the same promise to the readers of our edition and invite them to continue the great Shakespearean collaboration.

STEPHEN GREENBLATT
CAMBRIDGE, MASSACHUSETTS

Volume Editors' Acknowledgments

The creation of this edition has drawn heavily on the resources, experience, and skill of its remarkable publisher, W. W. Norton. Norton's record of success in academic publishing has sometimes made it seem like a giant, akin to the multinational corporations that dominate the publishing world, but it is in fact the only major publishing house that is employee-owned. Our principal guide has been our brilliant editor Julia Reidhead, whose calm intelligence, common sense, and steady focus have been essential in enabling us to reach our goal. With this Third Edition, we were blessed once again with the indispensable judgment and project-editorial expertise of Marian Johnson, managing editor, college department, as well as scrupulous manuscript editing by Alice Vigliani and Harry Haskell. Carly Fraser Doria, literature media editor, skillfully guided us through the new waters of the Digital Edition, following Cliff Landesman's innovative lead. Assistant editor Emily Stuart managed with remarkable skill and graciousness the complexities of manuscript preparation and review. Kim Yi, managing editor, digital media, and Kristin Sheerin, digital project editor, oversaw the monumental checking and proofing of files. In addition, we are deeply grateful to Cara Folkman, media assistant editor; JoAnn Simony and Elizabeth Audley, digital file coordinators; Eric Pier-Hocking, production manager; and Debra Morton Hoyt, corporate art director, who, along with designer Timothy Hsu, created our Ortelius-inspired cover design. Thanks also to Mary Jo Mecca for design and construction of the jester hat. For invaluable help in creating the Digital Edition, we would like to thank Jane Chu and Colleen Caffrey, digital designers, and Mateus Teixiera and Kristian Sanford, digital production.

The editors have, in addition, had the valuable—indeed, indispensable—support of a host of undergraduate and graduate research assistants, colleagues, friends, and family. Even a partial listing of those to whom we owe our heartfelt thanks is very long, but we are all fortunate enough to live in congenial and supportive environments, and the edition has been part of our lives for a long time. We owe special thanks for sustained dedication and learning to our colleagues, friends, and principal assistants:

Stephen Greenblatt wishes to thank his talented research assistants at Harvard, including Maria Devlin, Seth Herbst, Rhema Hokama, David Nee, Elizabeth Weckhurst, Benjamin Woodring, Catherine Woodring, and, above all, Misha Teramura. In addition, he is grateful for valuable assistance from Rebecca Cook and Aubrey Everett, along with advice and counsel from many friends, colleagues, and students. Thanks also go to C. Edward McGee (University of Waterloo), Barbara D. Palmer (late of the University of Mary Washington), Sylvia Thomas (the Yorkshire Archaeological Society), and John M. Wasson (late of Washington State University). He acknowledges a special and enduring debt to Ramie Targoff (Brandeis University).

Walter Cohen wishes to thank Marjorie Levinson (University of Michigan).

Jean Howard would like to acknowledge the help of each of her excellent research assistants at Columbia University: Bryan Lowrance, John Kuhn, Alexander Paulsson Lash, Chris McKeen, and especially Emily Shortslef, whose scholarly contributions have been indispensable and impeccable and whose good cheer is astonishingly unflagging.

We gratefully acknowledge the reviewers who provided thoughtful critiques for particular plays or of the project as a whole: Bernadette Andrea (University of Texas at San Antonio), John M. Archer (New York University), Oliver Arnold (University of California–Berkeley), Amanda Bailey (University of Connecticut), JoAnn D. Barbour

(Texas Woman's University), Catherine Belsey (Swansea University), Barbara Bono (University at Buffalo), Michael D. Bristol (McGill University), Karen Britland (University of Wisconsin–Madison), James C. Bulman (Allegheny College), William C. Carroll (Boston University), Kent Cartwright (University of Maryland, College Park), Joseph Cerami (Texas A&M University), Julie Crawford (Columbia University), Jonathan Crewe (Dartmouth College), Stephen Deng (Michigan State University), Christy Desmet (University of Georgia), Donald R. Dickson (Texas A&M University), Mario DiGangi (Graduate Center of the City University of New York), Tobias Doering (University of Munich), Frances Dolan (University of California–Davis), John Drakakis (University of Stirling), Heather Dubrow (Fordham University), Holly Dugan (George Washington University), Amy E. Earhart (Texas A&M University), Katherine E. Eggert (University of Colorado–Boulder), Lars D. Engle (University of Tulsa), Christopher John Fitter (Rutgers University), Mary Floyd-Wilson (University of North Carolina–Chapel Hill), Susan Caroline Frye (University of Wyoming), Brett Gamboa (Dartmouth College), Evelyn Gajowski (University of Nevada, Las Vegas), Hugh Hartridge Grady, Jr. (Arcadia University), Kenneth Gross (University of Rochester), Elizabeth Hanson (Queen's University), Jonathan Gil Harris (George Washington University), Michael Hattaway (New York University), Diana Henderson (Massachusetts Institute of Technology), Terence Allan Hoagwood (Texas A&M University), Lucia Kristina Hodgson (Texas A&M University), Peter Holbrook (The University of Queensland), Peter Holland (University of Notre Dame), John W. Huntington (University of Illinois at Chicago), Lorna Hutson (University of St. Andrews), Coppélia Kahn (Brown University), Jeffrey Knapp (University of California–Berkeley), Yu Jin Ko (Wellesley College), Paul A. Kottman (The New School), Bryon Lew (Trent University), Genevieve Love (Colorado College), Julia R. Lupton (University of California–Irvine), Ellen MacKay (Indiana University), Cristina Malcolmson (Bates College), Lawrence G. Manley (Yale University), Steven Mentz (St. John's University), Erin Minear (College of William and Mary), Arash Moradi (Shiraz University), Ian Moulton (Arizona State University), Steven Mullaney (University of Michigan), Cyrus Mulready (State University of New York–New Paltz), Karen Newman (Brown University), Mary A. O'Farrell (Texas A&M University), Laurie E. Osborne (Colby College), Simon Palfrey (Oxford University), Garry Partridge (Texas A&M University), Thomas Pendleton (Iona College), Peter G. Platt (Barnard College), Christopher Pye (Williams College), Phyllis R. Rackin (University of Pennsylvania), Sally Robinson (Texas A&M University), Mary Beth Rose (University of Illinois at Chicago), Suparna Roychoudhury (Mount Holyoke College), Elizabeth D. Samet (United States Military Academy at West Point), Melissa E. Sanchez (University of Pennsylvania), Michael Schoenfeldt (University of Michigan), Laurie J. Shannon (Northwestern University), Jyotsna Singh (Michigan State University), Elizabeth Spiller (Florida State University), Tiffany Stern (Oxford University), Richard Strier (University of Chicago), Ayanna Thompson (George Washington University), Douglas Trevor (University of Michigan), Henry S. Turner (Rutgers University), Brian Walsh (Yale University), Tiffany Jo Werth (Simon Fraser University), Adam Zucker (University of Massachusetts).

General Textual Editors' Acknowledgments

First and foremost, we are grateful to Stephen Greenblatt for inviting us to imagine, and then to create, a wholly new text of Shakespeare for the Third Edition of *The Norton Shakespeare*; to the volume editors—Jean Howard, Katharine Maus, and Walter Cohen—for working closely with us and for supporting the single text–editing principle we adopted; and to Julia Reidhead, the edition's publisher, for her gracious engagement and direction at every stage. And of course we are hugely grateful to the remarkable team of editors with whom we have worked, all of whom, without exception, accepted the invitation with alacrity, edited superbly, completed their work in timely fashion, and tolerated the necessary processes stemming from the need to ensure that each individual play functions both in its own right and as part of the edition as a whole. We want to thank and acknowledge them all. We also wish to thank Lacey Conley, who provided invaluable research assistance at crucial moments in the creation of the text. None of this would have been possible without the indefatigable work of the team at Norton. Marian Johnson, managing editor, college, provided invaluable wisdom and care for the newly edited text. Cliff Landesman's enthusiasm for the project and his willingness to explore—and help us understand—the digital possibilities were invaluable. Carly Fraser Doria and Emily Stuart responded with remarkable generosity, patience, and professionalism to our requests and anxieties. And we are particularly grateful to Norton's copy editors, Alice Vigliani and Harry Haskell, for their wonderfully precise work on the texts of the plays.

Editors tend to fight like cats in a sack over the choices they make when editing Shakespeare—they did this in the eighteenth century, and they try their best to keep up the tradition today—yet they also know that they are in fact highly mutually dependent, and it matters a great deal to us to note that we have had a second set of collaborators in the creation of this new text, none of whom has had actual direct involvement in *The Norton Shakespeare*, Third Edition—due in some cases to working on equivalent editions for other presses—but without whose textual and critical work we could not have acquired the knowledge we needed to create this edition. These include David Bevington, Peter Blayney, A. R. Braunmuller, R. A. Foakes, John Jowett, David Scott Kastan, Laurie Maguire, Sonia Massai, Eric Rasmussen, Tiffany Stern, Gary Taylor, Stanley Wells, and Martin Wiggins. And we would like in particular to acknowledge our considerable debt to Richard Proudfoot, who mentored us both in the fine art of editing and whose knowledge of the Shakespearean text and generosity with that knowledge are unsurpassed. We should acknowledge too certain key resources without which our editorial work would have been, practically speaking, impossible: these include the British Library's remarkable Shakespeare in Quarto website and the online text and facsimiles provided by the Internet Shakespeare Edition (a remarkable enterprise led by the generous and endlessly energetic Michael Best).

Finally, we should also note that any edition of Shakespeare is merely one in a very long line, and all modern Shakespearean editors are indebted to the extraordinary work of the earliest toilers in the field—from Shakespeare's friends Heminges and Condell assembling the First Folio and thus providing the crucial basis for all subsequent work on the Shakespeare canon, to the anonymous editors of the Second, Third, and Fourth Folios, to the crucial work of Rowe, Capell, Pope, Johnson, Theobald, and their successors in the eighteenth, nineteenth, and twentieth centuries. How they did any of it without word-processing software and the resources of the Internet we cannot for the life of us figure out.

GORDON MCMULLAN and SUZANNE GOSSETT

General Introduction

STEPHEN GREENBLATT

"He was not of an age, but for all time!"

There are writers whose greatness is recognized only long after they have vanished from the earth. There are writers championed by a coterie of devoted followers who tend the flame of admiration against the cold world's indifference. There are writers beloved in their native land but despised abroad, and others neglected at home yet celebrated on distant shores. Shakespeare is none of these. His genius was recognized almost immediately. The famous words with which we have begun were written by his friend and rival Ben Jonson. They have been echoed innumerable times, across the centuries, across national and linguistic boundaries, across the demarcation lines of race and class, religion and ideology. Shakespeare belongs not simply to a particular culture—English culture of the late sixteenth and early seventeenth centuries—but to world culture, the dense network of constraints and entitlements, dreams and practices that help to make us fully human. Indeed, so absolute is Shakespeare's achievement that he has himself come to seem like great creating nature. His works embody the imagination's power to transcend time-bound beliefs and assumptions, particular historical circumstances, and specific artistic conventions. If we should ever be asked as a species to bring forward one artist who has most fully expressed the human condition, we could with confidence elect Shakespeare to speak for us. As it is, when we do ask ourselves the most fundamental questions about life—about love and hatred, ambition, desire, and fear, the demand for justice and the longing for a second chance—we repeatedly turn to Shakespeare for the words we wish to hear.

The near-worship Shakespeare inspires is one of the salient facts about his art. But we must at the same time acknowledge that this art is the product of peculiar historical circumstances and specific conventions, four centuries distant from our own. The acknowledgment is important because Shakespeare the working dramatist did not typically lay claim to the transcendent, visionary truths attributed to him by his most fervent admirers; his characters more modestly say, in the words of the magician Prospero, that their project was "to please" (*The Tempest*, Epilogue, line 13). The starting point, and perhaps the ending point as well, in any encounter with Shakespeare is simply to enjoy him, to savor his imaginative richness, to take pleasure in his infinite delight in language.

"If then you do not like him," Shakespeare's first editors wrote in 1623, "surely you are in some manifest danger not to understand him." Over the years, accommodations have been devised to make liking Shakespeare easier for everyone. When aspects of his language began to seem difficult, texts were published with notes and glosses. When the historical events he depicted receded into obscurity, explanatory introductions were written. When the stage sank to melodrama and light opera, Shakespeare made his appearance in suitably revised dress. When the populace had a craving for hippodrama, plays performed entirely on horseback, *Hamlet* was dutifully rewritten and mounted. When audiences went mad for realism, live frogs croaked in productions of *A Midsummer Night's Dream*. When the stage was stripped

1

bare and given over to stark exhibitions of sadistic cruelty, Shakespeare was our contemporary. And when the theater ceded some of its cultural centrality to radio, film, and television, Shakespeare moved effortlessly to Hollywood and the sound stages of the BBC.

This virtually universal appeal is one of the most astonishing features of the Shakespeare phenomenon: plays that were performed before glittering courts thrive in junior high school auditoriums; enemies set on destroying one another laugh at the same jokes and weep at the same catastrophes; some of the richest and most complex English verse ever written migrates with spectacular success into German and Italian, Hindi, Swahili, and Japanese. Is there a single, stable, continuous object that underlies all of these migrations and metamorphoses? Certainly not. The global diffusion and long life of Shakespeare's works depend on their extraordinary malleability, their protean capacity to elude definition and escape secure possession. His art is the supreme manifestation of the mobility of culture. At the same time, this art is not without identifiable shared features: across centuries and continents, family resemblances link many of the wildly diverse manifestations of plays such as *Romeo and Juliet, Hamlet*, and *Twelfth Night*. Moreover, if there is no clear limit or end point, there is a reasonably clear beginning, the England of the late sixteenth and early seventeenth centuries, when the plays and poems collected in *The Norton Shakespeare* made their first appearance.

An art virtually without end or limit but with an identifiable, localized, historical origin: Shakespeare's achievement defies the facile opposition between transcendent and time-bound. It is not necessary to choose between an account of Shakespeare as the scion of a particular culture and an account of him as a universal genius who created works that continually renew themselves across national and generational boundaries. On the contrary: crucial clues to understanding his art's remarkable power to soar beyond the time and place of its origin lie in the very soil from which that art sprang.

Shakespeare's World

Life and Death

Life expectancy at birth in early modern England was exceedingly low by our standards: under thirty years, compared with over seventy today. Infant mortality rates were extraordinarily high, and it is estimated that in the poorer parishes of London only about half the children survived to the age of fifteen, while the children of aristocrats fared only a little better. In such circumstances, some parents must have developed a certain detachment—one of Shakespeare's contemporaries writes of losing "some three or four children"—but there are many expressions of intense grief, so that we cannot assume that the frequency of death hardened people to loss or made it routine.

Still, the spectacle of death, along with that other great threshold experience, birth, must have been far more familiar to Shakespeare and his contemporaries than to ourselves. There was no equivalent in early modern England to our hospitals, and most births and deaths occurred at home. Physical means for the alleviation of pain and suffering were extremely limited—alcohol might dull the terror, but it was hardly an effective anesthetic—and medical treatment was generally both expensive and worthless, more likely to intensify suffering than to lead to a cure. This was a world without a concept of antiseptics, with little actual understanding of disease, with few effective ways of treating earaches or venereal disease, let alone the more terrible instances of what Shakespeare calls "the thousand natural shocks that flesh is heir to."

The worst of these shocks was the bubonic plague, which repeatedly ravaged England, and particularly English towns, until the third quarter of the seventeenth

Bill recording plague deaths in London, 1609.

century. The plague was terrifyingly sudden in its onset, rapid in its spread, and almost invariably lethal. Physicians were helpless in the face of the epidemic, though they prescribed amulets, preservatives, and sweet-smelling substances (on the theory that the plague was carried by noxious vapors). In the plague-ridden year of 1564, the year of Shakespeare's birth, some 254 people died in his native Stratford-upon-Avon, out of a total population of 800. The year before, some 20,000 Londoners are thought to have died; in 1593, almost 15,000; in 1603, 36,000, or over a sixth of the city's inhabitants. The social effects of these horrible visitations were severe: looting, violence, and despair, along with an intensification of the age's perennial poverty, unemployment, and food shortages. The London plague regulations of 1583, reissued with modifications in later epidemics, ordered that the infected and their households should be locked in their homes for a month; that the streets should be kept clean; that vagrants should be expelled; and that funerals and plays (as occasions in which large numbers of people gathered and infection could be spread) should be restricted or banned entirely. Comparable restrictions were not placed on gatherings for religious observance, since it was hoped that God would heed the desperate prayers of his suffering people.

The plague, then, had a direct and immediate impact on Shakespeare's own profession. City officials kept records of the weekly number of plague deaths; when these surpassed a certain number, the theaters were peremptorily closed. The basic idea was not only to prevent contagion but also to avoid making an angry God still angrier with the spectacle of idleness. While restricting public assemblies may in fact have slowed the epidemic, other public policies in times of plague, such as killing the cats and dogs, may have made matters worse (since the disease was spread not by these animals but by the fleas that bred on the black rats that infested the poorer neighborhoods). Moreover, the playing companies, driven out of London by the closing of the theaters, may have carried plague to the provincial towns.

Even in good times, when the plague was dormant and the weather favorable for farming, the food supply in England was precarious. A few successive bad harvests, such as occurred in the mid-1590s, could cause serious hardship, even starvation. Not surprisingly, the poor bore the brunt of the burden: inflation, low wages, and rent increases left large numbers of people with very little cushion against disaster. Further, at its best, the diet of most people seems to have been seriously deficient. The lower classes then, as throughout most of history, subsisted on one or two foodstuffs, usually low in protein. The upper classes disdained green vegetables and milk and gorged themselves on meat. Illnesses that we now trace to vitamin deficiencies were rampant. Some but not much relief from pain was provided by the beer that Elizabethans, including children, drank almost incessantly. (Home brewing aside, enough beer was sold in England for every man, woman, and child to have consumed forty gallons a year.)

Wealth

Despite rampant disease, the population of England in Shakespeare's lifetime grew steadily, from approximately 3,060,000 in 1564 to 4,060,000 in 1600 and 4,510,000 in 1616. Though the death rate was more than twice what it is in England today, the birthrate was almost three times the current figure. London's population in particular soared, from 60,000 in 1520 to 120,000 in 1550, 200,000 in 1600, and 375,000 a half-century later, making it the largest and fastest-growing city not only in England but in all of Europe. Every year in the first half of the seventeenth century, about 10,000 people migrated to London from other parts of England—wages in London tended to be around 50 percent higher than in the rest of the country—and it is estimated that one in eight English people lived in London at some point in their lives. The economic viability of Shakespeare's profession was closely linked to this extraordinary demographic boom: between 1567 and 1642, theater historians have estimated, the London playhouses were paid anywhere between 50 and 75 million visits.

As these visits to the theater indicate, in the capital city and elsewhere a substantial number of English men and women, despite hardships that were never very distant, had money to spend. After the disorder and dynastic wars of the fifteenth century, England in the sixteenth and early seventeenth centuries was for the most part a nation at peace, and with peace came a measure of enterprise and prosperity: the landowning classes busied themselves building great houses, planting orchards and hop gardens, draining marshlands, bringing untilled acreage under cultivation. The artisans and laborers who actually accomplished these tasks, though they were generally paid very little, often managed to accumulate something, as did the small freeholding farmers, the yeomen, who are repeatedly celebrated in the period as the backbone of English national independence and well-being. William Harrison's *Description of Britain* (1577) lovingly itemizes the yeoman's precious possessions: "fair garnish of pewter on his cupboard, with so much more odd vessel going about the house, three or four featherbeds, so many coverlets and carpets of tapestry, a silver salt [cellar], a bowl for wine (if not a whole nest) and a dozen of spoons." There are comparable accounts of the hard-earned acquisitions of the city dwellers—masters and apprentices in small workshops, shipbuilders, wool merchants, cloth makers, chandlers, tradesmen, shopkeepers, along with lawyers, apothecaries, schoolteachers, scriveners, and the like—whose pennies from time to time enriched the coffers of the players.

The chief source of England's wealth in the sixteenth century was its textile industry, an industry that depended on a steady supply of wool. The market for English textiles was not only domestic. In 1565, woolen cloth alone made up more than three-fourths of England's exports. (The remainder consisted mostly of other textiles and raw wool, with some trade in lead, tin, grain, and skins.) The Company of Merchant Adventurers carried cloth not only to nearby countries like France, Holland, and Germany but also to distant ports on the Baltic and Mediterranean, establishing links with Russia and Morocco (each took about 2 percent of London's cloth in 1597–98). English lead and tin, as well as fabrics, were sold in Tuscany and Turkey, and merchants found a market for Newcastle coal on the island of Malta. In the latter half of the century, London, which handled more than 85 percent of all exports, regularly shipped abroad more than 100,000 woolen cloths a year, at a value of at least £750,000. This figure does not include the increasingly important and profitable trade in so-called New Draperies, including textiles that went by such exotic names as bombazines, callamancoes, damazellas, damizes, mockadoes, and virgenatoes. When the Earl of Kent in *King Lear* insults Oswald as a "filthy, worsted-stocking knave" (2.2.14–15) or when the aristocratic Biron in *Love's Labor's Lost* declares that he will give up "taffeta phrases, silken terms precise, / Three-piled hyperboles" and woo henceforth "in russet 'yeas,' and honest kersey 'noes'" (5.2.407–08, 414), Shakespeare is assuming that a substantial portion of his audience will be alert to the social significance of fabric.

There is amusing confirmation of this alertness from an unexpected source: the report of a visit made to the Fortune playhouse in London in 1614 by a foreigner, Father Orazio Busino, the chaplain of the Venetian embassy. Father Busino neglected to mention the name of the play he saw, but like many foreigners, he was powerfully struck by the presence of gorgeously dressed women in the audience. In Venice, there was a special gallery for courtesans, but socially respectable women would not have been permitted to attend plays, as they could in England. In London, not only could middle- and upper-class women go to the theater, but they could also wear masks and mingle freely with male spectators and women of ill repute. The bemused cleric was uncertain about the ambiguous social situation in which he found himself:

> These theaters are frequented by a number of respectable and handsome ladies, who come freely and seat themselves among the men without the slightest hesitation. On the evening in question his Excellency and the Secretary were pleased to play me a trick by placing me amongst a bevy of young women. Scarcely was I seated ere a very elegant dame, but in a mask, came and placed herself beside me. . . . She asked me for my address both in French and English; and, on my turning a deaf ear, she determined to honor me by showing me some fine diamonds on her fingers, repeatedly taking off not fewer than three gloves, which were worn one over the other. . . . This lady's bodice was of yellow satin richly embroidered, her petticoat of gold tissue with stripes, her robe of red velvet with a raised pile, lined with yellow muslin with broad stripes of pure gold. She wore an apron of point lace of various patterns: her head-tire was highly perfumed, and the collar of white satin beneath the delicately-wrought ruff struck me as extremely pretty.

Father Busino may have turned a deaf ear on this "elegant dame" but not a blind eye: his description of her dress is worthy of a fashion designer and conveys something of the virtual clothes cult that prevailed in England in the late sixteenth and early seventeenth centuries, a cult whose major shrine, outside the royal court, was the theater.

Imports, Patents, and Monopolies

England produced some luxury goods, but the clothing on the backs of the most fashionable theatergoers was likely to have come from abroad. By the late sixteenth century, the English were importing substantial quantities of silks, satins, velvets, embroidery, gold and silver lace, and other costly items to satisfy the extravagant tastes of the elite and of those who aspired to dress like the elite. The government tried to put a check on the sartorial ambitions of the upwardly mobile by passing sumptuary laws—that is, laws restricting to the ranks of the aristocracy the right to wear certain of the most precious fabrics. But the very existence of these laws, in practice almost impossible to enforce, only reveals the scope and significance of the perceived problem.

Sumptuary laws were in part a conservative attempt to protect the existing social order from upstarts. Social mobility was not widely viewed as a positive virtue, and moralists repeatedly urged people to stay in their place. Conspicuous consumption that was tolerated, even admired, in the aristocratic elite was denounced as sinful and monstrous in less exalted social circles. English authorities were also deeply concerned throughout the period about the effects of a taste for luxury goods on the balance of trade. One of the principal English imports was wine: the "sherris" whose virtues Falstaff extols in *2 Henry IV* came from Xeres in Spain; the malmsey in which poor Clarence is drowned in *Richard III* was probably made in Greece or in the Canary Islands (from whence came Sir Toby Belch's "cup of canary" in *Twelfth Night*); and the "flagon of rhenish" that Yorick in *Hamlet* had once poured on the Gravedigger's head came from the Rhine region of Germany. Other imports included canvas, linen, fish, olive oil, sugar, molasses, dates, oranges and lemons, figs, raisins, almonds, capers, indigo, ostrich feathers, and that increasingly popular drug tobacco.

Joint stock companies were established to import goods for the burgeoning English market. The Merchant Venturers of the City of Bristol (established in 1552) handled great shipments of Spanish sack, the light, dry wine that largely displaced the vintages of Bordeaux and Burgundy when trade with France was disrupted by war. The Muscovy Company (established in 1555) traded English cloth and manufactured goods for Russian furs, oil, and beeswax. The Venice Company and the Turkey Company—uniting in 1593 to form the wealthy Levant Company—brought silk and spices home from Aleppo and carpets from Constantinople. The East India Company (founded in 1600), with its agent at Bantam in Java, brought pepper, cloves, nutmeg, and other spices from East Asia, along with indigo, cotton textiles, sugar, and saltpeter from India. English privateers "imported" American products, especially sugar, fish, and hides, in huge quantities, along with more precious cargoes. In 1592, a privateering expedition principally funded by Sir Walter Ralegh captured a huge Portuguese carrack (sailing ship), the *Madre de Dios,* in the Azores and brought it back to Dartmouth. The ship, the largest that had ever entered any English port, held 536 tons of pepper, cloves, cinnamon, cochineal, mace, civet, musk, ambergris, and nutmeg, as well as jewels, gold, ebony, carpets, and silks. Before order could be established, the English seamen began to pillage this immensely rich prize, and witnesses said they could smell the spices on all the streets around the harbor. Such piratical expeditions were rarely officially sanctioned by the state, but the Queen had in fact privately invested £1,800, for which she received about £80,000.

In the years of war with Spain, 1586–1604, the goods captured by the privateers annually amounted to 10–15 percent of the total value of England's imports. But organized theft alone could not solve England's balance-of-trade problems. Statesmen were particularly worried that the nation's natural wealth was slipping away in exchange for unnecessary things. In his *Discourse of the Commonweal* (1549), the prominent humanist Sir Thomas Smith exclaims against the importation of such trifles as mirrors, paper, laces, gloves, pins, inkhorns, tennis balls, puppets, and playing cards. And more than a century later, the same fear that England was trading its riches for trifles and wasting away in idleness was expressed by the Bristol merchant John Cary. The solution, Cary argues in "An Essay on the State of England in Relation to Its Trade" (1695),

Forging a magnet, 1600. The metal on the anvil is aligned North/South (Septentrio/Auster). From *De Magnete* by William Gilbert.

is to expand productive domestic employment. "People are or may be the Wealth of a Nation," he writes, "yet it must be where you find Employment for them, else they are a Burden to it, as the Idle Drone is maintained by the Industry of the laborious Bee, so are all those who live by their Dependence on others, as Players, Ale-House Keepers, Common Fiddlers, and such like, but more particularly Beggars, who never set themselves to work."

Stage players, all too typically associated here with vagabonds and other idle drones, could have replied in their defense that they not only labored in their vocation but also exported their skills abroad: English actors routinely performed on the Continent. But their labor was not regarded as a productive contribution to the national wealth, and plays were in truth no solution to the trade imbalances that worried authorities.

The government attempted to stem the flow of gold overseas by establishing a patent system initially designed to encourage skilled foreigners to settle in England by granting them exclusive rights to produce particular wares by a patented method. Patents were granted for such things as the making of hard white soap (1561), ovens and furnaces (1563), window glass (1567), sailcloths (1574), drinking glasses (1574), sulfur, brimstone, and oil (1577), armor and horse harness (1587), starch (1588), white writing paper made from rags (1589), aqua vitae and vinegar (1594), playing cards (1598), and mathematical instruments (1598).

By the early seventeenth century, English men and women were working in a variety of new industries like soap making, pin making, knife making, and the brewing of alegar and beeregar (ale- and beer-based vinegar). But although the ostensible purpose of the government's economic policy was to increase the wealth of England, encourage technical innovation, and provide employment for the poor, the effect of patents was often the enrichment of a few and the hounding of poor competitors by wealthy monopolists, a group that soon extended well beyond foreign-born entrepreneurs to the favorites of the monarch who vied for the huge profits to be made. "If I had a monopoly out" on folly, the Fool in *King Lear* protests, glancing at the "lords and great men" around him, "they would have part in't." The passage appears only in the Quarto version of the play (*History of King Lear* 4.140–41); it may have been cut for political reasons from the Folio. For the issue of monopolies provoked bitter criticism and parliamentary debate for decades. In 1601, Elizabeth was prevailed upon to revoke a number of the most hated monopolies, including aqua vitae and vinegar, bottles, brushes, fish livers, the coarse sailcloth known as poldavis and mildernix, pots, salt, and starch. The whole system was revoked during the reign of James I by an act of Parliament.

Haves and Have-Nots

When in the 1560s Elizabeth's ambassador to France, Sir Thomas Smith, wrote a description of England, he saw the commonwealth as divided into four sorts of people: "gentlemen, citizens, yeomen artificers, and laborers." At the forefront of the class of gentlemen was the monarch, followed by a very small group of nobles—dukes, marquesses, earls, viscounts, and barons—who either inherited their exalted titles, as the eldest male heirs of their families, or were granted them by the monarch. Under Elizabeth, this aristocratic peerage numbered between 50 and 60 individuals; James's promotions increased the number to nearer 130. Strictly speaking, Smith notes, the younger sons of the nobility were only entitled to be called "esquires," but in common speech they were also called "lords."

Below this tiny cadre of aristocrats in the social hierarchy of gentry were the knights, a title of honor conferred by the monarch, and below them were the "simple gentlemen." Who was a gentleman? According to Smith, "whoever studieth the laws of the realm, who studieth in the universities, who professeth liberal sciences, and to be short, who can live idly and without manual labor, and will bear the port, charge and countenance of a gentleman, he shall be called master . . . and shall be taken for a gentleman." To "live idly and without manual labor": where in Spain, for example, the crucial mark of a gentleman was "blood," in England it was "idleness," in the sense of sufficient income to afford an education and to maintain a social position without having to work with one's hands.

For Smith, the class of gentlemen was far and away the most important in the kingdom. Below were two groups that had at least some social standing and claim to authority: the citizens, or burgesses, those who held positions of importance and responsibility in their cities, and yeomen, farmers with land and a measure of economic independence. At the bottom of the social order was what Smith calls "the fourth sort of men which do not rule." The great mass of ordinary people have, Smith writes, "no voice nor authority in our commonwealth, and no account is made of them but only to be ruled." Still, even they can bear some responsibility, he notes, since they serve on juries and are named to such positions as churchwarden and constable.

In everyday practice, as modern social historians have observed, the English tended to divide the population not into four distinct classes but into two: a very small empowered group—the "richer" or "wiser" or "better" sort—and all the rest who were without much social standing or power, the "poorer" or "ruder" or "meaner" sort. References to the "middle sort of people" remain relatively rare until after Shakespeare's lifetime; these people are absorbed into the rulers or the ruled, depending on speaker and context.

The source of wealth for most of the ruling class, and the essential measure of social status, was land ownership, and changes to the social structure in the sixteenth and seventeenth centuries were largely driven by the land market. The property that passed into private hands as the Tudors and early Stuarts sold off confiscated monastic estates and then their own crown lands for ready cash amounted to nearly a quarter of all the land in England. At the same time, the buying and selling of private estates was on the rise throughout the period. Land was bought up not only by established landowners seeking to enlarge their estates but also by successful merchants, manufacturers, and urban professionals; even if the taint of vulgar moneymaking lingered around such figures, their heirs would be taken for true gentlemen. The rate of turnover in land ownership was great; in many counties, well over half the gentle families in 1640 had appeared since the end of the fifteenth century. The class that Smith called "simple gentlemen" was expanding rapidly: in the fifteenth century, they had held no more than a quarter of the land in the country, but by the later seventeenth, they controlled almost half. Over the same period, the land held by the great aristocratic magnates held steady at 15–20 percent of the total.

Riot and Disorder

London was a violent place in the first half of Shakespeare's career. There were thirty-five riots in the city in the years 1581–1602, twelve of them in the volatile month of June 1595. These included protests against the deeply unpopular Lord Mayor Sir John Spencer, attempts to release prisoners, anti-alien riots, and incidents of "popular market regulation." There is an unforgettable depiction of a popular uprising in *Coriolanus*, along with many other glimpses in Shakespeare's works, including Jack Cade's grotesque rebellion in *2 Henry VI*, the plebeian violence in *Julius Caesar*, and Laertes' "riotous head" in *Hamlet*.

The London rioters were mostly drawn from the large mass of poor and discontented apprentices who typically chose as their scapegoats foreigners, prostitutes, and gentlemen's servingmen. Theaters were very often the site of the social confrontations that sparked disorder. For two days running in June 1584, disputes between apprentices and gentlemen triggered riots outside the Curtain Theater involving up to a thousand participants. On one occasion, a gentleman was said to have exclaimed that "the apprentice was but a rascal, and some there were little better than rogues that took upon them the name of gentlemen, and said the prentices were but the scum of the world." These occasions culminated in attacks by the apprentices on London's law schools, the Inns of Court.

The most notorious and predictable incidents of disorder came on Shrove Tuesday (the Tuesday before the beginning of Lent), a traditional day of misrule when apprentices ran riot. Shrove Tuesday disturbances involved attacks by mobs of young men on the brothels of the South Bank, in the vicinity of the Globe and other public theaters. The city authorities took precautions to keep these disturbances from getting completely out of control, but evidently did not regard them as serious threats to public order.

Of much greater concern throughout the Tudor and early Stuart years were the frequent incidents of rural rioting. Though in *The Winter's Tale* Shakespeare provides a richly comic portrayal of a rural sheepshearing festival, the increasingly intensive production of wool had its grim side. When a character in Thomas More's *Utopia* (1516) complains that "the sheep are eating the people," he is referring to the practice of enclosure: throughout the sixteenth and early seventeenth centuries, many acres of croplands once farmed in common by rural communities were fenced in by wealthy landowners and turned into pasturage. The ensuing misery, displacement, and food shortages led to repeated protests, some of them violent and bloody, along with a series of government proclamations, but the process of enclosure was not reversed. The protests were at their height during Shakespeare's career: in the years 1590–1610, the frequency of anti-enclosure rioting doubled from what it had been earlier in Elizabeth's reign.

Although they often became violent, anti-enclosure riots were usually directed not against individuals but against property. Villagers—sometimes several hundred, often fewer than a dozen—gathered to tear down newly planted hedges. The event often took place in a carnival atmosphere, with songs and drinking, that did not prevent the participants from acting with a good deal of political canniness and forethought. Especially in the Jacobean period, it was common for participants to establish a fund for legal defense before commencing their assault on the hedges. Women were frequently involved, and on a number of occasions wives alone participated in the destruction of the enclosure, since there was a widespread, though erroneous, belief that married women acting without the knowledge of their husbands were immune from prosecution. In fact, the powerful Court of Star Chamber consistently ruled that both the wives and their husbands should be punished.

Although Stratford was never the scene of serious rioting, enclosure controversies turned violent more than once in Shakespeare's lifetime. In January 1601, Shakespeare's friend Richard Quiney and others leveled the hedges of Sir Edward Greville, lord of Stratford manor. Quiney was elected bailiff of Stratford in September of that year but did not live to enjoy the office for long. He died from a blow to the head struck by one of Greville's men in a tavern brawl. Greville, responsible for the administration of justice, neglected to punish the murderer.

There was further violence in January 1615, when William Combe's men threw to the ground two local aldermen who were filling in a ditch by which Combe was enclosing common fields near Stratford. The task of filling in the offending ditch was completed the next day by the women and children of Stratford. Combe's enclosure scheme was eventually stopped in the courts. Though he owned land whose value would have been affected by this controversy, Shakespeare took no active role in it, since he had previously come to a private settlement with the enclosers insuring him against personal loss.

Most incidents of rural rioting were small, localized affairs, and with good reason: when confined to the village community, riot was a misdemeanor; when it spread outward to include multiple communities, it became treason, punishable by death. The greatest of

The Peddler. From Jost Amman, *The Book of Trades* (1568).

the anti-enclosure riots, those in which hundreds of individuals from a large area participated, commonly took place on the eve of full-scale regional rebellions. The largest of these disturbances, Kett's Rebellion, involved some 16,000 peasants, artisans, and townspeople who rose up in 1549 under the leadership of a Norfolk tanner and landowner, Robert Kett, to protest economic exploitation. The agrarian revolts in Shakespeare's lifetime were on a much smaller scale. In the abortive Oxfordshire Rebellion of 1596, a carpenter named Bartholomew Steer attempted to organize a rising against the hated enclosures. The optimistic Steer allegedly promised his followers that "it was but a month's work to overrun England" and informed them "that the commons long since in Spain did rise and kill all gentlemen . . . and since that time have lived merrily there." Steer expected several hundred men to join him on Enslow Hill on November 21, 1596, for the start of the rising; no more than twenty showed up. They were captured, imprisoned, and tortured. Several were executed, but Steer apparently cheated the hangman by dying in prison.

Rebellions, most often triggered by hunger and oppression, continued into the reign of James I. The Midland Revolt of 1607, which may be reflected in *Coriolanus*, consisted of a string of agrarian risings in the counties of Northamptonshire, Warwickshire, and Leicestershire, involving assemblies of up to five thousand rebels in various places. The best known of their leaders was John Reynolds, called "Captain Powch" because of the pouch he wore, whose magical contents were supposed to defend the rebels from harm. (According to the chronicler Edmund Howes, when Reynolds was captured and the pouch opened, it contained "only a piece of green cheese.") The rebels, who were called by themselves and others both "Levelers" and "Diggers," insisted that they had no quarrel with the King but only sought an end to injurious enclosures. But Robert Wilkinson, who preached a sermon against the leaders at their trial, credited them with the intention to "level all states as they leveled banks and ditches." Most of the rebels got off relatively lightly, but, along with other ringleaders, Captain Powch was executed.

The Legal Status of Women

English women were not under the full range of crushing constraints that afflicted women in some countries in Europe. Foreign visitors were struck by their relative freedom, as shown, for example, by the fact that respectable women could venture unchaperoned into the streets and attend the theater. Yet while England was ruled for over forty years by a powerful woman, the great majority of women in the kingdom had very restricted social, economic, and legal standing. To be sure, a tiny number of influential aristocratic women, such as the formidable Countess of Shrewsbury, Bess of Hardwick, wielded considerable power. But, these rare exceptions aside, women were denied any rightful claim to institutional authority or personal autonomy. When Sir Thomas Smith thinks of how he should describe his country's social order, he declares that "we do reject women, as those whom nature hath made to keep home and to nourish their family and children, and not to meddle with matters abroad, nor to bear office in a city or commonwealth." Then, with a kind of glance over his shoulder, he makes an exception of those few for whom "the blood is respected, not the age nor the sex": for example, the Queen.

Single women, whether widowed or unmarried, could, if they were of full age, inherit and administer land, make a will, sign a contract, possess property, sue and be sued, without a male guardian or proxy. But married women had no such rights under English common law, the system of law based on court decisions rather than on codified written laws. Early modern writings about women and the family constantly return to a political model of domination and submission, in which the husband and father justly rules over wife and children as the monarch rules over the state. The husband's dominance in the family was the justification for the common-law rule that prohibited married women from possessing property, administering land, signing contracts, or bringing lawsuits in their own names: married women were described as legally "covered" by their husbands. Yet this conception of a woman's role conveniently ignores the fact that a *majority* of the adult women at any time in Shakespeare's England were not married. They were either widows or spinsters (a term that was not yet pejorative), and thus for the most part managed their own affairs. Even within marriage, women typically had more control over certain spheres than moralizing writers on the family cared to admit. For example, village wives oversaw the production of eggs, cheese, and beer, and sold these goods in the market. As seamstresses, pawnbrokers, second-hand clothing dealers, peddlers and the like—activities not controlled by the all-male craft guilds–women managed to acquire some economic power of their own, and, of course, they participated as well in the unregulated, black-market economy of the age and in the underworld of thievery and prostitution.

Women were not in practice as bereft of property as, according to English common law, they should have been. Demographic studies indicate that the inheritance system called primogeniture, the orderly transmission of property from father to eldest male heir, was more often an unfulfilled wish than a reality. Some 40 percent of marriages failed to produce a son, and in such circumstances fathers often left their land to their daughters, rather than to brothers, nephews, or male cousins. In many families, the father died before his male heir was old enough to inherit property, leaving the land, at least temporarily, in the hands of the mother. And while they were less likely than their brothers to inherit land ("real property"), daughters normally inherited a substantial share of their parents' personal property (cash and movables).

In fact, the legal restrictions upon women, though severe in Shakespeare's time, actually worsened in subsequent decades. English common law was significantly less egalitarian in its approach to wives and daughters than were alternative legal codes (manorial, civil, and ecclesiastical) still in place in the late sixteenth century. The eventual triumph of common law stripped women of many traditional rights, slowly driving them out of economically productive trades and businesses.

Limited though it was, the economic freedom of Elizabethan and Jacobean women far exceeded their political and social freedom—the opportunity to receive a grammar school or university education, to hold office in church or state, to have a voice in public debates, or even simply to speak their mind fully and openly in ordinary conversation. Women who asserted their views too vigorously risked being perceived as shrewish and labeled "scolds." Both urban and rural communities had a horror of scolds. In the Elizabethan period, such women came to be regarded as a threat to public order, to be dealt with by the local authorities. The preferred methods of correction included public humiliation—of the sort Katherina endures in *The Taming of the Shrew*—and such physical abuse as slapping, bridling with a bit or muzzle, and half-drowning by means of a contraption called the "cucking stool" (or "ducking stool"). This latter punishment originated in the Middle Ages, but its use spread in the sixteenth century, when it became almost exclusively a punishment for women. From 1560 onward, cucking stools were built or renovated in many English provincial towns; between 1560 and 1600, the contraptions were installed by rivers or ponds in Norwich, Bridport, Shrewsbury, Kingston-upon-Thames, Marlborough, Devizes, Clitheroe, Thornbury, and Great Yarmouth.

Such punishment was usually intensified by a procession through the town to the sound of "rough music," the banging together of pots and pans. The same cruel festivity accompanied the "carting" or "riding" of those accused of being whores. In some parts of the country, villagers also took the law into their own hands, publicly shaming women who married men much younger than themselves or who beat or otherwise domineered over their husbands. One characteristic form of these charivaris, or rituals of shaming, was known in the West Country as the Skimmington Ride. Villagers would rouse the offending couple from bed with rough music and stage a raucous pageant in which a man, holding a distaff, would ride backward on a donkey, while his "wife" (another man dressed as a woman) struck him with a ladle. In these cases, the collective ridicule and indignation were evidently directed at least as much at the henpecked husband as at his transgressive wife.

Women and Print

Books published for a female audience surged in popularity in the late sixteenth century, reflecting an increase in female literacy. (It is striking how many of Shakespeare's women are shown reading.) This increase is probably linked to a Protestant longing for direct access to the Scriptures, and the new books marketed specifically for women included devotional manuals and works of religious instruction. But there were also practical guides to such subjects as female education (for example, Giovanni Bruto's *Necessary, Fit, and Convenient Education of a Young Gentlewoman*, 1598), midwifery (James Guillemeau's *Child-birth; or, the Happy Delivery of Women*, 1612), needlework (Federico di Vinciolo's *New and Singular Patterns and Works of Linen*, 1591), cooking (Thomas Dawson's *The Good Housewife's Jewel*, 1587), gardening (Pierre Erondelle's *The French Garden*, 1605), and married life (Patrick Hanney's *A Happy Husband; or, Directions for a Maid to Choose Her Mate*, 1619). As the authors' names suggest, many of these works were translations, and almost all were written by men.

Starting in the 1570s, writers and their publishers increasingly addressed works of recreational literature (romance, fiction, and poetry) partially or even exclusively to women. Some books, such as Robert Greene's *Mamillia, a Mirror or Looking-Glass for the Ladies of England* (1583), directly specified in the title their desired audience. Others, such as Sir Philip Sidney's influential and popular romance *Arcadia* (1590–93), solicited female readership in their dedicatory epistles. The ranks of Sidney's followers eventually included his own niece, Mary Wroth, whose romance *Urania* was published in 1621.

In the literature of Shakespeare's time, women readers were not only wooed but also frequently railed at, in a continuation of a popular polemical genre that had long inspired heated charges and countercharges. Both sides in the polemic generally agreed that it was the duty of women to be chaste, dutiful, and modest in demeanor; the argument was whether women fulfilled or fell short of this proper role. Ironically, then, a modern reader is more likely to find inspiring accounts of courageous women not in the books written in defense of female virtue but in attacks on those who refused to be silent and obedient.

The most famous English skirmish in this controversy took place in a rash of pamphlets at the end of Shakespeare's life. Joseph Swetnam's crude *Arraignment of Lewd, Idle, Froward, and Unconstant Women* (1615) provoked three fierce responses attributed to women: Rachel Speght's *A Muzzle for Melastomus*, Esther Sowernam's *Esther Hath Hang'd Haman*, and Constantia Munda's *Worming of a Mad Dog*, all in 1617. There was also an anonymous play, *Swetnam the Woman-Hater Arraigned by Women* (first performed around 1618), in which Swetnam, depicted as a braggart and a lecher, is put on trial by women and made to recant his misogynistic lies.

Prior to the Swetnam controversy, only one English woman, writing under the pseudonym "Jane Anger," had published a defense of women (*Jane Anger Her Protection for Women*, 1589). Learned women writers in the sixteenth century tended not to become involved in public debate but rather to undertake a project to which it was difficult for even obdurately chauvinistic males to object: the translation of devotional literature into English. Thomas More's daughter Margaret More Roper translated Erasmus (*A Devout Treatise upon the Pater Noster*, 1524); Francis Bacon's mother, Anne Cooke Bacon, translated Bishop John Jewel (*An Apology or Answer in Defence of the Church of England*, 1564); Anne Locke Prowse, a friend of John Knox, translated the *Sermons of John Calvin* in 1560; and Mary Sidney, the Countess of Pembroke, completed the metrical version of the Psalms that her brother Sir Philip

Sidney had begun. Elizabeth Tudor (the future queen) herself translated, at the age of eleven, Marguerite de Navarre's *Le Miroir de l'âme pécheresse* (*The Glass of the Sinful Soul*, 1544). The translation was dedicated to her stepmother, Katherine Parr, herself the author of a frequently reprinted book of prayers.

There was in the sixteenth and early seventeenth centuries a social stigma attached to print. Far from celebrating publication, authors, and particularly female authors, often apologized for exposing themselves to the public gaze. Nonetheless, a number of women ventured in print beyond pious translations. Some, including Elizabeth Tyrwhitt, Anne Dowriche, Isabella Whitney, Mary Sidney, and Aemilia Lanyer, composed and published their own poems. Aemilia Lanyer's *Salve Deus Rex Judaeorum*, published in 1611, is a poem in praise of virtuous women, from Eve and the Virgin Mary to her noble patron, the Countess of Cumberland. "A Description of Cookeham," appended to the poem, is one of the first English country house poems, a celebration in verse of an aristocrat's rural estate.

The first Tudor woman to translate a play was the learned Jane Lumley, who composed an English version of Euripides' *Iphigenia at Aulis* (ca. 1550). The first known original play in English by a woman was by Elizabeth Cary, Viscountess Falkland, whose *Tragedy of Mariam, the Fair Queen of Jewry* was published in 1613. This remarkable play, which was not intended to be performed, includes speeches in defense of women's equality, though the most powerful of these is spoken by the villainous Salome, who schemes to divorce her husband and marry her lover. Cary, who bore

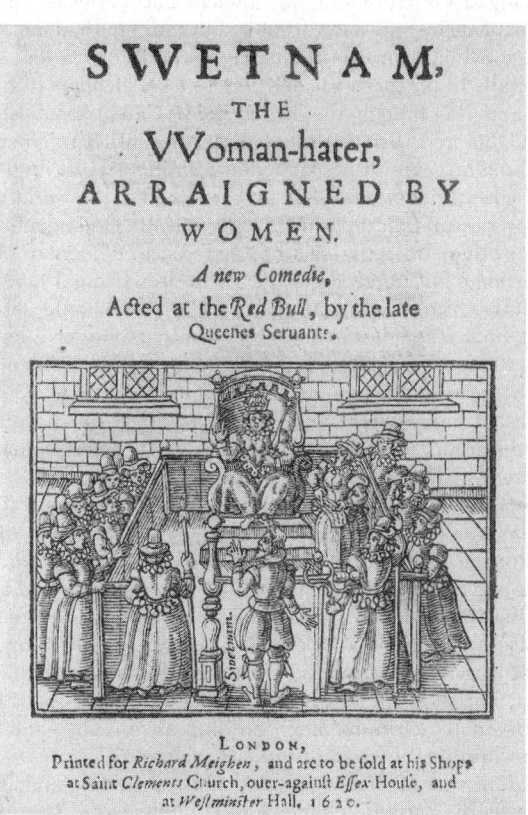

Title page of *Swetnam the Woman-Hater, Arraigned by Women* (1620), a play written in response to Joseph Swetnam's *The Arraignment of Lewd, Idle, Forward, and Unconstant Women* (1615); the woodcut depicts the trial of Swetnam in act 4.

eleven children, herself had a deeply troubled marriage, which effectively came to an end in 1625 when, defying her husband's staunchly Protestant family, she openly converted to Catholicism. Her biography was written by one of her four daughters, all of whom became nuns.

Henry VIII and the English Reformation

There had long been serious ideological and institutional tensions in the religious life of England, but officially, at least, England in the early sixteenth century had a single religion, Catholicism, whose acknowledged head was the pope in Rome. In 1517, drawing upon long-standing currents of dissent, Martin Luther, an Augustinian monk and professor of theology at the University of Wittenberg, challenged the authority of the pope and attacked several key doctrines of the Catholic Church. According to Luther, the Church, with its elaborate hierarchical structure centered in Rome, its rich monasteries and convents, and its enormous political influence, had become hopelessly corrupt, a conspiracy of venal priests who manipulated popular superstitions to enrich themselves and amass worldly power. Luther began by vehemently attacking the sale of indulgences—certificates promising the remission of punishments to be suffered in the afterlife by souls sent to purgatory to expiate their sins. These indulgences were a fraud, he argued; purgatory itself had no foundation in the Bible, which in his view was the only legitimate source of religious truth. Christians would be saved not by scrupulously following the ritual practices fostered by the Catholic Church—observing fast days, reciting the ancient Latin prayers, endowing chantries to say prayers for the dead, and so on—but by faith and faith alone.

This challenge, which came to be known as the Reformation, spread and gathered force, especially in northern Europe, where major leaders like the Swiss pastor Ulrich Zwingli and the French theologian John Calvin established institutional structures and elaborated various and sometimes conflicting doctrinal principles. Calvin, whose thought came to be particularly influential in England, emphasized the obligation of governments to implement God's will in the world. He advanced too the doctrine of predestination, by which, as he put it, "God adopts some to hope of life and sentences others to eternal death." God's "secret election" of the saved made Calvin uncomfortable, but his study of the Scriptures had led him to conclude that "only a small number, out of an incalculable multitude, should obtain salvation." It might seem that such a conclusion would lead to passivity or even despair, but for Calvin predestination was a mystery bound up with faith, confidence, and an active engagement in the fashioning of a Christian community.

The Reformation had a direct and powerful impact on those territories, especially in northern Europe, where it gained control. Monasteries, many of them fabulously wealthy, were sacked, their possessions and extensive landholdings seized by princes or sold off to the highest bidder; the monks and nuns, expelled from their cloisters, were encouraged to break their vows of chastity and find spouses, as Luther and his wife, a former nun, had done. In the great cathedrals and in hundreds of smaller churches and chapels, the elaborate altarpieces, bejeweled crucifixes, crystal reliquaries holding the bones of saints, and venerated statues and paintings were attacked as "idols" and often defaced or destroyed. Protestant congregations continued, for the most part, to celebrate the most sacred Christian ritual, the Eucharist, or Lord's Supper, but they did so in a profoundly different spirit from that of the Catholic Church—more as commemoration than as miracle—and they now prayed not in the ancient liturgical Latin but in the vernacular.

The Reformation was at first vigorously resisted in England. Indeed, with the support of his ardently Catholic chancellor, Thomas More, Henry VIII personally wrote (or at least lent his name to) a vehement, often scatological attack on Luther's character and views, an attack for which the pope granted him the honorific title "Defender of the Faith." Protestant writings, including translations of the Scriptures into English, were seized by officials of the church and state and burned. Protestants who made their views known were persecuted, driven to flee the country, or arrested, put on trial, and burned at the stake. But the situation changed drastically and decisively when in 1527 Henry decided to seek an annulment from his first wife, Catherine of Aragon, in order to marry Anne Boleyn.

Catherine had given birth to six children, but since only a daughter, Mary, survived infancy, Henry did not have the son he craved. Then as now, the Catholic Church did not ordinarily grant divorce, but Henry's lawyers argued on technical grounds that the marriage was invalid (and therefore, by extension, that Mary was illegitimate and hence unable to inherit the throne). Matters of this kind were far less doctrinal than diplomatic: Catherine, the daughter of Ferdinand of Aragon and Isabella of Castile, had powerful allies in Rome, and the pope ruled against Henry's petition. A series of momentous events followed, as England lurched away from the Church of Rome. In 1531, Henry charged the entire clergy of England with having usurped royal authority in the administration of canon law (the ecclesiastical law that governed faith, discipline, and morals, including such matters as divorce). Under extreme pressure, including the threat of mass confiscations and imprisonment, the Convocation of the Clergy begged for pardon, made a donation to the royal coffers of over £100,000, and admitted that the King was "supreme head of the English Church and clergy" (modified by the rider "as far as the law of Christ allows"). On May 15 of the next year, the convocation submitted to the demand that the King be the final arbiter of canon law; on the next day, Thomas More resigned his post.

In 1533, Henry's marriage to Catherine was officially declared null and void, and on June 1 Anne Boleyn was crowned queen (a coronation Shakespeare depicts in his late play *Henry VIII*). The King was promptly excommunicated by Pope Clement VII. In the following year, the parliamentary Act of Succession confirmed the effects of the annulment and required an oath from all adult male subjects confirming the new dynastic settlement. Thomas More and John Fisher, the Bishop of Rochester, were among the small number who refused. The Act of Supremacy, passed later in the year, formally declared the King to be "Supreme Head of the Church in England" and again required an oath to this effect. In 1535 and 1536, further acts made it treasonous to refuse the oath of royal supremacy or, as More had tried to do, to remain silent. The first victims were three Carthusian monks who rejected the oath—"How could the King, a layman," said one of them, "be Head of the Church of

The Pope as Antichrist riding the Beast of the Apocalypse. From *Fiery Trial of God's Saints* (1611; author unknown).

England?"—and in May 1535, they were duly hanged, drawn, and quartered. A few weeks later, Fisher and More were convicted and beheaded. Between 1536 and 1539, the monasteries were suppressed and their vast wealth seized by the crown.

Royal defiance of the authority of Rome was a key element in the Reformation but did not by itself constitute the establishment of Protestantism in England. On the contrary, in the same year that Fisher and More were martyred for their adherence to Roman Catholicism, twenty-five Protestants, members of a sect known as Anabaptists, were burned for heresy on a single day. Through most of his reign, Henry remained an equal-opportunity persecutor, ruthless to Catholics loyal to Rome but also hostile to some of those who espoused Reformation ideas, though many of these ideas gradually established themselves on English soil.

Even when Henry was eager to do so, it proved impossible to eradicate Protestantism, as it would later prove impossible for his successors to eradicate Catholicism. In large part this tenacity arose from the passionate, often suicidal heroism of men and women who felt that their souls' salvation depended on the precise character of their Christianity. It arose too from a mid-fifteenth-century technological innovation that made it almost impossible to suppress unwelcome ideas: the printing press. Early Protestants quickly grasped that with a few clandestine presses they could defy the Catholic authorities and flood the country with their texts. "How many printing presses there be in the world," wrote the Protestant polemicist John Foxe, "so many blockhouses there be against the high castle" of the pope in Rome, "so that either the pope must abolish knowledge and printing or printing at length will root him out." By the century's end, it was the Catholics who were using the clandestine press to propagate their beliefs in the face of Protestant persecution.

The greatest insurrection of the Tudor age was not over food, taxation, or land but over religion. On Sunday, October 1, 1536, stirred up by their vicar, the traditionalist parishioners of Louth in Lincolnshire, in the north of England, rose up in defiance of the ecclesiastical delegation sent to enforce royal supremacy. The rapidly spreading rebellion, which became known as the Pilgrimage of Grace, was led by the lawyer Robert Aske. The city of Lincoln fell to the rebels on October 6, and though it was soon retaken by royal forces, the rebels seized cities and fortifications throughout Yorkshire, Durham, Northumberland, Cumberland, Westmoreland, and northern Lancashire. Carlisle, Newcastle, and a few castles were all that were left to the King in the north. The Pilgrims soon numbered 40,000, led by some of the region's most prominent noblemen. The Duke of Norfolk, representing the crown, was forced to negotiate a truce, with a promise to support the rebels' demands that the King restore the monasteries, shore up the regional economy, suppress heresy, and dismiss his evil advisers. The Pilgrims kept the peace for the rest of 1536, on the naive assumption that their demands would be met. But Henry moved suddenly early in 1537 to impose order and capture the ringleaders; 130 people, including lords, knights, heads of religious houses, and, of course, Robert Aske, were executed.

In 1549, two years after the death of Henry VIII, the west and north of England were the sites of further unsuccessful risings for the restoration of Catholicism. The Western Rising is striking for its blend of Catholic universalism and intense regionalism among people who did not yet regard themselves as English. One of the rebels' articles, protesting against the imposition of the English Bible and religious service, declares, "We the Cornish men (whereof certain of us understand no English) utterly refuse this new English." The rebels besieged but failed to take the city of Exeter. As with almost all Tudor rebellions, the number of those executed in the aftermath of the failed rising was far greater than those killed in actual hostilities.

The Children of Henry VIII: Edward, Mary, and Elizabeth

Upon Henry's death in 1547, his ten-year-old son, Edward VI, came to the throne, with his maternal uncle Edward Seymour named as Duke of Somerset and Lord

Protector (regent while the King was still a minor). Both Edward and his uncle were staunch Protestants, and reformers hastened to transform the English church accordingly. During Edward's reign, Archbishop Thomas Cranmer formulated the forty-two articles of religion that became the core of Anglican orthodoxy and wrote the first Book of Common Prayer, which was officially adopted in 1549 as the basis of English worship services.

Somerset fell from power in 1549 and was replaced as Lord Protector by John Dudley, later Duke of Northumberland. When Edward fell seriously ill, probably of tuberculosis, Northumberland persuaded him to sign a will depriving his half-sisters Mary (the daughter of Catherine of Aragon) and Elizabeth (the daughter of Anne Boleyn) of their claim to royal succession. The Lord Protector was scheming to have his daughter-in-law, the Protestant Lady Jane Grey, a great-granddaughter of Henry VII, ascend to the throne. But when Edward died in 1553, Mary marshaled support, quickly secured the crown from Lady Jane (who had been titular queen for nine days), and had Lady Jane executed, along with her husband and Northumberland.

Queen Mary immediately took steps to return her kingdom to Roman Catholicism. Though she was unable to get Parliament to agree to return church lands seized under Henry VIII, she restored the Catholic Mass, once again affirmed the authority of the pope, and put down a rebellion that sought to depose her. Seconded by her ardently Catholic husband, Philip II, King of Spain, she initiated a series of religious persecutions that earned her (from her enemies) the name "Bloody Mary." Hundreds of Protestants took refuge abroad in cities such as Calvin's Geneva; almost three hundred less fortunate Protestants were condemned as heretics and burned at the stake.

Mary died childless in 1558, and her younger half-sister Elizabeth became queen. Elizabeth's succession had been by no means assured. For if Protestants regarded the marriage of Henry VIII to Catherine as invalid and hence deemed Mary illegitimate, so Catholics regarded his marriage to Anne Boleyn as invalid and deemed Elizabeth illegitimate. Henry VIII himself seemed to support both views, since only

The Family of Henry VIII: An Allegory of the Tudor Succession, by Lucas de Heere (ca. 1572). Henry, in the middle, is flanked by Mary to his right, and Edward and Elizabeth to his left.

three years after divorcing Catherine, he beheaded Anne Boleyn on charges of treason and adultery and urged Parliament to invalidate the marriage. Moreover, though
during her sister's reign Elizabeth outwardly complied with the official Catholic
religious observance, Mary and her advisers were deeply suspicious, and the young
princess's life was in grave danger. Poised and circumspect, Elizabeth warily evaded
the traps that were set for her. As she ascended the throne, her actions were scrutinized for some indication of the country's future course. During her coronation procession, when a girl in an allegorical pageant presented her with a Bible in English
translation—banned under Mary's reign—Elizabeth kissed the book, held it up reverently, and laid it to her breast; when the abbot and monks of Westminster Abbey
came to greet her in broad daylight with candles (a symbol of Catholic devotion) in
their hands, she briskly dismissed them with the telling words "Away with those
torches! We can see well enough." England had returned to the Reformation.

Many English men and women, of all classes, remained inwardly loyal to the old
Catholic faith; Shakespeare's father and mother may well have been among these.
But English authorities under Elizabeth moved steadily, if cautiously, toward ensuring at least an outward conformity to the official Protestant settlement. Recusants,
those who refused to attend regular Sunday services in their parish churches, were
fined heavily. Anyone who wished to receive a university degree, to be ordained as a
priest in the Church of England, or to be named as an officer of the state had to swear
an oath to the royal supremacy. Commissioners were sent throughout the land to
confirm that religious services were following the officially approved liturgy and to
investigate any reported backsliding into Catholic practice or, alternatively, any
attempts to introduce more radical reforms than the Queen and her bishops had chosen to embrace. For many of the Protestant exiles who streamed back to England
were eager not only to undo the damage Mary had done but to carry the Reformation
much further. They sought to dismantle the church hierarchy, to purge the calendar
of folk customs deemed pagan and the church service of ritual practices deemed
superstitious, to dress the clergy in simple garb, and, at the extreme edge, to smash
"idolatrous" statues, crucifixes, and altarpieces. Pressing for a stricter code of life
and a simplified system of worship, the religious radicals came to be called Puritans.
Throughout her long reign, however, Elizabeth herself remained cautiously conservative and determined to hold in check what she regarded as the religious zealotry of
Catholics, on the one side, and Puritans, on the other.

Shakespeare's plays tap into the ongoing confessional tensions: "sometimes," Maria
in *Twelfth Night* says of the sober, festivity-hating steward Malvolio, "he is a kind of
puritan" (2.3.129). But the plays tend to avoid the risks of direct engagement: "The devil
a puritan that he is, or anything constantly," Maria adds a moment later, "but a time-
pleaser" (2.3.135–36). *The Winter's Tale* features a statue that comes to life—exactly
the kind of magical image that Protestant polemicists excoriated as Catholic superstition and idolatry—but the play is set in the pre-Christian world of the Delphic Oracle.
And as if this careful distancing might not be enough, the play's ruler goes out of his
way to pronounce the wonder legitimate: "If this be magic, let it be an art / Lawful as
eating" (5.3.110–11).

In the space of a single lifetime, England had gone officially from Roman Catholicism, to Catholicism under the supreme headship of the English king, to a guarded
Protestantism, to a more radical Protestantism, to a renewed and aggressive Roman
Catholicism, and finally to Protestantism again. Each of these shifts was accompanied by danger, persecution, and death. It was enough to make some people wary. Or
skeptical. Or extremely agile.

The English Bible

Luther had undertaken a fundamental critique of the Catholic Church's sacramental
system, a critique founded on the twin principles of salvation by faith alone (*sola fide*)

and the absolute primacy of the Bible (*sola scriptura*). *Sola fide* contrasted faith with "works," by which was meant primarily the whole elaborate system of rituals sanctified, conducted, or directed by the priests. Protestants proposed to modify or reinterpret many of these rituals or, as with the rituals associated with purgatory, to abolish them altogether. *Sola scriptura* required direct lay access to the Bible, which meant in practice the widespread availability of vernacular translations. The Roman Catholic Church had not always and everywhere opposed such translations, but it generally preferred that the populace encounter the Scriptures through the interpretations of the priests, trained to read the Latin translation known as the Vulgate. In times of great conflict, this preference for clerical mediation hardened into outright prohibition of vernacular translation and into persecution and book burning.

Zealous Protestants set out, in the teeth of fierce opposition, to put the Bible into the hands of the laity. A remarkable translation of the New Testament, by an English Lutheran named William Tyndale, was printed on the Continent and smuggled into England in 1525; Tyndale's translation of the Pentateuch, the first five books of the Hebrew Bible, followed in 1530. Many copies of these translations were seized and burned, as was the translator himself, but the printing press made it extremely difficult for authorities to eradicate books for which there was a passionate demand. The English Bible was a force that could not be suppressed, and it became, in its various forms, the single most important book of the sixteenth century.

Tyndale's translation was completed by an associate, Miles Coverdale, whose rendering of the Psalms proved to be particularly influential. Their joint labor was the basis for the Great Bible (1539), the first authorized version of the Bible in English, a copy of which was ordered to be placed in every church in the kingdom. With the accession of Edward VI, many editions of the Bible followed, but the process was sharply reversed when Mary came to the throne in 1553. Along with people condemned as heretics, English Bibles were burned in great bonfires.

Marian persecution was indirectly responsible for what would become the most popular as well as most scholarly English Bible, the translation known as the Geneva Bible (1560), prepared, with extensive, learned, and often fiercely polemical marginal notes, by English exiles in Calvin's Geneva and widely diffused in England after Elizabeth came to the throne. In addition, Elizabethan church authorities ordered a careful revision of the Great Bible, and this version, known as the Bishops' Bible (1568), was the one read in the churches. The success of the Geneva Bible in particular prompted those Elizabethan Catholics who now in turn found themselves in exile to bring out a vernacular translation of their own in order to counter the Protestant readings and glosses. This Catholic translation, the so-called Rheims Bible (1582), may have been known to Shakespeare, but he seems to have been far better acquainted with the Geneva Bible, and he would also have repeatedly heard the Bishops' Bible read aloud. Scholars have identified over three hundred references to the Bible in Shakespeare's work; in one version or another, the Scriptures had a powerful impact on his imagination.

A Female Monarch in a Male World

In the last year of Mary's reign, 1558, the Scottish Calvinist minister John Knox thundered against what he called "the monstrous regiment of women." When the Protestant Elizabeth came to the throne the following year, Knox and his religious brethren were less inclined to denounce female rulers, but in England as elsewhere in Europe there remained a widespread conviction that women were unsuited to wield power over men. Many men seem to have regarded the capacity for rational thought as exclusively male; women, they assumed, were led only by their passions. While gentlemen mastered the arts of rhetoric and warfare, gentlewomen were expected to display the virtues of silence and good housekeeping. Among upper-class males, the will to dominate others was acceptable and indeed admired; the same will in women was condemned as a grotesque and dangerous aberration.

The Armada portrait: note Elizabeth's hand on the globe.

Apologists for the Queen countered these prejudices by appealing to historical precedent and legal theory. History offered inspiring examples of just female rulers, notably Deborah, the biblical prophetess who judged Israel. In the legal sphere, crown lawyers advanced the theory of "the king's two bodies." As England's crowned head, Elizabeth's person was mystically divided between her mortal "body natural" and the immortal "body politic." While the queen's natural body was inevitably subject to the failings of human flesh, the body politic was timeless and perfect. In political terms, therefore, Elizabeth's sex was a matter of no consequence, a thing indifferent.

Elizabeth, who had received a fine humanist education and an extended, dangerous lesson in the art of survival, made it immediately clear that she intended to rule in more than name only. She assembled a group of trustworthy advisers, foremost among them William Cecil (later named Lord Burghley), but she insisted on making many of the crucial decisions herself. Like many Renaissance monarchs, Elizabeth was drawn to the idea of royal absolutism, the theory that ultimate power was properly concentrated in her person and indeed that God had appointed her to be his deputy in the kingdom. Opposition to her rule, in this view, was not only a political act but also a kind of impiety, a blasphemous grudging against the will of God. Apologists for absolutism contended that God commands obedience even to manifestly wicked rulers whom he has sent to punish the sinfulness of humankind. Such arguments were routinely made in speeches and political tracts and from the pulpits of churches, where they were incorporated into the Book of Homilies, which clergymen were required to read out to their congregations.

In reality, Elizabeth's power was not absolute. The government had a network of spies, informers, and agents provocateurs, but it lacked a standing army, a national police force, an efficient system of communication, and an extensive bureaucracy. Above all, the Queen had limited financial resources and needed to turn periodically to an independent and often recalcitrant Parliament, which by long tradition had the sole right to levy taxes and to grant subsidies. Members of the House of Commons were elected from their boroughs, not appointed by the monarch, and though the Queen had considerable influence over their decisions, she could by no means dictate policy. Under these constraints, Elizabeth ruled through a combination of adroit political maneuvering and imperious command, all the while enhancing her authority in the eyes of both court and country by means of an extraordinary cult of love.

"We all loved her," Elizabeth's godson Sir John Harington wrote, with just a touch of irony, a few years after the Queen's death, "for she said she loved us." Ambassadors, courtiers, and parliamentarians all submitted to Elizabeth's cult of love, in which the Queen's gender was transformed from a potential liability into a significant asset. Those who approached her generally did so on their knees and were expected to address her with extravagant compliments fashioned from the period's most passionate love poetry; she in turn spoke, when it suited her to do so, in the language of love poetry. The court moved in an atmosphere of romance, with music, dancing, plays, and the elaborate, fancy-dress entertainments called masques. The Queen adorned herself in gorgeous clothes and rich jewels. When she went on one of her summer "progresses," ceremonial journeys through her land, she looked like an exotic, sacred image in a religious cult of love, and her noble hosts virtually bankrupted themselves to lavish upon her the costliest pleasures. England's leading artists, such as the poet Edmund Spenser and the painter Nicholas Hilliard, enlisted themselves in the celebration of Elizabeth's mystery, likening her to the goddesses of classical mythology: Diana, Astraea, Phoebe, Flora. Her cult drew its power from cultural discourses that ranged from the secular (her courtiers could pine for her as a chaste, unattainable maiden) to the sacred (the veneration that under Catholicism had been due to the Virgin Mary could now be directed toward England's semidivine queen).

There was a sober, even grim aspect to these poetical fantasies: Elizabeth was brilliant at playing one dangerous faction off against another, now turning her gracious smiles on one favorite, now honoring his hated rival, now suddenly looking elsewhere and raising an obscure upstart to royal favor. And when she was disobeyed or when she felt that her prerogatives had been challenged, she was capable of an anger that, as Harington put it, "left no doubtings whose daughter she was." Thus when Sir Walter Ralegh, one of the Queen's glittering favorites, married without her knowledge or consent, he found himself promptly imprisoned in the Tower of London. And when the Protestant polemicist John Stubbs ventured to publish a pamphlet stridently denouncing the Queen's proposed marriage to the French Catholic Duke of Alençon, Stubbs and his publisher were arrested and had their right hands chopped off. (After receiving the blow, the now prudent Stubbs lifted his hat with his remaining hand and cried, "God save the Queen!")

The Queen's marriage negotiations were a particularly fraught issue. When she came to the throne at twenty-five years old, speculation about a suitable match, already widespread, intensified and remained for decades at a fever pitch, for the stakes were high. If Elizabeth died childless, the Tudor line would come to an end. The nearest heir was her cousin Mary, Queen of Scots, a Catholic whose claim was supported by France and by the papacy and whose penchant for sexual and political intrigue confirmed the worst fears of English Protestants. The obvious way to avert the nightmare was for Elizabeth to marry and produce an heir, and the pressure upon her to do so was intense.

More than the royal succession hinged on the question of the Queen's marriage; Elizabeth's perceived eligibility was a vital factor in the complex machinations of international diplomacy. A dynastic marriage between the Queen of England and a foreign ruler would forge an alliance powerful enough to alter the balance of power in Europe. The English court hosted a steady stream of ambassadors from kings and princes eager to win the hand of the royal maiden, and Elizabeth, who prided herself on speaking fluent French and Italian (and on reading Latin and Greek), played her romantic part with exemplary skill, sighing and spinning the negotiations out for months and even years. Most probably, she never meant to marry any of her numerous foreign (and domestic) suitors. Such a decisive act would have meant the end of her independence, as well as the end of the marriage game by which she played one power off against another. One day she would seem to be on the verge of accepting a proposal; the next, she would vow never to forsake her virginity. "She is a princess," the French ambassador remarked, "who can act any part she pleases."

The Kingdom in Danger

Beset by Catholic and Protestant extremists, Elizabeth contrived to forge a moderate compromise that enabled her realm to avert the massacres and civil wars that poisoned France and other countries on the Continent. But menace was never far off, and there were constant fears of conspiracy, rebellion, and assassination. Many of the fears swirled around Mary, Queen of Scots, who had been driven from her own kingdom in 1568 by a powerful faction of rebellious nobles and had taken refuge in England. Her presence, under a kind of house arrest, was a source of intense anxiety and helped generate continual rumors of plots. Some of these plots were real enough, others imaginary, still others traps set in motion by the secret agents of the government's intelligence service under the direction of Sir Francis Walsingham. The situation worsened greatly after Spanish imperial armies invaded the Netherlands in order to stamp out Protestant rebels (1567), after the St. Bartholomew's Day Massacre of Protestants (Huguenots) in France (1572), and after the assassination there of Europe's other major Protestant leader, William of Orange (1584).

The Queen's life seemed to be in even greater danger after the proclamation of Pope Gregory XIII in 1580 that the assassination of the great heretic Elizabeth (who had been excommunicated a decade before) would not constitute a mortal sin. The immediate effect of the proclamation was to make existence more difficult for English Catholics, most of whom were loyal to the Queen but who fell under grave suspicion. Suspicion was intensified by the clandestine presence of English Jesuits, trained at seminaries abroad and smuggled back into England to serve the Roman Catholic cause. When Elizabeth's spymaster Walsingham unearthed an assassination plot in the correspondence between the Queen of Scots and the Catholic Anthony Babington, the wretched Mary's fate was sealed. After vacillating, a very reluctant Elizabeth signed the death warrant in February 1587, and her cousin was beheaded.

The long-anticipated military confrontation with Catholic Spain was now unavoidable. Elizabeth learned that Philip II, her former brother-in-law and onetime suitor, was preparing to send an enormous fleet against her island realm. It was to sail to the Netherlands, where a Spanish army would be waiting to embark and invade England. Barring its way was England's small fleet of well-armed and highly maneuverable fighting vessels, backed up by ships from the merchant navy. The Invincible Armada reached English waters in July 1588, only to be routed in one of the most famous and decisive naval battles in European history. Then, in what many viewed as an act of God on behalf of Protestant England, the Spanish fleet was dispersed and all but destroyed by violent storms.

As England braced itself to withstand the invasion that never came, Elizabeth appeared in person to review a detachment of soldiers assembled at Tilbury. Dressed in a white gown and a silver breastplate, she declared that though some among her councillors had urged her not to appear before a large crowd of armed men, she would never fail to trust the loyalty of her faithful and loving subjects. Nor did she fear the Spanish armies. "I know I have the body of a weak and feeble woman," Elizabeth declared, "but I have the heart and stomach of a king, and of England too." In this celebrated speech, Elizabeth displayed many of her most memorable qualities: her self-consciously histrionic command of grand public occasion, her subtle blending of magniloquent rhetoric and the language of love, her strategic appropriation of traditionally masculine qualities, and her great personal courage. "We princes," she once remarked, "are set on stages in the sight and view of all the world."

The English and Otherness

Shakespeare's London had a large population of resident aliens, mainly artisans and merchants and their families, from Portugal, Italy, Spain, Germany, and above all France and the Netherlands. Many of these people were Protestant refugees, and they were accorded some legal and economic protection by the government. But they were not always welcomed by the local populace. Throughout the sixteenth century, London was the site of repeated demonstrations and, on occasion, bloody riots against the communities of foreign artisans, who were accused of taking jobs away from Englishmen. There was widespread hostility as well toward the Welsh, the Scots, and especially the Irish, whom the English had for centuries been struggling unsuccessfully to subdue. The kings of England claimed to be rulers of Ireland, but in reality they effectively controlled only a small area known as the Pale, extending north from Dublin. The great majority of the Irish people remained stubbornly Catholic and, despite endlessly reiterated English repression, burning of villages, destruction of crops, and massacres, incorrigibly independent.

Shakespeare's *Henry V* (1598–99) seems to invite the audience to celebrate the conjoined heroism of English, Welsh, Scots, and Irish soldiers all fighting together as a "band of brothers" against the French. But such a way of imagining the national community must be set against the tensions and conflicting interests that often set these brothers at each other's throats. As Shakespeare's King Henry realizes, a feared or hated foreign enemy helps at least to mask these tensions, and indeed, in the face of the Spanish Armada, even the bitter gulf between Catholic and Protestant Englishmen seemed to narrow significantly. But the patriotic alliance was only temporary.

Another way of partially masking the sharp differences in language, belief, and custom among the peoples of the British Isles was to group these people together in contrast to the Jews. Medieval England's Jewish population, the recurrent object of persecution, extortion, and massacre, had been officially expelled by King Edward I in 1290. Therefore few if any of Shakespeare's contemporaries would have encountered on English soil Jews who openly practiced their religion. Elizabethan England probably did, however, harbor a small number of so-called Marranos, Spanish or Portuguese Jews who had officially converted to Christianity but secretly continued to observe Jewish practices. One of those suspected to be Marranos was Elizabeth's own physician, Roderigo Lopez, who was tried in 1594 for an alleged plot to poison the Queen. Convicted and condemned to the hideous execution reserved for traitors, Lopez went to his death, in the words of the Elizabethan historian

A Jewish man depicted poisoning a well. From Pierre Boaistuau, *Certain Secret Wonders of Nature* (1569).

William Camden, "affirming that he loved the Queen as well as he loved Jesus Christ; which coming from a man of the Jewish profession moved no small laughter in the standers-by." It is difficult to gauge the meaning here of the phrase "the Jewish profession," used to describe a man who never as far as we know professed Judaism, just as it is difficult to gauge the meaning of the crowd's cruel laughter.

Elizabethans appear to have been fascinated by Jews and Judaism but quite uncertain whether the terms referred to a people, a foreign nation, a set of strange practices, a living faith, a defunct religion, a villainous conspiracy, or a messianic inheritance. Protestant reformers brooded deeply on the Hebraic origins of Christianity; government officials ordered the arrest of those "suspected to be Jews"; villagers paid pennies to itinerant fortune-tellers who claimed to be descended from Abraham or masters of cabalistic mysteries; and London playgoers, perhaps including some who laughed at Lopez on the scaffold, enjoyed the spectacle of the downfall of the wicked Barabas in Christopher Marlowe's *Jew of Malta* (ca. 1589) and the forced conversion of Shylock in Shakespeare's *Merchant of Venice* (1596–97). Jews were not officially permitted to resettle in England until the middle of the seventeenth century, and even then their legal status was ambiguous.

Shakespeare's England also had a small African population whose skin color was the subject of pseudo-scientific speculation and theological debate. Some Elizabethans believed that Africans' blackness resulted from the climate of the regions in which they lived, where, as one traveler put it, they were "so scorched and vexed with the heat of the sun, that in many places they curse it when it riseth." Others held that blackness was a curse inherited from their forefather Chus, the son of Ham, who had, according to Genesis, wickedly exposed the nakedness of the drunken Noah. George Best, a proponent of this theory of inherited skin color, reported that "I myself have seen an Ethiopian as black as coal brought into England, who taking a fair English woman to wife, begat a son in all respects as black as the father was, although England were his native country, and an English woman his mother: whereby it seemeth this blackness proceedeth rather of some natural infection of that man."

As the word "infection" suggests, Elizabethans frequently regarded blackness as a physical defect, though the blacks who lived in England and Scotland throughout the sixteenth century were also treated as exotic curiosities. At his marriage to Anne of Denmark, James I entertained his bride and her family by commanding four naked black youths to dance before him in the snow. (The youths died of exposure shortly afterward.) In 1594, in the festivities celebrating the baptism of James's son, a "Black-Moor" entered pulling an elabo-

Man with head beneath his shoulders. From a Spanish edition of Mandeville's *Travels.* See *Othello* 1.3.144–45: "and men whose heads / Grew beneath their shoulders." Such men were frequently reported by medieval travelers to the East.

rately decorated chariot that was, in the original plan, supposed to be drawn in by a lion. There was a black trumpeter in the courts of Henry VII and Henry VIII, while Elizabeth had at least two black servants, one an entertainer and the other a page. Africans became increasingly popular as servants in aristocratic and gentle households in the last decades of the sixteenth century.

Some of these Africans were almost certainly slaves, though the legal status of slavery in England was ambiguous. In Cartwright's Case (1569), the court ruled "that England was too Pure an Air for Slaves to breathe in," but there is evidence that black slaves were owned in Elizabethan and Jacobean England. Moreover, by the mid-sixteenth century, the English had become involved in the profitable trade that carried African slaves to the New World. In 1562, John Hawkins embarked on his first slaving voyage, transporting some three hundred blacks from the Guinea coast to Hispaniola, where they were sold for £10,000. Elizabeth is reported to have said of this venture that it was "detestable, and would call down the Vengeance of Heaven upon the Undertakers." Nevertheless, she invested in Hawkins's subsequent voyages and loaned him ships.

English men and women of the sixteenth century experienced an unprecedented increase in knowledge of the world beyond their island, for a number of reasons. Religious persecution compelled both Catholics and Protestants to live abroad; wealthy gentlemen (and, in at least a few cases, ladies) traveled in France and Italy to view the famous cultural monuments; merchants published accounts of distant lands such as Turkey, Morocco, and Russia; and military and trading ventures took English ships to still more distant shores. In 1496, a Venetian tradesman living in Bristol, John Cabot, was granted a license by Henry VII to sail on a voyage of exploration; with his son Sebastian, he discovered Newfoundland and Nova Scotia. Remarkable feats of seamanship and reconnaissance soon followed: on his ship the *Golden Hind,* Sir Francis Drake circumnavigated the globe in 1579 and laid claim to California on behalf of the Queen; a few years later, a ship commanded by Thomas Cavendish also completed a circumnavigation. Sir Martin Frobisher explored bleak Baffin Island in search of a Northwest Passage to the Orient; Sir John Davis explored the west coast of Greenland and discovered the Falkland Islands off the coast of Argentina; Sir Walter Ralegh ventured up the Orinoco Delta, in what is now Venezuela, in search of the mythical land of El Dorado. Accounts of these and other exploits were collected by a clergyman and promoter of empire, Richard Hakluyt, and published as *The Principal Navigations* (1589; expanded edition 1599).

"To seek new worlds for gold, for praise, for glory," as Ralegh characterized such enterprises, was not for the faint of heart: Drake, Cavendish, Frobisher, and Hawkins all died at sea, as did huge numbers of those who sailed under their command. Elizabethans sensible enough to stay at home could do more than read written accounts of their fellow countrymen's far-reaching voyages. Expeditions brought back native plants (including, most famously, tobacco), animals, cultural artifacts, and, on occasion, samples of the native peoples themselves, most often seized against their will. There were exhibitions in London of a kidnapped Eskimo with his kayak and of Native Virginians with their canoes. Most of these miserable captives, violently uprooted and vulnerable to European diseases, quickly perished, but even in death they were evidently valuable property: when the English will not give one small coin "to relieve a lame beggar," one of the characters in *The Tempest* wryly remarks, "they will lay out ten to see a dead Indian" (2.2.30–31).

Perhaps most nations learn to define what they are by defining what they are not. This negative self-definition is, in any case, what Elizabethans seemed constantly to be doing, in travel books, sermons, political speeches, civic pageants, public exhibitions, and theatrical spectacles of otherness. The extraordinary variety of these exercises (which include public executions and urban riots, as well as more benign forms of curiosity) suggests that the boundaries of national identity were by no means clear and unequivocal. Even peoples whom English writers routinely, viciously stigmatize

An Indian dance. From Thomas Hariot, *A Brief and True Report of the New Found Land of Virginia* (1590).

as irreducibly alien—Italians, Indians, Turks, and Jews—have a surprising instability in the Elizabethan imagination and may appear for brief, intense moments as powerful models to be admired and emulated before they resume their place as emblems of despised otherness.

James I and the Union of the Crowns

Though under great pressure to do so, the aging Elizabeth steadfastly refused to name her successor. It became increasingly apparent, however, that it would be James Stuart, the son of Mary, Queen of Scots, and by the time Elizabeth's health began to fail, several of her principal advisers, including her chief minister, Robert Cecil, had been for several years in secret correspondence with him in Edinburgh. Crowned King James VI of Scotland in 1567 when he was but one year old, Mary's son had been raised as a Protestant by his powerful guardians, and in 1589 he married a Protestant princess, Anne of Denmark. When Elizabeth died on March 24, 1603, English officials reported that on her deathbed the Queen had named James to succeed her.

Upon his accession, James—now styled James VI of Scotland and James I of England—made plain his intention to unite his two kingdoms. As he told Parliament in 1604, "What God hath conjoined then, let no man separate. I am the husband, and all of the whole isle is my lawful wife; I am the head and it is my body; I am the

Funeral procession of Queen Elizabeth. From a watercolor sketch by an unknown artist (1603).

shepherd and it is my flock." But the flock was less perfectly united than James optimistically envisioned: English and Scottish were sharply distinct identities, as were Welsh and Cornish and other peoples who were incorporated, with varying degrees of willingness, into the realm.

Fearing that to change the name of the kingdom would invalidate all laws and institutions established under the name of England, a fear that was partly real and partly a cover for anti-Scots prejudice, Parliament balked at James's desire to be called "King of Great Britain" and resisted the unionist legislation that would have made Great Britain a legal reality. Though the English initially rejoiced at the peaceful transition from Elizabeth to her successor, there was a rising tide of resentment against James's advancement of Scots friends and his creation of new knighthoods. Lower down the social ladder, English and Scots occasionally clashed violently on the streets: in July 1603, James issued a proclamation against Scottish "insolencies," and in April 1604, he ordered the arrest of "swaggerers" waylaying Scots in London. The ensuing years did not bring the amity and docile obedience for which James hoped, and, though the navy now flew the Union Jack, combining the Scottish cross of St. Andrew and the English cross of St. George, the unification of the kingdoms remained throughout his reign an unfulfilled ambition.

Unfulfilled as well were James's lifelong dreams of ruling as an absolute monarch. Crown lawyers throughout Europe had long argued that a king, by virtue of his power to make law, must necessarily be above law. But in England sovereignty was identified not with the king alone or with the people alone but with the "King in Parliament." Against his absolutist ambitions, James faced the crucial power to raise taxes that was vested not in the monarch but in the elected members of the Parliament. He faced as well a theory of republicanism that traced its roots back to ancient Rome and that prided itself on its steadfast and, if necessary, violent resistance to tyranny. Shakespeare's fascination with monarchy is apparent throughout his work, but in his Roman plays in particular, as well as in his long poem *The Rape of Lucrece*, he manifests an intense imaginative interest in the idea of a republic.

The Jacobean Court

With James as with Elizabeth, the royal court was the center of diplomacy, ambition, intrigue, and an intense jockeying for social position. As always in monarchies, proximity to the king's person was a central mark of favor, so that access to the royal bedchamber was one of the highest aims of the powerful, scheming lords who followed James from his sprawling London palace at Whitehall to the hunting lodges and country estates to which he loved to retreat. A coveted office, in the Jacobean as in the Tudor court, was the Groom of the Stool, the person who supervised the disposal demanded an end to impositions before it would relieve the King and was angrily dissolved without completing its business.

James's Religious Policy and the Persecution of Witches

Before his accession to the English throne, the King had made known his view of Puritans, the general name for a variety of Protestant sects that were agitating for a radical reform of the church, the overthrow of its conservative hierarchy of bishops, and the rejection of a large number of traditional rituals and practices. In a book he wrote, *Basilikon Doron* (1599), James denounced "brainsick and heady preachers" who were prepared "to let King, people, law and all be trod underfoot." Yet he was not entirely unwilling to consider religious reforms. In religion, as in foreign policy, he was above all concerned to maintain peace.

On his way south to claim the throne of England in 1603, James was presented with the Millenary Petition (signed by one thousand ministers), which urged him as "our physician" to heal the disease of lingering "popish" ceremonies. He responded by calling a conference on the ceremonies of the Church of England, which duly took place at Hampton Court Palace in January 1604. The delegates who spoke for reform were moderates, and there was little in the outcome to satisfy Puritans. Nevertheless, while the Church of England continued to cling to such remnants of the Catholic past as wedding rings, square caps, bishops, and Christmas, the conference did produce some reform in the area of ecclesiastical discipline. It also authorized a new English translation of the Bible, known as the King James Bible, which was printed in 1611, too late to have been extensively used by Shakespeare. Along with Shakespeare's works, the King James Bible has probably had the profoundest influence on the subsequent history of English literature.

Having arranged this compromise, James saw his main task as ensuring conformity. He promulgated the 1604 Canons (the first definitive code of canon law since the Reformation), which required all ministers to subscribe to three articles. The first affirmed royal supremacy; the second confirmed that there was nothing in the Book of Common Prayer "contrary to the Word of God" and required ministers to use only the authorized services; the third asserted that the central tenets of the Church of England

The "swimming" of a suspected witch.

were "agreeable to the Word of God." There were strong objections to the second and third articles from those of Puritan leanings inside and outside the House of Commons. In the end, many ministers refused to conform or subscribe to the articles, but only about ninety of them, or 1 percent of the clergy, were deprived of their livings. In its theology and composition, the Church of England was little changed from what it had been under Elizabeth. In hindsight, what is most striking are the ominous signs of growing religious divisions that would by the 1640s burst forth in civil war and the execution of James's son Charles.

James seems to have taken seriously the official claims to the sacredness of kingship, and he certainly took seriously his own theories of religion and politics, which he had printed for the edification of his people. He was convinced that Satan, perpetually warring against God and His representatives on earth, was continually plotting against him. James thought moreover that he possessed special insight into Satan's wicked agents, the witches, and in 1597, while King of Scotland, he published his *Demonology*, a learned exposition of their malign threat to his godly rule. Hundreds of witches, he believed, were involved in a 1589 conspiracy to kill him by raising storms at sea when he was sailing home from Denmark with his new bride.

In the 1590s, Scotland embarked on a virulent witch craze of the kind that had since the fifteenth century repeatedly afflicted France, Switzerland, and Germany, where many thousands of women (and a much smaller number of men) were caught in a nightmarish web of wild accusations. Tortured into making lurid confessions of infant cannibalism, night flying, and sexual intercourse with the devil at huge, orgiastic "witches' Sabbaths," the victims had little chance to defend themselves and were routinely burned at the stake.

In England too there were witchcraft prosecutions, though on a much smaller scale and with significant differences in the nature of the accusations and the judicial procedures. Witch trials began in England in the 1540s; statutes against witchcraft were enacted in 1542, 1563, and 1604. English law did not allow judicial torture, stipulated lesser punishments in cases of "white magic," and mandated jury trials. Juries acquitted more than half of the defendants in witchcraft trials; in Essex, where the judicial records are particularly extensive, some 24 percent of those accused were executed, while the remainder of those convicted were pilloried and imprisoned or sentenced and reprieved. The accused were generally charged with *maleficium,* an evil deed—usually harming neighbors, causing destructive storms, or killing farm animals—but not with worshipping Satan.

After 1603, when James came to the English throne, he somewhat moderated his enthusiasm for the judicial murder of witches, for the most part defenseless, poor women resented by their neighbors. Though he did nothing to mitigate the ferocity of the ongoing witch hunts in his native Scotland, he did not try to institute Scottish-style persecutions and trials in his new realm. This relative waning of persecutorial eagerness principally reflects the differences between England and Scotland, but it may also bespeak some small, nascent skepticism on James's part about the quality of evidence brought against the accused and about the reliability of the "confessions" extracted from them. It is sobering to reflect that plays like Shakespeare's *Macbeth* (1606), Thomas Middleton's *Witch* (before 1616), and Thomas Dekker, John Ford, and William Rowley's *Witch of Edmonton* (1621) seem to be less the allies of skepticism than the exploiters of fear.

The Playing Field

Cosmic Spectacles

The first permanent, freestanding public theaters in England date only from Shakespeare's own lifetime: a London playhouse, the Red Lion, is mentioned in 1567, and

James Burbage's playhouse, The Theatre, was built in 1576. (The innovative use of these new stages, crucial to a full understanding of Shakespeare's achievement, is discussed in a separate essay in this volume, by the theater historian Holger Schott Syme.) But it is quite misleading to identify English drama exclusively with these specially constructed playhouses, for in fact there was a rich and vital theatrical tradition in England stretching back for centuries. Many towns in late medieval England were the sites of annual festivals that mounted elaborate cycles of plays depicting the great biblical stories, from the creation of the world to Christ's Passion and its miraculous aftermath. Most of these plays have been lost, but the surviving cycles, such as those from York, are magnificent and complex works of art. They are sometimes called "mystery plays," either because they were performed by the guilds of various crafts (known as "mysteries") or, more likely, because they represented the mysteries of the faith. The cycles were most often performed on the annual feast day instituted in the early fourteenth century in honor of the Corpus Christi, the sacrament of the Lord's Supper, which is perhaps the greatest of these religious mysteries.

The Feast of Corpus Christi, celebrated on the Thursday following Trinity Sunday, helped give the play cycles their extraordinary cultural resonance, but it also contributed to their downfall. For along with the specifically liturgical plays traditionally performed by religious confraternities and the "saints' plays," which depicted miraculous events in the lives of individual holy men and women, the mystery cycles were closely identified with the Catholic Church. Protestant authorities in the sixteenth century, eager to eradicate all remnants of popular Catholic piety, moved to suppress the annual procession of the Host, with its gorgeous banners, pageant carts, and cycle of visionary plays. In 1548, the Feast of Corpus Christi was abolished. Towns that continued to perform the mysteries were under increasing pressure to abandon them. It is sometimes said that the cycles were already dying out from neglect, but recent research has shown that many towns and their guilds were extremely reluctant to give them up. Desperate offers to strip away any traces of Catholic doctrine and to submit the play scripts to the authorities for their approval met with unbending opposition from the government. In 1576, the courts gave York permission to perform its cycle but only if

> in the said play no pageant be used or set forth wherein the Majesty of God the Father, God the Son, or God the Holy Ghost or the administration of either the Sacraments of baptism or of the Lord's Supper be counterfeited or represented, or anything played which tend to the maintenance of superstition and idolatry or which be contrary to the laws of God . . . or of the realm.

Such "permission" was tantamount to an outright ban. The local officials in the city of Norwich, proud of their St. George and the Dragon play, asked if they could at least parade the dragon costume through the streets, but even this modest request was refused. It is likely that as a young man Shakespeare had seen some of these plays: when Hamlet says of a noisy, strutting theatrical performance that it "out-Herods Herod," he is alluding to the famously bombastic role of Herod of Jewry in the mystery plays. But by the century's end, the cycles were no longer performed by live actors in great civic celebrations. They survived, if at all, in the debased form of puppet shows.

Early English theater was by no means restricted to these civic and religious festivals. Payments to professional and amateur performers appear in early records of towns and aristocratic households, though the Latin terms—*ministralli, histriones, mimi, lusores,* and so forth—are not used with great consistency and make it difficult to distinguish among minstrels, jugglers, stage players, and other entertainers. Performers acted in town halls and the halls of guilds and aristocratic mansions, on scaffolds erected in town squares and marketplaces, on pageant wagons in the streets, and in inn yards. By the fifteenth century, and probably earlier, there were organized companies of players traveling under noble patronage. Such companies earned a living providing amusement, while enhancing the prestige of the patron.

Panorama of London, showing two theaters, both round and both flying flags: a flying flag indicated that a performance was in progress. The Globe is in the foreground, and the Hope, or Beargarden, is to the left.

A description of a provincial performance in the late sixteenth century, written by one R. Willis, provides a glimpse of what seems to have been the usual procedure:

> In the City of Gloucester the manner is (as I think it is in other like corporations) that when the Players of Interludes come to town, they first attend the Mayor to inform him what nobleman's servant they are, and so to get license for their public playing; and if the Mayor like the Actors, or would show respect to their Lord and Master, he appoints them to play their first play before himself and the Aldermen and common Council of the City and that is called the Mayor's play, where everyone that will come in without money, the Mayor giving the players a reward as he thinks fit to show respect unto them.

In addition to their take from this "first play," the players would almost certainly have supplemented their income by performing in halls and inn yards, where they could on some occasions charge an admission fee. It was no doubt a precarious existence.

The "Interludes" mentioned in Willis's description of the Gloucester performances are likely plays that were, in effect, staged dialogues on religious, moral, and political themes. Such works could, like the mysteries, be associated with Catholicism, but they were also used in the sixteenth century to convey polemical Protestant messages, and they reached outside the religious sphere to address secular concerns as well. Henry Medwall's *Fulgens and Lucrece* (ca. 1490–1501), for example, pits a wealthy but dissolute nobleman against a virtuous public servant of humble origins, while John Heywood's *Play of the Weather* (ca. 1525–33) stages a debate among social rivals, including a gentleman, a merchant, a forest ranger, and two millers. The structure of such plays reflects the training in argumentation that students received in Tudor schools and, in particular, the sustained practice in examining all sides of a difficult question. Some of Shakespeare's amazing ability to look at critical issues from multiple perspectives may be traced back to this practice and the dramatic interludes it helped to inspire.

Another major form of theater that flourished in England in the fifteenth century and continued on into the sixteenth was the morality play. Like the mysteries, moralities addressed questions of the ultimate fate of the soul. They did so, however, not by rehearsing scriptural stories but by dramatizing allegories of spiritual struggle. Typically, a person named Human or Mankind or Youth is faced with a choice between a pious life in the company of such associates as Mercy, Discretion, and Good Deeds and a dissolute life among riotous companions like Lust or Mischief. Plays like *Mankind* (ca. 1465–70) and *Everyman* (ca. 1495) show how powerful these unpromising-sounding dramas could be, in part because of the extraordinary comic vitality of the story of social humiliation at a failure to perform that suggests that a well-educated Elizabethan was expected to be able to sing at sight. Even if this is an exaggeration in the interest of book sales, there is evidence of impressively widespread musical literacy, reflected in a splendid array of music for the lute, viol, recorder, harp, and virginal, as well as the marvelous vocal music.

Whether it is the aristocratic Orsino luxuriating in the dying fall of an exquisite melody or bully Bottom craving "the tongs and the bones," Shakespeare's characters frequently call for music. They also repeatedly give voice to the age's conviction that there was a deep relation between musical harmony and the harmonies of the well-ordered individual and state. "The man that hath no music in himself," warns Lorenzo in *The Merchant of Venice*, "nor is not moved with concord of sweet sounds, / Is fit for treasons, stratagems, and spoils" (5.1.83–85). This conviction in turn reflects a still deeper link between musical harmony and the divinely created harmony of the cosmos. When Ulysses in *Troilus and Cressida* wishes to convey the image of universal chaos, he speaks of the untuning of a string (1.3.108–09).

The playing companies must have regularly employed trained musicians, and many actors (like the actor who in playing Pandarus in *Troilus and Cressida* is supposed to accompany himself on the lute) must have possessed musical skill. When Shakespeare's company began to use an indoor theater, the Blackfriars, as a second venue, it became famous for its orchestra, and, among other composers, the King's Musician, Robert Johnson, seems to have written songs for the actors to sing. Unfortunately, we possess the original settings for very few of Shakespeare's songs, possibly because many of them may have been set to popular tunes of the time that everyone knew and no one bothered to write down.

Alternative Entertainments

Plays, music, and dancing were by no means the only shows in town. There were jousts, tournaments, royal entries, religious processions, pageants in honor of newly installed civic officials or ambassadors arriving from abroad; wedding masques, court masques, and costumed entertainments known as "disguisings" or "mummings"; juggling acts, fortune-tellers, exhibitions of swordsmanship, mountebanks, folk healers, storytellers, magic shows; bearbaiting, bullbaiting, cockfighting, and other blood sports; folk festivals such as Maying, the Feast of Fools, Carnival, and Whitsun Ales. For several years, Elizabethan Londoners were delighted by a trained animal—Banks's Horse—that performed elaborate dance steps and could, it was thought, do arithmetic and answer questions. And there was always the grim but compelling spectacle of public shaming, mutilation, and execution.

Most English towns had stocks and whipping posts. Drunks, fraudulent merchants, adulterers, and quarrelers could be placed in carts or mounted backward on asses and paraded through the streets for crowds to jeer and throw refuse at. Women accused of being scolds, as we have already remarked, could be publicly muzzled by an iron device called a "brank" or tied to a cucking stool and dunked in the river. Convicted criminals could have their ears cut off, their noses slit, their foreheads branded. Public beheadings (generally reserved for the elite) and hangings were common. Those convicted of treason were sentenced to be "hanged by the neck, and being alive cut down, and your privy members to be cut off, and your bowels to be taken out of your belly and there burned, you being alive."

Shakespeare occasionally takes note of these alternative entertainments: at the end of *Macbeth*, for example, with his enemies closing in on him, the doomed tyrant declares, "They have tied me to a stake. I cannot fly, / But bearlike I must fight the course" (5.7.1–2). The audience is reminded then that it is witnessing the human equivalent of a popular spectacle—a bear chained to a stake and attacked by fierce dogs—that they could have paid to watch at an arena near the Globe. And when, a few moments later, Macduff enters carrying Macbeth's head, the audience is seeing the theatrical equiva-

An Elizabethan hanging.

lent of the execution of criminals and traitors that they could have also watched in the flesh, as it were, nearby. In a different key, the audiences who paid to see *A Midsummer Night's Dream* or *The Winter's Tale* got to enjoy the comic spectacle of a Maying and a Whitsun Pastoral, while the spectators of *The Tempest* could gawk at what the Folio list of characters calls a "savage and deformed slave" and to enjoy an aristocratic magician's wedding masque in honor of his daughter.

The Enemies of the Stage

In 1624, a touring company of players arrived in Norwich and requested permission to perform. Permission was denied, but the municipal authorities, "in regard of the honorable respect which this City beareth to the right honorable the Lord Chamberlain," gave the players twenty shillings to get out of town. Throughout the sixteenth and early seventeenth centuries, there are many similar records of civic officials prohibiting performances and then, to appease a powerful patron, paying the actors to take their skills elsewhere. As early as the 1570s, there is evidence that the London authorities, while mindful of the players' influential protectors, were energetically trying to drive the theater out of the city.

Why should what we now regard as one of the undisputed glories of the age have aroused so much hostility? One answer, curiously enough, is traffic: plays drew large audiences—the public theaters could accommodate thousands—and residents objected to the crowds, the noise, and the crush of carriages. Other, more serious concerns were public health and crime. It was thought that numerous diseases, including the dreaded bubonic plague, were spread by noxious odors, and the packed playhouses were obvious breeding grounds for infection. (Patrons often tried to protect themselves by sniffing nosegays or stuffing cloves into their nostrils.) The large crowds drew pickpockets, cutpurses, and other scoundrels. On more than one occasion, if Shakespeare's fellow actor Will Kemp may be believed, pickpockets, caught in the act during a performance, were tied to a post onstage "for all people to wonder at." The theater was, moreover, a well-known haunt of prostitutes and, it was alleged, a place where innocent

Syphilis victim in tub. Frontispiece to the play *Cornelianum Dolium* (1638), possibly written by Thomas Randolph. The tub inscription translates as "I sit on the throne of love, I suffer in the tub"; and the banner as "Farewell, O sexual pleasures and lusts."

maids were seduced and respectable matrons corrupted. It was darkly rumored that "chambers and secret places" adjoined the theater galleries, and in any case, taverns, disreputable inns, and whorehouses were close at hand.

There were other charges as well. Plays in the public, outdoor amphitheaters were performed in the afternoon and therefore drew people, especially the young, away from their work. They were schools of idleness, luring apprentices from their trades, law students from their studies, housewives from their kitchens, and potentially pious souls from the sober meditations to which they might otherwise devote themselves. Wasting their time and money on disreputable shows, citizens exposed themselves to sexual provocation and outright political sedition. Even when the content of plays was morally exemplary—and, of course, few plays were so gratifyingly high-minded—the theater itself, in the eyes of most mayors and aldermen, was inherently disorderly.

The attack on the stage by civic officials was echoed and intensified by many of the age's moralists and religious leaders, especially those associated with Puritanism. While English Protestants earlier in the sixteenth century had attempted to counter the Catholic mystery cycles and saints' plays by mounting their own doctrinally correct dramas, by the century's end a fairly widespread consensus, even among those mildly sympathetic toward the theater, held that the stage and the pulpit were in tension with one another. After 1591, a ban on Sunday performances was strictly enforced, and in 1606, Parliament passed an act imposing a hefty fine of £10 on any person who shall "in any stage-play, interlude, show, May-game, or pageant, jestingly or profanely speak or use the holy name of God, or of Christ Jesus, or of the Holy Ghost, or of the Trinity (which are not to be spoken but with fear and reverence)." If changes in the printed texts are a reliable indication, the players seem to have complied at least to some degree with the ruling. The Folio (1623) text of *Richard III,* for example, omits the Quarto's (1597) four uses of "zounds" (for "God's wounds"), along with a mention of "Christ's dear blood shed for our grievous sins"; "God's my judge" in *The Merchant of Venice* becomes "well I know"; "By Jesu" in *Henry V* becomes a very proper "I say"; and in all the plays, "God" is from time to time metamorphosed to "Jove."

But for some of the theater's more extreme critics, these modest expurgations were tiny bandages on a gaping wound. In his huge book *Histriomastix* (1633), William Prynne regurgitates a half-century of frenzied attacks on the "sinful, heathenish, lewd, ungodly Spectacles." In the eyes of Prynne and his fellow antitheatricalists, stage plays were part of a demonic tangle of obscene practices proliferating like a cancer in the body of society. It is "manifest to all men's judgments," he writes, that effeminate mixed dancing, dicing, stage-plays, lascivious pictures, wanton fashions, face-painting, health-drinking, long hair, love-locks, periwigs, women's curling, powdering and cutting of their hair, bonfires, New-year's gifts, May-games, amorous pastorals, lascivious effeminate music, excessive laughter, luxurious disorderly Christmas-keeping, mummeries . . . [are] wicked, unchristian pastimes.

Given the anxious emphasis on effeminacy, it is not surprising that denunciations of this kind obsessively focused on the use of boy actors to play the female parts. The enemies of the stage charged that theatrical transvestism excited illicit sexual desires, both heterosexual and homosexual.

Since cross-dressing violated a biblical prohibition (Deuteronomy 22:5), religious antitheatricalists attacked it as wicked regardless of its erotic charge; indeed, they often seemed to consider any act of impersonation as inherently wicked. In their view, the theater itself was Satan's domain. Thus a Cambridge scholar, John Greene, reports the sad fate of "a Christian woman" who went to the theater to see a play: "She entered in well and sound, but she returned and came forth possessed of the devil. Whereupon certain godly brethren demanded Satan how he durst be so bold, as to enter into her a Christian. Whereto he answered, that *he found her in his own house,* and therefore took possession of her as his own" (italics in original). When the "godly brethren" came to power in the mid-seventeenth century, with the overthrow of Charles I, they saw to it that the playhouses, shut down in 1642 at the onset of the Civil War, remained closed. Public theater did not resume until the restoration of the monarchy in 1660.

Faced with enemies among civic officials and religious leaders, Elizabethan and Jacobean playing companies relied on the protection of their powerful patrons. As the liveried servants of aristocrats or of the monarch, the players could refute the charge that they were mere vagabonds, and they claimed, as a convenient legal fiction, that their public performances were necessary rehearsals in anticipation of those occasions when they would be called upon to entertain their noble masters. But harassment by the mayor and aldermen of the City of London—an area roughly one mile square, defined by the old Roman walls—continued unabated, and the players were forced to build their theaters outside the immediate jurisdiction of these authorities, either in the suburbs or in the areas known as the "liberties." A liberty was a piece of land within the City of London itself that was not directly subject to the authority of the Lord Mayor. The most significant liberty from the point of view of the theater was the area near St. Paul's Cathedral called "the Blackfriars," where, until the dissolution of the monasteries in 1538, there had been a Dominican priory. It was here that in 1608 Shakespeare's company, then called the King's Men, took over an indoor playhouse in which they performed during the winter months, reserving the open-air Globe in the suburb of Southwark for the warmer months.

Censorship and Regulation

In addition to those authorities who campaigned to shut down the theater, there were others whose task was to oversee, regulate, and censor it. Given the outright hostility of the former, the latter may have seemed to the London players equivocal allies rather than enemies. After all, plays that passed the censor were at least licensed to be performed and hence conceded to have some limited legitimacy. In April 1559, at the very start of her reign, Queen Elizabeth drafted a proposal that for the first time envisaged a system for the prior review and regulation of plays throughout her kingdom:

The Queen's Majesty doth straightly forbid all manner interludes to be played either openly or privately, except the same be notified beforehand, and licensed within any city or town corporate, by the mayor or other chief officers of the same, and within any shire, by such as shall be lieutenants for the Queen's Majesty in a license. In 1607, the system was significantly revised when Sir George Buc began to license plays for the press. When Buc succeeded to the post of Master of the Revels in 1610, the powers to license plays for the stage and the page were vested in one man.

Theatrical Innovations

The theater continued to flourish under this system of regulation after Shakespeare's death in 1616; by the 1630s, as many as five playhouses were operating daily in London. When the theater reemerged in 1660 after the eighteen-year hiatus imposed by Puritan rule, it quickly resumed its cultural importance, but not without a number of significant changes. Major innovations in staging resulted principally from continental influences on the English artists who accompanied the court of Charles II into exile in France, where they supplied it with masques and other theatrical entertainments.

The institutional conditions and business practices of the two companies chartered by Charles after the Restoration in 1660 also differed from those of Shakespeare's theater. In place of the more collective practice of Shakespeare's company, the Restoration theaters were controlled by celebrated actor-managers who not only assigned themselves starring roles, in both comedy and tragedy, but also assumed sole responsibility for many business decisions, including the setting of their colleagues' salaries. At the same time, the power of the actor-manager, great as it was, was limited by the new importance of outside capital. No longer was the theater, with all of its properties from script to costumes, owned by the "sharers," that is, by those actors who held shares in the joint stock company. Instead, entrepreneurs would raise capital for increasingly fantastic sets and stage machinery that could cost as much as £3,000, an astronomical sum, for a single production. This investment in turn not only influenced the kinds of new plays written for the theater but helped to transform old plays that were revived, including Shakespeare's.

In his diary entry for August 24, 1661, Samuel Pepys notes that he has been "to the Opera, and there saw Hamlet, Prince of Denmark, done with scenes very well, but above all, Betterton did the prince's part beyond imagination." This is Thomas Betterton's first review, as it were, and it is typical of the enthusiasm he would inspire throughout his fifty-year career on the London stage. Pepys's brief and scattered remarks on the plays he voraciously attended in the 1660s are precious because they are among the few records from the period of concrete and immediate responses to theatrical performances. Modern readers might miss the significance of Pepys's phrase "done with scenes": this production of *Hamlet* was only the third play to use the movable sets first introduced to England by its producer, William Davenant. The central historical fact that makes the productions of this period so exciting is that public theater had been banned altogether for eighteen years until the Restoration of Charles II.

A brief discussion of theatrical developments in the Restoration period will enable us at least to glance longingly at a vast subject that lies outside the scope of this introduction: the rich performance history that extends from Shakespeare's time to our own, involving tens of thousands of productions and adaptations for theater, opera, dance, Broadway musicals, and of course films. The scale of this history is vast in space as well as time: already in the late sixteenth and early seventeenth centuries, troupes of English actors performed as far afield as Poland and Bohemia.

While producing masques at the court of Charles I, the poet William Davenant had become an expert on stage scenery, and when the theaters reopened, he set to work on converting an indoor tennis court into a new kind of theater. He designed a broad open platform like that of the Elizabethan stage, but at the back of this platform he added or expanded a space, framed by a proscenium arch, in which scenes could be displayed. These elaborately painted scenes could be moved on and off, using grooves on the floor. The perspectival effect for a spectator of one central painted panel with two "wings" on either side was that of three sides of a room. This effect anticipated that of the familiar "picture frame" stage, developed fully in the nineteenth century, and began a subtle shift in theater away from the elaborate verbal descriptions that are so central to Shakespeare and toward the evocative visual poetry of the set designer's art.

Another convention of Shakespeare's stage, the use of boy actors for female roles, gave way to the more complete illusion of women playing women's parts. The King issued a decree in 1662 forcefully permitting, if not requiring, the use of actresses. The royal decree is couched in the language of social and moral reform: the introduction of actresses will require the "reformation" of scurrilous and profane passages in plays, and this in turn will help forestall some of the objections that shut the theaters down in 1642. In reality, male theater audiences, composed of a narrower range of courtiers and aristocrats than in Shakespeare's time, met this intended reform with the assumption that the new actresses were fair game sexually; most actresses (with the partial exception of those who married male members of their troupes) were regarded as, or actually became, whores. But despite the social stigma, and the fact that their salaries were predictably lower than those of their male counterparts, the stage saw some formidable female stars by the 1680s.

The first recorded appearance of an actress was that of a Desdemona in December 1660. Betterton's Ophelia in 1661 was Mary Saunderson (ca. 1637–1712), who became Mrs. Betterton a year later. The most famous Ophelia of the period was Susanna Mountfort, who appeared in that role for the first time at the age of fifteen in 1705. The performance by Mountfort that became legendary occurred in 1720, after a disappointment in love, or so it was said, had driven her mad. Hearing that *Hamlet* was being performed, Mountfort escaped from her keepers and reached the theater, where she concealed herself until the scene in which Ophelia enters in her state of insanity. At this point, Mountfort rushed onto the stage and, in the words of a contemporary, "was in truth Ophelia herself, to the amazement of the performers and the astonishment of the audience."

David Garrick and George Anne Bellamy in a celebrated production of *Romeo and Juliet* at Drury Lane, London. Engraving after a painting by Benjamin Wilson (1753).

That the character Ophelia became increasingly and decisively identified with the mad scene owes something to this occurrence, but it is also a consequence of the text used for Restoration performances of *Hamlet*. Having received the performance rights to a good number of Shakespeare's plays, Davenant altered them for the stage in the 1660s, and many of these acting versions remained in use for generations. In the case of *Hamlet*, neither Davenant nor his successors did what they so often did with other plays by Shakespeare, that is, alter the plot radically and interpolate other material. But many of the lines were cut or "improved." The cuts included most of Ophelia's sane speeches, such as her spirited retort to Laertes' moralizing; what remained made her part almost entirely an emblem of "female love melancholy."

Thomas Betterton (1635–1710), the prototype of the actor-manager, who would be the dominant figure in Shakespeare interpretation and in the English theater generally through the nineteenth century, made Hamlet his premier role. A contemporary who saw his last performance in the part (at the age of seventy-four, a rather old Prince of Denmark) wrote that to *read* Shakespeare's play was to encounter "dry, incoherent, & broken sentences," but that to see Betterton was to "prove" that the play was written "correctly." Spectators especially admired his reaction to the Ghost's appearance in the Queen's bedchamber: "his Countenance . . . thro' the violent and sudden Emotions of Amazement and Horror, turn[ed] instantly on the Sight of his fathers Spirit, as pale as his Neckcloath, when every Article of his Body seem's affected with a Tremor inexpressible." A piece of stage business in this scene, Betterton's upsetting his chair on the Ghost's entrance, became so thoroughly identified with the part that later productions were censured if the actor left it out. This business could very well have been handed down from Richard Burbage, the star of Shakespeare's original production, for Davenant, who had coached Betterton in the role, had known the performances of Joseph Taylor, who had succeeded Burbage in it. It is strangely gratifying to notice that Hamlets on stage and screen still occasionally upset their chairs.

Shakespeare's Life and Art

Playwrights, even hugely successful playwrights, were not ordinarily the objects of popular curiosity in early modern England. Many plays in this period were issued without the name of the author—there was no equivalent to our copyright system, and publishers were not required to specify on their title pages who wrote the texts they printed. Only occasionally were there significant exceptions, motivated by the pursuit of profit. Though by 1597 seven of Shakespeare's plays had been printed, the title pages did not identify him as the author. Beginning in 1598 Shakespeare's name, spelled in various ways, began to appear, and indeed several plays almost certainly not written by him were printed with his name. His name—Shakespeare, Shake-speare, Shakspeare, Shaxberd, Shakespere, and the like—had evidently begun to sell plays. During his lifetime more published plays were attributed to Shakespeare than to any other contemporary dramatist.

But this marketplace interest did not extend to the details of his life. It is both revealing and frustrating that the First Folio editors, John Heminges and Henry Condell—who knew Shakespeare well—were virtually silent about their friend's personal history. Though they included the author's picture, they did not bother to include his birth and death dates, his marital status, the names of his surviving children, his intellectual and social affiliations, his endearing or annoying quirks of character, let alone anything more psychologically revealing, such as the "table talk" carefully recorded by followers of Martin Luther. Shakespeare may have been a very private man, but, as he was dead when the edition was produced, it is unlikely to have been his own wishes that dictated the omissions. The editors evidently assumed that the potential buyers of the book—and this was an expensive commercial venture—would not be particularly interested in what we would now regard as essential biographical details.

Such presumed indifference is, in all likelihood, chiefly a reflection of Shakespeare's modest origins. He flew below the radar of ordinary Elizabethan and Jacobean social curiosity. In the wake of the death of the poet Sir Philip Sidney, Fulke Greville wrote a fascinating biography of his friend, but Sidney was a dashing aristocrat, linked by birth and marriage to the great families of the realm, and he died tragically of a wound he received on the battlefield. Writers of a less exalted station did not excite the same interest, unless, like Ben Jonson, they cultivated an extravagant public persona, or, like another of Shakespeare's contemporaries, Christopher Marlowe, they ran afoul of the authorities and got themselves murdered. The fact that there are no police reports, Privy Council orders, indictments, or postmortem inquests about Shakespeare, as there are about Marlowe, tells us something significant about Shakespeare's life—he possessed a gift for staying out of trouble—but it is not the kind of detail on which biographers thrive.

Yet Elizabethan England was a record-keeping society, and centuries of archival labor have turned up a substantial number of traces of its greatest playwright and his family. By themselves the traces would have relatively little interest, but in the light of Shakespeare's plays and poems, they have come to seem like precious relics and manage to achieve a considerable resonance.

Shakespeare's Family

William Shakespeare's grandfather, Richard, farmed land by the village of Snitterfield, near the small, pleasant market town of Stratford-upon-Avon, about ninety-six miles northwest of London. The playwright's father, John, moved in the mid-sixteenth century to Stratford, where he became a successful glover, landowner, moneylender, and dealer in wool and other agricultural goods. In or about 1557, he married Mary Arden, the daughter of a prosperous and well-connected farmer from the same area, Robert Arden of Wilmcote.

John Shakespeare was evidently highly esteemed by his fellow townspeople, for he held a series of important posts in local government. In 1556, he was appointed ale taster, an office reserved for "able persons and discreet," in 1558 was sworn in as a constable, and in 1561 was elected as one of the town's fourteen burgesses. As burgess, John served as one of the two chamberlains, responsible for administering borough property and revenues. In 1567, he was elected bailiff, Stratford's highest elective office and the equivalent of mayor. Though John Shakespeare signed all official documents with a cross or other sign, it is likely, though not certain, that he knew how to read and write. Mary, who also signed documents only with her mark, is less likely to have been literate.

According to the parish registers, which recorded baptisms and burials, the Shakespeares had eight children, four daughters and four sons, beginning with a daughter, Joan, born in 1558. A second daughter, Margaret, was born in December 1562 and died a few months later. William Shakespeare ("Gulielmus, filius Johannes Shakespeare"), their first son, was baptized on April 26, 1564. Since there was usually a few days' lapse between birth and baptism, it is conventional to celebrate Shakespeare's birthday on April 23, which happens to coincide with the Feast of St. George, England's patron saint, and with the day of Shakespeare's death fifty-two years later.

William Shakespeare had three younger brothers, Gilbert, Richard, and Edmund, and two younger sisters, Joan and Anne. (It was often the custom to recycle a name, so the first-born Joan must have died before the birth in 1569 of another daughter christened Joan, the only one of the girls to survive childhood.) Gilbert, who died in his forty-fifth year in 1612, is described in legal records as a Stratford haberdasher; Edmund followed William to London and became a professional actor, though evidently of no

Southeast Prospect of Stratford-upon-Avon, 1746. From *Gentleman's Magazine* (December 1792).

particular repute. He was only twenty-eight when he died in 1607 and was given an expensive funeral, perhaps paid for by his successful older brother.

At the high point of his public career, John Shakespeare, the father of this substantial family, applied to the Herald's College for a coat of arms, which would have marked his (and his family's) elevation from the ranks of substantial middle-class citizenry to that of the gentry. But the application went nowhere, for soon after he initiated what would have been a costly petitioning process, John apparently fell on hard times. The decline must have begun when William was still living at home, a boy of twelve or thirteen. From 1576 onward, John Shakespeare stopped attending council meetings. He became caught up in costly lawsuits, started mortgaging his land, and incurred substantial debts. In 1586, he was finally replaced on the council; in 1592, he was one of nine Stratford men listed as absenting themselves from church out of fear of being arrested for debt.

The reason for the reversal in John Shakespeare's fortunes is unknown. Some have speculated that it may have stemmed from adherence to Catholicism, since those who remained loyal to the old faith were subject to increasingly vigorous and costly discrimination. But if John Shakespeare was a Catholic, as seems possible, it would not necessarily explain his decline, since other Catholics (and Puritans) in Elizabethan Stratford and elsewhere managed to hold on to their offices. In any case, his fall from prosperity and local power, whatever its cause, was not absolute. In 1601, the last year of his life, his name was included among those qualified to speak on behalf of Stratford's rights. And he was by that time entitled to bear a coat of arms, for in 1596, some twenty years after the application to the Herald's office had been initiated, it was successfully renewed. There is no record of who paid for the bureaucratic procedures that made the grant possible, but it is likely to have been John's oldest son, William, by that time a highly successful London playwright. By elevating his father, he would have made himself a gentleman as well.

Education

Stratford was a small provincial town, but it had long been the site of an excellent free school, originally established by the church in the thirteenth century. The main purpose of such schools in the Middle Ages had been to train prospective clerics; since many aristocrats could neither read nor write, literacy by itself conferred no special distinction and was not routinely viewed as desirable. But the situation began to change markedly in the sixteenth century. Protestantism placed a far greater emphasis upon lay literacy: for the sake of salvation, it was crucially important to be intimately acquainted with the Holy Book, and printing made that book readily available. Schools became less strictly bound up with training for the church and more linked to the general acquisition of "literature," in the sense both of literacy and of cultural knowledge. In keeping with this new emphasis on reading and with humanist educational reform, the school was reorganized during the reign of Edward VI (1547–53). School records from the period have not survived, but it is almost certain that William Shakespeare attended the King's New School, as it was renamed in Edward's honor.

Scholars have painstakingly reconstructed the curriculum of schools of this kind and have even turned up the names and rather impressive credentials of the schoolmasters who taught at the King's New School when Shakespeare was of school age. (The principal teacher at that time was Thomas Jenkins, an Oxford graduate, who received £20 a year and a rent-free house.) A child's education in Elizabethan England began at age four or five with two years at what was called the "petty school," attached to the main grammar school. The little scholars carried a "hornbook," a sheet of paper or parchment framed in wood and covered, for protection, with a transparent layer of horn. On the paper was written the alphabet and the Lord's Prayer, which were reproduced as well in the slightly more advanced *ABC with the Catechism,* a combination primer and rudimentary religious guide.

After students demonstrated some ability to read, education for most girls came to a halt, but boys could go on, at about age seven, to the grammar school. Shakespeare's images of the experience are not particularly cheerful. In his famous account of the Seven Ages of Man, Jaques in *As You Like It* describes

> the whining schoolboy with his satchel
> And shining morning face, creeping like snail
> Unwillingly to school.
>
> (2.7.145–47)

The schoolboy would have crept quite early: the day began at 6:00 A.M. in summer and 7:00 A.M. in winter and continued until 5:00 P.M., with very few breaks or holidays.

At the core of the curriculum was the study of Latin, the mastery of which was in effect a prolonged male puberty rite involving much discipline and pain as well as pleasure. A late sixteenth-century Dutchman (whose name fittingly was Batty)

The Cholmondeley Ladies (ca. 1600–1610). Artist unknown. This striking image brings to mind Shakespeare's fascination with twinship, both identical (notably in *The Comedy of Errors*) and fraternal (in *Twelfth Night*).

proposed that God had created the human buttocks so that they could be severely beaten without risking permanent injury. Such thoughts dominated the pedagogy of the age, so that even an able young scholar, as we might imagine Shakespeare to have been, could scarcely have escaped recurrent flogging.

Shakespeare evidently reaped some rewards for the miseries he probably endured: his works are laced with echoes of many of the great Latin texts taught in grammar schools. One of his earliest comedies, *The Comedy of Errors,* is a brilliant variation on a theme by the Roman playwright Plautus, whom Elizabethan schoolchildren often performed as well as read; and one of his earliest tragedies, *Titus Andronicus,* is heavily indebted to Seneca. These are among the most visible of the classical influences that are often more subtly and pervasively interfused in Shakespeare's works. He seems to have had a particular fondness for *Aesop's Fables,* Apuleius's *Golden Ass,* and above all Ovid's *Metamorphoses.* His learned contemporary Ben Jonson remarked that Shakespeare had "small Latin and less Greek," but from this distance what is striking is not the limits of Shakespeare's learning but rather the unpretentious ease, intelligence, and gusto with which he draws upon what he must have first encountered as laborious study.

Traces of a Life

In November 1582, William Shakespeare, at the age of eighteen, married twenty-six-year-old Anne Hathaway, who came from the village of Shottery near Stratford. Their first daughter, Susanna, was baptized six months later. This circumstance, along with the fact that Anne was eight years Will's senior, has given rise to a mountain of speculation, all the more lurid precisely because there is no further evidence. Shakespeare depicts in several plays situations in which marriage is precipitated by a pregnancy, but he also registers, in *Measure for Measure* (1.2.133ff), the Elizabethan belief that a "true contract" of marriage could be legitimately made and then consummated simply by the mutual vows of the couple in the presence of witnesses.

On February 2, 1585, the twins Hamnet and Judith Shakespeare were baptized in Stratford. Hamnet died at the age of eleven, when his father was already living for much of the year in London as a successful playwright. These are Shakespeare's only known children, though in the mid-seventeenth century the playwright and impresario William Davenant hinted that he was Shakespeare's bastard son. Since people did not ordinarily advertise their illegitimacy, the claim, though impossible to verify, at least suggests the unusual strength of Shakespeare's posthumous reputation.

William Shakespeare's father, John, died in 1601; his mother died seven years later. They would have had the satisfaction of witnessing their eldest son's prosperity, and not only from a distance, for in 1597 William purchased New Place, the second-largest house in Stratford. In 1607, the playwright's daughter Susanna married a successful and well-known physician, John Hall. The next year, the Halls had a daughter, Elizabeth, Shakespeare's first grandchild. In 1616, the year of Shakespeare's death, his daughter Judith married a vintner, Thomas Quiney, with whom she had three children. Shakespeare's widow, Anne, died in 1623, at the age of sixty-seven. His first-born, Susanna, died at the age of sixty-six in 1649, the year that King Charles I was beheaded by the parliamentary army. Judith lived through Cromwell's Protectorate and on to the Restoration of the monarchy; she died in February 1662, at the age of seventy-seven. By the end of the century, the line of Shakespeare's direct heirs was extinct.

Patient digging in the archives has turned up other traces of Shakespeare's life as a family man and a man of means: assessments, small fines, real estate deeds, minor actions in court to collect debts. In addition to his fine Stratford house and a large garden and cottage facing it, Shakespeare bought substantial parcels of land in the vicinity. When in *The Tempest* the wedding celebration conjures up a vision of "barns and garners never empty," Shakespeare could have been glancing at what the legal documents record as his own "tithes of corn, grain, blade, and hay" in the fields near

Stratford. At some point after 1610, Shakespeare seems to have begun to shift his attention from the London stage to his Stratford properties, though the term "retirement" implies a more decisive and definitive break than appears to have been the case. By 1613, when the Globe Theater burned down during a performance of Shakespeare and Fletcher's *Henry VIII,* Shakespeare was probably residing for the most part in Stratford, but he retained his financial interest in the rebuilt playhouse and probably continued to have some links to his theatrical colleagues. Still, by this point, his career as a playwright was substantially over. Legal documents from his last years show him concerned to protect his real estate interests in Stratford.

A half-century after Shakespeare's death, a Stratford vicar and physician, John Ward, noted in his diary that Shakespeare and his fellow poets Michael Drayton and Ben Jonson "had a merry meeting, and it seems drank too hard, for Shakespeare died of a fever there contracted." It is not inconceivable that Shakespeare's last illness was somehow linked, if only coincidentally, to the festivities on the occasion of the wedding in February 1616 of his daughter Judith (who was still alive when Ward made his diary entry). In any case, on March 25, 1616, Shakespeare revised his will, and on April 23 he died. Two days later, he was buried in the chancel of Holy Trinity Church beneath a stone bearing an epitaph he is said to have devised:

> Good friend for Jesus' sake forbear,
> To dig the dust enclosed here:
> Blest be the man that spares these stones,
> And curst be he that moves my bones.

The verses are hardly among Shakespeare's finest, but they seem to have been effective: though bones were routinely dug up to make room for others—a fate imagined with unforgettable intensity in the graveyard scene in *Hamlet*—his own remains were undisturbed. Like other vestiges of sixteenth- and early seventeenth-century Stratford, Shakespeare's grave has for centuries now been the object of a tourist industry that borders on a religious cult.

Shakespeare's will has been examined with an intensity befitting this cult; every provision and formulaic phrase, no matter how minor or conventional, has borne a heavy weight of interpretation, none more so than the sole bequest to his wife, Anne, of "my second-best bed." Scholars have pointed out that Anne would in any case have been provided for by custom and that the terms are not necessarily a deliberate slight, but the absence of the customary words "my loving wife" or "my well-beloved wife" is difficult to ignore.

Portrait of the Playwright as Young Provincial

The great problem with the surviving traces of Shakespeare's life is not that they are few but that they are unspectacular. Christopher Marlowe was a double or triple agent, accused of brawling, sodomy, and atheism. Ben Jonson, who somehow clambered up from bricklayer's apprentice to classical scholar, served in the army in Flanders, killed a fellow actor in a duel, converted to Catholicism in prison in 1598, and returned to the Church of England in 1610. Provincial real estate investments and the second-best bed cannot compete with such adventurous lives. Indeed, the relative ordinariness of Shakespeare's social background and life has contributed to a persistent current of speculation that the glover's son from Stratford-upon-Avon was not in fact the author of the plays attributed to him.

The anti-Stratfordians, as those who deny Shakespeare's authorship are sometimes called, almost always propose as the real author someone who came from a higher social class and received a more prestigious education. Francis Bacon, the Earl of Oxford, the Earl of Southampton, even Queen Elizabeth, have been advanced, among many others, as glamorous candidates for the role of clandestine playwright. Several famous people, including Mark Twain and Sigmund Freud, have espoused these theories, though very few scholars have joined them. Since Shakespeare was quite well known in his own time as the author of the plays that bear his name, there would need to have been an extraordinary conspiracy to conceal the identity of the real master who (the theory goes) disdained to appear in the vulgarity of print or on the public stage. Like many conspiracy theories, the extreme implausibility of this one seems only to increase the fervent conviction of its advocates.

To the charge that a middle-class author from a small town could not have imagined the lives of kings and nobles, one can respond by citing the exceptional qualities that Ben Jonson praised in Shakespeare: "excellent *Phantsie*; brave notions, and gentle expressions." Even in ordinary mortals, the human imagination is a strange faculty; in Shakespeare, it seems to have been uncannily powerful, working its mysterious, transforming effects on everything it touched. His imagination was intensely engaged by what he found in books. He seems throughout his life to have been an intense, voracious reader, and it is fascinating to witness his creative encounters with Raphael Holinshed's *Chronicles of England, Scotland, and Ireland*, Plutarch's *Lives of the Noble Grecians and Romans*, Ovid's *Metamorphoses*, Montaigne's *Essays*, and the Bible, to name only some of his favorite books. But books were clearly not the only objects of Shakespeare's attention; like most artists, he drew upon the whole range of his life experiences.

To those accustomed to instant telecommunication, photography, film, and digital media, that range might seem narrowly circumscribed, but in fact something like the opposite was the case. Though we inhabit a vast virtual world, our experiential world is deliberately reduced, carefully screened, and tightly delimited. Most of us are born, sicken, and die in special institutions set apart from everyday life. We have invented means to quiet toothaches, heal wounds, and put us to sleep through painful surgeries. Those we condemn as criminals are penned up and punished behind high, windowless walls. We scarcely ever see our political representatives in person, and when we vote, we enter small, private booths. We take our entertainments most often in the dark or in the privacy of our homes, and those homes are generally walled off from the homes of others. Our meat bears little or no visible relation to the animal from which it comes; the slaughtering and butchering is discretely done out of sight. Our wastes disappear down drains; our rubbish is collected and disposed of; we live and move about in a well-lit, heavily policed, massively controlled environment.

None of this was the case in Shakespeare's world. Virtually anyone who grew up in the late sixteenth century would have had occasion to hear the sharp cries of childbirth and the groans of dying. There were a small number of hospitals and lazar houses (for lepers), but for the most part the sick, the maimed, and the mad mingled with everyone else in the crowded, muddy streets. The sufferings attendant on ordinary life were inescapable, and very few palliatives were available. (There were limits to the oblivion that the strongest ale could bring.) Malefactors, as we have seen, were most often punished in public, often hideously. There was nothing remotely equivalent to our taste for privacy. Servants were ubiquitous, and it was a rare person who had the privilege or perhaps the inclination to escape into solitude. Guests at an inn would often find themselves sharing a room or even a bed with a complete stranger. Smells and tastes—in a world without flush toilets and refrigeration—were intense, and so too were colors, for Elizabethans of any means favored vividly dyed and elaborately worked clothing. There were no streetlights, and the days faded into nights that were pitch dark and often dangerous.

Nothing here is particular to Shakespeare's biography; these were the conditions in this period of everyone's life. And what would astonish or appall us, if we were suddenly carried back into the past, would simply have been taken for granted as the way things are by most of those born into that world. But Shakespeare seems precisely not to have taken anything for granted: he seems to have carefully noted everything, from the carter who urinates in the chimney and complains of his fleabites (*1 Henry IV* 2.1.19–20) to the mad beggar who sticks sprigs of rosemary into his numbed arms (*King Lear* 2.2.177–79) to the merchant who keeps his money locked up in a desk that is covered with a Turkish tapestry (*Comedy of Errors* 4.1.103–04).

Shakespeare may have begun this practice of noting quite early in his life. When he was a very young boy—not quite four years old—his father was chosen by the Stratford council as the town bailiff. The bailiff of an Elizabethan town was a significant position; he served the borough as a justice of the peace and performed a variety of other functions, including coroner and clerk of the market. He dealt routinely with an unusually wide spectrum of local society, for on the one hand he distributed alms and on the other he negotiated with the lord of the manor. More to the point, for our purposes, the office was attended with considerable ceremony. The bailiff and his deputy were entitled to appear in public in furred gowns, attended by sergeants bearing maces before them. On Rogation Days (three days of prayer for the harvest, before Ascension Day), they would solemnly pace out the parish boundaries, and they would similarly walk in processions on market and fair days. On Sundays, the sergeants would accompany the bailiff to church, where he would sit with his wife in a front pew, and he would have a comparable seat of honor at sermons in the Guild Chapel. On special occasions, there would also be plays in the Guildhall, at which the bailiff would be seated in the front row.

On a precocious child (or even, for that matter, on an ordinary child), this ceremony must have had a significant impact. It would have conveyed irresistibly the power of clothes (the ceremonial gown of office) and of symbols (the mace) to transform identity as if by magic. It would have invested the official in question—Shakespeare's own father—with immense power, distinction, and importance, awakening what we may call a lifelong dream of high station. And perhaps, pulling slightly against this dream, it would have provoked an odd feeling that the father's clothes do not fit, a perception that the office is not the same as the man, and an intimate, firsthand knowledge that when the robes are put off, their wearer is inevitably glimpsed in a far different, less exalted light.

The honoring of the bailiff was only one of the political rituals that Shakespeare could easily have witnessed as a young man growing up in the provinces. As we have seen, Queen Elizabeth was fond of going on what were known as "progresses," triumphant ceremonial journeys around her kingdom. In 1574—when Shakespeare was ten years old—one of these progresses took her to Warwick, near Stratford-upon-Avon. The crowds that gathered to watch were participating in an elaborate celebration of charismatic power: the courtiers in their gorgeous clothes, the nervous local officials bedecked in velvets and silks, and at the center, carried in a special litter like a bejeweled icon, the virgin queen. The Queen cultivated this charisma, taking over in effect some of the iconography associated with the worship of the Virgin Mary, but she was also paradoxically fond of calling attention to the fact that she was after all quite human. For example, on this occasion at Warwick, after the trembling Recorder, presumably a local civil official of high standing, had made his official welcoming speech, Elizabeth offered her hand to him to be kissed: "Come hither, little Recorder," she said. "It was told me that you would be afraid to look upon me or to speak boldly; but you were not so afraid of me as I was of you; and I now thank you for putting me in mind of my duty." Of course, the charm of this royal "confession" of nervousness depends on its manifest implausibility: it is, in effect, a theatrical performance of humility by someone with immense confidence in her own histrionic power.

A royal progress was not the only form of spectacular political activity that Shakespeare might well have seen in the 1570s; it is still more likely that he would have witnessed parliamentary elections, particularly since his father was qualified to vote. In 1571, 1572, 1575, and 1578, there were shire elections conducted in Warwick, elections that would certainly have attracted well over a thousand voters. These were often memorable events: large crowds came together; there was usually heavy drinking and carnivalesque festivity; and at the same time, there was enacted, in a very different register from that of the monarchy, a ritual of empowerment. The people, those entitled to vote by virtue of meeting the property and residence requirements, chose their own representatives by giving their votes—their voices—to candidates for office. Here, legislative sovereignty was conferred not by God but by the consent of the community, a consent marked by shouts and applause.

Recent cultural historians have been so fascinated by the evident links between the spectacles of the absolutist monarchy and the theater that they have largely ignored the significance of this alternative public arena, one that generated intense excitement throughout the country. A child who was a spectator at a parliamentary election in the 1570s might well have found the occasion enormously compelling. It is striking, in any case, how often the adult Shakespeare returns to scenes of mass consent, and striking too how much the theater depends on assembling crowds and soliciting popular acclamation.

The most frequent occasions for the gathering together of crowds were neither elections nor theatrical performances, but rather the religious services that all Elizabethans were expected to attend at least once a week. (Recurrent absences were noted and investigated.) Protestant spokesmen routinely condemned the Catholic Mass as a form of perverse theatrical performance: a "play of sacred miracles," a "wonderful pageant," a "devil Theater." The Catholic Mass, as it had been celebrated for centuries, was outlawed, and with it a range of other Catholic rites. On occasion those rites were still practiced in secret, at considerable danger, and it is possible that Shakespeare could have been among those present. He was certainly present at the services of the English Church, whose ceremonies led by berobed priests, guided by the resonant prose of the Book of Common Prayer, and held in settings whose magnificence continues to astonish us, had their own intense histrionic power.

The young Shakespeare, whether true believer or skeptic or something in between ("So have I heard, and do in part believe it," says Hamlet's friend Horatio [1.1.164]), might have carried away from such ceremonies several impressions: an intimation of immense, cosmic forces that may impinge upon human life; a heightened understanding of the power of language to form and exalt the spirit; an awareness of intense, even murderous competition and rivalry among competing rituals; and perhaps a sense of the longing to believe that may be awakened and shaped in large crowds.

I have placed Shakespeare himself in each of these scenes—which together sketch the root conditions of the Elizabethan theater—because some people have found it difficult to conceive how this one man, with his provincial origins and his restricted range of experience, could have so rapidly and completely mastered the central imaginative themes of his times. Moreover, it is sometimes difficult to grasp how seeming abstractions such as market society, monarchical state, and theological doctrine were actually experienced directly by distinct individuals. Shakespeare's plays were social and collective events, but they also bore the stamp of a particular artist, one endowed with a remarkable capacity to craft lifelike illusions, a daring willingness to articulate an original vision, and a loving command, at once precise and generous, of language. These plays are stitched together from shared cultural experiences, inherited dramatic devices, and the pungent vernacular of the day, but we should not lose sight of the extent to which they articulate an intensely personal vision, a bold shaping of the available materials. Four centuries of feverish biographical speculation, much of it foolish, bear witness to a basic intuition: the richness of these plays, their inexhaustible openness, is the consequence not only of the auspicious collective conditions of the culture but also of someone's exceptional skill, inventiveness, and courage at taking those conditions and making of them something rich and strange.

The Theater of the Nation

What precisely were the collective conditions disclosed by the spectacles that Shakespeare would likely have witnessed? First, the growth of Stratford-upon-Avon, the bustling market town of which John Shakespeare was bailiff, is a small version of a momentous sixteenth-century development that made Shakespeare's career possible: the making of an urban "public." That development obviously depended on adequate numbers; the period experienced a rapid and still unexplained growth in population. With it came an expansion and elaboration of market relations: markets became less periodic, more continuous, and more abstract—centered, that is, not on the familiar materiality of goods but on the liquidity of capital and goods. In practical terms, this meant that it was possible to conceive of the theater not only as festive entertainment for special events—Lord Mayor's pageants, visiting princes, seasonal festivals, and the like—but as a permanent, year-round business venture. The venture relied on revenues from admission—it was an innovation of this period to have money advanced in the expectation of pleasure rather than offered to servants afterward as a reward—and counted on habitual playgoing, with a concomitant demand for new plays from competing theater companies: "But that's all one, our play is done," sings the Clown at the end of *Twelfth Night* and adds a glance toward the next afternoon's proceeds: "And we'll strive to please you every day" (5.1.393–94).

Second, the royal progress is an instance of what the anthropologist Clifford Geertz has called the Theater State, a state that manifests its power and meaning in exemplary public performances. Professional companies of players, like the one Shakespeare belonged to, understood well that they existed in relation to this Theater State and would, if they were fortunate, be called upon to serve it. Unlike Ben Jonson, Shakespeare did not, as far as we know, write royal entertainments on commission, but his plays were frequently performed before Queen Elizabeth and then before King James and Queen Anne, along with their courtiers and privileged guests. There are many fascinating glimpses of these performances, including a letter from Walter Cope to Robert Cecil, early in James's reign. "Burbage is come," Cope writes, referring to the leading actor of Shakespeare's company, "and says there is no new play that the Queen hath not seen, but they have revived an old one, called *Love's Labor's Lost*, which for wit and mirth he says will please her exceedingly. And this is appointed to be played tomorrow night at my Lord of Southampton's." Not only would such theatrical performances have given great pleasure—evidently, the Queen had already exhausted the company's new offerings—but they conferred prestige upon those who commanded them and those in whose honor they were mounted.

Monarchical power in the period was deeply allied to spectacular manifestations of the ruler's glory and disciplinary authority. The symbology of power depended on regal magnificence, reward, punishment, and pardon, all of which were heavily theatricalized. Indeed, the conspicuous public display does not simply serve the interests of power; on many occasions in the period, power seemed to exist in order to make pageantry possible, as if the nation's identity were only fully realized in theatrical performance. It would be easy to exaggerate this perception: the subjects of Queen Elizabeth and King James were acutely aware of the distinction between shadow and substance. But they were fascinated by the political magic through which shadows could be taken for substantial realities, and the ruling elite was largely complicit in the formation and celebration of a charismatic absolutism. At the same time, the claims of the monarch who professes herself or himself to be not the representative of the nation but its embodiment were set against the counterclaims of the House of Commons. And this institution too, as we have glimpsed, had its own theatrical rituals, centered on the crowd whose shouts of approval, in heavily stage-managed elections, chose the individuals who would stand for the polity and participate in deliberations held in a hall whose resemblance to a theater did not escape contemporary notice.

Third, in outlawing the Catholic Mass and banning the medieval mystery plays, along with pilgrimages and other rituals associated with holy shrines and sacred images, English Protestant authorities hoped to hold a monopoly on religious observances. But they inevitably left some people, perhaps substantial numbers of them, mourning what they had lost. Playing companies could satisfy at least some of the popular longings and appropriate aspects of the social energy no longer allowed a theological outlet. That is, official attacks on certain Catholic practices made it more possible for the public theater to appropriate and exploit their allure. Hence, for example, the plays that celebrated the solemn miracle of the Catholic Mass were banned, along with the most elaborate church vestments, but in *The Winter's Tale* Dion can speak in awe of what he witnessed at Apollo's temple:

> I shall report,
> For most it caught me, the celestial habits—
> Methinks I so should term them—and the reverence
> Of the grave wearers. Oh, the sacrifice!
> How ceremonious, solemn, and unearthly
> It was i'th' off'ring!
>
> (3.1.3–8)

And at the play's end, the statue of the innocent mother breathes, comes to life, and embraces her child.

The theater in Shakespeare's time, then, is intimately bound up with all three crucial cultural formations: market society, the Theater State, and the church. But it is important to note that the institution is not *identified* with any of them. The theater may be a market phenomenon, but it is repeatedly and bitterly attacked as the enemy of diligent, sober, productive economic activity. Civic authorities generally regarded the theater as a pestilential nuisance, a parasite on the body of the commonwealth, a temptation to students, apprentices, housewives, even respectable merchants to leave their serious business and lapse into idleness and waste. That waste, it might be argued, could be partially recuperated if it went for the glorification of a guild or the entertainment of an important dignitary, but the only group regularly profiting from the theater were the players and their disreputable associates.

For his part, Shakespeare made a handsome profit from the commodification of theatrical entertainment, but he seems never to have written "city comedy"—plays set in London and more or less explicitly concerned with market relations—and his characters express deep reservations about the power of money and commerce: "That smooth-faced gentleman, tickling commodity," Philip the Bastard observes in *King John*, "wins of all, / Of kings, of beggars, old men, young men, maids" (2.1.569–73). We could argue that the smooth-faced gentleman is none other than Shakespeare himself, for his drama famously mingles kings and clowns, princesses and panderers. But the mingling is set against a romantic current of social conservatism: in *Twelfth Night*, the aristocratic heiress Olivia falls in love with someone who appears far beneath her in wealth and social station, but it is revealed that he (and his sister Viola) are of noble blood; in *The Winter's Tale*, Leontes' daughter Perdita is raised as a shepherdess, but her noble nature shines through her humble upbringing, and she marries the Prince of Bohemia; the strange island maiden with whom Ferdinand, son of the King of Naples, falls madly in love in *The Tempest* turns out to be the daughter of the rightful Duke of Milan. Shakespeare pushes against this conservative logic in *All's Well That Ends Well*, but the noble young Bertram violently resists the unequal match thrust upon him by the King, and the play's mood is notoriously uneasy.

Similarly, Shakespeare's theater may have been patronized and protected by the monarchy—after 1603, his company received a royal patent and was known as the King's Men—but the two institutions were by no means identical in their interests or their ethos. To be sure, *Richard III* and *Macbeth* incorporate aspects of royal propaganda, but given the realities of censorship, Shakespeare's plays, and the period's drama as a whole, are surprisingly independent and complex in their political vision. There is, in any case, a certain inherent tension between kings and player kings: Elizabeth and James may both have likened themselves to actors onstage, but they were loath to admit their dependence on the applause and money, freely given or freely withheld, of the audience. The charismatic monarch insists that the sacredness of authority resides in the body of the ruler, not in a costume that may be worn and then discarded by an actor. Kings are not *representations* of power—or do not admit that they are—but claim to be the thing itself. The government institution that was actually based on the idea of representation, Parliament, had theatrical elements, as we have seen, but it significantly excluded any audience from its deliberations. And Shakespeare's oblique portraits of parliamentary representatives, the ancient Roman tribunes Sicinius Velutus and Junius Brutus in *Coriolanus,* are anything but flattering.

Finally, the theater drew significant energy from the liturgy and rituals of the late medieval church, but as Shakespeare's contemporaries widely remarked, the playhouse and the church were scarcely natural allies. Not only did the theater represent a potential competitor to worship services, and not only did ministers rail against prostitution and other vices associated with playgoing, but theatrical representation itself, even when ostensibly pious, seemed to many to empty out whatever it presented, turning substance into mere show. The theater could and did use the period's deep currents of religious feeling, but it had to do so carefully and with an awareness of conflicting interests.

Shakespeare Comes to London

How did Shakespeare decide to turn his prodigious talents to the stage? When did he make his way to London? How did he get his start? Concerning these and similar questions we have a mountain of speculation but no secure answers. There is not a single surviving record of Shakespeare's existence from 1585, when his twins were baptized in Stratford church, until 1592, when a rival London playwright made an envious remark about him. In the late seventeenth century, the delightfully eccentric collector of gossip John Aubrey was informed that prior to moving to London the young Shakespeare had been a schoolteacher in the country. Aubrey also recorded a story that Shakespeare had been a rather unusual apprentice butcher: "When he killed a calf, he would do it in a high style, and make a speech."

These and other legends, including one that has Shakespeare whipped for poaching game, fill the void until the unmistakable reference in Robert Greene's *Groatsworth of Wit Bought with a Million of Repentance* (1592). An inspired hack writer with a university education, a penchant for self-dramatization, a taste for wild living, and a strong streak of resentment, Greene, in his early thirties, was dying in poverty when he penned his last farewell, piously urging his fellow dramatists Christopher Marlowe, Thomas Nashe, and George Peele to abandon the wicked stage before they were brought low, as he had been, by a new arrival: "For there is an upstart crow, beautified with our feathers, that with his 'Tiger's heart wrapped in player's hide' supposes he is as well able to bombast out a blank verse as the best of you, and, being an absolute *Johannes Factotum,* is in his own conceit the only Shake-scene in a country." If "Shake-scene" is not enough to identify the object of his attack, Greene parodies a line from Shakespeare's early play 3 *Henry VI:* "O tiger's heart wrapped in a woman's hide" (1.4.137). Greene is accusing Shakespeare of being an upstart, a plagiarist, an egomaniacal jack-of-all-trades—and, above all perhaps, a popular success.

By 1592, then, Shakespeare had already arrived on the highly competitive London theatrical scene. He was successful enough to be attacked by Greene and, a few months later, defended by Henry Chettle, another hack writer who had seen Greene's manuscript through the press (or, some scholars speculate, had written the attack himself and passed it off as the dying Greene's). Chettle expresses his regret that he did not suppress Greene's diatribe and spare Shakespeare "because myself have seen his demeanor no less civil than he excellent in the quality he professes." Besides, Chettle adds, "divers of worship have reported his uprightness of dealing, which argues his honesty and his facetious [polished] grace in writing that approves his art." "Divers of worship": not only was Shakespeare established as an accomplished writer and actor, but he evidently had aroused the attention and the approbation of several socially prominent people. In Elizabethan England, aristocratic patronage, with the money, protection, and prestige it alone could provide, was probably a professional writer's most important asset.

This patronage, or at least Shakespeare's quest for it, is most visible in the dedications in 1593 and 1594 of his narrative poems *Venus and Adonis* and *The Rape of Lucrece* to the young nobleman Henry Wriothesley, Earl of Southampton. It may be glimpsed as well, perhaps, in the sonnets, with their extraordinary adoration of the fair youth, though the identity of that youth has never been determined. What return Shakespeare got for his exquisite offerings is likewise unknown. We do know that among wits and gallants, the narrative poems won Shakespeare a fine reputation as an immensely stylish and accomplished poet. An amateur play performed at Cambridge University at the end of the sixteenth century, *The Return from Parnassus*, makes fun of this vogue, as a foolish character effusively declares, "I'll worship sweet Mr. Shakespeare, and to honor him will lay his *Venus and Adonis* under my pillow." Many readers at the time may have done so: the poem went through sixteen editions before 1640, more than any other work by Shakespeare.

Patronage was crucially important not only for individual artists but also for the actors, playwrights, and investors who pooled their resources to form professional theater companies. The public playhouses had enemies, especially among civic and religious authorities, who wished greatly to curb performances or to ban them altogether. An Act of Parliament of 1572 included players among those classified as vagabonds, threatening them therefore with the horrible punishments meted out to those regarded as economic parasites. The players' escape route was to be nominally enrolled as apprentices in guilds, as if they were learning to be goldsmiths or grocers rather than actors. Alternatively, as we have noted, they could be officially listed as the servants of high-ranking noblemen.

When Shakespeare came to London, presumably in the late 1580s, there were more than a half-dozen of these companies operating under the patronage of various aristocrats. We do not know for which of these companies, several of which had toured in Stratford, he originally worked, nor whether he began, as legend has it, by holding gentlemen's horses outside the theater or by serving as a prompter's assistant and then graduated to acting and playwriting. Shakespeare is listed among the actors in Ben Jonson's *Every Man in His Humor* (performed in 1598) and *Sejanus* (performed in 1603), but we do not know for certain what roles he played, nor are there records of any of his other performances. Tradition has it that he played Adam in *As You Like It* and the Ghost in *Hamlet*, but he was clearly not one of the leading actors of the day.

Shakespeare may initially have been associated with the company of Ferdinando Stanley, Lord Strange; that company included actors with whom Shakespeare was later linked. Or he may have belonged to the Earl of Pembroke's Men, since there is evidence that they performed *The Taming of a Shrew* and a version of *3 Henry VI*. At any event, by 1594, Shakespeare was a member of the Chamberlain's Men, for his name, along with those of Will Kemp and Richard Burbage, appears on a record of those "servants to the Lord Chamberlain" paid for performance at the royal palace at Greenwich on December 26 and 28. Shakespeare stayed with this company, which during the reign of King James received royal patronage and became the King's Men, for the rest of his career.

Many playwrights in Shakespeare's time worked freelance, moving from company to company as opportunities arose, collaborating on projects, adding scenes to old plays, scrambling from one enterprise to another. But certain playwrights, among them the most successful, wrote for a single company, often agreeing contractually to give that company exclusive rights to their theatrical works. Shakespeare seems to have followed such a pattern. For the Chamberlain's Men, later the King's Men, he wrote an average of two plays per year. His company initially performed in The Theatre, a playhouse built in 1576 by an entrepreneurial actor and trained craftsman, James Burbage, the father of the actor Richard, who was to perform many of Shakespeare's greatest roles. When in 1597 their lease on this playhouse expired, the Chamberlain's Men passed through a difficult time, but they formed a joint stock company, raising sufficient capital to lease a site and put up a splendid new playhouse in the suburb of Southwark, on the south bank of the Thames. This playhouse, the Globe, opened in 1599. Shakespeare is listed in the legal agreement as one of the principal investors, and when the company began to use Blackfriars as their indoor playhouse around 1610, he was a major shareholder in that theater as well. The Chamberlain's Men dominated the theater scene, and the shares were quite valuable. Then as now, the theater was an extremely risky enterprise—most of those who wrote plays and performed in them made pathetically little money—but Shakespeare was a notable exception. The fine house in Stratford and the coat of arms he succeeded in acquiring were among the fruits of his multiple mastery, as actor, playwright, and investor of the London stage.

Edward Alleyn. Artist unknown. Alleyn was the great tragic actor of the Admiral's Men (the principal rival to Shakespeare's company). He was famous especially for playing the major characters of Christopher Marlowe.

The Shakespearean Trajectory

Though Shakespeare's England was in many ways a record-keeping society, no reliable record survives that details the performances, year by year, in the London theaters. Every play had to be licensed by the Master of the Revels, but the records kept by the relevant government officials from 1579 to 1621 have not survived. A major theatrical entrepreneur, Philip Henslowe, kept a careful account of his expenditures, including what he paid for the scripts he commissioned, but unfortunately Henslowe's main business was with the Rose and the Fortune theaters and not with the playhouses at which Shakespeare's company performed. A comparable ledger must have been kept by the shareholders of the Chamberlain's Men, but it has not survived. Shakespeare himself apparently did not undertake to preserve all his writings for posterity, let alone to clarify the chronology of his works or to specify which plays he wrote alone and which with collaborators.

The principal source for Shakespeare's works is the 1623 Folio volume of *Mr. William Shakespeares Comedies, Histories, & Tragedies.* The world owes this work,

IF YOV KNOW NOT ME,
You know no body.
OR,
The troubles of Queene ELIZABETH.

LONDON.
Printed by *B.A.* and *T.F.* for *Nathanaell Butter.* 1 6 3 2.

Title page of *If You Know Not Me, You Know Nobody; or, the Troubles of Queen Elizabeth* (1632).

lovingly edited after his death by two of the playwright's friends, an incalculable debt: without it, nearly half of Shakespeare's plays, including many of his greatest masterpieces, would have been lost forever. The edition does not, however, include any of Shakespeare's non-dramatic poems, and it omits four plays in which Shakespeare is now thought to have had a significant hand, *Edward III, Pericles, Cardenio,* and *The Two Noble Kinsmen,* along with his probable contribution to the multiauthored *Sir Thomas More.* (A number of other plays were attributed to Shakespeare, both before and after his death, but scholars have not generally accepted any of these into the established canon.) Moreover, the Folio edition does not print the plays in chronological order, nor does it attempt to establish a chronology. We do not know how much time would normally have elapsed between the writing of a play and its first performance, nor, with a few exceptions, do we know with any certainty the month or even the year of the first perfor-

mance of any of Shakespeare's plays. The quarto editions of those plays that were published during Shakespeare's lifetime obviously establish a date by which we know a given play had been written, but they give us little more than an end point, because there was likely to be a substantial though indeterminate gap between the first performance of a play and its publication.

With enormous patience and ingenuity, however, scholars have gradually assembled a considerable archive of evidence, both external and internal, for dating the composition of the plays. Besides actual publication, the external evidence includes explicit reference to a play, a record of its performance, or (as in the case of Greene's attack on the "upstart crow") the quoting of a line, though all of these can be maddeningly ambiguous. The most important single piece of external evidence appears in 1598 in *Palladis Tamia,* a long book of jumbled reflections by the churchman Francis Meres that includes a survey of the contemporary literary scene. Meres finds that "the sweet, witty soul of Ovid lives in mellifluous and honey-tongued Shakespeare, witness his *Venus and Adonis,* his *Lucrece,* his sugared Sonnets among his private friends, etc." Meres goes on to list Shakespeare's accomplishments as a playwright as well:

> As Plautus and Seneca are accounted the best for Comedy and Tragedy among the Latins: so Shakespeare among the English is the most excellent in both kinds for the stage; for Comedy, witness his *Gentlemen of Verona,* his *Errors,* his *Love labors lost,* his *Love labors won,* his *Midsummers night dream,* & his *Merchant of Venice:* for Tragedy his *Richard the 2, Richard the 3, Henry the 4, King John, Titus Andronicus* and his *Romeo and Juliet.*

Meres thus provides a date by which twelve of Shakespeare's plays had definitely appeared (including one, *Love's Labor's Won,* that appears either to have been lost or to be known to us by a different title). Unfortunately, Meres provides no clues about the order of appearance of these plays, and there are no other comparable lists.

Faced with the limitations of the external evidence, scholars have turned to a bewildering array of internal evidence, ranging from datable sources and topical allusions on the one hand to evolving stylistic features (ratio of verse to prose, percentage of rhyme to blank verse, colloquialisms, use of extended similes, and the like) on the other. Thus, for example, a cluster of plays with a high percentage of rhymed verse may follow closely upon Shakespeare's writing of the rhymed poems *Venus and Adonis* and *The Rape of Lucrece* and therefore be datable to 1594–95. Similarly, vocabulary overlap probably indicates proximity in composition, so if four or five plays share relatively "rare" vocabulary, it is likely that they were written in roughly the same period. Again, there seems to be a pattern in Shakespeare's use of colloquialisms, with a steady increase from *As You Like It* (1599–1600) to *Coriolanus* (1608), followed in the late romances by a retreat from the colloquial.

Ongoing computer analysis should provide further guidance in the future, though the precise order of the plays, still very much in dispute, is never likely to be settled to universal satisfaction. Still, certain broad patterns are now widely accepted. These patterns can be readily grasped in *The Norton Shakespeare*, which presents the plays according to our best estimate of their chronological order.

Shakespeare began his career, probably in the early 1590s, by writing both comedies and history plays. The attack by Greene suggests that he made his mark with the series of theatrically vital, occasionally brilliant, and often crude plays based on the foreign and domestic broils that erupted during the unhappy reign of the Lancastrian Henry VI. Modern readers and audiences are more likely to find the first sustained evidence of unusual power in *Richard III* (ca. 1592), a play that combines a richly imagined central character, a dazzling command of histrionic rhetoric, and an overarching moral vision of English history.

At virtually the same time that he was setting his stamp on the genre of the history play, Shakespeare was writing his first—or first surviving—comedies. Here, there are even fewer signs than in the histories of an apprenticeship. *The Comedy of Errors,* one of his early works in this genre, already displays a rare command of the resources of comedy: mistaken identity, madcap confusion, and the threat of disaster, giving way in the end to reconciliation, recovery, and love. Shakespeare's other comedies from the first half of the 1590s, *The Two Gentlemen of Verona, The Taming of the Shrew,* and *Love's Labor's Lost,* are no less remarkable for their sophisticated variations on familiar comic themes, their inexhaustible rhetorical inventiveness, and their poignant intimation, in the midst of festive celebration, of loss.

Successful as are these early histories and comedies, and indicative of an extraordinary theatrical talent, Shakespeare's achievement in the later 1590s would still have been all but impossible to foresee. Starting with *A Midsummer Night's Dream* (1595–96), Shakespeare wrote an unprecedented series of romantic comedies—*The Merchant of Venice, Much Ado About Nothing, The Merry Wives of Windsor, As You Like It,* and *Twelfth Night* (1600–1601)—whose poetic richness and emotional complexity remain unmatched. In the same period, he wrote a sequence of profoundly searching and ambitious history plays—*Richard II, 1* and *2 Henry IV,* and *Henry V*—which together explore the death throes of feudal England and the birth of the modern nation-state ruled by a charismatic monarch. Both the comedies and histories of this period are marked by their capaciousness, their ability to absorb characters who press up against the outermost boundaries of the genre: the comedy *The Merchant of Venice* somehow contains the figure, at once nightmarish and poignant, of Shylock, while the *Henry IV* plays, with their somber vision of crisis in the family and the state, bring to the stage one of England's greatest comic characters, Falstaff.

If in the mid- to late 1590s Shakespeare reached the summit of his art in two major genres, he also manifested a lively interest in a third. As early as 1592–93, he wrote the crudely violent tragedy *Titus Andronicus,* the first of several plays on themes from Roman history, and a few years later, in *Richard II,* he created in the protagonist a figure who achieves by the play's close the stature of a tragic hero. In the same year that Shakespeare wrote the wonderfully farcical "Pyramus and Thisbe" scene in *A Midsummer Night's Dream,* he probably also wrote the deeply tragic realization of the same story in *Romeo and Juliet.* But once again, the lyric anguish of *Romeo and Juliet* and the tormented self-revelation of *Richard II,* extraordinary as they are, could not have led anyone to predict the next phase of Shakespeare's career, the great tragic dramas that poured forth in the early years of the seventeenth century: *Hamlet, Othello, King Lear, Macbeth, Antony and Cleopatra,* and *Coriolanus.* These plays, written between 1600 and 1608, seem to mark a major shift in sensibility, an existential and metaphysical darkening that many readers think must have drawn upon a deep personal anguish, perhaps caused by the decline and death of Shakespeare's father, John, in 1601.

Whatever the truth of these speculations—and we have no direct, personal testimony either to support or to undermine them—there appears to have occurred in the same period a shift as well in Shakespeare's comic sensibility. The comedies written between 1601 and 1607, *Troilus and Cressida, Measure for Measure,* and *All's Well That Ends Well,* are sufficiently different from the earlier comedies—more biting in tone, more uneasy with comic conventions, more ruthlessly questioning of the values of the characters and the resolutions of the plots—that they led many twentieth-century scholars to classify them as "problem plays" or "dark comedies." This category has recently begun to fall out of favor, since Shakespeare criticism is perfectly happy to demonstrate that *all* of the plays are "problem plays." But there is another group of plays, among the last Shakespeare wrote, that continue to constitute a distinct category. *Pericles, Cymbeline, The Winter's Tale,* and *The Tempest*—written between 1607 and 1611, when the playwright had developed a remarkably fluid, dreamlike sense of plot and a poetic style that could veer, apparently effortlessly, from the tortured to the ineffably sweet—have been known since the late nineteenth century as the "romances." These plays share an interest in the moral and emotional life less of the adolescents who dominate the earlier comedies than of their parents. The romances are deeply concerned with patterns of loss and recovery, suffering and redemption, despair and renewal. They have seemed to many critics to constitute a deliberate conclusion to a career that began in histories and comedies and passed through the dark and tormented tragedies.

One effect of the practice of printing Shakespeare's plays in a reconstructed chronological order, as this edition does, is to produce a kind of authorial plot, a progress from youthful exuberance and a heroic grappling with history, through psychological anguish and radical doubt, to a mature serenity built upon an understanding of loss. The ordering of Shakespeare's "complete works" in this way reconstitutes the figure of the author as the beloved hero of his own, lived romance. There are numerous reasons to treat this romance with considerable skepticism: the precise order of the plays remains in dispute, the obsessions of the earliest plays crisscross with those of the last, the drama is a collaborative art form, and the relation between authorial consciousness and theatrical representation is murky. Yet a longing to identify Shakespeare's personal trajectory, to chart his psychic and spiritual as well as professional progress, is all but irresistible.

The Fetishism of Dress

Whatever the personal resonance of Shakespeare's own life, his art is deeply enmeshed in the collective hopes, fears, and fantasies of his time. For example, throughout his plays, Shakespeare draws heavily upon his culture's investment in costume, symbols of authority, visible signs of status—the fetishism of dress he must have witnessed from early childhood. Disguise in his drama is often assumed to be incredibly effective: when Henry V borrows a cloak, when Portia dresses in a jurist's robes, when Viola puts on a young man's suit, it is as if each has become unrecognizable, as if identity resided in clothing. At the end of *Twelfth Night,* even though Viola's true identity has been disclosed, Orsino continues to call her Cesario; he will do so, he says, until she resumes her maid's garments, for only then will she be transformed into a woman:

> Cesario, come—
> For so you shall be while you are a man—
> But when in other habits you are seen,
> Orsino's mistress and his fancy's queen.
> (5.1.371–74)

The pinnacle of this fetishism of costume is the royal crown, for whose identity-conferring power men are willing to die, but the principle is everywhere, from the filthy blanket that transforms Edgar into Poor Tom to the coxcomb that is the badge of the licensed fool. Antonio, wishing to express his utter contempt, spits on Shylock's "Jewish gaberdine," as if the clothing were the essence of the man; Kent, pouring insults on the loathsome Oswald, calls him a "filthy worsted-stocking knave"; and innocent Imogen, learning that her husband has ordered her murder, thinks of herself as an expensive cast-off dress, destined to be ripped at the seams:

> Poor I am stale, a garment out of fashion,
> And for I am richer than to hang by th' walls,
> I must be ripped: to pieces with me.
> (*Cymbeline* 3.4.50–52)

What can be said, thought, felt in this culture seems deeply dependent on the clothes one wears—clothes that one is, in effect, *permitted* or *compelled* to wear, since there is little freedom in dress. Shakespearean drama occasionally represents something like such freedom: after all, Viola in *Twelfth Night* chooses to put off her "maiden weeds," as does Rosalind, who declares, "We'll have a swashing and a martial outside" (*As You Like It* 1.3.116). But these choices are characteristically made under the pressure of desperate circumstances, here shipwreck and exile. Part of the charm of Shakespeare's heroines is their ability to transform distress into an opportunity for self-fashioning, but the plays often suggest that there is less autonomy than meets the eye. What looks like an escape from cultural determinism may be only a deeper form of constraint. We may take, as an allegorical emblem of this constraint, the transformation of the beggar Christopher Sly in the playful Induction to *The Taming of the Shrew* into a nobleman. The transformation seems to suggest that you are free to make of yourself whatever you choose to be—the play begins with the drunken Sly claiming the dignity of his pedigree ("Look in the Chronicles" [Induction 1.3–4])—but in fact he is only the subject of the mischievous lord's experiment, designed to demonstrate the interwovenness of clothing and identity. "What think you," the lord asks his huntsman,

> if he were conveyed to bed,
> Wrapped in sweet clothes, rings put upon his fingers,
> A most delicious banquet by his bed,
> And brave attendants near him when he wakes—
> Would not the beggar then forget himself?

To which the huntsman replies, in words that underscore the powerlessness of the drunken beggar, "Believe me, lord, I think he cannot choose" (Induction 1.33–38).

Petruccio's taming of Katherina is similarly constructed around an imposition of identity, an imposition closely bound up with the right to wear certain articles of clothing. When the haberdasher arrives with a fashionable lady's hat, Petruccio refuses it over his wife's vehement objections: "This doth fit the time, / And gentlewomen wear such caps as these." "When you are gentle," Petruccio replies, "you shall have one, too, /

And not till then" (4.3.70–73). At the play's close, Petruccio demonstrates his authority by commanding his tamed wife to throw down her cap: "Off with that bauble; throw it underfoot" (5.2.122). Here as elsewhere in Shakespeare, acts of robing and disrobing are intensely charged, a charge that culminates in the trappings of monarchy. When Richard II, in a scene that was probably censored during the reign of Elizabeth from the stage as well as the printed text, is divested of his crown and scepter, he experiences the loss as the eradication of his name, the symbolic melting away of his identity:

> Alack the heavy day,
> That I have worn so many winters out
> And know not now what name to call myself.
> Oh, that I were a mockery king of snow,
> Standing before the sun of Bolingbroke
> To melt myself away in water-drops.
>   (4.1.250–55)

When Lear tears off his regal "lendings" in order to reduce himself to the nakedness of the Bedlam beggar, he is expressing not only his radical loss of social identity but the breakdown of his psychic order as well, expressing therefore his reduction to the condition of the "poor bare forked animal" that is the primal form of undifferentiated existence. And when Cleopatra determines to kill herself in order to escape public humiliation in Rome, she magnificently affirms her essential being by arraying herself as she had once done to encounter Antony:

> Show me, my women, like a queen. Go, fetch
> My best attires. I am again for Cydnus
> To meet Mark Antony.
>   (5.2.226–28)

Such scenes are a remarkable intensification of the everyday symbolic practice of Renaissance English culture, its characteristically deep and knowing commitment to illusion: "I know perfectly well that the woman in her crown and jewels and gorgeous gown is an aging, irascible, and fallible mortal—she herself virtually admits as much—yet I profess that she is the virgin queen, timelessly beautiful, wise, and just." Shakespeare understood how close this willed illusion was to the spirit of the theater, to the actors' ability to work on what the chorus in *Henry V* calls the "imaginary forces" of the audience. But there is throughout Shakespeare's works a counterintuition that, while it does not exactly overturn this illusion, renders it poignant, vulnerable, fraught. The "masculine usurp'd attire" that is donned by Viola, Rosalind, Portia, Jessica, and other Shakespeare heroines alters what they can say and do, reveals important aspects of their character, and changes their destiny, but it is, all the same, not theirs and not all of who they are. They have, the plays insist, natures that are neither transformed nor altogether concealed by their dress: "Pray God defend me," exclaims the frightened Viola. "A little thing would make me tell them how much I lack of a man" (*Twelfth Night* 3.4.271–72).

The Paradoxes of Identity

The gap between costume and identity is not simply a matter of what women supposedly lack; virtually all of Shakespeare's major characters, men and women, convey the sense of both a *self-division* and an *inward expansion*. The belief in a complex inward realm beyond costumes and status is a striking inversion of the clothes cult: we know perfectly well that the characters have no inner lives apart from what we see on the stage, and yet we believe that they continue to exist when we do not see them, that they exist apart from their represented words and actions, that they have hidden dimensions. How is this conviction aroused and sustained? In part, it is the effect of what the characters themselves say: "My grief lies all within," Richard II tells Bolingbroke,

> And these external manner of laments
> Are merely shadows to the unseen grief
> That swells with silence in the tortured soul.
> (4.1.288–91)

Similarly, Hamlet, dismissing the significance of his outward garments, declares, "I have that within which passes show— / These but the trappings and the suits of woe" (1.2.85–86). And the distinction between inward and outward is reinforced throughout this play and elsewhere by an unprecedented use of the aside and the soliloquy.

The soliloquy is a continual reminder in Shakespeare that the inner life is by no means transparent to one's surrounding world. Prince Hal seems open and easy with his mates in Eastcheap, but he has a hidden reservoir of disgust:

> I know you all, and will a while uphold
> The unyoked humor of your idleness.
> Yet herein will I imitate the sun,
> Who doth permit the base contagious clouds
> To smother up his beauty from the world,
> That, when he please again to be himself,
> Being wanted he may be more wondered at
> By breaking through the foul and ugly mists
> Of vapors that did seem to strangle him.
> (I Henry IV 1.2.170–78)

"When he please again to be himself": the line implies that identity is a matter of free choice—you decide how much of yourself you wish to disclose—but Shakespeare employs other devices that suggest more elusive and intractable layers of inwardness. There is a peculiar, recurrent lack of fit between costume and character, in fools as in princes, that is not simply a matter of disguise and disclosure. If Hal's true identity is partially "smothered" in the tavern, it is not completely revealed either in his soldier's armor or in his royal robes, nor do his asides reach the bedrock of unimpeachable self-understanding.

Identity in Shakespeare repeatedly slips away from the characters themselves, as it does from Richard II after the deposition scene and from Lear after he has given away his land and from Macbeth after he has gained the crown. The slippage does not mean that they retreat into silence; rather, they embark on an experimental, difficult fashioning of themselves and the world, most often through role-playing. "I cannot do it," says the deposed and imprisoned Richard II. "Yet I'll hammer't out" (5.5.5). This could serve as the motto for many Shakespearean characters: Viola becomes Cesario, Rosalind calls herself Ganymede, Kent becomes Caius, Edgar presents himself as Poor Tom, Hamlet plays the madman that he has partly become, Hal pretends that he is his father and a highwayman and Hotspur and even himself. Even in comedy, these ventures into alternate identities are rarely matters of choice; in tragedy, they are always undertaken under pressure and compulsion. And often enough it is not a matter of role-playing at all, but of a drastic transformation whose extreme emblem is the harrowing madness of Lear and of Leontes.

There is a moment in Richard II in which the deposed king asks for a mirror and then, after musing on his reflection, throws it to the ground. The shattering of the glass serves to remind us not only of the fragility of identity in Shakespeare but of its characteristic appearance in fragmentary mirror images. The plays continually generate alternative reflections, identities that intersect with, underscore, echo, or otherwise set off that of the principal character. Hence, Desdemona and Iago are not only important figures in Othello's world—they also seem to embody partially realized aspects of himself; Falstaff and Hotspur play a comparable role in relation to Prince Hal, Fortinbras and Horatio in relation to Hamlet, Gloucester and the Fool in relation to Lear, and so forth. In many of these plays, the complementary and contrasting characters figure in subplots, subtly interwoven with the play's main plot and illuminating its concerns. The note so conspicuously sounded by Fortinbras at the close of *Hamlet*—what the hero might have been, "had he been put on"—is heard repeatedly in Shakespeare and contributes to the overwhelming intensity, poignancy, and complexity of the characters. This is a world in which outward appearance is everything and nothing, in which individuation is at once sharply etched and continually blurred, in which the victims of fate are haunted by the ghosts of the possible, in which everything is simultaneously as it must be and as it need not have been.

Are these alternatives signs of a struggle between contradictory and irreconcilable perspectives in Shakespeare? In certain plays—notably, *Measure for Measure, All's Well That Ends Well, Coriolanus,* and *Troilus and Cressida*—the tension seems both high and entirely unresolved. But Shakespearean contradictions are more often reminiscent of the capacious spirit of Montaigne, who refused any systematic order that would betray his sense of reality. Thus, individual characters are immensely important in Shakespeare—he is justly celebrated for his unmatched skill in the invention of particular dramatic identities, marked with distinct speech patterns, manifested in social status, and confirmed by costume and gesture—but the principle of individuation is not the rock on which his theatrical art is founded. After the masks are stripped away, the pretenses exposed, the claims of the ego shattered, there is a mysterious remainder; as the shamed but irrepressible Paroles declares in *All's Well That Ends Well,* "Simply the thing I am / Shall make me live" (4.3.316–17). Again and again the audience is made to sense a deeper energy, a source of power that at once discharges itself in individual characters and seems to sweep right through them.

The Poet of Nature

In *The Birth of Tragedy,* Nietzsche called a comparable source of energy that he found in Greek tragedy "Dionysos." But the god's name, conjuring up Bacchic frenzy, does not seem appropriate to Shakespeare. In the late seventeenth and eighteenth centuries, it was more plausibly called Nature: "The world must be peopled," says the delightful Benedict in *Much Ado About Nothing* (2.3.213), and there are frequent invocations elsewhere of the happy, generative power that brings couples together—

> Jack shall have Jill,
> Naught shall go ill,
> The man shall have his mare again, and all shall be well.
> (*A Midsummer Night's Dream* 3.2.461–63)

—and the melancholy, destructive power that brings all living things to the grave: "Golden lads and girls all must, / As chimney-sweepers, come to dust" (*Cymbeline* 4.2.261–62).

But the celebration of Shakespeare as a poet of nature—often coupled with an inane celebration of his supposedly "natural" (that is, untutored) genius—has its distinct limitations. For Shakespearean art brilliantly interrogates the "natural," refusing to take for granted precisely what the celebrants think is most secure. His comedies are endlessly inventive in showing that love is not simply natural: the playful hint of bestiality in the line quoted above, "the man shall have his mare again" (from a play in which the Queen of the Fairies falls in love with an ass-headed laborer), lightly unsettles the boundaries between the natural and the perverse. These boundaries are called into question throughout Shakespeare's work, from the cross-dressing and erotic crosscurrents that deliciously complicate the lives of the characters in *Twelfth Night* and *As You Like It* to the terrifying violence that wells up from the heart of the family in *King Lear* or from the sweet intimacy of sexual desire in *Othello.* Even the boundary between life and death is not secure, as the ghosts in *Julius Caesar, Hamlet,* and *Macbeth* attest, while the principle of natural death (given its most eloquent articulation by old Hamlet's murderer, Claudius!) is repeatedly tainted and disrupted.

Disrupted too is the idea of order that constantly makes its claim, most insistently in the history plays. Scholars have observed the presence in Shakespeare's works of the so-called Tudor myth—the ideological justification of the ruling dynasty as a restoration of national order after a cycle of tragic violence. The violence, Tudor apologists claimed, was divine punishment unleashed after the deposition of the anointed king, Richard II, for God will not tolerate violations of the sanctified order. Traces of this propaganda certainly exist in the histories—Shakespeare may, for all we know, have personally subscribed to its premises—but a closer scrutiny of his plays has disclosed so many ironic reservations and qualifications and subversions as to call into question any straightforward adherence to a political line. The plays manifest a profound fascination with the monarchy and with the ambitions of the aristocracy, but the fascination is never simply endorsement. There is always at least the hint of a slippage between the great figures, whether admirable or monstrous, who stand at the pinnacle of authority and the vast, miscellaneous mass of soldiers, scriveners, ostlers, poets, whores, gardeners, thieves, weavers, shepherds, country gentlemen, sturdy beggars, and the like who make up the commonwealth. And the idea of order, though eloquently articulated (most memorably by Ulysses in *Troilus and Cressida*), is always shadowed by a relentless spirit of irony.

The Play of Language

If neither the individual nor nature nor order will serve, can we find a single comprehensive name for the underlying force in Shakespeare's work? Certainly not. The work is too protean and capacious. But much of the energy that surges through this astonishing body of plays and poems is closely linked to the power of language. Shakespeare was the supreme product of a rhetorical culture, a culture steeped in the arts of persuasion and verbal expressiveness. In 1512, the great Dutch humanist Erasmus published a work called *De copia* that taught its readers how to cultivate "copiousness," verbal richness, in discourse. (Erasmus obligingly provides, as a sample, a list of 144 different ways of saying "Thank you for your letter.") Recommended modes of variation include putting the subject of an argument into fictional form, as well as the use of synonym, substitution, paraphrase, metaphor, metonymy, synecdoche, hyperbole, diminution, and a host of other figures of speech. To change emotional tone, he suggests trying *ironia, interrogatio, admiratio, dubitatio, abominatio*—the possibilities seem infinite.

In Renaissance England, certain syntactic forms or patterns of words known as "figures" (also called "schemes") were shaped and repeated in order to confer beauty or heighten expressive power. Figures were usually known by their Greek and Latin names, though in an Elizabethan rhetorical manual, *The Art of English Poesy,* George Puttenham made a valiant if short-lived attempt to give them English equivalents, such as "*Hyperbole,* or the Overreacher," "*Ironia,* or the Dry Mock," and "*Ploce,* or the Doubler." Those who received a grammar school education throughout Europe at almost any point between the Roman Empire and the eighteenth century probably knew by heart the names of up to one hundred such figures, just as they knew by heart their multiplication tables. According to one scholar's count, Shakespeare knew and made use of about two hundred.

As certain grotesquely inflated Renaissance texts attest, lessons from *De copia* and similar rhetorical guides could encourage mere prolixity and verbal self-display. But though he shared his culture's delight in rhetorical complexity, Shakespeare always understood how to swoop from baroque sophistication to breathtaking simplicity. Moreover, he grasped early in his career how to use figures of speech, tone, and rhythm not only to provide emphasis and elegant variety but also to articulate the inner lives of his characters. Take, for example, these lines from *Othello,* where, as scholars have noted, Shakespeare deftly combines four common rhetorical figures— *anaphora, parison, isocolon,* and *epistrophe*—to depict with painful vividness Othello's psychological torment:

> By the world,
> I think my wife be honest, and think she is not;
> I think that thou art just, and think thou art not.
> I'll have some proof.
>
> (3.3.380–83)

Anaphora is simply the repetition of a word at the beginning of a sequence of sentences or clauses ("I/I"). *Parison* is the correspondence of word to word within adjacent sentences or clauses, either by direct repetition ("think/think") or by the matching of noun with noun, verb with verb ("wife/thou"; "be/art"). *Isocolon* gives exactly the same length to corresponding clauses ("and think she is not/and think thou art not"), and *epistrophe* is the mirror image of *anaphora,* in that it is the repetition of a word at the end of a sequence of sentences or clauses ("not/not"). Do we need to know the Greek names for these figures in order to grasp the effectiveness of Othello's lines? Of course not. But Shakespeare and his contemporaries, convinced that rhetoric provided the most natural and powerful means by which feelings could be conveyed to readers and listeners, were trained in an analytical language that helped at once to promote and to account for this effectiveness. In his 1593 edition of *The Garden of Eloquence,* Henry Peacham remarks that *epistrophe* "serveth to leave a word of importance in the end of a sentence, that it may the longer hold the sound in the mind of the hearer," and in *Directions for Speech and Style* (ca. 1599), John Hoskins notes that *anaphora* "beats upon one thing to cause the quicker feeling in the audience."

Shakespeare also shared with his contemporaries a keen understanding of the ways that rhetorical devices could be used not only to express powerful feelings but to hide them: after all, the artist who created Othello also created Iago, Richard III, and Lady Macbeth. He could deftly skewer the rhetorical affectations of Polonius in *Hamlet* or the pedant Holofernes in *Love's Labor's Lost.* He could deploy stylistic variations to mark the boundaries not of different individuals but of different social realms; in *A Midsummer Night's Dream,* for example, the blank verse of Duke Theseus is played off against the rhymed couplets of the well-born young lovers, and both in turn contrast with the prose spoken by the artisans. At the same time that he thus marks boundaries between both individuals and groups, Shakespeare shows a remarkable ability to establish unifying patterns of imagery that knit together the diverse strands of his plot and suggest subtle links among characters who may be scarcely aware of how much they share with one another.

One of the hidden links in Shakespeare's own works is the frequent use he makes of a somewhat unusual rhetorical figure called *hendiadys.* An example from the Roman poet Virgil is the phrase *pateris libamus et auro,* "we drink from cups and gold" (*Georgics* 2.192). Rather than serving as an adjective or a dependent noun, as in "golden cups" or "cups of gold," the word "gold" serves as a substantive joined to another substantive, "cups," by a conjunction, "and." Shakespeare uses the figure over three hundred times in all, and since it does not appear in ancient or medieval lists of tropes and schemes and is treated only briefly by English rhetoricians, he may have come upon it directly in Virgil. *Hendiadys* literally means "one through two," though Shakespeare's versions often make us quickly, perhaps only subliminally, aware of the complexity of what ordinarily passes for straightforward perceptions. When Othello, in his suicide speech, invokes the memory of "a malignant and a turbaned Turk," the figure of speech at once associates enmity with cultural difference and keeps them slightly apart. And when Macbeth speaks of his "strange and self-abuse," the *hendiadys* seems briefly to hold both "strange" and "self" up for scrutiny. It would be foolish to make too much of any single feature in Shakespeare's varied and diverse creative achievement, and yet this curious rhetorical scheme has something of the quality of a fingerprint.

But all of his immense rhetorical gifts, though rich, beautiful, and supremely useful, do not adequately convey Shakespeare's relation to language, which is less strictly functional than a total immersion in the arts of persuasion may imply. An Erasmian admiration for copiousness cannot fully explain Shakespeare's astonishing vocabulary of some 25,000 words. (His closest rival among the great English poets of the period was John Milton, with about 12,000 words, and most major writers, let alone ordinary people, have much smaller vocabularies.) This immense word hoard, it is worth noting, was not the result of scanning a dictionary; in the late sixteenth century, there were no large-scale English dictionaries of the kind to which we are now accustomed. Shakespeare seems to have absorbed new words from virtually every discursive realm he ever encountered, and he experimented boldly and tirelessly with them. These experiments were facilitated by a flexibility in grammar, orthography, and diction that the more orderly, regularized English of the later seventeenth and eighteenth centuries suppressed.

Owing in part to the number of dialects in London, pronunciation was variable, and there were many opportunities for phonetic association between words: the words "bear," "barn," "bier," "bourn" "born," and "barne" could all sound like one another. Homonyms were given greater scope by the fact that the same word could be spelled so many different ways—Christopher Marlowe's name appears in the records as Marlowe, Marloe, Marlen, Marlyne, Merlin, Marley, Marlye, Morley, and Morle—and by the fact that a word's grammatical function could easily shift, from noun to verb, verb to adjective, and so forth. Since grammar and punctuation did not insist on relations of coordination and subordination, loose, nonsyntactic sentences were common, and etymologies were used to forge surprising or playful relations between distant words.

It would seem inherently risky for a popular playwright to employ a vocabulary so far in excess of what most mortals could possibly possess, but Shakespeare evidently counted on his audience's linguistic curiosity and adventurousness, just as he counted on its general and broad-based rhetorical competence. He was also usually careful to provide a context that in effect explained or translated his more arcane terms. For example, when Macbeth reflects with horror on his murderous hands, he shudderingly imagines that even the sea could not wash away the blood; on the contrary, his bloodstained hand, he says, "will rather / The multitudinous seas incarnadine." The meaning of the unfamiliar word "incarnadine" is explained by the next line: "Making the green one red" (2.2.64–66).

What is most striking is not the abstruseness or novelty of Shakespeare's language but its extraordinary vitality, a quality that the playwright seemed to pursue with a kind of passionate recklessness. Perhaps Samuel Johnson was looking in the right direction when he complained that the "quibble," or pun, was "the fatal Cleopatra for which [Shakespeare] lost the world, and was content to lose it." For the power that continually discharges itself throughout the plays, at once constituting and unsettling everything it touches, is the polymorphous power of language, language that seems both costume and that which lies beneath the costume, personal identity and that which challenges the merely personal, nature and that which enables us to name nature and thereby distance ourselves from it.

Shakespeare's language has an overpowering exuberance and generosity that often resembles the experience of love. Consider, for example, Oberon's description in *A Midsummer Night's Dream* of the moment when he saw Cupid shoot his arrow at the fair vestal: "Thou rememberest," he asks Puck,

> Since once I sat upon a promontory
> And heard a mermaid on a dolphin's back
> Uttering such dulcet and harmonious breath
> That the rude sea grew civil at her song

> And certain stars shot madly from their spheres
> To hear the sea-maid's music?
>
> (2.1.148–54)

Here, Oberon's composition of place, lightly alluding to a classical emblem, is infused with a fantastically lush verbal brilliance. This brilliance, the result of masterful alliterative and rhythmical technique, seems gratuitous; that is, it does not advance the plot, but rather exhibits a capacity for display and self-delight that extends from the fairies to the playwright who has created them. The rich music of Oberon's words imitates the "dulcet and harmonious breath" he is intent on recalling, breath that has, in his account, an oddly contradictory effect: it is at once a principle of order, so that the rude sea is becalmed like a lower-class mob made civil by a skilled orator, and a principle of disorder, so that celestial bodies in their fixed spheres are thrown into mad confusion. And this contradictory effect, so intimately bound up with an inexplicable, supererogatory, and intensely erotic verbal magic, is a key to *A Midsummer Night's Dream,* with its exquisite blend of confusion and discipline, lunacy and hierarchical ceremony.

The fairies in this comedy seem to embody a pervasive sense found throughout Shakespeare's work that there is something uncanny about language, something that is not quite human, at least in the conventional and circumscribed sense of the human that dominates waking experience. In the comedies, this intuition is alarming but ultimately benign: Oberon and his followers trip through the great house at the play's close, blessing the bride-beds and warding off the nightmares that lurk in marriage and parenthood. But there is in Shakespeare an alternative, darker vision of the uncanniness of language, a vision also embodied in creatures that test the limits of the human—not the fairies of *A Midsummer Night's Dream* but the weird sisters of *Macbeth.* When in the tragedy's opening scene the witches chant, "Fair is foul, and foul is fair," they unsettle through the simplest and most radical act of linguistic equation (x is y) the fundamental distinctions through which a moral order is established. And when Macbeth appears onstage a few minutes later, his first words unconsciously echo what we have just heard from the witches' mouths: "So foul and fair a day I have not seen" (1.3.39). What is the meaning of this linguistic "unconscious"? On the face of things, Macbeth presumably means only that the day of fair victory is also a day of foul weather, but the fact that he echoes the witches (something that we hear but that he cannot know) intimates an occult link between them, even before their direct encounter. It is difficult, perhaps impossible, to specify exactly what this link signifies—generations of emboldened critics have tried without notable success—but we can at least affirm that its secret lair is in the play's language, like a half-buried pun whose full articulation will entail the murder of Duncan, the ravaging of his kingdom, and Macbeth's own destruction.

Macbeth is haunted by half-buried puns, equivocations, and ambiguous grammatical constructions known as amphibologies. They manifest themselves most obviously in the words of the witches, from the opening exchanges to the fraudulent assurances that deceive Macbeth at the close, but they are also present in his most intimate and private reflections, as in his tortured broodings about his proposed act of treason:

> If it were done when 'tis done, then 'twere well
> It were done quickly. If th'assassination
> Could trammel up the consequence and catch
> With his surcease success—that but this blow
> Might be the be-all and the end-all!—here,
> But here, upon this bank and shoal of time,
> We'd jump the life to come.
>
> (1.7.1–7)

The dream is to reach a secure and decisive end, to catch as in a net (hence "trammel up") all of the slippery, unforeseen, and uncontrollable consequences of regicide, to hobble time as one might hobble a horse (another sense of "trammel up"), to stop the flow ("success") of events, to be, as Macbeth later puts it, "settled." But Macbeth's words themselves slip away from the closure he seeks; they slide into one another, trip over themselves, twist and double back and swerve into precisely the sickening uncertainties their speaker most wishes to avoid. And if we sense a barely discernible note of comedy in Macbeth's tortured language, a discordant playing with the senses of the word "done" and the hint of a childish tongue twister in the phrase "catch / With his surcease success," we are in touch with a dark pleasure to which Shakespeare was all his life addicted.

Look again at the couplet from *Cymbeline:* "Golden lads and girls all must, / As chimney-sweepers, come to dust." The playwright who insinuated a pun into the solemn dirge is the same playwright whose tragic heroine in *Antony and Cleopatra,* pulling the bleeding body of her dying lover into the pyramid, says, "Our strength is all gone into heaviness" (4.15.34). He is the playwright whose Juliet, finding herself alone on the stage, says, "My dismal scene I needs must act alone" (*Romeo and Juliet* 4.3.19), and the playwright who can follow the long, wrenching periodic sentence that Othello speaks, just before he stabs himself, with the remark "O bloody period!" (5.2.349). The point is not merely the presence of puns in the midst of tragedy (as there are stabs of pain in the midst of Shakespearean comedy); it is rather the streak of wildness that they so deliberately disclose, the sublimely indecorous linguistic energy of which Shakespeare was at once the towering master and the most obedient, worshipful servant.

From Page to Stage: Shakespeare at Work

Shakespeare's extraordinary imaginative and linguistic power left its mark, like a personal signature, on everything he wrote. But his plays became the property of the theatrical company in which he was a shareholder. The company could choose to sell its plays to printers who might hope to profit if the public was eager to read as well as to watch a popular hit. But relatively few plays excited that level of public interest. Moreover, playing companies did not always think it was in their interest to have their scripts circulating in print, at least while the plays were actively in repertory: players evidently feared competition from rival companies and thought that reading might dampen playgoing. Plays were on occasion printed quickly, in order to take advantage of their popularity, but they were most often sold to the printers when the theaters were temporarily closed by plague, or when the company was in need of capital (four of Shakespeare's plays were published in 1600, presumably to raise money to pay the debts incurred in building the new Globe), or when a play had grown too old to revive profitably. There is no conclusive evidence that Shakespeare disagreed with this professional caution. There was clearly a market for his plays in print as well as onstage, and he himself may have taken pride in what he wrote as suitable for reading as well as viewing. But unlike Jonson, who took the radical step of rewriting his own plays for publication in the 1616 folio of his *Works,* Shakespeare evidently never undertook to constitute his plays as a canon. If in the sonnets he imagines his verse achieving a symbolic immortality, this dream apparently did not extend to his plays, at least through the medium of print.

Moreover, there is no evidence that Shakespeare had an interest in asserting authorial rights over his scripts, or that he or any other working English playwright had a public "standing," legal or otherwise, from which to do so. (Jonson was ridiculed for his presumption.) There is no indication whatever that he could, for example, veto changes in his scripts or block interpolated scenes or withdraw a play from production if a particular interpretation, addition, or revision did not please him. To be sure, in his advice to the players, Hamlet urges that those who play the clowns "speak no more than is set down for them," but—apart from the question of whether the prince speaks for the playwright—the play-within-the-play in *Hamlet* is precisely an instance of a script altered to suit a particular occasion. It seems likely that Shakespeare would have routinely accepted the possibility of such alterations. Moreover, he would of necessity have routinely accepted the possibility, and in certain cases the virtual inevitability, of cuts in order to stage his plays in the two to two and one-half hours that was the normal performing time. There is an imaginative generosity in many of Shakespeare's scripts, as if he were deliberately offering his fellow actors more than they could use on any one occasion and hence giving them abundant materials with which to reconceive and revivify each play again and again, as they or their audiences liked it. The Elizabethan theater, like most theater in our own time, was a collaborative enterprise, and the collaboration almost certainly extended to decisions about selection, trimming, shifts of emphasis, and minor or major revision.

Writing for the theater for Shakespeare was never simply a matter of sitting alone at his desk and putting words on paper; it was a social process as well as individual act. We do not know the extent to which this process frustrated him; in Sonnet 66 he writes of "art made tongue-tied by authority." Shakespeare may have been forced on occasion to cut lines and even whole scenes to which he was attached; shifting political circumstances may have occasioned rewriting, possibly against his will; or his fellow players may have insisted that they could not successfully perform what he had written, compelling him to make changes he did not welcome. But compromise and collaboration are part of what it means to be in the theater, and Shakespeare was, supremely, a man of the theater.

As a man of the theater, Shakespeare understood that whatever he set down on paper was not the end of the story. It would inevitably be shaped by the words he spoke to his fellow actors and by their own ideas concerning emphasis, stage business, tone, pacing, possible cuts, and so forth. It could be modified too by the intervention of the government censor or by intimations that some powerful figure might take offense at something in the script. To the extent that the agreed-upon alterations were ever written down, they were recorded in the promptbook used for a particular performance, and that promptbook could in turn be modified for a subsequent performance in a different setting.

For many years, it was thought that Shakespeare himself did little or no revising. Some recent editors have argued persuasively that there are many signs of authorial revision, even wholesale rewriting. But there is no sign that Shakespeare sought through such revision to bring each of his plays to its "perfect," "final" form. On the contrary, many of the revisions seem to indicate that the scripts remained open texts that the playwright and his company expected to add to, cut, and rewrite as the occasion demanded.

Ralph Waldo Emerson once compared Shakespeare and his contemporary Francis Bacon in terms of the relative "finish" of their work. All of Bacon's work, wrote Emerson, "lies along the ground, a vast unfinished city." Each of Shakespeare's dramas, by contrast, "is perfect, hath an immortal integrity. To make Bacon's work complete, he must live to the end of the world." Recent scholarship suggests that Shakespeare was more like Bacon than Emerson thought. Neither the Folio nor the quarto texts of Shakespeare's plays bear the seal of final authorial intention, the mark of decisive closure that has served, at least ideally, as the guarantee of textual authenticity. We want to believe, as we read the text, "This is the play as Shakespeare himself wanted it read," but there is no license for such a reassuring sentiment. To be "not of an age, but for all time" means in Shakespeare's case not that the plays have achieved a static perfection, but that they are creatively, inexhaustibly unfinished.

The Status of the Artist

That we have been so eager to link certain admired scripts to a single known playwright is closely related to changes in the status of artists in the Renaissance, changes that led to a heightened interest in the hand of the individual creator. Like medieval painting, medieval drama gives us few clues as to the particular individuals who fashioned the objects we admire. We know something about the places in which these objects were made, the circumstances that enabled their creation, the spaces in which they were placed, but relatively little about the particular artists themselves. It is easy to imagine a wealthy patron or a civic authority in the late Middle Ages commissioning a play on a particular subject (appropriate, for example, to a seasonal ritual, a religious observance, or a political festivity) and specifying the date, place, and length of the performance, the number of actors, even the costumes to be used, but it is more difficult to imagine him specifying a particular playwright and still less insisting that the entire play be written by this dramatist alone. Only with the Renaissance do we find a growing insistence on the name of the maker, the signature that heightens the value and even the meaning of the work by implying that it is the emanation of a single, distinct shaping consciousness.

In the case of Renaissance painting, we know that this signature does not necessarily mean that every stroke was made by the master. Some of the work, possibly the greater part of it, may have been done by assistants, with only the faces and a few finishing touches from the hand of the illustrious artist to whom the work is confidently attributed. As the skill of individual masters became more explicitly valued, contracts began to specify how much was to come from the brush of the principal painter. Consider, for example, the Italian painter Luca Signorelli's contract of 1499 for frescoes in Orvieto Cathedral:

> The said master Luca is bound and promises to paint [1] all the figures to be done on the said vault, and [2] especially the faces and all the parts of the figures from the middle of each figure upwards, and [3] that no painting should be done on it without Luca himself being present. . . . And it is agreed [4] that all the mixing of colors should be done by the said master Luca himself.

Such a contract at once reflects a serious cash interest in the characteristic achievement of a particular artist and a conviction that this achievement is compatible with the presence of other hands, provided those hands are subordinate, in the finished work. For paintings on a smaller scale, it was more possible to commission an exclusive performance. Thus the contract for a small altarpiece by Signorelli's great teacher, Piero della Francesca, specifies that "no painter may put his hand to the brush other than Piero himself."

There is no record of any comparable concern for exclusivity in the English theater. Unfortunately, the contracts that Shakespeare and his fellow dramatists almost certainly signed have not, with one significant exception, survived. But plays written for the professional theater are by their nature an even more explicitly collective art form than paintings; they depend for their full realization on the collaboration of others, and that collaboration may well extend to the fashioning of the script. It seems that some authors may simply have been responsible for providing plots that others then dramatized; still others were hired to "mend" old plays or to supply prologues, epilogues, or songs. A particular playwright's name came to be attached to a certain identifiable style—a characteristic set of plot devices, a marked rhetorical range, a tonality of character—but this name may refer in effect more to a certain product associated with a particular playing company than to the individual artist who may or may not have written most of the script. The one contract whose details do survive, that entered into by Richard Brome and the actors and owners of the Salisbury Court Theater in 1635, does not stipulate that Brome's plays must be written by him alone or even that he must be responsible for a certain specifiable proportion of each script. Rather, it specifies that the playwright "should not nor would write any play or any part of a play to any other players or playhouse, but apply all his study and endeavors therein for the benefit of the said company of the said playhouse." The Salisbury Court players want rights to everything Brome writes for the stage; the issue is not that the plays associated with his name be exclusively *his* but rather that he be exclusively *theirs*.

Recent textual scholarship, then, has been moving steadily away from a conception of Shakespeare's plays as direct, unmediated emanations from the mind of the author and toward a conception of them as working scripts, composed and continually reshaped as part of a collaborative commercial enterprise in competition with other, similar enterprises. One consequence has been the progressive weakening of the idea of the solitary, inspired genius, in the sense fashioned by Romanticism and figured splendidly in the statue of Shakespeare in the public gardens in Germany's Weimar, the city of Goethe and Schiller: the poet, with his sensitive, expressive face and high domed forehead sitting alone and brooding, a skull at his feet, a long-stemmed rose in his crotch. In place of this projection of German Romanticism, we have now a playwright and sometime actor who is also (to his considerable financial advantage) a major shareholder in the company—the Chamberlain's Men, later the King's Men—to which he loyally supplies for most of his career an average of two plays per year.

As a shareholder Shakespeare had to concern himself with such matters as economic cycles, lists of plague deaths, the cost of costumes, government censorship, city ordinances, the hiring and firing of personnel, and innumerable other factors that affected his enterprise. Practical considerations did not merely affect the context of his writing for the stage; they also shaped the form of what he wrote. His plays were not monuments, fixed in every detail and immobilized forever. They were like living beings, destined to change as a condition for their very survival.

One of the very first biographical mentions of Shakespeare, in the Reverend Thomas Fuller's *History of the Worthies of England* (1662), seems to have grasped this principle of mobility. Fuller reports—or imagines—the "wit-combats" that Shakespeare and Jonson had at the Mermaid Tavern:

> which two I behold like a Spanish great galleon and an English man of war; Master Jonson (like the former) was built far higher in learning, solid but slow in his performances. Shakespeare, with the English man of war, lesser in bulk, but lighter in sailing, could turn with all tides, tack about, and take advantage of all winds by the quickness of his wit and invention.

The encounters Fuller describes may be apocryphal, but to "turn with all tides, tack about, and take advantage of all winds" is a canny description of the highly mobile texts that Shakespeare fashioned and bequeathed to posterity.

Conjuring Shakespeare

The Elizabethan and Jacobean public had an interest in reading plays as well as seeing them. There was a lively market in such texts, often rushed into print to catch public excitement, and there is even evidence that at certain performances it was possible for audiences at the playhouse to purchase a copy of the very play they were watching.

Shakespeare's attitude to this market is unclear. Unlike Ben Jonson, he never personally edited and oversaw the publication of his plays, either individually or as a collection, but he may, for all we know, have imagined some day doing so. Perhaps death simply overtook him before he reached that goal. Certainly the Folio editors, though they were themselves fellow actors, thought of his plays as literary works. In 1623, seven years after the playwright's death, Heminges and Condell believed they could sell copies of their expensive collection of Shakespeare's plays—"What euer you do," they urge their readers, "buy"—by insisting that their texts were "as he conceiued them."

"As he conceived them": potential readers in the early seventeenth century then were already interested in access to Shakespeare's "conceits"—his "wit," his imagination, and his creative power—and were willing to assign a high value to the products of his particular, identifiable skill, one distinguishable from that of his company and of his rival playwrights. After all, Jonson's dedicatory poem in the Folio praises Shakespeare not as the playwright of the incomparable King's Men but as the equal of Aeschylus, Sophocles, and Euripides. And if we now see Shakespeare's dramaturgy in the context of his contemporaries and of a collective artistic practice, readers continue to have little difficulty recognizing that most of the plays attached to his name tower over those of his rivals.

The First Folio included an engraving purporting to show what Shakespeare looked like, but in the little poem that accompanied this image Jonson urged the reader to "look / Not on his Picture, but his Book." The words on the page then should conjure up the author himself; they should ideally give the reader unmediated access to the astonishing forge of imaginative power that was the mind of the dramatist. Such is the vision—at its core closely related to the preservation of the divinely inspired text in the great scriptural religions—that has driven many of the great editors who have for centuries produced successive editions of Shakespeare's works. The vision was not yet fully formed in the First Folio, for Heminges and Condell still felt obliged to apologize to their noble patrons for dedicating to them a collection of mere "trifles." But by the eighteenth century, there were no longer any ritual apologies for Shakespeare; instead, there was growing recognition of the supreme artistic importance of his works.

At the same time, from the eighteenth century onward, there was growing recognition of the uncertain, conflicting, and in some cases corrupt state of the surviving texts. Every conceivable step, it was thought, must be undertaken to correct mistakes, strip away corruptions, and return the texts to their pure and unsullied form. Noticing that there were multiple texts of fully half of the plays and noticing too that these texts often contain significant variants, editors routinely conflated the distinct versions into a single text in an attempt to reconstruct the ideal, definitive, complete, and perfect copy that they imagined Shakespeare must have aspired to and eventually reached for each of his plays. In doing so they succeeded in producing something that Shakespeare himself never wrote.

Heminges and Condell, who knew the author and had access to at least some of his manuscripts, lamented the fact that Shakespeare did not live "to have set forth and overseen his own writings." But even had he done so—or, alternatively, even if a cache of his manuscripts were discovered in a Warwickshire attic tomorrow—all of the editorial problems would not be solved, though the textual landscape would change, nor would all of the levels of mediation be swept away. The written word has strange powers: it seems to hold onto something of the very life of the person who has written it, but it also seems to pry that life loose from the writer, exposing it to vagaries of history and chance quite independent of those to which the writer was personally subject. Moreover, with the passing of centuries, the language itself and the whole frame of reference within which language and symbols are understood have decisively changed. The most learned modern scholar still lives at a huge experiential remove from Shakespeare's world and, even holding a precious copy of the First Folio in hand, cannot escape having to read across a vast chasm of time what is, after all, an edited text. The rest of us cannot so much as indulge in the fantasy of direct access: our eyes inevitably wander to the glosses and the explanatory notes.

Abandoning the dream of direct access to Shakespeare's final and definitive intentions is not a cause for despair, nor should it lead us to throw our hands up and declare that one text is as good as another. What it does is to encourage us to be actively interested in the editorial principles that underlie the particular edition that we are using. It is said that the great artist Brueghel once told an inquisitive connoisseur who had come to his studio, "Keep your nose out of my paintings; the smell of the paint will poison you." In the case of Shakespeare, it is increasingly important to bring one's nose close to the page, as it were, and sniff the ink. More precisely, it is important to understand the rationale for the choices that the editors have made.

The rationale behind *The Norton Shakespeare* is described at length in the Textual Introduction to this volume. What should be stressed here is the fact that

Shakespeare was the master of the unfinished, the perpetually open. The notion of finding a perfectly fixed text of one of his plays, the copy that he directly handed over to the printer as his "final" version, goes against everything we know about his personal practice and about Elizabethan and Jacobean theater. Shakespeare wrote his plays to be performed by professional players in a range of different settings, at different times, and before different publics. The project required considerable flexibility. As a working playwright, he seems to have thought about the creation of "parts" or roles, often with specific actors in mind though always with the understanding that the personnel might change. Taken all together, of course, the parts made up a whole, but both the individual pieces and the larger structure they formed were and have remained open. The editors of *The Norton Shakespeare* have tried to record and preserve this openness.

Speaking only for myself, I will confess a further ambition: I would like to meet Shakespeare in person. I think that throughout his career Shakespeare produced in effect detachable parts of himself, parts that derived from his personhood (his social relationships, his acquired knowledge, his temperament, his memories, his inner life, and so forth) but that moved independently in the world. He created out of himself hundreds of secondary agents, his characters, some of whom seem even to float free of the particular narrative structures in which they perform their given roles and to take on an agency we ordinarily reserve for biological persons. As an artist he literally gave his life to these agents, transferring his personal energies to them.

I do not mean that Shakespeare's characters are all self-portraits in the sense of referring back to his individual existence (though some of them almost certainly do). I mean rather that Shakespeare's life is, in an unusually intense and vivid way, in his works. And therefore when I open the printed book or scroll through the Digital Edition, I feel his eerie presence and want to call out, with the words Ben Jonson wrote in his dedicatory poem to the First Folio, "My Shakespeare, rise!"

General Textual Introduction

GORDON McMULLAN AND SUZANNE GOSSETT

Most people read an edition of Shakespeare's plays and poems because they want to read the plays and poems, not because they wish to dwell on the material origins of the texts they are reading—where the texts came from, how the manuscripts looked, who printed them, for whom they were printed, how the publishing practices of the English Renaissance made them what they are. Yet attention to the text itself is, we believe, an integral part of understanding the meaning of Shakespeare's works, considerably enhancing the pleasure of the reading experience. Seeing Shakespeare in the theater, reading Shakespeare on the page: both can offer extraordinary, multiply layered experiences of entertainment and intellectual uplift, a sense of unparalleled access to the past, and often simply a great deal of fun. We have edited the text of Shakespeare with these pleasures, and the reader's choices, in mind, and we wish to share with you a sense of the further levels of engagement that close attention to the origins of the text itself can bring.

For us, first and foremost, the *textual* is inseparable from the *critical*. That is, the "themes" we locate in Shakespeare, the sense of the place of the plays and poems in Shakespeare's world and in our own, the ways in which these remarkable writings require us to reflect on being human, on being gendered, on living in community, on having an ethnicity and a class status, all have their foundation in the words we read—and if we don't know whether the words we are reading are the "right" ones, or if we don't have the tools to reflect on the challenges presented by the very idea of "right" words, then we may miss out on key aspects of the Shakespearean experience. The fantasies of the "anti-Stratfordians" (people who claim Shakespeare's works were written by one or another equally implausible candidate) serve to remind us of the obsession of our age with Shakespearean *authenticity,* with the urge to ensure that the Shakespeare we see performed, or that we read or study, is the *real* Shakespeare, the *authentic* Shakespeare. The primary question we address in our textual introduction is central to this debate—"How authentic is the text I am reading?"—and in order to do this we need to reflect on two things: on the nature of the Shakespearean text and on the complex idea of "authenticity." Once we have done that, we can begin to explain some of the decisions we made in editing the texts that together form *The Norton Shakespeare.*

The "Authentic" Shakespeare

For centuries, playgoers and readers had two questions answered for them in advance: which plays and poems to read as "Shakespeare's" (the reader logically assumed that if a play or poem was in the "complete works," then it was Shakespeare's, and if not, not), and, beyond that, which *text* of a given Shakespeare play or poem to read. This second question might seem odd. Surely there is only one *Hamlet* and that is the *Hamlet* Shakespeare wrote? Yet not only does more than one authoritative text of certain plays (above all, as it happens, of *Hamlet*) exist, some of which are very different from each other, but the word "authoritative" raises a third question—notably, "On what grounds do we decide that a printed text is close to what Shakespeare actually wrote?" Moreover, the first of these questions is itself not straightforward. The boundaries of the Shakespeare canon—those texts accepted as being written in whole or in part by Shakespeare—have always been porous. Neither *Pericles* nor *The Two Noble Kinsmen,* for instance, was included in the First Folio, yet both have long been attributed to Shakespeare (in each case, as it happens, to Shakespeare working jointly with another playwright, as pretty much all his fellow Elizabethan and Jacobean playwrights did), and both are now invariably included in "Complete Works" editions. Some plays have been considered part of the Shakespeare canon for far less time. *Edward III,* for instance, now appears in editions as a "Shakespeare and others" play, where a couple of decades ago it did not. Times change, evidence surfaces, and methods of attributing authorship develop. As a result, other plays continue to hover at the edges of the canon. At the time of writing, the newest contender for inclusion is a celebrated play by Thomas Kyd called *The Spanish Tragedy,* for which, it is suggested, Shakespeare supplied extra scenes, capitalizing on the play's success. *The Spanish Tragedy* does not appear in the present edition of *The Norton Shakespeare,* but if in due course we are sufficiently convinced by the arguments for its inclusion, then in it will come. What the French thinker Jacques Derrida called "the logic of the supplement" operates here: each time you add something to a volume called "Complete" you make it *more* complete, but the fact that you needed to add something to complete a volume already claiming to be "complete" has the effect of undermining the very possibility of completeness. For editors of Shakespeare, this is unavoidable—and to be celebrated, not resented.

It is not only the *external* borders of the Shakespeare canon that are fluid; the *internal* borders too—the choice of words within a given play or poem—have never, to the surprise of many readers, been firmly fixed. Shakespeare lovers are aware, perhaps, that Hamlet's flesh is too "solid," "sullied," or "sallied," depending on which version of the play one reads; they may also have wondered which of two "others"—"the base Judean" or "the base Indian"—is the one to which Othello really means to compare himself just before his suicide; but they may not realize that these celebrated instances of Shakespearean textual choice are part of a much broader canvas of instabilities, uncertainties, and options. This means that not only the choice of play, but the choice of *text* of that play, affects the reader's experience of Shakespeare.

The key question arising here is that of the "right" reading, the "authentic" reading, a status usually taken to require a direct relationship to the author. The mental adjustment needed is to accept that, quite often, there may be either *no* "right" reading or *more than one.* We cannot ever know exactly what Shakespeare wrote because (with one limited, debated exception) we do not have the holograph manuscript (a manuscript in his own handwriting) of any of his plays or poems. Shakespeare's own manuscripts of the plays in the First Folio or in the various quartos that predate the Folio have not survived, and so editors are unable to do the one thing they would most like to be able to do, which is to compare what Shakespeare actually wrote with what was printed. The apparent exception is the lines in the surviving manuscript of *Sir Thomas More* that are largely accepted as being in Shakespeare's hand—but, maddeningly, this is the one play in the Shakespeare canon as currently constituted that never found its way into print in the late sixteenth or early seventeenth century. So, even in the case of the one brief section of extant manuscript generally thought to be in Shakespeare's hand, we cannot make a direct comparison between what was written and what was printed.

It was long believed that Shakespeare never revised his texts (a myth prompted by the prefatory material to the First Folio) and therefore that there must have been one, and only one, lost master original from which all subsequent texts derive. But further complicating the notion of the "authentic Shakespeare" is the existence of short, variant quarto texts of several plays. Because certain of these are noticeably inferior to the Folio (or, sometimes, to a fuller quarto) text of the same play, they were traditionally referred to as "bad quartos." In recent years, scholars have sought to replace the unhelpful connotations of "bad" with neutral descriptive terms such as "short quartos," but the point of origin of these texts remains unclear. Are they "authentic"? One long-standing argument has it that they are "reported" texts, the product of "pirate" printers who sat a handful of actors down and persuaded them to recall not only their own lines but the entire play—this, it is claimed, explains the discrepancy in quality between the lines of certain characters in these quartos (e.g., Mercutio in the First Quarto of *Romeo and Juliet,* whose lines are nearly identical to those in the much fuller Second Quarto) and those of others. These quartos vary considerably, from the brief, highly problematic quarto of *The Merry Wives of Windsor* to the much more independent and interpretively convincing First Quarto of *Hamlet.* It has sometimes been proposed that these quartos may represent Shakespeare's early drafts. A further possibility, championed recently as a development of increasing editorial openness to the possibility that Shakespeare did occasionally revise his own work, is that the short quartos represent "theatrical" versions of the plays, whereas the lengthy Folio texts represent more overtly "literary" versions designed with readers in mind. It may be that we will never fully understand how these quartos came to be so different from the fuller, ostensibly more authoritative versions in the First Folio and elsewhere, but it seems essential to present them in all their intriguing difference. Our editorial principles and the technology we adopt in this edition allow us to include fully edited versions of all these quartos, so that the reader may understand the complexity of deciding what constitutes "authentic" Shakespeare.

The Text in the Print House

One reason it is hard to know what Shakespeare actually wrote is that all early modern printed texts include interpretations, adjustments, and misreadings of the manuscripts on which they are based (which may have been the author's own or a neater scribal copy), as well as mechanical errors made by the compositors in the process of setting the type for printing. Moreover, workers in the Renaissance print house did not simply transfer the words passively from writer to reader; they actively intervened in what they printed. There was no fixed way to spell words in Shakespeare's day—Shakespeare himself spelled his own name differently at different times when signing documents—and compositors made the most of this irregularity to even out or "justify" the line they were setting (for example, by adding or removing a final "e" on an individual word). Similarly, there was no sense that the printer's duty was to print exactly what he found in the manuscript with which he was working. On the contrary, since early modern play manuscripts typically included little or no punctuation, it was the job of the compositor setting the type to add punctuation so as to enable and enhance the reader's experience. One of the most misleading of Shakespearean myths, one prevalent among actors even today, is the claim that the punctuation in the First Folio expresses "Shakespeare's instructions to actors": those theater professionals who have carefully timed their pauses and breaths according to the arrangement of commas and semicolons in the First Folio may be sad to learn that they are almost certainly basing their practice on the habits of Compositor A or Compositor J (since we almost never know the names of the workers in the print houses, compositors are usually referred to by letter).

To understand how the printing process affected the texts we read, it helps to know how the two principal formats in which Shakespeare's plays were printed—folio and quarto—were put together. A folio is made up of standard-sized sheets of paper printed with two pages on each side, then folded in half and assembled with several other such folded sheets inserted inside each other to form a "gathering" or "quire"; these gatherings are then stitched together to form the book. A quarto is made of the same standard-sized sheets of paper but is printed with four pages on each side and then folded twice (so that it is a quarter the size of the original sheet and half the size of a folio); each set of four leaves is either stitched together with other sets or inserted into a number of others to form a gathering as with a folio; the gatherings are then sewn through the central fold to form a book (which is why, very occasionally, you might come across a book where some of the pages need cutting apart if the print is to be read; the folding of the sheet to form eight pages will always require two edges to be cut after binding). Try folding a sheet of paper and you will see how this works. If you write the page numbers from one to eight on the folded sheet and then unfold it again, you will see that pages 1, 4, 5, and 8 (the "outer forme") are on one side and 2, 3, 6, and 7 (the "inner forme") are on the other, and that only some pages on each side are printed consecutively. (Scholars in fact tend to specify locations in early printed texts not by page numbers, which are notoriously unreliable in books from Shakespeare's day, but by what are called "signatures," which express the physical construction of the book—that is, the number of leaves collected together as a gathering and the number of gatherings that make up the book. Thus B2, or B2r, signifies the front side—recto—of the second sheet in gathering B, while C3v means the reverse side—verso—of the third sheet in gathering C.) A compositor setting either an inner or an outer form was thus not setting the type in the order of the plot, and you can imagine the loss of understanding this might produce at moments of complication in the text, even in an experienced professional. And then of course there is the Elizabethan equivalent of the coffee break to consider: one compositor would at times take over from another and carry on setting the type, and you can see where this has happened because the new compositor has different habits—his own preferences for abbreviating speech prefixes, say—and in a context where there are two characters with similar names he might misunderstand the speech prefix for the one and set it as the other, thus attributing a speech to the wrong speaker—all of which makes it that much harder to determine the nature of the manuscript from which the compositors were working.

If you look at the illustration on the next page, you can see a visual summary of the print workers' tasks. In the right foreground a boy is examining a forme (the frame into which the type is locked for printing) that has been set with type; he seems to be doing a last check against the manuscript while waiting for the forme to be placed in the press. To the far left, a pair of compositors is setting type from typecases, with the manuscript copy from which they are working stuck to the wall in front of them; behind them, a worker is replacing used type into a typecase arranged alphabetically and vertically ("upper-case" letters, i.e., capitals, at the top, "lower-case" below); to his right, a bespectacled proofreader checks an as-yet-uncorrected sheet against copy; in the background, a figure who is just possibly a woman (there is evidence that women worked in, and sometimes even, as printers' widows, owned, print houses) is using absorbent, wool-stuffed leather balls to apply ink to the forme before it is placed on the bed of the press; and, finally, the pressman pulls the bar across to lower the central weight of press onto the conjunction of inked type and blank paper and thus imprint the sheet.

The first sheet pulled would be handed to the proofreader for checking, and he would mark errors for correction; when he finished, the press would be stopped, the (now very inky) type adjusted to make the corrections, and the process would then continue. The pressman would, however, keep printing sheets during the twenty minutes it might take the proofreader to work through the proof, and those uncorrected sheets (a hundred or so) would be stacked together indiscriminately with the corrected ones in the overall print run (which was 1,200 or so copies in the case of the First Folio), not separated or discarded. The result is that early printed books are a blend of uncorrected and corrected sheets, and no individual copy of a book such

Unknown engraver, after Stradanus (Jan van der Straet), *Invention of Book Printing*, from *Nova reperta* (New inventions and discoveries of modern times; ca. 1599–1603).

as the Folio is likely to be exactly the same as any other, given the random distribution of uncorrected sheets. If you look closely at the list of textual variants to this edition, you will see that editors sometimes note when they have selected a corrected reading from a copy of the base text other than the primary one from which they are working.

One printing-house factor likely to affect the text was the need for print workers to "cast off," that is, to work out how many lines of a given manuscript would fit on a printed page, and to make pencil annotations in the manuscript to mark where page breaks would fall in print. Occasionally mistakes would be made, and you can see in the printed text where either a compositor has realized that he still has a lot of words to set but little space to play with, and so keeps everything tight, or where he is, by contrast, running out of words yet still has a fair amount of page to fill, and so deploys white space, printers' ornaments, and the like. For examples of these composition strategies, see pages 80 and 81.

of Romeo and Iuliet.

On Thurſday next be married to the Countie.

  Iu: Tell me not Frier that thou hearſt of it,
Vnleſſe thou tell me how we may preuent it.
Giue me ſome ſudden counſell : els behold
Twixt my extreames and me, this bloodie Knife
Shall play the Vmpeere, arbitrating that
Which the Commiſsion of thy yeares and arte
Could to no iſſue of true honour bring.
Speake not, be briefe: for I deſire to die,
If what thou ſpeakſt, ſpeake not of remedie.

  Fr: Stay *Iuliet*, I doo ſpie a kinde of hope,
VVhich craues as deſperate an execution,
As that is deſperate we would preuent.
If rather than to marrie Countie *Paris*
Thou haſt the ſtrength or will to ſlay thy ſelfe,
Tis not vnlike that thou wilt vndertake
A thing like death to chyde away this ſhame,
That coapſt with death it ſelfe to flye from blame.
And if thou dooſt, Ile giue thee remedie,

  Iul: Oh bid me leape (rather than marrie *Paris*)
From off the battlements of yonder tower :
Or chaine me to ſome ſteepie mountaines top,
VVhere roaring Beares and ſauage Lions are :
Or ſhut me nightly in a Charnell-houſe,
VVith reekie ſhankes, and yeolow chaples ſculls :
Or lay me in tombe with one new dead :
Things that to heare them namde haue made me tremble ;
And I will doo it without feare or doubt,
To keep my ſelfe a faithfull vnſtaind VVife
To my deere Lord, my deereſt *Romeo*.

  Fr: Hold *Iuliet*, hie thee home, get thee to bed,
Let not thy Nurſe lye with thee in thy Chamber :
And when thou art alone, take thou this Violl,
And this diſtilled Liquor drinke thou off :
VVhen preſently through all thy veynes ſhall run
A dull and heauie ſlumber, which ſhall ſeaze

H 3

Each

Q1 *Romeo and Juliet*, H3r. An example of a "tight" page where the casting-off seems to have been efficient.

The excellent Tragedie

Each vitall fpirit: for no Pulfe fhall keepe
His naturall progreffe, but furceafe to beate:
No figne of breath fhall teftifie thou liuft,
And in this borrowed likenes of fhrunke death,
Thou fhalt remaine full two and fortie houres.
And when thou art laid in thy Kindreds Vault,
Ile fend in haft to *Mantua* to thy Lord,
And he fhall come and take thee from thy graue.

  Iul: Frier I goe, be fure thou fend for my deare *Romeo*.
             Exeunt.

   Enter olde Capolet, his Wife, Nurfe, and
        Seruingman.

  Capo: Where are you firra?
  Sor: Heere forfooth.
  Capo: Goe, prouide me twentie cunning Cookes.
  Ser: I warrant you Sir, let me alone for that, Ile knowe
them by licking their fingers.
  Capo: How canft thou know them fo?
  Ser: Ah Sir, tis an ill Cooke cannot licke his owne fin-
gers.
  Capo: Well get you gone.

      Exit Seruingman.

But wheres this Head-ftrong?
  Moth: Shees gone (my Lord) to Frier *Laurence* Cell
To be confeft.
  Capo: Ah, he may hap to doo fome good of her,
A headftrong felfewild harlotrie it is.

               Enter

Q1 *Romeo and Juliet*, H3v. An example of a "loose" page—note the white space and use of the ornament.

These moments of professional adjustment necessarily affect the texts we have inherited, and a close look at the early printed page may explain why lines that seem metrically regular have been set as prose, say, or as fragmented verse lines. Here from the First Quarto of *King Lear* is an example of verse lines that have been squeezed into prose in order to save space:

The Historie of King Lear.

like a riotous Inne,epicurisme,and lust make more like a tauerne or brothell, then a great pallace; the shame it selfe doth speake for instant remedie: be thou desired by her, that else will take the thing shee begs, a little to disquantitie your traine, and the remainder that shall still depend, to bee such men as may besort your age, that know themselues and you.

Lear. Darkenes,and Deuils! saddle my horses, call my traine together; degenerate bastard, ile not trouble thee; yet haue I left a daughter.

Gon. You strike my people;and your disordred rabble,make seruants of their betters. *Enter Duke.*

Lear. We that too late repent. O sir,are you come?is it your will that wee prepare any horses?ingratitude!thou marble harted fiend, more hideous when thou shewest thee in a child,then the Sea-monster: detested kite, thou lift my traine, and men of choise and rarest parts, that all particulars of dutie knowe, and in the most exact regard, support the worships of their name?O most small fault, how vgly did'st thou in *Cordelia* shewe, that like an engine wrencht my frame of nature from the fixt place; drew from my heart all loue,and added to the gall. O *Lear!Lear!* beat at this gate that let thy folly in, and thy deere iudgement out; goe,goe, my people.

Duke. My Lord,I am giltles,as I am ignorant.

Leir. It may be so my Lord: harke *Nature,*heare deere Goddesse; suspend thy purpose, if thou did'st intend to make this creature fruitful,into her wombe conuey sterility; drie vp in hir the organs of increase,and from her derogate body neuer spring a babe to honour her; if shee must teeme, create her childe of spleene, that it may liue and bee a thourt disnatur'd torment to her; let it stampe wrinckles in her brow of youth; with accent teares, fret channels in her cheeks;turne all her mothers paines and benefits to laughter and contempt, that shee may feele,that she may feele, how sharper then a serpents tooth it is, to haue a thanklesse child; goe, goe,my people.

Duke. Now Gods that we adore, whereof comes this!

Gon. Neuer afflict your selfe to know the cause, but let his disposition haue that scope that dotage giues it.

Lear. What,fiftie of my followers at a clap,within a fortnight?

D 2 *Duke.*

Q1 *King Lear*, D2r

And here from the First Quarto of *Henry V* is an example of prose that has been set as rough verse (notice how the first word of each line of Fluellen's speeches is capitalized) in order to stretch it out to fill the available space:

> *of Henry the fift.*
>
> So hath he fworne the like to me.
>
>   *K.* How think you *Flewellen*,is it lawfull he keep his oath?
>
>   *Fl.* And it pleafe your maiefty,tis lawful he keep his vow.
>
> If he be periur'd once,he is as arrant a beggerly knaue,
>
> As treads vpon too blacke fhues.
>
>   *Kin.* His enemy may be a gentleman of worth.
>
>   *Flew.* And if he be as good a gentleman as Lucifer
>
> And Belzebub,and the diuel himfelfe,
>
> Tis meete he keepe his vowe.
>
>   *Kin.* Well firrha keep your word.
>
> Vnder what Captain ferueft thou?
>
>   *Soul.* Vnder Captaine *Gower.*
>
>   *Flew.* Captaine *Gower* is a good Captaine
>
> And hath good littrature in the warres.
>
>   *Kin.* Go call him hither.
>
>   *Soul.* I will my Lord.
>
>   *Exit fouldier.*
>
>   *Kin.* Captain *Flewellen*,when *Alonfon* and I was
>
> Downe together,*I* tooke this gloue off from his helmet,
>
> Here *Flewellen*, weare it. If any do challenge it,
>
> He is a friend of *Alonfons,*
>
> And an enemy to mee.
>
>   *Fle.* Your maieftie doth me as great a fauour
>
> As can be defired in the harts of his fubiects.
>
> *I* would fee that man now that fhould chalenge this gloue:
>
> And it pleafe God of his grace,*I* would but fee him,
>
> That is all.
>
>   *Kin.* *Flewellen* knowft thou Captaine *Gower?*
>
>   *Fle.* Captaine *Gower* is my friend.
>
> And if it like your maieftie,*I* know him very well.
>
>   *Kin.* Go call him hither.
>
>   *Flew.* I will and it fhall pleafe your maieftie.
>
>   *Kin.* Follow *Flewellen* clofely at the heeles,
>
> The gloue he weares, it was the fouldiers:
>
>   F 2   It

Q1 *Henry V*, F2r

Understanding these print-house procedures clarifies how at each stage of the printing process error and variety may be introduced: at the stage of "casting off," at the stage of setting the type from manuscript (especially if the writer had difficult handwriting), at the stages of proofreading and press correction, and in the assembly of corrected and uncorrected sheets into the book itself. Clearly, we need to be wary of assuming that the material features of the early texts unconditionally transmit "authorial intention."

What Kind of Edition Is This?

Editions always exist for readers. There is no more fundamental question for an editor than "For whom am I editing?" because the answer determines very substantially the nature of the edition produced. No edition can be designed for every imaginable reader; on the contrary, specific kinds of editing are done with specific sets of readers in mind. "Diplomatic" editions, for instance, are designed for scholars: they reproduce all the features of the original text without correction or alteration, but for most readers they would make for an unappealing reading experience. An "old-spelling" edition is another possibility: it is edited (that is, an editor has emended the text where error is apparent and included other aids to reading, such as stage directions), but it remains in the spelling (and, perhaps, the punctuation) of Shakespeare's day and is thus again likely to be difficult going for most contemporary readers. Modern-spelling editions are designed to make early modern texts as accessible as possible: the editor makes necessary corrections to the text, adds stage directions where they are needed to clarify the action, makes consistent certain variable features of the original, and modernizes the spelling and punctuation of those texts (while keeping a close eye on moments when the modernizing of spelling or punctuation might change the actual meaning). It is this latter course—the modern-spelling edition designed to offer maximum accessibility for contemporary readers—that *The Norton Shakespeare* adopts, but with certain developments and enhancements and with a specific set of principles for editorial choice.

We—the team of editors who together created this edition—have edited the works of Shakespeare—that is, the existing early texts—from scratch on the basis of a set of principles known as "single-text editing." The first two editions of *The Norton Shakespeare* were based on the text created in 1986 for Oxford University Press—a groundbreaking edition that transformed the modern editing of Shakespeare—but editorial practice has changed since that time, and Norton has created a new text for the present moment. This text is new both in its physical construction and in its theoretical underpinnings.

First, this, the Third Edition of *The Norton Shakespeare,* is "born digital." That is, we have taken the opportunity offered by the interactive ebook format to offer readers and classroom teachers an unprecedented set of options that will allow them to engage with, not just be passive recipients of, the words before them. The Digital Edition allows readers to open textual and performance comments by clicking on icons in the margin next to the line they are reading; to toggle from the text to a facsimile of the original printed folio or quarto; to hear all the songs scattered through the plays; and to listen to eight hours of selected scenes read by professional actors. In addition, readers can view the Quarto and Folio versions of *King Lear* side by side, scrolling as they choose; side-by-side viewing is also available for selected scenes from six plays and for two versions of a sonnet. Readers using the print and electronic editions in combination will be able to move between thumbing through the printed book and navigating the ebook not only for added portability but also in order to find additional versions of fifteen plays plus many enhancements, not least a selection of Textual Comments designed to underline the interconnections of textual decisions and the meaning of the plays.

Second, this edition adopts a new approach to the Shakespearean text, one made possible in part by the opportunities offered by the digital platform. Our underlying editorial principle has been, at its simplest, to edit the *text,* not the *work.* Let us explain what we mean by this with reference in particular to the plays (though there are similar issues with the sonnets). Shakespeare's plays exist in imperfect ways— none of them ideal, none of them perfectly representing what Shakespeare wrote or what his first audiences heard. Editors have always recognized that these surviving printed texts vary in their origins, though all must bear in some way "traces" of the original literary works that Shakespeare wrote out with quill and paper. Lying behind the surviving texts are, variously, authorial drafts, "fair" or scribal copies, theatrical promptbooks, and occasionally unfinished materials—often a mixture of more than one of these. One older editorial tradition sought to address the imperfections present in the texts as a result of this variable provenance by reconstructing, to a greater or lesser extent, an imagined original, creating an edition that—drawing on their professional knowledge of the writing habits of Shakespeare and his contemporaries, of Elizabethan handwriting, and of the printing process—the editors believed to be nearer to what Shakespeare and his audiences would have known or wanted than the actual surviving text with its flaws and imperfections. Of course editors need to correct many of those flaws and imperfections: to give readers a comprehensible reading experience, you must address errors and other distractions. But we believe it is not necessary or even desirable to try to reconstruct a "perfect" work that may never have existed in this form. Consequently, we have made the decision not to do what editors have normally done for centuries, which is to emend at will by merging the differing elements of distinct early texts of a given play, but rather to provide carefully considered editions of each of the early authoritative texts of works for which more than one such text survives. Similarly, in dealing with plays for which only one text survives, we have stayed as close as possible to that text when sense can be made of it, not adopting a traditional emendation if it appears to us to be the product of editorial preference rather than necessary for sense. In other words, we have chosen to edit the *texts* we actually have, not the *play* or the *poem* we do not, to accept uncertainty, and to exercise a certain skepticism toward earlier claims that sometimes made the editor seem a substitute for Shakespeare.

As we have noted, this edition was "born digital"—that is, we set out to invert the prior hierarchy of page and screen by creating an edition that would reach its fullest potential in digital form. Both the print and the digital editions are, in different ways, "complete works." The print volume includes all the poems, some of which exist in various manuscripts and others in print; there is usually only one form of each of these, though we include the entire *Passionate Pilgrim*, which was falsely ascribed to Shakespeare alone but does include some of his poems in variant forms. It—the print volume—includes all the plays too, providing one text for each play (except for *Hamlet,* for which we offer two editions, the First Quarto and a text merging the Second Quarto with materials from the Folio, and *King Lear,* for which we offer editions of the Quarto and the Folio, plus a merged text including all materials in both: for an account of the inclusion of these merged editions, or "conflations," in an edition based on single-text editing principles, see page 87, below. In deciding which of several texts to include in the bound volume we have used a pragmatic and flexible measure. Rather than (as has been done in the past) claiming to be able to determine and present the text that was Shakespeare's "original" version—or his "final" version, or the one that the company probably performed—we have in the case of plays that exist in significantly different texts printed the text that is most complete and apparently most finished. This often means the text in the First Folio, where about half the plays appear for the first time in the only text we have. But when—as, for example, in the case of *Romeo and Juliet* or of *1 Henry IV*—the Folio text is itself derived from a good quarto, we choose that earlier quarto as the base text from which our print edition is created.

We encourage readers to work with both versions, digital and print, to gain the most possible from *The Norton Shakespeare*. Editing Shakespeare digitally enables us to offer readers the opportunity to read, compare, and contrast the two (or, in the case of *Hamlet*, three) early texts of each of the plays for which multiple texts exist. Whether the plays exist in one substantive text or several, we have taken the same approach to the editing—modernizing spelling and punctuation on principles that are consistent across the edition, providing additional stage directions where they are required to clarify the action, and trusting the original text wherever possible, emending only where absolutely necessary and not "reconstructing" material in addition to that provided by the surviving texts.

The primary impact of these choices is, naturally, on those plays for which more than one early substantive text exists. For instance, we provide (in the Digital Edition) edited texts of Quarto *Othello* and Folio *Othello*—two different texts representing, we believe, two subtly different plays. Even when two separate early texts are nearly identical, the differences can be fascinating. Thus, in *Othello*, the female protagonist, Desdemona, infuriates her father by marrying an older man who is both black and a convert from Islam. Her father, who initially voices a series of racist reasons for assuming that Othello had brainwashed his daughter into eloping with him, sees her as shy and almost worryingly asexual (she has shown no interest in the eligible men he has introduced her to), but Othello's narrative of the process by which he wooed her suggests that she is more actively aware of her sexuality than her father believes: "My story being done, / She gave me for my pains a world of sighs. / [. . .] She thanked me / And bade me, if I had a friend that loved her, / I should but teach him how to tell my story, / And that would woo her" (Q 1.3.145–46, 150–53).

Q1 *Othello*, C3v

So the Quarto. The slightly later Folio version of the play alters one key word: "My story being done, / She gave me for my pains a world of kisses" (F 1.3.158–59).

F *Othello*, ss5v

Thus there are two equally coherent versions of the same line, different in one small but significant way. By providing editions of both texts, we avoid the necessity of preferring the one reading over the other (male editors have typically preferred "sighs," just as the editorial tradition seems generally to assume, in the phrasing of inserted stage directions, that men kiss women, not that women and men kiss each other), and we open up for our readers a degree of choice—to read the Quarto with its sighing Desdemona or the Folio with its more ardent, kissing Desdemona—and their decision about which version to read will impact the way they see the tragedy unfolding and thus their interpretation of the play. In this way, the study of the material features of the text and of the meaning of the play are inseparable.

This tiny difference between Quarto *Othello* and Folio *Othello* may represent revised authorial intention or some incidental external influence; we cannot know for certain. But there is a category of difference between Quarto and Folio that reminds us that when we read Shakespeare's plays we are dealing with the substantially collaborative process that is theatrical production—and thus with texts that have in various ways gone through the performance process. The severe reduction in Emilia's and Desdemona's parts in act 4 of Quarto *Othello*—the cutting, for instance, of the "Willow Song" that Desdemona sings before she goes to bed for the last time or of Emilia's wry lines about husbands—may be due not to authorial choice, a decision on Shakespeare's part to reduce the prominence of the women at this late stage of the play, but to theatrical necessity, that is, the presumed absence from the King's Men at one point of boy actors with sufficient singing ability or stamina. Often we can only guess at the reasons for such changes, but the point is that they are very often material and environmental, not intentional in the sense of being deliberate changes made for artistic reasons by the author. Yet they cannot be dismissed simply as "inauthentic," not only because we do not know Shakespeare's role at such moments but also because all staged plays are necessarily constructed through collaborative engagement between text and actor. Furthermore, for readers and playgoers across subsequent centuries, these renegotiated texts, offering evidence of multiple inputs for a range of practical reasons, were the "real" Shakespeare. Knowing about the practical processes of playwriting, performance, and printing enables the reader to gain a fuller understanding of the nature of the Shakespearean text as an expression of the highly socialized process of dramatic creativity.

We have noted in passing that, across the centuries, the borders of the Shakespeare canon have been fluid. For a century and a half, the *King Lear* that audiences saw in the theater was not Shakespeare's *King Lear* as we know it, but an adaptation of the play created by Irish poet and playwright Nahum Tate in the late seventeenth century that radically cut and altered the original, even providing a happy ending that suited the theatrical expectations of the day but looks to us bewilderingly inappropriate. Once the popularity of the Tate version had faded, the *King Lear* that audiences began to see reverted to "Shakespeare's *King Lear*"—or, rather, to a particular version of that play, one that editors (and directors) assembled from the two markedly different early texts, Quarto and Folio, by including as many of the different lines as possible from each and merging or "conflating" them into a play a few hundred lines longer than either of the early texts. The paradox is obvious—in the process of trying to present the reader with a "Shakespearean" text, editors produced a text different from either of the ones for which Shakespeare was responsible—yet for readers from the mid-nineteenth to the late twentieth centuries, this elongated version of *King Lear* was the one they read and grew to know and love as "Shakespeare's" play.

This history underpins the decision of *The Norton Shakespeare* to include, alongside editions of the early texts of *Hamlet* and *King Lear*, a further, "scars and stitches" conflated edition of each—that is, an edition of each play that, by way of indentation and a distinctive yet quiet difference in font, makes the process of conflation visible without intruding excessively on the pleasure of the reading experience. We provide these multiple options because they will enable readers to see how these texts changed, developed, and were remade across time. In the case of *King Lear*, it is very possible that Shakespeare was involved in reworking his tragedy a couple of years after he had first written it and it had gone into regular production, and readers can reflect on that dynamic process by comparing the two early versions; equally, they can choose to read the "scars and stitches" edition, which both replicates the experience of nineteenth- and twentieth-century readers who came to know the play through traditional conflated editions and makes visible the process through which that conflation was achieved. Thus in the Digital Edition we offer three versions of *King Lear*—and four of *Hamlet*—so as to enable readers to witness the dynamic and contingent processes that go into the bringing-into-the-present of Shakespeare's plays.

"Single-Text Editing" and the Treatment of Error

The Norton Shakespeare seeks to minimize intervention by the editor, but there are nonetheless occasions when the editor must assist the reader in making sense of the text and where it is not immediately obvious how to do so. In order to explain our decision making at such moments, we will offer some examples. Readers will see that for all texts in this edition, both print and digital, we offer in the Digital Edition a set of Textual Variants, compressed notes in which editors mark each moment where the edited version is in some way different from the "base text," that is, from the original quarto or folio text from which the edition is formed, specifying where the preferred word or other feature originates—from another early text, or from the editorial tradition, or from our own choice. No edition of a Shakespeare play can simply present the exact words of its base text, because no early text is free from error or complication. How many times, after all, reading a modern printed book, have you spotted errors, omissions, or typos? Even with the vast technological transformations since Shakespeare's death, the printing process remains flawed; so you would expect that any text printed in (or somewhat after) Shakespeare's day—created on a manually operated press using fiddly metal type set by hand in wooden frames, in often cramped conditions, using toxic ink, and always under pressure to speed up the process to keep the business afloat—would include a fair number of such errors. As we have noted, the print-house workers were actively involved in the creation of the Shakespearean text, an involvement that is by no means limited to error—but human error is inevitable and pervasive.

Consequently, editors working on the basis of single-text editing must always balance their commitment to the text against the possibility of error. Our basic premise is that the editor should not attempt to alter or "improve"—by following a different text, the editorial tradition, or her own informed invention—any reading that can make sense, even if that meaning seems a little strained. While such difficulties may arise from print-house errors, they may instead be signs of the semantic or syntactical differences between our current version of the English language and that of the late sixteenth and early seventeenth centuries. Single-text editing compels editors— and their readers—to make an effort to understand the given text, rather than to slide into something apparently more familiar. This is known as the principle of the "harder reading" (in Latin, *lectio difficilior*), and it expresses our urge not to risk obliterating the powerful specificity and difference of Shakespeare's works, even as it remains the editor's task to address error when it is undoubtedly present.

The multiplicity of early authoritative texts sometimes confronts the editor adhering to single-text-editing principles with difficult decisions. For example, at one point in the Folio text of *Troilus and Cressida*, Thersites is abusing Patroclus: "Let thy bloud be thy direction till thy death," he sneers, "then, if she that laies thee out sayes thou art a fair coarse [i.e., corpse], I'll be sworne and sworne upon't, she never shrowded any but Lazars." The earlier Quarto reads the central section as follows: "if she that layes thee out sayes thou art not a fair course," and it seems clear that the Folio corrects the Quarto reading, since the "not" makes nonsense of the meaning ("You'll be so ugly by the time you die that if the person laying out your corpse says you're beautiful then the only possible conclusion would be that the dead bodies she usually buries must all be lepers"). The editor therefore emends by removing the "not" from her Quarto edition on the grounds that while single-text editing normally requires her to maintain differences between cognate texts—that is, between texts of the same play that have reached us through different processes of transmission— she must not do this at the expense of sense.

By contrast, the two texts of *King Lear* provide a fine instance of the presence or absence of a word—again, as it happens, "not"—offering equal sense in two cognate texts. At the very end of the long first scene in the Folio, Lear's daughters Goneril and Regan talk together about their aging father's increasingly erratic behavior, and

Goneril notes that "the obseruation we haue made of it hath beene little"—an expression of regret for not taking notice of these mood swings before they led to the current crisis:

> *Gon.* You fee how full of changes his age is, the ob-
> feruation we haue made of it hath beene little: he alwaies
> lou'd our Sifter moft, and with what poore iudgement he
> hath now caft her off, appeares too groffely.

F *King Lear*, qq3r

In the Quarto, however, Goneril notes that "the obseruation we haue made of it hath *not* bin little" (our italics)—that is, that the sisters have in fact been aware of the problem for quite a while:

> *Gon.* You fee how full of changes his age is the obferuation we
> haue made of it hath not bin little; hee alwaies loued our fifter
> moft, and with what poore iudgement hee hath now caft her
> off, appeares too groffe.

Q1 *King Lear*, C1r

It is this earlier version that is invariably chosen by conflating editors and is thus the reading that those who already know *King Lear* will recognize. Yet it is not the only meaningful option. Both readings make sense, even if one is less familiar, and the advantage of single-text editing is that the editor is not forced to choose one option and thus to dilute the possibilities for meaning on both page and stage.

We briefly mentioned earlier one of the best-known cruxes in *Othello,* the moment at which the protagonist, just prior to his suicide, compares himself to a racial other who also failed to recognize the extraordinary value of what he had until he lost it. In the Quarto, the lines read "one whose hand, / Like the base *Indian,* threw a pearle away, / Richer then all his Tribe"; this has, marginally, been the version preferred by editors across time:

> Perplext in the extreame ; of one whofe hand,
> Like the bafe *Indian*, threw a pearle away,
> Richer then all his Tribe : of one whofe fubdued eyes,

Q1 *Othello*, N2r

In the Folio, the lines read "one, whose hand / (Like the base Iudean) threw a Pearle away / Richer then all his Tribe"—the "Judean" here probably being associated with Christ's betrayer, Judas Iscariot, and thus, for Shakespeare's audiences, with Jews in general:

> Perplexed in the extreame : Of one, whofe hand
> (Like the bafe Iudean) threw a Pearle away
> Richer then all his Tribe: Of one, whofe fubdu'd Eyes,

F *Othello*, vv5v

Note two elements here. First, the punctuation differs; neither version can be said to be either *better* or *more authorial* than the other in this regard (the parentheses in the Folio, for instance, are probably the preference of the King's company scribe, Ralph Crane, who transcribed several plays for inclusion in the Folio). Second, the difference between *"Indian"* and "Iudean" could be attributed to two kinds of easy error: a misreading of a scratchy secretary-hand "i" for "e" (or vice versa)—

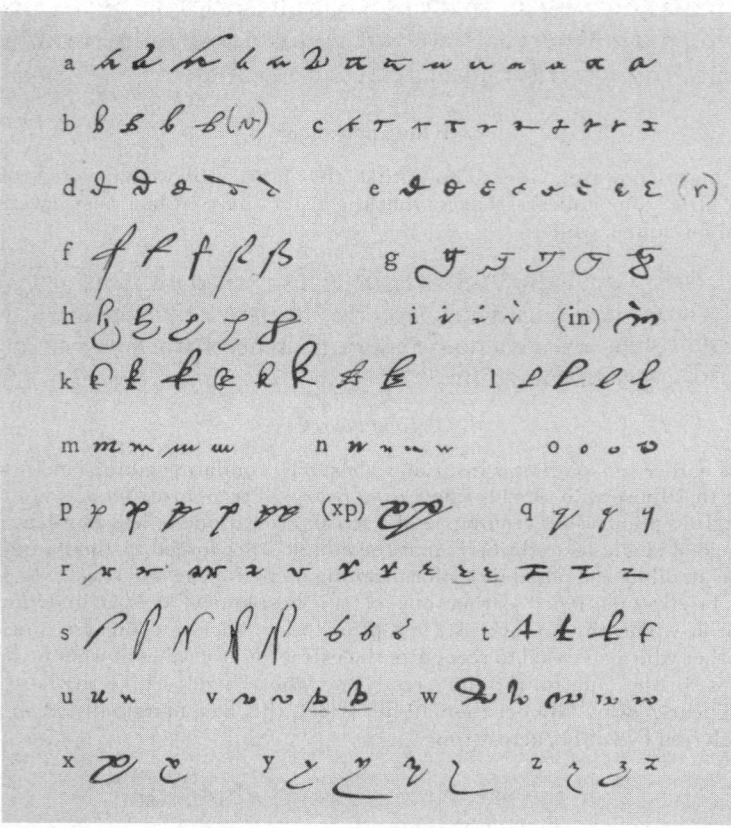

Sample minuscules in secretary hand from Ronald B. McKerrow, *An Introduction to Bibliography for Literary Students*, Oxford 1927.

—and an accidental inversion of the individual type "n" for "u" (or vice versa) by the compositor. The vice versas underline the impossibility of deciding which is "correct," and the presence in *The Norton Shakespeare* of editions of both early texts removes the need for the imposition of editorial preference.

   Single-text editing thus seeks to minimize editorial intervention while remaining aware of the needs of the reader and offering clarification (e.g., in the form of expanded or inserted stage directions, which we mark with square brackets) of action, speaker, or other elements of the original that may delay the reader's progress through the play. For these pragmatic reasons, we have chosen to maintain certain traditional overarching elements that could be considered to run counter to the theory of single-text editing. An instance is our division of almost all play texts into acts and scenes, an editorial practice that dates back to the eighteenth century. Such neat divisions are by no means always present in the base texts—either in the Folio, which is not always consistent or precise in its divisions (*Love's Labor's Lost*, for instance, has two different acts marked "*Actus Quartus*"; Folio *Hamlet* stops marking act divisions after act 2), or in the various quartos, many of which either mark scene divisions only or offer no divisions or numbers at all. Act divisions only became fully formalized with the development of indoor playhouses, where the necessity of trimming the candles every half-hour or so required breaks in the action; they thus apply far less to Elizabethan plays than to Jacobean. Our working premise for this edition, however, is that many of our readers will wish to locate scholarly discussions of these plays by critics who, almost without exception, cite speeches by act and scene number; thus, we offer act and scene numbers for all main texts and reserve scene divisions only for a handful of quartos that do not fall into the usual divisions.

The single-text editor's task is not necessarily more straightforward when she is dealing with plays with only one early authoritative text. One of the key questions anyone editing on single-text-editing principles has to ask is when to emend and when to leave alone. An instance comes in *All's Well That Ends Well*, which opens (in our modernized version) with this stage direction:

> *Enter young* BERTRAM, *Count of Roussillon, his mother [the Dowager* COUNTESS], *and* HELEN, *Lord* LAFEU, *all in black.*

The "*and*" seems to be in an odd place here; that is, you might expect it to be positioned between "HELEN" and "*Lord*," completing the list. Yet it comes instead between "*Mother*" and "HELEN." Is this simply a mistake by the compositor? It could easily be. Often, editors simply move the "*and*" to what seems to be the logical place between "HELEN" and "*Lord*." But what if there is a different logic to its positioning? It might be that Shakespeare is using the conjunction to separate two pairs: to connect Bertram and his mother on the one hand, and Helen and Lafeu on the other. Equally, the "*and*" might serve to connect the Countess and Helen, a connection that proves particularly resilient in the action to follow. Rather than limit the possibilities, we leave the stage direction as it is in the Folio, simply modernizing and standardizing the names and clarifying (with "dowager") that the Countess is the widow of Bertram's father. A theater director might wish to think about the staging options this stage direction offers.

All of these editorial challenges inevitably require the creation of something hybrid, something impure, despite the earnest intentions of the regularizing editor. Editing is always negotiation, and it is always compromise. This does not mean it is slapdash or arbitrary; on the contrary, it must be exceptionally precise, requiring a level of patience and concentration that is not everyone's forte. The paradox for editors is that the outcome of good work—words or lines or stage directions that took a great deal of experience, research, and agonizing to establish—will be simply, and rightly, invisible to the reader. In this, the editor's lot is not so very different—structurally, if not creatively—from that of the collaborating playwright. Effective collaboration is about effacing the joins between the work of different contributors—we presume that Shakespeare and Fletcher, composing *Henry VIII* and *The Two Noble Kinsmen* together, would not have wanted audience members to register when the writing of a given scene switched from the one to the other—and the quiet collaboration across time that is the work of the editor ought by definition to be hidden, at least in the case of editions created for the general reader and the advanced student who do not want or need the intrusion of the mediator.

Shakespeare and the Multiplication of Meaning

Most people, reading a Shakespeare poem or play, have in mind the question "What did Shakespeare mean here?" as they reflect on the words, especially if the words are not easy to make sense of. Despite the profound ways in which the Romantic construction of authorship as a process of untrammeled, transcendent individual inspiration has been questioned and deconstructed over the last half-century, the general understanding of the processes of writing, as of all forms of creativity, remains firmly bound up with ideas of intention, of textual "ownership," of the creative artist as "author"— that is, as the sole source of "authority" in respect of the form and meaning of a given text. We have tried in this introduction to suggest that the meanings of Shakespeare's plays and poems have a wider range of starting points, emerge from a more complex, varied, and fascinating creative base, than simply what the poet himself "meant"—in other words, that Shakespearean "authenticity" is a multivalent concept, one that includes at its core what the author meant but also a range of other, contiguous collaborations, negotiations, and origins for meaning. The Shakespearean text is fluid and multiple, and the nature of the engagement of both editor and reader with that text should, we believe, follow suit. We have much to gain by being open to the increased possibilities this transformed understanding can bring. The very words themselves are, in so many ways, unfixed in their meanings; the ways through which they came into the public domain in Shakespeare's own day—in manuscript, on the stage, in the various print formats available to those seeking to profit from publication—are also multiple; and the ways in which the plays and poems have been presented and re-presented in subsequent centuries make "multiple" seem a gross understatement. Shakespeare seems to have re-thought and re-imagined his own writings; his colleagues in the King's Men negotiated and adapted his work to suit conditions; publishers printed it in a range of ways, official and unofficial, working with Shakespeare himself on the poems if not on the plays (we have no evidence that Shakespeare—unlike his friend and rival Ben Jonson—oversaw the printing of his plays, whereas he clearly did pay attention to the publication of his poems), and his former colleagues gathered most, though not all, of the plays into a single, rather grandiose Folio in 1623, initiating the long tradition of editing the works to make them available for the "great variety of readers." *The Norton Shakespeare* offers its readers a set of options for reading and understanding Shakespeare that makes the most both of the digital technologies and of the editorial practices of the present, giving the reader choices—of text, of taxonomy, of glossarial support—and in the process providing the means for a new generation actively to discover, engage with, learn from, and—above all—be thrilled and moved by these astonishing works in all their fabulous multiplicity.

The Theater of Shakespeare's Time

HOLGER SCHOTT SYME

Early modern London was a theatrical city like no other, as the travel writer Fynes Moryson proudly proclaimed: "as there be, in my opinion, more plays in London than in all parts of the world I have seen, so do these players or comedians excel all others in the world." Moryson wrote just after Shakespeare's death, around 1619, but the world of playacting he described had thrived in and around England's capital long before Shakespeare arrived there. The decades between 1567, when the first theater built in England since the Romans opened its doors, and 1642, when playacting was prohibited by Parliament, saw an unprecedented and still unparalleled flourishing of theatrical artistry. Moryson's account emphasizes not just the quality of London's actors, but also the sheer quantity of plays on offer: as far as he was concerned, there was more theater in the city than anywhere else in the world. The historical record bears out his impression. English acting companies, driven by a constant hunger for new work, kept dozens of dramatists busy writing a staggering number of plays—more than 2,500 works, of which just over 500 survive. Theaters sprang up all around London in the 1570s. Throughout Shakespeare's career, there were never fewer than four acting venues in operation; some years, up to nine theaters were competing for audiences. Different spaces and different companies catered to different tastes and income brackets: the tiny indoor location of the Boys of St. Paul's, an acting company of youths, could accommodate fewer than 100 of the wealthy courtiers and law students who were their typical spectators; the Swan Theater, on the other hand, the largest of the open-air venues that were the most common type of theater in Shakespeare's London, had room for over 3,000 people from all social backgrounds. The theater was rich and varied, an engine of artistic experiment and a place where traditions flourished; it was an art form both elite and popular; it provided entertainment for kings and queens even as their governments worried that it was difficult to control, attracting large and boisterous crowds and posing a threat to public health during plague outbreaks.

In London, theater was everywhere. But *what* was it? Who performed it, where, under what circumstances, using what methods and techniques, and for whom?

History

Before we can approach these questions, a few words about historical evidence are in order. Theater is a transitory art, not designed to leave behind lasting records or traces; it is, as Shakespeare never tired of noting, a kind of dream. In Shakespeare's time, it was a pursuit about which the government cared only intermittently, and was therefore rarely the subject of official recordkeeping. Much of what we know about playhouses and acting companies derives from squabbles over money and the lawsuits that followed. What information survives is just enough to make theater historians realize how much has been lost. For instance, with few exceptions, we do not know who performed which roles. We cannot name a single character Shakespeare played. Even for the most famous actors of the age, we can list at most a handful of parts. Nor do we

93

know how popular most of Shakespeare's plays were. His history plays, more than his tragedies or comedies, sold well as books—but did they do as well on stage? We would like to think so, but without attendance records, we cannot know for sure. *Much Ado About Nothing* was never reprinted on its own after its initial publication in 1600. Does that mean it was a theatrical flop too? Probably not—else why print it at all? But we cannot be certain.

One extant document contains a tremendous amount of information: Philip Henslowe's business record, known as his *Diary*. Henslowe was a financier who owned three theaters and served as a financial manager of sorts for the acting companies that rented his venues. The *Diary* includes performance records from 1592 through 1597, mostly for the Lord Admiral's Men. It allows us to get a sense of this company's business practices, its repertory of plays, its inventory of props and costumes, and its dealings with playwrights and artisans. And the *Diary* makes us realize just how many plays have disappeared: it mentions about 280 titles, of which at most 31 survive.

This may all sound rather depressing, as if the story of Shakespeare's theater were ultimately irretrievable. But it is not. We can interpret archaeological discoveries; extrapolate from extant records such as Henslowe's or the accounts of court officials; trace contemporary responses to the theater in letters, diaries, satires, and polemics; and study plays and their stage directions to understand what features playwrights expected in playhouses and how they intended to use them. We can make the most of what survives to construct a tentative and careful, but not baseless, narrative of what this world may have been like.

Playhouses

Theater in Shakespeare's London was predominantly an outdoor activity. Most playhouses were open-air spaces much larger than the few indoor venues. The building simply called The Theatre, in the suburb of Shoreditch, north of the City of London, created a model in 1576 that many playhouses would follow for the next forty years. It was a fourteen-sided polygonal structure, nearly round, with an external diameter of about seventy-two feet; audiences stood in the open yard or sat in one of three galleries. There was probably a permanent stage, which thrust out into the yard, with the galleries behind it serving as a balcony over the performance area and, where they were walled off, providing a backstage area (the "tiring house" in early modern terminology). The Theatre may not have had a roof over its stage. The Rose Theater in Southwark, across the Thames from the City of London, was built without such a roof in 1587; one was added during renovations in 1592. The shape of the stage also changed over time: archaeological excavations have shown that the Rose's original stage was relatively shallow, not extending far into the yard. In 1592, the space was redesigned to allow the stage to thrust out farther, creating a deeper playing area surrounded by standing spectators on three sides. This model would be followed in later playhouses, but whereas the Rose's stage (and probably those of other early theaters as well) tapered toward the front, later ones were rectangular and thus quite large. Judging from the erosion around the stage area in the excavated Rose, audiences responded with enthusiasm to the new configuration, pressing as close to the action as possible.

This first generation of playhouses also included The Theatre's close neighbor in Shoreditch, the Curtain, built in 1577 and named not after a stage curtain, which these theaters did not have, but after its location, the "Curtain Estate." The Theatre, the Curtain, and the Rose resembled one another in size and shape and had room for 2,000–2,500 spectators. The next generation of theaters did not depart from the earlier model in shape, but anticipated larger crowds. The Swan (1595), the Globe (1599), and the last outdoor theater erected in London, the Hope (1613), had a capacity of about 3,000. They were impressive buildings not just because of their size but

This view of London's northern suburbs shows the Curtain playhouse (the three-story polygonal structure with the flag on the left). It aptly illustrates the almost rural location of these early theaters: the Curtain stands adjacent to farmhouses and windmills.

also because they were beautifully decorated, as foreign visitors reported. Johannes de Witt, a Dutchman, described the Swan in 1596 as an "amphitheater of obvious beauty," admiring its wooden columns painted to look like marble.

Although some of the later playhouses modified the formula set by The Theatre, all the open-air venues shared a common spatial and social logic. They all separated their audience into those standing in the yard (the "groundlings" or "understanders"), who paid a penny to enter the theater, and those who sat in one of the galleries, paying two pennies for the lower level or three for the upper levels, where the benches had cushions. The most exclusive seats, at sixpence, were in the "lords' rooms," probably located in the sections of the galleries closest to the stage, and possibly in the balcony over the stage. Fashionable gallants and wealthy show-offs could also sit on the stage itself, paying an additional sixpence for a stool. Neither the "lords' rooms" nor the stools onstage gave the best view of the play, but they provided unparalleled opportunities to put fancy clothes on display: these were seats for being seen. Stage-sitting was often satirized as a vain and foolish habit, and the groundlings evidently objected to the rich fops blocking their view. As Shakespeare's contemporary Thomas Dekker describes the scene at one of the outdoor theaters, the "scarecrows in the yard hoot at you, hiss at you, spit at you, yea, throw dirt even in your teeth: 'tis most Gentlemanlike patience to endure all this, and to laugh at the silly animals."

The theaters, though hierarchically structured, were unusually inclusive: audience members from all social spheres could gain admission and enjoy the same spectacles. Social hierarchies became dangerously porous in this shared space, as Dekker's stage-sitters experienced firsthand: the commoners in the yard could hurl abuse and even dirt at the gentle and noble audience members onstage. Lords had to suffer close proximity with their social inferiors. However, the playhouses' inclusiveness had limits, too: the poor and royalty were unlikely to enter a theater. Neither Queen Elizabeth I nor King James I ever did.

Purpose-built theaters were not the only places where plays were performed. From the mid-1570s on, four inns also regularly hosted acting companies: the Bell, the Bull, the Cross Keys, and the Bell Savage. Only one of them, the Bell, seems to have had an indoor hall for play performances; the others had yards in which a stage could be erected. These yards had open galleries to give guests access to rooms on the upper floors, so that the overall structure of the auditorium was similar to the theaters: an open yard surrounded by galleries, at least some of which would have had benches. Unlike the theaters, however, which stood in the suburbs surrounding London, the inns were within or just outside the city walls. This location made them favored acting sites in the winter, when the roads were unpredictable and the days

A Victorian photograph of the Elizabethan galleried yard of the White Hart Inn in Southwark, similar to the layout of the inns used for performing plays.

were short, making it difficult for audience members to return to the City before the gates were shut at nightfall. But the inns irked London authorities. No venues other than churches allowed for the assembly of as many people as inn yards did, and play performances could attract particularly unruly crowds. For the authorities, these places created a threat of public disorder right in the heart of the City, and for over two decades, Lord Mayors and aldermen made intermittent attempts to shut down acting at the inns. It seems they succeeded by 1596, since references to regular performances in those venues cease after that year.

No adult acting company regularly performed in an indoor space in London between 1576 and 1610. There were a number of such venues, though, notably a very small theater near St. Paul's Cathedral, with room for only a select few, and a somewhat larger space inside the former Blackfriars friary. Both were active in the 1570s and 1580s, when two children's companies used them—acting troupes made up of choirboys from the royal chapels and St. Paul's Cathedral. By the time Shakespeare arrived in London, however, the old Blackfriars had closed, and neither space was used during the 1590s. But the boys' companies started performing again around the turn of the century, acting exclusively indoors.

This reemergence lies behind the conversation between Rosencrantz and Hamlet about the "eyrie of children" that produce plays mocking "the common stages." Although the boys' companies could not seriously jeopardize the adult troupes' economic success, their reappearance around 1600 apparently made their grown-up competitors look unfashionable among the trendiest patrons. Exclusivity was the hallmark of these companies and their indoor theaters, which were referred to as "private" playhouses; unlike the "common" theaters, these venues kept the wider world out both architecturally and socially. Entrance fees were much higher, probably starting at sixpence (the price of the costliest seats in the open-air theaters) and going up to over two shillings.

The boys also performed less frequently than the adult companies. They made the most of their elite status, thriving on satirical plays and a willingness to court controversy that sometimes landed them in hot water with persons of influence. Their financial situation was as unstable as their favor with the authorities. When King James, in March 1608, shut down the children's company that was using a recently constructed theater inside the former Blackfriars monastery, he unwittingly made theater history. Soon thereafter, the decades-old division between outdoor adult and indoor boys' companies came to an end. In 1610, near the end of Shakespeare's career, the King's Men adopted the Blackfriars as a second venue. Even after that, however, most audiences would still have experienced plays in the outdoor playhouses that remained the most popular, accessible, and visible acting venues in and around London.

Companies and Repertories

What was an acting company in Shakespeare's time? Formally, a group of players serving a noble patron. A law of 1572 had forced performers to find official sponsors to avoid legal prosecution as "vagrants" and "masterless men." That is why the troupe with which Shakespeare was associated for most of his documented career was first known as the Lord Chamberlain's Servants, and after 1603 as the King's Servants: these actors were officially servants of the Lord Chamberlain (the member of the Privy Council in charge of the royal household), and later of King James I. (Modern scholars generally refer to these companies as the Lord Chamberlain's Men and the King's Men.) All companies resident in London for at least part of the year were associated with high-ranking noblemen. After 1603, most of these troupes came under royal patronage, formally serving the King, the Queen, or a member of their family.

In all likelihood, the connection between patrons and companies was fairly loose, although the players technically formed part of their patrons' households. Take the example of James's son-in-law, the Count Palatine: his troupe, the Palsgrave's Men, operated under that name from 1613 to 1632, although their supposed patron only lived in England for a few months from 1612 to 1613. Links may have been closer where companies were sponsored by nobles of lower rank, as was common throughout the kingdom. Dozens of these groups appear in contemporary records. They toured the towns, cities, and stately homes surrounding their lords' seats, returning at Christmas to entertain families and guests. Whether they visited London is unclear, as is the question of what plays they performed; but some of them were so active on the road that they probably traveled to the country's biggest city as well.

What most defined a company were its leading members: the actors who would typically take on all major roles and who jointly owned the troupe's stock of costumes, props, and, crucially, play scripts. There were between six and a dozen of these "sharers." They not only formed the heart of any acting company, but also had an immediate financial interest in its success, as they divided the weekly profits among themselves. But there was more to a troupe of actors than its sharers. When the King's Men received their royal patent, or license, in 1603, the document not only identified the nine sharers (Shakespeare among them) as "servants" of James I, but also recognized that those servants required further "associates" to stage plays. These hired actors could in some cases be as closely associated with a company as the sharers. John Sincklo, for example, was a member of the Chamberlain's Men for most of their existence and is mentioned by name in the stage directions to three of Shakespeare's plays. He was apparently an extraordinarily thin man and is often linked with very skinny characters—in *1 Henry IV* he played the Beadle whom Doll Tearsheet calls a "thin man in a censer." Sincklo was a fixture of Chamberlain's Men productions for playwrights and audiences alike, and an integral part of their identity. Yet despite this status,

Sincklo continued to be an employee rather than an owner of the company for the rest of his recorded life.

The theatrical power of one other set of actors likewise outstripped their institutional power within the company: the male youths who played all female roles. These "boys"—in reality, adolescents who would not have started acting before they were twelve or thirteen and sometimes continued into their early twenties—were associated with the companies as sharers' apprentices. In effect, therefore, none of the actors who played Shakespeare's great female roles, from Tamora to Lady Macbeth to Hermione, were officially members of an acting troupe; rather, they belonged to a sharer's household. Each boy was contracted to serve his master for at least seven years, in return for instruction, room, and board. But officially, they would not have been in training as actors, since there was no guild for actors (and thus no official training available). Instead, they formally became apprentices in the trade governed by the guild to which their master belonged. For example, John Heminges, one of the leading sharers in Shakespeare's troupe, was a member of the Company of Grocers, the guild that oversaw that trade. Over thirty years, he had about ten apprentices. Since Heminges did not actually work as a grocer, these youths were probably boy actors, being trained as stage performers. If they completed their term, though, they could pay a fee and become "freemen" of the Company of Grocers and citizens of London— positions that came with many legal advantages and privileges. Although many boy actors did not become leading men, the social status they gained by formally completing an apprenticeship left them free to make their way in life after their careers as players had ended.

Although increasingly integrated into London's social life over the course of Shakespeare's career, most acting companies also spent part of the year touring market towns and stately homes. Acting was frowned upon if not strictly forbidden in London during Lent, the forty days or so before Easter, and companies had to go elsewhere to secure an income then; there was also a long-standing custom of traveling during the summer, when days were longer and roads more reliable (see the map of touring routes in the map appendix, below). Many companies only knew this itinerant existence, and it was their work that the young Shakespeare may have seen in Stratford. But around the time he began working as a theater professional some companies had started to regard London as their home. By the 1590s, that group included Lord Strange's Men, the Admiral's Men, and the Earl of Pembroke's Men. They established long-term relationships with the owners of playhouses where they performed more or less permanently. The Admiral's Men became associated with the Rose and later the Fortune, both theaters belonging to Philip Henslowe. The Chamberlain's Men, founded in 1594, started at The Theatre, owned by James Burbage (whose son Richard would soon emerge as the troupe's young star). Pembroke's Men may have been the resident company at the Swan once that playhouse opened in 1595. A further troupe probably occupied the Curtain. By 1599 yet another company, the Earl of Derby's Men, took up residence at the Boar's Head. In fact, so many acting troupes

Money was collected in small, round earthenware containers that had to be smashed after a performance. Many fragments of these were found during the excavation of the Rose playhouse.

performed in London that there were never fewer than four venues in operation during Shakespeare's career, and in some years the city sustained nine theaters.

The proprietors of most of those playhouses rented their buildings to the actors for a share of the revenues: half the takings from the galleries belonged to the landlord, while the sharers in the company retained all income from the yard and the other half of the takings from the galleries. Troupes and theater owners thus divided profits as well as risk: if a play flopped, the landlord also lost income, just as he gained from popular offerings. Some owners, Henslowe in particular, acted as the company's financial manager, keeping stock of belongings and conducting transactions on the actors' behalf.

Despite the great variety of playhouses and acting companies, or perhaps because of it, some venues developed specific profiles. This happened surprisingly early in the history of London theater. Writing in 1579, the antitheatrical polemicist Stephen Gosson excluded some plays from his general criticism, praising two "shown at the Bull"; two others "usually brought into the Theater"; and especially "the two prose books played at the Bell Savage, where you shall find never a word without wit, never a line without pith, never a letter placed in vain." Within a few years of opening, then, two of the inns and The Theatre were already known for specific plays one could expect to see there—whereas the four venues Gosson does not mention may have staged precisely the kinds of plays of which he disapproved.

All the same, few playhouses or acting companies were famous exclusively for a handful of titles or a particular kind of drama. The repertories of most troupes, including the Chamberlain's Men and King's Men, were inclusive in their approach to themes and genres and combined old favorites with new and potentially challenging material. The King's Men's 1603 patent describes them as performing not only "comedies, tragedies, histories"—the kinds of plays we might expect from Shakespeare's company—but also "interludes, morals, pastorals." Shakespeare's works do not represent all these categories, and they likely do not represent the full range of shows his troupe staged. If Henslowe's *Diary* is a reliable model, companies commissioned ten to twenty plays each year, and new plays dominated their repertory. If a play failed to draw crowds, it disappeared quickly. If it had staying power, it would remain in circulation for a while, but few became recognized classics destined to be revived every couple of years. In general, it seems that audiences enjoyed periodically reencountering older scripts, but had a more voracious appetite for fresh material—although old stories might frequently return in novel versions. Companies would produce their own take on plays from competing repertories: the Admiral's Men paid Ben Jonson in 1602 for a script about Richard III, for instance; and the Chamberlain's Men bought Jonson's *Every Man in His Humor* in 1598, probably hoping to capitalize on a 1597 hit at the Rose, George Chapman's *Comedy of Humors*. Even a single troupe's repertory might feature multiple plays drawn from the same stories or materials. The King's Men owned another *Richard II* play, which they staged at the Globe in April 1611—within weeks of performances of *Macbeth*, *Cymbeline*, and *The Winter's Tale*. Of those three Shakespearean offerings, the latter two were then still quite new; but *Macbeth* would have been a revival, an indication that it was a success when first performed.

The repertory system required daily turnover. Staging the same play for days at a time, let alone for weeks, was practically unheard of. The nine consecutive performances of Thomas Middleton's *A Game at Chess* at the Globe in 1624 were described as extraordinary at the time—nowadays, of course, a run of nine nights would be notable for its brevity. We can get a glimpse of what a typical selection of shows would have looked like in Shakespeare's company from Henslowe's *Diary*, which contains the only surviving sample of the Chamberlain's Men's repertory (staged in collaboration with the Admiral's Men in June 1594):

MON 3 June	*Hesther and Ahasuerus*
TUE 4 June	*The Jew of Malta*
WED 5 June	*Titus Andronicus*

THU 6 June	*Cutlack*
SAT 8 June	*Belin Dun*
SUN 9 June	*Hamlet*
MON 10 June	*Hesther and Ahasuerus*
TUE 11 June	*The Taming of a Shrew*
WED 12 June	*Titus Andronicus*
THU 13 June	*The Jew of Malta*

The two companies performed seven different plays in ten days. Of those, two were tragedies based on fictional plots (*The Jew of Malta* and *Titus Andronicus*), two were tragedies set in the distant northern European past (*Cutlack* and *Hamlet*—the latter not Shakespeare's version), one was a biblical drama (*Hesther and Ahasuerus*), one was a history or tragedy drawn from the English chronicles (*Belin Dun*, about a highwayman hanged by King Henry I), and one was a comedy (*The Taming of a Shrew*—again, not Shakespeare's). One play was brand-new (*Belin Dun*); one recent (*Titus Andronicus*, first performed in January 1594); two quite old (*The Jew of Malta* and *The Taming of a Shrew* were probably written before 1590); and we know nothing about the others.

The two companies' combined offerings constitute a representative mixture of old and new; of different geographical settings and historical periods; of tragic, heroic, moral, and comedic entertainments. Variety was a predictable feature of any company's stock of plays. Predictability, however, was not. For theatergoers keen to see a performance of *Titus* after its successful June 5 outing, finding out when the play was going to be mounted next was neither easy nor straightforward (we now know that their next chance would have come on June 12). They may have relied on word of mouth, as the actors commonly announced the next day's play at the end of a show; they might have encountered the players marching through the City in the morning hours, advertising that day's performance; or they may have read the news on one of the playbills posted daily all over the City to inform audiences what was being staged where. But would-be spectators had to keep their eyes peeled: while repertories responded to popular demand, they did not follow an easily foreseeable schedule. Since *Titus* did well, it would certainly be back onstage soon. But exactly when was uncertain.

Why Shakespeare's Company Was Different

The playhouse in which the Chamberlain's Men and the King's Men performed after 1599, the Globe, was a unique building project. In 1597 James Burbage's lease for the land on which The Theatre stood ran out, and a year later the Chamberlain's Men were forced to vacate the premises and move to the neighboring Curtain. The building itself, however, still belonged to Burbage, and after his death in 1597, to his sons Cuthbert and Richard, the latter Shakespeare's fellow sharer. The Burbages therefore took the extraordinary step of having a carpenter dismantle the structure and use the salvaged timber to build a new playhouse. This would be erected on a plot of land on the other side of London, south of the river and across the street from Henslowe's Rose Theater. This new theater, the Globe, would be significantly bigger than its predecessor. As archaeological digs have revealed, it was probably a sixteen-sided polygon with a diameter of about eighty-five feet, nearly fourteen feet more than The Theatre's. It was operational by September 1599, when the Swiss traveler Thomas Platter saw a performance of *Julius Caesar* at what he called "the straw-thatched house"—almost certainly the Globe, which had a thatched roof over the galleries and stage.

Opening a new playhouse right next to the small and aging Rose might look like an aggressive gesture on the Burbages' part, bringing the Chamberlain's Men into direct competition with the Admiral's Men. In such a turf-war narrative, Burbage and company look like history's winners: Henslowe and his son-in-law Edward Alleyn almost immediately started building a new playhouse elsewhere. The Admiral's Men abandoned the Rose in 1600 and moved into their new home, the Fortune, in Clerkenwell, northwest of the City and far away from the Globe. But there is no reason to think that a desire to ramp up competition motivated the Burbages' decision. For one thing, this kind of thinking would have been out of step with the general atmosphere of mutual respect among London's acting companies. For another, the very speed with which Henslowe and Alleyn acted supports a different story. In fact, the Burbages may have chosen the Southwark location because they knew that Henslowe had started to look for a suitable site for a new playhouse and that the Admiral's Men would soon leave their old home.

What made the Globe a remarkable project was neither its builders' allegedly aggressive approach to the theatrical marketplace nor its size or design, which were no more impressive than the Swan's. The Globe was unique for the way it was financed: it belonged not to a separate landlord, but to members of the acting company itself.

How did this come about? It may be that when the Burbages decided to move their playhouse in 1598, they did not have sufficient funds for that enterprise. In 1596, their father had spent the very large sum of £600 to transform a medieval hall inside the former Blackfriars monastery into a theater. The purpose of this investment is uncertain: the doomed lease negotiations for The Theatre had not yet begun, so James Burbage might have been trying to expand his activities as a theater owner rather than replace his old playhouse. He had only been his son's company's landlord for a little over a year when he bought the Blackfriars, and may very well have had another company in mind for the new space. Whatever the case, the new venue was the largest indoor performance space in London, and probably the first hall theater designed for an adult company. But the undertaking failed. Almost instantly, a group of wealthy inhabitants of the Blackfriars precinct successfully protested against the plan. The composition of that group is enlightening: it contained Lord Hunsdon, the patron of Shakespeare's company; and Hunsdon's recently deceased father had tried to buy part of the same property Burbage was after the year before. If the new playhouse was meant for the Chamberlain's Men, it is certainly strange that both these patrons of the company attempted to prevent its construction.

In any event, the property was not a viable alternative when Richard Burbage and his fellows lost The Theatre. Whether for financial reasons or because neither Cuthbert nor Richard Burbage wanted to play the role of theater owner and landlord, the brothers devised a solution that would for the first time put a venue mostly in actors' hands. Half the enterprise belonged to the Burbages (since they contributed the timber from The Theatre), but the remaining 50 percent was divided equally among five of the seven or eight remaining sharers in the Chamberlain's Men: John Heminges, William Kemp, Augustine Phillips, Thomas Pope, and William Shakespeare. At Christmas 1598, this consortium signed the lease for the plot of land in Southwark. They subsequently covered the construction costs of £700, exactly what The Theatre had cost to build in 1576.

Having a playhouse owned by the majority of the sharers in an acting company was a unique business model. These sharers now were responsible for the upkeep of the building, but they also, as landlords, received a portion of the entire revenue from every show (the Globe used the same rental agreement as the Rose, splitting performance income between landlords and actors). Beyond economics, the agreement created an unparalleled strong bond between these actors and their venue. It practically ensured that the Globe became their default home, and that its joint owners would remain members of the same acting company. The Globe was made for the Chamberlain's Men—but the Chamberlain's Men, in a sense, were also made by the Globe.

What happened to the Blackfriars property in the meantime? It stood empty for three years; and then, in 1600, it became an active theater after all. That year, Richard Burbage, clearly unwilling to adopt his father's or Henslowe's business model, leased

This section of Wenceslaus Hollar's 1647 "Long View" of London, drawn from South-wark, shows the Globe in its rebuilt state. The Globe is the round building in the middle, misidentified as a "Beere bayting" arena. The round building to its right, mislabeled "The Globe," is in fact the Hope playhouse, which by the 1620s was used exclusively as a bearbaiting venue.

the Blackfriars venue outright to the manager of a boys' acting company—for a flat annual fee of £40, and for twenty-one years. No revenue sharing, no managerial services: Burbage washed his hands of his father's failed endeavor. (The boys' company did not face the same opposition as the 1596 venture, perhaps because it performed as rarely as once a week, or because it represented a more up-market kind of playing.)

Eventually, the Blackfriars would become the King's Men's second venue: they probably started performing plays there sometime in 1610, at the very end of Shakespeare's career. But neither the company nor the Burbages were in any rush to move indoors. In 1604, the boys' company's manager tried to return the building to them and cut the twenty-one-year lease short, but the Burbages were uninterested. Only after the King forced out the children's troupe in 1608 did they agree to terminate the lease. The brothers owned the property and certainly had no financial incentive to search for investors. And yet the Burbages immediately turned the Blackfriars into another shared venture, splitting costs and revenues equally among themselves, one outsider, and four King's Men's sharers, including Shakespeare. The idea here was evidently not to maximize personal gain, but to enhance the company's profile—and its leaders' fortunes.

Within a decade, the Blackfriars turned into *the* place for new, fashionable plays. But during Shakespeare's lifetime, it never outshone the older outdoor space. For the first years of the new theater's existence, references to King's Men plays mention only the Globe; prominent audience members, including foreign princes, still visited the open-air venue; and in 1613, the company emphatically reaffirmed its commitment to its traditional playhouse. That year, the building's cost-effective thatched roof caught

A different section of Hollar's panorama shows the Blackfriars precinct across the river from the Globe and Hope theaters. Just left off the center, next to the spire of St. Bride's Church, the long roof with two tall chimneys marks the probable location of the Blackfriars theater.

fire during the first performance of Shakespeare and Fletcher's *Henry VIII*. The Globe burned down, leaving the King's Men with only an indoor theater at their disposal. However, instead of redefining themselves as the Blackfriars company, they extended their lease on the Southwark plot, invested the enormous sum of £1,400, and rebuilt their playhouse—with decorations that made it, in the words of an eyewitness, "the fairest that ever was in England." This time, the galleries and stage had tiled roofs.

If the Chamberlain's/King's Men were unique in forming such a strong interconnection between actors and theaters, they also benefited from the unusual privilege of having an in-house playwright. No other company in the 1590s seems to have had a sharer who could also provide, on average, two plays a year. In addition, Shakespeare apparently performed other tasks for his company that would normally have been farmed out to hired dramatists, which included writing new scenes for old plays. The sheets in the *Sir Thomas More* manuscript that are probably in Shakespeare's handwriting are one example: there, he provided a long scene for a collaboratively authored text that needed major patching to be stageable. There is also evidence that additions to Thomas Kyd's *Spanish Tragedy* first printed in 1602 are by Shakespeare; if so, he wrote them for a Chamberlain's Men revival of this early classic (originally staged around 1587). The role of Hieronimo in the play was one of Richard Burbage's star turns, so we know the script found its way into the company's repertory at some point in the late 1590s or early 1600s.

Although the Chamberlain's Men were unusually fortunate to have Shakespeare as a sharer, we should not overestimate his place in their repertory. He was no Thomas Dekker, the dramatist who between 1597 and 1603 wrote or coauthored 41 new plays for a range of companies. Nor was Shakespeare as productive as Thomas Heywood, who claimed to have authored or cowritten more than 220 plays in a career spanning forty years. Given a need for at least ten fresh scripts a year, Shakespeare's contributions to his company's repertory were valuable, even indispensable—but they could never make up more than a fraction of the new material commissioned every year. Even if demand for new plays slowed in the 1620s, after the King's Men had accumulated a stock of reliably popular offerings, those of Shakespeare's works that had proved their lasting appeal would always be part of a much larger set of scripts. And the company treated Shakespeare's plays much like other authors' works, hiring play-wrights to spruce up the old texts and make them newly exciting for audiences; in Shakespeare's case, it was Thomas Middleton who revised *Measure for Measure*, *Macbeth*, and possibly others.

At Court

Thinking of theater as a commercial enterprise taking place in venues accessible to all who paid the price of admission means leaving out one important aspect of early modern theater: private performances for aristocratic audiences. Companies were occasionally paid to stage their plays inside the London houses of noble clients, but such interactions with the highest social ranks were intermittent and unpredict-able. The court, on the other hand, annually required actors to provide entertain-ments during lengthy revels between Christmas and Twelfth Night, and usually at Shrovetide (the three days before Ash Wednesday). Under Elizabeth I, there was only one court, her own, and theatrical activities were limited to those two holiday periods. With the ascension of James I, however, the number of royal courts multiplied—besides the King's own, Queen Anne, Prince Henry, and later Prince Charles also maintained courts with their own occasions for entertainment—and playing was no longer limited to holidays. The records show that the royally sponsored adult companies could be sum-moned to one of the palaces at any time. Officially, the courts' desire for theater justified the actors' need to play all year round in public venues, despite the City authorities' con-cerns: companies constantly had to rehearse and try out plays in front of live audiences so they could be ready to perform whenever a royal patron needed them.

The person in charge of organizing royal entertainments was the Master of the Revels, an officer who worked for the Lord Chamberlain. Under Elizabeth, the office was held by Sir Edmund Tilney. His job was not an easy one: he was responsible for choosing the appropriate companies and plays from the multitude available in London. In his early years, Tilney's approach seemed scattershot, with up to seven different troupes playing at court per season. The sheer complexity of keeping that many com-panies organized may have led to the foundation of an elite troupe under Elizabeth's own patronage, the Queen's Men, who dominated court entertainments for a few years after 1583. In 1594, the Master of the Revels apparently undertook a second effort to streamline holiday performances, this time relying not on a single troupe, but on a pair—and his superior, the Lord Chamberlain, adopted one of those compa-nies as his own. For five years thereafter, Tilney could draw on two consistently excellent groups of actors, the Chamberlain's Men and the Admiral's Men.

As in 1583, though, this approach gave the Queen's revels a rather different com-plexion from the popular theaters. The Queen's Men were the leading company for about ten years after their creation, but other troupes eventually reappeared in the court season. Similarly, Shakespeare's company and their colleagues at the Rose were prominent but far from alone in London, and their competitors also turned up on Tilney's payroll again before long. Derby's Men, Worcester's Men, Hertford's Men, and the boys' companies all performed at court within a few years of the establish-ment of the Lord Chamberlain's troupe in 1594. Tilney's tenure as Master of the Revels was marked by repeated, ultimately futile efforts to limit actors' access to courtly employment—efforts seemingly designed to shut out the unrestrained variety of the public theatrical marketplace.

Under James I, the Lord Chamberlain's office finally acknowledged the size and diversity of London's theater world. Abandoning the model of a separate set of privileged companies with access to the court, the crown instead brought all major London companies gradually under royal patronage. By 1615, five adult troupes were being officially sponsored by members of James's family. Only those companies were asked to perform at court, but they were probably also the only acting outfits remaining in London: there were not enough playhouses to accommodate more than five permanent adult companies.

Even if the diversity of companies performing at court came to reflect the situation in the public playhouses over the course of Shakespeare's career, the repertory the actors drew on for their courtly performances remained distinct in surprising ways. We might expect that kings and queens, princes, ambassadors, and wealthy courtiers would have made for the most discerning and demanding audience imaginable, but the records tell a different story. Often, the plays staged at court were already several years old; by the 1610s, Revels playlists begin to feel like compilations of the classics that had their place in every company's repertory but could not normally compete with the appeal of new material. The court's, or the Master of the Revels', taste was broadly on the conservative side.

Though the records list almost no specific play titles from Elizabeth's reign, those surviving from James's time suggest that the King and his inner circle liked their Shakespeare well aged. In 1604, there were *A Midsummer Night's Dream*, nine years old; *The Merry Wives of Windsor*, seven years old; and *The Comedy of Errors*, over ten years old. The next year, we have recorded performances of *Henry V*, six or seven years after its first staging; and of *The Merchant of Venice*, at least seven years old, but performed twice within three days in James's presence in February 1605. These were the typical Shakespearean offerings. Exceptions occurred, including the still-new *Tempest* and *Winter's Tale* in November 1611, but for the most part, the Master of the Revels assembled an unadventurous repertory in which certain favorites often reappear. *Twelfth Night*, *The Winter's Tale*, *Othello*, and *1 Henry IV* show up every few years, as do some of Ben Jonson's plays (*Volpone* and *The Alchemist* in particular) and titles whose continued popularity at court now seems puzzling (such as the anonymous *Greene's Tu Quoque* and *The Merry Devil of Edmonton*). A company that performed for the royal households as often as did the King's Men must have adjusted to their courtly audience's expectations to some degree, and may therefore have been less quick to follow the latest artistic fashions than a company less in demand at court. But even so, Shakespeare and his fellows probably saw acting for their royal patrons as quite a different challenge from playing for London audiences. And in spite of the unquestionable importance of their connection to the royal household, the fact that they performed publicly far more frequently and depended on the income from those performances probably meant that their day-to-day activities were less influenced by the preferences of the court than we might imagine.

The Regulation of Playing and Its Failures

Organizing court entertainments was the most important aspect of the Master of the Revels' job, but he had another major responsibility: the licensing of new plays. Every script had to be submitted to him for approval, and only manuscripts bearing his license and signature were allowed to be performed. In their censorship activities, Tilney and his successors concentrated mainly on three concerns: no actual persons could be slandered or attacked; plays had to steer clear of incendiary topics and language; and, after a law banning profanity onstage had been passed in 1606, actors were no longer allowed to utter oaths using the name of God in any form. In the main, though, the Master of the Revels was not the acting companies' antagonist. For instance, Tilney did not simply reject *Sir Thomas More*, although he found the play objectionable on a number of counts; instead, he suggested changes that would enable him to give the players his license.

That relatively benign mode of control could quickly shift into an aggressive register when the players crossed a line. Companies that staged plays without first having them licensed, if discovered, were severely reprimanded. Stricter actions followed whenever a performance offended a person of high rank and influence. Playhouses were sometimes shut down as a consequence, and actors and playwrights found themselves in prison while under investigation. When these perceived transgressions happened (and they happened infrequently), the state was typically unable to explain what had gone wrong, especially if the play had been licensed. Playwrights would routinely offer the likeliest theory: the actors had ad-libbed, adding content the Master of the Revels had not seen and the author(s) had not written. There was certainly a kernel of truth to those defenses. Live performance is invariably different from the script on which it is based. But although that insight was not unknown to Shakespeare's contemporaries, it never seemed to affect the official system of licensing, which continued to operate unchanged throughout the early modern period.

Beyond the licensing requirements, there are few signs that the state took any sustained interest in regulating the theatrical marketplace, in London or elsewhere in the country. Nor were such efforts especially effective when they did occur. One of the most significant interventions took place in July 1597, apparently in response to a now-lost play, *The Isle of Dogs*, performed by Pembroke's Men at the Swan. This performance caused a massive scandal, landed some actors and the playwright Ben Jonson in jail under investigation for sedition, shut down all the theaters, and ruined Pembroke's Men financially. We do not know what made the play so offensive, but it must have been a serious trespass. The Privy Council's reaction to what it regarded as the players' "lewd and mutinous behaviour" was unprecedentedly severe; an order went out to stop all performances and have all playhouses demolished within three months. As telling as this order, though, is what happened next: almost nothing. The company was broken up, but no theaters were destroyed. Henslowe's *Diary* shows no signs that he was concerned about loss of income, and before long a new London-based company established itself in a new theater, the Boar's Head. For the next few years, the Privy Council attempted to control the number of troupes and playhouses in London, but every one of its annual letters to the local authorities expresses frustration about the inefficient implementation of the previous set of orders. No letters on the subject written after 1602 survive.

The Privy Council's general indifference to tightly regulating the theaters and its relatively hands-off attitude, even in the brief period when it adopted restrictive policies, did not align well with the wishes of the Lord Mayor and aldermen of the City, for whom the theaters posed a perennial challenge to public order. However, even the City authorities were not consistent in their opposition: they habitually relied on actors and playwrights for the annual civic entertainments, especially the Lord Mayor's pageants. Some aldermen befriended players, and actors participated in parish-level government (Shakespeare's colleagues Henry Condell and John Heminges were church wardens; Edward Alleyn and Philip Henslowe served as members of the vestry, or parish council, of St. Saviour's Church in Southwark). And although opposition to regular performances at the inns in the City was fairly consistent over twenty years, this policy may not have been the reason that all the large playhouses were built in the suburbs. Rather, high property prices and the scarcity of plots of land large enough for an amphitheater-style structure inside the densely packed City probably forced theater-builders to look beyond the city walls. Having large gathering places close to their gates but beyond their control vexed London authorities, but their anger may have been fueled by more than a simple desire to prohibit playacting: the theaters made a lot of money, and none of that income could be taxed by the City—despite the fact that the vast majority of playgoers would have been Londoners. The Mayor and his aldermen thus had many reasons for feeling aggrieved. Not only did they have to suffer the threat of riots and public disturbances sparked at the theaters, but they could not even collect fees and taxes in return.

The one cause that brought the interests of City and Privy Council together was also the single biggest economic threat to the acting companies, and the most frequent reason for playhouse closures: the plague. While the transmission of diseases was not well understood in early modern England, the authorities knew that crowds spread illness. Hence the government would order the theaters to shut whenever plague deaths reached a certain level (these figures had to be recorded and reported parish by parish every week). Sometimes, such closures were a precaution and did not last long. But on a number of occasions during Shakespeare's career, the theaters were closed for many months, with disastrous consequences for the London-based companies. A plague outbreak in 1593 halted performances for almost the entire year, forced all companies to tour, and caused a major reorganization of the theatrical landscape—out of which the Chamberlain's Men emerged as a new troupe formed from the fragments of its disbanded predecessors. At least as devastating was the horrific eruption of plague that shut down all playing in London from March 1603 to September 1604, and the less severe but longer episode that kept the theaters closed from August 1608 to the end of 1610. The first decade of James's reign was an especially chaotic and challenging time for the London companies, as there were lengthy plague closures even in the years when the playhouses were periodically open. If the world of London theater changed fundamentally after Shakespeare's retirement in 1613, the great watershed may not have been the introduction of multiple royal patrons or of new indoor performance venues, but instead the comparative stability offered by an extended period without plague outbreaks. In any case, it seems clear that the greatest threat to an acting company's fortunes was not the Privy Council, the censor, or local authorities, but a mysterious, unpredictable, and lethal disease.

Casting

We have already glimpsed some of the details of how an early modern acting company was put together: at its core were the sharers, the actors who jointly owned the troupe's assets; then there were a number of male youths, usually apprenticed to the sharers, who played women and children; and then there was a group of hired men, who had no financial stake in the group's success, as they were paid a set salary, although some (such as John Sincklo) stayed loyally with the same troupe. Beyond those actors, most London companies employed someone who functioned like a modern stage manager, the book-holder. That person was responsible for maintaining play scripts and organizing the backstage action during performances; he likely also acted as a prompter. Finally, there were employees who collected admission fees, cleaned the theater, and probably doubled as stagehands. Some of these workers were women, a female presence in an otherwise entirely male business.

Senior actors developed a degree of professional specialization. The most obvious experts were the clowns or fools, often among the most prominent members of any company. Richard Tarlton was the first of the great and famous Elizabethan clowns, and he was the Queen's Men's undisputed star until his death in 1588. Will Kemp, a sharer in the Chamberlain's Men as well as, for a short while, in the Globe, took over Tarlton's crown as the funniest man on English stages. After Kemp left the company in 1599, Robert Armin inherited his role as clown. The styles of these comedic performers differed, with Tarlton famed as an improviser and singer, Kemp known for his athleticism, and Armin for his subtler verbal wit, but they all had one thing in common: their responsibilities included the comic entertainments performed after plays

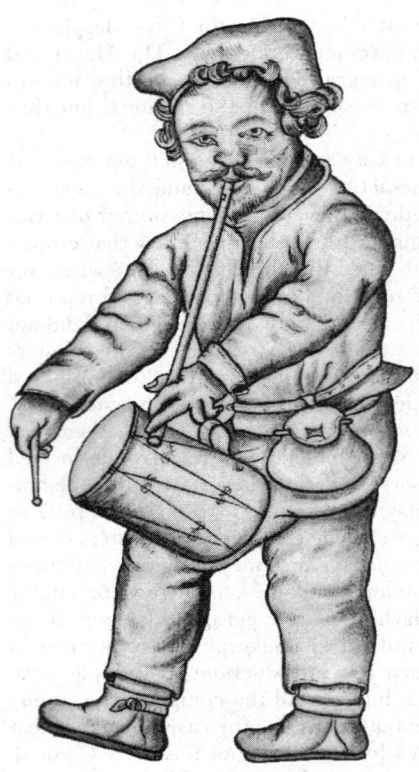

This portrait of Richard Tarlton, drawn by John Scottowe in or around 1588, shows Tarlton dressed as a jester, playing the tabor (a kind of drum) and pipe.

were done. Hence, they regularly appeared before audiences as themselves or as recognizable stage personae. They were certainly among the most readily identifiable faces of the company.

Unlike other roles, the clowns' parts in plays were often not fully scripted, and allowed for improvisation—the excessive use of which Hamlet criticizes when he tells the players to "let those that play your clowns speak no more than is set down for them." It is thus no coincidence that even as playwriting became a profession separate from acting, famous clowns still continued to be known as dramatists as well: Tarlton, Kemp, and Armin all wrote, as did John Shank, John Singer, and William Rowley. The line between the play and its performance, between the playwright's text and what the actors said and did, was particularly blurred in these performers' roles—and we should not assume that authors (or anyone else) found this especially troubling. It would be an error to read Hamlet's views as Shakespeare's, let alone the audience's: by all accounts, including Hamlet's, theatergoers enjoyed the clowns' ad-libbing and did not mind if such riffing delayed the progress of the play. We should, however, take seriously Hamlet's use of the plural "clowns." The company's specialist clown would never have been the only actor with comedic skills. *Hamlet* itself requires at least two clowns, the two gravediggers, even if Armin took on three of the plays' foolish roles and acted Polonius, Osric, and the first gravedigger (a casting choice the structure of the play allows). *Twelfth Night*, similarly, calls for a designated clown, but also needs another comically gifted actor as Sir Andrew Aguecheek. Shakespeare's company included a number of such performers. Thomas Pope, one of its founding sharers, had a reputation as a comedian, as did Richard Cowley, a hired man with the Chamberlain's Men who became a sharer in the King's Men.

If not all comic parts always went to the same performer, the same is true of dramatic leads. Two great tragic actors dominate all narratives of Shakespeare's stage: Edward Alleyn, the Admiral's Men's star, and Richard Burbage, the Chamberlain's and King's Men's leading player. Both rose to prominence in the 1590s. Alleyn, Burbage's senior by three years, gained fame first. However, although he led the longer life (Burbage died in 1619, Alleyn in 1626), his career as an actor lasted nowhere near as long as his colleague's: sometime before 1606, Alleyn retired from the stage to devote his attention to even more profitable ventures, whereas Burbage continued acting until his death. But even these two titans of the stage would not have taken the lead in every play: that is not how ensembles work. Alleyn certainly performed the title characters in Christopher Marlowe's *Tamburlaine* and *Doctor Faustus* and Barabas in *The Jew of Malta*, though he may not have originated those roles; beyond these, we know of five other parts in which he acted, four of them from lost plays. Burbage's list is not much longer. An elegy written shortly after his death laments that with him died characters that no other actor could bring to life as powerfully: "No more young Hamlet, old Hieronimo, / Kind Lear, the grievèd Moor." He was closely associated, then, with three of Shakespeare's plays and Kyd's *Spanish Tragedy*; notably, those works were at least ten years old when he died.

We might expect that Burbage, at the height of his fame, played all the largest parts, but the elegy suggests otherwise: Othello is a smaller role than Iago. What is more, when the Chamberlain's Men were established in 1594, Burbage was only twenty-five, the youngest sharer, and had not yet risen to the level of prominence he would later attain; and the company included other well-known actors: George Bryan, John Heminges, Augustine Phillips, and William Sly. Initially, Burbage's name would not have been the most recognizable among these, and even when his reputation ultimately eclipsed the others', he would—and could—not

A contemporary portrait of Richard Burbage. Burbage sometimes worked as a visual artist, and some scholars believe this painting to be a self-portrait.

have been the only choice for leads. Think of Shakespeare's plays from the mid-1590s: Burbage probably played Romeo, but what about *Richard II*? Would Burbage have been a better fit for the king or for the usurper Bolingbroke? In *The Merchant of Venice*, Shylock is the star turn nowadays, but Bassanio may have been the likelier role for Burbage, with older actors, like Bryan or Phillips, taking the roles of the other two male leads, Antonio and Shylock—or Thomas Pope, if Shylock was considered a comic part. Or take, as a final example, *Titus Andronicus*. Titus is the largest role, but Burbage may well have been a better fit for Aaron, a younger and more agile character.

Matching actors' ages to those of their characters, though, is a complicated business, and a casting consideration that was treated differently in Shakespeare's time from now. Burbage played Lear when he was no older than thirty-seven; and he was famous in the role of Hieronimo—an elderly father figure—by 1601, when he was just thirty-two. The same actor, then, might have acted the aged King Lear, "old Hieronimo," and "young Hamlet" within the span of a few days. And yet, despite this apparent disregard for verisimilitude, it was the supposedly lifelike quality of his acting that made Burbage famous. A writer in the 1660s reported on his ability to "wholly transfor[m] himself into his part, putting off himself with his clothes, as he never assumed himself again until the play was done." Part of Burbage's power was that he could seemingly become another person, even if that meant aging by decades. If the effect was a kind of make-believe, however, the means were an orator's, not those of modern psychological realism. What contemporary witnesses praise is Burbage's facility with speech, with finding the right vocal affect and the right quality of voice to express his character. As important was his aptitude at suiting his physical movement to the role, finding what were called the right "actions." That term probably referred to an elaborate arsenal of gestures and body positions that was systematic enough that audiences could read and make sense of actors' movements: putting a hand on the heart, holding one's face in one's hands, making a fist, and so on. Even if Burbage seemed able to go beyond conventions and give his actions an unusually personal or individual quality, though, it is clear that what seemed lifelike in Shakespeare's theater had little to do with a modern understanding of stage realism.

Burbage's specific talent may have been self-transformation; Alleyn, on the other hand, was known and remembered for his extraordinary stage presence. But both actors used a similar technical arsenal. Alleyn, like Burbage, was praised for his "excellent action"—as Thomas Nashe wrote in 1592, not even the greatest Roman actors "could ever perform more in action than famous Ned Alleyn." If Burbage disappeared into his roles, Alleyn was celebrated for the awe-inspiring quality he himself lent the characters he played. We do not know what his acting would have looked like onstage, but its outsized effect was not universally popular. Hamlet's criticism of players that "so strutted and bellowed" that "they imitated humanity so abominably" may refer to actors of Alleyn's ilk, perhaps an implicit statement that the Chamberlain's Men favored a different approach to performance. After Alleyn's death, in the reign of Charles I, the larger-than-life style associated with him was frowned upon by some writers and by spectators at some theaters. But there is no evidence that Burbage's brand of acting displaced Alleyn's within Shakespeare's lifetime. More probably, the two actors' particular aptitudes represented the pinnacles of two different but not incompatible acting techniques that in other players' work appeared in mixed forms. Both of these men were exceptional figures, after all. The Admiral's Men were not a company of many Alleyns, nor were the Chamberlain's Men a troupe of Burbages. What most performers and audiences probably understood "acting" (or "playing") to mean is captured vividly in these lines from *Richard III*:

> Come, cousin, canst thou quake, and change thy color,
> Murder thy breath in middle of a word,
> And then begin again, and stop again,
> As if thou wert distraught and mad with terror?

> (3.5.1–4)

What Richard is asking Buckingham here is whether he can act—and Buckingham replies that he can indeed "counterfeit the deep tragedian," in part because he can use the appropriate actions (looks, trembling, starts, smiles). Both characters describe a kind of performance that is highly codified, quite predictable, and not exactly lifelike; but both share the confidence that a talented actor can turn hackneyed gestures and tics into a convincing impression of reality.

If actors were capable of creating something like reality out of obvious fictions, and if those fictions could stretch to having an actor in his thirties play an old king one day and a young prince the next, then it cannot have been difficult for performers and audiences to come to terms with the widespread practice of doubling. All but the actors cast in the largest roles routinely played multiple characters, often leaving the stage as one person only to return shortly thereafter, wearing a new hat or a different cloak, as an entirely different character. Doubling meant that most early modern plays, although they may feature thirty or more characters, could be staged by around fourteen actors. In *The Merchant of Venice*, for example, the same player could take the parts of Old Gobbo, Tubal, the Jailer, and the Duke; or Morocco, Arragon, and the Duke—in either case, characters ranging widely in age and social status.

Like doubling, the casting of male youths in all female parts was a firmly established theatrical convention, though one that had less to do with pragmatic considerations than with a strong moral rationale. The idea of women putting their bodies on public display, even if fully clothed, was widely regarded as immoral and likened to prostitution. All-male casts were so deeply ingrained in English theatergoers' expectations that seeing actual women play female roles startled those who traveled abroad, where female actors were common. Some expressed their surprise that women could in fact act; others compared the Continental female performers critically to English boy players, whom they considered preferable not on moral but on artistic grounds. The women, these witnesses argued, played their characters too close to life, not artfully enough. A degree of artifice was as desirable in the boy actors' performances as in those delivered by the men. But as with the adult players, that artfulness did not diminish the potential impact of the show, as a famous account of a 1610 staging of *Othello* in Oxford attests. There, the scholar Henry Jackson recalls how Desdemona's death affected him: "although she always acted her whole part supremely well, yet when she was killed she was even more moving, for when she fell back upon the bed she implored the pity of the spectators by her very face." The boy player disappears behind the female pronouns, as if the artifice of the performance had become invisible. At the same time, Jackson registers that the body onstage, female or not, is not quite like a real corpse either; it responds to, and demands a response from, "the spectators." Yet, despite his recognition that the actor, or the character, is manipulating the audience's emotions, Jackson still responds emotionally and is in fact moved. The convention of using male youths for

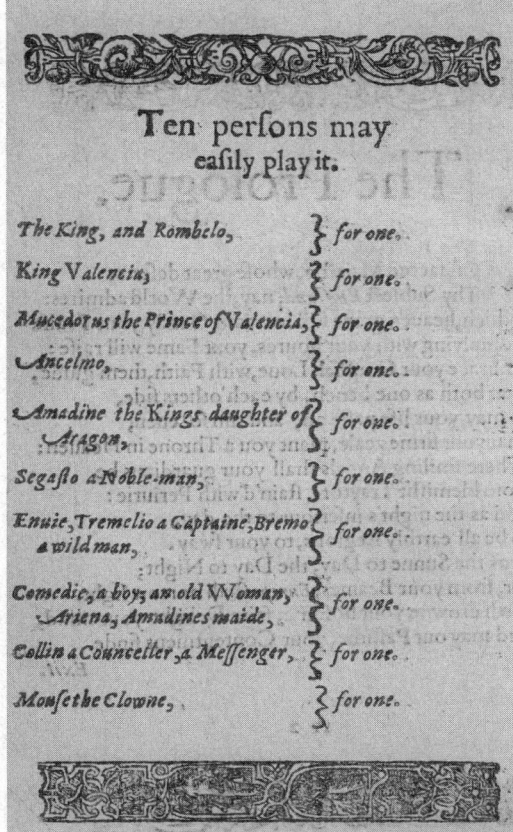

A chart from the second edition of the very popular anonymous play *Mucedorus* (1606), showing which actors can play more than one part.

female parts, then, was of a piece with the broader understanding of acting in Shakespeare's time as an art that deployed heightened artifice in order to create an affectively powerful semblance of real life.

Staging and Its Meanings

The staging of a new play in Shakespeare's time did not begin in a rehearsal room or in a theater, but in an actor's home. One of the first tasks of the company book-holder in readying a new script for performance was the preparation of the players' individual parts: each actor received only his own lines, along with the cues to which he was to respond and a handful of stage directions. Initially, then, most actors did not know who else was onstage with them, how many lines those other characters had, how much time passed between the scenes in which they appeared, or even who would give them their cues—nor what those characters said before the two or three words that made up the cue. Since companies performed together almost every day and actors often lived close to each other, informal discussions must have taken place to clarify relationships between characters, but any performer's primary duty would have been to learn

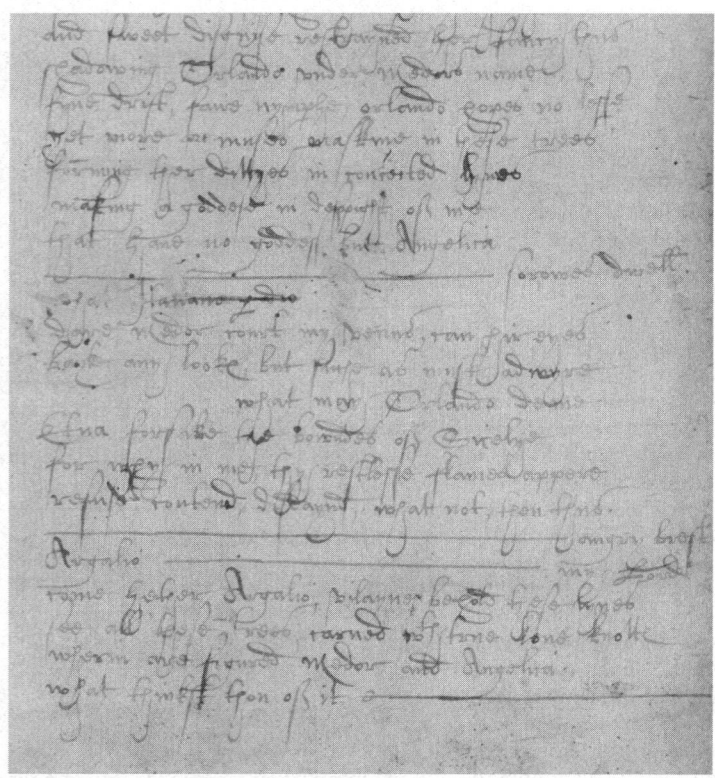

A section of Edward Alleyn's part for the role of Orlando in Robert Greene's *Orlando Furioso*. The long lines across the page mark breaks in Orlando's speech; at their end, the actor could find the cue for his next line.

his part in relative isolation, finding appropriate actions and intonations for his lines and memorizing cues. For leads, this was a formidable responsibility. Parts were written on strips of paper that were glued together to form a roll—which is why the terms "role" and "part" are synonymous. The scrolls for leads could reach remarkable length and heft. The one extant early modern part, Alleyn's copy of Orlando in Robert Greene's *Orlando Furioso*, is six inches wide and an impressive thirteen feet long, but its 530 lines probably did not overly tax an actor who had mastered more than 1,100 lines in *The Jew of Malta* and nearly 900 lines in the second part of *Tamburlaine*.

By Shakespeare's time, the solitary actor preparing his role could have predicted how the play would be staged with some certainty. The setup illustrated in the 1596 drawing of the Swan Theater is broadly representative of what a performer could expect in any venue: a rectangular, flat, largely empty stage; no sets in the modern sense, and few large furniture items; two pillars, probably set back from the edges of the stage by a few feet; at least two stage doors, and possibly a third in the center; and a balcony where scenes described as taking place "aloft" or "above" would be staged, though sections of it may also have offered additional audience seating, and part of it may have been used as a "music room." Even if there was no central stage door, there would have been an area between the two entrances that lay concealed behind an arras or a curtain that could be drawn to reveal pre-set tableaux, such as Hermione's statue in *The Winter's Tale*, Ferdinand and Miranda's chess game in *The Tempest*, or the caskets in *The Merchant of Venice*. There was also a trapdoor giving access to the space underneath the stage (sometimes called hell)—the place from which the ghost of Hamlet's father calls out to his son and his friends. In some theaters,

The interior of the Swan Theater, a sixteenth-century copy of a drawing by the Dutch traveler Johannes de Witt.

there was a pulley system that allowed objects, such as the figure of Jupiter in *Cymbeline*, to be lowered to the stage from the roof above it. That roof was often called the heavens, so that the stage as a whole represented a Christian microcosm, with hell, earth, and heaven enclosed in a round—*Hamlet*'s "distracted globe" or *Henry V*'s "wooden O."

This fairly stable, symbolically rich staging setup lent itself to an emblematic

The modern Globe on London's South Bank. This 1997 reconstruction is significantly larger than the original, but it captures the general idea of what an early modern theater may have looked like.

approach to performance. Figures appearing in the balcony are not always more powerful than those on the stage itself, but their position above could be dramatically exploited that way. When Tamora appears "aloft" alongside Saturninus in *Titus Andronicus*, for example, the staging suggests her elevation from prisoner of war to empress—a shift that officially does not take place until twenty lines later. The appearance of a prisoner and a foreigner in the location symbolically associated with supreme national power, however, also instantly signals how much of a topsy-turvy world Saturninus's Rome is about to become. This kind of visual logic of power returns in many plays that deal with the subjects of governance or rule: the descent of Richard II from the balcony to the stage when he surrenders to Bolingbroke is a particularly rich example. However, the emblematic use of the stage (where "above" means "powerful") could always be layered onto other modes of representation. In *Richard II*, the balcony also stands for an actual space "above," the battlements of Flint Castle; as the stage direction has it, Richard and his allies "enter on the walls." The stage to which he descends likewise is not simply "below" but also the "base court," the castle's lower court where Bolingbroke is waiting. From the perspective of the actor working with his part, the scene and its stage directions would have carried these various representational meanings—the text informed him both of Richard's movement from sun-like power to debasement before his enemy, and of the fact that the scene is taking place in two different locations in a castle. But the directions also had additional pragmatic value, as "on the walls" told the actor that he would have to enter on the balcony.

Stage directions such as these are explicit. Far more common are "internal" stage directions: textual references to actions characters perform. Often, these are straightforward: for instance, Bolingbroke's "there I throw my gage" in *Richard II*. But they can also be quite opaque. In *Hamlet*, when Polonius says, "Take this from this if this be otherwise," the line only tells the actor to perform some kind of gesture—he needs to indicate what "this" should be taken from what other "this" if Polonius is wrong. The most common interpretation is "my head from my shoulders" (indicated with appropriate gestures), but he may also be talking about his staff of office and his hand, or

A performance at the modern Globe.

his chain of office and his neck, or something else. The line requires actions to complete it, but it does not prescribe those actions.

Explicit and implicit stage directions allowed for a very short rehearsal period: they made it possible for the actor to conceive much of his performance alone. The text may not always tell him what to do, but it will often tell him when he needs to do *something*. However, there are also many cases where Shakespeare's plays seem to presuppose a good deal of back and forth between actors. For example, when Hamlet tells his mother to "leave wringing of your hands" in 3.4, the youth playing Gertrude would have needed to know to perform that action before Hamlet tells him to stop it—but there may have been no indication of this in his part. So while the part system allowed players to prepare for much, and while the established shape and features of playhouses by the 1590s made it possible for actors to anticipate many staging decisions before ever rehearsing a play, Shakespeare's texts also contain many instances where a successful performance depends on the players going beyond their individual parts.

Even if rehearsal periods were short, it is hard to imagine that the elaborate dumbshows, masques, and battle scenes featured in some plays were not carefully prepared. But rehearsal in the modern sense did not exist, mainly because the modern idea of character work did not exist. Renaissance actors did not spend long hours developing ideas about their characters' biographies, inner lives, or hidden feelings. Acting was primarily a physical and oratorical art and, in its conventionality, quite predetermined. What made any individual performance surprising and unpredictable were the specific effects achieved by bringing together a particular text with a conventionalized physical and vocal arsenal. But rehearsal also did not have to address many of the technological challenges that only came into being in the modern theater. In an outdoor venue without artificial lighting, actors do not need to hit their "marks"; an expansive stage lit only by sunlight allows for greater freedom of movement than one illuminated by an elaborate lighting design. Lastly, staging was determined in part by the architecture of the playhouses. Certain spots on stage worked especially well for certain set pieces. Soliloquies, for instance, were at their most powerful not when delivered front and center, but instead from a position farther away from the audience, off-center, and underneath the stage roof, which provided the greatest sense of acoustic intimacy. Therefore, an actor preparing a speech could predict with some certainty where onstage he would deliver it.

Of course there is more to staging a play than speaking lines and finding positions. Nowadays, sets are of paramount importance. In Shakespeare's time, they were all but nonexistent, except for some big-impact items: the Rose Theater owned a hell-mouth, probably covering the trapdoor, for devils to enter and exit in plays such as Marlowe's *Doctor Faustus*. Tombs, caves, and cages also appear in Henslowe's inventory, as do magical trees and severed heads. One other cost factor of modern productions, however, loomed similarly large in Shakespeare's time: costumes. Dresses in particular could be more expensive to commission than new plays, and companies maintained a rich stock of costumes; in 1598, the Admiral's Men owned at least eighty complete men's outfits. Most of these were generic items, but some were character-specific: "Harry the Fifth's velvet gown," "Longshanks' suit," or "Merlin's gown and cape."

What the actors wore was the most noteworthy visual aspect of staging. On a basic level, costumes identified characters. If the actor playing Tubal in *The Merchant of Venice* also played the jailor and the Duke, his three characters would have been distinguished initially and immediately by different garments. But costumes did more than facilitate identification. Dress signified social rank. It instantly allowed audiences to place characters, without having heard them speak or knowing anything else about them. More important, dress could set the scene: a nightgown signaled where and when an action took place; a forester's outfit told the audience to imagine a woodland setting; an innkeeper's costume moved the scene to a tavern. And dress denoted historical periods—as can be seen in Henry Peacham's famous illustration of *Titus Andronicus*. In this 1590s drawing, Titus's garments—Roman armor and a toga accessorized with a laurel wreath—immediately inform the viewer that this is a classical figure, and that the play is set in ancient Rome.

Yet Peacham's picture also shows that costume functioned in multiple registers on Shakespeare's stage. Titus wears Roman dress, and the short tunics of the three figures on the right also suggest quasiclassical costumes. But Tamora, on her knees in a flowing, embroidered gown and wearing a nonclassical crown, signifies less an ancient figure (Goth or Roman) than royalty. Her garments, unlike those of the characters beside her, are designed to situate her not in history, but in a particular social sphere. The outfits of the two leftmost characters follow a different logic yet again: they are Elizabethan soldiers, with breeches, halberds, and contemporary helmets. Their costume has no historical function; its sole purpose is to identify them as having a particular occupation. Dress, then, could signify in multiple, mutually contradictory ways at the same time on Shakespeare's stage. What Peacham's image

Henry Peacham's illustration of a scene from *Titus Andronicus* (ca. 1595).

suggests visually is that *Titus Andronicus*, while set in Rome, is also concerned with general questions of monarchic power and soldierly virtue. All three of those aspects of the play could be communicated through costume. If the picture portrays a kind of theater capable of sustaining anachronistic and logical contradictions in the pursuit of its thematic goals, it is representative of the broader, and pervasive, anachronism of Shakespearean drama, in which church bells ring and books rather than scrolls are read in *Julius Caesar*'s Rome, while the title character wears that most Elizabethan of male garments, a doublet. No matter how far back in historical time these plays were set, they also always took place in the present moment.

Audience members seem to have consumed a wide range of foods at the theater. Archaeologists found oyster shells, remnants of crab, and a large quantity of nutshells and fruit seeds at the Rose Theater site.

Impressive and expensive as the actors' costumes could be, their visual impact would necessarily have been lessened by the daylight playing conditions: performers were not isolated in space and light as they can be in modern theaters, but always competed for attention with the audience itself, with the equally splendid figures in the lords' rooms and on stage stools, and with whatever distracting things spectators chose to do while the play was in progress: play cards, smoke tobacco, solicit prostitutes (or johns). Aurally, too, Shakespeare's stage was not as insulated as a modern theater. Spectators were rowdier and more audibly present than audiences now. But the sounds of the city would also have infiltrated the open-air space: church bells, the noise of bears and hounds from the nearby bearbaiting arenas, the cries of street vendors, and perhaps even the sound of performances at neighboring playhouses might all have been heard. Going to a play in early modern London was never exclusively about the action and words onstage; it was always also about the theater itself, its temporary inhabitants, and the places where the theaters stood. Visually and aurally, the stage was in competition with the world, but it also found ways of integrating that world into its fictions.

Although the early modern theatrical experience was shaped by a host of immediate sensory perceptions, it equally depended on the audience's ability to refashion those impressions in their minds—even as plays insisted on drawing attention to the material reality of the stage. The Prologue to *Henry V* illustrates this condition perfectly. On the one hand, it mocks the apparent inadequacy of the theater, an "unworthy scaffold," a "cockpit" laughably ill suited to representing the "vasty fields of France"; it mercilessly reminds the audience where they are. At the same time, the Prologue also encourages the listeners to ignore all these carefully catalogued shortcomings and allow the play to work "on your imaginary forces," pleading with them to "piece out our imperfections with your thoughts." The Prologue seems to indulge in a risky game: it explains in detail why the theater should fail even as it dares the audience to make it work. But this risk lay at the heart of Shakespeare's theatrical art. We can detect it in the use of boy actors as much as in contradictory costuming choices and willful anachronisms. It found its most daring expression in the frequent use of narrative, seemingly the least theatrical form of writing. Antonio's tearful farewell to Bassanio in *The Merchant of Venice*; the deaths of the Dukes of Suffolk and York in *Henry V*; the reunion of Perdita and Leontes in *The Winter's Tale*; most remarkably, the death of as charismatic a character as Falstaff, in *Henry V*: again and again, Shakespeare chose to have events such as these reported by other characters rather than staging them before his spectators' eyes. In these scenes, the words and their demands on the audience's imagination do not just compete with what is visible, as they always did in the early modern playhouse. These narrations do more than that: they celebrate and rely on the power of words to take audiences out of the theater altogether, to transport them, without any visual aid whatsoever, to places and encounters that even the characters in the play itself only imagine.

And yet, despite placing such trust in language's capacity to transform reality, both the scenes and their author depended on their actors' ability to make audiences believe those words. If language's appeal to the imagination was meant to pull theatergoers out of their immediate sensory experience and into an engagement with a world of fiction, that goal could be achieved only by virtue of the very bodies, costumes, and props whose specific presence audiences were encouraged to transform into representations of an alternative reality. If a play worked, it enabled its viewers almost to forget the theaters whose splendor impressed so many visitors; allowed them to imagine for a moment that the words they heard did not come from a scroll of paper, that they had not been preapproved and licensed by a government official, purchased by a profit-hungry company, and written by a commercial playwright. Ultimately, then, in spite of the theater's undeniably powerful architectural, social, cultural, and visual presence in the lives of Shakespeare's contemporaries, its success in creating alternative, fictional worlds depended on an audience capable of understanding that all this splendor was not an end in itself. That is the marvelous paradox of Shakespeare's theater: it invested a great deal of goods, money, and physical labor in an effort to persuade people not to ignore those material realities altogether, but to use them as a means of accessing greater, still more wondrous, and wholly imaginary worlds beyond.

LATER
PLAYS AND POEMS

Hamlet

"Who's there?" Shakespeare's most famous play begins. The question, turned back on the tragedy itself, has haunted actors, audiences, and readers for centuries. *Hamlet* is an enigma. Mountains of feverish speculation have only deepened the interlocking mysteries: Why does Hamlet delay avenging the murder of his father by Claudius, his father's brother? How much guilt does Hamlet's mother, Gertrude, who has since married Claudius, bear in this crime? How trustworthy is the Ghost of Hamlet's father, who has returned from the grave to demand that Hamlet avenge his murder? Is vengeance morally justifiable in this play, or is it to be condemned? What exactly *is* the Ghost, and where has it come from? Why is the Ghost, visible to everyone in the first act, visible only to Hamlet in act 3? Is Hamlet's madness feigned or true, a strategy masquerading as a reality or a reality masquerading as a strategy? Does Hamlet, who once loved Ophelia, continue to love her in spite of his apparent cruelty? Does Ophelia, crushed by that cruelty and driven mad by Hamlet's murder of her father, Polonius, actually intend to drown herself, or does she die accidentally? What enables Hamlet to pass from thoughts of suicide to faith in God's providence, from "To be or not to be" to "Let be"? What is Hamlet trying to say before death stops his speech at the close?

It is tempting to think that when *Hamlet* was first performed at the Globe around 1600, the audiences possessed answers to many of these questions and that our perplexities result principally from the passage of time. Yet the play seems designed to provoke bafflement. "What art thou?" Horatio asks the Ghost, and the question, unanswered, is echoed again and again until it seems to touch on everything: "Is it not like the King?" (1.1.57);* "Why seems it so particular with thee?" (1.2.75); "What does this mean, my lord?" (1.4.7); "Whither wilt thou lead me?" (1.5.1); "What's Hecuba to him or he to her / That he should weep for her?" (2.2.478–79); "Why wouldst thou be a breeder of sinners?" (3.1.119–20); "What should such fellows as I do crawling between earth and heaven?" (3.1.125–26); "Do you see nothing there?" (3.4.131); "What is it you would see?" (5.2.340). The dream of getting answers to such questions tantalizes many of the play's characters and drives them to scrutinize one another. But the task is maddeningly difficult. When Hamlet repeatedly asks Guildenstern, one of the school friends whom his uncle has set to spy on him, to play the recorder, Guildenstern protests that he does not know how. "[Y]ou would play upon me," Hamlet returns, "you would seem to know my stops, you would pluck out the heart of my mystery. . . . [D]o you think I am easier to be played on than a pipe?" (3.2.339–44).

Hamlet at once invites and resists interrogation. He is, more than any theatrical character before and perhaps since, a figure constructed around an unseen or secret core. Such a figure in the theater is something of a paradox, since all that exists of any character onstage is what is seen and heard there. But from his place onstage at the center of a courtly world in which he is "the observed of all observers" and hence a person allowed virtually no privacy, Hamlet insists that he has "that within which passes show" (1.2.85). What is it that he has "within"? In the nineteenth century, following a suggestion by the German poet Johann Wolfgang von Goethe, critics frequently argued that Hamlet has within him the soul of a poet, too sensitive, delicate,

*All quotations are taken from the edited text of the Second Quarto with additions from the Folio (the "combined text"). The print edition also includes the edited First Quarto text. The Digital Edition includes both these texts plus the edited Second Quarto and Folio texts.

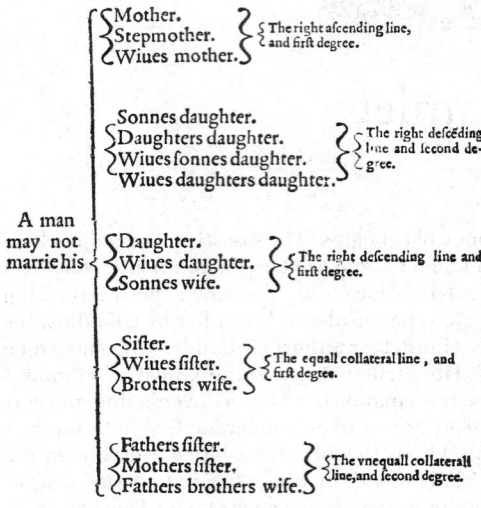

Mother. Stepmother. Wiues mother.	}	The right afcending line, and firft degree.
Sonnes daughter. Daughters daughter. Wiues fonnes daughter. Wiues daughters daughter.	}	The right defcending line and fecond degree.

A man may not marrie his

Daughter. Wiues daughter. Sonnes wife.	}	The right defcending line and firft degree.
Sifter. Wiues fifter. Brothers wife.	}	The equall collateral line, and firft degree.
Fathers fifter. Mothers fifter. Fathers brothers wife.	}	The vnequall collaterall line, and fecond degree.

30 Therfore fhall ye keepe mine ordinances, that ye doe not any of the abhominable cuftomes, which haue been done before you.

Table of prohibited marriages. From William Clerke, *The Trial of Bastardy* (London, 1594).

and complex to endure the cruel pressures of a coarse world. In the twentieth century, following a suggestion by the founder of psychoanalysis, Sigmund Freud, many critics have speculated that Hamlet has within him an unresolved Oedipus complex, a sexual desire for his mother that prevents him from taking decisive action against the man who has done in reality the thing that Hamlet unconsciously desires to do: kill his father and marry his mother. On occasion, this psychological speculation has been challenged by a political one: Hamlet hides within himself a spirit of political resistance, a subversive challenge to a corrupt, illegitimate regime shored up by lies, spies, and treachery.

These recurrent attempts to pluck out the heart of Hamlet's mystery are a modern continuation of an interpretive activity that goes on throughout the play itself. Attempting to solve the riddle of Hamlet's strange behavior, Polonius speculates that the Prince is desperately lovesick for his daughter, but Claudius concludes, after spying on Hamlet's conversation with Ophelia, that his "affections do not that way tend" (3.1.159). Rosencrantz and Guildenstern propose that Hamlet is suffering from ambition—after all, though Denmark is an elective monarchy, the Prince could have hoped to succeed his father on the throne—but Hamlet vehemently refutes the charge: "O God, I could be bounded in a nutshell and count myself a king of infinite space, were it not that I have bad dreams" (2.2.231.15–17). Claudius doubts that Hamlet is mad and, though he never directly articulates this suspicion, seems to fear that the Prince somehow knows of his secret crime, but Hamlet's painful interiority, his melancholy insistence that he has something "within," is already clear from his first appearance, before the Ghost's revelation. Gertrude therefore seems wiser to argue that her son's distemper at least originates in "[h]is father's death and our hasty marriage" (2.2.57).

As we first encounter him, Hamlet is a young man in deep mourning, which his mother and uncle both urge him to cease. The death of fathers is natural and inevitable, they point out, and while it is customary to grieve, it is unreasonable to persist obstinately in sorrow. Hamlet responds that his grief is not a theatrical performance, a mere costume to be put on and then discarded. When he is alone onstage a few moments later, he discloses, in the first of his famous soliloquies, a near-suicidal despair and a corrosive bitterness centered on the haste with which his mother has remarried. This bitterness is intensified by Hamlet's idealized image of his father and by painful memories of what had seemed to him his parents' perfect mutual love. Like any adolescent whose family has undergone unexpected and traumatic changes, Hamlet finds himself caught up in the painful process of reassessing his image of his parents and of himself, a process that spills over into his relationship with a new, unwelcome stepparent and with his peers. As he broods on the brief time between his father's death and his mother's remarriage, Hamlet's mind convulsively shortens the interval: "two months," "nay, not so much, not two," "within a month."

At such moments—and there are many in this play—the audience seems to have direct access to the protagonist's tormented inner life. That life appears startlingly raw and unscripted, but the impression is actually the consequence of Shakespeare's sophisticated poetic skills. Hamlet's soliloquies are carefully crafted rhetorical performances. Thus, for example, the celebrated lines that begin "To be or not to be: that is the question" (3.1.55ff) have the structure of a formal academic debate on the subject of suicide: prudently considering both sides of the question and rehearsing venerable commonplaces, Hamlet does not once use the words "I" or "me." Yet here and elsewhere his words manage with astonishing vividness to convey the spontaneous rhythms of a mind in motion. Shakespeare had anticipated this achievement in such plays as *Richard II, 1 Henry IV,* and *Julius Caesar*: King Richard, Prince Hal, and Brutus all have intimate moments in which they seem to disclose the troubled faces that are normally hidden behind expressionless social masks. But in its moral complexity, psychological depth, and philosophical power, *Hamlet* seems to mark an epochal shift not only in Shakespeare's own career but in Western drama; it is as if the play were giving birth to a whole new kind of literary subjectivity.

This subjectivity—the sense of being inside a character's psyche and following its twists and turns—is to a large degree an effect of language, the product of dramatic poetry and prose of unprecedented intensity. In order to convey a traumatized mind struggling to articulate perceptions of a shattered world, Shakespeare developed a complex syntax and a remarkably expanded diction. Take the moment, for example, in which Hamlet broods on the spectacle of Fortinbras's army marching off to fight to the death for a worthless piece of ground. Hamlet is struck by the absurd waste of lives and wealth, but then his agonized consciousness of his failure to act more quickly to avenge his father's death begins to transform his thinking:

> Rightly to be great
> Is not to stir without great argument
> But greatly to find quarrel in a straw
> When honor's at the stake.
> (4.1.52–55)

The strain in the syntax reflects the strain of a mind queasily in motion. For the sentence to be made fully coherent, we would need to add a missing "not" or otherwise change the wording, but the point is not coherence. Such strange twists in meaning, along with a host of words used in new or unfamiliar ways, give us intimate access to the vortex of moral principle and psychological compulsion that constitutes Hamlet's inner life. The innovative inwardness is not restricted to scenes in which Hamlet is alone onstage, nor is it restricted to the Prince himself; indeed, many of the deepest psychic revelations in the play are conveyed not in moments of isolation but in disturbing exchanges, intimate encounters in which love and poison are intertwined.

These innovations are not called for by the story itself. In *Hamlet,* as in so many of his plays, Shakespeare was recycling narratives long in circulation. The legendary tale of Hamlet (Amleth) had already been recounted at length in the late twelfth-century *Danish History* compiled in Latin by Saxo the Grammarian. (The tale was retold in French in François de Belleforest's 1570 collection *Histoires Tragiques.*) In Saxo's version the unscrupulous Feng ambushes and kills his brother Horwendil and marries Horwendil's wife, Gerutha. Horwendil and Gerutha had a son, Amleth, who undertakes to avenge his father. In doing so, the son suffers no pangs of conscience, since in pre-Christian Denmark revenge was not a violation of the moral or religious law but a filial obligation. And he needs no ghost to inform him of what happened and experiences no sickening uncertainty about his uncle's guilt, since the murder is public knowledge. Amleth's problem is survival: young and surrounded by Feng's henchmen, he finds his every move carefully watched. In order to avert suspicion and buy time, the cunning avenger pretends to be feebleminded. His strategy works: with the active assistance of his mother, Amleth eventually succeeds in killing his uncle, along with the uncle's followers, and is enthusiastically proclaimed King of Denmark. Amleth suffers no doubt about his uncle's guilt and no pangs of conscience over killing him.

This is the rough outline of the story Shakespeare inherited, along, it seems, with at least one other version about which we know tantalizingly little: by 1589, English audiences had evidently seen a play, now lost, on the theme of Hamlet. Apparently, this play—which scholars call the Ur (original)-*Hamlet*—featured a ghost who cried, "Hamlet, revenge!" On the basis of the barest shreds of contemporary evidence, scholars have constructed elaborate theories about this supposed source play, but there is little agreement among them. Assuming that there was an Elizabethan staging of the story that preceded Shakespeare's, its author remains unknown.

Shakespeare probably wrote *Hamlet* in 1600 (shortly after *Julius Caesar*, to which Polonius seems to allude at 3.2.94–95), but the precise date of composition is uncertain, and this uncertainty is compounded by the complex state of the text: Shakespeare's most famous tragedy is a monument of world literature, but it is a monument built on shifting sands. The two fullest early texts of the play are found in a quarto dated 1604–05 (the Second Quarto, Q2) and in the First Folio of 1623 (F). However, these texts differ in important ways, each including passages not found in the other. The edition of the play printed in *The Norton Shakespeare* is based on the Second Quarto text; lines that appear only in the Folio are also included but are made visually distinct, so that readers will be able to assess the major variations between the two. Those who want to read these early texts in their original forms can find fully edited versions of both the Second Quarto and the Folio texts in the Digital Edition of *The Norton Shakespeare*, which also offers side-by-side comparisons of selected scenes.

To further complicate the textual situation, there is yet a third version of *Hamlet*. This earliest known text appeared in 1603 and is therefore called the First Quarto (Q1). Much shorter and less reliable than either the Second Quarto or the Folio texts, it was long known as the "bad quarto" of *Hamlet*. (The Prince's celebrated soliloquy, for example, begins "To be, or not to be—ay, there's the point.") The First Quarto is nevertheless a fascinating document, theatrically effective in its own right, with valuable clues about what a severely cut and reshaped *Hamlet* might have looked like on the Elizabethan stage. For these reasons, a fully edited version of this earliest text is presented in *The Norton Shakespeare*—both print and digital—for the first time.

These early published texts, along with numerous early references to the play, suggest that *Hamlet* was a success from the beginning. The play may well have seemed radically innovative to its first audiences—after four hundred years it still seems startlingly fresh—but it also spoke to contemporary theatrical interests. One of the most successful and enduring Elizabethan plays was *The Spanish Tragedy* (ca. 1587), written by Thomas Kyd, who is a prime candidate for authorship of the lost Ur-*Hamlet*. *The Spanish Tragedy* itself has features that strikingly anticipate Shakespeare's tragedy, including a ghost impatient for revenge, a secret crime, a hero tormented by uncertainty and self-reproach, the strategic feigning of a madness that seems disturbingly close to real, a woman who goes mad from grief and commits suicide, a play-within-the-play, and a final slaughter that wipes out much of the royal family and court, along with the avenger himself. Kyd's play is entirely structured around the problem of revenge—"wild justice," in Francis Bacon's haunting phrase—and gave rise to a whole genre of revenge plays in which *Hamlet* participates.

These plays generally share certain conventional assumptions. First, revenge is an individual response to an intolerable wrong or a public insult. It is an unauthorized, violent action in a world whose institutions seem unable or unwilling to satisfy a craving for justice. Second, since institutional channels are closed and since the criminal is usually either hidden or well protected, revenge almost always follows a devious path toward its violent end. Third, the revenger is in the grip of an inner compulsion: his course of action may be motivated by institutional failure—for example, the mechanisms of justice are in the hands of the criminals themselves—but even if these mechanisms were operating perfectly, they would not allow the psychic satisfactions of revenge. Fourth, revengers generally need their victims to know what is happening and why: satisfaction depends on a moment of declaration and vindication. And fifth, revenge is a universal imperative more powerful than the pious injunctions of any particular belief system, including Christianity itself.

Shakespeare had already produced a sensationally violent version of these conventions in *Titus Andronicus.* In *Hamlet,* he at once reproduces them and calls them into question. The audience knows for certain—from Claudius's tortured attempt to pray in act 3—that there has been a "foul murder," a fratricide successfully covered over by the story that a serpent stung the sleeping King. But Hamlet does not overhear Claudius's confession and has only the questionable testimony of the Ghost. That testimony is open to question because the nature of the Ghost is open to question. The Ghost speaks as if he were condemned to a term of suffering in the realm Catholics called purgatory:

> Doomed for a certain term to walk the night
> And for the day confined to fast in fires
> Till the foul crimes done in my days of nature
> Are burnt and purged away.
>
> (1.5.10–13)

But Protestant theologians vehemently denied that purgatory existed and argued that spirits thought to be ghosts were in fact devils sent to lure humans into sinful actions. Hamlet responds at first as if he believes the Ghost to be the authentic spirit of his father returned from the dead. But he subsequently expresses serious doubts— "The spirit that I have seen / May be a dev'l" (2.2.517–18)—and in the play's most famous soliloquy he speaks of death as "[t]he undiscovered country from whose bourn / No traveler returns" (3.1.78–79).

The theatrical test Hamlet devises to authenticate the Ghost's accusation— carefully watching the reaction of his uncle to *The Mousetrap*—appears to resolve any doubts: "I'll take the Ghost's word," Hamlet exults, after the King has stormed out in a rage, "for a thousand pound" (3.2.265–66). Yet even here Shakespeare introduces an occasion for uncertainty: after all, the murderer in the play-within-the play is "one Lucianus, nephew to the King" (3.2.226). Claudius's anger could have arisen from the spectacle of the player-nephew killing his player-uncle and not from the spectacle of his own hidden crime. The effect on the audience is not so much to cast doubt on the Ghost's word as to uncouple Hamlet's inner life once again from the external world, even at the moment that he himself thinks they are at last securely linked.

This uncoupling, this sense of inward thoughts and feelings painfully cut off from the world around him, haunts virtually all of Hamlet's relationships. When he speaks with his old school friends Rosencrantz and Guildenstern, with the courtier Osric or with Polonius, he is deliberately evasive, but his exchanges with Ophelia are equally oblique and baffling. Even with his intimate friend Horatio, there is some gap across which Hamlet struggles to speak: "There are more things in heaven and earth, Horatio," Hamlet says after his first encounter with the Ghost, "[t]han are dreamt of in your philosophy" (1.5.168–69). When Hamlet directly confronts his mother with the charge of murder, she reacts with astonishment. The painful words that follow, Hamlet's weird, tormented admonition to his mother to shun her husband's bed, do indeed seem to strike home: "These words like daggers," Gertrude exclaims, "enter in mine ears" (3.4.95). But the Ghost's sudden reappearance, visible this time only to Hamlet (and, of course, to the audience), convinces his mother that her son is mad. "Do you see nothing there?" asks Hamlet, to which his mother, certain that her son is hallucinating, replies steadfastly, "Nothing at all, yet all that is I see" (3.4.131–32).

Ironically, the distance between what Hamlet sees and what those around him see is smallest in the case of Claudius, since both share a knowledge of the secret crime that has poisoned the kingdom, and each maneuvers against the other throughout the play. But their fatal opposition never rises to full, open view until the final

The man in prayer. By Mair von Landshut (1499).

violent seconds, nor does Hamlet ever establish unequivocal, unambiguous public confirmation of his uncle's guilt. It would have been easy for Shakespeare to provide such confirmation, for example in a last speech by the mortally wounded usurper, but he chooses instead to leave what Horatio calls "th' yet unknowing world" (5.2.357) in the dark. Until the explosion of treason and murder, the horrified bystanders know only a court in which the loving Claudius appeals to Hamlet as his "son" and wagers on his skill in fencing. Hamlet begins an explanation—"oh, I could tell you" (5.2.315)—but he is cut short by death. The effect is to extend Hamlet's tragic isolation, his gnawing inward pain, all the way to his final silence.

What would it take to get rid of this pain? The possibility of cleansing, definitive action at once continually tantalizes and eludes the Prince. Such action is embodied in the soldier Fortinbras, but if Hamlet finds some way of easing his mental anguish, it is not through any comparable martial exploit, nor is it through the secret plotting undertaken by Laertes. The fact that both Fortinbras and Laertes are also attempting to avenge the deaths of fathers only intensifies the contrast with Hamlet's spiritual journey. The calm to which he gives voice near the play's close—"There is special providence in the fall of a sparrow. If it be, 'tis not to come; if it be not to come, it will be now; if it be not now, yet it will come; the readiness is all" (5.2.191–94)—descends upon him *before,* not as a result of, his revenge. The act of revenge itself happens in a flash of rage, without planning, without any self-vindicating declaration by Hamlet to Claudius, and without any public confession of guilt by the usurper. Revenge leaves the Prince not with inner satisfaction but with intense anxiety over his "wounded name."

Swordsmen. From *Vincentio Saviolo his Practise* (London, 1595).

Standing on a stage littered with corpses, Horatio promises to fulfill Hamlet's dying request to tell his story, but his account of "carnal, bloody, and unnatural acts," though it may be accurate, must be inadequate to the play we have just witnessed. For *Hamlet* situates the need for revenge in a context that goes beyond any crime, however heinous, and that seems resistant to violent solutions. Before the Ghost disclosed his uncle's villainy, Hamlet was suffering from the traumas of mortality: the searing pain of his father's death, a troubled recognition of his mother's sexuality, a sickening awareness of the vulnerability and corruptibility of the flesh. There was a time, the play implies, when Hamlet embodied all the hopes and aspirations of his age and his own vision of human possibility was unbounded—"What piece of work is a man"— but that vision has given way to bitter disillusionment: "and yet to me what is this quintessence of dust?" (2.2.264–65, 268–69).

Renaissance psychologists had a word for Hamlet's condition: melancholy, a state of spiritual desolation akin to madness but also to literary and artistic genius. In Hamlet's melancholy consciousness, human existence has been reduced to dust at its dustiest. Though Claudius's secret crime is a political act that has poisoned the public sphere, the roots of Hamlet's despair seem to lie in a more intractably inward place, a place perhaps less consonant with revenge than with suicide. If there were only the evil usurper to depose, Hamlet might compass a straightforward course of action, but his soul-sickness has receding layers: beyond political corruption, there is the time-serving shallowness of his friends Rosencrantz and Guildenstern, and beyond this there is Ophelia's dismayingly compliant obedience to her father, and beyond this there is his mother's disturbing carnality, and beyond this there is the ongoing, endlessly transformative, morally indifferent cycle of life itself. For Hamlet, the quintessence of dust is not only the cold, inert matter produced by the nauseating triumph of death—the flesh of Alexander the Great metamorphosed into a plug of dirt stopping up a beer barrel—but also living matter pullulating with tenacious, meaningless vitality, produced by the equally nauseating triumph of life. "We fat all creatures else to fat us," Hamlet tells Claudius, "and we fat ourselves for maggots" (3.6.21–22).

In a world pervaded by decay, the process of natural renewal has come to seem grotesque and disgusting:

> 'tis an unweeded garden
> That grows to seed; things rank and gross in nature
> Possess it merely.
>
> (1.2.135–37)

These lines immediately give way to bitter reflections on his mother's sexual appetite: in Hamlet's diseased consciousness, the spectacle of nature run riot, of uncontrolled breeding and feeding, centers on the body of woman. His bitterness at his mother's remarriage spreads like a stain to touch all women, including the woman he had once ardently courted. "Get thee to a nunnery!" Hamlet urges Ophelia, as if the only virtuous course of action were renunciation of the flesh. "Why wouldst thou be a breeder of sinners?" (3.1.119–20). Even this desperate advice seems to be undermined by Hamlet's obsessive sense of rampant female sexuality and of his own corruption, since in Elizabethan slang "nunnery" could also be a term for "brothel."

Even before her father's murder causes her complete mental collapse, the fragile Ophelia begins to crack under the strain of Hamlet's misogynistic revulsion. Set up as a decoy to enable her father and the King to spy on Hamlet, she is treated humiliatingly by the Prince who had once passionately wooed her and now showers her with a blend of disgust and self-loathing. Gertrude, who also takes the full brunt of this misogyny, does not lose her wits, but when confronted alone by her son, she fears for her life. Both women sense the violence and despair seething in Hamlet beneath what he calls his "antic disposition" (1.5.173). That disposition, manifested in his disordered dress and in the "wild and whirling words" (1.5.135) that he begins to speak after encountering the Ghost, casts Hamlet in the strange role of jester in the court in which he is the mourning son and the heir apparent. Of all Shakespeare's tragic heroes, he is at once the saddest and the funniest. His blend of sarcasm, riddling, and sly wordplay initially strikes those around him as folly, but this first impression continually gives way to an uneasy awareness of hidden meanings: Claudius, alert to danger, notes that "[t]here's something in his soul / O'er which his melancholy sits on brood" (3.1.161–62). The "something" Claudius senses is in part the murderous design of the revenger, but it is also the philosophical meditation on life and death that haunts Hamlet throughout the play. This meditation reaches a climax in the graveyard, where Hamlet, trading zany quibbles with one of the gravediggers, directly confronts the corruption and decay that had obsessed him ever since his father's death. If there is any release for Hamlet from this obsession—and it is not clear that there is—it comes from an unflinching gaze at a skull, the skull of the jester Yorick, but also, by extension, his father's skull and his own.

STEPHEN GREENBLATT

SELECTED BIBLIOGRAPHY

Adelman, Janet. "Man and His Wife Is One Flesh: *Hamlet* and the Confrontation with the Maternal Body." *Suffocating Mothers: Fantasies of Maternal Origin in Shakespeare's Plays, "Hamlet" to "The Tempest."* New York: Routledge, 1992. 11–37. Argues that for Shakespeare, fully realized female sexuality (in the form of Gertrude) gives birth not only to fallen and contaminated man, but also to tragedy itself.

Bradley, A. C. *Shakespearean Tragedy: Lectures on "Hamlet," "Othello," "King Lear," "Macbeth."* 1904. 3rd ed. Basingstoke: Macmillan, 1992. Discusses how Hamlet's character—at the center of the tragedy that bears his name—is dominated by a morbid melancholy that weakens his ability to love and impedes his ability to act.

Cavell, Stanley. "Hamlet's Burden of Proof." *Disowning Knowledge in Seven Plays of Shakespeare*. Cambridge: Cambridge UP, 2003. 179–91. Explores how the play-within-the-play, interpreted with Freud's concept of the "primal scene," can be seen as a dreamlike expression of Hamlet's refusal to confront the burden of his own existence.

de Grazia, Margreta. *"Hamlet" without Hamlet*. Cambridge: Cambridge UP, 2007. Argues that the elusiveness of Hamlet's inner life is a largely modern critical invention, obscuring the dispossession that Renaissance audiences would have seen as the tragedy's central crisis.

Eliot, T. S. "Hamlet and His Problems." *The Sacred Wood: Essays on Poetry and Criticism*. London: Methuen, 1920. 87–94. Asserts that *Hamlet* proves deficient as a work of art: Hamlet's disproportionate confusion about his condition reflects Shakespeare's own confusion concerning the proper assembly of his diverse literary materials.

Garber, Marjorie. "*Hamlet*: Giving Up the Ghost." *Shakespeare's Ghost Writers: Literature as Uncanny Causality*. New York: Methuen, 1987. 124–76. Discusses how, simultaneously constituting and dissolving the self, the Ghost haunts the unstable relationship between action and memory, and argues that Shakespeare himself has a similarly haunting purchase on the modern imagination.

Greenblatt, Stephen. *Hamlet in Purgatory*. Princeton, NJ: Princeton UP, 2001. Examines how *Hamlet* exploits and transforms into theatrical ritual the fears and desires generated by the Catholic cult of purgatory, a cult banned by Tudor Protestantism.

Maguire, Laurie. "'Actions that a man might play': Mourning, Memory, Editing." *Performance Research* 7 (2002): 66–76. Argues that editors of Shakespeare searching for one "true" text of the play should take a hint from Hamlet himself: single viewpoints (whether ontological or editorial) ultimately bow to the daunting yet rich reality of multiplicity.

McGee, Arthur. *The Elizabethan Hamlet*. New Haven, CT: Yale UP, 1987. Sees Hamlet emerging as a sophisticated manifestation of Vice from the medieval morality-play tradition.

Showalter, Elaine. "Representing Ophelia: Women, Madness, and the Responsibilities of Feminist Criticism." *Shakespeare and the Question of Theory*. Ed. Patricia Parker and Geoffrey Hartman. New York: Methuen, 1985. 77–94. Surveys shifting cultural attitudes toward the representation of Ophelia and notes how they serve as a barometer of ideological conflict and contribute to the evolving discourse of feminist criticism.

Wilson, J. Dover. *What Happens in "Hamlet."* 3rd ed. Cambridge: Cambridge UP, 1951. Argues that in grappling with the play's dramatic difficulties, especially the problematic *Mousetrap* scene, we more nearly approach "the secret of Hamlet's character."

See also the creative uses of *Hamlet* in Johann Wolfgang von Goethe's *Wilhelm Meister's Apprenticeship* (1796), James Joyce's *Ulysses* (1922), Tom Stoppard's *Rosencrantz and Guildenstern Are Dead* (1967), Heiner Müller's *Hamletmachine* (1978), and John Updike's *Gertrude and Claudius* (2000).

FILMS

Hamlet. 1948. Dir. Laurence Olivier. UK. 155 min. Olivier's Hamlet is an oedipal prince, tormented by a desire to kill his father and sleep with his mother (played in the film by an actress only two years older than Olivier).

Gamlet. 1963. Dir. Grigori Kozintsev. USSR. 148 min. A powerful, black-and-white Cold War *Hamlet*, in Russian, set in a prisonlike Elsinore.

Hamlet. 1990. Dir. Franco Zeffirelli. UK. 135 min. Naturalistic medieval scenes, with Glenn Close's strong Gertrude in an oedipally charged relationship with Mel Gibson's Hamlet.

Hamlet. 1996. Dir. Kenneth Branagh. UK. 242 min. (cut version 150 min.). Opulent full-text epic rendered in the mirrored halls of a palatial nineteenth-century Austrian court.

Hamlet. 2000. Dir. Michael Almereyda. USA. 112 min. Inspired by director Akira Kurosawa, Almereyda updates the play to modern New York and draws on communications technologies such as video cameras and computers.

TEXTUAL INTRODUCTION

The textual situation of *Hamlet* is unusually intricate. The play survives in three distinct early versions: the First Quarto (Q1, 1603), the Second Quarto (Q2, 1604–05), and the Folio (F, 1623). The dates of publication are, however, misleading if we are trying to understand the provenance of the various texts; the different versions were not composed in the order in which they were printed. Most scholars now agree that the Q2 version predates that in F, which in turn preceded Q1. But we can't be sure. (Three other quartos, based closely on the second and hence without independent authority, were printed in 1611, ca. 1621, and 1637; Restoration quartos, emended and marked with cuts, also had no textual authority.)

There are many substantive differences between these early texts, and while there is general agreement among scholars about the outlines of the relations between them, there are many areas of disagreement, making it difficult to say anything definitive about the various tangles. Here is what most, though certainly not all, scholars believe: Somewhere around 1600–1601, Shakespeare wrote a play about Hamlet; a few years later, his manuscript, or a copy of it, served as the basis for Q2. In the period between the initial composing of the play and its printing in 1604–05, the text underwent a number of important transformations. It was streamlined somewhat, undergoing several cuts, probably with performance in mind, and at the same time many verbal substitutions and other minor revisions were made. It is likely, though by no means definite, that Shakespeare himself, perhaps in consultation with his theatrical colleagues, was responsible for most of these changes. A copy of this somewhat shorter and in many small ways different text may have served as the "playbook" used in performance, or at least a playbook was derived from it, perhaps having been further reduced. Much later, in 1623, this initial playbook manuscript, no doubt changed in various ways over the intervening years, became the basis for the text printed in F.

Meanwhile, back in 1601 or 1602, a radically cut and restructured version, based on the playhouse text that became F rather than on the authorial manuscript that became Q2, was put together, possibly for touring performance, by either Shakespeare's company or some smaller troupe of provincial players. In 1603 this much shorter text was made available by one or two of the players to the London publishers Nicholas Ling and John Trundle, and was printed as Q1. This text seems to have been reconstructed at least partially from memory by an actor working with a scribe; the man responsible appears to have doubled as Marcellus and Lucianus, and possibly played Voltemand as well, since those roles closely match the roles as they appear in Q2/F. A year later, Ling hired a different printer to produce a text (Q2) that he described on the title page as "enlarged to almost as much againe as it was, according to the true and perfect Coppie." This implies that Ling knew his initial offering (Q1) was defective and that he somehow had got hold of a much more complete and authoritative manuscript.

First Quarto

There are no act or scene divisions in Q1. Editors have usually divided the play into separate scenes, numbered consecutively, and this edition has adopted that policy.

The division is based on the usual Elizabethan practice of beginning a new scene after the stage is completely cleared and a new character or set of characters enters. The text is very short—not much more than half the length of Q2. The title page declares that it was acted by "his Highnesse seruants" (i.e., Shakespeare's company) in London, Oxford, Cambridge, "and else-where." How true this is we don't know, but many scholars believe that the text was at some point prepared for a London-based company, likely for a provincial tour, and later reconstructed for presentation to a publisher. A noteworthy feature of Q1 is that it frequently accords with F where the latter differs from Q2 (though, to complicate matters, it sometimes agrees with Q2 against F). This affinity between the two texts suggests that the Q1 manuscript was probably based on the manuscript that after further transcription became the basis for F, while Q2 derives from a different stem. F shows a closer relationship to the theater than does Q2, so perhaps some of the players, having acted in a version similar to F, used that as the basis for a shorter text they could take on tour.

However we explain its puzzling origins, we can appreciate that Q1 is a revenge drama, which, missing much of the speculation and philosophizing usually associated with *Hamlet,* has been shown to work remarkably well onstage. Though parts of it read like a garbled version of the play that we are used to (see, e.g., Q1 Textual Comment 4), other parts are coherent and effective (and some bits, notably in the first few scenes, are almost exactly the same as their counterparts in F). Whoever devised it knew something about theatrical value. For example, the complicated interweaving of themes and plots in 2.2 in Q2/F (the longest scene in the play) is simplified by separating the Ophelia plot from the business with the players. Thus the "To be or not to be" speech and the "nunnery scene" come earlier in Q1, before the arrival of the players; in this more "rational" scenario, Hamlet's enthusiastic decision to make the play the thing that will catch the conscience of the King *follows* rather than precedes the anomie of the "To be" soliloquy. (Because the order of events and interweaving of plots in Q1 differs so much from that in the other texts, *The Norton Shakespeare* does not give cross-references from scenes between Q1 and F or Q2.) A second example is the appearance of an entirely new scene (14) that firmly establishes the Queen's alliance with her son (clearing up an ambiguity in the longer versions and making her a more sympathetic character), and skillfully compresses information from several different scenes in the longer texts (see Q1 Textual Comments 6 and 8). Such adaptations allow the play to move more quickly and make it more immediately accessible to an audience.

Second Quarto and Folio

Except for some sections of act 1 where the compositor probably had recourse to a copy of Q1, Q2, scholars agree, was printed from Shakespeare's "foul papers" (a draft in his hand), or perhaps a copy of them. There are many signs that the underlying manuscript was difficult to read; there are numerous instances of what seem to be characteristically Shakespearean spellings; and, tellingly, there is an example of a "false start," an authorial second thought or revision of a passage where apparently unrevised text is printed beside revised:

> For women fear too much even as they love,
> And women's fear and love hold quantity:
> Either none, in neither aught or in extremity.
> (3.2.150–52)

The second line immediately revises the first (which is left without a corresponding rhyme line), and "in neither aught" revises "Either none"; but the compositor failed to note any deletion marks there may have been. F omits both "false starts." These features of Q2 suggest that it is based on Shakespeare's foul papers.

There is more debate about the provenance of F, though most scholars allow that it derives from a separate manuscript from that behind Q2 and, further, that that manuscript had some connection to performance. Most likely, a fair copy was made of the foul papers and that copy was then subjected to theatrical modification. F's stage directions are normally fuller and more precise than Q2's; its apparent cuts from Q2 seem aimed at speeding up the action; and many of its verbal substitutions help clarify obscurity. There has been debate about whether the many changes indicate theatrical "corruption" (for example, the phrase "Oh, vengeance!" in Hamlet's second soliloquy may well be an actorly interpolation) or whether they represent attempts at improvement in which Shakespeare may have taken an active part. No doubt both factors played a part.

Q2 contains some 220 lines that have no counterpart in F and which seem mostly to have been cut for performance. In act 1, Horatio's scholarly disquisition on portents and omens (Q2 1.111–24) and Hamlet's analysis of how a single blemish can poison the whole organism (Q2 4.17–38) are excised, doubtless because they distract from the growing excitement around the Ghost's appearances. Hamlet's extended attack on his mother in the "closet scene" is reduced by a total of 27 lines; almost the whole of 4.1 disappears, including Hamlet's final soliloquy (see F Textual Comment 7); 27 lines go from 4.3; and two passages (around 40 lines) from 5.2 disappear in the course of revision (see F Textual Comment 10). Conversely, Q2 lacks about 70 lines found in F, mostly in three extended passages. One of these is likely a deliberate addition, while the other two are more uncertain (see combined text Textual Comments 10 and 4).

There are puzzles and ambiguities associated with all these texts, and for that reason this Norton edition provides the reader with four different edited versions, Q2 and F in digital form and Q1 and a fourth, combined text in both digital and print editions. This fourth edition is based on the Q2 text, augmented by passages from F of a line or more; the latter are presented in a different typeface to indicate their addition. Yet this "scars-and-stitches" edition is *not* a conflated edition in the tradition of Shakespearean editing as it was practiced throughout the twentieth century— that is, one in which the editor chose, word by word, from the surviving texts, according to a view of which was better, and then as much as possible hid the joins between elements of text from different sources. By contrast, our decision to produce a "combined" text means that many individual lines from Q2 remain as they are in the source text and have not been emended by substituting the F reading. Sometimes this results in metrical irregularity. For example, at 1.5.47, Q2 (and thus our text) reads, "O Hamlet, what falling off was there," resulting in a metrically irregular line. F's reading, "O Hamlet, what a falling off was there," regularizes the meter and is typically adopted by editors. But the Q2 reading makes perfect sense and could be effectively spoken by a skilled actor. Thus, since we are operating on the principle of "single-text editing," we follow Q2. In essence, this edition is a hybrid designed to do two things: to provide as many as possible of the lines readers expect to find in *Hamlet* (for example, the long passage about the "eyrie of children" in 2.2, which is present only in F) and to demonstrate what most nineteenth- and twentieth-century readers understood to be *Hamlet*. Thus the edition gives the reader more *Hamlet* than any one of the early texts does, but, by making the seams obvious, reminds the reader that the conflation represents a *Hamlet* that never in fact existed in this form.

Two Notes on Editorial Procedure

Character names. For the three original texts, *The Norton Shakespeare* spells the names of the characters as they are most frequently spelled in the originals. However, for the Q2/F version, the proper names have been regularized so that they match the usual spellings in other modern editions.

Act and scene numbers. Q1 and Q2 have no act or scene designations. F marks only act 1, scenes 1–3 and both scenes in act 2. Editors have supplied the other act and scene numbers, but where act 3 should end has proven controversial. The traditional 3.4 ends with Hamlet "tugging" Polonius out, leaving his mother onstage to face a worried Claudius, who enters immediately. Gertrude does not leave the stage (none of the texts has an exit for her, though Q2 mistakenly includes her in the stage direction for the king's entry), and thus what follows is not a new scene. Commentators since the eighteenth century have noted the anomaly, though most editors have, for ease of reference, retained the traditional divisions that have been in place since 1676. This edition takes note of the continuous nature of the traditional 3.4 and 4.1 by running them together as a single scene, ending with Claudius's command to Rosencrantz and Guildenstern to find Hamlet and bring him to the King. The next two scenes (traditional 4.2 and 4.3) follow directly from that and therefore belong in the same act. So traditional 4.2 and 4.3 become 3.5 and 3.6. The next scene (Fortinbras, the Captain, and, in Q2 only, Hamlet and his guard) takes place sometime later and in a different location. It therefore seems a suitable place to begin a new act, so traditional 4.4 becomes in this edition 4.1, and the other scenes in what remains of traditional act 4 are renumbered accordingly. ANTHONY B. DAWSON

PERFORMANCE NOTE

Perhaps the foremost concern for directors of *Hamlet* is assembling a text for performance. Most companies cut the play substantially, as a full combination of the two primary sources (Q2 and F) can easily run four hours or longer. Cutting can help determine whether the tragedy takes on a more political or domestic character, and whether espionage, madness, theater, militarism, and the supernatural surface as dominant or momentary themes. Besides Hamlet (the longest role in Shakespeare) the more frequent targets of editing or elision are Fortinbras, Reynaldo, *The Mousetrap,* and Hamlet's final soliloquy ("How all occasions . . ."), though cutting is also employed to confer unity on the characters and plot, making Claudius a purer villain, for example, or Denmark a more palpably corrupt state.

There are at least as many approaches to the role of Hamlet as there are to the text, though most actors fall somewhere within the traditions of either the prince or the rebel. In one tradition (greatly simplified), Hamlet is a noble and capable successor to his father, slow to his revenge not from fear but prudence, using his soliloquies primarily to renew his commitment to the task at hand. In the other, Hamlet is an outcast, a disaffected student who scorns the politics at court yet likely would struggle to succeed there. This Hamlet is often a cynic and joker, indulging in playacting to escape the despair that pervades solitary moments. Within these broad contours, myriad further choices present themselves: Hamlet can loathe Gertrude or regard her with oedipal fascination; heap abuse on Ophelia or treat her with pity and restraint; condescend to Horatio or seem, admirably, without pretension. These and other choices can inform whether the production works to deliver a markedly sympathetic character or one whose theatrical appeal is complicated or undercut by moral deficiencies.

The portrayals of the supporting cast critically affect the audience's reception of Hamlet and the degree to which he dominates their awareness at play's end. Claudius can be the "bloat king" Hamlet describes or a respected ruler; Gertrude, an oversexed newlywed or a concerned mother; Polonius, a cunning politician or bumbling fool; Rosencrantz and Guildenstern, caring friends or sinister mercenaries; Laertes, a loyal brother and son or self-satisfied favorite; and Ophelia, a clever upstart or model of naïve obedience. Other dramaturgical considerations include representing the Ghost (see Digital Edition PC 1); determining Gertrude's complicity in the murder of King Hamlet and her awareness of Claudius's intentions for her son; placing "To be or not to be" and deciding on its audience; cultivating attention for some extremely familiar set pieces; clarifying Hamlet's awareness or ignorance of being watched in 3.1 (Digital Edition PC 5); sorting out textual confusion regarding the ship for England and the pirates; and determining whether Laertes' (and Fortinbras') return to Denmark is a private matter or a coup. BRETT GAMBOA

The Tragedy of Hamlet, Prince of Denmark

COMBINED TEXT*

[THE PERSONS OF THE PLAY

HAMLET, Prince of Denmark
KING Claudius of Denmark, brother to former King Hamlet
QUEEN Gertrude of Denmark, mother to Hamlet
GHOST of Hamlet, former King of Denmark and father to Prince Hamlet
POLONIUS, a royal counselor
OPHELIA, daughter to Polonius
LAERTES, son to Polonius
REYNALDO, servant to Polonius
FOLLOWERS of Laertes
HORATIO, companion to Hamlet
ROSENCRANTZ } school friends to Hamlet
GUILDENSTERN
CORNELIUS } Danish ambassadors
VOLTEMAND
English AMBASSADORS
FRANCISCO
BARNARDO } sentries
MARCELLUS
FIRST PLAYER, leader of the troupe
PLAYERS, playing roles of PROLOGUE, PLAYER KING, PLAYER QUEEN, and LUCIANUS
FORTINBRAS, Prince of Norway
Norwegian CAPTAIN
Soldiers in the Norwegian army
GRAVEDIGGER
SECOND MAN, his companion
PRIEST
OSRIC, a courtier
GENTLEMAN
LORDS
SAILORS
MESSENGER
Attendants, Officers, Servants]

1.1
Enter BARNARDO *and* FRANCISCO, *two sentinels.*

BARNARDO   Who's there?
FRANCISCO   Nay, answer me!¹ Stand and unfold° yourself.   *identify*
BARNARDO   Long live the King.
FRANCISCO   Barnardo?
BARNARDO   He.
FRANCISCO   You come most carefully° upon your hour.   *dutifully; cautiously*

---

*Text based on the Second Quarto, with interpolated
lines, passages, and scenes from the Folio.
1.1 Location: A guard platform at Elsinore Castle,
Denmark.
1. Francisco, as sentry on duty, is responsible for
challenging anyone who appears.

5 BARNARDO 'Tis now struck twelve—get thee to bed, Francisco.
FRANCISCO For this relief much thanks. 'Tis bitter cold,
And I am sick at heart.
BARNARDO Have you had quiet guard?
FRANCISCO   Not a mouse stirring.
BARNARDO Well, good night.
10   If you do meet Horatio and Marcellus,
The rivals° of my watch, bid them make haste.   *partners*
         Enter HORATIO *and* MARCELLUS.
FRANCISCO I think I hear them. —Stand ho! Who is there?
HORATIO Friends to this ground.°   *country*
MARCELLUS   And liegemen° to the Dane.[2]   *sworn servants*
FRANCISCO Give° you good night.   *God give*
15 MARCELLUS Oh, farewell, honest soldier. Who hath relieved
you?
FRANCISCO Barnardo hath my place. Give you good night.
                                         Exit.

MARCELLUS Holla, Barnardo!
BARNARDO Say, what, is Horatio there?
HORATIO   A piece of him.
BARNARDO Welcome, Horatio; welcome, good Marcellus.
20 HORATIO What, has this thing appeared again tonight?
BARNARDO I have seen nothing.
MARCELLUS Horatio says 'tis but our fantasy
And will not let belief take hold of him
Touching° this dreaded sight twice seen of us.   *Concerning*
25   Therefore I have entreated him along
With us to watch the minutes of this night,
That if again this apparition come
He may approve° our eyes and speak to it.[3]   *verify the evidence of*
HORATIO Tush, tush, 'twill not appear.
BARNARDO   Sit down awhile,
30   And let us once again assail your ears
That are so fortified against our story
What we have two nights seen.
HORATIO   Well, sit we down,
And let us hear Barnardo speak of this.
BARNARDO Last night of all,°   *Just last night*
35   When yond same star that's westward from the pole°   *polestar*
Had made his° course t'illume that part of heaven   *its*
Where now it burns, Marcellus and myself,
The bell then beating one—
         Enter GHOST.[4]
MARCELLUS Peace, break thee off—look where it comes
again!
40 BARNARDO In the same figure like the King that's dead.
MARCELLUS Thou art a scholar: speak to it, Horatio.
BARNARDO Looks 'a° not like the King? Mark it, Horatio!   *he*
HORATIO Most like; it harrows me with fear and wonder.

---

2. King of Denmark.
3. A ghost was believed to speak only when spoken
to. As a precaution, the experiment will be conducted
by an educated man (Horatio; see line 41) who knows
Latin (the language effective for exorcising demonic
spirits).

4. PERFORMANCE COMMENT Productions range widely
in how they choose to represent the Ghost, whether as
a figure who arouses terror or one who evokes pity; a
spectral image or a full-fleshed person; a radical alternative to Claudius or his uncanny double. For the
implications of these choices, see Digital Edition PC 1.

BARNARDO   It would° be spoke to.   *wishes to*

MARCELLUS   Speak to it, Horatio!

45 HORATIO   What art thou that usurp'st[5] this time of night
Together with that fair and warlike form
In which the majesty of buried Denmark°   *the buried King*
Did sometimes° march? By heaven, I charge thee, speak!   *formerly*

MARCELLUS   It is offended.

BARNARDO   See, it stalks away.

50 HORATIO   Stay! Speak, speak, I charge thee, speak!

                                        Exit GHOST.

MARCELLUS   'Tis gone and will not answer.

BARNARDO   How now, Horatio? You tremble and look pale:
Is not this something more than fantasy?
What think you on't?°   *of it*

55 HORATIO   Before my God, I might not this believe
Without the sensible° and true avouch°   *sensory / testimony*
Of mine own eyes.

MARCELLUS   Is it not like the King?

HORATIO   As thou art to thyself.
Such was the very armor he had on
60 When he the ambitious Norway° combated;   *King of Norway*
So frowned he once, when in an angry parle°   *encounter*
He smote the sledded Polacks[6] on the ice.
'Tis strange.

MARCELLUS   Thus twice before, and jump° at this dead hour,   *precisely*
65 With martial stalk° hath he gone by our watch.   *gait*

HORATIO   In what particular thought to work,[7] I know not,
But in the gross and scope of mine opinion[8]
This bodes some strange eruption° to our state.   *calamity*

MARCELLUS   Good now,° sit down, and tell me he that knows, *(an entreaty: Good sir, now)*
70 Why this same strict and most observant watch
So nightly toils the subject of the land,[9]
And with such daily cost of brazen cannon
And foreign mart° for implements of war—   *trade*
Why such impress° of shipwrights whose sore task   *drafting*
75 Does not divide the Sunday from the week?
What might be toward° that this sweaty haste   *impending*
Doth make the night joint laborer with the day—
Who is't that can inform me?

HORATIO   That can I.
At least the whisper goes so: our last king,
80 Whose image even but now appeared to us,
Was, as you know, by Fortinbras of Norway,
Thereto pricked° on by a most emulate° pride,   *spurred / rivalrous*
Dared to the combat, in which our valiant Hamlet—
For so this side of our known world esteemed him—
85 Did slay this Fortinbras, who, by a sealed compact[1]
Well ratified by law and heraldry,[2]
Did forfeit with his life all these his lands

---

5. Wrongfully seize (both the night and the shape of
the King). The familiar "thou" would be an inappropriate form of address for a real king.
6. Poles who traveled by sled.
7. *In . . . work:* What precise theory to follow.
8. But in my general opinion.

9. *So . . . land:* Requires the country's subjects to toil
every night.
1. A mutually agreed-upon contract ("compact") to
which each set his seal.
2. Properly ratified in accordance with civil law and
the law of arms.

Which he stood seized of° to the conqueror;   *held possession of*
Against the which a moiety competent°   *an equal portion*
90 Was gagèd° by our king, which had return³   *staked*
To the inheritance° of Fortinbras   *ownership*
Had he been vanquisher—as by the same co-mart⁴
And carriage of the article designed⁵
His fell to Hamlet. Now, sir, young Fortinbras,
95 Of unimprovèd° mettle hot and full,   *untested; untrained*
Hath in the skirts° of Norway here and there   *outlying parts*
Sharked up a list⁶ of lawless⁷ resolutes
For food and diet to some enterprise
That hath a stomach in't,⁸ which is no other,
100 As it doth well° appear unto our state,   *obviously*
But to recover of us by strong hand⁹
And terms compulsatory° those foresaid lands   *compulsory*
So by his father lost. And this, I take it,
Is the main motive of our preparations,
105 The source of this our watch, and the chief head°   *source*
Of this post-haste and rummage¹ in the land.²
BARNARDO   I think it be no other, but e'en so.
Well may it sort° that this portentous figure   *be fitting*
Comes armèd through our watch so like the King
110 That was and is the question° of these wars.   *cause*
HORATIO   A mote° it is to trouble the mind's eye.   *speck of dust*
In the most high and palmy° state of Rome,   *flourishing*
A little ere the mightiest Julius³ fell,
The graves stood tenantless and the sheeted° dead   *shrouded*
115 Did squeak and gibber in the Roman streets.
As stars with trains of fire and dews of blood,
Disasters⁴ in the sun; and the moist star,⁵
Upon whose influence Neptune's empire stands,°   *depends*
Was sick almost to doomsday with eclipse.⁶
120 And even the like precurse° of feared events,   *forerunner*
As harbingers preceding still° the fates   *always*
And prologue to the omen° coming on,   *disastrous event*
Have heaven and earth together demonstrated
Unto our climatures° and countrymen.   *regions*
      Enter GHOST.
125 But soft,° behold: lo, where it comes again!   *hush*
I'll cross⁷ it though it blast° me. —Stay, illusion!   *wither*
      It spreads his arms.
If thou hast any sound or use of voice,
Speak to me!

---

3. Which would have gone. *return:* returned.
4. Covenant. Q2's use of "co-mart" is unattested elsewhere.
5. And execution of the contract's provision.
6. Gathered together indiscriminately (as a shark takes prey) a band ("list").
7. F uses "landless," providing a more specific motive for their enlistment.
8. *For . . . in't:* The men will "feed" his enterprise; they are fed in return for their service. *stomach:* courageous action; challenge to the pride (of both the Prince and his men).
9. By main force (punning on the name "Fortinbras," literally "strong arm").

1. Of this feverish activity and commotion.
2. The following passage, lines 107–24, is omitted in F.
3. Julius Caesar, whose assassination Shakespeare dramatized in his play of that name.
4. Malevolent influences (astrological term).
5. The moon, thought to control tides by drawing water out of the sea ("Neptune's empire," line 118).
6. Eclipses of sun and moon would accompany Christ's return to earth on Judgment Day (see Revelation 6:12).
7. Confront, cross its path; also, make the sign of the cross (to counter its evil influence).

If there be any good thing to be done
130 That may to thee do ease and grace to me,
Speak to me!
If thou art privy to thy country's fate
Which happily° foreknowing may avoid,   *perhaps; fortunately*
Oh, speak!
135 Or if thou hast uphoarded in thy life
Extorted treasure in the womb of earth,
For which they say your spirits oft walk in death,
Speak of it.
     The cock crows.
     Stay and speak! Stop it, Marcellus!
MARCELLUS Shall I strike it with my partisan?°   *spear-handled blade*
HORATIO Do, if it will not stand.
BARNARDO   'Tis here.
140 HORATIO   'Tis here.
            [*Exit* GHOST.]
MARCELLUS 'Tis gone.
We do it wrong, being so majestical,
To offer it the show of violence,
For it is as the air, invulnerable,
145 And our vain blows malicious mockery.
BARNARDO It was about to speak when the cock crew.
HORATIO And then it started like a guilty thing
Upon a fearful summons. I have heard
The cock that is the trumpet to the morn
150 Doth with his lofty and shrill-sounding throat
Awake the god of day,[8] and at his warning,
Whether in sea or fire, in earth or air,
Th'extravagant and erring[9] spirit hies°   *hurries*
To his confine°—and of the truth herein   *enclosure*
155 This present object° made probation.°   *example / proof*
MARCELLUS It faded on the crowing of the cock.
Some say that ever 'gainst° that season comes   *always when*
Wherein our Savior's birth is celebrated,
This bird of dawning singeth all night long,
160 And then, they say, no spirit dare stir abroad,
The nights are wholesome, then no planets strike,[1]
No fairy takes,° nor witch hath power to charm,   *bewitches*
So hallowed and so gracious° is that time.   *full of God's grace*
HORATIO So have I heard and do in part believe it.
165 But look, the morn in russet mantle clad[2]
Walks o'er the dew of yon high eastward hill.
Break we our watch up and, by my advice,
Let us impart what we have seen tonight
Unto young Hamlet, for upon my life
170 This spirit, dumb to us, will speak to him.
Do you consent we shall acquaint him with it
As needful in our loves,[3] fitting our duty?
MARCELLUS Let's do't, I pray, and I this morning know
Where we shall find him most convenient.   *Exeunt.*

8. The sun god, Phoebus Apollo.
9. Wandering out of its boundaries.
1. When they were in certain unfavorable astrological positions, heavenly bodies were thought to exercise a negative influence on earthly events.
2. Dressed in a reddish-brown cloak.
3. As necessary because of the love we have for him.

1.2

Flourish. Enter Claudius, KING *of Denmark, Gertrude
the* QUEEN, *Council [members, such] as* POLONIUS *and
his son* LAERTES, HAMLET, *with others[, including*
VOLTEMAND *and* CORNELIUS].

KING   Though yet of Hamlet our[1] dear brother's death
    The memory be green, and that it us befitted
    To bear our hearts in grief and our whole kingdom
    To be contracted in one brow of woe,[2]
5   Yet so far hath discretion fought with nature°   *natural love*
    That we with wisest sorrow think on him
    Together with remembrance of ourselves.[3]
    Therefore our sometime° sister, now our queen,[4]   *former*
    Th'imperial jointress to° this warlike state,   *joint possessor of*
10   Have we as 'twere with a defeated joy,
    With an auspicious and a dropping eye,[5]
    With mirth in funeral and with dirge in marriage,
    In equal scale weighing delight and dole,°   *sorrow*
    Taken to wife. Nor have we herein barred°   *excluded; contradicted*
15   Your better wisdoms, which have freely gone
    With this affair along—for all, our thanks.
    Now follows that you know:° young Fortinbras,   *that which you should know*
    Holding a weak supposal° of our worth   *poor opinion*
    Or thinking by our late dear brother's death
20   Our state to be disjoint° and out of frame,°   *fractured / order*
    Co-leaguèd with this dream of his advantage,[6]
    He hath not failed to pester us with message
    Importing° the surrender of those lands   *Concerning*
    Lost by his father, with all bands° of law,   *obligations*
25   To our most valiant brother. So much for him.
    Now for ourself and for this time of meeting,
    Thus much the business is: we have here writ
    To Norway, uncle of young Fortinbras,
    Who, impotent and bedrid, scarcely hears
30   Of this his nephew's purpose, to suppress
    His further gait° herein, in that the levies,   *progress*
    The lists, and full proportions are all made
    Out of his subject;[7] and we here dispatch
    You, good Cornelius, and you, Voltemand,
35   For bearers of this greeting to old Norway,
    Giving to you no further personal power
    To business with the King more than the scope
    Of these delated° articles allow.   *spelled out; specific*

1.2 Location: The castle.

1. My. (Kings often referred to themselves in the plural, the royal "we," although in the lines that follow, Claudius may also be talking about Danes in general.)

2. To be drawn together into a collective expression of mourning (playing on the expression "the frowning brow of a mourner").

3. *we . . . ourselves:* "He is not wise that is not wise for himself" was proverbial.

4. English canon law forbade marriage between a former brother- and sister-in-law (Leviticus 18:16; Book of Common Prayer); it was on this ground that

Henry VIII annulled his marriage to his brother's widow and married Anne Boleyn, Queen Elizabeth's mother. The relationship between Claudius and Gertrude could thus be regarded as incestuous. In some early Germanic societies, however, a new king customarily married the late king's widow.

5. One eye looking hopefully, the other downcast, or "dropping" tears.

6. Reinforced by this illusion of his own advantageous position.

7. *in that . . . subject:* since the moneys, enlistments, and forces are made up of his (the King of Norway's) subjects.

Farewell, and let your haste commend your duty.[8]
40 CORNELIUS *and* VOLTEMAND   In that and all things will we
    show our duty.
    KING   We doubt it nothing;° heartily farewell.   *not at all*
                    [*Exeunt* VOLTEMAND *and* CORNELIUS.]
    And now, Laertes, what's the news with you?
    You told us of some suit°—what is't, Laertes?   *petition; request*
    You cannot speak of reason to the Dane°   *the Danish King*
45 And lose your voice. What wouldst thou beg, Laertes,
    That shall not be my offer, not thy asking?[9]
    The head is not more native[1] to the heart,
    The hand more instrumental to the mouth,
    Than is the throne of Denmark to thy father.
    What wouldst thou have, Laertes?
50 LAERTES   My dread° lord,   *revered*
    Your leave° and favor° to return to France,   *permission / approval*
    From whence, though willingly I came to Denmark
    To show my duty in your coronation,
    Yet now I must confess, that duty done,
55 My thoughts and wishes bend again toward France
    And bow them to your gracious leave and pardon.[2]
    KING   Have you your father's leave? —What says Polonius?
    POLONIUS   He hath, my lord, wrung from me my slow leave
    By laborsome petition, and at last
60 Upon his will° I sealed my hard° consent.   *desire / reluctant*
    I do beseech you give him leave to go.
    KING   Take thy fair hour,[3] Laertes; time be thine
    And thy best graces spend it at thy will.[4]
    But now, my cousin[5] Hamlet, and my son—
65 HAMLET   A little more than kin and less than kind.[6]
    KING   How is it that the clouds still hang on you?
    HAMLET   Not so much, my lord; I am too much in the sun.[7]
    QUEEN   Good Hamlet, cast thy nighted color[8] off
    And let thine eye look like a friend on Denmark.[9]
70 Do not forever with thy veilèd lids°   *downcast eyes*
    Seek for thy noble father in the dust—
    Thou know'st 'tis common, all that lives must die,
    Passing through nature to eternity.
    HAMLET   Ay, madam, it is common.[1]
    QUEEN   If it be,
75 Why seems it so particular° with thee?   *personal*
    HAMLET   "Seems," madam? Nay, it is. I know not "seems."
    'Tis not alone my inky cloak, cold mother,
    Nor customary suits of solemn black,
    Nor windy suspiration° of forced breath,   *sigh*

---

8. Let your swift departure (rather than elaborate speeches) show your loyalty.
9. *What wouldst . . . asking:* What could you ask of me that I would not offer before you asked?
1. Naturally connected; an allusion to the "body politic," headed by the King and having as its heart the King's council.
2. And humbly ask you to grant permission to depart.
3. Opportunity (while you are young).
4. *time . . . will:* your time is your own; use it in accordance with your best qualities.
5. Kinsman (outside one's immediate family).
6. "The nearer in kin the less in kindness" was pro-

verbial. Hamlet's riddling comment indicates first that there is little warmth in their new, only nominally closer relationship. Playing on "kind" in the sense of natural type or offspring, however, he also refers to the incestuousness of the marriage that has produced their unnatural kinship.
7. In the sunshine of Claudius's favor; also, punning on "son."
8. Black mourning garments and melancholic behavior.
9. Both the King of Denmark and the country.
1. Commonplace; crude (?).

80 No, nor the fruitful° river in the eye,   *copious*
    Nor the dejected 'havior° of the visage,   *expression*
    Together with all forms, moods, shapes of grief
    That can denote me truly. These indeed seem,
    For they are actions that a man might play,
85 But I have that within which passes show—
    These but the trappings and the suits of woe.
    KING 'Tis sweet and commendable in your nature, Hamlet,
    To give these mourning duties to your father,
    But you must know your father lost a father,
90 That father lost, lost his, and the survivor bound
    In filial obligation for some term
    To do obsequious sorrow;[2] but to persever
    In obstinate condolement° is a course   *lamenting*
    Of impious stubbornness—'tis unmanly grief;
95 It shows a will most incorrect° to heaven,   *unsubmissive*
    A heart unfortified or mind impatient,[3]
    An understanding simple° and unschooled—   *childish*
    For what we know must be and is as common
    As any the most vulgar thing to sense,[4]
100 Why should we in our peevish opposition
    Take it to heart? Fie, 'tis a fault to heaven,
    A fault against the dead, a fault to nature,
    To reason most absurd, whose common theme
    Is death of fathers and who still° hath cried   *always*
105 From the first corpse[5] till he that died today,
    "This must be so." We pray you throw to earth
    This unprevailing° woe and think of us   *unavailing*
    As of a father, for let the world take note
    You are the most immediate° to our throne,   *next in succession*
110 And with no less nobility° of love   *purity; generosity*
    Than that which dearest father bears his son
    Do I impart toward you. For your intent
    In going back to school in Wittenberg,[6]
    It is most retrograde° to our desire,   *contrary*
115 And we beseech you bend you° to remain   *yield; agree*
    Here in the cheer and comfort of our eye,
    Our chiefest courtier, cousin, and our son.
    QUEEN Let not thy mother lose her prayers, Hamlet:
    I pray thee stay with us; go not to Wittenberg.
120 HAMLET I shall in all my best obey you, madam.
    KING Why, 'tis a loving and a fair reply.[7]
    Be as ourself in Denmark. —Madam, come;
    This gentle and unforced accord of Hamlet
    Sits smiling to° my heart, in grace° whereof   *Pleases / honor*
125 No jocund health° that Denmark° drinks today   *toast / the King*
    But the great cannon to the clouds shall tell,°   *sound*
    And the King's rouse[8] the heaven shall bruit again,°   *loudly echo*

---

2. To mourn as befits obsequies, or funeral ceremonies.
3. A heart not strengthened (against emotion or misfortune), a mind unprepared to suffer.
4. As the most obvious and ordinary thing we perceive using our senses.
5. That of Abel, the first human to die, murdered by his brother, Cain.
6. The birthplace of Protestantism, the university of

Luther and Faustus; many Danes studied there.
7. PERFORMANCE COMMENT Whether the King's behavior merits the insult implicit in Hamlet's "loving" reply is a critical question for productions, which must decide how to depict the relationships in this scene. For discussion of the range of options, see Digital Edition PC 2.
8. Bout of drinking.

Re-speaking earthly thunder. Come away.

Flourish. Exeunt all but HAMLET.

HAMLET   Oh, that this too, too sallied[9] flesh would melt,
130 Thaw, and resolve° itself into a dew,   *dissolve*
Or that the Everlasting had not fixed
His canon° 'gainst self-slaughter. O God, God,   *law*
How weary, stale, flat, and unprofitable
Seem to me all the uses° of this world.   *customs; business*
135 Fie on't, ah, fie, 'tis an unweeded garden
That grows to seed; things rank and gross in nature
Possess it merely.° That it should come thus: *entirely*
But two months dead—nay, not so much, not two—
So excellent a king, that was to this
140 Hyperion to a satyr,[1] so loving to my mother
That he might not beteem° the winds of heaven   *permit*
Visit her face too roughly—heaven and earth,
Must I remember? Why, she would hang on him
As if increase of appetite had grown
145 By what it fed on. And yet within a month—
Let me not think on't—Frailty, thy name is woman—
A little month, or e'er° those shoes were old   *before*
With which she followed my poor father's body,
Like Niobe all tears,[2] why, she—
150 O God, a beast that wants discourse of reason[3]
Would have mourned longer—married with my uncle,
My father's brother, but no more like my father
Than I to Hercules.[4] Within a month,
Ere yet the salt of most unrighteous tears
155 Had left the flushing in her gallèd° eyes,   *irritated*
She married. Oh, most wicked speed, to post°   *hurry*
With such dexterity to incestuous sheets—
It is not, nor it cannot come to good.
But break, my heart, for I must hold my tongue.

Enter HORATIO, MARCELLUS, *and* BARNARDO.

HORATIO   Hail to your lordship!
160 HAMLET   I am glad to see you well—
Horatio, or I do forget myself.
HORATIO   The same, my lord, and your poor servant ever.
HAMLET   Sir, my good friend, I'll change° that name with   *exchange*
you.
And what make you from[5] Wittenberg, Horatio?
165 —Marcellus!
MARCELLUS   My good lord.
HAMLET   I am very glad to see you. [*to* BARNARDO] Good
even, sir.
[*to* HORATIO] But what in faith make you from Wittenberg?

---

9. TEXTUAL COMMENT Q1 and Q2 read "sallied,"
while F reads "solid." "Solid" fits with the imagery of
thawing, but "sallied" (meaning "assailed" or "sullied") also works well, evoking the themes of oppression and pollution that Hamlet explores elsewhere in
the play. See Digital Edition TC 1 (combined text).
1. *So . . . satyr:* That king was to this as the sun god
(Hyperion, a Titan) is to a lustful half goat (mythological companion of the wine god, Bacchus).

2. Niobe's fourteen children were killed by Apollo
and Artemis to punish her for boasting about them.
She continued to weep bitterly even after she was
turned to stone.
3. That lacks the faculty of rational thought.
4. In Greek and Roman mythology, a powerful demigod renowned for his strength, as exemplified in his
twelve famous "labors."
5. What are you doing away from.

HORATIO A truant disposition, good my lord.

170 HAMLET I would not hear your enemy say so,
Nor shall you do my ear that violence
To make it truster° of your own report   *believer*
Against yourself. I know you are no truant.
But what is your affair in Elsinore?

175 We'll teach you for to° drink ere you depart.   *for to = to*

HORATIO My lord, I came to see your father's funeral.

HAMLET I prithee° do not mock me, fellow student,   *pray thee*
I think it was to see my mother's wedding.

HORATIO Indeed, my lord, it followed hard upon.°   *quickly thereafter*

180 HAMLET Thrift, thrift, Horatio: the funeral baked meats°   *meat pies and pastries*
Did coldly° furnish forth the marriage tables.   *when cold*
Would I had met my dearest° foe in heaven   *most hated*
Or ever° I had seen that day, Horatio.   *Before*
My father—methinks I see my father.

HORATIO Where, my lord?

185 HAMLET   In my mind's eye, Horatio.

HORATIO I saw him once; 'a° was a goodly king.   *he*

HAMLET 'A was a man, take him for all in all;
I shall not look upon his like again.

HORATIO My lord, I think I saw him yesternight.

HAMLET Saw? Who?

190 HORATIO   My lord, the King your father.

HAMLET The King my father?

HORATIO Season° your admiration° for a while   *Moderate / amazement*
With an attent° ear till I may deliver,   *attentive*
Upon the witness of these gentlemen,
This marvel to you.

195 HAMLET   For God's love let me hear!

HORATIO Two nights together had these gentlemen,
Marcellus and Barnardo, on their watch
In the dead waste° and middle of the night,   *bleak stillness*
Been thus encountered: a figure like your father

200 Armed at point° exactly, cap-à-pie,°   *in readiness / head to foot*
Appears before them and with solemn march
Goes slow and stately by them. Thrice he walked
By their oppressed and fear-surprisèd eyes
Within his truncheon's[6] length, whilst they, distilled°   *dissolved*

205 Almost to jelly with the act° of fear,   *effect*
Stand dumb and speak not to him. This to me
In dreadful secrecy impart they did,
And I with them the third night kept the watch
Where, as they had delivered,° both in time,   *reported*

210 Form of the thing, each word made true and good,
The apparition comes. I knew your father:
These hands are not more like.[7]

HAMLET   But where was this?

MARCELLUS My lord, upon the platform where we watch.

HAMLET Did you not speak to it?

HORATIO   My lord, I did,

215 But answer made it none; yet once methought

---

6. Officer's baton.
7. These hands are not more like each other than the apparition was like King Hamlet.

It lifted up it° head and did address   *its*
Itself to motion like as it would speak.[8]
But even° then the morning cock crew loud,   *just*
And at the sound it shrunk in haste away
And vanished from our sight.
220 HAMLET   'Tis very strange.
HORATIO   As I do live, my honored lord, 'tis true,
And we did think it writ down° in our duty   *prescribed*
To let you know of it.
HAMLET   Indeed, sirs, but this troubles me—
Hold you the watch tonight?
225 BARNARDO *and* MARCELLUS   We do, my lord.
HAMLET   Armed, say you?
HORATIO, BARNARDO, *and* MARCELLUS   Armed, my lord.
HAMLET   From top to toe?
HORATIO, BARNARDO, *and* MARCELLUS   My lord, from head to foot.
HAMLET   Then saw you not his face.
HORATIO   Oh, yes, my lord, he wore his beaver° up.   *helmet's faceguard*
230 HAMLET   What, looked he frowningly?
HORATIO   A countenance more in sorrow than in anger.
HAMLET   Pale or red?
HORATIO   Nay, very pale.
HAMLET   And fixed his eyes upon you?
HORATIO   Most constantly.
HAMLET   I would I had been there.
235 HORATIO   It would have much amazed you.
HAMLET   Very like; stayed it long?
HORATIO   While one with moderate haste might tell° a   *count*
hundred.
BARNARDO *and* MARCELLUS   Longer, longer.
HORATIO   Not when I saw't.
HAMLET   His beard was grizzled,° no?   *gray*
240 HORATIO   It was as I have seen it in his life,
A sable silvered.[9]
HAMLET   I will watch tonight;
Perchance 'twill walk again.
HORATIO   I warr'nt° it will.   *guarantee*
HAMLET   If it assume my noble father's person,
I'll speak to it though hell itself should gape
245 And bid me hold my peace. I pray you all,
If you have hitherto concealed this sight,
Let it be tenable[1] in your silence still;
And whatsomever° else shall hap° tonight   *whatever / occur*
Give it an understanding but no tongue.
250 I will requite your loves. So fare you well.
Upon the platform twixt eleven and twelve
I'll visit you.
HORATIO, BARNARDO, *and* MARCELLUS   Our duty to your honor.
HAMLET   Your loves, as mine to you; farewell.
            Exeunt [HORATIO, BARNARDO, *and* MARCELLUS].
My father's spirit in arms! All is not well:

---

8. *address . . . speak:* start to move as though it wished
to speak.
9. Black sprinkled with white.
1. That is, able to be held. F's reading is "treble."

255 I doubt° some foul play. Would the night were come!   *suspect*
    Till then sit still, my soul. Foul deeds will rise,
    Though all the earth o'erwhelm them, to men's eyes.   *Exit.*

1.3

Enter LAERTES *and* OPHELIA, *his sister.*

LAERTES   My necessaries are embarked.° Farewell.   *aboard ship*
    And, sister, as the winds give benefit
    And convey is assistant,[1] do not sleep
    But let me hear from you.
OPHELIA   Do you doubt that?
5 LAERTES   For Hamlet and the trifling of his favor,
    Hold it a fashion and a toy in blood,
    A violet in the youth of primy nature,
    Forward,[2] not permanent, sweet, not lasting,
    The perfume and suppliance° of a minute,   *diversion*
    No more.
OPHELIA   No more but so?
10 LAERTES   Think it no more.
    For nature crescent° does not grow alone   *growing*
    In thews° and bulks, but as this temple° waxes,   *muscles / body*
    The inward service° of the mind and soul   *responsibility*
    Grows wide withal.° Perhaps he loves you now,   *along with it*
15   And now no soil° nor cautel° doth besmirch   *stain / deception*
    The virtue of his will.° But you must fear,   *intentions; desires*
    His greatness weighed,[3] his will is not his own:
    He may not, as unvalued° persons do,   *common*
    Carve for himself,[4] for on his choice depends
20   The safety and health of this whole state.
    And therefore must his choice be circumscribed
    Unto the voice° and yielding° of that body[5]   *vote / consent*
    Whereof he is the head. Then if he says he loves you,
    It fits° your wisdom so far to believe it   *befits*
25   As he in his particular act and place[6]
    May give his saying deed,[7] which is no further
    Than the main° voice of Denmark goes withal.   *collective*
    Then weigh what loss your honor may sustain
    If with too credent° ear you list° his songs,   *trusting / listen to*
30   Or lose your heart, or your chaste treasure open
    To his unmastered° importunity.   *uncontrolled*
    Fear it, Ophelia, fear it, my dear sister,
    And keep you in the rear of your affection[8]
    Out of the shot and danger of desire.
35   The chariest° maid is prodigal enough   *most careful; modest*
    If she unmask her beauty to the moon.[9]

1.3 Location: Polonius's apartments in the castle.
1. And means of transport is available.
2. *a toy . . . Forward:* a passing sexual fancy, a flower of his natural impulses in their prime, early blooming ("forward").
3. When his high rank is considered.
4. Help himself to his own choice of the roast (proverbially, to choose for himself).
5. Body politic; nation.
6. His power of action and social position.

7. May act on his promise.
8. And be restrained, despite the forward march of your feelings.
9. *prodigal . . . moon:* risk-taking enough if she exposes herself to the moon. (The suggestion here is that a maid can never be too cautious. Upper-class women wore masks to screen their complexions from the sun. The moon was classically figured as chaste, while the sun was traditionally associated with passion.)

Virtue itself scapes not calumnious strokes,
The canker galls the infants[1] of the spring
Too oft before their buttons be disclosed,°   *buds are open*
40 And in the morn and liquid dew of youth
Contagious blastments° are most imminent.   *blights*
Be wary, then: best safety lies in fear.
Youth to itself rebels, though none else near.[2]

OPHELIA   I shall the effect of this good lesson keep
45 As watchman to my heart. But, good my brother,
Do not as some ungracious° pastors do   *ungodly*
Show me the steep and thorny way to heaven
Whiles, a puffed° and reckless libertine,   *proud*
Himself the primrose path of dalliance treads
And recks° not his own rede.°   *heeds / advice*
50 LAERTES   Oh, fear me not.°   *fear not for me*

    Enter POLONIUS.

I stay too long—but here my father comes.
A double blessing is a double grace;
Occasion smiles upon a second leave.[3]

POLONIUS   Yet here, Laertes? Aboard, aboard for shame!
55 The wind sits in the shoulder° of your sail   *at the back*
And you are stayed° for. There, my blessing with thee,   *waited*
And these few precepts in thy memory
Look thou character:° give thy thoughts no tongue   *inscribe*
Nor any unproportioned° thought his act;   *unruly*
60 Be thou familiar but by no means vulgar;[4]
Those friends thou hast, and their adoption tried,[5]
Grapple them unto thy soul with hoops of steel,
But do not dull° thy palm with entertainment[6]   *callous*
Of each new-hatched, unfledged courage;° beware   *comrade*
65 Of entrance to a quarrel but, being in,
Bear't° that th'opposèd may beware of thee;   *Manage it so*
Give every man thy ear but few thy voice;
Take each man's censure,° but reserve thy judgment;   *opinion*
Costly thy habit° as thy purse can buy   *dress*
70 But not expressed in fancy,° rich not gaudy—   *showiness*
For the apparel oft proclaims the man,
And they in France of the best rank and station
Are of a most select and generous chief in that.[7]
Neither a borrower nor a lender be,
75 For loan oft loses both itself and friend,
And borrowing dulleth th'edge of husbandry.°   *economy*
This above all: to thine own self be true,
And it must follow as the night the day
Thou canst not then be false to any man.
80 Farewell, my blessing season° this in thee.   *mature*
LAERTES   Most humbly do I take my leave, my lord.
POLONIUS   The time invests° you—go, your servants tend.°   *presses / wait*
LAERTES   Farewell, Ophelia, and remember well

---

1. The cankerworm injures the shoots.
2. Young people are naturally rebellious, even without provocation.
3. Favorable circumstances provide us with a second farewell.
4. *Be . . . vulgar:* Be friendly but by no means indiscriminately social.
5. *Those . . . tried:* Those friends of yours who have proven true and reliable.
6. Greeting (handshaking).
7. Are of all people the most adept at displaying rank in fine appearance.

What I have said to you.

OPHELIA   'Tis in my memory locked,
85   And you yourself shall keep the key of it.
LAERTES   Farewell.   *Exit.*
POLONIUS   What is't, Ophelia, he hath said to you?
OPHELIA   So please you, something touching the Lord Hamlet.
POLONIUS   Marry,[8] well bethought.
90   'Tis told me he hath very oft of late
Given private time to you, and you yourself
Have of your audience° been most free and bounteous.   *attention*
If it be so, as so 'tis put on° me—   *suggested to*
And that in way of caution—I must tell you
95   You do not understand yourself so clearly
As it behooves my daughter and your honor.
What is between you? Give me up the truth.
OPHELIA   He hath, my lord, of late made many tenders°   *offers*
Of his affection to me.
100   POLONIUS   Affection! Pooh! You speak like a green girl
Unsifted° in such perilous circumstance.   *Inexperienced*
Do you believe his "tenders,"[9] as you call them?
OPHELIA   I do not know, my lord, what I should think.
POLONIUS   Marry, I will teach you: think yourself a baby
105   That you have ta'en these tenders for true pay
Which are not sterling.[1] Tender° yourself more dearly   *Value; protect*
Or—not to crack the wind of the poor phrase
Wronging it thus[2]—you'll tender me a fool.[3]
OPHELIA   My lord, he hath importuned me with love
110   In honorable fashion—
POLONIUS   Ay, "fashion"° you may call it. Go to,[4] go to!   *conventional flattery*
OPHELIA   And hath given countenance° to his speech,   *authority*
My lord, with almost all the holy vows of heaven.
POLONIUS   Ay, springes to catch woodcocks.[5] I do know
115   When the blood burns how prodigal° the soul   *lavishly*
Lends the tongue vows; these blazes, daughter,
Giving more light than heat, extinct° in both   *extinguished*
Even in their promise as it is a-making,
You must not take for fire. From this time
120   Be something scanter of your maiden presence;
Set your entreatments at a higher rate
Than a command to parle.[6] For Lord Hamlet,
Believe so much in° him that he is young,   *concerning*
And with a larger tether may he walk
125   Than may be given you. In few,° Ophelia,   *brief*
Do not believe his vows, for they are brokers°   *go-betweens*
Not of that dye which their investments° show   *clerical vestments*
But mere implorators° of unholy suits,   *solicitors*
Breathing° like sanctified and pious bonds°   *Speaking / promises*
130   The better to beguile. This is for all:
I would not, in plain terms, from this time forth

---

8. By the Virgin Mary, a mild oath.
9. *tenders*: offers of payment in compensation for something.
1. Genuine currency.
2. *crack . . . thus*: ruin the phrase with overworking (like a "broken-winded" horse).

3. A multiple pun: make me look foolish; seem yourself a fool; show me a baby (idiomatically, a "fool").
4. That's enough; come, come.
5. Traps for proverbially gullible birds.
6. *Set . . . parle*: Do not negotiate a surrender (of your chastity) just because he asks to speak with you.

Have you so slander° any moment leisure   *disgrace*
As to give words or talk with the Lord Hamlet.
Look to't, I charge you. Come your ways.°   *Come along*
135 OPHELIA   I shall obey, my lord.   *Exeunt.*

1.4

Enter HAMLET, HORATIO, *and* MARCELLUS.

HAMLET   The air bites shrewdly;° it is very cold.   *sharply*
HORATIO   It is nipping and an eager° air.   *a bitter*
HAMLET   What hour now?
HORATIO   I think it lacks of twelve.
MARCELLUS   No, it is struck.
HORATIO   Indeed? I heard it not—
5   It then draws near the season°   *time*
Wherein the spirit held his wont° to walk.   *was accustomed*
    A flourish of trumpets and two pieces° [*go*] *off.*   *cannons*
What does this mean, my lord?
HAMLET   The King doth wake tonight and takes his rouse,
Keeps wassail and the swaggering upspring reels,[1]
10   And as he drains his drafts of Rhenish° down   *Rhine wine*
The kettledrum and trumpet thus bray out
The triumph of his pledge.[2]
HORATIO   Is it a custom?
HAMLET   Ay, marry, is't,
But to my mind, though I am native here
15   And to the manner° born, it is a custom   *custom*
More honored in the breach than the observance.[3]
This heavy-headed revel east and west
Makes us traduced and taxed of other nations:
They clepe° us drunkards and with swinish phrase   *call*
20   Soil our addition,° and indeed it takes   *reputation*
From our achievements, though performed at height,°   *excellently*
The pith° and marrow of our attribute.°   *heart / attributed glory*
So oft it chances in particular men
That for some vicious mole of nature[4] in them,
25   As in their birth° wherein they are not guilty—   *parentage*
Since nature cannot choose his° origin—   *its*
By their o'er-growth of some complexion[5]
Oft breaking down the pales° and forts of reason,   *fences; boundaries*
Or by some habit that too much o'er-leavens
30   The form of plausive manners[6]—that these men,
Carrying, I say, the stamp of one defect—
Being nature's livery or fortune's star[7]—
His virtues else, be they as pure as grace,
As infinite as man may undergo,°   *sustain*
35   Shall in the general censure° take corruption   *the public opinion*

1.4 Location: The castle's battlements.
1. *The King . . . reels:* The King revels and carouses rather than sleeping, has a drinking party ("wassail"), and staggers ("reels") through a wild German dance.
2. His success in draining his cup upon making a toast.
3. Which is more honored in being broken than in being observed. The following passage, lines 17–38, is omitted in F.
4. Natural blemish that tends to vice.

5. By the disproportionate amount of one humor (see note to 2.2.280–81), and thus an unbalanced personality.
6. *o'er-leavens . . . manners:* changes the whole effect of otherwise pleasing ("plausive") manners for the worse (as too much yeast ruins a batch of bread).
7. Being a congenital defect (the "livery," or clothing, given by nature) or a blemish caused by fortune (the influence of chance astrological events).

From that particular fault: the dram of eale
Doth all the noble substance of a doubt
To his own scandal[8]—
    Enter GHOST.

HORATIO   Look, my lord, it comes.
HAMLET   Angels and ministers of grace defend us!
40   Be thou a spirit of health or goblin° damned,   *demon*
    Bring with thee airs° from heaven or blasts[9] from hell,   *gentle breezes*
    Be thy intents wicked or charitable,
    Thou com'st in such a questionable shape
    That I will speak to thee: I'll call thee Hamlet,
45   King, father, royal Dane. Oh, answer me!
    Let me not burst in ignorance, but tell
    Why thy canonized° bones, hearsed° in death,   *consecrated / coffined*
    Have burst their cerements,° why the sepulcher   *grave clothes*
    Wherein we saw thee quietly interred°   *entombed*
50   Hath oped his ponderous and marble jaws
    To cast thee up again. What may this mean
    That thou, dead corpse, again in complete steel°   *armor*
    Revisits thus the glimpses of the moon,[1]
    Making night hideous and we fools of nature[2]
55   So horridly to shake our disposition°   *mental foundations*
    With thoughts beyond the reaches of our souls?
    Say, why is this? Wherefore? What should we do?
        [*The* GHOST] *beckons.*
HORATIO   It beckons you to go away with it
    As if it some impartment° did desire   *communication*
    To you alone.
60 MARCELLUS   Look with what courteous action
    It waves° you to a more removèd ground—   *beckons*
    But do not go with it.
HORATIO   No, by no means.
HAMLET   It will not speak; then I will follow it.
HORATIO   Do not, my lord.
HAMLET   Why, what should be the fear?
65   I do not set my life at a pin's fee,°   *value*
    And for my soul, what can it do to that,
    Being a thing immortal as itself?
    It waves me forth again; I'll follow it.
HORATIO   What if it tempt you toward the flood,° my lord,   *sea*
70   Or to the dreadful summit of the cliff
    That beetles o'er° his base into the sea,   *overhangs*
    And there assume some other horrible form
    Which might deprive your sovereignty of reason
    And draw you into madness? Think of it:[3]
75   The very place puts toys of desperation,[4]
    Without more motive,° into every brain   *cause*
    That looks so many fathoms to the sea
    And hears it roar beneath.

---

8. *dram:* tiny amount (eighth of an ounce). *scandal:* shame. TEXTUAL COMMENT *the dram . . . scandal:* These famously obscure lines, absent from Q1 and F, are plagued by uncertain syntax and opaque words and phrases. See Digital Edition TC 2 (combined text).
9. Pestilent gusts.

1. *glimpses of the moon:* (earth lit by) flickering moonlight.
2. Mere mortals (terrified by encounters with the supernatural).
3. The following passage, lines 75–78, is omitted in F.
4. Imaginings of despair and suicide.

HAMLET   It waves me still. —Go on, I'll follow thee.

MARCELLUS   You shall not go, my lord.

80 HAMLET   Hold off your hands.

HORATIO   Be ruled; you shall not go.

HAMLET   My fate cries out

And makes each petty art'ry° in this body   *artery*

As hardy as the Nemean lion's[5] nerve.

[GHOST *beckons.*] Still am I called—unhand me, gentlemen!

85 By heaven, I'll make a ghost of him that lets me.°   *gets in my way*

I say, away! —Go on, I'll follow thee.

                              Exeunt GHOST *and* HAMLET.

HORATIO   He waxes desperate with imagination.

MARCELLUS   Let's follow. 'Tis not fit thus to obey him.

HORATIO   Have after.° To what issue° will this come?   *Go on / end*

90 MARCELLUS   Something is rotten in the state of Denmark.

HORATIO   Heaven will direct it.

MARCELLUS   Nay, let's follow him.

                                        Exeunt.

1.5

                    Enter GHOST *and* HAMLET.

HAMLET   Whither wilt thou lead me? Speak! I'll go no
    further.

GHOST   Mark me.

HAMLET   I will.

GHOST   My hour is almost come

When I to sulf'rous and tormenting flames

Must render up myself.

HAMLET   Alas, poor ghost.

5 GHOST   Pity me not, but lend thy serious hearing

To what I shall unfold.

HAMLET   Speak, I am bound to hear.

GHOST   So art thou to revenge, when thou shalt hear.

HAMLET   What?

GHOST   I am thy father's spirit,

10 Doomed for a certain term to walk the night

And for the day confined to fast° in fires   *do penance*

Till the foul crimes done in my days of nature°   *my natural life*

Are burnt and purged away. But that I am forbid

To tell the secrets of my prison house,

15 I could a tale unfold whose lightest word

Would harrow up° thy soul, freeze thy young blood,   *torment*

Make thy two eyes like stars start from their spheres,

Thy knotted and combinèd locks to part,

And each particular hair to stand on end

20 Like quills upon the fearful porcupine.

But this eternal blazon[1] must not be

To ears of flesh and blood. List,° list, oh, list.   *Listen*

If thou didst ever thy dear father love—

HAMLET   O God!

25 GHOST   Revenge his foul and most unnatural murder.

---

5. A ferocious beast killed by Hercules.   1. Catalogue or display of the afterlife's mysteries.

1.5 Location: Scene continues.

HAMLET   Murder?

GHOST   Murder most foul, as in the best it is,
But this most foul, strange, and unnatural.

HAMLET   Haste me to know't, that I with wings as swift

30   As meditation or the thoughts of love
May sweep to my revenge.

GHOST   I find thee apt,
And duller shouldst thou be than the fat° weed   *gross*
That roots itself[2] in ease on Lethe wharf,[3]
Wouldst thou not stir in this. Now, Hamlet, hear:

35   'Tis given out° that, sleeping in my orchard,   *It's being said*
A serpent stung me; so the whole ear of Denmark
Is by a forgèd process° of my death   *fabricated account*
Rankly abused.° But know, thou noble youth,   *deceived*
The serpent that did sting thy father's life

40   Now wears his crown.

HAMLET   Oh, my prophetic soul! My uncle!

GHOST   Ay, that incestuous, that adulterate° beast,   *adulterous*
With witchcraft of his wits, with traitorous gifts°—   *abilities; presents*
Oh, wicked wit and gifts that have the power

45   So to seduce!—won to his shameful lust
The will of my most seeming-virtuous queen.
O Hamlet, what falling off was there,
From me whose love was of that dignity
That it went hand in hand even with the vow

50   I made to her in marriage, and to decline°   *sink down*
Upon a wretch whose natural gifts were poor
To° those of mine.   *Compared to*
But virtue, as it never will be moved
Though lewdness court it in a shape of heaven,

55   So lust, though to a radiant angel linked,
Will sate itself[4] in a celestial bed
And prey on garbage.
But soft,[5] methinks I scent the morning air.
Brief let me be: sleeping within my orchard—

60   My custom always of the afternoon—
Upon my secure hour thy uncle stole
With juice of cursed hebona[6] in a vial
And in the porches° of my ears did pour   *entranceways*
The leprous distilment,[7] whose effect

65   Holds such an enmity with blood of man
That swift as quicksilver[8] it courses through
The natural gates and alleys of the body,
And with a sudden vigor it doth possess
And curd, like eager° droppings into milk,   *acid (like vinegar)*

70   The thin and wholesome blood. So did it mine,
And a most instant tetter° barked about,[9]   *scaly rash*
Most lazar-like,° with vile and loathsome crust   *leper-like*

---

2. F prints "rots itself," or decays under its own excessive growth.
3. In classical mythology, Lethe was the river of forgetfulness in Hades.
4. Will become satiated (and unable to find further
pleasure).
5. The Ghost urges himself quickly to wrap up his

speech.
6. A poison, possibly henbane.
7. Distillation causing skin to become scaly (as in
leprosy, a disease familiar in Elizabethan England).
8. Liquid mercury, noted for its capacity for rapid
motion.
9. Covered the body like bark.

All my smooth body.
Thus was I, sleeping, by a brother's hand
75 Of life, of crown, of queen at once dispatched,°   *deprived*
Cut off even in the blossoms of my sin,[1]
Unhouseled, disappointed, unaneled,[2]
No reck'ning made, but sent to my account
With all my imperfections on my head.[3]
80 Oh, horrible, oh, horrible, most horrible!
If thou hast nature° in thee, bear it° not;   *natural feeling / (this injustice)*
Let not the royal bed of Denmark be
A couch for luxury° and damned incest.   *lechery*
But howsomever° thou pursuest this act,   *however*
85 Taint not thy mind,[4] nor let thy soul contrive
Against thy mother aught;° leave her to heaven   *any (punishment)*
And to those thorns that in her bosom lodge
To prick and sting her. Fare thee well at once—
The glowworm shows the matin° to be near   *morning*
90 And 'gins° to pale his uneffectual fire.   *begins*
Adieu, adieu, adieu: remember me.   [*Exit.*]
HAMLET   O all you host of heaven! O earth! What else?
And shall I couple° hell? Oh, fie! Hold, hold, my heart,   *add*
And you, my sinews, grow not instant old,
95 But bear me swiftly up. Remember thee?
Ay, thou poor ghost, whiles memory holds a seat
In this distracted globe.[5] Remember thee?
Yea, from the table° of my memory   *tablet; book*
I'll wipe away all trivial fond° records,   *foolish*
100 All saws of books, all forms, all pressures past[6]
That youth and observation copied there,
And thy commandment all alone shall live
Within the book and volume of my brain
Unmixed with baser matter. Yes, by heaven!
105 O most pernicious woman!
O villain, villain, smiling damnèd villain—
My tables![7] Meet it is I set it down
That one may smile and smile and be a villain—
At least I am sure it may be so in Denmark.
    [*He writes.*]
110 So, uncle, there you are. Now to my word:°   *watchword; motto*
It is "Adieu, adieu, remember me."
I have sworn't.
    Enter HORATIO *and* MARCELLUS.
HORATIO   My lord, my lord!
MARCELLUS   Lord Hamlet!
HORATIO   Heavens secure him.
HAMLET   So be it.
115 MARCELLUS   Illo, ho, ho, my lord!

---

1. Cut off when my sins were full-blown, flourishing.
2. Without the sacrament of the Eucharist, without deathbed confession and absolution, and without extreme unction, the ritual anointing of those who are close to death.
3. *No . . . head:* Without having made restitution for my sins, but sent to the Last Judgment liable for all my faults.

4. Do not let yourself be corrupted.
5. Confused head; disordered world; often also taken as a reference to the Globe Theater and the audience.
6. All adages from books, all images or customs, all past impressions.
7. Scholars and others might carry two writing tablets hinged together, as a notebook.

HAMLET   Hillo, ho, ho, boy, come and come![8]
MARCELLUS   How is't, my noble lord?
HORATIO   What news, my lord?
HAMLET   Oh, wonderful!
120   HORATIO   Good my lord, tell it.
HAMLET   No, you will reveal it.
HORATIO   Not I, my lord, by heaven.
MARCELLUS   Nor I, my lord.
HAMLET   How say you, then, would heart of man once
    think it—
    But you'll be secret?
HORATIO *and* MARCELLUS   Ay, by heaven.
125   HAMLET   There's never a villain dwelling in all Denmark
    But he's an arrant° knave.   *a complete*
HORATIO   There needs no ghost, my lord, come from the grave
    To tell us this.
HAMLET   Why, right, you are in the right,
    And so without more circumstance° at all   *elaborate speech*
130   I hold it fit that we shake hands and part,
    You as your business and desire shall point you—
    For every man hath business and desire,
    Such as it is. And for my own poor part,
    I will go pray.
135   HORATIO   These are but wild and whirling words, my lord.
HAMLET   I am sorry they offend you. Heartily,
    Yes, faith, heartily.
HORATIO   There's no offense, my lord.
HAMLET   Yes, by Saint Patrick,[9] but there is, Horatio,
    And much offense too. Touching° this vision here,   *Concerning*
140   It is an honest° ghost, that let me tell you.   *a reliable; a genuine*
    For your desire to know what is between us,
    O'ermaster't as you may. And now, good friends,
    As you are friends, scholars, and soldiers,
    Give me one poor request.
145   HORATIO   What is't, my lord? We will.
HAMLET   Never make known what you have seen tonight.
HORATIO *and* MARCELLUS   My lord, we will not.
HAMLET   Nay, but swear't.
HORATIO   In faith, my lord, not I.[1]
MARCELLUS   Nor I, my lord, in faith.
HAMLET   Upon my sword.[2]
150   MARCELLUS   We have sworn, my lord, already.
HAMLET   Indeed, upon my sword, indeed.
GHOST (*cries under the stage*)   Swear.
HAMLET   Ha, ha, boy, say'st thou so? Art thou there,
    truepenny?°   *trusty fellow*
    Come on, you hear this fellow in the cellarage.°   *cellars*
    Consent to swear.
155   HORATIO   Propose the oath, my lord.
HAMLET   Never to speak of this that you have seen:
    Swear by my sword.

---

8. Hamlet parodies a falconer's call.   1. I will indeed not reveal it.
9. Perhaps because St. Patrick was thought to be keeper   2. Swearing on a sword was a fairly common practice
of purgatory.   because the hilt and blade form a cross.

GHOST [*under the stage*]   Swear.

HAMLET   *Hic et ubique?*[3] Then we'll shift our ground.
160   Come hither, gentlemen, and lay your hands
Again upon my sword. Swear by my sword
Never to speak of this that you have heard.

GHOST [*under the stage*]   Swear by his sword.

HAMLET   Well said, old mole: canst work i'th' earth so fast?
165   A worthy pioneer![4] —Once more remove,° good friends.   move

HORATIO   O day and night, but this is wondrous strange.

HAMLET   And therefore as a stranger give it welcome.[5]
There are more things in heaven and earth, Horatio,
Than are dreamt of in your philosophy.[6] But come,
170   Here, as before, never, so help you mercy,
How strange or odd some'er° I bear myself—   so ever
As I perchance hereafter shall think meet
To put an antic disposition on[7]—
That you at such times seeing me, never shall
175   With arms encumbered° thus, or this head-shake,   folded
Or by pronouncing of some doubtful° phrase,   ambiguous
As "Well, well, we know," or "We could an if° we would,"   an if = if
Or "If we list° to speak," or "There be an if they might,"[8]   liked
Or such ambiguous giving out, to note
180   That you know aught° of me[9]   anything
180.1   —*This not to do,*
So grace and mercy at your most need help you,
181.1   *Swear.*

GHOST [*under the stage*]   Swear.
[*They swear.*]

HAMLET   Rest, rest, perturbèd spirit. —So, gentlemen,
With all my love I do commend me to you,
185   And what so poor a man as Hamlet is
May do t'express his love and friending° to you,   friendship
God willing shall not lack.° Let us go in together—   be left undone
And still° your fingers on your lips, I pray.   always
The time is out of joint:° oh, cursèd spite   dislocated; disordered
190   That ever I was born to set it right.
Nay, come,[1] let's go together.   *Exeunt.*

2.1

Enter old POLONIUS, *with his man* [REYNALDO] *or two.*

POLONIUS   Give him this money and these notes, Reynaldo.

REYNALDO   I will, my lord.

POLONIUS   You shall do marv'lous wisely, good Reynaldo,
Before you visit him, to make inquire
Of his behavior.

5   REYNALDO   My lord, I did intend it.

POLONIUS   Marry, well said, very well said. Look you, sir:
Inquire me° first what Danskers° are in Paris,   for me / Danes

3. Here and everywhere (Latin).
4. Army trench digger.
5. As if it had a guest's right to courteous hospitality.
6. Human speculative knowledge; science. F prints "our philosophy."
7. To assume the behavior of a madman.
8. There are those who would speak if they were allowed.
9. Lines 180.1 and 181.1 are found only in F. Q2 reads: "This do swear, / So grace and mercy . . . ."
1. The others are politely waiting for Hamlet, the Prince, to lead the way; he insists on informality.
2.1 Location: Polonius's apartments in the castle.

And how, and who, what means,° and where they keep,°   *wealth; income / lodge*
What company, at what expense, and finding
10 By this encompassment and drift of question[1]
That they do know my son, come you more nearer
Than your particular demands will touch it.[2]
Take you° as 'twere some distant knowledge of him,   *Pretend*
As thus, "I know his father and his friends
15 And in part him." Do you mark this, Reynaldo?
REYNALDO   Ay, very well, my lord.
POLONIUS   "And in part him, but," you may say, "not well;
But if't be he I mean, he's very wild,
Addicted so and so," and there put on him°   *attribute to him*
20 What forgeries° you please—marry, none so rank[3]   *made-up tales*
As may dishonor him, take heed of that—
But, sir, such wanton,° wild, and usual slips   *unrestrained*
As are companions noted and most known
To youth and liberty.
REYNALDO   As gaming, my lord?
25 POLONIUS   Ay, or drinking, fencing, swearing,
Quarreling, drabbing°—you may go so far.   *whoring*
REYNALDO   My lord, that would dishonor him.
POLONIUS   Faith, as you may season° it in the charge.   *mitigate*
You must not put another scandal on him
30 That he is open° to incontinency;°   *inclined / sexual excess*
That's not my meaning. But breathe his faults so quaintly
That they may seem the taints of liberty,[4]
The flash and outbreak of a fiery mind,
A savageness in unreclaimèd° blood   *unchecked*
Of general assault.[5]
35 REYNALDO   But my good lord—
POLONIUS   Wherefore should you do this?
REYNALDO   Ay, my lord,
I would know that.
POLONIUS   Marry, sir, here's my drift—
And I believe it is a fetch of wit[6]—
You laying these slight sallies on my son,
40 As 'twere a thing a little soiled with working,[7]
Mark you, your party° in converse, him you would sound,°   *partner / sound out*
Having° ever seen in the prenominate crimes[8]   *If he has*
The youth you breathe of guilty, be assured
He closes° with you in this consequence:[9]   *confides*
45 "Good sir," or so, or "Friend," or "Gentleman,"
According to the phrase° or the addition[1]   *expression*
Of man and country—
REYNALDO   Very good, my lord.
POLONIUS   And then, sir, does 'a° this: 'a does—   *he*
What was I about to say? By the mass, I was about to say

---

1. By this roundabout and indirect way of inquiry.
2. *come . . . it:* you will come closer to the truth than by direct questions.
3. Excessive; foul.
4. Faults resulting from freedom of action.
5. That afflicts all young men.
6. *fetch of wit:* clever scheme. F has "fetch of war-

rant," or justifiable trick.
7. Stained by education in the ways of the world, "shop soiled."
8. Aforesaid faults.
9. To the following effect.
1. Title of address.

50 something—where did I leave?[2]
REYNALDO   At "closes in the consequence."
POLONIUS   At "closes in the consequence"—ay, marry.
He closes thus: "I know the gentleman,
I saw him yesterday"—or "th'other day,"
55 Or then, or then, with such or such°—"and as you say,   *such and such*
There was 'a gaming, there o'ertook in 's rouse,
There falling out° at tennis," or perchance   *quarreling*
"I saw him enter such a house of sale,"
Videlicet,° a brothel, or so forth. See you now,   *That is to say (Latin)*
60 Your bait of falsehood take this carp of truth,
And thus do we of wisdom and of reach°   *wide understanding*
With windlasses and with assays of bias[3]
By indirections find directions° out.   *real tendencies*
So by my former° lecture and advice   *preceding*
65 Shall you my son.[4] You have me,[5] have you not?
REYNALDO   My lord, I have.
POLONIUS   God b'wi'ye, fare ye well.
REYNALDO   Good my lord.
POLONIUS   Observe his inclination in° yourself.   *for*
REYNALDO   I shall, my lord.
POLONIUS   And let him ply° his music.   *work at*
70 REYNALDO   Well, my lord.
POLONIUS   Farewell.   *Exit* REYNALDO.
          Enter OPHELIA.
                              How now, Ophelia, what's the matter?
OPHELIA   O my lord, my lord, I have been so affrighted!
POLONIUS   With what, i'th' name of God?
OPHELIA   My lord, as I was sewing in my closet,°   *private chamber*
75 Lord Hamlet, with his doublet all unbraced,°   *jacket all unfastened*
No hat upon his head, his stockings fouled,
Ungartered, and down-gyvèd to his ankle,[6]
Pale as his shirt, his knees knocking each other,
And with a look so piteous in purport
80 As if he had been loosèd out of hell
To speak of horrors, he comes before me.
POLONIUS   Mad for thy love?
OPHELIA   My lord, I do not know,
But truly I do fear it.
POLONIUS   What said he?
OPHELIA   He took me by the wrist and held me hard,
85 Then goes he to the length of all his arm
And with his other hand thus o'er his brow,
He falls to such perusal of my face
As 'a° would draw it. Long stayed he so;   *As if he*
At last, a little shaking of mine arm
90 And thrice his head thus waving up and down,
He raised a sigh so piteous and profound
As it did seem to shatter all his bulk

---

2. PERFORMANCE COMMENT Productions can indicate quite different reasons for Polonius's forgetfulness, affecting the reception of the character and, sometimes, the stability of the dramatic experience. See Digital Edition PC 3.
3. And with indirect tests, like the curved line, or "bias," that a weighted bowling ball describes. *wind-*

lasses: roundabout paths (a hunter's circuit to intercept game).
4. And so shall you figure out what my son has been doing.
5. You get my meaning.
6. Fallen round his ankles, like a prisoner's fetters, or "gyves."

Say, Voltemand, what from our brother° Norway?   *fellow monarch*

60 VOLTEMAND   Most fair return of greetings and desires.°   *good wishes*

Upon our first,[8] he sent out to suppress

His nephew's levies,° which to him appeared   *raising of troops*

To be a preparation 'gainst the Polack,°   *King of Poland*

But, better looked into, he truly found

65 It was against your highness; whereat, grieved

That so his sickness, age, and impotence

Was falsely borne in hand,[9] sends out arrests

On Fortinbras,[1] which he in brief obeys,

Receives rebuke from Norway, and, in fine,°   *in the end*

70 Makes vow before his uncle never more

To give th'assay of arms[2] against your majesty.

Whereon old Norway, overcome with joy,

Gives him threescore thousand crowns in annual fee°   *income*

And his commission to employ those soldiers,

75 So levied as before, against the Polack,

With an entreaty herein further shown

That it might please you to give quiet pass

Through your dominions for this enterprise

On such regards of safety and allowance[3]

As therein are set down.

80 KING   It likes° us well,   *pleases*

And at our more considered° time we'll read,   *suitable for thought*

Answer, and think upon this business.

Meantime, we thank you for your well-took labor.

Go to your rest; at night we'll feast together.

Most welcome home.

            Exeunt Ambassadors [VOLTEMAND *and* CORNELIUS].

85 POLONIUS   This business is well ended.

My liege and madam, to expostulate°   *discuss; dilate*

What majesty should be, what duty is,

Why day is day, night night, and time is time,

Were nothing but to waste night, day, and time;

90 Therefore brevity is the soul of wit

And tediousness the limbs and outward flourishes.°   *rhetorical devices*

I will be brief. Your noble son is mad—

Mad call I it, for to define true madness,

What is't but to be nothing else but mad?

But let that go.

95 QUEEN   More matter with less art.

POLONIUS   Madam, I swear I use no art at all.

That he's mad 'tis true; 'tis true, 'tis pity,

And pity 'tis 'tis true—a foolish figure,°   *figure of speech*

But farewell it, for I will use no art.

100 Mad let us grant him, then, and now remains

That we find out the cause of this effect—

Or rather say the cause of this defect,

For this effect defective[4] comes by cause.

---

8. When we first raised the matter.
9. Disloyally taken advantage of; tricked.
1. *arrests / On Fortinbras:* orders commanding Fortinbras to stop his preparations and (presumably) present himself to explain them.

2. To mount a military challenge.
3. *On . . . allowance:* Following conditions regarding your realm's safety, subject to your approval.
4. This consequence shows a lack of something (Hamlet's reason).

Thus it remains, and the remainder thus:
105 Perpend.°   *Consider*
I have a daughter—have while she is mine°—   *until she marries*
Who in her duty and obedience, mark,
Hath given me this. Now gather and surmise:
[*Reads.*] "To the celestial and my soul's idol, the most beauti-
110 fied Ophelia"—that's an ill phrase, a vile phrase—"beautified"
is a vile phrase. But you shall hear—thus: "in her excellent
white bosom, these—" etc.
QUEEN   Came this from Hamlet to her?
POLONIUS   Good madam, stay° awhile; I will be faithful.[5]   *wait*
115 [*Reads.*] "Doubt thou the stars are fire,
        Doubt that the sun doth move,
        Doubt° truth to be a liar,   *Suspect*
        But never doubt I love.
O dear Ophelia, I am ill at these numbers.[6] I have not art to
120 reckon my groans,[7] but that I love thee best—oh, most best—
believe it. Adieu. Thine evermore, most dear lady, whilst this
machine is° to him, Hamlet."   *this body belongs*
This in obedience hath my daughter shown me,
And, more above,° hath his solicitings   *in addition*
125 As they fell out° by time, by means, and place,   *occurred*
All given to mine ear.
KING   But how hath she
Received his love?
POLONIUS   What do you think of me?
KING   As of a man faithful and honorable.
POLONIUS   I would fain° prove so. But what might you think,   *be glad to*
130 When I had seen this hot love on the wing—
As I perceived it (I must tell you that)
Before my daughter told me—what might you
Or my dear majesty, your queen here, think,
If I had played the desk or table-book,[8]
135 Or given my heart a working mute and dumb,[9]
Or looked upon this love with idle sight—
What might you think? No, I went round° to work,   *directly*
And my young mistress thus I did bespeak:°   *address*
"Lord Hamlet is a prince out of thy star.°   *above your sphere*
140 This must not be." And then I prescripts° gave her   *instructions*
That she should lock herself from his resort,°   *visits*
Admit no messengers, receive no tokens.
Which done, she took the fruits of my advice
And he, repelled—a short tale to make—
145 Fell into a sadness, then into a fast,
Thence to a watch,° thence into a weakness,   *an insomnia*
Thence to lightness,° and by this declension°   *dizziness / decline*
Into the madness wherein now he raves
And all we° mourn for.   *of us*
KING   Do you think this?
150 QUEEN   It may be, very like.

---

5. I will accurately read out the letter's contents.
6. I.e., I am inept at writing verse.
7. Count my groans; also, number my groans metrically.
8. If I had recorded the perception (in my memory) but kept it hidden.
9. Or made my heart effectively mute.

POLONIUS   Hath there been such a time—I would fain know
    that—
That I have positively said, "'Tis so"
When it proved otherwise?
KING   Not that I know.
POLONIUS [*indicating his head and torso*]   Take this from this,
    if this be otherwise.

155 If circumstances lead me, I will find
Where truth is hid, though it were hid indeed
Within the center.°   *middle of the earth*
KING   How may we try° it further?   *test*
POLONIUS   You know sometimes he walks four hours together
Here in the lobby.
QUEEN   So he does indeed.
160 POLONIUS   At such a time, I'll loose my daughter to him.
Be you and I behind an arras;° then   *a wall tapestry*
Mark the encounter—if he love her not
And be not from his reason fallen thereon,°   *on that account*
Let me be no assistant for a state
But keep a farm and carters.°   *wagon drivers*
165 KING   We will try it.
         Enter HAMLET.
QUEEN   But look where sadly° the poor wretch comes   *gravely*
    reading.
POLONIUS   Away, I do beseech you both, away.
I'll board him presently;° oh, give me leave.[1]   *accost him immediately*
        Exeunt KING *and* QUEEN [*and Attendants*].
How does my good lord Hamlet?
170 HAMLET   Well, God ha' mercy.[2]
POLONIUS   Do you know me, my lord?
HAMLET   Excellent well—you are a fishmonger.
POLONIUS   Not I, my lord.
HAMLET   Then I would you were so honest a man.
175 POLONIUS   Honest, my lord?
HAMLET   Ay, sir, to be honest as this world goes is to be one
    man picked out of ten thousand.
POLONIUS   That's very true, my lord.
HAMLET   For if the sun breed maggots in a dead dog, being a
180   good kissing carrion[3]—have you a daughter?
POLONIUS   I have, my lord.
HAMLET   Let her not walk i'th' sun.[4] Conception[5] is a blessing,
    but as your daughter may conceive, friend—look to't.°   *take care*
POLONIUS [*aside*]   How say you by that? Still harping on my
185   daughter. Yet he knew me not at first: 'a° said I was a fishmon-   *he*
    ger. 'A is far gone—and truly in my youth I suffered much
    extremity for love, very near this. I'll speak to him again.
    —What do you read, my lord?
HAMLET   Words, words, words.
190 POLONIUS   What is the matter,[6] my lord?
HAMLET   Between who?

---

1. Excuse me (politely asking the King and Queen to
leave).
2. Thank you (used with inferiors).
3. Piece of flesh good for kissing. Dead matter was
thought to breed maggots, especially in sunlight.

4. Walk out in public.
5. The ability to form ideas; pregnancy.
6. Content, although Hamlet deliberately takes it as
"subject of a quarrel."

POLONIUS   I mean the matter that you read, my lord.

HAMLET   Slanders, sir, for the satirical rogue says here that
old men have gray beards, that their faces are wrinkled, their
195 eyes purging° thick amber° and plumtree gum, and that they   *discharging / resin*
have a plentiful lack of wit° together with most weak hams.°   *intellect / thighs*
All which, sir, though I most powerfully and potently believe,[7]
yet I hold it not honesty° to have it thus set down. For your-   *honorable*
self, sir, shall grow old as I am, if like a crab you could go
200 backward.

POLONIUS   [aside] Though this be madness, yet there is
method in't. —Will you walk out of the air,[8] my lord?

HAMLET   Into my grave.

POLONIUS   Indeed, that's out of the air. [aside] How pregnant°   *meaningful*
205 sometimes his replies are—a happiness° that often madness   *an appropriateness*
hits on, which reason and sanctity[9] could not so prosperously°   *successfully*
be delivered of. I will leave him and[1]
207.1   *suddenly° contrive the means of meeting between him*   *immediately*
        and
my daughter. —My lord, I will take my leave of you.

HAMLET   You cannot take from me anything that I will not
210 more willingly part withal°—except my life, except my life,   *with*
except my life.

POLONIUS   Fare you well, my lord.

HAMLET   These tedious old fools.

Enter GUILDENSTERN *and* ROSENCRANTZ.

POLONIUS   You go to seek the Lord Hamlet? There he is.

215 ROSENCRANTZ   [to POLONIUS]   God save you, sir.

                              [*Exit* POLONIUS.]

GUILDENSTERN   My honored lord.

ROSENCRANTZ   My most dear lord.

HAMLET   My excellent good friends! How dost thou, Guildenstern? Ah, Rosencrantz! Good lads, how do you both?

220 ROSENCRANTZ   As the indifferent° children of the earth.   *ordinary*

GUILDENSTERN   Happy° in that we are not ever° happy—   *Fortunate / perpetually*
on Fortune's cap we are not the very button.°   *highest point*

HAMLET   Nor the soles of her shoe.

ROSENCRANTZ   Neither, my lord.

225 HAMLET   Then you live about her waist or in the middle of her
favors.

GUILDENSTERN   Faith, her privates[2] we.

HAMLET   In the secret parts of Fortune? Oh, most true, she is
a strumpet.° What news?   *whore*

230 ROSENCRANTZ   None, my lord, but the world's grown honest.

HAMLET   Then is doomsday near—but your news is not true.[3]

231.1   *Let me question more in particular: what have you, my*
        good friends, deserved at the hands of Fortune that she
        sends you to prison hither?

        GUILDENSTERN   *Prison, my lord?*

231.5   HAMLET   *Denmark's a prison.*

---

7. TEXTUAL COMMENT Q1 7.216 reads "believe not,"
which covers the sarcasm with superficial politeness.
See Digital Edition TC 3 (combined text).
8. Outdoor air was regarded as a hazard for the sick;
Polonius may mean "out of the drafts," since the
scene seems to be set indoors.
9. *sanctity*: virtue. F has "sanity."
1. F has the following lines, 207.1–207.2, not found

in Q2.
2. A triple pun: private persons holding no office;
intimate friends; private parts, genitalia.
3. TEXTUAL COMMENT The following passage (231.1–
231.30) occurs only in F. Its denigration of Denmark
leads some to believe that it is a missed cut rather than
an addition. See Digital Edition TC 4 (combined text).

ROSENCRANTZ *Then is the world one.*

HAMLET *A goodly*[4] *one, in which there are many confines,°*   *enclosures*
wards,° and dungeons, Denmark being one o'th' worst.   *cells*

ROSENCRANTZ *We think not so, my lord.*

231.10   HAMLET *Why, then 'tis none to you, for there is nothing*
either good or bad but thinking makes it so. To me it is a
prison.

ROSENCRANTZ *Why, then your ambition makes it one—*
'tis too narrow for your mind.

231.15   HAMLET *O God, I could be bounded in a nutshell and*
count myself a king of infinite space, were it not that I
have bad dreams.

GUILDENSTERN *Which dreams indeed are ambition: for*
the very substance of the ambitious is merely the shadow

231.20   *of a dream.*

HAMLET *A dream itself is but a shadow.*

ROSENCRANTZ *Truly, and I hold ambition of so airy and*
light a quality that it is but a shadow's shadow.

HAMLET *Then are our beggars bodies, and our monarchs*

231.25   *and outstretched heroes the beggars' shadows.*[5] *Shall*
we to th' court? For, by my fay,° I cannot reason.   *faith*

ROSENCRANTZ *and* GUILDENSTERN *We'll wait upon° you.*   *accompany*

HAMLET *No such matter.° I will not sort° you with the*   *Certainly not / class*
rest of my servants, for, to speak to you like an honest

231.30   *man, I am most dreadfully attended.°*   *waited upon*
But in the beaten way[6] of friendship, what make you° at   *are you doing*
Elsinore?

ROSENCRANTZ To visit you, my lord, no other occasion.

235   HAMLET Beggar that I am, I am ever poor in thanks, but I
thank you, and sure, dear friends, my thanks are too dear a
halfpenny.[7] Were you not sent for? Is it your own inclining?
Is it a free° visitation? Come, come, deal justly with me.   *voluntary*
Come, come, nay, speak.

240   GUILDENSTERN What should we say, my lord?

HAMLET Anything, but to th' purpose: you were sent for, and
there is a kind of confession in your looks which your mod-
esties[8] have not craft enough to color.° I know the good King   *disguise*
and Queen have sent for you.

245   ROSENCRANTZ To what end, my lord?

HAMLET That you must teach me. But let me conjure° you, by   *solemnly request*
the rights of our fellowship, by the consonancy° of our youth,   *harmonious friendship*
by the obligation of our ever-preserved love, and by what more
dear a better proposer can charge you withal, be even° and   *level*

250   direct with me whether you were sent for or no.

ROSENCRANTZ [*to* GUILDENSTERN] What say you?

HAMLET [*aside*] Nay, then, I have an eye of° you. —If you love   *on*
me, hold not off.

GUILDENSTERN My lord, we were sent for.

255   HAMLET I will tell you why—so shall my anticipation pre-

---

4. Spacious; fine.

5. *Then . . . shadows:* Then beggars, being without
ambition, are not shadows but have substance; if
monarchs and heroes (who ambitiously "stretch" too
far) are shadows and only substantial bodies can cast
shadows, they must be the beggars' shadows.

6. Well-worn track (plain words).

7. Too expensive at a halfpenny (not worth a halfpenny); perhaps also, too expensive by a halfpenny for
me to give in return for such worthless information.

8. Senses of decency.

310   hearer. That great baby you see there is not yet out of his
       swaddling clouts.°   *clothes*

ROSENCRANTZ   Happily° he is the second time come to them,   *Perhaps*
       for they say an old man is twice a child.

HAMLET   I will prophesy he comes to tell me of the players;
315   mark it. —You say right, sir, o'Monday morning, 'twas then
       indeed.

POLONIUS   My lord, I have news to tell you.

HAMLET   My lord, I have news to tell you: when Roscius[6] was
       an actor in Rome—

320 POLONIUS   The actors are come hither, my lord.

HAMLET   Buzz, buzz.[7]

POLONIUS   Upon my honor—

HAMLET   Then came each actor on his ass—

POLONIUS   The best actors in the world, either for tragedy, com-
325   edy, history, pastoral, pastoral-comical, historical-pastoral,[8]
325.1   *tragical-historical, tragical-comical-historical-pastoral,*
       scene individable[9] or poem unlimited.[1] Seneca cannot be
       too heavy, nor Plautus too light.[2] For the law of writ and the
       liberty,[3] these are the only men.

HAMLET   O Jephthah, judge of Israel, what a treasure hadst
330   thou![4]

POLONIUS   What a treasure had he, my lord?

HAMLET   Why,
[*Sings.*]   One fair daughter and no more,
              The which he lovèd passing° well.   *surpassingly*

335 POLONIUS [*aside*]   Still on my daughter.

HAMLET   Am I not i'th' right, old Jephthah?

POLONIUS   If you call me Jephthah, my lord, I have a daughter
       that I love passing well.

HAMLET   Nay, that follows not.[5]

340 POLONIUS   What follows then, my lord?

HAMLET   Why,
           As by lot,° God wot.°   *chance / knows*
    And then you know
           It came to pass, as most like° it was—   *probable*
345   The first row° of the pious chanson° will show you more, for   *stanza / ballad*
       look where my abridgment[6] comes.
       Enter the PLAYERS.
    You are welcome, masters, welcome all. I am glad to see thee
    well. Welcome, good friends; O old friend, why, thy face is
    valanced[7] since I saw thee last. Com'st thou to beard° me in   *defy*
350   Denmark? What, my young lady and mistress![8] By'r Lady,
    your ladyship is nearer to heaven than when I saw you last by

6. The most famous ancient Roman actor, a rather
dated news item.
7. A response to stale news.
8. F has the following line, 325.1, not found in Q2.
9. Probably, play with no breaks in performance, or
play observing the unity of place (and presumably the
other classical unities). Shakespeare parodies the
classifications of contemporary dramatic theorists.
1. (Dramatic) poem unrestricted by classical rules.
2. The best-known Roman playwrights, masters of
tragedy and comedy, respectively.
3. For plays where classical rules are either observed

or abandoned.
4. Jephthah vowed that if he defeated the Ammo-
nites, he would sacrifice the first living thing he saw
on his return. He won, and his daughter became the
sacrificial victim (Judges 11). *Jephthah, Judge of Israel*
was the title of a popular ballad, the "pious chanson"
from which Hamlet subsequently sings.
5. Polonius's having a daughter is not a logical consequence of Hamlet's calling him Jephthah.
6. Those who cut me short; also, entertainment.
7. Fringed (with beard).
8. The boy who played female roles.

the altitude of a chopine;° pray God your voice, like a piece of   *high platform shoe*
uncurrent gold, be not cracked within the ring.[9] Masters,
you are all welcome. We'll e'en to't like French falconers,[1] fly
355   at anything we see. We'll have a speech straight°—come, give   *right away*
us a taste of your quality.° Come, a passionate speech.   *professional skill*

FIRST PLAYER   What speech, my good lord?

HAMLET   I heard thee speak me a speech once, but it was
never acted, or if it was, not above once, for the play I
360   remember pleased not the million—'twas caviar to the general;° but it was, as I received it, and others whose judgments   *populace*
in such matters cried in the top of[2] mine, an excellent play,
well digested° in the scenes, set down with as much mod-   *organized*
esty° as cunning. I remember one said there were no salads[3]   *restraint*
365   in the lines to make the matter savory, nor no matter in the
phrase that might indict the author of affection,° but called it   *affectedness*
an honest method, as wholesome as sweet, and by very much
more handsome than fine.[4] One speech in't I chiefly loved:
'twas Aeneas' talk to Dido, and thereabout of it especially
370   when he speaks of Priam's slaughter.[5] If it live in your memory, begin at this line—let me see, let me see,
    "The rugged° Pyrrhus[6] like th' Hyrcanian beast"°—   *savage / tiger*
'Tis not so. It begins with Pyrrhus—
    "The rugged Pyrrhus, he whose sable° arms,   *black*
375   Black as his purpose, did the night resemble
When he lay couchèd° in th'ominous horse,[7]   *hidden*
Hath now this dread and black complexion° smeared   *appearance*
With heraldry° more dismal: head to foot   *heraldic colors*
Now is he total gules,° horridly tricked°   *all red / inked over*
380   With blood of fathers, mothers, daughters, sons,
Baked and impasted with° the parching° streets   *encrusted by / fiery*
That lend a tyrannous and a damnèd light
To their lord's murder. Roasted in wrath and fire
And thus o'ersizèd[8] with coagulate gore,
385   With eyes like carbuncles,[9] the hellish Pyrrhus
Old grandsire Priam seeks."
So, proceed you.

POLONIUS   Fore God, my lord, well spoken, with good accent
and good discretion.
390   FIRST PLAYER   "Anon° he finds him,   *Soon*
Striking too short at Greeks. His antique sword,
Rebellious to his arm, lies where it falls,
Repugnant° to command. Unequal matched,   *Resistant*
Pyrrhus at Priam drives, in rage strikes wide,
395   But with the whiff and wind of his fell° sword   *fierce*
Th'unnervèd° father falls. Then senseless Ilium,[1]   *strengthless*

9. A coin was no longer legal tender if the circle or
ring enclosing the monarch's head was broken (by
"clipping," or trimming off small amounts of gold).
1. We'll go to work at once. (French falconers seem to
have been regarded as experts, willing to try any
potential prey.)
2. *cried . . . of*: outweighed.
3. Seasoned dishes. I.e., deliberate attempts to vary
or embellish the style in order to make the lines more
pleasing ("savory").
4. Beautifully crafted rather than showy.
5. The murder of the Trojan king Priam, at the end

of the Trojan War; adapted from Virgil's *Aeneid*, possibly via Christopher Marlowe's *Dido, Queen of Carthage*. Aeneas recounts the story of Priam's slaughter
to his beloved, Dido.
6. Also known as Neoptolemus, he came to Troy to
avenge the death of his father, the Greek hero
Achilles.
7. The Trojan horse, full of Greek warriors.
8. As though coated with sizing, the thick liquid
used to prepare a canvas for painting.
9. Gems supposed to glow with their own light.
1. The citadel of Troy.

    Seeming to feel this blow, with flaming top
    Stoops to his° base and with a hideous crash   *its*
    Takes prisoner Pyrrhus' ear: for lo, his sword,
400   Which was declining° on the milky° head   *descending / white*
    Of reverend Priam, seemed i'th' air to stick.
    So as a painted tyrant[2] Pyrrhus stood
    Like a neutral to his will and matter,[3]
    Did nothing.
405   But as we often see against° some storm   *before*
    A silence in the heavens, the rack° stand still,   *cloud banks*
    The bold winds speechless, and the orb° below   *earth*
    As hush as death, anon the dreadful thunder
    Doth rend the region,° so after Pyrrhus' pause   *sky*
410   A rousèd vengeance sets him new a-work,
    And never did the Cyclops'[4] hammers fall
    On Mars's armor, forged for proof eterne,[5]
    With less remorse° than Pyrrhus' bleeding sword   *pity; hesitation*
    Now falls on Priam.
415   Out, out, thou strumpet Fortune! All you gods
    In general synod, take away her power,
    Break all the spokes and fellies from her wheel[6]
    And bowl the round nave° down the hill of heaven°   *wheel hub / Mount Olympus*
    As low as to the fiends."
420 POLONIUS   This is too long.
  HAMLET   It shall to the barber's with your beard.°   —Prithee   *It shall be cut short*
    say on; he's for a jig[7] or a tale of bawdry, or he sleeps. Say on;
    come to Hecuba.
  FIRST PLAYER   "But who, ah woe, had seen the mobled°   *veiled; muffled*
    Queen—"
425 HAMLET   "The mobled Queen"!
  POLONIUS   That's good.
  FIRST PLAYER   "—Run barefoot up and down, threat'ning the
    flames
    With bisson rheum,° a clout° upon that head   *blinding tears / cloth*
    Where late the diadem stood, and for a robe
430   About her lank and all-o'erteemèd[8] loins
    A blanket in the alarm of fear caught up—
    Who this had seen, with tongue in venom steeped,
    'Gainst Fortune's state° would treason have pronounced.   *rule*
    But if the gods themselves did see her then,
435   When she saw Pyrrhus make malicious sport
    In mincing with his sword her husband limbs,
    The instant burst of clamor that she made,
    Unless things mortal move them not at all,
    Would have made milch° the burning eyes of heaven   *milky; moist*
440   And passion° in the gods."   *suffering; pity*
  POLONIUS   Look where° he has not turned his color and has   *whether*
    tears in 's eyes! —Prithee, no more.

---

2. Tyrant depicted in a painting and so incapable of moving.
3. As one indifferent toward his intention and the action at hand.
4. The three one-eyed giants who served as armorers to the classical gods and heroes.
5. To remain impenetrable forever.
6. The power of Fortune's ever-turning wheel, rais-ing and lowering men in succession, was proverbial. *fellies:* curved sections of a wooden wheel rim.
7. A ridiculous piece of poetry, or the dance that fol-lowed many plays (unrelated to the drama).
8. Completely worn out with childbearing. (Hecuba was supposed to have borne seventeen or more children.)

HAMLET [*to* FIRST PLAYER] 'Tis well. I'll have thee speak out
the rest of this soon. [*to* POLONIUS] Good my lord, will you
445   see the players well bestowed?° Do you hear, let them be   *lodged*
well used,° for they are the abstract° and brief chronicles of   *treated / summary*
the time; after your death you were better have a bad epi-
taph than their ill report while you live.
POLONIUS   My lord, I will use them according to their desert.
450   HAMLET   God's bodkin,° man, much better! Use every man   *By God's dear body*
after° his desert and who shall scape whipping? Use them   *according to*
after your own honor and dignity—the less they deserve the
more merit is in your bounty. Take them in.
POLONIUS   Come, sirs.
455   HAMLET   Follow him, friends; we'll hear a play tomorrow.
[*As* POLONIUS *leads the* PLAYERS *off,* HAMLET *speaks*
aside to the FIRST PLAYER.]
Dost thou hear me, old friend—can you play *The Murder of*
Gonzago?
FIRST PLAYER   Ay, my lord.
HAMLET   We'll ha't° tomorrow night. You could, for need,°   *have it / if necessary*
460   study a speech of some dozen lines or sixteen lines which I
would set down and insert in't, could you not?
FIRST PLAYER   Ay, my lord.
HAMLET   Very well. Follow that lord, and look you mock
him not.   [*Exit* FIRST PLAYER.]
465   [*to* ROSENCRANTZ *and* GUILDENSTERN] My good friends, I'll
leave you till night. You are welcome to Elsinore.
ROSENCRANTZ   Good my lord.
HAMLET   Ay so, good-bye to you.
Exeunt [ROSENCRANTZ *and* GUILDENSTERN].
Now I am alone.
Oh, what a rogue and peasant slave am I!
470   Is it not monstrous that this player here,
But° in a fiction, in a dream of passion,   *Merely*
Could force his soul so to his own conceit[9]
That from her° working all the° visage wanned,°   *(the soul's) / his / grew pale*
Tears in his eyes, distraction in his aspect,
475   A broken voice, and his whole function suiting
With forms to his conceit?[1] And all for nothing!
For Hecuba!
What's Hecuba to him or he to her
That he should weep for her? What would he do
480   Had he the motive and that for passion
That I have? He would drown the stage with tears
And cleave the general ear[2] with horrid speech,
Make mad the guilty and appall the free,°   *innocent*
Confound the ignorant and amaze° indeed   *bewilder*
485   The very faculties of eyes and ears. Yet I,
A dull and muddy-mettled° rascal, peak°   *dull-spirited / mope*
Like John-a-dreams,° unpregnant of[3] my cause,   *a sleepy idler*
And can say nothing—no, not for a King

9. Could make his innermost being conform so well   in outward accord with his imagination.
with his imagined situation.   2. The ears of people generally.
1. *his whole . . . conceit:* the action of his whole body   3. Not quickened into action by.

Upon whose property° and most dear life   *rightful sovereignty*
490   A damned defeat[4] was made. Am I a coward?
Who calls me villain, breaks my pate° across,   *head*
Plucks off my beard and blows it in my face,
Tweaks me by the nose, gives me the lie i'th' throat
As deep as to the lungs?[5] Who does me this?
495   Ha? 'Swounds,° I should take it, for it cannot be   *By God's wounds*
But I am pigeon-livered and lack gall[6]
To make oppression bitter, or ere this
I should've fatted all the region kites[7]
With this slave's offal. Bloody, bawdy villain!
500   Remorseless, treacherous, lecherous, kindless° villain![8]   *unnatural*
500.1   *Oh, vengeance!*
Why, what an ass am I! This is most brave,°   *fine*
That I, the son of a dear murdered,°   *the dear murdered man*
Prompted to my revenge by heaven and hell,
Must like a whore unpack my heart with words
505   And fall a-cursing like a very drab,°   *whore*
A stallion![9] Fie upon't, foh!
About,° my brains! Hmm—I have heard   *Into action*
That guilty creatures sitting at a play
Have by the very cunning° of the scene   *artfulness*
510   Been struck so to the soul that presently°   *immediately*
They have proclaimed their malefactions.
For murder, though it have no tongue, will speak
With most miraculous organ. I'll have these players
Play something like the murder of my father
515   Before mine uncle. I'll observe his looks;
I'll tent° him to the quick. If 'a° do blench,   *probe (a wound) / he*
I know my course. The spirit that I have seen
May be a dev'l, and the dev'l hath power
T'assume a pleasing shape; yea, and perhaps
520   Out of my weakness and my melancholy,
As he is very potent with such spirits,[1]
Abuses° me to damn me. I'll have grounds   *Deceives*
More relative° than this. The play's the thing   *relevant*
Wherein I'll catch the conscience of the King.   *Exit.*

3.1

Enter KING, QUEEN, POLONIUS, OPHELIA,
ROSENCRANTZ, [*and*] GUILDENSTERN.[1]
KING   And can you by no drift of conference[2]
Get from him why he puts on this confusion,
Grating so harshly all his days of quiet
With turbulent and dangerous lunacy?

4. An act of overthrow worthy of damnation.
5. *gives . . . lungs:* calls me a thoroughgoing liar.
6. Pigeons were thought not to secrete gall, a bitter fluid produced by the liver and the supposed source of anger.
7. All the kites (birds of prey) in the sky ("region").
8. F has the following line, 500.1, not found in Q2.
9. *stallion:* a male prostitute. F has "scullion," a menial kitchen servant.
1. *Out of . . . spirits:* It was thought that those afflicted with too much black bile, a humor (fluid) or "spirit" (distillation), became melancholy and subject to hallu-

cinations, which in turn made them easily tricked by the devil. *potent with:* powerful over.
3.1 Location: The castle.
1. TEXTUAL COMMENT We have cut the entry of the "*Lords*" originally specified in F and Q2. There is no reasonable moment in the scene for the Lords to exit (unless it is with Rosencrantz and Guildenstern or the Queen), and the King's plans to spy on Hamlet are presumably meant to be secretive. See Digital Edition TC 5 (combined text).
2. By no carefully directed conversation.

5 ROSENCRANTZ He does confess he feels himself distracted,°   *confused; agitated*
    But from what cause 'a will by no means speak.
  GUILDENSTERN Nor do we find him forward° to be sounded,°   *eager / probed*
    But with a crafty madness keeps aloof
    When we would bring him on to some confession
    Of his true state.
10 QUEEN   Did he receive you well?
  ROSENCRANTZ Most like a gentleman—
  GUILDENSTERN But with much forcing of his disposition.°   *mood*
  ROSENCRANTZ Niggard of question,[3] but of° our demands   *to*
    Most free in his reply.
15 QUEEN Did you assay° him to any pastime?   *try to persuade*
  ROSENCRANTZ Madam, it so fell out that certain players
    We o'erraught° on the way; of these we told him,   *passed*
    And there did seem in him a kind of joy
    To hear of it. They are here about the court
20   And, as I think, they have already order
    This night to play before him.
  POLONIUS   'Tis most true,
    And he beseeched me to entreat your majesties
    To hear and see the matter.
  KING With all my heart! And it doth much content me
25   To hear him so inclined.
    Good gentlemen, give him a further edge,°   *stimulus; appetite*
    And drive his purpose into these delights.
  ROSENCRANTZ We shall, my lord.
             Exeunt ROSENCRANTZ *and* GUILDENSTERN.
  KING   Sweet Gertrude, leave us too,
    For we have closely° sent for Hamlet hither,   *privately*
30   That he, as 'twere by accident, may here
    Affront° Ophelia. Her father and myself,   *Confront*
    We'll so bestow ourselves that, seeing unseen,
    We may of their encounter frankly judge
    And gather by him as he is behaved
35   If't be th'affliction of his love or no
    That thus he suffers for.
  QUEEN   I shall obey you.
    And for your part, Ophelia, I do wish
    That your good beauties be the happy cause
    Of Hamlet's wildness; so shall I hope your virtues
40   Will bring him to his wonted° way again   *customary*
    To both your honors.
  OPHELIA   Madam, I wish it may.   *[Exit* QUEEN.*]*
  POLONIUS Ophelia, walk you here. *[to the* KING*]* Gracious,° so   *Your grace*
      please you,
    We will bestow ourselves. *[to* OPHELIA*]* Read on this book
    That show of such an exercise may color
45   Your lowliness.[4] We are oft to blame in this:
    'Tis too much proved° that with devotion's visage   *true in experience*
    And pious action we do sugar o'er
    The devil himself.
  KING   Oh, 'tis too true.

---

3. Reluctant to offer conversation.
4. *may . . . lowliness:* may show your humility, and

also give it a virtuous or pious look. The "book" is a
prayer book or devotional text.

OPHELIA Heavenly powers restore him!

HAMLET I have heard of your paintings° well enough. God *cosmetics*
140   hath given you one face and you make yourselves another;
you jig and amble and you lisp,[2] you nickname God's creatures[3] and make your wantonness ignorance.[4] Go to, I'll no
more on't°—it hath made me mad. I say we will have no *of it*
more marriage. Those that are married already—all but
145   one—shall live; the rest shall keep as they are. To a nunnery, go.   *Exit.*

OPHELIA Oh, what a noble mind is here o'erthrown!
The courtier's, soldier's, scholar's eye, tongue, sword,
Th'expectation° and rose of the fair state,   *The hope*
150   The glass° of fashion and the mold of form,[5]   *mirror image*
Th'observed of all observers, quite, quite down!
And I, of ladies most deject and wretched,
That sucked the honey of his musicked vows,
Now see what noble and most sovereign reason
155   Like sweet bells jangled out of time and harsh—
That unmatched form and stature of blown° youth,   *fully blossoming*
Blasted° with ecstasy.° Oh, woe is me   *Withered / madness*
T'have seen what I have seen, see what I see!
        KING *and* POLONIUS [*come forward*].
KING Love? His affections° do not that way tend,   *emotions*
160   Nor what he spake, though it lacked form a little,
Was not like madness. There's something in his soul
O'er which his melancholy sits on brood,
And I do doubt° the hatch and the disclose[6]   *fear*
Will be some danger—which for to prevent
165   I have in quick determination
Thus set it down:° he shall with speed to England   *resolved it*
For the demand of our neglected tribute.[7]
Haply° the seas and countries different   *Perhaps; with luck*
With variable objects[8] shall expel
170   This something-settled° matter in his heart,   *somewhat rooted*
Whereon his brains still° beating puts him thus   *constantly*
From fashion of himself.[9] What think you on't?
POLONIUS It shall do well. But yet do I believe
The origin and commencement of his grief
175   Sprung from neglected° love. How now, Ophelia?   *unrequited*
You need not tell us what Lord Hamlet said—
We heard it all. My lord, do as you please,
But if you hold it fit, after the play
Let his queen-mother all alone entreat him
180   To show his grief. Let her be round° with him,   *blunt*
And I'll be placed, so please you, in the ear°   *within earshot*
Of all their conference. If she find him not,[1]
To England send him, or confine him where

2. *you jig . . . lisp:* you dance (or sing), walk with an
affectedly easy gait, and speak artificially.
3. Use new and fashionable names instead of the
God-given ones.
4. *make . . . ignorance:* "play dumb" to excuse your
(seductive) affectations.
5. Pattern of decorum.

6. Public disclosure.
7. Although the play is set in a Renaissance world,
Claudius's words invoke a distant medieval past,
when England paid tribute to Denmark.
8. With different sights or interests.
9. *puts . . . himself:* makes him unlike his normal self.
1. If she fails to discover his secret.

Your wisdom best shall think.

KING   It shall be so.

185   Madness in great ones must not unmatched go.[2]   *Exeunt.*

3.2

Enter HAMLET *and three of the* PLAYERS.

HAMLET   Speak the speech, I pray you, as I pronounced it to
you, trippingly on the tongue. But if you mouth it[1] as many of
our players do, I had as lief° the town crier spoke my lines.   *willingly*
Nor do not saw the air too much with your hand thus, but
5   use all gently, for in the very torrent, tempest, and, as I may
say, whirlwind of your passion, you must acquire and beget a
temperance that may give it smoothness. Oh, it offends me
to the soul to hear a robustious° periwig-pated° fellow tear a   *bombastic / wig-wearing*
passion to tatters, to very rags, to split the ears of the ground-
10   lings,[2] who for the most part are capable of nothing but inexplicable dumb shows[3] and noise. I would have such a fellow
whipped for o'erdoing Termagant—it out-Herods Herod.[4]
Pray you avoid it.

PLAYER   I warrant your honor.[5]

15   HAMLET   Be not too tame neither, but let your own discretion
be your tutor. Suit the action to the word, the word to the
action, with this special observance: that you o'erstep not
the modesty° of nature. For anything so o'erdone is from°   *moderation / opposed to*
the purpose of playing, whose end both at the first and now
20   was and is to hold as 'twere the mirror up to nature, to
show virtue her feature, scorn her own image, and the very
age and body of the time his form and pressure.[6] Now this
overdone, or come tardy° off, though it makes the unskill-   *faultily*
ful° laugh, cannot but make the judicious grieve, the cen-   *undiscriminating*
25   sure of which one[7] must in your allowance o'erweigh a whole
theater of others. Oh, there be players that I have seen play,
and heard others praised, and that highly, not to speak it
profanely,[8] that neither having th'accent of Christians nor
the gait of Christian, pagan, nor man, have so strutted and
30   bellowed that I have thought some of nature's journeymen[9]
had made men, and not made them well, they imitated humanity so abominably.

PLAYER   I hope we have reformed that indifferently° with us.   *moderately well*

HAMLET   Oh, reform it altogether. And let those that play your
35   clowns speak no more than is set down for them; for there be
of° them that will themselves laugh to set° on some quantity   *some of / urge*
of barren° spectators to laugh too, though in the meantime   *unthinking*
some necessary question of the play be then to be consid-

---

2. Madness in great ones should not be left alone, or
unopposed.
3.2 Location: A stateroom of the castle.
1. If you speak exaggeratedly.
2. Spectators standing on the ground before the stage
(the cheapest area).
3. Pantomimes, featuring gestures without words.
By Shakespeare's time, this once-common device
was out of fashion.
4. It surpasses the excesses of Herod, who, as a character in medieval cycle plays, was famous for his
ranting. Termagant, an imaginary deity supposedly

worshipped by Muslims, takes the form of a violent
speaking idol in medieval drama.
5. I assure your honor (that we will avoid it).
6. *the very . . . pressure:* the true state of things at
present, in shape ("form") and likeness (as a stamp
pressed in wax).
7. The judgment of one of whom (judicious persons).
8. Meaning no blasphemy (by implying as he goes on
to do that some humans were not created by God).
9. Hirelings, those who have completed their apprenticeship but are not yet "masters" of their trade.

may outlive his life half a year—but by'r Lady, 'a must build
120   churches then, or else shall 'a suffer not thinking on,[7] with
the hobbyhorse whose epitaph is "For oh! For oh! The hobbyhorse is forgot."[8]

> *The trumpets sounds. Dumb show follows.*
> *Enter a* [PLAYER] KING *and a* [PLAYER] QUEEN, *the*
> QUEEN *embracing him and he her.* [*She kneels and*
> *makes show of protestation unto him.*] *He takes her*
> *up and declines*° *his head upon her neck. He lies him*   leans
> *down upon a bank of flowers; she, seeing him asleep,*
> *leaves him. Anon come in another man, takes off his*
> *crown, kisses it, pours poison in the sleeper's ears, and*
> *leaves him. The* QUEEN *returns, finds the* KING *dead,*
> *makes passionate action. The poisoner with some*
> *three or four come in again, seem to condole with her.*
> *The dead body is carried away. The poisoner woos the*
> QUEEN *with gifts. She seems harsh awhile but in the*
> *end accepts love.*   [*Exeunt.*]

OPHELIA   What means this, my lord?
HAMLET   Marry, this miching mallico?° It means mischief.   sneaking wrongdoing
125   OPHELIA   Belike this show imports the argument° of the play.   plot

> *Enter* PROLOGUE.

HAMLET   We shall know by this fellow. The players cannot
keep counsel°—they'll tell all.   a secret
OPHELIA   Will 'a tell us what this show meant?
HAMLET   Ay, or any show that you will show him. Be not you
130   ashamed to show, he'll not shame to tell you what it means.
OPHELIA   You are naught,° you are naught. I'll mark the play.   indecent
PROLOGUE   For us and for our tragedy

> Here stooping to your clemency,
> We beg your hearing patiently.   [*Exit.*]

135   HAMLET   Is this a prologue or the posy of a ring?[9]
OPHELIA   'Tis brief, my lord.
HAMLET   As woman's love.

> *Enter* [PLAYER] KING *and* [PLAYER] QUEEN.

PLAYER KING   Full thirty times hath Phoebus' cart[1] gone round

> Neptune's salt wash and Tellus' orbèd ground[2]
140   And thirty dozen moons with borrowed sheen°   reflected light
> About the world have times twelve thirties been
> Since love our hearts and Hymen° did our hands   god of marriage
> Unite commutual in most sacred bands.

PLAYER QUEEN   So many journeys may the sun and moon
145   Make us again count o'er ere love be done.

> But woe is me, you are so sick of late,
> So far from cheer and from our former state,
> That I distrust° you. Yet though I distrust,   am worried about
> Discomfort° you, my lord, it nothing must.[3]   Sadden
150   For women fear too much even as they love,
> And women's fear and love hold quantity°   are in equal proportions

---

7. He shall have to endure being forgotten.
8. The hobbyhorse, a man with a mock horse's body
strapped round his waist, was a figure in May Day
morris dances (under attack in Shakespeare's time by
religious reformers). "The hobbyhorse is forgot"
seems to have been a ballad refrain.

9. The motto engraved in a ring.
1. Apollo's chariot (the sun).
2. *Neptune's . . . ground:* The salty flood of the sea
god and the round foundation of Tellus (the earth).
3. The following line, 150, is omitted in F.

Either none, in neither aught or in extremity.[4]
Now what my love is, proof° hath made you know,   *experience*
And as my love is sized,° my fear is so.[5]   *in quantity*
155 Where love is great, the littlest doubts are fear;
Where little fears grow great, great love grows there.
PLAYER KING   Faith, I must leave thee, love, and shortly too.
My operant° powers their functions leave° to do,   *vital / cease*
And thou shalt live in this fair world behind,
160 Honored, beloved; and haply° one as kind   *perhaps*
For husband shalt thou—
PLAYER QUEEN   Oh, confound the rest!
Such love must needs be treason in my breast.
In second husband let me be accurst:
None wed the second but who killed the first.
165 HAMLET   That's wormwood.[6]
PLAYER QUEEN   The instances° that second marriage move°   *motives / prompt*
Are base respects of thrift° but none of love.   *economic considerations*
A second time I kill my husband dead
When second husband kisses me in bed.
170 PLAYER KING   I do believe you think what now you speak,
But what we do determine, oft we break.
Purpose is but the slave to[7] memory,
Of violent birth but poor validity,°   *enduring strength*
Which now like fruit unripe sticks on the tree
175 But fall unshaken when they mellow be.
Most necessary 'tis that we forget
To pay ourselves what to ourselves is debt;[8]
What to ourselves in passion we propose,
The passion ending, doth the purpose lose.
180 The violence of either grief or joy
Their own enactures with themselves destroy.[9]
Where joy most revels grief doth most lament,
Grief joys, joy grieves, on slender accident.[1]
This world is not for aye,° nor 'tis not strange   *eternity*
185 That even our loves should with our fortunes change—
For 'tis a question left us yet to prove
Whether love lead fortune or else fortune love.
The great man down, you mark his favorite flies;
The poor advanced° makes friends of enemies.   *promoted*
190 And hitherto° doth love on fortune tend,°   *to this extent / attend*
For who not needs shall never lack a friend,
And who in want a hollow friend doth try°   *test*
Directly seasons him[2] his enemy.
But orderly to end where I begun,
195 Our wills and fates do so contrary run[3]
That our devices still° are overthrown—   *our plans always*

4. *Either . . . extremity:* Either love and fear are both
absent, or both are extremely strong.
5. The following couplet, lines 155–56, is omitted in F.
6. A bitter herb taken medicinally (hence, "a bitter
pill to swallow").
7. *Purpose . . . slave to:* Our intentions serve and
depend on.
8. *Most . . . debt:* It is inevitable (or necessary for our
well-being) that we neglect to fulfill those promises

made to ourselves.
9. *The violence . . . destroy:* Extreme grief and joy
destroy themselves, and the motive for action vanishes
with them.
1. On account of a small, unforeseen event.
2. Immediately hardens him, as timber is seasoned
for use.
3. What we desire and what is destined to happen
are so opposed.

275 GUILDENSTERN Good my lord, vouchsafe me a word with you.
HAMLET Sir, a whole history.
GUILDENSTERN The King, sir—
HAMLET Ay, sir, what of him?
GUILDENSTERN Is in his retirement° marvelous distempered. *withdrawal*
280 HAMLET With drink, sir?
GUILDENSTERN No, my lord, with choler.[1]
HAMLET Your wisdom should show itself more richer° to sig- *resourceful*
nify this to the doctor, for for me to put him to his purgation[2]
would perhaps plunge him into more choler.
285 GUILDENSTERN Good my lord, put your discourse into some
frame° and start° not so wildly from my affair. *order / jump away*
HAMLET I am tame, sir. Pronounce.
GUILDENSTERN The Queen your mother, in most great affliction of spirit, hath sent me to you.
290 HAMLET You are welcome.
GUILDENSTERN Nay, good my lord, this courtesy is not of the
right breed.° If it shall please you to make me a wholesome° *kind; nobility / sane*
answer, I will do your mother's commandment. If not, your
pardon° and my return shall be the end of business. *permission to go*
295 HAMLET Sir, I cannot.
ROSENCRANTZ What, my lord?
HAMLET Make you a wholesome answer: my wit's diseased.
But sir, such answer as I can make, you shall command, or
rather, as you say, my mother. Therefore no more, but to the
300 matter. My mother, you say?
ROSENCRANTZ Then thus she says: your behavior hath struck
her into amazement and admiration.° *bewilderment*
HAMLET Oh, wonderful son that can so 'stonish a mother! But
is there no sequel at the heels of this mother's admiration?
305 Impart.° *Do tell*
ROSENCRANTZ She desires to speak with you in her closet° ere *private chamber*
you go to bed.
HAMLET We shall obey, were she ten times our mother. Have
you any further trade with us?
310 ROSENCRANTZ My lord, you once did love me.
HAMLET And do still, by these pickers and stealers.[3]
ROSENCRANTZ Good my lord, what is your cause of distemper? You do surely° bar the door upon your own liberty if *securely*
you deny your griefs to your friend.
315 HAMLET Sir, I lack advancement.
ROSENCRANTZ How can that be when you have the voice of
the King himself for your succession in Denmark?
Enter the PLAYERS *with recorders.*
HAMLET Ay, sir, but while the grass grows[4]—the proverb is
something° musty. —Oh, the recorders! Let me see one. *somewhat*
320 —To withdraw° with you: why do you go about to recover *speak privately*
the wind of me as if you would drive me into a toil?[5]

---

1. Both anger (Guildenstern's meaning) and indiges-
tion (Hamlet's). In Renaissance medical psychology,
each was a symptom of too much yellow bile—an
imbalance ("distemper") of the bodily fluids (humors).
2. A complicated pun: bloodletting; spiritual purging
(confession and absolution); legal purging (clearing
oneself of a crime).
3. Hands. (The catechism in the Book of Common

Prayer includes a promise to "keep my hands from
picking and stealing, and my tongue from evil speaking, lying, and slandering.")
4. "While the grass grows, the horse starves."
5. *go . . . toil*: contrive to get windward of me as if
you were hunters cunningly driving me toward a trap
("toil").

GUILDENSTERN   O my lord, if my duty be too bold, my love is
too unmannerly.[6]

HAMLET   I do not well understand that. Will you play upon
325   this pipe?

GUILDENSTERN   My lord, I cannot.

HAMLET   I pray you.

GUILDENSTERN   Believe me, I cannot.

HAMLET   I do beseech you.

330 GUILDENSTERN   I know no touch of it, my lord.

HAMLET   It is as easy as lying. Govern these ventages° with   *finger holes*
your fingers and thumb, give it breath with your mouth, and
it will discourse most eloquent music. Look you, these are
the stops.°   *finger holes; notes*

335 GUILDENSTERN   But these cannot I command to any utterance
of harmony. I have not the skill.

HAMLET   Why, look you now how unworthy a thing you make
of me: you would play upon me, you would seem to know my
stops, you would pluck out the heart of my mystery, you
340   would sound° me from my lowest note to my compass,° and   *fathom; play on / limit*
there is much music, excellent voice, in this little organ,° yet   *musical instrument*
cannot you make it speak. 'Sblood, do you think I am easier
to be played on than a pipe? Call me what instrument you
will, though you fret[7] me, you cannot play upon me.
       Enter POLONIUS.
345 God bless you, sir.

POLONIUS   My lord, the Queen would speak with you, and
presently.

HAMLET   Do you see yonder cloud that's almost in shape of a
camel?

350 POLONIUS   By th' mass, and 'tis like a camel indeed.

HAMLET   Methinks it is like a weasel.

POLONIUS   It is backed like a weasel.

HAMLET   Or like a whale.

POLONIUS   Very like a whale.

355 HAMLET   Then I will come to my mother by and by. [*aside*]
They fool me to the top of my bent.[8] —I will come by and by.
[*to* ROSENCRANTZ *and* GUILDENSTERN] Leave me, friends. [*to*
POLONIUS] I will—say so. "By and by" is easily said.
                          [*Exeunt all but* HAMLET.]
'Tis now the very witching time of night
360 When churchyards yawn and hell itself breaks out
Contagion to this world. Now could I drink hot blood
And do such business as the bitter day
Would quake to look on. Soft, now to my mother.
O heart, lose not thy nature,° let not ever   *natural affection*
365 The soul of Nero[9] enter this firm° bosom—   *resolved*
Let me be cruel, not unnatural.
I will speak daggers to her but use none.
My tongue and soul in this be hypocrites:[1]

6. If I have been discourteous in pursuing what is my
duty, my love for you is to blame.
7. Irritate, punning on frets of stringed instruments,
which regulate fingering and pitch.
8. They go along with my foolishness to its limit, or
to the limit of my endurance.
9. The Roman emperor Nero reputedly murdered his
mother, in one account, by cutting open her womb.
1. Let me appear and speak as if I intended violence
(though I do not).

How in my words somever[2] she be shent,°   *rebuked*
370 To give them seals[3] never my soul consent.   *Exit.*

3.3

Enter KING, ROSENCRANTZ, *and* GUILDENSTERN.

KING I like him not, nor stands it safe with us
To let his madness range. Therefore prepare you:
I your commission will forthwith dispatch
And he to England shall along with you.
5 The terms of our estate[1] may not endure
Hazard so near us as doth hourly grow
Out of his brows.[2]

GUILDENSTERN   We will ourselves provide.
Most holy and religious fear° it is   *care*
To keep those many many bodies safe
10 That live and feed upon your majesty.

ROSENCRANTZ The single° and peculiar° life is bound *individual / private*
With all the strength and armor of the mind
To keep itself from noyance,° but much more   *harm*
That spirit upon whose weal° depends and rests   *well-being*
15 The lives of many. The cease° of majesty   *decease*
Dies not alone but like a gulf° doth draw   *whirlpool*
What's near it with it, or it is a massy° wheel   *massive*
Fixed on the summit of the highest mount
To whose huge spokes ten thousand lesser things
20 Are mortised° and adjoined, which° when it falls *affixed / so that*
Each small annexment, petty consequence,
Attends° the boist'rous ruin. Never alone   *Accompanies*
Did the king sigh, but with a general groan.

KING Arm° you, I pray you, to this speedy voyage,   *Prepare*
25 For we will fetters put about this fear
Which now goes too free-footed.

ROSENCRANTZ   We will haste us.
Exeunt [ROSENCRANTZ *and* GUILDENSTERN].
Enter POLONIUS.

POLONIUS My lord, he's going to his mother's closet.
Behind the arras° I'll convey myself   *wall tapestry*
To hear the process.° I'll warrant she'll tax him home,[3] *proceedings*
30 And as you said—and wisely was it said—
'Tis meet° that some more audience than a mother,   *fitting*
Since nature makes them partial, should o'erhear
The speech of vantage.° Fare you well, my liege.   *in addition*
I'll call upon you ere you go to bed
And tell you what I know.

35 KING   Thanks, dear my lord.
Exit [POLONIUS].
Oh, my offense is rank, it smells to heaven;
It hath the primal eldest curse[4] upon't—

---

2. However much by my words.
3. To confirm them with visible deeds.
3.3 Location: The castle.
1. The responsibilities of our position.
2. An ambiguous term suggesting "brain," "expressions," or "effrontery." Instead of "brows," F has "lunacies."
3. I'm sure she will rebuke him thoroughly.
4. The first, oldest curse (God's curse on Cain for murdering his brother, Abel; see Genesis 4:10–12).

A brother's murder. Pray can I not:
Though inclination be as sharp as will,[5]
40 My stronger guilt defeats my strong intent
And like a man to double business bound[6]
I stand in pause where I shall first begin,
And both neglect. What if this cursèd hand
Were thicker than itself with brother's blood[7]—
45 Is there not rain enough in the sweet heavens
To wash it white as snow?[8] Whereto serves mercy
But to confront the visage of offense?[9]
And what's in prayer but this twofold force:
To be forestalled° ere we come to fall   *prevented*
50 Or pardoned, being down? Then I'll look up.
My fault is past, but, oh, what form of prayer
Can serve my turn? Forgive me my foul murder?
That cannot be, since I am still possessed
Of those effects for which I did the murder—
55 My crown, mine own ambition, and my queen.
May one be pardoned and retain th'offense?[1]
In the corrupted currents of this world
Offense's gilded° hand may shove by justice,   *bribing*
And oft 'tis seen the wicked prize[2] itself
60 Buys out the law, but 'tis not so above.
There is no shuffling,° there the action lies   *evasion*
In his true nature,[3] and we ourselves compelled
Even to the teeth and forehead of[4] our faults
To give in evidence.[5] What then? What rests?°   *remains to be done*
65 Try what repentance can—what can it not?
Yet what can it when one cannot repent?
Oh, wretched state; oh, bosom black as death;
Oh, limèd[6] soul that struggling to be free
Art more engaged!° Help, angels! Make assay°—   *entangled / some attempt*
70 Bow, stubborn knees, and heart with strings of steel,
Be soft as sinews of the newborn babe.
All may be well.
      Enter HAMLET [*behind him*].
HAMLET   Now might I do it, but now 'a° is a-praying.   *he*
And now I'll do't! [*He draws his sword.*] And so 'a goes to
    heaven,
75 And so am I revenged—that would be scanned:[7]
A villain kills my father, and for that
I, his sole son, do this same villain send
To heaven.
Why, this is base and silly, not revenge.

---

5. Though my desire (to pray) is as strong as my determination to do so.
6. Committed to two different goals.
7. Were covered with a layer of brother's blood deeper than the hand's thickness.
8. Compare Isaiah 1:15–18: "And though ye make many prayers, I will not hear: for your hands are full of blood. Wash you, make you clean; take away the evil of your works from before mine eyes. . . . though your sins were as crimson, they shall be made white as snow."
9. *Whereto . . . offense:* What purpose has mercy if not to oppose sin face to face?

1. And keep what was gained from the crime.
2. The profits from wickedness.
3. *the action . . . nature:* the deed appears in its true form; legal proceedings are properly conducted.
4. *Even . . . of:* Even face to face with. (English law provided for the confrontation of the accused and the witnesses.)
5. To testify. In English law, one cannot be forced to give evidence against oneself; heavenly justice is different.
6. Caught as if in birdlime, a sticky substance smeared on twigs to catch birds.
7. That needs careful evaluation.

80   'A took my father grossly, full of bread,[8]
    With all his crimes broad blown,[9] as flush° as May—   *vigorously thriving*
    And how his audit° stands, who knows save heaven?   *spiritual account*
    But in our circumstance and course of thought[1]
    'Tis heavy with him. And am I then revenged
85   To take him in the purging of his soul
    When he is fit and seasoned° for his passage?   *made ready*
    No.
        [*He sheathes his sword.*]
    Up, sword, and know thou a more horrid hent[2]—
    When he is drunk asleep, or in his rage,
90   Or in th'incestuous pleasure of his bed,
    At game, a-swearing, or about some act
    That has no relish° of salvation in't.   *trace*
    Then trip him that his heels may kick at heaven
    And that his soul may be as damned and black
95   As hell whereto it goes. My mother stays°—   *waits*
    This physic[3] but prolongs thy sickly days.   *Exit.*
KING   My words fly up, my thoughts remain below;
    Words without thoughts never to heaven go.   *Exit.*

3.4

Enter QUEEN *and* POLONIUS.
POLONIUS   'A will come straight.° Look you lay home to him:[1]   *immediately*
    Tell him his pranks have been too broad° to bear with   *outrageous*
    And that your grace hath screened and stood between
    Much heat and him. I'll silence me even here.
5   Pray you be round.[2]
5.1   HAMLET (*within*)   *Mother, mother, mother.*
QUEEN   I'll warr'nt you, fear° me not.   *doubt*
    Withdraw, I hear him coming.
        [POLONIUS *hides behind an arras.*]
        Enter HAMLET.
HAMLET   Now, mother, what's the matter?
QUEEN   Hamlet, thou hast thy father much offended.
10 HAMLET   Mother, you have my father much offended.
QUEEN   Come, come, you answer with an idle tongue.
HAMLET   Go, go, you question with a wicked tongue.
QUEEN   Why, how now,° Hamlet?   *what's this*
HAMLET   What's the matter now?
QUEEN   Have you forgot me?[3]
HAMLET   No, by the rood,° not so: *cross of Christ*
15   You are the Queen, your husband's brother's wife,
    And, would it were not so, you are my mother.
QUEEN   Nay, then I'll set those to you that can speak.[4]
HAMLET   Come, come and sit you down, you shall not budge;

---

8. Not spiritually prepared. Compare Ezekiel 16:49: "Behold, this was the iniquity of thy sister Sodom, pride, fullness of bread, and abundance of idleness."
9. With all his sins in full bloom.
1. But in our indirect and limited way of knowing on earth.
2. Design. Or, occasion (if "hent" is taken from "hint").
3. Medicine (both Claudius's prayer and Hamlet's postponement of the revenge).
3.4 Location: The Queen's private chamber.
1. Be sure to rebuke him thoroughly.
2. F has the following line, 5.1, omitted in Q2. *round*: blunt.
3. Forgotten the respect you owe to me as your mother.
4. *that can speak*: who can deal with someone as impossibly rude as you.

You go not till I set you up a glass° mirror
20 Where you may see the inmost part of you.
QUEEN What wilt thou do? Thou wilt not murder me?
Help, ho!
POLONIUS [behind the arras] What ho! Help!
HAMLET How now, a rat?
[He stabs through the arras and kills POLONIUS.]
Dead for a ducat, dead.⁵
POLONIUS Oh, I am slain!
25 QUEEN O me, what hast thou done?
HAMLET Nay, I know not. Is it the King?
[He parts the arras, discovering POLONIUS.]
QUEEN Oh, what a rash and bloody deed is this!
HAMLET A bloody deed—almost as bad, good mother,
As kill a king and marry with his brother.
QUEEN As kill a king?
30 HAMLET Ay, lady, it was my word.
[to POLONIUS] Thou wretched, rash, intruding fool,
farewell.
I took thee for thy better. Take thy fortune.
Thou find'st to be too busy° is some danger. nosy
—Leave wringing of your hands. Peace, sit you down
35 And let me wring your heart, for so I shall
If it be made of penetrable stuff,
If damnèd custom° have not brazed it so sinful habit
That it be proof and bulwark against sense.⁶
QUEEN What have I done that thou dar'st wag thy tongue
In noise so rude against me?
40 HAMLET Such an act
That blurs the grace and blush of modesty,
Calls virtue hypocrite, takes off the rose
From the fair forehead of an innocent love
And sets a blister there,⁷ makes marriage vows
45 As false as dicers' oaths—oh, such a deed
As from the body of contraction° plucks marriage contract
The very soul, and sweet religion makes
A rhapsody⁸ of words. Heaven's face does glow° blush
O'er this solidity and compound mass⁹
50 With heated visage as against the doom,¹
Is thought-sick at the act—
QUEEN Ay me, what act
That roars so loud and thunders in the index?²
HAMLET Look here upon this picture, and on this—
The counterfeit presentment° of two brothers. painted portrayal
55 See what a grace was seated on this brow,
Hyperion's° curls, the front° of Jove himself, The sun god's / forehead
An eye like Mars° to threaten and command, Roman god of war
A station like the herald Mercury³
New lighted° on a heaven-kissing hill, Newly alighted

5. I bet a ducat I have killed it.
6. brazed . . . sense: made it so brazen that it is impen-
etrably fortified against natural feeling ("sense").
7. Prostitutes, among other criminals, were branded
on the forehead during the sixteenth and seventeenth centuries.
8. Meaningless jumble.
9. Solid earth (a compound of the four elements).
1. As if preparing for the Last Judgment.
2. Table of contents; preface.
3. A stance like the winged herald of the gods.

HAMLET   My pulse as yours doth temperately keep time
    And makes as healthful music. It is not madness
    That I have uttered. Bring me to the test
    And I the matter will reword,° which madness   *repeat exactly*
145   Would gambol° from. Mother, for love of grace,   *skitter away*
    Lay not that flattering unction[4] to your soul
    That not your trespass but my madness speaks.
    It will but skin° and film the ulcerous place   *cover*
    Whiles rank corruption, mining° all within,   *undermining*
150   Infects unseen. Confess yourself to heaven,
    Repent what's past, avoid what is to come,
    And do not spread the compost on the weeds
    To make them ranker. Forgive me this my virtue,°   *virtuous exhortation*
    For in the fatness° of these pursy° times   *grossness / flabby*
155   Virtue itself of vice must pardon beg,
    Yea, curb° and woo for leave° to do him good.   *bow / permission*
  QUEEN   O Hamlet, thou hast cleft my heart in twain.
  HAMLET   Oh, throw away the worser part of it
    And live the purer with the other half.
160   Good night. But go not to my uncle's bed—
    Assume° a virtue if you have it not.[5]   *Put on (actions of)*
    That monster custom, who all sense doth eat,
    Of habits devil,° is angel yet in this,   *devilish*
    That to the use° of actions fair and good   *habitual practice*
165   He likewise gives a frock or livery
    That aptly° is put on. Refrain tonight,   *quickly*
    And that shall lend a kind of easiness
    To the next abstinence, the next more easy.
    For use almost can change the stamp of nature,
170   And either lodge the devil, or throw him out[6]
    With wondrous potency. Once more good night,
    And when you are desirous to be blessed,
    I'll blessing beg of you. For this same lord
    I do repent. But heaven hath pleased it so
175   To punish me with this and this with me,
    That I must be their scourge and minister.[7]
    I will bestow° him and will answer well[8]   *dispose of*
    The death I gave him. So again, good night.
    I must be cruel only to be kind.
180   This bad begins and worse remains behind.°   *to follow*
    One word more, good lady.
  QUEEN   What shall I do?
  HAMLET   Not this, by no means that I bid you do:
    Let the bloat King tempt you again to bed,
    Pinch wanton on your cheek, call you his mouse,
185   And let him for a pair of reechy° kisses,   *filthy*
    Or paddling° in your neck with his damned fingers, *fondly fingering*
    Make you to ravel° all this matter out   *disclose*
    That I essentially am not in madness

---

4. Do not apply an ointment that relieves pain but does not heal (contrasted to a sacramental unction that blesses the soul).
5. Lines 162–71 represent Q2's version of the passage, which is considerably shorter in F.
6. TEXTUAL COMMENT Q2's version of this line (which begins "And either the deuill") is clearly defective, and supplying a verb meant to contrast with "throwing out" seems the most sensible solution. See Digital Edition TC 6 (combined text).
7. Heaven's agent of punishment.
8. Will take responsibility for.

But mad in craft.° 'Twere good you let him know, *cunning*
190 For who that's but° a queen, fair, sober, wise, *only*
Would from a paddock,° from a bat, a gib,° *toad / tomcat*
Such dear concernings° hide? Who would do so? *vital affairs*
No, in despite of sense and secrecy,
Unpeg the basket on the house's top,
195 Let the birds fly and, like the famous ape,
To try conclusions, in the basket creep
And break your own neck down.[9]
QUEEN   Be thou assured, if words be made of breath
And breath of life, I have no life to breathe
200 What thou hast said to me.
HAMLET   I must to England, you know that.
QUEEN   Alack,
I had forgot; 'tis so concluded on.[1]
HAMLET   There's letters sealed and my two schoolfellows,
Whom I will trust as I will adders fanged,
205 They bear the mandate. They must sweep my way
And marshal me to knavery.[2] Let it work,° *proceed*
For 'tis the sport to have the enginer[3]
Hoist with his own petard[4]—and't shall go hard
But I will delve one yard below their mines° *military tunnels*
210 And blow them at the moon. Oh, 'tis most sweet
When in one line two crafts directly meet.[5]
[*He indicates* POLONIUS.] This man shall set me packing—
I'll lug the guts into the neighbor room.
Mother, good night indeed. This counselor
215 Is now most still, most secret, and most grave,
Who was in life a most foolish prating knave.
—Come, sir, to draw toward an end with you.[6]
—Good night, mother.   *Exit* [*with Polonius' body*].
                  Enter KING *with* ROSENCRANTZ *and* GUILDENSTERN.
KING   There's matter in these sighs; these profound heaves
220 You must translate—'tis fit we understand them.
Where is your son?
QUEEN   Bestow this place on us a little while.
                  [*Exeunt* ROSENCRANTZ *and* GUILDENSTERN.]
Ah, mine own lord, what have I seen tonight!
KING   What, Gertrude? How does Hamlet?
225 QUEEN   Mad as the sea and wind when both contend
Which is the mightier: in his lawless fit,
Behind the arras hearing something stir,
Whips out his rapier, cries, "A rat, a rat,"
And in this brainish apprehension° kills *brain-sick notion*
The unseen good old man.
230 KING   Oh, heavy deed!
It had been so with us° had we been there. *me (royal "we")*

---

9. *like . . . down:* A tale presumably involving an ape who opened a wicker cage full of birds and released them from the rooftop; after climbing into the basket, he tried to imitate their flight to freedom but died in the fall. *try conclusions:* test the results.
1. The following passage, lines 203–11, is omitted in F.
2. *sweep . . . knavery:* prepare my path and escort me into a trap (also, and provoke me to crime).

3. Designer and builder of "engines" (military devices).
4. Blown skyward by his own bomb (for breaching enemy fortifications).
5. That is, when two devious plots ("crafts") meet along the same path of tunneling (a standard technique in siege warfare).
6. To conclude my dealings with you (punning on "draw" as "drag").

His liberty is full of threats to all,
To you yourself, to us, to everyone.
Alas, how shall this bloody deed be answered?°   *accounted for*
235   It will be laid to° us whose providence°   *blamed on / foresight*
Should have kept short,° restrained, and out of haunt[7]   *closely tethered*
This mad young man. But so much was our love
We would not understand what was most fit,
But like the owner° of a foul disease,   *victim*
240   To keep it from divulging,° let it feed   *being seen*
Even on the pith of life. Where is he gone?
QUEEN   To draw apart the body he hath killed,
O'er whom his very madness, like some ore°   *vein of gold*
Among a mineral° of metals base,   *mine*
245   Shows itself pure: 'a° weeps for what is done.   *he*
KING   O Gertrude, come away.
The sun no sooner shall the mountains touch
But we will ship him hence, and this vile deed
We must with all our majesty and skill
250   Both countenance° and excuse. Ho, Guildenstern!   *condone*
        Enter ROSENCRANTZ *and* GUILDENSTERN.
Friends both, go join you with some further aid.
Hamlet in madness hath Polonius slain,
And from his mother's closet hath he dragged him.
Go seek him out, speak fair, and bring the body
255   Into the chapel. I pray you haste in this.
            [*Exeunt* ROSENCRANTZ *and* GUILDENSTERN.]
Come, Gertrude, we'll call up our wisest friends
And let them know both what we mean to do
And what's untimely done[8]—
Whose whisper[9] o'er the world's diameter,°   *whole extent*
260   As level as the cannon to his blank[1]
Transports his poisoned shot, may miss our name
And hit the woundless° air. Oh, come away,   *invulnerable*
My soul is full of discord and dismay.   *Exeunt.*

3.5

        Enter HAMLET.
HAMLET   Safely stowed.
        [*Shouts within, "Hamlet!"*]
But soft, what noise? Who calls on Hamlet? Oh, here they
come.
        Enter ROSENCRANTZ, [GUILDENSTERN,] *and others.*
ROSENCRANTZ   What have you done, my lord, with the dead
5   body?
HAMLET   Compound° it with dust whereto 'tis kin.   *Mix*
ROSENCRANTZ   Tell us where 'tis that we may take it thence
and bear it to the chapel.
HAMLET   Do not believe it.
10   ROSENCRANTZ   Believe what?

---

7. Public gatherings.
8. The following passage, lines 259–62, is omitted
in F.
9. The subject of "whisper" is unclear. Scholars have
conjectured that the passage is defective, perhaps
lacking a line that establishes "slander" as the subject

of "whisper."
1. As straight as the cannon at a target at point-blank
range. (The cannon would be tilted to aim at a distant target.)
3.5 Location: Scene continues.

HAMLET   That I can keep your counsel and not mine own.[1]
Besides, to be demanded of° a sponge, what replication°   *questioned by / reply*
should be made by the son of a king?

ROSENCRANTZ   Take you me for a sponge, my lord?

15   HAMLET   Ay, sir, that soaks up the King's countenance,° his   *favor*
rewards, his authorities. But such officers do the King best
service in the end. He keeps them like an ape in the corner
of his jaw—first mouthed to be last swallowed. When he
needs what you have gleaned, it is but squeezing you and,
20   sponge, you shall be dry again.

ROSENCRANTZ   I understand you not, my lord.

HAMLET   I am glad of it. A knavish speech sleeps in a foolish
ear.[2]

ROSENCRANTZ   My lord, you must tell us where the body is
25   and go with us to the King.

HAMLET   The body is with the King, but the King is not with
the body.[3] The King is a thing—

GUILDENSTERN   A thing, my lord?

HAMLET   Of nothing. Bring me to him.   *Exeunt.*

3.6

Enter KING *and two or three.*[1]

KING   I have sent to seek him and to find the body.
How dangerous is it that this man goes loose!
Yet must not we put the strong law on him—
He's loved of° the distracted° multitude,   *by / unreasonable*
5   Who like not in their judgment but their eyes,[2]
And where 'tis so, th'offender's scourge° is weighed   *punishment*
But never the offense. To bear° all smooth and even,   *manage*
This sudden sending him away must seem
Deliberate pause.° Diseases desperate grown   *Careful planning*
10   By desperate appliance° are relieved   *remedy*
Or not at all.
          Enter ROSENCRANTZ[, GUILDENSTERN,] *and all*
          the rest.
                    How now, what hath befallen?

ROSENCRANTZ   Where the dead body is bestowed, my lord,
We cannot get from him.

KING   But where is he?

ROSENCRANTZ   Without,° my lord, guarded, to know your   *Outside*
pleasure.

KING   Bring him before us.

15   ROSENCRANTZ   —Ho! Bring in the lord.
          Enter [HAMLET, *guarded*].

KING   Now, Hamlet, where's Polonius?

HAMLET   At supper.

---

1. Hamlet plays on two senses of "counsel": that I
can follow your advice and not keep my secret.
2. An insulting remark is not perceived by a fool.
3. A riddle. Hamlet may mean that Polonius is gone
to the afterlife with King Hamlet but Claudius is still
alive; or he may refer to the legal theory of the "king's
two bodies" (one the king's natural body, the other
the immortal abstract body of the state).
3.6 Location: Scene continues.
1. TEXTUAL COMMENT F's version of this stage direction, which has the King enter alone and speak his
opening lines as a soliloquy, makes better theatrical
sense than Q2's, which has the King enter with *"two
or three"* attendants. This and other confusions in this
scene's stage directions corroborate the view that Q2
was printed from Shakespeare's "foul papers." See
Digital Edition TC 7 (combined text).
2. Who choose not by reason but by external
appearance.

KING   At supper? Where?

HAMLET   Not where he eats, but where 'a is eaten:³ a certain
20 convocation of politic° worms are e'en° at him. Your worm is   *cunning / now*
your only emperor for diet.⁴ We fat all creatures else° to fat   *besides ourselves*
us, and we fat ourselves for maggots. Your fat king and your
lean beggar is but variable service,° two dishes but to one   *different courses*
table. That's the end.

25 KING   Alas, alas.

HAMLET   A man may fish with the worm that hath ate of a
king and eat of the fish that hath fed of that worm.

KING   What dost thou mean by this?

HAMLET   Nothing but to show you how a king may go a prog-
30 ress° through the guts of a beggar.   *royal journey*

KING   Where is Polonius?

HAMLET   In heaven. Send thither to see; if your messenger
find him not there, seek him i'th' other place yourself. But if
indeed you find him not within this month, you shall nose
35 him as you go up the stairs into the lobby.

KING [*to Attendants*]   Go seek him there.

HAMLET   'A will stay till you come.   [*Exeunt Attendants.*]

KING   Hamlet, this deed, for thine especial safety,
Which we do tender° as we dearly grieve   *value*
40 For that which thou hast done, must send thee hence.
Therefore prepare thyself:
The bark° is ready and the wind at help,   *ship*
The associates tend,° and everything is bent°   *companions wait / poised*
For England.

HAMLET   For England?

KING   Ay, Hamlet.

HAMLET   Good.

45 KING   So is it if thou knew'st our purposes.

HAMLET   I see a cherub⁵ that sees them. But come, for
England.
Farewell, dear mother.

KING   Thy loving father, Hamlet.

HAMLET   My mother: father and mother is man and wife,
Man and wife is one flesh,⁶ so my mother.
50 Come, for England.   *Exit.*

KING   Follow him at foot,° tempt him with speed aboard.   *his heel*
Delay it not—I'll have him hence tonight.
Away, for everything is sealed and done
That else leans° on th'affair. Pray you make haste.   *bears*
[*Exeunt all but* KING.]

55 And England,⁷ if my love thou hold'st at aught°—   *any value*
As my great power thereof may give thee sense,⁸
Since yet thy cicatrice° looks raw and red   *scar*
After the Danish sword, and thy free awe⁹

---

3. Possibly an allusion to the Eucharist (Lord's Supper), in which the body of Christ is consumed in the
form of bread.
4. *Your worm . . . diet:* The average worm is the only
creature with a diet superior to a king's. The Diet
(Council) of Emperor Charles V at Worms in 1521
called on Martin Luther to defend his new Protestant
doctrine. A scholar at Hamlet's university at Wittenberg, Luther maintained that faith alone, rather than

sacramental ritual, was the basis of salvation.
5. The keen-sighted second order of angels, cherubim symbolized heavenly knowledge.
6. As stated in Genesis 2:23–24 and the marriage
rite of the Book of Common Prayer.
7. King of England.
8. May give you a reason to feel the value of that love.
9. Your respect unconstrained (by an army of occupation).

Pays homage to us—thou mayst not coldly set°   *indifferently view*
60   Our sovereign process, which imports at full,[1]
By letters congruing to° that effect,   *according with*
The present° death of Hamlet. Do it, England,   *immediate*
For like the hectic° in my blood he rages   *fever*
And thou must cure me. Till I know 'tis done,
65   Howe'er my haps,° my joys will ne'er begin.   *Exit.*   *fortunes*

4.1

Enter FORTINBRAS [*and a* CAPTAIN] *with his army*
over the stage.

FORTINBRAS   Go, Captain, from me greet the Danish King.
Tell him that by his license° Fortinbras   *permission*
Craves the conveyance of° a promised march   *escort for*
Over his kingdom. You know the rendezvous.
5   If that his majesty would aught with us,
We shall express our duty in his eye°—   *presence*
And let him know so.
CAPTAIN   I will do't, my lord.
FORTINBRAS   Go softly° on.[1]   *slowly; circumspectly*
        [*Exeunt* FORTINBRAS *and his army.*
           The CAPTAIN *remains.*]
     Enter HAMLET, ROSENCRANTZ[, GUILDENSTERN,
     and others].
HAMLET   Good sir, whose powers° are these?   *forces*
CAPTAIN   They are of Norway, sir.
10   HAMLET   How purposed, sir, I pray you?
CAPTAIN   Against some part of Poland.
HAMLET   Who commands them, sir?
CAPTAIN   The nephew to old Norway, Fortinbras.
HAMLET   Goes it against the main° of Poland, sir,   *heart*
15   Or for some frontier?
CAPTAIN   Truly to speak, and with no addition,°   *exaggeration*
We go to gain a little patch of ground
That hath in it no profit but the name.
To pay five ducats—five—I would not farm° it,   *lease*
20   Nor will it yield to Norway or the Pole
A ranker rate should it be sold in fee.[2]
HAMLET   Why, then, the Polack never will defend it.
CAPTAIN   Yes, it is already garrisoned.
HAMLET   Two thousand souls and twenty thousand ducats
25   Will now debate the question of this straw.°   *trifle*
This is th'impostume° of much wealth and peace   *the abscess*
That inward breaks and shows no cause without[3]
Why the man dies. I humbly thank you, sir.
CAPTAIN   God b'wi'you, sir.   [*Exit* CAPTAIN.]
ROSENCRANTZ   Will't please you go, my lord?
30   HAMLET   I'll be with you straight. Go a little before.
       [ROSENCRANTZ, GUILDENSTERN, *and the others*
       move aside.]

---

1. Our sovereign command, which signifies in detailed instructions.
4.1 Location: The Danish coast.
1. The rest of the scene, lines 8–65, is omitted in F.

2. Sold outright as a freehold. *ranker rate*: more generous return.
3. That ruptures internally without external symptom.

KING   Pretty Ophelia—
OPHELIA   Indeed, without an oath I'll make an end on't:°   *of it*
  [*Sings.*]   By Gis° and by Saint Charity,   *Jesus*
            Alack and fie for shame,
60   Young men will do't if they come to't,
            By Cock[7] they are to blame.

            Quoth she, "Before you tumbled me
            You promised me to wed."
  He answers:
65   "So would I ha' done by yonder sun
            An° thou hadst not come to my bed."   *If*
KING   How long hath she been thus?
OPHELIA   I hope all will be well. We must be patient. But I cannot choose but weep to think they would lay him i'th' cold
70   ground. My brother shall know of it. And so I thank you for
  your good counsel. Come, my coach! Good night, ladies, good
  night, sweet ladies, good night, good night.   [*Exit.*]
KING [*to* HORATIO]   Follow her close. Give her good watch, I
  pray you.   [*Exit* HORATIO.]
  Oh, this is the poison of deep grief. It springs
75   All from her father's death—and now behold!
  O Gertrude, Gertrude,
  When sorrows come, they come not single spies°   *scouts*
  But in battalions: first her father slain;
  Next your son gone, and he most violent author
80   Of his own just remove; the people muddied,°   *confused*
  Thick and unwholesome in thoughts and whispers
  For good Polonius' death—and we have done but greenly°   *naively*
  In hugger-mugger° to inter him; poor Ophelia,   *secrecy*
  Divided from herself and her fair judgment,
85   Without the which we are pictures or mere beasts;
  Last, and as much containing° as all these,   *and as important*
  Her brother is in secret come from France,
  Feeds on this wonder, keeps himself in clouds,°   *his intentions obscure*
  And wants° not buzzers° to infect his ear   *lacks / scandalmongers*
90   With pestilent speeches of his father's death,
  Wherein necessity, of matter beggared,
  Will nothing stick our person to arraign
  In ear and ear.[8] O my dear Gertrude, this,
  Like to a murdering piece,[9] in many places
95   Gives me superfluous° death.   *redundant*
      A noise within.[1]
95.1   QUEEN   *Alack, what noise is this?*
KING   Attend!
  Where is my Switzers?[2] Let them guard the door.
      Enter a MESSENGER.
  What is the matter?
MESSENGER   Save yourself, my lord.

---

7. A corruption of "God" in very mild swearing (playing on "penis").
8. *Wherein . . . ear*: In which affair, because they
have no real information and need to give some
account, they will not hesitate to whisper accusations
against us.
9. Small cannon that fired shrapnel.
1. F has the following line, 95.1, not found in Q2.
2. Company of Swiss mercenaries (employed as royal
bodyguards in many European countries).

The ocean, overpeering of his list,[3]
100 Eats not the flats with more impiteous[4] haste
Than young Laertes in a riotous head°   *insurrection; tidal wave*
O'erbears your officers. The rabble call him lord
And, as° the world were now but° to begin,   *as if / only now*
Antiquity forgot, custom not known—
105 The ratifiers and props of every word[5]—
They cry, "Choose we: Laertes shall be king!"
Caps, hands, and tongues applaud it to the clouds,
"Laertes shall be king, Laertes king!"
        A noise within.
QUEEN   How cheerfully on the false trail they cry![6]
110 Oh, this is counter,[7] you false Danish dogs!
KING   The doors are broke.
        Enter LAERTES *with* [FOLLOWERS].
LAERTES   Where is this King? Sirs, stand you all without.
FOLLOWERS   No, let's come in.
LAERTES   I pray you give me leave.
FOLLOWERS   We will, we will.
LAERTES   I thank you. Keep° the door.   [*Exeunt* FOLLOWERS.]   *Guard*
115   O thou vile King,
Give me my father.
QUEEN [*restraining him*]   Calmly, good Laertes.
LAERTES   That drop of blood that's calm proclaims me
     bastard,
Cries "Cuckold!" to my father, brands the harlot
Even here between the chaste unsmirchèd brow
Of my true mother.
120 KING   What is the cause, Laertes,
That thy rebellion looks so giant-like?
—Let him go, Gertrude. Do not fear° our person: *fear for*
There's such divinity doth hedge a king
That treason can but peep to what it would,[8]
125 Acts little of his will. —Tell me, Laertes,
Why thou art thus incensed. —Let him go, Gertrude.
—Speak, man.
LAERTES   Where is my father?
KING   Dead.
QUEEN   But not by him.°   *(the King)*
KING   Let him demand his fill.
130 LAERTES   How came he dead? I'll not be juggled with.°   *deceived*
To hell allegiance, vows to the blackest devil,
Conscience and grace to the profoundest pit!
I dare damnation. To this point° I stand,   *resolve*
That both the worlds I give to negligence.[9]
135 Let come what comes, only I'll be revenged
Most throughly° for my father.   *thoroughly*

---

3. Rising over its boundary at the shore.
4. Probably meaning "merciless" as well as "rash." *flats:* low-lying countryside.
5. *Antiquity . . . word:* Ignoring history and traditional precedents, which give meaning, order, and stability to society by fixing the agreed-upon meaning of political contracts (and of any truth expressed in language).
6. How enthusiastically they run after the wrong

scent (like a pack of hounds hunting the murderer of Polonius).
7. This is following the quarry's trail, but in the wrong direction.
8. That treason can only glance furtively at what it would like to do.
9. That both this world and the next do not matter to me.

KING   Who shall stay° you?   *prevent*
LAERTES   My will, not all the world's.
And for my means I'll husband them so well
They shall go far with little.
KING   Good Laertes,
140   If you desire to know the certainty
Of your dear father,[1] is't writ in your revenge
That, sweepstake,[2] you will draw° both friend and foe,   *take from*
Winner and loser?
LAERTES   None but his enemies.
KING   Will you know them, then?
145   LAERTES   To his good friends thus wide I'll ope my arms
And, like the kind life-rend'ring pelican,
Repast them with my blood.[3]
KING   Why, now you speak
Like a good child and a true gentleman.
That I am guiltless of your father's death
150   And am most sensibly° in grief for it,   *sympathetically*
It shall as level° to your judgment 'pear   *directly*
As day does to your eye.
        A noise within. [OPHELIA *is heard singing.*]
        [*to an Attendant*]   Let her come in.
LAERTES   How now, what noise is that?
        Enter OPHELIA.
Oh, heat dry up my brains, tears seven times salt
155   Burn out the sense and virtue° of mine eye!   *natural power*
By heaven, thy madness shall be paid with weight
Till our scale turn the beam.[4] O rose of May,
Dear maid, kind sister, sweet Ophelia!
O Heavens, is't possible a young maid's wits
160   Should be as mortal as a poor man's life?[5]
160.1   *Nature is fine in love, and where 'tis fine*
        It sends some precious instance of itself
        After the thing it loves.[6]
OPHELIA (*sings*)   They bore him bare-faced on the bier[7]
161.1   *Hey non nonny, nonny, hey nonny,*
                And in his grave rained many a tear.
Fare you well, my dove.
LAERTES   Hadst thou thy wits and didst persuade° revenge,   *argue for*
165   It could not move thus.
OPHELIA   You must sing "a-down a-down" —and you "call him
a-down-a." Oh, how the wheel[8] becomes it. It is the false
steward that stole his master's daughter.[9]
LAERTES   This nothing's more than matter.[1]

---

1. That is, of his death.
2. Indiscriminately. (The winner of a sweepstake gained the stakes of all other players.)
3. The female pelican was supposed to feed, and even revive, its young with blood from a wound it pecked in its own breast. *Repast:* Feed.
4. *shall . . . beam:* shall be atoned for until vengeance outweighs the injury of madness (thus tilting the "scale" of justice).
5. F has the following passage, lines 160.1–160.3, not found in Q2.
6. *Nature . . . loves:* Human nature is made most ethe-

really pure by love and sends a precious token ("instance") of itself after the object of its love. Laertes struggles to say that because of Ophelia's great love for her father, her sanity departed with him.
7. F has the following line of verse, 161.1, not found in Q2.
8. Probably refrain, although possibly spinning wheel (at which women sang ballads) or Fortune's wheel. "A-down a-down" resembles the refrain of ballads of the period.
9. *false . . . daughter:* The tale is unknown.
1. This nonsense signifies more than coherent speech.

170 OPHELIA There's rosemary: that's for remembrance. Pray you,
love, remember. And there is pansies: that's for thoughts.[2]
LAERTES A document° in madness: thoughts and remembrance   *An object lesson*
fitted.
OPHELIA There's fennel for you and columbines;[3] there's rue
175 for you, and here's some for me. We may call it herb of grace
o'Sundays. You may wear your rue with a difference.[4] There's
a daisy. I would give you some violets,[5] but they withered all
when my father died. They say 'a made a good end.
[*Sings.*] For bonny sweet Robin is all my joy.
180 LAERTES Thought and afflictions, passion, hell itself
She turns to favor° and to prettiness.   *beauty*
OPHELIA (*sings*) And will 'a not come again,
     And will 'a not come again?
     No, no, he is dead.
185   Go to thy deathbed.
     He never will come again.

     His beard was as white as snow,
     Flaxen° was his poll.°   *White / head*
     He is gone, he is gone,
190   And we cast away moan.
     God ha' mercy on his soul—
and of all Christians' souls. God b'wi'you.   [*Exit.*]
LAERTES Do you see this, O God?
KING Laertes, I must commune with your grief
195 Or you deny me right. Go but apart,
Make choice of whom° your wisest friends you will,   *whichever of*
And they shall hear and judge twixt you and me:
If by direct or by collateral° hand   *an agent's*
They find us touched,° we will our kingdom give,   *involved in guilt*
200 Our crown, our life, and all that we call ours
To you in satisfaction;° but if not,   *recompense*
Be you content to lend your patience to us
And we shall jointly labor with your soul
To give it due content.
LAERTES   Let this be so.
205 His means of death, his obscure funeral—
No trophy, sword, nor hatchment[6] o'er his bones,
No noble rite, nor formal ostentation°—   *rite of grief*
Cry to be heard as 'twere from heaven to earth
That I must call't in question.[7]
KING   So you shall.
210 And where th'offense is, let the great ax fall.
I pray you go with me.   *Exeunt.*

---

2. *There's . . . thoughts:* Ophelia, recalling the flowers'
symbolic significance, distributes them to Laertes,
Gertrude, and Claudius.
3. Columbines were associated with ingratitude or
marital infidelity, fennel with flattery.
4. In heraldry, minor branches of a family were distinguished by a "difference," a variation or an addition
to the coat of arms. Ophelia probably means "for a
different reason." Rue is associated with repentance,
and Ophelia identifies it with the "herb of grace"

(wormwood), since penitence depended on and enabled
God's blessing.
5. Representing faithfulness; daisies could symbolize dissembling seduction.
6. Lozenge-shaped tablet bearing a coat of arms,
carried in funeral processions and deposited near the
tomb. *trophy:* memorial (often consisting of real or
symbolic weapons and armor).
7. I must demand an explanation of it.

4.3

Enter HORATIO *and* [*a* GENTLEMAN].

HORATIO What are they that would speak with me?

GENTLEMAN Seafaring men, sir. They say they have letters
for you.

HORATIO Let them come in.   [*Exit* GENTLEMAN.]

5   I do not know from what part of the world I should be
greeted, if not from Lord Hamlet.

Enter SAILORS.

SAILOR God bless you, sir.

HORATIO Let Him bless thee too.

SAILOR 'A shall, sir, an° please Him. There's a letter for you, sir.   *if it*

10   It came from th'ambassador that was bound for England—if
your name be Horatio, as I am let to know it is.

HORATIO [*reads the letter*] "Horatio, when thou shalt have
overlooked° this, give these fellows some means° to the King: *read / access*
they have letters for him. Ere we were two days old at sea, a

15   pirate of very warlike appointment° gave us chase. Finding   *equipment*
ourselves too slow of sail, we put on a compelled valor and in
the grapple I boarded them. On the instant, they got clear of
our ship, so I alone became their prisoner. They have dealt
with me like thieves of mercy, but they knew what they did:[1]

20   I am to do a turn for them. Let the King have the letters I
have sent and repair thou° to me with as much speed as thou   *come*
wouldst fly death. I have words to speak in thine ear will
make thee dumb, yet are they much too light for the bore° of   *caliber; size*
the matter. These good fellows will bring thee where I am.

25   Rosencrantz and Guildenstern hold their course for England.
Of them I have much to tell thee. Farewell.
He that thou knowest thine,   Hamlet."
Come, I will give you way° for these your letters,   *means of delivery*
And do't the speedier that you may direct me

30   To him from whom you brought them.   *Exeunt.*

4.4

Enter KING *and* LAERTES.

KING Now must your conscience my acquittance seal,[1]
And you must put me in your heart for friend
Sith° you have heard, and with a knowing ear,   *Since*
That he which hath your noble father slain
Pursued my life.

5   LAERTES   It well appears. But tell me
Why you proceed not against these feats,°   *acts*
So criminal and so capital° in nature,   *punishable by death*
As by your safety, greatness, wisdom, all things else,
You mainly° were stirred up.   *greatly*

KING   Oh, for two special reasons,

10   Which may to you perhaps seem much unsinewed,°   *uncompelling*

4.3 Location: The castle.
1. *They have . . . did:* They have been merciful, but
with the expectation of a return. Hamlet recalls the
thieves crucified next to Christ (one of whom he
blessed) and Christ's plea of forgiveness for those

who "know not what they do" (Luke 23:34–43).
4.4 Location: Claudius's private apartments.
1. *my acquittance seal:* affirm my innocence (of Polonius's death).

But yet to me they're strong. The Queen his mother
Lives almost by his looks and, for myself—
My virtue or my plague, be it either which—
She is so conjunct to my life and soul
15 That as the star moves not but in his sphere[2]
I could not but by her. The other motive
Why to a public count° I might not go · · · · · · · · · · · *accounting*
Is the great love the general gender° bear him, · · · · · · *common people*
Who, dipping all his faults in their affection,
20 Work like the spring that turneth wood to stone,[3]
Convert his gyves° to graces; so that my arrows, · · · *shortcomings (lit. fetters)*
Too slightly timbered for so loud a wind,
Would have reverted to my bow again
But not where I have aimed them.
25 LAERTES   And so have I a noble father lost,
A sister driven into desperate terms,
Whose worth, if praises may go back again,[4]
Stood challenger on mount of all the age
For her perfections.[5] But my revenge will come.
30 KING   Break not your sleeps for that. You must not think
That we are made of stuff so flat and dull
That we can let our beard be shook with danger[6]
And think it pastime. You shortly shall hear more.
I loved your father, and we love ourself,
35 And that, I hope, will teach you to imagine[7]—
      Enter a MESSENGER *with letters.*
35.1   *How now, what news?*
   MESSENGER   *Letters, my lord, from Hamlet;*
These to your majesty, this to the Queen.
KING   From Hamlet? Who brought them?
MESSENGER   Sailors, my lord, they say—I saw them not.
They were given me by Claudio; he received them
Of him that brought them.
40 KING   Laertes, you shall hear them.
—Leave us.   [*Exit* MESSENGER.]
[*He reads.*] "High and mighty, you shall know I am set naked° · · · *destitute*
on your kingdom. Tomorrow shall I beg leave to see your
kingly eyes, when I shall, first asking you pardon,° thereunto · · · *permission*
45 recount the occasion of my sudden return."
What should this mean? Are all the rest come back,
Or is it some abuse° and no such thing? · · · · · · · · · · · · · · *deception*
LAERTES   Know you the hand?
KING   'Tis Hamlet's character.° · · · · · · · · · · *handwriting*
"Naked"?
50 And in a postscript here he says "alone."
Can you devise° me? · *direct*
LAERTES   I am lost in it, my lord—but let him come.

---

2. According to Ptolemaic astronomy, heavenly bodies moved in hollow spheres. *conjunct* (line 14): closely united (as two planets were said astronomically to be "in conjunction" when they appeared close).
3. In limestone-rich areas (such as south Warwickshire), concentrations in spring water may be great enough to petrify absorbent objects.
4. May refer to what was (but is no longer).
5. *Stood . . . perfections:* Conspicuously challenged the world to match her perfections.
6. That I can allow anyone to endanger me with contemptuous behavior.
7. F has the following passage, lines 35.1–35.2, not found in Q2.

It warms the very sickness in my heart
That I live and tell him to his teeth,
"Thus didst thou."[8]

55 KING　　　　　　　　If it be so, Laertes—
As how should it be so, how otherwise?[9]—
Will you be ruled by me?

LAERTES　　　　　　　Ay, my lord,
　So° you will not o'errule me to a peace.　　　　　　　　*Provided that*

KING　To thine own peace. If he be now returned
60 As checking at[1] his voyage and that he means
No more to undertake it, I will work him
To an exploit now ripe in my device,°　　　　　　　　　*planning*
Under the which he shall not choose but fall.
And for his death no wind of blame shall breathe
65 But even his mother shall uncharge° the practice°　　*not accuse / connivance*
And call it accident.[2]

LAERTES　　　　　　　My lord, I will be ruled
The rather if you could devise it so
That I might be the organ.°　　　　　　　　　　　　　　*agent*

KING　　　　　　　　It falls right.
You have been talked of since your travel much,
70 And that in Hamlet's hearing, for a quality
Wherein they say you shine. Your sum of parts°　　　　*abilities*
Did not together pluck such envy from him
As did that one, and that in my regard
Of the unworthiest siege.°　　　　　　　　　　　　　　*lowest rank*

75 LAERTES　What part is that, my lord?

KING　A very ribbon in the cap of youth—
Yet needful too, for youth no less becomes°　　　　　　*is suited by*
The light and careless livery that it wears
Than settled age his sables and his weeds
80 Importing health and graveness.[3] Two months since
Here was a gentleman of Normandy.
I have seen myself, and served against, the French,
And they can well° on horseback, but this gallant　　　*are skilled*
Had witchcraft in't; he grew unto his seat
85 And to such wondrous doing brought his horse
As had he been incorpsed and demi-natured[4]
With the brave beast. So far he topped,° methought,　*surpassed*
That I in forgery of shapes and tricks[5]
Come short of what he did.

LAERTES　　　　　　　A Norman, was't?

90 KING　A Norman.

LAERTES　Upon my life, Lamord!

KING　　　　　　　　The very same.

LAERTES　I know him well—he is the brooch° indeed　　*ornament*
And gem of all the nation.

KING　He made confession° of you　　　　　　　　　　　*testimonial*

8. This which I do now to you, you did to my father.
9. As . . . otherwise: How could Hamlet be returning, and yet how else could he have sent this letter?
1. As one who has been diverted from ("checking at" is a term from falconry).
2. The following passage, lines 66–80, is omitted in F.

3. his sables . . . graveness: its rich gowns trimmed with sable, garments ("weeds") signifying concern for prosperity and dignity.
4. As if he had been in the same body and had half the nature of (the image of a centaur).
5. That I in my very imagination ("forgery") of figures and skillful feats of horsemanship.

95 And gave you such a masterly report
For art and exercise in your defense,
And for your rapier most especial,
That he cried out 'twould be a sight indeed
If one could match you. The scrimers° of their nation   *fencers*
100 He swore had neither motion, guard, nor eye,
If you opposed them. Sir, this report of his
Did Hamlet so envenom with his envy
That he could nothing do but wish and beg
Your sudden° coming o'er to play with you.   *immediate*
Now out of this—
105 LAERTES   What out of this, my lord?
KING   Laertes, was your father dear to you?
Or are you like the painting of a sorrow,
A face without a heart?
LAERTES   Why ask you this?
KING   Not that I think you did not love your father,
110 But that I know love is begun by time°   *circumstance*
And that I see in passages of proof[6]
Time qualifies° the spark and fire of it.[7]   *moderates*
There lives within the very flame of love
A kind of wick or snuff[8] that will abate it,
115 And nothing is at a like° goodness still°—   *an equal / always*
For goodness growing to a pleurisy[9]
Dies in his own too much.° That we would do   *overabundance*
We should do when we would: for this "would" changes
And hath abatements and delays as many
120 As there are tongues, are hands, are accidents,
And then this "should" is like a spendthrift's sigh
That hurts by easing.[1] But to the quick° of th'ulcer—   *center*
Hamlet comes back. What would you undertake
To show yourself indeed your father's son
More than in words?
125 LAERTES   To cut his throat i'th' church.
KING   No place indeed should murder sanctuarize;[2]
Revenge should have no bounds. But, good Laertes,
Will you do this: keep close within your chamber;
Hamlet, returned, shall know you are come home.
130 We'll put on those shall[3] praise your excellence
And set a double varnish on the fame
The Frenchman gave you, bring you in fine° together   *conclusion*
And wager o'er your heads. He being remiss,°   *unwary*
Most generous° and free from all contriving,   *noble*
135 Will not peruse the foils, so that with ease,
Or with a little shuffling, you may choose
A sword unbated, and in a pass of practice[4]
Requite him for your father.

---

6. From experiences that have tested this.
7. The following passage, lines 113–22, is omitted in F.
8. Burned part of the wick (which causes smoke and reduces light if not removed).
9. A chest inflammation, metaphorically like a fire in the heart; thought to take its name from the Latin for "more" (*plus*) and to be caused by an excess of humors (and so playing on "excess").

1. A sigh was thought to use up a drop of blood.
2. Give sanctuary to a murderer. In English tradition, a criminal remained temporarily (and in some cases, permanently) safe from arrest for most crimes (save sacrilege and treason) as long as he took refuge in a church.
3. *We'll . . . shall:* I shall incite some people to.
4. In a treacherous thrust. *unbated:* unblunted (recreational or practice foils were typically blunted).

LAERTES   I will do't,
And for purpose I'll anoint my sword.
140   I bought an unction° of a mountebank°   ointment / quack
So mortal that, but dip a knife in it,
Where it draws blood no cataplasm° so rare,   poultice
Collected from all simples° that have virtue°   herbs / potency
Under the moon, can save the thing from death
145   That is but scratched withal.° I'll touch my point   with it
With this contagion that if I gall° him slightly   prick
It may be death.
KING   Let's further think of this—
Weigh what convenience both of time and means
May fit us to our shape.⁵ If this should fail
150   And that our drift look° through our bad performance,   our intention be seen
'Twere better not essayed. Therefore this project
Should have a back or second⁶ that might hold
If this did blast in proof.⁷ Soft, let me see,
We'll make a solemn wager on your cunnings°—   skills
155   I ha't:
When in your motion° you are hot and dry,   exercise
As make your bouts more violent to that end,
And that he calls for drink, I'll have prepared him
A chalice for the nonce° whereon but sipping,   occasion
160   If he by chance escape your venomed stuck,°   thrust
Our purpose may hold there. But stay, what noise?
          Enter QUEEN.
QUEEN   One woe doth tread upon another's heel,
So fast they follow. Your sister's drowned, Laertes.
LAERTES   Drowned? Oh, where?
165   QUEEN   There is a willow grows askant° the brook   aslant
That shows his hoary leaves⁸ in the glassy stream;
Therewith fantastic garlands did she make
Of crowflowers, nettles, daisies, and long purples⁹
That liberal shepherds give a grosser¹ name
170   But our cold° maids do dead men's fingers call them.   chaste
There on the pendant boughs her crownet° weeds   garlanded
Clamb'ring to hang,² an envious sliver° broke,   a malicious twig
When down her weedy trophies and herself
Fell in the weeping brook. Her clothes spread wide
175   And mermaid-like awhile they bore her up,
Which time she chanted snatches of old lauds°   hymns
As one incapable° of her own distress,   uncomprehending
Or like a creature native and endued
Unto that element.³ But long it could not be
180   Till that her garments, heavy with their drink,
Pulled the poor wretch from her melodious lay°   song

5. May make us ready to put into effect our plot and
to assume the roles we are to play.
6. Should have something in reserve (military metaphor for the plotting).
7. Should blow up in our faces when put to the test
(like a cannon).
8. The willow leaf is gray-white ("hoary") on the under-
side (reflected from below by the water). The willow
was an emblem of mourning and of forsaken love.
9. Early purple orchids. *crowflowers*: common name

for several wildflowers, including Ragged Robin and
bluebells (often appearing beside long purples in
woodland and sharing their association with fertility).
1. More indecent. Among the recorded names for
the purple orchis are "priest's-pintle" (penis), "dog's
cullions" (testicles), "goat's cullions," and "fool's bal-
lochs." *liberal*: free-spoken.
2. Deserted lovers proverbially hung garlands on
willows.
3. *native . . . element*: naturally fit to live in water.

To muddy death.

LAERTES   Alas, then she is drowned.

QUEEN   Drowned, drowned.

LAERTES   Too much of water hast thou, poor Ophelia,
185 And therefore I forbid my tears. But yet
It is our trick°—nature her custom holds,   *characteristic way*
Let shame say what it will. [*He weeps.*] When these are
    gone
The woman will be out.[4] Adieu, my lord.
I have a speech o'fire that fain° would blaze   *gladly*
But that this folly drowns it.   *Exit.*

190 KING   Let's follow, Gertrude.
How much I had to do to calm his rage!
Now fear I this will give it start again.
Therefore let's follow.   *Exeunt.*

5.1

Enter two Clowns°[, *a* GRAVEDIGGER *and a*   *rustics; peasants*
SECOND MAN].

GRAVEDIGGER   Is she to be buried in Christian burial when
she willfully seeks her own salvation?[1]

SECOND MAN   I tell thee she is. Therefore make her grave
straight.° The crowner hath sat on her[2] and finds it Chris-   *right away*
5   tian burial.[3]

GRAVEDIGGER   How can that be, unless she drowned herself
in her own defense?

SECOND MAN   Why, 'tis found so.

GRAVEDIGGER   It must be "so offended";[4] it cannot be else, for
10   here lies the point: if I drown myself wittingly, it argues an
act, and an act hath three branches—it is to act, to do, to
perform. Argal,[5] she drowned herself wittingly.

SECOND MAN   Nay, but hear you, goodman delver[6]—

GRAVEDIGGER   Give me leave. Here lies the water, good; here
15   stands the man, good. If the man go to this water and drown
himself, it is, willy-nilly, he goes, mark you that. But if the
water come to him and drown him, he drowns not himself.
Argal, he that is not guilty of his own death shortens not his
own life.

20 SECOND MAN   But is this law?

GRAVEDIGGER   Ay, marry is't, crowner's 'quest° law.   *inquest*

SECOND MAN   Will you ha' the truth on't? If this had not been
a gentlewoman, she should have been buried out o' Christian burial.

25 GRAVEDIGGER   Why, there thou say'st,° and the more pity that   *how right you are*
great folk should have countenance° in this world to drown   *privilege*

---

4. *When . . . out:* When I have cried my tears, the
feminine side of my nature will be gone with them.
5.1 Location: A churchyard.
1. Probably the Gravedigger's mistake for "damnation"; suicide was a mortal sin. Ordinarily, suicides
would not receive a "Christian burial" (in consecrated ground with the church's blessing and ritual).
2. Conducted an inquest on the cause of her death.
crowner: coroner.
3. And has given the verdict that she is eligible for a
Christian burial (in effect, a decision that Ophelia

did not drown herself).
4. A mangled version of *se defendendo*, the legal term
for "killing in self-defense."
5. For "ergo," or "therefore." The argument parodies
a famous law case of 1554 concerning suicide by
drowning, in which the act was said to have three
parts: imagination, resolution, and perfection (accomplishment).
6. Master Digger ("Goodman" was the ordinary title
in addressing a man by his occupation).

or hang themselves more than their even°-Christian. Come,   *fellow*
my spade. There is no ancient gentlemen but gardeners,
ditchers, and gravemakers: they hold up° Adam's profession.   *carry on*

30 SECOND MAN   Was he a gentleman?

GRAVEDIGGER   'A was the first that ever bore arms.[7]

31.1   SECOND MAN   *Why, he had none.*

      GRAVEDIGGER   *What, art a heathen? How doth thou under-*
      stand the Scripture? The Scripture says Adam digged.
      Could he dig without arms?

I'll put another question to thee. If thou answerest me not to
the purpose, confess thyself.[8]

SECOND MAN   Go to.[9]

35 GRAVEDIGGER   What is he that builds stronger than either the
mason, the shipwright, or the carpenter?

SECOND MAN   The gallowsmaker, for that outlives a thousand
tenants.

GRAVEDIGGER   I like thy wit well, in good faith. The gallows
40 does° well, but how does it well? It does well to those that do   *serves*
ill. Now, thou dost ill to say the gallows is built stronger
than the church. Argal, the gallows may do well to thee. To't
again, come.

SECOND MAN   Who builds stronger than a mason, a shipwright,
45 or a carpenter?

GRAVEDIGGER   Ay, tell me that and unyoke.[1]

SECOND MAN   Marry, now I can tell—

GRAVEDIGGER   To't.

SECOND MAN   Mass,° I cannot tell.   *By the mass*

50 GRAVEDIGGER   Cudgel thy brains no more about it, for your
dull ass will not mend° his pace with beating; and when you   *improve*
are asked this question next, say "a gravemaker"—the houses
he makes lasts till doomsday. Go get thee in and fetch me a
stoup° of liquor.   [*Exit* SECOND MAN.]   *flagon*
    [*He digs and sings.*]
                    Song.

55   In youth when I did love, did love,
    Methought it was very sweet
    To contract°-a the time for-a my behove,°   *shorten / advantage*
    Oh, methought there a-was nothing a-meet.[2]

    Enter HAMLET *and* HORATIO.

HAMLET   Has this fellow no feeling of his business? 'A sings in
60 gravemaking.

HORATIO   Custom hath made it in him a property of easiness.[3]

HAMLET   'Tis e'en so, the hand of little employment hath the
daintier sense.[4]

GRAVEDIGGER (*sings*)   But age with his stealing steps
65   Hath clawed me in his clutch
    And hath shipped me into the land°   *earth*
    As if I had never been such.
    [*He tosses up a skull.*]

HAMLET   That skull had a tongue in it and could sing once.

---

7. Those bearing a family coat of arms were officially recognized as gentlemen; playing on "limbs."
8. "Confess thyself and be hanged" was proverbial.
9. An expression of impatience.
1. Rest your wits from work (like draft animals).
2. *meet:* suitable. The Gravedigger sings garbled snatches of Thomas Lord Vaux's poem "The Aged

Lover Renounceth Love," printed in *Tottel's Miscellany* (1557). The extrametrical "a"s are probably grunts while digging.
3. *a property of easiness:* something he can do without distress.
4. Has more delicate feeling (because not hardened by callouses).

How the knave jowls° it to the ground as if 'twere Cain's   *slams*
70   jawbone that did the first murder. This might be the pate of
a politician which this ass now o'erreaches[5]—one that would
circumvent God, might it not?

HORATIO   It might, my lord.

HAMLET   Or of a courtier which could say, "Good morrow,
75   sweet lord, how dost thou, sweet lord?" This might be my
lord Such-a-one that praised my lord Such-a-one's horse
when 'a went to beg it, might it not?

HORATIO   Ay, my lord.

HAMLET   Why, e'en so, and now my lady Worm's, chopless° and   *lacking a lower jaw*
80   knocked about the mazard° with a sexton's spade—here's fine   *head*
revolution[6] an° we had the trick° to see't. Did these bones cost   *if / ability*
no more the breeding but to play at loggets with them?[7] Mine
ache to think on't.

GRAVEDIGGER (*sings*)   A pickax and a spade, a spade,
85   For and° a shrouding sheet,   *And also*
               Oh, a pit of clay for to be made
               For such a guest is meet.
      [*He tosses up another skull.*]

HAMLET   There's another. Why, may not that be the skull of a
lawyer? Where be his quiddities[8] now, his quillets,° his   *quibbles*
90   cases, his tenures,° and his tricks? Why does he suffer this   *property titles*
mad knave now to knock him about the sconce° with a dirty   *head*
shovel, and will not tell him of his action of battery?[9] Hmm,
this fellow might be in 's time a great buyer of land, with his
statutes, his recognizances, his fines, his double vouchers,
95   his recoveries,[1] to have his fine° pate full of fine° dirt. Will   *subtle / fine-grained*
vouchers vouch° him no more of his purchases and dou-   *guarantee*
bles° than the length and breadth of a pair of indentures?[2]   *(duplicate purchases)*
The very conveyances° of his lands will scarcely lie in this   *deeds*
box,° and must th'inheritor° himself have no more, ha?   *deed box; coffin / owner*
100 HORATIO   Not a jot more, my lord.

HAMLET   Is not parchment made of sheepskins?

HORATIO   Ay, my lord, and of calves' skins too.

HAMLET   They are sheep and calves° which seek out assur-   *simpletons and fools*
ance[3] in that. I will speak to this fellow. —Whose grave's
105   this, sirrah?[4]

GRAVEDIGGER   Mine, sir.
    [*Sings.*]   Oh, a pit of clay for to be made[5]
107.1   *For such a guest is meet.*

HAMLET   I think it be thine indeed, for thou liest in't.

GRAVEDIGGER   You lie out on't, sir, and therefore 'tis not yours.
110   For my part I do not lie in't, yet it is mine.

---

5. *o'erreaches*: reaches over or overtakes. In Elizabethan England, a "politician" was a schemer for political advantage.
6. Reversal of fortune (literally, the turning of Fortune's wheel).
7. Was it so inexpensive and easy to bring these bones to maturity that they can be treated as loggets (small wooden clubs thrown at a stake)?
8. Subtle distinctions.
9. Legal prosecution for assault.
1. Fines and recoveries were both kinds of lawsuits brought to make legal an agreement to transfer land ownership. The "double voucher" summoned two wit-

nesses to attest to the land's ownership in these cases. *statutes:* mortgages on land, often linked with "recognizances" (bonds acknowledging a particular debt).
2. The two copies of a document (written on one sheet and separated by an irregular cut so that they could later be proved to be part of one transaction). The dead man's property (his grave) is hardly bigger than these elaborate papers.
3. Security, playing on the legal conveyance of a property title.
4. An address used with inferiors.
5. F has the following line of verse, 107.1, not found in Q2.

HAMLET   Thou dost lie in't to be in't and say it is thine—'tis
for the dead, not for the quick.° Therefore thou liest.

living

GRAVEDIGGER   'Tis a quick° lie, sir, 'twill away again from me
to you.

nimble

115   HAMLET   What man dost thou dig it for?

GRAVEDIGGER   For no man, sir.

HAMLET   What woman, then?

GRAVEDIGGER   For none neither.

HAMLET   Who is to be buried in't?

120   GRAVEDIGGER   One that was a woman, sir, but rest her soul,
she's dead.

HAMLET   How absolute° the knave is! We must speak by the
card[6] or equivocation will undo us. By the Lord, Horatio,
this three years I have took note of it, the age is grown so
125   picked° that the toe of the peasant comes so near the heel of
the courtier, he galls his kibe.° —How long hast thou been
gravemaker?

precise

punctilious
chafes his heel sore

GRAVEDIGGER   Of the days i'th' year, I came to't that day that
our last King Hamlet overcame Fortinbras.

130   HAMLET   How long is that since?

GRAVEDIGGER   Cannot you tell that? Every fool can tell that.
It was that very day that young Hamlet was born—he that is
mad and sent into England.

HAMLET   Ay, marry, why was he sent into England?

135   GRAVEDIGGER   Why, because 'a was mad. 'A shall recover his
wits there, or, if 'a do not, 'tis no great matter there.

HAMLET   Why?

GRAVEDIGGER   'Twill not be seen in him there—there the men
are as mad as he.

140   HAMLET   How came he mad?

GRAVEDIGGER   Very strangely, they say.

HAMLET   How, "strangely"?

GRAVEDIGGER   Faith, e'en with losing his wits.

HAMLET   Upon what ground?[7]

145   GRAVEDIGGER   Why, here in Denmark. I have been sexton
here, man and boy, thirty years.

HAMLET   How long will a man lie i'th' earth ere he rot?

GRAVEDIGGER   Faith, if 'a be not rotten before 'a die—as we
have many pocky corpses that will scarce hold the laying
150   in[8]—'a will last you some eight year or nine year. A tanner
will last you nine year.

HAMLET   Why he more than another?

GRAVEDIGGER   Why, sir, his hide is so tanned with his trade
that 'a will keep out water a great while, and your water is a
155   sore decayer of your whoreson° dead body. Here's a skull
now hath lain you i'th' earth twenty-three years.

vile

HAMLET   Whose was it?

GRAVEDIGGER   A whoreson mad fellow's it was—whose do you
think it was?

160   HAMLET   Nay, I know not.

---

6. With precisely defined meanings (literally, by the
directions marked on a mariner's compass card).
7. From what cause? (The Gravedigger takes him to
mean "In what country?")

8. *pocky . . . in:* bodies riddled with venereal disease
that hardly keep from disintegrating during their
burial rites.

GRAVEDIGGER A pestilence on him for a mad rogue. 'A poured
a flagon of Rhenish° on my head once. This same skull, sir,   *Rhine wine*
was, sir, Yorick's skull, the King's jester.
HAMLET [*taking the skull*] This?
165 GRAVEDIGGER E'en that.
HAMLET Alas, poor Yorick. I knew him, Horatio—a fellow of
infinite jest, of most excellent fancy. He hath bore me on his
back a thousand times and now how abhorred° in my imagi-   *disgusting*
nation it is. My gorge rises at it. Here hung those lips that I
170 have kissed I know not how oft. —Where be your gibes now,
your gambols, your songs, your flashes of merriment that
were wont to set the table on a roar? Not one now to mock
your own grinning? Quite chapfallen?[9] Now get you to my
lady's table and tell her, let her paint an inch thick, to this
175 favor° she must come—make her laugh at that. Prithee,   *appearance*
Horatio, tell me one thing.
HORATIO What's that, my lord?
HAMLET Dost thou think Alexander looked o'this fashion i'th'
earth?
180 HORATIO E'en so.
HAMLET And smelt so? Pah!
       [*He puts down the skull.*]
HORATIO E'en so, my lord.
HAMLET To what base uses we may return, Horatio. Why may
not imagination trace the noble dust of Alexander till 'a find
185 it stopping a bunghole?°   *opening of a cask*
HORATIO 'Twere to consider too curiously° to consider so.   *oversubtly*
HAMLET No, faith, not a jot. But to follow him thither with
modesty° enough and likelihood to lead it: Alexander died,   *reasonable speculation*
Alexander was buried, Alexander returneth to dust, the dust
190 is earth, of earth we make loam,[1] and why of that loam
whereto he was converted might they not stop a beer barrel?
Imperious Caesar, dead and turned to clay,
Might stop a hole to keep the wind away.
Oh, that that earth which kept the world in awe
195 Should patch a wall t'expel the water's flaw.°   *squall*
But soft, but soft awhile—
       Enter KING, QUEEN, LAERTES, *and the corpse* [*of*
       Ophelia, *with other* LORDS *and a* PRIEST].
                              here comes the King,
The Queen, the courtiers; who is this they follow,
And with such maimèd rites?[2] This doth betoken
The corpse they follow did with desperate hand
200 Fordo it° own life. 'Twas of some estate.[3]   *Bring down its*
Couch we° awhile and mark.   *Let's lie low*
       [HAMLET *and* HORATIO *stand aside.*]
LAERTES What ceremony else?[4]
HAMLET [*to* HORATIO] That is Laertes, a very noble youth—
mark.
LAERTES What ceremony else?
205 PRIEST Her obsequies have been as far enlarged

---

9. Dejected; also, with a dropped or lost lower jaw.   3. Someone of importance.
1. A mix of clay and straw used as plaster.   4. Laertes insists upon further funeral rites.
2. Truncated ceremonies; curtailed rituals.

As we have warranty.° Her death was doubtful,[5]   *proper sanction*
And, but that great command o'ersways the order,[6]
She should in ground unsanctified been lodged
Till the last trumpet. For° charitable prayers,   *Rather than*

210   Flints and pebbles should be thrown on her,
Yet here she is allowed her virgin crants,[7]
Her maiden strewments,[8] and the bringing home
Of bell and burial.[9]

LAERTES   Must there no more be done?

PRIEST   No more be done.

215   We should profane the service of the dead
To sing a requiem and such rest to her
As to peace-parted° souls.   *peacefully deceased*

LAERTES   Lay her i'th' earth,
And from her fair and unpolluted flesh
May violets spring. I tell thee, churlish priest,

220   A minist'ring angel shall my sister be
When thou liest howling.°   *(in hell)*
     [*Ophelia's body is laid in the grave.*]

HAMLET [*aside*]   What, the fair Ophelia?

QUEEN [*scattering flowers on the grave*]   Sweets to the sweet.
    Farewell.
I hoped thou shouldst have been my Hamlet's wife—
I thought thy bride-bed to have decked, sweet maid,
And not have strewed thy grave.

225 LAERTES   Oh, treble woe
Fall ten times double on that cursèd head
Whose wicked deed thy most ingenious sense[1]
Deprived thee of. Hold off the earth awhile[2]
Till I have caught her once more in mine arms.
    [*He leaps into the grave.*]

230   Now pile your dust upon the quick and dead
Till of this flat a mountain you have made
T'o'ertop old Pelion or the skyish head
Of blue Olympus.[3]

HAMLET [*coming forward*]   What is he whose grief
Bears such an emphasis,[4] whose phrase° of sorrow   *rhetoric*

235   Conjures the wand'ring stars° and makes them stand   *planets*
Like wonder-wounded° hearers? This is I,   *awestruck*
Hamlet the Dane.[5]

LAERTES   The devil take thy soul!
    [*He grapples with* HAMLET.][6]

---

5. That is, possibly suicide.
6. And if royal authority had not prevailed over the usual ecclesiastical procedure.
7. TEXTUAL COMMENT F has "Shardes" additionally strewn on Ophelia, while substituting "Rites" for Q2's "Crants." See Digital Edition TC 8 (combined text).
8. Flowers strewed over the casket or grave. Throughout northern Europe, funerary flowers of an unmarried girl often included a special wreath that was sometimes afterward hung in the church. *crants:* garlands.
9. *the bringing . . . burial:* the taking her to her resting place with the ritual passing bells and funeral service.
1. Quick, perceptive intelligence.

2. Stop filling the grave for a moment.
3. In Greek mythology, giants piled Pelion (a mountain in Thessaly) on top of Mount Ossa in an attempt to climb Mount Olympus.
4. A violent expression.
5. Normally the title of the king of Denmark.
6. TEXTUAL COMMENT The stage directions of F and Q1 make clear that Laertes jumps into the grave, whereas in Q2 the jump is only implied through a later line. But only Q1 specifies that Hamlet jumps into the grave after him. We omit any specific staging direction concerning whether Hamlet jumps, or how the ensuing fight takes place, because the scene's ambiguities admit multiple possible arrangements. See Digital Edition TC 9 (combined text).

HAMLET   Thou pray'st not well.
   I prithee take thy fingers from my throat,

240   For though I am not splenative° and rash,   *quick-tempered*
   Yet have I in me something dangerous
   Which let thy wisdom fear. Hold off thy hand.

KING   Pluck them asunder.

QUEEN   Hamlet, Hamlet!

LORDS   Gentlemen!

HORATIO [*to* HAMLET]   Good my lord, be quiet.

245 HAMLET   Why, I will fight with him upon this theme
   Until my eyelids will no longer wag.°   *blink*

QUEEN   O my son, what theme?

HAMLET   I loved Ophelia. Forty thousand brothers
   Could not with all their quantity of love

250   Make up my sum. What wilt thou do for her?

KING   Oh, he is mad, Laertes.

QUEEN   For love of God, forbear him.°   *let him alone*

HAMLET   'Swounds,° show me what thou'lt do—   *By Christ's wounds*
   Wilt weep, wilt fight, wilt fast, wilt tear thyself,

255   Wilt drink up eisel,° eat a crocodile?   *vinegar*
   I'll do't. Dost come here to whine,
   To outface me with leaping in her grave?
   Be buried quick° with her and so will I.   *alive*
   And if thou prate of mountains, let them throw

260   Millions of acres on us till our ground,
   Singeing his pate° against the burning zone,°   *head / sun's sphere*
   Make Ossa[7] like a wart. Nay, an° thou'lt mouth,°   *if / speak excessively*
   I'll rant as well as thou.

QUEEN   This is mere madness—
   And thus awhile the fit will work on him;

265   Anon,° as patient as the female dove   *Soon*
   When that her golden couplets are disclosed,°   *chicks are hatched*
   His silence will sit drooping.

HAMLET   Hear you, sir,
   What is the reason that you use me thus?
   I loved you ever—but it is no matter.

270   Let Hercules himself do what he may,
   The cat will mew and dog will have his day.[8]   *Exit.*

KING   I pray thee, good Horatio, wait upon him.

                                    Exit HORATIO.

   [*aside to* LAERTES] Strengthen your patience in° our last   *with*
     night's speech—
   We'll put the matter to the present push.°   *the test immediately*

275   —Good Gertrude, set some watch over your son.
   —This grave shall have a living monument.[9]
   An hour of quiet thereby shall we see;
   Till then in patience our proceeding be.   *Exeunt.*

5.2

Enter HAMLET *and* HORATIO.

HAMLET   So much for this, sir. Now shall you see the other:°   *other matter*
   You do remember all the circumstance?°   *state of things then*

---

7. Greek mountain (see note to line 233).
8. *Let . . . day:* Despite Laertes' Herculean ranting, my day will come.

9. A lasting memorial; hinting that Hamlet, now "living," will soon be sacrificed to Ophelia's memory.
5.2 Location: A stateroom of the castle.

HORATIO   Remember it, my lord?

HAMLET   Sir, in my heart there was a kind of fighting

5   That would not let me sleep; methought I lay
       Worse than the mutines in the bilbo.[1] Rashly°—   *Impulsively*
       And praised be rashness for it—let us know°   *acknowledge*
       Our indiscretion° sometime serves us well   *unreasoned action*
       When our deep plots do fall,[2] and that should learn us

10   There's a divinity that shapes our ends,
       Rough-hew them° how we will.   *Form them roughly*

HORATIO   That is most certain.

HAMLET   Up from my cabin,
       My sea-gown scarfed about me, in the dark
       Groped I to find out them, had my desire,

15   Fingered° their packet, and in fine° withdrew   *Stole / finally*
       To mine own room again, making so bold—
       My fears forgetting manners—to unfold
       Their grand commission; where I found, Horatio,
       A royal knavery: an exact command,

20   Larded° with many several° sorts of reasons   *Elaborated / different*
       Importing° Denmark's health and England's too,   *Concerning*
       With—ho!—such bugs and goblins in my life[3]
       That on the supervise,° no leisure bated°—   *reading / allowed*
       No, not to stay° the grinding of the ax—   *await*
       My head should be struck off.

25 HORATIO   Is't possible?

HAMLET   Here's the commission: read it at more leisure.
       But wilt thou hear now how I did proceed?

HORATIO   I beseech you.

HAMLET   Being thus benetted round with villains—

30   Ere I could make a prologue to my brains
       They had begun the play[4]—I sat me down,
       Devised a new commission, wrote it fair.[5]
       I once did hold it as our statists° do   *statesmen*
       A baseness to write fair and labored much

35   How to forget that learning,[6] but, sir, now
       It did me yeoman's service.[7] Wilt thou know
       Th'effect of what I wrote?

HORATIO   Ay, good my lord.

HAMLET   An earnest conjuration° from the King,   *appeal*
       As England was his faithful tributary,

40   As love between them like the palm might flourish,
       As peace should still her wheaten garland[8] wear
       And stand a comma[9] 'tween their amities,
       And many suchlike "as," sir, of great charge,[1]
       That on the view and knowing of these contents,

1. Worse than the mutineers in the ankle fetters.
2. When our best-laid plans fail.
3. Such fanciful horrors that would result were I to remain alive. *bugs:* bugbears.
4. *Ere . . . play:* Hamlet's brains "acted" before he consciously thought out a plan.
5. In the professional handwriting of finished (published) documents.
6. *I once . . . learning:* In the sixteenth century, the upper echelons of government became increasingly professionalized; Hamlet implies that these newly elevated officials are prone to snobbish pretensions,

covering up their education as common clerks, and he confesses that he once shared their snobbery.
7. It served me valiantly. English yeomen (free landholders) were famous for military strength, supposedly because they fought for their national interest rather than for base pay.
8. The wheaten garland, like the palm tree, is an emblem of peace and prosperity.
9. And hold their interests separate but still connected (unlike a period, which would cut off "amity").
1. Weighty clauses beginning with "as."

45 Without debatement further more or less,
He should those bearers put to sudden death,
Not shriving time² allowed.

HORATIO   How was this sealed?

HAMLET   Why, even in that was heaven ordinant;°   *guiding*
I had my father's signet in my purse,

50 Which was the model of that Danish seal;
Folded the writ up in the form of th'other,
Subscribed° it, gave't th'impression,° placed it safely,   *Signed / the seal (in wax)*
The changeling³ never known. Now, the next day
Was our sea fight, and what to this was sequent°   *subsequent*

55 Thou knowest already.

HORATIO   So Guildenstern and Rosencrantz go to't.⁴

56.1   HAMLET   *Why, man, they did make love to this employment.*
They are not near my conscience; their defeat°   *destruction*
Does by their own insinuation grow.
'Tis dangerous when the baser nature comes

60 Between the pass and fell incensèd points⁵
Of mighty opposites.°   *opponents*

HORATIO   Why, what a king is this!

HAMLET   Does it not, think thee, stand me now upon⁶—
He that hath killed my king and whored my mother,

65 Popped in between th'election and my hopes,
Thrown out his angle° for my proper° life,   *fishhook / own*
And with such coz'nage°— is't not perfect conscience⁷   *trickery*

67.1   *To quit° him with this arm? And is't not to be damned*   *requite*
To let this canker° of our nature come   *cancerous sore*
In° further evil?   *Into*

HORATIO   *It must be shortly known to him from England*

67.5   *What is the issue° of the business there.*   *result*

HAMLET   *It will be short; the interim's mine,*
*And a man's life's no more than to say "one."*⁸
But I am very sorry, good Horatio,
That to Laertes I forgot myself,

67.10   *For by the image° of my cause I see*   *mirror's reflection*
The portraiture of his. I'll court his favors.
But sure the bravery° of his grief did put me   *ostentation*
Into a tow'ring passion.

         Enter [OSRIC,] *a courtier.*

HORATIO   *Peace, who comes here?*

OSRIC   Your lordship is right welcome back to Denmark.

HAMLET   I humbly thank you, sir. [*aside to* HORATIO] Dost

70 know this water fly?

HORATIO   No, my good lord.

HAMLET   Thy state is the more gracious,° for 'tis a vice to know   *blessed*
him. He hath much land, and fertile. Let a beast be lord of

---

2. Time for final confession and absolution, a part of
the state ritual of legal executions.
3. A malicious elf child substituted for an infant, as
Hamlet swaps his counterfeit letter for their authentic one.
4. F has the following line, 56.1, not found in Q2.
5. *the pass . . . points:* fencing language; the thrust
("pass") and fiercely angry ("fell") rapiers.
6. Rest incumbent upon me.
7. TEXTUAL COMMENT F has the following passage,

lines 67.1–67.13, omitted in Q2. There is a similar passage in Q1 but not in Q2. These lines, combined with
F's omission of Hamlet's mean-spirited exchange with
Ostrick of Q2 (5.2.96–117), evoke a more sympathetic
protagonist who does not need Q2's subsequent
reminders of princely duty (5.2.178–80). See Digital
Edition TC 10 (combined text).
8. And life lasts no longer than it takes to pronounce
("say") the monosyllable "one."

beasts and his crib shall stand at the king's mess.⁹ 'Tis a

75 chough° but, as I say, spacious in the possession of dirt.   *rich boor; jackdaw*

OSRIC   Sweet lord, if your lordship were at leisure, I should
impart a thing to you from his majesty.

HAMLET   I will receive it, sir, with all diligence of spirit. Your
bonnet° to his right use—'tis for the head.   *hat*

80 OSRIC   I thank your lordship, it is very hot.

HAMLET   No, believe me, 'tis very cold: the wind is northerly.

OSRIC   It is indifferent° cold, my lord, indeed.   *rather*

HAMLET   But yet methinks it is very sultry and hot, or my
complexion°—   *constitution*

85 OSRIC   Exceedingly, my lord, it is very sultry, as 'twere—I cannot tell how. My lord, his majesty bade me signify to you
that 'a° has laid a great wager on your head. Sir, this is the   *he*
matter.

HAMLET   I beseech you, remember.¹

[*He gestures to* OSRIC *to put on his hat.*]

90 OSRIC   Nay, good my lord, for my ease, in good faith.² Sir,
here is newly come to court Laertes—believe me, an abso-
lute gentleman full of most excellent differences,° of very   *superior qualities*
soft° society and great showing.° Indeed, to speak feel-   *pleasing / appearance*
ingly° of him, he is the card or calendar of gentry,³ for you   *appreciatively*

95 shall find in him the continent of what part⁴ a gentleman
would see.

HAMLET   Sir, his definement suffers no perdition in you,⁵
though I know to divide him inventorially would dozy°   *dizzy*
th'arithmetic of memory, and yet but yaw neither in respect

100 of his quick sail;⁶ but in the verity of extolment,° I take   *in truthful praise*
him to be a soul of great article⁷ and his infusion° of such   *inborn essence*
dearth° and rareness as, to make true diction⁸ of him, his   *preciousness*
semblable° is his mirror, and who else would trace him,   *likeness*
his umbrage, nothing more.⁹

105 OSRIC   Your lordship speaks most infallibly of him.

HAMLET   The concernancy,° sir—why do we wrap the gentle-   *relevance (to us)*
man in our more rawer breath?¹

OSRIC   Sir?

HORATIO   Is't not possible to understand in another tongue?

110 You will to't, sir, really.²

HAMLET   What imports the nomination° of this gentleman?   *mention*

OSRIC   Of Laertes?

HORATIO   His purse is empty already—all 's golden words are
spent.

115 HAMLET   Of him, sir.

OSRIC   I know you are not ignorant—

9. *Let . . . mess:* If an animal owned enough herds, even
it might find a place at the king's table. *crib:* manger.
1. "Remember your courtesy," the conventional expression inviting a subordinate to put his hat back on.
2. A conventional expression declining Hamlet's
invitation. After "faith," the following passage, lines
91–118, is omitted in F.
3. The model of gentlemanly behavior. *card:* chart or
map. *calendar:* account book, directory.
4. Attribute or quality, playing on "region" (to which
Laertes is the "card"). *continent:* embodiment, continuing the geographical pun.
5. Your picture of him ("definement") loses none of
the man's real excellence.

6. *to divide . . . sail:* to list his qualities individually
would confuse the memory's reckoning up (through
recounting vast numbers), and yet only steer erratically ("yaw") around Laertes' skills—that is, the
description would only approximate his virtues.
7. An obscure phrase. Possibly, large scope; excellent
quality.
8. To speak truly.
9. And whoever imitates him is like his shadow
("umbrage"), not the real thing at all.
1. Our less refined words (since we are so much inferior to Laertes).
2. *Is't . . . really:* Can't he understand his words in
another man's mouth? You will have your joke, sir, truly.

HAMLET I would you did, sir. Yet, in faith, if you did, it would not much approve° me. Well, sir?   *commend*

OSRIC You are not ignorant of what excellence Laertes is.

120 HAMLET I dare not confess that, lest I should compare with him in excellence.[3] But to know a man well were to know himself.[4]

OSRIC I mean, sir, for his weapon; but in the imputation laid on him by them in his meed,° he's unfellowed.°   *merit / unmatched*

125 HAMLET What's his weapon?

OSRIC Rapier and dagger.

HAMLET That's two of his weapons, but well.

OSRIC The King, sir, hath wagered with him six Barbary horses, against the which he has impawned,° as I take it, six   *staked*

130 French rapiers and poniards with their assigns,° as girdle,°   *accessories / sword belt* hanger,[5] and so. Three of the carriages, in faith, are very dear to fancy, very responsive to the hilts, most delicate carriages and of very liberal conceit.[6]

HAMLET What call you the carriages?[7]

135 HORATIO I knew you must be edified by the margin[8] ere you had done.

OSRIC The carriages, sir, are the hangers.

HAMLET The phrase would be more germane to the matter if we could carry a cannon by our sides;[9] I would it might be

140 "hangers" till then. But on: six Barbary horses against six French swords, their assigns, and three liberal-conceited carriages—that's the French bet against the Danish. Why, is this all you call it?

OSRIC The King, sir, hath laid,° sir, that in a dozen passes   *placed his bet*

145 between yourself and him, he shall not exceed you three hits.[1] He hath laid on twelve for nine,[2] and it would come to immediate trial if your lordship would vouchsafe the answer.[3]

HAMLET How if I answer no?

OSRIC I mean, my lord, the opposition of your person in trial.

150 HAMLET Sir, I will walk here in the hall. If it please his majesty, it is the breathing° time of day with me—let the foils   *exercising* be brought. The gentleman willing and the King hold his purpose, I will win for him an° I can; if not, I will gain noth-   *if* ing but my shame and the odd hits.

155 OSRIC Shall I deliver you so?

HAMLET To this effect, sir, after what flourish your nature will.

OSRIC I commend my duty° to your lordship.   *dedicate my service*

HAMLET Yours.   [*Exit* OSRIC.]

'A does well to commend° it himself; there are no tongues   *recommend*

160 else for 's turn.°   *purpose*

---

3. Claim to match him (since, proverbially, only excellence recognizes excellence).
4. For in order to know another man truly, one must know oneself.
5. Attaching straps.
6. *are . . . conceit:* capture the imagination ("fancy") and match or echo ("responsive to") the ornamentation on the rapiers' hilts; further, they are finely wrought ("delicate") and of an elaborate ("liberal") design.
7. Osric's inflated term for "hangers," or straps.
8. Must be informed by an explanatory note (from the margin of a book). F omits Horatio's line.

9. A common definition of "carriage" at the time was a mount for a cannon.
1. Laertes must score three more "hits" than Hamlet out of twelve bouts of swordplay to win the wager.
2. If "he" is Laertes, Osric may mean "He has bet twelve passes for nine hits" (a greater challenge than the King's terms, by which he would only need eight hits to win).
3. Would accept the challenge (Osric's meaning, and the only honorable response). In the next line, Hamlet deliberately misunderstands "answer" as "(any) reply."

HORATIO   This lapwing runs away with the shell on his head.[4]

HAMLET   'A did so, sir, with his dug[5] before 'a sucked it. Thus
has he, and many more of the same breed that I know the
drossy° age dotes on, only got the tune of the time,[6] and out   *worthless*
165   of an habit of encounter, a kind of yeasty collection,[7] which
carries them through and through the most profane and
winnowed opinions[8]—and do but blow them to their trial,
the bubbles are out.[9]

Enter a LORD.

LORD   My lord, his majesty commended him to you by young
170   Osric, who brings back to him that you attend him in the
hall. He sends to know if your pleasure hold to play with
Laertes or that you will take longer time?

HAMLET   I am constant to my purposes. They follow the
King's pleasure; if his fitness speaks, mine is ready—now or
175   whensoever, provided I be so able as now.

LORD   The King and Queen and all are coming down.

HAMLET   In happy time.

LORD   The Queen desires you to use some gentle entertainment[1] to Laertes before you fall to play.

180   HAMLET   She well instructs me.   [*Exit* LORD.]

HORATIO   You will lose, my lord.

HAMLET   I do not think so. Since he went into France I have
been in continual practice. I shall win at the odds. Thou
wouldst not think how ill all's here about my heart, but it is
185   no matter.

HORATIO   Nay, good my lord.

HAMLET   It is but foolery, but it is such a kind of gaingiving°   *misgiving*
as would perhaps trouble a woman.

HORATIO   If your mind dislike anything, obey it. I will fore-
190   stall their repair° hither and say you are not fit.   *coming*

HAMLET   Not a whit. We defy augury. There is special providence[2] in the fall of a sparrow. If it be, 'tis not to come; if it
be not to come, it will be now; if it be not now, yet it will
come; the readiness is all. Since no man, of aught he leaves,
195   knows, what is't to leave betimes?[3] Let be.

A table prepared. [*Enter*] *trumpets, drums, and
Officers with cushions, foils,* [*and*] *daggers.* [*Then
enter*] KING, QUEEN, LAERTES, [OSRIC, LORDS,] *and
all the state.*

KING   Come, Hamlet, come and take this hand from me.
[*He puts Laertes' hand in Hamlet's.*]

---

4. The newly hatched chicks of the plover ("lapwing") were supposed to scurry about still wearing
their eggshells, a reference to the bonnet that Osric
has finally put back on, as well as to the courtier's
brainless chirping.
5. *'A did . . . dug:* He did the same to his mother's
breast. Obscure in Q2, the line in F—"He did comply
with his dug"—mocks Osric's obsequiousness.
6. *the tune of the time:* the fashionable turns of speech.
7. *and out . . . collection:* and from the formulas
("habit") of courteous conversation ("encounter")
they make a frothy and inflated repertoire of speech
and behavior ("yeasty collection").
8. *which . . . opinions:* their empty clichés get them
through or pass for the most carefully considered
wisdom (which is "winnowed" like wheat separated

from chaff during threshing).
9. And if you test them by blowing on them—as
Hamlet does by speaking to Osric—they pop and dissolve. The following passage, lines 169–80, is omitted in F.
1. To behave with conciliatory courtesy.
2. God's direction for a specific event (over and
above "general providence," the whole shape of God's
design). Compare Matthew 10:29: "Are not two sparrows sold for a farthing? and one of them shall not
fall on the ground without your Father."
3. Since no man fully understands what he's leaving
behind him, why does it matter to leave it early
("betimes")? F reads: "Since no man has aught of what
he leaves, what is't to leave betimes?"

HAMLET [*to* LAERTES] Give me your pardon, sir. I have done
    you wrong,
    But pardon't as you are a gentleman.
    This presence° knows, and you must needs have heard,   *royal company*
200   How I am punished with a sore distraction.°   *agitation; insanity*
    What I have done
    That might your nature, honor, and exception°   *disapproval*
    Roughly awake, I here proclaim was madness.
    Was't Hamlet wronged Laertes? Never Hamlet.
205   If Hamlet from himself be ta'en away,
    And when he's not himself does wrong Laertes,
    Then Hamlet does it not; Hamlet denies it.
    Who does it then? His madness. If't be so,
    Hamlet is of the faction that is wronged—
210   His madness is poor Hamlet's enemy.[4]
210.1   *Sir, in this audience,*
    Let my disclaiming from a purposed evil[5]
    Free me so far in your most generous thoughts
    That I have shot my arrow o'er the house
    And hurt my brother.[6]
215   LAERTES I am satisfied in nature,
    Whose motive in this case should stir me most
    To my revenge. But in my terms of honor[7]
    I stand aloof and will no reconcilement
    Till by some elder masters of known honor
220   I have a voice and precedent of peace[8]
    To keep my name ungored.° But all that time   *my reputation intact*
    I do receive your offered love like love
    And will not wrong it.
    HAMLET   I embrace it freely
    And will this brothers' wager frankly° play.   *freely*
    —Give us the foils.
225   LAERTES   Come, one for me.
    HAMLET I'll be your foil,[9] Laertes. In mine ignorance
    Your skill shall like a star i'th' darkest night
    Stick° fiery off indeed.   *Sparkle; jab*
    LAERTES   You mock me, sir.
    HAMLET No, by this hand.
230   KING Give them the foils, young Osric. Cousin Hamlet,
    You know the wager.
    HAMLET   Very well, my lord.
    Your grace has laid the odds o'th' weaker side.
    KING I do not fear it. I have seen you both.
    But since he is better,° we have therefore odds.°   *favored / handicapping*
235   LAERTES This is too heavy—let me see another.
    HAMLET This likes° me well. These foils have all a° length?   *pleases / the same*
    OSRIC Ay, my good lord.
        [*They prepare to play. Enter Servants with flagons*
        of wine.]

---

4. F has the following line, 210.1, not found in Q2.
5. Let my disavowal of evil intention.
6. F's reading is "mother."
7. But where my social standing as a man of honor is concerned.
8. *Till . . . peace:* Until the consensus of men of

authoritative standing, judging by the standards of tradition (precedent), holds that I can make an honorable peace.
9. Flattering contrast. Jewels were often set with a piece of metal foil under them to increase their glitter.

You that look pale and tremble at this chance,
That are but mutes° or audience to this act,   *nonspeaking actors*
Had I but time—as this fell sergeant,[7] Death,
315 Is strict in his arrest—oh, I could tell you—
But let it be. Horatio, I am dead.
Thou livest: report me and my cause aright
To the unsatisfied.
HORATIO   Never believe it:
I am more an antique Roman than a Dane;[8]
Here's yet some liquor left—
320 HAMLET   As thou'rt a man,
Give me the cup. Let go—by heaven I'll ha't!
O God, Horatio, what a wounded name,
Things standing thus unknown, shall I leave behind me!
If thou didst ever hold me in thy heart,
325 Absent thee from felicity awhile
And in this harsh world draw thy breath in pain
To tell my story.
            A march afar off.
            Enter OSRIC.
                    What warlike noise is this?
OSRIC Young Fortinbras, with conquest come from Poland,
To th'ambassadors of England gives this warlike volley.°   *military salute*
330 HAMLET Oh, I die, Horatio—
The potent poison quite o'ercrows[9] my spirit.
I cannot live to hear the news from England,
But I do prophesy th'election lights
On Fortinbras—he has my dying voice.[1]
335 So tell him, with th'occurrents° more and less   *events*
Which have solicited[2]—the rest is silence.
336.1   *Oh, oh, oh, oh.*[3]
            [*He dies.*]
HORATIO Now cracks a noble heart. Good night, sweet prince,
And flights of angels sing thee to thy rest.
            [*Drums sound within.*]
Why does the drum come hither?
            Enter FORTINBRAS *with* [*his train and*] *the* [*English*]
            AMBASSADORS.
FORTINBRAS Where is this sight?
340 HORATIO   What is it you would see?
If aught of woe or wonder, cease your search.
FORTINBRAS This quarry cries on havoc.[4] O proud Death,
What feast is toward° in thine eternal cell   *preparing*
That thou so many princes at a shot
So bloodily hast struck?
345 AMBASSADOR   The sight is dismal,

---

7. As this fierce sheriff's officer.
8. Ancient ("antique") Romans generally regarded suicide as preferable to dishonor; in particular, they believed that servants or retainers should not outlive their master's overthrow.
9. Announces triumph over, like the victorious rooster in a cockfight.
1. Vote. Because Denmark is an elective monarchy, Fortinbras can only become king by receiving the "voice," or vote, of electors like Hamlet.

2. Some editors assume that the sentence is grammatically incomplete, broken off by death. Hamlet seems to refer to the events that have moved ("solicited") him to have his story told and to give his support to Fortinbras.
3. These exclamations, which appear in F but not Q2, might be suggestive stage directions for death throes, rather than scripted cries.
4. All this slaughtered game ("quarry") proclaims a massacre.

And our affairs from England come too late.
The ears are senseless that should give us hearing
To tell him° his commandment is fulfilled　　　　　　　　　　*(Claudius)*
That Rosencrantz and Guildenstern are dead.
Where should we have our thanks?

350 HORATIO [*indicating* KING]　　　　Not from his mouth,
Had it th'ability of life to thank you:
He never gave commandment for their death.
But since so jump° upon this bloody question°　　　*immediately / matter*
You from the Polack wars and you from England
355 Are here arrived, give order that these bodies
High on a stage be placèd to the view,
And let me speak to th' yet unknowing world
How these things came about. So shall you hear
Of carnal, bloody, and unnatural acts,
360 Of accidental judgments,° casual° slaughters,　　　*retributions / chance*
Of deaths put on° by cunning and for no cause,　　　　　　　*instigated*
And in this upshot purposes mistook
Fall'n on th'inventors' heads. All this can I
Truly deliver.
FORTINBRAS　　Let us haste to hear it—
365 And call the noblest to the audience.
For° me, with sorrow I embrace my fortune.　　　　　　　　　*As for*
I have some rights of memory⁵ in this kingdom,
Which now to claim my vantage° doth invite me.　　*favorable opportunity*
HORATIO　Of that I shall have also cause to speak,
370 And from his mouth whose voice will draw no more.
But let this same be presently performed
Even while men's minds are wild, lest more mischance
On° plots and errors happen.　　　　　　　　　　　　　　　*On top of*
FORTINBRAS　　　　　　　　Let four captains
Bear Hamlet like a soldier to the stage,
375 For he was likely, had he been put on,°　　　　　　*put to the test*
To have proved° most royal. And for his passage　　*shown himself; acted*
The soldier's music and the rite of war
Speak loudly for him.
Take up the bodies. Such a sight as this
380 Becomes the field⁶ but here shows° much amiss.　　　　　　*appears*
Go, bid the soldiers shoot.　　　　　　　　　　　*Exeunt.*

---

5. *of memory:* unforgotten; traditional.　　　　6. Is most appropriate to a battlefield.

1603 HAMLET

In 1823 a British army officer and antiquary, Sir Henry Bunbury, found in a closet in his country estate a volume that, he thought, must have been acquired by his grandfather, an ardent collector of old dramas. The volume, which bound together twelve Shakespeare quartos, had a curious feature: the quarto of *Hamlet* that it contained did not correspond to any that Shakespeare scholars had previously known. The title page was dated 1603, and the text differed in crucial ways from both that printed in a quarto of 1604–05 (Q2) and that included in the 1623 First Folio (F). Bunbury exchanged his volume of quartos with a bookseller for books worth £180. In 1856 a second copy of the strange 1603 quarto of *Hamlet,* lacking the title page, was bought from a student for one shilling by a Dublin bookdealer, who turned a tidy profit by selling it for £70. The first of these copies is in the Huntington Library in California, the second in the British Library in London. Immensely valuable, they are the only two known surviving copies of what is called the First Quarto (Q1) of *Hamlet.*

The first and most striking difference between the 1603 Q1 and the other early texts of *Hamlet* is its length. The title page of the 1604–05 Q2 announced accurately that it was "[n]ewly imprinted" and that it was "enlarged to almost as much againe as it was" (that is, it is almost twice as long). With a further glance back at Q1, the Q2 title page advertised that it was printed from "the true and perfect Coppie," and, though there is no way to verify this claim (or even fully to understand what it means), the text of Q1 certainly has many moments of incoherence, awkwardness, and confusion.

When Q1 returned to circulation in the nineteenth century, many of its readers thought that they were encountering Shakespeare's first draft of his tragedy. They believed, for example, that he had initially written "To be, or not to be—ay, there's the point" (as the soliloquy begins in Q1), and then made the inspired revision that resulted in the version with which everyone is familiar. They assumed he had started with "Corambis" and "Montano" and then changed the names to "Polonius" and "Reynaldo." Or they thought he had first depicted Gertrude as Hamlet's ally in the plot against Claudius—for so she is in several scenes of Q1—and then decided to make the extent of her knowledge and her allegiance far more ambiguous.

But gradually another theory was advanced and gained ascendency. Q1, it was said, was one of those "stolen and surreptitious copies" that the Folio editors denounced, copies that were "maimed and deformed by the frauds and stealths of injurious impostors." It was a "bad quarto"—as A. W. Pollard termed it in 1909—defective, the theory went, because it had been pirated, possibly by an audience member good at shorthand, or more probably by one or more of the actors who had been paid to reconstruct from memory the whole script. Careful examination even seemed to reveal the principal culprit: the actor who played Marcellus. Hence the scenes in which Marcellus appears are relatively close in Q1 to those same scenes in Q2 and F; the further Marcellus gets from the stage, the more distorted the memorial reconstruction. But what of the *Mousetrap* scene in Q1, a scene without Marcellus and yet also fairly close to the other versions? The answer, it was proposed, lay in doubling: the performer who played Marcellus also played one or more of the minor characters elsewhere in the play.

Most (though not all) contemporary scholars accept some presence of memorial reconstruction in the Q1 *Hamlet.* But it is difficult to attribute all of the features of the text to the vagaries and inadequacies of memory. Whoever helped put together the text may have forgotten some lines, but the brevity and the rearrangement of several scenes seem to have at least as much to do with the exigencies of performance on the Elizabethan and Jacobean public stage. That is, both the "good" texts of *Hamlet*— the massive Q2 and even the somewhat shorter version printed in F—were too long to be performed in the ordinary circumstances of the times: an open-air stage without artificial lighting where in some seasons it begins to get dark by midafternoon. They would have had to be cut, and it is possible that the shape of Q1 reflects, in some way or other, one such theatrical abridgment.

This possibility would make Q1 a particularly fascinating trace, a trace not of Shakespeare's own manuscript but rather of a contemporary theater company's way of handling the play. (The title page calls attention to performance, claiming that it has been "diverse times acted by his Highnesse seruants in the City of London, as also in the two universities of Cambridge and Oxford, and else-where.") Since its recovery, Q1 has served as the basis for a number of productions, and its theatrical viability—its pace and momentum and compression—has found adherents. And even when Q1 is regarded as nothing but an interesting oddity, most productions of *Hamlet* have mined it for hints for performance. Thus Q2 brings on the mad Ophelia with the stage direction "*Enter Ophelia*," while Q1 says "*Enter Ofelia playing on a lute, and her hair down, singing.*" So too in the closet scene between Hamlet and his mother: Q2 and F have "*Enter Ghost*," while Q1 tells us "*Enter the Ghost in his nightgown.*" The nightgown—a striking change from the full armor of his initial appearance—seems to mark a crucial transformation in the Ghost's status.

Stephen Greenblatt

Selected Bibliography

Clayton, Thomas, ed. *The Hamlet First Published (Q1, 1603): Origins, Form, Intertextualities.* Newark: U of Delaware P; London and Toronto: Associated UP, 1992. How and why was the First Quarto composed, and what is its value? The twelve essays in this collection address these questions in wide-ranging and sometimes conflicting ways.

Craig, Hardin. *A New Look at Shakespeare's Quartos.* Stanford: Stanford UP, 1961. Shakespeare's "bad quartos" are not reconstructions by actors, but rather revisions or early versions made by the playwright himself.

Egan, Gabriel. *The Struggle for Shakespeare's Text: Twentieth-Century Editorial Theory and Practice.* Cambridge: Cambridge UP, 2010. Egan traces the twentieth-century debate between the New Bibliographers, with their author-centered approach, and the New Textualists, who focused instead on the socialized text, taking the side of the New Bibliographers.

Lesser, Zachary. *Hamlet after Q1.* Philadelphia: U of Pennsylvania P, 2015. A study of the reevaluation of *Hamlet* in text and performance after the 1823 discovery of Q1, which is consequently both the earliest and the latest text.

Maguire, Laurie E. *Shakespearean Suspect Texts: The "Bad" Quartos and Their Context.* Cambridge: Cambridge UP, 1996. Based on the examination of forty-one "suspect texts," Maguire argues that a case for memorial reconstruction can be made for only a few of the supposed "bad quartos," including Q1 of *Hamlet.*

Menzer, Paul. *The Hamlets: Cues, Qs, and Remembered Texts.* Newark: U of Delaware P, 2008. On the basis of an analysis of the cues, Menzer argues that Q1 was not intended as a memorial reconstruction of Shakespeare's *Hamlet* but rather as a separate project cobbled together out of a range of recollected *Hamlet* materials.

Sams, Eric. "Shakespeare's Hand in the Copy for the 1603 First Quarto of *Hamlet.*" *Hamlet Studies* 20 (1998): 80–88. An orthographical analysis of the Q1 and Q2 editions of *Hamlet* suggests that the First Quarto is a revision of an earlier Shakespearean text rather than a memorial reconstruction.

The Tragical History of Hamlet, Prince of Denmark

FIRST QUARTER

[THE PERSONS OF THE PLAY

HAMLET, Prince of Denmark
KING of Denmark and stepfather to Prince Hamlet
Gertred, QUEEN of Denmark
GHOST of Hamlet, former King of Denmark and father to Prince Hamlet
CORAMBIS, a royal counselor
OFELIA, daughter to Corambis
LEARTES, son to Corambis
MONTANO, servant to Corambis
BARNARDO ⎱ sentries
MARCELLUS ⎰
FIRST SENTINEL
HORATIO, friend to Hamlet
ROSSENCRAFT ⎱ school friends to Hamlet
GILDERSTONE ⎰
CORNELIUS ⎱ Danish ambassadors
VOLTEMAR ⎰
English AMBASSADORS
FIRST PLAYER, leader of the troupe
PLAYERS, who take on the roles of PROLOGUE, DUKE, DUCHESS, and LUCIANS
FORTENBRASSE, Prince of Norway
FIRST CLOWN, a gravedigger
SECOND CLOWN, companion to First Clown
PRIEST
Braggart GENTLEMAN
Lords, Norwegian Captain, Soldiers in the Norwegian army, Attendants]

Scene 1

Enter [FIRST SENTINEL *and* BARNARDO].

FIRST SENTINEL   Stand! Who is that?
BARNARDO   'Tis I.
FIRST SENTINEL   Oh, you come most carefully° upon your   *dutifully; cautiously*
    watch.
BARNARDO   An if° you meet Marcellus and Horatio,   *An if = If*
5   The partners of my watch, bid them make haste.
FIRST SENTINEL   I will. See, who goes there?
    Enter HORATIO *and* MARCELLUS.
HORATIO   Friends to this ground.°   *country*
MARCELLUS   And liegemen° to the Dane.[1]   *sworn servants*
    [*to* FIRST SENTINEL] Oh, farewell, honest soldier; who hath
    relieved you?

Scene 1 Location: A guard platform at Elsinore Castle, Denmark.
1. King of Denmark.

Speak to me!
If thou art privy to thy country's fate,
Which happily° foreknowing may prevent,   *perhaps; fortunately*
Oh, speak to me!
95   Or if thou hast extorted in thy life
Or hoarded treasure in the womb of earth,
For which they say you spirits oft walk in death,
Speak to me, stay and speak! Speak!
          [*The cock crows.*]
Stop it, Marcellus—

BARNARDO   'Tis here.
HORATIO   'Tis here.   *Exit* GHOST.
MARCELLUS   'Tis gone.
100   Oh, we do it wrong, being so majestical,
To offer it the show of violence,
For it is as the air invulnerable,
And our vain blows malicious mockery.

BARNARDO   It was about to speak when the cock crew.
105 HORATIO   And then it faded like a guilty thing
Upon a fearful summons. I have heard
The cock, that is the trumpet to the morning,
Doth with his early and shrill-crowing throat
Awake the god of day,[7] and at his sound,
110   Whether in earth or air, in sea or fire,
The extravagant and erring[8] spirit hies°   *hurries*
To his confines°—and of the truth hereof   *enclosure*
This present object° made probation.°   *example / proof*

MARCELLUS   It faded on the crowing of the cock.
115   Some say that ever 'gainst° that season comes   *always when*
Wherein our Savior's birth is celebrated,
The bird of dawning singeth all night long;
And then, they say, no spirit dare walk abroad,
The nights are wholesome, then no planet strikes,[9]
120   No fairy takes,° nor witch hath power to charm,   *bewitches*
So gracious° and so hallowed is that time.   *full of God's grace*

HORATIO   So have I heard and do in part believe it.
But see, the sun in russet mantle clad[1]
Walks o'er the dew of yon high mountaintop.
125   Break we our watch up and, by my advice,
Let us impart what we have seen tonight
Unto young Hamlet, for upon my life
This spirit, dumb to us, will speak to him.
Do you consent we shall acquaint him with it,
130   As needful in our love,[2] fitting our duty?

MARCELLUS   Let's do't, I pray, and I this morning know
Where we shall find him most conveniently.   [*Exeunt.*]

Scene 2

Enter KING, QUEEN, HAMLET, LEARTES, CORAMBIS, *and*
the two Ambassadors [CORNELIUS *and* VOLTEMAR],
with Attendants.

KING   Lords, we here have writ to Fortenbrasse,
  Nephew to old Norway, who, impotent
  And bedrid, scarcely hears of this his
  Nephew's purpose. And we here dispatch
5 You, good Cornelius, and you, Voltemar,
  For bearers of these greetings to old Norway,
  Giving to you no further personal power
  To business with the King
  Than those related articles do show.
10 Farewell, and let your haste commend your duty.
CORNELIUS *and* VOLTEMAR   In this and all things will we
    show our duty.
KING   We doubt it nothing;° heartily farewell.   *not at all*
                [*Exeunt* CORNELIUS *and* VOLTEMAR.]
  And now, Leartes, what's the news with you?
  You said you had a suit°—what is't, Leartes?   *petition; request*
15 LEARTES   My gracious lord, your favorable license,
  Now that the funeral rites are all performed,
  I may have leave° to go again to France;   *permission*
  For though the favor of your grace might stay me,
  Yet something is there whispers in my heart
20 Which makes my mind and spirits bend all for France.
KING   Have you your father's leave, Leartes?
CORAMBIS   He hath, my lord, wrung from me a forced grant,° *concession*
  And I beseech you grant your highness' leave.
KING   With all our heart, Leartes, fare thee well.
25 LEARTES   I in all love and duty take my leave.   *Exit.*
KING   And now, princely son Hamlet,
  What means these sad and melancholy moods?
  For° your intent going to Wittenberg,[1]   *As for*
  We hold it most unmeet° and unconvenient,   *unsuitable*
30 Being the joy and half-heart° of your mother.   *darling*
  Therefore let me entreat you stay in court,
  All Denmark's hope, our cousin[2] and dearest son.
HAMLET   My lord, 'tis not the sable° suit I wear,   *black*
  No, nor the tears that still stand in my eyes,
35 Nor the distracted 'havior° in the visage,   *expression*
  Nor all together mixed with outward semblance,
  Is equal to the sorrow of my heart.
  Him have I lost I must of force forgo,
  These but the ornaments and suits° of woe.   *trappings*
40 KING   This shows a loving care in you, son Hamlet,
  But you must think your father lost a father,
  That father dead lost his, and so shall be
  Until the general ending.°   *apocalypse*
  Therefore cease laments. It is a fault
45 'Gainst heaven, fault 'gainst the dead, a fault 'gainst nature,

---

Scene 2 Location: The castle.
1. The birthplace of Protestantism, the university of
Luther and Faustus; many Danes studied there.

Hamlet intends to resume his studies at the university in Wittenberg.
2. Kinsman (outside one's immediate family).

And in reason's common course most certain
None lives on earth but he is born to die.

QUEEN   Let not thy mother lose her prayers, Hamlet—
Stay here with us, go not to Wittenberg.

50 HAMLET   I shall in all my best obey you, madam.

KING   Spoke like a kind and a most loving son.
And there's no health° the King shall drink today   *toast*
But° the great cannon to the clouds shall tell°   *Unless / sound*
The rouse° the King shall drink unto Prince Hamlet.   *large cup of drink*

Exeunt all but HAMLET.

55 HAMLET   Oh, that this too much grieved and sallied[3] flesh
Would melt to nothing, or that the universal
Globe of heaven would turn all to a chaos!
O God, within two months—no, not two—married
Mine uncle—oh, let me not think of it—
60 My father's brother, but no more like
My father than I to Hercules.[4]
Within two months, ere° yet the salt of most   *before*
Unrighteous tears had left their flushing
In her galled° eyes, she married. O God, a beast   *distressed*
65 Devoid of reason would not have made
Such speed! Frailty, thy name is woman!
Why, she would hang on him as if increase
Of appetite had grown by what it looked on.
Oh, wicked, wicked speed, to make such
70 Dexterity to incestuous sheets!
Ere yet the shoes were old
With which she followed my dead father's corpse
Like Niobe, all tears[5]—married! Well, it is not,
Nor it cannot come to good.
75 But break, my heart, for I must hold my tongue.

Enter HORATIO, MARCELLUS[, *and* BARNARDO].

HORATIO   Health to your lordship!

HAMLET   I am very glad to see you—
Horatio, or I much forget myself.

HORATIO   The same, my lord, and your poor servant ever.

80 HAMLET   O my good friend, I change° that name with you.   *exchange*
But what make you from[6] Wittenberg, Horatio?
—Marcellus!

MARCELLUS   My good lord.

HAMLET   I am very glad to see you. Good even, sirs!
85 [*to* HORATIO] But what is your affair in Elsinore?
We'll teach you to drink deep ere you depart.

HORATIO   A truant disposition, my good lord.

HAMLET   Nor shall you make me truster°   *believer*
Of your own report against yourself—
90 Sir, I know you are no truant.
But what is your affair in Elsinore?

---

3. "Sallied" is a possible spelling of "sullied." Editors
have seen wordplay on "sallied," assailed, or, alternatively, salty, tear-soaked (salting was a method of preserving meat), and "sullied," or contaminated,
ill-used. F has "solid."
4. In Greek and Roman mythology, a powerful demigod renowned for his strength, as exemplified in his

twelve famous "labors."
5. Niobe's fourteen children were killed by Apollo
and Artemis to punish her for boasting about them.
She continued to weep bitterly even after she was
turned to stone.
6. What are you doing away from.

HORATIO   My good lord, I came to see your father's funeral.

HAMLET   Oh, I prithee do not mock me, fellow student,
    I think it was to see my mother's wedding.

95 HORATIO   Indeed, my lord, it followed hard upon.°   *quickly thereafter*

HAMLET   Thrift, thrift, Horatio: the funeral baked meats°   *meat pies and pastries*
    Did coldly° furnish forth the marriage tables.   *when cold*
    Would I had met my dearest° foe in heaven   *most hated*
    Ere ever I had seen that day, Horatio.

100   Oh, my father, my father, methinks I see my father.

HORATIO   Where, my lord?

HAMLET   Why, in my mind's eye, Horatio.

HORATIO   I saw him once: he was a gallant king.

HAMLET   He was a man, take him for all in all;

105   I shall not look upon his like again.

HORATIO   My lord, I think I saw him yesternight.

HAMLET   Saw? Who?

HORATIO   My lord, the King your father.

HAMLET   Ha! Ha! The King my father, kee° you?   *say*

HORATIO   Season° your admiration° for awhile   *Moderate / amazement*

110   With an attentive ear till I may deliver,
    Upon the witness of these gentlemen,
    This wonder to you.

HAMLET   For God's love let me hear it!

HORATIO   Two nights together had these gentlemen,

115   Marcellus and Barnardo, on their watch
    In the dead vast° and middle of the night,   *stillness*
    Been thus encountered by a figure like your father,
    Armed to point,[7] exactly, cap-à-pie,°   *head to foot*
    Appears before them. Thrice he walks

120   Before their weak and fear-oppressèd eyes
    Within his truncheon's[8] length while they, distilled°   *dissolved*
    Almost to jelly with the act° of fear,   *effect*
    Stand dumb and speak not to him. This to me
    In dreadful secrecy impart they did,

125   And I with them the third night kept the watch
    Where, as they had delivered°—form° of the thing,   *reported / the form*
    Each part made true and good—
    The apparition comes. I knew your father:
    These hands are not more like.[9]

HAMLET   'Tis very strange.

130 HORATIO   As I do live, my honored lord, 'tis true,
    And we did think it right done° in our duty   *prescribed*
    To let you know it.

HAMLET   Where was this?

MARCELLUS   My lord, upon the platform where we watched.

HAMLET   Did you not speak to it?

135 HORATIO   My lord, we did, but answer made it none;
    Yet once methought it was about to speak,
    And lifted up his head to motion
    Like as he would speak, but even° then   *just*
    The morning cock crew loud, and in all haste

7. Armed in each point or detail.
8. Officer's baton.

9. These hands are not more like each other than the apparition was like King Hamlet.

140   It shrunk in haste away, and vanishèd° our sight.   *vanished from*

HAMLET   Indeed, indeed, sirs—but this troubles me.
    Hold you the watch tonight?

BARNARDO *and* MARCELLUS   We do, my lord.

HAMLET   Armed, say ye?

HORATIO, BARNARDO, *and* MARCELLUS   Armed, my good lord.

145   HAMLET   From top to toe?

HORATIO, BARNARDO, *and* MARCELLUS   My good lord, from
    head to foot.

HAMLET   Why, then, saw you not his face?

HORATIO   Oh, yes, my lord, he wore his beaver° up.   *helmet's faceguard*

HAMLET   How looked he—frowningly?

150   HORATIO   A countenance more in sorrow than in anger.

HAMLET   Pale, or red?

HORATIO   Nay, very pale.

HAMLET   And fixed his eyes upon you?

HORATIO   Most constantly.

HAMLET   I would I had been there.

HORATIO   It would've much amazed you.

155   HAMLET   Yea, very like, very like—stayed it long?

HORATIO   While one with moderate pace might tell° a   *count*
    hundred.

MARCELLUS   Oh, longer, longer.

HAMLET   His beard was grizzled,° no?   *gray*

HORATIO   It was as I have seen it in his life,
    A sable silver.[1]

HAMLET   I will watch tonight;
    Perchance 'twill walk again.

160   HORATIO   I warrant° it will.   *guarantee*

HAMLET   If it assume my noble father's person,
    I'll speak to it, if hell itself should gape
    And bid me hold my peace. Gentlemen,
    If you have hitherto concealed this sight,

165   Let it be tenable° in your silence still;   *held*
    And whatsoever else shall chance tonight
    Give it an understanding but no tongue.
    I will requite your loves. So fare you well.
    Upon the platform twixt eleven and twelve
    I'll visit you.

170   ALL   Our duties to your honor.

HAMLET   Oh, your loves, your loves, as mine to you. Farewell.
        Exeunt [HORATIO, MARCELLUS, *and* BARNARDO].
    My father's spirit in arms! Well, all's not well:
    I doubt° some foul play. Would the night were come!   *suspect*
    Till then, sit still my soul. Foul deeds will rise,

175   Though all the world o'erwhelm them, to men's eyes.   *Exit.*

Scene 3
Enter LEARTES *and* OFELIA.

LEARTES   My necessaries are embarked°—I must aboard.   *on the ship*
    But, ere I part, mark what I say to thee:

---

1. Black sprinkled with white.
Scene 3 Location: Corambis's apartments in the castle.

I see Prince Hamlet makes a show of love—
Beware, Ofelia, do not trust his vows.
5 Perhaps he loves you now, and now his tongue
Speaks from his heart, but yet take heed, my sister:
The chariest° maid is prodigal enough   *most careful; modest*
If she unmask her beauty to the moon.[1]
Virtue itself scapes not calumnious thoughts—
10 Believe't, Ofelia—therefore keep aloof
Lest that he trip° thy honor and thy fame.°   *bring down / reputation*
OFELIA Brother, to this I have lent attentive ear
And doubt not but to keep my honor firm.
But, my dear brother, do not you,
15 Like to a cunning sophister,[2]
Teach me the path and ready way to heaven,
While you, forgetting what is said to me,
Yourself, like to a careless libertine,
Doth give his heart his appetite at full
20 And little recks° how that his honor dies.   *notices; cares*
LEARTES No, fear it not,° my dear Ofelia.   *fear not for me*
Here comes my father:
Occasion smiles upon a second leave.[3]
        Enter CORAMBIS.
CORAMBIS Yet here, Leartes? Aboard, aboard, for shame,
25 The wind sits in the shoulder° of your sail   *at the back*
And you are stayed° for. There [*laying his hand on Leartes'*   *waited*
        head], my blessing with thee,
And these few precepts in thy memory:
Be thou familiar but by no means vulgar;[4]
Those friends thou hast, and their adoptions tried,[5]
30 Grapple them to thee with a hoop of steel,
But do not dull° the palm with entertain°   *callous / the greeting (handshaking)*
Of every new unfledged courage;[6]
Beware of entrance into a quarrel, but, being in,
Bear it° that the opposed may beware of thee;   *Manage it so*
35 Costly thy apparel as thy purse can buy,
But not expressed in fashion°—   *showiness*
For the apparel oft proclaims the man,
And they of France, of the chief rank and station,
Are of a most select and general chief in that.
40 This above all: to thy own self be true,
And it must follow as the night the day
Thou canst not then be false to anyone.
Farewell, my blessing with thee.
LEARTES I humbly take my leave. Farewell, Ofelia,
45 And remember well what I have said to you.

---

1. *prodigal . . . moon:* risk-taking enough if she
exposes herself to the moon. (Upper-class women
wore masks to screen their complexions from the
sun.) The moon was classically figured as chaste,
while the sun was traditionally associated with passion. The suggestion here is that a maid can never be
too cautious.
2. *cunning sophister:* one using speech in a deceptive
or suspect manner.
3. Favorable circumstances provide us with a second

farewell.
4. *Be . . . vulgar:* Be friendly but by no means indiscriminately social.
5. *Those . . . tried:* Those friends of yours who have
proven true and reliable.
6. *Of . . . courage:* Of any given untried (and thus not
fully trusted) acquaintance. "Courage," meaning
heart or spirit here, is a synecdoche for a person, like
"soul" in "you must not tell a soul."

OFELIA It is already locked within my heart,
  And you yourself shall keep the key of it.   *Exit* [LEARTES].
CORAMBIS What is't, Ofelia, he hath said to you?
OFELIA Something touching the Prince Hamlet.
50 CORAMBIS Marry, well thought on; 'tis given me to
    understand
  That you have been too prodigal of your
  Maiden presence unto Prince Hamlet.
  If it be so—as so 'tis given to° me,   *suggested to*
  And that in way of caution—I must tell you,
55 You do not understand yourself so well
  As befits my honor and your credit.°   *reputation*
OFELIA My lord, he hath made many tenders° of   *offers*
  His love to me—
CORAMBIS "Tenders"? Ay, ay, "tenders"[7] you may call them—
60 OFELIA And withal° such earnest vows—   *also*
CORAMBIS Springes to catch woodcocks.[8]
  What, do not I know, when the blood doth burn,
  How prodigal° the heart lends the tongue vows?   *lavishly*
  In brief, be more scanter of your maiden presence,
65 Or, tendering thus, you'll tender me a fool.[9]
OFELIA I shall obey, my lord, in all I may.
CORAMBIS Ofelia, receive none of his letters,
  For lovers' lines are snares to entrap the heart;
  Refuse his tokens: both of them° are keys   *(lines and tokens)*
70 To unlock chastity unto desire.
  Come in, Ofelia. Such men often prove
  Great in their words but little in their love.
OFELIA I will, my lord.   *Exeunt.*

Scene 4
Enter HAMLET, HORATIO, *and* MARCELLUS.
HAMLET The air bites shrewd;°   *sharply*
  It is an eager° and a nipping wind.   *a bitter*
  What hour is't?
HORATIO   I think it lacks of twelve.
MARCELLUS No, 'tis struck.
HORATIO   Indeed? I heard it not.
    Sound trumpets[, *drums, and cannon*].
5 What doth this mean, my lord?
HAMLET Oh, the King doth wake tonight and takes his
    rouse,
  Keeps wassail and the swaggering upspring reels,[1]
  And as he drains his draughts of Rhenish° down   *Rhine wine*
  The kettledrum and trumpet thus bray out
10 The triumphs of his pledge.[2]
HORATIO Is it a custom here?
HAMLET Ay, marry, is't, and though I am

---

7. *tenders*: offers of payment in compensation for
something.
8. Traps for proverbially gullible birds.
9. A multiple pun: make me look foolish; seem yourself a fool; show me a baby (idiomatically, a "fool").
Scene 4 Location: The castle's battlements.

1. *the King . . . reels*: the King revels and carouses,
has a drinking party ("wassail"), and staggers ("reels")
through a wild German dance.
2. His success in draining his cup upon making a
toast.

Native here and to the manner° born,   *custom*
It is a custom more honored in the breach
Than in the observance.[3]
    Enter the GHOST.

15 HORATIO   Look, my lord, it comes.
HAMLET   Angels and ministers of grace defend us!
Be thou a spirit of health or goblin° damned,   *demon*
Bring with thee airs° from heaven or blasts[4] from hell,   *gentle breezes*
Be thy intents wicked or charitable,
20 Thou comest in such questionable shape
That I will speak to thee. I'll call thee Hamlet,
King, father, royal Dane. Oh, answer me!
Let me not burst in ignorance, but say
Why thy canonized° bones, hearsed° in death,   *consecrated / coffined*
25 Have burst their ceremonies,[5] why thy sepulcher
In which we saw thee quietly interred
Hath burst his° ponderous and marble jaws   *its*
To cast thee up again. What may this mean
That thou, dead corpse, again in complete steel°   *armor*
30 Revisits thus the glimpses of the moon,[6]
Making night hideous and we fools of nature[7]
So horridly to shake our disposition°   *mental foundations*
With thoughts beyond the reaches of our souls?
Say, speak: wherefore? What may this mean?
35 HORATIO   It beckons you, as though it had something
To impart to you alone.
MARCELLUS   Look with what courteous action
It waves you to a more removèd ground—
But do not go with it.
HORATIO   No, by no means, my lord.
40 HAMLET   It will not speak—then will I follow it.
HORATIO   What if it tempt you toward the flood,° my lord,   *sea*
That beckles[8] o'er his base into the sea,
And there assume some other horrible shape
Which might deprive your sovereignty of reason
45 And drive you into madness? Think of it.
HAMLET   Still am I called. —Go on, I'll follow thee.
HORATIO   My lord, you shall not go.
HAMLET   Why, what should be the fear?
I do not set my life at a pin's fee,°   *worth*
And for my soul, what can it do to that,
50 Being a thing immortal like itself?
—Go on, I'll follow thee.
MARCELLUS   My lord, be ruled, you shall not go.
HAMLET   My fate cries out and makes each petty artery
As hardy as the Nemean lion's[9] nerve.
55 Still am I called—unhand me, gentlemen!

---

3. Which is more honored in being broken than in
being observed.
4. Pestilent gusts.
5. Funeral ceremonies more generally, or perhaps
Q2 and F's "cerements," grave clothes.
6. *glimpses of the moon:* (earth lit by) flickering
moonlight.

7. Mere mortals (terrified by encounters with the
supernatural).
8. "Beckles" is unattested in the *OED*. Q2 and F have
"bettles" and "beetles," suggesting a protruding or
overhanging into the sea.
9. A ferocious beast killed by Hercules.

By heaven I'll make a ghost of him that lets° me.　　　　　　　　　*hinders*
Away, I say! —Go on, I'll follow thee.
                    [*Exeunt* GHOST *and* HAMLET.]
HORATIO　He waxeth desperate with imagination.
MARCELLUS　Something is rotten in the state of Denmark.
60　HORATIO　Have after!° To what issue° will this sort?　　　　　*Go on / end*
MARCELLUS　Let's follow; 'tis not fit thus to obey him.
                                        Exeunt.

Scene 5
        Enter GHOST *and* HAMLET.
HAMLET　I'll go no farther. Whither wilt thou lead me?
GHOST　Mark me.
HAMLET　　　　　　I will.
GHOST　　　　　　　　I am thy father's spirit,
    Doomed for a time to walk the night
    And all the day confined in flaming fire
5　Till the foul crimes done in my days of nature°　　　　*my natural life*
    Are purged and burnt away.
HAMLET　　　　　　Alas, poor ghost.
GHOST　Nay, pity me not, but to my unfolding
    Lend thy listening ear: but that I am forbid
    To tell the secrets of my prison house,
10　I would a tale unfold whose lightest word
    Would harrow up° thy soul, freeze thy young blood,　　　　*vex*
    Make thy two eyes like stars start from their spheres,
    Thy knotted and combinèd locks to part,
    And each particular hair to stand on end
15　Like quills upon the fretful porcupine.
    But this same blazon¹ must not be to ears
    Of flesh and blood. Hamlet,
    If ever thou didst thy dear father love—
HAMLET　O God!
20　GHOST　Revenge his foul and most unnatural murder.
HAMLET　Murder?
GHOST　　　　　Yea, murder in the highest degree—
    As in the least 'tis bad, but mine most foul,
    Beastly, and unnatural.
HAMLET　　　　　　Haste me to know it,
    That with wings as swift as meditation,
25　Or the thought of it, may sweep to my revenge.
GHOST　Oh, I find thee apt, and duller shouldst thou be
    Than the fat° weed which roots itself in ease　　　　　　*gross*
    On Lethe wharf.² Brief let me be:
    'Tis given out° that, sleeping in my orchard,　　　　　*It's being said*
30　A serpent stung me; so the whole ear of Denmark
    Is with a forgèd process° of my death　　　　　*a fabricated account*
    Rankly abused.° But know, thou noble youth,　　　　　　*deceived*
    He that did sting thy father's heart now wears
    His crown.
HAMLET　　　　Oh, my prophetic soul, my uncle!

Scene 5　Location: Scene continues.
1. Catalogue or display of the afterlife's mysteries.
2. In classical mythology, Lethe was the river of forgetfulness in Hades. The comparison as it stands
seems incomplete, as it is missing the "Wouldst thou
not stir in this" from Q2 and F.

35   My uncle!
      GHOST   Yea, he!
      That incestuous wretch won to his will with gifts°—   *abilities; presents*
      Oh, wicked will and gifts that have the power
      So to seduce—my most seeming-virtuous queen.
40   But virtue, as it never will be moved
      Though lewdness court it in a shape of heaven,
      So lust, though to a radiant angel linked,
      Would sate itself³ from a celestial bed
      And prey on garbage.
45   But soft,⁴ methinks I scent the morning's air.
      Brief let me be: sleeping within my orchard—
      My custom always in the afternoon—
      Upon my secure hour thy uncle came
      With juice of hebona⁵ in a vial
50   And through the porches° of my ears did pour   *entranceways*
      The leprous distilment,⁶ whose effect
      Holds such an enmity with blood of man
      That swift as quicksilver⁷ it posteth° through   *speeds*
      The natural gates and alleys of the body
55   And turns the thin and wholesome blood
      Like eager° droppings into milk,   *acid (like wine)*
      And all my smooth body barked and tettered⁸ over.
      Thus was I, sleeping, by a brother's hand
      Of crown, of queen, of life, of dignity
60   At once deprived, no reckoning made of,
      But sent unto my grave with all my accounts
      And sins upon my head.⁹ Oh, horrible, most horrible!
      HAMLET   O God!
      GHOST   If thou hast nature° in thee, bear it° not—   *natural feeling / (this injustice)*
65   But, howsoever, let not thy heart conspire
      Against thy mother aught;° leave her to heaven   *any (punishment)*
      And to the burden that her conscience bears.
      I must be gone:
      The glowworm shows the matin° to be near   *morning*
70   And 'gins° to pale his uneffectual fire.   *begins*
      Hamlet, adieu! Adieu, adieu, remember me!   *Exit.*
      HAMLET   O all you host of heaven! O earth! What else?
      And shall I couple° hell? Remember thee?   *add*
      Yes, thou poor ghost,
75   From the tables° of my memory I'll wipe away   *tablet; book*
      All saws of books, all trivial fond° conceits   *foolish*
      That ever youth or else observance noted,
      And thy remembrance all alone shall sit.
      Yes, yes, by heaven, a damned pernicious villain,
80   Murderous, bawdy, smiling, damnèd villain!

---

3. Will become satiated (and unable to find further
pleasure).
4. The Ghost urges himself quickly to wrap up his
speech.
5. A poison, possibly henbane.
6. Distillation causing skin to become scaly (as in
leprosy, a disease familiar in Elizabethan England).

7. Liquid mercury, noted for its capacity for rapid
motion.
8. *barked and tettered*: covered in a scaly barklike
rash.
9. *no . . . head*: without having made restitution for
my sins, but sent to the Last Judgment liable for all
my faults.

My tables[1]—[*He takes out his table-book and writes.*] Meet°   *Appropriate*
  it is I set it down
That one may smile and smile and be a villain—
At least I am sure it may be so in Denmark.
So, uncle, there you are, there you are.
85 Now to the words: it is "Adieu, adieu,
Remember me." So, 'tis enough, I have sworn.
       Enter HORATIO *and* MARCELLUS.
HORATIO My lord, my lord!
MARCELLUS Lord Hamlet!
HORATIO Illo, lo, ho, ho!
90 MARCELLUS Illo, lo, so, ho, so, come, boy, come![2]
HORATIO Heavens secure him.
MARCELLUS How is't, my noble lord?
HORATIO What news, my lord?
HAMLET Oh, wonderful, wonderful!
95 HORATIO Good my lord, tell it.
HAMLET No, not I, you'll reveal it.
HORATIO Not I, my lord, by heaven.
MARCELLUS Nor I, my lord.
HAMLET How say you, then—would heart of man once
  think it—
But you'll be secret?
100 HORATIO *and* MARCELLUS Ay, by heaven, my lord.
HAMLET There's never a villain dwelling in all Denmark
  But he's an arrant° knave.   *a complete*
HORATIO   There need no ghost
  Come from the grave to tell you this.
HAMLET Right, you are in the right; and therefore
105 I hold it meet, without more circumstance° at all,   *elaborate speech*
We shake hands and part, you as your business
And desires shall lead you—for, look you,
Every man hath business and desires
Such as it is—and, for my own poor part,
110 I'll go pray.
HORATIO These are but wild and whirling words, my lord.
HAMLET I am sorry they offend you. Heartily,
  Yes, faith, heartily.
HORATIO   There's no offense, my lord.
HAMLET Yes, by Saint Patrick,[3] but there is, Horatio,
115 And much offense too. Touching° this vision,   *Concerning*
It is an honest° ghost, that let me tell you.   *a reliable; a genuine*
For your desires to know what is between us,
O'ermaster it as you may. And now, kind friends,
As you are friends, scholars, and gentlemen,
Grant me one poor request.
120 HORATIO *and* MARCELLUS What is't, my lord?
HAMLET Never make known what you have seen tonight.
HORATIO *and* MARCELLUS My lord, we will not.
HAMLET Nay, but swear.
HORATIO   In faith, my lord, not I.[4]

---

1. Scholars and others might carry two writing tablets hinged together, as a notebook.
2. Marcellus parodies a falconer's call.

3. Perhaps because St. Patrick was thought to be
keeper of purgatory.
4. I will indeed not reveal it.

MARCELLUS   Nor I, my lord, in faith.
125   HAMLET   Nay, upon my sword;[5] indeed, upon my sword.
        The GHOST [*calls out*] *under the stage.*
      GHOST   Swear.
      HAMLET   Ha, ha! Come, you hear this fellow in the
        cellarage:°   *cellar*
        Here consent to swear.[6]
      HORATIO   Propose the oath, my lord.
130   HAMLET   Never to speak what you have seen tonight,
        Swear by my sword.
      GHOST   Swear.
      HAMLET   *Hic et ubique?*[7] Nay then, we'll shift our ground.
        Come hither, gentlemen, and lay your hands
135   Again upon this sword. Never to speak
        Of that which you have seen, swear by my sword.
      GHOST   Swear.
      HAMLET   Well said, old mole: canst work in the earth so fast?
        A worthy pioneer![8] —Once more remove.°   *move*
140   HORATIO   Day and night, but this is wondrous strange.
      HAMLET   And therefore as a stranger give it welcome:[9]
        There are more things in heaven and earth, Horatio,
        Than are dreamt of in your philosophy.[1]
        But come here: as before, you never shall,
145   How strange or odd soe'er I bear myself—
        As I perchance hereafter shall think meet
        To put an antic disposition on[2]—
        That you at such times seeing me never shall
        With arms encumbered° thus, or this head-shake,   *folded*
150   Or by pronouncing some undoubtful[3] phrase
        As "Well, well, we know," or "We could an if° we would,"   *an if = if*
        Or "There be an if they might,"[4] or such ambiguous
        Giving out, to note that you know aught° of me—   *anything*
        This not to do, so grace and mercy
155   At your most need help you, swear.
      GHOST   Swear.
        [*They swear.*]
      HAMLET   Rest, rest, perturbèd spirit. —So, gentlemen,
        In all my love I do commend me to you,
        And what so poor a man as Hamlet may
160   To pleasure you, God willing, shall not want.°   *be left undone*
        Nay, come, let's go together.
        But still° your fingers on your lips, I pray.   *always*
        The time is out of joint:° oh, cursèd spite,   *dislocated; disordered*
        That ever I was born to set it right.
165   Nay, come,[5] let's go together.   *Exeunt.*

5. Swearing on a sword was a fairly common practice because the hilt and blade form a cross.
6. TEXTUAL COMMENT This moment—exactly whom Hamlet is addressing and what he is saying—is treated differently in Q2 and F and admits multiple interpretations. See Digital Edition TC 2 (First Quarto edited text).
7. Here and everywhere (Latin).
8. Army trench digger.

9. As if it had a guest's right to courteous hospitality.
1. Human speculative knowledge; science.
2. To assume the behavior of a madman.
3. Q2 and F read "doubtfull."
4. There are those who would speak if they were allowed.
5. The others are politely waiting for Hamlet, the Prince, to lead the way; he insists on informality.

Scene 6

Enter CORAMBIS *and* MONTANO.

CORAMBIS   Montano, here, these letters to my son
And this same money with my blessing to him,
And bid him ply° his learning, good Montano.   *work at*
MONTANO   I will, my lord.
5   CORAMBIS   You shall do very well, Montano, to say thus: "I
knew the gentleman," or "know his father"; to inquire the
manner of his life, as thus: being amongst his acquaintance,[1]
you may say you saw him at such a time, mark you me, at
game, or drinking, swearing, or drabbing°—you may go so   *whoring*
10   far.
MONTANO   My lord, that will impeach his reputation.
CORAMBIS   I'faith, not a whit, no, not a whit. Now, happily, he
closeth° with you in the consequence[2]—as you may bridle it,   *confides*
not disparage him a jot—What was I about to say?
15   MONTANO   "He closeth with him in the consequence."
CORAMBIS   Ay, you say right, he closeth with him° thus: this   *(you)*
will he say—let me see what he will say—marry, this: "I saw
him yesterday," or t'other day, or then, or at such a time,
"a-dicing" or "at tennis," ay, or "drinking drunk" or "entering
20   of a house of lightness"—*videlicet,*° brothel. Thus, sir, do we   *that is to say*
that know the world, being men of reach,° by indirections   *wide understanding*
find directions° forth, and so shall you my son[3]—you ha'   *real tendencies*
me,° ha' you not?   *my meaning*
MONTANO   I have, my lord.
25   CORAMBIS   Well, fare you well: commend me to him.
MONTANO   I will, my lord.
CORAMBIS   And bid him ply his music.
MONTANO   My lord, I will.
CORAMBIS   Farewell.   *Exit* [MONTANO].
         Enter OFELIA.
30   How now, Ofelia? What's the news with you?
OFELIA   O my dear father, such a change in nature,
So great an alteration in a prince,
So pitiful to him, fearful to me,
A maiden's eye ne'er looked on.
35   CORAMBIS   Why, what's the matter, my Ofelia?
OFELIA   Oh, young Prince Hamlet, the only flower of
Denmark,
He is bereft of all the wealth he had.
The jewel that adorned his feature most
Is filched and stolen away: his wit's bereft him.
40   He found me walking in the gallery all alone—
There comes he to me with a distracted° look,   *deranged; mad*
His garters lagging down, his shoes untied,
And fixed his eyes so steadfast on my face
As if they had vowed this is their latest object.
45   Small while he stood, but grips me by the wrist
And there he holds my pulse till, with a sigh,

Scene 6 Location: Corambis's apartments in the
castle.
1. His acquaintances.

2. To the following effect.
3. And so shall you figure out what my son has been
doing.

He doth unclasp his hold and parts away,°   *departs*
Silent as is the mid-time of the night.
And as he went, his eye was still on me,
50   For thus his head over his shoulder looked.
He seemed to find the way without his eyes,
For out of doors he went without their help,
And so did leave me.
CORAMBIS   Mad for thy love.
What, have you given him any cross words of late?
55   OFELIA   I did repel his letters, deny his gifts,
As you did charge me.
CORAMBIS   Why, that hath made him mad.
By heav'n, 'tis as proper for our age to cast
Beyond ourselves as 'tis for the younger sort
To love their wantonness. Well, I am sorry
60   That I was so rash. But what remedy?
Let's to the King. This madness may prove,
Though wild awhile, yet more true to thy love.   *Exeunt.*

Scene 7
Enter KING, QUEEN, ROSSENCRAFT, *and* GILDERSTONE.
KING   Right noble friends, that our dear cousin Hamlet
Hath lost the very heart of all his sense
It is most right,° and we most sorry for him.   *true*
Therefore we do desire, even as you tender
5   Our care to him and our great love to you,
That you will labor but to wring from him
The cause and ground of his distemperance.
Do this, the King of Denmark shall be thankful.
ROSSENCRAFT   My lord, whatsoever lies within our power.
10   Your majesty may more command in words
Than use persuasions to your liegemen, bound
By love, by duty, and obedience.
GILDERSTONE   What we may do for both your majesties
To know the grief troubles the Prince your son,
15   We will endeavor all the best we may.
So, in all duty, do we take our leave.
KING   Thanks, Gilderstone and gentle Rossencraft.
QUEEN   Thanks, Rossencraft and gentle Gilderstone.
        [*Exeunt* ROSSENCRAFT *and* GILDERSTONE.]
    Enter CORAMBIS *and* OFELIA.
CORAMBIS   My lord, the ambassadors are joyfully
20   Returned from Norway.
KING   Thou still° hast been the father of good news.   *always*
CORAMBIS   Have I, my lord? I assure your grace
I hold my duty as I hold my life
Both to my God and to my sovereign king.
25   And I believe—or else this brain of mine
Hunts not the train of policy° so well   *cleverness*
As it had wont to do¹—but I have found
The very depth of Hamlet's lunacy.

Scene 7 Location: A stateroom in the castle.   1. As it had in the past.

QUEEN God grant he hath.
        Enter the Ambassadors [VOLTEMAR *and* CORNELIUS].
30 KING Now, Voltemar, what from our brother° Norway?   *fellow monarch*
VOLTEMAR Most fair returns of greetings and desires.°   *good wishes*
    Upon our first,[2] he sent forth to suppress
    His nephew's levies,° which to him appeared   *raising of troops*
    To be a preparation 'gainst the Polack,°   *King of Poland*
35   But, better looked into, he truly found
    It was against your highness; whereat, grieved
    That so his sickness, age, and impotence
    Was falsely borne in hand,[3] sends out arrests
    On Fortenbrasse,[4] which he in brief obeys,
40   Receives rebuke from Norway, and, in fine,°   *conclusion*
    Makes vow before his uncle never more
    To give the assay of arms[5] against your majesty.
    Whereon old Norway, overcome with joy,
    Gives him three thousand crowns in annual fee°   *income*
45   And his commission to employ those soldiers,
    So levied as before, against the Polack—
    With an entreaty herein further shown
    That it would please you to give quiet pass
    Through your dominions for that enterprise
50   On such regards of safety and allowances[6]
    As therein are set down.
KING   It likes° us well, and at fit time and leisure   *pleases*
    We'll read and answer these his articles.
    Meantime, we thank you for your well-took labor.
55   Go to your rest; at night we'll feast together.
    Right welcome home!
        Exeunt Ambassadors [VOLTEMAR *and* CORNELIUS].
CORAMBIS This business is very well dispatched.
    Now, my lord, touching the young Prince Hamlet,
    Certain it is that he is mad; mad let us grant him, then.
60   Now, to know the cause of this effect—
    Or else to say the cause of this defect,
    For this effect defective[7] comes by cause—
QUEEN Good my lord, be brief.
CORAMBIS   Madam, I will.
    My lord, I have a daughter—have while she's mine°—   *until she marries*
65   For that we think is surest we often lose.
    Now, to the Prince: my lord, but note this letter,
    The which my daughter in obedience
    Delivered to my hands.
KING   Read it, my lord.
CORAMBIS Mark, my lord:
70   [*Reads.*] "Doubt that in earth is fire,
        Doubt that the stars do move,
        Doubt° truth to be a liar,   *Suspect*
        But do not doubt I love.

---

2. When we first raised the matter.
3. Disloyally taken advantage of; tricked.
4. *arrests / On Fortenbrasse:* orders commanding Fortenbrasse to stop his preparations and (presumably) present himself to explain them.
5. To mount a military challenge.
6. *On . . . allowances:* Following conditions regarding your realm's safety, subject to your approval.
7. This consequence shows a lack of something (Hamlet's reason).

To the beautiful Ofelia: thine ever, the most unhappy Prince
75 Hamlet."
My lord, what do you think of me?
Ay, or what might you think when I saw this?
KING   As of a true friend and a most loving subject.
CORAMBIS   I would be glad to prove so.
80 Now, when I saw this letter, thus I bespake my maiden:
"Lord Hamlet is a prince out of your star°   *above your sphere*
And one that is unequal° for your love."   *not proper*
Therefore I did command her refuse his letters,
Deny his tokens, and to absent herself.
85 She, as my child, obediently obeyed me.
Now, since which time, seeing his love thus crossed—
Which I took to be idle and but sport—
He straightway grew into a melancholy,
From that unto a fast, then unto distraction,
90 Then into a sadness, from that unto a madness,
And so, by continuance and weakness of the brain,
Into this frenzy which now possesseth him.
An if this be not true, take this from this.
    [*He points to his head and shoulders.*]
KING   Think you 'tis so?
95 CORAMBIS   How? So? My lord, I would very fain know
That thing that I have said 'tis so, positively,
And it hath fallen out otherwise.
Nay, if circumstances lead me on
I'll find it out, if it were hid as deep
100 As the center of the earth.
KING   How should we try° this same?   *test*
CORAMBIS   Marry, my good lord, thus:
The Prince's walk is here in the gallery—
There let Ofelia walk until he comes.
105 Yourself and I will stand close in the study:
There shall you hear the effect° of all his heart,   *purpose; drift*
And if it prove any otherwise than love,
Then let my censure fail another time.
KING   See where he comes, poring upon a book.
    Enter HAMLET.
110 CORAMBIS   Madam, will it please your grace to leave us here?
QUEEN   With all my heart.   *Exit.*
CORAMBIS   And here, Ofelia, read you on this book
And walk aloof.° The King shall be unseen.   *at a distance*
    [KING *and* CORAMBIS *retire.*]
HAMLET[8]   To be, or not to be—ay, there's the point.°   *issue to debate*
115 To die, to sleep, is that all? Ay, all.
No, to sleep, to dream—ay, marry,[9] there it goes[1]—
For in that dream of death, when we awake

---

8. TEXTUAL COMMENT Hamlet's famous soliloquy
here seems to be recomposed from memory. This
process evidently caused some confusions and inconsistencies, but it also led to a more accessible and
distilled version than its rendering in Q2 and F. See
Digital Edition TC 3 (First Quarto edited text).
9. *marry*: used for emphasis, expressing astonish-

ment or outrage.
1. *there it goes*: the "point" or question "goes" toward
the potentially problematic consideration that dreams
by necessity accompany sleep. The line is confusing
because, unlike in Q2 and F, Hamlet does not subsequently explain why the question should pivot on
dreams.

And borne before an everlasting judge,
From whence no passenger ever returned,
120 The undiscovered country, at whose sight
The happy smile and the accursèd damned—
But for this, the joyful hope of this,
Who'd bear the scorns and flattery of the world—
Scorned by the right° rich (the rich cursed of the poor),   *downright*
125 The widow being oppressed, the orphan wronged,
The taste of hunger or a tyrant's reign,
And thousand more calamities besides—
To grunt and sweat under this weary life
When that he may his full quietus make[2]
130 With a bare bodkin?° Who would this endure,   *mere dagger*
But for a hope of something after death,
Which puzzles the brain and doth confound the sense,
Which makes us rather bear those evils we have
Than fly to others that we know not of?
135 Ay, that—oh, this conscience[3] makes cowards of us all.
—Lady, in thy orisons° be all my sins remembered.   *prayers*

OFELIA My lord, I have sought opportunity, which now I
have, to redeliver to your worthy hands a small remembrance: such tokens which I have received of you.
140 HAMLET Are you fair?
OFELIA My lord?
HAMLET Are you honest?°   *chaste; truthful*
OFELIA What means my lord?
HAMLET That if you be fair and honest, your beauty should
145 admit no discourse to[4] your honesty.
OFELIA My lord, can beauty have better privilege than with
honesty?
HAMLET Yea, marry, may it, for beauty may sooner transform
honesty from what she was into a bawd than honesty can
150 transform beauty. This was sometimes° a paradox, but now   *formerly*
the time gives it scope.[5] I never gave you nothing.
OFELIA My lord, you know right well you did, and with them
such earnest vows of love as would have moved the stoniest
breast alive.
155 But now too true I find
Rich gifts wax° poor when givers grow unkind.   *grow*
HAMLET I never loved you.
OFELIA You made me believe you did.
HAMLET Oh, thou shouldst not ha' believed me! Go to a nun-
160 nery,[6] go! Why shouldst thou be a breeder of sinners? I am
myself indifferent honest,° but I could accuse myself of such   *moderately virtuous*
crimes it had been better my mother had ne'er borne me.
Oh, I am very proud, ambitious, disdainful, with more sins
at my beck° than I have thoughts to put them in. What   *command*
165 should such fellows as I do, crawling between heaven and

---

2. A paid-off account was marked "Quietus est" (Latin: "It is laid to rest").
3. Both consciousness (introspective knowledge) and moral conscience.
4. No familiar conversation with.

5. *now . . . scope*: these days (this phenomenon) is given free range.
6. By entering a nunnery, Ofelia will take a vow of lifelong chastity. But in Elizabethan slang, "nunnery" could also mean "brothel."

earth? To a nunnery, go! We are arrant° knaves all—believe   *complete*
none of us. To a nunnery, go!

OFELIA   Oh, heavens secure him!

HAMLET   Where's thy father?

170 OFELIA   At home, my lord.

HAMLET   For God's sake, let the doors be shut on him. He
may play the fool nowhere but in his own house. To a nunnery, go!

OFELIA   Help him, good God!

175 HAMLET   If thou dost marry, I'll give thee this plague to thy
dowry:
Be thou as chaste as ice, as pure as snow,
Thou shalt not scape calumny. To a nunnery, go!

OFELIA   Alas, what change is this!

180 HAMLET   But if thou wilt needs marry, marry a fool, for wise
men know well enough what monsters[7] you° make of them.   *you women*
To a nunnery, go!

OFELIA   Pray God restore him!

HAMLET   Nay, I have heard of your paintings° too: God hath   *cosmetics*
185 given you one face and you make yourselves another. You
fig[8] and you amble and you nickname God's creatures,[9]
making your wantonness your ignorance.[1] A pox,[2] 'tis scurvy!
I'll no more of it—it hath made me mad. I'll no more marriages. All that are married, but one, shall live, the rest shall
190 keep as they are. To a nunnery, go. To a nunnery, go!   *Exit.*

OFELIA   Great God of heaven, what a quick change is this!
The courtier, scholar, soldier—all in him,
All dashed and splintered thence. Oh, woe is me,
To ha' seen what I have seen, see what I see.   *Exit.*
          KING *and* CORAMBIS [*come forward*].

195 KING   Love? No, no, that's not the cause:
Some deeper thing it is that troubles him.

CORAMBIS   Well, something it is. My lord, content you
    awhile,
I will myself go feel him. Let me work,
I'll try him every way.
      Enter HAMLET.
             See where he comes—
200 Send you those gentlemen. Let me alone
To find the depth of this—away, be gone.   *Exit* KING.
—Now, my good lord, do you know me?

HAMLET   Yea, very well, you're a fishmonger.

CORAMBIS   Not I, my lord.

205 HAMLET   Then, sir, I would you were so honest a man, for to
be honest as this age goes[3] is one man to be picked out of
ten thousand.

CORAMBIS   What do you read, my lord?

HAMLET   Words, words.

---

7. Alluding to the belief that cuckolds grew horns,
but Hamlet may mean a more spiritual or psychological transformation as well.
8. TEXTUAL COMMENT "Fig" is more obscene than
Q2's "gig" and F's "gidge." See Digital Edition TC 4
(First Quarto edited text).

9. Use new and fashionable names instead of the
God-given ones. *amble*: dance.
1. *making . . . ignorance*: "playing dumb" to excuse
your (seductive) affectations.
2. (An oath.)
3. These days.

210 CORAMBIS What's the matter,[4] my lord?

HAMLET Between who?

CORAMBIS I mean the matter you read, my lord.

HAMLET Marry, most vile heresy: for here the satirical satyr
writes that old men have hollow eyes, weak backs, gray
215 beards, pitiful weak hams,° gouty legs—all which, sir, I   *thighs*
most potently believe not.[5] For, sir, yourself shall be old as I
am if, like a crab, you could go backward.

CORAMBIS [aside] How pregnant° his replies are, and full of   *meaningful*
wit. Yet at first he took me for a fishmonger. All this comes
220 by love, the vehemency of love. And when I was young, I was
very idle and suffered much ecstasy in love, very near this.
—Will you walk out of the air,[6] my lord?

HAMLET Into my grave.

CORAMBIS By the mass, that's out of the air indeed. [aside]
225 Very shrewd answers! —My lord, I will take my leave of you.

HAMLET You can take nothing from me, sir, I will more willingly part withal.° [aside] Old doting fool!   *with*

    Enter GILDERSTONE *and* ROSSENCRAFT.

CORAMBIS You seek Prince Hamlet—see, there he is.   *Exit.*

GILDERSTONE Health to your lordship!

230 HAMLET What, Gilderstone and Rossencraft! Welcome, kind
schoolfellows, to Elsinore.

GILDERSTONE We thank your grace and would be very glad
you were as when we were at Wittenberg.

HAMLET I thank you. But is this visitation free° of yourselves,   *voluntary*
235 or were you not sent for? Tell me true. Come, I know the
good King and Queen sent for you. There is a kind of confession in your eye: come, I know you were sent for.

GILDERSTONE What say you?

HAMLET Nay then, I see how the wind sits: come, you were
240 sent for.

ROSSENCRAFT My lord, we were—and willingly. If we might
know the cause and ground of your discontent—

HAMLET Why, I want preferment.[7]

ROSSENCRAFT I think not so, my lord.

245 HAMLET Yes, faith, this great world you see contents me not—
no, nor the spangled heavens, nor earth, nor sea, no, nor man
that is so glorious a creature, contents not me—no, nor
woman too, though you laugh.

GILDERSTONE My lord, we laugh not at that.

250 HAMLET Why did you laugh then, when I said man did not
content me?

GILDERSTONE My lord, we laughed when you said man did
not content you, what entertainment the players shall have.
We boarded° them o'the way; they are coming to you.   *passed by*

255 HAMLET Players? What players be they?

ROSSENCRAFT My lord, the tragedians° of the city, those that   *actors*
you took delight to see so often.

---

4. Content, although Hamlet deliberately takes it as
"subject of a quarrel."
5. TEXTUAL COMMENT The "not," at once polite and
sarcastic, is absent from Q2 and F. See Digital Edi-

tion TC 5 (First Quarto edited text).
6. Outdoor air was regarded as a hazard for the sick.
7. I'm lacking a promotion; I'm being deprived of an
office.

Strikes wide; but with the whiff and wind
Of his fell° sword, th'unnervèd° father falls."   *fierce / strengthless*

CORAMBIS   Enough, my friend, 'tis too long.

345 HAMLET   It shall to the barber's with your beard°—a pox, he's   *It shall be cut short*
for a jig⁴ or a tale of bawdry,° or else he sleeps. Come on: to   *obscenity*
Hecuba,⁵ come.

FIRST PLAYER   "But who, oh, who had seen the moblèd°   *veiled; muffled*
queen—"

CORAMBIS   "Moblèd queen" is good, faith, very good—

350 FIRST PLAYER   "All in the alarum and fear of death rose up,
And o'er her weak and all o'er-teeming⁶ loins
A blanket, and a kercher° on that head   *kerchief*
Where late the diadem stood—who this had seen,
With tongue-envenomed speech would treason
      have pronounced.

355 For if the gods themselves had seen her then,
When she saw Pyrrhus with malicious strokes
Mincing her husband's limbs, it would have made milch°   *milky; moist*
The burning eyes of heaven and passion° in the gods."   *suffering; pity*

CORAMBIS   Look, my lord, if he hath not changed his color
360 and hath tears in his eyes. —No more, good heart, no more.

HAMLET   'Tis well, 'tis very well. I pray, my lord, will you see
the players well bestowed?° I tell you they are the chronicles   *lodged*
and brief abstracts° of the time. After your death, I can tell   *summaries*
you, you were better have a bad epitaph than their ill report
365 while you live.

CORAMBIS   My lord, I will use them according to their deserts.

HAMLET   Oh, far better, man! Use every man after° his deserts,   *according to*
then who should scape whipping? Use them after your own
370 honor and dignity: the less they deserve, the greater credit's
yours.

CORAMBIS   Welcome, my good fellows.   [*He begins to*] *exit.*

HAMLET   Come hither, masters. Can you not play *The Murder
of Gonzago?*

FIRST PLAYER   Yes, my lord.

375 HAMLET   And couldst not thou, for a need,° study me some   *if necessary*
dozen or sixteen lines which I would set down and insert?

FIRST PLAYER   Yes, very easily, my good lord.

HAMLET   'Tis well, I thank you. Follow that lord—and do you
hear, sirs, take heed you mock him not!
                    [*Exeunt* PLAYERS, *following* CORAMBIS.]

380 [*to* ROSSENCRAFT *and* GILDERSTONE] Gentlemen, for your
kindness I thank you, and for a time I would desire you
leave me.

GILDERSTONE   Our love and duty is at your command.
                    Exeunt [ROSSENCRAFT *and* GILDERSTONE].

HAMLET   Why, what a dunghill idiot slave am I!
385 Why, these players here draw water from eyes—
For Hecuba! Why, what is Hecuba to him,
Or he to Hecuba?

---

4. A ridiculous piece of poetry, or the dance that followed many plays (unrelated to the drama).
5. In Greek mythology, the wife of King Priam of
Troy, mother of Hector and Cassandra.

6. Completely worn out with childbearing. (Hecuba
was supposed to have borne seventeen or more
children.)

What would he do an if° he had my loss—   *an if = if*
His father murdered and a crown bereft him?
390   He would turn all his tears to drops of blood,
Amaze the standers-by with his laments,
Strike more than wonder in the judicial ears,
Confound the ignorant, and make mute the wise—
Indeed, his passion would be general.°   *felt by all*
395   Yet I, like to an ass and John-a-dreams,°   *a sleepy idler*
Having my father murdered by a villain,
Stand still and let it pass! Why, sure I am a coward!
Who plucks me by the beard or twits° my nose,   *taunts; makes fun of*
Gives me the lie i'th' throat down to the lungs?[7]
400   Sure I should take it. Or else I have no gall,[8]
Or by this I should've fatted all the region kites[9]
With this slave's offal—this damnèd villain,
Treacherous, bawdy, murderous villain!
Why, this is brave,° that I, the son of my dear father,   *fine*
405   Should like a scullion,° like a very drab,°   *kitchen servant / whore*
Thus rail in words! About,° my brain!   *Into action*
I have heard that guilty creatures sitting at a play
Hath by the very cunning° of the scene   *artfulness*
Confessed a murder committed long before.
410   This spirit that I have seen may be the devil,
And out of[1] my weakness and my melancholy,
As he is very potent with[2] such men,
Doth seek to damn me.
I will have sounder proofs: the play's the thing
415   Wherein I'll catch the conscience of the King.   *Exit.*

Scene 8

Enter the KING, QUEEN, *and Lords* [CORAMBIS,
ROSSENCRAFT, *and* GILDERSTONE].

KING   Lords, can you by no means find
The cause of our son Hamlet's lunacy?
You, being so near in love even from his youth,
Methinks should gain more than a stranger should.
5   GILDERSTONE   My lord, we have done all the best we could
To wring from him the cause of all his grief,
But still he puts us off and by no means
Would make an answer to that we exposed.[1]
ROSSENCRAFT   Yet was he something more inclined to mirth
10   Before we left him, and I take it
He hath given order for a play tonight,
At which he craves your highness' company.
KING   With all our heart: it likes us very well.
Gentlemen, seek still to increase his mirth.
15   Spare for no cost: our coffers shall be open,
And we unto yourselves will still be thankful.

---

7. *Gives . . . lungs*: Calls me a thoroughgoing liar.
8. A bitter fluid produced by the liver; the supposed source of anger.
9. All the kites (birds of prey) in the sky ("region").
1. *out of*: capitalizing upon.

2. *potent with*: powerful over.
Scene 8 Location: The castle.
1. "Exposed" functions here like a (now obsolete) use of "expostulate": to demand, question.

GILDERSTONE *and* ROSSENCRAFT   In all we can, be sure you
   shall command.
QUEEN   Thanks, gentlemen, and what the Queen of
   Denmark
   May pleasure you, be sure you shall not want.[2]
20 GILDERSTONE   We'll once again unto the noble Prince.
   KING   Thanks to you both.
          [*Exeunt* ROSSENCRAFT *and* GILDERSTONE.]
          Gertred, you'll see this play?
QUEEN   My lord, I will, and it joys me at the soul
   He is inclined to any kind of mirth.
CORAMBIS   Madam, I pray be ruled by me,
25 And, my good sovereign, give me leave to speak:
   We cannot yet find out the very ground
   Of his distemperance; therefore I hold it meet,
   If so it please you—else they shall not meet—and thus it is—
   KING   What is't, Corambis?
CORAMBIS   Marry, my good lord, this:
30 Soon when the sports° are done,   *entertainments*
   Madam, send you in haste to speak with him,
   And I myself will stand behind the arras.[3]
   There question you the cause of all his grief
   And then, in love and nature unto you,°   *natural feeling toward you*
35 He'll tell you all. My lord, how think you on't?
   KING   It likes us well.° Gertred, what say you?   *It pleases me*
QUEEN   With all my heart! Soon will I send for him.
CORAMBIS   Myself will be that happy messenger
   Who hopes his grief will be revealed to her.   *Exeunt.*

Scene 9
Enter HAMLET *and the* PLAYERS.

HAMLET   Pronounce me this speech trippingly o'the tongue
   as I taught thee. Marry, an you mouth it[1] as a many of your
   players do, I'd rather hear a town bull[2] bellow than such a
   fellow speak my lines. Nor do not saw the air thus with your
5 hands, but give everything his action with temperance. Oh,
   it offends me to the soul to hear a robustious° periwigged° *bombastic / wig-wearing*
   fellow to tear a passion in tatters, into very rags, to split the
   ears of the ignorant, who for the most part are capable of
   nothing but dumb shows[3] and noises. I would have such a fel-
10 low whipped for o'erdoing Termagant—it out-Herods Herod.[4]
FIRST PLAYER   My lord, we have indifferently° reformed that *moderately well*
   among us.
HAMLET   The better, the better. Mend it altogether. There be
   fellows that I have seen play—and heard others commend
15 them, and that highly too—that, having neither the gait of
   Christian, pagan, nor Turk, have so strutted and bellowed

---

2. *what . . . want:* you will not be lacking in anything
that the Queen may do for you.
3. A hanging screen of tapestry fabric placed around
the walls of a room.
Scene 9 Location: A stateroom of the castle.
1. If you speak exaggeratedly.
2. A bull shared in common by a village's cow-keepers.

3. Pantomimes, featuring gestures without words.
4. It surpasses the excesses of Herod, who, as a character in medieval cycle plays, was famous for his ranting. Termagant, an imaginary deity supposedly worshipped by Muslims, takes the form of a violent speaking idol in medieval drama.

that you would've thought some of nature's journeymen[5]
had made men, and not made them well, they imitated
humanity so abominably. Take heed, avoid it.

20 FIRST PLAYER I warrant° you, my lord.   assure

HAMLET And do you hear? Let not your clown speak more
than is set down. There be of° them, I can tell you, that will   some of
laugh themselves to set° on some quantity of barren° specta-   urge / unthinking
tors to laugh with them, albeit there is some necessary point

25 in the play then to be observed. Oh, 'tis vile and shows a
pitiful ambition in the fool that useth it. And then you have
some again that keeps one suit of jests, as a man is known
by one suit of apparel, and gentlemen quotes his jests down
in their tables before they come to the play, as thus: "Cannot

30 you stay till I eat my porridge?" and "You owe me a quarter's
wages" and "My coat wants a cullison"° and "Your beer is   badge
sour" and, blabbering with his lips and thus keeping in his
cinquepace[6] of jests, when, God knows, the warm° clown   warmed up; practiced
cannot make a jest unless by chance, as the blind man

35 catcheth a hare. Masters, tell him of it.

FIRST PLAYER We will, my lord.

HAMLET Well, go make you ready.   *Exeunt* PLAYERS.

      [*Enter* HORATIO.]

HORATIO Here, my lord.

HAMLET Horatio, thou art even as just° a man   honest; balanced

40 As e'er my conversation coped withal.[7]

HORATIO O my lord!

HAMLET   Nay, why should I flatter thee?
Why should the poor be flattered?
What gain should I receive by flattering thee
That nothing hath but thy good mind?

45 Let flattery sit on those time-pleasing[8] tongues,
To gloze° with them that loves to hear their praise,   flatter
And not with such as thou, Horatio.
There is a play tonight wherein one scene they have
Comes very near the murder of my father.

50 When thou shalt see that act afoot,
Mark thou the King; do but observe his looks,
For I mine eyes will rivet to his face.
And if he do not bleach° and change at that,   lose color
It is a damnèd ghost that we have seen.

55 Horatio, have a care, observe him well.

HORATIO My lord, mine eyes shall still° be on his face   always
And not the smallest alteration
That shall appear in him but I shall note it.

HAMLET Hark, they come.

      Enter KING, QUEEN, CORAMBIS[, OFELIA,
      ROSSENCRAFT, GILDERSTONE], *and other Lords.*

60 KING How now, son Hamlet, how fare you? Shall we have a
play?

HAMLET I'faith, the chameleon's dish—not capon-crammed,

---

5. Hirelings, those who have completed their apprenticeship but are not yet "master" of their trade.
6. A lively five-step dance.

7. As I ever encountered in my dealings with men.
8. Fawning upon whomever is powerful or popular at
the time.

feed o'the air.[9] Ay, father. [*to* CORAMBIS] My lord, you played in the university?

65 CORAMBIS   That I did, my lord, and I was counted a good actor.

HAMLET   What did you enact there?

CORAMBIS   My lord, I did act Julius Caesar. I was killed in the Capitol:[1] Brutus killed me.

70 HAMLET   It was a brute part of him to kill so capital a calf.°   *such a prize fool*
Come, be these players ready?

QUEEN   Hamlet, come sit down by me.

HAMLET   No, by my faith, mother, here's a mettle[2] more attractive. [*to* OFELIA] Lady, will you give me leave, and so
75 forth, to lay my head in your lap?

OFELIA   No, my lord.

HAMLET   Upon your lap. What do you think I meant, contrary matters?[3]

> *Enter in a dumb show the* [DUKE] *and the* [DUCHESS].
> *He sits down in an arbor; she leaves him.*
> *Then enters* LUCIANUS *with poison in a vial and*
> *pours it in his ears and goes away. Then the*
> [DUCHESS] *cometh and finds him dead, and goes*
> *away with the other.*
> [*The* PLAYERS *retire.*]

OFELIA   What means this, my lord?

80 HAMLET   This is miching mallico°—that means mischief.   *sneaking wrongdoing*

> *Enter the* PROLOGUE.

OFELIA   What doth this mean, my lord?

HAMLET   You shall hear anon—this fellow will tell you all.

OFELIA   Will he tell us what this show means?

HAMLET   Ay, or any show you'll show him. Be not afraid to
85 show, he'll not be afraid to tell. Oh, these players cannot keep counsel:° they'll tell all.   *a secret*

PROLOGUE   For us and for our tragedy,
Here stooping to your clemency,
We beg your hearing patiently.   [*Exit.*]

90 HAMLET   Is't a prologue or a posy for a ring?[4]

OFELIA   'Tis short, my lord.

HAMLET   As women's love.

> *Enter the* DUKE *and* DUCHESS.

DUKE   Full forty years are past, their date is gone,
Since happy time joined both our hearts as one.
95 And now the blood that filled my youthful veins
Runs weakly in their pipes, and all the strains
Of music which whilom° pleased mine ear   *at one time*
Is now a burden that age cannot bear—
And therefore, sweet, nature must pay his due:

---

9. Hamlet is addressing the King's first question, "how fare you?" by punning on "fare." The chameleon was supposed to live on air. Hamlet also puns on "heir," referring to the King's insubstantial promise of the succession. All of this he contrasts with the eating habits of the capon, a castrated cock, crammed or fattened for the table (and a term for a fool).
1. Perhaps an allusion to Shakespeare's own *Julius Caesar*; the actor who first played Corambis may also have played the part of Caesar.
2. A disposition (punning on magnetically attractive "metal").
3. F and Q2 have "country matters" (i.e., coarse or rustic, with an obscene pun on "cunt").
4. The motto engraved in a ring.

100　To heaven must I and leave the earth with you.
　　DUCHESS　Oh, say not so, lest that you kill my heart;
　　　When death takes you, let life from me depart.
　　DUKE　Content thyself. When ended is my date,
　　　Thou mayst perchance have a more noble mate,
105　　More wise, more youthful, and one—
　　DUCHESS　Oh, speak no more, for then I am accursed:
　　　None weds the second but she kills the first.
　　　A second time I kill my lord that's dead
　　　When second husband kisses me in bed.
110　HAMLET [aside]　Oh, wormwood,[5] wormwood!
　　DUKE　I do believe you, sweet, what now you speak,
　　　But what we do determine oft we break,
　　　For our devices still are overthrown.
　　　Our thoughts are ours, their ends° none of our own.　　　　　　　　*results*
115　　So think you will no second husband wed,
　　　But die thy thoughts when thy first lord is dead.
　　DUCHESS　Both here and there pursue me lasting strife
　　　If, once a widow, ever I be wife.
　　HAMLET　If she should break now—
120　DUKE　'Tis deeply sworn. Sweet, leave me here awhile:
　　　My spirits grow dull and fain° I would beguile　　　　　　　　　　*gladly*
　　　The tedious time with sleep.
　　DUCHESS　　　　　　　　　　Sleep rock thy brain,
　　　And never come mischance between us twain.
　　　　　　　　　　　　　　　　Exit [DUCHESS].
　　HAMLET　Madam, how do you like this play?
125　QUEEN　The lady protests too much.
　　HAMLET　Oh, but she'll keep her word.
　　KING　Have you heard the argument?° Is there no offense　　　*plot*
　　　in it?
　　HAMLET　No offense in the world—poison in jest, poison in
130　jest.
　　KING　What do you call the name of the play?
　　HAMLET　*Mousetrap*. Marry, how? Tropically.[6] This play is the
　　　image of a murder done in Guyana. Albertus was the Duke's
　　　name, his wife Baptista.[7] Father, it is a knavish piece o'work,
135　but what o'that, it toucheth not us—you and I that have
　　　free° souls. Let the galled jade[8] wince.　　　　　　　　　*guiltless*
　　　　　[*Enter* LUCIANUS.]
　　　This is one Lucianus, nephew to the king.[9]
　　OFELIA　You're as good as a chorus,[1] my lord.
　　HAMLET　I could interpret the love you bear, if I saw the poop-
140　ies[2] dallying.
　　OFELIA　You're very pleasant, my lord.
　　HAMLET　Who, I? Your only° jig-maker! Why, what should a　　　*preeminent*

5. A bitter herb taken medicinally (hence, "a bitter pill to swallow").
6. Punning on "tropically": figuratively.
7. Shakespeare seems to base *The Mousetrap* on an extremely muddled version of the Duke of Urbino's alleged murder by Luigi Gonzaga in 1538.
8. *galled jade*: chafed horse.
9. King = the Duke.

1. The chorus explained the forthcoming action. In puppet shows, a choric narrator, or "interpreter," announced the characters' names and spoke the dialogue.
2. Q2 and F have "puppets." "Poopies" could also mean puppet (though the *OED* does not have it attested before 1659) or a promiscuous woman.

man do but be merry? For look how cheerfully my mother
looks—my father died within these two hours.

OFELIA   Nay, 'tis twice two months, my lord.

HAMLET   Two months? Nay then, let the devil wear black, for
I'll have a suit of sables.³ Jesus, two months dead and not
forgotten yet? Nay, then, there's some likelihood a gentleman's death may outlive memory. But, by my faith, he must
build churches then, or else he must follow the old epithet:
"With ho, with ho, the hobbyhorse is forgot."⁴

OFELIA   Your jests are keen,° my lord.   sharp

HAMLET   It would cost you a groaning to take them off.⁵

OFELIA   Still better and worse.⁶

HAMLET   So you must take your husband.⁷ —Begin, murderer,
begin! A pox, leave thy damnable° faces and begin. Come: grimacing
"The croaking raven doth bellow for revenge."⁸

LUCIANUS   Thoughts black, hands apt, drugs fit, and time
  agreeing,
Confederate° season else no creature seeing.   Complicit
Thou mixture rank° of midnight weeds collected,   foul
With Hecate's bane⁹ thrice blasted, thrice infected,
Thy natural magic and dire property°   quality
One wholesome life usurps immediately.
            [He pours poison in the Duke's ear and] exit.

HAMLET   He poisons him for his estate.°   position; state

KING   Lights! I will to bed.

CORAMBIS   The King rises! Lights, ho!
                  Exeunt [all but HAMLET and HORATIO].

HAMLET   What, frighted with false fires?¹
Then let the stricken deer go weep,²
The hart ungallèd° play,   unafflicted
For some must laugh, while some must weep,
Thus runs the world away.³

HORATIO   The King is moved,° my lord.   vexed

HAMLET   Ay, Horatio, I'll take the Ghost's word for more than
all the coin in Denmark.
                  Enter ROSSENCRAFT and GILDERSTONE.

ROSSENCRAFT   Now, my lord, how is't with you?

HAMLET   An if° the King like not the tragedy,   An if = If
Why then, belike he likes it not, perdie.°   indeed (pardieu)

ROSSENCRAFT   We are very glad to see your grace so pleasant.
My good lord, let us again entreat to know of you the ground
and cause of your distemperature.

GILDERSTONE   My lord, your mother craves to speak with you.

HAMLET   We shall obey, were she ten times our mother.

---

3. Sable is both an expensive fur for cloaks and trim
and the heraldic term for "black"; Hamlet simultaneously forswears his ascetic mourning and vows to
continue it.
4. The hobbyhorse, a man with a mock horse's body
strapped around his waist, was a figure in May Day
morris dances (under attack in Shakespeare's time by
religious reformers). "The hobbyhorse is forgot" seems
to have been a ballad refrain.
5. To satisfy my sexual appetite (leading to groaning
in either sexual intercourse or childbirth).

6. Wittier, and more obscene.
7. The marriage vow compels one to take a husband
"for better and for worse."
8. Misquoted from The True Tragedy of Richard III
(ca. 1591; not to be confused with Shakespeare's own
Richard III).
9. Poison from the goddess of witchcraft.
1. Fireworks or blank cartridges.
2. A deer was thought to weep when mortally wounded.
These four lines are probably from a lost ballad.
3. That's the way of the world.

ROSSENCRAFT   But, my good lord, shall I entreat thus much?
HAMLET   I pray, will you play upon this pipe?[4]
185   ROSSENCRAFT   Alas, my lord, I cannot.
HAMLET [to GILDERSTONE]   Pray, will you?
GILDERSTONE   I have no skill, my lord.
HAMLET   Why, look, it is a thing of nothing: 'tis but stopping
    of these holes and, with a little breath from your lips, it will
190   give most delicate music.
GILDERSTONE   But this cannot we do, my lord.
HAMLET   Pray now, pray—heartily I beseech you.
ROSSENCRAFT   My lord, we cannot.
HAMLET   Why, how unworthy a thing would you make of me?
195   You would seem to know my stops,[5] you would play upon
    me, you would search the very inward part of my heart and
    dive into the secret of my soul. Zounds,[6] do you think I am
    easier to be played on than a pipe? Call me what instrument
    you will, though you can fret[7] me, yet you cannot play upon
200   me. Besides, to be demanded by a sponge—
ROSSENCRAFT   How? A sponge, my lord?
HAMLET   Ay, sir, a sponge that soaks up the King's counte-
    nance, favors, and rewards, that makes his liberality your
    storehouse. But such as you do the King in the end best ser-
205   vice: for he doth keep you as an ape doth nuts, in the corner
    of his jaw: first mouths you, then swallows you. So, when he
    hath need of you, 'tis but squeezing of you and, sponge, you
    shall be dry again—you shall.
ROSSENCRAFT   Well, my lord, we'll take our leave.
210   HAMLET   Farewell, farewell, God bless you.
            [Exeunt] ROSSENCRAFT and GILDERSTONE.
        Enter CORAMBIS.
CORAMBIS   My lord, the Queen would speak with you.
HAMLET   Do you see yonder cloud in the shape of a camel?
CORAMBIS   'Tis like a camel indeed.
HAMLET   Now methinks it's like a weasel.
215   CORAMBIS   'Tis backed like a weasel.
HAMLET   Or like a whale.
CORAMBIS   Very like a whale.
HAMLET   Why, then, tell my mother I'll come by and by.
                           Exit CORAMBIS.
    Good night, Horatio.
220   HORATIO   Good night unto your lordship.   Exit HORATIO.
HAMLET   My mother she hath sent to speak with me.
    O God, let ne'er the heart of Nero[8] enter
    This soft bosom.
    Let me be cruel, not unnatural.
225   I will speak daggers—those sharp words being spent,
    To do her wrong my soul shall ne'er consent.   Exit.

---

4. Hamlet appears to present them with a recorder.
5. Finger holes; notes.
6. By God's wounds, an oath.
7. Irritate, punning on frets of stringed instruments, which regulate fingering and pitch.
8. The Roman emperor Nero reputedly murdered his mother, in one account, by cutting open her womb.

Scene 10

Enter the KING.

KING   Oh, that this wet° that falls upon my face   *these tears*
    Would wash the crime clear from my conscience!
    When I look up to heaven I see my trespass.
    The earth doth still cry out upon my fact:°   *act*
5   Pay me the murder of a brother and a king
    And the adulterous fault I have committed.
    Oh, these are sins that are unpardonable.
    Why, say thy sins were blacker than is jet,[1]
    Yet may contrition make them as white as snow.[2]
10   Ay, but still to persever in a sin,
    It is an act 'gainst the universal power.
    Most wretched man, stoop, bend thee to thy prayer,
    Ask grace of heaven to keep thee from despair.

        He kneels. Enter HAMLET.

HAMLET   Ay, so. [*He draws his sword.*] Come forth and work
    thy last—
15   And thus he dies, and so am I revenged.
    No, not so:
    He took my father sleeping, his sins brimful,°   *overflowing*
    And how his soul stood to the state of heaven,
    Who knows save the immortal powers? And shall
20   I kill him now, when he is purging of his soul,
    Making his way for heaven?
    This is a benefit and not revenge.
    No, get thee up again. [*He sheathes his sword.*] When he's at
    game,
    Swearing, taking his carouse, drinking drunk,
25   Or in the incestuous pleasure of his bed,
    Or at some act
    That hath no relish° of salvation in't,   *trace*
    Then trip him that his heels may kick at heaven
    And fall as low as hell. My mother stays,°   *waits*
30   This physic° but prolongs thy weary days.   *Exit.*   *medicine*
KING   My words fly up, my sins remain below.
    No king on earth is safe if God's his foe.   *Exit.*

Scene 11

Enter QUEEN *and* CORAMBIS.

CORAMBIS   Madam, I hear young Hamlet coming: I'll shroud
    myself behind the arras.
QUEEN   Do so, my lord.
    CORAMBIS [*hides behind the arras*].
HAMLET [*within*]   Mother, mother!
    [*Enter* HAMLET.]
5   Oh, are you here? How is't with you, mother?
QUEEN   How is't with you?
HAMLET   I'll tell you, but first we'll make all safe.[1]

Scene 10 Location: The castle.
1. A glossy black stone.
2. Compare Isaiah 1:15–18: "And though ye make many prayers, I will not hear: for your hands are full of blood. Wash you, make you clean; take away the evil of your works from before mine eyes . . . though

your sins were as crimson, they shall be made white as snow."
Scene 11 Location: The Queen's private chamber.
1. Hamlet looks for a private ("safe") conversation with his mother.

QUEEN   Hamlet, thou hast thy father much offended.
HAMLET   Mother, you have my father much offended.
QUEEN   How now,° boy?   *What's this*
10   HAMLET   How now, mother?
    Come here. Sit down, for you shall hear me speak.
    QUEEN What wilt thou do? Thou wilt not murder me?
    Help, ho!
    CORAMBIS [*behind the arras*]   Help for the Queen!
    HAMLET   Ay, a rat!
        [*He stabs* CORAMBIS *through the arras.*]
    Dead for a ducat!² [*He looks behind the arras.*] Rash
        intruding fool,
15   Farewell. I took thee for thy better.
    QUEEN   Hamlet, what hast thou done?
    HAMLET   Not so much harm, good mother,
    As to kill a king and marry with his brother.
    QUEEN   How? Kill a king?
20   HAMLET   Ay, a king. Nay, sit you down, and ere you part,
    If you be made of penetrable stuff,
    I'll make your eyes look down into your heart
    And see how horrid there and black it shows.
    QUEEN   Hamlet, what mean'st thou by these killing words?
25   HAMLET   Why, this I mean: see here, behold this picture.
    It is the portraiture of your deceased husband.
    See here a face to outface Mars° himself,   *the Roman god of war*
    An eye at which his foes did tremble at,
    A front° wherein all virtues are set down   *forehead*
30   For to adorn a king and gild his crown,
    Whose heart went hand in hand even with that vow
    He made to you in marriage. And he is dead—
    Murdered, damnably murdered! This was your husband.
    Look you now:
35   Here is your husband, with a face like Vulcan,³
    A look fit for a murder and a rape,
    A dull, dead, hanging look, and a hell-bred eye
    To affright children and amaze the world.
    And this same have you left to change with this.
40   What devil thus hath cozened you at hob-man blind?⁴
    Ah! Have you eyes, and can you look on him
    That slew my father and your dear husband,
    To live in the incestuous pleasure of his bed?
    QUEEN   O Hamlet, speak no more.
45   HAMLET   To leave him that bare a monarch's mind
    For a king of clouts, of very shreds!⁵
    QUEEN   Sweet Hamlet, cease.
    HAMLET   Nay, but still to persist and dwell in sin,
    To sweat under the yoke of infamy,
50   To make increase of shame, to seal damnation—
    QUEEN   Hamlet, no more!

---

2. I bet a ducat I have killed it.
3. The Roman god of fire and metalworking.
4. In this way has cheated you in blindman's buff (as if her second husband had been put in her way while she was groping blindfolded).
5. *clouts . . . shreds:* a king of tattered clothing, possibly suggesting the costume of a jester.

HAMLET   Why, appetite with you is in the wane,
   Your blood runs backward now from whence it came.
   Who'll chide hot blood within a virgin's heart
55   When lust shall dwell within a matron's breast?
QUEEN   Hamlet, thou cleav'st my heart in twain.
HAMLET   Oh, throw away the worser part of it
   And keep the better.
          Enter the GHOST *in his nightgown.*
   Save me, save me, you gracious powers above,
60   And hover over me with your celestial wings!
   —Do you not come your tardy son to chide
   That I thus long have let revenge slip by?
   Oh, do not glare with looks so pitiful,
   Lest that my heart of stone yield to compassion
65   And every part that should assist revenge
   Forgo their proper powers and fall to pity.
GHOST   Hamlet, I once again appear to thee
   To put thee in remembrance of my death.
   Do not neglect nor long time put it off.
70   But I perceive by her distracted° looks   *distressed*
   Thy mother's fearful, and she stands amazed.
   Speak to her, Hamlet, for her sex is weak;
   Comfort thy mother, Hamlet. Think on me.
HAMLET   How is't with you, lady?
QUEEN   Nay, how is't with you
75   That thus you bend your eyes on vacancy
   And hold discourse with nothing but with air?
HAMLET   Why, do you nothing hear?
QUEEN   Not I.
HAMLET   Nor do you nothing see?
QUEEN   No, neither.
HAMLET   No?
   Why, see, the King, my father—
80   My father in the habit[6] as° he lived!   *when; as if*
   Look you how pale he looks—
   See how he steals away out of the portal!°   *door*
   Look, there he goes.   *Exit* GHOST.
QUEEN   Alas, it is the weakness of thy brain
85   Which makes thy tongue to blazon° thy heart's grief.   *describe in detail*
   But, as I have a soul, I swear by heaven
   I never knew of this most horrid murder.
   But, Hamlet, this is only fantasy,
   And for my love forget these idle° fits.   *delirious*
90 HAMLET   Idle? No, mother, my pulse doth beat like yours.
   It is not madness that possesseth Hamlet.
   O mother, if ever you did my dear father love,
   Forbear the adulterous bed tonight,
   And win yourself by little as you may.[7]
95   In time it may be you will loathe him quite.
   And mother, but assist me in revenge
   And in his death your infamy shall die.

6. Dress and bearing.
7. Wean yourself (i.e., away from sex with the King) and recover your virtue.

QUEEN[8] Hamlet, I vow by that Majesty
That knows our thoughts and looks into our hearts,
100   I will conceal, consent, and do my best,
What stratagem soe'er thou shalt devise.
HAMLET   It is enough. Mother, good night.
—Come, sir, I'll provide for you a grave,
Who was in life a foolish prating knave.

> *Exit* HAMLET *with the dead body.*
> *Enter the* KING *and* [ROSSENCRAFT *and*
> GILDERSTONE].

105   KING   Now, Gertred, what says our son? How do you find him?
QUEEN   Alas, my lord, as raging as the sea.
Whenas° he came, I first bespake him fair,   *When*
But then he throws and tosses me about
As one forgetting that I was his mother.
110   At last I called for help and, as I cried,
Corambis called, which Hamlet no sooner heard
But whips me out his rapier and cries,
"A rat, a rat!"
And in his rage the good old man he kills.
115   KING   Why, this his madness will undo our state.
Lords, go to him: inquire the body out.
GILDERSTONE   We will, my lord.

> *Exeunt* [ROSSENCRAFT *and* GILDERSTONE].

KING   Gertred, your son shall presently to England.
His shipping is already furnished,
120   And we have sent by Rossencraft and Gilderstone
Our letters to our dear brother of England
For Hamlet's welfare and his happiness:
Haply the air and climate of the country
May please him better than his native home.
125   See where he comes.

> *Enter* HAMLET *and the Lords* [ROSSENCRAFT *and*
> GILDERSTONE].

GILDERSTONE   My lord, we can by no means know of him
Where the body is.
KING   Now, son Hamlet, where is this dead body?
HAMLET   At supper—not where he is eating, but where he is
130   eaten.[9] A certain company of politic° worms are even now at   *cunning*
him. Father, your fat king and your lean beggar are but vari-
able services,° two dishes to one mess.° Look you, a man   *different courses / meal*
may fish with that worm that hath eaten of a king, and a
beggar eat that fish which that worm hath caught.
135   KING   What of this?
HAMLET   Nothing, father, but to tell you how a king may go a
progress° through the guts of a beggar.   *royal journey*
KING   But, son Hamlet, where is this body?
HAMLET   In heav'n. If you chance to miss him there, father,
140   you had best look in the other parts below for him, and if you
cannot find him there, you may chance to nose him as you
go up the lobby.

8. TEXTUAL COMMENT Gertred's lines here, unique
to Q1, make her pledge to support Hamlet far more
concrete and explicit than in Q2 or F. See Digital
Edition TC 6 (First Quarto edited text).

9. Possibly an allusion to the Eucharist (Lord's Supper), in which the body of Christ is consumed in the
form of bread.

KING [*to* ROSSENCRAFT *and* GILDERSTONE] Make haste and
  find him out.

145 HAMLET   Nay, do you hear? Do not make too much haste—I'll
  warrant you he'll stay till you come.
                         [*Exeunt* ROSSENCRAFT *and* GILDERSTONE.]

KING   Well, son Hamlet,
  We, in care of you, but specially
  In tender preservation of your health—

150 The which we prize even as our proper self[1]—
  It is our mind° you forthwith go for England.   *intention*
  The wind sits fair; you shall aboard tonight.
  Lord Rossencraft and Gilderstone shall go
  Along with you.

155 HAMLET   Oh, with all my heart. Farewell, mother.

KING   Your loving father, Hamlet.

HAMLET   My mother, I say: you married my mother, my
  mother is your wife, man and wife is one flesh[2]—and so, my
  mother. Farewell. For England, ho!   [*Exit.*][3]

160 KING   Gertred, leave me, and take your leave of Hamlet.
                                         [*Exit* QUEEN.]

  To England is he gone, ne'er to return.
  Our letters are unto the King of England
  That on the sight of them, on his allegiance,
  He presently,° without demanding why—   *immediately*

165 That Hamlet lose his head. For he must die:
  There's more in him than shallow eyes can see.
  He once being dead, why then our state is free.   *Exit.*

Scene 12

  Enter FORTENBRASSE, [*Captain,*] *Drum,°* and   *Drummer*
    Soldiers.

FORTENBRASSE   Captain, from us go greet the King of
    Denmark.
  Tell him that Fortenbrasse, nephew to old Norway,
  Craves a free pass and conduct over his land
  According to the articles agreed on.

5 You know our rendezvous, go. —March away!   *Exeunt.*

Scene 13

  Enter KING *and* QUEEN.

KING   Hamlet is shipped for England. Fare him well!
  I hope to hear good news from thence ere long,
  If everything fall out to our content,
  As I do make no doubt but so it shall.

5 QUEEN   God grant it may. Heav'ns keep my Hamlet safe!
  But this mischance of old Corambis' death
  Hath piercèd so the young Ofelia's heart
  That she, poor maid, is quite bereft her wits.

KING   Alas, dear heart! And on the other side,

---

1. Which we prize as much as our own health.
2. As stated in Genesis 2:23 and the marriage rite of
the Book of Common Prayer.
3. TEXTUAL COMMENT We have emended the stage
direction to account for the dramatic needs of the
scene. The "*Lordes*" (possibly Rossencraft and Gil-

derstone) would conceivably seek the dead body as a
unit, leaving the disturbed Hamlet to exit the stage
alone. See Digital Edition TC 7 (First Quarto edited
text).
Scene 12 Location: The Danish coast.
Scene 13 Location: A public room of the castle.

10   We understand her brother's come from France,
        And he hath half the heart of all our land,
        And hardly he'll forget his father's death
        Unless by some means he be pacified.
        QUEEN   Oh, see where the young Ofelia is!
        Enter OFELIA *playing on a lute, and her hair down,*
             singing.
15   OFELIA   How should I your true love know
        From another man?
        By his cockle hat, and his staff,
        And his sandal shoon.¹

        White his shroud as mountain snow,
20   Larded° with sweet flowers,   *Garnished*
        That bewept to the grave did not² go
        With true lovers' showers.°   *tears*

        He is dead and gone, lady,
        He is dead and gone:
25   At his head a grass green turf,
        At his heels a stone.
        KING   How is't with you, sweet Ofelia?
        OFELIA   Well, God yield° you. It grieves me to see how they   *God reward*
        laid him in the cold ground—I could not choose but weep.
30   [*Sings.*]   And will he not come again?
        And will he not come again?
        No, no, he is gone,
        And we cast away moan,
        And he never will come again.

35   His beard as white as snow,
        All flaxen° was his poll,°   *white / head*
        He is dead, he is gone,
        And we cast away moan:
        God ha' mercy on his soul.
40   And of all Christian souls, I pray God. God be with you,
        ladies, God be with you!   *Exit* OFELIA.
        KING   A pretty wretch! This is a change indeed.
        O Time, how swiftly runs our joys away!
        Content° on earth was never certain bred: *Contentment*
45   Today we laugh and live, tomorrow dead.
             A noise within.
        How now? What noise is that?
             Enter LEARTES.
        LEARTES [*to his followers offstage*]   Stay there until I come.
        —O thou vile king, give me my father! Speak! Say, where's
        my father?
50   KING   Dead.
        LEARTES   Who hath murdered him? Speak! I'll not be juggled
        with°—for he is murdered.   *deceived*
        QUEEN   True, but not by him.°   *(the King)*

---

1. Shoes. *cockle hat:* a cockleshell badge worn in the
hat was a pilgrim's memento of St. James's shrine at
Compostela in Spain.

2. By adding "not," Ofelia changes the song's words
and meter to fit the circumstances of Corambis's
burial.

LEARTES   By whom? By heav'n, I'll be resolved.
55 KING   Let him go, Gertred. Away, I fear him not.
    There's such divinity doth wall a king
    That treason dares not look on.
    Let him go, Gertred. —That your father is murdered
    'Tis true, and we most sorry for it,
60 Being the chiefest pillar of our state.
    Therefore, will you, like a most desperate gamester,
    Swoopstake-like,³ draw at° friend and foe and all?   *prepare to attack*
LEARTES   To his good friends thus wide I'll ope mine arms
    And lock them in my heart, but to his foes
65 I will no reconcilement but by blood.
    KING   Why, now you speak like a most loving son.
    And that in soul we sorrow for his death,
    Yourself ere long shall be a witness.
    Meanwhile, be patient and content yourself.
        Enter OFELIA *as before.*
70 LEARTES   Who's this? Ofelia? O my dear sister!
    Is't possible a young maid's life
    Should be as mortal as an old man's saw?⁴
    O heav'ns themselves! How now, Ofelia?
OFELIA   Well, God ha' mercy. I ha' been gathering of flowers:
75 here, here is rue for you: you may call it herb o'grace o'Sundays.
    Here's some for me too. You must wear your rue with a differ-
    ence.⁵ There's a daisy.⁶ Here, love, there's rosemary for
    you—for remembrance. I pray, love, remember. And there's
    pansy for thoughts.⁷
80 LEARTES   A document° in madness! Thoughts, remembrance!   *An object lesson*
    O God, God!
OFELIA   There is fennel for you: I would ha' giv'n you some
    violets,⁸ but they all withered when my father died. Alas,
    they say the owl was a baker's daughter.⁹ We see what we
85 are, but cannot tell what we shall be.
    [*Sings.*]   For bonny sweet Robin is all my joy.
LEARTES   Thoughts and afflictions—torments worse than
        hell!
OFELIA   Nay, love, I pray you make no words of this now. I
    pray now, you shall sing "a-down" and you "a-down-a." 'Tis
90 o'the king's daughter and the false steward¹—and if anybody
    ask you of anything, say you this:
    [*Sings.*]   Tomorrow is Saint Valentine's day,
                All in the morning betime,°   *early*
                And a maid at your window
95   To be your valentine.

---

3. Indiscriminately. (The winner of a sweepstake gained the stakes of all other players.)
4. Is it possible a young maid's life can be as dead as a worn-out saying?
5. In heraldry, minor branches of a family were distinguished by a "difference," a variation or an addition to the coat of arms. Ofelia probably means "for a different reason." Rue is associated with repentance, and Ofelia identifies it with the "herb of grace" (wormwood), since penitence depended on and enabled God's blessing.

6. Daisies could symbolize dissembling seduction.
7. there's . . . thoughts: Ofelia, recalling the flowers' symbolic significance, distributes them to Leartes, Gertred, and the King.
8. Representing faithfulness.
9. Referring to a folktale wherein Jesus visits a baker's shop asking for bread. The shop's mistress puts a generous piece in the oven but is reprimanded by her daughter, who is later turned into an owl for her stinginess.
1. The tale is unknown.

The young man rose and donned his clothes
And dupped° the chamber door,   *unlatched*
Let in the maid that out a maid
Never departed more.
100   Nay, I pray, mark now:
By Gis° and by Saint Charity,   *Jesus*
Away, and fie for shame!
Young men will do't when they come to't,
By Cock,[2] they are to blame.

105   Quoth she, "Before you tumbled me,
You promised me to wed."
"So would I ha' done, by yonder sun,
If thou hadst not come to my bed."
So God be with you all, God b'wi'y', ladies. God b'wi'you,
110   love.   *Exeunt* OFELIA [*and* QUEEN].
LEARTES   Grief upon grief:
My father murdered, my sister thus distracted.
Cursed be his soul that wrought this wicked act!
KING   Content you, good Leartes, for a time,
115   Although I know your grief is as a flood,
Brimful of sorrow; but forbear awhile
And think already the revenge is done
On him that makes you such a hapless son.
LEARTES   You have prevailed, my lord. Awhile I'll strive
120   To bury grief within a tomb of wrath
Which, once unhearsed, then the world shall hear
Leartes had a father he held dear.
KING   No more of that. Ere many days be done,
You shall hear that° you do not dream upon.   *Exeunt.*   *that which*

Scene 14[1]

Enter HORATIO *and the* QUEEN.
HORATIO   Madam, your son is safe arrived in Denmark.
This letter I even° now received of him   *just*
Whereas he writes how he escaped the danger
And subtle treason that the King had plotted.
5   Being crossed by the contention of the winds,
He found the packet sent to the King of England,
Wherein he saw himself betrayed to death—
As at his next conversing with your grace
He will relate the circumstance at full.
10   QUEEN   Then I perceive there's treason in his° looks   *(the King's)*
That seemed to sugar o'er his villainy.
But I will soothe and please him for a time,
For murderous minds are always jealous.
But know not you, Horatio, where he° is?   *(Hamlet)*
15   HORATIO   Yes, madam, and he hath appointed me
To meet him on the east side of the city

---

2. A corruption of "God" in very mild swearing (playing on "penis").
Scene 14 Location: The castle.
1. TEXTUAL COMMENT Q1 here condenses material concerning Hamlet's adventures treated elsewhere in

Q2 and F. It also differs from Q2 and F by having Gertred explicitly ally herself with Hamlet and plan to deceive her husband. See Digital Edition TC 8 (First Quarto edited text).

Tomorrow morning.

QUEEN   Oh, fail not, good Horatio.
And withal° commend me a mother's care to him;   *also*
Bid him awhile be wary of his presence
20   Lest that he fail in that he goes about.

HORATIO   Madam, never make doubt of that. I think by this
The news be come to court he is arrived:
Observe the King and you shall quickly find,
Hamlet being here, things fell not to his mind.

25 QUEEN   But what became of Gilderstone and Rossencraft?

HORATIO   He being set ashore,[2] they went for England
And in the packet there writ down that doom
To be performed on them 'pointed for him.
And by great chance° he had his father's seal,   *luck*
30   So all was done without discovery.[3]

QUEEN   Thanks be to heaven for blessing of the Prince![4]
Horatio, once again I take my leave,
With thousand mother's blessings to my son.

HORATIO   Madam, adieu.   [*Exeunt separately.*]

Scene 15

Enter KING *and* LEARTES.

KING   Hamlet from England! Is it possible?
What chance is this—they are gone and he come home?

LEARTES   Oh, he is welcome—by my soul, he is.
At it my jocund heart doth leap for joy
5   That I shall live to tell him, thus he dies.

KING   Leartes, content yourself. Be ruled by me,
And you shall have no let° for your revenge.   *hindrance*

LEARTES   My will, not all the world.[1]

KING   Nay, but Leartes, mark the plot I have laid:
10   I have heard him often with a greedy wish,
Upon some praise that he hath heard of you
Touching° your weapon, wish with all his heart   *Concerning*
He might be once tasked for to try your cunning.

LEARTES   And how for this?[2]

15 KING   Marry, Leartes, thus: I'll lay a wager—
Shall be on Hamlet's side and you shall give the odds
(The which will draw him with a more desire
To try the mastery)—that in twelve venies
You gain not three of him.[3] Now, this being granted,
20   When you are hot in midst of all your play,
Among the foils shall a keen rapier lie
Steeped in a mixture of deadly poison
That, if it draws but the least dram of blood
In any part of him, he cannot live.
25   This being done will free you from suspicion,

2. Hamlet is ultimately set ashore on account of the "contention of the winds" in line 5.
3. By editing the letter and giving it his father's official stamp, Hamlet transfers his "doom" (death sentence) to Gilderstone and Rossencraft.
4 Thanks be to heaven for saving the prince.
Scene 15 Location: The King's private apartments.

1. By my will, not all the world combined could hinder me.
2. Leartes is essentially asking, "What has this got to do with my revenge?"
3. In twelve venies, or rounds, of fencing, you do not top him by three.

And not the dearest friend that Hamlet loved
Will ever have Leartes in suspect.
LEARTES   My lord, I like it well.
But say Lord Hamlet should refuse this match?
30   KING   I'll warrant you, we'll put on you
Such a report of singularity°   *exceptional skill*
Will bring him on, although against his will.
And lest that all should miss,
I'll have a potion that shall ready stand,
35   In all his heat when that he calls for drink,
Shall be his period° and our happiness.   *end*
LEARTES   'Tis excellent. Oh, would the time were come!
          Enter the QUEEN.
Here comes the Queen.
KING   How now, Gertred? Why look you heavily?
40   QUEEN   O my lord, the young Ofelia,
Having made a garland of sundry sorts of flowers,
Sitting upon a willow by a brook,
The envious° sprig broke—into the brook she fell   *evil*
And for awhile her clothes, spread wide abroad,
45   Bore the young lady up. And there she sat
Smiling, even mermaid-like, twixt heaven and earth,
Chanting old sundry tunes—uncapable,°   *uncomprehending*
As it were, of her distress; but long it could not be
Till that her clothes, being heavy with their drink,
Dragged the sweet wretch to death.
50   LEARTES   So, she is drowned.
Too much of water hast thou, Ofelia—
Therefore I will not drown thee in my tears.
Revenge it is must yield this heart relief,
For woe begets woe, and grief hangs on grief.   *Exeunt.*

Scene 16

          *Enter [*FIRST *and* SECOND CLOWNS].°   *rustics; peasants*
FIRST CLOWN   I say no, she ought not to be buried in Chris-
tian burial.[1]
SECOND CLOWN   Why, sir?
FIRST CLOWN   Marry, because she's drowned.
5   SECOND CLOWN   But she did not drown herself.
FIRST CLOWN   No, that's certain, the water drowned her.
SECOND CLOWN   Yea, but it was against her will.
FIRST CLOWN   No, I deny that, for look you, sir—I stand here:
if the water come to me, I drown not myself, but if I go to
10   the water and am there drowned, ergo,[2] I am guilty of my
own death. You're gone,[3] go, you're gone, sir.
SECOND CLOWN   Ay, but see, she hath Christian burial because
she is a great° woman.   *important; powerful*
FIRST CLOWN   Marry, more's the pity that great folk should
15   have more authority to hang or drown themselves more than
other people. Go fetch me a stoup° of drink. But before thou   *flagon*

Scene 16 Location: A churchyard.
1. Ordinarily, suicides would not receive a "Christian burial" (in consecrated ground with the church's
blessing and ritual).
2. Therefore (Latin).
3. You lose.

goest, tell me one thing: who builds strongest of⁴ a mason, a
shipwright, or a carpenter?

SECOND CLOWN Why, a mason, for he builds all of stone and
20 will endure long.

FIRST CLOWN That's pretty! To't again, to't again.⁵

SECOND CLOWN Why then, a carpenter, for he builds the gallows and that brings many a one to his long home.

FIRST CLOWN Pretty again! The gallows doth° well—marry,   *serves*
25 how does it well? The gallows does well to them that do ill.
Go, get thee gone. And if anyone ask thee hereafter, say a
gravemaker, for the houses he builds last till doomsday.
Fetch me a stoup of beer, go.   [*Exit* SECOND CLOWN.]
      Enter HAMLET *and* HORATIO [*apart*].

[*Sings.*]   A pick-ax and a spade, a spade,
30   For and° a winding sheet,   *And also*
                          Most fit it is, for 'twill be made
                          For such a guest most meet.
      He throws up a [*skull*].

HAMLET Hath this fellow any feeling of himself that is thus
merry in making of a grave? See how the slave jowls° their   *slams*
35 heads against the earth.

HORATIO My lord, custom hath made it in him seem
nothing.

FIRST CLOWN [*sings*] A pickax and a spade, a spade,
                          For and a winding sheet,
40   Most fit it is for to be made,
                          For such a guest most meet.
      [*He throws up another skull.*]

HAMLET Look you, there's another, Horatio. Why, may't not
be the skull of some lawyer? Methinks he should indict that
fellow of an action of battery⁶ for knocking him about the
45 pate° with 's shovel. Now, where is your quirks and quillets°   *head / quibbles*
now, your vouchers and double vouchers,⁷ your leases and
freehold and tenements?⁸ Why, that same box° there will   *deed box; coffin*
scarce hold the conveyance° of his land, and must his honor   *deed*
lie there? Oh, pitiful transformance! I prithee tell me, Hora-
50 tio, is parchment made of sheepskins?

HORATIO Ay, my lord, and of calves' skins too.

HAMLET I'faith, they prove themselves sheep and calves° that   *simpletons and fools*
deal with them or put their trust in them.°   *(lawyers)*
      [FIRST CLOWN *throws up another skull.*]
There's another—why, may not that be Such-a-one's skull
55 that praised my lord Such-a-one's horse when he meant to
beg him? Horatio, I prithee let's question yonder fellow.
—Now, my friend, whose grave is this?

FIRST CLOWN Mine, sir.

HAMLET But who must lie in it?

60 FIRST CLOWN If I should say I should, I should lie in my
throat, sir.

---

4. The "of" functions something like a colon here, introducing the three types of men to be compared.
5. That's not bad, but try again.
6. Legal prosecution for assault.
7. "Vouchers" summoned witnesses to attest to a piece of land's ownership. A "double voucher" required two such witnesses.
8. *freehold*: a land or property held permanently with full rights of disposal. *tenements*: an umbrella term for properties in freehold (i.e., beyond land).

HAMLET   What man must be buried here?

FIRST CLOWN   No man, sir.

HAMLET   What woman?

65   FIRST CLOWN   No woman neither, sir—but indeed one that
was a woman.

HAMLET   An excellent fellow, by the Lord, Horatio. This seven
years have I noted it: the toe of the peasant comes so near
the heel of the courtier that he galls his kibe.° [*to* FIRST   *chafes his heel sore*

70   CLOWN] I prithee tell me one thing: how long will a man lie
in the ground before he rots?

FIRST CLOWN   I'faith, sir, if he be not rotten before he be laid
in—as we have many pocky° corpses—he will last you eight   *pox-riddled*
years. A tanner will last you eight years full out, or nine.

75   HAMLET   And why a tanner?

FIRST CLOWN   Why, his hide is so tanned with his trade that it
will hold out water—that's a parlous° devourer of your dead   *dangerous; awful*
body, a great soaker. Look you, here's a skull hath been here
this dozen year—let me see, ay, ever since our last King

80   Hamlet slew Fortenbrasse in combat—young Hamlet's
father, he that's mad.

HAMLET   Ay, marry—how came he mad?

FIRST CLOWN   I'faith, very strangely—by losing of his wits.

HAMLET   Upon what ground?[9]

85   FIRST CLOWN   O'this ground, in Denmark.

HAMLET   Where is he now?

FIRST CLOWN   Why, now they sent him to England.

HAMLET   To England? Wherefore?

FIRST CLOWN   Why, they say he shall have his wits there or, if

90   he have not, 'tis no great matter there—it will not be seen
there.

HAMLET   Why not there?

FIRST CLOWN   Why, there they say the men are as mad as he.

HAMLET   Whose skull was this?

95   FIRST CLOWN   This? A plague on him, a mad rogue's it was—
he poured once a whole flagon of Rhenish° on my head.   *Rhine wine*
Why, do not you know him? This was one Yorick's skull.

HAMLET   Was this? I prithee let me see it.

[*He takes the skull.*]

Alas, poor Yorick. I knew him, Horatio—a fellow of infinite

100   mirth. He hath carried me twenty times upon his back.
Here hung those lips that I have kissed a hundred times,
and, to see now, they abhor° me. Where's your jests now,   *disgust; frighten*
Yorick, your flashes of merriment? Now go to my lady's
chamber and bid her paint herself an inch thick, to this she

105   must come, Yorick. Horatio, I prithee tell me one thing: dost
thou think that Alexander looked thus?

HORATIO   Even so, my lord.

HAMLET   And smelt thus?

HORATIO   Ay, my lord, no otherwise.

110   HAMLET   No. Why might not imagination work, as thus, of
Alexander: Alexander died, Alexander was buried, Alexander became earth, of earth we make clay, and Alexander

---

9. From what cause? (The Clown takes him to mean "In what country?")

being but clay, why might not time bring to pass that he
might stop the bung-hole° of a beer barrel?   *opening*

115   Imperious Caesar, dead and turned to clay,
Might stop a hole to keep the wind away.
> *Enter* KING *and* QUEEN, LEARTES, *and other Lords,*
> *with a* PRIEST *after* [Ofelia's] *coffin.*

HAMLET   What funeral's this that all the court laments?
It shows to be some noble parentage.
Stand by awhile.

120   LEARTES   What ceremony else?[1] Say, what ceremony else?

PRIEST   My lord, we have done all that lies in us,
And more than well the church can tolerate.
She hath had a dirge sung for her maiden soul
And, but for favor of the King and you,

125   She had been° buried in the open fields,   *would have been*
Where° now she is allowed Christian burial.   *Whereas (instead)*

LEARTES   So! I tell thee, churlish priest,
A minist'ring angel shall my sister be
When thou liest howling.°   *(in hell)*

HAMLET [*aside*][2]   The fair Ofelia dead!

130   QUEEN [*scattering flowers*]   Sweets to the sweet. Farewell.
I had thought to adorn thy bridal bed, fair maid,
And not to follow thee unto thy grave.

LEARTES   Forbear the earth a while.[3] Sister, farewell!
> LEARTES *leaps into the grave.*
Now pour your earth on, Olympus-high,

135   And make a hill to o'ertop old Pelion.[4]
> HAMLET *leaps in after* LEARTES.[5]

HAMLET   What's he that conjures so? Behold, 'tis I,
Hamlet the Dane.[6]

LEARTES   The devil take thy soul!

HAMLET   Oh, thou prayest not well.
I prithee take thy hand from off my throat,

140   For there is something in me dangerous
Which let thy wisdom fear. Hold off thy hand!
I loved Ofelia as dear as twenty brothers could.
Show me what thou wilt do for her:
Wilt° fight? Wilt fast? Wilt pray?   *Wilt (thou)*

145   Wilt drink up vessels? Eat a crocodile?
I'll do't. Com'st thou here to whine?
And where thou talk'st of burying thee alive,
Here let us stand and let them throw on us
Whole hills of earth till with the height thereof

150   Make Ossa[7] as a wart.

KING   Forbear, Leartes. Now is he mad as is the sea,
Anon° as mild and gentle as a dove.   *Soon*

---

1. Leartes insists upon further funeral rites.
2. TEXTUAL COMMENT We have chosen to cast this
line as an aside rather than as a comment to Horatio,
in order to convey Hamlet's inward shock of grief.
See Digital Edition TC 9 (First Quarto edited text).
3. Stop filling the grave for a moment.
4. In Greek mythology, giants piled Pelion (a mountain in Thessaly) on top of Mount Ossa in an attempt
to climb Mount Olympus.

5. TEXTUAL COMMENT Q1 is the only edition to
direct specifically what form Hamlet's reaction to
Leartes' grieving should take. This active decision of
leaping into the grave after Leartes possibly squares
with earlier cultural conceptions of Hamlet's character. See Digital Edition TC 10 (First Quarto edited
text).
6. Normally the title of the King of Denmark.
7. Greek mountain (see note to line 135).

Therefore awhile give his wild humor scope.[8]

HAMLET   What is the reason, sir, that you wrong me thus?
155 I never gave you cause. But stand away,
A cat will mew, a dog will have a day.[9]

                        Exeunt HAMLET *and* HORATIO.

QUEEN   Alas, it is his madness makes him thus
And not his heart, Leartes.

KING   My lord, 'tis so. [*aside to* LEARTES] But we'll no longer
trifle—
160 This very day shall Hamlet drink his last,
For presently we mean to send to him.
Therefore, Leartes, be in readiness.

LEARTES [*aside to* KING]   My lord, till then my soul will not
be quiet.

KING   Come, Gertred, we'll have Leartes and our son
165 Made friends and lovers, as befits them both,
Even as they tender° us and love their country.   *care for*

QUEEN   God grant they may.   *Exeunt.*

Scene 17

Enter HAMLET *and* HORATIO.

HAMLET   Believe me, it grieves me much, Horatio,
That to Leartes I forgot myself.
For by myself methinks I feel his grief,
Though there's a difference in each other's wrong.

Enter a braggart GENTLEMAN.

5 Horatio, but mark yon water fly:
The court knows him, but he knows not the court.

GENTLEMAN   Now God save thee, sweet Prince Hamlet.

HAMLET   And you, sir. [*aside to* HORATIO] Foh, how the musk-
cod[1] smells!

10 GENTLEMAN   I come with an embassage from his majesty to
you.

HAMLET   I shall, sir, give you attention. By my troth, methinks
'tis very cold.

GENTLEMAN   It is indeed very rawish cold.

15 HAMLET   'Tis hot methinks.

GENTLEMAN   Very sweltery hot. The King, sweet Prince, hath
laid a wager on your side: six Barbary horse against six
French rapiers, with all their accoutrements, too, and the
carriages—in good faith, they are very curiously wrought.

20 HAMLET   The carriages,[2] sir? I do not know what you mean.

GENTLEMAN   The girdles and hangers,[3] sir, and suchlike.

HAMLET   The word had been more cousin-german° to the   *related; appropriate*
phrase if he could have carried the cannon by his side.[4] And
how's the wager? I understand you now.

25 GENTLEMAN   Marry, sir, that young Leartes, in twelve venies at
rapier and dagger, do not get three odds of you,[5] and on your
side the King hath laid and desires you to be in readiness.

---

8. Let his temper run its course.
9. Despite Leartes' ranting, my day will come.
Scene 17 Location: A stateroom of the castle.
1. An excessively perfumed gentleman.
2. The Gentleman's inflated term for "hangers," or straps.

3. Attaching straps.
4. A common definition of "carriage" at the time was a mount for a cannon.
5. Leartes must score three more "hits" than Hamlet out of twelve bouts of swordplay to win the wager.

HAMLET   Very well. If the King dare venture his wager, I dare
venture my skill. When must this be?

30   GENTLEMAN   My lord, presently—the King and her majesty,
with the rest of the best judgment in the court, are coming
down into the outward palace.

HAMLET   Go tell his majesty I will attend him.

GENTLEMAN   I shall deliver your most sweet answer.   *Exit.*

35   HAMLET   You may, sir, none better, for you're spiced°—else he   *fragrant*
had a bad nose could not smell a fool!

HORATIO   He will disclose himself without inquiry.

HAMLET   Believe me, Horatio, my heart is on the sudden very
sore all hereabout.

40   HORATIO My lord, forbear the challenge then.

HAMLET   No, Horatio, not I. If danger be now, why, then, it is
not to come. There's a predestinate providence[6] in the fall of
a sparrow. Here comes the King.

Enter KING, QUEEN, LEARTES, [*and*] *Lords.*

KING   Now, son Hamlet, we have laid upon your head[7]

45   And make no question but to have the best.[8]

HAMLET   Your majesty hath laid o'the weaker side.

KING   We doubt it not.[9] —Deliver them the foils.

HAMLET   First, Leartes, here's my hand and love,
Protesting° that I never wronged Leartes.   *Declaring*

50   If Hamlet in his madness did amiss,
That was not Hamlet but his madness did it.
And all the wrong I e'er did to Leartes
I here proclaim was madness.
Therefore let's be at peace and think I have shot

55   Mine arrow o'er the house and hurt my brother.

LEARTES   Sir, I am satisfied in nature, but
In terms of honor I'll stand aloof and will
No reconcilement till by some elder masters
Of our time[1] I may be satisfied.

KING   Give them the foils.

60   HAMLET   I'll be your foil,[2] Leartes.
These foils have all a° length? [*He chooses a foil.*] Come   *the same*
on, sir.

Here they play.

A hit!

LEARTES   No, none!

HAMLET   Judgment?

65   GENTLEMAN   A hit, a most palpable hit.

LEARTES   Well, come again.

They play again.

HAMLET   Another! Judgment?

LEARTES   Ay, I grant—a touch, a touch.

KING   Here, Hamlet, the King doth drink a health to thee.[3]

---

6. God's direction for a specific event (over and above "general providence," the whole shape of God's design). Compare Matthew 10:29: "Are not two sparrows sold for a farthing? and one of them shall not fall on the ground without your Father."
7. *we . . . head:* we have cast our bet on your side.
8. *but . . . best:* that we've picked the best.
9. We're not fearful of that being true.

1. *till . . . time:* until the consensus of men of authoritative standing holds that I can accept Hamlet's apology.
2. Flattering contrast. Jewels were often set with a piece of metal foil under them to increase their glitter.
3. Here in Q2 and F, the King drops a poisoned pearl into Hamlet's cup.

70 QUEEN   Here, Hamlet, take my napkin,° wipe thy face.   *handkerchief*
KING   Give him the wine.
HAMLET   Set it by. I'll have another bout first. I'll drink anon.°   *shortly*
QUEEN   Here, Hamlet, thy mother drinks to thee.
     She drinks.
KING   Do not drink, Gertred. [*aside*] Oh, 'tis the poisoned cup!
75 HAMLET   Leartes, come, you dally with me. I pray you pass°   *thrust*
with your most cunning'st play.
LEARTES   Ay, say you so? Have at you! I'll hit you now, my
lord. [*aside*] And yet it goes almost against my conscience.
HAMLET   Come on, sir.
     They catch one another's rapiers and both are
     wounded.
     LEARTES *falls down; the* QUEEN *falls down.*
80 KING   Look to the Queen.
QUEEN   Oh, the drink, the drink! Hamlet, the drink!
     [*She*] *dies.*
HAMLET   Treason, ho! Keep the gates!
GENTLEMAN   How is't, my lord Leartes?
LEARTES   Even as a coxcomb should[4]—foolishly slain with my
85 own weapon.
Hamlet,
Thou hast not in thee half an hour of life.
The fatal instrument is in thy hand,
Unbated° and envenomed. Thy mother's poisoned—   *Not blunted*
90 That drink was made for thee.
HAMLET   The poisoned instrument within my hand?
Then venom to thy venom: die, damned villain!
     [*He stabs the* KING.]
Come, drink: here lies thy union—here!
     [*He pours the drink down the King's throat and*] *the*
     KING *dies.*
LEARTES   Oh, he is justly served.
95 Hamlet, before I die, here take my hand
And withal° my love: I do forgive thee.   *with it*
     LEARTES *dies.*
HAMLET   And I thee.
Oh, I am dead, Horatio; fare thee well.
HORATIO   No, I am more an antique Roman
100 Than a Dane[5]—here is some poison left.
HAMLET   Upon my love I charge thee, let it go.
Oh fie, Horatio—an if° thou shouldst die,   *an if = if*
What a scandal wouldst thou leave behind!
What tongue should tell the story of our deaths
105 If not from thee? Oh, my heart sinks, Horatio,
Mine eyes have lost their sight, my tongue his use.
Farewell, Horatio: heaven receive my soul.
     HAMLET *dies.*

4. *Even . . . should:* Just like a coxcomb; in the manner of a coxcomb.
5. Ancient ("antique") Romans generally regarded

suicide as preferable to dishonor; in particular, they
believed that servants or retainers should not outlive
their master's overthrow.

Enter VOLTEMAR *and the* AMBASSADORS *from England.*
Enter [through a different door] FORTENBRASSE *with*
his train.

FORTENBRASSE   Where is this bloody sight?

HORATIO   If aught of woe or wonder you'd behold,

110   Then look upon this tragic spectacle.

FORTENBRASSE   O imperious Death, how many princes

    Hast thou at one draft° bloodily shot to death?   *draw of the bow*

AMBASSADOR   Our embassy that we have brought from

    England—

    Where be these princes that should hear us speak?

115   Oh, most unlooked-for time! Unhappy country!

HORATIO   Content yourselves. I'll show to all the ground,

    The first beginning of this tragedy.

    Let there a scaffold be reared up in the marketplace,

    And let the state of the world be there,

120   Where you shall hear such a sad story told

    That never mortal man could more unfold.

FORTENBRASSE   I have some rights of memory⁶ to this

    kingdom,

    Which now to claim my leisure doth invite me.

    Let four of our chiefest captains

125   Bear Hamlet like a soldier to his grave,

    For he was likely, had he lived,

    To've proved° most royal.   *shown himself ; acted*

    Take up the body; such a sight as this

    Becomes the fields,⁷ but here doth much amiss.   [*Exeunt.*]

---

6. *of memory:* unforgotten; traditional.   7. Is most appropriate to a battlefield.

Troilus and Cressida

Audiences or readers who come to *Troilus and Cressida* (written 1601–02) from the *Iliad* are in for a shock. Where Homer sings of heroic conflict culminating in the epic battle between Hector and Achilles, Shakespeare gives center stage to a love story that, like the events of the Trojan War itself, he treats skeptically. Where Homer finds tragic grandeur in the events he portrays, Shakespeare sees only carnage, a carnage unrelieved by the romantic plot, which ends—and indeed, arguably, begins—in disillusionment. This unfamiliar recasting of traditional material produces a modern, dark view of sexuality and politics.

Shakespeare knew Homer through George Chapman's *Seven Books of the Iliads of Homer* (1598) and perhaps through earlier English and French translations. (The frontispiece from Chapman's *Homer* suggests the era's standard view of the Trojan War; see p. 1983.) Moreover, the English monarchy had long traced its lineage back to Troy. For the titular figures and core narrative, Shakespeare almost certainly drew on Geoffrey Chaucer's *Troilus and Criseyde* (1380s), which views the central relationship through the code of courtly love and produces an aristocratic medieval tragedy from the failure of that love. Shakespeare was also indebted to a range of other texts: classical (Virgil's *Aeneid*, Ovid's *Metamorphoses,* perhaps several plays of Euripides), medieval (John Lydgate's *Troy Book*, early fifteenth century), and Renaissance (probably including Robert Greene's *Euphues His Censure to Philautus,* 1587). In *Doctor Faustus* (1592?), a tragedy that broadly influenced Shakespeare, Christopher Marlowe's titular figure lovingly apostrophizes Helen of Troy: "Was this the face that launched a thousand ships, / And burned the topless towers of Ilium?" And in 1599, a London theatrical company apparently performed Thomas Dekker and Henry Chettle's *Troilus and Cressida,* but only a fragmentary list of little more than stage entrances and exits survives today. The lost drama may have covered the same territory as *Troilus and Cressida* from an epic, didactic, and sentimental perspective to which Shakespeare's company, perceiving the commercial opportunities of a rival work on the topic, stingingly replied.

Troilus and Cressida achieves ironic effect by self-consciously retelling a familiar story. The lovers swear oaths of fidelity that, as audience members but not the characters realize, anticipate their quite different literary reputations. Cressida's uncle, the go-between Pandarus, provides a summary: "If ever you prove false one to another, . . . let all pitiful goers-between be called to the world's end after my name: call them all panders. Let all constant men be Troiluses, all false women Cressids, and all brokers-between panders" (3.2.185–90).* Pandarus's initial neutrality ("If ever you prove false one to another") reverts to the traditional sexual double standard, a shift predictive of the outcome and already voiced in the lovers' immediately preceding speeches, where only Cressida's faithfulness is in question.

Similarly, the military plot recalls attention to the very different Homeric version. Achilles is outfought by Hector and must appeal to the Trojan's chivalric generosity: "Pause if thou wilt" (5.6.14). Achilles then treacherously employs his soldiers, the Myrmidons, to ambush and kill Hector:

---

*All quotations are taken from the edited text of the Folio, printed here. The Digital Edition includes edited texts of both the Folio and the Quarto.

> HECTOR   I am unarmed. Forgo this vantage, Greek.
> ACHILLES   Strike, fellows, strike; this is the man I seek.
> . . . .
>
> On, Myrmidons, cry you all amain:
> "Achilles hath the mighty Hector slain!"
>
> (5.9.9–14)

The passage both deflates the epic account and explains how that false account arose in the first place. It thus reconciles conflicting interpretations while propelling a movement toward increasing bitterness.

The play equally breaks with the drama Shakespeare composed in the first half of his career. The romantic comedies from *Two Gentlemen of Verona* to *Twelfth Night* focus on romantic attachment and conclude in marriage. *Troilus and Cressida* moves from extramarital sex to infidelity, recriminations, deception, self-deception, venereal disease, and despair. The English history plays from *2 Henry VI* to *Henry V* usually turn on martial action in defense of the state. But *Troilus and Cressida* questions the moral legitimacy of war, viewed as an arena of mindless brutality.

The play's negativity is partly anticipated in the sources. The *Iliad* mixes nostalgic admiration for warrior culture with an awareness of human suffering. Robert Henryson's *Testament of Cresseid* (late fifteenth century) punishes Cressida's infidelity by the infliction of leprosy, and William Caxton's *Recuyell of the Historyes of Troye* (the first English printed book, about 1474) has a jaundiced view of the Trojan War. Similarly, Shakespeare's earlier comedies and histories hint at the dyspeptic vision of *Troilus and Cressida*.

More important, contemporary London stage practice provides a suggestive context. The children's theaters that reopened in 1599 popularized misogynistic dramatic satire, to which *Troilus and Cressida* responds. The play arguably participates in the battle of rival playwrights at the turn of the century, known as the Poets' War. The ridiculous figure of Ajax may satirize Ben Jonson, whose drama had criticized Shakespeare's works. And the railing Thersites perhaps points to John Marston, the most vituperative satiric playwright. Within Shakespeare's own oeuvre, *Troilus and Cressida*'s tone anticipates the so-called problem plays, *Measure for Measure* and *All's Well That Ends Well.* Further, beginning in 1599 with *Julius Caesar,* Shakespeare initiated a decade-long appropriation of classical history in which, generally, Rome is the subject of tragedy, Greece of satire. But satire and especially a disgust with women, sexuality, and the diseased body are important throughout Shakespeare's tragic period (1599–1608).

Finally, because the play is heterogeneous in tone, it sometimes connects with sunnier motifs in Shakespeare's earlier work. Troilus's initial state echoes the comically extravagant romantic excess in which Duke Orsino begins *Twelfth Night.* When asked by an attendant whether he will hunt the "hart" (deer, with a pun on "heart," line 16), the Duke explains that when he first saw Olivia, he was

> turned into a hart,
> And my desires, like fell and cruel hounds,
> E'er since pursue me.
>
> (1.1.20–22)

Lovesick Troilus also renounces the hunt:

> Why should I war without the walls of Troy
> That find such cruel battle here within?
> Each Trojan that is master of his heart,
> Let him to field. Troilus, alas, hath none.
>
> (1.1.2–5)

This opening follows the Prologue's military exposition and is succeeded by scenes of sexual comedy, cynical politics, satiric abuse, and perverse idealism. By the time any

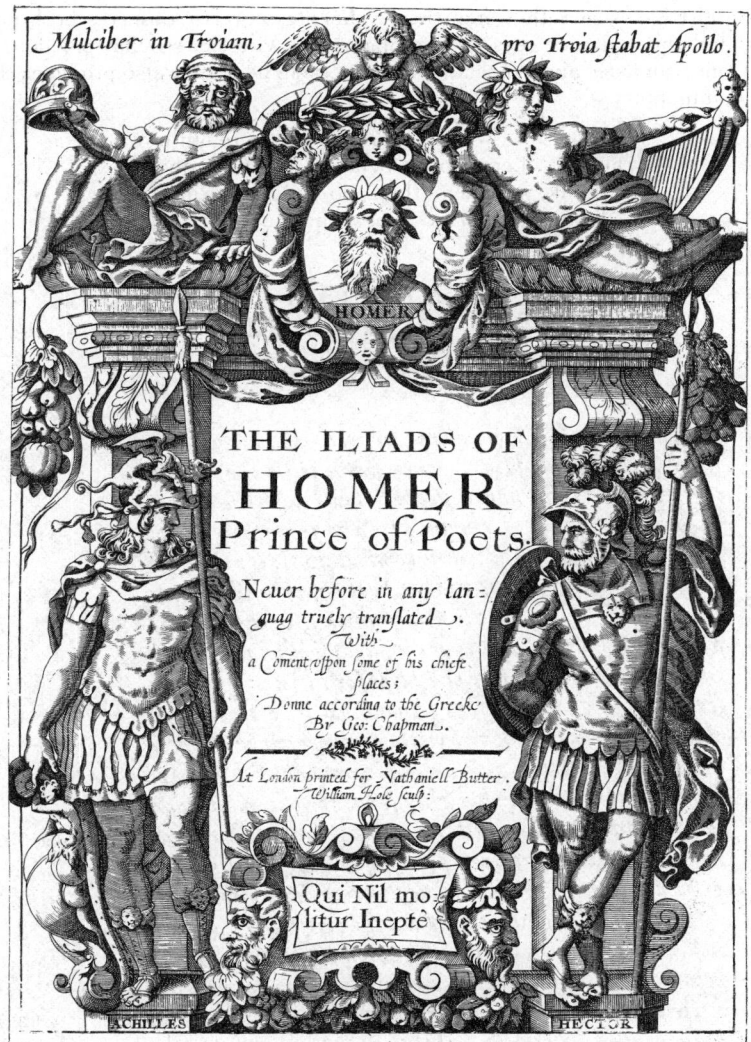

Title page of the *Iliad* of Homer in George Chapman's translation (1611?). Shakespeare probably used the less complete 1598 edition.

of these perspectives is repeated, one-third of the play is over. *Troilus and Cressida* thus presents multiple views: it is formally hybrid.

Hence, even though ironic disillusionment becomes increasingly pervasive, it does not subsume other perspectives. Accordingly, the nature of the work has always provoked disagreement. Early seventeenth-century references label it variously a history, a comedy, and a tragedy. By adding satire to the list, twentieth-century critics intensified the uncertainty. Although Shakespeare's career is marked by formal mixing, by the violation of neoclassical norms that separated comedy from tragedy, *Troilus and Cressida* represents an extreme. The play never adopts a consistent outlook in dismantling central aristocratic narrative forms—medieval chivalric romance and classical epic.

This disorientation extends to particular scenes. In 5.2, one of Shakespeare's most celebrated forays into eavesdropping, Diomedes and Cressida have an assignation,

Troilus and Ulysses secretly watch them, Thersites covertly observes both pairs of figures, and the audience sees all five characters. Cressida's behavior elicits judgments from Diomedes and especially from Cressida herself; it also produces the following commentary:

> ULYSSES   Cressid was here but now.
> TROILUS   Let it not be believed, for womanhood.
>   Think, we had mothers; do not give advantage
>   To stubborn critics, apt without a theme

This prefatory epistle (continued on the facing page) was added to the second state of the 1609 Quarto of *Troilus and Cressida* (Qc). It is not found in the first state (Qu) or in the First Folio (F).

> For deprivation, to square the general sex
> By Cressid's rule. Rather, think this not Cressid.
> ULYSSES   What hath she done, Prince, that can soil our mothers?
> TROILUS   Nothing at all, unless that this were she.
> THERSITES   Will he swagger himself out on 's own eyes?
>
> (5.2.128–36)

Troilus oscillates between misogynistic generalization and idealistic denial of Cressida's infidelity, Ulysses rejects extrapolation from individual to gender, and Thersites ridicules Troilus's willful blindness. Not only does staged action diverge from commentary on that action; one commentary is also at odds with the next. This pattern suggests that the play's view is broader than Thersites'. But what is that view? Although the audience occupies a privileged position, it must synthesize incompatible

THE EPISTLE.

. . . much as will make you thinke your testerne well bestowd) but for so much worth, as euen poore I know to be stuft in it. It deserues such a labour, as well as the best Commedy in Terence or Plautus. And beleeue this, that when hee is gone, and his Commedies out of sale, you will scramble for them, and set vp a new English Inquisition. Take this for a warning, and at the perrill of your pleasures losse, and Iudgements, refuse not, nor like this the lesse, for not being sullied, with the smoaky breath of the multitude; but thinke fortune for the scape it hath made amongst you. Since by the grand possessors wills I beleeue you should haue prayd for them rather then beene prayd. And so I leaue all such to bee prayd for (for the states of their wits healths) that will not praise it

Vale.

perspectives. Multiple eavesdropping onstage opens up an infinite regress that extends to the spectators, thereby undermining interpretive certainty. This uncertainty holds throughout *Troilus and Cressida*.

The play's philosophical rationales for even the most trivial actions intensify this effect. Characters disagree with one another and with themselves in the sense that their words diverge from their deeds. The linkage of policy questions to foundational principles thus highlights the practical irrelevance of those principles. Further, since there is almost no fighting until act 5, the play relies on talk and on decisions about how—or even whether—to prosecute the war. In the meeting of the Greek leaders (1.3), Ulysses treats Achilles' defection from the war as a disruption of "degree" (1.3.82)—of a hierarchically ordered world—by mere power. His speech, the most famous in the play, has often been read as Shakespeare's own orthodox credo.

The dramatic context undermines this judgment, however. Ulysses' humanely conservative political vision sits oddly with the manipulative scheme he immediately proposes to return Achilles to the fray. Similarly, Ulysses complains that Patroclus amuses Achilles by satirically impersonating other Greek leaders. To illustrate, he reproduces Patroclus's performances, thereby ridiculing Agamemnon and Nestor. And his own satiric voice is repeatedly heard, especially about Ajax. In this, the play echoes events of the previous dozen years, in which puritan satirical attacks on the official Church of England were answered, with the approval of the bishops, by satires on the satirists. As such, it dramatizes a cynical world antithetical to the norms of trust that are necessary, early modern political theorists argued, in any reasonably functioning society.

Slippage from lofty precept to dubious behavior also marks the corresponding Trojan council (2.2). Arguing that it is worth returning Helen to the Greeks to achieve peace, Hector asserts, "Every tithe soul 'mongst many thousand dismes [souls] / Hath been as dear as Helen" (2.2.19–20). This claim leads to a debate with Troilus:

> HECTOR   Brother, she [Helen] is not worth what she doth cost
> The holding.
> TROILUS   What's aught but as 'tis valued?
> HECTOR   But value dwells not in particular will;
> It holds his estimate and dignity
> As well wherein 'tis precious of itself
> As in the prizer.
>
> (2.2.51–56)

In response to Troilus's subjective view, then, Hector offers an equally weighty, objective standard of value. Hector's disabused view of Helen differs from at least three other positions staked out in the play. It is more bitterly refracted when Paris asks who deserves her more, "Myself or Menelaus" (4.1.55). Diomedes replies:

> He merits well to have her that doth seek her,
> Not making any scruple of her soilure,
> With such a hell of pain and world of charge;
> And you as well to keep her that defend her,
> Not palating the taste of her dishonor,
> With such a costly loss of wealth and friends.
> (4.1.56–61)

Accordingly, Helen is branded a "whore" by both Diomedes and Thersites (4.1.67, 2.3.65) before that term is attached to Cressida. Misogyny thus fuses with the play's dominant anti-war sentiment.

Second, when the Greek leaders snub Achilles to get him to fight, Ulysses tells the shaken warrior that value consists not in merit but in reputation—almost the opposite of Hector's position. Characteristically, the play provides no resolution to this implicit disagreement. And third, Troilus himself is undeterred by Hector's argument. Now appealing not to subjective attribution of value but to constancy of purpose, he rejects returning Helen to end the war:

> I take today a wife, and my election
> Is led on in the conduct of my will,
> . . . .
> . . . How may I avoid,
> Although my will distaste what it elected,
> The wife I chose? There can be no evasion
> To blench from this and to stand firm by honor.
> (2.2.61–68)

Troilus's defense of marital commitment unwittingly militates against his own position, however. Helen is Menelaus's wife, not Paris's, and Troilus himself gives no thought to marrying Cressida. Even Hector, the play's noblest character, cannot act on his words. Claiming that to keep Helen is self-destructive and immoral, he wins the debate with Troilus (and Paris). But partly inspired by desire for chivalric glory, he collapses intellectually, agreeing to fight for Trojan "dignities," the very aristocratic honor he had just scorned.

The romantic plot also holds contradictory outlooks in tension. Reacting against earlier criticism that identified with Troilus, recent discussions look skeptically at the male lover and sympathetically at the woman who apparently betrays him. Troilus has a mundane goal: "Her bed is India: there she lies, a pearl" (1.1.95). This sensual motivation turns Cressida into an object of exchange. The jarring juxtaposition ironizes the idealized image of love he articulates elsewhere: the metaphor parallels the businesslike enterprise of seduction in which Pandarus is instrumental. When Troilus calls himself "skill-less as unpracticed infancy" and "simpler than the infancy of truth" (1.1.12, 3.2.157), he continues his self-regarding rhetoric, distancing himself from his own sexually aggressive behavior and arguably imagining sexual intercourse between adults as the relationship between infant and mother. Troilus fears a subsequent letdown: "that the will is infinite and the execution confined, that the desire is boundless and the act a slave to limit" (3.2.75–76). Disappointment is Cressida's anxiety as well, although her concern is male inconstancy: "Yet hold I off. Women are angels, wooing; / Things won are done, joy's soul lies in the doing" (1.2.264–65). Cressida's ambivalence turns on the conviction, embedded in gender inequality, that female sexual surrender cools male ardor. She acts out of multiple motives—love and sexual desire, vulnerability, fear of betrayal, the possibility of self-betrayal from the need to protect herself, and the tendency to understand herself as others define her.

The play validates her worries. She has been abandoned by her father, and her remaining relative seeks to send her to bed with Troilus. Following their first and only night together, the lovers' common fear is realized. Troilus cheerfully gets up to leave, over Cressida's objections. The news that she will be swapped for Antenor—will become an object of exchange—elicits her passionate refusal but Troilus's immediate resignation. Although her reference to "the merry Greeks" (4.4.55) arouses Troilus's jealousy, Cressida interprets his renewed passion as further devaluation of her. Upon her arrival in the enemy camp, she is kissed by the Greek leaders in a scene that may reveal everything from her wantonness to near gang rape. Reunited with a father who delivers her to Diomedes, she acts with characteristic ambiguity, perhaps combining ambivalence, a sense of entrapment, desperation, weakness, desire, and manipulation.

But one should not simply reverse Troilus's self-understanding, seeing him as victimizer and Cressida as victim. The play offers competing interpretations without privileging any of them. In a way, this uncertainty does not matter. Troilus and Cressida's relationship is a zero-sum game: however one explains their behavior, the effect is to undermine ideals that have been overrated all along.

Ambiguity and degradation also mark the military climax. Hector compounds his

The friendly chivalric combat between two noble kinsmen, Hector and Ajax. From Geffrey Whitney, *A Choice of Emblems* (1586).

failure in the Trojan council by disastrous chivalric generosity. Driven by honor, he insists on fighting, although he is warned not to and the fate of Troy hangs on his health. Ulysses, Ajax, and Troilus remark on his habit of sparing a defeated foe. This habit depends on the assumption, despite clear evidence to the contrary, that others operate similarly. Thus, when Hector disarms before Achilles comes upon him, he proves an easy target. With this implicit judgment of Hector, the play universalizes its critique. The result is near moral vacuum. Although aristocratic norms retain some of their former appeal, the struggle to live by them is scarcely worth the effort. The play may thus gesture toward the political crisis at the end of Elizabeth's reign, highlighted by the execution of the Earl of Essex, whose ambitious factionalism (perhaps echoed in Achilles) and chivalric competitiveness (perhaps exemplified by Hector) more generally marked the behavior of competing groups of courtiers who sought royal favor.

The systematic ambiguity of *Troilus and Cressida* is intensified by the early publishing history of the play. (See the Textual Introduction.) The First Quarto emphasizes Troilus, Cressida, and Pandarus on the title page and is prefaced by an anonymous prose epistle that defines the work as a comedy. (See the facsimile reproduction of the epistle, pp. 1984–85, and the transcription in the Digital Edition of Q.) The First Folio version is called a tragedy and lacks the epistle, instead introducing the play by a verse Prologue that ignores the lovers while focusing on the Trojan War itself, treated in heroic terms. In other words, the two texts set up antithetical expectations for their readers.

The Quarto's satiric thrust and the epistle's claim that the work was never performed in a public theater have given rise to the theory that it was composed for elite private performance—possibly at one of the Inns of Court (law schools) or at Cambridge. This view, often supported by emphasis on the play's Latinate language, legal references, and philosophical argument, is unsupported by contemporary documents and is at odds with Shakespeare's normal practice. Possibly, however, *Troilus and Cressida* was relatively unsuccessful at the Globe; probably it was influenced by the Inns of Court; possibly it was performed there, at Cambridge, or in both locales. Whatever the truth, the debate about the nature and location of the early audience reproduces the generic ambiguity of *Troilus and Cressida*: coterie performance implies satire; the public stage, tragedy.

This uncertainty troubled neoclassical writers. In 1679, John Dryden removed "that heap of rubbish" that detracted from tragedy. His Cressida remains true to Troilus but commits suicide, and Achilles kills off Troilus. Dryden's adaptation was occasionally staged between 1679 and 1734. Thereafter, *Troilus and Cressida* went unperformed until 1898. Especially in the last fifty years, however, its incompatible meanings and bitter view of love and war have made it popular. Just as Shakespeare's history plays were mobilized to support patriotic sentiment, *Troilus and Cressida* has given expression to anti-war views—on the eve of both world wars, repeatedly during the Vietnam War in the 1960s and 1970s, and more recently with reference to the

Middle East. Consequently, Thersites sometimes becomes the play's central spokesman; Ulysses, advocate of traditional hierarchy, is ironized. Similarly, feminist-inspired sympathy for Cressida leads to depreciation of Troilus.

But does the play offer positive values, even if they cannot be openly articulated? The ceremonial exchanges between the rival military leaders suggest the lure of homosocial bonding, which simultaneously excludes women and drives men back into battle. Performances since the 1960s have frequently been sensitive to this motif. Hector challenges "the fair'st of Greece," by which he means not a woman but a man, and indeed a man who will "dare avow her [the man's mistress's] beauty and her worth / In other arms than hers" (1.3.262, 268–69). Ulysses resorts to similar wordplay when trying to persuade Achilles to overcome heterosexual love: "And better would it fit Achilles much / To throw down Hector than Polyxena" (3.3.206–07).

An ambivalent imagistic pattern connecting women, effeminacy, and sexual deviation comes closest to providing a countervision to this heroic ethos. Cassandra interrupts the Trojan council with prophecies of doom, a tactic she repeats—again unsuccessfully—in seconding Andromache's efforts to prevent Hector's fatal return to combat. Priam sums up the primarily female argument for inaction, telling Hector, "go back. / Thy wife hath dreamt, thy mother hath had visions, / Cassandra doth foresee" (5.3.62–64). Paris reports, "I would fain have armed today, but my Nell [Helen] would not have it so" (3.1.126–27). And Achilles' love for Polyxena keeps him sidelined: "Fall Greeks, fail fame, honor or go or stay, / My major vow lies here; this I'll obey" (5.1.38–39).

The warriors internalize the female perspective. Troilus cannot fight because his love for Cressida makes him "weaker than a woman's tear, / . . . Less valiant than the virgin in the night" (1.1.9–11). Here, sexual desire works against the instrumental use of women to further men's relations with one another. Only temporarily, however. The dispatch of Cressida to the Greek camp, ending her relationship with Troilus, partly counterbalances the earlier flight of Helen from the Greeks to the Trojans that establishes the (hostile) connection between the two groups of warriors in the first place. But Troilus's womanliness is a general phenomenon. Ajax calls the play's leading satirist "Mistress Thersites" (2.1.32). Hector opens his attack on the war by asserting: "There is no lady . . . / More ready to cry out, 'Who knows what follows?' / Than Hector is" (2.2.11–14).

Achilles has "a woman's longing, / . . . / To see great Hector in his weeds of peace" (3.3.237–39). Thersites, when faced in battle with "A bastard son of Priam's," makes an illogical, if life-saving, argument: "I am a bastard too. I love bastards! . . . Take heed, the quarrel's most ominous to us: if the son of a whore fight for a whore, he tempts judgment" (5.8.8–13). Here, Thersites' cowardice evokes a sexually illegitimate brotherhood opposed to meaningless slaughter. Finally, Patroclus is loathed as "an effeminate man" (3.3.217); he tells Achilles, owing to their enforced leisure:

> I stand condemned for this;
> They think my little stomach to the war
> And your great love to me restrains you thus.
> (3.3.218–20)

What "they think" may be true. Thersites calls Patroclus "Achilles' brach" (bitch hound, 2.1.108), later describing him as "Achilles' male varlet . . . his masculine whore" (5.1.14–16). The death of "My sweet Patroclus" (5.1.32) causes Achilles to break his vow and seek revenge, just as the loss of Cressida turns Troilus toward savagery. In a play about the most famous war in Western literature, opposition to battle brings disgrace. But in such moments—moments of sexual, romantic, or familial intimacy rooted in female or homoerotic experience—an alternative to both aristocratic values and their ironic deflation can be glimpsed.

WALTER COHEN

SELECTED BIBLIOGRAPHY

Charnes, Linda. "The Two Party System in *Troilus and Cressida*." *A Companion to Shakespeare's Works*. Vol. 4: *The Poems, Problem Comedies, Late Plays*. Ed. Richard Dutton and Jean E. Howard. Oxford: Blackwell, 2003. 302–15. Argues that the play begins from, rather than moves toward, disillusionment, with the characters accordingly exhibiting cynical idealism—passionate avowal of causes in which they don't believe.

Gil, Daniel Juan. "At the Limits of the Social World: Fear and Pride in *Troilus and Cressida*." *Shakespeare Quarterly* 52 (2001): 336–59. Investigates the contradiction between aristocratic, lineage-based relations and universalist, modern ones, focusing on the consequent disruption by sexuality of standard homosocial bonds, in which men use women to establish connections with other men.

Grady, Hugh. *Shakespeare's Universal Wolf: Studies in Early Modern Reification*. Oxford: Clarendon, 1996. 58–94. Argues that, philosophically, the play negates all value, seeing a world, from which it dissents, dominated by desire, power, capital, and instrumental reason unlinked to ethics.

James, Heather. *Shakespeare's Troy: Drama, Politics, and the Translation of Empire*. New York: Cambridge UP, 1997. 85–118. Explores Shakespeare's refusal to choose among alternative versions of the Troy legend, some of which trace a direct lineage from the Trojan to the English monarchy, the result being a conflicted play rooted in the late Elizabethan crisis.

Navitsky, Joseph. "Scurrilous Jests and Retaliatory Abuse in Shakespeare's *Troilus and Cressida*." *English Literary Renaissance* 42 (2012): 3–31. Argues that Ulysses' satiric response to Achilles' satire on the Greek leaders parallels the official clerical response to satire on the late Elizabethan church—in both instances thereby undermining the very values ostensibly being defended.

Scott, William O. "Risk, Distrust, and Ingratitude in Shakespeare's *Troilus and Cressida*." *Studies in English Literature* 52 (2012): 345–62. Contrasts Hobbes's understanding of the political basis of contractual trust with the cynical world of both the military and the sexual plots.

Shirley, Frances A., ed. *Troilus and Cressida*. New York: Cambridge UP, 2005. Presents a performance history, followed by a text of the play with notes on staging from various productions.

Traub, Valerie. *Desire and Anxiety: Circulations of Sexuality in Shakespearean Drama*. London: Routledge, 1992. 72–87. Connects militarism, sexual desire, and disease (syphilis) in the play—articulated by Thersites and Pandarus, projected onto Helen and especially Cressida, countered by bawdy, and undercut by homoeroticism.

Weimann, Robert. *Author's Pen and Actor's Voice: Playing and Writing in Shakespeare's Theatre*. Ed. Helen Higbee and William West. Cambridge: Cambridge UP, 2000. 62–70. Understands the play's "bifold authority" as a contrast between word and action, between mimetic performance and onstage commentary about it, and between performed and printed versions of the play.

Yachnin, Paul. "'The Perfection of Ten': Populuxe Art and Artisanal Value in *Troilus and Cressida*." *Shakespeare Quarterly* 56 (2005): 306–27. Sees *Troilus and Cressida* as an upscale, deluxe satire performed by a popular, artisan acting company whose need to win audience approval informs the play's debates about value and reputation.

FILM

Troilus and Cressida. 1981. Dir. Jonathan Miller. UK. 190 min. Relatively conservative BBC production that steers clear of homoeroticism but offers a spirited, rather than a debased, Cressida and effectively exploits television's resources by using both broad background shots and intimate close-ups.

TEXTUAL INTRODUCTION

Witnessing Cressida's interaction with Diomedes late in this play, Troilus cannot understand what he is seeing; thus, he famously laments that "This is and is not Cressid" (5.2.146). The same indeterminacy haunts the textual dimension of *Troilus and Cressida*, for every aspect of its printing history gives at least two alternatives, resulting in fundamental uncertainties that make this one of the most unsolvable textual puzzles in the Shakespearean canon.

First, there are two entries in the Stationers' Register. The earlier is dated February 7, 1603, when James Roberts entered "the Booke of Troilus and Cresseda as acted by the Lord Chamberlain's Men." Six years later, on January 28, 1609, Richard Bonion and Henry Walley (or Walleys) entered their copy of "the history of Troylus and Cressida." These entries suggest that Roberts gained the right to print but never undertook the financial risk of doing so, later selling the play to Bonion and Walley, who went on to publish *Troilus* in quarto form in 1609.

The resulting Quarto exists in two "states." Bonion and Walley engaged George Eld, who also printed Shakespeare's sonnets, as the printer for *Troilus*. The work commenced with a title page identifying the play as "The Historie of Troylus and Cresseida, As it was acted by the Kings Maiesties seruants at the Globe." However, this title page was replaced by another that says nothing about performance and adds a reference to "the conceited wooing of Pandarus Prince of Licia." A new epistle to the reader identifies the play as a comedy and claims that it has never been performed or "clapper-clawd with the palmes of the vulgar." Aside from the first three pages, the rest of the text is identical, yet the initial differences between the two states lead to a variety of questions: Was the play performed by Shakespeare's company? If so, was the performance at the Globe or somewhere else? If it was performed, why does the epistle claim otherwise? These questions about performance and printing history are inevitably tied to other issues, such as *Troilus*'s genre: Was it written as a history, a comedy, a satire, or, as it may seem, a tragedy?

No scholarly consensus has satisfactorily solved these problems, though one popular suggestion is that the play was written (or else revised) for a performance somewhere other than the Globe, such as the Inns of Court or Cambridge. This theory perhaps accounts for the contradictory claims about performance and may explain the satirical tone of the play. Unfortunately, however, there is no solid evidence for this claim. Furthermore, it is unlikely that Shakespeare would have gone to the trouble of writing a play not intended for performance, so unless there were problems with its political content—some scholars have suggested dangerous connections to the Essex rebellion—surely the King's (or Chamberlain's) Men would have attempted a performance at one or more venues. Nevertheless, the length of the play, as well as the second-issue title page and epistle, may suggest that the Quarto was intended for the reading public.

Even the 1623 Folio text tells an ambiguous story. *Troilus* was originally planned as part of the tragedies section, to be placed after *Romeo and Juliet*, and the printing was begun with this arrangement. After the first few pages, however, William Jaggard, the printer of the Folio, stopped the printing and canceled these pages, leaving a space in the tragedies section that *Timon of Athens* was selected to fill. Later, Jaggard apparently achieved or regained the right to print *Troilus*, placing it hurriedly between the histories and tragedies and inserting a Prologue not present in the previous version; *Troilus* did not even make it into the table of contents (the "Catalogue") of the Folio because of its late addition. The most insistent mystery about the Folio printing is the origin of the text from which it was printed. During the initial attempt to print *Troilus*, the Folio compositors were clearly using the Quarto as their base text, but after those pages were canceled and the printing resumed, they were also consulting another text of unknown origin.

The discrepancies between the Quarto and Folio texts are many: five thousand minor variants, but five hundred substantive ones. In most cases, both readings are viable. Despite theories that attribute variants to author, scribes, compositors, theatrical annotation, or revision, no explanation has been agreed upon. Arguments have been made that both texts derive from Shakespeare's foul papers or from transcriptions of them, yet no evidence conclusively proves that one text has earlier origins than the other. In the absence of any consensus about the relationship between these texts, *Troilus* emerges as one of the most compelling case studies for a two-text edition. Undoubtedly, many hands (those of actors, scribes, compositors, annotators) were involved in creating these two versions, yet too often previous editors have based their theories about their chosen base text on assumptions about certain readings being "better" or "more Shakespearean." However, allowing these two versions to stand as discrete examples of *Troilus* obviates the need for such adjudication. A close analysis reveals that the Folio version is more tragic and the Quarto more satiric, but the differences also offer performance alternatives that lend some weight to theories that these two versions were designed for different performances and venues.

The base text for the present printed edition is the Folio. This decision is not predicated upon assumptions about its aesthetic superiority or closeness to Shakespeare's intentions. Instead, the Folio is chosen because it was printed later and its provenance draws not just upon the Quarto but upon other sources as well. It also provides a somewhat expanded text, though we cannot know whether the additional passages and alterations of the Folio resulted from revisions by Shakespeare or by the theatrical companies. Revision does not ensure that the resulting play is necessarily "better"; nonetheless, one of the few certainties is that *Troilus* was a particularly volatile and indeterminate play from its inception, and the Folio text does the better job of illustrating this phenomenon.

GRETCHEN E. MINTON

PERFORMANCE NOTE

The sprawling, often stagnant plot of *Troilus and Cressida,* combined with its generic uncertainty, makes it one of Shakespeare's most difficult plays to produce. Directors can adapt the play so as to make it more uniformly tragic or satiric, and many strive to increase its relevance by substituting modern national or racial groups for the Trojans and Greeks. Yet actors are still challenged to facilitate engagement with characters that, in comparison to the heroic figures on which they are based, often appear distressingly inconsistent, obtuse, or morally deficient. They must also sustain interest in romantic and martial subplots amid scathing internal critiques of love and war, without allowing satire to eclipse Troilus's humanity or prevent audiences from becoming emotionally invested in his situation. Multiple passages of tortured syntax and drawn-out debate, meanwhile, make for a text that is unusually tricky to elucidate, as does the play's dubious and contested (non-)ending. Yet for all its challenges, *Troilus* can succeed brilliantly when directors recognize that fragmentation and irresolution lie at the heart of its dramatic logic.

Pandarus, Thersites, and Cressida, the main sources of dramatic interest and energy, are cases in point. The play seems to work best when audiences are in equal measure charmed and repulsed by each character, finding Pandarus as sentimental as he is sleazy; Thersites as fascinating, and convincing, as he is vile; and Cressida both wholly sympathetic and blameworthy. The potential for productive contradiction is there across the *dramatis personae*: Diomedes can be both chivalrous and menacing; Achilles the height of masculinity and an effeminate lover to Patroclus; Ulysses a moral compass and a trickster. Productions can even complicate Troilus's proverbial constancy, arguing Cressida's status as a tragic figure by implying that her indiscretions are forced by Troilus's jealousy and ready assent to her exchange for Antenor. Why Cressida yields to Diomedes is always a crucial consideration for productions, as is whether to stress the comparison between Pandarus (in wooing Cressida) and Ulysses (in wooing Achilles to battle). Other considerations include the casting of the Prologue (Pandarus and Thersites, "choral" presences throughout, are regular choices) and staging the many instances of onstage voyeurism (especially 5.2).

BRETT GAMBOA

The Tragedy of Troilus and Cressida

[THE PERSONS OF THE PLAY

Trojans:

PRIAM, King of Troy

HECTOR

PARIS

HELENUS, a priest } sons to Priam and Hecuba

DEIPHOBUS

TROILUS

Margarelon the BASTARD, illegitimate son to Priam

CASSANDRA, a prophetess, daughter to Priam and Hecuba

ANDROMACHE, wife to Hector

AENEAS }
Antenor } Trojan commanders

CALCHAS, a Trojan priest

CRESSIDA, daughter to Calchas

PANDARUS, uncle to Cressida

MAN (Alexander), servant to Cressida

Troilus' BOY

TROILUS' MAN

SERVANT to Paris

Attendants, Soldiers, Musicians, Trumpeter

Greeks:

AGAMEMNON, general of the Greek forces

MENELAUS, brother to Agamemnon

HELEN, wife to Menelaus, living in Troy with Paris

NESTOR

ULYSSES

ACHILLES } Greek commanders

AJAX

DIOMEDES

PATROCLUS, companion to Achilles

THERSITES, a scurrilous fool

SERVANT to Diomedes

MYRMIDONS

Servants, Soldiers, Attendants, Trumpeter

PROLOGUE]

The Prologue

[*Enter the* PROLOGUE *in armor.*][1]

PROLOGUE   In Troy, there lies the scene. From isles of Greece

---

Prologue

1. TEXTUAL COMMENT In armor (see line 23); perhaps referring to Ben Jonson's prologue to *Poetaster* (1601), where an armed figure defends Jonson's embattled reputation among playwrights. The Prologue first appeared in F. See Digital Edition TC 1 (Folio edited text) for its textual history and its differences from the opening of Q. For the epistle prefacing the second state of Q, see the facsimile on pp. 1984–85, as well as the electronic version of Q and Digital Edition TC 1 (Quarto edited text) for that text. See also the Textual Introduction.

The princes orgulous, their high blood chafed,[2]
Have to the port of Athens sent their ships,
Fraught° with the ministers and instruments   *Weighted down*
Of cruel war. Sixty and nine that wore
5   Their crownets° regal from th'Athenian bay   *coronets*
Put forth toward Phrygia,[3] and their vow is made
To ransack Troy, within whose strong immures°   *fortifications*
The ravishèd° Helen, Menelaus' queen,   *kidnapped (sexual)*
With wanton Paris sleeps—and that's the quarrel.°   *(petty) cause of complaint*
10 To Tenedos° they come,   *island near Troy*
And the deep-drawing barks[4] do there disgorge
Their warlike freightage. Now on Dardan[5] plains
The fresh and yet unbruisèd Greeks do pitch
15 Their brave pavilions.° Priam's six-gated city—   *finely arrayed tents*
Dardan, and Timbria, Helias, Chetas, Troien,
And Antenorides—with massy staples°   *bolt holes*
And corresponsive and fulfilling bolts
Spar up the sons of Troy.[6]
20 Now expectation, tickling skittish° spirits   *excitable*
On one and other side, Trojan and Greek,
Sets all on hazard.° And hither am I come,   *at stake*
A Prologue armed, but not in confidence
Of author's pen or actor's voice,[7] but suited
25 In like conditions as our argument,[8]
To tell you, fair beholders, that our play
Leaps o'er the vaunt° and firstlings of those broils,   *preliminaries*
Beginning in the middle,[9] starting thence away
To what may be digested in a play.
30 Like or find fault, do as your pleasures are,
Now good or bad, 'tis but the chance of war.   [*Exit.*]

1.1 (Q 1.1)

Enter PANDARUS *and* TROILUS.

TROILUS   Call here my varlet;° I'll unarm again.   *page (of genteel birth)*
Why should I war without° the walls of Troy   *outside*
That° find such cruel battle here within?°   *Who / in myself*
Each Trojan that is master of his heart,
5   Let him to field. Troilus, alas, hath none.[1]
PANDARUS   Will this gear° ne'er be mended?   *affair*
TROILUS   The Greeks are strong, and skillful to their
        strength,[2]
Fierce to their skill, and to their fierceness valiant;
But I am weaker than a woman's tear,

10   Tamer than sleep, fonder° than ignorance,   *sillier*
    Less valiant than the virgin in the night,
    And skill-less as unpracticed infancy.
    PANDARUS   Well, I have told you enough of this. For my part,
    I'll not meddle nor make° no farther. He that will have a   *be involved (proverbial)*
15   cake out of the wheat must needs tarry° the grinding.   *wait for*
    TROILUS   Have I not tarried?
    PANDARUS   Ay, the grinding, but you must tarry the bolting.°   *sifting*
    TROILUS   Have I not tarried?
    PANDARUS   Ay, the bolting, but you must tarry the leav'ning.
20   TROILUS   Still have I tarried.
    PANDARUS   Ay, to the leavening, but here's yet in the word°   *(tarry)*
    hereafter the kneading, the making of the cake, the heating
    of the oven, and the baking—nay, you must stay the cooling
    too, or you may chance to burn your lips.
25   TROILUS   Patience herself, what goddess e'er she be,
    Doth lesser blench at sufferance[3] than I do.
    At Priam's royal table do I sit,
    And when fair Cressid comes into my thoughts—
    So, traitor,[4] "when she comes"? When is she thence?
30   PANDARUS   Well, she looked yesternight fairer than ever I saw
    her look, or any woman else.
    TROILUS   I was about to tell thee: when my heart,
    As wedgèd° with a sigh, would rive° in twain,   *divided / tear apart*
    Lest Hector or my father should perceive me,
35   I have, as when the sun doth light a storm,
    Buried this sigh in wrinkle of a smile,
    But sorrow that is couched° in seeming gladness   *concealed*
    Is like that mirth fate turns to sudden sadness.
    PANDARUS   An° her hair were not somewhat darker than   *If*
40   Helen's[5]—well, go to,° there were no more comparison   *say no more*
    between the women. But, for my part, she is my kinswoman; I
    would not, as they term it, praise° her, but I would somebody   *compliment; appraise*
    had heard her talk yesterday as I did. I will not dispraise your
    sister Cassandra's wit, but—
45   TROILUS   O Pandarus, I tell thee, Pandarus,
    When I do tell thee there my hopes lie drowned,
    Reply not in how many fathoms deep
    They lie indrenched. I tell thee I am mad
    In Cressid's love; thou answer'st she is fair,
50   Pour'st in the open ulcer of my heart
    Her eyes, her hair, her cheek, her gait, her voice;
    Handlest in thy discourse—oh, that her hand,[6]
    In whose comparison all whites are ink
    Writing their own reproach, to° whose soft seizure°   *compared to / grasp*
55   The cygnet's down is harsh, and spirit of sense[7]
    Hard as the palm of plowman. This thou tell'st me,
    As true° thou tell'st me, when I say I love her.   *Truly*
    But saying thus, instead of oil and balm,

---

3. Shies away less from suffering. (Troilus presumably means more, not "lesser.")
4. Troilus considers himself a "traitor" to Cressida for ever forgetting her.
5. Pandarus shows the standard Elizabethan hostility to dark hair or a dark complexion.

6. *Handlest . . . hand:* You treat in your discussion—Oh, that hand of hers. (Troilus's use of "handlest" reminds him of Cressida's hand.)
7. The quintessential medium of feeling or touch that conveyed sense impressions from body to mind.

Thou lay'st in every gash that love hath given me
60 The knife that made it.
PANDARUS I speak no more than truth.
TROILUS   Thou dost not speak so much.
PANDARUS Faith, I'll not meddle in't. Let her be as she is. If
  she be fair, 'tis the better for her; an she be not, she has the
  mends° in her own hands.   *cure (cosmetics)*
65 TROILUS Good Pandarus—how now, Pandarus?
PANDARUS I have had my labor for my travail,° ill thought on   *my pains as payment*
  of her, and ill thought on of you, gone between and between,
  but small thanks for my labor.
TROILUS What, art thou angry, Pandarus? What, with me?
70 PANDARUS Because she's kin to me, therefore she's not so fair
  as Helen; an she were not kin to me, she would be as fair on
  Friday as Helen is on Sunday.[8] But what care I? I care not
  an she were a blackamoor—'tis all one to me.
TROILUS Say I she is not fair?
75 PANDARUS I do not care whether you do or no. She's a fool to
  stay behind her father;[9] let her to the Greeks, and so I'll tell
  her the next time I see her. For my part, I'll meddle nor make
  no more i'th' matter.
TROILUS Pandarus—
80 PANDARUS Not I.
TROILUS Sweet Pandarus—
PANDARUS Pray you, speak no more to me. I will leave all as
  I found it, and there an end.   *Exit.*
        Sound alarum.°   *trumpet call to arms*
TROILUS Peace, you ungracious clamors, peace, rude
  sounds!
85 Fools on both sides. Helen must needs be fair
When with your blood you daily paint° her thus.   *daub (as with rouge)*
I cannot fight upon this argument;°   *on these grounds*
It is too starved a subject° for my sword.   *too weak a reason*
But Pandarus—O gods, how do you plague me!
90 I cannot come to Cressid but by Pandar,
And he's as tetchy to be° wooed to woo   *touchy about being*
As she is stubborn, chaste against all suit.
Tell me, Apollo, for thy Daphne's love,[1]
What Cressid is, what Pandar, and what we.
95 Her bed is India:[2] there she lies, a pearl.
Between our Ilium° and where she resides   *(Priam's palace)*
Let it be called the wild and wand'ring flood,
Ourself the merchant, and this sailing Pandar
Our doubtful° hope, our convoy,° and our bark.   *uncertain / escort*
        Alarum. Enter AENEAS.
100 AENEAS How now, Prince Troilus? Wherefore not afield?
TROILUS Because not there. This woman's answer sorts,°   *is fitting*
For womanish it is to be from thence.
What news, Aeneas, from the field today?

8. *An . . . Sunday:* If she weren't my kinswoman
(with the result that my praise seems biased), she'd
be as beautiful in everyday dress as Helen is in her
finest clothes.
9. She's a fool not to leave with her father, Calchas, a
prophet who deserted to the Greeks, having foreseen

their victory.
1. For your love of Daphne. Daphne was a nymph
who prayed (successfully) to be turned into a bay tree
to escape the advances of Apollo, god of poetry.
2. Source of jewels, precious metals, exotic spices,
and rich fabrics.

AENEAS   That Páris is returnèd home, and hurt.
TROILUS   By whom, Aeneas?
105 AENEAS   Troilus, by Menelaus.
TROILUS   Let Paris bleed—'tis but a scar to scorn;
    Paris is gored with Menelaus' horn.[3]
        Alarum.
AENEAS   Hark, what good sport is out of town° today.   *outside Troy*
TROILUS   Better at home, if "would I might" were "may."[4]
110 But to the sport abroad—are you bound thither?
AENEAS   In all swift haste.
TROILUS   Come, go we then together.
                          Exeunt.

1.2 (Q 1.2)

Enter CRESSIDA *and her* MAN.

CRESSIDA   Who were those went by?
MAN   Queen Hecuba and Helen.
CRESSIDA   And whither go they?
MAN   Up to the eastern tower,
    Whose height commands as subject all the vale,°   *valley*
    To see the battle. Hector, whose patience
5   Is as a virtue fixed,° today was moved.°   *unwavering / angry*
    He chides Andromache and struck his armorer,
    And, like as there were husbandry in war,
    Before the sun rose[1] he was harnessed light,°   *in lightweight armor*
    And to the field goes he, where every flower
10   Did as a prophet weep° what it foresaw   *Was wet with dew at*
    In Hector's wrath.
CRESSIDA   What was his cause of anger?
MAN   The noise° goes this: there is among the Greeks   *rumor*
    A lord of Trojan blood, nephew° to Hector;   *relation*
    They call him Ajax.
CRESSIDA   Good,° and what of him?   *Well*
15 MAN   They say he is a very man *per se*° and stands alone.° *unique man / is preeminent*
CRESSIDA   So do all men, unless they are drunk, sick, or have
    no legs.
MAN   This man, lady, hath robbed many beasts of their partic-
    ular additions:° he is as valiant as the lion, churlish as the *characteristics*
20   bear, slow as the elephant—a man into whom nature hath so
    crowded humors[2] that his valor is crushed into folly, his folly
    sauced with discretion. There is no man hath a virtue that he
    hath not a glimpse° of, nor any man an attaint° but he carries *hint / a flaw*
    some stain of it. He is melancholy without cause and merry
25   against the hair;° he hath the joints of everything, but every- *against the grain*
    thing so out of joint that he is a gouty Briareus, many hands
    and no use; or purblinded Argus, all eyes and no sight.[3]

---

3. '*tis . . . horn:* it's just a trivial wound (or a wound given in return for Paris's scorn of Menelaus): Paris is wounded by the emblem of the cuckold (having seduced Helen, Menelaus's wife).
4. If what I wished for (an affair with Cressida) were what I could actually have.
1.2 Location: Troy.
1. *like . . . rose:* as if there were prudent management in war as in agriculture, where the conscientious laborer gets up before dawn. The comparison contin-

ues with "field" and "flower" (line 9).
2. Peculiarities. Humors were the four main bodily fluids, which were believed to determine a person's temperament.
3. He is put together with everything, but so badly that he is a giant (Briareus), whose hundred hands are ruined by gout, or totally blind Argus, whose hundred eyes Juno deprived of sight because he fell asleep guarding Io.

CRESSIDA   But how should this man that makes me smile
make Hector angry?

30   MAN   They say he yesterday coped° Hector in the battle and   *engaged*
struck him down, the disdain° and shame whereof hath ever   *indignation*
since kept Hector fasting and waking.

Enter PANDARUS.

CRESSIDA   Who comes here?

MAN   Madam, your uncle Pandarus.

35   CRESSIDA   Hector's a gallant man.

MAN   As may be in the world, lady.

PANDARUS   What's that? What's that?

CRESSIDA   Good morrow, uncle Pandarus.

PANDARUS   Good morrow, cousin° Cressid. What do you talk   *relation*
40   of? —Good morrow, Alexander. —How do you, cousin? When
were you at Ilium?

CRESSIDA   This morning, uncle.

PANDARUS   What were you talking of when I came? Was Hector armed and gone ere ye came to Ilium? Helen was not up,
45   was she?

CRESSIDA   Hector was gone, but Helen was not up.

PANDARUS   E'en so. Hector was stirring early.

CRESSIDA   That were we talking of, and of his anger.

PANDARUS   Was he angry?

50   CRESSIDA   So he° says here.   *(Alexander)*

PANDARUS   True, he was so. I know the cause too; he'll lay
about him today, I can tell them that.

[*He dismisses Cressida's* MAN.]

And there's Troilus will not come far behind him; let them
take heed of Troilus, I can tell them that too.

55   CRESSIDA   What, is he angry too?

PANDARUS   Who, Troilus? Troilus is the better man of the two.

CRESSIDA   O Jupiter, there's no comparison!

PANDARUS   What, not between Troilus and Hector? Do you
know a man if you see him?

60   CRESSIDA   Ay, if I ever saw him before and knew him.[4]

PANDARUS   Well, I say Troilus is Troilus.°   *(that special man)*

CRESSIDA   Then you say as I say, for I am sure he is not Hector.

PANDARUS   No, nor Hector is not Troilus in some degrees.°   *respects*

CRESSIDA   'Tis just to each of them: he is himself.

65   PANDARUS   Himself? Alas, poor Troilus, I would he were.

CRESSIDA   So he is.

PANDARUS   Condition I had gone barefoot to India.[5]

CRESSIDA   He is not Hector.

PANDARUS   Himself? No, he's not himself; would 'a° were   *he*
70   himself. Well, the gods are above; time must friend or end.°   *befriend or kill him*
Well, Troilus, well. I would my heart were in her body. No,
Hector is not a better man than Troilus.

CRESSIDA   Excuse me.[6]

PANDARUS   He is elder.

75   CRESSIDA   Pardon me, pardon me.

---

4. Here and in the following lines, Cressida obstinately takes Pandarus's figurative language literally.
Recognized him; met an ideal man; saw him from the
front ("before") and had sexual intercourse with
("knew") him.
5. If I'd gone barefoot (on pilgrimage) to India—an
impossibility.
6. Cressida disagrees, as in line 68.

PANDARUS Th'other's not come to't.° You shall tell me another   *his prime; intercource*
tale when th'other's come to't. Hector shall not have his will[7]
this year.
CRESSIDA He shall not need it if he have his own.
80 PANDARUS Nor his qualities.
CRESSIDA No matter.
PANDARUS Nor his beauty.
CRESSIDA 'Twould not become him; his own's better.
PANDARUS You have no judgment, niece. Helen herself swore
85 th'other day that Troilus, for a brown favor[8]—for so 'tis, I
must confess—not brown neither—
CRESSIDA No, but brown.
PANDARUS Faith, to say truth, brown and not brown.
CRESSIDA To say the truth, true and not true.
90 PANDARUS She praised his complexion above Paris'.
CRESSIDA Why, Paris hath color enough.
PANDARUS So he has.
CRESSIDA Then Troilus should° have too much. If she praised   *must therefore*
him above, his° complexion is higher than his;° he having   *(Troilus's) / (Paris's)*
95 color enough, and the other higher, is too flaming a praise for
a good complexion. I had as lief Helen's golden tongue had
commended Troilus for a copper nose.[9]
PANDARUS I swear to you I think Helen loves him better than
Paris.
100 CRESSIDA Then she's a merry Greek[1] indeed.
PANDARUS Nay, I am sure she does. She came to him th'other
day into the compassed° window—and you know he has not   *bay*
past three or four hairs on his chin—
CRESSIDA Indeed, a tapster's° arithmetic may soon bring his   *the simplest*
105 particulars therein to a total.
PANDARUS Why, he is very young, and yet will he within three
pound lift as much as his brother Hector.
CRESSIDA Is he so young a man and so old a lifter?°   *so practiced a thief*
PANDARUS But to prove to you that Helen loves him: she
110 came and puts me° her white hand to his cloven chin—   *puts me = puts*
CRESSIDA Juno have mercy! How came it cloven?
PANDARUS Why, you know 'tis dimpled. I think his smiling
becomes him better than any man in all Phrygia.
CRESSIDA Oh, he smiles valiantly.
115 PANDARUS Does he not?
CRESSIDA Oh, yes, an 'twere a cloud in autumn.[2]
PANDARUS Why, go to then! But to prove to you that Helen
loves Troilus—
CRESSIDA Troilus will stand to the proof[3] if you'll prove it so.
120 PANDARUS Troilus? Why, he esteems her no more than I esteem
an addle° egg.   *a rotten*
CRESSIDA If you love an addle egg as well as you love an idle
head, you would eat chickens i'th' shell.[4]

---

7. Troilus's resolve; Troilus's sexual desire.
8. Notwithstanding his (unfashionably) dark or
tanned face.
9. Red nose, caused by drinking; perhaps also an artificial nose, made necessary by the ravages of syphilis.
1. Slang for a reveler or wanton, implying good fellowship and superficiality; here, appropriately applied

to Helen and more generally to the Greeks, at least as
they treat Cressida.
2. As if he were a rain cloud.
3. Will uphold the proof; will have an erection.
4. An addled egg often resulted from the chick dying
during hatching.

PANDARUS   I cannot choose but laugh to think how she tick-
125   led his chin—indeed, she has a marvelous white hand, I
must needs confess.
CRESSIDA   Without the rack.°   *being tortured*
PANDARUS   And she takes upon her to spy a white hair on his
chin.
130   CRESSIDA   Alas, poor chin; many a wart is richer.°   *(in hairs)*
PANDARUS   But there was such laughing. Queen Hecuba
laughed that° her eyes ran o'er.   *so much that*
CRESSIDA   With millstones.[5]
PANDARUS   And Cassandra laughed.
135   CRESSIDA   But there was more temperate fire under the pot of
her eyes.[6] Did her eyes run o'er too?
PANDARUS   And Hector laughed.
CRESSIDA   At what was all this laughing?
PANDARUS   Marry,[7] at the white hair that Helen spied on Troi-
140   lus' chin.
CRESSIDA   An't had been a green hair I should have laughed
too.
PANDARUS   They laughed not so much at the hair as at his
pretty° answer.   *witty*
145   CRESSIDA   What was his answer?
PANDARUS   Quoth she, "Here's but two and fifty hairs on your
chin, and one of them is white."
CRESSIDA   This is her question.
PANDARUS   That's true, make no question of that. "Two and
150   fifty hairs," quoth he, "and one white. That white hair is my
father and all the rest are his sons.[8]" "Jupiter!" quoth she,
"Which of these hairs° is Paris, my husband?" "The forked[9]   *pun on "heirs"*
one," quoth he, "pluck't out and give it him." But there was
such laughing, and Helen so blushed, and Paris so chafed,°   *(was) so irritated*
155   and all the rest so laughed, that it passed.°   *surpassed description*
CRESSIDA   So let it now, for it has been a great while going by.
PANDARUS   Well, cousin, I told you a thing yesterday. Think
on't.
CRESSIDA   So I do.
160   PANDARUS   I'll be sworn 'tis true; he will weep you an 'twere°   *for you as if he were*
a man born in April.°   *month of showers*
CRESSIDA   And I'll spring up in his tears an 'twere° a nettle   *as if I were*
against° May.   *anticipating*
        Sound a retreat.
PANDARUS   Hark, they are coming from the field. Shall we
165   stand up here and see them as they pass toward Ilium, good
niece? Do, sweet niece Cressida.
CRESSIDA   At your pleasure.
PANDARUS   Here, here, here's an excellent place! Here we may

---

5. A hard-hearted person was proverbially said to
weep millstones rather than tears. Cressida doesn't
think the story is particularly funny.
6. Cassandra's tears are "more temperate" because
she was associated with mournful, doom-laden prophecy. Cressida imagines tears of laughter as a pot boiling over.

7. An oath based on the name of the Virgin Mary;
here, meaning "Why," elsewhere "Indeed."
8. Priam reputedly had fifty sons. The "forked" hair
(line 152) apparently counts as two.
9. Like a cuckold's horns, thereby suggesting Helen's
unfaithfulness to Paris.

170 see most bravely.° I'll tell you them all by their names as they   *very finely*
pass by, but mark Troilus above the rest.
    Enter AENEAS [*and passes over the stage*].
CRESSIDA   Speak not so loud.
PANDARUS   That's Aeneas. Is not that a brave° man? He's one   *splendid; courageous*
of the flowers° of Troy, I can tell you. But mark Troilus; you   *finest men*
shall see anon.
175 CRESSIDA   Who's that?
    Enter Antenor [*and passes over the stage*].
PANDARUS   That's Antenor. He has a shrewd wit, I can tell
you, and he's a man good enough. He's° one o'th' soundest   *He has*
judgments in Troy whosoever,° and a proper man of person.[1]   *of any man*
When comes Troilus? I'll show you Troilus anon. If he see
180 me, you shall see him nod at me.
CRESSIDA   Will he give you the nod?
PANDARUS   You shall see.
CRESSIDA   If he do, the rich shall have more.[2]
    Enter HECTOR [*and passes over the stage*].
PANDARUS   That's Hector—that, that, look you that, there's a
185 fellow! —Go thy way, Hector! —There's a brave man, niece.
O brave Hector! Look how he looks—there's a countenance.
Is't not a brave man?
CRESSIDA   O brave man!
PANDARUS   Is 'a° not? It does a man's heart good. Look you   *he*
190 what hacks are on his helmet; look you yonder, do you see?
Look you there, there's no jesting; laying on, take't off who
will,[3] as they say; there be hacks!
CRESSIDA   Be those with swords?
    Enter PARIS [*and passes over the stage*].
PANDARUS   Swords, anything, he cares not an the devil come
195 to him, it's all one.° By God's lid,° it does one's heart good.   *the same / eyelid*
Yonder comes Paris, yonder comes Paris! Look ye yonder,
niece, is't not a gallant° man too, is't not? Why, this is brave   *fine*
now. Who said he came hurt home today? He's not hurt.
Why, this will do Helen's heart good now, ha? Would I could
200 see Troilus now; you shall° Troilus anon.   *shall see*
CRESSIDA   Who's that?
    Enter HELENUS [*and passes over the stage*].
PANDARUS   That's Helenus. I marvel where Troilus is. That's
Helenus. I think he went not forth today. That's Helenus.
CRESSIDA   Can Helenus fight, uncle?
205 PANDARUS   Helenus? No. Yes, he'll fight indifferent° well. I   *fairly*
marvel where Troilus is. Hark, do you not hear the people
cry "Troilus"? Helenus is a priest.
CRESSIDA   What sneaking fellow comes yonder?
    Enter TROILUS [*and passes over the stage*].
PANDARUS   Where? Yonder? That's Deiphobus. 'Tis Troilus!
210 There's a man, niece. Hem! Brave Troilus, the prince of
chivalry!

---

1. Is a good-looking man.
2. If Troilus acknowledges Pandarus with a nod, this will make Pandarus even more of a noddy, a fool. "Give you the nod" (line 181) implies both personal recognition and recognition of folly.
3. There's hard fighting, denials notwithstanding (with sexual wordplay: "laying on" versus "take't off").

CRESSIDA Peace, for shame, peace.

PANDARUS Mark him, note him. O brave Troilus! Look well
upon him, niece. Look you how his sword is bloodied and
215 his helm more hacked than Hector's, and how he looks, and
how he goes.° O admirable youth! He ne'er saw three-and-   *walks*
twenty. —Go thy way, Troilus, go thy way. —Had I a sister
were a grace⁴ or a daughter a goddess, he should take his
choice. O admirable man! Paris? Paris is dirt to him, and I
220 warrant Helen to change° would give money to boot.   *exchange*

Enter common Soldiers [and pass over the stage].

CRESSIDA Here come more.

PANDARUS Asses, fools, dolts; chaff and bran, chaff and bran;
porridge° after meat. I could live and die i'th' eyes of Troilus.   *soup*
Ne'er look, ne'er look, the eagles are gone; crows and daws,°   *jackdaws; fools*
225 crows and daws. I had rather be such a man as Troilus than
Agamemnon and all Greece.

CRESSIDA There is among the Greeks Achilles, a better man
than Troilus.

PANDARUS Achilles? A drayman,° a porter, a very camel.   *cart driver*
230 CRESSIDA Well, well.

PANDARUS "Well, well"? Why, have you any discretion? Have
you any eyes? Do you know what a man is? Is not birth,°   *lineage*
beauty, good shape, discourse,° manhood, learning, gentle-   *eloquence*
ness,° virtue, youth, liberality, and so forth the spice and salt   *gentility*
235 that seasons a man?

CRESSIDA Ay, a minced⁵ man, and then to be baked with no
date in the pie, for then the man's date's out.⁶

PANDARUS You are such another woman!° One knows not at   *like other women*
what ward you lie.⁷

240 CRESSIDA Upon my back to defend my belly,⁸ upon my wit to
defend my wiles, upon my secrecy° to defend mine honesty,⁹   *privacy; genitals*
my mask to defend my beauty,° and you to defend all these.   *(from sun)*
And at all these wards I lie, at a thousand watches.¹

PANDARUS Say one of your watches.

245 CRESSIDA Nay, I'll watch you for that, and that's one of the
chiefest of them, too.² If I cannot ward what I would not
have hit,° I can watch you for° telling how I took the blow—   *(sexually) / from*
unless it swell past hiding,° and then it's past watching.   *(from pregnancy)*

Enter [Troilus'] BOY.

PANDARUS You are such another!

250 BOY Sir, my lord would instantly speak with you.

PANDARUS Where?

BOY At your own house.

PANDARUS Good boy, tell him I come.   [*Exit* BOY.]

---

4. The three Graces were goddesses of beauty and
charm.
5. Affected (punning on "mincemeat" to suggest the
multiple ingredients of Troilus and thus beginning to
develop Pandarus's "spice and salt" metaphor; also
hints at impotence).
6. The man is flavorless; out of date; past his sexual
prime; not in female genitalia.
7. One doesn't know what position of defense in fencing ("ward") you adopt. (A man doesn't know how to
deal with you.)

8. Vagina. Lying on one's back is not, of course, the
obvious way to defend one's virginity.
9. Reputation.
1. Ways of guarding; hours of the night; the duties of
a watchman (playing on "watch" and "ward," line 243);
devotional exercises (line 244). "Watch" as a verb is
also implied: observe (line 245); prevent (lines 246–
47); worry (line 248).
2. Presumably the immediately preceding phrase is
one of her chief devotional exercises.

I doubt° he be hurt. Fare ye well, good niece.   *fear*
255 CRESSIDA   Adieu, uncle.
     PANDARUS   I'll be with you, niece, by and by.
     CRESSIDA   To bring, uncle?
     PANDARUS   Ay, a token from Troilus.
     CRESSIDA   By the same token you are a bawd.°   *pander; pimp*

                        Exit PANDARUS.

260 Words, vows, gifts, tears, and love's full sacrifice
     He offers in another's enterprise,
     But more in Troilus thousandfold I see
     Than in the glass° of Pandar's praise may be.   *mirror*
     Yet hold I off. Women are angels, wooing;°   *when men woo them*
265 Things won are done, joy's soul lies in the doing.
     That she beloved° knows naught that knows not this: *A woman who is loved*
     Men prize the thing ungained more than it is.°   *is worth*
     That she was never yet that ever knew
     Love got so sweet as when desire did sue.³
270 Therefore this maxim out of° love I teach: *taken from*
     Achievement is command; ungained, beseech.⁴
     Then though my heart's contents⁵ firm love doth bear,
     Nothing of that shall from mine eyes appear.   *Exit.*

                        1.3 (Q 1.3)
         Sennet.° Enter AGAMEMNON, NESTOR, ULYSSES,   *Fanfare*
              DIOMEDES, MENELAUS, *with others.*
     AGAMEMNON   Princes, what grief hath set the jaundice° on   *sickliness*
          your cheeks?
     The ample proposition that hope makes
     In all designs begun on earth below
     Fails in the promised largeness; checks° and disasters   *obstacles*
5   Grow in the veins¹ of actions highest reared,
     As knots by the conflux° of meeting sap   *confluence*
     Infect the sound pine and divert his° grain,   *its*
     Tortive° and errant,° from his course of growth.   *Contorted / straying*
     Nor, princes, is it matter new to us
10   That we come short of our suppose° so far,   *intention*
     That after seven years' siege yet Troy walls stand,
     Sith° every action that hath gone before,   *Since*
     Whereof we have record, trial did draw
     Bias and thwart,² not answering° the aim   *living up to*
15   And that unbodied figure° of the thought   *theoretical design*
     That gave't surmisèd shape. Why, then, you princes,
     Do you with cheeks abashed behold our works
     And think them shame which are indeed naught else
     But the protractive trials of great Jove
20   To find persistive constancy in men,
     The fineness of which metal° is not found   *hard substance; mettle*

---

3. *That . . . sue:* No woman has ever known making love with a man to be as sweet as when it is still desired for the first time.
4. Once a woman yields, the man controls her; what the man doesn't have, he must plead for.
5. *contents: con-tents'*—happiness;   *con'tents*—substance.

1.3 Location: The Greek camp outside Troy.
1. It is assumed that trees have veins through which sap flows.
2. *trial . . . thwart:* the act of attempting the deed ("action") called it into being crookedly and in a manner at odds with the purpose.

115	Force should be right—or rather, right and wrong,	
	Between whose endless jar justice resides,⁵	
	Should lose their names, and so should justice too.	
	Then everything includes itself in° power,	comes down to
	Power into will,° will into appetite,°	egotism / lust
120	And appetite, an universal wolf,	
	So doubly seconded with will and power,	
	Must make perforce an universal prey,°	seizing
	And last eat up himself. Great Agamemnon,	
	This chaos, when degree is suffocate,	
125	Follows the choking.	
	And this neglection of degree is it	
	That by a pace goes backward in a purpose	
	It hath to climb.⁶ The general's disdained	
	By him one step below, he by the next,	
130	That next by him beneath—so every step,	
	Exampled by the first pace that is sick	
	Of his superior, grows to an envious fever	
	Of pale and bloodless emulation.°	sick rivalry
	And 'tis this fever that keeps Troy on foot,°	standing
135	Not her own sinews. To end a tale of length,	
	Troy in our weakness lives, not in her strength.	
	NESTOR Most wisely hath Ulysses here discovered°	revealed
	The fever whereof all our power is sick.	
	AGAMEMNON The nature of the sickness found, Ulysses,	
140	What is the remedy?	
	ULYSSES The great Achilles, whom opinion° crowns	consensus
	The sinew and the forehand° of our host,°	strongest / army
	Having his ear full of his airy° fame,	lofty; insubstantial
	Grows dainty of° his worth and in his tent	too conscious of
145	Lies mocking our designs. With him Patroclus,	
	Upon a lazy bed, the livelong day	
	Breaks scurrile° jests,	scurrilous
	And with ridiculous and awkward action°—	gesture
	Which, slanderer, he "imitation" calls—	
150	He pageants° us. Sometime, great Agamemnon,	mimics
	Thy topless deputation° he puts on,	supreme rank
	And, like a strutting player whose conceit	
	Lies in his hamstring⁷ and doth think it rich	
	To hear the wooden dialogue and sound	
155	Twixt his stretched footing and the scaffoldage,⁸	
	Such to-be-pitied and o'er-wrested seeming°	pitiful imitation
	He acts thy greatness in. And when he speaks	
	'Tis like a chime a-mending, with terms unsquared,⁹	
	Which from the tongue of roaring Typhon¹ dropped	
160	Would seem hyperboles. At this fusty° stuff	stale; bombastic
	The large Achilles, on his pressed° bed lolling,	(by Achilles' weight)
	From his deep chest laughs out a loud applause,	

---

5. Justice stands between the clashing ("jar") of the opposing contenders.
6. *That . . . climb:* That drops back step by step when it intends to climb.
7. *whose . . . hamstring:* whose brains are in his thighs.
8. *To hear . . . scaffoldage:* To hear the sound of his long, powerful strides (and dull speech?) on the platform stage.
9. Like bells being repaired (or tuned), with ill-fitting expressions.
1. Monster with a hundred heads, each uttering the cry of a different beast; eventually buried by Jupiter under (and so associated with) a volcano.

Cries, "Excellent! 'Tis Agamemnon just.°   *exactly*
Now play me Nestor—'hem'° and stroke thy beard   *(as in "ahem")*
165   As he being dressed to° some oration."   *preparing for*
That's done as near as the extremest ends
Of parallels, as like as Vulcan and his wife,[2]
Yet god° Achilles still cries, "Excellent!   *semidivine (ironic)*
'Tis Nestor right. Now play him me, Patroclus,
170   Arming to answer in° a night alarm."   *respond to*
And then, forsooth, the faint° defects of age   *weak*
Must be the scene of mirth: to cough and spit,
And, with a palsy fumbling on his gorget,°   *throat armor*
Shake in and out the rivet.° And at this sport   *fastening bolt*
175   Sir Valor dies,° cries, "Oh, enough, Patroclus,   *(laughing)*
Or give me ribs of steel! I shall split all
In pleasure of my spleen."° And in this fashion   *(seat of mirth)*
All our abilities, gifts, natures, shapes,
Severals and generals of grace exact,[3]
180   Achievements, plots, orders, preventions,°   *precautions*
Excitements° to the field, or speech for truce,   *Urgings*
Success or loss, what is or is not, serves
As stuff for these two to make paradoxes.°   *absurdities*
NESTOR   And in the imitation of these twain—
185   Who, as Ulysses says, opinion crowns
With an imperial voice—many are infect:°   *infected*
Ajax is grown self-willed and bears his head
In such a rein,° in full as proud a place   *So high*
As broad Achilles, and keeps° his tent like him;   *stays within*
190   Makes factious° feasts; rails on° our state of war,   *divisive / complains about*
Bold as an oracle; and sets Thersites,
A slave whose gall° coins slanders like a mint,   *rancor*
To match us in comparisons with dirt,
To weaken and discredit our exposure,°   *exposed position*
195   How rank° soever rounded in with° danger.   *densely / hemmed in by*
ULYSSES   They tax° our policy and call it cowardice,   *criticize*
Count wisdom as no member of the war,
Forestall prescience,° and esteem no act   *advance planning*
But that of hand.° The still and mental parts   *brute force*
200   That do contrive how many hands shall strike
When fitness° calls them on, and know by measure   *the right moment*
Of their observant toil the enemy's weight°—   *power*
Why, this hath not a finger's dignity!
They call this bed-work, mapp'ry,° closet-war,   *mere mapping; planning*
205   So that the ram that batters down the wall
For the great swing and rudeness of his poise[4]
They place before° his hand that made the engine°   *exalt above / (the ram)*
Or those that with the fineness° of their souls   *subtlety*
By reason guide his execution.°   *the ram's use*
210   NESTOR   Let this be granted, and Achilles' horse

---

2. *as near . . . wife:* as closely as the ends of parallel lines (which, since they are equidistant, never meet), and as the ugly, limping god Vulcan, the smith, resembles his beautiful wife, Venus. Ulysses is stressing how bad the acting is, while at the same time covertly belittling Agamemnon and Nestor.
3. Supreme merits, possessed individually and in common.
4. Because of the impetus and violence of its impact.

Makes many Thetis' sons.[5]
   Tucket.°   *Trumpet call*
AGAMEMNON What trumpet? Look, Menelaus.
MENELAUS   From Troy.
   Enter AENEAS [*with a Trumpeter*].
AGAMEMNON What would you fore° our tent?   *before*
AENEAS Is this great Agamemnon's tent, I pray you?
215 AGAMEMNON Even this.
AENEAS May one that is a herald and a prince
 Do a fair message to his kingly ears?
AGAMEMNON With surety° stronger than Achilles' arm   *security*
 Fore all the Greekish heads, which with one voice
220 Call Agamemnon head and general.
AENEAS Fair leave and large° security. How may   *generous*
 A stranger to those most imperial looks
 Know them from eyes of other mortals?
AGAMEMNON   How?
AENEAS Ay, I ask that I might waken reverence
225 And on the cheek be ready with a blush
 Modest as morning when she coldly eyes
 The youthful Phoebus.[6]
 Which is that god in office, guiding men?
 Which is the high and mighty Agamemnon?
230 AGAMEMNON This Trojan scorns us, or the men of Troy
 Are ceremonious courtiers.
AENEAS Courtiers as free,° as debonair,° unarmed, *generous / gracious*
 As bending° angels—that's their fame in peace—   *ministering*
 But when they would seem soldiers they have galls,[7]
235 Good arms, strong joints, true swords, and, Jove's accord,° *Jove willing*
 Nothing° so full of heart.° But peace, Aeneas, *No one / courage*
 Peace, Trojan, lay thy finger on thy lips;
 The worthiness of praise distains° his worth   *stains*
 If that the praised himself bring the praise forth.
240 But what the repining° enemy commends,   *grudging*
 That breath fame blows; that praise, sole pure,° transcends. *the only pure kind*
AGAMEMNON Sir, you of Troy, call you yourself Aeneas?
AENEAS Ay, Greek,° that is my name.   *cheater (slang)*
AGAMEMNON What's your affair, I pray you?
245 AENEAS Sir, pardon, 'tis for Agamemnon's ears.
AGAMEMNON He hears naught privately that comes from
  Troy.
AENEAS Nor I from Troy come not to whisper him.
 I bring a trumpet to awake his ear,
 To set his sense on the attentive bent,
 And then to speak.
250 AGAMEMNON   Speak frankly° as the wind;   *freely*
 It is not Agamemnon's sleeping hour.
 That thou shalt know, Trojan, he is awake,
 He tells thee so himself.
AENEAS   Trumpet,° blow loud!   *Trumpeter*

---

5. *Let . . . sons:* If this is true, then Achilles' horse is
worth many Achilleses. Thetis was the mother of
Achilles.
6. *Modest . . . Phoebus:* Modest as Aurora, the blushing dawn personified, when she coldly eyes Apollo,
the sun god ("youthful" because it is early morning).
7. But when it is time for them to be warriors, their
courageous tempers do not tolerate mistreatment.

Send thy brass voice through all these lazy tents,
255 And every Greek of mettle, let him know
What Troy means fairly shall be spoke aloud.
      [*Sound trumpet.*]
We have, great Agamemnon, here in Troy
A prince called Hector—Priam is his father—
Who in this dull and long-continued truce
260 Is rusty grown. He bade me take a trumpet
And to this purpose speak: "Kings, princes, lords,
If there be one amongst the fair'st of Greece
That holds his honor higher than his ease,
That seeks his praise more than he fears his peril,
265 That knows his valor and knows not his fear,
That loves his mistress more than in confession
With truant vows to her own lips he loves,[8]
And dare avow her beauty and her worth
In other arms than hers,° to him this challenge.   *armor; Hector's arms*
270 Hector in view of Trojans and of Greeks
Shall make it good, or do his best to do it:
He hath a lady wiser, fairer, truer
Than ever Greek did compass° in his arms,   *hold*
And will tomorrow with his trumpet call
275 Midway between your tents and walls of Troy
To rouse a Grecian that is true in love.
If any come, Hector shall honor him;
If none, he'll say in Troy when he retires
The Grecian dames are sunburnt° and not worth   *not fair-skinned*
280 The splinter° of a lance." Even so much.   *breaking; fragment*
AGAMEMNON   This shall be told our lovers, Lord Aeneas.
If none of them have soul in such a kind,
We left them all at home. But we are soldiers,
And may that soldier a mere recreant° prove   *coward*
285 That means not, hath not,[9] or is not in love.
If then one is, or hath, or means to be,
That one meets Hector; if none else, I'll be he.
NESTOR   Tell him of Nestor, one that was a man
When Hector's grandsire sucked. He is old now,
290 But if there be not in our Grecian mold°   *character; model*
One noble man that hath one spark of fire
To answer for his love, tell him from me
I'll hide my silver beard in a gold beaver°   *helmet's face guard*
And in my vambrace° put this withered brawn,°   *forearm armor / arm*
295 And, meeting him, will tell him that my lady
Was fairer than his grandam and as chaste
As may be in the world. His youth in flood,°   *Despite his youth*
I'll pawn this truth with my three drops of blood.
AENEAS   Now heavens forbid such scarcity of youth!
300 ULYSSES   Amen.
AGAMEMNON   Fair Lord Aeneas, let me touch° your hand;   *shake*
To our pavilion shall I lead you first.
Achilles shall have word of this intent,

---

8. *That loves . . . loves:* Who will declare his love
with stronger proof (deeds) than unreliable, private   promises.
9. Who does not aim (to be), has never been.

So shall each lord of Greece from tent to tent.
305 Yourself shall feast with us before you go
And find the welcome of a noble foe.

Exeunt. ULYSSES *and* NESTOR *remain.*

ULYSSES Nestor!
NESTOR What says Ulysses?
ULYSSES I have a young conception in my brain;
310 Be you my time¹ to bring it to some shape.
NESTOR What is't?
ULYSSES This 'tis:
Blunt wedges rive° hard knots; the seeded pride   split
That hath to this maturity blown° up   swelled
315 In rank° Achilles must or° now be cropped   overgrown / either
Or, shedding,° breed a nursery of like evil   dropping its seed
To over-bulk° us all.   overrun
NESTOR   Well, and how?
ULYSSES This challenge that the gallant Hector sends,
However it is spread in general name,
320 Relates in purpose only to Achilles.
NESTOR The purpose is perspicuous° even as substance°   easy to see / wealth
Whose grossness little characters sum up;²
And in the publication make no strain³
But that Achilles, were his brain as barren
325 As banks of Libya°—though, Apollo knows,   the Sahara Desert
'Tis dry° enough—will with great speed of judgment,   infertile; empty
Ay, with celerity, find Hector's purpose
Pointing on him.°   himself
ULYSSES And wake him to the answer, think you?
330 NESTOR Yes, 'tis most meet.° Who may you else oppose   fitting
That can from Hector bring his honor off
If not Achilles? Though't be a sportful combat,
Yet in this trial much opinion° dwells,   reputation
For here the Trojans taste our dear'st repute
335 With their fin'st palate. And trust to me, Ulysses,
Our imputation° shall be oddly poised⁴   reputation
In this wild° action, for the success,   uncontrollable
Although particular, shall give a scantling
Of good or bad unto the general;⁵
340 And in such indexes,° although small pricks   tables of contents
To° their subsequent volumes, there is seen   Compared to
The baby figure of the giant mass
Of things to come at large. It is supposed
He that meets Hector issues from our choice,
345 And choice, being mutual act of all our souls,
Makes merit her election° and doth boil,   grounds of choice
As 'twere from forth us all, a man distilled
Out of our virtues; who miscarrying,°   should he lose
What heart from hence receives the conqu'ring part

---

1. *conception . . . time:* The primary meaning (unfolding of a plan) metaphorically extended to pregnancy's
onset and gestation period, the latter associated with
the male and aged Nestor, who is oddly connected
with this female and ordinarily youthful activity, presumably because he embodies the passage of time.

2. Whose size is reckoned by small figures (on paper).
3. And, with the announcement, do not doubt.
4. Disproportionately judged.
5. *the success . . . general:* the outcome, although
relating only to one person, shall serve as an example
of the whole army's abilities.

350   To steel a strong opinion to themselves![6]
Which entertained, limbs are his instruments
In no less working than are swords and bows
Directive by the limbs.[7]

ULYSSES   Give pardon to my speech:
Therefore 'tis meet° Achilles meet not Hector.   *appropriate*

355   Let us, like merchants, show our foulest wares
And think perchance they'll sell; if not,
The luster of the better yet to show°   *not yet shown*
Shall show the better. Do not consent
That ever Hector and Achilles meet,

360   For both our honor and our shame in this
Are dogged with two strange followers.°   *unpleasant effects*

NESTOR   I see them not with my old eyes; what are they?

ULYSSES   What glory our Achilles shares° from Hector,   *gains*
Were he not proud, we all should wear° with him.   *share*

365   But he already is too insolent,
And we were better parch in Afric sun
Than in the pride and salt° scorn of his eyes   *bitter*
Should he scape Hector fair. If he were foiled,
Why, then we did our main opinion° crush   *common reputation*

370   In taint of° our best man. No, make a lott'ry,   *In the dishonor of*
And by device let blockish° Ajax draw   *blockheaded*
The sort° to fight with Hector. Among ourselves   *lot*
Give him allowance° as the worthier man,   *acknowledgment*
For that will physic the great Myrmidon,[8]

375   Who broils in° loud applause, and make him fall°   *is excited by / lower*
His crest that prouder than blue Iris[9] bends.
If the dull brainless Ajax come safe off,
We'll dress him up in voices;° if he fail,   *sing his praises*
Yet go we under our opinion still

380   That we have better men. But hit or miss,
Our project's life° this shape of sense° assumes: *success / rationale*
Ajax employed plucks down Achilles' plumes.

NESTOR   Now, Ulysses, I begin to relish thy advice,
And I will give a taste of it forthwith

385   To Agamemnon. Go we to him straight.°   *immediately*
Two curs shall tame each other; pride alone
Must tar the mastiffs on,[1] as 'twere° their bone.   *Exeunt.*   *if it were*

2.1 (Q 2.1)
Enter AJAX *and* THERSITES.

AJAX   Thersites!

THERSITES   Agamemnon. How° if he had boils, full,° all over,   *What / (of pus)*
generally?

AJAX   Thersites!

5   THERSITES   And those boils did run—say so—did not the general run?[1] Were not that a botchy core?°   *an ulcerous center*

---

6. *What . . . themselves:* What motivation will the Trojans get from this to make them feel more confident (with a play on "steel" = "steal")!

7. *Which . . . limbs:* Assuming that this confidence ("strong opinion") is received from the victory, the soldiers' limbs become the mechanisms ("instruments") of that confidence in the same way that swords and bows are subject to direction by the limbs themselves.

8. Will give medicine to (purge) Achilles, who led the Myrmidons.

9. Goddess of the rainbow; blue flower.

1. Must incite these large, aggressive dogs.

2.1 Location: The Greek camp.

1. *And . . . run:* And if those boils ran—let's say—wouldn't the general (Agamemnon, the whole army) have running sores (flee from battle)?

AJAX Dog!

THERSITES Then there would come some matter° from him. I   *pus; sense*
    see none now.

10 AJAX Thou bitch-wolf's son, canst thou not hear? Feel, then.
    [*He*] *strikes* [THERSITES].

THERSITES The plague of Greece upon thee, thou mongrel²
    beef-witted° lord!   *dumb as an ox*

AJAX Speak, then, you finewed'st leaven,³ speak. I will beat⁴
    thee into handsomeness.°   *decency; good looks*

15 THERSITES I shall sooner rail thee into wit and holiness; but I
    think thy horse will sooner con° an oration than thou learn   *memorize*
    a prayer without book.° Thou canst strike, canst thou? A red   *by heart*
    murrain o'thy jade's⁵ tricks!

AJAX Toadstool,⁶ learn me° the proclamation!   *instruct me (about)*

20 THERSITES Dost thou think I have no sense,° thou strik'st me   *feeling*
    thus?

AJAX The proclamation!

THERSITES Thou art proclaimed a fool, I think.

AJAX Do not, porcupine,⁷ do not; my fingers itch°—   *(to hit you)*

25 THERSITES I would thou didst itch from head to foot and I
    had the scratching of thee. I would make thee the loathsom'st
    scab in Greece.

AJAX I say, the proclamation.

THERSITES Thou grumblest and railest every hour on Achil-
30   les, and thou art as full of envy at his greatness as Cerberus
    is at Proserpina's⁸ beauty, ay, that° thou bark'st at him.   *so much so that*

AJAX Mistress⁹ Thersites!

THERSITES Thou shouldst strike him.°   *(Achilles)*

AJAX Cobloaf!°   *Small crusty loaf*

35 THERSITES He would pun° thee into shivers° with his fist, as   *pound / pieces*
    a sailor breaks a biscuit.

AJAX [*striking him*] You whoreson cur!

THERSITES Do, do.°   *Go on*

AJAX Thou stool° for a witch!   *privy*

40 THERSITES Ay, do, do, thou sodden-witted° lord. Thou hast no   *boiled-brained*
    more brain than I have in mine elbows—an asinego° may   *little ass*
    tutor thee. Thou scurvy-valiant ass! Thou art here but to
    thresh° Trojans, and thou art bought and sold¹ among those of   *harvest*
    any wit like a barbarian slave. If thou use° to beat me, I will   *continue*
45   begin at thy heel and tell what thou art by inches, thou thing
    of no bowels,° thou.   *with no pity*

AJAX You dog!

THERSITES You scurvy lord!

AJAX [*striking him*] You cur!

50 THERSITES Mars his idiot!° Do, rudeness; do, camel, do, do!   *God of war's jester*
    Enter ACHILLES *and* PATROCLUS.

---

2. Ajax's mother was Trojan; hence, he was of mixed breed, "mongrel."
3. *leaven:* fermenting agent, causing dough to rise. *finewed'st:* moldiest. Hence, Ajax accuses Thersites of being a pollutant.
4. Punning on the pounding of bread dough.
5. A bloody plague on your bad-tempered worn-out horse's (woman's).
6. Toadstools were once thought to be a toad's poisonous excrement (stool).

7. The porcupine's sharp quills were emblematic of the satirist (here, Thersites).
8. Cerberus was the monstrous three-headed dog who guarded the gate of Hades. Proserpina was Queen of Hades and wife of Pluto, god of the underworld.
9. Because a woman's only weapon was thought to be her tongue, because Thersites is a coward, or because he is believed to be homosexual.
1. You are traded like goods—hence, treated as an object, treated contemptuously.

ACHILLES Why, how now, Ajax? Wherefore do you this?
—How now, Thersites? What's the matter, man?

THERSITES You see him there, do you?

ACHILLES Ay, what's the matter?

55 THERSITES Nay, look upon him.

ACHILLES So I do. What's the matter?

THERSITES Nay, but regard him well.

ACHILLES Well, why I do so.

THERSITES But yet you look not well upon him,[2] for whosom-
60 ever you take him to be, he is Ajax.° *a jakes = toilet*

ACHILLES I know that, fool.

THERSITES Ay, but that fool knows not himself.[3]

AJAX Therefore I beat thee.[4]

THERSITES Lo,° lo, lo, lo, what modicums of wit he utters. *Behold (sarcastic)*
65 His evasions have ears thus long.[5] I have bobbed° his brain *thumped*
more than he has beat my bones; I will° buy nine sparrows *can*
for a penny, and his *pia mater*° is not worth the ninth part of *brain*
a sparrow. This lord, Achilles—Ajax, who wears his wit in
his belly and his guts in his head—I'll tell you what I say of
70 him.

ACHILLES What?

THERSITES I say, this Ajax—

ACHILLES [*holding* AJAX *back*] Nay, good Ajax.

THERSITES Has not so much wit—

75 ACHILLES Nay, I must hold° you. *restrain*

THERSITES As will stop the eye of Helen's needle,[6] for whom
he comes to fight.

ACHILLES Peace, fool.

THERSITES I would have peace and quietness, but the fool° *(Ajax)*
80 will not: he there, that he,° look you there. *(I mean Ajax)*

AJAX O thou damned cur, I shall—

ACHILLES Will you set your wit to° a fool's? *against*

THERSITES No, I warrant you, for a fool's will shame it.

PATROCLUS Good words,° Thersites. *Speak with restraint*

85 ACHILLES What's the quarrel?

AJAX I bade the vile owl[7] go learn me the tenor of the proclamation, and he rails upon me.

THERSITES I serve thee not.

AJAX Well, go to, go to.

90 THERSITES I serve here voluntary.° *as a volunteer*

ACHILLES Your last service was sufferance, 'twas not voluntary. No man is beaten voluntary. Ajax was here the voluntary, and you as under an impress.[8]

THERSITES E'en so; a great deal of your wit too lies in your
95 sinews, or else there be liars. Hector shall have a great catch
if he knock out either of your brains; he were as good° crack *might as well*
a fusty° nut with no kernel. *rotten*

---

2. Thersites is probably feigning amazement that
Achilles can look at Ajax and yet not see what a fool
he is; but he may also mean that Achilles does not do
well to favor ("look . . . upon") him.
3. Thersites deliberately understands Achilles' line
without the intended comma: "I know that fool"
(Ajax), rather than "I know that [fact], fool."
4. Ajax thinks Thersites is calling himself (rather

than Ajax) a "fool" who does not know himself.
5. His efforts to dodge witty rejoinders are like an
ass's—hence, asinine.
6. "Eye" perhaps alludes to "vagina"; "needle" is also
obscene. *stop:* fill.
7. The owl is associated with evil portent.
8. As a conscript; being hit as though with a stamp
(by Ajax).

ACHILLES   What, with me too, Thersites?

THERSITES   There's Ulysses and old Nestor, whose wit was
100   moldy ere your grandsires had nails on their toes, yoke you
like draft-oxen and make you plow up the war.°   *(pun on ware = crops)*

ACHILLES   What, what?

THERSITES   Yes, good sooth: To,° Achilles! To, Ajax! To—   *(urging on the oxen)*

AJAX   I shall cut out your tongue.

105   THERSITES   'Tis no matter; I shall speak as much as thou
afterwards.

PATROCLUS   No more words, Thersites.

THERSITES   I will hold my peace when Achilles' brach° bids   *bitch*
me, shall I?

110   ACHILLES   There's for you, Patroclus.

THERSITES   I will see you hanged like clodpolls° ere I come   *blockheads*
any more to your tents; I will keep where there is wit stirring
and leave the faction of fools.   *Exit.*

PATROCLUS   A good riddance.

115   ACHILLES *[to* AJAX*]*   Marry, this, sir, is proclaimed through all
our host:

That Hector by the fifth hour° of the sun   *11 A.M.*
Will with a trumpet twixt our tents and Troy
Tomorrow morning call some knight to arms
That hath a stomach,° and such a one that dare   *an appetite for combat*
120   Maintain—I know not what. 'Tis trash. Farewell.

AJAX   Farewell. Who shall answer him?

ACHILLES   I know not; 'tis put to lott'ry. Otherwise,
He knew his man.   *[Exeunt* ACHILLES *and* PATROCLUS.*]*

AJAX   Oh, meaning you? I will go learn more of it.   *Exit.*

2.2 (Q 2.2)

Enter PRIAM, HECTOR, TROILUS, PARIS, *and* HELENUS.

PRIAM   After so many hours, lives, speeches spent,
Thus once again says Nestor from the Greeks:
"Deliver Helen, and all damage else—
As° honor, loss of time, travail,° expense,   *Such as / hard labor*
5   Wounds, friends, and what else dear° that is consumed   *beloved; costly*
In hot digestion of this cormorant° war—   *rapacious*
Shall be struck off."° Hector, what say you to't?   *expunged*

HECTOR   Though no man lesser fears the Greeks than I
As far as touches my particular,°   *own concerns*
10   Yet, dread Priam,
There is no lady of more softer bowels,°   *compassion*
More spongy to suck in° the sense of fear,   *able to absorb*
More ready to cry out, "Who knows what follows?"
Than Hector is. The wound° of peace is surety°—   *danger / false confidence*
15   Surety secure—but modest doubt° is called   *precaution*
The beacon of the wise, the tent° that searches   *surgical probe*
To th' bottom of the worst. Let Helen go.
Since the first sword was drawn about this question
Every tithe soul 'mongst many thousand dismes
20   Hath been as dear as Helen[1]—I mean of ours.

2.2 Location: The palace in Troy.
1. *Every . . . Helen:* Every soul taken to pay the tithe
(a tenth of one's goods, paid as a tax), among many

thousand "dismes" (tenths; tithes paid, through soldiers' deaths), has been as valuable as Helen.

If we have lost so many tenths of ours
To guard a thing not ours, nor worth to us,
Had it our name, the value of one ten,[2]
What merit's in that reason which denies
The yielding of her up?
25 TROILUS   Fie, fie, my brother!
Weigh you the worth and honor of a king
So great as our dread father in a scale
Of common ounces? Will you with counters° sum   *worthless chips*
The past-proportion of his infinite[3]
30 And buckle in a waist most fathomless[4]
With spans° and inches so diminutive   *nine inches*
As fears and reasons?° Fie, for godly shame!   *(pun on "raisins")*
HELENUS   No marvel though you bite so sharp at reasons,
You are so empty of them. Should not our father
35 Bear the great sway of his affairs with reasons
Because your speech hath none that tell him so?
TROILUS   You are for dreams and slumbers, brother priest.
You fur your gloves with reason;[5] here are your reasons:
You know an enemy intends you harm,
40 You know a sword employed is perilous,
And reason flies the object of all harm.°   *any sight of danger*
Who marvels then, when Helenus beholds
A Grecian and his sword, if he do set
The very wings of reason to his heels
45 And fly like chidden Mercury[6] from Jove,
Or like a star disorbed?° Nay, if we talk of reason   *a shooting star*
Let's shut our gates and sleep. Manhood and honor
Should have hare° hearts would they but fat their thoughts   *timid*
With this crammed° reason. Reason and respect°   *fattened / deliberation*
50 Makes livers° pale and lustihood° deject.   *courage / energy*
HECTOR   Brother, she is not worth what she doth cost
The holding.°   *To keep*
TROILUS   What's aught but as 'tis valued?[7]
HECTOR   But value dwells not in particular will;°   *individual desire*
It holds his° estimate and dignity   *its*
55 As well wherein 'tis precious of itself
As in the prizer. 'Tis mad idolatry
To make the service° greater than the god,   *the devotion paid*
And the will dotes that is inclineable
To what infectiously itself affects
60 Without some image of th'affected merit.[8]
TROILUS   I take today a wife, and my election°   *choice*
Is led on in the conduct° of my will,   *under the guidance*
My will enkindled by mine eyes and ears,

2. Even if Helen were Trojan, the value of one-tenth (one of the men lost).
3. Add up the infinitude of his measurelessness.
4. Most immeasurable even in fathoms (6-foot lengths, used in calculating sea depths). "Waist" puns on "waste" as uninhabited expanse, especially the ocean, and as the squandering of resources (the second unintended by Troilus).
5. You rationalize your desire for comfort.
6. Messenger of the gods, usually pictured with wings on his heels. Mercury was once arraigned before Jove for stealing cattle and was ordered to go and return them.
7. No absolute measure of value exists; value refers only to the esteem that people grant to an object.
8. *the will . . . merit*: the will is foolishly dependent that accords value to what it likes in a sick way (having caught this desire like a disease), without some conception of that object's real value. The point is related to Jesus' attack on the scribes and Pharisees in Matthew 23—for instance, verse 19: "whether is greater, the offering, or the altar which sanctifieth the offering?"

Two traded° pilots twixt the dangerous shores   *experienced*
65   Of will and judgment. How may I avoid,
Although my will distaste what it elected,
The wife I chose? There can be no evasion
To blench° from this and to stand firm by honor.   *shy away*
We turn not back° the silks upon° the merchant   *don't return / to*
70   When we have spoiled them, nor the remainder viands°   *uneaten food*
We do not throw in unrespective° sieve   *undiscriminating*
Because we now are full. It was thought meet°   *appropriate that*
Paris should do some vengeance on the Greeks.
Your breath of full consent bellied° his sails;   *swelled*
75   The seas and winds, old wranglers,° took a truce   *opponents*
And did him service. He touched the ports desired,
And for an old aunt whom the Greeks held captive[9]
He brought a Grecian queen,° whose youth and freshness   *(pun on quean = whore?)*
Wrinkles Apollo's and makes stale the morning.[1]
80   Why keep we her? The Grecians keep our aunt.
Is she worth keeping? Why, she is a pearl
Whose price hath launched above a thousand ships[2]
And turned crowned kings to merchants.
If you'll avouch 'twas wisdom Paris went—
85   As you must needs, for you all cried "Go, go!"—
If you'll confess he brought home noble prize—
As you must needs, for you all clapped your hands
And cried "Inestimable!"—why do you now
The issue° of your proper° wisdoms rate°   *result / own / berate*
90   And do a deed that Fortune never did:[3]
Beggar the estimation[4] which you prized
Richer than sea and land? Oh, theft most base
That° we have stol'n what we do fear to keep!   *In that*
But thieves unworthy of a thing so stol'n
95   That in their country did them that disgrace
We fear to warrant in our native place.[5]
CASSANDRA [*within*]   Cry, Trojans, cry![6]
PRIAM   What noise? What shriek is this?
TROILUS   'Tis our mad sister; I do know her voice.
CASSANDRA [*within*]   Cry, Trojans!
100 HECTOR   It is Cassandra.
          Enter CASSANDRA[7] *with her hair about her ears.*
CASSANDRA   Cry, Trojans, cry! Lend me ten thousand eyes
And I will fill them with prophetic tears.
HECTOR   Peace, sister, peace.
CASSANDRA   Virgins and boys, mid-age and wrinkled old,°   *old people*
105 Soft infancy that nothing can° but cry,   *can do*
Add to my clamor. Let us pay betimes°   *in advance*

9. Hesione, Priam's sister, kidnapped by the Greeks;
"aunt" is also slang for "whore." The "vengeance"
(line 73) is for the kidnapping.
1. Helen's "youth and freshness" by comparison make
Apollo's (hence, also the sun's) "youth and freshness"
seem old, and rosy dawn seem dried out (but also,
unintentionally on Troilus's part, sluttish).
2. A well-worn phrase even when Marlowe used it in
Doctor Faustus: "Was this the face that launched a
thousand ships?" Here, given a mercantile turn.
3. And act more erratically than Fortune.

4. (Why do you) deem worthless the valued object?
5. *That . . . place:* (We Trojans) who in Greece dishonored the Greeks but back home are afraid to
stand up for what we did.
6. TEXTUAL COMMENT On the timing of Cassandra's
entrance and her appearance when she enters, see
Digital Edition TC 3 (Folio edited text).
7. Apollo gave Cassandra the gift of prophecy to win
her love, but because she rejected his wooing, he cursed
her by causing her prophecies to be disregarded.

A moiety° of that mass° of moan to come. *portion / sum*
Cry, Trojans, cry! Practice your eyes with tears.° *Learn to weep*
Troy must not be, nor goodly Ilium stand;
110 Our firebrand[8] brother, Paris, burns us all.
Cry, Trojans, cry—a Helen and a woe!
Cry, cry! Troy burns, or else let Helen go. *Exit.*
HECTOR   Now, youthful Troilus, do not these high strains
Of divination in our sister work
115 Some touches of remorse? Or is your blood
So madly hot that no discourse of reason
Nor fear of bad success° in a bad cause *outcome*
Can qualify° the same? *moderate*
TROILUS Why brother Hector,
We may not think the justness of each act
120 Such and no other than event doth form it,[9]
Nor once deject° the courage of our minds *reduce*
Because Cassandra's mad. Her brainsick raptures
Cannot distaste° the goodness of a quarrel *make distasteful*
Which hath our several honors all engaged
125 To make it gracious.° For my private part, *righteous; successful*
I am no more touched° than all Priam's sons, *implicated*
And Jove forbid there should be done amongst us
Such things as might offend the weakest spleen
To fight for and maintain.[1]
130 PARIS   Else might the world convince° of levity *convict*
As well my undertakings as your counsels.
But I attest° the gods: your full consent *call to witness*
Gave wings to my propension° and cut off *leaning*
All fears attending on so dire a project—
135 For what, alas, can these my single arms?° *can my arms do alone*
What propugnation° is in one man's valor *defense*
To stand the push° and enmity of those *thrust*
This quarrel would excite?° Yet I protest, *incite to battle*
Were I alone to pass° the difficulties *endure*
140 And had as ample power as I have will,
Paris should ne'er retract what he hath done,
Nor faint in the pursuit.
PRIAM Paris, you speak
Like one besotted° on your sweet delights: *drunk*
You have the honey still, but these the gall,
145 So° to be valiant is no praise at all. *In such circumstances*
PARIS   Sir, I propose not merely to myself° *for my own benefit*
The pleasures such a beauty brings with it,
But I would have the soil of her fair rape[2]
Wiped off in honorable keeping her.
150 What treason were it to the ransacked° queen, *carried off as plunder*
Disgrace to your great worths, and shame to me
Now to deliver her possession up
On terms of base compulsion! Can it be

---

8. When pregnant with Paris, Hecuba dreamed of giving birth to a firebrand.
9. *We . . . it:* We must not judge the "justness" of our cause only by the results.
1. *And Jove . . . maintain:* We ("Priam's sons") shouldn't undertake something unless even the least courageous of us is willing to fight to defend it.
2. The defilement (of Helen or Paris, or both) resulting from her proper (also, beautiful) abduction (also, sexual violation).

	That so degenerate a strain° as this	*an impulse*
155	Should once set footing in your generous° bosoms?	*noble*
	There's not the meanest spirit on our party	
	Without a heart to dare or sword to draw	
	When Helen is defended, nor none so noble	
	Whose life were ill bestowed or death unfamed	
160	Where Helen is the subject. Then, I say,	
	Well may we fight for her whom we know well	
	The world's large spaces cannot parallel.	

HECTOR Paris and Troilus, you have both said well,
And on the cause and question now in hand
165 Have glozed,° but superficially—not much   *commented*
Unlike young men whom Aristotle thought
Unfit to hear moral philosophy.[3]
The reasons you allege do more conduce
To the hot passion of distempered blood
170 Than to make up a free determination
Twixt right and wrong, for pleasure and revenge
Have ears more deaf than adders[4] to the voice
Of any true decision. Nature craves
All dues be rendered to their owners: now
175 What nearer debt in all humanity
Than wife is to the husband? If this law
Of nature be corrupted through affection,°   *lust*
And that great minds, of partial° indulgence   *through prejudiced*
To their benumbèd° wills, resist the same,°   *dulled / (law of nature)*
180 There is a law in each well-ordered nation
To curb those raging appetites that are
Most disobedient and refractory.°   *stubborn*
If Helen then be wife to Sparta's king,
As it is known she is, these moral laws
185 Of nature and of nation speak aloud
To have her back returned. Thus to persist
In doing wrong extenuates not wrong,
But makes it much more heavy. Hector's opinion
Is this in way of° truth. Yet ne'ertheless,   *with respect to*
190 My sprightly° brethren, I propend° to you   *spirited / incline*
In resolution to keep Helen still,
For 'tis a cause that hath no mean dependence
Upon our joint and several° dignities.   *separate*

TROILUS Why, there you touch the life of our design!
195 Were it not glory that we more affected°   *desired*
Than the performance of our heaving spleens,°   *acting on our anger*
I would not wish a drop of Trojan blood
Spent more in her defense. But, worthy Hector,
She is a theme of honor and renown,
200 A spur to valiant and magnanimous° deeds,   *noble*
Whose present courage may beat down our foes
And fame in time to come canonize° us;   *future fame glorify*
For I presume brave Hector would not lose

---

3. Political philosophy. This is an anachronistic reference to Aristotle's *Nicomachean Ethics* 1.3.
4. Adders were proverbially deaf. See Psalms 58:4–5:
"like the deaf adder that stoppeth his ear. Which heareth not the voice of the enchanter, though he be most expert in charming."

So rich advantage of a promised glory
205 As smiles upon the forehead° of this action   countenance
For° the wide world's revenue.   in return for
HECTOR   I am yours,
You valiant offspring of great Priamus.
I have a roisting° challenge sent amongst   boisterous
The dull and factious nobles of the Greeks
210 Will° strike amazement to their drowsy spirits.   That will
I was advertised their great general slept[5]
Whilst emulation° in the army crept;   jealous rivalry
This, I presume, will wake him.   *Exeunt.*

2.3 (Q 2.3)

Enter THERSITES *alone.*

THERSITES   How now, Thersites? What, lost in the labyrinth
of thy fury? Shall the elephant Ajax carry it° thus? He beats   get away with it
me, and I rail at him. Oh, worthy satisfaction. Would it were
otherwise: that I could beat him whilst he railed at me.
5 'Sfoot,° I'll learn to conjure and raise devils, but I'll see   God's foot
some issue of my spiteful execrations.[1] Then there's Achilles, a rare engineer.[2] If Troy be not taken till these two
undermine it, the walls will stand till they fall of themselves. O thou great thunder-darter of Olympus, forget that
10 thou art Jove, the king of gods; and Mercury, lose all the
serpentine craft of thy caduceus,[3] if thou take not that little,
little—less than little—wit from them that they have, which
short-armed ignorance[4] itself knows is so abundant° scarce   manifestly
it will not in circumvention deliver a fly from a spider with-
15 out drawing the massy irons and cutting the web.[5] After
this, the vengeance on the whole camp, or rather the bone-
ache,° for that, methinks, is the curse dependent° on those   syphilis / impending
that war for a placket.[6] I have said my prayers, and devil
Envy say "Amen." —What ho! My lord Achilles!

Enter PATROCLUS *[at the opening of the tent].*

20 PATROCLUS   Who's there? Thersites. Good Thersites, come in
and rail.   [PATROCLUS *withdraws.*]
THERSITES   If I could have remembered a gilt counterfeit thou
wouldst not have slipped out of my contemplation[7]—but it is
no matter. Thyself upon thyself;[8] the common curse of man-
25 kind, folly and ignorance, be thine in great revenue.° Heaven   amounts
bless° thee from a tutor, and discipline come not near thee.   save
Let thy blood° be thy direction° till thy death; then, if she   lust / guide
that lays thee out says thou art a fair corpse, I'll be sworn
and sworn upon't, she never shrouded any but lazars.° Amen.   lepers; sick bodies

[*Enter* PATROCLUS.]

---

5. I was told that Achilles (Agamemnon?) slept.
2.3 Location: The Greek camp, outside Achilles' tent.
1. *but I'll . . . execrations:* in order to get tangible results from my contemptuous (or, unintended, "malicious") curses.
2. Constructor of military earthworks and machines.
3. Mercury's emblem, a rod entwined by snakes. Known for "craft," Mercury was the patron of thieves.
4. "Short-armed" because most things are beyond its grasp.

5. *it will not . . . web:* it will use excessive, brute force. *Circumvention:* craftiness. *irons:* swords.
6. Petticoat; woman; woman's genitalia (obscene).
7. If I could have remembered a fake gold coin (worthless Patroclus), you wouldn't have been forgotten (punning on "slip," a counterfeit coin) in my devout meditation (which focused on Ajax and Achilles, but only to curse them).
8. To be Patroclus is the worst possible fate—hence, Thersites' curse on him is to be himself.

30   —Where's Achilles?

PATROCLUS   What, art thou devout? Wast thou in a prayer?

THERSITES   Ay, the heavens hear me.

     Enter ACHILLES.

ACHILLES   Who's there?

PATROCLUS   Thersites, my lord.

35 ACHILLES   Where? Where? —Art thou come? Why, my cheese,°   *digestive aid*
my digestion, why hast thou not served thyself in to my table
so many meals? Come, what's Agamemnon?

THERSITES   Thy commander, Achilles. Then tell me, Patroclus, what's Achilles?

40 PATROCLUS   Thy lord, Thersites. Then tell me, I pray thee,
what's thyself?

THERSITES   Thy knower, Patroclus. Then tell me, Patroclus,
what art thou?

PATROCLUS   Thou mayst tell that know'st.

45 ACHILLES   Oh, tell, tell.

THERSITES   I'll decline the whole question:[9] Agamemnon commands Achilles, Achilles is my lord, I am Patroclus' knower,
and Patroclus is a fool.

PATROCLUS   You rascal!

50 THERSITES   Peace, fool, I have not done.

ACHILLES   He is a privileged man.[1] Proceed, Thersites.

THERSITES   Agamemnon is a fool, Achilles is a fool, Thersites
is a fool, and, as aforesaid, Patroclus is a fool.

ACHILLES   Derive this,° come.   *Show your reasoning*

55 THERSITES   Agamemnon is a fool to offer to command Achilles, Achilles is a fool to be commanded of Agamemnon,
Thersites is a fool to serve such a fool, and Patroclus is a fool
positive.°   *absolute*

PATROCLUS   Why am I a fool?

60 THERSITES   Make that demand to the Creator; it suffices me
thou art. Look you, who comes here?

     Enter [at a distance] AGAMEMNON, ULYSSES, NESTOR,
       DIOMEDES, AJAX, *and* CALCHAS.

ACHILLES   Patroclus, I'll speak with nobody. Come in with
me, Thersites.   *Exit.*

THERSITES   Here is such patchery,° such juggling,° and such   *foolery / deception*
65 knavery. All the argument is a cuckold and a whore—a good
quarrel to draw[2] emulous° factions and bleed to death upon.   *envious*
Now the dry serpigo° on the subject, and war and lechery   *skin disease*
confound all!   *[Exit.]*

AGAMEMNON   Where is Achilles?

70 PATROCLUS   Within his tent, but ill-disposed,° my lord.   *unwell; bad-tempered*

AGAMEMNON   Let it be known to him that we are here.
He shent° our messengers, and we lay by   *shamed*
Our appertainments,° visiting of him.   *rights of rank*
Let him be told so, lest perchance he think
75 We dare not move the question of our place°   *assert our authority*
Or know not what we are.

---

9. I'll recite in order the entire subject under investigation. "The words decline," "Derive" (line 54), and
"positive" (line 58) are all grammatical terms.

1. An acknowledged fool could speak with impunity.
2. Attract to itself, like a magnet; extract, like a
sword; tear to pieces; drag to execution.

PATROCLUS   I shall so say to him.   [*Exit.*]

ULYSSES   We saw him at the opening of his tent;
He is not sick.

AJAX   Yes, lion-sick,° sick of proud heart. You may call it mel-   *sick with pride*
80   ancholy[3] if you will favor the man, but, by my head, it is
pride. But why? Why? Let him show us the cause. —A word,
my lord.

          [AJAX *takes* AGAMEMNON *aside.*]

NESTOR   What moves Ajax thus to bay at him?

ULYSSES   Achilles hath inveigled° his fool from him.   *enticed away*

85   NESTOR   Who, Thersites?

ULYSSES   He.

NESTOR   Then will Ajax lack matter,[4] if he have lost his
argument.°   *subject matter*

ULYSSES   No, you see he is his argument that has his argu-
90   ment:[5] Achilles.

NESTOR   All the better; their fraction° is more our wish than   *division*
their faction.° But it was a strong counsel that a fool could   *joint rebellion*
disunite.°   *(ironic)*

ULYSSES   The amity that wisdom knits not° folly may easily   *is not created by*
95   untie.   *wisdom*

          Enter PATROCLUS.

Here comes Patroclus.

NESTOR   No Achilles with him.

ULYSSES   The elephant hath joints, but none for courtesy.[6]
His legs are legs for necessity, not for flexure.°   *bending*

100   PATROCLUS   Achilles bids me say he is much sorry
If anything more than your sport and pleasure
Did move your greatness and this noble state°   *company*
To call upon him. He hopes it is no other
But for your health and your digestion sake—
An after-dinner's breath.°   *exercise*

105   AGAMEMNON   Hear you, Patroclus:
We are too well acquainted with these answers,
But his evasion, winged thus swift with scorn,
Cannot out-fly° our apprehensions.°   *escape / understanding*
Much attribute° he hath, and much the reason   *reputation*
110   Why we ascribe it to him. Yet all his virtues,
Not virtuously of his own part beheld,°   *performed by him*
Do in our eyes begin to lose their gloss—
Yea, and like fair fruit in an unwholesome dish
Are like to rot untasted. Go and tell him
115   We came to speak with him, and you shall not sin
If you do say we think him over-proud
And under-honest, in self-assumption° greater   *his own opinion*
Than in the note of judgment. And worthier° than himself   *one(s) worthier*
Here tends° the savage strangeness° he puts on,   *waits on / aloofness*
120   Disguise the holy strength of their command,

---

3. A fashionable philosophical malady.
4. Something to say; sense; pus.
5. Achilles is the person who is Ajax's argument.
Since Achilles has taken Thersites (who used to be
Ajax's object of derision) as the object of his derision,

Ajax has transferred his scorn from Thersites to
Achilles.
6. The elephant's supposed lack of knee joints made
it resemble a proud, unbowing man.

	And underwrite in an observing kind°	submit compliantly to
	His humorous predominance[7]—yea, watch	
	His pettish lines,° his ebbs, his flows, as if	sulky behavior
	The passage and whole carriage° of this action	means and ends
125	Rode on his tide. Go tell him this, and add	
	That if he overhold° his price so much	overestimate
	We'll none of him, but let him, like an engine	
	Not portable, lie under this report:	
	"Bring action hither; this cannot go to war.	
130	A stirring° dwarf we do allowance give	bustling
	Before a sleeping giant." Tell him so.	

PATROCLUS   I shall, and bring his answer presently.°   [*Exit.*]   *immediately*

AGAMEMNON   In second voice° we'll not be satisfied.   *By proxy (Patroclus)*

We come to speak with him. —Ulysses, enter you.

Exit ULYSSES.

135 AJAX   What is he more than another?

AGAMEMNON   No more than what he thinks he is.[8]

AJAX   Is he so much? Do you not think he thinks himself a
better man than I am?

AGAMEMNON   No question.

140 AJAX   Will you subscribe his thought and say he is?

AGAMEMNON   No, noble Ajax. You are as strong, as valiant, as
wise, no less noble, much more gentle, and altogether more
tractable.

AJAX   Why should a man be proud? How doth pride grow? I
145 know not what it is.

AGAMEMNON   Your mind is the clearer, Ajax, and your virtues
the fairer. He that is proud eats up himself; pride is his own
glass,° his own trumpet, his own chronicle, and whatever   *its own mirror*
praises itself but in the deed devours the deed in the praise.[9]

Enter ULYSSES.

150 AJAX   I do hate a proud man as I hate the engendering° of   *mating*
toads.

NESTOR [*aside*]   Yet he loves himself; is't not strange?

ULYSSES   Achilles will not to the field tomorrow.

AGAMEMNON   What's his excuse?

ULYSSES   He doth rely on none,
155 But carries on the stream of his dispose°   *disposition*
Without observance or respect of any,
In will peculiar and in self-admission.[1]

AGAMEMNON   Why will he not upon our fair request
Untent his person and share the air with us?

160 ULYSSES   Things small as nothing, for request's sake only,[2]
He makes important. Possessed° he is with greatness,   *Bewitched*
And speaks not to himself but with a pride
That quarrels at self-breath.[3] Imagined worth
Holds in his blood such swoll'n and hot discourse

---

7. His idiosyncratic assumption of superiority; the
domination of one particular "humor" (temperament)—
pride.
8. He's the only one with a high opinion of him; he's
worth as much as he thinks he is.
9. Whatever self-praise arises except from silently
performing the noble deed itself destroys the deed by

the act of praising it.
1. In self-will and in acknowledgment of only his
own authority.
2. Merely because they are asked for.
3. *And . . . self-breath:* Achilles is not even satisfied
with what he himself has to say in praise of his merits; he is too proud to talk even to himself.

165 That twixt his mental and his active parts
Kingdomed Achilles[4] in commotion° rages · *insurrection*
And batters 'gainst himself. What should I say?
He is so plaguy proud that the death-tokens of it[5]
Cry, "No recovery!"

AGAMEMNON · · · · · · · · · Let Ajax go to him.

170 —Dear lord, go you and greet him in his tent;
'Tis said he holds you well and will be led
At your request a little from himself.° · *from his self-conceit*

ULYSSES · · O Agamemnon, let it not be so.
We'll consecrate the steps that Ajax makes

175 When they go from Achilles. Shall the proud lord
That bastes his arrogance with his own seam[6]
And never suffers matter° of the world · *the affairs*
Enter his thoughts, save° such as do revolve · *except*
And ruminate° himself? Shall he be worshipped · *turn on*

180 Of that° we hold an idol more than he? · *By one who*
No, this thrice-worthy and right valiant lord
Must not so stale his palm° nobly acquired, · *sully his honor*
Nor by my will assubjugate° his merit, · *reduce to subjection*
As amply titled as Achilles' is,

185 By going to Achilles.
That were to enlard his fat-already pride
And add more coals to Cancer[7] when he burns
With entertaining great Hyperion.° · *the sun*
This lord go to him? Jupiter forbid,

190 And say in thunder: "Achilles, go to him!"

NESTOR [*aside*] · · Oh, this is well; he rubs the vein of him.° · · · · · · · · · · *stirs up Ajax*

DIOMEDES [*aside*] · · And how his silence drinks up this
     applause.

AJAX · If I go to him, with my armèd fist
I'll pash° him o'er the face. · *smash*

AGAMEMNON · · · · · · · · · Oh, no, you shall not go.

195 AJAX · An 'a° be proud with me, I'll feeze° his pride. · · · · · · · · · · *If he / take care of*
Let me go to him.

ULYSSES · Not for the worth that hangs upon our quarrel.° · · · · · · · · · · · · · *(with Troy)*

AJAX · A paltry, insolent fellow.

NESTOR [*aside*] · How he describes himself.

200 AJAX · Can he not be sociable?

ULYSSES [*aside*] · The raven chides blackness.

AJAX · I'll let his humors blood.[8]

AGAMEMNON [*aside*] · He will be the physician that should be
     the patient.

205 AJAX · An all men were o'my mind—

ULYSSES [*aside*] · Wit would be out of fashion.

AJAX · 'A should not bear it so; 'a should eat swords[9] first. Shall
pride carry it?

NESTOR [*aside*] · An 'twould, you'd carry half.

---

4. Achilles' body is imagined as a state at civil war.
5. He is so annoyingly (diseasedly) proud that the fatal signs of plague.
6. Fat; appearance (punning on "seam" as "seem"). Achilles is accused of feeding self-flattery to his already inflated arrogance.
7. And add fuel to the fire. Cancer is the sign of the

zodiac that begins on June 21—hence, a symbol of summer heat.
8. I'll cure his illness (pride) by bloodletting, as a doctor would do to get rid of surplus humors.
9. He wouldn't carry on so; he would be defeated in combat (eat his words).

210	ULYSSES [*aside*] 'A would have ten shares.[1]	
	AJAX I will knead him, I'll make him supple;° he's not yet	*compliant*
	through warm.°	*warm all through*
	NESTOR [*aside*] Farce° him with praises—pour in, pour in;	*Stuff; sauce*
	his ambition is dry.°	*thirsty*
215	ULYSSES [*to* AGAMEMNON] My lord, you feed too much on	
	this dislike.	
	NESTOR Our noble general, do not do so.	
	DIOMEDES You must prepare to fight without Achilles.	
	ULYSSES Why, 'tis this naming of him° doth him harm.	*(as our sole hope)*
	Here is a man°—but 'tis before his face;°	*(Ajax) / he's present*
	I will be silent.	
220	NESTOR Wherefore should you so?	
	He is not emulous,° as Achilles is.	*hungry for praise*
	ULYSSES Know the whole world,° he is as valiant.	*May the whole world know*
	AJAX A whoreson dog that shall palter° thus with us.	*deal evasively*
	Would he were a Trojan!	
225	NESTOR What a vice were it in Ajax now—	
	ULYSSES If he were proud.	
	DIOMEDES Or covetous of praise.	
	ULYSSES Ay, or surly borne.	
	DIOMEDES Or strange,° or self-affected.°	*aloof / egotistical*
	ULYSSES [*to* AJAX] Thank the heavens, lord, thou art of sweet	
	composure.°	*temperament*
	Praise him that got thee, she that gave thee suck;	
230	Famed be thy tutor, and thy parts of nature°	*natural attributes*
	Thrice-famed beyond, beyond all erudition;[2]	
	But he that disciplined thy arms to fight,	
	Let Mars divide eternity in twain	
	And give him half; and for thy vigor,	
235	Bull-bearing Milo[3] his addition° yield	*reputation*
	To sinewy Ajax. I will not praise thy wisdom,°	*(ironic)*
	Which, like a bourn, a pale, a shore, confines[4]	
	Thy spacious and dilated° parts. Here's Nestor,	*ample; famous*
	Instructed by the antiquary° times;	*ancient*
240	He must, he is, he cannot but be wise.	
	But pardon, father Nestor, were your days	
	As green[5] as Ajax' and your brain so tempered,°	*composed*
	You should not have the eminence of° him,	*be superior to*
	But be as° Ajax.	*equal to*
	AJAX Shall I call you father?°	*guide*
	ULYSSES Ay, my good son.	
245	DIOMEDES Be ruled by him, Lord Ajax.	
	ULYSSES There is no tarrying here; the hart Achilles	
	Keeps thicket.[6] Please it our general°	*(Agamemnon)*
	To call together all his state° of war.	*council*
	Fresh kings° are come to Troy; tomorrow	*Reinforcements*
250	We must with all our main of power° stand fast.	*utmost strength*
	And here's a lord—come knights from east to west°	*the whole world*

---

1. Probably alluding to the ten shares into which the assets of Shakespeare's company, the Lord Chamberlain's Men, were divided—hence, everything.
2. Ajax's glory exceeds anything scholars might say about it. Also, ironic: learning constitutes no part of it.
3. Famous Greek athlete who bore a four-year-old bull on his shoulders.
4. Which like a boundary, a fence, a shore, marks the extent of (probably ironic).
5. Young, fresh; immature; gullible.
6. Stays concealed (at home).

And cull their flower,[7] Ajax shall cope° the best.   *match*
AGAMEMNON   Go we to counsel. Let Achilles sleep;
  Light boats may sail swift, though greater hulks draw
  deep.[8]   *Exeunt.*

3.1 (Q 3.1)

Music sounds within. Enter PANDARUS *and a*
SERVANT[, *meeting*].

PANDARUS   Friend, you, pray you, a word: do not you follow
  the young Lord Paris?
SERVANT   Ay, sir, when he goes before me.
PANDARUS   You depend upon him,° I mean.   *serve him*
5 SERVANT   Sir, I do depend upon the Lord.°   *God; Paris*
PANDARUS   You depend upon a noble gentleman; I must needs
  praise him.
SERVANT   The Lord be praised!
PANDARUS   You know me, do you not?
10 SERVANT   Faith, sir, superficially.
PANDARUS   Friend, know me better: I am the Lord Pandarus.
SERVANT   I hope I shall know your honor better.[1]
PANDARUS   I do desire it.
SERVANT   You are in the state of grace?[2]
15 PANDARUS   Grace? Not so, friend; "honor" and "lordship" are
  my titles. What music is this?
SERVANT   I do but partly know, sir; it is music in parts.
PANDARUS   Know you the musicians?
SERVANT   Wholly, sir.
20 PANDARUS   Who play they to?
SERVANT   To the hearers, sir.
PANDARUS   At whose pleasure, friend?
SERVANT   At mine, sir, and theirs that love music.
PANDARUS   Command, I mean, friend.
25 SERVANT   Who shall I command, sir?
PANDARUS   Friend, we understand not one another: I am too
  courtly, and thou art too cunning. At whose request do
  these men play?
SERVANT   That's to't° indeed, sir. Marry, sir, at the request of   *to the point*
30 Paris, my lord, who's there in person, with him the mortal°   *living; fatal*
  Venus, the heart-blood of beauty, love's invisible soul.°   *(made visible)*
PANDARUS   Who, my cousin Cressida?
SERVANT   No, sir, Helen—could you not find out that by her
  attributes?
35 PANDARUS   It should seem, fellow, that thou hast not seen the
  lady Cressida. I come to speak with Paris from the Prince
  Troilus; I will make a complimental° assault upon him, for   *courteous*
  my business seethes.°   *boils; is pressing*

---

7. And choose their best men.
8. We will progress more swiftly without Achilles (perhaps alluding to the success of "light" English ships against the "greater hulks" of the Spanish Armada). Doubly ironic: Ajax is hardly a "light boat," and the Greeks are associated with "deep-drawing" boats in the Prologue (line 12).
3.1 Location: Troy's palace.
1. I hope to get to know you better. I hope to learn of an improvement in your spiritual health. The double

meaning here is typical of the servant's playful mockery of Pandarus, which partly contrasts Pandarus's secular concerns with more important, albeit anachronistic, Christian ones.
2. Theologically (deliberately misunderstanding Pandarus's "desire" in line 13 as a wish for moral improvement rather than social acquaintance). Pandarus proceeds to misunderstand "grace" as the status of being called "your grace" (a duke's title).

SERVANT Sodden business? There's a stewed[3] phrase indeed.

Enter PARIS *and* HELEN[, *with Attendants*].

40 PANDARUS Fair be to you, my lord, and to all this fair company. Fair desires in all fair measure fairly guide them—especially to you, fair Queen: fair thoughts be your fair pillow.

HELEN Dear lord, you are full of fair words.

45 PANDARUS You speak your fair pleasure, sweet Queen. Fair prince, here is good broken music.[4]

PARIS You have broke° it, cousin,[5] and by my life you shall   *interrupted* make it whole again; you shall piece it out° with a piece of   *repair it* your performance.° —Nell, he is full of harmony.   *performed by you*

50 PANDARUS Truly, lady, no.

HELEN O sir!

PANDARUS Rude,° in sooth; in good sooth, very rude.   *Unskilled; unmusical*

PARIS Well said, my lord; well, you say so in fits.[6]

PANDARUS I have business to my lord, dear Queen. —My lord, 55 will you vouchsafe me a word?

HELEN Nay, this shall not hedge° us out; we'll hear you sing,   *keep* certainly.

PANDARUS Well, sweet Queen, you are pleasant with° me.   *teasing* But marry, thus, my lord: my dear lord and most esteemed 60 friend, your brother Troilus—

HELEN My lord Pandarus, honey-sweet lord—

PANDARUS Go to, sweet Queen, go to! —commends himself most affectionately to you.

HELEN You shall not bob° us out of our melody. If you do, our   *swindle* 65 melancholy[7] upon your head.

PANDARUS Sweet Queen, sweet Queen, that's a sweet Queen, i'faith—

HELEN And to make a sweet lady sad is a sour offense.

PANDARUS Nay, that shall not serve your turn, that shall it 70 not in truth, la. Nay, I care not for such words, no, no. —And, my lord, he desires you that, if the King call for him at supper, you will make his excuse.

HELEN My lord Pandarus?

PANDARUS What says my sweet Queen, my very, very sweet 75 Queen?

PARIS What exploit's in hand? Where sups he tonight?

HELEN Nay, but my lord—

PANDARUS What says my sweet Queen? My cousin will fall out with you.[8]

80 HELEN [*to* PARIS] You must not° know where he sups.   *are not supposed to*

PARIS With my disposer[9] Cressida.

PANDARUS No, no, no such matter; you are wide.° Come, your   *off target* disposer° is sick.   *(Cressida)*

---

3. "Stewed" (overdone, literally and metaphorically; associated with stews, or brothels) puns on "sodden," which means "boiled" (picking up on "seethes," line 38); is stupid; is drunk; is being treated for venereal disease.

4. Music for instruments of different kinds—for example, strings and woodwind.

5. Kinsman (used especially by sovereigns to noblemen, whether or not related).

6. In sections of music (fits and starts; spasms of laughter).

7. May our "melancholy" mood (supposedly cured by music) be.

8. *What . . . you:* If you (Helen) keep interrupting, my "cousin" Paris (as in line 47) will be angry with you; if you keep inquiring about private affairs, my "cousin" Cressida will be angry with you.

9. Of uncertain meaning but perhaps suggesting that Paris is at Cressida's service, that Cressida can do what she likes with Troilus and Paris.

PARIS Well, I'll make excuse.°   *(for Troilus)*

85 PANDARUS Ay, good my lord. Why should you say Cressida?
No, your poor disposer's sick.

PARIS I spy[1]—

PANDARUS You spy? What do you spy? *[to an Attendant]*
Come, give me an instrument. Now, sweet Queen—

90 HELEN Why, this is kindly done!

PANDARUS My niece is horribly in love with a thing you have,
sweet Queen.

HELEN She shall have it, my lord, if it be not my lord Paris.

PANDARUS He? No, she'll none of him; they two are twain.°   *estranged*

95 HELEN Falling in[2] after falling out° may make them three.   *arguing*

PANDARUS Come, come, I'll hear no more of this. I'll sing you
a song now.

HELEN Ay, ay, prithee now; by my troth, sweet lord, thou hast
a fine forehead.[3]

100 PANDARUS Ay, you may, you may.°   *(go on)*

HELEN Let thy song be love: "This love will undo us all."
O Cupid, Cupid, Cupid!

PANDARUS Love? Ay, that it shall,° i'faith.   *(be); (undo us)*

PARIS Ay, good now:° "Love, love, nothing but love . . ."   *please*

105 PANDARUS In good troth, it° begins so.   *the song; love*

[*Sings.*] Love, love, nothing but love, still° more: *always*
For oh, love's bow shoots buck and doe.°   *male and female*
The shaft° confounds, not that it wounds,   *arrow; penis*
But tickles still the sore.[4]

110 These lovers cry "Oh! Oh!" they die;°   *perish; have an orgasm*
Yet that which seems the wound to kill°   *mortal wound*
Doth turn "Oh! Oh!" to "Ha ha he!",[5]
So dying love lives still.
"Oh! Oh!" awhile, but "Ha ha ha!"

115 "Oh! Oh!" groans out for "Ha ha ha!"
—Heigh-ho!

HELEN In love, i'faith, to the very tip of the nose.

PARIS He eats nothing but doves,° love, and that breeds hot   *emblem of true love*
blood, and hot blood begets hot thoughts, and hot thoughts

120 beget hot deeds, and hot deeds is love.

PANDARUS Is this the generation° of love: hot blood, hot   *genealogy; source*
thoughts, and hot deeds? Why, they are vipers. Is love a gen-
eration of vipers?[6]
[*Alarum.*]
Sweet lord, who's afield today?

125 PARIS Hector, Deiphobus, Helenus, Antenor, and all the gal-
lantry of Troy. I would fain have° armed today, but my Nell   *like to have*
would not have it so. How chance my brother Troilus went
not?

HELEN He hangs the lip° at something. —You know all, Lord   *looks despondent*

130 Pandarus.

PANDARUS Not I, honey-sweet Queen. I long to hear how they
sped today. —You'll remember your brother's excuse?

---

1. I understand what's going on between Troilus and
Cressida (alluding to a child's game).
2. "Falling in" sexually, so as to produce a child.
3. Impudence; modesty; sign of male beauty; hint of
cuckoldry.

4. Wound; four-year-old buck.
5. Turns pain to joy; turns ecstasy to derision.
6. Anachronistic allusion to a biblical phrase—for
instance, the "generation of vipers" in Matthew 23:33,
promising damnation.

PARIS   To a hair.°   *Exactly*
PANDARUS   Farewell, sweet Queen.
135   HELEN   Commend me to your niece.
PANDARUS   I will, sweet Queen.   [*Exit.*]
        Sound a retreat.
PARIS   They're come from field. Let us to Priam's hall
   To greet the warriors. Sweet Helen, I must woo you
   To help unarm our Hector. His stubborn buckles
140   With these, your white enchanting fingers, touched,
   Shall more obey than to the edge of steel°   *sword blade*
   Or force of Greekish sinews. You shall do more
   Than all the island kings:° disarm great Hector.   *Greek lords*
HELEN   'Twill make us proud to be his servant, Paris.
145   Yea, what he shall receive of us in duty
   Gives us more palm in° beauty than we have—   *fame for*
   Yea, overshines ourself.
   Sweet, above thought I love thee!⁷   *Exeunt.*

3.2 (Q 3.2)

Enter PANDARUS *and* TROILUS' MAN[, *meeting*].
PANDARUS   How now, where's thy master? At my cousin
   Cressida's?
TROILUS' MAN   No, sir, he stays for you to conduct him thither.
        Enter TROILUS.
PANDARUS   Oh, here he comes. —How now, how now?
5   TROILUS   Sirrah, walk off.   [*Exit* TROILUS' MAN.]
PANDARUS   Have you seen my cousin?
TROILUS   No, Pandarus. I stalk about her door
   Like a strange° soul upon the Stygian banks,   *newly arrived*
   Staying for waftage.¹ Oh, be thou my Charon
10   And give me swift transportance to those fields²
   Where I may wallow° in the lily-beds   *roll around*
   Proposed for° the deserver. O gentle Pandarus,   *Promised to*
   From Cupid's shoulder pluck his painted° wings   *brightly colored*
   And fly with me to Cressid!
15   PANDARUS   Walk here i'th' orchard;° I'll bring her straight.   *garden*
                                                          Exit.

TROILUS   I am giddy; expectation whirls me round.
   Th'imaginary relish° is so sweet   *pleasant anticipation*
   That it enchants my sense. What will it be
   When that the wat'ry° palates taste indeed   *watering*
20   Love's thrice-repurèd nectar?³ Death, I fear me,
   Swooning destruction, or some joy too fine,°   *exquisite*
   Too subtle-potent, and too sharp in sweetness°   *(musically)*
   For the capacity of my ruder powers.
   I fear it much, and I do fear besides
25   That I shall lose distinction in° my joys,   *power to distinguish among*
   As doth a battle° when they charge on heaps°   *an army / en masse*

7. TEXTUAL COMMENT For the different implications of Q's attribution of this line to Paris, where it ends with "her" rather than "thee," see Digital Edition TC 4 (Folio edited text).
3.2 Location: Cressida's garden.
1. Waiting to be ferried across. The dead were car-
ried across the river Styx into the underworld by the ferryman Charon.
2. The Elysian Fields, which were reserved for the blessed dead ("the deserver," line 12).
3. Thrice-purified drink of the gods (giving immortality).

The enemy flying.
    Enter PANDARUS.

PANDARUS She's making her ready; she'll come straight.° You   *immediately*
    must be witty° now; she does so blush and fetches her wind°   *clever; sane / breath*
30 so short, as if she were 'fraid with a sprite.[4] I'll fetch her. It
    is the prettiest villain;° she fetches her breath so short as a   *peasant (affectionate)*
    new-ta'en° sparrow.   *Exit.*   *just-captured*

TROILUS Even such a passion doth embrace my bosom:
    My heart beats thicker° than a feverous pulse,   *faster*
35 And all my powers do their bestowing° lose   *function*
    Like vassalage at unawares° encount'ring   *vassals unexpectedly*
    The eye of majesty.
        Enter PANDARUS *and* CRESSIDA[, *veiled*].

PANDARUS Come, come, what need you blush? Shame's a baby.
    —Here she is now; swear the oaths now to her that you have
40 sworn to me. [CRESSIDA *draws back*.] —What, are you gone
    again? You must be watched ere you be made tame,[5] must
    you? Come your ways, come your ways; an you draw back-
    ward we'll put you i'th' thills.[6] —Why do you not speak to
    her? —Come, draw this curtain, and let's see your picture.[7]
45 [*He unveils her.*] Alas, the day! How loath you are to offend
    daylight; an 'twere dark you'd close° sooner. —So, so, rub on,   *agree; unite*
    and kiss the mistress.[8] [TROILUS *kisses her.*] How now, a kiss in
    fee-farm?° Build there, carpenter; the air° is sweet. Nay, you *land tenure / her breath*
    shall fight your hearts out ere I part you, the falcon as the
50 tercel,[9] for° all the ducks i'th' river. Go to, go to.   *I'd bet*

TROILUS You have bereft me of all words, lady.

PANDARUS Words pay no debts; give her deeds. But she'll
    bereave you o'th' deeds° too if she call your activity° in ques- *wear you out / virility*
    tion. [*They kiss.*] What, billing° again? Here's "In witness   *kissing*
55 whereof the parties interchangeably[1]—" Come in, come in;
    I'll go get a fire.°   [*Exit.*]   *(for the bedroom)*

CRESSIDA Will you walk in, my lord?

TROILUS O Cressida, how often have I wished me thus!

CRESSIDA Wished, my lord? The gods grant—O my lord—

60 TROILUS What should they grant? What makes this pretty
    abruption?° What too curious dreg° espies my sweet lady in *pause / speck of dirt*
    the fountain of our love?

CRESSIDA More dregs than water, if my fears have eyes.

TROILUS Fears make devils of cherubim;° they never see truly. *predict the worst*
65 CRESSIDA Blind fear, that seeing° reason leads, finds safer   *clear-sighted*
    footing than blind reason, stumbling without fear. To fear
    the worst oft cures the worse.

TROILUS Oh, let my lady apprehend no fear; in all Cupid's
    pageant there is presented no monster.

70 CRESSIDA Nor nothing monstrous neither?

TROILUS Nothing but our undertakings° when we vow to weep   *promises*

---

4. Frightened by a ghost.
5. Hawks were kept awake at night to tame them.
6. If you back away, we'll back you, like a horse, into the shafts of a cart.
7. Cressida's face is veiled. Pictures were curtained for protection against light and dust.
8. Metaphor from the game of bowls: keep on course,

and touch gently the master ball (a small ball at which bowls were aimed).
9. The female hawk as (eagerly as) the male.
1. A garbled version of a betrothal; also, a contractual legal formula completed by the words "have set their hands and seals."

seas, live in fire, eat rocks, tame tigers, thinking it harder for
our mistress to devise imposition enough° than for us to   *a big enough challenge*
undergo any difficulty imposed. This is the monstrosity in
75   love, lady: that the will is infinite and the execution confined,
that the desire is boundless and the act° a slave to limit.   *(sex) act*

CRESSIDA   They say all lovers swear more performance than
they are able, and yet reserve an ability that they never perform, vowing more than the perfection of ten° and discharg-   *(lovers)*
80   ing less than the tenth part of one. They that have the voice
of lions and the act of hares—are they not monsters?

TROILUS   Are there such? Such are not we. Praise us as we are
tasted,° allow° us as we prove. Our head shall go bare till   *tested / praise*
merit crown it. No perfection in reversion shall have a praise
85   in present;[2] we will not name desert° before his° birth, and,   *mention merit / its*
being born, his addition° shall be humble. Few words to fair   *title*
faith.[3] Troilus shall be such to Cressid as what envy can say
worst shall be a mock for his truth,[4] and what truth can
speak truest not truer[5] than Troilus.

90 CRESSIDA   Will you walk in, my lord?

        Enter PANDARUS.

PANDARUS   What, blushing still? Have you not done talking
yet?

CRESSIDA   Well, uncle, what folly° I commit I dedicate to you.   *whatever indiscretion*

PANDARUS   I thank you for that. If my lord get a boy of you,
95   you'll give him me. Be true to my lord; if he flinch,° chide   *(sexually)*
me for it.

TROILUS   You know now your hostages:° your uncle's word and   *pledges*
my firm faith.

PANDARUS   Nay, I'll give my word for her too. Our kindred,
100 though they be long ere they are wooed, they are constant
being won. They are burrs, I can tell you—they'll stick where
they are thrown.°   *laid (sexual)*

CRESSIDA   Boldness comes to me now and brings me heart.
Prince Troilus, I have loved you night and day
105 For many weary months.

TROILUS   Why was my Cressid then so hard to win?

CRESSIDA   Hard to seem won; but I was won, my lord,
With the first glance that ever—pardon me:
If I confess much you will play the tyrant.
110 I love you now, but not, till now, so much
But I might master it. In faith, I lie;
My thoughts were like unbridled children grown
Too headstrong for their mother. See, we fools!
Why have I blabbed? Who shall be true to us°   *(women)*
115 When we are so unsecret to ourselves?°   *betray ourselves*
But though I loved you well, I wooed you not,
And yet, good faith, I wished myself a man,
Or that we women had men's privilege
Of speaking first. Sweet, bid me hold my tongue,
120 For in this rapture I shall surely speak

---

2. We won't count our chickens before they're
hatched.
3. Brevity goes with honesty (proverbial).

4. *as . . . truth:* that envy's most malicious comment
on Troilus can only be to mock him for constancy.
5. *not truer:* could not be more reliable.

The thing I shall repent. See, see, your silence,
Coming° in dumbness, from my weakness draws   *(forward)*
My soul of counsel° from me. Stop my mouth.   *most secret thoughts*

TROILUS   And shall, albeit sweet music issues thence.
    [*He kisses her.*]

125 PANDARUS   Pretty, i'faith.

CRESSIDA   My lord, I do beseech you, pardon me.
'Twas not my purpose thus to beg a kiss.
I am ashamed. O heavens, what have I done?
For this time will I take my leave, my lord.

130 TROILUS   Your leave, sweet Cressid?

PANDARUS   Leave? An you take leave till tomorrow morning—

CRESSIDA   Pray you, content you.°   *be quiet*

TROILUS   What offends you, lady?

CRESSIDA   Sir, mine own company.

TROILUS   You cannot shun yourself.

CRESSIDA   Let me go and try.

135   I have a kind of self resides with you,
But an unkind° self that itself will leave   *unnatural*
To be another's fool. Where is my wit?
I would be gone; I speak I know not what.

TROILUS   Well know they what they speak that speaks so
    wisely.

140 CRESSIDA   Perchance, my lord, I show more craft° than love   *cunning*
And fell so roundly° to a large° confession   *openly / full*
To angle for° your thoughts. But you are wise,   *fish for*
Or else you love not,[6] for to be wise and love
Exceeds man's might: that dwells with gods above.

145 TROILUS   Oh, that I thought it could be in a woman—
As if it can, I will presume in° you—   *it to be in*
To feed for aye° her lamp and flames of love,   *forever*
To keep her constancy in plight° and youth,   *as when first pledged*
Outliving beauty's outward° with a mind   *exterior*

150 That doth renew swifter than blood° decays;   *passion*
Or that persuasion could but thus convince me
That my integrity and truth to you
Might be affronted° with the match and weight°   *met / same amount*
Of such a winnowed[7] purity in love—

155 How were I then uplifted! But alas,
I am as true as truth's simplicity°   *truth itself*
And simpler° than the infancy of truth.   *more naive*

CRESSIDA   In that I'll war° with you.   *compete*

TROILUS   Oh, virtuous fight
When right with right wars who shall be most right!

160 True swains in love shall in the world to come
Approve° their truths by Troilus: when their rhymes,   *Attest*
Full of protest,° of oath and big compare,°   *protestation / comparison*
Wants° similes, truth tired with iteration°—   *Lack / repetition*
As true as steel, as plantage to the moon,[8]

165 As sun to day, as turtle° to her mate,   *turtledove*

---

6. Alternative explanations for why he has made no
"large confession" (line 141).
7. Grain is "winnowed" (separated from worthless

light chaff).
8. Plants were supposed to be affected in growth by
the moon.

As iron to adamant,° as earth to th' center⁹—   *a magnet*
Yet, after all comparisons of truth,
As truth's authentic author to be cited,
"As true as Troilus" shall crown up the verse
And sanctify the numbers.°   *verses*

170 CRESSIDA   Prophet may you be.
If I be false, or swerve a hair from truth,
When time is old and hath forgot itself,
When water drops have worn the stones of Troy,
And blind oblivion swallowed cities up,
175 And mighty states characterless are grated°   *are ground up unrecorded*
To dusty nothing, yet let memory,
From false° to false among false maids in love,   *falsehood*
Upbraid my falsehood. When they've said, "As false
As air, as water, as wind, as sandy earth,
180 As fox to lamb, as wolf to heifer's calf,
Pard° to the hind, or stepdame to her son"—   *Panther; leopard*
Yea, let them say, to stick the heart° of falsehood,   *hit the bullseye*
"As false as Cressid."
PANDARUS   Go to, a bargain made. Seal it, seal it! I'll be the
185 witness. Here I hold your hand, here my cousin's.¹ If ever
you prove false one to another, since I have taken such pains
to bring you together, let all pitiful goers-between be called
to the world's end after my name: call them all panders. Let
all constant men be Troiluses, all false women Cressids, and
190 all brokers-between° panders. Say "Amen."   *pimps*
TROILUS   Amen.
CRESSIDA   Amen.
PANDARUS   Amen. Whereupon I will show you a chamber,
which bed, because it shall not speak of your pretty encoun-
195 ters, press it to death.² Away!
                      [*Exeunt* TROILUS *and* CRESSIDA.]
And Cupid grant all tongue-tied maidens° here   *male or female virgins*
Bed, chamber, and pander to provide this gear.°   *Exit.*   *equipment*

3.3 (Q 3.3)

Flourish. Enter ULYSSES, DIOMEDES, NESTOR,
AGAMEMNON, [AJAX,] MENELAUS, *and* CALCHAS.¹

CALCHAS   Now, princes, for the service I have done you
Th'advantage° of the time prompts me aloud   *opportunity*
To call for recompense. Appear it° to your mind   *Let it appear*
That, through the sight I bear in things to come,
5 I have abandoned Troy, left my possession,°   *belongings*
Incurred a traitor's name, exposed myself
From certain and possessed conveniences
To doubtful fortunes, sequest'ring° from me all   *divorcing*
That time, acquaintance, custom, and condition°   *position*
10 Made tame° and most familiar to my nature,   *accustomed*
And here to do you service am become

---

9. The earth's surface to the earth's center, or axis.
1. Taking hands before a witness could be regarded
as a (civil) marriage.
2. Customary punishment for an accused person

who remained silent and would not plead.
3.3 Location: The Greek camp.
1. Calchas is Cressida's father, a Trojan priest siding
with the Greeks.

As new into the world, strange, unacquainted.
I do beseech you, as in way of taste,°   *a foretaste*
To give me now a little benefit
15 Out of those many registered in promise°   *many promised things*
Which you say live to come° in my behalf.   *wait to be fulfilled*

AGAMEMNON   What wouldst thou of us, Trojan? Make
    demand.

CALCHAS   You have a Trojan prisoner called Antenor,
Yesterday took; Troy holds him very dear.
20 Oft have you—often have you thanks therefore°—   *for it*
Desired my Cressid in right great exchange,²
Whom Troy hath still denied; but this Antenor
I know is such a wrest³ in their affairs
That their negotiations° all must slack,   *affairs of state*
25 Wanting his manage,° and they will almost   *guidance*
Give us a prince of blood,° a son of Priam,   *a royal prince*
In change of° him. Let him be sent, great princes,   *exchange for*
And he shall buy my daughter, and her presence
Shall quite strike off° all service I have done   *annul*
In most accepted° pain.   *willingly undertaken*
30 AGAMEMNON   Let Diomedes bear him,
And bring us Cressid hither. Calchas shall have
What he requests of us. Good Diomed,
Furnish you fairly° for this interchange;   *Completely ready yourself*
Withal° bring word if Hector will tomorrow   *At the same time*
35 Be answered in his challenge. Ajax is ready.

DIOMEDES   This shall I undertake, and 'tis a burden
Which I am proud to bear.

                    Exeunt [DIOMEDES *and* CALCHAS].
            Enter ACHILLES *and* PATROCLUS *in* [*the opening of*]
            their tent.

ULYSSES   Achilles stands i'th' entrance of his tent.
Please it our general to pass strangely° by him,   *aloofly*
40 As if he were forgot; and, princes all,
Lay negligent and loose° regard upon him.   *casual*
I will come last; 'tis like he'll question me
Why such unplausive° eyes are bent, why turned, on him.   *unapproving*
If so, I have derision medicinable°   *health-giving scorn*
45 To use° between your strangeness and his pride   *act as intermediary*
Which his own will shall have desire to drink.
It may do good: pride hath no other glass
To show itself but pride,⁴ for supple knees°   *bowing and scraping*
Feed arrogance and are the proud man's fees.°   *expected reward*
50 AGAMEMNON   We'll execute your purpose and put on
A form° of strangeness as we pass along;   *An appearance*
So do each lord, and either greet him not
Or else disdainfully, which shall shake him more
Than if not looked on. I will lead the way.

            [*They file past Achilles' tent.*]
55 ACHILLES   What, comes the general to speak with me?
You know my mind: I'll fight no more 'gainst Troy.

---

2. In return for someone important.
3. Tuning key for a stringed instrument (hence, probably related to "slack," line 24); peg for tighten-

ing a surgical ligature.
4. *pride . . . pride:* a proud person recognizes excessive pride only when shown it in others.

AGAMEMNON   What says Achilles? Would he aught with us?
NESTOR   Would you, my lord, aught with the general?
ACHILLES   No.
60 NESTOR   Nothing, my lord.
AGAMEMNON   The better. [*Exeunt* AGAMEMNON *and* NESTOR.]
ACHILLES   Good day, good day.
MENELAUS   How do you, how do you?   [*Exit.*]
ACHILLES   What? Does the cuckold scorn me?
65 AJAX   How now, Patroclus?
ACHILLES   Good morrow, Ajax.
AJAX   Ha?
ACHILLES   Good morrow.
AJAX   Ay, and good next day too.   *Exit.*
        [ULYSSES *remains behind, reading.*]
70 ACHILLES   What mean these fellows? Know they not
        Achilles?
PATROCLUS   They pass by strangely; they were used to bend,
        To send their smiles before them to Achilles,
        To come as humbly as they used° to creep   *are accustomed*
        To holy altars.
ACHILLES   What, am I poor° of late?   *insignificant*
75   'Tis certain, greatness, once fall'n out with fortune,
        Must fall out with men too. What the declined° is   *man who has sunk in life*
        He shall as soon read in the eyes of others
        As feel in his own fall, for men, like butterflies,
        Show not their mealy° wings but to the summer;   *powdery*
80   And not a man,° for being simply man,   *no man*
        Hath any honor but honored for⁵ those honors
        That are without° him, as place, riches, and favor⁶—   *external to*
        Prizes of accident° as oft as merit,   *that come by chance*
        Which, when they fall, as being slippery standers,°   *on an uncertain base*
85   The love that leaned on them, as slippery too,
        Doth one° pluck down another, and together   *The one doth*
        Die in the fall. But 'tis not so with me:
        Fortune and I are friends. I do enjoy
        At ample point° all that I did possess,   *Fully*
90   Save° these men's looks, who do, methinks, find out   *Except*
        Something not worth in me such rich beholding°   *attention*
        As they have often given. Here is Ulysses;
        I'll interrupt his reading.
        —How now, Ulysses?
ULYSSES   Now, great Thetis' son!
ACHILLES   What are you reading?
95 ULYSSES   A strange fellow here
        Writes me that man, how dearly ever parted,°   *however valuably endowed*
        How much in having, or without or in,⁷
        Cannot make boast to have that which he hath,
        Nor feels not what he owes,° but by reflection°—   *owns / how others respond*
100   As when his virtues, shining upon others,
        Heat them, and they retort° that heat again   *cast back*
        To the first giver.
ACHILLES   This is not strange, Ulysses.

5. *but honored for:* except.
6. Position, wealth, and popularity (or looks).

7. However much he possesses, either externally or
internally.

The beauty that is borne here in the face
The bearer knows not, but commends itself,
105 Not going from itself, but eye to eye opposed,
Salutes each other with each other's form;[8]
For speculation° turns not to itself   *sight*
Till it hath traveled and is mirrored there,
Where it may see itself. This is not strange at all.
110 ULYSSES   I do not strain at° the position°—   *question / thesis*
It is familiar—but at the author's drift,
Who in his circumstance expressly° proves   *in detail explicitly*
That no man is the lord of anything,
Though in and of him there is much consisting,°   *value*
115 Till he communicate his parts° to others;   *qualities*
Nor doth he of himself know them for aught°   *as valuable*
Till he behold them formed in th'applause
Where they are extended, who° like an arch° reverb'rate   *(the applauders) / a vault*
The voice again, or, like a gate of steel
120 Fronting° the sun, receives and renders back   *Facing*
His figure° and his heat. I was much rapt in this,   *Its appearance*
And apprehended here immediately
The unknown Ajax. Heavens, what a man is there!
A very horse that has he knows not what.°   *doesn't know himself*
125 Nature, what things there are
Most abject in regard and dear in use;°   *Despised but useful*
What things again most dear in the esteem
And poor in worth! Now shall we see tomorrow
An act that very° chance doth throw upon him.   *pure*
130 Ajax renowned? O heavens, what some men do,
While some men leave to do!°   *leave undone*
How some men° creep in° skittish Fortune's hall   *(like Ajax) / sneak into*
Whiles others play the idiots in her eyes;[9]
How one man° eats into another's° pride   *(Ajax) / (Achilles')*
135 While pride is fasting in his wantonness![1]
To see these Grecian lords—why, even already
They clap the lubber° Ajax on the shoulder   *lout*
As if his foot were on brave Hector's breast
And great Troy shrinking.°   *cowering; declining*
ACHILLES   I do believe it,
140 For they passed by me as misers do by beggars,
Neither gave to me good word nor look.
What, are my deeds forgot?
ULYSSES   Time hath, my lord, a wallet at° his back   *satchel on*
Wherein he puts alms for oblivion,
145 A great-sized monster[2] of ingratitudes.
Those scraps are good deeds past
Which are devoured as fast as they are made,
Forgot as soon as done. Perseverance, dear my lord,
Keeps honor bright. To have done° is to hang   *rely on past deeds*

---

8. *but commends . . . form:* unless it commends itself
(to others), since it is unable to leave itself, but two
eyes (in two people), looking at each other, can show
both people their images.
9. While others (like Achilles) foolishly squander the
opportunity provided by Fortune's attention.

1. While the second man in effect starves his pride,
and hence his reputation, through his conceitedness.
2. *alms for oblivion:* feats that won't be remembered.
Traditionally, if you wore your satchel behind you, it
contained your vices, which you in this way forgot.
monster: time or, more likely, oblivion.

150	Quite out of fashion, like a rusty mail,°	*coat of armor*
	In monumental mock'ry.° Take the instant way,	*a useless monument*
	For honor travels in a strait so narrow	
	Where one but goes abreast;° keep then the path,	*must go single file*
	For emulation hath a thousand sons	
155	That one by one pursue. If you give way	
	Or hedge aside from the direct forthright,°	*straightforward path*
	Like to an entered tide° they all rush by	*a tide that has entered*
	And leave you hindmost;	
	Or like a gallant horse fall'n in first rank	
160	Lie there for pavement to the abject rear,°	*worthless rearguard*
	O'er-run and trampled on. Then what they do in present,	
	Though less than yours in past, must o'er-top yours;	
	For Time is like a fashionable host	
	That slightly shakes his parting guest by th' hand	
165	And, with his arms outstretched as he would° fly,	*as if he wanted to*
	Grasps in the comer. The welcome ever smiles,	
	And farewells goes out sighing. Oh, let not virtue seek	
	Remuneration for the thing it was,	
	For beauty, wit,	
170	High birth, vigor of bone,° desert in service,°	*strength / worthy service*
	Love, friendship, charity are subjects all	
	To envious and calumniating Time.	
	One touch of nature° makes the whole world kin,°	*natural fault / similar*
	That all with one consent praise newborn gauds,°	*toys; (pun on "gods")*
175	Though they are made and molded of things past,	
	And give to dust that is a little gilt°	*gilded*
	More laud than gilt o'er-dusted.°	*older treasures*
	The present eye praises the present object.	
	Then marvel not, thou great and complete man,	
180	That all the Greeks begin to worship Ajax,	
	Since things in motion sooner catch the eye	
	Than what not stirs. The cry° went out on thee,	*approval*
	And still it might, and yet it may again,	
	If thou wouldst not entomb thyself alive	
185	And case° thy reputation in thy tent,	*shut up*
	Whose glorious deeds but in these fields of late	
	Made emulous missions 'mongst the gods themselves[3]	
	And drove great Mars to faction.°	*to take sides*

ACHILLES   Of this my privacy
I have strong reasons.

ULYSSES   But 'gainst your privacy
190 The reasons are more potent and heroical.
'Tis known, Achilles, that you are in love
With one of Priam's daughters.°   *(Polyxena)*

ACHILLES   Ha, known?

ULYSSES   Is that a wonder?
195 The providence that's in a watchful state[4]
Knows almost every grain of Pluto's gold,[5]
Finds bottom in th'uncomprehensive° deeps,   *unimaginable*

---

3. Caused the gods to join the fight on both sides in an effort to match Achilles.
4. Government foresight is compared to divine

"providence"—perhaps ironically.
5. That is, the gold of Pluto, god of the underworld (regularly identified with Plutus, god of wealth).

	Keeps place with thought,° and, almost like the gods,	*Stays on top of things*
	Do thoughts unveil in their dumb cradles.[6]	
200	There is a mystery (with whom relation°	*report*
	Durst never meddle) in the soul of state	
	Which hath an operation more divine	
	Than breath or pen can give expressure° to.	*expression*
	All the commerce° that you have had with Troy	*dealings*
205	As perfectly is ours as yours,[7] my lord.	
	And better would it fit Achilles much	
	To throw down° Hector than Polyxena.	*(in war); (in love)*
	But it must grieve young Pyrrhus,° now at home,	*(Achilles' son)*
	When Fame shall in our islands sound her trump,	
210	And all the Greekish girls shall tripping sing:	
	"Great Hector's sister did Achilles win,	
	But our great Ajax bravely beat down him!"°	*(Hector)*
	Farewell, my lord. I as your lover° speak;	*good friend*
	The fool slides o'er the ice that you should break.[8] [*Exit.*]	
215	PATROCLUS To this effect, Achilles, have I moved you.	
	A woman impudent° and mannish grown	*immodest*
	Is not more loathed than an effeminate° man	*cowardly*
	In time of action. I stand condemned for this;	
	They think my little stomach to° the war	*appetite for*
220	And your great love to me restrains you thus.	
	Sweet, rouse yourself, and the weak wanton Cupid	
	Shall from your neck unloose his amorous fold,°	*embrace*
	And, like a dewdrop from the lion's mane,	
	Be shook to airy air.	
225	ACHILLES Shall Ajax fight with Hector?	
	PATROCLUS Ay, and perhaps receive much honor by him.	
	ACHILLES I see my reputation is at stake;	
	My fame is shrewdly gored.°	*severely wounded*
	PATROCLUS Oh, then beware;	
	Those wounds heal ill that men do give themselves.	
230	Omission to do what is necessary	
	Seals a commission to a blank of danger,[9]	
	And danger, like an ague, subtly taints	
	Even then when we sit idly in the sun.[1]	
	ACHILLES Go call Thersites hither, sweet Patroclus.	
235	I'll send the fool to Ajax and desire him	
	T'invite the Trojan lords after the combat	
	To see us here unarmed. I have a woman's longing,	
	An appetite that I am sick withal,°	*with*
	To see great Hector in his weeds° of peace,	*garments*
240	To talk with him and to behold his visage,	
	Even to my full of view.°	*in full view*

          Enter THERSITES.

                     A labor saved.

THERSITES   A wonder.

6. *Do . . . cradles:* Discovers thoughts before they are spoken.
7. Is as well known to us (the other Greek leaders) as to you.
8. Perhaps: Ajax (the fool) can get away with what would be damaging to you; or, Ajax is engaged in superficial action, whereas only you can initiate real combat.
9. Gives danger free rein (literally, provides danger with a blank warrant to fill in as it pleases).
1. *danger . . . sun:* danger, like a fever, insidiously weakens (causes shivering) even when one is sitting in the sun. *ague:* fever; chills.

ACHILLES What?

245 THERSITES Ajax goes up and down the field, asking for himself.[2]

ACHILLES How so?

THERSITES He must° fight singly tomorrow with Hector, and   *is to*
is so prophetically proud of an heroical cudgeling° that he   *(by Hector)*
raves in saying nothing.

250 ACHILLES How can that be?

THERSITES Why, he stalks up and down like a peacock, a
stride and a stand;° ruminates like an hostess that hath no   *walking, then stopping*
arithmetic but her brain to set down her reckoning;[3] bites
his lip with a politic regard,° as who should say, "There were   *judicious expression*
255 wit in his head, an 'twould out"°—and so there is, but it lies *if it would only come out*
as coldly in him as fire in a flint, which will not show with-
out knocking.° The man's undone forever, for if Hector   *striking (into flame)*
break not his neck i'th' combat he'll break't himself in vainglory. He knows not me; I said, "Good morrow, Ajax," and he
260 replies, "Thanks, Agamemnon." What think you of this man
that takes me for the general? He's grown a very land-fish,°   *unnatural creature*
languageless, a monster. A plague of opinion! A man may
wear it on both sides like a leather jerkin.[4]

ACHILLES Thou must be my ambassador to him, Thersites.

265 THERSITES Who, I? Why, he'll answer nobody. He professes
not answering;° speaking is for beggars. He wears his tongue   *refuses to respond*
in 's arms. I will put on° his presence. Let Patroclus make   *imitate*
his demands to me; you shall see the pageant of Ajax.

ACHILLES To him, Patroclus. Tell him I humbly desire the val-
270 iant Ajax to invite the most valorous Hector to come unarmed
to my tent, and to procure safe-conduct for his person of° the   *for Hector from*
magnanimous and most illustrious six-or-seven-times-
honored captain-general of the Grecian army, Agamemnon,
et cetera. Do this.

275 PATROCLUS Jove bless great Ajax!

THERSITES Hum!

PATROCLUS I come from the worthy Achilles—

THERSITES Ha?

PATROCLUS Who most humbly desires you to invite Hector to
280 his tent—

THERSITES Hum!

PATROCLUS And to procure safe-conduct from Agamemnon.

THERSITES Agamemnon?

PATROCLUS Ay, my lord.

285 THERSITES Ha?

PATROCLUS What say you to't?

THERSITES God b'wi' you,° with all my heart.   *(dismissive)*

PATROCLUS Your answer, sir.

THERSITES If tomorrow be a fair day, by eleven o'clock it will
290 go one way or other; howsoever, he shall pay for me ere° he   *pay dearly before*
has me.

---

2. Punning on "Ajax" and "a jakes" (a toilet), the point
presumably being that Ajax is so terrified by battle, he
cannot help relieving himself.
3. Like the hostess at an inn whose mathematical

ineptitude makes it hard for her to work out the bill.
4. A plague on conceit (or reputation)! One can wear
it either way (conceit or reputation) like a reversible
jacket (but it's still the same pride).

PATROCLUS Your answer, sir.

THERSITES Fare you well, with all my heart.

ACHILLES Why, but he is not in this tune,° is he?   *mood*

295 THERSITES No, but he's out o'tune thus. What music will be
in him when Hector has knocked out his brains I know not,
but I am sure none, unless the fiddler Apollo get his sinews
to make catlings[5] on.

ACHILLES Come, thou shalt bear a letter to him straight.

300 THERSITES Let me carry another to his horse, for that's the
more capable° creature.   *intelligent*

ACHILLES My mind is troubled like a fountain stirred,
And I myself see not the bottom of it.

[*Exeunt* ACHILLES *and* PATROCLUS.]

THERSITES Would the fountain of your mind were clear
305 again, that I might water an ass at it. I had rather be a tick in
a sheep than such a valiant ignorance.°   [*Exit.*]   *puffed-up fool*

4.1 (Q 4.1)

Enter at one door AENEAS *with a torch, at another*
PARIS, DEIPHOBUS, *Antenor,* DIOMEDES *the Grecian,*
with torches.

PARIS See, ho! Who is that there?

DEIPHOBUS It is the Lord Aeneas.

AENEAS Is the Prince there in person?
Had I so good occasion to lie long
5 As you, Prince Paris, nothing but heavenly business
Should rob my bedmate of my company.

DIOMEDES That's my mind too. Good morrow, Lord Aeneas.

PARIS A valiant Greek, Aeneas; take his hand.
Witness the process of your speech[1] wherein
10 You told how Diomed, in a whole week by days,°   *every day*
Did haunt you in the field.

AENEAS   Health to you, valiant sir,
During all question of° the gentle truce,   *conversations during*
But when I meet you armed, as black defiance
As heart can think or courage execute.

15 DIOMEDES The one and other Diomed embraces.
Our bloods are now in calm, and so long, health;
But when contention and occasion meets,°   *it's time to fight*
By Jove, I'll play the hunter for thy life
With all my force, pursuit, and policy.°   *cunning*

20 AENEAS And thou shalt hunt a lion that will fly
With his face backward.[2] In humane gentleness,
Welcome to Troy. Now, by Anchises' life,
Welcome indeed! By Venus'[3] hand, I swear
No man alive can love in such a sort°   *to such an extent*
25 The thing he means to kill more excellently.

DIOMEDES We sympathize.° Jove, let Aeneas live—   *feel the same*
If to my sword his fate be not the glory—

---

5. Instrument strings made of catgut.
4.1 Location: A street in Troy.
1. *Witness . . . speech:* As the thrust of your narrative
made clear (that he is valiant).
2. In the imagery of heraldry for chivalric combat, a

lion walking and looking back over his shoulder; also,
Aeneas will still fight even as he retreats.
3. Anchises and Venus, the goddess of love, were
Aeneas's parents.

A thousand complete courses of the sun,
But in mine emulous honor[4] let him die
30 With every joint a wound, and that tomorrow.
AENEAS   We know each other well.
DIOMEDES   We do, and long to know each other worse.
PARIS   This is the most despiteful'st gentle greeting,
The noblest hateful love, that e'er I heard of.
35   —What business, lord, so early?
AENEAS   I was sent for to the King, but why I know not.
PARIS   His purpose meets you:° it was to bring this Greek   *I'll tell you why*
To Calchas' house, and there to render him,
For the enfreed Antenor, the fair Cressid.
40 Let's have your company, or, if you please,
Haste there before us. [*aside to* AENEAS] I constantly° do   *firmly*
    think—
Or rather call my thought a certain knowledge—
My brother Troilus lodges there tonight.
Rouse him and give him note of our approach,
45 With the whole quality° whereof. I fear   *cause*
We shall be much unwelcome.
AENEAS [*aside to* PARIS]   That I assure you.
Troilus had rather Troy were borne to Greece
Than Cressid borne from Troy.
PARIS [*aside to* AENEAS]   There is no help;
The bitter disposition of the time
50 Will have it so. —On, lord; we'll follow you.
AENEAS   Good morrow, all.   *Exit.*
PARIS   And tell me, noble Diomed, faith, tell me true,
Even in the soul of sound good fellowship:
Who in your thoughts merits fair Helen most,
Myself or Menelaus?
55 DIOMEDES   Both alike.
He merits well to have her that doth seek her,
Not making any scruple of her soilure,°   *issue of her dishonor*
With such a hell of pain and world of charge;°   *expense*
And you as well to keep her that defend her,
60 Not palating the taste of° her dishonor,   *Not even tasting*
With such a costly loss of wealth and friends.
He like a puling° cuckold would drink up   *whining*
The lees and dregs of a flat tamèd piece;[5]
You like a lecher out of whorish loins
65 Are pleased to breed out your inheritors.°   *produce your heirs*
Both merits poised,° each weighs no less nor more,   *weighed in the scales*
But he as he: which heavier for a whore?[6]
PARIS   You are too bitter to° your countrywoman.   *(given that Helen is)*
DIOMEDES   She's bitter to her country. Hear me, Paris:
70 For every false drop in her bawdy veins
A Grecian's life hath sunk; for every scruple°   *tiny unit of weight*
Of her contaminated carrion° weight   *putrid*
A Trojan hath been slain. Since she could speak
She hath not given so many good words breath

---

4. If his death will increase my honor.   6. But one the same as the other: which more deserves
5. Of a stale insipid (penetrated) cask of wine (woman).   (is made sadder by) the whore?

75   As for her Greeks and Trojans suffered death.

  PARIS   Fair Diomed, you do as chapmen° do: *merchants*

    Dispraise the thing that you desire to buy.

    But we in silence hold this virtue well:

    We'll not commend what we intend to sell.[7]

80   Here lies our way.   *Exeunt.*

4.2a (Q 4.2)

Enter TROILUS *and* CRESSIDA.

  TROILUS   Dear, trouble not yourself; the morn is cold.

  CRESSIDA   Then, sweet my lord, I'll call mine uncle down.

    He shall unbolt the gates.

  TROILUS   Trouble him not.

    To bed, to bed. Sleep kill those pretty eyes

5   And give as soft attachment° to thy senses   *imprisonment*

    As infants empty of all thought.

  CRESSIDA   Good morrow, then.

  TROILUS   I prithee now, to bed.

  CRESSIDA   Are you aweary of me?

  TROILUS   O Cressida! But that the busy day,

10   Waked by the lark, hath roused the ribald° crows,   *offensively noisy*

    And dreaming night will hide our eyes no longer,

    I would not from thee.

  CRESSIDA   Night hath been too brief.

  TROILUS   Beshrew the witch! With venomous wights[1] she

    stays

    As hideously as hell, but flies° the grasps of love   *flees*

15   With wings more momentary-swift than thought.

    You will catch cold and curse me.

  CRESSIDA   Prithee, tarry; you men will never tarry.

    O foolish Cressid! I might have still held off,

    And then you would have tarried. —Hark, there's one up.

20 PANDARUS *(within)*   What's° all the doors open here?   *Why are*

  TROILUS   It is your uncle.

         Enter PANDARUS.

  CRESSIDA   A pestilence on him! Now will he be mocking;

    I shall have such a life!

  PANDARUS   How now, how now? How go° maidenheads? Hear   *What's the price of*

25   you, maid: where's my cousin Cressid?[2]

  CRESSIDA   Go hang yourself, you naughty mocking uncle.

    You bring me to do°—and then you flout me too.   *have sex*

  PANDARUS   To do what, to do what? Let her say what. What

    have I brought you to do?

30 CRESSIDA   Come, come, beshrew° your heart; you'll ne'er be   *curses on*

    good,

    Nor suffer others.°   *let others be good*

---

7. Possibly: we don't intend to bargain for Helen and so won't praise her. But this is not what Paris says. If Diomed belittles Helen because he wants to buy her back (line 77), Paris as potential seller ought to negotiate by praising her. But he won't praise what he's trying to sell (line 79). The problem in interpreting this passage is that he won't consider giving, or selling, Helen back.

4.2a Location: Cressida's house.
1. Curse the night! With evil people (who are hateful to one another).
2. Pandarus pretends not to recognize Cressida, now that she is no longer a virgin. It is possible that he addresses her as "maid" because she is wearing a veil, which suggests a modesty appropriate to virgins.

PANDARUS Ha, ha! Alas, poor wretch. Ah, poor *chipochia°*—   *clitoris; vagina*
has't not slept tonight? Would he not, a naughty man, let it
sleep? A bugbear° take him!   *goblin*
35 CRESSIDA Did not I tell you? Would he were knocked i'th'
head.°   *killed*

> *One knocks.*

Who's that at door? Good uncle, go and see.
—My lord, come you again into my chamber.
You smile and mock me, as if I meant naughtily.
TROILUS Ha, ha!
40 CRESSIDA Come, you are deceived; I think of no such thing.

> *Knock.*

How earnestly they knock! Pray you, come in.
I would not for half Troy have you seen here.

> *Exeunt* [TROILUS *and* CRESSIDA].

PANDARUS Who's there? What's the matter? Will you beat
down the door? How now, what's the matter?

> [*Enter* AENEAS.]

45 AENEAS Good morrow, lord, good morrow.
PANDARUS Who's there? My lord Aeneas? By my troth, I knew
you not. What news with you so early?
AENEAS Is not Prince Troilus here?
PANDARUS Here? What should he do here?
50 AENEAS Come, he is here, my lord; do not deny him. It doth
import° him much to speak with me.   *concern*
PANDARUS Is he here, say you? 'Tis more than I know, I'll be
sworn. For my own part, I came in late. What should he do
here?
55 AENEAS Whoa, nay then! Come, come, you'll do him wrong
ere you're ware.° You'll be so true to him to be false to him.°   *aware / as to harm him*
Do not you know of him, but yet go fetch him hither. Go.

> [*Exit* PANDARUS.][3]

> *Enter* TROILUS.

TROILUS How now, what's the matter?
AENEAS My lord, I scarce have leisure to salute you,
60 My matter is so rash.° There is at hand   *urgent*
Paris your brother, and Deiphobus,
The Grecian Diomed, and our Antenor
Delivered to us, and for him° forthwith,   *(Antenor)*
Ere the first sacrifice, within this hour,
65 We must give up to Diomed's hand
The lady Cressida.
TROILUS   Is it concluded so?
AENEAS By Priam and the general state° of Troy.   *council*
They are at hand and ready to effect it.
TROILUS How my achievements mock me!
70 I will go meet them. And, my lord Aeneas,
We° met by chance—you did not find me here.   *(Pretend that) we*
AENEAS Good, good, my lord; the secrets of nature
Have not more gift in taciturnity.   *Exeunt.*

---

3. Editors usually keep him on and have Cressida enter alone at what is the beginning of 4.2b in this edition.

4.2b (Q 4.2)[1]

Enter PANDARUS *and* CRESSIDA.

PANDARUS Is't possible? No sooner got but lost? The devil
take Antenor! The young prince will go mad. A plague upon
Antenor! I would they had broke 's neck.

CRESSIDA How now? What's the matter? Who was here?

5   PANDARUS Ah, ah!

CRESSIDA Why sigh you so profoundly? Where's my lord?
Gone? Tell me, sweet uncle, what's the matter?

PANDARUS Would I were as deep under the earth as I am
above.

10 CRESSIDA O the gods, what's the matter?

PANDARUS Prithee, get thee in. Would thou hadst ne'er been
born! I knew thou wouldst be his death. Oh, poor gentleman. A plague upon Antenor!

CRESSIDA Good uncle, I beseech you, on my knees I beseech

15 you: what's the matter?

PANDARUS Thou must be gone, wench, thou must be gone.
Thou art changed° for Antenor; thou must to thy father and   exchanged
be gone from Troilus. 'Twill be his death, 'twill be his bane;
he cannot bear it.

20 CRESSIDA O you immortal gods, I will not go!

PANDARUS Thou must.

CRESSIDA I will not, uncle. I have forgot my father.
I know no touch of consanguinity—
No kin, no love, no blood, no soul so near me

25 As the sweet Troilus. O you gods divine,
Make Cressid's name the very crown° of falsehood   height
If ever she leave Troilus. Time, force, and death,
Do to this body what extremity you can,
But the strong base and building of my love

30 Is as the very center of the earth,
Drawing all things to it. I will go in and weep—

PANDARUS Do, do.

CRESSIDA Tear my bright hair and scratch my praisèd
cheeks,
Crack my clear voice with sobs, and break my heart

35 With sounding "Troilus." I will not go from Troy. *Exeunt.*

4.3 (Q 4.3)

Enter PARIS, TROILUS, AENEAS, DEIPHOBUS, *Antenor,*
and DIOMEDES.

PARIS It is great morning,° and the hour prefixed°   broad daylight / arranged
Of her delivery to this valiant Greek
Comes fast upon. Good my brother Troilus,
Tell you the lady what she is to do
And haste her to the purpose.

5   TROILUS   Walk into her house.
[*aside to* PARIS] I'll bring her to the Grecian presently,°   immediately
And to his hand, when I deliver her,

4.2b Location: Scene continues.
1. TEXTUAL COMMENT For the rationale behind the
partial scene division here, the thematic implica-

tions, and the difference from Q, see Digital Edition
TC 5 (Folio edited text).
4.3 Location: Outside Cressida's house.

Think it an altar, and thy brother Troilus
A priest there off'ring to it his heart.

10 PARIS [*aside to* TROILUS] I know what 'tis to love,
And would,° as I shall pity, I could help.   *wish*
—Please you walk in, my lords.   *Exeunt.*

4.4 (Q 4.4)
Enter PANDARUS *and* CRESSIDA.

PANDARUS Be moderate, be moderate.
CRESSIDA Why tell you me of moderation?
The grief is fine,° full, perfect that I taste,   *undiluted*
And no less in a sense° as strong   *in a manner*
5 As that which causeth it.° How can I moderate it?   *(her love)*
If I could temporize with° my affection,   *bargain with*
Or brew° it to a weak and colder palate,°   *dilute / taste*
The like allayment° could I give my grief.   *dilution*
My love admits no qualifying dross,°   *modifying impurity*
10 No more° my grief in such a precious loss.   *Any more than does*
    Enter TROILUS.
PANDARUS Here, here, here he comes—a sweet duck.
CRESSIDA O Troilus, Troilus!
PANDARUS What a pair of spectacles° is here! Let me embrace   *sights*
too. "O heart," as the goodly saying is:
15 "O heart, heavy heart,
Why sighest thou without breaking?"
Where he answers again:
"Because thou canst not ease thy smart
By friendship nor by speaking."
20 There was never a truer rhyme. Let us cast away nothing,
for we may live to have need of such a verse. We see it, we
see it. How now, lambs?
TROILUS Cressid, I love thee in so strange° a purity   *unusual*
That the blest gods, as° angry with my fancy,°   *as if / love*
25 More bright in zeal than the devotion which
Cold lips blow to their deities, take thee from me.
CRESSIDA Have the gods envy?
PANDARUS Ay, ay, ay, ay—'tis too plain a case.
CRESSIDA And is it true that I must go from Troy?
TROILUS A hateful truth.
30 CRESSIDA   What, and from Troilus too?
TROILUS From Troy and Troilus.
CRESSIDA   Is't possible?
TROILUS And suddenly°—where injury of° chance   *immediately / injurious*
Puts back° leave-taking, jostles roughly by°   *Prevents / past*
All time of pause, rudely beguiles° our lips   *deprives*
35 Of all rejoindure,° forcibly prevents   *joining again; reply*
Our locked embrasures, strangles our dear vows
Even in the birth of our own laboring breath°—   *(as in childbirth)*
We two, that with so many thousand sighs
Did buy each other, must poorly sell ourselves
40 With the rude brevity and discharge of one.°   *(sigh)*

4.4 Location: Inside Cressida's house.

Injurious time now with a robber's haste
Crams his rich thievery up he knows not how.[1]
As many farewells as be stars in heaven,
With distinct breath and consigned° kisses to them,   *ratifying*
45   He fumbles up° into a loose adieu   *clumsily combines*
And scants us with a single famished kiss,
Distasting[2] with the salt of broken° tears.   *interrupted*
AENEAS *(within)*   My lord, is the lady ready?
TROILUS   Hark, you are called. Some say the Genius° so   *guardian spirit*
50   Cries "Come!" to him that instantly must die.
[*to* PANDARUS] Bid them have patience; she shall come anon.
PANDARUS   Where are my tears? Rain to lay this wind,° or my   *allay my sighs*
heart will be blown up by the root.   [*Exit.*]
CRESSIDA   I must then to the Grecians?
TROILUS   No remedy.
55   CRESSIDA   A woeful Cressid 'mongst the merry Greeks.[3]
When shall we see again?
TROILUS   Hear me, my love: Be thou but true of heart—
CRESSIDA   I true? How now, what wicked deem° is this?   *thought*
TROILUS   Nay, we must use expostulation° kindly,   *conversation*
60   For it° is parting from us.   *the opportunity*
I speak not "Be thou true" as fearing thee—
For I will throw my glove to° Death himself   *challenge*
That there's no maculation° in thy heart—   *stain of infidelity*
But "Be thou true" say I to fashion in°   *introduce*
65   My sequent° protestation: Be thou true,   *following*
And I will see thee.
CRESSIDA   Oh, you shall be exposed, my lord, to dangers
As infinite as imminent, but I'll be true.
TROILUS   And I'll grow friend with danger. Wear this sleeve.[4]
70   CRESSIDA   And you this glove. When shall I see you?
TROILUS   I will corrupt the Grecian sentinels
To° give thee nightly visitation.   *In order that I may*
But yet be true.
CRESSIDA   O heavens, "Be true" again?
TROILUS   Hear why I speak it, love:
75   The Grecian youths are full of quality,
Their loving well composed with gifts of nature,
Flowing and swelling o'er with arts° and exercise.°   *education / practice*
How novelties may move, and parts with person,°   *talent and good looks*
Alas, a kind of godly° jealousy—   *divinely sanctioned*
80   Which, I beseech you, call a virtuous sin—
Makes me afraid.
CRESSIDA   O heavens, you love me not!
TROILUS   Die I a villain then.
In this I do not call your faith° in question   *fidelity*
So mainly° as my merit:[5] I cannot sing,   *much*
85   Nor heel the high lavolt, nor sweeten talk,[6]
Nor play at subtle games—fair virtues all,

---

1. Compresses his stolen goods (farewell kisses) into a short period, in disorganized fashion, distractedly.
2. Made distasteful.
3. Common phrase for licentious revelers; here, also meant literally.
4. Often detachable in Elizabethan dress.

5. Deserts; good works, deserving of salvation (picking up the religious language of the preceding lines, especially "faith," line 83).
6. Nor dance the "lavolt" (which involved spectacular jumps), nor flatter.

To which the Grecians are most prompt and pregnant;°   *ready*
But I can tell that in each grace of these
There lurks a still and dumb-discoursive° devil   *silently communicating*
90   That tempts most cunningly. But be not tempted.
CRESSIDA   Do you think I will?
TROILUS   No, but something may be done that we will not,°   *do not want; do not will*
And sometimes we are devils to ourselves
When we will tempt the frailty of our powers,
95   Presuming on their changeful potency.°   *unreliable strength*
AENEAS *(within)*   Nay, good my lord!
TROILUS   Come, kiss, and let us part.
PARIS *(within)*   Brother Troilus!
TROILUS   Good brother, come you hither,
And bring Aeneas and the Grecian with you.
CRESSIDA   My lord, will you be true?
100   TROILUS   Who, I? Alas, it is my vice, my fault.
Whiles others fish with craft° for great opinion,°   *guile / reputation*
I with great truth catch mere simplicity;[7]
Whilst some with cunning gild their copper crowns,°   *coins; heads*
With truth and plainness I do wear° mine bare.   *dress; erode*
105   Fear not my truth; the moral° of my wit   *maxim*
Is "plain and true"—there's all the reach of it.
        Enter [DIOMEDES, AENEAS, PARIS, DEIPHOBUS,
        and Antenor].
Welcome, Sir Diomed. Here is the lady
Which for Antenor we deliver you.
At the port,° lord, I'll give her to thy hand,   *gate of the city*
110   And by the way possess° thee what she is.   *instruct*
Entreat° her fair, and by my soul, fair Greek,   *Treat*
If e'er thou stand at mercy of my sword,
Name Cressid and thy life shall be as safe
As Priam is in Ilium.
DIOMEDES   Fair lady Cressid,
115   So please you, save the thanks this prince expects.[8]
The luster in your eye, heaven in your cheek
Pleads your fair usage,° and to Diomed   *treatment*
You shall be mistress and command him wholly.
TROILUS   Grecian, thou dost not use me courteously
120   To shame the seal of my petition to thee
I'praising her. I tell thee, lord of Greece:
She is as far high-soaring o'er thy praises
As thou unworthy to be called her servant.[9]
I charge thee, use her well, even for my charge,°   *simply at my command*
125   For, by the dreadful Pluto, if thou dost not,
Though the great bulk Achilles be thy guard,
I'll cut thy throat.
DIOMEDES   Oh, be not moved,° Prince Troilus.   *angry*
Let me be privileged by my place and message
To be a speaker free; when I am hence
130   I'll answer to my lust.° And know, my lord,   *do as I please*
I'll nothing do on charge°—to her own worth   *command*

---

7. Am known for complete sincerity (innocence).   for the good treatment I will give you.
8. *save . . . expects:* you won't need to thank Troilus   9. Like "mistress" (line 118), a cliché of courtly love.

She shall be prized; but that° you say "Be't so,"   *simply because*
I'll speak it in my spirit and honor: "No."
TROILUS   Come to the port. I'll tell thee, Diomed,
135   This brave° shall oft make thee to hide thy head.   *boast*
—Lady, give me your hand, and as we walk
To our own selves bend we our needful talk.
                    [*Exeunt* TROILUS, CRESSIDA, *and* DIOMEDES.]
                    Sound trumpet.
PARIS   Hark, Hector's trumpet!
AENEAS   How have we spent this morning!
The Prince must think me tardy and remiss
140   That swore to ride before him in the field.
PARIS   'Tis Troilus' fault. Come, come, to field with him.
DEIPHOBUS   Let us make ready straight.
AENEAS   Yea, with a bridegroom's fresh alacrity
Let us address° to tend on Hector's heels.   *prepare*
145   The glory of our Troy doth this day lie
On his fair worth and single chivalry.   *Exeunt.*

4.5a (Q 4.5)

Enter AJAX *armed,* ACHILLES, PATROCLUS,
AGAMEMNON, MENELAUS, ULYSSES, NESTOR[, *and*
a Trumpeter, with others].
AGAMEMNON   Here art thou in appointment° fresh and fair,   *equipment*
Anticipating time.[1] With starting° courage   *bounding*
Give with thy trumpet a loud note to Troy,
Thou dreadful° Ajax, that the appallèd air   *causing fear*
5   May pierce the head of the great combatant
And hale° him hither.   *draw*
AJAX   Thou, trumpet,° there's my purse.   *Trumpeter*
Now crack thy lungs and split thy brazen pipe;°   *trumpet; windpipe*
Blow, villain,° till thy spherèd bias° cheek   *servant / puffed-out*
Out-swell the colic of puffed Aquilon.[2]
10   Come, stretch thy chest and let thy eyes spout blood—
Thou blowest for Hector.
                    [*Trumpet sounds.*]
ULYSSES   No trumpet answers.
ACHILLES   'Tis but early days.°   *early in the day*
                    [*Enter* DIOMEDES *and* CRESSIDA.]
AGAMEMNON   Is not yon Diomed, with Calchas' daughter?
ULYSSES   'Tis he; I ken° the manner of his gait: *recognize*
15   He rises on the toe. That spirit of his
In aspiration lifts him from the earth.
AGAMEMNON   Is this the lady Cressid?
DIOMEDES   Even she.
AGAMEMNON   Most dearly welcome to the Greeks, sweet lady.
                    [AGAMEMNON *kisses her.*][3]
NESTOR   Our general doth salute you with a kiss.
20   ULYSSES   Yet is the kindness but particular;°   *from only one of us*

4.5a Location: Between the Greek camp and Troy.
1. Ajax has not waited for Hector to appear with his
challenge.
2. Outswells the intestinal pain (from bloating) of
the north wind (Aquilon). (Winds on contemporary

maps were represented as human heads blowing.)
3. PERFORMANCE COMMENT For the importance of
how the ensuing kisses are performed (respectful, lustful), see Digital Edition PC 1.

'Twere better she were kissed in general.
NESTOR   And very courtly counsel; I'll begin.
     [NESTOR *kisses her.*]
  So much for Nestor.
ACHILLES   I'll take that winter° from your lips, fair lady.   *(Nestor's old age)*
     [ACHILLES *kisses her.*]
25 Achilles bids you welcome.
MENELAUS   I had good argument° for kissing once—   *(Helen)*
PATROCLUS   But that's no argument for kissing now,
  For thus popped° Paris in his hardiment.[4]   *thrust in*
     [PATROCLUS *kisses her.*]
ULYSSES   Oh, deadly gall and theme of all our scorns,
30 For which we lose our heads to gild his horns.°   *cuckold's horns*
PATROCLUS   The first was Menelaus' kiss, this mine.
     [PATROCLUS *kisses her again.*]
  Patroclus kisses you.
MENELAUS   Oh, this is trim.°   *excellent*
PATROCLUS   Paris and I kiss evermore° for him.°   *always / (Menelaus)*
MENELAUS   I'll have my kiss, sir. Lady, by your leave—
35 CRESSIDA   In kissing do you render or receive?
MENELAUS   Both take and give.
CRESSIDA   I'll make my match to live,°   *bet my life*
  The kiss you take is better than you give;
  Therefore, no kiss.
MENELAUS   I'll give you boot:° I'll give you three for one.   *profit*
40 CRESSIDA   You are an odd[5] man; give even or give none.
MENELAUS   An odd man, lady? Every man is odd.
CRESSIDA   No, Paris is not, for you know 'tis true
  That you are odd and he is even° with you.   *has gotten even*
MENELAUS   You fillip me o'th' head.[6]
CRESSIDA   No, I'll be sworn.
45 ULYSSES   It were no match, your nail against his horn.[7]
  May I, sweet lady, beg a kiss of you?
CRESSIDA   You may.
ULYSSES   I do desire it.
CRESSIDA   Why, beg then.
ULYSSES   Why then, for Venus' sake, give me a kiss
  When Helen is a maid again and his.°   *(Menelaus's)*
50 CRESSIDA   I am your debtor; claim it when 'tis due.
ULYSSES   Never's my day,° and then a kiss of you.   *the due date*
DIOMEDES   Lady, a word: I'll bring you to your father.
NESTOR   A woman of quick sense.°   *intelligence; sexuality*
ULYSSES   Fie, fie upon her!
  There's a language in her eye, her cheek, her lip—
55 Nay, her foot speaks; her wanton spirits look out°   *are exposed*
  At every joint and motive° of her body.   *moving limb*
  Oh, these encounterers,° so glib of tongue,   *flirtatious women*
  That give a coasting° welcome ere it comes   *an indirect*
  And wide unclasp the tables° of their thoughts   *tablets*
60 To every tickling° reader. Set them down°   *lustful / Mark them*

---

4. Bold hardness; erection.
5. *odd* (lines 40–43): strange; unique; left out; single (lacking a partner); opposite of "even" (line 43).
6. You tease me about being a cuckold (literally, you flick your fingernail on my head).

7. No contest, Cressida's fingernail against Menelaus's cuckold's horn (which is far harder and for Ulysses therefore justifies Cressida's denial that she's tapping him on the head).

For sluttish spoils of opportunity°   *As easy sexual prey*
And daughters of the game.°   *prostitutes*

        Exeunt [DIOMEDES *and* CRESSIDA].
   Flourish. Enter all of Troy: HECTOR [*armed*], PARIS,
      AENEAS, [TROILUS,] HELENUS, *and Attendants.*

ALL   The Trojans' trumpet!°   *(Trojan strumpet)*

AGAMEMNON   Yonder comes the troop.

AENEAS   Hail, all you state° of Greece. What shall be done°   *noblemen / rewarded*
65   To him that victory commands? Or do you purpose
A victor shall be known? Will you° the knights   *Do you wish that*
Shall to the edge of all extremity°   *death*
Pursue each other or shall be divided
By any voice or order of the field?[8]
Hector bade ask.

70 AGAMEMNON   Which way would Hector have it?

AENEAS   He cares not; he'll obey conditions.°   *your choice*

AGAMEMNON   'Tis done like Hector—but securely° done,   *too boldly*
A little proudly and great deal disprizing°   *underestimating*
The knight opposed.

AENEAS   —If not Achilles, sir,
What is your name?

75 ACHILLES   If not Achilles, nothing.

AENEAS   Therefore Achilles. But whate'er, know this:
In the extremity of great and little,
Valor and pride excel themselves in Hector—
The one° almost as infinite as all,   *(valor)*
80 The other° blank as nothing. Weigh him well,   *(pride)*
And that which looks like pride is courtesy.
This Ajax is half made of Hector's blood,[9]
In love whereof half Hector stays at home;
Half heart, half hand, half Hector comes to seek
85 This blended knight, half Trojan and half Greek.

ACHILLES   A maiden° battle, then? Oh, I perceive you.   *bloodless*
    [*Enter* DIOMEDES.]

AGAMEMNON   Here is Sir Diomed. Go, gentle knight,
Stand by our Ajax. As you and Lord Aeneas
Consent° upon the order° of their fight,   *Decide / terms*
90 So be it—either to the uttermost,
Or else a breath.°   *bout of exercise*
    [*Exeunt* HECTOR, AJAX, AENEAS, *and* DIOMEDES.]
       The combatants being kin
Half stints their strife before their strokes begin.

ULYSSES   They are opposed already.[1]

AGAMEMNON   What Trojan is that same that looks so heavy?°   *sorrowful*
95 ULYSSES   The youngest son of Priam,
A true knight; they call him Troilus.[2]
Not yet mature, yet matchless firm of word,
Speaking in deeds, and deedless in his tongue;°   *not boastful*
Not soon provoked, nor, being provoked, soon calmed;

---

8. By any umpire or rules of combat?
9. Ajax was Priam's nephew.
1. TEXTUAL COMMENT For possible differences between the staging of the combat in F and in Q—offstage in F, onstage in Q—see Digital Edition

TC 6 (Folio edited text).
2. TEXTUAL COMMENT For the possible link between the repetition of "they call him Troilus" (lines 96, 108) and the different staging possibilities of this scene, see Digital Edition TC 7 (Folio edited text).

100 His heart and hand both open and both free,°   *generous*
For what he has he gives, what thinks he shows,
Yet gives he not till judgment guide his bounty,°   *generosity*
Nor dignifies an impare° thought with breath;   *uneven; unfit; harmful*
Manly as Hector, but more dangerous,
105 For Hector in his blaze of wrath subscribes°   *relents*
To tender objects, but he in heat of action
Is more vindicative° than jealous love.   *vindictive*
They call him Troilus and on him erect
A second hope, as fairly built as Hector.
110 Thus says Aeneas, one that knows the youth
Even to his inches and with private soul³
Did in great Ilium thus translate° him to me.   *describe*
    Alarum.
AGAMEMNON   They are in action.
NESTOR   Now, Ajax, hold thine own!
115 TROILUS   Hector, thou sleep'st; awake thee!
AGAMEMNON   His blows are well disposed. There, Ajax!
                      [*Exeunt.*]

4.5b (Q 4.5)¹

[*Enter* HECTOR *and* AJAX, *fighting, with* AENEAS *and*
DIOMEDES *attempting to stop them.*] *Trumpets cease.*
DIOMEDES   You must no more.
AENEAS   Princes, enough, so please you.
AJAX   I am not warm yet; let us fight again.
DIOMEDES   As Hector pleases.
HECTOR   Why, then will I no more.
Thou art, great lord, my father's sister's son,
5 A cousin-german° to great Priam's seed.   *first cousin*
The obligation of our blood forbids
A gory emulation° twixt us twain.   *competition*
Were thy commixtion° Greek and Trojan so°   *blending / such*
That thou couldst say: "This hand is Grecian all,
10 And this is Trojan; the sinews of this leg
All Greek, and this all Troy; my mother's blood
Runs on the dexter° cheek, and this sinister°   *right / left*
Bounds in my father's," by Jove multipotent,°   *most powerful*
Thou shouldst not bear from me a Greekish member°   *part of the body*
15 Wherein my sword had not impressure made
Of our rank° feud. But the just gods gainsay°   *heated / prohibit*
That any drop thou borrowed'st from thy mother,
My sacred aunt, should by my mortal sword
Be drained. Let me embrace thee, Ajax.
20 By him that thunders,° thou hast lusty arms!   *(Jupiter)*
Hector would have them fall upon him thus.°   *in an embrace*
Cousin, all honor to thee.
AJAX   I thank thee, Hector.
Thou art too gentle and too free a man.
I came to kill thee, cousin, and bear hence
25 A great addition° earnèd in thy death.   *title*

---

3. *Even . . . soul*: In utmost detail and in confidence.
4.5b Location: Scene continues.
1. TEXTUAL COMMENT Most modern editions do not
mark a scene break here; this affects the numbering
of the following lines. See Digital Edition TC 6 (Folio
edited text).

HECTOR Not Neoptolemus² so mirable°—	wonderful
On whose bright crest° Fame with her loud'st oyez°	helmet / hear ye
Cries, "This is he!"—couldst promise to himself	
A thought of added honor torn from Hector.	
30 AENEAS There is expectance here from both the sides	
What further you will do.	
HECTOR We'll answer it:	
The issue° is embracement. Ajax, farewell.	conclusion
AJAX If I might in entreaties find success,	
As seld° I have the chance, I would desire	seldom
35 My famous cousin to our Grecian tents.	
DIOMEDES 'Tis Agamemnon's wish, and great Achilles	
Doth long to see unarmed the valiant Hector.	
HECTOR Aeneas, call my brother Troilus to me	
And signify this loving interview	
40 To the expecters of our Trojan part;°	awaiting Trojans
Desire them home.° —Give me thy hand, my cousin;	to go home
I will go eat with thee and see your knights.	

  Enter AGAMEMNON *and the rest*[: ULYSSES, TROILUS,
        ACHILLES, MENELAUS, *and* NESTOR].

AJAX Great Agamemnon comes to meet us here.	
HECTOR The worthiest of them° tell me name by name—	(the Greeks)
45 But for Achilles, mine own searching eyes	
Shall find him by his large and portly size.	
AGAMEMNON Worthy of arms! As welcome as to° one	as you can be to
That would be rid of such an enemy.	
But that's no welcome. Understand more clear:	
50 What's past and what's to come is strewed with husks	
And formless ruin of oblivion;	
But in this extant° moment, faith and troth,	present
Strained purely from all hollow bias-drawing,³	
Bids thee with most divine integrity,	
55 From heart of very heart, great Hector, welcome.	
HECTOR I thank thee, most imperious° Agamemnon.	imperial
AGAMEMNON [*to* TROILUS] My well-famed lord of Troy, no	
less to you.	
MENELAUS Let me confirm my princely brother's greeting:	
You brace° of warlike brothers, welcome hither.	pair
HECTOR Who must we answer?	
60 AENEAS The noble Menelaus.	
HECTOR Oh, you, my lord. By Mars his° gauntlet, thanks.	Mars's
Mock not that I affect° th'untraded° oath:	choose / unfamiliar
Your quondam° wife swears still by Venus' glove.⁴	former
She's well, but bade me not commend her to you.	
65 MENELAUS Name her not now, sir; she's a deadly theme.	
HECTOR Oh, pardon, I offend.	
NESTOR I have, thou gallant Trojan, seen thee oft,	
Laboring for destiny,⁵ make cruel way	
Through ranks of Greekish youth; and I have seen thee,	
70 As hot as Perseus,° spur thy Phrygian steed;	(on winged Pegasus)

---

2. Achilles' son Pyrrhus (but Shakespeare may have thought Neoptolemus was Achilles' surname).
3. Freed from all insincerity and indirectness.
4. *Venus' glove*: contrasting with Mars's gauntlet and alluding to Venus's adultery with Mars; possibly with an obscene innuendo.
5. Doing the Fates' work for them.

And seen thee scorning forfeits and subduements[6]
When thou hast hung° thy advancèd sword i'th' air,   *kept high*
Not letting it decline° on the declined,°   *fall / fallen*
That I have said unto my standers by,
75 "Lo, Jupiter is yonder, dealing life."[7]
And I have seen thee pause and take thy breath
When that a ring of Greeks have hemmed thee in
Like an Olympian° wrestling. This have I seen,   *a god*
But this thy countenance, still° locked in steel,   *always*
80 I never saw till now. I knew thy grandsire[8]
And once fought with him; he was a soldier good,
But by great Mars, the captain of us all,
Never like thee. Let an old man embrace thee,
And, worthy warrior, welcome to our tents.

85 AENEAS   'Tis the old Nestor.

HECTOR   Let me embrace thee, good old chronicle°   *record of history*
That hast so long walked hand in hand with time.
Most reverend Nestor, I am glad to clasp thee.

NESTOR   I would my arms could match thee in contention°   *in battle*
90 As they contend with thee in courtesy.

HECTOR   I would they could.

NESTOR   Ha?
By this white beard, I'd fight with thee tomorrow.
Well, welcome, welcome. I have seen the time.[9]

95 ULYSSES   I wonder now how yonder city stands
When we have here her base and pillar by us.

HECTOR   I know your favor,° Lord Ulysses, well.   *face*
Ah, sir, there's many a Greek and Trojan dead
Since first I saw yourself and Diomed
100 In Ilium on your Greekish embassy.

ULYSSES   Sir, I foretold you then what would ensue.
My prophecy is but half his journey yet,
For yonder walls that pertly front your town,
Yon towers whose wanton° tops do buss° the clouds,   *reckless; (sexual) / kiss*
Must kiss their own feet.

105 HECTOR   I must not believe you.
There they stand yet, and modestly I think
The fall of every Phrygian stone will cost
A drop of Grecian blood. The end crowns all,
And that old common arbitrator, Time,
Will one day end it.

110 ULYSSES   So to him we leave it.
Most gentle and most valiant Hector, welcome.
After the general, I beseech you next
To feast with me and see me at my tent.

ACHILLES   I shall forestall thee, Lord Ulysses, thou.[1]
115 —Now, Hector, I have fed mine eyes on thee;
I have with exact view perused° thee, Hector,   *minutely looked over*
And quoted° joint by joint.   *taken note*

HECTOR   Is this Achilles?

---

6. Scorning those whose lives might have been forfeit and (possible) conquests.
7. Giving life being the gods' prerogative.
8. Laomedon, builder of Troy's walls.
9. That is, the time when I could have met you in combat. (Nestor takes Hector's "I would they could," line 91, as a put-down.)
1. Insulting use of the second person familiar—"thee" (Ulysses), "thou" (Hector).

ACHILLES I am Achilles.
HECTOR Stand fair,° I prithee; let me look on thee.   *open to view*
ACHILLES Behold thy fill.
120 HECTOR   Nay, I have done already.
ACHILLES Thou art too brief. I will the second time,
    As° I would buy thee, view thee limb by limb.   *As though*
HECTOR Oh, like a book of sport° thou'lt read me o'er;   *hunting manual*
    But there's more in me than thou understand'st.
125 Why dost thou so oppress² me with thine eye?
ACHILLES Tell me, you heavens, in which part of his body
    Shall I destroy him—whether there, or there, or there—
    That I may give the local wound a name
    And make distinct the very breach whereout
130 Hector's great spirit flew. Answer me, heavens.
HECTOR It would discredit the blest gods, proud man,
    To answer such a question. Stand again;°   *Let me look again*
    Think'st thou to catch my life so pleasantly°   *easily*
    As to prenominate° in nice° conjecture   *name in advance / exact*
    Where thou wilt hit me dead?
135 ACHILLES   I tell thee, yea.
HECTOR Wert thou the oracle to tell me so,
    I'd not believe thee. Henceforth guard thee well,
    For I'll not kill thee there, nor there, nor there,
    But, by the forge that stithied° Mars his helm,   *forged*
140 I'll kill thee everywhere—yea, o'er and o'er.
    You wisest Grecians, pardon me this brag;
    His insolence draws folly from my lips,
    But I'll endeavor deeds to match these words,
    Or may I never—
AJAX   Do not chafe thee,° cousin.   *get angry*
145 And you, Achilles, let these threats alone
    Till accident or purpose bring you to't.
    You may every day enough of Hector
    If you have stomach.° The general state, I fear,   *appetite*
    Can scarce entreat you to be odd with him.³
150 HECTOR I pray you, let us see you in the field.
    We have had pelting° wars since you refused   *paltry*
    The Grecians' cause.
ACHILLES   Dost thou entreat me, Hector?
    Tomorrow do I meet thee, fell as death.
    Tonight, all friends.
HECTOR   Thy hand upon that match.
155 AGAMEMNON First, all you peers of Greece, go to my tent—
    There in the full convive you.° Afterwards,   *feast together*
    As Hector's leisure and your bounties shall
    Concur together, severally entreat° him.   *individually invite*
    Beat loud the taborins,° let the trumpets blow,   *small drums*
160 That this great soldier may his welcome know.
        [*Trumpets and drums.*]
                Exeunt [*all but* TROILUS *and* ULYSSES].
TROILUS My lord Ulysses, tell me, I beseech you,

---

2. Molest; in heraldry, place a perpendicular or diago-
nal stripe across an animal (continuing the metaphor
of Hector as a hunted animal from "book of sport,"
line 123).
3. I fear that the Greek leaders can hardly get you to
oppose him.

In what place of the field doth Calchas keep?°   *reside*
ULYSSES   At Menelaus' tent, most princely Troilus.
There Diomed doth feast with him tonight,
165   Who neither looks on heaven nor on earth,
But gives all gaze and bent° of amorous view   *inclination*
On the fair Cressid.
TROILUS   Shall I, sweet lord, be bound to thee so much,
After we part from Agamemnon's tent,
To bring me thither?
170   ULYSSES   You shall command me, sir.
As gentle° tell me: of what honor was   *Just as courteously*
This Cressida in Troy? Had she no lover there
That wails her absence?
TROILUS   O sir, to such as boasting show their scars°   *brag of past wounds*
175   A mock is due. Will you walk on, my lord?
She was beloved, she loved, she is and doth;
But still sweet love is food for Fortune's tooth.   *Exeunt.*

5.1 (Q 5.1)
Enter ACHILLES *and* PATROCLUS.
ACHILLES   I'll heat his blood with Greekish wine tonight,
Which with my scimitar I'll cool° tomorrow.   *expose to air*
Patroclus, let us feast him to the height.
PATROCLUS   Here comes Thersites.
Enter THERSITES.
ACHILLES   How now, thou core° of envy,   *(of an ulcer)*
5   Thou crusty batch[1] of nature, what's the news?
THERSITES   Why, thou picture° of what thou seem'st and idol   *mere image*
of idiot-worshippers, here's a letter for thee.
ACHILLES   From whence, fragment?°   *scrap of leftovers*
THERSITES   Why, thou full dish of fool,[2] from Troy.
[ACHILLES *stands aside to read the letter.*]
10   PATROCLUS   Who keeps the tent now?[3]
THERSITES   The surgeon's box, or the patient's wound.
PATROCLUS   Well said, adversity.° And what need these tricks?   *perversity*
THERSITES   Prithee be silent, boy; I profit not by thy talk.
Thou art thought to be Achilles' male varlet.°   *servant; lover*
15   PATROCLUS   Male varlet, you rogue? What's that?
THERSITES   Why, his masculine whore. Now the rotten diseases of the south, guts-griping, ruptures, catarrhs, loads
o'gravel i'th' back, lethargies, cold palsies,[4] and the like, take
and take again such preposterous discoveries.°   *revealed sodomy*
20   PATROCLUS   Why, thou damnable box of envy, thou, what
mean'st thou to curse thus?
THERSITES   Do I curse thee?
PATROCLUS   Why, no,[5] you ruinous butt,° you whoreson indis-   *leaky tub*
tinguishable cur.°   *formless beast*

5.1. Location: The Greek camp, near Achilles' tent.
1. You scab-encrusted (bad-tempered) boil.
2. Punning on the name of a dessert, probably clotted cream or egg custard.
3. Who stays in the tent now? Thersites can no longer taunt Achilles for remaining indoors. But Thersites deliberately mistakes Patroclus to mean the surgeon's probe or lint used to clean a wound.
4. These may be separate diseases, but they can nearly

all be symptoms of venereal disease. *south*: referring to the arrival of venereal disease in Europe after the Crusades and its association with Italy, particularly Naples. *guts-griping*: colic. *ruptures*: hernias. *catarrhs*: nose or throat infections. *loads . . . back*: kidney stones. *lethargies*: inertia. *palsies*: paralysis.
5. Sarcastic, since Thersites obviously is cursing him; also, perhaps denying the charge of homosexuality.

25 THERSITES No? Why art thou then exasperate,° thou idle   *irritated*
       immaterial skein of sleaved silk, thou green sarcenet flap[6] for
       a sore eye,[7] thou tassel of a prodigal's purse, thou? Ah, how
       the poor world is pestered with such waterflies°—diminutives   *tiny, flashy insects*
       of nature.
30 PATROCLUS Out, gall!
    THERSITES Finch egg!°   *small, gaudy egg*
    ACHILLES [*coming forward*]   My sweet Patroclus, I am
       thwarted quite
    From my great purpose in tomorrow's battle.
    Here is a letter from Queen Hecuba,
35 A token from her daughter, my fair love,
    Both taxing° me and gaging° me to keep   *reproving / binding*
    An oath that I have sworn. I will not break it.
    Fall Greeks, fail fame, honor or° go or stay,   *either*
    My major vow lies here; this I'll obey.
40 Come, come, Thersites; help to trim° my tent.   *decorate*
    This night in banqueting must all be spent.
    Away, Patroclus.   *Exeunt* [ACHILLES *and* PATROCLUS].
    THERSITES With too much blood° and too little brain, these   *passion*
       two may run mad, but if with too much brain and too little
45   blood they do, I'll be a curer of madmen.[8] Here's° Agamem-   *Take*
       non, an honest fellow enough, and one that loves quails,° but   *(as food); prostitutes*
       he has not so much brain as earwax; and the goodly transfor-
       mation of Jupiter there—the bull,[9] the primitive°   *archetypal*
       statue and oblique° memorial of cuckolds, a thrifty shoeing-   *perverse*
50   horn in a chain, hanging at his brother's leg[1]—to what form
       but that° he is should wit larded with malice and malice   *other than what*
       farced° with wit turn him to?° To an ass were nothing—he is   *stuffed / transform*
       both ass and ox; to an ox were nothing—he is both ox and ass.   *him into*
       To be a dog, a mule, a cat, a fitchew,[2] a toad, a lizard, an owl,
55   a puttock,° or a herring without a roe° I would not care, but to *small hawk / of no value*
       be Menelaus I would conspire against destiny. Ask me not
       what I would be if I were not Thersites, for I care not to be°   *wouldn't mind being*
       the louse of a lazar, so[3] I were not Menelaus. Hey-day, spirits
       and fires![4]
              Enter HECTOR, [TROILUS,] AJAX, AGAMEMNON,
              [MENELAUS,] ULYSSES, NESTOR, DIOMEDES, *with lights.*
    AGAMEMNON We go wrong, we go wrong.
60 AJAX   No, yonder 'tis,
    There where we see the light.
    HECTOR   I trouble you.
    AJAX No, not a whit.
              Enter ACHILLES.
    ULYSSES   Here comes himself° to guide you.   *the man himself*
    ACHILLES Welcome, brave Hector; welcome, princes all.
    AGAMEMNON So now, fair prince of Troy, I bid good night.

---

6. *thou idle . . . flap:* you insubstantial fine silk thread,
you immature patch of silk fabric.
7. Possible symptom of venereal disease.
8. Paradoxes and improbabilities: Achilles and
Patroclus going mad from excess intellect and insuf-
ficient passion, and Thersites curing them.
9. Jupiter made himself into a bull to rape Europa;
but Menelaus is bull-like for almost the opposite reason—he has the horns of a cuckold.

1. A convenient tool (the shoehorn, suggested by the
cuckold's horn, was sometimes worn on "a chain")
available to serve Agamemnon; also, always underfoot.
2. Polecat (proverbially lecherous and stinking).
3. The louse of a leper, as long as.
4. The Greeks approach with torches, suggesting
night; Thersites imagines them to be light-bearing
spirits.

65   Ajax commands the guard to tend on you.
HECTOR   Thanks and good night to the Greeks' general.
MENELAUS   Good night, my lord.
HECTOR   Good night, sweet Lord Menelaus.
THERSITES [aside]   Sweet draft!⁵ "Sweet," quoth 'a?° Sweet sink,°   *he / cesspool*
70   sweet sewer.
ACHILLES   Good night and welcome, both at once, to those
    That go or tarry.
AGAMEMNON   Good night.   [*Exeunt* AGAMEMNON *and*
                                       MENELAUS.]
ACHILLES   Old Nestor tarries—and you too, Diomed,
75   Keep Hector company an hour or two.
DIOMEDES   I cannot, lord; I have important business,
    The tide° whereof is now. —Good night, great Hector.   *time*
HECTOR   Give me your hand.   [*Exit* DIOMEDES.]
ULYSSES [aside to TROILUS]   Follow his torch; he goes to
    Calchas' tent.
    I'll keep you company.
80 TROILUS   Sweet sir, you honor me.
                  [*Exeunt* TROILUS *and* ULYSSES.]
HECTOR   And so good night.
ACHILLES   Come, come, enter my tent.
        Exeunt [ACHILLES, HECTOR, AJAX, *and* NESTOR].
THERSITES   That same Diomed's a false-hearted rogue, a most
    unjust knave. I will no more trust him when he leers° than I   *smiles*
    will a serpent when he hisses. He will spend his mouth and
85   promise like Babbler the hound, but when he performs
    astronomers foretell it—that it is prodigious; there will come
    some change.⁶ The sun borrows of the moon⁷ when Diomed
    keeps his word. I will rather leave to see Hector than not to
    dog him.⁸ They say he keeps a Trojan drab° and uses the   *whore*
90   traitor Calchas his° tent. I'll after. Nothing but lechery—all   *Calchas's*
    incontinent varlets!   *Exit.*

5.2 (Q 5.2)

  Enter DIOMEDES.
DIOMEDES   What, are you up here, ho? Speak!
CALCHAS [within]   Who calls?
DIOMEDES   Diomed. Calchas, I think. Where's your daughter?
CALCHAS [within]   She comes to you.
  Enter TROILUS *and* ULYSSES [*at a distance, and after*
  them, THERSITES].
5 ULYSSES   Stand where the torch may not discover° us.   *disclose*
  Enter CRESSIDA.
TROILUS   Cressid comes forth to him.
DIOMEDES   How now, my charge?
CRESSIDA   Now, my sweet guardian, hark, a word with you.
    [*She whispers to him.*]

---

5. Drink; team of beasts used for pulling wagons; cesspool, toilet.
6. *He will . . . change:* He will bark and "promise" (that there is prey) like a hound that is noisy (quarrelsome), even when off the scent, but when he actually "performs" (acts in good faith, keeps his word), astronomers make predictions on that basis: it is such a rare event that they consider it an ominous warning of a cosmic happening (often indicative of massive political upheaval).
7. It was well known that the moon's light was merely a reflection of the sun's.
8. I'll stop seeing Hector rather than give up tailing Diomedes.
5.2 Location: Outside Calchas's tent.

TROILUS	Yea, so familiar?	
ULYSSES	She will sing any man at first sight.[1]	
10 THERSITES	And any man may sing her, if he can take her clef;	
	she's noted.[2]	
DIOMEDES	Will you remember?	
CRESSIDA	Remember? Yes.	
DIOMEDES	Nay, but do then,	
15	And let your mind be coupled with your words.	
TROILUS	What should she remember?	
ULYSSES	List!°	*Listen*
CRESSIDA	Sweet honey Greek, tempt me no more to folly.°	*promiscuity*
THERSITES	Roguery!	
20 DIOMEDES	Nay, then.	
CRESSIDA	I'll tell you what—	
DIOMEDES	Faugh, faugh, come, tell a pin;° you are a forsworn—	*tell me nothing*
CRESSIDA	In faith, I cannot.° What would you have me do?	*(do as I promised)*
THERSITES	A juggling trick, to be secretly open.[3]	
25 DIOMEDES	What did you swear you would bestow on me?	
CRESSIDA	I prithee do not hold me to mine oath;	
	Bid me do anything but that, sweet Greek.	
DIOMEDES	Good night.	
TROILUS	Hold, patience.	
30 ULYSSES	How now, Trojan?	
CRESSIDA	Diomed—	
DIOMEDES	No, no, good night. I'll be your fool no more.	
TROILUS	Thy better must.°	*(be Cressida's fool)*
CRESSIDA	Hark, one word in your ear.	
35 TROILUS	Oh, plague and madness!	
ULYSSES	You are moved, Prince. Let us depart, I pray you,	
	Lest your displeasure should enlarge itself	
	To wrathful terms. This place is dangerous,	
	The time right deadly; I beseech you, go.	
TROILUS	Behold, I pray you.	
40 ULYSSES	Nay, good my lord, go off.	
	You flow° to great distraction. Come, my lord.	*rise; flood*
TROILUS	I pray thee, stay.	
ULYSSES	You have not patience; come.	
TROILUS	I pray you, stay. By hell and hell-torments,	
	I will not speak a word.	
DIOMEDES	And so good night.	
CRESSIDA	Nay, but you part in anger.	
45 TROILUS	Doth that grieve thee?	
	Oh, withered truth!	
ULYSSES	Why, how now, lord?	
TROILUS	By Jove,	
	I will be patient.	
CRESSIDA	Guardian? Why, Greek—	
DIOMEDES	Faugh, faugh, adieu, you palter.°	*equivocate*
CRESSIDA	In faith, I do not. Come hither once again.	
50 ULYSSES	You shake, my lord, at something; will you go?	

---

1. As in sight-reading of music; Cressida does not need to know the man beforehand to play (upon) him. 2. *if . . . noted:* if he can find her musical key (also, her cleft, or pudenda). She's like music written down; she's note-orious. 3. *juggling:* often meant sexual dexterity. *open:* public; available for sexual intercourse.

You will break out.

TROILUS　　　　　　　She strokes his cheek!

ULYSSES　　　　　　　　　　　　　Come, come.

TROILUS　Nay, stay. By Jove, I will not speak a word.

There is between my will and all offenses°　　　　　*any bad deeds*

A guard° of patience. Stay a little while.　　　　　*barrier*

55　THERSITES　How the devil Luxury° with his fat rump and　　　*Lust*

potato[4] finger tickles these together. Fry, lechery, fry![5]

DIOMEDES　But will you, then?

CRESSIDA　In faith I will, la; never trust me else.

DIOMEDES　Give me some token for the surety of it.

60　CRESSIDA　I'll fetch you one.　　　　　　　　　*Exit.*

ULYSSES　You have sworn patience.

TROILUS　　　　　　　　　　　Fear me not, sweet lord.

I will not be myself, nor have cognition°　　　　　*awareness*

Of what I feel. I am all patience.

　　　Enter CRESSIDA [*with Troilus' sleeve*].

THERSITES　Now the pledge, now, now, now!

65　CRESSIDA　Here, Diomed, keep this sleeve.

　　　[*She gives him the sleeve.*]

TROILUS　O beauty, where is thy faith?

ULYSSES　　　　　　　　　　　My lord—

TROILUS　I will be patient; outwardly I will.

CRESSIDA　You look upon that sleeve; behold it well.

He loved me—O false wench! Give't me again.

　　　[*She takes it back from him.*]

70　DIOMEDES　Whose was't?

CRESSIDA　It is no matter, now I have't again.

I will not meet with you tomorrow night.

I prithee, Diomed, visit me no more.

THERSITES　Now she sharpens.[6] Well said, whetstone!

DIOMEDES　I shall have it.

CRESSIDA　　　　　　　What, this?

75　DIOMEDES　　　　　　　　　　　Ay, that.

CRESSIDA　O all you gods! Oh, pretty, pretty pledge.

Thy master now lies thinking in his bed

Of thee and me, and sighs, and takes my glove,

And gives memorial° dainty kisses to it,　　　　　*in remembrance*

As I kiss thee.

　　　[*As she is kissing the sleeve,* DIOMEDES *takes it from*

　　　her; she tries to get it back.]

80　DIOMEDES　　　　　　Nay, do not snatch it from me.

CRESSIDA　He that takes that takes my heart withal.

DIOMEDES　I had your heart before; this follows it.

TROILUS　I did swear patience.

CRESSIDA　You shall not have it, Diomed, faith, you shall not.

85　I'll give you something else.

DIOMEDES　I will have this. Whose was it?

CRESSIDA　It is no matter.

DIOMEDES　Come, tell me whose it was.

CRESSIDA　'Twas one that loved me better than you will.

---

4. The Spanish, or sweet, potato was thought to be　5. In the fires of lust and of hell.
an aphrodisiac.　　　　　　　　　　　　　　6. Becomes harsh; whets his desire.

. But now you have it, take it.

90 DIOMEDES   Whose was it?

CRESSIDA   By all Diana's waiting-women[7] yond,
  And by herself, I will not tell you whose.

DIOMEDES   Tomorrow will I wear it on my helm
  And grieve° his spirit that dares not challenge it.   afflict

95 TROILUS   Wert thou the devil and wor'st it on thy horn
  It should be challenged.

CRESSIDA   Well, well, 'tis done, 'tis past—and yet it is not;
  I will not keep my word.

DIOMEDES   Why then, farewell;
  Thou never shalt mock Diomed again.

100 CRESSIDA   You shall not go. One cannot speak a word
  But it straight starts you.°   makes you run off

DIOMEDES   I do not like this fooling.

THERSITES   Nor I, by Pluto, but that that likes not you° pleases   that which you dislike
  me best.

DIOMEDES   What, shall I come? The hour?

105 CRESSIDA   Ay, come. O Jove, do come! I shall be plagued.[8]

DIOMEDES   Farewell till then.

CRESSIDA   Good night. I prithee, come.
                                    Exit [DIOMEDES].

  Troilus, farewell. One eye yet looks on thee,
  But with my heart the other eye° doth see.°   *(pun on "I") / (Diomedes)*
  Ah, poor our° sex! This fault in us I find: our poor
110 The error of our eye directs our mind.
  What error° leads must err—oh, then conclude: wandering
  Minds swayed by eyes are full of turpitude.   *Exit.*

THERSITES   A proof of strength she could not publish more,[9]
  Unless she say, "My mind is now turned whore."

ULYSSES   All's done, my lord.

TROILUS   It is.

115 ULYSSES   Why stay we then?

TROILUS   To make a recordation to my soul
  Of every syllable that here was spoke.
  But if I tell how these two did co-act,
  Shall I not lie in publishing a truth,
120 Sith yet there is a credence in my heart,
  An esperance° so obstinately strong,   hope
  That doth invert th'attest° of eyes and ears,   reverse the testimony
  As if those organs had deceptious° functions,   deceptive
  Created only to calumniate?
  Was Cressid here?

125 ULYSSES   I cannot conjure,° Trojan.   produce a ghost

TROILUS   She was not, sure.

ULYSSES   Most sure she was.

TROILUS   Why, my negation hath no taste of madness.

ULYSSES   Nor mine, my lord: Cressid was here but now.

TROILUS   Let it not be believed, for° womanhood.   for the sake of
130 Think, we had mothers; do not give advantage

---

7. The stars (Diana being the goddess of the moon
and, ironically, of chastity).
8. Vexed; teased (but also alluding to her eventual
fate in late medieval narrative, as a leper). See the

Introduction.
9. She could not make a strong proof known more
clearly.

To stubborn critics, apt without a theme
For deprivation,[1] to square the general sex
By Cressid's rule.[2] Rather, think this not Cressid.

ULYSSES   What hath she done, Prince, that can soil our
    mothers?

135 TROILUS   Nothing at all, unless that this were she.

THERSITES   Will he swagger himself out on 's own eyes?[3]

TROILUS   This she? No, this is Diomed's Cressida.
If beauty have a soul, this is not she;
If souls guide vows, if vows are sanctimony,°   *sacred things*
140 If sanctimony° be the gods' delight,   *sanctity*
If there be rule in unity itself,°   *unity is indivisible*
This is not she. Oh, madness of discourse°   *reason*
That cause[4] sets up with and against itself—
Bifold authority, where reason can revolt
145 Without perdition and loss assume all reason
Without revolt.[5] This is and is not Cressid.
Within my soul there doth conduce° a fight   *come together*
Of this strange nature, that a thing inseparate°   *indivisible*
Divides more wider than the sky and earth,
150 And yet the spacious breadth of this division
Admits no orifex° for a point as subtle°   *orifice / fine*
As Ariachne's[6] broken woof° to enter.   *weaving thread*
Instance,° O instance, strong as Pluto's gates: *Evidence*
Cressid is mine, tied with the bonds of heaven.
155 Instance, O instance, strong as heaven itself:
The bonds of heaven are slipped, dissolved, and loosed,
And with another knot, five-finger-tied,[7]
The fractions° of her faith, orts° of her love,   *pieces / leftover scraps*
The fragments, scraps, the bits, and greasy relics
160 Of her o'er-eaten° faith are bound to Diomed. *eaten-away; surfeited*

ULYSSES   May worthy Troilus be half attached
    With that which here his passion doth express?[8]

TROILUS   Ay, Greek, and that shall be divulgèd well
In characters as red as Mars his° heart   *Mars's*
165 Inflamed with Venus. Never did young man fancy° *love*
With so eternal and so fixed a soul.
Hark, Greek: as much as I do Cressida love,
So much by weight hate I her Diomed.
That sleeve is mine that he'll bear in his helm;
170 Were it a casque° composed by Vulcan's[9] skill, *helmet*
My sword should bite it. Not the dreadful spout
Which shipmen do the hurricano° call,   *waterspout*

---

1. Depriving women of their reputation.
2. *to square . . . rule:* to measure all women by the standard of Cressida.
3. Will he bluster himself out of (the evidence of) his own eyes?
4. Case; plea (where, here, defendant and plaintiff are one).
5. *Bifold . . . revolt:* Perhaps: Divided authority, where reason (belief in the testimony of the senses) can revolt against itself (by claiming that this is not in fact Cressida) without being accused of loss of reason ("perdition"); and where loss of reason (inability to trust the senses), without rebelling against reason, can lay claim to being the highest form of reason precisely because the sensual evidence, which ought

to be the highest form of reason, lies (because this cannot be Cressida).
6. A conflation of Arachne the weaver, turned into a spider by Athena for overweening pride in her work, and Ariadne, who gave Theseus a ball of thread to mark his way out of the Labyrinth of her father.
7. United by human hands (Cressida's and Diomedes'), as opposed to "the bonds of heaven" (line 154); evilly consummated (alluding to the devil's five fingers, symbolizing the steps to lechery).
8. *May . . . express:* Can worthy Troilus be even half as affected as he seems to be?
9. Smith of the gods, Vulcan made armor for various classical heroes, most notably Achilles.

Constringed° in mass by the almighty sun,   *Drawn together*
Shall dizzy° with more clamor Neptune's ear   *stun*
175   In his descent than shall my prompted° sword   *eager*
Falling on Diomed.
THERSITES   He'll tickle it for his concupy!¹
TROILUS   O Cressid! O false Cressid—false, false, false!
Let all untruths stand by° thy stainèd name,   *be compared with*
And they'll seem glorious.
180   ULYSSES   Oh, contain yourself;
Your passion draws ears hither.
                    Enter AENEAS.
AENEAS   I have been seeking you this hour, my lord.
Hector by this° is arming him in Troy.   *by this time*
Ajax, your guard, stays to conduct you home.
185   TROILUS   Have° with you, Prince. —My courteous lord, adieu.   *I shall come*
[*aside*] Farewell, revolted fair, and Diomed,
Stand fast and wear a castle° on thy head.   *strong defense*
ULYSSES   I'll bring you to the gates.
TROILUS   Accept distracted thanks.
                    Exeunt TROILUS, AENEAS, *and* ULYSSES.
THERSITES   Would I could meet that rogue Diomed; I would
190   croak like a raven,² I would bode, I would bode.°   *foretell evil*
will give me anything for the intelligence° of this whore— *secret information*
the parrot will not do more for an almond³ than he for a
commodious drab.° Lechery, lechery, still wars and lechery;   *willing whore*
nothing else holds fashion. A burning devil° take them!   *venereal disease*
                                            [*Exit.*]

5.3 (Q 5.3)
Enter HECTOR *and* ANDROMACHE.

ANDROMACHE   When was my lord so much ungently
        tempered
To stop his ears against admonishment?
Unarm, unarm, and do not fight today.
HECTOR   You train° me to offend you; get you gone.   *teach*
5   By the everlasting gods, I'll go.
ANDROMACHE   My dreams will sure prove ominous to the day.°   *true omens of the day*
HECTOR   No more, I say.
                    Enter CASSANDRA.
CASSANDRA   Where is my brother Hector?
ANDROMACHE   Here, sister, armed and bloody in intent.
Consort° with me in loud and dear° petition;   *Join / earnest*
10   Pursue we him on knees, for I have dreamt
Of bloody turbulence, and this whole night
Hath nothing been but shapes and forms of slaughter.
CASSANDRA   Oh, 'tis true.
HECTOR   Ho! Bid my trumpet sound!
CASSANDRA   No notes of sally, for the heavens, sweet brother.
15   HECTOR   Begone, I say; the gods have heard me swear.
CASSANDRA   The gods are deaf to hot and peevish° vows;   *headstrong*
They° are polluted off'rings, more abhorred   *(Rash vows)*

---

1. (Probably) Troilus will "tickle" (beat [ironic]) Dio-   3. *the parrot . . . almond:* proverbial for a brainless
medes' helmet for his lust (his concubine).   passion for a trivial delicacy.
2. Proverbially, birds of ill omen.   5.3 Location: Priam's palace.

Than spotted livers° in the sacrifice.	*ruined offerings*
ANDROMACHE Oh, be persuaded; do not count it holy[1]	
20 To hurt by being just°—it is as lawful,	*true to your vow*
For we would° give much, to use violent thefts,	*Because we want to*
And rob in the behalf of charity.	
CASSANDRA It is the purpose that makes strong the vow,	
But vows to every purpose must not° hold.	*do not have to*
Unarm, sweet Hector.	
25 HECTOR Hold you still,° I say.	*Stop it*
Mine honor keeps the weather of° my fate;	*counts for more than*
Life every man holds dear, but the dear° man	*worthy*
Holds honor far more precious-dear than life.	

Enter TROILUS.

How now, young man, mean'st thou to fight today?	
30 ANDROMACHE Cassandra, call my father° to persuade.	*father-in-law*

Exit CASSANDRA.

HECTOR No, faith, young Troilus, doff thy harness,° youth.	*disarm*
I am today i'th' vein of° chivalry;	*mood for*
Let grow thy sinews till their knots be strong,	
And tempt not yet the brushes° of the war.	*encounters*
35 Unarm thee, go, and doubt thou not, brave boy,	
I'll stand today for thee and me and Troy.	
TROILUS Brother, you have a vice of mercy in you	
Which better fits a lion[2] than a man.	
HECTOR What vice is that? Good Troilus, chide me for it.	
40 TROILUS When many times the captive° Grecian falls,	*miserable*
Even in the fan and wind of your fair sword,[3]	
You bid them rise and live.	
HECTOR Oh, 'tis fair play.	
TROILUS Fool's play, by heaven, Hector.	
HECTOR How now? How now?	
TROILUS For th' love of all the gods,	
45 Let's leave the hermit Pity with our mothers,	
And when we have our armors buckled on,	
The venomed vengeance ride upon our swords,	
Spur them to ruthful° work, rein them from ruth.°	*woeful / pity*
HECTOR Fie, savage, fie!	
TROILUS Hector, then 'tis wars.°	*then it's a true war*
50 HECTOR Troilus, I would not have you fight today.	
TROILUS Who should withhold me?	
Not fate, obedience, nor the hand of Mars	
Beck'ning with fiery truncheon[4] my retire;	
Not Priamus and Hecuba on knees,	
55 Their eyes o'er-gallèd° with recourse° of tears;	*sore / repeated flow*
Nor you, my brother, with your true sword drawn	
Opposed to hinder me, should stop my way,	
But by my ruin.	

Enter PRIAM *and* CASSANDRA.

CASSANDRA Lay hold upon him, Priam. Hold him fast.	

---

1. TEXTUAL COMMENT For the differences between this passage (lines 19–28) and the equivalent lines in Q, see Digital Edition TC 8 (Folio edited text).
2. Lions were said not to attack any animal that submitted to them.
3. The rapidly moving sword is like a fan, blowing his enemies down before he reaches them.
4. Staff of office (carried by the marshal of a formal combat).

60 He is thy crutch. Now if thou lose thy stay,°   *prop*
Thou on him leaning, and all Troy on thee,
Fall all together.
PRIAM   Come, Hector, come; go back.
Thy wife hath dreamt, thy mother hath had visions,
Cassandra doth foresee, and I myself
65 Am like a prophet suddenly enrapt°   *inspired*
To tell thee that this day is ominous.
Therefore, come back.
HECTOR   Aeneas is afield,
And I do stand engaged to many Greeks,
Even in the faith of valor,° to appear   *warrior's honor*
This morning to them.
70 PRIAM   Ay, but thou shalt not go.
HECTOR   I must not break my faith.
You know me dutiful; therefore, dear sir,
Let me not shame respect,° but give me leave   *duty to a parent*
To take that course by your consent and voice
75 Which you do here forbid me, royal Priam.
CASSANDRA   O Priam, yield not to him!
ANDROMACHE   Do not, dear father.
HECTOR   Andromache, I am offended with you.
Upon the love you bear me, get you in.   *Exit* ANDROMACHE.
TROILUS   This foolish, dreaming, superstitious girl
Makes all these bodements.°   *warnings*
80 CASSANDRA   Oh, farewell, dear Hector.
Look how thou diest, look how thy eye turns pale,
Look how thy wounds do bleed at many vents!
Hark, how Troy roars, how Hecuba cries out,
How poor Andromache shrills her dolor forth.
85 Behold: distraction, frenzy, and amazement,
Like witless antics,° one another meet,   *buffoons*
And all cry, "Hector, Hector's dead! O Hector!"
TROILUS   Away, away.
CASSANDRA   Farewell—yes, soft.° Hector, I take my leave;   *wait a moment*
90 Thou dost thyself and all our Troy deceive.   *Exit.*
HECTOR   You are amazed, my liege, at her exclaim.°   *outcry*
Go in and cheer the town. We'll forth and fight,
Do deeds of praise, and tell you them at night.
PRIAM   Farewell. The gods with safety stand about thee.
                 [*Exeunt* HECTOR *and* PRIAM *separately.*]
          Alarum.
95 TROILUS   They are at it, hark! Proud Diomed, believe:
I come to lose my arm or win my sleeve.
          Enter PANDARUS.
PANDARUS   Do you hear, my lord? Do you hear?
TROILUS   What now?
PANDARUS   Here's a letter come from yond poor girl.
100 TROILUS   Let me read.
          [TROILUS *reads the letter.*]
PANDARUS   A whoreson phthisic,° a whoreson rascally phthisic   *consumptive cough*
so troubles me, and the foolish fortune of this girl, and what
one thing, what another, that I shall leave you one o'these
days. And I have a rheum° in mine eyes too, and such an   *watery discharge*

105 ache in my bones° that, unless a man were cursed, I cannot   *(suggesting syphilis)*
tell what to think on't. —What says she there?

TROILUS   Words, words, mere words, no matter from the
     heart—

Th'effect° doth operate another way.   *Her action*
     [*He tears the letter.*]

Go, wind, to wind, there turn and change together.[5]

110 My love with words and errors° still she feeds,   *lies*
But edifies another with her deeds.

PANDARUS   Why, but hear you!

TROILUS   Hence, broker-lackey!° Ignomy° and shame   *pimp / Ignominy*
Pursue thy life, and live aye with thy name.

                  Exeunt [*separately*].[6]

5.4 (Q 5.4)

Alarum. Enter THERSITES [*in the midst of an*]
excursion.°   *advancing troops*

THERSITES   Now they are clapper-clawing° one another; I'll   *thrashing*
go look on. That dissembling abominable varlet, Diomed,
has got that same scurvy, doting, foolish young knave's
sleeve of Troy° there in his helm. I would fain see them   *Trojan knave's sleeve*
5 meet,[1] that that same young Trojan ass that loves the whore
there might send that Greekish whore-masterly villain with
the sleeve back to the dissembling luxurious drab of a sleeve-
less errand.[2] O'th' t'other side, the policy° of those crafty   *statecraft; scheming*
swearing rascals—that stale old mouse-eaten dry cheese,
10 Nestor, and that same dog-fox,° Ulysses—is not proved   *crafty one*
worth a blackberry.° They set me up° in policy that mongrel   *proved worthless / set up*
cur, Ajax, against that dog of as bad a kind, Achilles; and
now is the cur Ajax prouder than the cur Achilles and will
not arm today, whereupon the Grecians began to proclaim
15 barbarism,[3] and policy grows into an ill opinion.[4]

         Enter DIOMEDES[, *followed by*] TROILUS.

Soft! Here comes sleeve and th'other.

TROILUS   Fly not, for shouldst thou take the river Styx,[5]
I would swim after.

DIOMEDES   Thou dost miscall retire;°   *mistake my retreat*
I do not fly, but advantageous care°   *tactical caution*
20 Withdrew me from the odds of multitude.
Have at thee!

THERSITES   Hold thy whore, Grecian! Now for thy whore, Trojan! Now the sleeve, now the sleeve!

            [*Exeunt* TROILUS *and* DIOMEDES, *fighting.*]

         Enter HECTOR.

---

5. Go, empty words, into the breeze: there, along with
the air, toss about ("turn" was often used of sexual
infidelity).

6. TEXTUAL COMMENT See Digital Edition TC 9
(Folio edited text) for the textual and associated
generic problems raised by lines 112–14, which are
absent from the comparable point in Q but are
repeated at F 5.11.32–34 and appear, similarly, at Q
5.11.31–33.

5.4 Location: The rest of the play takes place on the
battlefield.

1. *fain see them meet:* rejoice to have them fight.
2. To the lying, lecherous slut on a pointless errand
(punning on the actual sleeve).
3. Began to set up ignorance (or anarchy) in authority ("barbarism" being normally contrasted with
"Greek"-ness).
4. *policy . . . opinion:* statecraft (or, more negatively,
cunning) gets a bad reputation.
5. Even if you should enter the river of the underworld (as prey go into the water hoping to make the
hunter lose the scent).

HECTOR   What art thou, Greek? Art thou for Hector's match?
25   Art thou of blood° and honor?   *nobility*
THERSITES   No, no, I am a rascal, a scurvy railing knave, a
   very filthy rogue.
HECTOR   I do believe thee. Live.[6]   [*Exit.*]
THERSITES   God-a-mercy° that thou wilt believe me, but a   *Thank God*
30   plague break thy neck for frighting me! What's become of
   the wenching rogues? I think they have swallowed one
   another. I would laugh at that miracle—yet, in a sort, lechery eats itself. I'll seek them.   *Exit.*

5.5 (Q 5.5)

Enter DIOMEDES *and* [SERVANT].

DIOMEDES   Go, go, my servant, take thou Troilus' horse;
   Present the fair steed to my lady Cressid.
   Fellow, commend my service to her beauty;
   Tell her I have chastised the amorous Trojan
   And am her knight by proof.°   *(of deeds)*
5   SERVANT   I go, my lord.   [*Exit.*]
   Enter AGAMEMNON.
AGAMEMNON   Renew, renew! The fierce Polydamas
   Hath beat down Menon; bastard Margarelon
   Hath Doreus prisoner
   And stands colossus-wise, waving his beam°   *spearshaft*
10   Upon the pashèd° corpses of the kings   *smashed*
   Epistrophus and Cedius. Polyxenes is slain,
   Amphimacus and Thoas deadly hurt,
   Patroclus ta'en or slain, and Palamedes
   Sore hurt and bruised. The dreadful sagittary[1]
15   Appalls our numbers.° Haste we, Diomed,   *soldiers*
   To reinforcement, or we perish all.
   Enter NESTOR [*and others*].
NESTOR   Go bear Patroclus' body to Achilles,
   And bid the snail-paced Ajax arm for shame.
                                        [*Exeunt some.*]
   There is a thousand Hectors in the field:
20   Now here he fights on Galathe his horse,
   And there lacks work; anon he's there afoot,
   And there they fly or die like scalèd schools[2]
   Before the belching° whale; then is he yonder,   *spouting*
   And there the strawy Greeks, ripe for his edge,°   *sword blade*
25   Fall down before him like the mower's swath.
   Here, there, and everywhere he leaves and takes,[3]
   Dexterity so obeying appetite
   That what he will he does, and does so much
   That proof° is called impossibility.   *his achievement*
   Enter ULYSSES.
30   ULYSSES   Oh, courage, courage, princes! Great Achilles
   Is arming, weeping, cursing, vowing vengeance.
   Patroclus' wounds have roused his drowsy blood,

---

6. Here, Hector is at once contemptuous and merciful.
5.5
1. A legendary centaurlike beast, armed with bow

and arrows.
2. Scaly (armor-clad) schools of fish.
3. He spares and kills; possibly, he "leaves" the dead
and "takes" on the living.

Together with his mangled Myrmidons,
That noseless, handless, hacked, and chipped come to him,

35 Crying on° Hector. Ajax hath lost a friend   *Complaining of*
And foams at mouth, and he is armed and at it,
Roaring for Troilus, who hath done today
Mad and fantastic execution,
Engaging and redeeming of° himself   *Risking and saving*

40 With such a careless force and forceless care,°   *effortless diligence*
As if that luck, in very spite of cunning,°   *his foes' skill*
Bade him win all.
   Enter AJAX.
AJAX Troilus, thou coward Troilus!   *Exit.*
DIOMEDES   Ay, there, there! *Exit.*
NESTOR So, so, we draw together.°   *join forces*
   Enter ACHILLES.
ACHILLES   Where is this Hector?

45 Come, come, thou boy-queller, show thy face;
Know what it is to meet Achilles angry.
Hector! Where's Hector? I will none but Hector. *Exeunt.*

5.6 (Q 5.6)

   Enter AJAX.
AJAX Troilus, thou coward Troilus, show thy head!
   Enter DIOMEDES.
DIOMEDES Troilus, I say! Where's Troilus?
AJAX   What wouldst thou?
DIOMEDES I would correct° him.   *chastise*
AJAX   Were I the general
Thou shouldst have my office

5 Ere° that correction. —Troilus, I say! What, Troilus! *Before you should have*
   Enter TROILUS.
TROILUS O traitor Diomed! Turn thy false face, thou traitor,
And pay the life thou owest me for my horse.
DIOMEDES Ha, art thou there?
AJAX I'll fight with him alone. Stand, Diomed.

10 DIOMEDES He is my prize; I will not look upon.° *be a spectator*
TROILUS Come, both you cogging° Greeks, have at you both! *cheating*
   Enter HECTOR.
    Exit TROILUS[, *fighting with* AJAX *and* DIOMEDES].
HECTOR Yea, Troilus! Oh, well fought, my youngest brother!
   Enter ACHILLES.
ACHILLES Now do I see thee; have at thee, Hector!
   [*They fight, and* ACHILLES *is subdued.*]
HECTOR Pause if thou wilt.

15 ACHILLES I do disdain thy courtesy, proud Trojan.
Be happy that my arms are out of use;°   *practice*
My rest and negligence befriends thee now,
But thou anon shalt hear of me again,
Till when, go seek thy fortune.   *Exit.*
HECTOR   Fare thee well.

20 I would have been much more a fresher man
Had I expected thee.
   Enter TROILUS.
      How now, my brother?
TROILUS Ajax hath ta'en° Aeneas. Shall it be?   *taken captive*

No, by the flame of yonder glorious heaven,
He shall not carry him. I'll be ta'en too,
25　Or bring him off.° Fate, hear me what I say:　　　　　　　　　*rescue Aeneas*
　　I reck° not though thou end my life today.　　　*Exit.*　　　*care*
　　　　Enter one in armor.
HECTOR　Stand, stand, thou Greek. Thou art a goodly mark.°　　*target*
　　No? Wilt thou not? I like thy armor well;
　　I'll frush° it and unlock the rivets all,　　　　　　　　　*smash*
　　But I'll be master of it.　　　　　　*[Exit one in armor.]*
30　　　　　　　　　Wilt thou not, beast, abide?
　　Why, then, fly on; I'll hunt thee for thy hide.　　*Exit.*

5.7 (Q 5.7)
　　　Enter ACHILLES *with* MYRMIDONS.
ACHILLES　Come here about me, you my Myrmidons.
　　Mark what I say: attend me where I wheel;°　　　　　　　*range*
　　Strike not a stroke, but keep yourselves in breath,
　　And when I have the bloody Hector found
5　Empale° him with your weapons round about;　　　　　　　*Fence in*
　　In fellest° manner execute your arms.　　　　　　　　　*fiercest*
　　Follow me, sirs, and my proceedings eye;
　　It is decreed Hector the great must die.　　　*Exeunt.*

5.8 (Q 5.8)
　　　Enter THERSITES, *[watching]* MENELAUS *and*
　　　PARIS *[fight].*
THERSITES　The cuckold and the cuckold-maker are at it. Now,
　　bull! Now, dog! 'Loo, Paris,¹ 'loo! Now, my double-henned
　　sparrow!² 'Loo Paris, 'loo. The bull has the game°—'ware°　*is winning / beware*
　　horns, ho!　　　　　　　　*Exeunt* PARIS *and* MENELAUS.
　　　　Enter BASTARD *[Margarelon].*
5　BASTARD　Turn, slave, and fight.
THERSITES　What art thou?
BASTARD　A bastard son of Priam's.
THERSITES　I am a bastard too. I love bastards! I am a bastard
　　begot, bastard instructed, bastard in mind, bastard in valor,
10　in everything illegitimate. One bear will not bite another,
　　and wherefore should one bastard? Take heed, the quarrel's
　　most ominous to us: if the son of a whore fight for a whore,
　　he tempts judgment. Farewell, bastard.　　　　　*[Exit.]*
BASTARD　The devil take thee, coward!　　　　　*Exit.*

5.9 (Q 5.9)
　　　Enter HECTOR.
HECTOR　Most putrifièd core,¹ so fair without,
　　Thy goodly armor thus hath cost thy life.
　　Now is my day's work done; I'll take good breath.
　　Rest, sword, thou hast thy fill of blood and death.

5.8
1. *'Loo:* Halloo (shout to encourage dogs chasing game
or in bullbaiting). *Paris:* the character; Paris Garden,
site of bullbaiting.
2. Paris is meek as a "sparrow" and "double-henned"

in possessing both Helen and a rejected wife.
5.9
1. Pun on French *corps* ("body"); hence, the "corpse"
of the fallen Greek.

[*He disarms.*]
Enter ACHILLES *and his* MYRMIDONS.

5 ACHILLES   Look, Hector, how the sun begins to set,
How ugly night comes breathing at his heels.
Even with the vail² and dark'ning of the sun
To close the day up, Hector's life is done.
HECTOR   I am unarmed. Forgo this vantage, Greek.
10 ACHILLES   Strike, fellows, strike; this is the man I seek.
[*They kill* HECTOR.]
So, Ilium, fall thou. Now, Troy, sink down—
Here lies thy heart, thy sinews, and thy bone.
On, Myrmidons, cry you all amain:°   *with full force*
"Achilles hath the mighty Hector slain!"
Retreat [*sounded*].
15 Hark, a retreat upon our Grecian part.
[*Another retreat sounded.*]
A MYRMIDON   The Trojan trumpets sounds the like, my lord.
ACHILLES   The dragon wing of night o'erspreads the earth
And stickler°-like the armies separates.   *referee (in combat)*
My half-supped° sword that frankly° would have fed,   *half-satisfied / freely*
20 Pleased with this dainty bait,° thus goes to bed.   *snack*
[*He sheathes his sword.*]
Come, tie his body to my horse's tail;
Along the field I will the Trojan trail.   *Exeunt.*

5.10 (Q 5.10)

Sound retreat. Enter AGAMEMNON, AJAX, MENELAUS,
NESTOR, DIOMEDES, *and the rest, marching.*
Shout [*within*].

AGAMEMNON   Hark, hark, what shout is that?
NESTOR   Peace, drums.
SOLDIERS [*within*]   Achilles, Achilles! Hector's slain!
Achilles!
DIOMEDES   The bruit° is Hector's slain, and by Achilles.   *report*
5 AJAX   If it be so, yet bragless let it be;
Great Hector was a man as good as he.
AGAMEMNON   March patiently along. Let one be sent
To pray Achilles see us at our tent.
If in his death the gods have us befriended,
10 Great Troy is ours, and our sharp° wars are ended. *Exeunt.*   *fierce*

5.11 (Q 5.11)

Enter AENEAS, PARIS, *Antenor, and* DEIPHOBUS.

AENEAS   Stand ho! Yet are we masters of the field.
Never go home; here starve we out the night.¹
Enter TROILUS.
TROILUS   Hector is slain.
ALL   Hector? The gods forbid!
TROILUS   He's dead, and at the murderer's horse's tail

---

2. At the same time as the setting.
5.11
1. Wait in discomfort; outlast, kill by starvation (the
night being imagined as a city under siege). TEXTUAL

COMMENT For the different consequences of attributing this line to Aeneas, here, or to Troilus, in Q, see
Digital Edition TC 10 (Folio edited text).

5	In beastly sort° dragged through the shameful field.	*manner*
	Frown on, you heavens; effect your rage with speed.	
	Sit, gods, upon your thrones and smile at Troy.	
	I say at once: let your brief plagues be mercy,[2]	
	And linger not our sure destructions on.	
10	AENEAS My lord, you do discomfort all the host.°	*army*
	TROILUS You understand me not that tell me so.	
	I do not speak of flight, of fear, of death,	
	But dare all imminence that gods and men	
	Address their dangers in.[3] Hector is gone.	
15	Who shall tell Priam so, or Hecuba?	
	Let him that will a screech-owl aye° be called	*voice of doom always*
	Go into Troy and say there, "Hector's dead."	
	There is a word° will Priam turn to stone,	*sentence that*
	Make wells and Niobes[4] of the maids and wives,	
20	Cold statues of the youth, and, in a word,	
	Scare Troy out of itself. But march away.	
	Hector is dead; there is no more to say.	
	Stay yet, you vile abominable tents	
	Thus proudly pitched upon our Phrygian plains.	
25	Let Titan° rise as early as he dare,	*sun god Hyperion*
	I'll through and through you. And thou great-sized	
	coward,°	*(Achilles)*
	No space of earth shall sunder our two hates.	
	I'll haunt thee like a wicked° conscience still°	*guilty / continually*
	That moldeth goblins swift as frenzy's thoughts.[5]	
30	Strike a free march to Troy, with comfort° go;	*this one comfort*
	Hope of revenge shall hide our inward woe.	
	Enter PANDARUS.	
	PANDARUS But hear you, hear you!	
	TROILUS Hence, broker-lackey! [*He strikes him.*] Ignomy and	
	shame	
	Pursue thy life and live aye with thy name.	
	Exeunt [*all but* PANDARUS].	
35	PANDARUS A goodly medicine for mine aching bones. Oh,	
	world, world, world! Thus is the poor agent despised. O trai-	
	tors and bawds, how earnestly are you set a-work,° and how	*to work*
	ill requited. Why should our endeavor be so desired and the	
	performance so loathed? What verse for it? What instance°	*traditional saying*
40	for it? Let me see:	
	Full merrily the humble-bee doth sing,	
	Till he hath lost his honey and his sting;	
	And, being once subdued in armèd tail,[6]	
	Sweet honey and sweet notes together fail.	
45	Good traders in the flesh, set this in your painted cloths:[7]	
	As many as be here of panders' hall,°	*guild hall*
	Your eyes, half out,[8] weep out at Pandar's fall.	
	Or if you cannot weep, yet give some groans,	

---

2. Be mercifully quick in destruction.
3. *But . . . in:* But dare all impending danger that gods and men prepare for me.
4. Mythical Queen of Thebes, who wept so much at the murder of her children by the gods that the gods turned her into a statue that flowed with water.
5. Generates evil spirits (in the mind) as quickly as frenzy produces mad "thoughts."
6. And having lost his sting: alluding to impotence caused by venereal disease.
7. Inexpensive substitutes for tapestries, often including moralistic inscriptions.
8. Half-blinded by venereal disease.

Though not for me, yet for your aching bones.° *(from syphilis)*
50 Brethren and sisters of the hold-door trade,° *Pimps and bawds*
Some two months hence my will shall here be made.[9]
It should be now, but that my fear is this:
Some gallèd goose of Winchester would hiss.[1]
Till then I'll sweat[2] and seek about for eases,
55 And at that time bequeath you my diseases. *Exit.*

9. The word "here" is possibly a reference to the stage of the Globe and hence the promise of a sequel that never materialized; it has also been taken to refer to an Inn of Court, where young men studied law, a plausible place to make a "will" and thus hypothesized by some scholars to be the location of the first performance. See the Introduction.

1. A prostitute or customer afflicted with venereal disease, from the diocese of Winchester (which had jurisdiction over Southwark, home of both the brothels and the Globe), would disapprove—of the will and/or the play.
2. Usual treatment for venereal disease.

Othello

Othello (ca. 1601–03) has always been popular in performance, although—or per-haps, paradoxically, because—it is excruciating to watch. We look on helplessly as Iago tricks Othello into believing that Desdemona, Othello's beloved and loving wife, has committed adultery. We see the villain cunningly stage-manage appearances to "prove" her guilt. We witness Othello's psychic degeneration into insane jealousy. As mere spectators, we can say nothing to warn or exonerate her. We then watch Othello kill the innocent Desdemona, and finally we watch him, tormented with bafflement and remorse, kill himself.

Massive, collective, transhistorical forces—racism, ancient gender stereotypes, deep-rooted sexual and religious anxieties—conspire against Othello and Desdemona. These forces have by no means vanished from our own world. But Shakespeare depicts them in a highly specific form, shaped by the culture of the Venetian Republic and its outpost, Cyprus, at a moment of historical conflict with the Ottoman Turks. So too the central characters grapple with universal passions, but the passions are only set in fatal motion by circumstances particular to their place and time. *Othello* in consequence is a play that is at once utterly alien and utterly familiar.

Racism's persistence today offers an accessible path into *Othello*; at the same time, some of the play's racial markers are now unfamiliar and hence easily overlooked. The First Folio calls Othello "the Moor of Venice." In the Renaissance, the term "Moor" could designate an African (north or south of the Sahara), a Muslim, or even a South Asian Indian. While *Othello*'s Moorish protagonist, and much of its plot, derive from Giovanbattista Giraldi Cinthio's *De gli hecatommithi* (Hundred Tales, 1565), Shake-speare gives race far more attention than Cinthio does, and explores the issue in sustained and unsettling fashion.

How, then, does race function in *Othello*? Iago, the clever and audacious villain, incites horror of miscegenation when he informs Desdemona's father, Brabanzio, that "an old black ram / Is tupping [copulating with] your white ewe" (1.1.86–87).* Soon after, he adds: "you'll have your daughter covered with a Barbary [Arab, North African] horse" (1.1.108–09). These comments register Elizabethan prejudice toward black Africans resident in England and reflect the growing European participation in the African slave trade that had long been dominated by Arab merchants. Such racially charged language recurs throughout the play, reinforced by the conventional association of blackness with evil. Othello considers his "best judgment collied" (darkened; 2.3.185) by anger; Iago speaks of "the blackest sins," vowing to "turn" Desdemona's "virtue into pitch" (sticky black resin; 2.3.322, 331). But when Brabanzio accuses Othello of seducing his daughter by magic, Iago recognizes that the charges will fall on deaf ears: Venice needs Othello to repel the Turkish navy that has invaded Cyprus. And practical necessity is not the only mitigating factor. The Sen-ate's acceptance of his courtship of Desdemonda projects overtones of Christian universalism and the positive view of interracial love in the Song of Songs. As the Duke tells Brabanzio, in a backhanded compliment, "Your son-in-law is far more fair than black" (1.3.287).

The racist attack on Othello falters partly because the play initially obeys the logic of romantic comedy—nighttime encounters, an old but ineffectual father blocking

*Except where noted, all quotations are taken from the edited text of the Folio, printed here. The Digital Edition includes edited texts of both the Folio and the Quarto.

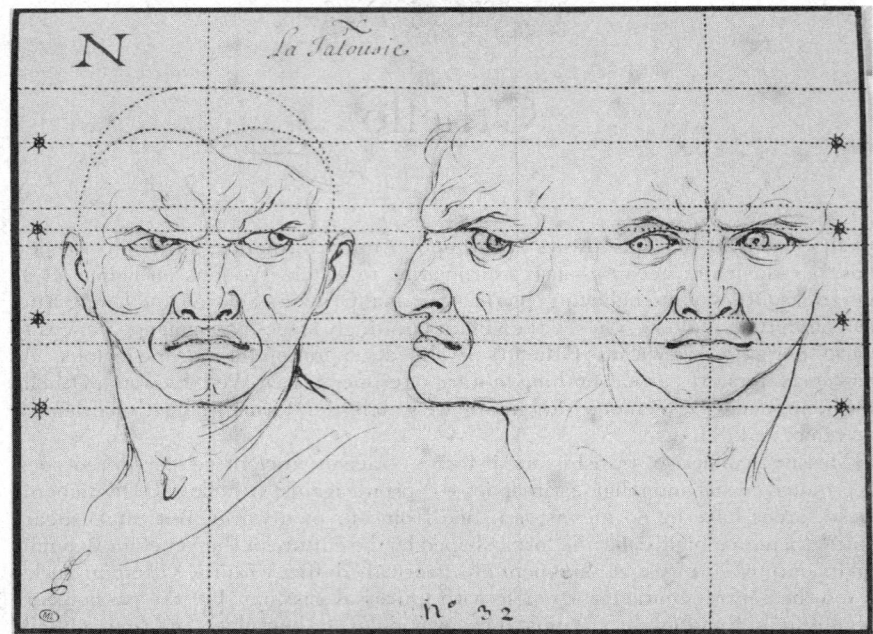

Jealousy. Charles Le Brun (1619–1690).

his daughter's marriage, and official ratification of the couple's marriage. It then modulates into romance, a form in which, characteristically, virtuous lovers are parted and face perilous adventures before happily reuniting. Here, Desdemona and Othello separately sail for Cyprus through bad weather to confront the Turks. But they arrive safely and a storm disperses the enemy fleet. Hence, the obstacles seem to have been overcome.

As the plot unfolds, however, less familiar racial discourses emerge, coincident with a generic shift to domestic tragedy—a wife's alleged adultery and her husband's response. Since we know that Desdemona is innocent, Othello's rush toward violence is horrific. Shakespeare offers various, sometimes incompatible, motivations for that swiftness. His portrait of Othello draws on a stereotype of African men's extreme jealousy that he likely took from *A Geographical History of Africa* (trans. 1600) by Leo Africanus, a Moroccan Muslim who converted to Catholicism after being captured by Christian pirates. The play owes a further debt to geohumoralism, a theory linking psychology ("humors") to geography or climate. For geohumoralists, Africans (unlike Italians) were not naturally jealous but, once provoked, responded fiercely. When Iago's wife Emilia comments on Othello's jealousy, Desdemona replies: "Who, he? I think the sun where he was born / Drew all such humors from him" (3.4.27–28). And Othello ultimately sees himself as "one not easily jealous but, being wrought, / Perplexed in the extreme" (5.2.338–39).

Iago invokes another racial stereotype—that of African naïveté—when he observes that Othello

> is of a free and open nature
> That thinks men honest that but seem to be so,
> And will as tenderly be led by th' nose
> As asses are.
>
> (1.3.377–80)

This gullibility went hand in hand, in European eyes, with the propensity of "uncivilized" Africans to fetishize—to overvalue or even attribute magical powers to—trivial objects. Thus, in act 3, Shakespeare has Othello chastise Desdemona for failing to produce the handkerchief he gave to her. (Iago planted it on Cassio, Othello's lieutenant, to suggest that he and Desdemona were lovers.) Othello explains that an Egyptian presented the handkerchief to his mother.

> To lose't or give't away were such perdition
> As nothing else could match. . . .
> There's magic in the web of it.
> . . . .
> And it was dyed in mummy, which the skillful
> Conserved of maidens' hearts.
> (3.4.64–72)

In short, *Othello* attributes Othello's susceptibility to Iago to multiple facets of his blackness and Africanness. As social mores have changed, so have interpretations of blackness in the play. Well into the twentieth century, audiences and critics often agreed with Brabanzio that Othello's barbaric African essence triumphs over his civilized European surface. Those who defended his nobility tended to argue that he was not black at all, but white, Oriental, or Arab. Historic performances by black actors have often seemed blows for freedom—for example, in Europe following the 1848 revolutions, in czarist Russia just before the liberation of the serfs, after the emancipation of American slaves in 1863, in World War II America, and in the final years of South African apartheid. Although commentators of African descent have sometimes worried that casting a black actor as Othello risks reinforcing racism, recent years have seen a return to the pre-1800 conviction that Othello is black. Directors have avoided casting white performers in the part, lest they conjure images of the blackface minstrel-shows that figured in nineteenth-century burlesques of the play—the charge made against Laurence Olivier's 1965 film portrayal. Additionally, the intertwining of race with gender and sexuality, especially the killing of a young white woman, has inspired adaptations of *Othello* by novelists of African descent—notably, the American Richard Wright in *Native Son* (1940) and the Sudanese Tayeb Salih in the Arabic-language *Season of Migration to the North* (1966).

Although race is an important issue in *Othello*, it does not solely drive the plot. Roderigo calls Othello an "old black ram" to highlight disparities not only of skin color but also of age. The allusion is to the farcical January–May marriage between an old man and a young woman who, sexually unsatisfied by her husband, looks elsewhere for gratification. In Venice, Iago says, such women "let heaven see the pranks / They dare not show their husbands" (3.3.200–201). Venice's reputation as a center of sexual license was a commonplace of Shakespeare's England, for instance in Thomas Coryat's *Coryat's Crudities* (1611). Coryat estimated that there were at least twenty thousand courtesans in Venice, "whereof many are esteemed so loose," as he put it, "that they are said to open their quivers to every arrow." And as in Venice, so in Cyprus. Once the storm scatters the Turks, the island loses its garrison status, recovering instead a traditional association with Venus, the classical goddess of love.

Othello registers Desdemona's threatening allure when they are reunited there: "If it were now to die, / 'Twere now to be most happy," where "to die" also means to have an orgasm (2.1.181–82). Christian doctrine sometimes considered excessive marital sexual pleasure a form of adultery, and Shakespeare hints that Othello experiences his own desire as adulterous, projecting this desire onto Cassio. Sex also connects with violence in the handkerchief, "[s]potted with strawberries" (3.3.431), that may evoke the blood Desdemona loses with her virginity. Othello anticipates that her "bed, lust-stained, shall with lust's blood be spotted" (5.1.36). Yet even as he prepares to murder his sleeping wife, he cannot resist kissing her. He recalls this necrophilic perversity at his own death: "I kissed thee ere I killed thee. No way but this: / Killing myself, to die upon a kiss" (5.2.351–52), where "die" again connotes sexual pleasure. Romance's reunion of long-separated lovers becomes postmortem embrace.

Desdemona seems entirely unaware of this dangerous current of male sexual anxiety. At the beginning of the play, she is frank and forthright about her own desires, declaring that she will "trumpet" her love for Othello "to the world" (1.3.247). At the end, Shakespeare emphasizes her innocent victimization, dramatizing her submission to Othello.

> DESDEMONA　　　　　　　　　Oh, falsely, falsely murdered!
> . . . .
> 　A guiltless death I die.
> EMILIA　　　　　　　　　　　Oh, who hath done this deed?
> DESDEMONA　Nobody. I myself. Farewell.
> 　Commend me to my kind lord. Oh, farewell!
> 　　　　　　　　　　　　　　　(5.2.115–22)

Desdemona's last words may indicate a submissiveness bordering on suicide, normally a mortal sin for Christians but here more like Christlike self-sacrifice. Her speech also increases Othello's guilt, underscoring the mistreatment of women that is seen as well in Iago's relationship with Emilia and Cassio's with Bianca, the courtesan who loves him.

In addition to racial and sexual anxieties, *Othello* is woven through with religious concerns. Iago's pleasure in the sport of destroying Othello descends from the earlier English morality plays' Vice figure, a semi-secularized devil out to damn the virtuous. Tellingly, Othello refers to his scheming ensign as "that demi-devil" who "hath thus ensnared my soul and body" (5.2.294–95). On the verge of stabbing his antagonist, he declares, "If that thou beest a devil, I cannot kill thee." To which Iago rejoins, "I bleed, sir, but not killed" (5.2.280–81).From a Christian perspective, Othello reenacts the Fall in repudiating Desdemona, his good "angel" (5.2.128), and succumbing to demonic temptation. Desdemona, by contrast, commends herself to her "kind lord"—Othello, but also God. The word "lord" runs through the final scene, as does religious language more generally, especially references to heaven. Iago is damned and Desdemona saved, but what of Othello? He believes that killing Desdemona protects her immortal "soul," is a "sacrifice," is "merciful" (5.2.32, 66, 86). Once disabused, however, he reverses himself: "This look of thine [Desdemona's] will hurl my soul from heaven, / And fiends will snatch at it" (5.2.268–69). In murdering his innocent wife, he has committed a mortal sin, and in committing suicide—another mortal sin—he compounds his damnation.

Othello's final act calls up another tension that has been present throughout the play: that between the Europeans and the Turks, whose ethnic difference underlies the political, military, and religious threats to Cyprus and beyond. For this material, absent from Cinthio, Shakespeare may have drawn on Richard Knolles's *General History of the Turks* (1603), which could have provided various details, along with an international resonance. Shakespeare borrows the storm in act 1 of *Othello*, which completes the fictitious defeat of the Turks, from England's destruction of the Spanish Armada in 1588. When Othello breaks up Cassio's fight, he asks,

> Are we turned Turks, and to ourselves do that
> Which heaven hath forbid the Ottomites?
> For Christian shame, put by this barbarous brawl.
> 　　　　　　　　　　　　　　　(2.3.149–51)

Othello speaks as the Christian he is. Although the passage refers to the providential storm that saves Christian Cyprus, "turning Turk" usually referred to captives of Muslim pirates who renounced Christianity for Islam. This fear seems remote until

Othello's final speech, in which he partially identifies with the non-Christian world. In the Quarto, Othello is culpably ignorant, "like the base Indian" who "threw a pearl away / Richer than all his tribe" (Q 5.2.319–20). But the Folio reads "base Judean" (F 5.2.340), perhaps alluding to Judas, betrayer of Christ, or to Herod the Great, jealous murderer of his wife.

In act 1, Othello leads Venice against the Turks—Muslims with whom Moors were linked. At the end of the play, he recalls his service in defending the Republic against "a malignant and a turbaned Turk" who "[b]eat a Venetian and traduced the state" (5.2.346–47). The deed divides him into agent and object of justice, servant and enemy of the Christian state. A "base Judean" and "circumcisèd dog" (5.2.348), he is both Jew and Turk. Othello internalizes the military conflict, half assuming ethnic and religious otherness

The manner of Turkish tyrannie over Christian slaves.

Woodcut, from F. Knight, *A Relation of Seven Years Slavery under the Turks of Argeire . . .* (1640). See Othello's speech before he kills himself (5.2.331–49).

to exorcise his guilt. Hence, the uneasy ending, with responsibility located both within and beyond Europe. But the last word on Othello's death is Cassio's: "This did I fear . . . / For he was great of heart" (5.2.353–54). The allusion to classical Roman suicide, rendered by Shakespeare earlier in *Julius Caesar* (1599), emphasizes Othello's nobility despite his damnation.

These social and cultural forces suggest why *Othello might* end tragically. But *must* it? Since it would take little to unmask Iago, we long for a happy ending. Yet audiences feel a helpless sense of inevitability. These contradictory perspectives coexist because *Othello* presents a world of guesswork misunderstood as proof, dramatizing characters who are driven by imperfect information, conjecture, and (im)probability. Yet what gives these considerations of likelihood, on which ordinary life depends, such destructive consequences? The answer seems to lie in the villain.

Iago wittily speaks to, not just before, the audience, and he speaks a lot, uttering two hundred more lines than Othello—more than any other Shakespearean character except Hamlet and Richard III. His verbal dominance is all the more evident in a play that deploys the smallest cast in Shakespearean tragedy and that, after the first act, almost conforms to the Aristotelian unities of time, place, and action, a convention that Shakespeare normally ignores but here turns to claustrophobic effect. Iago's verboseness is far from harmless. Indeed, destruction ensues in part because of Iago's ability to turn Othello's and Desdemona's noblest traits against them. Having invoked Othello's "constant, loving, noble nature" (2.1.272), he explains:

> 'tis most easy
> Th'inclining Desdemona to subdue

In any honest suit: she's framed as fruitful
As the free elements. And then for her
To win the Moor . . .
. . . .
His soul is so enfettered to her love
That she may make, unmake, do what she list.
                                    (2.3.310–17)

Othello's trustfulness and Desdemona's support of Cassio's "honest suit"—her persistent efforts to get Cassio reinstated after Othello dismisses him following a drunken brawl—thus become grist for "Honest Iago['s]" mill (1.3.291). And Iago seems honest to others because his blunt speech conceals his varied, impenetrable motives. Poet and critic Samuel Taylor Coleridge accordingly spoke of Iago's "motiveless malignity." That impenetrability persists even when it cannot help him. Captured, Iago refuses to explain himself—perhaps because he cannot—thereby leaving behind a sense of the mystery of things.

Othello also hurtles toward tragedy because Iago can manipulate other characters' belief in the debased cultural clichés by which he and they live. His sexual jealousy rests on the surmise that Emilia has committed adultery with Othello:

I know not if't be true,
But I, for mere suspicion in that kind,
Will do as if for surety.
                                    (1.3.366–68)

"Suspicion" functions as "surety," a destructive substitution. It is a dangerous surmise based on the clichéd fear of the adulterous wife. Iago must then convince Othello to share his belief in Desdemona's adultery with Cassio. The rhetorician par excellence, he repeats a commonplace—Brabanzio's warning that Desdemona "has deceived her father, and may thee" (1.3.290)—in order to persuade Othello to internalize the stereotype of the unfaithful woman:

She did deceive her father, marrying you;
And when she seemed to shake and fear your looks,
She loved them most.
                                    (3.3.204–06)

The same appeal to likelihood underpins Iago's presentation of "proof" in the form of "the fleers [sneers], the jibes, and notable scorns / That dwell in every region of his [Cassio's] face" (4.1.79–80). Similarly, to explain Desdemona's alleged betrayal, Othello echoes Roderigo's "old black ram":

Haply, for I am black
And have not those soft parts of conversation
That chamberers have, or for I am declined
Into the vale of years. . . .
                                    (3.3.261–64)

And after Iago considers Cassio and Desdemona "as prime as goats, as hot as monkeys" (3.3.400), Othello parrots his very words: "Goats and monkeys!" (4.1.250).

The play constantly warns against mere plausibility. Characters, as unstable as their own suspicions, are not what they seem. Iago confesses, "Were I the Moor, I would not be Iago" (1.1.55)—perhaps indicating a preference for Othello's lofty status, but also acknowledging their differences in character. In the same speech, he declares more elusively, "I am not what I am" (1.1.63). This reversal of God's words in Exodus—"I am what I am"—suggests Iago's psychic disunity. His self-presentation is not what he is, or he is not what he seems. Iago's explanation of Othello's jealousy is similar:

He's that he is . . . .
What he might be—if what he might, he is not—
I would to heaven he were.

(4.1.257–59)

The meaningless statement of psychic unity is promptly undermined as Iago seems to have it both ways: if Othello is not sane, I wish he were; on the other hand, if Othello is not insane, I wish he were (since that would explain his behavior). This duality returns at the end:

> LODOVICO   Where is this rash and most unfortunate man?
> OTHELLO   That's he that was Othello: here I am."
>
> (5.2.276–77)

Othello considers his former, third-person self "this rash and most unfortunate man"; the first-person Othello is someone else. And when Iago is asked for his own motives, he replies: "What you know, you know" (5.2.296). Self-identity reveals nothing; self-division reveals something, but what?

As the play demonstrates again and again, to act on suspicion is dangerous. The Duke is dismissive of Brabanzio's claims that Othello must have used witchcraft to win Desdemona:

> To vouch this is no proof
> Without more wider and more overt test
> Than these thin habits and poor likelihoods
> Of modern seeming do prefer against him.
>
> (1.3.106–09)

Emilia likewise repudiates Othello's charges against Desdemona, demanding evidence: "Why should he call her 'whore?' Who keeps her company? / What place, what time, what form, what likelihood?" (4.2.136–37). These challenges to surmise encourage in the audience a position of anguished superiority. But Shakespeare undermines this superiority by asking us to accept the plot's improbabilities. These include the love marriage of the older black foreigner to the young white woman, unlikely in Shakespeare's day; Iago's inconsistent motives, most opaque at the end; the lapses of memory and plausibility concerning the handkerchief; and the play's double time, in which events hurry forward, perhaps within a week, while Othello asserts that Desdemona "with Cassio hath the act of shame / A thousand times committed" (5.2.206–07). In seeing *Othello*, we impose reason on the incomprehensible, replicating the characters' behavior. We, too, operate via best guesses. This is the way of the world.

In *Othello*, however, Shakespeare makes us believe not that such behavior *may* lead to tragedy but that it *must*. It *must* because of the debased prejudices prevalent in society, Iago's remarkable skill in deploying them, and Desdemona's and Othello's equally remarkable nobility of soul and love for each other. It is a tragedy wrought of prejudice and of guesswork, and, most dangerously, of the two combined. Unable to intervene, we experience an overwhelming sense of loss at the destruction of something precious and rare. It is this that makes *Othello* so painfully moving.

WALTER COHEN

SELECTED BIBLIOGRAPHY

Altman, Joel. *The Improbability of Othello: Rhetorical Anthropology and Shakespearean Selfhood.* Chicago: U of Chicago P, 2010. Sees, especially in Iago and Othello, a classical and humanist exploration of probability, where a rhetorically multiple self (a dramatis persona) periodically coalesces into a dialectically fixed subject (a specific character).

Floyd-Wilson, Mary. *English Ethnicity and Race in Early Modern Drama.* Cambridge: Cambridge UP, 2003. Draws on classical geohumoral theory (linking character to climate and geography) to see Italian Iago as naturally jealous and African Othello as naturally calm—a theory modified by early racism, deployed by Iago to corrupt Othello.

Greenblatt, Stephen. *Renaissance Self-Fashioning: From More to Shakespeare.* Chicago: U of Chicago P, 1980. 222–54. Examines Othello's narrative self-fashioning and its subversion by Desdemona's submission and Iago's malice; a central essay for modern *Othello* scholarship and for New Historicist criticism generally.

Hall, Kim F. *Othello, the Moor of Venice: Texts and Contexts.* Boston: Bedford/St. Martin's, 2007. Presents a text of the play; contemporary primary sources on race and religion, cultural geography, marriage and the household, masculinity and military life, and passions; and critical and artistic responses from the past three centuries.

Korda, Natasha. *Shakespeare's Domestic Economies: Gender and Property in Early Modern England.* Philadelphia: U of Pennsylvania P, 2002. Links Othello's jealousy, focused on Desdemona's handkerchief, to contradictory discourses of private property manipulated by Iago—African fetishistic overvaluation of trifling objects, English household discipline, and European female extravagance.

Lupton, Julia Reinhard. "Othello Circumcised: Shakespeare and the Pauline Discourse of Nations." *Representations* 57 (Winter 1997): 73–89. Views Othello through the prism of St. Paul's distinction between pagans and Jews, seeing the Moor as both ex-barbarian and ex-Muslim, positions to which he partly returns.

Neill, Michael, ed. *Othello, the Moor of Venice.* Oxford: Oxford UP, 2006. Outstanding scholarly edition with a book-length critical introduction.

Orlin, Lena Cowen, ed. *Othello.* New York: Palgrave Macmillan, 2004. Collects leading essays since 1990, mostly on gender and marriage (Berger, Bristol, Sinfield) or race and reception (Bartels, Singh, Hodgdon, Albanese).

Vaughan, Virginia Mason. *Performing Blackness on English Stages, 1500–1800.* Cambridge: Cambridge UP, 2005. Reviews *Othello*'s stage and screen history, arguing that the text metatheatrically refers to blackface performance—a tradition that emphasizes the actor's artifice and raises ideological problems opposite to those of a black actor's apparently authentic impersonation.

Vitkus, Daniel. *Turning Turk: English Theater and the Multicultural Mediterranean, 1570–1630.* New York: Palgrave Macmillan, 2003. Argues for a Turkish Othello, emblematic of the Ottoman threat to Christian Europe, associated with unbridled sexuality and to some extent racial otherness—a position undermined early in the play but subsequently confirmed and resulting in Othello's damnation.

FILMS

Othello. 1952. Dir. Orson Welles. USA. 93 min. This black-and-white film stars Welles as Othello. Famous for its innovative and disorienting camera work more than for its acting.

Othello. 1965. Dir. Stuart Burge and John Dexter. UK. 165 min. Film of a stage performance, with Laurence Olivier as Othello and Maggie Smith as Desdemona.

Notable not only for the white actor's effort fully to impersonate a black African—seen at the time as both troubling and moving—but also for Smith's spirited Desdemona, a break with the prior stage tradition of representing the character as a passive victim.

Othello. 1988. Dir. Janet Suzman. South Africa/UK. 187 min. Film of the controversial South African stage performance (the first with a black African actor and a white actress) that became a form of anti-apartheid protest.

Othello. 1995. Dir. Oliver Parker. USA/UK. 123 min. First version made for film with an African American, Laurence Fishburne, as Othello. Kenneth Branagh as Iago dominates the play (as often happens with Iago). Ironically, racial issues are muted.

O. 2001. Dir. Tim Blake Nelson. USA. 95 min. Set in a contemporary high school, centered on a basketball player, Odin (Mekhi Phifer), in love with Desi (Julia Stiles), undone by Hugo (Josh Hartnett); also with Martin Sheen.

TEXTUAL INTRODUCTION

Othello's uncertain textual history shows the fluid processes by which a play moved between stage and printed page. *Othello* was written ca. 1601–03, and its first recorded performance was at court on November 1, 1604. Despite at least two revivals, at Oxford in 1610 and at court in 1612–13, *Othello* was not published during Shakespeare's lifetime. Twenty years after its composition, however, it was printed in swift succession in two distinct forms. It was entered in the Stationers' Register (the list of plays to be printed) on October 6, 1621, by the bookseller and publisher Thomas Walkley, who brought it out the following year. The play survives in two printed versions: Walkley's 1622 Quarto and the First Folio of 1623. No manuscript survives, and editors have expended considerable effort in trying to establish the relationships between the printed texts and whatever lost manuscripts may lie behind them, as well as their sequence of composition.

Othello's two early texts differ in ways that cumulatively seem significant. Perhaps the most obvious difference is found in 4.3. In the Folio, 4.3 contains dialogue, the "Willow Song," and Emilia's speech on husbands, all of which are missing from the Quarto. There has been speculation that the song was cut from the Quarto because when that text was solidified, the company lacked an actor—Desdemona was probably played by an adolescent male—capable of singing the part. (This casting issue has been used to support a proposed date of composition in 1602 rather than later [Honigmann 346–50]). The Folio's other unique passages include Desdemona's protestation of her innocence at 4.2.150–63 and Roderigo's account of Othello and Desdemona's elopement, when he famously describes Othello as "an extravagant and wheeling stranger" (1.1.132).

Most of the thousands of differences, though, are small. They are found at the most basic level: punctuation (the Quarto uses commas and colons, while the Folio favors periods); oaths (the Quarto is peppered with them, the Folio has few); and some seemingly arbitrary alternative choices (e.g., the Quarto's *coloquintida* is "acerb" [1.3.324–25], while the Folio's, less colorfully, is "bitter" [1.3.337–38]). These small differences slowly build to create two subtly different plays. So, for instance, when Othello describes at F 1.3.159 the "world of kisses" Desdemona gives him, she is characterized as more sexually active than the woman who offers him "a world of sighs" (Q 1.3.146). In all, the Folio has around 160 lines not in the Quarto; the Quarto, in its turn, has several unique lines.

Uncertainty about the history and nature of the two texts continues; each suggests a different relationship to the playhouse and to Shakespeare, and these differences may also reveal that while the two were published close in time, they derive from different periods in the play's life. The Folio, it has been argued, comes from a scribe's transcription of Shakespeare's own "fair copy" (Honigmann 1). Unique passages in the Folio, such as Othello's speech at 3.3.447–54, are thought to preserve Shakespeare's "second thoughts," though filtered by the work of a scribe who made changes of his own (Honigmann 58–76). When precisely these changes were made is unclear.

There is even less agreement about the history of the Quarto. The Quarto has much fuller stage directions than does the Folio, which suggests that it is at least partly the product of the early modern theater. Scott McMillin proposes that the Quarto derives from a scribe's transcription of a prompt book from a later Jacobean revival—even possibly after Shakespeare's death—and that the missing sections were cut to meet the constraints of performance (7–8). Following this logic, differences such as the Quarto's "muttering" (3.3.67) for the Folio's rare "mammering" (3.3.68) might be actors' adaptations. This would bring the Quarto very close to the stage indeed, although as Lukas Erne argues, the Quarto still might retain more of the play than just what was performed (183–84). Other scholars, while agreeing that the Quarto is a scribal copy, instead propose that it derives from Shakespeare's own draft manuscript or "foul papers"—not necessarily the same manuscript that gave us the Folio (Honigmann 1)—thereby drawing the Quarto closer to Shakespeare and in fact suggesting that the text it contains is earlier—not, as is normally assumed, later—than that of the Folio. One theory enshrines the author, the other collaborative theater: neither is watertight.

The differing history of the two texts may, in part, explain their differences in lineation. The Quarto's lineation has often been criticized as substandard. However, it has many more short lines that can be read as shared lines than does the Folio. McMillin proposes that these short lines, many clearly misplaced in the middle of speeches, are the result of a listening scribe mistakenly anticipating the end of an actor's speech. Nevertheless, the Folio also has lineation problems, sometimes making odd divisions between verse and prose. The Folio sets Iago's misogynistic proverbs at 2.1.108–11 as prose, though they fall neatly enough into slightly irregular iambic pentameter lines; in *The Norton Shakespeare* they are set as verse. The Quarto, too, also sometimes mistakes the shift between prose and verse, as in Cassio's lament over his "reputation" at 2.3.242–44. Here the Quarto mistakenly continues the verse form of the previous passage before belatedly shifting into prose at line 245; in *The Norton Shakespeare* the speech is all set as prose.

The two distinct forms of *Othello* reflect different moments in the play's development, and each has a coherent logic. Most editors use the Folio as their base text, drawing from the Quarto when the Folio seems corrupt or inadequate. The Folio apparently preserves more of the play and is probably closer to Shakespeare's final thoughts. The Quarto, however, may transmit a version that was seen on the stage in Shakespeare's time. Consequently, *The Norton Shakespeare* offers an edition of the Folio in the print volume and editions of both texts in the Digital Edition, in each case preserving distinctive features wherever possible.

Clare McManus

Textual Bibliography

Erne, Lukas. *Shakespeare as a Literary Dramatist.* Cambridge: Cambridge UP, 2003.
Honigmann, E. A. J. *The Texts of "Othello" and Shakespearian Revision.* London: Routledge, 1996.
McMillin, Scott, ed. *The First Quarto of "Othello."* Cambridge: Cambridge UP, 2001.

PERFORMANCE NOTE

Directors of *Othello* make critical decisions respecting the protagonist's assimilation and acceptance in Venice. Through choices of accent, expression, costume, and bearing, Othello can appear a well-acclimated emigrant or an insecure outsider; a dignified general or a repressed brute; a sincere Christian or a heathen—and the Venetians can treat the Moor with earnest respect, grudging tolerance, or contempt. Race is often (but not always) a major factor: Othello can appear suspicious or confrontational because of perceived slights over his skin color, or basically indifferent to them; Iago and Brabanzio can be conspicuous bigots or voices of the majority. Productions must further decide whether Cyprus is an extension of a palpably racist Venice or a refuge of civility, and whether the Venetian military represents a shield from Turkish invaders or a violent occupation in its own right.

Another prominent consideration in performance is Iago's motivation for villainy. Productions regularly implicate envy of Cassio, racism, homoerotic desire, or psychotic ambition; some, though, obscure his motives altogether, thus harnessing uncertainties that deepen the tragic outcome. Whatever the choice, Iago is consistently a favorite of audiences, who are teasingly made complicit in his treachery through his use of direct address and uncanny blend of humor, improvisation, and menace. Productions therefore face the challenge of facilitating his unique theatrical power without sidelining Othello and (effectively) his tragedy. Creating genuine sexual chemistry between Othello and Desdemona, thereby raising the stakes of what is lost, and exhibiting Othello's extremes of character (brutality and heroism, jealousy and tenderness, impulsiveness and eloquence) without qualifications, can help the Moor emerge as the clear star of the final acts. Desdemona must likewise maintain theatrical interest alongside Emilia, another audience favorite. Actors are challenged to portray the "fair warrior" who stands up to her father and banters with Iago, then convincingly sustain the persona despite her naïveté and apparent willing subjection to her persecutor in the late acts.

Emilia, for her part, can variously balance roles as wife, waiting woman, and confidante; treat Desdemona with sisterly tenderness or a rival's jealousy; suspect Iago from the beginning or seem desperate for his affection. Cassio can be an entitled intellectual or a modest soldier; Roderigo, a fop or a site of unexpected pathos; Brabanzio, comic in his ranting or gravely prophetic; Bianca, a savvy prostitute or an unfortunate innocent, a Venetian who chases the soldiers to Cypress or a Cypriot preyed upon by them. Other considerations in performance include Othello's race and religion (Digital Edition PC 1); managing the play's "double" time schemes; fixing the point at which Othello is convinced of the supposed adultery; motivating Emilia's participation in Iago's deception (PC 6); and solving problems posed by Desdemona's bed and Othello's third weapon (PC 7).

BRETT GAMBOA

The Tragedy of Othello, the Moor of Venice

THE PERSONS OF THE PLAY

OTHELLO, the Moor
BRABANZIO, father to Desdemona
DESDEMONA, wife to Othello
IAGO, a villain
EMILIA, wife to Iago
RODERIGO, a gulled gentleman
DUKE of Venice
MONTANO, Governor of Cyprus
Michael CASSIO, an honorable lieutenant
BIANCA, a courtesan
LODOVICO ⎫
GRAZIANO ⎭ two noble Venetians
FIRST SENATOR
SECOND SENATOR
OFFICERS
SAILOR
MESSENGERS
GENTLEMEN of Cyprus
HERALD
MUSICIANS
CLOWN
Servants, Attendants

1.1 (Q 1.1)

Enter RODERIGO *and* IAGO.[1]

RODERIGO   Never tell me!° I take it much unkindly   *(annoyance; disbelief)*
   That thou, Iago, who hast had my purse
   As if the strings were thine, shouldst know of this.
IAGO   But you'll not hear me. If ever I did dream
   Of such a matter, abhor me.
5 RODERIGO   Thou told'st me
   Thou didst hold him in thy hate.
IAGO   Despise me[2]
   If I do not. Three great ones of the city,
   In personal suit to make me his lieutenant,
   Off-capped° to him—and, by the faith of man,   *Took off their caps*
10   I know my price: I am worth no worse a place—
   But he, as loving his own pride and purposes,
   Evades them with a bombast circumstance[3]
   Horribly stuffed with epithets of war;°   *military jargon*

1.1 Location: A street in Venice.
1. Iago's name may be related to Santiago Matamoros, St. James the Moor Slayer, the patron saint of Spain. The potential irony lies in having a character with a foreign-sounding name express hatred for foreigners on behalf of Venice.
2. *abhor, hate, Despise* (lines 4–6): The language of

animosity here, largely undirected toward particular objects or persons, may suggest something about Iago or even the world of the play.
3. With an inflated circumlocution. *bombast:* cotton padding in clothes, a metaphor running through "stuffed" (line 13), and possibly "suit" (line 8) and "Nonsuits" (line 14).

	Nonsuits° my mediators. For, "Certes,"° says he,	*Denies / Certainly*
15	"I have already chose my officer."	
	And what was he?	
	Forsooth, a great arithmetician:[4]	
	One Michael Cassio, a Florentine,°	*(hence, a foreigner)*
	A fellow almost damned in a fair wife,[5]	
20	That° never set a squadron in the field,	*Who*
	Nor the division° of a battle° knows	*ordering / battalion*
	More than a spinster°—unless the bookish theoric,°	*housewife / learning*
	Wherein the tonguèd consuls can propose[6]	
	As masterly as he! Mere prattle without practice	
25	Is all his soldiership. But he, sir, had th'election	
	And I—of whom his° eyes had seen the proof	*(Othello's)*
	At Rhodes, at Cyprus, and on others' grounds,	
	Christened and heathen—must be be-leed° and calmed°	*without wind / becalmed*
	By debitor and creditor. This counter-caster,[7]	
30	He, in good time,° must his lieutenant be	*in timely fashion (ironic)*
	And I, bless the mark,° his moorship's ensign.[8]	*God help us*

RODERIGO   By heaven, I rather would have been his hangman!

IAGO   Why, there's no remedy. 'Tis the curse of service:

	Preferment goes by letter and affection[9]	
35	And not by old gradation,° where each second	*traditional seniority*
	Stood heir to th' first. Now, sir, be judge yourself	
	Whether I in any just term am affined°	*am bound in any just way*
	To love the Moor.[1]	

RODERIGO   I would not follow him, then.

IAGO   O sir, content you!°   *be content*

	I follow him to serve my turn upon him.°	*serve my own interests*
40	We cannot all be masters, nor all masters	
	Cannot be truly followed. You shall mark	
	Many a duteous and knee-crooking° knave	*(servilely) knee-bending*
	That, doting on his own obsequious bondage,	
45	Wears out his time,° much like his master's ass,	*Spends his years serving*
	For naught but provender,° and when he's old—cashiered.°	*animal feed / fired*
	Whip me° such honest knaves! Others there are	*I'd have whipped*
	Who, trimmed° in forms and visages of duty,	*outwardly decorated*
	Keep yet their hearts attending on themselves	
50	And, throwing but shows of service on their lords,	
	Do well thrive by them° and, when they have lined their°	*("shows," "lords") / (own)*
	coats,	
	Do themselves homage. These fellows have some soul	
	And such a one do I profess myself. For, sir,	
	It is as sure as you are Roderigo,	
55	Were I the Moor, I would not be Iago:[2]	

4. Implying that Cassio's knowledge of war is purely theoretical.

5. Obscure. Cassio has not yet met Bianca and is unmarried, although in Shakespeare's source he is. Perhaps Shakespeare's error, a reference to Cassio as a ladies' man, or an oblique, debatable anticipation of the main plot.

6. In which the talkative political leaders (of ancient Rome, but referring to modern Italy) can debate.

7. *debitor and creditor, counter-caster:* pejorative terms for an accountant (Cassio).

8. As "ensign," Iago is something like a standard-bearer or third-in-command, ranking below "lieuten-ant" Cassio, the second-in-command. "His moorship": the first indication of whom Iago is complaining about.

9. Promotion comes through connections and favor-itism.

1. TEXTUAL COMMENT For possible meanings of "Moor," see Digital Edition TC 1 (Folio edited text).

2. If I could have Othello's status, I would not want my own position. Or: if I were a person of Othello's (nobler) character—but occupied my current rank—I would not behave so self-servingly. The line perhaps also suggests both a deeper self-loathing and identifi-cation with Othello.

In following him, I follow but myself.
Heaven is my judge: not I for° love and duty,   *I am not driven by*
But seeming so for my peculiar° end.   *personal*
For when my outward action doth demonstrate
60 The native act and figure[3] of my heart
In complement extern,° 'tis not long after   *outward appearance*
But I will wear my heart upon my sleeve
For daws° to peck at. I am not what I am.[4]   *crowlike birds*
RODERIGO   What a full fortune does the thicklips owe°   *own*
If he can carry't thus?°   *succeed*
65 IAGO   Call up her° father: *(Desdemona's)*
Rouse him,[5] make after° him, poison his delight,   *hound*
Proclaim° him in the streets, incense her kinsmen,   *criminally accuse*
And, though he in a fertile climate dwell,
Plague him with flies. Though that his joy be joy,[6]
70 Yet throw such chances of vexation on't
As it may lose some color.[7]
RODERIGO   Here is her father's house. I'll call aloud.
IAGO   Do, with like timorous accent° and dire yell   *frightening tone*
As when, by night and negligence, the fire
75 Is spied in populous cities.
RODERIGO   What ho, Brabanzio! Signor Brabanzio, ho!
IAGO   Awake! What ho, Brabanzio! Thieves! Thieves!
Look to your house, your daughter, and your bags!
Thieves! Thieves!
          [*Enter*] BRABANZIO *above.*
80 BRABANZIO   What is the reason of this terrible summons?
What is the matter there?
RODERIGO   Signor, is all your family within?
IAGO   Are your doors locked?
BRABANZIO   Why? Wherefore ask you this?
IAGO   Sir, you're robbed. For shame, put on your gown.
85 Your heart is burst; you have lost half your soul:
Even now, now, very now, an old black ram[8]
Is tupping° your white ewe. Arise! Arise!   *copulating with*
Awake the snorting° citizens with the bell,   *snoring*
Or else the devil will make a grandsire of you.
Arise, I say!
90 BRABANZIO   What, have you lost your wits?
RODERIGO   Most reverend signor, do you know my voice?
BRABANZIO   Not I. What are you?
RODERIGO   My name is Roderigo.
BRABANZIO   The worser welcome.
I have charged thee not to haunt about my doors:

---

3. The internal operation (or motivation) and shape (or nature).
4. Probably: I am not in essence what I seem in appearance, or the opposite, though it comes to the same thing: I am not in appearance what I am in essence. Either way, the language reverses God's "I am what I am" (Exodus 3:14), while perhaps indicating Iago's divided self. See also 1.1.55 and n., 4.1.257–59 and n., 5.2.277, 5.2.296 and n., and Introduction.
5. *him, his, he* (lines 66–69): The pronouns can refer

either to Brabanzio, Desdemona's father, or to Othello, seemingly moving from the former to the latter as the passage proceeds.
6. Though his joy is real; also consistent with Iago's evocation of false equivalences (lines 55, 63).
7. Basis, plausibility, rationale, sign of good health; but perhaps more literally anticipating "old black ram" (line 86).
8. Connoting animalistic, monstrous, diabolical (horned) sexuality.

95	In honest plainness thou hast heard me say	
	My daughter is not for thee, and now in madness,	
	Being full of supper and distempering draughts,°	*inebriating beverages*
	Upon malicious knavery dost thou come	
	To start° my quiet?	*upset*

RODERIGO   Sir! Sir! Sir!

BRABANZIO   But thou must needs be sure:

100   My spirits and my place° have in their power   *rank*
        To make this bitter to thee.

RODERIGO   Patience, good sir.

BRABANZIO   What, tell'st thou me of robbing?
        This is Venice: my house is not a grange.°   *country house*

RODERIGO   Most grave Brabanzio,

105   In simple and pure soul I come to you—

IAGO   Sir, you are one of those that will not serve God if the
        devil bid you! Because we come to do you service and you
        think we are ruffians, you'll have your daughter covered with a
        Barbary horse;[9] you'll have your nephews° neigh to you; you'll   *grandsons*

110   have coursers for cousins and jennets for germans.[1]

BRABANZIO   What profane wretch art thou?

IAGO   I am one, sir, that comes to tell you your daughter and
        the Moor are making the beast with two backs.°   *copulating*

BRABANZIO   Thou art a villain!

IAGO   You are a senator.[2]

115   BRABANZIO   —This thou shalt answer:° I know thee, Roderigo.   *answer for*

RODERIGO   Sir, I will answer anything. But, I beseech you,
        If't be your pleasure and most wise consent[3]
        —As partly I find it is—that your fair daughter
        At this odd even° and dull° watch o'th' night   *(near midnight) / sleepy*

120   Transported with no worse nor better guard
        But with a knave of common° hire, a gondolier,   *public*
        To the gross clasps of a lascivious Moor—
        If this be known to you and your allowance,°   *allowed by you*
        We then have done you bold and saucy° wrongs.   *impudent*

125   But if you know not this, my manners tell me
        We have your wrong rebuke. Do not believe
        That, from° the sense of all civility,   *in opposition to*
        I thus would play and trifle with your reverence.
        Your daughter—if you have not given her leave,

130   I say again—hath made a gross° revolt,   *foul; brazen*
        Tying her duty, beauty, wit, and fortunes
        In an extravagant° and wheeling° stranger   *vagrant / restless*
        Of here and everywhere. Straight° satisfy yourself: *Immediately*
        If she be in her chamber or your house,

135   Let loose on me the justice of the state
        For thus deluding you.

BRABANZIO [*to Servants within*]   Strike on the tinder,° ho!   *A light*
        Give me a taper!° Call up all my people!   *candle*

---

9. Horse from northwest coastal Africa; an Arab;
suggesting Berbers or barbarians; *covered:* (sexually).
1. *coursers:* strong horses. *cousins:* kinsmen. *jennets:*
small Spanish horses. *germans:* close relatives.

2. *villain:* criminal; peasant. *senator:* ironically respectful, but perhaps also suggesting that both attributions
are accurate.
3. Lines 117–33 do not appear in Q.

[*aside*] This accident° is not unlike my dream;   *event*
Belief of it oppresses me already.
—Light, I say! Light!   *Exit* [*above*].
140 IAGO [*to* RODERIGO]   Farewell, for I must leave you.
It seems not meet° nor wholesome to my place   *proper*
To be produced°—as, if I stay, I shall—   *presented as witness*
Against the Moor. For I do know the state,
However this may gall him with some check,°   *reprimand*
145 Cannot with safety cast° him: for he's embarked°   *dismiss / committed*
With such loud reason° to the Cyprus wars,   *vociferous, just support*
Which even now stand in act° that, for° their souls,   *are taking place / to save*
Another of his fathom° they have none   *caliber*
To lead their business. In which regard,
150 Though I do hate him as I do hell pains,
Yet, for necessity of present life,°   *livelihood*
I must show out a flag and sign of love,
Which is indeed but sign. That you shall surely find him,
Lead to the Sagittary⁴ the raisèd search,°   *awakened searchers*
155 And there will I be with him. So, farewell.   *Exit.*
    Enter BRABANZIO *with Servants and torches.*
BRABANZIO   It is too true an evil: gone she is,
And what's to come of my despisèd time°   *lifetime*
Is naught but bitterness. Now, Roderigo,
Where didst thou see her? —O unhappy girl!
160 —With the Moor, say'st thou? —Who would be a father?
—How didst thou know 'twas she? —Oh, she deceives me
Past thought! —What said she to you? [*to Servants*] Get more
    tapers!
Raise all my kindred! —Are they married, think you?
RODERIGO   Truly, I think they are.
BRABANZIO   O heaven!
165 How got she out? Oh, treason of the blood!
Fathers, from hence trust not your daughters' minds
By what you see them act. Is there not charms°   *magic*
By which the property° of youth and maidhood°   *nature / virginity*
May be abused? Have you not read, Roderigo,
Of some such thing?
170 RODERIGO   Yes, sir, I have indeed.
BRABANZIO [*to Servants*]   Call up my brother! —Oh, would you
    had had her!
[*to Servants*] Some one way, some another. —Do you know
Where we may apprehend her and the Moor?
RODERIGO   I think I can discover him, if you please
175 To get good guard and go along with me.
BRABANZIO   Pray you, lead on. At every house I'll call:
I may command° at most.° [*to Servants*] Get   *demand help / most of them*
    weapons, ho!
And raise some special officers of might.
—On, good Roderigo: I will deserve° your pains.   *Exeunt.*   *reward*

4. Perhaps indicating an inn named for the astrological sign Sagittarius, where Othello and Desdemona are staying. It may also suggest Othello himself, since Sagittarius is depicted as a centaur (a mythological being part man, part horse), and Iago has already likened Othello to a "Barbary horse."

1.2 (Q 1.2)

Enter OTHELLO, IAGO, *[and] Attendants with torches.*

IAGO   Though in the trade of war I have slain men,
  Yet do I hold it very stuff° o'th' conscience   *essence*
  To do no contrived° murder. I lack iniquity   *premeditated*
  Sometime to do me service: nine or ten times
5   I had thought t'have yerked° him here under the ribs.   *struck with a dagger*

OTHELLO   'Tis better as it is.

IAGO   Nay, but he prated
  And spoke such scurvy and provoking terms
  Against your honor
  That, with the little godliness I have,
10   I did full hard forbear him.[1] But I pray you, sir,
  Are you fast° married? Be assured of this: *legitimately*
  That the magnifico° is much beloved,   *(Brabanzio)*
  And hath in his effect a voice potential°   *powerful*
  As double as the Duke's.[2] He will divorce you,
15   Or put upon you what restraint or grievance
  The law, with all his might to enforce it on,
  Will give him cable.°   *rope; scope*

OTHELLO   Let him do his spite:[3]
  My services which I have done the signory°   *Venetian government*
  Shall out-tongue his complaints. 'Tis yet to know°—   *It has never been shown*
20   Which, when I know that boasting is an honor,
  I shall promulgate—I fetch my life and being
  From men of royal siege,° and my demerits°   *rank / deserts*
  May speak unbonneted° to as proud a fortune   *with(out?) deference*
  As this that I have reached. For know, Iago,
25   But that° I love the gentle Desdemona,   *But for the fact that*
  I would not my unhousèd° free condition   *unconfined*
  Put into circumscription and confine
  For the sea's worth—

      Enter CASSIO *[and* OFFICERS*] with torches.*
             But look, what lights come yond?°   *yonder*

IAGO   Those are the raisèd father and his friends.
  You were best go in.

30 OTHELLO   Not I: I must be found.
  My parts,° my title, and my perfect soul[4]   *qualities*
  Shall manifest me rightly. Is it they?

IAGO   By Janus,° I think no.   *two-faced Roman god*

OTHELLO   The servants of the Duke's? And my lieutenant?
35   —The goodness of the night upon you, friends.
  What is the news?

CASSIO   The Duke does greet you, general,
  And he requires your haste-post-haste appearance
  Even on the instant.

OTHELLO   What is the matter, think you?

CASSIO   Something from Cyprus, as I may divine.
40   It is a business of some heat:° the galleys   *urgency*
  Have sent a dozen sequent° messengers   *successive*

1.2 Location: Another street in Venice, before Othello's lodgings.
1. I barely restrained myself from attacking him.
2. Like the Duke's, Brabanzio's influence is twice as great as that of any other senator.

3. PERFORMANCE COMMENT For the importance of Othello's physical appearance in this, his first, scene, as well as multiple options open to directors, see Digital Edition PC 1.
4. My clear conscience.

This very night at one another's heels,
And many of the consuls, raised and met,
Are at the Duke's already. You have been hotly called for:
45 When, being not at your lodging to be found,
The Senate hath sent about three several quests
To search you out.[5]

OTHELLO 'Tis well I am found by you.
I will but spend a word here in the house,
And go with you.   [Exit.]

CASSIO Ensign, what makes he here?

50 IAGO Faith, he tonight hath boarded a land carrack:°   large merchant ship
If it prove lawful prize, he's made for ever.

CASSIO I do not understand.

IAGO   He's married.

CASSIO   To who?

IAGO Marry,° to—   By Mary (wordplay)
        [Enter OTHELLO.]
        [to OTHELLO]   Come, captain, will you go?

OTHELLO   Have with you.°   Let's go
        Enter BRABANZIO, RODERIGO, with OFFICERS
        and torches.

CASSIO Here comes another troop to seek for you.

55 IAGO It is Brabanzio. —General, be advised:
He comes to bad intent.

OTHELLO [to BRABANZIO and RODERIGO] Holla, stand there!

RODERIGO Signor, it is the Moor.

BRABANZIO   Down with him, thief!

IAGO [drawing] You, Roderigo! Come, sir, I am for you.

OTHELLO Keep up° your bright swords, for the dew will rust   Put away
        them.
60 [to BRABANZIO] Good signor, you shall more command with
        years
Than with your weapons.

BRABANZIO O thou foul° thief! Where hast thou stowed my   (ethically); (in color)
        daughter?
Damned as thou art, thou hast enchanted her:
For I'll refer me to all things of sense,[6]
65 If she in chains of magic were not bound,
Whether a maid, so tender, fair, and happy,
So opposite to marriage that she shunned
The wealthy curlèd darling° of our nation,   darlings
Would ever have, t'incur a general mock,
70 Run from her guardage to the sooty bosom
Of such a thing as thou—to fear, not to delight.
Judge me the world if 'tis not gross in sense[7]
That thou hast practiced on her with foul charms,
Abused her delicate youth with drugs or minerals
75 That waken motion.[8] I'll have't disputed on:°   argued; looked into
'Tis probable, and palpable to thinking.

---

5. Cassio's speech suggests that the issue of Cyprus is a surprise to him and apparently to the Senate and Othello as well. But Iago (1.1.143–49) has already acknowledged that Othello is crucial to Venice's dealings with Cyprus. Either the point here is the immediacy of the danger or, more likely, the two pas- sages are not fully harmonized.
6. For I'll refer the matter to all rational beings.
7. Let the world judge me if it is not patently obvious. Lines 72–77 do not appear in Q.
8. Mental agitation.

I therefore apprehend and do attach° thee   *arrest*
For an abuser of the world, a practicer
Of arts inhibited and out of warrant.°   *prohibited and illegal*
80 [*to* OFFICERS] Lay hold upon him. If he do resist,
Subdue him at his peril.

OTHELLO   Hold your hands,
Both you of my inclining° and the rest!   *following*
Were it my cue to fight, I should have known it
Without a prompter. [*to* BRABANZIO] Whither will you that I go
To answer this your charge?

85 BRABANZIO   To prison, till fit time
Of law and course of direct session°   *court session*
Call thee to answer.

OTHELLO   What if I do obey?
How may the Duke be therewith satisfied,
Whose messengers are here about my side
90 Upon some present business of the state
To bring me to him?

OFFICER   'Tis true, most worthy signor:
The Duke's in council, and your noble self,
I am sure, is sent for.

BRABANZIO   How? The Duke in council?
In this time of the night? Bring him away!°   *along*
95 Mine's not an idle cause. The Duke himself,
Or any of my brothers of the state,
Cannot but feel this wrong as 'twere their own:
For if such actions may have passage free,
Bondslaves and pagans[9] shall our statesmen be.   *Exeunt.*

1.3 (Q 1.3)

Enter DUKE, [FIRST *and* SECOND] SENATORS,
and OFFICERS.

DUKE   There's no composition in this news
That gives them credit.[1]

FIRST SENATOR   Indeed, they are disproportioned:°   *inconsistent*
My letters say a hundred and seven galleys—

DUKE   And mine a hundred forty—

SECOND SENATOR   And mine two hundred.
5   But though they jump not on a just account°—   *don't exactly agree*
As in these cases where the aim reports,
'Tis oft with difference[2]—yet do they all confirm
A Turkish fleet, and bearing up to Cyprus.

DUKE   Nay, it is possible enough to judgment:°   *if one judges rationally*
10 I do not so secure me in the error
But the main article I do approve
In fearful sense.[3]

SAILOR (*within*)   What ho! What ho! What ho!

Enter SAILOR.

OFFICER   A messenger from the galleys.

---

9. Implicitly accusing Othello of being both slave
and non-Christian, though he is neither.
1.3 Location: A Venetian council room.
1. *There is . . . credit:* The reports lack the consistency that would make them believable.

2. *where . . . difference:* where the reports are esti-
mates, there are often discrepancies among them.
3. *I do not . . . sense:* I am not so reassured by the
discrepancies as to dismiss the main concern—the
approach of the Turkish fleet.

DUKE   —Now, what's the business?

SAILOR   The Turkish preparation° makes for Rhodes: *battle-ready fleet*
15   So was I bid report here to the state
        By Signor Angelo.[4]

DUKE [*to* SENATORS]   How say you by this change?

FIRST SENATOR   This cannot be
        By no assay° of reason: 'tis a pageant   *test*
        To keep us in false gaze. When we consider
20   Th'importancy of Cyprus to the Turk,
        And let ourselves again but understand
        That as it more concerns the Turk than Rhodes,
        So may he with more facile question bear it,[5]
        For that it stands not in such warlike brace,
25   But altogether lacks th'abilities
        That Rhodes is dressed in. If we make thought of this,
        We must not think the Turk is so unskillful
        To leave that latest° which concerns him first,   *last*
        Neglecting an attempt of ease and gain
30   To wake and wage° a danger profitless.   *risk*

DUKE   Nay, in all confidence, he's not for Rhodes.

OFFICER   Here is more news.

        Enter a MESSENGER.

MESSENGER   The Ottomites,° reverend and gracious,°   *Turks / (the Senators)*
        Steering with due course toward the isle of Rhodes,
35   Have there injointed them with an after° fleet.   *joined with another*

FIRST SENATOR   Ay, so I thought. How many, as you guess?

MESSENGER   Of thirty sail. And now they do restem°   *retrace*
        Their backward course, bearing with frank appearance
        Their purposes toward Cyprus. Signor Montano,
40   Your trusty and most valiant servitor,
        With his free duty recommends you thus,[6]
        And prays you to believe him.

DUKE   'Tis certain, then, for Cyprus.
        Marcus Luccicos,[7] is not he in town?

45 FIRST SENATOR   He's now in Florence.

DUKE   Write from us to him, post-post-haste.—Dispatch!
                        [*Exeunt* MESSENGER *and* SAILOR.]

FIRST SENATOR   Here comes Brabanzio and the valiant Moor.

        Enter BRABANZIO, OTHELLO, CASSIO, IAGO, RODERIGO,
        and OFFICERS.

DUKE   Valiant Othello, we must straight° employ you   *immediately*
        Against the general enemy° Ottoman.   *(of all Christendom)*
50   [*to* BRABANZIO] I did not see you. Welcome, gentle° signor;   *noble*
        We lacked your counsel and your help tonight.

BRABANZIO   So did I yours. Good your grace, pardon me:
        Neither my place° nor aught I heard of business   *official duty*
        Hath raised me from my bed; nor doth the general care
55   Take hold on me, for my particular grief
        Is of so floodgate° and o'er-bearing nature   *drenching*
        That it engluts and swallows other sorrows,

---

4. Not mentioned elsewhere in the play, Angelus Sorianus was a Venetian sea captain who received the Venetian ambassador bearing from Constantinople the Turkish ultimatum to surrender Cyprus shortly before its capture by the Turks in 1571.

5. So also can the Turkish fleet more easily win it. Lines 24–30 are not in Q.
6. With his freely given loyalty reports to you thus.
7. Not mentioned elsewhere in the play.

And it is still itself.[8]

DUKE	Why, what's the matter?
BRABANZIO	My daughter! Oh, my daughter!
FIRST *and* SECOND SENATORS	Dead?
BRABANZIO	Ay—to me.

60 She is abused,° stol'n from me, and corrupted°   *deluded / harmed bodily*
By spells and medicines bought of mountebanks:°   *quacks*
For nature so preposterously° to err,   *monstrously*
Being not deficient, blind, or lame of sense,
Sans° witchcraft could not.   *Without*

65 DUKE   Whoe'er he be that in this foul proceeding
Hath thus beguiled your daughter of herself
And you of her, the bloody book of law
You shall yourself read in the bitter letter
After your own sense, yea, though our proper son
Stood in your action.[9]

70 BRABANZIO   Humbly I thank your grace.
Here is the man: this Moor, whom now it seems
Your special mandate for the state affairs
Hath hither brought.

FIRST *and* SECOND SENATORS   We are very sorry for't.

DUKE [*to* OTHELLO]   What in your own part can you say to this?

75 BRABANZIO   Nothing, but this is so.

OTHELLO   Most potent, grave, and reverend signors,
My very noble and approved° good masters: *proven; experienced*
That I have ta'en away this old man's daughter,
It is most true; true I have married her.
80 The very head and front° of my offending   *height and breadth*
Hath this extent, no more. Rude° am I in my speech,   *Unpolished*
And little blessed with the soft phrase of peace
For, since these arms of mine had seven years' pith°   *strength*
Till now some nine moons wasted,° they have used   *nine months ago*
85 Their dearest° action in the tented° field,   *most valued / military*
And little of this great world can I speak
More than pertains to feats of broils° and battle;   *combats*
And, therefore, little shall I grace my cause
In speaking for myself. Yet, by your gracious patience,
90 I will a round° unvarnished tale deliver   *plain*
Of my whole course of love: what° drugs, what charms,   *with what*
What conjuration, and what mighty magic—
For such proceeding I am charged withal°—   *with*
I won his daughter.

95 BRABANZIO   A maiden never bold,
Of spirit so still and quiet that her motion
Blushed at herself;[1] and she, in spite of nature,
Of years, of country, credit,° everything,   *reputation*
To fall in love with what she feared to look on?
It is a judgment maimed and most imperfect
100 That will confess perfection so could err
Against all rules of nature, and must° be driven   *(we therefore) must*

---

8. *That . . . itself:* That my "grief" can incorporate
other "sorrows" without being affected.
9. *You shall . . . action:* You yourself shall interpret
the law as you see fit even if you are accusing my

own son.
1. *her . . . herself:* she blushed at her slightest display
of emotion.

To find out practices of cunning hell
Why this should be. I therefore vouch again
That with some mixtures powerful o'er the blood,°   *passions*
105   Or with some dram conjured° to this effect,   *enchanted dose*
        He wrought upon her.
DUKE   To vouch this is no proof
        Without more wider and more overt test
        Than these thin habits and poor likelihoods
        Of modern seeming do prefer against him.[2]
110   FIRST SENATOR   But, Othello, speak.
        Did you by indirect and forcèd courses°   *means*
        Subdue and poison this young maid's affections?
        Or came it by request and such fair question°   *conversation*
        As soul to soul affordeth?
OTHELLO   I do beseech you,
115   Send for the lady to the Sagittary,°   *(see 1.1.154 and note)*
        And let her speak of me before her father.
        If you do find me foul in her report,
        The trust, the office I do hold of you,
        Not only take away, but let your sentence
120   Even fall upon my life.
DUKE [*to* OFFICERS]   Fetch Desdemona hither.
OTHELLO   Ensign, conduct them: you best know the place.
               [*Exeunt* IAGO *and* OFFICERS.]
        —And till she come, as truly as to heaven
        I do confess the vices of my blood,°   *sins of passion*
125   So justly to your grave ears I'll present
        How I did thrive in this fair lady's love
        And she in mine.
DUKE   Say it, Othello.
OTHELLO   Her father loved me, oft invited me,
        Still° questioned me the story of my life   *Constantly*
130   From year to year: the battles, sieges, fortune,
        That I have passed.
        I ran it through, even from my boyish days
        To th' very moment that he bade me tell it,
        Wherein I spoke of most disastrous chances;°   *events*
135   Of moving accidents° by flood and field;   *events*
        Of hairbreadth scapes i'th' imminent deadly breach;[3]
        Of being taken by the insolent foe
        And sold to slavery; of my redemption thence,
        And portance° in my traveler's history;   *conduct*
140   Wherein of antres° vast and deserts idle,   *caves*
        Rough quarries, rocks, hills whose head touch heaven,
        It was my hint° to speak—such was my process°—   *occasion / story*
        And of the cannibals that each other eat—
        The *Anthropophagi*[4]—and men whose heads
145   Grew beneath their shoulders. These things to hear

---

2. *Without . . . him:* Without fuller and more direct testimony than mere appearances and conjecture based on current, shallow popular beliefs tell against him.
3. In the deadly gaps in a fortification.
4. Man-eaters. The term is from the ancient Roman writer Pliny the Elder. Shakespeare was also indebted to the travel literature of the Middle Ages (*Mandeville's Travels*) and the Renaissance (Hakluyt's *Principal Navigations*, among others), as well as to John Pory's English description of Leo Africanus's life in his translation of Leo's *Geographical History* (see the Introduction).

	Would Desdemona seriously incline;°	*eagerly lean (listen)*
	But still the house affairs would draw her hence,	
	Which ever as° she could with haste dispatch,	*Whenever*
	She'd come again, and with a greedy ear	
150	Devour up my discourse. Which I, observing,	
	Took once a pliant° hour, and found good means	*convenient*
	To draw from her a prayer of earnest heart	
	That I would all my pilgrimage dilate°	*relate*
	Whereof by parcels she had something heard	
155	But not instinctively.° I did consent,	*naturally*
	And often did beguile her of her tears	
	When I did speak of some distressful stroke	
	That my youth suffered. My story being done,	
	She gave me for my pains a world of kisses.[5]	
160	She swore, "In faith, 'twas strange, 'twas passing° strange.	*exceptionally*
	'Twas pitiful, 'twas wondrous pitiful."	
	She wished she had not heard it, yet she wished	
	That heaven had made her such a man.[6] She thanked me	
	And bade me, if I had a friend that loved her,	
165	I should but teach him how to tell my story,	
	And that would woo her. Upon this hint,° I spake.	*opportunity; suggestion*
	She loved me for the dangers I had passed,	
	And I loved her that she did pity them.	
	This only is the witchcraft I have used.	

Enter DESDEMONA, IAGO, [*and*] *Attendants.*

	Here comes the lady. Let her witness it.	
170		

DUKE I think this tale would win my daughter too.

—Good Brabanzio, take up this mangled matter at the best:° *as well as you can*
Men do their broken weapons rather use
Than their bare hands.

BRABANZIO   I pray you hear her speak.

175 If she confess that she was half the wooer,
Destruction° on my head if my bad blame *May destruction fall*
Light on the man. [*to* DESDEMONA] Come hither, gentle
   mistress:
Do you perceive in all this noble company
Where most you owe obedience?

DESDEMONA   My noble father,

180 I do perceive here a divided duty.
To you I am bound for life and education;
My life and education both do learn° me *teach*
How to respect you. You are the lord of duty;
I am, hitherto, your daughter. But here's my husband,
185 And so much duty as my mother showed
To you, preferring you before her father,
So much I challenge° that I may profess *assert*
Due to the Moor my lord.

BRABANZIO God be with you. I have done.

190 [*to* DUKE] Please it, your grace, on to the state affairs.
I had rather to adopt a child than get° it. *beget*
[*to* OTHELLO] Come hither, Moor.

---

5. F reads "kisses," Q "sighs." It is hard to explain "kisses" as a textual error.

6. Made such a man for her; made her into such a man.

I here do give thee that with all my heart
Which, but° thou hast already, with all my heart   *except that*
195   I would keep from thee. [*to* DESDEMONA] For your sake, jewel,
I am glad at soul I have no other child,
For thy escape would teach me tyranny,
To hang clogs[7] on them. [*to* DUKE] I have done, my lord.
DUKE   Let me speak like yourself, and lay a sentence°   *draw a moral*
200   Which as a grece° or step may help these lovers.   *flight of stairs*
"When remedies are past, the griefs are ended
By seeing the worst, which late on hopes depended.[8]
To mourn a mischief that is past and gone
Is the next way to draw new mischief on.
205   What cannot be preserved, when Fortune takes,
Patience her injury a mockery makes.[9]
The robbed that smiles steals something from the thief;
He robs himself that spends a bootless° grief."   *pointless*
BRABANZIO   So let the Turk of Cyprus us beguile:
210   We lose it not so long as we can smile.
He bears the sentence° well that nothing bears   *saying; judgment*
But the free comfort which from thence he hears;
But he bears both the sentence and the sorrow
That, to pay grief, must of poor patience borrow.
215   These sentences, to sugar or to gall,°   *both sweet and bitter*
Being strong on both sides, are equivocal.°   *equally apt*
But words are words: I never yet did hear
That the bruisèd heart was piercèd[1] through the ears.
I humbly beseech you, proceed to th'affairs of state.
220   DUKE   The Turk with a most mighty preparation makes for
Cyprus. Othello, the fortitude° of the place is best known to   *military layout*
you, and, though we have there a substitute of most allowed
sufficiency,° yet opinion, a more sovereign mistress of effects,   *known ability*
throws a more safer voice on you.[2] You must therefore be con-
225   tent to slubber° the gloss of your new fortunes with this more   *soil*
stubborn° and boisterous expedition.   *rougher*
OTHELLO   The tyrant custom, most grave senators,
Hath made the flinty and steel coach° of war   *captain's quarters*
My thrice-driven° bed of down. I do agnize°   *sifted / acknowledge*
230   A natural and prompt alacrity
I find in hardness,° and do undertake   *hardship*
This present war against the Ottomites.
Most humbly, therefore, bending to your state,°   *authority*
I crave fit disposition for my wife,
235   Due reference of place and exhibition[3]
With such accommodation and besort°   *suitable attendance*
As levels with° her breeding.   *fits*
DUKE   Why, at her father's.
BRABANZIO   I will not have it so.
OTHELLO   Nor I.
DESDEMONA   Nor would I there reside

---

7. Blocks of wood tied to criminals' legs to keep them from escaping.
8. By seeing those things come to pass that caused grief in anticipation, "griefs are ended." The Duke paints the moral in rhyming couplets, to which Brabanzio replies in kind.

9. Patience laughs at what cannot be helped (and thus reduces the "injury").
1. Surgically lanced (and presumably cured).
2. *opinion . . . you*: public opinion, which determines what gets done, finds greater security with you.
3. Proper accommodation and maintenance.

240   To put my father in impatient thoughts
    By being in his eye. —Most gracious Duke,
    To my unfolding° lend your prosperous° ear,   *proposal / receptive*
    And let me find a charter° in your voice   *an authorization*
    T'assist my simpleness.

    DUKE   What would you, Desdemona?

245 DESDEMONA   That I love the Moor to live with him
    My downright violence and storm of fortunes[4]
    May trumpet to the world. My heart's subdued
    Even to the very quality of my lord.[5]
    I saw Othello's visage in his mind,[6]
250   And to his honors and his valiant parts°   *qualities*
    Did I my soul and fortunes consecrate—
    So that, dear lords, if I be left behind
    A moth of peace, and he go to the war,
    The rites° for why I love him are bereft me,   *(of love or war); rights*
255   And I a heavy interim shall support°   *have to bear*
    By his dear absence. Let me go with him.

    OTHELLO   Let her have your voice.°   *agreement*
    Vouch with me, heaven, I therefore beg it not
    To please the palate of my appetite,
260   Nor to comply with heat° the young affects   *satisfy*
    In my defunct and proper satisfaction,[7]
    But to be free° and bounteous to her mind.   *liberal*
    And heaven defend your good souls that you think
    I will your serious and great business scant
265   When she is with me. No, when light-winged toys°   *diversions*
    Of feathered Cupid seal° with wanton dullness   *blind*
    My speculative and officed instrument[8]
    That° my disports° corrupt and taint my business,   *So that / sexual pleasures*
    Let housewives make a skillet of my helm,°   *helmet*
270   And all indign° and base adversities   *undignified*
    Make head against my estimation.[9]

    DUKE   Be it as you shall privately determine,
    Either for her stay or going. Th'affair cries haste,
    And speed must answer it.

    FIRST SENATOR   You must away tonight.

275 OTHELLO   With all my heart.

    DUKE   At nine i'th' morning here we'll meet again.
    Othello, leave some officer behind,
    And he shall our commission bring to you,
    And such things else of quality and respect°   *weight and importance*
    As doth import° you.   *concern*

280 OTHELLO   So please your grace, my ensign:
    A man he is of honesty[1] and trust.

---

4. My strong feelings and assault on the constraints I was fated to endure.
5. *My heart's . . . lord:* I love him for what he is (military, adventurous). Q reads "utmost pleasure" for "very quality"—a formulation that makes Desdemona's response one of subordination rather than of identification, sexual and otherwise.
6. I saw Othello as he sees himself; or: Othello's face expresses his character; or, perhaps: I looked past his outward appearance (age, skin color) to his inner

essence.
7. *Nor . . . satisfaction:* Nor to fulfill with passion youthful desires in the performed (though possibly suggesting defectiveness: "defunct") and fitting satisfaction (of marital relations).
8. My duty-bound faculties of sense.
9. Raise an army against my good reputation.
1. The first of many references to Iago's "honesty," all of them deeply ironic, some unwittingly so.

To his conveyance I assign my wife
With what else needful your good grace shall think
To be sent after me.

DUKE   Let it be so.
285 —Good night to everyone. [*to* BRABANZIO] And, noble signor,
If virtue no delighted° beauty lack,   *delightful*
Your son-in-law is far more fair than black.°   *(ethically); (racially)*

FIRST SENATOR Adieu, brave Moor;[2] use Desdemona well.
BRABANZIO Look to her,° Moor, if thou hast eyes to see: *Watch her carefully*
290 She has deceived her father, and may thee.
OTHELLO My life upon her faith.

               Exeunt [all except OTHELLO, DESDEMONA, IAGO,
                        and RODERIGO].

                  Honest Iago,
My Desdemona must I leave to thee.
I prithee let thy wife attend on her,
And bring them after in the best advantage.[3]
295 —Come, Desdemona, I have but an hour
Of love, of wordly matter, and direction°   *directives*
To spend with thee. We must obey the time.

            Exeunt [OTHELLO *and* DESDEMONA].

RODERIGO Iago?
IAGO   What say'st thou, noble heart?
RODERIGO What will I do, think'st thou?
IAGO   Why, go to bed and sleep.
300 RODERIGO I will incontinently° drown myself!   *immediately*
IAGO If thou dost, I shall never love thee after. Why, thou silly
gentleman!
RODERIGO It is silliness to live when to live is torment; and then
have we a prescription° to die when death is our physician.   *right; doctor's order*
305 IAGO Oh, villainous!° I have looked upon the world for four   *absurd; immoral(?)*
times seven years and, since I could distinguish betwixt a bene-
fit and an injury, I never found man that knew how to love
himself. Ere I would say I would drown myself for the love of a
guinea hen, I would change my humanity with a baboon.[4]
310 RODERIGO What should I do? I confess it is my shame to be so
fond, but it is not in my virtue° to amend it.   *native ability*
IAGO Virtue? A fig!° 'Tis in ourselves that we are thus, or thus.   *(obscenity)*
Our bodies are our gardens, to the which our wills are garden-
ers, so that if we will plant nettles or sow lettuce, set hyssop°   *mint herb*
315 and weed up thyme, supply it with one gender° of herbs or   *type*
distract it with many, either to have it sterile with idleness° or   *noncultivation*
manured with industry, why the power and corrigible authority°   *ability to improve*
of this lies in our wills. If the brain of our lives had not one
scale of reason to poise° another of sensuality, the blood and   *counterweigh*
320 baseness of our natures would conduct us to most preposterous conclusions.° But we have reason to cool our raging   *outcomes*
motions,° our carnal stings, or unbitted° lusts—whereof I take   *impulses / unrestrained*

---

2. TEXTUAL COMMENT *Moor* (line 288): an elastic term
referring to any or all Muslims, heretics, North Africans, or, by way of general association with blackness,
sub-Saharan Africans. Both F and Q foreground
Othello's blackness through abusive terms such as
"black ram," "sooty bosom," and the like (1.1.86, 1.2.70).
While F exclusively refers to Othello by name in stage
directions (though calling him "*Moor*" in its list of

roles), the Q stage directions sometimes substitute
"*Moor*" for Othello's name, thus perhaps emphasizing
the ways in which early modern English actors created the appearance of black skin. See Digital Edition TC 1 (Folio edited text).
3. And bring them along at the most favorable moment.
4. *guinea hen:* prostitute; perhaps a disparaging reference to Guinea in West Africa, picked up by "baboon."

this that you call "love" to be a sect or scion.°   *offshoot*

RODERIGO   It cannot be.

325   IAGO   It is merely a lust of the blood and a permission of the
will. Come, be a man! Drown thyself? Drown cats and blind
puppies! I have professed me thy friend, and I confess me knit
to thy deserving with cables of perdurable° toughness. I could   *durable*
never better stead° thee than now. Put money in thy purse!   *help*

330   Follow thou the wars; defeat thy favor with an usurped beard.[5]
I say, put money in thy purse! It cannot be long that Desdemona should continue her love to the Moor—put money in
thy purse!—nor he his to her. It was a violent commencement°   *an abruptly begun affair*
in her, and thou shalt see an answerable sequestration[6]—put

335   but money in thy purse! These Moors are changeable in their
wills—fill thy purse with money! The food that to him now is
as luscious as locusts[7] shall be to him shortly as bitter as *colo-*
quintida.[8] She must change for youth:° when she is sated with   *a youth*
his body, she will find the errors of her choice. Therefore put

340   money in thy purse! If thou wilt needs° damn thyself, do it a   *If you must*
more delicate way than drowning. Make all the money thou
canst. If sanctimony° and a frail vow betwixt an erring barbar-   *holy rite*
ian[9] and super-subtle° Venetian be not too hard for my wits   *deceptive*
and all the tribe of hell, thou shalt enjoy her. Therefore, make

345   money. A pox of drowning thyself! It is clean out of the way!°   *unacceptable*
Seek thou rather to be hanged in compassing° thy joy than to   *obtaining*
be drowned and go without her.

RODERIGO   Wilt thou be fast° to my hopes if I depend on the   *duty bound*
issue?°   *outcome*

350   IAGO   Thou art sure of me. Go, make money. I have told thee
often and I re-tell thee again and again: I hate the Moor. My
cause is hearted,° thine hath no less reason: let us be conjunc-   *heartfelt*
tive° in our revenge against him. If thou canst cuckold him,   *joined*
thou dost thyself a pleasure, me a sport. There are many events

355   in the womb of Time which will be delivered. Traverse,° go,   *Go (to arms)*
provide thy money: we will have more of this tomorrow. Adieu.

RODERIGO   Where shall we meet i'th' morning?

IAGO   At my lodging.

RODERIGO   I'll be with thee betimes.°   *early*

IAGO   Go to. Farewell. Do you hear, Roderigo?

360   RODERIGO   I'll sell all my land!   *Exit.*

IAGO   Thus do I ever make my fool my purse:
For I mine own gained knowledge should profane
If I would time expend with such snipe°   *fools*
But for my sport and profit. I hate the Moor,

365   And it is thought abroad° that twixt my sheets   *rumored*
He's done my office.° I know not if't be true,   *(sexual)*
But I, for mere suspicion in that kind,°   *regard*
Will do° as if for surety.° He holds° me well;   *act / it were true / likes*
The better shall my purpose work on him.

370   Cassio's a proper° man—let me see now: *handsome*
To get his place° and to plume up° my will   *position / gratify*
In double knavery? How? How? Let's see.

---

5. Disguise yourself to look more like a soldier with a
fake beard.
6. A correspondingly abrupt separation.
7. A sweet, exotic fruit, perhaps carob or honeysuckle.

8. Colocynth, a purgative—one of Iago's many references to the digestive tract.
9. Wandering (also mistaken) foreigner (savage; native
of Barbary in North Africa).

After some time, to abuse Othello's ears
That he is too familiar with his wife.[1]
375 He hath a person and a smooth dispose°   manner
To be° suspected, framed to make women false.   That are to be
The Moor is of a free° and open nature   liberal
That thinks men honest that but seem to be so,
And will as tenderly° be led by th' nose   easily
380 As asses are.
I have't! It is engendered. Hell and night
Must bring this monstrous birth to the world's light.[2]   [*Exit.*]

2.1 (Q 2.1)

Enter MONTANO, *and* [FIRST *and* SECOND]
GENTLEMEN.

MONTANO   What from the cape can you discern at sea?
FIRST GENTLEMAN   Nothing at all. It is a high-wrought flood:°   very rough sea
I cannot twixt the heaven and the main°   sea
Descry° a sail.   Discern
5 MONTANO   Methinks the wind hath spoke aloud at land;
A fuller blast ne'er shook our battlements.
If it hath ruffianed° so upon the sea,   raged
What ribs of oak, when mountains melt on them,
Can hold the mortise?[1] What shall we hear of this?
10 SECOND GENTLEMAN   A segregation° of the Turkish fleet: separation
For do but stand upon the foaming shore,
The chidden billow[2] seems to pelt the clouds,
The wind-shaked surge° with high and monstrous main°   fountain / open sea
Seems to cast water on the burning Bear
15 And quench the guards of th'ever-fixèd pole.[3]
I never did like molestation view°   see such a tumult
On the enchafèd° flood.   heated; tumultuous
MONTANO   If that the Turkish fleet
Be not ensheltered and embayed, they are drowned.
It is impossible to bear it out.

Enter [THIRD] GENTLEMAN.

20 THIRD GENTLEMAN   News, lads! Our wars are done.
The desperate tempest hath so banged the Turks
That their designment° halts. A noble ship of Venice   plan
Hath seen a grievous wreck and sufferance
On most part of their fleet.
MONTANO   How? Is this true?
25 THIRD GENTLEMAN   The ship is here put in,
A Veronese.[4] Michael Cassio,
Lieutenant to the warlike Moor, Othello,
Is come on shore; the Moor himself at sea,
And is in full commission here for Cyprus.
30 MONTANO   I am glad on't; 'tis a worthy governor.

---

1. "He" is Cassio (as in line 371), but "his" refers to Othello—a potential confusion of pronouns.
2. PERFORMANCE COMMENT. For some of the many ways of performing Iago's soliloquies, see Digital Edition PC 2.
2.1 Location: A seaport in Cyprus; outdoors near the harbor.
1. *What . . . mortise:* What ship (with "ribs of oak") can hold its joints ("mortise") together when "moun-

tains" of water pour on it?
2. The rising ocean, rebuked ("chidden") by the wind or repulsed by the land.
3. *burning Bear:* the constellation Ursa Minor. *guards:* probably two stars in the constellation that point in a line to the polestar, also in Ursa Minor.
4. Meaning unclear: originally from Verona, though now used by the Venetians; a cutter.

THIRD GENTLEMAN   But this same Cassio, though he speak of
   comfort
   Touching° the Turkish loss, yet he looks sadly°   *About / somberly*
   And prays the Moor be safe, for they were parted
   With foul and violent tempest.
MONTANO   Pray heavens he be!
35   For I have served him, and the man commands
   Like a full° soldier. Let's to the sea-side, ho,   *true*
   As well to see the vessel that's come in
   As to throw out our eyes for brave Othello,
   Even till we make the main and th'aerial blue
   An indistinct regard.[5]
40 THIRD GENTLEMAN   Come, let's do so,
   For every minute is expectancy
   Of more arrivancy.
         Enter CASSIO.
CASSIO   Thanks, you, the valiant of the warlike isle
   That so approve the Moor! Oh, let the heavens
45   Give him defense against the elements,
   For I have lost him on a dangerous sea.
MONTANO   Is he well shipped?
CASSIO   His bark is stoutly timbered, and his pilot
   Of very expert and approved allowance:°   *known ability*
50   Therefore my hopes, not surfeited to death,°   *not excessive*
   Stand in bold cure.°   *Are likely to be rewarded*
VOICES (*within*)   A sail! A sail! A sail!
CASSIO   What noise?
SECOND GENTLEMAN   The town is empty: on the brow° o'th' sea   *cliff at the edge*
   Stand ranks of people and they cry, "A sail!"
55 CASSIO   My hopes do shape him for° the governor.   *make it out to be*
     [*A shot is heard.*]
SECOND GENTLEMAN   They do discharge their shot of courtesy.
   Our friends, at least.
CASSIO [*to* SECOND GENTLEMAN]   I pray you, sir, go forth,
   And give us truth who 'tis that is arrived.
SECOND GENTLEMAN   I shall.   *Exit.*
60 MONTANO   But, good lieutenant, is your general wived?
CASSIO   Most fortunately! He hath achieved° a maid   *won*
   That paragons° description and wild fame,[6]   *stands above*
   One that excels the quirks of blazoning° pens   *praise-giving*
   And in th'essential vesture of creation
   Does tire the engineer.[7]
        Enter [SECOND] GENTLEMAN.
65   —How now? Who has put in?
SECOND GENTLEMAN   'Tis one Iago, ensign to the general.
CASSIO   He's had most favorable and happy speed.
   Tempests themselves, high seas, and howling winds,
   The guttered° rocks and congregated° sands—   *jagged / accumulated*
70   Traitors ensteeped° to enclog the guiltless keel—   *underwater*
   As having sense of beauty do omit°   *forgo*
   Their mortal° natures, letting go safely by   *deadly*
   The divine Desdemona.

---

5. *Even . . . regard:* Until we can't distinguish sea from
sky.
6. Unrestrained rumors.

7. *in . . . engineer:* whose natural beauty exhausts the
poet's capacity to invent praise.

MONTANO   What is she?

CASSIO   She that I spake of: our great captain's captain,
75   Left in the conduct of the bold Iago,
      Whose footing here anticipates our thoughts
      A sennight's speed.[8] Great Jove, Othello guard,°   guard Othello
      And swell his sail with thine own powerful breath,
      That he may bless this bay with his tall ship,
80   Make love's quick pants in Desdemona's arms,
      Give renewed fire to our extinguished spirits—

          Enter DESDEMONA, IAGO, RODERIGO, *and* EMILIA.

                                          Oh, behold!
      The riches of the ship is come on shore.
      You men of Cyprus, let her have your knees.
          [*He kneels.*]
      Hail to thee, lady, and the grace of heaven
85   Before, behind thee, and on every hand
      Enwheel thee round.

DESDEMONA   I thank you, valiant Cassio.
          [CASSIO *rises.*]
      What tidings can you tell of my lord?

CASSIO   He is not yet arrived, nor know I aught
      But that he's well and will be shortly here.

90 DESDEMONA   Oh, but I fear! How lost you company?

CASSIO   The great contention of sea and skies
      Parted our fellowship—

VOICES (*within*)   A sail! A sail!

CASSIO   But hark, a sail!
          [*A shot is heard.*]

SECOND GENTLEMAN   They give this greeting to the citadel;
      This likewise is a friend.

CASSIO [*to* SECOND GENTLEMAN]   See for the news.
                    [*Exit* SECOND GENTLEMAN.]
95   —Good ensign, you are welcome. [*He kisses* EMILIA.] Wel-
          come, mistress.
      —Let it not gall your patience, good Iago,
      That I extend my manners: 'tis my breeding
      That gives me this bold show of courtesy.

IAGO   Sir, would she give you so much of her lips
100   As of her tongue° she oft bestows on me,   (*scolding*); (*kissing*)
      You would have enough.

DESDEMONA   Alas, she has no speech![9]

IAGO   In faith, too much:
      I find it still when I have leave to sleep.
      Marry, before your ladyship I grant
105   She puts her tongue a little in her heart,[1]
      And chides with thinking.

EMILIA   You have little cause to say so.

IAGO   Come on! Come on! You are pictures out of door,
      Bells in your parlors, wildcats in your kitchens,
110   Saints in your injuries, devils being offended,

---

8. *Whose . . . speed:* Whose arrival predates our expectations by a week.
9. Perhaps: Alas, the accused scolding chatterbox is

not even rising to her own defense (both a defense of
Emilia and a prod for her to speak).
1. She keeps her (critical) thoughts to herself.

Players in your housewifery, and housewives in your beds.[2]
DESDEMONA Oh, fie upon thee, slanderer![3]
IAGO Nay, it is true, or else I am a Turk:
You rise to play, and go to bed to work.
EMILIA You shall not write my praise.
115 IAGO   No, let me not.
DESDEMONA What wouldst write of me, if thou shouldst
    praise me?
IAGO O gentle lady, do not put me to't,
For I am nothing if not critical.
DESDEMONA Come on: assay.° There's one gone to the harbor?   try
120 IAGO Ay, madam.
DESDEMONA I am not merry, but I do beguile°   disguise
The thing I am° by seeming otherwise.   (worried for Othello)
Come, how wouldst thou praise me?[4]
IAGO   I am about it,
But, indeed, my invention comes from my pate
125 As birdlime[5] does from frieze:° it plucks out brains and all.   coarse wool cloth
But my muse labors° and thus she is delivered: (in childbirth)
"If she be fair and wise, fairness and wit,
The one's for use, the other useth it."[6]
DESDEMONA Well praised. How if she be black and witty?
130 IAGO "If she be black and thereto have a wit,
She'll find a white that shall her blackness fit."[7]
DESDEMONA Worse and worse!
EMILIA   How if fair and foolish?
IAGO "She never yet was foolish that was fair,
For even her folly° helped her to an heir."   foolishness; lechery
135 DESDEMONA These are old fond° paradoxes to make fools laugh   foolish
i'th' alehouse. What miserable praise hast thou for her that's
foul° and foolish?   ugly
IAGO "There's none so foul and foolish thereunto°   to boot
But does foul° pranks which fair and wise ones do."   lascivious
140 DESDEMONA Oh, heavy ignorance: thou praisest the worst
best! But what praise couldst thou bestow on a deserving
woman indeed? One that in the authority of her merit did
justly put on the vouch° of very malice itself?   compel the approval
IAGO "She that was ever fair and never proud,
145 Had tongue at will and yet was never loud,
Never lacked gold and yet went never gay,°   lavishly clothed
Fled from her wish and yet said, 'Now I may';[8]
She that being angered, her revenge being nigh,
Bade her wrong stay° and her displeasure fly;   sense of injury end
150 She that in wisdom never was so frail

2. *You are . . . beds:* Iago shifts from Emilia to women generally in this speech. *pictures:* models of silent propriety. *Bells:* Noisy. *kitchens:* perhaps domestic affairs generally, rather than a specific room. *Saints:* Martyrs. *Players in your housewifery:* Deceptive in managing household expenses. *housewives:* wanton (perhaps businesslike, or sparing of sexual favors).
3. TEXTUAL COMMENT This line is part of Iago's speech in Q, where it may have been meant to be spoken by Emilia. For the different consequences of having Desdemona or Emilia utter this line, see Digital Edition TC 2 (Folio edited text).
4. PERFORMANCE COMMENT For the various issues raised by this scene in Cyprus's harbor—what appears onstage, relations between Venetians and Cypriots, possible sexual tension among the characters—see Digital Edition PC 3.
5. Sticky substance used to trap small birds.
6. *The one's . . . it:* Intelligence makes use of beauty.
7. *black:* dark-haired or dark-complexioned. *white:* fair-skinned person ("wight" means "person"). *blackness* (referring to hair or skin; also sexual). *fit:* (sexual).
8. Voluntarily withstood temptation even when given the choice.

To change the cod's head for the salmon's tail;[9]
She that could think and never disclose her mind,
See suitors following and not look behind;
She was a wight,° if ever such wights were"—   *(play on "white," line 131)*
155 DESDEMONA   To do what?
IAGO   "To suckle fools and chronicle small beer."[1]
DESDEMONA   Oh, most lame and impotent conclusion! —Do not
learn of him, Emilia, though he be thy husband. —How say
you, Cassio? Is he not a most profane and liberal° counselor?   *outspoken*
160 CASSIO   He speaks home,° madam: you may relish him   *forcefully*
More in° the soldier than in the scholar.   *as*
IAGO [*aside*]   He takes her by the palm. Ay, well said:° whisper!   *well done*
With as little a web as this will I ensnare as great a fly as
Cassio. Ay, smile upon her, do! I will give° thee in thine own   *shackle*
165 courtship.° [*to* CASSIO] You say true; 'tis so indeed. [*aside*] If   *courtliness*
such tricks as these strip you out of your lieutenantry, it had
been better you had not kissed your three fingers[2] so oft,
which now, again, you are most apt to play the sir° in. Very   *gentleman*
good: well kissed and excellent curtsy! [*to* CASSIO] 'Tis so
170 indeed. [*aside*] Yet again your fingers to your lips? Would they
were clyster-pipes° for your sake.   *enema tubes*
     [*Trumpets within.*]
—The Moor! I know his trumpet.
CASSIO   'Tis truly so.
DESDEMONA   Let's meet him and receive him.
          Enter OTHELLO *and Attendants.*
CASSIO   Lo, where he comes!
OTHELLO   O my fair warrior!
DESDEMONA   My dear Othello!
175 OTHELLO   It gives me wonder great as my content
To see you here before me. O my soul's joy!
If after every tempest come such calms,
May the winds blow till they have wakened death,
And let the laboring bark° climb hills of seas   *small ship*
180 Olympus-high,[3] and duck again as low
As hell's from heaven. If it were now to die,
'Twere now to be most happy—for I fear
My soul hath her content so absolute
That not another comfort like to this
Succeeds° in unknown fate.°   *Will follow / future*
185 DESDEMONA   The heavens forbid
But that our loves and comforts should increase
Even as our days do grow.
OTHELLO   Amen to that, sweet powers!
I cannot speak enough of this content;
It° stops me here.° It is too much of joy.   *(Emotion) / now; in my heart*
     [*They kiss.*]
190 And this, and this, the greatest discords be
That e'er our hearts shall make.
IAGO [*aside*]   Oh, you are well tuned now,

---

9. To make an unworthy exchange. Probably also suggesting sexual infidelity: "cod" means "penis," and "tail" equals "vulva."
1. To breast-feed babies and keep track of trivial domestic goods. That is, such perfect virtue suits only a dull, complacent, decidedly ungenteel housewife.
2. Kissing one's own hand was a common courtly gesture from a gentleman to a lady.
3. Mount Olympus, home of the Greek gods and hence too high for mortals.

But I'll set down the pegs that make this music,[4]
As honest as I am.

OTHELLO   Come, let us to the castle.
—News, friends! Our wars are done. The Turks are drowned.
195 How does my old acquaintance of this isle?
[*to* DESDEMONA] Honey, you shall be well desired° in Cyprus: *welcomed*
I have found great love amongst them. O my sweet,
I prattle out of fashion, and I dote
In mine own comforts. —I prithee, good Iago,
200 Go to the bay and disembark my coffers.
Bring thou the master° to the citadel: *captain*
He is a good one, and his worthiness
Does challenge° much respect. —Come, Desdemona.   *deserve*
—Once more, well met at Cyprus.

                    Exeunt [*all but* IAGO *and* RODERIGO].

205 IAGO   Do thou meet me presently at the harbor. Come thither.
If thou beest valiant—as they say base° men being in love   *lowly born*
have then a nobility in their natures more than is native to
them—list° me. The lieutenant tonight watches on the court   *listen to*
of guard.[5] First, I must tell thee this: Desdemona is directly
210 in love with him.

RODERIGO   With him? Why, 'tis not possible!

IAGO [*putting a finger to his lips*]   Lay thy finger thus, and let
thy soul be instructed. Mark me with what violence she first
loved the Moor but for bragging and telling her fantastical
215 lies. To love him still for prating? Let not thy discreet heart
think it. Her eye must be fed, and what delight shall she have
to look on the devil? When the blood is made dull with the act
of sport, there should° be a game° to inflame it and to give   *needs to / (sexual)*
satiety a fresh appetite: loveliness in favor,° sympathy in years,   *look; appearance*
220 manners, and beauties—all which the Moor is defective in.
Now, for want of these required conveniences,° her delicate   *agreements; advantages*
tenderness will find itself abused,[6] begin to heave the gorge,°   *feel nausea*
disrelish, and abhor the Moor: very nature will instruct her in
it, and compel her to some second choice. Now, sir, this
225 granted—as it is a most pregnant° and unforced position—   *obvious; (sexual)*
who stands so eminent in the degree of[7] this fortune as Cas-
sio does? A knave very voluble,° no further conscionable° than   *facile / no more ethical*
in putting on the mere form of civil and humane° seeming for   *courteous*
the better compass° of his salt° and most hidden loose affec-   *achievement / lewd*
230 tion. Why, none! Why, none! A slipper° and subtle knave, a   *slippery*
finder of occasion that has an eye can stamp and counterfeit
advantages, though true advantage[8] never present itself. A
devilish knave! Besides, the knave is handsome, young, and
hath all those requisites in him that folly° and green minds   *wantonness*
235 look after. A pestilent° complete knave, and the woman hath   *damnably*
found him already.

RODERIGO   I cannot believe that in her: she's full of most blessed
condition.

IAGO   Blessed fig's end!° The wine she drinks is made of   *(obscene)*
240 grapes. If she had been blessed, she would never have loved

---

4. I'll untune (by loosening) the "pegs" that hold the
strings of a musical instrument taut.
5. Cassio is in charge of the watch at the guardhouse.
6. Mistreated; deceived.

7. *in the degree of:* as next in line for.
8. Who can (like a counterfeiter) mint his own opportunities.

the Moor. Blessed pudding!° Didst thou not see her paddle   *sausage*
with the palm of his hand? Didst not mark that?

RODERIGO   Yes, that I did; but that was but courtesy.

IAGO   Lechery, by this hand. An index and obscure prologue to
245   the history of lust and foul thoughts.[9] They met so near
with their lips that their breaths embraced together. Villainous thoughts, Roderigo! When these mutabilities so marshal
the way, hard at hand comes the master and main exercise:[1]
th'incorporate° conclusion. Pish! But, sir, be you ruled by me.   *fleshly; physical*
250   I have brought you from Venice. Watch you tonight for the
command; I'll lay't upon you.[2] Cassio knows you not. I'll not
be far from you. Do you find some occasion to anger Cassio,
either by speaking too loud, or tainting° his discipline, or   *insulting*
from what other course you please, which the time shall more
255   favorably minister.°   *provide*

RODERIGO   Well?

IAGO   Sir, he's rash and very sudden in choler,° and happily°   *anger / to our benefit*
may strike at you. Provoke him that he may, for even out of
that will I cause these of Cyprus to mutiny, whose qualifica-
260   tion shall come into no true taste again[3] but by the displanting
of Cassio. So shall you have a shorter journey to your desires
by the means I shall then have to prefer° them, and the impedi-   *promote*
ment most profitably removed, without the which there were
no expectation of our prosperity.

265   RODERIGO   I will do this, if you can bring it to any opportunity.

IAGO   I warrant thee. Meet me by and by at the citadel. I must
fetch his necessaries° ashore. Farewell.   *Othello's possessions*

RODERIGO   Adieu.   *Exit.*

IAGO   That Cassio loves her, I do well believe't;
270   That she loves him, 'tis apt and of great credit.°   *likely and believable*
The Moor, howbeit that I endure him not,
Is of a constant, loving, noble nature,
And I dare think he'll prove to Desdemona
A most dear° husband. Now I do love her, too,   *affectionate; costly*
275   Not out of absolute lust—though, peradventure,°   *perhaps*
I stand accountant° for as great a sin—   *accountable*
But partly led to diet° my revenge,   *feed*
For that I do suspect the lusty Moor
Hath leaped into my seat,° the thought whereof   *slept with my wife*
280   Doth like a poisonous mineral gnaw my inwards,°   *innards*
And nothing can, or shall, content my soul
Till I am evened with him, wife for wife.
Or, failing so, yet that I put the Moor,
At least, into a jealousy so strong
285   That judgment cannot cure. Which thing to do,
If this poor trash of Venice, whom I trace
For his quick hunting, stand the putting-on,[4]
I'll have our Michael Cassio on the hip;°   *at my mercy*

9. *An . . . thoughts:* The analogy is to a dirty book.
index: table of contents. *obscure:* encoded. *history:*
story.
1. When these intimacies have cleared the way, the
main event follows close behind. Here, the analogy is
to an official procession.
2. Stand watch tonight. I'll see that you receive

orders.
3. *whose . . . again:* who will not be adequately
appeased.
4. *If . . . on:* If Roderigo, whom I follow (?), train (?),
puts weights on to slow him down (?), is successfully
set on the hunt when incited.

Abuse° him to the Moor in the right garb°—   *Slander / manner*
290 For I fear Cassio with my night-cape,° too—   *wife (sexual)*
Make the Moor thank me, love me, and reward me
For making him egregiously an ass
And practicing upon° his peace and quiet   *undermining*
Even to madness. 'Tis here,° but yet confused: *My plan is here*
295 Knavery's plain face is never seen till used.   *Exit.*

2.2 (Q 2.2)

Enter Othello's HERALD *with a proclamation.*

HERALD [*reads*] "It is Othello's pleasure, our noble and valiant
general, that upon certain tidings now arrived, importing the
mere perdition° of the Turkish fleet, every man put himself   *entire loss*
into triumph: some to dance, some to make bonfires, each
5 man to what sport and revels his addition° leads him. For,   *rank*
besides these beneficial news, it is the celebration of his nuptial." So much was his pleasure should be proclaimed. All
offices° are open, and there is full liberty of feasting from this   *storehouses*
present hour of five till the bell have told eleven. Bless the
10 isle of Cyprus and our noble general Othello!   *Exit.*

2.3 (Q 2.3)

Enter OTHELLO, DESDEMONA, CASSIO, *and Attendants.*

OTHELLO Good Michael, look you to the guard tonight.
Let's teach ourselves that honorable stop°   *self-restraint*
Not to out-sport° discretion.   *pass the limits of*
CASSIO Iago hath direction what to do,
5 But notwithstanding with my personal eye
Will I look to't.
OTHELLO   Iago is most honest.
Michael, good night: tomorrow with your earliest
Let me have speech with you. —Come, my dear love.
The purchase made, the fruits are to ensue:
10 That profit's yet to come tween me and you.[1]
—Good night.   *Exeunt* [OTHELLO *and* DESDEMONA].
          Enter IAGO.
CASSIO Welcome, Iago. We must to the watch.
IAGO Not this hour, lieutenant: 'tis not yet ten o'th' clock.
Our general cast° us thus early for the love of his Desde-   *dismissed*
15 mona, who let us not therefore blame: he hath not yet made
wanton the night with her, and she is sport for Jove.
CASSIO She's a most exquisite lady.
IAGO And, I'll warrant her, full of game.°   *spirit; (sexual?)*
CASSIO Indeed, she's a most fresh and delicate creature.
20 IAGO What an eye she has! Methinks it sounds a parley° to   *(military) call*
provocation.
CASSIO An inviting eye, and yet methinks right modest.
IAGO And when she speaks, is it not an alarum° to love?   *a call (to arms)*
CASSIO She is indeed perfection.
25 IAGO Well, happiness to their sheets. Come, lieutenant, I
have a stoup° of wine, and here without° are a brace of°   *bottle / outside / two*

2.2 Location: A street in Cyprus.   1. We haven't yet consummated our marriage.
2.3 Location: The citadel at Cyprus.

Cyprus gallants that would fain have a measure° to the health — *would like to drink*
of black Othello.

CASSIO Not tonight, good Iago. I have very poor and unhappy
30 brains for drinking: I could well wish courtesy would invent
some other custom of entertainment.

IAGO Oh, they are our friends! But one cup: I'll drink for you.

CASSIO I have drunk but one cup tonight—and that was craft-
ily qualified,° too—and behold what innovation° it makes — *well diluted / disorder*
35 here. I am infortunate in the infirmity, and dare not task my
weakness with any more.

IAGO What, man? 'Tis a night of revels. The gallants desire it.

CASSIO Where are they?

IAGO Here, at the door. I pray you call them in.

40 CASSIO I'll do't, but it dislikes me.°   *Exit.*   *I don't like doing it*

IAGO   If I can fasten but one cup upon him
With that which he hath drunk tonight already,
He'll be as full of quarrel and offense
As my young mistress' dog. Now, my sick fool Roderigo,
45 Whom love hath turned almost the wrong side out,
To Desdemona hath tonight caroused
Potations pottle-deep, and he's to watch.[2]
Three else of Cyprus—noble swelling° spirits — *proud*
That hold their honors in a wary distance,[3]
50 The very elements° of this warlike isle— — *character(istic)s*
Have I tonight flustered with flowing cups,
And they watch, too. Now 'mongst this flock of drunkards
Am I put to° our Cassio in some action° — *to put / fight*
That may offend the isle.
      Enter CASSIO, MONTANO, *and* [*three*] GENTLEMEN
      [*with wine*].
                              But here they come.
55 If consequence do but approve my dream,[4]
My boat sails freely both with wind and stream.° — *current*

CASSIO Fore heaven, they have given me a rouse° already! — *full draft*

MONTANO   Good faith, a little one: not past a pint, as I am a
soldier!

60 IAGO   —Some wine, ho!
[*sings*]   And let me the cannikin° clink, clink, — *drinking vessel*
            And let me the cannikin clink.
            A soldier's a man, oh, man's life's but a span,
            Why, then, let a soldier drink!
65 Some wine, boys!

CASSIO Fore heaven, an excellent song!

IAGO   I learned it in England, where indeed they are most
potent in potting.[5] Your Dane, your German, and your swag°- — *hanging*
bellied Hollander—drink, ho!—are nothing to your English.

70 CASSIO Is your Englishman so exquisite in his drinking?

IAGO   Why, he drinks you with facility° your Dane dead drunk; — *easily drinks*
he sweats not to overthrow your Almain;° he gives your Hol- — *German*
lander a vomit ere the next pottle° can be filled. — *tankard*

CASSIO To the health of our general!

---

2. *caroused . . . watch:* consumed drink to the bottom of the tankard, and he's set to watch Cassio.
3. Who are touchy about their honor.

4. If events turn out as I hope.
5. Most adept at drinking (self-referential joke).

75 MONTANO I am for it, lieutenant, and I'll do you justice.°   *match your drinking*

IAGO O sweet England!

    [*sings*]   King Stephen was and a worthy peer,

                  His breeches cost him but a crown;

                  He held them sixpence all too dear,

80   With that he called the tailor "loon."°   *lout*

                  He was a wight of high renown

                  And thou art but of low degree:

                  'Tis pride° that pulls the country down,   *ostentatious clothing*

                  And take thy old cloak about thee.

85   —Some wine, ho!

CASSIO Why, this is a more exquisite song than the other!

IAGO Will you hear't again?

CASSIO No, for I hold him to be unworthy of his place that does those things. Well, heaven's above all, and there be souls must
90 be saved, and there be souls must not be saved.[6]

IAGO It's true, good lieutenant.

CASSIO For mine own part, no offense to the general nor any man of quality,° I hope to be saved.   *rank*

IAGO And so do I, too, lieutenant.

95 CASSIO Ay, but by your leave, not before me! The lieutenant is   –climax
to be saved before the ensign. Let's have no more of this. Let's to our affairs. Forgive us our sins. —Gentlemen, let's look to our business. Do not think, gentlemen, I am drunk: this is my ensign, this is my right hand, and this is my left. I am not
100 drunk now: I can stand well enough and I speak well enough.

GENTLEMEN Excellent well.

CASSIO Why, very well, then: you must not think, then, that
I am drunk.   *Exit.*

MONTANO To th' platform, masters. Come, let's set the watch.

                              [*Exeunt* GENTLEMEN.]

105 IAGO You see this fellow that is gone before?

    He's a soldier fit to stand by Caesar

    And give direction; and do but see his vice:

    'Tis to his virtue a just equinox,°   *of equal size*

    The one as long as th'other. 'Tis pity of him.°   *It's a shame*

110   I fear the trust Othello puts him in

    On some odd time of his infirmity

    Will shake this island.

MONTANO   But is he often thus?

IAGO 'Tis evermore his prologue to his sleep:

    He'll watch the horologe a double set[7]

    If drink rock not his cradle.

115 MONTANO   It were well

    The general were put in mind of it.

    Perhaps he sees it not, or his good nature

    Prizes the virtue that appears in Cassio

    And looks not on his evils. Is not this true?—

    Enter RODERIGO.

120 IAGO [*aside*] How now, Roderigo?

    I pray you, after the lieutenant: go!   [*Exit* RODERIGO.]

MONTANO —And 'tis great pity that the noble Moor

---

6. Referring to the idea of predestination, the belief held by Calvinist Protestants that some souls are des-   tined from the outset to be saved and others damned.
7. He'll stay up twice around the clock.

Should hazard such a place as his own second
With one of an engraft° infirmity.   *ingrained*
125   It were an honest action to say so
To the Moor.
IAGO   Not I, for this fair island!
I do love Cassio well, and would do much
To cure him of this evil. But hark, what noise?
Enter CASSIO *pursuing* RODERIGO.
CASSIO   You rogue! You rascal!
MONTANO   What's the matter, lieutenant?
130   CASSIO   A knave teach me my duty?
I'll beat the knave into a twiggen bottle.⁸
RODERIGO   Beat me?
CASSIO   Dost thou prate, rogue?
MONTANO   Nay, good lieutenant!
I pray you, sir, hold your hand.
CASSIO   Let me go, sir,
Or I'll knock you o'er the mazard.°   *head*
MONTANO   Come, come! You're drunk.
135   CASSIO   Drunk?
        [*They fight.*]
IAGO [*aside to* RODERIGO]   Away, I say! Go out and cry a mutiny.
                                    [*Exit* RODERIGO.]
—Nay, good lieutenant. Alas, gentlemen!
—Help, ho! —Lieutenant! Sir! —Montano!
—Help, masters! —Here's a goodly watch indeed.
        [*A bell rings.*]
140   Who's that which rings the bell? *Diablo!*° Ho!   *Devil!*
The town will rise. —Fie, fie, lieutenant,
You'll be ashamed for ever.
        Enter OTHELLO *and Attendants.*
OTHELLO   What is the matter here?
MONTANO   I bleed still. I am hurt to th' death. He dies!
OTHELLO   Hold, for your lives!
145   IAGO   Hold, ho! Lieutenant! Sir! Montano! Gentlemen!
Have you forgot all place of sense and duty?
Hold! The general speaks to you. Hold, for shame!
OTHELLO   Why, how now? Ho! From whence ariseth this?
Are we turned Turks, and to ourselves do that
150   Which heaven hath forbid the Ottomites?°   (*by raising a storm*)
For Christian shame, put by this barbarous brawl.
He that stirs next to carve for his own rage°   *draw a sword in anger*
Holds his soul light: he dies upon his motion.
[*to Attendants*] Silence that dreadful bell: it frights the isle
From her propriety.   [*Exit Attendant.*]
155   —What is the matter, masters?
—Honest Iago, that looks dead with grieving,
Speak. Who began this? On thy love I charge thee.
IAGO   I do not know. Friends all but now; even now
In quarter° and in terms like bride and groom   *Under control*
160   Devesting them° for bed; and then but now,   *Getting undressed*

---

8. *twiggen:* wicker-cased. Hence, smash to pieces or, perhaps, produce wicker-like lashes on Roderigo's back.

As if some planet° had unwitted men,   *astrological influence*
Swords out, and tilting one at other's breasts
In opposition bloody. I cannot speak
Any beginning to this peevish odds,°   *capricious quarrel*
165   And would in action glorious I had lost
Those legs that brought me to a part of it.
OTHELLO   How comes it, Michael, you are thus forgot?°   *you thus forgot yourself*
CASSIO   I pray you, pardon me: I cannot speak.
OTHELLO   Worthy Montano, you were wont to be° civil: *you used to be*
170   The gravity and stillness of your youth
The world hath noted, and your name is great
In mouths of wisest censure.° What's the matter   *judgment*
That you unlace your reputation thus,
And spend your rich opinion° for the name   *reputation*
175   Of a night-brawler? Give me answer to it!
MONTANO   Worthy Othello, I am hurt to danger.
Your officer, Iago, can inform you
While I spare speech, which something now offends me,°   *somewhat now pains me*
Of all that I do know. Nor know I aught°   *anything*
180   By me that's said or done amiss this night,
Unless self-charity° be sometimes a vice,   *care of oneself*
And to defend ourselves it be a sin
When violence assails us.
OTHELLO   Now, by heaven,
My blood begins my safer guides to rule
185   And passion, having my best judgment collied,[9]
Assays to lead the way! If I once stir
Or do but lift this arm, the best of you
Shall sink in my rebuke. Give me to know
How this foul rout began, who set it on,
190   And he that is approved in° this offense,   *shown culpable of*
Though he had twinned with me, both at a birth,
Shall lose me. What, in a town of war
Yet° wild, the peoples' hearts brimful of fear,   *Still*
To manage° private and domestic quarrel   *carry on*
195   In night, and on the court and guard of safety?[1]
'Tis monstrous! Iago, who began't?
MONTANO [*to* IAGO]   If partially affined or league in office,[2]
Thou dost deliver more or less than truth,
Thou art no soldier.
IAGO   Touch me not so near.
200   I had rather have this tongue cut from my mouth
Than it should do offense to Michael Cassio.
Yet, I persuade myself, to speak the truth
Shall nothing wrong him. This it is, general:
Montano and myself being in speech,
205   There comes a fellow crying out for help
And Cassio following him with determined sword
To execute upon° him. Sir, this gentleman   *attack*
        [*indicating* MONTANO]
Steps in to Cassio and entreats his pause.

---

9. Obscured by anger (choler); darkened racially.   2. *If . . . office:* If biased (in favor of Cassio) by your
1. And at the place where safety and security are at   ties to him or (by) your holding office together.
stake (on the night watch).

Myself the crying fellow did pursue
210 Lest by his clamor, as it so fell out,
The town might fall in fright. He, swift of foot,
Outran my purpose, and I returned then rather
For that° I heard the clink and fall of swords   *especially since*
And Cassio high in oath, which till tonight
215 I ne'er might say before. When I came back—
For this was brief—I found them close together
At blow and thrust, even as again they were
When you yourself did part them.
More of this matter cannot I report.
220 But men are men: the best sometimes forget.
Though Cassio did some little wrong to him,
As men in rage strike those that wish them best,
Yet surely Cassio, I believe, received
From him that fled some strange indignity
Which patience could not pass.°   *let pass*
225 OTHELLO   I know, Iago,
Thy honesty and love doth mince° this matter,   *minimize*
Making it light to Cassio. —Cassio, I love thee,
But never more be officer of mine.
            Enter DESDEMONA [*and Attendants*].
Look if my gentle love be not raised up—
230 [*to* CASSIO] I'll make thee an example.
DESDEMONA   What is the matter, dear?
OTHELLO   All's well, sweeting.
Come away to bed. [*to* MONTANO] Sir, for your hurts
Myself will be your surgeon. [*to Attendants*] Lead him off.
—Iago, look with care about the town,
235 And silence those whom this vile brawl distracted.
—Come, Desdemona. 'Tis the soldier's life
To have their balmy slumbers waked with strife.
                Exeunt [*all but* IAGO *and* CASSIO].
IAGO   What, are you hurt, lieutenant?
CASSIO   Ay, past all surgery.
240 IAGO   Marry, heaven forbid!
CASSIO   Reputation, reputation, reputation! Oh, I have lost my
reputation! I have lost the immortal part of myself, and what
remains is bestial. My reputation, Iago, my reputation!
IAGO   As I am an honest man, I had thought you had received
245 some bodily wound; there is more sense in that than in reputa-
tion. Reputation is an idle and most false imposition,° oft got   *artificial notion*
without merit and lost without deserving. You have lost no
reputation at all, unless you repute yourself such a loser.
What, man, there are more ways to recover the general again!
250 You are but now cast in his mood; a punishment more in policy[3] than in malice, even so as one would beat his offenseless
dog to affright an imperious lion. Sue to° him again, and he's   *Petition*
yours.
CASSIO   I will rather sue to be despised than to deceive so good a
255 commander with so slight, so drunken, and so indiscreet an
officer. Drunk? And speak parrot?° And squabble, swagger,   *rant on*
swear? And discourse fustian° with one's own shadow? O thou   *nonsense*

---

3. *cast . . . policy:* dismissed in anger—a matter of policy (of public example).

invisible spirit of wine, if thou hast no name to be known by, let
us call thee "devil."

260 IAGO   What was he that you followed with your sword? What
had he done to you?

CASSIO   I know not.

IAGO   Is't possible?

CASSIO   I remember a mass of things, but nothing distinctly; a
265   quarrel, but nothing wherefore.° Oh, that men should put   *but not why*
an enemy in their mouths° to steal away their brains! That   *should drink*
we should with joy, pleasance, revel, and applause transform
ourselves into beasts!

IAGO   Why, but you are now well enough. How came you thus
270   recovered?

CASSIO   It hath pleased the devil drunkenness to give place to
the devil wrath: one unperfectness shows me another to
make me frankly despise myself.

IAGO   Come, you are too severe a moraler. As the time, the
275   place, and the condition of this country stands, I could heartily wish this had not befallen; but since it is as it is, mend it,
for your own good.

CASSIO   I will ask him for my place again; he shall tell me I am
a drunkard. Had I as many mouths as Hydra,[4] such an
280   answer would stop them all. To be now a sensible man, by
and by a fool, and presently a beast! Oh, strange! Every inordinate cup is unblessed, and the ingredient is a devil.

IAGO   Come, come: good wine is a good familiar creature, if it
be well used. Exclaim no more against it. And, good lieuten-
285   ant, I think you think I love you?

CASSIO   I have well approved° it, sir.—I, drunk?   *tested*

IAGO   You, or any man living, may be drunk at a time, man. I
tell you what you shall do. Our general's wife is now the
general—I may say so, in this respect, for that he hath
290   devoted and given up himself to the contemplation, mark,
and devotement of° her parts° and graces. Confess yourself   *devotion to / qualities*
freely to her; importune her help to put you in your place°   *office*
again. She is of so free, so kind, so apt, so blessed a disposition, she holds it a vice in her goodness not to do more than
295   she is requested.[5] This broken joint[6] between you and her
husband entreat her to splinter° and, my fortunes against   *heal with a splint*
any lay° worth naming, this crack of your love shall grow   *wager*
stronger than it was before.

CASSIO   You advise me well.

300 IAGO   I protest,° in the sincerity of love and honest kindness.   *insist*

CASSIO   I think it freely, and betimes° in the morning I will   *early*
beseech the virtuous Desdemona to undertake for me. I am
desperate of my fortunes if they check° me!   *stop*

IAGO   You are in the right. Good night, lieutenant. I must to
305   the watch.

---

4. A mythical serpent with many heads who grew
two more when one was cut off.
5. In these lines, Iago may covertly defame Desdemona, unbeknownst to Cassio; line 289: "general" (generally accessible sexually); line 292: "put you in your
place" (penetration in intercourse); line 293: "free"
(generous, erotically open), "kind" (good-humored
about agreeing to make love), "apt" (inclined to help, to
engage in amorous behavior). Similar undertones mark
his ensuing soliloquy, lines 307–33.
6. (Of a bone).

CASSIO   Good night, honest Iago.   *Exit* CASSIO.
IAGO   And what's he, then, that says I play the villain
        When this advice is free I give, and honest,
        Probal° to thinking, and indeed the course   *Wise*
310   To win the Moor again? For 'tis most easy
        Th'inclining° Desdemona to subdue   *The well-disposed*
        In any honest suit: she's framed as fruitful°   *generous*
        As the free elements.° And then for her   *unconstrained nature*
        To win the Moor—were° to renounce his baptism,   *even if it were*
315   All seals and symbols of redeemed sin—
        His soul is so enfettered to her love
        That she may make, unmake, do what she list,
        Even as her appetite⁷ shall play the god
        With his weak function.° How am I then a villain   *(intellectual?); (sexual)*
320   To counsel Cassio to this parallel° course   *suitable*
        Directly to his good? Divinity° of hell: *Theology*
        When devils will the blackest sins put on,
        They do suggest at first with heavenly shows,
        As I do now. For whiles this honest fool
325   Plies Desdemona to repair his fortune,
        And she for him pleads strongly to the Moor,
        I'll pour this pestilence into his° ear: *(Othello's)*
        That she repeals him° for her body's lust   *appeals for him*
        And, by how much she strives to do him good,
330   She shall undo her credit with the Moor.
        So will I turn her virtue into pitch⁸
        And out of her own goodness make the net
        That shall enmesh them all—
            Enter RODERIGO.
                          —How now, Roderigo?
RODERIGO   I do follow here in the chase, not like a hound that
335   hunts but one that fills up the cry.° My money is almost   *a pack follower*
        spent; I have been tonight exceedingly well cudgeled; and I
        think the issue will be I shall have so much° experience for *only this*
        my pains. And so, with no money at all and a little more wit,
        return again to Venice.
340   IAGO   How poor are they that have not patience!
        What wound did ever heal but by degrees?
        Thou know'st we work by wit and not by witchcraft,
        And wit depends on dilatory° time.   *drawn-out*
        Does't not go well? Cassio hath beaten thee,
345   And thou by that small hurt hath cashiered° Cassio.   *dismissed*
        Though other things grow fair against the sun,
        Yet fruits that blossom first will first be ripe.⁹
        Content thyself awhile. In troth, 'tis morning!
        Pleasure and action make the hours seem short.
350   Retire thee; go where thou art billeted.
        Away, I say! Thou shalt know more hereafter.
        Nay, get thee gone!   *Exit* RODERIGO.
                Two things are to be done:

---

7. *her appetite:* Despdemona's wishes or desire for
Othello; perhaps, his appetite for her.
8. Black, sticky substance used as a snare. The more
the thing caught in it tries to escape, the more stuck
it becomes.

9. *Though . . . ripe:* Although others prosper only
when fully in the sun, your plan will be successful even
earlier in the day (metaphorically) because started first
and allowed to develop slowly.

My wife must move for Cassio to her mistress—
I'll set her on;
355 Myself a while to draw the Moor apart
And bring him jump° when he may Cassio find   *exactly*
Soliciting his wife. Ay, that's the way.
Dull not device by coldness and delay.[1]   *Exit.*

3.1 (Q 3.1)

Enter CASSIO [*with*] MUSICIANS.

CASSIO Masters, play here—I will content° your pains—   *reward*
    Something that's brief, and bid "Good morrow, general."
    [MUSICIANS *play.*]
    [*Enter* CLOWN.]
CLOWN Why, masters, have your instruments been in Naples,
    that they speak i'th' nose thus?[1]
5 MUSICIAN How, sir? How?
CLOWN Are these, I pray you, wind instruments?[2]
MUSICIAN Ay, marry are they, sir.
CLOWN Oh, thereby hangs a tail!
MUSICIAN Whereby hangs a tale, sir?
10 CLOWN Marry, sir, by many a wind instrument that I know.
    But, masters, here's money for you, and the general so likes
    your music that he desires you, for love's sake,[3] to make no
    more noise with it.
MUSICIAN Well, sir, we will not!
15 CLOWN If you have any music that may not° be heard, to't   *cannot*
    again. But, as they say, to hear music the general does not
    greatly care.
MUSICIAN We have none such, sir.
CLOWN Then put up your pipes in your bag, for I'll away. Go,
20   vanish into air. Away!   *Exeunt* MUSICIANS.
CASSIO Dost thou hear, mine honest friend?
CLOWN No, I hear not your honest friend: I hear you.
CASSIO Prithee, keep up thy quillets.° There's a poor piece of   *pack up your puns*
    gold for thee. If the gentlewoman that attends the general
25   be stirring, tell her there's one Cassio entreats her a little
    favor of speech. Wilt thou do this?
CLOWN She is stirring, sir. If she will stir hither, I shall seem°   *arrange*
    to notify unto her.   *Exit* CLOWN.[4]
    Enter IAGO.
CASSIO In happy time,° Iago.   *I'm glad to see you*
IAGO   You have not been a-bed, then?
30 CASSIO Why, no: the day had broke before we parted.
    I have made bold, Iago, to send in to your wife:
    My suit to her is that she will to virtuous
    Desdemona procure me some access.
IAGO I'll send her to you presently,°   *immediately*
35   And I'll devise a mean to draw the Moor

---

1. Don't let sluggishness and slowness to act weaken the plot.
3.1 Location: Outside Othello and Desdemona's room.
1. That they sound so nasal; perhaps a reference to venereal disease, often associated with Naples, or a phallic or anal joke.
2. The exchange that follows depends on the con-
nections between wind instruments, flatulence, and "tale/tail."
3. Out of affection for him; so that his lovemaking won't be disturbed.
4. PERFORMANCE COMMENT For the consequences of cutting (or preserving) both the Clown's part (here and in 3.4) and the very brief 3.2, see Digital Edition PC 4.

Out of the way, that your converse and business
May be more free.

CASSIO   I humbly thank you for't.   *Exit* [IAGO].

                           I never knew
A Florentine° more kind and honest.   *Even a fellow Florentine*
    Enter EMILIA.

40   EMILIA   Good morrow, good lieutenant. I am sorry
For your displeasure,° but all will sure be well: *troubles*
The general and his wife are talking of it,
And she speaks for you stoutly. The Moor replies
That he you hurt is of great fame in Cyprus
45   And great affinity,° and that, in wholesome wisdom,   *well connected*
He might not but refuse you. But he protests he loves you,
And needs no other suitor but his likings
To bring you in again.

CASSIO   Yet, I beseech you,
If you think fit, or that it may be done,
50   Give me advantage of some brief discourse
With Desdemon alone.

EMILIA   Pray you, come in.
I will bestow you where you shall have time
To speak your bosom° freely.   *heart*

CASSIO   I am much bound to you.
                                      [Exeunt.]

3.2 (Q 3.2)
    Enter OTHELLO, IAGO, *and* GENTLEMEN.

OTHELLO   These letters give, Iago, to the pilot,
And by him do my duties° to the Senate.   *send my respects*
That done, I will be walking on the works.°   *fortifications*
Repair there to me.

IAGO   Well, my good lord, I'll do't.
5   OTHELLO   —This fortification, gentlemen, shall we see't?

GENTLEMEN   We'll wait upon your lordship.   *Exeunt.*

3.3 (Q 3.3)
    Enter DESDEMONA, CASSIO, *and* EMILIA.

DESDEMONA   Be thou assured, good Cassio, I will do
All my abilities in thy behalf.

EMILIA   Good madam, do. I warrant it grieves my husband
As if the cause were his.

5   DESDEMONA   Oh, that's an honest fellow. —Do not doubt,
    Cassio,
But I will have my lord and you again
As friendly as you were.

CASSIO   Bounteous madam,
Whatever shall become of Michael Cassio,
He's never anything but your true servant.

10   DESDEMONA   I know't. I thank you. You do love my lord;
You have known him long and, be you well assured,
He shall in strangeness stand no farther off

3.2 Location: The citadel.   3.3 Location: The citadel's garden.

Than in a politic distance.[1]

CASSIO   Ay, but, lady,
That policy may either last so long,
15   Or feed upon such nice and waterish diet,
Or breed itself so out of circumstances[2]
That, I being absent, and my place supplied,°   *filled*
My general will forget my love and service.

DESDEMONA   Do not doubt° that. Before Emilia here   *fear*
20   I give thee warrant° of thy place. Assure thee: *assurance*
If I do vow a friendship, I'll perform it
To the last article. My lord shall never rest:
I'll watch him tame, and talk him out of patience;[3]
His bed shall seem a school, his board a shrift;°   *confessional*
25   I'll intermingle everything he does
With Cassio's suit. Therefore be merry, Cassio,
For thy solicitor° shall rather die   *advocate*
Than give thy cause away.°   *up*

           Enter OTHELLO *and* IAGO.[4]

EMILIA   Madam, here comes my lord.

CASSIO   Madam, I'll take my leave.

DESDEMONA   Why, stay and hear me speak.
30 CASSIO   Madam, not now: I am very ill at ease,
Unfit for mine own purposes.

DESDEMONA   Well, do your discretion.   *Exit* CASSIO.

IAGO   Ha! I like not that.

OTHELLO   What dost thou say?

IAGO   Nothing, my lord, or if—I know not what.

35 OTHELLO   Was not that Cassio parted from my wife?

IAGO   Cassio, my lord? No, sure. I cannot think it
That he would steal away so guilty-like,
Seeing your coming.

OTHELLO   I do believe 'twas he.

DESDEMONA   How now, my lord?
40   I have been talking with a suitor here,
A man that languishes in your displeasure.

OTHELLO   Who is't you mean?

DESDEMONA   Why, your lieutenant, Cassio. Good my lord,
If I have any grace or power to move you,
45   His present reconciliation take:°   *Accept him now*
For if he be not one that truly loves you,
That errs in ignorance and not in cunning,°   *not knowingly*
I have no judgment in an honest face.
I prithee call him back.

OTHELLO   Went he hence now?
50 DESDEMONA   I'sooth,° so humbled   *Truly*
That he hath left part of his grief with me
To suffer with him. Good love, call him back.

OTHELLO   Not now, sweet Desdemon. Some other time.

DESDEMONA   But shall't be shortly?

---

1. *He . . . distance:* He will distance himself from you only as much as good diplomacy requires.
2. *Or feed . . . circumstances:* Or persist based on such unimportant and poor justifications (perhaps: such pampered and juicy fare), or continue by chance.
3. I'll keep him awake until he obeys me, and talk to him beyond his endurance.
4. TEXTUAL COMMENT For the difference between F's and Q's stage directions here, and the implications for understanding events as public or private, see Digital Edition TC 3 (Folio edited text).

	OTHELLO	The sooner, sweet, for you.
	DESDEMONA	Shall't be tonight at supper?
55	OTHELLO	No, not tonight.
	DESDEMONA	Tomorrow dinner,° then?

OTHELLO   I shall not dine at home:
     I meet the captains at the citadel.
DESDEMONA   Why, then, tomorrow night? On Tuesday morn?
     On Tuesday noon, or night? On Wednesday morn?
60   I prithee, name the time, but let it not
     Exceed three days. In faith, he's penitent,
     And yet his trespass, in our common reason°—
     Save that, they say, the wars must make example
     Out of her° best—is not almost a fault
65   T'incur a private check.[5] When shall he come?
     Tell me, Othello. I wonder in my soul
     What you would ask me that I should deny,
     Or stand so mammering° on? What, Michael Cassio
     That came a-wooing with you, and so many a time
70   When I have spoke of you dispraisingly
     Hath ta'en your part? To have so much to do
     To bring him in?° Trust me, I could do much.[6]
OTHELLO   Prithee, no more. Let him come when he will:
     I will deny thee nothing.
DESDEMONA   Why, this is not a boon.
75   'Tis as I should entreat you wear your gloves,
     Or feed on nourishing dishes, or keep you warm,
     Or sue to you to do a peculiar° profit
     To your own person. Nay, when I have a suit
     Wherein I mean to touch your love indeed,
80   It shall be full of poise° and difficult weight,
     And fearful to be granted.[7]
OTHELLO   I will deny thee nothing.
     Whereon, I do beseech thee, grant me this:
     To leave me but a little to myself.
85 DESDEMONA   Shall I deny you? No. Farewell, my lord.
OTHELLO   Farewell, my Desdemona. I'll come to thee straight.°
DESDEMONA   Emilia, come. [to OTHELLO] Be as your fancies
     teach° you:
     Whate'er you be, I am obedient.
                  Exeunt [DESDEMONA *and* EMILIA].
OTHELLO   Excellent wretch!° Perdition catch my soul
90   But I do love thee; and when I love thee not,
     Chaos is come again.
IAGO   My noble lord?
OTHELLO   What dost thou say, Iago?
IAGO   Did Michael Cassio,
     When you wooed my lady, know of your love?
OTHELLO   He did, from first to last. Why dost thou ask?
95 IAGO   But for a satisfaction of my thought,
     No further harm.
OTHELLO   Why of thy thought, Iago?

Right-margin glosses:
- *midday meal*
- *normal judgment*
- *(war's)*
- *hesitating*
- *into favor*
- *particular*
- *balanced judgment*
- *immediately*
- *as your whims lead*
- *(affectionate)*

5. *is . . . check:* is barely worth even private criticism.
6. Do much to make you regret your reluctance (?).
7. Desdemona argues that her request is trivial, that only a far more serious "suit" (line 78) would be a real test of his devotion.

IAGO   I did not think he had been acquainted with her.

OTHELLO   Oh, yes, and went between us very oft.

IAGO   Indeed?

100   OTHELLO   Indeed? Ay, indeed! Discern'st thou aught in that?
    Is he not honest?

IAGO   Honest, my lord?

OTHELLO   Honest? Ay, honest.

IAGO   My lord, for aught I know.

OTHELLO   What dost thou think?

IAGO   Think, my lord?

105   OTHELLO   "Think, my lord?" Alas, thou echo'st me
    As if there were some monster in thy thought
    Too hideous to be shown. Thou dost mean something.
    I heard thee say even now thou "lik'st not that"
    When Cassio left my wife. What didst not like?

110   And when I told thee he was of my counsel,°   *in my confidence*
    Of my whole course of wooing, thou cried'st "Indeed?"
    And didst contract and purse thy brow together
    As if thou then hadst shut up in thy brain
    Some horrible conceit.° If thou dost love me,   *conception*

115   Show me thy thought.

IAGO   My lord, you know I love you.

OTHELLO   I think thou dost.
    And, for° I know thou'rt full of love and honesty   *since*
    And weigh'st thy words before thou giv'st them breath,
    Therefore these stops° of thine fright me the more: *disruptive pauses*

120   For such things in a false, disloyal knave
    Are tricks of custom,° but in a man that's just   *habitual*
    They're close dilations[8] working from the heart
    That passion cannot rule.°   *control*

IAGO   For Michael Cassio,
    I dare be sworn, I think that he is honest.

OTHELLO   I think so too.

125   IAGO   Men should be what they seem,
    Or those that be not, would they might seem none.[9]

OTHELLO   Certain, men should be what they seem.

IAGO   Why, then, I think Cassio's an honest man.

OTHELLO   Nay, yet there's more in this.

130   I prithee, speak to me as to thy thinkings
    As thou dost ruminate, and give thy worst of thoughts
    The worst of words.

IAGO   Good my lord, pardon me.
    Though I am bound to every act of duty,
    I am not bound to that: all slaves are free.°   *(to hide their thoughts)*

135   Utter my thoughts? Why, say they are vile and false—
    As where's that palace whereinto foul things
    Sometimes intrude not?—who has that breast so pure?—
    Wherein uncleanly apprehensions
    Keep leets and law-days, and in sessions sit

140   With meditations lawful?[1]

---

8. Involuntary hesitations (expansions, censures) of interior, close-kept secrets.
9. *Or . . . none:* If only those who are not what they seem didn't seem to be what they are not.

1. *Wherein . . . lawful:* (Even in pure breasts) illegitimate thoughts meet in court ("leets") from time to time (on "law-days") and debate (in court "session") with legitimate ones.

OTHELLO   Thou dost conspire against thy friend,° Iago,   *(Othello)*
If thou but think'st him wronged and mak'st his ear
A stranger to thy thoughts.
IAGO   I do beseech you,
Though I perchance am vicious° in my guess—   *culpably mistaken*
145   As, I confess, it is my nature's plague
To spy into abuses and of my jealousy°   *suspicion; envy*
Shape faults that are not—that your wisdom
From one that so imperfectly conceits°   *imagines*
Would take no notice, nor build yourself a trouble
150   Out of his scattering° and unsure observance.   *incoherent*
It were not° for your quiet, nor your good,   *It would not be good*
Nor for my manhood, honesty, and wisdom
To let you know my thoughts.
OTHELLO   What dost thou mean?
IAGO   Good name in man and woman, dear my lord,
155   Is the immediate jewel of their souls.
Who steals my purse, steals trash: 'tis something, nothing;
'Twas mine, 'tis his, and has been slave to thousands.
But he that filches from me my good name
Robs me of that which not enriches him
And makes me poor indeed.
160   OTHELLO   I'll know thy thoughts.
IAGO   You cannot, if my heart were in your hand,
Nor shall not, whilst 'tis in my custody.
OTHELLO   Ha!
IAGO   Oh, beware, my lord, of jealousy!
It is the green-eyed monster which doth mock
165   The meat it feeds on.[2] That cuckold lives in bliss
Who, certain of his fate, loves not his wronger;[3]
But, oh, what damnèd minutes tells he o'er°   *does he note pass by*
Who dotes, yet doubts; suspects, yet soundly loves.
OTHELLO   Oh, misery![4]
170   IAGO   Poor and content is rich, and rich enough;
But riches fineless° is as poor as winter   *boundless*
To him that ever fears he shall be poor.
Good heaven, the souls of all my tribe defend
From jealousy!
OTHELLO   Why? Why is this?
175   Think'st thou I'd make a life of jealousy,
To follow still the changes of the moon°   *Always madly to waver*
With fresh suspicions? No, to be once in doubt
Is to be resolved.° Exchange me for a goat   *to be finally settled*
When I shall turn the business of my soul
180   To such exufflicate and blowed° surmises,   *inflated and blown-up*
Matching thy inference.° 'Tis not to make me jealous *implication*
To say my wife is fair, feeds well, loves company,
Is free of speech, sings, plays, and dances:
Where virtue is, these are more virtuous.
185   Nor from mine own weak merits will I draw
The smallest fear or doubt of her revolt,°   *or worry of her betrayal*

---

2. **which . . . on:** that tortures, as it consumes, the body and soul of the jealous person.
3. Who, knowing it is his fate to be cuckolded, doesn't love his wife.

4. PERFORMANCE COMMENT For different ways of playing Othello's psychological and physical response to Iago's temptation of him, see Digital Edition PC 5.

For she had eyes and chose me. No, Iago,
I'll see before I doubt; when I doubt, prove;
And, on the proof, there is no more but this:
190   Away at once with love or jealousy.
IAGO   I am glad of this, for now I shall have reason
To show the love and duty that I bear you
With franker spirit. Therefore, as I am bound,
Receive it from me, I speak not yet of proof:
195   Look to your wife; observe her well with Cassio.
Wear your eyes thus: not jealous, nor secure.
I would not have your free and noble nature
Out of self-bounty be abused.[5] Look to't.
I know our country° disposition well: *(obscene wordplay)*
200   In Venice they do let heaven see the pranks
They dare not show their husbands; their best conscience
Is not to leave't undone but kept unknown.
OTHELLO   Dost thou say so?
IAGO   She did deceive her father, marrying you;
205   And when she seemed to shake and fear your looks,
She loved them most.
OTHELLO   And so she did.
IAGO   Why, go to,° then!   *that's it*
She that so young could give out such a seeming
To seal her father's eyes up, close as oak[6]—
He thought 'twas witchcraft. But I am much to blame.
210   I humbly do beseech you of your pardon
For too much loving you.
OTHELLO   I am bound to thee for ever.
IAGO   I see this hath a little dashed your spirits.
OTHELLO   Not a jot, not a jot.
IAGO   Trust me, I fear it has.
215   I hope you will consider what is spoke
Comes from your love. But I do see you're moved.
I am to pray you not to strain my speech
To grosser issues,° nor to larger reach   *greater conclusions*
Than to suspicion.
OTHELLO   I will not.
220   IAGO   Should you do so, my lord,
My speech should fall into such vile success
Which my thoughts aimed not at. Cassio's my worthy friend.
My lord, I see you're moved.
OTHELLO   No, not much moved.
I do not think but Desdemona's honest.
225   IAGO   Long live she so, and long live you to think so.
OTHELLO   And yet, how nature erring from itself—
IAGO   Ay, there's the point! As, to be bold with you,
Not to affect° many proposed matches   *desire*
Of her own clime, complexion,° and degree,°   *nature, skin color / rank*
230   Whereto we see in all things nature tends.
Faugh!° One may smell in such a will most rank,   *(expressing disgust)*
Foul disproportions,° thoughts unnatural.   *abnormalities*
But pardon me, I do not in position°   *argument*

---

5. Be deceived on account of your own goodness.
6. Perhaps: To cover (the homonym "seel" means "to
blind") her father's eyes as tightly as oak (a fine-grained
wood).

Distinctly speak of her, though I may fear
235 Her will, recoiling to° her better judgment,   *resuming*
May fall to match you with her country forms,[7]
And happily° repent.   *perhaps*
OTHELLO   Farewell, farewell.
If more thou dost perceive, let me know more.
Set on thy wife to observe. Leave me, Iago.
240 IAGO My lord, I take my leave.
OTHELLO Why did I marry? This honest creature doubtless
Sees and knows more, much more, than he unfolds.
IAGO My lord, I would I might entreat your honor
To scan this thing no farther: leave it to time.
245 Although 'tis fit that Cassio have his place—
For, sure, he fills it up with great ability—
Yet if you please to hold him off awhile,
You shall by that perceive him and his means.°   *(of regaining his job)*
Note if your lady strain his entertainment°   *urge his reception*
250 With any strong or vehement importunity:
Much will be seen in that. In the meantime,
Let me be thought too busy° in my fears—   *meddlesome*
As worthy cause I have to fear I am—
And hold her free,° I do beseech your honor.   *believe her innocent*
OTHELLO Fear not my government.°   *self-conduct*
255 IAGO   I once more take my leave.
                                                                                                   Exit.
OTHELLO This fellow's of exceeding honesty,
And knows all quantities with a learned spirit
Of human dealings.[8] If I do prove her haggard,°   *wild (falconry)*
Though that her jesses were my dear heartstrings,
260 I'd whistle her off, and let her down the wind
To prey at fortune.[9] Haply, for° I am black   *Perhaps, because*
And have not those soft parts of° conversation°   *easy / manner; intercourse*
That chamberers° have, or for I am declined   *gallants; valets*
Into the vale of years—yet that's not much—
265 She's gone, I am abused,° and my relief   *deceived*
Must be to loathe her. O curse of marriage,
That we can call these delicate creatures ours
And not their appetites! I had rather be a toad
And live upon the vapor of a dungeon
270 Than keep a corner in the thing I love
For others' uses. Yet 'tis the plague to great ones:
Prerogatived° are they less than the base.°   *Privileged / lowborn*
'Tis destiny unshunnable, like death:
Even then, this forked plague is fated to us
When we do quicken.[1]
           Enter DESDEMONA *and* EMILIA.
275   Look where she comes!
If she be false, heaven mocked itself.
I'll not believe't.

---

7. May happen to compare you with Venetian (with obscene pun on "country") standards.
8. *quantities . . . of human dealings:* amounts of a commodity in civil commercial transactions (literal); characteristics of human behavior (metaphorical).
9. *Though . . . fortune:* Even if what tied her ("jesses"

were leg straps put on a hawk) were my own heart-strings, I'd set her loose downwind forever to hunt on her own.
1. *Even . . . quicken:* The "plague" of horns (imagined to grow from the forehead of a cuckold) is our fate as soon as we live.

DESDEMONA   How now, my dear Othello?
   Your dinner, and the generous° islanders   *noble*
   By you invited, do attend° your presence.   *wait for*
OTHELLO   I am to blame.
280 DESDEMONA   Why do you speak so faintly?
   Are you not well?
OTHELLO   I have a pain upon my forehead here.°   *(from cuckold's horns)*
DESDEMONA   Why, that's with watching;° 'twill away again.   *from lack of sleep*
   Let me but bind it hard, within this hour
   It will be well.
285 OTHELLO   Your napkin° is too little.   *handkerchief*
   Let it alone.
     [*They drop the handkerchief.*]
         Come, I'll go in with you.
DESDEMONA   I am very sorry that you are not well.
          Exeunt [OTHELLO *and* DESDEMONA].
EMILIA   I am glad I have found this napkin:
     [*She picks up the handkerchief.*]
   This was her first remembrance from the Moor.
290 My wayward husband hath a hundred times
   Wooed me to steal it, but she so loves the token—
   For he conjured her[2] she should ever keep it—
   That she reserves it evermore about her
   To kiss and talk to. I'll have the work ta'en out,°   *embroidery copied*
295 And giv't Iago. What he will do with it
   Heaven knows, not I.
   I nothing,° but to please his fantasy.   *do (know; intend) nothing*
     Enter IAGO.
IAGO   How now? What do you here alone?
EMILIA   Do not you chide: I have a thing for you.
300 IAGO   You have a thing for me? It is a common thing[3]—
EMILIA   Ha!
IAGO   —To have a foolish wife.
EMILIA   Oh, is that all? What will you give me now
   For that same handkerchief?[4]
IAGO   What handkerchief?
305 EMILIA   What handkerchief?
   Why, that the Moor first gave to Desdemona;
   That which so often you did bid me steal.
IAGO   Hast stolen it from her?
EMILIA   No, but she let it drop by negligence,
310 And to th'advantage° I, being here, took't up.   *taking the opportunity*
   Look, here 'tis.
IAGO   A good wench. Give it me.
EMILIA   What will you do with't, that you have been so earnest
   To have me filch it?
IAGO   Why, what is that to you?
EMILIA   If it be not for some purpose of import,
315 Give't me again. Poor lady, she'll run mad
   When she shall lack it.
IAGO   Be not acknown on't.°   *Conceal your role in it*

---

2. Made her swear; perhaps also an unwitting backward glance at Brabanzio's charge in 1.3 that Othello employed witchcraft to win Desdemona.
3. It is a vagina ("thing") available to all.

4. PERFORMANCE COMMENT For Emilia's behavior and various possible motives for taking the handkerchief and giving it to Iago, see Digital Edition PC 6.

I have use for it. Go, leave me.   *Exit* EMILIA.
I will in Cassio's lodging lose° this napkin,   *misplace; let loose*
And let him find it. Trifles light as air
320 Are to the jealous confirmations strong
As proofs of holy writ. This may do something.
The Moor already changes with my poison:
Dangerous conceits° are in their natures poisons   *ideas*
Which, at the first, are scarce found to distaste
325 But, with a little,° act upon the blood,   *(time)*
Burn like the mines of sulfur.⁵
          Enter OTHELLO.
                    I did say so!
Look where he comes! Not poppy, nor mandragora,⁶
Nor all the drowsy syrups of the world
Shall ever medicine thee to that sweet sleep
Which thou owed'st° yesterday.   *owned*
330 OTHELLO   Ha! Ha! False to me?
IAGO   Why, how now, general? No more of that.
OTHELLO   Avaunt!° Be gone! Thou hast set me on the rack.   *Leave me!*
I swear 'tis better to be much abused°   *mistreated; deceived*
Than but to know't a little.
IAGO   How now, my lord?
335 OTHELLO   What sense had I in her stolen hours of lust?
I saw't not, thought it not, it harmed not me;
I slept the next night well, fed well, was free and merry;
I found not Cassio's kisses on her lips.
He that is robbed, not wanting° what is stolen,   *missing*
340 Let him not know't, and he's not robbed at all.
IAGO   I am sorry to hear this.
OTHELLO   I had been happy if the general camp,
Pioneers° and all, had tasted her sweet body,   *Manual laborers*
So° I had nothing known. Oh, now forever   *If*
345 Farewell the tranquil mind; farewell content;
Farewell the plumèd troops and the big wars
That makes ambition virtue! Oh, farewell,
Farewell the neighing steed and the shrill trump,
The spirit-stirring drum, th'ear-piercing fife,
350 The royal banner, and all quality,°   *merit*
Pride,° pomp, and circumstance° of glorious war.   *Magnificence / ceremony*
And O you mortal engines,° whose rude throats   *deadly cannons*
Th'immortal Jove's dread clamors° counterfeit,   *thunderclaps*
Farewell. Othello's occupation's gone.
355 IAGO   Is't possible, my lord?
OTHELLO   Villain, be sure thou prove my love a whore;
Be sure of it! Give me the ocular proof
Or, by the worth of mine eternal soul,
Thou hadst been better have been born a dog
Than answer my waked wrath.
360 IAGO   Is't come to this?
OTHELLO   Make me to see't, or at the least so prove it
That the probation° bear no hinge nor loop   *proof*

---

5. Pliny the Elder describes two islands of sulfur   6. A sleep-inducing substance made from the man-
between mainland Italy and Sicily that were rumored   drake root.
to be always on fire.

To hang a doubt on, or woe upon thy life!

IAGO   My noble lord—

365 OTHELLO   If thou dost slander her and torture me,
Never pray more; abandon all remorse;
On horror's head horrors accumulate;
Do deeds to make heaven weep, all earth amazed;
For nothing canst thou to damnation add
Greater than that.

370 IAGO   O grace! O heaven forgive me!
Are you a man? Have you a soul, or sense?
God b'wi'you; take mine office.[7] O wretched fool°   (to himself)
That lov'st to make thine honesty a vice!°   fault
O monstrous world! Take note, take note, O world:

375 To be direct and honest is not safe.
I thank you for this profit° and, from hence,   profitable lesson
I'll love no friend, sith° love breeds such offense.   since

OTHELLO   Nay, stay: thou shouldst be honest.

IAGO   I should be wise, for honesty's a fool,
And loses that° it works for.   what

380 OTHELLO   By the world,[8]
I think my wife be honest, and think she is not;
I think that thou art just, and think thou art not.
I'll have some proof. My name, that was as fresh
As Dian's[9] visage, is now begrimed and black

385 As mine own face. If there be cords or knives,
Poison or fire, or suffocating streams,[1]
I'll not endure it. Would I were satisfied!

IAGO   I see you are eaten up with passion;
I do repent me that I put it to you.
You would be satisfied?

390 OTHELLO   Would? Nay, and I will!

IAGO   And may. But how? How satisfied, my lord?
Would you the supervision grossly gape on?[2]
Behold her topped?°   sexually mounted

OTHELLO   Death and damnation! Oh!

IAGO   It were a tedious° difficulty, I think,   disagreeable
395 To bring them to that prospect.° Damn them, then,   viewable position
If ever mortal eyes do see them bolster°   use a pillow
More° than their own. What, then? How, then?   Other
What shall I say? Where's satisfaction?
It is impossible you should see this,

400 Were they as prime° as goats, as hot as monkeys,   lustful
As salt as wolves in pride,[3] and fools as gross
As ignorance made drunk. But yet, I say,
If imputation and strong circumstances[4]—
Which lead directly to the door of truth—

405 Will give you satisfaction, you might have't.

OTHELLO   Give me a living° reason she's disloyal.   legitimate

7. Good-bye, I resign my official position (ensign).
8. Othello's speech (lines 380–87) does not appear
in Q.
9. Diana, goddess of chastity and of the (pale) moon.
1. *cords . . . streams*: methods of suicide or murder.
2. *Would you the supervision . . . gape on?*: Would

you look ("gape") at the sight ("vision") from above
("super")? Would you, the person in the observer's position ("the supervision"), look ("gape") on?
3. As lecherous as wolves in heat.
4. If attribution of fault and strong circumstantial
evidence.

IAGO   I do not like the office.
But, sith I am entered in this cause so far—
Pricked to't° by foolish honesty and love—   *Prodded on*
410   I will go on. I lay with Cassio lately
And, being troubled with a raging tooth,
I could not sleep. There are a kind of men
So loose of soul that in their sleeps will mutter
Their affairs: one of this kind is Cassio.
415   In sleep I heard him say, "Sweet Desdemona,
Let us be wary. Let us hide our loves."
And then, sir, would he grip and wring my hand,
Cry, "O sweet creature!" then kiss me hard
As if he plucked up kisses by the roots
420   That grew upon my lips; laid his leg o'er my thigh,
And sighed, and kissed, and then cried, "Cursèd fate,
That gave thee to the Moor!"
OTHELLO   Oh, monstrous! Monstrous!
IAGO   Nay, this was but his dream.
OTHELLO   But this denoted a foregone conclusion.°   *an earlier event*
425   'Tis a shrewd doubt,° though it be but a dream.   *reasonable fear*
IAGO   And this may help to thicken other proofs
That do demonstrate thinly.
OTHELLO   I'll tear her all to pieces!
IAGO   Nay, yet be wise; yet we see nothing done.
She may be honest yet. Tell me but this:
430   Have you not sometimes seen a handkerchief
Spotted with strawberries in your wife's hand?
OTHELLO   I gave her such a one. 'Twas my first gift.
IAGO   I know not that, but such a handkerchief—
I am sure it was your wife's—did I today
See Cassio wipe his beard with.
435   OTHELLO   If it be that—
IAGO   If it be that, or any, it was hers.
It speaks against her with the other proofs.
OTHELLO   Oh, that the slave° had forty thousand lives!   *(Cassio)*
One is too poor, too weak for my revenge.
440   Now do I see 'tis true. Look here, Iago:
All my fond love thus do I blow to heaven. 'Tis gone.
          [OTHELLO *kneels*.]
Arise, black vengeance, from the hollow hell;
Yield up, O love, thy crown and hearted throne°   *rule of the heart*
To tyrannous hate. Swell, bosom, with thy fraught,°   *burden*
For 'tis of aspics'° tongues.   *poisonous snakes'*
445   IAGO   Yet be content.
OTHELLO   Oh, blood! Blood! Blood!
IAGO   Patience, I say: your mind may change.
OTHELLO   Never, Iago! Like to the Pontic Sea,°   *Black Sea*
Whose icy current and compulsive course
Ne'er keeps retiring ebb, but keeps due on
450   To the Propontic and the Hellespont,[5]
Even so my bloody thoughts, with violent pace,

5. The Pontic, or Black, Sea was said by the ancient   straits of Bosphorus and the Dardanelles (Helles-
Roman writer Pliny to flow in only one direction—   pont), the latter strait leading to the Aegean.
into the Propontic, the body of water bounded by the

Shall ne'er look back, ne'er ebb to humble love
Till that a capable° and wide revenge   *capacious*
Swallow them up. Now, by yond marble heaven,
455   In the due reverence of a sacred vow
I here engage my words.
IAGO   Do not rise yet.
   [IAGO *kneels.*⁶]
Witness, you ever-burning lights above,
You elements that clip° us round about,   *embrace (sexual?)*
Witness that here Iago doth give up
460   The execution° of his wit, hands, heart,   *command*
To wronged Othello's service. Let him command,
And to obey shall be in me remorse,°   *pity (for Othello)*
What bloody business ever.
OTHELLO   I greet thy love
Not with vain thanks but with acceptance bounteous,
465   And will upon the instant put thee to't.°   *immediately test it*
Within these three days let me hear thee say
That Cassio's not alive.
IAGO   My friend is dead.
'Tis done at your request. But let her live.
OTHELLO   Damn her, lewd minx!° Oh, damn her! Damn her!   *wanton*
470   Come, go with me apart. I will withdraw
To furnish me with some swift means of death
For the fair devil. Now art thou my lieutenant.
IAGO   I am your own forever.   *Exeunt.*

3.4 (Q 3.4)

Enter DESDEMONA, EMILIA, *and* CLOWN.

DESDEMONA   Do you know, sirrah,¹ where lieutenant Cassio
lies?
CLOWN   I dare not say he lies anywhere.
DESDEMONA   Why, man?
5   CLOWN   He's a soldier, and for me to say a soldier lies, 'tis
stabbing.
DESDEMONA   Go to! Where lodges he?
CLOWN   To tell you where he lodges is to tell you where I lie.
DESDEMONA   Can anything be made of this?
10   CLOWN   I know not where he lodges, and for me to devise a
lodging and say, "He lies here," or "He lies there," were to lie
in mine own throat.°   *lie outrageously*
DESDEMONA   Can you inquire him out, and be edified by report?
CLOWN   I will catechize the world for him: that is, make ques-
15   tions and by them answer.°   *find the answer*
DESDEMONA   Seek him. Bid him come hither. Tell him I have
moved° my lord on his behalf, and hope all will be well.   *petitioned*
CLOWN   To do this is within the compass° of man's wit and,   *scope*
therefore, I will attempt the doing it.   *Exit* CLOWN.
20   DESDEMONA   Where should° I lose the handkerchief, Emilia?   *did*
EMILIA   I know not, madam.
DESDEMONA   Believe me, I had rather have lost my purse

---

6. Parody of the marriage ceremony.   1. A form of address to an inferior.
3.4 Location: Before the citadel.

Full of *crusados*.° And but° my noble Moor   *gold coins / but that*
Is true of mind and made of no such baseness
25   As jealous creatures are, it were enough
To put him to ill thinking.
EMILIA   Is he not jealous?
DESDEMONA   Who, he? I think the sun where he was born
Drew all such humors from him.[2]
         Enter OTHELLO.
EMILIA   Look where he comes.
DESDEMONA   I will not leave him now till Cassio be
30   Called to him. —How is't with you, my lord?
OTHELLO   Well, my good lady. [*aside*] Oh, hardness to dissemble!
—How do you, Desdemona?
DESDEMONA   Well, my good lord.
OTHELLO   Give me your hand. This hand is moist,° my lady.   *(sign of carnal desire)*
DESDEMONA   It hath felt no age, nor known no sorrow.
35   OTHELLO   This argues fruitfulness and liberal heart.[3]
Hot, hot, and moist: this hand of yours requires
A sequester from liberty, fasting, and prayer,
Much castigation, exercise devout,
For here's a young and sweating devil here
40   That commonly rebels. 'Tis a good hand,
A frank° one.   *(sexually) open*
DESDEMONA   You may indeed say so,
For 'twas that hand that gave away my heart.
OTHELLO   A liberal hand. The hearts of old gave hands,
But our new heraldry is hands, not hearts.[4]
45   DESDEMONA   I cannot speak of this. Come now, your
     promise.
OTHELLO   What promise, chuck?°   *woodchuck (affectionate)*
DESDEMONA   I have sent to bid Cassio come speak with you.
OTHELLO   I have a salt and sorry rheum° offends me.   *badly watering eyes*
Lend me thy handkerchief.
DESDEMONA   Here, my lord.
OTHELLO   That which I gave you.
50   DESDEMONA   I have it not about me.
OTHELLO   Not?
DESDEMONA   No, indeed, my lord.
OTHELLO   That's a fault. That handkerchief
Did an Egyptian to my mother give:
She was a charmer,° and could almost read   *sorceress*
55   The thoughts of people. She told her, while she kept it,
'Twould make her amiable,° and subdue my father   *desirable*
Entirely to her love; but if she lost it,
Or made a gift of it, my father's eye
Should hold her loathed, and his spirits should hunt
60   After new fancies. She, dying, gave it me,
And bid me, when my fate would have me wived,
To give it her.° I did so, and take heed on't;   *to my wife*
Make it a darling like° your precious eye;   *as dear to you as*

2. The four humors were bodily fluids, the mix of
which was believed by classical and Renaissance
thinkers to determine one's temperament. Desdemona
here repeats a standard position—that the climate of
Africa, in its effect on the bodily humors, prevented its
inhabitants from easily succumbing to jealousy.
3. This demonstrates fertility (perhaps, by implication, lust) and a generous (loose) heart.
4. These days the joining of hands doesn't signify the
joining of hearts.

To lose't or give't away were such perdition°   loss; damnation
As nothing else could match.

65 DESDEMONA   Is't possible?

OTHELLO   'Tis true. There's magic in the web of it.
A sibyl,° that had numbered in the world   female prophet
The sun to course two hundred compasses,[5]
In her prophetic fury sewed the work;

70 The worms were hallowed that did breed the silk;
And it was dyed in mummy,[6] which the skillful
Conserved of° maidens' hearts.   Preserved out of

DESDEMONA   Indeed? Is't true?

OTHELLO   Most veritable. Therefore look to't well.

DESDEMONA   Then would to heaven that I had never seen't!

75 OTHELLO   Ha! Wherefore?

DESDEMONA   Why do you speak so startingly° and rash?   impetuously

OTHELLO   Is't lost? Is't gone? Speak, is't out o'th' way?

DESDEMONA   Bless us!

OTHELLO   Say you?

80 DESDEMONA   It is not lost—but what an if° it were?   an if = if

OTHELLO   How?

DESDEMONA   I say it is not lost.

OTHELLO   Fetch't. Let me see't.

DESDEMONA   Why, so I can, but I will not now:
This is a trick to put me from my suit.

85 Pray you, let Cassio be received again.

OTHELLO   Fetch me the handkerchief! [aside] My mind misgives.

DESDEMONA   Come, come. You'll never meet a more sufficient°   complete
man.

OTHELLO   The handkerchief!

DESDEMONA   A man that all his time
Hath founded his good fortunes on your love,
Shared dangers with you—

90 OTHELLO   The handkerchief!

DESDEMONA   In sooth, you are to blame.

OTHELLO   Away!
                              Exit OTHELLO.

EMILIA   Is not this man jealous?

DESDEMONA   I ne'er saw this before.
Sure, there's some wonder in this handkerchief;
I am most unhappy in the loss of it.

95 EMILIA   'Tis not a year or two shows us a man:[7]
They are all but° stomachs, and we all but food;   nothing but
They eat us hungrily, and when they are full
They belch us.

                    Enter IAGO and CASSIO.
                         Look you, Cassio and my husband.

IAGO [to CASSIO]   There is no other way; 'tis she must do't.

100 [He indicates DESDEMONA.] And, lo, the happiness![8] Go and
importune her.

DESDEMONA   How now, good Cassio? What's the news with you?

CASSIO   Madam, my former suit. I do beseech you

---

5. that . . . compasses: who was two hundred years old.   7. Probably: It doesn't take long to see what men are
6. Fluid drained from mummified bodies, suppos-   made of.
edly magical.   8. What a happy coincidence (seeing Desdemona).

That by your virtuous means I may again
Exist, and be a member of his love
105 Whom I, with all the office of my heart,
Entirely honor. I would not be delayed.
If my offense be of such mortal° kind   *deadly*
That nor° my service past, nor present sorrows,   *neither*
Nor purposed° merit in futurity,°   *intended / the future*
110 Can ransom me into his love again,
But to know so° must be my benefit.   *Even to know this*
So° shall I clothe me in a forced content,   *If so*
And shut myself up in° some other course   *limit myself to*
To° Fortune's alms.   *To win*
DESDEMONA   Alas, thrice-gentle Cassio,
115 My advocation is not now in tune.[9]
My lord is not my lord, nor should I know him
Were he in favor° as in humor altered.   *appearance*
So help me every spirit sanctified,
As I have spoken for you all my best,
120 And stood within the blank of° his displeasure   *in the aim of*
For my free speech. You must awhile be patient:
What I can do, I will, and more I will
Than for myself I dare. Let that suffice you.
IAGO   Is my lord angry?
EMILIA   He went hence but now,
125 And certainly in strange unquietness.
IAGO   Can he be angry? I have seen the cannon
When it hath blown his ranks into the air
And, like the devil, from his very arm
Puffed his own brother[1]—and is he angry?
130 Something of moment, then. I will go meet him.
There's matter in't indeed, if he be angry.
DESDEMONA   I prithee, do so.   *Exit* [IAGO].
                 Something, sure, of state,°   *state business*
Either from Venice or some unhatched practice°   *unfinished plot*
Made demonstrable° here in Cyprus to him,   *Revealed*
135 Hath puddled° his clear spirit; and in such cases   *fouled; dirtied*
Men's natures wrangle with inferior things,
Though great ones are their object. 'Tis even so:
For let our finger ache, and it endues°   *induces*
Our other healthful members even to a sense
140 Of pain. Nay, we must think men are not gods,
Nor of them look for such observancy°   *careful attention*
As fits the bridal.° Beshrew me° much, Emilia,   *wedding / (mild curse)*
I was—unhandsome° warrior as I am—   *unskilled*
Arraigning his unkindness with my soul,
145 But now I find I had suborned the witness,
And he's indicted falsely.[2]
EMILIA   Pray heaven it be
State matters, as you think, and no conception
Nor no jealous toy° concerning you.   *whim*
DESDEMONA   Alas the day! I never gave him cause.

---

9. My advocacy isn't working properly.
1. Blew up his own brother (and Othello wasn't angry even then).
2. *suborned . . . falsely:* made the witness lie and so accused Othello falsely.

150 EMILIA   But jealous souls will not be answered so.
        They are not ever jealous for the cause,
        But jealous for they're jealous: it is a monster
        Begot upon itself, born on itself.
    DESDEMONA   Heaven keep the monster from Othello's mind!
155 EMILIA   Lady, amen.
    DESDEMONA   I will go seek him. —Cassio, walk here about.
        If I do find him fit, I'll move your suit,
        And seek to effect it to my uttermost.
    CASSIO   I humbly thank your ladyship.
                    Exeunt [DESDEMONA *and* EMILIA].
            Enter BIANCA.³
    BIANCA   Save you,° friend Cassio.   *God save you*
160 CASSIO   What make° you from home?   *brings*
        How is't with you, my most fair Bianca?
        Indeed, sweet love, I was coming to your house.
    BIANCA   And I was going to your lodging, Cassio.
        What, keep a week away? Seven days and nights,
165   Eight score eight hours—and lovers' absent hours
        More tedious than the dial eight score times!⁴
        Oh, weary reck'ning!°   *calculating*
    CASSIO   Pardon me, Bianca.
        I have this while with leaden thoughts been pressed,
        But I shall in a more continuate° time   *opportune*
170   Strike off° this score of absence. Sweet Bianca,   *Make up*
            [*He gives her the handkerchief.*]
        Take me this work out.°   *Copy this embroidery*
    BIANCA   O Cassio, whence came this?
        This is some token from a newer friend.
        To the felt absence now I feel a cause.
        Is't come to this? Well, well!
    CASSIO   Go to,° woman!   *Stop it*
175   Throw your vile guesses in the devil's teeth
        From whence you have them. You are jealous now
        That this is from some mistress some remembrance.
        No, in good troth, Bianca.
    BIANCA   Why, whose is it?
    CASSIO   I know not, neither. I found it in my chamber.
180   I like the work well: ere it be demanded,°   *sought out*
        As like° enough it will, I would have it copied.   *likely*
        Take it, and do't, and leave me for this time.
    BIANCA   Leave you? Wherefore?
    CASSIO   I do attend here on the general,
185   And think it no addition,° nor my wish,   *(to my cause)*
        To have him see me womaned.°   *with a woman*
    BIANCA   Why, I pray you?
    CASSIO   Not that I love you not.
    BIANCA   But that you do not love me.
        I pray you, bring me on the way a little,
        And say if I shall see you soon at night.
190 CASSIO   'Tis but a little way that I can bring you,

---

3. "Bianca" means "white" in Italian—perhaps part of the play's ironic reversal of conventional color imagery, given that Bianca is a "customer" (courte-san, 4.1.115).
4. *lovers'* . . . *times:* each hour lovers are parted is eight score (160) times more tedious than normal clock time.

For I attend here; but I'll see you soon.
BIANCA   'Tis very good. I must be circumstanced.[5]

Exeunt all.

4.1 (Q 4.1)

Enter OTHELLO *and* IAGO.

IAGO   Will you think so?
OTHELLO   Think so, Iago?
IAGO   What,
  To kiss in private?
OTHELLO   An unauthorized kiss!
IAGO   Or to be naked with her friend in bed
  An hour or more, not meaning any harm?
5 OTHELLO   Naked in bed, Iago, and not mean harm?
  It is hypocrisy against the devil.[1]
  They that mean virtuously, and yet do so,
  The devil their virtue tempts, and they tempt heaven.[2]
  IAGO   If they do nothing, 'tis a venial slip;°   *an excusable sin*
  But if I give my wife a handkerchief—
10 OTHELLO   What then?
  IAGO   Why, then 'tis hers, my lord, and, being hers,
  She may, I think, bestow't on any man.
  OTHELLO   She is protectress of her honor, too.
  May she give that?
15 IAGO   Her honor is an essence that's not seen:
  They° have it very oft that have it not.   *They are reputed to*
  But for the handkerchief—
  OTHELLO   By heaven, I would most gladly have forgot it!
  Thou said'st—oh, it comes o'er my memory
20 As doth the raven o'er the infectious house,[3]
  Boding to all—he had my handkerchief.
  IAGO   Ay, what of that?
  OTHELLO   That's not so good now.
  IAGO   What if I had said I had seen him do you wrong?
  Or heard him say—as knaves be such abroad,[4]
25 Who, having by their own importunate suit,
  Or voluntary dotage of some mistress,
  Convinced or supplied° them, cannot choose   *Seduced or satisfied*
  But they must blab—
  OTHELLO   Hath he said anything?
  IAGO   He hath, my lord, but be you well assured,
  No more than he'll unswear.
30 OTHELLO   What hath he said?
  IAGO   Why, that he did—I know not what he did.
  OTHELLO   What? What?
  IAGO   Lie.
  OTHELLO   With her?

---

5. Content with what circumstances offer.
4.1 Location: Before the citadel.
1. *Naked . . . devil:* By showing every sign of committing adultery but then stopping just in time, they deliberately mislead the devil, who wrongly takes their apparent intention to sin at face value (just as an ordinary hypocrite deceives by professing virtue).

2. *they . . . heaven:* Those who mean well ("virtuously") but act in this lascivious fashion ("so") make it easy for the devil successfully to tempt them, and they violate the biblical prohibition against tempting God.
3. The raven was thought to be an ill omen and a carrier of plague. *infectious:* plague-infested.
4. As such knaves do exist in the world.

IAGO   With her, on her, what you will.

OTHELLO   Lie with her? Lie on her? We say "lie on her"° when   *lie about her; (sexual)*
they belie° her. Lie with her? That's fulsome!° Handker-   *slander / nauseating*
35   chief! Confessions! Handkerchief! To[5] confess and be
hanged for his labor. First to be hanged and then to confess.
I tremble at it. Nature would not invest herself in such shadowing passion without some instruction.[6] It is not words
that shakes me thus—pish! Noses, ears, and lips! Is't possi-
40   ble? Confess? Handkerchief? Oh, devil!
          [*He*] *falls in a trance.*

IAGO   Work on,
My medicine works! Thus credulous fools are caught,
And many worthy and chaste dames, even thus
All guiltless, meet reproach. —What ho, my lord?
My lord, I say! Othello!
          Enter CASSIO.
45   —How now, Cassio?

CASSIO   What's the matter?

IAGO   My lord is fallen into an epilepsy.
This is his second fit; he had one yesterday.

CASSIO   Rub him about the temples.

50   IAGO   The lethargy° must have his° quiet course: *trance / its*
If not, he foams at mouth and, by and by,
Breaks out to savage madness. Look, he stirs.
Do you withdraw yourself a little while.
He will recover straight.° When he is gone,   *immediately*
55   I would on great occasion° speak with you.   [*Exit* CASSIO.]   *important matters*
—How is it, general? Have you not hurt your head?[7]

OTHELLO   Dost thou mock me?

IAGO   I mock you not, by heaven.
Would you would bear your fortune like a man.

OTHELLO   A hornèd man's a monster and a beast.

60   IAGO   There's many a beast, then, in a populous city,
And many a civil° monster.   *city-dwelling*

OTHELLO   Did he confess it?

IAGO   Good sir, be a man.
Think every bearded fellow that's but yoked
May draw with you?[8] There's millions now alive
65   That nightly lie in those unproper beds
Which they dare swear peculiar.[9] Your case is better.
Oh, 'tis the spite of hell, the fiend's arch-mock,°   *devil's greatest mock*
To lip° a wanton in a secure° couch   *kiss / an unsuspected*
And to suppose her chaste. No, let me know
70   And, knowing what I am,° I know what she shall be.   *(a cuckold)*

OTHELLO   Oh, thou art wise, 'tis certain.

IAGO   Stand you awhile apart.

---

5. Lines 35–40 do not appear in Q. Arguably, these
lines provide more time for Othello to drive himself
to distraction and hence make his collapse more
plausible.
6. *Nature . . . instruction:* It isn't natural that I would
feel such foreboding ("shadowing") emotion (jealousy) unless there were some cause for it.
7. Othello takes this as suggesting that he has grown

cuckold's horns.
8. *every . . . you:* every married man ("yoked," like an
ox, to his wife and hence to cuckoldry) labors ("draws")
under the same fate.
9. *That . . . peculiar:* Who lie in beds that don't belong
entirely to them but that they would swear are exclusively their own.

Confine yourself but in a patient list.°   *boundary; bearing; desire*
Whilst you were here, o'erwhelmed with your grief—
A passion most resulting° such a man—   *recoiling upon (?)*
75 Cassio came hither. I shifted him away,
And laid good 'scuses upon your ecstasy,°   *for your fit*
Bade him anon° return and here speak with me,   *soon*
The which he promised. Do but encave° yourself,   *Only hide*
And mark the fleers,° the jibes, and notable scorns   *sneers*
80 That dwell in every region of his face:
For I will make him tell the tale anew,
Where, how, how oft, how long ago, and when
He hath and is again to cope° your wife.   *copulate with*
I say but mark his gesture. Marry, patience!
85 Or I shall say you're all-in-all in spleen,°   *completely impulsive*
And nothing of a man.
OTHELLO   Dost thou hear, Iago?
I will be found most cunning in my patience,
But—dost thou hear?—most bloody.
IAGO   That's not amiss.
But yet keep time° in all. Will you withdraw?   *maintain control*
    [OTHELLO *withdraws*.]
90 Now will I question Cassio of Bianca,
A housewife that by selling her desires[1]
Buys herself bread and cloth. It is a creature
That dotes on Cassio, as 'tis the strumpet's plague
To beguile many and be beguiled by one.
95 He, when he hears of her, cannot restrain
From the excess of laughter.
    Enter CASSIO.
                  Here he comes.
As he shall smile, Othello shall go mad,
And his unbookish jealousy[2] must construe
Poor Cassio's smiles, gestures, and light behaviors
100 Quite in the wrong. [*to* CASSIO] How do you, lieutenant?
CASSIO   The worser that you give me the addition°   *title*
Whose want even° kills me.   *lack just*
IAGO   Ply Desdemona well, and you are sure on't.
Now, if this suit lay in Bianca's dower°   *dowry*
How quickly should you speed?
105 CASSIO   Alas, poor caitiff!°   *wretch*
OTHELLO [*apart*]   Look how he laughs already.
IAGO   I never knew woman love man so.
CASSIO   Alas, poor rogue. I think indeed she loves me.
OTHELLO [*apart*]   Now he denies it faintly, and laughs it out.
IAGO   Do you hear, Cassio?—
110 OTHELLO [*apart*]   Now he importunes him
To tell it o'er. Go to: well said, well said.
IAGO   —She gives it out that you shall marry her.
Do you intend it?
CASSIO   Ha, ha, ha!

---

1. *housewife . . . selling her desires:* housewife (or hussy = prostitute) selling her desired body.
2. Naïve; ignorant of the high level of suspiciousness appropriate to an educated Venetian man—given

Othello's refusal to be jealous of Desdemona merely because she "loves company, / Is free of speech, . . . and dances" (3.3.182–83); not conforming to the bookish notion of the unjealous African.

OTHELLO [*apart*]   Do ye triumph, Roman?[3] Do you triumph?

115 CASSIO   I marry! What, a customer!° Prithee bear some char-   *courtesan*
    ity to my wit.° Do not think it so unwholesome. Ha, ha, ha!   *sense*

OTHELLO [*apart*]   So, so, so, so. They laugh that wins.

IAGO   Why, the cry goes that you marry her.

CASSIO   Prithee say true.

IAGO   I am a very villain else.°   *if it's not true (ironic)*

120 OTHELLO [*apart*]   Have you scored me?[4] Well.

CASSIO   This is the monkey's own giving out.° She is per-   *Bianca's own story*
    suaded I will marry her out of her own love and flattery, not
    out of my promise.

OTHELLO [*apart*]   Iago beckons me. Now he begins the story.
        [OTHELLO *moves closer.*]

125 CASSIO   She was here even now; she haunts me in every place.
    I was the other day talking on the sea-bank with certain
    Venetians, and thither comes the bauble° and falls me thus   *toy*
    about my neck.

OTHELLO [*apart*]   Crying, "O dear Cassio!", as it were: his ges-
130   ture imports° it.   *indicates*

CASSIO   So hangs, and lolls, and weeps upon me; so shakes
    and pulls me. Ha, ha, ha!

OTHELLO [*apart*]   Now he tells how she plucked him to my
    chamber. Oh, I see that nose of yours, but not that dog I shall
135   throw it to.[5]

CASSIO   Well, I must leave her company.
        Enter BIANCA.

IAGO   Before me, look where she comes!

CASSIO   'Tis such another fitchew.[6] Marry, a perfumed one!
    [*to* BIANCA] What do you mean by this haunting of me?

140 BIANCA   Let the devil and his dam° haunt you! What did you   *mother*
    mean by that same handkerchief you gave me even now? I
    was a fine fool to take it. I must take out° the work? A likely   *copy*
    piece of work,° that you should find it in your chamber and   *An implausible story*
    know not who left it there. This is some minx's token—and
145   I must take out the work? There, give it° your hobby-horse!°   *it to / loose woman*
    Wheresoever you had it, I'll take out no work on't.

CASSIO   How now, my sweet Bianca? How now? How now?

OTHELLO [*apart*]   By heaven, that should° be my handkerchief!   *must*

BIANCA   If you'll come to supper tonight, you may: if you will
150   not, come when you are next prepared for.[7]   *Exit.*

IAGO   After her! After her!

CASSIO   I must: she'll rail in the streets else.

IAGO   Will you sup there?

CASSIO   Yes, I intend so.

155 IAGO   Well, I may chance to see you, for I would very fain°   *be very well pleased to*
    speak with you.

CASSIO   Prithee, come. Will you?

IAGO   Go to. Say no more.   [*Exit* CASSIO.]

---

3. Perhaps Othello draws on associations either with
Rome's imperial successes (and subsequent collapse)
or with the Roman practice of holding celebratory
processions.
4. Wounded me; sexually conquered at my expense.
5. *I see . . . to:* I'm envisioning my revenge, but the

time is not yet quite right. Cutting off the enemy's
nose was understood as a form of retribution.
6. Polecat, associated with prostitutes because of its
bad smell and presumed lecherousness.
7. Come next time I prepare for you (never).

	OTHELLO How shall I murder him, Iago?	
160	IAGO Did you perceive how he laughed at his vice?	

OTHELLO   How shall I murder him, Iago?

160 IAGO   Did you perceive how he laughed at his vice?

OTHELLO   O Iago!

IAGO   And did you see the handkerchief?

OTHELLO   Was that mine?

IAGO   Yours, by this hand. And to see how he prizes the foolish
165   woman, your wife: she gave it him, and he hath given it his
    whore.

OTHELLO   I would have him nine years a-killing.[8] A fine woman!
    A fair woman! A sweet woman!

IAGO   Nay, you must forget that.

170 OTHELLO   Ay, let her rot and perish, and be damned tonight,
    for she shall not live. No, my heart is turned to stone: I strike
    it, and it hurts my hand. Oh, the world hath not a sweeter
    creature: she might lie by an emperor's side, and command
    him tasks.

175 IAGO   Nay, that's not your way.°   *(the way to think)*

OTHELLO   Hang her! I do but say what she is: so delicate with
    her needle; an admirable musician—oh, she will sing the
    savageness out of a bear!—of so high and plenteous wit and
    invention°—   *imagination*

180 IAGO   She's the worse for all this.

OTHELLO   Oh, a thousand, a thousand times! And, then, of so
    gentle° a condition!   *highly born*

IAGO   Ay, too gentle.°   *generous (sexually)*

OTHELLO   Nay, that's certain.
185   But yet the pity of it, Iago. O Iago, the pity of it, Iago!

IAGO   If you are so fond° over her iniquity, give her patent° to   *foolish / license*
    offend; for if it touch not you, it comes near nobody.

OTHELLO   I will chop her into messes!° Cuckold me!   *pieces of food*

IAGO   Oh, 'tis foul in her.

190 OTHELLO   With mine officer!

IAGO   That's fouler.

OTHELLO   Get me some poison, Iago, this night. I'll not expos-
    tulate with her, lest her body and beauty unprovide my mind°   *weaken my resolve*
    again. This night, Iago.

195 IAGO   Do it not with poison. Strangle her in her bed, even the
    bed she hath contaminated.

OTHELLO   Good, good. The justice of it pleases. Very good.

IAGO   And for Cassio, let me be his undertaker.° You shall hear   *murderer*
    more by midnight.

OTHELLO   Excellent good.
    [*A trumpet sounds.*]
200   What trumpet is that same?

IAGO   I warrant, something from Venice.
        Enter LODOVICO, DESDEMONA, *and Attendants.*
    'Tis Lodovico: this comes from the Duke.
    See, your wife's with him.

LODOVICO   Save you, worthy general.

OTHELLO   With all my heart,° sir.   *Thank you*

205 LODOVICO   The Duke and the senators of Venice greet you.
        [*He gives* OTHELLO *a letter.*]

---

8. I would spend nine years killing him.

OTHELLO I kiss the instrument° of their pleasures.°   *bearer / commands*
DESDEMONA And what's the news, good cousin Lodovico?
IAGO I am very glad to see you, signor.
  Welcome to Cyprus.
210 LODOVICO I thank you. How does Lieutenant Cassio?
IAGO Lives, sir.
DESDEMONA Cousin, there's fallen between him and my lord
  An unkind° breach, but you shall make all well.   *unnatural; painful*
OTHELLO Are you sure of that?
215 DESDEMONA My lord?
OTHELLO [*reads*] "This fail you not to do, as you will—"
LODOVICO [*to* DESDEMONA] He did not call: he's busy in° the   *with*
  paper.
  Is there division twixt my lord and Cassio?
DESDEMONA A most unhappy one. I would do much
220 T'atone° them, for the love I bear to Cassio.   *To reconcile*
OTHELLO Fire and brimstone!
DESDEMONA   My lord?
OTHELLO   Are you wise?
DESDEMONA [*to* LODOVICO] What, is he angry?
LODOVICO   Maybe the letter moved him,
  For, as I think, they do command him home,
  Deputing Cassio in his government.°   *official position*
DESDEMONA Trust me, I am glad on't.
OTHELLO   Indeed?
225 DESDEMONA   My lord?
OTHELLO I am glad to see you mad.[9]
DESDEMONA   Why, sweet Othello?
OTHELLO Devil!
       [*He strikes her.*]
DESDEMONA I have not deserved this!
LODOVICO My lord! This would not be believed in Venice,
230 Though I should swear I saw't. 'Tis very much.°   *serious*
  Make her amends: she weeps.
OTHELLO   O devil! Devil!
  If that the earth could teem with° woman's tears,   *become pregnant by*
  Each drop she falls would prove a crocodile.[1]
  —Out of my sight!
DESDEMONA   I will not stay to offend you.
       [*She starts to leave.*]
235 LODOVICO Truly obedient, lady.
  —I do beseech your lordship, call her back.
OTHELLO Mistress.
DESDEMONA   My lord?
OTHELLO [*to* LODOVICO]   What would you° with her, sir?   *do you wish*
LODOVICO Who? I, my lord?
OTHELLO Ay, you did wish that I would make her turn.°   *return*
240 Sir, she can turn and turn,° and yet go on   *(sexually)*
  And turn again. And she can weep, sir, weep!

---

9. Perhaps Othello is pleased that she's rejoicing in Cassio's promotion and hence revealing their adulterous affair, which she would be "mad" to do in public and in front of him.

1. Each drop would cause the earth to conceive a crocodile (crocodiles proverbially wept false tears for their victims).

And she's obedient, as you say, obedient,
Very obedient. [*to* DESDEMONA] Proceed you in your tears.
[*to* LODOVICO] Concerning this, sir— [*to* DESDEMONA] Oh,
    well-painted passion!
245 —I am commanded home. [*to* DESDEMONA] Get you away.
I'll send for you anon. —Sir, I obey the mandate
And will return to Venice. [*to* DESDEMONA] Hence! Avaunt!°   Begone
                                    [*Exit* DESDEMONA.]
[*to* LODOVICO] Cassio shall have my place, and, sir, tonight
I do entreat that we may sup together.
250 You are welcome, sir, to Cyprus. —Goats and monkeys!²
                                                    Exit.
LODOVICO   Is this the noble Moor whom our full Senate
Call all-in-all sufficient? Is this the nature
Whom passion could not shake? Whose solid virtue
The shot of accident nor dart of chance
Could neither graze nor pierce?
255 IAGO   He is much changed.
LODOVICO   Are his wits safe? Is he not light of brain?
IAGO   He's that he is: I may not breathe my censure.
What he might be—if what he might, he is not—
I would to heaven he were.³
LODOVICO   What, strike his wife?
260 IAGO   Faith, that was not so well. Yet would I knew
That stroke would prove the worst.
LODOVICO   Is it his use?°   custom
Or did the letters work upon his blood,°   passions
And new create his fault?
IAGO   Alas, alas!
It is not honesty in me to speak
265 What I have seen and known. You shall observe him,
And his own courses° will denote him so   actions
That I may save my speech. Do but go after,
And mark how he continues.
LODOVICO   I am sorry that I am deceived in him.   *Exeunt.*

4.2 (Q 4.2)

Enter OTHELLO *and* EMILIA.
OTHELLO   You have seen nothing, then?
EMILIA   Nor ever heard, nor ever did suspect.
OTHELLO   Yes? You have seen Cassio and she together?
EMILIA   But then I saw no harm; and then I heard
5 Each syllable that breath made up between them.
OTHELLO   What, did they never whisper?
EMILIA   Never, my lord.
OTHELLO   Nor send you out o'th' way?
EMILIA   Never.
OTHELLO   To fetch her fan, her gloves, her mask, nor nothing?
EMILIA   Never, my lord.

---

2. Symbols of lust (borrowing Iago's language, 3.3.400).
3. *He's that . . . were:* He is what he is (as Iago says of himself, "I am not what I am," 1.1.63). I won't express my judgment on whether he is sane. What he might be

(sane)—if, though he might be (sane), he is not—I wish he were (sane). That is: if he is not sane, I wish he were. Alternatively: if he is sane, I wish he were insane (because only that would excuse his bad behavior).
4.2 Location: The citadel.

10   OTHELLO   That's strange.

EMILIA   I durst, my lord, to wager she is honest:
  Lay down my soul at stake. If you think other,
  Remove your thought: it doth abuse your bosom.
  If any wretch have put this in your head,

15   Let heaven requit° it with the serpent's curse,[1]   *requite*
  For if she be not honest, chaste, and true,
  There's no man happy: the purest of their wives
  Is foul as slander.

OTHELLO   Bid her come hither. Go.   *Exit* EMILIA.
  She says enough. Yet she's a simple bawd

20   That cannot say as much.[2] This is a subtle whore,
  A closet, lock, and key° of villainous secrets;   *A hider*
  And yet she'll kneel and pray—I have seen her do't.

      Enter DESDEMONA *and* EMILIA.

DESDEMONA   My lord, what is your will?

OTHELLO   Pray you, chuck, come hither.

DESDEMONA   What is your pleasure?

OTHELLO   Let me see your eyes.
  Look in my face.

25   DESDEMONA   What horrible fancy's this?

OTHELLO [*to* EMILIA]   Some of your function,[3] mistress.
  Leave procreants° alone, and shut the door.   *copulators*
  Cough or cry "hem!" if anybody come.
  Your mystery, your mystery° may dispatch![4]   *Exit* EMILIA.   *profession*

30   DESDEMONA [*kneeling*]   Upon my knee, what doth your speech
    import?
  I understand a fury in your words.

OTHELLO   Why, what art thou?

DESDEMONA   Your wife, my lord: your true and loyal wife.

OTHELLO   Come, swear it! Damn thyself, lest, being°   *appearing*

35   Like one of heaven, the devils themselves
  Should fear to seize thee. Therefore be double damned:
  Swear thou art honest.

DESDEMONA   Heaven doth truly know it.

OTHELLO   Heaven truly knows that thou art false as hell.

DESDEMONA   To whom, my lord? With whom? How am I false?

40   OTHELLO   Ah, Desdemon! Away! Away! Away!

DESDEMONA   Alas the heavy day, why do you weep?
  Am I the motive of these tears, my lord?
  If haply° you my father do suspect   *perhaps*
  An instrument of this your calling back,

45   Lay not your blame on me. If you have lost him,
  I have lost him too.

OTHELLO   Had it pleased heaven
  To try me with affliction; had they° rained   *the heavens*
  All kind of sores and shames on my bare head;
  Steeped me in poverty to the very lips;

50   Given to captivity me and my utmost hopes,
  I should have found in some place of my soul
  A drop of patience. But, alas, to make me

---

1. In Genesis, the curse that God laid on the serpent who deceived Eve.
2. *Yet . . . much:* Yet it would be a simpleminded go-between who can't say as much as she did.
3. Fulfill your bawd's function by guarding the door.
4. May send you to your destination.

The fixèd figure for the time of scorn
To point his slow and moving finger at!⁵
55 Yet could I bear that too, well, very well.
But there, where I have garnered° up my heart,   stored
Where either I must live, or bear no life,
The fountain⁶ from the which my current runs,
Or else dries up—to be discarded thence,
60 Or keep it as a cistern for foul toads
To knot and gender° in! Turn thy complexion there,   To couple and engender
Patience, thou young and rose-lipped cherubin:
I here look grim as hell.⁷

DESDEMONA I hope my noble lord esteems me honest.
65 OTHELLO Oh, ay. As summer flies are in the shambles,°   slaughter-house
That quicken even with blowing.⁸ O thou weed,
Who art so lovely fair and smell'st so sweet
That the sense aches at thee! Would thou hadst never been
born!

DESDEMONA Alas, what ignorant° sin have I committed?   unwitting
70 OTHELLO Was this fair paper, this most goodly book,
Made to write "whore" upon? "What committed?"
"Committed?"⁹ O thou public commoner!°   prostitute
I should make very forges of my cheeks
That would to cinders burn up modesty,
75 Did I but speak thy deeds. "What committed?"
Heaven stops the nose at it, and the moon winks;°   closes its eyes
The bawdy° wind, that kisses all it meets,   promiscuous
Is hushed within the hollow mine of earth,°   cave of the winds
And will not hear't. "What committed?"

80 DESDEMONA By heaven, you do me wrong!
OTHELLO Are not you a strumpet?
DESDEMONA   No, as I am a Christian!
If to preserve this vessel for my lord
From any other foul, unlawful touch
Be not to be a strumpet, I am none.

OTHELLO What, not a whore?
85 DESDEMONA   No, as I shall be saved!
OTHELLO Is't possible?
DESDEMONA   O heaven, forgive us!
OTHELLO I cry you mercy,° then;   I beg your pardon
I took you for that cunning whore of Venice
That married with Othello. [He calls EMILIA.] You, mistress,
Enter EMILIA.
90 That have the office opposite to Saint Peter,
And keeps the gate of hell. You, you! Ay, you!
We have done our course.° There's money for your pains.   business
[He gives EMILIA money.]
I pray you, turn the key, and keep our counsel.   Exit.

EMILIA Alas, what does this gentleman conceive?°   believe

---

5. *The fixèd . . . at:* The designated object of scorn
for this scornful time to point (as on a clock face) its
slowly moving hand at.
6. Spring. The language here imagines Desdemona
as the source of Othello's emotional vitality.
7. *Turn . . . / hell:* Look there (or change your look for
the worse) at the thought of that, Patience, and you

"cherubin": I (or: Ay) here look infernally forbidding.
8. Who come to life (or bring their offspring to life
and hence make the meat foul) as soon as the eggs are
deposited. The point seems to be the speed of breeding, inferred from Desdemona's supposed infidelity.
9. Lines 72–75 do not appear in Q.

95   —How do you, madam? How do you, my good lady?

DESDEMONA   Faith, half asleep.

EMILIA   Good madam, what's the matter with my lord?

DESDEMONA   With who?

EMILIA   Why, with my lord, madam.

DESDEMONA   Who is thy lord?

EMILIA   He that is yours, sweet lady.

100 DESDEMONA   I have none. Do not talk to me, Emilia.

    I cannot weep, nor answers have I none

    But what should go by water.° Prithee tonight   *appear in tears*

    Lay on my bed my wedding sheets. Remember,

    And call thy husband hither.

EMILIA   Here's a change indeed.   *Exit.*

105 DESDEMONA   'Tis meet° I should be used so, very meet.   *fitting*

    How have I been behaved, that he might stick

    The small'st opinion on my least misuse?[1]

       Enter IAGO *and* EMILIA.

IAGO   What is your pleasure, madam?

    How is't with you?

110 DESDEMONA   I cannot tell. Those that do teach young babes

    Do it with gentle means and easy tasks;

    He might have chid me so, for, in good faith,

    I am a child to chiding.°   *new to being reproached*

IAGO   What is the matter, lady?

EMILIA   Alas, Iago, my lord hath so bewhored her,°   *called her whore*

115   Thrown such despite° and heavy terms upon her,   *spite*

    That true hearts cannot bear it.

DESDEMONA   Am I that name, Iago?

IAGO   What name, fair lady?

DESDEMONA   Such as she said my lord did say I was.

EMILIA   He called her "whore." A beggar in his drink

120   Could not have laid such terms upon his callet.°   *whore*

IAGO   Why did he so?

DESDEMONA   I do not know; I am sure I am none such.

IAGO   Do not weep, do not weep. Alas the day!

EMILIA   Hath she forsook so many noble matches,

125   Her father, and her country, and her friends,

    To be called "whore"? Would it not make one weep?

DESDEMONA   It is my wretched fortune.

IAGO   Beshrew° him for't.   *Curse*

    How comes this trick° upon him?   *behavior*

DESDEMONA   Nay, heaven doth know.

EMILIA   I will be hanged if some eternal villain,

130   Some busy° and insinuating rogue,   *meddling*

    Some cogging,° cozening° slave, to get some office   *deceiving / cheating*

    Have not devised this slander—I will be hanged else.

IAGO   Fie, there is no such man: it is impossible.

DESDEMONA   If any such there be, heaven pardon him.

135 EMILIA   A halter° pardon him, and hell gnaw his bones!   *hangman's noose*

    Why should he call her "whore"? Who keeps her company?

    What place, what time, what form, what likelihood?

---

1. *that . . . misuse:* which would cause him to suspect even slightly my smallest fault. TEXTUAL COMMENT For the differences between F and Q in this, Desdemona's only soliloquy, see Digital Edition TC 4 (Folio edited text).

The Moor's abused by some most villainous knave,
Some base, notorious knave, some scurvy fellow.
140 O heavens, that° such companions thou'dst unfold,°   would that / reveal
And put in every honest hand a whip
To lash the rascals naked through the world,
Even from the East to th' West!

IAGO [*aside to* EMILIA]   Speak within door.°   more softly
EMILIA [*aside to* IAGO]   Oh, fie upon them! Some such squire°   fellow
    he was
145 That turned your wit the seamy-side without,°   wrong side out
And made you to suspect me with the Moor.

IAGO [*aside to* EMILIA]   You are a fool. Go to!

DESDEMONA   Alas, Iago,
What shall I do to win my lord again?
Good friend, go to him—for, by this light of heaven,
150 I know not how I lost him. Here I kneel:[2]
If e'er my will did trespass 'gainst his love,
Either in discourse of thought or actual deed;
Or that mine eyes, mine ears, or any sense
Delighted them, or any other form;[3]
155 Or that I do not yet° and ever did   still
And ever will—though he do shake me off
To beggarly divorcement—love him dearly,
Comfort forswear me.° Unkindness may do much,   Deny me (divine) solace
And his unkindness may defeat my life
160 But never taint my love. I cannot say "whore":
It doth abhor me[4] now I speak the word—
To do the act that might the addition° earn,   label
Not the world's mass of vanity° could make me.   all worldly splendor

IAGO   I pray you, be content: 'tis but his humor.°   mood
165 The business of the state does him offense.

DESDEMONA   If 'twere no other—

IAGO   It is but so, I warrant.
    [*Trumpets sound.*]
Hark how these instruments summon to supper:
The messengers of Venice stay the meat.°   are waiting to eat
Go in, and weep not: all things shall be well.
                        Exeunt DESDEMONA *and* EMILIA.
       Enter RODERIGO.
170 How now, Roderigo?

RODERIGO   I do not find that thou deal'st justly with me.

IAGO   What in the contrary?

RODERIGO   Every day thou dafts me with some device,[5] Iago,
    and rather, as it seems to me now, keep'st from me all conve-
175   niency° than suppliest me with the least advantage of hope.   opportunity
    I will indeed no longer endure it, nor am I yet persuaded to
    put up in peace what already I have foolishly suffered.

IAGO   Will you hear me, Roderigo?

RODERIGO   I have heard too much, and your words and per-
180   formances are no kin together.

---

2. Lines 150–63 (beginning with "Here") do not
appear in Q.
3. Took pleasure in anyone but him.

4. Fill me with abhorrence; make me abhorrent, with
a pun on "ab-whore."
5. You make a fool of me with some trick.

IAGO You charge me most unjustly.

RODERIGO With naught but truth. I have wasted myself out of my means: the jewels you have had from me to deliver Desdemona would half have corrupted a votarist.° You have told me *nun* she hath received them, and returned me expectations and comforts of sudden respect and acquaintance, but I find none.

IAGO Well, go to.° Very well. *(expresses remonstrance)*

RODERIGO "Very well"? "Go to"? I cannot go to,° man, nor 'tis *succeed sexually* not very well! Nay, I think it is scurvy,° and begin to find myself *shabby* fopped° in it. *made a fool*

IAGO Very well.

RODERIGO I tell you, 'tis not very well! I will make myself known to Desdemona: if she will return me my jewels, I will give over my suit, and repent my unlawful solicitation. If not, assure yourself I will seek satisfaction of you.

IAGO You have said° now. *finished*

RODERIGO Ay, and said nothing but what I protest intendment of doing.

IAGO Why, now I see there's mettle in thee, and even from this instant do build on thee a better opinion than ever before. Give me thy hand, Roderigo. Thou hast taken against me a most just exception, but yet, I protest, I have dealt most directly in thy affair.

RODERIGO It hath not appeared.

IAGO I grant indeed it hath not appeared, and your suspicion is not without wit and judgment. But, Roderigo, if thou hast that in thee indeed which I have greater reason to believe now than ever—I mean purpose, courage, and valor—this night show it. If thou, the next night following, enjoy not Desdemona, take me from this world with treachery, and devise engines for° my life. *plots against*

RODERIGO Well, what is it? Is it within reason and compass?° *possibility*

IAGO Sir, there is especial commission come from Venice to depute Cassio in Othello's place.

RODERIGO Is that true? Why, then Othello and Desdemona return again to Venice.

IAGO Oh, no. He goes into Mauretania[6] and taketh away with him the fair Desdemona, unless his abode be lingered here by some accident, wherein none can be so determinate° as *effectual* the removing of Cassio.

RODERIGO How do you mean, removing him?

IAGO Why, by making him uncapable of Othello's place: knocking out his brains!

RODERIGO And that you would have me to do?

IAGO Ay, if you dare do yourself a profit and a right. He sups tonight with a harlotry,° and thither will I go to him. He *prostitute* knows not yet of his honorable fortune.° If you will watch *promotion* his going thence, which I will fashion° to fall out between *arrange* twelve and one, you may take him at your pleasure. I will be near to second your attempt, and he shall fall between us. Come: stand not amazed at it, but go along with me; I will show you such a necessity in his death that you shall think

---

6. Country in the western Sahara.

yourself bound to put it on him. It is now high supper-time,
and the night grows to waste: about it!

235 RODERIGO I will hear further reason for this.

IAGO And you shall be satisfied. *Exeunt.*

4.3 (Q 4.3)

Enter OTHELLO, LODOVICO, DESDEMONA, EMILIA,
and Attendants.

LODOVICO I do beseech you, sir, trouble yourself no further.

OTHELLO Oh, pardon me. 'Twill do me good to walk.

LODOVICO —Madam, good night. I humbly thank your ladyship.

DESDEMONA Your honor is most welcome.

5 OTHELLO Will you walk, sir? —O Desdemona—

DESDEMONA My lord?

OTHELLO Get you to bed on th'instant: I will be returned
forthwith. Dismiss your attendant there. Look't be done.

DESDEMONA I will, my lord.

Exeunt [OTHELLO, LODOVICO, *and Attendants*].

10 EMILIA How goes it now? He looks gentler than he did.

DESDEMONA He says he will return incontinent,°   *immediately*
And hath commanded me to go to bed,
And bid me to dismiss you.

EMILIA   Dismiss me?

DESDEMONA It was his bidding: therefore, good Emilia,

15 Give me my nightly wearing, and adieu.
We must not now displease him.

EMILIA I would you had never seen him!

DESDEMONA So would not I: my love doth so approve him
That even his stubbornness, his checks, his frowns

20 —Prithee, unpin me—have grace and favor.

EMILIA I have laid those sheets you bade me on the bed.

DESDEMONA All's one.° —Good Father, how foolish are our   *It doesn't matter*
minds!
—If I do die before, prithee shroud me
In one of these same sheets.

EMILIA   Come, come: you talk!

25 DESDEMONA My mother had a maid called Barbary:[1]
She was in love, and he she loved proved mad
And did forsake her. She had a song of "willow":
An old thing 'twas, but it expressed her fortune,
And she died singing it. That song tonight

30 Will not go from my mind.[2] I have much to do
But to[3] go hang my head all at one side
And sing it like poor Barbary. Prithee dispatch.

EMILIA Shall I go fetch your nightgown?

DESDEMONA   No, unpin me here.
This Lodovico is a proper man.

EMILIA A very handsome man.

35 DESDEMONA   He speaks well.

4.3 Location: Scene continues.
1. Iago compares Othello to a "Barbary horse" (1.1.109).
2. TEXTUAL COMMENT Lines 30–49 ("I . . . next") do not appear in Q. For the significance of sexuality in

this passage, the only one in the play where women are alone together, see Digital Edition TC 5 (Folio edited text).
3. I can barely bring myself not to.

EMILIA I know a lady in Venice would have walked barefoot
   to Palestine for a touch of his nether lip.
DESDEMONA [*sings*]   The poor soul sat singing[4] by a sycamore
          tree:
          Sing all a green willow.[5]
40   Her hand on her bosom, her head on her knee:
          Sing willow, willow, willow.
          The fresh streams ran by her and murmured her
             moans:
          Sing willow, willow, willow.
          Her salt tears fell from her and softened the stones:
          Sing willow, willow, willow—
45 [*to* EMILIA]   Lay by these—
   [*sings*]   Willow, willow—
   [*to* EMILIA]   Prithee, hie thee:° he'll come anon.   *hurry*
   [*sings*]   "Sing all a green willow" must be my garland:
          Let nobody blame him, his scorn I approve—
   Nay, that's not next. —Hark, who is't that knocks?
50 EMILIA   It's the wind.
DESDEMONA [*sings*]   I called my love "false love" but what said he
             then?[6]
          Sing willow, willow, willow.
          "If I court more women, you'll couch with more men."
   [*to* EMILIA] So, get thee gone: good night. Mine eyes do itch.
   Doth that bode weeping?
55 EMILIA   'Tis neither here nor there.
 ✦ DESDEMONA   I have heard it said so. Oh, these men, these men![7]
   Dost thou in conscience think—tell me, Emilia—
   That there be women do abuse their husbands
   In such gross kind?°   *fashion*
   EMILIA   There be some such, no question.
60 DESDEMONA   Wouldst thou do such a deed for all the world?
   EMILIA   Why, would not you?
   DESDEMONA   No, by this heavenly light.
   EMILIA   Nor I neither by this heavenly light:
   I might do't as well i'the dark.
   DESDEMONA   Wouldst thou do such a deed for all the world?
65 ✦ EMILIA   The world's a huge thing; it is a great price
   For a small vice.
   DESDEMONA   In troth, I think thou wouldst not.
   EMILIA   In troth, I think I should, and undo't when I had
   done. Marry, I would not do such a thing for a joint ring,[8]
   nor for measures of lawn,° nor for gowns, petticoats, nor   *linen*
70   caps, nor any petty exhibition.° But for all the whole world?   *gift*
   Why, who would not make her husband a cuckold to make
   him a monarch? I should venture purgatory for't.
   DESDEMONA   Beshrew me if I would do such a wrong
   For the whole world!

4. TEXTUAL COMMENT For the gendered significance
of "singing" here, which replaces "sighing" in the popular version of this song, as well as its relationship to
printing house processes, see Digital Edition TC 6
(Folio edited text).

5. A conventional symbol of disappointed love.
6. Lines 51–53 do not appear in Q.
7. Lines 56–59 do not appear in Q.
8. A cheap ring in separable halves.

75 EMILIA   Why, the wrong is but a wrong i'the world and, hav-
     ing the world for your labor, 'tis a wrong in your own world,
     and you might quickly make it right!
DESDEMONA   I do not think there is any such woman.
EMILIA   Yes, a dozen! And as many to th' vantage as would
80   store the world they played for.⁹
     But I do think it is their husbands' faults¹
     If wives do fall. Say that they slack their duties,°   *marital duties*
     And pour our treasures into foreign laps;²
     Or else break out in peevish jealousies,
85   Throwing restraint upon us; or say they strike us,
     Or scant our former having in despite:³
     Why, we have galls,° and, though we have some grace,   *tempers*
     Yet have we some revenge. Let husbands know
     Their wives have sense like them: they see and smell,
90   And have their palates both for sweet and sour,
     As husbands have. What is it that they do
     When they change us for others? Is it sport?
     I think it is. And doth affection° breed it?   *lust*
     I think it doth. Is't frailty that thus errs?
95   It is so, too. And have not we affections,
     Desires for sport, and frailty, as men have?
     Then let them use us well. Else let them know
     The ills we do, their ills instruct us so.
DESDEMONA   Good night, good night. Heaven me such uses°   *habits*
     send
100 Not to pick bad from bad, but by bad, mend.⁴   *Exeunt.*

5.1 (Q 5.1)

Enter IAGO *and* RODERIGO.

IAGO   Here, stand behind this balk:° straight° will he come.   *timber beam / right away*
     Wear thy good rapier bare, and put it home.°   *drive it into him*
     Quick, quick! Fear nothing; I'll be at thy elbow.
     It makes us or it mars us. Think on that,
5   And fix most firm thy resolution.
RODERIGO   Be near at hand; I may miscarry in't.
IAGO   Here, at thy hand. Be bold, and take thy stand.
RODERIGO [*aside*]   I have no great devotion to the deed;
     And yet he hath given me satisfying reasons.
10   'Tis but a man gone. —Forth my sword: he dies!
          [*He draws.*]
          [IAGO *withdraws.*]
IAGO [*aside*]   I have rubbed this young quat° almost to the   *pimple*
     sense,°   *to the quick*
     And he grows angry. Now, whether he kill Cassio,
     Or Cassio him, or each do kill the other,
     Every way makes my gain. Live Roderigo,°   *If Roderigo lives*
15   He calls me to a restitution large
     Of gold and jewels that I bobbed from him°   *defrauded him of*
     As gifts to Desdemona—

---

9. *And . . . for:* and as many more as it would take to
populate the world they gained by doing it.
1. Lines 81–98 do not appear in Q.
2. And give the semen that belongs to us to other
women.

3. Or reduce our allowances out of spite.
4. Not to take bad behavior as an example, but to
know what to avoid.
5.1 Location: A street in Cyprus.

It must not be. If Cassio do remain,
He hath a daily beauty in his life
20   That makes me ugly; and, besides, the Moor
May unfold° me to him: there stand I in much peril.   *reveal*
No, he must die. But so:° I heard him coming.   *so be it*
    [*He draws.*]
    Enter CASSIO.
RODERIGO   I know his gait, 'tis he. —Villain, thou diest!
    [*He thrusts at* CASSIO.]
CASSIO   That thrust had been mine enemy indeed,
25   But that my coat is better° than thou know'st.   *thicker; more armored*
I will make proof of° thine.   *test*
    [*He stabs* RODERIGO.]
RODERIGO   Oh, I am slain!
    [IAGO *stabs* CASSIO.]
CASSIO   I am maimed forever! Help, ho! Murder! Murder!
                            [*Exit* IAGO.]
    Enter OTHELLO [*apart*].
OTHELLO   The voice of Cassio. Iago keeps his word!
RODERIGO   Oh, villain that I am!
OTHELLO   It is even so.
30 CASSIO   Oh, help, ho! Light! A surgeon!
OTHELLO   'Tis he. O brave Iago, honest and just,
That hast such noble sense of thy friend's wrong;
Thou teachest me. —Minion,° your dear lies dead,   *Hussy*
And your unblest fate hies.° Strumpet, I come: *damnation hurries on*
35   For of° my heart those charms, thine eyes, are blotted;   *out of*
Thy bed, lust-stained, shall with lust's blood be spotted.
                        Exit OTHELLO.
    Enter LODOVICO *and* GRAZIANO [*apart*].
CASSIO   What, ho? No watch? No passage?° Murder! Murder!   *passersby*
GRAZIANO [*to* LODOVICO]   'Tis some mischance. The voice is
very direful.
CASSIO   Oh, help!
40 LODOVICO [*to* GRAZIANO]   Hark!
RODERIGO   O wretched villain!
LODOVICO [*to* GRAZIANO]   Two or three groan! 'Tis heavy° night;   *dark*
These may be counterfeits. Let's think't unsafe
To come into° the cry without more help.   *go near*
45 RODERIGO   Nobody come? Then shall I bleed to death!
    Enter IAGO [*with a light*].
LODOVICO [*to* GRAZIANO]   Hark!
GRAZIANO [*to* LODOVICO]   Here's one comes in his shirt, with
light and weapons.
IAGO   Who's there? Whose noise is this that cries on murder?
LODOVICO   We do not know.
IAGO   Do not you hear a cry?
CASSIO   Here! Here! For heaven sake, help me!
50 IAGO [*to* CASSIO]   What's the matter?
GRAZIANO [*to* LODOVICO]   This is Othello's ensign, as I take it.
LODOVICO [*to* GRAZIANO]   The same indeed: a very valiant fellow.
IAGO [*to* CASSIO]   What are you here, that cry so grievously?
CASSIO   Iago? Oh, I am spoiled, undone by villains!
Give me some help.
55 IAGO   O me, lieutenant!

What villains have done this?

CASSIO   I think that one of them is hereabout

And cannot make° away.   get

IAGO   O treacherous villains!

[*to* LODOVICO *and* GRAZIANO] What are you there? Come in
   and give some help.

RODERIGO   Oh, help me there!

60   CASSIO   That's one of them!

IAGO [*to* RODERIGO]   O murd'rous slave! O villain!
       [*He stabs* RODERIGO.]

RODERIGO   O damned Iago! O inhuman dog!

IAGO   Kill men i'th' dark? Where be these bloody thieves?
   How silent is this town! Ho! Murder! Murder!

65   [*to* LODOVICO *and* GRAZIANO] What may you be? Are you of
   good or evil?

LODOVICO   As you shall prove us, praise us.

IAGO   Signor Lodovico?

LODOVICO   He, sir.

IAGO   I cry you mercy: here's Cassio hurt by villains.

GRAZIANO   Cassio?

IAGO [*to* CASSIO]   How is't, brother?

70   CASSIO   My leg is cut in two.

IAGO   Marry, heaven forbid.
  —Light, gentlemen! I'll bind it with my shirt.
      Enter BIANCA.

BIANCA   What is the matter, ho? Who is't that cried?

IAGO   Who is't that cried?

BIANCA   O my dear Cassio!

75   My sweet Cassio! O Cassio! Cassio! Cassio!

IAGO   O notable strumpet. —Cassio, may you suspect
  Who they should be that have thus mangled you?

CASSIO   No.

GRAZIANO   I am sorry to find you thus; I have been to seek you.

IAGO [*to* LODOVICO *and* GRAZIANO]   Lend me a garter. So.

80   [*He binds Cassio's leg.*]   Oh, for a chair°   litter
  To bear him easily hence.

BIANCA   Alas, he faints! O Cassio! Cassio! Cassio!

IAGO   Gentlemen all, I do suspect this trash°   (Bianca)
  To be a party in this injury.

85   —Patience awhile, good Cassio. [*to* LODOVICO *and* GRAZIANO]
   Come, come,

Lend me a light. [*He goes to* RODERIGO.] Know we this face
  or no?

Alas, my friend and my dear countryman,
  Roderigo! No? Yes, sure. Yes, 'tis Roderigo!

GRAZIANO   What, of Venice?

IAGO   Even he, sir. Did you know him?

90   GRAZIANO   Know him? Ay.

IAGO   Signor Graziano? I cry your gentle pardon;
  These bloody accidents must excuse my manners
  That so neglected you.

GRAZIANO   I am glad to see you.

IAGO   —How do you, Cassio? —Oh, a chair! A chair!

95   GRAZIANO   Roderigo?

IAGO   He, he. 'Tis he.

[*Enter Attendants with a chair.*]
                    Oh, that's well said:° the chair.   *carried out*
Some good man bear him carefully from hence.
I'll fetch the general's surgeon. [*to* BIANCA] For you, mistress,
Save you your labor. —He that lies slain here, Cassio,
100   Was my dear friend. What malice was between you?
CASSIO   None in the world, nor do I know the man.
IAGO   What, look you pale? [*to Attendants*] Oh, bear him o'th'
         air.[1]   [*Exeunt Attendants with* CASSIO *and* RODERIGO.]
   [*to* LODOVICO *and* GRAZIANO] Stay you, good gentlemen. [*to*
      BIANCA] Look you pale, mistress?
   [*to* LODOVICO *and* GRAZIANO] Do you perceive the gastness°   *terror*
      of her eye?
105   [*to* BIANCA] Nay, if you stare we shall hear more anon.
   [*to* LODOVICO *and* GRAZIANO] Behold her well. I pray you,
      look upon her:
Do you see, gentlemen? Nay, guiltiness will speak,
Though tongues were out of use.
            [*Enter* EMILIA.]
EMILIA   Alas, what is the matter?
What is the matter, husband?
110   IAGO   Cassio hath here been set on in the dark
By Roderigo and fellows that are scaped:
He's almost slain, and Roderigo quite dead.
EMILIA   Alas, good gentleman! Alas, good Cassio!
IAGO   This is the fruits of whoring. Prithee, Emilia,
115   Go know of Cassio where he supped tonight.
   [*to* BIANCA] What, do you shake at that?
BIANCA   He supped at my house, but I therefore shake not.
IAGO   Oh, did he so? I charge you go with me.
EMILIA   Oh, fie upon thee, strumpet!
120   BIANCA   I am no strumpet, but of life as honest
As you that thus abuse me.
EMILIA   As I? Fie upon thee!
IAGO   Kind gentlemen, let's go see poor Cassio dressed.°   *bandaged*
   [*to* BIANCA]   Come, mistress, you must tell's another tale.
   —Emilia, run you to the citadel
125   And tell my lord and lady what hath happed.
   [*to* LODOVICO *and* GRAZIANO] Will you go on afore?
      [*aside*] This is the night
That either makes me or fordoes° me quite.   *Exeunt.*   *undoes*

5.2 (Q 5.2)
Enter OTHELLO [*with a light,*] *and* DESDEMONA *in
her bed.*[1]
OTHELLO   It is the cause,[2] it is the cause, my soul.
Let me not name it to you, you chaste stars:
It is the cause. Yet I'll not shed her blood,
Nor scar that whiter skin of hers than snow
5   And smooth as monumental alabaster;°   *stone used in tombs*

1. Out of the open air (thought to be bad for wounds).
5.2 Location: Desdemona and Othello's bedroom.
1. PERFORMANCE COMMENT For the problem of where on stage to place Desdemona's bed, as well as how Desdemona, Othello, and Iago are to be played in this scene, see Digital Edition PC 7.
2. What matters is Desdemona's infidelity; the "cause" of justice, which Othello sees himself defending, as in the subsequent lines.

Yet she must die, else she'll betray more men.
Put out the light, and then put out the light.³
If I quench thee, thou flaming minister,°   *light that serves me*
I can again thy former light restore,
10   Should I repent me—but once put out thy light,
Thou cunning'st pattern of excelling nature,⁴
I know not where is that Promethean heat⁵
That can thy light relume.° When I have plucked thy rose,   *relight*
I cannot give it vital growth again:
15   It needs must wither. I'll smell thee on the tree.
        [*He kisses her.*]
Oh, balmy breath, that dost almost persuade
Justice to break her sword! One more, one more.
Be thus when thou art dead, and I will kill thee
And love thee after. One more, and that's the last.
        [*He kisses her.*]
20   So sweet was ne'er so fatal. I must weep,
But they are cruel tears. This sorrow's heavenly:
It strikes where it doth love.⁶ She wakes!
DESDEMONA   Who's there? Othello?
OTHELLO   Ay, Desdemona.
DESDEMONA   Will you come to bed, my lord?
OTHELLO   Have you prayed tonight, Desdemon?
25   DESDEMONA   Ay, my lord.
OTHELLO   If you bethink yourself of any crime
Unreconciled as yet to heaven and grace,
Solicit° for it straight.   *Ask forgiveness*
DESDEMONA   Alack, my lord,
What may you mean by that?
30   OTHELLO   Well, do it, and be brief. I will walk by.
I would not kill thy unpreparèd spirit;
No, heavens forfend, I would not kill thy soul.
DESDEMONA   Talk you of killing?
OTHELLO   Ay, I do.
DESDEMONA   Then heaven have mercy on me!
OTHELLO   Amen, with all my heart.
35   DESDEMONA   If you say,° I hope you will not kill me.   *Since you say "amen"*
OTHELLO   Hum!
DESDEMONA   And yet I fear you, for you're fatal then
When your eyes roll so. Why I should fear I know not,
Since guiltiness I know not, but yet I feel I fear.
OTHELLO   Think on thy sins.
40   DESDEMONA   They are loves I bear to you.
OTHELLO   Ay, and for that thou diest.
DESDEMONA   That death's unnatural that kills for loving.
Alas, why gnaw you so your nether lip?
Some bloody passion shakes your very frame.
45   These are portents, but yet I hope, I hope,
They do not point on me.
OTHELLO   Peace, and be still.

---

3. This and the following lines compare the light of
Othello's lamp or torch to Desdemona's "light" of life.
4. You most cleverly wrought example of nature's work.
5. Life-giving fire. In Greek mythology, Prometheus
stole fire from heaven to give it to humankind; in a
different tradition, he is credited with animating
humankind from clay.
6. See Hebrews 12:6: "For whom the Lord loveth, he
chasteneth."

DESDEMONA I will so. What's the matter?

OTHELLO   That handkerchief,
Which I so loved and gave thee, thou gav'st to Cassio.

DESDEMONA No, by my life and soul! Send for the man,
50 And ask him.

OTHELLO Sweet soul, take heed, take heed of perjury.
Thou art on thy death-bed.

DESDEMONA   I? But not yet to die?

OTHELLO Presently.°   *Immediately*
Therefore confess thee freely of thy sin,
55 For to deny each article with oath
Cannot remove nor choke the strong conception
That I do groan withal:[7] thou art to die.

DESDEMONA O heaven, have mercy on me!

OTHELLO   I say amen.

DESDEMONA And have you mercy, too. I never did
60 Offend you in my life, never loved Cassio
But with such general warranty of heaven
As I might love. I never gave him token.

OTHELLO By heaven, I saw my handkerchief in's hand!
O perjured woman, thou dost stone° my heart,   *harden*
65 And makest me call what I intend to do
A murder, which I thought a sacrifice.
I saw the handkerchief.

DESDEMONA   He found it, then.
I never gave it him. Send for him hither:
Let him confess a truth.

OTHELLO   He hath confessed.

DESDEMONA What, my lord?

OTHELLO   That he hath used thee.

70 DESDEMONA   How, unlawfully?

OTHELLO Ay.

DESDEMONA He will not say so.

OTHELLO   No, his mouth is stopped.
Honest Iago hath ta'en order for't.

DESDEMONA Oh, my fear interprets. What, is he dead?

OTHELLO Had all his hairs been lives, my great revenge
75 Had stomach for them all.

DESDEMONA Alas, he is betrayed, and I undone.

OTHELLO Out, strumpet! Weep'st thou for him to my face?

DESDEMONA Oh, banish me, my lord, but kill me not.

OTHELLO Down, strumpet!
          [*He attacks her.*]
80 DESDEMONA [*struggling*] Kill me tomorrow; let me live tonight!

OTHELLO Nay, if you strive—

DESDEMONA But half an hour!

OTHELLO   Being done, there is no pause.[8]

DESDEMONA But while I say one prayer!

OTHELLO   It is too late.
          [*He*] smothers her.

EMILIA (*at the door*) My lord! My lord! What ho, my lord! My
          lord!

---

7. *Cannot . . . withal:* Cannot stop the strong conviction I have in your guilt (or the firm plan to kill you),
which makes me groan so. The metaphor is from

childbirth.
8. Now that I've started, there's no stopping.

85 OTHELLO   What noise is this? —Not dead? Not yet quite dead?
    I, that am cruel, am yet merciful:
    I would not have thee linger in thy pain.
    So. So.
       [*He smothers* DESDEMONA *again.*]
EMILIA (*within*)   What ho, my lord! My lord!
OTHELLO   Who's there?
EMILIA [*within*]   O good my lord, I would speak a word with you.
90 OTHELLO   Yes. —'Tis Emilia. —By and by! —She's dead.
    'Tis like° she comes to speak of Cassio's death: *likely*
    The noise was high.° —Ha, no more moving?   *commotion was loud*
    Still as the grave. Shall she come in? Were't good?
    I think she stirs again! No. What's best to do?
95   If she come in, she'll sure speak to my wife.
    My wife! My wife! What wife? I have no wife.
    Oh, insupportable! Oh, heavy hour!
    Methinks it should be now a huge eclipse
    Of sun and moon, and that th'affrighted globe
    Did yawn at alteration.[9]
100 EMILIA [*within*]   I do beseech you
    That I may speak with you, O good my lord!
OTHELLO   I had forgot thee. —Oh, come in, Emilia.
    —Soft!° —By and by. —Let me the curtains draw.   *Quiet*
    —Where art thou? What's the matter with thee now?
       Enter EMILIA.
105 EMILIA   O my good lord, yonder's foul murders done.
OTHELLO   What? Now?
EMILIA   But° now, my lord.   *Just*
OTHELLO   It is the very error° of the moon: *deviation*
    She comes more nearer earth than she was wont,
    And makes men mad.
110 EMILIA   Cassio, my lord, hath killed
    A young Venetian called Roderigo.
OTHELLO   Roderigo killed? And Cassio killed?
EMILIA   No, Cassio is not killed.
OTHELLO [*aside*]   Not Cassio killed? Then murder's out of tune,
    And sweet revenge grows harsh.
115 DESDEMONA   Oh, falsely, falsely murdered!
EMILIA   Alas, what cry is that?
OTHELLO   That? What?
EMILIA   Out and alas, that was my lady's voice!
       [*She opens the bed curtains.*]
    Help! Help, ho! Help! —O lady, speak again!
    Sweet Desdemona! O sweet mistress, speak!
DESDEMONA   A guiltless death I die.
120 EMILIA   Oh, who hath done this deed?
DESDEMONA   Nobody. I myself. Farewell.
    Commend me to my kind lord. Oh, farewell!
       [*She dies.*]
OTHELLO   Why, how should she be murdered?
EMILIA   Alas, who knows?

---

9. Should gape at the change. Earthquakes were associated with eclipses.

OTHELLO You hear her say herself it was not I.

125 EMILIA She said so. I must needs report the truth.

OTHELLO She's like a liar gone to burning hell:
'Twas I that killed her.

EMILIA Oh, the more angel she, and you the blacker devil.

OTHELLO She turned to folly,° and she was a whore.   *wantonness*

130 EMILIA Thou dost belie her, and thou art a devil.

OTHELLO She was false as water.

EMILIA   Thou art rash as fire to say
That she was false. Oh, she was heavenly true!

OTHELLO Cassio did top her—ask thy husband else.°   *if you doubt it*
Oh, I were damned beneath all depth in hell

135 But that I did proceed upon just grounds
To this extremity. Thy husband knew it all.

EMILIA My husband?

OTHELLO   Thy husband.

EMILIA   That she was false to wedlock?

OTHELLO Ay, with Cassio. Had she been true,
If heaven would make me such another world

140 Of one entire and perfect chrysolite,°   *topaz*
I'd not have sold her for it.

EMILIA   My husband?

OTHELLO Ay, 'twas he that told me on her first.
An honest man he is, and hates the slime
That sticks on filthy deeds—

EMILIA   My husband?

145 OTHELLO What needs this iterance,° woman? I say, thy   *repetition*
husband.

EMILIA O mistress! Villainy hath made mocks with° love.[1]   *at*
—My husband say she was false?

OTHELLO   He, woman.
I say, thy husband. Dost understand the word?
My friend, thy husband, honest, honest Iago.

150 EMILIA If he say so, may his pernicious soul
Rot half a grain a day: he lies to th' heart.
She was too fond of her most filthy bargain.

OTHELLO Ha!

EMILIA Do thy worst!

155 This deed of thine is no more worthy heaven
Than thou wast worthy her.

OTHELLO   Peace, you were best.[2]

EMILIA Thou hast not half that power to do me harm
As I have to be hurt. O gull!° O dolt,   *fool*
As ignorant as dirt. Thou hast done a deed—

160 I care not for thy sword: I'll make thee known,
Though I lost twenty lives. —Help! Help, ho! Help!
The Moor hath killed my mistress. Murder! Murder!

Enter MONTANO, GRAZIANO, *and* IAGO.

MONTANO What is the matter? How now, general?

EMILIA Oh, are you come, Iago? You have done well

165 That men must lay their murders on your neck.

---

1. Lines 146–49 do not appear in Q.
2. It would be best for you (to remain silent).

GRAZIANO   What is the matter?

EMILIA [*to* IAGO]   Disprove this villain, if thou beest a man.
  He says thou told'st him that his wife was false.
  I know thou didst not: thou'rt not such a villain.
170   Speak, for my heart is full.

IAGO   I told him what I thought, and told no more
  Than what he found himself was apt and true.

EMILIA   But did you ever tell him she was false?

IAGO   I did.

175 EMILIA   You told a lie, an odious, damned lie!
  Upon my soul, a lie, a wicked lie!
  She false with Cassio? Did you say with Cassio?

IAGO   With Cassio, mistress. Go to, charm° your tongue.   silence

EMILIA   I will not charm my tongue: I am bound to speak:
180   My mistress here lies murdered in her bed.[3]

MONTANO *and* GRAZIANO   O heavens forfend!

EMILIA   And your reports have set the murder on.

OTHELLO   Nay, stare not, masters: it is true indeed.

GRAZIANO   'Tis a strange truth.

MONTANO   Oh, monstrous act!

185 EMILIA   Villainy! Villainy! Villainy!
  I think upon't; I think I smell't. Oh, villainy!
  I thought so, then. I'll kill myself for grief.
  Oh, villainy! Villainy!

IAGO   What, are you mad?
  I charge you, get you home.

190 EMILIA   Good gentlemen, let me have leave to speak.
  'Tis proper I obey him, but not now.
  —Perchance, Iago, I will ne'er go home.

OTHELLO   Oh! Oh! Oh!
  [OTHELLO *falls on the bed.*]

EMILIA   Nay, lay thee down and roar,
  For thou hast killed the sweetest innocent
  That e'er did lift up eye.°   (*to heaven*)

195 OTHELLO   Oh, she was foul!
  [*to* GRAZIANO] I scarce did know you, uncle. There lies your
      niece,
  Whose breath, indeed, these hands have newly stopped.
  I know this act shows° horrible and grim.   appears

GRAZIANO   Poor Desdemon. I am glad thy father's dead:
200   Thy match was mortal to him, and pure grief
  Shore his old thread in twain.[4] Did he live now,
  This sight would make him do a desperate turn,°   act
  Yea, curse his better angel from his side,
  And fall to reprobance.[5]

205 OTHELLO   'Tis pitiful, but yet Iago knows
  That she with Cassio hath the act of shame
  A thousand times committed. Cassio confessed it,
  And she did gratify his amorous works
  With that recognizance° and pledge of love   token

---

3. Lines 180–88 do not appear in Q.
4. Cut the thread of his life.
5. Reprobation, rejection by God—here for suicide,

the unforgivably sinful act of despair, leading to eternal damnation.

210 Which I first gave her. I saw it in his hand:
It was a handkerchief, an antique token
My father gave my mother.[6]

EMILIA   O heaven! O heavenly powers!

IAGO   Come, hold your peace!

EMILIA   'Twill out, 'twill out. I, peace?
No, I will speak as liberal as the north.[7]

215 Let heaven, and men, and devils, let them all,
All, all cry shame against me, yet I'll speak.

IAGO   Be wise, and get you home.

    [*He draws.*]

EMILIA   I will not.

GRAZIANO   Fie! Your sword upon a woman?

EMILIA   O thou dull Moor, that handkerchief thou speak'st of

220 I found by fortune, and did give my husband:
For often, with a solemn earnestness—
More than indeed belonged to such a trifle—
He begged of me to steal't.

IAGO   Villainous whore!

EMILIA   She give it Cassio? No, alas, I found it,
And I did give't my husband.

225 IAGO   Filth! Thou liest.

EMILIA   By heaven, I do not. I do not, gentlemen.

    [*to* OTHELLO] O murd'rous coxcomb!° What should such a   *fool*
    fool
Do with so good a wife?

OTHELLO   Are there no stones° in heaven   *thunderbolts*
But what serves for the thunder? [*to* IAGO] Precious° villain!   *Absolute*

    [OTHELLO *runs at* IAGO; MONTANO *disarms him.*

    IAGO *stabs* EMILIA.][8]

230 GRAZIANO   The woman falls! Sure, he hath killed his wife.

                        [*Exit* IAGO.]

EMILIA   Ay! Ay! Oh, lay me by my mistress' side.

    [GRAZIANO *puts her on the bed.*][9]

GRAZIANO   He's gone, but his wife's killed.

MONTANO   'Tis a notorious villain. [*to* GRAZIANO] Take you
    this weapon,
Which I have recovered from the Moor.

235 Come, guard the door without; let him not pass,
But kill him rather. I'll after that same villain,
For 'tis a damned slave.   *Exeunt* [MONTANO *and* GRAZIANO].

OTHELLO   I am not valiant, neither,
But every puny whipster° gets my sword.   *insignificant person*
But why should honor outlive honesty?[1]
Let it go all.

240 EMILIA [*to* DESDEMONA]   What did thy song bode, lady?[2]
Hark, canst thou hear me? I will play the swan

---

6. Earlier, however, Othello says that his mother got the handkerchief not from his father but from "an Egyptian . . . charmer" (3.4.53–54).
7. As freely as the north wind.
8. TEXTUAL COMMENT For the significance of Othello's use of swords, and the difference between F's and Q's treatment of the matter, see Digital Edition TC 7 (Folio edited text).

9. TEXTUAL COMMENT For the different consequences of having Graziano honor, or ignore, Emilia's dying request, "Lay me by my mistress' side," see Digital Edition TC 8 (Folio edited text).
1. Why should military reputation outlive integrity?
2. Lines 240–42 ("What . . . willow.'") do not appear in Q.

And die in music. [*She sings.*] "Willow, willow, willow."
—Moor, she was chaste. She loved thee, cruel Moor.
So come my soul to bliss as I speak true;
245 So, speaking as I think, alas, I die.
     [*She dies.*]
OTHELLO   I have another weapon in this chamber:
It was a sword of Spain, the ice-brook's temper.°   *tempered in icy water*
Oh, here it is. —Uncle, I must come forth.
GRAZIANO [*within*]   If thou attempt it, it will cost thee dear:
250 Thou hast no weapon, and perforce must suffer.
OTHELLO   Look in upon me, then, and speak with me
Or, naked° as I am, I will assault thee.   *unarmed*
     [*Enter* GRAZIANO.]
GRAZIANO   What is the matter?
OTHELLO   Behold, I have a weapon:
A better never did itself sustain
255 Upon a soldier's thigh. I have seen the day
That, with this little arm and this good sword,
I have made my way through more impediments
Than twenty times your stop.° But, oh, vain boast!   *power to stop*
Who can control his fate? 'Tis not so now.
260 Be not afraid, though you do see me weaponed:[3]
Here is my journey's end; here is my butt°   *goal*
And very sea-mark° of my utmost sail.°   *beacon / voyage's limit*
Do you go back dismayed? 'Tis a lost° fear: *an unnecessary*
Man but a rush° against Othello's breast,   *Aim even a reed*
265 And he retires. Where should Othello go?
[*to* DESDEMONA] Now, how dost thou look now? O ill-starred
    wench,
Pale as thy smock. When we shall meet at count,°   *Judgment Day*
This look of thine will hurl my soul from heaven,
And fiends will snatch at it. Cold, cold, my girl?
270 Even like thy chastity. O cursèd, cursèd slave!
Whip me, ye devils,
From the possession of this heavenly sight;
Blow me about in winds, roast me in sulfur,
Wash me in steep-down gulfs of liquid fire.
275 O Desdemon! Dead, Desdemon, dead! Oh! Oh![4]
     Enter LODOVICO, CASSIO [*in a chair*], MONTANO, *and*
      IAGO [*as a prisoner*], *with* OFFICERS.
LODOVICO   Where is this rash and most unfortunate man?
OTHELLO   That's he that was Othello: here I am.
LODOVICO   Where is that viper? [*to* OFFICERS] Bring the
    villain forth.
OTHELLO   I look down towards his feet,[5] but that's a fable.
280 [*to* IAGO] If that thou beest a devil, I cannot kill thee.
     [*He stabs* IAGO.]
LODOVICO [*to* OFFICERS]   Wrench his sword from him!
IAGO   I bleed, sir, but not killed.
OTHELLO   I am not sorry, neither: I'd have thee live,
For, in my sense,° 'tis happiness to die.   *state of feeling*

3. Lines 260–66 do not appear in Q.
4. TEXTUAL COMMENT For the consequences of the metrical differences between F and Q in rendering

Othello's grief in this line, see Digital Edition TC 9 (Folio edited text).
5. I look for the devil's cloven feet.

LODOVICO   O thou, Othello, that was once so good,
285   Fallen in the practice° of a cursèd slave,   *plot*
     What shall be said to thee?
OTHELLO   Why, anything.
     An honorable murderer, if you will,
     For naught I did in hate, but all in honor.
LODOVICO   This wretch hath part confessed his villainy.
290   Did you and he consent in Cassio's death?
OTHELLO   Ay.
CASSIO   Dear general, I never gave you cause!
OTHELLO   I do believe it, and I ask your pardon.
     Will you, I pray, demand that demi-devil
295   Why he hath thus ensnared my soul and body?
IAGO   Demand me nothing. What you know, you know:[6]
     From this time forth I never will speak word.
LODOVICO   What, not to pray?
GRAZIANO   Torments° will ope your lips.   *Tortures*
OTHELLO   Well, thou dost best.[7]
300   LODOVICO   Sir,
     You shall understand what hath befallen,
     Which, as I think, you know not. Here is a letter
     Found in the pocket of the slain Roderigo,
     And here another: the one of them imports
305   The death of Cassio, to be undertook
     By Roderigo.
OTHELLO   O villain!
CASSIO   Most heathenish and most gross!°   *monstrous*
LODOVICO   Now, here's another discontented paper°   *paper listing complaints*
     Found in his pocket, too, and this it seems
     Roderigo meant t' have sent this damnèd villain
310   But that, belike,° Iago in the interim   *most likely*
     Came in and satisfied him.
OTHELLO   O thou pernicious caitiff!°   *wretch*
     —How came you, Cassio, by that handkerchief
     That was my wife's?
CASSIO   I found it in my chamber,
     And he himself confessed it but even now
315   That there he dropped it for a special purpose
     Which wrought to his desire.
OTHELLO   O fool! Fool! Fool!
CASSIO   There is, besides, in Roderigo's letter
     How he upbraids Iago that he made him
     Brave° me upon the watch, whereon it came   *Defy*
320   That I was cast;° and even but now he spake,   *dismissed*
     After long seeming dead: Iago hurt him;
     Iago set him on.
LODOVICO [*to* OTHELLO]   You must forsake this room and go
          with us:
     Your power and your command is taken off,
325   And Cassio rules in Cyprus. For this slave,
     If there be any cunning cruelty

---

6. Iago's final pithy statement of identity or noniden-   7. Addressed to Lodovico and Graziano or, ironi-
tity. See 1.1.63, 4.1.257–59, and notes.   cally, to Iago.

That can torment him much and hold him° long,   *(alive)*

It shall be his. —You shall close° prisoner rest   *tightly confined*

Till that the nature of your fault be known

330 To the Venetian state. [*to* OFFICERS] Come, bring away.

OTHELLO   Soft you,° a word or two before you go.   *Wait*

I have done the state some service, and they know't—

No more of that. I pray you, in your letters,

When you shall these unlucky deeds relate,

335 Speak of me as I am; nothing extenuate,

Nor set down aught in malice. Then must you speak

Of one that loved not wisely, but too well;

Of one not easily jealous but, being wrought,

Perplexed in the extreme;[8] of one whose hand,

340 Like the base Judean,[9] threw a pearl away

Richer than all his tribe; of one whose subdued° eyes,   *(by grief)*

Albeit unusèd to the melting mood,

Drop tears as fast as the Arabian trees

Their medicinable gum.° Set you down this,   *myrrh*

345 And say, besides, that in Aleppo[1] once,

Where a malignant and a turbaned Turk

Beat a Venetian and traduced° the state,   *defamed*

I took by th' throat the circumcisèd dog

And smote him thus.

    [*He stabs himself.*]

LODOVICO   Oh, bloody period!°   *conclusion; sentence*

350 GRAZIANO   All that is spoke is marred.

OTHELLO [*to* DESDEMONA]   I kissed thee ere I killed thee. No

    way but this:

Killing myself, to die upon a kiss.

    [*He*] *dies*[.]

CASSIO   This did I fear—but thought he had no weapon—

For he was great of heart.

LODOVICO [*to* IAGO]   O Spartan dog,°   *(notoriously savage)*

355 More fell° than anguish, hunger, or the sea,   *cruel*

Look on the tragic loading of this bed:

This is thy work. The object poisons sight.

Let it be hid. —Graziano, keep° the house,   *guard*

And seize upon the fortunes of the Moor,

360 For they succeed on you. [*to* CASSIO] To you, Lord Governor,

Remains the censure° of this hellish villain: *sentence*

The time, the place, the torture—oh, enforce it.

Myself will straight aboard, and to the state

This heavy act with heavy heart relate.   *Exeunt.*

---

8. *not easily jealous . . . perplexed in the extreme*: The first of these two statements echoes Desdemona's earlier comment about Othello's disinclination to be jealous (3.4.27–28); the second, an accompanying geocultural belief of the time—that southern temperaments, when once that disinclination was overcome, became extremely jealous.

9. TEXTUAL COMMENT For the differences between F's anti-Semitic reading, "Judean," and Q's colonialist reading, "Indian," see Digital Edition TC 10 (Folio text).

1. Ottoman city in what later became Syria through which Venice traded with the East.

Sir Thomas More

How would you write a play sympathetic to a Catholic martyr who had been executed by the father (Henry VIII) of your Protestant queen (Elizabeth I)? And what if the execution was motivated by more than doctrinal differences, since it turned on the victim's refusal to recognize the king's—rather than the pope's—supremacy in church matters? In other words, is there a way of producing an ideologically acceptable play that celebrates a man whose actions challenge both church and state? This was the set of problems facing the authors of *Sir Thomas More*. Not surprisingly, the resulting manuscript was subjected to severe censorship by Edmund Tilney, who, as Queen Elizabeth's Master of the Revels, had the responsibility for such matters. But the passages Tilney rejected had nothing to do with the thorny religious controversy that lies behind the play's story line and is one of the defining features of the age. Rather, from Tilney's perspective the offending material concerned popular rebellion and xenophobic hostility to foreign residents of London. In due course, a revision of the original version was commissioned—perhaps, but not certainly, to meet the censor's objections, but undoubtedly to prepare the work for performance. It is not clear whether the revision succeeded: there is no evidence of performance in the early modern period or long after, and the play was not printed until the nineteenth century. Since then and until quite recently, critical discussion of *Sir Thomas More* has paid relatively little attention to these issues—religious, socioeconomic, and ethnic/national conflicts; censorship, revision, and collaboration—or to the aesthetic and dramaturgical challenges involved in dealing with such explosive material.

Instead, the spotlight has fallen on a manuscript passage from the revised version of the play included in the present edition as 2.3.1–157. (The complete edited text of the play appears in the Digital Edition of *The Norton Shakespeare*.) The reason for this interest is that the passage is almost certainly in Shakespeare's hand. As such, it represents by far the most extensive surviving sample of Shakespeare's handwriting, in the plays or anywhere else. It is therefore of considerable scholarly, as well as theatrical and literary, value. It shows what a Shakespearean draft looks like and, hence, some of the challenges a scribe or printer had to contend with. The attribution to Shakespeare is based on resemblances to his other extant handwriting (almost exclusively signatures), spelling similarities to printed texts that probably are directly based on manuscripts in Shakespeare's hand, word-frequency tests, parallel phrases in other plays by Shakespeare, metrical tests, and stylistic affinities. Shakespeare is probably responsible for 3.1.1–21 as well, though this passage is in Hand C, that of a playhouse scribe apparently assigned the task of putting the various pieces of the original and the revision together into a coherent play. Shakespeare might also be the author of most of 3.2.6–22, though this too is in Hand C.

The significance of Shakespeare's contributions may emerge by placing them primarily in the context of the play as a whole and secondarily in relation to his theatrical career more generally. *Sir Thomas More* was originally composed either in about 1593–94 or around 1600. The earlier date is traditional; but the later one, only recently proposed, may well have the stronger claim. The first version is entirely in the hand of Anthony Munday, who composed at least part of it. He may have been assisted by Henry Chettle and perhaps one or more other playwrights. Sometime later, almost certainly in 1603–04, Shakespeare seems to have participated in the revision of the play, along with Chettle, Thomas Dekker, Thomas Heywood, and Hand C (see the Textual Introduction).

Drawing primarily on Nicholas Harpsfield's Catholic *Life and Death of Sir Thomas More* (by 1575) and secondarily on Raphael Holinshed's Protestant *Chronicles of England, Scotland, and Ireland* (1587), the play conforms to the popular tragic model known in Latin as *de casibus virorum illustrium* (on the fall of illustrious men). It follows the career of More—leading English Renaissance humanist and author of the pathbreaking *Utopia*, Lord Chancellor of England and persecutor of Protestants, and, finally, Catholic martyr when the religious tide turned. The work focuses on his success as sheriff of London in peacefully quelling the anti-alien London riots of May Day 1517; his elevation to the post of Lord Chancellor; and his eventual execution for refusing to subscribe to certain of the king's articles. Throughout and especially at the end, the witty and wise protagonist is treated with almost uncritical admiration.

How do the playwrights wend their way through this ideological minefield? First, the work carefully converts the issue that led to More's death (papal versus royal supremacy of the church) into a less concrete conflict between worldly authority and individual conscience that would appeal to the Puritan-leaning audience of London, where More remained popular despite his Catholicism. This seems to have worked, at least from the perspective of the censor. Second, it shows More successfully preventing popular protest that historically he was unable to control. At least the original version also exploits the parallel between the 1517 unrest and contemporary antiforeign resentment, which was noticeable by late 1592 and led to rioting and harsh government reprisals between 1593 and 1595. It is the immediacy and prominence of this popular protest, as well as the parliamentary echoes of it, that provide the strongest argument for the earlier dating of the original manuscript. As we have seen, however, here the censor was unconvinced. Tilney demanded substantial rewriting, in particular a toning down of the attack on foreigners, the elimination of the scene dramatizing the 1517 rebellion against them, and hence a reduction in the analogies between past and present. Significantly, on neither issue does the absolute monarch—who never appears in the play—end up looking particularly good. Henry VIII insists on killing his honorable, talented, and loyal Lord Chancellor, and he shows less mercy toward his rebellious subjects than does More himself.

But if this original version really does date from around 1600, it forms part of a vogue for the national history play at the end of the century—onstage and in print— and in particular for national history plays not built around the reigns of particular monarchs. Thus, though *Sir Thomas More* echoes Shakespeare's earlier English history plays in various ways, it differs from them in conforming to the newly emergent subgenre of the nonmonarchical history play. Secondarily, and despite its tragic outcome, the play has affinities to another new dramatic genre—citizen comedy. This is a matter not only of the extensive use of popular prose—as in the *Henry IV* plays—but also of the restriction of the action to London and its immediate environs, and often of the setting of a scene in a particular street or neighborhood. Indeed, for most of the first two acts, and more mutedly in the remainder of the drama, the City of London itself seems the true protagonist of the play.

The revision may have followed hard upon James I's accession to the throne in 1603. A new monarch without much of a connection to Henry VIII and the greater distance from the dangerous political context of the 1590s may have allowed the revisers more flexibility than would have been the case just a few years before. The same goes for the presence on the throne of James's wife, Queen Anne, known for her pro-Catholic sympathies—a circumstance that leads to the possibility that the revision was undertaken for the acting company known as Queen Anne's Men. The revision significantly improved the quality of the play. The result, "The Booke of Sir Thomas Moore" (British Library, MS Harleian 7368)—where "Booke" means theatrical promptbook—is arguably the messiest and most extensively revised dramatic manuscript of the age. It highlights the frequency of both revision and collaboration.

Hans Holbein the Younger. Painting of Sir Thomas More as a member of the Privy Council, 1527. The Frick Collection, New York City.

Revision could serve a variety of purposes—not just as a response to censorship but also as a form of salesmanship, as an effort to bring a play up to date, as a claim that the new version was different from, and better than, the one you previously may have seen or read. Collaboration was routine in the theater of the time, a phenomenon that doesn't easily fit into the modern assumption of individual literary creation, especially when it comes to Shakespeare. But Shakespeare's contribution to *Sir Thomas More* forms part of a larger pattern in his career, in which collaboration and revision figure prominently, with the result that a number of Shakespeare's plays are not just by Shakespeare. Other works that may fall into this group—for different reasons and in different ways—include *1 Henry VI, Titus Andronicus, Edward III, Timon of Athens, Pericles,* the lost *Cardenio, Henry VIII,* and *The Two Noble Kinsmen.* In short, it is possible that almost a quarter of Shakespeare's plays involve collaboration of one sort or another.

What then did Shakespeare contribute to the revised version of *Sir Thomas More*? The question can be addressed from the perspectives of theme, form, and characterization. Early in the play, the citizens of London, angered by the high-handed, legally protected behavior of upper-class foreigners or "strangers" (1.1.25) who act with aristocratic contempt toward the native population, prepare to take bloody revenge. In act 2, scene 3, More, functioning on behalf of a state otherwise prepared to meet force with force, talks the assembled crowd out of violence and into submission to the King. Shakespeare's revision belittles the protesters, depriving them of an individuality and self-conscious purposefulness they possess earlier in the play, not least in the person of Doll—outspoken, fearless victim and foe of foreign sexual predation; threatener of sodomy-like revenge on aliens; and in the end aggressively faithful wife of an English carpenter. The citizens, tradesmen initially identified with merchants, are now associated with apprentices, a lowly and—as commonly understood—unruly lot. Their grievances, previously treated with sympathy, are reduced to the idiotic fear of disease-causing foreign vegetables (the parsnip and the pumpkin, 2.3.10–19). Even Lincoln, the leader of the uprising, comes to find his followers ungovernable, with the result that the subsequent singling of him out as the central malefactor loses some of its force.

The rhetoric of More's arguments for obedience is clever. It is also arresting in its evocation of "the wretched strangers" leaving England (2.3.82). Here More, and of course Shakespeare behind him, discards the earlier resentment of the citizens at their high-handed mistreatment by rapacious foreigners whom the Crown was protecting. Instead, we are presented with an image of miserable refugees, and indeed many of the foreigners in London were in fact Protestant fugitives from continental Catholic repression. This is a different way of seeing the phenomenon of immigration, but one not quite compatible with the action presented previously in the play. Shakespeare's position here may draw on speeches made in Parliament in the early 1590s that urged a tolerant attitude, though the House of Commons as a whole sided with the City's hostile position. In its evocation of what might happen to Londoners if they had to seek shelter abroad, the passage may also be indebted to the historical More's own exercise in hypothetical politics, *Utopia*, which denounces the enclosure of common land, and the resulting misery of landless laborers, from the perspective of a Christian communism. The overall effect, then, is to transform the rampaging citizens from the oppressed to the oppressors.

The fictional More's claims here are orthodox and traditional. They may represent changes from the original manuscript and, like the imagery, have parallels in Shakespeare's other plays, most tellingly in Ulysses' speech on degree in 1.3 of *Troilus and Cressida* (1601–02). Even though the lines seem at least partly designed to reassure the censor, their political implications also point in a different direction. Once the crowd has listened to More, whom they already trust and respect, they willingly submit to royal authority. The text demonstrates the fundamental decency of the common folk—a recurrent motif in Shakespearean drama. And More's brilliant success provides a plausible, if historically inaccurate, explanation of his appointment as Lord Chancellor.

Like Ulysses' speech, however, More's is undermined by the rest of the play. The passage engages in powerfully ironic foreshadowing at the expense of the monarchy. More promises,

> Submit you to these noble gentlemen;
> Entreat their mediation to the King;
> Give up yourself to form; obey the magistrate;
> And there's no doubt but mercy may be found
> If you so seek it.
>
> (2.3.153–57)

There is, however, a "doubt": the royal pardon arrives in time to save most of the citizens but not their leader, Lincoln, whose death sentence comes not from the City but from the court, and whose noble death anticipates More's own fate. More also insists that

> . . . to the King God hath his office lent
> . . . .
> . . . What do you then,
> Rising 'gainst him that God Himself installs,
> But rise 'gainst God?
> (2.3.109, 115–17)

But the equation of God and king, the divine sanction for royal authority—these are the principles that More repudiates at the cost of his life.

A similar effect is achieved in the opening of act 3, scene 1—another probable Shakespearean passage. Newly named Lord Chancellor, More, in the play's only soliloquy, meditates on the suddenness of his ascent, in which he sees evidence of a

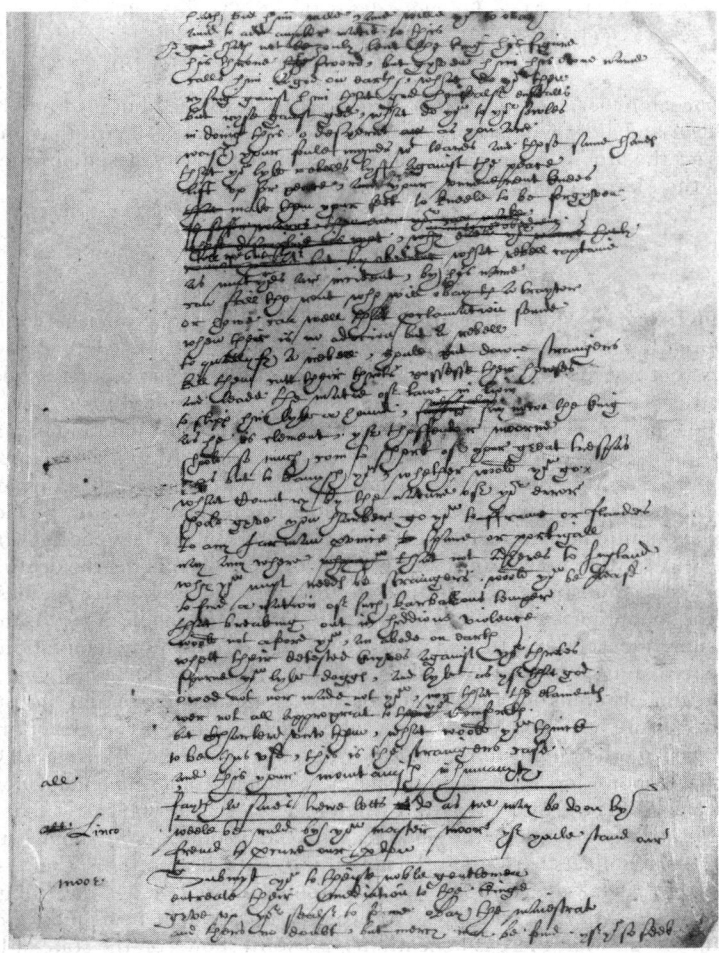

From Anthony Munday and others, "The Booke of Sir Thomas Moore" (British Library MS Harleian 7368), fol. 9a. This is the most legible of the pages believed to be in Shakespeare's hand.

providential force at odds with explanations based on "our fortunes" (3.1.2; Fortune is usually represented in *de casibus* tragedy by the image of the turning wheel). Instead, he argues, "It is in heaven that I am thus and thus" (3.1.1)—virtually a direct rebuttal of Iago's claim in *Othello* (1601–03), probably composed shortly before: "'Tis in ourselves that we are thus, or thus" (1.3.311). More's view leads him to predict, accurately, that "to be great / Is" to be "greatly undone" (3.1.19–21)—where the greatness of the undoing can refer both to the height from which he falls and to the stature of the cause for which he goes to his death.

The opening of act 3, scene 2, the final passage likely to be by Shakespeare, is less consequential. It first evokes More's sad parting from his friend Erasmus, the great Dutch humanist, who while visiting More in 1509 composed *The Praise of Folly*. Its Greek title, *Morias enkomion*, is a play on the Greek word for "folly" and More's name—and hence resonates not only with the endless wordplay of both the stage More and his historical model, but also and rather differently with the fictional character's sober final speech:

> Here More forsakes all mirth; good reason why:
> The fool of flesh must with her frail life die.
> (5.4.117–18)

More's speech in act 3, scene 2 then turns to the unexpected but glad news that the Lord Mayor and aldermen of London are coming for dinner—a visit that once again emphasizes the protagonist's profound connection to the City, despite his new Court rank. As the Mayor remarks soon after:

> My lord, you set a gloss on London's fame,
> And make it happy ever by your name.
> (3.2.101–02)

The lighter tone of More's lines in 3.2 notwithstanding, the passage connects up with the earlier Shakespearean revisions. In all three cases, More delivers long speeches that reveal a good deal about his character. This is important because in the end this is a play of character: indeed, at over eight hundred lines More's part is one of the longest in English Renaissance drama. It is about what kind of man More really is—in his public acts, in his private life, and, crucially, in his inner being.

It is here that More's wit plays a surprising role. At one level, the question is just that—a matter of role playing. *Sir Thomas More* is intensely aware of the fact that it is a play about a man extremely interested in theater. In act 1, scene 2, More helps save the life of Lifter, an appropriately named thief possibly facing the death penalty. The overly sure Suresby, who believes Lifter deserves hanging, partly blames Lifter's victim, the inappropriately named Smart, for carrying so much money in his purse that even an honest man is turned into a rogue by overwhelming temptation. This is More's cue. He has Lifter lift Suresby's equally overstuffed purse and give the proceeds to him, whereupon Suresby learns his lesson and moderates his stance of superiority. More formally, More has an actual play staged for the Mayor and aldermen as part of their entertainment. Its title, *The Marriage of Wit and Wisdom*, reflects back upon More, and when the acting company comes up a man short, More takes on a part—as the historical More often had as a youth. The part is that of Good Counsel, precisely the role More plays as Lord Chancellor. As in *Hamlet*, the play-within-the-play reflects back upon the larger plot of the drama. This, then, is serious play. But the crucial advice More offers as Good Counsel, "judge not things by the outward show" (3.2.275), though obviously of broad relevance, bears most directly on More himself, on what there is beneath his "outward show," on the state of his soul.

The function of wit here is paradoxical, however. The latter part of *Sir Thomas More* leads up to the protagonist's martyrdom. In most admiring sixteenth-century accounts of religious martyrs, the cheerful state of the condemned person on the

SIR THOMAS MORE ◆ 461

point of death is taken by the writer as a sign of inner peace, of a clear conscience, and, by implication, of the truth of the religion for which he or she is being executed. Most martyrs bear witness to their faith, but not More. Since the playwrights cannot actually say what he is dying for, cannot explain why his conscience prevents him from signing the royal document placed before him, the protagonist's relentless wit must do double duty. As in other tales of martyrs, More's good humor indicates his inner purity. But its pervasive display also serves to obscure the content of that purity. It is a sign of his inner inscrutability, oblique evidence that, like Hamlet, he has "that within which passes show" (*Hamlet*, 1600–1601, 1.2.85). More's mirth also stands in for the trial scene, which is reported rather than dramatized. From this perspective, moreover, it is important that More's soliloquy in 3.1 falls before, rather than during, his crisis of conscience, since in that earlier location it need not reflect upon the substantive issue. In like manner, his witty but gratuitously cruel toying with his family's desperate pleas that he accede to the King's demands suggests that their function in the play is to offer an emotionally powerful threat to the exercise of conscience—again, however, without specifying the issue. And heading to the scaffold he predicts: "And sure my memory is grown so ill, / I fear I shall forget my head behind me!" (5.4.26–27; see also lines 51–52).

Parallels with the citizen scenes accentuate this presentation of More's behavior as a matter of form (abstract conscience) rather than content (the specific dilemma facing that conscience). This is more than a matter of Lincoln's execution foreshadowing his own. Like More, Doll rebels against authority only to accept a higher authority—in one case, her husband; in the other, his Father (God). Similarly, when Falconer refuses to cut his hair because he has taken a vow not to for three years, More replies,

> Vows are recorded in the court of heaven,
> For they are holy acts. Young man, I charge thee
> And do advise thee, start not from that vow.
> (3.1.112–14)

More then sends Falconer to prison to honor his vow—a path he himself later takes. Falconer's sentence is three years, to be reduced to one month if he'll cut his hair. Falconer initially refuses: "I'll not lose a hair to be Lord Chancellor of Europe!" (3.1.122). But he quickly relents, gets his hair cut, and gains his release. As More says: "Thy head is for thy shoulders now more fit" (3.1.239). But Falconer is unhappy: "if I notch [cut] not that rogue Tom Barber that makes me look thus like a Brownist, hang me!" (3.1.245–47); "I'll go hang myself out for the poll [shaved] head" (3.1.255–56). These lines anticipate More's remarks to the hangman on the scaffold: "take heed thou cutt'st not off my beard. Oh, I forgot, execution passed upon that last night" (5.4.100–101). Most notably, More's unexplained behavior is repeatedly considered "strange," a characterization that links him to the foreigners he defends earlier in the play.

This isn't quite the whole story, however. We do learn what More will die for, but not from More and not in reality. Instead, More's family members have prophetic dreams of his downfall. Thus, one of his daughters recounts her vision of the Reformation's desecration of Catholic icons, an event that actually occurred after More's death:

> Methought I saw him here in Chelsea Church,
> Standing upon the rood [cross] loft, now defaced.
> And whilst he kneeled and prayed before the image,
> It fell with him into the upper choir,
> Where my poor father lay all stained in blood.
> (4.2.37–41)

The fall of More is thus the fall of Catholicism. In any case, one can approve or not of More's resistance to royal injunction on the grounds of conscience. Either way, however, More's fate is glorious. The final lines are Surrey's:

> A very learned, worthy gentleman
> Seals error with his blood. Come, we'll to the Court.
> Let's sadly hence to perfect unknown fates
> Whilst he tends progress to the state of states.
> (5.4.121–24)

It is unclear whether the "error" that More dies for is his own or King Henry's. But it is clear that More is a "very learned, worthy gentleman" and that he is going to heaven, "to the state of states." In *Sir Thomas More*, he is not the killer of Protestants but the man who helps free Lifter, the rioters, and Falconer. Surrey and the others, however, face "unknown fates"—an irony given that Surrey too was later executed on a charge of embracing Catholicism.

The original version of *Sir Thomas More* was never performed. As already noted, the revision may not have fared any better. Thereafter, it is almost certain that the play remained unstaged until the twentieth century. In the last hundred years, however, there have been almost fifteen known productions, most recently in 2005–06 by the Royal Shakespeare Company at Stratford-upon-Avon and elsewhere. As might be expected, the intellectual lacuna at the center of the play—the emptiness of More's steadfast appeal to conscience—has proven a recurrent problem in production. It is therefore interesting to juxtapose *Sir Thomas More* with modern "takes" on More. Robert Bolt's *A Man for All Seasons*, first a play and then an Academy Award–winning movie (1966) starring Paul Scofield, who also played More in the stage version, parallels *Sir Thomas More* in portraying its hero above all as a man of conscience. By contrast, Hilary Mantel's Man Booker Prize–winning novel *Wolf Hall* (2009) views More through the eyes of his early antagonist Thomas Cromwell and hence as a self-righteous murderer of Protestants. But as various scholars have noted, *Sir Thomas More* might leave one with a different final impression. Despite Shakespeare's relatively small contribution to the text of the play, this is the story of a man who, at his best, combined remarkable verbal wit with a capaciousness of vision in a fashion that resembles the effect produced by the plays of Shakespeare himself.

WALTER COHEN

SELECTED BIBLIOGRAPHY

Hill, Tracey. "'The Cittie is in an uproare': Staging London in *The Book of Sir Thomas More*." *Early Modern Literary Studies* 11.1 (May 2005): 2.1–19 http://purl.oclc.org/emls/11-1/more.htm. Traces the detailed account of London in the play, the sympathetic treatment of the citizens in the original version, and the less sympathetic rendering in the revisions.

Levine, Nina S. "Citizens' Games: Differentiating Collaboration and *Sir Thomas More*." *Shakespeare Quarterly* 58 (2007): 31–64. Investigates the analogy between collaborative authorship and the subject of that collaboration, rebellious citizen solidarity.

Masten, Jeffrey. "More or Less: Editing the Collaborative." *Shakespeare Studies* 29 (2001): 109–31. Argues for including the full play, rather than just the Shakespearean portions, in editions of Shakespeare, thus avoiding a practice that underemphasizes the unity of the work.

Monta, Susannah Brietz. "*The Book of Sir Thomas More* and Laughter of the Heart." *Sixteenth Century Journal* 34 (2003): 107–21. Argues that the play deviates from most sixteenth-century accounts of martyrs in using the protagonist's humor and joy in the face of martyrdom to conceal, rather than reveal, his beliefs, a strategy designed to obscure the religious divide of the era.

Munday, Anthony, and Henry Chettle. *Sir Thomas More*. Censored by Edmund Tilney. Revisions coordinated by Hand C. Revised by Henry Chettle, Thomas Dekker,

Thomas Heywood, and William Shakespeare. Ed. John Jowett. London: Methuen, 2011. Fullest scholarly edition of the play, dating the original to 1600 and the revisions to 1603–04.

Schülting, Sabine. "'What country, friends, is this?': The Performance of Conflict in Shakespeare's Drama of Migration." *Shakespeare and Conflict: A European Perspective.* Ed. Carla Dente, Sara Sancini, and Ton Hoenselaars. New York: Palgrave Macmillan, 2013. 24–39. Places Shakespeare's manuscript revision in the context of other scenes of the arrival of destitute migrants in Shakespeare's career, seeing in it a transformation of the play's earlier conflict between citizens and upper-class foreigners "into tensions between citizens and migrants."

Tudeau-Clayton, Margaret. "'This is the strangers' case': The Utopic Dissonance of Shakespeare's Contribution to *Sir Thomas More.*" *Shakespeare Survey* 65 (2013): 239–54. Finds in Shakespeare's manuscript lines echoes of the 1593 sympathetic parliamentary comments on foreigners in London and the critique of enclosure in More's own *Utopia*—both placing the passage at odds with the rest of the play.

Watt, Timothy Irish. "The Authorship of the Hand-D Addition to *The Book of Sir Thomas More.*" *Shakespeare, Computers, and the Mystery of Authorship.* Ed. Hugh Craig and Arthur Kinney. Cambridge: Cambridge UP, 2009. 134–61. Concludes on the basis of computational stylistics that the "identification of Hand-D with Shakespeare now seems one of the better established facts about his canon, and among the surest facts of his biography."

Wentersdorf, Karl P. "On 'Momtanish Inhumanyty' in *Sir Thomas More.*" *Studies in Philology* 103 (2006): 178–85. Argues that More criticizes the citizens' hostility to foreigners as Muslim inhumanity.

Woods, Gillian. "'Strange Discourse': The Controversial Subject of *Sir Thomas More.*" *Renaissance Drama* n.s. 39 (2011): 3–35. Argues in a detailed reading of the play for a pervasive link between "strangers" (foreigners) and the strangeness of More's behavior as a Catholic—a strangeness rooted in the oblique representation of the religious conflict behind More's fatal act of conscience.

TEXTUAL INTRODUCTION

The manuscript known as *The Book of Sir Thomas More* records the collaborative activities of a large group of playwrights and professionals associated with the theater. A large part of the document is in the hand of Anthony Munday, who authored or transcribed most of the original version of the play, either around 1593–94 or around 1600 (scholars have not reached consensus on this question). That version was heavily edited by the Master of the Revels, Edmund Tilney, who left his own traces in the manuscript in the form of deletion marks and marginal demands. But the manuscript also contains a second, later set of authors' attempts to revise the play, undertaken most likely in 1603 or 1604—not necessarily in response to Tilney's comments. These writers included Henry Chettle, Thomas Dekker, Thomas Heywood, a playhouse scribe usually identified as Hand C—and Shakespeare.

This later effort, organized in the document by Hand C's annotating and editing pen, forms the basis of the present edition. In keeping with *The Norton Shakespeare*'s single-text editing principles, this edition takes the revised version of the play as its base text, assuming that Hand C had authority to shape the various playwrights' contributions and Munday's original script into a coherent whole. In conceiving of the play as a unified text, however, we largely gloss over the composite nature of the manuscript. Consequently, changes such as Hand C's corrections to the speech prefixes in what is now 2.3 are not noted, because we base our edition on the "Hand C version" of the play, not on Shakespeare's unrevised manuscript. Deletions are treated as such and are not included in the body of the text. Changes that are clearly authorial self-corrections or instant revisions made while writing are not recorded in the textual variants either. In the interest of still providing as much of the text as possible to readers, though, substantive deletions by Hand C or in an ink other than the original writer's are recorded (in the case of single lines, in the textual variants; in the case of longer passages, in the Appendix).

For the purposes of this edition, Tilney's demands are not considered part of the creative collaboration (but they are recorded in Appendix C). Thus 1.1, a scene he wanted cut in its entirety, is included in our text—partly because there is no indication that Hand C or any of the revisers considered it obsolete or unusable. Similarly, several of his proposed deletions remain in 1.3 and elsewhere. Omission marks in other hands, however, have been observed, and the cut passages can now be found in Appendices A and B. In fact, the play as it survives only makes sense if passages Tilney wanted deleted are included, as the revisers provided nothing to replace them. What is more, the single replacement for a scene censored by the Master of the Revels (2.1) flatly ignores Tilney's major objections: it still stages a popular rebellion and still focuses on xenophobic resentment among London's citizens. Why that scene was revised is unclear. Thomas Heywood's new version uses passages from the original, but greatly expands the Clown's part—which may reflect the company's sense of what audiences might look for in a "popular" scene.

One major exception to this rule needs to be noted. Passage 1B in Appendix B is a scene that was marked for deletion by Tilney. In its surviving form, the scene is fragmentary and unfinished, and the manuscript as it now stands gives no indication that the revising team considered this passage part of the play's new version. No effort was made to edit or rewrite it. We have excluded this scene from the body of the text, not because Tilney censored it, but because it appears to have been discarded in the course of the revisions. It likely survives in the manuscript only because the sheet on which it is written also contains the end of 1.3 and the opening stage directions for 2.1.

The physical state of the manuscript poses certain editorial challenges. Every sheet of the book, which is housed in the British Library, is now encased in its own individual plexiglas frame. However, prior to these conservation efforts, the manuscript suffered serious deterioration, and many lines that we know used to be legible are now unreadable, some of them having disappeared altogether. The edges of some of the pages are more frayed than they were when the text was first examined, and some of the earliest conservation efforts rendered other parts of the manuscript illegible. In more than a few spots, therefore, all modern editors of the text depend on the earliest transcriptions prepared prior to the destruction of some of the text, especially Alexander Dyce's 1844 version.

The present edition does not highlight instances in the body of the text where Dyce's transcript stands in for parts of the manuscript that no longer exist, but all such cases are recorded in the textual variants. These are treated as a mediated form of access to the original text. In some cases, Dyce and later editors also suggested words to fill gaps that were already present in the mid-nineteenth century; where the present edition accepts such suggestions, they are recorded as emendations in the textual variants (marked as "not in ms"). Lastly, as with any manuscript, different transcribers disagree about how to decipher specific words. In such cases, particular readings have been silently adopted without identifying the range of possible interpretations.

Only parts of the manuscript are in holograph. Although the entire surviving text of the first version is in Munday's hand, he may not have been the sole author; and the scribe known as Hand C transcribed large parts of the revised scenes from his authors' originals. Following is a list of whose handwriting is represented where in the manuscript (excluding brief annotations in Chettle's, Heywood's, and the scribe's hands):

1.1–2.1.0 SD	Anthony Munday (original version)
2.1.1–66	Thomas Heywood ("Addition II")

2.2.1–2.3.0 SD	Hand C ("Addition II")
2.3.1–157	Hand D (probably William Shakespeare)
2.3.158–3.1.0 SD	Anthony Munday (original version)
3.1.1–21	Hand C ("Addition III")
3.1.21 SD–248	Hand C ("Addition IV")
3.1.249–76	Thomas Dekker ("Addition IV")
3.2.1–22	Hand C ("Addition V")
3.2.23–305	Anthony Munday (original version)
3.2.306–58	Thomas Heywood ("Addition VI")
4.1.1–4.4.50	Anthony Munday (original version)
4.4.51–99	Henry Chettle ("Addition I")
4.4.100–5.4.124	Anthony Munday (original version)

All the passages in Appendix B are part of the original version and in Munday's hand.

HOLGER SCHOTT SYME

PERFORMANCE NOTE

While several early modern plays have shaped our ideas about historical figures (*Henry V, Richard III*), *Sir Thomas More* has not. The play is produced so rarely that directors and audiences typically approach it free from any sense of precedent, unless it comes from Robert Bolt's play, *A Man for All Seasons* (1960). In Bolt's play, More maintains his political and spiritual convictions in the face of frequent threats from Henry VIII and Cardinal Wolsey; *Sir Thomas More*, by contrast, complicates matters for actors and directors by failing to stage these antagonists, as well as omitting any direct reference to Catherine of Aragon, Henry's first queen, or to Henry's affair with Anne Boleyn. Consequently, the actor playing More is challenged to create a sense of tragedy despite the absence of tangible opposition to him or any identifiable internal flaw, in a play that sometimes feels more like biography than drama. Furthermore, the character must arrive at his tragic end after several comic scenes of his own devising, most of them seemingly immaterial to the action's progress.

Productions sometimes attempt to unify the play as tragedy by reducing or omitting the comedy while clarifying the articles that More refuses to sign. Surrey and, especially, Shrewsbury can be sinister figures, their jealousy over More's rise at court making them appear as hostile proxies for Henry. In the most effective productions, though, More infuses his celebrated faith with inner turmoil, hesitancy, and doubt, his practical joking concealing deep-seated fears and doubts about not only the earthly punishment that awaits him, but also the "good God" who motivates him to choose it. Ian McKellen, who admired the role's versatility and centrality enough to play it twice, made More's personal misgivings about the saintliness ascribed to him a source of awkwardness, suggesting thereby the human fallibility that makes tragedy possible.

Much rests with the central character, yet *More* has nearly sixty speaking roles, making ensemble casting and doubling roles distinctively tricky in production. Directors must also account for textual gaps; manage Latin phrases; differentiate the acting style of the play-within-the-play from the acting in the rest of the play; stage executions; and decide whether to translate the crowd's revolts over unwelcome immigration to a contemporary setting.

BRETT GAMBOA

Measure for Measure

A young man is in grave trouble with the law, and his beautiful sister goes to the magistrate to plead for mercy. The magistrate offers to remit the penalty if the sister will sleep with him. It is an old story in more ways than one. Shakespeare knew several sixteenth-century versions: the Italian Giovanbattista Giraldi Cinthio produced both prose and dramatic renderings, and in 1578 the English playwright George Whetstone published *Promos and Cassandra,* the most important source for *Measure for Measure.* Shakespeare's play was first performed in 1603 or 1604, though the text we have is probably derived from a revival staged in 1621 and likely contains some material by the younger playwright Thomas Middleton.

In the mid-to-late 1590s and the first years of the seventeenth century, Shakespeare wrote a series of comedies that explore complex issues of sex, marriage, and personal identity. *Measure for Measure* is the last play in this group. Its tone, themes, and methods of characterization veer close to tragedy, the genre that largely, though not exclusively, preoccupied Shakespeare in the years immediately following. Many critics, therefore, classify *Measure for Measure* as a "problem" comedy. The designation attests both to the difficult moral issues that the play confronts and to the boldness with which it stretches—some would say shatters—the normal limits of comic form. In *Measure for Measure,* Shakespeare considers the often-vexed relationship between civic life and human passion, and between religious commitment and the conduct of secular affairs. Is it possible or advisable to regulate sexual behavior through the courts? How do religious convictions affect the experience of sexual desire? These concerns resonate in an era like our own, characterized by a lack of consensus in religion and in sexual mores, by widespread transformations in the institution of marriage, and by debates over the extent to which the state ought to monitor the sexual behavior of citizens.

The play's distinctiveness becomes evident almost immediately. In act 1, scene 2, Claudio and his pregnant lover, Juliet, appear in the custody of the Provost, being led away to prison. Their crime is premarital sex; the penalty, for Claudio at least, is death. Claudio's initial description of his plight is quite remarkable:

> LUCIO   Why, how now, Claudio? Whence comes this restraint?
> CLAUDIO   From too much liberty, my Lucio, liberty.
>   As surfeit is the father of much fast,
>   So every scope by the immoderate use
>   Turns to restraint. Our natures do pursue,
>   Like rats that raven down their proper bane,
>   A thirsty evil, and when we drink, we die.
>
> (1.2.113–19)

Claudio likens his passion for his beloved to a rat's craving for poison: compulsive, irrational, and self-destructive. Excessive indulgence, or "surfeit," inevitably brings regret and punishment in its train. Claudio sounds as if he is describing the most arrant kind of lust, although, as he will subsequently explain, he is actually "precontracted" to Juliet—bound by a promise of marriage that many in Renaissance England saw as providing conjugal privileges. (Shakespeare himself may have subscribed to this view, since his wife gave birth to their daughter five months after their wedding. More pertinent, the Duke, in his guise as a friar, affirms that the precontract sanctions

Mariana's intimacy with Angelo later in the play.) It is interesting, however, that neither Claudio nor Juliet argues that their devotion to each other mitigates their guilt. Instead, they admit that they have committed "fornication," a severely condemnatory term that conflates all kinds of sex outside of marriage under the same rubric, recognizing no difference between long-term relationships and sheerest promiscuity.

As the play continues, it becomes clear that Claudio's imagery of suicidal animalism, havoc, and pollution is not merely the consequence of his immediate agitation, but expresses a profound assumption of the society in which he lives. For his sister, Isabella, sexual intercourse is "what I abhor to name" (3.1.101). The Duke deplores Pompey's "filthy vice" and Juliet's "most offenseful act." The wise Escalus acknowledges Claudio's "error" even as he attempts to alleviate his punishment. Few doubt that human sexuality is an essentially sordid matter, a sign of degradation rather than a means of creativity or love. Occasional glimpses of an alternative vision—Lucio's brief, radiant analogy between Juliet's pregnancy and agricultural fertility, for instance—by their very rarity reinforce the prevailing pessimism.

Such austere views of human sexuality have ancient roots. When the Duke calls Vienna's sex laws "needful bits and curbs to headstrong jades" (1.3.20), he recalls an image from Plato, who compared the desiring part of the soul to a useful but refractory horse, which the rational part of the soul needs to keep strictly bridled and under firm control. When Isabella refers to erotic desire as a "natural guiltiness" (2.2.140), she draws upon a traditional Christian connection between sexuality and original sin, the disobedience committed by Adam and Eve in the Garden of Eden and passed on to all their offspring as a kind of intrinsic pollution.

To say that a view is traditional, however, is not to say that it is inevitable. What makes sexuality so troublesome in this particular play? In Shakespeare's earlier, more optimistic comedies, the prospect of heterosexual consummation usually seems automatically to entail marriage, so that the weddings with which the plays conclude seem to follow spontaneously from the eroticism that fuels the plot. By marrying and establishing a family, the young couples satisfy their mutual yearning for one another as well as their community's demand for clear kinship structures and for orderly means of transferring property to "legitimate" members of a new generation. In *Measure for Measure,* however, the link between heterosexual desire and marriage seems to have snapped. Claudio and Juliet defer their wedding day; Angelo abandons Mariana; Lucio refuses to support his child or marry the mother. Prostitution flourishes. Rampant promiscuity makes syphilis a familiar ailment and a standard topic for nervous jokes.

Once carnal desire comes unhinged from the institution of marriage, it begins to seem subversive of personal and civic order. And if one believes that one's sexuality is intrinsically antisocial and depraved, then complete sexual renunciation might seem the wisest course. In *Measure for Measure,* the morally ambitious characters—the Duke, Angelo, and Isabella—initially assume that their virtue is tied up with, perhaps even identical with, their chastity. "Believe not that the dribbling dart of love / Can pierce a complete bosom," the Duke

Charioteer with two galloping horses. From Geffrey Whitney, *A Choice of Emblems* (1586).

boasts to the Friar (1.3.2–3). Angelo attempts to protect his reputation for austerity even as he hopelessly compromises his scruples in secret. Isabella believes that sleeping with Angelo will defile her forever, even if she does so in order to save her brother's life.

The value of celibacy is endorsed by characters who do not themselves aspire to such high standards of conduct. Lucio is a libertine, but he believes that Isabella's intention to enter a nunnery renders her "a thing enskied and sainted" (1.4.35). Likewise, Pompey admits that his life as a pimp "does stink in some sort, sir" (3.1.282). A few of those who cannot be chaste themselves are, like Claudio, capable of moments of shame or self-loathing; others, like Lucio, shruggingly accept their lack of saintliness. The Vienna of *Measure for Measure* is full of people unlikely to be enlisted for projects of social or spiritual improvement: the moronic Elbow, the impenitent Pompey, the unregenerate Bawd, the "gravel-hearted" Barnardine, the heedless First and Second Gentlemen, the gullible Froth. These people are part of the commonwealth, subject to the law. They are willy-nilly part, too, of a Roman Catholic Church that aspires—as the Church of England did as well in Shakespeare's day—to include the entire community. Should the laws of this community reflect its stringent ideals or the actual behavior of most of its members? Throughout *Measure for Measure*, those who aspire to belong to a principled moral elite deplore the weaknesses of the reprobate. At the same time, because the rascals are so vividly memorable, the play also suggests that moral failure is often at least as humanly compelling as moral excellence is—at least moral excellence defined in the narrow, self-denying terms that prevail in Vienna.

For the intransigent majority unable or unwilling to control the horses of lust, the "needful bits and curbs" of which the Duke speaks (1.3.20) impose an external system of repression. Such a system would not have been unfamiliar to Shakespeare's original audience. Courts administered by the Church of England prosecuted many sexual infractions: among them fathering or giving birth to a bastard, committing adultery or bigamy, deserting a spouse, reneging on a wedding engagement, or groundlessly accusing others of such transgressions. Convicted individuals could be fined, whipped, displayed in the marketplace, or made to announce their sins in church. (Thus, Claudio and Juliet are paraded about the streets of Vienna before being taken to prison, to humiliate them and to serve as an example for others.) Repeat offenders were excommunicated, or cast out of the church.

Underlying such proceedings was the assumption, as in *Measure for Measure*, that morality could and should be legislated; that the sexual conduct of individuals was the business of the entire community. Indeed, in the early seventeenth century, when Shakespeare was writing *Measure for Measure*, an increasingly powerful group of Puritans, or "precisians," argued that the church courts' punishments were far too mild. Threats of disgrace and excommunication failed to deter the worst offenders, who had no reputation to lose and were unlikely to fret at their exclusion from church. Moreover, shaming punishments worked less well in the increasingly busy, heterogeneous neighborhoods of Jacobean London than they had in the smaller rural communities for which they were originally designed.

In *Measure for Measure*, the repeated characterization of Angelo as "precise" associates him with the rigorists of Shakespeare's time; and since Viennese justice treats Claudio more strictly than it does professionals in the sex trade, the question of what constitutes adequate severity is certainly at issue. Perhaps, then, the play constitutes Shakespeare's reflection on an issue of contemporary concern: what would happen if, as some argued, sexual misconduct could be punished with death? At the same time, Shakespeare carefully distinguishes the world of his play from that of seventeenth-century England, most obviously by making Vienna a Roman Catholic city peopled with the nuns and friars who had been eliminated from Protestant England over half a century earlier. For despite obvious connections between *Measure for Measure* and some of the issues of its own day, Shakespeare's play hardly constitutes a clear policy recommendation.

In *Measure for Measure,* Angelo's disastrous career suggests one possible effect of strict sexual self-denial: that the habits of restraint can themselves provoke sexual excitement. Rigid and self-righteous, Angelo seems not to have experienced the violence of desire until Isabella's first visit on behalf of her brother awakens his appetite:

> What's this, what's this? Is this her fault or mine?
> The tempter or the tempted, who sins most, ha?
> Not she, nor doth she tempt. But it is I
> That, lying by the violet in the sun,
> Do as the carrion does, not as the flower,
> Corrupt with virtuous season.
>
> (2.2.165–70)

Like Claudio, Angelo thinks of passion in terms of death and decay, but the resemblance between the two men ends there. Angelo imagines himself as tainted meat rotting all the faster under the very sun that gives life to innocent, lovely things. What ought to improve Angelo—his keen appreciation for the presence of virtue—makes him worse.

Angelo is sexually aroused by prohibition. Mariana loves him, and his relationship with her breaches no social norms; he discards her. Isabella is ostentatiously pristine, and her nun's habit marks her as taboo; he finds her irresistible. In order to extract pleasure from the encounter, however, Angelo must force himself to remain

Poor Clare nun. From Jost Amman, *Cleri totius Romanae ecclesiae subjecti* (1585).

aware of the principles he attempts so flagrantly to violate. If he rationalized his behavior or blamed it on Isabella, he would lose the nearly sensual luxury of self-hatred. Therefore, the lucidity with which Angelo analyzes his own motives leads not to penitence or self-restraint, but to an increasing recklessness. His inclination to categorize all sexual conduct as transgressive actually makes his offense easier to commit. Propositioning Isabella in their second meeting together, he tells her: "I have begun, / And now I give my sensual race the rein" (2.4.156–57). Angelo explains why he cannot govern himself with the same image of horsemanship that the Duke used to underscore the necessity of control. Once embarked on the "sensual race," Angelo imagines, there is no alternative to utter abandon.

For Isabella, however, sleeping with Angelo is out of the question. Some modern critics have found her defiance heroic, others chilling or selfish. Probably in Shakespeare's time she elicited a similarly mixed response. Shakespeare alters his source story considerably to expand Isabella's role and to specify its implications more exactly. In Whetstone's *Promos and Cassandra,* the sister has no plans to enter a convent, and she eventually goes to bed with the deputy in order to save her brother's life. For Isabella, by contrast, virginity is a principled choice, not an accident of youth. The vow of lifelong, religiously dedicated chastity she plans to take is a matter about which Shakespeare's contemporaries had conflicting feelings. One effect of England's break with the Catholic Church had been a spectacular change in official attitudes toward celibacy. While Catholics honored sexual renunciation and demanded that their clergy remain chaste, Protestants discouraged veneration of the Virgin Mary, abolished convents and monasteries, and urged clergy to marry. Despite these alterations, however, a powerful appreciation for virginity and belief in its semimagical powers persisted in Reformation England. The effect of Shakespeare's innovations on Whetstone, then, is both to heighten the ambivalence of the story and to focus the moral spotlight on Isabella's convictions and the choices that follow from them.

Isabella believes that she would damn herself by sleeping with Angelo.

> Better it were a brother died at once
> Than that a sister by redeeming him
> Should die forever.
>
> (2.4.103–05)

Is she right? There is a long tradition of considering such questions. St. Augustine, the most influential Christian writer on sexual morality, insists that since sin is a property of the will, not a physical state, persons who are forced to perform sexual acts are blameless. Chastity, he argues, is a state of mind. In that case, the fate of Isabella's body is possibly independent of, and irrelevant to, the fate of her soul. Perhaps, in fact, by acquiescing to Angelo, Isabella would perform an act of charity, generously sacrificing her own preferences for Claudio's benefit. However, female "virtue" has traditionally been defined in physical as well as mental terms, so that chastity, the spiritual attitude, is hard to separate from virginity, the bodily condition. Moreover, Isabella is not the victim of forcible rape; she must, as Angelo says, "fit her consent" to his proposal. Does that consent, however reluctant, contaminate her with his sin? Quite possibly. Would it permanently unsuit her for her religious vocation? Quite possibly. Clearly, it is reasonable, then, for Isabella to be cautious; and no one, says Augustine, is obliged to put him- or herself in eternal peril merely in order to save the life of another person.

Since, however, Shakespeare characteristically translates sweeping moral questions into scrupulously personal terms, apparently reasonable general maxims do not entirely suffice to explain Isabella's motives. On the one hand, her obstinacy seems justified after the fact, when Angelo decides to execute Claudio, because clearly her capitulation would not have saved her brother's life. On the other hand, Isabella's obsession with her own purity seems excessive, especially in 3.1, when it manifests itself in gross insensitivity to her plaintive, terrified brother. Moreover, her fervent yearning for constraint, like Angelo's, seems luridly tinged with sadomasochism.

> were I under the terms of death,
> Th'impression of keen whips I'd wear as rubies,
> And strip myself to death as to a bed
> That longing have been sick for, ere I'd yield
> My body up to shame.
>
> (2.4.97–101)

At such moments, Isabella seems not to be exterminating or transcending her own sexuality, but redirecting it in ways of which she is not entirely conscious. She not only shares Angelo's assumption that the sexual act is a defilement, but like him she finds discipline exciting. With all our disapproval of Angelo's abuse of power and our sympathy with Isabella's indignation, we can still see how the conflict between them arises as much from their similarities as from their differences.

Isabella's difficulty is hard to resolve because it is unclear how much her chastity is worth. Is it more valuable than her brother's life? Is it more valuable than her own life, which she would throw down for Claudio, she claims, "as frankly as a pin" (3.1.105)? Is it only fair, as Angelo claims, to yield him her body as compensation for overlooking Claudio's offense, or is "lawful mercy . . . nothing kin to foul redemption" (2.4.109–10)? Shakespeare provides no answer to these questions, but the conflict they produce yields the play's most vividly realized interactions. As the title suggests, *Measure for Measure* is obsessed with problems of equivalence, asking us to reflect on which things are commensurable to, or equal in value to, or might be substituted for, which other things. We see this preoccupation in the opening scene in which Angelo takes over as the Duke's deputy, in Angelo's proposal that Isabella vindicate Claudio by committing his sin herself, in the bed trick that replaces Isabella with Mariana, in the Provost's exchange of Ragozine's head for Claudio's. Even the most apparently trivial comic interchanges persistently echo the concern with equivalence, proportionality, and relative priority: the Gentlemen argue about whether they are cut from lists or velvet; Pompey and Abhorson debate the relative standing of bawd and hangman.

Questions of equivalence seem to underlie the very possibility of justice, even the possibility of any ethical thinking. A wrongdoer ought, we feel, either to make adequate restitution for his or her misdeeds or to suffer in rough proportion to the anguish he or she has caused. Who can assess those penalties, who is subject to them, and how rigorous they ought to be—these become pressing issues again and again in *Measure for Measure*. Shakespeare takes the title of the play from Jesus' Sermon on the Mount: "Judge not, that ye be not judged. For with what judgment you judge, you shall be judged, and with what measure you mete, it shall be meted unto you again" (Matthew 7:1–2). The Bible passage is a complex one: even while assuring believers that ultimately, strict justice will be served, Jesus advises believers not to pass judgment at all. What would it mean to "judge not" in practical terms, given that some kind of justice system seems necessary for an orderly society?

In sexual matters, problems of just equivalence are especially murky, because there is no consensus regarding how apparently straightforward bodily acts ought to be interpreted. Angelo compares Claudio's offense to murder and counterfeiting; Lucio thinks it is trivial, "a game of tick-tack" (1.2.178). What seem to be the same actions can be evaluated in wildly different ways, depending on one's frame of reference: to the abstemious Angelo, Claudio's behavior looks like gross debauchery, while to the Bawd's dissolute patrons, it looks positively restrained. Motives alter what seem to be the same actions, so that we are inclined to regard Claudio more leniently than Lucio, who abandoned his mistress after making her pregnant. So do outcomes: the bed trick means that Angelo, intending to commit an impermissible act, in fact performs a licit one, unknowingly laying the groundwork for his pardon in the final scene.

The commitment of several characters to a Christian religious vocation further complicates the possibility of establishing some consensus about proper equivalence. Isabella, especially, assumes that spiritual goods like honor and purity are infinitely more important than secular, visible possessions. In her system of values, a promise of ardent prayer constitutes the most potent bribe she can offer Angelo, beside which gold is barren and trivial. Isabella's counterintuitive otherworldliness is central to Christianity, a religion founded on the spectacularly lopsided substitution of the blameless Christ for sinful humanity in the system of God's justice. But since such religious convictions are not subject to the verification of the senses, they are open to challenge by those more firmly attached to the things of this world. For Claudio, any fate seems better than death. His hierarchy of priorities is different from Isabella's.

How are such drastic discrepancies between the various characters' moral and social outlooks to be reconciled? The agent for bringing order and justice is Duke Vincentio, a concealed authority who learns everybody's secrets in the course of the play. Far from providing an authoritative solution to the play's ethical impasse, however, the Duke has elicited almost as much controversy as Isabella. Some critics see him as a version of God, "like power divine," as Angelo declares in the final scene (5.1.371). Some have suggested that the Duke was meant to compliment the diffident King James I, who at the time of the play's first performance had recently ascended the English throne after the death of his extroverted predecessor, Elizabeth I. More skeptical critics see the Duke as a schemer who foists his dirty work onto political subordinates and meddles impudently, even sacrilegiously, with the lives of his subjects.

Controversy over the Duke's role perhaps reflects the fact that the task he needs to accomplish requires him to wield two ordinarily distinct forms of power. The problems of Measure for Measure can be solved only by someone who can obtain access to the concealed realm of motives and intentions, a privilege usually reserved for a confessor. But merely knowing such information will not bring practical redress of injustice. So at the same time, unlike a clergyman, the Duke must retain the secular ruler's ability to mandate changes in the world. A prince disguised as a friar, the Duke bridges, however unsteadily, the gap between power and knowledge. His sweeping authority conveniently enables him to impose a resolution.

There are limits, however, even to Vincentio's power. Not even a duke can sequester erotic fervor from the cruelty and disorder with which it seems, in this play, to be so intimately and insidiously allied. Not even a duke can make passion tractable. The best he can manage is to introduce his subjects to some socially sanctioned medium between celibacy and abandon. Marriage in Measure for Measure is thus patently not a happy aspiration but a stopgap measure imposed on reluctant or noncommittal individuals, for whom the alternative in several cases is death. Indeed, Lucio, forthright as usual, complains that marriage is a worse fate than hanging; the others are distinctly muted in their response to the Duke's nuptial stratagems. Claudio and Juliet are given no lines in which to celebrate their reunion; nor do we hear that Angelo, who claims to "crave death more willingly than mercy" (5.1.480), is grateful to be preserved as Mariana's husband. Isabella remains silent in the face of the Duke's unexpected proposal of marriage, leaving it an open question whether she is overwhelmed with joy or gripped with horror. Does the Duke provide her with a socially and personally satisfying alternative to the cloister, or does he, from Isabella's point of view, merely recapitulate Angelo's harassment?

The pro forma quality of the coupling with which Measure for Measure concludes suggests that marital union is not, finally, the resolution toward which the play most convincingly moves. In quick succession, the Duke's trial in the last scene rehearses the normal outcome of Isabella's complaint—her condemnation and

Angelo's exoneration—and then demonstrates that in this instance, almost miraculously, Angelo's secret vice will be made manifest after all. But this disclosure does not end the play, for the Duke's plan demands that Isabella plead for Angelo's life "against all sense" (5.1.436), as the Sermon on the Mount commands her to do. The simple asceticism of the flesh with which *Measure for Measure* begins is displaced at last by a more subtle and exacting asceticism of the spirit, as Isabella renounces the hunger for vengeance in favor of a forgiveness that goes very much against the grain. Only this principled willingness to overlook injury and tolerate difference, the play seems to imply, can still the jostling among heterogeneous moral perspectives that endlessly complicate life in Vienna.

KATHARINE EISAMAN MAUS

SELECTED BIBLIOGRAPHY

Adelman, Janet. "Bed Tricks: On Marriage as the End of Comedy in *All's Well That Ends Well* and *Measure for Measure*." *Shakespeare's Personality*. Ed. Norman H. Holland, Sidney Homan, and Bernard J. Paris. Berkeley: U of California P, 1989. 151–74. Explores sexuality as defilement and marriage as punishment in *Measure for Measure*.

Beckwith, Sara. "Medieval Penance, Reformation Repentance, and *Measure for Measure*." *Reading the Medieval in Early Modern England*. Ed. Gordon McMullan and David Matthews. Cambridge: Cambridge UP, 2007. 193–204. Examines changing ways of thinking about confession, repentance, and the role of church and state, as reflected in *Measure for Measure*.

Bennett, Josephine Waters. *"Measure for Measure" as Royal Entertainment*. New York: Columbia UP, 1966. An examination of the play as it reflects James I's court, political philosophy, and royal persona.

Bloom, Harold, ed. *William Shakespeare's "Measure for Measure."* New York: Chelsea House, 1987. An anthology of critical essays.

Engle, Lars. "*Measure for Measure* and Modernity: The Problem of the Skeptic's Authority." *Shakespeare and Modernity: Early Modern to Millennium*. Ed. Hugh Grady. New York: Routledge, 2000. 85–104. Discusses ethical relativism and difficulties of judgment.

Jowett, John. "*Measure for Measure*: A Genetic Text." *Thomas Middleton: The Collected Works*. Oxford: Clarendon, 2007. 1542–85. Makes the case that Middleton revised *Measure for Measure* in 1621 and analyzes the significance of the changes he may have introduced.

Maus, Katharine Eisaman. "Sexual Secrecy in *Measure for Measure*." *Inwardness and Theater in the English Renaissance*. Chicago: U of Chicago P, 1995. 157–81. Examines sexual privacy as a challenge for legal supervision and as the grounds for character in *Measure for Measure*.

Shell, Marc. *The End of Kinship: "Measure for Measure," Incest, and the Ideal of Universal Siblinghood*. Stanford: Stanford UP, 1988. An analysis of proper and improper exchanges in the Christian world of *Measure for Measure*, in which everyone is a brother or sister to everyone else.

Shuger, Debora Kuller. *Political Theologies in Shakespeare's England: The Sacred and the State in "Measure for Measure."* New York: Palgrave, 2001. Argues that *Measure for Measure* shows the intimate connection between problems of governance and religion in early modern Europe.

Wheeler, Richard P. *Shakespeare's Development and The Problem Comedies: Turn and Counter-Turn*. Berkeley: U of California P, 1981. 1–33; 92–153. Offers a detailed psychoanalytic interpretation.

FILM

Measure for Measure. 1979. Dir. Desmond Davis. UK. This BBC-TV production features nuanced performances from the entire ensemble, particularly Tim Pigott-Smith (Angelo), Kenneth Colley (Duke), Kate Nelligan (Isabella), and Frank Middlemass (Pompey).

TEXTUAL INTRODUCTION

Measure for Measure was first printed in the 1623 First Folio. It is one of a group of plays occurring at the start of the Folio, including *The Tempest,* for which there is reason to think that the printers were working not from Shakespeare's own papers directly but from a now-lost transcript prepared by the professional scribe Ralph Crane. All subsequent printings derive from the Folio, which is the sole authoritative text for this play.

There are some internal inconsistencies, of which the clearest example occurs in 1.2, where the Bawd seems suddenly to forget the news that she has told everyone about Claudio's misfortune. These loose ends suggest revision of some sort. Furthermore, the song that appears in 4.1 also appears, in a more complete version, in *Rollo Duke of Normandy, or The Bloody Brother,* a play by John Fletcher, Philip Massinger, and possibly others, first performed around 1617; this fact might suggest that revision of *Measure for Measure* took place later than 1603–04, when it was first performed. The most developed version of this theory, put forward by the Oxford editors of *Measure for Measure* and articulated at greater length in the 2007 edition of Thomas Middleton's *Collected Works,* is that the play as we have it is a version substantially revised by Middleton for performance by the King's Men after Shakespeare's death. The Middleton theory remains unproven but persuasive.

If the Middleton hypothesis is correct, then there might be an argument for offering an edition of the play that attempts to purge it of its later revisions and return it to something like the state in which it might have existed in 1604. However, such an edition would be highly conjectural, because the play is only known through the 1623 version. Instead, the text of *Measure for Measure* offered here follows closely that of the First Folio, resisting the temptation to restructure the text we have so as to resolve apparent inconsistencies such as that noted in 1.2. In accordance with the policy of the edition as a whole, it also retains the character names in the forms favored by the First Folio: thus, CLOWN and BAWD are found in this edition as speech prefixes rather than POMPEY and MISTRESS OVERDONE.

Measure for Measure contains a number of passages that are so difficult to interpret that editors have suspected the text has become corrupt, either through mistakes in manuscript copying or through errors made by the compositors. Over the centuries, a large critical literature has built up around these cruces, as they are called, the most famous of which is perhaps the "brakes of ice / brakes of vice" passage (2.1.39). Each crux has attracted different attempts to make sense of it as it stands, as well as competing emendations that attempt to diagnose and correct errors in the text.

In making decisions about which emendations or explanations to adopt in each case, this edition is one of the first to be able to use the computer database *Early English Books Online,* which searches an electronic full-text database of (currently) around 30,000 early modern texts. For instance, *EEBO* finds hitherto unnoticed examples of Shakespeare's contemporaries using metaphorical phrases such as "brakes of vanity" or "brakes of sensuality." The same search currently finds no other instances of "brakes of" being followed by a word relating to ice. That result has informed this edition's decision to prefer the emendation "brakes of vice" at 2.1.39. *EEBO* similarly underpins decisions about the other cruces, as well as informing the three entirely new emendations offered in this text at 2.4.75, 4.1.53, and 4.4.24. For further details, see Digital Edition TC 3 and TC 8.

MATTHEW STEGGLE

TEXTUAL BIBLIOGRAPHY

Murphy, Andrew, ed. A *Concise Companion to Shakespeare and the Text*. Chichester: Wiley-Blackwell, 2010.
Shakespeare, William. *Measure for Measure*. Ed. Mark Eccles. New York: MLA, 1980.
Stewart, Alan. *Shakespeare's Letters*. Oxford: Oxford UP, 2008.

PERFORMANCE NOTE

Productions of *Measure for Measure* can convince audiences that any of the play's three leads—the Duke of Vienna, Isabella, or Angelo—occupies its central position, and each role can be played so as to deserve sympathy or condemnation, so performances can feel revelatory even to those already intimately familiar with the play. Whatever balance is struck among attention to the Duke's motives for abandoning authority, Isabella's moral dilemmas regarding sin and self-sacrifice, and Angelo's decline under the influence of power, each production must decide whether its Duke will appear more as a benevolent savior or a machiavel, whether Isabella performs piety or lives it, and whether Angelo is a victim of temptation or a vicious hypocrite. Productions must also determine how Isabella will react to the Duke's proposal and whether to indicate any romantic chemistry between the two beforehand.

Like its characters, the play's contrasting settings of state and street accommodate widely different interpretations. In some productions, a totalitarian government oppresses an attractive and pleasure-loving populace, often with signs of institutional control in the form of prison gates and crucifixes looming large. In others, benign leaders toil on behalf of a city wholly devoted to its own dissolution. Religion can be an oppressive or a vitalizing force, according to the production's emphasis on the prudery and self-righteousness of the nobles or the vulgarity of the masses. To these ends, many directors have opted for a Victorian setting that complements church and state efforts to legislate morality, while others have taken the play's illicit expressions of sexuality as grounds to portray Vienna as one big red light district.

BRETT GAMBOA

Measure for Measure

Vincentio, DUKE of Vienna
ANGELO, the deputy
ESCALUS, an ancient lord
CLAUDIO, a young gentleman
JULIET, beloved of Claudio
ISABELLA, sister to Claudio
LUCIO, a fantastic°   *an impulsive eccertric*
Two other like GENTLEMEN
FROTH, a foolish gentleman
Mistress Overdone, a BAWD
Pompey, her tapster, the CLOWN
The PROVOST
ELBOW, a simple constable
A JUSTICE
ABHORSON, an executioner
BARNARDINE, a dissolute prisoner
MARIANA, betrothed to Angelo
A BOY, Mariana's servant
FRIAR Thomas
Friar PETER
Francisca, a NUN
MESSENGER
SERVANTS
Varrius, a lord
Lords, Officers, Citizens

1.1

Enter DUKE, ESCALUS, *[and] Lords.*[1]

DUKE Escalus.
ESCALUS   My lord.
DUKE   Of government the properties to unfold°   *explain*
   Would seem in me to affect° speech and discourse,   *love; show off*
5 Since I am put° to know that your own science°   *obliged / knowledge*
   Exceeds in that the lists° of all advice   *limits*
   My strength can give you. Then no more remains
   But that, to° your sufficiency,° as your worth is able,   *rely on / ability*
   And let them[2] work. The nature of our people,
10 Our city's institutions, and the terms°   *procedures*
   For common justice, you're as pregnant° in   *expert*
   As art° and practice hath enrichèd any   *learning*
   That we remember. There is our commission,
   From which we would not have you warp.°   *deviate*

1.1 Location: The play takes place in Vienna. Some scene locations can merely be inferred. This scene may be set in the Duke's palace.
1. TEXTUAL COMMENT In the Folio (F) text, the Duke is called "Vincentio" only in the cast list; stage directions and speech prefixes refer to him as "Duke." See Digital Edition TC 1 for a discussion on the different implications of these ways of referring to this character.
2. The referent of "them" is unclear. Perhaps a line is missing.

[*He gives* ESCALUS *a paper.*]
                                          Call hither,
15   I say bid come before us, Angelo.
     What figure of us, think you, he will bear?[3]
     For you must know, we have with special soul°   deliberation
     Elected° him our absence to supply:°   Chosen / make up for
     Lent him our terror, dressed him with our love,
20   And given his deputation° all the organs°   deputyship / instruments
     Of our own power. What think you of it?
     ESCALUS   If any in Vienna be of worth
     To undergo° such ample grace° and honor,   sustain / favor
     It is Lord Angelo.
              Enter ANGELO.
     DUKE   Look where he comes.
25   ANGELO   Always obedient to your grace's will,
     I come to know your pleasure.
     DUKE   Angelo,
     There is a kind of character[4] in thy life
     That to th'observer doth thy history°   life story
     Fully unfold. Thyself and thy belongings°   endowments
30   Are not thine own so proper° as to waste   exclusively
     Thyself upon thy virtues, they on thee.
     Heaven doth with us as we with torches do,
     Not light them for themselves. For if our virtues
     Did not go forth of° us, 'twere all alike   from
35   As if we had them not.[5] Spirits are not finely touched
     But to fine issues,[6] nor nature never lends
     The smallest scruple° of her excellence,   bit
     But like a thrifty goddess she determines°   ordains
     Herself the glory of a creditor,
40   Both thanks and use.° But I do bend° my speech   interest / direct
     To one that can my part in him advertise.°   make known
     Hold,[7] therefore, Angelo.
     In our remove be thou at full ourself.
     Mortality° and mercy in Vienna   Power to kill
45   Live in thy tongue and heart. Old Escalus,
     Though first in question, is thy secondary.[8]
     Take thy commission.
     ANGELO   Now, good my lord,
     Let there be some more test made of my mettle°   punning on "metal"
     Before so noble and so great a figure
     Be stamped upon it.
50   DUKE   No more evasion.
     We have with a leavened° and preparèd choice   fermented (mature)
     Proceeded to you; therefore take your honors.
              [*He gives* ANGELO *a paper.*]
     Our haste from hence is of so quick condition
     That it prefers itself and leaves unquestioned[9]
55   Matters of needful value. We shall write to you,

---

3. How do you think he will represent me (with the
royal plural)? Angelo is imagined bearing his ruler's
image like a coin; compare "mettle" (metal) in line 48.
4. Handwriting; engraved pattern.
5. *Heaven . . . not:* similarly, Jesus, in Matthew 5:14–
16, tells his followers not to hide their light under a

bushel.
6. *Spirits . . . issues:* Spirits are not made fine except
to do fine deeds.
7. Silence; take (this commission).
8. Though first to be addressed, is your subordinate.
9. That it takes precedence and leaves unconsidered.

As time and our concernings° shall importune,°   *affairs / demand*
How it goes with us, and do look° to know   *expect*
What doth befall you here. So fare you well.
To th' hopeful execution do I leave you
Of your commissions.

60 ANGELO   Yet give leave, my lord,
That we may bring you something° on the way.   *some distance*
DUKE   My haste may not admit° it.   *permit*
Nor need you, on mine honor, have to do
With[1] any scruple. Your scope is as mine own,
65 So to enforce or qualify° the laws   *mitigate*
As to your soul seems good. Give me your hand.
I'll privily away. I love the people,
But do not like to stage me° to their eyes.   *display myself*
Though it do well,° I do not relish well   *is politically useful*
70 Their loud applause and aves° vehement,   *salutations*
Nor do I think the man of safe discretion°   *sound judgment*
That does affect° it. Once more, fare you well.   *desire*
ANGELO   The heavens give safety to your purposes!
ESCALUS   Lead forth and bring you back in happiness!
75 DUKE   I thank you. Fare you well.[2]   *Exit.*
ESCALUS   I shall desire you, sir, to give me leave
To have free° speech with you, and it concerns me   *frank*
To look into the bottom of my place.[3]
A power I have, but of what strength and nature
80 I am not yet instructed.°   *informed*
ANGELO   'Tis so with me. Let us withdraw together,
And we may soon our satisfaction have
Touching that point.
ESCALUS   I'll wait upon° your honor.   *Exeunt.*   *accompany*

1.2

Enter LUCIO, *and two other* GENTLEMEN.[1]

LUCIO   If the Duke with the other dukes come not to compo-
sition° with the king of Hungary, why then all the dukes fall   *agreement*
upon° the King.   *attack*
FIRST GENTLEMAN   Heaven grant us its peace, but not the king
5   of Hungary's!
SECOND GENTLEMAN   Amen.
LUCIO   Thou conclud'st like the sanctimonious pirate, that went to
sea with the ten commandments but scraped° one out of   *erased*
the table.°   *tablet*
10 SECOND GENTLEMAN   Thou shalt not steal?
LUCIO   Ay, that he razed.
FIRST GENTLEMAN   Why, 'twas a commandment to command
the captain and all the rest from their functions. They put forth
to steal! There's not a soldier of us all that, in the thanksgiving
15 before meat,° do relish the petition well that prays for peace.   *food*
SECOND GENTLEMAN   I never heard any soldier dislike° it.   *express aversion to*

---

1. *have to do / With:* worry about.
2. PERFORMANCE COMMENT The part of the Duke
presents many challenges to the actor; for a discussion
of the options in performance, see Digital Edition PC 1.
3. To examine my duties thoroughly.

1.2. Location: A street or public place.
1. TEXTUAL COMMENT Various inconsistencies in this
scene suggest textual corruption or, perhaps, a revision that is not completely thorough. See Digital Edition TC 2.

LUCIO   I believe thee, for I think thou never wast where grace
was said.

SECOND GENTLEMAN   No, a dozen times at least.

20 FIRST GENTLEMAN   What? In meter?

LUCIO   In any proportion,° or in any language.   *meter*

FIRST GENTLEMAN   I think, or in any religion!

LUCIO   Ay, why not? Grace is grace, despite of all controversy.[2] [*to*
FIRST GENTLEMAN] As, for example, thou thyself art a wicked
25 villain, despite of all grace.

FIRST GENTLEMAN   Well, there went but a pair of shears
between us.[3]

LUCIO   I grant, as there may between the lists° and the velvet.   *selvages*
Thou art the list.

30 FIRST GENTLEMAN   And thou the velvet. Thou art good velvet;
thou'rt a three-piled[4] piece, I warrant thee. I had as lief° be a   *had rather*
list of an English kersey° as be piled, as thou art piled,[5] for a   *wool cloth*
French velvet. Do I speak feelingly° now?   *to the point; painfully*

LUCIO   I think thou dost, and indeed with most painful feeling°   *conviction*
35 of thy speech. I will, out of thine own confession, learn to begin°   *drink to*
thy health, but, whilst I live, forget to drink after thee.°   *(to avoid infection)*

FIRST GENTLEMAN   I think I have done myself wrong,° have I   *laid myself open to that*
not?

SECOND GENTLEMAN   Yes, that thou hast, whether thou art
40 tainted or free.°   *sick or well*

        Enter BAWD.

LUCIO   Behold, behold, where Madam Mitigation° comes. I   *(of sexual desire)*
have purchased as many diseases under her roof as come
to—

SECOND GENTLEMAN   To what, I pray?

45 LUCIO   Judge.°   *Guess*

SECOND GENTLEMAN   To three thousand dolors° a year.   *pains; dollars*

FIRST GENTLEMAN   Ay, and more.

LUCIO   A French crown° more.   *coin; syphilitic sore*

FIRST GENTLEMAN   Thou art always figuring° diseases in me,   *imagining*
50 but thou art full of error. I am sound.°   *healthy*

LUCIO   Nay, not, as one would say, healthy, but so sound° as   *resounding*
things that are hollow. Thy bones are hollow.[6] Impiety° has   *Wickedness*
made a feast of thee.

FIRST GENTLEMAN [*to* BAWD]   How now? Which of your hips
55 has the most profound sciatica?[7]

BAWD   Well, well. There's one yonder arrested and carried to
prison was worth five thousand of you all.

SECOND GENTLEMAN   Who's that, I pray thee?

BAWD   Marry,° sir, that's Claudio, Signor Claudio.   *By the Virgin Mary*

60 FIRST GENTLEMAN   Claudio to prison? 'Tis not so.

BAWD   Nay, but I know 'tis so. I saw him arrested, saw him

---

2. Referring to the religious controversy over
whether human beings are saved by divine grace or
by good works. *grace:* divine favor; prayer before a
meal.
3. We are cut from the same cloth.
4. Very plush; full of rectal sores (a symptom of
syphilis). Lucio accuses the First Gentleman of being
a "list," a selvage or edging of inferior cloth; the Gentleman retorts that he'd rather be a plain selvage

than an expensively "piled" velvet like Lucio. Lucio
then uses the Gentleman's knowledge of "piles" to
score a point against him.
5. Ruined; made bald (a sign of syphilis, the "French
pox"). Syphilitic sores were covered with velvet
patches.
6. Syphilis causes bones to become brittle.
7. Ache in the sciatic vein of the hip, associated with
venereal disease.

carried away, and which is more, within these three days his
head to be chopped off.

LUCIO But, after° all this fooling, I would not have it so. Art   *despite*
65 thou sure of this?

BAWD I am too sure of it, and it is for getting Madam Julietta
with child.

LUCIO Believe me, this may be. He promised to meet me two
hours since, and he was ever precise in promise-keeping.

70 SECOND GENTLEMAN Besides, you know, it draws° something   *approaches*
near to the speech we had to such a purpose.

FIRST GENTLEMAN But most of all agreeing with the proclamation.

LUCIO Away, let's go learn the truth of it.

Exeunt [LUCIO *and the* GENTLEMEN].

BAWD Thus, what with the war, what with the sweat,° what   *plague*
75 with the gallows, and what with poverty, I am custom-
shrunk.°   *short on customers*

Enter [*Pompey the*] CLOWN.

—How now? What's the news with you?

CLOWN Yonder man is carried to prison.

BAWD Well, what has he done?

80 CLOWN A woman.

BAWD But what's his offense?

CLOWN Groping for trouts in a peculiar river.

BAWD What? Is there a maid with child by him?

CLOWN No, but there's a woman with maid by him. You have
85 not heard of the proclamation, have you?

BAWD What proclamation, man?

CLOWN All houses in the suburbs[8] of Vienna must be plucked°   *torn*
down.

BAWD And what shall become of those in the city?

90 CLOWN They shall stand for seed.[9] They had gone down too,
but that a wise burgher put in° for them.   *citizen interceded*

BAWD But shall all our houses of resort in the suburbs be
pulled down?

CLOWN To the ground, mistress.

95 BAWD Why, here's a change indeed in the commonwealth!
What shall become of me?

CLOWN Come, fear not you. Good counselors° lack no cli-   *attorneys*
ents. Though you change your place, you need not change
your trade. I'll be your tapster° still. Courage, there will be   *bartender*
100 pity taken on you; you that have worn your eyes almost out
in the service,[1] you will be considered.°   *recompensed*

[*A noise within.*]

BAWD What's to do° here, Thomas tapster?[2] Let's withdraw.   *the matter*

Enter PROVOST,° CLAUDIO, JULIET,[3] *Officers,* LUCIO,   *jailer*
and [*the*] *two* GENTLEMEN.

CLOWN Here comes Signor Claudio, led by the Provost to
prison, and there's Madam Juliet.

[*Exeunt* BAWD *and* CLOWN.]

---

8. London brothels ("houses") were located outside
the city walls, where civic authorities had difficulty
controlling them.
9. Grain for the next crop; semen.
1. "Eye" was slang for "female genital"; blindness is

another symptom of syphilis.
2. Stock name for a tapster.
3. Claudio and Juliet are perhaps wearing white
sheets of penance; such public humiliations were
common punishments for sexual transgressions.

105 CLAUDIO Fellow, why dost thou show me thus to th' world?
      Bear me to prison, where I am committed.
    PROVOST I do it not in evil disposition,
      But from Lord Angelo by special charge.
    CLAUDIO Thus can the demigod Authority
110   Make us pay down for our offense by weight.°   *fully*
      The words of° heaven; on whom it will, it will,[4]   *judgment of*
      On whom it will not, so; yet still 'tis just.
    LUCIO Why, how now, Claudio? Whence comes this restraint?
    CLAUDIO From too much liberty,° my Lucio, liberty.   *looseness*
115   As surfeit is the father of much fast,°   *gluttony precedes fasting*
      So every scope° by the immoderate use   *freedom*
      Turns to restraint. Our natures do pursue,
      Like rats that raven° down their proper bane,°   *devour / poison*
      A thirsty evil, and when we drink, we die.
120 LUCIO If I could speak so wisely under an arrest, I would
    send for certain of my creditors.[5] And yet, to say the truth, I
    had as lief have the foppery° of freedom as the morality of   *folly*
    imprisonment. What's thy offense, Claudio?
    CLAUDIO What but to speak of would offend again.
125 LUCIO What, is't murder?
    CLAUDIO No.
    LUCIO Lechery?
    CLAUDIO Call it so.
    PROVOST Away, sir, you must go.
    CLAUDIO   One word, good friend.
130   [*to* LUCIO] Lucio, a word with you.
    LUCIO A hundred, if they'll do you any good. Is lechery so
    looked after?
    CLAUDIO Thus stands it with me: upon a true contract[6]
      I got possession of Julietta's bed.
135   You know the lady. She is fast° my wife,   *nearly; entirely*
      Save that we do the denunciation° lack   *declaration*
      Of outward order.° This we came not to,   *public ceremony*
      Only for propagation° of a dower   *enlargement*
      Remaining in the coffer of her friends,°   *relatives*
140   From whom we thought it meet° to hide our love   *appropriate*
      Till time had made them for° us. But it chances   *favorably disposed to*
      The stealth of our most mutual° entertainment   *reciprocal; intimate*
      With character too gross° is writ on Juliet.   *writing too large*
    LUCIO With child, perhaps?
    CLAUDIO   Unhappily, even so.
145   And the new deputy now for the Duke,
      Whether it be the fault and glimpse° of newness,   *glitter*
      Or whether that the body public be
      A horse whereon the governor doth ride,
      Who, newly in the seat, that it may know
150   He can command, lets it straight° feel the spur—   *immediately*
      Whether the tyranny be in his place°   *office*

---

4. Paul has God say in Romans 9:15: "I will have mercy on him, to whom I will show mercy: and will have compassion on him, on whom I will have compassion."
5. Who, Lucio implies, would have him arrested for nonpayment of debts.
6. A secret plighting of troth, as opposed to public nup-

tials; in seventeenth-century England, such a contract could constitute legal marriage if made in the present tense ("I marry you" rather than "I will marry you") and followed by sexual consummation. The nature of the contract between Claudio and Juliet is unclear.

Or in his eminence that fills it up,
I stagger in.° But this new governor   *hesitate to say*
Awakes me all the enrolled° penalties   *recorded*
155 Which have like unscoured armor hung by th' wall
So long that nineteen zodiacs° have gone round   *years*
And none of them been worn; and, for a name,°   *reputation*
Now puts the drowsy and neglected act
Freshly on me. 'Tis surely for a name.
160 LUCIO   I warrant° it is. And thy head stands so tickle° on thy   *I'm sure / insecurely*
shoulders that a milkmaid, if she be in love, may sigh it off.[7]
Send after the Duke, and appeal to him.
CLAUDIO   I have done so, but he's not to be found.
I prithee, Lucio, do me this kind service:
165 This day my sister should the cloister enter
And there receive her approbation.°   *become a novice*
Acquaint her with the danger of my state,
Implore her, in my voice, that she make friends
To the strict deputy, bid herself assay° him.   *try*
170 I have great hope in that, for in her youth
There is a prone° and speechless dialect,   *eager; submissive*
Such as move men. Beside, she hath prosperous art°   *skill*
When she will play with reason and discourse,
And well she can persuade.
175 LUCIO   I pray she may, as well for the encouragement of the
like,° which else would stand under grievous imposition,° as   *those like you / burden*
for the enjoying of thy life, who I would be sorry should be
thus foolishly lost at a game of tick-tack.[8] I'll to her.
CLAUDIO   I thank you, good friend Lucio.
LUCIO   Within two hours.
180 CLAUDIO   Come, officer, away.   *Exeunt.*

1.3

Enter DUKE *and* FRIAR *Thomas.*
DUKE   No, holy father, throw away that thought.
Believe not that the dribbling[1] dart of love
Can pierce a complete° bosom. Why I desire thee   *an invulnerable*
To give me secret harbor hath a purpose
5 More grave and wrinkled° than the aims and ends   *(suggesting aged wisdom)*
Of burning youth.
FRIAR   May your grace speak of it?
DUKE   My holy sir, none better knows than you
How I have ever loved the life removed,°   *retired*
And held in idle price° to haunt assemblies   *thought it frivolous*
10 Where youth and cost, witless bravery° keeps.   *pointless ostentation*
I have delivered to Lord Angelo,
A man of stricture° and firm abstinence,   *self-restraint*
My absolute power and place here in Vienna,
And he supposes me traveled to Poland;
15 For so I have strewed it in the common ear,°   *ears of common people*

---

7. That a milkmaid's lovesick sigh may blow it off
(with wordplay on "maidenhead").
8. A kind of backgammon scored by placing pegs
into holes; with sexual innuendo.

1.3 Location: A friar's cell.
1. Inadequate, like an arrow shot without sufficient
force.

And so it is received.° Now, pious sir,   *believed*
You will demand of me why I do this.
FRIAR Gladly, my lord.
DUKE We have strict statutes and most biting laws,
20 The needful bits and curbs to headstrong jades,°   *horses*
Which for this fourteen years we have let slip,°   *slide*
Even like an o'ergrown lion in a cave
That goes not out to prey. Now, as fond° fathers,   *doting*
Having bound up the threatening twigs of birch
25 Only to stick it in their children's sight
For terror, not to use, in time the rod
More mocked than feared becomes; so our decrees,
Dead to infliction,° to themselves are dead,   *Never inflicted*
And liberty plucks justice by the nose,[2]
30 The baby beats the nurse, and quite athwart
Goes all decorum.
FRIAR   It rested in° your grace *remained possible for*
To unloose this tied-up justice when you pleased,
And it in you more dreadful would have seemed
Than in Lord Angelo.
DUKE   I do fear, too dreadful.
35 Sith° 'twas my fault to give the people scope,   *Since*
'Twould be my tyranny to strike and gall° them   *chafe*
For what I bid them do. For we bid this be done,
When evil deeds have their permissive pass° *unhindered passage*
And not the punishment. Therefore indeed, my father,
40 I have on Angelo imposed the office,
Who may in th'ambush° of my name strike home,   *under cover*
And yet my nature never in the fight
To do in slander.° And to behold his sway° *To permit slander / rule*
I will, as 'twere a brother of your order,
45 Visit both prince° and people. Therefore, I prithee,   *ruler*
Supply me with the habit, and instruct me
How I may formally in person bear° *behave in character*
Like a true friar. More reasons for this action
At our more leisure shall I render you.
50 Only this one: Lord Angelo is precise,°   *puritanical*
Stands at a guard with envy,° scarce confesses *on guard against desire*
That his blood flows or that his appetite
Is more to bread than stone. Hence shall we see
If power change purpose, what our seemers be. *Exit.*

1.4

Enter ISABELLA *and Francisca, a* NUN.
ISABELLA And have you nuns no farther privileges?
NUN Are not these large° enough?   *generous*
ISABELLA Yes, truly; I speak not as desiring more,
But rather wishing a more strict restraint
5 Upon the sisterhood, the votarists of Saint Clare.
LUCIO (*within*) Ho! Peace be in this place.
ISABELLA Who's that which calls?
NUN It is a man's voice. Gentle Isabella,

---

2. Licentiousness insults the administration of law.
1.4 Location: A convent of St. Clare, an order known for austere discipline.

Turn you the key, and know° his business of° him. *find out / from*
10 You may, I may not: you are yet unsworn.
When you have vowed, you must not speak with men
But in the presence of the prioress.
Then, if you speak, you must not show your face,
Or if you show your face, you must not speak.
15 He calls again. I pray you, answer him.
    [ISABELLA *opens the door.*]
ISABELLA   Peace and prosperity! Who is't that calls?
    [*Enter* LUCIO.]
LUCIO   Hail, virgin, if you be, as those cheek-roses° *glowing cheeks*
Proclaim you are no less. Can you so stead° me *help*
As bring me to the sight of Isabella,
20 A novice of this place, and the fair sister
To her unhappy° brother Claudio? *unfortunate*
ISABELLA   Why "her unhappy brother," let me ask?
The rather for I now must make you know
I am that Isabella and his sister.
25 LUCIO   Gentle and fair, your brother kindly greets you.
Not to be weary° with you, he's in prison. *tedious*
ISABELLA   Woe me! For what?
LUCIO   For that which, if myself might be his judge,
He should receive his punishment in thanks.
30 He hath got his friend° with child. *lover*
ISABELLA   Sir, make me not your story.° *don't tell me tales*
LUCIO   'Tis true.
I would not, though 'tis my familiar° sin *habitual*
With maids to seem the lapwing[1] and to jest,
Tongue far from heart, play with all virgins so.
35 I hold you as a thing enskied° and sainted *placed in heaven*
By your renouncement, an immortal spirit,
And to be talked with in sincerity,
As with a saint.
ISABELLA   You do blaspheme the good in mocking me.
40 LUCIO   Do not believe it. Fewness° and truth, 'tis thus. *In few words*
Your brother and his lover have embraced.
As those that feed, grow full; as blossoming time
That from the seedness° the bare fallow° brings *sowing / plowland*
To teeming foison;° even so her plenteous womb *abundance*
45 Expresseth his full tilth° and husbandry.[2] *tillage*
ISABELLA   Someone with child by him? My cousin Juliet?
LUCIO   Is she your cousin?
ISABELLA   Adoptedly,° as school-maids change° their names *By choice / exchange*
By vain° though apt affection. *foolish*
LUCIO   She it is.
ISABELLA   Oh, let him marry her.
50 LUCIO   This is the point.
The Duke is very strangely gone from hence;
Bore many gentlemen, myself being one,
In hand and hope of action.[3] But we do learn,
By those that know the very nerves° of state, *sinews (innermost secrets)*
55 His giving-out° were of an infinite distance *What he proclaimed*

---

1. A bird that cries alarm when far from its nest, a common figure for deception.
2. Cultivation (punning on "husband").
3. *Bore . . . action:* Deceived us into hoping for some military action.

From his true-meant design. Upon° his place | *In*
And with full line° of his authority | *extent*
Governs Lord Angelo, a man whose blood
Is very snow-broth,° one who never feels | *melted snow*
60 The wanton stings and motions° of the sense | *stimulants and impulses*
But doth rebate° and blunt his natural edge | *dull*
With profits of the mind, study and fast.
He, to give fear to use° and liberty, | *custom*
Which have for long run by the hideous law
65 As mice by lions, hath picked out an act° | *a statute*
Under whose heavy° sense your brother's life | *oppressive*
Falls into forfeit. He arrests him on it,
And follows close the rigor of the statute
To make him an example. All hope is gone
70 Unless you have the grace by your fair prayer
To soften Angelo. And that's my pith° of business | *essence*
Twixt you and your poor brother.

ISABELLA   Doth he so
Seek his life?

LUCIO   Has censured° him already, | *sentenced*
And, as I hear, the Provost hath a warrant
For 's execution.

75 ISABELLA   Alas! What poor
Ability's in me to do him good?

LUCIO   Assay the power you have.

ISABELLA   My power? Alas, I doubt.

LUCIO   Our doubts are traitors
And makes us lose the good we oft might win,
80 By fearing to attempt. Go to Lord Angelo,
And let him learn to know, when maidens sue
Men give like gods, but when they weep and kneel,
All their petitions are as freely theirs
As° they themselves would owe° them. | *As if / were to own*

ISABELLA   I'll see what I can do.

85 LUCIO   But speedily.

ISABELLA   I will about it straight,° | *immediately*
No longer staying but to give the mother° | *Mother Superior*
Notice of my affair.° I humbly thank you. | *business*
Commend me to my brother. Soon at night
90 I'll send him certain word of my success.° | *fortune (good or bad)*

LUCIO   I take my leave of you.

ISABELLA   Good sir, adieu.[4]   *Exeunt.*

2.1

Enter ANGELO, ESCALUS, *a* JUSTICE, *and Servants.*

ANGELO   We must not make a scarecrow of the law,
Setting it up to fear° the birds of prey | *frighten*
And let it keep one shape till custom make it
Their perch and not their terror.

ESCALUS   Ay, but yet
5 Let us be keen, and rather cut a little
Than fall and bruise to death. Alas, this gentleman

---

4. PERFORMANCE COMMENT Isabella's sexuality, and the degree to which she is aware of it, has been variously imagined in different productions; for a discussion of the options in performance, see Digital Edition PC 2.
2.1 Location: The court of justice.

Whom I would save had a most noble father.
Let but your honor know—
Whom I believe to be most strait° in virtue—   rigorous
10 That in the working of your own affections,°   passions
Had time cohered with place, or place with wishing,
Or that the resolute acting of your blood°   desire
Could have attained th'effect° of your own purpose,   fulfillment
Whether you had not sometime in your life
15 Erred in this point which now you censure° him,   condemn in
And pulled the law upon you.
ANGELO   'Tis one thing to be tempted, Escalus,
Another thing to fall. I not° deny   do not
The jury passing on the prisoner's life
20 May in the sworn twelve have a thief or two
Guiltier than him they try. What's open° made to justice,   evident
That justice seizes. What knows the laws[1]
That thieves do pass on thieves? 'Tis very pregnant,°   clear
The jewel that we find, we stoop and take't,
25 Because we see it; but what we do not see
We tread upon and never think of it.
You may not so extenuate his offense
For° I have had such faults; but rather tell me   Because
When I, that censure him, do so offend,
30 Let mine own judgment pattern out° my death,   give precedent for
And nothing come in partial.° Sir, he must die.   no allowances be made
      Enter PROVOST.
ESCALUS   Be it as your wisdom will.
ANGELO   Where is the Provost?
PROVOST   Here, if it like your honor.
ANGELO   See that Claudio
Be executed by nine tomorrow morning.
35 Bring him his confessor, let him be prepared,
For that's the utmost of his pilgrimage.°   [*Exit* PROVOST.]   life's journey
ESCALUS [*aside*]   Well, heaven forgive him, and forgive us all!
Some rise by sin, and some by virtue fall.
Some run from brakes of vice,[2] and answer none,°   not at all
40 And some condemnèd for a fault alone.°   single imperfection
      Enter ELBOW, FROTH, CLOWN, [*and*] *Officers.*
ELBOW   Come, bring them away. If these be good people in a
commonweal, that do nothing but use their abuses° in com-   do their bad deeds
mon houses,° I know no law. Bring them away.   brothels
ANGELO   How now, sir, what's your name? And what's the matter?
45 ELBOW   If it please your honor, I am the poor Duke's constable,
and my name is Elbow. I do lean° upon justice, sir, and do   depend
bring in here before your good honor two notorious benefactors.[3]
ANGELO   Benefactors? Well! What benefactors are they? Are
50 they not malefactors?
ELBOW   If it please your honor, I know not well what they are.
But precise[4] villains they are, that I am sure of, and void of all
profanation° in the world that good Christians ought to have.   (for "reverence")

---

1. What does the law know; who knows what law.
2. *brakes:* thickets. TEXTUAL COMMENT F has "brakes of Ice," a famous crux; often amended as here. For a fuller discussion of the textual problem, and for a suggestion about how the mistake might have occurred,
see Digital Edition TC 3.
3. Elbow comically misuses words; here he means "malefactors," criminals.
4. Elbow means "precious"; "precise" (morally scrupulous) is elsewhere applied to Angelo.

ESCALUS This comes off° well! Here's a wise officer.		*turns out*
55	ANGELO Go to. What quality° are they of? [*to* ELBOW] Elbow is your name? Why dost thou not speak, Elbow?	*rank*
	CLOWN He cannot, sir. He's out at elbow.[5]	
	ANGELO [*to* CLOWN] What are you, sir?	
	ELBOW He, sir? A tapster, sir, parcel bawd.° One that serves a	*part-time pimp*
60	bad woman, whose house, sir, was, as they say, plucked down in the suburbs. And now she professes a hothouse,° which I	*pretends to run a sauna*
	think is a very ill house, too.	
	ESCALUS How know you that?	
	ELBOW My wife, sir, whom I detest° before heaven and your honor—	*(for "protest")*
65	ESCALUS How? Thy wife?	
	ELBOW Ay, sir, whom I thank heaven is an honest woman—	
	ESCALUS Dost thou detest her therefore?	
	ELBOW I say, sir, I will detest myself also, as well as she, that this house, if it be not a bawd's house, it is pity of her life,° for	*a great pity*
70	it is a naughty° house.	*wicked*
	ESCALUS How dost thou know that, constable?	
	ELBOW Marry, sir, by my wife, who, if she had been a woman cardinally° given, might have been accused in fornication,	*(for "carnally")*
	adultery, and all uncleanliness there.	
75	ESCALUS By the woman's means?	
	ELBOW Ay, sir, by Mistress Overdone's means; but as she° spit in his° face, so she defied him.	*(Elbow's wife)* *(the Clown's)*
	CLOWN Sir, if it please your honor, this is not so.	
	ELBOW Prove it before these varlets° here, thou honorable	*villains*
80	man, prove it.	
	ESCALUS [*to* ANGELO] Do you hear how he misplaces?°	*confuses his words*
	CLOWN Sir, she came in great with child, and longing, saving your honor's reverence,° for stewed prunes,[6] sir; we had but	*excuse the expression*
	two in the house, which at that very distant° time stood, as	*(for "instant")*
85	it were in a fruit dish,[7] a dish of some threepence; your honors have seen such dishes—they are not china dishes, but	
	very good dishes.	
	ESCALUS Go to, go to. No matter for the dish, sir.	
	CLOWN No, indeed, sir, not of° a pin; you are therein in the	*worth*
90	right, but to the point. As I say, this Mistress Elbow, being, as I say, with child, and being great-bellied, and longing, as	
	I said, for prunes; and having but two in the dish, as I said, Master Froth here, this very man, having eaten the rest, as I	
	said, and, as I say, paying for them very honestly —for, as	
95	you know, Master Froth, I could not give you threepence again.°	*in change*
	FROTH No, indeed.	
	CLOWN Very well. You being then, if you be remembered, cracking the stones of the foresaid prunes—	
100	FROTH Ay, so I did indeed.	
	CLOWN Why, very well! I telling you then, if you be remembered, that such a one, and such a one, were past cure of the thing you wot of,[8] unless they kept very good diet, as I told you—	

---

5. Ragged; perplexed at the sound of his name. The Clown loves to play on the double meanings of words.
6. Commonly served in brothels; also suggesting

"testicles" in the series of double-entendres that follows.
7. Slang term for "female genital."
8. Euphemism for syphilis. *wot:* know.

FROTH   All this is true.

105 CLOWN   Why, very well then—

ESCALUS   Come, you are a tedious fool! To the purpose: what
was done to Elbow's wife that he hath cause to complain of?
Come me° to what was done to her.   *Get*

CLOWN   Sir, your honor cannot come to that yet.[9]

110 ESCALUS   No, sir, nor I mean it not.°   *I don't mean that*

CLOWN   Sir, but you shall come to it, by your honor's leave.
And I beseech you, look into° Master Froth here, sir, a man   *consider*
of fourscore pound a year,[1] whose father died at Hallow-
mas° —was't not at Hallowmas, Master Froth?   *Nov. 1, All Saints' Day*

115 FROTH   All Hallow Eve.°   *Halloween*

CLOWN   Why, very well! I hope here be truths. He, sir, sitting,
as I say, in a lower° chair, sir —'twas in the Bunch of Grapes,[2]   *reclining?*
[to FROTH] where indeed you have a delight to sit, have you
not?

120 FROTH   I have so, because it is an open room[3] and good for
winter.

CLOWN   Why, very well then. I hope here be truths.

ANGELO   This will last out a night in Russia
When nights are longest there. I'll take my leave,

125 And leave you to the hearing of the cause,°   *case*
Hoping you'll find good cause to whip them all.

ESCALUS   I think no less. Good morrow to your lordship.

                                            Exit ANGELO.

[to CLOWN] Now, sir, come on. What was done to Elbow's
wife, once more?

130 CLOWN   Once, sir? There was nothing done to her once.

ELBOW [to ESCALUS]   I beseech you, sir, ask him what this
man did to my wife.

CLOWN [to ESCALUS]   I beseech your honor, ask me.

ESCALUS [to CLOWN]   Well, sir, what did this gentleman to her?

135 CLOWN   I beseech you, sir, look in this gentleman's face. Good
Master Froth, look upon his honor, 'tis for a good purpose.
Doth your honor mark° his face?   *note*

ESCALUS   Ay, sir, very well.

CLOWN   Nay, I beseech you, mark it well.

140 ESCALUS   Well, I do so.

CLOWN   Doth your honor see any harm in his face?

ESCALUS   Why, no.

CLOWN   I'll be supposed° upon a book,° his face is the worst   *(for "deposed") / Bible*
thing about him. Good, then, if his face be the worst thing

145 about him, how could Master Froth do the constable's wife
any harm? I would know that of your honor.

ESCALUS   He's in the right. Constable, what say you to it?

ELBOW   First, an it like° you, the house is a respected[4] house;   *if it please*
next, this is a respected fellow; and his mistress is a respected

150 woman.

CLOWN   By this hand, sir, his wife is a more respected person
than any of us all.

---

9. Taking "done" in the sexual sense, the Clown pretends shock at Escalus's salaciousness.
1. Eighty pounds was a low income for a gentleman.
The father's recent death means that Froth has just

come into his inheritance.
2. A room in a tavern.
3. A public room (where fires were kept burning).
4. For "suspected."

ELBOW Varlet, thou liest, thou liest, wicked varlet! The time
is yet to come that she was ever respected with man, woman,
155 or child.

CLOWN Sir, she was respected with him before he married with
her.

ESCALUS [aside] Which is the wiser here, Justice or Iniquity?
—Is this true?

160 ELBOW O thou caitiff, O thou varlet, O thou wicked Hannibal![5] I respected with her before I was married to her? [to
ESCALUS] If ever I was respected with her, or she with me,
let not your worship think me the poor Duke's officer. [to
CLOWN] Prove this, thou wicked Hannibal, or I'll have mine
165 action of battery° on thee.   (for "slander")

ESCALUS If he took° you a box o'th' ear, you might have your   struck
action of slander too.

ELBOW Marry, I thank your good worship for it. What is't your
worship's pleasure I shall do with this wicked caitiff?°   knave

170 ESCALUS Truly, officer, because he hath some offenses in him
that thou wouldst discover° if thou couldst, let him continue   expose
in his courses° till thou know'st what they are.   conduct

ELBOW Marry, I thank your worship for it. —Thou seest, thou
wicked varlet now, what's come upon thee. Thou art to con-
175 tinue now, thou varlet, thou art to continue.

ESCALUS [to FROTH] Where were you born, friend?

FROTH Here in Vienna, sir.

ESCALUS Are you of fourscore pounds a year?

FROTH Yes, an't please you, sir.

180 ESCALUS So. [to CLOWN] What trade are you of, sir?

CLOWN A tapster, a poor widow's tapster.

ESCALUS Your mistress' name?

CLOWN Mistress Overdone.

ESCALUS Hath she had any more than one husband?

185 CLOWN Nine, sir. Overdone by the last.[6]

ESCALUS Nine? [to FROTH] Come hither to me, Master Froth.
Master Froth, I would not have you acquainted with tap-
sters. They will draw you,[7] Master Froth, and you will hang
them.° Get you gone, and let me hear no more of you.   get them hanged

190 FROTH I thank your worship. For mine own part, I never
come into any room in a taphouse, but I am drawn in.

ESCALUS Well, no more of it, Master Froth. Farewell.
                                                        [Exit FROTH.]
Come you hither to me, Master Tapster. What's your name,
Master Tapster?

195 CLOWN Pompey.

ESCALUS What else?

CLOWN Bum, sir.

ESCALUS Troth, and your bum is the greatest thing about you,
so that in the beastliest sense, you are Pompey the Great.[8]
200 Pompey, you are partly a bawd, Pompey, howsoever you color
it in being a tapster, are you not? Come, tell me true, it shall
be the better for you.

---

5. Blunder for "cannibal"; also, both Hannibal and
Pompey were famous generals of ancient times.
6. She takes her name from Overdone, her last husband; her last husband wore her out.

7. Get you beer; steal your substance; convey you to
execution.
8. The Roman general Pompey was surnamed "the
Great."

CLOWN   Truly, sir, I am a poor fellow that would live.

ESCALUS   How would you live, Pompey? By being a bawd?
205   What do you think of the trade, Pompey? Is it a lawful trade?

CLOWN   If the law would allow it, sir.

ESCALUS   But the law will not allow it, Pompey, nor it shall
not° be allowed in Vienna.   *nor shall it*

CLOWN   Does your worship mean to geld and splay all the
210   youth of the city?

ESCALUS   No, Pompey.

CLOWN   Truly, sir, in my poor opinion, they will to't then. If
your worship will take order° for the drabs° and the knaves,   *measures / whores*
you need not to fear the bawds.

215   ESCALUS   There is pretty orders beginning, I can tell you. It is
but heading° and hanging.   *beheading*

CLOWN   If you head and hang all that offend that way but for
ten year together, you'll be glad to give out a commission°   *an order*
for more heads. If this law hold° in Vienna ten year, I'll rent   *remain*
220   the fairest house in it after threepence a bay.⁹ If you live to
see this come to pass, say Pompey told you so.

ESCALUS   Thank you, good Pompey, and in requital of° your   *return for*
prophecy, hark you: I advise you let me not find you before me
again upon any complaint whatsoever, no, not for° dwelling   *even for*
225   where you do. If I do, Pompey, I shall beat you to your tent
and prove a shrewd Caesar to you.¹ In plain dealing, Pompey, I shall have you whipped. So for this time, Pompey, fare
you well.

CLOWN   I thank your worship for your good counsel; [*aside*]
230   but I shall follow it as the flesh and fortune shall better determine. Whip me? No, no, let carman° whip his jade.°   *cart driver / horse*
The valiant heart's not whipped out of his trade.

                                        Exit [*guarded*].

ESCALUS   Come hither to me, Master Elbow. —Come hither,
Master Constable. How long have you been in this place of
235   constable?

ELBOW   Seven year and a half, sir.

ESCALUS   I thought, by the readiness in the office, you had
continued in it some time. You say seven years together.

ELBOW   And a half, sir.

240   ESCALUS   Alas, it hath been great pains to you. They do you
wrong to put you so oft upon't. Are there not men in your ward
sufficient° to serve it?   *fit*

ELBOW   Faith, sir, few of any wit in such matters. As they are
chosen, they are glad to choose me for them; I do it for some
245   piece of money, and go through withal.

ESCALUS   Look° you bring me in the names of some six or   *See that*
seven, the most sufficient of your parish.

ELBOW   To your worship's house, sir?

ESCALUS   To my house. Fare you well.

                              [*Exeunt* ELBOW *and Officers.*]

---

9. Townhouse rental fees were based on the number   1. Julius Caesar defeated Pompey in 48 B.C.E. *shrewd:*
of front windows ("bays").   harsh.

250 —What's o'clock, think you?
JUSTICE   Eleven, sir.
ESCALUS   I pray you home to dinner with me.[2]
JUSTICE   I humbly thank you.
ESCALUS   It grieves me for the death of Claudio,
255   But there's no remedy.
JUSTICE   Lord Angelo is severe.
ESCALUS   It is but needful.
   Mercy is not itself that oft looks so;
   Pardon is still° the nurse of second woe.   *always*
   But yet, poor Claudio! There is no remedy.
260   Come, sir.   *Exeunt.*

2.2
   Enter PROVOST [*and*] SERVANT.
SERVANT   He's hearing a cause.° He will come straight.° I'll   *case / right away*
   tell him of you.
PROVOST   Pray you, do.   [*Exit* SERVANT.]
                          I'll know
   His pleasure; maybe he will relent. Alas,
5   He° hath but as offended in a dream.   *(Claudio)*
   All sects,° all ages smack° of this vice, and he   *kinds of people / partake*
   To die for't?
          Enter ANGELO.
ANGELO   Now, what's the matter, Provost?
PROVOST   Is it your will Claudio shall die tomorrow?
ANGELO   Did not I tell thee yea? Hadst thou not order?
   Why dost thou ask again?
10   PROVOST   Lest I might be too rash.
   Under your good correction, I have seen
   When after execution, judgment hath
   Repented o'er his doom.°   *sentence*
ANGELO   Go to; let that be mine.°   *my concern*
   Do you your office, or give up your place,
   And you shall well be spared.°   *easily be done without*
15   PROVOST   I crave your honor's pardon.
   What shall be done, sir, with the groaning Juliet?
   She's very near her hour.°   *(of childbirth)*
ANGELO   Dispose of her
   To some more fitter place, and that with speed.
          [*Enter* SERVANT.]
SERVANT   Here is the sister of the man condemned
   Desires access to you.
20   ANGELO   Hath he a sister?
PROVOST   Ay, my good lord, a very virtuous maid,
   And to be shortly of a sisterhood,
   If not already.
ANGELO   Well, let her be admitted.   [*Exit* SERVANT.]
   —See you the fornicatress be removed.
25   Let her have needful, but not lavish means.
   There shall be order° for't.   *written direction*
          Enter LUCIO *and* ISABELLA.

2. Dinner was served at midday. *pray:* invite.   2.2 Location: A room in the court of justice.

PROVOST   Save your honor.

ANGELO [*to* PROVOST]   Stay a little while. [*to* ISABELLA] You're
     welcome; what's your will?

ISABELLA   I am a woeful suitor to your honor,
     Please° but your honor hear me.   *If it please*

ANGELO   Well, what's your suit?

30 ISABELLA   There is a vice that most I do abhor
     And most desire should meet the blow of justice;
     For which I would not plead, but that I must;
     For which I must not plead, but that I am
     At war 'twixt will and will not.

ANGELO   Well, the matter?

35 ISABELLA   I have a brother is condemned to die.
     I do beseech you, let it be his fault,°   *his fault be condemned*
     And not my brother.

PROVOST [*aside*]   Heaven give thee moving graces.°   *the gift of persuasion*

ANGELO   Condemn the fault and not the actor° of it?   *doer*
     Why, every fault's condemned ere it be done.

40   Mine were the very cipher of a function
     To fine° the faults, whose fine° stands in record,   *condemn / penalty*
     And let go by° the actor.   *leave unpunished*

ISABELLA   Oh, just but severe law!
     I had a brother then. Heaven keep your honor.

LUCIO [*aside to* ISABELLA]   Give't not o'er° so. To him again,   *Don't give up*
     entreat him,

45   Kneel down before him, hang upon° his gown.   *cling to*
     You are too cold. If you should need a pin,
     You could not with more tame a tongue desire it;
     To him, I say.

ISABELLA   Must he needs° die?   *necessarily*

ANGELO   Maiden, no remedy.

50 ISABELLA   Yes. I do think that you might pardon him,
     And neither heaven nor man grieve at the mercy.

ANGELO   I will not do't.

ISABELLA   But can you if you would?

ANGELO   Look, what° I will not, that I cannot do.   *Whatever*

ISABELLA   But might you do't and do the world no wrong,

55   If so your heart were touched with that remorse°   *pity*
     As mine is to him?

ANGELO   He's sentenced. 'Tis too late.

LUCIO [*aside to* ISABELLA]   You are too cold.

ISABELLA   Too late? Why, no. I that do speak a word
     May call° it again. Well, believe this: *retract*

60   No ceremony° that to great ones 'longs,   *symbolic accessory*
     Not the king's crown, nor the deputed sword,
     The marshal's truncheon, nor the judge's robe
     Become them with one half so good a grace
     As mercy does.

65   If he had been as you, and you as he,
     You would have slipped like him, but he like you
     Would not have been so stern.

ANGELO   Pray you be gone.

ISABELLA   I would to heaven I had your potency°   *power*
     And you were Isabel. Should it then be thus?

70   No. I would tell what 'twere to be a judge,

And what a prisoner.

LUCIO [*aside to* ISABELLA]   Ay, touch him:[1] there's the vein.°   *that's the style*

ANGELO   Your brother is a forfeit of the law,
And you but waste your words.

ISABELLA   Alas, alas.
Why, all the souls that were, were forfeit[2] once,
75   And He that might the vantage° best have took   *advantage*
Found out° the remedy.[3] How would you be   *Procured*
If He, which is the top° of judgment, should   *highest pattern or source*
But judge you as you are? Oh, think on that,
And mercy then will breathe within your lips
Like man new made.°   *renewed by faith*
80   ANGELO   Be you content, fair maid.°   *(with play on "new made")*
It is the law, not I, condemn your brother.
Were he my kinsman, brother, or my son,
It should be thus with him. He must die tomorrow.

ISABELLA   Tomorrow? Oh, that's sudden. Spare him, spare him.
85   He's not prepared for death. Even for our kitchens
We kill the fowl of season.° Shall we serve heaven   *at the proper time*
With less respect than we do minister
To our gross selves? Good, good my lord, bethink you:
Who is it that hath died for this offense?
There's many have committed it.
90   LUCIO [*aside to* ISABELLA]   Ay, well said.

ANGELO   The law hath not been dead, though it hath slept.
Those many had not dared to do that evil
If the first that did th'edict infringe
Had answered for his deed. Now 'tis awake,
95   Takes note of what is done, and like a prophet
Looks in a glass° that shows what future evils   *mirror*
Either new,° or by remissness new-conceived   *unripe*
And so in progress to be hatched and born,
Are now to have no successive degrees,[4]
But ere they live to end.
100   ISABELLA   Yet show some pity.

ANGELO   I show it most of all when I show justice,
For then I pity those I do not know
Which a dismissed° offense would after gall,°   *Whom a pardoned / hurt*
And do him right that answering° one foul wrong   *paying for*
105   Lives not to act another. Be satisfied
Your brother dies tomorrow; be content.

ISABELLA   So you must be the first that gives this sentence,
And he, that suffers. Oh, it is excellent
To have a giant's strength, but it is tyrannous
To use it like a giant.
110   LUCIO [*aside to* ISABELLA]   That's well said.

ISABELLA   Could great men thunder
As Jove[5] himself does, Jove would never be quiet,
For every pelting° petty officer   *paltry*
Would use his heaven for thunder, nothing but thunder.
115   Merciful heaven!

---

1. Influence him; but perhaps Isabella touches Angelo's arm or garment here.
2. Lost (as a result of Adam and Eve's disobedience).
3. By saving all humankind in the person of Christ.
4. Future stages of development.
5. King of the Roman gods, whose weapon was the thunderbolt.

Thou rather with thy sharp and sulphurous° bolt   *fiery*
Splits the unwedgeable and gnarlèd oak
Than the soft myrtle. But man, proud man,
Dressed in a little brief authority,
120 Most ignorant of what he's most assured—
His glassy° essence—like an angry ape[6]   *fragile; illusory*
Plays such fantastic tricks before high heaven
As makes the angels weep, who with our spleens[7]
Would all themselves laugh mortal.
125 LUCIO [*aside to* ISABELLA] Oh, to him, to him, wench,° he   *girl*
    will relent.
He's coming,° I perceive't.   *yielding*
PROVOST [*aside*]   Pray heaven she win him!
ISABELLA We cannot weigh our brother with ourself.[8]
Great men may jest with saints; 'tis wit in them,
But in the less,° foul profanation.   *ordinary people*
130 LUCIO [*aside to* ISABELLA] Thou'rt i'th' right, girl, more o'that.
ISABELLA That in the captain's but a choleric word
Which in the soldier is flat blasphemy.
LUCIO [*aside to* ISABELLA] Art advised o'that?° More on't!   *So you know about that*
ANGELO Why do you put° these sayings upon me?   *impose*
135 ISABELLA Because authority, though it err like others,
Hath yet a kind of medicine in itself
That skins the vice o'th' top.[9] Go to your bosom,
Knock there, and ask your heart what it doth know
That's like my brother's fault; if it confess
140 A natural guiltiness such as is his,
Let it not sound a thought upon your tongue
Against my brother's life.
ANGELO [*aside*]   She speaks, and 'tis such sense°   *sound advice*
That my sense breeds° with it. —Fare you well.   *desire increases*
ISABELLA Gentle my° lord, turn back.   *My gracious*
145 ANGELO I will bethink me.° Come again tomorrow.   *consider*
ISABELLA Hark how I'll bribe you. Good my lord, turn back.
ANGELO How! Bribe me?
ISABELLA Ay, with such gifts that° heaven shall share with° you.   *as / apportion to*
LUCIO [*aside*] You had marred all, else.
150 ISABELLA Not with fond° shekels of the tested° gold,   *foolish / refined*
Or stones° whose rate° are either rich or poor   *jewels / value*
As fancy values them, but with true prayers
That shall be up at heaven and enter there
Ere sunrise, prayers from preservèd° souls,   *protected*
155 From fasting maids, whose minds are dedicate
To nothing temporal.
ANGELO   Well, come to me tomorrow.
LUCIO [*to* ISABELLA] Go to;° 'tis well; away.   *Come on*
ISABELLA   Heaven keep your honor[1] safe.
ANGELO [*aside*] Amen.
For I am that way going to temptation,
Where prayers cross.°   *corrupt; frustrate*

---

6. A figure of grotesque mimicry.
7. Thought to be the seat of laughter.
8. We cannot judge others as we judge ourselves.
9. That causes a skin to grow over the sore.

1. Isabella calls Angelo "your honor" as a term of respect; Angelo understands the phrase as referring to his virtue.

160 ISABELLA   At what hour tomorrow
     Shall I attend your lordship?
    ANGELO   At any time fore noon.
    ISABELLA   Save° your honor.   *God save (a farewell)*
               [*Exeunt* ISABELLA, LUCIO, *and* PROVOST.]
    ANGELO   From thee, even from thy virtue.
165   What's this, what's this? Is this her fault or mine?
     The tempter or the tempted, who sins most, ha?
     Not she, nor doth she tempt. But it is I
     That, lying by the violet in the sun,
     Do as the carrion does, not as the flower,
170   Corrupt with virtuous season.° Can it be   *Rot in fine weather*
     That modesty may more betray our sense°   *seduce our appetite*
     Than woman's lightness?° Having waste ground enough,   *licentiousness*
     Shall we desire to raze the sanctuary
     And pitch° our evils there? Oh, fie, fie, fie!   *hurl; set up*
175   What dost thou, or what art thou, Angelo?
     Dost thou desire her foully for those things
     That make her good? Oh, let her brother live:
     Thieves for their robbery have authority
     When judges steal themselves. What, do I love her,
180   That I desire to hear her speak again
     And feast upon her eyes? What is't I dream on?
     O cunning enemy,° that to catch a saint°   *(Satan) / holy person*
     With saints dost bait thy hook. Most dangerous
     Is that temptation that doth goad us on
185   To sin in loving virtue. Never could the strumpet
     With all her double vigor,° art and nature,   *twofold power*
     Once stir my temper,° but this virtuous maid   *excite me*
     Subdues me quite. Ever till now
     When men were fond,° I smiled and wondered how.   *Exit.*   *infatuated*

2.3

Enter DUKE [*disguised as a friar*] *and* PROVOST.
    DUKE   Hail to you, Provost, so I think you are.
    PROVOST   I am the Provost. What's your will, good Friar?
    DUKE   Bound by my charity and my blessed order,
     I come to visit the afflicted spirits
5   Here in the prison.[1] Do me the common right°   *right of all clerics*
     To let me see them and to make me know
     The nature of their crimes, that I may minister
     To them accordingly.
    PROVOST   I would do more than that, if more were needful.
           Enter JULIET.
10   Look, here comes one, a gentlewoman of mine,°   *in my care*
     Who, falling in the flaws° of her own youth,   *faults; gusts of passion*
     Hath blistered her report.° She is with child,   *reputation*
     And he that got° it, sentenced; a young man   *begot*
     More fit to do another such offense
15   Than die for this.

2.3 Location: The prison.
1. Echoing 1 Peter 3:19: "He . . . went, and preached unto the spirits that were in prison."

DUKE When must he die?
PROVOST   As I do think, tomorrow.
    [*to* JULIET] I have provided for you. Stay a while,
    And you shall be conducted.
DUKE Repent you, fair one, of the sin you carry?
20 JULIET I do, and bear the shame most patiently.
DUKE I'll teach you how you shall arraign° your conscience   *accuse*
    And try your penitence, if it be sound
    Or hollowly put on.
JULIET   I'll gladly learn.
DUKE Love you the man that wronged you?
25 JULIET Yes, as I love the woman that wronged him.
DUKE So then it seems your most offenseful act
    Was mutually committed.
JULIET   Mutually.
DUKE Then was your sin of heavier° kind than his.   *graver*
JULIET I do confess it and repent it, Father.
30 DUKE 'Tis meet° so, daughter, but lest you do repent   *appropriate*
    As that° the sin hath brought you to this shame,   *Because*
    Which sorrow is always toward ourselves, not heaven,
    Showing we would not spare heaven[2] as we love it
    But as we stand in fear—
35 JULIET I do repent me as it is an evil,
    And take the shame with joy.
DUKE   There rest.°   *remain*
    Your partner, as I hear, must die tomorrow,
    And I am going with instruction to him.
    Grace go with you. *Benedicite.*°   *Exit.*   *Bless you*
40 JULIET Must die tomorrow? O injurious love,
    That respites me a life[3] whose very comfort
    Is still a dying horror.
PROVOST   'Tis pity of° him.   *Exeunt.*   *for*

2.4

    Enter ANGELO.
ANGELO When I would pray and think, I think and pray
    To several° subjects. Heaven hath my empty words,   *different*
    Whilst my invention,° hearing not my tongue,   *imagination*
    Anchors on Isabel. Heaven in my mouth,
5   As if I did but only chew his name,
    And in my heart the strong and swelling evil
    Of my conception.[1] The state° whereon I studied   *statecraft; dignity*
    Is like a good thing being often read,
    Grown feared° and tedious. Yea, my gravity   *disliked*
10 Wherein, let no man hear me, I take pride,
    Could I with boot° change for an idle plume[2]   *advantage*
    Which the air beats for vain. O place,° O form,°   *rank / formality*
    How often dost thou with thy case,° thy habit,°   *appearance / dress*

---

2. Relieve heaven from distress.
3. Pregnant women were spared the death penalty, at least until after childbirth.
2.4 Location: A room in the court of justice.

1. *the strong . . . conception:* the wickedness of my idea; original sin, inherited through the parents.
2. A frivolous feather, as worn in the hats of rakish youths.

Wrench awe from fools and tie the wiser souls
15 To thy false seeming! Blood, thou art blood.[3]
Let's write "good angel"[4] on the devil's horn;
'Tis not the devil's crest.°   *heraldic device*
          [*Enter* SERVANT.]
                    How now? Who's there?
SERVANT   One Isabel, a sister, desires access to you.
ANGELO   Teach her the way.   [*Exit* SERVANT.]
                    O heavens!
20 Why does my blood thus muster° to my heart,   *crowd*
Making both it unable° for itself   *weak*
And dispossessing all my other parts
Of necessary fitness?
So play° the foolish throngs with one that swoons: *act*
25 Come all to help him, and so stop the air
By which he should revive; and even so
The general subject° to a well-wished king   *common people*
Quit their own part° and in obsequious fondness°   *place / foolish love*
Crowd to his presence, where their untaught° love   *ignorant*
Must needs appear offense.
          Enter ISABELLA.
30   —How now, fair maid?
ISABELLA   I am come to know your pleasure.
ANGELO [*aside*]   That you might know[5] it would much better
          please me
Than to demand° what 'tis. [*to* ISABELLA] Your brother cannot live.   *ask*
ISABELLA   Even so.° Heaven keep your honor.[6]   *So be it*
35 ANGELO   Yet may he live a while, and it may be
As long as you or I; yet he must die.
ISABELLA   Under your sentence?
ANGELO   Yea.
ISABELLA   When, I beseech you? That in his reprieve
Longer or shorter, he may be so fitted°   *prepared*
40 That his soul sicken not.
ANGELO   Ha! Fie, these filthy vices! It were as good
To pardon him that hath from nature stolen
A man already made,[7] as to remit°   *excuse*
Their saucy sweetness that do coin heaven's image
45 In stamps that are forbid.[8] 'Tis all as easy
Falsely° to take away a life true° made   *Wrongly / legitimately*
As to put metal[9] in restrainèd° means   *forbidden*
To make a false one.
ISABELLA   'Tis set down so in heaven, but not in earth.
50 ANGELO   Say you so? Then I shall pose° you quickly.   *ask*
Which had you rather, that the most just law
Now took your brother's life, or to redeem him
Give up your body to such sweet uncleanness
As she that he hath stained?
ISABELLA   Sir, believe this:

---

3. That is, basic passions cannot be eradicated (contrasts with 1.4.56–62).
4. With pun on Angelo's name.
5. With pun on "carnal knowledge."
6. A form of farewell.
7. *hath . . . made*: has committed murder.

8. *coin . . . forbid*: counterfeit God's image (by begetting illegitimate children).
9. Variant spelling of "mettle" (spirit). Some people thought the child's spirit was conveyed in his or her father's semen.

55   I had rather give my body than my soul.
        ANGELO   I talk not of your soul. Our compelled sins
        Stand more for number than for account.[1]
        ISABELLA   How say you?
        ANGELO   Nay, I'll not warrant that,[2] for I can speak
        Against the thing I say. Answer to this:

60   I, now the voice of the recorded law,
        Pronounce a sentence on your brother's life.
        Might there not be a charity in sin
        To save this brother's life?
        ISABELLA   Please° you to do't,   *If it please*
        I'll take it as a peril to my soul

65   It is no sin at all, but charity.
        ANGELO   Pleased you to do't, at peril of your soul,
        Were equal poise° of sin and charity.   *balance*
        ISABELLA   That I do beg his life, if it be sin,
        Heaven let me bear it. You granting of° my suit,   *Supposing you grant*

70   If that be sin, I'll make it my morn prayer
        To have it added to the faults of mine,
        And nothing of your answer.
        ANGELO   Nay, but hear me.
        Your sense pursues not mine.[3] Either you are ignorant
        Or seem so craftily, and that's not good.

75   ISABELLA   Let it be ignorant, and in nothing good,
        But graciously° to know I am no better.   *by God's grace*
        ANGELO   Thus wisdom wishes to appear most bright
        When it doth tax° itself, as these black masks[4]   *reprove*
        Proclaim an enshield° beauty ten times louder   *a shielded*

80   Than beauty could, displayed. But mark me.
        To be receivèd° plain, I'll speak more gross.°   *understood / clearly*
        Your brother is to die.
        ISABELLA   So.°   *Yes*
        ANGELO   And his offense is so, as it appears,
        Accountant° to the law upon that pain.°   *Accountable / penalty*
        ISABELLA   True.

85   ANGELO   Admit° no other way to save his life   *Suppose*
        —As I subscribe not° that, nor any other,   *agree to neither*
        But in the loss of question[5]—that you, his sister,
        Finding yourself desired of such a person
        Whose credit with the judge, or own great place,°   *rank*

90   Could fetch your brother from the manacles
        Of the all-binding law; and that there were
        No earthly mean to save him but that either
        You must lay down the treasures of your body
        To this supposed,° or else to let him suffer;   *supposed man*

95   What would you do?
        ISABELLA   As much for my poor brother as myself;
        That is, were I under the terms° of death,   *sentence*
        Th'impression of keen whips I'd wear as rubies,
        And strip myself to death as to a bed

---

1. *Our . . . account:* Sins we are forced to commit fill out the list but are not held against us.
2. I'll not guarantee that to be true.
3. You don't follow my meaning; your desire is not aroused by mine.
4. Worn at court entertainments.
5. For the sake of discussion.

100   That longing have been sick for, ere I'd yield
         My body up to shame.
ANGELO   Then must your brother die.
ISABELLA   And 'twere the cheaper way.
         Better it were a brother died at once
         Than that a sister by redeeming him
105   Should die forever.°   be eternally damned
ANGELO   Were not you then as cruel as the sentence
         That you have slandered so?
ISABELLA   Ignomy in ransom and free pardon
         Are of two houses;° lawful mercy   different families
110   Is nothing kin to foul redemption.
ANGELO   You seemed of late to make the law a tyrant,
         And rather proved° the sliding of your brother   argued
         A merriment than a vice.
ISABELLA   Oh, pardon me, my lord, it oft falls out
115   To have what we would° have, we speak not what we mean.   wish to
         I something° do excuse the thing I hate   to some extent
         For his advantage that I dearly love.
ANGELO   We are all frail.[6]
ISABELLA   Else° let my brother die,   Otherwise
         If not a fedary° but only he   confederate
120   Owe and succeed thy weakness.[7]
ANGELO   Nay, women are frail too.
ISABELLA   Ay, as the glasses° where they view themselves,   mirrors
         Which are as easy broke as they make forms.
         Women? Help, heaven! Men their creation° mar   origin
125   In profiting by them. Nay, call us ten times frail,
         For we are soft as our complexions are
         And credulous to false prints.[8]
ANGELO   I think it well,°   agree completely
         And from this testimony of your own sex
         —Since I suppose we are made to be no stronger
130   Than faults may shake our frames—let me be bold:°   presumptuous
         I do arrest° your words. Be that you are,   seize upon
         That is, a woman; if you be more,° you're none.   (that is, better)
         If you be one, as you are well expressed°   shown to be
         By all external warrants,° show it now   evidence
135   By putting on the destined livery.[9]
ISABELLA   I have no tongue° but one. Gentle my lord,   speech
         Let me entreat you speak the former language.
ANGELO   Plainly conceive, I love you.
ISABELLA   My brother did love Juliet,
140   And you tell me that he shall die for't.
ANGELO   He shall not, Isabel, if you give me love.
ISABELLA   I know your virtue hath a license[1] in't
         Which seems a little fouler than it is,
         To pluck on° others.   test; mislead
ANGELO   Believe me on mine honor,

---

6. Echoing Ecclesiastes 8:5: "We are all worthy
blame."
7. Own and inherit the weakness under discussion,
or the weakness that you possess.
8. And receptive to false impressions; referring to

Angelo's counterfeiting imagery, lines 44ff.
9. That is, by accepting women's sexual destiny and
subjection to men. *livery:* servant's uniform.
1. Liberty to seem licentious.

145 My words express my purpose.
   ISABELLA   Ha! Little honor, to be much believed,
   And most pernicious purpose. Seeming, seeming!
   I will proclaim° thee, Angelo, look for't.   *denounce*
   Sign me a present° pardon for my brother,   *an immediate*
150 Or with an outstretched throat I'll tell the world aloud
   What man thou art.
   ANGELO   Who will believe thee, Isabel?
   My unsoiled name, th'austereness of my life,
   My vouch° against you, and my place i'th' state,   *attestation*
   Will so your accusation overweigh
155 That you shall stifle in your own report°   *story; reputation*
   And smell of calumny. I have begun,
   And now I give my sensual race the rein.
   Fit thy consent to my sharp appetite,
   Lay by all nicety and prolixious° blushes   *coyness and excessive*
160 That banish what they sue for. Redeem thy brother
   By yielding up thy body to my will,
   Or else he must not only die the death,
   But thy unkindness° shall his death draw out   *unnaturalness*
   To lingering sufferance.° Answer me tomorrow,   *torment*
165 Or by the affection° that now guides me most,   *passion*
   I'll prove a tyrant to him. As for you,
   Say what you can; my false o'erweighs your true.   *Exit.*
   ISABELLA   To whom should I complain? Did I tell this,
   Who would believe me? Oh, perilous mouths,
170 That bear in them one and the selfsame tongue
   Either of condemnation or approof,°   *approval*
   Bidding the law make curtsy° to their will,   *submit*
   Hooking both right and wrong to th'appetite,
   To follow as it draws! I'll to my brother.
175 Though he hath fallen by prompture° of the blood,   *instigation*
   Yet hath he in him such a mind of honor
   That had he twenty heads to tender° down   *pay*
   On twenty bloody blocks, he'd yield them up
   Before his sister should her body stoop
180 To such abhorred pollution.
   Then, Isabel, live chaste, and brother, die;
   More than our brother is our chastity.
   I'll tell him yet of Angelo's request,
   And fit his mind to death for his soul's rest.   *Exit.*

3.1

Enter DUKE [*disguised as a friar*], CLAUDIO, *and* PROVOST.
   DUKE   So then you hope of pardon from Lord Angelo?
   CLAUDIO   The miserable have no other medicine
   But only hope.
   I've hope to live, and am prepared to die.
5 DUKE   Be absolute° for death; either death or life   *resolved*
   Shall thereby be the sweeter. Reason thus with life:
   If I do lose thee, I do lose a thing
   That none but fools would keep. A breath thou art,
   Servile to all the skyey influences[1]

3.1 Location: The prison.   1. Subject to all the influences of the heavenly bodies.

10	That dost this habitation where thou keep'st°	*lives*
	Hourly afflict. Merely° thou art death's fool,°	*Utterly / dupe*
	For him thou labor'st by thy flight to shun,	
	And yet runn'st toward him still.° Thou art not noble,	*always*
	For all th'accommodations° that thou bear'st	*material comforts*
15	Are nursed by baseness.[2] Thou'rt by no means valiant,	
	For thou dost fear the soft and tender fork°	*forked tongue*
	Of a poor worm.° Thy best of rest is sleep,	*snake*
	And that thou oft provok'st,° yet grossly fear'st	*summons*
	Thy death, which is no more. Thou art not thyself,°	*self-contained*
20	For thou exists on many a thousand grains	
	That issue out of dust.° Happy thou art not,	*grow from the ground*
	For what thou hast not, still thou striv'st to get,	
	And what thou hast, forget'st. Thou art not certain,°	*stable*
	For thy complexion° shifts to strange effects	*temperament*
25	After° the moon. If thou art rich, thou'rt poor,[3]	*Following*
	For like an ass whose back with ingots bows,	
	Thou bear'st thy heavy riches but a journey,	
	And death unloads thee. Friend hast thou none.	
	For thine own bowels° which do call thee sire,	*offspring*
30	The mere effusion° of thy proper° loins,	*very emission / own*
	Do curse the gout, serpigo,° and the rheum°	*skin disease / congestion*
	For ending thee no sooner. Thou hast nor youth, nor age,	
	But as it were an after-dinner's sleep	
	Dreaming on both, for all thy blessèd youth	
35	Becomes as agèd° and doth beg the alms°	*as if old / for money*
	Of palsied eld;° and when thou art old and rich,	*old people*
	Thou hast neither heat,° affection, limb,° nor beauty	*desire / strength*
	To make thy riches pleasant. What's in this	
	That bears the name of life? Yet in this life	
40	Lie hid more thousand° deaths; yet death we fear,	*a thousand more*
	That makes these odds° all even.	*irregularities*

CLAUDIO   I humbly thank you.
> To sue° to live, I find I seek to die,   *ask*
> And seeking death find life.[4] Let it come on.

Enter ISABELLA.

ISABELLA   What ho! Peace here, grace, and good company.
45 PROVOST   Who's there? Come in; the wish deserves a welcome.
DUKE [*to* CLAUDIO]   Dear sir, ere long I'll visit you again.
CLAUDIO   Most holy sir, I thank you.
ISABELLA   My business is a word or two with Claudio.
PROVOST   And very welcome. Look, signor, here's your sister.
50 DUKE [*aside to* PROVOST]   Provost, a word with you.
PROVOST   As many as you please.
DUKE   Bring me to hear them speak where I may be concealed.
> > > > > [*Exeunt* DUKE *and* PROVOST.]

CLAUDIO   Now, sister, what's the comfort?
ISABELLA   Why,
55   As all comforts are: most good, most good indeed.

---

2. Are grown from plants and animals; made by lower-class people.
3. From Revelation 3:17: "For thou sayest, I am rich and increased with goods, and have need of nothing, and knowest not how thou art wretched and misera-ble, and poor, and blind, and naked."
4. Echoing Matthew 16:25: "For whosoever will save his life, shall lose it: and whosoever shall lose his life for my sake, shall find it."

Lord Angelo, having affairs to heaven,
Intends you for his swift ambassador,
Where you shall be an everlasting ledger.°   *resident ambassador*
Therefore your best appointment° make with speed;   *preparation*
Tomorrow you set on.°   *forward*

60 CLAUDIO   Is there no remedy?
ISABELLA   None but such remedy as, to save a head,
To cleave a heart in twain.
CLAUDIO   But is there any?
ISABELLA   Yes, brother, you may live.
There is a devilish mercy in the judge,
65 If you'll implore it, that will free your life,
But fetter you till death.
CLAUDIO   Perpetual durance?°   *imprisonment*
ISABELLA   Ay, just,° perpetual durance; a restraint,   *exactly so*
Though all the world's vastidity° you had,   *vastness*
To a determined scope.[5]
CLAUDIO   But in what nature?
70 ISABELLA   In such a one as, you consenting to't,
Would bark[6] your honor from that trunk° you bear   *body; tree trunk*
And leave you naked.
CLAUDIO   Let me know the point.
ISABELLA   Oh, I do fear thee, Claudio, and I quake
Lest thou a feverous° life shouldst entertain,°   *feverish / cherish*
75 And six or seven winters more respect°   *esteem*
Than a perpetual honor. Dar'st thou die?
The sense° of death is most in apprehension,°   *awareness / anticipation*
And the poor beetle that we tread upon
In corporal sufferance° finds a pang as great   *bodily suffering*
As when a giant dies.
80 CLAUDIO   Why give you me this shame?
Think you I can a resolution fetch°   *derive*
From flow'ry° tenderness? If I must die,   *florid*
I will encounter darkness as a bride
And hug it in mine arms.
85 ISABELLA   There spake my brother; there my father's grave
Did utter forth a voice. Yes, thou must die.
Thou art too noble to conserve a life
In base appliances.° This outward-sainted deputy,   *ignoble means*
Whose settled° visage and deliberate word   *composed*
90 Nips youth i'th' head,[7] and follies doth enew°   *drive into hiding*
As falcon doth the fowl, is yet a devil.
His filth within being cast,[8] he would appear
A pond as deep as hell.
CLAUDIO   The precise[9] Angelo?
ISABELLA   Oh, 'tis the cunning livery of hell,
95 The damn'dest body to invest° and cover   *dress*
In precise guards!° Dost thou think, Claudio,   *trimmings*
If I would yield him my virginity

---

5. Constricted space (by the awareness of the means by which he had been saved).
6. Strip off, like bark from a tree.
7. As a hawk kills a bird.
8. Cleaned out; measured; vomited.

9. **TEXTUAL COMMENT** F has the nonsense word "prenzie" here and in line 96; some editors emend (as here) to "precise," others to "princely" or "priestly." See Digital Edition TC 4.

Thou mightst be freed?

CLAUDIO   O heavens, it cannot be.

ISABELLA   Yes, he would give't thee, from this rank offense,
100   So to offend him still.[1] This night's the time
       That I should do what I abhor to name,
       Or else thou diest tomorrow.

CLAUDIO   Thou shalt not do't.

ISABELLA   Oh, were it but my life,
       I'd throw it down for your deliverance
       As frankly° as a pin.   freely

105 CLAUDIO   Thanks, dear Isabel.

ISABELLA   Be ready, Claudio, for your death tomorrow.

CLAUDIO   Yes. Has he affections in him,
       That thus can make him bite the law by th' nose°   flout the law
       When he would force it? Sure it is no sin,
110   Or of the deadly seven[2] it is the least.

ISABELLA   Which is the least?

CLAUDIO   If it were damnable, he being so wise,
       Why would he for the momentary trick°   trifle
       Be perdurably fined?° O Isabel—   eternally punished

115 ISABELLA   What says my brother?

CLAUDIO   Death is a fearful thing.

ISABELLA   And shamèd life a hateful.

CLAUDIO   Ay, but to die, and go we know not where,
       To lie in cold obstruction° and to rot,   congealment
120   This sensible warm motion° to become   conscious warm body
       A kneaded clod; and the delighted° spirit   expansive; released
       To bathe in fiery floods or to reside
       In thrilling° region of thick-ribbèd ice,   bitterly cold
       To be imprisoned in the viewless° winds   unseeing; invisible
125   And blown with restless violence round about
       The pendent° world, or to be worse than worst   hanging in space
       Of those that lawless and incertain thought[3]
       Imagine howling—'tis too horrible!
       The weariest and most loathed worldly life
130   That age, ache, penury, and imprisonment
       Can lay on nature, is a paradise
       To what we fear of death.

ISABELLA   Alas, alas.

CLAUDIO   Sweet sister, let me live.
       What sin you do to save a brother's life,
135   Nature dispenses with° the deed so far   excuses
       That it becomes a virtue.

ISABELLA   O you beast!
       O faithless coward, O dishonest wretch!
       Wilt thou be made a man° out of my vice?   given life
       Is't not a kind of incest to take life
140   From thine own sister's shame? What should I think?
       Heaven shield° my mother played my father fair,   forbid
       For such a warpèd slip of wilderness°   shoot of wild stock

---

1. *give't thee . . . still:* grant you freedom in return for his foul sin, so that you might continue offending him.
2. Seven deadly sins (pride, lechery, envy, anger, covetousness, gluttony, and sloth).
3. Of those whom unbridled and dubious conjecture.

Ne'er issued from his blood. Take my defiance;°   *rejection*
Die, perish! Might but my bending down
145   Reprieve thee from thy fate, it should proceed.
I'll pray a thousand prayers for thy death,
No word to save thee.
CLAUDIO   Nay, hear me, Isabel—
ISABELLA   Oh, fie, fie, fie!
Thy sin's not accidental,° but a trade.°   *casual / habit*
150   Mercy to thee would prove itself a bawd.[4]
'Tis best that thou diest quickly.
CLAUDIO   Oh, hear me, Isabella—
     [*Enter* DUKE, *disguised as a friar.*]
DUKE   Vouchsafe a word, young sister, but one word.
ISABELLA   What is your will?
155   DUKE   Might you dispense with your leisure,° I would by and   *spare the time*
by have some speech with you. The satisfaction I would
require is likewise your own benefit.
ISABELLA   I have no superfluous leisure; my stay must be stolen out of other affairs. But I will attend° you a while.   *await*
160   DUKE [*aside to* CLAUDIO]   Son, I have overheard what hath
passed between you and your sister. Angelo had never the
purpose to corrupt her; only he hath made an assay° of her   *a trial*
virtue, to practice his judgment with the disposition of
natures. She, having the truth of honor° in her, hath made   *chastity*
165   him that gracious° denial which he is most glad to receive. I   *virtuous*
am confessor to Angelo, and I know this to be true; there-
fore prepare yourself to death. Do not satisfy your resolu-
tion° with hopes that are fallible. Tomorrow you must die.   *buck yourself up*
Go to your knees and make ready.
170   CLAUDIO   Let me ask my sister pardon. I am so out of love with
life that I will sue to be rid of it.
DUKE   Hold you there.° Farewell.   [*Exit* CLAUDIO.]   *Remain so resolved*
           Provost, a word with you.
     [*Enter* PROVOST.]
PROVOST   What's your will, father?
DUKE   That now you are come, you will be gone. Leave me a
175   while with the maid. My mind° promises with my habit,° no   *intention / friar's gown*
loss shall touch her by my company.
PROVOST   In good time.°   *Exit.*   *Very well*
DUKE   The hand that hath made you fair hath made you good.
The goodness[5] that is cheap in beauty makes beauty brief in
180   goodness, but grace,° being the soul of your complexion,°   *virtue / constitution*
shall keep the body of it ever fair. The assault that Angelo
hath made to you, fortune hath conveyed to my understand-
ing; and but that frailty hath examples° for his falling, I   *precedents*
should wonder at Angelo. How will you do to content this
185   substitute° and to save your brother?   *deputy*
ISABELLA   I am now going to resolve him. I had rather my
brother die by the law than my son should be unlawfully born.
But oh, how much is the good Duke deceived in Angelo! If

---

4. By facilitating sinful behavior.
5. The goodness that is little valued by the beautiful makes beauty short-lived.

ever he return, and I can speak to him, I will open my lips in
190 vain or discover° his government.[6]　　　　　　　　　　　　　　　*expose*

DUKE　That shall not be much amiss. Yet, as the matter now
stands, he will avoid° your accusation: he "made trial of you"　　　*quash*
only. Therefore fasten your ear on my advisings; to the love
I have in doing good a remedy presents itself. I do make
195 myself believe that you may most uprighteously do a poor
wronged lady a merited benefit; redeem your brother from
the angry law; do no stain to your own gracious person; and
much please the absent Duke, if peradventure he shall ever
return to have hearing of this business.

200 ISABELLA　Let me hear you speak farther. I have spirit to do
anything that appears not foul in the truth of my spirit.

DUKE　Virtue is bold, and goodness never fearful. Have you
not heard speak of Mariana, the sister of Frederick, the
great soldier who miscarried° at sea?　　　　　　　　　　　　*perished*

205 ISABELLA　I have heard of the lady, and good words went with
her name.

DUKE　She should this Angelo have married; was affianced to
her oath, and the nuptial appointed;° between which time of　　*wedding day set*
the contract and limit° of the solemnity, her brother Freder-　　*date*
210 ick was wrecked at sea, having in that perished vessel the
dowry of his sister. But mark how heavily this befell to the
poor gentlewoman. There she lost a noble and renowned
brother, in his love toward her ever most kind and natural;
with him, the portion and sinew° of her fortune, her mar-　　*mainstay*
215 riage dowry; with both, her combinate° husband, this well-　　*betrothed*
seeming Angelo.

ISABELLA　Can this be so? Did Angelo so leave her?

DUKE　Left her in her tears, and dried not one of them with
his comfort; swallowed° his vows whole, pretending° in her　　*retracted / alleging*
220 discoveries of dishonor;° in few, bestowed her on her own　　*unchastity*
lamentation, which she yet wears for his sake; and he, a
marble° to her tears, is washed with them but relents not.　　*impervious*

ISABELLA　What a merit were it in death to take this poor
maid from the world! What corruption in this life, that it
225 will let this man live? But how out of this can she avail?°　　*profit*

DUKE　It is a rupture that you may easily heal, and the cure of
it not only saves your brother, but keeps you from dishonor
in doing it.

ISABELLA　Show me how, good father.

230 DUKE　This forenamed maid hath yet in her the continuance
of her first affection.° His unjust unkindness, that in all rea-　　*passion*
son should have quenched her love, hath, like an impedi-
ment in the current, made it more violent and unruly. Go you
to Angelo, answer his requiring with a plausible obedience,
235 agree with his demands to the point.° Only refer yourself to　　*exactly*
this advantage: first, that your stay with him may not be long;
that the time may have all shadow° and silence in it; and the　　*darkness*
place answer to convenience. This being granted in course,
and now follows all: we shall advise this wronged maid to
240 stead up° your appointment, go in your place. If the encoun-　　*fulfill*

6. Conduct; mode of governing.

ter acknowledge itself° hereafter, it may compel him to her   *becomes known*
recompense. And here, by this is your brother saved, your
honor untainted, the poor Mariana advantaged, and the corrupt deputy scaled.[7] The maid will I frame° and make fit for   *prepare*
245 his attempt. If you think well to carry this as you may, the
doubleness of the benefit defends the deceit from reproof.
What think you of it?

ISABELLA The image of it gives me content already, and I
trust it will grow to a most prosperous perfection.°   *completion*
250 DUKE It lies much in your holding up. Haste you speedily to
Angelo. If for this night he entreat you to his bed, give him
promise of satisfaction. I will presently to Saint Luke's.
There at the moated grange° resides this dejected[8] Mariana.   *country house*
At that place call upon me, and dispatch° with Angelo that it   *settle*
255 may be quickly.

ISABELLA I thank you for this comfort. Fare you well, good
father.   *Exit.*

     Enter ELBOW, CLOWN, *and Officers.*[9]

ELBOW Nay, if there be no remedy for it, but that you will
needs° buy and sell men and women like beasts, we shall   *you must*
260 have all the world drink brown and white bastard.°   *sweet wine (with pun)*
DUKE O heavens, what stuff is here?
CLOWN 'Twas never merry world since of two usuries[1] the
merriest was put down, and the worser allowed by order of
law[2] a furred gown° to keep him warm; and furred with fox   *(worn by usurers)*
265 and lambskins, too, to signify that craft,° being richer than   *cunning*
innocency, stands for the facing.[3]
ELBOW Come your way, sir. Bless you, good Father Friar.[4]
DUKE And you, good brother father. What offense hath this
man made you, sir?
270 ELBOW Marry, sir, he hath offended the law; and, sir, we take
him to be a thief too, sir; for we have found upon him, sir, a
strange picklock,° which we have sent to the deputy.   *skeleton key*
DUKE Fie, sirrah, a bawd,° a wicked bawd!   *pimp*
The evil that thou causest to be done,
275 That is thy means to live. Do thou but think
What 'tis to cram a maw or clothe a back
From such a filthy vice; say to thyself,
From their abominable and beastly touches
I drink, I eat, array° myself, and live.   *dress*
280 Canst thou believe thy living is a life,
So stinkingly depending?° Go mend, go mend.   *dependent*
CLOWN Indeed, it does stink in some sort, sir, but yet, sir, I
would prove—
DUKE Nay, if the devil have given thee proofs for sin
285 Thou wilt prove° his. Take him to prison, officer.   *prove to be*
Correction° and instruction must both work   *Punishment*
Ere this rude° beast will profit.°   *barbarous / improve*

---

7. Overreached; weighed (and found wanting).
8. Depressed; rejected.
9. The rest of the scene takes place on the street.
Some editors begin a new scene here, though the
Duke remains onstage.
1. Lending of money at interest; prostitution.

2. A statute of 1570 allowed interest of 10 percent or
less.
3. Is used to trim the garment; displays itself to the
world.
4. Absurd, since "friar" means "brother"; hence the
Duke's reply.

ELBOW   He must before the deputy, sir, he has given him
warning. The deputy cannot abide a whoremaster. If he be a
290   whoremonger, and comes before him, he were as good go a
mile on his errand.[5]

DUKE   That° we were all, as some would seem to be,   *Would that*
Free from our faults, as faults from seeming free!°   *free from seeming*

ELBOW   His neck will come to° your waist—a cord,[6] sir.   *end up like*
Enter LUCIO.

295   CLOWN   I spy comfort, I cry bail! Here's a gentleman, and a
friend of mine.

LUCIO   How now, noble Pompey? What, at the wheels of Caesar? Art thou led in triumph?[7] What, is there none of Pygmalion's images[8] newly made woman to be had now, for
300   putting the hand in the pocket and extracting clutched?[9]
What reply, ha? What sayest thou to this tune, matter, and
method?[1] Is't not drowned i'th' last rain,[2] ha? What sayest
thou, trot?° Is the world as it was, man? Which is the way? Is   *bawd*
it sad and few words? Or how? The trick° of it?   *style*

305   DUKE   Still° thus and thus; still worse!   *Always*

LUCIO   How doth my dear morsel, thy mistress? Procures she
still? Ha?

CLOWN   Troth, sir, she hath eaten up° all her beef,° and she is   *worn out / prostitutes*
herself in the tub.[3]

310   LUCIO   Why, 'tis good! It is the right of it, it must be so. Ever
your fresh whore and your powdered[4] bawd, an unshunned°   *unavoidable*
consequence; it must be so. Art going to prison, Pompey?

CLOWN   Yes, faith, sir.

LUCIO   Why, 'tis not amiss, Pompey. Farewell. Go say I sent
315   thee thither. For debt, Pompey, or how?

ELBOW   For being a bawd, for being a bawd.

LUCIO   Well, then, imprison him. If imprisonment be the due
of a bawd, why, 'tis his right. Bawd is he doubtless, and of
antiquity° too, bawd born.° Farewell, good Pompey. Com-   *long standing / at birth*
320   mend me to the prison, Pompey; you will turn good hus-
band° now, Pompey; you will keep the house.   *householder*

CLOWN   I hope, sir, your good worship will be my bail?

LUCIO   No, indeed will I not, Pompey, it is not the wear.° I will   *fashion*
pray, Pompey, to increase your bondage; if you take it not
325   patiently, why, your mettle° is the more. Adieu, trusty Pom-   *spirit; shackles*
pey. Bless you, Friar.

DUKE   And you.

LUCIO   Does Bridget paint° still, Pompey, ha?   *use cosmetics*

ELBOW   Come your ways, sir, come.

330   CLOWN   You will not bail me then, sir?

LUCIO   Then, Pompey, nor now. What news abroad,° Friar?   *in the world*
What news?

---

5. *he were . . . errand:* he would be better doing anything rather than that.
6. Encircled by a rope, as the friar's cord encircles
his waist.
7. After Roman victories, vanquished generals were
paraded behind the chariot wheels of their
conquerors.
8. In classical legend, the sculptor Pygmalion fell in
love with one of his statues, who was given life by

Venus, the goddess of love; with a play on "become a
woman" (lose one's virginity).
9. Clenched, with money for bail.
1. This style, topic, and sequence of thought.
2. Overwhelmed with recent misfortune.
3. Pickling tub for preserving ("powdering") beef;
sweating tub for curing venereal disease.
4. Pickled; covered with cosmetic powder.

ELBOW   Come your ways, sir, come.

LUCIO   Go to kennel, Pompey,[5] go.

[*Exeunt* ELBOW, CLOWN, *and Officers.*]

335   What news, Friar, of the Duke?

DUKE   I know none. Can you tell me of any?

LUCIO   Some say he is with the Emperor of Russia; other   *some others*
some,° he is in Rome; but where is he, think you?

DUKE   I know not where, but wheresoever, I wish him well.

340 LUCIO   It was a mad fantastical trick° of him to steal from the   *eccentric caprice*
state and usurp the beggary he was never born to. Lord Angelo
dukes it° well in his absence; he puts transgression to't.[6]   *plays the Duke*

DUKE   He does well in't.

LUCIO   A little more lenity to lechery would do no harm in
345 him. Something too crabbed° that way, Friar.   *Somewhat too harsh*

DUKE   It is too general a vice, and severity must cure it.

LUCIO   Yes, in good sooth, the vice is of a great° kindred, it is   *an extensive; powerful*
well allied;° but it is impossible to extirp° it quite, Friar, till   *connected / extirpate*
eating and drinking be put down. They say this Angelo was
350 not made by man and woman after this downright[7] way of
creation. Is it true, think you?

DUKE   How should he be made then?

LUCIO   Some report a sea-maid° spawned him; some, that he   *mermaid*
was begot between two stockfishes.° But it is certain that   *dried fish*
355 when he makes water, his urine is congealed ice; that I know
to be true. And he is a motion generative,[8] that's infallible.°   *certain*

DUKE   You are pleasant,° sir, and speak apace.°   *merry / unrestrainedly*

LUCIO   Why, what a ruthless thing is this in him, for the rebellion of a codpiece[9] to take away the life of a man? Would the
360 Duke that is absent have done this? Ere he would have
hanged a man for the getting° a hundred bastards, he would   *begetting*
have paid for the nursing a thousand. He had some feeling of
the sport, he knew the service,° and that instructed him to   *(of prostitution)*
mercy.

365 DUKE   I never heard the absent Duke much detected° for   *accused*
women; he was not inclined that way.

LUCIO   O sir, you are deceived.

DUKE   'Tis not possible.

LUCIO   Who, not the Duke? Yes, your beggar of fifty, and his
370 use° was to put a ducat in her clack-dish.[1] The Duke had   *custom*
crotchets° in him. He would be drunk, too, that let me inform   *odd notions*
you.

DUKE   You do him wrong, surely.

LUCIO   Sir, I was an inward° of his. A shy fellow was the Duke,   *intimate*
375 and I believe I know the cause of his withdrawing.

DUKE   What, I prithee, might be the cause?

LUCIO   No, pardon. 'Tis a secret must be locked within the
teeth and the lips. But this I can let you understand, the
greater file of the subject° held the Duke to be wise.   *majority of the people*

380 DUKE   Wise? Why, no question but he was.

---

5. "Pompey" was a common name for a dog.   8. An impotent puppet.
6. He prosecutes lawbreaking vigorously.   9. Padded pouch worn over a man's breeches.
7. In accordance with this straightforward.   1. Begging bowl (with sexual innuendo).

LUCIO   A very superficial, ignorant, unweighing° fellow.   *injudicious*
DUKE   Either this is envy° in you, folly, or mistaking. The very   *malice*
   stream° of his life, and the business he hath helmed,° must   *course / steered*
   upon a warranted need° give him a better proclamation.°   *necessarily / reputation*
385   Let him be but testimonied° in his own bringings forth,°   *proven / public actions*
   and he shall appear to the envious a scholar, a statesman,
   and a soldier. Therefore you speak unskillfully,° or, if your   *ignorantly*
   knowledge be more, it is much darkened in your malice.
LUCIO   Sir, I know him, and I love him.
390   DUKE   Love talks with better knowledge, and knowledge with
   dearer love.
LUCIO   Come, sir. I know what I know.
DUKE   I can hardly believe that, since you know not what you
   speak. But if ever the Duke return, as our prayers are he
395   may, let me desire you to make your answer before him. If it
   be honest you have spoke, you have courage to maintain it. I
   am bound to call upon° you, and I pray you, your name.   *accuse*
LUCIO   Sir, my name is Lucio, well known to the Duke.
DUKE   He shall know you better, sir, if I may live to report you.
400   LUCIO   I fear you not.
DUKE   Oh, you hope the Duke will return no more, or you
   imagine me too unhurtful an opposite.° But indeed I can do   *adversary*
   you little harm. You'll forswear this again.°   *at another time*
LUCIO   I'll be hanged first. Thou art deceived in me, Friar. But
405   no more of this. Canst thou tell if Claudio die tomorrow, or
   no?
DUKE   Why should he die, sir?
LUCIO   Why? For filling a bottle with a tundish.° I would the   *funnel (with innuendo)*
   Duke we talk of were returned again. This ungenitured
410   agent° will unpeople the province with continency. Sparrows[2]   *sexless deputy*
   must not build in his house eaves, because they are lecher-   *(proverbially lustful)*
   ous. The Duke yet would have dark deeds darkly answered;°   *secretly requited*
   he would never bring them to light. Would he were returned.
   Marry, this Claudio is condemned for untrussing.° Farewell,   *undoing his leggings*
415   good Friar, I prithee pray for me. The Duke, I say to thee
   again, would eat mutton on Fridays.[3] He's now past it, and yet
   I say to thee he would mouth° with a beggar, though she   *kiss*
   smelt° brown bread and garlic.[4] Say that I said so! Farewell.   *smelled of*
                                                                                        Exit.
DUKE   No might, nor greatness in mortality°   *mortal existence*
420   Can censure scape.° Back-wounding calumny[5]   *escape censure*
   The whitest virtue strikes. What king so strong,
   Can tie the gall° up in the slanderous tongue?   *rancor*
   But who comes here?
      Enter ESCALUS, PROVOST, BAWD[, *and Officers*].
ESCALUS   Go, away with her to prison.
425   BAWD   Good my lord, be good to me; your honor is accounted
   a merciful man, good my lord.

---

2. Sparrows were proverbially lustful.
3. *mutton*: prostitute (slang); it was forbidden to eat
meat on Fridays.

4. The food of the poor.
5. *Back-wounding calumny*: slander ("calumny") is
cowardly because it is not said to the victim's face.

ESCALUS Double and treble admonition,[6] and still forfeit in
the same kind!° This would make mercy swear[7] and play the   *way*
tyrant.

430 PROVOST A bawd of eleven years' continuance, may it please
your honor.

BAWD My lord, this is one Lucio's information° against me.   *accusation*
Mistress Kate Keepdown was with child by him in the
Duke's time, he promised her marriage. His child is a year

435 and a quarter old come Philip and Jacob.[8] I have kept it
myself, and see how he goes about° to abuse° me.   *out of his way / injure*

ESCALUS That fellow is a fellow of much license. Let him be
called before us. Away with her to prison, go to, no more
words.   *[Exeunt* BAWD *and Officers.]*

440 Provost, my brother° Angelo will not be altered: Claudio   *colleague*
must die tomorrow. Let him be furnished with divines and
have all charitable preparation.[9] If my brother wrought by°   *acted according to*
my pity, it should not be so with him.

PROVOST So please you, this friar hath been with him and

445 advised him for th'entertainment° of death.   *acceptance*

ESCALUS Good even, good father.

DUKE Bliss and goodness on you.

ESCALUSLUS Of whence are you?

DUKE Not of this country, though my chance° is now   *fortune*

450 To use it for my time.° I am a brother   *dwell here at present*
Of gracious order, late come from the See°   *Vatican*
In special business from his Holiness.

ESCALUS What news abroad i'th' world?

DUKE None, but that there is so great a fever on goodness that

455 the dissolution of it must cure it.[1] Novelty is only in request,°   *alone in demand*
and it is as dangerous to be aged in° any kind of course, as it   *habituated to*
is virtuous to be constant in any undertaking. There is
scarce truth° enough alive to make societies secure, but   *honesty; loyalty*
security[2] enough to make fellowships° accursed. Much   *partnerships*

460 upon° this riddle runs the wisdom of the world. This news is   *According to*
old enough, yet it is every day's news. I pray you, sir, of what
disposition was the Duke?

ESCALUS One that above all other strifes contended especially
to know himself.[3]

465 DUKE What pleasure was he given to?

ESCALUS Rather rejoicing to see another merry, than merry
at anything which professed° to make him rejoice. A gentle-   *attempted*
man of all temperance. But leave we him to his events,° with   *affairs*
a prayer they may prove prosperous, and let me desire to

470 know° how you find Claudio prepared. I am made to under-   *ask*
stand that you have lent him visitation.°   *visited him*

---

6. Exceeding that recommended by Paul in Titus
3:10: "Reject him that is an heretic, after once or
twice admonition."
7. Varying the proverbial "make a saint swear."
8. May 1 was the Feast of St. Philip and St. James
(Jacob), but also the time of sexually licentious May
Day festivities, when the child was presumably
conceived.

9. Spiritual preparation enjoined by Christian
charity.
1. *there is . . . it:* that is, goodness is so sick that only
death will "cure" it.
2. Financial bonds liable to forfeit; blind trustfulness. *societies:* association with others.
3. "Know thyself" was proverbial advice.

DUKE He professes to have received no sinister measure° from
 his judge, but most willingly humbles himself to the deter-
 mination° of justice. Yet had he framed° to himself, by the
475 instruction of his frailty, many deceiving promises of life,
 which I by my good leisure° have discredited to him, and
 now is he resolved to die.

ESCALUS You have paid the heavens your function, and the
 prisoner the very debt of your calling.[4] I have labored for the
480 poor gentleman to the extremest shore° of my modesty, but
 my brother justice have I found so severe that he hath forced
 me to tell him, he is indeed Justice.[5]

DUKE If his own life answer° the straitness° of his proceeding,
 it shall become him well; wherein if he chance to fail he hath
485 sentenced° himself.

ESCALUS I am going to visit the prisoner. Fare you well.

DUKE Peace be with you.   *Exit* ESCALUS.
 He who the sword of heaven[6] will bear
 Should be as holy as severe;
490 Pattern in himself to know,
 Grace to stand, and virtue, go;[7]
 More nor less to others paying
 Than by self-offenses° weighing.
 Shame to him whose cruel striking
495 Kills for faults of his own liking;
 Twice treble shame on Angelo
 To weed my vice[8] and let his grow.
 Oh, what may man within him hide,
 Though angel on the outward side?
500 How may likeness made in crimes,[9]
 Making practice on the times,
 To draw with idle spiders' strings
 Most ponderous and substantial things?[1]
 Craft against vice I must apply.
505 With Angelo tonight shall lie
 His old betrothèd, but despisèd;
 So disguise shall by th' disguisèd[2]
 Pay with falsehood false exacting,
 And perform an old contracting.   *Exit.*

4.1

Enter MARIANA *and* BOY *singing.*

BOY [*sings*] Take, oh, take those lips away
    That so sweetly were forsworn,°
    And those eyes, the break of day,
    Lights° that do mislead° the morn;

Right margin glosses:

unjust treatment

sentence / imagined

gradually

utmost limit

correspond to / strictness

condemned

his own offenses

perjured

Suns / falsely guide

---

4. You have repaid the heavens for giving you your vocation, and given the prisoner all he can expect of a friar.
5. Absolute justice personified.
6. The authority of a ruler, conferred by God.
7. When to stand firm, and when to take action (?).
8. The Duke speaks as a representative sinner.
9. How can the similarity between Claudio's and Angelo's offenses . . . (see also note 1).
1. *To draw . . . things:* the law was proverbially compared to a spider's web, which caught small insects

but which large insects could break through. *idle:* ineffectual. TEXTUAL COMMENT The text of 500–503 is clearly corrupt, but it is not clear how to fix it, so *The Norton Shakespeare* prints the passage as it appears in F. For a discussion of the problem, see Digital Edition TC 5.
2. Mariana, "disguised" as Isabella.
4.1 Location: Mariana's house. Probably Mariana and the Boy are "discovered" by drawing back a curtain to reveal the characters within an alcove at the back of the stage.

5	But my kisses bring again, bring again,°	*return*
	Seals of love, but sealed in vain, sealed in vain.	

Enter DUKE [*disguised as a friar*].

	MARIANA Break off thy song and haste thee quick away.	
	Here comes a man of comfort whose advice	
	Hath often stilled my brawling° discontent. [*Exit* BOY.]	*clamorous*
10	—I cry you mercy,° sir, and well could wish	*beg your pardon*
	You had not found me here so musical.	
	Let me excuse me, and believe me so:°	*in this*
	My mirth it much displeased, but pleased my woe.[1]	
	DUKE 'Tis good, though music oft hath such a charm°	*magic spell*
15	To make bad good° and good provoke to harm.	*bad appear good*
	I pray you tell me, hath anybody inquired for me here today?	
	Much upon° this time have I promised here to meet.	*At about*
	MARIANA You have not been inquired after. I have sat here	
	all day.	

Enter ISABELLA [*carrying two keys*].

20	DUKE I do constantly° believe you. The time is come even	*assuredly*
	now. I shall crave your forbearance° a little. Maybe I will	*departure; patience*
	call upon you anon for some advantage to yourself.	
	MARIANA I am always bound to you. *Exit.*	
	DUKE [*to* ISABELLA] Very well met, and welcome.	
25	What is the news from this good deputy?	
	ISABELLA He hath a garden circummured° with brick,	*walled about*
	Whose western side is with a vineyard backed,	
	And to that vineyard is a planchèd° gate	*made of planks*
	That makes his opening with this bigger key.	
30	This other doth command a little door	
	Which from the vineyard to the garden leads.	
	There have I made my promise	
	Upon the heavy° middle of the night	*In the gloomy*
	To call upon him.	
35	DUKE But shall you on your knowledge° find this way?	*with this information*
	ISABELLA I have ta'en a due and wary note upon't.	
	With whispering and most guilty diligence,	
	In action all of precept,° he did show me	*With explanatory gestures*
	The way twice o'er.	
	DUKE Are there no other tokens°	*signs*
40	Between you 'greed concerning her observance?[2]	
	ISABELLA No. None but only a repair° i'th' dark,	*journey to the place*
	And that I have possessed° him my most° stay	*informed / longest*
	Can be but brief, for I have made him know	
	I have a servant comes with me along	
45	That stays upon° me, whose persuasion is	*waits for*
	I come about my brother.	
	DUKE 'Tis well borne up.°	*maintained*
	I have not yet made known to Mariana	
	A word of this. —What ho, within, come forth!	

Enter MARIANA.

	I pray you be acquainted with this maid.	
50	She comes to do you good.	
	ISABELLA I do desire the like.	

---

1. The music drove away mirth but nurtured melancholy.   2. That she (Mariana) must observe.

DUKE   Do you persuade yourself° that I respect you?   *believe*
MARIANA   Good friar, I know you do, and have so found it.
DUKE   Take then this your companion° by the hand,   *partner*
55   Who hath a story ready for your ear.
I shall attend your leisure,° but make haste,   *wait until you are ready*
The vaporous night approaches.
MARIANA   Will't please you walk aside?
               [*Exeunt* MARIANA *and* ISABELLA.]
DUKE   O place° and greatness! Millions of false° eyes   *rank / misjudging*
60   Are stuck° upon thee. Volumes of report°   *fixed / rumors*
Run with their false and most contrarious quest°   *misguided inquiry*
Upon thy doings. Thousand escapes° of wit   *sallies*
Make thee the father° of their idle dream°   *subject / fantasy*
And rack³ thee in their fancies.
               Enter MARIANA *and* ISABELLA.
                         —Welcome, how agreed?
65   ISABELLA   She'll take the enterprise upon her, father,
If you advise it.
DUKE   It is not my consent,
But my entreaty too.
ISABELLA   Little have you to say
When you depart from him, but soft and low,
"Remember now my brother."
MARIANA   Fear me not.⁴
70   DUKE   Nor, gentle daughter, fear you not at all.
He is your husband on a precontract.°   *formal betrothal*
To bring you thus together 'tis no sin,
Sith that° the justice of your title to him   *Since*
Doth flourish° the deceit. Come, let us go;   *give propriety to*
75   Our corn's to reap, for yet our tilth's° to sow.   *Exeunt.*   *tilled land*

4.2

               Enter PROVOST *and* CLOWN.
PROVOST   Come hither, sirrah. Can you cut off a man's head?
CLOWN   If the man be a bachelor, sir, I can. But if he be a
married man, he's his wife's head,¹ and I can never cut off a
woman's head.²
5   PROVOST   Come, sir, leave me° your snatches,° and yield me a   *stop / quips*
direct answer. Tomorrow morning are to die Claudio and
Barnardine. Here is in our prison a common executioner
who in his office lacks a helper. If you will take it on you to
assist him, it shall redeem you from your gyves.° If not, you   *fetters*
10   shall have your full time of imprisonment and your deliver-
ance with an unpitied° whipping, for you have been a noto-   *unmerciful*
rious bawd.
CLOWN   Sir, I have been an unlawful bawd time out of mind,
but yet I will be content to be a lawful hangman. I would be
15   glad to receive some instruction from my fellow partner.
PROVOST   What ho, Abhorson! Where's Abhorson there?
               Enter ABHORSON.
ABHORSON   Do you call, sir?

---

3. Misrepresent (literally, "torture by stretching").
4. Rely upon me; but the Duke takes "fear" in its
modern sense.
4.2 Location: The prison.

1. Alluding to Paul's doctrine that "the husband is
the wife's head," Ephesians 5:23.
2. Playing on "married woman's maidenhead," an
improbability.

PROVOST   Sirrah, here's a fellow will help you tomorrow in your execution. If you think it meet, compound with him by
20   the year,[3] and let him abide here with you; if not, use him for the present and dismiss him. He cannot plead his esti- mation° with you; he hath been a bawd.   *reputation*

ABHORSON   A bawd, sir? Fie upon him, he will discredit our mystery.[4]

25 PROVOST   Go to, sir, you weigh equally. A feather will turn the scale.   *Exit.*

CLOWN   Pray, sir, by your good favor°—for surely, sir, a good   *permission* favor° you have, but that you have a hanging look[5]—do you   *face* call, sir, your occupation a mystery?

30 ABHORSON   Ay, sir, a mystery.

CLOWN   Painting,[6] sir, I have heard say, is a mystery; and your whores, sir, being members of my occupation, using painting, do prove my occupation a mystery. But what mystery there should be in hanging, if I should be hanged I cannot imagine.

35 ABHORSON   Sir, it is a mystery.

CLOWN   Proof.

ABHORSON   Every true man's apparel fits your thief.[7]

CLOWN   If it be too little for your thief, your true man thinks it big enough.° If it be too big for your thief, your thief   *a big enough loss*
40   thinks it little enough.° So, every true man's apparel fits   *a small enough gain* your thief.

           Enter PROVOST.

PROVOST   Are you agreed?

CLOWN   Sir, I will serve him, for I do find your hangman is a more penitent trade than your bawd. He doth oftener ask
45   forgiveness.[8]

PROVOST   You, sirrah, provide your block and your ax tomorrow, four o'clock.

ABHORSON   Come on, bawd, I will instruct thee in my trade. Follow.

50 CLOWN   I do desire to learn, sir. And I hope, if you have occasion to use me for your own turn, you shall find me yare.° For truly, sir, for your kindness, I owe you a good   *skillful; eager* turn.[9]

PROVOST   Call hither Barnardine and Claudio.

             [Exeunt ABHORSON *and* CLOWN.]

55 Th'one has my pity, not a jot the other,
Being a murderer, though he were my brother.

           Enter CLAUDIO.

Look, here's the warrant, Claudio, for thy death.
'Tis now dead midnight, and by eight tomorrow
Thou must be made immortal. Where's Barnardine?

60 CLAUDIO   As fast locked up in sleep as guiltless labor
When it lies starkly° in the traveler's° bones.   *stiffly / worker's*
He will not wake.

---

3. Settle regular terms of employment with him.
4. Profession, requiring specialized skills and training.
5. Downcast expression; hangman's face.
6. Artist's occupation; use of cosmetics.
7. Abhorson implies that the thief assumes the character of an honest man by stealing his clothing; he

also suggests an analogy between the thief and the hangman, who was awarded the clothes of his victims.
8. Executioners customarily asked forgiveness of their victims before killing them.
9. Favor; turning off the scaffold.

PROVOST   Who can do good on him?
Well, go prepare yourself. [*Knocking within.*] But hark,
    what noise?
Heaven give your spirits comfort.   [*Exit* CLAUDIO.]
    [*Knocking within.*]
                                    By and by!
65 I hope it is some pardon or reprieve
    For the most gentle Claudio.
              Enter DUKE [*disguised as a friar*].
                          Welcome, Father.
DUKE   The best and wholesom'st spirits of the night
    Envelop you, good Provost! Who called here of late?
PROVOST   None since the curfew[1] rung.
70 DUKE   Not Isabel?
PROVOST   No.
DUKE   They will, then, ere't be long.
PROVOST   What comfort is for Claudio?
DUKE   There's some in hope.
75 PROVOST   It is a bitter° deputy.   *cruel*
DUKE   Not so, not so. His life is paralleled
    Even with the stroke and line[2] of his great justice.
    He doth with holy abstinence subdue
    That in himself which he spurs on his power
80 To qualify° in others. Were he mealed° with that   *moderate / stained*
    Which he corrects, then were he tyrannous,
    But this being so, he's just. [*Knocking within.*] Now are they
        come.   [*Exit* PROVOST.]
    This is a gentle provost. Seldom-when°   *Rarely*
    The steelèd° jailer is the friend of men.   *hard-hearted*
              [*Enter* PROVOST. *Knocking within.*]
85 How now? What noise? That spirit's possessed with haste
    That wounds th'unresisting postern° with these strokes.   *unyielding door*
PROVOST   There he° must stay until the officer   *(the messenger)*
    Arise to let him in. He° is called up.   *(the officer)*
DUKE   Have you no countermand for Claudio yet,
90 But he must die tomorrow?
PROVOST   None, sir, none.
DUKE   As near the dawning, Provost, as it is,
    You shall hear more ere morning.
PROVOST   Haply°   *Perhaps*
    You something know, yet I believe there comes
    No countermand. No such example° have we.   *precedent*
95 Besides, upon the very siege° of justice   *seat*
    Lord Angelo hath to the public ear
    Professed the contrary.
              Enter a MESSENGER.
DUKE   This is his lordship's man.
PROVOST   And here comes Claudio's pardon.[3]

---

1. Evening bell, rung at 9:00 P.M.
2. Exact course; also suggesting ax blows and hanging ropes.
3. TEXTUAL COMMENT Some editors have argued
that the end of line 97 makes more sense coming

from the Provost and that the Duke ought to utter
the following line. The Norton text retains the F
speech prefixes. For an account of the problem, see
Digital Edition TC 6.

MESSENGER My lord hath sent you this note, and by me this
further charge: that you swerve not from the smallest article
of it, neither in time, matter, or other circumstance. Good
morrow, for as I take it, it is almost day.

PROVOST I shall obey him.   [*Exit* MESSENGER.]

DUKE This is his pardon purchased by such sin
For which the pardoner himself is in.
Hence hath offense his° quick celerity   *its*
When it is born in high authority.
When vice makes mercy, mercy's so extended
That for the fault's love[4] is th'offender friended.°   *befriended*
—Now, sir, what news?

PROVOST I told you: Lord Angelo, belike thinking me remiss
in mine office, awakens me with this unwonted putting on,°   *urging*
methinks strangely, for he hath not used° it before.   *practiced*

DUKE Pray you, let's hear.

PROVOST [*reads the letter*][5] "Whatsoever you may hear to the
contrary, let Claudio be executed by four of the clock, and in
the afternoon Barnardine. For my better satisfaction, let me
have Claudio's head sent me by five. Let this be duly performed with a thought that more depends on it than we
must yet deliver.° Thus fail not to do your office, as you will   *make known*
answer it at your peril." What say you to this, sir?

DUKE What is that Barnardine who is to be executed in
th'afternoon?

PROVOST A Bohemian born, but here nursed up and bred, one
that is a prisoner nine years old.°   *nine years a prisoner*

DUKE How came it that the absent Duke had not either delivered him to his liberty or executed him? I have heard it was
ever his manner to do so.

PROVOST His friends still° wrought reprieves for him, and   *continually*
indeed his fact° till now in the government of Lord Angelo   *crime*
came not to an undoubtful° proof.   *a certain*

DUKE It is now apparent?

PROVOST Most manifest, and not denied by himself.

DUKE Hath he borne himself penitently in prison? How
seems he to be touched?°   *affected*

PROVOST A man that apprehends death no more dreadfully
but as a drunken sleep; careless, reckless, and fearless of
what's past, present, or to come; insensible of mortality, and
desperately mortal.[6]

DUKE He wants° advice.   *needs*

PROVOST He will hear none. He hath evermore had the liberty of the prison. Give him leave to escape hence, he would
not. Drunk many times a day, if not many days entirely°   *continuously*
drunk. We have very oft awaked him, as if to carry him to
execution, and showed him a seeming warrant for it. It hath
not moved him at all.

DUKE More of him anon. There is written in your brow, Provost, honesty and constancy. If I read it not truly, my ancient
skill beguiles me; but in the boldness° of my cunning,° I will   *confidence / skill*

---

4. For love of the fault.
5. TEXTUAL COMMENT In F, it is unclear who reads
the letter aloud; modern editors assign it to the Pro-

vost. The Textual Comment explores the significance
of the ambiguity. See Digital Edition TC 7.
6. Reckless of death, and in a state of mortal sin.

150   lay myself in hazard.[7] Claudio, whom here you have warrant
       to execute, is no greater forfeit to the law than Angelo who
       hath sentenced him. To make you understand this in a mani-
       fested effect,° I crave but four days' respite, for the which you   *clear demonstration*
       are to do me both a present° and a dangerous courtesy.°   *an immediate / favor*
155 PROVOST   Pray, sir, in what?
       DUKE   In the delaying death.
       PROVOST   Alack, how may I do it? Having the hour limited,
       and an express command, under penalty, to deliver his head
       in the view of Angelo? I may make my case as Claudio's to
160   cross° this in the smallest.   *oppose*
       DUKE   By the vow of mine order, I warrant you. If my instruc-
       tions may be your guide, let this Barnardine be this morning
       executed, and his head borne to Angelo.
       PROVOST   Angelo hath seen them both and will discover° the   *discern*
165   favor.
       DUKE   Oh, death's a great disguiser, and you may add to it.
       Shave the head, and tie the beard, and say it was the desire
       of the penitent to be so bared before his death; you know the
       course is common. If anything fall to you upon° this more   *as a result of*
170   than thanks and good fortune, by the saint whom I profess,[8]
       I will plead against it with my life.
       PROVOST   Pardon me, good Father; it is against my oath.
       DUKE   Were you sworn to the Duke, or to the deputy?
       PROVOST   To him and to his substitutes.
175 DUKE   You will think you have made no offense, if the Duke
       avouch° the justice of your dealing?   *vouch for*
       PROVOST   But what likelihood is in that?
       DUKE   Not a resemblance,° but a certainty. Yet since I see you   *likelihood*
       fearful that neither my coat,° integrity, nor persuasion can   *religious garb*
180   with ease attempt you,° I will go further than I meant, to   *win you over*
       pluck all fears out of you. Look you, sir, here is the hand and
       seal of the Duke. You know the character,° I doubt not, and   *handwriting*
       the signet is not strange to you.
       PROVOST   I know them both.
185 DUKE   The contents of this is the return of the Duke. You
       shall anon° over-read it at your pleasure, where you shall   *right away*
       find within these two days he will be here. This is a thing
       that Angelo knows not, for he this very day receives letters
       of strange tenor, perchance of the Duke's death, perchance
190   entering into some monastery, but by chance nothing of
       what is writ.° Look, th'unfolding star[9] calls up the shepherd.   *written here*
       Put not yourself into amazement° how these things should   *perplexity*
       be; all difficulties are but easy when they are known. Call
       your executioner, and off with Barnardine's head. I will
195   give him a present shrift[1] and advise him for a better
       place. Yet° you are amazed, but this° shall absolutely   *Still / (the letter)*
       resolve you.° Come away, it is almost clear dawn.   *Exeunt.*   *free you from doubt*

---

7. I will bet on it; I will put myself in peril.   safely release the sheep from the fold).
8. The patron saint of my order.   1. An immediate confession.
9. Morning star (which tells the shepherd he may

4.3

Enter CLOWN.

CLOWN I am as well acquainted here as I was in our house of
profession.[1] One would think it were Mistress Overdone's
own house, for here be many of her old customers. First,
here's young Master Rash. He's in for a commodity[2] of brown
paper and old ginger, nine score and seventeen pounds, of
which he made five marks ready money.[3] Marry, then ginger[4] was not much in request, for the old women were all
dead.[5] Then is there here one Master Caper,° at the suit of   *fashionable dance*
Master Three-pile[6] the mercer,° for some four suits of   *cloth dealer*
peach-colored satin which now peaches° him a beggar. Then   *impeaches; declares*
have we here young Dizzy, and young Master Deep-vow,
and Master Copper-spur, and Master Starve-lackey[7] the
rapier and dagger man,[8] and young Drop-heir[9] that killed
lusty Pudding,° and Master Forthright the tilter,° and brave   *Stuffed Guts / fencer*
Master Shoe-tie the great traveler,[1] and wild Half-can that
stabbed Pots,[2] and I think forty more, all great doers in our
trade, and are now "for the Lord's sake."[3]

Enter ABHORSON.

ABHORSON Sirrah, bring Barnardine hither.
CLOWN Master Barnardine, you must rise[4] and be hanged,
Master Barnardine.
ABHORSON What ho, Barnardine!
BARNARDINE [*within*] A pox o'your throats! Who makes that
noise there? What are you?
CLOWN Your friends, sir—the hangman. You must be so
good, sir, to rise and be put to death.
BARNARDINE [*within*] Away, you rogue, away, I am sleepy.
ABHORSON Tell him he must awake, and that quickly too.
CLOWN Pray, Master Barnardine, awake till you are executed
and sleep afterwards.
ABHORSON Go in to him and fetch him out.
CLOWN He is coming, sir, he is coming. I hear his straw rustle.

Enter BARNARDINE.

ABHORSON Is the ax upon the block, sirrah?
CLOWN Very ready, sir.
BARNARDINE How now, Abhorson? What's the news with you?
ABHORSON Truly, sir, I would desire you to clap into[5] your
prayers, for look you, the warrant's come.
BARNARDINE You rogue, I have been drinking all night. I am
not fitted for't.
CLOWN Oh, the better, sir. For he that drinks all night and is
hanged betimes° in the morning, may sleep the sounder all   *early*
the next day.

Enter DUKE [*disguised as a friar*].

4.3 Location: Scene continues.
1. Religious house ("nunnery" was slang for "brothel").
2. To evade the statutory limit on interest, usurers
would give borrowers part of their loan in practically
worthless "commodities," which they were supposed
to sell for ready money. *He's in for:* He's in for falling
into debt over.
3. Rash paid 197 pounds for the "commodity," a very
large sum, and sold it for about 3.3 pounds.
4. Used to make warming tonics.
5. Presumably victims of the 1603 plague, men-

tioned earlier by Mistress Overdone.
6. Richest sort of velvet.
7. One who fails to feed his servants.
8. Suggesting a reputation for brawling.
9. With a pun on dropping hair, a sign of syphilis.
1. Observer of foreign fashions (probably ironic).
2. Suggesting drinking cups.
3. The cry of prisoners begging from the prison grate.
Prisoners had to pay for their own food and lodging.
4. Get out of bed; mount the scaffold.
5. Immediately begin; join your hands for.

ABHORSON Look you, sir, here comes your ghostly° father. Do   *spiritual*
we jest now, think you?

DUKE Sir, induced by my charity, and hearing how hastily
45 you are to depart, I am come to advise you, comfort you, and
pray with you.

BARNARDINE Friar, not I. I have been drinking hard all night,
and I will have more time to prepare me, or they shall beat
out my brains with billets.° I will not consent to die this day,   *thick sticks*
50 that's certain.

DUKE O sir, you must, and therefore I beseech you look
forward on the journey you shall go.

BARNARDINE I swear I will not die today for any man's persuasion.

DUKE But hear you—

55 BARNARDINE Not a word. If you have anything to say to me,
come to my ward,° for thence will not I today.   *Exit.*   *cell*

                Enter PROVOST.

DUKE Unfit to live or die! O gravel° heart.   *(i.e., hard)*
After him, fellows, bring him to the block.

                [*Exeunt* POMPEY *and* ABHORSON.]

PROVOST Now, sir, how do you find the prisoner?

60 DUKE A creature unprepared, unmeet° for death,   *unfit*
And to transport° him in the mind he is   *execute (euphemistic)*
Were damnable.

PROVOST   Here in the prison, father,
There died this morning of a cruel fever
One Ragozine, a most notorious pirate,

65 A man of Claudio's years, his beard and head
Just of his color. What if we do omit°   *disregard*
This reprobate till he were well inclined,
And satisfy the deputy with the visage
Of Ragozine, more like to Claudio?

70 DUKE Oh, 'tis an accident that heaven provides.
Dispatch it presently. The hour draws on
Prefixed° by Angelo. See this be done,   *Designated in advance*
And sent according to command, whiles I
Persuade this rude° wretch willingly to die.   *uncivilized*

75 PROVOST This shall be done, good Father, presently,
But Barnardine must die this afternoon.
And how shall we continue° Claudio,   *maintain*
To save me from the danger that might come
If he were known alive?

DUKE   Let this be done:

80 Put them in secret holds,° both Barnardine   *cells*
And Claudio.
Ere twice the sun hath made his journal° greeting   *daily*
To yonder generation,[6] you shall find
Your safety manifested.

PROVOST   I am your free dependent.°   *willing servant*

85 DUKE Quick, dispatch, and send the head to Angelo.

                Exit PROVOST.

Now will I write letters to Angelo[7]—
The Provost he shall bear them—whose contents

6. That is, the people outside the prison.
7. "Angelo" may be an error for "Varrius," whom the Duke meets outside the city in 4.5.

Shall witness to him I am near at home,
And that by great injunctions° I am bound — *for compelling reasons*
90   To enter publicly. Him I'll desire
To meet me at the consecrated fount
A league below the city, and from thence,
By cold gradation° and well-balanced form, — *deliberate degrees*
We shall proceed with Angelo.

Enter PROVOST [*with a severed head*].

95   PROVOST   Here is the head. I'll carry it myself.
DUKE   Convenient° is it. Make a swift return, — *Suitable*
For I would commune° with you of such things — *confer*
That want no ear but yours.
PROVOST   I'll make all speed.   *Exit.*
ISABELLA (*within*)   Peace, ho, be here!
100 DUKE   The tongue of Isabel. She's come to know
If yet her brother's pardon be come hither.
But I will keep her ignorant of her good,
To make her heavenly comforts of° despair — *out of*
When it is least expected.

Enter ISABELLA.

105 ISABELLA   Ho, by your leave!
DUKE   Good morning to you, fair and gracious daughter.
ISABELLA   The better given me° by so holy a man. — *so greeted*
Hath yet the deputy sent my brother's pardon?
DUKE   He hath released him, Isabel, from the world.
110 His head is off and sent to Angelo.
ISABELLA   Nay, but it is not so.
DUKE   It is no other.
Show your wisdom, daughter, in your close° patience. — *silent*
ISABELLA   Oh, I will to° him, and pluck out his eyes! — *will go to*
DUKE   You shall not be admitted to his sight.
115 ISABELLA   Unhappy Claudio, wretched Isabel,
Injurious world, most damnèd Angelo!
DUKE   This nor° hurts him, nor profits you a jot. — *neither*
Forbear it therefore; give your cause° to heaven. — *grievance*
Mark what I say, which you shall find
120 By every syllable a faithful verity.
The Duke comes home tomorrow. Nay, dry your eyes.
One of our convent, and his confessor,
Gives me this instance.° Already he hath carried — *indication*
Notice to Escalus and Angelo,
125 Who do prepare to meet him at the gates
There to give up their power. If you can, pace° your wisdom — *train to walk*
In that good path that I would wish it go,
And you shall have your bosom° on this wretch, — *desire*
Grace° of the Duke, revenges to your heart, — *Favor*
And general honor.
130 ISABELLA   I am directed by you.
DUKE [*giving* ISABELLA *a letter*]   This letter then to Friar Peter
give;
'Tis that he sent me of the Duke's return.
Say, by this token, I desire his company
At Mariana's house tonight. Her cause and yours
135 I'll perfect° him withal, and he shall bring you — *fully instruct*
Before the Duke, and to the head of° Angelo — *and directly to*

Accuse him home and home.° For my poor self,   *to the utmost*
I am combinèd° by a sacred vow   *bound*
And shall be absent. Wend you° with this letter;   *Depart*
140 Command these fretting° waters from your eyes   *agitated; corrosive*
With a light heart; trust not my holy order
If I pervert° your course. —Who's here?   *lead astray*
    Enter LUCIO.
LUCIO   Good even.° —Friar, where's the Provost?   *evening*
DUKE   Not within, sir.
145 LUCIO   O pretty Isabella, I am pale at mine heart to see thine
eyes so red; thou must be patient. I am fain to dine and sup
with water and bran;[8] I dare not for my head fill my belly.
One fruitful° meal would set me to't.[9] But they say the Duke   *plentiful*
will be here tomorrow. By my troth, Isabel, I loved thy
150 brother. If the old fantastical° Duke of dark corners° had *capricious / secret places*
been at home, he had lived.
DUKE   Sir, the Duke is marvelous° little beholden to your   *remarkably*
reports, but the best is, he lives not° in them.   *is not to be found*
LUCIO   Friar, thou knowest not the Duke so well as I do: he's
155 a better woodman[1] than thou tak'st him for.
DUKE   Well, you'll answer° this one day. Fare ye well.   *account for*
LUCIO   Nay, tarry, I'll go along with thee. I can tell thee pretty
tales of the Duke.
DUKE   You have told me too many of him already, sir, if they
160 be true. If not true, none were enough.
LUCIO   I was once before him for getting a wench with child.
DUKE   Did you such a thing?
LUCIO   Yes, marry did I. But I was fain to forswear it. They
would else° have married me to the rotten medlar.[2]   *otherwise*
165 DUKE   Sir, your company is fairer° than honest. Rest you well. *more speciously pleasant*
LUCIO   By my troth, I'll go with thee to the lane's end. If
bawdy talk offend you, we'll have very little of it. Nay, Friar,
I am a kind of burr, I shall stick.   *Exeunt.*

4.4

Enter ANGELO *and* ESCALUS.
ESCALUS   Every letter he hath writ hath disvouched other.°   *repudiated the others*
ANGELO   In most uneven and distracted manner. His actions
show much like to madness. Pray heaven his wisdom be not
tainted.° And why meet him at the gates and reliver° our   *impaired / hand over*
5 authorities there?
ESCALUS   I guess not.
ANGELO   And why should we proclaim it in an hour before his
entering, that if any crave redress of injustice they should
exhibit° their petitions in the street?   *present*
10 ESCALUS   He shows his reason for that: to have a dispatch° of   *prompt settlement*
complaints, and to deliver us from devices° hereafter, which   *contrivances*
shall then have no power to stand against us.
ANGELO   Well, I beseech you, let it be proclaimed betimes°   *early*
i'th' morn. I'll call you at your house. Give notice to such
15 men of sort and suit° as are to meet him.   *rank and retinue*

8. Diet thought to suppress lust.
9. Would incite me to lechery.
1. Hunter (literally, of game; here, of women).

2. Kind of pear eaten when rotten; slang for "prostitute."
4.4 Location: Vienna.

ESCALUS   I shall, sir. Fare you well.   *Exit.*

ANGELO   Good night.

  This deed unshapes° me quite, makes me unpregnant°   *destroys / unready*

  And dull to all proceedings. A deflowered maid,

20 And by an eminent body[1] that enforced°   *exerted; raped*

  The law against it? But that her tender shame

  Will not proclaim against her maiden loss,°   *loss of virginity*

  How might she tongue° me? Yet reason dares her no,[2]   *reproach*

  For my authority bears so far credent bulk[3]

25 That no particular° scandal once can touch   *private; single*

  But it confounds° the breather. He should have lived,   *confutes; overthrows*

  Save that his riotous youth with dangerous sense°   *sensibility; sensuality*

  Might in the times to come have ta'en revenge

  By° so receiving a dishonored life   *Because of*

30 With ransom of such shame. Would yet he had lived.

  Alack, when once our grace we have forgot,

  Nothing goes right. We would, and we would not.   *Exit.*

4.5

Enter DUKE [*as himself*] *and Friar* PETER.

DUKE   These letters at fit time deliver me.

  The Provost knows our purpose and our plot.

  The matter being afoot, keep° your instruction   *observe*

  And hold you ever to our special drift,°   *purpose*

5 Though sometimes you do blench° from this to that   *swerve*

  As cause doth minister.° Go call at Flavius' house   *serve*

  And tell him where I stay. Give the like notice

  To Valencius, Rowland, and to Crassus,

  And bid them bring the trumpets° to the gate.   *trumpeters*

  But send me Flavius first.

10 PETER   It shall be speeded well.°   *quickly done*

Enter Varrius.

DUKE   I thank thee, Varrius, thou hast made good haste.

  Come, we will walk.° There's other of our friends   *withdraw*

  Will greet us here anon, my gentle° Varrius.   *Exeunt.*   *noble*

4.6

Enter ISABELLA *and* MARIANA.

ISABELLA   To speak so indirectly° I am loath.   *evasively*

  I would say the truth, but to accuse him so—

  That is your part, yet I am advised to do it,

  He says, to veil full purpose.

MARIANA   Be ruled by him.

5 ISABELLA   Besides, he tells me that if peradventure

  He speak against me on the adverse side

  I should not think it strange, for 'tis a physic°   *medicine*

  That's bitter to sweet end.

Enter [*Friar*] PETER.

MARIANA   I would Friar Peter—

---

1. Person (also suggesting the physical body).
2. Makes her dare not.
3. Sustains such massive credibility. TEXTUAL COM-MENT The F text reads "For my Authoritie bears of a credent bulke," which probably involves a printing error. *The Norton Shakespeare* emends the passage; for a justification of this change, see Digital Edition TC 8.

4.5 Location: Outside the city.
4.6 Location: A street near the city gates.

<table>
<tr><td>10</td><td>ISABELLA Oh, peace, the friar is come.</td><td></td></tr>
<tr><td></td><td>PETER Come. I have found you out a stand° most fit</td><td>place</td></tr>
<tr><td></td><td>Where you may have such vantage° on the Duke</td><td>advantageous position</td></tr>
<tr><td></td><td>He shall not pass you. Twice have the trumpets sounded.[1]</td><td></td></tr>
<tr><td></td><td>The generous° and gravest citizens</td><td>noble</td></tr>
<tr><td>15</td><td>Have hent° the gates, and very near upon</td><td>reached</td></tr>
<tr><td></td><td>The Duke is entering. Therefore hence, away!   *Exeunt.*</td><td></td></tr>
</table>

5.1

[Flourish.] Enter DUKE, *Varrius, Lords,* ANGELO, ESCALUS,
LUCIO, [PROVOST, *Officers, and] Citizens at several doors.*

<table>
<tr><td></td><td>DUKE [*to* ANGELO] My very worthy cousin,° fairly met.</td><td>fellow nobleman</td></tr>
<tr><td></td><td>[*to* ESCALUS] Our old and faithful friend, we are glad to see you.</td><td></td></tr>
<tr><td></td><td>ANGELO *and* ESCALUS Happy return be to your royal grace.</td><td></td></tr>
<tr><td></td><td>DUKE Many and hearty thankings to you both.</td><td></td></tr>
<tr><td>5</td><td>[*to* ANGELO] We have made inquiry of you, and we hear</td><td></td></tr>
<tr><td></td><td>Such goodness of your justice that our soul</td><td></td></tr>
<tr><td></td><td>Cannot but yield you forth to public thanks,</td><td></td></tr>
<tr><td></td><td>Forerunning more requital.°</td><td>greater reward</td></tr>
<tr><td></td><td>ANGELO You make my bonds° still greater.</td><td>obligations</td></tr>
<tr><td>10</td><td>DUKE Oh, your desert speaks loud, and I should wrong it</td><td></td></tr>
<tr><td></td><td>To lock it in the wards° of covert bosom</td><td>prison cells</td></tr>
<tr><td></td><td>When it deserves with characters° of brass</td><td>letters</td></tr>
<tr><td></td><td>A forted° residence 'gainst the tooth of time</td><td>fortified</td></tr>
<tr><td></td><td>And razure° of oblivion. Give me your hand</td><td>erasure</td></tr>
<tr><td>15</td><td>And let the subject° see, to make them know</td><td>people</td></tr>
<tr><td></td><td>That outward courtesies would fain proclaim</td><td></td></tr>
<tr><td></td><td>Favors that keep° within. —Come, Escalus,</td><td>dwell</td></tr>
<tr><td></td><td>You must walk by us on our other hand;</td><td></td></tr>
<tr><td></td><td>And good supporters[1] are you.</td><td></td></tr>
<tr><td></td><td>Enter [Friar] PETER and ISABELLA.</td><td></td></tr>
<tr><td>20</td><td>PETER Now is your time.</td><td></td></tr>
<tr><td></td><td>Speak loud, and kneel before him.</td><td></td></tr>
<tr><td></td><td>ISABELLA Justice, O royal Duke! vail your regard°</td><td>look down</td></tr>
<tr><td></td><td>Upon a wronged—I would fain° have said a maid.</td><td>like to</td></tr>
<tr><td></td><td>O worthy prince, dishonor not your eye</td><td></td></tr>
<tr><td>25</td><td>By throwing it on any other object</td><td></td></tr>
<tr><td></td><td>Till you have heard me in my true complaint</td><td></td></tr>
<tr><td></td><td>And given me justice, justice, justice, justice.</td><td></td></tr>
<tr><td></td><td>DUKE Relate your wrongs: in what, by whom? Be brief.</td><td></td></tr>
<tr><td></td><td>Here is Lord Angelo shall give you justice.</td><td></td></tr>
<tr><td></td><td>Reveal yourself° to him.</td><td>(your complaint)</td></tr>
<tr><td>30</td><td>ISABELLA   O worthy Duke,</td><td></td></tr>
<tr><td></td><td>You bid me seek redemption of the devil.</td><td></td></tr>
<tr><td></td><td>Hear me yourself, for that which I must speak</td><td></td></tr>
<tr><td></td><td>Must either punish me, not being believed,</td><td></td></tr>
<tr><td></td><td>Or wring redress from you.</td><td></td></tr>
<tr><td>35</td><td>Hear me, oh, hear me, here.</td><td></td></tr>
<tr><td></td><td>ANGELO My lord, her wits I fear me are not firm.</td><td></td></tr>
<tr><td></td><td>She hath been a suitor to me for her brother</td><td></td></tr>
<tr><td></td><td>Cut off° by course of justice.</td><td>Executed</td></tr>
</table>

	ISABELLA	By course of justice!	
40	ANGELO	And she will speak most bitterly and strange.	
	ISABELLA	Most strange, but yet most truly will I speak.	

ISABELLA   By course of justice!

40 ANGELO And she will speak most bitterly and strange.

ISABELLA Most strange, but yet most truly will I speak.
  That Angelo's forsworn, is it not strange?
  That Angelo's a murderer, is't not strange?
  That Angelo is an adulterous thief,

45   An hypocrite, a virgin-violator,
  Is it not strange and strange?

DUKE Nay, it is ten times strange.

ISABELLA It is not truer he is Angelo
  Than this is all as true as it is strange.

50   Nay, it is ten times true, for truth is truth
  To th'end of reck'ning.[2]

DUKE   Away with her. Poor soul,
  She speaks this in th'infirmity of sense.

ISABELLA O prince, I conjure° thee, as thou believ'st   *appeal to*
  There is another comfort than this world,

55   That thou neglect me not with that opinion
  That I am touched with madness. Make not impossible
  That which but seems unlike.° 'Tis not impossible   *unlikely*
  But° one the wicked'st caitiff° on the ground   *That / villain*
  May seem as shy,° as grave, as just, as absolute°   *reserved / perfect*

60   As Angelo. Even so may Angelo
  In all his dressings, caracts,[3] titles, forms,°   *formalities*
  Be an arch-villain. Believe it, royal prince.
  If he be less, he's nothing, but he's more,
  Had I more name for badness.

DUKE   By mine honesty,

65   If she be mad, as I believe no other,
  Her madness hath the oddest frame° of sense,   *shape*
  Such a dependency° of thing on thing,   *connected sequence*
  As e'er I heard in madness.

ISABELLA   O gracious Duke,
  Harp not on that, nor do not banish reason

70   For inequality,[4] but let your reason serve
  To make the truth appear where it seems hid
  And hide the false seems° true.   *that seems*

DUKE   Many that are not mad
  Have sure more lack of reason. What would you say?

ISABELLA I am the sister of one Claudio,

75   Condemned upon the act of° fornication   *decree against*
  To lose his head, condemned by Angelo.
  I, in probation of a sisterhood,
  Was sent to by my brother; one Lucio
  As° then the messenger—   *Being*

80 LUCIO That's I, an't like your grace.
  I came to her from Claudio and desired her
  To try her gracious fortune with Lord Angelo
  For her poor brother's pardon.

ISABELLA   That's he indeed.

---

2. *for truth . . . reck'ning:* echoing 1 Ezra 4:38: "But truth doth abide, and is strong forever, and liveth and reigneth for ever and ever." *reck'ning:* day of reckoning.

3. Signs (of office).

4. Difference in rank (between Isabella and Angelo); discrepancy (between my report and what seems true).

DUKE You were not bid to speak.

LUCIO   No, my good lord,
  Nor wished to hold my peace.

85 DUKE   I wish you now then.
  Pray you take note of it, and when you have
  A business for yourself, pray heaven you then
  Be perfect.

LUCIO   I warrant° your honor.   assure

DUKE The warrant's⁵ for yourself. Take heed to't.

90 ISABELLA This gentleman told somewhat of my tale.

LUCIO Right.

DUKE It may be right, but you are i'the wrong
  To speak before your time. [to ISABELLA] Proceed.

ISABELLA   I went
  To this pernicious caitiff deputy—

DUKE That's somewhat madly spoken.

95 ISABELLA   Pardon it,
  The phrase is to the matter.°   appropriate

DUKE Mended again. The matter; proceed.

ISABELLA In brief, to set the needless process by⁶—
  How I persuaded, how I prayed and kneeled,

100 How he refelled° me, and how I replied,   repelled
  For this was of much length—the vile conclusion
  I now begin with grief and shame to utter.
  He would not but by gift of my chaste body
  To his concupiscible° intemperate lust   desirous

105 Release my brother; and after much debatement,
  My sisterly remorse confutes° mine honor,   overcomes
  And I did yield to him. But the next morn betimes,
  His purpose surfeiting,° he sends a warrant   having been satisfied
  For my poor brother's head.

DUKE   This is most likely!

110 ISABELLA Oh, that it were as like° as it is true.   probable

DUKE By heaven, fond° wretch, thou know'st not what thou   foolish
    speak'st,
  Or else thou art suborned against his honor
  In hateful practice.° First, his integrity   conspiracy
  Stands without blemish. Next, it imports no reason°   makes no sense

115 That with such vehemency he should pursue
  Faults proper° to himself. If he had so offended,   belonging
  He would have weighed thy brother by himself
  And not have cut him off. Someone hath set you on.°   incited you
  Confess the truth, and say by whose advice
  Thou cam'st here to complain.

120 ISABELLA   And is this all?
  Then, O you blessed ministers° above,   angels
  Keep me in patience, and with ripened time
  Unfold the evil which is here wrapped up
  In countenance!⁷ Heaven shield your grace from woe,

125 As I thus wrongèd hence unbelievèd go.

DUKE I know you'd fain be gone. An officer!
  To prison with her!

---

5. That is, for arrest, punning on the verb in line 88.   7. In false appearance; in royal favor.
6. To skip unnecessary parts of the story.

[*An Officer arrests* ISABELLA.] Shall we thus permit
  A blasting° and a scandalous breath to fall   *blighting*
  On him so near us? This needs must be a practice.°   *conspiracy*
130 Who knew of your intent and coming hither?
ISABELLA One that I would were here, Friar Lodowick.[8]
                          [*Exit, guarded.*]
DUKE A ghostly father, belike! Who knows that Lodowick?
LUCIO My lord, I know him; 'tis a meddling friar.
  I do not like the man. Had he been lay, my lord,
135 For certain words he spake against your grace
  In your retirement I had swinged° him soundly.   *beat*
DUKE Words against me? This'° a good friar belike.   *This is*
  And to set on this wretched woman here
  Against our substitute! Let this friar be found.
140 LUCIO But yesternight, my lord, she and that friar,
  I saw them at the prison. A saucy friar,
  A very scurvy fellow.
PETER   Blessed be your royal grace!
  I have stood by, my lord, and I have heard
  Your royal ear abused. First hath this woman
145 Most wrongfully accused your substitute,
  Who is as free from touch or soil with her
  As she from one ungot.°   *not yet begotten*
DUKE   We did believe no less.
  Know you that Friar Lodowick that she speaks of?
PETER I know him for a man divine and holy,
150 Not scurvy, nor a temporary meddler[9]
  As he's reported by this gentleman,
  And on my trust, a man that never yet
  Did, as he vouches,° misreport your grace.   *asserts*
LUCIO My lord, most villainously, believe it.
155 PETER Well, he in time may come to clear himself,
  But at this instant he is sick, my lord,
  Of a strange fever. Upon his mere° request,   *Solely at his*
  Being come to knowledge that there was complaint
  Intended 'gainst Lord Angelo, came I hither
160 To speak as from his mouth what he doth know
  Is true and false, and what he with his oath
  And all probation° will make up full clear   *proof*
  Whensoever he's convented.° First, for this woman,   *summoned*
  To justify° this worthy nobleman   *vindicate*
165 So vulgarly and personally accused,
  Her shall you hear disprovèd to her eyes,
  Till she herself confess it.
DUKE   Good Friar, let's hear it.
                   [*Exit Friar* PETER.]
  —Do you not smile at this, Lord Angelo?
  O heaven, the vanity of wretched fools.
170 Give us some seats. Come, cousin Angelo,
  In this I'll be impartial; be you judge
  Of your own cause.[1]

---

8. Evidently the Duke's name when in disguise.
9. Meddler in temporal matters.

1. Ironically recalling the principle that no one ought to judge his or her own cause.

[*The* DUKE *and* ANGELO *sit.*]
Enter [*Friar* PETER *with*] MARIANA[, *veiled*].
Is this the witness, Friar?
First, let her show her face, and after, speak.

MARIANA   Pardon, my lord, I will not show my face
175   Until my husband bid me.

DUKE   What, are you married?

MARIANA   No, my lord.

DUKE   Are you a maid?°   *an unmarried woman; a virgin*

MARIANA   No, my lord.

180   DUKE   A widow, then?

MARIANA   Neither, my lord.

DUKE   Why, you are nothing then: neither maid, widow, nor wife?

LUCIO   My lord, she may be a punk,° for many of them are   *prostitute*
neither maid, widow, nor wife.

185   DUKE   Silence that fellow! I would° he had some cause to prat-   *wish*
tle for himself.°   *(in his own defense)*

LUCIO   Well, my lord.

MARIANA   My lord, I do confess I ne'er was married,
And I confess besides I am no maid.
190   I have known[2] my husband, yet my husband
Knows not that ever he knew me.

LUCIO   He was drunk, then, my lord; it can be no better.

DUKE   For the benefit of silence, would thou wert so too.

LUCIO   Well, my lord.

195   DUKE   This is no witness for Lord Angelo.

MARIANA   Now I come to't, my lord.
She that accuses him of fornication
In selfsame manner doth accuse my husband,
And charges him, my lord, with such a time
200   When I'll depose° I had him in mine arms   *testify*
With all th'effect° of love.   *manifestations*

ANGELO   Charges she more than me?

MARIANA   Not that I know.

DUKE   No? You say your husband.

205   MARIANA   Why, just,° my lord, and that is Angelo,   *just so*
Who thinks he knows that he ne'er knew my body,
But knows, he thinks, that he knows Isabel's.

ANGELO   This is a strange abuse!° Let's see thy face.   *imposture*

MARIANA   My husband bids me, now I will unmask.
210   This is that face, thou cruel Angelo,
Which once thou swor'st was worth the looking on.
This is the hand which with a vowed contract
Was fast belocked in thine. This is the body
That took away the match° from Isabel,   *assignation*
215   And did supply° thee at thy garden-house   *satisfy*
In her imagined person.

DUKE   Know you this woman?

LUCIO   Carnally, she says.

DUKE   Sirrah, no more.

220   LUCIO   Enough, my lord.

ANGELO   My lord, I must confess I know this woman,
And five years since there was some speech of marriage

2. Had sexual intercourse with.

	Betwixt myself and her, which was broke off,	
	Partly for that her promised proportions°	*dowry*
225	Came short of composition,° but in chief	*the agreed sum*
	For that her reputation was disvalued°	*discredited*
	In levity.° Since which time of five years	*For wantonness*
	I never spake with her, saw her, nor heard from her	
	Upon my faith and honor.	

MARIANA [*kneeling*]   Noble prince,
230   As there comes light from heaven and words from breath,
     As there is sense° in truth and truth in virtue,   *significance*
     I am affianced this man's wife as strongly
     As words could make up vows. And, my good lord,
     But Tuesday night last gone, in 's garden-house
235   He knew me as a wife. As this is true,
     Let me in safety raise me from my knees,
     Or else forever be confixèd° here   *fixed firmly*
     A marble monument.[3]

ANGELO   I did but smile till now.
240   Now, good my lord, give me the scope° of justice;   *extent*
     My patience here is touched.° I do perceive   *irritated*
     These poor informal° women are no more   *disorderly*
     But instruments° of some more mightier member°   *agents / power*
     That sets them on. Let me have way, my lord,
     To find this practice out.

245 DUKE   Ay, with my heart,
     And punish them to your height of pleasure.
     Thou foolish friar, and thou, pernicious woman,
     Compact with° her that's gone, think'st thou thy oaths,   *In league with*
     Though they would swear down each particular saint,
250   Were testimonies against his worth and credit
     That's sealed in approbation?° You, Lord Escalus,   *ratified by proof*
     Sit with my cousin; lend him your kind pains
     To find out this abuse, whence 'tis derived.
     There is another friar that set them on.
255   Let him be sent for.

PETER   Would he were here, my lord, for he indeed
     Hath set the women on to this complaint.
     Your provost knows the place where he abides,
     And he may fetch him.

DUKE   Go, do it instantly.   [*Exit* PROVOST.]
260   —And you, my noble and well-warranted cousin,
     Whom it concerns to hear this matter forth,°   *out*
     Do with your injuries as seems you best
     In any chastisement. I for a while
     Will leave you, but stir not you till you have
265   Well determined° upon these slanderers.   *Passed judgment*

ESCALUS   My lord, we'll do it throughly.°   *Exit* [DUKE].   *thoroughly*
     [ESCALUS *sits in the Duke's place.*]
     Signior Lucio, did not you say you knew that Friar Lodowick
     to be a dishonest person?

LUCIO   *Cucullus non facit monachum.*[4] Honest in nothing but

---

3. TEXTUAL COMMENT F leaves it unclear exactly when, in this scene, Mariana kneels and when she gets up again, so the modern editor must decide where to insert stage directions. For a justification of the Norton editor's decision, see Digital Edition TC 9.
4. The hood does not make the monk (proverbial).

270   in his clothes, and one that hath spoke most villainous
       speeches of the Duke.
ESCALUS   We shall entreat you to abide here till he come and
       enforce° them against him. We shall find this friar a notable   urge
       fellow.
275 LUCIO   As any in Vienna, on my word.
ESCALUS   Call that same Isabel here once again, I would
       speak with her. [*to* ANGELO] Pray you, my lord, give me leave
       to question. You shall see how I'll handle her.
LUCIO   Not better than he, by her own report.
280 ESCALUS   Say you?
LUCIO   Marry, sir, I think if you handled her privately she
       would sooner confess. Perchance publicly she'll be ashamed.
              Enter ISABELLA [*guarded*].
ESCALUS   I will go darkly° to work with her.   *privately; soberly*
LUCIO   That's the way, for women are light[5] at midnight.
285 ESCALUS   Come on, mistress, here's a gentlewoman denies all
       that you have said.
              Enter DUKE [*disguised as a friar*] *and* PROVOST.
LUCIO   My lord, here comes the rascal I spoke of, here, with
       the Provost.
ESCALUS   In very good time. Speak not you to him till we call
290   upon you.
LUCIO   Mum.
ESCALUS   Come, sir, did you set these women on to slander Lord
       Angelo? They have confessed you did.
DUKE   'Tis false.
295 ESCALUS   How? Know you where you are?
DUKE   Respect to your great place; and let the devil
       Be sometime honored for his burning throne.[6]
       Where is the Duke? 'Tis he should hear me speak.
ESCALUS   The Duke's in° us, and we will hear you speak.   *The Duke's power is vested in*
300   Look you speak justly.°   *accurately*
DUKE   Boldly, at least. [*to* ISABELLA *and* MARIANA] But, O
       poor souls,
       Come you to seek the lamb here of the fox?
       Good night to your redress. Is the Duke gone?
       Then is your cause gone too. The Duke's unjust
305   Thus to retort° your manifest appeal°   *cast back / accusation*
       And put your trial in the villain's mouth
       Which here you come to accuse.
LUCIO   This is the rascal, this is he I spoke of.
ESCALUS   Why, thou unreverend and unhallowed° friar,   *impious*
310   Is't not enough thou hast suborned these women
       To accuse this worthy man, but in foul mouth,
       And in the witness of his proper° ear,   *own*
       To call him villain, and then to glance° from him   *ricochet*
       To th' Duke himself, to tax° him with injustice?   *reproach*
315   Take him hence! To th' rack with him. We'll touse° you   *tear*
       Joint by joint, but we will know his[7] purpose.

5. Licentious; exploiting the unintentional sexual
suggestion of Escalus's "go darkly to work."
6. *let . . . throne*: that is, the devil, too, seated on his
throne in hell, seems a figure of honor.
7. The friar's; the confusion of pronouns suggests
Escalus's fury.

What? Unjust?

DUKE   Be not so hot. The Duke dare
No more stretch this finger of mine than he
Dare rack his own. His subject am I not,
320   Nor here provincial.[8] My business in this state
Made me a looker-on here in Vienna,
Where I have seen corruption boil and bubble
Till it o'errun the stew:° laws for all faults,   *cauldron; brothel*
But faults so countenanced that the strong statutes
325   Stand like the forfeits[9] in a barber's shop,
As much in mock as mark.

ESCALUS   Slander to th' state! Away with him to prison.

ANGELO   What can you vouch against him, Signor Lucio? Is
this the man you did tell us of?

330   LUCIO   'Tis he, my lord. Come hither, Goodman Bald-pate.[1]
Do you know me?

DUKE   I remember you, sir, by the sound of your voice.[2] I met
you at the prison, in the absence of the Duke.

LUCIO   Oh, did you so? And do you remember what you said of
335   the Duke?

DUKE   Most notedly, sir.

LUCIO   Do you so, sir? And was the Duke a fleshmonger,° a   *whoremaster*
fool, and a coward, as you then reported him to be?

DUKE   You must, sir, change persons with me, ere you make
340   that my report. You indeed spoke so of him, and much more,
much worse.

LUCIO   O thou damnable fellow! Did I not pluck thee by the
nose° for thy speeches?   *(gesture of contempt)*

DUKE   I protest I love the Duke as I love myself.

345   ANGELO   Hark how the villain would close[3] now after his trea-
sonable abuses.

ESCALUS   Such a fellow is not to be talked withal. Away with
him to prison. Where is the Provost? Away with him to
prison! Lay bolts° enough upon him. Let him speak no more.   *fetters*
350   Away with those giglets° too, and with the other confederate   *strumpets*
companion.[4]

[*The* PROVOST *attempts to lead the* DUKE *away.*]

DUKE   Stay, sir, stay a while.

ANGELO   What, resists he? Help him, Lucio.

LUCIO   Come, sir, come, sir, come, sir. Faugh,° sir! Why, you   *(expression of disgust)*
355   bald-pated lying rascal, you must be hooded, must you? Show
your knave's visage, with a pox to you. Show your sheep-
biting face,[5] and be hanged an hour.[6] Will't not off?

[LUCIO *pulls off the Duke's hood.*]

DUKE   Thou art the first knave that e'er mad'st a duke.
—First, Provost, let me bail these gentle three.
360   [*to* LUCIO] Sneak not away, sir, for the friar and you

---

8. Subject to local ecclesiastical authorities.
9. Jocular list of penalties for minor infractions.
1. "Mr. Bald-head." "Goodman" was a form of address for a man below the rank of gentleman; friars shaved their heads.
2. The friar's hood presumably covers his face so that he cannot see Lucio.

3. Conclude; hide himself; come to a settlement.
4. Fellow (contemptuous).
5. Like the wolf in sheep's clothing.
6. Jocular way of saying "be hanged." Animals were sometimes executed like human beings for destroying life or property.

Must have a word anon. [*to Officers*] Lay hold on him!
LUCIO   This may prove worse than hanging.
DUKE [*to* ESCALUS]   What you have spoke, I pardon. Sit you down,
   We'll borrow place° of him. [*to* ANGELO] Sir, by your leave.   *seat; office*
   [*The* DUKE *takes Angelo's seat.*]
365   Hast thou or° word, or wit, or impudence,   *either*
   That yet can do thee office?° If thou hast,   *service*
   Rely upon it till my tale be heard,
   And hold no longer out.
ANGELO   O my dread lord,
   I should be guiltier than my guiltiness
370   To think I can be undiscernible
   When I perceive your grace like power divine
   Hath looked upon my passes.[7] Then, good prince,
   No longer session° hold upon my shame,   *inquiry*
   But let my trial be mine own confession.
375   Immediate sentence then and sequent° death   *thereafter*
   Is all the grace I beg.
DUKE   Come hither, Mariana.
   [MARIANA *rises.*]
   Say, wast thou e'er contracted to this woman?
ANGELO   I was, my lord.
380 DUKE   Go, take her hence, and marry her instantly.
   —Do you the office, Friar, which consummate,°   *finished*
   Return him here again. —Go with him, Provost.
       Exeunt [ANGELO, MARIANA, *Friar* PETER, *and* PROVOST].
ESCALUS   My lord, I am more amazed at his dishonor
   Than at the strangeness of it.°   *(the situation)*
DUKE   Come hither, Isabel.
385   Your friar is now your prince. As I was then
   Advertising° and holy to your business,   *Attentive*
   Not changing heart with habit, I am still
   Attorneyed° at your service.   *Engaged as advocate*
ISABELLA   Oh, give me pardon
   That I, your vassal, have employed and pained°   *troubled*
   Your unknown sovereignty.
390 DUKE   You are pardoned, Isabel.
   And now, dear maid, be you as free° to us.   *generous*
   Your brother's death I know sits at your heart,
   And you may marvel why I obscured myself
   Laboring to save his life, and would not rather
395   Make rash remonstrance° of my hidden power   *demonstration*
   Than let him so be lost. O most kind maid,
   It was the swift celerity of his death,
   Which I did think with slower foot came on,
   That brained° my purpose. But peace be with him!   *killed*
400   That life is better life past fearing death,
   Than that which lives to fear. Make it your comfort,
   So happy is your brother.
      Enter ANGELO, MARIANA, [*Friar*] PETER, *and* PROVOST.
ISABELLA   I do, my lord.
DUKE   For this new-married man approaching here,

---

7. Actions, trespasses; recalling Job 34:21: "For his eyes are upon the ways of man, and he seeth all his goings."

Whose salt° imagination yet hath wronged   *salacious*
405 Your well-defended honor, you must pardon
For Mariana's sake. But as he adjudged° your brother,   *condemned*
Being criminal in double violation
Of sacred chastity and of promise-breach,
Thereon dependent for your brother's life,
410 The very mercy° of the law cries out   *Even the merciful aspect*
Most audible even from his proper° tongue: *its own*
"An Angelo for Claudio, death for death.
Haste still° pays haste, and leisure° answers leisure;   *always / deliberation*
Like doth quit° like, and measure still for measure."⁸   *requite*
415 Then, Angelo, thy fault's thus manifested
Which, though° thou wouldst deny, denies thee vantage.°   *even if / (i.e., clemency)*
We do condemn thee to the very block
Where Claudio stooped to death, and with like haste.
Away with him.
MARIANA   O my most gracious lord,
420 I hope you will not mock me with a husband.
DUKE   It is your husband mocked you with a husband.
Consenting to the safeguard of your honor
I thought your marriage fit, else imputation°   *censure*
For that he knew you might reproach your life
425 And choke your good to come.° For his possessions,   *ruin your prospects*
Although by confiscation they are ours,⁹
We do instate and widow you° withal   *give you widow's rights*
To buy you a better husband.
MARIANA   O my dear lord,
I crave no other nor no better man.
430 DUKE   Never crave him, we are definitive.°   *resolute*
MARIANA [*kneeling*]   Gentle my liege—
DUKE   You do but lose your labor.
Away with him to death. [*to* LUCIO] Now, sir, to you—
MARIANA   O my good lord! Sweet Isabel, take my part.
Lend me your knees, and all my life to come
435 I'll lend you all my life to do you service.
DUKE   Against all sense you do importune her.
Should she kneel down in mercy of this fact,°   *crime*
Her brother's ghost his pavèd bed° would break   *stone-covered grave*
And take her hence in horror.
MARIANA   Isabel!
440 Sweet Isabel, do yet but kneel by me.
Hold up your hands, say nothing, I'll speak all.
They say best men are molded out of faults,
And for the most,° become much more the better   *most part*
For being a little bad. So may my husband.
445 O Isabel, will you not lend a knee?
DUKE   He dies for Claudio's death.
ISABELLA [*kneeling*]   Most bounteous sir,
Look, if it please you, on this man condemned
As if my brother lived. I partly think
A due sincerity governed his deeds

---

8. TEXTUAL COMMENT The F punctuation leaves it unclear at what point the Duke stops quoting "the law" and begins speaking in his own person; for the signifi- cance of this ambiguity, see Digital Edition TC 10.
9. Because a felon's property was forfeit to the Crown.

450   Till he did look on me. Since it is so,
Let him not die. My brother had but justice,
In that he did the thing for which he died.
For Angelo, his act did not o'ertake his bad intent
And must be buried° but as an intent   *(i.e., forgotten)*
455   That perished by the way. Thoughts are no subjects,[1]
Intents but merely thoughts.

MARIANA   Merely, my lord.

DUKE   Your suit's unprofitable. Stand up, I say.
        [MARIANA *and* ISABELLA *rise.*]
    I have bethought me of another fault.
    Provost, how came it Claudio was beheaded
    At an unusual hour?

460 PROVOST   It was commanded so.

DUKE   Had you a special warrant for the deed?

PROVOST   No, my good lord. It was by private message.

DUKE   For which I do discharge you of your office.
    Give up your keys.

PROVOST   Pardon me, noble lord.
465   I thought it was a fault but knew it not,
    Yet did repent me after more advice,°   *deliberation*
    For° testimony whereof one in the prison   *As*
    That should by private order else° have died   *otherwise*
    I have reserved alive.

470 DUKE   What's he?

PROVOST   His name is Barnardine.

DUKE   I would thou hadst done so by Claudio.
    Go fetch him hither, let me look upon him.   [*Exit* PROVOST.]

ESCALUS   I am sorry one so learnèd and so wise
475   As you, Lord Angelo, have still° appeared,   *always*
    Should slip so grossly both in the heat of blood
    And lack of tempered judgment afterward.

ANGELO   I am sorry that such sorrow I procure,°   *cause*
    And so deep sticks it in my penitent heart
480   That I crave death more willingly than mercy.
    'Tis my deserving, and I do entreat it.
        Enter PROVOST, BARNARDINE, CLAUDIO [*muffled*],°   *with his face wrapped*
        and JULIET.

DUKE   Which is that Barnardine?

PROVOST   This, my lord.

DUKE   There was a friar told me of this man.
    Sirrah, thou art said to have a stubborn soul
485   That apprehends no further than this world,
    And squar'st° thy life according. Thou'rt condemned,   *frames*
    But for those earthly faults,[2] I quit° them all,   *pardon*
    And pray thee take this mercy to provide
    For better times to come. Friar, advise him,
490   I leave him to your hand. What muffled fellow's that?

PROVOST   This is another prisoner that I saved,
    Who should have died when Claudio lost his head,
    As like almost to Claudio as himself.
        [*Claudio's disguise is removed.*]

---

1. Thoughts are not subject to prosecution.   2. Offenses subject to earthly punishment.

DUKE [*to* ISABELLA]   If he be like your brother, for his sake
495   Is he pardoned, and for your lovely sake
  Give me your hand, and say you will be mine,[3]
  He is my brother° too—but fitter time for that.   *(as a brother-in-law)*
  By this Lord Angelo perceives he's safe:
  Methinks I see a quick'ning in his eye.
500   Well, Angelo, your evil quits° you well.   *recompenses*
  Look that you love your wife, her worth worth° yours.   *being equal to*
  I find an apt remission° in myself,   *inclination to mercy*
  And yet here's one in place° I cannot pardon.   *present*
  [*to* LUCIO] You, sirrah, that knew me for a fool, a coward,
505   One all of luxury,° an ass, a madman;   *lasciviousness*
  Wherein have I so deserved of you
  That you extol me thus?
LUCIO   'Faith, my lord, I spoke it but according to the trick.° If   *fashion*
  you will hang me for it you may, but I had rather it would
510   please you I might be whipped.
DUKE   Whipped first, sir, and hanged after.
  Proclaim it, Provost, round about the city,
  If any woman wronged by this lewd fellow—
  As I have heard him swear himself there's one
515   Whom he begot with child—let her appear,
  And he shall marry her. The nuptial finished,
  Let him be whipped and hanged.
LUCIO   I beseech your highness, do not marry me to a whore.
  Your highness said even now I made you a duke. Good my
520   lord, do not recompense me in making me a cuckold.
DUKE   Upon mine honor thou shalt marry her.
  Thy slanders I forgive, and therewithal
  Remit thy other forfeits.° Take him to prison,   *punishments*
  And see our pleasure herein executed.
525 LUCIO   Marrying a punk, my lord, is pressing to death,[4] whip-
  ping, and hanging.
DUKE   Slandering a prince deserves it.
  —She, Claudio, that you wronged, look you restore.[5]
  —Joy to you, Mariana. —Love her, Angelo;
530   I have confessed her,° and I know her virtue.   *heard her confession*
  —Thanks, good friend Escalus, for thy much goodness,
  There's more behind° that is more gratulate.°   *to come / gratifying*
  —Thanks, Provost, for thy care and secrecy;
  We shall employ thee in a worthier place.
535   —Forgive him, Angelo, that brought you home
  The head of Ragozine for Claudio's—
  Th'offense pardons itself. Dear Isabel,
  I have a motion° much imports your good,   *proposal*
  Whereto if you'll a willing ear incline,
540   What's mine is yours, and what is yours is mine.
  So bring° us to our palace, where we'll show   *accompany*
  What's yet behind that's meet° you all should know.   *suitable*

                                [*Exeunt.*]

---

3. PERFORMANCE COMMENT It is not clear from Shakespeare's text how Isabella responds to the Duke's proposal of marriage; for some performance options, see Digital Edition PC 3.

4. Executing by crushing under heavy weights.
5. To her good name, by marrying her publicly and being a good husband.

The Sonnets

Shakespeare's plays often seem indifferent to high-cultural rules of construction. His sonnets (composed from about 1592 to 1604, possibly revised thereafter, and published in 1609) are the opposite: they belong to an international tradition inspired by the fourteenth-century Italian poet Petrarch. The very strictness of sonnet structure provides the basis for originality. The form's fixed length of fourteen lines, rigorous rhyme scheme, and relatively unvarying metrical structure encourage a logical approach to the standard topic of the Renaissance sonnet—love and its emotions (desire, jealousy, etc.). In Shakespeare, the conflict between passionate feelings and an intellect often skeptical of those feelings becomes a central theme of the poems. And that skepticism is conveyed through a linguistic virtuosity marked by metaphors and puns (only a fraction of which are identified in the notes) that work both with and against the larger structure of the sonnet.

Thematically, the sonnets are equally distinctive. The typical object of love—the unapproachable lady—is replaced by a daring representation of homoerotic and adulterous passions. Almost the entire sequence can be divided along these lines. Sonnets 1–126 recount the speaker's initially idealized but sometimes painful love for a femininely beautiful, well-born male youth; 127–152 discuss his unidealized, ultimately bitter affair with a darkly attractive, unaristocratic "mistress"—where this term invokes, ironically, courtly love rather than the derogatory modern meaning. The two love relationships are complicated by a lovers' triangle (40–42, 133–134, 144) and a poetic rival for the youth's affections (78–80, 82–86). These topics provide the occasion for meditation upon time, nature, mortality, economics, perhaps class and race, and, not least, artistic immortality.

The poems may be approached by locating their formal specificity within the sonnet tradition. The Petrarchan version ends in "feminine rhyme"—a stressed syllable followed by an unstressed one, both of which must rhyme with one or more other line endings. English offers possibilities ("mother-brother," "wonder-thunder"); but in Shakespeare and most other English Renaissance sonneteers, feminine rhyme is rare. The tendency is to stick to ten-syllable iambic pentameter lines and hence to conclude on a stressed syllable, usually a monosyllabic word. This preference may indicate a conventional difference between the treatment of rhymed and unrhymed poetry. In the second half of his career, Shakespeare frequently resorted to feminine endings in blank verse but not in rhyme. Yet the aversion to feminine rhyme is also rooted in the English language, where the erosion of word endings increased the percentage of monosyllabic words and reduced the opportunities of rhyme, especially of polysyllabic rhyme. Feminine rhyme can sound sing-song or comical—hence, its use in limericks.

Shakespeare does, however, occasionally rhyme polysyllabic words on their secondary stress:

> Not marble nor the gilded monuments
> Of princes shall outlive this powerful rhyme,
> But you shall shine more bright in these contents
> Than unswept stone besmeared with sluttish time.
>
> (55.1–4)

Here, Shakespeare is after the durability, the immortality of his art. Subsequent rhyme words in the sonnet include "overturn," "masonry," "memory," "enmity," and "posterity" (lines 5, 6, 8, 9, 11). The rhymes' stately sound effects reinforce the sonnet's semantic thrust.

The structure of English also helps explain Shakespeare's rhyme scheme. The Petrarchan sonnet is divided into two frequently contrasting units, an octave (eight lines) and a sestet (six lines), by its rhymes—*abbaabba* (rarely varied) *cdcdcd* (often varied), where each letter represents a line and a repeated letter indicates a rhyme. The Petrarchan mode reached England by the early sixteenth century in the works of Thomas Wyatt and Henry Howard, Earl of Surrey, the latter of whom pioneered the modified rhyme scheme later taken over by Shakespeare (*abab cdcd efef gg*). Because English is a relatively rhyme-poor language, there are more rhyme sounds in the Shakespearean sonnet—seven rather than Petrarch's four or five. Thus, Shakespeare never has to find more than two words that rhyme on a given sound, whereas Petrarch needs up to four.

The Shakespearean rhyme scheme divides the sonnet into three quatrains (four-line groupings) and a couplet. This organization offers greater conceptual range than does Petrarch's. The quatrains can operate in parallel, represent steps in an argument, or contradict each other. They may be grouped into larger units of eight-and-four lines or eight-and-six (if the couplet is included) that are set against each other. In turn, the epigrammatic concluding couplet, whose conceptual tendencies contrast with the more experiential approach of at least the first two quatrains, can summarize, generalize, draw appropriate inferences, contribute a new thought, or even reverse the preceding argument.

Sonnet structure often guides Shakespeare's pervasive use of imagery and metaphor. In Sonnet 73, each quatrain pursues a different metaphor as part of a single argument:

> That time of year thou mayst in me behold
> When yellow leaves, or none, or few do hang
> Upon those boughs which shake against the cold,
> Bare ruined choirs where late the sweet birds sang.
> 5 In me thou seest the twilight of such day
> As after sunset fadeth in the west,
> Which by and by black night doth take away,
> Death's second self that seals up all in rest.
> In me thou seest the glowing of such fire
> 10 That on the ashes of his youth doth lie,
> As the deathbed whereon it must expire,
> Consumed with that which it was nourished by.
>   This thou perceiv'st, which makes thy love more strong,
>   To love that well which thou must leave ere long.

The evocation of fall in the opening quatrain nostalgically communicates the sadness of aging. Enjambment supports the imagistic pattern: it causes meaning to "hang" in the balance at the end of the line, just as "yellow leaves . . . do hang / Upon those boughs." The "yellow leaves" are also leaves of a book, "bare ruined choirs," or quires (manuscript gatherings). Similarly, the birds' former song, together with the primary meaning of "choirs" (the part of a church where the choir sings), may refer to the speaker's own voice and hence to a lost poetic creativity. In short, aging is compared to the annual movement toward colder seasons and to the decline of artistic inspiration. In the second quatrain, duration constricts: "That time of year" is replaced by "the twilight of such day." Although, like autumn, sunset is a natural process, it is not organic. Emphasis accordingly shifts away from bodily degeneration. These lines also look forward, unlike the first quatrain. Twilight is taken away by "black night . . . , / Death's second self that seals up all in rest." Nighttime rest brings comfort, but night is compared with death, and the syntax, at odds with the literal meaning, suggests that it is death rather than night "that seals up all in [eternal] rest."

The third quatrain opens like the second, with "In me thou seest," a phrase also partly anticipated in the poem's opening line. This repetition reinforces the parallelism among the quatrains: the poem proceeds less by narrative progression than by thematic variation. This quatrain, highlighting the transition from aging to mortality, narrows time further, to the "glowing" fire (line 9), thereby abandoning the previous temporal model for a spatial metaphor. Only ashes remain from the fire's and the speaker's "youth" (line 10); they are also the fire's and the speaker's "death-bed" (line 11). Although the fire of old age no longer rages, it is still "glowing." The present thus continues the past. Furthermore, the metaphorical relationship becomes reciprocal. The dying fire is a metaphor for aging, but aging is a metaphor for the dying fire.

The fire is "[c]onsumed with that which it was nourished by"; it is "consumed" (or choked) by—and along with—the ashes that, as fuel, previously "nourished" it. Normally, the fire consumes the fuel, not the other way around. Both "consumed" and "nourished" metaphorically explain the already metaphorical fire, which their allusions to eating connect to humanity. The speaker's fiery passion for the youth he addresses nourished him when he was young but consumes him now. The line structurally enacts this tacit rejection of temporal decline. It is an example of chiasmus, in which the elements of the first half ("Consumed . . . that") are repeated in reverse order in the second ("which . . . nourished"), thus producing an *abba* semantic pattern. Accordingly, this quatrain does not echo the earlier "cold" or "night" metaphorically responsible for the approach of death. Life and death have the same source.

All three quatrains use cyclical metaphors of life, death, and rebirth. But the cycle remains incomplete. Autumn does not lead to spring or night to day. The "long-lived phoenix" (19.4), the self-resurrecting bird that dies in flames and is reborn from the ashes, doesn't appear. Perhaps these suppressed allusions to cyclical patterns raise, then frustrate expectations, denying the consolation of the future. The concluding couplet, which abandons metaphor for a new idea, suggests this interpretation. Recognizing the speaker's passion makes the youth's "love more strong" (line 13). The youth, therefore, loves "well" what he "must leave ere long" (line 14)—explicitly, the speaker; implicitly, his own life, partly because what he "must leave" recalls the earlier "yellow leaves." The destructive power of time is only partly counteracted by love.

Sonnet 73 suggests how conformity to sonnet convention can enable a thoughtful interplay among time, love, death, and art. But Sonnet 81 offers a radical disjunction of syntax and rhyme scheme: almost any two consecutive lines can produce a complete sentence, depending on how you punctuate:

> And toungs to be, your beeing shall rehearse,
> When all the breathers of this world are dead,
> You still shall liue (such vertue hath my Pen).
> (81.11–13)

This three-line sequence, presented as it appears in the first edition, the Quarto of 1609, runs over the end of a quatrain but nonetheless produces two possible sentences (lines 11–12 or 12–13). The unorthodox move is the implicit equation of the speaker with his social superior, the youth. The poet's literary prowess promises enduring renown for both writer and subject matter. Or does it? If you take lines 11 and 12 together, as modern editions do, the emphasis falls on "dead." But if you connect lines 12 and 13, "liue" and "my Pen" are emphasized. The poem thus promises both death and immortality, just as "rehearse" (line 11) predicts a future where the youth is still spoken about and re-hearsed.

The relationship between formal and thematic innovation can also be approached by considering the sonnets as a sequence. English enthusiasm for such sequences was triggered by the posthumous printing of Philip Sidney's *Astrophel and Stella* (1591). Sonnets also circulated in manuscript, since print was often considered undignified by (would-be) gentlemen or courtier-poets. The vogue for sonnet sequences responded to poets' ambitions as well as to the gender politics of the late Elizabethan court. Middle-class writers sought financial assistance for their work by praising their aristocratic patrons. Expressions of love may be less indications of deep feeling than competitive strategies of advancement. Shakespeare's "rival poet" sonnets seem to convert this competition into a literary theme. It is thus often hard to determine where sentiment ends and calculation begins.

Further, given uncertainties about Shakespeare's role in the publication of the sonnets, their ordering may or may not represent the poet's final intent. (See the Textual Introduction.) It is also easy to overstate the internal organization of the sonnets as we have them. The division of the sequence into two main groups is arguably unwarranted. Most of the poems are not explicitly about either the youth or the mistress, not even designating the sex of the person discussed. Only their relative position in the collection has produced the standard simplification adopted here. Furthermore, the sequence as a whole is relatively uninterested in plot. The poems to the mistress in particular show little organization or process, combining occasional affection with frequent disgust. Perhaps, in 1609, they had not yet been placed in a particular order; perhaps they were intended for a separate collection. But the first 126 sonnets, too, evince only intermittent interest in linear movement, anticipating both the desire and the anguish of the subsequent poems.

Nonetheless, many of the sonnets *are* ordered in pairs or longer groups. The lovers' triangle and rival poet sonnets, noted above, are examples. Others are identified in the notes. More important, the two main sections of the sequence are thematically compelling. For the two centuries ending a generation ago, the homoerotic attachment to the youth, now routine in critical discussion, provoked revulsion or denial. Sonnet 20 was—and still is—the center of the debate:

> A woman's face with Nature's own hand painted
> Hast thou, the master-mistress of my passion;
> A woman's gentle heart, but not acquainted
> With shifting change as is false women's fashion;
> 5   An eye more bright than theirs, less false in rolling,
> Gilding the object whereupon it gazeth;
> A man in hue, all hues in his controlling,
> Which steals men's eyes and women's souls amazeth.
> And for a woman wert thou first created,
> 10   Till Nature as she wrought thee fell a-doting,
> And by addition me of thee defeated
> By adding one thing to my purpose nothing.
>   But since she pricked thee out for women's pleasure,
>   Mine be thy love, and thy love's use their treasure.

Nature originally intended the youth to be female (the octave). But she fell in love with her creation and hence made him a man, a change that benefited her but forced the speaker to limit himself to love without sexual consummation (the sestet). The poem plays with gender boundaries—"master-mistress," "A woman's face," "one thing" (a penis), "A man in hue" (further sexualized if "hue" was pronounced like "you"; lines 2, 1, 12, 7). "Acquainted" and "controlling" pun on "cunt"; "nothing" and "treasure" also refer to the female sexual organ (lines 3, 7, 12, 14). As someone "pricked . . . out for women's pleasure" (line 13), the youth can both give and receive women's pleasure (be "pricked"). Moreover, this is the only sonnet in which all the rhymes have feminine endings—a thematically resonant stylistic joke. Finally, the poem's misogynistic complaint about "false" women (lines 4, 5) is consistent with its homoeroticism. Women are resented because the speaker prefers the youth, and because they can enjoy "love's use," while he gets only "love" (line 14)—where "love" carries both its

Renaissance meaning of "friendship" and its modern sense of romantic and sexual desire.

Sonnet 20 looks forward to poems that express erotic love for the youth, apparently without sexual fulfillment. But it also looks back to the opening seventeen sonnets, in which the speaker urges the youth to marry and produce an heir. The speaker solicits the youth's love for someone else, since the point is procreation and, therefore, immortality comparable to the artistic immortality promised later in the sequence. The exhortation cuts against both the love sonnet's conventional aspirations and the speaker's unconventional aim of winning the youth. But this is because the multiple possible meanings of "love" in Sonnet 20 generally characterize the poems to the youth.

"Thy beauty's form in table of my heart" (24.2). Here a man is holding a "table" (tablet) in front of his heart while another man engraves the first man's portrait on it. From Geffrey Whitney, *A Choice of Emblems* (1586).

How the case for marriage is argued in the early sonnets is instructive. Shakespeare's reversal of the metaphorical relationship in Sonnet 73, it will be recalled, removes any fixed point of reference. A comparable reversal also marks economic imagery of the initial sonnets, and beyond. As in Sonnet 20 (line 14), that imagery frequently turns on usury. Long denounced, Renaissance English usury was beginning its conversion into the respectable financial category of interest. Shakespeare shared the prevailing dislike of making money out of money. The speaker condemns his mistress for her affair with the young man, represented as collecting a debt:

> The statute of thy beauty thou wilt take—
> Thou usurer that putt'st forth all to use.
> (134.9–10)

She will "take" the "statute of" her "beauty"—what's owed to her financially (sexually)—because, like a "usurer," she employs "all" her wealth (her body) for profit (where "use" means "engage in usury" and "engage in sexual activity"). Elsewhere, ambivalently, the youth is criticized as, paradoxically, both "unthrifty" and a "niggard" (4.1, 5):

> Profitless usurer, why dost thou use
> So great a sum of sums, yet canst not live?
> (4.7–8)

Here, "use" antithetically means "use up" and "lend at interest." Literally, how can the youth lend vast "sums" for profit and be poor? Metaphorically, he acts in a "profitless" manner in wasting his personal endowments. Hence, he cannot "live" on in his children. By implication, a usurer is valueless.

But the lines also imagine the opposite. A profitless usurer implies a profitable one. This good usurer predominates elsewhere:

> That use is not forbidden usury
> Which happies those that pay the willing loan.
> (6.5–6)

Is all, or just unallowable, usury "forbidden"? Keeping one's "treasure" to oneself merits only "thriftless praise"; "beauty's use" deserves "much more praise" if a child results (2.6–9). At least "an unthrift" allows the world to enjoy his wealth; "beauty's waste" is indefensible—"kept unused the user so destroys it" (9.9–12). And Sonnet 20 ends, as we've seen, with the speaker getting the youth's love, whereas the "treasure" women enjoy is merely the "use" (metaphorically, children) of that love. He obtains the principal, they the interest. These passages activate metaphorical meanings of "use" to promote marriage and family. In so doing, they connect the proper use of beauty with usury, which is understood as the economic equivalent of human reproduction, the early sonnets' highest ideal. Neofeudal celebration of traditional lineage smuggles in economic behavior destructive of tradition. Usury becomes potentially noble. Through metaphor, Shakespeare entertains ideas that were less accessible as bald statements.

The poems to the speaker's mistress are also unconventional—in depicting sordid adultery with an unfaithful woman marked by passionate desire and recrimination. Even serene sonnets in this section undermine convention:

> My mistress' eyes are nothing like the sun;
> . . . .
> And yet, by heaven, I think my love as rare
> As any she belied with false compare.
> (130.1, 13–14)

The target is standard Petrarchan praise and, more generally, falsely idealizing rhetoric:

> When my love swears that she is made of truth,
> I do believe her though I know she lies,
> . . . .
> Therefore I lie with her, and she with me,
> And in our faults by lies we flattered be.
> (138.1–2, 13–14)

In Sonnet 130, true love requires the speaker to reject "false compare." In Sonnet 138, love paradoxically requires the speaker to "credit . . . false-speaking," to suppress "simple truth" (lines 7–8), and to embrace "lies." The sequence ends, however, with the disabused deployment of the same rhetoric against speaker and woman alike:

> For I have sworn thee fair—more perjured eye,
> To swear against the truth so foul a lie.
> (152.13–14)

This couplet recalls the opening poem on the mistress:

> In the old age black was not counted fair,
> . . . .
> But now is black beauty's successive heir.
> (127.1, 3)

Black is the color of the woman's eyes, eyebrows, breasts, hair (127.9–10, 132.3, 130.3–4), and skin:

> Then I will swear beauty herself is black,
> And all they foul that thy complexion lack.
> (132.13–14)

This anticonventional praise of blackness echoes the biblical Song of Songs as well as sixteenth-century Continental and English poetry, including Sidney's. The praise is often inseparable from misogynistic denunciation of cosmetics' artificial beauty (127.4–12). Black hair and eyes gained prestige in the 1590s through a shift in fashion. Thus, the speaker's views accord with broader social change.

The mistress's color may or may not be racialized, since dark skin might merely distinguish her from falsely idealized women or aristocratic ladies who avoided the sun. Nonetheless, *Titus Andronicus, Othello, Antony and Cleopatra,* and *The Tempest* feature actual or threatened interracial coupling. The mistress's blackness and promiscuity may thus provoke desire and fear of exotic female sexuality. Blackness accordingly moves from paradox to cliché: "In nothing art thou black save in thy deeds" (131.13); "For I have sworn thee fair, and thought thee bright, / Who art as black as hell, as dark as night" (147.13–14). Like usury, then, blackness oscillates between convention and innovation. Such is the case with the sonnets generally.

Finally, the intense emotion associated with the "I" of the sonnets, the psychological complexity with which that emotion is scrutinized, the unconventional subject matter, the sense that one is overhearing snatches of conversation, the first-person speaker, that speaker's self-conscious identification with Shakespeare (135 and 136)—all encourage biographical interpretation. For two centuries, such interpretation has proven risky to undertake—or to avoid. Scholars have failed to discover the real people whom Shakespeare presumably discusses but does not name. (See the Textual Introduction.) This outcome led mid-twentieth-century critics to focus on formal concerns. But the resulting advances often entailed evading the biographical material that the poems seem to provide. Shakespeare's sonnets, like his plays, combine verbal artistry and conceptual unorthodoxy with psychological exploration. Their special fascination, however, is that the soul they examine may be Shakespeare's own.

WALTER COHEN

SELECTED BIBLIOGRAPHY

Booth, Stephen, ed. *Shakespeare's Sonnets.* New Haven, CT: Yale UP, 1977. Provides the 1609 Quarto of the sonnets and a modernized version, with a commentary detailing multiple overlapping structures within individual sonnets, structures that expand possible meaning without cohering into a unified whole.

Dubrow, Heather. *Echoes of Desire: English Petrarchism and Its Counterdiscourses.* Ithaca, NY: Cornell UP, 1995. 119–34. Argues that Shakespeare's sonnets both follow many Petrarchan conventions and, especially beginning with Sonnet 127, challenge those conventions as well.

Empson, William. *Some Versions of Pastoral.* London: Chatto & Windus, 1935. 89–101. Shows, in a classic close reading, that the ironies of Sonnet 94 result in complex, multiple meanings that center on the speaker advocating a hypocritical, but dangerous, Machiavellianism on the part of the youth.

Flesch, William. "Personal Identity and Vicarious Experience in Shakespeare's Sonnets." *A Companion to Shakespeare's Sonnets.* Ed. Michael Schoenfeldt. Malden, MA: Blackwell, 2007. 383–401. Investigates the poems' account of the limitations of one's access to another's subjectivity through discussion of the sonnets' elusive descriptions of the youth, appeals to the youth's vanity, and emphasis on our vicarious interest in others.

Gregerson, Linda. "Open Voicing: Wyatt and Shakespeare." *The Oxford Handbook of Shakespeare's Poetry.* Ed. Jonathan F. S. Post. Oxford: Oxford UP, 2013. 151–67. Traces to Wyatt's lyrics a discontinuous subjectivity that produces psychological complexity and is then taken up by Shakespeare in his sonnets and plays.

Halpern, Richard. *Shakespeare's Perfume: Sodomy and Sublimity in the Sonnets, Wilde, Freud, and Lacan.* Philadelphia: U of Pennsylvania P, 2002. 11–31. Links sodomy, aesthetics, sublimation, and the sublime.

Kalas, Rayna. *Frame, Glass, Verse: The Technology of Poetic Invention in the English Renaissance.* Ithaca, NY: Cornell UP, 2007. 166–98. Finds in the sonnets a craft of poetic production tied to contemporary production in glass—the mirror, window, and hourglass—and thereby also to matters of property and social status.

Schoenfeldt, Michael. "The Sonnets." *The Cambridge Companion to Shakespeare's Poetry.* Ed. Patrick Cheney. Cambridge: Cambridge UP, 2007. 125–43. Presents an overview of the sonnets, emphasizing erotic and emotional desire, its frustration, and the limited resources (progeny, poetry) for mitigating the ravages of time.

Trevor, Douglas. "Shakespeare's Love Objects." *A Companion to Shakespeare's Sonnets.* Ed. Michael Schoenfeldt. Malden, MA: Blackwell, 2007. 225–41. Proposes that Shakespeare rejects transcendence and places his faith less in the objects of his love than in his poetic creation.

Vendler, Helen. *The Art of Shakespeare's Sonnets.* Cambridge: Belknap P, 1997. Offers a detailed sonnet-by-sonnet interpretation, focusing on formal considerations, together with the 1609 Quarto and a modernized version of the text, as well as a CD-ROM of Vendler reading the poems.

TEXTUAL INTRODUCTION

On May 20, 1609, the publisher Thomas Thorpe entered "Shakespeares sonnetts" in the Stationers' Register. The Quarto (Q) was printed in the same year by George Eld, the only edition until John Benson's *Poems* (1640). Along with 154 sonnets, Q includes the separately titled "A Lover's Complaint," also identified as "by William Shakespeare." Thirteen surviving copies preserve two states, some identifying John Wright and others William Aspley as bookseller.

The size and prominence of "SHAKE-SPEARES SONNETS" on the title page suggest the value Thorpe placed on the writer's name as advertising copy, but it is not clear if Q was printed with Shakespeare's consent or knowledge. Shakespeare provided dedicatory epistles for *Venus and Adonis* and *The Rape of Lucrece* but not for the sonnets. Thorpe set his own initials to a stylized dedication on the second leaf, visually reminiscent of a monument inscription: "TO.THE.ONLIE.BEGETTER.OF.THESE.INSVING. SONNETS. M^r. W. H."

The present edition emends Thorpe's dedication, accepting scholarly arguments that the "only begetter" is meant to be Shakespeare and "M^r. W. H." in Q is a misprint for "M^r. W. S." (or "SH."). Error is assumed on the grounds that the unexpected letter "H" obscures a straightforward message (Foster, "Master W. H., R.I.P."; see Digital Edition TC 1). A compositor setting type from Thorpe's manuscript epigraph could plausibly have mistaken a malformed "S" for an "h" in secretary hand or a "sh" with indistinct long "s" for "H"—or he could simply have picked up the wrong piece of type. This error could have gone uncorrected in an edition that shows only cursory signs of proofreading. The H/S error has a precedent: "*Hyn.*" for "*Syn.*" (the character Sindefy) goes uncorrected in Eld's print shop in the first edition of *Eastward Ho*, published by Aspley and Thorpe in 1605 (sig. C1r).

Efforts to make sense of "M^r. W. H." have rested on insecure premises. Although poems as author's progeny is a standard trope, most current interpretations associate "the only begetter" with the young man of Sonnets 1–126. Often, they gloss over the unlikeliness of a complimentary address to a nobleman (the earls of Pembroke and Southampton being leading contenders) omitting "the right honorable . . . Earl of . . ." and substituting "M[aster]," a form of respectful address appropriate to no rank higher than gentleman or esquire. Indeed, in 1610 and 1616 Thorpe addressed dedications to the Earl of Pembroke using his titles and elaborately deferential language. In contrast, when respectful admirers praised Shakespeare in poems accompanying the 1623 First Folio, "Master" was the address term they chose.

Questions remain about the extent of Thorpe's or an intermediary's editorial intervention. We cannot be sure if the manuscript he acquired consisted of a single sequence in the Quarto's order, nor do we know whether Shakespeare capped his sonnets with "A Lover's Complaint" or Thorpe filled out a short volume with the narrative poem. The authorship of "A Lover's Complaint" remains in doubt.

Date and time span of composition are uncertain. External evidence establishes that some sonnets were extant in the 1590s. In 1599, Sonnets 138 and 144 were printed in *The Passionate Pilgrim*. In 1598, Francis Meres's *Palladis Tamia* mentioned Shakespeare's "sugared Sonnets among his private friends," suggesting that some had circulated in manuscript. However, while over twenty existing manuscripts include Shakespeare sonnets or excerpts, these generally date ca. 1620–60 and derive from the 1609 Quarto or the 1640 edition. Research comparing linguistic elements like rare vocabulary with phases of Shakespeare's corpus provides a speculative chronology for composition and possible revision of discrete sonnet groupings (Jackson, "Vocabulary"). The final "mistress" grouping, 127–154, is likely the earliest written (ca. 1592–95); the concluding group to the youth (104–126) probably latest (ca. 1598–1604). The mid-1590s (ca. 1594–96) is the likeliest period for other "young man" sonnets (1–103), with the "marriage" subgroup (1–17) sometimes dated earlier and the "rival poet" sonnets (78–80, 82–86) later.

Scribal copy almost certainly served as the copy-text, placing Q at least two removes from an authorial manuscript. A recurring error in Q ("their" printed for "thy") evidently derives from the manuscript copy. Not replicated elsewhere in Shakespeare's canon, it is not attributable to his handwriting; nor to compositor idiosyncrasy, given MacDonald P. Jackson's demonstration ("Punctuation") that at least two compositors worked on Q, both setting "their" for "thy." Jackson identified distinctive spelling and punctuation patterns for each compositor. For example, Compositor B preferred "O" rather than "Oh" spellings in interjections and punctuated 53 percent of third quatrain endings with full stops, while Compositor A used "Oh" exclusively and closed quatrain 3 with heavier punctuation (70 percent full stop).

This modernized edition preserves only the more significant of Q's features. While Elizabethan spellings may suggest puns unavailable in modern spelling, Q reflects compositorial rather than authorial spelling. In contrast to Q's heavy line-end punctuation, Hand D of *Sir Thomas More* (possibly Shakespeare's) exhibits virtually no line-end punctuation but moderate mid-line punctuation, usually commas marking caesuras or intonation shifts. Some mid-line commas in Q may serve these functions but do not invariably produce credible readings. On the principle that some Shakespeare sonnets tend to reflection and longer sentence or utterance units, while others are strongly dramatic or dialogic, this edition introduces more short sentences in the latter (e.g., 58.9–12).

Q is attuned to prosody, using apostrophe for poetic elision. Its use of capitals and italics is not systematic. In 135 and 136, these devices cue punning on the name "Will," but capital letters only sometimes signal personification, and this edition uses capitals only for sustained personification. Finally, Q's readings are retained in some cases where editorial tradition has favored emendation (e.g., "steeled" 24.1, "worth" 25.9, "there" 31.8, "loss" 34.12, "by" 54.14). In other cases, this edition reinterprets Q by repunctuating (e.g., 6.9, 16.12, 51.11, 131.9, 142.7).

LYNNE MAGNUSSON

TEXTUAL BIBLIOGRAPHY

Foster, Donald W. "Master W. H., R.I.P." *PMLA* 102 (1987): 42–54.
Jackson, MacDonald P. "Punctuation and the Compositors of Shakespeare's *Sonnets*, 1609." *Library* 5th ser. 30 (1975): 1–24.
———. "Vocabulary and Chronology: The Case of Shakespeare's Sonnets." *Review of English Studies* n.s. 52 (2001): 59–75.

Sonnets

1

From fairest creatures° we desire increase,°   *living things / offspring*
That° thereby beauty's rose¹ might never die,   *So that*
But as the riper should by time decease
His tender heir² might bear his memory.°   *(in his look)*
5 But thou, contracted° to thine own bright eyes,   *engaged; reduced*
Feed'st thy light's flame with self-substantial fuel,³
Making a famine where abundance lies,
Thyself thy foe, to thy sweet self too cruel.
Thou, that art now the world's fresh° ornament   *young*
10 And only herald to the gaudy° spring,   *ornate*
Within thine own bud buriest thy content°   *offspring; happiness*
And, tender churl,° mak'st waste in niggarding.°   *young old miser / (paradox)*
Pity the world,° or else this glutton be,   *Have a child*
To eat the world's due, by the grave and thee.⁴

2

When forty winters shall besiege thy brow
And dig deep trenches° in thy beauty's field,   *wrinkles*
Thy youth's proud livery,° so gazed on now,   *uniform; appearance*

Dedication

1. TEXTUAL COMMENT The identity of the Quarto's W. H. has generated much speculation. For the interpretation of the initials as a misprint for "W. S." or "W. SH." (William Shakespeare), see the Textual Introduction and Digital Edition TC 1.
2. TEXTUAL COMMENT Perhaps God, literally "ever-living," who promises eternity to Shakespeare (if "W. H." refers to Shakespeare); or perhaps Shakespeare, who promises "eternity" to the young man. See Digital Edition TC 1.
3. Thomas Thorpe, the printer, is the "well-wishing adventurer."

Sonnet 1

1. In Q, "rose," unlike most other nouns, is always capitalized (35.2; 54.3, 6, 11; 67.8; 95.2; 98.10; 99.8; 109.14; and 130.5, 6). Here, in Q, it is also italicized. These printing conventions, combined with the place-ment of the word near the beginning of the first sonnet and its frequent repetition thereafter, suggest that "rose" is the poet's name for the object of his desire, on the model of, for instance, Stella in Sidney's influential sonnet sequence *Astrophel and Stella* (published 1591). The rose had long been associated with female genitalia, most notably in the thirteenth-century French narrative poem *The Romance of the Rose*, by Guillaume de Lorris and Jean de Meun. In Shakespeare's case, however, the object of desire is male. He is most frequently referred to as "youth," almost never as "boy" or "man." Shakespeare's "mistress" is later contrasted with "roses" (130.5, 6).
2. The rose's (that is, the youth's) young child.
3. Are consuming yourself like a candle.
4. *or else . . . thee:* otherwise you'll be a glutton by causing your posterity, which is due to the world, to be consumed both by the grave and within yourself.

Will be a tattered weed° of small worth held.   *clothing; plant*
5 Then being asked where all thy beauty lies,
Where all the treasure of thy lusty days,
To say within thine own deep-sunken eyes
Were an all-eating shame and thriftless praise.[1]
How much more praise deserved thy beauty's use[2]
10 If thou couldst answer, "This fair child of mine
Shall sum my count and make my old excuse,"[3]
Proving his beauty by succession thine.°   *inherited from you*
    This were° to be new made when thou art old   *would be*
    And see thy blood warm when thou feel'st it cold.

3

Look in thy glass,° and tell the face thou viewest,   *mirror; hourglass (?)*
Now is the time that face should form another,
Whose° fresh repair,° if now thou not renewest,   *(the face's) / state; (pun on "pair")*
Thou dost beguile° the world, unbless° some mother.   *swindle / leave childless*
5 For where is she so fair whose uneared° womb   *unplowed; unheired*
Disdains the tillage of thy husbandry?[1]
Or who is he so fond will be the tomb
Of his self-love to stop posterity?[2]
Thou art thy mother's glass, and she in thee
10 Calls back the lovely April of her prime;
So thou through windows of thine age[3] shalt see,
Despite of wrinkles, this thy golden time.°   *youth*
    But if thou live remembered not to be,[4]
    Die single, and thine image dies with thee.

4

Unthrifty loveliness, why dost thou spend
Upon thyself thy beauty's legacy?[1]
Nature's bequest gives nothing but doth lend,
And being frank she lends to those are free.[2]
5 Then, beauteous niggard, why dost thou abuse
The bounteous largesse given thee to give?
Profitless usurer, why dost thou use°   *lend for profit; spend*
So great a sum of sums, yet canst not live?[3]
For having traffic° with thyself alone,   *(commercial); (sexual)*
10 Thou of thyself thy sweet self dost deceive.°   *defraud (of offspring)*
Then how, when nature calls thee to be gone—
What acceptable audit canst thou leave?
    Thy unused[4] beauty must be tombed with thee,
    Which usèd lives th'executor to be.

Sonnet 2
1. Would be an all-consuming shame and praise that brings no profit.
2. How much more would the use (employment; investment or usurious lending) of your beauty merit.
3. Shall make my accounts balance and defend (or absolve) me in my age.
Sonnet 3
1. Cultivation; acting as a husband.
2. *who . . . posterity:* who is so foolish that he will selfishly deny posterity a child?
3. Eyes weakened by old age; your children.
4. But if you live to be forgotten.
Sonnet 4
1. *legacy:* both from your parents and to your children.
2. And being generous, she lends to those who (also) are generous.
3. Make a living; live on in your children.
4. Not put to use; not interest-bearing.

5

Those hours that with gentle work did frame°   *form*
The lovely gaze° where every eye° doth dwell   *face / (pun on "I"?)*
Will play the tyrants to the very same
And that unfair which fairly doth excel.[1]
5 For never-resting time leads summer on
To hideous winter and confounds him° there,   *destroys summer*
Sap checked with frost and lusty leaves quite gone,
Beauty o'er-snowed and bareness everywhere.
Then were not summer's distillation left
10 A liquid prisoner pent in walls of glass,
Beauty's effect with beauty were bereft,[2]
Nor° it nor no remembrance what it was.   *Neither*
  But flowers distilled, though they with winter meet,
  Lose[3] but their show; their substance still lives sweet.

6[1]

Then let not winter's ragged° hand deface[2]   *rough*
In thee thy summer ere thou be distilled.°   *(in children)*
Make sweet some vial;° treasure° thou some place *womb / enrich*
With beauty's treasure ere it be self-killed.
5 That use° is not forbidden usury   *lending for profit*
Which happies those that pay the willing loan:[3]
That's for thyself° to breed another thee,   *So you would do*
Or ten times happier, be it ten for one.°   *1,000 percent interest*
Ten times thyself were happier than thou art:
10 If ten of thine ten times refigured° thee,   *copied*
Then what could death do if thou shouldst depart,
Leaving thee living in posterity?
  Be not self-willed,[4] for thou art much too fair
  To be death's conquest and make worms thine heir.

7

Lo, in the orient° when the gracious light°   *East / sun*
Lifts up his burning head, each under° eye   *earthly*
Doth homage to his new-appearing sight,
Serving with looks his sacred majesty;
5 And having climbed the steep-up heavenly hill,
Resembling strong youth in his middle age,°   *noon*
Yet mortal looks adore his beauty still,
Attending on his golden pilgrimage.
But when from highmost pitch with weary car° *sun god's chariot*
10 Like feeble age he reeleth from the day,
The eyes, fore duteous, now converted° are   *turned away*
From his low tract° and look another way.   *path*

Sonnet 5
1. Will make unattractive that which now excels in beauty.
2. *Then . . . bereft:* Then if there were no perfume distilled from flowers bottled in glass vials, both beauty and its effect would be lost. *pent:* (with pun on "penned").
3. Q has "Leese," thus allowing a pun on "lease." See 13.5.

Sonnet 6
1. This sonnet links with 5.
2. Disfigure; de-face, through death.
3. Which makes happy those who willingly lend, or who willingly repay the loan with interest (in the form of children).
4. Stubborn; leaving everything in a will to yourself alone.

So thou, thyself outgoing in thy noon,[1]
Unlooked on diest unless thou get° a son.°   *beget / (sun)*

8

Music to hear,[1] why hear'st thou music sadly?
Sweets° with sweets war not, joy delights in joy.   *Sweet things*
Why lov'st thou that which thou receiv'st not gladly,
Or else receiv'st with pleasure thine annoy?°   *pun on "ennui" (boredom)*
5 If the true concord of well-tunèd sounds,
By unions° married, do offend thine ear,   *harmony*
They do but sweetly chide thee, who confounds°   *destroys*
In singleness the parts[2] that thou shouldst bear.
Mark how one string, sweet husband to another,
10 Strikes each in each° by mutual ordering,   *Resonates*
Resembling sire and child and happy mother,
Who all in one one pleasing note do sing;
    Whose speechless° song (being many, seeming one)   *The strings' wordless*
    Sings this to thee: "Thou single wilt prove none."[3]

9

Is it for fear to wet a widow's eye
That thou consum'st thyself in single life?
Ah, if thou issueless° shalt hap to die,   *childless*
The world will wail thee like a makeless° wife.   *widowed*
5 The world will be thy widow and still° weep   *continually*
That thou no form of thee hast left behind,
When every private° widow well may keep,   *individual*
By children's eyes, her husband's shape in mind.
Look what° an unthrift in the world doth spend   *Whatever*
10 Shifts but his° place, for still the world enjoys it;   *its*
But beauty's waste hath in the world an end,
And kept unused the user° so destroys it.   *spender; lender*
    No love toward others in that bosom sits
    That on himself such murd'rous shame commits.

10

For° shame deny that thou bear'st love to any,   *Out of*
Who for thyself art so unprovident.°   *not foreseeing the future*
Grant, if thou wilt, thou art beloved of many,
But that thou none lov'st is most evident.
5 For thou art so possessed with murd'rous hate
That 'gainst thyself thou stick'st not to conspire,°   *don't balk at conspiring*
Seeking that beauteous roof° to ruinate   *house (family); head*
Which to repair should be thy chief desire.
Oh, change thy thought, that I may change my mind!°   *judgment*
10 Shall hate be fairer lodged than gentle love?
Be as thy presence° is, gracious and kind,   *appearance*
Or to thyself at least kind-hearted prove.
    Make thee another self for love of me,
    That beauty still may live in thine or thee.

Sonnet 7
1. Declining from the high point of your youth; going out (like a light).
Sonnet 8
1. You whose voice is music.

2. Musical parts; roles as husband and father; children.
3. Without an heir, death will render you nothing (alluding to the proverb "One is no number").

11

As fast as thou shalt wane, so fast thou grow'st
In one of thine from that which thou departest,[1]
And that fresh blood which youngly thou bestow'st
Thou mayst call thine when thou from youth convertest.°   *turn away*
5 Herein lives wisdom, beauty, and increase;°   *offspring*
Without this, folly, age, and cold decay.
If all were minded so, the times should cease,
And threescore year would make the world away.
Let those whom Nature hath not made for store°—   *breeding*
10 Harsh,° featureless,° and rude°—barrenly perish.   *Rough / ugly / unrefined*
Look whom she best endowed she gave the more,[2]
Which bounteous gift thou shouldst in bounty° cherish.   *by using bountifully*
     She carved thee for her seal,° and meant thereby   *stamp of authority*
     Thou shouldst print more, not let that copy die.

12

When I do count the clock° that tells the time,   *hours as they strike*
And see the brave° day sunk in hideous night;   *fine*
When I behold the violet° past prime   *(the flower)*
And sable curls° ensilvered o'er with white;   *black hair*
5 When lofty trees I see barren of leaves,
Which erst° from heat did canopy the herd,   *once*
And summer's green, all girded up in sheaves,
Borne on the bier with white and bristly beard;[1]
Then of thy beauty do I question make
10 That thou among the wastes of time must go,
Since sweets° and beauties do themselves forsake   *sweet things*
And die as fast as they see others grow;
     And nothing 'gainst Time's scythe can make defense
     Save breed, to brave him° when he takes thee hence.   *children, to defy time*

13

Oh, that you were yourself! But, love, you are
No longer yours than you yourself here live.
Against° this coming end you should prepare   *For*
And your sweet semblance to some other give.
5 So should that beauty which you hold in lease
Find no determination.° Then you were°   *Never end / would be*
Yourself again after your self's decease,
When your sweet issue your sweet form should bear.
Who lets so fair a house fall to decay,
10 Which husbandry[1] in honor might uphold
Against the stormy gusts of winter's day
And barren rage of death's eternal cold?
     Oh, none but unthrifts!° Dear my love, you know   *spendthrifts*
     You had a father; let your son say so.

Sonnet 11
1. *As . . . departest:* As you decline with age, so you become youthful through your child.
2. Nature gave extra reproductive abilities to whomever nature made best-looking. "Best endowed" and "more" allude to Matthew 25:29, the paradoxical parable of the talents: "For unto every man that hath, it shall be given."
Sonnet 12
1. *And . . . beard:* And sheaves of mature ("bearded") grain carried away on the harvest cart; old man borne on a funeral bier.
Sonnet 13
1. Stewardship; being a husband.

14

Not from the stars do I my judgment pluck,
And yet methinks I have astronomy,°   *astrological knowledge*
But not to tell of good or evil luck,
Of plagues, of dearths, or seasons' quality;
5   Nor can I fortune to brief minutes° tell,   *precisely*
Pointing to each his thunder, rain, and wind,
Or say with princes if it shall go well
By oft predict° that I in heaven find;   *numerous signs*
But from thine eyes my knowledge I derive,
10 And, constant stars,° in them I read such art   *the eyes; (astrological)*
As[1] truth and beauty shall together thrive
If from thyself to store thou wouldst convert[2]—
     Or else, of thee this I prognosticate:
     Thy end is truth's and beauty's doom and date.°   *final judgment and end*

15

When I consider every thing that grows
Holds° in perfection but a little moment,   *Remains*
That this huge stage presenteth naught but shows
Whereon the stars in secret influence° comment;   *(astrologically)*
5   When I perceive that men as plants increase,
Cheerèd and checked even by the selfsame sky,
Vaunt° in their youthful sap,° at height decrease,   *Gloat / strength*
And wear their brave state out of memory;[1]
Then the conceit° of this inconstant stay°   *imagination / (on earth)*
10 Sets you most rich in youth before my sight,
Where wasteful Time debateth° with Decay   *competes*
To change your day of youth to sullied night;
     And all in war with Time for love of you,
     As he takes from you, I engraft you new.[2]

16[1]

But wherefore do not you a mightier way
Make war upon this bloody tyrant Time,
And fortify yourself in your decay
With means more blessèd than my barren rhyme?
5   Now stand you on the top of happy hours,°   *in your prime*
And many maiden gardens, yet unset,°   *unplanted*
With virtuous wish would bear your living flowers,
Much liker° than your painted counterfeit.°   *more like you / portrait*
So should the lines of life that life repair,[2]
10 Which this time's pencil or my pupil pen[3]
Neither in inward worth nor outward fair°   *beauty*
Can make° you. —Live yourself° in eyes of men!   *do for / as yourself*

Sonnet 14
1. *such art / As:* such predictions as that.
2. If you would provide for the future.
Sonnet 15
1. Wear their splendid clothing until they are forgotten (with a sense of "wearing out").
2. *And . . . new:* And I, in competition with time because I love you, restore you to life with (re-plant you via; rejuvenate you by grafting you to) my verse.
Sonnet 16
1. This sonnet links with 15.

2. *So . . . repair:* So ought (or would) your appearance (or facial wrinkles, lineage, descendants, palm's life-lines)—in short, living lines, unlike those of poet or painter—restore your life. Or vice versa: "So should" your life restore "the lines of life."
3. *this . . . pen:* today's painters ("pencil" means "paintbrush") nor I, who imitate painting in my verse. TEXTUAL COMMENT For the significance of the punctuation of this line and of line 12, see Digital Edition TC 2.

To give away yourself keeps yourself still,°　　　　　*(as children)*
And you must live, drawn by your own sweet skill.

17

Who will believe my verse in time to come
If it were filled with your most high deserts?
Though yet, heaven knows, it is but as a tomb
Which hides your life and shows not half your parts.°　　　　*attributes*
5　If I could write the beauty of your eyes
And in fresh numbers° number all your graces,　　　　*lively verses*
The age to come would say, "This poet lies:
Such heavenly touches ne'er touched earthly faces."
So should my papers, yellowed with their age,
10　Be scorned, like old men of less truth than tongue,
And your true rights° be termed a poet's rage°　　　*praises / hyperbole*
And stretchèd meter° of an antique song.　　　　*overwrought poetry*
　　　But were some child of yours alive that time,
　　　You should live twice—in it and in my rhyme.

18

Shall I compare thee to a summer's day?
Thou art more lovely and more temperate.
Rough winds do shake the darling buds of May,
And summer's lease° hath all too short a date.　　　*fixed span of time*
5　Sometime too hot the eye of heaven shines
And often is his° gold complexion dimmed,　　　　　*its*
And every fair from fair¹ sometime declines,
By chance or nature's changing course untrimmed.°　　*rendered ordinary*
But thy eternal summer shall not fade
10　Nor lose possession of that fair° thou ow'st,°　　　*beauty / own*
Nor shall Death brag thou wand'rest in his shade,
When in eternal lines to time thou grow'st.²
　　　So long as men can breathe or eyes can see,
　　　So long lives this, and this gives life to thee.

19

Devouring Time, blunt thou the lion's paws,
And make the earth devour° her own sweet brood.　　*(in death)*
Pluck the keen teeth from the fierce tiger's jaws,
And burn the long-lived phoenix¹ in her blood.°　　　*alive*
5　Make glad and sorry seasons as thou fleet'st,
And do whate'er thou wilt, swift-footed Time,
To the wide world and all her fading sweets.°　　　*sweet things*
But I forbid thee one most heinous crime:
Oh, carve not with thy hours my love's fair brow,
10　Nor draw no lines there with thine antique° pen;　　　*old*
Him in thy course untainted do allow
For° beauty's pattern to succeeding men.　　　　　*As*
　　　Yet do thy worst, old Time. Despite thy wrong,
　　　My love shall in my verse ever live young.

Sonnet 18
1. Lovely thing from loveliness.
2. When in immortal poetry you become engrafted to time.

Sonnet 19
1. Legendary, self-resurrecting bird believed to live in cycles of several centuries, dying in flames and being reborn from the ashes. See also 73.9–12.

20[1]

<table>
<tr><td></td><td>A woman's face with Nature's own hand° painted</td><td style="text-align:right">(without cosmetics)</td></tr>
<tr><td></td><td>Hast thou, the master-mistress of my passion;[2]</td><td></td></tr>
<tr><td></td><td>A woman's gentle heart, but not acquainted°</td><td style="text-align:right">(pun on "quaint," "cunt")</td></tr>
<tr><td></td><td>With shifting change as is false women's fashion;</td><td></td></tr>
<tr><td>5</td><td>An eye more bright than theirs, less false in rolling,°</td><td style="text-align:right">wandering (sexually)</td></tr>
<tr><td></td><td>Gilding the object whereupon it gazeth;</td><td></td></tr>
<tr><td></td><td>A man in hue, all hues in his controlling,[3]</td><td></td></tr>
<tr><td></td><td>Which steals men's eyes and women's souls amazeth.°</td><td style="text-align:right">overwhelms</td></tr>
<tr><td></td><td>And for° a woman wert thou first created,</td><td style="text-align:right">to be; to be with</td></tr>
<tr><td>10</td><td>Till Nature as she wrought thee fell a-doting,°</td><td style="text-align:right">behaved foolishly</td></tr>
<tr><td></td><td>And by addition me of thee defeated°</td><td style="text-align:right">cheated me of you</td></tr>
<tr><td></td><td>By adding one thing to my purpose nothing.[4]</td><td></td></tr>
<tr><td></td><td>But since she pricked° thee out for women's pleasure,[5]</td><td style="text-align:right">chose; (sexual)</td></tr>
<tr><td></td><td>Mine be thy love, and thy love's use their treasure.[6]</td><td></td></tr>
</table>

21

<table>
<tr><td></td><td>So is it not with me as with that muse°</td><td style="text-align:right">poet</td></tr>
<tr><td></td><td>Stirred by a painted° beauty to his verse,</td><td style="text-align:right">(with cosmetics)</td></tr>
<tr><td></td><td>Who° heaven itself for ornament° doth use</td><td style="text-align:right">(the poet) / poetic imagery</td></tr>
<tr><td></td><td>And every fair with his fair doth rehearse,[1]</td><td></td></tr>
<tr><td>5</td><td>Making a couplement of proud compare[2]</td><td></td></tr>
<tr><td></td><td>With sun and moon, with earth and sea's rich gems,</td><td></td></tr>
<tr><td></td><td>With April's firstborn flowers and all things rare</td><td></td></tr>
<tr><td></td><td>That heaven's air in this huge rondure hems.°</td><td style="text-align:right">globe surrounds</td></tr>
<tr><td></td><td>Oh, let me true in love but truly write,</td><td></td></tr>
<tr><td>10</td><td>And then, believe me, my love is as fair</td><td></td></tr>
<tr><td></td><td>As any mother's child, though not so bright</td><td></td></tr>
<tr><td></td><td>As those gold candles° fixed in heaven's air.</td><td style="text-align:right">(the stars)</td></tr>
<tr><td></td><td>Let them say more that like of hearsay° well;</td><td style="text-align:right">clichés</td></tr>
<tr><td></td><td>I will not praise that purpose not° to sell.</td><td style="text-align:right">since I don't intend</td></tr>
</table>

22

<table>
<tr><td></td><td>My glass° shall not persuade me I am old</td><td style="text-align:right">mirror</td></tr>
<tr><td></td><td>So long as youth and thou are of one date,°</td><td style="text-align:right">While you're young</td></tr>
<tr><td></td><td>But when in thee time's furrows I behold,</td><td></td></tr>
<tr><td></td><td>Then look I° death my days should expiate.°</td><td style="text-align:right">I expect / conclude</td></tr>
<tr><td>5</td><td>For all that beauty that doth cover thee</td><td></td></tr>
<tr><td></td><td>Is but the seemly° raiment of my heart,</td><td style="text-align:right">fitting</td></tr>
<tr><td></td><td>Which in thy breast doth live as thine in me:</td><td></td></tr>
<tr><td></td><td>How can I then be elder than thou art?</td><td></td></tr>
<tr><td></td><td>O therefore, love, be of thyself so wary</td><td></td></tr>
<tr><td>10</td><td>As I not for myself but for thee will,[1]</td><td></td></tr>
</table>

Sonnet 20
1. The only sonnet in exclusively feminine rhyme.
2. *master . . . passion:* The hyphenated words designate the youth's feminine looks and position as patron and (homoerotic) sexual mistress. Hence, object or controller of my love or passionate poetry.
3. A man whose looks enable him to attract and dominate all others; a man whose looks encompass all other appearances (both male and female). "Hue" may pun on "you" with possible sexual connotations. "Hues" may pun on "use"; see line 14 and note 6. "Controlling" puns on "cunt."
4. *one . . . nothing:* something (a penis) of no use to me; "thing" meant male sexual organ; "nothing" meant

female sexual organ.
5. To give women pleasure; to have the pleasure women have.
6. I'll have the main part of your love (the capital or principal), while women get just the "use" (interest; pleasure; children) of it (or: while you use women sexually).
Sonnet 21
1. And compares every beautiful thing with his beloved.
2. Making a link in proud comparison.
Sonnet 22
1. *be . . . will:* care for yourself as much as I do for myself, which I do not for myself but for you.

Bearing thy heart, which I will keep so chary°   *cautiously*
As tender nurse her babe from faring ill.
   Presume not on[2] thy heart when mine is slain.
   Thou gav'st me thine not to give back again.

23

As an unperfect actor on the stage
Who with his fear is put besides° his part,   *forgets*
Or° some fierce thing replete with too much rage   *Or like*
Whose strength's abundance weakens his own heart,
5 So I, for fear of trust,° forget to say   *lack of confidence*
The perfect ceremony of love's rite,[1]
And in mine own love's strength seem to decay,
O'ercharged with burden of mine own love's might.
Oh, let my books be then the eloquence
10 And dumb presagers° of my speaking breast,   *mute presenters*
Who plead for love and look for recompense
More than that tongue that more hath more expressed.[2]
   Oh, learn to read what silent love hath writ!
   To hear with eyes belongs to love's fine wit.

24

Mine eye hath played the painter[1] and hath steeled[2]
Thy beauty's form in table° of my heart;   *the painted tablet*
My body is the frame wherein 'tis held,°   *(pun on "healed"?)*
And perspective it is best painter's art.[3]
5 For through° the painter must you see his skill   *by means of; by looking in*
To find where your true image pictured lies,°   *rests; fibs*
Which in my bosom's shop° is hanging still,   *heart's workshop*
That hath his windows glazèd with thine eyes.[4]
Now see what good turns eyes for eyes have done:
10 Mine eyes have drawn thy shape, and thine for me
Are windows to my breast, wherethrough the sun
Delights to peep, to gaze therein on thee.
   Yet eyes this cunning want° to grace their art: *lack this talent*
   They draw but what they see, know not the heart.°   *(of the youth)*

25

Let those who are in favor with their stars
Of public honor and proud titles boast,
Whilst I, whom fortune of such triumph bars,
Unlooked for joy in that I honor most.[1]
5 Great princes' favorites their fair leaves spread

2. Do not expect to get back.
Sonnet 23
1. Q reads "right," suggesting love's due as well as ritual. Lines 5–6 pick up the comparison to "an unperfect actor" (lines 1–2); lines 7–8 to "some fierce thing"
(lines 3–4).
2. More than that (rival) speaker who has more extrav-
agantly and more often spoken.
Sonnet 24
1. The running conceit is of the speaker and addressee
looking into each other's eyes, seeing both the other
and himself reflected.
2. Engraved. Editors often emend Q's "steeld" to
"stell'd" ("fixed," "placed") for a better fit with "painter."

3. *perspective . . . art:* seen from the proper angle
(through my painter's eyes), your form is an excellent
work of art. A "perspective" was a distorted painting
that looked right only if viewed from the correct
angle. The meter of the line is similarly distorted.
4. The addressee looks into the speaker's eyes ("windows"), which seem fitted with glass ("glazèd") by the
reflection there of the addressee's own eyes. The eyes
are the heart's ("his" [its], referring to "bosom's shop,"
line 7) windows, through which the addressee can
therefore see his own image in the speaker's heart.
Sonnet 25
1. Unexpectedly (or privately) take pleasure in what I
most esteem (the youth).

But as the marigold at the sun's eye,[2]
And in themselves their pride lies° burièd,   *will lie*
For at a frown they in their glory die.
The painful warrior famousèd for worth,[3]
10 After a thousand victories once foiled,
Is from the book of honor razèd° quite   *deleted*
And all the rest forgot for which he toiled.
    Then happy I, that love and am beloved
    Where I may not remove nor be removed.

26

Lord of my love, to whom in vassalage°   *feudal allegiance*
Thy merit hath my duty strongly knit,
To thee I send this written embassage°   *missive*
To witness duty, not to show my wit;
5 Duty so great, which wit so poor as mine
May make seem bare, in wanting° words to show it,   *lacking*
But that I hope some good conceit° of thine   *opinion; ingenuity*
In thy soul's thought (all naked)[1] will bestow° it,   *provide a place for*
Till whatsoever star that guides my moving°   *actions*
10 Points on me graciously with fair aspect°   *astrological influence*
And puts apparel on my tattered loving
To show me worthy of thy[2] sweet respect.
    Then may I dare to boast how I do love thee;
    Till then, not show my head where thou mayst prove° me.   *test*

27

Weary with toil, I haste me to my bed,
The dear repose for limbs with travel° tired,   *work; journeying*
But then begins a journey in my head
To work my mind, when body's work's expired.
5 For then my thoughts (from far where I abide)
Intend a zealous pilgrimage to thee,
And keep my drooping eyelids open wide,
Looking on darkness which the blind do see;
Save that my soul's imaginary sight
10 Presents thy shadow° to my sightless view,   *picture*
Which like a jewel hung in ghastly night
Makes black night beauteous and her old face new.
    Lo thus, by day my limbs, by night my mind,
    For° thee, and for myself, no quiet find.   *Because of*

28[1]

How can I then return in happy plight°   *condition*
That am debarred the benefit of rest,
When day's oppression is not eased by night,
But day by night and night by day oppressed?
5 And each (though enemies to either's° reign)   *each other's*

---

2. Only at the princes' pleasure or whim.
3. TEXTUAL COMMENT For the retention here of Q's uncharacteristic absence of rhyme between lines 9 and 11, see Digital Edition TC 3.
Sonnet 26
1. Refers to his "bare"-seeming "duty."

2. TEXTUAL COMMENT For the emendation of Q's "their" to "thy" here and elsewhere, based on Elizabethan handwriting, see Digital Edition TC 4.
Sonnet 28
1. This sonnet links with 27.

Do in consent shake hands to torture me,
The one by toil, the other to complain[2]
How far I toil, still farther off from thee.
I tell the day, to please him, thou art bright
10 And dost him grace when clouds do blot the heaven;[3]
So flatter I the swart°-complexioned night,   dark
When sparkling stars twire not thou gild'st the even.[4]
    But day doth daily draw my sorrows longer,
    And night doth nightly make grief's length seem stronger.

29

When in disgrace with fortune and men's eyes,
I all alone beweep my outcast state,
And trouble deaf heaven with my bootless° cries,   fruitless
And look upon myself and curse my fate;
5 Wishing me like to one more rich in hope,
Featured like him, like him with friends possessed,[1]
Desiring this man's art° and that man's scope,°   skill / range
With what I most enjoy° contented least;   like; own
Yet in these thoughts myself almost despising,
10 Haply[2] I think on thee, and then my state°   mood; fortunes
Like to the lark at break of day arising
From sullen earth sings hymns at heaven's gate.
    For thy sweet love remembered such wealth brings
    That then I scorn to change my state with kings.

30

When to the sessions° of sweet silent thought   court sittings
I summon° up remembrance of things past,   (play on court summons)
I sigh° the lack of many a thing I sought   mourn
And with old woes new wail my dear time's waste.[1]
5 Then can I drown an eye, unused to flow,
For precious friends hid in death's dateless° night,   endless
And weep afresh love's long-since-canceled° woe,   repaid (with sorrow)
And moan th'expense° of many a vanished sight.   passing
Then can I grieve at grievances foregone,°   bygone
10 And heavily° from woe to woe tell° o'er   sadly / say; count
The sad account° of fore-bemoanèd moan,   story; finances
Which I new pay as if not paid before.
    But if the while I think on thee, dear friend,
    All losses are restored and sorrows end.

31

Thy bosom is endearèd with° all hearts   loved by; enriched by
Which I by lacking have supposèd dead,
And there reigns love, and all love's loving parts,
And all those friends which I thought burièd.
5 How many a holy and obsequious° tear   dutifully mourning

2. *one:* day. *other:* night, making me "complain."
3. And confer beauty on him as a substitute for the sun.
4. By saying that when stars aren't twinkling, you brighten the evening.
Sonnet 29
1. *Wishing . . . possessed:* Three people he wants to
be like—"like to one" with better prospects, better looking "like him," and having friends "like him."
2. By chance; also, pun on "happily."
Sonnet 30
1. *my . . . waste:* the frittering or wasting away of my precious time.

Hath dear religious° love stol'n from mine eye   *devoted*
As interest of° the dead, which° now appear   *due payment to / who*
But things removed° that hidden in there lie!   *absent*
Thou art the grave where buried love doth live,
10 Hung with the trophies° of my lovers[1] gone,   *memorials*
Who all their parts° of me to thee did give: *shares*
That due of many[2] now is thine alone.
    Their images I loved I view in thee,
    And thou, all they,[3] hast all the all of me.

32

If thou survive my well-contented day[1]
When that churl death my bones with dust shall cover,
And shalt by fortune° once more resurvey   *chance*
These poor rude° lines of thy deceasèd lover,   *rough*
5 Compare them with the bett'ring° of the time,   *progress; better art*
And though they be outstripped by every pen,
Reserve° them for my love,° not for their rhyme,   *keep / out of love for me*
Exceeded by the height of happier men.[2]
Oh, then vouchsafe me but this loving thought:
10 "Had my friend's muse grown with this growing age,
A dearer birth° than this his love had brought   *worthier poem*
To march in ranks of better equipage;°   *poems*
    But since he died and poets better prove,°   *have improved*
    Theirs for their style I'll read, his for his love."

33

Full many a glorious morning have I seen
Flatter the mountain tops with sovereign eye,°   *sunlight*
Kissing with golden face the meadows green,
Gilding pale streams with heavenly alchemy,
5 Anon° permit the basest° clouds to ride   *(But) soon / darkest*
With ugly rack° on his celestial face   *cloudy mask*
And from the forlorn world his visage hide,
Stealing unseen to west° with this disgrace.   *to the west*
Even so my sun one early morn did shine
10 With all triumphant splendor on my brow,
But, out alack,° he was but one hour mine: *alas*
The region° cloud hath masked him from me now.   *high*
    Yet him for this my love no whit disdaineth;
    Suns° of the world may stain,° when heaven's sun staineth.   *(pun on "sons") / darken*

34[1]

Why didst thou promise such a beauteous day
And make me travel forth without my cloak,
To let base clouds o'ertake me in my way,
Hiding thy brav'ry° in their rotten smoke?°   *finery / noxious mists*
5 'Tis not enough that through the cloud thou break

Sonnet 31
1. Paramours; friends.
2. That love which was owed to many.
3. And you, who are made up of all of them.
Sonnet 32
1. Day of my death (possibly also: my span of life),
which I shall willingly accept.
2. *Exceeded . . . men:* Which is surpassed by poets
more fortunate in their talent.
Sonnet 34
1. This sonnet links with 33.

To dry the rain on my storm-beaten face,
For no man well of such a salve can speak
That heals the wound and cures not the disgrace.[2]
Nor can thy shame° give physic to° my grief: remorse / cure
10 Though thou repent, yet I have still the loss;
Th' offender's sorrow lends but weak relief
To him that bears the strong offense's loss.
    Ah, but those tears are pearl which thy love sheds,
    And they are rich and ransom° all ill deeds.   atone for

35

No more be grieved at that which thou hast done.
Roses have thorns, and silver fountains mud;
Clouds and eclipses stain° both moon and sun,   darken
And loathsome canker° lives in sweetest bud.   (worm)
5   All men make faults, and even I in this,
Authorizing thy trespass with compare,[1]
Myself corrupting salving thy amiss,[2]
Excusing thy sins more than thy sins are;[3]
For to thy sensual fault I bring in sense[4]—
10 Thy adverse party° is thy advocate°—   plaintiff / defender
And 'gainst myself a lawful plea commence.
Such civil war is in my love and hate
    That I an accessory needs must be
    To that sweet thief which sourly° robs from me.   cruelly; bitterly

36

Let me confess that we two must be twain,[1]
Although our undivided loves are one;
So shall those blots° that do with me remain   flaws; sources of shame
Without thy help by me be borne alone.
5   In our two loves there is but one respect,°   mutual affection
Though in our lives a separable spite,[2]
Which, though it alter not love's sole° effect,   single-minded
Yet doth it steal sweet hours from love's delight.
I may not evermore acknowledge thee
10 Lest my bewailèd guilt° should do thee shame,   (the poet's, or youth's)
Nor thou with public kindness honor me
Unless thou take° that honor from thy name.°   lose / family name
    But do not so. I love thee in such sort°   such a way
    As thou being mine, mine is thy good report.[3]

37

As a decrepit father takes delight
To see his active child do deeds of youth,
So I, made lame by fortune's dearest° spite,   direst
Take all my comfort of° thy worth and truth.   in

---

2. Disfigurement; dishonor done the poet by the youth's neglect.
Sonnet 35
1. Justifying your offense with comparisons.
2. Corrupting myself in minimizing your transgression.
3. Excusing you (overindulgently) from worse sins than the ones you've committed.

4. I use reason to defend your sensual offense.
Sonnet 36
1. Separated; but also, paradoxically, two of a kind or bound together.
2. Separation that causes vexation; vexation that causes separation.
3. *mine . . . report:* your good reputation is also mine. This couplet also ends Sonnet 96.

5 For whether beauty, birth, or wealth, or wit,
Or any of these all, or all, or more,
Entitled in their parts,[1] do crownèd sit,
I make my love engrafted to this store.[2]
So then I am not lame, poor, nor despised
10 Whilst that this shadow° doth such substance give   *idea*
That I in thy abundance am sufficed,
And by a part of all thy glory live.
      Look what° is best, that best I wish in thee.   *Whatever*
      This° wish I have—then ten times happy me!   *When this*

38

How can my muse want subject to invent°   *lack subject matter*
While thou dost breathe, that pour'st into my verse
Thine own sweet argument,° too excellent   *theme*
For every vulgar paper to rehearse?[1]
5 Oh, give thyself the thanks if aught in me
Worthy perusal stand against thy sight.[2]
For who's so dumb that cannot write to thee
When thou thyself dost give invention light?
Be thou the tenth muse—ten times more in worth
10 Than those old nine which rhymers invocate—
And he that calls on thee, let him bring forth
Eternal numbers° to outlive long° date.   *verses / a distant*
      If my slight muse do please these curious° days,   *finicky*
      The pain° be mine, but thine shall be the praise.   *pains; effort*

39

Oh,[1] how thy worth with manners° may I sing   *modesty*
When thou art all the better part of me?
What can mine own praise to mine own self bring,
And what is't but mine own when I praise thee?
5 Even for° this, let us divided live,   *Because of*
And our dear love lose name of single one,°   *the reputation of unity*
That by this separation I may give
That due to thee which thou deserv'st alone.
O[2] absence, what a torment wouldst thou prove,
10 Were it not° thy sour leisure gave sweet leave   *not that*
To entertain° the time with thoughts of love   *enliven*
(Which time and thoughts so sweetly doth deceive)
      And that thou° teachest how to make one twain,   *(absence)*
      By praising him here° who doth hence remain.   *in this poem*

Sonnet 37
1. Enrolled among your good qualities.
2. I engraft my love onto this abundance (of good qualities).
Sonnet 38
1. Every ordinary, commonplace piece of writing to set forth.
2. *if . . . sight:* if you see anything in my writing worth reading.
Sonnet 39
1. TEXTUAL COMMENT For the spellings "Oh" and "O" in this edition and their possible meanings, see Digital Edition TC 5.
2. TEXTUAL COMMENT For the same spellings in Q, see Digital Edition TC 6.

40[1]

Take all my loves, my love, yea, take them all!
What hast thou then more than thou hadst before?
No love, my love, that thou mayst true love call:
All mine was thine before thou hadst this more.
5 Then if for my love thou my love receivest,[2]
I cannot blame thee, for my love thou usest.[3]
But yet be blamed, if thou this self[4] deceivest
By willful taste of what thyself° refusest.   *your better nature*
I do forgive thy robb'ry, gentle thief,
10 Although thou steal thee all my poverty;°   *what little I own*
And yet love knows it is a greater grief
To bear love's wrong than hate's known injury.
     Lascivious grace,° in whom all ill well shows,   *Charming one*
     Kill me with spites,° yet we must not be foes.   *offenses*

41

Those pretty° wrongs that liberty° commits   *minor / licentiousness*
When I am sometime absent from thy heart,
Thy beauty and thy years full well befits,
For still° temptation follows where thou art.   *continually*
5 Gentle° thou art, and therefore to be won;   *Tender; upper-class*
Beauteous thou art, therefore to be assailed;
And when a woman woos, what woman's son
Will sourly leave her till he have prevailed?°   *(sexually)*
Ay me, but yet thou mightst my seat° forbear,   *(sexual) place*
10 And chide thy beauty and thy straying youth,
Who lead thee in their riot° even there   *depraved conduct*
Where thou art forced to break a twofold truth:
     Hers—by thy beauty tempting her to thee;
     Thine—by thy beauty being false to me.

42

That thou hast her it is not all my grief,
And yet it may be said I loved her dearly;
That she hath thee is of my wailing chief,°   *chief reason*
A loss in love that touches me more nearly.
5 Loving offenders, thus I will excuse ye:
Thou dost love her because thou know'st I love her,
And for my sake even so doth she abuse° me,   *mistreat*
Suff'ring my friend for my sake to approve her.[1]
If I lose thee, my loss is my love's gain,
10 And, losing° her, my friend hath found that loss;   *I losing*
Both find each other, and I lose both twain,
And both for my sake lay on me this cross.°   *affliction*
     But here's the joy: my friend and I are one.
     Sweet flattery!° Then she loves but me alone.   *Pleasing delusion*

Sonnet 40
1. Sonnets 40–42 concern a situation that may be identical to the love triangle described in 133–134 and 144.
2. Then if for/in place of love of me you host/take my beloved.

3. *for . . . usest:* because you use my beloved (sexually).
4. The poet (often emended, perhaps rightly, to "thyself").
Sonnet 42
1. To put her to the test (sexually).

43

When most I wink,° then do mine eyes best see,   *shut my eyes*
For all the day they view things unrespected,°   *unheeded; unworthy*
But when I sleep, in dreams they look on thee,
And, darkly bright, are bright in dark directed.[1]
5 Then thou, whose shadow shadows doth make bright[2]—
How would thy shadow's form° form happy show°   *substance / sight*
To the clear day, with thy much clearer light,
When to unseeing eyes[3] thy shade shines so!
How would (I say) mine eyes be blessèd made
10 By looking on thee in the living day,
When in dead night thy fair imperfect shade°   *incorporeal shadow*
Through heavy sleep on sightless eyes doth stay!°   *remain*
  All days are nights to see till I see thee,
  And nights bright days when dreams do show thee me.°   *to me*

44

If the dull° substance of my flesh were thought,   *heavy*
Injurious distance should not stop my way,
For then despite of space I would be brought,
From limits° far remote, where° thou dost stay.   *places / to where*
5 No matter then, although my foot did stand
Upon the farthest earth removed from thee,
For nimble thought can jump both sea and land
As soon as think the place where he° would be.   *(thought)*
But ah, thought kills me that I am not thought,
10 To leap large lengths of miles when thou art gone,
But that, so much of earth and water wrought,[1]
I must attend time's leisure[2] with my moan,
  Receiving naught by elements so slow
  But heavy tears, badges of either's woe.[3]

45[1]

The other two,[2] slight° air and purging fire,   *light*
Are both with thee, wherever I abide,
The first my thought, the other my desire:
These present-absent[3] with swift motion slide.
5 For when these quicker° elements are gone   *livelier*
In tender embassy of love to thee,
My life, being made of four, with two alone
Sinks down to death, oppressed with melancholy,
Until life's composition° be recured°   *mix of elements / restored*
10 By those swift messengers returned from thee,
Who even but now come back again assured
Of thy fair health, recounting it to me.
  This told, I joy; but then, no longer glad,
  I send them back again and straight° grow sad.   *at once*

Sonnet 43
1. (My eyes) seeing in the dark turn toward your bright eyes in the dark.
2. Whose image lightens darkness.
3. Because closed in sleep.
Sonnet 44
1. Being compounded of so much earth and water (the heavy elements).
2. I must wait humbly (as if on a great man) for time to reunite us.
3. Emblems of the grief of each of the poet's elements (earth because heavy [sad], water because wet).
Sonnet 45
1. This sonnet links with 44.
2. Of the poet's four elements. See 44.11.
3. Now present, now absent; constantly coming and going.

46

Mine eye and heart are at a mortal° war   *lethal*
How to divide the conquest of thy sight.[1]
Mine eye my° heart thy picture's sight would bar,   *to my*
My heart mine° eye the freedom° of that right.   *to my / free enjoyment*
5 My heart doth plead that thou in him° dost lie   *(the heart)*
(A closet° never pierced with crystal eyes),   *room*
But the defendant° doth that plea deny   *the eyes*
And says in him thy fair appearance lies.
To 'cide° this title is impanelèd°   *decide / enrolled*
10 A quest° of thoughts, all tenants to the heart,   *jury*
And by their verdict is determinèd
The clear eye's moiety° and the dear heart's part,   *share*
    As thus: mine eye's due is thy outward part,
    And my heart's right, thy inward love of heart.°   *the love from your heart*

47[1]

Betwixt mine eye and heart a league is took,°   *truce is made*
And each doth good turns now unto the other.
When that mine eye is famished for a look,
Or heart in love with sighs himself doth smother,[2]
5 With my love's picture then my eye doth feast
And to the painted banquet bids my heart;
Another time mine eye is my heart's guest,
And in his thoughts of love doth share a part.
So either by thy picture or my love,
10 Thyself, away, art present still° with me,   *always*
For thou no farther than my thoughts canst move,
And I am still with them, and they with thee;
    Or if they sleep, thy picture in my sight
    Awakes my heart, to heart's and eye's delight.

48

How careful was I when I took my way°   *set off*
Each trifle under truest bars° to thrust,   *strongest barriers*
That to my use° it might unusèd stay°   *benefit / remain safe*
From hands of falsehood, in sure wards° of trust!   *certain guards*
5 But thou, to° whom my jewels trifles are,   *compared to*
Most worthy comfort, now my greatest grief,[1]
Thou best of dearest, and mine only care,
Art left the prey of every vulgar thief.
Thee have I not locked up in any chest,
10 Save where thou art not, though I feel thou art,
Within the gentle closure of my breast,
From whence at pleasure thou mayst come and part;°   *go*
    And even thence thou wilt be stol'n, I fear,
    For truth° proves thievish for a prize so dear.   *even honesty*

49

Against° that time (if ever that time come)   *In preparation for*
When I shall see thee frown on my defects,

Sonnet 46
1. The spoils of the sight of you (possibly in a painting; see 47.5–14).
Sonnet 47
1. This sonnet links with 46.
2. Or when my loving heart smothers itself with sighs.

Sonnet 48
1. Because absent and in danger of being stolen.

Whenas thy love hath cast his utmost sum,[1]
Called to that audit by advised respects;°   *judicious reasons*
5   Against that time when thou shalt strangely° pass   *as a stranger*
And scarcely greet me with that sun, thine eye,
When love converted from the thing it was
Shall reasons find of settled gravity;[2]
Against that time do I ensconce me° here   *secure myself*
10   Within the knowledge of mine own desert,[3]
And this my hand against myself uprear°   *testify against myself*
To guard the lawful reasons on thy part.°   *defend your case*
    To leave poor me, thou hast the strength of laws,
    Since why to love° I can allege no cause.   *why you should love*

50

How heavy° do I journey on the way   *wearily*
When what I seek, my weary travel's end,
Doth teach that ease and that repose to say,[1]
"Thus far the miles are measured from thy friend."
5   The beast that bears me, tired with my woe,
Plods dully on to bear° that weight in me,   *while bearing*
As if by some instinct the wretch did know
His rider loved not speed being made[2] from thee.
The bloody spur cannot provoke him on
10   That sometimes anger thrusts into his hide,
Which heavily he answers with a groan
More sharp to me than spurring to his side,
    For that same groan doth put this in my mind:
    My grief lies onward and my joy behind.

51[1]

Thus can my love excuse the slow offense°   *offense of slowness*
Of my dull bearer when from thee I speed:
"From where thou art why should I haste me thence?
Till I return, of posting° is no need."   *riding quickly*
5   Oh, what excuse will my poor beast then find
When swift extremity° can seem but slow?   *extreme (return) speed*
Then should I spur, though mounted on the wind;
In wingèd speed no motion shall I know![2]
Then can no horse with my desire keep pace.
10   Therefore desire (of perfect'st love being made)
Shall neigh (no dull flesh in his fiery race!);[3]
But love, for love,° thus shall excuse my jade:°   *on love's behalf / horse*
    "Since from thee going he went willful slow,
    Towards thee I'll run, and give him leave to go."°   *walk*

Sonnet 49
1. When your love has calculated the bottom line.
2. Shall find reasons for a dignified reserve; shall find reasons of well-established seriousness (for leaving me).
3. My (lack of?) worthiness to be loved.
Sonnet 50
1. Teach the comforts at the end of the road to remind me that.
2. *speed being made:* hastening away; haste, when and because it is.

Sonnet 51
1. This sonnet links with 50.
2. I will feel no motion when desire carries me back through the air. See line 11 and Sonnets 44–45 for the association of fire and air with desire and thought, and of earth and water with dull, slow flesh.
3. TEXTUAL COMMENT For the retention of Q's wording but not its punctuation of this line, see Digital Edition TC 7.

52

So am I as the rich° whose blessèd key   *rich man*
Can bring him to his sweet up-lockèd treasure,
The which he will not ev'ry hour survey
For° blunting the fine point of seldom° pleasure.   *To avoid / occasional*
5 Therefore are feasts° so solemn° and so rare,   *feast days / dignified*
Since, seldom coming, in the long year set
Like stones of worth they thinly placèd are,
Or captain° jewels in the carcanet.°   *chief / jeweled collar*
So is the time that keeps you as° my chest,°   *like / jewel case*
10 Or as the wardrobe,° which the robe doth hide   *room for costly clothes*
To make some special instant special blest
By new unfolding his imprisoned pride.
    Blessèd are you whose worthiness gives scope,
    Being had, to triumph; being lacked, to hope.[1]

53

What is your substance, whereof are you made,
That millions of strange shadows on you tend,°   *attend*
Since everyone hath, every one, one shade,[1]
And you, but one, can every shadow lend?[2]
5 Describe° Adonis, and the counterfeit°   *Draw / likeness*
Is poorly imitated after you.°   *Is a poor imitation of you*
On Helen's cheek all art of beauty set,
And you in Grecian tires are painted new.[3]
Speak of the spring and foison° of the year: *harvest time*
10 The one doth shadow of your beauty show,
The other as your bounty doth appear,
And you° in every blessèd shape we know.°   *you are / recognize*
    In all external grace you have some part,
    But you like none, none you,° for constant heart.°   *like you / (pun on "art")*

54

Oh, how much more doth beauty beauteous seem
By° that sweet ornament which truth doth give!   *Because of*
The rose looks fair, but fairer we it deem
For that sweet odor which doth in it live.
5 The canker blooms[1] have full as deep a dye
As the perfumèd tincture° of the roses,   *color*
Hang on such thorns, and play as wantonly°   *flatter as playfully*
When summer's breath their maskèd buds discloses;
But, for° their virtue only is° their show,   *since / lies wholly in*
10 They live unwooed, and unrespected° fade,   *unappreciated*
Die to themselves.° Sweet roses do not so;   *alone; without influence*
Of their sweet deaths are sweetest odors made.
    And so of you, beauteous and lovely youth:
    When that° shall vade, by verse distills your truth.[2]   *beauty*

Sonnet 52
1. *gives . . . hope:* allows me to exult when with you and to hope when not with you.
Sonnet 53
1. Since each person has an individual shadow.
2. Can cast all shadows (are visible in every beautiful image).
3. *On . . . new:* If one were to use every art to reproduce the beauty of Helen of Troy (or use artful cos-

metics on Helen's cheek), it would look like you in Grecian headgear.
Sonnet 54
1. Dog roses (having little scent)—hence, run-of-the-mill people, but also with the connotation of the cankerworm that destroys the rose.
2. *vade . . . truth:* "vade" is a variant of "fade" but also means "depart," from the Latin *vadere*. By my verse your truth is distilled. See Sonnet 5 for distilling.

55

Not marble nor the gilded monuments
Of princes shall outlive this powerful rhyme,
But you shall shine more bright in these contents
Than unswept stone besmeared with sluttish° time.   *slovenly*
5   When wasteful war shall statues overturn
And broils° root out the work of masonry,   *battles*
Nor Mars his° sword nor war's quick fire shall burn   *Neither Mars's*
The living record of your memory.
'Gainst death and all oblivious enmity
10 Shall you pace forth. Your praise shall still find room
Even in the eyes of all posterity
That wear this world out to the ending doom.[1]
    So till the judgment that yourself arise,
    You live in this, and dwell in lovers' eyes.

56

Sweet love,° renew thy force. Be it not said   *(the feeling, not the lover)*
Thy edge should blunter be than appetite,
Which, but° today, by feeding is allayed,   *only for*
Tomorrow sharpened in his former might.
5   So, love, be thou. Although today thou fill
Thy hungry eyes even till they wink° with fullness,   *close (to sleep)*
Tomorrow see again and do not kill
The spirit of love with a perpetual dullness.
Let this sad int'rim like the ocean be
10 Which parts the shore° where two, contracted new,°   *shores / newly betrothed*
Come daily to the banks, that when they see
Return of love,° more blessed may be the view—   *the other lover*
    Or call it winter, which, being full of care,
    Makes summer's welcome thrice more wished, more rare.° *valuable*

57

Being your slave, what should I do but tend°   *wait*
Upon the hours and times of your desire?
I have no precious time at all to spend
Nor services to do till you require.°   *(my services)*
5   Nor dare I chide the world-without-end° hour   *endless*
Whilst I, my sovereign,° watch the clock for you,   *you (directly addressed)*
Nor think the bitterness of absence sour
When you have bid your servant once adieu.
Nor dare I question with my jealous thought
10 Where you may be, or your affairs suppose,°   *speculate on*
But like a sad slave stay and think of naught
Save, where you are, how happy you make those.°   *(who are with you)*
    So true a fool is love that in your will,[1]
    Though you do anything, he thinks no ill.

Sonnet 55
1. Doomsday: in Christianity, the Day of Judgment, when dead bodies are supposed to "arise" (line 13) from the grave and be united with their souls.

Sonnet 57
1. Desire (including sexual desire); capitalized in Q, perhaps punning on Shakespeare's first name—Will, nickname for William. See 135–136, 143.

58[1]

That° god forbid that made me first your slave   *May that*
I should in thought control your times of pleasure,
Or at your hand th'account of hours to crave,[2]
Being your vassal° bound to stay° your leisure.   *slave (and) / wait upon*
Oh, let me suffer, being at your beck,   5
Th'imprisoned absence of your liberty,[3]
And patience, tame to sufferance, bide each check[4]
Without accusing you of injury.
Be where you list.° Your charter° is so strong   *wish / freedom*
That you yourself may privilege° your time   *allocate*   10
To what you will. To you it doth belong
Yourself to pardon of self-doing° crime.   *committed by you*
    I am to wait, though waiting so be hell,
    Not blame your pleasure, be it ill or well.

59

If there be nothing new, but that which is
Hath been before, how are our brains beguiled,°   *cheated*
Which, laboring for° invention, bear amiss   *working at; giving birth to*
The second burden of a former child?[1]
Oh, that record° could with a backward look   *if only written memory*   5
Even of five hundred courses of the sun
Show me your image in some antique book,
Since mind at first in character was done,[2]
That I might see what the old world could say
To this composèd wonder of your frame:[3]   10
Whether we are mended,° or whe'er better they,   *improved*
Or whether revolution be the same.[4]
    Oh, sure I am the wits° of former days   *clever writers*
    To subjects worse have given admiring praise.

60

Like as the waves make towards the pebbled shore,
So do our minutes hasten to their end,
Each changing place with that which goes before;
In sequent toil all forwards do contend.[1]
Nativity,° once in the main of light,°   *A newborn / in the world*   5
Crawls to maturity, wherewith being crowned,
Crookèd° eclipses 'gainst his glory fight,   *Pernicious*
And Time that gave doth now his gift confound.°   *ruin*
Time doth transfix the flourish[2] set on youth
And delves the parallels° in beauty's brow,   *carves the wrinkles*   10
Feeds on the rarities of nature's truth,[3]
And nothing stands but for his scythe to mow.
    And yet to times in hope° my verse shall stand,   *future days*
    Praising thy worth, despite his° cruel hand.   *(Time's)*

Sonnet 58
1. This sonnet links with 57.
2. Or seek an account of how you pass your time.
3. The imprisoned feeling caused by your licentiousness when you're away.
4. And (let me) patiently, acquiescent in suffering, endure each setback.
Sonnet 59
1. *bear . . . child:* mistakenly give birth for a second time to a (brain-)child that has already been born.
2. Since writing was invented.

3. To the wonderful composition of your form (perhaps referring to the sonnet itself as well).
4. Whether the revolving of the ages makes no difference.
Sonnet 60
1. Toiling one after the other, all seek to move forward.
2. Time pierces and destroys the ornament (beauty).
3. On the most precious products of nature's perfection.

61

Is it thy will thy image should keep open
My heavy eyelids to the weary night?
Dost thou desire my slumbers should be broken,
While shadows° like to thee do mock my sight?   *visions*
5 Is it thy spirit that thou send'st from thee
So far from home into my deeds to pry,
To find out shames and idle hours in me,°   *my leisure-time misdeeds*
The scope and tenor of thy jealousy?[1]
Oh no, thy love, though much, is not so great;
10 It is my love that keeps mine eye awake,
Mine own true love that doth my rest defeat
To play the watchman ever for thy sake.
  For thee watch I,° whilst thou dost wake elsewhere, *I remain awake*
  From me far off, with others all too near.

62

Sin of self-love possesseth all mine eye,
And all my soul, and all my every part;
And for this sin there is no remedy,
It is so grounded inward in my heart.
5 Methinks no face so gracious is as mine,
No shape so true,° no truth of such account,   *perfect*
And for myself mine own worth do define
As° I all other° in all worths surmount.   *As if / others*
But when my glass° shows me myself indeed,   *mirror*
10 Beated and chopped with tanned antiquity,
Mine own self-love quite contrary I read:
Self so self-loving were iniquity.
  'Tis thee (my self)° that for° myself I praise, *you, my other self / as*
  Painting my age with beauty of thy days.

63

Against° my love shall be as I am now,   *Preparing for when*
With Time's injurious hand crushed and o'erworn,
When hours have drained his blood and filled his brow
With lines and wrinkles, when his youthful morn
5 Hath traveled° on to age's steepy[1] night   *progressed; toiled*
And all those beauties whereof now he's king
Are vanishing, or vanished out of sight,
Stealing away the treasure of his spring—
For such a time do I now fortify
10 Against confounding° age's cruel knife,   *devastating*
That he° shall never cut from memory   *(age)*
My sweet love's beauty, though° my lover's life. *though he will sever*
  His beauty shall in these black lines be seen,
  And they shall live, and he in them still green.° *perpetually youthful*

Sonnet 61
1. (Which are) the object and intent of your distrust (that is, the "shames and idle hours," line 7).

Sonnet 63
1. Precipitous (like the path of the setting sun).

64

When I have seen by Time's fell° hand defaced   *fierce*
The rich proud cost° of outworn buried age,   *expense*
When sometime° lofty towers I see down razed   *once*
And brass eternal slave to mortal rage;[1]
5 When I have seen the hungry ocean gain
Advantage on the kingdom of the shore
And the firm soil win of° the wat'ry main,   *win ground from*
Increasing store with loss, and loss with store;[2]
When I have seen such interchange of state,
10 Or state[3] itself confounded to decay,°   *reduced to ruins*
Ruin hath taught me thus to ruminate
That Time will come and take my love away.
      This thought is as a death, which° cannot choose   *(thought)*
      But weep to have° that which it fears to lose.   *at having*

65

Since° brass, nor stone, nor earth, nor boundless sea,   *Since there is neither*
But sad mortality o'ersways their power,
How with this rage shall beauty hold a plea,[1]
Whose action is no stronger than a flower?
5 Oh, how shall summer's honey breath hold out
Against the wrackful° siege of batt'ring days,   *damaging*
When rocks impregnable are not so stout,
Nor gates of steel so strong, but Time decays?°   *decays them*
Oh, fearful meditation; where, alack,
10 Shall Time's best jewel° from Time's chest[2] lie hid?   *(the beloved)*
Or what strong hand can hold his° swift foot back,   *(Time's)*
Or who his spoil° of beauty can forbid?   *destruction*
      Oh, none, unless this miracle have might,
      That in black ink my love may still shine bright.

66

Tired with all these,° for restful death I cry: *(the ensuing wrongs)*
As to behold desert a beggar born,
And needy nothing trimmed in jollity,[1]
And purest faith unhappily forsworn,°   *betrayed; perjured*
5 And gilded honor shamefully misplaced,
And maiden virtue rudely strumpeted,
And right perfection wrongfully disgraced,
And strength by limping sway° disabled,   *feeble leaders*
And art made tongue-tied° by authority,   *learning silenced*
10 And folly (doctor-like) controlling skill,[2]
And simple truth miscalled simplicity,°   *naïveté*
And captive good attending° captain ill.   *serving*
      Tired with all these, from these would I be gone,
      Save that to die I leave my love alone.

Sonnet 64
1. And eternal brass forever succumbs to death's violence.
2. Adding to the stock of one by loss of the other, and vice versa.
3. *state* (line 9): condition; sovereign territory. *state* (line 10): pomp.
Sonnet 65
1. How can beauty make a (legal) case against such a power to destroy?

2. (Miser's) treasure chest; coffin.
Sonnet 66
1. *As . . . jollity:* For example, to see merit (a worthy person) born in poverty (and hence without prospects) / And talentless (or impoverished) worthlessness adorned with finery.
2. And folly, feigning erudition, dominating true wisdom or ability. Before modern medicine, doctors were often portrayed as fools or con artists.

67

Ah, wherefore with infection[1] should he live
And with his presence grace impiety,
That° sin by him advantage should achieve   *So that*
And lace° itself with his society?   *decorate*
5   Why should false painting imitate his cheek
And steal dead seeing of[2] his living hue?
Why should poor° beauty indirectly seek   *lesser; aged*
Roses of shadow,° since his rose is true?   *Cosmetic beauty*
Why should he live, now Nature bankrupt is,
10   Beggared° of blood to blush° through lively veins,   *Bereft / flow red*
For she hath no exchequer° now but his   *treasury*
And, proud of many, lives upon his gains?[3]
　　Oh, him she stores,° to show what wealth she had   *keeps*
　　In days long since, before these last so bad.

68[1]

Thus is his cheek the map° of days outworn   *image*
When beauty lived and died as flowers do now,
Before these bastard signs of fair° were borne°   *cosmetics / worn; born*
Or durst inhabit on a living brow;
5   Before the golden tresses of the dead,
The right of sepulchers,[2] were shorn away
To live a second life on second head;
Ere beauty's dead fleece made another gay.
In him those holy antique hours° are seen   *good old days*
10   Without all ornament, itself and true,
Making no summer of another's green,
Robbing no old to dress his beauty new;
　　And him as for a map doth Nature store,°   *keep*
　　To show false Art what beauty was of yore.

69

Those parts of thee that the world's eye doth view
Want° nothing that the thought of hearts can mend;°   *Lack / imagine better*
All tongues (the voice of souls) give thee that due,
Utt'ring bare truth, even so as foes commend.[1]
5   Thy outward thus with outward praise is crowned,
But those same tongues that give thee so thine own°   *your due*
In other accents° do this praise confound°   *words / undermine*
By seeing farther than the eye hath shown.
They look into the beauty of thy mind,
10   And that in guess they measure by thy deeds.
Then, churls, their thoughts (although their eyes were kind)
To thy fair flower add the rank smell of weeds.
　　But why thy odor matcheth not thy show,°   *appearance*
　　The soil is this, that thou dost common grow.[2]

Sonnet 67
1. The world's ills (as in 66).
2. *dead seeing of*: an inanimate outward resemblance from.
3. Though (falsely, nostalgically) taking pride in her abundance (of lesser or former beauties), lives off the interest he earns (from his endowment of true beauty).
Sonnet 68
1. This sonnet links with 67.

2. Properly belonging to tombs (wigs were made from the hair of corpses).
Sonnet 69
1. Uttering minimal truth, in the way that enemies praise.
2. The ground (reason; also, stain) is this: you are becoming low (promiscuous).

70[1]

That thou art blamed shall not be thy defect,

For slander's mark° was ever yet the fair.   *target*

The ornament of beauty is suspect,°   *suspicion*

A crow that flies in heaven's sweetest air.

5 So° thou be good, slander doth but approve   *So long as*

Thy worth the greater, being wooed of time,[2]

For canker vice[3] the sweetest buds doth love,

And thou present'st a pure unstainèd prime.°   *youth*

Thou hast passed by the ambush of young days

10 Either not assailed or victor being charged;°   *defeating an attack*

Yet this thy praise cannot be so° thy praise   *enough*

To tie up envy, evermore enlarged.°   *forever at large; growing*

    If some suspect° of ill masked not thy show,°   *suspicion / appearance*

    Then thou alone kingdoms of hearts shouldst owe.°   *own*

71[1]

No longer mourn for me when I am dead

Than you shall hear the surly sullen bell

Give warning to the world that I am fled

From this vile world with vilest[2] worms to dwell.

5 Nay, if you read this line, remember not

The hand that writ it, for I love you so

That I in your sweet thoughts would be forgot

If thinking on me then should make you woe.

Oh, if, I say, you look upon this verse

10 When I, perhaps, compounded am° with clay,   *am mixed*

Do not so much as my poor name rehearse,°   *repeat; rebury*

But let your love even with my life decay,

    Lest the wise world should look into your moan

    And mock you with me° after I am gone.   *for loving me*

72

Oh, lest the world should task you to recite

What merit lived in me that you should love,

After my death, dear love, forget me quite,

For you in me can nothing worthy prove°—   *provide evidence of*

5 Unless you would devise some virtuous lie

To do more for me than mine own desert,

And hang more praise upon deceasèd I

Than niggard truth would willingly impart.

Oh, lest your true love may seem false in this,

10 That you for love speak well of me untrue,°   *untruthfully*

My° name be buried where my body is   *Let my*

And live no more to shame nor me nor you;

    For I am shamed by that which I bring forth,[1]

    And so should you,° to love things nothing worth.   *you be*

Sonnet 70
1. This sonnet links with 69.
2. *slander . . . time:* the gossip merely proves that because you're so popular ("wooed of time"), you're worth even more.
3. Slander, like a cankerworm.
Sonnet 71
1. The first of four linked sonnets.

2. Q's "vildest" is an archaic form of "vilest" that may also carry the connotation of "most reviled."
Sonnet 72
1. Presumably alluding to the writer's poems or to his profession as actor and playwright.

73

That time of year thou mayst in me behold
When yellow leaves, or none, or few do hang
Upon those boughs which shake against the cold,
Bare ruined choirs where late the sweet birds sang.[1]
5 In me thou seest the twilight of such day
As after sunset fadeth in the west,
Which by and by black night doth take away,
Death's second self that seals up all in rest.
In me thou seest the glowing of such fire
10 That° on the ashes of his youth[2] doth lie,   *As*
As the deathbed whereon it must expire,
Consumed with that which it was nourished by.[3]
    This thou perceiv'st, which makes thy love more strong,
    To love that° well which thou must leave ere long.   *(the speaker); (life)*

74

But be contented when that fell arrest°   *fearful death*
Without all bail shall carry me away.
My life hath in this line° some interest,°   *verse / legal claim*
Which for memorial still with thee shall stay.
5 When thou reviewest° this, thou dost review   *reread*
The very part° was consecrate° to thee: *part of me that / devoted*
The earth can have but earth, which is his° due;   *its*
My spirit is thine, the better part of me.
So then thou hast but lost the dregs of life,
10 The prey of worms, my body being dead,
The coward conquest of a wretch's knife,[1]
Too base of° thee to be rememberèd.   *by*
    The worth of that° is that which it contains,   *(the body)*
    And that is this,° and this with thee remains.   *the spirit (his poetry)*

75

So are you to my thoughts as food to life
Or as sweet seasoned° showers are to the ground,   *spring*
And for the peace of you° I hold such strife   *you provide*
As twixt a miser and his wealth is found:
5 Now proud as an enjoyer, and anon°   *soon; immediately*
Doubting the filching age[1] will steal his treasure;
Now counting° best to be with you alone,   *estimating*
Then bettered° that the world may see my pleasure;   *better contented*
Sometime all full with feasting on your sight
10 And by and by clean° starvèd for a look;   *wholly*
Possessing or pursuing no delight
Save what is had° or must° from you be took.   *(already) / (later)*
    Thus do I pine and surfeit day by day,
    Or° gluttoning on all, or all away.°   *Either / having nothing*

Sonnet 73
1. *choirs:* the area in a church where the choir ("sweet birds") sings; gatherings of manuscript "leaves" (line 2), or quires ("quiers" in Q).
2. Perhaps referring to the phoenix, a legendary self-resurrecting bird believed to live in cycles of several centuries, dying in flames and being reborn from the ashes. See also 19.4 and Shakespeare's "The Phoenix and Turtle."

3. Ironically, the fire is choked ("consumed") by (along with) the ashes, which are the residue of the fuel that the fire previously fed upon ("was nourished by").
Sonnet 74
1. The cowardly conquest of a wretch such as Death (who was thought to carry a scythe).
Sonnet 75
1. Fearing that these dishonest times.

76

Why is my verse so barren of new pride,°   *adornments*
So far from variation or quick° change?   *lively*
Why with the time° do I not glance aside   *following the fashion*
To new-found methods and to compounds[1] strange?
5   Why write I still all one, ever the same,
And keep invention in a noted weed,[2]
That every word doth almost tell my name,
Showing their birth, and where° they did proceed?   *whence*
Oh, know, sweet love, I always write of you,
10 And you and love are still my argument.°   *always my topic*
So all my best is dressing old words new,
Spending again what is already spent,
    For as the sun is daily new and old,
    So is my love still telling what is told.

77[1]

Thy glass° will show thee how thy beauties wear,[2]   *mirror*
Thy dial° how thy precious minutes waste,   *sundial*
The vacant leaves thy mind's imprint° will bear,   *written ideas*
And of this book this learning° mayst thou taste: *(what you write)*
5   The wrinkles which thy glass will truly show
Of mouthèd° graves will give thee memory;°   *gaping / remind you*
Thou by thy dial's shady stealth° mayst know   *stealing shadow*
Time's thievish progress to eternity.
Look what° thy memory cannot contain   *Whatever*
10 Commit to these waste blanks,° and thou shalt find   *empty pages*
Those children nursed,° delivered from thy brain,   *preserved*
To take a new acquaintance of thy mind.°   *strike you afresh*
    These offices,° so oft as thou wilt look,   *functions*
    Shall profit thee and much enrich thy book.

78[1]

So oft have I invoked thee for my muse
And found such fair assistance in my verse
As every alien pen hath got my use,[2]
And under thee° their poesy disperse.   *with you as patron*
5   Thine eyes, that taught the dumb on high° to sing   *aloud*
And heavy ignorance aloft to fly,
Have added feathers to the learned's wing[3]
And given grace° a double majesty.   *excellence*
Yet be most proud of that which I compile,°   *write*
10 Whose influence° is thine and born of thee.   *power to move*
In others' works thou dost but mend° the style,   *improve*
And arts° with thy sweet graces gracèd be.   *(their) artistry*
    But thou art all my art, and dost advance
    As high as learning my rude ignorance.

Sonnet 76
1. *compounds:* stylistic or formal mixtures; compound words; elaborate medicines (with "methods," which also refers to both literary and medical treatments).
2. And keep literary creativity in such familiar clothing.
Sonnet 77
1. This sonnet is presented as accompanying the gift of a notebook.
2. Last; wear away; "were" (Q's spelling).
Sonnet 78
1. This sonnet begins the rival poet sequence (78–80, 82–86).
2. That every other poet imitates me.
3. Have improved the poetic "flights" of even accomplished poets.

79

Whilst I alone did call upon thy aid,
My verse alone had all thy gentle grace;
But now my gracious numbers are decayed,
And my sick muse doth give another place.°   *way to another poet*
5   I grant, sweet love, thy lovely argument[1]
Deserves the travail° of a worthier pen,   *labor*
Yet what of thee thy poet° doth invent   *(the writer or his rival)*
He robs thee of and pays it thee again.
He lends thee virtue, and he stole that word
10 From thy behavior; beauty doth he give
And found it in thy cheek: he can afford°   *extend*
No praise to thee but what in thee doth live.
      Then thank him not for that which he doth say,
      Since what he owes thee thou thyself dost pay.

80

Oh, how I faint° when I of you do write,   *get discouraged*
Knowing a better spirit° doth use your name   *(the rival poet)*
And, in the praise thereof, spends all his might
To make me tongue-tied speaking of your fame.
5   But since your worth, wide as the ocean is,
The humble as° the proudest sail doth bear,   *as well as*
My saucy bark,° inferior far to his,   *impudent boat*
On your broad main° doth willfully appear.   *waters*
Your shallowest help will hold me up afloat
10 Whilst he upon your soundless° deep doth ride,   *bottomless*
Or, being wrecked, I am a worthless boat,
He of tall building° and of goodly pride.°   *strong build / magnificence*
      Then if he thrive and I be cast away,
      The worst was this: my love was my decay.

81[1]

Or° I shall live your epitaph to make,   *Either*
Or you survive when I in earth am rotten;
From hence° your memory death cannot take,   *the world; my poetry*
Although in me each part° will be forgotten.   *each of my attributes*
5   Your name from hence° immortal life shall have,   *henceforth; my poetry*
Though I, once gone, to all the world must die;
The earth can yield me but a common grave,
When you entombèd in men's eyes shall lie.
Your monument shall be my gentle verse,
10 Which eyes not yet created shall o'er-read,
And tongues to be° your being shall rehearse°   *future tongues / recite*
When all the breathers of this world are dead.
      You still shall live—such virtue° hath my pen—   *power*
      Where breath most breathes, even in° the mouths of men.   *right in*

Sonnet 79
1. The subject of your loveliness.

Sonnet 81
1. Except for lines 2–3 and 10–11, any two consecutive lines in this sonnet form a complete sentence.

82

I grant thou wert not married to my muse,
And therefore mayst without attaint o'erlook°   *dishonor read*
The dedicated[1] words which writers° use   *other writers*
Of their fair subject, blessing[2] every book.
5 Thou art as fair in knowledge as in hue,°   *appearance*
Finding thy worth a limit° past my praise,   *region*
And therefore art enforced to seek anew
Some fresher stamp of the time-bettering days.[3]
And do so, love! Yet when they have devised
10 What strainèd touches rhetoric can lend,
Thou, truly fair, wert truly sympathized[4]
In true plain words by thy true-telling friend,
   And their gross painting° might be better used   *cosmetics; flattery*
   Where cheeks need blood. In thee, it is abused.°   *used wrongly*

83

I never saw that you did painting° need,   *cosmetics; exaggeration*
And therefore to your fair° no painting set.   *beauty*
I found—or thought I found—you did exceed
The barren tender° of a poet's debt;   *payment*
5 And therefore have I slept in your report,[1]
That° you yourself, being extant, well might show   *So that*
How far a modern° quill doth come too short,   *trite; fashionable*
Speaking of worth, what worth[2] in you doth grow.
This silence for° my sin you did impute,   *to be*
10 Which shall be most my glory, being dumb,
For I impair not beauty, being mute,
When others would give life and bring a tomb.[3]
   There lives more life in one of your fair eyes
   Than both your poets can in praise devise.

84

Who is it that says most which[1] can say more
Than this rich praise—that you alone are you;
In whose confine immurèd is the store
Which should example where your equal grew?[2]
5 Lean penury within that pen doth dwell
That to his subject lends not some small glory;
But he that writes of you, if he can tell
That you are you, so dignifies his story.
Let him but copy what in you is writ,
10 Not making worse what nature made so clear,°   *purely excellent*
And such a counterpart shall fame° his wit,   *copy will make famous*
Making his style admirèd everywhere.
   You to your beauteous blessings add a curse,[3]
   Being fond on praise, which makes your praises worse.[4]

Sonnet 82
1. Devoted; referring to a prefatory dedication.
2. Either the writers or the youth is "blessing," just as either the poet or the youth is "finding" (line 6).
3. Some more recent imprint (commendation) of these culturally progressive times.
4. Would be accurately represented.
Sonnet 83
1. Neglected to sing your praises.
2. In speaking of value of the worth that.
3. When others who try to make you live in their writings only end up burying you.
Sonnet 84
1. *Who . . . which*: What hyperbolical enthusiast.
2. *In . . . grew*: Within whom is contained the stock that would be needed to produce your equal?
3. Personality flaw; vexation (for those who would praise you).
4. Being (too) fond of praise, which makes the praise seem like flattery; being (too) fond of the sort of praise that detracts from you (because you're better than it).

85

My tongue-tied muse in manners holds her still,°   *tactfully says nothing*
While comments of° your praise, richly compiled,   *commentaries in*
Reserve their character° with golden quill   *Hoard up your features*
And precious phrase by all the muses filed.°   *polished*
5 I think good thoughts, whilst other° write good words,   *others*
And like unlettered clerk still cry "Amen"[1]
To every hymn[1] that able spirit affords°   *offers*
In polished form of well-refinèd pen.
Hearing you praised, I say, "'Tis so, 'tis true,"
10 And to the most° of praise add something more—   *highest*
But that is in my thought,° whose love to you,   *unspoken*
Though words come hindmost, holds his rank before.°   *before all others*
    Then others for the breath of words respect,°   *hold in esteem*
    Me for my dumb thoughts, speaking in effect.°   *in reality*

86

Was it the proud full sail of his° great verse,   *(a rival poet's)*
Bound for the prize° of all-too-precious you,   *pirate's spoils*
That did my ripe thoughts in my brain inhearse,°   *bury*
Making their tomb the womb wherein they grew?
5 Was it his spirit, by spirits taught to write
Above a mortal pitch,° that struck me dead?   *height*
No, neither he, nor his compeers[1] by night
Giving him aid, my verse astonishèd.°   *made silent*
He, nor that affable familiar ghost°   *spirit*
10 Which nightly gulls° him with intelligence,°   *fools / ideas*
As victors of my silence cannot boast:
I was not sick of any fear from thence.
    But when your countenance filled up[2] his line,
    Then lacked I matter. That enfeebled mine.

87

Farewell! Thou art too dear° for my possessing,   *costly*
And like° enough thou know'st thy estimate.°   *it is likely / value*
The charter of thy worth gives thee releasing;[1]
My bonds in thee are all determinate.°   *terminated*
5 For how do I hold thee but by thy granting,
And for that riches where is my deserving?
The cause° of° this fair gift in me is wanting,   *reason; legal case / for*
And so my patent back again is swerving.[2]
Thyself thou gav'st, thy own worth then not knowing,
10 Or me, to whom thou gav'st it, else mistaking;°   *overestimating*
So thy great gift, upon misprision growing,°   *based on error*
Comes home again on better judgment making.[3]
    Thus have I had thee as a dream doth flatter:°   *creates an illusion*
    In sleep a king, but waking no such matter.

Sonnet 85
1. *like . . . hymn:* like an illiterate parish clerk reflexively approve ("cry 'Amen'" after) every poem ("hymn") of praise.
Sonnet 86
1. Colleagues (the "spirits" in line 5).
2. Your features gave the entire subject-matter to; your approval made up for any lack in.
Sonnet 87
1. The privilege you derive from your worth releases you from love's bonds.
2. My rights of possession revert to you.
3. *on . . . making:* when you realize your error.

88

When thou shalt be disposed to set me light°   *value me little*
And place my merit in the eye of scorn,
Upon thy side against myself I'll fight
And prove thee virtuous, though thou art forsworn.
5 With mine own weakness being best acquainted,
Upon thy part° I can set down a story   *On your behalf*
Of faults concealed wherein I am attainted°   *charged; tainted*
That° thou, in losing me, shalt win much glory;   *So that*
And I by this will be a gainer too,
10 For, bending all my loving thoughts on thee,
The injuries that to myself I do,
Doing thee vantage,° double vantage me.[1]   *advantage*
    Such is my love, to thee I so belong,
    That for thy right myself will bear° all wrong.   *suffer; reveal (bare)*

89

Say that thou didst forsake me for some fault,
And I will comment° upon that offense.   *elaborate*
Speak of my lameness, and I straight will halt,[1]
Against thy reasons making no defense.
5 Thou canst not, love, disgrace me half so ill,
To set a form upon desirèd change,[2]
As I'll myself disgrace, knowing thy will.
I will acquaintance strangle and look strange,[3]
Be absent from thy walks,° and in my tongue,   *familiar places*
10 Thy sweet belovèd name no more shall dwell,
Lest I, too much profane, should do it wrong
And haply° of our old acquaintance tell.   *by chance*
    For thee, against myself I'll vow debate,°   *combat*
    For I must ne'er love him whom thou dost hate.

90[1]

Then hate me when thou wilt—if ever, now!
Now, while the world is bent my deeds to cross,°   *foil*
Join with the spite of fortune, make me bow,
And do not drop in for an after-loss.[2]
5 Ah, do not, when my heart hath scaped this sorrow,
Come in the rearward of a conquered woe;[3]
Give not a windy night a rainy morrow
To linger out a purposed overthrow.[4]
If thou wilt leave me, do not leave me last,
10 When other petty griefs have done their spite,
But in the onset come. So shall I taste
At first the very worst of fortune's might,
    And other strains° of woe, which now seem woe,   *types; burdens*
    Compared with loss of thee, will not seem so.

Sonnet 88
1. "Double" because the speaker is now being honest and because he takes pleasure in benefiting his beloved; but perhaps "double" also means "duplicitous."
Sonnet 89
1. Talk of my disability (perhaps alluding to the lame meter of line 2), and I at once will limp (stop objecting).
2. To lend justification to the change you seek.

3. I will end our familiarity and act like a stranger.
Sonnet 90
1. This sonnet links with 89.
2. Do not fall upon me to inflict a later disaster.
3. Assault me again after I have overcome my present grief.
4. *To . . . overthrow:* By protracting or delaying your intended assault.

91

Some glory in their birth, some in their skill,
Some in their wealth, some in their body's force,
Some in their garments (though new-fangled ill),°   *fashionably ugly*
Some in their hawks and hounds, some in their horse;°   *horses*
5   And every humor hath his° adjunct pleasure   *temperament has its*
Wherein it finds a joy above the rest.
But these particulars are not my measure;°   *(of joy)*
All these I better° in one general best.   *exceed*
Thy love is better than high birth to me,
10   Richer than wealth, prouder than garments' cost,
Of more delight than hawks or horses be;
And having thee, of all men's pride[1] I boast—
        Wretched in this alone, that thou mayst take
        All this away, and me most wretched make.

92[1]

But do thy worst to steal thyself away,
For term of° life thou art assurèd mine,   *the duration of my*
And life no longer than thy love will stay,
For it depends upon that love of thine.
5   Then need I not to fear the worst of wrongs,
When in the least of them[2] my life hath end;
I see a better state° to me belongs   *condition; situation*
Than that which on thy humor° doth depend.   *mood*
Thou canst not vex me with inconstant mind,
10   Since that my life on thy revolt doth lie.[3]
Oh, what a happy title[4] do I find:
Happy to have thy love, happy to die!
        But what's so blessèd fair that fears no blot?
        Thou mayst be false, and yet I know it not.

93[1]

So shall I live supposing thou art true,
Like a deceivèd husband; so love's face°   *appearance*
May still seem love to me, though altered new—
Thy looks with me, thy heart in other place.
5   For there can live no hatred in thine eye;
Therefore in that I cannot know thy change.
In many's looks, the false heart's history
Is writ in moods and frowns and wrinkles strange,[2]
But heaven in thy creation did decree
10   That in thy face sweet love should ever dwell;
Whate'er thy thoughts or thy heart's workings be,
Thy looks should nothing thence but sweetness tell.
        How like Eve's apple doth thy beauty grow,
        If thy sweet virtue answer not thy show.[3]

Sonnet 91
1. Of everything in which others take pride.
Sonnet 92
1. This sonnet links with 91.
2. In the slightest sign of your displeasure.
3. Since change in your affections would kill me.

4. What a claim to be considered happy.
Sonnet 93
1. This sonnet links with 92.
2. In signs of anger and frowns and displeased expressions.
3. Does not correspond to your looks.

94

They that have power to hurt and will do none,
That do not do the thing they most do show,[1]
Who, moving others, are themselves as stone,
Unmovèd, cold,° and to temptation slow—   *composed*
5   They rightly° do inherit heaven's graces   *truly*
And husband nature's riches from expense;[2]
They are the lords and owners of their faces,
Others but stewards° of their excellence.   *hired managers*
The summer's flower is to the summer sweet,
10 Though to itself it only live and die,[3]
But if that flower with base infection meet,
The basest weed outbraves his dignity:[4]
      For sweetest things turn sourest by their deeds;
      Lilies that fester smell far worse than weeds.[5]

95

How sweet and lovely dost thou make the shame
Which, like a canker° in the fragrant rose,   *cankerworm*
Doth spot the beauty of thy budding name!°   *fame*
Oh, in what sweets dost thou thy sins enclose!
5   That tongue that tells the story of thy days,
Making lascivious comments on thy sport,°   *amorous adventures*
Cannot dispraise but in a kind of praise:
Naming thy name blesses° an ill report.   *makes positive*
Oh, what a mansion have those vices got
10 Which for their habitation chose out thee,
Where beauty's veil doth cover every blot
And all things turns to fair that eyes can see!
      Take heed, dear heart, of this large privilege;
      The hardest knife ill used doth lose his° edge.   *its*

96

Some say thy fault is youth, some wantonness;°   *promiscuity; frivolity*
Some say thy grace is youth and gentle sport.[1]
Both grace and faults are loved of more and less;°   *by people of all ranks*
Thou mak'st faults graces that to thee resort.
5   As on the finger of a thronèd queen
The basest jewel will be well esteemed,
So are those errors that in thee are seen
To truths translated° and for true things deemed.   *converted*
How many lambs might the stern° wolf betray   *vicious*
10 If like° a lamb he could his looks translate?   *into*
How many gazers mightst thou lead away
If thou wouldst use the strength of all thy state?°   *power*
      But do not so. I love thee in such sort
      As, thou being mine, mine is thy good report.[2]

Sonnet 94
1. *they most do show*: that their appearance implies.
2. And protect nature's rich endowment from waste.
3. *is . . . die*: emits its sweetness to others even though it lives and dies only for itself and in apparent isolation (unpollinated: compare 54.5–11).
4. Exceeds the flower in magnificence.

5. This line also occurs in *Edward III*, a play printed anonymously in 1596 and probably written in part by Shakespeare.
Sonnet 96
1. Gentlemanly conduct (including sexual license).
2. See 36.13–14 and note 3 for the same couplet. *such sort*: such a way.

97

How like a winter hath my absence been
From thee, the° pleasure of the fleeting year!   *(who are) the*
What freezings have I felt, what dark days seen,
What old December's bareness everywhere!
5   And yet this time removed° was summer's time,   *away*
The teeming autumn big° with rich increase,   *pregnant*
Bearing the wanton burden of the prime°   *harvest of wanton spring*
Like widowed wombs after their lords' decease.
Yet this abundant issue seemed[1] to me
10 But hope of orphans and unfathered fruit,
For summer and his° pleasures wait° on thee,   *its / attend*
And, thou away, the very birds are mute;
    Or if they sing, 'tis with so dull a cheer,°   *such a dismal mood*
    That leaves look pale, dreading the winter's near.

98

From you have I been absent in the spring
When proud-pied° April, dressed in all his trim,°   *multicolored / finery*
Hath put a spirit of youth in everything,
That° heavy Saturn[1] laughed and leapt with him.   *So that*
5   Yet nor the lays° of birds nor the sweet smell   *not the songs*
Of different flowers° in odor and in hue   *flowers differing*
Could make me any summer's story tell,°   *speak (write) happily*
Or from their proud lap° pluck them where they grew.   *(the ground)*
Nor did I wonder at the lily's white,
10 Nor praise the deep vermilion in the rose;
They were but sweet, but figures° of delight,   *merely emblems*
Drawn after you, you pattern of all those.
    Yet seemed it winter still, and, you away,
    As with your shadow I with these did play.[2]

99[1]

The forward° violet thus did I chide: *early*
"Sweet thief, whence didst thou steal thy sweet° that smells   *perfume*
If not from my love's breath? The purple pride°   *beauty*
Which on thy soft cheek for complexion dwells
5   In my love's veins thou hast too grossly° dyed."[2]   *obviously*
The lily I condemnèd for thy hand,[3]
And buds of marjoram[4] had stol'n thy hair.
The roses fearfully on thorns did stand,
One blushing shame, another white despair;
10 A third, nor red, nor white, had stol'n of both,°   *(making it pink)*
And to° his robb'ry had annexed thy breath,   *in addition to*
But for his theft in pride of all his growth
A vengeful canker° ate him up to death.   *cankerworm*
    More flowers I noted, yet I none could see,
15   But sweet° or color it had stol'n from thee.   *perfume*

Sonnet 97.
1. Offspring seemed in prospect.
Sonnet 98
1. The planet Saturn was regarded as cold and slow, exerting a melancholy influence.
2. As if with your image I played with these flowers.
Sonnet 99
1. This sonnet has an extra opening line.

2. The violet has been dyed purple in "my love's veins," with a play on "died": the blood of the dead beloved nourishes the flower.
3. For stealing whiteness from your (the beloved's) hand.
4. The herb, sweet of scent and auburn in color.

100

Where art thou, Muse, that thou forgett'st so long
To speak of that which gives thee all thy might?
Spend'st thou thy fury[1] on some worthless song,
Dark'ning° thy power to lend base subjects light?   *Debasing*
5 Return, forgetful Muse, and straight° redeem   *immediately*
In gentle numbers° time so idly spent.   *noble poetry*
Sing to the ear that doth thy lays° esteem   *songs*
And gives thy pen both skill and argument.°   *substance*
Rise, resty° Muse, my love's sweet face survey   *lazy*
10 If° Time have any wrinkle graven there;   *To see if*
If any, be a satire to° decay   *satirist of*
And make Time's spoils despisèd everywhere.
      Give my love fame faster than Time wastes life;
      So° thou prevent'st° his scythe and crooked knife.   *Thereby / impede*

101[1]

O truant Muse, what shall be thy amends
For thy neglect of truth in beauty dyed?
Both truth and beauty on my love depends;
So dost thou too, and therein° dignified.   *therein are you*
5 Make answer, Muse. Wilt thou not haply° say,   *perhaps*
"Truth needs no color with his color fixed,[2]
Beauty no pencil beauty's truth to lay,[3]
But best is best if never intermixed"?°   *(with cosmetics)*
Because he needs no praise, wilt thou be dumb?
10 Excuse not silence so, for't lies in thee
To make him much outlive a gilded tomb
And to be praised of° ages yet to be.   *by*
      Then do thy office,° Muse. I teach thee how   *duty*
      To make him seem long° hence as he shows° now.   *a long time / appears*

102

My love is strengthened though more weak in seeming;°   *appearance*
I love not less, though less the show appear.
That love is merchandized[1] whose rich esteeming°   *appraisal*
The owner's tongue doth publish everywhere.
5 Our love was new, and then but in the spring°   *just beginning*
When I was wont to greet it with my lays,
As Philomel[2] in summer's front° doth sing   *beginning*
And stops her pipe in growth of riper days—
Not that the summer is less pleasant now
10 Than when her mournful hymns did hush the night,
But that wild music burdens[3] every bough,
And sweets grown common lose their dear delight.
      Therefore, like her, I sometime hold my tongue,
      Because I would not dull° you with my song.   *overfeed*

Sonnet 100
1. Inspiration (the "poet's rage" of 17.11).
Sonnet 101
1. This sonnet links with 100.
2. Truth needs no artificial color to be added to his natural coloring.
3. True beauty needs no cosmetics brush.
Sonnet 102
1. (Debased by being) turned into merchandise for sale.

2. Nightingale; with ambiguous hints of the myth of Philomela, whose brother-in-law raped her and ripped out her tongue to ensure her silence. See Book 6 of Ovid's *Metamorphoses*.
3. Loads; provides a musical refrain (probably from many other poets) on.

103

Alack, what poverty my muse brings forth,
That, having such a scope to show her pride,[1]
The argument all bare° is of more worth   *subject in itself*
Than when it hath my added praise beside.
5 Oh, blame me not if I no more can write.
Look in your glass,° and there appears a face   *mirror*
That overgoes my blunt invention[2] quite,
Dulling° my lines and doing me disgrace.   *Deadening (by contrast)*
Were it not sinful then, striving to mend,°   *improve*
10 To mar the subject that before was well?
For to no other pass° my verses tend   *end*
Than of your graces and your gifts to tell;
     And more—much more than in my verse can sit—
     Your own glass shows you when you look in it.

104

To me, fair friend, you never can be old,
For as you were when first your eye I eyed,
Such seems your beauty still. Three winters cold
Have from the forests shook three summers' pride;°   *splendor*
5 Three beauteous springs to yellow autumn turned
In process° of the seasons have I seen;   *the progress*
Three April perfumes in three hot Junes burned
Since first I saw you fresh, which yet° are green.   *who still*
Ah, yet doth beauty, like a dial hand,
10 Steal from his figure, and no pace perceived;[1]
So your sweet hue,° which methinks still doth stand,[2]   *appearance*
Hath motion,° and mine eye may be deceived.   *changes*
     For fear of which, hear this, thou age unbred:°   *future age*
     Ere you were born was beauty's summer dead.

105

Let not my love be called idolatry,
Nor my belovèd as an idol show,[1]
Since all alike my songs and praises be
To one,° of one, still° such, and ever so.   *the beloved / continually*
5 Kind is my love[2] today, tomorrow kind,
Still constant in a wondrous excellence.
Therefore my verse, to constancy confined,
One thing expressing, leaves out[3] difference.°   *diversity (of theme)*
"Fair, kind, and true" is all my argument;
10 "Fair, kind, and true," varying to other words—
And in this change is my invention spent[4]—
     Three themes in one, which wondrous° scope affords.   *(with pun on "one")*
        "Fair," "kind," and "true" have often lived alone,°   *separately*
        Which three, till now, never kept seat° in one.   *dwelt permanently*

Sonnet 103
1. Considering that she has such opportunity (in you) to display her skill (her pride in you).
2. That surpasses my dull powers of invention.
Sonnet 104
1. *doth . . . perceived:* beauty imperceptibly "steals" (departs stealthily from; robs from) the youthful appearance ("figure") of the beloved as the hand of the watch ("dial") stealthily progresses ("steals") away from the number ("figure") on the watch face.

2. Is unchanged or motionless (in contrast with "pace," line 10, and "motion," line 12).
Sonnet 105
1. Seem like an idol; seem idle.
2. The youth; the speaker's feelings.
3. Omits; perhaps "leaves" of paper, referring to "verse," line 7. See 73.2.
4. And in varying the words alone my inventiveness is expended.

106

When in the chronicle of wasted° time   *past*
I see descriptions of the fairest wights,°   *people*
And beauty making beautiful old rhyme
In praise of ladies dead and lovely knights,
5   Then in the blazon[1] of sweet beauty's best—
Of hand, of foot, of lip, of eye, of brow—
I see their antique pen would have expressed
Even such a beauty as you master° now.   *possess*
So all their praises are but prophecies
10   Of this our time, all you prefiguring;
And for° they looked but with divining° eyes,   *as / prophetic*
They had not skill enough your worth to sing;
    For we,° which now behold these present days,   *even we*
    Have eyes to wonder, but lack tongues to praise.

107

Not mine own fears, nor the prophetic soul
Of the wide world,° dreaming on° things to come,   *people / predicting*
Can yet the lease° of my true love° control,   *allotted term / affection*
Supposed as forfeit to a confined doom.[1]
5   The mortal moon hath her eclipse endured,[2]
And the sad augurs mock their own presage;[3]
Incertainties now crown themselves assured,[4]
And peace proclaims olives of endless age.[5]
Now with the drops[6] of this most balmy time,
10   My love looks fresh, and Death to me subscribes,°   *submits*
Since spite of him° I'll live in this poor rhyme,   *(death)*
While he insults° o'er dull and speechless tribes.[7]   *prevails*
    And thou in this shalt find thy monument,
    When tyrants' crests and tombs of brass are spent.°   *ruined*

108

What's in the brain that ink may character°   *express*
Which hath not figured° to thee my true spirit?   *shown*
What's new to speak, what now to register,°   *record*
That may express my love or thy dear merit?
5   Nothing, sweet boy. But yet, like prayers divine,
I must each day say o'er° the very same—   *repeat*
Counting no old thing old, thou mine, I thine,
Even as when first I hallowed thy fair name—
So that eternal love in love's fresh case°   *covering*
10   Weighs not° the dust and injury of age,   *Overlooks*
Nor gives to necessary° wrinkles place,°   *inevitable / priority*
But makes antiquity for aye his page,[1]

Sonnet 106
1. Poetic catalog of virtues.
Sonnet 107
1. Wrongly imagined as limited to a finite term.
2. Survived. Referring to an eclipse of the moon or perhaps to an event in the life (or 1603 death) of Queen Elizabeth (often known as Diana, the moon goddess).
3. And prophets of doom now ridicule their own prophecies.
4. Desired but doubtful possibilities now celebrate their realization—possibly alluding to the accession

of James I in 1603.
5. And peace declares the olive branches that symbolize it to be everlasting. Perhaps a reference to the peace treaty with Spain signed by James.
6. Soothing drops of dew, rain, or balm. Balm was used in the coronation ceremony.
7. Over those legions of dead who have no poetic legacy.
Sonnet 108
1. But makes (old) age forever the (youthful) servant to love; perhaps referring to the pages of poetry written when the "sweet boy" (line 5) was still young.

Finding the first conceit of love there bred[2]
Where time and outward form would° show it dead.   *want to*

109

Oh, never say that I was false of heart,
Though absence seemed my flame to qualify;°   *reduce*
As easy might I from myself depart
As from my soul, which in thy breast doth lie.
5   That is my home of love. If I have ranged,
Like him that travels, I return again,
Just to the time,° not with the time exchanged,[1]   *Punctually*
So that myself bring water for my stain.[2]
Never believe, though in my nature reigned
10 All frailties that besiege all kinds of blood,°   *disposition*
That it could so preposterously be stained
To leave for° nothing all thy sum of good: *exchange for*
      For nothing this wide universe I call,
      Save thou, my rose; in it thou art my all.

110

Alas, 'tis true, I have gone here and there,
And made myself a motley to the view;[1]
Gored° mine own thoughts, sold cheap what is most dear,   *Injured*
Made old offenses of affections new.[2]
5   Most true it is that I have looked on truth°   *fidelity*
Askance and strangely.° But by all above,   *coldly*
These blenches° gave my heart another youth,   *alterations*
And worse essays° proved thee my best of love.   *experiments*
Now all is done. Have what shall have no end.[3]
10 Mine appetite I never more will grind[4]
On newer proof, to try° an older friend,   *test*
A god in love, to whom I am confined.
      Then give me welcome, next my heaven the best,°   *next best to heaven*
      Even to thy pure and most most loving breast.

111

Oh, for my sake do you with[1] Fortune chide,
The guilty goddess of my harmful deeds,
That did not better for my life provide
Than public means, which public manners breeds.[2]
5   Thence comes it that my name receives a brand,°   *stigma*
And almost thence my nature is subdued
To what it works in, like the dyer's hand.
Pity me then, and wish I were renewed,°   *cured*

---

2. Recovering the first feeling (poetic expression) of love generated in that place (the beloved; the past; the poem).
Sonnet 109
1. Not changed by the times (or passage of time).
2. *water for my stain:* tears to cleanse the stain of my absence.
Sonnet 110
1. Referring to the multicolored outfit of the fool, clown, or jester—onstage and off—and hence probably to Shakespeare's theatrical career, including acting. *motley to the view:* clown to the world.

2. Repeated the traditional misbehavior of infidelity (or offended old friends) in (my treatment of) new attachments.
3. *Have . . . end:* Take that (my love) which will not expire.
4. *grind:* sharpen with new experience.
Sonnet 111
1. Q has "wish," which gives a more problematic array of alternative meanings.
2. Probably: Than employment as an actor, which requires one to curry favor with the public.

Whilst, like a willing patient, I will drink
10 Potions of eisel° 'gainst my strong infection;   *medicinal vinegar*
No° bitterness that I will bitter think,   *There is no*
Nor double penance to correct correction.°   *correct me twice over*
    Pity me then, dear friend, and I assure ye
    Even that your pity is enough to cure me.

112[1]

Your love and pity doth th'impression fill°   *eliminates the scar*
Which vulgar° scandal stamped upon my brow;   *public*
For what care I who calls me well or ill,
So you o'er-green my bad, my good allow?[2]
5 You are my all the world, and I must strive
To know my shames and praises from your tongue;
None else to me, nor I to none alive,
That my steeled sense or changes right or wrong.[3]
In so profound abysm I throw all care
10 Of others' voices that my adder's sense°   *deaf ears*
To critic and to flatterer stoppèd are.
Mark how with my neglect I do dispense:[4]
    You are so strongly in my purpose bred[5]
    That all the world besides methinks are dead.

113

Since I left you, mine eye is in my mind,[1]
And that which governs me to go about°   *And my real sight*
Doth part his° function, and is partly blind,   *Divides its (the eye's)*
Seems seeing, but effectually is out.°   *blind*
5 For it no form delivers to the heart
Of bird, of flower, or shape which it doth latch;°   *catch sight of*
Of his quick objects° hath the mind no part,   *the eye's fleeting sights*
Nor his own vision holds[2] what it doth catch.
For if it see the rud'st or gentlest° sight—   *coarsest or noblest*
10 The most sweet favor[3] or deformed'st creature,
The mountain or the sea, the day or night,
The crow or dove—it shapes them to your feature.[4]
    Incapable of more, replete with you,
    My most true mind thus makes mine eye untrue.

114[1]

Or whether doth my mind, being crowned with you,[2]
Drink up the monarch's plague, this flattery?
Or whether shall I say mine eye saith true,
And that your love taught it this alchemy,[3]
5 To make of monsters and things indigest°   *chaotic*

Sonnet 112
1. This sonnet links with 111.
2. So long as you allow new growth to cover what is bad in me, and give credit for what is good.
3. *None . . . wrong:* No one else is alive to me, or I to them, who can change my hardened disposition rightly or wrongly.
4. How I excuse my neglect (of "others' voices," line 10).
5. Nurtured in all my plans.
Sonnet 113
1. I see with my mind's eye.

2. Nor does the eye's vision hold on to.
3. Face; perhaps Q's "sweet-favor" means "sweet-favored" or "good-looking."
4. It makes them look like you.
Sonnet 114
1. This sonnet links with 113.
2. Being made a king by having you. "Or whether" (lines 1, 3) introduces alternatives.
3. And that love of you taught my eye how thus to transform things.

Such cherubins° as your sweet self resemble,   *angels*
Creating every° bad a perfect best   *from every*
As fast as objects to his beams assemble?[4]
Oh, 'tis the first! 'Tis flatt'ry in my seeing,
10 And my great° mind most kingly drinks it up.   *pompous*
Mine eye well knows what with his gust is 'greeing[5]
And to his palate doth prepare the cup.
    If it be poisoned, 'tis the lesser sin
    That mine eye loves it and doth first begin.[6]

115

Those lines that I before have writ do lie,
Even those that said I could not love you dearer;
Yet then my judgment knew no reason why
My most full flame should afterwards burn clearer.
5 But reckoning time,[1] whose millioned accidents
Creep in twixt vows° and change decrees of kings,   *(and their performance)*
Tan° sacred beauty, blunt the sharp'st intents,   *Darken*
Divert strong minds to th' course of alt'ring things—
Alas, why, fearing of time's tyranny,
10 Might I not then say,[2] "Now I love you best,"
When I was certain o'er° incertainty,   *beyond*
Crowning° the present, doubting of the rest?   *Exalting*
    Love is a babe. Then might I not say so,[3]
    To give° full growth to that which still doth grow.   *Thereby giving*

116

Let me not to the marriage of true minds
Admit impediments.° Love is not love   *legal barriers to marriage*
Which alters when it alteration finds
Or bends with the remover to remove.[1]
5 Oh no, it is an ever-fixèd mark,[2]
That looks on tempests and is never shaken;
It is the star to every wand'ring bark,
Whose worth's unknown, although his height be taken.[3]
Love's not Time's fool,° though rosy lips and cheeks   *plaything*
10 Within his bending sickle's compass[4] come;
Love alters not with his° brief hours and weeks,   *its*
But bears it out even to the edge of doom.[5]
    If this be error and upon° me proved,   *against*
    I never writ, nor no man ever loved.

4. As fast as objects come before its gaze. (The eye was thought to emit beams of light.)
5. What pleases the mind's appetite.
6. And drinks first (like a king's taster).
Sonnet 115
1. But taking time into account; but time, which settles accounts.
2. Was I not then right to have said.
3. Thus I shouldn't say, "Now I love you best" (line 10).
Sonnet 116
1. Or abandons the relationship when the loved one is unfaithful or has departed or died, or when time

("the remover") alters things for the worse.
2. An unmoving sea mark, such as a lighthouse or a beacon, that provides a constant reference point for sailors.
3. *Whose . . . taken:* The star's (great) intrinsic value cannot be assessed, although navigators at sea can measure height above the horizon.
4. Within range of time's curved (and hostile) scythe. "Compass" also recalls the imagery of the second quatrain. *his:* (Time's).
5. But endures until the eve of doomsday.

117

Accuse me thus: that I have scanted° all   *neglected*
Wherein I should your great deserts repay;
Forgot upon your dearest love to call,
Whereto all bonds do tie me day by day;
5 That I have frequent° been with unknown minds°   *friendly / strangers*
And given to time your own dear-purchased right;[1]
That I have hoisted sail to all the winds
Which should° transport me farthest from your sight.   *were likely to*
Book both my willfulness and errors down,
10 And on just proof surmise accumulate.[2]
Bring me within the level° of your frown,   *aim*
But shoot not at me in your wakened hate,
    Since my appeal says I did strive to prove[3]
    The constancy and virtue of your love.

118

Like° as to make our appetites more keen   *Just*
With eager° compounds we our palate urge,°   *sharp / stimulate*
As to prevent° our maladies unseen   *forestall*
We sicken to shun sickness when we purge;[1]
5 Even so, being full of your ne'er-cloying sweetness,
To bitter sauces did I frame° my feeding,   *adjust*
And, sick of welfare,[2] found a kind of meetness°   *suitability*
To be diseased ere that there was true needing.
Thus policy° in love, t'anticipate   *strategy*
10 The ills that were not, grew to faults assured,
And brought to[3] medicine a healthful state
Which, rank of goodness, would by ill be cured.[4]
    But thence I learn and find the lesson true:
    Drugs poison him that so° fell sick of you.   *thus; so badly*

119

What potions have I drunk of siren[1] tears
Distilled from limbecks° foul as hell within,   *stills*
Applying° fears to hopes, and hopes to fears,   *(as a medicine)*
Still° losing when I saw myself° to win?   *Always / expected*
5 What wretched errors hath my heart committed
Whilst it hath thought itself so blessèd never?°   *more blessed than ever*
How have mine eyes out of their spheres been fitted[2]
In the distraction° of this madding° fever?   *delirium / fit-inducing*
Oh, benefit of ill! Now I find true
10 That better is by evil still made better,
And ruined love, when it is built anew,
Grows fairer than at first, more strong, far greater.
    So I return rebuked to my content,
    And gain by ills thrice more than I have spent.

Sonnet 117
1. And wasted idly what should have been your right (rite) because acquired by your great worth and affection (because acquired at your great cost).
2. And pile suspicion on top of your proof.
3. Since my defense is that I was trying to test.
Sonnet 118
1. We sicken ourselves with medicine that causes vomiting or bowel movements so as to prevent greater illness.

2. Made ill by good food.
3. Treated with; brought to the need of.
4. Overfull with goodness (health, the beloved), sought to be cured by disease (evil).
Sonnet 119
1. Deceitfully and dangerously alluring. Sirens were mythological creatures, part bird, part woman, said to lure sailors to their death with their songs.
2. Been driven convulsively out of their sockets.

120

That you were once unkind befriends me now,
And, for° that sorrow which I then did feel,   *because of*
Needs must I under my transgression bow,
Unless my nerves° were brass or hammered steel.   *sinews*
5   For if you were by my unkindness shaken
As I by yours, you've passed a hell of time,
And I, a tyrant, have no leisure taken
To weigh° how once I suffered in° your crime.   *contemplate / from*
Oh, that our night of woe[1] might have remembered°   *reminded*
10 My deepest sense how hard true sorrow hits,
And soon to you, as you to me then, tendered°   *offered*
The humble salve, which wounded bosoms fits![2]
     But that your trespass° now becomes a fee:°   *offense / payment*
     Mine ransoms° yours, and yours must ransom me.   *absolves*

121

'Tis better to be vile than vile esteemed°   *reputed vile*
When not to be receives reproach of being,°   *being vile*
And the just pleasure lost, which is so deemed
Not by our feeling but by others' seeing.[1]
5   For why should others' false adulterate° eyes   *corrupted*
Give salutation to my sportive blood?[2]
Or on my frailties why are frailer spies,
Which in their wills[3] count bad what I think good?
No, I am that I am,[4] and they that level°   *aim*
10 At my abuses reckon up their own.
I may be straight though they themselves be bevel;°   *crooked*
By their rank° thoughts my deeds must not be shown°— *foul / measured*
     Unless this general evil they maintain:
     All men are bad and in their badness reign.°   *thrive*

122

Thy gift, thy tables,° are° within my brain   *notebook / are already*
Full charactered° with lasting memory,   *written*
Which shall above that idle rank[1] remain
Beyond all date, even to eternity—
5   Or at the least so long as brain and heart
Have faculty° by nature to subsist;   *power*
Till each to razed° oblivion yield his part   *demolished*
Of thee, thy record never can be missed.°   *lost*
That poor retention[2] could not so much hold,
10 Nor need I tallies thy dear love to score.[3]
Therefore to give them° from me was I bold,   *(the "tables")*
To trust those tables° that receive thee more.   *memory*
     To keep an adjunct° to remember thee   *aid*
     Were to import° forgetfulness in me.   *imply*

Sonnet 120
1. Our earlier time of suffering (caused by the youth's unfaithfulness).
2. The salve of apology that is just the thing for an injured heart.
Sonnet 121
1. *And . . . seeing:* And we are denied the appropriate, innocent pleasure, which is considered sinful not by us but by others.
2. Greet me as a fellow sinner owing to my sexual behavior.

3. *Or . . . wills:* Why should my failings be pried into by even more culpable people, who willfully (who licentiously; who in Will Shakespeare).
4. God's words, Exodus 3:14.
Sonnet 122
1. Trivial status (of the "tables" as opposed to "memory").
2. That inadequate container (the "tables").
3. Nor do I need the notched sticks used in calculating sums (to which the "tables" are contemptuously compared) to reckon up your precious love.

123

No! Time, thou shalt not boast that I do change.
Thy pyramids built up with newer might[1]
To me are nothing° novel, nothing strange.   *in no way*
They are but dressings of a former sight.[2]
5   Our dates° are brief, and therefore we admire   *lives*
What thou dost foist upon us that is old,
And rather make them born to our desire[3]
Than think that we before have heard them told.°   *described*
Thy registers° and thee I both defy,   *records*
10 Not wond'ring at the present nor the past,
For thy records and what we see doth lie,
Made more or less by thy continual haste.[4]
      This I do vow and this shall ever be:
      I will be true despite thy scythe and thee.

124

If my dear love° were but the child of state,[1]   *(for you)*
It might for fortune's bastard be unfathered,[2]
As subject to time's love or to time's hate,
Weeds among weeds, or flowers with flowers gathered.[3]
5   No, it was builded far from accident;°   *chance*
It suffers° not in smiling pomp, nor falls   *changes*
Under the blow of thrallèd° discontent,   *captive*
Whereto th'inviting time our fashion calls.[4]
It fears not policy,° that heretic,   *expediency*
10 Which works on leases of short-numbered hours,°   *short-term contracts*
But all alone stands hugely politic,°   *prudent*
That it nor° grows with heat° nor drowns with showers.   *neither / prosperity*
      To this I witness call the fools of time,
      Which die for goodness, who have lived for crime.[5]

125

Were't aught to me I bore the canopy,[1]
With my extern° the outward honoring,   *exterior action*
Or laid great bases for eternity,[2]
Which proves more short than waste° or ruining?   *decay*
5   Have I not seen dwellers on form and favor[3]
Lose all, and more, by paying too much rent,°   *overdoing homage*
For compound sweet forgoing simple savor,[4]
Pitiful thrivers, in their gazing spent?[5]

Sonnet 123
1. Grand buildings constructed by more modern means. Possibly referring to structures erected in Rome in 1586 or in London in 1603 (for James's coronation), but retaining a sense of almost timeless Egyptian antiquity.
2. Replicas of what's been seen before.
3. And consider them made just for us.
4. Raised and destroyed by time's swift passage; made to seem more or less majestic by virtue of newness or antiquity and the tastes of the times.
Sonnet 124
1. Were simply the result of circumstances (or of your high position).
2. It might be disinherited as a passing fancy, a product of fortune (chance, wealth).
3. *As . . . gathered:* Regarded as useless or valuable as time and fortune decide.
4. To which ("pomp" and "discontent") we are driven by the latest trend ("fashion").
5. *To . . . crime:* I call as witness those playthings of time who, having lived wicked lives, reform or repent at death.
Sonnet 125
1. Would I care if I enhanced my status by carrying a ceremonial canopy for a royal person?
2. Laid foundations for eternal monuments.
3. Seen those who depend (linger) on ceremony and appearance.
4. For obsequious praise (or fleeting worldly concerns) giving up plain candor (or true values).
5. Pitiful in their empty achievements, ruined by love of show.

No, let me be obsequious° in thy heart,   *dutiful*
10 And take thou my oblation,° poor but free,°   *offering / freely given*
Which is not mixed with seconds,⁶ knows no art,°   *artifice*
But mutual render°—only me for thee.   *exchange*
    Hence, thou suborned informer!⁷ A true soul,
    When most impeached,° stands least in thy control.   *accused*

126¹

O thou, my lovely boy, who in thy power
Dost hold Time's fickle glass,² his sickle hour;°   *reaping time*
Who hast by waning grown,³ and therein show'st
Thy lover's withering as thy sweet self grow'st—
5 If Nature, sovereign mistress over wrack,°   *decay*
As thou goest onwards still° will pluck thee back,   *constantly*
She keeps thee to this purpose: that her skill
May Time disgrace and wretched minute° kill.   *life's miserable brevity*
Yet fear her, O thou minion° of her pleasure!   *darling*
10 She may detain, but not still° keep, her treasure.   *always*
Her audit,° though delayed, answered° must be,   *debt (to time) / paid*
And her quietus° is to render° thee.   *settlement / relinquish*
    (   )
    (   )

127¹

In the old age° black was not counted fair,²   *old days*
Or if it were, it bore not beauty's name;°   *reputation*
But now is black beauty's successive heir,°   *heir by succession*
And beauty slandered with a bastard shame.³
5 For since each hand hath put on° nature's power,   *usurped*
Fairing° the foul with art's false borrowed face,   *Beautifying*
Sweet beauty hath no name, no holy bower,
But is profaned, if not lives in disgrace.
Therefore my mistress' eyes are raven black,
10 Her brows so suited,⁴ and they mourners seem
At such who, not born fair, no beauty lack,
Sland'ring creation with a false esteem.⁵
    Yet so° they mourn, becoming of° their woe,   *in such a way / adorning*
    That every tongue says beauty should look so.

---

6. The second-rate.
7. Paid spy: jealousy or the detractor whose charges the poem answers.
Sonnet 126
1. TEXTUAL COMMENT This "sonnet" or envoi, of six couplets, concludes the part of the sequence apparently addressed to the youth and formally signals a change in tone and subject matter in the remaining sonnets. For the distinctive form of this poem, the only one in the sequence with twelve lines, see Digital Edition TC 8.
2. Hourglass from which the sands of life run out; mirror showing decay.
3. Become more beautiful with age. As the sand in the top half of an hourglass wanes, the sand in the bottom part grows.

Sonnet 127
1. Sonnets 127–152 have been traditionally known as the "dark lady" group, although their subject matter is not uniform and their object is only once called "dark" (147.14) and never a "lady." She is referred to as the poet's "mistress" (127.9; 130.1, 8, 12), however, and is often described as "black" (127.1, 3, 9; 130.4; 131.12, 13; 132.3, 13; 147.14). The celebration of black beauty goes back to the biblical Song of Songs 1:4: "I am blacke . . . but comelie." See the Introduction.
2. Beautiful; light-colored.
3. And (fair) beauty accused of illegitimacy (by use of cosmetics).
4. Her brow dressed (or matched) in an eyebrow black like her eyes (and for the same reason).
5. *At . . . esteem:* Because of those who, not being fair, make up for it with cosmetics, so that even natural beauty is presumed artificial.

128

How oft, when thou, my music, music play'st
Upon that blessèd wood whose motion° sounds   *mechanism*
With thy sweet fingers when thou gently sway'st°   *govern*
The wiry concord that mine ear confounds,°   *amazes (with delight)*
5 Do I envy those jacks[1] that nimble leap
To kiss the tender inward of thy hand,
Whilst my poor lips, which should that harvest reap,
At the wood's boldness by thee blushing stand!
To be so tickled they would change their state
10 And situation with those dancing chips,
O'er whom thy fingers walk with gentle gait,
Making dead wood more blest than living lips.
    Since saucy° jacks so happy are in this,   *impudent*
    Give them thy fingers, me thy lips to kiss.

129

Th'expense of spirit in a waste of shame
Is lust in action;[1] and till action, lust
Is perjured, murd'rous, bloody, full of blame,
Savage, extreme, rude,° cruel, not to trust;°   *harsh / be trusted*
5 Enjoyed no sooner but despisèd straight;°   *immediately*
Past reason° hunted, and no sooner had,   *Madly*
Past reason hated, as a swallowed bait
On purpose laid to make the taker mad;
Mad in pursuit and in possession so;°   *(mad)*
10 Had, having, and in quest to have, extreme;
A bliss in proof, and proved,[2] a very woe;
Before, a joy proposed; behind, a dream.
    All this the world well knows, yet none knows well
    To shun the heaven that leads men to this hell.

130

My mistress' eyes are nothing like the sun;
Coral is far more red than her lips' red;
If snow be white, why then her breasts are dun;°   *grayish brown*
If hairs be wires,[1] black wires grow on her head.
5 I have seen roses damasked,° red and white,   *dappled*
But no such roses see I in her cheeks;
And in some perfumes is there more delight
Than in the breath that from my mistress reeks.°   *issues; smells*
I love to hear her speak, yet well I know
10 That music hath a far more pleasing sound.
I grant I never saw a goddess go;°   *walk*
My mistress when she walks treads on the ground.
    And yet, by heaven, I think my love as rare
    As any she belied with false compare.[2]

Sonnet 128
1. Keys of the virginal, a harpsichord-like instrument; fellows.
Sonnet 129
1. Th'expense . . . action: The expenditure of vital energy (including semen) in a shameful waste (waist) is consummated lust.
2. in proof: while being experienced. proved: having been experienced.

Sonnet 130
1. Elizabethan poets often compared women's hair to golden wires.
2. As any woman misrepresented by falsely flattering comparison. (Despite the apparent contrast signaled by "yet," line 13, the speaker continues the poem's ironic repudiation of the hyperbole conventional in love poetry, calling his beloved "as rare," not "more rare," and hence no more attractive than any woman overpraised for her beauty.)

131

Thou art as tyrannous, so as thou art,[1]
As those whose beauties proudly make them cruel;
For well thou know'st to my dear° doting heart   *fond(ly)*
Thou art the fairest and most precious jewel.
5 Yet, in good faith, some say that thee behold,
Thy face hath not the power to make love groan;
To say they err I dare not be so bold,
Although I swear it to myself alone.
And, to be sure,° that is not false I swear: *for proof; surely*
10 A thousand groans, but thinking on° thy face,   *just thinking about*
One on another's neck° do witness bear   *In quick succession*
Thy black° is fairest in my judgment's place.[2]   *dark appearance*
    In nothing art thou black° save in thy deeds,   *ugly*
    And thence this slander,[3] as I think, proceeds.

132

Thine eyes I love, and they, as° pitying me—   *as if*
Knowing thy heart torment° me with disdain—   *to torment*
Have put on black, and loving mourners be,
Looking with pretty ruth° upon my pain.   *pity*
5 And truly not the morning sun of heaven
Better becomes° the gray cheeks° of the east,   *beautifies / clouds*
Nor that full star that ushers in the even°   *(Venus, the evening star)*
Doth° half that glory to the sober west   *Imparts*
As those two mourning° eyes become thy face.   *(pun on "morning")*
10 Oh, let it then as well beseem° thy heart   *become*
To mourn for me, since mourning doth thee grace,
And suit thy pity like in every part.[1]
    Then will I swear beauty herself is black,
    And all they foul° that thy complexion lack.   *ugly*

133

Beshrew° that heart that makes my heart to groan   *Curse (a mild term)*
For that deep wound it gives my friend and me.
Is't not enough to torture me alone,
But slave to slavery° my sweet'st friend must be?   *utterly enslaved*
5 Me from myself thy cruel eye hath taken,
And my next self thou harder hast engrossed;[1]
Of him, myself, and thee I am forsaken,
A torment thrice threefold thus to be crossed.°   *afflicted*
Prison° my heart in thy steel bosom's ward,°   *Imprison / cell*
10 But then my friend's heart let my poor heart bail.
Whoe'er keeps° me, let my heart be his guard;[2]   *guards*
Thou canst not then use rigor° in my jail.   *severity*
    And yet thou wilt, for I, being pent° in thee,   *locked up*
    Perforce am thine, and° all that is in me.   *as is*

Sonnet 131
1. As cruel as you are dark (hence, not conventionally beautiful).
2. In my opinion.
3. See line 6 for "this slander."
Sonnet 132
1. And dress (or soot, blacken, playing on "suit")
your pity similarly, in heart as well as eyes.

Sonnet 133
1. And my second self, or closest friend, you have
even more cruelly monopolized.
2. My friend's prison.

134[1]

So now° I have confessed that he is thine   *now that*
And I myself am mortgaged to thy will,°   *intent; sexual desire*
Myself I'll forfeit, so that other mine[2]
Thou wilt restore to be my comfort still.
5 But thou wilt not, nor he will not° be free,   *doesn't want to*
For thou art covetous, and he is kind.
He learned but surety-like° to write° for me   *as guarantor / sign*
Under that bond° that him as fast[3] doth bind.   *(of infatuation)*
The statute[4] of thy beauty thou wilt take—
10 Thou usurer that putt'st forth all to use°—   *at interest; for sex*
And sue a friend came° debtor for my sake;   *who became*
So him I lose through my unkind abuse.[5]
    Him have I lost, thou hast both him and me;
    He pays the whole,° and yet am I not free.   *(pun on "hole")*

135[1]

Whoever hath her wish, thou hast thy Will,
And Will to boot,° and Will in overplus.   *in addition*
More than enough am I that vex thee still,°   *always (by wooing)*
To thy sweet will making addition° thus.   *increasing your pleasure*
5 Wilt thou, whose will is large and spacious,
Not once vouchsafe to hide my will in thine?°   *(sexual)*
Shall will in others° seem right gracious,   *others' wills*
And in my will no fair acceptance shine?[2]
The sea, all water, yet receives rain still,
10 And in abundance addeth to his° store;   *its*
So° thou, being rich in Will, add° to thy Will   *Similarly / should add*
One will of mine° to make thy large Will more.   *the poet; (sexual)*
    Let "no," unkind, no fair beseechers kill;[3]
    Think all but one,° and me in that one Will.   *one suitor*

136[1]

If thy soul check° thee that I come so near,[2]   *chide*
Swear to thy blind soul that I was thy Will,[3]
And will, thy soul knows, is admitted there.
Thus far for love my love-suit, sweet, fulfill.°   *grant*
5 Will will fulfill the treasure° of thy love;   *fill up the treasury*
Ay, fill it full with wills, and my will one.°   *one of them*
In things of great receipt° with ease we prove   *volume*
Among a number one is reckoned none.[4]
Then in the number let me pass untold,°   *uncounted*
10 Though in thy store's account° I one must be;   *tally (of lovers)*
For nothing hold me, so it please thee hold

Sonnet 134
1. This sonnet links with 133.
2. So long as my other self.
3. As firmly as myself.
4. The total guaranteed by the bond.
5. Through your ill treatment of me; perhaps: through my ill treatment of the youth.
Sonnet 135
1. This sonnet, as well as 136, 143, and "A Lover's Complaint," lines 126–33, puns elaborately on different senses of "will": wishes, sexual desire, futurity, testament, the name "Will" (applied to one or more

persons, including Shakespeare, and capitalized and sometimes italicized in Q), and the male and female sexual organs. See also 57.13 and note 1.
2. And my will not be greeted with a kind reception.
3. Do not ungenerously say "no," an act that would kill your honorable (or good-looking) suitors.
Sonnet 136
1. This sonnet links with 135.
2. I am so forthright; I am so physically close.
3. See Sonnet 135, note 1.
4. Proverbially, one is no number.

That nothing me a something sweet to thee.[5]
    Make but my name thy love,[6] and love that still,°   *always*
    And then thou lovest me, for my name is Will.°   *(the speaker); lust*

137

Thou blind fool love, what dost thou to mine eyes,
That they behold and see not what they see?
They know what beauty is, see where it lies,
Yet what the best is take the worst to be.[1]
5 If eyes corrupt° by over-partial° looks   *corrupted / overly doting*
Be anchored in the bay where all men ride,[2]
Why of eyes' falsehood hast thou forgèd hooks
Whereto the judgment of my heart is tied?
Why should my heart think that° a several plot°   *that place / private land*
10 Which my heart knows the wide world's common place?[3]
Or° mine eyes, seeing this, say this is not,   *Or why should*
To put fair truth upon so foul a face?
    In things right true my heart and eyes have erred,
    And to this false plague[4] are they now transferred.

138[1]

When my love swears that she is made of truth,
I do believe her though I know she lies,
That° she might think me some untutored youth,   *So that*
Unlearnèd in the world's false subtleties.
5 Thus vainly° thinking that she thinks me young,   *in vain; with vanity*
Although she knows my days are past the best,
Simply I credit[2] her false-speaking tongue.
On both sides thus is simple truth suppressed.
But wherefore says she not she is unjust?°   *unfaithful*
10 And wherefore say not I that I am old?
Oh, love's best habit is in seeming trust,[3]
And age in love loves not to have years told.°   *counted*
    Therefore I lie° with her, and she with me,   *tell lies; lie down*
    And in our faults by lies we flattered be.

139

Oh, call° not me to justify° the wrong   *ask / approve*
That thy unkindness° lays upon my heart.   *infidelity*
Wound me not with thine eye,[1] but with thy tongue;
Use power with power,[2] and slay me not by art.°   *by deceit*
5 Tell me thou lov'st elsewhere; but in my sight,
Dear heart, forbear to glance thine eye aside.
What° need'st thou wound with cunning, when thy might   *Why*

---

5. *For . . . thee:* Think me worthless so long as, my darling, you treasure worthless me (sexually).
6. Love only my name, "Will"; that is, act on your desire.
Sonnet 137
1. Yet take the worst to be the best.
2. Harbor for general use (suggesting a promiscuous woman).
3. *the wide . . . place:* common land, open to all (also, the mistress's vagina).
4. This plague of false perception; this deceitful woman.

Sonnet 138
1. TEXTUAL COMMENT Another version of this sonnet appears as Poem 1 in *The Passionate Pilgrim.* For the differences between the two versions, see Textual Comment 1 to that work.
2. Naively (foolishly; giving the appearance of folly) I (pretend to) believe.
3. Love is best dressed in (also, love's best behavior is) apparent fidelity.
Sonnet 139
1. By looking elsewhere, at other men (see line 6).
2. Use power frankly; fairly.

Is more than my o'erpressed defense can bide?°   *endure*
Let me excuse thee: "Ah, my love well knows
10   Her pretty looks have been mine enemies,
And therefore from my face she turns my foes,°   *her looks*
That they elsewhere might dart their injuries."
      Yet do not so; but since I am near slain,
      Kill me outright with looks, and rid° my pain.   *put an end to*

140

Be wise as thou art cruel; do not press
My tongue-tied patience with too much disdain,
Lest sorrow lend me words, and words express
The manner of my pity-wanting[1] pain.
5   If I might teach thee wit,° better it were,   *wisdom*
Though not to love, yet, love, to tell me so—
As testy sick men when their deaths be near
No news but health from their physicians know.°   *learn*
For if I should despair I should grow mad,
10   And in my madness might speak ill of thee;
Now this ill-wresting world[2] is grown so bad
Mad slanderers by mad ears believèd be.
      That I may not be so, nor thou belied,°   *maligned*
      Bear thine eyes straight,[3] though thy proud heart go wide.° *astray*

141

In faith, I do not love thee with mine eyes,
For they in thee a thousand errors note,
But 'tis my heart that loves what they despise,
Who in despite of view° is pleased to dote;   *despite what it sees*
5   Nor are mine ears with thy tongue's tune delighted,
Nor tender feeling to base touches prone,[1]
Nor taste, nor smell, desire to be invited
To any sensual feast with thee alone;
But my five wits[2] nor my five senses can
10   Dissuade one foolish heart from serving thee,
Who leaves unswayed the likeness of a man,[3]
Thy proud heart's slave and vassal wretch to be.
      Only my plague thus far° I count my gain,   *to this extent*
      That she that makes me sin awards me pain.[4]

142[1]

Love is my sin, and thy dear virtue hate,
Hate of my sin, grounded on sinful loving.[2]
Oh, but with mine, compare thou thine own state,
And thou shalt find it° merits not reproving;   *(my state)*

Sonnet 140
1. Unpitied; desiring pity; pitiable.
2. Now this world, which tends to interpret in the worst light.
3. Keep looking only at me (see 139).
Sonnet 141
1. Nor is my keen sense of touch susceptible to "base" sexual contact.
2. Mental faculties (common sense, imagination, fancy, judgment, memory).
3. Which (the heart, serving you) leaves without a commander (the five wits or senses) what is therefore the mere semblance of a man.
4. By making me sin, she causes me to suffer punitive penance, which will reduce my sufferings after death (or she just makes me suffer).
Sonnet 142
1. This sonnet links with 141.
2. *Love . . . loving:* My only sin is love, and your most valuable virtue is hatred, hatred of my sin in loving you (but also, your most valuable virtue is the haughty rejection of my wooing) based on (your) immoral sexual affairs.

5   Or if it do, not from those lips of thine,
    That have profaned their scarlet ornaments,[3]
    And sealed false bonds of love as oft as mine
    Robbed others' beds' revenues of their rents.[4]
    Be it lawful° I love thee as thou lov'st those   *Let it be lawful that*
10 Whom thine eyes woo as mine importune thee.
    Root pity in thy heart, that, when it grows,
    Thy pity may deserve to pitied be.°   *make you pitiable*
        If thou dost seek to have what thou dost hide,°   *(pity)*
        By self-example mayst thou be denied.

143

    Lo, as a careful° housewife runs to catch   *busy*
    One of her feathered creatures broke° away,   *that has broken*
    Sets down her babe, and makes all swift dispatch°   *hurries*
    In pursuit of the thing she would have stay,
5   Whilst her neglected child holds her in chase,°   *pursues her*
    Cries to catch her whose busy care is bent
    To follow that which flies before her face,
    Not prizing° her poor infant's discontent;   *regarding*
    So runn'st thou after that which flies from thee,
10 Whilst I, thy babe, chase thee afar behind.
    But if thou catch thy hope, turn back to me
    And play the mother's part: kiss me, be kind.
        So will I pray that thou mayst have thy Will,[1]
        If thou turn back and my loud crying still.°   *quiet*

144[1]

    Two loves I have, of comfort and despair,
    Which like two spirits do suggest° me still: *entice*
    The better angel is a man right fair,
    The worser spirit a woman colored ill.°   *darkly*
5   To win me soon to hell my female evil
    Tempteth my better angel from my side,
    And would corrupt my saint to be a devil,
    Wooing his purity with her foul pride.
    And whether that my angel be turned fiend
10 Suspect I may, yet not directly tell;
    But being both from me, both to each friend,[2]
    I guess one angel in another's hell.[3]
        Yet this shall I ne'er know, but live in doubt,
        Till my bad angel fire my good one out.[4]

---

3. Lips, which are scarlet, like a cardinal's robe.
4. And kissed others' lips as often as I have stolen the sexual and emotional intimacy ("rents" paid by a tenant) from others' marriages by committing adultery, thus reducing the possibility that these marriages will result in children ("revenues," estates that yield income). Q has a comma after "mine" that, if retained, would mean that the mistress is guilty both of kissing others' lips as often as those of the poet and of robbing "others' beds' revenues." "Sealed" with a kiss: comparing the mistress's lips to the red wax used to seal official documents.

Sonnet 143
1. A pun; see Sonnet 135, note 1.

Sonnet 144
1. TEXTUAL COMMENT Another version of this sonnet appears as Poem 2 in *The Passionate Pilgrim.* For the differences between the two versions, see Digital Edition TC 2 to that work.
2. Both away from me and lovers to one another.
3. Each torments the other; they are in the "hell," or middle den, of a (sexual) game called barley-break; the man occupies the sex organ ("hell") of the woman.
4. Until my bad angel expels my good one, who has become an animal to be smoked out of a burrow; until my bad angel infects my good one with venereal disease; until bad money ("angel" = gold coin) drives out good.

145[1]

Those lips that love's own hand did make
Breathed forth the sound that said "I hate"
To me that languished for her sake;
But when she saw my woeful state,
5 Straight in her heart did mercy come,
Chiding that tongue that, ever sweet,
Was used in giving gentle doom,°   *mild judgment*
And taught it thus anew to greet:
"I hate" she altered with an end
10 That followed it as gentle day
Doth follow night, who, like a fiend,
From heaven to hell is flown away.
　　"I hate" from hate away she threw,[2]
　　And saved my life, saying "not you."

146

Poor soul, the center of my sinful earth,
Shamed by these rebel powers that thee array,[1]
Why dost thou pine within and suffer dearth,
Painting thy outward walls so costly gay?
5 Why so large cost, having so short a lease,
Dost thou upon thy fading mansion° spend?   *(the body)*
Shall worms, inheritors of this excess,
Eat up thy charge?° Is this thy body's end?   *expense*
Then, soul, live thou upon thy servant's° loss,   *(the body's)*
10 And let that pine to aggravate thy store.[2]
Buy terms divine° in selling hours of dross;°   *eternal life / waste*
Within be fed, without be rich no more.
　　So shalt thou feed on death, that feeds on men,
　　And death once dead, there's no more dying then.

147

My love is as a fever, longing still°   *continually*
For that which longer nurseth° the disease,   *nourishes*
Feeding on that which doth preserve° the ill,   *prolong*
Th'uncertain° sickly appetite to please.   *capricious*
5 My reason, the physician to my love,
Angry that his prescriptions are not kept,
Hath left me, and I desperate now approve
Desire is death, which physic did except.[1]
Past cure I am, now reason is past care,[2]
10 And frantic mad with ever more° unrest.   *constant*
My thoughts and my discourse as madmen's are,

Sonnet 145
1. Unlike the other sonnets, which are in iambic pentameter, 145 is composed of eight-syllable (iambic tetrameter) lines.
2. She converted the normal meaning of the phrase "I hate" away from "hate." A pun on "hate away" and "(Anne) Hathaway," Shakespeare's wife, is possible.
Sonnet 146
1. This rebellious body in which you are clothed. TEXTUAL COMMENT At the beginning of the line, Q repeats "My sinful earth" from the previous line. There is no way of discovering with certainty what

Shakespeare wrote. For the emendation adopted here, see Digital Edition TC 9.
2. And let the body dwindle to add to your wealth.
Sonnet 147
1. *now . . . except:* now discover that desire, which medicine rejected (or, possibly, which rejected medicine), is fatal.
2. Medical care: inverting the proverb "Past cure, past care" (don't worry about what you can't control). In the proverb, you don't care because you can't cure; here, because you don't care, you can't cure.

At random from° the truth, vainly° expressed,   *unconnected to / idly*
    For I have sworn thee fair, and thought thee bright,
    Who art as black as hell, as dark as night.

148

Oh, me! What eyes hath love put in my head,
Which have no correspondence with true sight?
Or if they have, where is my judgment fled,
That censures falsely[1] what they see aright?
5 If that be fair whereon my false eyes dote,
What means the world to say it is not so?
If it be not, then love doth well denote[2]
Love's eye is not so true as all men's "no."[3]
How can it? Oh, how can love's eye be true,
10 That is so vexed with watching° and with tears?   *staying awake*
No marvel then though I° mistake my view;   *that I (eye)*
The sun itself sees not till heaven clears.
    O cunning love, with tears thou keep'st me blind,
    Lest eyes, well seeing, thy foul faults should find.

149

Canst thou, O cruel, say I love thee not
When I against myself with thee partake?°   *take sides*
Do I not think on thee when I forgot
Am of myself—all, tyrant,[1] for thy sake?
5 Who hateth thee that I do call my friend?
On whom frown'st thou that I do fawn upon?
Nay, if thou lour'st° on me, do I not spend°   *scowl / wreak*
Revenge upon myself with present moan?°   *instant anguish*
What merit do I in myself respect°   *value; note*
10 That is so proud thy service to despise,[2]
When all my best° doth worship thy defect,°   *best qualities / flaws*
Commanded by the motion of thine eyes?
    But, love, hate on, for now I know thy mind:
    Those that can see thou lov'st, and I am blind.[3]

150

Oh, from what power hast thou this powerful might
With insufficiency° my heart to sway,   *By your flaws*
To make me give the lie to my true sight
And swear that brightness doth not grace the day?[1]
5 Whence hast thou this becoming of things ill,[2]
That in the very refuse of thy deeds°   *your basest behavior*
There is such strength and warrantise° of skill   *guarantee*
That in my mind thy worst all best exceeds?

Sonnet 148
1. That judges inaccurately (dishonestly). "False" (line 5) has similar meanings.
2. Then my self-delusion in love proves that.
3. Not so true as all other men's denial, suggesting a pun on "eye/ay" (yes).
Sonnet 149
1. *when . . . all, tyrant:* when I neglect myself—doing all of this, you tyrant.
2. So proud as to scorn to serve you.
3. You love those who see you accurately and thus admire you, but I am blinded (by love and, thus, from your point of view, unworthy of being loved). The first clause may have the opposite sense, however: you love those who see your defects well enough not to love you.
Sonnet 150
1. *To . . . day:* The speaker is so blindly in love that he finds beauty only in the blackness he associates with his mistress.
2. This capacity to render the ugly attractive.

Who taught thee how to make me love thee more,
10   The more I hear and see just cause of hate?
Oh, though I love what others do abhor,°   *(pun on "whore")*
With others thou shouldst not abhor my state.
    If thy unworthiness raised° love in me,   *(sexual)*
    More worthy I to be beloved of thee.³

151

Love is too young° to know what conscience is;   *(Cupid being a boy)*
Yet who knows not conscience¹ is born of love?
Then, gentle cheater, urge° not my amiss,°   *stress / fault*
Lest guilty of my faults thy sweet self prove.
5   For, thou betraying me, I do betray
My nobler part° to my gross body's treason.   *(the soul)*
My soul doth tell my body that he° may   *(the body)*
Triumph in love; flesh stays no farther reason,²
But, rising at thy name, doth point out thee
10   As his triumphant prize. Proud of this pride,³
He is contented thy poor drudge to be—
To stand° in thy affairs, fall by thy side.   *assist; be erect*
    No want of conscience hold it that I call
    Her "love," for whose dear love I rise and fall.

152

In loving thee thou know'st I am forsworn,¹
But thou art twice forsworn, to me love swearing:°   *in swearing love to me*
In act thy bed-vow° broke, and new faith torn   *to husband (or lover)*
In vowing new hate after new love bearing.²
5   But why of two oaths' breach do I accuse thee,
When I break twenty? I am perjured most,
For all my vows are oaths but to misuse° thee;   *deceive*
And all my honest faith in thee is lost.
For I have sworn deep oaths of thy deep kindness—
10   Oaths of thy love, thy truth, thy constancy—
And to enlighten thee gave eyes to blindness,³
Or made them swear against the thing they see.
    For I have sworn thee fair—more perjured eye,°   *(punning on "I")*
    To swear against the truth so foul a lie.

---

3. Love me owing to my generosity; perhaps: love me because my bad judgment makes me a suitable match.
Sonnet 151
1. Moral sense; carnal knowledge.
2. Flesh, specifically the sexual organ, needs no further encouragement.
3. Swelling with pride (and lust).
Sonnet 152
1. Forsworn presumably in breaking loving vows—

perhaps to his wife, to the youth to whom he promised unswerving devotion in earlier sonnets, or to both.
2. *new faith . . . bearing*: the "new faith" followed by "new hate" may be addressed either to the speaker's young friend or to the speaker himself.
3. And to make you fair (give you insight), I looked blindly on your failings (pretended to see what I couldn't).

153[1]

	Cupid[2] laid by his brand° and fell asleep.	*torch; (phallic)*
	A maid of Dian's[3] this advantage found,°	*seized*
	And his love-kindling fire did quickly steep	
	In a cold valley-fountain of that ground,	
5	Which borrowed from this holy fire of Love	
	A dateless° lively heat still° to endure,	*An endless / always*
	And grew a seething bath, which yet men prove	
	Against strange maladies a sovereign cure.[4]	
	But at my mistress' eye Love's brand new fired,°	*being newly lit*
10	The boy for trial° needs would touch my breast.	*to test it*
	I, sick withal,° the help of bath desired,	*from it*
	And thither hied, a sad distempered° guest,	*seriously ill*
	But found no cure. The bath for my help lies	
	Where Cupid got new fire: my mistress' eyes.	

154[1]

	The little love-god, lying once asleep,	
	Laid by his side his heart-inflaming brand,°	*torch*
	Whilst many nymphs that vowed chaste life to keep	
	Came tripping by; but in her maiden hand,	
5	The fairest votary° took up that fire	*religious adherent*
	Which many legions of true hearts° had warmed,	*lovers*
	And so the general° of hot desire	*commander (Cupid)*
	Was, sleeping, by a virgin hand disarmed.	
	This brand she quenchèd in a cool well by,°	*close by*
10	Which from Love's fire took heat perpetual,	
	Growing a bath and healthful remedy	
	For men diseased. But I, my mistress' thrall,°	*slave*
	Came there for cure, and this° by that I prove:	*the following*
	Love's fire heats water, water cools not love.	

Sonnet 153
1. This and the following sonnet derive indirectly from classical fifth-century Greek epigrams.
2. God of love (especially erotic desire), a boy, son of Venus, goddess of love—associated with the speaker's mistress rather than with the male youth.
3. Diana, goddess of chastity.
4. *And grew . . . cure:* And became a boiling-hot medicinal bath (used, among other purposes, for the treatment of venereal disease), which men still find to be an outstanding remedy for foreign illnesses (venereal diseases were associated with foreigners). There may be an allusion here and in Sonnet 154 to the town of Bath, which became a famous health spa in the eighteenth century.
Sonnet 154
1. This sonnet varies the topic of 153.

A Lover's Complaint

Shakespeare's sonnets first appeared in print in the Quarto of 1609, but they did not appear alone. In that volume, they were followed by "A Lover's Complaint," a poem probably from the first years of the seventeenth century and possibly by Shakespeare. (See the Textual Introduction). In complaint poetry, a woman laments her (usually) sexual ruin amid doleful reflections on life. Between 1593 and 1596, six poets published works consisting of a sonnet sequence, a brief intermediate piece usually based on ancient Greek form or subject matter (Cupid, for example), and a concluding complaint. The sonnets section of one such work, Richard Barnfield's *Cynthia* (1595), from which Shakespeare probably borrowed, is addressed to an attractive male youth. Another poet anticipates Shakespeare's sequence in dividing his sonnets into two main groups. It would be wrong to overstate the homogeneity of this mini-tradition. Nonetheless, the 1609 Quarto—a sonnet sequence plausibly divided into two parts, the first concerning a beautiful male youth and the second a woman; two concluding sonnets on Cupid; and a poetic complaint—is less miscellaneous collection than multigeneric form.

That form is characterized by its links between the sonnets and the complaint. The voyeuristic poems dealing with the affair between the male youth and the speaker's mistress anticipate "A Lover's Complaint." In a conventional pastoral landscape, the "Complaint's" narrator overhears a young woman tell an old man of her seduction and abandonment by an attractive young man. The "double voice" (line 3) the narrator hears—explicitly, an echo—also anticipates the young woman's extended quotation of the young man inside her own tale, the young man's duplicitous method of wooing (using poetry and theater), and even the uncertain veracity of the woman, the old man, and the narrator. Except for the old man, the characters resemble the three central figures in the sonnet sequence.

Yet in "A Lover's Complaint," but only ambiguously if at all in the sonnets, the male youth seduces the woman, and both seemingly get to speak for themselves. The first-person voice—the only one heard in the sonnets—is denied even the concluding comment promised by the opening frame. Instead, the betrayed woman closes the poem, whose ornamental, archaic diction, partly modeled on the works of Shakespeare's older contemporary Edmund Spenser, contrasts with the sonnets' mixture of down-to-earth colloquialism and metaphorical density. Again, though written (like the sonnets) in rhymed iambic pentameter, "A Lover's Complaint" has a different form—rime royal, a seven-line stanza rhyming *ababbcc* used extensively by Chaucer, occasionally by Spenser, and by Shakespeare himself in *The Rape of Lucrece*. As in *Lucrece*, enjambment is more common than in the sonnets, perhaps owing to the greater emphasis on narrative in "A Lover's Complaint." Finally, the woman's voice, rather than the first person, is employed as elsewhere in complaint poetry to ventriloquize the male poet's views. But here, the self-referential turn emphasizes not the memorializing but the destructive power of poetry.

WALTER COHEN

SELECTED BIBLIOGRAPHY

Cheney, Patrick. "'Deep-Brained Sonnets' and 'Tragic Shows': Shakespeare's Late Ovidian Art in *A Lover's Complaint*." *Critical Essays on Shakespeare's "A Lover's Complaint*." Ed. Shirley Sharon-Zisser. Aldershot, Hampshire: Ashgate, 2006. 55–77. Reads the poem as a self-referential attempt to reconcile competing literary traditions (lyrical-tragic vs. pastoral-epic) and views of nationhood (liberty vs. monarchy), in which the female protagonist is both agent and victim of the seductiveness of art.

Rowe, Katherine. "A Lover's Complaint." *The Cambridge Companion to Shakespeare's Poetry*. Ed. Patrick Cheney. Cambridge: Cambridge UP, 2007. 144–60. Places the poem in relation to the tradition of complaint poetry, to treatment of the emotions, and to the use of ostentatiously artificial language.

TEXTUAL INTRODUCTION

"A Louers complaint. | BY | WILLIAM SHAKE-SPEARE" follows the "FINIS." of Shakespeare's sonnets in the 1609 Quarto, filling out the last eleven pages of the brief volume (sigs. K1–L2). Neither publisher Thomas Thorpe's entry of the sonnets in the Stationers' Register on May 20, 1609, nor the Quarto's title page and dedication of "INSVING.SONNETS" mentions this complaint poem, written in the seven-line rime royal stanza that is also used in *The Rape of Lucrece*. Despite the Quarto's attribution of the poem to Shakespeare, its authorship has been widely debated. It was questioned in the first half of the twentieth century as awkward in expression (e.g., "sawn" as past participle of "see" to fit the rhyme at line 91) and un-Shakespearean in vocabulary. New arguments in the 1960s, however, turned the tide back in favor of Shakespeare's authorship: even the high proportion of "non-Shakespearean" vocabulary, for instance, was reconceived in quantitative studies as positive evidence when set in comparison with rates of new vocabulary in other Shakespearean works (Jackson 169–83). Positive critical evaluations, often claiming the complaint poem as an integral coda to the sonnets, suggested an emerging consensus about the poem's authenticity over the next few decades, but the authorship debate has since been rekindled, especially in response to Brian Vickers's proposal of John Davies of Hereford as a candidate. Some recent approaches emphasize recognizable collocation and phrasal patterns, rhetorical figures, metrical characteristics (including stress profiles and syntactic breaks), and distinctive spellings, and the poem has also become a testing ground for computer-assisted stylometric analysis synthesizing complex variables. Definitive conclusions do, however, remain elusive.

LYNNE MAGNUSSON

TEXTUAL BIBLIOGRAPHY

Jackson, MacDonald P. *Determining the Shakespeare Canon*: Arden of Faversham *and* A Lover's Complaint. Oxford: Oxford UP, 2014.

Vickers, Brian. *Shakespeare, "A Lover's Complaint," and John Davies of Hereford*. Cambridge: Cambridge UP, 2007.

A Lover's Complaint

From off a hill whose concave womb reworded°   *hollow side echoed*
A plaintful story from a sist'ring° vale,   *nearby*
My spirits t'attend° this double voice accorded,°   *hear / agreed*
And down I laid to list° the sad-tuned tale;   *listen to*
5 Ere long espied a fickle° maid full pale,   *disturbed*
Tearing of papers, breaking rings a-twain,°   *in two*
Storming her world with sorrow's wind and rain.

Upon her head a plaited hive° of straw,   *hat*
Which fortified° her visage from the sun,   *protected*
10 Whereon the thought° might think sometime it saw   *imagination*
The carcass° of a beauty spent and done.   *dead remainder*
Time had not scythèd all that youth begun,
Nor youth all quit,° but spite° of heaven's fell° rage,   *gone / in spite / fierce*
Some beauty peeped through lattice of seared° age.   *withered*

15 Oft did she heave her napkin to her eyne,[1]
Which on it had conceited characters,°   *imaginative designs*
Laund'ring the silken figures in the brine
That seasoned° woe had pelleted in tears,   *experienced; salted*
And often reading° what contents it bears;   *(the "figures," line 17)*
20 As often shrieking undistinguished° woe   *inarticulate*
In clamors of all size, both high and low.

Sometimes her leveled eyes their carriage ride[2]
As° they did batt'ry to the spheres° intend;   *As if / planets*
Sometime diverted, their poor balls° are tied   *eyeballs; cannonballs*
25 To th'orbèd° earth; sometimes they do extend   *spherical*
Their view right on;° anon their gazes° lend   *straight / the eyes*
To every place at once and nowhere fixed,
The mind and sight distractedly commixed.°   *confused*

Her hair, nor° loose nor tied in formal plait,   *neither*
30 Proclaimed in her a careless hand of pride;[3]
For some, untucked, descended her sheaved hat,°   *fell from her straw hat*
Hanging her pale and pinèd cheek beside;
Some in her threaden fillet° still did bide   *headband*
And, true to bondage, would not break from thence,
35 Though slackly braided in loose negligence.

A thousand favors° from a maund° she drew,   *love tokens / basket*
Of amber, crystal, and of beaded jet,°   *beads of black stone*

---

1. Often did she raise her handkerchief to her eyes.
2. Sometimes her eyes, aimed (like a cannon), glare (are mounted on a swivel).
3. A hand careless of pride; a hand proud in its carelessness (knowing that she could attract with no effort).

Which one by one she in a river threw,
Upon whose weeping margin she was set,°   *seated*
40   Like usury applying wet to wet,[4]
Or monarch's hands that lets not bounty fall
Where want cries some, but where excess begs all.[5]

Of folded schedules° had she many a one,   *letters*
Which she perused, sighed, tore, and gave the flood;
45   Cracked many a ring of posied gold and bone,[6]
Bidding them find their sepulchers in mud;
Found yet more letters, sadly penned in blood,
With sleided silk feat and affectedly
Enswathed[7] and sealed to curious° secrecy.   *careful*

50   These often bathed she in her fluxive° eyes,   *flowing*
And often kissed, and often gave to tear,
Cried, "O false blood, thou register° of lies,   *record*
What unapprovèd° witness dost thou bear!   *unreliable*
Ink would have seemed more black and damnèd here!"
55   This said, in top of rage the lines she rents,°   *rips*
Big° discontent so breaking their contents.   *Powerful*

A reverend man that grazed his cattle nigh
(Sometime a blusterer that the ruffle knew[8]
Of court, of city, and had let go by
60   The swiftest hours observèd as they flew[9])
Towards this afflicted fancy fastly[1] drew
And, privileged by age, desires to know
In brief the grounds and motives of her woe.

So slides he down upon his grainèd bat[2]
65   And, comely° distant, sits he by her side,   *politely*
When he again desires her, being sat,
Her grievance with his hearing to divide.°   *share*
If that from him there may be aught° applied   *anything*
Which may her suffering ecstasy° assuage,   *grief*
70   'Tis promised in the charity of age.

"Father," she says, "though in me you behold
The injury of many a blasting° hour,   *disfiguring*
Let it not tell your judgment I am old:
Not age, but sorrow, over me hath power.
75   I might as yet have been a spreading° flower,   *blooming*
Fresh to myself, if I had self-applied
Love to myself, and to no love beside.

4. Like usury making wealth wealthier (by adding tears to the stream).
5. *Or . . . all:* Or like the monarch who, rather than give a little to the truly needy, gives a great deal to those who already have plenty.
6. A ring of gold and ivory inscribed with messages (of love).
7. *With . . . / Enswathed:* Delicately and affectionately wrapped in strands of separated ("sleided") silk.
8. Once a loudmouthed man of the world who was accustomed to the busier life.
9. *had . . . flew:* was past the prime of life, but had learned from experience.
1. Toward this person afflicted by love rapidly (close by).
2. So he comes down the bank with the help of his forked herdsman's staff.

"But woe is me, too early I attended
A youthful suit—it was° to gain my grace°—   *was designed / favor*
80   Oh, one by nature's outwards° so commended   *external appearance*
That maidens' eyes stuck over all° his face.   *were glued to*
Love lacked a dwelling and made him her place,
And when in his fair parts she did abide,
She was new lodged and newly deified.

85   "His browny locks did hang in crooked curls,
And every light occasion° of the wind   *chance stirring*
Upon his lips their silken parcels° hurls.   *(of hair)*
What's sweet to do, to do will aptly find:[3]
Each eye that saw him did enchant the mind,
90   For on his visage was in little° drawn   *miniature*
What largeness thinks in paradise was sawn.[4]

"Small show of man was yet upon his chin:
His phoenix° down began but to appear,   *singularly lovely*
Like unshorn velvet, on that termless skin[5]
95   Whose bare out-bragged the web[6] it seemed to wear;
Yet showed his visage by that cost more dear,[7]
And nice affections° wavering stood in doubt   *discriminating tastes*
If best were as it was, or best without.°   *(shaven)*

"His qualities° were beauteous as his form,   *skills; manners*
100 For maiden-tongued° he was and thereof free;°   *modest of speech / fluent*
Yet if men moved° him, was he such a storm   *angered*
As oft twixt May and April is to see
When winds breathe sweet, unruly though they be.
His rudeness so with his authorized youth
105 Did livery falseness in a pride of truth.[8]

"Well could he ride, and often men would say,
'That horse his mettle from his rider takes:
Proud of subjection, noble by the sway,°   *control*
What rounds, what bounds, what course,° what stop he makes!'   *gallop*
110 And controversy hence a question takes:
Whether the horse by him became his deed,
Or he his manage by th' well-doing steed.[9]

"But quickly on this side the verdict went:
His real habitude° gave life and grace   *royal manner (or attire)*
115 To appertainings° and to ornament—   *external outfits*
Accomplished in himself, not in his case;°   *mere appearance; clothes*
All aids, themselves made fairer by their place,

---

3. Ways are easily found to do pleasant things (look, love).
4. What one would imagine seeing on a larger scale in paradise.
5. Like velvet with its nap unclipped, on that indescribable (invulnerable to time) skin.
6. Whose naked surface showed more beautiful than the down covering.
7. Yet his face looked more precious (attractive) because of its rich clothing.
8. *His . . . truth:* His roughness, sanctioned by his "youth," employed falseness in truth's uniform.
9. *Whether . . . steed:* Whether he performed so well because of his horsemanship or because his grace in horsemanship (French: *manège*) was a result of the horse's skill.

Came for additions;[1] yet their purposed trim
Pieced not[2] his grace, but were all graced by him.

120   "So on the tip of his subduing tongue
All kind of arguments and question deep,
All replication prompt,° and reason strong   *quick reply*
For his advantage still did wake and sleep.[3]
To make the weeper laugh, the laugher weep,
125   He had the dialect and different skill,[4]
Catching all passions in his craft of will,[5]

"That° he did in the general bosom° reign   *So that / all hearts*
Of young, of old, and sexes both° enchanted   *both sexes*
To dwell with him in thoughts, or to remain
130   In personal duty, following where he haunted.°   *often went*
Consents,[6] bewitched, ere he desire° have granted,   *before he asks*
And dialogued for him what° he would say,   *anticipated what words*
Asked their own wills and made their wills obey.

"Many there were that did his picture get
135   To serve their eyes, and in it put their mind,
Like fools that in th'imagination set
The goodly objects° which abroad° they find   *sights / traveling*
Of lands and mansions, theirs in thought assigned,
And laboring in more pleasures to bestow them[7]
140   Than the true gouty landlord which doth owe° them.   *own*

"So many have, that never touched his hand,
Sweetly supposed them mistress of his heart.
My woeful self, that did in freedom stand
And was my own fee-simple[8] (not in part),
145   What with his art in youth and youth in art
Threw my affections in his charmèd° power,   *magical; songlike*
Reserved the stalk and gave him all my flower.

"Yet did I not, as some my equals° did,   *young girls of my rank*
Demand of him; nor, being desired, yielded.°   *yielded sexual favors*
150   Finding my self in honor so forbid,
With safest distance I mine honor° shielded.   *chastity*
Experience° for me many bulwarks builded   *(of "my equals")*
Of proofs new bleeding, which remained the foil[9]
Of this false jewel and his amorous spoil.

155   "But ah, who ever shunned by precedent
The destined ill she must herself assay?°   *try out*

---

1. Attempted to increase his worth.
2. *their . . . not:* their anticipated decorative effect did not increase (or: mend—continuation of the stanza's ostensibly denied emphasis on external garments).
3. *For . . . sleep:* (Like servants) adjusted their waking and sleeping hours for the benefit of their master.
4. The manner of speech and versatile skill.
5. His faculty of persuasion. Here and in the next stanza, there are suggestions of other senses of "will," including the author's name. See Sonnets 135 and 136.
6. (Sexually) consenting people.
7. *theirs . . . them:* imagining the "lands and mansions"

their own, they try harder to use them pleasurably.
8. And had absolute control of myself (as of land in freehold).
9. *Of . . . foil:* Fresh examples of seduction, which remained the defense (or sword—picking up the military, specifically fencing, imagery of "distance," "shielded," "bulwarks," "bleeding," lines 151–53). But "foil" as the dark material in which gems are set to make them look more brilliant also works with "false jewel" in the following line, to suggest that the young man's sexual escapades made him more attractive.

Or forced examples 'gainst her own content
To put the bypast perils in her way?[1]
Counsel may stop awhile what will not stay,°   *stop for good*
160 For when we rage,° advice is often seen   *(with lust)*
By blunting° us to make our wits more keen.   *repressing*

"Nor gives it satisfaction to our blood°   *sexuality*
That we must curb it upon others' proof°—   *experience*
To be forbid° the sweets that seems so good   *forbidden*
165 For fear of harms that preach in our behoof.°   *for our benefit*
O appetite, from judgment stand aloof!
The one a palate hath that needs will taste,
Though reason weep and cry, 'It is thy last!'

"For further I could say, 'This man's untrue';[2]
170 And knew the patterns° of his foul beguiling,   *instances*
Heard where his plants in others' orchards° grew,   *(wombs)*
Saw how deceits were gilded in his smiling,
Knew vows were ever brokers° to defiling,   *go-betweens*
Thought characters and words merely but art,[3]
175 And bastards of his foul adulterate heart.

"And long upon these terms I held my city,°   *chastity*
Till thus he gan° besiege me: 'Gentle maid,   *began to*
Have of my suffering youth some feeling pity,
And be not of my holy vows afraid.
180 That's° to ye sworn to none was ever said: *What is*
For feasts of love I have been called unto,
Till now, did° ne'er invite nor never woo.   *(I) did*

"'All my offenses that abroad° you see°   *in the world / learn of*
Are errors of the blood,° none of the mind.   *sexual passion*
185 Love made them not; with acture they may be,[4]
Where neither party is nor true nor kind.°   *faithful or loving*
They sought their shame that so° their shame did find,   *who in this way*
And so much less of shame in me remains
By how much of me their reproach contains.[5]

190 "'Among the many that mine eyes have seen,
Not° one whose flame my heart so much as warmèd   *There is not*
Or my affection put to th' smallest teen°   *pain*
Or any of my leisures° ever charmèd.   *hours of leisure*
Harm have I done to them but ne'er was harmèd;
195 Kept hearts in liveries,° but mine own was free   *in uniform (service)*
And reigned commanding in his monarchy.

"'Look here what tributes wounded fancies° sent me   *lovers*
Of pallid pearls and rubies red as blood,
Figuring° that they their passions likewise lent me   *Showing*

---

1. *Or . . . way:* Or reminded herself, to counter her present inclinations, of bygone dangers. *forced:* urged.
2. I am able to say more about this man's perfidy.
3. Written and spoken words were merely instruments of skill (in seduction).
4. *with . . . be:* by a mere physical act they may be performed.
5. *By . . . contains:* The more they name me in their reproaches (thus revealing that they are unchaste and, hence, by this logic, to blame).

Of grief and blushes, aptly understood
In bloodless white and the encrimsoned mood°—   *form (of rubies)*
Effects of terror and dear modesty,
Encamped in hearts, but fighting outwardly.[6]

"'And lo, behold these talents° of their hair   *riches*
With twisted metal amorously impleached[7]
I have received from many a several fair°   *a different beauty*
(Their kind acceptance weepingly beseeched),
With th'annexions° of fair gems enriched   *additions*
And deep-brained sonnets that did amplify°   *expound; increase*
Each stone's dear° nature, worth, and quality.   *precious*

"'The diamond? Why, 'twas beautiful and hard,
Whereto his invised[8] properties did tend;
The deep green em'rald, in whose fresh regard
Weak sights their sickly radiance do amend;[9]
The heaven-hued sapphire and the opal blend[1]
With objects manifold: each several° stone,   *distinct*
With wit well blazoned,° smiled or made some moan.   *described*

"'Lo, all these trophies of affections° hot,   *passions*
Of pensive° and subdued desires the tender,°   *saddened / gifts*
Nature hath charged me that I hoard them not,
But yield them up where I myself must render:
That is to you, my origin and ender;°   *alpha and omega; all*
For these of force must your oblations be,[2]
Since I their altar, you enpatron me.[3]

"'Oh, then, advance of yours that phraseless° hand   *beyond description*
Whose white weighs down the airy scale of praise.[4]
Take all these similes[5] to your own command,
Hallowed with sighs that burning° lungs did raise.   *(with love)*
What me, your minister, for you obeys,
Works under you,[6] and to your audit° comes   *account*
Their distract parcels° in combinèd sums.   *component parts*

"'Lo, this device was sent me from a nun,
Or sister sanctified of holiest note,°   *reputation*
Which late her noble suit° in court did shun,   *attendance; suitors*
Whose rarest havings° made the blossoms° dote;   *qualities / young nobles*
For she was sought by spirits of richest coat,°   *coat of arms*
But kept cold distance and did thence remove
To spend her living° in eternal love.°   *life / (of God)*

200, 205, 210, 215, 220, 225, 230, 235

---

6. *Effects . . . outwardly:* White ("terror") and red (blushing "modesty") fighting on their faces.
7. With metal clasps lovingly intertwined.
8. Its unseen—referring to the diamond but also, perhaps, to the equally "beautiful and hard" young man.
9. *in . . . amend:* which, when looked at, can heal weak vision.
1. Blended: many-colored; accompanying other "objects" (line 216).
2. For these necessarily must be offerings at your

altar.
3. Since I am the altar (on which they were offered), you must necessarily be the patron saint of the altar (me).
4. Whose white exceeds any measure of praise.
5. These emblematic gifts and the sonnets that explain them.
6. *What . . . under you:* Whatever pays homage to me, your agent, serves you.

"'But oh, my sweet, what labor is't to leave
240 The thing we have not, mast'ring what not strives,°   *does not resist*
Planing° the place which did no form[7] receive,   *Smoothing*
Playing patient sports in unconstrainèd gyves?[8]
She that her fame so to herself contrives[9]
The scars of battle scapeth° by the flight,   *escapes*
245 And makes her absence valiant, not her might.[1]

"'Oh, pardon me in that my boast is true!
The accident which brought me to her eye
Upon the moment° did her force° subdue,   *Immediately / resolve*
And now she would the cagèd cloister fly:
250 Religious° love put out religion's eye.   *Devoted (sexual)*
Not to be tempted would she be immured,°   *walled up*
And now, to tempt, all liberty procured.

"'How mighty then you are, oh, hear me tell!
The broken bosoms° that to me belong   *hearts*
255 Have emptied all their fountains in my well,
And mine I pour° your ocean all among: *pour into*
I strong o'er them, and you o'er me being strong,
Must for your victory us all congest,°   *gather*
As compound° love, to physic° your cold breast.   *medicinal / treat*

260 "'My parts° had power to charm a sacred nun,   *attributes; limbs; roles*
Who, disciplined, ay, dieted in° grace,   *sustained by*
Believed her eyes when they t'assail begun,[2]
All vows and consecrations giving place.°   *yielding*
O most potential love! Vow, bond, nor space
265 In thee hath neither sting, knot, nor confine,[3]
For thou art all, and all things else are thine.

"'When thou impressest,[4] what are precepts worth
Of stale example? When thou wilt inflame,
How coldly those impediments stand forth
270 Of wealth, of filial fear, law, kindred, fame!°   *reputation*
Love's arms are° peace, 'gainst rule, 'gainst sense, 'gainst   *Love's power compels*
     shame;
And° sweetens in the suff'ring pangs it bears   *And love*
The aloes° of all forces, shocks, and fears.   *bitterness*

"'Now all these hearts that do on mine depend,
275 Feeling it break, with bleeding groans they pine,[5]
And, supplicant,° their sighs to you extend   *as supplicants*
To leave° the batt'ry that you make 'gainst mine,   *cease*
Lending soft audience to my sweet design[6]

---

7. No impression (of love, on the heart).
8. Pretending to patiently endure shackles ("gyves") that have not been forced upon one and that can be removed (or that do not constrain). (The entire sentence is ironic.)
9. She who thus contrives for herself the reputation of disinterest in love.
1. And achieves a reputation for valor by avoiding the temptation of love, not by strongly resisting it.
2. When my attributes ("parts") began to assail her

heart.
3. *potential . . . confine:* powerful love: a "vow" has no force ("sting"), a "bond" does not tie ("knot"), and "space" does not restrain ("confine").
4. When you draft someone into your (military) service; make an impression on the heart.
5. Because each sigh supposedly robbed the heart of a drop of blood.
6. Looking favorably on my good intentions.

And credent° soul to that strong bonded oath   *trustful*
280 That shall prefer and undertake° my troth.'   *advance and guarantee*

"This said, his wat'ry eyes he did dismount,°   *lower (military)*
Whose sights till then were leveled° on my face.   *aimed*
Each cheek, a river running from a fount,
With brinish current downward flowed apace.
285 Oh, how the channel° to the stream° gave grace,   *cheeks / tears*
Who, glazed with crystal, 'gat the glowing roses
That flame through water which their hue encloses.[7]

"O father, what a hell of witchcraft lies
In the small orb of one particular° tear!   *single*
290 But, with the inundation of the eyes,
What rocky heart to° water will not wear?°   *eroded by / wear away*
What breast so cold that is not warmèd here?
Or cleft° effect—cold modesty, hot wrath°—   *divided / passion*
Both fire from hence and chill extincture hath?[8]

295 "For lo, his passion,° but an art of craft,   *passionate speech*
Even there resolved° my reason into tears.   *dissolved*
There my white stole of chastity I daffed,°   *took off*
Shook off my sober guards and civil° fears;   *respectable; sober*
Appear to him as he to me appears—
300 All melting, though our drops this diff'rence bore:
His poisoned me, and mine did him restore.

"In him a plenitude of subtle matter,°   *raw material; cunning*
Applied to cautels,° all strange forms receives[9]—   *tricky devices*
Of burning blushes, or of weeping water,
305 Or swooning paleness; and he takes and leaves°   *uses this and shuns that*
In either's aptness° as it best deceives: *As each is appropriate*
To blush at speeches rank,° to weep at woes,   *offensive*
Or to turn white and swoon at tragic shows;

"That not a heart which in his level° came   *range (of fire)*
310 Could scape the hail of his all-hurting aim,
Showing fair nature is° both kind and tame;   *Pretending his nature is*
And, veiled in them,° did win whom he would maim.   *(kindness and tameness)*
Against the thing he sought he would exclaim:
When he most burned in heart-wished luxury,°   *lust*
315 He preached pure maid° and praised cold chastity.   *virginal purity*

"Thus, merely with the garment of a grace[1]
The naked and concealèd fiend° he covered,   *devil*
That th'unexperient° gave the tempter place,°   *inexperienced / entry*
Which° like a cherubin above them hovered.°   *(The tempter) / (ironic)*
320 Who, young and simple, would not be so lovered?[2]

---

7. *Who . . . encloses:* The stream (of tears) is seen as a kind of glass covering ("crystal") over the cheeks ("roses"), to which it imparts a passionate color that shines through the "water," like a jewel enclosed in glass. *Who:* (the stream).
8. *Both . . . hath:* Tears heat up "cold modesty" and extinguish "hot" passion (as the following stanza elaborates).
9. *all . . . receives:* is shaped into novel forms.
1. With (merely) external appeal; also part of the religious language of the stanza, while looking back to earlier uses of "grace" with a variety of meanings.
2. Would not desire such a lover.

Ay me, I fell, and yet do question make°   *wonder*
What I should do again for such a sake.°   *person; pleasure*

"Oh, that infected° moisture of his eye!   *tainted*
Oh, that false fire which in his cheek so glowed!
325 Oh, that forced thunder from° his heart did fly!   *that from*
Oh, that sad breath his spongy lungs bestowed!°   *emitted*
Oh, all that borrowed motion, seeming owed,[3]
Would yet again betray the fore-betrayed
And new pervert a reconcilèd° maid."   *penitent*

---

3. That emotion apparently his own.

King Lear

You have, King James told his eldest son a few years before Shakespeare wrote *King Lear,* a double obligation to love God: first because He made you a man, and second because He made you "a little God to sit on his Throne, and rule over other men." Whatever the realities of Renaissance kingship—realities that included the stern necessity of compromise, reciprocity, and restraint—the idea of sovereignty was closely linked to fantasies of divine omnipotence. From his exalted height, the sovereign looked down upon the tiny figures of the ordinary mortals below him. Their hopes, the material conditions of their miserable existence, their names, were of little interest, and yet the King knew that they too were looking back up at him. "For kings being public persons," James uneasily acknowledged, are set "upon a public stage, in the sight of all the people; where all the beholders' eyes are attentively bent to look and pry in the least circumstance of their secretest drifts." Under such circumstances, the sovereign's dream was to command, like God, not only unquestioning obedience but unqualified love.

In *King Lear,* Shakespeare explores the dark consequences of this dream not only in the state but also in the family, where the Renaissance father increasingly styled himself "a little God." If, as the play opens, the aged Lear, exercising his imperious will and demanding professions of devotion, is every inch a king, he is also by the same token every inch a father, the absolute ruler of a family that conspicuously lacks the alternative authority of a mother. Shakespeare's play invokes this royal and paternal sovereignty only to chronicle its destruction in scenes of astonishing cruelty and power. The very words "every inch a king" are spoken not by the confident figure of supreme authority whom we glimpse in the first moments but by the ruined old man who perceives in his feverish rage and madness that the fantasy of omnipotence is a fraud: "When the rain came to wet me once, and the wind to make me chatter, when the thunder would not peace at my bidding, there I found 'em, there I smelt 'em out. Go to, they are not men o'their words. They told me I was everything. 'Tis a lie. I am not ague-proof" (*The Tragedy of King Lear* [Folio text] 4.5.100–105; cf. *The History of King Lear* [Quarto text] 4.6.100–105).

"They told me I was everything": Shakespeare's culture continually staged public rituals of deference to authority. These rituals—kneeling, bowing, uncovering the head, and so forth—enacted respect for wealth, caste, power, and, at virtually every level of society, age. Jacobean England had a strong official regard for the rights and privileges of age. It told itself that, by the will of God and the natural order of things, authority gravitated to the old, particularly to old men, and it contrived to ensure that this proper, sanctified arrangement of society be everywhere respected.

"'Tis a lie": Shakespeare's culture continually told itself at the same time that without the control of property and the threat of punishment, any claim to authority was chillingly vulnerable to the ruthless ambitions of the young, the restless, and the discontented. The incessant, ritualized spectacles of sovereignty have a nervous air, as if no one quite believed all the grand claims to divine sanction for the rule of kings and fathers, as if those who ruled both states and families harbored a half-conscious fear that the elaborate hierarchical structure could vanish like a mirage, exposing their shivering, defenseless bodies.

In ordinary circumstances, the tension between the extravagant claim to divinely sanctioned authority and the queasy sense that this claim was baseless lay far below the surface. Men and women went about their lives making the quiet compromises people usually make: rulers understood that they were not in fact God omnipotent; wives and children found ways to make their wishes felt without rising in open rebellion; social rituals were observed with the blend of deference, light irony, and flexibility that enables the social order to maintain its equilibrium.

But *King Lear* is emphatically not about ordinary circumstances, quiet compromises, and equilibrium. It is about a crisis in which latent contradictions become all too manifest, polite fictions give way to unbearable truths, and all veils are stripped away. *King Lear* relentlessly stages a horrifying descent toward what the ruined King, contemplating the filthy, naked body of a mad beggar, calls "the thing itself": "Unaccommodated man is no more but such a poor, bare, forked animal as thou art" (F 3.4.98–100; cf. Q 3.4.93–95). Lear and the Earl of Gloucester, another old man whose terrible fate closely parallels Lear's, repeatedly look up at the heavens and call upon the gods for help, but the gods are silent. The despairing Gloucester concludes that the universe is actively malevolent—"As flies to wanton boys are we to th' gods: / They kill us for their sport" (F 4.1.38–39; cf. Q 4.1.37–38)—but the awful silence of the gods may equally be a sign of their indifference or their nonexistence.

The story of King Lear and his three daughters had been often told when Shakespeare undertook to make it the subject of a tragedy. The play, performed at court in December 1606, was probably written and first performed somewhat earlier, though not before 1603, since it contains allusions to a florid piece of anti-Catholic propaganda published in that year: Samuel Harsnett's *Declaration of Egregious Popish Imposture* (the source of the colorful names of the "foul fiends" by whom Shakespeare's mad beggar claims to be possessed). Thus, scholars generally assign Shakespeare's composition of *King Lear* to 1604–05, shortly after *Othello* (ca. 1601–03) and before *Macbeth* (ca. 1606): an astounding succession of tragic masterpieces.

King Lear first appeared in print in a Quarto published in 1608 entitled the *True Chronicle Historie of the life and death of King Lear;* a substantially different text, entitled *The Tragedie of King Lear* and grouped with the other tragedies, was printed in the 1623 First Folio. From the eighteenth century, when the difference between the two texts was first noted, editors, assuming that the texts were imperfect versions of the identical play, customarily conflated them, blending together the approximately one hundred Folio lines not printed in the Quarto with the approximately three hundred Quarto lines not printed in the Folio and selecting as best they could among the hundreds of particular alternative readings.

There is, however, a growing scholarly consensus that the 1608 text of *Lear* represents the play as Shakespeare first wrote it and that the 1623 text represents a substantial revision. The changes include what appears to be a serious rethinking of the armed struggle—whether it is to be imagined principally as a foreign invasion or a civil war—that brings about the denouement, as well as a reconsideration of the play's final moments. (See the Textual Introduction for further discussion.) Since this revision includes significant structural changes as well as many local details, the two texts provide a precious opportunity to glimpse Shakespeare's creative process as an artist and the collaborative work of his theater company. Accordingly, *The Norton Shakespeare* prints *The History of King Lear* (Q) and *The Tragedy of King Lear* (F) on facing pages, and the plays can be read independently of one another in the Digital Edition. In addition, we include a modern combined version of the play, so that readers will be able to judge for themselves the effects of the familiar editorial practice of stitching together the two texts. The combined text also provides readers with access to the version that has for centuries formed the basis for innumerable stage and, more recently, film productions.

When *King Lear* was first performed, it may have struck contemporaries as strangely timely in the wake of a lawsuit that had occurred in late 1603. The two elder daughters of a doddering gentleman named Sir Brian Annesley had attempted to get their father legally certified as insane, thereby enabling themselves to take over his estate, while his youngest daughter vehemently protested on her father's behalf. The youngest daughter's name happened to be Cordell, a name uncannily close to that of Lear's youngest daughter, Cordelia, who tries to save her father from the malevolent designs of her older sisters.

The Annesley case is worth invoking not only because the weird coincidence may have caught Shakespeare's attention but also because it directs our own attention to the ordinary family tensions and fears around which *King Lear,* for all of its wildness, violence, and strangeness, is constructed.

Cordeilla Queene. From Raphael Holinshed, *Chronicles of England, Scotland, and Ireland* (1577).

Though the Lear story has the mythic quality of a folktale (specifically, it resembles both the tale of Cinderella and the tale told in many cultures of a daughter who falls into disfavor for telling her father she loves him as much as salt), it was rehearsed in Shakespeare's time as a piece of authentic British history from the very ancient past (ca. 800 B.C.E.) and as an admonition to contemporary fathers not to put too much trust in the flattery of their children: "Remember what happened to old King Lear. . . ." In some versions of the story, including Shakespeare's, the warning centers on a decision to retire.

Retirement has come to seem a routine event, but in the patriarchal, gerontocratic culture of Tudor and Stuart England, it was generally shunned. When through illness or extreme old age it became unavoidable, retirement put a severe strain on the politics and psychology of deference by driving a wedge between status—what Lear at society's pinnacle calls "[t]he name and all th'addition to a king" (F 1.1.133; cf. Q 1.1.121)—and power. In both the state and the family, the strain could be somewhat eased by transferring power to the eldest legitimate male successor, but as the families of both the legendary Lear and the real Brian Annesley showed, such a successor did not always exist.

In the absence of a male heir, the aged Lear, determined to "shake all cares and business" from himself and confer them on "younger strengths," attempts to divide his kingdom equally among his daughters so that, as he puts it, "future strife / May be prevented now" (F 1.1.37–38, 42–43; cf. Q 1.1.37–38). This attempt is a disastrous failure. Critics have often argued that the roots of the failure lie in the division of the kingdom, that any parceling out of the land on a map would itself have provoked in the audience an ominous shudder, as it is clearly meant to do when the rebels spread out a map in anticipation of a comparable division in *1 Henry IV.* But perhaps to some observers at least, Lear's intended plan, under the circumstances, might have seemed to make strategic sense. After all, the play opens with the Earl of Gloucester and the Earl of Kent commenting without apparent disapproval on the King's scrupulous distribution of the shares. The plan is not, in any case, put to the test, and the principal focus of the tragedy lies elsewhere. Lear's folly is not (or not only) that he retires or even that he divides his kingdom, but rather that he rashly disinherits the only child who truly loves him—his youngest daughter.

Shakespeare contrives moreover to show that the problem of generational transition—and the related tensions in the family and the state—with which his characters are grappling does not simply result from the absence of a son and heir. In his most brilliant and complex use of a double plot, he intertwines the story of Lear and his three daughters with the story of Gloucester and his two sons, a tale he adapted from an episode in Philip Sidney's prose romance *Arcadia*. The fact that this second story is given unusually full and intense treatment, almost equal to the main plot, has the effect of suggesting that what is at stake extends beyond the royal family alone, that the roots of the tragedy lie deep in the nature of things. Gloucester has a legitimate heir, his elder son, Edgar, as well as an illegitimate son, Edmund, and in this family the tragic conflict originates not in an unusual manner of transferring property from one generation to another but rather in the reverse: Edmund seethes with murderous resentment at the disadvantage entirely customary for someone in his position, both as a younger son and as what was called a "base" or "natural" child. "Thou, Nature, art my goddess," he declares:

> Wherefore should I
> Stand in the plague of custom and permit
> The curiosity of nations to deprive me,
> For that I am some twelve or fourteen moonshines
> Lag of a brother? Why "bastard"? Wherefore "base" . . . ?
> (F 1.2.1–6; cf. Q 1.2.1–6)

For the seductive and ruthlessly ambitious Edmund, the social order and the language used to articulate it are merely arbitrary constraints, obstacles to the triumph of his will. He schemes to tear down the obstacles by playing on his father's fears, cleverly planting a forged letter in which his older brother appears to be plotting against his father's life. The letter's chilling sentences express Edmund's own impatience, his hatred of the confining power of custom, his disgusted observation of "the oppression of aged tyranny, who sways not as it hath power but as it is suffered" (F 1.2.48–49; cf. Q 1.2.47–48). Gloucester is predictably horrified and incensed; these are, as Edmund cunningly knows, the cold sentiments that the aged fear lie just beneath the surface of deference and flattery. The forged letter reflects back as well on the scene that has just concluded and on whose outcome Gloucester is brooding: a scene in which everyone, with the exception of the Earl of Kent, has tamely suffered a tyrannical old man to banish his youngest daughter for her failure to flatter him.

Stargazing. From John Cypriano, *A Most Strange and Wonderful Prophesy* (1595). "I should have been that I am had the maidenliest star in the firmament twinkled on my bastardizing" (F 1.2.118–20).

Why does Lear, who has already drawn up the map dividing the kingdom, stage the love test? In Shakespeare's principal source, an anonymous play called *The True Chronicle History of King Leir* (published in 1605 but dating from 1594 or earlier), there is a gratifyingly clear answer. Leir's strong-willed daughter Cordella has vowed that she will only marry a man whom she herself loves; Leir wishes her to marry the man he chooses for his own dynastic purposes. He stages the love test, anticipating that in competing with her sisters Cordella will declare that she loves her father best, at which point Leir will demand that she prove her love by marrying the suitor of his choice. The stratagem backfires, but its purpose is clear.

By stripping his character of a comparable motive, Shakespeare makes

Lear's act seem stranger, at once more arbitrary and more rooted in deep psychological needs. His Lear is a man who has determined to retire from power but who cannot endure dependence. Unwilling to lose his identity as an absolute authority both in the state and in the family, he arranges a public ritual—"Which of you shall we say doth love us most . . . ?" (F 1.1.49; cf. Q 1.1.43)—whose aim seems to be to allay his own anxiety by arousing it in his children. Since the shares have already been apportioned, Lear evidently wants his daughters to engage in a symbolic competition for his bounty without having to endure any of the actual consequences of such a competition; he wants, that is, to produce in them something like the effect of theater, where emotions run high and their practical effects are negligible. But in this absolutist theater—whose formal, ceremonial character Goneril and Regan perfectly understand—Cordelia refuses to perform: "What shall Cordelia speak? Love, and be silent" (F 1.1.60; cf. Q 1.1.54). When she says "Nothing," a word that echoes darkly throughout the play, Lear hears what he most dreads: emptiness, loss of respect, the extinction of identity. And when, under further interrogation, she declares that she loves her father "[a]ccording to my bond" (F 1.1.91; cf. Q 1.1.79), Lear understands these words too to be the equivalent of "nothing."

As Cordelia's subsequent actions demonstrate, his youngest daughter's bond is in reality something substantial and deep. It is linked to the primary sense of obligation that keeps the Fool from abandoning the fallen King, leads Gloucester to commit what is regarded as treason, and drives Kent to put his life at risk to serve his royal master. In the case of Cordelia, this bond extends beyond duty and service to include a sustaining, generous love, but it is a love that ultimately leads to her death. Here Shakespeare makes an even more startling departure not only from *The True Chronicle History of King Leir* but from all his known sources. The earliest of these, the account in Geoffrey of Monmouth's twelfth-century *Historia Regum Britanniae*, sets the pattern repeated in John Higgins's *Mirror for Magistrates* (1574 edition), William Warner's *Albions England* (1586), Raphael Holinshed's *Chronicles of England, Scotland, and Ireland* (2nd ed., 1587), and Edmund Spenser's *Faerie Queene* (1590, 2.10.27–32): the aged Lear is overthrown by his wicked daughters and their husbands, but he is restored to the throne by the army of his good daughter's husband, the King of France. The story then is one of loss and restoration: Lear resumes his reign, and when, "made ripe for death" by old age, as Spenser puts it, he dies, he is succeeded by Cordelia. The conclusion is not unequivocally happy; in all of the known chronicles, Cordelia rules worthily for several years and then, after being deposed and imprisoned by her nephews, in despair commits suicide. But Shakespeare's ending is unprecedented in its tragic devastation. When in act 5 Lear suddenly enters with the lifeless body of Cordelia in his arms, the original audience, secure in the expectation of a very different resolution, must have been doubly shocked, a shock cruelly reinforced when the signs that she might be reviving—"This feather stirs. She lives!" (F 5.3.239; cf. Q 5.3.261)—all prove false. In the Folio *Tragedy of King Lear*, the father apparently dies in the grip of the illusion that he detects some breath on his daughter's lips, but we know that Cordelia will, as he says a moment earlier, "come no more, / Never, never, never, never, never!" (F 5.3.283–84; cf. Q 5.3.303–04).

Those five reiterated words, the bleakest pentameter line Shakespeare ever wrote, are the climax of an extraordinary poetics of despair that is set in motion when Lear disinherits Cordelia and when Gloucester credits Edmund's lies about Edgar. *King Lear* has seemed to many modern readers and audiences the greatest of Shakespeare's tragedies precisely because of its anguished look into the heart of darkness, but its vision of suffering and evil has not always commanded unequivocal admiration. In the eighteenth century, Samuel Johnson wrote, "I was many years ago so shocked by Cordelia's death that I know not whether I ever endured to read again the last scenes of the play till I undertook to revise them as an editor." Johnson's contemporaries preferred a revision of Shakespeare's tragedy undertaken in 1681 by Nahum Tate. Finding the play "a Heap of Jewels, unstrung, and unpolisht," Tate proceeded to restring them in order to save Cordelia's life and to produce the unambiguous and happy triumph of the forces of good.

Only in the nineteenth century was Shakespeare's deeply pessimistic ending—the old generation dead or dying, the survivors shaken to the core, the ruling families all broken with no impending marriage to promise renewal—generally restored to theatrical performance and the tragedy's immense power fully acknowledged. Even passionate admirers of *King Lear,* however, continued to express deep uneasiness, repeatedly noting not only its unbearably painful close but also what Johnson first called the "improbability of Lear's conduct" and what Samuel Taylor Coleridge termed the plot's "glaring absurdity." Above all, critics questioned whether the tragedy was suitable for the stage. Coleridge compared the suffering Lear to one of Michelangelo's titanic figures, but the grandeur invoked by the comparison led his contemporary Charles Lamb to conclude flatly that "Lear is essentially impossible to be represented on stage." "To see Lear acted," Lamb wrote, "to see an old man tottering about the stage with a walking stick, turned out of doors by his daughters in a rainy night, has nothing in it but what is painful and disgusting." In such a view, *King Lear* could only be staged successfully in the imagination; there alone would Lear's passion be perceived not like ordinary human suffering but rather, in the marvelous characterization of another Romantic critic, William Hazlitt, "like a sea, swelling, chafing, raging, without bound, without hope, without beacon, or anchor." In the theater of the mind, Shakespeare's play could assume its true, stupendous proportions, enabling the reader to grasp its ultimate meaning. That meaning, the great early twentieth-century critic A. C. Bradley wrote, is that we must "renounce the world, hate it, and lose it gladly. The only real thing in it is the soul, with its courage, patience, devotion. And nothing outward can touch that." These are stirring words, but what about the body?

Brilliant modern stage performances and, more recently, films belying the view that *King Lear* is unactable have underscored not only the play's acute theatrical sophistication and self-awareness but also its emphasis on the body's inescapable centrality. If Shakespeare explores the extremes of the mind's anguish and the soul's devotion, he never forgets that his characters have bodies as well, bodies that have needs, cravings, and vulnerabilities.

Then as now, those vulnerabilities are at their most terrible in the poor, and *King Lear* insists with singular urgency on the crucial importance of noticing what those who are wrapped in their "[r]obes and furred gowns" (F 4.5.159; cf. Q 4.6.158) rarely if ever register. The world is full of people who have almost nothing to shield them from the harshness of the elements and the grotesque inequities of the state. When those in power see the bodies of what the play calls "unaccommodated man," they look away or merely pretend to see what in reality they ignore. "Get thee glass eyes," Lear says bitterly, "And, like a scurvy politician, / Seem to see the things thou dost not" (F 4.5.164–66; cf. Q 4.6.158–60).

Lear himself was blind in precisely this way, but he has been forced, as he puts it, "to feel what wretches feel" (F 3.4.35; cf. Q 3.4.31). When in this tragedy characters fall from high station, they plunge unprotected into a world of violent storms, murderous cruelty, and physical horror. The old King wanders raging on the heath, through a wild night of thunder and rain. Disguised as Poor Tom, a mad beggar possessed by demons, Gloucester's son Edgar enacts a life of utmost degradation: "Poor Tom, that eats the swimming frog, the toad, the tadpole, the wall-newt, and the water, that in the fury of his heart, when the foul fiend rages, eats cow dung for salads, swallows the old rat and the ditch dog, drinks the green mantle of the standing pool" (F 3.4.118–22; cf. Q 3.4.114–18). Gloucester's fate is even more terrible: betrayed by his son Edmund, he is seized in his own house by Lear's sadistic daughter Regan and her husband, Cornwall, tied to a chair, brutally interrogated, blinded, and then thrust bleeding out of doors.

Mental anguish in *King Lear,* then, is closely intertwined with physical anguish; the terrifying forces that are released by Lear's folly crash down upon both body and soul, just as the storm that rages on the heath seems at once an objective event and a symbolic representation of Lear's innermost being. The greatest expression of this intertwining in the play is Lear's madness, which brings together a devastating loss of identity; a relentless, radical assault on the hypocrisies of authority; and a demented, nauseated loathing of female sexuality. The loathing culminates in a fit of retching— "Fie, fie, fie! Pah, pah!"—followed by Lear's delusional attempt to find a physical remedy for his psychic pain: "Give me an ounce of civet, good apothecary; / Sweeten my imagination" (F 4.5.127–29; cf. Q 4.6.126–28). In fact, relief from the chaotic rage of madness comes in the wake of a deep, restorative sleep and a change of garments.

The body in *King Lear* is a site not only of abject misery, nausea, and pain but of care and a nascent moral and political awareness. In the midst of his mad ravings, Lear turns to the shivering Fool and asks, "Art cold?" (F 3.2.68; cf. Q 3.2.71). The simple question anticipates his recognition a few moments later that there is more suffering in the world than his own:

> Poor naked wretches, wheresoe'er you are,
> That bide the pelting of this pitiless storm,
> How shall your houseless heads and unfed sides,
> Your looped and windowed raggedness defend you
> From seasons such as these? Oh, I have ta'en
> Too little care of this!
> (F 3.4.29–34; cf. Q 3.4.25–30)

And if the world seems largely unjust and indifferent to human suffering, there are nonetheless throughout the play constant manifestations of generosity of body as well as soul. "Help me, help me!" cries the frightened Fool, to which Kent (disguised in order to serve the King, who has banished him) says simply, "Give me thy hand" (F 3.4.39–41; cf. Q 3.4.34–36). "What are you?" says the blind Gloucester to the son he has unjustly disinherited, to which the son, also in disguise, replies similarly, "Give me your hand" (F 4.5.213, 216; cf. Q 4.6.66). (In a moving moment from the Quarto, absent from the Folio version, two of Glouces- ter's servants not only react with horror to their master's blinding but also resolve to assist him: "Go thou. I'll fetch some flax and whites of eggs to apply to his bleeding face. Now, heaven help him!" [Q 3.7.105–06].) Such signs of goodness and empathy do not outweigh the harshness of the physical world of the play, let alone cancel out the vicious cru- elty of certain of its inhabitants, but they do qualify its moral bleakness.

It is possible to detect in *King Lear* one of the great structural

Tom Durie (1614). By Marcus Gheeraerts the Younger. Durie was the jester of Anne of Denmark, who was married to James I.

rhythms of Christianity: a passage through suffering, humiliation, and pain to a transcendent wisdom and love. Lear's initial actions were blind and selfish, but he comes to acknowledge his folly and, in an immensely poignant scene, to kneel down before the daughter he has wronged. Gloucester too learns that he was blind, even when his eyes could see, and he passes, by means of Edgar's strange deception at the imaginary cliff, from suicidal despair to patient resignation. "Men must endure / Their going hence even as their coming hither," Edgar wisely counsels his father. "Ripeness is all" (F 5.2.9–11; cf. Q 5.2.9–11).

But "ripeness," as the play shows, may entail resistance as well as resignation. For a time, evil seems to flourish in the world, but the forces of decency regroup themselves, and the wicked do not ultimately triumph. Edmund is killed by the brother he had tried to destroy; the loathsome Oswald is clubbed to death trying to murder Gloucester; one wicked sister poisons the other and then kills herself. And in an astonishing moment, radical in its political implications, the sadistic Duke of Cornwall is wounded by an upright servant. The anonymous servant—a nobody in the social world of the play—is Cornwall's own, but there are moments in which deference to authority is not enough, in which it is not acceptable merely to stand by and watch, in which the will to serve paradoxically requires violent disobedience. The servant is stabbed to death by the shocked and outraged Regan—"A peasant stand up thus?" (F 3.7.80; cf. Q 3.7.79)—but the Duke does not survive his wound, and the balance of power at that point in the play begins to shift.

Against self-interest and in the face of intolerable pressure, goodness and moral courage repeatedly shine forth. The Earl of Kent, banished by the rash Lear, dons a disguise in order to serve his king and master, and there are comparable acts of devoted service, political resolve, and self-sacrificing love from Edgar, Gloucester, Cordelia, and that remarkable figure the Fool. In one of the comic masterpieces of the sixteenth century, *The Praise of Folly,* the great Dutch humanist Erasmus used the fool as an emblem of the deepest Christian wisdom, revealed only when the pride, cruelty, and ambition of the world are shattered by a cleansing laughter. The shattering in *King Lear* is tragically violent and deadly, but the presence of the truth-telling Fool seems to point toward a comparable revelation.

Yet *King Lear,* set in a pagan world, resists the redemptive optimism that underlies the Christian vision (an optimism that led Dante to call his poem of damnation and salvation *The Divine Comedy*). The Fool's unnervingly perceptive observations sound far more corrosive than loving—he is, in Lear's words, "A bitter fool" (F 1.4.124; cf. Q 1.4.125)—and he disappears altogether in the third act. His moments of insight and those of all the other characters in the play are radically unstable, like brilliant flashes of lightning in a vast, dark landscape. Hence, for example, Lear's recognition of his folly in banishing Cordelia for her "most small fault" (F 1.4.232; cf. Q 1.4.250) is immediately followed by his hideous cursing of Goneril. His moving acknowledgment of the suffering of the poor, naked wretches is immediately followed by his inability to see the poor, naked wretch before him in any terms but his own: "Didst thou give all to thy daughters, and art thou come to this?" (F 3.4.48–49; cf. Q 3.4.43–44). And his appeal to patient resignation—"When we are born, we cry that we are come / To this great stage of fools" (F 4.5.176–77; cf. Q 4.6.170–71)—is immediately followed by a mad fantasy of revenge: "Then kill, kill, kill, kill, kill, kill!" (F 4.5.181; cf. Q 4.6.174). Every time we seem to have reached firm moral ground, the ground shifts, and we are kept, as Johnson observed, in "a perpetual tumult of indignation, pity, and hope." There are moments of apparent resolution: "Come, let's away to prison," says Lear to the weeping Cordelia, when they are captured by the enemy. "We two alone will sing like birds i'th' cage" (F 5.3.8–9; cf. Q 5.3.8–9). But a more terrible fate lies before them. "Some good I mean to do," says the dying Edmund, "Despite of mine own nature" (F 5.3.218–19; cf. Q 5.3.239–40). But his attempt to send a reprieve and therefore in some measure to redeem himself comes too late.

The play's nightmarish events continually lurch ahead of intentions, and even efforts to say "I have seen the worst" are frustrated.

The tragedy is not only that the intervals of moral resolution, mental lucidity, and spiritual calm are so brief, continually giving way to feverish grief and rage, but also that the modest human understandings, moving in their simplicity, cost such an enormous amount of pain. Edgar saves his father from despair but also in some sense breaks his father's heart. Cordelia's steadfast honesty, her refusal to flatter the father she loves, may be admirable but has disastrous consequences, and her attempt to save Lear only leads to her own death. For a sublime moment, Lear actually *sees* his daughter, understands her separateness, acknowledges her existence—"Do not laugh at me, / For as I am a man, I think this lady / To be my child Cordelia"—but it has taken the destruction of virtually his whole world for him to reach this recognition (F 4.6.65–67; cf. Q 4.7.69–71).

An apocalyptic dream of last judgment and redemption hovers over the entire tragedy, but it is a dream forever deferred. At the sight of the howling Lear with the dead Cordelia in his arms, the bystanders can only ask a succession of stunned questions:

> KENT   Is this the promised end?
> EDGAR   Or image of that horror.
>   (F 5.3.237–38; cf. Q 5.3.259–60)

Lear's own question a moment later seems the most terrible and the most important: "Why should a dog, a horse, a rat have life, / And thou no breath at all?" (F 5.3.282–83; cf. Q 5.3.302–03). It is a sign of *King Lear*'s astonishing freedom from orthodoxy that it refuses to offer any of the conventional answers to this question, answers that largely serve to conceal or deflect the mourner's anguish. Shakespeare's tragedy asks us not to turn away from evil, folly, and unbearable human pain but, seeing them face-to-face, to strengthen our capacity to speak the truth, to seek justice, and to love.

STEPHEN GREENBLATT

SELECTED BIBLIOGRAPHY

Cavell, Stanley. "The Avoidance of Love: A Reading of *King Lear*." *Disowning Knowledge in Six Plays of Shakespeare*. Cambridge: Cambridge UP, 1987. 39–124. To face the frightening isolation of all humans, to grasp the difference between the knowledge of love and the acknowledgment of love, to understand that in order to see one must also allow oneself to be seen, to endure the shame of exposure—these are among *King Lear*'s radical insights.

de Grazia, Margreta. "The Ideology of Superfluous Things: *King Lear* as Period Piece." *Subject and Object in Renaissance Culture*. Ed. Margreta de Grazia, Maureen Quilligan, and Peter Stallybrass. Cambridge: Cambridge UP, 1996. 17–42. Asserts that far from being protomodern, the play depicts a world in which persons and things cannot be separated and superfluity is a sign of apocalypse.

Greenblatt, Stephen. "Shakespeare and the Exorcists." *Shakespearean Negotiations: The Circulation of Social Energy in Renaissance England*. Berkeley: U of California P, 1988. 94–128. Argues that Shakespeare draws theatrical energy from the contemporary practice of exorcism, a ritualized encounter with evil attacked by Protestant officials as a vicious, histrionic fraud.

Holland, Peter, ed. *"King Lear" and Its Afterlife. Shakespeare Survey* 55 (2002). Treating four centuries of adaptations, appropriations, performances, and interpretations, this essay collection focuses on plays, songs, and novels that draw on *King Lear*.

Jones, John. *Shakespeare at Work*. Oxford: Oxford UP, 1995. Points out that close attention to the Folio revisions of the Quarto text discloses a cunning symbolic design that links Lear's craziness to his obsession with quantity.

Kronenfeld, Judy. *"King Lear" and the Naked Truth: Rethinking the Language of Religion and Resistance*. Durham, NC: Duke UP, 1998. Claims that the play should be understood not through deconstruction or new historicism but through the common Christian culture that gave its terms meaning outside a polemical context.

Leggatt, Alexander. *King Lear*. 2nd ed. Manchester: Manchester UP, 2004. Explores interpretive problems through the history of twentieth-century stage and film productions.

Nuttall, A. D. *"King Lear." Why Does Tragedy Give Pleasure?* Oxford: Clarendon, 1996. 81–105. Argues that the play gives pleasure not by sealing off suffering in poetic form but by destroying the expected recognition and closure of tragedy.

Strier, Richard. *Resistant Structures: Particularity, Radicalism, and Renaissance Texts*. Berkeley: U of California P, 1995. 165–202. Asserts that in *King Lear* Shakespeare endorses a radical political position that, in extreme circumstances, counseled resistance to authority as the highest form of "good service."

Taylor, Gary, and Michael Warren, eds. *The Division of the Kingdoms: Shakespeare's Two Versions of "King Lear."* Oxford: Clarendon, 1983. This essay collection presents the case for the Quarto and Folio texts as distinct works and explores the consequences for interpreting *King Lear*.

FILMS

King Lear. 1953. Dir. Andrew McCullough, with Peter Brook. US. 73 min. Heavily cut—entirely without the Edgar–Edmund subplot—this version, filmed for live television, features the powerful presence of Orson Welles, along with a fine performance of the Fool by the Irish actor Michael MacLiammoir.

Korol Lir. 1969. Dir. Grigori Kozintsev and Iosif Shapiro. USSR. 139 min. This black-and-white film presents a wizened but childlike Lear in a peasant-filled wasteland; a romantic fable set in the Christian Middle Ages.

King Lear. 1971. Dir. Peter Brook. UK. 137 min. Men in pelts wander in a primitive tundra. Breaks in cinematic realism signal Lear's decline. With Paul Scofield and Jack MacGowran.

King Lear. 1982. Dir. Jonathan Miller. UK. 180 min. Michael Hordern's Lear draws upon director Miller's background in neurology to depict his character's mental deterioration.

King Lear. 1983. Dir. Michael Elliott. UK. 158 min. Laurence Olivier, nearly eighty years old, in his final *Lear*. A television production that opens at Stonehenge.

Ran. 1985. Dir. Akira Kurosawa. Japan. 160 min. Set in sixteenth-century feudal Japan, the story, loosely adapted from Shakespeare, is noted for its elegiac battle sequences and orgies of red. With Tatsuya Nakadai and Akira Terao.

King Lear. 1998. Dir. Richard Eyre. UK. 150 min. Garish hues and torch-lit interiors for an especially cruel Lear, with equally vicious Regan and Goneril. With Ian Holm and Victoria Hamilton.

King Lear. 2008. Dir. Trevor Nunn. UK. 172 min. Set in a vaguely Hapsburg-era Central European court, this production features a commanding Ian McKellen tormented by the discovery that he cannot compel love from his daughters.

TEXTUAL INTRODUCTION

King Lear presents the most fascinating, important, and contentious textual issues of the entire Shakespeare canon. The play exists in two early authoritative texts, the Quarto (Q1) of 1608 and the Folio (F) of 1623. For many years, it was presumed that each text was an imperfect and incomplete version of a lost, longer original. Consequently, *King Lear* was usually printed in a "conflated" text: that is, in an attempt to give readers and audiences as many as possible of Shakespeare's words, editors combined the two texts into a version of the play that was longer than either of the early texts. However, by the end of the twentieth century there was a general consensus that the two texts were sequential—that is, that the Quarto represents a first complete stage of the play and the Folio represents a later stage, which may be Shakespeare's revision of his own play. This consensus informs the decision of *The Norton Shakespeare* to print both texts, so as to enable readers to compare them, and in addition to print a text that merges material from both (discussed below).

The Quarto, as Peter Blayney argued in *The Texts of "King Lear" and Their Origins* (1982), was most probably printed from Shakespeare's "foul papers," or draft. Such drafts typically fail to provide necessary directions, use inconsistent speech prefixes, and include "false starts"—i.e., inconsistencies in the development of plot, structure, or characters. An instance of Shakespeare's characteristic patterns of composition in the Quarto text includes his use of generic speech prefixes (e.g., Edmund is "*Bastard*" in the speech prefixes). There are also signs of rapid revision. Such revisions may be signaled in verse by a hypermetric line (one with too many syllables for a pentameter) and in a prose line by a crowded right margin. Shakespeare may also have made further refinements and alterations as the play moved from the draft to the version used for performance. Q1, then, based as it appears to be on foul papers, most likely reflects the play as originally written and corrected; it may have been further revised before a "fair copy" was made that could serve as the basis for the "promptbook," or script from which the play was performed.

The Q1 text has acquired a second layer of alteration through correction during the printing process, as revealed by variant copies of Q1: for example, at 4.6.253, some copies read "my gayle" and others have been corrected to "my iayle." Occasionally, "corrections" of one word during printing have created errors in other words, as when Gonorill warns her husband, Albany, of the impending threat of attack by Cordelia's army: "*France* . . . With plumed helme, thy slayer begins threats" is corrected to "*France* . . . With plumed helm, thy state begins thereat" (4.2.58ff). Since the lines do not appear in the Folio text, we cannot know which parts of these first and second versions in Q1 are Shakespeare's own. While we have no proof that Shakespeare or his acting company authorized the printing of Q1, the use of his foul papers in its printing may suggest that the King's Men participated to some degree in this text's transmission.

The second significant version of the play is the text printed in the 1623 First Folio. The printer's copy for this text seems to have been the Second Quarto, one of the so-called Pavier Quartos, which were printed by the publisher Thomas Pavier without the authority of the King's Men in what seems to have been a first stab at a collection of Shakespeare's plays. The title page bears the false date of 1608, but in fact Q2 was printed eleven years later. This 1619 Q2 is largely identical to Q1, and printers of the First Folio evidently collated it against a King's Men theatrical manuscript.

The Folio contains about one hundred lines that do not appear in the Q1 text of the play, while the Q1 text contains about three hundred lines that do not appear in the F text. F intensifies the action in the last two acts through heavy cutting, particularly to focus on Lear himself. F deletes Q1's entire scene 4.3, in which Kent and a Gentleman discuss Cordelia's return, and, even more remarkably, cuts the "mock-trial" scene of Q1, in which Lear puts his daughters Gonorill and Regan on trial in absentia. It is above all the coherence of the changes from Q that has persuaded scholars that the Folio was a deliberate revision by Shakespeare of his own play.

Some of the streamlining of characters and action was probably done for stage economy. For example, the three Gentlemen in Q1 who chase the mad Lear in 4.6 are reduced to one Gentleman in the parallel scene (4.5) in F, and such Q1 characters as the Doctor are reduced to a generic Gentleman in F. But other economies notably alter the action, as in the blinding of Gloucester in 3.7, which concludes in Q1 with the decision of the two servants to follow and comfort him—lines not in F. In addition, the consolatory (if generic) final lines of the play, spoken by Albany in Q1, are given to Edgar here. This reassignment of lines, along with the omission of the mock-trial and all of 4.3, seems to suggest a carefully planned attempt by Shakespeare to alter the play's theatrical impact.

In addition to its reassigned speeches and omitted or cut scenes, the Folio text offers dozens of small, and seemingly minor, corrections and revisions. A striking example occurs in Cordelia's aside at F 1.1.60 (cf. Q1 1.1.54):

> F: What shall *Cordelia* speake? Loue, and be silent.
> Q1: What shall *Cordelia* doe, loue and be silent.

Throughout the play, Cordelia places an emphasis on action in Q1 and on language in F, and this type of consistent revision in characterization is also apparent in the presentations of Edmund, Kent, Edgar, and Gloucester.

Some editors attribute F's alterations to external censorship, noting, for example, the cuts of numerous references to France. However, enough references to France remain in F to suggest that censorship cannot have been the primary factor. The substantive variants between Q1 and F suggest the kinds of clear, coherent patterns of revision typical of an author. Whether this revision was done to suit a new venue, such as the Blackfriars indoor playhouse, or a changing group of personnel is not certain, and it is possible that Shakespeare may simply have wished to revise his tragedy.

Audiences and editors have traditionally been reluctant to entertain the idea that Shakespeare revised, particularly in the case of so great a play as *King Lear*. The Quarto, which has a substantial number of incoherent or misprinted lines, was thus labeled "bad" by a generation of editors, and the Folio, regarded as the sole authoritative text of the play, served as base text for their editions. Nonetheless, in an attempt to save passages that appeared only in Q1, editors produced texts that interpolated words, lines, passages, scenes, and characters from Q1 into F, even when these variants appeared contradictory, as in Kent's main speech in 3.1, in which, in Q1, he discusses the foreign war with France, whereas in F his subject is the civil war between Albany and Cornwall. Despite the conflict, such conflated editions included both sets of lines.

The Norton Shakespeare offers separate editions of Q1 and F *King Lear*. These editions attempt to present both Q1 and F in a form that makes them accessible to readers, ensuring that the differences between the texts are maintained but emending where necessary to address error. Whenever possible, Q1 has been emended on the basis of either Q2 or F. F's very occasional errors are corrected through emendation (from Q1 or Q2 when possible). Lineation has occasionally been silently corrected. Because printers did not discard sheets that had been printed before the proofreader corrected them and the press was stopped for corrections, all early modern books, including the First Folio, contain a mixture of uncorrected and corrected pages. These variants have been recorded unless they involve only changes in punctuation.

Because conflations of *King Lear* have been for three centuries the basis of performance, criticism, and interpretation, we also provide a "scars-and-stitches" edition of the play, based on the Folio. Unless they cannot structurally coexist with the material in F, lines, passages, and scenes (but not single words or phrases) that appear only in the Quarto have been interpolated into this base text. To signal their insertion, these interpolations are indented, printed in a slightly different typeface, and given different line numbers. Indifferent or disputable variants follow F; F's character names have been regularized to the spelling that has become standard in modern editions; and stage directions that appear in Q but not in F have been interpolated. In addition, as has been conventional practice, the long scene of 2.2, which continues in F until the end of the act, is divided into two further scenes, 2.3 and 2.4.

GRACE IOPPOLO

TEXTUAL BIBLIOGRAPHY

Blayney, Peter W. M. *The Texts of "King Lear" and Their Origins.* Cambridge: Cambridge UP, 1982.
Ioppolo, Grace. *Revising Shakespeare.* Cambridge: Harvard UP, 1991.
Taylor, Gary, and Michael Warren, eds. *The Division of the Kingdoms: Shakespeare's Two Versions of "King Lear."* Oxford: Clarendon, 1983.

PERFORMANCE NOTE

Though Shakespeare wrote longer plays than *King Lear* (*Hamlet, Cymbeline*), no other work so taxes the playgoer's emotional reserves, or so thoroughly implicates his or her sense of personal endurance in the experience of tragedy. Consequently, directors face unusual risks when cutting *Lear* for performance, a task already complicated by significant variants between the Quarto and Folio texts (see the Textual Introduction). Each production's handling of the play's length and textual cruxes can vary its balance between domestic and political concerns, and can determine whether audiences see a man journeying toward moral redemption or foundering, tormented, in a world void of morals or meaning.

Historically, Lear has most often been portrayed as a man "more sinned against than sinning," a rash yet loving father victimized by ungrateful daughters (F 3.2.60; cf. Q 3.2.61). Productions featuring sympathetic treatments sometimes give religious significance to Lear's atonement and death, or present a fractured fairy tale pitting Lear and Cordelia against a pair of matching harpies. Such choices clarify the audience's moral sympathies and can deepen the impact of a tragic outcome so contrary to its sense of justice. Increasingly, however, directors take more neutral positions, showing Lear's peremptory dismissals of Kent and Cordelia as more characteristic than anomalous, and letting Goneril and Regan act upon legitimate grievances. Such productions may show Cordelia as more prig than princess, and moderate her sisters' cruelty by giving them distinct personalities, affections, and insecurities. Whatever the approach, each production must strike balances between Lear's majesty and dotage, suffering and tyranny, reason and lunacy.

Gloucester, meanwhile, can charm or alienate audiences when discussing Edmund's bastardy, and Edgar can be an entitled favorite or a devoted brother and son. Such choices may condemn or almost justify Edmund, whose birth story can seem a source of anguish or a transparent excuse for villainy. Meanwhile, Kent can be a trusty servant or a bully; Lear's knights can be decorous guests or hooligans; the Fool can be a light-hearted jester or a bitter cynic. Other considerations for directors include staging the storm; accounting for the Fool's disappearance; extracting Gloucester's eyes; determining Edmund's familiarity with Goneril; representing Dover and explaining Edgar's reluctance to confide in his father; and devising a setting for a play that seems to demand cosmic grandeur and familial intimacy, timelessness, and specificity.

BRETT GAMBOA

The History of King Lear[1]

QUARTO

[THE PERSONS OF THE PLAY

LEAR, King of Britain
GONORILL, eldest daughter to Lear
Duke of ALBANY, husband to Gonorill
REGAN, second daughter to Lear
Duke of CORNWALL, husband to Regan
CORDELIA, youngest daughter to Lear
King of FRANCE, suitor to Cordelia
Duke of BURGUNDY, suitor to Cordelia
FOOL, Lear's jester
Earl of GLOUCESTER
EDGAR, legitimate son to Gloucester, later disguised as Poor Tom
Edmund the BASTARD, illegitimate son to Gloucester
Earl of KENT, later disguised as Caius
Oswald, STEWARD to Gonorill
OLD MAN, a tenant of Gloucester
CURAN, a servant of Gloucester
SERVANTS to Cornwall
DOCTOR
CAPTAIN OF THE GUARD
CAPTAIN
HERALD
MESSENGER
KNIGHTS
GENTLEMEN
SERVANTS
Soldiers]

1.1[2] (F 1.1)
Enter KENT, GLOUCESTER,[3] *and* [*Edmund the*] BASTARD.

KENT   I thought the King had more affected° the Duke of   *favored*
   Albany° than Cornwall.   *Scotland*
GLOUCESTER   It did always seem so to us. But now, in the divi-
   sion of the kingdoms, it appears not° which of the Dukes he   *is not clear*
5   values most, for equalities° are so weighed° that curiosity in   *shares / equal*
   neither can make choice of either's moiety.[4]
KENT   Is not this your son, my lord?

---

1. TEXTUAL COMMENT The first readers of the Quarto and Folio versions of *King Lear* would have confronted not only very different material books but also two different plays, as suggested by the titles of the earliest printed copies of the play. *King Lear* is either a "history" or a "tragedy," depending on which book one is reading. See Digital Edition TC 1 (Quarto edited text).
1.1 Location: King Lear's court.
2. TEXTUAL COMMENT One major difference between the Quarto and Folio texts is that the latter provides act and scene divisions while the former marks no such breaks. These notations suggest that Q1 of *King Lear* was printed from Shakespeare's "foul papers" (or first draft) and that the Folio text was printed from a later "fair copy" (or theatrical manuscript) written out by a scribe and checked against Q2. See Digital Edition TC 2 (Quarto edited text).
3. Pronounced "Gloster."
4. *that . . . moiety:* that careful scrutiny ("curiosity") of both parts cannot determine which portion ("moiety") is preferable.

The Tragedy of King Lear[1]

FOLIO

[THE PERSONS OF THE PLAY

LEAR, King of Britain
GONERILL, eldest daughter to Lear
Duke of ALBANY, husband to Gonerill
REGAN, second daughter to Lear
Duke of CORNWALL, husband to Regan
CORDELIA, youngest daughter to Lear
King of FRANCE, suitor to Cordelia
Duke of BURGUNDY, suitor to Cordelia
FOOL, Lear's jester
Earl of GLOUCESTER
EDGAR, legitimate son to Gloucester, later disguised as Poor Tom
EDMOND, illegitimate son to Gloucester
Earl of KENT, later disguised as Caius
Oswald, STEWARD to Gonerill
OLD MAN, a tenant of Gloucester
CURAN, a servant of Gloucester
SERVANTS to Cornwall
CAPTAIN
HERALD
MESSENGER
GENTLEMEN
KNIGHTS
Attendants, Servants, Soldiers]

1.1[2] (Q 1.1)

Enter KENT, GLOUCESTER,[3] *and* EDMOND.

KENT I thought the King had more affected° the Duke of   *favored*
Albany° than Cornwall.   *Scotland*

GLOUCESTER It did always seem so to us. But now, in the division of the kingdom, it appears not° which of the Dukes he   *is not clear*
5   values most, for qualities° are so weighed° that curiosity in   *shares / equal*
neither can make choice of either's moiety.[4]

KENT Is not this your son, my lord?

---

1. TEXTUAL COMMENT The first readers of the Quarto and Folio versions of *King Lear* would have confronted not only very different material books but also two different plays, as suggested by the titles of the earliest printed copies of the play. *King Lear* is either a "history" or a "tragedy," depending on which book one is reading. See Digital Edition TC 1 (Folio edited text).
1.1 Location: King Lear's court.
2. TEXTUAL COMMENT One major difference between the Quarto and Folio texts is that the latter provides act and scene divisions while the former marks no

such breaks. These notations suggest that Q1 of *King Lear* was printed from Shakespeare's "foul papers" (or first draft) and that the Folio text was printed from a later "fair copy" (or theatrical manuscript) written out by a scribe and checked against Q2. See Digital Edition TC 2 (Folio edited text).
3. Pronounced "Gloster."
4. *for . . . moiety*: because their qualities are so evenly weighted that careful scrutiny ("curiosity") of both parts cannot determine which portion ("moiety") is preferable.

GLOUCESTER   His breeding,° sir, hath been at my charge.[5] I have   upbringing
so often blushed to acknowledge him that now I am brazed°   hardened
10   to it.
KENT   I cannot conceive° you.   comprehend
GLOUCESTER   Sir, this young fellow's mother could,[6] where-
upon she grew round-wombed and had indeed, sir, a son for
her cradle ere she had a husband for her bed. Do you smell
15   a fault?[7]
KENT   I cannot wish the fault undone, the issue° of it being so   offspring; result
proper.°   handsome; right
GLOUCESTER   But I have, sir, a son by order of law,° some year   a legitimate son
elder than this, who yet is no dearer in my account.° Though   estimation
20   this knave° came something saucily[8] into the world before   scamp; fellow
he was sent for, yet was his mother fair, there was good sport
at his making, and the whoreson° must be acknowledged. —Do   rogue; bastard
you know this noble gentleman, Edmund?
BASTARD   No, my lord.
25   GLOUCESTER   My lord of Kent. Remember him hereafter as
my honorable friend.
BASTARD   My services to your lordship.
KENT   I must love you and sue° to know you better.   seek
BASTARD   Sir, I shall study deserving.°   shall learn to deserve
30   GLOUCESTER   He hath been out° nine years, and away he shall   away; abroad
again. The King is coming.
        Sound a sennet.° Enter one bearing a coronet, then   fanfare of trumpets
        LEAR, *then the Dukes of* ALBANY *and* CORNWALL,
        next GONORILL, REGAN, CORDELIA, *with followers*
        [*and* SERVANTS].
LEAR   Attend° my lords of France and Burgundy, Gloucester.   Attend upon; escort
GLOUCESTER   I shall, my liege.°   [*Exit.*]   feudal superior
LEAR   Meantime we° will express our darker° purposes.   (royal "we") / more secret
35   [*He points to map.°*]   The map there. Know we have divided
In three our kingdom, and 'tis our first intent
To shake all cares and business of our state,°   position (as King)
Confirming them on younger years.
The two great princes, France and Burgundy,
40   Great rivals in our youngest daughter's love,
Long in our court have made their amorous sojourn
And here are to be answered. Tell me, my daughters,

Which of you shall we say doth love us most,
That° we our largest bounty° may extend   So that / generosity
45   Where merit doth most challenge it?°   best claim it
Gonorill, our eldest born, speak first.

5. My responsibility; at my cost.   7. Sin, wrongdoing; female genitals.
6. Could conceive; punning on biological conception.   8. Somewhat rudely; somewhat shamefully.

GLOUCESTER   His breeding,° sir, hath been at my charge.[5] I   *upbringing*
have so often blushed to acknowledge him that now I am
10   brazed° to't.   *hardened*
KENT   I cannot conceive° you.   *comprehend*
GLOUCESTER   Sir, this young fellow's mother could,[6] whereupon she grew round-wombed, and had indeed, sir, a son for
her cradle ere she had a husband for her bed. Do you smell
15   a fault?[7]
KENT   I cannot wish the fault undone, the issue° of it being so   *offspring; result*
proper.°   *handsome; right*
GLOUCESTER   But I have a son, sir, by order of law,° some year   *a legitimate son*
elder than this, who yet is no dearer in my account.° Though   *estimation*
20   this knave° came something saucily[8] to the world before he   *scamp; fellow*
was sent for, yet was his mother fair, there was good sport at
his making, and the whoreson° must be acknowledged.   *rogue; bastard*
—Do you know this noble gentleman, Edmond?
EDMOND   No, my lord.
25   GLOUCESTER   My lord of Kent. Remember him hereafter as
my honorable friend.
EDMOND   My services to your lordship.
KENT   I must love you and sue° to know you better.   *seek*
EDMOND   Sir, I shall study deserving.°   *shall learn to deserve*
30   GLOUCESTER   He hath been out° nine years, and away he shall   *away; abroad*
again. The King is coming.
　　　Sennet.° Enter [one bearing a coronet,] King LEAR,   *Fanfare of trumpets*
　　　CORNWALL, ALBANY, GONERILL, REGAN, CORDELIA,
　　　and Attendants.
LEAR   Attend° the lords of France and Burgundy, Gloucester.   *Attend upon; escort*
GLOUCESTER   I shall, my lord.   *Exit.*
LEAR   Meantime we° shall express our darker° purpose.   *(royal "we") / more secret*
35   Give me the map there. Know that we have divided
In three our kingdom, and 'tis our fast° intent   *fixed*
To shake all cares and business from our age,
Conferring them on younger strengths, while we
Unburdened crawl toward death. Our son° of Cornwall,   *son-in-law*
40   And you, our no-less-loving son of Albany,
We have this hour a constant will to publish[9]
Our daughters' several dowers,° that future strife   *individual dowries*
May be prevented now. The princes, France and Burgundy,
Great rivals in our youngest daughter's love,
45   Long in our court have made their amorous sojourn
And here are to be answered. Tell me, my daughters,
Since now we will divest us both of rule,
Interest° of territory, cares of state,   *Legal title*
Which of you shall we say doth love us most,
50   That° we our largest bounty° may extend   *So that / generosity*
Where nature doth with merit challenge?[1] Gonerill,
Our eldest born, speak first.

---

5. My responsibility; at my cost.
6. Could conceive; punning on biological conception.
7. Sin, wrongdoing; female genitals.
8. Somewhat rudely; somewhat shamefully.

9. A fixed determination to announce publicly.
1. *Where . . . challenge:* To the one whose natural
love and deserving lay claim (to our generosity).

GONORILL   Sir, I do love you more than words can wield° the   *convey*
   matter:
Dearer than eyesight, space,° or liberty,   *freedom of movement*
Beyond what can be valued rich or rare,
50   No less than life, with grace, health, beauty, honor,
As much a child e'er loved, or father friend,
A love that makes breath° poor and speech unable.   *language*
Beyond all manner of so much° I love you.   *Beyond all comparison*
CORDELIA [*aside*]   What shall Cordelia do? Love and be
   silent.
55   LEAR [*pointing to map*]   Of all these bounds,° even from this   *regions*
   line to this,
With shady forests and wide-skirted meads,°   *broad meadows*
We make thee lady. To thine and Albany's issue°   *children; heirs*
Be this perpetual. [*to* REGAN] What says our second
   daughter,
Our dearest Regan, wife to Cornwall? Speak.
60   REGAN   Sir, I am made of the selfsame metal° that my sister is   *spirit; substance*
And prize me at her worth.° In my true heart   *believe myself her equal*
I find she names my very deed of love, only she came short,
That° I profess myself an enemy to all other joys   *In that*
Which the most precious square of sense possesses,[9]
65   And find I am alone felicitate° in your dear highness' love.   *am only made happy*

CORDELIA [*aside*]   Then poor Cordelia, and yet not so, since I
   am sure
My love's more richer than my tongue.
LEAR [*pointing to map*]   To thee and thine hereditary ever
Remain this ample third of our fair kingdom,
70   No less in space, validity,° and pleasure   *value*
Than that confirmed° on Gonorill. [*to* CORDELIA] But now,   *fixed*
   our joy,
Although the last, not least in our dear love,

What can you say to win a third more opulent
Than your sisters'?
75   CORDELIA   Nothing, my lord.
LEAR   How? Nothing can come of nothing.[1] Speak again.

---

9. *Which . . . possesses:* That the body can enjoy. *pre-cious square of sense:* measure of sensibility; or, perhaps, balanced and sensitive perception. The square may represent the even mixture of the body's four fluids, or humors.

1. *Ex nihilo nihil fit,* a maxim derived from Aristotle, was accepted by the Christian Middle Ages with the single exception of God having created the world out of nothing.

GONERILL   Sir, I love you more than word can wield° the   *convey*
    matter:
    Dearer than eyesight, space,° and liberty,   *freedom of movement*
55 Beyond what can be valued rich or rare,
    No less than life, with grace, health, beauty, honor,
    As much as child e'er loved or father found,
    A love that makes breath° poor and speech unable.   *language*
    Beyond all manner of so much° I love you.   *Beyond all comparison*
60 CORDELIA [*aside*]   What shall Cordelia speak? Love, and be
    silent.
    LEAR [*pointing to map*]   Of all these bounds,° even from this   *regions*
    line to this,
    With shadowy forests and with champaigns riched,°   *enriched plains*
    With plenteous rivers and wide-skirted meads,°   *broad meadows*
    We make thee lady. To thine and Albany's issues°   *children; heirs*
65 Be this perpetual. [*to* REGAN] What says our second
    daughter,
    Our dearest Regan, wife of Cornwall?
    REGAN   I am made of that self-mettle° as my sister   *same spirit; substance*
    And prize me at her worth.° In my true heart   *believe myself her equal*
    I find she names my very deed of love,
70 Only she comes too short, that° I profess   *in that*
    Myself an enemy to all other joys
    Which the most precious square of sense professes,[2]
    And find I am alone felicitate°   *am only made happy*
    In your dear highness' love.
    CORDELIA [*aside*]   Then, poor Cordelia,
75 And yet not so, since I am sure my love's
    More ponderous° than my tongue.   *weighty*
    LEAR [*pointing to map*]   To thee and thine hereditary ever,
    Remain this ample third of our fair kingdom,
    No less in space, validity,° and pleasure   *value*
80 Than that conferred on Gonerill. [*to* CORDELIA] Now, our
    joy,
    Although our last and least,° to whose young love   *youngest; smallest*
    The vines of France and milk of Burgundy
    Strive to be interest,° what can you say to draw   *admitted*
    A third more opulent than your sisters'? Speak.
85 CORDELIA   Nothing, my lord.
    LEAR   Nothing?
    CORDELIA   Nothing.
    LEAR   Nothing will come of nothing.[3] Speak again.

---

2. *Which . . . professes:* That the body can enjoy. *precious square of sense:* measure of sensibility; or, perhaps, balanced and sensitive perception. The square may represent the even mixture of the body's four fluids, or humors.

3. *Ex nihilo nihil fit,* a maxim derived from Aristotle, was accepted by the Christian Middle Ages with the single exception of God having created the world out of nothing.

CORDELIA   Unhappy that I am, I cannot heave
 My heart into my mouth.[2] I love your majesty
 According to my bond,° nor more nor less.   *filial duty*
80 LEAR   Go to, go to. Mend your speech a little,
 Lest it may mar your fortunes.
CORDELIA   Good my lord,
 You have begot me, bred me, loved me.
 I return those duties back as are right fit:
 Obey you, love you, and most honor you.
85 Why have my sisters husbands if they say they love you all?° *exclusively*
 Happily,° when I shall wed, that lord whose hand *Perhaps; if lucky*
 Must take my plight° shall carry half my love with him, *marriage vow; condition*
 Half my care and duty. Sure, I shall never
 Marry like my sisters, to love my father all.
LEAR   But goes this with thy heart?
90 CORDELIA   Ay, good my lord.
LEAR   So young and so untender?
CORDELIA   So young, my lord, and true.°   *honest; faithful*
LEAR   Well, let it be so! Thy truth then be thy dower,[3]
 For by the sacred radiance of the sun,
95 The mistress of Hecate,[4] and the might;
 By all the operation of the orbs,
 From whom we do exist and cease to be;[5]
 Here I disclaim all my paternal care,
 Propinquity,° and property of blood,°   *Closeness / kinship*
100 And as a stranger to my heart and me
 Hold thee from this° forever. The barbarous Scythian,[6] *this time*
 Or he that makes his generation
 Messes[7] to gorge his appetite,
 Shall be as well neighbored, pitied, and relieved
105 As thou my sometime° daughter.   *former*

---

2. *I cannot heave . . . mouth:* Cf. "The heart of fools is in their mouth: but the mouth of the wise is in their heart" (Ecclesiastes 1:26).
3. PERFORMANCE COMMENT The opening sequence of *King Lear,* from Lear's entrance to his banishment of Cordelia, involves crucial interpretive choices for directors and performers, choices that center on the motivations of the central characters. See Digital Edition PC 1.
4. A classical goddess of the moon and the patron of witchcraft, she was associated with the underworld, Hades.
5. *By all . . . be:* referring to the belief that the movements of stars and planets ("orbs") corresponded to physical and spiritual motions in a person and thus controlled his or her fate.
6. Notoriously savage Crimean nomads of classical antiquity.
7. *he . . . Messes:* he who makes meals of his children.

CORDELIA   Unhappy that I am, I cannot heave
90   My heart into my mouth.[4] I love your majesty
   According to my bond,° no more nor less.   *filial duty*
LEAR   How, how, Cordelia? Mend your speech a little,
   Lest you may mar your fortunes.
CORDELIA   Good my lord,
   You have begot me, bred me, loved me.
95   I return those duties back as are right fit:
   Obey you, love you, and most honor you.
   Why have my sisters husbands if they say
   They love you all?° Happily,° when I shall wed,   *completely / Perhaps; if lucky*
   That lord whose hand must take my plight° shall carry   *marriage vow; condition*
100   Half my love with him, half my care and duty.
   Sure, I shall never marry like my sisters.
LEAR   But goes thy heart with this?
CORDELIA   Ay, my good lord.
LEAR   So young and so untender?
CORDELIA   So young, my lord, and true.°   *honest; faithful*
105 LEAR   Let it be so: thy truth, then, be thy dower![5]
   For by the sacred radiance of the sun,
   The mysteries of Hecate[6] and the night,
   By all the operation of the orbs
   From whom we do exist and cease to be,[7]
110   Here I disclaim all my paternal care,
   Propinquity° and property of blood,°   *Closeness / kinship*
   And as a stranger to my heart and me
   Hold thee from this° forever. The barbarous Scythian,[8]   *this time*
   Or he that makes his generation messes[9]
115   To gorge his appetite, shall to my bosom
   Be as well neighbored, pitied, and relieved
   As thou my sometime° daughter.   *former*

---

4. *I cannot heave . . . mouth:* Cf. "The heart of fools is in their mouth: but the mouth of the wise is in their heart" (Ecclesiastes 1:26).
5. PERFORMANCE COMMENT The opening sequence of *King Lear*, from the Lear's entrance to his banishment of Cordelia, involves crucial interpretive choices for directors and performers, choices that center on the motivations of the central characters. See Digital Edition PC 1.
6. A classical goddess of the moon and the patron of

witchcraft, she was associated with the underworld, Hades.
7. *By all . . . be:* referring to the belief that the movements of stars and planets ("orbs") corresponded to physical and spiritual motions in a person and thus controlled his or her fate.
8. Notoriously savage Crimean nomads of classical antiquity.
9. *he . . . messes:* he who makes meals of his children.

KENT   Good my liege—

LEAR   Peace, Kent! Come not between the dragon and his
      wrath!
      I loved her most and thought to set my rest[8]
      On her kind nursery.° Hence and avoid my sight.   *care*
110   So be my grave my peace,[9] as here I give
      Her father's heart from her. Call France! Who stirs?[1]
      Call Burgundy!   [*Exeunt some* SERVANTS.]
                      Cornwall and Albany,
      With my two daughters' dower digest° this third.   *incorporate*
      Let pride, which she calls "plainness,"° marry her.   *directness*
115   I do invest you jointly in my power,
      Preeminence, and all the large effects°   *outward shows; trappings*
      That troop with° majesty. Ourself by monthly course,   *accompany*
      With reservation of° an hundred knights,   *legal right to retain*
      By you to be sustained, shall our abode
120   Make with you by due turns. Only we still retain
      The name and all the additions° to a king.   *prerogatives*
      The sway,° revenue, execution of the rest,   *power*
      Beloved sons, be yours, which to confirm,
      This coronet[2] part betwixt you. [*He hands them a coronet.*]

KENT   Royal Lear,
125   Whom I have ever honored as my king,
      Loved as my father, as my master followed,
      As my great patron thought on in my prayers—

LEAR   The bow is bent and drawn; make from° the shaft.   *get clear of*

KENT   Let it fall° rather, though the fork° invade   *strike here / arrowhead*
130   The region of my heart. Be Kent unmannerly
      When Lear is mad. What wilt thou do, old man?
      Think'st thou that duty shall have dread to speak
      When power to flattery bows? To plainness° honor's bound   *plain speaking*
      When majesty stoops to folly. Reverse thy doom,°   *Revoke your sentence*
135   And in thy best consideration check°   *halt*
      This hideous rashness. Answer my life my judgment:[3]
      Thy youngest daughter does not love thee least,
      Nor are those empty-hearted whose low sound
      Reverbs no hollowness.°   *Echoes no insincerity*

---

8. To secure my repose; to stake my all, as in the
card game known as primero.
9. So may I rest in peace (probably an oath).
1. Does nobody stir? An order, with the force of "Get
moving."

2. Cordelia's crown, symbol of the endowment she
has forsworn.
3. *Answer . . . judgment:* I'll stake my life on my
opinion.

KENT   Good my liege—

LEAR   Peace, Kent!

    Come not between the dragon and his wrath!

120   I loved her most and thought to set my rest[1]

    On her kind nursery.° Hence and avoid my sight.   *care*

    So be my grave my peace,[2] as here I give

    Her father's heart from her. Call France! Who stirs?[3]

    Call Burgundy!   [*Exeunt some Attendants.*]

               Cornwall and Albany,

125   With my two daughters' dowers digest° the third.   *incorporate*

    Let pride, which she calls plainness,° marry her.   *directness*

    I do invest you jointly with my power,

    Preeminence, and all the large effects°   *outward shows; trappings*

    That troop with° majesty. Ourself by monthly course,   *accompany*

130   With reservation of° an hundred knights,   *legal right to retain*

    By you to be sustained, shall our abode

    Make with you by due turn. Only we shall retain

    The name and all th'addition° to a king. The sway,°   *the prerogatives / power*

    Revenue, execution of the rest,

135   Beloved sons, be yours, which to confirm,

    This coronet[4] part between you. [*He hands them a coronet.*]

KENT   Royal Lear,

    Whom I have ever honored as my king,

    Loved as my father, as my master followed,

    As my great patron thought on in my prayers—

140   LEAR   The bow is bent and drawn; make from° the shaft.   *get clear of*

KENT   Let it fall° rather, though the fork° invade   *strike here / arrowhead*

    The region of my heart. Be Kent unmannerly

    When Lear is mad. What wouldst thou do, old man?

    Think'st thou that duty shall have dread to speak

145   When power to flattery bows?

    To plainness° honor's bound   *plain speaking*

    When majesty falls to folly. Reserve° thy state,°   *Retain / rule; position*

    And in thy best consideration check°   *halt*

    This hideous rashness. Answer my life my judgment:[5]

150   Thy youngest daughter does not love thee least,

    Nor are those empty-hearted whose low sounds

    Reverb no hollowness.°   *Echo no insincerity*

---

1. To secure my repose; to stake my all, as in the card game known as primero.
2. So may I rest in peace (probably an oath).
3. Does nobody stir? An order, with the force of "Get moving."
4. Cordelia's crown, symbol of the endowment she has forsworn.
5. *Answer . . . judgment:* I'll stake my life on my opinion.

140   LEAR   Kent, on thy life, no more!

KENT   My life I never held but as a pawn°   *chess piece; stake*
     To wage° against thy enemies, nor fear to lose it   *wager*
     Thy safety being the motive.

LEAR   Out of my sight!

145   KENT   See better, Lear, and let me still° remain   *always*
     The true blank° of thine eye.   *precise bull's-eye*

LEAR   Now, by Apollo—

KENT   Now, by Apollo, King, thou swearest thy gods in vain.[4]

LEAR   Vassal, recreant!°   *traitor*

150   KENT   Do, kill thy physician,
     And the fee bestow upon the foul disease.[5]
     Revoke thy doom, or whilst I can vent clamor
     From my throat I'll tell thee thou dost evil.

LEAR   Hear me! On thy allegiance, hear me!

155   Since thou hast sought to make us break our vow,
     Which we durst never yet; and with strayed° pride   *wayward; erring*
     To come between our sentence and our power,
     Which nor our nature nor our place[6] can bear,
     Our potency made good,° take thy reward.   *demonstrated*

160   Four days we do allot thee for provision,
     To shield thee from diseases° of the world,   *discomforts*
     And on the fifth to turn thy hated back
     Upon our kingdom. If, on the tenth day following,
     Thy banished trunk° be found in our dominions,   *body*

165   The moment is thy death. Away! By Jupiter,
     This shall not be revoked.

KENT   Why, fare thee well, King. Since thus thou wilt appear,
     Friendship lives hence, and banishment is here.
     [*to* CORDELIA] The gods to their protection take thee,
           maid,

170   That rightly thinks and hast most justly said.
     [*to* GONORILL *and* REGAN] And your large speeches may
          your deeds approve,[7]
     That good effects may spring from words of love.
     Thus, Kent, O princes, bids you all adieu;
     He'll shape his old course in a country new.
           Enter FRANCE *and* BURGUNDY *with* GLOUCESTER.

175   GLOUCESTER   Here's France and Burgundy, my noble lord.

LEAR   My lord of Burgundy, we first address towards you,
     Who with a king hath rivaled for our daughter.
     What in the least will you require in present
     Dower with her or cease your quest of love?

---

4. You invoke your gods falsely and without effect.
5. *kill . . . disease:* you would not only kill the doctor but also hand his fee over to the disease.
6. Which neither my temperament nor my royal position.
7. And let your actions live up to your fine words.

LEAR   Kent, on thy life, no more!

KENT   My life I never held but as pawn°   *chess piece; stake*
To wage° against thine enemies; ne'er fear to lose it,   *wager*
Thy safety being motive.°   *(my) motivation*

155 LEAR   Out of my sight!

KENT   See better, Lear, and let me still° remain   *always*
The true blank° of thine eye.   *precise bull's-eye*

LEAR   Now, by Apollo—

KENT   Now, by Apollo, King,
Thou swear'st thy gods in vain.[6]

LEAR   O vassal! Miscreant!°   *Villain; unbeliever*

160 ALBANY *and* CORNWALL   Dear sir, forbear.

KENT   Kill thy physician and thy fee bestow
Upon the foul disease.[7] Revoke thy gift,
Or whilst I can vent clamor from my throat
I'll tell thee thou dost evil.

165 LEAR   Hear me, recreant!° On thine allegiance, hear me!   *traitor*
That thou hast sought to make us break our vows,
Which we durst never yet; and with strained° pride   *overblown*
To come betwixt our sentences and our power,
Which nor our nature nor our place[8] can bear,

170 Our potency made good,° take thy reward.   *demonstrated*
Five days we do allot thee for provision,
To shield thee from disasters of the world,
And on the sixth to turn thy hated back
Upon our kingdom. If, on the tenth day following,

175 Thy banished trunk° be found in our dominions,   *body*
The moment is thy death. Away! By Jupiter,
This shall not be revoked.

KENT   Fare thee well, King. Sith° thus thou wilt appear,   *Since*
Freedom lives hence, and banishment is here.

180 [*to* CORDELIA] The gods to their dear shelter take thee,
maid,
That justly think'st and hast most rightly said.
[*to* GONERILL *and* REGAN] And your large speeches may
your deeds approve.[9]
That good effects may spring from words of love.
Thus Kent, O princes, bids you all adieu.

185 He'll shape his old course in a country new.   *Exit.*
Flourish.° Enter GLOUCESTER *with* FRANCE *and*   *Fanfare of trumpets*
BURGUNDY [*and*] *Attendants.*

CORNWALL   Here's France and Burgundy, my noble lord.

LEAR   My lord of Burgundy,
We first address toward you, who with this king
Hath rivaled for our daughter. What in the least

190 Will you require in present dower with her
Or cease your quest of love?

---

6. You invoke your gods falsely and without effect.
7. *Kill . . . disease:* You would not only kill the doctor
but also hand his fee over to the disease.

8. Which neither my temperament nor my royal
position.
9. And let your actions live up to your fine words.

180	BURGUNDY Royal majesty, I crave no more than what	
	Your highness offered, nor will you tender° less.	*offer*
	LEAR Right noble Burgundy, when she was dear to us	
	We did hold her so, but now her price is fallen.	
	Sir, there she stands. If aught within that little	
185	Seeming substance,[8] or all of it with our displeasure	
	pieced°	*joined*
	And nothing else, may fitly like° your grace,	*please*
	She's there, and she is yours.	
	BURGUNDY I know no answer.	
	LEAR Sir, will you with those infirmities she owes,°	*owns*
	Unfriended, new-adopted to our hate,	
190	Covered with our curse and strangered° with our oath,	*estranged*
	Take her or leave her?	
	BURGUNDY Pardon me, royal sir, election makes not up	
	On such conditions.[9]	
	LEAR Then leave her, sir, for, by the power that made me,	
195	I tell you° all her wealth. [*to* FRANCE] For° you, great King,	*inform you of / As for*
	I would not from your love make such a stray°	*stray so far*
	To° match you where I hate. Therefore, beseech you	*As to*
	To avert your liking° a more worthier way	*To turn your affections*
	Than on a wretch whom Nature is ashamed	
200	Almost to acknowledge hers.	
	FRANCE This is most strange, that she, that even but now	
	Was your best object, the argument° of your praise,	*theme*
	Balm of your age, most best, most dearest,	
	Should in this trice° of time commit a thing	*moment*
205	So monstrous to dismantle° so many folds of favor.	*as to strip off; disrobe*
	Sure, her offense must be of such unnatural degree	
	That monsters it,° or you, for vouched affections,	*makes it monstrous*
	Fallen into taint,[1] which to believe of her	
	Must be a faith that reason without miracle	
210	Could never plant in me.	
	CORDELIA I yet beseech your majesty—	
	If for I want° that glib and oily art	*because I lack*
	To speak and purpose not,° since what I well intend	*and not intend*
	I'll do't before I speak—that you may know°	*acknowledge*
215	It is no vicious blot, murder, or foulness,	
	No unclean action or dishonored step	
	That hath deprived me of your grace and favor,	
	But even for want of that for which I am rich:	
	A still soliciting° eye and such a tongue	*An always-begging*
220	As I am glad I have not, though not to have it	
	Hath lost me in your liking.	
	LEAR Go to, go to. Better thou hadst not been born	
	Than not to have pleased me better.	

---

8. *little / Seeming substance*: one who appears insubstantial; one who will not pretend.
9. A choice cannot be made under those terms.
1. *or . . . taint*: or else the love you earlier swore for

Cordelia must be regarded with suspicion. "Or" may also mean "before," in which case the phrase would mean "before the love you once proclaimed could have decayed."

BURGUNDY   Most royal majesty,
I crave no more than hath your highness offered,
Nor will you tender° less.   *offer*
LEAR   Right noble Burgundy,
When she was dear to us we did hold her so,
195   But now her price is fallen. Sir, there she stands.
If aught within that little-seeming substance,[1]
Or all of it with our displeasure pieced°   *joined*
And nothing more, may fitly like° your grace,   *please*
She's there, and she is yours.
BURGUNDY   I know no answer.
200   LEAR   Will you with those infirmities she owes,°   *owns*
Unfriended, new-adopted to our hate,
Dow'red with our curse and strangered° with our oath,   *estranged*
Take her or leave her?
BURGUNDY   Pardon me, royal sir,
Election makes not up in such conditions.[2]
205   LEAR   Then leave her, sir, for, by the power that made me,
I tell you° all her wealth. [*to* FRANCE] For° you, great King,   *inform you of / As for*
I would not from your love make such a stray°   *stray so far*
To° match you where I hate. Therefore, beseech you   *As to*
T'avert your liking° a more worthier way   *To turn your affections*
210   Than on a wretch whom Nature is ashamed
Almost t'acknowledge hers.
FRANCE   This is most strange,
That she, whom even but now was your object,
The argument° of your praise, balm of your age,   *theme*
The best, the dearest, should in this trice° of time   *moment*
215   Commit a thing so monstrous to dismantle°   *as to strip off; disrobe*
So many folds of favor. Sure, her offense
Must be of such unnatural degree
That monsters it,° or your fore-vouched affection   *makes it monstrous*
Fall into taint,[3] which to believe of her
220   Must be a faith that reason without miracle
Should never plant in me.
CORDELIA   I yet beseech your majesty—
If for I want° that glib and oily art   *because I lack*
To speak and purpose not,° since what I will intend,   *and not intend*
I'll do't before I speak—that you make known
225   It is no vicious blot, murder, or foulness,
No unchaste action or dishonored step
That hath deprived me of your grace and favor,
But even for want of that for which I am richer:
A still soliciting° eye and such a tongue   *An always begging*
230   That I am glad I have not, though not to have it
Hath lost me in your liking.
LEAR   Better thou hadst
Not been born than not t'have pleased me better.

---

1. *little-seeming substance:* one who appears insubstantial; one who will not pretend.
2. A choice cannot be made under those terms.
3. *or . . . taint:* or else the love you earlier swore for

Cordelia must be regarded with suspicion. "Or" may
also mean "before," in which case the phrase would
mean "before the love you once proclaimed could
have decayed."

FRANCE   Is it no more but this, a tardiness in nature,
225   That often leaves the history unspoke that it intends to do?[2]
         My lord of Burgundy, what say you to the lady?
         Love is not love when it is mingled with
         Respects° that stands aloof from the entire point.   *Considerations*
         Will you have her? She is herself and dower.
230   BURGUNDY   Royal Lear, give but that portion
         Which yourself proposed, and here I take Cordelia
         By the hand, Duchess of Burgundy,
      LEAR   Nothing, I have sworn.
      BURGUNDY [*to* CORDELIA]   I am sorry, then, you have so lost a
         father
235   That you must lose a husband.
      CORDELIA   Peace be with Burgundy. Since that respects
         Of fortune are his love, I shall not be his wife.
      FRANCE   Fairest Cordelia, that art most rich being poor,
         Most choice forsaken, and most loved despised,
240   Thee and thy virtues here I seize upon.
         Be it lawful I take up what's cast away.
         Gods, gods! 'Tis strange, that from their cold'st neglect
         My love should kindle to inflamed respect.°   *ardent regard*
         Thy dowerless daughter, King, thrown to my chance,
245   Is queen of us, of ours, and our fair France.
         Not all the dukes in wat'rish° Burgundy   *irrigated; watery; weak*
         Shall buy this unprized° precious maid of me.   *unappreciated*
         Bid them farewell, Cordelia; though unkind,°   *though they are unkind*
         Thou losest here° a better where° to find.   *this place / place*
250   LEAR   Thou hast her, France. Let her be thine,
         For we have no such daughter, nor shall ever see
         That face of hers again. Therefore be gone
         Without our grace, our love, our benison.°   *blessing*
         Come, noble Burgundy.
                  Exeunt LEAR *and* BURGUNDY[, *Dukes of* ALBANY
                     and CORNWALL, GLOUCESTER, *Edmund the*
                                    BASTARD, *and* SERVANTS].
255   FRANCE   Bid farewell to your sisters.
      CORDELIA   The jewels of our father,
         With washèd eyes Cordelia leaves you.
         I know you what you are
         And like a sister am most loath to call your faults
260   As they are named.° Use well our father;   *are properly called*
         To your professed bosoms° I commit him.   *publicly proclaimed love*
         But yet, alas, stood I within his grace,
         I would prefer° him to a better place.   *promote; recommend*
         So farewell to you both.

---

2. *a tardiness . . . do:* a natural reserve that inhibits voicing one's intentions.

FRANCE   Is it but this, a tardiness in nature,
Which often leaves the history unspoke
235   That it intends to do?[4] My lord of Burgundy,
What say you to the lady? Love's not love
When it is mingled with regards° that stands   *considerations*
Aloof from th'entire point. Will you have her?
She is herself a dowry.
BURGUNDY   Royal King,
240   Give but that portion which yourself proposed,
And here I take Cordelia by the hand,
Duchess of Burgundy.
LEAR   Nothing, I have sworn; I am firm.
BURGUNDY [*to* CORDELIA]   I am sorry, then, you have so lost
   a father
That you must lose a husband.
245   CORDELIA   Peace be with Burgundy.
Since that respect and fortunes are his love,
I shall not be his wife.
FRANCE   Fairest Cordelia, that art most rich being poor,
Most choice forsaken, and most loved despised,
250   Thee and thy virtues here I seize upon.
Be it lawful I take up what's cast away.
Gods, gods! 'Tis strange, that from their cold'st neglect
My love should kindle to enflamed respect.°   *ardent regard*
Thy dowerless daughter, King, thrown to my chance,
255   Is Queen of us, of ours, and our fair France.
Not all the dukes of wat'rish° Burgundy   *irrigated; watery; weak*
Can buy this unprized,° precious maid of me.   *unappreciated*
Bid them farewell, Cordelia; though unkind,°   *though they are unkind*
Thou losest here° a better where° to find.   *this place / place*
260   LEAR   Thou hast her, France. Let her be thine, for we
Have no such daughter, nor shall ever see
That face of hers again. Therefore be gone
Without our grace, our love, our benison.°   *blessing*
—Come, noble Burgundy.
            Flourish. Exeunt [*all but* FRANCE, CORDELIA,
                        GONERILL, *and* REGAN].
265   FRANCE   Bid farewell to your sisters.
CORDELIA   The jewels of our father, with washed eyes
Cordelia leaves you. I know you what you are
And like a sister am most loath to call
Your faults as they are named.° Love well our father;   *are properly called*
270   To your professed bosoms° I commit him.   *publicly proclaimed love*
But yet, alas, stood I within his grace,
I would prefer° him to a better place.   *promote; recommend*
So farewell to you both.

---

4. *a tardiness . . . do*: a natural reserve that inhibits voicing one's intentions.

265 GONORILL   Prescribe not us our duties.
   REGAN   Let your study be to content your lord,
     Who hath received you at fortune's alms.[3]
     You have obedience scanted°   *neglected*
     And well are worth the worth that you have wanted.[4]
270 CORDELIA   Time shall unfold what pleated cunning hides;
     Who covers faults, at last shame them derides.[5]
     Well may you prosper.
   FRANCE   Come, fair Cordelia.
               Exeunt FRANCE *and* CORDELIA.
   GONORILL   Sister, it is not a little I have to say of what most
     nearly appertains to us both. I think our father will hence to-
275   night.
   REGAN   That's most certain, and with you; next month with us.
   GONORILL   You see how full of changes° his age is; the obser-   *fickleness*
     vation we have made of it hath not been little.[6] He always
     loved our sister most, and with what poor judgment he hath
280   now cast her off appears too gross.°   *blatant*
   REGAN   'Tis the infirmity of his age, yet he hath ever but slen-
     derly known himself.
   GONORILL   The best and soundest of his time hath been but
     rash.[7] Then° must we look to receive from his age not alone   *Therefore*
285   the imperfection of long engrafted condition,° but there- *deep-rooted habit*
     withal unruly waywardness that infirm and choleric years
     bring with them.
   REGAN   Such unconstant starts[8] are we like° to have from him   *likely*
     as this of Kent's banishment.
290 GONORILL   There is further compliment° of leave-taking between   *ceremony*
     France and him. Pray, let's hit° together. If our father carry   *join; strike*
     authority with such dispositions[9] as he bears, this last surren-
     der° of his will but offend° us.   *abdication / harm*
   REGAN   We shall further think on't.
295 GONORILL   We must do something, and i'th' heat.°   *Exeunt.*   *quickly*

---

3. As a charitable gift from fortune.
4. And you deserve to get no more love (from your husband) than you have given (to your father). "Want" plays on its alternative meanings of "lack" and "desire."
5. *Who . . . derides:* Those who hide their faults will in the end be put to shame.
6. We have observed it more than a little.
7. *The . . . rash:* Even in the prime of his life he was impetuous.
8. Such impulsive outbursts.
9. Frame of mind.

REGAN   Prescribe not us our duty.

GONERILL   Let your study

275   Be to content your lord, who hath received you
      At fortune's alms.[5] You have obedience scanted°   *neglected*
      And well are worth the want that you have wanted.[6]

CORDELIA   Time shall unfold what plighted cunning hides;
      Who covers faults, at last with shame derides.[7]
      Well may you prosper.

280   FRANCE   Come, my fair Cordelia.

                              Exeunt FRANCE *and* CORDELIA.

GONERILL   Sister, it is not little I have to say of what most
      nearly appertains to us both. I think our father will hence
      tonight.

REGAN   That's most certain, and with you; next month with us.

285   GONERILL   You see how full of changes° his age is; the obser-   *fickleness*
      vation we have made of it hath been little.°   *in the smallest detail*
      our sister most, and with what poor judgment he hath now
      cast her off appears too grossly.°   *blatantly*

REGAN   'Tis the infirmity of his age, yet he hath ever but slen-
290   derly known himself.

GONERILL   The best and soundest of his time hath been but
      rash.[8] Then° must we look from his age to receive not alone   *Therefore*
      the imperfections of long engraffed condition,° but there-   *deep-rooted habit*
      withal the unruly waywardness that infirm and choleric
295   years bring with them.

REGAN   Such unconstant starts[9] are we like° to have from   *likely*
      him as this of Kent's banishment.

GONERILL   There is further compliment° of leave-taking   *ceremony*
      between France and him. Pray you let us sit together. If our
300   father carry authority with such disposition[1] as he bears,
      this last surrender° of his will but offend° us.   *abdication / harm*

REGAN   We shall further think of it.

GONERILL   We must do something, and i'th' heat.°   *Exeunt.*   *quickly*

---

5. As a charitable gift from fortune.
6. And you deserve to get no more love (from your husband) than you have given (to your father). "Want" plays on its alternative meanings of "lack" and "desire."
7. *Time . . . derides:* Time eventually exposes and shames all hidden faults.
8. *The . . . rash:* Even in the prime of his life he was impetuous.
9. Such impulsive outbursts.
1. Frame of mind.

1.2 (F 1.2)

Enter [Edmund the] BASTARD *alone.*

BASTARD Thou, Nature, art my goddess; to thy law
My services are bound.[1] Wherefore° should I   *Why*
Stand in the plague of custom[2] and permit
The curiosity° of nations to deprive me,   *legal niceties*
5 For that° I am some twelve or fourteen moonshines°   *Because / months*
Lag of° a brother? Why "bastard"? Wherefore "base,"   *Younger than*
When my dimensions are as well compact,°   *composed*
My mind as generous,° and my shape as true   *noble*
As honest° madam's issue?   *married; chaste*
10 Why brand they us with "base," "base bastardy"?
Who, in the lusty stealth of nature, take
More composition and fierce quality[3]
Than doth within a stale, dull-eyed bed go
To the creating of a whole tribe of fops°   *fools*
15 Got° 'tween a sleep and wake? Well, the   *Begotten*
"Legitimate" Edgar, I must have your land.
Our father's love is to° the bastard Edmund   *as much to*
As to the legitimate. Well, my legitimate, if
This letter speed° and my invention° thrive,   *succeed / plot*
20 Edmund the base shall to° th' legitimate.   *match up to; usurp*
I grow, I prosper. Now, gods, stand up for bastards!

Enter GLOUCESTER.

GLOUCESTER Kent banished thus? And France in choler
parted?°   *in anger departed*
And the King gone tonight,° subscribed° his power,   *last night / limited*
Confined to exhibition?[4] All this done
25 Upon the gad?° —Edmund, how now, what news?   *spur of the moment*
BASTARD *[putting up a letter]* So please your lordship, none.
GLOUCESTER Why so earnestly seek you to put up that letter?
BASTARD I know no news, my lord.
GLOUCESTER What paper were you reading?

1.2 Location: The Earl of Gloucester's house.
1. Edmund declares the raw force of unsocialized and unregulated existence, as opposed to human law, to be his ruler; ironically, "nature" also means "natural filial affection." A "natural" was another word for a "bastard" (illegitimate child).
2. Submit to the imposition of inheritance law.
3. *Who . . . quality:* Whose begetting, by reason of its furtiveness and heightened excitement, requires bet-

ter execution and more vigor. Alternatively (with "take" meaning "give"), whose begetting produces (a person of) more mixture and vigor. "Composition," or mixture, may refer to the belief that the perfect offspring was conceived from an equal quantity of male and female essence and that physical and mental abnormalities were caused by a predominance of one or the other.
4. Pension; mere show without force.

1.2 (Q 1.2)

Enter EDMOND.

EDMOND Thou, Nature, art my goddess; to thy law
　　　My services are bound.[1] Wherefore° should I   *Why*
　　　Stand in the plague of custom[2] and permit
　　　The curiosity° of nations to deprive me,   *legal niceties*
5　　For that° I am some twelve or fourteen moonshines°   *Because / months*
　　　Lag of° a brother? Why "bastard"? Wherefore "base,"   *Younger than*
　　　When my dimensions are as well compact,°   *composed*
　　　My mind as generous,° and my shape as true   *noble*
　　　As honest° madam's issue? Why brand they us   *married; chaste*
10　With "base"? With "baseness," "bastardy"? Base? Base?
　　　Who, in the lusty stealth of nature, take
　　　More composition and fierce quality[3]
　　　Than doth within a dull, stale, tired bed
　　　Go to th' creating a whole tribe of fops°   *fools*
15　Got° 'tween a sleep and wake? Well, then,   *Begotten*
　　　Legitimate Edgar, I must have your land.
　　　Our father's love is to° the bastard Edmond   *as much to*
　　　As to th' legitimate. Fine word: "legitimate"!
　　　Well, my legitimate, if this letter speed°   *succeed*
20　And my invention° thrive, Edmond the base   *plot*
　　　Shall to° th' legitimate. I grow. I prosper.   *match up to; usurp*
　　　Now, gods, stand up for bastards!
　　　　　Enter GLOUCESTER.
GLOUCESTER Kent banished thus? And France in choler
　　　parted?°   *in anger departed*
　　　And the King gone tonight,° prescribed° his power,   *last night / limited*
25　Confined to exhibition?[4] All this done
　　　Upon the gad?° —Edmond, how now? What news?   *spur of the moment*
EDMOND [*putting up a letter*] So please your lordship, none.
GLOUCESTER Why so earnestly seek you to put up that letter?
EDMOND I know no news, my lord.
30　GLOUCESTER What paper were you reading?

1.2 Location: The Earl of Gloucester's house.
1. Edmond declares the raw force of unsocialized and unregulated existence, as opposed to human law, to be his ruler; ironically, "nature" also means "natural filial affection." A "natural" was another word for a "bastard" (illegitimate child).
2. Submit to the imposition of inheritance law.
3. *Who . . . quality:* Whose begetting, by reason of its furtiveness and heightened excitement, requires bet-

ter execution and more vigor. Alternatively (with "take" meaning "give"), whose begetting produces (a person of) more mixture and vigor. "Composition," or mixture, may refer to the belief that the perfect offspring was conceived from an equal quantity of male and female essence and that physical and mental abnormalities were caused by a predominance of one or the other.
4. Pension; mere show without force.

30 BASTARD Nothing, my lord,

GLOUCESTER No? What needs then that terrible dispatch° of   *frightened haste*
it into your pocket? The quality of nothing hath not such
need to hide itself. Let's see. Come, if it be nothing, I shall
not need spectacles.

35 BASTARD I beseech you, sir, pardon me. It is a letter from my
brother that I have not all o'er-read. For so much as I have
perused, I find it not fit for your liking.°   *pleasure*

GLOUCESTER Give me the letter, sir.

BASTARD I shall offend either to detain or give it. The con-
40 tents, as in part I understand them, are to blame.

GLOUCESTER Let's see, let's see.

BASTARD [*giving him a letter*] I hope, for my brother's justification, he wrote this but as an essay or taste[5] of my virtue.

GLOUCESTER ([*reading*] *a letter*) "This policy of age makes the
45 world bitter to the best of our times,[6] keeps our fortunes
from us till our oldness cannot relish them. I begin to find an
idle and fond° bondage in the oppression of aged tyranny,   *a useless and foolish*
who sways not as it hath power but as it is suffered.[7] Come to
me, that of this I may speak more. If our father would sleep
50 till I waked him, you should enjoy half his revenue forever
and live the beloved of your brother. Edgar." Hum, conspiracy! "Slept till I waked him, you should enjoy half his revenue"! My son Edgar, had he a hand to write this, a heart and
brain to breed it in? When came this to you? Who brought it?

55 BASTARD It was not brought me, my lord. There's the cunning
of it. I found it thrown in at the casement° of my closet.°   *window / private room*

GLOUCESTER You know the character° to be your brother's?   *handwriting*

BASTARD If the matter° were good, my lord, I durst swear it   *content*
were his, but in respect of that, I would fain° think it were not.   *gladly*

60 GLOUCESTER It is his?

BASTARD It is his hand, my lord, but I hope his heart is not in
the contents.

GLOUCESTER Hath he never heretofore sounded you° in this   *sounded you out*
business?

65 BASTARD Never, my lord. But I have often heard him maintain
it to be fit that, sons at perfect age° and fathers declining, his   *at maturity*
father should be as ward[8] to the son, and the son manage the
revenue.

GLOUCESTER Oh, villain, villain! His very opinion in the let-
70 ter! Abhorred villain! Unnatural, detested, brutish villain;
worse than brutish! Go, sir, seek him. Ay, apprehend him.
Abominable villain! Where is he?

---

5. *but . . . taste:* simply as a proof or test. Both terms
derive from metallurgy.
6. The established primacy of the elderly embitters
us at the prime of our lives. *policy:* statecraft; craftiness; established order.

7. *who . . . suffered:* which rules not because it is
powerful but because it is permitted to ("suffered").
8. A child under eighteen years of age who was
legally dependent, often orphaned.

EDMOND Nothing, my lord.

GLOUCESTER No? What needed then that terrible dispatch° *frightened haste*
of it into your pocket? The quality of nothing hath not such
need to hide itself. Let's see. Come, if it be nothing, I shall
35   not need spectacles.

EDMOND I beseech you, sir, pardon me. It is a letter from my
brother that I have not all o'er-read, and, for so much as I
have perused, I find it not fit for your o'erlooking.

GLOUCESTER Give me the letter, sir.

40   EDMOND I shall offend either to detain or give it. The contents,
as in part I understand them, are to blame.

GLOUCESTER Let's see, let's see.

EDMOND [*giving him a letter*] I hope, for my brother's justification, he wrote this but as an essay or taste⁵ of my virtue.

45   GLOUCESTER (*reads*) "This policy and reverence of age makes
the world bitter to the best of our times,⁶ keeps our fortunes
from us till our oldness cannot relish them. I begin to find an
idle and fond° bondage in the oppression of aged tyranny, *a useless and foolish*
who sways not as it hath power but as it is suffered.⁷ Come to
50   me, that of this I may speak more. If our father would sleep
till I waked him, you should enjoy half his revenue forever
and live the beloved of your brother. Edgar." Hum, conspiracy! "Sleep till I wake him, you should enjoy half his revenue"! My son Edgar, had he a hand to write this, a heart and
55   brain to breed it in? When came you to this? Who brought it?

EDMOND It was not brought me, my lord; there's the cunning
of it. I found it thrown in at the casement° of my closet.° *window / private room*

GLOUCESTER You know the character° to be your brother's? *handwriting*

EDMOND If the matter° were good, my lord, I durst swear it *content*
60   were his, but in respect of that, I would fain° think it were not. *gladly*

GLOUCESTER It is his?

EDMOND It is his hand, my lord, but I hope his heart is not in
the contents.

GLOUCESTER Has he never before sounded you° in this busi- *sounded you out*
65   ness?

EDMOND Never, my lord. But I have heard him oft maintain it
to be fit that, sons at perfect age° and fathers declined, the *at maturity*
father should be as ward⁸ to the son, and the son manage his
revenue.

70   GLOUCESTER Oh, villain, villain! His very opinion in the
letter! Abhorred villain! Unnatural, detested, brutish villain;
worse than brutish. Go, sirrah,⁹ seek him. I'll apprehend
him. Abominable villain! Where is he?

---

5. *but . . . taste:* simply as a proof or test. Both terms
derive from metallurgy.
6. The established primacy of the elderly embitters
us at the prime of our lives. *policy:* statecraft; craftiness; established order.
7. *who . . . suffered:* which rules not because it is

powerful but because it is permitted to ("suffered").
8. A child under eighteen years of age who was legally
dependent, often orphaned.
9. A form of address used with children or social
inferiors.

BASTARD   I do not well know, my lord. If it shall please you to
suspend your indignation against my brother till you can
75   derive from him better testimony of this intent, you should
run a certain° course; where,° if you violently proceed against   *safe; reliable / whereas*
him, mistaking his purpose, it would make a great gap in
your own honor and shake in pieces the heart of his obedi-
ence. I dare pawn down° my life for him, he hath wrote this   *I dare stake*
80   to feel° my affection to your honor and to no further pretense   *feel out*
of danger.[9]
GLOUCESTER   Think you so?
BASTARD   If your honor judge it meet,° I will place you where   *appropriate*
you shall hear us confer of this and by an auricular° assur-   *audible*
85   ance have your satisfaction, and that without any further delay
than this very evening.
GLOUCESTER   He cannot be such a monster—
BASTARD   Nor is not, sure.
GLOUCESTER   —To his father, that so tenderly and entirely loves
90   him. Heaven and earth! Edmund, seek him out; wind me
into him.[1] I pray you, frame° your business after your own   *arrange*
wisdom. I would unstate myself to be in a due resolution.[2]
BASTARD   I shall seek him, sir, presently,° convey° the busi-   *immediately / carry out*
ness as I shall see means, and acquaint you withal.°   *therewith*
95   GLOUCESTER   These late° eclipses in the sun and moon por-   *recent*
tend no good to us.[3] Though the wisdom of Nature can rea-
son thus and thus, yet Nature finds itself scourged by the
sequent effects.[4] Love cools, friendship falls off, brothers
divide; in cities, mutinies; in countries, discords; palaces,
100   treason; the bond cracked between son and father. Find out
this villain, Edmund. It shall lose thee nothing. Do it carefully. And the noble and true-hearted Kent banished, his
offense honest. Strange, strange!   [*Exit.*]
BASTARD   This is the excellent foppery° of the world, that when   *foolishness*
105   we are sick in fortune, often the surfeit° of our own behavior,   *excesses*
we make guilty of° our disasters the sun, the moon, and the   *we hold responsible for*
stars, as if we were villains by necessity, fools by heavenly
compulsion, knaves, thieves, and treacherers° by spiritual   *traitors*
predominance,[5] drunkards, liars, and adulterers by an
110   enforced obedience of planetary influence, and all that we
are evil in by a divine thrusting-on.° An admirable° evasion   *imposition / amazing*
of whoremaster man, to lay his goatish disposition to the

9. No further intention to do harm.
1. Worm your way into his confidence (with "me" as
an intensifier); worm your way into his confidence for
me ("me" as a dative of respect).
2. I would give up my rank and property to have my
doubts resolved.
3. The lunar and solar eclipses that were seen in London between September and October 1605, about a
year before the play's first recorded performance,

would have added spice to this superstitious belief in
the role of heavenly bodies as augurs of misfortune.
4. *Though . . . effects:* Though natural science may
explain the eclipses this way or that, Nature (and
family bonds) suffers in the effects that follow.
5. By the ascendancy of a particular planet. In the
universe as conceived by the second-century astronomer Ptolemy, the planets revolved about the earth on
crystalline spheres.

EDMOND   I do not well know, my lord. If it shall please you to
suspend your indignation against my brother till you can
derive from him better testimony of his intent, you should
run a certain° course; where,° if you violently proceed against   *safe; reliable / whereas*
him, mistaking his purpose, it would make a great gap in your
own honor and shake in pieces the heart of his obedience. I
dare pawn down° my life for him that he hath writ this to   *I dare stake*
feel° my affection to your honor and to no other pretense of   *feel out*
danger.[1]

GLOUCESTER   Think you so?

EDMOND   If your honor judge it meet,° I will place you where   *appropriate*
you shall hear us confer of this and by an auricular° assur-   *audible*
ance have your satisfaction, and that without any further
delay than this very evening.

GLOUCESTER   He cannot be such a monster. Edmond, seek
him out; wind me into him,[2] I pray you. Frame° the business   *Arrange*
after your own wisdom. I would unstate myself to be in a
due resolution.[3]

EDMOND   I will seek him, sir, presently,° convey° the business   *immediately / carry out*
as I shall find means, and acquaint you withal.°   *therewith*

GLOUCESTER   These late° eclipses in the sun and moon por-   *recent*
tend no good to us.[4] Though the wisdom of Nature can
reason it thus and thus, yet Nature finds itself scourged by
the sequent effects.[5] Love cools, friendship falls off,
brothers divide; in cities, mutinies; in countries, discord;
in palaces, treason; and the bond cracked twixt son and
father. This villain of mine comes under the prediction:
there's son against father. The King falls from bias of
nature:[6] there's father against child. We have seen the best
of our time. Machinations, hollowness,° treachery, and all   *insincerity*
ruinous disorders follow us disquietly to our graves. Find
out this villain, Edmond. It shall lose thee nothing. Do it
carefully. And the noble and true-hearted Kent banished,
his offense: honesty! 'Tis strange!   *Exit.*

EDMOND   This is the excellent foppery° of the world, that when   *foolishness*
we are sick in fortune, often the surfeits° of our own behav-   *excesses*
ior, we make guilty of° our disasters the sun, the moon, and   *we hold responsible for*
stars, as if we were villains on necessity, fools by heavenly
compulsion, knaves, thieves, and treacherers° by spherical pre-   *traitors*
dominance,[7] drunkards, liars, and adulterers by an enforced
obedience of planetary influence, and all that we are evil in
by a divine thrusting-on.° An admirable° evasion of whore-   *imposition / amazing*
master man, to lay his goatish disposition on the charge of a

---

1. No other intention to do harm.
2. Worm your way into his confidence (with "me" as an intensifier); worm your way into his confidence for me ("me" as a dative of respect).
3. I would give up my rank and property to have my doubts resolved.
4. The lunar and solar eclipses that were seen in London between September and October 1605, about a year before the play's first recorded performance, would have added spice to this superstitious belief in the role of heavenly bodies as augurs of misfortune.

5. *Though . . . effects:* Though natural science may explain the eclipses this way or that, nature (and family bonds) suffers in the effects that follow.
6. The King deviates from his natural inclination. In the game of bowls, the "bias" ("course") is the eccentric path taken by the weighted ball when thrown.
7. By the ascendancy of a particular planet. In the universe as conceived by the second-century astronomer Ptolemy, the planets revolved about the earth on crystalline spheres.

charge of stars!⁶ My father compounded° with my mother   coupled
under the dragon's tail, and my nativity was under Ursa
115   Major,⁷ so that it follows I am rough and lecherous. Fut!° I   By Christ's foot
should have been that° I am had the maidenliest star of the   what
firmament twinkled on my bastardy.
         Enter EDGAR.
[*aside*] Edgar! And out he comes like the catastrophe° of the old   resolution
comedy. Mine° is villainous melancholy, with a sigh like them   My cue; my role
120   of Bedlam.⁸ —Oh, these eclipses do portend these divisions.
   EDGAR   How now, brother Edmund, what serious contemplation are you in?
   BASTARD   I am thinking, brother, of a prediction I read this
other day what should follow these eclipses.
125   EDGAR   Do you busy yourself about that?
   BASTARD   I promise you, the effects he writ of succeed° unhap-   follow
pily, as of unnaturalness between the child and the parent,
death, dearth, dissolutions of ancient amities, divisions in
state, menaces and maledictions against king and nobles,
130   needless diffidences,° banishment of friends, dissipation of   baseless suspicions
cohorts,⁹ nuptial breaches, and I know not what.
   EDGAR   How long have you been a sectary astronomical?°   a devotee of astrology
   BASTARD   Come, come, when saw you my father last?
   EDGAR   Why, the night gone by.
135   BASTARD   Spake you with him?
   EDGAR   Two hours together.
   BASTARD   Parted you in good terms? Found you no displea-
sure in him by word or countenance?°   appearance; demeanor
   EDGAR   None at all.
140   BASTARD   Bethink yourself wherein you may have offended
him and at my entreaty forbear° his presence till some little   avoid
time hath qualified° the heat of his displeasure, which at   moderated
this instant so rageth in him that with the mischief of your
person it would scarce allay.¹
145   EDGAR   Some villain hath done me wrong.
   BASTARD   That's my fear, brother. I advise you to the best: go
armed. I am no honest man if there be any good meaning
towards you. I have told you what I have seen and heard but
faintly, nothing like the image and horror of it. Pray you,
150   away!

---

6. *to lay . . . stars*: to hold the stars responsible for his
lustful desires. In Greek mythology, the satyr, a creature with goat-like characteristics, was notoriously
lecherous.
7. Constellations: "dragon's tail" = Draco and "Ursa
Major" = Great Bear.
8. Like the inmates of Bedlam. "Bethlehem," shortened to "Bedlam," was the name of the oldest and
best-known London madhouse.
9. Scattering of forces.
1. *with . . . allay*: even harming you bodily would
hardly relieve his anger; alternatively, with the irritant of your presence, it (Gloucester's anger) would
not be abated.

star!⁸ My father compounded° with my mother under the   *coupled*
dragon's tail, and my nativity was under Ursa Major,⁹ so that
it follows I am rough and lecherous. I should have been
120   that° I am had the maidenliest star in the firmament twin-   *what*
kled on my bastardizing.

     Enter EDGAR.

  [*aside*] Pat,° he comes like the catastrophe° of the old com-   *On cue / resolution*
edy. My cue is villainous melancholy, with a sigh like Tom
o'Bedlam.¹ —Oh, these eclipses do portend these divisions.
125   [*Sings.*] Fa, sol, la, mi.²

EDGAR   How now, brother Edmond, what serious contemplation are you in?

EDMOND   I am thinking, brother, of a prediction I read this
other day what should follow these eclipses.

130 EDGAR   Do you busy yourself with that?

EDMOND   I promise you, the effects he writes of succeed°   *follow*
unhappily. When saw you my father last?

EDGAR   The night gone by.

EDMOND   Spake you with him?

135 EDGAR   Ay, two hours together.

EDMOND   Parted you in good terms? Found you no displeasure in him by word nor countenance?°   *appearance; demeanor*

EDGAR   None at all.

EDMOND   Bethink yourself wherein you may have offended
140   him, and at my entreaty forbear° his presence until some   *avoid*
little time hath qualified° the heat of his displeasure, which   *moderated*
at this instant so rageth in him that with the mischief of
your person it would scarcely allay.³

EDGAR   Some villain hath done me wrong.

145 EDMOND   That's my fear. I pray you, have a continent forbear-
ance° till the speed of his rage goes slower, and, as I say, retire   *restrained absence*
with me to my lodging, from whence I will fitly° bring you to   *when suitable*
hear my lord speak. Pray ye go; there's my key. If you do stir
abroad, go armed.

150 EDGAR   Armed, brother?

EDMOND   Brother, I advise you to the best. I am no honest
man if there be any good meaning toward you. I have told
you what I have seen and heard but faintly, nothing like the
image and horror of it. Pray you, away!

8. *to lay . . . star:* to hold a star responsible for his
lustful desires. In Greek mythology, the satyr, a creature with goat-like characteristics, was notoriously
lecherous.
9. Constellations: "dragon's tail" = Draco and "Ursa
Major" = Great Bear.
1. The usual name for lunatic beggars; "Bethlehem,"
shortened to "Bedlam," was the name of the oldest
and best-known London madhouse.

2. The portion of the scale that Edmond sings is an
augmented fourth, an interval considered at this time
very discordant; it was sometimes referred to as
diabolus in musica ("the devil in music"). *divisions:*
social fractures; melodic embellishments.
3. *with . . . allay:* even harming you bodily ("mischief") would hardly relieve his anger; alternatively,
with the irritant of your presence, it (Gloucester's
anger) would not be abated.

EDGAR Shall I hear from you anon?
BASTARD I do serve you in this business.   *Exit* EDGAR.
  A credulous father and a brother noble,
  Whose nature is so far from doing harms
155 That he suspects none; on whose foolish honesty
  My practices° ride easy. I see the business.[2]   plots
  Let me, if not by birth, have lands by wit.°   intelligence
  All with me's meet that I can fashion fit.[3]   *Exit.*

1.3 (F 1.3)

Enter GONORILL *and* GENTLEMAN.

GONORILL Did my father strike my gentleman
  For chiding of his fool?
GENTLEMAN Yes, madam.
GONORILL By day and night he wrongs me;
5 Every hour he flashes into one gross crime° or other   offense
  That sets us all at odds. I'll not endure it.
  His knights grow riotous, and himself upbraids us
  On every trifle. When he returns from hunting
  I will not speak with him. Say I am sick.
10 If you come slack of former services,[1]
  You shall do well; the fault of it I'll answer.°   answer for
GENTLEMAN He's coming, madam, I hear him.
GONORILL Put on what weary negligence you please,
  You and your fellow servants. I'd have it come
15 In° question. If he dislike it, let him   Into
  To our sister, whose mind and mine I know
  In that are one, not to be overruled.
  Idle° old man, that still would manage those   Foolish
  Authorities that he hath given away!
20 Now, by my life, old fools are babes again
  And must be used with checks as flatteries when
  They are seen abused.[2] Remember what I tell you.
GENTLEMAN Very well, madam.
GONORILL And let his knights have colder looks among you.
25 What grows of it no matter; advise your fellows so.
  I would breed from hence occasions, and I shall.
  That I may speak,[3] I'll write straight° to my sister   straightaway
  To hold my very° course. Go prepare for dinner.   exact
            Exeunt [*severally*].°   separately

---

2. It is now clear to me what needs to be done.
3. Anything is fine by me as long as I can make it serve my purpose. *meet:* justifiable; appropriate.
1.3 Location: The Duke of Albany's castle.
1. If you offer him less service (and respect) than before.

2. *old . . . abused:* When foolish old men act like children, rebukes are the kindest treatment when kind treatment is abused.
3. *I would . . . speak:* I wish to foster situations, and I shall, in which to speak my mind.

155 EDGAR   Shall I hear from you anon?
EDMOND   I do serve you in this business.   *Exit* EDGAR.
   A credulous father and a brother noble,
   Whose nature is so far from doing harms
   That he suspects none; on whose foolish honesty
160   My practices° ride easy. I see the business.[4]   *plots*
   Let me, if not by birth, have lands by wit.°   *intelligence*
   All with me's meet that I can fashion fit.[5]   *Exit.*

1.3 (Q 1.3)

Enter GONERILL, *and* [Oswald the] STEWARD.

GONERILL   Did my father strike my gentleman
   For chiding of his fool?
STEWARD   Ay, madam.
GONERILL   By day and night he wrongs me; every hour
   He flashes into one gross crime° or other   *offense*
5   That sets us all at odds. I'll not endure it.
   His knights grow riotous, and himself upbraids us
   On every trifle. When he returns from hunting,
   I will not speak with him. Say I am sick.
   If you come slack of former services,[1]
10   You shall do well; the fault of it I'll answer.°   *answer for*
STEWARD   He's coming, madam, I hear him.
GONERILL   Put on what weary negligence you please,
   You and your fellows.° I'd have it come to question.   *other servants*
   If he distaste° it, let him to my sister,   *dislike*
15   Whose mind and mine I know in that are one.

   Remember what I have said.
STEWARD   Well, madam.
GONERILL   And let his knights have colder looks among you.
   What grows of it no matter; advise your fellows so.
   I'll write straight° to my sister to hold my course.   *straightaway*
20   Prepare for dinner.   *Exeunt* [*severally*].°   *separately*

---

4. It is now clear to me what needs to be done.
5. Anything is fine by me as long as I can make it serve my purpose. *meet:* justifiable; appropriate.

1.3 Location: The Duke of Albany's castle.
1. If you offer him less service (and respect) than before.

1.4 (F 1.4)

Enter KENT [*disguised as Caius*].

KENT   If but as well[1] I other accents borrow,
    That can my speech diffuse,° my good intent   *disguise*
    May carry through itself to that full issue°   *result*
    For which I razed my likeness.[2] Now, banished Kent,
5   If thou canst serve where thou dost stand condemned,
    Thy master, whom thou lovest, shall find thee full of labor.°   *ready for work*

Enter LEAR [*and* SERVANTS].

LEAR   Let me not stay° a jot for dinner; go get it ready.   *wait*

[*Exit a* SERVANT.]

[*to* KENT] How now, what° art thou?   *who*

KENT   A man, sir.

10 LEAR   What dost thou profess?[3] What wouldst thou with us?

KENT   I do profess to be no less than I seem, to serve him
    truly that will put me in trust, to love him that is honest, to
    converse° with him that is wise and says little, to fear judg-   *associate*
    ment, to fight when I cannot choose,° and to eat no fish.[4]   *when I must*

15 LEAR   What art thou?

KENT   A very honest-hearted fellow and as poor as the King.

LEAR   If thou be as poor for a subject as he is for a king, thou'rt
    poor enough. What wouldst thou?

KENT   Service.

20 LEAR   Who wouldst thou serve?

KENT   You.

LEAR   Dost thou know me, fellow?

KENT   No, sir, but you have that in your countenance which I
    would fain° call master.   *gladly*

25 LEAR   What's that?

KENT   Authority.

LEAR   What services canst do?

KENT   I can keep honest counsel,° ride, run, mar a curious   *keep secrets*
    tale in telling it[5] and deliver a plain message bluntly. That
30   which ordinary men are fit for, I am qualified in, and the
    best of me is diligence.

LEAR   How old art thou?

KENT   Not so young to love a woman for singing, nor so old to
    dote on her for anything. I have years on my back forty-eight.

35 LEAR   Follow me. Thou shalt serve me if I like thee no worse
    after dinner. I will not part from thee yet. —Dinner, ho, din-
    ner! Where's my knave, my fool? [*to a* SERVANT] Go you and
    call my fool hither.   [*Exit a* SERVANT.]

Enter [*Oswald the*] STEWARD.

    You, sirrah, where's my daughter?

40 STEWARD   So please you—   [*Exit.*]

1.4 Location: As before.
1. As well as disguising my appearance.
2. Disguised my appearance; shaved off my beard.
3. What is your job (profession)? Kent, in reply, uses "profess" punningly to mean "claim."

4. And not to be a Catholic or penitent (Catholics were obliged to eat fish on specified occasions and as penance); alternatively, to be a manly man, a meat eater.
5. That is, Kent's plain, blunt speech would make him ill suited to tell a convoluted ("curious") tale.

1.4 (Q 1.4)

Enter KENT [*disguised as Caius*].

KENT If but as well[1] I other accents borrow
That can my speech diffuse,° my good intent   *disguise*
May carry through itself to that full issue°   *result*
For which I razed my likeness.[2] Now, banished Kent,

5   If thou canst serve where thou dost stand condemned,
So may it come° thy master, whom thou lov'st,   *come to pass*
Shall find thee full of labors.°   *helpful; keen*
       Horns within.° *Enter* LEAR *and* [KNIGHTS *as*]   *Hunting horns offstage*
       Attendants.

LEAR Let me not stay° a jot for dinner; go get it ready. [*to* KENT]   *wait*
How now, what° art thou?   *who*

10 KENT A man, sir.

LEAR What dost thou profess?[3] What wouldst thou with us?

KENT I do profess to be no less than I seem, to serve him
truly that will put me in trust, to love him that is honest,
to converse° with him that is wise and says little, to fear   *associate*

15 judgment, to fight when I cannot choose,° and to eat no   *when I must*
fish.[4]

LEAR What art thou?

KENT A very honest-hearted fellow and as poor as the King.

LEAR If thou be'st as poor for a subject as he's for a king, thou

20 art poor enough. What wouldst thou?

KENT Service.

LEAR Who wouldst thou serve?

KENT You.

LEAR Dost thou know me, fellow?

25 KENT No, sir, but you have that in your countenance which I
would fain° call master.   *gladly*

LEAR What's that?

KENT Authority.

LEAR What services canst thou do?

30 KENT I can keep honest counsel,° ride, run, mar a curious tale   *keep secrets*
in telling it,[5] and deliver a plain message bluntly. That which
ordinary men are fit for I am qualified in, and the best of me
is diligence.

LEAR How old art thou?

35 KENT Not so young, sir, to love a woman for singing, nor
so old to dote on her for anything. I have years on my back
forty-eight.

LEAR Follow me. Thou shalt serve me if I like thee no worse
after dinner. I will not part from thee yet. —Dinner, ho, din-

40 ner! Where's my knave? My fool? Go you and call my fool
hither.   [*Exit a* KNIGHT.]
       Enter [*Oswald the*] STEWARD.
You, you, sirrah, where's my daughter?

STEWARD So please you—   *Exit.*

1.4 Location: As before.
1. As well as disguising my appearance.
2. Disguised my appearance; shaved off my beard.
3. What is your job (profession)? Kent, in reply, uses "profess" punningly to mean "claim."
4. And not to be a Catholic or penitent (Catholics were obliged to eat fish on specified occasions and as penance); alternatively, to be a manly man, a meat eater.
5. That is, Kent's plain, blunt speech would make him ill suited to tell a convoluted ("curious") tale.

LEAR What says the fellow there? Call the clotpoll° back.   blockhead
                    [*Exeunt* KENT *and a* SERVANT.]
        Where's my fool, ho? I think the world's asleep.
                    [*Enter* KENT *and a* SERVANT.]
        How now, where's that mongrel?
KENT He says, my lord, your daughter is not well.
45 LEAR Why came not the slave back to me when I called him?
SERVANT Sir, he answered me in the roundest° manner, he   bluntest; rudest
        "would not."
LEAR 'A° would not?   He
SERVANT My lord, I know not what the matter is, but to my
50   judgment, your highness is not entertained with that cere-
        monious affection as you were wont.° There's a great abate-   accustomed to
        ment appears as well in the general dependents° as in the   servants
        Duke himself also and your daughter.
LEAR Ha? Say'st thou so?
55 SERVANT I beseech you pardon me, my lord, if I be mistaken,
        for my duty cannot be silent when I think your highness
        wronged.
LEAR Thou but remember'st° me of mine own conception.° I   remind / perception
        have perceived a most faint neglect of late, which I have
60   rather blamed as mine own jealous curiosity[6] than as a very
        pretense° and purport of unkindness. I will look further   a true intention
        into't. But where's this fool? I have not seen him this two
        days.
SERVANT Since my young lady's going into France, sir, the
65   fool hath much pined away.
LEAR No more of that, I have noted it. [*to* SERVANT] Go you
        and tell my daughter I would speak with her. [*to another*
        SERVANT] Go you, call hither my fool.
                                        [*Exeunt two* SERVANTS.]
                    [*Enter Oswald the* STEWARD.]
        Oh, you, sir, you, sir, come you hither. Who am I, sir?
70 STEWARD My lady's father.
LEAR "My lady's father"? My lord's knave! You whoreson dog,
        you slave, you cur!
STEWARD I am none of this, my lord. I beseech you pardon me.
LEAR [*striking the* STEWARD] Do you bandy looks with me,
75   you rascal?
STEWARD I'll not be struck, my lord,
KENT [*tripping the* STEWARD] Nor tripped neither, you base
        football player.[7]
LEAR I thank thee, fellow! Thou serv'st me, and I'll love thee.
80 KENT [*to* STEWARD] Come, sir, I'll teach you differences.°   (of rank)
        Away, away. If you will measure your lubber's length again,[8]
        tarry. But away, you have wisdom.   [*Exit* STEWARD.]

---

6. *jealous curiosity:* paranoid concern with niceties.   8. If you will be stretched out by me again. *lubber:*
7. Football was a rough street game played by the poor.   clumsy oaf.

LEAR   What says the fellow there? Call the clotpoll° back.   blockhead
            [*Exit* SECOND KNIGHT.]
45   Where's my fool? Ho, I think the world's asleep.
        [*Enter* SECOND KNIGHT.]
    How now? Where's that mongrel?
SECOND KNIGHT   He says, my lord, your daughter is not well.
LEAR   Why came not the slave back to me when I called him?
SECOND KNIGHT   Sir, he answered me in the roundest° manner,   bluntest; rudest
50   he would not.
LEAR   He would not?
SECOND KNIGHT   My lord, I know not what the matter is, but
    to my judgment your highness is not entertained with that
    ceremonious affection as you were wont.° There's a great   accustomed to
55   abatement of kindness appears as well in the general depen-
    dents° as in the Duke himself also and your daughter.   servants
LEAR   Ha? Say'st thou so?
SECOND KNIGHT   I beseech you pardon me, my lord, if I be
    mistaken, for my duty cannot be silent when I think your
60   highness wronged.
LEAR   Thou but rememberest° me of mine own conception.° I   remind / perception
    have perceived a most faint neglect of late, which I have
    rather blamed as mine own jealous curiosity[6] than as a very
    pretense° and purpose of unkindness. I will look further   a true intention
65   into't. But where's my fool? I have not seen him this two days.
SECOND KNIGHT   Since my young lady's going into France, sir,
    the fool hath much pined away.
LEAR   No more of that, I have noted it well. [*to* SECOND KNIGHT]
    Go you and tell my daughter I would speak with her. [*to*
70   *another* KNIGHT] Go you, call hither my fool.
                    [*Exeunt two* KNIGHTS.]
       Enter [*Oswald the*] STEWARD.
    Oh, you, sir, you, come you hither, sir. Who am I, sir?
STEWARD   My lady's father.
LEAR   "My lady's father"? My lord's knave! You whoreson dog,
    you slave, you cur!
75   STEWARD   I am none of these, my lord. I beseech your pardon.
LEAR [*striking him*]   Do you bandy looks with me, you rascal?
STEWARD   I'll not be strucken, my lord.
KENT [*tripping him*]   Nor tripped, neither, you base football
    player.[7]
80   LEAR   I thank thee, fellow. Thou serv'st me, and I'll love thee.
KENT [*to* STEWARD]   Come, sir, arise, away. I'll teach you
    differences.° Away, away. If you will measure your lubber's   (of rank)
    length again,[8] tarry. But away, go to; have you wisdom, so.
                    [*Exit* STEWARD.]

---

6. *jealous curiosity:* paranoid concern with niceties.   8. If you will be stretched out by me again. *lubber:*
7. Football was a rough street game played by the poor.   clumsy oaf.

LEAR [*to* KENT] Now, friendly knave, I thank thee. [*He gives him money.*] There's earnest of° thy service.   *downpayment for*
    Enter FOOL.[9]

85 FOOL Let me hire him too. [*He hands* KENT *his cap.*] Here's my coxcomb.°   *fool's cap*

LEAR How now, my pretty knave, how dost thou?

FOOL [*to* KENT] Sirrah, you were best take my coxcomb.

KENT Why, Fool?

90 FOOL Why, for taking one's part that's out of favor. Nay, an° thou canst not smile as the wind sits, thou'lt catch cold shortly.[1] There, take my coxcomb. Why, this fellow hath banished two on 's daughters[2] and done the third a blessing against his will. If thou follow him, thou must needs wear

95 my coxcomb. How now, nuncle?° Would I had two coxcombs and two daughters.   *(mine) uncle*   *if*

LEAR Why, my boy?

FOOL If I gave them any living,° I'd keep my coxcombs myself.[3] [*He hands him his cap.*] There's mine; beg another of thy   *goods*

100 daughters.

LEAR Take heed, sirrah, the whip.

FOOL Truth is a dog that must to° kennel; he must be whipped out, when the Lady Brach[4] may stand by the fire and stink.   *go to*

LEAR A pestilent gull° to me.   *annoyance; bitterness*

105 FOOL Sirrah, I'll teach thee a speech.

LEAR Do.

FOOL Mark it, uncle:
  Have more than thou showest,
  Speak less than thou knowest,

110   Lend less than thou owest,°   *own*
  Ride more than thou goest,°   *walk*
  Learn° more than thou trowest,°   *Hear / believe*
  Set less than thou throwest;[5]
  Leave thy drink and thy whore,

115   And keep in a-door,
  And thou shalt have more
  Than two tens to a score.[6]

LEAR This is nothing, Fool.

FOOL Then like the breath° of an unfeed° lawyer, you gave   *speech / unpaid*

120 me nothing for't. Can you make no use of nothing, uncle?

LEAR Why, no, boy, nothing can be made out of nothing.

---

9. PERFORMANCE COMMENT The Fool and Cordelia never meet onstage, making it possible in some productions for one actor to play both roles. Some other productions cast an older actor as the Fool, thus providing a third aging figure alongside Lear and Gloucester. See Digital Edition PC 2.
1. *an . . . shortly:* if you can't keep in favor with those in power, you will soon find yourself left out in the cold.
2. By abdicating, Lear has in effect prevented his eldest daughters from any longer being his subjects,

just as if he had "banished" them.
3. I'd be twice as much a fool.
4. *Lady Brach:* Lady Bitch. Pet dogs were often called "Lady" such and such. The allusion is to Regan and Gonorill, who are now being preferred to truthful Cordelia.
5. Don't gamble everything on a single cast of the dice.
6. *And thou . . . score:* And there will be more than two tens in your twenty—that is, you will become richer.

LEAR Now, my friendly knave, I thank thee. [*He gives him*
85   *money.*] There's earnest of° thy service.   *downpayment for*
       Enter FOOL.[9]
FOOL   Let me hire him too. [*He hands* KENT *his cap.*] Here's my
       coxcomb.°   *fool's cap*
LEAR   How now, my pretty knave, how dost thou?
FOOL [*to* KENT] Sirrah, you were best take my coxcomb.
90 LEAR Why, my boy?
FOOL   Why, for taking one's part that's out of favor. Nay, an thou
       canst not smile as the wind sits, thou'lt catch cold shortly.[1]
       There, take my coxcomb. Why, this fellow has banished two
       on 's daughters[2] and did the third a blessing against his will. If
95   thou follow him, thou must needs wear my coxcomb. How
       now, nuncle?° Would I had two coxcombs and two daughters.   *(mine) uncle*
LEAR   Why, my boy?
FOOL   If I gave them all my living,° I'd keep my coxcombs   *goods*
       myself.[3] [*He hands him his cap.*] There's mine; beg another of
100   thy daughters.
LEAR   Take heed, sirrah, the whip.
FOOL   Truth's a dog must to° kennel; he must be whipped out,   *go to*
       when the lady brach[4] may stand by th' fire and stink.
LEAR   A pestilent gall° to me.   *annoyance; bitterness*
105 FOOL Sirrah, I'll teach thee a speech.
LEAR   Do.
FOOL   Mark it, nuncle:
       Have more than thou showest,
       Speak less than thou knowest,
110   Lend less than thou owest,°   *own*
       Ride more than thou goest,°   *walk*
       Learn° more than thou trowest,°   *Hear / believe*
       Set less than thou throwest;[5]
       Leave thy drink and thy whore,
115   And keep in a-door,
       And thou shalt have more
       Than two tens to a score.[6]
KENT   This is nothing, Fool.
FOOL   Then 'tis like the breath° of an unfeed° lawyer: you gave   *speech / unpaid*
120   me nothing for't. Can you make no use of nothing, nuncle?
LEAR   Why, no, boy, nothing can be made out of nothing.

---

9. PERFORMANCE COMMENT The Fool and Cordelia
never meet onstage, making it possible in some productions for one actor to play both roles. Some other
productions cast an older actor as the Fool, thus providing a third aging figure alongside Lear and Gloucester. See Digital Edition PC 2.
1. *an . . . shortly:* if you can't keep in favor with those
in power, you will soon find yourself left out in the cold.
2. By abdicating, Lear has in effect prevented his

eldest daughters from any longer being his subjects,
just as if he had "banished" them.
3. I'd be twice as much a fool.
4. Lady bitch. Pet dogs were often called "Lady" such
and such. The allusion is to Regan and Gonerill, who
are now being preferred to truthful Cordelia.
5. Don't gamble everything on a single cast of the dice.
6. *And thou . . . score:* And there will be more than two
tens in your twenty—that is, you will become richer.

FOOL Prithee, tell him so much the rent of his land comes
    to.[7] He will not believe a fool.
LEAR A bitter fool.
125 FOOL Dost know the difference, my boy, between a bitter fool
    and a sweet fool?
LEAR No, lad, teach me.
FOOL That lord that counseled thee
    To give away thy land,
130   Come place him here by me;
    Do thou for him stand.°   *represent him*
    The sweet and bitter fool
    Will presently appear,
    The one in motley[8] here,
135   [*pointing to* LEAR] The other found out there.
LEAR Dost thou call me fool, boy?
FOOL All thy other titles thou hast given away; that thou wast
    born with.
KENT This is not altogether fool,[9] my lord.
140 FOOL No, faith, lords and great men will not let me. If I had a
    monopoly out, they would have part in't, and ladies too. They
    will not let me have all the fool to myself; they'll be snatch-
    ing. Give me an egg, nuncle, and I'll give thee two crowns.
LEAR What two crowns shall they be?
145 FOOL Why, after I have cut the egg in the middle and ate up
    the meat,° the two crowns of the egg. When thou clovest°   *edible part / cleaved*
    thy crown i'th' middle and gavest away both parts, thou bor-
    est[1] thy ass a'th'° back o'er the dirt. Thou hadst little wit° in   *on your / sense*
    thy bald crown when thou gavest thy golden one away. If I
150   speak like myself° in this, let him be whipped that first finds   *(like a fool)*
    it so.[2]
    [*Sings.*]   Fools had ne'er less wit in a year,
                   For wise men are grown foppish;[3]
                   They know not how their wits do wear,
155   Their manners are so apish.°   *stupid; imitative*
LEAR When were you wont° to be so full of songs, sirrah?   *accustomed*
FOOL I have used° it, nuncle, ever since thou mad'st thy daugh-   *practiced*
    ters thy mother. For when thou gavest them the rod and putt'st
    down thine own breeches,
160   [*Sings.*]   Then they for sudden joy did weep,
                   And I for sorrow sung,
                   That such a king should play bo-peep,°   *(a child's game)*
                   And go the fools among.
    Prithee, nuncle, keep a schoolmaster that can teach thy
165   Fool to lie. I would fain learn to lie.

---

7. Remind him that no land means no rent; with a
pun on "rent" meaning "torn," "divided."
8. Multicolored dress of a court jester.
9. Foolish, folly. In the next line, the Fool takes
"altogether fool" to mean "one who has cornered the
market on folly."

1. *thou borest:* you carried.
2. *that . . . so:* who first discovers for himself that
this is true; who first considers this to be foolish.
3. *Fools . . . foppish:* Professional fools have never
been as witless since wise men have lately outdone
them in idiocy.

FOOL   Prithee, tell him so much the rent of his land comes
to.[7] He will not believe a fool.

LEAR   A bitter fool.

125   FOOL   Dost thou know the difference, my boy, between a bitter fool and a sweet one?

LEAR   No, lad, teach me.

FOOL   Nuncle, give me an egg, and I'll give thee two crowns.

LEAR   What two crowns shall they be?

130   FOOL   Why, after I have cut the egg i'th' middle and ate up the
meat,° the two crowns of the egg. When thou clovest° thy
crown i'th' middle and gav'st away both parts, thou bor'st°
thine ass on thy back o'er the dirt. Thou hadst little wit° in thy
bald crown when thou gav'st thy golden one away. If I speak
135   like myself° in this, let him be whipped that first finds it so.[8]

[Sings.]   Fools had ne'er less grace in a year,
                For wise men are grown foppish;[9]
                And know not how their wits to wear,
                Their manners are so apish.°

140   LEAR   When were you wont° to be so full of songs, sirrah?

FOOL   I have used° it, nuncle, e'er since thou mad'st thy daughters thy mothers. For when thou gav'st them the rod and putt'st
down thine own breeches,

[Sings.]   Then they for sudden joy did weep,
145   And I for sorrow sung,
                That such a king should play bo-peep,°
                And go the fool among.

Prithee, nuncle, keep a schoolmaster that can teach thy fool
to lie. I would fain learn to lie.

edible part / cleaved
you carried
sense

(like a fool)

stupid; imitative
accustomed
practiced

(a child's game)

7. Remind him that no land means no rent; with a
pun on "rent" meaning "torn," "divided."
8. *that . . . so:* who first discovers for himself that
this is true; who first considers this to be foolish.

9. *Fools . . . foppish:* Professional fools have never
been as witless since wise men have lately outdone
them in idiocy.

LEAR   An° you lie, we'll have you whipped.   *If*

FOOL   I marvel what kin° thou and thy daughters are! They'll   *how alike*
have me whipped for speaking true, thou wilt have me
whipped for lying, and sometime I am whipped for holding
170   my peace. I had rather be any kind of thing than a fool, and
yet I would not be thee, nuncle. Thou hast pared thy wit
o'both sides and left nothing in the middle. Here comes one
of the parings.

       Enter GONORILL.

LEAR   How now, daughter, what makes that frontlet[4] on?
175   Methinks you are too much o'late i'th' frown.

FOOL   Thou wast a pretty fellow when thou hadst no need to
care for her frown. Now thou art an O without a figure.[5] I
am better than thou art now: I am a fool, thou art nothing.
—Yes, forsooth, I will hold my tongue. So your face bids me,
180   though you say nothing.
    [*Sings.*]   Mum, mum,
                He that keeps neither crust nor crumb,
                Weary of all, shall want° some.   *lack; be in need of*
    [*He points to* GONORILL.] That's a shelled peascod.°   *empty pea pod; nothing*

185   GONORILL   Not only, sir, this, your all-licensed° Fool,   *unrestrained*
But other of your insolent retinue
Do hourly carp and quarrel, breaking forth
In rank° and not-to-be-endurèd riots.   *foul; spreading*
Sir, I had thought by making this well known unto you
190   To have found a safe° redress, but now grow fearful   *sure*
By what yourself too late° have spoke and done,   *recently*
That you protect this course and put it on°   *encourage it*
By your allowance; which if you should, the fault
Would not scape censure, nor the redress sleep;
195   Which in the tender of a wholesome weal[6]
Might in their working do you that offense
That else were shame, that then necessity
Must call discreet proceedings.[7]

FOOL   For you trow, nuncle,
200   [*Sings.*]   The hedge-sparrow fed the cuckoo[8] so long
                That it had it head bit off by't young,°   *(the young cuckoo)*
                So out went the candle,
                And we were left darkling.°   *in the dark*

---

4. A headband; here, a metaphor for "frown."
5. A zero without a preceding digit to give it value;
nothing.
6. *tender of a wholesome weal*: maintenance of a
well-ordered commonwealth.
7. *which if you . . . proceedings*: if you do approve (of
your attendants' behavior), you will not escape criticism, nor will it be without retribution, which for the
common good will cause you pain. While this would
otherwise be improper, it will be seen as a prudent
("discreet") action under the circumstances.
8. The cuckoo lays its eggs in the nests of other
birds, which then hatch and feed their offspring.

150   LEAR   An° you lie, sirrah, we'll have you whipped.   *If*

FOOL   I marvel what kin° thou and thy daughters are. They'll   *how alike*
have me whipped for speaking true, thou'lt have me whipped
for lying, and sometimes I am whipped for holding my peace.
I had rather be any kind o'thing than a fool, and yet I would
155   not be thee, nuncle. Thou hast pared thy wit o'both sides and
left nothing i'th' middle. Here comes one o'th' parings.
          Enter GONERILL.

LEAR   How now, daughter? What makes that frontlet¹ on? You
are too much of late i'th' frown.

FOOL   Thou wast a pretty fellow when thou hadst no need to
160   care for her frowning. Now thou art an O without a figure.²
I am better than thou art now: I am a fool, thou art nothing.
—Yes, forsooth, I will hold my tongue, so your face bids me,
though you say nothing.
     [*Sings.*]   Mum, mum,
165   He that keeps nor crust, nor crumb,
                          Weary of all, shall want° some.   *lack; be in need of*
     [*He points to* GONERILL.] That's a shelled peascod.°   *empty pea pod; nothing*

GONERILL   Not only, sir, this, your all-licensed° fool,   *unrestrained*
But other of your insolent retinue
170   Do hourly carp and quarrel, breaking forth
In rank° and not-to-be-endured riots. Sir,   *foul; spreading*
I had thought by making this well known unto you
To have found a safe° redress, but now grow fearful,   *sure*
By what yourself too late° have spoke and done,   *recently*
175   That you protect this course and put it on°   *encourage it*
By your allowance; which if you should, the fault
Would not scape censure, nor the redresses sleep;
Which in the tender of a wholesome weal³
Might in their working do you that offense
180   Which else were shame, that then necessity
Will call discreet proceeding.⁴

FOOL   For you know, nuncle,
     [*Sings.*]   The hedge-sparrow fed the cuckoo⁵ so long
                          That its had its head bit off by its young;°   *(the young cuckoo)*
185   So out went the candle,
                          And we were left darkling.°   *in the dark*

---

1. A headband; here, a metaphor for "frown."
2. A zero without a preceding digit to give it value;
nothing.
3. *tender of a wholesome weal:* maintenance of a
well-ordered society.
4. *which if you . . . proceeding:* if you do approve (of
your attendants' behavior), you will not escape criti-

cism, nor will it be without retribution, which for the
common good will cause you pain. While this would
otherwise be improper, it will be seen as a prudent
("discreet") action under the circumstances.
5. The cuckoo lays its eggs in the nests of other
birds, which then hatch and feed their offspring.

LEAR Are you our daughter?

205 GONORILL Come, sir, I would° you would make use of that   *wish*
  Good wisdom whereof I know you are fraught°   *full*
  And put away these dispositions,° that   *moods; attitudes*
  Of late transform you from what you rightly are.

FOOL May not an ass know when the cart draws the horse?

210 [*Sings.*] Whoop-jug,[9] I love thee.

LEAR Doth any here know me? Why, this is not Lear.
  Doth Lear walk thus? Speak thus? Where are his eyes?
  Either his notion,° weakness, or his discernings   *intellect*
  Are lethargied. Sleeping or waking, ha!

215 Sure, 'tis not so. Who is it that can tell me who I am?
  Lear's shadow? I would° learn that, for by the marks°   *wish to / evidence*
  Of sovereignty, knowledge, and reason,
  I should be false persuaded I had daughters.

FOOL Which° they will make an obedient father.   *Whom*

220 LEAR [*to* GONORILL] Your name, fair gentlewoman?

GONORILL Come, sir, this admiration° is much of the savor   *excessive amazement*
  Of other your new pranks. I do beseech you,
  Understand my purposes aright:
  As you are old and reverend, should° be wise.   *you should*

225 Here do you keep a hundred knights and squires,
  Men so disordered,° so deboist° and bold,   *disorderly / debauched*
  That this our court, infected with their manners,
  Shows° like a riotous inn; epicurism° and lust   *Appears / gluttony*
  Make more like a tavern or brothel

230 Than a great palace.[1] The shame itself doth speak
  For instant remedy. Be thou desired
  By her, that else will take the thing she begs,
  A little to disquantity your train,°   *to reduce your retinue*
  And the remainder that shall still depend°   *be retained*

235 To be such men as may besort° your age,   *befit*
  That know themselves° and you.   *Who know their place*

LEAR Darkness and devils! [*to his* SERVANTS] Saddle my
    horses;
  Call my train together. [*to* GONORILL] Degenerate bastard,
  I'll not trouble thee. Yet° have I left a daughter.   *Still*

240 GONORILL You strike my people, and your disordered rabble
  Make servants of their betters!

---

9. Nickname for "Joan"; sobriquet for a whore.
1. PERFORMANCE COMMENT Productions must decide whether the king's followers are well-behaved "men of choicest parts," as Lear puts it, or a "disordered rabble," as Gonorill describes them. See Digital Edition PC 3.

LEAR   Are you our daughter?

GONERILL   I would° you would make use of your good   *wish*
     wisdom,
     Whereof I know you are fraught,° and put away   *full*
190 These dispositions,° which of late transport you   *moods; attitudes*
     From what you rightly are.

FOOL   May not an ass know when the cart draws the horse?
     [*Sings.*]   Whoop, jug,[6] I love thee.

LEAR   Does any here know me? This is not Lear.
195 Does Lear walk thus? Speak thus? Where are his eyes?
     Either his notion° weakens, his discernings   *intellect*
     Are lethargied. Ha! Waking?° 'Tis not so.   *Am I awake*
     Who is it that can tell me who I am?

FOOL   Lear's shadow.

200 LEAR [*to* GONERILL]   Your name, fair gentlewoman?

GONERILL   This admiration,° sir, is much o'th' savor   *excessive amazement*
     Of other your new pranks. I do beseech you
     To understand my purposes aright:
     As you are old and reverend, should° be wise.   *you should*
205 Here do you keep a hundred knights and squires,
     Men so disordered,° so debauched and bold,   *disorderly*
     That this our court, infected with their manners,
     Shows° like a riotous inn. Epicurism° and lust   *Appears / Gluttony*
     Makes it more like a tavern or a brothel
210 Than a graced° palace.[7] The shame itself doth speak   *an honored*
     For instant remedy. Be then desired
     By her, that else will take the thing she begs,
     A little to disquantity your train,°   *to reduce your retinue*
     And the remainders that shall still depend°   *be retained*
215 To be such men as may besort° your age,   *befit*
     Which know themselves° and you.   *Who know their place*

LEAR   Darkness and devils!
     Saddle my horses; call my train together.
     Degenerate bastard, I'll not trouble thee.
220 Yet° have I left a daughter.   *Still*

GONERILL   You strike my people, and your disordered rabble
     Make servants of their betters.

---

6. Nickname for "Joan"; sobriquet for a whore.
7. PERFORMANCE COMMENT Productions must
decide whether the king's followers are well-behaved
"men of choicest parts," as Lear puts it, or a "disordered rabble," as Gonerill describes them. See Digital Edition PC 3.

Enter [Duke of] ALBANY.

LEAR We that too late repent 's! [*to* ALBANY] O sir, are you
    come?
    Is it your will that we prepare any horses?
    [*to* GONORILL] Ingratitude! Thou marble-hearted fiend,
245   More hideous when thou showest thee in a child
    Than the sea-monster! Detested kite,° thou liest!   *carrion-eating hawk*
    My train and men of choice and rarest parts°   *qualities*
    That all particulars of duty know,
    And in the most exact regard support
250   The worships of° their name. —O most small fault,   *honor accorded*
    How ugly didst thou in Cordelia show,
    That like an engine wrenched my frame of nature
    From the fixed place,[2] drew from my heart all love
    And added to the gall. O Lear, Lear!
255   Beat at this gate° that let thy folly in   *(his head)*
    And thy dear° judgment out. [*to his* SERVANTS] Go, go, my   *precious*
    people.   [*Exeunt* SERVANTS.]
ALBANY   My lord, I am guiltless as I am ignorant.
LEAR   It may be so, my lord. Hark, Nature, hear,
    Dear goddess! Suspend thy purpose if thou
260   Didst intend to make this creature fruitful.
    Into her womb convey sterility,
    Dry up in her the organs of increase,
    And from her derogate° body never spring   *debased*
    A babe to honor her. If she must teem,°   *breed*
265   Create her child of spleen,° that it may live   *malice*
    And be a thwart dis-utered° torment to her.   *a perverse unnatural*
    Let it stamp wrinkles in her brow of youth;
    With cadent° tears, fret° channels in her cheeks;   *flowing / carve*
    Turn all her mother's pains and benefits°   *cares and kind actions*
270   To laughter and contempt, that she may feel—
    That she may feel
    How sharper than a serpent's tooth it is
    To have a thankless child. —Go, go, my people!
ALBANY   Now, gods that we adore, whereof comes this?
275 GONORILL   Never afflict yourself to know the cause,
    But let his disposition have that scope
    That dotage gives it.
LEAR   What, fifty of my followers at a clap,
    Within a fortnight?
ALBANY   What is the matter, sir?
280 LEAR   I'll tell thee: life and death! [*to* GONORILL] I am
    ashamed
    That thou hast power to shake my manhood thus;
    That these hot tears that break from me perforce°   *against my will*
    Should make the worst blasts and fogs upon thee.

---

2. *like . . . place:* as a machine (or lever) dislocated my natural affections from their proper foundations.

Enter [Duke of] ALBANY.

LEAR   Woe that° too late repents!   *Woe to him who*

[*to* ALBANY] Is it your will? Speak, sir. Prepare my horses.

225   [*to* GONERILL] Ingratitude! Thou marble-hearted fiend,

More hideous when thou show'st thee in a child

Than the sea-monster.

ALBANY   Pray, sir, be patient.

LEAR [*to* GONERILL]   Detested kite,° thou liest!   *carrion-eating hawk*

My train are men of choice and rarest parts°   *qualities*

230   That all particulars of duty know,

And in the most exact regard support

The worships of° their name. —O most small fault,   *honors accorded*

How ugly didst thou in Cordelia show,

Which, like an engine, wrenched my frame of nature

235   From the fixed place,[8] drew from my heart all love,

And added to the gall. O Lear, Lear, Lear!

Beat at this gate° that let thy folly in   *(his head)*

And thy dear° judgment out. [*to his* KNIGHTS] Go, go, my   *precious*

people.   [*Exeunt* KNIGHTS.]

ALBANY   My lord, I am guiltless as I am ignorant

Of what hath moved you.

240   LEAR   It may be so, my lord.

Hear, Nature, hear, dear goddess, hear:

Suspend thy purpose if thou didst intend

To make this creature fruitful.

Into her womb convey sterility,

245   Dry up in her the organs of increase,

And from her derogate° body never spring   *debased*

A babe to honor her. If she must teem,°   *breed*

Create her child of spleen,° that it may live   *malice*

And be a thwart disnatured° torment to her.   *a perverse unnatural*

250   Let it stamp wrinkles in her brow of youth;

With cadent° tears fret° channels in her cheeks;   *flowing / carve*

Turn all her mother's pains and benefits°   *cares and kind actions*

To laughter and contempt, that she may feel

How sharper than a serpent's tooth it is

255   To have a thankless child. Away, away.

                 Exeunt [LEAR *and* KENT].

ALBANY   Now gods that we adore,

Whereof comes this?

GONERILL   Never afflict yourself to know more of it,

But let his disposition have that scope

260   As° dotage gives it.   *Which*

        Enter LEAR.

LEAR   What, fifty of my followers at a clap?

Within a fortnight?

ALBANY   What's the matter, sir?

LEAR   I'll tell thee:

Life and death! [*to* GONERILL] I am ashamed

265   That thou hast power to shake my manhood thus,

That these hot tears, which break from me perforce,°   *against my will*

Should make thee worth them.

Blasts and fogs upon thee!

---

8. *like . . . place:* as a machine (or lever), dislocated my natural affections from their proper foundations.

Untented woundings° of a father's curse,   *Undressed wounds*
285 Pierce every sense about thee! Old fond° eyes,   *foolish*
Beweep° this cause again, I'll pluck you out   *If you weep over*
And cast you with the waters that you make
To temper° clay. Yea, is't come to this? Yet   *soften*
Have I left a daughter, whom I am sure
290 Is kind and comfortable.°   *comforting*
When she shall hear this of thee, with her nails
She'll flay thy wolvish visage. Thou shalt find
That I'll resume the shape which thou dost think
I have cast off forever. Thou shalt, I warrant thee.
                              [*Exeunt* LEAR *and* KENT.]
295 GONORILL   Do you mark that, my lord?
ALBANY   I cannot be so partial,° Gonorill,   *biased*
To° the great love I bear you—   *Because of*
GONORILL   Come, sir, no more.—
[*to* FOOL] You, more knave than fool, after your master.
300 FOOL   Nuncle Lear, nuncle Lear, tarry and take the Fool
      with.
   A fox when one has caught her,
   And such a daughter
   Should sure° to the slaughter,   *surely be sent*
   If my cap would buy a halter,°   *collar; noose*
305 So the Fool follows after.   [*Exit.*]

GONORILL   What, Oswald, ho!
            [*Enter Oswald the* STEWARD.]
STEWARD   Here, madam,
GONORILL   What, have you writ this letter to my sister?
STEWARD   Yes, madam.
GONORILL   Take you some company and away to horse.
310 Inform her full of my particular fears,
   And thereto add such reasons of your own
   As may compact° it more. Get you gone   *compound*
   And hasten your return.   [*Exit* STEWARD.]
                       Now, my lord,
   This milky gentleness and course of yours,
315 Though I dislike not, yet under pardon,°   *begging your pardon*
   You're much more attasked° for want of wisdom   *taken to task; censured*
   Than praise for harmful mildness.
ALBANY   How far your eyes may pierce,° I cannot tell;   *foresee*
   Striving to better aught,° we mar what's well.   *anything*
GONORILL   Nay, then—
320 ALBANY   Well, well, the event.°   *Exeunt.*   *let's see the outcome*

Th'untented woundings° of a father's curse   *The undressed wounds*
270 Pierce every sense about thee. Old fond° eyes,   *foolish*
Beweep° this cause again, I'll pluck ye out   *If you weep over*
And cast you with the waters that you lose°   *let loose*
To temper° clay. Ha? Let it be so.   *soften*
I have another daughter
275 Who I am sure is kind and comfortable.°   *comforting*
When she shall hear this of thee, with her nails
She'll flay thy wolvish visage. Thou shalt find
That I'll resume the shape which thou dost think
I have cast off forever.   *Exit.*

GONERILL   Do you mark that?
280 ALBANY   I cannot be so partial,° Gonerill,   *biased*
To° the great love I bear you—   *Because of*
GONERILL   Pray you, content.° What, Oswald, ho?   *be quiet*
[*to* FOOL] You, sir, more knave than fool, after your master.
FOOL   Nuncle Lear, nuncle Lear,
285 Tarry, take the fool with thee.
A fox when one has caught her,
And such a daughter
Should sure° to the slaughter   *surely be sent*
If my cap would buy a halter.°   *collar; noose*
290 So the fool follows after.   *Exit.*
GONERILL   This man hath had good counsel. A hundred
knights?
'Tis politic° and safe to let him keep   *prudent*
At point° a hundred knights; yes, that on every dream   *Armed*
Each buzz,° each fancy, each complaint, dislike.   *rumor*
295 He may enguard° his dotage with their powers   *protect*
And hold our lives in mercy. Oswald, I say!
ALBANY   Well, you may fear too far.
GONERILL   Safer than trust too far.
Let me still° take away the harms I fear,   *always*
300 Not° fear still to be taken. I know his heart;   *Rather than*
What he hath uttered I have writ my sister.
If she sustain him and his hundred knights
When I have showed th'unfitness—
          Enter [*Oswald the*] STEWARD.
How now, Oswald?
305 What, have you writ that letter to my sister?
STEWARD   Ay, madam.
GONERILL   Take you some company and away to horse.
Inform her full of my particular fear
And thereto add such reasons of your own
310 As may compact° it more. Get you gone   *compound*
And hasten your return.   [*Exit* STEWARD.]
[*to* ALBANY]   No, no, my lord,
This milky gentleness and course of yours,
Though I condemn not, yet under pardon,°   *begging your pardon*
You are much more at task° for want of wisdom   *taken to task; censured*
315 Than praised for harmful mildness.
ALBANY   How far your eyes may pierce,° I cannot tell;   *foresee*
Striving to better, oft we mar what's well.
GONERILL   Nay, then—
ALBANY   Well, well, th'event.°   *Exeunt.*   *let's see the outcome*

1.5 (F 1.5)

Enter LEAR[, KENT, FOOL, *and a* SERVANT].

LEAR Go you before° to Gloucester[1] with these letters; acquaint *on ahead*
my daughter no further with anything you know than comes
from her demand out of the letter.[2] If your diligence be not
speedy, I shall be there before you.

5 KENT I will not sleep, my lord, till I have delivered your
letter.   *Exit.*

FOOL If a man's brains were in his heels, were't not in danger
of kibes?°   *chilblains*

LEAR Ay, boy.

10 FOOL Then I prithee, be merry; thy wit shall ne'er go slipshod.[3]

LEAR Ha, ha, ha.

FOOL Shalt° see thy other daughter will use thee kindly, for *Thou shalt*
though she's as like this as a crab[4] is like an apple, yet I con° *know*
what I can tell.

15 LEAR Why, what canst thou tell, my boy?

FOOL She'll taste as like this as a crab doth to a crab. Thou
canst not tell why one's nose stand in the middle of his face?

LEAR No.

FOOL Why, to keep his eyes on either side 's nose, that what a
20 man cannot smell out 'a° may spy into.   *he*

LEAR I did her wrong.

FOOL Canst tell how an oyster makes his shell?

LEAR No.

FOOL Nor I, neither, but I can tell why a snail has a house.

25 LEAR Why?

FOOL Why, to put his head in, not to give it away to his
daughter and leave his horns without a case.[5]

LEAR I will forget my nature.[6] So kind a father! Be my horses
ready?

30 FOOL Thy asses° are gone about them. The reason why the *(servants)*
seven stars° are no more than seven is a pretty reason. *the Pleiades*

LEAR Because they are not eight.

FOOL Yes, thou wouldst make a good fool.

LEAR To take't again, perforce.[7] Monster ingratitude!

35 FOOL If thou wert my fool, nuncle, I'd have thee beaten for
being old before thy time.

LEAR How's that?

FOOL Thou shouldst not have been old before thou hadst
been wise.

40 LEAR Oh, let me not be mad, sweet heaven! I would not be
mad! Keep me in temper.° I would not be mad! —Are the *sane*
horses ready?

1.5 Location: Before Albany's castle.
1. To Gloucestershire, where Cornwall and Regan
reside.
2. *than . . . letter:* other than such questions as are
prompted by the letter.
3. Literally, your brains will not wear slippers (to
warm feet that are afflicted with chilblains); feet of
any intelligence would not walk toward Regan.
4. *crab:* crab apple; sour apple.

5. Protective covering for his head, or concealment
for his horns (horns were the conventional sign of a
cuckold). The Fool may be slyly implying that Lear's
wife cheated on him.
6. Lose my fatherly feelings. *nature:* character.
7. To take it back by force. Lear may refer to Gonorill's treachery, or he may be contemplating resuming
his authority.

1.5 (Q 1.5)

Enter LEAR, KENT [*disguised as Caius*], GENTLEMAN, *and* FOOL.

LEAR [*to* KENT]   Go you before° to Gloucester[1] with these let-   *on ahead*
ters; acquaint my daughter no further with anything you
know than comes from her demand out of the letter.[2] If your
diligence be not speedy, I shall be there afore you.

5   KENT   I will not sleep, my lord, till I have delivered your letter.

Exit.

FOOL   If a man's brains were in 's heels, were't not in danger
of kibes?°   *chilblains*

LEAR   Ay, boy.

FOOL   Then, I prithee, be merry; thy wit shall not go slipshod.[3]

10   LEAR   Ha, ha, ha.

FOOL   Shalt° see thy other daughter will use thee kindly, for   *Thou shalt*
though she's as like this as a crab's° like an apple, yet I can   *crab apple; sour apple*
tell what I can tell.

LEAR   What canst tell, boy?

15   FOOL   She will taste as like this as a crab does to a crab. Thou
canst tell why one's nose stands i'th' middle on 's° face?   *of one's*

LEAR   No.

FOOL   Why, to keep one's eyes of either side 's nose, that what
a man cannot smell out he may spy into.

20   LEAR   I did her wrong.

FOOL   Canst tell how an oyster makes his shell?

LEAR   No.

FOOL   Nor I, neither, but I can tell why a snail has a house.

LEAR   Why?

25   FOOL   Why, to put 's head in, not to give it away to his daughters and leave his horns without a case.[4]

LEAR   I will forget my nature.[5] So kind a father! Be my horses
ready?

FOOL   Thy asses° are gone about 'em; the reason why the   *(servants)*
30   seven stars° are no more than seven is a pretty reason.   *the Pleiades*

LEAR   Because they are not eight.

FOOL   Yes, indeed; thou wouldst make a good fool.

LEAR   To take't again perforce.[6] Monster ingratitude!

FOOL   If thou wert my fool, nuncle, I'd have thee beaten for
35   being old before thy time.

LEAR   How's that?

FOOL   Thou shouldst not have been old till thou hadst been
wise.

LEAR   Oh, let me not be mad, not mad. Sweet heaven, keep me
40   in temper;° I would not be mad. —How now, are the horses   *sane*
ready?

1.5 Location: Before Albany's castle.
1. To Gloucestershire, where Cornwall and Regan reside.
2. *than . . . letter:* other than such questions as are prompted by the letter.
3. Literally, your brains will not wear slippers (to warm feet that are afflicted with chilblains); feet of any intelligence would not walk toward Regan.

4. Protective covering for his head, or concealment for his horns (horns were the conventional sign of a cuckold). The Fool may be slyly implying that Lear's wife cheated on him.
5. Lose my fatherly feelings. *nature:* character.
6. To take it back by force. Lear may refer to Gonerill's treachery, or he may be contemplating resuming his authority.

SERVANT   Ready, my lord.

LEAR [*to* FOOL]   Come, boy.   [*Exeunt* LEAR *and* SERVANT.]

45   FOOL   She that is maid now and laughs at my departure,
      Shall not be a maid long, except things be cut shorter.[8]

                                               Exit.

2.1 (F 2.1)

Enter [Edmund the] BASTARD *and* CURAN, *meeting.*

BASTARD   Save° thee, Curan.   *God save*

CURAN   And you, sir. I have been with your father and given
      him notice that the Duke of Cornwall and his duchess will
      be here with him tonight.

5   BASTARD   How comes that?

CURAN   Nay, I know not. You have heard of the news abroad.
      I mean the whispered ones, for there are yet but ear-bussing[1]
      arguments.

BASTARD   Not I. Pray you, what are they?

10   CURAN   Have you heard of no likely wars towards° twixt the   *impending*
      two Dukes of Cornwall and Albany?

BASTARD   Not a word.

CURAN   You may, then, in time. Fare you well, sir.   [*Exit.*]

BASTARD   The Duke be here tonight! The better best!

15   This weaves itself perforce° into my business.   *necessarily*
      My father hath set guard to take my brother,
      And I have one thing of a queasy question,[2]
      Which must ask briefness and Fortune help.

            Enter EDGAR [*above*].

      Brother, a word! Descend, brother, I say!

      [EDGAR *descends*.]

20   My father watches. Oh, fly this place!
      Intelligence is given where you are hid.
      You have now the good advantage of the night.
      Have you not spoken 'gainst the Duke of Cornwall aught?°   *anything*
      He's coming hither now in the night, i'th' haste,

25   And Regan with him. Have you nothing said
      Upon his party° against the Duke of Albany?   *On his (Cornwall's) side*
      Advise your—°   *Consider carefully*

EDGAR   I am sure on't,° not a word.   *of it*

BASTARD   I hear my father coming. Pardon me:
      [*He draws his sword*.] In cunning I must draw my sword
          upon you.

30   Seem to defend yourself; now quit you° well.   *acquit yourself*
      [*He shouts*.] Yield, come before my father. —Light here,
         here!
      [*to* EDGAR] Fly, brother, fly! —Torches, torches! [*to* EDGAR]
      So farewell!   [*Exit* EDGAR.]

---

8. *She . . . shorter:* A girl who would laugh at my leaving would be so foolish that she could not remain a virgin for long; "things" refers both to the unfolding event and to penises.
2.1 Location: Gloucester's castle.

1. *ear-bussing:* ear-kissing, from "buss" meaning "to kiss." Perhaps also a pun on "buzz" (rumor). Compare to Lear's use of the term in 1.4.294 in F.
2. And I have a hazardous and delicate problem.

GENTLEMAN   Ready, my lord.

LEAR   Come, boy.

FOOL   She that's a maid now and laughs at my departure,

45   Shall not be a maid long, unless things be cut shorter.[7]

Exeunt.

2.1 (Q 2.1)

Enter [EDMOND the] bastard, and CURAN, severally.° — separately

EDMOND   Save° thee, Curan. — God save

CURAN   And you, sir. I have been with your father and given
him notice that the Duke of Cornwall and Regan, his duchess, will be here with him this night.

5   EDMOND   How comes that?

CURAN   Nay, I know not. You have heard of the news abroad,
I mean the whispered ones, for they are yet but ear-kissing
arguments.[1]

EDMOND   Not I. Pray you, what are they?

10   CURAN   Have you heard of no likely wars toward° twixt the — impending
Dukes of Cornwall and Albany?

EDMOND   Not a word.

CURAN   You may do, then, in time. Fare you well, sir.   *Exit.*

EDMOND   The Duke be here tonight? The better best!

15   This weaves itself perforce° into my business. — necessarily
My father hath set guard to take my brother,
And I have one thing of a queasy question[2]
Which I must act. Briefness and fortune work.° — be with me

Enter EDGAR [above].

Brother, a word! Descend, brother, I say.

[EDGAR *descends.*]

20   My father watches. O sir, fly this place!
Intelligence is given where you are hid.
You have now the good advantage of the night.
Have you not spoken 'gainst the Duke of Cornwall?
He's coming hither now, i'th' night, i'th' haste,

25   And Regan with him. Have you nothing said
Upon his party° 'gainst the Duke of Albany? — On his (Cornwall's) side
Advise yourself.° — Consider carefully of it

EDGAR   I am sure on't,° not a word. — of it

EDMOND   I hear my father coming. Pardon me:
[*He draws his sword.*] In cunning, I must draw my sword
upon you.

30   Draw, seem to defend yourself. Now quit you° well. — acquit yourself
[*He shouts.*] Yield, come before my father. —Light, ho, here!
[*to EDGAR*] Fly, brother! —Torches, torches! [*to EDGAR*] So
farewell!   [*Exit EDGAR.*]

---

7. *She . . . shorter:* A girl who would laugh at my leaving would be so foolish that she could not remain a
virgin for long; "things" refers both to the unfolding
event and to penises.

2.1 Location: Gloucester's castle.
1. Barely whispered affairs.
2. And I have a hazardous and delicate problem.

[*He wounds his arm.*] Some blood drawn on me would
         beget opinion°   *produce the impression*
Of my more fierce endeavor. I have seen
35   Drunkards do more than this in sport. [*He shouts.*] Father,
         father!
Stop, stop! No help?
              Enter GLOUCESTER [*and* SERVANTS].
GLOUCESTER   Now, Edmund, where is the villain?
BASTARD   Here stood he in the dark, his sharp sword out,
     Warbling of wicked charms, conjuring the moon
     To stand 's° auspicious mistress.   *To act as his*
40   GLOUCESTER   But where is he?
BASTARD   Look, sir, I bleed.
GLOUCESTER   Where is the villain, Edmund?
BASTARD   Fled this way, sir, when by no means he could—
GLOUCESTER   Pursue him, go after!   [*Exeunt* SERVANTS.]
                    By no means—what?
BASTARD   —Persuade me to the murder of your lordship,
45   But that° I told him the revengive° gods   *In response to that / revenging*
     'Gainst parricides did all their thunders bend;
     Spoke with how manifold and strong a bond
     The child was bound to the father. Sir,
     In a fine,° seeing how loathly opposite° I stood   *Finally / opposed*
50   To his unnatural purpose, with fell° motion   *deadly*
     With his preparèd sword he charges home°   *strikes to the heart of*
     My unprovided° body, lanced° mine arm,   *unprotected / struck*
     But when he saw my best alarumed spirits,
     Bold in the quarrel's rights,[3] roused to the encounter,
55   Or° whether gasted° by the noise I made,[4]   *Either / frightened*
     But suddenly he fled.
GLOUCESTER   Let him fly far.
     Not in this land shall he remain uncaught,
     And found, dispatch.° The noble Duke, my master,   *And once found, killed*
     My worthy arch° and patron, comes tonight.   *lord*
60   By his authority I will proclaim it
     That he which finds him shall deserve our thanks,
     Bringing the murderous caitiff° to the stake.[5]   *wretch*
     He that conceals him, death.
BASTARD   When I dissuaded him from his intent
65   And found him pight° to do it, with cursed° speech   *resolved / bitter*
     I threatened to discover° him. He replied,   *expose*
     "Thou unpossessing bastard, dost thou think,
     If I would stand against thee, could the reposure°   *placing*
     Of any trust, virtue, or worth in thee
70   Make thy words faithed?° No. What I should deny—   *credible*
     As this I would, ay, though thou didst produce
     My very character[6]—I'd turn it all
     To[7] thy suggestion, plot, and damned pretence,°   *intent*
     And thou must make a dullard of the world
75   If they not thought the profits of my death

3. *my best . . . rights:* that I was fully roused to action,   one could be burned.
made brave by righteousness.   6. Handwriting; but also, a true summary of my
4. From the jumbled syntax, it appears likely that Q   character.
has accidentally omitted a verse line.   7. *I'd . . . To:* I'd blame it all on.
5. Treachery and rebellion were crimes for which

[*He wounds his arm.*] Some blood drawn on me would beget
    opinion°   *produce the impression*
  Of my more fierce endeavor. I have seen drunkards
35 Do more than this in sport. [*He shouts.*] Father, father!
  Stop, stop! No help?
               Enter GLOUCESTER *and* SERVANTS, *with torches.*
GLOUCESTER   Now, Edmond, where's the villain?
EDMOND   Here stood he in the dark, his sharp sword out,
  Mumbling of wicked charms, conjuring the moon
40 To stand° auspicious mistress.   *To act as his*
GLOUCESTER   But where is he?
EDMOND   Look, sir, I bleed.
GLOUCESTER   Where is the villain, Edmond?
EDMOND   Fled this way, sir, when by no means he could—
GLOUCESTER   Pursue him, ho, go after.   [*Exeunt* SERVANTS.]
45   —By no means—what?
EDMOND   —Persuade me to the murder of your lordship,
  But that° I told him the revenging gods   *In response to that*
  'Gainst parricides did all the thunder bend;
  Spoke with how manifold and strong a bond
50 The child was bound to th' father. Sir, in fine,°   *finally*
  Seeing how loathly opposite° I stood   *opposed*
  To his unnatural purpose, in fell° motion   *deadly*
  With his preparèd sword he charges home°   *strikes to the heart of*
  My unprovided° body, latched° mine arm,   *unprotected / struck*
55 And when he saw my best alarumed spirits
  Bold in the quarrel's right,[3] roused to th'encounter,
  Or whether gasted° by the noise I made,   *frightened*
  Full suddenly he fled.
GLOUCESTER   Let him fly far.
  Not in this land shall he remain uncaught,
60 And found, dispatch.° The noble Duke, my master,   *And once found, killed*
  My worthy arch° and patron, comes tonight.   *lord*
  By his authority I will proclaim it,
  That he which finds him shall deserve our thanks,
  Bringing the murderous coward to the stake.[4]
65 He that conceals him, death.
EDMOND   When I dissuaded him from his intent,
  And found him pight° to do it, with curst° speech   *resolved / bitter*
  I threatened to discover° him. He replied,   *expose*
  "Thou unpossessing bastard, dost thou think,
70 If I would stand against thee, would the reposal°   *placing*
  Of any trust, virtue, or worth in thee
  Make thy words faithed?° No, what should I deny—   *credible*
  As this I would, though thou didst produce
  My very character[5]—I'd turn it all
75 To[6] thy suggestion, plot, and damnèd practice,°   *scheming*
  And thou must make a dullard of the world,
  If they not thought the profits of my death

---

3. *my best . . . right:* that I was fully roused to action, made brave by righteousness.
4. Treachery and rebellion were crimes for which one could be burned.
5. Handwriting; but also, a true summary of my character.
6. *I'd . . . To:* I'd blame it all on.

Were very pregnant and potential spurs
To make thee seek it."[8]
GLOUCESTER   Strong° and fastened° villain,   *Flagrant / incorrigible*
Would he deny his letter? I never got° him!   *begot*
    [*A sennet sounds.*]
Hark, the Duke's trumpets! I know not why he comes.
80   All ports° I'll bar. The villain shall not scape;   *seaports; exits*
The Duke must grant me that. Besides, his picture
I will send far and near, that all the kingdom
May have note of him[9] and of my land.
Loyal and natural° boy, I'll work the means   *loving; illegitimate*
85   To make thee capable.°   *legally able to inherit*
       Enter the Duke of CORNWALL [*and* REGAN].
CORNWALL How now, my noble friend? Since I came hither,
Which I can call but now, I have heard strange news.
REGAN If it be true, all vengeance comes too short
Which can pursue the offender. How dost my lord?
90   GLOUCESTER Madam, my old heart is cracked, is cracked.
REGAN What, did my father's godson seek your life?
He whom my father named, your Edgar?
GLOUCESTER Ay, lady, lady; shame would have it hid.
REGAN Was he not companion with the riotous knights
95   That tends° upon my father?   *attend*
GLOUCESTER I know not, madam. 'Tis too bad, too bad.
BASTARD Yes, madam, he was.
REGAN No marvel, then, though° he were ill affected.°   *that / ill disposed*
'Tis they have put him on° the old man's death   *have urged him to seek*
100   To have the waste and spoil of his revenues.
I have this present evening from my sister
Been well informed of them, and with such cautions
That if they come to sojourn at my house,
I'll not be there.
CORNWALL   Nor I, assure thee, Regan.
105   Edmund, I heard that you have shown your father
A childlike office.°   *filial service*
BASTARD   'Twas my duty, sir.
GLOUCESTER He did betray his practice° and received   *uncover his (Edgar's) plot*
This hurt you see, striving to apprehend him.
CORNWALL Is he pursued?
GLOUCESTER   Ay, my good lord.
110   CORNWALL If he be taken, he shall never more
Be feared of doing harm. Make your own purpose
How in my strength you please.[1] For you, Edmund,
Whose virtue and obedience doth this instant
So much commend itself, you shall be ours.
115   Natures of such deep trust we shall much need;
You we first seize on.
BASTARD I shall serve you truly, however else.°   *if nothing else*
GLOUCESTER For him, I thank your grace.

---

8. *And thou . . . it:* And do you think the world so stupid that it could not see the benefit you would get from
my death (and thus a motive for plotting to kill me)?
pregnant: full. *potential spurs:* powerful temptations.
9. Likenesses of outlaws were drawn up, printed,
and publicly displayed, sometimes with an offer of
reward as in "Wanted" posters.
1. *Make . . . please:* Devise your plots making use of
my forces and authority as you see fit.

Were very pregnant and potential spirits
To make thee seek it."[7]

GLOUCESTER   Oh, strange° and fastened° villain,   *unnatural / incorrigible*
80 Would he deny his letter, said he?
              Tucket° within.   *Flourish of trumpets*
Hark, the Duke's trumpets. I know not where he comes.
All ports° I'll bar. The villain shall not scape;   *seaports; exits*
The Duke must grant me that. Besides, his picture
I will send far and near, that all the kingdom
85 May have due note of him,[8] and of my land,
Loyal and natural° boy, I'll work the means   *loving; illegitimate*
To make thee capable.°   *legally able to inherit*
              Enter CORNWALL, REGAN, *and Attendants.*
CORNWALL   How now, my noble friend? Since I came hither,
Which I can call but now, I have heard strangeness.
90 REGAN   If it be true, all vengeance comes too short
Which can pursue th'offender. How dost my lord?
GLOUCESTER   O madam, my old heart is cracked; it's cracked.
REGAN   What, did my father's godson seek your life?
He whom my father named, your Edgar?
95 GLOUCESTER   O lady, lady, shame would have it hid.
REGAN   Was he not companion with the riotous knights
That tended° upon my father?   *attend*
GLOUCESTER   I know not, madam. 'Tis too bad, too bad.
EDMOND   Yes, madam, he was of that consort.°   *company*
100 REGAN   No marvel, then, though° he were ill affected.°   *that / ill disposed*
'Tis they have put him on° the old man's death   *have urged him to seek*
To have th'expense° and waste of his revenues.   *use*
I have this present evening from my sister
Been well informed of them, and with such cautions
105 That if they come to sojourn at my house,
I'll not be there.
CORNWALL   Nor I, assure thee, Regan.
Edmond, I hear that you have shown your father
A childlike office.°   *filial service*
EDMOND   It was my duty, sir.
GLOUCESTER   He did bewray his practice° and received   *uncover his (Edgar's) plot*
110 This hurt you see, striving to apprehend him.
CORNWALL   Is he pursued?
GLOUCESTER   Ay, my good lord.
CORNWALL   If he be taken, he shall never more
Be feared of doing harm. Make your own purpose
How in my strength you please.[9] For you, Edmond,
115 Whose virtue and obedience doth this instant
So much commend itself, you shall be ours.
Natures of such deep trust we shall much need;
You we first seize on.
EDMOND   I shall serve you, sir, truly, however else.°   *if nothing else*
120 GLOUCESTER   For him, I thank your grace.

---

7. *And thou . . . it:* And do you think the world so stupid that it could not see the benefit you would get from my death (and thus a motive for plotting to kill me)? *pregnant:* full. *potential spirits:* powerful temptations.
8. Likenesses of outlaws were drawn up, printed, and publicly displayed, sometimes with an offer of reward as in "Wanted" posters.
9. *Make . . . please:* Devise your plots making use of my forces and authority as you see fit.

CORNWALL   You know not why we came to visit you?

120 REGAN   Thus out of season—threat'ning dark-eyed night—

Occasions, noble Gloucester, of some poise,°   weight

Wherein we must have use of your advice.

Our father he hath writ—so hath our sister—

Of differences,° which I best thought it fit   quarrels

125 To answer from° our home. The several° messengers   away from / various

From hence attend° dispatch. Our good old friend,   await

Lay comforts to your bosom and bestow your needful°   badly needed

  counsel

To our business, which craves the instant use.[2]

GLOUCESTER   I serve you, madam. Your graces are right

  welcome.   *Exeunt.*

2.2 (F 2.2)

Enter KENT [*disguised as Caius*] *and* [*Oswald the*]
STEWARD.

STEWARD   Good even° to thee, friend. Art° of the house?   *evening / Are you a servant*

KENT   Ay.

STEWARD   Where may we set our horses?

KENT   I'th' mire.

5 STEWARD   Prithee, if thou love me,° tell me.   *if you will be so kind*

KENT   I love thee not.

STEWARD   Why, then, I care not for thee.

KENT   If I had thee in Lipsbury pinfold,[1] I would make thee
  care for me.

10 STEWARD   Why dost thou use° me thus? I know thee not.   *treat*

KENT   Fellow, I know thee.

STEWARD   What dost thou know me for?

KENT   A knave, a rascal, an eater of broken meats,° a base,   *scraps*
  proud, shallow, beggarly, three-suited, hundred pound, filthy,

15 worsted-stocking knave,[2] a lily-livered, action-taking knave,
  a whoreson, glass-gazing, superfinical rogue, one-trunk-
  inheriting slave,[3] one that wouldst be a bawd in way of good
  service[4] and art nothing but the composition° of a knave,   *combination*
  beggar, coward, pander, and the son and heir of a mongrel

20 bitch, whom I will beat into clamorous whining if thou deny
  the least syllable of the addition.[5]

STEWARD   What a monstrous fellow art thou thus to rail on
  one that's neither known of° thee nor knows thee.   *by*

KENT   What a brazen-faced varlet° art thou to deny thou   *rascal*

25 knowest me! Is it two days ago since I beat thee and tripped
  up thy heels before the King? [*He draws his sword.*] Draw,

---

2. Which requires immediate attention.
2.2 Location: Before Gloucester's house.
1. If I had you in the enclosure of my mouth (gripped
in my teeth). Lipsbury is probably an invented place-
name. *pinfold:* pen, animal enclosure.
2. *three-suited . . . knave:* Oswald is being called a poor
imitation of a gentleman. Servants were permitted
three suits a year; one hundred pounds was the minimum qualification for the purchase of one of King
James's knighthoods; a gentleman would wear stock-

ings of silk, not "worsted" (thick woolen material).
3. *lily-livered:* cowardly. *action-taking:* litigious, one
who would rather use the law than his fists. *glass-
gazing:* mirror-gazing. *superfinical:* overly finicky, fastidious. *one-trunk-inheriting:* owning only what would
fill one trunk.
4. *one that . . . service:* one who would even be a
pimp if called upon.
5. Of the descriptions Kent has just applied to him.
addition: title (used ironically).

CORNWALL   You know not why we came to visit you?

REGAN   Thus out of season, threading dark-eyed night?
Occasions, noble Gloucester, of some prize,°   *weight*
Wherein we must have use of your advice.

125   Our father, he hath writ—so hath our sister—
Of differences,° which I best thought it fit   *quarrels*
To answer from° our home. The several° messengers   *away from / various*
From hence attend° dispatch. Our good old friend,   *await*
Lay comforts to your bosom and bestow

130   Your needful° counsel to our businesses,   *badly needed*
Which craves the instant use.[1]

GLOUCESTER   I serve you, madam.
Your graces are right welcome.   *Exeunt. Flourish.*

2.2 (Q 2.2)

Enter KENT [*disguised as Caius*] *and* [*Oswald the*]
STEWARD *severally.*°   *separately*

STEWARD   Good dawning to thee, friend. Art° of this house?   *Are you a servant*

KENT   Ay.

STEWARD   Where may we set our horses?

KENT   I'th' mire.

5   STEWARD   Prithee, if thou lov'st me,° tell me.   *if you will be so kind*

KENT   I love thee not.

STEWARD   Why, then, I care not for thee.

KENT   If I had thee in Lipsbury pinfold,[1] I would make thee
care for me.

10   STEWARD   Why dost thou use° me thus? I know thee not.   *treat*

KENT   Fellow, I know thee.

STEWARD   What dost thou know me for?

KENT   A knave, a rascal, an eater of broken meats,° a base,   *scraps*
proud, shallow, beggarly, three-suited, hundred pound, filthy,

15   worsted-stocking knave,[2] a lily-livered, action-taking, whoreson, glass-gazing, super-serviceable finical rogue, one-trunk-
inheriting slave,[3] one that wouldst be a bawd in way of good
service[4] and art nothing but the composition° of a knave,   *combination*
beggar, coward, pander, and the son and heir of a mongrel

20   bitch. One whom I will beat into clamors whining if thou
deny'st the least syllable of thy addition.[5]

STEWARD   Why, what a monstrous fellow art thou thus to rail
on one that is neither known of° thee nor knows thee!   *by*

KENT   What a brazen-faced varlet° art thou to deny thou know-   *rascal*

25   est me! Is it two days since I tripped up thy heels and beat
thee before the King? [*He draws his sword.*] Draw, you rogue, for

---

1. Which requires immediate attention.
2.2 Location: Before Gloucester's house.
1. If I had you in the enclosure of my mouth (gripped
in my teeth). Lipsbury is probably an invented place-
name. *pinfold:* pen, animal enclosure.
2. *three-suited . . . knave:* Oswald is being called a poor
imitation of a gentleman. Servants were permitted
three suits a year; one hundred pounds was the minimum qualification for the purchase of one of King
James's knighthoods; a gentleman would wear stockings of silk, not "worsted" (thick woolen material).

3. *lily-livered:* cowardly. *action-taking:* litigious; one
who would rather use the law than his fists. *glass-
gazing:* mirror-gazing. *super-serviceable:* overly officious, or too ready to serve. *finical:* finicky, fastidious.
one-trunk-inheriting: owning only what would fill one
trunk.
4. *one that . . . service:* one who would even be a
pimp if called upon.
5. Of the descriptions Kent has just applied to him.
addition: title (used ironically).

you rogue, for though it be night, the moon shines. I'll make
a sop of the moonshine[6] o'you. Draw, you whoreson, cullionly barber-monger![7] Draw!

30 STEWARD   Away, I have nothing to do with thee.

KENT   Draw, you rascal! You bring letters against the King,
and take Vanity the puppet's part against the royalty of her
father.[8] Draw, you rogue, or I'll so carbonado[9] your shanks—
Draw, you rascal! Come your ways!°   *Come forward*
  [*He beats him.*]

35 STEWARD   Help, ho, murder, help!

KENT   Strike, you slave! Stand, rogue! Stand, you neat° slave.   *elegant; foppish*
Strike!

STEWARD   Help, ho, murder, help!
  Enter Edmund [the BASTARD] *with his rapier drawn,*
  GLOUCESTER, *the Duke and Duchess [*CORNWALL
  and REGAN].

BASTARD   How now, what's the matter?

40 KENT   With you, goodman boy, an't° you please. Come, I'll   *if*
flesh you.[1] Come on, young master!

GLOUCESTER   Weapons? Arms? What's the matter here?

CORNWALL   Keep peace, upon your lives. He dies that strikes
again! What's the matter?

45 REGAN   The messengers from our sister and the King?

CORNWALL   What's your difference?° Speak.   *quarrel*

STEWARD   I am scarce in breath, my lord.

KENT   No marvel; you have so bestirred your valor, you
cowardly rascal. Nature disclaims° in thee. A tailor made   *disowns her part*
50 thee![2]

CORNWALL   Thou art a strange fellow! A tailor make a man?

KENT   Ay, a tailor, sir. A stonecutter or a painter could not
have made him so ill,° though he had been but two hours at   *so badly*
the trade.

55 GLOUCESTER   Speak yet: how grew your quarrel?

STEWARD   This ancient ruffian, sir, whose life I have spared at
suit of° his gray beard—   *on account of*

KENT [*to* STEWARD]   Thou whoreson zed,[3] thou unnecessary
letter! —My lord, if you'll give me leave, I will tread this
60 unbolted° villain into mortar and daub the walls of a jakes°   *unsifted; coarse /*
with him. [*to* STEWARD] "Spare my gray beard," you wag-tail![4]   *privy; toilet*

CORNWALL   Peace, sir! You beastly knave, you have no
reverence.°   *respect*

KENT   Yes, sir, but anger has a privilege.

65 CORNWALL   Why art thou angry?

---

6. Kent proposes to skewer and pierce Oswald so that
his body might be made into something insubstantial
(like moonshine). Alternatively, perhaps Kent is proposing to scramble Oswald's body into a substance
resembling the popular sixteenth- and seventeenth-
century pudding called "eggs in moonshine." *sop*:
piece of bread to be steeped or dunked in soup.
7. *cullionly barber-monger*: despicable frequenter of
hairdressers. *cullion*: testicle.
8. *and take . . . father*: and support Gonorill, here
depicted as a dressed-up doll whose pride is contrasted with Lear's kingliness.
9. Slash or score as one would the surface of meat in
preparation for broiling.

1. I'll initiate you into fighting, as a hunting dog is
given the taste of blood to rouse it for the chase.
2. Tailors, considered effeminate, were stock objects
of mockery. Kent has suggested that Oswald is
worthless apart from the value he derives from his
external garments.
3. The letter Z (zed) was considered superfluous
because it could be replaced by S; consequently, it
was omitted from many dictionaries.
4. A common English bird that takes its name from
the up-and-down flicking of its tail; this, and its
characteristic hopping from foot to foot, causes it to
appear nervous. Alternatively, a contemptuous term
for a harlot.

though it be night, yet the moon shines. I'll make a sop o'th'
moonshine of you,[6] you whoreson, cullionly barber-monger.[7]
Draw!

30 STEWARD   Away, I have nothing to do with thee.

KENT   Draw, you rascal! You come with letters against the
King and take Vanity the puppet's part against the royalty
of her father?[8] Draw, you rogue, or I'll so carbonado[9] your
shanks—Draw, you rascal! Come your ways!°   *Come forward*
[*He beats him.*]

35 STEWARD   Help, ho, murder, help!

KENT   Strike, you slave! Stand, rogue! Stand, you neat° slave!   *elegant; foppish*
Strike!

STEWARD   Help, ho, murder, murder!

Enter [EDMOND *the*] *bastard*, CORNWALL, REGAN,
GLOUCESTER, SERVANTS.

EDMOND   How now, what's the matter? Part!

40 KENT [*to* STEWARD]   With you, goodman boy, if you please.
Come, I'll flesh ye.[1] Come on, young master.

GLOUCESTER   Weapons? Arms? What's the matter here?

CORNWALL   Keep peace, upon your lives! He dies that strikes
again! What is the matter?

45 REGAN   The messengers from our sister and the King?

CORNWALL   What is your difference?° Speak.   *quarrel*

STEWARD   I am scarce in breath, my lord.

KENT   No marvel; you have so bestirred your valor, you
cowardly rascal. Nature disclaims° in thee. A tailor[2] made   *disowns her part*

50 thee!

CORNWALL   Thou art a strange fellow. A tailor make a man?

KENT   A tailor, sir. A stonecutter or a painter could not have
made him so ill,° though they had been but two years o'th'°   *so badly / at the*
trade.

55 CORNWALL   Speak yet: how grew your quarrel?

STEWARD   This ancient ruffian, sir, whose life I have spared at
suit of° his gray beard—   *on account of*

KENT [*to* STEWARD]   Thou whoreson zed,[3] thou unnecessary
letter! —My lord, if you will give me leave, I will tread

60 this unbolted° villain into mortar and daub the wall of a   *unsifted; coarse*
jakes° with him. [*to* STEWARD] "Spare my gray beard," you   *privy; toilet*
wagtail![4]

CORNWALL   Peace, sirrah!

You beastly knave, know you no reverence?°   *respect*

65 KENT   Yes, sir, but anger hath a privilege.

CORNWALL   Why art thou angry?

---

6. Kent proposes to skewer and pierce Oswald so that
his body might be made into something insubstantial
(like moonshine). Alternatively, perhaps Kent is proposing to scramble Oswald's body into a substance
resembling the popular sixteenth- and seventeenth-
century pudding called "eggs in moonshine." *sop*:
piece of bread to be steeped or dunked in soup.
7. *cullionly barber-monger*: despicable frequenter of
hairdressers. *cullion*: testicle.
8. *and take . . . father*: and support Gonerill, here
depicted as a dressed-up doll whose pride is contrasted with Lear's kingliness.
9. Slash or score, as one would the surface of meat in
preparation for broiling.

1. I'll initiate you into fighting, as a hunting dog is
given the taste of blood to rouse it for the chase.
2. Tailors, considered effeminate, were stock objects
of mockery. Kent has suggested that Oswald is worthless apart from the value he derives from his external
garments.
3. The letter Z (zed) was considered superfluous
because it could be replaced by S; consequently, it was
omitted from many dictionaries.
4. A common English bird that takes its name from
the up-and-down flicking of its tail; this, and its
characteristic hopping from foot to foot, causes it to
appear nervous. Alternatively, a contemptuous term
for a harlot.

KENT   That such a slave as this should wear a sword
    That° wears no honesty. Such smiling rogues   *Who*
    As these like rats oft bite those cords⁵ in twain
    Which are too entrench° to unloose; smooth° every passion   *intricate / flatter*
70   That in the natures of their lords rebel,
    Being oil to fire, snow to their colder moods,
    Renege,° affirm, and turn their halcyon beaks⁶   *Deny*
    With every gale and vary° of their masters,   *mood*
    Knowing naught like days but following.
75   A plague upon your epileptic° visage!   *distorted; grimacing*
    Smoile you° my speeches as° I were a fool?   *Do you smile at / as if*
    Goose, an I had you upon Sarum plain,
    I'd send you cackling home to Camelot.⁷
CORNWALL   What, art thou mad, old fellow?
80 GLOUCESTER   How fell you out? Say that.
KENT   No contraries° hold more antipathy   *opposites*
    Than I and such a knave.
CORNWALL   Why dost thou call him knave? What's his
        offense?
KENT   His countenance likes° me not.   *pleases*
85 CORNWALL   No more perchance does mine, or his, or hers.
KENT   Sir, 'tis my occupation to be plain.
    I have seen better faces in my time
    Than stands on any shoulder that I see
    Before me at this instant.
90 CORNWALL   This is a fellow who, having been praised
    For bluntness, doth affect a saucy roughness
    And constrains the garb quite from his nature.⁸
    He cannot flatter, he; he must be plain;
    He must speak truth, an they will take't so;
95   If not, he's plain.⁹ These kind of knaves I know,
    Which in this plainness harbor more craft
    And more corrupter ends than twenty silly ducking
    Observants that stretch their duties nicely.¹
KENT   Sir, in good sooth, or in sincere verity,
100   Under the allowance of your grand aspect,²
    Whose influence like the wreath of radiant fire
    In flickering Phoebus' front°—   *the sun god's forehead*
CORNWALL   What mean'st thou by this?
KENT   To go out of my dialogue,° which you discommend so *normal mode of speech*
105   much. I know, sir, I am no flatterer. He that beguiled you in
    a plain accent was a plain knave, which for my part I will not

---

5. Bonds of kinship, affection, marriage, or rank.
6. It was believed that the kingfisher (in Greek, *halcyon*) could be used as a weather vane when dead: suspended by a fine thread, its beak would turn whatever way the wind blew.
7. *Goose . . . Camelot:* Comparing him to a cackling goose, Kent tells Oswald that if he had him on Salisbury Plain, he would drive him all the way to Camelot, the legendary home of King Arthur.
8. *And constrains . . . nature:* and assumes the appearance although it is untrue to his real self. Alternatively (with "his" meaning "its"): and distorts the true shape

of plainness from what it naturally is (by turning it into disrespect).
9. If they will accept (Kent's attitude), well and good; if not, he is a plainspoken man (and does not care).
1. *than . . . nicely:* than twenty obsequious attendants who constantly bow idiotically and who perform their functions with excessive diligence ("nicely").
2. With the permission of your great countenance. "Aspect" also refers to the astrological position of a planet; Kent's bombastic language here raises Cornwall to the mock-heroic proportions of a heavenly body.

KENT   That such a slave as this should wear a sword
    Who wears no honesty. Such smiling rogues as these
    Like rats oft bite the holy cords[5] a-twain,
70   Which are t'intrince° t'unloose; smooth° every passion   *too intricate / flatter*
    That in the natures of their lords rebel,
    Being oil to fire, snow to the colder moods,
    Revenge affirm, and turn their halcyon beaks[6]
    With every gall and vary° of their masters,   *irritation and mood*
75   Knowing naught, like dogs, but following.
    A plague upon your epileptic° visage!   *distorted; grimacing*
    Smoile you° my speeches as° I were a fool?   *Do you smile at / as if*
    Goose, if I had you upon Sarum Plain,
    I'd drive ye cackling home to Camelot.[7]
80   CORNWALL   What, art thou mad, old fellow?
    GLOUCESTER   How fell you out? Say that.
    KENT   No contraries° hold more antipathy   *opposites*
    Than I and such a knave.
    CORNWALL   Why dost thou call him knave? What is his
      fault?°   *offense*
85   KENT   His countenance likes° me not.   *pleases*
    CORNWALL   No more, perchance, does mine, nor his, nor
      hers.
    KENT   Sir, 'tis my occupation to be plain.
    I have seen better faces in my time
    Than stands on any shoulder that I see
    Before me at this instant.
90   CORNWALL   This is some fellow
    Who, having been praised for bluntness, doth affect
    A saucy roughness and constrains the garb
    Quite from his nature.[8] He cannot flatter, he.
    An honest mind and plain, he must speak truth
95   An they will take it so; if not, he's plain.[9]
    These kind of knaves I know, which in this plainness
    Harbor more craft and more corrupter ends
    Than twenty silly-ducking observants
    That stretch their duties nicely.[1]
100 KENT   Sir, in good faith, in sincere verity,
    Under th'allowance of your great aspect,[2]
    Whose influence like the wreath of radiant fire
    On flick'ring Phoebus' front°—   *the sun god's forehead*
    CORNWALL   What mean'st by this?
    KENT   To go out of my dialect,° which you discommend so   *normal mode of speech*
105   much. I know, sir, I am no flatterer. He that beguiled you in
    a plain accent was a plain knave, which for my part I will not

---

5. Bonds of kinship, affection, marriage, or rank.
6. It was believed that the kingfisher (in Greek, *halcyon*) could be used as a weather vane when dead: suspended by a fine thread, its beak would turn whatever way the wind blew.
7. *Goose . . . Camelot:* Comparing him to a cackling goose, Kent tells Oswald that if he had him on Salisbury Plain, he would drive him all the way to Camelot, the legendary home of King Arthur.
8. *and constrains . . . nature:* and assumes the appearance although it is untrue to his real self. Alternatively (with "his" meaning "its"): and distorts the true

shape of plainness from what it naturally is (by turning it into disrespect).
9. If they will accept (Kent's attitude), well and good; if not, he is a plainspoken man (and does not care).
1. *Than . . . nicely:* Than twenty obsequious attendants who constantly bow idiotically and who perform their functions with excessive diligence ("nicely").
2. With the permission of your great countenance. "Aspect" also refers to the astrological position of a planet; Kent's bombastic language here raises Cornwall to the mock-heroic proportions of a heavenly body.

be, though I should win your displeasure to entreat me to't.[3]

CORNWALL [to STEWARD]   What's the offense you gave him?

STEWARD   I never gave him any.

110 It pleased the King his master very late°   lately
To strike at me upon his misconstruction,°   misunderstanding (me)
When he, conjunct° and flattering his displeasure,   in league with
Tripped me behind; being down, insulted,° railed,   I being down, he insulted
And put upon him such a deal of man that,

115 That worthied him,[4] got praises of the King;
For him attempting who was self-subdued,[5]
And in the fleshment° of this dread exploit   excitement; flush
Drew on me here again.

KENT   None of these rogues and cowards, but Ajax is their
120 fool.[6]

CORNWALL   Bring forth the stocks, ho!
You stubborn miscreant knave, you reverend° braggart,   old; revered
We'll teach you.

KENT   I am too old to learn.
Call not your stocks for me. I serve the King,
125 On whose employments I was sent to you.
You should do small respect, show too bold malice,
Against the grace° and person° of my master,   majesty / personal honor
Stopping° his messenger.   By stocking

CORNWALL   Fetch forth the stocks! As I have life and honor,
130 There shall he sit till noon.

REGAN   Till noon? Till night, my lord, and all night too.

KENT   Why, madam, if I were your father's dog,
You could not use me so.

REGAN   Sir, being° his knave, I will.   since you are

135 CORNWALL   This is a fellow of the selfsame nature
Our sister° speak of. —Come, bring away the stocks.   sister-in-law
[Enter a SERVANT with the stocks.]

GLOUCESTER   Let me beseech your grace not to do so;
His fault is much, and the good King his master
Will check° him for't. Your purposed° low correction   reprimand / intended
140 Is such as basest and 'temnest° wretches   condemnest; most condemned
For pilf'rings and most common trespasses
Are punished with. The King must take it ill
That he's so slightly valued in his messenger,
Should have him thus restrained.

CORNWALL   I'll answer° that.   be responsible for

145 REGAN   My sister may receive it much more worse
To have her gentlemen abused, assaulted,
For following° her affairs. —Put in his legs.   carrying out
[KENT is put in the stocks.]
Come, my good lord, away.
[Exeunt all but GLOUCESTER and KENT.]

GLOUCESTER [to KENT]   I am sorry for thee, friend. 'Tis the
Duke's pleasure,
150 Whose disposition all the world well knows
Will not be rubbed° nor stopped. I'll entreat for thee.   obstructed

---

3. He that . . . to't: The person who tried to hood-wink you with plain speaking was, indeed, a pure knave—something I won't be, even if you were to beg me to be one (a plain knave, or flatterer).
4. And put . . . worthied him: And put on such a show of manliness that he was thought a worthy fellow.

5. For attacking a man who had already surrendered (Kent attacking Oswald).
6. None . . . fool: Such rogues and cowards as these talk as if they were greater warriors (and blusterers) than Ajax; such rogues always make even mighty Ajax out to be a fool.

be, though I should win your displeasure to entreat me to't.[3]

CORNWALL [*to* STEWARD]   What was th'offense you gave him?

STEWARD   I never gave him any.

110 It pleased the King his master very late°   *lately*
    To strike at me upon his misconstruction,°   *misunderstanding (me)*
    When he, compact° and flattering his displeasure,   *in league with*
    Tripped me behind; being down, insulted,° railed,   *I being down, he insulted*
    And put upon him such a deal of man
115 That worthied him,[4] got praises of the King,
    For him attempting who was self-subdued,[5]
    And in the fleshment° of this dread exploit,   *excitement; flush*
    Drew on me here again.

KENT   None of these rogues and cowards
    But Ajax is their fool.[6]

120 CORNWALL   Fetch forth the stocks!

                       [*Exit a* SERVANT.]

    You stubborn, ancient knave, you reverend° braggart,   *old; revered*
    We'll teach you.

KENT   Sir, I am too old to learn.
    Call not your stocks for me. I serve the King,
    On whose employment I was sent to you.

125 You shall do small respects, show too bold malice
    Against the grace° and person° of my master,   *majesty / personal honor*
    Stocking° his messenger.   *By stocking*

CORNWALL   Fetch forth the stocks.
    As I have life and honor, there shall he sit till noon.

REGAN   Till noon? Till night, my lord, and all night too.

130 KENT   Why, madam, if I were your father's dog,
    You should not use me so.

REGAN   Sir, being° his knave, I will.   *since you are*

        Stocks brought out [*by a* SERVANT].

CORNWALL   This is a fellow of the selfsame color°   *character*
    Our sister° speaks of. —Come, bring away the stocks.   *sister-in-law*

135 GLOUCESTER   Let me beseech your grace not to do so;
    The King his master needs must take it ill
    That he, so slightly valued in his messenger,
    Should have him thus restrained.

CORNWALL   I'll answer° that.   *be responsible for*

REGAN   My sister may receive it much more worse
140 To have her gentleman abused, assaulted.

CORNWALL   Come, my lord, away.

        Exeunt [CORNWALL *and* REGAN].

GLOUCESTER   I am sorry for thee, friend. 'Tis the Duke's
    pleasure,
    Whose disposition, all the world well knows,
    Will not be rubbed° nor stopped. I'll entreat for thee.   *obstructed*

---

3. *He that . . . to't:* The person who tried to hood-wink you with plain speaking was, indeed, a pure knave—something I won't be, even if you were to beg me to be one (a plain knave, or flatterer).
4. *And put . . . worthied him:* And put on such a show of manliness that he was thought a worthy fellow.

5. For attacking a man who had already surrendered (Kent attacking Oswald).
6. *None . . . fool:* Such rogues and cowards as these talk as if they were greater warriors (and blusterers) than Ajax; such rogues always make even mighty Ajax out to be a fool.

KENT   Pray you, do not, sir. I have watched° and traveled   *gone without sleep*
        hard;
        Sometime I shall sleep on't, the rest I'll whistle.
        A good man's fortune may grow out at heels.[7]
155   Give° you good morrow.   *God give*
GLOUCESTER   The Duke's to blame in this; 'twill be ill
        took.   [*Exit.*]
KENT   Good King, that must approve° the common saw,°   *prove / saying*
        Thou out of heaven's benediction comest
        To the warm sun.[8]
160   [*He takes out a letter.*] Approach, thou beacon[9] to this
             underglobe,
        That by thy comfortable beams I may
        Peruse this letter. Nothing almost sees my wrack
        But misery.[1] I know 'tis from Cordelia,
        Who hath most fortunately been informed
165   Of my obscurèd° course and shall find time   *hidden; disguised*
        From this enormous state,° seeking to give   *awful state of affairs*
        Losses their remedies. All weary and overwatch,°   *too long awake*
        Take vantage,° heavy eyes, not to behold   *the opportunity*
        This shameful lodging. Fortune, good night;
170   Smile; once more turn thy wheel.[2]
             [*He*] *sleeps* [*and remains onstage*].
             Enter EDGAR.
EDGAR   I hear myself proclaimed°   *declared an outlaw*
        And by the happy° hollow of a tree   *opportune*
        Escaped the hunt. No port° is free; no place   *seaport; exit*
        That guard and most unusual vigilance
175   Dost not attend my taking.° While° I may scape   *await my capture / Until*
        I will preserve myself and am bethought°   *resolved*
        To take the basest and most poorest shape
        That ever penury in contempt of° man   *for*
        Brought near to beast. My face I'll grime with filth,
180   Blanket my loins, elf all my hair with knots,[3]
        And with presented° nakedness outface   *exposed*
        The wind and persecution of the sky.
        The country gives me proof and precedent
        Of Bedlam beggars, who, with roaring voices,
185   Strike° in their numbed and mortified° bare arms   *Stick / deadened*
        Pins, wooden pricks, nails, sprigs of rosemary,
        And with this horrible object° from low service,   *spectacle*
        Poor pelting° villages, sheepcotes, and mills,   *paltry; contemptible*
        Sometime with lunatic bans,° sometime with prayers,   *curses*
190   Enforce their charity. Poor Turlygod,[4] poor Tom!
        That's something yet. Edgar I nothing am.[5]   *Exit.*
             Enter King [LEAR, FOOL, *and a* KNIGHT].
LEAR   'Tis strange that they should so depart from hence
        And not send back my messenger.

---

7. The fortunes of even good men sometimes wear
thin.
8. *Thou . . . sun:* You come from the blessing of
heaven into the heat of the sun (go from good to bad).
9. That is, the sun.
1. *Nothing . . . misery:* Only those suffering misery
are granted miracles; any comfort seems miraculous
to those who are miserable.
2. The goddess Fortune was traditionally depicted

with a wheel to signify her mutability and caprice.
She was believed to take pleasure in arbitrarily lowering those at the top of her wheel and raising those
at the bottom.
3. Tangle the hair into "elf locks," supposed to be a
favorite trick of malicious elves.
4. A word of unknown origin.
5. Edgar, I am nothing; I am no longer Edgar.

145 KENT   Pray, do not, sir. I have watched° and traveled hard;   *gone without sleep*
　　　　Some time I shall sleep out, the rest I'll whistle.
　　　　A good man's fortune may grow out at heels.[7]
　　　　Give° you good morrow.   *God give*
　　GLOUCESTER   The Duke's to blame in this; 'twill be ill
　　　　taken.   *Exit.*
150 KENT   Good King, that must approve° the common saw,°   *prove / saying*
　　　　Thou out of heaven's benediction com'st
　　　　To the warm sun.[8]
　　　　Approach, thou beacon[9] to this under-globe,
　　　　That by thy comfortable beams I may
155 　　　Peruse this letter. Nothing almost sees miracles
　　　　But misery.[1] I know 'tis from Cordelia,
　　　　Who hath most fortunately been informed
　　　　Of my obscurèd° course and shall find time   *hidden; disguised*
　　　　From this enormous state,° seeking to give   *awful state of affairs*
160 　　　Losses their remedies. All weary and o'er-watched,°   *too long awake*
　　　　Take vantage,° heavy eyes, not to behold   *the opportunity*
　　　　This shameful lodging. Fortune, goodnight,
　　　　Smile once more; turn thy wheel.[2]
　　　　　[*Sleeps and remains onstage.*]
　　　　　Enter EDGAR.
　　EDGAR   I heard myself proclaimed°   *declared an outlaw*
165 　　And by the happy° hollow of a tree   *opportune*
　　　　Escaped the hunt. No port° is free; no place   *seaport; exit*
　　　　That guard and most unusual vigilance
　　　　Does not attend my taking.° Whiles° I may scape,   *await my capture / Until*
　　　　I will preserve myself and am bethought°   *resolved*
170 　　To take the basest and most poorest shape
　　　　That ever penury in contempt of° man   *for*
　　　　Brought near to beast. My face I'll grime with filth,
　　　　Blanket my loins, elf all my hairs in knots,[3]
　　　　And with presented° nakedness outface   *exposed*
175 　　The winds and persecutions of the sky.
　　　　The country gives me proof and precedent
　　　　Of Bedlam beggars who, with roaring voices,
　　　　Strike° in their numbed and mortified° arms   *Stick / deadened*
　　　　Pins, wooden pricks, nails, sprigs of rosemary,
180 　　And with this horrible object° from low farms,   *spectacle*
　　　　Poor pelting° villages, sheepcotes, and mills,   *paltry; contemptible*
　　　　Sometimes with lunatic bans,° sometime with prayers,   *curses*
　　　　Enforce their charity. Poor Turlygod,[4] poor Tom.
　　　　That's something yet. Edgar I nothing am.[5]   *Exit.*
　　　　　Enter LEAR, FOOL, *and* GENTLEMAN.[6]
185 LEAR   'Tis strange that they should so depart from home
　　　　And not send back my messengers.

7. The fortunes of even good men sometimes wear thin.
8. *Thou . . . sun:* You come from the blessing of heaven into the heat of the sun (go from good to bad).
9. That is, the sun.
1. *Nothing . . . misery:* Only those suffering misery are granted miracles; any comfort seems miraculous to those who are miserable.
2. The goddess Fortune was traditionally depicted with a wheel to signify her mutability and caprice.

She was believed to take pleasure in arbitrarily lowering those at the top of her wheel and raising those at the bottom.
3. Tangle the hair into "elf locks," supposed to be a favorite trick of malicious elves.
4. A word of unknown origin.
5. Edgar, I am nothing; I am no longer Edgar.
6. F seems to reserve "Gentleman" for this particular character, who returns in 5.3.

KNIGHT As I learned, the night before there was
195 No purpose° of his remove.°   *intention / change of*
                                                                    residence
KENT Hail to thee, noble master.
LEAR How, mak'st thou this shame thy pastime?
FOOL Ha, ha, look, he wears crewel garters.[6]
      Horses are tied by the heels, dogs and bears
200 By th' neck, monkeys by th' loins, and men
      By th' legs. When a man's overlusty at legs,[7]
      Then he wears wooden netherstocks.°   *knee socks*
LEAR What's° he that hath so much thy place° mistook   *Who's / position*
      To set thee here?
205 KENT It is both he and she: your son° and daughter.   *son-in-law*
LEAR No.
KENT   Yes.
LEAR No, I say.
KENT   I say yea.
LEAR No, no, they would not.
KENT   Yes, they have.
LEAR By Jupiter, I swear no. They durst not do't;
210 They would not, could not do't. 'Tis worse than murder
      To do upon respect[8] such violent outrage.
      Resolve° me with all modest° haste which way   *Inform / reasonable*
      Thou mayst deserve or they purpose this usage
      Coming from us.
KENT   My lord, when at their home
215 I did commend° your highness' letters to them,   *deliver*
      Ere I was risen from the place that showed
      My duty kneeling, came there a reeking° post,°   *sweating / messenger*
      Stewed in his haste, half breathless, panting forth,
      From Gonorill his mistress, salutations,
220 Delivered letters 'spite of intermission,[9]
      Which presently° they read. On whose contents   *immediately*
      They summoned up their men,° straight° took horse,   *retinue / straightaway*
      Commanded me to follow and attend the leisure
      Of their answer, gave me cold looks,
225 And meeting here the other messenger,
      Whose welcome I perceived had poisoned mine—
      Being the very° fellow that of late   *same*
      Displayed so saucily° against your highness—   *Acted so insolently*
      Having more man° than wit° about me, drew.   *courage / sense*
230 He raised the house with loud and coward cries.
      Your son and daughter found this trespass worth°   *deserving of*
      This shame which here it suffers.

---

6. Worsted garters, punning on "cruel." Crewel is a
thin yarn made of twisted fibers. The Fool is actually
referring to the stocks in which Kent's feet are held.
7. When a man's liable to run away.

8. To do to one who deserves respect.
9. Regardless of interrupting me; despite the inter-
ruptions in his account (as he gasped for breath).

GENTLEMAN   As I learned,
   The night before there was no purpose in them°   *they had no intention*
   Of this remove.°   *change of residence*
KENT   Hail to thee, noble master.
LEAR   Ha? Mak'st thou this shame thy pastime?
KENT   No, my lord.
190 FOOL   Ha, ha, he wears cruel garters![7] Horses are tied by the
   heads, dogs and bears by th' neck, monkeys by th' loins, and
   men by th' legs. When a man's overlusty at legs,[8] then he
   wears wooden nether-stocks.°   *knee socks*
LEAR   What's° he that hath so much thy place° mistook   *Who's / position*
   To set thee here?
195 KENT   It is both he and she:
   Your son° and daughter.   *son-in-law*
LEAR   No.
KENT   Yes.
LEAR   No, I say.
200 KENT   I say yea.
LEAR   By Jupiter, I swear no.
KENT   By Juno,[9] I swear ay.
LEAR   They durst not do't;
   They could not, would not do't. 'Tis worse than murder
205 To do upon respect[1] such violent outrage.
   Resolve° me with all modest° haste which way   *Inform / reasonable*
   Thou mightst deserve, or they impose, this usage,
   Coming from us.
KENT   My lord, when at their home
   I did commend° your highness' letters to them,   *deliver*
210 Ere I was risen from the place that showed
   My duty kneeling, came there a reeking° post,°   *sweating / messenger*
   Stewed in his haste, half breathless, painting° forth   *panting*
   From Gonerill, his mistress, salutations,
   Delivered letters 'spite of intermission,[2]
215 Which presently° they read. On those contents   *immediately*
   They summoned up their meiny,° straight° took horse,   *retinue / straightaway*
   Commanded me to follow and attend
   The leisure of their answer, gave me cold looks,
   And meeting here the other messenger,
220 Whose welcome I perceived had poisoned mine—
   Being the very° fellow which of late   *same*
   Displayed so saucily° against your highness—   *Acted so insolently*
   Having more man° than wit° about me, drew.   *courage / sense*
   He raised the house with loud and coward cries.
225 Your son and daughter found this trespass worth°   *deserving of*
   The shame which here it suffers.

---

7. Worsted garters, punning on "crewel," a thin yarn.
The Fool is actually referring to the stocks in which
Kent's feet are held.
8. When a man's liable to run away.
9. Queen of the Roman gods and wife of Jupiter,

with whom she constantly quarreled.
1. To do to one who deserves respect.
2. Regardless of interrupting me; despite the inter-
ruptions in his account (as he gasped for breath).

LEAR   Oh, how this mother° swells up toward my heart!   *hysteria*
          Hysterica passio, down, thou climbing sorrow,[1]
235   Thy element's° below! Where is this daughter?   *natural place is*
KENT   With the Earl, sir: within.
LEAR   Follow me not; stay there.   [*Exit.*]
KNIGHT   Made you no more offense than what you speak of?
KENT   No. How chance the King comes with so small a train?
240 FOOL An° thou hadst been set in the stocks for that question,   *If*
          thou hadst well deserved it.
KENT   Why, Fool?
FOOL   We'll set thee to school to an ant, to teach thee there's
          no laboring in the winter.[2] All that follow their noses are led
245   by their eyes but blind men, and there's not a nose among a
          hundred but can smell him that's stinking.° Let go thy hold   *(as his fortunes decay)*
          when a great wheel runs down a hill, lest it break thy neck
          with following it. But the great one that goes up the hill,[3] let
          him draw thee after. When a wise man gives thee better
250   counsel, give me mine again. I would have none but knaves
          follow it, since a fool gives it.
          [*Sings.*]   That sir that serves for gain,
                              And follows but for form,
                              Will pack° when it begin to rain,   *pack up and go*
255   And leave thee in the storm.
                              But I will tarry; the Fool will stay,
                              And let the wise man fly.
                              The knave turns fool that runs away,[4]
                              The fool no knave, pardie.°   *by God (pardieu)*
260 KENT Where learned you this, Fool?
FOOL   Not in the stocks.
                    Enter LEAR *and* GLOUCESTER.
LEAR   Deny to speak with me? They're sick, they're weary?
          They traveled hard tonight? Mere justice.
          Ay, the images of revolt and flying off![5]
          Fetch me a better answer.

---

1. Hysterica . . . *sorrow: Hysterica passio* (a Latin expression originating in the Greek *steiros,* "suffering in the womb") was an inflammation of the senses. In Renaissance medicine, vapors from the abdomen were thought to rise up through the body, and in women, the uterus itself was thought to wander around.
2. Ants, proverbially prudent, store food in the summer and thus do not work in the winter. Implicitly, a wise person should know better than to look for sustenance to an old man who has fallen on wintry times.
3. A great wheel is a figure for Lear and of Fortune's wheel itself, which has swung downward.
4. The scoundrel who runs away is the real fool.
5. *images of:* signs of. *flying off:* desertion; insurrection.

FOOL   Winter's not gone yet, if the wild geese fly that way.[3]
    Fathers that wear rags
    Do make their children blind.[4]
230   But fathers that bear bags
    Shall see their children kind.
    Fortune, that arrant whore,
    Ne'er turns the key° to th' poor.   *opens the door*
    But for all this, thou shalt have as many dolors[5] for thy
235   daughters as thou canst tell° in a year.   *count*
LEAR   Oh, how this mother° swells up toward my heart!   *hysteria*
    Hysterica passio, down, thou climbing sorrow,[6]
    Thy element's° below! Where is this daughter?   *natural place is*
KENT   With the Earl, sir, here within.
240 LEAR   Follow me not. Stay here.   *Exit.*
GENTLEMAN   Made you no more offense but what you
    speak of?
KENT   None. How chance the King comes with so small a
    number?
245 FOOL   An thou hadst been set i'th' stocks for that question,
    thou'dst well deserved it.
KENT   Why, Fool?
FOOL   We'll set thee to school to an ant, to teach thee there's
    no laboring i'th' winter.[7] All that follow their noses are led
250   by their eyes but blind men, and there's not a nose among
    twenty but can smell him that's stinking.° Let go thy hold   *(as his fortunes decay)*
    when a great wheel runs down a hill,[8] lest it break thy neck
    with following. But the great one that goes upward, let him
    draw thee after. When a wise man gives thee better counsel,
255   give me mine again. I would have none but knaves follow it
    since a fool gives it.
    [*Sings.*]   That sir which serves and seeks for gain,
                   And follows but for form,
                   Will pack° when it begins to rain,   *pack up and go*
260   And leave thee in the storm,
                 But I will tarry; the Fool will stay,
                 And let the wise man fly.
                 The knave turns fool that runs away,[9]
                 The Fool no knave, pardie.°   *by God (pardieu)*
       Enter LEAR *and* GLOUCESTER.
265 KENT   Where learned you this, Fool?
FOOL   Not i'th' stocks, Fool.
LEAR   Deny to speak with me?
    They are sick? They are weary?
    They have traveled all the night? Mere fetches,°   *ruses; pretexts*
270   The images of revolt and flying off.[1]
    Fetch me a better answer.

---

3. Things will get worse according to such omens.
4. Blind to their father's needs.
5. Pains, sorrows; punning on "dollar," the English term for the German "thaler," a large silver coin.
6. Hysterica . . . *sorrow*: *Hysterica passio* (a Latin expression originating in the Greek *steiros*, "suffering in the womb") was an inflammation of the senses. In Renaissance medicine, vapors from the abdomen were thought to rise up through the body, and in women, the uterus itself was thought to wander around.

7. Ants, proverbially prudent, store food in the summer and thus do not work in the winter. Implicitly, a wise person should know better than to look for sustenance to an old man who has fallen on wintry times.
8. A great wheel is a figure for Lear and of Fortune's wheel itself, which has swung downward.
9. The scoundrel who runs away is the real fool.
1. *images of*: signs of. *flying off*: desertion; insurrection.

265 GLOUCESTER   My dear lord,
    You know the fiery quality° of the Duke,   *disposition*
    How unremoveable and fixed he is
    In his own course.
    LEAR   Vengeance, death, plague, confusion!°   *destruction*
270   What "fiery quality"? Why, Gloucester, Gloucester,
    I'd speak with the Duke of Cornwall and his wife.

    GLOUCESTER   Ay, my good lord.
    LEAR   The King would speak with Cornwall, the dear father
    Would with his daughter speak, commands her service.
275   "Fiery Duke"? Tell the hot Duke that Lear—
    No, but not yet, maybe he is not well.
    Infirmity doth still° neglect all office°   *always / obligation*
    Whereto our health is bound. We are not ourselves
    When nature, being oppressed, command the mind
280   To suffer with the body. I'll forbear,
    And am fallen out with my more headier will[6]
    To take° the indisposed and sickly fit   *mistake*
    For the sound man. Death on my state![7] Wherefore°   *Why*
    Should he sit here? This act persuades me
285   That this remotion° of the Duke and her   *remoteness; aloofness*
    Is practice° only. Give me my servant forth.   *trickery*
    Tell the Duke and 's wife I'll speak with them
    Now, presently.° Bid them come forth and hear me,   *at once*
    Or at their chamber door I'll beat the drum
290   Till it cry sleep to death.[8]
    GLOUCESTER   I would have all well betwixt you.
    LEAR   Oh, my heart, my heart!
    FOOL   Cry to it, nuncle, as the Cockney° did to the eels when *Londoner (city woman)*
    she put 'em i'th' paste° alive. She rapped 'em o'th' coxcombs°   *pie; pastry / heads*
295   with a stick and cried, "Down, wantons,° down!" 'Twas her   *rogues*
    brother that, in pure kindness to his horse, buttered his hay.[9]
               Enter Duke [of CORNWALL] *and* REGAN.
    LEAR   Good morrow to you both.
    CORNWALL   Hail to your grace.
        [KENT *here set at liberty.*]
    REGAN   I am glad to see your highness.
    LEAR   Regan, I think you are. I know what reason
300   I have to think so. If thou shouldst not be glad,
    I would divorce me from thy mother's tomb,
    Sepulch'ring° an adultress. [*to* KENT] Yea, are you free?   *Because it entombed*
    Some other time for that. —Beloved Regan,
    Thy sister is naught.° O Regan, she hath tied   *wicked; nothing*
305   Sharp-toothed unkindness, like a vulture, here.[1]
    I can scarce speak to thee. Thou'lt not believe

---

6. And disagree with my (earlier) more rash intention.
7. May my royal authority end (an oath). Ironically, this has already happened.
8. Till the noise kills sleep.
9. Like that of his sister (who wanted to make eel pie without killing the eels), his kindness was misplaced:

horses will not eat buttered hay. The anecdote about the eels is reminiscent of Lear's attempt earlier in the scene to quell his grieving heart: "*Hysterica passio*, down, thou climbing sorrow."
1. Lear probably gestures to his heart.

GLOUCESTER My dear lord,
You know the fiery quality° of the Duke, *disposition*
How unremovable and fixed he is
In his own course.
LEAR Vengeance, plague, death, confusion!° *destruction*
275 "Fiery"? What "quality"? Why, Gloucester, Gloucester,
I'll speak with the Duke of Cornwall and his wife.
GLOUCESTER Well, my good lord, I have informed them so.
LEAR Informed them? Dost thou understand me, man?
GLOUCESTER Ay, my good lord.
280 LEAR The King would speak with Cornwall. The dear father
Would with his daughter speak, commands, tends° service. *awaits*
Are they informed of this? My breath and blood!
Fiery? The fiery Duke? Tell the hot Duke that—
No, but not yet; maybe he is not well.
285 Infirmity doth still° neglect all office° *always / obligation*
Whereto our health is bound. We are not ourselves
When nature, being oppressed, commands the mind
To suffer with the body. I'll forbear
And am fallen out with my more headier will,[2]
290 To take° the indisposed and sickly fit *mistake*
For the sound man. Death on my state![3] Wherefore° *Why*
Should he sit here? This act persuades me
That this remotion° of the Duke and her *remoteness; aloofness*
Is practice° only. Give me my servant forth. *trickery*
295 Go tell the Duke and 's wife I'd speak with them
Now, presently.° Bid them come forth and hear me, *at once*
Or at their chamber door I'll beat the drum
Till it cry sleep to death.[4]
GLOUCESTER I would have all well betwixt you. *Exit.*
300 LEAR Oh, me, my heart! My rising heart! But down.
FOOL Cry to it, nuncle, as the Cockney° did to the eels when *Londoner (city woman)*
she put 'em i'th' paste° alive. She knapped 'em o'th' cox- *pie; pastry*
combs° with a stick and cried, "Down, wantons,° down!" *heads / rogues*
'Twas her brother that, in pure kindness to his horse, but-
305 tered his hay.[5]
Enter CORNWALL, REGAN, GLOUCESTER, [*and*]
SERVANTS.
LEAR Good morrow to you both.
CORNWALL Hail to your grace.
KENT *here set at liberty.*
REGAN I am glad to see your highness.
LEAR Regan, I think you are. I know what reason
I have to think so. If thou shouldst not be glad,
310 I would divorce me from thy mother's tomb,
Sepulch'ring° an adultress. [*to* KENT] Oh, are you free? *Because it entombed*
Some other time for that. —Beloved Regan,
Thy sister's naught!° O Regan, she hath tied *wicked; nothing*
Sharp-toothed unkindness, like a vulture, here.[6]
315 I can scarce speak to thee. Thou'lt not believe

2. And disagree with my (earlier) more rash intention.
3. May my royal authority end (an oath). Ironically, this has already happened.
4. Till the noise kills sleep.
5. Like that of his sister (who wanted to make eel pie without killing the eels), his kindness was misplaced:
horses will not eat buttered hay. The anecdote about the eels is reminiscent of Lear's attempt earlier in the scene to quell his grieving heart: "*Hysterica passio,* down, thou climbing sorrow."
6. Lear probably gestures to his heart.

Of how deprived a quality—O Regan!
REGAN   I pray, sir, take patience. I have hope
    You less know how to value her desert
310   Than she to slack her duty.[2]

LEAR   My curses on her!
REGAN   O sir, you are old;
    Nature° on you stands on the very verge   *Life*
    Of her confine.° You should be ruled and led   *Of its limit*
    By some discretion° that discerns your state   *discreet person*
315   Better than you yourself. Therefore, I pray
    That to our sister you do make return.
    Say you have wronged her, sir.
LEAR   Ask her forgiveness?
    Do you mark how this becomes the house?[3]
    Dear daughter, I confess that I am old;
320   Age° is unnecessary. [*He kneels.*] On my knees, I beg   *An old man*
    That you'll vouchsafe me raiment,° bed, and food.   *promise me clothing*
REGAN   Good sir, no more; these are unsightly tricks.
    Return you to my sister.
LEAR [*rising*]   No, Regan,
    She hath abated° me of half my train,   *deprived*
325   Looked black upon me, struck me with her tongue
    Most serpent-like upon the very heart.
    All° the stored vengeances of heaven fall   *Let all*
    On her ungrateful top.° Strike her young bones,   *head*
    You taking° airs, with lameness.   *infectious; malignant*
CORNWALL   Fie, fie, sir.
330 LEAR   You nimble lightnings, dart your blinding flames
    Into her scornful eyes. Infect her beauty,
    You fen-sucked fogs, drawn by the powerful sun[4]
    To fall and blast her pride.
REGAN   Oh, the blest gods! So will you wish on me
335   When the rash mood—
LEAR   No, Regan, thou shalt never have my curse;
    The tender-hested° nature shall not give thee o'er   *pledged to tenderness*
    To harshness. Her eyes are fierce, but thine
    Do comfort and not burn. 'Tis not in thee
340   To grudge my pleasures, to cut off my train,
    To bandy hasty words, to scant my sizes,°   *reduce my allowances*
    And, in conclusion, to oppose the bolt°   *lock the door*
    Against my coming in. Thou better knowest
    The offices° of nature, bond of childhood,   *duties*
345   Effects° of courtesy, dues of gratitude.   *Actions*
    Thy half of the kingdom hast thou not forgot,
    Wherein I thee endowed.

---

2. *I have . . . duty:* I expect that you are worse at valuing her merit than she is at neglecting her duty. The double negative here ("less," "slack") is acceptable Jacobean usage.

3. Do you see how appropriate this is among members of a family (spoken ironically)?
4. The sun was thought to suck poisonous vapors from marshy ground.

With how depraved a quality—O Regan!
REGAN   I pray you, sir, take patience. I have hope
You less know how to value her desert
Than she to scant her duty.[7]
LEAR   Say? How is that?
320 REGAN   I cannot think my sister in the least
Would fail her obligation. If, sir, perchance
She have restrained the riots of your followers,
'Tis on such ground and to such wholesome end
As clears her from all blame.
LEAR   My curses on her!
325 REGAN   O sir, you are old;
Nature° in you stands on the very verge   *Life*
Of his confine.° You should be ruled and led   *Of its limit*
By some discretion° that discerns your state   *discreet person*
Better than you yourself. Therefore, I pray you
330 That to our sister you do make return.
Say you have wronged her.
LEAR   Ask her forgiveness?
Do you but mark how this becomes the house?[8]
Dear daughter, I confess that I am old;
Age° is unnecessary. [*He kneels.*] On my knees I beg   *An old man*
335 That you'll vouchsafe me raiment,° bed, and food.   *promise me clothing*
REGAN   Good sir, no more; these are unsightly tricks.
Return you to my sister.
LEAR [*rising*]   Never, Regan.
She hath abated° me of half my train,   *deprived*
Looked black upon me, struck me with her tongue
340 Most serpent-like upon the very heart.
All° the stored vengeances of heaven fall   *Let all*
On her ingrateful top.° Strike her young bones,   *head*
You taking° airs, with lameness.   *infectious; malignant*
CORNWALL   Fie, sir, fie!
LEAR   You nimble lightnings, dart your blinding flames
345 Into her scornful eyes. Infect her beauty,
You fen-sucked fogs, drawn by the pow'rful sun[9]
To fall and blister.
REGAN   Oh, the blest gods!
So will you wish on me when the rash mood is on.
LEAR   No, Regan, thou shalt never have my curse.
350 Thy tender-hafted[1] nature shall not give
Thee o'er to harshness. Her eyes are fierce, but thine
Do comfort and not burn. 'Tis not in thee
To grudge my pleasures, to cut off my train,
To bandy hasty words, to scant my sizes,°   *reduce my allowances*
355 And, in conclusion, to oppose the bolt°   *lock the door*
Against my coming in. Thou better know'st
The offices° of nature, bond of childhood,   *duties*
Effects° of courtesy, dues of gratitude.   *Actions*
Thy half o'th' kingdom hast thou not forgot,
Wherein I thee endowed.

---

7. *I have . . . duty:* I expect that you are worse at valuing her merit than she is at neglecting her duty. The
double negative here ("less," "scant") is acceptable
Jacobean usage.
8. Do you see how appropriate this is among mem-

bers of a family (spoken ironically)?
9. The sun was thought to suck poisonous vapors
from marshy ground.
1. Tenderly placed; firmly set in a tender disposition
(as a knife blade into its haft).

REGAN　Good sir, to th' purpose.°　　　　　　　　　　*get to the point*

LEAR　　　　　　　　　　　Who put my man i'th' stocks?

[*A sennet sounds.*]

CORNWALL　What trumpet's that?

　　　　Enter [*Oswald the*] STEWARD.

350　REGAN　I know't my sister's; this approves° her letters　　　*confirms*
　　　That she would soon be here. [*to* STEWARD] Is your lady
　　　　come?

LEAR　This is a slave whose easy-borrowed pride[5]
　　　Dwells in the fickle grace of her 'a° follows.　　　　　　　　*he*
　　　[*He strikes* STEWARD.] Out, varlet,° from my sight!　　　*wretch*

　　　　　　　　　　　　[*Exit* STEWARD.]

CORNWALL　　　　　　　　　What means your grace?

　　　　Enter GONORILL.

355　GONORILL　Who struck my servant? Regan, I have good hope
　　　Thou didst not know on't.°　　　　　　　　　　　　　　　*of it*

LEAR　　　　　　　　Who comes here? O heavens,
　　　If you do love old men, if your sweet sway allow
　　　Obedience, if yourselves are old, make it your cause;
　　　Send down and take my part.

360　[*to* GONORILL] Art not ashamed to look upon this beard?
　　　O Regan, wilt thou take her by the hand?

GONORILL　Why not by the hand, sir? How have I offended?
　　　All's not offense that indiscretion finds
　　　And dotage terms so.

LEAR　　　　　　　O sides,[6] you are too tough!
365　Will you yet hold? How came my man i'th' stocks?

CORNWALL　I set him there, sir, but his own disorders°　　　*disorderly behavior*
　　　Deserved much less advancement.[7]

LEAR　　　　　　　　　　You, did you?

REGAN　I pray you, father, being weak, seem so.°　　　　　*behave so*
　　　If till the expiration of your month
370　You will return and sojourn with my sister,
　　　Dismissing half your train, come then to me.
　　　I am now from home and out of that provision
　　　Which shall be needful for your entertainment.

LEAR　Return to her, and fifty men dismissed?
375　No, rather I abjure all roofs and choose
　　　To wage against the enmity of the air,
　　　To be a comrade with the wolf and owl,
　　　Necessity's sharp pinch.[8] Return with her?
　　　Why, the hot blood in France that dowerless
380　Took our youngest born, I could as well be brought
　　　To knee° his throne and squire-like pension beg,　　　*kneel to*
　　　To keep base life afoot. Return with her?
　　　Persuade me rather to be slave and sumpter°　　　　*packhorse*
　　　To this detested groom.°　　　　　　　　　　　　*(the Steward)*

GONORILL　　　　　　　At your choice, sir.
385　LEAR　Now, I prithee, daughter, do not make me mad.
　　　I will not trouble thee, my child; farewell.
　　　We'll no more meet, no more see one another.
　　　But yet thou art my flesh, my blood, my daughter,

5. Unmerited and unpaid-for arrogance; "pride" may
also refer to Oswald's fine clothing received for his
services to Gonorill.
6. Chest, where Lear's heart is swelling with emotion.

7. Deserved far worse treatment.
8. *To wage . . . pinch:* To counter the harshness of
the elements with the hardness brought on by necessity. *pinch:* stress, pressure.

360 REGAN   Good sir, to th' purpose.°   *get to the point*

LEAR   Who put my man i'th' stocks?

     Enter [Oswald the] STEWARD. *Tucket within.*

CORNWALL   What trumpet's that?

REGAN   I know't my sister's; this approves° her letter   *confirms*

 That she would soon be here. [*to* STEWARD] Is your lady

  come?

LEAR   This is a slave whose easy borrowed pride[2]

365 Dwells in the sickly grace of her he follows.

 [*to* STEWARD] Out, varlet,° from my sight.   *wretch*

CORNWALL   What means your grace?

LEAR   Who stocked my servant? Regan, I have good hope

 Thou didst not know on't.°   *of it*

    Enter GONERILL.

      Who comes here? O heavens,

 If you do love old men, if your sweet sway

370 Allow obedience, if you yourselves are old,

 Make it your cause: send down and take my part.

 [*to* GONERILL] Art not ashamed to look upon this beard?

 O Regan, will you take her by the hand?

GONERILL   Why not by th' hand, sir? How have I offended?

375 All's not offense that indiscretion finds

 And dotage terms so.

LEAR   O sides,[3] you are too tough! Will you yet hold?

 How came my man i'th' stocks?

CORNWALL   I set him there, sir, but his own disorders°   *disorderly behavior*

 Deserved much less advancement.[4]

380 LEAR   You, did you?

REGAN   I pray you, father, being weak, seem so.°   *behave so*

 If till the expiration of your month

 You will return and sojourn with my sister,

 Dismissing half your train, come then to me.

385 I am now from home and out of that provision

 Which shall be needful for your entertainment.

LEAR   Return to her, and fifty men dismissed?

 No, rather I abjure all roofs and choose

 To wage against the enmity o'th' air,

390 To be a comrade with the wolf and owl,

 Necessity's sharp pinch.[5] Return with her?

 Why, the hot-blooded France, that dowerless took

 Our youngest born, I could as well be brought

 To knee° his throne and squire-like pension beg,   *kneel to*

395 To keep base life afoot. Return with her?

 Persuade me rather to be slave and sumpter°   *packhorse*

 To this detested groom.°   *(Oswald)*

GONERILL   At your choice, sir.

LEAR   I prithee, daughter, do not make me mad.

 I will not trouble thee, my child; farewell.

400 We'll no more meet, no more see one another.

 But yet thou art my flesh, my blood, my daughter,

---

2. Unmerited and unpaid-for arrogance; "pride" may also refer to Oswald's fine clothing received for his services to Gonerill.
3. Chest, where Lear's heart is swelled with emotion.
4. Deserved far worse treatment.
5. *To wage . . . pinch:* To counter the harshness of the elements with the hardness brought on by necessity. *pinch:* stress, pressure.

Or rather a disease that lies within my flesh,
390 Which I must needs call mine. Thou art a boil,
A plague sore, an embossed° carbuncle in my   *a swollen*
Corrupted blood. But I'll not chide thee.
Let shame come when it will; I do not call° it.   *call upon*
I do not bid the thunder-bearer° shoot,   *(Jove)*
395 Nor tell tales of thee to high-judging Jove.
Mend° when thou canst; be better at thy leisure.   *Make amends*
I can be patient; I can stay with Regan,
I and my hundred knights.
REGAN   Not altogether so, sir. I look not for° you yet,   *I did not expect*
400 Nor am provided for your fit welcome.
Give ear, sir, to my sister, for those
That mingle reason with your passion[9]
Must be content to think you are old, and so.
But she knows what she does.
405 LEAR   Is this well° spoken now?   *earnestly*
REGAN   I dare avouch° it, sir. What, fifty followers?   *vouch for*
Is it not well? What should you need of more?
Yea, or so many, sith° that both charge° and danger *since / expense*
Speaks 'gainst so great a number? How in a house
410 Should many people under two commands
Hold amity? 'Tis hard, almost impossible.
GONORILL   Why might not you, my lord, receive attendance
From those that she calls servants or from mine?
REGAN   Why not, my lord? If then they chanced to slack°   *neglect*
    you,
415 We could control them. If you will come to me—
For now I spy a danger—I entreat you
To bring but five-and-twenty; to no more
Will I give place or notice.°   *acknowledgment*
LEAR   I gave you all—
REGAN   And in good time° you gave it.   *it was about time*
420 LEAR   —Made you my guardians, my depositaries,°   *trustees*
But kept a reservation° to be followed   *reserved a right*
With such a number. What, must I come to you
With five-and-twenty, Regan? Said you so?
REGAN   And speak't again, my lord: no more with me.
425 LEAR   Those wicked creatures yet do seem well-favored°   *attractive*
When others are more wicked; not being the worst
Stands in some rank of praise.[1] [*to* GONORILL] I'll go with
    thee:
Thy fifty yet doth double five-and-twenty,
And thou art twice her love.
GONORILL   Hear me, my lord.
430 What need you five-and-twenty, ten, or five
To follow in a house where twice so many
Have a command to tend you?
REGAN   What needs one?
LEAR   Oh, reason not the need! Our basest beggars
Are in the poorest thing superfluous.[2]
435 Allow not° nature more than nature needs,   *If you don't allow*
Man's life is cheap as beast's. Thou art a lady:

---

9. For those who temper your passionate argument
with their own calm reasoning.
1. Deserves some degree ("rank") of praise.

2. *Our . . . superfluous:* Even the lowliest beggars
have something more than the barest minimum.

Or rather a disease that's in my flesh
Which I must needs call mine. Thou art a boil,
A plague sore, or embossèd° carbuncle   *swollen*
405   In my corrupted blood. But I'll not chide thee.
Let shame come when it will; I do not call° it.   *call upon*
I do not bid the thunder-bearer° shoot,   *(Jove)*
Nor tell tales of thee to high-judging Jove.
Mend° when thou canst; be better at thy leisure.   *Make amends*
410   I can be patient: I can stay with Regan,
I and my hundred knights.

REGAN   Not altogether so.
I looked not for° you yet, nor am provided   *I did not expect*
For your fit welcome. Give ear, sir, to my sister,
For those that mingle reason with your passion[6]
415   Must be content to think you old and so.
But she knows what she does.

LEAR   Is this well° spoken?   *earnestly*

REGAN   I dare avouch° it, sir. What, fifty followers?   *vouch for*
Is it not well? What should you need of more?
Yea, or so many, sith° that both charge° and danger   *since / expense*
420   Speak 'gainst so great a number? How in one house
Should many people under two commands
Hold amity? 'Tis hard, almost impossible.

GONERILL   Why might not you, my lord, receive attendance
From those that she calls servants, or from mine?
425   REGAN   Why not, my lord?
If then they chanced to slack° ye,   *neglect*
We could control them. If you will come to me—
For now I spy a danger—I entreat you
To bring but five-and-twenty; to no more
430   Will I give place or notice.°   *acknowledgment*

LEAR   I gave you all—

REGAN   And in good time° you gave it.   *it was about time*

LEAR   —Made you my guardians, my depositaries,°   *trustees*
But kept a reservation° to be followed   *reserved a right*
With such a number. What, must I come to you
435   With five-and-twenty, Regan? Said you so?

REGAN   And speak't again, my lord; no more with me.

LEAR   Those wicked creatures yet do look well-favored°   *attractive*
When others are more wicked; not being the worst
Stands in some rank of praise.[7] [to GONERILL] I'll go with thee:
440   Thy fifty yet doth double five-and-twenty,
And thou art twice her love.

GONERILL   Hear me, my lord.
What need you five-and-twenty? Ten? Or five?
To follow in a house where twice so many
Have a command to tend you?

REGAN   What need one?
445   LEAR   Oh, reason not the need! Our basest beggars
Are in the poorest thing superfluous.[8]
Allow not° nature more than nature needs,   *If you don't allow*
Man's life is cheap as beast's. Thou art a lady:

---

6. For those who temper your passionate argument with their own calm reasoning.
7. Deserves some degree ("rank") of praise.
8. *Our . . . superfluous:* Even the lowliest beggars have something more than the barest minimum.

If only to go warm were gorgeous,
Why, nature needs not what thou gorgeous wearest,
Which scarcely keeps thee warm.³ But for true need,
440 You heavens, give me that patience,° patience I need.   *endurance*
You see me here, you gods, a poor old fellow,
As full of grief as age, wretched in both.
If it be you that stirs these daughters' hearts
Against their father, fool me not too much
445 To bear it lamely.⁴ Touch me with noble anger.
Oh, let not women's weapons, water drops,
Stain my man's cheeks. No, you unnatural hags,
I will have such revenges on you both
That all the world shall—I will do such things—
450 What they are, yet I know not, but they shall be
The terrors of the earth! You think I'll weep.
No, I'll not weep. I have full cause of weeping,
But this heart shall break in a hundred thousand flows,°   *fragments*
Or e'er° I'll weep. O Fool, I shall go mad.   *Before*
       Exeunt LEAR, [GLOUCESTER,] KENT, *and* FOOL.
455 CORNWALL   Let us withdraw, 'twill be a storm.
REGAN   This house is little; the old man and his people
Cannot be well bestowed.°   *lodged*
GONORILL   'Tis his own blame hath put himself from° rest   *deprived himself of*
And must needs taste his folly.
460 REGAN   For his particular,° I'll receive him gladly,   *single self*
But not one follower.
CORNWALL   So am I purposed. Where is my lord of Gloucester?
REGAN   Followed the old man forth.
       Enter GLOUCESTER.
               He is returned.
GLOUCESTER   The King is in high rage and will° I know not   *will go*
whither.
465 REGAN   'Tis good to give him way; he leads himself.
GONORILL   My lord, entreat him by no means to stay.
GLOUCESTER   Alack, the night comes on, and the bleak winds
Do sorely rustle. For many miles about there's not a bush.
REGAN   O sir, to willful men
470 The injuries that they themselves procure
Must be their schoolmasters. Shut up your doors.
He is attended with a desperate° train,   *violent*
And what they may incense° him to, being apt   *incite*
To have his ear abused,° wisdom bids fear.   *deceived*
475 CORNWALL   Shut up your doors, my lord. 'Tis a wild night.
My Regan counsels well. Come out o'th' storm.   *Exeunt.*

---

3. *If . . . thee warm:* If gorgeousness in clothes is measured by the warmth they provide, your elaborate clothes are superfluous, for they barely cover your body.
4. *fool . . . lamely:* do not make me so foolish as to accept it meekly.

If only to go warm were gorgeous,
450 Why, nature needs not what thou gorgeous wear'st,
Which scarcely keeps thee warm.[9] But for true need,
You heavens, give me that patience,° patience I need!   *endurance*
You see me here, you gods, a poor old man,
As full of grief as age, wretched in both.
455 If it be you that stirs these daughters' hearts
Against their father, fool me not so much
To bear it tamely.[1] Touch me with noble anger,
And let not women's weapons, water drops,
Stain my man's cheeks. No, you unnatural hags,
460 I will have such revenges on you both
That all the world shall—I will do such things—
What they are, yet I know not, but they shall be
The terrors of the earth! You think I'll weep.
No, I'll not weep. I have full cause of weeping.
        Storm and tempest.
465 But this heart shall break into a hundred thousand flaws°   *fragments*
Or e'er° I'll weep. O Fool, I shall go mad.   *Before*
        Exeunt [with GLOUCESTER, KENT, FOOL,
                and Attendants].

CORNWALL   Let us withdraw; 'twill be a storm.
REGAN   This house is little; the old man and 's people
Cannot be well bestowed.°   *lodged*
470 GONERILL   'Tis his own blame hath put himself from° rest   *deprived himself of*
And must needs taste his folly.
REGAN   For his particular,° I'll receive him gladly,   *single self*
But not one follower.
GONERILL   So am I purposed.
Where is my lord of Gloucester?
        Enter GLOUCESTER.
475 CORNWALL   Followed the old man forth; he is returned.
GLOUCESTER   The King is in high rage.
CORNWALL   Whither is he going?
GLOUCESTER   He calls to horse, but will° I know not whither.   *will go*
CORNWALL   'Tis best to give him way; he leads himself.
480 GONERILL   My lord, entreat him by no means to stay.
GLOUCESTER   Alack, the night comes on, and the high winds
Do sorely ruffle.° For many miles about   *bluster*
There's scarce a bush.
REGAN   O sir, to willful men
The injuries that they themselves procure
485 Must be their schoolmasters. Shut up your doors:
He is attended with a desperate° train,   *violent*
And what they may incense° him to, being apt   *incite*
To have his ear abused,° wisdom bids fear.   *deceived*
CORNWALL   Shut up your doors, my lord; 'tis a wild night.
490 My Regan counsels well: come out o'th' storm.   *Exeunt.*

---

9. *If . . . thee warm:* If gorgeousness in clothes is measured by the warmth they provide, your elaborate clothes are superfluous, for they barely cover your body.
1. *fool . . . tamely:* do not make me so foolish as to accept it meekly.

3.1 (F 3.1)

Enter KENT [*disguised as Caius*] *and a* GENTLEMAN *at*
   several° doors.   separate

KENT   What's here beside foul weather?

GENTLEMAN   One minded like the weather, most unquietly.

KENT   I know you. Where's the King?

GENTLEMAN   Contending with the fretful element;

5   Bids the wind blow the earth into the sea,

   Or swell the curlèd waters 'bove the main,°   mainland

   That things might change or cease; tears his white hair,

   Which the impetuous blasts, with eyeless rage,

   Catch in their fury and make nothing of;

10   Strives in his little world of man to outscorn

   The to-and-fro conflicting wind and rain

   This night, wherein the cub-drawn bear would couch,[1]

   The lion and the belly-pinchèd wolf

   Keep their fur dry. Unbonneted° he runs   Hatless; uncrowned

   And bids what will take all.

15 KENT   But who is with him?

GENTLEMAN   None but the Fool, who labors to out-jest

   His heart-struck injuries.[2]

KENT   Sir, I do know you

   And dare upon the warrant of my art[3]

   Commend a dear° thing to you. There is division,   Entrust a crucial

20   Although as yet the face of it be covered

   With mutual cunning, twixt Albany and Cornwall.

   But true it is, from France[4] there comes a power

   Into this scattered kingdom, who, already wise in° our   aware of

      negligence,

   Have secret feet in some of our best ports,

25   And are at point° to show their open banner.   ready

   Now to you: if on my credit you dare build° so far   if you trust me

   To make your speed to Dover, you shall find

   Some that will thank you, making just° report   accurate

   Of how unnatural and bemadding° sorrow   maddening

30   The King hath cause to plain.°   complain

   I am a gentleman of blood and breeding

   And from some knowledge and assurance

   Offer this office° to you.   role; duty

GENTLEMAN   I will talk farther with you.

KENT   No, do not.

35   For confirmation that I am much more

   Than my out-wall,° open this purse and take   outward appearance

   What it contains. If you shall see Cordelia—

   As fear not but you shall—show her this ring,

   And she will tell you who your fellow° is   (Kent himself)

3.1 Location: Bare, open country.
1. In which even the bear, though starving, having been sucked dry ("drawn") by its cub, would not go out to forage.
2. *to out-jest*: to relieve with laughter; to exorcise through ridicule. *heart-struck injuries*: injuries (from the betrayal of his paternal love) that penetrated to the heart.
3. On the basis of my skill (at judging people).

4. TEXTUAL COMMENT There is substantial variation between the Quarto and Folio texts in Kent's speech in 3.1 about the sources of political unrest. While Kent points to French foreign invasion in the Quarto, the Folio text presents a vision of civil unrest between Cornwall and Albany. Some scholars have proposed political censorship as a possible explanation for the stark difference between Kent's speeches. See Digital Edition TC 3 (Quarto edited text).

3.1 (Q 3.1)

Storm still. Enter KENT [*disguised as Caius*] *and a*
GENTLEMAN, *severally.°*   *separately*

KENT   Who's there besides foul weather?

GENTLEMAN   One minded like the weather, most unquietly.

KENT   I know you. Where's the King?

GENTLEMAN   Contending with the fretful elements;

5   Bids the wind blow the earth into the sea,
       Or swell the curlèd waters 'bove the main,°   *mainland*
       That things might change or cease.

KENT   But who is with him?

GENTLEMAN   None but the Fool, who labors to out-jest
       His heart-struck injuries.[1]

10   KENT   Sir, I do know you
       And dare upon the warrant of my note[2]
       Commend a dear° thing to you. There is division,   *Entrust a crucial*
       Although as yet the face of it is covered
       With mutual cunning, twixt Albany and Cornwall,[3]

15   Who have—as who have not that their great stars
       Throned and set high[4]—servants, who seem no less,°   *who appear as such*
       Which are to France the spies and speculations°   *observers*
       Intelligent of[5] our state. What hath been seen,
       Either in snuffs and packings° of the Dukes,   *quarrels and plots*

20   Or the hard rein° which both of them hath borne   *treatment*
       Against the old kind King, or something deeper,
       Whereof, perchance, these are but furnishings.°   *pretexts*

GENTLEMAN   I will talk further with you.

KENT   No, do not.
       For confirmation that I am much more

25   Than my out-wall,° open this purse and take   *outward appearance*
       What it contains. If you shall see Cordelia—
       As fear not but you shall—show her this ring,
       And she will tell you who that fellow° is   *(Kent himself)*

3.1 Location: Bare, open country.

1. *to out-jest*: to relieve with laughter; to exorcise through ridicule. *heart-struck injuries*: injuries (from the betrayal of his paternal love) that penetrated to the heart.

2. On the basis of my skill (at judging people).

3. TEXTUAL COMMENT There is substantial variation between the Quarto and Folio texts in Kent's speech in 3.1 about the sources of political unrest. While

Kent points to French foreign invasion in the Quarto, the Folio text presents a vision of civil unrest between Cornwall and Albany. Some scholars have proposed political censorship as a possible explanation for the stark difference between Kent's speeches. See Digital Edition TC 3 (Folio edited text).

4. *as . . . high:* as has everybody who has been favored by destiny.

5. Supplying intelligence about; too well informed of.

40   That yet you do not know. Fie on this storm!
        I will go seek the King.
GENTLEMAN   Give me your hand. Have you no more to say?
KENT   Few words, but to effect° more than all yet: *but in importance*
        That when we have found the King—
45   I'll° this way, you that—he that first lights   *I'll go*
        On him holla the other.   *Exeunt [severally].*°   *separately*

3.2 (F 3.2)
Enter LEAR *and* FOOL.

LEAR   Blow wind and crack your cheeks! Rage, blow,
        You cataracts° and hurricanos, spout   *waterspouts*
        Till you have drenched the steeples, drowned the cocks!°   *weather vanes*
        You sulphurous and thought-executing fires,[1]
5   Vaunt-couriers° to oak-cleaving thunderbolts,   *Forerunners*
        Singe my white head. And thou, all-shaking thunder,
        Smite flat the thick rotundity of the world,
        Crack Nature's mold, all germens° spill at once   *seeds*
        That make ingrateful man.
10 FOOL   O nuncle, court holy water[2] in a dry house is better
        than this rainwater out a-door. Good nuncle, in, and ask thy
        daughter's blessing. Here's a night pities neither wise man
        nor fool.
LEAR   Rumble thy bellyful! Spit fire, spout rain!
15   Nor rain, wind, thunder, fire are my daughters.
        I task° not you, you elements, with unkindness;   *blame*
        I never gave you kingdom, called you children.
        You owe me no subscription.° Why, then, let fall   *obedience; allegiance*
        Your horrible pleasure. Here I stand your slave,
20   A poor, infirm, weak, and despised old man.
        But yet I call you servile ministers,°   *agents*
        That have with two pernicious daughters joined
        Your high-engendered battle° 'gainst a head   *heaven-bred force*
        So old and white as this. Oh, 'tis foul!
25 FOOL   He that has a house to put his head in has a good
        headpiece.°   *hat; brain*
        The codpiece that will house
        Before the head has any,
        The head and he shall louse;
30   So beggars marry many.[3]
        The man that makes his toe
        What he his heart should make,
        Shall have a corn, cry "Woe,"
        And turn his sleep to wake.[4]
35   For there was never yet fair woman but she made mouths in
        a glass.[5]

3.2 Location: As before.
1. *thought-executing fires:* Either meaning lightning
that strikes as swiftly as thought or lightning that
puts an end to thought.
2. Sprinkled blessings of a courtier, flattery.
3. *The codpiece . . . many:* Whoever finds his penis a
lodging before providing shelter for his head will end
up in lice-infested poverty and live in married beggary.
codpiece: a pouchlike covering for the male genitals,
often conspicuous, particularly in the costume of a

fool.
4. *The man . . . wake:* The man who values an inferior part of his body over the part that is truly valuable will suffer from and lose sleep over that inferior
part.
5. She practiced making pretty faces in a mirror. The
Fool probably refers to Regan's and Gonorill's vanity,
or the line may be thrown in to soften the harshness
of his satire.

That yet you do not know. Fie on this storm!
I will go seek the King.

30 GENTLEMAN   Give me your hand.
Have you no more to say?

KENT   Few words, but to effect° more than all yet: *but in importance*
That when we have found the King—in which your pain
That way, I'll this⁶—he that first lights on him
35 Holla the other.   *Exeunt [severally].°*   *separately*

3.2 (Q 3.2)
Storm still. Enter LEAR *and* FOOL.

LEAR   Blow winds and crack your cheeks! Rage, blow,
You cataracts° and hurricanos, spout   *waterspouts*
Till you have drenched our steeples, drowned the cocks.°   *weather vanes*
You sulph'rous and thought-executing fires,¹
5 Vaunt-couriers° of oak-cleaving thunderbolts,   *Forerunners*
Singe my white head. And thou, all-shaking thunder,
Strike flat the thick rotundity o'th' world,
Crack Nature's molds, all germens° spill at once   *seeds*
That makes ingrateful man.

10 FOOL   O nuncle, court holy water² in a dry house is better
than this rainwater out o'door. Good nuncle, in! Ask thy
daughters' blessing. Here's a night pities neither wise men
nor fools.

LEAR   Rumble thy bellyful! Spit fire, spout rain!
15 Nor rain, wind, thunder, fire are my daughters.
I tax° not you, you elements, with unkindness: *blame*
I never gave you kingdom, called you children.
You owe me no subscription.° Then let fall   *obedience; allegiance*
Your horrible pleasure. Here I stand your slave,
20 A poor, infirm, weak, and despised old man.
But yet I call you servile ministers,°   *agents*
That will with two pernicious daughters join
Your high-engendered battles° 'gainst a head   *heaven-bred forces*
So old and white as this. Oh, ho! 'Tis foul.

25 FOOL   He that has a house to put 's head in has a good
headpiece.°   *hat; brain*
The codpiece that will house
Before the head has any,
The head and he shall louse;
30 So beggars marry many.³
The man that makes his toe
What he his heart should make,
Shall of a corn cry woe
And turn his sleep to wake.⁴
35 For there was never yet fair woman but she made mouths in
a glass.⁵

---

6. *in which . . . this:* in which effort you will go that
way and I this way.
3.2 Location: As before.
1. *thought-executing fires:* meaning either lightning
that strikes as swiftly as thought or lightning that
puts an end to thought.
2. Sprinkled blessings of a courtier; flattery.
3. *The codpiece . . . many:* Whoever finds his penis a
lodging before providing shelter for his head will end
up in lice-infested poverty and live in married beggary.

codpiece: a pouchlike covering for the male genitals,
often conspicuous, particularly in the costume of a
fool.
4. *The man . . . wake:* The man who values an inferior part of his body over the part that is truly valuable
will suffer from and lose sleep over that inferior part.
5. She practiced making pretty faces in a mirror. The
Fool probably refers to Regan's and Gonerill's vanity,
or the line may be thrown in to soften the harshness
of his satire.

LEAR [*sitting down*]   No, I will be the pattern of all patience.
        Enter KENT [*disguised as Caius*].
    I will say nothing.
KENT   Who's there?
40 FOOL   Marry, here's grace and a codpiece: that's a wise man
    and a fool.[6]
KENT   Alas, sir, sit you here?
    Things that love night love not such nights as these.
    The wrathful skies gallow° the very wanderer   *frighten*
45 Of the dark and makes them keep° their caves.   *keep inside*
    Since I was man, such sheets of fire,
    Such bursts of horrid thunder, such groans of
    Roaring wind and rain I ne'er remember
    To have heard. Man's nature cannot carry°   *bear*
    The affliction, nor the force.
50 LEAR   Let the great gods
    That keep this dreadful pother° o'er our heads   *commotion*
    Find out their enemies now. Tremble, thou wretch,
    That hast within thee undivulgèd crimes
    Unwhipped of° justice. Hide thee, thou bloody hand,   *Unpunished by*
55 Thou perjured and thou simular° man of virtue   *simulating; pretending*
    That art incestuous. Caitiff,° in pieces shake,   *Wretch*
    That under covert and convenient seeming°   *fitting hypocrisy*
    Hast practiced on° man's life.   *against*
    Close° pent-up guilts, rive° your concealed centers   *Secret / split open*
60 And cry these dreadful summoners grace.[7]
    I am a man more sinned against than sinning.
KENT   Alack, bareheaded?
    Gracious my lord, hard by here is a hovel.
    Some friendship will it lend you 'gainst the tempest.
65 Repose you there whilst I to this hard house°—   *household*
    More hard than is the stone whereof 'tis raised,
    Which° even but now demanding after me,   *Who*
    Denied me to come in—return and force
    Their scanted° courtesy.   *grudging*
70 LEAR   My wit begins to turn.
    [*to* FOOL] Come on, my boy. How dost, my boy? Art cold?
    I am cold myself. Where is this straw, my fellow?
    The art° of our necessities is strange   *skill; alchemy*
    That can make vile things precious. Come, your hovel.
75 Poor fool and knave, I have one part of my heart
    That sorrows yet for thee.
FOOL [*sings*][8]   He that has a little tiny wit,°   *sense*
                    With heigh-ho, the wind and the rain,
                    Must make content with his fortunes fit,
80   For the rain it raineth every day.
LEAR   True, my good boy. Come, bring us to this hovel.
                                        [*Exeunt.*]

---

6. The supposedly wise King is symbolized by royal
grace, the Fool by his codpiece (here, slang for
"penis"). The Fool speaks ironically: the King, as he
has pointed out, is now the foolish one. *Marry*: By the
Virgin Mary (a mild oath).

7. *And cry . . . grace*: And pray for mercy from these
elements that bring you to justice.
8. The following song is an adaptation of one sung by
the Clown at the end of *Twelfth Night*.

Enter KENT [*disguised as Caius*].

LEAR [*sitting down*]   No, I will be the pattern of all
    patience.
  I will say nothing.

KENT   Who's there?

40   FOOL   Marry, here's grace and a codpiece: that's a wise man
  and a fool.[6]

KENT   Alas, sir, are you here? Things that love night
  Love not such nights as these. The wrathful skies
  Gallow° the very wanderers of the dark   *Frighten*

45   And make them keep° their caves. Since I was man,   *keep inside*
  Such sheets of fire, such bursts of horrid thunder,
  Such groans of roaring wind and rain I never
  Remember to have heard. Man's nature cannot carry°   *bear*
  Th'affliction nor the fear.

LEAR   Let the great gods

50   That keep this dreadful pudder° o'er our heads   *commotion*
  Find out their enemies now. Tremble, thou wretch,
  That hast within thee undivulgèd crimes
  Unwhipped of° justice. Hide thee, thou bloody hand,   *Unpunished by*
  Thou perjured and thou simular° of virtue   *simulator; pretender*

55   That art incestuous. Caitiff,° to pieces shake,   *Wretch*
  That under covert and convenient seeming°   *fitting hypocrisy*
  Has practiced on° man's life. Close° pent-up guilts,   *against / Secret*
  Rive° your concealing continents° and cry   *Split open / coverings*
  These dreadful summoners grace.[7] I am a man
  More sinned against than sinning.

60   KENT   Alack, bareheaded?
  Gracious my lord, hard by here is a hovel;
  Some friendship will it lend you 'gainst the tempest.
  Repose you there, while I to this hard house°—   *household*
  More harder than the stones whereof 'tis raised,

65   Which° even but now, demanding° after you,   *Who / I demanding*
  Denied me to come in—return and force
  Their scanted° courtesy.   *grudging*

LEAR   My wits begin to turn.
  Come on, my boy. How dost, my boy? Art cold?
  I am cold myself. Where is this straw, my fellow?

70   The art° of our necessities is strange   *skill; alchemy*
  And can make vile things precious. Come, your hovel.
  Poor fool and knave, I have one part in my heart
  That's sorry yet for thee.

FOOL [*sings*][8]   He that has and° a little tiny wit,°   *even / sense*

75   With heigh-ho, the wind and the rain,
          Must make content with his fortunes fit,
          Though the rain it raineth every day.

LEAR   True, boy. Come, bring us to this hovel.

                        Exeunt [LEAR *and* KENT].

---

6. The supposedly wise King is symbolized by royal grace, the Fool by his codpiece (here, slang for "penis"). The Fool speaks ironically: the King, as he has pointed out, is now the foolish one. *Marry*: By the Virgin Mary (a mild oath).

7. *and cry . . . grace*: and pray for mercy from these elements that bring you to justice.
8. The following song is an adaptation of one sung by the Clown at the end of *Twelfth Night*.

3.3 (F 3.3)

Enter GLOUCESTER *and [Edmund] the* BASTARD *with
lights.*

GLOUCESTER   Alack, alack, Edmund, I like not this unnatural
dealing. When I desired their leave that I might pity° him,   *relieve*
they took from me the use of mine own house, charged me
on pain of their displeasure neither to speak of him, entreat
5   for him, nor any way sustain him.

BASTARD   Most savage and unnatural!

GLOUCESTER   Go to,° say you nothing. There's a division betwixt   *(an expletive)*
the Dukes and a worse matter than that. I have received a
letter this night—'tis dangerous to be spoken. I have locked
10   the letter in my closet.° These injuries the King now bears will   *private chamber*
be revenged home:° there's part of a power° already landed.   *to the hilt / an army*
We must incline to[1] the King. I will seek him and privily°   *secretly; privately*
relieve him. Go you and maintain talk with the Duke, that
my charity be not of him perceived. If he ask for me, I am ill
15   and gone to bed. Though I die for't, as no less is threatened
me, the King my old master must be relieved. There is some
strange thing toward.° Edmund, pray you be careful.   *Exit.*   *coming*

BASTARD   This courtesy,° forbid° thee, shall the Duke   *act of kindness / forbidden*
Instantly know, and of that letter too.
20   This seems a fair deserving[2] and must draw me
That which my father loses: no less than all.
Then younger rises when the old do fall.   *Exit.*

3.3 Location: At Gloucester's castle.
1. We must take the side of.

2. This seems an action that deserves to be rewarded.

FOOL   This is a brave night to cool a courtesan.[9] I'll speak a
80   prophecy ere I go:[1]
        When priests are more in word than matter,°   *real virtue*
        When brewers mar their malt with water,
        When nobles are their tailors' tutors,[2]
        No heretics burned but wenches' suitors,[3]
85   When every case in law is right,°   *just*
        No squire in debt, nor no poor knight,
        When slanders do not live in tongues,
        Nor cutpurses° come not to throngs,   *pickpockets*
        When usurers tell their gold i'th' field,[4]
90   And bawds and whores do churches build,
        Then shall the realm of Albion° come to great confusion.°   *Britain / decay*
        Then comes the time, who lives to see't,
        That going° shall be used° with feet.   *walking / practiced*
        This prophecy Merlin shall make, for I live before his time.[5]
                                                                    Exit.

                        3.3 (Q 3.3)
                Enter GLOUCESTER *and* EDMOND.
GLOUCESTER   Alack, alack, Edmond, I like not this unnatural
        dealing. When I desired their leave that I might pity° him,   *relieve*
        they took from me the use of mine own house, charged me
        on pain of perpetual displeasure neither to speak of him,
5   entreat for him, or any way sustain him.
EDMOND   Most savage and unnatural!
GLOUCESTER   Go to,° say you nothing. There is division between   *(an expletive)*
        the Dukes and a worse matter than that. I have received a
        letter this night—'tis dangerous to be spoken. I have locked
10   the letter in my closet.° These injuries the King now bears will   *private chamber*
        be revenged home.° There is part of a power already footed.[1]   *to the hilt*
        We must incline to[2] the King; I will look him and privily°   *secretly; privately*
        relieve him. Go you and maintain talk with the Duke, that my
        charity be not of him perceived. If he ask for me, I am ill and
15   gone to bed. If I die for it, as no less is threatened me, the King
        my old master must be relieved. There is strange things
        toward,° Edmond. Pray you be careful.   *Exit.*   *coming*
EDMOND   This courtesy,° forbid° thee, shall the Duke   *act of kindness / forbidden*
        Instantly know and of that letter too.
20   This seems a fair deserving[3] and must draw me
        That which my father loses: no less than all.
        The younger rises when the old doth fall.   *Exit.*

---

9. To cool even the hot lusts of a prostitute.
1. What follows is a parody of the pseudo-Chaucerian
"Merlin's Prophecy" from *The Art of English Poesy.*
2. When noblemen follow fashion more closely than
their tailors do.
3. When the only heretics burned are faithless lovers, who burn from venereal disease.
4. When usurers can count their profits openly

(because they have no shady dealings to hide).
5. Merlin was the great wizard at the legendary
court of King Arthur. Lear's Britain is set in an even
more distant past.
3.3 Location: At Gloucester's castle.
1. Part of an army already on the move.
2. We must take the side of.
3. This seems an action that deserves to be rewarded.

3.4 (F 3.4)

Enter LEAR, KENT [*disguised as Caius*], *and* FOOL.

KENT   Here is the place, my lord. Good my lord, enter.
    The tyranny of the open night's too rough
    For nature° to endure.   *human weakness*

LEAR   Let me alone.

KENT   Good my lord, enter.

LEAR   Wilt break my heart?

5   KENT   I had rather break mine own. Good my lord, enter.

LEAR   Thou think'st 'tis much that this tempestuous storm
    Invades us to the skin; so 'tis to thee.
    But where the greater malady is fixed,°   *rooted*
    The lesser is scarce felt. Thou'dst shun a bear,

10   But if thy flight lay toward the roaring sea,
    Thou'dst meet the bear i'th' mouth. When the mind's free,°   *unburdened*
    The body's delicate.° This tempest in my mind   *sensitive*
    Doth from my senses take all feeling else,
    Save° what beats: their filial ingratitude.   *Except*

15   Is it not as° this mouth should tear this hand   *as if*
    For lifting food to't? But I will punish sure.
    No, I will weep no more— In such a night as this!
    O Regan, Gonorill, your old kind father
    Whose frank heart gave you all! Oh, that way madness lies.

20   Let me shun that; no more of that.

KENT   Good my lord, enter.

LEAR   Prithee, go in thyself; seek thy own ease.   [*Exit* FOOL.]
    This tempest will not give me leave to° ponder   *allow me to*
    On things would hurt me more. But I'll go in.

25   Poor naked wretches, wheresoe'er you are,
    That bide° the pelting of this pitiless night,   *endure; dwell in*
    How shall your houseless heads and unfed sides,°   *starved ribs*
    Your looped and windowed[1] raggedness defend you
    From seasons such as these? Oh, I have ta'en

30   Too little care of this! Take physic, pomp;[2]
    Expose thyself to feel what wretches feel,
    That thou mayst shake the superflux[3] to them
    And show the heavens more just.

[Enter FOOL.]

FOOL   Come not in here, nuncle. Here's a spirit! Help me,

35   help me!

KENT   Give me thy hand. Who's there?

FOOL   A spirit. He says his name's Poor Tom.

KENT   What art thou that dost grumble there in the straw?
    Come forth.

3.4 Location: Open country, before a cattle shed.
1. *looped and windowed:* full of holes and vents;
"windowed" could also refer to cloth worn through to
semitransparency, like the oilcloth window "panes"
of the poor.

2. Cure yourself, pompous person.
3. Superfluity; bodily discharge, suggested by
"physic" (which also has the meaning of "purgative")
in line 30. Excess here is also excess of wealth.

3.4 (Q 3.4)

Enter LEAR, KENT *[disguised as Caius], and* FOOL.

KENT   Here is the place, my lord. Good my lord, enter.
The tyranny of the open night's too rough
For nature° to endure.   *human weakness*
     Storm still.

LEAR   Let me alone.

KENT   Good my lord, enter here.

LEAR   Wilt break my heart?

5   KENT   I had rather break mine own.
    Good my lord, enter.

LEAR   Thou think'st 'tis much that this contentious storm
Invades us to the skin; so 'tis to thee.
But where the greater malady is fixed,°   *rooted*
10 The lesser is scarce felt. Thou'dst shun a bear,
But if thy flight lay toward the roaring sea,
Thou'dst meet the bear i'th' mouth. When the mind's free,°   *unburdened*
The body's delicate.° The tempest in my mind   *sensitive*
Doth from my senses take all feeling else,
15 Save° what beats there: filial ingratitude.   *Except*
Is it not as° this mouth should tear this hand   *as if*
For lifting food to't? But I will punish home.°   *thoroughly*
No, I will weep no more. In such a night
To shut me out? Pour on, I will endure.
20 In such a night as this? O Regan, Gonerill,
Your old kind father, whose frank heart gave all!
Oh, that way madness lies. Let me shun that;
No more of that.

KENT   Good my lord, enter here.

LEAR   Prithee, go in thyself; seek thine own ease.
25 This tempest will not give me leave to° ponder   *allow me to*
On things would hurt me more, but I'll go in.
[to FOOL*]* In, boy, go first. You houseless poverty,°   *poor*
Nay, get thee in; I'll pray, and then I'll sleep.   *Exit [*FOOL*].*
Poor naked wretches, wheresoe'er you are,
30 That bide° the pelting of this pitiless storm,   *endure; dwell in*
How shall your houseless heads and unfed sides,°   *starved ribs*
Your looped and windowed[1] raggedness defend you
From seasons such as these? Oh, I have ta'en
Too little care of this! Take physic, pomp;[2]
35 Expose thyself to feel what wretches feel,
That thou mayst shake the superflux[3] to them
And show the heavens more just.

EDGAR *[within]*   Fathom and half,[4] fathom and half. Poor Tom!
     Enter FOOL.

FOOL   Come not in here, nuncle. Here's a spirit! Help me,
40 help me!

KENT   Give me thy hand. Who's there?

FOOL   A spirit, a spirit! He says his name's Poor Tom.

KENT   What art thou that dost grumble there i'th' straw?
Come forth.

3.4 Location: Open country, before a cattle shed.
1. *looped and windowed:* full of holes and vents; "windowed" could also refer to cloth worn through to semitransparency, like the oilcloth window "panes" of the poor.
2. Cure yourself, pompous person.

3. Superfluity; bodily discharge, suggested by "physic" (which also has the meaning of "purgative") in line 34. Excess here is also excess of wealth.
4. "Nine feet," a sailor's cry when taking soundings to gauge the depth of water.

[*Enter* EDGAR *disguised as Poor Tom.*]

40 EDGAR   Away, the foul fiend follows me! Through the sharp
hawthorn blows the cold wind.[4] Go to thy cold bed and
warm thee.[5]

LEAR   Hast thou given all to thy two daughters, and art thou
come to this?

45 EDGAR   Who gives anything to Poor Tom, whom the foul fiend
hath led through fire, and through ford and whirlpool, o'er
bog and quagmire, that has laid knives under his pillow and
halters in his pew, set ratsbane by his pottage,[6] made him
proud of heart to ride on a bay trotting horse over four-
50 inched bridges,[7] to course° his own shadow for° a traitor.   *hunt / as*
Bless thy five wits![8] Tom's a-cold. Bless thee from whirlwinds, star-blasting, and taking.[9] Do Poor Tom some charity, whom the foul fiend vexes. There could I have him now,
and there, and there again.[1]

55 LEAR   What, his daughters brought him to this pass?
—Couldst thou save nothing? Didst thou give them all?

FOOL   Nay, he reserved a blanket, else we had been all
shamed.

LEAR   Now all the plagues that in the pendulous° air   *overhanging; portentous*
60 Hang fated o'er men's faults fall on thy daughters.

KENT   He hath no daughters, sir.

LEAR   Death, traitor! Nothing could have subdued nature
To such a lowness but his unkind daughters.
Is it the fashion that discarded fathers
65 Should have thus little mercy on their flesh?
Judicious punishment! 'Twas this flesh
Begot those pelican[2] daughters.

EDGAR [*sings*]   Pilicock sat on pilicock's hill, a lo, lo, lo.[3]

FOOL   This cold night will turn us all to fools and madmen.

70 EDGAR   Take heed o'th' foul fiend, obey thy parents, keep thy
words justly, swear not, commit not with man's sworn spouse,
set not thy sweetheart on proud array.[4] Tom's a-cold.

LEAR   What hast thou been?

EDGAR   A servingman, proud in heart and mind, that curled
75 my hair, wore gloves in my cap,[5] served the lust of my mistress' heart, and did the act of darkness with her. Swore as
many oaths as I spake words and broke them in the sweet
face of heaven. One that slept in the contriving of lust and
waked to do it. Wine loved I deeply, dice dearly, and in
80 woman out-paramoured the Turk.[6] False of heart, light of

---

4. *Through . . . wind:* Perhaps a fragment from a
ballad.
5. *Go . . . thee:* This expression is also used by the
drunken beggar Christopher Sly in *The Taming of the
Shrew,* Induction 1.
6. *laid knives . . . potage:* these are all means by which
the foul fiend tempts Tom to commit suicide. *halters:*
nooses. *ratsbane:* rat poison. *pottage:* soup.
7. Impossibly narrow, and probably suicidal to
attempt without diabolical help.
8. The five wits were common wit, imagination, fantasy, estimation, and memory (from medieval and
Renaissance cognitive theory).
9. *whirlwinds, star-blasting:* malign astrological
influences capable of causing sickness or death. *tak-*

ing: infection; bewitchment.
1. As Edgar speaks this sentence, he might kill vermin on his body as if they were devils.
2. Greedy. Young pelicans were reputed to feed on
blood from the wounds they made in their mother's
breast; in some versions, they first killed their father.
3. A fragment of an old rhyme, followed by hunting
cries or a ballad refrain; "Pilicock" was both a term
of endearment and a euphemism for "penis."
4. *obey . . . array:* these are fragments from the Ten
Commandments.
5. Favors from his mistress. In Petrarchan poetry,
wooers are "servants" to their ladies.
6. And had more women than the Turkish sultan had
in his royal harem.

Enter EDGAR [*disguised as Poor Tom*].

45 EDGAR Away, the foul fiend follows me! Through the sharp
hawthorn blow the winds.[5] Hum, go to thy bed and warm
thee.[6]

LEAR Didst thou give all to thy daughters, and art thou come
to this?

50 EDGAR Who gives anything to Poor Tom, whom the foul fiend
hath led through fire and through flame, through sword and
whirlpool, o'er bog and quagmire, that hath laid knives under
his pillow and halters in his pew, set ratsbane by his porridge,[7]
made him proud of heart to ride on a bay trotting horse over
55 four-inched[8] bridges, to course° his own shadow for° a traitor.   hunt / as
Bless thy five wits![9] Tom's a-cold. Oh, do, de, do, de, do, de,
bless thee from whirlwinds, star-blasting, and taking![1] Do
Poor Tom some charity, whom the foul fiend vexes. There
could I have him now, and there, and there again, and there![2]
Storm still.

60 LEAR Has his daughters brought him to this pass?
—Couldst thou save nothing? Wouldst thou give 'em all?

FOOL Nay, he reserved a blanket, else we had been all
shamed.

LEAR Now all the plagues that in the pendulous° air   overhanging; portentous
65 Hang fated o'er men's faults light on thy daughters.

KENT He hath no daughters, sir.

LEAR Death, traitor! Nothing could have subdued nature
To such a lowness but his unkind daughters.
Is it the fashion that discarded fathers
70 Should have thus little mercy on their flesh?
Judicious punishment! 'Twas this flesh begot
Those pelican[3] daughters.

EDGAR [*sings*] Pillicock sat on Pillicock hill, alow, alow,
loo, loo.[4]

FOOL This cold night will turn us all to fools and madmen.

75 EDGAR Take heed o'th' foul fiend, obey thy parents, keep thy
word's justice, swear not, commit not with man's sworn
spouse, set not thy sweetheart on proud array.[5] Tom's a-cold.

LEAR What hast thou been?

EDGAR A servingman, proud in heart and mind, that curled
80 my hair, wore gloves in my cap,[6] served the lust of my mistress' heart and did the act of darkness with her. Swore as
many oaths as I spake words and broke them in the sweet
face of heaven. One that slept in the contriving of lust and
waked to do it. Wine loved I dearly, dice dearly, and in
85 woman out-paramoured the Turk.[7] False of heart, light of

---

5. *Through . . . winds:* Perhaps a fragment from a
ballad.
6. *go . . . thee:* This expression is also used by the
drunken beggar Christopher Sly in *The Taming of the
Shrew,* Induction 1.
7. *laid knives . . . porridge:* these are all means by
which the foul fiend tempts Tom to commit suicide.
halters: nooses. *ratsbane:* rat poison.
8. Impossibly narrow, and probably suicidal to attempt
without diabolical help.
9. The five wits were common wit, imagination, fantasy, estimation, and memory (from medieval and
Renaissance cognitive theory).
1. *whirlwinds, star-blasting:* malign astrological
influences capable of causing sickness or death. *tak-*

ing: infection; bewitchment.
2. As Edgar speaks this sentence, he might kill vermin on his body as if they were devils.
3. Greedy. Young pelicans were reputed to feed on
blood from the wounds they made in their mother's
breast; in some versions, they first killed their father.
4. A fragment of an old rhyme, followed by hunting
cries or a ballad refrain; "Pillicock" was both a term
of endearment and a euphemism for "penis."
5. *obey . . . array:* these are fragments from the Ten
Commandments.
6. Favors from his mistress. In Petrarchan poetry,
wooers are "servants" to their ladies.
7. And had more women than the Turkish sultan had
in his royal harem.

ear,° bloody of hand. Hog in sloth, fox in stealth, wolf in   *rumor-hungry*
greediness, dog in madness, lion in prey. Let not the creaking of shoes[7] nor the rustlings of silks betray thy poor heart
to women. Keep thy foot[8] out of brothel, thy hand out of
85   placket,[9] thy pen from lender's book, and defy the foul fiend.
Still through the hawthorn blows the cold wind.
[*Sings.*]   Heigh, no, nonny.
Dolphin, my boy, my boy! Cease! Let him trot by.[1]

LEAR   Why, thou wert better in thy grave than to answer°   *encounter*
90   with thy uncovered body this extremity of the skies.° Is man   *violent weather*
no more but this? Consider him well. Thou owest the worm
no silk, the beast no hide, the sheep no wool, the cat[2] no
perfume. Here's three on 's° are sophisticated. Thou art the   *of us*
thing itself. Unaccommodated[3] man is no more but such a
95   poor, bare, forked° animal as thou art. [*He begins to undress.*]   *two-legged*
Off, off, you lendings!° Come on.   *borrowed clothes*

FOOL   Prithee, nuncle, be content. This is a naughty° night to   *foul*
swim in. Now a little fire in a wild° field were like an old   *barren; lustful*
lecher's heart: a small spark, all the rest in° body cold. Look,   *of his*
100   here comes a walking fire.

Enter GLOUCESTER [*with a torch*].

EDGAR   This is the foul fiend Fliberdegibek.[4] He begins at
curfew° and walks till the first cock.° He gives the web and   *9:00 P.M. / midnight*
the pin,[5] squeans° the eye and makes the harelip, mildews   *causes squints in*
the white° wheat, and hurts the poor creature of earth.   *nearly ripe*
105   Swithold footed thrice the old,[6]
He met the night mare and her nine-fold[7]
Bid her "Oh, light,"
And her troth plight°   *And gave her word*
And aroint thee,° witch, aroint thee!   *begone*
110   KENT   How fares your grace?
LEAR   What's° he?   *Who's*
KENT   Who's there? What is't you seek?
GLOUCESTER   What are you there? Your names?
EDGAR   Poor Tom, that eats the swimming frog, the toad, the
115   tadpole, the wall-newt, and the water,° that in the fury of his   *water newt*
heart, when the foul fiend rages, eats cow dung for salads,
swallows the old rat and the ditch dog,[8] drinks the green
mantle° of the standing pool, who is whipped from tithing°   *scum / parish*
to tithing and stock-punished° and imprisoned, who hath   *put in stocks*
120   had three suits to his back, six shirts to his body.
Horse to ride, and weapon to wear.
But mice and rats and such small deer[9]
Hath been Tom's food for seven long year.
Beware my follower! Peace, snulbug!° Peace, thou fiend!   *(a Harsnett devil)*

7. Creaking shoes were a fashionable affectation.
8. Punning on the French *foutre* ("fuck").
9. Slits in skirts or petticoats.
1. These phrases are probably from songs and proverbs. *Dolphin*: dauphin; the heir to the French throne,
sometimes identified with the devil by the English.
2. Civet, in Shakespeare's time the major source of
musk for perfume.
3. Naked; without the trappings of civilization.
4. A devil drawn from folk beliefs but famous for his
prominent place in Samuel Harsnett's *Declaration of
Egregious Popish Impostures* (1603); the frequent borrowings from Harsnett in *King Lear* set the earliest

possible composition date for the play.
5. *web and the pin*: cataract.
6. Swithald (or St. Withold), an early English saint
famous for healing, traversed the hilly countryside
three times.
7. *night mare*: a demon, not necessarily in the shape
of a horse; *nine-fold* might suggest an entourage of
demons and familiars, or the many folds (coils) of a
snake.
8. A dog found dead in a ditch.
9. *deer*: animals. These verses are adapted from a
romance popular in Shakespeare's time, *Bevis of
Hampton*.

ear,° bloody of hand. Hog in sloth, fox in stealth, wolf in   *rumor-hungry*
greediness, dog in madness, lion in prey. Let not the creaking of shoes[8] nor the rustling of silks betray thy poor heart
to woman. Keep thy foot[9] out of brothels, thy hand out of
90 plackets,[1] thy pen from lenders' books, and defy the foul
fiend. Still through the hawthorn blows the cold wind, says
suum, mun, nonny. Dolphin, my boy, boy, cease. Let him
trot by.[2]
     Storm still.
LEAR Thou wert better in a grave than to answer° with thy   *encounter*
95 uncovered body this extremity of the skies.° Is man no more   *violent weather*
than this? Consider him well. Thou ow'st the worm no silk,
the beast no hide, the sheep no wool, the cat[3] no perfume.
Ha? Here's three on 's° are sophisticated. Thou art the thing   *of us*
itself. Unaccommodated[4] man is no more but such a poor,
100 bare, forked° animal as thou art. [*He begins to undress.*] Off,   *two-legged*
off, you lendings.° Come, unbutton here.   *borrowed clothes*
     Enter GLOUCESTER, *with a torch.*
FOOL Prithee, nuncle, be contented. 'Tis a naughty° night to   *foul*
swim in. Now a little fire in a wild° field were like an old   *barren; lustful*
lecher's heart: a small spark, all the rest on 's° body cold.   *of his*
105 Look, here comes a walking fire.
EDGAR This is the foul Flibbertigibbet![5] He begins at curfew°   *9:00 p.m.*
and walks at first cock.° He gives the web and the pin,[6]   *midnight*
squints the eye and makes the harelip, mildews the white°   *near-ripe*
wheat, and hurts the poor creature of earth.
110 Swithold footed thrice the old,[7]
He met the night mare and her nine-fold;[8]
Bid her alight and her troth plight,°   *and gave her word*
And aroint thee,° witch, aroint thee.   *begone*
KENT How fares your grace?
115 LEAR What's° he?   *Who's*
KENT Who's there? What is't you seek?
GLOUCESTER What are you there? Your names?
EDGAR Poor Tom, that eats the swimming frog, the toad, the
tadpole, the wall-newt, and the water,° that in the fury of his   *water newt*
120 heart, when the foul fiend rages, eats cow dung for salads,
swallows the old rat and the ditch dog,[9] drinks the green
mantle° of the standing pool, who is whipped from tithing°   *scum / parish*
to tithing and stocked,° punished, and imprisoned, who   *put in stocks*
hath three suits to his back, six shirts to his body.
125 Horse to ride, and weapon to wear.
But mice and rats and such small deer[1]
Have been Tom's food for seven long year.
Beware my follower! Peace, Smulkin!° Peace, thou fiend.   *(a Harsnett devil)*

8. Creaking shoes were a fashionable affectation.
9. Punning on the French *foutre* ("fuck").
1. Slits in skirts or petticoats.
2. These phrases are probably from songs and proverbs. *Dolphin:* dauphin; the heir to the French
throne, sometimes identified with the devil by the
English.
3. Civet, in Shakespeare's time the major source of
musk for perfume.
4. Naked; without the trappings of civilization.
5. A devil drawn from folk beliefs but famous for his
prominent place in Samuel Harsnett's *Declaration of
Egregious Popish Impostures* (1603); the frequent borrowings from Harsnett in *King Lear* set the earliest

possible composition date for the play.
6. *web and the pin:* cataract.
7. Swithin (or St. Withold), an early English saint
famous for healing, traversed the hilly countryside
three times. *old:* wold; uplands.
8. *night mare:* a demon, not necessarily in the shape
of a horse; *nine-fold* might suggest an entourage of
demons and familiars, or the many folds (coils) of a
snake.
9. A dog found dead in a ditch.
1. *deer:* animals. These verses are adapted from a
romance popular in Shakespeare's time, *Bevis of
Hampton.*

125 GLOUCESTER [*to* LEAR]   What, hath your grace no better
    company?
    EDGAR   The prince of darkness is a gentleman, Modo he's
    called and Mahu.[1]
    GLOUCESTER   Our flesh and blood is grown so vile, my lord,
130   That it doth hate what gets° it.   *begets*
    EDGAR   Poor Tom's a-cold.
    GLOUCESTER   Go in with me. My duty cannot suffer°   *permit me*
    To obey in all your daughters' hard commands.
    Though their injunction be to bar my doors
135   And let this tyrannous night take hold upon you,
    Yet have I ventured to come seek you out
    And bring you where both food and fire is ready.
    LEAR   First let me talk with this philosopher,
    [*to* EDGAR] What is the cause of thunder?
140 KENT   My good lord, take his offer; go into the house.
    LEAR   I'll talk a word with this most learned Theban.°   *(Greek sage)*
    What is your study?°   *field of expertise*
    EDGAR   How to prevent the fiend and to kill vermin.
    LEAR   Let me ask you one word in private.
145 KENT [*to* GLOUCESTER]   Importune him to go, my lord; his wits
    Begin to unsettle.
    GLOUCESTER   Canst thou blame him?
    His daughters seek his death. O that good Kent,
    He said it would be thus, poor banished man!
    Thou sayest the King grows mad. I'll tell thee, friend,
150 I am almost mad myself. I had a son
    Now outlawed° from my blood, 'a° sought my life   *disowned / he*
    But lately, very late.° I loved him, friend,   *recently*
    No father his son dearer. True to tell thee,
    The grief hath crazed my wits.
155 What a night's this! I do beseech your grace—
    LEAR   Oh, cry you mercy.° —Noble philosopher, your   *beg your pardon*
    company.
    EDGAR   Tom's a-cold.
    GLOUCESTER [*to* EDGAR]   In, fellow, there, in th' hovel. Keep
    thee warm.
    LEAR   Come, let's in all.
    KENT   This way, my lord.
160 LEAR   With him I will keep still, with my philosopher.
    KENT   Good my lord, soothe° him. Let him take the fellow.   *humor*
    GLOUCESTER   Take him you on.°   *on ahead*
    KENT [*to* EDGAR]   Sirrah, come on, go along with us.
    LEAR   Come, good Athenian.°   *Greek philosopher*
165 GLOUCESTER   No words, no words, hush.
    EDGAR   Child Rowland[2] to the dark town come,
    His word° was still° "Fie, fo, and fum,   *motto / always*
    I smell the blood of a British[3] man."   [*Exeunt.*]

---

1. Modo and Mahu, more Harsnett devils, were
commanding generals of the hellish troops.
2. *Child:* an aspirant to knighthood. Rowland is the
famous hero of the Charlemagne legends.

3. "An Englishman" usually appears in this rhyme
from the cycle of tales of which "Jack and the
Beanstalk" is the best known. The alteration befits
Lear's ancient Britain.

GLOUCESTER What, hath your grace no better company?

130 EDGAR The Prince of Darkness is a gentleman. Modo he's
called and Mahu.[2]

GLOUCESTER Our flesh and blood, my lord, is grown so vile
That it doth hate what gets° it.   *begets*

EDGAR Poor Tom's a-cold.

135 GLOUCESTER Go in with me. My duty cannot suffer°   *permit me*
T'obey in all your daughters' hard commands.
Though their injunction be to bar my doors
And let this tyrannous night take hold upon you,
Yet have I ventured to come seek you out

140 And bring you where both fire and food is ready.

LEAR First let me talk with this philosopher.
[*to* EDGAR] What is the cause of thunder?

KENT Good my lord, take his offer;
Go into th' house.

145 LEAR I'll talk a word with this same learned Theban.°   *(Greek sage)*
What is your study?°   *field of expertise*

EDGAR How to prevent the fiend and to kill vermin.

LEAR Let me ask you one word in private.

KENT [*to* GLOUCESTER] Importune him once more to go, my
lord,
His wits begin t'unsettle.

150 GLOUCESTER   Canst thou blame him?
     Storm still.
His daughters seek his death. Ah, that good Kent,
He said it would be thus, poor banished man!
Thou sayest the King grows mad. I'll tell thee, friend,
I am almost mad myself. I had a son,

155 Now outlawed° from my blood. He sought my life   *disowned*
But lately, very late.° I loved him, friend,   *recently*
No father his son dearer. True to tell thee,
The grief hath crazed my wits. What a night's this?
I do beseech your grace—

LEAR   Oh, cry you mercy,° sir.   *beg your pardon*

160 —Noble philosopher, your company.

EDGAR Tom's a-cold.

GLOUCESTER [*to* EDGAR] In, fellow, there: into th' hovel.
Keep thee warm.

LEAR Come, let's in all.

KENT   This way, my lord.

LEAR   With him
I will keep still, with my philosopher.

165 KENT [*to* GLOUCESTER] Good my lord, soothe° him.   *humor*
Let him take the fellow.

GLOUCESTER   Take him you on.°   *on ahead*

KENT Sirrah, come on. Go along with us.

LEAR Come, good Athenian.°   *Greek philosopher*

GLOUCESTER No words, no words, hush.

170 EDGAR Child Rowland[3] to the dark tower came,
His word° was still° "Fie, fo, and fum;   *motto / always*
I smell the blood of a British[4] man."   *Exeunt.*

---

2. Modo and Mahu, more Harsnett devils, were
commanding generals of the hellish troops.
3. *Child:* an aspirant to knighthood. Roland is the
famous hero of the Charlemagne legends.

4. "An Englishman" usually appears in this rhyme
from the cycle of tales of which "Jack and the
Beanstalk" is the best known. The alteration befits
Lear's ancient Britain.

3.5 (F 3.5)

Enter CORNWALL *and* [*Edmund the*] BASTARD.

CORNWALL   I will have my revenge ere I depart the house.

BASTARD   How, my lord, I may be censured,° that nature° thus   *judged / kinship*
    gives way to loyalty, something fears me° to think of.   *I am somewhat afraid*

CORNWALL   I now perceive it was not altogether your brother's

5   evil disposition made him seek his° death, but a provoking   *(Gloucester's)*
    merit set a-work by a reprovable badness in himself.[1]

BASTARD   How malicious is my fortune that I must repent to
    be just! This is the letter he spoke of, which approves him an
    intelligent party to the advantages of France.[2] O heavens,

10   that his treason were not, or not I the detector.

CORNWALL   Go with me to the Duchess.

BASTARD   If the matter of this paper be certain, you have
    mighty business in hand.

CORNWALL   True or false, it hath made thee Earl of Gloucester.

15   Seek out where thy father is, that he may be ready for our
    apprehension.°   *arrest*

BASTARD [*aside*]   If I find him comforting the King, it will
    stuff his° suspicion more fully. [*to* CORNWALL] I will per-   *(Cornwall's)*
    severe in my course of loyalty, though the conflict be sore

20   between that and my blood.°   *filial duty*

CORNWALL   I will lay trust upon thee, and thou shalt find a
    dearer father in my love.   *Exeunt.*

3.6 (F 3.6)

Enter GLOUCESTER *and* LEAR, KENT [*disguised as*
Caius], FOOL, *and* [EDGAR *disguised as Poor*] *Tom.*

GLOUCESTER   Here is better than the open air; take it thank-
    fully. I will piece out° the comfort with what addition I can.   *augment*
    I will not be long from you.

KENT   All the power of his wits have given way to impatience.[1]

5   The gods° deserve your kindness.   [*Exit* GLOUCESTER.]   *May the gods*

EDGAR   Fratereto° calls me and tells me Nero is an angler in   *(a Harsnett devil)*
    the lake of darkness.[2] Pray, innocent, beware the foul fiend.

FOOL   Prithee, nuncle, tell me whether a madman be a
    gentleman or a yeoman.[3]

10 LEAR   A king, a king! To have a thousand with red burning
    spits come hissing in upon them.

3.5 Location: At Gloucester's castle.
1. *a provoking . . . himself*: Gloucester's own wickedness deservedly triggered the blameworthy evil in
Edgar.
2. *which . . . France*: which proves him a spy and an
informer in the aid of France; "party," or faction, was
usually a term of opprobrium in the Renaissance.
3.6 Location: Within an outbuilding of Gloucester's.

1. Rage; inability to bear more suffering.
2. In Chaucer's *Monk's Tale*, the infamously cruel
Roman emperor Nero is found fishing in hell (lines
485–86).
3. A free landowner but not a member of the gentry,
lacking official family arms and the distinctions they
confer. Shakespeare seems to have procured a coat of
arms for his father in 1596.

3.5 (Q 3.5)

Enter CORNWALL *and* EDMOND.

CORNWALL   I will have my revenge ere I depart his house.

EDMOND   How, my lord, I may be censured,° that nature° thus   *judged / kinship*
gives way to loyalty, something fears me° to think of.   *I am somewhat afraid*

CORNWALL   I now perceive it was not altogether your brother's

5   evil disposition made him seek his° death, but a provoking   *(Gloucester's)*
merit set a-work by a reprovable badness in himself.[1]

EDMOND   How malicious is my fortune that I must repent to
be just! This is the letter which he spoke of, which approves
him an intelligent party to the advantages of France.[2] O

10   heavens, that this treason were not, or not I the detector.

CORNWALL   Go with me to the Duchess.

EDMOND   If the matter of this paper be certain, you have mighty
business in hand.

CORNWALL   True or false, it hath made thee Earl of Glouces-

15   ter. Seek out where thy father is, that he may be ready for our
apprehension.°   *arrest*

EDMOND [*aside*]   If I find him comforting the King, it will stuff
his° suspicion more fully. [*to* CORNWALL] I will persevere in   *(Cornwall's)*
my course of loyalty, though the conflict be sore between

20   that and my blood.°   *filial duty*

CORNWALL   I will lay trust upon thee, and thou shalt find a
dear father in my love.   *Exeunt.*

3.6 (Q 3.6)

Enter KENT [*disguised as Caius*] *and* GLOUCESTER.

GLOUCESTER   Here is better than the open air; take it thankfully. I will piece out° the comfort with what addition I can.   *augment*
I will not be long from you.

KENT   All the power of his wits have given way to his impa-

5   tience.[1] The gods° reward your kindness.   *May the gods*

                        Exit [GLOUCESTER].

Enter LEAR, EDGAR [*disguised as Poor Tom*],
and FOOL.

EDGAR   Frateretto° calls me and tells me Nero is an angler in   *(a Harsnett devil)*
the lake of darkness.[2] Pray, innocent, and beware the foul
fiend.

FOOL   Prithee, nuncle, tell me whether a madman be a gentle-

10   man or a yeoman.[3]

LEAR   A king, a king.

FOOL   No, he's a yeoman that has a gentleman to° his son, for   *for*
he's a mad yeoman that sees his son a gentleman before
him.

15 LEAR   To have a thousand with red burning spits
Come hizzing in upon 'em.

3.5 Location: At Gloucester's castle.

1. *a provoking . . . himself:* Gloucester's own wickedness deservedly triggered the blameworthy evil in
Edgar.

2. *which . . . France:* which proves him a spy and an
informer in the aid of France; "party," or faction, was
usually a term of opprobrium in the Renaissance.

3.6 Location: Within an outbuilding of Gloucester's.

1. Rage; inability to bear more suffering.

2. In Chaucer's *Monk's Tale,* the infamously cruel
Roman emperor Nero is found fishing in hell (lines
485–86).

3. A free landowner but not a member of the gentry,
lacking official family arms and the distinctions they
confer. Shakespeare seems to have procured a coat of
arms for his father in 1596.

EDGAR The foul fiend bites my back.

FOOL He's mad that trusts in the tameness of a wolf, a horse's
health, a boy's love, or a whore's oath.

15 LEAR It shall be done;[4] I will arraign° them straight.°   prosecute / immediately
[*to* EDGAR] Come, sit thou here, most learned Justice.
[*to the* FOOL] Thou, sapient sir, sit here —No, you she-foxes—

EDGAR Look where he stands and glares. Want'st thou eyes[5]
at trial, madam?

20 [*Sings.*]   Come o'er the broom, Bessy, to me.[6]

FOOL [*sings*] Her boat hath a leak,
And she must not speak,
Why she dares not come over to thee.

EDGAR The foul fiend haunts poor Tom in the voice of a
25 nightingale. Hoppedance° cries in Tom's belly for two white°   (a demon) / fresh
herring. Croak° not, black angel. I have no food for thee.   Growl

KENT [*to* LEAR] How do you, sir? Stand you not so amazed.
Will you lie down and rest upon the cushions?

LEAR I'll see their trial first: bring in their evidence.
30 [*to* EDGAR] Thou robèd man of justice, take thy place,
[*to the* FOOL] And thou, his yokefellow of equity,°   partner of law
Bench° by his side. You are o'th' commission:° sit you too.   Sit / judiciary

EDGAR Let us deal justly.
[*Sings.*]   Sleepest or wakest, thou jolly shepherd?
35 Thy sheep be in the corn,°   grain
And for one blast of thy minikin° mouth,   dainty
Thy sheep shall take no harm.
Purr, the cat is gray.[7]

LEAR Arraign her first: 'tis Gonorill, I here take my oath
40 before this honorable assembly, kicked the poor King her
father.

FOOL Come hither, mistress. Is your name Gonorill?

LEAR She cannot deny it.

FOOL Cry you mercy, I took you for a joint-stool.[8]

45 LEAR And here's another whose warped looks proclaim
What store° her heart is made on.° Stop her there.   material / of
Arms, arms, sword, fire, corruption in the place!
False Justicer, why hast thou let her scape?

---

4. Textual Comment Lear's "mock-trial" of Gonorill and Regan, in absentia, appears only in Q1
(3.6.15–48). The trial does not appear in F and was
probably cut by Shakespeare rather than omitted
due to a printer's error. See Digital Edition TC 4
(Quarto edited text).
5. *eyes:* eyeballs (?).

6. From an old song.
7. Purr the cat is another devil; such devils in the
shape of cats were the familiars of witches.
8. I beg your pardon, I mistook you for a stool. An
idiom of the day expressing annoyance at being
slighted. Here, the part of Gonorill is actually being
played by a stool.

EDGAR   Bless thy five wits.
50 KENT   Oh, pity. Sir, where is the patience now
That you so oft have boasted to retain?
EDGAR [*aside*]   My tears begin to take his part so much
They'll mar my counterfeiting.
LEAR   The little dogs and all,°   *Even the little dogs*
55 Trey, Blanche, and Sweetheart, see, they bark at me.
EDGAR   Tom will throw his head at° them; avaunt,° you curs!   *will threaten (?) / begone*
Be thy mouth or° black or white,   *either*
Tooth that poisons° if it bite,   *gives rabies*
Mastiff, greyhound, mongrel grim,
60 Hound or spaniel, brach° or him,   *bitch*
Bobtail tyke, or trundle-tail,⁹
Tom will make them weep and wail;
For with throwing thus my head,
Dogs leap the hatch¹ and all are fled.
65 Loudla, doodla, come march to wakes,° and fairs,   *parish festivals*
And market towns. Poor Tom, thy horn is dry.²
LEAR   Then let them anatomize° Regan, see what breeds about   *dissect*
her heart. Is there any cause in nature that makes this hard-
ness? [*to* EDGAR] You, sir, I entertain° you for one of my hun-   *retain*
70 dred, only I do not like the fashion of your garments. You'll
say they are Persian° attire, but let them be changed.   *oriental; splendid*
KENT   Now, good my lord, lie here awhile.
LEAR   Make no noise, make no noise. Draw the curtains,° so,   *bed curtains*
so, so. We'll go to supper i'th' morning, so, so, so.
[*He falls asleep.*]
Enter GLOUCESTER.
75 GLOUCESTER   Come hither, friend. Where is the King my
master?
KENT   Here, sir, but trouble him not. His wits are gone.
GLOUCESTER   Good friend, I prithee, take him in thy arms.
I have o'erheard a plot of death upon° him,   *against*
There is a litter ready; lay him in't
80 And drive towards Dover, friend, where thou shalt meet
Both welcome and protection. Take up thy master;
If thou shouldst dally half an hour, his life
With thine and all that offer to defend him
Stand in assurèd loss.° Take up the King   *Are certainly doomed*
85 And follow me, that will to some provision
Give thee quick conduct.³

---

9. Short-tailed mongrel, or long-tailed.
1. Dogs leap over the lower half of a divided door.
2. A begging formula that refers to the horn vessel
that vagabonds carried for drink; the covert sense is
that Edgar has run out of Bedlamite inspiration.
3. *that . . . conduct:* who will quickly guide you to
some supplies.

EDGAR   Bless thy five wits.[4]

KENT   Oh, pity. Sir, where is the patience now
That you so oft have boasted to retain?

20   EDGAR [*aside*]   My tears begin to take his part so much
They mar my counterfeiting.

LEAR   The little dogs and all,°   *Even the little dogs*
Trey, Blanche, and Sweetheart, see, they bark at me.

EDGAR   Tom will throw his head at° them. Avaunt,° you curs!   *will threaten (?) / Begone*
25   Be thy mouth or° black or white,   *either*
Tooth that poisons° if it bite,   *gives rabies*
Mastiff, greyhound, mongrel grim,
Hound or spaniel, brach° or him,   *bitch*
Or bobtail tyke, or trundle tail,[5]
30   Tom will make him weep and wail;
For with throwing thus my head,
Dogs leapt the hatch[6] and all are fled.
Do, de, de, de. Sessa.[7] Come, march to wakes,° and fairs,   *parish festivals*
and market towns. Poor Tom, thy horn is dry.[8]

35   LEAR   Then let them anatomize° Regan, see what breeds   *dissect*
about her heart. Is there any cause in nature that makes
these hard hearts? [*to* EDGAR] You, sir, I entertain° for one of   *retain*
my hundred, only I do not like the fashion of your garments.
You will say they are Persian,° but let them be changed.   *oriental; splendid*

40   KENT   Now, good my lord, lie here and rest awhile.

LEAR   Make no noise, make no noise. Draw the curtains,° so,   *bed curtains*
so. We'll go to supper i'th' morning.

FOOL   And I'll go to bed at noon.

Enter GLOUCESTER.

GLOUCESTER   Come hither, friend. Where is the King my
master?

45   KENT   Here, sir, but trouble him not. His wits are gone.

GLOUCESTER   Good friend, I prithee, take him in thy arms.
I have o'erheard a plot of death upon° him.   *against*
There is a litter ready: lay him in't
And drive toward Dover, friend, where thou shalt meet
50   Both welcome and protection. Take up thy master;
If thou shouldst dally half an hour, his life
With thine and all that offer to defend him
Stand in assurèd loss.° Take up, take up,   *Are certainly doomed*
And follow me, that will to some provision
55   Give thee quick conduct.[9] Come, come, away.   *Exeunt.*

---

4. TEXTUAL COMMENT Lear's "mock-trial" of Gonerill and Regan, in absentia, appears only in Q1
(3.6.12–49). The trial does not appear in F and was
probably cut by Shakespeare rather than omitted due
to a printer's error. See Digital Edition TC 4 (Folio
edited text).
5. Short-tailed mongrel, or long-tailed.
6. Dogs leaped over the lower half of a divided door.

7. Apparently nonsense, although "Sessa" may be a
version of the French *cessez* ("stop" or "hush").
8. A begging formula that refers to the horn vessel
that vagabonds carried for drink; the covert sense is
that Edgar has run out of Bedlamite inspiration.
9. *that . . . conduct:* who will quickly guide you to
some supplies.

KENT   Oppressed nature sleeps.
This rest might yet have balmed° thy broken sinews,°   *soothed / nerves*
Which, if convenience° will not allow,   *circumstances*
Stand in hard cure.° [*to the* FOOL] Come, help to bear thy   *Will be hard to cure*
   master.
90 Thou must not stay behind.
GLOUCESTER   Come, come away.   *Exeunt [all but* EDGAR].
EDGAR   When we our betters see bearing our° woes,   *our same*
We scarcely think our miseries our foes.
Who alone suffers, suffers most i'th' mind,
95 Leaving free° things and happy shows° behind.   *carefree / scenes*
But then the mind much sufferance doth o'erskip,
When grief hath mates and bearing° fellowship.   *pain; suffering*
How light and portable my pain seems now,
When that which makes me bend makes the King bow:
100 He° childed as I fathered. Tom, away.   *He is*
Mark the high noises° and thyself bewray°   *important rumors / reveal*
When false opinion, whose wrong thoughts defile thee,
In thy just proof repeals and reconciles thee.[4]
What° will hap° more tonight, safe scape the King,   *Whatever / chance*
105 Lurk, lurk.   [*Exit.*]

---

4. *In . . . thee:* When true evidence pardons you and reconciles you (with your father).

3.7 (F 3.7)

Enter CORNWALL, REGAN, GONORILL, [*Edmund the*]
BASTARD[, *and three* SERVANTS].

CORNWALL [*to* GONORILL]   Post° speedily to my lord your hus-   Ride
band; show him this letter. The army of France is landed. [*to*
SERVANTS] Seek out the villain Gloucester!

[*Exeunt two or three* SERVANTS.]

REGAN   Hang him instantly.

5 GONORILL   Pluck out his eyes.

CORNWALL   Leave him to my displeasure. Edmund, keep you
our sister° company. The revenge we are bound[1] to take upon   sister-in-law
your traitorous father are not fit for your beholding. Advise
the Duke where you are going to a most festinate prepara-
10 tion.[2] We are bound° to the like. Our post° shall be swift and   committed / messengers
intelligence° betwixt us. Farewell, dear sister. Farewell, my   convey information
lord of Gloucester.

Enter STEWARD.

How now, where's the King?

STEWARD   My lord of Gloucester hath conveyed him hence.
15 Some five- or six-and-thirty of his° knights,   (Lear's)
Hot questrists° after him, met him at gate,   searchers
Who, with some other of the lord's° dependents,   (Gloucester's)
Are gone with him towards Dover, where they boast
To have well-armed friends.

20 CORNWALL   Get horses for your mistress.   [*Exit* STEWARD.]

GONORILL   Farewell, sweet lord and sister.

CORNWALL   Edmund, farewell.

Exeunt GONORILL *and* [*Edmund the*] BASTARD.

Go seek the traitor Gloucester.
Pinion him° like a thief; bring him before us.   Tie his arms
Though we may not pass° upon his life   pass sentence
25 Without the form° of justice, yet our power   official proceedings
Shall do a courtesy[3] to our wrath, which men may blame
But not control. Who's there, the traitor?

Enter GLOUCESTER *brought in by two or three*
[SERVANTS].

REGAN   Ingrateful fox, 'tis he.

CORNWALL   Bind fast his corky° arms.   withered

[SERVANTS *bind* GLOUCESTER.]

GLOUCESTER   What means your graces? Good my friends,
consider
30 You are my guests. Do me no foul play, friends.

CORNWALL   Bind him, I say.

REGAN   Hard, hard! O filthy traitor!

GLOUCESTER   Unmerciful lady, as you are, I am true.

CORNWALL   To this chair bind him. —Villain, thou shalt find—

GLOUCESTER   By the kind gods, 'tis most ignobly done
35 To pluck me by the beard.°   (an extreme insult)

REGAN   So white° and such a traitor?   white-haired; venerable

---

3.7 Location: At Gloucester's castle.   tell the Duke to prepare quickly.
1. Bound by duty; expected by destiny.   3. Shall allow a courtesy or an indulgence; shall
2. *Advise . . . preparation:* When you reach Albany,   bow to.

3.7 (Q 3.7)

Enter CORNWALL, REGAN, GONERILL, [EDMOND *the*]
bastard, and SERVANTS.

CORNWALL [*to* GONERILL]   Post° speedily to my lord, your hus-   Ride
band; show him this letter. The army of France is landed. [*to*
SERVANTS] Seek out the traitor Gloucester.
                                      [*Exeunt* SERVANTS.]

REGAN   Hang him instantly.

5   GONERILL   Pluck out his eyes.

CORNWALL   Leave him to my displeasure. Edmond, keep you
our sister° company. The revenges we are bound[1] to take   sister-in-law
upon your traitorous father are not fit for your beholding.
Advise the Duke where you are going to a most festinate
10   preparation.[2] We are bound° to the like. Our posts° shall be   committed / messengers
swift and intelligent° betwixt us. Farewell, dear sister. Fare-   well informed
well, my lord of Gloucester.
        Enter [*Oswald the*] STEWARD.
How now? Where's the King?

STEWARD   My lord of Gloucester hath conveyed him hence.

15   Some five- or six-and-thirty of his° knights,   (Lear's)
Hot questrists° after him, met him at gate,   searchers
Who, with some other of the lord's° dependents,   (Gloucester's)
Are gone with him toward Dover, where they boast
To have well-armed friends.

20   CORNWALL   Get horses for your mistress.

GONERILL   Farewell, sweet lord and sister.

CORNWALL   Edmond, farewell.
        Exeunt GONERILL [*and* EDMOND].
        Go seek the traitor Gloucester;
Pinion him° like a thief; bring him before us.   Tie his arms
Though well we may not pass° upon his life   pass sentence
25   Without the form° of justice, yet our power   official proceedings
Shall do a court'sy[3] to our wrath, which men
May blame but not control.
        Enter GLOUCESTER *and* SERVANTS.
                Who's there? The traitor?

REGAN   Ingrateful fox, 'tis he.

CORNWALL   Bind fast his corky° arms.   withered

GLOUCESTER   What means your graces? Good my friends,
        consider
30   You are my guests. Do me no foul play, friends.

CORNWALL   Bind him, I say.
        [SERVANTS *bind* GLOUCESTER.]

REGAN   Hard, hard! O filthy traitor!

GLOUCESTER   Unmerciful lady, as you are, I'm none.

CORNWALL   To this chair bind him. —Villain, thou shalt find—

GLOUCESTER   By the kind gods, 'tis most ignobly done
35   To pluck me by the beard.°   (an extreme insult)

REGAN   So white° and such a traitor?   white-haired; venerable

---

3.7 Location: At Gloucester's castle.
1. Bound by duty; expected by destiny.
2. *Advise . . . preparation:* When you reach Albany,

tell the Duke to prepare quickly.
3. Shall allow a courtesy or an indulgence; shall
bow to.

GLOUCESTER   Naughty° lady,   *Wicked*
These hairs which thou dost ravish from my chin
Will quicken° and accuse thee. I am your host;   *come alive*
With robbers' hands my hospitable favors°   *features*
40   You should not ruffle° thus. What will you do?   *snatch at*
CORNWALL   Come, sir, what letters had you late° from   *lately*
    France?
REGAN   Be simple,° answerer, for we know the truth.   *direct*
CORNWALL   And what confederacy have you with the traitors
    Late-footed° in the kingdom?   *Recently on the move*
45   REGAN   To whose hands you have sent the lunatic King?
    Speak.
GLOUCESTER   I have a letter guessingly set down,[4]
Which came from one that's of a neutral heart
And not from one opposed.
CORNWALL   Cunning.
REGAN   And false.
CORNWALL   Where hast thou sent the King?
GLOUCESTER   To Dover.
50   REGAN   Wherefore° to Dover? Wast thou not charged° at   *Why / commanded*
    peril—
CORNWALL   Wherefore to Dover? Let him first answer that!
GLOUCESTER   I am tied to th' stake, and I must stand the
    course.[5]
REGAN   Wherefore to Dover, sir?
GLOUCESTER   Because I would not see thy cruel nails
55   Pluck out his poor old eyes, nor thy fierce sister
In his anointed[6] flesh, rash° boarish fangs.   *slash; cut*
The sea, with such a storm on his loved head
In hell-black night endured, would have laid° up   *risen*
And quenched the stellèd° fires. Yet, poor old heart,   *stars'*
60   He holped° the heavens to rage.   *helped*
If wolves had at thy gate heard that dern° time   *dreary; dreadful*
Thou shouldst have said, "Good Porter, turn the key."°   *(to open the door)*
All cruels else subscribed,[7] but I shall see
The wingèd vengeance[8] overtake such children.
65   CORNWALL   See't shalt thou never. Fellows,° hold the chair.   *Servants*
    —Upon those eyes of thine, I'll set my foot.
GLOUCESTER   He that will think° to live till he be old,   *Whoever hopes*
Give me some help! —Oh, cruel! O ye gods!
        [CORNWALL *plucks out Gloucester's eye.*]
REGAN   One side will mock another: t'other too.
70   CORNWALL   If you see vengeance—
FIRST SERVANT   Hold your hand, my lord.
I have served ever since I was a child,
But better service have I never done you
Than now to bid you hold.
REGAN   How now, you dog?

---

4. Written without confirmation; speculative.
5. An image from bearbaiting, in which a bear on a short tether had to fight off an assault by dogs.
6. Consecrated with holy oils (as part of a king's coronation).

7. All other cruel beasts would have pity, but not you; I can accept the cruelty of all creatures, but not yours.
8. Swift or heaven-sent revenge; either an angel of God or the Furies, who were flying executors of divine vengeance in classical mythology.

GLOUCESTER   Naughty° lady,   *Wicked*
These hairs which thou dost ravish from my chin
Will quicken° and accuse thee. I am your host;   *come alive*
With robbers' hands my hospitable favors°   *features*
40   You should not ruffle° thus. What will you do?   *snatch at*
CORNWALL   Come, sir, what letters had you late° from   *lately*
France?
REGAN   Be simple-answered,° for we know the truth.   *straightforward*
CORNWALL   And what confederacy have you with the traitors
Late footed° in the kingdom?   *Recently on the move*
REGAN   To whose hands
45   You have sent the lunatic King? Speak.
GLOUCESTER   I have a letter guessingly set down[4]
Which came from one that's of a neutral heart
And not from one opposed.
CORNWALL   Cunning.
REGAN   And false.
CORNWALL   Where hast thou sent the King?
50   GLOUCESTER   To Dover.
REGAN   Wherefore° to Dover?   *Why*
Wast thou not charged° at peril—   *commanded*
CORNWALL   Wherefore to Dover? Let him answer that.
GLOUCESTER   I am tied to th' stake, and I must stand the
course.[5]
55   REGAN   Wherefore to Dover?
GLOUCESTER   Because I would not see thy cruel nails
Pluck out his poor old eyes, nor thy fierce sister
In his anointed[6] flesh stick boarish fangs.
The sea, with such a storm as his bare head
60   In hell-black night endured, would have buoyed° up   *risen*
And quenched the stellèd° fires,   *stars'*
Yet poor old heart, he holp° the heavens to rain.   *helped*
If wolves had at thy gate howled that stern° time,   *dreary; dreadful*
Thou shouldst have said, "Good porter, turn the key,°   *(to open the door)*
65   All cruels else subscribe."[7] But I shall see
The wingèd vengeance[8] overtake such children.
CORNWALL   See't shalt thou never. Fellows,° hold the chair.   *Servants*
—Upon these eyes of thine, I'll set my foot.
         [*He plucks out Gloucester's eye.*]
GLOUCESTER   He that will think° to live till he be old,   *Whoever hopes*
70   Give me some help! —Oh, cruel! O you gods!
REGAN   One side will mock another: th'other too.
CORNWALL   If you see vengeance—
FIRST SERVANT   Hold your hand, my lord.
I have served you ever since I was a child,
But better service have I never done you
Than now to bid you hold.
75   REGAN   How now, you dog?

---

4. Written without confirmation; speculative.
5. An image from bearbaiting, in which a bear on a short tether had to fight off an assault by dogs.
6. Consecrated with holy oils (as part of a king's coronation).

7. All other cruel beasts would have pity, but not you; I can accept the cruelty of all creatures, but not yours.
8. Swift or heaven-sent revenge; either an angel of God or the Furies, who were flying executors of divine vengeance in classical mythology.

75 FIRST SERVANT   If you did wear a beard upon your chin,
    I'd shake it on this quarrel.[9] What do you mean?°   *intend*
    CORNWALL   My villein?°   *servant; villain*
    FIRST SERVANT   Why, then, come on and take the chance of
        anger![1]
        [*They*] *draw and fight.*
    REGAN   Give me thy sword. A peasant stand up thus?
        She takes a sword and runs at him behind.
80 FIRST SERVANT   Oh, I am slain! [*to* GLOUCESTER] My lord, yet
        have you one eye left
    To see some mischief° on him. Oh!   *injury*
        [*He dies.*]
    CORNWALL   Lest it see more, prevent it. Out, vile jelly![2]
        [*He plucks out Gloucester's other eye.*]
    Where is thy luster now?
    GLOUCESTER   All dark and comfortless? Where's my son
        Edmund?
85 Edmund, unbridle all the sparks of Nature[3]
    To quit° this horrid act.   *requite; avenge*
    REGAN   Out, villain!
    Thou call'st on him that hates thee. It was he
    That made the overture of° thy treasons to us,   *revealed*
    Who is too good to pity thee.
90 GLOUCESTER   Oh, my follies! Then Edgar was abused.°   *slandered*
    Kind gods, forgive me that and prosper him.
    REGAN   Go thrust him out at gates, and let him smell
    His way to Dover. How is't my lord? How look you?°   *How do you feel*
    CORNWALL   I have received a hurt. Follow me, lady.
95   [*to* SERVANTS] Turn out that eyeless villain; throw this
        slave
    Upon the dunghill.
                        [*Exeunt* SERVANTS *with* GLOUCESTER *and*
                                        First Servant's body.]
                    Regan, I bleed apace;
    Untimely comes this hurt. Give me your arm.
                        Exeunt [CORNWALL *and* REGAN].[4]
    SECOND SERVANT   I'll never care what wickedness I do if this
        man come to good.[5]
100 THIRD SERVANT   If she live long, and in the end meet the old°   *usual*
        course of death, women will all turn monsters.
    SECOND SERVANT   Let's follow the old Earl and get the Bed-
        lam° to lead him where he would. His madness allows itself   *madman*
        to anything.
105 THIRD SERVANT   Go thou. I'll fetch some flax and whites of
        eggs to apply to his bleeding face. Now, heaven help him!
                        Exeunt [*severally*].°   *separately*

---

9. I'd pluck it over this point; I'd issue a challenge.
1. Take the risk of fighting when angry; take the fortune of one who is governed by his anger.
2. PERFORMANCE COMMENT Should a production
minimize gore in this shocking scene, or emphasize
it? For the implications of the staging, see Digital
Edition PC 4.
3. All the warmth of filial love; all the anger that
your father has received such treatment.
4. TEXTUAL COMMENT Some critics have called the

play's blinding scene the "cruelest" in all of English
literature. Yet the two texts differ in their portrayals
of this cruelty. Notably, the Quarto version culminates
with Cornwall's two servants pledging to avenge
Gloucester's blinding. Their absence in the Folio version denies the audience even this brief expression of
sympathy. See Digital Edition TC 5 (Quarto edited
text).
5. I'll . . . good: Because this may be a sign that evil
goes unpunished. *this man*: Cornwall.

FIRST SERVANT   If you did wear a beard upon your chin,
  I'd shake it on this quarrel.[9] What do you mean?°   *intend*
CORNWALL [*drawing his sword*]   My villein?°   *servant; villain*
FIRST SERVANT   Nay, then, come on, and take the chance of
    anger.[1]
      [*They fight, and* CORNWALL *is wounded.*]
80 REGAN   Give me thy sword. A peasant stand up thus?
      [*She*] *kills him.*
FIRST SERVANT   Oh, I am slain! [*to* GLOUCESTER] My lord, you
    have one eye left
  To see some mischief° on him. Oh!   *injury*
      [*He dies.*]
CORNWALL   Lest it see more, prevent it. Out, vile jelly![2]
      [*He plucks out Gloucester's other eye.*]
  Where is thy luster now?
85 GLOUCESTER   All dark and comfortless?
  Where's my son Edmond?
  Edmond, enkindle all the sparks of nature[3]
  To quit° this horrid act.   *requite; avenge*
REGAN   Out, treacherous villain!
  Thou call'st on him that hates thee. It was he
90 That made the overture of° thy treasons to us,   *revealed*
  Who is too good to pity thee.
GLOUCESTER   Oh, my follies! Then Edgar was abused!°   *slandered*
  Kind gods, forgive me that, and prosper him.
REGAN   Go, thrust him out at gates, and let him smell
95 His way to Dover. How is't, my lord? How look you?°   *How do you feel*
CORNWALL   I have received a hurt. Follow me, lady.
  [*to* SERVANTS] Turn out that eyeless villain. Throw this slave
  Upon the dunghill.
            Exeunt [SERVANTS] *with* GLOUCESTER [*and First*
                                    Servant's body].
          Regan, I bleed apace;
  Untimely comes this hurt. Give me your arm.
            Exeunt [CORNWALL *and* REGAN].[4]

---

9. I'd pluck it over this point; I'd issue a challenge.
1. Take the risk of fighting when angry; take the fortune of one who is governed by his anger.
2. PERFORMANCE COMMENT Should a production
minimize gore in this shocking scene, or emphasize
it? For the implications of the staging, see Digital
Edition PC 4.
3. All the warmth of filial love; all the anger that
your father has received such treatment.

4. TEXTUAL COMMENT Some critics have called the
play's blinding scene the "cruelest" in all of English
literature. Yet the two texts differ in their portrayals
of this cruelty. Notably, the Quarto version culminates with Cornwall's two servants pledging to avenge
Gloucester's blinding. Their absence in the Folio version denies the audience even this brief expression of
sympathy. See Digital Edition TC 5 (Folio edited text).

4.1 (F 4.1)

Enter EDGAR *[disguised as Poor Tom].*

EDGAR Yet better thus and known to be contemned,°   despised
    Than still° contemned and flattered to be worst.   always
    The lowest and most dejected thing of Fortune
    Stands still in experience, lives not in fear.[1]
5   The lamentable change is from the best,
    The worst returns to laughter.[2]

Enter GLOUCESTER, *led by an* OLD MAN.
    Who's here? My father, parti-eyed![3] World, world, O world!
    But that thy strange mutations make us hate thee,
    Life would not yield to age.[4]

OLD MAN   O my good lord,
10   I have been your tenant and your father's
    Tenant this fourscore—
GLOUCESTER Away, get thee away! Good friend, be gone.
    Thy comforts° can do me no good at all;   assistance
    Thee they may hurt.
15 OLD MAN Alack, sir, you cannot see your way.
GLOUCESTER I have no way and therefore want no eyes.
    I stumbled when I saw. Full oft 'tis seen
    Our means secure us, and our mere defects
    Prove our commodities.[5] Ah, dear son Edgar,
20   The food° of thy abusèd° father's wrath,   fuel; prey / deceived
    Might I but live to see thee in° my touch,   through
    I'd say I had eyes again.
OLD MAN How now, who's there?
EDGAR *[aside]* O gods! Who is't can say, "I am at the worst"?
25   I am worse than e'er I was.
OLD MAN 'Tis poor mad Tom.
EDGAR *[aside]* And worse I may be yet. The worst is not
    As long as we can say, "This is the worst."
OLD MAN Fellow, where goest?
30 GLOUCESTER Is it a beggar man?
OLD MAN Madman and beggar too.
GLOUCESTER 'A° has some reason, else he could not beg.   He
    In the last night's storm, I such a fellow saw,
    Which made me think a man a worm. My son
35   Came then into my mind, and yet my mind
    Was then scarce friends with him. I have heard more since.
    As flies are to th' wanton° boys are we to th' gods: playful; careless
    They bit us for their sport.

4.1 Location: Open country.
1. *Stands . . . fear:* Remains calmly upright because there is no fear of falling further.
2. *The lamentable . . . laughter:* The change to be lamented is one that alters the best of circumstances; the worst luck can only improve.
3. Multicolored like a fool's costume (red with blood under white dressings).
4. *But . . . age:* If there were no strange reversals of fortune to make the world hateful, we would not consent to aging and death.
5. *Our means . . . commodities:* Our wealth makes us overconfident, and our utter deprivation proves to be beneficial.

4.1 (Q 4.1)

Enter EDGAR [*disguised as Poor Tom*].

EDGAR   Yet better thus and known to be contemned°   *despised*
Than still° contemned and flattered. To be worst,   *always*
The lowest and most dejected thing of fortune
Stands still in esperance, lives not in fear.[1]
5   The lamentable change is from the best,
The worst returns to laughter.[2] Welcome, then,
Thou unsubstantial air that I embrace.
The wretch that thou hast blown unto the worst
Owes nothing° to thy blasts.   *(because he can't pay)*

Enter GLOUCESTER *and an* OLD MAN.

10   But who comes here? My father, poorly led?
World, world, O world!
But that thy strange mutations make us hate thee,
Life would not yield to age.[3]
OLD MAN   O my good lord, I have been your tenant
15   And your father's tenant these fourscore years.
GLOUCESTER   Away, get thee away! Good friend, be gone.
Thy comforts° can do me no good at all;   *assistance*
Thee, they may hurt.
OLD MAN   You cannot see your way.
GLOUCESTER   I have no way and therefore want no eyes.
20   I stumbled when I saw. Full oft 'tis seen
Our means secure us, and our mere defects
Prove our commodities.[4] O dear son Edgar,
The food° of thy abusèd° father's wrath,   *fuel; prey / deceived*
Might I but live to see thee in° my touch,   *through*
I'd say I had eyes again.
25   OLD MAN   How now? Who's there?
EDGAR [*aside*]   O gods! Who is't can say, "I am at the worst"?
I am worse than e'er I was.
OLD MAN   'Tis poor mad Tom.
EDGAR [*aside*]   And worse I may be yet; the worst is not
So long as we can say, "This is the worst."
OLD MAN   Fellow, where goest?
30   GLOUCESTER   Is it a beggar man?
OLD MAN   Madman and beggar too.
GLOUCESTER   He has some reason, else he could not beg.
I'th' last night's storm, I such a fellow saw
Which made me think a man a worm. My son
35   Came then into my mind, and yet my mind
Was then scarce friends with him.
I have heard more since.
As flies to wanton° boys are we to th' gods: *playful; careless*
They kill us for their sport.

4.1 Location: Open country.
1. *Stands . . . fear:* Remains in hope ("esperance")
because there is no fear of falling further.
2. *The lamentable . . . laughter:* The change to be
lamented is one that alters the best of circumstances;
the worst luck can only improve.

3. *But . . . age:* If there were no strange reversals of
fortune to make the world hateful, we would not
consent to aging and death.
4. *Our means . . . commodities:* Our wealth makes us
overconfident, and our utter deprivation proves to be
beneficial.

EDGAR [*aside*]   How should this be?
  Bad is the trade that must play the fool to sorrow,[6]
40   Ang'ring itself and others. [*to* GLOUCESTER] Bless thee,
      master.
GLOUCESTER   Is that the naked fellow?
OLD MAN   Ay, my lord.
GLOUCESTER   Then prithee, get thee gone. If for my sake
  Thou wilt o'ertake us here a mile or twain
  I'th' way toward Dover, do it for ancient love,[7]
45   And bring some covering for this naked soul,
  Who I'll entreat to lead me.
OLD MAN   Alack, sir, he is mad.
GLOUCESTER   'Tis the time's plague when[8] madmen lead the
    blind.
  Do as I bid thee, or rather do thy pleasure.
50   Above the rest, be gone.
OLD MAN   I'll bring him the best 'parrel° that I have,   *apparel; clothing*
  Come on't what will.   [*Exit.*]
GLOUCESTER   Sirrah, naked fellow.
EDGAR   Poor Tom's a-cold. [*aside*] I cannot dance it farther.[9]
GLOUCESTER   Come hither, fellow.
55   EDGAR   Bless thy sweet eyes, they bleed.
GLOUCESTER   Know'st thou the way to Dover?
EDGAR   Both stile and gate, horse-way, and footpath. Poor Tom
    hath been scared out of his good wits. Bless the good man
    from the foul fiend. Five fiends have been in poor Tom at
60   once: of lust, as Obidicut; Hobbididence, prince of dumb-
    ness; Mahu of stealing; Modo of murder; Stiberdigebit of
    mopping and mowing,[1] who since possesses chambermaids
    and waiting women. So bless thee, master.
GLOUCESTER   Here, take this purse, thou whom the heavens'
    plagues
65   Have humbled to all strokes.° That I am wretched   *to accept all blows*
  Makes thee the happier. Heavens deal so still.°   *always*
  Let the superfluous and lust-dieted man[2]
  That stands° your ordinance,° that will not see   *resists / authority*
  Because he does not feel, feel your power quickly.
70   So distribution should undo excess,
  And each man have enough. Dost thou know Dover?
EDGAR   Ay, master.
GLOUCESTER   There is a cliff whose high and bending° head   *overhanging*
  Looks firmly in the confinèd deep.[3]
75   Bring me but to the very brim of it,
  And I'll repair the misery thou dost bear
  With something rich about me.
  From that place I shall no leading need.
EDGAR   Give me thy arm. Poor Tom shall lead thee.
                [*Exit* GLOUCESTER *led by* EDGAR.]

---

6. It is a bad business to have to play the fool in the face of sorrow.
7. For the sake of our long and loyal relationship (as master and servant).
8. The time is truly sick when.
9. I cannot continue the charade.
1. Grimacing and making faces.
2. Let the overprosperous man who indulges his appetite.
3. Looks fearsomely into the straits below.

EDGAR [*aside*]   How should this be?
40   Bad is the trade that must play fool to sorrow,[5]
     Ang'ring itself and others. [*to* GLOUCESTER] Bless thee,
       master.
GLOUCESTER   Is that the naked fellow?
OLD MAN   Ay, my lord.
GLOUCESTER   Get thee away. If for my sake
     Thou wilt o'ertake us hence a mile or twain
45   I'th' way toward Dover, do it for ancient love,[6]
     And bring some covering for this naked soul,
     Which I'll entreat to lead me.
OLD MAN   Alack, sir, he is mad.
GLOUCESTER   'Tis the time's plague when[7] madmen lead the
       blind.
     Do as I bid thee, or rather do thy pleasure.
50   Above the rest, be gone.
OLD MAN   I'll bring him the best 'parrel° that I have,   *apparel; clothing*
     Come on't what will.   *Exit.*
GLOUCESTER   Sirrah, naked fellow—
EDGAR   Poor Tom's a-cold. [*aside*] I cannot daub it further.[8]
55   GLOUCESTER   Come hither, fellow.
EDGAR [*aside*]   And yet I must. —Bless thy sweet eyes, they
       bleed.
GLOUCESTER   Know'st thou the way to Dover?
EDGAR   Both stile and gate, horse-way and footpath. Poor
60   Tom hath been scared out of his good wits. Bless thee, good-
       man's° son, from the foul fiend.   *householder's*
GLOUCESTER   Here, take this purse, thou whom the heav'ns'
       plagues
     Have humbled to all strokes.° That I am wretched   *to accept all blows*
     Makes thee the happier. Heavens deal so still.°   *always*
65   Let the superfluous and lust-dieted man,[9]
     That slaves° your ordinance,° that will not see   *defers to / authority*
     Because he does not feel, feel your power quickly.
     So distribution should undo excess,
     And each man have enough. Dost thou know Dover?
70   EDGAR   Ay, master.
GLOUCESTER   There is a cliff whose high and bending° head   *overhanging*
     Looks fearfully in the confinèd deep.[1]
     Bring me but to the very brim of it,
     And I'll repair the misery thou dost bear
75   With something rich about me. From that place
     I shall no leading need.
EDGAR   Give me thy arm;
     Poor Tom shall lead thee.   *Exeunt.*

---

5. It is a bad business to have to play the fool in the face of sorrow.
6. For the sake of our long and loyal relationship (as master and servant).
7. The time is truly sick when.

8. I cannot continue the charade. *daub:* mask, plaster.
9. Let the overprosperous man who indulges his appetite.
1. Looks fearsomely into the straits below.

4.2 (F 4.2)

Enter GONORILL *and* [*Edmund the*] BASTARD.

GONORILL Welcome, my lord. I marvel our mild husband
    Not° met us on the way.   *Has not*

Enter [*Oswald the*] STEWARD.

                    Now, where's your master?

STEWARD Madam, within, but never man so changed.
    I told him of the army that was landed;
5   He smiled at it. I told him you were coming;
    His answer was, "The worse." Of Gloucester's treachery,
    And of the loyal service of his son,
    When I informed him, then he called me "sot"°   *fool*
    And told me I had turned the wrong side out.[1]
10   What he should most dislike seems pleasant to him;
    What like, offensive.
GONORILL [*to* BASTARD]   Then shall you go no further.
    It is the cowish° terror of his spirit   *cowardly*
    That dares not undertake. He'll not feel wrongs
    Which tie him to an answer.[2] Our wishes on the way
15   May prove effects.[3] Back, Edmund, to my brother;°   *brother-in-law*
    Hasten his musters° and conduct his powers.°   *call-up of troops / armies*
    I must change arms at home and give the distaff[4]
    Into my husband's hands. This trusty servant
    Shall pass between us. Ere long, you are like° to hear—   *likely*
20   If you dare venture in your own behalf—
    A mistress's° command. Wear this; spare speech;[5]   *(playing on "lover's")*
    Decline your head. This kiss, if it durst speak,
    Would stretch thy spirits up into the air.
    Conceive,° and fare you well.   *Understand (my meaning)*
25 BASTARD Yours in° the ranks of death.   *even in*
GONORILL My most dear Gloucester, to thee woman's
      services are due.   [*Exit* BASTARD.]
    A fool usurps my bed.[6]
STEWARD Madam, here comes my lord.   *Exit.*
    [*Enter* ALBANY.]
GONORILL I have been worth the whistling.[7]
30 ALBANY O Gonorill,
    You are not worth the dust which the rude wind
    Blows in your face. I fear your disposition.
    That nature which contemns i'th'° origin   *despises its*
    Cannot be bordered certain° in itself.   *defended securely*
35   She that herself will sliver and disbranch°   *split*
    From her material sap, perforce must wither
    And come to deadly use.[8]

Scene 4.2 Location: Before Albany's castle.
1. I had reversed things (by mistaking loyalty for treachery).
2. *He'll . . . answer:* He'll ignore insults that would provoke him to retaliate.
3. May be put into action.
4. A device used in spinning and thus emblematic of the female role. To "change arms," therefore, is to swap the male and female identities.
5. TEXTUAL COMMENT The printing of 4.2 in Q1 shows an unusual amount of stop-press correction in the lines of Gonorill and Albany from 21 to 61. While such correction should improve the text, here the "corrections" often confuse the lines further. Editors have proposed various reasons for the scene's

textual problems (what editors would call a "textual crux"), ranging from printer errors to Shakespeare's own emendation of the text. See Digital Edition TC 6 (Quarto edited text).
6. Continuing the inversion of roles, Albany, who should be the head of the family, is seen by Gonorill as a subservient member with no right to control her.
7. At one time, you would have come to welcome me home; referring to the proverb "It is a poor dog that is not worth the whistling."
8. *She . . . use:* The allusion is probably biblical: "But that which beareth thorns and briers is reproved, and is near unto cursing; whose end is to be burned" (Hebrews 6:8). *come to deadly use:* be destroyed; be used for burning.

4.2 (Q 4.2)

Enter GONERILL, [EDMOND *the*] *bastard, and* [*Oswald the*] STEWARD.

GONERILL   Welcome, my lord. I marvel our mild husband
Not° met us on the way. [*to* STEWARD] Now, where's your   *Has not*
    master?

STEWARD   Madam, within, but never man so changed.
I told him of the army that was landed;
5   He smiled at it. I told him you were coming;
His answer was, "The worse." Of Gloucester's treachery,
And of the loyal service of his son,
When I informed him, then he called me "sot"°   *fool*
And told me I had turned the wrong side out.[1]
10   What most he should dislike seems pleasant to him;
What like, offensive.

GONERILL [*to* EDMOND]   Then shall you go no further.
It is the cowish° terror of his spirit   *cowardly*
That dares not undertake. He'll not feel wrongs
Which tie him to an answer.[2] Our wishes on the way
15   May prove effects.[3] Back, Edmond, to my brother;°   *brother-in-law*
Hasten his musters° and conduct his powers.°   *call-up of troops / armies*
I must change names° at home and give the distaff[4]   *exchange roles*
Into my husband's hands. This trusty servant
Shall pass between us. Ere long you are like° to hear—   *likely*
20   If you dare venture in your own behalf—
A mistress's° command. Wear this; spare speech;   *(playing on "lover's")*
Decline your head. This kiss, if it durst speak,
Would stretch thy spirits up into the air.
Conceive,° and fare thee well.   *Understand (my meaning)*

EDMOND   Yours in° the ranks of death.   *Exit.*   *even in*

25   GONERILL   My most dear Gloucester!
Oh, the difference of man and man!
To thee a woman's services are due;
My fool usurps my body.[5]

STEWARD   Madam, here comes my lord.   [*Exit.*]

        Enter ALBANY.

GONERILL   I have been worth the whistle.[6]

30   ALBANY   O Gonerill,
You are not worth the dust which the rude wind
Blows in your face.

4.2 Location: Before Albany's castle.
1. I had reversed things (by mistaking loyalty for treachery).
2. *He'll . . . answer:* He'll ignore insults that would provoke him to retaliate.
3. May be put into action.
4. A device used in spinning and thus emblematic of the female role. To "change names," therefore, is to swap the marking of male and female identities.
5. My idiot husband presumes to possess me.
6. At one time, you would have come to welcome me home; referring to the proverb "It is a poor dog that is not worth the whistling."

GONORILL   No more, the text is foolish.

ALBANY   Wisdom and goodness to the vile seem vile;

40   Filths savor but themselves. What have you done?

   Tigers, not daughters, what have you performed?

   A father and a gracious agèd man,

   Whose reverence even the head-lugged° bear would lick,   *dragged by the head*

   Most barbarous, most degenerate, have you madded.°   *driven mad*

45   Could my good brother° suffer you to do it?   *brother-in-law*

   A man, a prince, by him so benefited!

   If that the heavens do not their visible spirits

   Send quickly down to tame the vile offenses,

   It will come.

50   Humanity must perforce° prey on itself   *inevitably*

   Like monsters of the deep.

GONORILL   Milk-livered° man,   *Cowardly*

   That bearest a cheek for blows, a head for wrongs,[9]

   Who hast not in thy brows an eye discerning

   Thine honor from thy suffering,[1] that not know'st

55   Fools do those villains pity who are punished

   Ere they have done their mischief. Where's thy drum?°   *(to muster troops)*

   France spreads his banners in our noiseless° land   *peaceful*

   With plumèd helm. Thy state begins thereat

   Whilst thou, a moral° fool, sits still and cries,   *moralizing*

   "Alack, why does he so?"

60 ALBANY   See thyself, devil!

   Proper deformity seems not in the fiend

   So horrid as in woman.[2]

GONORILL   O vain° fool!   *useless*

ALBANY   Thou changèd and self-covered[3] thing, for shame!

   Bemonster not thy feature. Were't my fitness°   *If it were appropriate*

65   To let these hands obey my blood,

   They are apt enough to dislocate and tear

   Thy flesh and bones. Howe'er° thou art a fiend,   *Although*

   A woman's shape doth shield thee.

GONORILL   Marry, your manhood, mew[4]—

     Enter a GENTLEMAN.

70 ALBANY   What news?

GENTLEMAN   O my good lord, the Duke of Cornwall's dead,

   Slain by his servant, going to put out

   The other eye of Gloucester.

ALBANY   Gloucester's eyes?

GENTLEMAN   A servant that he bred, 'thralled with remorse,°   *shaken with pity*

75   Opposed against the act, bending° his sword   *directing*

   To° his great master, who, thereat enraged,   *Against*

---

9. *for wrongs*: fit for abuse; ready for cuckold's horns.
1. *discerning . . . suffering*: that can distinguish
between an insult to your honor and something you
should patiently endure.
2. *Proper . . . woman*: Deformity (of morals) is appropriate in the devil and so less horrid than in woman,
from whom virtue is expected. Albany may hold a
mirror in front of Gonorill, since Jacobean women

sometimes wore small mirrors attached to their
dresses.
3. Altered and with your true (womanly) self concealed.
4. Assert your feeble masculinity (with a derisive catcall, "mew"). Alternatively: get control of your manhood; restrain ("mew") it. *Marry*: By the Virgin Mary.

GONERILL   Milk-livered° man,   *Cowardly*
    That bear'st a cheek for blows, a head for wrongs,[7]
    Who hast not in thy brows an eye discerning
35   Thine honor from thy suffering.[8]

ALBANY   See thyself, devil!
    Proper deformity seems not in the fiend
    So horrid as in woman.[9]
GONERILL   O vain° fool!   *useless*
    Enter a MESSENGER.

MESSENGER   O my good lord, the Duke of Cornwall's dead,
40   Slain by his servant, going to put out
    The other eye of Gloucester.
ALBANY   Gloucester's eyes?
MESSENGER   A servant that he bred, thrilled with remorse,°   *shaken with pity*
    Opposed against the act, bending° his sword   *directing*
    To° his great master, who, threat-enragèd,   *Against*

---

7. *for wrongs:* fit for abuse; ready for cuckold's horns.
8. *discerning . . . suffering:* that can distinguish between an insult to your honor and something you should patiently endure.
9. *Proper . . . woman:* Deformity (of morals) is appro-priate in the devil and so less horrid than in woman, from whom virtue is expected. Albany may hold a mir-ror in front of Gonerill, since Jacobean women some-times wore small mirrors attached to their dresses.

Flew on him and amongst them felled him dead,
But not without that harmful stroke which since
Hath plucked him after.[5]

80 ALBANY   This shows you are above, you Justices,°   *Judges*
That these our nether crimes[6] so speedily can venge.
But, oh, poor Gloucester! Lost he his other eye?

GENTLEMAN   Both, both, my lord.
This letter, madam, craves a speedy answer.
'Tis from your sister.

85 GONORILL [*aside*]   One way I like this well:[7]
But being° widow, and my Gloucester with her,   *her being*
May all the building on my fancy pluck
Upon my hateful life.[8] Another way the news is not so took.[9]
[*to* GENTLEMAN] I'll read and answer.   *Exit.*

90 ALBANY   Where was his son when they did take his eyes?

GENTLEMAN   Come with my lady hither.

ALBANY   He is not here.

GENTLEMAN   No, my good lord, I met him back° again.   *returning*

ALBANY   Knows he the wickedness?

GENTLEMAN   Ay, my good lord. 'Twas he informed against
him

95 And quit the house on purpose that their punishment
Might have the freer course.

ALBANY   Gloucester, I live
To thank thee for the love thou showed'st the King
And to revenge thy eyes. Come hither, friend;
Tell me what more thou knowest.   *Exeunt.*

4.3
Enter KENT [*disguised as Caius*] *and a* GENTLEMAN.

KENT   Why the King of France is so suddenly gone back,
know you no reason?

GENTLEMAN   Something he left imperfect° in the state, which   *unsettled*
since his coming forth is thought of,° which imports° to the   *remembered / portends*
5 kingdom so much fear and danger that his personal return
was most required and necessary.

KENT   Who hath he left behind him general?

GENTLEMAN   The Marshal of France, Monsieur la Far.

KENT   Did your letters pierce the Queen to any demonstration
10 of grief?

GENTLEMAN   I say she took them, read them in my presence,
And now and then an ample tear trilled down
Her delicate cheek. It seemed she was a queen
Over her passion, who,° most rebel-like,   *which*
Sought to be king o'er her.

---

5. Has sent him to follow his servant into death.
6. Lower crimes, and so committed on earth, but also suggesting that the deeds smack of the netherworld of hell.
7. Because a political rival has been eliminated.
8. *May . . . life:* May pull down all of my built-up fantasies and thus make my life hateful.
9. The news may be taken otherwise.

45 Flew on him and amongst them felled him dead,
  But not without that harmful stroke which since
  Hath plucked him after.[1]
ALBANY   This shows you are above,
  You Justices,° that these our nether crimes[2]   *Judges*
  So speedily can venge. But oh, poor Gloucester!
  Lost he his other eye?
50 MESSENGER   Both, both, my lord.
  This letter, madam, craves a speedy answer:
  'Tis from your sister.
GONERILL [*aside*]   One way I like this well;[3]
  But being° widow, and my Gloucester with her,   *her being*
  May all the building in my fancy pluck
55 Upon my hateful life.[4] Another way
  The news is not so tart.° I'll read and answer.   *bitter*
ALBANY Where was his son when they did take his eyes?
MESSENGER Come with my lady hither.
ALBANY   He is not here.
MESSENGER No, my good lord, I met him back° again.   *returning*
60 ALBANY Knows he the wickedness?
MESSENGER Ay, my good lord. 'Twas he informed against
  him
  And quit the house on purpose, that their punishment
  Might have the freer course.
ALBANY   Gloucester, I live
  To thank thee for the love thou showed'st the King
65 And to revenge thine eyes. Come hither, friend;
  Tell me what more thou know'st.   *Exeunt.*

---

1. Has sent him to follow his servant into death.
2. Lower crimes, and so committed on earth, but also suggesting that the deeds smack of the nether-world of hell.
3. Because a political rival has been eliminated.
4. *May . . . life:* May pull down all of my built-up fantasies and thus make my life hateful.

15 KENT   Oh, then, it moved her.
GENTLEMAN   Not to a rage. Patience and sorrow stream
Who should express her goodliest.[1] You have seen
Sunshine and rain at once; her smiles and tears
Were like a better way. Those happy smilets
20 That played on her ripe lip seem not to know
What guests were in her eyes, which parted thence
As pearls from diamonds dropped. In brief,
Sorrow would be a rarity° most beloved,   gem
If all could so become it.[2]
25 KENT   Made she no verbal question?
GENTLEMAN   Faith, once or twice she heaved the name of
        father
Pantingly forth, as if it pressed her heart,
Cried, "Sisters, sisters, shame of ladies, sisters!
Kent, father, sisters! What, i'th' storm, i'th' night?
30 Let pity not be believed."[3] There she shook
The holy water from her heavenly eyes,
And clamor° moistened her. Then away she started,°   crying / sprang
To deal with grief alone.
KENT   It is the stars,
The stars above us, govern our conditions.
35 Else one self mate and make[4] could not beget
Such different issues.° You spoke not with her since?   offspring
GENTLEMAN   No.
KENT   Was this before the King returned?
GENTLEMAN   No, since.
KENT   Well, sir, the poor distressèd Lear's i'th' town,
40 Who sometime in his better tune° remembers   state of mind
What we are come about, and by no means
Will yield° to see his daughter.   consent
GENTLEMAN   Why, good sir?
KENT   A sovereign shame so elbows° him: his own   prods; nudges
        unkindness,
That stripped her from his benediction, turned her
45 To foreign casualties,° gave her dear rights   risks
To his dog-hearted daughters. These things sting his mind
So venomously that burning shame
Detains him from Cordelia.
GENTLEMAN   Alack, poor gentleman!
50 KENT   Of Albany's and Cornwall's powers you heard not?
GENTLEMAN   'Tis so, they are afoot.
KENT   Well, sir, I'll bring you to our master Lear
And leave you to attend him. Some dear cause°   Some important reason
Will in concealment wrap me up awhile.
55 When I am known aright, you shall not grieve°   regret
Lending me this acquaintance.° I pray you   news
Go along with me.   Exeunt.

4.3 Location: Near the French camp at Dover.   3. Never believe in pity; compassion cannot exist.
1. Which should best express her feelings.   4. Or else the same pair of spouses; "mate" and "make"
2. If everyone wore it so beautifully.   may describe either partner.

4.4 (F 4.3)

Enter CORDELIA, DOCTOR, *and others* [*including*
GENTLEMEN].

CORDELIA   Alack, 'tis he! Why, he was met even now,
As mad as the vent sea, singing aloud,
Crowned with rank fumitor and furrow weeds,[1]
With burdocks, hemlock, nettles, cuckoo flowers,

5   Darnell, and all the idle° weeds that grow   *useless*
In our sustaining corn. A century° is sent forth.   *battalion*
Search every acre in the high-grown field
And bring him to our eye.   [*Exeunt three* GENTLEMEN.]
                      What can man's wisdom
In the restoring° his bereaved sense? He that can help him   *Do to restore*

10   Take all my outward° worth.   *material*
DOCTOR   There is means, madam.
Our foster nurse of nature[2] is repose,
The which he lacks. That to provoke in him
Are many simples operative,[3] whose power
Will close the eye of anguish.

15   CORDELIA   All blest secrets,
All you unpublished virtues° of the earth,   *obscure healing plants*
Spring with my tears; be aidant and remediate°   *healing and remedial*
In the good man's distress. Seek, seek for him,
Lest his ungoverned rage dissolve the life
That wants° the means to lead it.   *lacks*
            Enter MESSENGER.

20   MESSENGER   News, madam:
The British powers° are marching hitherward.   *armies*
CORDELIA   'Tis known before; our preparation stands
In expectation of them. O dear father,
It is thy business that I go about![4]

25   Therefore great France
My mourning and important° tears hath pitied.   *urgent; solicitous*
No blown° ambition doth our arms incite,   *inflated*
But love, dear love, and our aged father's right.[5]
Soon may I hear and see him!   *Exeunt.*

4.4 Location: The French camp at Dover.
1. Fumitor was used against brain sickness. Furrow
weeds, like the other weeds in the following lines,
grow in the furrows of plowed fields.
2. *Our . . . nature:* That which comforts and nourishes human nature.
3. *That . . . operative:* To induce that ("repose") in

him, there are many effective medicinal herbs.
4. The line echoes Christ's explanation of his mission
in Luke 2:49: "I must go about my father's business."
5. *No . . . right:* 1 Corinthians 13:4–5 in the Bishops'
Bible (1568) says that love "swelleth not, dealeth not
dishonestly, seeketh not her own."

4.3 (Q 4.4)

Enter with drum and colors, CORDELIA, GENTLEMEN,
and Soldiers.

CORDELIA   Alack, 'tis he. Why, he was met even now,
As mad as the vexèd sea, singing aloud.
Crowned with rank fumitor and furrow weeds,[1]
With burdocks, hemlock, nettles, cuckoo flowers,
5   Darnel, and all the idle° weeds that grow   *useless*
In our sustaining corn. A century° send forth; *battalion (100 men)*
Search every acre in the high-grown field
And bring him to our eye.   [*Exit a* GENTLEMAN.]
       What can man's wisdom
In the restoring° his bereaved sense? He that helps him, *Do to restore*
Take all my outward° worth.   *material*
10 GENTLEMAN   There is means, madam.
Our foster nurse of nature[2] is repose,
The which he lacks. That to provoke in him
Are many simples operative,[3] whose power
Will close the eye of anguish.
CORDELIA   All blest secrets,
15   All you unpublished virtues° of the earth, *obscure healing plants*
Spring with my tears; be aidant and remediate° *healing and remedial*
In the good man's desires. Seek, seek for him,
Lest his ungoverned rage dissolve the life
That wants° the means to lead it.   *lacks*
   Enter MESSENGER.
MESSENGER   News, madam:
20   The British powers° are marching hitherward. *armies*
CORDELIA   'Tis known before. Our preparation stands
In expectation of them. O dear father,
It is thy business that I go about![4] Therefore great France
My mourning and importuned° tears hath pitied. *importunate; solicitous*
25   No blown° ambition doth our arms incite,   *inflated*
But love, dear love, and our aged father's right.[5]
Soon may I hear and see him!   *Exeunt.*

4.3 Location: The French camp at Dover.
1. Fumitor was used against brain sickness. Furrow weeds, like the other weeds in the following lines, grow in the furrows of plowed fields.
2. *Our . . . nature:* That which comforts and nourishes human nature.
3. *That . . . operative:* To induce that ("repose") in

him, there are many effective medicinal herbs.
4. The line echoes Christ's explanation of his mission in Luke 2:49: "I must go about my father's business."
5. *No . . . right:* 1 Corinthians 13:4–5 in the Bishops' Bible (1568) says that love "swelleth not, dealeth not dishonestly, seeketh not her own."

4.5 (F 4.4)

Enter REGAN *and* [*Oswald the*] STEWARD.

REGAN	But are my brother's powers° set forth?	*(Albany's forces)*
STEWARD	Ay, madam.	
REGAN	Himself in person?	
STEWARD	Madam, with much ado;°	*trouble*
	Your sister is the better soldier.	
REGAN	Lord Edmund spake not with your lady at home?	

5   STEWARD   No, madam.

REGAN   What might import° my sister's letters to him?   *mean*

STEWARD   I know not, lady.

REGAN   Faith, he is posted° hence on serious matter—   *sent*
It was great ignorance, Gloucester's eyes being out,
10   To let him live. Where he arrives, he moves
All hearts against us—and now, I think, is gone
In pity of his misery° to dispatch his nighted° life,   *(ironic)* / *darkened*
Moreover to descry° the strength o'th' army.   *investigate*

STEWARD   I must needs after° him with my letters.   *go after*

15   REGAN   Our troop sets forth tomorrow; stay with us.
The ways are dangerous.

STEWARD   I may not, madam;
My lady charged° my duty in this business.   *commanded*

REGAN   Why should she write to Edmund? Might not you
Transport her purposes by word? Belike°   *Perhaps*
20   Something—I know not what. I'll love° thee much: *reward*
Let me unseal the letter.

STEWARD   Madam, I'd rather—

REGAN   I know your lady does not love her husband.
I am sure of that, and at her late° being here   *recently*
She gave strange oeillades° and most speaking looks   *amorous glances*
25   To noble Edmund. I know you are of her bosom.°   *in her confidence*

STEWARD   Ay, madam.

REGAN   I speak in understanding,° for I know't.   *with certainty*
Therefore, I do advise you take this note.°   *take note of this*
My lord is dead. Edmund and I have talked,
30   And more convenient° is he for my hand   *appropriate*
Than for your lady's. You may gather° more.   *infer*
If you do find him, pray you give him this,[1]
And, when your mistress hears thus much from you,
I pray, desire her call her wisdom to her.[2] So, farewell.
35   If you do chance to hear of that blind traitor,
Preferment falls on him that cuts him off.°   *cuts his life short*

STEWARD   Would I could meet him, madam, I would show
What lady I do follow.

REGAN   Fare thee well.   *Exeunt* [*severally*].°   *separately*

4.5 Location: At Gloucester's castle.
1. This information, but possibly another letter or   token.
2. *desire . . . to her:* tell her to come to her senses.

4.4 (Q 4.5)

Enter REGAN *and* [*Oswald the*] STEWARD.

REGAN	But are my brother's powers° set forth?		*(Albany's forces)*
STEWARD	Ay, madam.		
REGAN	Himself in person there?		
STEWARD	Madam, with much ado;°		*trouble*

Your sister is the better soldier.

REGAN   Lord Edmond spake not with your lord at home?

5   STEWARD   No, madam.

REGAN   What might import° my sister's letter to him?   *mean*

STEWARD   I know not, lady.

REGAN   Faith, he is posted° hence on serious matter—   *sent*
It was great ignorance, Gloucester's eyes being out,

10   To let him live. Where he arrives, he moves
All hearts against us. Edmond, I think, is gone,
In pity of his misery,° to dispatch   *(ironic)*
His nighted° life; moreover to descry°   *darkened / investigate*
The strength o'th' enemy.

15   STEWARD   I must needs after° him, madam, with my letter.   *go after*

REGAN   Our troops set forth tomorrow; stay with us.
The ways are dangerous.

STEWARD   I may not, madam:
My lady charged° my duty in this business.   *commanded*

REGAN   Why should she write to Edmond?

20   Might not you transport her purposes by word? Belike°   *Perhaps*
Some things—I know not what. I'll love° thee much: *reward*
Let me unseal the letter.

STEWARD   Madam, I had rather—

REGAN   I know your lady does not love her husband.
I am sure of that, and at her late° being here,   *recently*

25   She gave strange oeillades° and most speaking looks   *amorous glances*
To noble Edmond. I know you are of her bosom.°   *in her confidence*

STEWARD   I, madam?

REGAN   I speak in understanding.° Y'are; I know't.   *with certainty*
Therefore I do advise you take this note.°   *take note of this*

30   My lord is dead. Edmond and I have talked,
And more convenient° is he for my hand   *appropriate*
Than for your lady's. You may gather° more.   *infer*
If you do find him, pray you give him this,[1]
And when your mistress hears thus much from you,

35   I pray, desire her call her wisdom to her.[2]
So, fare you well.
If you do chance to hear of that blind traitor,
Preferment falls on him that cuts him off.°   *cuts his life short*

STEWARD   Would I could meet, madam; I should show
What party I do follow.

40   REGAN   Fare thee well.   *Exeunt* [*severally*].°   *separately*

4.4 Location: At Gloucester's castle.
1. This information, but possibly another letter or

token.
2. *desire . . . to her*: tell her to come to her senses.

4.6 (F 4.5)

Enter GLOUCESTER *and* [EDGAR *disguised as a peasant*].

GLOUCESTER   When shall we come to th' top of that same°   agreed-upon
hill?
EDGAR   You do climb it up now. Look how we labor.
GLOUCESTER   Methinks the ground is even.
EDGAR   Horrible steep; hark, do you hear the sea?
5 GLOUCESTER   No, truly.
EDGAR   Why, then, your other senses grow imperfect
By your eyes' anguish.
GLOUCESTER   So may it be indeed.
Methinks thy voice is altered, and thou speakest
With better phrase and matter° than thou didst.   sense
10 EDGAR   You're much deceived. In nothing am I changed
But in my garments.
GLOUCESTER   Methinks you're better spoken.
EDGAR   Come on, sir. Here's the place. Stand still. How
fearful
And dizzy 'tis to cast one's eyes so low!
15 The crows and choughs° that wing the midway air[1]   jackdaws
Show° scarce so gross° as beetles. Halfway down   Appear / big
Hangs one that gathers samphire;° dreadful trade!   seaweed
Methinks he seems no bigger than his head.
The fishermen that walk upon the beach
20 Appear like mice, and yon tall anchoring bark°   ship
Diminished to her cock;° her cock a buoy   dinghy
Almost too small for sight. The murmuring surge,
That on the unnumbered° idle pebble chafes,   innumerable
Cannot be heard. It's so high, I'll look no more,
25 Lest my brain turn and the° deficient sight   my
Topple° down headlong.   Topple me
GLOUCESTER   Set me where you stand.
EDGAR   Give me your hand; you are now within a foot
Of th'extreme verge. For all beneath the moon
Would I not leap upright.[2]
GLOUCESTER   Let go my hand.
30 Here, friend, 's another purse, in it a jewel
Well worth a poor man's taking. Fairies and gods
Prosper it[3] with thee. Go thou farther off.
Bid me farewell, and let me hear thee going.
EDGAR   Now, fare you well, good sir.
GLOUCESTER   With all my heart.
35 EDGAR [*aside*]   Why I do trifle thus with his despair
Is done to cure it.
GLOUCESTER (*kneels*)   O you mighty gods,
This world I do renounce, and in your sights
Shake patiently my great affliction off.

4.6 Location: Near Dover.   my balance).
1. The air between cliff and sea.   3. Make it increase. Fairies were sometimes believed
2. I would not jump up and down (for fear of losing   to hoard and multiply treasure.

4.5 (Q 4.6)

Enter GLOUCESTER *and* EDGAR [*disguised as a peasant*].

GLOUCESTER   When shall I come to th' top of that same° hill?   *agreed-upon*

EDGAR   You do climb up it now. Look how we labor.

GLOUCESTER   Methinks the ground is even.

EDGAR   Horrible steep.
Hark, do you hear the sea?

GLOUCESTER   No, truly.

5 EDGAR   Why, then your other senses grow imperfect
By your eyes' anguish.

GLOUCESTER   So may it be indeed.
Methinks thy voice is altered, and thou speak'st
In better phrase and matter° than thou didst.   *sense*

EDGAR   You're much deceived. In nothing am I changed
10 But in my garments.

GLOUCESTER   Methinks you're better spoken.

EDGAR   Come on, sir,
Here's the place. Stand still. How fearful
And dizzy 'tis to cast one's eyes so low!
The crows and choughs° that wing the midway air[1]   *jackdaws*
15 Show° scarce so gross° as beetles. Halfway down   *Appear / big*
Hangs one that gathers samphire:° dreadful trade!   *seaweed*
Methinks he seems no bigger than his head.
The fishermen that walked upon the beach
Appear like mice, and yond tall anchoring bark°   *ship*
20 Diminished to her cock;° her cock, a buoy   *dinghy*
Almost too small for sight. The murmuring surge,
That on th'unnumbered° idle pebble chafes,   *innumerable*
Cannot be heard so high. I'll look no more,
Lest my brain turn and the° deficient sight   *my*
25 Topple° down headlong.   *Topple me*

GLOUCESTER   Set me where you stand.

EDGAR   Give me your hand.
You are now within a foot of th'extreme verge.
For all beneath the moon would I not leap upright.[2]

GLOUCESTER   Let go my hand.
30 Here, friend, 's another purse. In it, a jewel
Well worth a poor man's taking. Fairies and gods
Prosper it[3] with thee. Go thou further off.
Bid me farewell, and let me hear thee going.

EDGAR   Now, fare ye well, good sir.

GLOUCESTER   With all my heart.

35 EDGAR [*aside*]   Why I do trifle thus with his despair
Is done to cure it.

GLOUCESTER   O you mighty gods!
          [*He kneels.*]
This world I do renounce, and in your sights
Shake patiently my great affliction off.

4.5 Location: Near Dover.
1. The air between cliff and sea.
2. I would not jump up and down (for fear of losing
my balance).
3. Make it increase. Fairies were sometimes believed
to hoard and multiply treasure.

	If I could bear it longer and not fall	
40	To quarrel° with your great opposeless wills,	*Into conflict*
	My snuff and loathèd part of nature[4] should	
	Burn itself out. If Edgar live, oh, bless!	
	Now fellow, fare thee well.	

He falls.

EDGAR   Gone, sir; farewell,
And yet I know not how conceit may rob

45	The treasury of life, when life itself	
	Yields to the theft.[5] Had he been where he thought,	
	By this° had thought been past. Alive or dead?[6]	*now*
	[*to* GLOUCESTER] Ho, you, sir! Hear you, sir? Speak.	
	Thus might he pass° indeed, yet he revives.	*pass away*
	—What are you, sir?	
50	GLOUCESTER Away and let me die.	
	EDGAR Hadst thou been aught° but goss'mer, feathers, air,	*anything*
	So many fathom down precipitating,°	*plunging*
	Thou hadst shivered° like an egg. But thou dost breathe,	*shattered*
	Hast heavy substance, bleed'st not, speakest, art sound.	
55	Ten masts at each° make not the altitude	*end to end*
	Which thou hast perpendicularly fell.	
	Thy life's a miracle. Speak yet again.	
	GLOUCESTER But have I fallen or no?	
	EDGAR From the dread summons of this chalky bourn.[7]	
60	Look up a-height, the shrill gorged° lark so far	*shrill-voiced*
	Cannot be seen or heard. Do but look up.	
	GLOUCESTER Alack, I have no eyes.	
	Is wretchedness deprived° that benefit	*deprived of*
	To end itself by death? 'Twas yet some comfort	
65	When misery could beguile° the tyrant's rage	*cheat*
	And frustrate his proud will.	
	EDGAR Give me your arm.	
	Up, so; how feel you your legs? You stand.	
	GLOUCESTER Too well, too well.	
	EDGAR This is above all strangeness.	
	Upon the crown of the cliff, what thing was that	
	Which parted from you?	
70	GLOUCESTER A poor unfortunate beggar.	
	EDGAR As I stood here below, methoughts his eyes	
	Were two full moons, 'a had a thousand noses,	
	Horns whelked° and waved like the enridgèd sea.	*twisted*
	It was some fiend. Therefore, thou happy father,°	*lucky old man*
75	Think that the clearest° gods, who made their honors	*purest; most illustrious*
	Of men's impossibilities,[8] have preserved thee.	
	GLOUCESTER I do remember now. Henceforth I'll bear	
	Affliction till it do cry out itself,	
	"Enough, enough," and die. That thing you speak of,	
80	I took it for a man. Often would it say,	

---

4. The scorched and hateful remnant of my lifetime. *snuff*: end of a candlewick.

5. *And yet . . . theft*: Edgar worries that the imagined scenario ("conceit") he has invented may be enough to kill his father, particularly as Gloucester wishes for ("yields to") his own death.

6. PERFORMANCE COMMENT Like readers, audiences cannot initially be certain whether the cliff is "real"

(within the play's fictive world) or imaginary, and the resulting tension makes for one of Shakespeare's most fascinating scenes. See Digital Edition PC 5.

7. The white chalk cliffs of Dover, which make a boundary ("bourn") between land and sea.

8. *who . . . impossibilities*: who attained honor for themselves by performing deeds impossible to men.

    If I could bear it longer and not fall
40 To quarrel° with your great opposeless wills,   *Into conflict*
    My snuff and loathèd part of nature[4] should
    Burn itself out. If Edgar live, oh, bless him!
    Now, fellow, fare thee well.
EDGAR   Gone, sir. Farewell.
        [GLOUCESTER *falls down*.]
    And yet I know not how conceit may rob
45 The treasury of life, when life itself
    Yields to the theft.[5] Had he been where he thought,
    By this° had thought been past. Alive or dead?[6]   *now*
    [*to* GLOUCESTER] Ho, you, sir! Friend, hear you, sir? Speak.
    Thus might he pass° indeed. Yet he revives.   *pass away*
    —What are you, sir?
50 GLOUCESTER   Away and let me die.
    EDGAR   Hadst thou been aught° but goss'mer, feathers, air,   *anything*
    So many fathom down precipitating,°   *plunging*
    Thou'dst shivered° like an egg. But thou dost breathe,   *shattered*
    Hast heavy substance, bleed'st not, speak'st, art sound.
55 Ten masts at each° make not the altitude   *end to end*
    Which thou hast perpendicularly fell.
    Thy life's a miracle. Speak yet again.
    GLOUCESTER   But have I fall'n or no?
    EDGAR   From the dread summit of this chalky bourn.[7]
60 Look up a-height, the shrill-gorged° lark so far   *shrill-voiced*
    Cannot be seen or heard. Do but look up.
    GLOUCESTER   Alack, I have no eyes.
    Is wretchedness deprived° that benefit   *deprived of*
    To end itself by death? 'Twas yet some comfort
65 When misery could beguile° the tyrant's rage   *cheat*
    And frustrate his proud will.
    EDGAR   Give me your arm.
    Up, so. How is't? Feel you your legs? You stand.
    GLOUCESTER   Too well, too well.
    EDGAR   This is above all strangeness.
    Upon the crown o'th' cliff, what thing was that
    Which parted from you?
70 GLOUCESTER   A poor unfortunate beggar.
    EDGAR   As I stood here below, methought his eyes
    Were two full moons. He had a thousand noses,
    Horns whelked° and waved like the enragèd sea.   *twisted*
    It was some fiend. Therefore, thou happy father,°   *lucky old man*
75 Think that the clearest° gods, who make them honors   *purest; most illustrious*
    Of men's impossibilities,[8] have preserved thee.
    GLOUCESTER   I do remember now. Henceforth I'll bear
    Affliction till it do cry out itself,
    "Enough, enough," and die. That thing you speak of,
80 I took it for a man. Often 'twould say,

---

4. The scorched and hateful remnant of my lifetime. *snuff*: end of a candlewick.
5. *And yet . . . theft*: Edgar worries that the imagined scenario ("conceit") he has invented may be enough to kill his father, particularly as Gloucester wishes for ("yields to") his own death.
6. PERFORMANCE COMMENT Like readers, audiences cannot initially be certain whether the cliff is "real"

(within the play's fictive world) or imaginary, and the resulting tension makes for one of Shakespeare's most fascinating scenes. See Digital Edition PC 5.
7. The white chalk cliffs of Dover, which make a boundary ("bourn") between land and sea.
8. *who . . . impossibilities*: who attain honor for themselves by performing deeds impossible to men.

"The fiend, the fiend." He led me to that place.

EDGAR Bear free and patient thoughts.

    Enter LEAR *mad.*

                                      But who comes here?

The safer sense will ne'er accommodate

His master thus.[9]

85   LEAR No, they cannot touch me for coining,[1] I am the King
himself.

EDGAR [*aside*] O thou side-piercing sight!

LEAR Nature is above art in that respect.[2] There's your press
money.[3] That fellow handles his bow like a crow-keeper.[4]

90   Draw me a clothier's yard.[5] Look, look, a mouse. Peace, peace,
this toasted cheese will do it.° There's my gauntlet; I'll prove it   *(lure the mouse)*
on a giant.[6] Bring up the brown-bills.[7] Oh, well flown, bird,°   *arrow*
in the air. Ha, give the word.°   *password*

EDGAR Sweet marjoram.[8]

95   LEAR Pass.

GLOUCESTER I know that voice.

LEAR Ha, Gonorill, ha, Regan! They flattered me like a dog°   *fawningly*
and told me I had white hairs in my beard ere the black ones
were there.[9] To say "Ay" and "No" to everything I said "Ay"

100   and "No" to was no good divinity.[1] When the rain came to
wet me once, and the wind to make me chatter, when the
thunder would not peace at my bidding, there I found°   *understood*
them, there I smelt them out. Go to, they are not men of
their words. They told me I was everything. 'Tis a lie. I am

105   not ague-proof.°   *immune to illness*

GLOUCESTER The trick° of that voice I do well remember,   *peculiarity*
Is't not the King?

LEAR   Ay, every inch a king!

When I do stare, see how the subject quakes.

I pardon that man's life. —What was thy cause,°   *crime*

110   Adultery? Thou shalt not die for adultery.

No, the wren goes to't, and the small gilded fly

Do lecher in my sight.

Let copulation thrive, for Gloucester's bastard son

Was kinder to his father than my daughters

115   Got 'tween the lawful sheets. To't, luxury,° pell-mell,   *lechery*

For I lack soldiers. Behold yon simp'ring dame,

Whose face between her forks presageth snow,[2]

That minces° virtue, and do shake the head   *affects*

To hear of° pleasure's name.   *even of*

120   The fitchew nor the soiled horse[3] goes to't

With a more riotous appetite. Down from the waist

---

9. *The . . . thus:* A sane mind would never allow its
possessor to dress up in this way.
1. Because minting money was the prerogative of the
King, nobody could overtake or equal ("touch") him.
2. My true feelings will always outvalue others' hypocrisy; my natural supremacy surpasses any attempt to
create a false new reign. This image may also be based
on coining (see note 1, above).
3. Fee paid to a soldier impressed, or forced, into the
army.
4. A person hired as a scarecrow and thus unfit for
anything else.
5. Draw the bowstring the full length of the arrow (a
standard English arrow was a cloth yard [37 inches]

long).
6. I'll defend my stand even against a giant. To throw
down an armored glove ("gauntlet") was to issue a
challenge.
7. Brown painted pikes; the soldiers carrying them.
8. Used medicinally against madness.
9. Told me I had wisdom before age.
1. *no good divinity:* poor theology (because insincere);
from James 5:12: "Let your yea be yea; nay, nay."
2. Whose expression implies cold chastity. "Face"
refers to the area between her legs ("forks"), as well as
to her literal facial expression as framed by the aristocratic lady's starched headpiece, also called a "fork."
3. Neither the polecat nor a horse full of fresh grass.

"The fiend, the fiend." He led me to that place.

EDGAR Bear free and patient thoughts.

Enter LEAR.

But who comes here?

The safer sense will ne'er accommodate

His master thus.[9]

85 LEAR No, they cannot touch me° for crying. I am the King   *lay hands on me*
himself.

EDGAR [*aside*] O thou side-piercing sight!

LEAR Nature's above art in that respect.[1] There's your press
money.[2] That fellow handles his bow like a crow-keeper.[3]

90 Draw me a clothier's yard.[4] Look, look, a mouse! Peace, peace,
this piece of toasted cheese will do't.° There's my gauntlet; I'll   *(lure the mouse)*
prove it on a giant.[5] Bring up the brown bills.[6] Oh, well flown,
bird!° I'th' clout, i'th' clout! Whew. Give the word.°   *arrow / password*

EDGAR Sweet marjoram.[7]

95 LEAR Pass.

GLOUCESTER I know that voice.

LEAR Ha! Gonerill with a white beard? They flattered me like
a dog° and told me I had the white hairs in my beard ere the   *fawningly*
black ones were there.[8] To say "Ay" and "No" to everything

100 that I said "Ay" and "No" to was no good divinity.[9] When the
rain came to wet me once, and the wind to make me chatter,
when the thunder would not peace at my bidding, there I
found° 'em, there I smelt 'em out. Go to, they are not men   *understood*
o'their words. They told me I was everything. 'Tis a lie. I am

105 not ague-proof.°   *immune to illness*

GLOUCESTER The trick° of that voice, I do well remember.   *peculiarity*
Is't not the King?

LEAR   Ay, every inch a king!

When I do stare, see how the subject quakes.

I pardon that man's life. —What was thy cause?°   *crime*

110 Adultery? Thou shalt not die. Die for adultery?

No, the wren goes to't, and the small gilded fly

Does lecher in my sight. Let copulation thrive,

For Gloucester's bastard son was kinder to his father

Than my daughters got 'tween the lawful sheets.

115 To't, luxury,° pell-mell, for I lack soldiers.   *lechery*

Behold yond simp'ring dame,

Whose face between her forks presages snow,[1]

That minces° virtue and does shake the head   *affects*

To hear of° pleasure's name.   *even of*

120 The fitchew nor the soiled horse[2] goes to't

With a more riotous appetite.

Down from the waist they are centaurs,[3]

9. *The . . . thus:* A sane mind would never allow its possessor to dress up in this way.
1. My true feelings will always outvalue others' hypocrisy; my natural supremacy surpasses any attempt to create a false new reign.
2. Fee paid to a soldier impressed, or forced, into the army.
3. A person hired as a scarecrow and thus unfit for anything else.
4. Draw the bowstring the full length of the arrow (a standard English arrow was a cloth yard [37 inches] long).
5. I'll defend my stand even against a giant. To throw down an armored glove ("gauntlet") was to issue a

challenge.
6. Brown painted pikes; the soldiers carrying them.
7. Used medicinally against madness.
8. Told me I had wisdom before age.
9. *no good divinity:* poor theology (because insincere); from James 5:12: "Let your yea be yea; nay, nay."
1. Whose expression implies cold chastity. "Face" refers to the area between her legs ("forks") as well as to her literal facial expression as framed by the aristocratic lady's starched headpiece, also called a "fork."
2. Neither the polecat nor a horse full of fresh grass.
3. Lecherous mythological creatures that have a human body above the waist and the legs and torso of a horse below.

They're centaurs,[4] though women all above.
But° to the girdle° do the gods inherit;°   *Only / waist / own*
Beneath is all the fiend's. There's hell,[5] there's darkness,
125   There's the sulfury pit: burning, scalding,
Stench, consummation. Fie, fie, fie, pah, pah!
—Give me an ounce of civet,[6] good apothecary,
To sweeten my imagination. There's money for thee.
GLOUCESTER   Oh, let me kiss that hand.
130   LEAR   Here, wipe it first. It smells of mortality.
GLOUCESTER   O ruined piece° of nature, this great world   *masterpiece*
Should so wear out to naught.[7] Do you know me?
LEAR   I remember thy eyes well enough. Dost thou squiny° on   *squint*
me? No, do thy worst, blind Cupid, I'll not love. Read thou
135   that challenge; mark the penning of't.
GLOUCESTER   Were all the letters suns, I could not see one.
EDGAR [*aside*]   I would not take° this from report; it is,   *believe*
And my heart breaks at it.
LEAR   Read.
140   GLOUCESTER   What, with the case° of eyes?   *sockets*
LEAR   Oh, ho, are you there with me?[8] No eyes in your head,
nor no money in your purse? Your eyes are in a heavy case,[9]
your purse in a light, yet you see how this world goes.
GLOUCESTER   I see it feelingly.°   *by touch; painfully*
145   LEAR   What, art mad? A man may see how the world goes with
no eyes. Look with thy ears. See how yon justice rails upon
yon simple° thief. Hark in thy ear. Handy, dandy,[1] which is   *lowly; innocent*
the thief, which is the justice? Thou hast seen a farmer's dog
bark at a beggar?
150   GLOUCESTER   Ay, sir.
LEAR   And the creature run from the cur. There thou mightst
behold the great image of authority; a dog's obeyed in office.
—Thou rascal beadle,[2] hold° thy bloody hand.   *restrain*
Why dost thou lash that whore? Strip thine own back;
155   Thy blood hotly lusts to use her in that kind°   *way*
For which thou whip'st her. The usurer hangs the cozener.[3]
Through tattered rags small vices do appear;
Robes and furred gowns hides all. Get thee glass eyes,
And, like a scurvy politician,[4]
160   Seem to see the things thou dost not. No, now,
Pull off my boots, harder, harder, so.
EDGAR [*aside*]   Oh, matter and impertinency° mixed!   *sense and nonsense*
Reason in madness.

---

4. Lecherous mythological creatures that have a human body above the waist and the legs and torso of a horse below.
5. Shakespeare's frequent term for female genitals. Cf. Sonnets 129 and 144.
6. Perfume derived from the anal gland of the civet.
7. Shall decay to nothing in the same way. In Renaissance philosophy, humans were analogous to the cosmos, standing for the whole in miniature and as its

masterpiece.
8. Is that what you are telling me?
9. In a sad condition; playing on "case" as "sockets."
1. Pick a hand, as in a child's guessing game.
2. The parish officer responsible for whippings.
3. The ruinous moneylender, prosperous enough to be made a judge, convicts the ordinary cheat.
4. A vile schemer. In early modern England, "politician" meant an ambitious, even Machiavellian, upstart.

Though women all above.
But° to the girdle° do the gods inherit;°   *Only / waist / own*
125 Beneath is all the fiend's. There's hell,[4] there's darkness,
There is the sulphurous pit: burning, scalding,
Stench, consumption. Fie, fie, fie! Pah, pah!
—Give me an ounce of civet,[5] good apothecary;
Sweeten my imagination. There's money for thee.
GLOUCESTER   Oh, let me kiss that hand.
130 LEAR   Let me wipe it first.
It smells of mortality.
GLOUCESTER   O ruined piece° of nature, this great world   *masterpiece*
Shall so wear out to naught.[6] Dost thou know me?
LEAR   I remember thine eyes well enough. Dost thou squiny°   *squint*
135 at me? No, do thy worst, blind Cupid. I'll not love. Read
thou this challenge; mark but the penning of it.
GLOUCESTER   Were all thy letters suns, I could not see.
EDGAR [*aside*]   I would not take° this from report;   *believe*
It is, and my heart breaks at it.
140 LEAR   Read.
GLOUCESTER   What, with the case° of eyes?   *socket*
LEAR   Oh, ho, are you there with me?[7] No eyes in your head,
nor no money in your purse? Your eyes are in a heavy case,[8]
your purse in a light, yet you see how this world goes.
145 GLOUCESTER   I see it feelingly.°   *by touch; painfully*
LEAR   What, art mad? A man may see how this world goes with
no eyes. Look with thine ears. See how yond justice rails
upon yond simple° thief. Hark in thine ear. Change places,   *lowly; innocent*
and handy-dandy,[9] which is the justice, which is the thief?
150 Thou hast seen a farmer's dog bark at a beggar?
GLOUCESTER   Ay, sir.
LEAR   And the creature° run from the cur. There thou mightst *wretch*
behold the great image of authority; a dog's obeyed in office.
—Thou rascal beadle,[1] hold° thy bloody hand.   *restrain*
155 Why dost thou lash that whore? Strip thy own back;
Thou hotly lusts to use her in that kind°   *way*
For which thou whipp'st her. The usurer hangs the
    cozener.[2]
Through tattered clothes great vices do appear;
Robes and furred gowns hide all. Plate° sins with gold,   *Armor; gild*
160 And the strong lance of justice hurtless° breaks.   *harmlessly*
Arm it in rags, a pigmy's straw does pierce it.
None does offend; none, I say, none. I'll able° 'em.   *authorize*
Take that of me, my friend, who have the power
To seal th'accuser's lips. Get thee glass eyes,
165 And, like a scurvy politician,[3]
Seem to see the things thou dost not. Now, now, now, now.
Pull off my boots, harder, harder, so.
EDGAR [*aside*]   Oh, matter and impertinency° mixed!   *sense and nonsense*
Reason in madness.

---

4. Shakespeare's frequent term for female genitals.
Cf. Sonnets 129 and 144.
5. Perfume derived from the anal gland of the civet.
6. Shall decay to nothing in the same way. In Renaissance philosophy, humans were analogous to the cosmos, standing for the whole in miniature and as its
masterpiece.
7. Is that what you are telling me?

8. In a sad condition; playing on "case" as "sockets."
9. Pick a hand, as in a child's guessing game.
1. The parish officer responsible for whippings.
2. The ruinous moneylender, prosperous enough to
be made a judge, convicts the ordinary cheat.
3. A vile schemer. In early modern England, "politician" meant an ambitious, even Machiavellian, upstart.

LEAR   If thou wilt weep my fortune, take my eyes.
165   I know thee well enough: thy name is Gloucester.
      Thou must be patient. We came crying hither.
      Thou knowest the first time that we smell the air
      We wail and cry. I will preach to thee, mark me.
GLOUCESTER   Alack, alack the day!
170 LEAR   When we are born, we cry that we are come
      To this great stage of fools. This° a good block.[5]   *This is*
      It were a delicate° stratagem to shoe   *subtle*
      A troop of horse with fell,[6] and when I have stole upon
      These son-in-laws, then kill, kill, kill, kill, kill, kill!
         Enter three GENTLEMEN.
175 FIRST GENTLEMAN   Oh, here he is. Lay hands upon him, sirs.
      [*to* LEAR] Your most dear—
      LEAR   No rescue? What, a prisoner? I am e'en
      The natural fool[7] of fortune. Use° me well;   *Treat*
      You shall have ransom. Let me have a surgeon:
180   I am cut to the brains.
FIRST GENTLEMAN   You shall have anything.
      LEAR   No seconds?° All myself?   *supporters*
      Why, this would make a man of salt[8] to use
      His eyes for garden water-pots, ay, and
      Laying° autumn's dust.   *Settling*
FIRST GENTLEMAN   Good sir—
185 LEAR   I will die bravely,[9] like a bridegroom.
      What? I will be jovial. Come, come,
      I am a king, my masters. Know you that?
FIRST GENTLEMAN   You are a royal one, and we obey you.
      LEAR   Then there's life° in't, nay, an° you get it,   *hope / if*
190   You shall get it with running.
         Exit King [LEAR] *running*[, *pursued by*
                  two GENTLEMEN].
FIRST GENTLEMAN   A sight most pitiful in the meanest wretch,
      Past speaking of in a king. Thou hast one daughter
      Who redeems nature from the general curse
      Which twain hath brought her to.[1]
      EDGAR   Hail, gentle° sir.   *noble*
195 FIRST GENTLEMAN   Sir, speed you.° What's your will?   *God speed you*
      EDGAR   Do you hear aught of a battle toward?°   *coming*
FIRST GENTLEMAN   Most sure and vulgar,° everyone hears   *commonly known*
         that
      That can distinguish sense.°   *Who can understand*
      EDGAR   But by your favor, how near's the other army?
200 FIRST GENTLEMAN   Near and on speed for't; the main°   *main army*
         descries°   *scouts*
      Stand'st on the hourly thoughts.°   *Are expected forthwith*
      EDGAR   I thank you, sir. That's all.

5. Stage (often called "scaffold" and hence linked to an executioner's block); block used to shape a felt hat (such as the hat removed by a preacher before a sermon); mounting block (such as the stump or stock Lear may have sat on to remove his boots).
6. The skin or hide of an animal, to muffle the sound of the approaching cavalry.
7. Born plaything; playing on "natural" as "mentally deficient."
8. A man reduced to nothing but the salt his tears

deposit.
9. "Die" plays on the Renaissance sense of "have an orgasm."
1. *Who . . . to:* Who restores proper meaning and order to a universe plagued by the crimes of the other two daughters; alluding to the fall of humankind and the natural world caused by the sin of Adam and Eve and to the universal redemption brought about by Christ's sacrifice.

170 LEAR   If thou wilt weep my fortunes, take my eyes.
     I know thee well enough: thy name is Gloucester.
     Thou must be patient. We came crying hither.
     Thou know'st the first time that we smell the air
     We wail and cry. I will preach to thee. Mark.

175 GLOUCESTER   Alack, alack the day.

     LEAR   When we are born, we cry that we are come
     To this great stage of fools. This° a good block.[4]   *This is*
     It were a delicate° stratagem to shoe   *subtle*
     A troop of horse with felt.[5] I'll put't in proof,°   *to the test*
180 And when I have stol'n upon these son-in-laws,
     Then kill, kill, kill, kill, kill, kill!
              Enter a GENTLEMAN.

     GENTLEMAN   Oh, here he is. Lay hand upon him. [*to* LEAR] Sir,
     Your most dear daughter—

     LEAR   No rescue? What, a prisoner? I am even
185 The natural fool[6] of fortune. Use° me well;   *Treat*
     You shall have ransom. Let me have surgeons:
     I am cut to th' brains.

     GENTLEMAN   You shall have anything.

     LEAR   No seconds?° All myself?   *supporters*
     Why, this would make a man a man of salt,[7]
190 To use his eyes for garden water-pots. I will die bravely,[8]
     Like a smug° bridegroom. What? I will be jovial.   *an elegant*
     Come, come, I am a king, masters. Know you that?

     GENTLEMAN   You are a royal one, and we obey you.

     LEAR   Then there's life° in't. Come; an° you get it,   *hope / if*
195 You shall get it by running. Sa, sa, sa, sa.[9]   *Exit.*

     GENTLEMAN   A sight most pitiful in the meanest wretch,
     Past speaking of in a king. Thou hast a daughter
     Who redeems nature from the general curse,
     Which twain have brought her to.[1]

     EDGAR   Hail, gentle° sir.   *noble*

200 GENTLEMAN   Sir, speed you.° What's your will?   *God speed you*

     EDGAR   Do you hear aught, sir, of a battle toward?°   *coming*

     GENTLEMAN   Most sure and vulgar:°   *commonly known*
     Everyone hears that which can distinguish sound.

     EDGAR   But, by your favor, how near's the other army?

205 GENTLEMAN   Near and on speedy foot; the main descry°   *appearance*
     Stands on the hourly thought.°   *Is expected forthwith*

     EDGAR   I thank you, sir, that's all.

---

4. Stage (often called "scaffold" and hence linked to an executioner's block); block used to shape a felt hat (such as the hat removed by a preacher before a sermon); mounting block (such as the stump or stock Lear may have sat on to remove his boots).
5. Hat material, to muffle the sound of the approaching cavalry.
6. Born plaything; playing on "natural" as "mentally deficient."
7. A man reduced to nothing but the salt his tears deposit.
8. With courage; showily. "Die" plays on the Renaissance sense of "have an orgasm."
9. A cry to encourage dogs in the hunt.
1. *Who . . . to:* Who restores proper meaning and order to a universe plagued by the crimes of the other two daughters; alluding to the fall of humankind and the natural world caused by the sin of Adam and Eve and to the universal redemption brought about by Christ's sacrifice.

FIRST GENTLEMAN   Though that the Queen on° special
    cause° is here,   *for*
    Her army is moved on.   *reason*
EDGAR   I thank you, sir.
                         Exit [FIRST GENTLEMAN].

205 GLOUCESTER   You ever gentle gods, take my breath from me.
    Let not my worser spirit[2] tempt me again
    To die before you please.
EDGAR   Well pray you, father.[3]
GLOUCESTER   Now, good sir, what are you?
EDGAR   A most poor man, made lame by fortune's blows,
210   Who by the art of known and feeling° sorrows   *profound*
    Am pregnant to° good pity. Give me your hand;   *disposed to feel*
    I'll lead you to some biding.°   *resting place*
GLOUCESTER   Hearty thanks,
    The bounty and benison of heaven to boot, to boot.[4]
        Enter [Oswald the] STEWARD.
STEWARD   A proclaimed prize![5] Most happy!°   *lucky*
215   That eyeless head of thine was first framed° flesh   *made of*
    To raise my fortunes. Thou most unhappy traitor,
    Briefly thyself remember.[6] [*He draws his sword.*] The sword
        is out
    That must destroy thee.
GLOUCESTER   Now let thy friendly hand
    Put strength enough to't.
STEWARD [*to* EDGAR]   Wherefore, bold peasant,
220   Durst thou support a published° traitor? Hence,   *proclaimed*
    Lest the infection° of his fortune take   *(deathly) sickness*
    Like° hold on thee. Let go his arm.   *The same*
EDGAR [*drawing his sword and speaking in a country accent*]
    Chill[7] not let go, sir, without 'cagion.°   *occasion*
STEWARD   Let go, slave, or thou diest!
225 EDGAR   Good gentleman, go your gait.° Let poor voke pass.   *be on your way*
    An chud° have been swaggered out of my life, it would not   *If I could*
    have been so long by a vortnight. Nay, come not near the old
    man! Keep out, che vore ye, or I'll try whether your costard
    or my bat be the harder.[8] I'll be plain with you.
230 STEWARD   Out, dunghill!
        They fight.
EDGAR   Chill pick your teeth, sir; come, no matter for your
    foins.°   *sword thrusts*
STEWARD   Slave, thou hast slain me! Villain, take my purse.
    If ever thou wilt thrive, bury my body;
235   And give the letters which thou find'st about me
    To Edmund, Earl of Gloucester. Seek him out upon°   *within*
    The British party. Oh, untimely death! Death!
        He dies.

---

2. Wicked inclination; bad angel.
3. A term of respect for an elderly man.
4. To send you reward in addition to my thanks.
5. A wanted man, with a bounty on his life.
6. Recollect and pray forgiveness for your sins.

7. I will; dialect from Somerset was a stage convention for peasant dialogue.
8. *che vor ye . . . harder:* I warrant you, or I'll test whether your head or my cudgel is harder. *costard:* a kind of apple.

GENTLEMAN   Though that the Queen on° special cause° is   *for / reason*
    here,
    Her army is moved on.
EDGAR   I thank you, sir.   *Exit* [GENTLEMAN].
210 GLOUCESTER   You ever gentle gods, take my breath from me.
    Let not my worser spirit[2] tempt me again
    To die before you please.
EDGAR   Well pray you, father.[3]
GLOUCESTER   Now, good sir, what are you?
EDGAR   A most poor man, made tame to fortune's blows,
215 Who by the art of known and feeling° sorrows,   *profound*
    Am pregnant to° good pity. Give me your hand;   *disposed to feel*
    I'll lead you to some biding.°   *resting place*
GLOUCESTER   Hearty thanks.
    The bounty and the benison of heaven
    To boot and boot.[4]
        Enter [*Oswald the*] STEWARD.
STEWARD   A proclaimed prize![5] Most happy!°   *lucky*
220 That eyeless head of thine was first framed° flesh   *made of*
    To raise my fortunes. Thou old unhappy traitor,
    Briefly thyself remember.[6] [*He draws his sword.*] The sword
      is out
    That must destroy thee.
GLOUCESTER   Now let thy friendly hand
    Put strength enough to't.
STEWARD [*to* EDGAR]   Wherefore, bold peasant,
225 Dar'st thou support a published° traitor? Hence,   *proclaimed*
    Lest that th'infection° of his fortune take   *(deathly) sickness*
    Like° hold on thee. Let go his arm.   *The same*
EDGAR [*drawing his sword and speaking in a country accent*]
    Chill[7] not let go, zir, without vurther 'casion.°   *further occasion*
STEWARD   Let go, slave, or thou diest.
230 EDGAR   Good gentleman, go your gait,° and let poor volk pass.   *be on your way*
    An chud ha'° been zwaggered out of my life, 'twould not ha'   *If I could have*
    been zo long as 'tis by a vortnight. Nay, come not near th'old
    man! Keep out, che vor' ye, or I'll try whither your costard or
    my ballow be the harder.[8] Chill be plain with you.
235 STEWARD   Out, dunghill!
EDGAR   Chill pick your teeth, zir! Come, no matter vor your
    foins.°   *sword thrusts*
        [*They fight.*]
STEWARD   Slave, thou hast slain me! Villain, take my purse.
    If ever thou wilt thrive, bury my body,
240 And give the letters which thou find'st about me
    To Edmond, Earl of Gloucester. Seek him out
    Upon° the English party. Oh, untimely death, death!   *Within*
        [*He dies.*]

---

2. Wicked inclination; bad angel.
3. A term of respect for an elderly man.
4. In addition to my thanks, and may it bring you
some worldly reward.
5. A wanted man, with a bounty on his life.
6. Recollect and pray forgiveness for your sins.

7. I will; dialect from Somerset was a stage convention for peasant dialogue.
8. *che vor' ye . . . harder:* I warrant you, or I shall test
whether your head or my cudgel is harder. *costard:* a
kind of apple.

EDGAR   I know thee well: a serviceable° villain,   *an officious*
    As duteous to the vices of thy mistress
    As badness would desire.
240 GLOUCESTER   What, is he dead?
EDGAR   Sit you down, father, rest you.
    Let's see his pockets. These letters that he speaks of
    May be my friends. He's dead; I am only sorry
    He had no other deathsman.° [*He opens the letter.*] Let us see.   *executioner*
245 Leave,° gentle wax,[9] and manners blame us not.   *By your leave*
    To know our enemy's minds, we'd rip their hearts.
    Their° papers is more lawful.   *To rip their*
    ([*Reads*] *a letter.*) "Let your reciprocal vows be remembered.
    You have many opportunities to cut him off. If your will
250 want° not, time and place will be fruitfully offered. There is   *lacks*
    nothing done° if he return the conqueror; then am I the   *accomplished*
    prisoner and his bed my jail, from the loathed warmth
    whereof deliver me and supply° the place for your labor.[1]   *fill*
    Your wife (so I would say), your affectionate servant, and for
255 you her own for venture,[2] Gonorill."
    Oh, indistinguished space of woman's wit![3]
    A plot upon her virtuous husband's life,
    And the exchange° my brother. Here in the sands   *substitute*
    Thee I'll rake up,° the post unsanctified°   *cover up / unholy messenger*
260 Of murderous lechers, and in the mature time°   *when the time is ripe*
    With this ungracious° paper strike the sight   *ungodly*
    Of the death-practiced Duke.[4] For him, 'tis well
    That of thy death and business I can tell.
GLOUCESTER   The King is mad. How stiff is my vile sense[5]
265 That I stand up and have ingenious feeling[6]
    Of my huge sorrows? Better I were distract;°   *mad*
    So should my thoughts be fencèd from my griefs,
    And woes by wrong° imaginations lose   *false*
    The knowledge of themselves.
        A drum afar off.
EDGAR   Give me your hand.
270 Far off methinks I hear the beaten drum.
    Come, father, I'll bestow° you with a friend.   *Exeunt.*   *lodge*

---

9. The wax seal on the letter.
1. *for your labor*: as a reward for your endeavors, and for further sexual exertion.
2. *for you . . . venture*: one willing to risk all for you; all yours, if you dare be so bold.

3. Limitless extent of woman's cunning.
4. Of the Duke whose death is plotted.
5. How obstinate is my unwanted power of reason.
6. That I remain upright and firm in my sanity and have rational perceptions.

EDGAR   I know thee well: a serviceable° villain,   *an officious*
　　As duteous to the vices of thy mistress
　　As badness would desire.
245　GLOUCESTER　　　　　　　What, is he dead?
EDGAR　Sit you down, father; rest you.
　　Let's see these pockets. The letters that he speaks of
　　May be my friends. He's dead; I am only sorry
　　He had no other deathsman.° [*He opens the letter.*] Let   *executioner*
　　us see.
250　Leave,° gentle wax,[9] and manners blame us not.   *By your leave*
　　To know our enemies' minds, we rip their hearts;
　　Their° papers is more lawful.   *To rip their*
　　　　[*He*] *reads the letter.*
　　"Let our reciprocal vows be remembered. You have many
　　opportunities to cut him off. If your will want° not, time and   *lacks*
255　place will be fruitfully offered. There is nothing done° if he   *accomplished*
　　return the conqueror; then am I the prisoner and his bed my
　　jail, from the loathed warmth whereof deliver me, and sup-
　　ply° the place for your labor.[1] Your (wife, so I would say)   *fill*
　　affectionate servant, Gonerill."
260　Oh, indistinguished space of woman's will![2]
　　A plot upon her virtuous husband's life,
　　And the exchange° my brother! Here in the sands   *substitute*
　　Thee I'll rake up,° the post unsanctified°   *cover up / unholy messenger*
　　Of murderous lechers, and in the mature time°   *when the time is ripe*
265　With this ungracious° paper strike the sight   *ungodly*
　　Of the death-practiced Duke.[3] For him, 'tis well
　　That of thy death and business I can tell.
GLOUCESTER　The King is mad. How stiff is my vile sense[4]
　　That I stand up and have ingenious feeling[5]
270　Of my huge sorrows? Better I were distract;°   *mad*
　　So should my thoughts be severed from my griefs,
　　　　Drum afar off.
　　And woes by wrong° imaginations lose   *false*
　　The knowledge of themselves.
EDGAR　　　　　　　　　　　　Give me your hand.
　　Far off methinks I hear the beaten drum.
275　Come, father, I'll bestow° you with a friend.　　*Exeunt.*   *lodge*

9. The wax seal on the letter.
1. *for your labor:* as a reward for your endeavors, and
for further sexual exertion.
2. Limitless extent of woman's willfulness. As with
"hell" in line 125, "will" might also refer to a woman's

genitals.
3. Of the Duke whose death is plotted.
4. How obstinate is my unwanted power of reason.
5. That I remain upright and firm in my sanity and
have rational perceptions.

4.7 (F 4.6)

Enter CORDELIA, KENT [*dressed as Caius*], *and*
DOCTOR[, *and* GENTLEMAN].

CORDELIA O thou good Kent, how shall I live and work
To match thy goodness? My life will be too short
And every measure° fail me.   attempt

KENT To be acknowledged, madam, is o'erpaid.°   is more than enough
5   All my reports go¹ with the modest truth,
Nor more, nor clipped, but so.²

CORDELIA   Be better suited;°   attired
These weeds° are memories of those worser hours.   clothes
I prithee, put them off.

KENT Pardon me, dear madam.
10   Yet to be known shortens my made intent.³
My boon I make it⁴ that you know° me not   acknowledge
Till time and I think meet.°   suitable

CORDELIA Then be't so. [*to* DOCTOR] My good lord, how does
the King?

DOCTOR Madam, sleeps still.

15   CORDELIA O you kind gods,
Cure this great breach in his abusèd nature.
The untuned and hurrying senses, oh, wind up⁵
Of this child-changèd⁶ father.

DOCTOR So please your majesty
20   That we may wake the King? He hath slept long.

CORDELIA Be governed by your knowledge and proceed
I'th' sway° of your own will. Is he arrayed?°   By the authority / clothed

DOCTOR Ay, madam. In the heaviness of his sleep
We put fresh garments on him.

25   GENTLEMAN Good madam, be by when we do awake him;
I doubt not of his temperance.°   calmness

CORDELIA   Very well.
[*Music plays.*]

DOCTOR Please you draw near; louder the music there.
[*Enter* LEAR *in a chair carried by* SERVANTS.]

CORDELIA O my dear father, restoration
Hang thy medicine on my lips, and let this kiss
30   Repair those violent harms that my two sisters
Have in thy reverence° made.   aged dignity

KENT   Kind and dear princess.

CORDELIA Had you not⁷ been their father, these white
flakes°   locks of hair
Had challenged° pity of them. Was this a face   Would have provoked
To be exposed against the warring winds,

4.7 Location: The French camp at Dover.
1. May all accounts of me agree.
2. Not greater or less, but exactly the modest amount
I deserve.
3. Revealing myself now would abort my designs.
4. The reward I beg is.

5. *The . . . up:* Reorder his confused and delirious
mind. The image is of tightening the strings of a lute.
6. Changed by his children; changed into a child;
playing on a musical key change.
7. Even if you had not.

4.6 (Q 4.7)

Enter CORDELIA, KENT *[dressed as Caius], and*
GENTLEMAN.

CORDELIA   O thou good Kent, how shall I live and work
To match thy goodness? My life will be too short
And every measure° fail me.   *attempt*

KENT   To be acknowledged, madam, is o'erpaid.°   *is more than enough*

5   All my reports go[1] with the modest truth,
Nor more, nor clipped, but so.[2]

CORDELIA   Be better suited;°   *attired*
These weeds° are memories of those worser hours.   *clothes*
I prithee, put them off.

KENT   Pardon, dear madam,
Yet to be known shortens my made intent.[3]

10   My boon I make it[4] that you know° me not   *acknowledge*
Till time and I think meet.°   *suitable*

CORDELIA   Then be't so, my good lord.
—How does the King?

GENTLEMAN   Madam, sleeps still.

CORDELIA   O you kind gods,
Cure this great breach in his abusèd nature.

15   Th'untuned and jarring senses, oh, wind up[5]
Of this child-changed[6] father.

GENTLEMAN   So please your majesty
That we may wake the King? He hath slept long.

CORDELIA   Be governed by your knowledge and proceed
I'th' sway° of your own will. Is he arrayed?°   *By the authority / clothed*

Enter LEAR *in a chair carried by* SERVANTS.

20   GENTLEMAN   Ay, madam. In the heaviness of sleep,
We put fresh garments on him.
Be by, good madam, when we do awake him;
I doubt of his temperance.°   *calmness*

CORDELIA   O my dear father, restoration hang

25   Thy medicine on my lips, and let this kiss
Repair those violent harms that my two sisters
Have in thy reverence° made.   *aged dignity*

KENT   Kind and dear princess.

CORDELIA   Had you not[7] been their father, these white
flakes°   *locks of hair*
Did challenge° pity of them. Was this a face   *Would have provoked*

30   To be opposed against the jarring winds?

4.6 Location: The French camp at Dover.
1. May all accounts of me agree.
2. Not greater or less, but exactly the modest amount
I deserve.
3. Revealing myself now would abort my designs.
4. The reward I beg is.

5. *Th'untuned . . . up*: Reorder his confused and
delirious mind. The image is of tightening the strings
of a lute.
6. Changed by his children; changed into a child;
playing on a musical key change.
7. Even if you had not.

35 To stand against the deep dread-bolted thunder,
 In the most terrible and nimble stroke
 Of quick cross lightning to watch° —poor *perdu*![8]—   *to stand guard*
 With this thin helm?° Mine injurious dog,   *helmet (of hair)*
 Though he had bit me, should have stood that night
40 Against my fire. And wast thou fain,° poor father,   *obliged*
 To hovel thee with swine and rogues forlorn
 In short° and musty straw? Alack, alack,   *scant; broken*
 'Tis wonder that thy life and wits at once
 Had not concluded all!° —He wakes. Speak to him.   *altogether*
45 DOCTOR Madam, do you, 'tis fittest.
 CORDELIA How does my royal lord? How fares your majesty?
 LEAR You do me wrong to take me out o'th' grave.
 Thou art a soul in bliss, but I am bound
 Upon a wheel of fire, that mine own tears
 Do scald like molten lead.[9]
50 CORDELIA   Sir, know me.
 LEAR You're a spirit, I know. Where did you die?
 CORDELIA Still, still, far wide.°   *unbalanced*
 DOCTOR He's scarce awake. Let him alone a while.
 LEAR Where have I been? Where am I? Fair daylight?
55 I am mightily abused.° I should e'en die with pity   *wronged; deceived*
 To see another thus. I know not what to say.
 I will not swear these are my hands. Let's see,
 I feel this pin prick. Would I were assured
 Of my condition.
 CORDELIA [*kneeling*] Oh, look upon me, sir,
60 And hold your hands in benediction o'er me.
    [LEAR *kneels*.]
 No, sir, you must not kneel.
 LEAR [*rising*]   Pray do not mock.
 I am a very foolish fond° old man,   *silly*
 Fourscore and upward, and, to deal plainly,
 I fear I am not in my perfect mind.
65 Methinks I should know you and know this man.
 Yet I am doubtful, for I am mainly° ignorant   *entirely*
 What place this is, and all the skill I have
 Remembers not these garments, nor I know not
 Where I did lodge last night. Do not laugh at me,
70 For as I am a man, I think this lady
 To be my child Cordelia.
 CORDELIA   And so I am.
 LEAR Be your tears wet?[1] Yes, faith. I pray, weep not.
 If you have poison for me I will drink it.
 I know you do not love me, for your sisters
75 Have, as I do remember, done me wrong.
 You have some cause; they have not.
 CORDELIA   No cause, no cause.

---

8. Lost one; in military terms, a dangerously exposed sentry.
9. *but I . . . lead:* Lear puts himself in either hell or purgatory, both places of such punishment in medi-

eval accounts. Compare also to the classical myth of Ixion, bound by Zeus to a spinning wheel of fire.
1. Are your tears real? Is this really happening?

Mine enemy's dog, though he had bit me,
Should have stood that night against my fire.
And wast thou fain,° poor father, ⟶ *obliged*
To hovel thee with swine and rogues forlorn
35 In short° and musty straw? Alack, alack, ⟶ *scant; broken*
'Tis wonder that thy life and wits at once
Had not concluded all.° —He wakes; speak to him. ⟶ *altogether*
GENTLEMAN Madam, do you, 'tis fittest.
CORDELIA How does my royal lord?
40 How fares your majesty?
LEAR You do me wrong to take me out o'th' grave.
Thou art a soul in bliss, but I am bound
Upon a wheel of fire, that mine own tears
Do scald like molten lead.[8]
CORDELIA Sir, do you know me?
45 LEAR You are a spirit, I know. Where did you die?
CORDELIA Still, still, far wide.° ⟶ *unbalanced*
GENTLEMAN He's scarce awake. Let him alone a while.
LEAR Where have I been? Where am I? Fair daylight?
I am mightily abused.° I should e'en die with pity ⟶ *wronged; deceived*
50 To see another thus. I know not what to say.
I will not swear these are my hands. Let's see,
I feel this pin prick. Would I were assured
Of my condition.
CORDELIA [*kneeling*] Oh, look upon me, sir,
And hold your hand in benediction o'er me.
[LEAR *kneels.*]
You must not kneel.
55 LEAR [*rising*] Pray do not mock me.
I am a very foolish, fond° old man, ⟶ *silly*
Fourscore and upward,
Not an hour more nor less,
And to deal plainly,
60 I fear I am not in my perfect mind.
Methinks I should know you and know this man.
Yet I am doubtful, for I am mainly° ignorant ⟶ *entirely*
What place this is, and all the skill I have
Remembers not these garments, nor I know not
65 Where I did lodge last night. Do not laugh at me,
For as I am a man, I think this lady
To be my child Cordelia.
CORDELIA And so I am. I am.
LEAR Be your tears wet?[9] Yes, faith. I pray, weep not.
If you have poison for me, I will drink it.
70 I know you do not love me, for your sisters
Have, as I do remember, done me wrong.
You have some cause; they have not.
CORDELIA No cause, no cause.

---

8. *but I . . . lead:* Lear puts himself in either hell or purgatory, both places of such punishment in medieval accounts. Compare also to the classical myth of Ixion, bound by Zeus to a spinning wheel of fire.
9. Are your tears real? Is this really happening?

LEAR   Am I in France?

KENT   In your own kingdom, sir.

LEAR   Do not abuse° me.   *deceive; mock*

DOCTOR   Be comforted, good madam. The great rage
80   You see is cured in him, and yet it is
        Danger to make him even o'er° the time   *go over*
        He has lost. Desire him to go in;
        Trouble him no more till further settling.°   *until his mind eases*

CORDELIA   Will't please your highness walk?

85 LEAR   You must bear with me. Pray now, forget and forgive.
        I am old and foolish.

                        Exeunt [LEAR *and* CORDELIA]; KENT *and*
                                    GENTLEMAN *remain.*

GENTLEMAN   Holds it true, sir, that the Duke of Cornwall was
        so slain?

KENT   Most certain, sir.

90 GENTLEMAN   Who is conductor° of his people?   *commander*

KENT   As 'tis said, the bastard son of Gloucester.

GENTLEMAN   They say Edgar, his banished son, is with the
        Earl of Kent in Germany.

KENT   Report° is changeable. 'Tis time to look about.° The   *Rumor / prepare defenses*
95   powers of the kingdom approach apace.

GENTLEMAN   The arbitrament° is like to be bloody. Fare you   *encounter*
        well, sir.   [*Exit.*]

KENT   My point and period[2] will be thoroughly wrought,
        Or° well or ill as this day's battle's fought.   *Exit.*   *For*

5.1 (F 5.1)

                Enter Edmund [*the* BASTARD], REGAN, *and their
                powers.*

BASTARD   Know° of the Duke if his last purpose hold,[1]   *Inquire*
        Or whether since he is advised by aught[2]
        To change the course. He's full of alteration[3]
        And self reproving. Bring his constant pleasure.°   *his settled intent*

5   REGAN   Our sister's man is certainly miscarried.[4]

BASTARD   'Tis to be doubted,° madam,   *feared*

REGAN   Now, sweet lord,
        You know the goodness I intend upon you.
        Tell me but truly, but then speak the truth:
        Do you not love my sister?

BASTARD   Ay, honored° love.   *honorable*

10 REGAN   But have you never found my brother's way
        To the forfended[5] place?

---

2. The purpose and end of my life; literally, the full
stop.
5.1 Location: The British camp near Dover.
1. If his previous intention (to wage war) remains firm.
2. Since then anything has persuaded him.

3. A tendency to give up his intentions or put aside
his responsibilities.
4. Has surely come to grief by some accident.
5. Forbidden, by the prohibition against adultery.

LEAR Am I in France?

KENT   In your own kingdom, sir.

LEAR Do not abuse° me.   *deceive; mock*

75 GENTLEMAN Be comforted, good madam; the great rage
You see is killed in him. Desire him to go in;
Trouble him no more till further settling.°   *until his mind eases*

CORDELIA Will't please your highness walk?

LEAR   You must bear with me.
Pray you now, forget and forgive.

80 I am old and foolish.   *Exeunt.*

5.1 (Q 5.1)

Enter with drum and colors,° EDMOND, REGAN,   *regimental flags*
GENTLEMEN, *and Soldiers.*

EDMOND Know° of the Duke if his last purpose hold,[1]   *Inquire*
Or whether since he is advised by aught[2]
To change the course. He's full of alteration[3]
And self-reproving. Bring his constant pleasure.°   *his settled intent*

5 REGAN Our sister's man is certainly miscarried.[4]

EDMOND 'Tis to be doubted,° madam.   *feared*

REGAN   Now, sweet lord,
You know the goodness I intend upon you.
Tell me but truly, but then speak the truth:
Do you not love my sister?

EDMOND   In honored° love.   *honorable*

10 REGAN But have you never found my brother's way
To the forfended[5] place?

5.1 Location: The British camp near Dover.
1. If his previous intention (to wage war) remains firm.
2. Since then anything has persuaded him.

3. A tendency to give up his intentions or put aside his responsibilities.
4. Has surely come to grief by some accident.
5. Forbidden, by the prohibition against adultery.

BASTARD   That thought abuses° you.   *deceives*
REGAN   I am doubtful° that you have been conjunct°   *suspicious / complicit*
  And bosomed with° her—as far as we call hers.[6]   *enamored of*
BASTARD   No, by mine honor, madam.
15 REGAN   I never shall endure her. Dear my lord,
  Be not familiar° with her.   *intimate*
BASTARD   Fear° me not. She and the Duke, her husband—   *Doubt*
        Enter ALBANY *and* GONORILL *with troops.*
GONORILL [*aside*]   I had rather lose the battle than that sister
  Should loosen° him and me.   *disunite*
20 ALBANY   Our very loving sister, well be-met.°   *met*
  For this I hear: the King is come to his daughter,
  With others whom the rigor° of our state°   *harshness / government*
  Forced to cry out. Where I could not be honest°   *honorable*
  I never yet was valiant. For this business,
25 It touches° us as France invades our land,   *concerns*
  Not bolds° the King, with others whom I fear   *Does not embolden*
  Most just and heavy causes make oppose.[7]
BASTARD   Sir, you speak nobly.
REGAN   Why is this reasoned?[8]
GONORILL   Combine together 'gainst the enemy,
30 For these domestic poor particulars°   *minor details*
  Are not to° question here.   *the*
ALBANY   Let us, then, determine with the ancient° of war   *experienced officer(s)*
  On our proceedings.
BASTARD   I shall attend you presently° at your tent.   *in a moment*
35 REGAN   Sister, you'll go with us?
GONORILL   No.
REGAN   'Tis most convenient;° pray you go with us.[9]   *suitable*
GONORILL   Oh, ho, I know the riddle.° I will go.   *disguised meaning*
        Enter EDGAR [*disguised*].
EDGAR [*to* ALBANY]   If e'er your grace had speech with man
    so poor,
  Hear me one word.
ALBANY [*to the others*] I'll overtake you.
                        Exeunt [BASTARD, GONORILL, *and* REGAN
                              with their troops and powers].
40   Speak.
EDGAR   Before you fight the battle, ope this letter.
  If you have victory, let the trumpet sound
  For him that brought it. Wretched though I seem,
  I can produce a champion that will prove°   *defend*
45 What is avouchèd° there. If you miscarry,°   *asserted / perish*
  Your business of the world hath so an end.
  Fortune love you.
ALBANY   Stay till I have read the letter.

---

6. In total intimacy; all the way.
7. *It . . . oppose:* The invasion concerns us only insofar as France has invaded Britain, not because it has
emboldened Lear, who has just cause to attack.

8. What is the point of this kind of speech?
9. Regan wants Gonorill to go with Albany and her,
rather than with Edmund.

EDMOND   No, by mine honor, madam.

REGAN   I never shall endure her. Dear my lord,
  Be not familiar° with her.   *intimate*
EDMOND   Fear° not. She and the Duke, her husband—   *Doubt*
  Enter with drum and colors, ALBANY, GONERILL,
  Soldiers.

15 ALBANY   Our very loving sister, well be-met.°   *met*
  —Sir, this I heard: the King is come to his daughter,
  With others whom the rigor° of our state°   *harshness / government*
  Forced to cry out.

REGAN   Why is this reasoned?[6]
GONERILL   Combine together 'gainst the enemy.
20 For these domestic and particular broils°   *minor details*
  Are not the question here.
  ALBANY   Let's then determine with th'ancient° of war   *experienced officer(s)*
  On our proceeding.
  REGAN   Sister, you'll go with us?[7]
25 GONERILL   No.
  REGAN   'Tis most convenient;° pray go with us.   *suitable*
  GONERILL   Oh, ho, I know the riddle!° I will go.   *disguised meaning*
                 Exeunt both the armies.
      Enter EDGAR *[disguised].*
  EDGAR *[to* ALBANY*]*   If e'er your grace had speech with man
    so poor,
  Hear me one word.
  ALBANY *[to the others]*   I'll overtake you.
      [Exeunt EDMOND, GONERILL, *and* REGAN.*]*
            Speak.
30 EDGAR   Before you fight the battle, ope this letter.
  If you have victory, let the trumpet sound
  For him that brought it. Wretched though I seem,
  I can produce a champion that will prove°   *defend*
  What is avouchèd° there. If you miscarry,°   *asserted / perish*
35 Your business of the world hath so an end,
  And machination° ceases. Fortune loves you.   *plotting*
  ALBANY   Stay till I have read the letter.

---

6. What is the point of this kind of speech?
7. Regan wants Gonerill to go with Albany and her, rather than with Edmond.

EDGAR   I was forbid it.
When time shall serve, let but the herald cry
50   And I'll appear again.
ALBANY   Why, fare thee well. I will o'erlook the paper.
                                        Exit [EDGAR].

        Enter Edmund [the BASTARD].
BASTARD   The enemy's in view; draw up your powers.°   troops
Hard is the guess° of their great strength and forces   estimate
By diligent discovery,° but your haste is now urged on you.   spying
55   ALBANY   We will greet the time.[1]   *Exit.*
BASTARD   To both these sisters have I sworn my love,
Each jealous° of the other, as the stung   suspicious
Are of the adder. Which of them shall I take?
Both, one, or neither? Neither can be enjoyed
60   If both remain alive. To take the widow
Exasperates, makes mad, her sister Gonorill,
And hardly° shall I carry out my side,°   with difficulty / plan
Her husband being alive. Now, then, we'll use
His countenance[2] for the battle, which being done,
65   Let her that would be rid of him devise
His speedy taking-off. As for his mercy
Which he intends to Lear and to Cordelia,
The battle done, and they within our power,
Shall° never see his pardon. For my state°   They shall / condition
70   Stands on° me to defend, not to debate.   *Exit.*   Obliges

5.2 (F 5.2)

        Alarum.[1] *Enter the powers of France over the stage,*
        CORDELIA *with her father in her hand[, and exeunt].*
        Enter EDGAR [*disguised as a peasant*] *and*
        GLOUCESTER.
EDGAR   Here, father,[2] take the shadow of this bush
For your good host.° Pray that the right may thrive.   shelter
If ever I return to you again, I'll bring you comfort.   *Exit.*
GLOUCESTER   Grace go with you, sir.
        Alarum° and retreat. [*Enter* EDGAR.]   Trumpet signal
5   EDGAR   Away, old man! Give me thy hand, away!
King Lear hath lost: he and his daughter ta'en.
Give me thy hand, come on.
GLOUCESTER   No farther, sir, a man may rot even° here.   right
EDGAR   What, in ill thoughts again? Men must endure
10   Their going hence even as their coming hither.
Ripeness is all.[3] Come on.   [*Exeunt.*]

---

1. We will be ready to meet the occasion.
2. Authority or backing; also suggesting "face," to be used like a mask for Edmund's ambition.
5.2 Location: The rest of the play takes place near the battlefield.
1. Trumpet call to battle.

2. See note to 4.6.207.
3. To await the destined time is the most important thing, as fruit falls only when ripe (playing on Gloucester's "rot," line 8); readiness for death is our only duty (compare *Hamlet* 5.2.194, "The readiness is all").

EDGAR   I was forbid it.
When time shall serve, let but the herald cry,
And I'll appear again.   *Exit.*

40   ALBANY   Why, fare thee well. I will o'erlook thy paper.
       Enter EDMOND.

EDMOND   The enemy's in view; draw up your powers.°   *troops*
Here is the guess° of their true strength and forces   *estimate*
By diligent discovery,° but your haste   *spying*
Is now urged on you.

ALBANY   We will greet the time.[8]   *Exit.*

45   EDMOND   To both these sisters have I sworn my love,
Each jealous° of the other, as the stung   *suspicious*
Are of the adder. Which of them shall I take?
Both? One? Or neither? Neither can be enjoyed
If both remain alive. To take the widow

50   Exasperates, makes mad, her sister Gonerill,
And hardly° shall I carry out my side,°   *with difficulty / plan*
Her husband being alive. Now, then, we'll use
His countenance[9] for the battle, which being done,
Let her who would be rid of him devise

55   His speedy taking-off. As for the mercy
Which he intends to Lear and to Cordelia,
The battle done, and they within our power,
Shall° never see his pardon. For my state°   *They shall / condition*
Stands on° me to defend, not to debate.   *Exit.*   *Obliges*

5.2 (Q 5.2)

Alarum within.[1] *Enter with drum and colors,* LEAR,
CORDELIA, *and Soldiers, over the stage, and exeunt.*
Enter EDGAR [*disguised as a peasant*] *and*
GLOUCESTER.

EDGAR   Here, father,[2] take the shadow of this tree
For your good host.° Pray that the right may thrive.   *shelter*
If ever I return to you again,
I'll bring you comfort.

GLOUCESTER   Grace go with you, sir.   *Exit* [EDGAR].
       Alarum° and retreat within.   *Trumpet signal*
       Enter EDGAR.

5   EDGAR   Away, old man, give me thy hand, away!
King Lear hath lost: he and his daughter ta'en.
Give me thy hand. Come on.

GLOUCESTER   No further, sir, a man may rot even° here.   *right*

EDGAR   What, in ill thoughts again? Men must endure

10   Their going hence even as their coming hither;
Ripeness is all.[3] Come on.

GLOUCESTER   And that's true too.   *Exeunt.*

---

8. We will be ready to meet the occasion.
9. Authority or backing; also suggesting "face," to be used like a mask for Edmond's ambition.
5.2 Location: The rest of the play takes place near the battlefield.
1. Trumpet call to battle (backstage).

2. See note to 4.5.212.
3. To await the destined time is the most important thing, as fruit falls only when ripe (playing on Gloucester's "rot," line 8); readiness for death is our only duty (compare *Hamlet* 5.2.199, "The readiness is all").

5.3 (F 5.3)

Enter Edmund [the BASTARD, *and* CAPTAIN OF THE
GUARD], *with* LEAR *and* CORDELIA *prisoners[,
guarded].*[1]

BASTARD   Some officers! Take them away. Good guard,
 Until their greater pleasures[2] best be known
 That are to censure° them.   *judge*
CORDELIA   We are not the first
 Who with best meaning° have incurred the worst. *intention*
5 For thee, oppressèd King, am I cast down;° *(into unhappiness)*
 Myself could else out-frown false fortune's frown.[3]
 Shall we not see these daughters and these sisters?
LEAR   No, no, come, let's away to prison.
 We two alone will sing like birds i'th' cage.
10 When thou dost ask me blessing, I'll kneel down
 And ask of thee forgiveness. So we'll live,
 And pray, and sing, and tell old tales and laugh
 At gilded butterflies,[4] and hear poor rogues
 Talk of court news, and we'll talk with them too—
15 Who loses, and who wins, who's in, who's out—
 And take upon 's the mystery of things
 As if we were God's spies. And we'll wear out° *outlast*
 In a walled prison packs and sects of great ones
 That ebb and flow by th' moon.[5]
BASTARD   Take them away.
20 LEAR   Upon such sacrifices,[6] my Cordelia,
 The gods themselves throw incense. Have I caught thee?
 He that parts us shall bring a brand from heaven
 And fire us hence like foxes.[7] Wipe thine eyes.
 The good shall devour 'em, flesh and fell,[8]
25 Ere they shall make us weep. We'll see 'em starve first. Come.
    [*Exit with* CORDELIA, *guarded by* GENTLEMEN.]
BASTARD   Come hither, Captain. Hark.
 Take thou this note; go follow them to prison.
 One step I have advanced° thee; if thou dost *promoted*
 As this instructs thee, thou dost make thy way
30 To noble fortunes. Know thou this: that men
 Are as the time is. To be tender-minded
 Does not become a sword;° thy great employment *befit a swordsman*
 Will not bear question.° Either say thou'lt do't *discussion*
 Or thrive by other means.
CAPTAIN OF THE GUARD   I'll do't, my lord.
35 BASTARD   About it, and write happy when thou hast done.[9]
 Mark, I say, instantly, and carry it° so *carry it out*
 As I have set it down.

5.3
1. TEXTUAL COMMENT There are differences between
the entrance and exit directions in the Quarto and
Folio versions of 5.3. Q1's entrance of the "Captain"
late in the scene is replaced by the entrance of the
"Messenger" in F. The deletion of extraneous roles is
not unusual in the later revisions of plays, but this
scene's revision in F suggests that too many "Captains" are wandering the stage in Q1. See Digital Edition TC 7 (Quarto edited text).
2. *Good . . . pleasures:* Guard them well until the
desires of those greater persons.

3. Otherwise, I could be defiant in the face of bad
fortune.
4. Gaudy courtiers.
5. *packs . . . moon:* followers and factions of important people whose position at court varies as the tide.
6. Upon such sacrifices as we are or as you have made.
7. *shall . . . foxes:* must have divine aid to do so. The
image is of using a torch to smoke foxes out of their
holes—or, in the case of Lear and Cordelia, prison
cells.
8. *flesh and fell:* meat and skin; entirely.
9. Go to it, and call yourself happy when you are done.

5.3 (Q 5.3)

Enter in conquest with drum and colors, EDMOND;
LEAR *and* CORDELIA *as prisoners; Soldiers,* CAPTAIN.[1]

EDMOND   Some officers! Take them away. Good guard
Until their greater pleasures[2] first be known
That are to censure° them.   *judge*

CORDELIA   We are not the first
Who with best meaning° have incurred the worst.   *intention*
5   For thee, oppressèd King, I am cast down.°   *(into unhappiness)*
Myself could else out-frown false fortune's frown.[3]
Shall we not see these daughters and these sisters?

LEAR   No, no, no, no. Come, let's away to prison.
We two alone will sing like birds i'th' cage.
10   When thou dost ask me blessing, I'll kneel down
And ask of thee forgiveness. So we'll live,
And pray, and sing, and tell old tales, and laugh
At gilded butterflies,[4] and hear poor rogues
Talk of court news, and we'll talk with them too—
15   Who loses, and who wins; who's in, who's out—
And take upon 's the mystery of things,
As if we were God's spies. And we'll wear out,°   *outlast*
In a walled prison, packs and sects of great ones,
That ebb and flow by th' moon.[5]

EDMOND   Take them away.
20   LEAR   Upon such sacrifices,[6] my Cordelia,
The gods themselves throw incense. Have I caught thee?
He that parts us shall bring a brand from heaven,
And fire us hence like foxes.[7] Wipe thine eyes.
The good years shall devour them, flesh and fell,[8]
25   Ere they shall make us weep.
We'll see 'em starved first. Come.

Exeunt [*Soldiers with* LEAR *and* CORDELIA].

EDMOND   Come hither, Captain. Hark.
Take thou this note; go follow them to prison.
One step I have advanced° thee; if thou dost   *promoted*
30   As this instructs thee, thou dost make thy way
To noble fortunes. Know thou this: that men
Are as the time is. To be tender-minded
Does not become a sword;° thy great employment   *befit a swordsman*
Will not bear question.° Either say thou'lt do't   *discussion*
Or thrive by other means.

35   CAPTAIN   I'll do't, my lord.

EDMOND   About it, and write happy when th' hast done.[9]
Mark, I say instantly, and carry it so°   *carry it out*
As I have set it down.   *Exit* CAPTAIN.

5.3
1. TEXTUAL COMMENT There are differences between
the entrance and exit directions in the Q1 and F versions of 5.3. Q1's entrance of the "Captain" late in the
scene is replaced by the entrance of the "Messenger"
in F. The deletion of extraneous roles is not unusual
in the later revisions of plays, but this scene's revision
in F suggests that too many "Captains" are wandering
the stage in Q1. See Digital Edition TC 6 (Folio
edited text).
2. *Good . . . pleasures:* Guard them well until the
desires of those greater persons.
3. Otherwise, I could be defiant in the face of bad
fortune.

4. Gaudy courtiers.
5. *packs . . . moon:* followers and factions of important people whose position at court varies as the tide.
6. Upon such sacrifices as we are or as you have
made.
7. *shall . . . foxes:* must have divine aid to do so. The
image is of using a torch to smoke foxes out of their
holes—or, in the case of Lear and Cordelia, prison
cells.
8. *flesh and fell:* meat and skin; entirely. The precise
meaning of "good years" has not been explained; it
may signify simply the passage of time or may suggest
some ominous, destructive power.
9. Go to it, and call yourself happy when you are done.

CAPTAIN OF THE GUARD   I cannot draw a cart, nor eat dried
  oats;°   *(like a horse)*
  If it be man's work, I'll do't.   [*Exit.*]
    Enter [the] Duke [of ALBANY], *the two Ladies*
    [GONORILL *and* REGAN, *another* CAPTAIN], *and others.*

40 ALBANY Sir, you have showed today your valiant strain,° *qualities; heritage*
  And Fortune led you well. You have the captives
  That were the opposites° of this day's strife.   *opponents*
  We do require them of you, so to use° them   *treat*
  As we shall find their merits and our safety
  May equally determine.
45 BASTARD   Sir, I thought it fit
  To send the old and miserable King
  To some retention° and appointed guard,   *confinement*
  Whose° age has charms in it, whose title more,   *(Lear's)*
  To pluck the common bosom[1] of his side
50 And turn our impressed lances° in our eyes   *conscripted lancers*
  Which[2] do command them. With him I sent the Queen.
  My reason all the same, and they are ready
  Tomorrow or at further space° to appear   *at a future point*
  Where you shall hold your session.° At this time, *court of judgment*
55 We sweat and bleed. The friend hath lost his friend,
  And the best quarrels, in the heat, are cursed
  By those that feel their sharpness.[3]
  The question of Cordelia and her father
  Requires a fitter place.
  ALBANY   Sir, by your patience,
60 I hold you but a subject of° this war,   *in waging*
  Not as a brother.
  REGAN   That's as we list° to grace him.   *choose*
  Methinks our pleasure should have been demanded[4]
  Ere you had spoke so far. He led our powers,°   *armies*
  Bore the commission of my place and person,
65 The which immediate° may well stand up   *close connection*
  And call itself your brother.
  GONORILL   Not so hot.°   *Not so fast*
  In his own grace° he doth exalt himself   *merit*
  More than in your advancement.[5]
  REGAN   In my right,
  By me invested, he compeers° the best.   *equals*
70 GONORILL That were the most[6] if he should husband you.
  REGAN Jesters do oft prove prophets.
  GONORILL   Holla, holla!
  That eye that told you so looked but asquint.[7]
  REGAN Lady, I am not well, else I should answer
  From a full-flowing stomach.° —General,   *anger*
75 Take thou my soldiers, prisoners, patrimony.
  Witness the world that I create thee here
  My lord and master.

1. To garner the affection of the populace.
2. *in our eyes / Which:* in the eyes of us who.
3. *And . . . sharpness:* And in the heat of battle, even
the most just wars are cursed by those who must suffer the fighting.
4. I think you should have inquired into my wishes.

5. In the honors you confer upon him.
6. That investiture would be complete.
7. Squinting was a proverbial effect of jealousy,
because of the tendency to look suspiciously at
potential rivals.

Flourish. Enter ALBANY, GONERILL, REGAN, *Soldiers.*

ALBANY   Sir, you have showed today your valiant strain,°   *qualities; heritage*
40   And fortune led you well. You have the captives
          Who were the opposites° of this day's strife.   *opponents*
          I do require them of you, so to use° them   *treat*
          As we shall find their merits and our safety
          May equally determine.

EDMOND   Sir, I thought it fit
45   To send the old and miserable King to some retention,°   *confinement*
          Whose° age had charms in it, whose title more,   *(Lear's)*
          To pluck the common bosom[1] on his side
          And turn our impressed lances° in our eyes   *conscripted lancers*
          Which[2] do command them. With him I sent the Queen,
50   My reason all the same, and they are ready
          Tomorrow or at further space° t'appear   *at a future point*
          Where you shall hold your session.°   *court of judgment*

ALBANY   Sir, by your patience,
          I hold you but a subject of° this war,   *in waging*
          Not as a brother.

REGAN   That's as we list° to grace him.   *choose*
55   Methinks our pleasure might have been demanded[3]
          Ere you had spoke so far. He led our powers,°   *armies*
          Bore the commission of my place and person,
          The which immediacy° may well stand up   *close connection*
          And call itself your brother.

GONERILL   Not so hot.°   *Not so fast*
60   In his own grace° he doth exalt himself   *merit*
          More than in your addition.[4]

REGAN   In my rights,
          By me invested, he compeers° the best.   *equals*

ALBANY   That were the most[5] if he should husband you.

REGAN   Jesters do oft prove prophets.

GONERILL   Holla, holla!
65   That eye that told you so looked but asquint.[6]

REGAN   Lady, I am not well, else I should answer
          From a full-flowing stomach.° —General,   *anger*
          Take thou my soldiers, prisoners, patrimony;
          Dispose of them, of me. The walls° is thine.   *fortress of my heart*
70   Witness the world that I create thee here
          My lord and master.

1. To garner the affection of the populace.
2. *in our eyes / Which:* in the eyes of us who.
3. I think you should have inquired into my wishes.
4. In the honors you confer upon him.
5. That investiture would be complete.
6. Squinting was a proverbial effect of jealousy, because of the tendency to look suspiciously at potential rivals.

GONORILL   Mean you to enjoy him, then?
ALBANY   The let-alone° lies not in your good will.   veto
BASTARD   Nor in thine, lord.
ALBANY   Half-blooded° fellow, yes.   Bastard
80   BASTARD   Let the drum strike,⁸ and prove my title good.
ALBANY   Stay, yet; hear reason. Edmund, I arrest thee
     On capital treason, and in thine attaint⁹
     This gilded serpent. [to REGAN] For your claim, fair sister,°   sister-in-law
     I bar it in the interest of my wife.
85   'Tis she is subcontracted to this lord,
     And I her husband contradict the banns.°   marriage announcement
     If you will marry, make your love to me:
     My lady is bespoke. —Thou art armed, Gloucester;
     If none appear to prove upon thy head
90   Thy heinous, manifest, and many treasons,
     There is my pledge. [He throws down his gauntlet.] I'll prove
          it on thy heart
     Ere I taste bread, thou art in nothing less°   in no way less guilty
     Than I have here proclaimed thee.
REGAN   Sick, oh, sick!
GONORILL [aside]   If not, I'll ne'er trust poison.
95   BASTARD [throwing down his gauntlet]   There's my exchange.
     What° in the world he is   Whoever
     That names me traitor, villain-like he lies.
     Call by thy trumpet; he that dares approach
     On him, on you—who not—I will maintain
     My truth and honor firmly.
ALBANY   A herald, ho!
100 BASTARD   A herald, ho, a herald.
ALBANY   Trust to thy single virtue,° for thy soldiers,   your unassisted power
     All levied in my name, have in my name
     Took their discharge.
REGAN   This sickness grows upon me.
ALBANY   She is not well; convey her to my tent.
                         [Exit REGAN with GENTLEMEN.]
          [Enter a HERALD.]
105 Come hither, Herald. Let the trumpet sound,
     And read out this. [He hands him a letter.]

---

8. Perhaps to announce the betrothal or a challenge.
9. And in order to accuse you; and as one who shares your corruption or crime.

GONERILL   Mean you to enjoy him?

ALBANY   The let-alone° lies not in your good will.   *veto*

EDMOND   Nor in thine, lord.

ALBANY   Half-blooded° fellow, yes.   *Bastard*

REGAN   Let the drum strike,[7] and prove my title thine.

75 ALBANY   Stay yet; hear reason. Edmond, I arrest thee
        On capital treason, and in thy arrest[8]
        This gilded serpent. [*to* REGAN] For your claim, fair sister,°   *sister-in-law*
        I bar it in the interest of my wife.
        'Tis she is subcontracted to this lord,

80   And I her husband contradict your banns.°   *marriage announcement*
        If you will marry, make your loves to me:
        My lady is bespoke.

GONERILL   An interlude!°   *A farce*

ALBANY   Thou art armed, Gloucester. Let the trumpet sound.
        If none appear to prove upon thy person

85   Thy heinous, manifest, and many treasons,
        There is my pledge. I'll make° [*He throws down his gaunt-*   *prove*
        let.] it on thy heart,
        Ere I taste bread, thou art in nothing less°   *in no way less guilty*
        Than I have here proclaimed thee.

REGAN   Sick, oh, sick!

GONERILL [*aside*]   If not, I'll ne'er trust medicine.°   *poison (euphemistic)*

90 EDMOND [*throwing down his gauntlet*]   There's my exchange.
        What° in the world he's   *Whoever*
        That names me traitor, villain-like he lies.
        Call by the trumpet. He that dares approach
        On him, on you—who not—I will maintain
        My truth and honor firmly.

ALBANY   A herald, ho!

        Enter a HERALD.

95   Trust to thy single virtue,° for thy soldiers,   *your unassisted power*
        All levied in my name, have in my name
        Took their discharge.

REGAN   My sickness grows upon me.

ALBANY   She is not well; convey her to my tent.
                    [*Exit* REGAN, *attended.*]
        Come hither, Herald; let the trumpet sound,

100   And read out this. [*He hands him a letter.*]

---

7. Perhaps to announce the betrothal or a challenge.
8. And in order to accuse you; and as one who shares your corruption or crime.

CAPTAIN   Sound trumpet!
 [*A trumpet sounds.*]
HERALD [*reads*] "If any man of quality or degree, in the host
 of the army, will maintain upon Edmund, supposed Earl of
 Gloucester, that he's a manifold traitor, let him appear at
110 the third sound of the trumpet. He is bold in his defense."
BASTARD Sound!
 [*A trumpet sounds.*]
 Again!
 [*A trumpet sounds.*]
 Enter EDGAR [*in armor*] *at the third sound, a trumpet*
 before him.
ALBANY Ask him his purposes: why he appears
 Upon this call o'th' trumpet.
115 HERALD What° are you? Your name and quality°   *Who / degree; rank*
 And why you answer this present summons?
EDGAR Oh, know my name is lost, by treason's tooth
 Bare-gnawn and canker-bit.[1] Yet ere I move't,°   *make my declaration*
 Where is the adversary I come to cope withal?°   *to encounter with*
120 ALBANY Which is that adversary?
EDGAR What's he that speaks for Edmund, Earl of
 Gloucester?
BASTARD Himself. What sayest thou to him?
EDGAR   Draw thy sword,
 That° if my speech offend a noble heart, thy arm   *So that*
 May do thee justice. [*He draws his sword.*] Here is mine.
125 Behold, it is the privilege of my tongue,
 My oath, and my profession. I protest,
 Maugre° thy strength, youth, place, and eminence,   *Despite*
 Despite thy victor-sword and fire-new° fortune,   *newly minted*
 Thy valor and thy heart,° thou art a traitor,   *courage*
130 False to thy gods, thy brother, and thy father,
 Conspirant 'gainst this high illustrious prince,
 And from th'extremest upward° of thy head,   *top*
 To the descent° and dust beneath thy feet,   *lowest part; sole*
 A most toad-spotted[2] traitor. Say thou no,
135 This sword, this arm, and my best spirits
 Are bent° to prove upon thy heart, whereto I speak, *ready*
 Thou liest.
BASTARD   In wisdom I should ask thy name,
 But since thy outside looks so fair and warlike,
 And that° thy being some say[3] of breeding breathes, *since*
140 By right of knighthood,° I disdain and spurn.   *(to ask your name)*
 Here do I toss those treasons to thy head.
 With the hell-hated° lie o'erturned thy heart,   *hated as much as hell*

1. *canker-bit:* worm-eaten.   3. Taste (from "assay"); utterance.
2. Venomous, like a toad; spotted with disgrace.

A trumpet sounds.

HERALD (*reads*) "If any man of quality or degree, within the
lists of the army, will maintain upon Edmond, supposed
Earl of Gloucester, that he is a manifold traitor, let him
appear by the third sound of the trumpet. He is bold in his
105   defense."

        First trumpet [*sounds*].

Again!

        Second trumpet [*sounds*].

Again!

        Third trumpet [*sounds*].
        Trumpet answers within.
        Enter EDGAR, *armed.*

ALBANY   Ask him his purposes: why he appears
Upon this call o'th' trumpet.

HERALD   What° are you?   *Who*
110   Your name, your quality,° and why you answer   *degree; rank*
This present summons?

EDGAR   Know my name is lost,
By treason's tooth bare-gnawn and canker-bit,°   *worm-eaten*
Yet am I noble as the adversary
I come to cope.°   *to encounter*

ALBANY   Which is that adversary?

115   EDGAR   What's he that speaks for Edmond, Earl of
    Gloucester?

EDMOND   Himself. What say'st thou to him?

EDGAR   Draw thy sword,
That° if my speech offend a noble heart,   *So that*
Thy arm may do thee justice. [*He draws his sword.*] Here is
    mine.
Behold, it is my privilege,
120   The privilege of mine honors,
My oath, and my profession. I protest,
Maugre° thy strength, place, youth, and eminence,   *Despite*
Despite thy victor-sword and fire-new° fortune,   *newly minted*
Thy valor and thy heart,° thou art a traitor,   *courage*
125   False to thy gods, thy brother, and thy father,
Conspirant 'gainst this high illustrious prince,
And from th'extremest upward° of thy head   *top*
To the descent° and dust below thy foot   *lowest part; sole*
A most toad-spotted[9] traitor. Say thou no,
130   This sword, this arm, and my best spirits are bent°   *ready*
To prove upon thy heart, whereto I speak,
Thou liest.

EDMOND   In wisdom I should ask thy name,
But since thy outside looks so fair and warlike,
And that° thy tongue some say[1] of breeding breathes,   *since*
135   What safe and nicely I might well delay
By rule of knighthood, I disdain and spurn.[2]
Back do I toss these treasons to thy head,
With the hell-hated° lie o'erwhelm thy heart,   *hated as much as hell*

---

9. Venomous, like a toad; spotted with disgrace.
1. Taste (from "assay"); utterance.
2. *And . . . spurn:* And since your speech may suggest high birth, I will not stick safely and meticulously to the rules of knighthood (which do not
require a knight to fight an unknown opponent) and
refuse to fight you.

Which, for° they yet glance by and scarcely bruise, *since*
This sword of mine shall give them instant way° *access*
145 Where they shall rest forever. —Trumpets, speak.
    [*Alarums. They fight, and* EDGAR *vanquishes*
    BASTARD.]
ALBANY[4]   Save° him, save him! *Spare*
GONORILL   This is mere practice,° Gloucester! *trickery*
By the law of arms thou art not bound to answer
An unknown opposite.° Thou art not vanquished, *opponent*
But cozened and beguiled.° *cheated and deceived*
ALBANY [*showing her a letter*]   Stop your mouth, dame,
150 Or with this paper shall I stopple° it. *plug*
Thou worse than anything, read thine own evil!
Nay, no tearing, lady; I perceive you know't.
GONORILL   Say if I do, the laws are mine, not thine.
Who shall arraign° me for't? *prosecute*
155 ALBANY   Most monstrous! Know'st thou this paper?
GONORILL   Ask me not what I know.   *Exit.*
ALBANY   Go after her, she's desperate; govern° her. *restrain*
    [*Exeunt some* SERVANTS.]
BASTARD   What you have charged me with, that have I done,
And more, much more; the time will bring it out.
160 'Tis past, and so am I. But what art thou
That hast this fortune on me?[5] If thou beest noble,
I do forgive thee.
EDGAR   Let's exchange charity.° *forgiveness*
[*He removes his helmet.*] I am no less in blood than thou
    art, Edmund;
If more, the more thou hast wronged me.
165 My name is Edgar and thy father's son.
The gods are just, and of our pleasant virtues
Make instruments to scourge us:
The dark and vicious place where thee he got[6]
Cost him his eyes.
BASTARD   Thou hast spoken truth.
170 The wheel° is come full circled; I am here.[7] *Fortune's wheel*
ALBANY [*to* EDGAR]   Methought thy very gait did prophesy
A royal nobleness. I must embrace thee.
Let sorrow split my heart if I did ever hate
Thee or thy father.
EDGAR   Worthy prince, I know't.
175 ALBANY   Where have you hid yourself?
How have you known the miseries of your father?
EDGAR   By nursing them, my lord. List° a brief tale, *Listen to*
And, when 'tis told, oh, that my heart would burst!
The bloody proclamation to escape[8]
180 That followed me so near—oh, our lives' sweetness,

---

4. Both Q and F give this speech to "*Alb.*" (for "Albany"), which may be a compositor's mistake for "*All.*"
5. Who have this good fortune at my expense.
6. The adulterous bed in which you were conceived; or, possibly, the vagina. *got:* begot.
7. Back at the lowest point.
8. In order to escape the sentence of death.

Which, for° they yet glance by and scarcely bruise, *since*
140 This sword of mine shall give them instant way° *access*
  Where they shall rest for ever. —Trumpets, speak.
   Alarums. Fights.
 ALBANY[3] Save° him, save him! *Spare*
 GONERILL   This is practice,° Gloucester! *trickery*
  By th' law of war thou wast not bound to answer
  An unknown opposite.° Thou art not vanquished, *opponent*
  But cozened and beguiled.° *cheated and deceived*
145 ALBANY [*showing her a letter*] Shut your mouth, dame,
  Or with this paper shall I stop° it. Hold,° sir, *plug / Behold*
  Thou worse than any name, read thine own evil.
  No tearing, lady; I perceive you know it.
 GONERILL Say if I do, the laws are mine, not thine.
150 Who can arraign° me for't?   *Exit.* *prosecute*
 ALBANY [*to* EDMOND] Most monstrous! Oh, know'st thou this
  paper?
 EDMOND Ask me not what I know.
 ALBANY Go after her. She's desperate; govern° her. *restrain*
      [*Exeunt some Soldiers.*]
 EDMOND What you have charged me with, that have I done,
155 And more, much more; the time will bring it out.
  'Tis past, and so am I. But what art thou
  That hast this fortune on me?[4] If thou'rt noble,
  I do forgive thee.
 EDGAR   Let's exchange charity.° *forgiveness*
  [*He removes his helmet.*] I am no less in blood than thou
   art, Edmond;
160 If more, the more th' hast wronged me.
  My name is Edgar and thy father's son.
  The gods are just, and of our pleasant vices
  Make instruments to plague us:
  The dark and vicious place where thee he got[5]
  Cost him his eyes.
165 EDMOND   Th' hast spoken right, 'tis true:
  The wheel° is come full circle. I am here.[6] *Fortune's wheel*
 ALBANY [*to* EDGAR] Methought thy very gait did prophesy
  A royal nobleness. I must embrace thee.
  Let sorrow split my heart if ever I
  Did hate thee or thy father.
170 EDGAR   Worthy prince, I know't.
 ALBANY Where have you hid yourself?
  How have you known the miseries of your father?
 EDGAR By nursing them, my lord. List° a brief tale, *Listen to*
  And when 'tis told, oh, that my heart would burst!
175 The bloody proclamation to escape,[7]
  That followed me so near—oh, our lives' sweetness,

---

3. Both Q and F give this speech to "*Alb.*" (for "Albany"), which may be a compositor's mistake for "*All.*"
4. Who have this good fortune at my expense.
5. The adulterous bed in which you were conceived; or, possibly, the vagina. *got:* begot.
6. Back at the lowest point.
7. In order to escape the sentence of death.

That with the pain of death would hourly die,
Rather than die at once⁹—taught me to shift
Into a madman's rags, to assume a semblance
That very° dogs disdained, and in this habit   even
185 Met I my father with his bleeding rings° —   sockets
The precious stones° new lost—became his guide,   eyes
Led him, begged for him, saved him from despair.
Never—O father—revealed myself unto him
Until some half hour past, when I was armed.
190 Not sure, though hoping of this good success,°   conclusion
I asked his blessing and from first to last
Told him my pilgrimage. But his flawed° heart,   cracked
Alack, too weak the conflict to support,
Twixt two extremes of passion, joy and grief,
Burst smilingly.
195 BASTARD   This speech of yours hath moved me
And shall perchance do good. But speak you on;
You look as you had something more to say.
ALBANY   If there be more, more woeful, hold it in,
For I am almost ready to dissolve,°   melt into tears
200 Hearing of this.
EDGAR   This would have seemed a period° to such   conclusion
As love not sorrow, but another to amplify° too much   enlarge; extend
Would make much more and top extremity.
Whilst I was big in clamor,° came there in a man,   lamenting loudly
205 Who having seen me in my worst estate
Shunned my abhorred society, but then finding
Who 'twas that so endured, with his strong arms
He fastened on my neck and bellowed out
As he'd burst heaven, threw me on my father,
210 Told the most piteous tale of Lear and him°   himself
That ever ear received, which, in recounting,
His grief grew puissant,° and the strings of life   powerful
Began to crack twice. Then the trumpets sounded.
And there I left him tranced.
ALBANY   But who was this?
215 EDGAR   Kent, sir, the banished Kent, who in disguise
Followed his enemy king¹ and did him service
Improper° for a slave.   Unfit even
              Enter one [a GENTLEMAN] *with a bloody knife.*
GENTLEMAN   Help, help!
ALBANY   What kind of help? What means that bloody knife?
GENTLEMAN   It's hot! It smokes! It came even from the heart of—
220 ALBANY   Who, man? Speak!
GENTLEMAN   —Your lady, sir, your lady—and her sister
By her is poisoned; she hath confessed it.

---

9. *our . . . once:* how sweet must life be that we prefer the constant pain of dying to death itself.

1. Because Lear had previously banished him. *enemy:*
hostile.

That we the pain of death would hourly die
Rather than die at once[8]—taught me to shift
Into a madman's rags, t'assume a semblance
180 That very° dogs disdained, and in this habit   *even*
Met I my father with his bleeding rings°—   *sockets*
Their precious stones° new lost—became his guide,   *eyes*
Led him, begged for him, saved him from despair.
Never—oh, fault—revealed myself unto him
185 Until some half hour past, when I was armed.
Not sure, though hoping of this good success,°   *conclusion*
I asked his blessing and from first to last
Told him our pilgrimage. But his flawed° heart,   *cracked*
Alack, too weak the conflict to support,
190 Twixt two extremes of passion, joy and grief,
Burst smilingly.

EDMOND   This speech of yours hath moved me
And shall perchance do good. But speak you on;
You look as you had something more to say.

ALBANY   If there be more, more woeful, hold it in,
195 For I am almost ready to dissolve,°   *melt into tears*
Hearing of this.

Enter a GENTLEMAN [*with a bloody knife*].

GENTLEMAN   Help, help! Oh, help!

EDGAR   What kind of help?

ALBANY   Speak, man.

EDGAR   What means this bloody knife?

GENTLEMAN   'Tis hot! It smokes! It came even from the
heart of—
Oh, she's dead.

200 ALBANY   Who dead? Speak, man.

GENTLEMAN   Your lady, sir, your lady—and her sister
By her is poisoned; she confesses it.

---

8. *our . . . once:* how sweet must life be that we prefer the constant pain of dying to death itself.

BASTARD   I was contracted to them both; all three
   Now marry° in an instant.   *unite (in death)*

225 ALBANY   Produce their bodies, be they alive or dead.
   This justice of the heavens that makes us tremble
   Touches us not with pity.
          Enter KENT.
EDGAR   Here comes Kent, sir.
ALBANY   Oh, 'tis he. The time will not allow
   The compliment that very manners urges.[2]

230 KENT   I am come to bid my king and master
   Aye° good night. Is he not here?   *Forever*
ALBANY   Great thing of° us forgot!   *by*
   Speak, Edmund, where's the King? And where's Cordelia?
       The bodies of GONORILL *and* REGAN *are brought in.*
   See'st thou this object,° Kent?   *spectacle*
KENT   Alack, why thus?
235 BASTARD   Yet° Edmund was beloved: *Despite all*
   The one the other poisoned for my sake
   And after slew herself.
ALBANY   Even so; cover their faces.
BASTARD   I pant for life. Some good I mean to do
240   Despite of my own nature. Quickly send—
   Be brief° —into th' castle, for my writ[3]   *speedy*
   Is on the life of Lear and on Cordelia.
   Nay, send in time!
ALBANY   Run, run, oh, run!
EDGAR   To who, my lord? —Who hath the office?° Send   *commission*
245   Thy token of reprieve.
BASTARD   Well thought on! Take my sword. The Captain,
   Give it the° Captain!   *to the*
ALBANY [*to* EDGAR]   Haste thee for thy life.   [*Exit* EDGAR.]
BASTARD   He hath commission from thy wife and me
   To hang Cordelia in the prison and to lay
250   The blame upon her own despair,
   That she fordid herself.[4]
ALBANY   The gods defend her! Bear him hence awhile.
               [*Edmund the* BASTARD *is carried out by*
                       CAPTAIN *and some* SERVANTS.]
     Enter LEAR *with* CORDELIA *in his arms*[, EDGAR, *and*
     CAPTAIN OF THE GUARD].
LEAR   Howl, howl, howl, howl! Oh, you are men of stones!
   Had I your tongues and eyes, I would use them so
255   That heaven's vault should crack! She's gone forever.
   I know when one is dead and when one lives;
   She's dead as earth. Lend me a looking glass.

2. *The compliment . . . urges:* the ceremony that barest custom demands.
3. Order of execution.

4. Destroyed herself. In most of Shakespeare's source texts for the play, Cordelia does in fact kill herself after reigning for some years.

EDMOND   I was contracted to them both; all three
   Now marry° in an instant.   *unite (in death)*
      Enter KENT.
EDGAR   Here comes Kent.
205 ALBANY   Produce the bodies, be they alive or dead.
      Gonerill and Regan's bodies brought out.
   This judgment of the heavens that makes us tremble
   Touches us not with pity. Oh, is this he?
   The time will not allow the compliment
   Which very manners urges.⁹
KENT   I am come
210 To bid my king and master aye° good night.   *forever*
   Is he not here?
ALBANY   Great thing of° us forgot!   *by*
   Speak, Edmond, where's the King? And where's Cordelia?
   Seest thou this object,° Kent?   *spectacle*
KENT   Alack, why thus?
EDMOND   Yet° Edmond was beloved: *Despite all*
215 The one the other poisoned for my sake
   And after slew herself.
ALBANY   Even so. Cover their faces.
EDMOND   I pant for life. Some good I mean to do
   Despite of mine own nature. Quickly send—
220 Be brief° in it—to th' castle, for my writ¹   *speedy*
   Is on the life of Lear and on Cordelia.
   Nay, send in time.
ALBANY   Run, run, oh, run!
EDGAR   To who, my lord? —Who has the office?°   *commission*
   Send thy token of reprieve.
EDMOND   Well thought on. Take my sword,
   Give it the° Captain.   *to the*
225 EDGAR   Haste thee for thy life!
                    [*Exit* GENTLEMAN.]
EDMOND   He hath commission from thy wife and me
   To hang Cordelia in the prison and
   To lay the blame upon her own despair,
   That she fordid herself.²
230 ALBANY   The gods defend her! Bear him hence awhile.
             [EDMOND *is carried out by Soldiers.*]
      Enter LEAR, *with* CORDELIA *in his arms[, and*
      GENTLEMAN].
LEAR   Howl, howl, howl! Oh, you are men of stones!
   Had I your tongues and eyes, I'd use them so
   That heaven's vault should crack. She's gone forever.
   I know when one is dead and when one lives;
235 She's dead as earth. Lend me a looking glass,

---

9. *the compliment . . . urges:* the ceremony that barest custom demands.
1. Order of execution.

2. Destroyed herself. In most of Shakespeare's
source texts for the play, Cordelia does in fact kill
herself after reigning for some years.

If that her breath will mist or stain the stone,[5]
Why, then, she lives.
KENT   Is this the promised end?[6]
EDGAR   Or image of that horror?
260   ALBANY   Fall and cease.[7]
LEAR   This feather stirs. She lives![8] If it be so,
It is a chance which does redeem all sorrows
That ever I have felt.
KENT   Ay, my good master.
LEAR   Prithee, away.
EDGAR   'Tis noble Kent, your friend.
265   LEAR   A plague upon your murderous traitors all!
I might have saved her; now she's gone forever.
Cordelia, Cordelia, stay a little. Ha,
What is't thou sayest? Her voice was ever soft,
Gentle, and low, an excellent thing in women.
270   —I killed the slave that was a-hanging thee.
CAPTAIN OF THE GUARD   'Tis true, my lords, he did.
LEAR   Did I not, fellow? I have seen the day,
With my good biting falchion° I would   light sword
Have made them skip. I am old now,
275   And these same crosses spoil me.[9] Who are you?
Mine eyes are not o'the best, I'll tell you straight.°   recognize you soon
KENT   If Fortune bragged of two she loved or hated,
One of them we behold.[1]
LEAR   Are not you Kent?
KENT   The same: your servant Kent. Where is your servant
Caius?°   (Kent's pseudonym)
280   LEAR   He's a good fellow, I can tell that;
He'll strike, and quickly, too. He's dead and rotten.
KENT   No, my good lord, I am the very man—
LEAR   I'll see that straight.[2]
KENT   —That from your life of difference and decay[3]
Have followed your sad steps.
285   LEAR   You're welcome hither.
KENT   Nor no man else.[4] All's cheerless, dark and deadly.°   deathly
Your eldest daughters have fordone° themselves   destroyed
And desperately° are dead.   in despair
LEAR   So think I, too.

5. Mica, or stone polished to a mirror finish.
6. Doomsday; expected end of the play. In no version of the story previous to Shakespeare's does Cordelia die at this point.
7. Let the world collapse and end.
8. PERFORMANCE COMMENT Each production must determine whether to sustain suspense regarding the possibility that Cordelia is still alive or to make it clear that her father is raving over a corpse. See Digital Edition PC 6.
9. And these recent adversities have weakened me; and these parries I could once match would now

destroy me.
1. *If . . . behold:* If there were only two supreme examples in the world of Fortune's ability to raise up and cast down, Lear would be one; alternatively, we are each of us one (Lear and Kent are here looking at each other).
2. I'll attend to that shortly; I'll comprehend that in a moment.
3. Who from the beginning of your alteration and deterioration.
4. No, neither I nor anyone else is welcome. Alternatively, I am that man, not disguised as anyone else.

If that her breath will mist or stain the stone,[3]
Why, then, she lives.

KENT   Is this the promised end?[4]

EDGAR   Or image of that horror.

ALBANY   Fall and cease.[5]

LEAR   This feather stirs. She lives![6] If it be so,
240   It is a chance which does redeem all sorrows
That ever I have felt.

KENT   O my good master.

LEAR   Prithee, away.

EDGAR   'Tis noble Kent, your friend.

LEAR   A plague upon you murderers, traitors all!
I might have saved her; now she's gone forever.
245   Cordelia, Cordelia, stay a little. Ha,
What is't thou say'st? Her voice was ever soft,
Gentle, and low, an excellent thing in woman.
—I killed the slave that was a-hanging thee.

GENTLEMAN   'Tis true, my lords, he did.

LEAR   Did I not, fellow?
250   I have seen the day, with my good biting falchion°   light sword
I would have made him skip. I am old now,
And these same crosses spoil me.[7] Who are you?
Mine eyes are not o'th' best, I'll tell you straight.°   recognize you soon

KENT   If Fortune brag of two she loved and hated,
255   One of them we behold.[8]

LEAR   This is a dull sight;[9] are you not Kent?

KENT   The same: your servant Kent.
Where is your servant Caius?°   (Kent's pseudonym)

LEAR   He's a good fellow, I can tell you that;
260   He'll strike, and quickly, too. He's dead and rotten.

KENT   No, my good lord, I am the very man—

LEAR   I'll see that straight.[1]

KENT   —That from your first of difference and decay[2]
Have followed your sad steps.

LEAR   You are welcome hither.

265 KENT   Nor no man else.[3]
All's cheerless, dark, and deadly.°   deathly
Your eldest daughters have fordone° themselves   destroyed
And desperately° are dead.   in despair

LEAR   Ay, so I think.

3. Mica, or stone polished to a mirror finish.
4. Doomsday; expected end of the play. In no version of the story previous to Shakespeare's does Cordelia die at this point.
5. Let the world collapse and end.
6. PERFORMANCE COMMENT Each production must determine whether to sustain suspense regarding the possibility that Cordelia is still alive or to make it clear that her father is raving over a corpse. See Digital Edition PC 6.
7. And these recent adversities have weakened me; and these parries I could once match would now destroy me.

8. *If . . . behold:* If there were only two supreme examples in the world of Fortune's ability to raise up and cast down, Lear would be one; alternatively, we are each of us one (Lear and Kent are here looking at each other).
9. This is a sad sight; my vision is failing.
1. I'll attend to that shortly; I'll comprehend that in a moment.
2. Who from the beginning of your alteration and deterioration.
3. No, neither I nor anyone else is welcome. Alternatively, I am that man, not disguised as anyone else.

ALBANY   He knows not what he sees, and vain° it is   *in vain*
　　That we present us to him.
290　EDGAR   Very bootless.°   *futile*
　　　　Enter CAPTAIN.
CAPTAIN   Edmund is dead, my lord.
ALBANY   That's but a trifle here.
　　You lords and noble friends, know our intent:
　　What comfort to this decay° may come   *ruin; destruction*
　　Shall be applied. For us, we will resign
295　During the life of this old majesty
　　To him our absolute power; [*to* EDGAR] you to your rights,
　　With boot° and such addition° as your honor   *reward / distinction*
　　Have more than merited. All friends shall taste
　　The wages of their virtue and all foes
300　The cup of their deservings. Oh, see, see!
LEAR   And my poor fool[5] is hanged. No, no life.
　　Why should a dog, a horse, a rat have life
　　And thou no breath at all? Oh, thou wilt come no more.
　　Never, never, never! —Pray you, undo
305　This button. Thank you, sir. Oh, oh, oh, oh![6]
　　　　[*He faints.*]
EDGAR   He faints. My lord, my lord?
LEAR   Break, heart, I prithee, break!
　　　　[*He dies.*]
EDGAR   Look up, my lord!
KENT   Vex not his ghost.[7] Oh, let him pass!
　　He hates him that would upon the rack[8]
310　Of this tough world stretch him out longer.
EDGAR   Oh, he is gone indeed.
KENT   The wonder is he hath endured so long.
　　He but usurped his life.[9]
ALBANY   Bear them from hence. Our present business
315　Is to general woe. [*to* KENT *and* EDGAR] Friends of my soul,
　　　　you twain
　　Rule in this kingdom and the gored° state sustain.   *wounded; bloody*
KENT   I have a journey, sir, shortly to go.
　　My master calls, and I must not say no.
ALBANY[1]   The weight of this sad time we must obey;
320　Speak what we feel, not what we ought to say.
　　The oldest have borne most; we that are young
　　Shall never see so much, nor live so long.   [*Exeunt.*]

---

5. A term of endearment, here used for Cordelia, though it also recalls the disappearance of Lear's Fool after 3.6.
6. TEXTUAL COMMENT All the source plays for the King Lear story show Lear and Cordelia prevailing, with Cordelia surviving and accepting the role of Lear's successor as monarch. In the Folio text, unlike in the Quarto text, Lear apparently thinks that his attempts to revive her are successful. See Digital Edition TC 8 (Quarto edited text).
7. Do not disturb his departing soul.
8. Instrument of torture, used to stretch its victims.

9. From death, which already had a claim on it.
1. TEXTUAL COMMENT One of the apparently minor but nevertheless significant differences between the two early texts of *King Lear* is that in the Quarto 1 text the last lines of the play are given to Albany, whereas in the Folio they are given to Edgar. These powerful lines suggest that their speaker will inherit political leadership, and editors who conflate the two texts face the challenge of selecting which character should stand as the moral and political spokesperson at the end of the play. See Digital Edition TC 9 (Quarto edited text).

ALBANY He knows not what he says, and vain° is it   *in vain*
    That we present us to him.
        Enter a MESSENGER.
270 EDGAR   Very bootless.°   *futile*
MESSENGER   Edmond is dead, my lord.
ALBANY   That's but a trifle here.
    You lords and noble friends, know our intent:
    What comfort to this great decay° may come   *ruin; destruction*
    Shall be applied. For us, we will resign
275   During the life of this old majesty
    To him our absolute power; [*to* EDGAR] you to your rights,
    With boot° and such addition° as your honors   *reward / distinction*
    Have more than merited. All friends shall
    Taste the wages of their virtue and all foes
280   The cup of their deservings. Oh, see, see!
LEAR   And my poor fool[4] is hanged. No, no, no life?
    Why should a dog, a horse, a rat have life,
    And thou no breath at all? Thou'lt come no more,
    Never, never, never, never, never!
285   Pray you, undo this button. Thank you, sir.
    Do you see this? Look on her! Look, her lips,
    Look there. Look there![5]
        He dies.
EDGAR   He faints. My lord, my lord.
KENT   Break, heart, I prithee, break.
EDGAR   Look up, my lord.
KENT   Vex not his ghost.[6] Oh, let him pass! He hates him
290   That would upon the rack[7] of this tough world
    Stretch him out longer.
EDGAR   He is gone indeed.
KENT   The wonder is he hath endured so long.
    He but usurped his life.[8]
ALBANY   Bear them from hence. Our present business
295   Is general woe. [*to* KENT *and* EDGAR] Friends of my soul,
      you twain
    Rule in this realm and the gored° state sustain.   *wounded; bloody*
KENT   I have a journey, sir, shortly to go.
    My master calls me. I must not say no.
EDGAR[9]   The weight of this sad time we must obey;
300   Speak what we feel, not what we ought to say.
    The oldest hath borne most; we that are young
    Shall never see so much, nor live so long.
            Exeunt with a dead march.

---

4. A term of endearment, here used for Cordelia, though it also recalls the disappearance of Lear's Fool after 3.6.

5. TEXTUAL COMMENT All the source plays for the King Lear story show Lear and Cordelia prevailing, with Cordelia surviving and accepting the role of Lear's successor as monarch. In F, unlike in Q, Lear apparently thinks that his attempts to revive her are successful. See Digital Edition TC 7 (Folio edited text).

6. Do not disturb his departing soul.

7. Instrument of torture, used to stretch its victims.

8. From death, which already had a claim on it.

9. TEXTUAL COMMENT One of the apparently minor but nevertheless significant differences between the two early texts of *King Lear* is that in Q1 the last lines of the play are given to Albany, whereas in F they are given to Edgar. These powerful lines suggest that their speaker will inherit political leadership, and editors who conflate the two texts face the challenge of selecting which character should stand as the moral and political spokesperson at the end of the play. See Digital Edition TC 8 (Folio edited text).

King Lear[1]

COMBINED TEXT*

[THE PERSONS OF THE PLAY

LEAR, King of Britain
GONERIL, eldest daughter to Lear
Duke of ALBANY, husband to Goneril
REGAN, second daughter to Lear
Duke of CORNWALL, husband to Regan
CORDELIA, youngest daughter to Lear
King of FRANCE, suitor to Cordelia
Duke of BURGUNDY, suitor to Cordelia
FOOL, Lear's jester
Earl of GLOUCESTER
EDGAR, legitimate son to Gloucester, later disguised as Poor Tom
EDMUND, illegitimate son to Gloucester
Earl of KENT, later disguised as Caius
OSWALD, steward to Goneril
OLD MAN, a tenant of Gloucester
CURAN, a servant of Gloucester
SERVANTS to Cornwall
CAPTAIN
HERALD
MESSENGER
GENTLEMEN
KNIGHTS
SERVANTS
Attendants, Soldiers]

1.1[2]

Enter KENT, GLOUCESTER,[3] *and* EDMUND.

KENT I thought the King had more affected° the Duke of   *favored*
    Albany° than Cornwall.   *Scotland*

GLOUCESTER It did always seem so to us. But now, in the divi-
    sion of the kingdom, it appears not° which of the Dukes he   *is not clear*
5   values most, for qualities° are so weighed° that curiosity in   *shares / equal*
    neither can make choice of either's moiety.[4]

KENT Is not this your son, my lord?

GLOUCESTER His breeding,° sir, hath been at my charge.[5] I   *upbringing*

---

1. TEXTUAL COMMENT The first readers of the Quarto and Folio versions of *King Lear* would have confronted not only very different material books but also two different plays, as suggested by the titles of the earliest printed copies of the play. *King Lear* is either a "history" or a "tragedy," depending on which book one is reading. See Digital Edition TC 1 (combined text).
*Text based on the Folio, with interpolated lines, passages, and scenes from Q1.
2. TEXTUAL COMMENT One major difference between the Quarto and Folio texts is that the latter provides act and scene divisions while the former marks no

such breaks. These notations suggest that Q1 of *King Lear* was printed from Shakespeare's "foul papers" (or first draft) and that F was printed from a later "fair copy" (or theatrical manuscript) written out by a scribe and checked against Q2. See Digital Edition TC 2 (combined text).
1.1 Location: King Lear's court.
3. Pronounced "Gloster."
4. for . . . *moiety*: their qualities are so evenly weighted that careful scrutiny ("curiosity") of both parts cannot determine which portion ("moiety") is preferable.
5. My responsibility; at my cost.

have so often blushed to acknowledge him that now I am
10 brazed° to't.

KENT   I cannot conceive° you.

GLOUCESTER   Sir, this young fellow's mother could,[6] whereupon she grew round-wombed, and had, indeed, sir, a son for
her cradle ere she had a husband for her bed. Do you smell a
15 fault?[7]

KENT   I cannot wish the fault undone, the issue° of it being so   *offspring; result*
proper.°   *handsome; right*

GLOUCESTER   But I have a son, sir, by order of law,° some year   *a legitimate son*
elder than this, who yet is no dearer in my account.° Though   *estimation*
20 this knave° came something saucily[8] to the world before he   *scamp; fellow*
was sent for, yet was his mother fair, there was good sport at
his making, and the whoreson° must be acknowledged. —Do   *rogue; bastard*
you know this noble gentleman, Edmund?

EDMUND   No, my lord.

25 GLOUCESTER   My lord of Kent. Remember him hereafter as
my honorable friend.

EDMUND   My services to your lordship.

KENT   I must love you and sue° to know you better.   *seek*

EDMUND   Sir, I shall study deserving.°   *shall learn to deserve*

30 GLOUCESTER   He hath been out° nine years, and away he shall   *away; abroad*
again. The King is coming.

        Sennet.° Enter [one bearing a coronet,] King LEAR,   *Fanfare of trumpets*
        CORNWALL, ALBANY, GONERIL, REGAN, CORDELIA,
        and Attendants.

LEAR   Attend the lords of France and Burgundy, Gloucester.

GLOUCESTER   I shall, my lord.°   *Exit.*   *feudal superior*

LEAR   Meantime we° shall express our darker° purpose.   *(royal "we") / more secret*

35 Give me the map there. Know that we have divided
In three our kingdom, and 'tis our fast° intent   *fixed*
To shake all cares and business from our age,
Conferring them on younger strengths, while we
Unburdened crawl toward death. Our son° of Cornwall   *son-in-law*
40 And you, our no-less-loving son of Albany,
We have this hour a constant will to publish[9]
Our daughters' several dowers,° that future strife   *individual dowries*
May be prevented now. The princes, France and Burgundy,
Great rivals in our youngest daughter's love,
45 Long in our court have made their amorous sojourn
And here are to be answered. Tell me, my daughters,
Since now we will divest us both of rule,
Interest° of territory, cares of state,   *Legal title*
Which of you shall we say doth love us most,
50 That° we our largest bounty° may extend   *So that / generosity*
Where nature doth with merit challenge?[1] Goneril,
Our eldest born, speak first.

GONERIL   Sir, I love you more than word can wield° the   *convey*
matter;
Dearer than eyesight, space,° and liberty,   *freedom of movement*
55 Beyond what can be valued rich or rare,
No less than life, with grace, health, beauty, honor,

---

6. Could conceive; punning on biological conception.   9. A fixed determination to announce publicly.
7. Sin, wrongdoing; female genitals.   1. *Where . . . challenge:* To the one whose natural
8. Somewhat rudely; somewhat shamefully.   love and deserving lay claim (to our generosity).

As much as child e'er loved or father found,
A love that makes breath° poor and speech unable.   *language*
Beyond all manner of so much° I love you.   *Beyond all comparison*
60 CORDELIA [*aside*]   What shall Cordelia speak? Love, and be
    silent.
    LEAR [*pointing to map*]   Of all these bounds,° even from this   *regions*
    line to this,
    With shadowy forests and with champaigns riched°   *enriched plains*
    With plenteous rivers and wide-skirted meads,°   *broad meadows*
    We make thee lady. To thine and Albany's issues°   *children; heirs*
65 Be this perpetual. [*to* REGAN] What says our second daughter,
    Our dearest Regan, wife of Cornwall?
    REGAN   I am made of that self-mettle° as my sister   *same spirit; substance*
    And prize me at her worth.° In my true heart   *believe myself her equal*
    I find she names my very deed of love,
70 Only she comes too short, that° I profess   *in that*
    Myself an enemy to all other joys
    Which the most precious square of sense professes,[2]
    And find I am alone felicitate°   *am only made happy*
    In your dear highness' love.
    CORDELIA [*aside*]   Then, poor Cordelia,
75 And yet not so, since I am sure my love's
    More ponderous° than my tongue.   *weighty*
    LEAR [*pointing to map*]   To thee and thine hereditary ever,
    Remain this ample third of our fair kingdom,
    No less in space, validity,° and pleasure   *value*
80 Than that conferred on Goneril. [*to* CORDELIA] Now, our joy,
    Although our last and least,° to whose young love   *youngest; smallest*
    The vines of France and milk of Burgundy
    Strive to be interest,° what can you say to draw   *admitted*
    A third more opulent than your sisters'? Speak.
85 CORDELIA   Nothing, my lord.
    LEAR   Nothing?
    CORDELIA   Nothing.
    LEAR   Nothing will come of nothing.[3] Speak again.
    CORDELIA   Unhappy that I am, I cannot heave
90 My heart into my mouth.[4] I love your majesty
    According to my bond,° no more nor less.   *filial duty*
    LEAR   How, how, Cordelia? Mend your speech a little,
    Lest you may mar your fortunes.
    CORDELIA   Good my lord,
    You have begot me, bred me, loved me.
95 I return those duties back as are right fit:
    Obey you, love you, and most honor you.
    Why have my sisters husbands if they say
    They love you all?° Happily,° when I shall wed,   *completely / Perhaps; if lucky*
    That lord whose hand must take my plight° shall carry *marriage vow; condition*
100 Half my love with him, half my care and duty.
    Sure, I shall never marry like my sisters,
101.1   *To love my father all.*

2. *Which . . . professes:* That the body can enjoy. *pre-cious square of sense:* measure of sensibility; or, perhaps, balanced and sensitive perception. The square may represent the even mixture of the body's four fluids, or humors.
3. *Ex nihilo nihil fit,* a maxim derived from Aristotle, was accepted by the Christian Middle Ages with the single exception of God having created the world out of nothing.
4. *I cannot heave . . . mouth:* Cf. "The heart of fools is in their mouth: but the mouth of the wise is in their heart" (Ecclesiastes 1:26).

LEAR   But goes thy heart with this?

CORDELIA   Ay, my good lord.

LEAR   So young and so untender?

CORDELIA   So young, my lord, and true.°   honest; faithful

105 LEAR   Let it be so: thy truth, then, be thy dower!⁵
     For by the sacred radiance of the sun,
     The mysteries of Hecate⁶ and the night;
     By all the operation of the orbs,
     From whom we do exist and cease to be;⁷

110 Here I disclaim all my paternal care,
     Propinquity° and property of blood,°   Closeness / kinship
     And as a stranger to my heart and me,
     Hold thee from this° forever. The barbarous Scythian,⁸   this time
     Or he that makes his generation messes⁹

115 To gorge his appetite, shall to my bosom
     Be as well neighbored, pitied, and relieved
     As thou my sometime° daughter.   former

KENT   Good my liege—

●LEAR   Peace, Kent!
     Come not between the dragon and his wrath!

120 I loved her most and thought to set my rest¹
     On her kind nursery.° Hence and avoid my sight.   care
     So be my grave my peace,² as here I give
     Her father's heart from her. Call France! Who stirs?³
     Call Burgundy!   [Exeunt some Attendants.]

                    Cornwall and Albany,

125 With my two daughters' dowers digest° the third.   incorporate
     Let pride, which she calls plainness,° marry her.   directness
     I do invest you jointly with my power,
     Preeminence, and all the large effects°   outward shows; trappings
     That troop with° majesty. Ourself by monthly course,   accompany

130 With reservation of° an hundred knights,   legal right to retain
     By you to be sustained, shall our abode
     Make with you by due turn. Only we shall retain
     The name and all th'addition° to a king. The sway,°   the prerogatives / power
     Revenue, execution of the rest,

135 Beloved sons, be yours, which to confirm,
     This coronet⁴ part between you. [He hands them the
     coronet.]

KENT   Royal Lear,
     Whom I have ever honored as my king,
     Loved as my father, as my master followed,
     As my great patron thought on in my prayers—

140 LEAR   The bow is bent and drawn; make from° the shaft.   get clear of

KENT   Let it fall° rather, though the fork° invade   strike home / arrowhead
     The region of my heart. Be Kent unmannerly

5. PERFORMANCE COMMENT The opening sequence of *King Lear*, from the king's entrance to his banishment of Cordelia, involves crucial interpretive choices for directors and performers, choices that center on the motivations of the central characters. See Digital Edition PC 1.
6. A classical goddess of the moon and the patron of witchcraft, she was associated with the underworld, Hades.
7. *By all . . . be*: Referring to the belief that the movements of stars and planets ("orbs") corresponded to physical and spiritual motions in a person and thus controlled his or her fate.
8. Notoriously savage nomads of classical antiquity.
9. *he . . . messes*: he who makes meals of his parents or his children.
1. To secure my repose; to stake my all, as in the card game known as primero.
2. So may I rest in peace (probably an oath).
3. Does nobody stir? An order, with the force of "Get moving."
4. Cordelia's crown, symbol of the endowment she has forsworn.

When Lear is mad. What wouldst thou do, old man?
Think'st thou that duty shall have dread to speak
145 When power to flattery bows?
To plainness° honor's bound   *plain speaking*
When majesty falls to folly. Reserve° thy state,°   *Retain / rule; position*
And in thy best consideration check°   *halt*
This hideous rashness. Answer my life my judgment:[5]
150 Thy youngest daughter does not love thee least,
Nor are those empty-hearted whose low sounds
Reverb no hollowness.°   *Echo no insincerity*
LEAR   Kent, on thy life, no more!
KENT   My life I never held but as pawn°   *chess piece; stake*
To wage° against thine enemies; ne'er fear to lose it,   *wager*
Thy safety being motive.°   *(my) motivation*
155 LEAR   Out of my sight!
KENT   See better, Lear, and let me still° remain   *always*
The true blank° of thine eye.   *precise bull's-eye*
LEAR   Now, by Apollo—
KENT   Now, by Apollo, King,
Thou swear'st thy gods in vain.[6]
LEAR   O vassal! Miscreant!°   *Villain; unbeliever*
160 ALBANY *and* CORNWALL   Dear sir, forbear.
KENT   Kill thy physician and thy fee bestow
Upon the foul disease.[7] Revoke thy gift,
Or whilst I can vent clamor from my throat
I'll tell thee thou dost evil.
165 LEAR   Hear me, recreant!° On thine allegiance, hear me!   *traitor*
That thou hast sought to make us break our vows,
Which we durst never yet; and with strained° pride   *overblown*
To come betwixt our sentences and our power,
Which nor our nature nor our place[8] can bear.
170 Our potency made good,° take thy reward.   *demonstrated*
Five days we do allot thee for provision,
To shield thee from disasters of the world,
And on the sixth to turn thy hated back
Upon our kingdom. If, on the tenth day following,
175 Thy banished trunk° be found in our dominions,   *body*
The moment is thy death. Away! By Jupiter,
This shall not be revoked.
KENT   Fare thee well, King. Sith° thus thou wilt appear,   *Since*
Freedom lives hence, and banishment is here.
180 [*to* CORDELIA] The gods to their dear shelter take thee, maid,
That justly think'st and hast most rightly said.
[*to* GONERIL *and* REGAN] And your large speeches may your
  deeds approve,[9]
That good effects may spring from words of love.
Thus Kent, O princes, bids you all adieu.
185 He'll shape his old course in a country new.   *Exit.*
        Flourish.° Enter GLOUCESTER *with* FRANCE *and*   *Fanfare of trumpets*
        BURGUNDY [*and*] *Attendants.*

---

5. *Answer . . . judgment:* I'll stake my life on my opinion.
6. You invoke your gods falsely and without effect.
7. *Kill . . . disease:* You would not only kill the doctor

but also hand his fee over to the disease.
8. Which neither my temperament nor my royal position.
9. And let your actions live up to your fine words.

CORNWALL   Here's France and Burgundy, my noble lord.
LEAR   My lord of Burgundy,
We first address toward you, who with this king
Hath rivaled for our daughter. What in the least
190   Will you require in present dower with her
Or cease your quest of love?
BURGUNDY   Most royal majesty,
I crave no more than hath your highness offered,
Nor will you tender° less.   offer
LEAR   Right noble Burgundy,
When she was dear to us we did hold her so,
195   But now her price is fallen. Sir, there she stands.
If aught within that little-seeming substance,[1]
Or all of it with our displeasure pieced°   joined
And nothing more, may fitly like° your grace,   please
She's there, and she is yours.
BURGUNDY   I know no answer.
200   LEAR   Will you with those infirmities she owes,°   owns
Unfriended, new-adopted to our hate,
Dow'red with our curse and strangered° with our oath,   estranged
Take her or leave her?
BURGUNDY   Pardon me, royal sir,
Election makes not up in such conditions.[2]
205   LEAR   Then leave her, sir, for, by the power that made me,
I tell you° all her wealth. [to FRANCE] For° you, great King,   inform you of / As for
I would not from your love make such a stray°   stray so far
To° match you where I hate. Therefore, beseech you   As to
T'avert your liking° a more worthier way   To turn your affections
210   Than on a wretch whom Nature is ashamed
Almost t'acknowledge hers.
FRANCE   This is most strange,
That she, whom even but now was your object,
The argument° of your praise, balm of your age,   theme
The best, the dearest, should in this trice° of time   moment
215   Commit a thing so monstrous to dismantle°   as to strip off; disrobe
So many folds of favor. Sure, her offense
Must be of such unnatural degree
That monsters it,° or your fore-vouched affection   makes it monstrous
Fall into taint,[3] which to believe of her
220   Must be a faith that reason without miracle
Should never plant in me.
CORDELIA   I yet beseech your majesty—
If for I want° that glib and oily art   because I lack
To speak and purpose not,° since what I will intend,   and not intend
I'll do't before I speak—that you make known
225   It is no vicious blot, murder, or foulness,
No unchaste action or dishonored step
That hath deprived me of your grace and favor,
But even for want of that for which I am richer:

---

1. *little-seeming substance:* one who appears insubstantial; one who will not pretend.
2. A choice cannot be made under those terms.
3. *or . . . taint:* or else the love you earlier swore for

Cordelia must be regarded with suspicion. "Or" may also mean "before," in which case the phrase would mean "before the love you once proclaimed could have decayed."

A still soliciting° eye and such a tongue   *An always-begging*
230   That I am glad I have not, though not to have it
        Hath lost me in your liking.
      LEAR   Better thou hadst
        Not been born than not t'have pleased me better.
      FRANCE   Is it but this, a tardiness in nature,
        Which often leaves the history unspoke
235   That it intends to do?[4] My lord of Burgundy
        What say you to the lady? Love's not love
        When it is mingled with regards° that stands   *considerations*
        Aloof from th'entire point. Will you have her?
        She is herself a dowry.
      BURGUNDY   Royal King,
240   Give but that portion which yourself proposed
        And here I take Cordelia by the hand,
        Duchess of Burgundy.
      LEAR   Nothing, I have sworn; I am firm.
      BURGUNDY [*to* CORDELIA]   I am sorry, then, you have so lost a
            father
        That you must lose a husband.
245   CORDELIA   Peace be with Burgundy.
        Since that respect and fortunes are his love,
        I shall not be his wife.
      FRANCE   Fairest Cordelia, that art most rich being poor,
        Most choice forsaken, and most loved despised,
250   Thee and thy virtues here I seize upon.
        Be it lawful I take up what's cast away.
        Gods, gods! 'Tis strange, that from their cold'st neglect
        My love should kindle to enflamed respect.°   *ardent regard*
        Thy dowerless daughter, King, thrown to my chance,
255   Is Queen of us, of ours, and our fair France.
        Not all the dukes of wat'rish° Burgundy   *irrigated; watery; weak*
        Can buy this unprized,° precious maid of me.   *unappreciated*
        Bid them farewell, Cordelia; though unkind,°   *though they are unkind*
        Thou losest here° a better where° to find.   *this place / place*
260   LEAR   Thou hast her, France. Let her be thine, for we
        Have no such daughter, nor shall ever see
        That face of hers again. Therefore be gone
        Without our grace, our love, our benison.°   *blessing*
        —Come, noble Burgundy.
                        Flourish. Exeunt [*all but* FRANCE, CORDELIA,
                                    GONERIL, *and* REGAN].
265   FRANCE   Bid farewell to your sisters.
      CORDELIA   The jewels of our father, with washed eyes
        Cordelia leaves you. I know you what you are
        And like a sister am most loath to call
        Your faults as they are named.° Love well our father;   *are properly called*
270   To your professed bosoms° I commit him.   *publicly proclaimed love*
        But yet, alas, stood I within his grace,
        I would prefer° him to a better place.   *promote; recommend*
        So farewell to you both.
      REGAN   Prescribe not us our duty.

4. *a tardiness . . . do:* a natural reserve that inhibits voicing one's intentions.

GONERIL   Let your study

275 Be to content your lord, who hath received you
At fortune's alms.[5] You have obedience scanted°   *neglected*
And well are worth the want that you have wanted.[6]

CORDELIA   Time shall unfold what plighted cunning hides;
Who covers faults, at last with shame derides.[7]
Well may you prosper.

280 FRANCE   Come, my fair Cordelia.

                         Exeunt FRANCE *and* CORDELIA.

GONERIL   Sister, it is not little I have to say of what most nearly
appertains to us both. I think our father will hence tonight.

REGAN   That's most certain and with you; next month with us.

GONERIL   You see how full of changes° his age is; the observa-   *fickleness*
tion we have made of it hath been little.° He always loved our   *in the smallest detail*
sister most, and with what poor judgment he hath now cast
her off appears too grossly.°   *blatantly*

REGAN   'Tis the infirmity of his age, yet he hath ever but slen-
derly known himself.

290 GONERIL   The best and soundest of his time hath been but
rash.[8] Then° must we look from his age to receive not alone   *Therefore*
the imperfections of long engraffed condition,° but there-   *deep-rooted habit*
withal the unruly waywardness that infirm and choleric
years bring with them.

295 REGAN   Such unconstant starts[9] are we like° to have from   *likely*
him as this of Kent's banishment.

GONERIL   There is further compliment° of leave-taking between   *ceremony*
France and him. Pray you let us sit together. If our father
carry authority with such disposition[1] as he bears, this last
300 surrender° of his will but offend° us.   *abdication / harm*

REGAN   We shall further think of it.

GONERIL   We must do something, and i'th' heat.°   *Exeunt.*   *quickly*

1.2

       Enter EDMUND.

EDMUND   Thou, Nature, art my goddess; to thy law
My services are bound.[1] Wherefore° should I   *Why*
Stand in the plague of custom[2] and permit
The curiosity° of nations to deprive me,   *legal niceties*
5 For that° I am some twelve or fourteen moonshines°   *Because / months*
Lag of° a brother? Why "bastard"? Wherefore "base,"   *Younger than*
When my dimensions are as well compact,°   *composed*
My mind as generous° and my shape as true   *noble*
As honest° madam's issue? Why brand they us   *married; chaste*
10 With "base"? With "baseness," "bastardy"? Base? Base?
Who, in the lusty stealth of nature, take

---

5. As a charitable gift from fortune.
6. And you deserve to get no more love (from your husband) than you have given (to your father). "Want" plays on its alternative meanings of "lack" and "desire."
7. *Time . . . derides:* Time eventually exposes and shames all hidden faults.
8. *The . . . rash:* Even in the prime of his life he was impetuous.

9. Such impulsive outbursts.
1. Frame of mind.
1.2 Location: The Earl of Gloucester's house.
1. Edmund declares the raw force of unsocialized and unregulated existence, as opposed to human law, to be his ruler; ironically, "nature" also means "natural filial affection." A "natural" was another word for "bastard" (illegitimate child).
2. Submit to the imposition of inheritance law.

More composition and fierce quality[3]
Than doth within a dull, stale, tired bed
Go to th' creating a whole tribe of fops°   *fools*
15   Got° 'tween a sleep, and wake? Well, then,   *Begotten*
Legitimate Edgar, I must have your land.
Our father's love is to° the bastard Edmund   *as much to*
As to th' legitimate. Fine word: "legitimate"!
Well, my legitimate, if this letter speed°   *succeed*
20   And my invention° thrive, Edmund the base   *plot*
Shall to° th' legitimate. I grow. I prosper.   *match up to; usurp*
Now, gods, stand up for bastards!
          Enter GLOUCESTER.
GLOUCESTER   Kent banished thus? And France in choler
      parted?°   *in anger departed*
And the King gone tonight,° prescribed° his power,   *last night / limited*
25   Confined to exhibition?[4] All this done
Upon the gad?° —Edmund, how now? What news?   *spur of the moment*
EDMUND [*putting up a letter*]   So please your lordship, none.
GLOUCESTER   Why so earnestly seek you to put up that letter?
EDMUND   I know no news, my lord.
30   GLOUCESTER   What paper were you reading?
EDMUND   Nothing, my lord.
GLOUCESTER   No? What needed then that terrible dispatch°   *frightened haste*
of it into your pocket? The quality of nothing hath not such
need to hide itself. Let's see. Come, if it be nothing, I shall
35   not need spectacles.
EDMUND   I beseech you, sir, pardon me. It is a letter from my
brother that I have not all o'er-read, and, for so much as I
have perused, I find it not fit for your o'erlooking.
GLOUCESTER   Give me the letter, sir.
40   EDMUND   I shall offend either to detain or give it. The contents, as in part I understand them, are to blame.
GLOUCESTER   Let's see; let's see.
EDMUND [*giving him a letter*]   I hope, for my brother's justification, he wrote this but as an essay or taste[5] of my virtue.
45   GLOUCESTER (*reads*)   "This policy and reverence of age makes
the world bitter to the best of our times,[6] keeps our fortunes
from us till our oldness cannot relish them. I begin to find an
idle and fond° bondage in the oppression of aged tyranny,   *a useless and foolish*
who sways not as it hath power but as it is suffered.[7] Come to
50   me, that of this I may speak more. If our father would sleep
till I waked him, you should enjoy half his revenue forever
and live the beloved of your brother. Edgar." Hum, conspiracy! "Sleep till I wake him, you should enjoy half his revenue"! My son Edgar, had he a hand to write this, a heart and
55   brain to breed it in? When came you to this? Who brought it?

---

3. *Who . . . quality:* Whose begetting, by reason of its
furtiveness and heightened excitement, requires better execution and more vigor. Alternatively (with
"take" meaning "give"), whose begetting produces (a
person of) more mixture and vigor. "Composition," or
mixture, may refer to the belief that the perfect offspring was conceived from an equal quantity of male
and female essence and that physical and mental
abnormalities were caused by a predominance of one

or the other.
4. Pension; mere show without force.
5. *but . . . taste:* simply as a proof or test. Both terms
derive from metallurgy.
6. The established primacy of the elderly embitters
us at the prime of our lives. *policy:* statecraft; craftiness; established order.
7. *who . . . suffered:* which rules not because it is
powerful but because it is permitted to ("suffered").

EDMUND   It was not brought me, my lord; there's the cunning
of it. I found it thrown in at the casement° of my closet.°   *window / private room*

GLOUCESTER   You know the character° to be your brother's?   *handwriting*

EDMUND   If the matter° were good, my lord, I durst swear it   *content*
60   were his, but in respect of that, I would fain° think it were not.   *gladly*

GLOUCESTER   It is his?

EDMUND   It is his hand, my lord, but I hope his heart is not in
the contents.

GLOUCESTER   Has he never before sounded you° in this   *sounded you out*
65   business?

EDMUND   Never, my lord. But I have heard him oft maintain it
to be fit that, sons at perfect age° and fathers declined, the   *at maturity*
father should be as ward[8] to the son, and the son manage his
revenue.

70   GLOUCESTER   Oh, villain, villain! His very opinion in the letter! Abhorred villain! Unnatural, detested, brutish villain;
worse than brutish! Go, sirrah,[9] seek him. I'll apprehend
him. Abominable villain! Where is he?

EDMUND   I do not well know, my lord. If it shall please you to
75   suspend your indignation against my brother till you can derive
from him better testimony of his intent, you should run a cer-
tain° course; where,° if you violently proceed against him,   *safe; reliable / whereas*
mistaking his purpose, it would make a great gap in your own
honor and shake in pieces the heart of his obedience. I dare
80   pawn down° my life for him that he hath writ this to feel° my   *I dare stake / feel out*
affection to your honor and to no other pretense of danger.[1]

GLOUCESTER   Think you so?

EDMUND   If your honor judge it meet,° I will place you where   *appropriate*
you shall hear us confer of this and by an auricular° assur-   *audible*
85   ance have your satisfaction, and that without any further
delay than this very evening.

GLOUCESTER   He cannot be such a monster—

87.1   EDMUND   *Nor is not, sure.*

GLOUCESTER   *—To his father that so tenderly and entirely*
loves him. Heaven and earth!
Edmund, seek him out; wind me into him,[2] I pray you.
Frame° the business after your own wisdom. I would unstate   *Arrange*
90   myself to be in a due resolution.[3]

EDMUND   I will seek him, sir, presently,° convey° the business   *immediately / carry out*
as I shall find means and acquaint you withal.°   *therewith*

GLOUCESTER   These late° eclipses in the sun and moon por-   *recent*
tend no good to us.[4] Though the wisdom of Nature can rea-
95   son it thus and thus, yet Nature finds itself scourged by the
sequent effects.[5] Love cools, friendship falls off, brothers
divide; in cities, mutinies; in countries, discord; in palaces,
treason; and the bond cracked twixt son and father. This
villain of mine comes under the prediction: there's son against

---

8. A child under eighteen years of age who was legally
dependent, often orphaned.
9. A form of address used with children or social
inferiors.
1. No further intention to do harm.
2. Worm your way into his confidence (with "me" as
an intensifier); worm your way into his confidence for
me ("me" as a term of respect).
3. I would give up my rank and property to have my

doubts resolved.
4. The lunar and solar eclipses that were seen in
London between September and October 1605, about
a year before the play's first recorded performance,
would have added spice to this superstitious belief in
the role of heavenly bodies as augurs of misfortune.
5. *Though . . . effects:* Though natural science may
explain the eclipses this way or that, nature (and family bonds) suffers in the effects that follow.

100 father. The King falls from bias of nature:[6] there's father
against child. We have seen the best of our time. Machina-
tions, hollowness,° treachery and all ruinous disorders fol-   *insincerity*
low us disquietly to our graves. Find out this villain,
Edmund. It shall lose thee nothing. Do it carefully. And the
105 noble and true-hearted Kent banished, his offense: honesty!
'Tis strange!   *Exit.*

EDMUND   This is the excellent foppery° of the world, that when   *foolishness*
we are sick in fortune, often the surfeits° of our own behavior,   *excesses*
we make guilty of° our disasters the sun, the moon, and stars,   *we hold responsible for*
110 as if we were villains on necessity, fools by heavenly compul-
sion, knaves, thieves, and treacherers° by spherical predomi-   *traitors*
nance,[7] drunkards, liars, and adulterers by an enforced
obedience of planetary influence, and all that we are evil in
by a divine thrusting-on.° An admirable° evasion of whore-   *imposition / amazing*
115 master man to lay his goatish disposition on the charge of a
star![8] My father compounded° with my mother under the   *coupled*
dragon's tail, and my nativity was under Ursa Major,[9] so that
it follows I am rough and lecherous. I should have been that°   *what*
I am had the maidenliest star in the firmament twinkled on
120 my bastardizing.

          Enter EDGAR.

[*aside*] Pat,° he comes like the catastrophe° of the old com-   *On cue / resolution*
edy. My cue is villainous melancholy, with a sigh like Tom
o'Bedlam.[1] —Oh, these eclipses do portend these divisions.
[*Sings.*]   Fa, sol, la, mi.[2]

125 EDGAR   How now, brother Edmund, what serious contemplation are you in?

EDMUND   I am thinking, brother, of a prediction I read this
other day what should follow these eclipses.

EDGAR   Do you busy yourself with that?

130 EDMUND   I promise you, the effects he writes of succeed°   *follow*
unhappily,
131.1   *as of unnaturalness between the child and the parent,*
death, dearth, dissolutions of ancient amities, divisions in
state, menaces and maledictions against king and nobles,
needless diffidences,° banishment of friends, dissipation   *baseless suspicions*
131.5   *of cohorts,[3] nuptial breaches, and I know not what.*

EDGAR   *How long have you been a sectary astronomical?°*   *a devotee of astrology*
BASTARD   *Come, come,*
EDMUND   when saw you my father last?
EDGAR   The night gone by.
EDMUND   Spake you with him?
135 EDGAR   Ay, two hours together.
EDMUND   Parted you in good terms? Found you no displea-
sure in him by word nor countenance?°   *appearance; demeanor*

---

6. The King deviates from his natural inclination. In
the game of bowls, the "bias" ("course") is the eccentric path taken by the weighted ball when thrown.
7. By the ascendancy of a particular planet. In the
universe as conceived by the second-century astronomer, Ptolemy, the planets revolved about the earth on
crystalline spheres.
8. *to lay . . . star:* to hold a star responsible for his
lustful desires. In Greek mythology, the satyr, a creature with goat-like characteristics, was notoriously
lecherous.

9. Constellations: "dragon's tail" = Draco and "Ursa
Major" = Great Bear.
1. The usual name for lunatic beggars; "Bethlehem,"
shortened to "Bedlam," was the name of the oldest
and best-known London madhouse.
2. The portion of the scale Edmund sings is an augmented fourth, an interval considered at this time
very discordant; it was sometimes referred to as
diabolus in musica ("the devil in music"). *divisions:*
social fractures; melodic embellishments.
3. Scattering of forces.

EDGAR   None at all.

EDMUND   Bethink yourself wherein you may have offended
140   him, and at my entreaty forbear° his presence until some   *avoid*
little time hath qualified° the heat of his displeasure, which   *moderated*
at this instant so rageth in him that with the mischief of
your person it would scarcely allay.⁴

EDGAR   Some villain hath done me wrong.

145   EDMUND   That's my fear. I pray you, have a continent forbear-
ance° till the speed of his rage goes slower, and, as I say,   *restrained absence*
retire with me to my lodging, from whence I will fitly° bring   *when suitable*
you to hear my lord speak. Pray ye go; there's my key. If you
do stir abroad, go armed.

150   EDGAR   Armed, brother?

EDMUND   Brother, I advise you to the best. I am no honest man
if there be any good meaning toward you. I have told you
what I have seen and heard but faintly, nothing like the image
and horror of it. Pray you, away!

155   EDGAR   Shall I hear from you anon?

EDMUND   I do serve you in this business.   *Exit* EDGAR.
A credulous father and a brother noble,
Whose nature is so far from doing harms
That he suspects none; on whose foolish honesty
160   My practices° ride easy. I see the business.⁵   *plots*
Let me, if not by birth, have lands by wit.°   *intelligence*
All with me's meet that I can fashion fit.⁶   *Exit.*

1.3

Enter GONERIL *and [Oswald the]* STEWARD.

GONERIL   Did my father strike my gentleman
For chiding of his fool?

STEWARD   Ay, madam.

GONERIL   By day and night he wrongs me; every hour
He flashes into one gross crime° or other   *offense*
5   That sets us all at odds. I'll not endure it.
His knights grow riotous, and himself upbraids us
On every trifle. When he returns from hunting,
I will not speak with him. Say I am sick.
If you come slack of former services,¹
10   You shall do well; the fault of it I'll answer.°   *answer for*

STEWARD   He's coming, madam, I hear him.

GONERIL   Put on what weary negligence you please,
You and your fellows.° I'd have it come to question.   *the other servants*
If he distaste it, let him to my sister,
15   Whose mind and mine I know in that are one,
15.1   *Not to be overruled. Idle° old man,*   *Foolish*
That still would manage those authorities
That he hath given away! Now, by my life,
Old fools are babes again and must be used
15.5   *With checks as flatteries when they are seen abused.²*

---

4. *with . . . allay:* even harming you bodily ("mischief") would hardly relieve his anger; alternatively, with the irritant of your presence, it (Gloucester's anger) would not be abated.
5. It is now clear to me what needs to be done.
6. Anything is fine by me as long as I can make it serve my purpose. *meet:* justifiable; appropriate.

1.3 Location: The Duke of Albany's castle.
1. If you offer him less service (and respect) than before.
2. *Old . . . abused:* When foolish old men act like children, rebukes are the kindest treatment when kind treatment is abused.

Remember what I have said.

STEWARD   Well, madam.

GONERIL   And let his knights have colder looks among you.
What grows of it no matter; advise your fellows so.
I'll write straight° to my sister to hold my course.   *straightaway*
20 Prepare for dinner.   *Exeunt* [*severally*].°   *separately*

1.4
Enter KENT [*disguised as Caius*].
KENT   If but as well[1] I other accents borrow
That can my speech diffuse,° my good intent   *disguise*
May carry through itself to that full issue°   *result*
For which I razed my likeness.[2] Now, banished Kent,
5   If thou canst serve where thou dost stand condemned,
So may it come° thy master, whom thou lov'st,   *come to pass*
Shall find thee full of labors.°   *helpful; keen*
          Horns within.° Enter LEAR *and* [KNIGHTS *as*]   *Hunting horns offstage*
          Attendants.
LEAR   Let me not stay° a jot for dinner; go get it ready.   *wait*
[*to* KENT] How now, what° art thou?   *who*
10 KENT   A man, sir.
LEAR   What dost thou profess?[3] What wouldst thou with us?
KENT   I do profess to be no less than I seem, to serve him
truly that will put me in trust, to love him that is honest, to
converse° with him that is wise and says little, to fear judg-   *associate*
15 ment, to fight when I cannot choose,° and to eat no fish.[4]   *when I must*
LEAR   What art thou?
KENT   A very honest-hearted fellow and as poor as the King.
LEAR   If thou be'st as poor for a subject as he's for a king, thou
art poor enough. What wouldst thou?
20 KENT   Service.
LEAR   Who wouldst thou serve?
KENT   You.
LEAR   Dost thou know me, fellow?
KENT   No, sir, but you have that in your countenance which I
25 would fain° call master.   *gladly*
LEAR   What's that?
KENT   Authority.
LEAR   What services canst thou do?
KENT   I can keep honest counsel,° ride, run, mar a curious tale   *keep secrets*
30 in telling it,[5] and deliver a plain message bluntly. That which
ordinary men are fit for I am qualified in, and the best of me
is diligence.
LEAR   How old art thou?
KENT   Not so young, sir, to love a woman for singing, nor so
35 old to dote on her for anything. I have years on my back
forty-eight.
LEAR   Follow me. Thou shalt serve me if I like thee no worse
after dinner. I will not part from thee yet. —Dinner, ho,

1.4 Location: As before.
1. As well as disguising my appearance.
2. Disguised my appearance; shaved off my beard.
3. What is your job (profession)? Kent, in reply, uses
"profess" punningly to mean "claim."
4. And not to be a Catholic or penitent (Catholics

were obliged to eat fish on specified occasions and as
penance); alternatively, to be a manly man, a meat
eater.
5. That is, Kent's plain, blunt speech would make
him ill suited to tell a convoluted ("curious") tale.

dinner! Where's my knave? My fool? Go you and call my fool
40   hither.   [*Exit a* KNIGHT.]
          Enter [*Oswald the*] STEWARD.
      You, you, sirrah, where's my daughter?
STEWARD   So please you—   *Exit.*
LEAR   What says the fellow there? Call the clotpoll° back.   *blockhead*
                                          [*Exit* SECOND KNIGHT.]
      Where's my fool? Ho, I think the world's asleep.
          [*Enter* SECOND KNIGHT.]
45   How now? Where's that mongrel?
SECOND KNIGHT   He says, my lord, your daughter is not well.
LEAR   Why came not the slave back to me when I called him?
SECOND KNIGHT   Sir, he answered me in the roundest° man-   *bluntest; rudest*
      ner, he would not.
50   LEAR   He would not?
SECOND KNIGHT   My lord, I know not what the matter is, but
      to my judgment your highness is not entertained with that
      ceremonious affection as you were wont.° There's a great   *accustomed to*
      abatement of kindness appears as well in the general depen-
55   dents° as in the Duke himself also and your daughter.   *servants*
LEAR   Ha? Say'st thou so?
SECOND KNIGHT   I beseech you pardon me, my lord, if I be mis-
      taken, for my duty cannot be silent when I think your high-
      ness wronged.
60   LEAR   Thou but rememberest° me of mine own conception.° I   *remind / perception*
      have perceived a most faint neglect of late, which I have
      rather blamed as mine own jealous curiosity[6] than as a very
      pretense° and purpose of unkindness. I will look further   *a true intention*
      into't. But where's my fool? I have not seen him this two days.
65   SECOND KNIGHT   Since my young lady's going into France, sir,
      the fool hath much pined away.
LEAR   No more of that, I have noted it well. [*to* SECOND KNIGHT]
      Go you and tell my daughter I would speak with her. [*to
      another* KNIGHT] Go you, call hither my fool.
                                          [*Exeunt both* KNIGHTS.]
          Enter [*Oswald the*] STEWARD.
70   Oh, you, sir, you, come you hither, sir. Who am I, sir?
STEWARD   My lady's father.
LEAR   "My lady's father"? My lord's knave! You whoreson dog,
      you slave, you cur!
STEWARD   I am none of these, my lord. I beseech your pardon.
75   LEAR [*striking him*]   Do you bandy looks with me, you rascal?
STEWARD   I'll not be strucken, my lord.
KENT [*tripping him*]   Nor tripped, neither, you base football
      player.[7]
LEAR   I thank thee, fellow. Thou serv'st me, and I'll love thee.
80   KENT [*to* STEWARD]   Come, sir, arise, away. I'll teach you dif-
      ferences.° Away, away. If you will measure your lubber's   *(of rank)*
      length again,[8] tarry. But away, go to; have you wisdom, so.

6. *jealous curiosity:* paranoid concern with niceties.   8. If you will be stretched out by me again. *lubber:*
7. Football was a rough street game played by the   clumsy oaf.
poor.

LEAR   Now, my friendly knave, I thank thee. [*He gives him money.*] There's earnest of° thy service.   *downpayment for*
  Enter FOOL.[9]

85   FOOL   Let me hire him too. [*He hands* KENT *his cap.*] Here's my coxcomb.°   *fool's cap*

LEAR   How now, my pretty knave, how dost thou?

FOOL [*to* KENT]   Sirrah, you were best take my coxcomb.

LEAR   Why, my boy?

90   FOOL   Why, for taking one's part that's out of favor. Nay, an°   *if*
  thou canst not smile as the wind sits, thou'lt catch cold
  shortly.[1] There, take my coxcomb. Why, this fellow has banished two on 's daughters[2] and did the third a blessing against
  his will. If thou follow him, thou must needs wear my coxcomb. How now, nuncle?° Would I had two coxcombs and   *(mine) uncle*
  two daughters.

LEAR   Why, my boy?

FOOL   If I gave them all my living,° I'd keep my coxcombs   *goods*
  myself.[3] [*He hands him his cap.*] There's mine; beg another of
100   thy daughters.

LEAR   Take heed, sirrah, the whip.

FOOL   Truth's a dog that must to° kennel; he must be whipped   *go to*
  out, when the lady brach[4] may stand by th' fire and stink.

LEAR   A pestilent gall° to me.   *annoyance; bitterness*

105   FOOL   Sirrah, I'll teach thee a speech.

LEAR   Do.

FOOL   Mark it, nuncle:
  Have more than thou showest,
  Speak less than thou knowest,
110   Lend less than thou owest,°   *own*
  Ride more than thou goest,°   *walk*
  Learn° more than thou trowest,°   *Hear / believe*
  Set less than thou throwest;[5]
  Leave thy drink and thy whore,
115   And keep in a-door,
  And thou shalt have more
  Than two tens to a score.[6]

KENT   This is nothing, Fool.

FOOL   Then 'tis like the breath° of an unfeed° lawyer: you gave   *speech / unpaid*
120   me nothing for't. Can you make no use of nothing, nuncle?

LEAR   Why, no, boy, nothing can be made out of nothing.

FOOL   Prithee, tell him so much the rent of his land comes
  to.[7] He will not believe a fool.

LEAR   A bitter fool.

125   FOOL   Dost thou know the difference, my boy, between a bitter fool and a sweet one?

LEAR   No, lad, teach me.

---

9. PERFORMANCE COMMENT The Fool and Cordelia never meet onstage, making it possible in some productions for one actor to play both roles. Some other productions cast an older actor as the Fool, thus providing a third aging figure alongside Lear and Gloucester. See Digital Edition PC 2.
1. *an . . . shortly:* if you can't keep in favor with those in power, you will soon find yourself left out in the cold.
2. By abdicating, Lear has in effect prevented his eldest daughters from any longer being his subjects, just as if he had "banished" them.

3. I'd be twice as much a fool.
4. Lady bitch. Pet dogs were often called "Lady" such and such. The allusion is to Regan and Goneril, who are now being preferred to truthful Cordelia.
5. Don't gamble everything on a single cast of the dice.
6. *And thou . . . score:* And there will be more than two tens in your twenty—that is, you will become richer.
7. Remind him that no land means no rent; with a pun on "rent" meaning "torn," "divided."

127.1   FOOL   *That lord that counseled thee*
               To give away thy land,
               Come place him here by me;
               Do thou for him stand.°   *represent him*

127.5   *The sweet and bitter fool*
               Will presently appear,
               The one in motley[8] *here,*
               [pointing to LEAR*] The other found out there.*
    LEAR   *Dost thou call me fool, boy?*

127.10   FOOL   *All thy other titles thou hast given away; that thou*
      wast born with.
    KENT   *This is not altogether fool,*[9] *my lord.*
    FOOL   *No, faith, lords and great men will not let me. If I*
      had a monopoly out, they would have part in't, and
127.15   *ladies too. They will not let me have all the fool to*
      myself, they'll be snatching.
        Nuncle, give me an egg, and I'll give thee two crowns.
    LEAR   *What two crowns shall they be?*

130 ● FOOL   *Why, after I have cut the egg i'th' middle and ate up the*
      meat,° the two crowns of the egg. When thou clovest° thy   *edible part / cleaved*
      crowns i'th' middle and gav'st away both parts, thou bor'st°   *you carried*
      thine ass on thy back o'er the dirt. Thou hadst little wit° in   *sense*
135   *thy bald crown when thou gav'st thy golden one away. If I*
      speak like myself° in this, let him be whipped that first finds   *(like a fool)*
      it so.[1]
      [Sings.]   *Fools had ne'er less grace in a year,*
                   For wise men are grown foppish;[2]
                   And know not how their wits to wear,
140   *Their manners are so apish.°*   *stupid; imitative*
    LEAR   *When were you wont° to be so full of songs, sirrah?*   *accustomed*
    FOOL   *I have used° it, nuncle, e'er since thou mad'st thy daugh-*   *practiced*
      ters thy mothers. For when thou gav'st them the rod and
      putt'st down thine own breeches,
145   *[Sings.]*   *Then they for sudden joy did weep,*
                   And I for sorrow sung,
                   That such a king should play bo-peep,°   *(a child's game)*
                   And go the fool among.
        Prithee, nuncle, keep a schoolmaster that can teach thy fool
150   *to lie. I would fain learn to lie.*
    LEAR   *An° you lie, sirrah, we'll have you whipped.*   *If*
    FOOL   *I marvel what kin° thou and thy daughters are. They'll*   *how alike*
      have me whipped for speaking true, thou'lt have me whipped
      for lying, and sometimes I am whipped for holding my peace.
155   *I had rather be any kind o'thing than a fool, and yet I would*
      not be thee, nuncle. Thou hast pared thy wit o'both sides and
      left nothing i'th' middle. Here comes one o'th' parings.
        Enter GONERIL.
    LEAR   *How now, daughter? What makes that frontlet*[3] *on?*
    You are too much of late i'th' frown.

---

8. Multicolored dress of a court jester.
9. Foolish, folly. In the next line, the Fool takes "altogether fool" to mean "one who has cornered the market on folly."
1. *that . . . so:* who first discovers for himself that this

is true; who first considers this to be foolish.
2. *Fools . . . foppish:* Professional fools have never been as witless since wise men have lately outdone them in idiocy.
3. A headband; here, a metaphor for "frown."

160   FOOL   Thou wast a pretty fellow when thou hadst no need to
      care for her frowning. Now thou art an O without a figure.[4]
      I am better than thou art now: I am a fool, thou art nothing.
      —Yes, forsooth, I will hold my tongue, so your face bids me,
      though you say nothing.
165   [*Sings.*]   Mum, mum,
               He that keeps nor crust, nor crumb,
               Weary of all, shall want° some.   *lack; be in need of*
    [*He points to* GONERIL.] That's a shelled peascod.°   *empty pea pod; nothing*
    GONERIL   Not only, sir, this, your all-licensed° fool,   *unrestrained*
170   But other of your insolent retinue
      Do hourly carp and quarrel, breaking forth
      In rank° and not-to-be-endured riots. Sir,   *foul; spreading*
      I had thought by making this well known unto you
      To have found a safe° redress, but now grow fearful   *sure*
175   By what yourself too late° have spoke and done,   *recently*
      That you protect this course and put it on°   *encourage it*
      By your allowance; which if you should, the fault
      Would not scape censure, nor the redresses sleep;
      Which in the tender of a wholesome weal[5]
180   Might in their working do you that offense
      Which else were shame, that then necessity
      Will call discreet proceeding.[6]
    FOOL   For you know, nuncle,
    [*Sings.*] The hedge-sparrow fed the cuckoo[7] so long
185   That its had its head bit off by its young;°   *(the young cuckoo)*
           So out went the candle,
           And we were left darkling.°   *in the dark*
    LEAR   Are you our daughter?
    GONERIL   I would° you would make use of your good   *wish*
      wisdom,
190   Whereof I know you are fraught,° and put away   *full*
      These dispositions,° which of late transport you   *moods; attitudes*
      From what you rightly are.
    FOOL   May not an ass know when the cart draws the horse?
    [*Sings.*]   Whoop, jug,[8] I love thee.
195   LEAR   Does any here know me? This is not Lear.
      Does Lear walk thus? Speak thus? Where are his eyes?
      Either his notion° weakens, his discernings   *intellect*
      Are lethargied. Ha! Waking?° 'Tis not so.   *Am I awake*
      Who is it that can tell me who I am?
200   FOOL   Lear's shadow.
    LEAR [*to* GONERIL]   Your name, fair gentlewoman?
    GONERIL   This admiration,° sir, is much o'th' savor   *excessive amazement*
      Of other your new pranks. I do beseech you
      To understand my purposes aright:
205   As you are old and reverend, should be wise.
      Here do you keep a hundred knights and squires,

---

4. A zero without a preceding digit to give it value; nothing.
5. *tender of a wholesome weal*: maintenance of a well-ordered commonwealth.
6. *which if you . . . proceeding*: if you do approve (of your attendants' behavior), you will not escape criticism, nor will it be without retribution, which for the common good will cause you pain. While this would otherwise be improper, it will be seen as a prudent ("discreet") action under the circumstances.
7. The cuckoo lays its eggs in the nests of other birds, which then hatch and feed their offspring.
8. Nickname for "Joan"; sobriquet for a whore.

Men so disordered,° so debauched and bold,   *disorderly*
That this our court, infected with their manners,
Shows° like a riotous inn. Epicurism° and lust   *Appears / Gluttony*
210 Makes it more like a tavern or a brothel
Than a graced° palace.[9] The shame itself doth speak   *an honored*
For instant remedy. Be then desired
By her, that else will take the thing she begs,
A little to disquantity your train,°   *to reduce your retinue*
215 And the remainders that shall still depend,°   *be retained*
To be such men as may besort° your age,   *befit*
Which know themselves° and you.   *Who know their place*
  LEAR   Darkness and devils!
Saddle my horses; call my train together.
220 Degenerate bastard, I'll not trouble thee.
Yet° have I left a daughter.   *Still*
  GONERIL   You strike my people, and your disordered rabble
Make servants of their betters.
     Enter [Duke of] ALBANY.
  LEAR   Woe that° too late repents!   *Woe to him who*
225 [*to* ALBANY] Is it your will? Speak, sir. Prepare my horses.
[*to* GONERIL] Ingratitude! Thou marble-hearted fiend,
More hideous when thou show'st thee in a child
Than the sea-monster!
  ALBANY   Pray, sir, be patient.
  LEAR [*to* GONERIL]   Detested kite,° thou liest!   *carrion-eating hawk*
230 My train are men of choice and rarest parts°   *qualities*
That all particulars of duty know,
And in the most exact regard support
The worships of° their name. —O most small fault,   *honors accorded*
How ugly didst thou in Cordelia show,
235 Which, like an engine, wrenched my frame of nature
From the fixed place,[1] drew from my heart all love,
And added to the gall. O Lear, Lear, Lear!
Beat at this gate° that let thy folly in   *(his head)*
And thy dear° judgment out. [*to his* KNIGHTS] Go, go, my   *precious*
    people.   [*Exeunt* KNIGHTS.]
240 ALBANY   My lord, I am guiltless as I am ignorant
Of what hath moved you.
  LEAR   It may be so, my lord.
Hear, Nature, hear, dear goddess, hear:
Suspend thy purpose, if thou didst intend
To make this creature fruitful.
245 Into her womb convey sterility,
Dry up in her the organs of increase,
And from her derogate° body never spring   *debased*
A babe to honor her. If she must teem,°   *breed*
Create her child of spleen,° that it may live   *malice*
250 And be a thwart disnatured° torment to her.   *a perverse unnatural*
Let it stamp wrinkles in her brow of youth;
With cadent° tears fret° channels in her cheeks;   *flowing / carve*
Turn all her mother's pains and benefits°   *cares and kind actions*

9. PERFORMANCE COMMENT Productions must decide whether the king's followers are well-behaved "men of choicest parts," as Lear puts it, or a "disordered rabble," as Goneril describes them. See Digital Edition PC 3.

1. *like . . . place*: as a machine (or lever), dislocated my natural affections from their proper foundations.

To laughter and contempt, that she may feel
255 How sharper than a serpent's tooth it is
To have a thankless child. Away, away.

Exeunt [LEAR *and* KENT].

ALBANY   Now gods that we adore,
Whereof comes this?

GONERIL   Never afflict yourself to know more of it,
260 But let his disposition have that scope
As° dotage gives it.   Which

Enter LEAR.

LEAR   What, fifty of my followers at a clap?
Within a fortnight?

ALBANY   What's the matter, sir?

LEAR   I'll tell thee:
265 Life and death! [*to* GONERIL] I am ashamed
That thou hast power to shake my manhood thus,
That these hot tears, which break from me perforce,°   against my will
Should make thee worth them.
Blasts and fogs upon thee!
270 Th'untented woundings° of a father's curse   The undressed wounds
Pierce every sense about thee. Old fond° eyes,   foolish
Beweep° this cause again, I'll pluck ye out   If you weep over
And cast you with the waters that you lose°   let loose
To temper° clay. Ha? Let it be so.   soften
275 I have another daughter
Who I am sure is kind and comfortable.°   comforting
When she shall hear this of thee, with her nails
She'll flay thy wolvish visage. Thou shalt find
That I'll resume the shape which thou dost think
I have cast off forever.   *Exit.*
280 GONERIL   Do you mark that?

ALBANY   I cannot be so partial,° Goneril,   biased
To° the great love I bear you—   Because of

GONERIL   Pray you, content.° What, Oswald, ho?   be quiet
[*to* FOOL] You, sir, more knave than fool, after your master.
285 FOOL   Nuncle Lear, nuncle Lear,
Tarry, take the fool with thee.
A fox when one has caught her,
And such a daughter
Should sure° to the slaughter   surely be sent
290 If my cap would buy a halter.°   collar; noose
So the fool follows after.   *Exit.*

GONERIL   This man hath had good counsel. A hundred
knights?
'Tis politic° and safe to let him keep   prudent
At point° a hundred knights; yes, that on every dream   Armed
295 Each buzz,° each fancy, each complaint, dislike.   rumor
He may enguard° his dotage with their powers   protect
And hold our lives in mercy. Oswald, I say!

ALBANY   Well, you may fear too far.

GONERIL   Safer than trust too far.
300 Let me still° take away the harms I fear,   always
Not° fear still to be taken. I know his heart;   Rather than
What he hath uttered I have writ my sister.

If she sustain him and his hundred knights
When I have showed th'unfitness.—
    Enter [Oswald the] STEWARD.
305 How now, Oswald?
What, have you writ that letter to my sister?
STEWARD Ay, madam.
GONERIL Take you some company and away to horse.
Inform her full of my particular fear
310 And thereto add such reasons of your own
As may compact° it more. Get you gone   *compound*
And hasten your return.   [*Exit* STEWARD.]
[*to* ALBANY]   No, no, my lord,
This milky gentleness and course of yours,
Though I condemn not, yet under pardon°   *begging your pardon*
315 You are much more at task° for want of wisdom *taken to task; censured*
Than praised for harmful mildness.
ALBANY How far your eyes may pierce,° I cannot tell; *foresee*
Striving to better, oft we mar what's well.
GONERIL Nay, then—
ALBANY   Well, well, th'event.° *Exeunt.* *let's see the outcome*

1.5

Enter LEAR, KENT [*disguised as Caius*], GENTLEMAN,
 and FOOL.

LEAR [*to* KENT] Go you before° to Gloucester[1] with these let- *on ahead*
ters; acquaint my daughter no further with anything you
know than comes from her demand out of the letter.[2] If your
diligence be not speedy, I shall be there afore you.
5 KENT I will not sleep, my lord, till I have delivered your letter.
                 Exit.
FOOL If a man's brains were in 's heels were't not in danger of
kibes?°   *chilblains*
LEAR Ay, boy.
FOOL Then, I prithee, be merry; thy wit shall not go slipshod.[3]
10 LEAR Ha, ha, ha.
FOOL Shalt° see thy other daughter will use thee kindly, for *Thou shalt*
though she's as like this as a crab's° like an apple, yet I can *crab apple; sour apple*
tell what I can tell.
LEAR What canst tell, boy?
15 FOOL She will taste as like this as a crab does to a crab. Thou
canst tell why one's nose stands i'th' middle on 's° face? *of one's*
LEAR No.
FOOL Why, to keep one's eyes of either side 's nose, that what
a man cannot smell out he may spy into.
20 LEAR I did her wrong.
FOOL Canst tell how an oyster makes his shell?
LEAR No.
FOOL Nor I, neither, but I can tell why a snail has a house.
LEAR Why?

1.5 Location: Before Albany's castle.
1. To Gloucestershire, where Cornwall and Regan
reside.
2. *than . . . letter:* other than such questions as are

prompted by the letter.
3. Literally, your brains will not wear slippers (to
warm feet that are afflicted with chilblains); feet of
any intelligence would not walk toward Regan.

25 FOOL Why, to put 's head in, not to give it away to his daughters and leave his horns without a case.[4]

LEAR I will forget my nature.[5] So kind a father! Be my horses
ready?

FOOL Thy asses° are gone about 'em; the reason why the seven   (servants)
30 stars° are no more than seven is a pretty reason.   the Pleiades

LEAR Because they are not eight.

FOOL Yes, indeed, thou wouldst make a good fool.

LEAR To tak't again perforce.[6] Monster ingratitude!

FOOL If thou wert my fool, nuncle, I'd have thee beaten for
35 being old before thy time.

LEAR How's that?

FOOL Thou shouldst not have been old till thou hadst been
wise.

LEAR Oh, let me not be mad, not mad. Sweet heaven, keep me
40 in temper;° I would not be mad. —How now, are the horses   sane
ready?

GENTLEMAN Ready, my lord.

LEAR Come, boy.

FOOL She that's a maid now and laughs at my departure,
45 Shall not be a maid long, unless things be cut shorter.[7]

                                                    Exeunt.

2.1

Enter [EDMUND *the*] *Bastard, and* CURAN, *severally.°*   separately

EDMUND Save° thee, Curan.   God save

CURAN And you, sir. I have been with your father and given
him notice that the Duke of Cornwall and Regan, his duchess, will be here with him this night.

5 EDMUND How comes that?

CURAN Nay, I know not. You have heard of the news abroad,
I mean the whispered ones, for they are yet but ear-kissing
arguments.[1]

EDMUND Not I. Pray you, what are they?

10 CURAN Have you heard of no likely wars toward° twixt the   impending
Dukes of Cornwall and Albany?

EDMUND Not a word.

CURAN You may do, then, in time. Fare you well, sir.   *Exit.*

EDMUND The Duke be here tonight? The better best!
15 This weaves itself perforce° into my business.   necessarily
My father hath set guard to take my brother,
And I have one thing of a queasy question[2]
Which I must act. Briefness and fortune work.°   be with me
        Enter EDGAR [*above*].
Brother, a word! Descend, brother, I say.

---

4. Protective covering for his head or concealment
for his horns (horns were the conventional sign of a
cuckold). The Fool may be slyly implying that Lear's
wife cheated on him.
5. Lose my fatherly feelings. *nature*: character.
6. To take it back by force. Lear may refer to Goneril's treachery, or he may be contemplating resuming
his authority.

7. *She . . . shorter:* A girl who would laugh at my leaving would be so foolish that she could not remain a
virgin for long; "things" refers both to the unfolding
event and to penises.
2.1 Location: Gloucester's castle.
1. Barely whispered affairs.
2. And I have a hazardous and delicate problem.

[EDGAR *descends.*]

20 My father watches. O sir, fly this place!
Intelligence is given where you are hid.
You have now the good advantage of the night.
Have you not spoken 'gainst the Duke of Cornwall?
He's coming hither now, i'th' night, i'th' haste
25 And Regan with him. Have you nothing said
Upon his party° 'gainst the Duke of Albany?   *On his (Cornwall's) side*
Advise yourself.°   *Consider carefully*
EDGAR   I am sure on't,° not a word.   *of it*
EDMUND   I hear my father coming. Pardon me:
[*He draws his sword.*] In cunning, I must draw my sword
upon you.
30 Draw, seem to defend yourself. Now quit you° well.   *acquit yourself*
[*He shouts.*] Yield, come before my father. —Light, ho, here!
[*to* EDGAR] Fly, brother! —Torches, torches! [*to* EDGAR] So
farewell.   [*Exit* EDGAR.]
[*He wounds his arm.*] Some blood drawn on me would beget
opinion°   *produce the impression*
Of my more fierce endeavor. I have seen drunkards
35 Do more than this in sport. [*He shouts.*] Father, father!
Stop, stop! No help?
            Enter GLOUCESTER *and* SERVANTS, *with torches.*
GLOUCESTER   Now, Edmund, where's the villain?
EDMUND   Here stood he in the dark, his sharp sword out,
Mumbling of wicked charms, conjuring the moon
40 To stand° auspicious mistress.   *To act as his*
GLOUCESTER   But where is he?
EDMUND   Look, sir, I bleed.
GLOUCESTER   Where is the villain, Edmund?
EDMUND   Fled this way, sir, when by no means he could—
GLOUCESTER   Pursue him, ho, go after.   [*Exeunt* SERVANTS.]
45   —By no means—what?
EDMUND   —Persuade me to the murder of your lordship,
But that° I told him the revenging gods   *In response to that*
'Gainst parricides did all the thunder bend;
Spoke with how manifold and strong a bond
50 The child was bound to th' father. Sir, in fine,°   *finally*
Seeing how loathly opposite° I stood   *opposed*
To his unnatural purpose, in fell° motion   *deadly*
With his preparèd sword he charges home°   *strikes to the heart of*
My unprovided° body, latched° mine arm,   *unprotected / struck*
55 And when he saw my best alarumed spirits
Bold in the quarrel's right,[3] roused to th'encounter,
Or whether gasted° by the noise I made,   *frightened*
Full suddenly he fled.
GLOUCESTER   Let him fly far.
Not in this land shall he remain uncaught;
60 And found, dispatch.° The noble Duke, my master,   *And once found—killed*
My worthy arch° and patron, comes tonight.   *lord*
By his authority I will proclaim it,
That he which finds him shall deserve our thanks,

3. *my best . . . right:* that I was fully roused to action, made brave by righteousness.

Bringing the murderous coward to the stake.[4]
65 He that conceals him, death.
EDMUND   When I dissuaded him from his intent,
And found him pight° to do it, with curst° speech   *resolved / bitter*
I threatened to discover° him. He replied,   *expose*
"Thou unpossessing bastard, dost thou think,
70 If I would stand against thee, would the reposal°   *placing*
Of any trust, virtue, or worth in thee
Make thy words faithed?° No, what should I deny—   *credible*
As this I would, though thou didst produce
My very character[5]—I'd turn it all
75 To[6] thy suggestion, plot, and damnèd practice,°   *scheming*
And thou must make a dullard of the world,
If they not thought the profits of my death
Were very pregnant and potential spirits
To make thee seek it."[7]
GLOUCESTER   Oh, strange° and fastened° villain,   *unnatural / incorrigible*
80 Would he deny his letter, said he?
80.1   *I never got° him!*   *begot*
                    Tucket° within.   *Flourish of trumpets*
Hark, the Duke's trumpets. I know not where he comes.
All ports° I'll bar. The villain shall not scape.   *seaports; exits*
The Duke must grant me that. Besides, his picture
I will send far and near that all the kingdom
85 May have due note of him,[8] and of my land,
Loyal and natural° boy, I'll work the means   *loving; illegitimate*
To make thee capable.°   *legally able to inherit*
                 Enter CORNWALL, REGAN, *and Attendants.*
CORNWALL   How now, my noble friend? Since I came hither,
Which I can call but now, I have heard strangeness.
90 REGAN   If it be true, all vengeance comes too short
Which can pursue th'offender. How dost my lord?
GLOUCESTER   O madam, my old heart is cracked; it's cracked.
REGAN   What, did my father's godson seek your life?
He whom my father named, your Edgar?
95 GLOUCESTER   O lady, lady, shame would have it hid.
REGAN   Was he not companion with the riotous knights
That tended° upon my father?   *attend*
GLOUCESTER   I know not, madam. 'Tis too bad, too bad.
EDMUND   Yes, madam, he was of that consort.°   *company*
100 REGAN   No marvel, then, though° he were ill affected.°   *that / ill disposed*
'Tis they have put him on° the old man's death   *have urged him to seek*
To have th'expense° and waste of his revenues.   *the use*
I have this present evening from my sister
Been well informed of them and with such cautions
105 That if they come to sojourn at my house,
I'll not be there.
CORNWALL   Nor I, assure thee, Regan.
Edmund, I hear that you have shown your father

4. Treachery and rebellion were crimes for which one could be burned.
5. Handwriting; but also, a true summary of my character.
6. *I'd . . . To:* I'd blame it all on.
7. *And thou . . . it:* And do you think the world so stu-pid that it could not see the benefit you would get from my death (and thus a motive for plotting to kill me)? *pregnant:* full. *potential spirits:* powerful temptations.
8. Likenesses of outlaws were drawn up, printed, and publicly displayed, sometimes with an offer of reward as in "Wanted" posters.

A childlike office.°   *filial service*

EDMUND   It was my duty, sir.

GLOUCESTER   He did bewray his practice° and received   *uncover his (Edgar's) plot*

110 This hurt you see, striving to apprehend him.

CORNWALL   Is he pursued?

GLOUCESTER   Ay, my good lord.

CORNWALL   If he be taken, he shall never more
     Be feared of doing harm. Make your own purpose
     How in my strength you please.⁹ For you, Edmund,

115 Whose virtue and obedience doth this instant
     So much commend itself, you shall be ours.
     Natures of such deep trust we shall much need;
     You we first seize on.

EDMUND   I shall serve you, sir, truly, however else.°   *if nothing else*

120 GLOUCESTER   For him, I thank your grace.

CORNWALL   You know not why we came to visit you?

REGAN   Thus out of season, threading dark-eyed night?
     Occasions, noble Gloucester, of some prize,°   *weight*
     Wherein we must have use of your advice.

125 Our father, he hath writ, so hath our sister,
     Of differences,° which I best thought it fit   *quarrels*
     To answer from° our home. The several° messengers   *away from / various*
     From hence attend° dispatch. Our good old friend,   *await*
     Lay comforts to your bosom and bestow

130 Your needful° counsel to our businesses,   *badly needed*
     Which craves the instant use.¹

GLOUCESTER   I serve you, madam.
     Your graces are right welcome.   *Exeunt. Flourish.*

2.2

Enter KENT *[disguised as Caius] and [Oswald the]*
STEWARD severally.°   *separately*

STEWARD   Good dawning to thee, friend. Art° of this house?   *Are you a servant*

KENT   Ay.

STEWARD   Where may we set our horses?

KENT   I'th' mire.

5   STEWARD   Prithee, if thou lov'st me,° tell me.   *if you will be so kind*

KENT   I love thee not.

STEWARD   Why, then, I care not for thee.

KENT   If I had thee in Lipsbury pinfold,¹ I would make thee
     care for me.

10 STEWARD   Why dost thou use° me thus? I know thee not.   *treat*

KENT   Fellow, I know thee.

STEWARD   What dost thou know me for?

KENT   A knave, a rascal, an eater of broken meats,° a base,   *scraps*
     proud, shallow, beggarly, three-suited, hundred pound, filthy,

15   worsted-stocking knave,² a lily-livered, action-taking, whore-
     son, glass-gazing, super-serviceable finical rogue, one-trunk-

---

9. *Make . . . please:* Devise your plots making use of
my forces and authority as you see fit.
1. Which requires immediate attention.
2.2 Location: Before Gloucester's house.
1. If I had you in the enclosure of my mouth (gripped
in my teeth). Lipsbury is probably an invented place-
name. *pinfold:* pen, animal enclosure.

2. *three-suited . . . knave:* Oswald is being called a poor
imitation of a gentleman. Servants were permitted
three suits a year; one hundred pounds was the minimum qualification for the purchase of one of King
James's knighthoods; a gentleman would wear stockings of silk, not "worsted" (thick woolen material).

inheriting slave,[3] one that wouldst be a bawd in way of good
service[4] and art nothing but the composition° of a knave, beg-   *combination*
gar, coward, pander, and the son and heir of a mongrel bitch.
20   One whom I will beat into clamors whining if thou deny'st
the least syllable of thy addition.[5]

STEWARD   Why, what a monstrous fellow art thou thus to rail
on one that is neither known of° thee nor knows thee!   *by*

KENT   What a brazen-faced varlet° art thou to deny thou know-   *rascal*
25   est me! Is it two days since I tripped up thy heels and beat
thee before the King? [*He draws his sword.*] Draw, you rogue,
for though it be night, yet the moon shines. I'll make a sop
o'th' moonshine[6] of you, you whoreson, cullionly barber-
monger.[7] Draw!

STEWARD   Away, I have nothing to do with thee.

30 KENT   Draw, you rascal! You come with letters against the
King and take Vanity the puppet's part against the royalty of
her father?[8] Draw, you rogue, or I'll so carbonado[9] your
shanks—Draw, you rascal! Come your ways!°   *Come forward*
[*He beats him.*]

STEWARD   Help, ho, murder, help!

35 KENT   Strike, you slave! Stand, rogue! Stand, you neat° slave!   *elegant; foppish*
Strike!

STEWARD   Help, ho, murder, murder!
Enter [EDMUND *the*] *Bastard,* CORNWALL, REGAN,
GLOUCESTER, SERVANTS.

EDMUND   How now, what's the matter? Part!

KENT [*to* STEWARD]   With you, goodman boy, if you please.
40   Come, I'll flesh ye.[1] Come on, young master.

GLOUCESTER   Weapons? Arms? What's the matter here?

CORNWALL   Keep peace, upon your lives! He dies that strikes
again! What is the matter?

REGAN   The messengers from our sister and the King?

45 CORNWALL   What is your difference?° Speak.   *quarrel*

STEWARD   I am scarce in breath, my lord.

KENT   No marvel; you have so bestirred your valor, you cow-
ardly rascal. Nature disclaims° in thee. A tailor[2] made thee!   *disowns her part*

CORNWALL   Thou art a strange fellow. A tailor make a man?

50 KENT   A tailor, sir. A stonecutter or a painter could not have
made him so ill,° though they had been but two years o'th'   *so badly*
trade.

CORNWALL   Speak yet: how grew your quarrel?

---

3. *lily-livered:* cowardly. *action-taking:* litigious, one
who would rather use the law than his fists. *glass-
gazing:* mirror-gazing. *super-serviceable:* overly officious, or too ready to serve. *finical:* finicky, fastidious.
one-trunk-inheriting: owning only what would fill
one trunk.
4. *one that . . . service:* one who would even be a pimp
if called upon.
5. Of the descriptions Kent has just applied to him.
addition: title (used ironically).
6. Kent proposes to skewer and pierce Oswald so that
his body might be made into something insubstantial
(like moonshine). Alternatively, perhaps Kent is proposing to scramble Oswald's body into a substance
resembling the popular sixteenth- and seventeenth-

century pudding called "eggs in moonshine." *sop:*
piece of bread to be steeped or dunked in soup.
7. *cullionly barber-monger:* despicable frequenter of
hairdressers. *cullion:* testicle.
8. *and take . . . father:* and support Goneril, here
depicted as a dressed-up doll whose pride is contrasted
with Lear's kingliness.
9. Slash or score as one would the surface of meat in
preparation for broiling.
1. I'll initiate you into fighting, as a hunting dog is
given the taste of blood to rouse it for the chase.
2. Tailors, considered effeminate, were stock objects
of mockery. Kent has suggested that Oswald is worthless apart from the value he derives from his external
garments.

STEWARD   This ancient ruffian, sir, whose life I have spared at
55   suit of° his gray beard—   *on account of*
KENT [*to* STEWARD]   Thou whoreson zed,[3] thou unnecess-
      ary letter! —My lord, if you will give me leave, I will tread
      this unbolted° villain into mortar and daub the wall of a   *unsifted; coarse*
      jakes° with him. [*to* STEWARD] "Spare my gray beard," you   *privy; toilet*
60   wagtail![4]
CORNWALL   Peace, sirrah!
      You beastly knave, know you no reverence?°   *respect*
KENT   Yes, sir, but anger hath a privilege.
CORNWALL   Why art thou angry?
65   KENT   That such a slave as this should wear a sword
      Who wears no honesty. Such smiling rogues as these
      Like rats oft bite the holy cords[5] a-twain,
      Which are t'intrince° t'unloose; smooth° every passion   *too intricate / flatter*
      That in the natures of their lords rebel,
70   Being oil to fire, snow to the colder moods,
      Revenge, affirm, and turn their halcyon beaks[6]
      With every gall and vary° of their masters,   *irritation and mood*
      Knowing naught, like dogs, but following.
      A plague upon your epileptic° visage!   *distorted; grimacing*
75   Smile you° my speeches as° I were a fool?   *Do you smile at / as if*
      Goose, if I had you upon Sarum Plain,
      I'd drive ye cackling home to Camelot.[7]
CORNWALL   What, art thou mad, old fellow?
GLOUCESTER   How fell you out? Say that.
80   KENT   No contraries° hold more antipathy   *opposites*
      Than I and such a knave.
CORNWALL   Why dost thou call him knave? What is his fault?°   *offense*
KENT   His countenance likes° me not.   *pleases*
CORNWALL   No more, perchance, does mine, nor his, nor hers.
85   KENT   Sir, 'tis my occupation to be plain.
      I have seen better faces in my time
      Than stands on any shoulder that I see
      Before me at this instant.
CORNWALL   This is some fellow
      Who, having been praised for bluntness, doth affect
90   A saucy roughness and constrains the garb
      Quite from his nature.[8] He cannot flatter, he.
      An honest mind and plain, he must speak truth
      An they will take it so; if not, he's plain.[9]
      These kind of knaves I know, which in this plainness
95   Harbor more craft and more corrupter ends
      Than twenty silly-ducking observants

---

3. The letter Z (zed) was considered superfluous
because it could be replaced by S; consequently, it
was omitted from many dictionaries.
4. A common English bird that takes its name from
the up-and-down flicking of its tail; this, and its characteristic hopping from foot to foot, causes it to appear
nervous. Alternatively, a contemptuous term for a
harlot.
5. Bonds of kinship, affection, marriage, or rank.
6. It was believed that the kingfisher (in Greek, *halcyon*) could be used as a weather vane when dead:
suspended by a fine thread, its beak would turn what-

ever way the wind blew.
7. *Goose . . . Camelot*: Comparing him to a cackling
goose, Kent tells Oswald that if he had him on Salisbury Plain, he would drive him all the way to Camelot,
the legendary home of King Arthur.
8. *and constrains . . . nature*: and assumes the appearance although it is untrue to his real self. Alternatively
(with "his" meaning "its"): and distorts the true shape
of plainness from what it naturally is (by turning it
into disrespect).
9. If they will accept (Kent's attitude), well and good;
if not, he is a plainspoken man (and does not care).

That stretch their duties nicely.[1]
KENT   Sir, in good faith, in sincere verity,
 Under th'allowance of your great aspect,[2]
100 Whose influence like the wreath of radiant fire
 On flick'ring Phoebus' front°—   *the sun god's forehead*
CORNWALL   What mean'st by this?
KENT   To go out of my dialect,° which you discommend so *normal mode of speech*
 much. I know, sir, I am no flatterer. He that beguiled you in
 a plain accent was a plain knave, which for my part I will not
105 be, though I should win your displeasure to entreat me to't.[3]
CORNWALL [*to* STEWARD]   What was th'offense you gave him?
STEWARD   I never gave him any.
 It pleased the King his master very late°   *lately*
 To strike at me upon his misconstruction,°   *misunderstanding (me)*
110 When he, compact° and flattering his displeasure,   *in league with*
 Tripped me behind; being down, insulted,° railed, *I being down, he insulted*
 And put upon him such a deal of man
 That worthied him,[4] got praises of the King,
 For him attempting who was self-subdued,[5]
115 And in the fleshment° of this dread exploit,   *excitement; flush*
 Drew on me here again.
KENT   None of these rogues and cowards
 But Ajax is their fool.[6]
CORNWALL   Fetch forth the stocks!
       [*Exit a* SERVANT.]
 You stubborn, ancient knave, you reverend° braggart, *old; revered*
 We'll teach you.
120 KENT   Sir, I am too old to learn.
 Call not your stocks for me. I serve the King,
 On whose employment I was sent to you.
 You shall do small respects, show too bold malice
 Against the grace° and person° of my master,   *majesty / personal honor*
 Stocking° his messenger.   *By stocking*
125 CORNWALL   Fetch forth the stocks.
 As I have life and honor, there shall he sit till noon.
REGAN   Till noon? Till night, my lord, and all night too.
KENT   Why, madam, if I were your father's dog,
 You should not use me so.
130 REGAN Sir, being° his knave, I will.   *since you are*
    Stocks brought out [*by a* SERVANT].
CORNWALL   This is a fellow of the selfsame color°   *character*
 Our sister° speaks of. —Come, bring away the stocks. *sister-in-law*
GLOUCESTER   Let me beseech your grace not to do so;
133.1 *His fault is much, and the good King his master*
 Will check° him for't. Your purposed° low correction *reprimand / intended*
 Is such as basest and 'temnest[7] wretches

---

1. *Than . . . nicely:* Than twenty obsequious attendants who constantly bow idiotically and who perform
their functions with excessive diligence ("nicely").
2. With the permission of your great countenance.
"Aspect" also refers to the astrological position of a
planet; Kent's bombastic language here raises Cornwall to the mock-heroic proportions of a heavenly body.
3. *He that . . . to't:* The person who tried to hoodwink
you with plain speaking was, indeed, a pure knave—
something I won't be, even if you were to beg me to be

one (a plain knave, or flatterer).
4. *And put . . . worthied him:* And put on such a show
of manliness that he was thought a worthy fellow.
5. For attacking a man who had already surrendered
(Kent attacking Oswald).
6. *None . . . fool:* Such rogues and cowards as these
talk as if they were greater warriors (and blusterers)
than Ajax; such rogues always make even mighty Ajax
out to be a fool.
7. Condemnest; most condemned.

<table>
<tr><td>133.5</td><td colspan="2">For pilf'rings and most common trespasses
Are punished with.</td></tr>
</table>

133.5   *For pilf'rings and most common trespasses*
        Are punished with.
    The King his master needs must take it ill
135   That he, so slightly valued in his messenger,
     Should have him thus restrained.
   CORNWALL   I'll answer° that.   *be responsible for*
   REGAN   My sister may receive it much more worse
     To have her gentleman abused, assaulted,
138.1   *For following° her affairs. —Put in his legs.*   *carrying out*
   CORNWALL   Come, my lord, away.
                      Exeunt [CORNWALL *and* REGAN].
140   GLOUCESTER   I am sorry for thee, friend. 'Tis the Duke's
       pleasure,
     Whose disposition, all the world well knows,
     Will not be rubbed° nor stopped. I'll entreat for thee.   *obstructed*
   KENT   Pray, do not, sir. I have watched° and traveled hard;   *gone without sleep*
     Some time I shall sleep out, the rest I'll whistle.
145   A good man's fortune may grow out at heels.[8]
     Give° you good morrow.   *God give*
   GLOUCESTER   The Duke's to blame in this; 'twill be ill taken.
                                Exit.
   KENT   Good King, that must approve° the common saw,°   *prove / saying*
     Thou out of heaven's benediction com'st
150   To the warm sun.[9]
     Approach, thou beacon[1] to this under-globe,
     That by thy comfortable beams I may
     Peruse this letter. Nothing almost sees miracles
     But misery.[2] I know 'tis from Cordelia,
155   Who hath most fortunately been informed
     Of my obscurèd° course and shall find time   *hidden; disguised*
     From this enormous state,° seeking to give   *awful state of affairs*
     Losses their remedies. All weary and o'er-watched,°   *too long awake*
     Take vantage,° heavy eyes, not to behold   *the opportunity*
160   This shameful lodging. Fortune, good night,
     Smile once more; turn thy wheel.[3]
       [*Sleeps and remains onstage.*]

2.3

     Enter EDGAR.
   EDGAR   I heard myself proclaimed°   *declared an outlaw*
     And by the happy° hollow of a tree   *opportune*
     Escaped the hunt. No port° is free; no place   *seaport; exit*
     That guard and most unusual vigilance
5   Does not attend my taking.° Whiles° I may scape,   *await my capture / Until*
     I will preserve myself and am bethought°   *resolved*
     To take the basest and most poorest shape
     That ever penury in contempt of° man   *for*
     Brought near to beast. My face I'll grime with filth,

---

8. The fortunes of even good men sometimes wear thin.
9. *Thou . . . sun:* You come from the blessing of heaven into the heat of the sun (go from good to bad).
1. That is, the sun.
2. *Nothing . . . misery:* Only those suffering misery are granted miracles; any comfort seems miraculous to those who are miserable.
3. The goddess Fortune was traditionally depicted with a wheel to signify her mutability and caprice. She was believed to take pleasure in arbitrarily lowering those at the top of her wheel and raising those at the bottom.
2.3 Location: As before.

10   Blanket my loins, elf all my hairs in knots,[1]
      And with presented° nakedness outface   *exposed*
      The winds and persecutions of the sky.
      The country gives me proof and precedent
      Of Bedlam beggars who, with roaring voices,
15   Strike° in their numbed and mortified° arms   *Stick / deadened*
      Pins, wooden pricks, nails, sprigs of rosemary,
      And with this horrible object° from low farms,   *spectacle*
      Poor pelting° villages, sheepcotes, and mills,   *paltry; contemptible*
      Sometimes with lunatic bans,° sometime with prayers,   *curses*
20   Enforce their charity. Poor Turlygod,[2] poor Tom:
      That's something yet. Edgar I nothing am.[3]   *Exit.*

2.4
Enter LEAR, FOOL, *and* GENTLEMAN.

LEAR   'Tis strange that they should so depart from home
      And not send back my messengers.
GENTLEMAN   As I learned,
      The night before there was no purpose in them°   *they had no intention*
      Of this remove.°   *change of residence*
KENT   Hail to thee, noble master.
LEAR   Ha? Mak'st thou this shame thy pastime?
5 KENT   No, my lord.
FOOL   Ha, ha, he wears cruel garters![1] Horses are tied by the
      heads, dogs and bears by th' neck, monkeys by th' loins, and
      men by th' legs. When a man's overlusty at legs,[2] then he
      wears wooden nether-stocks.°   *knee socks*
10 LEAR   What's° he that hath so much thy place° mistook *Who's / position*
      To set thee here?
KENT   It is both he and she:
      Your son° and daughter.   *son-in-law*
LEAR   No.
KENT   Yes.
15 LEAR   No, I say.
KENT   I say yea.
LEAR   By Jupiter, I swear no.
KENT   By Juno,[3] I swear ay.
LEAR   They durst not do't;
20   They could not, would not do't. 'Tis worse than murder
      To do upon respect[4] such violent outrage.
      Resolve° me with all modest° haste, which way   *Inform / reasonable*
      Thou mightst deserve, or they impose, this usage,
      Coming from us.
KENT   My lord, when at their home
25   I did commend° your highness' letters to them,   *deliver*
      Ere I was risen from the place, that showed
      My duty kneeling, came there a reeking° post,° *sweating / messenger*
      Stewed in his haste, half breathless, painting° forth   *panting*

---

1. Tangle the hair into "elf locks," supposed to be a
favorite trick of malicious elves.
2. A word of unknown origin.
3. Edgar, I am nothing; I am no longer Edgar.
2.4 Location: As before.
1. Worsted garters, punning on "crewel." Crewel is a

thin yarn made of twisted fibers. The Fool is actually
referring to the stocks in which Kent's feet are held.
2. When a man's liable to run away.
3. Queen of the Roman gods and wife of Jupiter,
with whom she constantly quarreled.
4. To do to one who deserves respect.

From Goneril, his mistress, salutations,
30 Delivered letters 'spite of intermission,[5]
Which presently° they read. On those contents   *immediately*
They summoned up their meiny,° straight° took horse,   *retinue / straightaway*
Commanded me to follow and attend
The leisure of their answer, gave me cold looks,
35 And meeting here the other messenger,
Whose welcome I perceived had poisoned mine—
Being the very° fellow which of late   *same*
Displayed so saucily° against your highness—   *Acted so insolently*
Having more man° than wit° about me, drew.   *courage / sense*
40 He raised the house with loud and coward cries.
Your son and daughter found this trespass worth°   *deserving of*
The shame which here it suffers.
FOOL   Winter's not gone yet, if the wild geese fly that way.[6]
Fathers that wear rags
45 Do make their children blind.[7]
But fathers that bear bags
Shall see their children kind.
Fortune, that arrant whore,
Ne'er turns the key° to th' poor.   *opens the door*
50 But for all this, thou shalt have as many dolors[8] for thy daugh-
ters as thou canst tell° in a year.   *count*
LEAR   Oh, how this mother° swells up toward my heart!   *hysteria*
Hysterica passio, down, thou climbing sorrow,[9]
Thy element's° below! Where is this daughter?   *natural place is*
55 KENT   With the Earl, sir, here within.
LEAR   Follow me not. Stay here.   *Exit.*
GENTLEMAN   Made you no more offense but what you speak of?
KENT   None. How chance the King comes with so small a
number?
60 FOOL   An° thou hadst been set i'th' stocks for that question,   *If*
thou'dst well deserved it.
KENT   Why, Fool?
FOOL   We'll set thee to school to an ant, to teach thee there's
no laboring i'th' winter.[1] All that follow their noses are led by
65 their eyes but blind men, and there's not a nose among twenty
but can smell him that's stinking.° Let go thy hold when a   *(as his fortunes decay)*
great wheel runs down a hill,[2] lest it break thy neck with fol-
lowing. But the great one that goes upward, let him draw thee
after. When a wise man gives thee better counsel, give me
70 mine again. I would have none but knaves follow it since a
fool gives it.
[*Sings.*]   That sir which serves and seeks for gain,
And follows but for form,
Will pack° when it begins to rain,   *pack up and go*

5. Regardless of interrupting me; despite the inter-ruptions in his account (as he gasped for breath).
6. Things will get worse according to such omens.
7. Blind to their father's needs.
8. Pains, sorrows; punning on "dollar," the English term for the German "thaler," a large silver coin.
9. Hysterica . . . *sorrow*: *Hysterica passio* (a Latin expression originating in the Greek *steiros*, "suffering in the womb") was an inflammation of the senses. In

Renaissance medicine, vapors from the abdomen were thought to rise up through the body, and in women, the uterus itself was thought to wander around.
1. Ants, proverbially prudent, store food in the sum-mer and thus do not work in the winter. Implicitly, a wise person should know better than to look for suste-nance to an old man who has fallen on wintry times.
2. A great wheel is a figure for Lear and of Fortune's wheel itself, which has swung downward.

75	And leave thee in the storm,	
	But I will tarry; the Fool will stay,	
	And let the wise man fly.	
	The knave turns fool that runs away,³	
	The Fool no knave, pardie.°	*by God (pardieu)*
	Enter LEAR *and* GLOUCESTER.	
80	KENT Where learned you this, Fool?	
	FOOL Not i'th' stocks, Fool.	
	LEAR Deny to speak with me?	
	They are sick? They are weary?	
	They have traveled all the night? Mere fetches,°	*ruses; pretexts*
85	The images of revolt and flying off.⁴	
	Fetch me a better answer.	
	GLOUCESTER My dear lord,	
	You know the fiery quality° of the Duke,	*disposition*
	How unremoveable and fixed he is	
	In his own course.	
	LEAR Vengeance, plague, death, confusion!°	*destruction*
90	"Fiery"? What "quality"? Why, Gloucester, Gloucester,	
	I'll speak with the Duke of Cornwall and his wife.	
	GLOUCESTER Well, my good lord, I have informed them so.	
	LEAR Informed them? Dost thou understand me, man?	
	GLOUCESTER Ay, my good lord.	
95	LEAR The King would speak with Cornwall. The dear father	
	Would with his daughter speak, commands, tends° service.	*awaits*
	Are they informed of this? My breath and blood!	
	Fiery? The fiery Duke? Tell the hot Duke that—	
	No, but not yet; maybe he is not well.	
100	Infirmity doth still° neglect all office°	*always / obligation*
	Whereto our health is bound. We are not ourselves	
	When nature, being oppressed, commands the mind	
	To suffer with the body. I'll forbear	
	And am fallen out with my more headier will,⁵	
105	To take° the indisposed and sickly fit	*mistake*
	For the sound man. Death on my state!⁶ Wherefore°	*Why*
	Should he sit here? This act persuades me	
	That this remotion° of the Duke and her	*remoteness; aloofness*
	Is practice° only. Give me my servant forth.	*trickery*
110	Go tell the Duke and 's wife I'd speak with them	
	Now, presently.° Bid them come forth and hear me,	*at once*
	Or at their chamber door I'll beat the drum	
	Till it cry sleep to death.⁷	
	GLOUCESTER I would have all well betwixt you. *Exit.*	
115	LEAR Oh, me, my heart! My rising heart! But down.	
	FOOL Cry to it, nuncle, as the Cockney° did to the eels when	*Londoner (city woman)*
	she put 'em i'th' paste° alive. She knapped 'em o'th' coxcombs°	*pie; pastry / heads*
	with a stick and cried, "Down, wantons,° down!" 'Twas her	*rogues*
	brother that, in pure kindness to his horse, buttered his hay.⁸	

---

3. The scoundrel who runs away is the real fool.
4. *images of:* signs of. *flying off:* desertion; insurrection.
5. And disagree with my (earlier) more rash intention.
6. May my royal authority end (an oath). Ironically, this has already happened.

7. Till the noise kills sleep.
8. Like that of his sister (who wanted to make eel pie without killing the eels), his kindness was misplaced: horses will not eat buttered hay. The anecdote about the eels is reminiscent of Lear's attempt earlier in the scene to quell his grieving heart: "*Hysterica passio,* down, thou climbing sorrow."

Enter CORNWALL, REGAN, GLOUCESTER, [*and*]
    SERVANTS.

LEAR   Good morrow to you both.

120 CORNWALL   Hail to your grace.
    KENT *here set at liberty.*

REGAN   I am glad to see your highness.

LEAR   Regan, I think you are. I know what reason
   I have to think so. If thou shouldst not be glad,
   I would divorce me from thy mother's tomb,

125   Sepulch'ring° an adultress. [*to* KENT] Oh, are you free?   *Because it entombed*
   Some other time for that. —Beloved Regan,
   Thy sister's naught!° O Regan, she hath tied   *wicked; nothing*
   Sharp-toothed unkindness, like a vulture, here.[9]
   I can scarce speak to thee. Thou'lt not believe

130   With how depraved a quality—O Regan!

REGAN   I pray you, sir, take patience. I have hope
   You less know how to value her desert
   Than she to scant her duty.[1]

LEAR   Say? How is that?

REGAN   I cannot think my sister in the least

135   Would fail her obligation. If, sir, perchance
   She have restrained the riots of your followers,
   'Tis on such ground and to such wholesome end
   As clears her from all blame.

LEAR   My curses on her!

REGAN   O sir, you are old;

140   Nature° in you stands on the very verge   *Life*
   Of his confine.° You should be ruled and led   *Of its limit*
   By some discretion° that discerns your state   *discreet person*
   Better than you yourself. Therefore I pray you
   That to our sister you do make return.
   Say you have wronged her.

145 LEAR   Ask her forgiveness?
   Do you but mark how this becomes the house?[2]
   Dear daughter, I confess that I am old;
   Age° is unnecessary. [*He kneels.*] On my knees I beg   *An old man*
   That you'll vouchsafe me raiment,° bed, and food.   *promise me clothing*

150 REGAN   Good sir, no more; these are unsightly tricks.
   Return you to my sister.

LEAR [*rising*]   Never, Regan.
   She hath abated° me of half my train,   *deprived*
   Looked black upon me, struck me with her tongue
   Most serpent-like upon the very heart.

155   All° the stored vengeances of heaven fall   *Let all*
   On her ingrateful top.° Strike her young bones,   *head*
   You taking° airs, with lameness.   *infectious; malignant*

CORNWALL   Fie, sir, fie!

LEAR   You nimble lightnings, dart your blinding flames
   Into her scornful eyes. Infect her beauty,

160   You fen-sucked fogs, drawn by the pow'rful sun[3]

---

9. Lear probably gestures to his heart.
1. *I have . . . duty:* I expect that you are worse at
valuing her merit than she is at neglecting her duty.
The double negative here ("less," "scant") is acceptable Jacobean usage.

2. Do you see how appropriate this is among members of a family (spoken ironically)?
3. The sun was thought to suck poisonous vapors
from marshy ground.

To fall and blister.

REGAN   O the blest gods!
So will you wish on me when the rash mood is on.
LEAR   No, Regan, thou shalt never have my curse.
Thy tender-hafted⁴ nature shall not give
165   Thee o'er to harshness. Her eyes are fierce, but thine
Do comfort and not burn. 'Tis not in thee
To grudge my pleasures, to cut off my train,
To bandy hasty words, to scant my sizes,°   *reduce my allowances*
And, in conclusion, to oppose the bolt°   *lock the door*
170   Against my coming in. Thou better know'st
The offices° of nature, bond of childhood,   *duties*
Effects° of courtesy, dues of gratitude.   *Actions*
Thy half o'th' kingdom hast thou not forgot,
Wherein I thee endowed.
REGAN   Good sir, to th' purpose.°   *get to the point*
LEAR   Who put my man i'th' stocks?
          Enter [Oswald the] STEWARD. Tucket within.
175   CORNWALL   What trumpet's that?
REGAN   I know't my sister's; this approves° her letter   *confirms*
That she would soon be here. [*to* STEWARD] Is your lady come?
LEAR   This is a slave whose easy borrowed pride⁵
Dwells in the sickly grace of her he follows.
[*to* STEWARD] Out, varlet,° from my sight.   *wretch*
180   CORNWALL   What means your grace?
LEAR   Who stocked my servant? Regan, I have good hope
Thou didst not know on't.°   *of it*
          Enter GONERIL.
                          Who comes here? O heavens,
If you do love old men, if your sweet sway
Allow obedience, if you yourselves are old,
185   Make it your cause: send down and take my part.
[*to* GONERIL] Art not ashamed to look upon this beard?
O Regan, will you take her by the hand?
GONERIL   Why not by th' hand, sir? How have I offended?
All's not offense that indiscretion finds
190   And dotage terms so.
LEAR   O sides,⁶ you are too tough! Will you yet hold?
How came my man i'th' stocks?
CORNWALL   I set him there, sir, but his own disorders°   *disorderly behavior*
Deserved much less advancement.⁷
LEAR   You, did you?
195   REGAN   I pray you, father, being weak, seem so.°   *behave so*
If till the expiration of your month
You will return and sojourn with my sister,
Dismissing half your train, come then to me.
I am now from home and out of that provision
200   Which shall be needful for your entertainment.
LEAR   Return to her, and fifty men dismissed?
No, rather, I abjure all roofs and choose

---

4. Tenderly placed; firmly set in a tender disposition
(as a knife blade into its haft).
5. Unmerited and unpaid-for arrogance; "pride" may
also refer to Oswald's fine clothing received for his
services to Goneril.
6. Chest, where Lear's heart is swelling with emotion.
7. Deserved far worse treatment.

To wage against the enmity o'th' air,
To be a comrade with the wolf and owl,
205 Necessity's sharp pinch.[8] Return with her?
Why, the hot-blooded France, that dowerless took
Our youngest born, I could as well be brought
To knee° his throne and squire-like pension beg,   kneel to
To keep base life afoot. Return with her?
210 Persuade me rather to be slave and sumpter°   packhorse
To this detested groom.°   the Steward
GONERIL   At your choice, sir.
LEAR   I prithee, daughter, do not make me mad.
I will not trouble thee, my child; farewell.
We'll no more meet, no more see one another.
215 But yet thou art my flesh, my blood, my daughter,
Or rather a disease that's in my flesh
Which I must needs call mine. Thou art a boil,
A plague sore, or embossèd° carbuncle   a swollen
In my corrupted blood. But I'll not chide thee.
220 Let shame come when it will; I do not call° it.   call upon
I do not bid the thunder-bearer° shoot,   (Jove)
Nor tell tales of thee to high-judging Jove.
Mend° when thou canst; be better at thy leisure.   Make amends
I can be patient: I can stay with Regan,
I and my hundred knights.
225 REGAN   Not altogether so.
I looked not for° you yet, nor am provided   I did not expect
For your fit welcome. Give ear, sir, to my sister,
For those that mingle reason with your passion[9]
Must be content to think you old and so.
But she knows what she does.
230 LEAR   Is this well° spoken?   earnestly
REGAN   I dare avouch° it, sir. What, fifty followers?   vouch for
Is it not well? What should you need of more?
Yea, or so many, sith° that both charge° and danger   since / expense
Speak 'gainst so great a number? How in one house
235 Should many people under two commands
Hold amity? 'Tis hard, almost impossible.
GONERIL   Why might not you, my lord, receive attendance
From those that she calls servants, or from mine?
REGAN   Why not, my lord?
240 If then they chanced to slack° ye,   neglect
We could control them. If you will come to me—
For now I spy a danger—I entreat you
To bring but five-and-twenty; to no more
Will I give place or notice.°   acknowledgment
LEAR   I gave you all—
245 REGAN   And in good time° you gave it.   it was about time
LEAR   —Made you my guardians, my depositaries,°   trustees
But kept a reservation° to be followed   reserved a right
With such a number. What, must I come to you
With five-and-twenty, Regan? Said you so?

---

8. *To wage . . . pinch:* To counter, like predators, the   9. For those who temper your passionate argument
harshness of the elements with the hardness brought   with their own calm reasoning.
on by necessity. *pinch:* stress, pressure.

250 REGAN   And speak't again, my lord; no more with me.

LEAR   Those wicked creatures yet do look well-favored°   *attractive*
   When others are more wicked; not being the worst
   Stands in some rank of praise.[1] I'll go with thee:
   Thy fifty yet doth double five-and-twenty,
   And thou art twice her love.

255 GONERIL   Hear me, my lord.
   What need you five-and-twenty? Ten? Or five?
   To follow in a house where twice so many
   Have a command to tend you?

REGAN   What need one?

LEAR   Oh, reason not the need! Our basest beggars
260   Are in the poorest thing superfluous.[2]
   Allow not° nature more than nature needs,   *If you don't allow*
   Man's life is cheap as beast's. Thou art a lady:
   If only to go warm were gorgeous,
   Why, nature needs not what thou gorgeous wear'st,
265   Which scarcely keeps thee warm.[3] But for true need,
   You heavens, give me that patience,° patience I need!   *endurance*
   You see me here, you gods, a poor old man,
   As full of grief as age, wretched in both.
   If it be you that stirs these daughters' hearts
270   Against their father, fool me not so much
   To bear it tamely.[4] Touch me with noble anger,
   And let not women's weapons, water drops,
   Stain my man's cheeks. No, you unnatural hags,
   I will have such revenges on you both
275   That all the world shall—I will do such things—
   What they are, yet I know not, but they shall be
   The terrors of the earth! You think I'll weep.
   No, I'll not weep. I have full cause of weeping.
                    Storm and tempest.
   But this heart shall break into a hundred thousand flaws°   *fragments*
280   Or e'er° I'll weep. O Fool, I shall go mad.   *Before*
                    Exit [with GLOUCESTER, KENT, FOOL,
                         and Attendants].

CORNWALL   Let us withdraw; 'twill be a storm.

REGAN   This house is little; the old man and 's people
   Cannot be well bestowed.°   *lodged*

GONERIL   'Tis his own blame hath put himself from° rest   *deprived himself of*
285   And must needs taste his folly.

REGAN   For his particular,° I'll receive him gladly,   *single self*
   But not one follower.

GONERIL   So am I purposed.
   Where is my lord of Gloucester?
                    Enter GLOUCESTER.

CORNWALL   Followed the old man forth; he is returned.

290 GLOUCESTER   The King is in high rage.

CORNWALL   Whither is he going?

GLOUCESTER   He calls to horse, but will° I know not whither.   *will go*

CORNWALL   'Tis best to give him way; he leads himself.

---

1. Deserves some degree ("rank") of praise.
2. *Our . . . superfluous:* Even the lowliest beggars
have something more than the barest minimum.
3. *If . . . thee warm:* If gorgeousness in clothes is
measured by the warmth they provide, your elabo-

rate clothes are superfluous, for they barely cover
your body.
4. *fool . . . tamely:* do not make me so foolish as to
accept it meekly.

GONERIL   My lord, entreat him by no means to stay.
295   GLOUCESTER   Alack, the night comes on, and the high winds
Do sorely ruffle.° For many miles about   *bluster*
There's scarce a bush.
REGAN   O sir, to willful men,
The injuries that they themselves procure
Must be their schoolmasters. Shut up your doors:
300   He is attended with a desperate° train,   *violent*
And what they may incense° him to, being apt   *incite*
To have his ear abused,° wisdom bids fear.   *deceived*
CORNWALL   Shut up your doors, my lord; 'tis a wild night.
My Regan counsels well: come out o'th' storm.   *Exeunt.*

3.1

Storm still. Enter KENT [*disguised as Caius*] *and a*
GENTLEMAN, severally.°   *separately*
KENT   Who's there besides foul weather?
GENTLEMAN   One minded like the weather, most unquietly.
KENT   I know you. Where's the King?
GENTLEMAN   Contending with the fretful elements:
5   Bids the wind blow the earth into the sea,
Or swell the curlèd waters 'bove the main,°   *mainland*
That things might change or cease;
7.1   *tears his white hair,*
Which the impetuous blasts, with eyeless rage,
Catch in their fury and make nothing of;
Strives in his little world of man to outscorn
7.5   *The to-and-fro conflicting wind and rain*
This night, wherein the cub-drawn bear would couch,[1]
The lion and the belly-pinchèd wolf
Keep their fur dry. Unbonneted° *he runs*   *Hatless; uncrowned*
And bids what will take all.
KENT   But who is with him?
GENTLEMAN   None but the Fool, who labors to out-jest
His heart-struck injuries.[2]
10   KENT   Sir, I do know you
And dare upon the warrant of my note[3]
Commend a dear° thing to you. There is division,   *Entrust a crucial*
Although as yet the face of it is covered
With mutual cunning, twixt Albany and Cornwall,[4]
15   Who have—as who have not that their great stars
Throned and set high[5]—servants, who seem no less,°   *who appear as such*
Which are to France the spies and speculations°   *observers*
Intelligent[6] of our state. What hath been seen,
Either in snuffs and packings° of the Dukes,   *quarrels and plots*
20   Or the hard rein° which both of them hath borne   *treatment*

3.1 Location: Bare, open country.
1. In which even the bear, though starving, having
been sucked dry ("drawn") by its cub, would not go
out to forage.
2. *to out-jest:* to relieve with laughter; to exorcise
through ridicule. *heart-struck injuries:* injuries (from
the betrayal of his paternal love) that penetrated to
the heart.
3. On the basis of my skill (at judging people).
4. TEXTUAL COMMENT There is substantial variation
between the Quarto and Folio texts in Kent's speech

in 3.1 about the sources of political unrest. While
Kent points to French foreign invasion in the Quarto,
the Folio text presents a vision of civil unrest between
Cornwall and Albany. Some scholars have proposed
political censorship as a possible explanation for the
stark difference between Kent's speeches. See Digital Edition TC 3 (combined text).
5. *as . . . high:* as has everybody who has been favored
by destiny.
6. Supplying intelligence about; too well informed of.

Against the old kind King, or something deeper,
Whereof, perchance, these are but furnishings.°   *pretexts*
22.1   *But true it is, from France there comes a power*
         Into this scattered kingdom, who, already wise in° our   *aware of*
         negligence,
         Have secret feet in some of our best ports,
         And are at point° to show their open banner.   *ready*
22.5   *Now to you: if on my credit you dare build° so far*   *if you trust me*
         To make your speed to Dover, you shall find
         Some that will thank you, making just° report   *accurate*
         Of how unnatural and bemadding° sorrow   *maddening*
         The King hath cause to plain.°   *complain*
22.10   *I am a gentleman of blood and breeding*
         And from some knowledge and assurance
         Offer this office° to you.   *role; duty*
GENTLEMAN   I will talk further with you.
KENT   No, do not.
         For confirmation that I am much more
25   Than my out-wall,° open this purse and take   *outward appearance*
         What it contains. If you shall see Cordelia—
         As fear not but you shall—show her this ring,
         And she will tell you who that fellow° is   *(Kent himself)*
         That yet you do not know. Fie on this storm!
         I will go seek the King.
30   GENTLEMAN   Give me your hand.
         Have you no more to say?
         KENT   Few words, but to effect° more than all yet: *but in importance*
         That when we have found the King—in which your pain
         That way, I'll this[7]—he that first lights on him
35   Holla the other.   *Exeunt* [*severally*].

                              3.2
                 Storm still. Enter LEAR *and* FOOL.
         LEAR   Blow winds and crack your cheeks! Rage, blow,
         You cataracts° and hurricanos, spout   *waterspouts*
         Till you have drenched our steeples, drowned the cocks.°   *weather vanes*
         You sulph'rous and thought-executing fires,[1]
5   Vaunt-couriers° of oak-cleaving thunderbolts,   *Forerunners*
         Singe my white head. And thou, all-shaking thunder,
         Strike flat the thick rotundity o'th' world,
         Crack Nature's molds, all germens° spill at once   *seeds*
         That makes ingrateful man.
10   FOOL   O nuncle, court holy water[2] in a dry house is better
         than this rainwater out o' door. Good nuncle, in! Ask thy
         daughters' blessing. Here's a night pities neither wise men
         nor fools.
         LEAR   Rumble thy bellyful! Spit fire, spout rain!
15   Nor rain, wind, thunder, fire are my daughters.
         I tax° not you, you elements, with unkindness;   *blame*
         I never gave you kingdom, called you children.

---

7. *in which . . . this:* in which effort you will go that
way and I this way.
3.2 Location: As before.
1. *thought-executing fires:* either meaning lightning

that strikes as swiftly as thought or lightning that
puts an end to thought.
2. Sprinkled blessings of a courtier; flattery.

You owe me no subscription.° Then let fall   *obedience; allegiance*
Your horrible pleasure. Here I stand your slave,
20   A poor, infirm, weak, and despised old man.
But yet I call you servile ministers,°   *agents*
That will with two pernicious daughters join
Your high-engendered battles° 'gainst a head   *heaven-bred forces*
So old and white as this. Oh, ho! 'Tis foul.
25   FOOL   He that has a house to put 's head in has a good
     headpiece.°   *hat; brain*
     The codpiece that will house
     Before the head has any,
     The head and he shall louse;
30   So beggars marry many.[3]
     The man that makes his toe
     What he his heart should make,
     Shall of a corn cry woe
     And turn his sleep to wake.[4]
35   For there was never yet fair woman but she made mouths in
     a glass.[5]
                 Enter KENT [*disguised as Caius*].
LEAR [*sitting down*]   No, I will be the pattern of all patience.
     I will say nothing.
KENT   Who's there?
40   FOOL   Marry, here's grace and a codpiece: that's a wise man
     and a fool.[6]
KENT   Alas, sir, are you here? Things that love night
     Love not such nights as these. The wrathful skies
     Gallow° the very wanderers of the dark   *Frighten*
45   And make them keep° their caves. Since I was man,   *keep inside*
     Such sheets of fire, such bursts of horrid thunder,
     Such groans of roaring wind and rain I never
     Remember to have heard. Man's nature cannot carry°   *bear*
     Th'affliction, nor the fear.
     LEAR   Let the great gods
50   That keep this dreadful pudder° o'er our heads,   *commotion*
     Find out their enemies now. Tremble, thou wretch,
     That hast within thee undivulgèd crimes
     Unwhipped of° justice. Hide thee, thou bloody hand,   *Unpunished by*
     Thou perjured and thou simular° of virtue   *simulator; pretender*
55   That art incestuous. Caitiff,° to pieces shake,   *Wretch*
     That under covert and convenient seeming°   *fitting hypocrisy*
     Has practiced on° man's life. Close° pent-up guilts,   *against / Secret*
     Rive° your concealing continents° and cry   *Split open / coverings*
     These dreadful summoners grace.[7] I am a man
     More sinned against than sinning.

---

3. *The codpiece . . . many:* Whoever finds his penis a
lodging before providing shelter for his head will end
up in lice-infested poverty and live in married beggary. *codpiece:* a pouchlike covering for the male
genitals, often conspicuous, particularly in the costume of a fool.
4. *The man . . . wake:* The man who values an inferior part of his body over the part that is truly valuable will suffer from and lose sleep over that inferior
part.
5. She practiced making pretty faces in a mirror. The

Fool probably refers to Regan's and Goneril's vanity,
or the line may be thrown in to soften the harshness
of his satire.
6. The supposedly wise King is symbolized by royal
grace, the Fool by his codpiece (here, slang for "penis").
The Fool speaks ironically: the King, as he has pointed
out, is now the foolish one. *Marry:* By the Virgin Mary
(a mild oath).
7. *and cry . . . grace:* and pray for mercy from these
elements that bring you to justice.

60	KENT Alack, bareheaded?	

KENT   Alack, bareheaded?
    Gracious my lord, hard by here is a hovel;
    Some friendship will it lend you 'gainst the tempest.
    Repose you there, while I to this hard house°—   *household*
    More harder than the stones whereof 'tis raised,
65   Which° even but now, demanding° after you,   *Who / I demanding*
    Denied me to come in—return and force
    Their scanted° courtesy.   *grudging*
    LEAR   My wits begin to turn.
    Come on, my boy. How dost, my boy? Art cold?
    I am cold myself. Where is this straw, my fellow?
70   The art° of our necessities is strange   *skill; alchemy*
    And can make vile things precious. Come, your hovel.
    Poor fool and knave, I have one part in my heart
    That's sorry yet for thee.
    FOOL [*sings*][8]   He that has and° a little tiny wit,°   *even / sense*
75   With heigh-ho, the wind and the rain,
                Must make content with his fortunes fit,
                Though the rain it raineth every day.
    LEAR   True, boy. Come, bring us to this hovel.
                             Exeunt [LEAR *and* KENT].
    FOOL   This is a brave night to cool a courtesan.[9] I'll speak a
80   prophecy ere I go:[1]
    When priests are more in word than matter,°   *real virtue*
    When brewers mar their malt with water,
    When nobles are their tailors' tutors,[2]
    No heretics burned, but wenches' suitors,[3]
85   When every case in law is right,°   *just*
    No squire in debt, nor no poor knight,
    When slanders do not live in tongues,
    Nor cutpurses° come not to throngs,   *pickpockets*
    When usurers tell their gold i'th' field,[4]
90   And bawds and whores do churches build,
    Then shall the realm of Albion° come to great confusion.°   *Britain / decay*
    Then comes the time, who lives to see't,
    That going° shall be used° with feet.   *walking / practiced*
    This prophecy Merlin shall make, for I live before his time.[5]
                                 Exit.

3.3

Enter GLOUCESTER *and* EDMUND.

GLOUCESTER   Alack, alack, Edmund, I like not this unnatural
    dealing. When I desired their leave that I might pity° him,   *relieve*
    they took from me the use of mine own house, charged me
    on pain of perpetual displeasure neither to speak of him,
5   entreat for him, or any way sustain him.
    EDMUND   Most savage and unnatural!

---

8. The following song is an adaptation of one sung by the Clown at the end of *Twelfth Night*.
9. To cool even the hot lusts of a prostitute.
1. What follows is a parody of the pseudo-Chaucerian "Merlin's Prophecy" from *The Art of English Poesy*.
2. When noblemen follow fashion more closely than their tailors do.
3. When the only heretics burned are faithless lov-

ers, who burn from venereal disease.
4. When usurers can count their profits openly (because they have no shady dealings to hide).
5. Merlin was the great wizard at the legendary court of King Arthur. Lear's Britain is set in an even more distant past.
3.3 Location: At Gloucester's castle.

GLOUCESTER Go to,° say you nothing. There is division between   *(an expletive)*
    the Dukes and a worse matter than that. I have received a let-
    ter this night—'tis dangerous to be spoken. I have locked the
10   letter in my closet.° These injuries the King now bears will be   *private chamber*
    revenged home.° There is part of a power already footed.[1]   *to the hilt*
    We must incline to[2] the King; I will look him and privily°   *secretly; privately*
    relieve him. Go you and maintain talk with the Duke, that
    my charity be not of him perceived. If he ask for me, I am ill
15   and gone to bed. If I die for it, as no less is threatened me,
    the King my old master must be relieved. There is strange
    things toward,° Edmund. Pray you, be careful.   *Exit.*   *coming*
EDMUND This courtesy,° forbid° thee, shall the Duke   *act of kindness / forbidden*
    Instantly know, and of that letter too.
20   This seems a fair deserving[3] and must draw me
    That which my father loses: no less than all.
    The younger rises when the old doth fall.   *Exit.*

3.4

Enter LEAR, KENT [*disguised as Caius,*] *and* FOOL.
KENT Here is the place, my lord. Good my lord, enter.
    The tyranny of the open night's too rough
    For nature° to endure.   *human weakness*
         Storm still.
LEAR   Let me alone.
KENT Good my lord, enter here.
LEAR   Wilt break my heart?
5   KENT I had rather break mine own.
    Good my lord, enter.
LEAR Thou think'st 'tis much that this contentious storm
    Invades us to the skin; so 'tis to thee.
    But where the greater malady is fixed,°   *rooted*
10   The lesser is scarce felt. Thou'dst shun a bear,
    But if thy flight lay toward the roaring sea,
    Thou'dst meet the bear i'th' mouth. When the mind's free,°   *unburdened*
    The body's delicate.° The tempest in my mind   *sensitive*
    Doth from my senses take all feeling else,
15   Save° what beats there: filial ingratitude.   *Except*
    Is it not as° this mouth should tear this hand   *as if*
    For lifting food to't? But I will punish home.°   *thoroughly*
    No, I will weep no more. In such a night
    To shut me out? Pour on, I will endure.
20   In such a night as this? O Regan, Goneril,
    Your old kind father, whose frank heart gave all!
    Oh, that way madness lies. Let me shun that,
    No more of that.
KENT   Good my lord, enter here.
LEAR Prithee, go in thyself; seek thine own ease.
25   This tempest will not give me leave to° ponder   *allow me to*
    On things would hurt me more, but I'll go in.
    [*to* FOOL] In, boy, go first. You houseless poverty,°   *poor*
    Nay, get thee in; I'll pray, and then I'll sleep.   *Exit* [FOOL].

---

1. Part of an army already on the move.   3. This seems an action that deserves to be rewarded.
2. We must take the side of.   3.4 Location: Open country, before a cattle shed.

•Poor naked wretches, wheresoe'er you are,
30 That bide° the pelting of this pitiless storm,   *endure; dwell in*
    How shall your houseless heads and unfed sides,°   *starved ribs*
•Your looped and windowed[1] raggedness defend you
    From seasons such as these? Oh, I have ta'en
    Too little care of this! Take physic, pomp;[2]
35 Expose thyself to feel what wretches feel,
    That thou mayst shake the superflux[3] to them
    And show the heavens more just.

EDGAR [*within*]   Fathom and half,[4] fathom and half. Poor Tom!

          Enter FOOL.

FOOL   Come not in here, nuncle. Here's a spirit! Help me, help
40 me!

KENT   Give me thy hand. Who's there?

FOOL   A spirit, a spirit! He says his name's Poor Tom.

KENT   What art thou that dost grumble there i'th' straw? Come
    forth.

          Enter EDGAR [*disguised as Poor Tom*].

45 EDGAR   Away, the foul fiend follows me! Through the sharp haw-
    thorn blow the winds.[5] Hum, go to thy bed and warm thee.[6]

LEAR   Didst thou give all to thy daughters, and art thou come
    to this?

EDGAR   Who gives anything to Poor Tom, whom the foul fiend
50 hath led through fire and through flame, through sword and
    whirlpool, o'er bog and quagmire, that hath laid knives under
    his pillow and halters in his pew, set ratsbane by his porridge,[7]
    made him proud of heart to ride on a bay trotting horse over
    four-inched bridges,[8] to course° his own shadow for° a traitor.   *hunt / as*
55 Bless thy five wits![9] Tom's a-cold. Oh, do, de, do, de, do, de,
    bless thee from whirlwinds, star-blasting, and taking![1] Do
    Poor Tom some charity, whom the foul fiend vexes. There
    could I have him now, and there, and there again, and there.[2]
          Storm still.

LEAR   Has his daughters brought him to this pass?
60 —Couldst thou save nothing? Wouldst thou give 'em all?

FOOL   Nay, he reserved a blanket, else we had been all
    shamed.

LEAR   Now all the plagues that in the pendulous° air   *overhanging; portentous*
    Hang fated o'er men's faults light on thy daughters!
65 KENT   He hath no daughters, sir.

LEAR   Death, traitor! Nothing could have subdued nature
    To such a lowness but his unkind daughters.
    Is it the fashion that discarded fathers

---

1. *looped and windowed:* full of holes and vents; "windowed" could also refer to cloth worn through to semitransparency, like the oilcloth window "panes" of the
poor.
2. Cure yourself, pompous person.
3. Superfluity; bodily discharge, suggested by "physic"
(which also has the meaning of "purgative") in line
34. Excess here is also excess of wealth.
4. "Nine feet," a sailor's cry when taking soundings
to gauge the depth of water.
5. *Through . . . winds:* Perhaps a fragment from a
ballad.
6. *go . . . thee:* this expression is also used by the
drunken beggar Christopher Sly in *The Taming of*

the Shrew, Induction 1.
7. *laid knives . . . porridge:* these are all means by
which the foul fiend tempts Tom to commit suicide.
halters: nooses. *ratsbane:* rat poison.
8. Impossibly narrow, and probably suicidal to attempt
without diabolical help.
9. The five wits were common wit, imagination, fantasy, estimation, and memory (from medieval and
Renaissance cognitive theory).
1. *whirlwinds, star-blasting:* malign astrological influences capable of causing sickness or death. *taking:*
infection; bewitchment.
2. As Edgar speaks this sentence, he might kill vermin on his body as if they were devils.

Should have thus little mercy on their flesh?
70 Judicious punishment! 'Twas this flesh begot
Those pelican[3] daughters.
EDGAR [*sings*]   Pillicock sat on Pillicock hill, alow,
alow, loo, loo.[4]
FOOL   This cold night will turn us all to fools and madmen.
EDGAR   Take heed o'th' foul fiend, obey thy parents, keep thy
75 word's justice, swear not, commit not with man's sworn
spouse, set not thy sweetheart on proud array.[5] Tom's a-cold.
LEAR   What hast thou been?
EDGAR   A serving man, proud in heart and mind, that curled
my hair, wore gloves in my cap,[6] served the lust of my mis-
80 tress' heart and did the act of darkness with her. Swore as
many oaths as I spake words and broke them in the sweet
face of heaven. One that slept in the contriving of lust and
waked to do it. Wine loved I dearly, dice dearly, and in woman
out-paramoured the Turk.[7] False of heart, light of ear,° bloody   *rumor-hungry*
85 of hand. Hog in sloth, fox in stealth, wolf in greediness, dog
in madness, lion in prey. Let not the creaking of shoes[8] nor
the rustling of silks betray thy poor heart to woman. Keep thy
foot[9] out of brothels, thy hand out of plackets,[1] thy pen from
lender's books, and defy the foul fiend. Still through the haw-
90 thorn blows the cold wind, says suum, mun, nonny. Dolphin,
my boy, boy, cease. Let him trot by.[2]
        Storm still.
LEAR   Thou wert better in a grave than to answer° with thy   *encounter*
uncovered body this extremity of the skies.° Is man no more   *violent weather*
than this? Consider him well. Thou ow'st the worm no silk,
95 the beast no hide, the sheep no wool, the cat[3] no perfume.
Ha? Here's three on 's° are sophisticated. Thou art the thing   *of us*
itself. Unaccommodated[4] man is no more but such a poor,
bare, forked° animal as thou art. [*He begins to undress.*] Off,   *two-legged*
off, you lendings.° Come, unbutton here.   *borrowed clothes*
        Enter GLOUCESTER, *with a torch.*
100 FOOL   Prithee, nuncle, be contented. 'Tis a naughty° night to   *foul*
swim in. Now a little fire in a wild° field were like an old   *barren; lustful*
lecher's heart: a small spark, all the rest on 's° body cold.   *of his*
Look, here comes a walking fire.
EDGAR   This is the foul Flibbertigibbet![5] He begins at curfew°   *9:00 p.m.*
105 and walks at first cock.° He gives the web and the pin,[6]   *midnight*
squints the eye and makes the harelip, mildews the white°   *near-ripe*
wheat, and hurts the poor creature of earth.

---

3. Greedy. Young pelicans were reputed to feed on blood from the wounds they made in their mother's breast; in some versions, they first killed their father.
4. A fragment of an old rhyme, followed by hunting cries or a ballad refrain; "Pillicock" was both a term of endearment and a euphemism for "penis."
5. *obey . . . array:* these are fragments from the Ten Commandments.
6. Favors from his mistress. In Petrarchan poetry, wooers are "servants" to their ladies.
7. And had more women than the Turkish sultan had in his royal harem.
8. Creaking shoes were a fashionable affectation.
9. Punning on the French *foutre* ("fuck").

1. Slits in skirts or petticoats.
2. These phrases are probably snatches from songs and proverbs. *Dolphin:* dauphin; the heir to the French throne, sometimes identified with the devil by the English.
3. Civet, in Shakespeare's time the major source of musk for perfume.
4. Naked; without the trappings of civilization.
5. A devil drawn from folk beliefs but famous for his prominent place in Samuel Harsnett's *Declaration of Egregious Popish Impostures* (1603); the frequent borrowings from Harsnett in *King Lear* set the earliest possible composition date for the play.
6. *web and the pin:* cataract.

Swithold footed thrice the old,[7]
He met the night mare and her nine-fold;[8]
110 Bid her alight and her troth plight,°   *and gave her word*
And aroint thee,° witch, aroint thee.   *begone*

KENT   How fares your grace?
LEAR   What's° he?   *Who's*
KENT   Who's there? What is't you seek?
115 GLOUCESTER   What are you there? Your names?
EDGAR   Poor Tom, that eats the swimming frog, the toad, the
tadpole, the wall-newt, and the water,° that in the fury of his   *water newt*
heart, when the foul fiend rages, eats cow dung for salads,
swallows the old rat and the ditch dog,[9] drinks the green
120 mantle° of the standing pool, who is whipped from tithing°   *scum / parish*
to tithing and stocked,° punished, and imprisoned, who hath   *put in stocks*
three suits to his back, six shirts to his body.
Horse to ride, and weapon to wear.
But mice and rats and such small deer[1]
125 Have been Tom's food for seven long year.
Beware my follower! Peace, Smulkin!° Peace, thou fiend.   *(a Harsnett devil)*
GLOUCESTER   What, hath your grace no better company?
EDGAR   The Prince of Darkness is a gentleman. Modo he's
called and Mahu.[2]
130 GLOUCESTER   Our flesh and blood, my lord, is grown so vile
That it doth hate what gets° it.   *begets*
EDGAR   Poor Tom's a-cold.
GLOUCESTER   Go in with me. My duty cannot suffer°   *permit me*
T'obey in all your daughters' hard commands.
135 Though their injunction be to bar my doors
And let this tyrannous night take hold upon you,
Yet have I ventured to come seek you out
And bring you where both fire and food is ready.
LEAR   First let me talk with this philosopher.
140 [*to* EDGAR] What is the cause of thunder?
KENT   Good my lord, take his offer;
Go into th' house.
LEAR   I'll talk a word with this same learned Theban.°   *(Greek sage)*
What is your study?°   *field of expertise*
145 EDGAR   How to prevent the fiend and to kill vermin.
LEAR   Let me ask you one word in private.
KENT [*to* GLOUCESTER]   Importune him once more to go, my lord,
His wits begin t'unsettle.
GLOUCESTER   Canst thou blame him?
       Storm still.
His daughters seek his death. Ah, that good Kent,
150 He said it would be thus, poor banished man!
Thou sayest the King grows mad. I'll tell thee, friend,
I am almost mad myself. I had a son,
Now outlawed° from my blood. He sought my life   *disowned*

---

7. St. Swithin (or Withold), an early English saint
famous for healing, traversed the hilly countryside
three times. *old:* wold; uplands.
8. *night mare:* a demon, not necessarily in the shape
of a horse; *nine-fold* might suggest an entourage of
demons and familiars, or the many folds (coils) of a
snake.

9. A dog found dead in a ditch.
1. *deer:* animals. These verses are adapted from a
romance popular in Shakespeare's time, *Bevis of
Hampton.*
2. Modo and Mahu, more Harsnett devils, were commanding generals of the hellish troops.

But lately, very late.° I loved him, friend,   *recently*
155   No father his son dearer. True to tell thee,
The grief hath crazed my wits. What a night's this?
I do beseech your grace—

LEAR   Oh, cry you mercy,° sir.   *beg your pardon*
—Noble philosopher, your company.

EDGAR   Tom's a-cold.

GLOUCESTER [*to* EDGAR]   In, fellow, there: into th' hovel.
160   Keep thee warm.

LEAR   Come, let's in all.

KENT   This way, my lord.

LEAR   With him
I will keep still, with my philosopher.

KENT [*to* GLOUCESTER]   Good my lord, soothe° him.   *humor*
Let him take the fellow.

GLOUCESTER   Take him you on.°   *on ahead*
165 KENT   Sirrah, come on. Go along with us.

LEAR   Come, good Athenian.°   *Greek philosopher*

GLOUCESTER   No words, no words, hush.

EDGAR   Child Rowland[3] to the dark tower came,
His word° was still° "Fie, fo, and fum;   *motto / always*
170   I smell the blood of a British[4] man."   *Exeunt.*

3.5

Enter CORNWALL *and* EDMUND.

CORNWALL   I will have my revenge ere I depart his house.

EDMUND   How, my lord I may be censured,° that nature° thus   *judged / kinship*
gives way to loyalty, something fears me° to think of.   *I am somewhat afraid*

5 CORNWALL   I now perceive it was not altogether your brother's
evil disposition made him seek his° death, but a provoking   *(Gloucester's)*
merit set a-work by a reproveable badness in himself.[1]

EDMUND   How malicious is my fortune that I must repent to
be just! This is the letter which he spoke of, which approves
him an intelligent party to the advantages of France.[2]
10   O heavens, that this treason were not, or not I the detector.

CORNWALL   Go with me to the Duchess.

EDMUND   If the matter of this paper be certain, you have mighty
business in hand.

CORNWALL   True or false, it hath made thee Earl of Glouces-
15   ter. Seek out where thy father is that he may be ready for our
apprehension.°   *arrest*

EDMUND [*aside*]   If I find him comforting the King, it will
stuff his° suspicion more fully. [*to* CORNWALL] I will per-   *(Cornwall's)*
severe in my course of loyalty, though the conflict be sore
20   between that and my blood.°   *filial duty*

CORNWALL   I will lay trust upon thee, and thou shalt find a
dear father in my love.   *Exeunt.*

---

3. *Child*: an aspirant to knighthood. Roland is the famous hero of the Charlemagne legends.
4. "An Englishman" usually appears in this rhyme from the cycle of tales of which "Jack and the Beanstalk" is the best known. The alteration befits Lear's ancient Britain.
3.5 Location: At Gloucester's castle.

1. *a provoking . . . himself*: Gloucester's own wickedness deservedly triggered the blameworthy evil in Edgar.
2. *which . . . France*: which proves him a spy and an informer in the aid of France; "party," or faction, was usually a term of opprobrium in the Renaissance.

3.6

Enter KENT *[disguised as Caius] and* GLOUCESTER.

GLOUCESTER   Here is better than the open air; take it thankfully. I will piece out° the comfort with what addition I can.   *augment*
I will not be long from you.

KENT   All the power of his wits have given way to his impa-
5   tience.[1] The gods° reward your kindness.   *May the gods*

Exit [GLOUCESTER].

Enter LEAR, EDGAR *[disguised as Poor Tom,]*
and FOOL.

EDGAR   Fraterretto° calls me and tells me Nero is an angler in   *(a Harsnett devil)*
the lake of darkness.[2] Pray, innocent, and beware the foul
fiend.

FOOL   Prithee, nuncle, tell me whether a madman be a gentle-
10   man or a yeoman.[3]

LEAR   A king, a king.

FOOL   No, he's a yeoman that has a gentleman to° his son, for   *for*
he's a mad yeoman that sees his son a gentleman before him.

LEAR   To have a thousand with red burning spits
15   Come hizzing in upon 'em.

15.1   EDGAR   *The foul fiend bites my back.[4]*

FOOL   *He's mad that trusts in the tameness of a wolf, a*
horse's health, a boy's love, or a whore's oath.

LEAR   *It shall be done; I will arraign° them straight.°*   *prosecute / immediately*
15.5   *[to* EDGAR*] Come, sit thou here, most learned Justice.*
[to the FOOL*] Thou, sapient sir, sit here —No, you she-foxes—*

EDGAR   *Look where he stands and glares. Want'st thou*
eyes° at trial, madam?   *observers*
[Sings.]   *Come o'er the broom, Bessy, to me.[5]*

15.10   FOOL *[sings]*   *Her boat hath a leak,[6]*
And she must not speak,
Why she dares not come over to thee.

EDGAR   *The foul fiend haunts poor Tom in the voice of a*
nightingale. Hoppedance° cries in Tom's belly for two   *(a demon)*
15.15   *white° herring. Croak° not, black angel. I have no food*   *fresh / Growl*
for thee.

KENT *[to* LEAR*]   How do you, sir? Stand you not so amazed.*
Will you lie down and rest upon the cushions?

LEAR   *I'll see their trial first: bring in their evidence.*
15.20   *[to* EDGAR*] Thou robèd man of justice, take thy place,*
[to the FOOL*] And thou, his yokefellow of equity,°*   *partner of law*
Bench° by his side. You are o'th' commission:° sit you too.   *Sit / judiciary*

EDGAR   *Let us deal justly.*
[Sings.]   *Sleepest or wakest, thou jolly shepherd?*
15.25   *Thy sheep be in the corn,°*   *grain*
And for one blast of thy minikin° mouth,   *dainty*
Thy sheep shall take no harm.

3.6 Location: Within an outbuilding of Gloucester's.
1. Rage; inability to bear more suffering.
2. In Chaucer's *Monk's Tale*, the infamously cruel
Roman emperor Nero is found fishing in hell (lines
485–86).
3. A free landowner but not a member of the gentry,
lacking official family arms and the distinctions they
confer. Shakespeare seems to have procured a coat of
arms for his father in 1596.

4. TEXTUAL COMMENT Lear's "mock-trial" of Goneril
and Regan, in absentia, appears only in Q1 (3.6.12
–48). The trial does not appear in F and was probably
cut by Shakespeare rather than omitted due to a
printer's error. See Digital Edition TC 4 (combined
text).
5. From an old song. *broom*: a small stream.
6. She has venereal disease.

Purr, the cat is gray.[7]

15.30   LEAR   *Arraign her first: 'tis Goneril: I here take my oath*
        before this honorable assembly, kicked the poor King
        her father.

    FOOL   *Come hither, mistress. Is your name Goneril?*

    LEAR   *She cannot deny it.*

    FOOL   *Cry you mercy, I took you for a joint-stool.*[8]

15.35   LEAR   *And here's another whose warped looks proclaim*
        What store° her heart is made on.° Stop her there.   *material / of*
        Arms, arms, sword, fire, corruption in the place!
        False Justicer, why hast thou let her scape?

    EDGAR   Bless thy five wits.

    KENT   Oh, pity. Sir, where is the patience now
        That you so oft have boasted to retain?

    EDGAR *[aside]*   My tears begin to take his part so much

20   They mar my counterfeiting.

    LEAR   The little dogs and all,°   *Even the little dogs*
        Trey, Blanche, and Sweetheart, see, they bark at me.

    EDGAR   Tom will throw his head at° them. Avaunt,° you curs!   *will threaten (?) / Begone*
        Be thy mouth or° black or white,   *either*

25   Tooth that poisons° if it bite,   *gives rabies*
        Mastiff, greyhound, mongrel grim,
        Hound or spaniel, brach,° or him,   *bitch*
        Or bobtail tyke, or trundle tail,[9]
        Tom will make him weep and wail;

30   For with throwing thus my head,
        Dogs leapt the hatch[1] and all are fled.
        Do, de, de, de. Sessa.[2] Come, march to wakes,° and fairs, and   *parish festivals*
        market towns. Poor Tom, thy horn is dry.[3]

    LEAR   Then let them anatomize° Regan, see what breeds about   *dissect*
35   her heart. Is there any cause in nature that makes these
        hard hearts? *[to* EDGAR*]* You, sir, I entertain° for one of my   *retain*
        hundred, only I do not like the fashion of your garments.
        You will say they are Persian,° but let them be changed.   *oriental; splendid*

    KENT   Now, good my lord, lie here and rest awhile.

40   LEAR   Make no noise, make no noise. Draw the curtains,° so,   *bed curtains*
        so. We'll go to supper i'th' morning.

    FOOL   And I'll go to bed at noon.

           Enter GLOUCESTER.

    GLOUCESTER   Come hither, friend. Where is the King my master?

    KENT   Here, sir, but trouble him not. His wits are gone.

45   GLOUCESTER   Good friend, I prithee, take him in thy arms.
        I have o'erheard a plot of death upon° him.   *against*
        There is a litter ready: lay him in't
        And drive toward Dover, friend, where thou shalt meet
        Both welcome and protection. Take up thy master;

50   If thou shouldst dally half an hour, his life
        With thine and all that offer to defend him

---

7. Purr the cat is another devil; such devils in the shape of cats were the familiars of witches.

8. I beg your pardon, I mistook you for a stool. An idiom of the day expressing annoyance at being slighted. Here the part of Goneril is actually being played by a stool.

9. Short-tailed mongrel, or long-tailed.

1. Dogs leap over the lower half of a divided door.

2. Apparently nonsense, although "Sessa" may be a version of the French *cessez* ("stop" or "hush").

3. A begging formula that refers to the horn vessel that vagabonds carried for drink; the covert sense is that Edgar has run out of Bedlamite inspiration.

Stand in assurèd loss.° Take up, take up,   *Are certainly doomed*
And follow me, that will to some provision
Give thee quick conduct.⁴

54.1   KENT   *Oppressed nature sleeps.*
This rest might yet have balmed° thy broken sinews,°   *soothed / nerves*
Which, if convenience will not allow,
Stand in hard cure.° [to the FOOL] *Come, help to bear*   *Will be hard to cure*
thy master.

54.5   *Thou must not stay behind.*

55   GLOUCESTER   *Come, come away.*   *Exeunt [all but* EDGAR].

55.1   EDGAR   *When we our betters see bearing our° woes,*   *our same*
We scarcely think our miseries our foes.
Who alone suffers, suffers most i'th' mind,
Leaving free° things and happy shows° behind.   *carefree / scenes*

55.5   *But then the mind much sufferance doth o'er-skip,*
When grief hath mates and bearing° fellowship.   *pain; suffering*
How light and portable my pain seems now,
When that which makes me bend makes the King bow:
He° childed as I fathered. Tom, away.   *He is*

55.10   *Mark the high noises° and thyself bewray°*   *important rumors / reveal*
When false opinion, whose wrong thoughts defile thee,
In thy just proof repeals and reconciles thee.⁵
What° will hap° more tonight, safe scape the King.   *Whatever / chance*
Lurk, lurk.   [*Exit.*]

3.7

Enter CORNWALL, REGAN, GONERIL, [EDMUND *the*]
bastard, and SERVANTS.

CORNWALL [*to* GONERIL]   Post° speedily to my lord, your hus-   *Ride*
band; show him this letter. The army of France is landed.
[*to* SERVANTS] Seek out the traitor Gloucester.

[*Exeunt* SERVANTS.]

REGAN   Hang him instantly.

5   GONERIL   Pluck out his eyes.

CORNWALL   Leave him to my displeasure. Edmund, keep you
our sister° company. The revenges we are bound¹ to take   *sister-in-law*
upon your traitorous father are not fit for your beholding.
Advise the Duke where you are going to a most festinate

10   preparation.² We are bound° to the like. Our posts° shall be   *committed / messengers*
swift and intelligent° betwixt us. Farewell, dear sister. Fare-   *well informed*
well, my lord of Gloucester.

Enter [Oswald the] STEWARD.

How now? Where's the King?

STEWARD   My lord of Gloucester hath conveyed him hence.

15   Some five- or six-and-thirty of his° knights,   *(Lear's)*
Hot questrists° after him, met him at gate,   *searchers*
Who, with some other of the lord's° dependents,   *(Gloucester's)*
Are gone with him toward Dover, where they boast
To have well-armed friends.

20   CORNWALL   Get horses for your mistress.

---

4. *that . . . conduct:* who will quickly guide you to
some supplies.
5. *In . . . thee:* When true evidence pardons you and
reconciles you (with your father).

3.7 Location: At Gloucester's castle.
1. Bound by duty; expected by destiny.
2. *Advise . . . preparation:* When you reach Albany,
tell the Duke to prepare quickly.

GONERIL   Farewell, sweet lord and sister.

CORNWALL   Edmund, farewell.

Exeunt GONERIL [*and* EDMUND].

Go seek the traitor Gloucester;

Pinion him° like a thief, bring him before us.   *Tie his arms*

Though well we may not pass° upon his life   *pass sentence*

25   Without the form° of justice, yet our power   *official proceedings*

Shall do a court'sy³ to our wrath, which men

May blame but not control.

Enter GLOUCESTER *and* SERVANTS.

Who's there? The traitor?

REGAN   Ingrateful fox, 'tis he.

CORNWALL   Bind fast his corky° arms.   *withered*

GLOUCESTER   What means your graces? Good my friends, consider

30   You are my guests. Do me no foul play, friends.

CORNWALL   Bind him, I say.

[SERVANTS *bind* GLOUCESTER.]

REGAN   Hard, hard! O filthy traitor!

GLOUCESTER   Unmerciful lady, as you are, I'm none.

CORNWALL   To this chair bind him. —Villain, thou shalt find—

GLOUCESTER   By the kind gods, 'tis most ignobly done

35   To pluck me by the beard.°   *(an extreme insult)*

REGAN   So white° and such a traitor?   *white-haired; venerable*

GLOUCESTER   Naughty° lady,   *Wicked*

These hairs which thou dost ravish from my chin

Will quicken° and accuse thee. I am your host;   *come alive*

With robbers' hands my hospitable favors°   *features*

40   You should not ruffle° thus. What will you do?   *snatch at*

CORNWALL   Come, sir, what letters had you late° from France?   *lately*

REGAN   Be simple-answered,° for we know the truth.   *straightforward*

CORNWALL   And what confederacy have you with the traitors

Late footed° in the kingdom?   *Recently on the move*

REGAN   To whose hands

45   You have sent the lunatic King? Speak.

GLOUCESTER   I have a letter guessingly set down⁴

Which came from one that's of a neutral heart

And not from one opposed.

CORNWALL   Cunning.

REGAN   And false.

CORNWALL   Where hast thou sent the King?

50   GLOUCESTER   To Dover.

REGAN   Wherefore° to Dover?   *Why*

Wast thou not charged° at peril—   *commanded*

CORNWALL   Wherefore to Dover? Let him answer that.

GLOUCESTER   I am tied to th' stake, and I must stand the course.⁵

55   REGAN   Wherefore to Dover?

GLOUCESTER   Because I would not see thy cruel nails

Pluck out his poor old eyes, nor thy fierce sister

---

3. Shall allow a courtesy or an indulgence; shall bow to.   5. An image from bearbaiting, in which a bear on a
4. Written without confirmation; speculative.   short tether had to fight off an assault by dogs.

In his anointed[6] flesh stick boarish fangs.
The sea, with such a storm as his bare head
60 In hell-black night endured, would have buoyed° up   risen
And quenched the stellèd° fires.   stars'
Yet poor old heart, he holp° the heavens to rain.   helped
If wolves had at thy gate howled that stern° time,   dreary; dreadful
Thou shouldst have said, "Good porter, turn the key,"°   (to open the door)
65 All cruels else subscribe."[7] But I shall see
The wingèd vengeance[8] overtake such children.
CORNWALL   See't shalt thou never. Fellows,° hold the chair.   Servants
    —Upon these eyes of thine, I'll set my foot.
        [*He plucks out Gloucester's eye.*]
GLOUCESTER   He that will think° to live till he be old,   Whoever hopes
70 Give me some help! —Oh, cruel! O you gods!
REGAN   One side will mock another: th'other too.
CORNWALL   If you see vengeance—
FIRST SERVANT   Hold your hand, my lord.
    I have served you ever since I was a child,
    But better service have I never done you
    Than now to bid you hold.
75 REGAN   How now, you dog?
FIRST SERVANT   If you did wear a beard upon your chin,
    I'd shake it on this quarrel.[9] What do you mean?°   intend
CORNWALL [*drawing his sword*]   My villein?°   servant; villain
FIRST SERVANT   Nay, then, come on and take the chance of
        anger.[1]
        [*They fight, and* CORNWALL *is wounded.*]
80 REGAN   Give me thy sword. A peasant stand up thus?
        [*She*] kills him.
FIRST SERVANT   Oh, I am slain! [*to* GLOUCESTER] My lord, you
        have one eye left
    To see some mischief° on him. Oh!   injury
        [*He dies.*]
CORNWALL   Lest it see more, prevent it. Out, vile jelly![2]
        [*He plucks out Gloucester's other eye.*]
    Where is thy luster now?
85 GLOUCESTER   All dark and comfortless?
    Where's my son Edmund?
    Edmund, enkindle all the sparks of nature[3]
    To quit° this horrid act.   requite; avenge
REGAN   Out, treacherous villain!
    Thou call'st on him that hates thee. It was he
90 That made the overture of° thy treasons to us,   revealed
    Who is too good to pity thee.
GLOUCESTER   Oh, my follies! Then Edgar was abused!°   slandered
    Kind gods, forgive me that, and prosper him.
REGAN   Go, thrust him out at gates, and let him smell
95 His way to Dover. How is't, my lord? How look you?°   How do you feel

6. Consecrated with holy oils (as part of a king's coronation).
7. All other beasts would have pity, but not you; I can accept the cruelty of all creatures, but not yours.
8. Swift or heaven-sent revenge; either an angel of God or the Furies, who were flying executors of divine vengeance in classical mythology.
9. I'd pluck it over this point; I'd issue a challenge.

1. Take the risk of fighting when angry; take the fortune of one who is governed by his anger.
2. PERFORMANCE COMMENT Should a production minimize gore in this shocking scene, or emphasize it? For the implications of the staging, see Digital Edition PC 4.
3. All the warmth of filial love; all the anger that your father has received such treatment.

CORNWALL   I have received a hurt. Follow me, lady.
    [*to* SERVANTS] Turn out that eyeless villain. Throw this slave
    Upon the dunghill.
                                    Exeunt [SERVANTS] *with* GLOUCESTER
                                        [*and First Servant's body*].
                        Regan, I bleed apace;
    Untimely comes this hurt. Give me your arm.
                                    Exeunt [CORNWALL *with* REGAN].[4]

99.1   SECOND SERVANT   *I'll never care what wickedness I do if*
        this man come to good.[5]
        THIRD SERVANT   *If she live long, and in the end meet the*
            old° course of death, women will all turn monsters.   usual
99.5   SECOND SERVANT   *Let's follow the old Earl and get the*
            Bedlam° to lead him where he would. His madness   madman
            allows itself to anything.
        THIRD SERVANT   *Go thou. I'll fetch some flax and whites of*
            eggs to apply to his bleeding face. Now, heaven help him!
                                    Exeunt [*severally*].°   separately

4.1
        Enter EDGAR [*disguised as Poor Tom*].
    EDGAR   Yet better thus and known to be contemned°   despised
        Than still° contemned and flattered. To be worst,   always
        The lowest and most dejected thing of fortune
        Stands still in esperance, lives not in fear.[1]
5   The lamentable change is from the best,
        The worst returns to laughter.[2] Welcome, then,
        Thou unsubstantial air that I embrace.
        The wretch that thou hast blown unto the worst
        Owes nothing° to thy blasts.   (*because he can't pay*)
            Enter GLOUCESTER *and an* OLD MAN.
10   But who comes here? My father, poorly led?
        World, world, O world!
        But that thy strange mutations make us hate thee,
        Life would not yield to age.[3]
    OLD MAN   O my good lord, I have been your tenant
15   And your father's tenant these fourscore years.
    GLOUCESTER   Away, get thee away! Good friend, be gone.
        Thy comforts° can do me no good at all;   assistance
        Thee, they may hurt.
    OLD MAN   You cannot see your way.
    GLOUCESTER   I have no way and therefore want no eyes.
20   I stumbled when I saw. Full oft 'tis seen
        Our means secure us, and our mere defects
        Prove our commodities.[4] O dear son Edgar,
        The food° of thy abusèd° father's wrath,   fuel; prey / despised

---

4. TEXTUAL COMMENT Some critics have called the play's blinding scene the "cruelest" in all of English literature. Yet the two texts differ in their portrayals of this cruelty. Notably, the Quarto version culminates with Cornwall's two servants pledging to avenge Gloucester's blinding. Their absence in the Folio version denies the audience even this brief expression of sympathy. See Digital Edition TC 5 (combined text).
5. *I'll . . . good*: because this may be a sign that evil goes unpunished. *this man*: Cornwall.
4.1 Location: Open country.

1. *Stands . . . fear*: Remains in hope ("esperance") because there is no fear of falling further.
2. *The lamentable . . . laughter*: The change to be lamented is one that alters the best of circumstances; the worst luck can only improve.
3. *But . . . age*: If there were no strange reversals of fortune to make the world hateful, we would not consent to aging and death.
4. *Our means . . . commodities*: Our wealth makes us overconfident, and our utter deprivation proves to be beneficial.

Might I but live to see thee in° my touch,   *through*
I'd say I had eyes again.
25 OLD MAN   How now? Who's there?
EDGAR [*aside*]   O gods! Who is't can say, "I am at the worst"?
I am worse than e'er I was.
OLD MAN   'Tis poor mad Tom.
EDGAR [*aside*]   And worse I may be yet; the worst is not
So long as we can say, "This is the worst."
OLD MAN   Fellow, where goest?
30 GLOUCESTER   Is it a beggar man?
OLD MAN   Madman and beggar too.
GLOUCESTER   He has some reason, else he could not beg.
I'th' last night's storm, I such a fellow saw
Which made me think a man a worm. My son
35 Came then into my mind, and yet my mind
Was then scarce friends with him.
I have heard more since.
As flies to wanton° boys are we to th' gods: *playful; careless*
They kill us for their sport.
EDGAR [*aside*]   How should this be?
40 Bad is the trade that must play fool to sorrow,[5]
Ang'ring itself and others. [*to* GLOUCESTER] Bless thee,
master.
GLOUCESTER   Is that the naked fellow?
OLD MAN   Ay, my lord.
GLOUCESTER   Get thee away. If for my sake
Thou wilt o'ertake us hence a mile or twain
45 I'th' way toward Dover, do it for ancient love,[6]
And bring some covering for this naked soul,
Which I'll entreat to lead me.
OLD MAN   Alack, sir, he is mad.
GLOUCESTER   'Tis the time's plague when[7] madmen lead the
blind.
Do as I bid thee, or rather do thy pleasure.
50 Above the rest, be gone.
OLD MAN   I'll bring him the best 'parrel° that I have,   *apparel; clothing*
Come on't what will.   *Exit.*
GLOUCESTER   Sirrah, naked fellow—
EDGAR   Poor Tom's a-cold. [*aside*] I cannot daub it further.[8]
55 GLOUCESTER   Come hither, fellow.
EDGAR [*aside*]   And yet I must. —Bless thy sweet eyes, they
bleed.
GLOUCESTER   Know'st thou the way to Dover?
EDGAR   Both stile and gate, horse-way and footpath. Poor
60 Tom hath been scared out of his good wits. Bless thee, goodman's° son, from the foul fiend.   *householder's*
61.1   *Five fiends have been in*
poor Tom at once: of lust, as Obidicut; Hobbididence,
prince of dumbness; Mahu of stealing; Modo of mur-
der; Stiberdigebit of mopping and mowing,[9] who since
61.5   *possesses chambermaids and waiting women. So bless*
thee, master.

---

5. It is a bad business to have to play the fool in the
face of sorrow.
6. For the sake of our long and loyal relationship (as
master and servant).

7. The time is truly sick when.
8. I cannot continue the charade. *daub*: mask, plaster.
9. Grimacing and making faces.

GLOUCESTER   Here, take this purse, thou whom the heav'ns'
 plagues
 Have humbled to all strokes.° That I am wretched   *to accept all blows*
 Makes thee the happier. Heavens deal so still.°   *always*
65 Let the superfluous and lust-dieted man,[1]
 That slaves° your ordinance,° that will not see   *defers to / authority*
 Because he does not feel, feel your power quickly.
 So distribution should undo excess,
 And each man have enough. Dost thou know Dover?
70 EDGAR   Ay, master.
 GLOUCESTER   There is a cliff whose high and bending° head   *overhanging*
 Looks fearfully in the confinèd deep.[2]
 Bring me but to the very brim of it,
 And I'll repair the misery thou dost bear
75 With something rich about me. From that place
 I shall no leading need.
 EDGAR   Give me thy arm;
 Poor Tom shall lead thee.   *Exeunt.*

4.2

Enter GONERIL, [EDMUND *the*] *bastard, and* [Oswald
the] STEWARD.

GONERIL   Welcome, my lord. I marvel our mild husband
 Not° met us on the way. [*to* STEWARD] Now, where's your *Has not*
 master?
 STEWARD   Madam, within, but never man so changed.
 I told him of the army that was landed:
5 He smiled at it. I told him you were coming.
 His answer was, "The worse." Of Gloucester's treachery,
 And of the loyal service of his son,
 When I informed him, then he called me "sot"°   *fool*
 And told me I had turned the wrong side out.[1]
10 What most he should dislike seems pleasant to him;
 What like, offensive.
 GONERIL [*to* EDMUND] Then shall you go no further.
 It is the cowish° terror of his spirit   *cowardly*
 That dares not undertake. He'll not feel wrongs
 Which tie him to an answer.[2] Our wishes on the way
15 May prove effects.[3] Back, Edmund, to my brother;° *brother-in-law*
 Hasten his musters° and conduct his powers.° *call-up of troops / armies*
 I must change names° at home and give the distaff[4] *exchange roles*
 Into my husband's hands. This trusty servant
 Shall pass between us. Ere long you are like° to hear— *likely*
20 If you dare venture in your own behalf—
 A mistress's° command. Wear this; spare speech; *(playing on "lover's")*
 Decline your head. This kiss, if it durst speak,
 Would stretch thy spirits up into the air.
 Conceive,° and fare thee well.   *Understand my meaning*
 EDMUND   Yours in° the ranks of death.   *Exit.* *even in*

---

1. Let the overprosperous man who indulges his
appetite.
2. Looks fearsomely into the straits below.
4.2 Location: Before Albany's castle.
1. I had reversed things (by mistaking loyalty for
treachery).

2. *He'll . . . answer:* He'll ignore insults that would
provoke him to retaliate.
3. May be put into action.
4. A device used in spinning and thus emblematic of
the female role. To "change names," therefore, is to
swap the marking of male and female identities.

25 GONERIL   My most dear Gloucester!
     Oh, the difference of man and man!
     To thee a woman's services are due;
     My fool usurps my body.[5]
   STEWARD   Madam, here comes my lord.   [*Exit.*]
             Enter ALBANY.
   GONERIL   I have been worth the whistle.[6]
30 ALBANY   O Goneril,
     You are not worth the dust which the rude wind
     Blows in your face.
32.1   *I fear your disposition.*
     That nature which contemns i'th' origin°   despises its origin
     Cannot be bordered certain° *in itself.*   be defended securely
     She that herself will sliver and disbranch°   split
32.5 *From her material sap, perforce must wither*
     And come to deadly use.[7]
   GONERIL   *No more, the text is foolish.*
   ALBANY   *Wisdom and goodness to the vile seem vile;*
     Filths savor but themselves. What have you done?
32.10 *Tigers, not daughters, what have you performed?*
     A father and a gracious agèd man,
     Whose reverence even the head-lugged° *bear would lick,*   dragged by the head
     Most barbarous, most degenerate, have you madded.°   driven mad
     Could my good brother° *suffer you to do it?*   brother-in-law
32.15 *A man, a prince, by him so benefited!*
     If that the heavens do not their visible spirits
     Send quickly down to tame the vile offenses,
     It will come.
     Humanity must perforce° *prey on itself*   inevitably
32.20 *Like monsters of the deep.*
   GONERIL   Milk-livered° man,   Cowardly
     That bear'st a cheek for blows, a head for wrongs,[8]
35   Who hast not in thy brows an eye discerning
     Thine honor from thy suffering,[9]
36.1   *that not know'st*
     Fools do those villains pity who are punished
     Ere they have done their mischief. Where's thy drum?°   (to muster troops)
     France spreads his banners in our noiseless° *land*   peaceful
36.5 *With plumèd helm. Thy state begins thereat*
     Whilst thou, a moral° *fool, sits still and cries,*   moralizing
     "Alack, why does he so?"
   ALBANY   See thyself, devil!
     Proper deformity seems not in the fiend
     So horrid as in woman.[1]
   GONERIL   O vain° fool!   useless
39.1   ALBANY   *Thou changèd, and self-covered*[2] *thing, for shame!*
     Bemonster not thy feature. Were't my fitness°   If it were appropriate

---

5. My idiot husband presumes to possess me.
6. At one time, you would have come to welcome me
home; referring to the proverb "It is a poor dog that is
not worth the whistling."
7. *She . . . use:* The allusion is probably biblical: "But
that which beareth thorns and briers is reproved, and
is near unto cursing; whose end is to be burned"
(Hebrews 6:8). *come to deadly use:* be destroyed; be
used for burning.
8. *for wrongs:* fit for abuse; ready for cuckold's horns.

9. *discerning . . . suffering:* that can distinguish
between an insult to your honor and something you
should patiently endure.
1. *Proper . . . woman:* Deformity (of morals) is appropriate in the devil and so less horrid than in woman,
from whom virtue is expected. Albany may hold a mirror in front of Goneril, since Jacobean women sometimes wore small mirrors attached to their dresses.
2. Altered and with your true (womanly) self concealed.

> To let these hands obey my blood,
> They are apt enough to dislocate and tear
39.5   Thy flesh and bones. Howe'er° thou art a fiend,   *Although*
> A woman's shape doth shield thee.

GONERIL   *Marry, your manhood, mew³—*
     Enter a GENTLEMAN.⁴

ALBANY   *What news?*

40 MESSENGER   O my good lord, the Duke of Cornwall's dead,
Slain by his servant, going to put out
The other eye of Gloucester.

ALBANY   Gloucester's eyes?

MESSENGER   A servant that he bred, thrilled with remorse,°   *shaken with pity*
Opposed against the act, bending° his sword   *directing*
45 To° his great master, who, threat-enragèd,   *Against*
Flew on him and amongst them felled him dead,
But not without that harmful stroke which since
Hath plucked him after.⁵

ALBANY   This shows you are above,
You justices,° that these our nether crimes⁶   *Judges*
50 So speedily can venge. But oh, poor Gloucester!
Lost he his other eye?

MESSENGER   Both, both, my lord.
This letter, madam, craves a speedy answer:
'Tis from your sister.

GONERIL [*aside*]   One way I like this well:⁷
But being° widow, and my Gloucester with her,   *her being*
55 May all the building in my fancy pluck
Upon my hateful life.⁸ Another way
The news is not so tart.° I'll read and answer.   *bitter*

ALBANY   Where was his son when they did take his eyes?

MESSENGER   Come with my lady hither.

ALBANY   He is not here.

60 MESSENGER   No, my good lord, I met him back° again.   *returning*

ALBANY   Knows he the wickedness?

MESSENGER   Ay, my good lord. 'Twas he informed against him
And quit the house on purpose, that their punishment
Might have the freer course.

ALBANY   Gloucester, I live
65 To thank thee for the love thou showed'st the King
And to revenge thine eyes. Come hither, friend;
Tell me what more thou know'st.   *Exeunt.*

4.3

Enter KENT [*disguised as Caius*] *and a* GENTLEMAN.

KENT   *Why the King of France is so suddenly gone back,*
     know you no reason?

GENTLEMAN   *Something he left imperfect° in the state,*   *unsettled*
     which since his coming forth is thought of,° which   *remembered*

---

3. Assert your feeble masculinity (with a derisive catcall, "mew"). Alternatively, get control of your manhood; restrain ("mew") it. *Marry:* By the Virgin Mary.
4. Q's Gentleman becomes a Messenger in F.
5. Has sent him to follow his servant into death.
6. Lower crimes, and so committed on earth, but also suggesting that the deeds smack of the netherworld of hell.
7. Because a political rival has been eliminated.
8. *May . . . life:* May pull down all of my built-up fantasies and thus make my life hateful.
4.3 Location: Near the French camp at Dover.

5   *imports°* to the kingdom so much fear and danger that   *portends*
        his personal return was most required and necessary.
    KENT   *Who hath he left behind him general?*
    GENTLEMAN   *The Marshal of France, Monsieur la Far.*
    KENT   *Did your letters pierce the Queen to any demon-*
10   *stration of grief?*
    GENTLEMAN   *I say she took them, read them in my presence,*
        And now and then an ample tear trilled down
        Her delicate cheek. It seemed she was a queen
        Over her passion, who,° most rebel-like,   *which*
        Sought to be king o'er her.
15   KENT   *Oh, then, it moved her.*
    GENTLEMAN   *Not to a rage. Patience and sorrow stream*
        Who should express her goodliest.[1] You have seen
        Sunshine and rain at once; her smiles and tears
        Were like a° better way. Those happy smilets   *Were similar in a*
20   *That played on her ripe lip seem not to know*
        What guests were in her eyes, which parted thence
        As pearls from diamonds dropped. In brief,
        Sorrow would be a rarity° most beloved,   *gem*
        If all could so become it.[2]
25   KENT   *Made she no verbal question?*
    GENTLEMAN   *Faith, once or twice she heaved the name*
         of father
        Pantingly forth, as if it pressed her heart,
        Cried, "Sisters, sisters, shame of ladies, sisters!
        Kent, father, sisters! What, i'th' storm, i'th' night?
30   *Let pity not be believed."[3] There she shook*
        The holy water from her heavenly eyes,
        And clamor° moistened her. Then away she started,°   *crying / sprang*
        To deal with grief alone.
    KENT   *It is the stars,*
        The stars above us, govern our conditions.
35   *Else one self mate and make[4] could not beget*
        Such different issues.° You spoke not with her since?   *offspring*
    GENTLEMAN   *No.*
    KENT   *Was this before the King returned?*
    GENTLEMAN   *No, since.*
    KENT   *Well, sir, the poor distressèd Lear's i'th' town,*
40   *Who sometime in his better tune° remembers*   *state of mind*
        What we are come about, and by no means
        Will yield° to see his daughter.   *consent*
    GENTLEMAN   *Why, good sir?*
    KENT   *A sovereign shame so elbows° him: his own*   *prods; nudges*
         unkindness,
        That stripped her from his benediction, turned her
45   *To foreign casualties,° gave her dear rights*   *risks*
        To his dog-hearted daughters. These things sting his mind
        So venomously that burning shame
        Detains him from Cordelia.
    GENTLEMAN   *Alack, poor gentleman!*

---

1. Which should best express her feelings.
2. If everyone wore it so beautifully.
3. Never believe in pity; compassion cannot exist.
4. Or else the same pair of spouses; "mate" and "make" may describe either partner.

50 KENT *Of Albany's and Cornwall's powers you heard not?*
GENTLEMAN *'Tis so, they are afoot.*
KENT *Well, sir, I'll bring you to our master Lear*
 And leave you to attend him. Some dear cause°   Some important reason
 Will in concealment wrap me up awhile.
55 *When I am known aright, you shall not grieve°*   regret
 Lending me this acquaintance.° I pray you   news
 Go along with me.   Exeunt.

4.4
Enter with drum and colors, CORDELIA, GENTLEMEN,
and Soldiers.

CORDELIA Alack, 'tis he. Why, he was met even now
As mad as the vexèd sea, singing aloud.
Crowned with rank fumitor and furrow weeds,[1]
With burdocks, hemlock, nettles, cuckoo flowers,
5 Darnel, and all the idle° weeds that grow   useless
In our sustaining corn. A century° send forth;   battalion (100 men)
Search every acre in the high-grown field
And bring him to our eye.   [*Exit a* GENTLEMAN.]
 What can man's wisdom
In the restoring° his bereavèd sense? He that helps him,   Do to restore
Take all my outward° worth.   material
10 GENTLEMAN   There is means, madam.
Our foster nurse of nature[2] is repose,
The which he lacks. That to provoke in him
Are many simples operative,[3] whose power
Will close the eye of anguish.
CORDELIA   All blest secrets,
15 All you unpublished virtues° of the earth,   obscure healing plants
Spring with my tears; be aidant and remediate°   healing and remedial
In the good man's desires. Seek, seek for him,
Lest his ungoverned rage dissolve the life
That wants° the means to lead it.   lacks
 Enter MESSENGER.
MESSENGER   News, madam:
20 The British powers° are marching hitherward.   armies
CORDELIA 'Tis known before. Our preparation stands
In expectation of them. O dear father,
It is thy business that I go about![4] Therefore great France
My mourning and importuned° tears hath pitied.   importunate; solicitous
25 No blown° ambition doth our arms incite,   inflated
But love, dear love, and our agèd father's right.[5]
Soon may I hear and see him!   Exeunt.

4.5
Enter REGAN *and* [*Oswald the*] STEWARD.
REGAN But are my brother's powers° set forth?   (Albany's forces)

4.4 Location: The French camp at Dover.
1. Fumitor was used against brain sickness. Furrow weeds, like the other weeds in the following lines, grow in the furrows of plowed fields.
2. *Our . . . nature:* That which comforts and nourishes human nature.
3. *That . . . operative:* To induce that ("repose") in

him, there are many effective medicinal herbs.
4. The line echoes Christ's explanation of his mission in Luke 2:49: "I must go about my father's business."
5. *No . . . right:* 1 Corinthians 13:4–5 in the Bishops' Bible (1568) says that love "swelleth not, dealeth not dishonestly, seeketh not her own."
4.5 Location: At Gloucester's castle.

STEWARD   Ay, madam.

REGAN   Himself in person there?

STEWARD   Madam, with much ado;°   *trouble*
Your sister is the better soldier.

REGAN   Lord Edmund spake not with your lord at home?

5   STEWARD   No, madam.

REGAN   What might import° my sister's letter to him?   *mean*

STEWARD   I know not, lady.

REGAN   Faith, he is posted° hence on serious matter—   *sent*
It was great ignorance, Gloucester's eyes being out,

10   To let him live. Where he arrives, he moves
All hearts against us. Edmund, I think, is gone,
In pity of his misery,° to dispatch   *(ironic)*
His nighted° life, moreover to descry°   *darkened / investigate*
The strength o'th' enemy.

15   STEWARD   I must needs after° him, madam, with my letter.   *go after*

REGAN   Our troops set forth tomorrow; stay with us.
The ways are dangerous.

STEWARD   I may not, madam:
My lady charged° my duty in this business.   *commanded*

REGAN   Why should she write to Edmund?

20   Might not you transport her purposes by word? Belike°   *Perhaps*
Some things—I know not what. I'll love° thee much: *reward*
Let me unseal the letter.

STEWARD   Madam, I had rather—

REGAN   I know your lady does not love her husband.
I am sure of that, and at her late° being here,   *recently*

25   She gave strange oeillades° and most speaking looks   *amorous glances*
To noble Edmund. I know you are of her bosom.°   *in her confidence*

STEWARD   I, madam?

REGAN   I speak in understanding.° Y'are; I know't.   *with certainty*
Therefore I do advise you take this note.°   *take note of this*

30   My lord is dead. Edmund and I have talked,
And more convenient° is he for my hand   *appropriate*
Than for your lady's. You may gather° more.   *infer*
If you do find him, pray you give him this,[1]
And when your mistress hears thus much from you,

35   I pray, desire her call her wisdom to her.[2]
So, fare you well.
If you do chance to hear of that blind traitor,
Preferment falls on him that cuts him off.°   *cuts his life short*

STEWARD   Would I could meet, madam; I should show
What party I do follow.

40   REGAN   Fare thee well.   *Exeunt [severally].*°   *separately*

4.6

Enter GLOUCESTER *and* EDGAR [*disguised as
a peasant*].

GLOUCESTER   When shall I come to th' top of that same° hill?   *agreed-upon*

EDGAR   You do climb up it now. Look how we labor.

GLOUCESTER   Methinks the ground is even.

---

1. This information, but possibly another letter or
token.
2. *desire . . . to her:* tell her to come to her senses.
4.6 Location: Near Dover.

EDGAR Horrible steep.
   Hark, do you hear the sea?

GLOUCESTER No, truly.

5 EDGAR Why, then, your other senses grow imperfect
   By your eyes' anguish.

GLOUCESTER So may it be indeed.
   Methinks thy voice is altered, and thou speak'st
   In better phrase and matter° than thou didst.   *sense*

EDGAR You're much deceived. In nothing am I changed
10   But in my garments.

GLOUCESTER Methinks you're better spoken.

EDGAR Come on, sir,
   Here's the place. Stand still. How fearful
   And dizzy 'tis to cast one's eyes so low!
   The crows and choughs° that wing the midway air[1]   *jackdaws*
15   Show° scarce so gross° as beetles. Halfway down   *Appear / big*
   Hangs one that gathers samphire:° dreadful trade!   *seaweed*
   Methinks he seems no bigger than his head.
   The fishermen that walked upon the beach
   Appear like mice, and yond tall anchoring bark°   *ship*
20   Diminished to her cock;° her cock a buoy   *dinghy*
   Almost too small for sight. The murmuring surge,
   That on th'unnumbered° idle pebble chafes,   *innumerable*
   Cannot be heard so high. I'll look no more,
   Lest my brain turn and the° deficient sight   *my*
25   Topple° down headlong.   *Topple me*

GLOUCESTER Set me where you stand.

EDGAR Give me your hand.
   You are now within a foot of th'extreme verge.
   For all beneath the moon would I not leap upright.[2]

GLOUCESTER Let go my hand.
30   Here, friend, 's another purse. In it, a jewel
   Well worth a poor man's taking. Fairies and gods
   Prosper it[3] with thee. Go thou further off.
   Bid me farewell, and let me hear thee going.

EDGAR Now, fare ye well, good sir.

GLOUCESTER With all my heart.

35 EDGAR [*aside*] Why I do trifle thus with his despair
   Is done to cure it.

GLOUCESTER O you mighty gods!
      [*He kneels.*]
   This world I do renounce, and in your sights
   Shake patiently my great affliction off.
   If I could bear it longer and not fall
40   To quarrel° with your great opposeless wills,   *Into conflict*
   My snuff and loathèd part of nature[4] should
   Burn itself out. If Edgar live, oh, bless him!
   Now, fellow, fare thee well.

EDGAR Gone, sir. Farewell.
      [GLOUCESTER *falls down.*]

---

1. The air between cliff and sea.
2. I would not jump up and down (for fear of losing my balance).
3. Make it increase. Fairies were sometimes believed to hoard and multiply treasure.
4. The scorched and hateful remnant of my lifetime. *snuff:* end of a candlewick.

And yet I know not how conceit may rob
45　The treasury of life, when life itself
Yields to the theft.[5] Had he been where he thought,
By this° had thought been past. Alive or dead?[6]　　　　　*now*
[*to* GLOUCESTER] Ho, you, sir! Friend, hear you, sir? Speak.
Thus might he pass° indeed. Yet he revives.　　　　　*pass away*
—What are you, sir?
50　GLOUCESTER　　　　Away and let me die.
EDGAR　Hadst thou been aught° but goss'mer, feathers, air,　　　　　*anything*
So many fathom down precipitating,°　　　　　*plunging*
Thou'dst shivered° like an egg. But thou dost breathe,　　　　　*shattered*
Hast heavy substance, bleed'st not, speak'st, art sound.
55　Ten masts at each° make not the altitude　　　　　*end to end*
Which thou hast perpendicularly fell.
Thy life's a miracle. Speak yet again.
GLOUCESTER　But have I fall'n or no?
EDGAR　From the dread summit of this chalky bourn.[7]
60　Look up a-height, the shrill-gorged° lark so far　　　　　*shrill-voiced*
Cannot be seen or heard. Do but look up.
GLOUCESTER　Alack, I have no eyes.
Is wretchedness deprived° that benefit　　　　　*deprived of*
To end itself by death? 'Twas yet some comfort
65　When misery could beguile° the tyrant's rage　　　　　*cheat*
And frustrate his proud will.
EDGAR　　　　　　　　　Give me your arm.
Up, so. How is't? Feel you your legs? You stand.
GLOUCESTER　Too well, too well.
EDGAR　　　　　　　　　This is above all strangeness.
Upon the crown o'th' cliff, what thing was that
Which parted from you?
70　GLOUCESTER　　　　　　A poor unfortunate beggar.
EDGAR　As I stood here below, methought his eyes
Were two full moons. He had a thousand noses,
Horns whelked° and waved like the enragèd sea.　　　　　*twisted*
It was some fiend. Therefore, thou happy father,°　　　　　*lucky old man*
75　Think that the clearest° gods, who make them honors　　　　　*purest; most illustrious*
Of men's impossibilities,[8] have preserved thee.
GLOUCESTER　I do remember now. Henceforth I'll bear
Affliction till it do cry out itself,
"Enough, enough," and die. That thing you speak of,
80　I took it for a man. Often 'twould say
"The fiend, the fiend." He led me to that place.
EDGAR　Bear free and patient thoughts.
　　　　　Enter LEAR.
　　　　　　　　　　　　But who comes here?
The safer sense will ne'er accommodate
His master thus.[9]

---

5. *And yet . . . theft:* Edgar worries that the imagined scenario ("conceit") he has invented may be enough to kill his father, particularly as Gloucester wishes for ("yields to") his own death.
6. PERFORMANCE COMMENT Like readers, audiences cannot initially be certain whether the cliff is "real" (within the play's fictive world) or imaginary, and the resulting tension makes for one of Shakespeare's most fascinating scenes. See Digital Edition PC 5.
7. The white chalk cliffs of Dover, which make a boundary ("bourn") between land and sea.
8. *who . . . impossibilities:* who attain honor for themselves by performing deeds impossible to men.
9. *The . . . thus:* A sane mind would never allow its possessor to dress up in this way.

85   LEAR   No, they cannot touch me° for crying. I am the King   *lay hands on me*
     himself.
     EDGAR *[aside]*   O thou side-piercing sight!
     LEAR   Nature's above art in that respect.[1] There's your press
     money.[2] That fellow handles his bow like a crow-keeper.[3] Draw
90   me a clothier's yard.[4] Look, look, a mouse! Peace, peace, this
     piece of toasted cheese will do't.° There's my gauntlet; I'll prove   *(lure the mouse)*
     it on a giant.[5] Bring up the brown bills.[6] Oh, well-flown, bird!°   *arrow*
     I'th' clout,° i'th' clout! Whew. Give the word.°   *bull's-eye / password*
     EDGAR   Sweet marjoram.[7]
95   LEAR   Pass.
     GLOUCESTER   I know that voice.
     LEAR   Ha! Goneril with a white beard? They flattered me like
     a dog° and told me I had the white hairs in my beard ere the   *fawningly*
     black ones were there.[8] To say "Ay" and "No" to everything
100   that I said "Ay" and "No" to was no good divinity.[9] When the
     rain came to wet me once, and the wind to make me chatter,
     when the thunder would not peace at my bidding, there I
     found° 'em, there I smelt 'em out. Go to, they are not men   *understood*
     o'their words. They told me I was everything. 'Tis a lie. I am
105   not ague-proof.°   *immune to illness*
     GLOUCESTER   The trick° of that voice, I do well remember.   *peculiarity*
     Is't not the King?
     LEAR   Ay, every inch a king!
     When I do stare, see how the subject quakes.
     I pardon that man's life. —What was thy cause?°   *crime*
110   Adultery? Thou shalt not die. Die for adultery?
     No, the wren goes to't, and the small gilded fly
     Does lecher in my sight. Let copulation thrive,
     For Gloucester's bastard son was kinder to his father
     Than my daughters got 'tween the lawful sheets.
115   To't, luxury,° pell-mell, for I lack soldiers.   *lechery*
     Behold yond simp'ring dame,
     Whose face between her forks presages snow,[1]
     That minces° virtue and does shake the head   *affects*
     To hear of° pleasure's name.   *even of*
120   The fitchew nor the soiled horse[2] goes to't
     With a more riotous appetite.
     Down from the waist they are centaurs,[3]
     Though women all above.
     But° to the girdle° do the gods inherit;°   *Only / waist / own*

---

1. My true feelings will always outweigh others' hypocrisy; my natural supremacy surpasses any attempt to create a false new reign.
2. Fee paid to a soldier impressed, or forced, into the army.
3. A person hired as a scarecrow and thus unfit for anything else.
4. Draw the bowstring the full length of the arrow (a standard English arrow was a cloth yard [37 inches] long).
5. I'll defend my stand even against a giant. To throw down an armored glove ("gauntlet") was to issue a challenge.
6. Brown painted pikes; the soldiers carrying them.
7. Used medicinally against madness.
8. Told me I had wisdom before age.
9. *no good divinity:* poor theology (because insincere); from James 5:12: "Let your yea be yea; nay, nay."
1. Whose expression implies cold chastity. "Face" refers to the area between her legs ("forks"), as well as to her literal facial expression as framed by the aristocratic lady's starched headpiece, also called a "fork."
2. Neither the polecat nor a horse full of fresh grass.
3. Lecherous mythological creatures that have a human body above the waist and the legs and torso of a horse below.

125 Beneath is all the fiend's. There's hell,[4] there's darkness,
There is the sulphurous pit: burning, scalding,
Stench, consumption. Fie, fie, fie! Pah, pah!
—Give me an ounce of civet,[5] good apothecary;
Sweeten my imagination. There's money for thee.
GLOUCESTER   Oh, let me kiss that hand.
130 LEAR   Let me wipe it first.
It smells of mortality.
GLOUCESTER   O ruined piece° of nature, this great world   *masterpiece*
Shall so wear out to naught.[6] Dost thou know me?
LEAR   I remember thine eyes well enough. Dost thou squiny°   *squint*
135 at me? No, do thy worst, blind Cupid. I'll not love. Read
thou this challenge; mark but the penning of it.
GLOUCESTER   Were all thy letters suns, I could not see.
EDGAR [*aside*]   I would not take° this from report;   *believe*
It is, and my heart breaks at it.
140 LEAR   Read.
GLOUCESTER   What, with the case° of eyes?   *socket*
LEAR   Oh, ho, are you there with me?[7] No eyes in your head,
nor no money in your purse? Your eyes are in a heavy case,[8]
your purse in a light, yet you see how this world goes.
145 GLOUCESTER   I see it feelingly.°   *by touch; painfully*
LEAR   What, art mad? A man may see how this world goes
with no eyes. Look with thine ears. See how yond justice
rails upon yond simple° thief. Hark in thine ear. Change   *lowly; innocent*
places, and handy-dandy,[9] which is the justice, which is the
150 thief? Thou hast seen a farmer's dog bark at a beggar?
GLOUCESTER   Ay, sir.
LEAR   And the creature° run from the cur. There thou mightst   *wretch*
behold the great image of authority; a dog's obeyed in office.
—Thou rascal beadle,[1] hold° thy bloody hand.   *restrain*
155 Why dost thou lash that whore? Strip thy own back;
Thou hotly lusts to use her in that kind°   *way*
For which thou whipp'st her. The usurer hangs the
cozener.[2]
Through tattered clothes great vices do appear.
Robes and furred gowns hide all. Plate° sins with gold,   *Armor; gild*
160 And the strong lance of justice hurtless° breaks.   *harmlessly*
Arm it in rags; a pigmy's straw does pierce it.
None does offend; none, I say, none. I'll able° 'em.   *authorize*
Take that of me, my friend, who have the power
To seal th'accuser's lips. Get thee glass eyes,
165 And, like a scurvy politician,[3]
Seem to see the things thou dost not. Now, now, now, now.
Pull off my boots, harder, harder, so.
EDGAR [*aside*]   Oh, matter and impertinency° mixed!   *sense and nonsense*
Reason in madness.

---

4. Shakespeare's frequent term for female genitals.
Cf. Sonnets 129 and 144.
5. Perfume derived from the anal gland of the civet.
6. Shall decay to nothing in the same way. In Renaissance philosophy, humans were perfectly analogous
to the cosmos, standing for the whole in miniature
and as its masterpiece.
7. Is that what you are telling me?

8. In a sad condition; playing on "case" as "sockets."
9. Pick a hand, as in a child's guessing game.
1. The parish officer responsible for whippings.
2. The ruinous moneylender, prosperous enough to
be made a judge, convicts the ordinary cheat.
3. A vile schemer. In early modern England, "politician" meant an ambitious, even Machiavellian, upstart.

170 LEAR If thou wilt weep my fortunes, take my eyes.
I know thee well enough: thy name is Gloucester.
Thou must be patient. We came crying hither.
Thou know'st, the first time that we smell the air
We wail and cry. I will preach to thee. Mark.

175 GLOUCESTER Alack, alack the day.
LEAR When we are born, we cry that we are come
To this great stage of fools. This° a good block.[4]   *This is*
It were a delicate° stratagem to shoe   *subtle*
A troop of horse with felt.[5] I'll put't in proof,°   *to the test*
180 And when I have stol'n upon these son-in-laws,
Then kill, kill, kill, kill, kill, kill!

Enter a GENTLEMAN.

GENTLEMAN Oh, here he is. Lay hand upon him. [*to* LEAR] Sir,
Your most dear daughter—
LEAR No rescue? What, a prisoner? I am even
185 The natural fool[6] of fortune. Use° me well;   *Treat*
You shall have ransom. Let me have surgeons:
I am cut to th' brains.
GENTLEMAN   You shall have anything.
LEAR No seconds?° All myself?   *supporters*
Why, this would make a man a man of salt,[7]
190 To use his eyes for garden water-pots. I will die[8] bravely,
Like a smug° bridegroom. What? I will be jovial.   *an elegant*
Come, come, I am a king, masters. Know you that?
GENTLEMAN You are a royal one, and we obey you.
LEAR Then there's life° in't. Come; an° you get it,   *hope / if*
195 You shall get it by running. Sa, sa, sa, sa.[9]   *Exit.*
GENTLEMAN A sight most pitiful in the meanest wretch,
Past speaking of in a king. Thou hast a daughter
Who redeems nature from the general curse,
Which twain have brought her to.[1]
EDGAR Hail, gentle° sir.   *noble*
200 GENTLEMAN   Sir, speed you.° What's your will?   *God speed you*
EDGAR Do you hear aught, sir, of a battle toward?°   *coming*
GENTLEMAN Most sure and vulgar:°   *commonly known*
Everyone hears that which° can distinguish sound.   *who*
EDGAR But, by your favor, how near's the other army?
205 GENTLEMAN Near and on speedy foot; the main descry°   *appearance*
Stands on the hourly thought.°   *Is expected forthwith*
EDGAR I thank you, sir, that's all.
GENTLEMAN Though that the Queen on° special cause° is here,   *for / reason*
Her army is moved on.
EDGAR   I thank you, sir. *Exit* [GENTLEMAN].
210 GLOUCESTER You ever gentle gods, take my breath from me.

---

4. Stage (often called "scaffold" and hence linked to an executioner's block); block used to shape a felt hat (such as the hat removed by a preacher before a sermon); mounting block (such as the stump or stock Lear may have sat on to remove his boots).
5. Hat material, to muffle the sound of the approaching cavalry.
6. Born plaything; playing on "natural" as "mentally deficient."
7. A man reduced to nothing but the salt his tears deposit.
8. "Die" plays on the Renaissance sense of "have an orgasm."
9. A cry to encourage dogs in the hunt.
1. *Who . . . to:* Who restores proper meaning and order to a universe plagued by the crimes of the other two daughters; alluding to the fall of humankind and the natural world caused by the sin of Adam and Eve and to the universal redemption brought about by Christ's sacrifice.

Let not my worser spirit[2] tempt me again
To die before you please.
EDGAR　　　　　　　　　　Well pray you, father.[3]
GLOUCESTER　　Now, good sir, what are you?
EDGAR　　A most poor man, made tame to fortune's blows,
215　Who, by the art of known and feeling° sorrows,　　　　　　*profound*
Am pregnant to° good pity. Give me your hand,　　　　　*disposed to feel*
I'll lead you to some biding.°　　　　　　　　　　　　　*resting place*
GLOUCESTER　　　　　　　　Hearty thanks.
The bounty and the benison of heaven
To boot and boot.[4]
　　　　　Enter [Oswald the] STEWARD.
STEWARD　　　　　　　　A proclaimed prize![5] Most happy!°　　*lucky*
220　That eyeless head of thine was first framed° flesh　　　　*made of*
To raise my fortunes. Thou old unhappy traitor,
Briefly thyself remember.[6] [*He draws his sword.*] The sword
　　is out
That must destroy thee.
GLOUCESTER　　　　　　　Now let thy friendly hand
Put strength enough to't.
STEWARD [*to* EDGAR]　　　　Wherefore, bold peasant,
225　Dar'st thou support a published° traitor? Hence,　　　　*proclaimed*
Lest that th'infection° of his fortune take　　　　　　*(deathly) sickness*
Like° hold on thee. Let go his arm.　　　　　　　　　*The same*
EDGAR [*drawing his sword and speaking in a country accent*]
Chill[7] not let go, zir, without vurther 'casion.°　　　　*further occasion*
STEWARD　　Let go, slave, or thou diest.
230　EDGAR　　Good gentleman, go your gait,° and let poor volk pass.　*be on your way*
An chud ha'° been zwaggered out of my life, 'twould not ha'　*If I could have*
been zo long as 'tis by a vortnight. Nay, come not near th'old
man! Keep out, che vor' ye, or I'll try whither your costard or
my ballow be the harder.[8] Chill be plain with you.
235　STEWARD　　Out, dunghill.
EDGAR　　Chill pick your teeth, zir! Come, no matter vor your
foins.°　　　　　　　　　　　　　　　　　　　　*sword thrusts*
　　　　　[*They fight.*]
STEWARD　　Slave, thou hast slain me! Villain, take my purse.
If ever thou wilt thrive, bury my body,
240　And give the letters which thou find'st about me
To Edmund, Earl of Gloucester. Seek him out
Upon° the English party. Oh, untimely death, death!　　*Within*
　　　　　[*He dies.*]
EDGAR　　I know thee well: a serviceable° villain,　　　　*an officious*
As duteous to the vices of thy mistress
As badness would desire.
245　GLOUCESTER　　　　　　　What, is he dead?
EDGAR　　Sit you down, father; rest you.
Let's see these pockets. The letters that he speaks of
May be my friends. He's dead; I am only sorry

2. Wicked inclination; bad angel.
3. A term of respect for an elderly man.
4. In addition to my thanks, and may it bring you
some worldly reward.
5. A wanted man, with a bounty on his life.
6. Recollect and pray forgiveness for your sins.

7. I will; dialect from Somerset was a stage convention for peasant dialogue.
8. *che vor' ye . . . harder:* I warrant you, or I shall test
whether your head or my cudgel is harder. *costard:* a
kind of apple.

He had no other deathsman.° [*He opens the letter.*] Let
    us see;   *executioner*

250 Leave,° gentle wax,[9] and manners blame us not.   *By your leave*
To know our enemies' minds, we rip their hearts;
Their° papers is more lawful.   *To rip their*
    [*He*] *reads the letter.*
"Let our reciprocal vows be remembered. You have many
opportunities to cut him off. If your will want° not, time and   *lacks*
255 place will be fruitfully offered. There is nothing done° if he   *accomplished*
return the conqueror; then am I the prisoner and his bed my
jail, from the loathed warmth whereof deliver me, and supply°   *fill*
the place for your labor.[1] Your (wife, so I would say), affectionate servant,
259.1   *and for you her own for venture,*
260 Goneril."
Oh, indistinguished space of woman's will![2]
A plot upon her virtuous husband's life,
And the exchange° my brother! Here in the sands   *substitute*
Thee I'll rake up,° the post unsanctified°   *cover up / unholy messenger*
265 Of murderous lechers, and in the mature time°   *when the time is ripe*
With this ungracious° paper strike the sight   *ungodly*
Of the death-practiced Duke.[3] For him, 'tis well
That of thy death and business I can tell.
GLOUCESTER   The King is mad. How stiff is my vile sense[4]
270 That I stand up and have ingenious feeling[5]
Of my huge sorrows? Better I were distract;°   *mad*
So should my thoughts be severed from my griefs,
      Drum afar off.
And woes by wrong° imaginations lose   *false*
The knowledge of themselves.
EDGAR   Give me your hand.
275 Far off methinks I hear the beaten drum.
Come, father, I'll bestow° you with a friend.   *Exeunt.*   *lodge*

4.7

Enter CORDELIA, KENT [*dressed as Caius*], *and*
  GENTLEMAN.
CORDELIA   O thou good Kent, how shall I live and work
To match thy goodness? My life will be too short
And every measure° fail me.   *attempt*
KENT   To be acknowledged, madam, is o'erpaid.°   *is more than enough*
5 All my reports go[1] with the modest truth,
Nor more, nor clipped, but so.[2]
CORDELIA   Be better suited;°   *attired*
These weeds° are memories of those worser hours.   *clothes*
I prithee, put them off.
KENT   Pardon, dear madam,
Yet to be known shortens my made intent.[3]

---

9. The wax seal on the letter.
1. *for your labor:* as a reward for your endeavors, and
for further sexual exertion.
2. Limitless extent of woman's willfulness. As with
"hell" in line 125, "will" might also refer to a woman's
genitals.
3. Of the Duke whose death is plotted.
4. How obstinate is my unwanted power of reason.

5. That I remain upright and firm in my sanity and
have rational perceptions.
4.7 Location: The French camp at Dover.
1. May all accounts of me agree.
2. Not greater or less, but exactly the modest amount
I deserve.
3. Revealing myself now would abort my designs.

10　My boon I make it[4] that you know° me not　　　　　　　　*acknowledge*
　　Till time and I think meet.°　　　　　　　　　　　　　　　　*suitable*
CORDELIA　　　　　　　　　Then be't so, my good lord.
　　—How does the King?
GENTLEMAN　　　　　　　　Madam, sleeps still.
CORDELIA　　O you kind gods,
　　Cure this great breach in his abusèd nature.
15　Th'untuned and jarring senses, oh, wind up[5]
　　Of this child-changed[6] father.
GENTLEMAN　　　　　　　　So please your majesty,
　　That we may wake the King? He hath slept long.
CORDELIA　　Be governed by your knowledge and proceed
　　I'th' sway° of your own will. Is he arrayed?°　　　*By the authority / clothed*
　　　　　　Enter LEAR *in a chair carried by* SERVANTS.
20　GENTLEMAN　　Ay, madam. In the heaviness of sleep,
　　We put fresh garments on him.
　　Be by, good madam, when we do awake him;
　　I doubt of his temperance.°　　　　　　　　　　　　　*calmness*
CORDELIA　　O my dear father, restoration hang
25　Thy medicine on my lips, and let this kiss
　　Repair those violent harms that my two sisters
　　Have in thy reverence° made.　　　　　　　　　　　*aged dignity*
KENT　　　　　　　　　　　Kind and dear princess.
CORDELIA　　Had you not[7] been their father, these white flakes°　　*locks of hair*
　　Did challenge° pity of them. Was this a face　　　　*Would provoke*
30　To be opposed against the jarring winds,
30.1　　*To stand against the deep dread-bolted thunder,*
　　　In the most terrible and nimble stroke
　　　Of quick cross lightning to watch°—poor perdu![8]—　　　*to stand guard*
　　　With this thin helm?°　　　　　　　　　　　　　*helmet (of hair)*
　　Mine enemy's dog, though he had bit me,
　　Should have stood that night against my fire.
　　And wast thou fain,° poor father,　　　　　　　　　　*obliged*
　　To hovel thee with swine and rogues forlorn
35　In short° and musty straw? Alack, alack,　　　　　　*scant; broken*
　　'Tis wonder that thy life and wits at once
　　Had not concluded all.° —He wakes; speak to him.　　*altogether*
GENTLEMAN　　Madam, do you, 'tis fittest.
CORDELIA　　How does my royal lord?
40　How fares your majesty?
LEAR　　You do me wrong to take me out o'th' grave.
　　Thou art a soul in bliss, but I am bound
　　Upon a wheel of fire, that mine own tears
　　Do scald like molten lead.[9]
CORDELIA　　　　　　　　Sir, do you know me?
45　LEAR　　You are a spirit, I know. Where did you die?
CORDELIA　　Still, still, far wide.°　　　　　　　　　　*unbalanced*
GENTLEMAN　　He's scarce awake. Let him alone a while.

LEAR   Where have I been? Where am I? Fair daylight?
      I am mightily abused.° I should e'en die with pity   *wronged; deceived*
50   To see another thus. I know not what to say.
      I will not swear these are my hands. Let's see,
      I feel this pin prick. Would I were assured
      Of my condition.
CORDELIA [*kneeling*]   Oh, look upon me, sir,
      And hold your hand in benediction o'er me.
            [LEAR *kneels.*]
      You must not kneel.
55   LEAR [*rising*]   Pray, do not mock me.
      I am a very foolish, fond° old man,   *silly*
      Fourscore and upward,
      Not an hour more nor less,
      And to deal plainly,
60   I fear I am not in my perfect mind.
      Methinks I should know you and know this man,
      Yet I am doubtful, for I am mainly° ignorant   *entirely*
      What place this is, and all the skill I have
      Remembers not these garments, nor I know not
65   Where I did lodge last night. Do not laugh at me,
      For, as I am a man, I think this lady
      To be my child Cordelia.
CORDELIA   And so I am. I am.
LEAR   Be your tears wet?[1] Yes, faith. I pray, weep not.
      If you have poison for me, I will drink it.
70   I know you do not love me, for your sisters
      Have, as I do remember, done me wrong.
      You have some cause; they have not.
CORDELIA   No cause, no cause.
LEAR   Am I in France?
KENT   In your own kingdom, sir.
LEAR   Do not abuse° me.   *deceive; mock*
75   GENTLEMAN   Be comforted, good madam; the great rage
      You see is killed in him. Desire him to go in;
      Trouble him no more till further settling.°   *until his mind eases*
CORDELIA   Will't please your highness walk?
LEAR   You must bear with me.
      Pray you now, forget and forgive,
80   I am old and foolish.
                    Exeunt [LEAR *and* CORDELIA;
                    KENT *and* GENTLEMAN *remain*].
80.1 GENTLEMAN   *Holds it true, sir, that the Duke of Corn-*
      wall was so slain?
KENT   *Most certain, sir.*
GENTLEMAN   *Who is conductor° of his people?*   *commander*
80.5 KENT   *As 'tis said, the bastard son of Gloucester.*
GENTLEMAN   *They say Edgar, his banished son, is with*
      the Earl of Kent in Germany.
KENT   *Report° is changeable. 'Tis time to look about.°*   *Rumor / prepare defenses*
      The powers of the kingdom approach apace.

---

1. Are your tears real? Is this really happening?

80.10 GENTLEMEN *The arbitrament° is like to be bloody. Fare*   *encounter*
    you well, sir. [*Exit.*]
  KENT *My point and period*[2] *will be thoroughly wrought,*
    Or° well or ill as this day's battle's fought. Exit.   *For*

5.1

Enter with drum and colors,° EDMUND, REGAN,   *regimental flags*
  GENTLEMEN, *and Soldiers.*
  EDMUND   Know° of the Duke if his last purpose hold,[1]   *Inquire*
  Or whether since he is advised by aught[2]
  To change the course. He's full of alteration[3]
  And self-reproving. Bring his constant pleasure.°   *his settled intent*
5   REGAN   Our sister's man is certainly miscarried.[4]
  EDMUND   'Tis to be doubted,° madam.   *feared*
  REGAN   Now, sweet lord,
  You know the goodness I intend upon you.
  Tell me but truly, but then speak the truth:
  Do you not love my sister?
  EDMUND   In honored° love.   *honorable*
10   REGAN   But have you never found my brother's way
  To the forfended[5] place?
11.1   EDMUND   *That thought abuses° you.*   *deceives*
     REGAN   *I am doubtful° that you have been conjunct°*   *suspicious / complicit*
    And bosomed with° her—as far as we call hers.[6]   *enamored of*
  EDMUND   No, by mine honor, madam.
  REGAN   I never shall endure her. Dear my lord,
  Be not familiar° with her.   *intimate*
15   EDMUND   Fear° not. She and the Duke her husband—   *Doubt*
    Enter with drum and colors, ALBANY, GONERIL,
    Soldiers.
15.1   GONERIL [*aside*]   *I had rather lose the battle than that sister*
    Should loosen° him and me.   *disunite*
  ALBANY   Our very loving sister, well be-met.
  —Sir, this I heard: the King is come to his daughter
  With others, whom the rigor° of our state°   *harshness / government*
  Forced to cry out.
19.1   *Where I could not be honest°*   *honorable*
    I never yet was valiant. For this business,
    It touches° us as France invades our land,   *concerns*
    Not bolds° the King, with others whom I fear   *Does not embolden*
19.5   *Most just and heavy causes make oppose.*[7]
  EDMUND   *Sir, you speak nobly.*
20   REGAN   Why is this reasoned?[8]
  GONERIL   Combine together 'gainst the enemy.
  For these domestic and particular broils°   *minor details*
  Are not the question here.
  ALBANY   Let's then determine with th'ancient° of war   *experienced officer(s)*
25   On our proceeding.

---

2. The purpose and end of my life; literally, the full stop.
5.1 Location: The British camp near Dover.
1. If his previous intention (to wage war) remains firm.
2. Since then anything has persuaded him.
3. A tendency to give up his intentions or put aside his responsibilities.

4. Has surely come to grief by some accident.
5. Forbidden, by the prohibition against adultery.
6. In total intimacy; all the way.
7. *It . . . oppose:* The invasion concerns us only insofar that France has invaded Britain, not because it has emboldened Lear, who has just cause to attack.
8. What is the point of this kind of speech?

REGAN   Sister, you'll go with us?[9]
GONERIL   No.
REGAN   'Tis most convenient;° pray go with us.   *suitable*
GONERIL   Oh, ho, I know the riddle!° I will go.   *disguised meaning*
                                            Exeunt both the armies.
                    Enter EDGAR [*disguised*].
30   EDGAR [*to* ALBANY]   If e'er your grace had speech with man
          so poor,
        Hear me one word.
     ALBANY [*to the others*]   I'll overtake you.
                              [*Exeunt* EDMUND, GONERIL, *and* REGAN.]
                              Speak.
     EDGAR   Before you fight the battle, ope this letter.
        If you have victory, let the trumpet sound
        For him that brought it. Wretched though I seem,
35   I can produce a champion that will prove°   *defend*
        What is avouchèd° there. If you miscarry,°   *asserted / perish*
        Your business of the world hath so an end,
        And machination° ceases. Fortune loves you.   *plotting*
     ALBANY   Stay till I have read the letter.
     EDGAR   I was forbid it.
40   When time shall serve, let but the herald cry,
        And I'll appear again.   *Exit.*
     ALBANY   Why, fare thee well. I will o'erlook thy paper.
                    Enter EDMUND.
     EDMUND   The enemy's in view; draw up your powers.°   *troops*
        Here is the guess° of their true strength and forces   *estimate*
45   By diligent discovery,° but your haste   *spying*
        Is now urged on you.
     ALBANY   We will greet the time.[1]   *Exit.*
     EDMUND   To both these sisters have I sworn my love,
        Each jealous° of the other, as the stung   *suspicious*
        Are of the adder. Which of them shall I take?
50   Both? One? Or neither? Neither can be enjoyed
        If both remain alive. To take the widow
        Exasperates, makes mad, her sister Goneril,
        And hardly° shall I carry out my side,°   *with difficulty / plan*
        Her husband being alive. Now, then, we'll use
55   His countenance[2] for the battle, which being done,
        Let her who would be rid of him devise
        His speedy taking-off. As for the mercy
        Which he intends to Lear and to Cordelia,
        The battle done, and they within our power,
60   Shall° never see his pardon. For my state°   *They shall / condition*
        Stands on° me to defend, not to debate.   *Exit.*   *Obliges*

---

9. Regan wants Goneril to go with Albany and her,   2. Authority or backing; also suggesting "face," to be
rather than with Edmund.   used like a mask for Edmund's ambition.
1. We will be ready to meet the occasion.

5.2

Alarum within.[1] *Enter with drum and colors,* LEAR,
CORDELIA, *and Soldiers, over the stage, and exeunt.*
Enter EDGAR [*disguised as a peasant*] *and*
GLOUCESTER.

EDGAR Here, father,[2] take the shadow of this tree
For your good host.° Pray that the right may thrive.   *shelter*
If ever I return to you again,
I'll bring you comfort.
GLOUCESTER   Grace go with you, sir. *Exit* [EDGAR].
Alarum and retreat° within.   *trumpet signal*
Enter EDGAR.
5 EDGAR Away, old man, give me thy hand, away!
King Lear hath lost; he and his daughter ta'en.
Give me thy hand. Come on.
GLOUCESTER No further, sir, a man may rot even° here.   *right*
EDGAR What, in ill thoughts again? Men must endure
10 Their going hence even as their coming hither;
Ripeness is all.[3] Come on.
GLOUCESTER   And that's true too. *Exeunt.*

5.3

Enter in conquest with drum and colors, EDMUND;
LEAR *and* CORDELIA, *as prisoners; Soldiers,* CAPTAIN.[1]

EDMUND Some officers! Take them away. Good guard,
Until their greater pleasures[2] first be known
That are to censure° them.   *judge*
CORDELIA   We are not the first
Who with best meaning° have incurred the worst.   *intention*
5 For thee, oppressèd King, I am cast down.°   *(into unhappiness)*
Myself could else out-frown false fortune's frown.[3]
Shall we not see these daughters and these sisters?
LEAR No, no, no, no. Come, let's away to prison.
We two alone will sing like birds i'th' cage.
10 When thou dost ask me blessing, I'll kneel down
And ask of thee forgiveness. So we'll live,
And pray, and sing, and tell old tales, and laugh
At gilded butterflies,[4] and hear poor rogues
Talk of court news, and we'll talk with them too—
15 Who loses, and who wins; who's in, who's out—
And take upon 's the mystery of things,
As if we were God's spies. And we'll wear out,°   *outlast*
In a walled prison, packs and sects of great ones,
That ebb and flow by th' moon.[5]
EDMUND   Take them away.
20 LEAR Upon such sacrifices,[6] my Cordelia,

5.2 Location: The rest of the play takes place near
the battlefield.
1. Trumpet call to battle (backstage).
2. See note to 4.6.212.
3. To await the destined time is the most important
thing, as fruit falls only when ripe (playing on Gloucester's "rot," line 8); readiness for death is our only duty
(compare *Hamlet* 5.2.194, "the readiness is all").
5.3
1. TEXTUAL COMMENT There are differences between
the entrance and exit directions in the First Quarto
and the Folio versions of 5.3. Q1's entrance of the
"Captain" late in the scene is replaced by the entrance

of the "Messenger" in F. The deletion of extraneous
roles is not unusual in the later revisions of plays, but
this scene's revision in F suggests that too many
"Captains" are wandering the stage in Q1. See Digital
Edition TC 6 (combined text).
2. *Good . . . pleasures:* Guard them well until the
desires of those greater persons.
3. Otherwise, I could be defiant in the face of bad
fortune.
4. Gaudy courtiers.
5. *packs . . . moon:* followers and factions of important people whose positions at court vary as the tide.
6. Upon such sacrifices as we are or as you have made.

The gods themselves throw incense. Have I caught thee?
He that parts us shall bring a brand from heaven
And fire us hence like foxes.[7] Wipe thine eyes.
The good years shall devour them, flesh and fell,[8]

25 Ere they shall make us weep.
We'll see 'em starved first. Come.

Exeunt [Soldiers with LEAR *and* CORDELIA].

EDMUND   Come hither, Captain. Hark.
Take thou this note; go follow them to prison.
One step I have advanced° thee; if thou dost   *promoted*

30 As this instructs thee, thou dost make thy way
To noble fortunes. Know thou this: that men
Are as the time is. To be tender-minded
Does not become a sword;° thy great employment   *befit a swordsman*
Will not bear question.° Either say thou'lt do't   *discussion*
Or thrive by other means.

35 CAPTAIN   I'll do't, my lord.

EDMUND   About it, and write happy when th' hast done.[9]
Mark, I say, instantly, and carry it° so   *carry it out*
As I have set it down.

38.1 CAPTAIN   *I cannot draw a cart, nor eat dried oats;°*   *(like a horse)*
If it be man's work, I'll do't.   *Exit* CAPTAIN.

Flourish. Enter ALBANY, GONERIL, REGAN, *Soldiers.*

ALBANY   Sir, you have showed today your valiant strain,°   *qualities; heritage*

40 And fortune led you well. You have the captives
Who were the opposites° of this day's strife.   *opponents*
I do require them of you, so to use° them   *treat*
As we shall find their merits and our safety
May equally determine.

EDMUND   Sir, I thought it fit

45 To send the old and miserable King to some retention,°   *confinement*
Whose° age had charms in it, whose title more,   *(Lear's)*
To pluck the common bosom[1] on his side
And turn our impressed lances° in our eyes   *conscripted lancers*
Which[2] do command them. With him I sent the Queen,

50 My reason all the same, and they are ready
Tomorrow or at further space° t'appear   *at a future point*
Where you shall hold your session.°   *court of judgment*

52.1   *At this time*
We sweat and bleed. The friend hath lost his friend,
And the best quarrels, in the heat, are cursed
By those that feel their sharpness.[3]

52.5 *The question of Cordelia and her father*
Requires a fitter place.

ALBANY   Sir, by your patience,
I hold you but a subject of° this war,   *in waging*
Not as a brother.

55 REGAN   That's as we list° to grace him.   *choose*

---

7. *shall . . . foxes:* must have divine aid to do so. The image is of using a torch to smoke foxes out of their holes—or, in the case of Lear and Cordelia, prison cells.
8. *flesh and fell:* meat and skin; entirely. The precise meaning of "good years" has not been explained; it may signify simply the passage of time or may suggest some ominous, destructive power.
9. Go to it, and call yourself happy when you are done.
1. To garner the affection of the populace.
2. *in our eyes / Which:* in the eyes of us who.
3. *And . . . sharpness:* And in the heat of battle, even the most just wars are cursed by those who must suffer the fighting.

Methinks our pleasure might have been demanded[4]
Ere you had spoke so far. He led our powers,°   *armies*
Bore the commission of my place and person,
The which immediacy° may well stand up   *close connection*
And call itself your brother.

60 GONERIL   Not so hot.°   *Not so fast*
In his own grace° he doth exalt himself   *merit*
More than in your addition.[5]

REGAN   In my rights,
By me invested, he compeers° the best.   *equals*

ALBANY   That were the most[6] if he should husband you.

REGAN   Jesters do oft prove prophets.

65 GONERIL   Holla, holla!
That eye that told you so looked but asquint.[7]

REGAN   Lady, I am not well, else I should answer
From a full-flowing stomach.° —General,   *anger*
Take thou my soldiers, prisoners, patrimony;

70 Dispose of them, of me. The walls° is thine.   *fortress of my heart*
Witness the world that I create thee here
My lord and master.

GONERIL   Mean you to enjoy him?

ALBANY   The let-alone° lies not in your good will.   *veto*

EDMUND   Nor in thine, lord.

ALBANY   Half-blooded° fellow, yes.   *Bastard*

75 REGAN   Let the drum strike,[8] and prove my title thine.

ALBANY   Stay yet; hear reason. Edmund, I arrest thee
On capital treason, and in thy arrest[9]
This gilded serpent. [*to* REGAN] For your claim, fair sister,°   *sister-in-law*
I bar it in the interest of my wife.

80 'Tis she is subcontracted to this lord,
And I her husband contradict your banns.°   *marriage announcement*
If you will marry, make your loves to me:
My lady is bespoke.

GONERIL   An interlude!°   *A farce*

ALBANY   Thou art armed, Gloucester. Let the trumpet sound.

85 If none appear to prove upon thy person
Thy heinous, manifest, and many treasons,
There is my pledge. [*He throws down his gauntlet.*] I'll make
    it on thy heart,
Ere I taste bread, thou art in nothing less°   *in no way less guilty*
Than I have here proclaimed thee.

REGAN   Sick, oh, sick!

90 GONERIL [*aside*]   If not, I'll ne'er trust medicine.°   *poison (euphemistic)*

EDMUND [*throwing down his gauntlet*]   There's my exchange.
    What° in the world he's   *Whoever*
That names me traitor, villain-like he lies.
Call by the trumpet. He that dares approach
On him, on you—who not—I will maintain
My truth and honor firmly.

95 ALBANY   A herald, ho!

---

4. I think you should have inquired into my wishes.
5. In the honors you confer upon him.
6. That investiture would be complete.
7. Squinting was a proverbial effect of jealousy, because of the tendency to look suspiciously at poten-

tial rivals.
8. Perhaps to announce the betrothal or a challenge.
9. And in order to accuse you; and as one who shares your corruption or crime.

Enter a HERALD.

Trust to thy single virtue,° for thy soldiers,   *your unassisted power*
All levied in my name, have in my name
Took their discharge.

REGAN   My sickness grows upon me.

ALBANY   She is not well; convey her to my tent.

                     [*Exit* REGAN, *attended.*]

100   Come hither, Herald; let the trumpet sound,
And read out this. [*He hands him a letter.*]
     A trumpet sounds.

HERALD (*reads*)   "If any man of quality or degree, within the
lists of the army, will maintain upon Edmund, supposed Earl
of Gloucester, that he is a manifold traitor, let him appear by
105   the third sound of the trumpet. He is bold in his defense."
     First trumpet [*sounds*].

Again!
     Second trumpet [*sounds*].

Again!
     Third trumpet [*sounds*].
     Trumpet answers within.
     Enter EDGAR, *armed.*

ALBANY   Ask him his purposes; why he appears
Upon this call o'th' trumpet.

HERALD   What° are you?   *Who*
110   Your name, your quality,° and why you answer   *degree; rank*
This present summons?

EDGAR   Know my name is lost,
By treason's tooth bare-gnawn and canker-bit,°   *worm-eaten*
Yet am I noble as the adversary
I come to cope.°   *to encounter*

ALBANY   Which is that adversary?

115 EDGAR   What's he that speaks for Edmund, Earl of
Gloucester?

EDMUND   Himself. What say'st thou to him?

EDGAR   Draw thy sword,
That° if my speech offend a noble heart,   *So that*
Thy arm may do thee justice. [*He draws his sword.*] Here is
mine.
Behold, it is my privilege,
120   The privilege of mine honors,
My oath, and my profession. I protest,
Maugre° thy strength, place, youth, and eminence,   *Despite*
Despite thy victor-sword, and fire-new° fortune,   *newly minted*
Thy valor and thy heart,° thou art a traitor,   *courage*
125   False to thy gods, thy brother, and thy father,
Conspirant 'gainst this high illustrious prince,
And from th'extremest upward° of thy head   *top*
To the descent° and dust below thy foot   *lowest part; sole*
A most toad-spotted[1] traitor. Say thou no,
130   This sword, this arm, and my best spirits are bent°   *ready*
To prove upon thy heart, whereto I speak,
Thou liest.

---

1. Venomous, like a toad; spotted with disgrace.

EDMUND   In wisdom I should ask thy name,
But since thy outside looks so fair and warlike,
And that thy tongue some say² of breeding breathes,
135 What safe and nicely I might well delay
By rule of knighthood, I disdain and spurn.³
Back do I toss these treasons to thy head,
With the hell-hated° lie o'erwhelm thy heart,   *hated as much as hell*
Which for° they yet glance by and scarcely bruise,   *since*
140 This sword of mine shall give them instant way°   *access*
Where they shall rest for ever. —Trumpets, speak.
        Alarums. Fights, and EDGAR *vanquishes* BASTARD.
ALBANY⁴   Save° him, save him!   *Spare*
GONERIL   This is practice,° Gloucester!   *trickery*
By th' law of war thou wast not bound to answer
An unknown opposite.° Thou art not vanquished   *opponent*
But cozened and beguiled.°   *cheated and deceived*
145 ALBANY [*showing her a letter*]   Shut your mouth, dame,
Or with this paper shall I stop° it. Hold,° sir,   *plug / Behold*
Thou worse than any name, read thine own evil.
No tearing, lady; I perceive you know it.
GONERIL   Say if I do, the laws are mine, not thine.
150 Who can arraign° me for't?   *Exit.*   *prosecute*
ALBANY [*to* EDMUND]   Most monstrous! Oh, know'st thou this
        paper?
EDMUND   Ask me not what I know.
ALBANY   Go after her. She's desperate; govern° her.   *restrain*
                    [*Exeunt some Soldiers.*]
EDMUND   What you have charged me with, that have I done,
155 And more, much more; the time will bring it out.
'Tis past, and so am I. But what art thou
That hast this fortune on me?⁵ If thou'rt noble,
I do forgive thee.
EDGAR   Let's exchange charity.°   *forgiveness*
[*He removes his helmet.*] I am no less in blood than thou
        art, Edmund;
160 If more, the more th' hast wronged me.
My name is Edgar and thy father's son.
The gods are just and of our pleasant vices
Make instruments to plague us:
The dark and vicious place where thee he got⁶
Cost him his eyes.
165 EDMUND   Th' hast spoken right, 'tis true:
The wheel° is come full circle. I am here.⁷   *Fortune's wheel*
ALBANY [*to* EDGAR]   Methought thy very gait did prophesy
A royal nobleness. I must embrace thee.
Let sorrow split my heart if ever I
Did hate thee or thy father.
170 EDGAR   Worthy prince, I know't.

2. Taste (from "assay"); utterance.
3. *And . . . spurn*: And since your speech may suggest high birth, I will not stick safely and meticulously to the rules of knighthood (which do not
require a knight to fight an unknown opponent) and
refuse to fight you.

4. Both F and Q give this speech to "*Alb.*" (for
Albany), which may be a compositor's error for "*All.*"
5. Who have this good fortune at my expense.
6. The adulterous bed in which you were conceived;
or, possibly, the vagina. *got*: begot.
7. Back at the lowest point.

ALBANY   Where have you hid yourself?
How have you known the miseries of your father?
EDGAR   By nursing them, my lord. List° a brief tale,   *Listen to*
And when 'tis told, oh, that my heart would burst!
175 The bloody proclamation to escape,[8]
That followed me so near—oh, our lives' sweetness,
That we the pain of death would hourly die
Rather than die at once[9]—taught me to shift
Into a madman's rags, t'assume a semblance
180 That very° dogs disdained, and in this habit   *even*
Met I my father with his bleeding rings°—   *sockets*
Their precious stones° new lost—became his guide,   *eyes*
Led him, begged for him, saved him from despair.
Never—oh, fault—revealed myself unto him
185 Until some half hour past, when I was armed.
Not sure, though hoping of this good success,°   *conclusion*
I asked his blessing and from first to last
Told him our pilgrimage. But his flawed° heart,   *cracked*
Alack, too weak the conflict to support,
190 Twixt two extremes of passion, joy and grief,
Burst smilingly.
EDMUND   This speech of yours hath moved me
And shall perchance do good. But speak you on;
You look as you had something more to say.
ALBANY   If there be more, more woeful, hold it in,
195 For I am almost ready to dissolve,°   *melt into tears*
Hearing of this.
196.1   EDGAR   *This would have seemed a period° to such*   *conclusion*
As love not sorrow, but another to amplify° too much   *enlarge; extend*
Would make much more and top extremity.
Whilst I was big in clamor,° came there in a man,   *lamenting loudly*
196.5   *Who having seen me in my worst estate*
Shunned my abhorred society, but then finding
Who 'twas that so endured, with his strong arms
He fastened on my neck and bellowed out
As he'd burst heaven, threw me on my father,
196.10   *Told the most piteous tale of Lear and him°*   *himself*
That ever ear received, which, in recounting,
His grief grew puissant,° and the strings of life   *powerful*
Began to crack twice. Then the trumpets sounded.
And there I left him tranced.
ALBANY   *But who was this?*
196.15   EDGAR   *Kent, sir, the banished Kent, who in disguise*
Followed his enemy king[1] and did him service
Improper° for a slave.   *Unfit even*
          Enter a GENTLEMAN [*with a bloody knife*].
GENTLEMAN   Help, help! Oh, help!
EDGAR   What kind of help?
ALBANY   Speak, man.
EDGAR   What means this bloody knife?
GENTLEMAN   'Tis hot! It smokes! It came even from the heart of—

---

8. In order to escape the sentence of death.   1. Because Lear had previously banished him. *enemy:*
9. *our . . . once:* how sweet must life be that we pre-   hostile.
fer the constant pain of dying to death itself.

Oh, she's dead.
200 ALBANY   Who dead? Speak, man.
GENTLEMAN   Your lady, sir, your lady—and her sister
    By her is poisoned; she confesses it.
EDMUND   I was contracted to them both; all three
    Now marry° in an instant.   unite (in death)
        Enter KENT.
EDGAR   Here comes Kent.
205 ALBANY   Produce the bodies, be they alive or dead.
        Goneril and Regan's bodies brought out.
    This judgment of the heavens that makes us tremble
    Touches us not with pity. Oh, is this he?
    The time will not allow the compliment
    Which very manners urges.[2]
KENT   I am come
210 To bid my king and master aye° good night.   forever
    Is he not here?
ALBANY   Great thing of° us forgot!   by
    Speak, Edmund, where's the King? And where's Cordelia?
    Seest thou this object,° Kent?   spectacle
KENT   Alack, why thus?
EDMUND   Yet° Edmund was beloved: Despite all
215 The one the other poisoned for my sake
    And after slew herself.
ALBANY   Even so. Cover their faces.
EDMUND   I pant for life. Some good I mean to do
    Despite of mine own nature. Quickly send—
220 Be brief° in it—to th' castle, for my writ[3]   speedy
    Is on the life of Lear and on Cordelia.
    Nay, send in time.
ALBANY   Run, run, oh, run!
EDGAR   To who, my lord? —Who has the office?°   commission
    Send thy token of reprieve.
EDMUND   Well thought on. Take my sword,
    Give it the° Captain.   to the
225 EDGAR   Haste thee for thy life!
                          [*Exit* GENTLEMAN.]
EDMUND   He hath commission from thy wife and me
    To hang Cordelia in the prison and
    To lay the blame upon her own despair,
    That she fordid herself.[4]
230 ALBANY   The gods defend her! Bear him hence awhile.
                          [EDMUND *is carried out by Soldiers.*]
        Enter LEAR, *with* CORDELIA *in his arms*[*, and*
        GENTLEMAN].
LEAR   Howl, howl, howl! Oh, you are men of stones!
    Had I your tongues and eyes, I'd use them so
    That heaven's vault should crack. She's gone forever.
    I know when one is dead and when one lives;
235 She's dead as earth. Lend me a looking glass,

---

2. *the compliment . . . urges:* the ceremony that barest custom demands.
3. Order of execution.

4. Destroyed herself. In most of Shakespeare's
source texts for the play, Cordelia does in fact kill
herself after reigning for some years.

If that her breath will mist or stain the stone,[5]
Why, then, she lives.[6]
KENT   Is this the promised end?[7]
EDGAR   Or image of that horror.
ALBANY   Fall and cease.[8]
LEAR   This feather stirs. She lives! If it be so,
240 It is a chance which does redeem all sorrows
That ever I have felt.
KENT   O my good master.
LEAR   Prithee, away.
EDGAR   'Tis noble Kent, your friend.
LEAR   A plague upon you murderers, traitors all!
I might have saved her; now she's gone forever.
245 Cordelia, Cordelia, stay a little. Ha,
What is't thou say'st? Her voice was ever soft,
Gentle, and low, an excellent thing in woman.
—I killed the slave that was a-hanging thee.
GENTLEMAN   'Tis true, my lords, he did.
LEAR   Did I not, fellow?
250 I have seen the day, with my good biting falchion°   light sword
I would have made him skip. I am old now,
And these same crosses spoil me.[9] Who are you?
Mine eyes are not o'th' best, I'll tell you straight.°   recognize you soon
KENT   If Fortune brag of two she loved and hated,
255 One of them we behold.[1]
LEAR   This is a dull sight;[2] are you not Kent?
KENT   The same: your servant Kent.
Where is your servant Caius?°   (Kent's pseudonym)
LEAR   He's a good fellow, I can tell you that;
260 He'll strike, and quickly, too. He's dead and rotten.
KENT   No, my good lord, I am the very man—
LEAR   I'll see that straight.[3]
KENT   —That from your first of difference and decay[4]
Have followed your sad steps.
LEAR   You are welcome hither.
265 KENT   Nor no man else.[5]
All's cheerless, dark, and deadly.°   deathly
Your eldest daughters have fordone° themselves   destroyed
And desperately° are dead.   in despair
LEAR   Ay, so I think.
ALBANY   He knows not what he says, and vain° is it   in vain
That we present us to him.
          Enter a MESSENGER.
270 EDGAR   Very bootless.°   futile
MESSENGER   Edmund is dead, my lord.

---

5. Mica, or stone polished to a mirror finish.
6. PERFORMANCE COMMENT Each production must determine whether to sustain suspense regarding the possibility that Cordelia is still alive or to make it clear that her father is raving over a corpse. See Digital Edition PC 6.
7. Doomsday; expected end of the play. In no version of the story previous to Shakespeare's does Cordelia die at this point.
8. Let the world collapse and end.
9. And these recent adversities have weakened me; and these parries I could once match would now destroy me.

1. *If . . . behold*: If there were only two supreme examples in the world of Fortune's ability to raise up and cast down, Lear would be one; alternatively, we are each of us one (Lear and Kent are here looking at each other).
2. This is a sad sight; my vision is failing.
3. I'll attend to that shortly; I'll comprehend that in a moment.
4. Who from the beginning of your alteration and deterioration.
5. No, neither I nor anyone else is welcome. Alternatively, I am that man, not disguised as anyone else.

ALBANY   That's but a trifle here.
You lords and noble friends, know our intent:
What comfort to this great decay° may come   ruin; destruction
Shall be applied. For us, we will resign
275   During the life of this old majesty
To him our absolute power; [*to* EDGAR] you to your rights,
With boot° and such addition° as your honors   reward / distinction
Have more than merited. All friends shall
Taste the wages of their virtue and all foes
280   The cup of their deservings. Oh, see, see!
LEAR   And my poor fool[6] is hanged. No, no, no life?
Why should a dog, a horse, a rat have life,
And thou no breath at all? Thou'lt come no more,
Never, never, never, never, never!
285   Pray you, undo this button. Thank you, sir.
Do you see this? Look on her! Look, her lips,
Look there. Look there![7]
          He dies.
EDGAR   He faints. My lord, my lord.
KENT   Break, heart, I prithee, break.
EDGAR   Look up, my lord.
KENT   Vex not his ghost.[8] Oh, let him pass! He hates him
290   That would upon the rack[9] of this tough world
Stretch him out longer.
EDGAR   He is gone indeed.
KENT   The wonder is he hath endured so long.
He but usurped his life.[1]
ALBANY   Bear them from hence. Our present business
295   Is general woe. [*to* KENT *and* EDGAR] Friends of my soul,
          you twain
Rule in this realm and the gored° state sustain.   wounded; bloody
KENT   I have a journey, sir, shortly to go.
My master calls me. I must not say no.
EDGAR[2]   The weight of this sad time we must obey;
300   Speak what we feel, not what we ought to say.
The oldest hath borne most; we that are young
Shall never see so much, nor live so long.
                    Exeunt with a dead march.

6. A term of endearment, here used for Cordelia, though it also recalls the disappearance of Lear's Fool after 3.6.
7. Textual Comment All the source plays for the King Lear story show Lear and Cordelia prevailing, with Cordelia surviving and accepting the role of Lear's successor as monarch. In the Folio text, unlike in the Quarto text, Lear apparently thinks that his attempts to revive her are successful. See Digital Edition TC 7 (combined text).
8. Do not disturb his departing soul.
9. Instrument of torture, used to stretch its victims.

1. From death, which already had a claim on it.
2. Textual Comment One of the apparently minor but nevertheless significant differences between the two early texts of *King Lear* is that in the First Quarto text the last lines of the play are given to Albany, whereas in the Folio they are given to Edgar. These powerful lines suggest that their speaker will inherit political leadership, and conflating editors face the challenge of selecting which character should stand as the moral and political spokesperson at the end of the play. See Digital Edition TC 8 (combined text).

Timon of Athens

In a jewelry advertisement, a handsome man and a beautiful woman share a rapturous embrace. A large diamond sparkles on the woman's finger; apparently, the impressive ring symbolizes a love equally magnificent. Although the deliberate confusion of emotional and financial investments seems crass once it is explicitly recognized, the ad can only be effective at selling jewelry if it captures something people know, or wish, to be true. What does love have to do with money? How closely entwined are friendship and material self-interest? Are persons esteemed for intrinsic personal characteristics or for the glamor of their possessions? Are affluent communities or prosperous individuals especially likely to confuse sheer wealth with other forms of value? *Timon of Athens* asks such questions with a fierce relentlessness unusual for Shakespeare. In the past four decades its tale of debt-fueled extravagance followed by ruin has inspired a series of memorable productions that have drawn connections between the world of the play and our own society, with its rampant consumerism and its precarious reliance upon borrowed funds.

It is probably no coincidence that *Timon's* schematic plot and static characters seem closer to the satiric drama of Shakespeare's contemporaries than to the other tragedies that Shakespeare was writing around 1605–08, the probable date of its composition. Recent scholarship strongly suggests that *Timon* is a collaborative work, about a third of which was written by Shakespeare's fellow dramatist Thomas Middleton. (Middleton seems to have been responsible for act 1, scene 2, the long party scene, and for most of the third act, when Timon's fortunes turn; he may have contributed to other parts of the play as well.) In many of his comedies, Middleton addresses the selfishness and hypocrisy of the commercial London of his day. He frequently portrays young spendthrifts struggling, as Timon does, in the clutches of predatory lenders. At the same time, the connections between *Timon* and Shakespeare's other plays are clear enough. The plot derives from that Shakespearean favorite, Plutarch's *Lives,* which also provided the sources for *Julius Caesar, Antony and Cleopatra,* and *Coriolanus. Timon* has strong affinities to *The Merchant of Venice* in its concern with the connections between material and intangible goods, and between friendship and moneylending. The play's jaundiced view of ancient Greece recalls *Troilus and Cressida,* as does its evasion of ordinary generic categories: although its protagonist dies at the end, its title does not promise a tragedy but merely a "life." The hero's sensational degradation from preeminence to utter penury, and his ferociously misanthropic reaction to that humiliation, has often prompted comparison with *King Lear.*

Timon opens on a panorama of glittering abundance. Purveyors of luxury goods—art, poems, jewels, textiles—flock to Timon's palace in hope of reward. Like advertisers today, they claim that their goods have a symbolic significance that goes beyond their obvious beauty or utility: these items give concrete expression to the ineffable virtues of their possessor. "Things of like value differing in the owners / Are prizèd by their masters," fawns the Jeweler. "You mend the jewel by the wearing it" (1.1.172–73, 174). The guests at Timon's sumptuous banquet are likewise loud in their admiration for their host. Their conversation turns almost obsessively upon Timon's apparently inexhaustible fortune.

And no wonder—for Timon seems not merely rich but unique. His generosity is characterized by what the Poet calls "magic of bounty," an outflow uncannily unbalanced by any apparent countereffort at acquisition. While ordinary owners have the power merely to transfer, not actually to generate, new goods, Timon seems freed from such basic material laws. He dispenses his "bounty" as if he were a god empowered to create wealth from nothing. But Timon's "magic" relies on a trick that he himself resolutely ignores. Using his lands as collateral, he borrows the money he needs to buy expensive presents and keep a lavish table. The recipients of his hospitality are often the same men to whom he is indebted.

To Timon's surprise, but hardly to the audience's, his elaborate charade collapses in the play's second act. Why has he behaved so self-destructively? We are given clues to his motives when, in the course of his banquet, he and his guests explicitly and implicitly offer several theories about the relationship of his "bounty" both to the social weal and to his own self-conception. Timon desires love and admiration, and in Athenian society, as in many others, money proves a potent way of getting both. The adjectives "good," "worthy," "free," "kind," "gentle," and "noble" echo through the first act—their simultaneously economic and moral significance tending to break down any difference between the two domains. When Ventidius offers to return the large sum that Timon has spent releasing him from prison, Timon refuses:

> You mistake my love.
> I gave it freely ever, and there's none
> Can truly say he gives if he receives.
> (1.2.9–11)

Typically, love and money are here almost inextricable. Is the "it" that Timon freely gives the love to which he refers in the previous line or the money he has bestowed upon Ventidius? Moreover, Timon's generosity is entangled with a desire for mastery. By always giving, never receiving, Timon attempts to force his beneficiaries into an endlessly grateful and therefore subordinate role. His conduct recalls that of the chiefs of the Native American tribes of the Pacific Northwest, who consolidated their status by "potlatches," great parties at which they would give away virtually all their possessions, thus compelling their guests to serve them in the future. In such a system, divesting oneself of wealth, not accumulating it, is the primary mode of acquiring status.

In the socioeconomic world of the potlatch, in which the recipient of a gift is profoundly obliged to the donor, Timon might well escape serious financial danger. His "courtiers" would have to repay him somehow, in kind or in service. Timon briefly imagines such a system when he rhapsodizes at his dinner party: "We are born to do benefits, and what better or properer can we call our own than the riches of our friends? Oh, what a precious comfort 'tis to have so many like brothers commanding one another's fortunes!" (1.2.97–100). Unfortunately, not only is this communitarian vision at odds with Timon's insistence on entirely unilateral gift-giving, but it is grossly out of kilter with the covetous society in which he actually lives. When Timon pays Ventidius's debt, Ventidius's messenger declares that "Your lordship ever binds him" (1.1.106); likewise the First Lord claims to be "virtuously bound" by Timon's generosity (1.2.223). Yet by the middle of act 2, they have already lost any sense of commitment to their erstwhile benefactor. Timon's "bonds," the legal instruments that enable his lenders to seize his lands when he forfeits cash repayment, turn out to be more "binding" than the unwritten ties of gratitude. In Athens, tangible goods are considered more real than intangible ones, legal commitments more real than obligations informally imposed.

Apemantus, hovering on the margins of Timon's dinner party, introduces an alternative economic language early in the play: the audience's perception of the entire banquet extravaganza is filtered through his commentary. Apemantus is a Cynic, that is, a follower of a Greek philosophical school that repudiated conventional desires for wealth and social prominence and regarded many forms of human interaction as hypocritical and self-serving. For Timon, magnanimity apparently comes naturally and gifts express sociability. For Apemantus, by contrast, people are naturally greedy and antisocial: protestations of friendship and gratitude conceal an impulse to accumulate wealth at the expense of another, just as lavishness conceals a desire for adulation. In such circumstances, the Cynic philosopher preserves his safety and integrity by repudiating his need both for property and for other people:

> Immortal gods, I crave no pelf.
> I pray for no man but myself.
> Grant I may never prove so fond
> To trust a man on his oath or bond,
> Or a harlot for her weeping,
> Or a dog that seems a-sleeping,
> Or a keeper with my freedom,
> Or my friends if I should need 'em.
> (1.2.62–69)

To Timon's generous trustfulness, Apemantus counterpoises a self-protective suspicion. The difference in the way the two men conceive of human nature correlates with a difference in the way they imagine the material world. Timon believes that wealth is endlessly renewable and thus endlessly sharable without decrease. Apemantus believes that resources are strictly limited and that one person's gain must entail another person's loss. Thus what Timon sees as banquet pleasantries amount, in Apemantus's view, to a form of cannibalism. "O you gods! What a number of men eats Timon, and he sees 'em not? It grieves me to see so many dip their meat in one man's blood" (1.2.40–42). Both of these apparently opposite attitudes, however— Timon's romanticism and Apemantus's reductiveness—are actually rooted in a conviction that one's possessions, or the lack of them, centrally determine the way one thinks of oneself and interacts with other people. Arguably, Apemantus's cannibal imagery makes the shared materialism of the two men's attitudes especially obvious to a Christian audience; for that vision of Timon's banquet parodies, in grotesquely literal terms, the dispersal of Christ's spiritual body in the Communion ceremony.

Most scholars believe that *Timon of Athens* was written between 1606 and 1608, several years after the accession of James I to the English throne. There are good reasons why Timon's particular economic dilemma would interest dramatists observing the contemporary scene in these years. If the play was, as many argue, left unfinished and unproduced, perhaps it was too incendiary to be safely performed in Jacobean England: although most of Shakespeare's plays reflect to some extent the time in which they were written, *Timon* is unusual in its brutally direct topical relevance. In the first decade of the seventeenth century, the traditional aristocratic virtues of openhanded generosity and carelessness of expense were coming into increasingly acute conflict with the limited means upon which the great nobles could actually draw. As England became an international trading power, luxuries once unheard of became available to people with the money to buy them. As tastes grew more sophisticated, noblemen who wished to impress peers and subordinates with the splendor of their "bounty" were forced into ever greater expenditures. The result was an extraordinary expansion in the credit markets. The worst offender in this respect was King James, who—like Timon—showered his favorites with expensive gifts, a habit that created staggering deficits in the Royal Exchequer. By 1608, royal indebtedness had reached crisis proportions, and other members of the upper aristocracy were likewise floating on a sea of debt and credit.

Shakespeare, or Shakespeare and Middleton, thus bears witness to a society in the process of a crucial economic transition—a transition that affects more than financial matters narrowly defined. In the first act, Timon assumes that his money transactions are accompanied by affection on the part of the giver and gratitude on the part of the recipient. In an informal, small-scale credit system, the difference between love and money, and between loans and gifts, may indeed become blurred, for friends may help one another financially on occasion. In Jacobean England, however, the inability of the upper classes to live within their means overstrained the limits of "friendly understanding": for few people then or now lend really substantial sums of money out of sheer amiability. Borrowing and lending thus increasingly became business matters transacted between relative strangers, divorced from rather than continuous with friendship and patronage relationships. Usury, a practice traditionally deplored and even illegal, was nonetheless widespread and increasingly accepted as a necessary fact of life.

A fiscally prudent, hardworking businessman, Shakespeare may well have been shocked on occasion at the profligacy of the patrons upon whose expansiveness he and his theater company partly depended. Certainly he recognized acutely that the motives of the Poet and the Painter do not differ from the motives of the other courtiers: "artists" in Athens are as venal as everybody else. What seems to have intrigued him most, however, is the way in which an apparently rather limited social phenomenon—aristocratic reliance on credit—necessarily affects social and even biological relations that seem far removed from moneylending. Uniquely among Shakespeare's plays, *Timon* is nearly bereft of women. The few who do briefly appear—the Amazons of act 1, Alcibiades' whores in act 4—are pointedly excluded from the "normal" marital relationships in which most socially useful reproductive activity traditionally takes place. In this nearly all-male world, the language of erotic intimacy is reserved for interactions among men. Exchanges of money and commodities take over some of the functions of procreative sexual intimacy, an appropriation that can easily be construed as perverse or depraved. Lending money at interest seems especially corrupt: *Timon of Athens* draws upon an ancient tradition of imagining usury to be a form of unnatural "breeding." After his disillusionment, Timon continually and deliberately conflates lust with greed, the venereal with the venal. Syphilis and its symptoms are not merely analogies for, but are perhaps even the consequences of, economic iniquity.

Despite the virtual absence of

Penthesilea, Queen of the Amazons. Drawing by Inigo Jones. From *The Masque of Queens* (1609), by Ben Jonson.

Dame Fortune, blind, standing on a ball with wings (to show how quickly her favors may fly away). From George Wither, *A Collection of Emblems* (1635).

actual women, allegorical representations of female power play an important rhetorical role in *Timon of Athens*. The first half of the play is dominated by the allegorical figure of Fortune. The Poet describes her as a "sovereign lady" enthroned "upon a high and pleasant hill" (1.1.69, 64), huge, omnipotent, and whimsical, raising and crushing her struggling male subjects for no apparent reason. In the second half of the play, "Mother Earth" has some of the same threatening demeanor. The ruined Timon forsakes Athens for the wilderness outside it, rather as Shakespeare's lovers had done in that drastically different play *A Midsummer Night's Dream*. In *Dream*, the woods outside Athens are a lushly sexual place, but in *Timon*, roughly the same geographical locale is unusually harsh and minimalist. Like the whores to whom Timon compares her, Mother Earth is barren, refusing to surrender the roots for which Timon digs and instead yielding only the gold he had hoped to flee. Thus, for all the energy spent exposing the "unnaturalness" of Athenians' economic relations, a potentially restorative "natural" alternative is wholly lacking.

In many respects, Timon's disillusioned ferocity simply inverts, recoils from, the generous courtesy he had manifested throughout act 1. Yet not everything changes: there is a clear continuity to Timon's personality in the first and second halves of the play. Initially, as a wealthy patron and benefactor, Timon isolates himself from others by making himself a god of generosity. Later, as an indigent, he similarly sets himself apart, cursing mankind with all the immoderation with which he once blessed it. Shakespeare was fascinated throughout his career by self-absorbed, almost solipsistic characters: Adonis in *Venus and Adonis,* the young man of the sonnets, Malvolio in *Twelfth Night* "sick of self-love." Timon exemplifies an extreme version of this egocentrism, his sense of his own separateness untouched even after his conception of human nature has been poisoned at its source. He not only dies alone, but—in the possibly corrupt text that has come down to us—mysteriously manages to bury himself and engrave his own epitaph: an epitaph that typically, and perversely, both demands that passersby remember him and orders them to "Seek not my name" (5.5.71).

The necessarily social medium of the drama finds true hermits impossible to accommodate. For most of acts 4 and 5, various acquaintances crowd to Timon's cave as they once crowded to his palace, some to commiserate or to offer advice, some to investigate rumors that Timon had discovered gold while digging for roots to eat. The disillusioned Timon no longer wants gold, because it has value only insofar as it can be exchanged, and thus requires that its users form relationships with other human beings. So, ironically, the man who once blessed his "friends" with treasure once again gives it away to them, this time with his curses. The sense of separateness Timon has always possessed makes satiric alienation congenial to him; but, like many satirists, he is an ambiguous figure. The satirist can tell truths about society because his disengagement gives him the standing to criticize practices he regards as corrupt. At the same time, his observational acuteness—his refusal to accept the complacencies of the majority—bespeaks a certain imbalance. The satirist's misanthropy coexists curiously with an inability to mind his own business. The tone of the play's latter acts thus becomes profoundly equivocal. Are we supposed to agree with Timon that virtually all human values and activities can be plausibly reduced to money and the greed for it? Certainly the action of the play gives us ample reason to share his disgust at his erstwhile friends. Or is his rage disproportionate to the adversities he endures? Just as the Timon of the early acts can be variously characterized as noble and foolish, the later Timon has seemed to some critics a sublimely disappointed idealist, to others a petulant whiner.

A few characters suggest that Timon's unmitigated misanthropy is too simple and incomplete. The steward Flavius's loyalty to his former master defies the terms of Timon's blanket condemnation of all humankind, as Timon reluctantly acknowledges. Throughout *Timon,* low-ranking characters—having less to gain from greed— display an acute sense of gratitude and obligation sadly lacking in their "betters." All Timon's servants, not merely Flavius, seem dismayed by their master's ruin; and in 3.4, the usurers' servants, talking among themselves, freely condemn the commands they are forced to carry out. But Timon prefers to believe that rapacity is a universal human trait, not a more limited, class-linked phenomenon. Reduced to rags and roots though he is, Timon cannot help being a snob. And to some extent, his status consciousness seems justified: for if the servants are kindhearted, they are also ineffectual. Their lack of resources prevents them from remedying the social problems they witness.

Alcibiades provides a more formidable alternative to the Athenian usurers, although the connection between this subplot and the main action is sketchy. Certainly he does not escape, or seek to disentangle, the interconnections between love and money that eventually seem so poisonous to Timon: when he visits Timon in the cave, he comes with a prostitute on each arm. Nonetheless, in his brief appearances, Alcibiades testifies to the existence of a less restricted, more complex sociopolitical world than the one we witness for most of the play. Whereas, for instance, Timon's function in Athens seems mainly to give expensive dinner parties, Alcibiades insists that Timon has performed important military services for the state: that his "bounty" has had a political and executive, as well as a sheerly economic, aspect. Unfortunately, the relationship between Timon and Alcibiades, as well as the relationship between the city's politics and its social organization, is left largely undeveloped in the text of the play as it has come down to us. The soldier, pursuing his vocation in the bleak world beyond the city walls, is imagined as partly outside the economic system in which other characters are enmeshed. Like the hermit-satirist, he has the special credibility that comes with distance. But whereas Timon's detachment is the product of a merely negative disgust, Alcibiades' involves allegiance to a different set of positive values. In 3.6, not only does he risk himself to defend a friend, but the terms of his defense hint at a code of behavior divorced from cash rewards and penalties.

At the end of the play, after Timon's death, the Athenian senators invite Alcibiades and his army back into the city. He will, they hope, "Approach the fold and cull th'infected forth" (5.5.43), as a shepherd kills the sick animals of his flock in order to keep disease from spreading to the remainder. The senators argue that greed is merely the failing of a degenerate few, not the universal human trait Timon had believed it to be. Alcibiades seems to accept this claim, agreeing to renounce the indiscriminate violence of a war against all Athens in favor of the more targeted punishment of particular offenders. But the play entertains this alternative view of Timon's plight too late and too hastily to carry much conviction, and the apparent optimism of the conclusion thus seems unearned. How Alcibiades' invasion will reform Athens is hard to imagine.

KATHARINE EISAMAN MAUS

SELECTED BIBLIOGRAPHY

Bailey, Amanda. "*Timon of Athens*, Forms of Payback, and the Genre of Debt." *English Literary Renaissance* 41 (2011): 375–400. Examines *Timon*'s connection to the system of credit and debt in early modern England.

Chorost, Michael. "Biological Finance in Shakespeare's *Timon of Athens*." *English Literary Renaissance* 21 (1991): 349–70. Looks at gift and money economies in *Timon* and the language of biological reproduction in which they are described.

Jowett, John. "Middleton and Debt in *Timon of Athens*." *Money and the Age of Shakespeare: Essays in New Economic Criticism*. Ed. Linda Woodbridge. New York: Palgrave Macmillan, 2003. Argues that the play reflects the economic attitudes of Thomas Middleton, Shakespeare's probable collaborator.

Kahn, Coppélia. "'Magic of Bounty': *Timon of Athens*, Jacobean Patronage, and Maternal Power." *Shakespeare Quarterly* 38 (1987): 34–57. Analyzes *Timon*'s links to the contradictory practices of Jacobean court patronage.

Lupton, Julia. "Job of Athens, Timon of Uz." *Thinking with Shakespeare: Essays on Politics and Life*. Chicago: U of Chicago P, 2011. 131–61. Compares reversals of fortune in the stories of Timon and the biblical Job.

Nuttall, A. D. *Timon of Athens*. Harvester New Critical Introductions to Shakespeare. Hemel Hempstead: Harvester Wheatsheaf, 1989. Offers chapters on stage history and critical reception, followed by a detailed commentary on the play.

Paster, Gail Kern. *The Idea of the City in the Age of Shakespeare*. Athens: U of Georgia P, 1985. 99–108. Looks at *Timon*'s bleak vision of urban life, as enacted in the hero's transformation from philanthropist to misanthrope.

Scott, Alison V. *Selfish Gifts: The Politics of Exchange and English Courtly Literature, 1580–1628*. Madison, NJ: Fairleigh Dickinson UP, 2005. Describes the culture of patronage and self-seeking upon which *Timon* comments.

FILM

Timon of Athens. 1981. Dir. Jonathan Miller. UK. 128 min. Sepia-toned BBC-TV production featuring Athenians in Jacobean dress. Jonathan Pryce stars as an initially clueless and eventually very battered Timon. Effectively slimy performances in the subsidiary roles.

TEXTUAL INTRODUCTION

The survival of *Timon of Athens* is largely a matter of chance, as evidence suggests that it was not originally to be included in the 1623 Folio. The Folio marks the play's first appearance in print, together with seventeen other Shakespeare plays that had not been published in an earlier quarto edition.

The play's initial textual history is tied to a dispute over the rights to Shakespeare's *Troilus and Cressida*. The printing syndicate that united to publish the First Folio had planned to include the latter play, but came into difficulties over ownership of the text. As a stopgap, *Timon of Athens* was brought in to fill up the pages left available by the missing *Troilus and Cressida*. This sequence of events is suggested by the fact that *Timon* occupies less space in the Folio than was allotted to it. The run of signatures, or pages, is too short, and the play was printed with an unusual degree of "white space," suggesting that the printers were trying to stretch it to cover more pages. Further, the initial "Catalogue" or list of plays does not include *Troilus*, which is located between the tragedies and histories in a run of signatures that is out of place. But the strongest evidence that *Timon* replaced *Troilus* occurs in a canceled sheet, which prints the first two pages of *Troilus*, that survives in a handful of copies following *Romeo and Juliet*. *Timon* is placed after *Romeo and Juliet* in most copies of the Folio. The canceled sheet indicates that early plans had gone awry.

So we are lucky that *Timon* survives at all, which raises a question as to why those collecting the Folio's plays—Shakespeare's fellow actors John Hemminges and Henry Condell—would initially seek to exclude the text. The answer probably lies in the likelihood that *Timon of Athens* was a collaborative effort, almost certainly written in part by Thomas Middleton. Similarly coauthored plays, *Pericles* and *The Two Noble Kinsmen*, were also left out of the Folio. That being said, other coauthored Shakespeare plays were included, so the exact reasons for excluding *Timon* from the initial conception of the volume cannot be fully determined.

Another possible reason for not including the play is the unsatisfactory nature of the text itself. *Timon* as it stands seems to lack the tidiness required to bring a play onto the stage, and as such it might reflect an early authorial draft, rather than a working theatrical copy. It is full of false starts and repetitions. Famously, Timon's epitaph at the end of the play includes two mutually contradictory rhyming couplets (see Digital Edition TC 9). The names of characters are frequently altered, as when Ventidius becomes Ventigius in 1.2, or when Apemantus is described as Apermantus in 1.1 and 1.2. The play also has several confusing moments in which servants are called by their masters' names. While the characters cause confusion in places, the dialogue can be said to be even more difficult to follow. The text contains patchy verse and errant lineation, with prose set as verse and verse set as prose. Characters switch between the two in a way that is uncharacteristic of Shakespeare, but does happen in Middleton's works. The dialogue also can be very opaque, and editors make frequent emendations to try to bring sense to seemingly corrupt passages. The text therefore poses challenges to readers attempting to make sense of its language and constant stream of thinly developed characters. Yet the text is not so corrupt as to disguise the obvious rhetorical and emotive power of the protagonist, and its inconsistencies make for a surprisingly contemporary play, one whose sometimes jarring scenic cadences have been well received on the stage.

EUGENE GIDDENS

PERFORMANCE NOTE

In general, directors of *Timon of Athens* view the protagonist predominantly as either a reckless prodigal bringing misery on himself or a magnanimous benefactor driven to desperation by parasitic Athenians. While productions can incorporate elements of both characterizations, they must decide how responsible Timon is for his downfall, a decision that impacts the second half's representation of his misanthropy. Some productions present Timon's generosity as transparently egocentric, his subsequent degradation then seeming a just punishment for vanity. Others make clear that Timon's vice is not self-love but excessive, guileless love for others, his fall the more tragic for proceeding from overabundant faith in his friends. In either case, Timon can deliver his invectives as a disconsolate wretch, a raging madman, or a visionary, depending on whether directors and actors see sadness, regret, or spiritual abnegation mingled with his cynicism. Timon's apparent lack of familial ties has also inspired productions to explain his wild generosity as founded on a desperate need for emotional intimacy, thus helping to excuse the fault and ennoble the character.

Though *Timon* is rarely produced, its preoccupations with wealth and greed give it urgent contemporary relevance, and productions commonly use modern dress and present-day substitutes for Athens. Nicholas Hytner's 2012 production, for example, began with Timon dedicating a room in a London art gallery while an Occupy-style protest took place nearby, the second half reducing him to a homeless figure pushing a cart under a bridge. Productions can use such contemporary parallels to dignify Timon—for example, by indicating that a market crash, rather than personal extravagance, is responsible for Timon's ruin. Like Timon, the secondary characters are often treated analogically or allegorized, but all productions must decide whether Apemantus is a well-meaning sage or a surly cynic, and whether Alcibiades is Athens' great hope or a new form of devourer. Both characters can seem pained by or indifferent to Timon's afflictions, while Flavius can remain a loyal steward or grasp after gold as eagerly as the rest. Other considerations in performance include staging the masque, the physical prominence of the gold and other gifts, and settling the text's contradictory versions of Timon's epitaph.

BRETT GAMBOA

The Life of Timon of Athens

THE PERSONS OF THE PLAY

TIMON of Athens
POET
PAINTER
JEWELER
MERCHANT
OLD ATHENIAN
LUCIUS ⎱
LUCULLUS ⎰ flattering lords and senators
SEMPRONIUS ⎱
VENTIDIUS, false friend to Timon
APEMANTUS, a churlish philosopher
ALCIBIADES, an Athenian captain
CUPID, a character in the masque
Masquers, LADIES as Amazons
FLAMINIUS ⎱
SERVILIUS ⎰ servants to Timon
LUCILIUS ⎱
Flavius, Timon's STEWARD
CAPHIS, a servant
Two of VARRO'S SERVANTS
TITUS, a servant
HORTENSIUS, a servant
PHILOTUS, a servant
LUCIUS' SERVANT
ISIDORE'S SERVANT
Other SERVANTS and Attendants
Four of Timon's FRIENDS
LORDS
SENATORS
BANDITTI, or thieves
MESSENGERS
FOOL
PAGE
Three STRANGERS
PHRYNIA
TIMANDRA
SOLDIERS

1.1

Enter POET, PAINTER, JEWELER, [*and*] MERCHANT *at
several doors.*[1]

POET   Good day, sir.
PAINTER   I am glad you're well.
POET   I have not seen you long. How goes the world?

1.1 Location: Timon's house, Athens.
1. TEXTUAL COMMENT The stage direction in the Folio

text leaves it unclear how many people enter at this
juncture; see Digital Edition TC 1 for clarification.

PAINTER   It wears,° sir, as it grows.°   *wears out / ages*
POET   Ay, that's well known.
   But what particular rarity, what strange,
5   Which manifold record° not matches? See,   *all recorded history*
   Magic of bounty,° all these spirits thy power   *generosity*
   Hath conjured to attend—I know the merchant.
PAINTER   I know them both: th'other's a jeweler.
MERCHANT [*to* JEWELER]   Oh, 'tis a worthy lord.°   *(Timon)*
JEWELER   Nay, that's most fixed.°   *definite*
10 MERCHANT   A most incomparable man, breathed° as it were,   *trained; inspired*
   To an untirable and continuate° goodness: *habitual*
   He passes.°   *excels*
JEWELER [*showing the jewel*]   I have a jewel here.
MERCHANT   Oh, pray let's see it. For the Lord Timon, sir?
15 JEWELER   If he will touch the estimate.° But for that—   *meet the price*
POET [*to himself*]   When we for recompense have praised the vile,
   It stains the glory in that happy° verse,   *appropriate*
   Which aptly sings the good.
MERCHANT   'Tis a good form.°   *shape*
JEWELER   And rich. Here is a water,° look ye.   *luster*
20 PAINTER [*to* POET]   You are rapt, sir, in some work, some dedication
   To the great lord.[2]
POET   A thing slipped idly from me.
   Our poesy is as a gum° which oozes   *sap*
   From whence 'tis nourished. The fire i'th' flint
   Shows not till it be struck. Our gentle flame
25   Provokes° itself, and like the current flies   *Generates*
   Each bound it chases.[3] What have you there?
PAINTER   A picture, sir. When comes your book forth?
POET   Upon the heels of my presentment,[4] sir.
   Let's see your piece.
PAINTER [*showing the painting*]   'Tis a good piece.
30 POET   So 'tis. This comes off well and excellent.
PAINTER   Indifferent.°   *So-so*
POET   Admirable! How this grace
   Speaks his own standing;[5] what a mental power
   This eye shoots forth! How big imagination
   Moves in this lip! To th' dumbness° of the gesture   *muteness*
35   One might interpret.°   *supply words*
PAINTER   It is a pretty mocking° of the life.   *imitation*
   Here is a touch: is't good?
POET   I will say of it,
   It tutors nature. Artificial strife°   *The striving of art*
   Lives in these touches livelier than life.
         Enter certain SENATORS.
40 PAINTER   How this lord is followed.
POET   The senators of Athens, happy men.
PAINTER   Look, more.
          [*More* SENATORS *pass over the stage,*
            and all the SENATORS *exeunt.*]

---

2. Poets dedicated their volumes to wealthy patrons
in hopes of financial reward.
3. *like . . . chases:* like the river overflows its banks.
4. As soon as I have presented it formally (to Timon).
5. Imparts the dignity of his estate.

POET   You see this confluence, this great flood of visitors.
      I have in this rough work shaped out a man
45   Whom this beneath[6] world doth embrace and hug
      With amplest entertainment.° My free drift°   *hospitality / meaning*
      Halts not particularly[7] but moves itself
      In a wide sea of wax.[8] No leveled malice
      Infects one comma in the course I hold
50   But flies an eagle flight, bold, and forth° on,   *straight*
      Leaving no tract° behind.   *trace*
PAINTER   How shall I
      Understand you?
POET   I will unbolt° to you.   *disclose*
      You see how all conditions, how all minds,
      As well of glib and slipp'ry creatures as
55   Of grave and austere quality, tender° down   *give*
      Their services to Lord Timon. His large fortune,
      Upon his good and gracious nature hanging,
      Subdues and properties° to his love and tendance°   *appropriates / attendance*
      All sorts of hearts. Yea, from the glass-faced[9] flatterer
60   To Apemantus, that few things loves better
      Than to abhor himself, even he drops down
      The knee before him and returns° in peace   *leaves*
      Most rich in Timon's nod.
PAINTER   I saw them speak together.
POET   Sir, I have upon a high and pleasant hill
65   Feigned° Fortune to be throned. The base o'th' mount   *Imagined*
      Is ranked with all deserts,[1] all kind of natures
      That labor on the bosom of this sphere
      To propagate their states.° Amongst them all   *improve their fortunes*
      Whose eyes are on this sovereign lady fixed,
70   One do I personate° of Lord Timon's frame,   *depict*
      Whom Fortune with her ivory hand wafts° to her,   *beckons*
      Whose present grace° to present slaves and servants   *graciousness*
      Translates his rivals.[2]
PAINTER   'Tis conceived to scope.°   *correctly*
      This throne, this Fortune, and this hill, methinks,
75   With one man beckoned from the rest below,
      Bowing his head against the sleepy mount
      To climb his happiness,° would be well expressed   *good fortune*
      In our condition.[3]
POET   Nay, sir, but hear me on:
      All those which were his fellows° but of late,   *equals*
80   Some better than his value, on the moment
      Follow his strides, his lobbies fill with tendance,[4]
      Rain sacrificial° whisperings in his ear,   *respectful*

6. Sublunar (in Ptolemaic astronomy, the earth was the center of the universe and the moon its closest satellite; things beyond the moon were eternally fixed, but things in the sublunar "sphere" died or changed).
7. Does not criticize individuals.
8. "Wide sea of wax" is perhaps a misprint in the Folio text, but possibly the Poet is contrasting the breadth of his inspiration with the small size of the wax tablets on which poems were written in classical times.

leveled: aimed (at a particular person).
9. Reflecting his patron's moods.
1. Is lined with people of all degrees of virtue.
2. *to present . . . rivals:* instantly converts Timon's rivals to his slaves and servants.
3. *would . . . condition:* would be a good expression of the human condition; would make a good design for a painter.
4. *his . . . tendance:* crowd his rooms to visit him.

Make sacred even his stirrup,[5] and through him
Drink the free air.
PAINTER   Ay, marry, what of these?
85 POET   When Fortune in her shift and change of mood
Spurns° down her late belovèd, all his dependents   *Kicks*
Which labored after him to the mountain's top,
Even on their knees and hands, let him set down,
Not one accompanying his declining foot.
90 PAINTER   'Tis common:
A thousand moral paintings I can show
That shall demonstrate these quick blows of Fortune's
More pregnantly° than words. Yet you do well   *forcibly*
To show Lord Timon that mean° eyes have seen   *base people's*
95 The foot above the head.
              Trumpets sound.
              Enter Lord TIMON, *addressing himself courteously*
              to every suitor[, *with* MESSENGER *from* VENTIDIUS,
              LUCILIUS, *and* SERVANTS].
TIMON [*to* MESSENGER]   Imprisoned is he, say you?
MESSENGER   Ay, my good lord, five talents[6] is his debt,
His means most short, his creditors most strait.°   *severe*
Your honorable letter he desires
100 To those° have shut him up, which failing,   *those who*
Periods° his comfort.   *Ends*
TIMON   Noble Ventidius, well!
I am not of that feather° to shake off   *sort*
My friend when he must need me. I do know him
A gentleman that well deserves a help,
105 Which he shall have. I'll pay the debt and free him.
MESSENGER   Your lordship ever binds° him.   *obligates*
TIMON   Commend me to him. I will send his ransom,
And, being enfranchised,° bid him come to me.   *set free*
'Tis not enough to help the feeble up
110 But to support him after. Fare you well.
MESSENGER   All happiness to your honor.   *Exit.*
              Enter an OLD ATHENIAN.
OLD ATHENIAN   Lord Timon, hear me speak.
TIMON   Freely, good father.
OLD ATHENIAN   Thou hast a servant named Lucilius.
TIMON   I have so. What of him?
115 OLD ATHENIAN   Most noble Timon, call the man before thee.
TIMON   Attends he here or no? Lucilius!
LUCILIUS   Here, at your lordship's service.
OLD ATHENIAN   This fellow here, Lord Timon, this thy creature,
By night frequents my house. I am a man
120 That from my first have been inclined to thrift,
And my estate deserves an heir more raised°   *exalted*
Than one which holds a trencher.[7]

---

5. By holding it reverently as he mounts.
6. A large unit of money, usually taken as equivalent
to several thousand dollars. The value of a "talent" is
inconsistent from scene to scene in *Timon*; these dis-

crepancies are often cited as evidence for incomplete
revision of the text.
7. Platter (one who waits on table).

TIMON   Well, what further?

OLD ATHENIAN   One only daughter have I, no kin else,
  On whom I may confer what I have got.
125 The maid is fair, o'th' youngest for a bride,
  And I have bred her° at my dearest cost   *brought her up*
  In qualities of the best. This man of thine
  Attempts her love. I prithee, noble lord,
  Join with me to forbid him her resort.°   *company*
  Myself have spoke in vain.

130 TIMON   The man is honest.

OLD ATHENIAN   Therefore he will be,[8] Timon.
  His honesty rewards him in itself;
  It must not bear° my daughter.   *carry off*

TIMON   Does she love him?

OLD ATHENIAN   She is young and apt.°   *impressionable*
135 Our own precedent° passions do instruct us   *former*
  What levity's in youth.

TIMON [*to* LUCILIUS]   Love you the maid?

LUCILIUS   Ay, my good lord, and she accepts of it.

OLD ATHENIAN   If in her marriage my consent be missing,
  I call the gods to witness, I will choose
140 Mine heir from forth the beggars of the world
  And dispossess her all.

TIMON   How shall she be endowed°   *What dowry will she have*
  If she be mated with an equal husband?

OLD ATHENIAN   Three talents on the present; in future, all.

TIMON   This gentleman of mine hath served me long.
145 To build his fortune I will strain a little,
  For 'tis a bond° in men. Give him thy daughter.   *duty of friendship*
  What you bestow, in him I'll counterpoise
  And make him weigh with her.

OLD ATHENIAN   Most noble lord,
  Pawn me to this your honor,[9] she is his.

150 TIMON   My hand to thee, mine honor on my promise.

LUCILIUS   Humbly I thank your lordship. Never may
  That state or fortune fall into my keeping
  Which is not owed to you.   *Exit* [*with* OLD ATHENIAN].

POET [*to* TIMON]   Vouchsafe° my labor   *Accept*
  And long live your lordship!

155 TIMON   I thank you. You shall hear from me anon.°   *soon*
  Go not away. —What have you there, my friend?

PAINTER   A piece of painting which I do beseech
  Your lordship to accept.

TIMON   Painting is welcome.
  The painting is almost the natural° man.   *actual*
160 For since dishonor traffics° with man's nature,   *has dealings*
  He is but outside.° These penciled figures are   *only superficial*
  Even such as they give out.[1] I like your work,
  And you shall find I like it. Wait attendance

8. He will behave honorably (and chastely).   1. Just what they profess to be.
9. If you pledge your honor to do this.

Till you hear further from me.

PAINTER   The gods preserve ye.

165 TIMON   Well fare you, gentleman. [*to* JEWELER] Give me your
      hand.
      We must needs dine together. Sir, your jewel
      Hath suffered under² praise.

JEWELER   What, my lord, dispraise?

TIMON   A mere° satiety of commendations.   *An utter*
      If I should pay you for't as 'tis extolled,
      It would unclew° me quite.   *ruin*

170 JEWELER   My lord, 'tis rated
      As those which sell would give.³ But you well know
      Things of like value differing in the owners
      Are prizèd by their masters.⁴ Believe't, dear lord,
      You mend° the jewel by the wearing it.   *improve*

TIMON   Well mocked.°   *You're kidding*

      Enter APEMANTUS.

175 MERCHANT   No, my good lord, he speaks the common tongue,°   *general opinion*
      Which all men speak with him.

TIMON   Look who comes here. Will you be chid?°   *scolded*

JEWELER   We'll bear° with your lordship.   *suffer*

MERCHANT   He'll spare none.

TIMON   Good morrow to thee, gentle Apemantus.

180 APEMANTUS   Till I be gentle, stay thou for thy good morrow—
      When thou art Timon's dog and these knaves honest.⁵

TIMON   Why dost thou call them knaves? Thou know'st them not.

APEMANTUS   Are they not Athenians?

TIMON   Yes.

185 APEMANTUS   Then I repent not.

JEWELER   You know me, Apemantus?

APEMANTUS   Thou know'st I do. I called thee by thy name.

TIMON   Thou art proud, Apemantus!

APEMANTUS   Of nothing so much as that I am not like Timon.

190 TIMON   Whither art going?

APEMANTUS   To knock out an honest Athenian's brains.

TIMON   That's a deed thou'lt die for.

APEMANTUS   Right, if doing nothing⁶ be death by th' law.

TIMON   How lik'st thou this picture, Apemantus?

195 APEMANTUS   The best for the innocence.⁷

TIMON   Wrought he not well that painted it?

APEMANTUS   He wrought better that made the painter, and
      yet he's but a filthy piece of work.

PAINTER   You're a dog.⁸

200 APEMANTUS   Thy mother's of my generation. What's she, if I
      be a dog?

TIMON   Wilt dine with me, Apemantus?

---

2. Has been inundated by (but the Jeweler
misunderstands).
3. At what a merchant would pay (the wholesale price).
4. Are valued as their owners are valued.
5. *stay . . . honest:* wait for a polite greeting until you
are changed into your own dog or (an equally unlikely

prospect) until these crooks become honest.
6. Since there are no honest Athenians.
7. For its inability to harm anyone.
8. "Dog" is not merely a term of contempt; Apemantus is a Cynic philosopher, a school whose name
derived from the Greek *kynē,* "dog."

APEMANTUS No, I eat not[9] lords.

TIMON An° thou shouldst, thou'dst anger ladies.   *If*

205 APEMANTUS Oh, they eat lords. So they come by great bellies.

TIMON That's a lascivious apprehension.[1]

APEMANTUS So thou apprehend'st it, take it for thy labor.

TIMON How dost thou like this jewel, Apemantus?

APEMANTUS Not so well as plain-dealing, which will not cost

210   a man a doit.°   *tiny coin*

TIMON What dost thou think 'tis worth?

APEMANTUS Not worth my thinking.

   How now, poet?

POET How now, philosopher?

APEMANTUS Thou liest.

POET Art not one?

APEMANTUS Yes.

POET Then I lie not.

APEMANTUS Art not a poet?

POET Yes.

APEMANTUS Then thou liest.

215   Look in thy last work, where thou hast feigned him° a worthy   *(Timon)*

   fellow.

POET That's not feigned. He is so.

APEMANTUS Yes, he is worthy of thee and to pay thee for thy

   labor. He that loves to be flattered is worthy o'th' flatterer.

220   Heavens, that I were a lord!

TIMON What wouldst do then, Apemantus?

APEMANTUS E'en as Apemantus does now: hate a lord with

   my heart.

TIMON What, thyself?

225 APEMANTUS Ay.

TIMON Wherefore?

APEMANTUS That I had no angry wit[2] to be a lord. —Art not

   thou a merchant?

MERCHANT Ay, Apemantus.

230 APEMANTUS Traffic confound° thee, if the gods will not.   *May business ruin*

MERCHANT If traffic do it, the gods do it.

APEMANTUS Traffic's thy god, and thy god confound thee.

     Trumpet sounds. Enter a MESSENGER.

TIMON What trumpet's that?

MESSENGER 'Tis Alcibiades and some twenty horse,°   *horsemen*

235   All of companionship.°   *in one group*

TIMON [*to* SERVANT] Pray, entertain them; give them guide to us.

               [*Exit* SERVANT.]

   You must needs dine with me. Go not you hence

   Till I have thanked you. [*to* PAINTER] When dinner's done

   Show me this piece. I am joyful of your sights.°   *to see you*

     Enter ALCIBIADES *with* [SOLDIERS *on horseback*].

240   —Most welcome, sir!

APEMANTUS [*aside*] So, so, there! Aches contract and starve°   *ruin*

   your supple joints. That there should be small love amongst

---

9. I do not devour the substance of.   2. Foresight (so I could avoid it).

1. Interpretation; grasping.

these sweet knaves and all this courtesy! The strain of man's
bred out° into baboon and monkey.   *degenerated*

245 ALCIBIADES [*to* TIMON]   Sir, you have saved my longing,° and I   *anticipated my desire*
feed
Most hungerly on your sight.
TIMON   Right welcome, sir!
Ere we depart we'll share a bounteous time
In different pleasures. Pray you, let us in.
                                Exeunt [all but APEMANTUS].
                    Enter two LORDS.
FIRST LORD   What time o'day is't, Apemantus?
APEMANTUS   Time to be honest.
250 FIRST LORD   That time serves still.°   *always*
APEMANTUS   The most accursèd thou that still omitt'st° it.   *do not take advantage of*
SECOND LORD   Thou art going to Lord Timon's feast?
APEMANTUS   Ay, to see meat fill knaves and wine heat fools.
SECOND LORD   Fare thee well, fare thee well.
255 APEMANTUS   Thou art a fool to bid me farewell twice.
SECOND LORD   Why, Apemantus?
APEMANTUS   Shouldst have kept one to thyself, for I mean to
give thee none.
FIRST LORD   Hang thyself!
260 APEMANTUS   No, I will do nothing at thy bidding. Make thy
requests to thy friend.
SECOND LORD   Away, unpeaceable dog, or I'll spurn° thee hence.   *kick*
APEMANTUS   I will fly like a dog the heels o'th' ass.
FIRST LORD   He's opposite° to humanity.   *antagonistic*
265 Come, shall we in and taste Lord Timon's bounty?
He outgoes° the very heart° of kindness.   *surpasses / essence*
SECOND LORD   He pours it out. Plutus, the god of gold,
Is but his steward. No meed° but he repays   *gift*
Sevenfold above itself; no gift to him
270 But breeds the giver a return exceeding
All use of quittance.°   *customary interest rates*
FIRST LORD   The noblest mind he carries
That ever governed man.
SECOND LORD   Long may he live in fortunes. Shall we in?
FIRST LORD   I'll keep you company.   *Exeunt.*

1.2

Oboes playing loud music.
A great banquet served in [by Flavius the STEWARD
and SERVANTS], *and then enter Lord* TIMON, *the*
[SENATORS], *the Athenian* LORDS, [ALCIBIADES, *and*]
VENTIDIUS *which Timon redeemed from prison. Then*
comes dropping° after all APEMANTUS *discontentedly*   *entering casually*
like himself.°   *in everyday clothes*
VENTIDIUS   Most honored Timon,
It hath pleased the gods to remember
My father's age and call him to long peace.°   *eternal rest*
He is gone happy and has left me rich.

1.2 Location: Timon's banqueting room.

5   Then, as in grateful virtue I am bound
To your free° heart, I do return those talents,   *generous*
Doubled with thanks and service, from whose help
I derived liberty.

TIMON   Oh, by no means,
Honest Ventidius. You mistake my love.

10   I gave it freely ever, and there's none
Can truly say he gives if he receives.
If our betters play at that game,° we must not dare   *pretend generosity*
To imitate them. Faults that are rich° are fair.   *of rich people*

VENTIDIUS   A noble spirit!
          [The LORDS *stand.]*

15   TIMON   Nay, my lords,
Ceremony was but devised at first
To set a gloss on[1] faint deeds, hollow welcomes,
Recanting goodness,[2] sorry ere 'tis shown.
But where there is true friendship, there needs none.°   *no ceremony*

20   Pray, sit. More welcome are ye to my fortunes
Than my fortunes to me.
          [They sit.]

FIRST LORD   My lord, we always have confessed it.

APEMANTUS   Ho, ho, confessed it? Hanged it, have you not?

TIMON   O Apemantus, you are welcome!

25   APEMANTUS   No. You shall not make me welcome:
I come to have thee° thrust me out of doors.   *provoke you to*
                                         rude one

TIMON   Fie, thou'rt a churl.° Ye've got a humor there
Does not become a man. 'Tis much to blame.
They say, my lords, *Ira furor brevis est*,[3]

30   But yond man is ever angry.
Go, let him have a table by himself,
For he does neither affect° company,   *like*
Nor is he fit for't, indeed.

APEMANTUS   Let me stay at thine apperil,° Timon.   *risk*

35   I come to observe; I give thee warning on't.

TIMON   I take no heed of thee. Thou'rt an Athenian,
Therefore welcome. I myself would have no power;[4]
Prithee, let my meat make thee silent.

APEMANTUS   I scorn thy meat. 'Twould choke me, for I should

40   ne'er flatter thee. O you gods! What a number of men eats
Timon, and he sees 'em not! It grieves me to see so many dip
their meat in one man's blood, and all° the madness is, he   *the height of*
cheers them up,° too.   *encourages them*
I wonder men dare trust themselves with men.

45   Methinks they should invite them without knives:[5]
Good for their meat, and safer for their lives.
There's much example for't. The fellow that sits next him,
now parts° bread with him, pledges the breath of him in a   *shares*
divided draft,[6] is the readiest man to kill him. 'T has been

50   proved. If I were a huge° man, I should fear to drink at meals,   *great*

---

1. To give a fine appearance to.
2. Generosity that demands repayment or that is immediately revoked.
3. Anger is brief insanity (Latin).
4. Wish no power to silence you.
5. Renaissance dinner guests brought their own silverware.
6. *pledges . . . draft*: toasts his health in a shared cup.

Lest they should spy my windpipe's dangerous notes.[7]
Great men should drink with harness° on their throats.   *armor*
TIMON [*drinking to a* LORD]   My lord, in heart. And let the
    health° go round.   *shared cup*
SECOND LORD   Let it flow° this way, my good lord.   *circulate*
55 APEMANTUS   "Flow this way"? A brave° fellow. He keeps his   *fine (ironic)*
    tides[8] well. Those healths will make thee and thy state look ill,
    Timon.
    Here's that which is too weak to be a sinner:
    Honest water, which ne'er left man i'th' mire.
60   This and my food are equals; there's no odds.
    Feasts are too proud to give thanks to the gods.
             Apemantus' grace.
      Immortal gods, I crave no pelf.°   *property (contemptuous)*
      I pray for no man but myself.
      Grant I may never prove so fond°   *foolish*
65   To trust man on his oath or bond,
      Or a harlot for her weeping,
      Or a dog that seems a-sleeping,
      Or a keeper° with my freedom,   *jailer*
      Or my friends if I should need 'em.
70   Amen. So fall to't.
      Rich men sin, and I eat root.
    Much good dich° thy good heart, Apemantus.   *may it do*
TIMON   Captain Alcibiades, your heart's in the field° now.   *battlefield*
ALCIBIADES   My heart is ever at your service, my lord.
75 TIMON   You had rather be at a breakfast of enemies° than a   *(at a battle)*
    dinner of friends.
ALCIBIADES   So they were bleeding new, my lord, there's no
    meat like 'em. I could wish my best friend at such a feast.
APEMANTUS   Would all those flatterers were thine enemies
    then,
80   That then thou mightst kill 'em and bid me to 'em.
FIRST LORD   Might we but have that happiness, my lord, that
    you would once use our hearts,[9] whereby we might express
    some part of our zeals,° we should think ourselves forever   *love*
    perfect.°   *happy*
85 TIMON   Oh, no doubt, my good friends, but the gods them-
    selves have provided that I shall have much help from you.
    How had you been my friends else? Why have you that
    charitable title° from thousands?[1] Did not you chiefly belong   *loving name*
    to my heart? I have told more of you to myself than you can
90   with modesty speak in your own behalf, and thus far I con-
    firm you.[2] O you gods, think I, what need we have any
    friends, if we should ne'er have need of 'em? They were the
    most needless creatures living, should we ne'er have use for
    'em, and would most resemble sweet instruments hung up in
95   cases that keeps their sounds to themselves. Why, I have
    often wished myself poorer that I might come nearer to you.

---

7. *my . . . notes:* the indications, when I drink, of where my windpipe is (so they can cut my throat).
8. He observes his opportunity (joking, with word-play on "flow," that the Second Lord is ensuring that he gets plenty to drink).
9. Would test of our affection.

1. Timon seems to mean, "Why are you, of all the thousands of Athenians, called my friends?" but also possibly, "Why do so many thousands of people call you their friends?"
2. In your claim to be my friends.

We are born to do benefits, and what better or properer° can   *more suitably*
we call our own than the riches of our friends? Oh, what a
precious comfort 'tis to have so many like brothers
100 commanding³ one another's fortunes! Oh, joy's e'en made
away° ere't can be born. Mine eyes cannot hold out water,   *destroyed (by tears)*
methinks. To forget their° faults, I drink to you.   *(my eyes')*

APEMANTUS   Thou weep'st to make them drink, Timon.

SECOND LORD   Joy had the like° conception in our eyes   *same kind of*
105 And, at that instant, like a babe sprung up.

APEMANTUS   Ho, ho! I laugh to think that babe a bastard.⁴

THIRD LORD [*to* TIMON]   I promise you, my lord, you moved me
much.

APEMANTUS   Much.
Sound tucket.°   *trumpet flourish*

TIMON   What means that trump? How now?
Enter SERVANT.

110 SERVANT   Please you, my lord, there are certain ladies most
desirous of admittance.

TIMON   Ladies? What are their wills?

SERVANT   There comes with them a forerunner, my lord,
which bears that office,° to signify their pleasures.°   *function / desires*
115 TIMON   I pray let them be admitted.
Enter CUPID.

CUPID   Hail to thee, worthy Timon, and to all
That of his bounties taste. The five best senses
Acknowledge thee their patron and come freely
To gratulate° thy plenteous bosom.°   *greet / generous heart*
120 There taste, touch, all, pleased from thy table rise.
They° only now come but to feast thine eyes.   *(the masquers)*

TIMON   They're welcome all! Let 'em have kind admittance.
Music make their welcome.

FIRST LORD   You see, my lord, how ample you're beloved.
Enter the masque of LADIES [*as*] *Amazons with lutes in
their hands, dancing and playing.*⁵

125 APEMANTUS   Hoy-day, what a sweep of vanity comes this way!
They dance? They are madwomen.
Like madness is the glory° of this life   *vain display*
As this pomp shows to a little oil and root.⁶
We make ourselves fools to disport° ourselves   *amuse*
130 And spend our flatteries to drink° those men   *toast; drink up*
Upon whose age we void° it up again   *old age we spit*
With poisonous spite and envy.
Who lives that's not depraved or depraves?
Who dies that bears not one spurn° to their graves   *insult*
135 Of their friends' gift?°   *giving*
I should fear those that dance before me now
Would one day stamp upon me. 'T has been done.
Men shut their doors against a setting sun.
The LORDS *rise from table with much adoring of
TIMON, and to show their loves each single out an
Amazon, and all dance, men with women, a lofty
strain or two to the oboes and cease.*

---

3. *commanding*: having at their command.
4. That is, the guests' tears are illegitimate.
5. TEXTUAL COMMENT The masque is a courtly entertainment. For information on the masque genre in the
early seventeenth century, see Digital Edition TC 2.
6. As this feast compares to a meager meal.

TIMON   You have done our pleasures much grace, fair ladies,
140   Set a fair fashion on° our entertainment,   *Made elegant*
Which was not half so beautiful and kind.
You have added worth unto't and luster,
And entertained me with mine own device.[7]
I am to thank you for't.
145   FIRST LADY   My lord, you take us even at the best.[8]
APEMANTUS   Faith, for the worst is filthy and would not hold
taking,[9] I doubt me.
TIMON   Ladies, there is an idle° banquet attends you.   *a trifling*
Please you to dispose° yourselves.   *seat*
150   ALL LADIES   Most thankfully, my lord.
                         Exeunt [LADIES *and* CUPID].
TIMON   Flavius.
STEWARD   My lord.
TIMON   The little casket bring me hither.
STEWARD   Yes, my lord. [*aside*] More jewels yet?
155   There is no crossing him in 's humor,°   *whim*
Else I should tell him well, i'faith I should,
When all's spent, he'd be crossed[1] then, an° he could.   *if*
'Tis pity bounty had not eyes behind,[2]
That man might ne'er be wretched for his mind.[3]   *Exit.*
160   FIRST LORD   Where be our men?
SERVANT   Here, my lord, in readiness.
SECOND LORD   Our horses.   [*Exit* SERVANT.]
TIMON   O my friends, I have one word to say to you—
Look you, my good lord,
165   I must entreat you honor me so much
As to advance° this jewel. Accept it and wear it,   *improve (by your worth)*
Kind my lord.
         [TIMON *gives the jewel.*]
FIRST LORD   I am so far already in your gifts.
ALL LORDS   So are we all.
         Enter [FIRST] SERVANT.
170   FIRST SERVANT   My lord, there are certain nobles of the Sen-
ate newly alighted and come to visit you.
TIMON   They are fairly° welcome.   [*Exit* FIRST SERVANT.]   *graciously*
         Enter Flavius [*the* STEWARD].
STEWARD   I beseech your honor, vouchsafe me a word; it does
concern you near.
175   TIMON   Near? Why, then, another time I'll hear thee. I prithee,
let's be provided to show them entertainment.
STEWARD   I scarce know how.
         Enter [*a* SECOND] SERVANT.
SECOND SERVANT   May it please your honor, Lord Lucius
Out of his free love hath presented to you
180   Four milk-white horses trapped° in silver.   *bedecked*
TIMON   I shall accept them fairly. Let the presents

---

7. Plan. Timon may be implying that he himself
arranged the entertainment, or merely that it was
designed for him by his admirers.
8. You consider our efforts in the best possible light.
9. Would not be worth noting; would not endure sex-

ual penetration (because of venereal disease).
1. He'd want to have his debts canceled.
2. 'Tis a pity generosity is not more careful.
3. *for his mind:* because of his (generous) intentions.

Be worthily entertained.°   [*Exit* SECOND SERVANT.]   *accepted*
          Enter a THIRD SERVANT.
                              How now, what news?
THIRD SERVANT   Please you, my lord, that honorable gentle-
          man Lord Lucullus entreats your company tomorrow to
185   hunt with him, and he's sent your honor two brace° of   *pairs*
          greyhounds.
TIMON   I'll hunt with him, and let them be received
          Not without fair reward.   [*Exit* THIRD SERVANT.]
STEWARD [*aside*]   What will this come to?
          He commands us to provide and give great gifts,
190   And all out of an empty coffer;
          Nor will he know his purse, or yield° me this: *allow*
          To show him what a beggar his heart is,
          Being of no power to make his wishes good.
          His promises fly so beyond his state°   *estate*
195   That what he speaks is all in debt. He owes
          For every word. He is so kind that he now
          Pays interest for't. His land's put to their books.°   *mortgaged*
          Well, would I were gently put out of office
          Before I were forced out.
200   Happier is he that has no friend to feed
          Than such that do e'en enemies exceed.[4]
          I bleed inwardly for my lord.   *Exit.*
TIMON [*to* LORDS]   You do yourselves
          Much wrong; you bate° too much of your own merits.   *undervalue*
          [*to* SECOND LORD] Here, my lord, a trifle of our love.
205   SECOND LORD   With more than common thanks I will receive it.
THIRD LORD   Oh, he's the very soul of bounty.
TIMON [*to* FIRST LORD]   And now I remember, my lord, you gave
          Good words the other day of a bay courser°   *horse*
          I rode on. 'Tis yours because you liked it.
210   FIRST LORD   Oh, I beseech you, pardon me, my lord, in that.[5]
TIMON   You may take my word, my lord; I know no man
          Can justly praise but what he does affect.°   *desire*
          I weigh my friends' affection with mine own.
          I'll tell you true, I'll call to° you.   *on*
ALL LORDS   Oh, none so welcome.
215   TIMON   I take all and your several visitations
          So kind to heart. 'Tis not enough to give.
          Methinks I could deal kingdoms to my friends
          And ne'er be weary. Alcibiades,
          Thou art a soldier, therefore seldom rich.
220   It comes in charity to thee, for all thy living
          Is 'mongst the dead, and all the lands thou hast
          Lie in a pitched field.
ALCIBIADES   Ay, defiled[6] land, my lord.
FIRST LORD   We are so virtuously bound.
TIMON   And so am I to you.

---

4. Who ruin themselves faster than enemies could.
5. That is, I wasn't hinting for the horse.
6. Lined with ranks of soldiers; punning on Ecclesias-

ticus 13:1, "He that toucheth pitch, shall be defiled with it."

225   SECOND LORD   So infinitely endeared.°   *obliged*

TIMON   All to you. —Lights, more lights!

FIRST LORD   The best of happiness, honor, and fortunes
    Keep with you, Lord Timon.

TIMON   Ready for his friends.

              Exeunt [all but TIMON *and* APEMANTUS].

APEMANTUS   What a coil's° here,   *commotion is*

230   Serving of becks° and jutting out of bums.   *bowing*

  I doubt whether their legs° be worth the sums   *curtsies*

  That are given for 'em. Friendship's full of dregs.

  Methinks false hearts should never have sound legs.

  Thus honest fools lay out their wealth on curtsies.

235   TIMON   Now, Apemantus, if thou wert not sullen,
    I would be good to thee.

APEMANTUS   No, I'll nothing. For if I should be bribed too,
    there would be none left to rail upon thee, and then thou
    wouldst sin the faster. Thou giv'st so long, Timon, I fear me

240   thou wilt give away thyself in paper° shortly. What needs   *promissory notes*
    these feasts, pomps, and vainglories?

TIMON   Nay, an you begin to rail on society once, I am sworn
    not to give regard° to you.   *pay attention*

    Farewell, and come with better music.   *Exit.*

APEMANTUS   So.

245   Thou wilt not hear me now; thou shalt not then.

  I'll lock thy heaven° from thee. Oh, that men's ears   *(my redemptive guidance)*
    should be

  To counsel deaf, but not to flattery.   *Exit.*

2.1

Enter a SENATOR.

SENATOR   And late five thousand. To Varro and to Isidore
  He owes nine thousand, besides my former sum,
  Which makes it five-and-twenty. Still in motion
  Of raging waste?[1] It cannot hold,° it will not.   *last*

5   If I want gold, steal but a beggar's dog
  And give it Timon, why, the dog coins gold!
  If I would sell my horse and buy twenty more
  Better than he, why, give my horse to Timon.
  Ask nothing, give it him; it foals me straight

10   And able horses.[2] No porter[3] at his gate,
  But rather one that smiles and still invites
  All that pass by. It cannot hold. No reason
  Can sound his state in safety.[4] —Caphis, ho!
  Caphis, I say!

      Enter CAPHIS.

CAPHIS   Here, sir, what is your pleasure?

15   SENATOR   Get on your cloak, and haste you to Lord Timon.
  Importune him for my moneys. Be not ceased°   *put off*
  With slight denial, nor then silenced when

2.1 Location: A Senator's house.
1. *Still . . . waste:* Still keeping up unending extravagance.
2. *it . . . horses:* it immediately "gives birth to" full-

grown horses (not "foals," baby horses).
3. Gatekeeper (who restricts entrance).
4. *No reason . . . safety:* No rational person can investigate his financial situation and believe it safe.

"Commend me to your master," and the cap
Plays in the right hand[5] thus, but tell him
20 My uses cry to me. I must serve my turn
Out of mine own.[6] His days and times are past,
And my reliances on his fracted° dates   *broken*
Have smit° my credit. I love and honor him   *hurt*
But must not break my back to heal his finger.
25 Immediate are my needs, and my relief
Must not be tossed and turned[7] to me in words
But find supply immediate. Get you gone.
Put on a most importunate aspect,
A visage of demand, for I do fear
30 When every feather sticks in his own wing[8]
Lord Timon will be left a naked gull,°   *an unfledged bird; dupe*
Which flashes now a phoenix. Get you gone!
CAPHIS   I go, sir.
SENATOR   "I go, sir"? [*He gives him bonds.*] Take the bonds
    along with you,
And have the dates in. Come.
CAPHIS   I will, sir.
35 SENATOR   Go.   *Exeunt.*

2.2

Enter STEWARD *with many bills in his hand.*
STEWARD   No care, no stop—so senseless of expense
That he will neither know how to maintain it
Nor cease his flow of riot,° takes no account   *his wastefulness*
How things go from him, nor resume° no care   *takes*
5 Of what is to continue. Never mind
Was to be so unwise to be so kind.[1]
What shall be done? He will not hear till feel.°   *he suffers*
I must be round° with him, now he comes from hunting.   *frank*
Fie, fie, fie, fie!
        Enter CAPHIS, ISIDORE['S SERVANT], *and* VARRO['S
        SERVANT].
10 CAPHIS   Good even, Varro. What, you come for money?
VARRO'S SERVANT   Is't not your business too?
CAPHIS   It is—and yours too, Isidore?
ISIDORE'S SERVANT   It is so.
CAPHIS   Would we were all dischargèd.
VARRO'S SERVANT   I fear it.
CAPHIS   Here comes the lord.
        Enter TIMON *and his train* [*of* LORDS, *with* ALCIBIADES].
15 TIMON   So soon as dinner's done we'll forth again,
My Alcibiades—
        [CAPHIS *approaches* TIMON.]
                    —With me? What is your will?
CAPHIS   My lord, here is a note of certain dues.°   *debts*

---

5. *when . . . hand:* that is, with friendly speech and gestures.
6. *serve . . . own:* pay for my needs with my own money.
7. Returned (like a tennis ball).

8. When everything is returned to its proper owner.
2.2 Location: Before Timon's house.
1. *Never . . . kind:* Never was anyone so idiotically generous.

TIMON   Dues? Whence are you?

CAPHIS   Of Athens here, my lord.

TIMON   Go to my steward.

20   CAPHIS   Please it your lordship, he hath put me off

To the succession of new days this month.°   *Every day for a month*

My master is awaked° by great occasion°   *driven / need*

To call upon his own° and humbly prays you   *own money*

That, with your other noble parts, you'll suit[2]

In giving him his right.

25   TIMON   Mine honest friend,

I prithee but repair° to me next morning.   *come back*

CAPHIS   Nay, good my lord.

TIMON   Contain thyself, good friend.

VARRO'S SERVANT [*giving bond to* TIMON]   One Varro's servant,

my good lord.

ISIDORE'S SERVANT [*giving bond to* TIMON]   From Isidore. He

humbly prays your speedy payment.

30   CAPHIS   If you did know, my lord, my master's wants.

VARRO'S SERVANT   'Twas due on forfeiture,[3] my lord, six weeks

and past.

ISIDORE'S SERVANT   Your steward puts me off, my lord, and I

Am sent expressly to your lordship.

TIMON   Give me breath.

—I do beseech you, good my lords, keep on.°   *go ahead*

I'll wait upon you instantly.

[*Exeunt* LORDS *with* ALCIBIADES.]

35   [*to* STEWARD]   Come hither, pray you.

How goes the world that I am thus encountered

With clamorous demands of debt, broken bonds,

And the detention of° long-since-due debts   *failure to pay*

Against my honor?

STEWARD [*to* SERVANTS]   Please you, gentlemen,

40   The time is unagreeable to this business.

Your importunacy cease till after dinner,

That I may make his lordship understand

Wherefore you are not paid.

TIMON [*to* SERVANTS]   Do so, my friends. [*to* STEWARD] See them

well entertained.   [*Exit.*]

45   STEWARD   Pray, draw near.   *Exit.*

Enter APEMANTUS *and* FOOL.

CAPHIS   Stay, stay, here comes the Fool with Apemantus.

Let's ha' some sport with 'em.

VARRO'S SERVANT   Hang him, he'll abuse us.

ISIDORE'S SERVANT   A plague upon him, dog.

50   VARRO'S SERVANT   How dost, Fool?

APEMANTUS   Dost dialogue with thy shadow?[4]

VARRO'S SERVANT   I speak not to thee.

APEMANTUS   No, 'tis to thyself. [*to* FOOL] Come away.

ISIDORE'S SERVANT   There's the Fool[5] hangs on your back

55   already.

---

2. That you'll act in accordance with your noble qualities.
3. On penalty of forfeiting the security.
4. With your reflection (implying that Varro's Ser-

vant is also a fool).
5. The name "fool." In Renaissance England, wrongdoers were punished by being made to wear signs declaring their offenses.

APEMANTUS   No, thou stand'st single.° Thou'rt not on him yet.   *alone (in being a fool)*

CAPHIS   Where's the Fool now?

APEMANTUS   He last asked the question. Poor rogues and usurers' men, bawds between gold and want.[6]

60   ALL SERVANTS   What are we, Apemantus?

APEMANTUS   Asses.

ALL SERVANTS   Why?

APEMANTUS   That you ask me what you are and do not know
yourselves. —Speak to 'em, Fool.

65   FOOL   How do you, gentlemen?

ALL SERVANTS   Gramercies,° good Fool. How does your mistress?   *Many thanks*

FOOL   She's e'en° setting on water to scald such chickens[7] as   *just now*
you are. Would we could see you at Corinth.[8]

APEMANTUS   Good, gramercy.

Enter PAGE.

70   FOOL   Look you, here comes my master's page.

PAGE   [*to* FOOL]   Why, how now, captain? What do you in this
wise company? —How dost thou, Apemantus?

APEMANTUS   Would I had a rod[9] in my mouth that I might
answer thee profitably.

75   PAGE   Prithee, Apemantus, read me the superscription° of   *address*
these letters. I know not which is which.

APEMANTUS   Canst not read?

PAGE   No.

APEMANTUS   There will little learning die, then, that day thou
80   art hanged. This is to Lord Timon, this to Alcibiades. Go,
thou wast born a bastard, and thou'lt die a bawd.

PAGE   Thou wast whelped a dog, and thou shalt famish° a   *die*
dog's death. Answer not; I am gone.   *Exit.*

APEMANTUS   E'en so thou outrunn'st grace.[1] —Fool, I will go
85   with you to Lord Timon's.

FOOL   Will you leave me there?

APEMANTUS   If Timon stay at home.[2] —You three serve three
usurers?

ALL SERVANTS   Ay, would they served us.°   *treated us well*

90   APEMANTUS   So would I: as good a trick as ever hangman
served thief.

FOOL   Are you three usurers' men?

ALL SERVANTS   Ay, Fool.

FOOL   I think no usurer but has a fool to his servant. My mis-
95   tress is one,[3] and I am her fool. When men come to borrow
of your masters, they approach sadly and go away merry, but
they enter my master's house merrily and go away sadly.[4]
The reason of this?

VARRO'S SERVANT   I could render one.

---

6. *bawds . . . want:* go-betweens making deals
between moneylenders and those who need loans.

7. In order to remove the feathers (a "plucked bird"
was a hoodwinked fool; compare 2.1.31); also, syphi-
litics were "sweated" in tubs of very hot water.

8. Greek city famous for prostitution.

9. From Proverbs 26:3–4: "Unto the horse belongeth
a whip, to the ass a bridle, and a rod to the fool's
back. Answer not a fool according to his foolishness,

lest thou also be like him."

1. You run away from profitable instruction.

2. There will be a fool at Timon's house as long as he
is at home.

3. She is a "usurer" in the sense that she lends her
body for financial gain; the connection between usury
and prostitution was traditional.

4. According to Aristotle, all creatures are sad after
sexual intercourse.

100 APEMANTUS Do it then, that we may account thee a whoremaster and a knave, which notwithstanding thou shalt be
no less esteemed.

VARRO'S SERVANT What is a whoremaster, Fool?

FOOL A fool in good clothes, and something like thee. 'Tis a
105 spirit. Sometime't appears like a lord, sometime like a lawyer, sometime like a philosopher, with two stones[5] more
than 's° artificial one. He is very often like a knight, and   *than his*
generally in all shapes that man goes up and down in from
fourscore to thirteen, this spirit walks in.

110 VARRO'S SERVANT Thou art not altogether a fool.

FOOL Nor thou altogether a wise man. As much foolery as I
have, so much wit thou lack'st.

APEMANTUS That answer might have become° Apemantus.   *suited*

ALL SERVANTS Aside, aside! Here comes Lord Timon.

    Enter TIMON *and* STEWARD.

115 APEMANTUS Come with me, Fool, come.

FOOL I do not always follow lover, elder brother, and woman:[6]
sometime the philosopher. [*Exeunt* APEMANTUS *and* FOOL.]

STEWARD [*to* SERVANTS] Pray you, walk near. I'll speak with
  you anon.   *Exeunt* [SERVANTS].

TIMON You make me marvel wherefore ere this time
120 Had you not fully laid my state before me,[7]
That I might so have rated° my expense   *regulated*
As I had leave of means.°   *As means permitted*

STEWARD   You would not hear me.
At many leisures I proposed.

TIMON   Go to.°   *(impatient exclamation)*
Perchance some single vantages° you took *isolated opportunities*
125 When my indisposition° put you back,   *disinclination*
And that unaptness made your minister°   *allowed you*
Thus to excuse yourself.

STEWARD   O my good lord,
At many times I brought in my accounts,
Laid them before you. You would throw them off
130 And say you found them in mine honesty.[8]
When for some trifling present you have bid me
Return so much,° I have shook my head and wept, *a large sum*
Yea, 'gainst th'authority of manners,° prayed you *with rude bluntness*
To hold your hand more close. I did endure
135 Not seldom nor no slight checks° when I have *rebukes*
Prompted you in° the ebb of your estate   *Urged you to note*
And your great flow of debts. My lovèd lord,
Though you hear now too late, yet now's a time° *by now*
The greatest of your having[9] lacks a half
To pay your present debts.

140 TIMON   Let all my land be sold.

STEWARD 'Tis all engaged,° some forfeited and gone, *mortgaged*
And what remains will hardly stop the mouth

---

5. Testicles. In alchemy, the "philosopher's stone"
was thought to turn base metals into gold.
6. All figures associated with folly.

7. Described my financial status.
8. You gauged their accuracy by my honesty.
9. The most generous estimate of your wealth.

Of present dues.° The future comes apace.   *debts*
What shall defend the interim, and at length°   *in the long term*
145   How goes our reckoning?
       TIMON   To Lacedaemon° did my land extend.   *Sparta*
       STEWARD   O my good lord, the world is but a word.
       Were it all yours to give it in a breath,
       How quickly were it gone.
       TIMON   You tell me true.
150   STEWARD   If you suspect my husbandry° or falsehood,   *household management*
       Call me before th'exactest auditors
       And set me on the proof. So the gods bless me,
       When all our offices° have been oppressed   *kitchens and workrooms*
       With riotous feeders, when our vaults have wept
155   With drunken spilth° of wine, when every room   *spilling*
       Hath blazed with lights and brayed with minstrelsy,
       I have retired me to a wasteful cock[1]
       And set mine eyes at flow.
       TIMON   Prithee, no more.
       STEWARD   "Heavens," have I said, "the bounty of this lord!
160   How many prodigal bits° have slaves and peasants   *extravagant morsels*
       This night englutted? Who is not Timon's?°   *devoted to Timon*
       What heart, head, sword, force, means, but is Lord Timon's?
       Great Timon, noble, worthy, royal Timon!"
       Ah, when the means are gone that buy this praise,
165   The breath is gone whereof this praise is made.
       Feast won, fast° lost. One cloud of winter showers: *quickly; while fasting*
       These flies are couched.°   *lying unseen*
       TIMON   Come, sermon me no further.
       No villainous° bounty yet hath passed my heart.   *shameful*
       Unwisely, not ignobly, have I given.
170   Why dost thou weep? Canst thou the conscience° lack   *conviction*
       To think I shall lack friends? Secure thy heart.
       If I would broach° the vessels of my love   *tap (like a wine barrel)*
       And try the argument° of hearts by borrowing,   *test the contents*
       Men and men's fortunes could I frankly° use   *as freely*
       As I can bid thee speak.
175   STEWARD   Assurance bless your thoughts.[2]
       TIMON   And in some sort° these wants of mine are crowned°   *respect / exalted*
       That I account them blessings. For by these
       Shall I try friends. You shall perceive how you
       Mistake my fortunes: I am wealthy in my friends.
180   —Within there, Flaminius, Servilius?
                   Enter three SERVANTS [*including* FLAMINIUS *and*
                   SERVILIUS].
       ALL SERVANTS   My lord, my lord.
       TIMON   I will dispatch you severally:° [*to* SERVILIUS] you to   *separately*
       Lord Lucius, [*to* FLAMINIUS] to Lord Lucullus you—I hunted
       with his honor today— [*to third* SERVANT] you to Sempro-
185   nius. Commend me to their loves, and I am proud, say, that
       my occasions° have found time° to use 'em toward a supply   *needs / occasion*
       of money. Let the request be fifty talents.°   *(a huge sum)*

---

1. I have sat down beside a wine spout, left waste-   2. May your hopes be well founded.
fully flowing.

FLAMINIUS As you have said, my lord.   [*Exeunt* SERVANTS.]
STEWARD   Lord Lucius and Lucullus? Humph!
190 TIMON   Go you, sir, to the senators,
     Of whom, even to the state's best health,[3] I have
     Deserved this hearing. Bid 'em send o'th' instant
     A thousand talents to me.
STEWARD   I have been bold,
     For that I knew it the most general° way,   *usual*
195 To them to use your signet[4] and your name,
     But they do shake their heads, and I am here
     No richer in return.
TIMON   Is't true? Can 't be?
STEWARD   They answer in a joint and corporate voice
     That now they are at fall,° want° treasure, cannot   *low ebb / lack*
200 Do what they would, are sorry. You are honorable,
     But yet they could have wished—they know not—
     Something hath been amiss; a noble nature
     May catch a wrench;° would all were well; 'tis pity.   *suffer a misfortune*
     And so intending° other serious matters,   *pretending; attending to*
205 After distasteful looks and these hard fractions,°   *phrases*
     With certain half-caps° and cold-moving nods,   *reluctant salutations*
     They froze me into silence.
TIMON   You gods, reward them!
     Prithee, man, look cheerily.° These old fellows   *cheerful*
     Have their ingratitude in them hereditary.
210 Their blood is caked, 'tis cold, it seldom flows.
     'Tis lack of kindly[5] warmth they are not kind.
     And nature, as it grows again toward earth,°   *the grave*
     Is fashioned for the journey dull and heavy.
     Go to Ventidius. Prithee, be not sad;
215 Thou art true and honest. Ingeniously I speak;
     No blame belongs to thee. Ventidius lately
     Buried his father, by whose death he's stepped
     Into a great estate. When he was poor,
     Imprisoned, and in scarcity of friends
220 I cleared him with five talents. Greet him from me.
     Bid him suppose some good° necessity   *urgent*
     Touches his friend, which craves to be remembered
     With° those five talents. That had, give't these fellows   *By return of*
     To whom 'tis instant due. Never speak or think
225 That Timon's fortunes 'mong his friends can sink.
STEWARD   I would I could not think it. That thought is bounty's
     foe;
     Being free° itself, it thinks all others so.   *Exeunt.*   *generous*

3.1

     [*Enter*] FLAMINIUS *waiting to speak with a lord*[,
          LUCULLUS]. *From his master enters a* SERVANT *to him.*
SERVANT   I have told my lord of you. He is coming down to you.
FLAMINIUS   I thank you, sir.
          Enter LUCULLUS.
SERVANT   Here's my lord.

---

3. Greatest welfare (see 4.3.92–95).   5. Natural, caring.
4. Signet ring (token of authorization).   3.1 Location: Lucullus's house.

LUCULLUS [aside] One of Lord Timon's men? A gift, I war-
5   rant. Why, this hits right: I dreamt of a silver basin and ewer°   *pitcher*
    tonight. —Flaminius, honest Flaminius, you are very respec-
    tively° welcome, sir! [*to* SERVANT] Fill me some wine.   *respectfully*
                                  [*Exit* SERVANT.]
    And how does that honorable, complete, freehearted gentle-
    man of Athens, thy very bountiful good lord and master?
10 FLAMINIUS His health is well, sir.
LUCULLUS I am right glad that his health is well, sir. And what
    hast thou there under thy cloak, pretty Flaminius?
FLAMINIUS Faith, nothing but an empty box, sir, which in my
    lord's behalf I come to entreat your honor to supply, who,
15   having great and instant° occasion to use fifty talents, hath   *urgent*
    sent to your lordship to furnish him, nothing doubting your
    present° assistance therein.   *immediate*
LUCULLUS La, la, la, la, "nothing doubting," says he? Alas,
    good lord! A noble gentleman 'tis, if he would not keep so
20   good a house.° Many a time and often I ha' dined with him   *such lavish hospitality*
    and told him on't, and come again to supper to him of pur-
    pose to have him[1] spend less, and yet he would embrace no
    counsel, take no warning by my coming. Every man has his
    fault, and honesty° is his. I ha' told him on't, but I could   *generosity*
25   ne'er get him from't.
          Enter SERVANT *with wine.*
SERVANT Please your lordship, here is the wine.
LUCULLUS Flaminius, I have noted thee always wise. Here's
    to thee!
        [*He drinks.*]
FLAMINIUS Your lordship speaks your pleasure.°   *It pleases you to say so*
30 LUCULLUS I have observed thee always for a towardly° prompt   *promising*
    spirit, give thee thy due, and one that knows what belongs
    to reason° and canst use the time well, if the time use thee   *is reasonable*
    well[2]—good parts in thee![3] [*to* SERVANT] Get you gone,
    sirrah.   [*Exit* SERVANT.]
35   Draw nearer, honest Flaminius. Thy lord's a bountiful gen-
    tleman, but thou art wise, and thou know'st well enough,
    although thou com'st to me, that this is no time to lend
    money, especially upon bare° friendship without security.   *mere*
    [*He gives coins.*] Here's three solidares° for thee. Good boy,   *shillings*
40   wink at me,[4] and say thou saw'st me not. Fare thee well.
FLAMINIUS Is't possible the world should so much differ,°   *alter*
    And we alive that lived? [*He throws back the coins.*] Fly,
      damned baseness,
    To him that worships thee.
LUCULLUS Ha! Now I see thou art a fool and fit for thy master.
                                      Exit.
45 FLAMINIUS May these add to the number that may scald thee.°   *(in hell)*
    Let molten coin be thy damnation,
    Thou disease of a friend, and not himself.°   *not a true friend*
    Has friendship such a faint and milky heart
    It turns° in less than two nights? O you gods!   *curdles*

---

1. *of . . . him:* in order to persuade him to.   3. To your good qualities (a toast).
2. *canst . . . thee well:* know how to use an   4. Close your eyes to me.
opportunity.

50 I feel my master's passion.° This slave   *suffering*
    Unto this hour has my lord's meat in him.
    Why should it thrive and turn to nutriment,
    When he is turned to poison?
    Oh, may diseases only work upon't,
55 And when he's sick to death, let not that part of nature
    Which my lord paid for be of any power
    To expel sickness, but prolong his hour.°   *Exit.*   *(of suffering)*

3.2

Enter LUCIUS *with three* STRANGERS.

LUCIUS Who, the Lord Timon? He is my very good friend and
    an honorable gentleman.

FIRST STRANGER We know him for no less, though we are but
    strangers to him. But I can tell you one thing, my lord, and
5   which I hear from common rumors: now Lord Timon's happy
    hours are done and past, and his estate shrinks from him.

LUCIUS Fie, no, do not believe it! He cannot want for money.

SECOND STRANGER But believe you this, my lord, that not
    long ago one of his men was with the Lord Lucullus to bor-
10 row so many talents, nay urged extremely for't, and showed
    what necessity belonged to't, and yet was denied.

LUCIUS How?

SECOND STRANGER I tell you, denied, my lord.

LUCIUS What a strange case was that! Now before the gods,
15 I am ashamed on't. Denied that honorable man? There was
    very little honor showed in't. For my own part, I must needs
    confess I have received some small kindnesses from him, as
    money, plate, jewels, and such like trifles—nothing compar-
    ing to his. Yet had he mistook him¹ and sent to me, I should
20 ne'er have denied his occasion so many talents.

Enter SERVILIUS.

SERVILIUS [*aside*] See, by good hap yonder's my lord. I have
    sweat° to see his honor. [*to* LUCIUS] My honored lord.   *hurried*

LUCIUS Servilius? You are kindly met, sir. [*He starts to leave.*]
    Fare thee well. Commend me to thy honorable virtuous
25 lord, my very exquisite° friend.   *extraordinary*

SERVILIUS May it please your honor, my lord hath sent—

LUCIUS Ha? What has he sent? I am so much endeared° to   *obliged*
    that lord; he's ever sending. How shall I thank him, think'st
    thou? And what has he sent now?

30 SERVILIUS He's only sent his present occasion now, my lord,
    requesting your lordship to supply his instant use with so
    many talents.

LUCIUS I know his lordship is but merry with me.
    He cannot want fifty, five hundred² talents.

35 SERVILIUS But in the meantime he wants less, my lord.
    If his occasion were not virtuous,
    I should not urge it half so faithfully.

LUCULLUS Dost thou speak seriously, Servilius?

SERVILIUS Upon my soul 'tis true, sir.

3.2 Location: A public place.   2. This number possibly retains Shakespeare's revi-
1. Not overestimated Lucullus's generosity.   sion from "five hundred" to "fifty" or vice versa.

40 LUCIUS   What a wicked beast was I to disfurnish myself against
such a good time³ when I might ha' shown myself honorable!
How unluckily it happened that I should purchase the day
before for a little part° and undo a great deal of honor! Ser-   *small investment*
vilius, now before the gods, I am not able to do, the more
45 beast, I say! I was sending to use° Lord Timon myself—   *make use of*
these gentlemen can witness—but I would not for the
wealth of Athens I had done't now. Commend me bountifully to his good lordship, and I hope his honor will conceive
the fairest° of me, because I have no power to be kind. And   *think the best*
50 tell him this from me: I count it one of my greatest afflictions, say, that I cannot pleasure° such an honorable gentle-   *gratify*
man. Good Servilius, will you befriend me so far as to use
mine own words to him?
SERVILIUS   Yes, sir, I shall.
55 LUCIUS   I'll look you out° a good turn, Servilius.   *seek to do you*

Exit SERVILIUS.⁴

—True as you said: Timon is shrunk indeed,
And he that's once denied will hardly speed.°   *Exit.*   *prosper*
FIRST STRANGER   Do you observe this, Hostilius?
SECOND STRANGER   Ay, too well.
FIRST STRANGER   Why, this is the world's soul,° and just of the   *essence*
same piece°   *(of cloth)*
60 Is every flatterer's spirit. Who can call him his friend
That dips in the same dish?⁵ For in my knowing
Timon has been this lord's father,°   *patron*
And kept his° credit with his purse,   *sustained (Lucius's)*
Supported his estate, nay, Timon's money
65 Has paid his men their wages. He ne'er drinks
But Timon's silver treads upon his lip,
And yet (oh, see the monstrousness of man
When he looks out° in an ungrateful shape!)   *shows himself*
He does deny him, in respect of his,⁶
70 What charitable men afford to beggars.
THIRD STRANGER   Religion groans at it.
FIRST STRANGER   For mine own part,
I never tasted° Timon in my life,   *had experience of*
Nor came any of his bounties over me
To mark me for his friend. Yet, I protest,
75 For his right noble mind, illustrious virtue,
And honorable carriage,°   *conduct*
Had his necessity made use of me,
I would have put my wealth into donation,°   *given my wealth*
And the best half should have returned to him,
80 So much I love his heart. But I perceive
Men must learn now with pity to dispense,
For policy° sits above conscience.   *Exeunt.*   *calculation*

---

3. *disfurnish . . . time:* be unprepared for such a fine
occasion.
4. TEXTUAL COMMENT In the Folio this stage direction is placed one line earlier, suggesting that Lucius
speaks to Servilius as he is going out. See Digital

Edition TC 3 for a discussion of this change.
5. Alluding to Judas's betrayal of Christ after the
Last Supper.
6. In proportion to what he owns.

3.3

Enter [Timon's] third SERVANT *with* SEMPRONIUS,
another of Timon's friends.

SEMPRONIUS   Must he needs trouble me in't? Humph! 'Bove
        all others?
    He might have tried Lord Lucius, or Lucullus,
    And now Ventidius is wealthy too,
    Whom he redeemed from prison. All these
5   Owes their estates unto him.
SERVANT   My lord,
    They have all been touched° and found base metal,   *tested for purity*
    For they have all denied him.
SEMPRONIUS   How!¹ Have they denied him?
    Has Ventidius and Lucullus denied him,
    And does he send to me? Three? Humph!
10 It shows but little love or judgment in him.
    Must I be his last refuge? His friends like physicians
    Thrive, give him over.² Must I take th' cure upon me?
    He's much disgraced me in't. I'm angry at him,
    That might have known my place.³ I see no sense for't,
15 But his occasions might have wooed me first.
    For in my conscience,° I was the first man   *on my word*
    That ere received gift from him,
    And does he think so backwardly of me now
    That I'll requite it last? No!
20 So it may prove an argument° of laughter   *a subject*
    To th' rest, and 'mongst lords be thought a fool.
    I'd rather than the worth of thrice the sum
    He'd sent to me first, but for my mind's sake;⁴
    I'd such a courage to do him good. But now return,
25 And with their faint reply this answer join:
    Who bates° mine honor shall not know my coin.   *Exit.*   *undervalues*
SERVANT   Excellent. Your lordship's a goodly villain. The devil
        knew not what he did when he made man politic.° He   *calculating*
        crossed⁵ himself by't, and I cannot think but in the end the
30   villainies of man will set him clear.⁶ How fairly° this lord   *fully; speciously*
        strives to appear foul, takes virtuous copies° to be wicked.   *precepts*
        Like those⁷ that under hot ardent zeal would set whole
        realms on fire, of such a nature is his politic love.
        This was my lord's best hope. Now all are fled
35   Save only the gods. Now his friends are dead.
        Doors that were ne'er acquainted with their wards°   *locks*
        Many a bounteous year must be employed
        Now to guard sure° their master.   *safely*
        And this is all a liberal° course allows: *generous*
40   Who cannot keep his wealth must keep his house.⁸   *Exit.*

3.3 Location: Sempronius's house.
1. TEXTUAL COMMENT The exclamation point is a
question mark in the Folio. The two forms of punctuation were not always distinguished in the early
modern period, so a modernized edition must often
choose between them. See Digital Edition TC 4.
2. Thrive, while abandoning him to death.
3. That is, his place in Timon's list of friends.
4. If only on account of my disposition to him.

5. Thwarted (by making men his equal); canceled
from the list of debtors.
6. Will make him look innocent; will free him from
debt.
7. Religious fanatics; perhaps alludes to the Catholic
Gunpowder Plot to blow up King James I and Parliament in 1605.
8. Must stay indoors (for fear of arrest).

3.4

*Enter [two of] VARRO'S [SERVANTS] meeting others, all
[servants of] Timon's creditors, to wait for his coming
out. Then enter LUCIUS' [SERVANT,] HORTENSIUS, and
[TITUS].*

VARRO'S FIRST SERVANT Well met. Good morrow, Titus and
 Hortensius.

TITUS The like to you, kind Varro.

HORTENSIUS Lucius, what, do we meet together?

LUCIUS' SERVANT Ay, and I think one business does command
 us all.
   For mine is money.

5 TITUS   So is theirs and ours.
  Enter PHILOTUS.

LUCIUS' SERVANT And Sir Philotus, too!

PHILOTUS   Good day, at once.

LUCIUS' SERVANT Welcome, good brother!
   What do you think the hour?

PHILOTUS   Laboring for° nine.   *Approaching*

LUCIUS' SERVANT So much?

PHILOTUS   Is not my lord° seen yet?   *(Timon)*

LUCIUS' SERVANT   Not yet.

10 PHILOTUS I wonder on't. He was wont to shine° at seven.   *used to rise*

LUCIUS' SERVANT Ay, but the days are waxed shorter with him.
   You must consider that a prodigal course
   Is like the sun's,[1]
   But not like his° recoverable, I fear.   *(the sun's)*

15 'Tis deepest winter in Lord Timon's purse. That is:
   One may reach deep enough and yet find little.

PHILOTUS I am of° your fear for that.   *I share*

TITUS I'll show you how t'observe a strange event:
   [*to* HORTENSIUS] Your lord sends now for money?

HORTENSIUS   Most true, he does.

20 TITUS And he wears jewels now of Timon's gift,
   For° which I wait for money.   *For the purchase of*

HORTENSIUS   It is against my heart.°   *desire*

LUCIUS' SERVANT Mark how strange it shows:
   Timon in this should pay more than he owes;
   And e'en° as if your lord should wear rich jewels   *just*

25 And send for money for 'em.[2]

HORTENSIUS I'm weary of this charge,° the gods can witness.   *task*
   I know my lord hath spent of Timon's wealth,
   And now ingratitude makes it worse than stealth.°   *stealing*

VARRO'S FIRST SERVANT Yes, mine's three thousand crowns.
   What's yours?

30 LUCIUS' SERVANT Five thousand, mine.

VARRO'S FIRST SERVANT 'Tis much° deep, and it should seem   *very*
   by th' sum
   Your master's confidence was above mine.°   *(my master's)*
   Else surely his° had equaled.   *(my master's loan)*
  Enter FLAMINIUS.

TITUS One of Lord Timon's men.

3.4 Location: Timon's house.
1. That is, waning after the summer solstice.

2. And demand payment from Timon for supplying
them.

35 LUCIUS' SERVANT   Flaminius! Sir, a word. Pray, is my lord
　　Ready to come forth?
　FLAMINIUS   No, indeed he is not.
　TITUS   We attend his lordship. Pray, signify so much.
　FLAMINIUS   I need not tell him that; he knows you are
　　Too diligent.   [*Exit.*]
　　　　Enter STEWARD *in a cloak, muffled.*
40 LUCIUS' SERVANT   Ha! Is not that his steward muffled so?
　　He goes away in a cloud.° Call him, call him!　　　　　　*concealed; in trouble*
　TITUS [*to* STEWARD]   Do you hear, sir?
　VARRO'S SECOND SERVANT [*to* STEWARD]   By your leave, sir.
　STEWARD   What do ye ask of me, my friend?
　TITUS   We wait for certain money here, sir.
45 STEWARD   Ay,
　　If money were as certain as your waiting,
　　'Twere sure enough.
　　Why then preferred° you not your sums and bills　　　　*brought forward*
　　When your false masters ate of my lord's meat?
50 　Then they could smile and fawn upon his debts
　　And take down th'interest into their gluttonous maws.
　　You do yourselves but wrong to stir me up.
　　Let me pass quietly.
　　Believe't, my lord and I have made an end;°　　　　*finished with each other*
55 　I have no more to reckon, he to spend.
　LUCIUS' SERVANT   Ay, but this answer will not serve.
　STEWARD   If 'twill not serve,³ 'tis not so base as you,
　　For you serve knaves.   [*Exit.*]
　VARRO'S FIRST SERVANT   How? What does his cashiered° wor-　　*dismissed*
60 　ship mutter?⁴
　VARRO'S SECOND SERVANT   No matter what. He's poor, and
　　that's revenge enough. Who can speak broader⁵ than he that
　　has no house to put his head in? Such may rail against great
　　buildings.
　　　　Enter SERVILIUS.
65 TITUS   Oh, here's Servilius. Now we shall know some answer.
　SERVILIUS   If I might beseech you, gentlemen, to repair° some　　*return*
　　other hour, I should derive° much from't. For take't of my　　*gain*
　　soul, my lord leans wondrously to discontent. His comfort-
　　able° temper has forsook him; he's much out of health and　　*cheerful*
70 　keeps his chamber.
　LUCIUS' SERVANT   Many do keep their chambers are not sick,⁶
　　And, if it be so far beyond his health,
　　Methinks he should the sooner pay his debts
　　And make a clear way to the gods.
　SERVILIUS   Good gods!
75 TITUS   We cannot take this for answer, sir.
　FLAMINIUS (*within*)   Servilius, help! My lord, my lord!
　　　　Enter TIMON *in a rage.*
　TIMON   What, are my doors opposed against my passage?
　　Have I been ever free,° and must my house　　　　*at liberty; generous*

---

3. Suffice (but in line 58, "wait on").
4. TEXTUAL COMMENT This line, like many in *Timon*,
is set as prose but has a pattern of stresses suggestive
of blank verse. For a discussion of the way the language of the play often hovers between verse and
prose, see Digital Edition TC 5.
5. More freely; more out of doors.
6. That is, they are avoiding arrest for debt.

Be my retentive° enemy? My jail?   *confining; niggardly*
80   The place which I have feasted, does it now
Like all mankind show me an iron heart?

LUCIUS' SERVANT Put in° now, Titus.   *Make your claim*

TITUS   My lord, here is my bill.

LUCIUS' SERVANT Here's mine.

VARRO'S FIRST SERVANT   And mine, my lord.

VARRO'S SECOND SERVANT   And ours, my lord.

PHILOTUS All our bills.

85   TIMON Knock me down with 'em; cleave me to the girdle.[7]

LUCIUS' SERVANT Alas, my lord.

TIMON Cut my heart in° sums.   *into*

TITUS Mine, fifty talents.

TIMON Tell° out my blood.   *Count*

LUCIUS' SERVANT   Five thousand crowns, my lord.

90   TIMON Five thousand drops pays that. [*to* VARRO'S SERVANTS]
What yours? And yours?

VARRO'S FIRST SERVANT My lord—

VARRO'S SECOND SERVANT My lord—

TIMON Tear me, take me, and the gods fall upon you.

                               Exit TIMON.

HORTENSIUS Faith, I perceive our masters may throw their
95   caps at° their money. These debts may well be called desper-   *cease pursuing*
ate° ones, for a madman owes 'em.   *Exeunt.*   *hopeless; insane*

3.5

Enter TIMON [*and* STEWARD].

TIMON They have e'en put[1] my breath from me, the slaves.
Creditors? Devils!

STEWARD My dear lord—

TIMON What if it should be so?[2]

5   STEWARD My lord—

TIMON I'll have it so. —My steward!

STEWARD   Here, my lord.

TIMON So fitly?° Go, bid all my friends again,   *conveniently*
Lucius, Lucullus, and Sempronius, usurers all.[3]
I'll once more feast the rascals.

STEWARD   O my lord,
10   You only speak from your distracted soul.
There's not so much left to furnish out
A moderate table.

TIMON   Be it not in thy care.°   *your responsibility*
Go, I charge thee, invite them all. Let in the tide
Of knaves once more. My cook and I'll provide.   *Exeunt.*

---

7. Timon puns on "bills" (line 84) as weapons (halberds).
3.5 Location: Scene continues.
1. Have taken (referring to Timon's breathlessness and to the proverb "Air is free").

2. Timon is referring to a plan he has just thought of.
3. TEXTUAL COMMENT The Folio reads "*Vllorxa*," probably a compositor's error, emended here to "usurers." For the rationale behind the emendation, see Digital Edition TC 6.

3.6

Enter three SENATORS *at one door,* ALCIBIADES
meeting them, with Attendants.

FIRST SENATOR My lord, you have my voice to't.° The fault's°   *vote for it / crime is*
    bloody;
    'Tis necessary he should die.
    Nothing emboldens sin so much as mercy.

SECOND SENATOR Most true. The law shall bruise 'em.

5 ALCIBIADES Honor, health, and compassion to the Senate.

FIRST SENATOR Now, captain—

ALCIBIADES I am an humble suitor to your virtues.
    For pity is the virtue° of the law,   *essence*
    And none but tyrants use it cruelly.

10   It pleases time and fortune to lie heavy
    Upon a friend of mine, who in hot blood
    Hath stepped into° the law, which is past depth   *(as into quicksand)*
    To those that without heed do plunge into't.
    He is a man, setting his fate° aside, of comely virtues,   *deed*

15   Nor did he soil the fact with cowardice—
    An honor in him which buys out his fault°—   *redeems his crime*
    But with a noble fury and fair spirit.
    Seeing his reputation touched to death,°   *fatally besmirched*
    He did oppose his foe:

20   And with such sober and unnoted[1] passion
    He did behoove° his anger, ere 'twas spent,   *control*
    As if he had but proved an argument.

FIRST SENATOR You undergo° too strict a paradox,   *undertake*
    Striving to make an ugly deed look fair.

25   Your words have took such pains as if they labored
    To bring manslaughter into form[2] and set quarreling
    Upon the head° of valor, which indeed   *In the category of*
    Is valor misbegot and came into the world
    When sects and factions were newly born.

30   He's truly valiant that can wisely suffer
    The worst that man can breathe,° and make his wrongs his   *utter*
        outsides,°   *merely external things*
    To wear them like his raiment, carelessly,
    And ne'er prefer° his injuries to his heart,   *promote*
    To bring it into danger.

35   If wrong be evils and enforce us kill,
    What folly 'tis to hazard life for ill.

ALCIBIADES My lord—

FIRST SENATOR   You cannot make gross sins look clear;
    To revenge is no valor, but to bear.°   *endure (is valor)*

ALCIBIADES My lords, then, under favor,° pardon me   *by your leave*

40   If I speak like a captain.
    Why do fond° men expose themselves to battle   *foolish*
    And not endure all threats, sleep upon't,
    And let the foes quietly cut their throats
    Without repugnancy?° If there be   *resistance*

---

2. To make manslaughter legal.

45	Such valor in the bearing,° what make we	*enduring*
	Abroad?³ Why, then, women are more valiant	
	That stay at home, if bearing carry it,°	*wins the day*
	And the ass more captain than the lion,	
	The fellow loaden with irons° wiser than the judge,	*shackles*
50	If wisdom be in suffering. O my lords,	
	As you are great, be pitifully good.°	*good in showing pity*
	Who cannot condemn rashness in cold blood?	
	To kill, I grant, is sin's extremest gust,°	*outburst*
	But in defense, by mercy,⁴ 'tis most just.	
55	To be in anger is impiety,	
	But who is man that is not angry?	
	Weigh but the crime with this.	

SECOND SENATOR　　　　　　　　You breathe in vain.

ALCIBIADES　In vain?

His service done at Lacedaemon and Byzantium
60 Were a sufficient briber for his life.

FIRST SENATOR　What's that?

	ALCIBIADES　Why, I say, my lords, he's done fair° service	*fine*
	And slain in fight many of your enemies.	
	How full of valor did he bear himself	
65	In the last conflict and made plenteous wounds!	

SECOND SENATOR　He has made too much plenty with him.

	He's a sworn rioter;° he has a sin	*committed reveler*
	That often drowns him and takes his valor prisoner.⁵	
	If there were no foes, that were enough	
70	To overcome him. In that beastly fury	
	He has been known to commit outrages	
	And cherish factions.° 'Tis inferred° to us	*foster dissension / alleged*
	His days are foul and his drink dangerous.	

FIRST SENATOR　He dies.

ALCIBIADES　　　　　　　　Hard fate! He might have died in war.

75	My lords, if not for any parts° in him—	*good qualities*
	Though his right arm might purchase his own time⁶	
	And be in debt to none—yet, more to move you,	
	Take° my deserts to his and join 'em both.	*Combine*
	And for I know your reverend ages love security,⁷	
80	I'll pawn my victories, all my honor, to you	
	Upon his good returns.°	*repayment (of your trust)*
	If by this crime he owes the law his life,	
	Why, let the war receive't in valiant gore;	
	For law is strict, and war is nothing more.	

85	FIRST SENATOR　We are for law. He dies. Urge it no more	
	On height of our° displeasure. Friend or brother,	*At risk of our highest*
	He forfeits his own blood that spills another.	

ALCIBIADES　Must it be so? It must not be.
My lords, I do beseech you know me.

SECOND SENATOR　　　　　　　　How?

ALCIBIADES　Call me to your remembrances.

90 THIRD SENATOR　　　　　　　　What?

---

3. *what make we / Abroad:* why do we (men) go outdoors?
4. But self-defense, considered mercifully.
5. *sin . . . prisoner:* that is, drunkenness.

6. Though performance in battle might redeem him for the duration of his life.
7. Collateral (as on a loan); safety.

ALCIBIADES   I cannot think but your age has forgot me.
It could not else° be I should prove so base   *otherwise*
To sue and be denied such common grace.
My wounds ache at you.
FIRST SENATOR   Do you dare our anger?
95   'Tis in few words but spacious° in effect: *great*
We banish thee forever.
ALCIBIADES   Banish me?
Banish your dotage, banish usury
That makes the Senate ugly.
FIRST SENATOR   If after two-days' shine Athens contain thee,
100   Attend our weightier judgment, and, not to swell our spirit,°   *anger*
He shall be executed presently.°   *Exeunt* [SENATORS].   *immediately*
ALCIBIADES   Now the gods keep you old enough that you may
        live
Only in bone,° that none may look on you!   *as skeletons*
I'm worse than mad; I have kept back their foes
105   While they have told° their money and let out   *counted*
Their coin upon large interest, I myself
Rich only in large hurts. All those, for this?
Is this the balsam° that the usuring Senate   *ointment*
Pours into captains' wounds? Banishment!
110   It comes not ill; I hate not to be banished.
It is a cause worthy my spleen and fury
That I may strike at Athens. I'll cheer up
My discontented troops and lay for hearts.°   *win their support*
'Tis honor with most lands° to be at odds;   *the richest*
115   Soldiers should brook° as little wrongs as gods.   *Exit.*   *endure*

3.7

Enter diverse [of Timon's] FRIENDS, *[*SENATORS
including LUCIUS, LUCULLUS, *and* SEMPRONIUS,*]*
at several doors.[1]

FIRST FRIEND   The good time of day to you, sir.
SECOND FRIEND   I also wish it to you. I think this honorable
        lord did but try° us this other day.   *test*
FIRST FRIEND   Upon that were my thoughts tiring[2] when we
5   encountered.° I hope it is not so low with him as he made it   *met*
        seem in the trial of his several friends.
SECOND FRIEND   It should not be, by the persuasion° of his   *evidence*
        new feasting.
FIRST FRIEND   I should think so. He hath sent me an earnest
10   inviting, which many my near occasions° did urge me to put   *my many urgent affairs*
        off, but he hath conjured me beyond them, and I must needs
        appear.
SECOND FRIEND   In like manner was I in debt° to my importu-   *I needed to attend*
        nate business, but he would not hear my excuse. I am sorry
15   when he sent to borrow of me that my provision was out.

3.7 Location: Timon's house.
1. TEXTUAL COMMENT The individual friends are not
named in the stage directions to this scene, nor in
the speech prefixes, although Lucius, Sempronius,

and Lucullus were invited to Timon's party in 3.5.
See Digital Edition TC 7 for a discussion of their
anonymity in this scene.
2. Feeding (as a hawk tears flesh).

FIRST FRIEND   I am sick of that grief, too, as I understand how
all things go.³

SECOND FRIEND   Every man hears so. What would he have
borrowed of you?

20 FIRST FRIEND   A thousand pieces.

SECOND FRIEND   A thousand pieces?

FIRST FRIEND   What of you?

SECOND FRIEND   He sent to me, sir—here he comes.
              Enter TIMON *and Attendants.*

TIMON   With all my heart, gentlemen both, and how fare you?

25 FIRST FRIEND   Ever at the best, hearing well of your lordship.

SECOND FRIEND   The swallow follows not summer more willing than we your lordship.

TIMON [*aside*]   Nor more willingly leaves winter; such summer
birds are men. —Gentlemen, our dinner will not recom-

30 pense this long stay. Feast your ears with the music a while,
if they will fare° so harshly o'th' trumpet's sound. We shall   sustain themselves
to't presently.

FIRST FRIEND   I hope it remains not unkindly with your lordship that I returned you an empty messenger.

35 TIMON   O sir, let it not trouble you.

SECOND FRIEND   My noble lord—

TIMON   Ah, my good friend, what cheer?
              The banquet brought in.

SECOND FRIEND   My most honorable lord, I am e'en° sick of   utterly
shame that when your lordship this other day sent to me I

40 was so unfortunate a beggar.

TIMON   Think not on't, sir.

SECOND FRIEND   If you had sent but two hours before—

TIMON   Let it not cumber° your better remembrance. [*He*   burden
calls.] Come, bring in all together.
              [*Enter* SERVANTS *with dishes.*]

45 SECOND FRIEND   All covered dishes.

FIRST FRIEND   Royal cheer,° I warrant you.   dining

THIRD FRIEND   Doubt not that, if money and the season can
yield it.

FIRST FRIEND   How do you? What's the news?

50 THIRD FRIEND   Alcibiades is banished. Hear you of it?

BOTH   Alcibiades banished?

THIRD FRIEND   'Tis so, be sure of it.

FIRST FRIEND   How? How?

SECOND FRIEND   I pray you upon what?°   what grounds

55 TIMON   My worthy friends, will you draw near?

THIRD FRIEND   I'll tell you more anon. Here's a noble feast
toward.°   coming up

SECOND FRIEND   This is the old⁴ man still.

THIRD FRIEND   Wilt hold? Wilt hold?°   last

60 SECOND FRIEND   It does, but time will,° and so—   *"time will tell"*

THIRD FRIEND   I do conceive.°   understand

TIMON   Each man to his stool with that spur° as he would to   speed
the lip of his mistress. Your diet shall be in all places alike.

---

3. *as . . . go:* now that I understand the real situation.   4. Familiar (in his generosity).

Make not a city feast[5] of it, to let the meat cool ere we can
65 agree upon the first place.° Sit, sit.   *place of honor*
     [*They sit.*]
The gods require our thanks:
You great benefactors, sprinkle our society with thankfulness. For your own gifts make yourselves praised. But reserve
still[6] to give, lest your deities be despised. Lend to each man
70 enough that one need not lend to another. For were your
godheads to borrow of men, men would forsake the gods.
Make the meat be beloved more than the man that gives it.
Let no assembly of twenty be without a score of villains. If
there sit twelve women at the table, let a dozen of them be as
75 they are.° The rest of your foes, O gods, the senators of Ath-   *(that is, unchaste)*
ens, together with the common leg° of people, what is amiss   *mob*
in them, you gods, make suitable for destruction. For these
my present friends, as they are to me nothing, so in nothing
bless them, and to nothing are they welcome. —Uncover,
80 dogs, and lap!
     [*The dishes, containing only hot water, are uncovered.*]
SOME FRIEND   What does his lordship mean?
SOME OTHER   I know not.
TIMON   May you a better feast never behold,
     You knot of mouth-friends.[7] Smoke and lukewarm water
85 Is your perfection. This is Timon's last,
     Who stuck and spangled you with flatteries,
     Washes it off and sprinkles in your faces
     Your reeking° villainy. [*He throws water at them.*] Live loathed   *steaming; stinking*
          and long,
     Most smiling, smooth, detested parasites,
90 Courteous destroyers, affable wolves, meek bears,
     You fools of fortune, trencher-friends,° time's flies,[8]   *mealtime friends*
     Cap-and-knee° slaves, vapors, and minute-jacks.[9]   *Sycophantic*
     Of man and beast, the infinite malady[1]
     Crust you quite o'er. What, dost thou go?
          [*He beats them.*]
95 Soft,° take thy physic° first—thou, too, and thou: *Wait / medicine*
     Stay, I will lend thee money, borrow none.
     What, all in motion?   [*Exeunt* FRIENDS *and* SENATORS.]
               Henceforth be no feast
     Whereat a villain's not a welcome guest.
     Burn, house! Sink, Athens! Henceforth hated be
100 Of Timon, man, and all humanity.   *Exit* [with SERVANTS].
          Enter the SENATORS, [*Timon's* FRIENDS,] *with other*
          LORDS.
FIRST FRIEND   How now, my lords?
SECOND FRIEND   Know you the quality° of Lord Timon's fury?   *nature*
THIRD FRIEND   Push,° did you see my cap?   *(impatient expression)*
FOURTH FRIEND   I have lost my gown.

---

5. Feast as given by London dignitaries, in which seating arrangements were thought socially significant.
6. But always hold back something.
7. You group of insincere (or gluttonous) friends.

8. That is, vanishing in cold weather.
9. Mannequins that strike bells on medieval clocks;
hence, timeservers.
1. May every disease of man and beast.

FIRST FRIEND He's but a mad lord, and naught but humors°   *unstable moods*
105   sways him. He gave me a jewel th'other day, and now he has
    beat it out of my hat.
    Did you see my jewel?
SECOND FRIEND   Did you see my cap?
THIRD FRIEND   Here 'tis.
FOURTH FRIEND   Here lies my gown.
FIRST FRIEND   Let's make no stay.
SECOND FRIEND   Lord Timon's mad.
THIRD FRIEND   I feel't upon my bones.
110 FOURTH FRIEND   One day he gives us diamonds, next day stones.

        Exeunt the SENATORS[, *other* LORDS, *and*
               Timon's FRIENDS].

4.1

    Enter TIMON.
TIMON   Let me look back upon thee. O thou wall
    That girdles in those wolves, dive in the earth
    And fence not Athens. Matrons, turn incontinent.°   *unchaste*
    Obedience, fail in children. Slaves and fools,
5   Pluck the grave-wrinkled Senate from the bench
    And minister in their steads. To general filths°   *common whores*
    Convert o'th' instant green[1] virginity.
    Do't in your parents' eyes! Bankrupts, hold fast:°   *refuse to pay*
    Rather than render back, out with your knives
10   And cut your trusters'° throats. Bound° servants, steal;   *creditors' / Indentured*
    Large-handed robbers your grave masters are
    And pill° by law. Maid, to thy master's bed;   *plunder*
    Thy mistress is o'th' brothel. Son of sixteen,
    Pluck the lined° crutch from thy old limping sire;   *padded*
15   With it, beat out his brains. Piety and fear,
    Religion to the gods, peace, justice, truth,
    Domestic awe,[2] night-rest and neighborhood,°   *neighborliness*
    Instruction, manners, mysteries,° and trades,   *crafts*
    Degrees,° observances,[3] customs, and laws,   *Social ranks*
20   Decline to your confounding° contraries,   *destroying*
    And yet confusion live. Plagues incident to men,
    Your potent and infectious fevers heap
    On Athens ripe for stroke.° Thou cold sciatica,°   *to be struck / nerve pain*
    Cripple our senators that their limbs may halt°   *limp*
25   As lamely as their manners. Lust and liberty,°   *licentiousness*
    Creep in the minds and marrows[4] of our youth,
    That 'gainst the stream of virtue they may strive
    And drown themselves in riot.° Itches, blains,°   *debauchery / sores*
    Sow all th'Athenian bosoms, and their crop
30   Be general leprosy. Breath infect breath,
    That their society,° as their friendship, may   *company*
    Be merely° poison. Nothing I'll bear from thee   *wholly*
    But nakedness, thou detestable town.
    Take thou that too, with multiplying bans.°   *curses*

4.1 Location: Outside the walls of Athens.
1. Young, newly menstruating girls often suffered anemia, then called "greensickness" and thought to be curable by sexual satisfaction.

2. Household government.
3. Respectful customs.
4. Thought to be the site of vigor; proverbially melted by lust.

35 Timon will to the woods, where he shall find
Th'unkindest beast more kinder⁵ than mankind.
The gods confound—hear me, you good gods all!—
Th'Athenians both within and out that wall,
And grant as Timon grows his hate may grow
40 To the whole race of mankind, high and low.
Amen.   *Exit.*

4.2

Enter STEWARD *with two or three* SERVANTS.
FIRST SERVANT   Hear you, Master Steward, where's our master?
  Are we undone, cast off, nothing remaining?
STEWARD   Alack, my fellows, what should I say to you?
  Let me be recorded by the righteous gods,
  I am as poor as you.
5 FIRST SERVANT   Such a house broke?
  So noble a master fallen? All gone, and not
  One friend to take his° fortune by the arm   (Timon's)
  And go along with him?
SECOND SERVANT   As we do turn our backs
  From our companion thrown into his grave,
10 So his familiars to¹ his buried fortunes
  Slink all away, leave their false vows with him
  Like empty purses picked. And his poor self,
  A dedicated° beggar to the air,   *Abandoned as a*
  With his disease of all-shunned poverty,
15 Walks like contempt alone.—More of our fellows.
        Enter other SERVANTS.
STEWARD   All broken implements of a ruined house.
THIRD SERVANT   Yet do our hearts wear Timon's livery,°   *servants' uniforms*
  That see I by our faces we are fellows still,
  Serving alike in sorrow. Leaked is our bark,°   *sailboat*
20 And we poor mates stand on the dying° deck,   *sinking*
  Hearing the surges threat.° We must all part   *waves threaten*
  Into this sea of air.
STEWARD   Good fellows all,
  The latest° of my wealth I'll share amongst you.   *last bit*
  Wherever we shall meet, for Timon's sake
25 Let's yet be fellows. Let's shake our heads and say,
  As 'twere a knell unto our master's fortunes,
  "We have seen better days." [*He gives them money.*] Let each
      take some.
  Nay, put out all your hands. Not one word more.
  Thus part we rich in sorrow, parting poor.
        Embrace and [SERVANTS] *part several ways.*
30 Oh, the fierce° wretchedness that glory brings us!   *excessive*
  Who would not wish to be from wealth exempt,
  Since riches point to misery and contempt?
  Who would be so mocked with glory, or to live
  But in a dream of friendship,

---

5. Gentler; more nearly akin.
4.2 Location: Timon's house.

1. So his intimate friends from (a "familiar" could
also be a flattering devil).

35   To have his pomp and all what state compounds[2]
       But only painted like his varnished friends?
       Poor honest lord, brought low by his own heart,
       Undone by goodness. Strange unusual blood,°   *disposition*
       When man's worst sin is he does too much good.
40   Who then dares to be half so kind again?
       For bounty that makes° gods do still mar men.   *characterizes*
       My dearest lord, blest to be most accursed,
       Rich only to be wretched. Thy great fortunes
       Are made thy chief afflictions. Alas, kind lord,
45   He's flung in rage from this ingrateful seat°   *residence*
       Of monstrous friends.
       Nor has he with him to supply° his life,   *resources to maintain*
       Or that° which can command it.   *(money)*
       I'll follow and inquire him out.
50   I'll ever serve his mind with my best will;
       Whilst I have gold, I'll be his steward still.   *Exit.*

                           4.3
                Enter TIMON *in the woods.*
       TIMON O blessèd breeding sun,[1] draw from the earth
       Rotten° humidity. Below thy sister's[2] orb   *Putrid*
       Infect the air. Twinned brothers of one womb,
       Whose procreation, residence,° and birth   *time in the womb*
5   Scarce is dividant,° touch them with several° fortunes: *separable / different*
       The greater scorns the lesser. Not nature,
       To whom all sores° lay siege, can bear great fortune, *afflictions*
       But by contempt of nature.[3]
       Raise me[4] this beggar, and deny't that lord,
10   The senators shall bear contempt hereditary,°   *as if he had inherited it*
       The beggar native° honor.   *inborn*
       It is the pasture lards[5] the brother's sides,
       The want that makes him lean. Who dares, who dares
       In purity of manhood stand upright
15   And say, "This man's a flatterer"? If one be,
       So are they all, for every grece° of fortune   *step on the staircase*
       Is smoothed by that below.[6] The learnèd pate°   *head*
       Ducks° to the golden fool. All's obliquy.°   *Bows / deviousness*
       There's nothing level° in our cursèd natures   *straight; consistent*
20   But direct villainy. Therefore be abhorred,
       All feasts, societies, and throngs of men.
       His semblable,° yea himself, Timon disdains.   *His own image*
       Destruction, fang° mankind. [*He digs.*] Earth, yield me roots. *seize*
       Who seeks for better of thee, sauce his palate
25   With thy most operant° poison. [*He discovers gold.*] What is *potent*
          here?
       Gold? Yellow, glittering, precious gold?

---

2. And all that splendor is made of.
4.3 Location: Outside Athens.
1. The sun was supposed to be able to generate vermin spontaneously and to foment infection.
2. The moon's; see note to 1.1.45.
3. Without scorning those of like nature.

4. This "me" is an example of the so-called ethic dative
("for me"), used to emphasize the verb. See also line
113.
5. Fattens ("pasture" suggests both owning and eating from the land).
6. By the people standing on the step below.

No, gods, I am no idle° votarist—   *frivolous*
Roots, you clear heavens! Thus much of this will make
Black white, foul fair, wrong right,
30   Base noble, old young, coward valiant.
Ha, you gods! Why this? What, this, you gods? Why, this
Will lug your priests and servants from your sides,
Pluck stout men's pillows from below their heads.°   *(to kill them)*
This yellow slave
35   Will knit and break religions, bless th'accursed,
Make the hoar° leprosy adored, place° thieves   *gray / appoint to office*
And give them title, knee,° and approbation   *reverence*
With senators on the bench. This is it
That makes the wappered° widow wed again.   *worn out*
40   She whom the spittle-house° and ulcerous sores   *hospital*
Would cast the gorge° at, this embalms and spices   *vomit*
To th'April day[7] again. Come, damnèd earth,°   *gold*
Thou common whore of mankind that puts odds°   *quarrels*
Among the rout° of nations, I will make thee   *rabble*
Do[8] thy right nature.
           March afar off.
45   Ha, a drum? Thou'rt quick.[9]
But yet I'll bury thee. [*He buries gold.*] Thou'lt go, strong
    thief,
When gouty keepers of thee cannot stand—
Nay, stay thou out for earnest.°   *as a pledge*
          Enter ALCIBIADES *with* [SOLDIERS *marching to*]
          drum and fife in warlike manner, and PHRYNIA
          and TIMANDRA.
ALCIBIADES   What art thou there? Speak.
TIMON   A beast as thou art. The canker[1] gnaw thy heart
50   For showing me again the eyes of man.
ALCIBIADES   What is thy name? Is man so hateful to thee,
    That art thyself a man?
TIMON   I am *Misanthropos*° and hate mankind.   *man-hater (Greek)*
    For thy part, I do wish thou wert a dog,
    That I might love thee something.°   *somewhat*
55   ALCIBIADES   I know thee well,
But in thy fortunes am unlearned and strange.[2]
TIMON   I know thee, too, and more than that I know thee
    I not desire° to know. Follow thy drum.   *do not desire*
    With man's blood paint the ground gules,° gules.   *red (heraldic term)*
60   Religious canons, civil laws are cruel.
Then what should war be? This fell° whore of thine   *dreadful*
Hath in her more destruction than thy sword,
For all her cherubin look.
PHRYNIA   Thy lips rot off!°   *(as in syphilis)*
TIMON   I will not kiss thee; then the rot returns
65   To thine own lips again.
ALCIBIADES   How came the noble Timon to this change?

---

7. To youthful freshness.
8. Act according to (by concealing gold and yielding roots).
9. Swift to bring strife; alive.
1. Spreading ulcer; cankerworm.
2. Am ignorant and unacquainted.

TIMON   As the moon does, by wanting° light to give.   *lacking*
    But then renew I could not like the moon;
    There were no suns to borrow of.

70 ALCIBIADES   Noble Timon, what friendship may I do thee?
TIMON   None, but to maintain my opinion.
ALCIBIADES   What is it, Timon?
TIMON   Promise me friendship, but perform none. If thou wilt
    not promise, the gods plague thee, for thou art a man. If
75 thou dost perform, confound° thee, for thou art a man.   *damn*
ALCIBIADES   I have heard in some sort° of thy miseries.   *to some extent*
TIMON   Thou saw'st them when I had prosperity.
ALCIBIADES   I see them now. Then was a blessèd time.
TIMON   As thine is now, held with a brace° of harlots.   *pair*
80 TIMANDRA   Is this th'Athenian minion° whom the world   *favorite*
    Voiced° so regardfully?   *Spoke of*
TIMON   Art thou Timandra?
TIMANDRA   Yes.
TIMON   Be a whore still. They love thee not that use thee.
    Give them diseases, leaving with thee their lust.
85 Make use of thy salt° hours. Season° the slaves   *lecherous / Prepare*
    For tubs and baths;³ bring down rose-cheeked youth
    To the tub-fast and the diet.
TIMANDRA   Hang thee, monster!
ALCIBIADES   Pardon him, sweet Timandra, for his wits
    Are drowned and lost in his calamities.
90 I have but little gold of late, brave Timon,
    The want whereof doth daily make° revolt   *cause*
    In my penurious band. I have heard and grieved
    How cursèd Athens, mindless of thy worth,
    Forgetting thy great deeds, when neighbor states
95 But for thy sword and fortune trod upon them⁴—
TIMON   I prithee, beat thy drum, and get thee gone.
ALCIBIADES   I am thy friend and pity thee, dear Timon.
TIMON   How dost thou pity him whom thou dost trouble?
    I had rather be alone.
ALCIBIADES   Why, fare thee well.
    [*He offers* TIMON *gold.*] Here is some gold for thee.
100 TIMON   Keep it; I cannot eat it.
ALCIBIADES   When I have laid proud Athens on a heap—
TIMON   Warr'st thou 'gainst Athens?
ALCIBIADES   Ay, Timon, and have cause.
TIMON   The gods confound them all in thy conquest,
    And thee after when thou hast conquerèd.
105 ALCIBIADES   Why me, Timon?
TIMON   That by killing of villains thou wast born to conquer
    my country.
    Put up thy gold.
            [*He offers* ALCIBIADES *gold.*]
            Go on, here's gold, go on!

---

3. Used, with "diet" (line 87), to treat venereal
disease.

4. Alcibiades suggests that Timon's money and military expertise saved Athens in the past.

Be as a planetary plague,[5] when Jove
110 Will o'er some high-viced city hang his poison
In the sick air. Let not thy sword skip one.
Pity not honored age for his white beard;
He is an usurer. Strike me° the counterfeit matron: Strike for me
It is her habit° only that is honest; attire
115 Herself's a bawd. Let not the virgin's cheek
Make soft thy trenchant° sword, for those milk paps° cutting / breasts
That through the window-bars° bore at men's eyes openwork bodice
Are not within the leaf° of pity writ, page
But set them down horrible traitors. Spare not the babe
120 Whose dimpled smiles from fools exhaust° their mercy. draw out
Think it a bastard, whom the oracle
Hath doubtfully° pronounced the throat shall cut, ambiguously
And mince it sans° remorse. Swear against objects;[6] without
Put armor on thine ears and on thine eyes,
125 Whose proof° nor yells of mothers, maids, nor babes, strength
Nor sight of priests in holy vestments bleeding
Shall pierce a jot. There's gold to pay thy soldiers.
Make large confusion and, thy fury spent,
Confounded be thyself. Speak not, be gone.
130 ALCIBIADES [taking gold]   Hast thou gold yet? I'll take the gold
      thou givest me,
      Not all thy counsel.
    TIMON   Dost thou or dost thou not, heaven's curse upon thee.
    PHRYNIA and TIMANDRA   Give us some gold, good Timon; hast
      thou more?
    TIMON   Enough to make a whore forswear her trade
135 And to make whores a bawd. Hold up, you sluts,
Your aprons mountant.[7] [He gives them gold.] You are not
      oathable,[8]
Although I know you'll swear, terribly swear
Into strong shudders and to heavenly agues° fevers
Th'immortal gods that hear you. Spare your oaths;
140 I'll trust to your conditions.° Be whores still, occupations; characters
And he whose pious breath seeks to convert you,
Be strong in whore, allure him, burn him up.° inflame him; infect him
Let your close° fire predominate his smoke,[9] secret
And be no turncoats. Yet may your pains six months
145 Be quite contrary,° and thatch your poor thin roofs Make you suffer intensely
With burdens of the dead[1]—some that were hanged—
No matter. Wear them, betray with them, whore still.
Paint° till a horse may mire° upon your face. Use cosmetics / get stuck
A pox of wrinkles!
    PHRYNIA and TIMANDRA   Well, more gold, what then?
150 Believe't that we'll do anything for gold.
    TIMON   Consumptions° sow Diseases
      In hollow bones of man, strike their sharp shins,[2]

---

5. Plagues were thought to be caused by the influence of the other planets.
6. Vow not to listen to protests.
7. Your skirts lifted ("mountant," a heraldic term, puns on "sexual mounting").

8. Capable of being bound on oath.
9. Overcome his "pious breath" (line 141).
1. thatch . . . dead: wear wigs made of corpses' hair to cover your syphilitic baldness.
2. Syphilis causes bone degeneration.

And mar men's spurring![3] Crack the lawyer's voice
That he may never more false title plead,
155 Nor sound his quillets° shrilly. Hoar the flamen[4]   *quibbles*
That scold'st against the quality° of flesh   *nature*
And not believes himself. Down with the nose,
Down with it flat,[5] take the bridge quite away
Of him that his particular° to foresee   *self-interest*
160 Smells from the general weal.[6] Make curled-pate ruffians
    bald,
And let the unscarred braggarts of the war
Derive some pain from you. Plague all,
That your activity may defeat and quell
The source of all erection.[7] There's more gold.
165 Do you damn others, and let this damn you,
And ditches grave you all.[8]
PHRYNIA *and* TIMANDRA   More counsel with more money,
    bounteous Timon!
TIMON   More whore, more mischief first. I have given you
    earnest.°   *a down payment*
ALCIBIADES   Strike up the drum towards Athens. Farewell,
    Timon.
170 If I thrive well, I'll visit thee again.
TIMON   If I hope well, I'll never see thee more.
ALCIBIADES   I never did thee harm.
TIMON   Yes, thou spok'st well of me.
ALCIBIADES   Call'st thou that harm?
TIMON   Men daily find it.° Get thee away,   *discover it to be so*
And take thy beagles° with thee.   *fawning curs (the whores)*
175 ALCIBIADES   We but offend him.
    [*to drummers*] Strike!   *Exeunt* [*all but* TIMON].
TIMON [*digging*]   That nature being sick of° man's unkindness   *through excess of*
Should yet be hungry! Common° mother, thou   *Universal*
Whose womb unmeasurable and infinite breast
180 Teems° and feeds all, whose selfsame mettle°   *Breeds / substance*
Whereof thy proud child, arrogant man, is puffed,
Engenders the black toad and adder blue,
The gilded newt and eyeless venomed worm,
With all th'abhorrèd births below crisp° heaven,   *clear*
185 Whereon Hyperion's quick'ning° fire doth shine,   *the sun's life-giving*
Yield him who all the human sons do hate
From forth thy plenteous bosom one poor root.
Ensear° thy fertile and conceptious womb;   *Dry up*
Let it no more bring out ingrateful man.
190 Go great° with tigers, dragons, wolves, and bears;   *pregnant*
Teem with new monsters, whom thy upward° face   *upturned*
Hath to the marbled mansion° all above   *heavens*
Never presented.—Oh, a root! Dear thanks.
Dry up thy marrows,° vines, and plough-torn leas,°   *pulpy fruits / fields*
195 Whereof ingrateful man with liquorish drafts[9]

3. Horseback riding; sexual intercourse. *Crack:* Ruin
(an ulcerous larynx is an effect of syphilis).
4. Whiten the priest (with syphilis or leprosy).
5. Syphilis sometimes causes the bridge of the nose
to collapse.

6. The image suggests a dog leaving the pack to pursue its own quarry.
7. Sexual erection; social advancement.
8. May you all suffer squalid deaths.
9. Sweet, lust-inducing drinks.

And morsels unctuous° greases his pure mind,   *oily*
That from it all consideration° slips.   *rationality*
    Enter APEMANTUS.
More man? Plague, plague!
APEMANTUS   I was directed hither. Men report
200   Thou dost affect° my manners and dost use them.   *like; imitate*
TIMON   'Tis, then, because thou dost not keep a dog
Whom I would imitate. Consumption catch thee!
APEMANTUS   This is in thee a nature but infected,[1]
A poor unmanly melancholy sprung
205   From change of future. Why this spade, this place,
This slave-like habit,° and these looks of care?   *costume*
Thy flatterers yet wear silk, drink wine, lie soft,
Hug their diseased perfumes,° and have forgot   *perfumed women*
That ever Timon was. Shame not these woods
210   By putting on the cunning of a carper.[2]
Be thou a flatterer now, and seek to thrive
By that which has undone thee. Hinge thy knee,
And let his very breath whom thou'lt observe°   *pay court to*
Blow off thy cap. Praise his most vicious strain,°   *trait*
215   And call it excellent. Thou wast told thus.
Thou gav'st thine ears like tapsters° that bade welcome   *bartenders*
To knaves and all approachers. 'Tis most just
That thou turn rascal.° Hadst thou wealth again,   *knave; solitary deer*
Rascals should have't. Do not assume my likeness.
220 TIMON   Were I like thee, I'd throw away myself.
APEMANTUS   Thou hast cast away thyself being like thyself,
A madman so long, now a fool. What think'st—
That the bleak air, thy boisterous chamberlain,°   *personal servant*
Will put thy shirt on warm? Will these moist trees,
225   That have outlived the eagle, page° thy heels   *follow at*
And skip when thou point'st out?[3] Will the cold brook,
Candied° with ice, caudle thy morning taste[4]   *Encrusted*
To cure thy o'ernight's surfeit? Call the creatures
Whose naked natures live in° all the spite   *exposed to*
230   Of wreakful° heaven, whose bare unhousèd trunks°   *vengeful / bodies*
To the conflicting elements exposed
Answer° mere nature. Bid them flatter thee.   *Obey*
Oh, thou shalt find—
TIMON   A fool of thee. Depart!
APEMANTUS   I love thee better now than ere I did.
TIMON   I hate thee worse.
APEMANTUS   Why?
235 TIMON   Thou flatter'st misery.
APEMANTUS   I flatter not but say thou art a caitiff.°   *wretch*
TIMON   Why dost thou seek me out?
APEMANTUS   To vex thee.
TIMON   Always a villain's office, or a fool's.
Dost please thyself in't?
APEMANTUS   Ay.
TIMON   What, a knave, too?

---

1. That is, not innately misanthropic or converted by philosophical argument.
2. The knowledge of a faultfinder.
3. And jump to get whatever you indicate.
4. Give you a hot drink in the morning.

240	APEMANTUS If thou didst put this sour cold habit° on	*dress; disposition*
	To castigate thy pride, 'twere well. But thou	
	Dost it enforcèdly.° Thou'dst courtier be again	*by compulsion*
	Wert thou not beggar. Willing misery	
	Outlives incertain° pomp, is crowned[5] before.	*insecure*
245	The one° is filling still,° never complete;	("incertain pomp") / always
	The other at high wish.[6] Best state, contentless,[7]	
	Hath a distracted and most wretched being,	
	Worse than the worst, content.[8]	
	Thou shouldst desire to die, being miserable.	
250	TIMON Not by his breath that is more miserable.[9]	
	Thou art a slave, whom Fortune's tender arm	
	With favor never clasped, but bred a dog.	
	Hadst thou like us from our first swathe proceeded[1]	
	The sweet degrees[2] that this brief world affords	
255	To such as° may the passive drudges of it	*To those who*
	Freely command, thou wouldst have plunged thyself	
	In general riot,° melted down thy youth	*debauchery*
	In different beds of lust, and never learned	
	The icy precepts of respect,° but followed	*restraint; judgment*
260	The sugared game° before thee. But myself,	*sweet quarry*
	Who had the world as my confectionary,	
	The mouths, the tongues, the eyes, and hearts of men	
	At duty° more than I could frame° employment—	*my service / provide*
	That numberless upon me stuck as leaves	
265	Do on the oak—have with one winter's brush	
	Fell from their boughs and left me open, bare,	
	For every storm that blows. I to bear this,	
	That never knew but better,° is some burden.	*anything but good fortune*
	Thy nature did commence in sufferance;° time	*suffering*
270	Hath made thee hard° in't. Why shouldst thou hate men?	*hardened*
	They never flattered thee. What hast thou given?	
	If thou wilt curse, thy father, that poor rag,°	*wretch*
	Must be thy subject, who in spite put stuff	
	To[3] some she-beggar and compounded° thee	*constituted*
275	Poor rogue hereditary.° Hence, be gone!	*by birth*
	If thou hadst not been born the worst of men,	
	Thou hadst been a knave and flatterer.	
	APEMANTUS Art thou proud yet?	
	TIMON Ay, that I am not thee.	
	APEMANTUS I that I was no prodigal.	
280	TIMON I that I am one now.	
	Were all the wealth I have shut up° in thee,	*contained*
	I'd give thee leave to hang it. Get thee gone.	
	That° the whole life of Athens were in this,	*Would that*
	Thus would I eat it.	
	[*He bites the root.*]	
	APEMANTUS [*offering food*] Here, I will mend° thy feast.	*improve*
285	TIMON First mend thy company. Take away thyself.	

5. Finds fulfillment.
6. (Misery) at the height of its wish.
7. The greatest prosperity, if not contented.
8. The least prosperity, living contented.
9. Not at the command of someone even unhappier

than I.
1. From our swaddling clothes mounted.
2. Social ranks; steps on Fortune's ladder.
3. *put stuff / To:* ejaculated into.

APEMANTUS   So I shall mend mine own, by th' lack of thine.
TIMON   'Tis not well mended so; it is but botched.⁴
   If not, I would it were.
APEMANTUS   What wouldst thou have to⁵ Athens?
TIMON   Thee thither in a whirlwind. If thou wilt,
290   Tell them there I have gold. Look, so I have.
APEMANTUS   Here is no use for gold.
TIMON   The best and truest.
   For here it sleeps and does no hired harm.
APEMANTUS   Where liest a-nights, Timon?
TIMON   Under that's above me.°   Where feed'st thou a-days,   (the sky)
295   Apemantus?
APEMANTUS   Where my stomach finds meat,° or rather where   food
   I eat it.
TIMON   Would poison were obedient and knew my mind.
APEMANTUS   Where wouldst thou send it?
300   TIMON   To sauce thy dishes.
APEMANTUS   The middle of humanity thou never knewest,
   but the extremity of both ends. When thou wast in thy gilt
   and thy perfume, they mocked thee for too much curiosity;°   delicacy
   in thy rags thou know'st none, but art despised for the con-
305   trary. There's a medlar⁶ for thee. Eat it.
TIMON   On what I hate I feed not.
APEMANTUS   Dost hate a medlar?
TIMON   Ay, though it look like thee.
APEMANTUS   An° thou'dst hated meddlers sooner, thou shouldst   If
310   have loved thyself better now. What man didst thou ever
   know unthrift° that was beloved after⁷ his means?   prodigal
TIMON   Who, without those means thou talk'st of, didst thou
   ever know beloved?
APEMANTUS   Myself.
315   TIMON   I understand thee. Thou hadst some means to keep a
   dog.⁸
APEMANTUS   What things in the world canst thou nearest
   compare to thy flatterers?
TIMON   Women nearest, but men, men are the things them-
320   selves. What wouldst thou do with the world, Apemantus, if
   it lay in thy power?
APEMANTUS   Give it° the beasts to be rid of the men.   Give it to
TIMON   Wouldst thou have thyself fall in the confusion° of   overthrow
   men and remain a beast with the beasts?
325   APEMANTUS   Ay, Timon.
TIMON   A beastly ambition, which the gods grant thee t'attain
   to. If thou wert the lion, the fox would beguile thee. If thou
   wert the lamb, the fox would eat thee. If thou wert the fox,
   the lion would suspect thee when peradventure° thou wert   perchance
330   accused by the ass. If thou wert the ass, thy dullness would
   torment thee, and still° thou lived'st but as a breakfast to   always
   the wolf. If thou wert the wolf, thy greediness would afflict

---

4. It is fixed badly (because Apemantus will still
have to endure himself).
5. Have conveyed to (but Timon changes the
meaning).
6. A pear eaten when rotten; with puns in the fol-

lowing lines on "lecher," "whore," and "interfering
person."
7. In proportion to; after losing. *means*: money.
8. Which flattered its master for meager reward (or
perhaps "dog" refers to Apemantus himself).

thee and oft thou shouldst hazard thy life for thy dinner.
Wert thou the unicorn, pride and wrath would confound
335   thee and make thine own self the conquest of thy fury.⁹
Wert thou a bear, thou wouldst be killed by the horse.¹ Wert
thou a horse, thou wouldst be seized by the leopard. Wert
thou a leopard, thou wert german° to the lion, and the spots   *related*
of thy kindred² were jurors on thy life. All thy safety were
340   remotion,° and thy defense absence. What beast couldst   *remaining away*
thou be that were not subject to a beast, and what a beast
art thou already, that seest not thy loss in transformation?³

APEMANTUS   If thou couldst please me with speaking to me,
thou mightst have hit upon it here.⁴ The commonwealth of
345   Athens is become a forest of beasts.

TIMON   How, has the ass broke the wall, that thou art out of
the city?

APEMANTUS   Yonder comes a poet and a painter.⁵ The plague
of company light upon thee! I will fear to catch it and give
350   way.° When I know not what else to do, I'll see thee again.   *go away*

TIMON   When there is nothing living but thee, thou shalt be
welcome. I had rather be a beggar's dog than Apemantus.

APEMANTUS   Thou art the cap⁶ of all the fools alive.

TIMON   Would thou wert clean enough to spit upon.

355 APEMANTUS   A plague on thee. Thou art too bad to curse.

TIMON   All villains that do stand by thee are pure.°   *(by comparison)*

APEMANTUS   There is no leprosy but what thou speak'st.

TIMON   If I name thee, I'll beat thee, but I should
Infect my hands.

APEMANTUS   I would my tongue could rot them off.

360 TIMON   Away, thou issue° of a mangy dog!   *offspring; discharge*
Choler does kill me that thou art alive.
I swoon to see thee.

APEMANTUS   Would thou wouldst burst.

TIMON   Away, thou tedious rogue!
       [*He throws a stone at* APEMANTUS.]
I am sorry I shall lose a stone by thee.

365 APEMANTUS   Beast!

TIMON   Slave!

APEMANTUS   Toad!

TIMON   Rogue, rogue, rogue!
I am sick of this false world and will love naught
370   But even° the mere necessities upon't.   *Except*
Then, Timon, presently° prepare thy grave.   *at once*
Lie where the light foam of the sea may beat
Thy gravestone daily; make thine epitaph,
That death in° me at others' lives may laugh.   *through*
       [*He looks at his gold.*]
375 O thou sweet king-killer and dear divorce
Twixt natural sun and fire, thou bright defiler

---

9. The legendary unicorn could be trapped by a hunter who stood in front of a tree; when the unicorn charged, the hunter stepped aside and the unicorn's horn stuck fast in the tree.
1. Bears were supposedly hated by horses.
2. Lion's crimes; leopard's spots.

3. Being transformed to a beast.
4. *thou . . . here:* what you've just said would please me.
5. They do not appear until 5.1 (perhaps a sign of revision).
6. Supreme instance (with wordplay on "fool's cap").

Of Hymen's° purest bed, thou valiant Mars,[7]   god of marriage
Thou ever-young, fresh, loved, and delicate wooer,
Whose blush° doth thaw the consecrated snow[8]   glow
380 That lies on Dian's lap, thou visible god,
That sold'rest close impossibilities[9]
And mak'st them kiss, that speak'st with every tongue
To every purpose, O thou touch° of hearts,   touchstone
Think thy slave, man, rebels, and by thy virtue°   power
385 Set them into confounding odds,° that beasts   men at ruinous strife
May have the world in empire.

APEMANTUS   Would 'twere so,
But not till I am dead. I'll say thou'st gold:
Thou wilt be thronged to shortly.

TIMON   Thronged to?

APEMANTUS   Ay.

TIMON   Thy back,[1] I prithee.

APEMANTUS   Live, and love thy misery.

390 TIMON   Long live so, and so die. I am quit.°   rid of you

      Enter the BANDITTI.

APEMANTUS   More things like men. Eat, Timon, and abhor
      them.   *Exit.*

FIRST BANDIT   Where should he have° this gold? It is some   have obtained; have put
      poor fragment, some slender ort° of his remainder. The   scrap
      mere want of gold and the falling from of his friends drove
395 him into this melancholy.

SECOND BANDIT   It is noised° he hath a mass of treasure.   rumored

THIRD BANDIT   Let us make the assay° upon him. If he care   test; assault
      not for't, he will supply us easily; if he covetously reserve it,
      how shall's get it?

400 SECOND BANDIT   True, for he bears it not about him. 'Tis hid.

FIRST BANDIT   Is not this he?

SECOND *and* THIRD BANDITS   Where?

SECOND BANDIT   'Tis his description.

THIRD BANDIT   He! I know him.

405 ALL   Save° thee, Timon.   God save

TIMON   Now, thieves—

ALL   Soldiers, not thieves.

TIMON   Both, too, and women's sons.

ALL   We are not thieves, but men that much do want.°   are very needy

TIMON   Your greatest want is you want much of meat.°   food
410 Why should you want? Behold, the earth hath roots.
Within this mile break forth a hundred springs.
The oaks bear mast,° the briars scarlet hips.[2]   acorns (fed to swine)
The bounteous housewife Nature on each bush
Lays her full mess° before you. Want? Why want?   serving

415 FIRST BANDIT   We cannot live on grass, on berries, water,
As beasts and birds and fishes.

TIMON   Nor on the beasts themselves, the birds, and fishes:
You must eat men. Yet thanks I must you con°   render

---

7. Adulterous lover of Venus and the god of war.
8. The snow of chastity, of which the goddess Diana
was patroness.

9. That tightly solders together incompatible things.
1. Show me your back (go away).
2. Rose hips (sour fruit).

That you are thieves professed, that you work not
420 In holier shapes, for there is boundless theft
In limited° professions. [*He gives them gold.*] Rascal thieves,   *legitimate*
Here's gold. Go, suck the subtle° blood o'th' grape   *delicate; deceptive*
Till the high fever seethe° your blood to froth,   *boil (by drunkenness)*
And so scape hanging.° Trust not the physician.   *(by dying of a fever)*
425 His antidotes are poison, and he slays
More than you rob. Take wealth and lives together—
Do, villain, do. Since you protest° to do't   *openly profess*
Like workmen,° I'll example you with³ thievery: *skilled artisans*
The sun's a thief and with his great attraction°   *power to draw up*
430 Robs the vast sea. The moon's an arrant⁴ thief,
And her pale fire she snatches from the sun.
The sea's a thief, whose liquid surge resolves°   *melts*
The moon into salt tears.⁵ The earth's a thief,
That feeds and breeds by a composture° stolen   *manure*
435 From general° excrement. Each thing's a thief.   *universal*
The laws, your curb and whip,° in their rough power   *restraint and punishment*
Has unchecked theft.⁶ Love not yourselves. Away!
Rob one another. There's more gold; cut throats.
All that you meet are thieves. To Athens go;
440 Break open shops. Nothing can you steal
But thieves do lose it. Steal less for° this I give you,   *because of*
And gold confound you howsoe'er.° Amen.   *whatever you do*

THIRD BANDIT   He's almost charmed me from my profession
by persuading me to it.

445 FIRST BANDIT   'Tis in the malice° of mankind that he thus   *out of hatred*
advises us, not to have us thrive in our mystery.°   *profession*

SECOND BANDIT   I'll believe him as an enemy⁷ and give over
my trade.

FIRST BANDIT   Let us first see peace in Athens.° There is no   *(an unlikely prospect)*
450 time so miserable but a man may be true.°   *may repent*
Exeunt [BANDITTI].

      Enter the STEWARD *to* TIMON.

STEWARD   O you gods!
Is yond despised and ruinous° man my lord?   *ruined*
Full of decay and failing? Oh, monument
And wonder of good deeds evilly bestowed!⁸
455 What an alteration of honor has desperate want made.
What viler thing upon the earth than friends,
Who can bring noblest minds to basest ends.
How rarely does it meet with this time's guise,
When man was wished to love his enemies.⁹
460 Grant I may ever love, and rather woo,
Those that would mischief me than those that do.¹
He's caught me in his eye. I will present
My honest grief unto him, and as my lord
Still serve him with my life. —My dearest master.

---

3. I'll give you precedents for.
4. Unmitigated; wandering (errant). The moon was considered auspicious to thieves.
5. Tides supposedly resulted from the sea drawing moisture from the moon.
6. Have unlimited power to steal.
7. As I would an enemy (that is, not at all).

8. Bestowed on ungrateful people.
9. *How . . . enemies:* How perfectly it accords with the customary exhortation to love one's enemies (since friends are one's undoing).
1. Those who would like to injure me, rather than those who really do so.

TIMON   Away, what art thou?

465 STEWARD   Have you forgot me, sir?

TIMON   Why dost ask that? I have forgot all men.
  Then, if thou grunt'st, thou'rt a man. I have forgot thee.

STEWARD   An honest poor servant of yours.

TIMON   Then I know thee not.
  I never had honest man about me. Ay, all

470 I kept were knaves to serve in meat° to villains.   *serve food*

STEWARD   The gods are witness,
  Ne'er did poor steward wear a truer grief
  For his undone lord than mine eyes for you.

TIMON   What, dost thou weep? Come nearer. Then I love thee

475 Because thou art a woman° and disclaim'st   *(in weeping)*
  Flinty mankind, whose eyes do never give°   *succumb*
  But through lust and laughter. Pity's sleeping.
  Strange times that weep with laughing, not with weeping.

STEWARD   I beg of you to know me, good my lord,

480 T'accept my grief, [*showing* TIMON *money*] and whilst this
      poor wealth lasts
  To entertain° me as your steward still.   *employ*

TIMON   Had I a steward
  So true, so just, and now so comfortable?°   *comforting*
  It almost turns my dangerous° nature wild.   *savage*

485 Let me behold thy face. Surely, this man
  Was born of woman.
  Forgive my general and exceptless° rashness,   *indiscriminate*
  You perpetual sober gods. I do proclaim
  One honest man. Mistake me not, but one—

490 No more, I pray—and he's a steward.
  How fain° would I have hated all mankind,   *willingly*
  And thou redeem'st thyself. But all save thee,
  I fell° with curses.   *cut down*
  Methinks thou art more honest now than wise,

495 For, by oppressing and betraying me,
  Thou mightst have sooner got another service.
  For many so arrive at second masters
  Upon° their first lord's neck. But tell me true—   *By stepping on*
  For I must ever doubt though ne'er so sure—

500 Is not thy kindness subtle,° covetous,   *treacherous*
  If not a usuring kindness, and, as rich men deal gifts,
  Expecting in return twenty for one?

STEWARD   No, my most worthy master, in whose breast
  Doubt and suspect,° alas, are placed too late.   *suspicion*

505 You should have feared false times when you did feast.
  Suspect still° comes where an estate is least.   *always*
  That which I show, heaven knows, is merely love,
  Duty, and zeal to your unmatched mind,
  Care of your food and living, and believe it,

510 My most honored lord,
  For° any benefit that points to me,   *As for*
  Either in hope,° or present, I'd exchange   *the future*
  For this one wish: that you had power and wealth
  To requite° me by making rich yourself.   *repay*

515 TIMON [*offering gold*]   Look thee, 'tis so, thou singly honest
      man.

Here, take. The gods out of my misery
Has sent thee treasure. Go, live rich and happy,
But thus conditioned:[2] thou shalt build from° men,   *away from*
Hate all, curse all, show charity to none,
520 But let the famished flesh slide from the bone
Ere thou relieve the beggar. Give to dogs
What thou deniest to men. Let prisons swallow 'em,
Debts wither 'em to nothing; be men° like blasted woods,   *let men be*
And may diseases lick up their false bloods.
525 And so farewell and thrive.
STEWARD Oh, let me stay and comfort you, my master.
TIMON If thou hat'st curses,
Stay not. Fly, whilst thou art blest and free;
Ne'er see thou man, and let me ne'er see thee.
        Exeunt [TIMON *to his cave and* STEWARD *separately*].

5.1

        Enter POET *and* PAINTER.
PAINTER As I took note of the place, it cannot be far where he
abides.
POET What's to be thought of him? Does the rumor hold for
true that he's so full of gold?
5 PAINTER Certain. Alcibiades reports it. Phrynia and Timandra had gold of him. He likewise enriched poor straggling
soldiers with great quantity. 'Tis said he gave unto his steward a mighty sum.
POET Then this breaking° of his has been but a try° for his   *bankruptcy / test*
10 friends?
PAINTER Nothing else. You shall see him a palm[1] in Athens
again and flourish with the highest. Therefore, 'tis not amiss
we tender our loves to him in this supposed distress of his. It
will show honestly in us and is very likely to load our purposes°   *to reward our efforts*
15 with what they travail° for, if it be a just and true report that   *labor; travel*
goes° of his having.°   *circulates / property*
POET What have you now to present unto him?
PAINTER Nothing at this time but my visitation. Only I will
promise him an excellent piece.
20 POET I must serve him so too, tell him of an intent that's
coming toward him.
PAINTER Good as the best.° Promising is the very air° o'th'   *That's excellent / fashion*
time. It opens the eyes of expectation. Performance is ever
the duller for his° act, and, but in the plainer and simpler   *its*
25 kind of people, the deed of saying° is quite out of use. To   *doing what one says*
promise is most courtly and fashionable; performance is a
kind of will or testament which argues a great sickness in
his judgment that makes it.[2]
        Enter TIMON *from his cave.*[3]
TIMON [*aside*] Excellent workman! Thou canst not paint a
30 man so bad as is thyself.

---

2. But on this condition.
5.1 Location: Outside Athens.
1. The highest tree: alluding to Psalm 92:12, "The
righteous shall flourish like a palm tree."
2. That is, only those close to death worry about ful-

filling their vows.
3. TEXTUAL COMMENT This stage direction suggests
that Timon's cave is either a stage door or a curtained
alcove at the back of the stage; see Digital Edition
TC 8 for a discussion of the theatrical possibilities.

POET   I am thinking what I shall say I have provided for him.
  It must be a personating° of himself—a satire against the   *representation*
  softness of prosperity, with a discovery° of the infinite flat-   *revelation*
  teries that follow youth and opulency.

35   TIMON [*aside*]   Must thou needs stand° for a villain in thine   *model*
  own work? Wilt thou whip thine own faults in other men?
  Do so; I have gold for thee.

POET   Nay, let's seek him.
  Then do we sin against our own estate,°   *condition in life*
40   When we may profit meet° and come too late.   *make a profit*

PAINTER   True.
  When the day serves° before black-cornered night,   *allows*
  Find what thou want'st by free and offered light.
  Come.

45   TIMON [*aside*]   I'll meet you at the turn.[4]
  What a god's gold that he is worshippèd
  In a baser temple than where swine feed?
  'Tis thou that rigg'st the bark° and plow'st the foam,   *puts sails on the boat*
  Settlest admired reverence in a slave.[5]
50   To thee be worship and thy saints for aye;°   *ever*
  Be crowned with plagues that thee alone obey.
  Fit° I meet them.   *It is fit*
        [*He comes forward.*]

POET   Hail, worthy Timon!

PAINTER   Our late noble master!

TIMON   Have I once° lived to see two honest men?   *really*

55   POET   Sir,
  Having often of your open bounty tasted,
  Hearing you were retired,° your friends fall'n off,   *had gone away*
  Whose thankless natures—oh, abhorrèd spirits!—
  Not all the whips of heaven are large enough—
60   What, to you,
  Whose star-like nobleness gave life and influence[6]
  To their whole being!—I am rapt° and cannot cover   *overwhelmed*
  The monstrous bulk of this ingratitude
  With any size[7] of words.

65   TIMON   Let it go naked. Men may see't the better.
  You that are honest, by being what you are,
  Make them° best seen and known.   *(the "abhorrèd spirits")*

PAINTER   He and myself
  Have travailed° in the great shower of your gifts   *worked*
  And sweetly felt it.

TIMON   Ay, you are honest men.

70   PAINTER   We are hither come to offer you our service.

TIMON   Most honest men, why, how shall I requite you?
  Can you eat roots and drink cold water? No?

BOTH   What we can do, we'll do to do you service.

TIMON   You're honest men. You've heard that I have gold.
75   I am sure you have. Speak truth; you're honest men.

---

4. I'll meet you when you come around the corner;
I'll trick you in return.
5. Makes an unworthy person be revered.
6. Explained astrologically, "influence" was a sub-

stance thought to stream forth from stars and affect
events on earth.
7. Amount; sizing, a layer applied to walls prior to
painting.

PAINTER   So it is said, my noble lord, but therefore
　　Came not my friend, nor I.
TIMON   Good honest men. [to PAINTER] Thou draw'st a
　　counterfeit°   *picture; fake*
　　Best in all Athens. Thou'rt indeed the best;
　　Thou counterfeit'st most lively.
80   PAINTER   So, so, my lord.
TIMON   E'en so, sir, as I say. [to POET] And for thy fiction,°   *poetry; lying*
　　Why, thy verse swells with stuff so fine and smooth
　　That thou art even natural° in thine art.   *lifelike; idiotic*
　　But for all this, my honest-natured friends,
85   I must needs say you have a little fault—
　　Marry, 'tis not monstrous in you, neither wish I
　　You take much pains to mend.
BOTH   Beseech your honor
　　To make it known to us.
TIMON   You'll take it ill.
BOTH   Most thankfully, my lord.
TIMON   Will you indeed?
90   BOTH   Doubt it not, worthy lord.
TIMON   There's never a one of you but trusts a knave
　　That mightily deceives you.
BOTH   Do we, my lord?
TIMON   Ay, and you hear him cog,° see him dissemble,   *cheat*
　　Know his gross patchery,° love him, feed him,   *roguery*
95   Keep° in your bosom, yet remain assured   *Keep him*
　　That he's a made-up° villain.   *complete*
PAINTER   I know none such, my lord.
POET   Nor I.
TIMON   Look you, I love you well. I'll give you gold.
100   Rid me these villains from your companies.
　　Hang them or stab them, drown them in a draft,°   *stream; cesspool*
　　Confound° them by some course, and come to me,   *Destroy*
　　I'll give you gold enough.
BOTH   Name them, my lord. Let's know them.
105   TIMON   You that way and you this, but two in company.
　　Each man apart, all single and alone,
　　Yet an archvillain keeps him company.[8]
　　[to one] If where thou art two villains shall not be,
　　Come not near him. [to the other] If thou wouldst not reside
110   But where one villain is, then him abandon.
　　　　　[TIMON attacks them.]
　　Hence, pack,° there's gold. You came for gold, ye slaves.   *go away*
　　You have work for me; there's payment, hence!
　　You are an alchemist;[9] make gold of that!
　　Out, rascal dogs!
　　　　　Exeunt [POET *and* PAINTER. *Exit* TIMON *to his cave*].

8. That is, both of you are archvillains.
9. That is, one who can translate base metal (the beating) into gold.

5.2

Enter STEWARD *and two* SENATORS.

STEWARD   It is vain that you would speak with Timon,
    For he is set so only to himself°   *so self-isolated*
    That nothing but himself which looks like man
    Is friendly with° him.   *congenial to*
FIRST SENATOR   Bring us to his cave.
5   It is our part and promise to th'Athenians
    To speak with Timon.
SECOND SENATOR   At all times alike
    Men are not still° the same. 'Twas time and griefs   *always*
    That framed him thus. Time with his fairer hand
    Offering the fortunes of his former days,
10   The former man may make him. Bring us to him
    And chance it as it may.
STEWARD   Here is his cave.
    [*He calls.*] Peace and content be here! Lord Timon, Timon,
    Look out and speak to friends. Th'Athenians
    By two of their most reverend Senate greet thee.
15   Speak to them, noble Timon.
             Enter TIMON *out of his cave.*
TIMON   Thou sun that comforts, burn! —Speak, and be hanged.
    For each true word, a blister, and each false°   *let each false word*
    Be as a cantherizing° to the root o'th' tongue,   *cauterizing*
    Consuming it with speaking.
FIRST SENATOR   Worthy Timon—
20 TIMON   Of none but such as you, and you of Timon.[1]
FIRST SENATOR   The senators of Athens greet thee, Timon.
TIMON   I thank them and would send them back the plague,
    Could I but catch it for them.
FIRST SENATOR   Oh, forget
    What we are sorry for ourselves in thee![2]
25   The senators with one consent of° love   *unanimous*
    Entreat thee back to Athens, who have thought
    On special dignities,° which vacant lie   *titles; offices*
    For thy best use and wearing.
FIRST SENATOR   They confess
    Toward thee forgetfulness too general gross,°   *obvious and extreme*
30   Which now the public body,° which doth seldom   *republic*
    Play the recanter,° feeling in itself   *Change its mind*
    A lack of Timon's aid, hath sense withal
    Of its own fall,° restraining° aid to Timon,   *failure / withholding*
    And send forth us to make their sorrowed render,°   *to apologize sadly*
35   Together with a recompense more fruitful
    Than their offense can weigh down by the dram,[3]
    Ay, even such heaps and sums of love and wealth
    As shall to thee blot out what wrongs were theirs
    And write in thee the figures[4] of their love,
    Ever to read them thine.
40 TIMON   You witch° me in it,   *bewitch*

5.2 Location: Scene continues.
1. That is, we deserve each other.
2. In the injuries we did you.

3. Can outweigh even by painstaking calculation.
4. Distinctive marks; numbers in an account book.

Surprise me to the very brink of tears.
Lend me a fool's heart and a woman's eyes,
And I'll beweep these comforts, worthy senators.
FIRST SENATOR   Therefore so please thee to return with us,
45   And of our Athens, thine and ours, to take
The captainship. Thou shalt be met with thanks,
Allowed° with absolute power, and thy good name   *Vested*
Live with authority. So soon we shall drive back
Of Alcibiades th'approaches wild,
50   Who like a boar too savage doth root up
His country's peace.
SECOND SENATOR   And shakes his threat'ning sword
Against the walls of Athens.
FIRST SENATOR   Therefore, Timon—
TIMON   Well, sir, I will. Therefore I will, sir, thus:
If Alcibiades kill my countrymen,
55   Let Alcibiades know this of Timon:
That Timon cares not. But if he sack fair Athens
And take our goodly agèd men by th' beards,
Giving our holy virgins to the stain°   *(by rape)*
Of contumelious,° beastly, mad-brained war,   *insolent*
60   Then let him know, and tell him Timon speaks it,
In pity of our agèd and our youth,
I cannot choose but tell him that I care not,
And let him take't at worst.[5] For their knives care not,
While you have throats to answer.° For myself,   *suitable for cutting*
65   There's not a whittle° in th'unruly camp   *pocketknife*
But I do prize it at my love before
The reverend'st throat in Athens. So I leave you
To the protection of the prosperous gods,
As thieves to keepers.
STEWARD   Stay not. All's in vain.
70   TIMON   Why, I was writing of my epitaph.
It will be seen tomorrow. My long sickness
Of health and living now begins to mend,
And nothing° brings me all things. Go, live still.   *oblivion*
Be Alcibiades your plague, you his,
And last so long enough.
75   FIRST SENATOR   We speak in vain.
TIMON   But yet I love my country and am not
One that rejoices in the common wrack,°   *ruin*
As common bruit° doth put it.   *rumor*
FIRST SENATOR   That's well spoke.
TIMON   Commend me to my loving countrymen.
80   FIRST SENATOR   These words become your lips as they pass
        through them.
SECOND SENATOR   And enter in our ears like great triumphers[6]
In their applauding gates.[7]
TIMON   Commend me to them,
And tell them that to ease them of their griefs,
Their fears of hostile strokes, their aches, losses,

---

5. Interpret what I say in the worst possible way.
6. Like conquerors returning home.

7. Gates full of applauding fellow citizens.

85	Their pangs of love, with other incident throes°	*natural torments*
	That nature's fragile vessel doth sustain	
	In life's uncertain voyage, I will some kindness do them.	
	I'll teach them to prevent° wild Alcibiades' wrath.	*forestall*
	FIRST SENATOR I like this well. He will return again.	
90	TIMON I have a tree which grows here in my close,°	*enclosure*
	That mine own use° invites me to cut down,	*purpose*
	And shortly must I fell it. Tell my friends,	
	Tell Athens, in the sequence of degree°	*in order of rank*
	From high to low throughout, that, whoso please	
95	To stop affliction, let him take his haste,	
	Come hither ere my tree hath felt the ax,	
	And hang himself. I pray you, do my greeting.	
	STEWARD Trouble him no further. Thus you still shall find him.	
	TIMON Come not to me again, but say to Athens	
100	Timon hath made his everlasting mansion°	*(his grave)*
	Upon the beachèd verge° of the salt flood,°	*edge / sea*
	Who once a day with his embossèd° froth	*foaming*
	The turbulent surge shall cover. Thither come,	
	And let my gravestone be your oracle.°	*source of revelation*
105	Lips, let four° words go by and language end;	*(that is, few)*
	What is amiss, plague and infection mend.	
	Graves only be men's works and death their gain.	
	Sun, hide thy beams. Timon hath done his reign. *Exit.*	
	FIRST SENATOR His discontents are unremovably	
110	Coupled to nature.°	*Intrinsic to his nature*
	SECOND SENATOR Our hope in him is dead. Let us return	
	And strain what other means is left unto us	
	In our dear peril.	
	FIRST SENATOR It requires swift foot. *Exeunt.*	

5.3

Enter two other SENATORS *with a* MESSENGER.

	THIRD SENATOR Thou hast painfully discovered.[1] Are his files°	*troops*
	As full as thy report?	
	MESSENGER I have spoke the least.°	*estimated low*
	Besides, his expedition° promises present° approach.	*speed / immediate*
	FOURTH SENATOR We stand much hazard if they bring not	
	Timon.	
5	MESSENGER I met a courier, one mine ancient friend,	
	Whom though in general part° we were opposed,	*public matters*
	Yet our old love made° a particular force	*exerted*
	And made us speak like friends. This man was riding	
	From Alcibiades to Timon's cave	
10	With letters of entreaty, which imported°	*urged*
	His fellowship i'th' cause against your city,	
	In part for his sake moved.	
	Enter the other SENATORS.	
	THIRD SENATOR Here come our brothers.	
	FIRST SENATOR No talk of Timon. Nothing of him expect.	
	The enemy's drum is heard, and fearful scouring°	*hostile action*

5.3 Location: Outside the walls of Athens.   1. Carefully reconnoitered; told us painful news.

15 Doth choke the air with dust. In and prepare.
    Ours is the fall, I fear, our foes the snare.   *Exeunt.*

5.4

Enter a SOLDIER *in the woods, seeking* TIMON.
SOLDIER By all description this should be the place.
  Who's here? Speak, ho! No answer? What is this?
      "Timon is dead, who hath outstretched his span.
      Some beast read this; there does not live a man."
5 Dead, sure, and this his grave. What's on this tomb
  I cannot read. The character I'll take with wax.[1]
  Our captain hath in every figure° skill,   *kind of writing*
  An aged° interpreter, though young in days.   *experienced*
  Before proud Athens he's set down by this,°   *laid siege by this time*
10 Whose fall the mark° of his ambition is.   *Exit.*   *goal*

5.5

Trumpets sound. Enter ALCIBIADES *with his powers*°   *army*
before Athens.
ALCIBIADES   Sound° to this coward and lascivious town   *Proclaim*
  Our terrible approach.
      Sounds a parley.[1]
      The SENATORS *appear upon the walls.*[2]
  Till now you have gone on and filled the time
  With all licentious measure,[3] making your wills
5 The scope of justice.[4] Till now myself and such
  As slept° within the shadow of your power   *dwelled*
  Have wandered with our traversed[5] arms and breathed
  Our sufferance[6] vainly. Now the time is flush,
  When crouching marrow° in the bearer strong   *latent vigor*
10 Cries of itself, "No more." Now breathless° wrong   *exhausted*
  Shall sit and pant in your great chairs of ease,
  And pursy° insolence shall break his wind°   *short-winded / pant; fart*
  With fear and horrid° flight.   *terrified*
FIRST SENATOR   Noble and young,
  When thy first griefs were but a mere conceit,°   *merely imagined*
15 Ere thou hadst power or we had cause of fear,
  We sent to thee to give thy rages balm,
  To wipe out our ingratitude, with loves
  Above their quantity.[7]
SECOND SENATOR   So did we woo
  Transformèd Timon to our city's love
20 By humble message and by promised means.°   *wealth*
  We were not all unkind, nor all deserve
  The common° stroke of war.   *indiscriminate*
FIRST SENATOR   These walls of ours
  Were not erected by their hands from whom

5.4 Location: Outside Athens.
1. By making an impression of the letters. The soldier is evidently reading a notice of some kind in
lines 3–4, yet in lines 5–6 he claims to be unable to
read the writing on the tombstone, perhaps because
the script is unfamiliar, or because the epitaph is in a
foreign language (later translated by Alcibiades).
5.5 Location: Outside the walls of Athens.
1. Trumpet call to negotiate.

2. Probably on the upper gallery at stage rear.
3. All kinds of licentious conduct.
4. *making . . . justice:* making justice conform to
your whims.
5. Crossed (as part of military training).
6. *breathed / Our sufferance:* voiced our grievances.
7. *loves . . . quantity:* friendly gestures greater than
your grievances.

You have received your grief. Nor are they such
25 That these great towers, trophies,° and schools⁸ should fall   *monuments*
For private faults in them.°   *(the offenders)*
SECOND SENATOR   Nor are they living
Who were the motives that you first went out.⁹
Shame, that they wanted° cunning, in excess   *lacked*
Hath broke their hearts. March, noble lord,
30 Into our city with thy banners spread.
By decimation and a tithèd death,¹
If thy revenges hunger for that food
Which nature loathes, take thou the destined tenth,
And by the hazard of the spotted die
35 Let die the spotted.²
FIRST SENATOR   All have not offended.
For those that were,° it is not square° to take   *(living) / fair*
On those that are, revenge. Crimes like lands
Are not inherited. Then, dear countryman,
Bring in thy ranks, but leave without° thy rage.   *outside*
40 Spare thy Athenian cradle° and those kin   *birthplace*
Which in the bluster of thy wrath must fall
With those that have offended. Like a shepherd
Approach the fold and cull th'infected forth,°   *pick out the corrupt*
But kill not altogether.
SECOND SENATOR   What thou wilt,
45 Thou rather shalt enforce it with thy smile
Than hew to't with thy sword.
FIRST SENATOR   Set but thy foot
Against our rampired° gates, and they shall ope,   *barricaded*
So° thou wilt send thy gentle heart before   *If*
To say thou'lt enter friendly.
SECOND SENATOR   Throw thy glove
50 Or any token° of thine honor else   *pledge*
That thou wilt use the wars as thy redress
And not as our confusion.° All thy powers°   *ruin / army*
Shall make their harbor° in our town till we   *lodging*
Have sealed° thy full desire.   *satisfied*
ALCIBIADES [*throwing his glove*]   Then there's my glove.
55 Descend and open your unchargèd ports.°   *unattacked gates*
Those enemies of Timon's and mine own,
Whom you yourselves shall set out for reproof,°   *select for punishment*
Fall, and no more. And to atone° your fears   *allay*
With my more noble meaning, not a man°   *soldier*
60 Shall pass his quarter° or offend the stream   *leave his assigned place*
Of regular justice³ in your city's bounds
But shall be remedied to° your public laws   *punished according to*
At heaviest answer.°   *penalty*
BOTH SENATORS   'Tis most nobly spoken.
ALCIBIADES   Descend, and keep your words.
        Enter a [SOLDIER].

---

8. Public buildings.
9. Who were those who prompted your banishment.
1. Killing one of every ten persons, chosen by lot.

2. Corrupt (punning on the spots of dice).
3. *offend . . . justice:* violate the ordinary laws.

65 SOLDIER My noble general, Timon is dead,
Entombed upon the very hem° o'th' sea, — edge
And on his gravestone this insculpture,° which — inscription
With wax I brought away, whose soft impression
Interprets for my poor ignorance.

ALCIBIADES *reads the epitaph.*[4]

70 "Here lies a wretchèd corpse of wretchèd soul bereft.
Seek not my name. A plague consume you wicked
caitiffs° left. — wretches
Here lie I, Timon, who alive all living men did hate.
Pass by and curse thy fill, but pass and stay not here
thy gait."
These well express in thee thy latter spirits.° — sentiments
75 Though thou abhorred'st in us our humane griefs,
Scorned'st our brain's flow,[5] and those our droplets which
From niggard[6] nature fall, yet rich conceit° — imagination
Taught thee to make vast Neptune weep for aye° — ever
On thy low grave, on faults forgiven. Dead
80 Is noble Timon, of whose memory
Hereafter more. Bring me into your city,
And I will use the olive° with my sword, — (symbol of peace)
Make war breed peace, make peace stint° war, make each — stop
Prescribe to other as each other's leech.[7]
85 Let our drums strike. *Exeunt.*

---

4. TEXTUAL COMMENT The epitaph seems to consist
of two mutually contradictory couplets, perhaps suggesting incomplete revision or collaboration, or perhaps indicating Timon's profoundly conflicted state
of mind. See Digital Edition TC 9 for a fuller
discussion.

5. Tears were thought to exude from the brain.
6. "Niggard" because teardrops are tiny compared
with the sea, Neptune (line 78).
7. Physician (because war purges peace of its
decadence, and peace purges war of its violence).

All's Well That Ends Well

In innumerable old folktales, an unknown or lowborn young man of great courage, intelligence, or expertise addresses himself to a serious peril: a dragon no one can slay, a riddle no one can solve, a wound no one can cure. The grateful recipient of his aid—a king or mighty duke—rewards the youth with marriage to a princess who would ordinarily be far above his station. *All's Well That Ends Well* retells this popular tale of fantastic upward mobility, but with the genders reversed: the resourceful young quester is female, the marital prize male. Shakespeare did not invent the reversal; he adapted his plot from a story in Boccaccio's *Decameron* that is itself a retelling of a traditional tale. But *All's Well That Ends Well* considerably heightens the heroine's risk-taking initiative, making Helen's adventures in the first two acts correspond more precisely, in sexually transposed form, to the masculine pattern.

Even today, this reversal makes the story seem problematic. In the customary version, no one inquires into the feelings of the noblewoman who is the champion's prize. But in *All's Well,* when a man becomes a reward, he reacts with astonished anger:

> BERTRAM   My wife, my liege? I shall beseech your highness:
>   In such a business give me leave to use
>   The help of mine own eyes.
> KING   Know'st thou not, Bertram,
>   What she has done for me?
> BERTRAM   Yes, my good lord,
>   But never hope to know why I should marry her.
>
> (2.3.104–08)

After the wedding ceremony, Bertram flees without consummating the union. He leaves behind a letter detailing for Helen two apparently impossible conditions she must satisfy before he will consider her his wife: "When thou canst get the ring upon my finger, which never shall come off, and show me a child begotten of thy body that I am father to, then call me husband" (3.2.53–55).

Folklorists have traced the second part of the play, in which Helen ingeniously fulfills Bertram's stipulations, to yet another old tale, that of the "clever wench" who ultimately wins a reluctant husband's affection by turning his recalcitrance to her own benefit. In Helen's case, however, her "unfeminine" audacity both before and after her wedding has repelled some commentators. Others have expressed doubts about Helen's bed trick, wherein she secretly substitutes herself for another woman and becomes pregnant by the spouse who thinks he loathes her. How, they wonder, could such a maneuver possibly convert anyone, much less Bertram, into a loving husband?

The gender reversals in the plot of *All's Well That Ends Well*, then, make the difference in conventional expectations for men and women vividly clear. The deviations from comic norms in *All's Well* might be taken as reflecting badly on the hero and heroine. At the same time, these deviations implicitly challenge conventional gender roles, making them seem artificial and restrictive. The generic uneasiness of the play has led some critics to classify it as a "problem comedy," a category that also includes *Measure for Measure* and sometimes *Troilus and Cressida*. Editors conjecture that all three plays were written between 1602 and

931

1607, a period in which Shakespeare was largely preoccupied with tragedy: *Hamlet, Othello, King Lear, Timon of Athens, Macbeth,* and *Antony and Cleopatra* are roughly contemporaneous compositions. The "problem comedies" often seem closer in theme and tone to these tragedies than to the sunnier romantic comedies Shakespeare wrote in the 1590s.

Nonetheless, *All's Well* has obvious connections to Shakespeare's earlier achievements. In *The Merchant of Venice, As You Like It,* and *Much Ado About Nothing,* Shakespeare had gradually developed the dramatic possibilities of an articulate, assertive, and sympathetic heroine. Helen is recognizably one of this company: generally beloved by those around her, premaritally chaste but intensely sexual, tenacious in pursuit of the man she desires. Bertram is likewise a version of a standard Shakespearean type: the immature youth who finds aggressively "masculine" enterprises like hunting or war emotionally easier to negotiate than the complications of heterosexual intimacy. Bertram's predecessors include the unwilling Adonis in *Venus and Adonis,* the naive Claudio in *Much Ado About Nothing,* the edgily unself-conscious Hotspur of *1 Henry IV,* and the narcissistic young man of the sonnets. Both Helen and Bertram, however, "push the envelope" of their generic type. No previous comic heroine need show herself as relentless as Helen in pursuing her man. And Bertram is surely the most perfidious, and the most thoroughly disgraced, of Shakespeare's callow males. His initial protest at being married off against his will does not seem unreasonable. Yet his objections to Helen seem purely snobbish and his contemptuous treatment of her entirely unwarranted. As the play continues he subjects Diana, the woman he claims to love, to even worse treatment, breaking his promises to her and then defaming her reputation.

In its portrayal of older characters, too, *All's Well* seems to develop out of Shakespeare's previous romantic plays. In much Greek and Roman comedy, parents or parent surrogates attempt to hinder their children's sexual happiness, and as a young playwright Shakespeare adhered to this ancient convention. In *A Midsummer Night's Dream* and *Romeo and Juliet,* written in the mid-1590s, parents are killjoys who block the glorious passions of youth out of mere peevishness. But in *The Merchant of Venice,* written a year or two later, Shylock's paternal possessiveness contrasts with the wise policy of Portia's father, whose strict constraints upon his daughter's marital options in fact ensure her happiness. In *Much Ado About Nothing* (1598), the sexually anxious young couples seem incapable of forming heterosexual pairs without the intervention of elders and friends. In *All's Well That Ends Well,* the marriage between Helen and Bertram is unthinkable without the support of the Countess and the King; the match is also roundly endorsed by the elderly courtier Lafeu. If the oldsters are culpable, it is for pushing the young people together prematurely, not for keeping them apart.

Arguably, this change in perspective is a consequence of Shakespeare's own aging. By the time he wrote *All's Well,* he was the father of two marriageable daughters, and surviving records indicate that he had strong opinions about the men they wed. At any rate, the role of family members in Shakespeare's romantic plays becomes more benign, even essential for the pairing-off with which the comedies conclude; by the time of the late romances, in fact, the primary dramatic emphasis tends to be less on the young couple than on their parents. Seen in such a light, *All's Well* marks an important transition in the generational dynamics of Shakespearean comedy.

At the same time, the expanded role of family and friends in "making a match" seems to reflect an increasing pessimism about sex. In both *All's Well* and *Measure for Measure,* mutual desire fails to flower spontaneously between eligible bachelors and maidens. Moreover, even when desire is somehow kindled, its relationship to the institution of lifelong monogamy seems difficult. In *All's Well,* erotic passion burns hottest not when it is gratified but when its goal is still unattained. Bertram wants Diana only so long as she rebuffs him:

Madding my eagerness with her restraint,
As all impediments in fancy's course
Are motives of more fancy.

(5.3.212–14)

Once he imagines he has deflowered her, he deserts her without compunction. Bertram behaves reprehensibly, and yet Helen's more steadfast love, too, seems at least in part an effect of distance and difficulty. In act 1, she declares Bertram to be a "bright particular star," fascinating although inaccessible, and perhaps *because* inaccessible. The obstacles Bertram places in the way of their union seem to make him all the more precious in Helen's eyes and to stimulate her extraordinary efforts to win his affections. But the more resolutely she strives to catch him, the more difficult it becomes to imagine her content with him once he is caught.

In sexual matters, apparently, as soon as one gets what one thinks one wants, it no longer seems so intensely appealing. "Success" brings disillusion in its train. In *All's Well*, this unfortunate arrangement is reflected in passages and episodes that oscillate painfully between imagined extremes of distance and intimacy. In act 2, Helen frets about the social gap that separates her from Bertram: he seems too alien for her. But when the Countess pleads that Helen consider her a "mother," Helen suffers a paroxysm of anxiety on the opposite count: that she and Bertram may be all too closely allied. "God's mercy, maiden," exclaims the Countess, "does it curd thy blood / To say I am thy mother?" (1.3.134–35). Helen's hysterical overreaction suggests that she fears being "too close" at the same time she fears being "too remote." Later in *All's Well*, the bed trick rehearses, in another key, a similar paradox of intimacy and distance. Fleeing his home and a spouse closely associated with his upbringing, Bertram lusts after a foreign woman. But this foreigner turns out, unbeknownst to him, to be interchangeable with his own wife.

Thus the fundamental structure of sexual desire seems inimical to a durably happy marriage, but marriage nonetheless remains the only socially approved arena for sexual expression. Caught in this dilemma, lovers simply cannot be trusted to make proper arrangements among themselves. The community therefore assumes a new prominence in initiating and regulating marriages. In *All's Well*, two means of such regulation are central to the plot. The first is the institution of wardship, a remnant of the feudal system. Minors who inherited estates automatically fell into the care of their feudal superiors: the King in Bertram's case. The guardian's powers included the right to specify a marriage partner of suitable social rank for the "ward." The ward could not refuse the match except by forfeiting much of his property; thus the tense exchange in 2.3 between Bertram and the King about Helen's qualifications in this respect.

Another form of external pressure is brought to bear upon Bertram at the end of the play, when Helen once again appeals to the King to enforce her claim. The hearing that ensues resembles those of the ecclesiastical courts, judicial bodies that settled complaints of sexual misconduct in early modern England. The conflicting testimony of Diana and Bertram painfully recalls the proceedings of the "bawdy courts," as they were popularly known: interminable prosecutions and counterprosecutions for premarital fornication, breach of promise, adultery, child support, and sexual slander—cases in which, as here, evidence was often hard to come by and truth difficult to unearth.

In the early seventeenth century, both wardship and the judicial regulation of sexual conduct were topics of considerable controversy. Some people fiercely resented any meddling in their domestic and sexual affairs, but others wanted the courts to monitor such behavior even more aggressively. Likewise, some attacked wardship on the grounds that guardians often trampled on the personal inclinations of the ward, while others argued that young heirs and heiresses required close supervision to prevent their seduction by unscrupulous gold diggers. In both cases, the point at issue is whether sexual conduct is an essentially personal matter or a

Drummers before an encampment. From
Geffrey Whitney, *A Choice of Emblems* (1586).

matter for public concern. By making both the custom of wardship and the procedures of the bawdy courts crucial to the plot of *All's Well*, Shakespeare seems to endorse the assumption upon which both institutions are premised: that individuals are not competent to manage their own sexual lives, and that stern legal measures are required to coerce the likes of Bertram into matrimony.

A comedy normally depicts the progress of young lovers toward marriage, and in *All's Well* Bertram's stubborn resistance to his generically mandated fate has important consequences. The protagonists of almost all comedies undergo some kind of suffering in the middle acts of the play, but that suffering is overcome. The happy ending retrospectively makes the hardships that preceded it seem worthwhile; conversely, pain validates and gives an appropriate significance to the concluding felicities. Despite its cheerful once-and-for-all title, *All's Well That Ends Well* does not conform to this timeworn pattern. Instead, the play constantly derails narrative expectations and promises endings that turn out to be mirages. Helen cures the King and weds Bertram, but the story is not yet over. She must then encounter Bertram somehow (whether by accident or design is unclear) and arrange to bed him. Then she must make sure she is pregnant; then she must return to France to beg justice of the King. The action continues past the point where one would expect it to terminate, again and again requiring the expenditure of additional effort and ingenuity on Helen's part. Early in act 5, even the King turns out to be surprisingly difficult to locate: Helen, Diana, and Diana's widowed mother arrive at Marseilles only to find that the court has just removed to Roussillon.

Helen's stamina is not demanded of the other characters, but they, too, persist willy-nilly after one might have expected them to subside, and they resurface after one might have expected them to vanish. The King is preparing for his own death when Helen's arrival returns him to the life he had resigned himself to losing. Later, Bertram believes that by fleeing Italy for France he has left Helen behind; similarly, returning to France from Italy, he forsakes Diana. But the two women decline to evaporate. They reappear together in a scene that begins with the King announcing that "the nature of [Bertram's] great offense is dead" (5.3.23), then revives and exacerbates his offense, then declares it buried once more.

These aborted endings, continual deferrals, unanticipated reemergences, and surprising persistences inevitably make the actual end of the play seem rather arbitrary. Eventually it becomes hard to credit the permanence of any resolution, any happy ending. When, in the play's final lines, the King blithely promises Diana her choice of husbands from among his stable of remaining wards, *All's Well* may seem not to be drawing to a close, but merely to be forecasting its own reiteration. The play's open-endedness has generated both dismay and appreciation, depending on the temperament of the critic and, often, on his or her convictions about literary form. Those who prefer celebratory and romantic modes often find the play's lack of convincing closure a disturbing flaw. Those who find the happy endings of most comedies wishful and unrealistic tend to applaud Shakespeare's eschewal of easy answers.

Once again, *All's Well's* apparent noncompliance with "normal" comic practice implicitly suggests limitations inherent in the comic forms it forsakes. At the beginning of 2.4, when Helen asks the Clown whether the Countess is well, he replies that "she is not well," despite the fact that "she's very well and wants nothing i'th' world." To the baffled Helen, the Clown goes on to explain that he does not consider the Countess well because "she's not in heaven, whither God send her quickly." In the Clown's mind, only the dead are happy, a notion that gives a distinctly uncomical twist to the concept of ending well. Consciously or not, the Clown echoes a long tradition of classical and Christian thought that emphasizes the misery of this world and defers true happiness until after death. In 4.3, the First Lord Dumaine relates this apparently

Occasion with her forelock. From Geffrey Whitney, *A Choice of Emblems* (1586). She must be taken "by the forward top"—that is, at the moment when she presents herself; the back of her head is bald to signify that once she is past, she can no longer be grasped. See *All's Well That Ends Well* 5.3.39.

misery to the intransigence of human passions, an intransigence imagined in the Christian tradition in terms of original sin. "As we are ourselves, what things are we!" (lines 19–20). Only divine grace can remedy the defects of human nature in general and of human sexuality in particular. Only another world can offer the prospect of true, lasting felicity. But comedy is a secular mode, lacking the means to represent heaven or divine intervention, and to that extent its happy endings must be partial or temporary. *All's Well* is not unique among Shakespearean comedies in gesturing beyond the mundane, imperfect world with which plays are necessarily concerned, to an ideal world that cannot be directly represented in the theater. Lorenzo's discussion of the music of the spheres in *The Merchant of Venice* and Isabella's acute conviction of divine mentorship in *Measure for Measure* likewise have the effect of implicitly contrasting the limited bliss of comic endings with an unlimited, indescribable counterpart.

But although absolute fulfillment may be impossible in this world, relative improvements are surely feasible. In *All's Well*, it seems that a community can constructively intervene to correct, at least provisionally, some of the grosser imperfections of individuals. In act 4, Bertram acknowledges that he has misjudged Paroles and at the end of the play begs pardon for his behavior, finally promising to love his wife "ever, ever, dearly" (5.3.310). These apparent changes of heart are not motivated by an instinctive sense of regret for his past actions or by a spontaneous upwelling of love for Helen. Rather, the vigorous efforts of his mother, his king, his friends, and his wife force Bertram onto the path that seems best for him whether he likes it or not. Those critics who find his apparent reformation at the end of the play unconvincing are often those skeptical of whether this kind of social pressure will suffice to rescue Bertram from himself. If, however, we are to believe that Bertram is salvageable, as the play implies, then we must acknowledge the effectiveness of the community's efforts to rectify him.

Obviously, a society can have these beneficial effects on its more wayward members only if its moral intuitions are fundamentally sound, and only if its coercive resources have the potential to induce heartfelt, lasting change. The King can force

Bertram to marry Helen and to acknowledge the legitimacy of the child in her womb. But such decrees will ensure Bertram's *love* of Helen only if his inner convictions somehow follow from, or develop out of, his external submission to the King's commands. How actual—not merely apparent—compliance might be achieved is suggested in a speech in which the King warmly remembers Bertram's father, the late Count Roussillon. The old Count, according to the King, adhered to a traditional aristocratic code: he was careful to speak no more than he was willing to defend with his sword. Thought, word, and deed were thus inextricable. The King characterizes this inextricability as "honor," for honor and its corollary, shame, bridge the gap between external behavior and private states of mind, internalizing social scruples so that the aristocrat behaves well even in the absence of obvious incentives or punishments. At best, honor is thus a "clock to itself," a self-regulating mechanism. Only when that clock fails to function properly—as it fails in Bertram's case—must the same results be compelled by clumsier, more obviously extrinsic means.

In his comments on the old Count, the King claims that the up-and-coming generation has an insufficiently vivid conception of honor and its importance:

> Such a man
> Might be a copy to these younger times,
> Which followed well would demonstrate them now
> But goers backward.
>
> (1.2.45–48)

The danger of such a regression is embodied in Paroles, whose name means "words." Paroles exhibits all the superficial signs of courtiership—wit, lavish dress, a familiarity with military and courtly jargons—without any of the real skills or virtues those signs are supposed to indicate. Paroles endangers the social processes by which the world of *All's Well* is imagined to operate, estranging externals from inner substance and subversively demonstrating limitations in the courtly code of honor. He is tightly connected to Bertram, not merely through their friendship but by similarities in their circumstances. The staged drum trick on Paroles coincides temporally with the unstageable bed trick on Bertram, and there are clear thematic parallels as well: both victims are blind, morally as well as literally, to plots perpetrated by close acquaintances masquerading as strangers.

Still, Paroles' menace should not be overestimated. Everyone except Bertram sees through him instantly, and Bertram's inability to discern Paroles' pretenses is a telling mark of his immaturity. Once Bertram finally recognizes that Paroles is a "counterfeit model," moreover, he recoils violently from his former friend and adviser. Bertram may be gauche and inattentive, but he recognizes gross cowardice when he sees it, and in that rudimentary recognition of the difference between honorable and dishonorable conduct may lay the groundwork for his improvement.

Paroles, then, both incarnates Bertram's flaws and diminishes Bertram's culpability. "Your son was misled with a snipped taffeta fellow there," opines Lafeu indignantly to the Countess, "whose villainous saffron would have made all the unbaked and doughy youth of a nation in his color" (4.5.1–3). If, in the world of *All's Well,* good associates and benign forms of institutional duress can maneuver Bertram in the right direction, then bad associates and bad customs likewise have the power to exacerbate his worst impulses. On the other hand, unlike a sterner and more principled character, the "unbaked" Bertram retains the capacity to be reformed, like a lump of dough, despite his unpromising shape.

In less obvious ways, Paroles' presence in *All's Well* also deflects criticism from Helen. Helen's marital plans involve, as she herself admits, quite startling social ambitions. Marrying Bertram will elevate her from the relatively large gentry class to a tiny elite at the pinnacle of the social pyramid. In a hierarchically stratified society where people are supposed to "know their places," such aspirations might well seem disruptive. But Paroles, a cruder and less principled social climber, helps clarify the actually *conservative* nature of Helen's desires. In marked contrast to the craven Paroles, Helen is willing to certify her words with her body as honorable aristocrats are supposed to do, proposing to sacrifice life and reputation if her promises to cure the King prove empty. Helen's conviction that words must suit actions, that her tongue must obey her hand, marks her as "noble" despite her lack of material resources, and gains her the respect of the older members of the nobility, such as the King, the Countess, and Lafeu. Thus marriage to Bertram seems to remedy an unaccountable lapse in the proper social order, rather than to create a breach in that order.

Left deliberately vague is what relationship, if any, merit really has with birth. On the one hand, Helen's excellence seems to belie her humble origins; on the other hand, although both Helen and Diana are poor, it is carefully specified that they are not "base" persons of artisan or peasant stock. Their gentility, however modest, seems

Foppish camp follower. Peter Flötner (mid-sixteenth century).

to lend their upward mobility a respectability that Paroles' attempts at self-promotion can never possess. Paroles thus draws off criticism that Helen might otherwise attract for violating class boundaries. Similarly, his presence in the play serves partially to allay criticism of Helen's sexual transgressiveness: his boastful inaction is so obviously worse than Helen's vigorous but possibly "unfeminine" enterprise that once again he seems an instructive example that tells in Helen's favor.

Although Paroles functions as a scapegoat of sorts, at the end of the play he does not suffer the scapegoat's usual cruel fate. After his disgrace, his dramatic function as corrupter of Bertram and foil to Helen is evidently complete, and we might imagine that we have seen the last of him. But like so many other characters in *All's Well,* good and bad, Paroles has a surprising durability. "Simply the thing I am," he declares, "shall make me live" (4.3.316–17). Like Helen and Diana, he reappears in the final scenes, reinserting himself, in a reduced capacity, into a world that had scorned him. The partial, incremental improvement promised by the conclusion of *All's Well That Ends Well* may from some points of view seem disappointing. But its pessimism inspires a certain tolerance, a forbearance that allows even the ridiculous or debased to find a home.

KATHARINE EISAMAN MAUS

SELECTED BIBLIOGRAPHY

Donaldson, Ian. "*All's Well That Ends Well*: Shakespeare's Play of Endings." *Essays in Criticism* 27 (1977): 34–55. Discusses the play's preoccupation with endings and its problematic final scene.

Harris, Jonathan Gil. "All Swell That End Swell: Dropsy, Phantom Pregnancy, and the Sound of Deconception in *All's Well That Ends Well*." *Renaissance Drama* 35 (2006): 169–89. Swollen bodies: the King's illness, Paroles' empty inflation, Helen's pregnancy.

Hodgdon, Barbara. "The Making of Virgins and Mothers: Sexual Signs, Substitute Scenes, and Doubled Presences in *All's Well That Ends Well*." *Philological Quarterly* 66 (1987): 47–72. Examines the character of Helen, as Shakespeare develops it from the source story in Boccaccio's *Decameron*.

Huston, J. Dennis. "'Some Stain of Soldier': The Functions of Paroles in *All's Well That Ends Well*." *Shakespeare Quarterly* 21 (1970): 431–38. Compares Paroles with Helen.

Parker, Patricia. "*All's Well That Ends Well*: Increase and Multiply." *Creative Imitation: New Essays on Renaissance Literature in Honor of Thomas M. Greene*. Ed. David Quint, Margaret Ferguson, G. W. Pigman, and Wayne Rebhorn. Binghamton, NY: Medieval and Renaissance Texts and Studies, 1992. 355–90. Looks at linguistic and sexual deferral and displacement as the key to abundance in the play.

Schwarz, Kathryn. "'My Intents Are Fixed': Constant Will in *All's Well That Ends Well*." *Shakespeare Quarterly* 58 (2007): 200–27. Argues that Helen's admirable but disconcerting constancy shows how male privilege is contingent upon the active support of the women subjected to it.

Sullivan, Garrett. "'Be This Sweet Helen's Knell, and Now Forget Her': Forgetting, Memory, and Identity in *All's Well That Ends Well*." *Shakespeare Quarterly* 50 (1999): 51–69. Analyzes how the forgetfulness associated with sexual desire both threatens and produces identity in *All's Well That Ends Well*.

Traister, Barbara Howard. "'Doctor She': Healing and Sex in *All's Well That Ends Well*." *A Companion to Shakespeare's Works*, IV: *Poems, Problem Comedies, Late Plays*. Blackwell Companions to Literature and Culture 20. Ed. Richard Dutton and Jean E. Howard. Malden, MA: Blackwell, 2003. 333–47. Looks at Helen as lovesick physician.

Wheeler, Richard P. "Imperial Love and the Dark House: *All's Well That Ends Well*." *Shakespeare's Development and the Problem Comedies: Turn and Counter-Turn*. Berkeley: U of California P, 1981. 35–91. Offers a detailed psychoanalytic reading.

Zitner, Sheldon P. *All's Well That Ends Well*. Boston: Twayne, 1989. Stage and reception histories as well as critical commentary on the play.

FILM

All's Well That Ends Well. 1981. Dir. Elijah Moshinsky. UK. 142 min. From BBC-TV. An elegant production, with sets and lighting that recall the paintings of Vermeer and Caravaggio. Compelling performances from Angela Down (Helen), Celia Johnson (Countess), Donald Sinden (King), and Ian Charleson (Bertram).

TEXTUAL INTRODUCTION

The only text of *All's Well That Ends Well* is that in the Folio. It was set primarily by Compositor B, but pages V3 recto and verso were set by Compositor D and V4 recto and verso by Compositor C. The play is divided into acts, but scenes are not numbered. Since division into acts occurred only once the King's Men started acting at the Blackfriars, this division may, if the play is from as late as 1607 rather than the traditional date of 1604–05 or earlier, anticipate the move. Otherwise the divisions may have been imposed later, either for a performance or for printing.

The text of *All's Well That Ends Well* offers a number of notorious difficulties. Aside from some verbal cruxes, these include variation in the names of characters, confusion of the two lords eventually identified as the brothers Dumaine, and some unusually worded stage directions. Initially, the Countess of Roussillon is called *"Mother"*; in the course of the play she is also identified as *"Countess," "Old Countess," "Lady,"* and *"Old Lady."* Her son is sometimes *"Count Roussillon,"* sometimes *"Roussillon,"* sometimes *"Bertram"*; Lafeu is *"Lord Lafeu," "Old Lafeu,"* and *"Old Lord"*; Helen is *"Helena"* once in dialogue and several times in stage directions. More troublesome is the confusion of the *"two French Lords,"* as they are called in the Folio's opening stage direction to 5.3, or *"the two Frenchmen"* (3.1.0 SD), or *"the Frenchmen, as at first"* (3.6.0 SD), or *"the two French Captaines"* (4.3.0 SD). We learn they are brothers only at 3.6.98 and that their name is Dumaine only at 4.3.172. In speech prefixes they are sometimes identified as *"1. Lo. G."* and *"2. Lo. E."* (1.2), sometimes differentiated only with numbers, e.g., *"1 Lord"* (3.1), sometimes with such abbreviated terms as *"French E."* (3.1), *"Cap. G.,"* or *"Cap. E."* (3.6). More important, the parts of the two characters seem to have become confused. The difficulties begin at the end of 3.6, when *"Cap. E."* has been urging Bertram to allow him to surprise Paroles. As Captain E. (in this edition called *"Second Lord Dumaine"*) says he will "go look my twigs"—presumably meaning that he will leave to prepare the ambush—Bertram responds, "Your brother, he shall go along with me," and *"Cap. G."* (or *"First Lord Dumaine"*) says, "As't please your lordship, I'll leave you." Captain E. remains with Bertram, who offers to "show [him] the lass [he] spoke of," i.e., Diana (3.6.96–102). Later, at 4.3.14–15, E. accordingly tells G. the details of how Bertram "hath perverted a young gentlewoman." Nevertheless, in Folio 4.1, it is E., not G., who leads the capture of Paroles. At the beginning of 4.3, E. reports to Bertram on Paroles' behavior once captured, but in the rest of 4.3 it is G. who leads the interrogation.

Different explanations have been offered for these variations. Traditionally it has been thought that they reflect Shakespeare's developing vision of his characters or their roles at particular moments (e.g., "mother"), and hence that these variations indicate that the play was set from Shakespeare's "foul papers" or working draft. The lack of consistency, along with the confusion over the French "lords Dumaine," perhaps suggests that there may have been interruptions in the writing during which Shakespeare lost track of the titles he had earlier given some characters. Changes of speech prefix within certain scenes—for example, the switch from *"Coun."* to *"Old Cou."* in 1.3 from lines 113 to 152—may indicate that some sections where new speech prefixes appear were additions originally written on separate sheets or in the margin.

Further support for the idea of interrupted composition comes from a number of stage directions in which what seem to be private notations have crept into the text. Two striking examples are F 2.3.181 SD, *"Parolles and Lafew stay behind, commenting of this wedding,"* and F 3.6.0, *"Enter Count Rossillion and the Frenchmen, as at first."* "Commenting of this wedding" and "as at first" are not directions that would be visible on the stage, and they can perhaps be understood as Shakespeare's notes to himself.

On the other hand, certain textual oddities have been attributed to collaboration. Laurie Maguire and Emma Smith propose that the play was written by Shakespeare and Thomas Middleton soon after their joint work on *Timon of Athens*. The play would thus date from 1606–07—a suggestion made on other grounds by scholars including McDonald P. Jackson and accepted in the *Norton Shakespeare* chronology—and collaboration might also explain the "notes to author" style of some of the stage directions, the variation in character names, and the confusion of the two French lords. Maguire and Smith find Middleton's hand in certain scenes (1.1, 1.3, 2.1, 2.3, 4.1, 4.3, and 5.3) or parts of scenes—for instance, at the switch of speech prefixes in 1.3. They cite a variety of characteristics of Middleton's style in sections of *All's Well*, including the high proportion of rhyming lines; characteristic contractions, exclamations, and vocabulary; and numerous

LAFEU He hath abandoned his physicians,[4] madam, under
whose practices he hath persecuted time with hope[5] and
finds no other advantage in the process but only the losing
15 of hope by time.

COUNTESS This young gentlewoman had a father—oh, that
"had," how sad a passage° 'tis!—whose skill was almost as   *expression; passing away*
great as his honesty;° had it° stretched so far, would have   *integrity / (his skill)*
made nature immortal, and death should have play for lack
20 of work. Would for the King's sake he were living: I think it
would be the death of the King's disease.

LAFEU How called you the man you speak of, madam?

COUNTESS He was famous, sir, in his profession, and it was
his great right to be so: Gerard de Narbonne.[6]

25 LAFEU He was excellent indeed, madam; the King very lately
spoke of him admiringly and mourningly. He was skillful
enough to have lived still, if knowledge could be set up
against mortality.

BERTRAM What is it, my good lord, the King languishes of?

30 LAFEU A fistula,° my lord.   *abscess (often anal)*

BERTRAM I heard not of it before.

LAFEU I would it were not notorious.° [*He indicates* HELEN.]   *known to everyone*
Was this gentlewoman the daughter of Gerard de Narbonne?

COUNTESS His sole child, my lord, and bequeathed to my
35 overlooking.[7] I have those hopes of her good that her edu-
cation° promises her dispositions she inherits, which   *upbringing*
makes fair gifts° fairer.[8] For where an unclean mind car-   *abilities*
ries virtuous qualities,° there commendations go with   *acquired skills*
pity:° they are virtues and traitors, too.[9] In her they are the *mingle with regret*
40 better for their simpleness;° she derives° her honesty and   *purity / inherits*
achieves her goodness.

LAFEU Your commendations, madam, get from her tears.

COUNTESS 'Tis the best brine a maiden can season° her praise   *preserve (as with salt)*
in. The remembrance of her father never approaches her
45 heart but the tyranny of her sorrows takes all livelihood°   *liveliness*
from her cheek. —No more of this, Helena: go to, no more,
lest it be rather thought you affect° a sorrow than to have—   *make a show of*

HELEN I do affect a sorrow, indeed, but I have it, too.

LAFEU Moderate lamentation is the right of the dead, exces-
50 sive grief the enemy to the living.

COUNTESS If the living be not enemy to the grief, the excess
makes it soon mortal.°   *fatal*

BERTRAM Madam, I desire your holy wishes.°   *blessing*

LAFEU How understand we that?[1]

55 COUNTESS Be thou blest, Bertram, and succeed thy father
In manners° as in shape. Thy blood and virtue[2]   *behavior*
Contend for empire in thee, and thy goodness
Share with thy birthright. Love all, trust a few,

---

4. Playing on the usual "his physicians have abandoned him" (given up hope of his cure).
5. Afflicted his days by hoping for a cure.
6. Town just north of Roussillon.
7. Guardianship (Helen is the Countess's ward, as
Bertram is the King's).
8. TEXTUAL COMMENT Editors often add a semicolon
after "promises," but *The Norton Shakespeare* does

not for reasons explained in Digital Edition TC 2.
9. Because the skills are used for evil purposes.
1. TEXTUAL COMMENT Possibly a misplaced line;
possibly Lafeu thinks Bertram's interruption discourteous. For a fuller discussion, see Digital Edition TC 3.
2. (May) your noble birth and acquired goodness.

Do wrong to none. Be able° for thine enemy   *a match for*

60 Rather in power than use,[3] and keep thy friend
Under thy own life's key.[4] Be checked° for silence   *criticized*
But never taxed for speech.° What heaven more will   *rebuked for chatter*
That thee may furnish° and my prayers pluck down,   *embellish*
Fall on thy head. [*to* LAFEU] Farewell, my lord.

65 'Tis an unseasoned° courtier. Good my lord,   *immature*
Advise him.

LAFEU   He cannot want the best
That shall attend his love.[5]

COUNTESS   Heaven bless him! —Farewell, Bertram.

BERTRAM   The best wishes that can be forged° in your   *fashioned*
70 thoughts be servants to you.°   [*Exit* COUNTESS.]   *assist you*
[*to* HELEN] Be comfortable° to my mother, your mistress,   *comforting*
and make much of her.

LAFEU   Farewell, pretty lady, you must hold the credit° of your   *uphold the reputation*
father.   [*Exeunt* BERTRAM *and* LAFEU.]

75 HELEN   Oh, were that all! I think not on my father,
And these great tears grace his remembrance more
Than those I shed for him.[6] What was he like?
I have forgot him. My imagination
Carries no favor° in't but Bertram's.   *face; liking; love token*
80 I am undone. There is no living, none,
If Bertram be away. 'Twere all one
That° I should love a bright particular star   *It is just as if*
And think to wed it, he is so above me.
In his bright radiance and collateral[7] light
85 Must I be comforted, not in his sphere.
Th'ambition in my love thus plagues itself:
The hind° that would be mated by the lion   *doe*
Must die for love. 'Twas pretty, though a plague,
To see him every hour, to sit and draw
90 His archèd brows, his hawking° eye, his curls,   *sharp*
In our heart's table°—heart too capable°   *drawing table / receptive*
Of every line and trick° of his sweet favor!°   *trait / face*
But now he's gone, and my idolatrous fancy°   *love*
Must sanctify his relics.[8] Who comes here?

     Enter PAROLES.

95 One that goes with him. I love him for his sake,
And yet I know him a notorious liar,
Think him a great way° fool, solely° a coward.   *mostly a / completely*
Yet these fixed evils sit so fit in him°   *fit him so well*
That they take place[9] when virtue's steely bones°   *rigid severity*
100 Looks bleak i'th' cold wind withal. Full oft we see
Cold wisdom waiting on superfluous folly.

PAROLES   Save° you, fair queen.   *God save*

HELEN   And you, monarch.

PAROLES   No.

105 HELEN   And no.

---

3. By having power, rather than using it.
4. *keep . . . key:* safeguard your friend's life as you do your own.
5. *He . . . love:* He will not lack the best advice my affection for him can supply.
6. *grace . . . him:* are a better tribute to my father

than those (few) tears I actually shed for him.
7. Rotating in a separate orbit (in Ptolomaic astronomy).
8. Must worship what reminds me of him.
9. Take precedence.

PAROLES Are you meditating on virginity?

HELEN Ay. You have some stain° of soldier in you; let me ask   *tinge*
you a question. Man is enemy to virginity: how may we
barricado° it against him?   *barricade*

110 PAROLES Keep him out.

HELEN But he assails, and our virginity, though valiant in the
defense, yet is weak. Unfold to us some warlike resistance.

PAROLES There is none. Man setting down before° you will   *laying siege to*
undermine you and blow you up.[1]

115 HELEN Bless our poor virginity from underminers and
blowers-up! Is there no military policy° how virgins might   *strategy*
blow up men?

PAROLES Virginity being blown down, man will quicklier be
blown up.° Marry,[2] in blowing him down again, with the   *have an erection*
120 breach yourselves made you lose your city. It is not politic°   *expedient*
in the commonwealth of nature to preserve virginity. Loss
of virginity is rational increase,[3] and there was never virgin
got° till virginity was first lost. That° you were made of is   *begotten / What*
mettle° to make virgins. Virginity, by being once lost, may   *substance*
125 be ten times found;° by being ever kept, it is ever lost. 'Tis   *reproduced tenfold*
too cold a companion: away with't!

HELEN I will stand for't° a little, though therefor I die a virgin.   *defend it*

PAROLES There's little can be said in't:° 'tis against the rule of   *for it*
nature. To speak on the part of virginity is to accuse your
130 mothers, which is most infallible disobedience. He that
hangs himself is a virgin.[4] Virginity murders itself and
should be buried in highways out of all sanctified limit,[5] as a
desperate offendress against nature. Virginity breeds mites
much like a cheese,[6] consumes itself to the very paring, and
135 so dies with feeding his own stomach.° Besides, virginity is   *pride*
peevish, proud, idle, made of self-love—which is the most
inhibited° sin in the canon.° Keep it not; you cannot choose   *prohibited / scriptures*
but lose by't. Out with't:[7] within t'one year it will make itself
two, which is a goodly increase, and the principal[8] itself not
140 much the worse. Away with't!

HELEN How might one do, sir, to lose it to her own liking?

PAROLES Let me see. Marry, ill, to like him that ne'er it likes.[9]
'Tis a commodity will lose the gloss with lying:° the longer   *remaining idle*
kept, the less worth. Off with't while 'tis vendible;° answer   *salable*
145 the time of request.[1] Virginity, like an old courtier, wears
her cap out of fashion, richly suited° but unsuitable,° just   *dressed / inappropriate*
like the brooch and the toothpick, which wear not now.[2]
Your date° is better in your pie and your porridge than in   *fruit; age*
your cheek, and your virginity, your old virginity, is like one
150 of our French withered pears:[3] it looks ill, it eats drily—
marry, 'tis a withered pear. It was formerly better, marry, yet
'tis a withered pear. Will you anything with it?

1. *undermine you*: dig tunnels under you (to plant
explosives). *blow you up*: punning on "inflate," "make
you pregnant."
2. By Mary (a mild oath).
3. *rational increase*: judicious growth in the human
("rational") population.
4. A suicide, like a virgin, is a self-destroyer.
5. Consecrated ground (in which suicides were
denied burial).

6. Cheese was thought to generate spontaneously
the mites that fed on it.
7. Get rid of it; put it out at interest.
8. Original investment (the woman's body).
9. To please him who doesn't appreciate virginity.
1. Respond to demand (greatest in youth).
2. Which are no longer in fashion.
3. Dried pears (suggesting aged female genitals).

HELEN   Not my virginity yet[4]—
There° shall your master have a thousand loves,   *(At court)*
155   A mother, and a mistress, and a friend,
A phoenix,[5] captain, and an enemy,
A guide, a goddess, and a sovereign,
A counselor, a traitress, and a dear.
His humble ambition, proud humility;
160   His jarring concord, and his discord dulcet;[6]
His faith, his sweet disaster, with a world
Of pretty fond adoptious christendoms
That blinking Cupid gossips.[7] Now shall he—
I know not what he shall. God send him well.
165   The court's a learning place, and he is one—
PAROLES   What one, i'faith?
HELEN   —That I wish well. 'Tis pity—
PAROLES   What's pity?
HELEN   —That wishing well had not a body in't
Which might be felt,° that we the poorer born,   *perceived*
170   Whose baser stars do shut us up in wishes,[8]
Might with effects of them follow our friends
And show what we alone must° think, which never   *must only*
Returns us thanks.°   *Wins us gratitude*
                    Enter PAGE.
PAGE   Monsieur Paroles, my lord calls for you.   [*Exit.*]
175   PAROLES   Little Helen, farewell. If I can remember thee, I will
think of thee at court.
HELEN   Monsieur Paroles, you were born under a charitable
star.
PAROLES   Under Mars,[9] I.
180   HELEN   I especially think under Mars.
PAROLES   Why under Mars?
HELEN   The wars hath so kept you under, that you must needs
be born under Mars.
PAROLES   When he was predominant.°   *in the ascendant*
185   HELEN   When he was retrograde,[1] I think rather.
PAROLES   Why think you so?
HELEN   You go so much backward when you fight.
PAROLES   That's for advantage.°   *tactical gain*
HELEN   So is running away when fear proposes the safety. But
190   the composition° that your valor and fear makes in you is a   *truce; mixture*
virtue of a good wing,[2] and I like the wear° well.   *habit; fashion*
PAROLES   I am so full of businesses I cannot answer thee
acutely. I will return perfect courtier, in the which my
instruction shall serve to naturalize° thee, so thou wilt be   *familiarize*
195   capable of a courtier's counsel and understand what advice
shall thrust upon thee; else thou diest in thine unthankfulness,

---

4. Not with *my* virginity: not my virginity *yet* (but soon).
5. The mythical phoenix was a one-of-a-kind bird; hence, marvelous, unique being.
6. Harmonious (all these oxymorons were typical of courtly love poetry).
7. *pretty . . . gossips:* foolish nicknames given when blind Cupid is godfather at a christening.

8. Whose less elevated destinies confine us merely to wishing.
9. The planet was identified with the god of war.
1. Retreating (said of a planet's apparent movement relative to the zodiac).
2. *of a good wing:* that is, rapid in flight; also, with large shoulder flaps. Paroles is foppishly dressed.

and thine ignorance makes thee away.° Farewell. When   *puts an end to you*
thou hast leisure, say thy prayers; when thou hast none,
remember thy friends.[3] Get thee a good husband, and use°   *treat*
200 him as he uses thee. So farewell.   [*Exit.*]
HELEN   Our remedies oft in ourselves do lie
Which we ascribe to heaven. The fated° sky   *destiny-ordaining*
Gives us free scope, only doth backward pull
Our slow designs when we ourselves are dull.°   *sluggish*
205 What power is it which mounts my love so high,[4]
That makes me see and cannot feed mine eye?
The mightiest space in fortune nature brings
To join like likes and kiss like native things.[5]
Impossible be strange° attempts to those   *unusual*
210 That weigh their pains in sense[6] and do suppose
What hath been cannot be. Who ever strove
To show her merit that did miss° her love?   *fail to achieve*
The King's disease—my project may deceive me,
But my intents are fixed and will not leave me.   *Exit.*

1.2

Flourish cornetts.°   *Wind-instrument fanfare*
Enter the KING *of France with letters and diverse*
ATTENDANTS[, *including the two* LORDS DUMAINE].[1]
KING   The Florentines and Sienese are by th'ears,°   *quarreling*
Have fought with equal fortune and continue
A braving° war.   *defiant; gallant*
FIRST LORD DUMAINE   So 'tis reported, sir.
KING   Nay, 'tis most credible. We here receive it
5 A certainty, vouched from our cousin Austria,[2]
With caution that the Florentine will move° us   *entreat*
For speedy aid, wherein our dearest friend°   *(the Duke of Austria)*
Prejudicates° the business and would seem   *Prejudges*
To have us make denial.
FIRST LORD DUMAINE   His love and wisdom,
10 Approved° so to your majesty, may plead   *Proven*
For amplest credence.
KING   He hath armed° our answer,   *hardened*
And Florence is denied before he comes.
Yet for our gentlemen that mean to see
The Tuscan service, freely have they leave
To stand on either part.°   *fight on either side*
15 SECOND LORD DUMAINE   It well may serve
A nursery to[3] our gentry, who are sick°   *pining*
For breathing° and exploit.   *exercise*
KING   What's he comes here?
Enter BERTRAM, LAFEU, *and* PAROLES.

---

3. Unclear: perhaps, Say your prayers when you have
the chance, and when you're too busy, rely on your
friends instead.
4. Which elevates my love to so lofty an object.
5. *The mightiest . . . things:* Natural affect brings
persons greatly distant in rank together as if they
were similar and conjoins them as if they had a common origin.

6. Who vividly imagine the difficulties.
1.2 Location: The King's court at Paris.
1. TEXTUAL COMMENT The roles of the two Lords
Dumaine are unclear in the original text. See Digital
Edition TC 4.
2. My kinsman, the Duke of Austria.
3. As a training school for.

FIRST LORD DUMAINE   It is the Count Roussillon, my good lord,
　　Young Bertram.
KING　　　　　　　　Youth, thou bear'st thy father's face.
20　Frank° nature, rather curious° than in haste,　　　　　　　*Generous / meticulous*
　　Hath well composed thee. Thy father's moral parts°　　　　　　*qualities*
　　Mayst thou inherit too. Welcome to Paris!
BERTRAM   My thanks and duty are your majesty's.
KING   I would I had that corporal soundness now
25　As when thy father and myself, in friendship,
　　First tried our soldiership. He did look far°　　　　　　　　*see deeply*
　　Into the service° of the time and was　　　　　　　　　　*military service*
　　Discipled of° the bravest. He lasted long,　　　　　　*Followed by; taught by*
　　But on us both did haggish° age steal on　　　　　　*witchlike; malevolent*
30　And wore us out of act.° It much repairs me　　　　　　　　*action*
　　To talk of your good father. In his youth
　　He had the wit which I can well observe
　　Today in our young lords, but they may jest
　　Till their own scorn return to them unnoted[4]
35　Ere they can hide their levity in honor.[5]
　　So like a courtier,° contempt nor bitterness　　　　　　*paradigm of courtesy*
　　Were in his pride° or sharpness;[6] if they were,　　　　　　*self-esteem*
　　His equal had awaked them,[7] and his honor,
　　Clock to itself,° knew the true minute when　　　　　　*Self-regulating*
40　Exception° bid him speak, and at this time　　　　　　*Disapproval*
　　His tongue obeyed his hand.[8] Who were below him,
　　He used as creatures of another place[9]
　　And bowed his eminent top° to their low ranks,　　　　　　*head*
　　Making them proud of his humility;
45　In their poor praise he humbled.[1] Such a man
　　Might be a copy° to these younger times,　　　　　　*model*
　　Which followed well would demonstrate them now
　　But goers backward.°　　　　　　*backsliders*
BERTRAM　　　　　　His good remembrance, sir,
　　Lies richer in your thoughts than on his tomb.
50　So in approof° lives not his epitaph　　　　　　*confirmation*
　　As in your royal speech.
KING   Would I were with him! He would always say—
　　Methinks I hear him now; his plausive° words　　　　　　*praiseworthy*
　　He scattered not in ears, but grafted them[2]
55　To grow there and to bear—"Let me not live"—
　　This his good melancholy oft began
　　On the catastrophe° and heel of pastime　　　　　　*end*
　　When it was out°—"Let me not live," quoth he,　　　　　　*finished*
　　"After my flame lacks oil, to be the snuff[3]
60　Of younger spirits, whose apprehensive° senses　　　　　　*quick*
　　All but new things disdain; whose judgments are
　　Mere fathers of their garments;[4] whose constancies°　　　　　　*loyalties*

4. *they may . . . unnoted:* their ridicule merely rebounds upon them, ignored by others.
5. Before they can compensate for their frivolity with noble acts.
6. Keenness of wit.
7. *if they were . . . them:* if ever he spoke bitterly or contemptuously, it was to a social equal.
8. He said no more than he would back up with action.
9. He treated as people of a higher station.

1. He willingly humbled himself to praise their poor selves.
2. He did not strew (words) superficially among his hearers (like seed), but planted them permanently (as twigs of fruit trees are grafted to a tree trunk).
3. Burned upper wick, which if not trimmed keeps the lower part from burning properly.
4. *whose judgments . . . garments:* whose mental prowess creates only new clothes.

Expire before their fashions." This he wished.
I after him do after° him wish too,   *in harmony with*
65   Since I nor wax nor honey can bring home,
I quickly were dissolvèd° from my hive   *removed*
To give some laborers room.
SECOND LORD DUMAINE   You're loved, sir;
They that least lend it you° shall lack° you first.   *grant you love / miss*
KING   I fill a place, I know't. How long is't, Count,
70   Since the physician at your father's died?
He was much famed.
BERTRAM   Some six months since, my lord.
KING   If he were living, I would try him yet.
—Lend me an arm. —The rest have worn me out
With several applications.° Nature and sickness   *various treatments*
75   Debate it at their leisure.[5] Welcome, Count;
My son's no dearer.
BERTRAM   Thank your majesty.   *Flourish. Exeunt.*

1.3

Enter COUNTESS, STEWARD, *and* CLOWN.

COUNTESS   I will now hear. What say you of this gentlewoman?
STEWARD   Madam, the care I have had to even your content[1]
I wish might be found in the calendar° of my past endeavors,   *record*
for then we wound our modesty and make foul the clearness
5   of our deservings, when of ourselves we publish° them.   *advertise*
COUNTESS   What does this knave here? [*to* CLOWN] Get you
gone, sirrah! The complaints I have heard of you I do not all
believe. 'Tis my slowness that I do not, for I know you lack
not folly to commit them, and have ability enough to make
10   such knaveries yours.
CLOWN   'Tis not unknown to you, madam, I am a poor fellow.
COUNTESS   Well, sir?
CLOWN   No, madam, 'tis not so well that I am poor, though
many of the rich are damned. But if I may have your lady-
15   ship's good will to go to the world,° Isbel the woman° and I   *marry / maidservant*
will do as we may.[2]
COUNTESS   Wilt thou needs be a beggar?
CLOWN   I do beg your good will in this case.
COUNTESS   In what case?
20   CLOWN   In Isbel's case and mine own. Service is no heritage,[3]
and I think I shall never have the blessing of God till I have
issue o'my body. For they say bairns° are blessings.   *children*
COUNTESS   Tell me thy reason why thou wilt marry.
CLOWN   My poor body, madam, requires it; I am driven on by
25   the flesh, and he must needs go that the devil drives.
COUNTESS   Is this all your worship's reason?
CLOWN   Faith, madam, I have other holy reasons,[4] such as they
are.

---

5. Argue over my condition at length.
1.3 Location: Roussillon.
1. To meet your desires.
2. Will do our best (with sexual pun on "do").
3. A servant has little to leave his children (prover-

bial; with sexual pun on "service").
4. Other motives sanctified by the marriage ceremony; with puns on "holy" ("hole-y") and "reasons"
("raisings").

COUNTESS   May the world know them?

30   CLOWN   I have been, madam, a wicked creature, as you and
all flesh and blood are, and indeed I do marry that I may
repent.⁵

COUNTESS   Thy marriage sooner than thy wickedness.

CLOWN   I am out o'friends, madam, and I hope to have friends
35   for my wife's sake.

COUNTESS   Such friends are thine enemies, knave.

CLOWN   You're shallow,° madam, in great friends, for the   *a superficial judge*
knaves come to do that for me which I am aweary of. He
that ears° my land spares my team and gives me leave to in°   *plows / harvest*
40   the crop. If I be his cuckold, he's my drudge. He that comforts my wife is the cherisher of my flesh and blood; he that
cherishes my flesh and blood loves my flesh and blood; he
that loves my flesh and blood is my friend; *ergo*, he that
kisses my wife is my friend. If men could be contented to be
45   what they are,° there were no fear in marriage, for young   *(cuckolds)*
Chairbonne the puritan and old Poisson the papist,⁶
howsome'er their hearts are severed in religion, their heads
are both one:° they may jowl° horns together like any deer   *identical / bump*
i'th' herd.⁷

50   COUNTESS   Wilt thou ever be a foul-mouthed and calumnious
knave?

CLOWN   A prophet I, madam, and I speak the truth the next°   *most direct*
way.
[*Sings*.]   For I the ballad will repeat,
55   Which men full true shall find:
            "Your marriage comes by destiny,
            Your cuckoo sings by kind."⁸

COUNTESS   Get you gone, sir; I'll talk with you more anon.

STEWARD   May it please you, madam, that he bid Helen come
60   to you. Of her I am to speak.

COUNTESS   Sirrah, tell my gentlewoman I would speak with
her—Helen, I mean.

CLOWN [*sings*]   "Was this fair face the cause," quoth she,⁹
                "Why the Grecians sackèd Troy,
65   Fond° done, done fond, was this¹ King Priam's joy?"   *Foolishly; lovingly*
                With that she sighèd as she stood, *bis*°   *(repeat)*
                And gave this sentence° then: *maxim*
                "Among nine bad if one be good,
                Among nine bad if one be good,
70   There's yet one good in ten."

COUNTESS   What, one good in ten? You corrupt² the song,
sirrah.

CLOWN   One good woman in ten, madam, which is a purify-
ing o'th' song. Would God would serve the world so all the

---

5. That I may make my illicit sexual activity lawful
(but alluding to the proverb "Marry in haste and
repent at leisure").
6. *chair bonne*: good meat (French). *poisson*: fish.
Catholics ate fish on fast days, but puritans rejected
the custom.
7. Cuckolds were supposed to have horns in their
foreheads.
8. *by kind*: according to its nature (the cuckoo's song

was supposed to mock cuckolds).
9. The Clown is reminded of the "fair face" of Helen
of Troy, the most famous cuckold maker. *she*: probably Hecuba, wife of Priam and mother of Paris, Hel-
en's lover.
1. *this*: probably refers to Paris.
2. Debase (the original presumably had "one bad in
ten," referring to Paris, Priam's only bad son).

75   year, we'd find no fault with the tithe woman[3] if I were the
      parson. One in ten, quoth 'a?° An° we might have a good   did he say / If
      woman born but or every blazing star° or at an earthquake,   comet
      'twould mend the lottery° well. A man may draw his heart   improve the odds
      out ere 'a pluck[4] one.
80   COUNTESS   You'll be gone, sir knave, and do as I command you?
      CLOWN   That man should be at woman's command, and yet
      no hurt done! Though honesty be no puritan,[5] yet it will do
      no hurt;° it will wear the surplice of humility over the black   harm
      gown of a big heart.[6] I am going, forsooth. The business is
85   for Helen to come hither.   *Exit.*
      COUNTESS   Well, now.
      STEWARD   I know, madam, you love your gentlewoman
      entirely.
      COUNTESS   Faith, I do. Her father bequeathed her to me, and
90   she herself, without other advantage,[7] may lawfully make title
      to° as much love as she finds. There is more owing her than is   claim
      paid, and more shall be paid her than she'll demand.
      STEWARD   Madam, I was very late° more near her than I think   recently
      she wished me. Alone she was, and did communicate to her-
95   self her own words to her own ears. She thought, I dare vow
      for her, they touched not any stranger sense.[8] Her matter°   subject
      was, she loved your son. Fortune, she said, was no goddess,
      that had put such difference betwixt their two estates;° Love   social stations
      no god, that would not extend his might only where qualities
100   were level;[9] Dian° no queen of virgins, that would suffer her   Diana, goddess of chastity
      poor knight surprised[1] without rescue in the first assault
      or ransom afterward. This she delivered in the most bitter
      touch° of sorrow that e'er I heard virgin exclaim in, which I   strain
      held my duty speedily to acquaint you withal, sithence° in   since
105   the loss that may happen, it concerns you something to
      know it.
      COUNTESS   You have discharged this honestly. Keep it to your-
      self. Many likelihoods informed me of this before, which
      hung so tottering in the balance that I could neither believe
110   nor misdoubt.° Pray you leave me. Stall° this in your bosom,   doubt / Enclose
      and I thank you for your honest care. I will speak with you
      further anon.   *Exit* STEWARD.
              Enter HELEN.
      COUNTESS [*aside*]   Even so it was with me when I was young.
      If ever we are nature's, these° are ours. This thorn   (love pangs)
115   Doth to our rose of youth rightly belong;
      Our blood° to us, this to our blood is born: passions
      It is the show° and seal of nature's truth   sign
      Where love's strong passion is impressed in youth.
      By our remembrances of days forgone,
120   Such were our faults, or° then we thought them none.   although
      Her eye is sick on't;° I observe her now.   with it

---

3. One-tenth of the parish produce was tithed to the church.
4. Before he draws (as from a lottery).
5. Though my honest self is not morally strict.
6. *it will wear . . . heart:* that is, the Clown will con-ceal his pride under apparent meekness. Some Puri-tan ministers obeyed English ecclesiastical law by wearing the surplice, or priestly garment, but with a black Calvinist gown underneath.
7. Even without any interest accrued (Helen being regarded as the "principal" bequeathed by her father).
8. Any other person's hearing.
9. Would not exercise his power except where rank was equal.
1. Would allow her poor devotee to be captured.

HELEN What is your pleasure, madam?

COUNTESS   You know, Helen,
I am a mother to you.

HELEN Mine honorable mistress.

COUNTESS   Nay, a mother.
125 Why not a mother? When I said "a mother"
Methought you saw a serpent. What's in "mother"
That you start at it? I say I am your mother,
And put you in the catalogue of those
That were enwombèd mine. 'Tis often seen
130 Adoption strives with nature, and choice breeds
A native slip to us from foreign seeds.[2]
You ne'er oppressed me with a mother's groan,°   *(in childbirth)*
Yet I express to you a mother's care.
God's mercy, maiden, does it curd thy blood
135 To say I am thy mother? What's the matter,
That this distempered° messenger of wet,°   *disturbed / rain; tears*
The many-colored Iris,[3] rounds thine eye?
Why? That you are my daughter?

HELEN   That I am not.

COUNTESS I say I am your mother.

HELEN   Pardon, madam.
140 The Count Roussillon cannot be my brother:
I am from humble, he from honored name;
No note° upon my parents, his all noble.   *distinction*
My master, my dear lord he is, and I
His servant live and will his vassal die.
He must not be my brother.

145 COUNTESS   Nor I your mother?

HELEN You are my mother, madam; would you were—
So° that my lord your son were not my brother—   *Provided*
Indeed my mother! Or were you both our mothers°   *mother of us both*
I care no more for than I do for heaven,
150 So I were not his sister. Can 't no other
But, I your daughter, he must be my brother?

COUNTESS Yes, Helen, you might be my daughter-in-law.
God shield you mean it not![4] "Daughter" and "mother"
So strive upon your pulse. What, pale again?
155 My fear hath catched your fondness!° Now I see   *love; folly*
The mystery of your loneliness and find
Your salt tears' head;° now to all sense 'tis gross:°   *source / obvious*
You love my son. Invention[5] is ashamed
Against° the proclamation of thy passion   *In the face of*
160 To say thou dost not. Therefore tell me true,
But tell me then 'tis so, for look, thy cheeks
Confess it t'one to th'other, and thine eyes
See it so grossly shown in thy behaviors
That in their kind° they speak it. Only sin   *after their fashion*
165 And hellish obstinacy tie thy tongue,
That truth should be suspected.° Speak, is't so?   *doubted*

---

2. *choice . . . seeds:* a twig chosen from foreign seed becomes, once engrafted, part of our plant.
3. Goddess of rainbows (Helen's tear-filled eyes are iridescent).
4. PERFORMANCE COMMENT The actor playing the Countess might pitch this speech as a stern prohibition or as a teasing fake-scolding; there are also a variety of ways Helen might respond. For a fuller discussion, see Digital Edition PC 1.
5. (Your) capacity to invent excuses.

If it be so, you have wound a goodly clew;[6]
If it be not, forswear't.° Howe'er,° I charge thee,   deny it / In any case
As heaven shall work in me for thine avail,°   benefit
To tell me truly.
170 HELEN   Good madam, pardon me.
COUNTESS Do you love my son?
HELEN   Your pardon, noble mistress.
COUNTESS Love you my son?
HELEN   Do not you love him, madam?
COUNTESS Go not about;[7] my love hath in't a bond
Whereof the world takes note.° Come, come: disclose   society recognizes
175 The state of your affection, for your passions
Have to the full appeached.°   informed against you
HELEN   Then I confess
Here on my knee, before high heaven and you,
That before you° and next unto high heaven,   even more than I love you
I love your son.
180 My friends° were poor but honest; so's my love.   relatives
Be not offended, for it hurts not him
That he is loved of me; I follow him not
By any token° of presumptuous suit,°   manifestations / wooing
Nor would I have him till I do deserve him,
185 Yet never know how that desert should be.
I know I love in vain, strive against hope:
Yet in this captious° and intenible° sieve   receptive / unretentive
I still° pour in the waters of my love   continually
And lack not to lose still.° Thus, Indian-like,   And keep losing it
190 Religious in mine error, I adore
The sun that looks upon his worshipper
But knows of him no more. My dearest madam,
Let not your hate encounter with° my love   oppose
For loving where you do; but if yourself,
195 Whose agèd honor cites° a virtuous youth,   testifies to
Did ever, in so true a flame of liking,
Wish chastely and love dearly, that your Dian
Was both herself and Love[8]—oh, then give pity
To her whose state is such that cannot choose
200 But lend and give where she is sure to lose;
That seeks not to find that° her search implies,   what
But riddle-like[9] lives sweetly where she dies.
COUNTESS Had you not lately an intent—speak truly—
To go to Paris?
HELEN   Madam, I had.
COUNTESS   Wherefore? Tell true.
205 HELEN I will tell truth; by grace itself I swear.
You know my father left me some prescriptions
Of rare and proved effects, such as his reading
And manifest° experience had collected   obvious
For general sovereignty;° and that he willed me   effectiveness
210 In heedfullest reservation° to bestow them,   With most sparing care
As notes whose faculties inclusive were

6. You have made a fine tangle of thread (mess).
7. Don't beat around the bush.
8. Venus, goddess of erotic love, is usually the antag-

onist of Diana, goddess of chastity; Helen's love reconciles them.
9. Paradoxically; retaining her secret.

More than they were in note.[1] Amongst the rest
There is a remedy, approved,° set down,   *tested*
To cure the desperate languishings whereof
215   The King is rendered lost.°   *held to be dying*
COUNTESS   This was your motive for Paris, was it? Speak.
HELEN   My lord your son made me to think of this;
Else Paris, and the medicine, and the King
Had from the conversation of my thoughts
Haply° been absent then.   *Perhaps*
220 COUNTESS   But think you, Helen,
If you should tender° your supposèd aid   *offer*
He would receive it? He and his physicians
Are of a° mind: he, that they cannot help him;   *one*
They, that they cannot help. How shall they credit
225 A poor unlearnèd virgin when the schools,
Emboweled° of their doctrine, have left off   *Emptied*
The danger to itself?
HELEN   There's something in't
More than my father's skill, which was the greatest
Of his profession, that his good receipt°   *prescription*
230 Shall for my legacy be sanctified
By th' luckiest stars in heaven. And would your honor
But give me leave to try success,° I'd venture   *test the outcome*
The well-lost life of mine on his grace's cure
By such a day, an hour.
COUNTESS   Dost thou believe't?
235 HELEN   Ay, madam, knowingly.[2]
COUNTESS   Why, Helen, thou shalt have my leave and love,
Means and attendants, and my loving greetings
To those of mine in court. I'll stay at home
And pray God's blessing into thy attempt.
240 Begone tomorrow, and be sure of this:
What I can help thee to, thou shalt not miss.°   *Exeunt.*   *lack*

2.1

Enter the KING *with diverse young* LORDS, *taking leave for
the Florentine war[, including* BERTRAM,] *Count Roussillon,*
PAROLES[, *and the two* LORDS DUMAINE]. *Flourish cornetts.*

KING   Farewell, young lords: these warlike principles°   *military precepts*
Do not throw from you. —And you, my lords,[1] farewell.
Share the advice betwixt you; if both gain all,
The gift doth stretch itself as 'tis received
And is enough for both.
5 FIRST LORD DUMAINE   'Tis our hope, sir,
After well-entered soldiers,[2] to return
And find your grace in health.
KING   No, no, it cannot be; and yet my heart
Will not confess he owes° the malady   *it owns*
10 That doth my life besiege. Farewell, young lords.

---

1. *As . . . note:* As prescriptions of greater powers
than were recognized.
2. Fully aware of what I am doing.
2.1 Location: The King's palace.

1. Presumably leaving to take the opposite side in
the war.
2. After we are well initiated as soldiers.

Whether I live or die, be you the sons
Of worthy Frenchmen. Let higher° Italy—   *northern*
Those bated° that inherit but the fall   *dwindled peoples*
Of the last monarchy³—see that you come
15   Not to woo honor but to wed it, when
The bravest questant° shrinks. Find what you seek,   *seeker*
That fame may cry you loud.° I say farewell.   *acclaim you loudly*
FIRST LORD DUMAINE   Health at your bidding serve your majesty.
KING   Those girls of Italy, take heed of them!
20   They say our French lack language to deny
If they demand.° Beware of being captives⁴   *request*
Before you serve.°   *(militarily)*
BOTH LORDS DUMAINE   Our hearts receive your warnings.
KING   Farewell. [*to some* LORDS *as he is helped aside*] Come
hither to me.
FIRST LORD DUMAINE [*to* BERTRAM]   O my sweet lord, that you
will stay behind us!
PAROLES   'Tis not his fault, the spark.°   *spirited person*
25   SECOND LORD DUMAINE   Oh, 'tis brave° wars!   *splendid*
PAROLES   Most admirable; I have seen those wars.
BERTRAM   I am commanded° here, and kept a coil° with   *(to stay) / fussed over*
"Too young," and "the next year," and "'tis too early."
PAROLES   An° thy mind stand to't, boy, steal away bravely.   *If*
30   BERTRAM   I shall stay here, the forehorse to a smock,⁵
Creaking my shoes on the plain masonry,⁶
Till honor be bought up° and no sword worn   *all acquired (by others)*
But one to dance with. By heaven, I'll steal away!
FIRST LORD DUMAINE   There's honor in the theft.
PAROLES   Commit it, Count.
35   SECOND LORD DUMAINE   I am your accessory,° and so farewell.   *accomplice*
BERTRAM   I grow° to you, and our parting is a tortured body.   *am deeply attached*
FIRST LORD DUMAINE   Farewell, Captain.
SECOND LORD DUMAINE   Sweet Monsieur Paroles!
PAROLES   Noble heroes, my sword and yours are kin, good
sparks and lustrous. A word, good mettles.° You shall find *spirits; sword blades*
40   in the regiment of the Spinii one Captain Spurio, with his
cicatrice,° an emblem of war, here on his sinister° cheek; it   *scar / left*
was this very sword entrenched it. Say to him I live, and
observe his reports° for me.   *note his reply*
FIRST LORD DUMAINE   We shall, noble captain.
45   PAROLES   Mars dote on you for his novices.
[*Exeunt the* LORDS DUMAINE.]
[*to* BERTRAM] What will ye do?
BERTRAM   Stay° the King.   *Await*
PAROLES   Use a more spacious ceremony° to the noble lords;   *expansive courtesy*
you have restrained yourself within the list° of too cold an   *limit*
50   adieu. Be more expressive to them. For they wear themselves in the cap of the time;⁷ there do muster true gait;⁸
eat, speak, and move under the influence of the most
received° star; and, though the devil lead the measure,°   *fashionable / dance*

3. Perhaps the Holy Roman Empire, the Medici, or   6. Level stonework (of the palace floors, in contrast
the papacy.   to the rough battlefield).
4. Of your mistresses.   7. Are ornaments of fashion.
5. Lead horse of a team driven by a woman (figura-   8. Display grace of movement.
tively, part of a dancing couple).

such are to be followed. After them, and take a more dilated°   *extended*
55   farewell.

BERTRAM   And I will do so.

PAROLES   Worthy fellows, and like to prove most sinewy
swordmen.   *Exeunt* [BERTRAM *and* PAROLES].

     Enter LAFEU [*to the* KING, *who is brought forward*].

LAFEU [*kneeling*]   Pardon, my lord, for me and for my tidings.

60   KING   I'll fee[9] thee to stand up.

LAFEU [*standing*]   Then here's a man stands that has brought
    his pardon.
I would you had kneeled, my lord, to ask me mercy,
And that at my bidding you could so stand up.

KING   I would I had, so I had broke thy pate°   *head*
And asked thee mercy for't.

65   LAFEU   Good faith, across![1]
But my good lord, 'tis thus. Will you be cured
Of your infirmity?

KING   No.

LAFEU   Oh, will you eat
No grapes, my royal fox?[2] Yes, but you will:
My noble grapes, an if° my royal fox   *an if = if*
70   Could reach them. I have seen a medicine°   *physician; remedy*
That's able to breathe life into a stone,
Quicken° a rock, and make you dance canary°   *Animate / a lively dance*
With sprightly fire and motion; whose simple° touch   *mere; medicinal herb*
Is powerful to araise King Pépin,[3] nay,
75   To give great Charlemagne[4] a pen in 's hand
And write to her a love line.

KING   What "her" is this?

LAFEU   Why, Doctor She. My lord, there's one arrived,
If you will see her—now by my faith and honor,
If seriously I may convey my thoughts
80   In this my light deliverance,° I have spoke   *mode of speaking*
With one that in her sex, her years, profession,°   *claims of skill*
Wisdom, and constancy, hath amazed me more
Than I dare blame my weakness.° Will you see her—   *(as an old man)*
For that is her demand—and know her business?
That done, laugh well at me.

85   KING   Now, good Lafeu,
Bring in the admiration,° that we with thee   *marvel*
May spend our wonder too, or take off thine
By wondering how thou took'st° it.   *came by*

LAFEU   Nay, I'll fit° you,   *satisfy*
And not be all day neither.

90   KING   Thus he his special nothing° ever prologues.   *trifles*

LAFEU [*going to the door*]   Nay, come your ways.°   *come along*

     Enter HELEN.

KING   This haste hath wings indeed.

LAFEU   Nay, come your ways.
This is his majesty; say your mind to him.
A traitor[5] you do look like, but such traitors

---

9. Pay (not merely "pardon").
1. A weak jest: in tilting, a blow "across" is a bad hit.
2. In Aesop, a fox pretends not to want a bunch of grapes he cannot reach.

3. Eighth-century French king.
4. Pépin's son, founder of the Holy Roman Empire.
5. Because she avoids the King's gaze.

95 His majesty seldom fears. I am Cressid's uncle,[6]
That dare leave two together. Fare you well.

Exeunt [all but KING *and* HELEN*]*.

KING Now, fair one, does your business follow us?

HELEN Ay, my good lord.
Gerard de Narbonne was my father,
In what he did profess, well found.°   *found to be good*

100 KING   I knew him.

HELEN The rather will I spare my praises towards him;
Knowing him is enough. On 's° bed of death   *On his*
Many receipts he gave me, chiefly one,
Which as the dearest issue[7] of his practice

105 And of his old experience th'only darling,
He bade me store up as a triple° eye,   *third*
Safer than mine own two. More dear I have so,
And hearing your high majesty is touched
With that malignant cause wherein the honor

110 Of my dear father's gift stands chief in power,[8]
I come to tender it and my appliance°   *treatment*
With all bound° humbleness.   *dutiful*

KING   We thank you, maiden,
But may not be so credulous of cure
When our most learnèd doctors leave us, and

115 The congregated college[9] have concluded
That laboring art° can never ransom nature   *medical skill*
From her inaidable estate.° I say we must not   *condition*
So stain our judgment or corrupt our hope
To prostitute° our past-cure malady   *submit*

120 To empirics,[1] or to dissever so
Our great self and our credit[2] to esteem
A senseless help,° when help past sense we deem.   *An unbelievable cure*

HELEN My duty then shall pay me for my pains.
I will no more enforce mine office° on you,   *service*

125 Humbly entreating from your royal thoughts
A modest one[3] to bear me back again.

KING I cannot give thee less to be called grateful.
Thou thought'st to help me, and such thanks I give
As one near death to those that wish him live.

130 But what at full I know, thou know'st no part:°   *not at all*
I knowing all my peril, thou art.

HELEN What I can do can do no hurt to try,
Since you set up your rest° 'gainst remedy.   *stake everything*
He that of greatest works is finisher

135 Oft does them by the weakest minister.
So Holy Writ in babes hath judgment shown
When judges have been babes.[4] Great floods have flown

---

6. Pandarus, the go-between for Troilus and Cressida and archetypal pimp.
7. Best product; favorite child.
8. *malignant . . . power:* disease for which my father's honored gift is most effective.
9. Assembled College of Physicians.
1. Physicians whose methods were based on experience rather than on medical theory. In early modern Europe, "theoretical" practitioners, like the members of the French College of Physicians, often considered their "empirical" colleagues mere quacks; the "empirics" usually hailed from lower social classes and had less formal education.
2. *to dissever . . . credit:* to open such a gap between my royal station and my gullibility.
3. A favorable thought appropriate to a woman and a subject.
4. *So . . . babes:* "Thou hast hid these things from the wise and men of understanding, and hast opened them unto babes" (Matthew 11:25).

From simple sources, and great seas have dried
When miracles have by the greatest been denied.
140 Oft expectation fails, and most oft there
Where most it promises; and oft it hits°   succeeds
Where hope is coldest and despair most fits.
KING   I must not hear thee. Fare thee well, kind maid;
Thy pains not used must by thyself be paid.
145 Proffers not took reap thanks° for their reward.   only thanks
HELEN   Inspired merit so by breath is barred.[5]
It is not so with Him that all things knows
As 'tis with us that square our guess by shows.[6]
But most it is presumption in us when
150 The help of heaven we count the act of men.
Dear sir, to my endeavors give consent;
Of heaven, not me, make an experiment.
I am not an impostor that proclaim
Myself against the level of mine aim,[7]
155 But know I think, and think I know most sure,
My art is not past° power, nor you past cure.   without
KING   Art thou so confident? Within what space
Hop'st thou my cure?
HELEN   The greatest grace lending grace,
Ere twice the horses of the sun shall bring
160 Their fiery torcher his diurnal ring;°   daily round
Ere twice in murk and occidental damp
Moist Hesperus° hath quenched her sleepy lamp,   the evening star
Or four-and-twenty times the pilot's glass°   hourglass
Hath told the thievish minutes, how they pass,
165 What is infirm from your sound parts shall fly;
Health shall live free and sickness freely die.
KING   Upon thy certainty and confidence
What dar'st thou venture?°   risk
HELEN   Tax° of impudence;   Accusation
A strumpet's boldness; a divulgèd shame
170 Traduced by odious ballads; my maiden's name
Seared.[8] Otherwise, no worse of worst, extended[9]
With vilest torture let my life be ended.
KING   Methinks in thee some blessèd spirit doth speak
His powerful sound within an organ weak,
175 And what impossibility would slay
In common sense, sense saves another way.[1]
Thy life is dear, for all that life can rate
Worth name of life in thee hath estimate:°   is present
Youth, beauty, wisdom, courage, all
180 That happiness and prime[2] can happy call.
Thou this to hazard needs must intimate[3]
Skill infinite or monstrous desperate.
Sweet practicer,° thy physic I will try   practitioner; schemer
That ministers thine own death if I die.

5. Divinely inspired virtue is thus denied by human
speech.
6. Who base our conjectures on appearances.
7. *proclaim . . . aim:* boast in advance of the accuracy
of my aim; declare myself to be different from what I
am.

8. Branded (like a criminal).
9. Prolonged; stretched on the rack.
1. *sense . . . way:* makes sense in another, uncommon
way.
2. That good fortune and the springtime of life.
3. For you to risk this must suggest.

185 HELEN If I break time or flinch in property[4]
        Of what I spoke, unpitied let me die,
        And well deserved. Not helping, death's my fee,
        But if I help, what do you promise me?
      KING Make thy demand.
      HELEN   But will you make it even?°   *satisfy it*
190   KING Ay, by my scepter and my hopes of heaven.
      HELEN Then shalt thou give me with thy kingly hand
        What husband in thy power I will command.
        Exempted be from me the arrogance
        To choose from forth the royal blood of France,
195   My low and humble name to propagate
        With any branch or image of thy state;°   *royal place*
        But such a one, thy vassal, whom I know
        Is free for me to ask, thee to bestow.
      KING Here is my hand. The premises observed,°   *conditions fulfilled*
200   Thy will by my performance shall be served.
        So make the choice of thy own time, for I,
        Thy resolvèd patient, on thee still° rely.   *always*
        More should I question thee, and more I must,
        Though more to know could not be more to trust—
205   From whence thou cam'st? how tended on?°—but rest   *attended*
        Unquestioned[5] welcome and undoubted blest.
        [*He calls.*] Give me some help here, ho! —If thou proceed
        As high as word, my deed shall match thy deed.
                                        Flourish. Exeunt.

2.2

Enter COUNTESS *and* CLOWN.

      COUNTESS Come on, sir, I shall now put you to the height of
        your breeding.[1]
      CLOWN I will show myself highly fed and lowly taught.[2] I
        know my business is but to the court.
5   COUNTESS To the court! Why, what place make you special,
        when you put off° that with such contempt? "But to the   *dismiss*
        court"!
      CLOWN Truly, madam, if God have lent a man any manners,
        he may easily put it off° at court. He that cannot make a leg,   *lose it; take it off*
10   put off 's cap, kiss his hand, and say nothing, has neither
        leg,° hands, lip, nor cap; and indeed such a fellow, to say   *bow*
        precisely, were not for the court. But for me, I have an
        answer will serve all men.
      COUNTESS Marry, that's a bountiful answer that fits all
15   questions.
      CLOWN It is like a barber's chair that fits all buttocks: the pin° *pointed*
        buttock, the quatch°-buttock, the brawn buttock, or any   *fat*
        buttock.
      COUNTESS Will your answer serve fit to all questions?
20   CLOWN As fit as ten groats is for the hand of an attorney, as
        your French crown[3] for your taffeta punk,° as Tib's rush[4]   *prostitute*

---

4. If I fail to meet the deadline or fall short in the
particulars.
5. Not having been asked; unquestionably.
2.2 Location: Bertram's palace.
1. Make you display your best manners.
2. Spoiled children were called "better fed than

taught."
3. Coin; bald head (from syphilis, the "French
disease").
4. Reed twisted into a ring for use in folk marriage,
with sexual innuendo.

for Tom's forefinger, as a pancake[5] for Shrove Tuesday, a
morris° for May Day, as the nail to his hole, the cuckold to   *morris dance*
his horn, as a scolding quean° to a wrangling knave, as the   *whore*
25 nun's lip to the friar's mouth—nay, as the pudding° to his   *sausage*
skin.
COUNTESS Have you, I say, an answer of such fitness for all
questions?
CLOWN From below your duke to beneath your constable, it
30 will fit any question.
COUNTESS It must be an answer of most monstrous size that
must fit all demands.
CLOWN But a trifle neither,° in good faith, if the learned   *No, just a trifle*
should speak truth of it. Here it is, and all that belongs to't.
35 Ask me if I am a courtier: it shall do you no harm to learn.
COUNTESS To be young again if we could! I will be a fool in
question, hoping to be the wiser by your answer. I pray you,
sir, are you a courtier?
CLOWN O Lord, sir![6] —There's a simple putting off. More,
40 more, a hundred of them.
COUNTESS Sir, I am a poor friend of yours that loves you.
CLOWN O Lord, sir! —Thick,° thick, spare not me.   *Quick*
COUNTESS I think, sir, you can eat none of this homely° meat.   *plain*
CLOWN O Lord, sir. —Nay, put me to't, I warrant you.
45 COUNTESS You were lately whipped, sir, as I think.
CLOWN O Lord, sir. —Spare not me.
COUNTESS Do you cry "O Lord, sir" at your whipping, and
"Spare not me"? Indeed your "O Lord, sir" is very sequent[7]
to your whipping; you would answer very well[8] to a whipping
50 if you were but bound to't.[9]
CLOWN I ne'er had worse luck in my life in my "O Lord, sir." I
see things may serve long but not serve ever.
COUNTESS I play the noble housewife° with the time, to   *good steward (ironic)*
entertain it so merrily with a fool.
55 CLOWN O Lord, sir! Why, there't serves well again.
COUNTESS An end, sir. To your business.
        [*She hands him a letter.*]
                                          Give Helen this,
And urge her to a present° answer back.   *immediate*
Commend me to my kinsmen and my son.
This is not much.
60 CLOWN Not much commendation to them.
COUNTESS Not much employment for you. You understand me?
CLOWN Most fruitfully. I am there before my legs.
COUNTESS Haste you again.°   *Exeunt.*   *back again*

2.3

Enter Count [BERTRAM], LAFEU [*holding a broadside*],°   *paper proclamation*
and PAROLES.

LAFEU They say miracles are past, and we have our philosophical persons to make modern and familiar things supernatural

---

5. Traditionally eaten on Shrove Tuesday, the day
before the beginning of Lent.
6. A voguish catchphrase that evades an answer by
appearing to wonder at the question. *putting off:*
evasion.

7. Follows naturally upon (as a plea for mercy).
8. Reply cleverly to; be a fitting recipient of.
9. Required to answer; tied to a whipping post.
2.3 Location: The King's palace.

and causeless.[1] Hence is it that we make trifles of terrors,
ensconcing ourselves into° seeming knowledge when we   *sheltering ourselves with*
5   should submit ourselves to an unknown fear.°   *awe of the unknown*

PAROLES   Why, 'tis the rarest argument° of wonder that hath   *best instance*
shot out in our latter° times.   *recent*

BERTRAM   And so 'tis.

LAFEU   To be relinquished of the artists[2]—

10 PAROLES   So I say, both of Galen and Paracelsus[3]—

LAFEU   Of all the learned and authentic fellows[4]—

PAROLES   Right, so I say.

LAFEU   That gave him out incurable—

PAROLES   Why, there 'tis! So say I too.

15 LAFEU   Not to be helped—

PAROLES   Right, as 'twere a man assured of a—

LAFEU   Uncertain life and sure death.

PAROLES   Just.° You say well. So would I have said.   *Exactly*

LAFEU   I may truly say it is a novelty to the world.

20 PAROLES   It is indeed. If you will have it in showing,° you shall   *demonstrated*
read it in what-do-ye-call there.

LAFEU [*reading from the broadside*]   "A showing of a heavenly
effect in an earthly actor."

PAROLES   That's it. I would have said the very same.

25 LAFEU   Why, your dolphin[5] is not lustier.° For me, I speak in   *more sportive*
respect°—   *respectfully*

PAROLES   Nay, 'tis strange, 'tis very strange, that is the brief°   *short*
and the tedious° of it, and he's of a most facinorous° spirit   *long / wicked*
that will not acknowledge it to be the—

30 LAFEU   Very hand of heaven.

PAROLES   Ay, so I say.

LAFEU   In a most weak—

PAROLES   And debile minister,° great power, great transcen-   *feeble agent*
dence, which should indeed give us a further use to be made
35 than alone the recovery of the King, as to be—

LAFEU   Generally° thankful.   *Universally*

Enter KING, HELEN, *and* ATTENDANTS.

PAROLES   I would have said it; you say well. Here comes the
King.

LAFEU   *Lustig,*° as the Dutchman says. I'll like a maid the bet-   *Frolicsome*
40 ter whilst I have a tooth in my head.[6] Why, he's able to lead
her a coranto.°   *running dance*

PAROLES   *Mort du vinaigre,*[7] is not this Helen?

LAFEU   Fore God, I think so.

KING   Go, call before me all the lords in court.

[*Exit an* ATTENDANT.]

45   Sit, my preserver, by thy patient's side,
And with this healthful hand whose banished sense°   *sense of feeling*
Thou hast repealed,° a second time receive   *restored*
The confirmation of my promised gift,
Which but attends° thy naming.   *awaits*

---

1. To make supernatural things, without apparent
cause, seem commonplace and easily explained.
2. Abandoned by the scholars.
3. Galen was a second-century Greek physician, the
traditional medical authority; Paracelsus was a
sixteenth-century Swiss physician who tried to reform
Galen's teachings.

4. Accredited members of the College of Physicians.
5. Punning on "dauphin," heir to the French throne.
6. *whilst . . . head:* so long as I have a taste for pleasure ("sweet tooth"); until I've degenerated into complete senility.
7. Death of the vinegar—a pseudo-French oath.

Enter four LORDS.

50 Fair maid, send forth thine eye. This youthful parcel°   *group*
Of noble bachelors stand at my bestowing,[8]
O'er whom both sovereign power and father's voice
I have to use. Thy frank election° make;   *free choice*
Thou hast power to choose, and they none to forsake.

55 HELEN   To each of you, one fair and virtuous mistress
Fall[9] when love please; marry, to each but one.
LAFEU   I'd give bay Curtal and his furniture[1]
My mouth no more were broken[2] than these boys'
And writ° as little beard.   *laid claim to*
KING   Peruse them well:
60 Not one of those but had a noble father.
She addresses her to a LORD.[3]
HELEN   Gentlemen,
Heaven hath through me restored the King to health.
ALL LORDS   We understand it, and thank heaven for you.
HELEN   I am a simple maid, and therein wealthiest
65 That I protest I simply am a maid.
—Please it your majesty, I have done already.
The blushes in my cheeks thus whisper me,
"We blush that thou shouldst choose but, be° refused,   *if you are*
Let the white death sit on thy cheek for ever,
We'll ne'er come there again."
70 KING   Make choice and see;
Who shuns thy love shuns all his love in me.
HELEN   Now Dian from thy altar do I fly,
And to imperial Love, that god most high,
Do my sighs stream. [*to* FIRST LORD] Sir, will you hear my suit?
FIRST LORD   And grant it.
75 HELEN   Thanks, sir; all the rest is mute.°   *I will say no more*
LAFEU [*aside*]   I had rather be in this choice than throw
ambsace[4] for my life.
HELEN [*to* SECOND LORD]   The honor, sir, that flames in your
fair eyes,[5]
Before I speak too threat'ningly replies.
80 Love make your fortunes twenty times above
Her that so wishes,° and her humble love.   *makes this wish*
SECOND LORD   No better, if you please.
HELEN   My wish receive,
Which great love grant; and so I take my leave.
LAFEU [*aside*]   Do all they deny her?[6] An they were sons of
85 mine, I'd have them whipped, or I would send them to th'
Turk to make eunuchs of.
HELEN [*to* THIRD LORD]   Be not afraid that I your hand should take;
I'll never do you wrong for your own sake.
Blessing upon your vows,° and in your bed   *marriage vows*
90 Find fairer fortune if you ever wed.

---

8. Are in my power to bestow (because they are his wards).
9. Befall, with the suggestion of a sexual "fall."
1. I'd give my dock-tailed bay horse and his trappings.
2. Contained broken teeth; of a boy's voice, "broken" at puberty; of a horse, "broken" to the bit.
3. TEXTUAL COMMENT In the Folio text this stage direction is possibly misplaced. See Digital Edition

TC 5.
4. Two aces (the lowest throw in dice); a joking understatement.
5. The pride of rank that shows in your look.
6. Either Lafeu, standing apart, misunderstands what is happening, or (less probably) the Lords' polite replies are belied by their evident relief when Helen rejects them.

LAFEU [*aside*]   These boys are boys of ice, they'll none have
her. Sure they are bastards to the English; the French ne'er
got° 'em.　　　　　　　　　　　　　　　　　　　　　　　　　　*begot*

HELEN [*to* FOURTH LORD]   You are too young, too happy, and
too good

95　　To make yourself a son out of my blood.

FOURTH LORD   Fair one, I think not so.

LAFEU [*aside*]   There's one grape° yet! I am sure thy father　　*fruit of a noble stock*
drunk wine.[7] But if thou be'st not an ass, I am a youth of
fourteen: I have known° thee already.　　　　　　　　　　　　　*found out*

100　HELEN [*to* BERTRAM]   I dare not say I take you, but I give
Me and my service, ever whilst I live,
Into your guiding power. [*to the* KING] This is the man.

KING   Why, then, young Bertram, take her; she's thy wife.

BERTRAM   My wife, my liege? I shall beseech your highness:

105　　In such a business give me leave to use
The help of mine own eyes.

KING　　　　　　　　　　　　Know'st thou not, Bertram,
What she has done for me?

BERTRAM　　　　　　　　　Yes, my good lord,
But never hope° to know why I should marry her.　　　　　　　*expect*

KING   Thou know'st she has raised me from my sickly bed.

110　BERTRAM   But follows it, my lord, to bring me down
Must answer for your raising? I know her well:
She had her breeding° at my father's charge.　　　　　　　　*upbringing*
A poor physician's daughter my wife? Disdain
Rather corrupt° me ever!　　　　　　　　　　　　　　　　　　　*ruin*

115　KING   'Tis only title° thou disdain'st in her, the which　　　　*rank*
I can build up. Strange is it that our bloods
Of color, weight, and heat, poured all together,
Would quite confound distinction,[8] yet stands off°　　　　　*is separated*
In differences so mighty. If she be

120　All that is virtuous, save what thou dislik'st—
"A poor physician's daughter"—thou dislik'st
Of virtue for the name.° But do not so:　　　　　　　　　　*(lack of) a title*
From lowest place when virtuous things proceed
The place is dignified by th' doer's deed.

125　Where great additions swell 's° and virtue none,　　　　　*titles swell us up*
It is a dropsied[9] honor. Good alone°　　　　　　　　　　　*in itself*
Is good without a name. Vileness is so;
The property° by what it is should go,　　　　　　　　　　　*quality*
Not by the title. She is young, wise, fair;

130　In these to nature she's immediate heir,
And these breed honor. That is honor's scorn
Which challenges° itself as honor's born　　　　　　　　　　*makes claims for*
And is not like the sire. Honors thrive
When rather from our acts we them derive

135　Than our foregoers. The mere word's a slave
Debauched° on every tomb, on every grave　　　　　　　　　*Debased*
A lying trophy,° and as oft is dumb　　　　　　　　　　　　　*memorial*
Where dust and damned° oblivion is the tomb　　　　　　　　*stopped-up*

---

7. Was red-blooded (wine was supposed to turn
directly into blood).　　　　　　8. Confuse the effort to distinguish.
　　　　　　　　　　　　　　　　9. Unhealthily swollen.

140　Of honored bones indeed. What should be said?
If thou canst like this creature as a maid,
I can create the rest. Virtue and she
Is her own dower;[1] honor and wealth from me.

BERTRAM　I cannot love her, nor will strive° to do't.　　　　*attempt*

KING　Thou wrong'st thyself if thou shouldst strive to choose.

145　HELEN　That you are well restored, my lord, I'm glad.
Let the rest go.

KING　My honor's at the stake, which to defeat
I must produce my power. Here, take her hand,
Proud, scornful boy, unworthy this good gift,

150　That dost in vile misprision° shackle up　　　　*wrongful disdain*
My love and her desert; that canst not dream
We, poising us in her defective scale,
Shall weigh thee to the beam;[2] that wilt not know
It is in us° to plant thine honor where　　　　*in our power*

155　We please to have it grow. Check° thy contempt;　　　　*Restrain*
Obey our will, which travails in° thy good;　　　　*labors for*
Believe not thy disdain, but presently
Do thine own fortunes that obedient right
Which both thy duty owes and our power claims,

160　Or I will throw thee from my care forever
Into the staggers[3] and the careless lapse°　　　　*fall; ruin*
Of youth and ignorance, both my revenge and hate
Loosing upon thee in the name of justice,
Without all terms of° pity. Speak! Thine answer!　　　　*any concessions to*

165　BERTRAM　Pardon, my gracious lord, for I submit
My fancy° to your eyes. When I consider　　　　*perceptions; affection*
What great creation[4] and what dole° of honor　　　　*portion*
Flies where you bid it, I find that she which late
Was in my nobler thoughts most base is now

170　The praisèd of the King, who, so ennobled,
Is as 'twere born so.

KING　　　　　　Take her by the hand
And tell her she is thine, to whom I promise
A counterpoise, if not to thy estate,
A balance more replete.[5]

BERTRAM　　　　　　I take her hand.

175　KING　Good fortune and the favor of the King
Smile upon this contract, whose ceremony
Shall seem expedient on the now-born brief[6]
And be performed tonight; the solemn feast
Shall more attend upon the coming space,

180　Expecting absent friends.[7] As thou lov'st her,
Thy love's to me religious:° else, does err.　　　　*properly devoted*

*Exeunt [all but] PAROLES and LAFEU[, who] stay
behind, commenting of this wedding.*

LAFEU　Do you hear, monsieur? A word with you.

---

1. *Virtue . . . dower:* Her own marriage gift is virtue and herself.
2. *We . . . beam:* Adding my weight to her deficient side of the balance shall raise your (lighter) side. (The King uses the royal plural.)
3. Confusion (literally, a horse disease).
4. Creating of greatness.
5. *A counterpoise . . . replete:* A dowry equal to, if not greater than, your own estate.
6. Shall expedite this newly made decree.
7. *the solemn . . . friends:* The wedding reception will be postponed until relatives and friends can arrive.

PAROLES   Your pleasure, sir.

LAFEU   Your lord and master did well to make his recantation.

185   PAROLES   Recantation? My lord? My master?

LAFEU   Ay. Is it not a language I speak?

PAROLES   A most harsh one, and not to be understood without bloody succeeding.° My master? — consequences

LAFEU   Are you companion to the Count Roussillon?

190   PAROLES   To any count; to all counts; to what is man.° — whatever is manly

LAFEU   To what is count's man;° count's master is of another style. — servant

PAROLES   You are too old, sir; let it satisfy you,[8] you are too old!

LAFEU   I must tell thee, sirrah, I write man,[9] to which title
195   age cannot bring thee.

PAROLES   What I dare too well do, I dare not do.[1]

LAFEU   I did think thee, for two ordinaries,° to be a pretty — meals
wise fellow; thou didst make tolerable vent° of thy travel—it — talk passably
might pass. Yet the scarves and the bannerets[2] about thee
200   did manifoldly dissuade me from believing thee a vessel of
too great a burden.° I have now found thee;[3] when I lose — tonnage
thee again, I care not. Yet art thou good for nothing but taking up,[4] and that thou'rt scarce worth.

PAROLES   Hadst thou not the privilege of antiquity[5] upon thee—

205   LAFEU   Do not plunge thyself too far in anger, lest thou hasten thy trial; which if, lord have mercy on thee for a hen! So,
my good window of lattice,[6] fare thee well; thy casement I
need not open, for I look through thee. Give me thy hand.

PAROLES   My lord, you give me most egregious indignity.

210   LAFEU   Ay, with all my heart, and thou art worthy of it.

PAROLES   I have not, my lord, deserved it.

LAFEU   Yes, good faith, ev'ry dram° of it, and I will not bate° — one-eighth of
thee a scruple.° — an ounce / remit
 — one-third of a dram

PAROLES   Well, I shall be wiser.

215   LAFEU   E'en as soon as thou canst, for thou hast to pull at a
smack o'th' contrary.[7] If ever thou be'st bound in thy scarf
and beaten, thou shall find what it is to be proud of thy
bondage. I have a desire to hold° my acquaintance with — maintain
thee, or rather my knowledge, that I may say in the default,° — in the event
220   "He is a man I know."

PAROLES   My lord, you do me most insupportable vexation.

LAFEU   I would it were hell-pains for thy sake, and my poor
doing[8] eternal. For doing[9] I am past—as I will by thee, in
what motion age will give me leave.   *Exit.*

225   PAROLES   Well, thou hast a son shall take this disgrace off
me. Scurvy, old, filthy, scurvy lord! Well, I must be patient;
there is no fettering of authority. I'll beat him, by my life, if
I can meet him with any convenience, an° he were double — if
and double a lord. I'll have no more pity of his age than I

---

8. Don't force me to avenge your insult.
9. I claim myself to be a man.
1. What I have the courage for (that is, fighting), your age prevents me from doing.
2. Streamers (which remind Lafeu of a ship's pennants).
3. Discovered what you are.
4. Rebuking; arresting; drafting as a soldier.

5. Exemption (from combat) because of age.
6. Paroles is easily seen through despite his affectation; his fancy "latticework" of scarves suggests a lattice window.
7. *pull . . . contrary:* drink a quantity of the opposite quality.
8. My poor attempt to vex you.
9. Activity (with sexual suggestion).

230 would have of—I'll beat him, an if I could but meet him
again!

        Enter LAFEU.

LAFEU   Sirrah, your lord and master's married; there's news
for you! You have a new mistress.

PAROLES   I most unfainedly beseech your lordship to make
235 some reservation of your wrongs.° He is my good lord; whom   *restrain your abuse*
I serve above is my master.

LAFEU   Who? God?

PAROLES   Ay, sir.

LAFEU   The devil it is that's thy master. Why dost thou garter
240 up[1] thy arms o'this fashion? Dost make hose of thy sleeves?
Do other servants so? Thou wert best set thy lower part
where thy nose stands. By mine honor, if I were but two
hours younger, I'd beat thee. Methink'st thou art a general
offense,° and every man should beat thee. I think thou wast   *public nuisance*
245 created for men to breathe° themselves upon thee.   *exercise*

PAROLES   This is hard and undeserved measure, my lord.

LAFEU   Go to, sir: you were beaten in Italy for picking a kernel
out of a pomegranate.[2] You are a vagabond and no true traveler. You are more saucy with lords and honorable person-
250 ages than the commission° of your birth and virtue gives you   *warrant*
heraldry.° You are not worth another word, else I'd call you   *entitles you*
knave. I leave you.   *Exit.*

        Enter [BERTRAM,] *Count Roussillon.*

PAROLES   Good, very good. It is so, then. Good, very good. Let
it be concealed awhile.

255 BERTRAM   Undone and forfeited to cares forever!

PAROLES   What's the matter, sweet heart?

BERTRAM   Although before the solemn priest I have sworn,
I will not bed her.

PAROLES   What? What, sweet heart?

BERTRAM   O my Paroles, they have married me!
260 I'll to the Tuscan wars and never bed her.

PAROLES   France is a dog-hole, and it no more merits
The tread of a man's foot. To th' wars!

BERTRAM   There's letters from my mother: what th'import is,
I know not yet.

PAROLES   Ay, that would be known.
265 To th' wars, my boy, to th' wars!
He wears his honor in a box unseen°   *(with sexual innuendo)*
That hugs his kicky-wicky° here at home,   *darling*
Spending his manly marrow in her arms
Which should sustain the bound and high curvet°   *leap*
270 Of Mars's fiery steed. To other regions!
France is a stable, we that dwell in't jades;[3]
Therefore, to th' war.

BERTRAM   It shall be so. I'll send her to my house;
Acquaint my mother with my hate to her
275 And wherefore I am fled; write to the King

---

1. Tie up (commenting again on Paroles' outfit).
2. *for picking . . . pomegranate:* on the slightest
pretext.
3. Worthless horses; sluts. Paroles considers staying
in France effeminating.

That which I durst not speak. His present gift[4]
Shall furnish me to° those Italian fields   *equip me for*
Where noble fellows strike. Wars is no strife
To° the dark house and the detested wife.   *Compared to*
280   PAROLES   Will this capriccio° hold in thee, art sure?   *caprice*
      BERTRAM   Go with me to my chamber and advise me.
      I'll send her straight away. Tomorrow
      I'll to the wars, she to her single sorrow.
      PAROLES   Why, these balls bound;[5] there's noise in it. 'Tis hard:
285   A young man married is a man that's marred.
      Therefore away and leave her bravely. Go.
      The King has done you wrong, but hush 'tis so.°   *Exeunt.*   *but don't say so*

2.4

Enter HELEN[, *with a letter,*] *and* CLOWN.
      HELEN   My mother greets me kindly. Is she well?
      CLOWN   She is not well,[1] but yet she has her health. She's very
      merry, but yet she is not well. But, thanks be given, she's very
      well and wants° nothing i'th' world. But yet she is not well.   *lacks*
5   HELEN   If she be very well, what does she ail that she's not
      very well?
      CLOWN   Truly, she's very well indeed, but for two things.
      HELEN   What two things?
      CLOWN   One, that she's not in heaven, whither God send her
10   quickly; the other, that she's in earth, from whence God
      send her quickly.
      Enter PAROLES.
      PAROLES   Bless you, my fortunate lady.
      HELEN   I hope, sir, I have your good will to have mine own
      good fortunes.
15   PAROLES   You had my prayers to lead them° on, and to keep   *(your good fortunes)*
      them on have them still. —O my knave, how does my old
      lady?
      CLOWN   So that you had her wrinkles and I her money, I
      would she did[2] as you say.
20   PAROLES   Why, I say nothing.
      CLOWN   Marry, you are the wiser man, for many a man's°   *servant's*
      tongue shakes out[3] his master's undoing. To say nothing, to
      do nothing, to know nothing, and to have nothing, is to be
      a great part of your title,[4] which is within a very little of
25   nothing.
      PAROLES   Away, thou'rt a knave.
      CLOWN   You should have said, sir, "Before[5] a knave, thou'rt a
      knave"; that's "before me[6] thou'rt a knave." This had been
      truth, sir.
30   PAROLES   Go to, thou art a witty fool. I have found° thee.   *seen through*
      CLOWN   Did you find me in yourself, sir, or were you taught to
      find me?
      PAROLES   In[7] myself.

---

4. Wedding present just bestowed.
5. Are bouncing now (from tennis); that is, that's how it should be done.
2.4 Location: Scene continues.
1. The dead were said to be well, because in heaven.
2. Perhaps playing on "died."
3. Inadvertently tumbles out.

4. Status; playing on "tittle," "tiny amount."
5. Even in comparison with; in the presence of.
6. An expression like "Upon my soul"; the Clown insinuates that Paroles is another knave.
7. By (reinterpreted in lines 34–35 by the Clown). This speech is not in F, but clearly some such reply should go here.

CLOWN   The search, sir, was profitable, and much fool may
35   you find in you, even to the world's pleasure and the increase
of laughter.
PAROLES   A good knave, i'faith, and well fed.°   *"better fed than taught"*
—Madam, my lord will go away tonight;
A very serious business calls on him.
40   The great prerogative and rite of love,
Which as your due time claims, he does acknowledge,
But puts it off to a compelled restraint,
Whose want, and whose delay, is strewed with sweets
Which they distill now in the curbèd time,[8]
45   To make the coming hour o'erflow with joy
And pleasure drown the brim.
HELEN   What's his will else?
PAROLES   That you will take your instant leave o'th' King
And make° this haste as your own good proceeding,   *represent*
Strengthened with what apology you think
May make it probable need.[9]
50   HELEN   What more commands he?
PAROLES   That having this obtained, you presently
Attend° his further pleasure.°   *Await / command*
HELEN   In everything I wait upon his will.
PAROLES   I shall report it so.   *Exit* PAROLES.
55   HELEN   I pray you come, sirrah.   *Exeunt.*

2.5

Enter LAFEU *and* BERTRAM.

LAFEU   But I hope your lordship thinks not him a soldier.
BERTRAM   Yes, my lord, and of very valiant approof.°   *proven value*
LAFEU   You have it from his own deliverance.°   *report*
BERTRAM   And by other warranted testimony.
5   LAFEU   Then my dial° goes not true. I took this lark for a   *clock*
bunting.[1]
BERTRAM   I do assure you, my lord, he is very great in knowl-
edge and accordingly° valiant.   *correspondingly*
LAFEU   I have, then, sinned against his experience and trans-
10   gressed against his valor, and my state that way is dangerous,[2] since I cannot yet find in my heart to repent. Here he
comes. I pray you make us friends: I will pursue the amity.

Enter PAROLES.

PAROLES [*to* BERTRAM]   These things shall be done, sir.
LAFEU   Pray you, sir, who's his tailor?[3]
15   PAROLES   Sir?
LAFEU   Oh, I know him well.[4] Ay, "Sir," he. Sir's a good work-
man, a very good tailor.
BERTRAM [*aside to* PAROLES]   Is she gone to the King?
PAROLES [*aside to* BERTRAM]   She is.
20   BERTRAM [*aside to* PAROLES]   Will she away tonight?
PAROLES [*aside to* BERTRAM]   As you'll have her.

---

8. *whose delay . . . time:* the delay of which multiplies
its sweetness, as distillation intensifies perfumes.
9. May make the need for haste probable.
2.5 Location: Scene continues.
1. I underestimated him (since the bunting looks

like a lark but does not sing).
2. In that respect risks damnation.
3. Mocking Paroles' clothes.
4. Lafeu pretends "Sir" is the tailor's name.

BERTRAM [*aside to* PAROLES]　I have writ my letters, casketed
　　　my treasure,
　　Given order for our horses, and tonight,
　　When I should take possession of the bride,
25　End ere I do begin.
LAFEU [*aside*]　A good traveler is something° at the latter end　　　*an asset*
　　of a dinner,[5] but one that lies three thirds° and uses a　　　*i.e., in all things*
　　known truth to pass a thousand nothings with should be
　　once heard and thrice beaten. —God save you, captain.
30　BERTRAM [*to* PAROLES]　Is there any unkindness between my
　　lord and you, monsieur?
PAROLES　I know not how I have deserved to run into my
　　lord's displeasure.
LAFEU　You have made shift° to run into't, boots and spurs and　　　*arranged*
35　all. Like him that leaped into the custard[6] and out of it, you'll
　　run again rather than suffer question for your residence.[7]
BERTRAM　It may be you have mistaken him, my lord.
LAFEU　And shall do so ever, though I took him at 's prayers.
　　Fare you well, my lord, and believe this of me: there can be
40　no kernel in this light nut. The soul of this man is his
　　clothes; trust him not in matter of heavy° consequence. I　　　*serious*
　　have kept of them tame[8] and know their natures. —Fare-
　　well, monsieur, I have spoken better of you than you have
　　or will[9] to deserve at my hand, but we must do good against
45　evil.　　　　　　　　　　　　　　　　　　　　　　[*Exit.*]
PAROLES　An idle lord, I swear.
BERTRAM　I think not so.
PAROLES　Why, do you not know him?
BERTRAM　Yes, I do know him well, and common speech
　　Gives him a worthy pass.°　　　　　　　　　　　　　　*report*
　　　　　　　Enter HELEN.
50　　　　　　　　　　　　Here comes my clog.[1]
HELEN　I have, sir, as I was commanded from you,
　　Spoke with the King and have procured his leave
　　For present parting. Only he desires
　　Some private speech with you.
BERTRAM　　　　　　　　　　　I shall obey his will.
55　You must not marvel, Helen, at my course,
　　Which holds not color° with the time nor does　　　*is not in keeping*
　　The ministration and required office
　　On my particular.[2] Prepared I was not
　　For such a business; therefore am I found
60　So much unsettled. This drives me to entreat you
　　That presently you take your way for home
　　And rather muse° than ask why I entreat you,　　　*wonder*
　　For my respects° are better than they seem,　　　*reasons*
　　And my appointments° have in them a need　　　*purposes*
65　Greater than shows itself at the first view
　　To you that know them not. [*He gives her a letter.*] This
　　　to my mother;
　　'Twill be two days ere I shall see you. So

5. When stories are welcome.
6. At the annual Lord Mayor's feast in London, a jester leaped into an enormous custard pie.
7. Rather than explain how you got there.
8. These kinds of tame animals.

9. The intelligence or intention.
1. Weighty fetter, "ball and chain."
2. *The ministration . . . particular:* The particular duty incumbent on me (as a husband).

I leave you to your wisdom.

HELEN   Sir, I can nothing say
But that I am your most obedient servant—

BERTRAM   Come, come, no more of that.

70 HELEN   And ever shall
With true observance° seek to eke out that   dutiful service
Wherein toward me my homely stars° have failed   humble birth
To equal my great fortune.

BERTRAM   Let that go.
My haste is very great. Farewell. Hie° home.   Hurry

HELEN   Pray, sir, your pardon.

75 BERTRAM   Well, what would you say?

HELEN   I am not worthy of the wealth I owe,°   own
Nor dare I say 'tis mine—and yet it is—
But like a timorous thief most fain° would steal   gladly
What law does vouch mine own.

BERTRAM   What would you have?

80 HELEN   Something and scarce so much; nothing, indeed;
I would not tell you what I would, my lord.
Faith, yes:
Strangers and foes do sunder° and not kiss.³   separate

BERTRAM   I pray you, stay° not, but in haste to horse.   delay

85 HELEN   I shall not break your bidding, good my lord.
Where are my other men? [to PAROLES] Monsieur, farewell.
                                                    Exit.

BERTRAM   Go thou toward home, where I will never come
Whilst I can shake my sword or hear the drum.
Away, and for our flight.

PAROLES   Bravely! Coraggio!°   [Exeunt.]   Courage (Italian)

3.1

Flourish. Enter the DUKE *of Florence, the two
Frenchmen [the* LORDS DUMAINE], *with a troop of*
SOLDIERS.

DUKE   So that from point to point now have you heard
The fundamental reasons of this war,
Whose great decision° hath much blood let forth   process of resolution
And more thirsts after.

FIRST LORD DUMAINE   Holy seems the quarrel
5 Upon your grace's part; black and fearful
On the opposer.

DUKE   Therefore we marvel much our cousin France
Would in so just a business shut his bosom
Against our borrowing prayers.°   entreaties for aid

SECOND LORD DUMAINE   Good my lord,
10 The reasons of our state I cannot yield,
But° like a common and an outward man,°   Except / an outsider
That the great figure° of a council frames   image
By self-unable motion,° therefore dare not   inadequate guess
Say what I think of it, since I have found
15 Myself in my incertain grounds° to fail   conjectures
As often as I guessed.

---

3. PERFORMANCE COMMENT The text does not indicate whether Helen and Bertram eventually kiss;
whether and how they do has been used in different
performances to forecast various possibilities for
their relationship. For a discussion of some of the
options, see Digital Edition PC 2.
3.1 Location: Florence.

DUKE   Be it his pleasure.
FIRST LORD DUMAINE   But I am sure the younger of our nature,
That surfeit on° their ease, will day by day   *have had too much of*
Come here for physic.[1]
DUKE   Welcome shall they be,
20   And all the honors that can fly° from us   *proceed*
Shall on them settle. You know your places well;
When better fall,[2] for your avails they fell.
Tomorrow to the field.   *Flourish. [Exeunt.]*

3.2
Enter COUNTESS *and* CLOWN[*, with a letter*].

COUNTESS   It hath happened all as I would have had it, save
that he comes not along with her.
CLOWN   By my troth, I take my young lord to be a very melancholy man.
5   COUNTESS   By what observance, I pray you?
CLOWN   Why, he will look upon his boot and sing; mend° the   *adjust*
ruff° and sing; ask questions and sing; pick his teeth and   *boot's cuff*
sing. I know a man that had this trick of melancholy sold a
goodly manor for a song.
10   COUNTESS   Let me see what he writes and when he means to
come.
        [*She takes the letter and reads to herself.*]
CLOWN   I have no mind to Isbel since I was at court. Our old
lings[1] and our Isbels o'th' country are nothing like your old
ling and your Isbels o'th' court. The brains of my Cupid's
15   knocked out, and I begin to love as an old man loves money,
with no stomach.°   *appetite*
COUNTESS   What have we here?
CLOWN   E'en that you have there.   *Exit.*
COUNTESS [*reads a letter*]   "I have sent you a daughter-in-law.
20   She hath recovered° the King and undone me. I have wedded   *cured*
her, not bedded her, and sworn to make the "not"° eternal.   *punning on "knot"*
You shall hear I am run away; know it before the report come.
If there be breadth enough in the world, I will hold a long
distance. My duty to you.
25   Your unfortunate son, Bertram."
This is not well, rash and unbridled boy:
To fly the favors of so good a king,
To pluck° his indignation on thy head   *pull down*
By the misprizing° of a maid too virtuous   *undervaluing*
30   For the contempt of empire°—   *an emperor*
        Enter CLOWN.
CLOWN   O madam, yonder is heavy° news within between two   *sad*
soldiers and my young lady.
COUNTESS   What is the matter?
CLOWN   Nay, there is some comfort in the news, some comfort:
35   your son will not be killed so soon as I thought he would.
COUNTESS   Why should he be killed?
CLOWN   So say I, madam—if he run away, as I hear he does.
The danger is in standing to't:[2] that's the loss of men, though

---

1. Cure (through bloodletting).   1. Salt cod (slang for "penis").
2. When better places fall vacant.   2. In standing one's ground (in love and war).
3.2 Location: Roussillon, Bertram's palace.

it be the getting° of children. Here they come will tell you   *begetting*
40   more. For my part I only hear your son was run away. [*Exit.*]
       Enter HELEN *and two Gentlemen*[, *the* LORDS DUMAINE].
SECOND LORD DUMAINE   Save you, good madam.
HELEN   Madam, my lord is gone, forever gone.
FIRST LORD DUMAINE   Do not say so.
COUNTESS   Think upon patience, pray you. —Gentlemen,
45   I have felt so many quirks of joy and grief
  That the first face° of neither on the start°   *appearance / suddenly*
  Can woman me unto't.[3] Where is my son, I pray you?
FIRST LORD DUMAINE   Madam, he's gone to serve the Duke of
    Florence.
  We met him thitherward,° for thence we came,   *going there*
50   And after some dispatch° in hand at court   *business*
  Thither we bend again.
HELEN   Look on his letter, madam: here's my passport.°   *vagabond's license*
  [*She reads.*] "When thou canst get the ring upon my finger,
  which never shall come off, and show me a child begotten
55   of thy body that I am father to, then call me husband, but
  in such a 'then' I write a 'never.'"
  This is a dreadful sentence.
COUNTESS   Brought you this letter, gentlemen?
FIRST LORD DUMAINE   Ay, madam,
  And for the contents' sake are sorry for our pains.
60 COUNTESS   I prithee, lady, have a better cheer.
  If thou engrossest° all the griefs are thine,   *monopolize*
  Thou robb'st me of a moiety.° He was my son,   *share*
  But I do wash his name out of my blood,
  And thou art all my° child. Towards Florence is he?   *my only*
FIRST LORD DUMAINE   Ay, madam.
65 COUNTESS   And to be a soldier?
FIRST LORD DUMAINE   Such is his noble purpose, and believe't,
  The Duke will lay upon him all the honor
  That good convenience claims.°   *That is suitable*
COUNTESS   Return you thither?
SECOND LORD DUMAINE   Ay, madam, with the swiftest wing of speed.
70 HELEN [*reads*]   "Till I have no wife, I have nothing in France."
  'Tis bitter.
COUNTESS   Find you that there?
HELEN   Ay, madam.
SECOND LORD DUMAINE   'Tis but the boldness of his hand,
    haply,°
  Which his heart was not consenting to.   *perhaps*
COUNTESS   Nothing in France until he have no wife!
75   There's nothing here that is too good for him
  But only she, and she deserves a lord
  That twenty such rude boys might tend upon
  And call her hourly mistress. Who was with him?
SECOND LORD DUMAINE   A servant only, and a gentleman
80   Which I have sometime known.
COUNTESS   Paroles, was it not?
SECOND LORD DUMAINE   Ay, my good lady, he.

---

3. Can make me weep like a woman.

COUNTESS A very tainted fellow, and full of wickedness.
My son corrupts a well-derivèd° nature   *nobly born*
With his inducement.
85 SECOND LORD DUMAINE Indeed, good lady,
The fellow has a deal of that too much
Which holds him much to have.[4]
COUNTESS   You're welcome, gentlemen.
I will entreat you, when you see my son,
To tell him that his sword can never win
90 The honor that he loses. More I'll entreat
You written to bear along.
FIRST LORD DUMAINE   We serve you, madam,
In that and all your worthiest affairs.
COUNTESS Not so, but° as we change° our courtesies.   *except / exchange*
Will you draw near?   *Exeunt [all but* HELEN].
95 HELEN "Till I have no wife, I have nothing in France."
Nothing in France until he has no wife!
Thou shalt have none, Roussillon, none in France;
Then hast thou all again. Poor lord, is't I
That chase thee from thy country and expose
100 Those tender limbs of thine to the event°   *outcome*
Of the none-sparing war? And is it I
That drive thee from the sportive court, where thou
Wast shot at with fair eyes, to be the mark
Of smoky muskets? O you leaden messengers°   *(bullets)*
105 That ride upon the violent speed of fire,
Fly with false aim, move the still-piecing air[5]
That sings with piercing; do not touch my lord!
Whoever shoots at him, I set him there.
Whoever charges on his forward° breast,   *brave; proud; advancing*
110 I am the caitiff° that do hold him to't,   *wretch*
And though I kill him not I am the cause
His death was so effected. Better 'twere
I met the ravin° lion when he roared   *ravenous*
With sharp constraint of hunger; better 'twere
115 That all the miseries which nature owes°   *human nature possesses*
Were mine at once. No, come thou home, Roussillon,
Whence honor but of danger wins a scar[6]
As oft it loses all. I will be gone;
My being here it is that holds thee hence.
120 Shall I stay here to do't? No, no, although
The air of paradise did fan the house
And angels officed all.[7] I will be gone,
That pitiful° rumor may report my flight   *pitying*
To consolate° thine ear. Come, night; end, day;   *console*
125 For with the dark, poor thief, I'll steal away.   *Exit.*

---

4. Has all too much persuasive power, which greatly profits him.
5. Air that is constantly repairing itself.

6. *Whence . . . scar:* From where honor at best can win a scar.
7. Performed all household tasks.

3.3

Flourish. Enter the DUKE *of Florence,* [BERTRAM, *Count*]
Roussillon, drum and trumpets, SOLDIERS, [*and*] PAROLES.

DUKE The general of our horse° thou art, and we,   cavalry
   Great in our hope, lay° our best love and credence°   wager / trust
   Upon thy promising fortune.
BERTRAM   Sir, it is
   A charge° too heavy for my strength, but yet   load
5   We'll strive to bear it for your worthy sake
   To th'extreme edge of hazard.°   limit of danger
DUKE   Then go thou forth,
   And fortune play upon thy prosperous helm
   As thy auspicious mistress.
BERTRAM   This very day,
   Great Mars, I put myself into thy file.°   line of soldiers
10 Make me but like my thoughts, and I shall prove
   A lover of thy drum, hater of love.   *Exeunt all.*

3.4

Enter COUNTESS *and* STEWARD[, *with a letter*].

COUNTESS Alas! And would you take the letter of her?
   Might you not know she would do as she has done
   By sending me a letter? Read it again.
STEWARD [*reads the letter*[1]] "I am Saint Jacques' pilgrim,[2]
     thither gone.
5   Ambitious love hath so in me offended
   That barefoot plod I the cold ground upon
   With sainted vow my faults to have amended.
   Write, write, that from the bloody course of war
   My dearest master, your dear son, may hie.°   hurry
10 Bless him at home in peace, whilst I from far
   His name with zealous fervor sanctify.°   (in prayer)
   His taken° labors bid him me forgive.   undertaken
   I, his despiteful Juno,[3] sent him forth
   From courtly friends with camping foes to live,
15 Where death and danger dogs the heels of worth.
   He is too good and fair for death and me,
   Whom[4] I myself embrace to set him free."
COUNTESS Ah, what sharp stings are in her mildest words!
   Rinaldo, you did never lack advice° so much   discretion
20 As letting her pass so. Had I spoke with her
   I could have well diverted her intents,
   Which thus she hath prevented.
STEWARD   Pardon me, madam.
   If I had given you this at overnight,°   last night
   She might have been o'erta'en, and yet she writes
   Pursuit would be but vain.
25 COUNTESS   What angel shall
   Bless this unworthy husband? He cannot thrive

3.3 Location: Florence.
3.4 Location: Roussillon. Bertram's palace.
1. The letter forms a sonnet.
2. A pilgrim to the shrine of St. James (presumably in Santiago de Compostela, in Spain).

3. Cruel goddess of marriage (who oppressed Hercules by assigning him twelve supposedly impossible tasks).
4. Death (but the suggestion "Bertram" may be deliberate).

Unless her prayers, whom heaven delights to hear
And loves to grant, reprieve him from the wrath
Of greatest justice. Write, write, Rinaldo,
30 To this unworthy husband of his wife.
Let every word weigh heavy of° her worth   *emphasize*
That he does weigh too light. My greatest grief,
Though little he do feel it, set down sharply.
Dispatch the most convenient messenger.
35 When haply° he shall hear that she is gone   *Perhaps when*
He will return, and hope I may that she,
Hearing so much, will speed her foot again,
Led hither by pure love. Which of them both
Is dearest to me, I have no skill in sense
40 To make distinction. Provide° this messenger.   *Make ready*
My heart is heavy and mine age is weak;
Grief would have tears, and sorrow bids me speak.   *Exeunt.*

3.5

A tucket° afar off. Enter [an] old WIDOW *of Florence,*   *trumpet call*
*her daughter [*DIANA], *and* MARIANA, *with other citizens.*
WIDOW   Nay, come, for if they do approach the city we shall
lose° all the sight.   *miss*
DIANA   They say the French count has done most honorable
service.
5 WIDOW   It is reported that he has taken their° great'st com-   *(of the Sienese)*
mander, and that with his own hand he slew the Duke's
brother. We have lost our labor; they are gone a contrary
way. Hark, you may know by their trumpets.
MARIANA   Come, let's return° again and suffice ourselves with   *go home*
10 the report of it. Well, Diana, take heed of this French earl.
The honor of a maid is her name,° and no legacy is so rich as   *reputation*
honesty.°   *chastity*
WIDOW [*to* DIANA]   I have told my neighbor how you have been
solicited by a gentleman, his companion.
15 MARIANA   I know that knave, hang him! One Paroles: a filthy
officer° he is in those suggestions° for the young earl. Beware   *agent / solicitings*
of them, Diana: their promises, enticements, oaths, tokens,
and all these engines° of lust are not the things they go[1]   *devices*
under. Many a maid hath been seduced by them, and the
20 misery is example that so terrible shows in the wreck of
maidenhood cannot for all that dissuade succession but that
they are limed with the twigs that threatens them.[2] I hope I
need not to advise you further, but I hope your own grace°   *virtue*
will keep you where you are, though there were no further
25 danger° known but the modesty which is so lost.   *(pregnancy)*
DIANA   You shall not need to fear° me.   *fear for*
Enter HELEN[, *dressed as a pilgrim*].
WIDOW   I hope so. Look, here comes a pilgrim. I know she
will lie at my house; thither they send one another. I'll question her.

3.5 Location: Florence.
1. Conceal themselves.
2. *the misery is . . . threatens them:* Unfortunately,
the example of those women ruined by the loss of

their virginity does not prevent others from falling
victim to the same deceptions. (Sticky lime was applied
to twigs to catch birds.)

30 —God save you, pilgrim, whither are you bound?

HELEN   To Saint Jacques le Grand.

Where do the palmers° lodge, I do beseech you?   *pilgrims*

WIDOW   At the Saint Francis, here beside the port.°   *city gate*

HELEN   Is this the way?

A march afar.

35 WIDOW   Ay, marry, is't. Hark you, they come this way.

If you will tarry, holy pilgrim,

But till the troops come by,

I will conduct you where you shall be lodged,

The rather for I think I know your hostess

40 As ample° as myself.   *well*

HELEN   Is it yourself?

WIDOW   If you shall please so, pilgrim.

HELEN   I thank you and will stay upon° your leisure.   *await*

WIDOW   You came, I think, from France?

HELEN   I did so.

45 WIDOW   Here you shall see a countryman of yours

That has done worthy service.

HELEN   His name, I pray you?

DIANA   The Count Roussillon. Know you such a one?

HELEN   But by the ear that hears most nobly of him;

His face I know not.

DIANA   Whatsome'er° he is,   *Whatever kind of man*

50 He's bravely taken° here. He stole from France,   *highly regarded*

As 'tis reported, for the King had married him

Against his liking. Think you it is so?

HELEN   Ay, surely, mere° the truth. I know his lady.   *simply*

DIANA   There is a gentleman that serves the Count

Reports but coarsely of her.

55 HELEN   What's his name?

DIANA   Monsieur Paroles.

HELEN   Oh, I believe with him.

In argument of praise,[3] or to° the worth   *compared to*

Of the great Count himself, she is too mean°   *lowly*

To have her name repeated. All her deserving°   *Her only merit*

60 Is a reservèd honesty,° and that   *preserved chastity*

I have not heard examined.°   *questioned*

DIANA   Alas, poor lady!

'Tis a hard bondage to become the wife

Of a detesting lord.

WIDOW   I warrant, good creature, wheresoe'er she is,

65 Her heart weighs sadly. This young maid might do her

A shrewd turn° if she pleased.   *nasty trick*

HELEN   How do you mean?

Maybe the amorous Count solicits her

In the unlawful purpose.

WIDOW   He does indeed,

And brokes° with all that can in such a suit   *bargains*

70 Corrupt the tender honor of a maid.

But she is armed for him and keeps her guard

In honestest defense.

___

3. As a topic of praise.

Drum and colors. Enter [BERTRAM,] *Count Roussillon,*
PAROLES, *and the whole army.*

MARIANA   The gods forbid else.

WIDOW   So, now they come.
That is Antonio, the Duke's eldest son;
That Escalus.

HELEN   Which is the Frenchman?

75 DIANA   He,
That with the plume. 'Tis a most gallant fellow;
I would he loved his wife. If he were honester[4]
He were much goodlier.
Is't not a handsome gentleman?

HELEN   I like him well.

80 DIANA   'Tis pity he is not honest. Yond's that same knave
That leads him to these places. Were I his lady,
I would poison that vile rascal.

HELEN   Which is he?

DIANA   That jackanapes° with scarves. Why is he melancholy?   monkey

HELEN   Perchance he's hurt i'th' battle.

85 PAROLES   Lose our drum?[5] Well!

MARIANA   He's shrewdly° vexed at something. [PAROLES *bows*   badly
to them.] Look, he has spied us.

WIDOW [*to* PAROLES]   Marry, hang you!

MARIANA [*to* PAROLES]   And your courtesy,° for a ring-carrier.°   bow / go-between
                    Exeunt [BERTRAM, PAROLES, *and the army*].

90 WIDOW   The troop is passed. Come, pilgrim, I will bring you
Where you shall host.° Of enjoined penitents[6]   lodge
There's four or five to great Saint Jacques bound
Already at my house.

HELEN   I humbly thank you.
Please it° this matron and this gentle maid   If it please
95 To eat with us tonight, the charge and thanking
Shall be for me, and to requite you further
I will bestow some precepts of° this virgin   advice on
Worthy the note.

MARIANA *and* DIANA   We'll take your offer kindly.°   *Exeunt.*   gratefully

3.6

Enter [BERTRAM,] *Count Roussillon, and the* [two]
Frenchmen [*the* LORDS DUMAINE], *as at first.*

SECOND LORD DUMAINE   Nay, good my lord, put him to't.° Let   (to the test)
him have his way.

FIRST LORD DUMAINE   If your lordship find him not a hilding,°   worthless wretch
hold me no more in your respect.

5 SECOND LORD DUMAINE   On my life, my lord, a bubble.

BERTRAM   Do you think I am so far deceived in him?

SECOND LORD DUMAINE   Believe it, my lord, in mine own direct
knowledge, without any malice, but to speak of him as° my   as if he were
kinsman, he's a most notable coward, an infinite and endless
10 liar, an hourly promise breaker, the owner of no one good
quality worthy your lordship's entertainment.°   patronage

---

4. More honorable (and chaste).   6. Those sworn to a penitential pilgrimage.
5. A military disgrace.   3.6 Location: The Florentine camp.

FIRST LORD DUMAINE   It were fit you knew him, lest reposing° _trusting_
too far in his virtue—which he hath not—he might at some
great and trusty business in a main danger fail you.

15 BERTRAM   I would I knew in what particular action to try him.

FIRST LORD DUMAINE   None better than to let him fetch off° his _back_
drum, which you hear him so confidently undertake to do.

SECOND LORD DUMAINE   I, with a troop of Florentines, will
suddenly surprise° him; such I will have whom I am sure he _ambush_
20 knows not from the enemy. We will bind and hoodwink° _blindfold_
him so that he shall suppose no other but that he is carried
into the leaguer° of the adversaries when we bring him to _camp_
our own tents. Be but your lordship present at his examination: if he do not, for the promise of his life, and in the high-
25 est compulsion of base fear, offer to betray you and deliver
all the intelligence° in his power against you, and that with _information_
the divine forfeit of his soul upon oath, never trust my judgment in anything.

FIRST LORD DUMAINE   Oh, for the love of laughter, let him
30 fetch his drum! He says he has a stratagem for't. When your
lordship sees the bottom° of his success in't, and to what _entirety_
metal this counterfeit lump of ore will be melted, if you give
him not John Drum's entertainment[1] your inclining° cannot _partiality_
be removed. Here he comes.

Enter PAROLES.

35 SECOND LORD DUMAINE [_aside to_ BERTRAM]   Oh, for the love of
laughter, hinder not the honor of his design! Let him fetch
off his drum in any hand.° _case_

BERTRAM   How now, monsieur? This drum sticks sorely in
your disposition.° _troubles you sorely_

40 FIRST LORD DUMAINE   A pox on't, let it go, 'tis but a drum.

PAROLES   But a drum! Is't "but a drum"? A drum so lost!
There was excellent command, to charge in with our horse° _cavalry_
upon our own wings° and to rend our own soldiers! _flank units_

FIRST LORD DUMAINE   That was not to be blamed in the com-
45 mand of the service. It was a disaster° of war that Caesar _an accident_
himself could not have prevented if he had been there to
command.

BERTRAM   Well, we cannot greatly condemn our success.[2]
Some dishonor we had in the loss of that drum, but it is not
50 to be recovered.

PAROLES   It might have been recovered.

BERTRAM   It might, but it is not now.

PAROLES   It is to be recovered. But that the merit of service is
seldom attributed to the true and exact performer, I would
55 have that drum or another, or _hic iacet._[3]

BERTRAM   Why, if you have a stomach° to't, monsieur, if you _an inclination_
think your mystery in stratagem° can bring this instrument _tactical skill_
of honor again into his native quarter,° be magnanimous° _back home / valiant_
in the enterprise and go on; I will grace° the attempt for a _honor_

---

1. _John Drum's entertainment:_ ignominious dismissal
(proverbial).
2. The general success of the battle.

3. Here lies (Latin): Paroles imagines himself dying
in an attempt to recover the drum.

60 worthy exploit. If you speed° well in it, the Duke shall both   *succeed*
speak of it and extend to you what further becomes his
greatness, even to the utmost syllable of your worthiness.

PAROLES   By the hand of a soldier, I will undertake it.

BERTRAM   But you must not now slumber in it.

65 PAROLES   I'll about it this evening, and I will presently pen
down my dilemmas,[4] encourage myself in my certainty, put
myself into my mortal preparation,[5] and by midnight look to
hear further from me.

BERTRAM   May I be bold to acquaint his grace you are gone
70 about it?

PAROLES   I know not what the success will be, my lord, but
the attempt I vow.

BERTRAM   I know thou'rt valiant, and to the possibility° of thy   *utmost capacity*
soldiership will subscribe° for thee. Farewell.   *vouch*

75 PAROLES   I love not many words.   *Exit.*

SECOND LORD DUMAINE   No more than a fish loves water. Is
not this a strange fellow, my lord, that so confidently seems
to undertake this business which he knows is not to be
done, damns himself to do, and dares better be damned
80 than to do't?

FIRST LORD DUMAINE   You do not know him, my lord, as we
do. Certain it is that he will steal himself into a man's favor
and for a week escape a great deal of discoveries,[6] but when
you find him out, you have° him ever after.   *understand*

85 BERTRAM   Why, do you think he will make no deed° at all of   *endeavor*
this that so seriously he does address himself unto?

SECOND LORD DUMAINE   None in the world, but return with
an invention° and clap upon you two or three probable° lies.   *tall tale / plausible*
But we have almost embossed[7] him. You shall see his fall
90 tonight, for indeed he is not for your lordship's respect.

FIRST LORD DUMAINE   We'll make you some sport with the fox
ere we case° him. He was first smoked[8] by the old lord   *skin*
Lafeu. When his disguise and he is parted, tell me what a
sprat° you shall find him, which you shall see this very   *tiny fish*
95 night.

SECOND LORD DUMAINE   I must go look my twigs.° He shall be   *see to my bird trap*
caught.

BERTRAM [*to* FIRST LORD DUMAINE]   Your brother, he shall go
along with me.

100 FIRST LORD DUMAINE   As't please your lordship. I'll leave you.
[*Exit.*]

BERTRAM   Now will I lead you to the house and show you
The lass I spoke of.

SECOND LORD DUMAINE   But you say she's honest.°   *chaste*

BERTRAM   That's all the fault. I spoke with her but once
And found her wondrous cold. But I sent to her
105 By this same coxcomb that we have i'th' wind°   *are stalking*
Tokens and letters, which she did resend,°   *return*

---

4. I will immediately reflect on my difficulties.
5. Spiritual preparation for death; readying of fatal
weapons.
6. *escape . . . discoveries:* largely get away with it.

7. Cornered; run to exhaustion (hunting term).
8. Forced into the open, like a fox smoked from its
hole.

And this is all I have done. She's a fair creature.
Will you go see her?
SECOND LORD DUMAINE   With all my heart, my lord.   *Exeunt.*

3.7

Enter HELEN *and* WIDOW.

HELEN   If you misdoubt° me that I am not she,   *doubt*
    I know not how I shall assure you further
    But I shall lose the grounds I work upon.[1]
WIDOW   Though my estate° be fallen, I was well born,   *fortune*
5   Nothing acquainted with these businesses,
    And would not put my reputation now
    In any staining act.
HELEN   Nor would I wish you.
    First give me trust° the Count he is my husband,   *trust me that*
    And what to your sworn counsel° I have spoken   *secrecy*
10   Is so° from word to word, and then you cannot,   *true*
    By° the good aid that I of you shall borrow,   *With respect to*
    Err in bestowing it.
WIDOW   I should believe you,
    For you have showed me that which well approves°   *confirms*
    You're great in fortune.
HELEN   Take this purse of gold,
15   And let me buy your friendly help thus far,
    Which I will overpay and pay again
    When I have found it.° The Count he woos your daughter;   *succeeded*
    Lays down his wanton siege before her beauty;
    Resolves to carry° her. Let her in fine° consent,   *conquer / in the end*
20   As we'll direct her how 'tis best to bear° it.   *manage*
    Now his important blood° will naught deny   *importunate passion*
    That she'll demand. A ring the County° wears   *Count*
    That downward hath succeeded in his house
    From son to son some four or five descents°   *generations*
25   Since the first father wore it. This ring he holds
    In most rich choice,° yet in his idle° fire   *estimation / crazy*
    To buy his will° it would not seem too dear,   *lust*
    Howe'er repented after.
WIDOW   Now I see the bottom of your purpose.
30 HELEN   You see it lawful, then. It is no more
    But that your daughter, ere she seems as won,
    Desires this ring; appoints him an encounter;
    In fine, delivers me to fill the time,°   *keep the appointment*
    Herself most chastely absent. After,
35   To marry her,° I'll add three thousand crowns   *As her dowry*
    To what is passed already.
WIDOW   I have yielded.
    Instruct my daughter how she shall persever[2]
    That time and place with this deceit so lawful
    May prove coherent.° Every night he comes   *fitting*
40   With musics of all sorts and songs composed

3.7 Location: The Widow's house, Florence.
1. *But . . . upon:* Unless I give up what my plot depends upon (and reveal my identity to Bertram).

2. Follow through, persevere (obsolete); pronounced with the accent on the second syllable.

To her unworthiness.[3] It nothing steads° us   *avails*
To chide him from our eaves, for he persists
As if his life lay on't.

HELEN   Why, then, tonight
45   Let us assay° our plot, which if it speed°   *attempt / succeed*
Is wicked meaning° in a lawful deed   *intention (Bertram's)*
And lawful meaning° in a lawful act,   *intention (Helen's)*
Where both not sin, and yet a sinful fact.[4]
But let's about it.

4.1

Enter one of the Frenchmen [the FIRST LORD
DUMAINE], *with five or six other* SOLDIERS *in ambush.*

FIRST LORD DUMAINE   He can come no other way but by this
hedge corner. When you sally° upon him, speak what terri-   *rush*
ble° language you will. Though you understand it not your-   *ferocious*
selves, no matter, for we must not seem to understand him,
5   unless° someone among us, whom we must produce for an   *except*
interpreter.

FIRST SOLDIER   Good captain, let me be th'interpreter.

FIRST LORD DUMAINE   Art not acquainted with him? Knows
he not thy voice?

10 FIRST SOLDIER   No, sir, I warrant you.

FIRST LORD DUMAINE   But what linsey-woolsey[1] hast thou to
speak to us again?

FIRST SOLDIER   E'en such as you speak to me.

FIRST LORD DUMAINE   He must think us some band of strang-
15   ers° i'th' adversary's entertainment.° Now, he hath a smack[2]   *foreigners / service*
of all neighboring languages; therefore we must everyone be
a man of his own fancy, not to know what we speak one to
another. So° we seem to know is to know straight° our pur-   *Provided / suffices for*
pose. Choughs'° language, gabble enough, and good enough.   *Crows'*
20   As for you, interpreter, you must seem very politic.° But   *cunning*
couch,° ho! Here he comes, to beguile° two hours in a sleep   *hide / while away*
and then to return and swear the lies he forges.

Enter PAROLES.

PAROLES   Ten o'clock. Within these three hours 'twill be time
enough to go home. What shall I say I have done? It must
25   be a very plausive° invention that carries it. They begin to   *plausible*
smoke° me, and disgraces have of late knocked too often at   *suspect*
my door. I find my tongue is too foolhardy, but my heart hath
the fear of Mars before it, and of his creatures, not daring
the reports of my tongue.[3]

30 FIRST LORD DUMAINE *[aside]*   This is the first truth that e'er
thine own tongue was guilty of.

PAROLES   What the devil should move me to undertake the
recovery of this drum, being not ignorant of the impossibility
and knowing I had no such purpose? I must give myself some
35   hurts and say I got them in exploit. Yet slight ones will not
carry it. They will say, "Came you off with so little?" And

---

3. To my humble daughter; to persuade my daughter
to unworthy deeds.
4. Deed (as Bertram intends it).
4.1 Location: Outside the Florentine camp.
1. Hodgepodge (literally, cloth of mixed linen and

wool fibers).
2. Smattering.
3. *my heart . . . tongue:* I am frightened by the god of
war and his followers, not daring to do what I have
boasted.

great ones I dare not give. Wherefore, what's the instance?°   *evidence*
Tongue, I must put you into a butter-woman's[4] mouth and buy
myself another of Bajazeth's mute,[5] if you prattle me into
40   these perils.
FIRST LORD DUMAINE [*aside*]   Is it possible he should know
  what he is and be that he is?
PAROLES   I would the cutting of my garments would serve the
  turn, or the breaking of my Spanish sword.
45 FIRST LORD DUMAINE [*aside*]   We cannot afford° you so.   *accommodate*
PAROLES   Or the baring° of my beard, and to say it was in   *shaving*
  stratagem.
FIRST LORD DUMAINE [*aside*]   'Twould not do.
PAROLES   Or to drown my clothes and say I was stripped.
50 FIRST LORD DUMAINE [*aside*]   Hardly serve.
PAROLES   Though I swore I leapt from the window of the citadel—
FIRST LORD DUMAINE [*aside*]   How deep?
PAROLES   Thirty fathom.°   *180 feet*
FIRST LORD DUMAINE [*aside*]   Three great oaths would scarce
55   make that be believed.
PAROLES   I would I had any drum of the enemy's: I would
  swear I recovered it.
FIRST LORD DUMAINE [*aside*]   You shall hear one anon.°   *immediately*
PAROLES   A drum, now, of the enemy's—
        Alarum° within.   *Call to arms*
60 FIRST LORD DUMAINE   *Throca movousus, cargo, cargo, cargo.*
ALL   *Cargo, cargo, cargo, villianda par corbo, cargo.*
        [*They seize* PAROLES *and blindfold him.*]
PAROLES   Oh, ransom, ransom! Do not hide mine eyes.
FIRST SOLDIER   *Boskos thromuldo boskos.*
PAROLES   I know you are the Moscows'° regiment,   *Russian*
65   And I shall lose my life for want of language.
  If there be here German or Dane, Low Dutch,
  Italian, or French, let him speak to me.
  I'll discover° that which shall undo the Florentine.   *reveal*
FIRST SOLDIER   *Boskos vauvado.* I understand thee and can
70   speak thy tongue. *Kerelybonto.* Sir, betake thee to thy faith,°   *say your prayers*
  for seventeen poniards° are at thy bosom.   *daggers*
PAROLES   Oh!
FIRST SOLDIER   Oh, pray, pray, pray! —*Manka reuania*
  dulche.
75 FIRST LORD DUMAINE   *Oscorbidulchos volivorco.*
FIRST SOLDIER   The general is content to spare thee yet,
  And hoodwinked[6] as thou art will lead thee on[7]
  To gather from thee. Haply° thou mayst inform   *Perhaps*
  Something to save thy life.
PAROLES   Oh, let me live,
80   And all the secrets of our camp I'll show—
  Their force, their purposes. Nay, I'll speak that
  Which you will wonder at.
FIRST SOLDIER   But wilt thou faithfully?[8]

---

4. Proverbially talkative.
5. *of Bajazeth's mute:* from the Turkish sultan's servant (whose tongue was cut off to ensure his discretion). TEXTUAL COMMENT The Folio text reads
"mule," not "mute," almost certainly a misprint. See

Digital Edition TC 6.
6. Blindfolded; punning on "deceived."
7. Will take you elsewhere; will deceive you further.
8. Truthfully; loyally (ironic).

PAROLES   If I do not, damn me.

FIRST SOLDIER   Acordo linta.
—Come on, thou art granted space.°   *breathing space*

Exit [FIRST SOLDIER *with* PAROLES].
A short alarum within.

85 FIRST LORD DUMAINE   Go tell the Count Roussillon and my
brother
We have caught the woodcock[9] and will keep him muffled°   *blindfolded*
Till we do hear from them.

SECOND SOLDIER   Captain, I will.

FIRST LORD DUMAINE   'A° will betray us all unto ourselves: *He*
Inform on° that.   *Report*

SECOND SOLDIER   So I will, sir.

90 FIRST LORD DUMAINE   Till then I'll keep him dark and safely
locked.

                                           Exeunt.

4.2

Enter BERTRAM *and the maid called* DIANA.

BERTRAM   They told me that your name was Fontibel.

DIANA   No, my good lord, Diana.

BERTRAM   Titled° goddess,   *Called*
And worth it with addition.[1] But, fair soul,
In your fine frame hath love no quality?

5 If the quick° fire of youth light not your mind   *vital*
You are no maiden but a monument.°   *statue*
When you are dead you should be such a one
As you are now. For you are cold and stern,
And now you should be as your mother was
When your sweet self was got.°   *begotten*

10 DIANA   She then was honest.

BERTRAM   So should you be.

DIANA   No.
My mother did but duty: such, my lord,
As you owe to your wife.

BERTRAM   No more o'that.
I prithee do not strive against my vows.[2]

15 I was compelled to her, but I love thee
By love's own sweet constraint and will forever
Do thee all rights of service.

DIANA   Ay, so you serve us
Till we serve you.° But when you have our roses,   *(sexually)*
You barely° leave our thorns to prick ourselves,   *only; nakedly*
And mock us with our bareness.

20 BERTRAM   How have I sworn!

DIANA   'Tis not the many oaths that makes the truth
But the plain single vow that is vowed true.
What is not holy, that we swear not by,
But take the high'st to witness. Then pray you, tell me:

9. Proverbially stupid bird.
4.2 Location: The Widow's house, Florence.
1. *worth it with addition:* you more than deserve to
be called a goddess; with wordplay on "addition" as
an honorific title. The goddess Diana was the patroness of chastity, an "addition" that hardly bodes well
for Bertram.
2. Do not quarrel with me about my wedding vows.

25   If I should swear by Jove's great attributes
        I loved you dearly, would you believe my oaths
        When I did love you ill?° This has no holding,[3]   *poorly; irreligiously*
        To swear by him whom I protest to love
        That I will work against him. Therefore your oaths
30   Are words and poor conditions but unsealed,[4]
        At least in my opinion.
    BERTRAM   Change it, change it!
        Be not so holy cruel. Love is holy,
        And my integrity ne'er knew the crafts°   *deceptive plays*
        That you do charge men with. Stand no more off,
35   But give thyself unto my sick desires,
        Who then recovers. Say thou art mine, and ever
        My love, as it begins, shall so persever.
    DIANA   I see that men may rope's in such a snare[5]
        That we'll forsake ourselves. Give me that ring.
40   BERTRAM   I'll lend it thee, my dear, but have no power
        To give it from me.
    DIANA   Will you not, my lord?
    BERTRAM   It is an honor 'longing to our house,°   *family line*
        Bequeathèd down from many ancestors,
        Which were the greatest obloquy° i'th' world   *disgrace*
        In me to lose.
45   DIANA   Mine honor's such a ring;
        My chastity's the jewel of our house,
        Bequeathèd down from many ancestors,
        Which were the greatest obloquy i'th' world
        In me to lose. Thus your own proper wisdom[6]
50   Brings in the champion, Honor, on my part,°   *side*
        Against your vain assault.
    BERTRAM   Here, take my ring.
        My house, mine honor, yea, my life be thine,
        And I'll be bid° by thee.   *commanded*
    DIANA   When midnight comes,
        Knock at my chamber window;
55   I'll order take my mother shall not hear.
        Now will I charge you in the band of truth,
        When you have conquered my yet maiden bed
        Remain there but an hour, nor speak to me.
        My reasons are most strong, and you shall know them
60   When back again this ring shall be delivered.
        And on your finger in the night I'll put
        Another ring, that what° in time proceeds   *whatever*
        May token° to the future our past deeds.   *betoken*
        Adieu till then; then fail not. You have won
65   A wife of° me, though there my hope be done.[7]   *in; through*
    BERTRAM   A heaven on earth I have won by wooing thee.
    DIANA   For which, live long to thank both heaven and me.
                            [*Exit* BERTRAM.]

---

3. Consistency; binding power.
4. *words . . . unsealed:* contracts without the validating seal.
5. I see that men may entrap us with such trifles.
TEXTUAL COMMENT The Folio text is corrupt here and

has been emended in various ways; for the rationale behind the Norton version, see Digital Edition TC 7.
6. Wisdom in your own affairs.
7. My marriage hopes are ruined; my hope of aiding Helen is accomplished.

You may so in the end.
My mother told me just how he would woo,
70   As if she sat in 's heart. She says all men
Have the like oaths. He has sworn to marry me
When his wife's dead; therefore I'll lie with him
When I am buried. Since Frenchmen are so braid,°   *deceitful*
Marry° that will, I live and die a maid.   *Let those marry*
75   Only in this disguise I think 't no sin
To cozen° him that would unjustly win.   *Exit.*   *cheat*

4.3

Enter the two French captains [the LORDS DUMAINE*],
and some two or three* SOLDIERS.

FIRST LORD DUMAINE You have not given him his mother's
letter?

SECOND LORD DUMAINE I have delivered it an hour since.
There is something in't that stings his nature, for on the
5   reading it he changed almost into another man.

FIRST LORD DUMAINE He has much worthy° blame laid upon   *deserved*
him for shaking off so good a wife and so sweet a lady.

SECOND LORD DUMAINE Especially he hath incurred the everlasting displeasure of the King, who had even tuned his
10   bounty to sing happiness to him.[1] I will tell you a thing, but
you shall let it dwell darkly° with you.   *secretly*

FIRST LORD DUMAINE When you have spoken it 'tis dead, and
I am the grave of it.

SECOND LORD DUMAINE He hath perverted a young gentle-
15   woman here in Florence of a most chaste renown,° and this   *reputation*
night he fleshes his will[2] in the spoil of her honor. He hath
given her his monumental° ring and thinks himself made in   *memorial*
the unchaste composition.°   *bargain*

FIRST LORD DUMAINE Now God delay our rebellion!° As we   *stifle our unruliness*
20   are ourselves,° what things are we!   *without divine aid*

SECOND LORD DUMAINE Merely° our own traitors. And as in   *Absolutely*
the common course of all treasons we still° see them reveal   *always*
themselves,° till they attain to their abhorred ends, so he   *(their true nature)*
that in this action contrives° against his own nobility, in his   *plots*
25   proper stream o'erflows himself.[3]

FIRST LORD DUMAINE Is it not meant damnable° in us to be   *meant to be mortal sin*
trumpeters of our unlawful intents? We shall not then have
his company tonight?

SECOND LORD DUMAINE Not till after midnight, for he is
30   dieted° to his hour.   *restricted*

FIRST LORD DUMAINE That approaches apace. I would gladly
have him see his company anatomized,° that he might take   *companion exposed*
a measure of his own judgments, wherein so curiously° he   *carefully*
had set this counterfeit.[4]

35   SECOND LORD DUMAINE We will not meddle with him° till   *(Paroles)*
he° come, for his presence must be the whip of the other.   *(Bertram)*

4.3 Location: The Florentine camp.
1. Who had previously readied his generosity to
make him happy (with musical metaphor).
2. He feeds his lust (hounds were "fleshed," or
rewarded, with a piece of meat from their prey, or

"spoil").
3. *in his . . . himself:* dissipates himself outside his
appropriate channel.
4. False jewel (Paroles).

FIRST LORD DUMAINE In the meantime, what hear you of these wars?

SECOND LORD DUMAINE I hear there is an overture of peace.

40 FIRST LORD DUMAINE Nay, I assure you, a peace concluded.

SECOND LORD DUMAINE What will Count Roussillon do then? Will he travel higher° or return again into France? | *farther*

FIRST LORD DUMAINE I perceive by this demand you are not altogether of his counsel.° | *in his confidence*

45 SECOND LORD DUMAINE Let it be forbid, sir. So should I be a great deal of his act.[5]

FIRST LORD DUMAINE Sir, his wife some two months since fled from his house. Her pretense° is a pilgrimage to Saint | *purpose*
Jacques le Grand, which holy undertaking with most aus-
50 tere sanctimony° she accomplished. And, there residing, the | *piety*
tenderness of her nature became as a prey to her grief; in
fine,° made a groan of her last breath, and now she sings in | *in conclusion*
heaven.

SECOND LORD DUMAINE How is this justified?° | *verified*

55 FIRST LORD DUMAINE The stronger part of it by her own letters, which makes her story true even to the point of her
death; her death itself, which could not be her office to say is
come, was faithfully confirmed by the rector of the place.

SECOND LORD DUMAINE Hath the Count all this intelligence?

60 FIRST LORD DUMAINE Ay, and the particular confirmations,
point from point, to the full arming° of the verity.° | *corroboration / truth*

SECOND LORD DUMAINE I am heartily sorry that he'll be glad of this.

FIRST LORD DUMAINE How mightily sometimes we make us
65 comforts of our losses!

SECOND LORD DUMAINE And how mightily some other times
we drown our gain in tears! The great dignity that his valor
hath here acquired for him shall at home be encountered° | *opposed*
with a shame as ample.

70 FIRST LORD DUMAINE The web° of our life is of a mingled | *fabric*
yarn, good and ill together: our virtues would be proud if
our faults whipped them not, and our crimes would despair
if they were not cherished by our virtues.

*Enter a [*SERVANT as*] Messenger.*
—How now? Where's your master?

75 SERVANT He met the Duke in the street, sir, of whom he hath
taken a solemn leave. His lordship will° next morning for | *intends to leave*
France. The Duke hath offered him letters of commenda-
tions to the King.

SECOND LORD DUMAINE They shall be no more than needful
80 there, if they were more than they can commend.[6]

*Enter [*BERTRAM,*] Count Roussillon.*

FIRST LORD DUMAINE They cannot be too sweet for the King's
tartness. Here's his lordship now. —How now, my lord, is't
not after midnight?

BERTRAM I have tonight dispatched sixteen businesses a
85 month's length apiece. By an abstract of success:° I have | *list of items*

---

5. An accessory to his deeds.
6. Even if they were more commendatory than they possibly could be.

congéd with° the Duke, done my adieu with his nearest,   *taken leave of*
buried a wife, mourned for her, writ to my lady mother I am
returning, entertained my convoy,° and between these main   *arranged my transport*
parcels of dispatch° effected many nicer° needs. The last *business / more delicate*
90   was the greatest, but that I have not ended yet.
SECOND LORD DUMAINE   If the business be of any difficulty,
    and this morning your departure hence, it requires haste of
    your lordship.
BERTRAM   I mean the business is not ended as fearing to
95   hear of it hereafter. But shall we have this dialogue
    between the Fool and the Soldier? Come, bring forth this
    counterfeit model;° he's deceived me like a double-   *image (of soldiership)*
    meaning° prophesier.   *ambiguous*
SECOND LORD DUMAINE   Bring him forth. [*Exeunt* SOLDIERS.]
100   He's sat i'th' stocks all night, poor gallant knave.
BERTRAM   No matter. His heels have deserved it in usurping
    his spurs[7] so long. How does he carry himself?
SECOND LORD DUMAINE   I have told your lordship already: the
    stocks carry him. But to answer you as you would be under-
105   stood, he weeps like a wench that had shed° her milk. He   *spilled*
    hath confessed himself to Morgan, whom he supposes to be
    a friar, from the time of his remembrance[8] to this very
    instant° disaster of his setting i'th' stocks. And what think   *present*
    you he hath confessed?
110 BERTRAM   Nothing of me, has 'a?°   *he*
SECOND LORD DUMAINE   His confession is taken, and it shall
    be read to his face. If your lordship be in't, as I believe you
    are, you must have the patience to hear it.
          Enter PAROLES, [*blindfolded,*] *with his*
          interpreter[, *the* FIRST SOLDIER].
BERTRAM   A plague upon him! Muffled!° He can say nothing   *Blindfolded*
115   of me.
FIRST LORD DUMAINE [*aside*]   Hush, hush! Hoodman[9] comes.
    —Portotartarossa.
FIRST SOLDIER   He calls for the tortures. What will you say
    without 'em?
120 PAROLES   I will confess what I know without constraint. If ye
    pinch me like a pasty° I can say no more.   *piecrust*
FIRST SOLDIER   *Bosko chimurcho.*
FIRST LORD DUMAINE   *Boblibindo chicurmurco.*
FIRST SOLDIER   You are a merciful general. —Our general
125   bids you answer to what I shall ask you out of a note.
PAROLES   And truly, as I hope to live.
FIRST SOLDIER [*reads*]   "First demand of him how many horse°   *horsemen*
    the Duke is strong." —What say you to that?
PAROLES   Five or six thousand, but very weak and unser-
130   viceable. The troops are all scattered and the commanders
    very poor rogues, upon my reputation and credit and as I
    hope to live.
FIRST SOLDIER   Shall I set down your answer so?

7. Symbolic of knightly valor.   9. The blindfolded player in blindman's buff.
8. As far back as he can recall.

PAROLES   Do. I'll take the sacrament on't, how and which way
135   you will.[1]
BERTRAM [*aside*]   All's one to him. What a past-saving slave is
this!
FIRST LORD DUMAINE [*aside*]   You're deceived, my lord. This
is Monsieur Paroles, the gallant militarist—that was his
140   own phrase—that had the whole theoric° of war in the   theory
knot of his scarf and the practice in the chape° of his   scabbard tip
dagger.
SECOND LORD DUMAINE [*aside*]   I will never trust a man again
for keeping his sword clean, nor believe he can have every-
145   thing in him by wearing his apparel neatly.
FIRST SOLDIER   Well, that's set down.
PAROLES   Five or six thousand horse, I said. I will say true.
"Or thereabouts" set down, for I'll speak truth.
FIRST LORD DUMAINE [*aside*]   He's very near the truth in this.
150   BERTRAM [*aside*]   But I con him no thanks° for't in the nature°   feel no gratitude / manner
he delivers it.
PAROLES   Poor rogues, I pray you say.
FIRST SOLDIER   Well, that's set down.
PAROLES   I humbly thank you, sir. A truth's a truth: the rogues
155   are marvelous poor.
FIRST SOLDIER [*reads*]   "Demand of him of what strength they
are a-foot." —What say you to that?
PAROLES   By my troth, sir, if I were to live but this present hour,
I will tell true. Let me see: Spurio a hundred and fifty, Sebas-
160   tian so many,° Corambus so many, Jacques so many; Guiltian,   the same number
Cosmo, Lodowick, and Gratii, two hundred fifty each; mine
own company, Chitopher, Vaumond, Bentii, two hundred fifty
each. So that the muster file, rotten and sound,[2] upon my
life amounts not to fifteen thousand poll,° half of the which   heads
165   dare not shake the snow from off their cassocks° lest they   cloaks
shake themselves to pieces.
BERTRAM [*aside*]   What shall be done to him?
FIRST LORD DUMAINE [*aside*]   Nothing, but let him have
thanks. [*aside to* FIRST SOLDIER] Demand of him my condi-
170   tion and what credit I have with the Duke.
FIRST SOLDIER   Well, that's set down. [*He pretends to read.*]
"You shall demand of him whether one Captain Dumaine be
i'th' camp, a Frenchman: what his reputation is with the
Duke, what his valor, honesty, and expertness in wars, or
175   whether he thinks it were not possible with well-weighing°   heavy; persuasive
sums of gold to corrupt him to a revolt." What say you to
this? What do you know of it?
PAROLES   I beseech you, let me answer to the particular of the
interrogatories.° Demand them singly.   judicial questions
180   FIRST SOLDIER   Do you know this Captain Dumaine?
PAROLES   I know him. 'A was a botcher's° prentice in Paris,   clothes mender's
from whence he was whipped for getting the sheriff's fool[3]
with child, a dumb innocent° that could not say him nay.   idiot

---

1. According to whatever rite you prefer.   3. Mentally retarded girl.
2. The total roll, sick and able-bodied.

BERTRAM [*to* FIRST LORD DUMAINE] Nay, by your leave, hold
185   your hands, though I know his brains are forfeit to the next
       tile that falls.⁴
FIRST SOLDIER Well, is this captain in the Duke of Florence's
       camp?
PAROLES Upon my knowledge he is, and lousy.
190 FIRST LORD DUMAINE [*aside*] Nay, look not so upon me; we
       shall hear of your lordship anon.
FIRST SOLDIER What is his reputation with the Duke?
PAROLES The Duke knows him for no other but a poor officer
       of mine, and writ to me this other day to turn him out o'th'
195   band. I think I have his letter in my pocket.
FIRST SOLDIER Marry, we'll search.
PAROLES In good sadness,° I do not know; either it is there or   all seriousness
       it is upon a file with the Duke's other letters in my tent.
FIRST SOLDIER Here 'tis, here's a paper. Shall I read it to you?
200 PAROLES I do not know if it be it or no.
BERTRAM [*aside*] Our interpreter does it well.
FIRST LORD DUMAINE [*aside*] Excellently.
FIRST SOLDIER "Dian, the Count's a fool and full of gold."
PAROLES That is not the Duke's letter, sir. That is an adver-
205   tisement° to a proper maid in Florence, one Diana, to take   admonition
       heed of the allurement of one Count Roussillon, a foolish,
       idle boy, but for all that very ruttish.° I pray you, sir, put it up   lecherous
       again.
FIRST SOLDIER Nay, I'll read it first, by your favor.
210 PAROLES My meaning in't, I protest, was very honest in the
       behalf of the maid, for I knew the young Count to be a dan-
       gerous and lascivious boy who is a whale to virginity and
       devours up all the fry° it finds.   tiny fish
BERTRAM [*aside*] Damnable both-sides rogue!
FIRST SOLDIER [*reads the*] *letter*
215 "When he swears oaths, bid him drop gold and take it;
       After he scores he never pays the score.°   bill
       Half-won is match well made; match and well make it.⁵
       He ne'er pays after-debts;⁶ take it before.
       And say a soldier, Dian, told thee this:
220   Men are to mell° with, boys are not to kiss.   meddle (sexually)
       For count° of this: the Count's a fool, I know it,   on account
       Who pays before° but not when he does owe it.   in advance
       Thine as he vowed to thee in thine ear,
                         Paroles."
225 BERTRAM [*aside*] He shall be whipped through the army with
       this rhyme in 's⁷ forehead.
SECOND LORD DUMAINE [*aside*] This is your devoted friend,
       sir, the manifold linguist and the armipotent° soldier.   mighty-in-arms
BERTRAM [*aside*] I could endure anything before but a cat,⁸
230   and now he's a cat to me.
FIRST SOLDIER I perceive, sir, by the general's looks, we shall
       be fain° to hang you.   obliged

---

4. I know he's close to sudden death.
5. Negotiating a good bargain is half the battle, so be
sure to bargain well.
6. Debts payable after receipt of goods.
7. On his (whores and their customers, when pun-

ished by public whipping, were often made to wear
signs indicating their transgressions).
8. A common phobia, but "cat" is also a term of contempt, usually referring to a spiteful or sluttish
woman.

PAROLES My life, sir, in any case! Not that I am afraid to die,
but that my offenses being many, I would repent out the
235 remainder of nature.° Let me live, sir, in a dungeon, i'th'   *my natural life*
stocks, or anywhere, so I may live.

FIRST SOLDIER We'll see what may be done, so you confess
freely. Therefore once more to this Captain Dumaine. You
have answered to his reputation with the Duke and to his
240 valor. What is his honesty?

PAROLES He will steal, sir, an egg out of a cloister. For rapes
and ravishments he parallels Nessus.[9] He professes° not   *makes a practice of*
keeping of oaths; in breaking 'em he is stronger than Her-
cules. He will lie, sir, with such volubility that you would
245 think truth were a fool. Drunkenness is his best virtue, for
he will be swine-drunk, and in his sleep he does little harm
save to his bedclothes about him—but they know his condi-
tions° and lay him in straw. I have but little more to say, sir,   *habits*
of his honesty. He has everything that an honest man
250 should not have; what an honest man should have, he has
nothing.

FIRST LORD DUMAINE [*aside*] I begin to love him for this.

BERTRAM [*aside*] For this description of thine honesty? A pox
upon him! For me, he's more and more a cat.

255 FIRST SOLDIER What say you to his expertness in war?

PAROLES Faith, sir, he's led the drum before the English tragedians.[1] To belie him I will not, and more of his soldiership
I know not, except in that country he had the honor to be
the officer at a place there called Mile End,[2] to instruct for
260 the doubling of files.[3] I would do the man what honor I can,
but of this I am not certain.

SECOND LORD DUMAINE [*aside*] He hath out-villained villainy
so far that the rarity° redeems him.   *uniqueness*

BERTRAM [*aside*] A pox on him! He's a cat still.

265 FIRST SOLDIER His qualities being at this poor price, I need
not to ask you if gold will corrupt him to revolt.

PAROLES Sir, for a *quart d'écu*[4] he will sell the fee-simple° of   *absolute ownership*
his salvation, the inheritance of it, and cut th'entail from all
remainders,[5] and a perpetual succession for it perpetually.

270 FIRST SOLDIER What's his brother, the other Captain Dumaine?

SECOND LORD DUMAINE [*aside*] Why does he ask him of me?

FIRST SOLDIER What's he?

PAROLES E'en a crow o'th' same nest: not altogether so great
as the first in goodness, but greater a great deal in evil. He
275 excels his brother for a coward, yet his brother is reputed
one of the best that is. In a retreat he outruns any lackey;[6]
marry, in coming on° he has the cramp.   *advancing*

FIRST SOLDIER If your life be saved, will you undertake to
betray the Florentine?

280 PAROLES Ay, and the captain of his horse, Count Roussillon.

FIRST SOLDIER I'll whisper with the general and know his
pleasure.

---

9. Centaur who attempted to rape Hercules' wife.
1. He's banged the drum to help advertise plays.
2. Where the London citizen militia drilled.
3. Simple drill exercise, in which the men stand in

two rows.
4. Quarter-crown, French coin of small value.
5. Prevent its succession to any future heirs.
6. Footman who runs before his master's coach.

PAROLES [*aside*]   I'll no more drumming. A plague of all
drums! Only to seem to deserve well, and to beguile the sup-
285 position° of that lascivious young boy the Count, have I run   *judgment*
into this danger. Yet who would have suspected an ambush
where I was taken?
FIRST SOLDIER   There is no remedy, sir, but you must die. The
general says you that have so traitorously discovered° the   *revealed*
290 secrets of your army and made such pestiferous reports of
men very nobly held° can serve the world for no honest use.   *regarded*
Therefore you must die. Come, headsman, off with his head.
PAROLES   O Lord, sir, let me live, or let me see my death.
FIRST SOLDIER   That shall you, and take your leave of all your
295 friends. [*He removes the blindfold.*] So, look about you.
Know you any here?
BERTRAM   Good morrow, noble captain.
SECOND LORD DUMAINE   God bless you, Captain Paroles.
FIRST LORD DUMAINE   God save you, noble captain.
300 SECOND LORD DUMAINE   Captain, what greeting will you° to   *do you desire*
my lord Lafeu? I am for° France.   *off to*
FIRST LORD DUMAINE   Good captain, will you give me a copy
of the sonnet you writ to Diana in behalf of the Count Rous-
sillon? An° I were not a very coward, I'd compel it of you, but   *If*
305 fare you well.   *Exeunt [all but* FIRST SOLDIER *and* PAROLES].
FIRST SOLDIER   You are undone, captain, all but your scarf;
that has a knot on't yet.
PAROLES   Who cannot be crushed with a plot?
FIRST SOLDIER   If you could find out a country where but
310 women were that had received so much shame, you might
begin an impudent° nation. Fare ye well, sir, I am for France   *a shameless*
too. We shall speak of you there.   *Exit.*
PAROLES   Yet am I thankful. If my heart were great
'Twould burst at this. Captain I'll be no more,
315 But I will eat, and drink, and sleep as soft
As captain shall. Simply the thing I am
Shall make me live.° Who knows himself a braggart,   *sustain me*
Let him fear this; for it will come to pass
That every braggart shall be found an ass.
320 Rust sword, cool blushes, and Paroles live
Safest in shame. Being fooled, by fool'ry thrive;
There's place and means for every man alive.
I'll after them.   *Exit.*

4.4

Enter HELEN, WIDOW, *and* DIANA.
HELEN   That you may well perceive I have not wronged you,
One of the greatest in the Christian world
Shall be my surety,° fore whose throne 'tis needful,   *guarantee*
Ere I can perfect mine intents, to kneel.
5 Time was I did him a desired office
Dear almost as his life, which gratitude

4.4 Location: The Widow's house, Florence.

Through flinty Tartar's bosom[1] would peep forth
And answer thanks. I duly am informed
His grace is at Marseilles, to which place
10 We have convenient convoy.° You must know   *suitable transport*
I am supposèd dead. The army breaking,°   *disbanding*
My husband hies him home, where heaven aiding,
And by the leave of my good lord, the King,
We'll be before our welcome.°   *before we're expected*
 WIDOW   Gentle madam,
15 You never had a servant to whose trust
Your business was more welcome.
 HELEN   Nor you, mistress,
Ever a friend whose thoughts more truly labor
To recompense your love. Doubt not but heaven
Hath brought me up to be your daughter's dower,
20 As it hath fated her to be my motive°   *means*
And helper to a husband. But, oh, strange men,
That can such sweet use make of what they hate!
When saucy trusting of the cozened° thoughts   *deceived*
Defiles the pitchy night,[2] so lust doth play
25 With what it loathes for° that which is away.   *in the place of*
But more of this hereafter. You, Diana,
Under my poor instructions yet must suffer
Something in my behalf.
 DIANA   Let death and honesty°   *chastity*
Go with your impositions, I am yours,
Upon° your will to suffer.   *At*
30 HELEN   Yet,° I pray you,   *A little longer*
But with the word° "the time will bring on summer," *("Yet")*
When briars shall have leaves as well as thorns
And be as sweet° as sharp. We must away.   *fragrant*
Our wagon is prepared, and time revives us.
35 All's well that ends well; still the fine's° the crown. *end*
Whate'er the course, the end is the renown.° *Exeunt.* *what is remembered*

4.5

Enter CLOWN, *old Lady* [COUNTESS], *and* LAFEU.

LAFEU No, no, no, your son was misled with a snipped taffeta[1] fellow there, whose villainous saffron[2] would have made
all the unbaked and doughy youth of a nation in his color.
Your daughter-in-law had been alive at this hour, and your
5 son here at home, more advanced by the King than by that
red-tailed humble-bee[3] I speak of.

COUNTESS I would I had not known him. It was the death of
the most virtuous gentlewoman that ever Nature had praise
for creating. If she had partaken of my flesh and cost me the
10 dearest groans of a mother I could not have owed her a more
rooted love.

LAFEU 'Twas a good lady, 'twas a good lady! We may pick a
thousand salads ere we light on such another herb.

---

1. Even from a savage's stony heart (Tartars, residents of central Asia, were considered barbaric by
western Europeans).
2. *When . . . night:* When lascivious yielding to
deceit defiles even the black night.

4.5 Location: Bertram's palace.
1. Silk slashed to show a contrasting lining.
2. Yellow dye, used for pastry; the coward's color.
3. Bumblebee (noisy, colorful, and useless).

CLOWN   Indeed, sir, she was the sweet marjoram of the salad,
15   or rather the herb of grace.°   *rue*
LAFEU   They are not salad-herbs,[4] you knave, they are nose-herbs.°   *fragrant plants*
CLOWN   I am no great Nebuchadnezzar,[5] sir: I have not much
        skill in grass.
LAFEU   Whether° dost thou profess thyself, a knave or a fool?   *Which*
20   CLOWN   A fool, sir, at a woman's service, and a knave at a
        man's.
LAFEU   Your distinction?
CLOWN   I would cozen° the man of his wife and do his service.   *cheat*
LAFEU   So you were a knave at his service indeed.
25   CLOWN   And I would give his wife my bauble,[6] sir, to do her
        service.
LAFEU   I will subscribe° for thee: thou art both knave and fool.   *vouch*
CLOWN   At your service.
LAFEU   No, no, no.
30   CLOWN   Why, sir, if I cannot serve you, I can serve as great a
        prince as you are.
LAFEU   Who's that, a Frenchman?
CLOWN   Faith, sir, 'a has an English name, but his physiog-
        nomy[7] is more hotter in France than there.
35   LAFEU   What prince is that?
CLOWN   The Black Prince,[8] sir, alias the prince of darkness,
        alias the devil.
LAFEU   Hold thee, there's my purse. I give thee not this to sug-
        gest° thee from thy master thou talk'st of. Serve him still.   *lure*
40   CLOWN   I am a woodland fellow, sir, that always loved a great
        fire, and the master I speak of ever keeps a good fire. But
        sure he is the prince of the world. Let his nobility remain in
        's court. I am for the house with the narrow gate,[9] which I
        take to be too little for pomp to enter. Some that humble
45   themselves may, but the many will be too chill and tender,[1]
        and they'll be for the flowery way that leads to the broad
        gate and the great fire.
LAFEU   Go thy ways, I begin to be a-weary of thee, and I tell thee
        so before° because I would not fall out with thee. Go thy ways.   *in advance*
50   Let my horses be well looked to without any tricks.
CLOWN   If I put any tricks upon 'em, sir, they shall be jades'
        tricks,[2] which are their own right by the law of nature.
                                                                Exit.
LAFEU   A shrewd° knave and an unhappy.   *bitter*
COUNTESS   So 'a is. My lord that's gone made himself much
55   sport out of him. By his authority he remains here, which he
        thinks is a patent° for his sauciness, and indeed he has no   *license*
        pace° but runs where he will.   *restraint*

---

4. Misconstruing "grace" as "grass."
5. In Daniel 4:28–34, the King of Babylon who, lacking spiritual "grace," went mad and ate "grass."
6. Fool's rod (suggesting "penis").
7. Physiognomy, face (in Elizabethan pronunciation,
punning on "nomy" and "name").
8. Punning on the nickname of Edward III's eldest
son, who conquered the French, and whom the Clown
equates to the devil, also as "black prince."
9. "Enter in at the strait gate; for it is the wide gate,

and broad way that leadeth to destruction, and many
there be which go in thereat. Because the gate is
strait and the way narrow that leadeth unto life, and
few there be that find it" (Matthew 7:13–14; see also
Luke 13:24). The devil is called the "prince of this
world" in John 12:31 and elsewhere.
1. Fainthearted and self-indulgent.
2. Contemptible tricks; playing on the sense "tricks
played on horses."

LAFEU   I like him well; 'tis not amiss. And I was about to tell
you: since I heard of the good lady's death, and that my lord
60   your son was upon his return home, I moved the King my
master to speak in the behalf of my daughter, which in the
minority of them both his majesty out of a self-gracious
remembrance[3] did first propose. His highness hath promised me to do it, and to stop up the displeasure he hath
65   conceived against your son there is no fitter matter. How
does your ladyship like it?
COUNTESS   With very much content, my lord, and I wish it
happily effected.
LAFEU   His highness comes post° from Marseilles, of as able   *speedily*
70   body as when he numbered thirty. 'A will be here tomorrow,
or I am deceived by him° that in such intelligence° hath sel-   *someone / information*
dom failed.
COUNTESS   It rejoices me that I hope I shall see him ere I die.
I have letters that my son will be here tonight. I shall
75   beseech your lordship to remain with me till they meet
together.
LAFEU   Madam, I was thinking with what manners I might
safely be admitted.°   *invited to be present*
COUNTESS   You need but plead your honorable privilege.[4]
80   LAFEU   Lady, of that I have made a bold charter,[5] but I thank
my God it holds yet.
         Enter CLOWN.
CLOWN   O madam, yonder's my lord your son with a patch of
velvet[6] on 's face. Whether there be a scar under't or no, the
velvet knows, but 'tis a goodly patch of velvet. His left cheek
85   is a cheek of two pile and a half,[7] but his right cheek is worn
bare.
LAFEU   A scar nobly got, or a noble scar, is a good liv'ry° of   *uniform*
honor. So belike° is that.   *probably*
CLOWN   But it is your carbonadoed[8] face.
90   LAFEU   Let us go see your son, I pray you. I long to talk with
the young noble soldier.
CLOWN   'Faith, there's a dozen of 'em, with delicate fine hats
and most courteous feathers, which bow the head and nod
at every man.   *Exeunt.*

5.1

Enter HELEN, WIDOW, *and* DIANA, *with two* ATTENDANTS.
HELEN   But this exceeding posting° day and night   *this hasty riding*
Must wear your spirits low. We cannot help it.
But since you have made the days and nights as one
To wear° your gentle limbs in my affairs,   *tire*
5   Be bold° you do so grow in my requital°   *confident / repayment*
As nothing can unroot you.
         Enter a GENTLE[MAN] *austringer.*[1]
         In happy time!°   *Just at the right time*

---

3. Recollection prompted by his own graciousness.
4. Privilege due your honor.
5. Made as bold a claim as I dare.
6. Used to cover a battle wound or a facial sore from syphilis.
7. The thickest velvet was three-piled; the Clown invents an imaginary next-best.

8. Slashed (like meat for broiling) in battle or by a surgeon, to treat a syphilitic eruption.
5.1 Location: Marseilles.
1. TEXTUAL COMMENT An austringer is a falconer, or keeper of hunting hawks. For a discussion of this unusual stage direction, see Digital Edition TC 8.

This man may help me to his majesty's ear
If he would spend his power. —God save you, sir.
GENTLEMAN   And you.
10   HELEN   Sir, I have seen you in the court of France.
GENTLEMAN   I have been sometimes there.
HELEN   I do presume, sir, that you are not fallen
From the report that goes upon your goodness;
And therefore goaded with most sharp occasions,°   urgent circumstances
15   Which lay nice° manners by, I put° you to   scrupulous / urge
The use of your own virtues, for the which
I shall continue thankful.
GENTLEMAN   What's your will?
HELEN   That it will please you
To give this poor petition to the King,
20   And aid me with that store of power you have
To come into his presence.
GENTLEMAN   The King's not here.
HELEN   Not here, sir?
GENTLEMAN   Not indeed.
He hence removed° last night, and with more haste   departed
Than is his use.°   custom
WIDOW   Lord, how we lose our pains!
25   HELEN   All's well that ends well yet,
Though time seem so adverse and means unfit.
—I do beseech you, whither is he gone?
GENTLEMAN   Marry, as I take it, to Roussillon,
Whither I am going.
HELEN   I do beseech you, sir,
30   Since you are like to see the King before me,
Commend° the paper to his gracious hand,   Present
Which I presume shall render you no blame
But rather make you thank your pains for it.
I will come after you with what good speed
Our means will make us means.°   resources will permit
35   GENTLEMAN   This I'll do for you.
HELEN   And you shall find yourself to be well thanked,
Whate'er falls more.   [Exit GENTLEMAN.]
We must to horse again. [to ATTENDANTS] Go, go, provide.
                                                    [Exeunt.]

5.2

Enter CLOWN *and* PAROLES.
PAROLES   Good Monsieur Lavache, give my lord Lafeu this
letter. I have ere now, sir, been better known to you, when I
have held familiarity with fresher clothes. But I am now, sir,
muddied in Fortune's mood and smell somewhat strong of
5   her strong displeasure.
CLOWN   Truly, Fortune's displeasure is but sluttish if it smell
so strongly as thou speak'st of. I will henceforth eat no fish
of Fortune's butt'ring.° Prithee, allow the wind.[1]   prepared by Fortune
PAROLES   Nay, you need not to stop your nose, sir. I spake but
10   by a metaphor.

5.2 Location: Roussillon.   1. Stand downwind of me.

CLOWN   Indeed, sir, if your metaphor stink I will stop my nose,
or against any man's metaphor. Prithee, get thee further.

PAROLES   Pray you, sir, deliver me this paper.

CLOWN   Foh! Prithee, stand away. A paper from Fortune's
15   close-stool,° to give to a nobleman! Look, here he comes   toilet
himself.

      Enter LAFEU.

Here is a pur² of Fortune's, sir, or of Fortune's cat—but not
a musk cat³—that has fallen into the unclean fishpond of
her displeasure and, as he says, is muddied withal. Pray you,
20   sir, use the carp⁴ as you may, for he looks like a poor,
decayed, ingenious, foolish, rascally knave. I do pity his
distress in my similes of comfort and leave him to your
lordship.

PAROLES   My lord, I am a man whom Fortune hath cruelly
25   scratched.

LAFEU   And what would you have me to do? 'Tis too late to
pare her nails now. Wherein have you played the knave with
Fortune that she should scratch you, who of herself is a good
lady and would not have knaves thrive long under her? There's
30   a *quart d'écu* for you. Let the justices⁵ make you and Fortune
friends; I am for other business.

PAROLES   I beseech your honor to hear me one single word.

LAFEU   You beg a single penny more. Come, you shall ha't.
Save your word.°   breath

35   PAROLES   My name, my good lord, is Paroles.

LAFEU   You beg more than one word,⁶ then. Cox my passion,°   By God's passion
give me your hand! How does your drum?

PAROLES   Oh, my good lord, you were the first that found me.

LAFEU   Was I, in sooth? And I was the first that lost thee.

40   PAROLES   It lies in you, my lord, to bring me in some grace,⁷
for you did bring me out.°   out of favor

LAFEU   Out upon thee, knave, dost thou put upon me at once
both the office of God and the devil? One brings thee in
grace and the other brings thee out. The King's coming; I
45   know by his trumpets. Sirrah, inquire further after me. I had
talk of you last night. Though you are a fool and a knave,
you shall eat. Go to, follow.

PAROLES   I praise God for you.   [*Exeunt.*]

5.3

Flourish. Enter KING, *old Lady* [COUNTESS], LAFEU,
the two French LORDS [DUMAINE], *with* ATTENDANTS.

KING   We lost a jewel of° her, and our esteem°   in / (own) worth
Was made much poorer by it, but your son,
As mad in folly, lacked the sense to know
Her estimation home.°   value to the full

COUNTESS   'Tis past, my liege,
5   And I beseech your majesty to make° it   consider

---

2. Piece of dung; cat's purr; knave (in the card game
post and pair).
3. Civet cat, a source of perfume.
4. Fish often bred in mud ponds; chatterbox.
5. Of the peace, responsible for beggars.

6. Playing on "Paroles," "words."
7. Into some favor (but Lafeu takes "grace" in its
religious sense).
5.3 Location: Scene continues.

Natural rebellion, done i'th' blade° of youth,   *greenness*
When oil and fire, too strong for reason's force,
O'erbears it and burns on.
KING   My honored lady,
 I have forgiven and forgotten all,
10 Though my revenges were high[1] bent upon him
 And watched° the time to shoot.   *vigilantly awaited*
LAFEU   This I must say,
 But first I beg my pardon. The young lord
 Did to his majesty, his mother, and his lady
 Offense of mighty note, but to himself
15 The greatest wrong of all. He lost a wife
 Whose beauty did astonish the survey°   *observation*
 Of richest° eyes; whose words all ears took captive;   *most experienced*
 Whose dear perfection hearts that scorned to serve
 Humbly called mistress.
KING   Praising what is lost
20 Makes the remembrance dear. [*to* ATTENDANT] Well, call him
  hither.
 We are reconciled, and the first view shall kill
 All repetition.[2] Let him not ask our pardon.
 The nature of his great offense is dead,
 And deeper than oblivion we do bury
25 Th'incensing relics° of it. Let him approach   *infuriating reminders*
 A stranger, no offender, and inform him
 So 'tis our will he should.
ATTENDANT   I shall, my liege.   [*Exit.*]
KING [*to* LAFEU] What says he to your daughter? Have you
  spoke?
LAFEU All that he is hath reference° to your highness.   *is submitted*
30 KING Then shall we have a match. I have letters sent me
 That sets him high in fame.
     Enter Count BERTRAM.
LAFEU   He looks well on't.
KING I am not a day of season,°   *constant weather*
 For thou mayst see a sunshine and a hail
 In me at once. But to the brightest beams
35 Distracted° clouds give way. So stand thou forth; *Agitated; broken*
 The time is fair again.
BERTRAM   My high repented blames,° *much-repented faults*
 Dear sovereign, pardon to me.
KING   All is whole.°   *healed*
 Not one word more of the consumèd time.
 Let's take the instant by the forward top,[3]
40 For we are old, and on our quick'st decrees
 Th'inaudible and noiseless foot of time
 Steals ere we can effect them. You remember
 The daughter of this lord?
BERTRAM Admiringly, my liege. At first
45 I stuck° my choice upon her, ere my heart   *fixed*
 Durst make too bold a herald of my tongue;
 Where the impression of mine eye infixing,[4]

---

1. To the utmost (like a taut bow).
2. Rehearsal of past grievances.
3. Let's seize time by the forelock; proverbial for

"taking a present opportunity."
4. Once the impression of Lafeu's daughter was implanted in my heart.

Contempt his scornful perspective[5] did lend me,
Which warped the line of every other favor,°   *face*
50 Scorned a fair color° or expressed it stolen,[6]   *complexion*
Extended or contracted all proportions
To a most hideous object. Thence it came
That she° whom all men praised, and whom myself   *(Helen)*
Since I have lost have loved, was in mine eye
The dust that did offend it.
55 KING   Well excused.
That thou didst love her strikes some scores° away   *debits*
From the great count.° But love that comes too late,   *reckoning*
Like a remorseful° pardon slowly carried,   *compassionate; regretful*
To the great sender turns a sour offense,
60 Crying, "That's good that's gone." Our rash faults
Make trivial price of° serious things we have,   *Underestimate*
Not knowing them until we know their grave.°   *lose them forever*
Oft our displeasures, to ourselves unjust,
Destroy our friends and after weep° their dust.   *mourn over*
65 Our own love waking° cries to see what's done,   *coming to its senses*
While shameful hate sleeps out the afternoon.
Be this sweet Helen's knell, and now forget her.
Send forth your amorous token for fair Maudlin.°   *Lafeu's daughter*
The main consents are had, and here we'll stay
70 To see our widower's second marriage day.
COUNTESS[7] Which better than the first, O dear heaven, bless
Or, ere they meet, in me, O Nature, cease.[8]
LAFEU Come on, my son, in whom my house's name
Must be digested,[9] give a favor from you
75 To sparkle in the spirits of my daughter,
That she may quickly come. [BERTRAM *offers a ring.*] By my
  old beard
And ev'ry hair that's on't! Helen that's dead
Was a sweet creature; such a ring as this,
The last° that ere I took her leave at court,   *last time*
I saw upon her finger.[1]
80 BERTRAM   Hers it was not.
KING Now pray you, let me see it. For mine eye,
While I was speaking, oft was fastened to't.
This ring was mine, and when I gave it Helen
I bade her if her fortunes ever stood
85 Necessitied to° help, that by this token   *In need of*
I would relieve her. Had you that craft to reave° her   *deprive*
Of what should stead° her most?   *aid*
BERTRAM   My gracious sovereign,
Howe'er it pleases you to take it so,
The ring was never hers.
COUNTESS   Son, on my life
90 I have seen her wear it, and she reckoned it
At her life's rate.°   *value*

---

5. Distorting optical glass.
6. Declared it artificial.
7. In F, the King speaks these lines.
8. Before they come to resemble one another, let me

die.
9. Absorbed (because Maudlin is his only child and will take Bertram's name).
1. See 4.2.61–64.

LAFEU   I am sure I saw her wear it.
BERTRAM   You are deceived, my lord; she never saw it.
In Florence was it from a casement thrown me,
Wrapped in a paper which contained the name
95   Of her that threw it. Noble she was, and thought
I stood engaged,[2] but when I had subscribed
To mine own fortune,° and informed her fully   admitted my situation
I could not answer in that course of honor
As she had made the overture, she ceased
100 In heavy satisfaction° and would never   sad acceptance
Receive the ring again.
KING   Plutus° himself,   god of riches
That knows the tinct and multiplying med'cine,[3]
Hath not in nature's mystery more science°   expertise
Than I have in this ring. 'Twas mine, 'twas Helen's,
105 Whoever gave it you. Then if you know
That you are well acquainted with yourself,[4]
Confess 'twas hers and by what rough enforcement
You got it from her. She called the saints to surety°   guarantee
That she would never put it from her finger,
110 Unless she gave it to yourself in bed,
Where you have never come, or sent it us
Upon° her great disaster.   On the occasion of
BERTRAM   She never saw it.
KING   Thou speak'st it falsely, as I love mine honor,
And mak'st conjectural fears to come into me
115 Which I would fain° shut out. If it should prove   gladly
That thou art so inhuman—'twill not prove so—
And yet I know not. Thou didst hate her deadly
And she is dead, which nothing but to close
Her eyes myself could win me to believe
120 More than to see this ring. —Take him away!
—My forepassed proofs,[5] howe'er the matter fall,°   befalls
Shall tax° my fears of little vanity,°   accuse / foolishness
Having vainly feared too little. —Away with him!
We'll sift this matter further.
BERTRAM   If you shall prove
125 This ring was ever hers, you shall as easy
Prove that I husbanded her bed in Florence,
Where yet she never was.   [Exit, guarded.]
        Enter a GENTLEMAN [austringer].
KING   I am wrapped in dismal thinkings.
GENTLEMAN   Gracious sovereign.
Whether I have been to blame or no, I know not.
130 Here's a petition from a Florentine,
Who hath for four or five removes come short
To tender it herself.[6] I undertook it,
Vanquished thereto by the fair grace and speech
Of the poor suppliant, who by this° I know   now
135 Is here attending. Her business looks° in her   shows itself

---

2. Pledged to her (alternatively, "ungaged," not
promised to anyone else).
3. Alchemical elixir for turning other metals into
gold.
4. That you know who you are; that you are willing

to admit your actions.
5. My evidence already in hand.
6. Who . . . herself: Who has for four or five changes
of royal residence failed to arrive in time to deliver it
herself.

With an importing° visage, and she told me   *urgent*
In a sweet verbal brief° it did concern   *summary*
Your highness with herself.

KING [*reads the*] *letter*   "Upon his many protestations to marry
140   me when his wife was dead, I blush to say it, he won me. Now
is the Count Roussillon a widower. His vows are forfeited to
me,[7] and my honors paid to him. He stole from Florence,
taking no leave, and I follow him to his country for justice.
Grant it me, O King; in you it best lies. Otherwise a seducer
145   flourishes and a poor maid is undone.

                         Diana Capilet."

LAFEU   I will buy me a son-in-law in a fair[8] and toll for this.[9]
I'll none of him.

KING   The heavens have thought well on thee, Lafeu,
150   To bring forth this discov'ry. —Seek these suitors.

                  [*Exit* GENTLEMAN *austringer.*]

—Go speedily, and bring again the Count.

                  [*Exit an* ATTENDANT.]

I am a-feared the life of Helen, lady,
Was foully snatched.

COUNTESS   Now justice on the doers!

      Enter BERTRAM.

KING   I wonder, sir, since wives are monsters to you,
155   And that° you fly them as you swear them lordship,[1]   *since*
Yet you desire to marry.

      Enter WIDOW [*and*] DIANA.

                    What woman's that?

DIANA   I am, my lord, a wretched Florentine,
Derivèd° from the ancient Capilet.   *Descended*
My suit, as I do understand, you know,
160   And therefore know how far I may be pitied.

WIDOW   I am her mother, sir, whose age and honor
Both suffer under this complaint we bring,
And both° shall cease without your remedy.   *(age and honor)*

KING   Come hither, Count. Do you know these women?
165 BERTRAM   My lord, I neither can nor will deny
But that I know them. Do they charge me further?

DIANA   Why do you look so strange upon your wife?

BERTRAM   She's none of mine, my lord.

DIANA   If you shall marry
You give away this° hand, and that is mine;   *(Bertram's)*
170   You give away heaven's vows, and those are mine;
You give away myself, which is known mine.
For I by vow am so embodied yours
That she which marries you must marry me,
Either both or none.

175 LAFEU   Your reputation comes too short for my daughter. You
are no husband for her.

BERTRAM   My lord, this is a fond° and desp'rate creature   *foolish*
Whom sometime I have laughed with. Let your highness
Lay a more noble thought upon mine honor
180   Than for to think that I would sink it here.

---

7. His promises have fallen due.   (Bertram).
8. Notorious for unreliable merchandise.   1. As soon as you vow to wed them.
9. Pay a tax for the privilege of selling this one

KING   Sir, for my thoughts, you have them ill to friend[2]
  Till your deeds gain them. Fairer prove your honor
  Than in my thought it lies!
DIANA   Good my lord,
  Ask him upon his oath if he does think
185 He had not my virginity.
KING   What say'st thou to her?
BERTRAM   She's impudent, my lord,
  And was a common gamester° to the camp.   prostitute
DIANA   He does me wrong, my lord. If I were so
  He might have bought me at a common price.
190 Do not believe him. Oh, behold this ring,
  Whose high respect° and rich validity°   worth / value
  Did lack a parallel. Yet for all that
  He gave it to a commoner o'th' camp
  If I be one.
COUNTESS   He blushes, and 'tis hit.°   it hit the mark
195 Of six preceding ancestors that gem,
  Conferred by testament to th' sequent issue,°   following generation
  Hath it been owed° and worn. This is his wife;   owned
  That ring's a thousand proofs.
KING   Methought you said°   (perhaps in the letter)
  You saw one here in court could witness it.
200 DIANA   I did, my lord, but loath am to produce
  So bad an instrument. His name's Paroles.
LAFEU   I saw the man today, if man he be.
KING   —Find him and bring him hither. [*Exit an* ATTENDANT.]
BERTRAM   What of him?
  He's quoted° for a most perfidious slave   noted
205 With all the spots o'th' world, taxed and debauched,
  Whose nature sickens but to speak a truth.
  Am I or° that or this for what he'll utter   either
  That will speak anything?
KING   She hath that ring of yours.
BERTRAM   I think she has. Certain it is I liked her
210 And boarded° her i'th' wanton way of youth.   made advances to
  She knew her distance and did angle for me,
  Madding° my eagerness with her restraint,   Maddening
  As all impediments in fancy's° course   love's
  Are motives° of more fancy. And in fine,°   causes / the end
215 Her infinite cunning with her modern° grace   commonplace
  Subdued me to her rate.° She got the ring,   price
  And I had that which any inferior might
  At market price have bought.
DIANA   I must be patient:
  You that have turned off a first so noble wife
220 May justly diet° me. I pray you yet—   starve (of favor)
  Since you lack virtue, I will lose a husband—
  Send for your ring, I will return it home,
  And give me mine again.
BERTRAM   I have it not.
KING   What ring was yours, I pray you?
225 DIANA   Sir, much like the same upon your finger.

---

2. *you . . . friend:* they are no friends of yours.

KING Know you this ring? This ring was his of late.

DIANA And this was it I gave him being abed.

KING The story then goes false you threw it him
Out of a casement.

DIANA   I have spoke the truth.

Enter PAROLES.

230 BERTRAM My lord, I do confess the ring was hers.

KING You boggle shrewdly;³ every feather starts° you.   startles
—Is this the man you speak of?

DIANA   Ay, my lord.

KING Tell me, sirrah—but tell me true, I charge you,
Not fearing the displeasure of your master,

235 Which on your just proceeding I'll keep off—
By° him and by this woman here, what know you?   About

PAROLES So please your majesty, my master hath been
an honorable gentleman. Tricks he hath had in him which
gentlemen have.

240 KING Come, come, to th' purpose. Did he love this woman?

PAROLES Faith, sir, he did love her, but how?

KING How, I pray you?

PAROLES He did love her, sir, as a gentleman loves a woman.

KING How is that?

245 PAROLES He loved her, sir, and loved her not.

KING As thou art a knave and no knave. —What an equivocal
companion is this!

PAROLES I am a poor man and at your majesty's command.

LAFEU He's a good drum,⁴ my lord, but a naughty° orator.   bad

250 DIANA Do you know he promised me marriage?

PAROLES Faith, I know more than I'll speak.

KING But wilt thou not speak all thou know'st?

PAROLES Yes, so please your majesty. I did go between them,
as I said, but more than that, he loved her. For indeed he

255 was mad for her, and talked of Satan, and of limbo, and of
furies, and I know not what. Yet I was in that° credit with   so much
them at that time that I knew of their going to bed, and of
other motions,° as promising her marriage, and things which   proposals
would derive me ill will to speak of. Therefore I will not

260 speak what I know.

KING Thou hast spoken all already, unless thou canst say
they are married. But thou art too fine° in thy evidence: hairsplitting
therefore stand aside.

[*to* DIANA] This ring, you say, was yours.

DIANA   Ay, my good lord.

265 KING Where did you buy it? Or who gave it you?

DIANA It was not given me, nor I did not buy it.

KING Who lent it you?

DIANA   It was not lent me neither.

KING Where did you find it then?

DIANA   I found it not.

KING If it were yours by none of all these ways,
How could you give it him?

---

3. You take fright violently; you attempt to evade the
point wickedly (or incompetently).

4. Capable only of noise; Lafeu probably also refers
to Paroles' earlier adventures.

270 DIANA   I never gave it him.

LAFEU   This woman's an easy glove, my lord: she goes off and
on at pleasure.

KING   This ring was mine. I gave it his first wife.

DIANA   It might be yours or hers for aught I know.

275 KING   Take her away; I do not like her now.
To prison with her! And away with him!
[*to* DIANA] Unless thou tell'st me where thou hadst this ring,
Thou diest within this hour.

DIANA   I'll never tell you.

KING   Take her away!

DIANA   I'll put in bail, my liege.

280 KING   I think thee now some common customer.°   *prostitute*

DIANA   By Jove, if ever I knew° man, 'twas you.   *(carnally)*

KING   Wherefore hast thou accused him all this while?

DIANA   Because he's guilty and he is not guilty.
He knows I am no maid and he'll swear to't;

285 I'll swear I am a maid and he knows not.
Great King, I am no strumpet, by my life;
I am either maid or else [*pointing at* LAFEU] this old man's° wife.   *(Lafeu's)*

KING   She does abuse our ears. To prison with her!

DIANA   Good mother, fetch my bail.   [*Exit* WIDOW.]
—Stay, royal sir.

290 The jeweler that owes° the ring is sent for   *owns*
And he shall surety me.° But for this lord,   *be my security*
Who hath abused me as he knows himself,
Though yet he never harmed me, here I quit° him.   *acquit; repay; leave*
He knows himself my bed he hath defiled,

295 And at that time he got his wife with child.
Dead though she be, she feels her young one kick.
So there's my riddle: one that's dead is quick.°   *alive; pregnant*
And now behold the meaning.
Enter HELEN *and* WIDOW.

KING   Is there no exorcist°   *conjurer*
Beguiles the truer office° of mine eyes?   *function*
Is't real that I see?

300 HELEN   No, my good lord.
'Tis but the shadow° of a wife you see,   *ghost; imitation*
The name and not the thing.

BERTRAM   Both, both! Oh, pardon!

HELEN   O my good lord, when I was like° this maid   *in the place of*
I found you wondrous kind. There is your ring,

305 And look you, here's your letter. This it says:
"When from my finger you can get this ring,
And are by me with child," etc. This is done,
Will you be mine now you are doubly won?

BERTRAM   If she, my liege, can make me know this clearly,

310 I'll love her dearly, ever, ever, dearly.

HELEN   If it appear not plain and prove untrue,
Deadly divorce step between me and you.
O my dear mother, do I see you living?

LAFEU [*to* PAROLES]   Mine eyes smell onions; I shall weep anon.

315 Good Tom Drum, lend me a handkerchief.
So. I thank thee. Wait on me home, I'll make sport with
thee. Let thy curtsies alone, they are scurvy ones.

KING   Let us from point to point this story know
   To make the even° truth in pleasure flow.   *plain*
320   [*to* DIANA] If thou beest yet a fresh uncroppèd flower,
   Choose thou thy husband and I'll pay thy dower.
   For I can guess that by thy honest aid
   Thou kept'st a wife herself, thyself a maid.
   Of that and all the progress more and less[5]
325   Resolvedly° more leisure shall express.   *So questions are resolved*
   All yet seems well, and if it end so meet,°   *properly*
   The bitter passed, more welcome is the sweet.
      Flourish.
   The King's a beggar now the play is done.
   All is well ended if this suit be won,
330   That you express content,° which we will pay   *(by applause)*
   With strife° to please you, day exceeding° day.   *trying / after*
   Ours be your patience, then, and yours our parts;[6]
   Your gentle hands lend us, and take our hearts.   *Exeunt.*

---

5. The course of events, great and small.
6. *Ours . . . parts:* We will wait patiently, like an audience, while you take the active part.

Macbeth

On May 19, 1603, a scant two months after the death of Queen Elizabeth and the accession to the English throne of the Scottish King James, Shakespeare's company, the Chamberlain's Men, was formally declared to be the King's Men. The players had every reason to be grateful to their royal master for this lucrative distinction and to be attentive to his pleasure and interest. It has long been argued that one of the most striking signs of their gratitude is *Macbeth*, based on a story from Scottish history particularly apt for a monarch who traced his line back to Banquo, the noble thane whose murder Macbeth orders after he has killed King Duncan. Shakespeare's Scottish play is far too complex about the nature of power—and far too frightening—to have served as a simple piece of flattery. But the King's Men must have calculated that the Jacobean court, where the play was frequently performed, would find the tragedy's vision gripping.

As so often with Shakespeare, we do not have a secure date for either the composition or the first performance of *Macbeth*. The first printed text is in the 1623 First Folio, but the play, usually dated 1606, has always seemed the most topical of Shakespeare's great tragedies, cannily alert at once to King James's personal obsessions and to contemporary events. The most unnerving of those events was the 1605 Gunpowder Plot, an assassination attempt that riveted the attention of the entire kingdom and had long-term political and psychological consequences. A small group of conspirators, embittered by what they perceived as James's unwillingness to extend toleration to Roman Catholics, smuggled barrels of gunpowder into the basement beneath the House of Lords and allegedly planned to set off a massive explosion that would blow up the King and his family, along with most of the government, at the ceremonial opening of England's Parliament. According to the official account, the King himself saved the day by brilliantly interpreting a subtle hint in an intercepted letter. On the night before the intended attempt, officers arrested one of the principal conspirators, Guy Fawkes, who revealed under torture the names of his collaborators.

How is it possible to confront and triumph over terror? What are the dark roots of treason? Whom can you trust? Surface appearances may deceive; apparently straightforward statements may conceal dangerous ambiguities; it is important to read between the lines. Among those hunted down and brought to trial was Father Henry Garnet, head of the clandestine Jesuit mission in England. Swearing that he was innocent, Garnet pointed out that there was no evidence against him, but the government prosecutors made much of the fact that he was the author of *A Treatise of Equivocation*, a book showing how to give misleading answers under oath. Convicted of treason, he was hanged, drawn, and quartered, and his head was set on a pole on London Bridge.

Written in the wake of this national trauma, Shakespeare's whole play is haunted by equivocation. At a harrowing moment in *Macbeth*, in the immediate wake of the murder of the sleeping King Duncan, an insistent knocking is heard at the castle gate. (The knocking is a simple device, but in performance it almost always has a thrilling effect, famously characterized by the Romantic critic Thomas de Quiney as the first reflux of the ordinary human world upon the fiendish.) A porter, roused by the hammering on the door but still half drunk from the evening's revelry, appears, and the play lurches suddenly toward macabre comedy. As he grumblingly goes to unlock the gate, the porter imagines that he is the gatekeeper in hell, opening the door to new arrivals. "Here's an equivocator," he says of one of these imaginary sinners, "that could swear in both the scales against either scale, who committed treason enough for God's sake, yet could not equivocate to heaven. Oh, come in, equivocator" (2.3.7–10). This treasonous equivocator knocking on hell's gate is almost certainly an allusion to the recently executed Henry Garnet.

The Gunpowder Plot was only one of the King's sources of anxiety. Not surprising for someone whose mother and father had both been killed, James had a horror of assassination and was convinced that there were many plots against his life. He also held a powerful conviction that a king was a sacred figure, God's own representative on earth. Regicide, in this view, was close to the ultimate crime, a demonic assault not simply on an individual and a community but on the fundamental order of the universe. James, who had written a learned book on witchcraft, suspected the hand of the devil in any plot against an anointed king, believed that witches had at various points in his own life conspired to harm him or render him impotent, and feared the existence of occult, invisible forces bent on bringing all things to ruin.

In several of his earlier plays, most notably *Richard II*, Shakespeare's characters give voice to the theory that the king is God's deputy on earth and consequently that attacks upon him are evil. The theory is by no means simply endorsed in any of these plays, and it jostles up against a thoroughly secular analysis of power politics and the manipulation of ideology. But kingship's claim to sacred authority is voiced exceptionally powerfully in *Macbeth* (not in Scotland alone, but also in neighboring England, where, as Malcolm tells Macduff, the touch of the pious King Edward cures disease). Exceptionally powerful too in this play is the metaphysical horror of regicide. The murder of Duncan is marked in the natural world with dreadful signs and portents, and in the human world with an overpowering sense of devastation ironically given its most eloquent expression by the murderer Macbeth:

> Renown and grace is dead.
> The wine of life is drawn, and the mere lees
> Is left this vault to brag of.
>
> (2.3.91–93)

Macbeth is speaking hypocritically—"Look like th'innocent flower," his wife had counseled him, "But be the serpent under't" (1.5.63–64)—and yet, at least in one interpretation of the part, he is saying what he himself knows to be the grim truth. Far more than any other of Shakespeare's villains, more than the homicidal Richard III, the treacherous Claudius in *Hamlet*, and the cold-hearted Iago in *Othello*, Macbeth is tormented by an awareness of the wickedness of what he is doing. Endowed with a clear-eyed grasp of the difference between good and evil, he chooses evil, even though the choice mystifies and sickens him.

Before he has taken the irrevocable step, Macbeth tries to recover his moral bearings. The deed he is contemplating, he begins by telling himself, would work only if he could control all consequences, so that his blow "Might be the be-all and the end-all" (1.7.5). But he grasps that there is no possibility of such complete control and therefore no hope of practical success. His thoughts then turn to the overwhelming ethical arguments against the murder: he is not only the King's kinsman and subject but also his host, "Who should against his murderer shut the door, / Not bear the knife myself" (1.7.15–16). And from these considerations, practical and ethical, Macbeth's restless, brooding mind rises higher, imagining that the murdered Duncan's virtues will plead like angels against the "deep damnation of his taking-off";

> And Pity, like a naked newborn babe
> Striding the blast, or heaven's cherubim horsed
> Upon the sightless couriers of the air,
> Shall blow the horrid deed in every eye,
> That tears shall drown the wind.
>
> (1.7.20–25)

Henry IV of France (1553–1610) administers the royal touch, thought to cure scrofula. An etching by Pierre Firens, in André Du Laurens' *De mirabili strumas sanandi vi solis Galliae regibus . . .* (Paris, 1609). See *Macbeth* 4.3.141–59.

No one else in the play has a moral sensibility so intense or so visionary, no one else imagines so vividly the forces that lie beyond the ordinary and familiar horizon of human experience. Macbeth understands exactly what is at stake and what he must do: "We will," he tells his wife decisively, "proceed no further in this business" (1.7.31).

Why, then, does he change his mind and commit a crime he cannot even contemplate without horror? A significant part of the answer lies in the instigation of his formidable wife. When we first glimpse Lady Macbeth, she is reading a letter. (Reading was by no means a universal achievement for women of the early seventeenth century, let alone the eleventh, when the play's events are set, but Shakespeare frequently represents it in his plays in a variety of contexts.) The letter makes her burn with visions of the "golden round" that "fate and metaphysical aid" (1.5.26–27) seem to have conferred upon her husband. But though she speaks of the crown as if it were already on Macbeth's head, she fears that he is too full of the "milk of human kindness" (1.5.15) to seize what has been promised him. She resolves then to "chastise" her husband, to urge him, in a phrase taken from archery that has a strong sexual undercurrent, to screw his courage to the sticking place. Lady Macbeth manipulates him in two principal ways. The first is through sexual taunting:

> Art thou afeard
> To be the same in thine own act and valor
> As thou art in desire?
> . . . .
> When you durst do it, then you were a man.
> (1.7.39–41, 49)

And the second is through the terrible force of her determination:

> I have given suck and know
> How tender 'tis to love the babe that milks me;
> I would, while it was smiling in my face,
> Have plucked my nipple from his boneless gums
> And dashed the brains out, had I so sworn as you
> Have done to this.
>
> (1.7.54–59)

These words, and the gestures that viscerally intensify them onstage, cannot by themselves account for Macbeth's decision. He counters his wife's sexual taunting with a clear sense of the proper boundaries of his identity as a male and as a human being: "I dare do all that may become a man; / Who dares do more is none" (1.7.46–47). As for Lady Macbeth's fantasy of murdering her infant, its horror might have served rather to deter Macbeth from his unnatural crime than to spur him toward it.

Virtually everyone is subject to terrible dreams and lawless fantasies—"Merciful powers," Banquo prays, "Restrain in me the cursèd thoughts that nature / Gives way to in repose" (2.1.7–9)—but not everyone crosses the fatal line from criminal desire to criminal act. That in crossing this line Macbeth murders a man toward whom he should be grateful, loyal, and protective deepens the mystery of his crime, linking it to a long current of theological and philosophical brooding on the nature of evil. For St. Augustine, the great fourth-century Church Father, evil in its most radical form is gratuitous—that is, without an explicable rationale or motivation—and this notion of gratuitousness haunts subsequent thinkers, including those far from Christian orthodoxy. Thus the Florentine Niccolò Machiavelli, notorious in the sixteenth century for free-thinking, writes in chapter 37 of his *Discourses* that "when men are no longer obliged to fight from necessity, they fight from ambition, which passion is so powerful in the hearts of men that it never leaves them, no matter to what height they may rise." The reason for this, Machiavelli proposes, is that "nature has created men so that they desire everything, but are unable to attain it; desire being thus always greater than the faculty of acquiring, discontent with what they have and dissatisfaction with themselves result from it."

Macbeth and Lady Macbeth act on ambition, restless desire, and a will to power normally kept in check by the pragmatic, ethical, and religious considerations to which the wavering Macbeth initially gives voice. Lady Macbeth in effect works to liberate that will to power in her husband, freeing him from his "sickly" fears of damnation so that he can act with a ruthless blend of murderous violence and cunning. In her radically disenchanted, coolly skeptical view, the murder of the King can be undertaken without fear of guilty conscience, vengeful ghosts, or divine judgment: "The sleeping and the dead," she tells her shaken husband, "Are but as pictures; 'tis the eye of childhood / That fears a painted devil" (2.2.56–58).

This reassurance, Shakespeare's tragedy shows, is hopelessly shallow. As the spectral dagger, the ghost sitting in Macbeth's chair, and the indelible bloodstains on Lady Macbeth's hands all chillingly demonstrate, the secure distinction between representation and reality, the dead and the living, repeatedly breaks down, not simply for the characters but for the spectators as well. In most productions, the dagger and the blood are visible only to the diseased minds of the murderers, but Banquo's ghost is almost always palpably present onstage, visible to the audience as well as to the unhinged Macbeth, though invisible to everyone around him. Moreover, the dream of a "clean" regicide proves psychologically untenable. Lady Macbeth, who had vaunted that she would readily kill her own infant in the pursuit of her ambition, finds that a family resemblance prevents her from sticking a dagger in the sleeping King: "Had he not resembled / My father as he slept, I had done't" (2.2.12–13).

The seizure of the crown brings with it feverish sleeplessness, brooding anxiety about security, and an overwhelming sense of defilement. Macbeth and Lady Macbeth are equally devastated, but the psychological trajectory in the wake of the crime is not the same for the two conspirators. Initially frozen in moral numbness, Lady Macbeth experiences a gradual decomposition, a growing horror that breaks forth unforgettably in the sleepwalking scene with her compulsive attempts to free herself of the smell and stain of blood: "All the perfumes of Arabia will not sweeten this little hand" (5.1.44–45). Initially gripped by a heightened sensitivity to fear, a dread that threatens inward decomposition, Macbeth experiences a gradual hardening and deadening of the self:

> Tomorrow and tomorrow and tomorrow
> Creeps in this petty pace from day to day
> To the last syllable of recorded time. . . .
> (5.5.19–21)

Macbeth's murderous attempt to make himself "perfect" (3.4.22), as he puts it, leads by a grim irony to a state of absolute numbness, so that his life story, indeed any life story, seems to him in the end "a tale / Told by an idiot, full of sound and fury, / Signifying nothing" (5.5.26–28).

The assassination also proves, as Macbeth had foreseen, politically untenable. There is always someone who escapes the murderer's net, someone who poses a threat or seeks to redress an injury or simply remembers what it felt like to be free and unafraid. It is impossible to tie up all the loose ends, to break the chain of action and reaction, to reach a stable resting place. There are no clean murders. One crime leads to another and then to another, without bringing the criminal any closer to the security or contentment that each desperate act is meant to achieve. Macbeth cannot stop the bloody acts; instead he must multiply and extend them. Where Lady Macbeth had only fantasized the murder of children, Macbeth actually undertakes that and other crimes until he dreams, in his half-crazed words to the "secret, black, and midnight hags" (4.1.47), of universal destruction.

It is Macbeth's first encounter with these hags—the weird (or, in the original spelling, "weyward" or "weyard") sisters—that seems to initiate his descent toward murder and tyranny. But what kind of power do these malevolent bearded women have over Macbeth? Are they responsible, by magical influence or by planting the idea in his mind, for his decision to kill Duncan? Are they somehow privy to a predestined fate, as if they have seen the script of the tragedy before it is performed? Or, alternatively, are they uncanny emblems of Macbeth's psychological condition, a kind of screen onto which he projects his "horrible imaginings" (1.3.140)? The word "weird," in one of its etymologies, derives from the Old English word for "fate," but do the women Shakespeare depicts, trafficking in ambiguous prophecies, fretting over village squabbles, mumbling charms, actually control destiny (or, what amounts to the same thing, the tragedy's plot)? What is the nature of these strange creatures that "look not like th'inhabitants o'th' earth," as Banquo observes, "And yet are on't" (1.3.42–43)?

Actors' responses to these questions have ranged wildly, though virtually all productions have recognized that the witches' scenes are among the most theatrically powerful and compelling in the play and that it matters a great deal whether they are made up to look grotesque or stately, perversely comical or terrifying. Scholarly responses have been complicated by the high probability that not all of the witchcraft scenes are by Shakespeare himself: it appears that 3.5 and part of 4.1, the scenes featuring the goddess Hecate, were added to the play sometime after its first performance and incorporate songs derived from Thomas Middleton's play *The Witch*. (The Folio text of Macbeth, and hence *The Norton Shakespeare*, cites only the first words of these songs, but they were probably sung in full onstage: recordings of these songs can be found in the Digital Edition.) But even if we set aside the problems raised by these interpolated scenes, the status of the witches in Shakespeare's play remains uncertain and seems to be so by design. "What are you?" asks Macbeth when he first encounters the eerie, sexually ambiguous figures, and he receives in reply his

Macbeth and Banquo encounter the weird sisters (1.3). From Raphael Holinshed, *The First Volume of the Chronicles of England, Scotland, and Ireland* (1577).

own name: "All hail, Macbeth!" (1.3.48–49). Banquo urgently renews the inquiry, asking the creatures before his eyes if they truly exist or are only figments of his imagination; but his question, too, remains unanswered. When Macbeth and Banquo demand to know more, the witches vanish: "what seemed corporal / Melted as breath into the wind" (1.3.82–83). "As breath into the wind"—*Macbeth* is a tragedy of meltings, vanishing boundaries, and liminal states.

Much of the play transpires on the border between fantasy and reality, a sickening betwixt-and-between where a "horrid image" in the mind has the uncanny power to produce bodily effects "Against the use of nature" (1.3.137, 139), where one mind is present to the innermost fantasies of another, where manhood threatens to vanish and murdered men walk and blood cannot be washed off. If these effects could be unequivocally attributed to the agency of the witches, the audience would at least have the security of a defined and focused fear. Alternatively, if the witches could be definitively dismissed as fantasy or fraud, the audience would at least have the clear-eyed certainty of witnessing human causes in an altogether secular world. But instead, it remains fascinatingly difficult to determine how much agency either Macbeth or his wife actually possesses, how much their choices are governed by political calculations in a radically unstable kingdom, how much they are in the grip of forces they barely understand.

Shakespeare achieves the remarkable effect of a nebulous infection, a bleeding of the demonic into the secular and the secular into the demonic. The most famous instance of this effect is Lady Macbeth's great invocation of the "spirits / That tend on mortal thoughts" (1.5.38–39) to unsex her, fill her with cruelty, make thick her blood, and exchange her milk for gall. The speech appears to be a conjuration of demonic powers, an act of witchcraft in which the "murdering ministers" are directed to bring about a set of changes in her body. She calls these ministers "sightless substances" (1.5.47): though invisible, they are—as she conceives them—not figures of speech or projections of her mind, but objective, substantial beings or forces. (Macbeth similarly seems to imagine invisible but objective forces when he speaks of "the sightless couriers of the air," 1.7.23.) But the fact that the spirits she invokes are "sightless" already moves this passage away from the literal existence of the weird sisters and toward the metaphorical use of "spirits" in her speech of a few moments earlier: "Hie thee hither, / That I may pour my spirits in thine ear" (1.5.23–24). The spirits she

Witchcraft in Scotland. From *News from Scotland* (1591).

speaks of here are manifestly figurative—they refer to the bold words, the undaunted mettle, and the sexual taunts with which she intends to incite Macbeth to murder Duncan—but, like all of her expressions of will and passion, they strain toward bodily realization, even as they convey a psychic and hence invisible inwardness. That is, there is something uncannily literal about Lady Macbeth's influence on her husband, as if marital intimacy were akin to demonic possession, as if she had contrived to inhabit his mind, as if, in other words, she had literally poured her spirits in his ear. Conversely, there is something uncannily figurative about the "sightless substances" she invokes, as if the spirit world, the realm of "fate and metaphysical aid," were only a metaphor for her blind and murderous desires, as if the weird sisters were condensations of her own breath.

In Shakespeare's plays, as in those of his contemporaries, evildoers may wreak havoc for a time, but in the final restoration of order and justice, they and their principal accomplices are almost inevitably punished. Thus, at the close of *Macbeth*, not only are Macbeth and Lady Macbeth dead, but the victorious Malcolm also speaks of settling scores with "the cruel ministers / Of this dead butcher and his fiend-like Queen" (5.7.98–99). Yet though the play has deeply implicated the witches in Macbeth's monstrous assault on the fabric of civilized life, there is no gesture toward punishing them, no sign that the victors are even aware of their existence. This omission is the more striking if we recall that at the time Shakespeare wrote his play, the authorities in England and Scotland were bringing women to trial on charges of witchcraft and executing them. The theatrical power of *Macbeth* seems bound up with its refusal to resolve the questions raised by the witches. At once marginal and central to the play, they are only briefly and intermittently onstage, but they are still suggestively present when we cannot see them, when the threats they embody are absorbed in the ordinary relations of everyday life.

"There's no art / To find the mind's construction in the face" (1.4.11–12), says the baffled Duncan about a man who had betrayed his trust, but Macbeth confronts a deeper perplexity, an appalling mystery within himself:

> My thought, whose murder yet is but fantastical,
> Shakes so my single state of man
> That function is smothered in surmise,
> And nothing is but what is not.
>
> (1.3.141–44)

The witches have something to do with this inner torment, but what that something is remains as elusive as the dagger that Macbeth sees before him, handle toward his hand. Scotland is sick, "Almost afraid to know itself" (4.3.165). But the sickness cannot be isolated in a conspiracy of witches. If violence stirs in the hinterlands, where marauding armies struggle, it breeds more murderously still in the inmost circles of the realm, where the ruler feels most secure: "This castle hath a pleasant seat," says Duncan, going unwittingly to his death. "The air nimbly and sweetly recommends itself / Unto our gentle senses" (1.6.1–3).

If there is sexual disturbance out on the heath, where the bearded hags stir the ingredients of their hideous cauldron, there is deeper sexual disturbance at home, in the murderous intimacy of the marriage bond: "When you durst do it, then you were a man" (1.7.49). If the mind is subject to "supernatural soliciting" (1.3.132) from some bizarre place, it is gripped still more terribly and irresistibly by "horrible imaginings" (1.3.140) from within. If you are anxious about your future, scrutinize your best friends. If you are worried about losing your manhood, it is not enough to hunt for witches; look to your wife. If you are worried about demonic temptation, fear your own dreams. And if you fear spiritual desolation, turn your eyes on the contents not only of the cauldron but of your skull: "Oh, full of scorpions is my mind, dear wife!" (3.2.35).

The men who persecuted witches in Shakespeare's age were determined to compel full confessions, to pass judgment, and to escape from the terror of the inexplicable, the unforeseen, the aimlessly malignant. In *Macbeth*, the audience is given something better than confession, for it has visible proof of the demonic in action, but this visibility turns out to be as maddeningly equivocal or frustrating as the witches' riddling words. The "wayward" witches appear and disappear, their promises and prophecies all tricks, like practical jokes with appalling consequences. The ambiguous language of the play subverts the illusory certainties of sight, and the forces of renewed order, Malcolm and Macduff, are themselves strangely unstable. Malcolm, who spins an elaborate fantasy of his own viciousness, and Macduff, who abandons his wife and children to their slaughter, are peculiar emblems of a renewed, divinely sanctioned order. Shakespeare may have set out to please the king, but it is difficult to see how the king, if he paid any attention to the tragedy that the King's Men offered him, could be reassured. The ambiguities of demonic agency are never resolved, and its horror spreads like a mist through a murky landscape. "What is't you do?" Macbeth asks the weird sisters, who answer, "A deed without a name" (4.1.48).

By the play's close, Macbeth has begun "To doubt th'equivocation of the fiend / That lies like truth" (5.5.43–44). Equivocations are lies with mental reservations, words with double meanings, puns, twists of emphasis, and plays on false interpretations (such as the meaning of the phrase "not of woman born"). Like the witches— and, for that matter, like concepts of gender and authority and social order—language in *Macbeth* is a boundary-stalker, neither a trustworthy guide nor a manifest illusion. Words sit dangerously in a middle ground; they must be brought under control, but they always threaten to slide into lies or magic charms or riddles or sheer emptiness. It is this emptiness with which Macbeth seems haunted at the end, with his vision of life as "a tale told by an idiot." If the closing moments of the play invite us to recoil from this black hole—after all, the tyrant is killed and his severed head held up for all to see—they also invite us to recoil from too confident and simple a celebration of the triumph of grace. For somewhere beyond the immediate circle of order restored, the witches are dancing around the cauldron, and, the play seems to imply, the cauldron is in every one of us.

STEPHEN GREENBLATT

SELECTED BIBLIOGRAPHY

Adelman, Janet. "'Born of Woman': Fantasies of Maternal Power in *Macbeth.*" *Cannibals, Witches, and Divorce: Estranging the Renaissance.* Ed. Marjorie Garber. Baltimore, MD: Johns Hopkins UP, 1987. 90–121. Argues that *Macbeth* represents dueling fantasies of absolute, destructive female power and of escape from that power; masculine authority is consolidated in the end by eliminating the feminine.

Bradley, A. C. *Shakespearean Tragedy: Lectures on "Hamlet," "Othello," "King Lear," "Macbeth."* London: Macmillan, 1905. Presents *Macbeth* as the most concentrated, classical, and fast-paced of Shakespeare's great tragedies, producing unequaled dread with its dark atmosphere and sublime central characters.

Calderwood, James L. *If It Were Done: "Macbeth" and Tragic Action.* Amherst: U of Massachusetts P, 1986. Looks at how *Macbeth* subverts the models of *Hamlet* and Aristotelian poetics, interrogating the nature of tragedy and the role of violence as both a threat to and a source of social order.

Greenblatt, Stephen. "Shakespeare Bewitched." *New Historical Literary Study: Essays on Reproducing Texts, Representing History.* Ed. Jeffrey N. Cox and Larry J. Reynolds. Princeton, NJ: Princeton UP, 1993. 108–35. Examines how in writing *Macbeth* Shakespeare drew upon both the king's belief in witchcraft and a skeptical critique of such belief by Reginald Scot.

Harris, Jonathan Gil. "The Smell of *Macbeth.*" *Shakespeare Quarterly* 58 (2007): 465–86. Reflects on the smell of gunpowder used for stage effects in the early performances of *Macbeth* and the associations that smell would have had for the audience.

Howard, Jean E. "Shakespeare, Geography, and the Work of Genre on the Early Modern Stage." *Modern Language Quarterly* 64.3 (2003): 299–322. Analyzes how Scotland's mingled contemporary reputation for nobility and savagery allowed Shakespeare to desacralize kingship.

Kastan, David Scott. "*Macbeth* and the 'Name of the King.'" *Shakespeare After Theory.* New York: Routledge, 1999. 165–82. Explores how insistent doubling, blending the figures of the king and tyrant, undermines the attempt in *Macbeth* to contain violence by restoring moral order.

Mullaney, Steven. "Lying Like Truth: Riddle, Representation, and Treason." *The Place of the Stage: License, Play, and Power in Renaissance England.* Chicago: U of Chicago P, 1988. 116–34. Argues that, like the Jacobean spectacle of a traitor on the scaffold, *Macbeth* reveals the generative power of equivocation, challenging the absolutes of royal authority.

Norbrook, David. "*Macbeth* and the Politics of Historiography." *Politics of Discourse: The Literature and History of Seventeenth-Century England.* Ed. Kevin Sharpe and Steven Zwicker. Berkeley: U of California P, 1987. 78–116. Argues that, embroiled in seventeenth-century debates over writing Scottish history, Shakespeare raised the specter of justified regicide even as he drew on King James's monarchist views.

Orgel, Stephen. "Macbeth and the Antic Round." *The Authentic Shakespeare and Other Problems of the Early Modern Stage.* New York: Routledge, 2002. 159–72. Analyzes how revisions to the witches' scenes link theatrical spectacle to psychological inwardness and heighten the paradoxical role of women.

FILMS

Macbeth. 1948. Dir. Orson Welles. USA. 107 mins. Expressionist, low-budget production, starring Welles and Jeanette Nolan.

Throne of Blood. 1957. Dir. Akira Kurosawa. Japan. 105 mins. Kabuki-influenced production set in feudal Japan stars Toshiro Mifune and Isuzu Yamada.

Macbeth. 1971. Dir. Roman Polanski. UK. 140 mins. Bleak, misty, bloody vision, with strikingly young leads, Jon Finch and Francesca Annis.

Macbeth. 1979. Dir. Philip Casson. UK. 146 mins. Minimalist production for television with doubling actors and simple sets. Ian McKellen and Judi Dench star.

Men of Respect. 1989. Dir. William Reilly. USA. 113 mins. John Turturro stars as a mafia hitman who murders his boss (Rod Steiger). With Stanley Tucci as Malcolm and Peter Boyle as Macduff.

Maqbool. 2003. Dir. Vishal Bhardwaj. India. 132 mins. Set in the Mumbai underworld, with the witches as two corrupt, fortune-telling policemen.

Macbeth. 2010. Dir. Rupert Goold. UK. 160 mins. Patrick Stewart and Kate Fleetwood star in a production that evokes the Soviet Union in the time of Stalin and his henchmen. The witches are murderous hospital nurses.

TEXTUAL INTRODUCTION

The sole early modern text for *The Tragedy of Macbeth* appears in Shakespeare's First Folio (1623, sigs. ll6–nn4) between *Julius Caesar* and *Hamlet*. At 2,084 lines, *Macbeth* is one of Shakespeare's shortest plays (longer only than *The Comedy of Errors* and *The Tempest*) and by far the shortest of Shakespeare's tragedies, which average 3,030 lines, excluding the collaborative and possibly incomplete *Timon of Athens* at 2,299 lines. The text is about 95 percent verse and 5 percent prose and shows minimal proof correction. The Second Folio (1632) has no independent textual authority, but it presents some suggested alternative readings.

The brevity of *Macbeth* suggests that the play may be an abridgment. Many have noted inconsistencies in the action, which suggest revision or at least complicated transmission: Ross, for example, reports that Cawdor's betrayal began the conflict (1.2.55) but Macbeth knows nothing of his treachery (1.3.73–74). Lennox tells of Macduff's flight to England and Macbeth's rebuffed messenger to him in 3.6, but Macbeth is shocked and angry in 4.1 to discover that Macduff is gone, "Fled to England?" (line 141).

The copy text for the Folio may have been a promptbook or a transcription of one. The relatively complete record of entrances and exits and the relatively clear designation of characters may signal origins in the theater, though many scholars now regard such signals as inconclusive. A. R. Braunmuller (263) notes some additional evidence of theatrical provenance: in his view the Folio erroneously incorporates a theatrical instruction—"Ring the bell!" (2.3.75)—and contains numerous "professionally terse" stage directions for sound and lighting ("*Hautboys. Torches*," 1.7.0 SD) and for supernumeraries ("*Drum and colors*," 5.2.0 SD, 5.4.0 SD, 5.5.0 SD, 5.6.0 SD, 5.7.64 SD4). The printed text divides the play into acts and scenes, though modern editors have questioned the division between 2.2 and 2.3 because the location remains the same, Macbeth's castle, and the action is continuous; some have also argued for more scenic divisions in act 5 (see Digital Edition TC 10 at 5.7.64 SD). Two workmen, dubbed Compositor A and Compositor B, competently set the type to convert the manuscript to print, but A sometimes arranged blank verse into irregular lines and B sometimes set prose as verse (see Digital Edition TC 5 at 3.1.75).

As Braunmuller explains (275–79), scholars generally agree that Folio *Macbeth* shows signs of theatrical interpolation. The text includes instances of "repetition brackets," identical lines in close proximity that may mark an addition between them.

The repeated command, "Look to the lady" (2.3.116, 122; see Digital Edition TC 4 at 2.3.115 SD) brackets Malcolm and Donaldbain's worried conversation about their future, a possible addition. Gary Taylor argues that the repeated phrase "How wilt thou do for a father?" (4.2.38, 56–57) brackets a conversation inserted to reflect the Overbury trials and hangings of 1615–16 (Taylor and Lavagnino, pp. 394–97). Malcolm's dialogue with the English Doctor (4.3, a curiously otiose anticipation of the Scottish Doctor of Physic, 5.1), including the discussion on the "king's evil" (140–59), occurs between lines that may be linked to make up a pentameter ("'Tis hard to reconcile" and "See who comes here"). Many have thought the dialogue a digressive addition by Shakespeare or another for a court performance; others have defended the passage as developing the contrast between the good King Edward, a miraculous healer, and the evil tyrant Macbeth. Others have questioned Malcolm and Macduff's previous dialogue in this scene because it raises doubts about the character of the heir apparent and does not advance the action. (Actors who play Macbeth are grateful for the break before the closing action, however.) Most also believe the Hecate speeches (3.5 and 4.1.39ff), so different in style from the other witches' verse, are additions by another playwright for later performance; others believe them to be Shakespearean.

The leading candidate for that other playwright, a collaborator or adaptor of Shakespeare's *Macbeth*, is Thomas Middleton. Evidence for the identification consists mainly in the cues for two songs, "Come away, come away" (3.5.35 SD) and "Black spirits" (4.1.43 SD), which appear in full in Middleton's *The Witch* (1616?) (see Digital Edition TC 8 at 3.5.35 SD). Gary Taylor has argued that Middleton revised Shakespeare's play in 1616 and wrote an additional 151 lines, as well as 72 lines with Shakespeare, for a total of about 11 percent of the Folio text (Taylor and Lavagnino, pp. 383–97). For this reason he and John Lavagnino include *Macbeth* in the Oxford edition of Thomas Middleton's *Collected Works* (2007). In a *TLS* article (2010) and in a study with Marcus Dahl and Marina Tarlinskaya (2010), Brian Vickers has argued against Middleton's presence in *Macbeth*. Using software programs to detect three-word collocations in the canons of Shakespeare and Middleton, and examining diction and syntax, Vickers argues that the lines attributed to Middleton are demonstrably Shakespearean. Responding that the Vickers–Dahl–Tarlinskaya databases are incomplete and their methods flawed, Taylor and others have defended the Middleton attributions. The debate is ongoing.

ROBERT S. MIOLA

TEXTUAL BIBLIOGRAPHY

Braunmuller, A. R., ed. *Macbeth*. Cambridge: Cambridge UP, 1997, rev. 2008.
Taylor, Gary. "*Macbeth* and Middleton." *Macbeth*. Ed. Robert S. Miola. 2nd ed. New York: Norton, 2014. 296–305.
Taylor, Gary, and John Lavagnino, eds. *Thomas Middleton and Early Modern Textual Culture: A Companion to the Collected Works*. Oxford: Oxford UP, 2007.
Vickers, Brian. "Disintegrated: Did Thomas Middleton Really Adapt *Macbeth*?" *Times Literary Supplement*, 28 May 2010, 13–14.
Vickers, Brian, Marcus Dahl, and Marina Tarlinskaya. "An Enquiry into Middleton's Supposed 'Adaptation' of *Macbeth*." *London Forum for Authorship Studies* (2010), seminar paper: http://ies.sas.ac.uk/events/seminars/LFAS/index.htm.

PERFORMANCE NOTE

Macbeth generates considerable theatrical energy by exploiting tensions and intersections between fate and human agency. While directors typically strive to maintain the sense of moral uncertainty that makes tragedy possible, they cannot sidestep questions regarding Macbeth's responsibility for Duncan's murder. Do the witches plant the seed of ambition or invite Macbeth to act on existing desires? Do they foretell fate or set the sequence of gruesome events in motion? Is Lady Macbeth an accessory to murder or its chief architect? Do the dagger, Banquo's ghost, and the divining apparitions portend supernatural intrusion or a tormented conscience? Each production's answers determine the level of sympathy or dread the audience feels for the protagonist, and can decide whether the witches appear as earthly hags, ghostly temptresses, or disembodied voices; Lady Macbeth as an ambitious partner, controlling mother, or fourth witch; Macbeth as a man tortured from within or without.

The title role requires actors to oscillate convincingly between hero and tyrant, portraying a man whose savagery and coldness are as genuine as his hesitancy and remorse. The challenge intensifies in the play's second half, when the protagonist diminishes considerably in dramatic opportunity, influence, and psychological depth, even as the play slackens its invigorating pace, compression, and conflict. Productions can attempt to maintain interest and stave off anticlimax by underplaying the early acts; spectacularly staging the supernatural phenomena; cutting Siward, trimming Malcolm, and focusing on Macduff's revenge plot; assigning political topicality to Macbeth's fall; or emphasizing the inverse developmental arcs of the Macbeths, or their parallel descents into madness. However addressed, the challenges help explain why no other play has seen so many celebrated actors disappoint in—or simply avoid—the title role.

The portrayals of the supporting cast further influence audiences' reception of the Macbeths. Duncan can be a martyr or an imperious warlord; Malcolm, a worthy successor or naïve underling; the Porter, a comic or an ominous figure; and Macduff, like Banquo, can personify loyalty and valor, or compromise his virtues with jealousy or self-loathing. Other dramaturgical considerations include clarifying the muddled events discussed in 3.6; motivating Ross's reticence and sudden disclosure (see Digital Edition PC 6); deciding whether Macbeth dies onstage or off, and representing his severed head; and determining whether notes of optimism, despair, or tragic irony dominate the play's final moments.

BRETT GAMBOA

The Tragedy of Macbeth

[THE PERSONS OF THE PLAY

KING Duncan of Scotland
MALCOLM, later Prince of Cumberland, eldest son to King Duncan
DONALDBAIN, son to King Duncan
CAPTAIN in King Duncan's army

MACBETH, Thane of Glamis, later Thane of Cawdor, later King of Scotland
LADY MACBETH
Three MURDERERS
PORTER at Macbeth's castle
SEYTON, servant to Macbeth
GENTLEWOMAN, servant to Lady Macbeth
DOCTOR OF PHYSIC, attending Lady Macbeth

Six WITCHES, including the three weird sisters
HECATE, queen of the witches

BANQUO, a thane
FLEANCE, son to Banquo

MACDUFF, Thane of Fife
WIFE to Macduff
SON to Macduff and Wife

LENNOX
ROSS
MENTEITH } thanes
ANGUS
CAITHNESS

English DOCTOR
OLD MAN
SIWARD, Earl of Northumberland
YOUNG SIWARD
Three APPARITIONS: an armed head, a bloody child, a child crowned
MESSENGER
LORDS
SERVANTS
SOLDIERS

Lords, Attendants, Drummers, a Sewer, a show of eight kings]

1.1

Thunder and lightning. Enter three WITCHES.[1]

FIRST WITCH   When shall we three meet again?

1.1 Location: An open place.
1. PERFORMANCE COMMENT Stage productions often include novel or spectacular approaches to representing the witches, but the most urgent decisions concern their ontological status—supernatural visionaries or earthly psychics?—and the extent of their power to influence the action. See Digital Edition PC 1.

In thunder, lightning, or in rain?[2]
SECOND WITCH   When the hurly-burly's° done,   *tumult is*
  When the battle's lost and won.
5   THIRD WITCH   That will be ere the set of sun.
FIRST WITCH   Where the place?
SECOND WITCH   Upon the heath.
THIRD WITCH   There to meet with Macbeth.
FIRST WITCH   I come, Grimalkin!
10   ALL   Paddock[3] calls anon!°   *at once*
  Fair is foul, and foul is fair,
  Hover through the fog and filthy air.   *Exeunt.*

1.2

Alarum within. Enter KING [*Duncan*], MALCOLM,
DONALDBAIN, LENNOX, *with Attendants, meeting a*
bleeding CAPTAIN.°   *staff officer*

KING   What bloody man is that? He can report,
  As seemeth by his plight, of the revolt
  The newest state.
MALCOLM   This is the sergeant
  Who like a good and hardy soldier fought
5   'Gainst my captivity. —Hail, brave friend!
  Say to the King the knowledge of the broil°   *battle*
  As thou didst leave it.
CAPTAIN   Doubtful it stood,
  As two spent° swimmers that do cling together   *exhausted*
  And choke their art.[1] The merciless Macdonald—
10   Worthy to be a rebel, for to that°   *that end*
  The multiplying villainies of nature[2]
  Do swarm upon him—from the Western Isles°   *Hebrides and Ireland*
  Of kerns and galloglasses[3] is supplied;
  And Fortune, on his damnèd quarrel[4] smiling,
15   Showed° like a rebel's whore. But all's too weak,   *Appeared*
  For brave Macbeth—well he deserves that name°—   *epithet*
  Disdaining Fortune with his brandished steel,
  Which smoked with bloody execution,
  Like valor's minion° carved out his passage   *favorite*
20   Till he faced the slave,°   *(Macdonald)*
  Which° ne'er shook hands nor bade farewell to him,   *Who*
  Till he unseamed him from the nave to th' chops,[5]
  And fixed his head upon our battlements.
KING   O valiant cousin,° worthy gentleman!   *kinsman*
25   CAPTAIN   As whence the sun 'gins his reflection,[6]
  Shipwrecking storms and direful thunders,
  So from that spring° whence comfort seemed to come,   *source; (season)*
  Discomfort swells.° Mark, King of Scotland, mark: *wells up*
  No sooner justice had, with valor armed,
30   Compelled these skipping° kerns to trust their heels,   *mobile; fleeing*
  But the Norwegian lord, surveying vantage,°   *seeing his chance*

---

2. Witches were thought to be able to cause bad weather.
3. Paddock, a toad, and Grimalkin, a gray cat, are the witches' familiars, or attendant evil spirits.
1.2 Location: A camp near the battlefield.
1. And confound their skill in swimming.
2. The evil aspects of his own nature; the villainous progeny of nature (the mercenaries).

3. *kerns:* lightly armed Irish foot soldiers. *galloglasses:* ax-wielding horsemen.
4. Macdonald's cursed rebellion.
5. Ripped him open from the navel to the jaw, as one would rip open the seam of a garment.
6. Begins its return after the spring equinox, thought to cause turbulent weather. F2 adds "breaking" to the end of line 26.

With furbished° arms and new supplies of men   *polished*
Began a fresh assault.
KING   Dismayed not this our captains, Macbeth and Banquo?
35 CAPTAIN   Yes, as sparrows eagles or the hare the lion.
If I say sooth, I must report they were
As cannons overcharged with double cracks;[7]
So they doubly redoubled strokes upon the foe.
Except° they meant to bathe in reeking wounds,   *Unless*
40 Or memorize another Golgotha,[8]
I cannot tell—
But I am faint. My gashes cry for help.
KING   So well thy words become thee as thy wounds;
They smack of honor both. —Go, get him surgeons.
                     [*Exit* CAPTAIN, *attended.*]
          Enter ROSS *and* ANGUS.
Who comes here?
45 MALCOLM   The worthy Thane[9] of Ross.
LENNOX   What a haste looks through his eyes!
So should he look that seems to° speak things strange.   *seems about to*
ROSS   God save the King!
KING   Whence cam'st thou, worthy thane?
50 ROSS   From Fife, great King,
Where the Norwegian banners flout° the sky   *mock*
And fan our people cold.°   *cold with fear*
Norway° himself, with terrible numbers,   *The King of Norway*
Assisted by that most disloyal traitor,
55 The Thane of Cawdor, began a dismal° conflict,   *an ominous*
Till that° Bellona's bridegroom,[1] lapped in proof,[2]   *Until*
Confronted him with self-comparisons,°   *comparable deeds*
Point° against point, rebellious arm 'gainst arm,   *Swordpoint*
Curbing his lavish° spirit. And to conclude,   *wild*
The victory fell on us—
KING   Great happiness!—
60 ROSS   —That now Sweno,
The Norways'° king, craves composition.°   *Norwegians' / a truce*
Nor would we deign him burial of his men
Till he disbursèd at Saint Colme's Inch[3]
Ten thousand dollars[4] to our general use.
65 KING   No more that Thane of Cawdor shall deceive
Our bosom interest.[5] Go pronounce his present° death,   *immediate*
And with his former title greet Macbeth.
ROSS   I'll see it done.
KING   What he hath lost noble Macbeth hath won.   *Exeunt.*

1.3
Thunder. Enter the three WITCHES.

FIRST WITCH   Where hast thou been, sister?
SECOND WITCH   Killing swine.
THIRD WITCH   Sister, where thou?

---

7. Overloaded with double charges of gunpowder.
8. Or make the battlefield as memorable as Golgotha, the "place of skulls" where Jesus was crucified.
9. Title of Scottish nobility.
1. Macbeth, imagined as husband to Bellona, the Roman goddess of war.
2. Clad in tested armor.

3. Incholm, the island of St. Columba in the Firth of Forth.
4. German and Spanish coins (first minted in the sixteenth century, 500 years after the events of the play).
5. Our closest concerns.
1.3 Location: An open place.

FIRST WITCH   A sailor's wife had chestnuts in her lap,
5   And munched, and munched, and munched.
       "Give me," quoth I.
       "Aroint thee,° witch!" the rump-fed runnion[1] cries.   Begone
       Her husband's to Aleppo gone, master o'the *Tiger*,
       But in a sieve I'll thither sail,
10   And like a rat without a tail,
       I'll do, I'll do, and I'll do.
SECOND WITCH   I'll give thee a wind.
FIRST WITCH   Thou'rt kind.
THIRD WITCH   And I another.
15 FIRST WITCH   I myself have all the other,°   others
       And the very ports they blow,°   blow from
       All the quarters° that they know   directions
       I'th' shipman's card.°   compass card
       I'll drain him dry as hay.
20   Sleep shall neither night nor day
       Hang upon his penthouse lid;[2]
       He shall live a man forbid.°   cursed
       Weary sennights° nine times nine   weeks
       Shall he dwindle, peak,° and pine.   waste away
25   Though his bark cannot be lost,
       Yet it shall be tempest-tossed.
       Look what I have.
SECOND WITCH   Show me, show me.
FIRST WITCH   Here I have a pilot's thumb,
30   Wrecked as homeward he did come.
              Drum within.
THIRD WITCH   A drum, a drum!
       Macbeth doth come!
ALL [*dancing in a circle*]   The weird[3] sisters, hand in hand,
       Posters° of the sea and land,   Swift travelers
35   Thus do go, about, about,
       Thrice to thine, and thrice to mine,
       And thrice again to make up nine.
       Peace, the charm's wound up.
              Enter MACBETH *and* BANQUO.
MACBETH   So foul and fair a day I have not seen.
40 BANQUO   How far is't called° to Forres? What are these,   said to be
       So withered and so wild in their attire,
       That look not like th'inhabitants o'th' earth,
       And yet are on't? —Live you? Or are you aught
       That man may question?° You seem to understand me   interrogate
45   By each at once her choppy° finger laying   chapped
       Upon her skinny lips. You should be women,
       And yet your beards forbid me to interpret
       That you are so.
MACBETH   Speak, if you can. What are you?
FIRST WITCH   All hail, Macbeth! Hail to thee, Thane of Glamis!
50 SECOND WITCH   All hail, Macbeth! Hail to thee, Thane of Cawdor!
   THIRD WITCH   All hail, Macbeth, that shalt be king hereafter!

---

1. The fat-rumped, mangy slut.
2. Eyelid, which projects out over the eye like the sloping roof of a penthouse.
3. TEXTUAL COMMENT This crucial word appears throughout F as both "weyard" and "weyward." For further details on the issue of its ambiguous spelling and meaning, see Digital Edition TC 1.

BANQUO   Good sir, why do you start and seem to fear
   Things that do sound so fair? —I'th' name of truth,
   Are ye fantastical° or that indeed   *imaginary*
55   Which outwardly ye show? My noble partner
   You greet with present grace° and great prediction   *title*
   Of noble having° and of royal hope   *estate*
   That he seems rapt withal.[4] To me you speak not.
   If you can look into the seeds of time
60   And say which grain will grow and which will not,
   Speak then to me, who neither beg nor fear
   Your favors nor your hate.
FIRST WITCH   Hail!
SECOND WITCH   Hail!
65 THIRD WITCH   Hail!
FIRST WITCH   Lesser than Macbeth, and greater.
SECOND WITCH   Not so happy,° yet much happier.   *fortunate*
THIRD WITCH   Thou shalt get° kings, though thou be none.   *beget*
   So all hail, Macbeth and Banquo!
70 FIRST WITCH   Banquo and Macbeth, all hail!
MACBETH   Stay, you imperfect° speakers, tell me more.   *incomplete*
   By Finel's° death I know I am Thane of Glamis,   *Macbeth's father's*
   But how of Cawdor? The Thane of Cawdor lives,
   A prosperous gentleman, and to be king
75   Stands not within the prospect of belief,
   No more than to be Cawdor. Say from whence
   You owe° this strange intelligence,° or why   *possess / information*
   Upon this blasted° heath you stop our way   *blighted*
   With such prophetic greeting. Speak, I charge you.
                            WITCHES *vanish.*
80 BANQUO   The earth hath bubbles as the water has,
   And these are of them. Whither are they vanished?
MACBETH   Into the air. And what seemed corporal°   *corporeal*
   Melted as breath into the wind. Would they had stayed.
BANQUO   Were such things here as we do speak about?
85   Or have we eaten on the insane root[5]
   That takes the reason prisoner?
MACBETH   Your children shall be kings.
BANQUO   You shall be king.
MACBETH   And Thane of Cawdor too. Went it not so?
BANQUO   To th' selfsame tune and words. —Who's here?
      Enter ROSS *and* ANGUS.
90 ROSS   The King hath happily received, Macbeth,
   The news of thy success; and when he reads°   *considers*
   Thy personal venture° in the rebels' fight,   *exploits*
   His wonders and his praises do contend
   Which should be thine or his. Silenced with that,[6]
95   In viewing o'er the rest o'th' selfsame day,
   He finds thee in the stout Norwegian ranks,
   Nothing° afeard of what thyself didst make,   *Not at all*
   Strange images° of death. As thick as hail   *forms*
   Came post° with post, and every one did bear   *messenger*
100 Thy praises in his kingdom's great defense

---

4. He seems entranced by these predictions.
5. Of the root causing insanity, possibly hemlock.
6. *His wonders . . . that:* Duncan does not know
whether to speak of his astonishment or his admiration, and so is silent.

And poured them down before him.

ANGUS   We are sent
To give thee from our royal master thanks,
Only to herald thee into his sight,
Not pay thee.

105 ROSS   And for an earnest° of a greater honor,   *a pledge*
He bade me, from him, call thee Thane of Cawdor;
In which addition,° hail, most worthy thane,   *title*
For it is thine.

BANQUO   What, can the devil speak true?

MACBETH   The Thane of Cawdor lives. Why do you dress me
In borrowed robes?

110 ANGUS   Who was the thane lives yet,
But under heavy judgment bears that life
Which he deserves to lose.
Whether he was combined° with those of Norway,   *allied*
Or did line the rebel° with hidden help   *support Macdonald*

115 And vantage,° or that with both he labored   *benefit*
In his country's wrack,[7] I know not.
But treasons capital, confessed and proved,
Have overthrown him.

MACBETH [*aside*]   Glamis, and Thane of Cawdor!
The greatest is behind.° —Thanks for your pains.   *to come*

120 [*aside to* BANQUO]   Do you not hope your children shall be kings,
When those that gave the Thane of Cawdor to me
Promised no less to them?

BANQUO [*aside to* MACBETH]   That trusted home°   *completely*
Might yet enkindle° you unto the crown,   *encourage*
Besides the Thane of Cawdor. But 'tis strange,

125 And oftentimes to win us to our harm,
The instruments of darkness tell us truths,
Win us with honest trifles, to betray's°   *betray us*
In deepest consequence.
—Cousins, a word, I pray you.
       [*He converses apart with* ROSS *and* ANGUS.]

MACBETH [*aside*]   Two truths are told,
130 As happy prologues to the swelling act[8]
Of th'imperial theme. —I thank you, gentlemen.
[*aside*] This supernatural soliciting°   *temptation*
Cannot be ill, cannot be good. If ill,
Why hath it given me earnest of success

135 Commencing in a truth? I am Thane of Cawdor.
If good, why do I yield to that suggestion
Whose horrid image doth unfix my hair
And make my seated heart knock at my ribs
Against the use° of nature? Present fears   *custom*

140 Are less than horrible imaginings.
My thought, whose murder yet is but fantastical,[9]
Shakes so my single state of man[1]
That function° is smothered in surmise,°   *capacity to act / speculation*
And nothing is but what is not.

145 BANQUO   Look how our partner's rapt.

---

7. He worked to bring about his country's ruin.
8. To the developing action, or climactic dramatic
action.
9. In which murder is so far only a fantasy.

1. My undivided self. Macbeth feels that his wholeness
is coming apart under the pressure of his criminal
thought.

MACBETH [*aside*]   If chance will have me king, why, chance
    may crown me
    Without my stir.°   *effort*
BANQUO   New honors come upon him,
    Like our strange° garments, cleave not to their mold°   *new / wearer's form*
    But with the aid of use.
MACBETH [*aside*]   Come what come may,
150   Time and the hour runs through the roughest day.[2]
BANQUO   Worthy Macbeth, we stay° upon your leisure.   *wait; attend*
MACBETH   Give me your favor.° My dull brain was wrought°   *pardon / agitated*
    With things forgotten. Kind gentlemen, your pains
    Are registered° where every day I turn   *recorded (in my memory)*
155   The leaf to read them. Let us toward the King.
    [*aside to* BANQUO] Think upon what hath chanced, and at
    more time,
    The interim having weighed it, let us speak
    Our free hearts° each to other.   *unconcealed thoughts*
BANQUO [*aside to* MACBETH]   Very gladly.
MACBETH [*aside to* BANQUO]   Till then, enough. —Come, friends.
                             Exeunt.

1.4

Flourish. Enter KING, LENNOX, MALCOLM,
DONALDBAIN, *and Attendants.*

KING   Is execution done on Cawdor? Or° not   *Or are*
    Those in commission[1] yet returned?
MALCOLM   My liege,
    They are not yet come back. But I have spoke
    With one that saw him die, who did report
5   That very frankly he confessed his treasons,
    Implored your highness' pardon, and set forth
    A deep repentance. Nothing in his life
    Became him like the leaving it. He died
    As one that had been studied° in his death   *practiced*
10   To throw away the dearest thing he owed°   *owned*
    As 'twere a careless° trifle.   *an uncared-for*
KING   There's no art
    To find the mind's construction in the face.
    He was a gentleman on whom I built
    An absolute trust.
        Enter MACBETH, BANQUO, ROSS, *and* ANGUS.
              O worthiest cousin!
15   The sin of my ingratitude even now
    Was heavy on me. Thou art so far before°   *ahead*
    That swiftest wing of recompense is slow
    To overtake thee. Would thou hadst less deserved,
    That the proportion both of thanks and payment
20   Might have been mine.[2] Only I have left to say,
    More is thy due than more than all can pay.
MACBETH   The service and the loyalty I owe
    In doing it pays itself. Your highness' part
    Is to receive our duties, and our duties

---

2. *Come . . . day:* What must happen will happen one   1. Those charged to execute Cawdor.
way or another.   2. *That . . . mine:* That the King's rewards would be
1.4 Location: A camp near the battlefield.   generously proportional to Macbeth's desert.

25 Are to your throne and state, children and servants,
Which do but what they should by doing everything
Safe toward° your love and honor.   *To safeguard*
KING   Welcome hither.
I have begun to plant thee and will labor
To make thee full of growing. —Noble Banquo,
30 That hast no less deserved nor must be known
No less to have done so, let me enfold thee
And hold thee to my heart.   There if I grow,
BANQUO
The harvest is your own.
KING   My plenteous joys,
Wanton° in fullness, seek to hide themselves   *Unrestrained*
35 In drops of sorrow. —Sons, kinsmen, thanes,
And you whose places are the nearest,° know   *nearest to the throne*
We will establish our estate[3] upon
Our eldest, Malcolm, whom we name hereafter
The Prince of Cumberland;[4] which honor must
40 Not unaccompanied invest him only,[5]
But signs of nobleness, like stars, shall shine
On all deservers. [*to* MACBETH] From hence to Inverness,°   *Macbeth's castle*
And bind us further to you.[6]
MACBETH   The rest is labor which is not used for you.[7]
45 I'll be myself the harbinger[8] and make joyful
The hearing of my wife with your approach.
So humbly take my leave.
KING   My worthy Cawdor!
MACBETH [*aside*]   The Prince of Cumberland! That is a step
On which I must fall down or else o'erleap,
50 For in my way it lies. Stars, hide your fires,
Let not light see my black and deep desires;
The eye wink at the hand;[9] yet let that be°   *be done*
Which the eye fears, when it is done, to see.   *Exit.*
KING   True, worthy Banquo, he is full so valiant,[1]
55 And in his commendations I am fed;
It is a banquet to me. Let's after him,
Whose care is gone before to bid us welcome.
It is a peerless kinsman.   *Flourish. Exeunt.*

1.5

Enter Macbeth's Wife [LADY MACBETH][1] *alone with
a letter.*

LADY MACBETH [*reading*]   "They met me in the day of success,
and I have learned by the perfect'st° report they have more   *most accurate*
in them than mortal knowledge. When I burnt in desire to
question them further, they made themselves air, into which
5 they vanished. Whiles I stood rapt in the wonder of it came

---

3. We will settle the succession of the kingdom. At the time, the Scottish crown was not hereditary.
4. Title of the Scottish heir apparent.
5. *which . . . only:* honors will not be bestowed on Malcolm alone.
6. And make me further indebted to you by your hospitality.
7. Even repose seems wearisome when it is not dedicated to your purposes.

8. Forerunner; messenger sent ahead to arrange royal lodgings.
9. Let the eye deliberately ignore what the hand does.
1. As valiant as you say.
1.5 Location: Inverness, Macbeth's castle.
1. TEXTUAL COMMENT Surprisingly to modern readers, this character is never named "Lady Macbeth" throughout F. For more on the issue of naming and character, see Digital Edition TC 2.

missives° from the King, who all-hailed me 'Thane of Caw-   *messengers*
dor,' by which title before these weird sisters saluted me and
referred me to the coming on of time with 'Hail, king that
shalt be!' This have I thought good to deliver° thee, my dear-   *inform*
10   est partner of greatness, that thou mightst not lose the dues
of rejoicing by being ignorant of what greatness is promised
thee. Lay it to thy heart, and farewell."
Glamis thou art, and Cawdor, and shalt be
What thou art promised. Yet do I fear° thy nature;   *doubt*
15   It is too full o'th' milk of human kindness
To catch the nearest° way. Thou wouldst be great,   *most expedient*
Art not without ambition, but without
The illness° should attend it. What thou wouldst highly,   *wickedness (that)*
That wouldst thou holily; wouldst not play false,
20   And yet wouldst wrongly win. Thou'dst have, great Glamis,
That which cries, "Thus thou must do" if thou have it,
And that which rather thou dost fear to do
Than wishest should be undone. Hie° thee hither,   *Hasten*
That I may pour my spirits in thine ear
25   And chastise with the valor of my tongue
All that impedes thee from the golden round,°   *crown*
Which fate and metaphysical° aid doth seem   *supernatural*
To have thee crowned withal.°   *with*
         Enter MESSENGER.
                    What is your tidings?
MESSENGER   The King comes here tonight.
LADY MACBETH   Thou'rt mad to say it!
30   Is not thy master with him, who, were't so,
Would have informed for preparation?
MESSENGER   So please you, it is true. Our thane is coming.
One of my fellows had the speed of° him,   *outdistanced*
Who, almost dead for breath, had scarcely more
Than would make up his message.
35   LADY MACBETH   Give him tending;
He brings great news.   *Exit* MESSENGER.
                 The raven[2] himself is hoarse
That croaks the fatal entrance of Duncan
Under my battlements. Come, you spirits
That tend on mortal° thoughts, unsex me here,   *attend deadly*
40   And fill me from the crown to the toe top-full
Of direst cruelty! Make thick my blood,
Stop up th'access and passage to remorse,°   *pity*
That no compunctious visitings of nature
Shake my fell° purpose nor keep peace° between   *cruel / intervene*
45   Th'effect and it.[3] Come to my woman's breasts
And take my milk for° gall, you murd'ring ministers,°   *in exchange for / agents*
Wherever in your sightless° substances   *invisible*
You wait on° nature's mischief. Come, thick night,   *assist*
And pall° thee in the dunnest° smoke of hell,   *envelop / darkest*
50   That my keen knife see not the wound it makes,
Nor heaven peep through the blanket of the dark
To cry, "Hold, hold!"[4]

---

2. The raven was considered a bird of ill omen.   Macbeth can choose to emphasize or downplay the
3. My purpose and its accomplishment.   witchlike implication of her summoning of spirits.
4. PERFORMANCE COMMENT Actors playing Lady   See Digital Edition PC 2.

Enter MACBETH.

                                    Great Glamis, worthy Cawdor,
                 Greater than both by the all-hail hereafter!
                 Thy letters have transported me beyond
55   This ignorant present, and I feel now
                 The future in the instant.
    MACBETH   My dearest love,
                 Duncan comes here tonight.
    LADY MACBETH   And when goes hence?
    MACBETH   Tomorrow, as he purposes.
    LADY MACBETH   Oh, never
                 Shall sun that morrow see!
60   Your face, my thane, is as a book where men
                 May read strange matters. To beguile the time,
                 Look like the time;⁵ bear welcome in your eye,
                 Your hand, your tongue. Look like th'innocent flower,
                 But be the serpent under't. He that's coming
65   Must be provided for. And you shall put
                 This night's great business into my dispatch,°   *management*
                 Which shall to all our nights and days to come
                 Give solely sovereign sway and masterdom.
    MACBETH   We will speak further.
    LADY MACBETH   Only look up clear.°   *appear innocent*
70   To alter favor⁶ ever is to fear.
                 Leave all the rest to me.   *Exeunt.*

1.6

                 Hautboys° and torches. Enter KING, MALCOLM,   *Oboes*
                 DONALDBAIN, BANQUO, LENNOX, MACDUFF, ROSS,
                 ANGUS, *and Attendants.*
    KING   This castle hath a pleasant seat.°   *location*
                 The air nimbly and sweetly recommends itself
                 Unto our gentle senses.
    BANQUO   This guest of summer,
                 The temple-haunting martlet,¹ does approve°   *prove*
5   By his loved mansionry° that the heavens' breath   *nest building*
                 Smells wooingly here. No jutty,° frieze,   *projection*
                 Buttress, nor coign of vantage,° but this bird   *convenient corner*
                 Hath made his pendent bed and procreant° cradle.   *for breeding*
                 Where they must breed and haunt, I have observed,
                 The air is delicate.
                 Enter LADY MACBETH.
10 KING   See, see, our honored hostess!
                 —The love that follows us sometime is our trouble,
                 Which still we thank as love.² Herein I teach you
                 How you shall bid God 'ield us for your pains,
                 And thank us for your trouble.³
    LADY MACBETH   All our service,
15   In every point twice done and then done double,

---

5. *To . . . like the time:* To deceive the world, match
your expression to the occasion.
6. To alter your facial expression and thereby arouse
suspicion.
1.6 Location: Outside Macbeth's castle.
1. A bird, the martin, that often built its nest in

churches.
2. *The . . . love:* Love bestowed upon us sometimes
causes us inconvenience, but we are still grateful
for it.
3. *bid . . . trouble:* ask God to reward ("yield") me for
the trouble I cause you.

Were° poor and single° business to contend   *Would be / small*
Against those honors deep and broad wherewith
Your majesty loads our house. For those of old,
And the late dignities heaped up to them,
We rest your hermits.[4]

20 KING   Where's the Thane of Cawdor?
We coursed him at the heels° and had a purpose   *followed him closely*
To be his purveyor;[5] but he rides well,
And his great love, sharp as his spur, hath holp° him   *helped*
To his home before us. Fair and noble hostess,
We are your guest tonight.

25 LADY MACBETH   Your servants ever
Have theirs, themselves, and what is theirs in count°   *account*
To make their audit at your highness' pleasure,
Still to return your own.[6]

KING   Give me your hand;
Conduct me to mine host. We love him highly
30 And shall continue our graces towards him.
By your leave,[7] hostess.   *Exeunt.*

1.7

Hautboys. Torches. Enter a Sewer,° and divers   *Butler*
SERVANTS *with dishes and service over the stage.*
Then enter MACBETH.

MACBETH   If it were done when 'tis done, then 'twere well
It were done quickly. If th'assassination
Could trammel up the consequence and catch
With his surcease success[1]—that but this blow
5   Might be the be-all and the end-all!—here,°   *in this world*
But here, upon this bank and shoal[2] of time,
We'd jump° the life to come. But in these cases   *risk*
We still have judgment[3] here, that° we but teach   *in that*
Bloody instructions which, being taught, return
10 To plague th'inventor. This even-handed° justice   *impartial*
Commends th'ingredients° of our poisoned chalice   *the contents*
To our own lips. He's here in double trust:
First, as I am his kinsman and his subject,
Strong both against the deed; then, as his host,
15 Who should against his murderer shut the door,
Not bear the knife myself. Besides, this Duncan
Hath borne his faculties° so meek, hath been   *authority*
So clear° in his great office, that his virtues   *blameless*
Will plead like angels, trumpet-tongued, against
20 The deep damnation of his taking-off;°   *murder*
And Pity, like a naked newborn babe

4. We remain your beadsmen (monks hired to pray for their employers).
5. Attendant who preceded the King when he traveled and procured foodstuffs for the royal party.
6. *Your servants . . . own:* Your servants hold all that they have in trust from you, and they are always ready to settle accounts and return to you what is yours.
7. By your permission. A request for permission to enter, or perhaps for a formal kiss.
1.7 Location: A courtyard or an anteroom in Macbeth's castle.

1. *If th'assassination . . . success:* If only I could gain success with Duncan's death (his "surcease"); if only the assassination were the end of the matter. *trammel up the consequence:* restrain the subsequent sequence of events, as in a trammel, or net.
2. Sandbar. The mortal span is seen as a narrow piece of land in the river of time. F has "Schoole," and "bank" may also mean "bench," suggesting that life is a time of instruction and probation.
3. We are invariably punished.

Striding the blast,[4] or heaven's cherubim horsed
Upon the sightless couriers[5] of the air,
Shall blow the horrid deed in every eye,
25 That tears shall drown the wind.[6] I have no spur
To prick the sides of my intent, but only
Vaulting ambition, which o'erleaps itself
And falls on th'other[7]—
        Enter LADY MACBETH.
                                How now? What news?
LADY MACBETH   He has almost supped. Why have you left the
    chamber?
MACBETH   Hath he asked for me?
30 LADY MACBETH   Know you not he has?
MACBETH   We will proceed no further in this business.
    He hath honored me of late, and I have bought°   won
    Golden opinions from all sorts of people,
    Which would be worn now in their newest gloss,
    Not cast aside so soon.
35 LADY MACBETH   Was the hope drunk
    Wherein you dressed yourself? Hath it slept since?
    And wakes it now to look so green° and pale   sickly
    At what it did so freely? From this time
    Such I account thy love. Art thou afeard
40 To be the same in thine own act and valor
    As thou art in desire? Wouldst thou have that°   (the crown)
    Which thou esteem'st the ornament of life,
    And live a coward in thine own esteem,
    Letting "I dare not" wait upon "I would,"
    Like the poor cat i'th' adage?[8]
45 MACBETH   Prithee, peace!
    I dare do all that may become a man;
    Who dares do more is none.
LADY MACBETH   What beast was't, then,
    That made you break° this enterprise to me?   broach
    When you durst do it, then you were a man;
50 And to be more than what you were, you would
    Be so much more the man. Nor time nor place
    Did then adhere,° and yet you would make both.   agree
    They have made themselves, and that their fitness now
    Does unmake you. I have given suck and know
55 How tender 'tis to love the babe that milks me;
    I would, while it was smiling in my face,
    Have plucked my nipple from his boneless gums
    And dashed the brains out, had I so sworn as you
    Have done to this.
MACBETH   If we should fail?
LADY MACBETH   We fail?[9]
60 But° screw your courage to the sticking-place,[1]   Just

4. Astride the storm provoked by Duncan's death.
5. The invisible runners, the winds.
6. Tears will fall like heavy rain, which was believed
to still the wind.
7. That is, the other side. The image is of a rider
vaulting over his horse instead of into his saddle, or
of a horseman who clears a high obstacle but falls on
the other side.
8. Proverbial: "The cat would eat fish but does not

dare to wet her feet."
9. TEXTUAL COMMENT F's version of this speech may
be understood either as a question ("We fail?") or as a
declaration ("We fail!"). For more on the issue of
early modern typography and its interpretative flexibility, see Digital Edition TC 3.
1. The notch on a crossbow that holds the string,
which is cranked or screwed taut.

And we'll not fail. When Duncan is asleep—
Whereto the rather shall his day's hard journey
Soundly invite him—his two chamberlains°   *bedroom attendants*
Will I with wine and wassail° so convince°   *carousing / overpower*
65 That memory, the warder° of the brain,   *guard*
Shall be a fume, and the receipt° of reason   *receptacle*
A limbeck[2] only. When in swinish sleep
Their drenchèd natures lies as in a death,
What cannot you and I perform upon
70 Th'unguarded Duncan? What not put upon
His spongy officers, who shall bear the guilt
Of our great quell?°   *murder*
MACBETH   Bring forth men-children only,
For thy undaunted mettle° should compose   *substance*
Nothing but males. Will it not be received,°   *believed*
75 When we have marked with blood those sleepy two
Of his own chamber and used their very daggers,
That they have done't?
LADY MACBETH   Who dares receive it other,
As we shall make our griefs and clamor roar
Upon his death?
MACBETH   I am settled, and bend up
80 Each corporal° agent to this terrible feat.[3]   *bodily*
Away, and mock° the time with fairest show;   *deceive*
False face must hide what the false heart doth know. *Exeunt*.

2.1

Enter BANQUO *and* FLEANCE, *with a torch before him.*
BANQUO How goes the night, boy?[1]
FLEANCE The moon is down; I have not heard the clock.
BANQUO And she goes down at twelve.
FLEANCE   I take't 'tis later, sir.
BANQUO Hold, take my sword. There's husbandry° in heaven; *thrift*
5 Their candles are all out. Take thee that,[2] too.
A heavy summons° lies like lead upon me, *summons to sleep*
And yet I would not sleep. Merciful powers,[3]
Restrain in me the cursèd thoughts that nature
Gives way to in repose.
Enter MACBETH *and a* SERVANT *with a torch.*
       Give me my sword!
10 —Who's there?
MACBETH A friend.
BANQUO What, sir, not yet at rest? The King's abed.
He hath been in unusual pleasure
And sent forth great largesse° to your offices.[4] *gifts*
15 This diamond he greets your wife withal,
By the name of most kind hostess, and shut up° *concluded*
In measureless content.
   [*He gives a diamond.*]
MACBETH   Being unprepared,

---

2. Alembic, the upper part of a still to which fumes rise. The wine will make the memory a fume that will fill and cloud the brain, the "receptacle of reason."
3. PERFORMANCE COMMENT Productions must consider why Macbeth agrees to undertake Duncan's murder so soon after resolving against it and how

Lady Macbeth manages to instigate him to do so. See Digital Edition PC 3.
2.1 Location: The courtyard of Macbeth's castle.
1. How much of the night has passed?
2. Some article of clothing or armor.
3. Angels invoked as protection against demons.
4. Household departments.

Our will became the servant to defect,
Which else should free have wrought.[5]

BANQUO   All's well.
20   I dreamt last night of the three weird sisters.
To you they have showed some truth.

MACBETH   I think not of them.
Yet, when we can entreat an hour to serve,
We would spend it in some words upon that business,
If you would grant the time.

BANQUO   At your kind'st leisure.
25   MACBETH   If you shall cleave to my consent, when 'tis,[6]
It shall make honor for you.

BANQUO   So° I lose none   *Provided*
In seeking to augment it, but still keep
My bosom franchised° and allegiance clear,°   *guiltless / unstained*
I shall be counseled.°   *receptive*

MACBETH   Good repose the while.
30   BANQUO   Thanks, sir; the like to you.

                         Exit BANQUO [*with* FLEANCE].

MACBETH   Go bid thy mistress, when my drink is ready,
She strike upon the bell. Get thee to bed.   *Exit* [SERVANT].
Is this a dagger which I see before me,
The handle toward my hand? Come, let me clutch thee.[7]
35   I have thee not, and yet I see thee still.
Art thou not, fatal vision, sensible°   *perceptible*
To feeling as to sight? Or art thou but
A dagger of the mind, a false creation,
Proceeding from the heat-oppressèd° brain?   *fevered*
40   I see thee yet in form as palpable
As this which now I draw.
         [*He draws a dagger.*]
Thou marshall'st° me the way that I was going,   *guide*
And such an instrument I was to use.
Mine eyes are made the fools o'th' other senses,
45   Or else worth all the rest. I see thee still,
And on thy blade and dudgeon° gouts° of blood,   *handle / drops*
Which was not so before. There's no such thing.
It is the bloody business which informs°   *creates shapes*
Thus to mine eyes. Now o'er the one half world
50   Nature seems dead, and wicked dreams abuse°   *deceive*
The curtained sleep. Witchcraft celebrates
Pale Hecate's off'rings,[8] and withered Murder,
Alarumed° by his sentinel the wolf,   *Roused*
Whose howl's his watch,° thus with his stealthy pace,   *watchword*
55   With Tarquin's[9] ravishing strides, towards his design°   *prey*
Moves like a ghost. Thou sure and firm-set earth,
Hear not my steps, which way they walk, for fear
Thy very stones prate of my whereabout
And take the present horror° from the time,   *i.e., terrible stillness*
60   Which now suits with it. Whiles I threat, he lives;

---

5. *Being . . . wrought:* Our desire to entertain the King liberally was constrained by the fact that we were unprepared. *defect:* deficiency. *free:* freely.
6. If you will support my opinion or my cause when the time comes.
7. PERFORMANCE COMMENT Whether or not the dagger that Macbeth attempts to clutch appears to the

audience is a decision that every director of the play needs to make. See Digital Edition PC 4.
8. Sacrificial rites offered to Hecate, Greek goddess of witchcraft and of the moon.
9. A Roman prince who ravished the chaste matron Lucrece. Shakespeare tells the story in *The Rape of Lucrece.*

Words to the heat of deeds too cold breath gives.
>*A bell rings.*
I go, and it is done. The bell invites me.
Hear it not, Duncan, for it is a knell
That summons thee to heaven or to hell.   *Exit.*

2.2

Enter LADY MACBETH.

LADY MACBETH   That which hath made them drunk hath
  made me bold;
What hath quenched them hath given me fire.
  [*An owl shrieks.*]

                                    Hark! Peace!

It was the owl that shrieked, the fatal bellman°   *night watchman*
Which gives the stern'st good-night.[1] He is about it.
5   The doors are open, and the surfeited grooms°   *attendants*
Do mock their charge° with snores. I have drugged their   *duty*
  possets,°   *mulled milk and wine*
That death and nature do contend about them
Whether they live or die.
      Enter MACBETH [*with bloody daggers*].[2]
MACBETH   Who's there? What ho!
LADY MACBETH [*to herself*]   Alack, I am afraid they have awaked,
10   And 'tis not done. Th'attempt and not the deed
Confounds° us. Hark! I laid their daggers ready;   *Ruins*
He could not miss 'em. Had he not resembled
My father as he slept, I had done't. —My husband?
MACBETH   I have done the deed. Didst thou not hear a noise?
15 LADY MACBETH   I heard the owl scream and the crickets cry.
  Did not you speak?
MACBETH   When?
LADY MACBETH   Now.
MACBETH   As I descended?
20 LADY MACBETH   Ay.
MACBETH   Hark, who lies i'th' second chamber?
LADY MACBETH   Donaldbain.
MACBETH   This is a sorry sight.
LADY MACBETH   A foolish thought to say a sorry sight.
25 MACBETH   There's one did laugh in 's sleep, and one cried
    "Murder!"
That they did wake each other. I stood and heard them.
But they did say their prayers and addressed them°   *settled themselves*
Again to sleep.
LADY MACBETH   There are two lodged together.
MACBETH   One cried, "God bless us!" and "Amen" the other,
30 As° they had seen me with these hangman's[3] hands.   *As if*
List'ning their fear, I could not say "Amen"
When they did say, "God bless us!"
LADY MACBETH   Consider it not so deeply.
MACBETH   But wherefore could not I pronounce "Amen"?
35   I had most need of blessing, and "Amen"

2.2 Location: Scene continues with only a brief pause.
1. A bell was rung outside the cells of condemned prisoners the night before they were to be executed.
2. Some editors have Macbeth first enter onto the upper stage space (line 8), then exit to descend the inner stairs during Lady Macbeth's speech before entering again onto the main stage at line 13.
3. Bloodstained. The hangman had to disembowel and quarter his victims.

Stuck in my throat.

LADY MACBETH   These deeds must not be thought°   *thought on*
After these ways; so, it will make us mad.

MACBETH   Methought I heard a voice cry, "Sleep no more!
Macbeth does murder sleep"—the innocent sleep,
40 Sleep that knits up the raveled° sleeve of care,   *unraveled*
The death of each day's life, sore labor's bath,
Balm of hurt minds, great nature's second course,[4]
Chief nourisher in life's feast—

LADY MACBETH   What do you mean?

MACBETH   Still it cried, "Sleep no more!" to all the house;
45 "Glamis hath murdered sleep, and therefore Cawdor
Shall sleep no more! Macbeth shall sleep no more!"

LADY MACBETH   Who was it that thus cried? Why, worthy thane,
You do unbend° your noble strength to think   *slacken*
So brainsickly of things. Go get some water,
50 And wash this filthy witness° from your hand.   *evidence*
Why did you bring these daggers from the place?
They must lie there. Go, carry them and smear
The sleepy grooms with blood.

MACBETH   I'll go no more.
I am afraid to think what I have done.
Look on't again I dare not.

55 LADY MACBETH   Infirm of purpose!
Give me the daggers. The sleeping and the dead
Are but as pictures; 'tis the eye of childhood
That fears a painted devil. If he do bleed,
I'll gild[5] the faces of the grooms withal,
For it must seem their guilt.   *Exit [with the daggers].*
        Knock within.
60 MACBETH   Whence is that knocking?
How is't with me, when every noise appalls me?
What hands are here? Ha, they pluck out mine eyes!
Will all great Neptune's ocean wash this blood
Clean from my hand? No, this my hand will rather
65 The multitudinous seas incarnadine,°   *turn red*
Making the green one red.[6]
        Enter LADY MACBETH.

LADY MACBETH   My hands are of your color, but I shame
To wear a heart so white. (*Knock.*) I hear a knocking
At the south entry. Retire we to our chamber.
70 A little water clears us of this deed.
How easy is it then. Your constancy
Hath left you unattended.[7] (*Knock.*) Hark, more knocking.
Get on your nightgown, lest occasion call us
And show us to be watchers.[8] Be not lost
75 So poorly in your thoughts.

MACBETH   To know my deed 'twere best not know myself.[9]
        (*Knock.*)
Wake Duncan with thy knocking. I would thou couldst!
                                Exeunt.

---

4. Second, and most nourishing, course of a meal;
second, or alternative, habit or practice.
5. Coat as if with gold leaf. Gold was often called
red; compare 2.3.109.
6. *one red:* entirely red.

7. *Your . . . unattended:* Your resolve has deserted you.
8. Those who have stayed awake.
9. It is better that I lose consciousness altogether
than face my deed.

2.3

Enter a PORTER. *Knocking within.*

PORTER Here's a knocking indeed! If a man were porter of hell
gate, he should have old° turning the key. (*Knock.*) Knock,   *plenty of*
knock, knock. Who's there, i'th' name of Beelzebub?° Here's a   *(a devil)*
farmer that hanged himself on th'expectation of plenty.[1] Come
in time![2] Have napkins° enough about you; here you'll sweat   *handkerchiefs*
for't. (*Knock.*) Knock, knock. Who's there, in th'other devil's
name? Faith, here's an equivocator[3] that could swear in both
the scales against either scale, who committed treason enough
for God's sake, yet could not equivocate to heaven. Oh, come
in, equivocator. (*Knock.*) Knock, knock, knock. Who's there?
Faith, here's an English tailor come hither for stealing out of a
French hose.[4] Come in, tailor. Here you may roast your goose.[5]
(*Knock.*) Knock, knock. Never at quiet? What are you? But
this place is too cold for hell. I'll devil-porter it no further. I
had thought to have let in some of all professions that go the
primrose way to th'everlasting bonfire. (*Knock.*) Anon, anon.
[*He opens the gate.*] —I pray you, remember° the porter.   *tip*

Enter MACDUFF *and* LENNOX.

MACDUFF Was it so late, friend, ere you went to bed,
That you do lie so late?

PORTER Faith, sir, we were carousing till the second cock,°   *3:00 A.M.*
and drink, sir, is a great provoker of three things.

MACDUFF What three things does drink especially provoke?

PORTER Marry,° sir, nose-painting,[6] sleep, and urine. Lech-   *Indeed*
ery, sir, it provokes and unprovokes: it provokes the desire
but it takes away the performance. Therefore, much drink
may be said to be an equivocator with lechery: it makes him
and it mars him; it sets him on and it takes him off; it persuades him and disheartens him, makes him stand to° and   *maintain an erection*
not stand to; in conclusion, equivocates him in a sleep[7] and,
giving him the lie,[8] leaves him.

MACDUFF I believe drink gave thee the lie last night.

PORTER That it did, sir, i'the very throat on me.[9] But I requited
him for his lie and, I think, being too strong for him, though
he took up my legs sometime, yet I made a shift to cast him.[1]

MACDUFF Is thy master stirring?

Enter MACBETH.

Our knocking has awaked him. Here he comes.

[*Exit* PORTER.]

LENNOX Good morrow, noble sir.

2.3 Location: Scene continues, perhaps after a short
pause.
1. *Here's . . . plenty:* A farmer had hoarded grain to
sell at high prices but was ruined by a crop surplus
that forced prices down.
2. Good timing.
3. One who speaks ambiguously. An allusion to the
Jesuit doctrine that a seemingly false statement was
not a lie (and therefore not repugnant to God) if the
speaker had in mind a different meaning in which
the utterance was true. Possibly an allusion to the
1606 trial of the Jesuit Henry Garnet for involvement
in the Gunpowder Plot to blow up the Houses of Parliament; Father Garnet had written a treatise defending equivocation for Catholics being persecuted for
their beliefs.

4. Tight-fitting breeches, which would easily reveal
the tailor's attempt to skimp on the cloth supplied
him for their manufacture. He had apparently been
able to do so undetected when loose-fitting breeches
were in fashion.
5. Heat your smoothing iron.
6. Reddening of the nose through drink.
7. Gives him an erotic experience in dreams only.
8. An elaborate pun: calling him a liar; laying him
out flat; making him urinate ("lye," or urine).
9. *i'the . . . me:* provoking a duel by insulting me with
a deliberate lie.
1. *being . . . cast him:* the effects of drunkenness are
described in the language of a wrestling match. *cast:*
throw off; vomit.

MACBETH   Good morrow, both.

MACDUFF   Is the King stirring, worthy thane?

MACBETH   Not yet.

MACDUFF   He did command me to call timely° on him.   *early*

  I have almost slipped the hour.

40 MACBETH   I'll bring you to him.

MACDUFF   I know this is a joyful trouble to you,

  But yet 'tis one.

MACBETH   The labor we delight in physics pain.[2]

  This is the door.

MACDUFF   I'll make so bold to call,

45 For 'tis my limited° service.   *Exit* MACDUFF.   *appointed*

LENNOX   Goes the King hence today?

MACBETH   He does; he did appoint so.

LENNOX   The night has been unruly. Where we lay,

  Our chimneys were blown down and, as they say,

50 Lamentings heard i'th' air, strange screams of death,

  And prophesying with accents terrible

  Of dire combustion° and confused events,   *tumult*

  New hatched to th' woeful time. The obscure bird[3]

  Clamored the livelong night. Some say the earth

  Was feverous and did shake.

◉ 55 MACBETH   'Twas a rough night.

LENNOX   My young remembrance cannot parallel

  A fellow to it.

        Enter MACDUFF.

MACDUFF   Oh, horror, horror, horror!

  Tongue nor heart cannot conceive nor name thee!

60 MACBETH *and* LENNOX   What's the matter?

MACDUFF   Confusion° now hath made his masterpiece!   *Ruin*

  Most sacrilegious murder hath broke ope

  The Lord's anointed temple° and stole thence   *(the King's body)*

  The life o'th' building!

MACBETH   What is't you say? The life?

65 LENNOX   Mean you his majesty?

MACDUFF   Approach the chamber and destroy your sight

  With a new Gorgon.[4] Do not bid me speak.

  See, and then speak yourselves.

                  Exeunt MACBETH *and* LENNOX.

                  —Awake, awake!

  Ring the alarum bell! Murder and treason!

70 Banquo and Donaldbain, Malcolm, awake!

  Shake off this downy sleep, death's counterfeit,

  And look on death itself! Up, up, and see

  The great doom's image!° Malcolm, Banquo,   *replica of Doomsday*

  As from your graves rise up and walk like sprites

75 To countenance° this horror! —Ring the bell![5]   *suit; behold*

        Bell rings. Enter LADY MACBETH.

LADY MACBETH   What's the business

  That such a hideous trumpet calls to parley

  The sleepers of the house? Speak, speak!

---

2. Pleasure in labor mitigates its laboriousness.
3. The owl, bird of darkness.
4. A mythical monster with a woman's figure and snakes for hair, the sight of whose face turned beholders to stone. Medusa was one of the three Gorgons.
5. Macduff's imperative to ring the bell may have been a stage direction mistakenly incorporated into his speech. For more, see the Textual Introduction.

MACDUFF   O gentle lady,
80 'Tis not for you to hear what I can speak.
The repetition° in a woman's ear   *report*
Would murder as it fell.
     Enter BANQUO.
—O Banquo, Banquo! Our royal master's murdered!
LADY MACBETH   Woe, alas! What, in our house?
85 BANQUO   Too cruel anywhere.
Dear Duff, I prithee, contradict thyself,
And say it is not so.
     Enter MACBETH, LENNOX, *and* ROSS.
MACBETH   Had I but died an hour before this chance,°   *occurrence*
I had lived a blessèd time, for from this instant
90 There's nothing serious in mortality.°   *worth living for*
All is but toys.° Renown and grace is dead.   *trifles*
The wine of life is drawn, and the mere lees
Is left this vault° to brag of.   *wine vault; world*
     Enter MALCOLM *and* DONALDBAIN.
DONALDBAIN   What is amiss?
MACBETH   You are and do not know't.
95 The spring, the head, the fountain of your blood
Is stopped, the very source of it is stopped.
MACDUFF   Your royal father's murdered.
MALCOLM   Oh! By whom?
LENNOX   Those of his chamber, as it seemed, had done't.
Their hands and faces were all badged° with blood;   *marked*
100 So were their daggers, which unwiped we found
Upon their pillows. They stared and were distracted;
No man's life was to be trusted with them.
MACBETH   Oh, yet I do repent me of my fury
That I did kill them.
MACDUFF   Wherefore did you so?
105 MACBETH   Who can be wise, amazed, temp'rate and furious,
Loyal and neutral in a moment? No man.
Th'expedition° of my violent love   *haste*
Outran the pauser,° reason. Here lay Duncan,   *delayer*
His silver skin laced with his golden blood,
110 And his gashed stabs looked like a breach in nature
For ruin's wasteful° entrance; there the murderers,   *destructive*
Steeped in the colors of their trade, their daggers
Unmannerly breeched with gore.[6] Who could refrain
That had a heart to love, and in that heart
Courage to make's love known?
115 LADY MACBETH [*fainting*][7]   Help me hence, ho!
MACDUFF   Look to the lady!
MALCOLM [*aside to* DONALDBAIN]   Why do we hold our tongues,
That most may claim this argument° for ours?   *subject*
DONALDBAIN [*aside to* MACBETH]   What should be spoken here,
    where our fate,
Hid in an auger-hole,° may rush and seize us?   *in a cranny (in ambush)*
120 Let's away. Our tears are not yet brewed.

---

6. Covered—as if with breeches—with blood.
7. TEXTUAL COMMENT Since the seventeenth century, performers and editors have had Lady Macbeth
faint at this moment; however, F lacks an explicit
stage direction to indicate what exactly happens. For
more on this issue, see Digital Edition TC 4.

MALCOLM [*aside to* DONALDBAIN]   Nor our strong sorrow upon
    the foot of motion.[8]
BANQUO   Look to the lady.   [*Exit* LADY MACBETH, *attended.*]
    And when we have our naked frailties hid,°   *clothed*
    That suffer in exposure, let us meet
125   And question° this most bloody piece of work   *discuss*
    To know it further. Fears and scruples° shake us.   *doubts*
    In the great hand of God I stand, and thence
    Against the undivulged pretense I fight
    Of treasonous malice.[9]
MACDUFF   And so do I.
ALL   So, all!
130 MACBETH   Let's briefly° put on manly readiness,°   *quickly / clothes; resolve*
    And meet i'th' hall together.
ALL   Well contented.
         Exeunt [*all but* MALCOLM *and* DONALDBAIN].
MALCOLM   What will you do? Let's not consort with them.
    To show an unfelt sorrow is an office
    Which the false man does easy. I'll to England.
135 DONALDBAIN   To Ireland, I. Our separated fortune
    Shall keep us both the safer. Where we are,
    There's daggers in men's smiles. The nearer in blood,
    The nearer bloody.[1]
MALCOLM   This murderous shaft that's shot
    Hath not yet lighted,° and our safest way   *fallen*
140   Is to avoid the aim. Therefore, to horse,
    And let us not be dainty of° leave-taking,   *polite about*
    But shift° away. There's warrant° in that theft   *slip / justification*
    Which steals itself[2] when there's no mercy left.   *Exeunt.*

2.4

Enter ROSS *with an* OLD MAN.
OLD MAN   Threescore and ten I can remember well,
    Within the volume of which time I have seen
    Hours dreadful and things strange, but this sore night
    Hath trifled former knowings.[1]
ROSS   Ha, good father,
5   Thou seest the heavens, as troubled with man's act,
    Threatens his bloody stage. By th' clock 'tis day,
    And yet dark night strangles the traveling lamp.°   *sun*
    Is't night's predominance° or the day's shame   *ascendancy*
    That darkness does the face of earth entomb
    When living light should kiss it?
10 OLD MAN   'Tis unnatural,
    Even like the deed that's done. On Tuesday last
    A falcon, tow'ring in her pride of place,[2]
    Was by a mousing owl[3] hawked at and killed.
ROSS   And Duncan's horses—a thing most strange and certain—

---

8. *Nor . . . motion:* Nor has our strong sorrow yet
begun to express itself.
9. *Against . . . malice:* I will fight against the hidden
purpose behind this treasonous act.
1. *The nearer . . . bloody:* The closer the kinship, the
nearer the danger of murder.
2. *Which steals itself:* Malcolm alludes to the fact that

he and Donaldbain intend to "steal" away from the
castle.
2.4 Location: Not far from Macbeth's castle.
1. Has made previous experiences seem trifling.
2. Mounting to her highest point in the sky before
swooping down.
3. An owl that usually feeds on mice.

15 Beauteous and swift, the minions° of their race,   *darlings*
Turned wild in nature, broke their stalls, flung out,
Contending 'gainst obedience, as° they would   *as if*
Make war with mankind.
OLD MAN   'Tis said they ate each other.
ROSS   They did so, to th'amazement of mine eyes
That looked upon't.
         Enter MACDUFF.
20   Here comes the good Macduff.
How goes the world, sir, now?
MACDUFF   Why, see you not?
ROSS   Is't known who did this more than bloody deed?
MACDUFF   Those that Macbeth hath slain.
ROSS   Alas, the day!
What good could they pretend?[4]
MACDUFF   They were suborned.°   *bribed*
25 Malcolm and Donaldbain, the King's two sons,
Are stol'n away and fled, which puts upon them
Suspicion of the deed.
ROSS   'Gainst nature still!
Thriftless ambition that will ravin up°   *devour*
Thine own life's means! Then 'tis most like
30 The sovereignty will fall upon Macbeth.
MACDUFF   He is already named and gone to Scone[5]
To be invested.
ROSS   Where is Duncan's body?
MACDUFF   Carried to Colmekill,[6]
The sacred storehouse of his predecessors
And guardian of their bones.
35 ROSS   Will you to Scone?
MACDUFF   No, cousin, I'll to Fife.[7]
ROSS   Well, I will thither.
MACDUFF   Well may you see things well done there. Adieu,
Lest our old robes sit easier than our new.
ROSS   Farewell, father.
40 OLD MAN   God's benison° go with you and with those   *blessing*
That would make good of bad and friends of foes.
                         Exeunt all.

3.1

         Enter BANQUO.
BANQUO   Thou hast it now—King, Cawdor, Glamis, all
As the weird women promised, and I fear
Thou play'dst most foully for't. Yet it was said
It should not stand in thy posterity[1]
5 But that myself should be the root and father
Of many kings. If there come truth from them—
As upon thee, Macbeth, their speeches shine°—   *smile favorably*
Why by the verities on thee made good
May they not be my oracles as well
10 And set me up in hope? But hush, no more.

---

4. What good could they expect to gain from the murder?
5. Ancient royal city where Scottish kings were invested with the ceremonial symbols of authority.
6. Iona, the burial place of Scottish kings.
7. Macduff is the Thane of Fife.
3.1 Location: The royal palace at Forres.
1. It should not pass to your descendants.

Sennet° sounded. Enter MACBETH *as King,* LADY   *Trumpet call*
[MACBETH *as Queen*], LENNOX, ROSS, LORDS, *and*
Attendants.

MACBETH   Here's our chief guest.

LADY MACBETH   If he had been forgotten,
  It had been as a gap in our great feast,
  And all-thing° unbecoming.   *entirely*

MACBETH   Tonight we hold a solemn° supper, sir,   *formal*
  And I'll request your presence.

15   BANQUO   Let your highness
  Command upon me, to the which my duties
  Are with a most indissoluble tie
  Forever knit.

MACBETH   Ride you this afternoon?

BANQUO   Ay, my good lord.

20   MACBETH   We should have else desired your good advice,
  Which still° hath been both grave° and prosperous,   *always / weighty*
  In this day's council; but we'll take² tomorrow.
  Is't far you ride?

BANQUO   As far, my lord, as will fill up the time
25   Twixt this and supper. Go not my horse the better,³
  I must become a borrower of the night
  For a dark hour or twain.

MACBETH   Fail not our feast.

BANQUO   My lord, I will not.

MACBETH   We hear our bloody cousins are bestowed°   *lodged*
30   In England and in Ireland, not confessing
  Their cruel parricide, filling their hearers
  With strange invention.° But of that tomorrow,   *falsehood*
  When therewithal we shall have cause of state
  Craving us jointly.⁴ Hie you to horse. Adieu,
35   Till you return at night. Goes Fleance with you?

BANQUO   Ay, my good lord. Our time does call upon's.

MACBETH   I wish your horses swift and sure of foot,
  And so I do commend° you to their backs.   *entrust*
  Farewell.   *Exit* BANQUO.
40   —Let every man be master of his time
  Till seven at night. To make society
  The sweeter welcome, we will keep ourself
  Till supper-time alone. While° then, God be with you.   *Till*

Exeunt LORDS [*and all but* MACBETH *and a* SERVANT].
  —Sirrah, a word with you: attend those men
45   Our pleasure?

SERVANT   They are, my lord, without° the palace gate.   *outside*

MACBETH   Bring them before us.   *Exit* SERVANT.
  To be thus is nothing, but to be safely thus.⁵
  Our fears in° Banquo stick° deep,   *of / prick*
50   And in his royalty of nature° reigns   *natural nobility*
  That which would be feared. 'Tis much he dares;
  And to° that dauntless temper of his mind   *added to*
  He hath a wisdom that doth guide his valor
  To act in safety. There is none but he
55   Whose being I do fear, and under him

---

2. Take it (Banquo's advice).   attention.
3. If my horse does not go faster than I expect.   5. *To be thus . . . thus:* To be a king is no good unless
4. *cause . . . jointly:* state business demanding our joint   one can reign in safety ("thus" refers to "king").

My genius° is rebuked, as it is said[6]   *tutelary spirit*
Mark Antony's was by Caesar.° He chid the sisters   *Octavius Caesar*
When first they put the name of king upon me,
And bade them speak to him; then, prophet-like,
60   They hailed him father to a line of kings.
Upon my head they placed a fruitless crown
And put a barren scepter in my grip,
Thence to be wrenched with° an unlineal hand,   *by*
No son of mine succeeding. If't be so,
65   For Banquo's issue have I filed° my mind,   *defiled*
For them the gracious° Duncan have I murdered,   *full of grace*
Put rancors° in the vessel of my peace   *bitterness*
Only for them, and mine eternal jewel°   *soul*
Given to the common enemy of man°   *(the devil)*
70   To make them kings—the seeds of Banquo kings!
Rather than so, come fate into the list,°   *arena*
And champion me to th'utterance![7] —Who's there!
      Enter SERVANT *and two* MURDERERS.
  [*to* SERVANT] Now go to the door, and stay there till we call.
                    Exit SERVANT.

  —Was it not yesterday we spoke together?
MURDERERS   It was, so please your highness.
75 MACBETH   Well, then; now,[8]
Have you considered of my speeches? Know
That it was he in the times past which held you
So under° fortune, which you thought had been   *out of favor with*
Our innocent self. This I made good to you
80   In our last conference, passed in probation° with you   *reviewed the proof*
How you were borne in hand,° how crossed,° the instruments,[9] *deceived / thwarted*
Who wrought with them, and all things else that might
To half a soul and to a notion crazed[1]
Say, "Thus did Banquo."
FIRST MURDERER   You made it known to us.
85 MACBETH   I did so, and went further, which is now
Our point of second meeting. Do you find
Your patience so predominant in your nature
That you can let this go? Are you so gospeled[2]
To pray for this good man and for his issue,
90   Whose heavy hand hath bowed you to the grave
And beggared yours° for ever?   *your family*
FIRST MURDERER   We are men, my liege.
MACBETH   Ay, in the catalogue ye go for men,
As hounds and greyhounds, mongrels, spaniels, curs,
Shoughs, water-rugs, and demi-wolves[3] are clept°   *called*
95   All by the name of dogs. The valued file[4]
Distinguishes the swift, the slow, the subtle,
The housekeeper,° the hunter—every one   *watchdog*

---

6. Said by Plutarch. Shakespeare paraphrases him in *Antony and Cleopatra* (2.3).
7. And fight with me in single combat to the death (i.e., the uttermost).
8. TEXTUAL COMMENT In F, lines 75–79 appear highly metrically irregular, which this edition has attempted to rearrange. For more on the issue of F's erratic lineation and the work of textual editing, see Digital Edition TC 5.
9. Agents.
1. Even to a half-wit or to a crazed mind.
2. Imbued with the gospel spirit.
3. Shaggy lapdogs, water dogs (for fowling), and crossbreeds between wolf and dog.
4. List specifying the value of the catalogued items.

According to the gift which bounteous nature
Hath in him closed,° whereby he does receive   *enclosed*
100   Particular addition from the bill
That writes them all alike;[5] and so of men.
Now, if you have a station° in the file,   *position*
Not i'th' worst rank of manhood, say't,
And I will put that business in your bosoms
105   Whose execution takes your enemy off,
Grapples you to the heart and love of us,
Who wear our health but sickly in his life,
Which in his death were perfect.
SECOND MURDERER   I am one, my liege,
Whom the vile blows and buffets of the world
110   Have so incensed that I am reckless what
I do to spite the world.
FIRST MURDERER   And I another,
So weary with disasters, tugged with° fortune,   *mauled by*
That I would set° my life on any chance   *risk*
To mend it or be rid on't.°   *of it*
MACBETH   Both of you
Know Banquo was your enemy.
115   MURDERERS   True, my lord.
MACBETH   So is he mine, and in such bloody distance°   *enmity*
That every minute of his being thrusts
Against my near'st of life.[6] And though I could
With barefaced power sweep him from my sight
120   And bid my will avouch° it, yet I must not,   *warrant*
For° certain friends that are both his and mine,   *Because of*
Whose loves I may not drop, but wail° his fall   *must bewail*
Who I myself struck down. And thence it is
That I to your assistance do make love,°   *I crave your aid*
125   Masking the business from the common eye
For sundry weighty reasons.
SECOND MURDERER   We shall, my lord,
Perform what you command us.
FIRST MURDERER   Though our lives—
MACBETH   Your spirits shine through you. Within this hour, at most,
I will advise you where to plant yourselves,
130   Acquaint you with the perfect spy o'th' time,
The moment on't,[7] for't must be done tonight,
And something° from the palace, always thought°   *at some distance / remember*
That I require a clearness.[8] And with him—
To leave no rubs° nor botches in the work—   *flaws*
135   Fleance, his son that keeps him company,
Whose absence is no less material to me
Than is his father's, must embrace the fate
Of that dark hour. Resolve yourselves apart.[9]
I'll come to you anon.
MURDERERS   We are resolved, my lord.
140   MACBETH   I'll call upon you straight; abide within.
                         Exeunt [MURDERERS].

5. *Particular . . . alike:* Distinction apart from a catalogue that lists them indiscriminately.
6. My most vital part, the heart.
7. *Acquaint . . . on't:* I will give you full and precise

instructions as to when it is to be done.
8. A clearance (from suspicion).
9. Make up your minds privately.

It is concluded. Banquo, thy soul's flight,
If it find heaven, must find it out tonight.　　　　　　　　[*Exit*.]

3.2

Enter LADY MACBETH *and a* SERVANT.

LADY MACBETH　Is Banquo gone from court?

SERVANT　Ay, madam, but returns again tonight.

LADY MACBETH　Say to the King I would attend his leisure
For a few words.

SERVANT　　　　　　　Madam, I will.　　　　　　　*Exit*.

LADY MACBETH　　　　　　　Naught's had, all's spent,

5　Where our desire is got without content.°　　　　　　*happiness*
'Tis safer to be that which we destroy
Than by destruction dwell in doubtful joy.

Enter MACBETH.

How now, my lord? Why do you keep alone,
Of sorriest° fancies your companions making,　　　　*most wretched*

10　Using° those thoughts which should indeed have died　*Entertaining*
With them they think on? Things without all remedy
Should be without regard.° What's done is done.　　*not considered*

MACBETH　We have scorched° the snake, not killed it.　*slashed*
She'll close° and be herself, whilst our poor malice　*heal*

15　Remains in danger of her former tooth.[1]
But let the frame of things disjoint, both the worlds suffer,[2]
Ere we will eat our meal in fear, and sleep
In the affliction of these terrible dreams
That shake us nightly. Better be with the dead,

20　Whom we, to gain our peace, have sent to peace,
Than on the torture° of the mind to lie　　　　　　　*rack*
In restless ecstasy.° Duncan is in his grave.　　　　　*frenzy*
After life's fitful fever he sleeps well.
Treason has done his worst; nor steel, nor poison,

25　Malice domestic, foreign levy,[3] nothing
Can touch him further.

LADY MACBETH　　　　　　Come on, gentle my lord,
Sleek o'er your rugged looks. Be bright and jovial
Among your guests tonight.

MACBETH　　　　　　　　So shall I, love,
And so, I pray, be you. Let your remembrance

30　Apply° to Banquo; present him eminence°　　　　　　*Be given / favor*
Both with eye and tongue—unsafe the while, that we
Must lave our honors in these flattering streams[4]
And make our faces vizards° to our hearts,　　　　　*masks*
Disguising what they are.

LADY MACBETH　　　　　　You must leave this.

35　MACBETH　Oh, full of scorpions is my mind, dear wife!
Thou know'st that Banquo and his Fleance lives.

LADY MACBETH　But in them nature's copy's[5] not eterne.°　*everlasting*

MACBETH　There's comfort yet; they are assailable.

3.2 Location: The palace.
1. *our . . . tooth:* we remain in danger of her fangs,
which are as dangerous as they were before she was
slashed. *poor malice:* weak enmity.
2. Let the universe fall apart, and heaven and earth
suffer destruction.
3. An army levied abroad against Scotland.

4. *unsafe . . . streams:* we are unsafe at present, so we
must make our reputations look clean by flattering
others; we are unsafe as long as we must flatter.
5. Lease on life (a copyhold lease was subject to can-
cellation and therefore "not eterne"); the individual
human cast from nature's mold.

Then be thou jocund. Ere the bat hath flown
40 His cloistered° flight, ere to black Hecate's summons   *restricted*
The shard-born[6] beetle with his drowsy hums
Hath rung night's yawning peal,[7] there shall be done
A deed of dreadful note.

LADY MACBETH   What's to be done?

MACBETH   Be innocent of the knowledge, dearest chuck,[8]
45 Till thou applaud the deed. —Come, seeling[9] night,
Scarf up° the tender eye of pitiful day,   *Blindfold*
And with thy bloody and invisible hand
Cancel and tear to pieces that great bond°   *(Banquo's lease on life)*
Which keeps me pale! Light thickens,
50 And the crow makes wing to th' rooky° wood;   *full of rooks*
Good things of day begin to droop and drowse,
Whiles night's black agents to their preys do rouse.
—Thou marvel'st at my words, but hold thee still.
Things bad begun make strong themselves by ill.
55 So, prithee, go with me.   *Exeunt.*

3.3

Enter three MURDERERS.

FIRST MURDERER   But who did bid thee join with us?

THIRD MURDERER   Macbeth.

SECOND MURDERER [*to* FIRST MURDERER]   He needs not our
     mistrust, since he delivers
Our offices and what we have to do
To the direction just.[1]

FIRST MURDERER [*to* THIRD MURDERER]   Then stand with us.
5 The West yet glimmers with some streaks of day.
Now spurs the lated° traveler apace   *belated*
To gain the timely inn, and near approaches
The subject of our watch.

THIRD MURDERER   Hark, I hear horses.

BANQUO (*within*)   Give us a light there, ho!

SECOND MURDERER   Then 'tis he. The rest
10 That are within the note of expectation°   *list of expected guests*
Already are i'th' court.

FIRST MURDERER   His horses go about.[2]

THIRD MURDERER   Almost a mile, but he does usually.
So all men do from hence to th' palace gate
Make it their walk.

Enter BANQUO *and* FLEANCE, *with a torch.*

15 SECOND MURDERER   A light, a light!

THIRD MURDERER   'Tis he.

FIRST MURDERER   Stand to't.

BANQUO   It will be rain tonight.

FIRST MURDERER   Let it come down![3]

[*They attack.* FIRST MURDERER *puts out the light.*]

BANQUO   Oh, treachery!

---

6. Born in dung ("shards"); carried on scaly wings ("shard-borne").
7. Macbeth likens the beetle's humming to a bell, signaling the time for sleep.
8. Chick (term of endearment).
9. Eye-closing. Falcons' eyelids were sewn shut ("seeled") as part of their training.

3.3 Location: Near the palace.
1. *He . . . just:* We need not mistrust this man, since he knows perfectly Macbeth's instructions to us.
2. Are led (by servants) to the stables.
3. TEXTUAL COMMENT For the variety of ways that Shakespeare's short lines can be read or performed, see Digital Edition TC 6.

20   Fly, good Fleance, fly, fly, fly!
        Thou mayst revenge. —O slave!
                    [BANQUO *dies.* FLEANCE *escapes.*]
        THIRD MURDERER   Who did strike out the light?
        FIRST MURDERER   Was't not the way?°   *proper thing*
        THIRD MURDERER   There's but one down. The son is fled.
        SECOND MURDERER   We have lost best half of our affair.
25   FIRST MURDERER   Well, let's away and say how much is done.
                            Exeunt [*with Banquo's body*].

                            3.4
                Banquet prepared. Enter MACBETH, LADY MACBETH,
                ROSS, LENNOX, LORDS, *and Attendants.*
        MACBETH   You know your own degrees;° sit down.   *ranks; places*
        At first and last,[1] the hearty welcome.
        LORDS   Thanks to your majesty.
        MACBETH   Ourself will mingle with society
5   And play the humble host.
        Our hostess keeps her state,° but in best time   *chair of state*
        We will require° her welcome.   *request*
        LADY MACBETH   Pronounce it for me, sir, to all our friends,
        For my heart speaks they are welcome.
                Enter FIRST MURDERER [*and stands aside*].
10   MACBETH   See, they encounter° thee with their hearts' thanks.   *answer*
        Both sides are even. Here I'll sit, i'th' midst.
        Be large° in mirth; anon we'll drink a measure   *unrestrained*
        The table round.
                [*He converses apart with the* FIRST MURDERER.]
                            There's blood upon thy face.
        FIRST MURDERER   'Tis Banquo's, then.
15   MACBETH   'Tis better thee without than he within.[2]
        Is he dispatched?
        FIRST MURDERER   My lord, his throat is cut. That I did for him.
        MACBETH   Thou art the best o'th' cutthroats.
        Yet he's good that did the like for Fleance;
20   If thou didst it, thou art the nonpareil.°   *paragon (without equal)*
        FIRST MURDERER   Most royal sir, Fleance is scaped.
        MACBETH   Then comes my fit again. I had else been perfect,
        Whole as the marble, founded° as the rock,   *immovable*
        As broad and general° as the casing° air,   *unconstrained / surrounding*
25   But now I am cabined, cribbed,° confined, bound in   *penned up*
        To saucy° doubts and fears. But Banquo's safe?   *importunate*
        FIRST MURDERER   Ay, my good lord, safe in a ditch he bides,
        With twenty trenchèd gashes on his head,
        The least a death to nature.
        MACBETH   Thanks for that.
30   There the grown serpent lies; the worm° that's fled   *young serpent*
        Hath nature that in time will venom breed,
        No teeth for th' present. Get thee gone. Tomorrow
        We'll hear ourselves° again.   *Exit* FIRST MURDERER.   *confer*
        LADY MACBETH   My royal lord,
        You do not give the cheer.° The feast is sold   *entertain*

3.4 Location: The palace.   2. Better on you than inside him.
1. To one and all.

35 That is not often vouched, while 'tis a-making,
    'Tis given with welcome.³ To feed° were best at home;   *Mere eating*
    From thence° the sauce to meat is ceremony: *Away from home*
    Meeting were° bare without it.   *Company would be*

            Enter the Ghost of BANQUO *and sits in* MACBETH'*s place.*⁴

MACBETH   Sweet remembrancer.°   *reminder*
    —Now, good digestion wait on appetite,
    And health on both.
40 LENNOX   May't please your highness, sit.
MACBETH   Here had we now our country's honor roofed,⁵
    Were the graced person of our Banquo present,
    Who may I rather challenge for° unkindness   *accuse of*
    Than pity for mischance.
ROSS   His absence, sir,
45 Lays blame upon his promise. Please't your highness
    To grace us with your royal company?
MACBETH [*seeing his place occupied*]   The table's full.
LENNOX   Here is a place reserved, sir.
MACBETH   Where?
LENNOX   Here, my good lord. What is't that moves your highness?
MACBETH   Which of you have done this?
50 LORDS   What, my good lord?
MACBETH [*to Ghost of* BANQUO]   Thou canst not say I did it.
        Never shake
    Thy gory locks at me!
ROSS   Gentlemen, rise. His highness is not well.
LADY MACBETH   Sit, worthy friends. My lord is often thus
55 And hath been from his youth. Pray you, keep seat.
    The fit is momentary; upon a thought°   *in a moment*
    He will again be well. If much you note him,
    You shall offend him and extend his passion.°   *prolong his suffering*
    Feed, and regard him not.
            [*She converses apart with* MACBETH.]
                        Are you a man?
60 MACBETH   Ay, and a bold one that dare look on that
    Which might appall the devil!
LADY MACBETH   Oh, proper stuff!°   *mere nonsense*
    This is the very painting of your fear;
    This is the air-drawn dagger⁶ which you said
    Led you to Duncan. Oh, these flaws° and starts,   *outbursts*
65 Impostors to° true fear, would well become   *compared with*
    A woman's story at a winter's fire,
    Authorized by her grandam. Shame itself!
    Why do you make such faces? When all's done,
    You look but on a stool.
MACBETH   Prithee, see there!
70 Behold, look, lo! How say you?
    Why, what care I? [*to Ghost of* BANQUO] If thou canst nod,
        speak too.
    If charnel houses and our graves must send

---

3. *The . . . welcome:* A feast is like a purchased ("sold") meal if it is not often affirmed ("vouched") to the guests, while the feast is taking place, that they are welcome.
4. TEXTUAL COMMENT F's stage direction for the Ghost of Banquo's entrance leaves some uncertainty about when precisely he appears on the stage, with

implications for the scene's theatrical effect. For further details on the issue of early modern stage directions, see Digital Edition TC 7.
5. All the Scottish nobility under one roof.
6. The dagger drawn on, or carried on, the air (2.1.33ff).

Those that we bury back, our monuments
Shall be the maws of kites.[7]   [*Exit Ghost of* BANQUO.][8]

75   LADY MACBETH   What, quite unmanned in folly?
MACBETH   If I stand here, I saw him.
LADY MACBETH   Fie, for shame!
MACBETH   Blood hath been shed ere now, i'th' olden time,
Ere humane statute purged the gentle weal;[9]
Ay, and since, too, murders have been performed,
80   Too terrible for the ear. The times has been
That, when the brains were out, the man would die,
And there an end. But now they rise again,
With twenty mortal murders° on their crowns,°   *deadly wounds / heads*
And push us from our stools. This is more strange
Than such a murder is.
85   LADY MACBETH   My worthy lord,
Your noble friends do lack you.
MACBETH   I do forget.
—Do not muse° at me, my most worthy friends.   *wonder*
I have a strange infirmity, which is nothing
To those that know me. Come, love and health to all;
90   Then I'll sit down. Give me some wine; fill full.
              Enter Ghost [*of* BANQUO].
I drink to th' general joy o'th' whole table
And to our dear friend Banquo, whom we miss.
Would he were here! To all and him we thirst,°   *drink*
And all to all.[1]
LORDS   Our duties and the pledge.°   *toast*
        [*They drink.*]
95   MACBETH [*to Ghost of* BANQUO]   Avaunt, and quit my sight!
Let the earth hide thee!
Thy bones are marrowless, thy blood is cold;
Thou hast no speculation° in those eyes   *sight*
Which thou dost glare with.
LADY MACBETH   Think of this, good peers,
But as a thing of custom; 'tis no other,
100   Only it spoils the pleasure of the time.
MACBETH   What man dare, I dare.
Approach thou like the rugged Russian bear,
The armed° rhinoceros, or th' Hyrcan[2] tiger!   *armored*
Take any shape but that,° and my firm nerves°   *(Banquo's) / sinews*
105   Shall never tremble. Or be alive again,
And dare me to the desert° with thy sword.   *deserted place*
If trembling I inhabit then,[3] protest me
The baby of a girl.[4] Hence, horrible shadow,
Unreal mock'ry, hence!   [*Exit Ghost of* BANQUO.]
              Why, so. Being gone,
110   I am a man again. —Pray you, sit still.
LADY MACBETH   You have displaced the mirth, broke the good
        meeting
With most admired° disorder.   *wondered at*

7. *If . . . kites:* If the dead return from their graves,
nothing will prevent them from being consumed by
birds of prey, making graves of their stomachs.
8. PERFORMANCE COMMENT Productions have to
decide how to stage the appearance of Banquo's ghost
at the banquet, or indeed whether to bring the figure
of Banquo on stage at all. See Digital Edition PC 5.

9. Before human or humane (Elizabethans did not
spell the two words differently) law cleansed the
commonwealth and made it peaceable.
1. All good wishes to everyone.
2. From Hyrcania, a region near the Caspian Sea.
3. If then I tremble; if, trembling, I stay indoors.
4. A baby girl; a girl's doll.

MACBETH   Can such things be,
And overcome° us like a summer's cloud,   *pass over*
Without our special wonder? You make me strange
115   Even to the disposition that I owe,[5]
When now I think you can behold such sights
And keep the natural ruby of your cheeks
When mine is blanched with fear.

ROSS   What sights, my lord?

LADY MACBETH   I pray you, speak not; he grows worse and worse.
120   Question enrages° him. At once, good night.   *Talk aggravates*
Stand not upon the order of your going,
But go at once.[6]

LENNOX   Good night, and better health
Attend his majesty.

LADY MACBETH   A kind good night to all.
                        Exeunt LORDS [*and Attendants*].

MACBETH   It will have blood, they say; blood will have blood.
125   Stones have been known to move and trees to speak;
Augurs° and understood relations[7] have   *Auguries*
By maggot-pies and choughs and rooks[8] brought forth°   *revealed*
The secret'st man of blood.° What is the night?[9]   *murderer*

LADY MACBETH   Almost at odds with morning, which is which.

130 MACBETH   How say'st thou[1] that Macduff denies his person
At our great bidding?

LADY MACBETH   Did you send to him, sir?

MACBETH   I hear it by the way,° but I will send.   *indirectly*
There's not a one of them but in his house
I keep a servant fee'd.° I will° tomorrow—   *paid to spy / will go*
135   And betimes° I will—to the weird sisters.   *early*
More shall they speak, for now I am bent° to know   *determined*
By the worst means the worst. For mine own good
All causes° shall give way. I am in blood   *other concerns*
Stepped in so far that, should I° wade no more,°   *were I to / no farther*
140   Returning were° as tedious as go° o'er.   *would be / going*
Strange things I have in head that will to hand,
Which must be acted ere they may be scanned.[2]

LADY MACBETH   You lack the season° of all natures, sleep.   *preservative*

MACBETH   Come, we'll to sleep. My strange and self-abuse°   *self-delusion*
145   Is the initiate fear that wants hard use.[3]
We are yet but young in deed.°   *Exeunt.*   *crime*

3.5

Thunder. Enter the three WITCHES, *meeting* HECATE.

FIRST WITCH   Why, how now, Hecate? You look angerly.

HECATE   Have I not reason, beldams,° as you are   *hags*
Saucy and overbold? How did you dare
To trade and traffic with Macbeth
5   In riddles and affairs of death,
And I, the mistress of your charms,

---

5. *You . . . owe:* You make me a stranger to my own nature, which I had supposed brave.
6. *Stand . . . once:* Do not follow the order of precedence in departing, but all go at once.
7. Formerly hidden, now revealed relationships between causes and effects.
8. Magpies, traditionally sacrificed by augurers, and birds (choughs and rooks) of the crow family.

9. What time of night is it?
1. What do you think of the fact.
2. *ere . . . scanned:* at once, before they can be considered.
3. Is the fear of a novice who lacks toughening experience.
3.5 Location: An open place.

The close° contriver of all harms,   *secret*
Was never called to bear my part,
Or show the glory of our art?
10   And, which is worse, all you have done
Hath been but for a wayward son,
Spiteful and wrathful, who, as others do,
Loves for his own ends, not for you.
But make amends now. Get you gone,
15   And at the pit of Acheron°   *a river in hell*
Meet me i'th' morning. Thither he
Will come to know his destiny.
Your vessels and your spells provide,
Your charms and everything beside.
20   I am for th'air. This night I'll spend
Unto a dismal and a fatal end.¹
Great business must be wrought ere noon.
Upon the corner of the moon
There hangs a vap'rous drop profound;²
25   I'll catch it ere it come to ground.
And that, distilled by magic sleights,
Shall raise such artificial sprites³
As by the strength of their illusion
Shall draw him on to his confusion.
30   He shall spurn fate, scorn death, and bear
His hopes 'bove wisdom, grace, and fear.
And you all know security°   *overconfidence*
Is mortals' chiefest enemy.
          Music and a song.
Hark, I am called. My little spirit, see,
35   Sits in a foggy cloud and stays for me.   [*Exit.*]
          Sing within:° "*Come away, come away,*" etc.⁴   *offstage*
FIRST WITCH   Come, let's make haste. She'll soon be back again.
                                        Exeunt.

3.6

Enter LENNOX *and another* LORD.

LENNOX   My former speeches have but hit your thoughts,
Which can interpret farther.¹ Only I say
Things have been strangely borne.° The gracious Duncan   *carried on*
Was pitied of Macbeth; marry, he was dead.²
5   And the right valiant Banquo walked too late,
Whom you may say, if't please you, Fleance killed,
For Fleance fled; men must not walk too late.
Who cannot want the thought° how monstrous   *can help thinking*
It was for Malcolm and for Donaldbain
10   To kill their gracious father? Damnèd fact,°   *deed*
How it did grieve Macbeth! Did he not straight
In pious° rage the two delinquents tear,   *loyal*
That were the slaves of drink and thralls° of sleep?   *slaves*

---

1. Working toward a disastrous and fateful end.
2. Of deep or hidden significance; ready to fall.
3. Spirits produced by magic art.
4. TEXTUAL COMMENT F's directions for the witches' song might indicate that *Macbeth* was revised, perhaps by Thomas Middleton, whose play *The Witch* includes an elaborately staged performance of a song with the same first line. For more on the issue, along with musical recordings, see Digital Edition TC 8.

3.6 Location: Somewhere in Scotland.
1. *My . . . farther:* What I have said has coincided with your thoughts. I need not say more; you can draw your own further conclusions.
2. *The . . . dead:* Macbeth pitied Duncan after he was dead, but not before. *of:* by.

Was not that nobly done? Ay, and wisely, too,
15   For 'twould have angered any heart alive
To hear the men deny't. So that I say
He has borne all things well. And I do think
That had he Duncan's sons under his key—
As, an't° please heaven, he shall not—they should find   *if it*
20   What 'twere to kill a father. So should Fleance.
But peace. For from broad words³ and 'cause he failed
His presence at the tyrant's feast, I hear
Macduff lives in disgrace. Sir, can you tell
Where he bestows himself?°   *lodges*

LORD   The son of Duncan,
25   From whom this tyrant holds° the due of birth,°   *withholds / birthright*
Lives in the English court and is received
Of the most pious Edward⁴ with such grace
That the malevolence of fortune nothing
Takes from his high respect.⁵ Thither Macduff
30   Is gone to pray the holy King, upon his aid,°   *in aid of Malcolm*
To wake Northumberland and warlike Siward,
That by the help of these, with Him above
To ratify the work, we may again
Give to our tables meat,° sleep to our nights,   *food*
35   Free from our feasts and banquets bloody knives,⁶
Do faithful homage, and receive free⁷ honors—
All which we pine for now. And this report
Hath so exasperate the King⁸ that he
Prepares for some attempt of war.

40   LENNOX   Sent he to Macduff?

LORD   He did, and with° an absolute "Sir, not I,"   *on receiving*
The cloudy messenger turns me his back
And hums, as who should say, "You'll rue the time
That clogs me with this answer."⁹

LENNOX   And that well might
45   Advise him to a caution, t'hold what distance
His wisdom can provide.¹ Some holy angel
Fly to the court of England and unfold
His message ere he come, that a swift blessing
May soon return to this our suffering country
Under a hand accursed.²

50   LORD   I'll send my prayers with him.   *Exeunt.*

4.1

Thunder. Enter the three WITCHES.

FIRST WITCH   Thrice the brinded° cat hath mewed.   *brindled; streaked*

SECOND WITCH   Thrice, and once the hedge-pig° whined.   *hedgehog*

---

3. As a result of his plain speaking.
4. *received . . . Edward:* received by the saintly King
Edward (Edward the Confessor, reigned 1042–1066).
5. *nothing . . . takes:* does not deprive Malcolm of
respect.
6. Free our feasts from bloody knives.
7. Freely given; enjoyed in freedom.
8. TEXTUAL COMMENT "Has so exasperated Macbeth."
F, however, reads "their King." For more on the issue
of textual confusions and how editors propose solutions, see Digital Edition TC 9.

9. *He did . . . answer:* Macduff says, "Sir, not I." The
scowling ("cloudy") messenger from Macbeth turns
his back and hums. His rudeness seems to say omi-
nously, "You'll rue the time that burdens ('clogs') me
with this answer."
1. *Advise . . . provide:* Warn Macduff to keep as far
from Macbeth as he can.
2. *suffering . . . accursed:* country suffering under an
accursed hand.
4.1 Location: A cave with a boiling cauldron.

THIRD WITCH Harpier° cries, "'Tis time, 'tis time!"		*(her familiar)*

FIRST WITCH   Round about the cauldron go;
5   In the poisoned entrails throw.
    Toad, that under cold stone
    Days and nights has thirty-one
    Sweltered venom sleeping got,[1]
    Boil thou first i'th' charmèd pot.
10   ALL   Double, double, toil and trouble;
    Fire burn, and cauldron bubble.

SECOND WITCH Fillet° of a fenny° snake	*Slice / from the swamps*

    In the cauldron boil and bake;
    Eye of newt and toe of frog,

15 Wool of bat and tongue of dog,	
    Adder's fork° and blind-worm's sting, | *forked tongue* |

    Lizard's leg and owlet's wing,
    For a charm of powerful trouble,
    Like a hell-broth boil and bubble.
20   ALL   Double, double, toil and trouble;
    Fire burn, and cauldron bubble.
    THIRD WITCH   Scale of dragon, tooth of wolf,

Witches' mummy,° maw and gulf[2]	*mummified flesh*
    Of the ravined° salt-sea shark, | *ravenous; glutted* |

25   Root of hemlock digged i'th' dark,
    Liver of blaspheming Jew,
    Gall of goat, and slips of yew

Slivered° in the moon's eclipse,	*Cut off*

    Nose of Turk and Tartar's[3] lips,
30   Finger of birth-strangled babe

Ditch-delivered by a drab,°	*whore*
    Make the gruel thick and slab.° | *viscous* |
    Add thereto a tiger's chawdron,° | *entrails* |

    For th'ingredients of our cauldron.
35   ALL   Double, double, toil and trouble;
    Fire burn, and cauldron bubble.
    SECOND WITCH   Cool it with a baboon's blood;
    Then the charm is firm and good.
        Enter HECATE *and the other three* WITCHES.
    HECATE   Oh, well done. I commend your pains,
40   And every one shall share i'th' gains.
    And now about the cauldron sing,
    Live elves and fairies in a ring,
    Enchanting all that you put in.
        Music and a song, "Black spirits," etc.
    SECOND WITCH   By the pricking of my thumbs,
45   Something wicked this way comes.
    Open, locks, whoever knocks!
        Enter MACBETH.
    MACBETH   How now, you secret, black, and midnight hags?
    What is't you do?
    ALL WITCHES   A deed without a name.

MACBETH I conjure you by that which you profess,°	*(the black arts)*

50   Howe'er you come to know it, answer me.

---

1. *has . . . got:* has for thirty-one days and nights   2. Stomach and gullet.
exuded poison formed during sleep.   3. Both thought of as cruel pagans.

Though you untie the winds and let them fight
Against the churches, though the yeasty° waves   *foamy*
Confound° and swallow navigation up,   *Defeat*
Though bladed corn° be lodged° and trees blown down,   *ripe wheat / beaten down*
55 Though castles topple on their warders' heads,
Though palaces and pyramids do slope°   *bend*
Their heads to their foundations, though the treasure
Of nature's germens⁴ tumble all together
Even till destruction sicken,° answer me   *be surfeited*
To what I ask you.
FIRST WITCH   Speak.
SECOND WITCH   Demand.
60 THIRD WITCH   We'll answer.
FIRST WITCH   Say if thou'dst rather hear it from our mouths,
Or from our masters.
MACBETH   Call 'em; let me see 'em.
FIRST WITCH   Pour in sow's blood that hath eaten
Her nine farrow;° grease that's sweaten°   *litter of nine / sweated*
65 From the murderer's gibbet° throw   *gallows*
Into the flame.
ALL WITCHES   Come high or low,
Thyself and office° deftly show!⁵   *function*
      Thunder. FIRST APPARITION, *an armed° head.*   *armored*
MACBETH   Tell me, thou unknown power—
FIRST WITCH   He knows thy thought.
Hear his speech, but say thou naught.
70 FIRST APPARITION   Macbeth, Macbeth, Macbeth. Beware
Macduff,
Beware the Thane of Fife. Dismiss me. Enough.
                              He descends.
MACBETH   Whate'er thou art, for thy good caution, thanks;
Thou hast harped° my fear aright. But one word more—   *guessed*
FIRST WITCH   He will not be commanded. Here's another,
75 More potent than the first.
      Thunder. SECOND APPARITION, *a bloody child.*
SECOND APPARITION   Macbeth, Macbeth, Macbeth.
MACBETH   Had I three ears, I'd hear thee.
SECOND APPARITION   Be bloody, bold, and resolute; laugh to
scorn
The power of man, for none of woman born
80 Shall harm Macbeth.
                              [He] descends.
MACBETH   Then live, Macduff. What need I fear of thee?
But yet I'll make assurance double sure
And take a bond of fate.⁶ Thou shalt not live,
That I may tell pale-hearted fear it lies,
And sleep in spite of thunder.
      Thunder. THIRD APPARITION, *a child crowned, with a*
      *tree in his hand.*⁷
85   What is this

---

4. Seeds from which all nature grows. According to
Renaissance theories of biology, if they were tumbled
together, they would become barren or produce only
monsters.
5. PERFORMANCE COMMENT No scene in *Macbeth*
raises more dramaturgical questions and challenges

than 4.1, which features Hecate, a trio of apparitions,
the return of Banquo's ghost, and at least eight spectral
kings. See Digital Edition PC 6.
6. Make a contract with fate.
7. Signifying Malcolm. The tree anticipates 5.5.33ff.

That rises like the issue of a king,
And wears upon his baby brow the round
And top of sovereignty?°   *(crown)*
ALL WITCHES   Listen, but speak not to't.
THIRD APPARITION   Be lion-mettled, proud, and take no care
90   Who chafes, who frets, or where conspirers are.
Macbeth shall never vanquished be until
Great Birnam Wood to high Dunsinane Hill
Shall come against him.
                                                    [*He*] *descends.*

MACBETH   That will never be.
Who can impress° the forest, bid the tree   *force into service*
95   Unfix his earth-bound root? Sweet bodements,° good.   *omens*
Rebellious dead,⁸ rise never till the Wood
Of Birnam rise, and our high-placed Macbeth
Shall live the lease of nature,° pay his breath   *natural life span*
To time and mortal custom.⁹ Yet my heart
100   Throbs to know one thing: tell me, if your art
Can tell so much, shall Banquo's issue ever
Reign in this kingdom?
ALL WITCHES   Seek to know no more.
MACBETH   I will be satisfied. Deny me this,
And an eternal curse fall on you! Let me know.
          [*The cauldron descends.*] *Hautboys.*
105   Why sinks that cauldron? And what noise° is this?   *music*
FIRST WITCH   Show!
SECOND WITCH   Show!
THIRD WITCH   Show!
ALL WITCHES   Show his eyes, and grieve his heart;
110   Come like shadows, so depart.
          A show of eight kings, and BANQUO *last;* [*the eighth*
          king] *with a glass° in his hand.*   *mirror*
MACBETH   Thou art too like the spirit of Banquo. Down!
Thy crown does sear mine eyeballs! And thy heir,
Thou other gold-bound brow, is like the first.
A third is like the former. —Filthy hags,
115   Why do you show me this? —A fourth! Start,° eyes!   *Bulge out*
What, will the line stretch out to th' crack of doom?
Another yet? A seventh! I'll see no more.
And yet the eighth appears, who bears a glass
Which shows me many more; and some I see
120   That two-fold balls and treble scepters¹ carry.
Horrible sight! Now, I see 'tis true,
For the blood-boltered² Banquo smiles upon me,
And points at them for his.³
          [*The show of kings and* BANQUO *vanish.*]
                    What, is this so?
FIRST WITCH   Ay, sir, all this is so. But why
125   Stands Macbeth thus amazedly?°   *entranced*
Come, sisters, cheer we up his sprites,°   *spirits*

---

8. Perhaps Banquo. Some editors emend to "Rebellious head" or "Rebellion's head," where "head" means
"army."
9. The custom of mortality; natural death.
1. James I was crowned twice, once as King of Scotland and later as King of England. He carried one orb
at each coronation. "Treble scepters" refers to the fact

that he held two scepters in the English coronation
and one in the Scottish, or perhaps to his claim to be
King of Britain, France, and Ireland.
2. Having hair matted with blood.
3. Banquo was the legendary founder of the Stuart
dynasty.

And show the best of our delights.
I'll charm the air to give a sound,
While you perform your antic round,°   *fantastic dance*
130   That this great king may kindly say
Our duties did his welcome pay.[4]
                 Music. The WITCHES *dance and vanish.*
MACBETH   Where are they? Gone? Let this pernicious hour
Stand aye° accursèd in the calendar!   *ever*
Come in, without there.
       Enter LENNOX.
LENNOX   What's your grace's will?
MACBETH   Saw you the weird sisters?
135   LENNOX   No, my lord.
MACBETH   Came they not by you?
LENNOX   No, indeed, my lord.
MACBETH   Infected be the air whereon they ride,
And damned all those that trust them! I did hear
The galloping of horse. Who was't came by?
140   LENNOX   'Tis two or three, my lord, that bring you word
Macduff is fled to England.
MACBETH   Fled to England?
LENNOX   Ay, my good lord.
MACBETH *[aside]*   Time, thou anticipat'st° my dread exploits.   *forestall*
The flighty purpose never is o'ertook
145   Unless the deed go with it.[5] From this moment
The very firstlings° of my heart shall be   *first notions*
The firstlings° of my hand. And even now,   *first acts*
To crown my thoughts with acts, be it thought and done.
The castle of Macduff I will surprise,
150   Seize upon Fife, give to th'edge o'th' sword
His wife, his babes, and all unfortunate souls
That trace him in his line. No boasting like a fool;
This deed I'll do before this purpose cool.
But no more sights. —Where are these gentlemen?
155   Come, bring me where they are.   *Exeunt.*

4.2

Enter Macduff's WIFE, *her* SON, *and* ROSS.
WIFE   What had he done to make him fly the land?
ROSS   You must have patience, madam.
WIFE   He had none;
His flight was madness. When our actions do not,
Our fears do make us traitors.[1]
ROSS   You know not
5   Whether it was his wisdom or his fear.
WIFE   Wisdom? To leave his wife, to leave his babes,
His mansion, and his titles° in a place   *estates*
From whence himself does fly? He loves us not;
He wants° the natural touch.° For the poor wren,   *lacks / affection*
10   The most diminutive of birds, will fight,
Her young ones in her nest, against the owl.

---

4. Our service repaid the welcome he gave us.
5. *The flighty . . . it:* The fleeting intention is never realized unless the deed is done immediately.
4.2 Location: Macduff's castle in Fife.

1. *When . . . traitors:* Even when we have committed no treason, our fear of suspicion makes us behave as though we are guilty.

All is the fear and nothing is the love,
As little is the wisdom, where the flight
So runs against all reason.

ROSS   My dearest coz,°   *kinswoman*

15   I pray you, school° yourself. But, for your husband,   *control*
He is noble, wise, judicious, and best knows
The fits o'th' season.[2] I dare not speak much further,
But cruel are the times when we are traitors
And do not know ourselves;[3] when we hold rumor

20   From what we fear, yet know not what we fear,[4]
But float upon a wild and violent sea,
Each way and none.[5] I take my leave of you;
Shall° not be long but° I'll be here again.   *It shall / before*
Things at the worst will cease or else climb upward

25   To what they were before. [*to the* SON] My pretty cousin,
Blessing upon you.

WIFE   Fathered he is, and yet he's fatherless.

ROSS   I am so much a fool, should I stay longer
It would be my disgrace and your discomfort.[6]
I take my leave at once.   *Exit* ROSS.

30 WIFE   Sirrah, your father's dead.
And what will you do now? How will you live?

SON   As birds do, mother.

WIFE   What, with worms and flies?

SON   With what I get, I mean, and so do they.

WIFE   Poor° bird, thou'dst never fear the net nor lime,[7]   *Pitiful*

35   The pitfall nor the gin.°   *snare*

SON   Why should I, mother? Poor° birds they are not set for.   *Worthless*
My father is not dead, for all your saying.

WIFE   Yes, he is dead. How wilt thou do for a father?

SON   Nay, how will you do for a husband?

40 WIFE   Why, I can buy me twenty at any market.

SON   Then you'll buy 'em to sell again.

WIFE   Thou speak'st with all thy wit, and yet, i'faith, with wit
enough for thee.

SON   Was my father a traitor, mother?

45 WIFE   Ay, that he was.

SON   What is a traitor?

WIFE   Why, one that swears and lies.[8]

SON   And be all traitors that do so?

WIFE   Every one that does so is a traitor and must be hanged.

50 SON   And must they all be hanged that swear° and lie?   *speak profanely*

WIFE   Every one.

SON   Who must hang them?

WIFE   Why, the honest men.

SON   Then the liars and swearers are fools, for there are liars and

55   swearers enough to beat the honest men and hang up them.

WIFE   Now, God help thee, poor monkey! But how wilt thou
do for a father?

---

2. The violent convulsions of the present time; what befits the time.
3. *we . . . ourselves:* we are denounced as traitors but do not know why; we have no self-knowledge.
4. *when . . . fear:* when we believe rumors inspired by our fears, but those fears are themselves vague.

5. In every direction, and so finally in none.
6. I would disgrace myself and embarrass you by weeping (or perhaps by lingering).
7. Birdlime, a sticky substance smeared on twigs to catch small birds.
8. Takes an oath and breaks it.

son   If he were dead, you'd weep for him; if you would not, it
        were a good sign that I should quickly have a new father.
60 wife   Poor prattler, how thou talk'st!
                Enter a messenger.
    messenger   Bless you, fair dame. I am not to you known,
        Though in your state of honor I am perfect.[9]
        I doubt° some danger does approach you nearly.   *fear*
        If you will take a homely° man's advice,   *plain*
65   Be not found here; hence with your little ones.
        To fright you thus, methinks, I am too savage;
        To do worse to you were fell cruelty,[1]
        Which is too nigh your person.[2] Heaven preserve you.
        I dare abide no longer.   *Exit* messenger.
    wife   Whither should I fly?
70   I have done no harm. But I remember now
        I am in this earthly world, where to do harm
        Is often laudable, to do good sometime
        Accounted dangerous folly. Why, then, alas,
        Do I put up that womanly defense,
        To say I have done no harm?
                Enter murderers.
75   What are these faces?
    murderer   Where is your husband?
    wife   I hope in no place so unsanctified
        Where such as thou mayst find him.
    murderer   He's a traitor.
    son   Thou liest, thou shag-haired villain!
    murderer [*stabbing him*]   What, you egg!
        Young fry° of treachery.   *spawn*
80 son   He has killed me, mother.
        Run away, I pray you!
                [*He dies.*]

                Exit [wife] *crying* "Murder!" [*followed by*
                    murderers *with Son's body.*]

4.3
                Enter malcolm *and* macduff.
    malcolm   Let us seek out some desolate shade and there
        Weep our sad bosoms empty.
    macduff   Let us rather
        Hold fast the mortal° sword and like good men   *deadly*
        Bestride our downfall birthdom.[1] Each new morn
5   New widows howl, new orphans cry, new sorrows
        Strike heaven on the face, that° it resounds   *so that*
        As if it felt with Scotland and yelled out
        Like syllable of dolor.°   *A similar cry of pain*
    malcolm   What I believe, I'll wail;
        What know, believe; and what I can, redress;
10   As I shall find the time to friend,° I will.   *favorable*
        What you have spoke, it may be so, perchance.
        This tyrant, whose sole° name blisters our tongues,   *mere*

9. Though I know perfectly well your high rank (an apology for bursting in).
1. *To fright . . . cruelty:* Even to frighten you by speaking of such danger is savage; actually to harm you would be brutal ("fell") cruelty.
2. Such cruelty is already too near you.
4.3 Location: England, before King Edward's palace.
1. Stand in defense over our downfallen native land.

Was once thought honest. You have loved him well;
He hath not touched° you yet. I am young, but something   *injured*
15 You may deserve of him through me,[2] and wisdom°   *it's prudent*
To offer up a weak, poor, innocent lamb
T'appease an angry god.

MACDUFF   I am not treacherous.

MALCOLM   But Macbeth is.
A good and virtuous nature may recoil
20 In an imperial charge.[3] But I shall crave your pardon.
That which you are my thoughts cannot transpose;°   *transform*
Angels are bright still though the brightest° fell.   *(Lucifer)*
Though all things foul would wear the brows of grace,
Yet grace must still look so.[4]

MACDUFF   I have lost my hopes.[5]

25 MALCOLM   Perchance even there where I did find my doubts.[6]
Why in that rawness° left you wife and child,   *unprotected condition*
Those precious motives,° those strong knots of love,   *inducements to devotion*
Without leave-taking? I pray you,
Let not my jealousies° be your dishonors   *suspicions*
30 But mine own safeties.° You may be rightly just,   *safeguards*
Whatever I shall think.

MACDUFF   Bleed, bleed, poor country!
Great tyranny, lay thou thy basis° sure,   *foundation*
For goodness dare not check thee; wear thou thy wrongs,°   *wrongful gains*
The title is affeered.° —Fare thee well, lord.   *confirmed*
35 I would not be the villain that thou think'st
For the whole space that's in the tyrant's grasp
And the rich East to boot.°   *as well*

MALCOLM   Be not offended.
I speak not as in absolute fear° of you.   *complete distrust*
I think our country sinks beneath the yoke;
40 It weeps, it bleeds, and each new day a gash
Is added to her wounds. I think withal°   *nonetheless*
There would be hands uplifted in my right,
And here from gracious England° have I offer   *the King of England*
Of goodly thousands. But, for all this,
45 When I shall tread upon the tyrant's head
Or wear it on my sword, yet my poor country
Shall have more vices than it had before,
More suffer and more sundry° ways than ever,   *in more various*
By him that shall succeed.

MACDUFF   What° should he be?   *Who*

50 MALCOLM   It is myself I mean, in whom I know
All the particulars° of vice so grafted   *varieties*
That, when they shall be opened,° black Macbeth   *disclosed*
Will seem as pure as snow, and the poor state
Esteem him as a lamb, being compared
With my confineless° harms.   *infinite*

55 MACDUFF   Not in the legions
Of horrid hell can come a devil more damned

---

2. *I . . . me:* I am inexperienced, but you might gain
favor with Macbeth by betraying me. *deserve:* F reads
"discerne."
3. *recoil . . . charge:* give way to a royal command.
4. *Though . . . so:* Though everything evil disguises

itself as virtue, virtue still looks like itself.
5. Hopes of Malcolm's help in a campaign against
Macbeth.
6. Doubts of Macduff's loyalty, because he has left
his wife and children.

In evils to top Macbeth.

MALCOLM   I grant him bloody,
Luxurious,° avaricious, false, deceitful,   *Lecherous*
Sudden,° malicious, smacking of every sin   *Violent*
60   That has a name. But there's no bottom, none,
In my voluptuousness: your wives, your daughters,
Your matrons, and your maids could not fill up
The cistern of my lust, and my desire
All continent° impediments would o'erbear   *restraining; chaste*
65   That did oppose my will. Better Macbeth
Than such an one to reign.

MACDUFF   Boundless intemperance
In nature° is a tyranny. It hath been   *human nature*
Th'untimely emptying of the happy throne
And fall of many kings. But fear not yet°   *nevertheless*
70   To take upon you what is yours. You may
Convey° your pleasures in a spacious plenty   *Manage secretly*
And yet seem cold;° the time° you may so hoodwink.° *chaste / age / deceive*
We have willing dames enough. There cannot be
That vulture in you to devour so many
75   As will to greatness dedicate themselves,
Finding it so inclined.

MALCOLM   With this there grows
In my most ill-composed affection° such   *character*
A stanchless° avarice that, were I king,   *An insatiable*
I should cut off the nobles for their lands,
80   Desire his jewels and this other's house,
And my more-having would be as a sauce
To make me hunger more, that I should forge
Quarrels unjust against the good and loyal,
Destroying them for wealth.

MACDUFF   This avarice
85   Sticks deeper, grows with more pernicious root
Than summer-seeming[7] lust, and it hath been
The sword° of our slain kings. Yet do not fear;   *undoing*
Scotland hath foisons° to fill up your will   *plenty*
Of your mere own.[8] All these are portable,
90   With other graces weighed.[9]

MALCOLM   But I have none. The king-becoming graces—
As justice, verity, temp'rance, stableness,
Bounty, perseverance, mercy, lowliness,°   *humility*
Devotion, patience, courage, fortitude—
95   I have no relish° of them, but abound   *trace*
In the division° of each several° crime,   *variations / separate*
Acting it many ways. Nay, had I power, I should
Pour the sweet milk of concord into hell,
Uproar the universal peace, confound
All unity on earth.

MACDUFF   O Scotland, Scotland!
100
MALCOLM   If such a one be fit to govern, speak.
I am as I have spoken.

---

7. Appropriate to youth ("summer") but passing with age, unlike avarice; summerlike.
8. *Scotland . . . own:* Scotland is bountiful enough to satisfy your greed with your own royal property alone.
9. *All . . . weighed:* All the vices you have described are bearable, when counterbalanced with your other graces.

MACDUFF   Fit to govern?
No, not to live. O nation miserable,
With an untitled° tyrant, bloody-sceptered!   *a usurping*
105   When shalt thou see thy wholesome days again,
Since that the truest issue of thy throne
By his own interdiction° stands accused   *declaration of unfitness*
And does blaspheme his breed?° —Thy royal father   *disgrace his heritage*
Was a most sainted king; the queen that bore thee,
110   Oft'ner upon her knees than on her feet,
Died[1] every day she lived. Fare thee well.
These evils thou repeat'st upon thyself
Hath banished me from Scotland. —O my breast,
Thy hope ends here.
MALCOLM   Macduff, this noble passion,
115   Child of integrity, hath from my soul
Wiped the black scruples,° reconciled my thoughts   *dark suspicions*
To thy good truth and honor. Devilish Macbeth
By many of these trains° hath sought to win me   *stratagems*
Into his power, and modest wisdom° plucks me   *prudent moderation*
120   From over-credulous haste. But God above
Deal between thee and me. For even now
I put myself to thy direction and
Unspeak° mine own detraction, here abjure   *Retract*
The taints and blames I laid upon myself
125   For° strangers to my nature. I am yet   *As*
Unknown to woman, never was forsworn,
Scarcely have coveted what was mine own,
At no time broke my faith, would not betray
The devil to his fellow, and delight
130   No less in truth than life. My first false speaking
Was this upon myself. What I am truly
Is thine and my poor country's to command,
Whither, indeed, before thy here-approach,
Old Siward with ten thousand warlike men
135   Already at a point° was setting forth.   *prepared*
Now we'll together, and the chance of goodness
Be like our warranted quarrel.[2] Why are you silent?
MACDUFF   Such welcome and unwelcome things at once
'Tis hard to reconcile.
Enter a[n English] DOCTOR.
140   MALCOLM   Well, more anon. [*to the* DOCTOR] Comes the King
forth, I pray you?
DOCTOR   Ay, sir. There are a crew of wretched souls
That stay° his cure. Their malady convinces   *await*
The great assay of art,[3] but at his touch—
Such sanctity hath heaven given his hand—
They presently amend.°   *heal*
145   MALCOLM   I thank you, Doctor. *Exit* [DOCTOR].
MACDUFF   What's the disease he means?
MALCOLM   'Tis called the Evil.[4]

1. Was dead to the world. ("By your rejoicing which I
have in Christ Jesus our Lord, I die daily," 1 Corinthians 15:31.)
2. *the . . . quarrel*: may the chance of success be equal
to the justice of our cause.

3. *convinces . . . art*: defeats the best efforts of medical skill.
4. "The king's evil," scrofula, thought to be cured by
the royal touch.

A most miraculous work in this good King,
Which often since my here-remain in England
I have seen him do. How he solicits° heaven   *moves by entreaty*
150   Himself best knows; but strangely visited° people,   *afflicted*
All swoll'n and ulcerous, pitiful to the eye,
The mere° despair of surgery, he cures,   *utter*
Hanging a golden stamp° about their necks,   *coin*
Put on with holy prayers; and, 'tis spoken,
155   To the succeeding royalty he leaves
The healing benediction. With this strange virtue,°   *power*
He hath a heavenly gift of prophecy,
And sundry blessings hang about his throne
That speak him full of grace.°   *divine grace*
       Enter ROSS.

MACDUFF   See who comes here.
160   MALCOLM   My countryman, but yet I know° him not.   *recognize*
MACDUFF   My ever gentle cousin, welcome hither.
MALCOLM   I know him now. Good God, betimes° remove   *quickly*
The means that makes us strangers.
ROSS   Sir, amen.
MACDUFF   Stands Scotland where it did?
ROSS   Alas, poor country,
165   Almost afraid to know itself. It cannot
Be called our mother, but our grave, where nothing
But who knows nothing is once seen to smile;[5]
Where sighs and groans and shrieks that rend the air
Are made, not marked;° where violent sorrow seems   *noticed*
170   A modern ecstasy.° The dead man's knell   *commonplace emotion*
Is there scarce asked for who,[6] and good men's lives
Expire before the flowers in their caps,
Dying or ere° they sicken.   *before*
MACDUFF   Oh, relation°   *report*
Too nice° and yet too true!   *detailed*
MALCOLM   What's the newest grief?
175   ROSS   That of an hour's age doth hiss the speaker;[7]
Each minute teems° a new one.   *yields*
MACDUFF   How does my wife?
ROSS   Why, well.
MACDUFF   And all my children?
ROSS   Well too.
MACDUFF   The tyrant has not battered at their peace?
ROSS   No, they were well at peace when I did leave 'em.
180   MACDUFF   Be not a niggard of your speech. How goes't?
ROSS   When I came hither to transport the tidings
Which I have heavily° borne, there ran a rumor   *gravely*
Of many worthy fellows that were out,[8]
Which was to my belief witnessed the rather°   *made more credible*
185   For that I saw the tyrant's power° afoot.   *army*
Now is the time of° help. [*to* MALCOLM] Your eye in Scotland   *moment for*
Would create soldiers, make our women fight
To doff° their dire distresses.   *remove*
MALCOLM   Be't their comfort

---

5. No one smiles except he who knows nothing.   7. Cause the speaker to be hissed for telling old news.
6. Scarcely anyone asks for whom it is rung.   8. Out in the field, in arms to rebel.

We are coming thither. Gracious England hath
190 Lent us good Siward and ten thousand men—
An older and a better soldier none°   *there is none*
That Christendom gives out.°   *proclaims; provides*
ROSS   Would I could answer
This comfort with the like. But I have words
That would be howled out in the desert air,
Where hearing should not latch° them.   *catch*
195 MACDUFF   What concern they?
The general cause, or is it a fee-grief°   *private woe*
Due to° some single breast?   *Owned by*
ROSS   No mind that's honest
But in it shares some woe, though the main part
Pertains to you alone.
MACDUFF   If it be mine,
200 Keep it not from me; quickly let me have it.
ROSS   Let not your ears despise my tongue forever,
Which shall possess them with the heaviest sound
That ever yet they heard.
MACDUFF   Hum—I guess at it.
ROSS   Your castle is surprised, your wife and babes
205 Savagely slaughtered. To relate the manner
Were, on the quarry of these murdered deer,
To add the death of you.[9]
MALCOLM   Merciful heaven!
What, man, ne'er pull your hat upon your brows.°   *conceal your grief*
Give sorrow words. The grief that does not speak
210 Whispers the o'er-fraught° heart and bids it break.   *overburdened*
MACDUFF   My children too?
ROSS   Wife, children, servants—
All that could be found.
MACDUFF   And I must be° from thence?   *had to be*
My wife killed too?
ROSS   I have said.
MALCOLM   Be comforted.
Let's make us med'cines of our great revenge
215 To cure this deadly grief.
MACDUFF   He has no children. All my pretty ones?
Did you say all? Oh, hell-kite! All?
What, all my pretty chickens and their dam
At one fell swoop?
MALCOLM   Dispute° it like a man.   *Fight*
220 MACDUFF   I shall do so.
But I must also feel it as a man.
I cannot but remember such things were
That were most precious to me. Did heaven look on
And would not take their part? Sinful Macduff,
225 They were all struck for° thee. Naught° that I am,   *on account of / Wicked*
Not for their own demerits but for mine
Fell slaughter on their souls. Heaven rest them now.
MALCOLM   Be this the whetstone of your sword. Let grief
Convert° to anger; blunt not the heart, enrage it.   *Be changed*

---

9. To tell how they were murdered would be to add
your death to the heap of slaughtered game ("quarry").
PERFORMANCE COMMENT In performance Ross's
reluctant delivery of the news about Macduff's wife
and children involves several interpretive questions
for directors, beginning with why Ross initially lies
when asked about the family. See Digital Edition
PC 7.

230   MACDUFF   Oh, I could play the woman with mine eyes
      And braggart with my tongue. But, gentle heavens,
      Cut short all intermission.° Front to front°   *delay / Face-to-face*
      Bring thou this fiend of Scotland and myself.
      Within my sword's length set him. If he scape,
      Heaven forgive him too.
235   MALCOLM   This tune goes manly.
      Come, go we to the King. Our power° is ready;   *army*
      Our lack is nothing but our leave.[1] Macbeth
      Is ripe for shaking, and the powers above
      Put on their instruments.[2] Receive what cheer you may;
240   The night is long that never finds the day.   *Exeunt.*

5.1

    Enter a DOCTOR OF PHYSIC° *and a waiting*   *Physician*
    GENTLEWOMAN.

  DOCTOR OF PHYSIC   I have two nights watched with you but can
    perceive no truth in your report. When was it she last walked?

  GENTLEWOMAN   Since his majesty went into the field,° I have   *battlefield*
    seen her rise from her bed, throw her nightgown upon her,
5   unlock her closet,° take forth paper, fold it, write upon't, read   *chest*
    it, afterwards seal it, and again return to bed, yet all this
    while in a most fast sleep.

  DOCTOR OF PHYSIC   A great perturbation in nature, to receive at
    once the benefit of sleep and do the effects of watching.° In   *act as if awake*
10   this slumbery agitation,° besides her walking and other actual°   *movement / active*
    performances, what at any time have you heard her say?

  GENTLEWOMAN   That, sir, which I will not report after her.

  DOCTOR OF PHYSIC   You may to me, and 'tis most meet° you should.   *proper*

  GENTLEWOMAN   Neither to you nor anyone, having no witness
15   to confirm my speech.

    Enter LADY MACBETH *with a taper.*

    Lo, you, here she comes. This is her very guise° and, upon   *exact habit*
    my life, fast asleep. Observe her; stand close.°   *concealed*

  DOCTOR OF PHYSIC   How came she by that light?

  GENTLEWOMAN   Why, it stood by her. She has light by her
20   continually; 'tis her command.

  DOCTOR OF PHYSIC   You see her eyes are open.

  GENTLEWOMAN   Ay, but their sense are shut.

  DOCTOR OF PHYSIC   What is it she does now? Look how she
    rubs her hands.

25   GENTLEWOMAN   It is an accustomed action with her to seem
    thus washing her hands. I have known her continue in this
    a quarter of an hour.

  LADY MACBETH   Yet here's a spot.

  DOCTOR OF PHYSIC   Hark, she speaks. I will set down what
30   comes from her to satisfy° my remembrance the more strongly.   *support*

  LADY MACBETH   Out, damned spot! Out, I say! One, two, why,
    then, 'tis time to do't. Hell is murky. Fie, my lord, fie, a sol-
    dier and afeard? What need we fear? Who knows it when
    none can call our power to account? Yet who would have
35   thought the old man to have had so much blood in him?

---

1. We have only to take leave of the King.
2. Arm themselves; set us to work as their agents.

5.1 Location: Macbeth's castle in Dunsinane.

DOCTOR OF PHYSIC   Do you mark that?

LADY MACBETH   The Thane of Fife had a wife. Where is she
now? What, will these hands ne'er be clean? No more o'that,
my lord, no more o'that. You mar all with this starting.°   *startled movement*

40 DOCTOR OF PHYSIC   Go to, go to.° You have known what you   *(expression of reproof)*
should not.

GENTLEWOMAN   She has spoke what she should not, I am sure
of that. Heaven knows what she has known.

LADY MACBETH   Here's the smell of the blood still. All the per-
45 fumes of Arabia will not sweeten this little hand. Oh, oh, oh!

DOCTOR OF PHYSIC   What a sigh is there! The heart is sorely
charged.°   *burdened*

GENTLEWOMAN   I would not have such a heart in my bosom
for the dignity° of the whole body.   *high rank (as Queen)*

50 DOCTOR OF PHYSIC   Well, well, well.

GENTLEWOMAN   Pray God it be, sir.

DOCTOR OF PHYSIC   This disease is beyond my practice.° Yet I   *skill*
have known those which have walked in their sleep who
have died holily in their beds.

55 LADY MACBETH   Wash your hands, put on your nightgown,
look not so pale. I tell you yet again, Banquo's buried; he
cannot come out on 's° grave.   *of his*

DOCTOR OF PHYSIC   Even so?

LADY MACBETH   To bed, to bed. There's knocking at the gate.
60 Come, come, come, come, give me your hand. What's done
cannot be undone. To bed, to bed, to bed.   *Exit.*

DOCTOR OF PHYSIC   Will she go now to bed?

GENTLEWOMAN   Directly.

DOCTOR OF PHYSIC   Foul whisp'rings are abroad. Unnatural
deeds
65 Do breed unnatural troubles. Infected minds
To their deaf pillows will discharge their secrets.
More needs she the divine° than the physician.   *priest*
God, God, forgive us all. Look after her;
Remove from her the means of all annoyance,°   *self-injury*
70 And still keep eyes upon her. So, good night.
My mind she has mated,° and amazed my sight.   *bewildered*
I think but dare not speak.

GENTLEWOMAN   Good night, good Doctor.   *Exeunt.*

5.2

Drum and colors.° Enter MENTEITH, CAITHNESS,   *flag-bearers*
ANGUS, LENNOX, *Soldiers.*

MENTEITH   The English power is near, led on by Malcolm,
His uncle Siward, and the good Macduff.
Revenges burn in them, for their dear causes
Would to the bleeding° and the grim alarm°   *bloody / call to battle*
Excite° the mortified° man.   *Rouse / insensible; dead*

5 ANGUS   Near Birnam Wood
Shall we well° meet them; that way are they coming.   *doubtless*

CAITHNESS   Who knows if Donaldbain be with his brother?

LENNOX   For certain, sir, he is not. I have a file°   *roster*
Of all the gentry. There is Siward's son

5.2 Location: The country near Dunsinane.

10   And many unrough° youths that even now   *beardless*
       Protest their first of manhood.[1]

MENTEITH   What does the tyrant?

CAITHNESS   Great Dunsinane he strongly fortifies.
       Some say he's mad; others that lesser hate him
       Do call it valiant fury, but for certain
15   He cannot buckle his distempered° cause   *disease-swollen*
       Within the belt° of rule.   *restraint*

ANGUS   Now does he feel
       His secret murders sticking on his hands;
       Now minutely° revolts upbraid his faith-breach.   *every minute*
       Those he commands move only in command,°   *under constraint*
20   Nothing in love. Now does he feel his title
       Hang loose about him, like a giant's robe
       Upon a dwarfish thief.

MENTEITH   Who then shall blame
       His pestered° senses to recoil and start,   *tormented*
       When all that is within him does condemn
       Itself for being there?

25 CAITHNESS   Well, march we on
       To give obedience where 'tis truly owed.
       Meet we the med'cine° of the sickly weal,°   *(Malcolm) / state*
       And with him pour we in our country's purge
       Each drop of us.

LENNOX   Or so much as it needs
30   To dew° the sovereign° flower and drown the weeds.   *bedew / royal; curative*
       Make we our march towards Birnam.   *Exeunt, marching.*

5.3

Enter MACBETH, DOCTOR [OF PHYSIC], *and Attendants.*

MACBETH   Bring me no more reports. Let them fly all.°   *Let all thanes desert*
       Till Birnam Wood remove to Dunsinane
       I cannot taint° with fear. What's the boy Malcolm?   *be infected*
       Was he not born of woman? The spirits that know
5   All mortal consequences° have pronounced me thus: *human destinies*
       "Fear not, Macbeth. No man that's born of woman
       Shall e'er have power upon thee." Then fly, false thanes,
       And mingle with the English epicures![1]
       The mind I sway° by and the heart I bear   *rule myself*
10   Shall never sag with doubt nor shake with fear.
       Enter SERVANT.
       The devil damn thee black, thou cream-faced loon!°   *rogue*
       Where gott'st thou that goose look?

SERVANT   There is ten thousand—

MACBETH   Geese, villain?

SERVANT   Soldiers, sir.

MACBETH   Go prick thy face and over-red thy fear,[2]
15   Thou lily-livered[3] boy. What soldiers, patch?°   *fool*
       Death of° thy soul! Those linen cheeks of thine   *on*
       Are counselors to fear.° What soldiers, whey-face?   *Teach others to fear*

SERVANT   The English force, so please you.

---

1. Declare for the first time that they are men.
5.3 Location: Macbeth's castle in Dunsinane.
1. Lovers of easy, luxurious living.

2. Redden your fearful pallor.
3. Lacking blood in your liver (thought to be the seat of courage); cowardly.

MACBETH   Take thy face hence.   [*Exit* SERVANT.]
                              —Seyton! —I am sick at heart,
20   When I behold —Seyton, I say! —This push°   *crisis*
     Will cheer[4] me ever or disseat° me now.   *dethrone*
     I have lived long enough. My way of life
     Is fall'n into the sere,° the yellow leaf,   *withered*
     And that which should accompany old age,
25   As° honor, love, obedience, troops of friends,   *Such as*
     I must not look to have, but in their stead
     Curses, not loud but deep, mouth-honor,° breath,   *lip service*
     Which the poor heart would fain deny and dare not.
          —Seyton!
                    Enter SEYTON.
SEYTON   What's your gracious pleasure?
30   MACBETH   What news more?
SEYTON   All is confirmed, my lord, which was reported.
MACBETH   I'll fight till from my bones my flesh be hacked.
     Give me my armor.
SEYTON   'Tis not needed yet.
MACBETH   I'll put it on.
35   Send out more horses, skirr° the country round,   *scour*
     Hang those that talk of fear. Give me mine armor.
          —How does your patient, Doctor?
DOCTOR OF PHYSIC   Not so sick, my lord,
     As she is troubled with thick-coming fancies
     That keep her from her rest.
MACBETH   Cure her of that.
40   Canst thou not minister to a mind diseased,
     Pluck from the memory a rooted sorrow,
     Raze out the written troubles of[5] the brain,
     And with some sweet oblivious° antidote   *causing forgetfulness*
     Cleanse the stuffed bosom of that perilous stuff
     Which weighs upon the heart?
45   DOCTOR OF PHYSIC   Therein the patient
     Must minister to himself.
MACBETH   Throw physic° to the dogs! I'll none of it.   *medicine*
     —Come, put mine armor on; give me my staff.°   *lance*
     —Seyton, send out. —Doctor, the thanes fly from me.
50   —Come, sir, dispatch.° —If thou couldst, Doctor, cast   *hurry*
     The water[6] of my land, find her disease,
     And purge it to a sound and pristine health,
     I would applaud thee to the very echo
     That should applaud again. —Pull't off, I say.[7]
55   —What rhubarb, senna,° or what purgative drug   *(medicinal plant)*
     Would scour° these English hence? Hear'st thou of them?   *purge*
DOCTOR OF PHYSIC   Ay, my good lord. Your royal preparation
     Makes us hear something.
MACBETH   —Bring it[8] after me.
     I will not be afraid of death and bane°   *destruction*

---

4. Comfort; enthrone or establish (punning on "cheer/chair").
5. Erase the troubles engraved in.
6. *cast / The water:* analyze the urine as a method of diagnosis.
7. A piece of armor is not properly fitted; Macbeth orders the attendant to take it off.
8. The armor not yet on Macbeth.

60　Till Birnam forest come to Dunsinane.

　　　　　　　　　　　　Exeunt [all but the DOCTOR OF PHYSIC].

DOCTOR OF PHYSIC　Were I from Dunsinane away and clear,
　Profit again should hardly draw me here.[9]　　　　　[*Exit.*]

5.4

Drum and colors. Enter MALCOLM, SIWARD, MACDUFF,
YOUNG SIWARD, MENTEITH, CAITHNESS, ANGUS, *and*
SOLDIERS, *marching.*

MALCOLM　Cousins, I hope the days are near at hand
　That chambers° will be safe.　　　　　　　　　　　　　*bedrooms*
MENTEITH　　　　　　　　　　We doubt it nothing.°　　　*not at all*
SIWARD　What wood is this before us?
MENTEITH　　　　　　　　　　　The Wood of Birnam.
MALCOLM　Let every soldier hew him down a bough
5　And bear't before him. Thereby shall we shadow°　　　*conceal*
　The numbers of our host and make discovery°　　　*reconnaissance*
　Err in report of us.
SOLDIER　　　　　　　It shall be done.
SIWARD　We learn no other but the confident tyrant
　Keeps still in Dunsinane and will endure
　Our setting down before't.°　　　　　　　　　*laying siege to it*
10　MALCOLM　　　　　　　　'Tis his main hope.
　For where there is advantage to be given,[1]
　Both more and less° have given him the revolt,　　*great and lowly*
　And none serve with him but constrainèd things
　Whose hearts are absent too.
MACDUFF　　　　　　　　　Let our just censures
15　Attend the true event,[2] and put we on
　Industrious soldiership.
SIWARD　　　　　　　　　The time approaches
　That will with due decision make us know
　What we shall say we have and what we owe.
　Thoughts speculative their unsure hopes relate,
20　But certain issue strokes must arbitrate[3]—
　Towards which, advance the war.　　*Exeunt, marching.*

5.5

Enter MACBETH, SEYTON, *and* SOLDIERS, *with drum
and colors.*

MACBETH　Hang out our banners on the outward walls.
　The cry is still, "They come!" Our castle's strength
　Will laugh a siege to scorn. Here let them lie
　Till famine and the ague° eat them up.　　　　　　　*fever*
5　Were they not forced° with those that should be ours,　*reinforced*
　We might have met them dareful,° beard to beard,　　*boldly*
　And beat them backward home.
　　　A cry within of women.
　　　　　　　　　　　What is that noise?

---

9. No large fees could lure me back.
5.4 Location: The country near Birnam Wood.
1. Where the opportunity presents itself.
2. *Let . . . event:* Let our judgments await the actual
outcome.

3. *Thoughts . . . arbitrate:* Speculation produces hopes
and unconfirmed optimism, but the issue will only be
decided by action.
5.5 Location: Macbeth's castle.

SEYTON   It is the cry of women, my good lord.   [*Exit.*]

MACBETH   I have almost forgot the taste of fears.

10   The time has been my senses would have cooled°   *been chilled with terror*
To hear a night-shriek, and my fell of hair°   *hair on my skin*
Would at a dismal treatise° rouse and stir   *story*
As life were in't. I have supped full with horrors.
Direness, familiar to my slaughterous thoughts,
Cannot once start° me.   *startle*
          [*Reenter* SEYTON.]

15   Wherefore was that cry?

SEYTON   The Queen, my lord, is dead.

MACBETH   She should have died hereafter;[1]
There would have been a time for such a word.
Tomorrow and tomorrow and tomorrow
20   Creeps in this petty pace from day to day
To the last syllable of recorded time,
And all our yesterdays have lighted fools
The way to dusty death. Out, out, brief candle.
Life's but a walking shadow, a poor player
25   That struts and frets his hour upon the stage
And then is heard no more. It is a tale
Told by an idiot, full of sound and fury,
Signifying nothing.
          Enter a MESSENGER.
Thou com'st to use thy tongue; thy story quickly.

30   MESSENGER   Gracious my lord,
I should report that which I say I saw,
But know not how to do't.

MACBETH   Well, say, sir.

MESSENGER   As I did stand my watch upon the hill,
I looked toward Birnam, and anon methought
The wood began to move.

35   MACBETH   Liar and slave!

MESSENGER   Let me endure your wrath if't be not so.
Within this three mile may you see it coming,
I say, a moving grove.

MACBETH   If thou speak'st false,
Upon the next tree shall thou hang alive
40   Till famine cling° thee; if thy speech be sooth,°   *wither / truth*
I care not if thou dost for me as much.
I pull in° resolution and begin   *rein in*
To doubt th'equivocation of the fiend
That lies like truth. "Fear not, till Birnam Wood
45   Do come to Dunsinane"—and now a wood
Comes toward Dunsinane. Arm, arm, and out!
If this which he avouches does appear,
There is nor flying hence nor tarrying here.
I 'gin to be aweary of the sun,
50   And wish th'estate° o'th' world were now undone.   *ordered structure*
Ring the alarum bell! Blow, wind, come, wrack!°   *ruin*
At least we'll die with harness° on our back.   *Exeunt.*   *armor*

---

1. She would certainly have died someday; she should have died at another, more peaceful time.

5.6

Drum and colors. Enter MALCOLM, SIWARD, MACDUFF,
and their army, with boughs.

MALCOLM   Now near enough. Your leafy screens throw down
And show° like those you are. You, worthy uncle,   *appear*
Shall with my cousin, your right noble son,
Lead our first battle.° Worthy Macduff and we   *battalion*
5   Shall take upon's what else remains to do,
According to our order.°   *battle plan*
SIWARD   Fare you well.
Do we but find the tyrant's power° tonight,   *army*
Let us be beaten if we cannot fight.
MACDUFF   Make all our trumpets speak. Give them all breath,
10   Those clamorous harbingers of blood and death!
                                Exeunt. Alarums continued.

5.7

Enter MACBETH.

MACBETH   They have tied me to a stake. I cannot fly,
But bearlike I must fight the course.[1] What's he
That was not born of woman? Such a one
Am I to fear, or none.
                    Enter YOUNG SIWARD.
YOUNG SIWARD   What is thy name?
5   MACBETH   Thou'lt be afraid to hear it.
YOUNG SIWARD   No, though thou call'st thyself a hotter name
Than any is in hell.
MACBETH   My name's Macbeth.
YOUNG SIWARD   The devil himself could not pronounce a title
More hateful to mine ear.
MACBETH   No, nor more fearful.
10   YOUNG SIWARD   Thou liest, abhorrèd tyrant! With my sword
I'll prove the lie thou speak'st.
                    Fight, and YOUNG SIWARD *slain.*
MACBETH   Thou wast born of woman.
But swords I smile at, weapons laugh to scorn,
Brandished by man that's of a woman born.
                                Exit [with the body].
                    Alarums. Enter MACDUFF.
15   MACDUFF   That way the noise is. Tyrant, show thy face!
If thou beest slain and with° no stroke of mine,   *by*
My wife and children's ghosts will haunt me still.°   *always*
I cannot strike at wretched kerns,° whose arms   *Irish foot soldiers*
Are hired to bear their staves.° Either thou, Macbeth,   *spears*
20   Or else my sword with an unbattered edge
I sheathe again, undeeded.[2] There thou shouldst be;
By this great clatter one of greatest note
Seems bruited.° Let me find him, Fortune,   *announced*
And more I beg not.   *Exit. Alarums.*
                    Enter MALCOLM *and* SIWARD.
25   SIWARD   This way, my lord. The castle's gently rendered.°   *surrendered*

5.6 Location: Scene continues.
5.7 Location: Scene continues.
1. Referring to the practice of bearbaiting, in which a

bear was tied to a stake and set upon by dogs. *course:*
round of bearbaiting.
2. Having accomplished no deeds.

The tyrant's people on both sides do fight;
The noble thanes do bravely in the war;
The day almost itself professes yours,
And little is to do.
MALCOLM   We have met with foes
That strike beside us.[3]
30 SIWARD   Enter, sir, the castle.   *Exeunt. Alarums.*
        Enter MACBETH.
MACBETH   Why should I play the Roman fool° and die   *the suicide*
On mine own sword? Whiles I see lives, the gashes
Do better upon them.
        Enter MACDUFF.
MACDUFF   Turn, hellhound, turn!
MACBETH   Of all men else I have avoided thee.
35 But get thee back. My soul is too much charged
With blood of thine already.
MACDUFF   I have no words.
My voice is in my sword, thou bloodier villain
Than terms can give thee out!°   *words can describe*
        Fight. Alarums.
MACBETH   Thou losest labor.°   *waste effort*
As easy mayst thou the intrenchant° air   *incapable of being cut*
40 With thy keen sword impress° as make me bleed.   *mark*
Let fall thy blade on vulnerable crests.
I bear a charmèd life which must not yield
To one of woman born.
MACDUFF   Despair° thy charm,   *Despair of*
And let the angel° whom thou still hast served   *(evil) spirit*
45 Tell thee, Macduff was from his mother's womb
Untimely° ripped.   *Prematurely*
MACBETH   Accursèd be that tongue that tells me so,
For it hath cowed° my better part of man.   *intimidated*
And be these juggling fiends no more believed,
50 That palter° with us in a double sense,   *equivocate*
That keep the word of promise to our ear
And break it to our hope. I'll not fight with thee.
MACDUFF   Then yield thee, coward,
And live to be the show and gaze° o'th' time.   *spectacle*
55 We'll have thee, as our rarer monsters° are,   *prodigies*
Painted upon a pole[4] and underwrit,
"Here may you see the tyrant."
MACBETH   I will not yield,
To kiss the ground before young Malcolm's feet,
And to be baited° with the rabble's curse.   *harassed*
60 Though Birnam Wood be come to Dunsinane,
And thou opposed, being of no woman born,
Yet I will try the last.° Before my body   *last resort*
I throw my warlike shield. Lay on, Macduff,
And damned be him that first cries, "Hold, enough!"
        Exeunt fighting. Alarums.

---

3. Fight on our side; deliberately miss us.
4. Painted on a cloth or board supported by a pole as a form of advertisement.

Enter [MACBETH *and* MACDUFF] *fighting, and*
MACBETH *slain.*[5]
[*Exit* MACDUFF *with Macbeth's body.*]
Retreat[6] *and flourish. Enter, with drum and colors,*
MALCOLM, SIWARD, ROSS, *Thanes, and* SOLDIERS.

65 MALCOLM   I would° the friends we miss were safe arrived.   *wish*

SIWARD   Some must go off;° and yet, by these[7] I see   *die*
So great a day as this is cheaply bought.

MALCOLM   Macduff is missing, and your noble son.

ROSS   Your son, my lord, has paid a soldier's debt.

70 He only lived but till he was a man,
The which no sooner had his prowess confirmed
In the unshrinking station[8] where he fought,
But like a man he died.

SIWARD   Then he is dead?

ROSS   Ay, and brought off the field. Your cause of sorrow

75 Must not be measured by his worth, for then
It hath no end.

SIWARD   Had he his hurts before?°   *on his front*

ROSS   Ay, on the front.

SIWARD   Why, then, God's soldier be he.
Had I as many sons as I have hairs,
I would not wish them to a fairer death.
And so, his knell is knolled.

80 MALCOLM   He's worth more sorrow,
And that I'll spend for him.

SIWARD   He's worth no more.
They say he parted° well and paid his score,   *departed*
And so, God be with him. Here comes newer comfort.

Enter MACDUFF *with Macbeth's head.*

MACDUFF   Hail, King, for so thou art. Behold where stands[9]

85 Th'usurper's cursèd head. The time is free.°   *free from tyranny*
I see thee compassed with thy kingdom's pearl,[1]
That speak my salutation in their minds,
Whose voices I desire aloud with mine:
Hail, King of Scotland!

ALL   Hail, King of Scotland!

Flourish.

90 MALCOLM   We shall not spend a large expense of time
Before we reckon with° your several loves   *make an accounting of*
And make us even with you.° My thanes and kinsmen,   *reward your loyalty*
Henceforth be earls, the first that ever Scotland
In such an honor named. What's more to do,

95 Which would be planted newly with the time,[2]
As calling home our exiled friends abroad
That fled the snares of watchful tyranny,
Producing forth[3] the cruel ministers°   *agents*
Of this dead butcher and his fiend-like queen—

100 Who, as 'tis thought, by self and violent hands°   *her own violent hands*

5. TEXTUAL COMMENT F's stage directions for the
fight between Macbeth and Macduff can be interpreted in different ways, with implications for the
play's dramatic structure. For more on this issue, see
Digital Edition TC 10.
6. A trumpet call signaling the end of the battle.
7. To judge from those who are present.

8. Post from which he did not shrink.
9. Presumably upon a pole or lance.
1. I see you surrounded by your nobles, here called
the "pearl" of the kingdom.
2. Which should be performed at the beginning of
this new era.
3. Bringing forward for trial.

Took off her life—this, and what needful else
That calls upon us, by the grace of grace,
We will perform in measure, time, and place.[4]
So, thanks to all at once and to each one
105 Whom we invite to see us crowned at Scone.

Flourish. Exeunt all.

4. In due order, at the proper time and place.

Antony and Cleopatra

What if Shakespeare had had second thoughts about *Romeo and Juliet*? He might have tried something different. In this version, the lovers, neither youthful nor married to each other, conduct a long-standing, adulterous relationship. Romeo, thinking Juliet dead because she has sent a messenger with that lie, kills himself—though with a sword rather than poison. He partly bungles the job, however, and hence takes a while to expire. Juliet resolves to follow suit but delays for the entire fifth act before killing herself—though with poison rather than a sword. And when they are both finally dead, the audience may be less likely to lament the loss of "star-crossed lovers" than celebrate the fulfillment of heroic passion.

Shakespeare did have second thoughts about *Romeo and Juliet*; he called these second thoughts *Antony and Cleopatra* (1606–early 1607). The last of Shakespeare's three love tragedies, the play also rewrites *Othello,* the middle work of this group, converting its threat from the East, there represented by Turks, into both threat and opportunity from the East, here represented by Egyptians. All three tragedies set their domestic concerns thematically against the backdrop of bloody political conflict, but formally against the expectations of romantic comedy. All three seem like derailed comedies. But *Antony and Cleopatra* replaces the emphasis on youth of romantic comedy, of *Romeo and Juliet,* and even of Desdemona in *Othello,* with the most complex portrayal of mature love in Shakespeare's dramatic career.

In the romantic comedies, problem plays, and romances, the female protagonist often dominates the scene. But in the tragedies that Shakespeare composed from roughly 1599 to 1608, *Antony and Cleopatra* is the only such candidate. Moreover, following a series of tragedies—*Hamlet, Othello, King Lear,* and *Macbeth*—in which the protagonist's psychology is consistently probed, *Antony and Cleopatra* almost completely avoids soliloquy. Antony's and Cleopatra's motives often remain opaque—arguably, even to themselves. We never learn why Antony thinks marriage to Octavia will solve his political problems, why Cleopatra flees at Actium, why she negotiates with Caesar in the last act. Instead of self-revelation, the play offers contradictory framing commentary by minor figures, who try to rein in their masters with a mix of praise and ridicule, usually without success, and who are accordingly victims of Antony's and Cleopatra's tragic extravagance. These external perspectives help impart an epic feel, as do the geographical and scenic shifts, which also produce a loose, fragmentary, and capacious structure alien to classically inspired notions of dramatic form. *Antony and Cleopatra* is thus a new kind of tragedy. Its restlessness is of a piece with that of *Pericles,* perhaps the next play Shakespeare wrote and the first of his late romances. And the intimations of transcendence with which *Antony and Cleopatra* ends point toward the magical or supernatural resolutions of the romances more generally.

The play may also be compared to Shakespeare's other Roman tragedies, *Julius Caesar* and *Coriolanus.* All are based on Thomas North's translation of *Plutarch's Lives of the Noble Grecians and Romans* (1579)—Shakespeare's favorite source, with the exception of Raphael Holinshed's *Chronicles of England, Scotland, and Ireland,* and one that he follows closely here. All three plays rely heavily on blank verse while almost entirely avoiding rhyme, though in *Antony and Cleopatra* (and *Coriolanus*) the heavy use of enjambment imparts a naturalistic, sometimes even colloquial, feel to poetic dialogue. Still, the use of blank verse for serious subjects is introduced into English by the Earl of Surrey's sixteenth-century translation of part of the *Aeneid* (19 B.C.E.), Virgil's epic of

Octavius Caesar, later known as Augustus, as on this medal. From Guillaume Du Choul, *Discours de la Religion des Anciens Romains* (1567 ed.).

the legendary founding of Rome, itself understood in the poet's own day as an allegory of the city-state's bloody transition from republic (rule by senatorial aristocracy) to empire (monarchical power).

It is this transition that Shakespeare dramatizes in *Julius Caesar* and *Antony and Cleopatra*. Chronologically, *Antony* picks up where *Julius Caesar* leaves off. That earlier play focuses on Caesar's assassination by republicans, led by Brutus and Cassius, and the assassins' subsequent defeat at the hands of Mark Antony (Caesar's lieutenant) and Octavius Caesar (Caesar's young grandnephew and adoptive son). *Antony and Cleopatra*, which covers the period from 40 to 30 B.C.E., completes the narrative of Roman civil war and the final destruction of the Republic. The Mediterranean's dominant military power, Rome is ruled by the triumvirate of Lepidus, Octavius Caesar, and Mark Antony, who govern, respectively, the Mediterranean portions of Africa, Europe, and Asia. Accordingly, *Antony and Cleopatra* turns away from *Julius Caesar*'s emphasis on Rome's internal political system, looking instead to its imperial domains. The stylistic restraint befitting Brutus's republican austerity yields to hyperbolic verse corresponding to the Empire's grandeur. This would seem the theater for legendary, even mythic, performance: Antony is associated with Hercules, and Antony and Cleopatra with Mars and Venus.

Yet *Antony and Cleopatra* investigates the possibility of such performance in a postheroic world. It offers an epic view of the political arena but deprives that arena of heroic significance. Mark Antony and Octavius Caesar contend for political supremacy, but the love between Antony and Cleopatra occupies center stage. The work then asks whether heroism can be transplanted to the private terrain of love. Much of the play's fascination arises from this intertwining of empire and sexuality. Plutarch and other classical writers were preoccupied with what for them was the opposition between the virtue of the conquering West and the luxury of the subjugated East. This understanding of empire re-emerged in the Renaissance during a new era of Western expansion, marked by an increasingly racialized and still-sexualized view of non-European peoples. Just months before the probable first performance of the play, King James authorized the establishment of an English colony in North America—an undertaking that resulted in the founding of Jamestown the following year. As in other Western European countries at the time, Rome was the central model of empire. The view of Egypt was more mixed: preeminent source of ancient wisdom, it threatened to transmit its decadence to the victors, even though Rome had defeated it.

Accordingly, *Antony and Cleopatra* elicits complicated judgments. Rendering this complexity has often proven difficult in performance. Long supplanted on the stage by John Dryden's *All for Love* (1678), which recasts Shakespeare's story as a tragedy of private life, the play came into its own only after 1800 in the heyday of the British Empire, with Cleopatra embodying Oriental sexual vice. The text seems to justify this interpretation: Rome is contrasted to Egypt, West to East, the conquerors to the conquered. Rapid shifts of scene across enormous distances accentuate this division. A sober, masculine military ethos opposes a frivolous, feminized, sexualized court. Opportunism drives Antony's marriage to Octavia, while love and sexual desire drive his relationship with Cleopatra; he chooses between fidelity to a chaste, white wife and adultery with a promiscuous, "tawny," "black" seductress (1.1.6, 1.5.28). That seductress has a smaller political role than in Plutarch. Though Cleopatra's political maneuvering remains considerable, this change accentuates the basic conflict. Where Caesar follows rational self-interest (he is the "universal landlord," 3.13.72), Antony revels in extravagant generosity and challenges Caesar to one-on-one combat. Young Caesar is a bureaucrat of the future, old Antony a warrior of the past. Caesar's concerns are public, Antony's private. Antony is guilty by association with his brother and his previous wife, Fulvia, who attack Caesar. By contrast, Caesar promises that "The time of universal peace is near" (4.6.5), an assertion that anticipates the Pax Romana (Roman Peace) he instituted throughout the Empire and the birth of Christ in a Roman province during his rule.

Yet the play seems to create such dichotomies only to undermine them. Antony boasts of his valor at Philippi, while Caesar "alone / Dealt on lieutenantry" (battled exclusively through his officers; 3.11.38–39). Earlier, however, Antony's "officer" Ventidius remarks, "Caesar and Antony have ever won / More in their officer than person" (3.1.16–17). Caesar's promise of "universal peace" is anticipated in a version of Christ's Last Supper that Antony shares with his followers:

> Tend me tonight.
> May be it is the period of your duty.
> Haply you shall not see me more, or if,
> A mangled shadow. Perchance tomorrow
> You'll serve another master.
> (4.2.24–28)

Enobarbus, who functions like a skeptical chorus, criticizes Antony for moving his friends to tears. But that skepticism is itself challenged. It leads Enobarbus to become a Judas figure who betrays his master by defecting to Caesar and who dies shortly thereafter, his heart broken by Antony's generosity.

Even the geographical contrast of the play partly dissolves into parallelisms: Roman war is eroticized, Egyptian love militarized. The external representation of the lovers' relationship, the absence of scenes of them alone, and their pride in exhibiting their affair intensify the feeling that love and war influence each other, that there is no distinction between public and private. Furthermore, love is on both sides of the divide, albeit with a difference. When the work opens, Antony's neglect of military command is criticized as "this dotage of our general's" (1.1.1) by Philo (a name that means "love in friendship"), a figure invented by Shakespeare. Late in the play, Antony, focused exclusively on Cleopatra, is heroically preceded in suicide by his aptly named servant Eros (romantic love), a figure from Plutarch.

The eroticization of Rome also takes the form of powerful feelings directed toward Antony. Octavius Caesar at times acts almost as if he were the son—rather than grandnephew and adopted son—of Cleopatra's former lover, Julius Caesar, whose paternal role Antony has usurped. Caesar is disgusted by Antony and Cleopatra's theatrical coronation:

> At the feet sat
> Caesarion, whom they call my father's son,
> And all the unlawful issue that their lust
> Since then hath made between them.
> (3.6.5–8)

Note the possible confusion between Antony and the older Caesar and the definite one between Caesarion and the younger Caesar, both of whom are "my father's son." At Antony's death, Caesar movingly recalls his foe:

> thou, my brother, my competitor
> In top of all design, my mate in empire,

> Friend and companion in the front of war,
> The arm of mine own body, and the heart
> Where mine his thoughts did kindle. . . .
>
> (5.1.42–46)

By calling Antony his "brother" and "mate," and by invoking a meeting of "heart" and mind, Caesar suggests an intimacy between the two men that recalls Renaissance celebrations of male friendship but that also borders on the erotic. But he neutralizes any filial anxiety he may feel by describing Antony first as "my brother" and then as a subordinate, "The arm of mine own body."

Most important, this strategy of undermining distinctions drains the political world of meaning. *Julius Caesar*'s struggle between republic and empire arises only peripherally in *Antony and Cleopatra,* where it is voiced by Pompey (2.6.10–19), who is bought off, attacked, and finally murdered by the triumvirs. The Republic is thus virtually dead when *Antony and Cleopatra* opens. Egypt's independence is at stake, although this occurs only to Cleopatra. That leaves just the conflict between Antony and Caesar, two ambitious men. The end of the Roman civil war is important, but it is hard either to celebrate Caesar's victory or to lament Antony's defeat. The consequent disabused view of political power might be an implicit critique of the centralizing monarchs of Shakespeare's own time.

Still, the political symbolism of the two men is antithetical. Caesar astutely adopts republican style, whereas Antony offends Roman sensibilities with his monarchical trappings (3.6.1–19). Antony's antagonist does not emulate the older Caesar, whose sexual and military conquests were intertwined (3.13.83–86). Hence, the younger Caesar represents not the preservation but the diminution of Roman values, a constriction of a heroic culture of which Antony is the last survivor. The play insists that politics and sex (or any kind of grandeur) are sundered, that one can no longer have it both ways.

Certainly, Antony and Cleopatra cannot. The play characterizes them through a language of greatness, shared by protagonists and minor figures alike, only to subvert that rhetoric through other commentary and especially the behavior of Antony and Cleopatra themselves. Although Shakespeare makes them more sympathetic than does Plutarch, they remain self-absorbed and self-destructive—lying, ignoring urgent business, acting impulsively, bullying underlings, reveling in vulgarity, betraying each other. They are also militarily peripheral, as the fighting scenes, except for the first Battle of Alexandria, testify. Shakespeare's uncharacteristic decision to follow classical theater and keep all combat offstage leaves a feeling of being let down, as observers report on the debacle. Enobarbus laments at Actium:

> Naught, naught, all naught! I can behold no longer:
> Th'Antoniad, the Egyptian admiral,
> With all their sixty fly and turn the rudder.
>
> (3.10.1–3)

At the play's last battle, it is Antony's turn:

> All is lost!
> This foul Egyptian hath betrayed me!
> My fleet hath yielded to the foe, and yonder
> They cast their caps up and carouse together
> Like friends long lost.
>
> (4.12.9–13)

But this is not the whole story. Antony and Cleopatra are great not despite their failings but because of them. Inability to fit into Caesar's narrowed world of self-discipline sets them apart. Their grandeur can be described only through paradoxical hyperbole. Antony's heart "is become the bellows and the fan / To cool a gypsy's lust": his heart is a fan that cools Cleopatra's lust by satisfying it, but in so doing he rekindles her passion, as if his heart were also a bellows (1.1.9–10). Similarly, when Cleopatra meets Antony, "pretty dimpled boys" (2.2.214) attend her

> With divers colored fans whose wind did seem
> To glow the delicate cheeks which they did cool,
> And what they undid did.
>
> (2.2.215–17)

When told that marriage to Octavia will force Antony to abandon Cleopatra, Enobarbus demurs in the play's most famous lines:

> Never, he will not.
> Age cannot wither her, nor custom stale
> Her infinite variety. Other women cloy
> The appetites they feed, but she makes hungry
> Where most she satisfies.
>
> (2.2.246–50)

These passages might be considered accounts of middle-aged lust. The trick of the play is to convince the audience that they are about love. Antony's feelings are easier to believe than Cleopatra's: he is the one who gives up an empire. By contrast, Cleopatra's teasing frivolity, comic jealousy, and cold calculation render her motives suspect. Yet Shakespeare gives her passages of extraordinary dignity early in the play, when Antony decides to leave her upon hearing of his wife Fulvia's death:

> Courteous lord, one word.
> Sir, you and I must part, but that's not it.
> Sir, you and I have loved, but there's not it—
> That you know well. Something it is I would—
> Oh, my oblivion is a very Antony,
> And I am all forgotten.
>
> (1.3.87–92)

Cleopatra experiences something more than she can express. Its articulation thus takes the form of a failure to articulate. There is an echo of this when Enobarbus describes her to his fellow Romans: "her own person . . . beggared all description" (2.2.209–10). Here, however, Cleopatra tries to convey her meaning through a witticism: her forgetfulness makes her like Antony, who is forgetful of her. She forgets and is forgotten. But when Antony misses the point, thinking he has merely witnessed idle wordplay, she corrects him:

> 'Tis sweating labor
> To bear such idleness so near the heart
> As Cleopatra this. But, sir, forgive me,
> . . . .
> . . . be deaf to my unpitied folly,
> And all the gods go with you.
>
> (1.3.94–100)

In short, Cleopatra's playfulness is the surface of her essential depth, her "sweating labor" like that of childbirth.

The last two acts test that depth, ultimately making Cleopatra the play's central character. The protagonists' sphere of activity is reduced to Alexandria. Cleopatra sends Antony a manipulative report of her death, he botches his suicide in response, and she then refuses to leave her monument to attend him as he lies dying. Instead, she hoists him up to her with the comment, "Here's sport indeed. How heavy weighs my lord!" (4.15.33), where "sport" is both playful and bitter, where "weighs" carries both physical and psychological meaning, and, hence, where the scene combines comedy with pathos. Antony's politically climactic death proves a false ending that shifts central significance to the final act. Egypt and Cleopatra are what matter.

Egypt is associated throughout with the overflowing that Antony is faulted for at the outset. Antony declares his love for Cleopatra by rejecting the state he rules: "Let Rome in Tiber melt and the wide arch / Of the ranged empire fall!" (1.1.34–35). Upon hearing of Antony's marriage to Octavia, Cleopatra prays, "Melt Egypt into Nile, and kindly creatures / Turn all to serpents!" (2.5.79–80). This apocalyptic imagery dissolves all distinction. It is tied to the play's account of spontaneous generation: "Your serpent of Egypt is bred now of your mud by the operation of your sun. So is your crocodile" (2.7.26–27). More generally, it contributes to the play's insistence on the inseparability of the human and natural worlds, perhaps with a gesture toward the new notion of an infinite universe, clothed in the language of the Christian Bible: "Then must thou needs find out new heaven, new earth" (1.1.17).

Psychologically, this language anticipates Antony's loss of self when he thinks Cleopatra has betrayed him. His body seems to him as "indistinct / As water is in water" (4.14.10–11). The language of liquefaction is also connected to the confusion of gender identity. Antony "is not more manlike / Than Cleopatra, nor the queen of Ptolemy / More womanly than he" (1.4.5–7). And Cleopatra reports, "I . . . put my tires and mantles on him, whilst / I wore his sword Philippan" (2.5.21–23). This behavior either confuses gender roles, thereby leading to Antony's flight at Actium, or overcomes a destructive opposition.

Cleopatra, who metaphorically overflows boundaries, is literally linked to Egypt and specifically to the Egyptian goddess Isis (3.6.17), who is invoked several times, probably owing to Plutarch's *On Isis and Osiris*. Isis is the sister-wife of Osiris, whom she restores after he is pursued to his death by his brother-rival, Typhon. The conclusion thus seeks the regenerative powers of the Nile in Cleopatra. It asks whether she is the equivalent of Isis, whether she is the wife of Antony (Osiris), whether she restores him after he is pursued to his death by his brother (Caesar).

This is the work of Cleopatra's suicide, which justifies these imagistic patterns and Antony's decision to die for her. In Shakespeare's earlier tragedies, we may desire the protagonists' deaths because life has lost its meaning for them. But *Antony and Cleopatra* goes further, convincing us that the two lovers' suicides are a heroic achievement, that anything less would constitute failure. The ending also evokes the synthesis precluded by the play's dichotomies but implied by its subtler patterns. Cleopatra dies the death of a Roman man:

> My resolution's placed, and I have nothing
> Of woman in me. Now from head to foot
> I am marble constant. Now the fleeting moon
> No planet is of mine.
> (5.2.237–40)

She also dies the death of a faithful Roman wife:

> Methinks I hear
> Antony call. I see him rouse himself
> To praise my noble act. . . .
> . . . .
> . . . Husband, I come.
> Now to that name, my courage prove my title.
> (5.2.279–84)

By taking the poisonous asp to her breast, she becomes a Roman mother as well, in a passage that recalls her earlier intense feeling in the language of childbirth:

> Peace, peace.
> Dost thou not see my baby at my breast,

That sucks the nurse asleep.

· ·

As sweet as balm, as soft as air, as gentle.
O Antony! Nay, I will take thee too.
            [*She applies another asp.*]
                                    (5.2.304–08)

Since the Folio lacks the stage direction included here, the final line can mean that
she takes Antony to her breast, like a mother comforting her infant son.

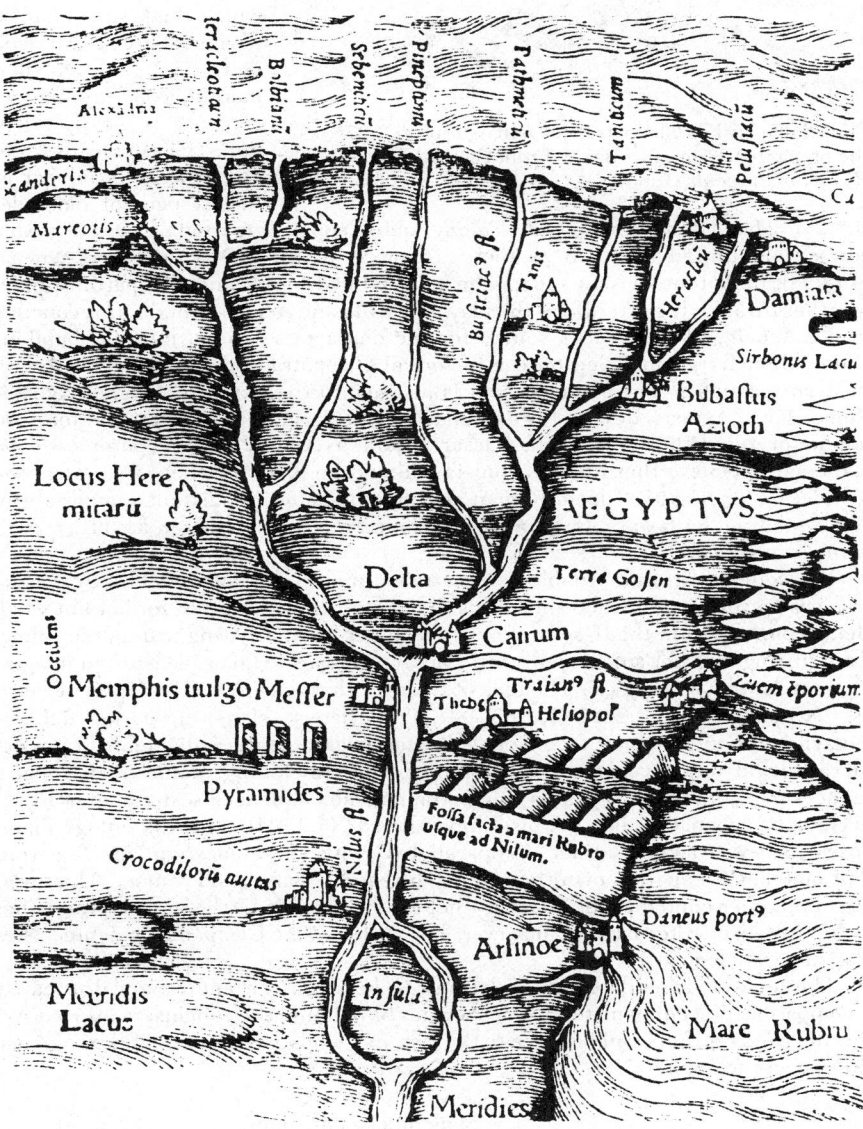

The Nile delta, showing the northern end of the river as it flows into the Mediterranean Sea. Alexandria is visible near the upper left-hand corner. From a map in
Sebastian Münster's *Cosmographia universalis* (1550).

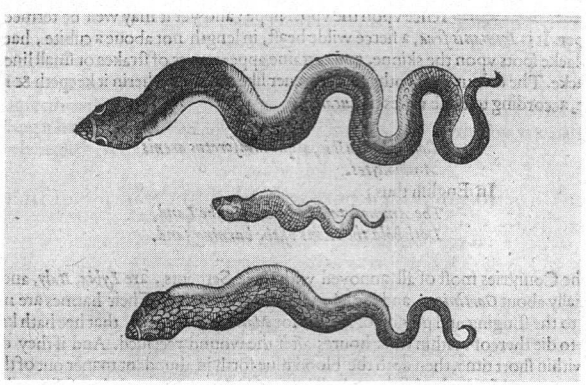

The Clown wishes Cleopatra "joy o'th' worm" (5.2.275) as she prepares to commit suicide. From Edward Topsell's *History of Serpents* (1608).

But "O Antony" is also a cry of orgasm that recalls Cleopatra's earlier sexual assertions, "I am again for Cydnus / To meet Mark Antony" (5.2.227–28) and "Husband, I come" (5.2.283), and looks ahead to Charmian's sexually ecstatic dying words, which Shakespeare added to his source: "Ah, soldier!" (5.2.324). Furthermore, Cleopatra's manner of death is clearly Egyptian. The asp recalls Antony's description of her as "my serpent of old Nile" (1.5.25). Thus, Rome and Egypt, Antony and Cleopatra, martial valor and sexual ecstasy are united in death as they cannot be in life. "Dido and her Aeneas" (4.14.53), in Antony's vision soon to be eclipsed by himself and Cleopatra, wander together through the afterlife of the play. But Dido and Aeneas remain unreconciled in the *Aeneid,* Shakespeare's source for the characters. There, Aeneas abandons Dido, whom Virgil modeled on the historical Cleopatra and thus associated with Eastern sensuality. The abandonment is justified in the name of a higher cause— Rome. Thus, Aeneas, despite his extramarital affair, functions as fictional forerunner not of Antony but of Octavius Caesar. Insofar as *Antony and Cleopatra* leads the audience to believe that its protagonists will end up together, then, it answers the *Aeneid,* distancing itself from Roman and, by extension, Renaissance imperialism. You *can* have it both ways. East and West, conquered and conqueror, are affirmed in a final synthesis.

Yet countercurrents trouble Cleopatra's "Immortal longings" (5.2.277). She resolves on suicide not when she learns that Antony killed himself for her but when she becomes certain that Caesar plans to lead her in humiliating triumph in Rome. Recognizing that her suicide will ruin Caesar's plans, she takes pleasure in imagining that Antony will "mock / The luck of Caesar," that the asp will "call great Caesar ass / Unpolicied" (5.2.281–82, 303–04). This rhetoric cleans up earlier dubious behavior and puts the best face on defeat. Heroic aristocratic individualism can act in the world only by leaving it. Moreover, the concluding, domestic Cleopatra reduces to a conventional gender role a woman who challenged sexual hierarchy. At her death, Cleopatra "lies / A lass unparalleled" (5.2.311–12). This eulogy juxtaposes the extravagant Latinate "unparalleled" with the homespun "lass," a word that matches Cleopatra's own rhetoric—"Husband," "baby," and "nurse." Moreover, in echoing her contempt for "Caesar [the] ass / Unpolicied," the phrase praises her at his expense. Alternatively, however, has *Antony and Cleopatra* presented "lies alas unparalleled"?

The answer depends on the relationship between the ending and the partly incompatible preceding material. Most critics have found the conclusion affirmative. But the work registers ambivalence to the last, in Cleopatra's account of the response she expects at Rome:

> The quick comedians
> Extemporally will stage us and present
> Our Alexandrian revels. Antony
> Shall be brought drunken forth, and I shall see

> Some squeaking Cleopatra boy my greatness
> I'th' posture of a whore.
>
> (5.2.215–20)

Cleopatra shudders at the absurdity of a boy actor badly impersonating her, yet the part of Cleopatra in *Antony and Cleopatra* was originally performed by a boy. This reminder punctures the dramatic illusion just when it seems most essential. It looks back to Cleopatra's blurring of gender division. It emphasizes Cleopatra's own artifice—a veteran actress in her final performance. Shakespeare here flaunts his medium. But if it is impossible to "boy" Cleopatra's "greatness," to represent her adequately, perhaps that is an invitation, as she has earlier suggested, to look beyond what can be shown, to take seriously her "immortal longings."

WALTER COHEN

SELECTED BIBLIOGRAPHY

Archer, John Michael. "Antiquity and Degeneration in *Antony and Cleopatra*." *Race, Ethnicity, and Power in the Renaissance.* Ed. Joyce Green MacDonald. Madison, NJ: Fairleigh Dickinson UP, 1997. 145–64. Explores the ambivalent image of Egypt in the Renaissance, combining reverence for its antique wisdom with anxiety about contagious decadence.

Deats, Sara Munson, ed. *Antony and Cleopatra: New Critical Essays.* New York: Routledge, 2005. Presents fourteen new essays, including Munson's own opening survey of criticism and performance.

Egan, Gabriel. *Green Shakespeare: From Ecopolitics to Ecocriticism.* London: Routledge, 2006. 108–19. Examines Antony and Cleopatra's sex without generation versus the Nile's generation without sex (spontaneous generation), the latter seen as an exceeding of bounds that levels humans with the rest of the natural world.

Geisweidt, Edward. "'The Nobleness of Life': Spontaneous Generation and Excremental Life in *Antony and Cleopatra*." *Ecocritical Shakespeare.* Ed. Lynne Bruckner and Dan Brayton. Farnham, Surrey: Ashgate, 2011. 89–103. Discusses erosion of the hierarchy between human and animal through the Nile's ability to produce life from its fertile dung and comparison of Antony and Caesar to excrement.

Loomba, Ania. *Shakespeare, Race, and Colonialism.* Oxford: Oxford UP, 2002. 112–34. Explores links of empire, gender ambiguity, skin color, gypsies, and role playing.

Madeleine, Richard, ed. *Antony and Cleopatra.* Cambridge: Cambridge UP, 1998. Offers a book-length history of productions of *Antony and Cleopatra*, combined with an edition of the play annotated with accounts of various performance decisions.

Oates, Joyce Carol. "The Tragedy of Imagination in *Antony and Cleopatra*." *Living with Shakespeare: Essays by Writers, Actors, and Directors.* Ed. Susannah Carson. New York: Vintage, 2013. 418–32. Sees the play as an atypical tragedy in which the protagonists' illusions, sustained by comic and hyperbolic language, are never demystified by reality.

Singh, Jyotsna G. "The Politics of Empathy in *Antony and Cleopatra*: A View from Below." *A Companion to Shakespeare's Works.* Ed. Richard Dutton and Jean E. Howard. Vol. 1: *The Tragedies.* Oxford: Blackwell, 2003. 411–29. Presents a critique of character-based scholarship and performances focusing on Cleopatra, in favor of a broader view of tragedy centered on the sufferings of the minor characters and drawing on Brecht's theory of alienation, or distancing, effects.

Weil, Judith. *Service and Dependency in Shakespeare's Plays.* Cambridge: Cambridge UP, 2005. 91–104. Examines Enobarbus and Charmian's flattery, combined with mockery, aimed at Antony and Cleopatra, and Cleopatra's similar strategy with Antony.

Wofford, Susanne L., ed. *Shakespeare's Late Tragedies: A Collection of Critical Essays.* Upper Saddle River, NJ: Prentice-Hall, 1996. Presents five essays on *Antony and Cleopatra* from the 1980s and 1990s, plus substantial discussion of the play in three other more general pieces; primarily issues of subjectivity, race, gender, empire, and performance.

FILM

Antony and Cleopatra. 1974. Dir. Jon Scoffield. UK. 161 min. Based on the 1972 Royal Shakespeare Company production starring Janet Suzman as an intelligent, "tawny," feminist Cleopatra. Focuses on love at the expense of politics.

TEXTUAL INTRODUCTION

The Tragedy of Anthonie, and Cleopatra was entered in the Stationers' Register on May 20, 1608, by the book publisher Edward Blount as if it were soon to be published, but for some reason the play was not printed until its inclusion in the First Folio of Shakespeare's plays in 1623. The comparatively clean Folio text requires very little emendation and serves as the base text for this edition. The text is likely drawn from a transcript of Shakespeare's original draft. The initial stage direction for 1.2 announces the entrance of Lamprius, Rannius, and Lucilius, but they have no speaking lines. Such "ghost characters" suggest an authorial manuscript rather than the kind of copy marked by a prompter who would normally note the specific entrances and exits required of the actors. This may explain why in the Folio Dolabella is mistakenly directed to enter at 5.2.315 and then again, properly, at 5.2.325. Some of the stage directions are descriptive, indicating the playwright's conception of what the action should look like. The initial stage direction for 3.1, "*Enter Ventidius as it were in triumph, the dead body of Pacorus borne before him,*" for example, gives an impression of the scene but no details about the actual staging. Other stage directions permissively direct three or four characters to enter, leaving the exact number of soldiers, attendants, or servants to be decided by the actors. At other places, the Folio has no stage directions where modern editors supply them, as in 5.2.35–36, where the dialogue indicates that Caesar's soldiers suddenly seize Cleopatra but no stage direction is provided. Because many of the Folio spellings are uncharacteristic of Shakespeare's usual practice, editors believe the copy used was not his own manuscript but a transcript very close to the original.

The central challenge in editing *Antony and Cleopatra* is to determine how lines in the Folio should be organized in a modernized version. The compositors who set the original manuscript copy into print worked from a handwritten draft that economized on paper by running lines of poetry together. As dialogue moved from one speaker to another, the compositors set each speech without indentation, regardless of whether the iambic pentameter line was to be shared between two speakers. In some places they were careless, and in other spots, finding a line too long to fit tidily in their half-page column, they cut it in two. But problems with lineation cannot all be laid at the compositors' feet. In the latter part of Shakespeare's career when *Antony and Cleopatra* was written, the dramatist used a high proportion of short and shared lines, often eschewing metrical regularity for a more realistic representation of the way people speak. Sometimes Shakespeare uses a series of short lines to heighten a scene's emotional effect, as in 2.2.169–75 when Antony, Caesar, and Lepidus discuss the military threat posed by Pompey. At other times it is difficult to distinguish prose from verse. In 1.2, for example, Charmian, Alexas, and Iras conduct their bawdy repartee in prose, but the Soothsayer's lines are metrically regular. The alternation of verse lines with prose in this scene sets up the characters' opposing perspectives until the mood shifts again with Cleopatra's entrance and a return to consistent blank verse.

With so many variables, it is not surprising that the arrangement of *Antony and Cleopatra*'s lines of text often varies from edition to edition. *The Norton Shakespeare* takes a conservative approach, adopting many traditional changes to the Folio lineation. When the dialogue moves rapidly back and forth between characters, as in Cleopatra's confrontation with the Messenger in 2.5, it employs split lines to indicate the dialogue's rhythm. In other passages, especially when short lines are metrically irregular, they are printed as single lines of text.

Ever since the eighteenth century, it has been customary to regularize Shakespeare's character names in accordance with his source, Thomas North's English translation of *Plutarch's Lives of the Noble Greeks and Romans*. While a few recent editions have returned to the Folio's spellings—"Anthony" instead of "Antony," for example—*The Norton Shakespeare* adheres to the speech prefixes most commonly associated with the play.

The Folio provides a heading for act 1, scene 1, but offers no act and scene divisions after that. As performed by the King's Company in the Globe, *Antony and Cleopatra* would have been staged continuously, with action flowing rapidly from Rome to Egypt, from battlefield to palace—all without interruption. Shakespeare's eighteenth-century editors imposed a five-act structure on the text and divided each act into separate scenes. Although *The Norton Shakespeare* follows that tradition in its assignment of act and scene numbers, the action should be conceived of as continuous.

VIRGINIA MASON VAUGHAN

PERFORMANCE NOTE

Theater companies frequently avoid *Antony and Cleopatra*, a widely admired but tremendously challenging play with a history of disappointing the audience. Its sixty speaking roles and ever-shifting locations can tax the resources of any company; its abundance of short scenes, some little more than fragments, frustrates efforts at abridgment or adaptation. Furthermore, as the plot concerns legendary tragic figures and world-shaping events, yet progresses mostly through scenes appropriate to satire (comic exchanges, domestic situations), directors must strike difficult balances between epic and intimate aspects and between competing genres. The more successful productions in recent years emphasize the lovers' fading glories and ultimate transcendence over the political events and favor designs that facilitate fluid transitions between scenes—complemented often by actors cast in multiple roles—over attempts to evoke the grandeur of ancient cities. But there are no easy solutions.

All of the foregoing challenges seem trivial, though, when compared to those presented by the title roles. In commending Cleopatra for "her infinite variety," Enobarbus efficiently summarizes the role's challenges: it seems to want an actor both calculating and rash, coquettish and queenly, aging and yet irresistible, one who can perform passions both feigned and sincere and who can ensure that spectators are able to tell the difference. The actor playing Antony has the even more unreasonable task of justifying his reputation as a brave soldier, brilliant tactician, and constant lover, despite a glaring lack of scenes or soliloquies centered on love or war. In addition, he must appear a mythic figure and a fallen one, at once, and must earn attention while continually being overshadowed by his scene partners (especially Cleopatra, but also Caesar, Enobarbus, and Eros). Both roles, then, require extreme versatility while providing limitless possibilities for emphasis. Versatility benefits lesser roles, too—Caesar combines callous efficiency with moments of tenderness for Lepidus and Octavia; Enobarbus is a center of lyricism, cynicism, and pathos, both character and choric figure. Other considerations in production include Antony's motives for marrying and hastily abandoning Octavia; Cleopatra's purpose in negotiating with Thidias in 3.13; hoisting Antony at the monument (see Digital Edition PC 3); and Cleopatra's spectacular suicide.

BRETT GAMBOA

The Tragedy of
Antony and Cleopatra

[THE PERSONS OF THE PLAY

MARK ANTONY (Marcus Antonius), triumvir of Rome

Antony's friends and followers:
PHILO
DEMETRIUS
Domitius ENOBARBUS
VENTIDIUS
SILIUS
EROS
CANIDIUS
SCARUS
DERCETUS
Lamprius
Rannius
Lucilius

OCTAVIUS CAESAR, triumvir of Rome

Caesar's friends and followers:
MAECENAS
AGRIPPA
TAURUS
DOLABELLA
THIDIAS
PROCULEIUS
Gallus

LEPIDUS, triumvir of Rome

CLEOPATRA, Queen of Egypt

Attendants to Cleopatra:
CHARMIAN
IRAS
ALEXAS
MARDIAN, a eunuch
EGYPTIAN
DIOMEDES
SELEUCUS, treasurer to Cleopatra

POMPEY (Sextus Pompeius)

Pompey's supporters:
MENAS
VARRIUS
Menecrates

OCTAVIA, sister to Caesar, wife to Antony
SOOTHSAYER
AMBASSADOR from Antony

SENTRY
WATCHMEN
MESSENGERS
CAPTAINS
SOLDIERS
BOY
GUARDSMEN
ATTENDANTS
CLOWN
SERVITORS *or* SERVANTS]

1.1

Enter DEMETRIUS *and* PHILO.

PHILO   Nay, but this dotage° of our general's   *absurd infatuation*
O'erflows the measure.[1] Those his goodly eyes,
That o'er the files and musters° of the war   *lines of troops*
Have glowed like plated° Mars, now bend, now turn   *armored*
5   The office° and devotion of their view   *duty*
Upon a tawny front.[2] His captain's heart,
Which in the scuffles of great fights hath burst
The buckles on his breast, reneges all temper[3]
And is become the bellows and the fan
To cool a gypsy's° lust.   *Egyptian's; hussy's*
    Flourish.° Enter ANTONY, CLEOPATRA, *her ladies*   *Trumpet fanfare*
    [CHARMIAN *and* IRAS, *and*] *the train°* with eunuchs   *retinue*
    fanning her.
10   Look where they come!
Take but good note, and you shall see in him
The triple pillar of the world[4] transformed
Into a strumpet's fool. Behold and see.
CLEOPATRA   If it be love indeed, tell me how much.
15 ANTONY   There's beggary° in the love that can be reckoned.   *little value*
CLEOPATRA   I'll set a bourn° how far to be beloved.   *boundary*
ANTONY   Then must thou needs find out new heaven, new earth.[5]
    Enter a MESSENGER.
MESSENGER   News, my good lord, from Rome.
ANTONY   Grates° me! The sum.°   *Irks / summary*
20 CLEOPATRA   Nay, hear them, Antony.
Fulvia° perchance is angry. Or, who knows   *(Antony's wife)*
If the scarce-bearded Caesar[6] have not sent
His powerful mandate to you: "Do this, or this;

1.1 Location: Cleopatra's palace, Alexandria.
1. Goes beyond suitable bounds.
2. A face or forehead of dark complexion (referring to Cleopatra; see the Introduction); military "front," or battle line.
3. Abandons all temperance ("temper" is also the hardness of tempered steel).
4. Antony, Octavius Caesar, and Lepidus were the three triumvirs ruling the Roman Empire (most of the known world, for Romans).

5. Alluding anachronistically to Revelation 21:1 ("I saw a new heaven, and a new earth"), and perhaps both to the cosmological revolution initiated by Copernicus and to the discovery of the New World. This second meaning may connect to the imperial theme of the play—its sense of geographical expansiveness and European geographical expansion.
6. The opening of the play is set in 40 B.C.E., when Octavius Caesar was twenty-three years old; Antony was almost twenty years his senior.

Take in° that kingdom, and enfranchise° that!   *Annex / liberate*
Perform't, or else we damn thee.'"
25 ANTONY   How,° my love?   *What*
  CLEOPATRA   Perchance? Nay, and most like!⁷
You must not stay here longer. Your dismission°   *marching orders*
Is come from Caesar; therefore hear it, Antony.
Where's Fulvia's process?°—Caesar's, I would say—both?   *summons*
30 Call in the messengers. As I am Egypt's queen,
Thou blushest, Antony, and that blood of thine
Is Caesar's homager°—else so° thy cheek pays shame   *Pays Caesar homage / or else*
When shrill-tongued Fulvia scolds. The messengers!
  ANTONY   Let Rome in Tiber melt and the wide arch
35 Of the ranged° empire fall! Here is my space.   *orderly; extensive*
Kingdoms are clay. Our dungy° earth alike   *made of manure*
Feeds beast as man. The nobleness of life
Is to do thus,° when such a mutual⁸ pair   *act as we do*
And such a twain can do't, in which I bind—
40 On pain of punishment—the world to weet°   *recognize*
We stand up peerless.
  CLEOPATRA   Excellent falsehood!
Why did he marry Fulvia and not love her?
I'll seem the fool I am not. Antony
Will be himself.⁹
  ANTONY   But stirred¹ by Cleopatra.
45 Now for the love of love and her soft hours,
Let's not confound° the time with conference° harsh.   *ruin / conversation*
There's not a minute of our lives should stretch
Without some pleasure now. What sport° tonight?   *entertainment*
  CLEOPATRA   Hear the ambassadors!
  ANTONY   Fie, wrangling Queen!
50 Whom every thing becomes—to chide, to laugh,
To weep; whose every passion fully strives
To make itself in thee fair and admired.
No messenger but thine,² and all alone
Tonight we'll wander through the streets and note
55 The qualities of people. Come, my queen,
Last night you did desire it. [*to the* MESSENGER] Speak not
  to us.   *Exeunt [the* MESSENGER, ANTONY,
                    and CLEOPATRA] *with the train.*
  DEMETRIUS   Is Caesar with° Antonius prized° so slight?   *by / esteemed*
  PHILO   Sir, sometimes when he is not Antony,
He comes too short of that great property°   *unique characteristic*
Which still° should go with Antony.   *always*
60 DEMETRIUS   I am full sorry
That he approves° the common liar who   *proves correct*
Thus speaks of him at Rome, but I will hope
Of better deeds tomorrow. Rest you happy.   *Exeunt.*

---

7. It is most likely, rather than merely possible, that Fulvia is angry or Caesar has sent orders.
8. Having the same feelings for each other; well-matched.
9. *I'll . . . himself*: I'll appear to believe Antony's falsehood, although I am really not so credulous; he will continue in his folly. (But Antony construes the words he hears as a compliment. It is also possible that Antony hears Cleopatra's entire speech.)
1. Aroused; motivated; disturbed.
2. I will hear only what you have to say.

1.2[1]

Enter ENOBARBUS, *Lamprius, a* SOOTHSAYER, *Rannius,*
Lucilius, CHARMIAN, IRAS, MARDIAN *the eunuch,*
and ALEXAS.[2]

CHARMIAN   Lord Alexas, sweet Alexas, most anything Alexas,
   almost most absolute° Alexas, where's the Soothsayer that   *perfect*
   you praised so to th' Queen? Oh, that I knew this husband,
   which you say must change his horns[3] with garlands.

5   ALEXAS   Soothsayer!

SOOTHSAYER   Your will?

CHARMIAN   Is this the man? —Is't you, sir, that know things?

SOOTHSAYER   In nature's infinite book of secrecy
   A little I can read.

10   ALEXAS   Show him your hand.

ENOBARBUS   Bring in the banquet° quickly; wine enough   *light meal; dessert*
   Cleopatra's health to drink.

CHARMIAN [*giving her hand to the* SOOTHSAYER] Good sir,
   give me good fortune.

15   SOOTHSAYER   I make not, but foresee.

CHARMIAN   Pray then, foresee me one.

SOOTHAYER   You shall be yet far fairer than you are.

CHARMIAN   He means in flesh.°   *(by getting fatter)*

IRAS   No, you shall paint° when you are old.   *use cosmetics*

20   CHARMIAN   Wrinkles forbid.

ALEXAS   Vex not his prescience; be attentive.

CHARMIAN   Hush.

SOOTHSAYER   You shall be more beloving than beloved.

CHARMIAN   I had rather heat my liver with drinking.[4]

25   ALEXAS   Nay, hear him.

CHARMIAN   Good now,° some excellent fortune! Let me be   *Please; fine; begin*
   married to three kings in a forenoon and widow them all; let
   me have a child at fifty, to whom Herod of Jewry[5] may do
   homage. Find me° to marry me with Octavius Caesar, and   *Find in my palm*

30   companion me° with my mistress.   *make me equal*

SOOTHSAYER   You shall outlive the lady whom you serve.

CHARMIAN   Oh, excellent! I love long life better than figs.[6]

SOOTHSAYER   You have seen and proved° a fairer former fortune   *undergone*
   Than that which is to approach.

35   CHARMIAN   Then belike° my children shall have no names.° *likely / be bastards*
   Prithee, how many boys and wenches must I have?

SOOTHSAYER   If every of your wishes had a womb
   And fertile every wish, a million.

CHARMIAN   Out, fool! I forgive thee for a witch.[7]

40   ALEXAS   You think none but your sheets are privy to your wishes?

CHARMIAN [*to* SOOTHSAYER] Nay, come, tell Iras hers.

1.2 Location: Scene continues.
1. TEXTUAL COMMENT For the rationale behind the
division of the play into scenes, despite the likelihood
that the play presents continuous action, see Digital
Edition TC 1.
2. TEXTUAL COMMENT The presence of "ghost
characters"—those with no speaking part—suggests
that the play was printed from a manuscript not yet
revised for performance. See Digital Edition TC 2.
3. Must adorn his (proverbial) cuckold's horns.
4. Both falling in love and excessive drinking were
thought to inflame the liver, the seat of the passions.

5. Anachronistic: Charmian wants homage to her
child even from Herod, Cleopatra's enemy, who was
to become proverbial for his brutality to children for
his Massacre of the Innocents in an effort to kill the
infant Jesus.
6. Genitalia (possibly proverbial); lines 31–32 also
foreshadow 5.2.232–324.
7. Since you are a soothsayer, I will let you speak
freely and will not persecute you as a witch; I will
forgive your outlandish prognostications because
they are unlikely to come true.

ALEXAS   We'll know all our fortunes.

ENOBARBUS   Mine, and most of our fortunes tonight, shall be drunk to bed.

45   IRAS   [*giving her hand to* SOOTHSAYER]   There's a palm pre-
sages chastity,° if nothing else.   *(a dry palm)*

CHARMIAN   E'en as the o'erflowing Nilus presageth famine.[8]

IRAS   Go, you wild° bedfellow, you cannot soothsay.   *licentious*

CHARMIAN   Nay, if an oily palm° be not a fruitful prognostica-   *(sign of sensuality)*
50   tion,° I cannot scratch mine ear. [*to* SOOTHSAYER] Prithee,   *sign of fertility*
tell her but a workaday° fortune.   *an everyday*

SOOTHSAYER   Your fortunes are alike.

IRAS   But how, but how? Give me particulars!

SOOTHSAYER   I have said.

55   IRAS   Am I not an inch of fortune better than she?

CHARMIAN   Well, if you were but an inch of fortune better than
I, where would you choose it?

IRAS   Not in my husband's nose!°   *(sexual innuendo)*

CHARMIAN   Our worser° thoughts heavens mend. Alexas—   *lascivious*
60   come, his fortune, his fortune. Oh, let him marry a woman
that cannot go, sweet Isis,[9] I beseech thee, and let her die,
too, and give him a worse, and let worse follow worse, till
the worst of all follow him laughing to his grave, fiftyfold a
cuckold. Good Isis, hear me this prayer, though thou deny
65   me a matter of more weight, good Isis, I beseech thee.

IRAS   Amen, dear goddess, hear that prayer of the people!
For, as it is a heartbreaking to see a handsome man loose-
wived,° so it is a deadly sorrow to behold a foul knave uncuck-   *wedded to an adulteress*
olded. Therefore, dear Isis, keep decorum° and fortune him   *do the right thing*
70   accordingly.

CHARMIAN   Amen.

ALEXAS   Lo now, if it lay in their hands to make me a cuckold,
they would make themselves whores, but they'd do't.°   *in order to do so*

Enter CLEOPATRA.

ENOBARBUS   Hush, here comes Antony.

75   CHARMIAN   Not he, the Queen.

CLEOPATRA   Saw you my lord?

ENOBARBUS   No, lady.

CLEOPATRA   Was he not here?

CHARMIAN   No, madam.

80   CLEOPATRA   He was disposed to mirth, but on the sudden
A Roman° thought hath struck him. Enobarbus!   *of Rome; serious*

ENOBARBUS   Madam.

CLEOPATRA   Seek him, and bring him hither. Where's Alexas?

ALEXAS   Here, at your service. My lord approaches.

Enter ANTONY *with a* MESSENGER.

85   CLEOPATRA   We will not look upon him: Go with us.

Exeunt [*all but* ANTONY *and the* MESSENGER].

MESSENGER   Fulvia, thy wife, first came into the field.°   *battlefield*

ANTONY   Against my brother Lucius?[1]

MESSENGER   Ay,
But soon that war had end, and the time's state°   *situation at the time*

---

8. Ironic: the silt brought down by the flooding Nile
each year gave Egypt its fertile soil.
9. Egyptian goddess of fertility, as well as of the earth

and moon. For the comparison of Cleopatra to Isis, see
the Introduction. go: come (sexual); bear children.
1. Lucius Antonius, Roman consul.

90 Made friends of them, jointing their force 'gainst Caesar,
Whose better issue° in the war from Italy   *greater success*
Upon the first encounter drave them.°   *drove them out*
ANTONY   Well, what worst?
MESSENGER   The nature of bad news infects the teller.[2]
95 ANTONY   When it concerns the fool or coward. On.
Things that are past are done with me. 'Tis thus:
Who tells me true, though in his tale lie death,
I hear him as° he flattered.   *as if*
MESSENGER   Labienus[3]—
This is stiff news—hath with his Parthian force
100 Extended° Asia. From Euphrates   *Seized*
His conquering banner shook, from Syria
To Lydia, and to Ionia,
Whilst—
ANTONY   Antony, thou wouldst say.
MESSENGER   O my lord!
ANTONY   Speak to me home,° mince not the general tongue.[4]   *plainly*
105 Name Cleopatra as she is called in Rome;
Rail thou in Fulvia's phrase,° and taunt my faults   *words*
With such full license as both truth and malice
Have power to utter. Oh, then we bring forth weeds
When our quick winds lie still, and our ills told us
110 Is as our earing.[5] Fare thee well awhile.
MESSENGER   At your noble pleasure.   *Exit* MESSENGER.
      Enter SECOND MESSENGER.
ANTONY   From Sicyon,[6] ho, the news! Speak there.
SECOND MESSENGER   The man from Sicyon—
ANTONY   Is there such a one?
SECOND MESSENGER   He stays upon° your will.   *He attends*
ANTONY   Let him appear.
      [*Exit* SECOND MESSENGER.]
115 These strong Egyptian fetters I must break,
Or lose myself in dotage.
      Enter THIRD MESSENGER *with a letter.*
          What are you?
THIRD MESSENGER   Fulvia, thy wife, is dead.
ANTONY   Where died she?
MESSENGER   In Sicyon.
Her length of sickness, with what else more serious
Importeth thee° to know, this bears.   *Is important for you*
    [*He gives* ANTONY *the letter.*]
120 ANTONY   Forbear° me.   *Leave*
    [*Exit* THIRD MESSENGER.]

---

2. Makes the teller hated by the hearer. For examples, see 2.5 and 3.13.
3. Quintus Labienus, who was sent by Brutus and Cassius following their killing of Julius Caesar (see *Julius Caesar*) to garner support from the Parthians, an Asian people whose empire came to include much of Mesopotamia (Iraq) and Persia (Iran) and who regularly warred with Rome. After Brutus's and Cassius's defeat at Philippi by Antony, Octavius Caesar, and Lepidus, Labienus defected to take command of the Parthian army and began a war against the Romans, conquering some of their provinces in what is now the Middle East (lines 100–102)—provinces Antony was supposed to protect.
4. Do not play down common opinion.
5. *Oh . . . earing:* Antony compares his recent behavior to an unplowed field: just as the field sprouts weeds when it remains untilled (by hand or) by a "quick" (fertile) wind, he falls into "ill" habits when he is not forced to face criticism (to undergo "earing," plowing).
6. City in Greece where Antony left Fulvia.

There's a great spirit gone. Thus did I desire it.
What our contempts doth often hurl from us,
We wish it ours again. The present pleasure,
By revolution low'ring,[7] does become
125 The opposite of itself. She's° good, being gone.   *Fulvia is*
The hand could° pluck her back that shoved her on.   *would wish to*
I must from this enchanting° queen break off.   *spellbinding*
Ten thousand harms, more than the ills I know,
My idleness doth hatch. How now, Enobarbus!

      Enter ENOBARBUS.

ENOBARBUS   What's your pleasure, sir?
130 ANTONY   I must with haste from hence.
ENOBARBUS   Why, then we kill[8] all our women. We see how
    mortal an unkindness is to them; if they suffer our depar-
    ture, death's the word.
ANTONY   I must be gone.
135 ENOBARBUS   Under a compelling occasion, let women die. It
    were pity to cast them away for nothing, though between
    them and a great cause, they should be esteemed nothing.
    Cleopatra, catching but the least noise of this, dies instantly.
    I have seen her die twenty times upon far poorer moment.°   *for far less reason*
140   I do think there is mettle° in death, which commits some   *(sexual) potency; courage*
    loving act upon her, she hath such a celerity° in dying.   *speed*
ANTONY   She is cunning past man's thought.
ENOBARBUS   Alack, sir, no! Her passions are made of nothing
    but the finest part of pure love. We cannot call her winds
145   and waters, sighs and tears—they are greater storms and
    tempests than almanacs can report. This cannot be cunning
    in her; if it be, she makes a shower of rain as well as Jove.[9]
ANTONY   Would I had never seen her!
ENOBARBUS   O sir, you had then left unseen a wonderful piece
150   of work,° which not to have been blest withal° would have   *masterpiece / with*
    discredited your travel.[1]
ANTONY   Fulvia is dead.
ENOBARBUS   Sir.
ANTONY   Fulvia is dead.
155 ENOBARBUS   Fulvia?
ANTONY   Dead.
ENOBARBUS   Why, sir, give the gods a thankful sacrifice.
    When it pleaseth their deities to take the wife of a man from
    him, it shows to man the tailors of the earth, comforting
160   therein, that when old robes° are worn out, there are mem-   *clothes; women*
    bers[2] to make new. If there were no more women but Fulvia,
    then had you indeed a cut, and the case to be lamented.
    This grief is crowned with consolation; your old smock brings
    forth a new petticoat, and indeed, the tears live in an onion
165   that should water this sorrow.°   *don't shed any real tears*

---

7. Growing lower by turning (as of a wheel, such as
Fortune's).
8. Alluding to achieving an orgasm. Throughout the
scene, the words "kill," "death," and "dying" all carry
this bawdy resonance. "Nothing," which Enobarbus
repeats, may refer to the female genitals.
9. Jupiter; ruler of the gods: one of his duties was to
govern rain.

1. Would have cast doubt on your success as a traveler. "Travel" also suggests "travail," or work, as in
"piece of work" (lines 149–50).
2. Limbs; sexual organs. The sexual innuendo is continued in "cut" (line 162: severe blow; slash in a garment; vagina), "case" (line 162: situation; set of clothes;
vagina), and "broachèd" (lines 166, 168: opened or
pricked).

ANTONY   The business she hath broachèd in the state,
    Cannot endure my absence.
ENOBARBUS   And the business you have broached here cannot
    be without you, especially that of Cleopatra's, which wholly
170   depends on your abode.°   *staying on here*
ANTONY   No more light answers. Let our officers
    Have notice what we purpose. I shall break
    The cause of our expedience° to the Queen   *haste*
    And get her leave to part. For not alone
175   The death of Fulvia, with more urgent touches°   *concerns*
    Do strongly speak to us, but the letters, too,
    Of many our contriving friends[3] in Rome
    Petition us at home.° Sextus Pompeius   *to go home*
    Hath given the dare to Caesar and commands
180   The empire of the sea.[4] Our slippery° people,   *inconstant*
    Whose love is never linked to the deserver
    Till his deserts are past, begin to throw°   *ascribe (the title of)*
    Pompey the Great and all his dignities
    Upon his son, who, high in name and power—
185   Higher than both in blood and life°—stands up   *vitality and energy*
    For the main soldier;° whose quality going on,   *acts like the top soldier*
    The sides o'th' world may danger.[5] Much is breeding,
    Which like the courser's hair hath yet but life,
    And not a serpent's poison.[6] Say our pleasure,
190   To such whose place° is under us, requires   *rank*
    Our quick remove from hence.
ENOBARBUS   I shall do't.

1.3

Enter CLEOPATRA, CHARMIAN, ALEXAS, *and* IRAS.

CLEOPATRA   Where is he?
CHARMIAN   I did not see him since.°   *recently*
CLEOPATRA   See where he is, who's with him, what he does.
    I did not send you.[1] If you find him sad,°   *serious*
    Say I am dancing; if in mirth, report
5   That I am sudden sick. Quick and return.   [*Exit* ALEXAS.]
CHARMIAN   Madam, methinks if you did love him dearly,
    You do not hold the method° to enforce   *act appropriately*
    The like from him.
CLEOPATRA   What should I do, I do not?°   *What else should I do?*
CHARMIAN   In each thing give him way. Cross him in nothing.
10 CLEOPATRA   Thou teachest like a fool the way to lose him.
CHARMIAN   Tempt° him not so too far. I wish—forbear°—   *Test / that you'd forbear*
    In time we hate that which we often fear.

        Enter ANTONY.

    But here comes Antony.
CLEOPATRA   I am sick and sullen.°   *dispirited*
ANTONY   I am sorry to give breathing° to my purpose.   *voice*

---

3. Of many friends acting on our behalf.
4. Sextus Pompey was the younger son of Pompey the Great, who was a foe of Julius Caesar (see *Julius Caesar* 1.1). Previously an outlaw, the Pompey of the play had gained control of the shipping routes around Sicily.
5. *whose . . . danger*: whose accomplishments and char-

acter, should they continue to succeed, might endanger the entire arrangement of the world.
6. A horse's ("courser's," line 188) hair was believed to become a live snake if put in water.
1.3 Location: Scene continues.
1. Do not say I sent you.

15 CLEOPATRA   Help me away, dear Charmian, I shall fall.
    It cannot be thus long; the sides of nature[2]
    Will not sustain it.
  ANTONY   Now, my dearest queen—
  CLEOPATRA   Pray you, stand farther from me.
  ANTONY   What's the matter?
  CLEOPATRA   I know by that same eye there's some good news.

20   What? Says the married woman° you may go?   *(Fulvia)*
    Would she had never given you leave to come!
    Let her not say 'tis I that keep you here.
    I have no power upon you. Hers you are.
  ANTONY   The gods best know—
  CLEOPATRA   Oh, never was there queen

25   So mightly betrayed! Yet at the first
    I saw the treasons planted.
  ANTONY   Cleopatra—
  CLEOPATRA   Why should I think you can be mine and true—
    Though you in swearing shake the thronèd gods[3]—
    Who have been false to Fulvia? Riotous madness,

30   To be entangled with those mouth-made° vows,   *hypocritical*
    Which break themselves in swearing.°   *as they are made*
  ANTONY   Most sweet queen—
  CLEOPATRA   Nay, pray you seek no color° for your going,   *excuse*
    But bid farewell, and go. When you sued staying,°   *entreated to remain*
    Then was the time for words. No going then;

35   Eternity was in our° lips and eyes,   *(royal plural)*
    Bliss in our brows' bent,° none our parts° so poor   *curve / of our parts was*
    But was a race of heaven. They are so still,
    Or thou, the greatest soldier of the world,
    Art turned the greatest liar.
  ANTONY   How now, lady?

40 CLEOPATRA   I would I had thy inches;° thou shouldst know   *size (phallic)*
    There were a heart in Egypt.[4]
  ANTONY   Hear me, Queen.
    The strong necessity of time commands
    Our services awhile, but my full heart
    Remains in use° with you. Our Italy   *in trust*

45   Shines o'er with civil swords.° Sextus Pompeius   *swords of civil war*
    Makes his approaches to the port of Rome;°   *Ostia (sixteen miles away)*
    Equality of two domestic powers
    Breed scrupulous faction.° The hated, grown to strength,   *distrustful dissent*
    Are newly grown to love.° The condemnèd° Pompey,   *popularity / banished*

50   Rich in his father's honor, creeps° apace   *insinuates himself*
    Into the hearts of such as have not thrived
    Upon the present state,° whose numbers threaten,   *government*
    And quietness grown sick of rest would purge
    By any desperate change.[5] My more particular,°   *personal motivation*

55   And that which most with you should safe° my going,   *sanction*
    Is Fulvia's death.
  CLEOPATRA   Though age from folly could not give me freedom

---

2. This cannot go on much longer; the bodily frame.
3. When Jupiter swore an oath, Mount Olympus, home of the gods, was supposed to shake.
4. There were courage (to respond to such insults) in the country (Queen) of Egypt.
5. *And . . . change:* And peace, made ill by inactivity, wishes to purge itself of impurities by a violently acting remedy.

It does from childishness. Can Fulvia die?
ANTONY   She's dead, my queen.
          [*He shows the letters.*]
60   Look here, and at thy sovereign leisure read
      The garboils° she awaked; at the last, best[6]—   *upheavals*
      See when and where she died.
CLEOPATRA   Oh, most false love!
      Where be the sacred vials[7] thou shouldst fill
      With sorrowful water? Now I see, I see,
65   In Fulvia's death how mine received shall be.
ANTONY   Quarrel no more, but be prepared to know
      The purposes I bear, which are, or cease°   *continue, or not*
      As you shall give th'advice. By the fire°   *sun*
      That quickens Nilus' slime,[8] I go from hence
70   Thy soldier-servant, making peace or war
      As thou affects.°   *choose*
CLEOPATRA   Cut my lace,[9] Charmian, come—
      But let it be. I am quickly ill and well,
      So[1] Antony loves.
ANTONY   My precious queen, forbear
      And give true evidence° to his love which stands   *be an honest witness*
      An honorable trial.
75   CLEOPATRA   So Fulvia told me.
      I prithee, turn aside and weep for her,
      Then bid adieu to me and say the tears
      Belong to Egypt.° Good now, play one scene   *Cleopatra*
      Of excellent dissembling, and let it look
80   Like perfect honor.
ANTONY   You'll heat my blood° no more!   *make me angry*
CLEOPATRA   You can do better yet: but this is meetly.°   *fairly good (acting)*
ANTONY   Now, by my sword!
CLEOPATRA   And target.[2] Still he mends.°   *improves*
      But this is not the best. Look, prithee, Charmian,
      How this Herculean Roman does become
85   The carriage of his chafe.°   *His posture of rage*
ANTONY   I'll leave you, lady.
CLEOPATRA   Courteous lord, one word.
      Sir, you and I must part, but that's not it.
      Sir, you and I have loved, but there's not it—
90   That you know well. Something it is I would—
      Oh, my oblivion is a very Antony,
      And I am all forgotten.[3]
ANTONY   But that your royalty
      Holds idleness your subject, I should take you
      For idleness itself.[4]
CLEOPATRA   'Tis sweating labor°   *work; birth pains*

6. The best news last; Fulvia was at her best at the end of her life.
7. Renaissance writers thought that the Romans filled small bottles with tears to place in graves; also, where are your sad and watery eyes ("vials")?
8. That causes plants to grow in the silt that the Nile deposits.
9. Cutting the strings would be quicker than untying the lace on her bodice to relieve her from her feigned fainting spell.

1. As long as; thus (falsely).
2. Shield. Cleopatra parodies the blustering oaths of heroic drama.
3. *my . . . forgotten*: my memory has deserted me as you are doing, and I have forgotten everything (am totally forgotten—by Antony).
4. *But . . . itself*: If you were not queen over your flippancy and hence in full control of it, I would think that you were flippancy itself.

95	To bear such idleness° so near the heart	*flippancy; laziness*
	As Cleopatra this. But, sir, forgive me,	
	Since my becomings° kill me when they do not	*transformations; graces*
	Eye° well to you. Your honor calls you hence;	*Look*
	Therefore be deaf to my unpitied folly,	
100	And all the gods go with you. Upon your sword	
	Sit laurel victory,° and smooth success	*the laurels of victory*
	Be strewed before your feet.	

ANTONY   Let us go. Come.
Our separation so abides and flies,[5]
That thou residing here goes yet with me,
105   And I hence fleeting here remain with thee.
Away.   *Exeunt.*

1.4

Enter Octavius [CAESAR] *reading a letter,* LEPIDUS,
and their train.

	CAESAR You may see, Lepidus, and henceforth know,	
	It is not Caesar's natural vice to hate	
	Our great competitor.° From Alexandria	*ally; rival*
	This is the news: he fishes, drinks, and wastes	
5	The lamps of night in revel; is not more manlike	
	Than Cleopatra, nor the queen of Ptolemy[1]	
	More womanly than he; hardly gave audience[2] or	
	Vouchsafed to think he had partners. You shall find there°	*(in the letter); (in Egypt)*
	A man who is th'abstract° of all faults	*the paradigm*
	That all men follow.	
10	LEPIDUS I must not think there are	
	Evils enough to darken all his goodness.	
	His faults in him seem as the spots of heaven,°	*stars*
	More fiery by night's blackness—hereditary,	
	Rather than purchased,° what he cannot change,	*acquired*
15	Than° what he chooses.	*Rather than*
	CAESAR You are too indulgent. Let's grant it is not	
	Amiss to tumble on the bed of Ptolemy,	
	To give a kingdom for a mirth,° to sit	*joke*
	And keep the turn of° tippling with a slave,	*take turns at*
20	To reel the streets at noon, and stand the buffet°	*come to blows*
	With knaves that smell of sweat. Say° this becomes him—	*Even if*
	As his composure° must be rare indeed	*And his character*
	Whom these things cannot blemish—yet must Antony	
	No way excuse his foils° when we do bear	*faults*
25	So great weight in° his lightness. If he filled	*as a result of*
	His vacancy° with his voluptuousness,	*leisure*
	Full surfeits and the dryness of his bones[3]	
	Call on° him for't. But to confound° such time	*Afflict / waste*
	That drums° him from his sport and speaks as loud	*summons*
30	As his own state° and ours, 'tis to be chid	*public responsibility*

5. Consists so much of both remaining together and
being separated (in that we are united by the shared
experience of it).
1.4 Location: Rome.
1. Julius Caesar had commanded Cleopatra to marry
her half brother Ptolemy XIV (acceptable within the

Egyptian royal family); she was said to have had Ptolemy poisoned.
2. Hardly listened (to Octavius's messenger, in 1.1).
3. *Full . . . bones:* Ill health caused by overeating and
venereal disease.

As we rate° boys who, being mature in knowledge,   *upbraid*
Pawn their experience to their present pleasure
And so rebel to judgment.[4]
    Enter a MESSENGER.
LEPIDUS   Here's more news.
MESSENGER   Thy biddings have been done, and every hour,
35   Most noble Caesar, shalt thou have report
How 'tis abroad. Pompey is strong at sea,
And it appears he is beloved of those
That only have feared Caesar.[5] To the ports
The discontents° repair, and men's reports   *discontented people*
Give him° much wronged.   *Say he is*
40 CAESAR   I should have known no less.
It hath been taught us from the primal state[6]
That he which is was wished until he were,[7]
And the ebbed° man, ne'er loved till ne'er worth love,   *fallen*
Comes feared° by being lacked. This common body,°   *Is revered / The people*
45 Like to a vagabond flag° upon the stream,   *drifting reed*
Goes to and back, lackeying° the varying tide   *following slavishly*
To rot itself with motion.
    [*Enter a* SECOND MESSENGER.]
SECOND MESSENGER   Caesar, I bring thee word:
Menecrates and Menas, famous pirates,°   *(allied with Pompey)*
Makes the sea serve them, which they ear° and wound   *plow*
50 With keels of every kind. Many hot inroads
They make in Italy; the borders maritime°   *coastal territories*
Lack blood° to think on't, and flush° youth revolt.   *Go pallid / spirited*
No vessel can peep forth but 'tis as soon
Taken as seen—for Pompey's name strikes more
Than could his war resisted.[8]
55 CAESAR   Antony,
Leave thy lascivious wassails.° When thou once   *drunken revels*
Was beaten from Modena,[9] where thou slew'st
Hirsius and Pansa, consuls, at thy heel
Did famine follow, whom thou fought'st against,
60 Though daintily brought up, with patience more
Than savages could suffer. Thou didst drink
The stale° of horses and the gilded° puddle   *urine / slime-covered*
Which beasts would cough at.° Thy palate then did deign°   *refuse (to drink) / accept*
The roughest berry on the rudest hedge.
65 Yea, like the stag when snow the pasture sheets,°   *covers*
The barks of trees thou browsèd.° On the Alps   *fed upon*
It is reported thou didst eat strange flesh
Which some did die to look on. And all this—
It wounds thine honor that I speak it now—
70 Was borne so like a soldier that thy cheek
So much as lanked° not.   *grew thin*

---

4. *being . . . judgment:* being old enough to know better, abandon their wisdom in favor of momentary pleasure and thus act against their better judgment.
5. That obeyed Caesar only out of fear.
6. Since the first society was organized.
7. That man who rules was supported until he began to rule.

8. *Pompey's . . . resisted:* Pompey's name alone is more powerful than his forces would be if confronted in battle.
9. Site of a battle in which Antony was defeated by the combined armies of Octavius Caesar and the Roman Senate, at the instigation of Cicero.

LEPIDUS   'Tis pity of him.

CAESAR   Let his shames quickly
Drive him to Rome. 'Tis time we twain
Did show ourselves i'th' field, and to that end
75 Assemble we immediate council. Pompey
Thrives in our idleness.

LEPIDUS   Tomorrow, Caesar,
I shall be furnished to inform you rightly
Both what° by sea and land I can be able°   *what forces / assemble*
To front° this present time.   *To confront the enemy at*

CAESAR   Till which encounter,
80 It is my business too. Farewell.

LEPIDUS   Farewell, my lord. What you shall know meantime
Of stirs° abroad, I shall beseech you, sir,   *incidents*
To let me be partaker.

CAESAR   Doubt not, sir.
I knew it for my bond.°   *Exeunt.*   *responsibility*

1.5

Enter CLEOPATRA, CHARMIAN, IRAS, *and* MARDIAN.

CLEOPATRA   Charmian!

CHARMIAN   Madam?

CLEOPATRA   Ha, ha! Give me to drink mandragora.[1]

CHARMIAN   Why, madam?

5 CLEOPATRA   That I might sleep out this great gap of time
My Antony is away.

CHARMIAN   You think of him too much.

CLEOPATRA   Oh, 'tis treason.

CHARMIAN   Madam, I trust not so.

CLEOPATRA   Thou, eunuch Mardian!

MARDIAN   What's your highness' pleasure?

CLEOPATRA   Not now to hear thee sing.[2] I take no pleasure
10 In aught[3] an eunuch has. 'Tis well for thee
That, being unseminared,° thy freer thoughts   *castrated*
May not fly forth of Egypt. Hast thou affections?°   *desires*

MARDIAN   Yes, gracious madam.

CLEOPATRA   Indeed?

15 MARDIAN   Not in deed, madam, for I can do° nothing   *(sexually)*
But what indeed is honest° to be done.   *chaste; moral*
Yet have I fierce affections and think
What Venus did with Mars.[4]

CLEOPATRA   O Charmian,
Where think'st thou he is now? Stands he, or sits he?
20 Or does he walk? Or is he on his horse?
Oh, happy horse to bear the weight of Antony!
Do bravely, horse, for wot'st° thou whom thou mov'st,   *know*
The demi-Atlas[5] of this earth, the arm°   *champion*
And burgonet° of men. He's speaking now   *helmet; guardian*

1.5 Location: Alexandria.
1. A narcotic, made from the mandrake plant.
2. Castrati were used in Italian music from the end of the sixteenth century, and Shakespeare associates singing eunuchs with the eastern Mediterranean in *Twelfth Night* and *A Midsummer Night's Dream;* they are not thought to have been used as singers in ancient Rome.

3. In anything; in the nothing. The eunuch has nothing instead of testicles.
4. Venus, goddess of love (married to Vulcan), and Mars, god of war, were lovers.
5. Octavius and Antony between them rule the world—Lepidus having conveniently been forgotten—as Atlas bore it on his shoulders.

25 Or murmuring, "Where's my serpent of old Nile?"[6]
(For so he calls me). Now I feed myself
With most delicious poison. Think on me
That am with Phoebus'° amorous pinches black   *the sun god's*
And wrinkled deep in time. Broad-fronted° Caesar,°   *Broad-browed / (Julius)*
30 When thou wast here above the ground, I was
A morsel for a monarch, and great Pompey[7]
Would stand and make his eyes grow in my brow;
There would he anchor his aspect° and die°   *gaze / (sexual)*
With looking on his life.
     Enter ALEXAS *from* [ANTONY].
35 ALEXAS   Sovereign of Egypt, hail!
CLEOPATRA   How much unlike art thou Mark Antony!
Yet coming from him, that great med'cine[8] hath
With his tinct° gilded thee.   *power; color*
How goes it with my brave° Mark Antony?   *magnificent*
40 ALEXAS   Last thing he did, dear queen,
He kissed—the last of many doubled kisses—
This orient[9] pearl. His speech sticks in my heart.
CLEOPATRA   Mine ear must pluck it thence.
ALEXAS   "Good friend," quoth he,
"Say the firm° Roman to great Egypt° sends   *loyal; resolute / Cleopatra*
45 This treasure of an oyster: at whose foot,
To mend° the petty present, I will piece°   *improve / add to*
Her opulent throne with kingdoms. All the East,"
Say thou, "shall call her mistress." So he nodded,
And soberly did mount an arm-gaunt steed,[1]
50 Who neighed so high that what I would have spoke
Was beastly dumbed° by him.   *drowned out*
CLEOPATRA   What was he, sad or merry?
ALEXAS   Like to the time o'th' year between th'extremes
Of hot and cold, he was nor° sad nor merry.   *neither*
55 CLEOPATRA   Oh, well-divided° disposition! Note him,   *balanced*
Note him, good Charmian, 'tis the man, but note him.
He was not sad, for he would shine on those
That make their looks by his;[2] he was not merry,
Which seemed to tell them his remembrance lay
60 In Egypt with his joy—but between both.
Oh, heavenly mingle! Be'st thou sad or merry,
The violence of either thee becomes,
So does it no man else. —Mett'st thou my posts?°   *messengers*
ALEXAS   Ay, madam, twenty several° messengers.   *separate*
Why do you send so thick?
65 CLEOPATRA   Who's° born that day   *Whoever is*
When I forget to send to Antony,
Shall die a beggar. Ink and paper, Charmian.
Welcome, my good Alexas! Did I, Charmian,
Ever love Caesar so?

6. See 2.7.26–27 for the superstition that snakes formed spontaneously in the Nile mud; the asp in particular was associated with Isis, with whom Cleopatra identifies herself.
7. Gneius Pompey, older brother of Sextus Pompey (the character in this play) and son of Pompey the Great. But Cleopatra's phrasing makes him sound like the father.

8. Elixir of life: sought by alchemists, it was thought to be able to turn base metals to gold and cure all disease.
9. From India (more lustrous than European pearls).
1. Thin but fiery war horse. TEXTUAL COMMENT For Shakespeare's invention of compound words like this one, see Digital Edition TC 3.
2. Who are dependent on his mood; who reflect his appearance in their own.

CHARMIAN   Oh, that brave Caesar!

70   CLEOPATRA   Be choked with such another emphasis,
Say "the brave Antony."

CHARMIAN   The valiant Caesar.

CLEOPATRA   By Isis, I will give thee bloody teeth,
If thou with Caesar paragon° again   *compare*
My man of men.

CHARMIAN   By your most gracious pardon,
I sing but after you.

75   CLEOPATRA   My salad days,
When I was green° in judgment, cold in blood,°   *immature / feeling*
To say as I said then. But come, away;
Get me ink and paper.
He shall have every day a several greeting

80   Or I'll unpeople Egypt.³   *Exeunt.*

2.1

Enter POMPEY, Menecrates, *and* MENAS,¹ *in
warlike manner.*

POMPEY   If the great gods be just, they shall assist
The deeds of justest men.

MENAS   Know, worthy Pompey,
That what they do delay they not deny.

POMPEY   Whiles we are suitors to their throne, decays
The thing we sue for.²

5   MENAS   We, ignorant of ourselves,
Beg often our own harms, which the wise powers
Deny us for our° good. So find we profit   *our own*
By losing of our prayers.

POMPEY   I shall do well.
The people love me, and the sea is mine;

10   My powers are crescent,° and my auguring° hope   *growing / prophesying*
Says it° will come to th' full.³ Mark Antony   *(my military power)*
In Egypt sits at dinner and will make
No wars without doors.⁴ Caesar gets money where
He loses hearts. Lepidus flatters both,

15   Of° both is flattered; but he neither loves,°   *By / loves neither*
Nor either cares for him.

MENAS   Caesar and Lepidus
Are in the field. A mighty strength they carry.

POMPEY   Where have you this? 'Tis false.

MENAS   From Silvius, sir.

POMPEY   He dreams. I know they are in Rome together

20   Looking° for Antony. But all the charms° of love,   *Waiting / incantations*
Salt° Cleopatra, soften thy waned⁵ lip!   *Lecherous*
Let witchcraft join with beauty, lust with both;
Tie up the libertine in a field of feasts;

---

3. If not, it will be only because I have run out of
Egyptians to act as messengers (or: because I have
killed all Egyptians).
2.1 Location: Pompey's headquarters (in Sicily).
1. TEXTUAL COMMENT For the assignment to Menas
of all dialogue with the speech prefix *Mene* in F, see
Digital Edition TC 4.
2. *Whiles . . . for:* While we are beseeching the gods,

what we request is losing its value.
3. Like the "crescent" moon.
4. Outside doors. Antony is concerned only with the
wars of love, conducted indoors.
5. Withered; decreased, like the moon, perhaps in
implicit contrast to the "crescent" and potentially
"full" moon of Pompey's "powers" (lines 10–11).

Keep his brain fuming.° Epicurean[6] cooks,   *drunk*
25 Sharpen with cloyless sauce[7] his appetite,
That sleep and feeding may prorogue° his honor   *postpone*
Even till a Lethe'd dullness[8]—
    Enter VARRIUS.
                How now, Varrius?
VARRIUS   This is most certain that I shall deliver:
Mark Antony is every hour in Rome
30 Expected. Since he went from Egypt 'tis
A space for farther travel.[9]
POMPEY   I could have given less° matter   *less crucial*
A better ear. Menas, I did not think
This amorous surfeiter would have donned his helm°   *helmet*
35 For such a petty war. His soldiership
Is twice the other twain. But let us rear°   *elevate*
The higher our opinion,° that our stirring   *(of ourselves)*
Can from the lap of Egypt's widow° pluck   *(see note to 1.4.6)*
The ne'er-lust-wearied Antony.
MENAS   I cannot hope°   *suppose*
40 Caesar and Antony shall well greet together.
His wife that's dead did trespasses to° Caesar;   *offended against*
His brother warred upon him, although I think
Not moved° by Antony.   *prompted*
POMPEY   I know not, Menas,
How lesser enmities may give way to greater.
45 Were't not that we stand up against them all,
'Twere pregnant° they should square° between themselves,   *evident / argue*
For they have entertainèd° cause enough   *sustained*
To draw their swords. But how the fear of us
May cement their divisions° and bind up   *unite them*
50 The petty difference, we yet not know.
Be't as our gods will have't! It only stands
Our lives upon to use[1] our strongest hands.
Come, Menas.   *Exeunt.*

2.2

    Enter ENOBARBUS *and* LEPIDUS.
LEPIDUS   Good Enobarbus, 'tis a worthy deed,
And shall become you well, to entreat your captain
To soft and gentle speech.
ENOBARBUS   I shall entreat him
To answer like himself.[1] If Caesar move° him,   *angers*
5 Let Antony look over Caesar's head
And speak as loud as Mars. By Jupiter,
Were I the wearer of Antonio's beard,
I would not shave't today.[2]
LEPIDUS   'Tis not a time for private stomaching.°   *quarrels*
10 ENOBARBUS   Every time serves for the matter that is then born in't.

---

6. The philosopher Epicurus and his followers believed that the gods took no interest in humans' actions and that the only aim of life was to seek pleasure.
7. Sauce that never wearies or disgusts.
8. Drinking the water of Lethe, one of the rivers bounding Hades, was believed to cause total loss of memory.
9. Sufficient time to have traveled even farther (than between Egypt and Rome).
1. *It . . . use:* Our lives depend entirely on the use of.
2.2 Location: Rome.
1. To answer in a manner appropriate to his character.
2. Plucking a man's beard was an insult; Enobarbus wants Antony to give Octavius the chance to insult him. Possibly, Enobarbus is suggesting not that Antony act heroically but that he merely look the part.

LEPIDUS But small to greater matters must give way.
ENOBARBUS Not if the small come first.
LEPIDUS Your speech is passion.° But pray you stir   °not reasoned
No embers° up. Here comes the noble Antony.   °old resentments
    Enter ANTONY *and* VENTIDIUS.
15 ENOBARBUS And yonder Caesar.
    Enter CAESAR, MAECENAS, *and* AGRIPPA.
ANTONY [*to* VENTIDIUS] If we compose° well here, to Parthia.   °reach agreement
Hark, Ventidius.
    [*They confer apart.*]
CAESAR I do not know, Maecenas, ask Agrippa.
LEPIDUS Noble friends.
20 That which combined us was most great, and let not
A leaner° action rend us. What's amiss,   °less important
May it be gently heard. When we debate
Our trivial difference loud,° we do commit   °loudly; violently
Murder in° healing wounds. Then, noble partners,   °in the process of
25 The rather for° I earnestly beseech,   °Especially because
Touch you the sourest points with sweetest terms,
Nor curstness grow° to th' matter.   °Do not let ill temper add
ANTONY   'Tis spoken well.
Were we° before our armies, and to° fight,   °If we were / about to
I should do thus.³
    Flourish.
30 CAESAR Welcome to Rome.
ANTONY Thank you.
CAESAR Sit.
ANTONY Sit, sir.
    [*They sit.*]
CAESAR Nay, then.
35 ANTONY I learn you take things ill which are not so,
Or being,° concern you not.   °being ill
CAESAR   I must be laughed at,
If or° for nothing, or a little, I   °either
Should say myself offended, and with you
Chiefly i'th'° world; more laughed at, that I should   °Of all the
40 Once name you derogately° when to sound   °censoriously
Your name it not concerned me.
ANTONY My being in Egypt, Caesar, what was't to you?
CAESAR No more than my residing here at Rome
Might be to you in Egypt. Yet if you there
45 Did practice on° my state, your being in Egypt   °scheme against
Might be my question.°   °concern
ANTONY   How intend you, practiced?
CAESAR You may be pleased to catch at° mine intent   °grasp
By what did here befall me. Your wife and brother
Made wars upon me, and their contestation
50 Was theme for you—you were the word of war.⁴
ANTONY You do mistake your business. My brother never
Did urge me in his act.⁵ I did inquire° it,   °inquire into
And have my learning from some true reports°   °reliable sources

---

3. Formally embrace you, as I do now; possibly, speak as you request.
4. *contestation . . . war:* war was meant as an exam-
ple for you to follow (had you as its theme)—your name was the war cry (war was waged in your name).
5. Claimed to be acting as my proxy.

That drew their swords with you. Did he not rather
55 Discredit my authority with yours
And make the wars alike against my stomach,°   *wish*
Having alike° your cause? Of this, my letters   *Since I shared*
Before did satisfy you. If you'll patch a quarrel,
As matter whole you have to make it with,[6]
It must not be with this.

60 CAESAR   You praise yourself
By laying defects of judgment to me, but
You patched up your excuses.

ANTONY   Not so, not so!
I know you could not lack—I am certain on't—
Very necessity of this thought,[7] that I,
65 Your partner in the cause 'gainst which he fought,
Could not with graceful eyes attend[8] those wars
Which fronted° mine own peace. As for my wife,   *opposed*
I would you had her spirit in such another.
The third o'th' world is yours, which with a snaffle[9]
70 You may pace° easy, but not such a wife.   *train to walk*

ENOBARARBUS   Would we had all such wives, that the men
might go to wars with the women.

ANTONY   So much uncurbable,° her garboils,° Caesar,   *uncontrollable / tumults*
Made out of her impatience—which not wanted°   *did not lack*
75 Shrewdness of policy too—I grieving grant
Did you too much disquiet. For that you must
But° say I could not help it.   *Only*

CAESAR   I wrote to you,
When rioting in Alexandria you
Did pocket up my letters and with taunts
80 Did gibe my missive out of audience.[1]

ANTONY   Sir, he fell upon° me ere admitted then.   *broke in on*
Three kings I had newly feasted, and did want
Of what I was[2] i'th' morning. But next day
I told him of myself,° which was as much   *my situation*
85 As to have asked him pardon. Let this fellow
Be nothing° of our strife; if we contend   *Be no part*
Out of our question° wipe him.   *dispute*

CAESAR   You have broken
The article° of your oath, which you shall never   *terms*
Have tongue to charge me with.

90 LEPIDUS   Soft, Caesar!

ANTONY   No, Lepidus, let him speak.
The honor is sacred which he talks on now,
Supposing that I lacked it.[3] But on, Caesar—
The article of my oath?

95 CAESAR   To lend me arms and aid when I required them,
The which you both denied.

ANTONY   Neglected rather—

---

6. *If . . . with*: If you'll patch together an old quarrel with trivia, when you have enough material to make a new one (or, possibly, as if you had enough material to make one).

7. *I know . . . thought*: I'm confident that you must have been aware.

8. Could not look with approval on.

9. Bridle (one without a curb, for good-tempered horses).

1. Scoffed my messenger out of your (public) hearing (referring to 1.1).

2. *did . . . was*: was not myself.

3. *The honor . . . it*: What Caesar speaks of now is my sacred honor, which he assumes I lack (even assuming I lack it).

And then when poisoned hours had bound me up
From mine own knowledge.[4] As nearly as I may,
I'll play the penitent to you. But mine honesty
100 Shall not make poor my greatness, nor my power
Work without it.[5] Truth is that Fulvia,
To have me out of Egypt, made war here,
For which myself, the ignorant motive, do
So far ask pardon as befits mine honor°   dignity
To stoop in such a case.
105 LEPIDUS   'Tis noble spoken.
MAECENAS   If it might please you to enforce no further
The griefs° between ye; to forget them quite   grievances
Were to remember that the present need
Speaks to atone you.°   Is to reconcile you
LEPIDUS   Worthily spoken, Maecenas.
110 ENOBARBUS   Or if you borrow one another's love for the instant,
you may, when you hear no more words of Pompey, return it
again. You shall have time to wrangle in when you have noth-
ing else to do.
ANTONY   Thou art a soldier only. Speak no more.
115 ENOBARBUS   That truth should be silent I had almost forgot.
ANTONY   You wrong this presence;° therefore speak no more!   (noble) company
ENOBARBUS   Go to, then. Your considerate stone.[6]
CAESAR   I do not much dislike the matter° but   content
The manner of his speech, for't cannot be
120 We shall remain in friendship, our conditions°   dispositions
So diff'ring in their acts. Yet if I knew
What hoop should hold us staunch,° from edge to edge   watertight; bound
O'th' world I would pursue it.
AGRIPPA   Give me leave, Caesar.
125 CAESAR   Speak, Agrippa.
AGRIPPA   Thou hast a sister by the mother's side,
Admired Octavia. Great Mark Antony
Is now a widower.
CAESAR   Say not so, Agrippa;
If Cleopatra heard you, your reproof
130 Were well deserved of rashness.[7]
ANTONY   I am not married, Caesar. Let me hear
Agrippa further speak.
AGRIPPA   To hold you in perpetual amity,
To make you brothers, and to knit your hearts
135 With an unslipping knot, take Antony°   let Antony take
Octavia to° his wife, whose beauty claims   for
No worse a husband than the best of men,
Whose virtue and whose general graces speak
That which none else can utter.[8] By this marriage
140 All little jealousies,° which now seem great,   mistrusts
And all great fears, which now import° their dangers,   bring along
Would then be nothing. Truths would be tales,

---

4. *bound . . . knowledge:* prevented me from realizing what I was doing.
5. *mine . . . it:* my honorable behavior (in admitting a
fault) will not diminish my power, nor shall my power
operate without honor.
6. Very well, then; still and silent, but capable of

thought.
7. *your . . . rashness:* the reproof you would receive
would befit your rashness.
8. *speak . . . utter:* speak for themselves; speak more
powerfully than in any other woman.

Where now half-tales be truths.⁹ Her love to both
Would each to other and all loves to both
145 Draw after her. Pardon what I have spoke,
For 'tis a studied, not a present° thought,   *sudden*
By duty ruminated.

ANTONY   Will Caesar speak?
CAESAR   Not till he hears how Antony is touched°   *reacts*
With° what is spoke already.   *To*
150 ANTONY   What power is in Agrippa,
If I would say, "Agrippa, be it so,"
To make this good?

CAESAR   The power of Caesar, and
His power unto Octavia.

ANTONY   May I never
To this good purpose, that so fairly shows,
155 Dream of impediment!¹ Let me have thy hand.
Further this act of grace, and from this hour
The heart of brothers govern in our loves
And sway our great designs.

CAESAR   There's my hand.
A sister I bequeath° you, whom no brother   *hand over to*
160 Did ever love so dearly. Let her live
To join our kingdoms and our hearts, and never
Fly off our loves again.²

LEPIDUS   Happily, amen!

ANTONY   I did not think to draw my sword 'gainst Pompey,
For he hath laid strange° courtesies and great   *uncommon*
165 Of late upon me. I must thank him, only°   *at least*
Lest my remembrance° suffer ill report—   *gratitude*
At heel of° that, defy him.   *Right after*

LEPIDUS   Time calls upon 's.
Of° us must Pompey presently° be sought,   *By / immediately*
Or else he seeks out us.

170 ANTONY   Where lies he?
CAESAR   About the Mount Misena.³
ANTONY   What is his strength by land?
CAESAR   Great, and increasing,
But by sea he is an absolute master.

175 ANTONY   So is the fame.°   *report*
Would we had spoke together!° Haste we for it,   *(earlier)*
Yet ere we put ourselves in arms, dispatch we
The business we have talked of.

CAESAR   With most gladness,
And do° invite you to my sister's view,   *I do*
180 Whither straight I'll lead you.

ANTONY   Let us, Lepidus, not lack your company.
LEPIDUS   Noble Antony, not sickness should detain me.

Flourish. Exeunt [CAESAR, ANTONY, LEPIDUS,
and VENTIDIUS]. ENOBARBUS, AGRIPPA,
and MAECENAS *remain*.

---

9. *Truths . . . truths:* True reports, even if they were
disturbing, could be passed over, regarded as hear-
say, where now incomplete rumors are accepted as
truth.
1. *May . . . impediment:* alluding to the Anglican
marriage service, as does Sonnet 116: "Let me not to

the marriage of true minds / Admit impediments." *so
fairly shows:* appears so attractive.
2. *never . . . again:* may our love for each other never
again desert us.
3. Misenum, a hilly outcropping at the northern end
of the Bay of Naples.

MAECENAS Welcome from Egypt, sir.

ENOBARBUS Half the heart° of Caesar, worthy Maecenas. —My   *Beloved friend*
185 honorable friend, Agrippa!

AGRIPPA Good Enobarbus!

MAECENAS We have cause to be glad that matters are so well
   digested.° You stayed well by't[4] in Egypt.   *settled*

ENOBARBUS Ay, sir, we did sleep day out of countenance[5] and
190 made the night light° with drinking.   *bright; merry*

MAECENAS Eight wild boars roasted whole at a breakfast and
   but twelve persons there. Is this true?

ENOBARBUS This was but as a fly by° an eagle. We had much   *compared with*
   more monstrous matter of feast, which worthily deserved
195 noting.

MAECENAS She's a most triumphant° lady, if report be square°   *magnificent / fair*
   to her.

ENOBARBUS When she first met Mark Antony, she pursed up
   his heart upon the river of Cydnus.[6]

200 AGRIPPA There she appeared indeed, or my reporter devised°   *imagined*
   well for her.

ENOBARBUS I will tell you.
   The barge° she sat in, like a burnished throne   *oar-driven ship*
   Burned on the water. The poop° was beaten gold,   *upper deck*
205 Purple° the sails, and so perfumèd that   *(royal dye)*
   The winds were lovesick with them. The oars were silver,
   Which to the tune of flutes kept stroke and made
   The water which they beat to follow faster,
   As° amorous of their strokes. For° her own person,   *As if / As for*
210 It beggared all description. She did lie
   In her pavilion—cloth of gold, of tissue[7]—
   O'er-picturing that Venus where we see
   The fancy outwork nature.[8] On each side her
   Stood pretty dimpled boys, like smiling Cupids,
215 With divers colored fans whose wind did seem
   To glow° the delicate cheeks which they did cool,   *make glow*
   And what they undid did.

AGRIPPA   Oh, rare for Antony.

ENOBARBUS Her gentlewomen like the Nereides,°   *sea nymphs*
   So many mermaids, tended her i'th' eyes°   *under her watchful eyes*
220 And made their bends adornings.[9] At the helm
   A seeming mermaid steers. The silken tackle°   *sails and ropes*
   Swell with the touches of those flower-soft hands
   That yarely frame° the office. From the barge   *artfully carry out*
   A strange invisible perfume hits the sense
225 Of the adjacent wharfs.° The city cast   *banks*
   Her people out upon° her, and Antony,   *toward*
   Enthroned i'th' marketplace, did sit alone
   Whistling to th'air, which, but for vacancy,[1]
   Had° gone to gaze on Cleopatra too,   *Would have*
   And made a gap in nature.

---

4. You hung in there; you had a high old time.
5. We disconcerted day by sleeping through it and did not see what it looked like.
6. She took possession of his heart on the Cydnus River in Cilicia, Asia Minor (Turkey), on which the city of Tarsus stood.
7. Fabric interwoven with gold thread.

8. *O'er-picturing . . . nature:* Outdoing even the picture of Venus in which the artist outdid nature.
9. Made their curtsies additions to the decoration.
1. Which, if not for the fact that its absence would have left a vacuum (already in Shakespeare's time proverbially impossible in nature).

230 AGRIPPA   Rare Egyptian!
ENOBARBUS   Upon her landing, Antony sent to her,
    Invited her to supper. She replied,
    It should be better he became her guest,
    Which she entreated. Our courteous Antony,
235   Whom ne'er the word of "No" woman heard speak,
    Being barbered ten times o'er, goes to the feast,
    And for his ordinary° pays his heart   public meal at an inn
    For what his eyes eat only.
AGRIPPA   Royal wench!
    She made great Caesar° lay his sword to bed;   (Julius)
    He ploughed her, and she cropped.[2]
240 ENOBARBUS   I saw her once
    Hop forty paces through the public street
    And, having lost her breath, she spoke and panted
    That° she did make defect° perfection,   So that / her panting
    And breathless pour breath forth.
245 MAECENAS   Now Antony must leave her utterly.
ENOBARBUS   Never, he will not.
    Age cannot wither her, nor custom stale°   familiarity diminish
    Her infinite variety. Other women cloy
    The appetites they feed, but she makes hungry
250   Where most she satisfies. For vilest things
    Become themselves° in her, that° the holy priests   Are becoming / so that
    Bless her when she is riggish.°   acts like a slut
MAECENAS   If beauty, wisdom, modesty can settle
    The heart of Antony, Octavia is
    A blessèd lottery° to him.   prize
255 AGRIPPA   Let us go.
    Good Enobarbus, make yourself my guest
    Whilst you abide here.
ENOBARBUS   Humbly, sir, I thank you.   *Exeunt.*

2.3

Enter ANTONY, CAESAR, OCTAVIA *between them.*

ANTONY   The world and my great office will sometimes
    Divide me from your bosom.
OCTAVIA   All which time,
    Before the gods my knee shall bow my prayers
    To them for you.
ANTONY   Good night, sir. —My Octavia,
5   Read not my blemishes in the world's report.
    I have not kept my square,° but that° to come   stayed in line / what's
    Shall all be done by th' rule.[1] Good night, dear lady.
    —Good night, sir.
CAESAR   Good night.   *Exeunt* [CAESAR *and* OCTAVIA].
              Enter SOOTHSAYER.
10 ANTONY   Now, sirrah,[2] you do wish yourself in Egypt?

---

2. She bore Caesarion. After the assassination of
Julius Caesar in 44 B.C.E., Cleopatra returned from
Rome, where she had accompanied him, to Egypt.
There she reigned with their son, who became Ptolemy XV, after she ordered the death of her half
brother. See 1.4.6 with note and 2.1.38. On Antony
and Cleopatra's plans for Ptolemy XV, see 3.6.1–16.

On Ptolemy XV's fate, see note to 5.2.358.
2.3 Location: Scene continues.
1. Regulation; ruler, as unit of measure (picking up
"square," line 6, a measuring tool).
2. Term by which a subordinate or social inferior is
addressed.

SOOTHSAYER   Would I had never come from thence,
Nor you thither!
ANTONY   If you can, your reason?
SOOTHSAYER   I see it in my motion,° have it not in my tongue;   *intuition*
But yet hie° you to Egypt again.   *hurry*
ANTONY   Say to me,
15   Whose fortunes shall rise higher: Caesar's or mine?
SOOTHSAYER   Caesar's.
Therefore, O Antony, stay not by his side.
Thy demon—that thy spirit[3] which keeps thee—is
Noble, courageous, high, unmatchable,
20   Where Caesar's is not. But near him thy angel
Becomes afeard, as° being o'er-powered. Therefore   *as if*
Make space enough between you.
ANTONY   Speak this no more.
SOOTHSAYER   To none but thee—no more but when° to thee.   *not at all except*
If thou dost play with him at any game,
25   Thou art sure to lose, and of° that natural luck   *by*
He beats thee 'gainst the odds. Thy luster thickens°   *Your brightness dims*
When he shines by. I say again, thy spirit
Is all afraid to govern thee near him,
But he away, 'tis noble.
ANTONY   Get thee gone.
30   Say to Ventidius I would speak with him.
                                        Exit [SOOTHSAYER].
He shall to Parthia. Be it art or hap,°   *talent or luck*
He° hath spoken true. The very dice obey him,°   *(the soothsayer) / (Caesar)*
And in our sports my better cunning° faints   *capability*
Under his chance.° If we draw lots, he speeds;°   *luck / succeeds*
35   His cocks do win the battle still of° mine   *always against*
When it is all to naught, and his quails ever
Beat mine, inhooped, at odds.[4] I will to Egypt.
And though I make this marriage for my peace,
I'th' East my pleasure lies.
                                        Enter VENTIDIUS.
                                        Oh, come, Ventidius.
40   You must to Parthia; your commission's ready.
Follow me and receive't.   *Exeunt.*

2.4

Enter LEPIDUS, MAECENAS, *and* AGRIPPA.
LEPIDUS   Trouble yourselves no further. Pray you hasten
Your generals after.[1]
AGRIPPA   Sir, Mark Antony
Will e'en but° kiss Octavia, and we'll follow.   *merely*
LEPIDUS   Till I shall see you in your soldiers' dress,
Which will become you both, farewell.
5   MAECENAS   We shall,
As I conceive the journey, be at the Mount°   *Mount Misenum*
Before you, Lepidus.
LEPIDUS   Your way is shorter.

---

3. *Thy demon . . . spirit*: Your guardian angel, which is the spirit.
4. *When . . . odds*: When the odds completely favor me, and when our quails are placed in a round enclo-

sure to make them fight, his always beat mine, against all odds.
2.4 Location: Scene continues.
1. *hasten . . . after*: follow your leaders.

My purposes do draw me° much about;   *force me to go*
    You'll win two days upon me.
  MAECENAS *and* AGRIPPA   Sir, good success.
10 LEPIDUS   Farewell.   *Exeunt.*

2.5

Enter CLEOPATRA, CHARMIAN, IRAS, *and* ALEXAS.

CLEOPATRA   Give me some music—music, moody° food   *melancholy*
    Of us that trade in love.
CHARMIAN, IRAS, *and* ALEXAS   The music, ho!
    Enter MARDIAN *the eunuch.*
CLEOPATRA   Let it alone. Let's to billiards. Come, Charmian.
CHARMIAN   My arm is sore. Best play with Mardian.
5 CLEOPATRA   As well a woman with an eunuch played
    As with a woman. Come, you'll play with me, sir?
MARDIAN   As well as I can, madam.
CLEOPATRA   And when good will is showed, though't come too
    short[1]
    The actor may plead pardon. I'll none now.°   *I won't play now*
10   Give me mine angle.° We'll to th' river. There,   *fishing rod*
    My music playing far off, I will betray°   *catch*
    Tawny-finned fishes. My bended hook shall pierce
    Their slimy jaws, and as I draw them up,
    I'll think them every one an Antony
    And say, "Aha! You're caught!"
15 CHARMIAN   'Twas merry when
    You wagered on your angling, when your diver
    Did hang a salt° fish on his hook which he   *preserved*
    With fervency drew up.
CLEOPATRA   That time? Oh, times!
    I laughed him out of patience, and that night
20   I laughed him into patience, and next morn,
    Ere the ninth hour, I drunk him to his bed,
    Then put my tires and mantles° on him, whilst   *headdresses and robes*
    I wore his sword Philippan.[2]
    Enter a MESSENGER.
                     Oh, from Italy!
    Ram thou thy fruitful tidings in mine ears
    That long time have been barren.
25 MESSENGER   Madam, madam!
CLEOPATRA   Antonio's dead? If thou say so, villain,
    Thou kill'st thy mistress; but well and free—
    If thou so yield° him—there is gold, and here   *report*
    My bluest veins to kiss, a hand that kings
30   Have lipped and trembled kissing.
MESSENGER   First, madam, he is well.
CLEOPATRA   Why, there's more gold. But, sirrah, mark, we use
    To say the dead are well. Bring it to that,
    The gold I give thee will I melt and pour
35   Down thy ill-uttering throat.
MESSENGER   Good madam, hear me.
CLEOPATRA   Well, go to, I will.

2.5 Location: Alexandria.
1. Referring to Mardian's sexual incapacity.

2. The sword with which Antony had beaten Brutus
and Cassius at Philippi.

But there's no goodness in thy face. If Antony
Be free and healthful, so tart a favor°   *so sour an expression*
40 To trumpet such good tidings! If not well,
Thou shouldst come like a fury[3] crowned with snakes,
Not like a formal° man.   *Not in the shape of a*
MESSENGER   Will't please you hear me?
CLEOPATRA   I have a mind to strike thee ere thou speak'st.
Yet if thou say Antony lives, 'tis well,
45 Or friends with Caesar, or not captive to him,
I'll set thee in a shower of gold and hail
Rich pearls upon thee.
MESSENGER   Madam, he's well.
CLEOPATRA   Well said.
MESSENGER   And friends with Caesar.
CLEOPATRA   Thou'rt an honest man.
MESSENGER   Caesar and he are greater friends than ever.
CLEOPATRA   Make thee a fortune from me.
50 MESSENGER   But yet, madam—
CLEOPATRA   I do not like "But yet." It does allay°   *dissipate*
The good precedence.° Fie upon "But yet"!   *preceding good news*
"But yet" is as a jailor to bring forth
Some monstrous malefactor. Prithee, friend,
55 Pour out the pack of matter to mine ear,°   *Give me all the news*
The good and bad together. He's friends with Caesar,
In state of health, thou say'st, and thou say'st, free.
MESSENGER   Free, madam, no! I made no such report.
He's bound unto Octavia.
CLEOPATRA   For what good turn?°   *good deed*
MESSENGER   For the best turn i'th' bed.
60 CLEOPATRA   I am pale, Charmian.
MESSENGER   Madam, he's married to Octavia.
CLEOPATRA   The most infectious pestilence upon thee!
        [*She*] *strikes him down.*
MESSENGER   Good madam, patience!
CLEOPATRA   What say you?
        [*She*] *strikes him.*
Hence, horrible villain, or I'll spurn° thine eyes   *kick*
65 Like balls before me! I'll unhair thy head;
        She hales° him up and down.   *drags*
Thou shalt be whipped with wire and stewed in brine,
Smarting in ling'ring pickle.°   *salt water*
MESSENGER   Gracious madam,
I that do bring the news made not the match!
CLEOPATRA   Say 'tis not so! A province I will give thee
70 And make thy fortunes proud. The blow thou hadst
Shall make thy peace for moving me to rage,
And I will boot° thee with what° gift beside   *compensate / whatever*
Thy modesty can beg.
MESSENGER   He's married, madam.
CLEOPATRA   Rogue, thou hast lived too long.
        [*She*] *draws a knife.*
MESSENGER   Nay, then I'll run.
75 What mean you, madam? I have made no fault.   *Exit.*

---

3. In Greek mythology, a female avenging spirit.

CHARMIAN   Good madam, keep yourself within yourself.°   *restrain yourself*
    The man is innocent.
CLEOPATRA   Some innocents scape° not the thunderbolt.   *escape*
    Melt Egypt into Nile, and kindly° creatures   *harmless*
80   Turn all to serpents! Call the slave again.
    Though I am mad, I will not bite him. Call!
CHARMIAN   He is afeard to come.
CLEOPATRA   I will not hurt him.
    These hands do lack nobility that they strike
    A meaner° than myself, since I myself   *One of lower rank*
    Have given myself the cause.°   *(by loving Antony)*
        Enter the MESSENGER *again.*
85   Come hither, sir.
    Though it be honest, it is never good
    To bring bad news. Give to a gracious message
    An host° of tongues, but let ill tidings tell   *A multitude*
    Themselves when they be felt.[4]
MESSENGER   I have done my duty.
90 CLEOPATRA   Is he married?
    I cannot hate thee worser than I do
    If thou again say "Yes."
MESSENGER   He's married, madam.
CLEOPATRA   The gods confound° thee. Dost thou hold there still?   *destroy*
MESSENGER   Should I lie, madam?
CLEOPATRA   Oh, I would thou didst,
95   So° half my Egypt were submerged and made   *Even if*
    A cistern° for scaled snakes. Go, get thee hence!   *reservoir; chamber pot*
    Hadst thou Narcissus[5] in thy face, to me
    Thou wouldst appear most ugly. He is married?
MESSENGER   I crave your highness' pardon.
CLEOPATRA   He is married?
100 MESSENGER   Take no offense that I would not° offend you;   *since I don't want to*
    To punish me for what you make me do
    Seems much unequal.° He's married to Octavia.   *most unfair*
CLEOPATRA   Oh, that his fault should make a knave° of thee,   *villain*
    That art not what thou'rt sure of![6] Get thee hence.
105   The merchandise which thou hast brought from Rome
    Are all too dear for me. Lie they upon thy hand,[7]
    And be undone° by 'em.   [*Exit* MESSENGER.]   *ruined (financially)*
CHARMIAN   Good your highness, patience!
CLEOPATRA   In praising Antony, I have dispraised Caesar.
CHARMIAN   Many times, madam.
110 CLEOPATRA   I am paid for't now. Lead me from hence.
    I faint. O Iras, Charmian—'tis no matter.
    Go to the fellow, good Alexas. Bid him
    Report the feature° of Octavia, her years,   *appearance*
    Her inclination.° Let him not leave out   *disposition*
115   The color of her hair. Bring me word quickly.
                    [*Exit* ALEXAS.]
    Let him forever go—let him not! Charmian,
    Though he be painted one way like a Gorgon,

---

4. *let . . . felt*: bad news is best revealed by letting the
victim feel the effects.
5. In Greek mythology, a surpassingly beautiful young
man.

6. Who are not bad, unlike the offense you know
about.
7. Leave with your goods unsold.

The other way's a Mars.[8] [*to* MARDIAN] Bid you Alexas
Bring me word how tall she is. Pity me, Charmian,
120   But do not speak to me. Lead me to my chamber.   *Exeunt.*

2.6

Flourish. Enter POMPEY *and* MENAS *at one door with*
drum and trumpet. At another [*door enter*] CAESAR,
LEPIDUS, ANTONY, ENOBARBUS, MAECENAS, *and*
AGRIPPA *with* SOLDIERS *marching.*

POMPEY   Your hostages I have, so have you mine,
And we shall talk before we fight.

CAESAR   Most meet°   *fitting*
That first we come to words, and therefore have we
Our written purposes° before us sent,   *offers*
5   Which if thou hast considered, let us know
If 'twill tie up° thy discontented sword   *lead you to put aside*
And carry back to Sicily much tall° youth   *courageous*
That else must perish here.

POMPEY   To you all three,
The senators alone° of this great world,   *sole governors*
10   Chief factors° for the gods: I do not know   *agents*
Wherefore° my father[1] should revengers want,°   *why / lack*
Having a son and friends, since Julius Caesar,
Who at Philippi the good Brutus ghosted,[2]
There saw you laboring for him.° What was't   *on his behalf*
15   That moved pale Cassius to conspire? And what
Made all-honored, honest,° Roman Brutus,   *honorable*
With the armed rest, courtiers° of beauteous freedom,   *seekers*
To drench° the Capitol, but that they would   *(in blood)*
Have one man but a man?° And that is it   *(and not a king)*
20   Hath made me rig° my navy. At whose burden   *equip*
The angered ocean foams, with which I meant
To scourge th'ingratitude that despiteful Rome
Cast on my noble father.

CAESAR   Take your time.

ANTONY   Thou canst not fear° us, Pompey, with thy sails.   *intimidate*
25   We'll speak with° thee at sea. At land thou know'st   *engage*
How much we do o'ercount° thee.   *outnumber*

POMPEY   At land indeed
Thou dost o'ercount me of my father's house.[3]
But, since the cuckoo builds not for himself,[4]
Remain in't as thou mayst.°   *as long as you can*

LEPIDUS   Be pleased to tell us,

---

8. Cleopatra imagines Antony as a figure in a perspective painting: popular in Shakespeare's time, they showed different images according to the angle from which they were viewed. In classical mythology, a Gorgon was one of three female monsters with snakes for hair whose horrific appearance could turn others to stone.
2.6 Location: Near Misenum, Italy.
1. Pompey the Great. After being defeated by Julius Caesar at Pharsalia, Pompey the Great fled to Egypt and was there assassinated by agents of Ptolemy, Cleopatra's half brother (prior to the events in *Julius Caesar*; see note to 1.4.6). In *Julius Caesar*, Julius

Caesar is then himself assassinated by the Roman republican conspirators, including Cassius and Brutus, who are in turn killed by the triumvirs (see note to 1.2.98). The younger Pompey thus believes that by making war on the triumvirate, he avenges his father's death and the deaths of Brutus and Cassius (and, therefore, fights for the Republic).
2. Caesar appeared as a ghost to Brutus at the Battle of Philippi.
3. Plutarch records that Antony agreed to buy the elder Pompey's house but ultimately refused to pay for it.
4. The cuckoo lays eggs in the nests of other birds, rather than building a nest of its own.

30 For this is from the present,° how you take   *beside the point*
The offers we have sent you.
CAESAR   There's the point.
ANTONY   Which do not be entreated to,° but weigh   *convinced unfairly of*
What it is worth embraced.°   *if you consent*
CAESAR   And what may follow
To try a larger fortune.⁵
POMPEY   You have made me offer
35 Of Sicily, Sardinia, and I must
Rid all the sea of pirates; then, to send
Measures of wheat to Rome. This 'greed upon,
To part with unhacked edges° and bear back   *unused swords*
Our targes undinted.°   *shields untouched*
CAESAR, ANTONY, *and* LEPIDUS   That's our offer.
POMPEY   Know, then,
40 I came before you here a man prepared
To take this offer. But Mark Antony
Put me to some impatience. Though I lose
The praise of it by telling, you must know,
When Caesar and your brother were at blows,
45 Your mother came to Sicily and did find
Her welcome friendly.
ANTONY   I have heard it, Pompey,
And am well studied for° a liberal thanks,   *intend to offer*
Which I do owe you.
POMPEY   Let me have your hand.
       [*They shake hands.*]
I did not think, sir, to have met you here.
50 ANTONY   The beds i'th' East are soft, and thanks to you
That called me timelier° than my purpose° hither,   *earlier / intention*
For I have gained by't.
CAESAR   Since I saw you last,
There's a change upon you.
POMPEY   Well, I know not
What counts harsh fortune casts upon my face,⁶
55 But in my bosom shall she never come
To make my heart her vassal.
LEPIDUS   Well met here.
POMPEY   I hope so, Lepidus. Thus we are agreed.
I crave our composition° may be written   *pact*
And sealed between us.
CAESAR   That's the next to do.
60 POMPEY   We'll feast each other ere we part, and let's
Draw lots who shall begin.°   *act as host*
ANTONY   That will I, Pompey.
POMPEY   No, Antony, take the lot, but first or last,
Your fine Egyptian cookery shall have
The fame. I have heard that Julius Caesar
Grew fat with feasting there.
65 ANTONY   You have heard much.
POMPEY   I have fair° meaning, sir.   *amicable*
ANTONY   And fair° words to them.   *(ironic)*

---

5. If you try (by fighting us) for a still larger fortune than we have offered.   6. What accounts cruel fortune calculates (by marking notches, like wrinkles).

POMPEY   Then so much have I heard,
  And I have heard Apollodorus carried[7]—
ENOBARBUS   No more that. He did so.
70 POMPEY   What, I pray you?
ENOBARBUS   A certain queen to Caesar in a mattress.
POMPEY   I know thee now. How far'st thou, soldier?
ENOBARBUS   Well, and well am like to do, for I perceive
  Four feasts are toward.°   *to come*
POMPEY   Let me shake thy hand,
75 I never hated thee. I have seen thee fight
  When I have envied thy behavior.
ENOBARBUS   Sir,
  I never loved you much, but I ha' praised ye,
  When you have well deserved ten times as much
  As I have said you did.
POMPEY   Enjoy thy plainness;°   *matter-of-fact speech*
80 It nothing ill becomes thee.
  Aboard my galley I invite you all.
  Will you lead, lords?
CAESAR, ANTONY, *and* LEPIDUS   Show 's the way, sir.
POMPEY   Come.
                Exeunt all but ENOBARBUS *and* MENAS.
MENAS [*aside*]   Thy father, Pompey, would ne'er have made
  this treaty. [*to* ENOBARBUS] You and I have known,° sir.   *met each other*
85 ENOBARBUS   At sea, I think.
MENAS   We have, sir.
ENOBARBUS   You have done well by water.
MENAS   And you by land.
ENOBARBUS   I will praise any man that will praise me, though
90 it cannot be denied what I have done by land.
MENAS   Nor what I have done by water.
ENOBARBUS   Yes, something you can deny for your own safety.
  You have been a great thief by sea.
MENAS   And you by land.
95 ENOBARBUS   There I deny my land service, but give me your
  hand, Menas. If our eyes had authority,° here they might   *(to make an arrest)*
  take two thieves kissing.[8]
MENAS   All men's faces are true,° whatsoe'er their hands are.   *honest*
ENOBARBUS   But there is never a fair woman has a true° face.   *(without makeup)*
100 MENAS   No slander°—they steal hearts.   *That's true*
ENOBARBUS   We came hither to fight with you.
MENAS   For my part, I am sorry it is turned to a drinking.
  Pompey doth this day laugh away his fortune.
ENOBARBUS   If he do, sure he cannot weep't back again.
105 MENAS   You've said,° sir. We looked not for Mark Antony here.   *spoken truly*
  Pray you, is he married to Cleopatra?
ENOBARBUS   Caesar's sister is called Octavia.
MENAS   True, sir. She was the wife of Caius Marcellus.
ENOBARBUS   But she is now the wife of Marcus Antonius.
110 MENAS   Pray ye,° sir?   *Really*
ENOBARBUS   'Tis true.

---

7. Alluding to the story that Cleopatra gained access
to her lover, Julius Caesar, by having herself rolled up
in a sleeping mat that Apollodorus carried into the
palace (told in Plutarch).
8. Arrest two thieves embracing; catch two thieving
hands in a handshake, plotting together.

MENAS   Then is Caesar and he forever knit together.

ENOBARBUS   If I were bound to divine° of this unity, I would
not prophesy so.   *make predictions*

115 MENAS   I think the policy of that purpose made more⁹ in the
marriage than the love of the parties.

ENOBARBUS   I think so too. But you shall find the band that
seems to tie their friendship together will be the very strangler
of their amity. Octavia is of a holy, cold, and still conversation.°   *disposition*

120 MENAS   Who would not have his wife so?

ENOBARBUS   Not he that himself is not so, which is Mark
Antony. He will to his Egyptian dish again. Then shall the
sighs of Octavia blow the fire up in Caesar, and—as I said
before—that which is the strength of their amity shall prove
125 the immediate author° of their variance.° Antony will use his   *cause / enmity*
affection where it is. He married but his occasion here.¹

MENAS   And thus it may be. Come, sir, will you aboard? I have
a health° for you.   *toast*

ENOBARBUS   I shall take it, sir; we have used our throats in Egypt.

130 MENAS   Come, let's away.   *Exeunt.*

2.7

Music plays.
Enter two or three SERVANTS *with a banquet.*¹

FIRST SERVANT   Here they'll be, man. Some o'their plants are
ill-rooted² already. The least wind i'th' world will blow them
down.

SECOND SERVANT   Lepidus is high-colored.

5 FIRST SERVANT   They have made him drink alms-drink.³

SECOND SERVANT   As they pinch one another by the disposition,⁴ he cries out, "No more," reconciles them to his
entreaty,° and himself to th' drink.   *(to stop arguing)*

FIRST SERVANT   But it raises the greater war between him and
10 his discretion.

SECOND SERVANT   Why, this it is to have a name° in great men's   *only a nominal place*
fellowship. I had as lief° have a reed that will do me no service *just as soon*
as a partisan I could not heave.⁵

FIRST SERVANT   To be called into a huge sphere, and not to be
15 seen to move in't, are the holes where eyes should be, which
pitifully disaster the cheeks.⁶

A sennet° sounded.   *flourish of trumpets*
Enter CAESAR, ANTONY, POMPEY, LEPIDUS, AGRIPPA,
MAECENAS, ENOBARBUS, [*and*] MENAS, *with other*
CAPTAINS [*and a* BOY].

ANTONY   Thus do they, sir. They take the flow° o'th' Nile   *measure the depth*
By certain scales i'th'° pyramid. They know   *marks on the*

---

9. I think the politics of that "unity" weighed more
heavily.
1. *Antony . . . here:* Antony will act on his desire
where it really is located (Egypt). He married out of
self-interest here.
2.7 Location: Pompey's galley, off Misenum.
1. One of the courses of the feast, possibly dessert.
2. *their . . . rooted:* the soles of the feet of the (drunken)
leaders are unsteady; the alliance between Antony and
Caesar is shaky.
3. Drink given out of charity; in this case, extra
rounds given to reconcile the parties each time they

quarrel; one too many.
4. As they irritate one another according to their
natures.
5. As a spear I could not lift (position without power).
6. *To be . . . cheeks:* To be placed in high circles
where one is incapable of moving is like having,
instead of eyes, empty eye sockets that disfigure one's
face. (In Ptolemaic astronomy, a planet "moves"
within its "sphere," one of a series of concentric circles of which the universe is formed, with the earth at
the center. A planet's ill influence causes "disaster"—
literally, "bad star.")

By th' height, the lowness, or the mean° if dearth   *middle position*
20   Or foison° follow. The higher Nilus swells,   *abundance*
The more it promises; as it ebbs, the seedsman
Upon the slime and ooze scatters his grain,
And shortly comes to harvest.
LEPIDUS   You've strange serpents there?
25   ANTONY   Ay, Lepidus.
LEPIDUS   Your serpent of Egypt is bred now of your mud by
the operation of your sun. So is your crocodile.
ANTONY   They are so.
POMPEY   Sit, and some wine. A health to Lepidus!
30   LEPIDUS   I am not so well as I should be, but I'll ne'er out.°   *leave; miss a round*
ENOBARBUS [*aside*]   Not till you have slept. I fear me you'll be
in° till then.   *remain; be drunk*
LEPIDUS   Nay, certainly, I have heard the Ptolemies' pyramises[7]
are very goodly things. Without contradiction I have heard
35   that.
MENAS [*aside to* POMPEY]   Pompey, a word.
POMPEY [*aside to* MENAS]   Say in mine ear. What is't?
MENAS   Forsake thy seat, I do beseech thee, captain,
And hear me speak a word.
40   POMPEY (*whispering in* [*Menas'*] *ear*)   Forbear° me till anon.   *Wait for*
—This wine for Lepidus!
LEPIDUS   What manner o'thing is your crocodile?
ANTONY   It is shaped, sir, like itself, and it is as broad as it hath
breadth. It is just so high as it is, and moves with it° own   *its*
45   organs. It lives by that which nourisheth it, and the elements
once out of it, it transmigrates.[8]
LEPIDUS   What color is it of?
ANTONY   Of it own color, too.
LEPIDUS   'Tis a strange serpent.
50   ANTONY   'Tis so, and the tears of it are wet.°   *deceitful crocodile tears*
CAESAR   Will this description satisfy him?
ANTONY   With the health that Pompey gives him, else he is a
very epicure.°   *an insatiable glutton*
[MENAS *whispers to* POMPEY.]
POMPEY   Go hang, sir, hang! Tell me of that? Away!
55   Do as I bid you. —Where's this cup I called for?
MENAS [*aside to* POMPEY]   If for the sake of merit° thou wilt   *past deeds*
hear me, rise from thy stool.
POMPEY   I think thou'rt mad. [*They step aside.*] The matter?
MENAS   I have ever held my cap off to° thy fortunes.   *ever served*
60   POMPEY   Thou hast served me with much faith. What's else to
say? —Be jolly, lords.
ANTONY   These quicksands, Lepidus, keep off them, for you sink.
MENAS   Wilt thou be lord of all the world?
POMPEY   What say'st thou?
MENAS   Wilt thou be lord of the whole world? That's twice.
POMPEY   How should that be?
65   MENAS   But entertain° it,   *consider*
And though thou think me poor, I am the man
Will give thee all the world.

---

7. Pyramids (drunken speech).
8. Passes into other forms of life: referring to
Pythagoras's theory, apparently of Egyptian origin,
that at death the soul moves into another newborn
living thing.

POMPEY   Hast thou drunk well?

MENAS   No, Pompey, I have kept me from the cup.
　　Thou art, if thou dar'st be, the earthly Jove.
70　　Whate'er the ocean pales° or sky inclips°   *encloses / embraces*
　　Is thine, if thou wilt ha't.

POMPEY   Show me which way?

MENAS   These three world-sharers, these competitors°   *allies*
　　Are in thy vessel. Let me cut the cable,
　　And when we are put off,° fall to their throats.   *(from shore)*
　　All there is thine.

75 POMPEY   Ah, this thou shouldst have done
　　And not have spoke on't. In me 'tis villainy;
　　In thee't had been good service. Thou must know,
　　'Tis not my profit that does lead mine honor,
　　Mine honor it.⁹ Repent that e'er thy tongue
80　　Hath so betrayed thine act.¹ Being done unknown,
　　I should have found it afterwards well done,
　　But must condemn it now. Desist, and drink.

MENAS [*aside*]   For this, I'll never follow thy palled° fortunes   *diminished*
　　more.
　　Who seeks and will not take when once 'tis offered
　　Shall never find it more.

85 POMPEY   This health to Lepidus.

ANTONY   Bear him ashore. I'll pledge it° for him, Pompey.   *drink the toast*

ENOBARBUS   Here's to thee, Menas.

MENAS   Enobarbus, welcome.

POMPEY   Fill till the cup be hid.

ENOBARBUS [*pointing to the servant carrying* LEPIDUS]   There's
　　a strong fellow, Menas.

90 MENAS   Why?

ENOBARBUS   'A° bears the third part of the world, man. See'st not?   *He*

MENAS   The third part then he is drunk—would it were all,
　　That it might go on wheels!°   *easily; out of control*

ENOBARBUS   Drink thou. Increase the reels.°   *revels; spinning*

95 MENAS   Come.

POMPEY   This is not yet an Alexandrian feast.

ANTONY   It ripens towards it. Strike the vessels,° ho!   *Open more casks*
　　Here's to Caesar!

CAESAR   I could well forbear't.
　　It's monstrous° labor when I wash my brain   *unnatural*
　　And° it grow fouler.   *If as a result*

100 ANTONY   Be a child o'th' time.

CAESAR   Possess it. I'll make answer,²
　　But I had rather fast from all° four days   *for all of*
　　Than drink so much in one.

ENOBARBUS   Ha, my brave emperor,
　　Shall we dance now the Egyptian bacchanals³
105　　And celebrate our drink?

POMPEY   Let's ha't, good soldier.

ANTONY   Come, let's all take hands,

---

9. *'Tis . . . it:* It is my honor that precedes or is the
basis of my profit.
1. Treacherously disclosed your intentions and so
made it impossible to carry them out.

2. Take it, and I'll drink, too; be in command of the
time, I say.
3. Wild, drunken revels in honor of Bacchus, god of
wine and revelry.

Till that the conquering wine hath steeped our sense
In soft and delicate Lethe.°   *oblivion*

ENOBARBUS   All take hands.

110   Make battery to° our ears with the loud music,   *Besiege*
The while I'll place you; then the boy shall sing.
The holding° every man shall beat° as loud   *refrain / beat out*
As his strong sides can volley.°   *fire off*
     Music plays. ENOBARBUS *places them hand in hand.*
                The Song.

BOY [*sings*]   Come thou monarch of the vine,
115   Plumpy Bacchus with pink eyne!⁴
               In thy fats our cares be drowned,
               With thy grapes our hairs be crowned.
                    Cup us till the world go round;
                    Cup us till the world go round.

120   **CAESAR**   What would you more? Pompey, good night. —Good
     brother,°   *Brother-in-law*
Let me request you off.° Our graver business   *to come ashore*
Frowns at this levity. Gentle lords, let's part.
You see we have burned° our cheeks. Strong Enobarb   *flushed*
Is weaker than the wine, and mine own tongue
125   Splits° what it speaks. The wild disguise° hath almost *Deforms / drunkenness*
Anticked us all.° What needs more words? Good night.   *Made us all clowns*
Good Antony, your hand.

POMPEY   I'll try you° on the shore.   *test your drinking*

ANTONY   And shall, sir—give's your hand.

POMPEY   O Antony, you have my father's house.
130   But what? We are friends! Come down into the boat.

ENOBARBUS   Take heed you fall not.
               [*Exeunt all but* ENOBARBUS *and* MENAS.]
                Menas, I'll not° on shore.   *not go*

MENAS   No, to my cabin. These drums, these trumpets, flutes!
What!
Let Neptune hear we bid a loud farewell
To these great fellows. Sound and be hanged. Sound out!
     Sound a flourish with drums.
135   **ENOBARBUS**   Hoo! Says 'a.° There's my cap!   *he*
     [*He throws his cap in the air.*]

MENAS   Hoo! Noble captain, come.   *Exeunt.*

3.1

     Enter VENTIDIUS *as it were in triumph, the dead body*
     of Pacorus borne before him[*, with* SILIUS *and other*
     SOLDIERS].

VENTIDIUS   Now, darting Parthia,¹ art thou struck, and now
Pleased fortune does of Marcus Crassus'² death
Make me revenger. Bear the King's son's body
Before our army. Thy° Pacorus, Orades,   *Your son*
Pays this for Marcus Crassus.
5   **SILIUS**   Noble Ventidius,

---

4. Half-closed and red from drinking.
3.1 Location: Syria.
1. Parthian cavalry advanced while flinging darts,
then retreated while shooting arrows. "Parthia" here
refers to both the nation and its king, Orodes.
2. A member, with Pompey the Great and Julius
Caesar, of the first triumvirate, treacherously and
cruelly killed in defeat by Orodes in 53 B.C.E.

Whilst yet with Parthian blood thy sword is warm,
The fugitive Parthians follow.³ Spur through Media,⁴
Mesopotamia, and the shelters whither
The routed fly. So thy grand captain Antony
10 Shall set thee on triumphant° chariots and   *triumphal*
Put garlands on thy head.
VENTIDIUS   O Silius, Silius,
I have done enough. A lower place,° note well,   *man of low rank*
May make too great an act. For learn this, Silius;
Better to leave undone than by our deed
15 Acquire too high a fame when him we serve's away.
Caesar and Antony have ever won
More in their officer than person.⁵ Sossius,
One of my place in Syria, his° lieutenant,   *(Antony's)*
For quick accumulation of renown,
20 Which he achieved by th' minute,° lost his favor.   *more of every minute*
Who does i'th' wars more than his captain can
Becomes his captain's captain, and ambition,
The soldier's virtue, rather makes choice of loss
Than gain which darkens him.°   *eclipses his renown*
25 I could do more to do Antonius good,
But 'twould offend him. And in his offense
Should my performance perish.°   *lose its value*
SILIUS   Thou hast, Ventidius, that°   *(discretion)*
Without the which a soldier and his sword
30 Grants scarce° distinction. Thou wilt write to Antony?   *Scarcely admits of*
VENTIDIUS   I'll humbly signify what in his name—
That magical word of war—we have effected;
How with his banners and his well-paid ranks
The ne'er-yet-beaten horse° of Parthia   *cavalry*
We have jaded° out o'th' field.   *chased like tired nags*
35 SILIUS   Where is he now?
VENTIDIUS   He purposeth to Athens, whither with what haste
The weight we must convey with 's will permit,
We shall appear before him. —On there! Pass along!
                      Exeunt.

3.2
Enter AGRIPPA *at one door,* ENOBARBUS *at another.*
AGRIPPA   What, are the brothers parted?°   *brothers-in-law gone*
ENOBARBUS   They have dispatched° with Pompey. He is gone;   *finished the business*
The other three are sealing.° Octavia weeps   *signing their pact*
To part from Rome. Caesar is sad, and Lepidus,
5 Since Pompey's feast—as Menas says—is troubled
With the greensickness.¹
AGRIPPA   'Tis a noble Lepidus.
ENOBARBUS   A very fine one. Oh, how he loves Caesar!
AGRIPPA   Nay, but how dearly he adores Mark Antony!

---

3. Chase the fleeing Parthians.
4. The land between Persia and Armenia, east of Mesopotamia—part of the Parthian Empire.
5. Owing more to the skill of their officers than to their own skill.

3.2 Location: Rome.
1. Anemia in adolescent, lovesick girls (hence, a feminizing attribute): here, used humorously for Lepidus's hangover and its effect, as well as ironically for his overblown affection for Caesar and Antony.

ENOBARBUS   Caesar? Why, he's the Jupiter of men.
10 AGRIPPA   What's Antony? The god of Jupiter?
ENOBARBUS   Spake you of Caesar? How, the nonpareil?°   *incomparable*
AGRIPPA   O Antony! O thou Arabian bird!²
ENOBARBUS   Would you praise Caesar? Say "Caesar." Go no
    further.
AGRIPPA   Indeed, he plied them both with excellent praises.
15 ENOBARBUS   But he loves Caesar best, yet he loves Antony.
    Hoo! Hearts, tongues, figures,° scribes, bards, poets cannot   *(of speech); numbers*
    Think, speak, cast,° write, sing, number!° Hoo!   *calculate / make verses*
    His love to Antony. But as for Caesar—
    Kneel down, kneel down, and wonder.
AGRIPPA   Both he loves.
ENOBARBUS   They are his shards³ and he their beetle.
    [*Trumpets sound within.*]
20   So,
    This is° to horse. Adieu, noble Agrippa.   *calls us*
AGRIPPA   Good fortune, worthy soldier, and farewell.
        Enter CAESAR, ANTONY, LEPIDUS, *and* OCTAVIA.
ANTONY   No further, sir.
CAESAR   You take from me a great part of myself.
25 Use me well in't. —Sister, prove such a wife
    As my thoughts make thee, and as my farthest band
    Shall pass on thy approof.⁴ —Most noble Antony,
    Let not the piece° of virtue which is set   *paragon*
    Betwixt us as the cement of our love
30 To keep it builded, be the ram to batter
    The fortress of it. For better might we
    Have loved without this mean° if on both parts   *intermediary*
    This be not cherished.
ANTONY   Make me not offended
    In° your distrust.   *By*
CAESAR   I have said.
ANTONY   You shall not find,
35 Though you be therein curious,° the least cause   *overly probing*
    For what you seem to fear. So the gods keep you
    And make the hearts of Romans serve your ends.
    We will here part.
CAESAR   Farewell, my dearest sister, fare thee well.
40 The elements be kind to thee and make
    Thy spirits all of comfort. Fare thee well.
OCTAVIA   My noble brother.
ANTONY   The April's in her eyes;° it is love's spring,   *She weeps*
    And these the showers to bring it on. Be cheerful.
45 OCTAVIA   Sir, look well to my husband's° house, and—   *(Antony's)*
CAESAR   What, Octavia?
OCTAVIA   I'll tell you in your ear.
ANTONY   Her tongue will not obey her heart, nor can
    Her heart inform her tongue. The swansdown feather

---

2. The phoenix, a legendary, self-resurrecting bird, only one of which existed at a time. It was believed to live for several centuries, to die in flames, and to be reborn from its own ashes.
3. Dung patches (between which the beetle crawls to feed and breed); perhaps, wing cases (with which the beetle flies).
4. *and as . . . approof:* and (such a wife) as to make my largest contractual commitment (also, my closest tie of affection: here, Caesar's to Octavia) approved on the basis of what you will prove to be.

That stands upon the swell at the full of tide
And neither way inclines.[5]

50 ENOBARBUS [*aside to* AGRIPPA]   Will Caesar weep?

AGRIPPA   He has a cloud in 's face.

ENOBARBUS   He were the worse for that were he a horse;[6]
So is he being a man.

AGRIPPA   Why, Enobarbus,
When Antony found Julius Caesar dead,
55 He cried almost to roaring. And he wept
When at Philippi he found Brutus slain.

ENOBARBUS   That year, indeed, he was troubled with a rheum.°   *flu; watery eyes*
What willingly he did confound° he wailed,°   *destroy / mourned*
Believe't, till I weep too.

CAESAR   No, sweet Octavia,
60 You shall hear from me still.° The time shall not   *constantly*
Outgo[7] my thinking on° you.   *of*

ANTONY   Come, sir, come,
I'll wrestle with you in my strength of love.
Look, here I have you. [*He embraces* CAESAR.] Thus I let you go,
And give you to the gods.

CAESAR   Adieu. Be happy.

65 LEPIDUS   Let all the number of the stars give light
To thy fair way.

CAESAR   Farewell, farewell.
      ([*He*] *kisses* OCTAVIA.)

ANTONY   Farewell.
                                         Trumpets sound. Exeunt.

3.3

Enter CLEOPATRA, CHARMIAN, IRAS, *and* ALEXAS.

CLEOPATRA   Where is the fellow?

ALEXAS   Half afeard to come.

CLEOPAPTRA   Go to, go to! Come hither, sir.
      Enter the MESSENGER *as before.*

ALEXAS   Good majesty,
Herod of Jewry[1] dare not look upon you
But when you are well pleased.

CLEOPATRA   That Herod's head
5 I'll have, but how, when Antony is gone
Through whom I might command it? —Come thou near.

MESSENGER   Most gracious majesty.

CLEOPATRA   Didst thou behold Octavia?

MESSENGER   Ay, dread queen.

CLEOPATRA   Where?

MESSENGER   Madam, in Rome.
I looked her in the face and saw her led
10 Between her brother and Mark Antony.

CLEOPATRA   Is she as tall as me?

MESSENGER   She is not, madam.

CLEOPATRA   Didst hear her speak? Is she shrill-tongued or low?

---

5. *the swansdown . . . inclines:* (she is like) the feather of a swan's down that floats in still water, unmoving (just as she can't speak) when the tide is about to turn. Octavia's emotions, balanced between brother and husband, are too strong to allow speech.
6. A horse with a cloud—a dark rather than a white star—on its face was supposedly ill tempered.
7. *The . . . / Outgo:* Even time will not endure beyond.
3.3 Location: Alexandria.
1. Renowned for his irrational cruelty. See note to 1.2.28.

MESSENGER   Madam, I heard her speak; she is low voiced.

CLEOPATRA   That's not so good.° He cannot like her long.   *favorable to Octavia*

15   CHARMIAN   Like her? O Isis, 'tis impossible!

CLEOPATRA   I think so, Charmian—dull of tongue and dwarfish!
What majesty is in her gait? Remember,
If ere thou look'st on majesty.

MESSENGER   She creeps.
Her motion and her station° are as one.   *standing still*

20   She shows° a body rather than a life,   *seems to be*
A statue than° a breather.   *rather than*

CLEOPAPTRA   Is this certain?

MESSENGER   Or I have no observance.°   *powers of observation*

CHARMIAN   Three in Egypt cannot make better note.[2]

CLEOPATRA   He's very knowing; I do perceive't.

25   There's nothing in her yet.
The fellow has good judgment.

CHARMIAN   Excellent.

CLEOPATRA   Guess at her years, I prithee.

MESSENGER   Madam, she was a widow.

CLEOPATRA   Widow? Charmian, hark.

30   MESSENGER   And I do think she's thirty.°   *(Cleopatra was 38)*

CLEOPATRA   Bear'st thou her face in mind? Is't long or round?

MESSSENGER   Round, even to faultiness.

CLEOPATRA   For the most part, too, they are foolish that are so.
Her hair, what color?

MESSENGER   Brown, madam, and her forehead
As low as she would wish it.[3]

35   CLEOPATRA   There's gold for thee.
Thou must not take my former sharpness ill.
I will employ thee back° again. I find thee   *to go back to Rome*
Most fit for business. Go, make thee ready.
Our letters are prepared.   [*Exit* MESSENGER.]

CHARMIAN   A proper° man.   *An admirable*

40   CLEOPATRA   Indeed, he is so. I repent me much
That so I harried him. Why, methinks by him°   *by his account*
This creature's no such thing.°   *nothing special*

CHARMIAN   Nothing, madam.

CLEOPATRA   The man hath seen some majesty and should know.

CHARMIAN   Hath he seen majesty? Isis else defend,

45   And serving you so long.[4]

CLEOPATRA   I have one thing more to ask him yet, good Charmian.
But 'tis no matter; thou shalt bring him to me
Where I will write. All may be well enough.

CHARMIAN   I warrant you, madam.   *Exeunt.*

3.4

Enter ANTONY *and* OCTAVIA.

ANTONY   Nay, nay, Octavia, not only that—
That were excusable, that and thousands more
Of semblable° import—but he hath waged   *like*
New wars 'gainst Pompey; made his will and read it

---

2. *Three . . . note:* There are not three better witnesses
in all Egypt.
3. So that she would wish it no lower: high foreheads
were admired.

4. *Isis . . . long:* He surely has, considering how long
he's served you. *else defend:* May Isis prevent it from
being otherwise.
3.4 Location: Athens.

5   To public ear;[1] spoke scantly° of me.   *meanly*
When perforce he could not
But pay me terms of honor, cold and sickly
He vented them—most narrow measure° lent me.   *little credit*
When the best hint° was given him, he not took't   *opportunity*
Or did it from his teeth.°   *insincerely*

10 OCTAVIA   O my good lord,
Believe not all, or, if you must believe,
Stomach° not all. A more unhappy lady,   *Resent*
If this division chance, ne'er stood between
Praying for both parts.

15   The good gods will mock me presently:°   *at once*
When I shall pray, "Oh, bless my lord and husband,"
Undo° that prayer by crying out as loud,   *I'll then undo*
"Oh, bless my brother." Husband win, win brother,
Prays and destroys the prayer[2]—no midway
Twixt these extremes at all.

20 ANTONY   Gentle Octavia,
Let your best love draw to that point which seeks
Best to preserve it.[3] If I lose mine honor,
I lose myself. Better I were not yours
Than yours so branchless.° But as you requested,   *amputated*
25   Yourself shall go between 's. The meantime, lady,
I'll raise the preparation of a war
Shall stain your brother.° Make your soonest haste,   *dim his luster*
So° your desires are yours.   *In this way; If*
OCTAVIA   Thanks to my lord.
The Jove of power make me, most weak, most weak,
30   Your reconciler. Wars twixt you twain would be
As if the world should cleave and that slain men
Should solder up the rift.[4]
ANTONY   When it appears to you where this begins,°   *who started this*
Turn your displeasure that way, for our faults
35   Can never be so equal that your love
Can equally move with° them. Provide° your going, *judge / Prepare for*
Choose your own company, and command what cost
Your heart has mind to.   *Exeunt.*

3.5

Enter ENOBARBUS *and* EROS.

ENOBARBUS   How now, friend Eros?
EROS   There's strange news come, sir.
ENOBARBUS   What, man?
EROS   Caesar and Lepidus have made wars upon Pompey.
5 ENOBARBUS   This is old. What is the success?°   *outcome*
EROS   Caesar, having made use of him° in the wars 'gainst Pom- *(Lepidus)*
pey, presently denied him rivality,° would not let him partake *equal partnership*
in the glory of the action, and not resting° here, accuses him *stopping*
of letters he had formerly wrote to Pompey. Upon his° own *(Caesar's)*
10 appeal° seizes him, so the poor third is up° till death enlarge *accusation / imprisoned*
his confine.

1. Caesar's act implies promises to the public.
2. Wishing well for husband and then brother is to
pray and then to undermine the prayer.
3. *Let . . . it:* Choose the one of us (Antony or Caesar)

who best strives to preserve your love.
4. *that . . . rift:* many deaths would be needed to repair
the breach.
3.5 Location: Scene continues.

ENOBARBUS   Then, world, thou hast a pair of chaps,° no more,°   jaws / (than two)
And throw° between them all the food thou hast,   if you should throw
They'll grind the one the other. Where's Antony?

15   EROS   He's walking in the garden, thus, and spurns°   kicks
The rush° that lies before him; cries, "Fool Lepidus!"   rushes
And threats the throat of that his officer°   of that officer of his
That murdered Pompey.[1]

ENOBARBUS   Our great navy's rigged.°   prepared

EROS   For Italy and Caesar. More,° Domitius: There's more (to say)

20   My lord desires you presently. My news
I might have told hereafter.

ENOBARBUS   'Twill be naught[2]—
But let it be. Bring me to Antony.

EROS   Come, sir.   *Exeunt.*

3.6

Enter AGRIPPA, MAECENAS, *and* CAESAR.

CAESAR   Contemning° Rome, he has done all this and more   Despising
In Alexandria. Here's the manner of't:
I'th' marketplace on a tribunal° silvered,   platform
Cleopatra and himself in chairs of gold

5   Were publicly enthroned. At the feet sat
Caesarion, whom they call my father's[1] son,
And all the unlawful issue that their lust
Since then hath made between them. Unto her
He gave the stablishment° of Egypt, made her   full possession

10   Of lower Syria, Cyprus, Lydia,[2]
Absolute queen.

MAECENAS   This in the public eye?

CAESAR   I'th' common showplace where they exercise,[3]
His sons were there proclaimed the kings of kings;
Great Media, Parthia, and Armenia

15   He gave to Alexander. To Ptolemy he assigned
Syria, Cilicia, and Phoenicia. She
In th' habiliments° of the goddess Isis   costume
That day appeared, and oft before gave audience,
As 'tis reported, so.°   in this costume

20   MAECENAS   Let Rome be thus informed.

AGRIPPA   Who, queasy with° his insolence already,   sick of
Will their good thoughts call° from him.   remove

CAESAR   The people knows it and have now received
His accusations.

AGRIPPA   Who does he accuse?

25   CAESAR   Caesar, and that having in Sicily
Sextus Pompeius spoiled,° we had not rated° him   ransacked / allotted
His part o'th' isle.° Then does he say he lent me   (Sicily)
Some shipping unrestored.° Lastly, he frets   not returned (by me)
That Lepidus of the triumvirate

---

1. Historically, though Shakespeare leaves Antony's responsibility for the killing unclear, Pompey was said to have been murdered at the command of Antony, who here regrets the death because Pompey might have been a useful ally against Caesar.
2. Of no consequence; extremely harmful.
3.6 Location: Rome.
1. Julius Caesar (who adopted his grandnephew

Octavius as his son). See 2.2.239–40 with note and note to 5.2.358.
2. District on the western coast of Asia Minor. Shakespeare took the name from North's translation of Plutarch, but the original has "Libya."
3. In the arena (theater) where they engage in sports (perform).

30	Should be deposed, and being that,° we detain	*being deposed*
	All his revenue.	

AGRIPPA　　　　　Sir, this should be answered.

CAESAR　'Tis done already and the messenger gone.
I have told him Lepidus was grown too cruel,
That he his high authority abused

35 And did deserve his change. For° what I have conquered,   *As for*
I grant him part; but then in his Armenia
And other of his conquered kingdoms, I
Demand the like.

MAECENAS　　　　He'll never yield to that.

CAESAR　Nor must not then be yielded to in this.

　　　　　Enter OCTAVIA *with her train.*

40 OCTAVIA　Hail, Caesar, and my lord. Hail, most dear Caesar!

CAESAR　That ever I should call thee castaway!

OCTAVIA　You have not called me so, nor have you cause.

CAESAR　Why have you stol'n upon us thus? You come not
Like Caesar's sister. The wife of Antony

45 Should have an army for an usher and
The neighs of horse to tell of her approach
Long ere she did appear. The trees by th' way
Should have borne men, and expectation fainted,
Longing for what it had not. Nay, the dust

50 Should have ascended to the roof of heaven,
Raised by your populous troops. But you are come
A market maid to Rome, and have prevented°   *(by coming too early)*
The ostentation° of our love, which, left unshown,   *public display*
Is often left unloved.[4] We should have met you

55 By sea and land, supplying every stage°   *(of the voyage)*
With an augmented greeting.

OCTAVIA　　　　　　　　Good my lord,
To come thus was I not constrained, but did it
On my free will. My lord, Mark Antony,
Hearing that you prepared for war, acquainted

60 My grievèd ear withal, whereon I begged
His pardon for° return.   *permission to*

CAESAR　　　　　　　　Which soon he granted,
Being an abstract 'tween his lust and him.

OCTAVIA　Do not say so, my lord.

CAESAR　　　　　　　　I have eyes upon him,
And his affairs come to me on the wind.
Where is he now?

65 OCTAVIA　　　　　　My lord, in Athens.

CAESAR　No, my most wrongèd sister. Cleopatra
Hath nodded him to her. He hath given his empire
Up to a whore, who° now are levying   *both of them*
The kings o'th' earth for war. He hath assembled

70 Bocchus, the King of Libya; Archelaus
Of Cappadocia; Philadelphos, King
Of Paphlagonia; the Thracian king, Adallas;
King Manchus of Arabia; King of Pont;
Herod of Jewry; Mithridates, King

4. Is often thought not to be love at all. Or, *which . . . unloved:* lack of opportunity to demonstrate love often leads to its actual decline.

75   Of Comagene; Polemon and Amintas,
       The Kings of Mede and Lycaonia,[5]
       With a more larger° list of scepters.   *yet longer*
OCTAVIA Ay me, most wretched,
       That have my heart parted betwixt two friends
       That does afflict each other.
80 CAESAR   Welcome hither.
       Your letters did withhold our° breaking forth   *restrain me from*
       Till we perceived both how you were wrong° led   *wrongly*
       And we in negligent danger.° Cheer your heart.   *danger from negligence*
       Be you not troubled with the time,° which drives   *present business*
85   O'er your content° these strong necessities,   *contentment*
       But let determined things to destiny
       Hold unbewailed their way.[6] Welcome to Rome,
       Nothing more dear to me. You are abused
       Beyond the mark° of thought, and the high gods   *limits*
90   To do you justice makes his ministers°   *agents*
       Of us and those that love you. Best of comfort,
       And ever welcome to us.
AGRIPPA   Welcome, lady.
MAECENAS Welcome, dear madam.
       Each heart in Rome does love and pity you.
95   Only th'adulterous Antony, most large°   *unlimited*
       In his abominations, turns you off
       And gives his potent regiment° to a trull°   *powerful rule / whore*
       That noises it° against us.   *cries out*
OCTAVIA   Is it so, sir?
CAESAR Most certain. Sister, welcome. Pray you,
100 Be ever known to patience. My dear'st sister!   *Exeunt.*

3.7
Enter CLEOPATRA *and* ENOBARBUS.

CLEOPATRA I will be° even with thee, doubt it not.   *get*
ENOBARBUS But why, why, why?
CLEOPATRA Thou hast forespoke° my being in these wars   *opposed*
       And say'st it is not fit.
ENOBARBUS   Well, is it, is it?
5 CLEOPATRA If not denounced° against us, why should not we   *If war is declared*
       Be there in person?
ENOBARBUS   Well, I could reply:
       If we should serve with horse and mares together,
       The horse were merely lost.[1] The mares would bear°   *seduce; carry*
       A soldier and his horse.
CLEOPATRA   What is't you say?
10 ENOBARBUS Your presence needs must puzzle° Antony,   *distract*
       Take from his heart, take from his brain, from 's time,
       What should not then be spared. He is already
       Traduced° for levity, and 'tis said in Rome   *Slandered*
       That Photinus, an eunuch, and your maids
       Manage this war.
15 CLEOPATRA   Sink Rome,° and their tongues rot   *To hell with Rome*

---

5. All kings from the East.
6. *let . . . way:* let predetermined events go to their destined conclusions without complaint.
3.7 Location: Antony's camp, near Actium, Greece.

1. *If . . . lost:* If we take both male and female horses (whores) to the wars, the males would have no hope of triumphing, because of the females ("merely" equals "mare-ly").

That speak against us! A charge° we bear i'th' war,   *An expense; duty*
And as the president of my kingdom will
Appear there for° a man. Speak not against it;   *as if I were*
I will not stay behind.
       Enter ANTONY *and* CANIDIUS.
20 ENOBARBUS   Nay, I have done. Here comes the Emperor.
ANTONY   Is it not strange, Canidius,
  That from Tarentum and Brundusium[2]
  He could so quickly cut° the Ionian° Sea   *cut across / Adriatic*
  And take in° Toryne?° —You have heard on't, sweet?   *overrun / (near Actium)*
25 CLEOPATRA   Celerity is never more admired°   *wondered at*
  Than by the negligent.
ANTONY   A good rebuke,
  Which might have well becomed the best of men
  To taunt at slackness. Canidius, we
  Will fight with him by sea.
CLEOPATRA   By sea, what else?
CANIDIUS   Why will my lord do so?
30 ANTONY   For that he dares us to't.
ENOBARBUS   So hath my lord dared him to single fight.
CANIDIUS   Ay, and to wage this battle at Pharsalia,°   *(near Actium)*
  Where Caesar fought with Pompey. But these offers
  Which serve not for his vantage, he shakes off,
  And so should you.
35 ENOBARBUS   Your ships are not well manned,
  Your mariners are muleteers,° reapers, people   *mule drivers*
  Engrossed° by swift impress.° In Caesar's fleet   *Amassed / conscription*
  Are those that often have 'gainst Pompey fought.
  Their ships are yare,° yours heavy. No disgrace   *smooth running*
40   Shall fall° you for refusing him at sea,   *befall*
  Being prepared for land.
ANTONY   By sea, by sea.
ENOBARBUS   Most worthy sir, you therein throw away
  The absolute soldiership you have by land,
  Distract° your army, which doth most consist   *Divert*
45   Of war-marked footmen, leave unexecuted°   *untapped*
  Your own renownèd knowledge, quite forgo
  The way which promises assurance,° and   *victory*
  Give up yourself merely° to chance and hazard   *completely*
  From firm security.
ANTONY   I'll fight at sea.
50 CLEOPATRA   I have sixty sails, Caesar none better.
ANTONY   Our overplus of shipping will we burn,[3]
  And with the rest full manned, from th' head° of Actium   *promontory*
  Beat th'approaching Caesar. But if we fail,
  We then can do't at land.
       Enter a MESSENGER.
               Thy business?
55 MESSENGER   The news is true, my lord. He is descried;°   *He has been seen*
  Caesar has taken Toryne.   [*Exit* MESSENGER.]
ANTONY   Can he be there in person? 'Tis impossible!

---

2. Ports in southeastern Italy.
3. Antony seems to have burned his excess ("over-plus") ships because he did not have enough sailors
to man them adequately and feared that they could easily be taken by Octavius Caesar.

Strange, that his power° should be. Canidius,   *his entire army*
Our nineteen legions thou shalt hold by land,
60 And our twelve thousand horse. We'll to our ship.
—Away, my Thetis.[4]
        Enter a SOLDIER.[5]
                        How now, worthy soldier?
SOLDIER   O noble emperor, do not fight by sea.
Trust not to rotten planks. Do you misdoubt
This sword and these my wounds? Let th'Egyptians
65 And the Phoenicians go a-ducking.° We   *to sea*
Have used to conquer standing on the earth
And fighting foot to foot.
ANTONY   Well, well, away!
        Exeunt ANTONY, CLEOPATRA, *and* ENOBARBUS.
SOLDIER   By Hercules, I think I am i'th' right.
CANIDIUS   Soldier, thou art, but his whole action grows
70 Not in the power on't.[6] So our leader's led,
And we are women's men.
SOLDIER   You keep by land
The legions and the horse whole, do you not?
CANIDIUS   Marcus Octavius, Marcus Justeius,
Publicola, and Caelius are for sea,
75 But we keep whole° by land. This speed of Caesar's   *stay undivided*
Carries beyond° belief.   *Exceeds*
SOLDIER   While he was yet in Rome,
His power went out in such distractions° as   *separate detachments*
Beguiled all spies.
CANIDIUS   Who's his lieutenant, hear you?
SOLDIER   They say one Taurus.
CANIDIUS   Well I know the man.
        Enter a MESSENGER.
80 MESSENGER   The Emperor calls, Canidius.
CANIDIUS   With news the time's with labor and throws forth
Each minute, some.[7]   *Exeunt.*

3.8
        Enter CAESAR *with his army, marching*[*, and* TAURUS].
CAESAR   Taurus?
TAURUS   My lord?
CAESAR   Strike not by land; keep whole.° Provoke not battle   *stay in reserve*
Till we have done at sea. Do not exceed
5 The prescript° of this scroll. Our fortune lies   *written orders*
Upon this jump.°   *Exeunt.*   *ploy*

3.9
        Enter ANTONY *and* ENOBARBUS.
ANTONY   Set we our squadrons on yond side o'th' hill
In eye° of Caesar's battle,° from which place   *view / battle line*
We may the number of the ships behold
And so proceed accordingly.   *Exeunt.*

---

4. Sea goddess, mother of the Greek hero Achilles.
5. TEXTUAL COMMENT For the significance of the
possible identification of this unnamed soldier with
the character Scarus in 3.10, see Digital Edition TC 5.
6. His entire plan is made without taking into account

his resources.
7. *throws . . . some:* each minute, more news is born.
3.8 Location: Near Actium.
3.9 Location: Scene continues.

3.10

CANIDIUS *marcheth with his land army one way over
the stage, and* TAURUS, *the lieutenant of Caesar, the
other way. After their going in is heard the noise of a
sea fight. Alarum. Enter* ENOBARBUS.

ENOBARBUS Naught, naught, all naught!° I can behold no longer: *lost; ruined*
Th'Antoniad, the Egyptian admiral,°   *flagship*
With all their sixty fly and turn the rudder.
To see't mine eyes are blasted.°   *(as if by lightning)*

Enter SCARUS.

SCARUS   Gods and goddesses,
All the whole synod° of them!   *assembly*
5   ENOBARBUS   What's° thy passion?   *What provokes*
SCARUS The greater cantle° of the world is lost   *corner; portion*
With° very ignorance.° We have kissed away   *Through / idiocy*
Kingdoms and provinces.
ENOBARBUS   How appears the fight?
SCARUS On our side, like the tokened pestilence,[1]
10 Where death is sure. Yon ribald nag of Egypt—
Whom leprosy o'ertake—i'th' midst o'th' fight,
When vantage like a pair of twins appeared
Both as the same[2]—or rather, ours the elder°—   *ours the stronger*
The breeze upon her[3] like a cow in June,
Hoists sails and flies.
15 ENOBARBUS   That I beheld.
Mine eyes did sicken at the sight and could not
Endure a further view.
SCARUS   She once being loofed,[4]
The noble ruin° of her magic, Antony,   *casualty*
Claps on his sea-wing,° and—like a doting mallard°—   *sails / male duck*
20 Leaving the fight in° height, flies after her!   *at its*
I never saw an action of such shame.
Experience, manhood, honor ne'er before
Did violate so itself.
ENOBARBUS   Alack, alack!

Enter CANIDIUS.

CANIDIUS Our fortune on the sea is out of breath
25 And sinks most lamentably. Had our general
Been what he knew himself,° it had gone well.   *(to be)*
Oh, he has given example for our flight
Most grossly by his own!
ENOBARBUS Ay, are you thereabouts?° Why, then, good night   *of the same mind*
indeed.
30 CANIDIUS Toward Peloponnesus are they fled.
SCARUS 'Tis easy to't,° and there I will attend   *to reach that place*
What further comes.
CANIDIUS   To Caesar will I render
My legions and my horse. Six kings already
Show me the way of yielding.
ENOBARBUS   I'll yet follow

3.10 Location: Scene continues.
1. Plague manifested in tokens (red spots presaging
death).
2. When the fight could have gone either way.

3. Bitten by a gadfly; driven by a breeze.
4. Luffed—prepared to sail close to the wind (ready
to leave); aloof.

35 The wounded chance° of Antony, though my reason   *fortune*
    Sits in the wind against me.°   [*Exeunt.*]   *Opposes*

3.11

Enter ANTONY *with* ATTENDANTS.

ANTONY   Hark, the land bids me tread no more upon't.
It is ashamed to bear me. Friends, come hither.
I am so lated° in the world that I   *lost in the dark*
Have lost my way forever. I have a ship
5   Laden with gold. Take that; divide it. Fly,
And make your peace with Caesar.

ATTENDANTS   Fly? Not we.

ANTONY   I have fled myself, and have instructed cowards
To run and show their shoulders.° Friends, begone!   *backs*
I have myself resolved upon a course
10 Which has no need of you. Begone!
My treasure's in the harbor. Take it. Oh,
I followed that° I blush to look upon.   *that which*
My very hairs do mutiny, for the white
Reprove the brown for rashness, and they them°   *they the others*
15 For fear and doting. Friends, begone! You shall
Have letters from me to some friends that will
Sweep° your way for you. Pray you, look not sad,   *Clear*
Nor make replies of loathness.° Take the hint°   *reluctance / chance*
Which my despair proclaims. Let that be left
20 Which leaves° itself. To the seaside straightway!   *ceases to be; flees*
I will possess you of that ship and treasure.
Leave me, I pray, a little°—pray you now,   *for a brief time*
Nay, do so, for indeed I have lost command;°   *the right to command you*
Therefore I pray you. I'll see you by and by.
                                    [*Exeunt* ATTENDANTS.]
    [ANTONY] *sits down.*
    Enter CLEOPATRA, *led by* CHARMIAN, [IRAS,] *and* EROS.
25 EROS   Nay, gentle madam, to him, comfort him.
IRAS   Do, most dear queen.
CHARMIAN   Do, why, what else?
CLEOPATRA   Let me sit down. O Juno!
ANTONY   No, no, no, no, no.
30 EROS   See you here, sir?
ANTONY   Oh, fie, fie, fie!
CHARMIAN   Madam.
IRAS   Madam, oh, good empress!
EROS   Sir, sir.
35 ANTONY   Yes, my lord, yes! He° at Philippi kept   *(Octavius)*
His sword e'en like a dancer,° while I struck   *(for decoration only)*
The lean and wrinkled Cassius, and 'twas I
That the mad Brutus ended.° He alone   *defeated*
Dealt on lieutenantry° and no practice had   *Fought through others*
40 In the brave squares° of war, yet now—no matter.   *fine formations*
CLEOPATRA   Ah, stand by.
EROS   The Queen, my lord! The Queen!
IRAS   Go to him, madam. Speak to him;
He's unqualitied° with very shame.   *lost his sense of self*

3.11 Location: Alexandria.

45 CLEOPATRA [*rising*]   Well, then, sustain me. Oh!

EROS   Most noble sir, arise. The Queen approaches;
   Her head's declined, and death will seize her but°   *unless*
   Your comfort makes the rescue.

ANTONY   I have offended reputation,
   A most unnoble swerving.°   *slippage*

50 EROS   Sir, the Queen.

ANTONY   Oh, whither hast thou led me, Egypt? See
   How I convey my shame out of° thine eyes,   *out of sight of; from*
   By looking back° what I have left behind   *recalling*
   'Stroyed° in dishonor.   *Destroyed*

CLEOPATRA   O my lord, my lord!

55   Forgive my fearful sails. I little thought
   You would have followed.

ANTONY   Egypt, thou knew'st too well
   My heart was to thy rudder tied by th' strings,
   And thou shouldst tow me after. O'er my spirit
   Thy full supremacy thou knew'st and that
60   Thy beck° might from the bidding of the gods   *call*
   Command me.

CLEOPATRA   Oh, my pardon.

ANTONY   Now I must
   To the young man[1] send humble treaties,° dodge   *appeals*
   And palter in the shifts of lowness,[2] who
   With half the bulk o'th' world played as I pleased,
65   Making and marring fortunes. You did know
   How much you were my conqueror, and that
   My sword, made weak by my affection,° would   *desire*
   Obey it on all cause.°   *for any reason*

CLEOPATRA   Pardon, pardon!

ANTONY   Fall° not a tear, I say. One of them rates°   *Weep / is worth*
70   All that is won and lost. Give me a kiss.
      [*They kiss.*]
   Even this repays me.
   We sent our schoolmaster.° Is 'a° come back? *tutor to our children / he*
   Love, I am full of lead. —Some wine
   Within there, and our viands!° Fortune knows   *food*
75   We scorn her most when most she offers blows.   *Exeunt.*

3.12

Enter CAESAR, [THIDIAS,] AGRIPPA, *and* DOLABELLA,
   with others.

CAESAR   Let him appear that's come from Antony.
   Know you him?

DOLABELLA   Caesar, 'tis his schoolmaster—
   An argument° that he is plucked, when hither   *A proof*
   He sends so poor a pinion° of his wing,   *an outer feather*
5   Which° had superfluous kings for messengers   *He who*
   Not many moons gone by.

      Enter AMBASSADOR *from Antony.*

CAESAR   Approach and speak.

---

1. Octavius Caesar at this time (31 B.C.E.) was thirty-two years old, Antony fifty-one.
2. *dodge . . . lowness:* shuffle and play fast and loose in the shifty ways of a man brought low.

3.12 Location: Caesar's camp, Egypt.

AMBASSADOR   Such as I am, I come from Antony.
I was of late as petty° to his ends   *inconsequential*
As is the morn dew on the myrtle leaf
To his grand sea.[1]
10 CAESAR   Be't so. Declare thine office.°   *business*
AMBASSADOR   Lord of his fortunes, he salutes thee and
Requires° to live in Egypt, which not granted,   *Asks*
He lessens his requests and to thee sues
To let him breathe between the heavens and earth
15 A private man in Athens. This for him.
Next, Cleopatra does confess thy greatness,
Submits her to thy might, and of thee craves
The circle° of the Ptolomies for her heirs,   *crown*
Now hazarded to thy grace.°   *placed at your mercy*
CAESAR   For Antony,
20 I have no ears to his request. The Queen
Of audience nor desire shall fail, so[2] she
From Egypt drive her all-disgracèd friend
Or take his life there. This if she perform
She shall not sue unheard. So to them both.
AMBASSADOR   Fortune pursue thee!
25 CAESAR   Bring° him through the bands.°   *Escort / ranks*
                    [*Exit* AMBASSADOR, *attended.*]
[*to* THIDIAS] To try thy eloquence, now 'tis time. Dispatch;
From Antony win Cleopatra. Promise,
And in our name, what she requires; add more
(From thine invention°) offers. Women are not   *imagination*
30 In° their best fortunes strong, but want will perjure   *While in*
The ne'er-touched vestal.[3] Try thy cunning, Thidias;
Make thine own edict° for thy pains, which we   *Command your reward*
Will answer as a law.
THIDIAS   Caesar, I go.
CAESAR   Observe how Antony becomes his flaw,°   *reacts to his fall*
35 And what thou think'st his very action speaks
In every power that moves.[4]
THIDIAS   Caesar, I shall.   *Exeunt.*

3.13

Enter CLEOPATRA, ENOBARBUS, CHARMIAN, *and* IRAS.

CLEOPATRA   What shall we do, Enobarbus?
ENOBARBUS   Think,° and die.   *(about our misery)*
CLEOPATRA   Is Antony or we in fault for this?
ENOBARBUS   Antony only, that would make his will°   *lust*
Lord of his reason. What though° you fled   *What if*
5 From that great face of war, whose several ranges°   *battle lines*
Frighted each other? Why should he follow?
The itch of his affection should not then
Have nicked° his captainship at such a point,   *bettered (gambling term)*
When half to half the world opposed, he being
10 The merèd° question? 'Twas a shame no less   *disputed*

---

1. In relation to the great sea, ultimate source of
dew, that is Antony.
2. Shall not fail to receive either a hearing or fulfillment of her wishes, as long as.
3. *want . . . vestal:* need will make the purest virgin
break her vows.
4. *his very . . . moves:* his actions themselves reveal
in every move he makes.
3.13 Location: Alexandria.

Than was his loss to course° your flying flags   *chase*
And leave his navy gazing.

CLEOPATRA   Prithee, peace.

        Enter the AMBASSADOR *with* ANTONY.

ANTONY   Is that his answer?

AMBASSADOR   Ay, my lord.

15   ANTONY   The Queen shall then have courtesy, so° she   *as long as*
Will yield us up.

AMBASSADOR   He says so.

ANTONY   Let her know't.
—To the boy Caesar send this grizzled head,
And he will fill thy wishes to the brim
With principalities.

CLEOPATRA   That head, my lord?

20   ANTONY   To him again. Tell him he wears the rose
Of youth upon him, from which the world should note
Something particular.° His coin, ships, legions,   *anticipate the remarkable*
May be a coward's,[1] whose ministers° would prevail   *aides; underlings*
Under the service of a child as soon°   *as well*
25   As i'th' command of Caesar. I dare him therefore
To lay his gay caparisons° apart   *showy adornments*
And answer me declined,[2] sword against sword,
Ourselves alone. I'll write it. Follow me.

        [Exeunt ANTONY *and* AMBASSADOR.]

ENOBARBUS [*aside*]   Yes, like enough. High-battled° Caesar will   *With many troops*
30   Unstate° his happiness and be staged to th' show[3]   *Overthrow*
Against a sworder! I see men's judgments are
A parcel of° their fortunes, and things outward   *Consistent with*
Do draw the inward quality after them
To suffer all alike.° That he should dream,   *To decay together*
35   Knowing all measures,[4] the full Caesar will
Answer° his emptiness. Caesar, thou hast subdued   *Fight; reply to*
His judgment too.[5]

        Enter a SERVANT.

SERVANT   A messenger from Caesar.

CLEOPATRA   What, no more ceremony? See, my women,
Against the blown° rose may they stop their nose   *decaying*
40   That° kneeled unto the buds. —Admit him, sir.   *Who once*

ENOBARBUS [*aside*]   Mine honesty° and I begin to square.°   *honor / square off; argue*
The loyalty well held° to fools does make   *given*
Our faith mere° folly. Yet he that can endure   *complete*
To follow with allegiance a fall'n lord
45   Does conquer him that did his master conquer
And earns a place i'th' story.

        Enter THIDIAS.

CLEOPATRA   Caesar's will?

THIDIAS   Hear it apart.

CLEOPATRA   None but friends. Say boldly.

---

1. Could just as well be a coward's (unless he does something special by himself).
2. And meet me past my prime, in my misfortune.
3. Be displayed to the public gaze (as in the London theater or Roman gladiatorial combat).
4. Having known the best and worst of times ("all measures" of fortune, both "full[ness]" and "empti-

ness," lines 35–36).
5. PERFORMANCE COMMENT For the consequences of treating Enobarbus's speech here as an aside (as the stage direction indicates), as a private address to Cleopatra, or as an aside overheard by Cleopatra, see Digital Edition PC 1.

THIDIAS   So haply° are they friends to Antony.   *possibly*
ENOBARBUS   He needs as many, sir, as Caesar has,
50   Or needs not us.[6] If Caesar please, our master
     Will leap to be his friend. For us, you know,
     Whose he is we are, and that is Caesar's.
THIDIAS   So,
     Thus then, thou most renowned: Caesar entreats,
     Not to consider° in what case thou stand'st   *be concerned*
     Further than he is Caesar.[7]
55   CLEOPATRA   Go on; right royal.°   *most generous*
THIDIAS   He knows that you embrace not Antony
     As you did love, but as you feared him.
CLEOPATRA   Oh.
THIDIAS   The scars upon your honor, therefore, he
     Does pity as constrainèd° blemishes,   *involuntary*
     Not as deserved.
60   CLEOPATRA   He is a god and knows
     What is most right. Mine honor was not yielded,
     But conquered merely.
ENOBARBUS [*aside*]   To be sure of that,
     I will ask Antony. Sir, sir, thou art so leaky
     That we must leave thee to thy sinking, for
     Thy dearest quit thee.   *Exit* ENOBARBUS.
65   THIDIAS   Shall I say to Caesar
     What you require° of him? For he partly begs   *request*
     To be desired to give. It much would please him,
     That of his fortunes you should make a staff
     To lean upon. But it would warm his spirits
70   To hear from me you had left Antony
     And put yourself under his shroud,°   *protection; burial sheet*
     The universal landlord.
CLEOPATRA   What's your name?
THIDIAS   My name is Thidias.
CLEOPATRA   Most kind messenger,
     Say to great Caesar this in deputation:°   *as my representative*
75   I kiss his conqu'ring hand. Tell him I am prompt
     To lay my crown at 's feet and there to kneel.
     Tell him from his all-obeying° breath I hear   *which all obey*
     The doom of Egypt.[8]
THIDIAS   'Tis your noblest course.
     Wisdom and fortune combating together,
80   If that the former dare but what it can,[9]
     No chance may shake it. Give me grace to lay
     My duty on your hand.
        [*He kisses her hand.*]
CLEOPATRA   Your Caesar's father oft,
     When he hath mused of taking kingdoms in,°   *subduing kingdoms*
85   Bestowed his lips on that unworthy place
     As° it rained kisses.   *As if*
        Enter ANTONY *and* ENOBARBUS.

6. *Or needs not us:* If the situation is truly hopeless,
he doesn't even need our friendship.
7. Beyond remembering that he is Caesar—and hence
nobly generous in forgiving insult and injury (but with
a more sinister undertone as well).
8. What he destines for Egypt and its queen.
9. If the wise man confines his daring to what is
possible.

ANTONY   Favors? By Jove that thunders!¹
    What art thou, fellow?
THIDIAS   One that but performs
    The bidding of the fullest° man and worthiest   *most successful*
    To have command obeyed.
ENOBARBUS   You will be whipped.
90 ANTONY   Approach there! Ah, you kite!° Now gods and devils!   *bird of prey; whore*
    Authority melts from me. Of late, when I cried, "Ho!"
    Like boys unto a muss² kings would start forth
    And cry, "Your will?" Have you no ears? I am
    Antony yet.
            Enter SERVANT[S].
                    Take hence this jack° and whip him.   *knave*
95 ENOBARBUS [*aside*]   'Tis better playing with a lion's whelp°   *cub*
    Than with an old one dying.
ANTONY   Moon and stars,
    Whip him! Were't twenty of the greatest tributaries
    That do acknowledge Caesar, should I find them
    So saucy with the hand of she here—what's her name
100 Since she was Cleopatra?³ Whip him, fellows,
    Till like a boy you see him cringe° his face   *distort*
    And whine aloud for mercy. Take him hence.
THIDIAS   Mark Antony!
ANTONY   Tug him away! Being whipped,
    Bring him again; the jack of Caesar's shall
105 Bear us an errand to him.
                    Exeunt [SERVANTS] *with* THIDIAS.
    You were half blasted° ere I knew you! Ha?   *decayed*
    Have I my pillow left unpressed in Rome,
    Forborne the getting° of a lawful race,   *begetting*
    And by a gem of women, to be abused
    By one that looks on feeders?°   *parasites; servants*
110 CLEOPATRA   Good my lord.
ANTONY   You have been a boggler° ever,   *fickle one*
    But when we in our viciousness grow hard
    (Oh, misery on't), the wise gods seal⁴ our eyes
    In our own filth, drop our clear judgments, make us
115 Adore our errors, laugh at 's while we strut
    To our confusion.
CLEOPATRA   Oh, is't come to this?
ANTONY   I found you as a morsel cold upon
    Dead Caesar's trencher.° Nay, you were a fragment°   *plate / leftover*
    Of Gneius Pompey's⁵—besides what hotter hours
120 Unregistered in vulgar fame° you have   *base gossip*
    Luxuriously° picked out. For I am sure,   *Wantonly*
    Though you can guess what temperance should be,
    You know not what it is.
CLEOPATRA   Wherefore is this?

1. PERFORMANCE COMMENT For the different views
of both Cleopatra and Antony that follow from having
Cleopatra's response to Thidias seem a betrayal of
Antony or, at the other extreme, an effort to protect
her defeated lover, see Digital Edition PC 2.
2. Game in which small items were tossed to the
ground for children to snatch and grab.

3. Antony's question suggests that since Cleopatra's
behavior has changed, her name must have changed
as well.
4. Blind: hawks' eyes were sealed (sewn up) to tame
them.
5. Older brother of the Pompey of the play and son of
Pompey the Great. See note to 1.5.31.

ANTONY To let a fellow that will take rewards
125 And say, "God quit° you" be familiar with   *repay*
My playfellow, your hand, this kingly seal
And plighter° of high hearts. Oh, that I were   *pledger*
Upon the hill of Basan to outroar
The hornèd herd,[6] for I have savage cause,
130 And to proclaim it civilly were like
A haltered° neck which does the hangman thank   *in the noose*
For being yare° about him.   *swift*
    Enter a SERVANT *with* THIDIAS.
               Is he whipped?
SERVANT Soundly, my lord.
ANTONY Cried he? and begged a pardon?
135 SERVANT He did ask favor.
ANTONY If that thy father live, let him repent
Thou wast not made his daughter, and be thou sorry
To follow Caesar in his triumph, since
Thou hast been whipped for following him. Henceforth
140 The white hand of a lady fever thee;[7]
Shake thou to look on't. Get thee back to Caesar.
Tell him thy entertainment.° Look° thou say   *treatment / See that*
He makes me angry with him, for he seems
Proud and disdainful, harping on what I am,
145 Not what he knew I was. He makes me angry,
And at this time most easy 'tis to do't,
When my good stars that were my former guides
Have empty left their orbs° and shot their fires   *spheres*
Into th'abysm of hell. If he mislike
150 My speech and what is done, tell him he has
Hipparchus, my enfranchèd° bondman, whom   *emancipated*
He may at pleasure whip, or hang, or torture,
As he shall like to quit° me. Urge it thou.   *requite*
Hence with thy stripes.° Begone!   *wounds*
    Exeunt [SERVANT *and*] THIDIAS.
CLEOPATRA   Have you done yet?
155 ANTONY Alack, our terrene moon[8] is now eclipsed,
And it portends alone the fall of Antony.
CLEOPATRA I must stay his time.[9]
ANTONY To flatter Caesar, would you mingle eyes
With one that ties his points.[1]
CLEOPATRA   Not know me yet?
ANTONY Cold-hearted toward me?
160 CLEOPATRA   Ah, dear, if I be so,
From my cold heart let heaven engender hail,
And poison it in the source, and the first stone
Drop in my neck.° As it determines,° so   *throat / turns to liquid*
Dissolve my life; the next Caesarion smite;
165 Till by degrees the memory of my womb,°   *my children*
Together with my brave Egyptians all,

---

6. Alluding to the bulls of the hill of Basan (Bashan) in Psalms 68:15 and 22:12; Antony sees himself as a cuckold (a man whose wife has committed adultery), conventionally imagined with horns.
7. May the white hand of a lady make you shiver with fear, as from a fever.

8. Terrestrial moon goddess—Cleopatra.
9. I must hold my tongue until he is over his rage.
1. *would . . . points*: would you flirt with one of his servants? *points*: laces (attaching stockings to other clothing).

By the discandying° of this pelleted storm   *dissolving*
Lie graveless till the flies and gnats of Nile
Have buried them for prey!

ANTONY   I am satisfied.

170   Caesar sets down in° Alexandria, where   *besieges*
I will oppose his fate.[2] Our force by land
Hath nobly held, our severed navy too
Have knit again, and fleet,° threat'ning most sealike.   *are afloat*
Where hast thou been, my heart?° Dost thou hear, lady?   *bravery*

175   If from the field I shall return once more
To kiss these lips, I will appear in blood.°   *bloody; vigorous*
I and my sword will earn our chronicle.°   *historical reputation*
There's hope in't yet.

CLEOPATRA   That's my brave lord.

ANTONY   I will be treble-sinewed, -hearted, -breathed,
180   And fight maliciously.° For when mine hours   *furiously*
Were nice[3] and lucky, men did ransom° lives   *buy their*
Of° me for jests.° But now I'll set my teeth   *From / trinkets*
And send to darkness all that stop me. Come,
Let's have one other gaudy° night. Call to me   *merry*
185   All my sad captains. Fill our bowls once more;
Let's mock the midnight bell.[4]

CLEOPATRA   It is my birthday.
I had thought t'have held it poor,° but since my lord   *modestly commemorated it*
Is Antony again, I will be Cleopatra.

ANTONY   We will yet do well.

190   CLEOPATRA   Call all his noble captains to my lord.

ANTONY   Do so. We'll speak to them, and tonight I'll force
The wine peep through their scars. Come on, my queen,
There's sap in't° yet. The next time I do fight   *vigor in (our cause)*
I'll make death love me, for I will contend°   *do battle*
195   Even with his pestilent° scythe.   *plague-dealing*

Exeunt [all but ENOBARBUS].

ENOBARBUS   Now he'll outstare° the lightning. To be furious°   *stare down / in a frenzy*
Is to be frighted out of fear, and in that mood
The dove will peck the estridge;° and I see still°   *a kind of hawk / always*
A diminution in our captain's brain
200   Restores his heart. When valor preys on reason,
It eats the sword it fights with. I will seek
Some way to leave him.   *Exit.*

4.1

Enter CAESAR, AGRIPPA, *and* MAECENAS, *with his
army,* CAESAR *reading a letter.*

CAESAR   He calls me "boy" and chides as° he had power   *as though*
To beat me out of Egypt. My messenger
He hath whipped with rods—dares me to personal combat,
Caesar to Antony! Let the old ruffian know
5   I have many other ways to die; meantime
Laugh at° his challenge.   *Mock*

MAECENAS   Caesar must think,

---

2. I will resist his apparently destined victory.
3. *Were nice:* Permitted me to pick and choose, to act with noble generosity; were lascivious; were pampered.
4. Let's make a mockery of the hour by revelry; let's mock the death knell that fate seems to ring for us.
4.1 Location: Caesar's camp, before Alexandria.

When one so great begins to rage, he's hunted
Even to falling. Give him no breath,° but now   *time to catch breath*
Make boot° of his distraction.° Never anger   *Take advantage / fury*
Made good guard for itself.

10 CAESAR   Let our best heads°   *officers*
Know that tomorrow the last of many battles
We mean to fight. Within our files° there are   *troops*
Of those that served Mark Antony but late,
Enough to fetch him in.° See it done,   *capture him*
15 And feast the army. We have store to do't,
And they have earned the waste.° Poor Antony!   *Exeunt.*   *expense*

4.2

Enter ANTONY, CLEOPATRA, ENOBARBUS, CHARMIAN,
IRAS, ALEXAS, *with others.*

ANTONY   He will not fight with me, Domitius?
ENOBARBUS   No.
ANTONY   Why should he not?
ENOBARBUS   He thinks, being twenty times of better fortune,
He is twenty men to one.
ANTONY   Tomorrow, soldier,
5 By sea and land I'll fight. Or° I will live,   *Either*
Or bathe my dying honor in the blood
Shall make it live again. Woo't thou° fight well?   *Will you*
ENOBARBUS   I'll strike, and cry, "Take all!"°   *Winner take all*
ANTONY   Well said. Come on;
Call forth my household servants.

Enter [some] SERVITORS.

                         Let's tonight
10 Be bounteous at our meal. Give me thy hand;
Thou hast been rightly honest. So hast thou,
Thou, and thou, and thou. You have served me well,
And kings have been your fellows.°   *companions*
CLEOPATRA [*aside to* ENOBARBUS]   What means this?
ENOBARBUS [*aside to* CLEOPATRA]   'Tis one of those odd tricks
which sorrow shoots
Out of the mind.
15 ANTONY   And thou art honest, too.
I wish I could be made° so many men,   *split up into*
And all of you clapped up together in
An Antony, that I might do you service
So good as you have done.
SERVITORS   The gods forbid.
20 ANTONY   Well, my good fellows, wait on me tonight.
Scant not my cups, and make as much of me
As when mine empire was your fellow° too   *fellow servant*
And suffered° my command.   *obeyed*
CLEOPATRA [*aside to* ENOBARBUS]   What does he mean?
ENOBARBUS [*aside to* CLEOPATRA]   To make his followers weep.
ANTONY   Tend me tonight.
25 May be it is the period° of your duty.   *end*
Haply° you shall not see me more, or if,°   *Maybe / if you do*

4.2 Location: Alexandria.

A mangled shadow.° Perchance tomorrow   *phantom*
You'll serve another master. I look on you
As one that takes his leave. Mine honest friends,
30   I turn you not away, but, like a master
Married to your good service, stay till death.[1]
Tend me tonight two hours—I ask no more—
And the gods yield° you for't!   *reward*
ENOBARBUS   What mean you, sir,
To give them this discomfort? Look, they weep,
35   And I, an ass, am onion-eyed.° For shame!   *weepy*
Transform us not to women.
ANTONY   Ho, ho, ho!
Now the witch take° me if I meant it thus.   *bewitch*
Grace grow where those drops fall! My hearty friends,
You take me in too dolorous a sense,
40   For I spake to you for your comfort, did desire you
To burn this night with torches. Know, my hearts,
I hope well of tomorrow, and will lead you
Where rather I'll expect victorious life
Than death and honor. Let's to supper. Come,
45   And drown consideration.°   *Exeunt.*   *serious thoughts*

4.3

Enter a company of SOLDIERS.
FIRST SOLDIER   Brother, goodnight. Tomorrow is the day.
SECOND SOLDIER   It will determine one way. Fare you well.°   *Good luck*
Heard you of nothing strange about° the streets?   *in*
FIRST SOLDER   Nothing. What news?
5   SECOND SOLDIER   Belike° 'tis but a rumor. Good night to you.   *Most likely*
FIRST SOLDIER   Well, sir, good night.
    [Enter] other SOLDIERS *[to meet them].*
SECOND SOLDIER   Soldiers, have careful watch.
THIRD SOLDIER   And you. Good night, good night.
    They place themselves in every corner of the stage.
SECOND SOLDIER   Here we,[1] and if tomorrow
10   Our navy thrive, I have an absolute hope
Our landmen will stand up.°   *make a stand*
FIRST SOLDIER   'Tis a brave army and full of purpose.
    Music of the hautboys° is under the stage.   *oboes*
SECOND SOLDIER   Peace, what noise?
FIRST SOLDIER   List, list.
15   SECOND SOLDIER   Hark.
FIRST SOLDIER   Music i'th' air.
THIRD SOLDIER   Under the earth.
FOURTH SOLDIER   It signs° well, does it not?   *bodes*
THIRD SOLDIER   No.
20   FIRST SOLDIER   Peace, I say! What should this mean?
SECOND SOLDIER   'Tis the god Hercules whom Antony loved
Now leaves him.
FIRST SOLDIER   Walk. Let's see if other watchmen
Do hear what we do.

---

1. Antony considers himself a good "master" because
he will remain loyal to ("stay" with) his followers until
his (imminent) death.

4.3 Location: Outside Cleopatra's palace, Alexandria.
1. Here are our positions.

SECOND SOLDIER How now, masters?°   *good sirs*
[*They*] *speak together.*[2]
25 ALL How now? How now? Do you hear this?
FIRST SOLDIER Ay, is't not strange?
THIRD SOLDIER Do you hear, masters? Do you hear?
FIRST SOLDIER Follow the noise so far as we have quarter.[3]
Let's see how it will give off.°   *end*
ALL   Content. 'Tis strange. *Exeunt.*

4.4

Enter ANTONY *and* CLEOPATRA, *with* [CHARMIAN
and] *others.*
ANTONY Eros, mine armor, Eros!
CLEOPATRA   Sleep a little.
ANTONY No, my chuck.° Eros, come, mine armor, Eros!   *my dear*
Enter EROS.
Come, good fellow, put thine iron on.[1]
If fortune be not ours today, it is
Because we brave° her. Come.   *dare*
5   CLEOPATRA   Nay, I'll help too.
What's this for?
ANTONY   Ah, let be, let be. Thou art
The armorer of my heart. False, false.° This, this.   *wrong*
CLEOPATRA Sooth,° la. I'll help. Thus it must be.   *Truly*
ANTONY   Well, well,
We shall thrive now. —See'st thou, my good fellow?
Go, put on thy defenses.°   *armor*
10 EROS   Briefly,° sir.   *Soon*
CLEOPATRA Is not this buckled well?
ANTONY   Rarely, rarely.°   *very well*
He that unbuckles this, till we do please
To daff't° for our repose, shall hear a storm.   *remove it*
—Thou fumblest, Eros, and my queen's a squire°   *attendant to a knight*
15 More tight° at this than thou. Dispatch.° —O love,   *able / Finish*
That thou couldst see my wars today, and knew'st
The royal occupation, thou shouldst see
A workman° in't.   *An expert*
Enter an armed SOLDIER.
Good morrow to thee. Welcome.
Thou look'st like him that knows a warlike charge.°   *purpose*
20 To business that we love we rise betime°   *early*
And go to't with delight.
SOLDIER   A thousand, sir,
Early though't be, have on their riveted trim°   *armor*
And at the port expect you.
Shout. Trumpets flourish.
Enter CAPTAINS *and* SOLDIERS.
CAPTAIN The morn is fair. Good morrow, general.
SOLDIERS Good morrow, general.
25 ANTONY   'Tis well blown,[2] lads.

---

2. Individual soldiers probably address different questions and comments to one another rather than speaking in chorus.
3. As far as the limit of our watch.
4.4 Location: Cleopatra's palace.

1. Clothe me in that piece of armor of mine that
you have.
2. Well sounded (of the trumpet); well started (of the
morning).

This morning, like the spirit of a youth
That means to be of note, begins betimes.
[*to* CLEOPATRA] So, so. Come, give me that. This way. Well
   said.°   *Well done*
Fare thee well, dame. Whate'er becomes of me,
30 This is a soldier's kiss. Rebukable,
And worthy shameful check° it were to stand   *reprimand*
On more mechanic° compliment. I'll leave thee   *coarse*
Now like a man of steel. —You that will fight,
Follow me close. I'll bring you to't. —Adieu.
        Exeunt [ANTONY, EROS, CAPTAINS, *and* SOLDIERS].
CHARMIAN   Please you retire to your chamber?
35 CLEOPATRA   Lead me.
He goes forth gallantly. That he and Caesar might
Determine this great war in single fight,
Then Antony—but now —Well, on.   *Exeunt.*

4.5

    Trumpets sound. Enter ANTONY, EROS[, *and a* SOLDIER].
SOLDIER   The gods make this a happy° day to Antony!   *fortunate*
ANTONY   Would thou and those thy scars had once° prevailed   *earlier*
To make me fight at land!
SOLDIER   Hadst thou done so,
The kings that have revolted° and the soldier   *deserted*
5 That has this morning left thee would have still
Followed thy heels.
ANTONY   Who's gone this morning?
SOLDIER   Who?
One ever near thee. Call for Enobarbus;
He shall not hear thee, or from Caesar's camp
Say, "I am none of thine."
ANTONY   What sayest thou?
SOLDIER   Sir,
He is with Caesar.
10 EROS   Sir, his chests and treasure
He has not with him.
ANTONY   Is he gone?
SOLDIER   Most certain.
ANTONY   Go, Eros; send his treasure after. Do it.
Detain no jot, I charge thee. Write to him—
I will subscribe°—gentle adieus and greetings.   *sign my name*
15 Say that I wish he never find more cause
To change a master. Oh, my fortunes have
Corrupted honest men. Dispatch. —Enobarbus!   *Exeunt.*

4.6

    Flourish. Enter AGRIPPA, CAESAR, *with* ENOBARBUS
      and DOLABELLA.
CAESAR   Go forth, Agrippa, and begin the fight.
Our will is Antony be took alive.
Make it so known.
AGRIPPA   Caesar, I shall.   [*Exit* AGRIPPA.]

4.5 Location: Antony's camp, Alexandria.   **4.6** Location: Caesar's camp, Alexandria.

5 CAESAR The time of universal peace is near.[1]
Prove this° a prosp'rous day, the three-nooked world[2]   *If this proves*
Shall bear the olive° freely.   *sign of peace*
    Enter a MESSENGER.
MESSENGER   Antony
Is come into the field.
CAESAR   Go charge Agrippa
Plant those that have revolted in the van,°   *front lines*
10 That Antony may seem to spend his fury
Upon himself.°   *Exeunt [all but* ENOBARBUS].   *On his former troops*
ENOBARBUS Alexas did revolt and went to Jewry on
Affairs of Antony; there did dissuade°   *persuade*
Great Herod to incline himself to Caesar
15 And leave his master Antony. For this pains,
Caesar hath hanged him. Canidius and the rest
That fell away have entertainment° but   *employment*
No honorable trust. I have done ill,
Of which I do accuse myself so sorely
20 That I will joy no more.
    Enter a SOLDIER *of Caesar's.*
SOLDIER Enobarbus, Antony
Hath after thee sent all thy treasure, with
His bounty overplus. The messenger
Came on my guard° and at thy tent is now   *on my watch*
Unloading of his mules.
25 ENOBARBUS   I give it you.
SOLDIER   Mock not, Enobarbus,
I tell you true. Best you safed the bringer
Out of the host.[3] I must attend mine office,°   *look after my duties*
Or would have done't myself. Your emperor
30 Continues still a Jove.   *Exit.*
ENOBARBUS I am alone the° villain of the earth   *the single greatest*
And feel I am so most.[4] O Antony,
Thou mine of bounty, how wouldst thou have paid
My better service when my turpitude
35 Thou dost so crown with gold! This blows° my heart.   *swells; bursts*
If swift thought° break it not, a swifter mean°   *regret / means (suicide)*
Shall outstrike thought; but thought will do't, I feel.
I fight against thee? No, I will go seek
Some ditch wherein to die. The foul'st best fits
40 My latter part of life.   *Exit.*

4.7

Alarum, drums, and trumpets.
Enter AGRIPPA *[and* SOLDIERS].
AGRIPPA Retire!° We have engaged ourselves too far.   *Sound the retreat*
Caesar himself has work,° and our oppression°   *is beset / what we face*

---

1. Octavius Caesar, later the Emperor Augustus, was known for the Pax Romana—Roman peace—of his reign; the phrase also alludes to the birth of Christ, which occurred while Augustus was emperor. See the Introduction.
2. Three-cornered world. Referring (in descending order of probability) to Europe, Asia, Africa (the triumvirate's holdings); the three races descended from Noah's sons (Japhet, Shem, Ham); earth, sea, sky. The

three races of Noah can to an extent be superimposed on the three continents and may connect with the later religious connotations of the Roman Empire. See the previous note.
3. *Best . . . host:* It would be best if you ensured safe conduct through the lines for the messenger who brought the treasure.
4. I, more than anyone else, know this to be true of me.
4.7 Location: The battlefield, Alexandria.

Exceeds what we expected.   *Exeunt.*
    Alarums. Enter ANTONY *and* SCARUS, *wounded.*

SCARUS O my brave emperor, this is fought indeed!
5 Had we done so at first, we had droven them home
  With clouts° about their heads.   bandages; blows
ANTONY   Thou bleed'st apace.
SCARUS I had a wound here that was like a T,
  But now 'tis made an H.[1]
    [*Sound retreat*] *far off.*
ANTONY   They do retire.
SCARUS We'll beat 'em into bench-holes.° I have yet   latrine holes
10 Room for six scotches° more.   gashes
    Enter EROS.
EROS They are beaten, sir, and our advantage serves
  For a fair victory.
SCARUS   Let us score° their backs,   slash
  And snatch 'em up, as° we take hares—behind!   in the same way as
  'Tis sport to maul a runner.°   coward
ANTONY   I will reward thee
15 Once for thy sprightly° comfort, and tenfold   cheerful
  For thy good valor. Come thee on!
SCARUS I'll halt° after.   *Exeunt.*   limp

4.8

    Alarum. Enter ANTONY *again in a march;* SCARUS,
    with others.

ANTONY We have beat him to his camp. Run one before,
  And let the Queen know of our gests.°   [*Exit a* SOLDIER.]   deeds
                      Tomorrow
  Before the sun shall see 's, we'll spill the blood
  That has today escaped. I thank you all,
5 For doughty-handed° are you, and have fought   brave
  Not as° you served the cause, but as't had been   as though
  Each man's like mine. You have shown all Hectors.[1]
  Enter the city, clip° your wives, your friends;   embrace
  Tell them your feats, whilst they with joyful tears
10 Wash the congealment from your wounds and kiss
  The honored gashes whole.
    Enter CLEOPATRA.
  [*to* SCARUS]   Give me thy hand;
  To this great fairy° I'll commend thy acts,   enchantress
  Make her thanks bless thee. [*to* CLEOPATRA] O thou day° o'th'   light
    world,
  Chain mine armed neck. Leap thou, attire and all,
15 Through proof of harness° to my heart, and there   impenetrable armor
  Ride on the pants° triumphing.   heartbeats
CLEOPATRA   Lord of lords!
  O infinite virtue,° com'st thou smiling from   valor
  The world's great snare uncaught?
ANTONY   My nightingale,
  We have beat them to their beds. What, girl, though gray

---

1. *wound . . . H:* The wound was originally shaped
like a T, but another gash across its bottom has made
it look like an H turned sideways (punning on "ache,"
pronounced "aitch").

4.8 Location: Scene continues.
1. You have all fought like Hector (the greatest of the
Trojan warriors).

20 Do something° mingle with our younger brown, yet ha' we   *somewhat*
   A brain that nourishes our nerves° and can   *muscles*
   Get goal for goal of youth.² Behold this man.
   Commend unto his lips thy favoring hand.
     [*She offers* SCARUS *her hand.*]
   —Kiss it, my warrior. —He hath fought today
25 As if a god in hate of mankind had
   Destroyed in such a shape.
   CLEOPATRA   I'll give thee, friend,
   An armor all of gold. It was a king's.
   ANTONY   He has deserved it, were it carbuncled°   *bejeweled*
   Like holy Phoebus' car.° Give me thy hand.   *the sun god's chariot*
30 Through Alexandria make a jolly march.
   Bear our hacked targets like° the men that owe° them.   *shields as befits / own*
   Had our great palace the capacity
   To camp° this host, we all would sup together   *put up*
   And drink carouses to the next day's fate,
35 Which promises royal° peril. —Trumpeters,   *great*
   With brazen din blast you the city's ear.
   Make mingle with our rattling taborins,°   *small drums*
   That heaven and earth may strike their sounds together,
   Applauding our approach.   [*Trumpets sound.*] *Exeunt.*

4.9

Enter a SENTRY *and his company* [*of* WATCH];
ENOBARBUS *follows.*

   SENTRY   If we be not relieved within this hour,
   We must return to th' court of guard.° The night   *guardroom*
   Is shiny,° and they say we shall embattle°   *bright / go to battle*
   By th' second hour i'th' morn.
5 FIRST WATCH   This last day was a shrewd° one to 's.   *bad*
   ENOBARBUS   Oh, bear me witness, night—
   SECOND WATCH   What man is this?
   FIRST WATCH   Stand close,° and list° him.   *hidden / listen to*
     [*They stand aside.*]
   ENOBARBUS   —Be witness to me, O thou blessèd moon,
   When men revolted° shall upon record   *deserters*
10 Bear hateful memory, poor Enobarbus did
   Before thy face repent.
   SENTRY   Enobarbus?
   SECOND WATCH   Peace! Hark further.
   ENOBARBUS   O sovereign mistress of true melancholy,°   *(the moon)*
   The poisonous damp of night disponge° upon me,   *pour down*
15 That life, a very rebel to my will,
   May hang no longer on me. Throw my heart
   Against the flint and hardness of my fault,
   Which,° being dried with grief, will break to powder   *(his heart)*
   And finish all foul thoughts. O Antony,
20 Nobler than my revolt is infamous,
   Forgive me in thine own particular,¹
   But let the world rank me in register°   *its records*

---

2. Compete with any youth. Antony is clearly referring here to the "boy" Caesar, but also, possibly, to his
own boyhood.

4.9 Location: Caesar's camp.
1. In whatever aspects of this business concern
only you.

A master-leaver and a fugitive.°   *deserter*
O Antony! O Antony!
    [*He dies.*]²
FIRST WATCH   Let's speak to him.
25   SENTRY Let's hear him, for the things he speaks
    May concern Caesar.
SECOND WATCH   Let's do so. But he sleeps.
SENTRY Swoons rather, for so bad a prayer as his
    Was never yet for° sleep.   *in preparation for*
FIRST WATCH   Go we to him.
SECOND WATCH   Awake, sir, awake! Speak to us.
FIRST WATCH   Hear you, sir?
30   SENTRY   The hand of death hath raught° him.   *taken*
    Drums afar off.
    Hark, the drums demurely° wake the sleepers.   *with subdued sound*
    Let us bear him to th' court of guard.
    He is of note. Our hour is fully out.°   *expired*
SECOND WATCH   Come on, then. He may recover yet.
                   Exeunt [*with the body*].

4.10

    Enter ANTONY *and* SCARUS *with their army.*
ANTONY Their preparation is today by sea;
    We please them not by land.
SCARUS   For both, my lord.
ANTONY I would they'd fight i'th' fire, or i'th' air;
    We'd fight there too.¹ But this it is: our foot°   *foot soldiers*
5   Upon the hills adjoining to the city
    Shall stay with us—order for sea is given;
    They have put forth° the haven—   *departed from*
    Where their appointment° we may best discover   *purpose; battle plan*
    And look on their endeavor.   *Exeunt.*

4.11

    Enter CAESAR *and his army.*
CAESAR But being° charged, we will be still° by land—   *Unless we're / inactive*
    Which, as I take't, we shall, for his best force
    Is forth to man his galleys. To the vales,°   *valleys*
    And hold our best advantage.°   *Exeunt.*   *take the best position*

4.12

    Alarum afar off, as at a sea fight.
    Enter ANTONY *and* SCARUS.
ANTONY Yet they are not joined.° Where yond pine does stand,   *(in battle)*
    I shall discover all. I'll bring thee word
    Straight° how 'tis like° to go.   *Exit.*   *Promptly / likely*
SCARUS   Swallows have built
    In Cleopatra's sails their nests. The augurs°   *soothsayers*
5   Say they know not, they cannot tell; look grimly
    And dare not speak their knowledge. Antony
    Is valiant and dejected, and by starts

---

2. Enobarbus's death is not yet obvious to those onstage and, depending on how the moment is played, may not be to the audience either.
4.10 Location: The battlefield.

1. As well as in the other elements, earth and water.
4.11 Location: Scene continues.
4.12 Location: Scene continues.

His fretted° fortunes give him hope and fear   *diminished*
Of what he has and has not.
      Enter ANTONY.
ANTONY   All is lost!
10   This foul Egyptian hath betrayed me!
       My fleet hath yielded to the foe, and yonder
       They cast their caps up and carouse together
       Like friends long lost. Triple-turned whore![1] 'Tis thou
       Hast sold me to this novice, and my heart
15   Makes only wars on thee. Bid them all fly,
       For when I am revenged upon my charm,°   *sorceress*
       I have done all. Bid them all fly! Be gone!   [*Exit* SCARUS.]
       O sun, thy uprise shall I see no more.
       Fortune and Antony part here; even here
20   Do we shake hands.° All come to this? The hearts   *(before parting)*
       That spanieled° me at heels, to whom I gave   *fawned upon*
       Their wishes, do discandy,° melt their sweets   *melt*
       On blossoming Caesar, and this pine° is barked[2]   *(Antony)*
       That overtopped them all. Betrayed I am.
25   Oh, this false soul of Egypt! This grave° charm,   *deadly*
       Whose eye becked° forth my wars and called them home,   *beckoned*
       Whose bosom was my crownet,° my chief end,°   *coronet / reward*
       Like a right° gypsy, hath at fast and loose[3]   *true*
       Beguiled° me to the very heart of loss.°   *Cheated / ruin*
       What, Eros, Eros!
          Enter CLEOPATRA.
30   Ah, thou spell! Avaunt.°   *Leave me*
CLEOPATRA   Why is my lord enraged against his love?
ANTONY   Vanish, or I shall give thee thy deserving
       And blemish Caesar's triumph.° Let him take thee   *triumphal procession*
       And hoist thee up to the shouting plebeians!
35   Follow his chariot like the greatest spot°   *taint*
       Of all thy sex. Most monster-like be shown
       For poor'st diminutives,[4] for dolts, and let
       Patient Octavia plough thy visage up
       With her preparèd° nails!   *Exit* CLEOPATRA.   *specially sharpened*
                  'Tis well thou'rt gone,
40   If it be well to live. But better 'twere
       Thou fell'st into° my fury, for one death   *a victim to*
       Might have prevented many. Eros, ho!
       The shirt of Nessus[5] is upon me. Teach me,
       Alcides, thou mine ancestor, thy rage.
45   Let me lodge Lichas on the horns o'th' moon,
       And with those hands that grasped the heaviest club
       Subdue my worthiest self.° The witch shall die!   *commit suicide*
       To the young Roman boy she hath sold me, and I fall
       Under this plot. She dies for't. Eros, ho!   *Exit.*

---

1. Cleopatra is "triple-turned" because disloyal to three (Julius Caesar, Pompey, and Antony); alluding to her changing political allegiances.
2. Stripped of its bark (and so killed).
3. *fast and loose:* a cheating game played by gypsies.
4. For the benefit of (in place of) the lowest people (dwarfs).
5. Hercules, also known as Alcides (line 44), with whom Antony is repeatedly compared, fatally wounded the centaur Nessus with poisoned arrows for trying to rape his wife, Deianira. Nessus gave her some of his blood, falsely claiming that it would act as a love potion. Years later, she smeared some of the deadly blood on a shirt and sent it to Hercules, for whom it produced an agonizing death. Before succumbing and blaming Lichas (line 45), who had brought the shirt, Hercules cast him into the sea. When Deianira realized what she had done, she killed herself.

4.13

Enter CLEOPATRA, CHARMIAN, IRAS[, *and*] MARDIAN.

CLEOPATRA   Help me, my women! Oh, he's more mad
Than Telamon for his shield;[1] the boar of Thessaly[2]
Was never so embossed.[3]

CHARMIAN   To th' monument![4]
There lock yourself, and send him word you are dead.
5   The soul and body rive° not more in parting   separate
Than greatness going off.°   leaving someone

CLEOPATRA   To th' monument!
Mardian, go tell him I have slain myself.
Say that the last I spoke was "Antony,"
And word it, prithee, piteously. Hence, Mardian,
10   And bring me° how he takes my death. To th' monument!   bring me word
                              Exeunt.

4.14

Enter ANTONY *and* EROS.

ANTONY   Eros, thou yet behold'st me?

EROS   Ay, noble lord.

ANTONY   Sometime we see a cloud that's dragonish,°   in a dragon's shape
A vapor sometime like a bear or lion,
A towered citadel, a pendant° rock,   hanging
5   A forkèd mountain or blue promontory
With trees upon't that nod unto the world
And mock our eyes with air. Thou hast seen these signs.
They are black vesper's pageants.[1]

EROS   Ay, my lord.

ANTONY   That which is now a horse, even with a thought
10   The rack dislimns° and makes it indistinct   cloud dims
As water is in water.

EROS   It does, my lord.

ANTONY   My good knave° Eros, now thy captain is   boy
Even such a body. Here I am Antony,
Yet cannot hold this visible shape, my knave.
15   I made these wars for Egypt and the Queen,
Whose heart I thought I had, for she had mine,
Which, whilst it was mine, had annexed unto't
A million more, now lost. She, Eros, has
Packed cards° with Caesar and false played my glory   Stacked the deck
20   Unto an enemy's triumph.°   victory; trump card
Nay, weep not, gentle Eros, there is left us
Ourselves to end ourselves.

                    Enter MARDIAN.
                              Oh, thy vile lady,
She has robbed me of my sword.°   valor; manhood

MARDIAN   No, Antony,

4.13 Location: Alexandria.
1. Ajax, also known as Telamon, went mad and killed himself after the capture of Troy when he was not awarded Achilles' shield.
2. Sent by Diana to lay waste Calydon (killed by Meleager).
3. Was never so exhaustedly foaming at the mouth—that is, was never driven to such extremity (a hunt-

ing term).
4. The tomb that Cleopatra, foreseeing her death, had built.
4.14 Location: Scene continues.
1. Illusory spectacles heralding the approach of night—with a probable allusion to funerals and death. (Pageants were originally moving stages on which miracle plays were presented.)

My mistress loved thee, and her fortunes mingled
With thine entirely.
25   ANTONY   Hence, saucy° eunuch! Peace!   *disrespectful*
She hath betrayed me and shall die the death.
MARDIAN   Death of one person can be paid but once,
And that she has discharged. What thou wouldst do
Is done unto thy hand.° The last she spake   *for you*
30   Was, "Antony, most noble Antony!"
Then in the midst a tearing groan did break
The name of Antony. It was divided
Between her heart and lips.[2] She rendered° life   *gave up*
Thy name so° buried in her.   *With thy name in this way*
ANTONY   Dead then?
MARDIAN   Dead.
35   ANTONY   Unarm, Eros. The long day's task is done,
And we must sleep. [*to* MARDIAN] That thou depart'st hence safe
Does pay thy labor richly. Go.   *Exit* MARDIAN.
                              Off, pluck off!
        [EROS *unarms him.*]
The sevenfold shield[3] of Ajax cannot keep
The battery° from my heart. Oh, cleave my sides!   *onslaught*
40   Heart, once be stronger than thy continent°—   *container*
Crack thy frail case. Apace,° Eros, apace!   *Quickly*
No more a soldier. —Bruisèd pieces,° go!   *(of armor)*
You have been nobly borne. —From me awhile.   *Exit* EROS.
I will o'ertake thee, Cleopatra, and
45   Weep for my pardon. So it must be, for now
All length° is torture. Since the torch° is out,   *longer life* / *(Cleopatra)*
Lie down and stray no farther. Now all labor
Mars what it does. Yea, very force entangles
Itself with strength.[4] Seal° then, and all is done.   *Finish the deed*
50   Eros! —I come, my queen. —Eros! —Stay for me,
Where souls do couch on flowers;[5] we'll hand in hand,
And with our sprightly port° make the ghosts gaze.   *cheerful stance*
Dido and her Aeneas shall want troops,[6]
And all the haunt° be ours. —Come, Eros, Eros!   *place; ghosts*
        Enter EROS.
EROS   What would my lord?
55   ANTONY   Since Cleopatra died,
I have lived in such dishonor that the gods
Detest my baseness. I, that with my sword
Quartered the world and o'er green Neptune's back°   *on the sea*
With ships made cities,[7] condemn myself to lack°   *for lacking*
60   The courage of a woman—less noble mind
Than she which by her death our Caesar tells,
"I am conqueror of myself." Thou art sworn, Eros,
That when the exigent° should come, which now   *urgent need*

2. *It . . . lips:* It was half-uttered.
3. A shield made of brass lined with six thicknesses
of oxhide.
4. *very . . . strength:* strength defeats itself by its own
exertions.
5. Lie ("couch") in the Elysian Fields of the blessed
dead in the mythological underworld.
6. Shall lack followers. Dido, Queen of Carthage,
commits suicide after being abandoned by her lover,

Aeneas, legendary Trojan founder of Rome, in Virgil's
Aeneid; they are not reconciled in the underworld.
Dido, who originally hailed from Phoenicia, is meant
to recall Cleopatra. In leaving her, Aeneas places
public responsibility above personal desire—unlike
Antony but very much like Octavius Caesar, whom
Virgil intended him to resemble.
7. Put so many ships to sea that the fleet resembled
a city.

Is come indeed, when I should see behind me
65 Th'inevitable prosecution° of   *pursuit*
Disgrace and horror, that on my command
Thou then wouldst kill me. Do't. The time is come.
Thou strik'st not me—'tis Caesar thou defeat'st.
Put color in thy cheek.

EROS   The gods withhold me!°   *God forbid*
70 Shall I do that which all the Parthian darts,
Though enemy, lost aim and could not?

ANTONY   Eros,
Wouldst thou be windowed° in great Rome and see   *looking from a window*
Thy master thus with pleached° arms, bending down   *tied*
His corrigible° neck, his face subdued   *submissive*
75 To penetrative° shame; whilst the wheeled seat°   *piercing / chariot*
Of fortunate Caesar, drawn before him, branded
His baseness that ensued?[8]

EROS   I would not see't.

ANTONY   Come, then, for with a wound I must be cured.
Draw that thy honest° sword, which thou hast worn   *honorable*
Most useful for thy country.

80 EROS   O sir, pardon me.

ANTONY   When I did make thee free, swor'st thou not then
To do this when I bade thee? Do it at once,
Or thy precedent° services are all   *earlier*
But accidents unpurposed.° Draw, and come.   *But pointless events*

85 EROS   Turn from me then that noble countenance
Wherein the worship° of the whole world lies.   *esteem; worth*

ANTONY   Lo thee!
        [*He turns away.*]

EROS   My sword is drawn.

ANTONY   Then let it do at once
The thing why thou hast drawn it.

EROS   My dear master,
90 My captain and my emperor, let me say,
Before I strike this bloody stroke, farewell.

ANTONY   'Tis said, man, and farewell.

EROS   Farewell, great chief. Shall I strike now?

ANTONY   Now, Eros.

EROS   Why, there, then! ([*He*] *kills himself.*) Thus I do escape
    the sorrow
Of Antony's death.

95 ANTONY   Thrice-nobler than myself,
Thou teachest me, O valiant Eros, what
I should and thou couldst not. My queen and Eros
Have by their brave instruction got upon° me   *gained ahead of*
A nobleness in record.° But I will be   *history*
100 A bridegroom in my death and run into't
As to a lover's bed.[9] Come, then, and Eros,
Thy master dies thy scholar; to do thus
I learned of thee. [*He falls on his sword.*] How, not dead?
    Not dead?

8. *branded . . . ensued:* indicated, as if by a criminal's   union or climax, with Antony as the bridegroom and
brand, the humiliation of the man who followed.   death (and Cleopatra) the bride.
9. *But . . . bed:* Death is here treated as a form of erotic

The guard, ho! Oh, dispatch° me!   *finish*
     Enter a [company of the] GUARD[*, one of them*
     DERCETUS].
FIRST GUARD   What's the noise?
105   ANTONY   I have done my work ill, friends. Oh, make an end
     Of what I have begun.
SECOND GUARD   The star is fall'n.
FIRST GUARD   And time is at his period.°   *its end*
ALL THE GUARD   Alas, and woe.
ANTONY   Let him that loves me, strike me dead.
FIRST GUARD   Not I.
110   SECOND GUARD   Nor I.
THIRD GUARD   Nor anyone.
               Exeunt [all the GUARD *but* DERCETUS].
DERCETUS   Thy death and fortunes bid thy followers fly.
     [*He takes Antony's sword.*]
   This sword, but shown to Caesar with this tidings,
   Shall enter me° with him.   *gain me favor*
     Enter DIOMEDES.
115   DIOMEDES   Where's Antony?
DERCETUS   There, Diomed, there.
DIOMEDES   Lives he? Wilt thou not answer, man?
                      [*Exit* DERCETUS.]
ANTONY   Art thou there, Diomed? Draw thy sword and give me
   Sufficing° strokes for death.   *Enough*
DIOMEDES   Most absolute lord,
120   My mistress Cleopatra sent me to thee.
ANTONY   When did she send thee?
DIOMEDES   Now, my lord.
ANTONY   Where is she?
DIOMEDES   Locked in her monument. She had a prophesying
   fear
   Of what hath come to pass; for when she saw—
   Which never shall be found°—you did suspect   *(to be true)*
125   She had disposed° with Caesar, and that your rage   *made an alliance*
   Would not be purged, she sent you word she was dead.
   But fearing since how it might work, hath sent
   Me to proclaim the truth, and I am come,
   I dread, too late.
130   ANTONY   Too late, good Diomed. Call my guard, I prithee.
DIOMEDES   What ho! The Emperor's guard! The guard, what ho!
   Come, your lord calls.
     Enter [some] of the GUARD *of Antony.*
ANTONY   Bear me, good friends, where Cleopatra bides.°   *waits; dwells*
   'Tis the last service that I shall command you.
135   FIRST GUARD   Woe, woe are we, sir, you may not live to wear
   All your true followers out.°   *outlive your followers*
ALL THE GUARD   Most heavy day!
ANTONY   Nay, good my fellows, do not please sharp fate
   To grace° it with your sorrows. Bid that welcome   *By gracing*
   Which comes to punish us, and we punish it
140   Seeming to bear it lightly. Take me up.
   I have led you oft; carry me now, good friends,
   And have my thanks for all.
     Exeunt, bearing ANTONY [*and* EROS].

4.15

Enter CLEOPATRA *and her maids aloft, with* CHARMIAN
and IRAS.

CLEOPATRA   O Charmian, I will never go from hence.

CHARMIAN   Be comforted, dear madam.

CLEOPATRA   No, I will not.
All strange and terrible events are welcome,
But comforts we despise. Our size of sorrow
5   Proportioned to our cause must be as great
As that which makes it.
        Enter DIOMEDES [*below*].
                        How now? Is he dead?

DIOMEDES   His death's upon him, but not dead.
Look out o'th' other side your monument;
His guard have brought him thither.
        Enter ANTONY [*below*] *and the* GUARD [*bearing him*].

10   CLEOPATRA   O sun,
Burn the great sphere thou mov'st in; darkling¹ stand
The varying shore o'th' world. O Antony,
Antony, Antony! Help, Charmian, help Iras, help!
Help friends below! Let's draw him hither.

ANTONY   Peace!
15   Not Caesar's valor hath o'erthrown Antony,
But Antony's hath triumphed on itself.

CLEOPATRA   So it should be that none but Antony
Should conquer Antony, but woe 'tis so!

ANTONY   I am dying, Egypt, dying. Only
20   I here importune death° awhile until   *ask death to wait*
Of many thousand kisses, the poor last
I lay upon thy lips.

CLEOPATRA   I dare not,° dear.   *dare not come down*
Dear my lord, pardon! I dare not
Lest I be taken. Not th'imperious show°   *triumphal procession*
25   Of the full-fortuned Caesar ever shall
Be brooched° with me; if knife, drugs, serpents have   *decorated*
Edge, sting, or operation,° I am safe.   *power*
Your wife Octavia, with her modest eyes
And still conclusion,° shall acquire no honor   *silent judgment*
30   Demuring° upon me. But come, come Antony.   *Gazing solemnly*
—Help me, my women! —We must draw thee up.
Assist, good friends!
        [*They begin lifting* ANTONY.]

ANTONY   Oh, quick, or I am gone.

CLEOPATRA   Here's sport indeed. How heavy weighs my lord!
Our strength is all gone into heaviness°—   *sadness; weight*
35   That makes the weight. Had I great Juno's power,
The strong-winged Mercury should fetch thee up
And set thee by Jove's side. Yet, come a little.
Wishers were ever fools. Oh, come, come, come!
        They heave ANTONY *aloft to* CLEOPATRA.²

4.15 Location: Cleopatra's monument, Alexandria.
1. O . . . *darkling*: For the spheres in which the sun,
like the planets and stars, was thought to move around
the earth, see note to 2.7.16. If the sun burned its
sphere, presumably it would move out of orbit, thus

leaving the earth in darkness ("darkling").
2. TEXTUAL COMMENT For the problem of visualizing
this as stage action, see Digital Edition TC 6. PERFOR-
MANCE COMMENT For how modern productions have
dealt with this problem, see Digital Edition PC 3.

And welcome, welcome. Die when thou hast lived;°   *lived again*
40   Quicken° with kissing. Had my lips that power,   *Revive*
    Thus would I wear them out.
      [*She kisses him.*]
   ALL   A heavy sight.
   ANTONY   I am dying, Egypt, dying.
    Give me some wine and let me speak a little.
45   CLEOPATRA   No, let me speak, and let me rail so high
    That the false hussy Fortune break her wheel,
    Provoked by my offense.°   *insults*
   ANTONY   One word, sweet queen.
    Of Caesar seek your honor with your safety. Oh!
   CLEOPATRA   They do not go together.
   ANTONY   Gentle, hear me.
50   None about Caesar trust but Proculeius.
   CLEOPATRA   My resolution and my hands I'll trust,
    None about Caesar.
   ANTONY   The miserable change now at my end
    Lament° nor sorrow at, but please your thoughts   *Neither lament*
55   In feeding them with those my former fortunes,
    Wherein I lived the greatest prince o'th' world,
    The noblest, and do now not basely die,
    Not cowardly put off my helmet to
    My countryman—a Roman by a Roman
60   Valiantly vanquished. Now my spirit is going.
    I can no more.
   CLEOPATRA   Noblest of men, woo't° die?   *will you*
    Hast thou no care of me? Shall I abide
    In this dull world, which in thy absence is
    No better than a sty? —Oh, see, my women,
65   The crown o'th' earth doth melt. —My lord?
      [ANTONY *dies.*]
    Oh, withered is the garland° of the war;   *crowning glory*
    The soldier's pole[3] is fall'n. Young boys and girls
    Are level now with men. The odds° is gone,   *distinction among humans*
    And there is nothing left remarkable
    Beneath the visiting moon.
70   CHARMIAN   Oh, quietness, lady.
   IRAS   She's dead, too, our sovereign.
   CHARMIAN   Lady!
   IRAS   Madam!
   CHARMIAN   O madam, madam, madam!
75   IRAS   Royal Egypt! Empress!
   CHARMIAN   Peace, peace, Iras!
   CLEOPATRA   No more but e'en° a woman and commanded   *just (no longer Queen)*
    By such poor passion as the maid that milks
    And does the meanest chores. It were for° me   *would befit*
80   To throw my scepter at the injurious gods
    To tell them that this world did equal theirs
    Till they had stol'n our jewel. All's but naught.
    Patience is sottish,° and impatience does   *foolish*
    Become a dog that's mad. Then is it sin
85   To rush into the secret house of death
    Ere death dare come to us? How do you, women?

---

3. Polestar; military standard; phallus.

What, what, good cheer! Why, how now, Charmian?
My noble girls! Ah, women, women! Look!
Our lamp is spent; it's out. Good sirs,° take heart.   (to the women)
90   We'll bury him, and then, what's brave,° what's noble,   fine
Let's do't after the high Roman fashion
And make death proud to take us. Come, away!
This case of that huge spirit now is cold.
Ah, women, women! Come, we have no friend
95   But resolution and the briefest° end.   fastest

             Exeunt, bearing off Antony's body.

5.1

Enter CAESAR *with* AGRIPPA, DOLABELLA,
[MAECENAS, GALLUS, *and* PROCULEIUS,]
his council of war.

CAESAR   Go to him, Dolabella, bid him yield.
Being so frustrate, tell him he mocks
The pauses that he makes.[1]
DOLABELLA   Caesar, I shall.
                                    [*Exit* DOLABELLA.]
Enter DERCETUS *with the sword of Antony.*
CAESAR   Wherefore is that? And what art thou that dar'st
Appear thus° to us?   (with a drawn weapon)
5   DERCETUS   I am called Dercetus.
Mark Antony I served, who best was worthy
Best to be served. Whilst he stood up and spoke
He was my master, and I wore my life
To spend° upon his haters. If thou please   expend
10   To take me to thee, as I was to him
I'll be to Caesar; if thou pleasest not,
I yield thee up my life.
CAESAR   What is't thou say'st?
DERCETUS   I say, O Caesar, Antony is dead.
CAESAR   The breaking° of so great a thing should make   end; telling
15   A greater crack!° The round world   noise; fracture
Should have shook lions into civil° streets   city
And citizens to their° dens. The death of Antony   (the lions')
Is not a single doom—in the name lay
A moiety° of the world.   half
DERCETUS   He is dead, Caesar,
20   Not by a public minister of justice,
Nor by a hired knife, but that self° hand   same
Which writ his honor in the acts it did
Hath, with the courage which the heart did lend it,
Splitted the heart. This is his sword.
25   I robbed his wound of it. Behold it stained
With his most noble blood.
CAESAR   Look you sad, friends?
The gods rebuke me,° but it is tidings   (for my tears)
To wash the eyes of kings.
DOLABELLA   And strange it is,
That nature must compel us to lament
Our most persisted deeds.°   What we persevered in

---

1. *he mocks . . . makes:* his delays are a mere mockery.

30 MAECENAS His taints and honors
Waged° equal with° him. Fought as if / in
DOLABELLA A rarer spirit never
Did steer humanity,° but you gods will give us govern (any) man
Some faults to make us men. Caesar is touched.
MAECENAS When such a spacious mirror's set before him,
He needs must see himself.
35 CAESAR O Antony,
I have followed° thee to this, but we do lance° pursued / wound to cure
Diseases in our bodies. I must perforce
Have shown to thee such a declining day[2]
Or look on thine. We could not stall° together live in peace
40 In the whole world. But yet let me lament
With tears as sovereign° as the blood of hearts as efficacious
That thou, my brother, my competitor° comrade; foe
In top of all design,° my mate in empire, In the greatest ventures
Friend and companion in the front of war,
45 The arm of mine own body, and the heart
Where mine his° thoughts did kindle—that our stars its
Unreconcilable should divide
Our equalness° to this. Hear me, good friends— partnership
Enter an EGYPTIAN.
But I will tell you at some meeter season.° fitter time
50 The business of this man looks out of him.
We'll hear him what he says. —Whence are you?
EGYPTIAN A poor Egyptian yet. The Queen, my mistress,
Confined in all she has—her monument—
Of thy intents desires instruction,
55 That she preparedly may frame herself
To th' way she's forced to.
CAESAR Bid her have good heart.
She soon shall know of us by some of ours
How honorable and how kindly we
Determine for her. For Caesar cannot live
To be ungentle.
60 EGYPTIAN So. The gods preserve thee. *Exit.*
CAESAR Come hither, Proculeius. Go and say
We purpose her no shame. Give her what comforts
The quality° of her passion° shall require, strength / grief
Lest in her greatness by some mortal stroke
65 She do defeat us. For her life in Rome
Would be eternal in our triumph.[3] Go,
And with your speediest bring us what she says
And how you find of her.
PROCULEIUS Caesar, I shall. *Exit.*
CAESAR Gallus, go you along. [*Exit* GALLUS.]
Where's Dolabella,
To second Proculeius?
70 ALL BUT CAESAR Dolabella!
CAESAR Let him alone, for I remember now
How he's employed. He shall in time be ready.

---

2. *I must . . . day:* I would have had to exhibit my
demise to you. *perforce:* necessarily.
3. *her life . . . triumph:* her presence alive in Rome
would bring eternal renown to my triumphal
procession.

Go with me to my tent, where you shall see
How hardly° I was drawn into this war,   *unwillingly*
75 How calm and gentle I proceeded still
In all my writings.° Go with me and see   *(letters to Antony)*
What I can show in this.   *Exeunt.*

5.2

Enter CLEOPATRA, CHARMIAN, IRAS, *and* MARDIAN.

CLEOPATRA   My desolation does begin to make
A better life. 'Tis paltry to be Caesar;
Not being Fortune, he's but Fortune's knave,°   *servant*
A minister of her will. And it is great
5   To do that thing° that ends all other deeds,   *(suicide)*
Which shackles accidents and bolts up change,
Which sleeps and never palates more the dung,
The beggar's nurse and Caesar's.[1]
                 Enter PROCULEIUS.[2]
PROCULEIUS   Caesar sends greeting to the Queen of Egypt,
10 And bids thee study on° what fair demands   *give thought to*
Thou mean'st to have him grant thee.
CLEOPATRA   What's thy name?
PROCULEIUS   My name is Proculeius.
CLEOPATRA   Antony
Did tell me of you, bade me trust you, but
I do not greatly care to be deceived
15 That° have no use for trusting.[3] If your master   *(I) who*
Would have a queen his beggar, you must tell him
That majesty to keep decorum must
No less beg than a kingdom. If he please
To give me conquered Egypt for my son,
20 He gives me so much of mine own as° I   *that*
Will kneel to him with thanks.
PROCULEIUS   Be of good cheer.
You're fall'n into a princely hand. Fear nothing.
Make your full reference° freely to my lord,   *case*
Who is so full of grace that it flows over
25 On all that need. Let me report to him
Your sweet dependency,° and you shall find   *meek obeisance*
A conqueror that will pray in aid for kindness[4]
Where he for grace is kneeled to.
CLEOPATRA   Pray you, tell him
I am his fortune's vassal, and I send him
30 The greatness he has got.[5] I hourly learn
A doctrine of obedience and would gladly
Look him i'th' face.
PROCULEIUS   This I'll report, dear lady.
Have comfort, for I know your plight is pitied

5.2 Location: Cleopatra's monument.
1. *Which sleeps . . . Caesar's:* Which brings a sleep in which we no longer taste the produce of the earth ("dung"), nourisher of all from beggar to emperor.
2. Cleopatra and her women are inside the monument, the others outside it.
3. Cleopatra claims not to care whether she is deceived, in the hope that Proculeius will relax his guard and

reveal Caesar's intentions. But she may also mean that she doesn't like being deceived, knowing as she does the perils of misplaced trust.
4. Who will beg help in finding new ways to be kind.
5. *I am . . . got:* I do homage to his good fortune, and I acknowledge the great position he has won. "Send him" may suggest Cleopatra's sense of superiority in conferring greatness upon Caesar.

Of° him that caused it.   *By*

[*Enter Roman* SOLDIERS, *who seize* CLEOPATRA
   from behind.][6]

35 [*to* SOLDIERS] You see how easily she may be surprised.
      Guard her till Caesar come.

IRAS   Royal Queen!

CHARMIAN   O Cleopatra, thou art taken, Queen!

CLEOPATRA [*drawing a dagger*]   Quick, quick, good hands.

PROCULEIUS [*seizing the dagger*]   Hold, worthy lady, hold!
      Do not yourself such wrong, who are in this
      Relieved° but not betrayed.   *Rescued*

40 CLEOPATRA   What, of° death, too,   *deprived of*
      That rids our dogs of languish?[7]

PROCULEIUS   Cleopatra,
      Do not abuse my master's bounty by
      Th'undoing of yourself. Let the world see
      His nobleness well acted, which your death
      Will never let come forth.°   *allow to be displayed*

45 CLEOPATRA   Where art thou, death?
      Come hither, come! Come, come, and take a queen
      Worth many babes and beggars![8]

PROCULEIUS   Oh, temperance, lady!

CLEOPATRA   Sir, I will eat no meat,° I'll not drink, sir;   *food*
      If idle talk will once be necessary[9]

50   I'll not sleep, neither. This mortal house° I'll ruin,   *My body*
      Do Caesar what he can. Know, sir, that I
      Will not wait pinioned[1] at your master's court,
      Nor once be chastised with the sober eye
      Of dull Octavia. Shall they hoist me up

55   And show me to the shouting varletry°   *rabble*
      Of censuring Rome? Rather a ditch in Egypt
      Be gentle grave unto me; rather on Nilus' mud
      Lay me stark naked and let the water-flies
      Blow me into abhorring![2] Rather make

60   My country's high pyramids my gibbet,°   *gallows*
      And hang me up in chains!

PROCULEIUS   You do extend
      These thoughts of horror further than you shall
      Find cause in Caesar.

                  Enter DOLABELLA.

DOLABELLA   Proculeius,
      What thou hast done, thy master Caesar knows,

65   And he hath sent for thee. For the Queen,
      I'll take her to my guard.

PROCULEIUS   So, Dolabella,
      It shall content me best. Be gentle to her.
      —To Caesar I will speak what° you shall please,   *whatever*
      If you'll employ me to him.

---

6. TEXTUAL COMMENT For the difficulty of understanding what happens in lines 33–37, perhaps
because intervening material has been lost, see Digital Edition TC 7.
7. Which rids even our dogs of protracted demise.
8. *babes and beggars*: death's cheapest victims; those
most often "Relieved" (line 39) by the great.

9. (Even) if useless words are at times needed (to
keep me awake); if I am forced to engage in pointless
chatter.
1. Will not serve shackled (or: will not wait like a
bird with clipped wings).
2. Lay their eggs on me (thereby breeding maggots)
so that I become disgusting, abhorrent.

	CLEOPATRA	Say, I would die.	

                           Exit PROCULEIUS [*with* SOLDIERS].

70   DOLABELLA   Most noble empress, you have heard of me?

        CLEOPATRA   I cannot tell.

        DOLABELLA   Assuredly you know me.

        CLEOPATRA   No matter, sir, what I have heard or known.

    You laugh when boys or women tell their dreams,

    Is't not your trick?°   *custom*

        DOLABELLA   I understand not, madam.

75   CLEOPATRA   I dreamt there was an emperor Antony.

    Oh, such another sleep, that I might see

    But such another man.

        DOLABELLA   If it might please ye—

        CLEOPATRA   His face was as the heav'ns, and therein stuck°   *were stuck*

    A sun and moon, which kept their course and lighted

    The little O, th'earth.

80   DOLABELLA   Most sovereign creature!

        CLEOPATRA   His legs bestrid° the ocean; his reared arm   *straddled*

    Crested[3] the world. His voice was propertied

    As all the tunèd spheres,[4] and that to friends.

    But when he meant to quail° and shake the orb,°   *awe / globe*

85   He was as rattling thunder. For his bounty,

    There was no winter in't. An Antony it was,

    That grew the more by reaping. His delights

    Were dolphin-like; they showed his back above°   *they rose above*

    The element they lived in.[5] In his livery°   *service*

90   Walked crowns and crownets.° Realms and islands were *kings and princes*

    As plates° dropped from his pocket.   *silver coins*

        DOLABELLA   Cleopatra—

        CLEOPATRA   Think you there was or might be such a man

    As this I dreamt of?

        DOLABELLA   Gentle madam, no.

        CLEOPATRA   You lie up to the hearing of the gods!

95   But if there be, nor ever were one such,

    It's past the size of dreaming.[6] Nature wants stuff

    To vie strange forms with fancy, yet t'imagine

    An Antony were nature's piece 'gainst fancy,

    Condemning shadows quite.[7]

        DOLABELLA   Hear me, good madam.

100   Your loss is as yourself, great, and you bear it

    As answering to the° weight. Would I might never   *Appropriately, given its*

    O'ertake° pursued success, but° I do feel   *Achieve / unless*

    By the rebound° of yours a grief that suits   *reflection*

    My very heart at root!

        CLEOPATRA   I thank you, sir.

105   Know you what Caesar means to do with me?

        DOLABELLA   I am loath to tell you what I would you knew.

        CLEOPATRA   Nay, pray you, sir.

        DOLABELLA   Though he be honorable—

---

3. Formed a crest over (as in heraldry).

4. *was . . . spheres:* sounded like the music of the spheres, supposedly produced by the harmonious structure of the universe. See note to 2.7.16.

5. Just as the dolphin's back appears above the water.

6. My vision of him surpasses what can be dreamed.

7. *Nature . . . quite:* Nature lacks material to compete with the remarkable visions of the imagination in creating fantastic forms; but by imagining and creating Antony, nature has produced a masterpiece that outstrips even fancy and thus discredits imaginary conceptions.

CLEOPATRA He'll lead me then in triumph?
DOLABELLA Madam, he will; I know't.
      Flourish.
      Enter PROCULEIUS, CAESAR, GALLUS, MAECENAS, *and*
      others of his train.
110 ALL° Make way there! Caesar!   *(Caesar's train)*
CAESAR Which is the Queen of Egypt?
DOLABELLA It is the Emperor, madam.
      CLEOPATRA *kneels.*
CAESAR Arise. You shall not kneel.
  I pray you rise. Rise, Egypt.
CLEOPATRA   Sir, the gods
115 Will have it thus.° My master and my lord,   *(that I obey you)*
  I must obey.
      [*She rises.*]
CAESAR   Take to you no hard thoughts.
  The record of what injuries you did us,
  Though written in our flesh, we shall remember
  As things but done by chance.
CLEOPATRA   Sole sir° o'th' world,   *lord*
120 I cannot project° mine own cause so well   *lay out*
  To make it clear,° but do confess I have   *innocent seeming*
  Been laden with like frailties, which before
  Have often shamed our sex.
CAESAR   Cleopatra, know,
  We will extenuate rather than enforce.°   *emphasize (faults)*
125 If you apply yourself° to our intents,   *conform*
  Which towards you are most gentle, you shall find
  A benefit in this change. But if you seek
  To lay on me a cruelty° by taking   *charge of cruelty*
  Antony's course, you shall bereave yourself
130 Of my good purposes and put your children
  To that destruction which I'll guard them from,
  If thereon you rely. I'll take my leave.
CLEOPATRA And may through all the world.[8] 'Tis yours, and we
  Your scutcheons° and your signs of conquest shall   *captured shields*
135 Hang in what place you please. Here, my good lord.
      [*She holds out a paper.*]
CAESAR You shall advise me in all for° Cleopatra.   *concerning*
CLEOPATRA This is the brief° of money, plate, and jewels   *summary*
  I am possessed of. 'Tis exactly valued,
  Not petty things admitted.° Where's Seleucus?   *Except trivial things*
      [*Enter* SELEUCUS.]
140 SELEUCUS Here, madam.
CLEOPATRA This is my treasurer. Let him speak, my lord,
  Upon his peril that I have reserved
  To myself nothing. Speak the truth, Seleucus.
SELEUCUS Madam, I had rather seal° my lips   *sew up*
145 Than to my peril speak that which is not.
CLEOPATRA What have I kept back?
SELEUCUS Enough to purchase what you have made known.
CAESAR Nay, blush not, Cleopatra. I approve
  Your wisdom in the deed.

---

8. As you may (take your leave and go) anywhere (as ruler of the world).

CLEOPATRA	See, Caesar! Oh, behold,	
150	How pomp is followed!⁹ Mine° will now be yours,	*My followers*
And should we shift estates,° yours would be mine.	*change positions*
The ingratitude of this Seleucus does	
Even make me wild. —O slave, of no more trust	
Than love that's hired! What, goest thou back? Thou shalt	
155	Go back, I warrant thee, but I'll catch thine eyes,	
Though° they had wings. Slave! Soulless villain!	*Even if*
Dog! Oh, rarely° base!	*exceptionally*
CAESAR	Good queen, let us entreat you—	
CLEOPATRA	O Caesar, what a wounding shame is this,	
That thou vouchsafing° here to visit me,	*stooping to come*
160	Doing the honor of thy lordliness	
To one so meek, that mine own servant should	
Parcel° the sum of my disgraces by	*Particularize; add to*
Addition of his envy!° Say, good Caesar,	*spite*
That I some lady° trifles have reserved,	*ladylike*
165	Immoment toys,° things of such dignity	*Worthless trinkets*
As we greet modern° friends withal,° and say	*everyday / with*
Some nobler token I have kept apart	
For Livia° and Octavia to induce	*(Caesar's wife)*
Their mediation, must I be unfolded	
170	With° one that I have bred! The gods! It smites me	*turned in by*
Beneath the fall I have. —Prithee, go hence,	
Or I shall show the cinders° of my spirits	*smoldering coals*
Through th'ashes of my chance.° Wert thou a man,	*fortune*
Thou wouldst have mercy on me.	
CAESAR	Forbear, Seleucus.	

[*Exit* SELEUCUS.]

175	CLEOPATRA	Be it known that we, the greatest, are misthought°	*misjudged*
For things that others do; and when we fall,	
We answer others' merits in our name¹—	
Are therefore to be pitied.	
CAESAR	Cleopatra,	
Not what you have reserved nor what acknowledged	
180	Put we i'th' roll of conquest. Still be't yours.	
Bestow° it at your pleasure, and believe	*Dispense*
Caesar's no merchant to make prize° with you	*haggle*
Of things that merchants sold. Therefore be cheered;	
Make not your thoughts your prisons.² No, dear Queen,	
185	For we intend so to dispose you as	
Yourself shall give us counsel. Feed and sleep.	
Our care and pity is so much upon you	
That we remain your friend. And so, adieu.	
CLEOPATRA	My master and my lord!	
CAESAR	Not so. Adieu.	

Flourish. Exeunt CAESAR *and his train*
[*including* DOLABELLA].

190	CLEOPATRA He words me, girls, he words me, that I should not
Be noble to myself.³ But hark thee, Charmian.

---

9. How the great are served.
1. We are responsible for the deeds committed by others in our names (an effort to shift the blame to Seleucus).

2. Don't think yourself a prisoner; don't be imprisoned by (or in) your thoughts.
3. *He words . . . myself:* He puts me off from committing suicide with mere words.

IRAS Finish, good lady. The bright day is done,
 And we are for the dark.
CLEOPATRA [*to* CHARMIAN] Hie thee again.°   *Hurry back*
 I have spoke already, and it is provided.
 Go, put it to the haste.°   *Do it quickly*
195 CHARMIAN   Madam, I will.
    Enter DOLABELLA.
DOLABELLA Where's the Queen?
CHARMIAN   Behold, sir.
         [*Exit* CHARMIAN.]
CLEOPATRA   Dolabella!
DOLABELLA Madam, as thereto sworn by your command,
 Which my love makes religion° to obey,   *compels me*
 I tell you this: Caesar through Syria
200 Intends his journey, and within three days
 You with your children will he send before.
 Make your best use of this. I have performed
 Your pleasure and my promise.
CLEOPATRA   Dolabella,
 I shall remain your debtor.
DOLABELLA   I your servant.
205 Adieu, good Queen. I must attend on Caesar.
CLEOPATRA Farewell, and thanks.   *Exit* [DOLABELLA].
     Now, Iras, what think'st thou?
 Thou, an Egyptian puppet, shall be shown
 In Rome as well as I. Mechanic slaves°   *Laborers*
 With greasy aprons, rules,° and hammers shall *measuring sticks*
210 Uplift us to the view. In their thick° breaths,   *foul*
 Rank° of gross diet,° shall we be enclouded *Stinking / coarse food*
 And forced to drink° their vapor.   *inhale*
IRAS   The gods forbid!
CLEOPATRA Nay, 'tis most certain, Iras. Saucy lictors° *Insolent law officers*
 Will catch at us like strumpets, and scald° rhymers *scurvy*
215 Ballad us out o'tune. The quick comedians
 Extemporally° will stage us and present   *In improvised manner*
 Our Alexandrian revels. Antony
 Shall be brought drunken forth, and I shall see
 Some squeaking Cleopatra boy[4] my greatness
 I'th' posture of a whore.
220 IRAS   O the good gods!
CLEOPATRA Nay, that's certain.
IRAS I'll never see't! For I am sure my nails
 Are stronger than mine eyes.
CLEOPATRA   Why, that's the way
 To fool their preparation and to conquer
 Their most absurd intents.
    Enter CHARMIAN.
225   Now, Charmian!
 Show° me, my women, like a queen. Go, fetch *Display*
 My best attires. I am again for Cydnus
 To meet Mark Antony.[5] Sirrah Iras, go!
 Now, noble Charmian, we'll dispatch° indeed, *hurry; finish*

---

4. Cleopatra's part will be played by a boy (as it was 5. See 2.2.198–238.
in Shakespeare's day).

230 And when thou hast done this chore, I'll give thee leave
To play till doomsday. Bring our crown and all.

                                            [*Exit* IRAS.]

         A noise within.
Wherefore's this noise?
       Enter a GUARDSMAN.
GUARDSMAN   Here is a rural fellow
That will not be denied your highness' presence.
He brings you figs.
CLEOPATRA   Let him come in.   *Exit* GUARDSMAN.
235   What° poor an instrument   *How*
May do a noble deed! He brings me liberty.
My resolution's placed,° and I have nothing   *unwavering*
Of woman in me. Now from head to foot
I am marble constant. Now the fleeting° moon   *changeable*
No planet is of mine.
      Enter GUARDSMAN *and* CLOWN° [*with basket*].   *a rustic*
240 GUARDSMAN   This is the man.
CLEOPATRA   Avoid,° and leave him.   *Exit* GUARDSMAN.   *Withdraw*
Hast thou the pretty worm[6] of Nilus there
That kills and pains not?
CLOWN   Truly I have him, but I would not be the party that
245   should desire you to touch him, for his biting is immortal.[7]
Those that do die of it do seldom or never recover.
CLEOPATRA   Remember'st thou any that have died on't?°   *of it*
CLOWN   Very many; men and women too! I heard of one of
them no longer than yesterday—a very honest° woman, but   *truthful; chaste*
250   something given to lie,° as a woman should not do but in the   *fib; lie with men*
way of honesty—how she died° of the biting of it, what pain *perished; had an orgasm*
she felt. Truly, she makes a very good report o'th' worm. But
he that will believe all that they say shall never be saved by
half that they do.[8] But this is most falliable;° the worm's an *(error for "infallible")*
255   odd worm.
CLEOPATRA   Get thee hence, farewell.
CLOWN   I wish you all joy of the worm.
CLEOPATRA   Farewell.
CLOWN   You must think this, look you, that the worm will do
260   his kind.°   *what's in its nature*
CLEOPATRA   Ay, ay, farewell.
CLOWN   Look you, the worm is not to be trusted but in the
keeping of wise people. For indeed, there is no goodness in
the worm.
265 CLEOPATRA   Take thou no care; it shall be heeded.
CLOWN   Very good. Give it nothing, I pray you, for it is not worth
the feeding.
CLEOPATRA   Will it eat me?
CLOWN   You must not think I am so simple but I know the
270   devil himself will not eat a woman. I know that a woman is
a dish for the gods, if the devil dress° her not. But truly, *prepare (food); clothe*

---

6. Snake or serpent. In the Clown's description (lines 244–52), the "worm" also suggests the penis.
7. Comic error: the Clown means the opposite, but as so often occurs with such malapropisms in Shakespeare, the mistake reveals an unintended truth. See Cleopatra's "Immortal longings" (line 277).

8. Perhaps the point is that a woman "given to lie" (line 250) is not to be believed. If Cleopatra acts on this "good report o'th' worm," she will "never be saved" (lines 252–53): she will die and, in Christian terms, will lose hope of salvation by committing suicide.

these same whoreson° devils do the gods great harm in their   *accursed*
women. For in every ten that they make, the devils mar five.
CLEOPATRA   Well, get thee gone. Farewell.
275 CLOWN   Yes, forsooth. I wish you joy o'th' worm.   *Exit.*
    [*Enter* IRAS *with robe and crown.*]
CLEOPATRA   Give me my robe; put on my crown. I have
  Immortal longings in me. Now no more
  The juice of Egypt's grape shall moist this lip.
  Yare,° yare, good Iras. Quick! Methinks I hear   *Briskly*
280 Antony call. I see him rouse himself
  To praise my noble act. I hear him mock
  The luck of Caesar, which the gods give men
  To excuse their° after wrath. Husband, I come.   *(the gods')*
  Now to that name, my courage prove my title.
285 I am fire and air. My other elements
  I give to baser life.[9] So, have you done?
  Come, then, and take the last warmth of my lips.
  Farewell, kind Charmian, Iras, long farewell.
    [*She kisses* CHARMIAN *and* IRAS, *who falls and dies.*]
  Have I the aspic° in my lips? Dost fall?   *asp*
290 If thou and nature can so gently part,
  The stroke of death is as a lover's pinch,
  Which hurts and is desired. Dost thou lie still?
  If thus thou vanishest, thou tell'st the world,
  It is not worth leave-taking.
295 CHARMIAN   Dissolve, thick cloud, and rain, that I may say
  The gods themselves do weep.
CLEOPATRA   This proves me base.°   *ignoble*
  If she first meet the curlèd° Antony,   *curly-haired*
  He'll make demand of° her and spend that kiss   *question; (sexual)*
  Which is my heaven to have. Come, thou mortal wretch;°   *deadly creature*
    [*She applies an asp.*]
300 With thy sharp teeth this knot intrinsicate°   *intricate*
  Of life at once untie. Poor venomous fool,
  Be angry and dispatch. Oh, couldst thou speak
  That I might hear thee call great Caesar ass
  Unpolicied.°   *Outsmarted*
CHARMIAN   O eastern star!°   *(Venus; Cleopatra)*
CLEOPATRA   Peace, peace.
305 Dost thou not see my baby at my breast,
  That sucks the nurse asleep.
CHARMIAN   Oh, break! Oh, break!
CLEOPATRA   As sweet as balm, as soft as air, as gentle.
  O Antony! Nay, I will take thee too.
    [*She applies another asp.*]
  What° should I stay—   *Why*
    [*She*] *dies.*
310 CHARMIAN   In this wild world? So, fare thee well.
  Now boast thee, death, in thy possession lies
  A lass unparalleled. Downy windows° close,   *eyelids*

---

9. *I am . . . life:* The "other elements" (line 285) are
earth and water, the lower and heavier elements traditionally linked to women and thought to explain their
fickleness. Cleopatra is particularly associated with
these elements through her equation with (the mud
of) Egypt. By asserting that she is only "fire and air,"
she is claiming to be manly (as in lines 237–38) and is
also referring to the separation of the soul from the
body at death.

And golden Phoebus never be beheld
Of eyes again so royal. Your crown's awry.
315 I'll mend it,° and then play—   *set it right*
        Enter the GUARD *rustling*° *in.*   *clattering*
FIRST GUARD Where's the Queen?
CHARMIAN   Speak softly. Wake her not.
FIRST GUARD Caesar hath sent—
CHARMIAN   Too slow a messenger.
        [*She applies an asp.*]
    Oh, come apace, dispatch. I partly feel thee.
FIRST GUARD Approach, ho! All's not well. Caesar's beguiled.°   *deceived*
320 SECOND GUARD There's Dolabella sent from Caesar. Call him.
                                        [*Exit a* GUARD.]
FIRST GUARD What work is here, Charmian? Is this well done?
CHARMIAN It is well done and fitting for a princess
    Descended of so many royal kings.
    Ah, soldier!
            CHARMIAN *dies.*
            Enter DOLABELLA.
DOLABELLA How goes it here?
SECOND GUARD   All dead.
325 DOLABELLA   Caesar, thy thoughts
    Touch their effects° in this. Thyself art coming   *Are realized*
    To see performed the dreaded act which thou
    So sought'st to hinder.
            Enter CAESAR *and all his train, marching.*
ALL   A way there, a way for Caesar!
330 DOLABELLA   O sir, you are too sure an augurer.
    That° you did fear is done.   *What*
CAESAR   Bravest at the last,
    She leveled at° our purposes and, being royal,   *discerned rightly*
    Took her own way. The manner of their deaths?
    I do not see them bleed.
DOLABELLA   Who was last with them?
335 FIRST GUARD A simple countryman that brought her figs.
    This was his basket.
CAESAR   Poisoned then.
FIRST GUARD   O Caesar,
    This Charmian lived but now; she stood and spake.
    I found her trimming up the diadem
    On her dead mistress. Tremblingly she stood,
    And on the sudden dropped.
340 CAESAR   Oh, noble weakness!
    If they had swallowed poison, 'twould appear
    By external swelling; but she looks like sleep,
    As° she would catch another Antony   *As if*
    In her strong toil° of grace.   *snare*
DOLABELLA   Here on her breast
345 There is a vent of blood and something blown;°   *emitted; swollen*
    The like is on her arm.
FIRST GUARD This is an aspic's trail, and these fig leaves
    Have slime upon them, such as th'aspic leaves
    Upon the caves of Nile.
CAESAR   Most probable
350 That so she died, for her physician tells me

She hath pursued conclusions° infinite   *trial outcomes*
Of easy ways to die. Take up her bed,
And bear her women from the monument.
She shall be buried by her Antony.
355 No grave upon the earth shall clip° in it   *embrace*
A pair so famous. High events as these
Strike° those that make° them, and their story is   *Afflict / cause*
No less in pity than his glory[1] which
Brought them to be lamented. Our army shall
360 In solemn show attend this funeral,
And then to Rome. Come, Dolabella, see
High order in this great solemnity.
        Exeunt all[, *the* GUARDS *bearing the dead bodies*].

---

1. *their . . . glory:* there is no less pity in their story than there is glory in the exploits of Caesar. The immodesty of these lines, in the guise of praise, recalls Caesar's ambiguous grief, his combination of calculation and sentiment, at the news of Antony's death in 5.1. The historical Octavius Caesar went on to order the murder of Ptolemy XV (Caesarion), Cleopatra's son by Julius Caesar. Since Julius Caesar was Octavius's great-uncle and adoptive father, this act, which ended the Ptolemaic dynasty, might be seen as fratricide. See 2.2.239–40, with note, and 3.6.1–16, with note to line 6. By contrast, after Antony and Cleopatra's deaths, the historical Octavia, over her brother Octavius's objections, raised Antony's children by Fulvia and Cleopatra, as well as her own five children by Antony and a previous husband.

Pericles

Pericles, Prince of Tyre (1607–08) was one of the most popular plays of its time and has proven effective in modern productions as well. Coherent and innovative, it brought a new dramatic genre—romance—into Shakespeare's work and, arguably, onto the English stage in general. As a written text, however, *Pericles* has proven problematic. It is not clear whether the difficulty is intrinsic to the play or results from a tendency to interpret it in light of Shakespeare's earlier works and thus to make unwarranted assumptions about plot, characterization, morality, dramaturgy, and style. Does the romance pattern succeed in mastering the play's messy materials? Does the play raise but not resolve social, political, and sexual anxieties, despite its structural and thematic unity? Are these even the right questions to ask?

Shakespeare's younger contemporary Ben Jonson spoke for many subsequent critics in disparaging *Pericles* as "a mouldy tale . . . and stale" and in attributing its success on the stage to its use of "scraps out of every dish." It is easy to see why. In *Pericles,* a king adorns his palace walls with his victims' skulls. A princess commits incest with her father. Another princess is kidnapped by pirates and sold to a brothel. Famine brings a city to its knees. An entire crew is lost in a storm. Two royal families are sent to fiery destruction. And Pericles is almost deposed by members of his restless nobility.

From the perspective of genre, *Pericles* enacts a transition from one kind of romance to another. Pericles first looks like a knight-errant risking death to win the beautiful maiden. But this standard medieval romance plot quickly gives way to late antique Greek romance narrative, in which faithful, virtuous lovers suffer separation and misfortune before their triumphant reunion. Pericles, then, does not act; he is acted upon. Bad things (as well as good) just happen to him. Every member of his family narrowly escapes death: two evade assassins sent by murderous monarchs, and the third survives burial at sea. Each is reported dead, only to experience apparently miraculous rebirth. The play eschews the probing of the protagonist's psyche that marks Shakespeare's immediately preceding tragic period in favor of clear-cut moral oppositions and emphatic poetic justice. By its end, the good are rewarded and the bad annihilated, but generally not owing to the protagonist's efforts.

Indeed, Pericles does not even get to act out significant portions of his destiny. Much of the story is told by Gower, the onstage presence of the fourteenth-century writer John Gower, whose major work, *Confessio Amantis,* is the most important direct source of *Pericles*. The eighth book of this verse narrative is devoted primarily to the tale of Apollonius of Tyre, which, via medieval intermediaries dating back to a fifth- or sixth-century Latin text, derives from a now-lost late classical Latin or, more probably, Greek romance influenced by *The Odyssey*. A different route through the medieval sources, this time incorporating the lives of early Christian saints who suffered persecution in brothels, leads to the other proximate source of the play, Laurence Twine's *Pattern of Painful Adventures* (written by 1576; published 1594?). *Pericles* is the first dramatization of these lengthy traditions. The shift in the protagonist's name from "Apollonius" to "Pericles" may derive from still other strains in the Apollonius tradition; from Sir Philip Sidney's *Arcadia* (1590), one of whose protagonists is named Pyrocles; or from one of Shakespeare's favorite sources, Plutarch's *Lives,* which perhaps provides still other characters' names. In addition to praising the renowned fifth-century B.C.E. Athenian statesman Pericles—head of the most famous of ancient city-states and

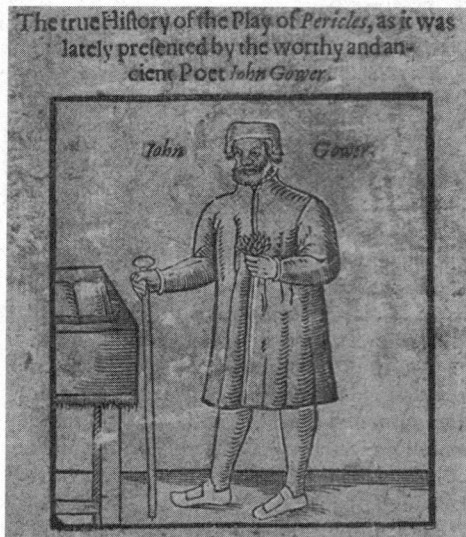

The true Hiftory of the Play of *Pericles*, as it was lately prefented by the worthy and ancient Poet *John Gower*.

Woodcut of John Gower, from the title page of *The Painful Adventures of Pericles Prince of Tyre*, by George Wilkins (1608).

hence appropriate to the play's world of city-states—it harshly judges his rival and successor, Cleon, as well as the fourth-century B.C.E. general Lysimachus, all names of characters in the play.

Pericles follows its sources more faithfully than do many of Shakespeare's works—for instance, by retaining an episodic plot. More striking still is the appearance of Gower himself as a character. His role as Chorus is broadly anticipated in *Henry V* (1599), but Gower also gives a specifically (pseudo-) medieval feel to the action—a feel connected to the antiquarian efforts of the time to recover the distant origins of England. Although Gower eventually reverts to standard pentameter lines, he starts out primarily in the rhymed tetrameter couplets in which *Confessio Amantis* is written: "To sing a song that old was sung / From ashes ancient Gower is come" (1.0.1–2). In addition, the theatrical Gower's diction often echoes the medieval poet's, extending even to antiquated language ("iwis" for "certainly," for example, at 2.0.2). His moralizing speeches are frequently graced by an unrealistic theatrical device—the dumb show. Further, Gower recounts much of the action in his eight monologues, as if to emphasize that poet's authorship of what sometimes feels like narrative, rather than dramatic, material. These metatheatrical strategies undermine the naturalistic illusion of the play, encouraging the audience to view events from a distance, to grasp the larger pattern rather than becoming emotionally engaged. Yet *Pericles* ultimately elicits that emotional engagement as well.

Gower's monologues structure the play more effectively than does the division into five acts introduced by later editors. The scene often shifts within each of the seven main groupings, but there is always a central focus. Gower introduces Antioch and incest (1.0), Pentapolis and Pericles' wooing of Thaisa (2.0), Ephesus and the saving of Thaisa (3.0), Tarsus and the attempted murder of Marina (4.0), Mytilene and Marina's virtuous life in the brothel (4.4), Mytilene again and Marina's reunion with Pericles (5.0), and Ephesus and the reunion with Thaisa (5.2), before providing the brief, concluding Epilogue.

The problematic authorship of *Pericles* is treated in the Textual Introduction. In brief, George Wilkins probably wrote at least the first two acts and Shakespeare most of the remaining three. The stylistic differences between the two parts of the play have long been recognized. Wilkins's dialogue is closer to Gower's language than is Shakespeare's. He also uses far more end-stopped rhyming couplets than does Shakespeare. By contrast, Shakespeare's predilection for blank-verse enjambment, in which the phrase or idea does not conclude at the end of the line, produces a tension between syntax and verse form.

Thus, Wilkins's Pericles decorously repudiates the incestuous Daughter of Antiochus:

> Fair glass of light, I loved you, and could still,
> Were not this glorious casket stored with ill.

> . . . .
> For he's no man on whom perfections wait
> That, knowing sin within, will touch the gate.
> . . . .
> But being played upon before your time,
> Hell only danceth at so harsh a chime.
>   (1.1.77–86)

Shakespeare's Pericles reacts to a storm in more complex but also more colloquial verse:

>   Oh, still
> Thy deafening dreadful thunders; gently quench
> Thy nimble sulphurous flashes! . . .
> . . . .
>   . . . The seaman's whistle
> Is as a whisper in the ears of death,
> Unheard. —Lychorida! —Lucina, O
> Divinest patroness and midwife gentle
> To those that cry by night, convey thy deity
> Aboard our dancing boat, make swift the pangs
> Of my queen's travails! —Now, Lychorida!
>   (3.1.4–14)

As a result, Shakespeare's section of the play is theatrically livelier, the contrast with Gower's increasingly frequent monologues sharper. Pericles' meeting with the Fishermen is Wilkins's only episode of a piece with such later parts of the play as the second tempest; the revival of Pericles' wife, Thaisa; the two brothel scenes; and the first recognition scene. And structurally, *Pericles* breaks neatly in two: in the first two acts, Pericles moves from felicity to misfortune and back to felicity; in the remaining three, he repeats this pattern more intensely.

Yet such distinctions are misleading. Many Renaissance plays were written by more than one dramatist; Shakespeare collaborated on about a fifth of his plays, mostly near the beginning and end of his career. Especially in performance, such works do not necessarily seem any less unified than single-author pieces. Even though its "feel" shifts, *Pericles'* motifs remain consistent—Pericles as noble tree, his jewel-like family, destructive eating, providential storms, divine music.

Its episodes also echo one another, within and across the play's two parts. The deadly skulls at Antiochus's palace are answered by the harmless jousting at Simonides' court; the bad potential marriage to Antiochus's Daughter is echoed by the good real one to Simonides'. The incestuous relationship between Antiochus and his Daughter is contrasted with the lovingly innocent one between Pericles and Marina. Thaliard's foiled attempt to assassinate Pericles at Antiochus's behest anticipates Leonine's failed effort to murder Marina at Dionyza's. Cleon calls down the "curse of heaven and men" (1.4.103) should his family prove ungrateful to Pericles, and when his family does so prove, "him and his they [his subjects] in his palace burn" (Epilogue 14). The storm that costs Pericles his men but leads him to Thaisa is paralleled by the later tempest that apparently disposes of Thaisa. The vigorous popular culture of the Fishermen is set against the degraded popular culture of the brothel. The vow of chastity that Simonides attributes to Thaisa to dismiss all her suitors except Pericles is fulfilled in her vow of chastity when she thinks Pericles is gone forever and in Marina's successful defense of her chastity in the brothel. The apparent burial of Thaisa is duplicated in the apparent interment of her daughter. And the excessive love of Antiochus for his daughter and, in a different way, of Dionyza for hers contrasts with the defective love of Cleon for his daughter and, arguably, of Pericles for Marina—until the end of the play, when Pericles demonstrates the appropriate love of father for daughter.

Throughout, the play insists that the miseries inflicted on Pericles and his family ultimately lead to higher felicity. As noted earlier, this is the structure of tragicomic romance, the genre of nearly all of Shakespeare's final plays. Typically, *Pericles* recapitulates Shakespeare's previous work while reversing its chronology: the tragic mood of the early seventeenth century precedes the comic tone of the 1590s. The play echoes *King Lear* in its storm scenes and its reunion of ravaged father and redemptive daughter, who gives "another life / To Pericles thy father" (5.1.196–97); it then duplicates *The Comedy of Errors,* which draws on the same sources as *Pericles* in its concluding retrieval of the missing wife-turned-priestess from Diana's temple at Ephesus.

Gower emphasizes this larger pattern—"I'll show you those in troubles reign, / Losing a mite, a mountain gain" (2.0.7–8)—which becomes especially prominent in Shakespeare's scenes owing to Diana's presiding benevolence. She is first mentioned when, according to Simonides, Thaisa opts for continued virginity (2.5.10). Thaisa invokes her upon awakening in an opened coffin (3.2.102–03), as does Pericles when he vows not to cut his hair until his baby, Marina, is married (3.3.28–30). Thaisa becomes Diana's priestess (3.4.12, 4.0.4), and Marina places her virginity in the goddess's protection (4.2.136). Finally, after Pericles is reunited with Marina, Diana appears to him in a dream, promising him happiness only if he goes to her temple in Ephesus and publicly recounts his loss of Thaisa (5.1.226–36). This supernatural moment recalls Thaisa's quasi-magical preservation by Cerimon (of whom Pericles says, "The gods can have no mortal officer / More like a god than you," 5.3.62–63), anticipates Pericles' actual meeting with Thaisa in the final scene (where Diana is repeatedly mentioned), and follows hard upon Pericles' perhaps unique ability to hear "the music of the spheres" (5.1.217)—a heavenly harmony that extends to human affairs below. Sensitivity to music has marked Pericles' family throughout.

The Temple of Diana at Ephesus (from the series The Eight Wonders of the World) after Maarten van Heemskerck, 1572. Found in the collection of the Museum Boijmans Van Beuningen, Rotterdam.

Pericles is "music's master," Thaisa awakens to "rough and woeful music," and, most telling, Marina "sings like one immortal" (2.5.30, 3.2.86, 5.0.3).

These signs of a divine providence guiding the destiny of Pericles' family are pagan in form but Christian in content. They draw on Catholic traditions, only partially reworked along Protestant lines. Tragicomedy's movement from tribulation to triumph is modeled on the *felix culpa*, Adam and Eve's fortunate fall that led to the redemptive coming of Christ. Antioch recalls Eden's sinister side: Pericles will "taste the fruit of yon celestial tree / Or die in th'adventure"; Antiochus praises the "golden fruit, but dangerous to be touched" and later warns, "touch not, upon thy life" (1.1.22–23, 29, 88). *Pericles*' eastern Mediterranean of late Greek antiquity also evokes Judaism and early Christianity. Tyre, connected with the reigns of David and Solomon, was later captured by the Christians in the First Crusade and was seen during the Renaissance as the home of Britain's first colonizers. Antioch recalls the Maccabee rebellion; in addition, Peter and Paul preached there. Paul was born in Tarsus and had a ministry in Ephesus. The Fishermen of Pentapolis are literally, like St. Peter, fishers of men. Amid talk of devouring whales (2.1.28–42), they fish out Pericles, whom "the sea hath cast upon [their] coast" (2.1.55) in a manner that recalls the biblical Jonah, understood in Christian allegory to prefigure Christ's resurrection. Thaisa later undergoes a similar resurrection; and at Mytilene, the Pander laments, "Neither is our profession any . . . calling" (4.2.35)—where "calling" has religious reverberations.

In a final, typically moralistic speech, Gower tells the audience:

> In Pericles, his queen, and daughter seen,
> Although assailed with fortune fierce and keen,
> Virtue preserved from fell destruction's blast,
> Led on by heaven and crowned with joy at last.
> (Epilogue 3–6)

Although there is no ambiguity here, the play as a whole leaves room for doubts. Despite the triumph over a pagan "fortune" by an implicitly Christian "heaven," Pericles' sufferings feel arbitrary. It is hard to understand, except by fairy-tale logic, why his predecessors cannot solve Antiochus's riddle or why the King advertises the very secret he wants to preserve. Similarly, the play does not explain why Pericles leaves his daughter at Tarsus or why Dionyza, eager to be rid of Marina, does not consider sending her home instead of murdering her. More important, the misfortunes in *Pericles* seem unrelenting, unconnected, and unrelated to the behavior of their victims. Yet this disjunction fails to inspire any Job-like reflections on injustice. In short, divine providence is not fully integrated with secular misfortune. Perhaps the play reveals a contingent relationship between human vicissitude and redemptive transcendence, thereby unsettling its own ostensible program.

Second, *Pericles* bears a complicated relationship to its social and political material. Popular culture provides some of the play's most engaging scenes without, however, linking up to the larger movement of the plot. The initial storm leaves Pericles "[be]reft of ships and men" (2.3.81). The Fishermen who help him receive his praise:

> FIRST FISHERMAN . . . I can compare our rich misers to nothing so fitly as to a whale; 'a plays and tumbles, driving the poor fry before him, and at last devours them all at a mouthful. . . .
> PERICLES [*aside*] A pretty moral.　　　　　　　　　　　　　　(2.1.29–35)

This account, which may echo the language of the 1607 Midlands Uprising against landlord enclosures of the common lands, leads to a rebuke of the monarch: "if the good King Simonides were of my mind . . . We would purge the land of these drones that rob the bee of her honey" (2.1.42–46). But the complaint quickly disappears, leaving only the positive image of Pericles' future father-in-law. Similarly, although

Pericles promises the fishermen "if that ever my low fortune's better, / I'll pay your bounties; till then, rest your debtor" (2.1.140–41), the debt, which is usually honored in previous tales of Apollonius (including Twine's), is not recalled when Pericles' fortunes quickly improve.

The anticommercial outlook implicit in the Fisherman's denunciation of "rich misers" also informs the brothel scenes, which, like Pericles' encounter with the Fishermen, peoples the Greek Mediterranean setting with English characters. Prostitution is the only market-driven activity depicted in the play. The Bawd advises Marina in economic terms: "You have fortunes coming upon you. Mark me: you must seem to do that fearfully which you commit willingly, despise profit where you have most gain. To weep that you live as ye do makes pity in your lovers. Seldom but that pity begets you a good opinion, and that opinion a mere profit" (4.2.105–10). Marina is thus urged to perform like an actor in London's professional theaters. With commerce almost reduced to the oldest profession, a profession practiced in the neighborhoods around the theaters, the play implicitly links itself to the very activity that it depicts Marina nobly resisting.

Further, despite exploiting popular culture for theatrical effect, *Pericles* excludes that culture from the final reconciliation, concluding with a purely aristocratic and royal circle. This ending is tacitly anticipated by the linguistic divisions of the popular scenes: the Fishermen and brothel-keepers speak prose, whereas Pericles and Marina favor blank verse. Nevertheless, *Pericles* is the only Shakespearean romance written before the King's Men began performing during the winter at Blackfriars, a "private," elite, commercial theater. It was acted at the Globe, the preeminent "public" theater, and its success in the early seventeenth century attests to the at least partly popular appeal of its traditional romance plot.

Pericles also seems critical of absolute monarchy. This makes sense: the value of such leadership is questionable. Antioch has been ruled by an incestuous murderer, with no indication of his successor. The Governor of Tarsus lets his city slip into famine; his wife is an attempted murderer. Although the inhabitants eventually kill the couple, their own earlier behavior does not inspire confidence: "All poverty was scorned, and pride so great, / The name of help grew odious to repeat" (1.4.30–31). Under duress, they are even worse:

> Those mothers who to nuzzle up their babes
> Thought naught too curious are ready now
> To eat those little darlings whom they loved.
> (1.4.42–44)

The passage echoes in reverse the riddle's equation of cannibalism with incest—"I feed / On mother's flesh" (1.1.65–66)—while also recalling other moments where "to eat" is to devour. The Fishermen express dissatisfaction with the state of things, which their good King does nothing to remedy. Ephesus's future remains unspecified: Lord Cerimon acts as a private figure. Lysimachus, the Governor of Mytilene, frequents a brothel until Marina converts him; at the play's end, the brothel remains, while Lysimachus, betrothed to Marina, leaves Mytilene in uncertain hands and goes off to rule Tyre. In so doing, does he bring syphilis into Pericles' family? The verbal juxtapositions upon his initial entry allow for this possibility: "there's no way to be rid on't [Marina's virginity] but by the way to the pox [syphilis]. Here comes the Lord Lysimachus disguised" (4.6.13–14).

Earlier, Pericles' departure from Tyre inspires aristocratic "mutiny" (3.0.29) and begins the practice of absentee landlordism that reaches its climax near the end when his deputy, Helicanus, appoints Escanes as *his* deputy and sets out with Pericles. Shortly thereafter, Pericles and Thaisa accede to the throne of Pentapolis, a society whose defects the Fishermen have dissected. The death of Thaisa's father, "the good Simonides," is not an occasion for grief but an opportunity to dole out kingdoms and divide a family only just reunited. This outcome may parallel the isolation of James I's family members, an isolation emblematized by James's failure to come to the deathbeds of two of his children. Pericles' absenteeism could also reflect on James's style of governing. Alternatively, it might simply recognize the necessity of intergenerational separation for dynastic continuity, just as Marina's redemptive role may reflect upon Shakespeare's relationship with his own daughter.

Here, *Pericles* also raises sexual doubts. Although the protagonists are subjected to debased sexuality only to demonstrate their Diana-like purity, perhaps they do not escape unpolluted. In Gower's *Confessio Amantis*, Pericles' daughter is not Marina but Thaisa. From an extradramatic perspective, then, sexual relations with Thaisa, which in Gower would have been incest, become appropriate marital intimacy. It is as if the name change allowed Pericles to have the experience castigated in Antioch under the protection of the marriage bond. When the catatonic Pericles reaches Mytilene, Lysimachus agrees that Marina might be the cure:

> She questionless, with her sweet harmony
> And other choice attractions, would allure
> And make a batt'ry through his deafened ports.
> (5.1.37–39)

Hence, Lysimachus, ignorant of Marina's parentage, suggests through "choice attractions" and "allure" an unfamilial relationship between father and daughter. So, too, does Pericles. He addresses Marina as "Thou that begett'st him that did thee beget" (5.1.185)—a line that expresses gratitude but that also recalls the generational reversals of Antiochus's incestuous riddle: "He's father, son, and husband mild; / I, mother, wife, and yet his child" (1.1.69–70).

Tragicomic romance often provides a nontragic resolution to the tale of Oedipus, Pericles' predecessor in solving murderous riddles. Do Pericles' words to Marina reverse or repeat Antiochus's riddle? Ambiguities such as this one trouble the providential pattern. By name, Pericles recalls an Athenian virtue at odds with the quasi-allegorical landscape through which he travels, a landscape of Asiatic luxury and decadence, of an incest associated with tyranny whose primary alternative seems to be anarchy. In other words, the various social, political, and sexual ambiguities of *Pericles* bear less on the psychology or morality of the protagonist than on the overall import of the play.

Modern performances of *Pericles* embrace the challenge posed by this pattern. Although some productions attempt naturalistic settings and complex characters, most respect *Pericles*' indifference to such matters by exploiting what's unrealistic about the play and Renaissance theater generally. The doubling of parts has led to the same actress playing Antiochus's Daughter and Marina, Marina and Thaisa, or Thaisa and Dionyza. This procedure can accentuate the differences between the paired characters; more often, however, it generates overtones of incest. Relatedly, when one actor plays all the Mediterranean kings, the stage captures the similarity, the repetitiousness, of Pericles' adventures and, hence, the ritualistic quality of the work. Second, although Gower can establish intimacy between audience and action, the tendency has been to follow the German dramatist Bertolt Brecht in resisting empathy and identification. Gower's role thus underscores the play's theatricality: it has been sung, treated as a voice-over, and played by a street performer. The dramatized action itself has been represented as street theater, as the work of a traveling troupe, as Chinese opera, as an African American boatswain's sea chantey to his fellow sailors aboard ship, as a child's picture book, as events in an asylum, as the floor show in a gay brothel. Sometimes the result is an ironic, farcical approach to the plot's absurdities. The price, however, is the failure of the climactic recognition scenes, which thrive on psychological nuance. Similar problems may arise with overtly political interpretations, though a feminist or multiethnic perspective can be suggestive. Perhaps the solution is to refuse to level the unevenness of the play, remaining faithful to its various registers.

WALTER COHEN

SELECTED BIBLIOGRAPHY

Frye, Susan. "Incest and Authority in *Pericles, Prince of Tyre.*" *Incest and the Literary Imagination.* Ed. Elizabeth Barnes. Gainesville: UP of Florida, 2002. 39–58. Focuses on three key scenes (incest, tournament, reunion) to argue that incest—understood physically, politically, and psychologically—is tied to questions of the royal family's legitimacy.

Gossett, Suzanne. "'You not your child well loving': Text and Family Structure in *Pericles.*" *A Companion to Shakespeare's Works.* Vol. 4: *Poems, Problem Comedies, Late Plays.* Ed. Richard Dutton and Jean E. Howard. Malden, MA: Blackwell, 2003. 348–64. Treats the play as an exploration of the proper love between parent and daughter (neither excessive nor deficient), perhaps rooted in Shakespeare's own family experience.

Halpern, Richard. *Shakespeare among the Moderns.* Ithaca, NY: Cornell UP, 1997. 140–58. Explores the weak internal causal logic of the plot combined with the transcendent romance plan as a symptomatic response to the decaying older social order.

Healy, Margaret. "*Pericles* and the Pox." *Shakespeare's Late Plays: New Readings.* Ed. Jennifer Richards and James Knowles. Edinburgh: Edinburgh UP, 1999. 92–107. Argues that the original audience, recognizing that Lysimachus carried venereal disease, would have been horrified by the marriage of Marina to pox-ridden Lysimachus.

Hiscock, Andrew. "*Pericles, Prince of Tyre* and the Appetite for Narrative." *Late Shakespeare, 1608–1613.* Ed. Andrew J. Power and Rory Loughnane. Cambridge: Cambridge UP, 2013. 16–36. Considers the importance of narrative at the expense of character, with Gower and, later, Marina as the key narrators among many.

Orkin, Martin. *Local Shakespeares: Proximations and Power.* London: Routledge, 2005. 63–81. Describes *Pericles* as a meditation on male unruliness, in this way providing a partial critique of its own patriarchal romance resolution.

Roebuck, Thomas, and Laurie Maguire. "*Pericles* and the Language of National Origins." *This England, That Shakespeare: New Angles on Englishness and the Bard.* Ed. Willy Maley and Margaret Tudeau-Clayton. Farnham, Surrey: Ashgate, 2010. 23–48. Examines the play's pattern of loss and recovery as a means of constructing national identity through, for instance, Gower's link with Welsh and Catholic heritages, or Phoenicians as the original settlers of Britain.

Skeele, David, ed. *"Pericles": Critical Essays.* New York: Garland, 2000. A collection of criticism beginning with Ben Jonson in the early seventeenth century and of theatrical reviews beginning in the mid-nineteenth. Modern critics include Knight, Felperin, Barber and Wheeler, Kahn, Mullaney, Adelman, and Novy, among others.

Tanner, Tony. *Prefaces to Shakespeare.* Cambridge: Harvard UP, 2010. 695–721. Presents a general interpretation of the play focusing on the relationship between father and daughter and drawing on religion (saints' lives, pagan gods) and ritual (incest and cannibalism taboos).

Werth, Tiffany Jo. *The Fabulous Dark Cloister: Romance in England after the Reformation.* Baltimore, MD: Johns Hopkins UP, 2011. 80–96. Explores *Pericles* as a romance drawing on the tradition of saints' miracles, treated in Catholic terms in Thaisa's resurrection, in Protestant terms in Marina's behavior, and ambiguously in the conclusion at Diana's temple.

FILM

Pericles, Prince of Tyre. 1984. Dir. David Hugh Jones. UK. 177 min. Generally praised BBC production, naturalistic by TV-studio standards but not by those of big-budget movies.

TEXTUAL INTRODUCTION

Since *Pericles* was not printed in the Folio of 1623, the basis for all editions is the quarto published by Henry Gosson in 1609 (Q1). This was the work of two printing houses and three different compositors, which speeded up the process and helped spread employment but seems to have led to a poor printing job, perhaps because Gosson's workmen had never printed a play before. The mixture of verse and prose made it hard to estimate how many lines to allocate to each sheet, and verse is sometimes set as prose to save space. Speech prefixes and stage directions seem to have been written in italics, and the compositors could not always tell the one from the other, sometimes omitting speech prefixes altogether. But while some of the textual problems may result from compositor error, others are consistent across the work of all three compositors and probably originated with complex manuscript copy.

Differences in literary quality between the first two acts and the rest led the play's earliest editors to suggest that the play might be collaborative. Recent studies, particularly those of MacDonald P. Jackson, argue that at least the first two acts are by George Wilkins, a minor writer. His part of *Pericles* shares mannerisms with his other writings, not least a tendency to omit relative pronouns for the sake of meter (e.g., the implied "what" in "Since I have here my father gave in his will" [2.1.132]).

The King's Men had originally registered the play with the Stationers' Company in 1608, the same year that Wilkins published a prose novel called *The Painful Adventures of Pericles Prince of Tyre, Being the True History of the Play of Pericles, as it was lately presented by the worthy and ancient Poet John Gower*, which begins, like a play, with a cast of characters and presents itself as "the book of the play" successfully performed "by the Kings Majesties Players." It may be that the publication of a pamphlet claiming a direct connection made it difficult for the company to proceed with publication of their play, and scholars believe that the manuscript Gosson used was not the official playbook.

One view is that the manuscript was based on what "reporters" could remember about the play in performance. Actors in Shakespeare's theaters received only their own "parts," consisting of lines and cues; the authors may have retained only the sections of the play they themselves had written. Judging by the lines apparently best remembered, Gary Taylor has suggested that the main "reporter" was a boy actor playing Lychorida, Marina, and the Third Fisherman. If this boy were apprenticed to the actor playing Gower, this might explain why the choruses seem mostly accurate. However, this theory assumes that the boy actor was "fired" when his voice broke or because of the frequent plague closures of the public theaters between 1604 and 1611. The King's Men continued to play privately, however, and a boy good enough to play leading female roles might have tried to sustain his career. The evidence is not clear-cut. The boy's absence from the scenes at Tyre could explain their incoherence, but not the apparent discrepancy at 4.6, where Lysimachus first behaves like a familiar visitor to the brothel and then rapidly backtracks.

The culprit may be Wilkins. That he had already published with Gosson raises suspicions: *The Painful Adventures* may be an attempt to make money out of a play that had been a huge financial success for the King's Men while earning its co-writer only a flat fee. However, certain misreadings do seem to be the result of mishearing and are less likely to come from Wilkins than from someone taking down the lines in shorthand. And it remains possible that the manuscript behind Gosson's edition came from the King's Men themselves. If they could not print the play without Gosson lodging a complaint against them for harming sales of the Wilkins novel, they may have decided to cut their losses by selling the play to him. If so, then the manuscript might have been copied quickly and carelessly, and there may also have been censorship, particularly in the scenes at Tyre that suggest a threat of mutiny among Pericles' subjects. The scene between Lysimachus and Marina might have been revised to avoid showing a man in high office visiting a brothel.

The main question for an editor is how much—or *how*—to use the Wilkins novel. Directors have often drawn on it to supplement the text in performance; some editors have printed passages from it in footnotes or appendices, and the Oxford edition "reconstructed" the play by importing material from the novel into both dialogue and stage directions. The first part of *The Painful Adventures* can help clarify the first two acts of the play, which are often verbally close to it (the novel even falls into blank verse at times). Unlike the play, the novel gives full details about the five princes who compete with Pericles in the tournament. Some editions and productions transfer this information to the speeches of Thaisa and Simonides, assuming that the ritual presentation remains consistent throughout, yet it is possible that the scene was deliberately truncated to avoid repetition. Additions based on Wilkins may make the play more attractive to modern tastes—for instance, by giving Thaisa and Marina more dialogue—but have no textual justification.

The Norton Shakespeare takes the view that, for students of Shakespeare, it is better to acknowledge rather than conceal textual problems. We correct obvious printers' errors and print as verse passages that have a basic blank verse rhythm, while recognizing that there can be no certainty about lineation and that it is hard to distinguish between errors and bad or hasty writing. We insert minimal stage directions, but we do not attempt to direct the play. *Pericles* works well in the theater precisely because it leaves so much to the imagination.

LOIS POTTER

TEXTUAL BIBLIOGRAPHY

Gossett, Suzanne. "'To foster is not always to preserve': Feminist Inflections in Editing *Pericles*." In *Arden: Editing Shakespeare*. Ed. Ann Thompson and Gordon McMullan. London: Thompson Learning, 2003: 65–80.

Jackson, Macdonald P. *Defining Shakespeare: Pericles as Test Case*. Oxford: Oxford UP, 2003.

Taylor, Gary. "The Transmission of *Pericles*." *Publications of the Bibliographical Society of America* 80 (1986): 193–217.

PERFORMANCE NOTE

Forty-six of *Pericles*' fifty-four speaking roles are limited to one act or scene, so a foremost concern for directors is how to redeploy actors throughout its many episodes. Doubling roles can lend coherence to the play's distinct halves and complement its pronounced artificiality, while reinforcing (or destabilizing) initial archetypes and hierarchies. Productions can easily reprise kings and courtiers at each new setting; additionally, the murderers Thaliard and Leonine can be played by one actor, the fishermen can return as sailors and pirates, and Dionyza, doubled as the Bawd, can continue harassing Marina. Doubling can also enhance the quality of the play's resolution, if, for example, the incestuous Antiochus and his Daughter progress to the more acceptably coupled Lysimachus and Marina. Gower, too, can assume minor roles within scenes, or his role can be divided among several performers, as indeed can Pericles', productions sometimes working through two or three substitutions to literalize the length of the protagonist's suffering.

Directors must also determine how to portray Gower and how to build psychological depth in Pericles: dramaturgical challenges that are, in fact, closely intertwined. Gower can appear well integrated into the play's Mediterranean world in costume and presentational manner; or he can stand apart from the action, presenting a calm naturalism against the artifice otherwise prevalent. A blatant performer, increasing the audience's sense of spectacle, may help Pericles seem comparatively human and sympathetic, while an unaffected Gower can earn support for Pericles through plain, credible accounts of his misfortunes. Productions can also "deepen" Pericles by lingering over his brief soliloquies, or making his and Marina's tormentors less cartoonish, though some exploit his two-dimensionality to increase audience surprise at his moving recognition scene with Marina. Productions also must decide how complicit Antiochus's Daughter is; whether Bolt and the brothel keepers are comic pragmatists or genuine threats; whether Marina's innocence is genuine or cleverly affected. They also must determine the nature and audibility of the "music of the spheres" (see Digital Edition PC 1) and resolve the staging for Simonides' tournament, Thaisa's burial at sea, and the appearance of Diana.

BRETT GAMBOA

The Play of Pericles, Prince of Tyre

[THE PERSONS OF THE PLAY

John GOWER, Presenter and Chorus

PERICLES, Prince of Tyre
MARINA, daughter to Pericles and Thaisa

In Antioch:
ANTIOCHUS, King of Antioch
DAUGHTER to Antiochus
THALIARD, attendant to Antiochus

In Tyre:
HELICANUS, counselor in Tyre
ESCANES, counselor in Tyre
Three LORDS of Tyre

In Tarsus:
CLEON, Governor of Tarsus
DIONYZA, wife to Cleon
LORD of Tarsus
LEONINE, servant to Cleon and Dionyza
Three PIRATES

In Pentapolis:
Three FISHERMEN
SIMONIDES, King of Pentapolis
THAISA, daughter to Simonides
FIRST KNIGHT, of Sparta
SECOND KNIGHT, of Macedon
THIRD KNIGHT, of Antioch
FOURTH KNIGHT
FIFTH KNIGHT
MARSHALL
LYCHORIDA, a nurse
Five Squires

MASTER of a ship
SAILORS

In Ephesus:
CERIMON, a gentleman of Ephesus
PHILEMON, his servant
Two VISITING SERVANTS
SERVANTS to Cerimon
Two GENTLEMEN of Ephesus

In Mytilene:
PANDER
BAWD, wife to Pander

BOLT, servant in the brothel
Two GENTLEMEN of Mytilene
LYSIMACHUS, Governor of Mytilene
LORD of Mytilene
Maid, companion to Marina

DIANA, Goddess of chastity

Lords, Ladies, Attendants, Messengers, Sailors, Pages, Priestesses of Diana,
Worshippers at the Temple of Diana]

1.0

Enter GOWER [as Chorus].[1]

GOWER[2] To sing a song that old° was sung		*of old*
From ashes ancient Gower is come,[3]		
Assuming man's infirmities°		*Donning mortal flesh*
To glad your ear and please your eyes.		
It hath been sung at festivals,		
On ember eves and holy ales,[4]		
And lords and ladies in their lives		
Have read it for restoratives.°		*as a medicine*
The purchase° is to make men glorious,		*benefit*
Et bonum quo antiquius eo melius.[5]		
If you, born in these latter times		
When wit's more ripe,° accept my rhymes,		*poetry's more advanced*
And that° to hear an old man sing		*And if*
May to your wishes pleasure bring,		
I life would wish, and that I might		
Waste it° for you like taper° light.		*Use it up / candle*

[*He indicates the stage setting.*]

This° Antioch, then. Antiochus the great[6]		*This is*
Built up this city for his chiefest seat,°		*capital*
The fairest in all Syria.		
I tell you what mine authors° say.		*sources*
This king unto him took a fere°		*mate*
Who died and left a female heir		
So buxom,° blithe, and full of face°		*lively / attractive (?)*
As° heaven had lent her all his° grace,		*As if / its*
With whom the father liking took		
And her to incest did provoke.		
Bad child, worse father, to entice his own		
To evil should° be done by none.		*that should*
By custom what they did begin		
Was with long use accounted no sin.[7]		
The beauty of this sinful dame		
Made many princes thither frame°		*go*
To seek her as a bedfellow,		
In marriage pleasures playfellow.		
Which to prevent, he made a law		

Line numbers: 5, 10, 15, 20, 25, 30, 35

1.0

1. TEXTUAL COMMENT For the role of Gower and the division of the play into acts and scenes, see Digital Edition TC 1.
2. Gower's story of Apollonius of Tyre is an important source of the play. See the Introduction.
3. Like most of Gower's choruses in the play, this one is mainly in rhyming tetrameter couplets.

4. *ember eves:* evenings before periods of religious fasting. *holy ales:* country festivals.
5. And the older something good is, the better (Latin).
6. *Antioch . . . Antiochus:* Recalling the Maccabee rebellion and the missions of Peter and Paul.
7. *By . . . sin:* When what they started (incest) became a habit, they no longer experienced it as a sin.

To keep her still,° and men in awe,   *always*
That whoso asked her for his wife,
His riddle told not,[8] lost his life.
So for her many a wight° did die—   *fellow*
   [*He indicates a display of severed heads.*]
40   As yon grim looks do testify.
What now ensues, to the judgment of your eye
I give my cause who best can justify.[9]   *Exit.*

1.1

Enter ANTIOCHUS, *Prince* PERICLES,[1] *and followers.*

ANTIOCHUS Young Prince of Tyre,[2] you have at large received°   *fully understood*
   The danger of the task you undertake.
PERICLES I have, Antiochus, and with a soul
   Emboldened with the glory of her praise
5   Think death no hazard in this enterprise.
ANTIOCHUS Music!
   [*Music plays.*][3]
   Bring in our daughter, clothèd like a bride
   For the embracements even of Jove himself,
   At whose conception, till Lucina reigned,
10   Nature this dowry gave: to glad her presence,[4]
   The senate house of planets all did sit
   To knit in her their best perfections.[5]
   Enter Antiochus' DAUGHTER.
PERICLES See where she comes, appareled like the spring,
   Graces her subjects[6] and her thoughts the king
15   Of every virtue gives[7] renown to men;
   Her face the book of praises[8] where is read
   Nothing but curious° pleasures, as° from thence   *delicate / as if*
   Sorrow were ever razed, and testy wrath
   Could never be her mild° companion.   *(modifies "her")*
20   You gods that made me man, and sway° in love,   *hold sway*
   That have enflamed desire in my breast
   To taste the fruit of yon celestial tree
   Or die in th'adventure, be my helps,
   As I am son and servant to your will,
25   To compass° such a boundless happiness.   *attain*
ANTIOCHUS Prince Pericles—
PERICLES That would be son to great Antiochus—
ANTIOCHUS Before thee stands this fair Hesperides
   With golden fruit, but dangerous to be touched,
30   For deathlike dragons here affright thee hard.[9]

8. If he failed to explain Antiochus's riddle.
9. *to . . . justify:* I present my case ("cause") to your judgment—you who can best legally excuse me of lying (or perceive the truth of my story).
1.1 Location: The palace at Antioch.
1. *Pericles:* Named after Pericles, the fifth-century B.C.E. Athenian leader, from Plutarch's *Lives,* or Pyrocles, a protagonist in Sidney's *Arcadia* (1590).
2. *Tyre:* Associated with David and Solomon; captured by a Christian army in the First Crusade.
3. TEXTUAL COMMENT On the role of music in the play, in relationship to both textual and performance issues, see Digital Edition TC 2.
4. *At . . . presence:* From my daughter's conception until she was born (Lucina was the Roman goddess of childbirth, often equated with Diana), nature gave

her this dowry: to make her presence welcome (or to make her happy).
5. *The . . . perfections:* Astrological forces arranged to give her every perfection.
6. With mastery of all human graces.
7. *virtue gives:* virtue that gives. Shakespeare's co-author, Wilkins, who likely wrote this part of the play, often omits "that," "which," or "who" in such phrases.
8. The anthology of all that is commendable.
9. *Before . . . hard:* The Hesperides (here representing Antiochus's Daughter) were daughters of Hesperus inhabiting a garden where golden apples grew, whose entrance was patrolled by a dragon. The "golden fruit, but dangerous to be touched," like "the fruit of yon celestial tree" (line 22), also evokes Eden.

Her face like heaven enticeth thee to view
Her countless° glory, which desert must gain,   *(like the stars)*
And which without desert, because thine eye
Presumes to reach, all the whole heap° must die.   *your whole body*
    [*He indicates the severed heads.*]
35 Yon sometimes° famous princes, like thyself   *at one time*
Drawn by report, adventurous by° desire,   *taking a risk out of*
Tell thee with speechless tongues and semblance° pale   *appearances*
That, without covering save yon field of stars,
Here they stand martyrs slain in Cupid's wars,
40 And with dead cheeks advise thee to desist
From going on° death's net whom none resist.   *into*
PERICLES   Antiochus, I thank thee, who hath taught
My frail mortality to know itself
And by those fearful objects to prepare
45 This body, like to them, to what I must.°   *to die*
For death remembered should be like a mirror
Who tells us life's but breath, to trust it, error.
I'll make my will then, and, as sick men do
Who know the world, see heaven, but, feeling woe,
50 Grip not at earthly joys as erst° they did.   *previously*
So I bequeath a happy peace to you
And all good men, as every prince should do;
My riches to the earth, from whence they came;
[*to* DAUGHTER] But my unspotted fire of love to you.
55 Thus ready for the way of life or death,
I wait the sharpest blow, Antiochus.
ANTIOCHUS   Scorning advice, read the conclusion,° then.   *riddle*
    [*He gives* PERICLES *the riddle.*]
Which read and not expounded, 'tis decreed,
As these before thee, thou thyself shalt bleed.
60 DAUGHTER   Of all 'sayed° yet, mayst thou prove prosperous.   *who have tried ("assayed")*
Of all 'sayed yet, I wish thee happiness.
PERICLES   Like a bold champion I assume the lists,°   *enter combat*
Nor ask advice of any other thought
But faithfulness and courage.
    [*He reads*] *the riddle.*
65   "I am no viper, yet I feed
        On mother's flesh which did me breed.[1]
        I sought a husband, in which labor
        I found that kindness° in a father.   *kinship; affection*
        He's father, son, and husband mild;
70   I, mother, wife, and yet his child.
        How they may be, and yet in two,°   *only two people*
        As you will live resolve it you."
Sharp physic° is the last! ° [*aside*] But, O you powers   *Harsh medicine / (threat)*
That gives heaven countless eyes° to view men's acts!   *(the stars)*
75 Why cloud they not their sights perpetually,
If this be true, which makes me pale to read it?
Fair glass° of light,° I loved you, and could still,   *image / (the Daughter)*
Were not this glorious casket stored with ill.[2]

---

1. Vipers were thought to eat their way out of their   2. If your beautiful body did not contain a sinful soul.
mother's body at birth.

But I must tell you, now my thoughts revolt.
80 For he's no man on whom perfections wait°   *(as servants)*
That, knowing sin within, will touch the gate.
You are a fair viol, and your sense° the strings   *senses*
Who,° fingered to make man his lawful music,   *(strings; daughter)*
Would draw heaven down, and all the gods to hearken.
85 But being played upon before your time,
Hell only danceth at so harsh a chime.
Good sooth,° I care not for you.   *Truly*
       [*He approaches the* DAUGHTER.]
ANTIOCHUS   Prince Pericles, touch not,[3] upon thy life,
For that's an article within our law
90 As dangerous as the rest. Your time's expired.
Either expound now or receive your sentence.
PERICLES   Great King,
Few love to hear the sins they love to act.
'Twould 'braid° yourself too near° for me to tell it.   *upbraid / plainly*
95 Who° has a book of all that monarchs do,   *Whoever*
He's more secure to keep it shut than shown.
For vice repeated is like the wand'ring wind
Blows dust in others' eyes to spread itself.
And yet the end of all is bought thus dear:
100 The breath is gone and the sore eyes see clear
To stop the air would hurt them.[4] The blind mole casts
Copped° hills towards heaven, to tell° the earth is thronged   *Peaked / tell that*
By man's oppression, and the poor worm doth die for't.[5]
Kings are earth's gods; in vice, their law's their will,
105 And, if Jove stray, who dares say Jove doth ill?
It is enough you know,° and it is fit,   *(that I know)*
What being more known grows worse,[6] to smother° it.   *conceal*
All love the womb that their first being bred[7]—
Then give my tongue like leave to love my head.
110 ANTIOCHUS [*aside*]   Heaven, that I had thy head! He has found
    the meaning.
But I will gloze° with him. —Young prince of Tyre,   *dissemble*
Though by the tenor of our strict edict,
Your exposition misinterpreting,°   *since you misinterpreted*
We might proceed to cancel° of your days,   *to the termination*
115 Yet hope, succeeding from so fair a tree[8]
As your fair self, doth tune° us otherwise.   *move*
Forty days longer we do respite you,
If by which time our secret be undone,
This mercy shows we'll joy in such a son.
120 And until then your entertain° shall be   *entertainment*
As doth befit our honor and your worth.

---

3. Perhaps Pericles makes some movement that Antiochus misinterprets (further Edenic overtones).
4. *For vice . . . them:* For with the breath used to speak word of others' sins, one blows irritating dust in the eyes of the offenders. But the consequence is merely the speaker's death, since the offenders nevertheless see well enough to stop the news-spreading breath.
5. *The blind . . . for't:* When we blindly protest against the injustice of our superiors, we die (with "mole" meaning "worm"), or, less likely, innocent creatures suffer (here, the "mole" is different from the "worm" and may even destroy it).
6. Since bad deeds become worse for being known.
7. All love the daughter they raised when young (hence, hinting at incest). The obvious meaning is: all love their mother's womb.
8. Hope of a correct answer (an heir), with the successful answer (succession) coming from such a fine specimen (Pericles' regal lineage).

[*Exeunt* ANTIOCHUS *and his* DAUGHTER.]
PERICLES *remains alone.*

PERICLES How courtesy would seem° to cover sin,   lie
  When what is done is like an hypocrite,
  The which is good in nothing but in sight!°   appearance
125 If it be true that I interpret false,
  Then were it certain you were not so bad
  As with foul incest to abuse your soul.
  Where now you're both a father and a son
  By your untimely claspings with your child—
130 Which pleasures fits a husband, not a father—
  And she an eater of her mother's flesh
  By the defiling of her parents' bed,
  And both like serpents are, who, though they feed
  On sweetest flowers, yet they poison breed.
135 Antioch, farewell, for wisdom sees those men°   men who
  Blush not in actions blacker than the night
  Will shun no course° to keep them from the light.   means
  One sin, I know, another doth provoke:
  Murder's as near to lust as flame to smoke.
140 Poison and treason are the hands of sin—
  Ay, and the targets° to put off the shame.   shields
  Then, lest my life be cropped to keep you clear,°   (of blame)
  By flight I'll shun the danger which I fear.   *Exit.*
    Enter ANTIOCHUS.
ANTIOCHUS He hath found the meaning—for which we mean
145 To have his head.
  He must not live to trumpet forth my infamy
  Nor tell the world Antiochus doth sin
  In such a loathèd manner.
  And therefore instantly this prince must die,
150 For by his fall my honor must keep high.
  —Who attends us there?
    Enter THALIARD.
THALIARD   Doth your highness call?
ANTIOCHUS Thaliard!
  You are of our chamber,° Thaliard, and our mind   my chamberlain
  Partakes° her° private actions to your secrecy,   Imparts / its
155 And for your faithfulness we will advance you.
  Thaliard, behold:
  Here's poison, and here's gold.
  We hate the prince of Tyre, and thou must kill him.
  It fits° thee not to ask the reason why.   befits
160 Because we bid it.
  Say, is it done?
THALIARD   My lord, 'tis done.
    Enter a MESSENGER.
ANTIOCHUS   Enough.
  [*to* MESSENGER] Let your breath cool yourself, telling your
    haste.[9]
MESSENGER My lord,
  Prince Pericles is fled.   [*Exit* MESSENGER.]
ANTIOCHUS [*to* THALIARD] As thou wilt live,

9. Use your rapid breathing to cool yourself by explaining the reason for your haste.

165   Fly after, and, like an arrow shot
    From a well experienced archer hits the mark
    His eye doth level° at, so thou—never return   *aim*
    Unless thou say, "Prince Pericles is dead."
  THALIARD   My lord, if I can get him within my pistol's[1] length,°   *range*
170   I'll make him sure° enough. So farewell to your highness.   *unthreatening (dead)*
  ANTIOCHUS   Thaliard, adieu.   [*Exit* THALIARD.]
                        Till Pericles be dead,
    My heart can lend no succor to my head.   [*Exit.*]

1.2

    Enter PERICLES *with his* LORDS[, HELICANUS *among*
    them*].[1]
  PERICLES   Let none disturb us.
    [LORDS *wait at a distance.*]
                  Why should this change of thoughts,°   *changed state of mind*
    The sad companion, dull-eyed melancholy,
    Be my so used° a guest as not an hour   *accustomed*
    In the day's glorious walk or peaceful night—
5   The tomb where grief should sleep—can breed me quiet?
    Here pleasures court mine eyes, and mine eyes shun them,
    And danger, which I feared, is at Antioch,
    Whose arm seems far too short to hit me here.
    Yet neither pleasure's art can joy my spirits
10   Nor yet the other's° distance comfort me.   *(danger's)*
    Then it is thus: the passions of the mind,°   *obsessions*
    That have their first conception by misdread,°   *fear*
    Have after-nourishment and life by care,°   *worry*
    And what was first but fear what might be done,
15   Grows elder now and cares it be not done.[2]
    And so with me. The great Antiochus,
    'Gainst whom I am too little to contend,
    Since he's so great can° make his will his act,   *that he can*
    Will think me speaking though I swear to silence.
20   Nor boots it° me to say I honor him,   *does it help*
    If he suspect I may dishonor him.
    And what may make him blush in being known,
    He'll stop the course by which it might be known.
    With hostile forces he'll o'erspread the land,
25   And with the ostent° of war will look so huge   *display*
    Amazement° shall drive courage from the state,   *Terror*
    Our men be vanquished ere they do resist,
    And subjects punished that ne'er thought offense—
    Which care of them, not pity of myself,
30   Who am no more but as the tops of trees
    Which fence° the roots they grow by and defend them,   *shield*
    Makes both my body pine and soul to languish,
    And punish that° before that he would punish.[3]   *(myself)*
    All the LORDS *come forward.*
  FIRST LORD   Joy and all comfort in your sacred breast!

---

1. Anachronism: assassination by pistol is a sixteenth-century development, depicted in many plays of the period.
1.2 Location: The palace at Tyre.
1. TEXTUAL COMMENT For the problematic relation-ship between these Lords and the ones at line 33, see Digital Edition TC 3.
2. *And what . . . done:* And what starts out as simple fear matures into a more rational concern for safety.
3. *before . . . punish:* before he punishes me ("that").

35   SECOND LORD   And keep your mind, till you return to us,
     Peaceful and comfortable!
   HELICANUS   Peace, peace, and give experience tongue!
     They do abuse the King that flatter him.
     For flattery is the bellows blows up° sin—   *that blows up*
40   The thing the which° is flattered but° a spark   *which / is but*
     To which that wind gives heat and stronger glowing,
     Whereas reproof, obedient and in order,
     Fits kings as they are men, for they may err.
     When Signor Sooth[4] here does proclaim "peace,"
45   He flatters you, makes war upon your life.
     [*He kneels.*]   Prince, pardon me, or strike me if you please—
     I cannot be much lower than my knees.
   PERICLES [*to the other* LORDS]   All leave us else°—but let your   *except Helicanus*
     cares o'erlook
     What shipping and what lading's[5] in our haven,
     And then return to us.   [*Exeunt* LORDS.]
50   Helicanus, thou
     Hast movèd us. What seest thou in our looks?
   HELICANUS   An angry brow, dread lord.
   PERICLES   If there be such a dart° in princes' frowns,   *danger*
     How durst thy tongue move anger to our face?
55   HELICANUS   How dares the plants look up to heaven from
        whence
     They have their nourishment?
   PERICLES   Thou knowest I have power
     To take thy life from thee.
   HELICANUS   I have ground the ax myself;
     Do but you strike the blow.
   PERICLES   Rise! Prithee, rise. [*He raises* HELICANUS.] Sit down.
     Thou art no flatterer.
60   I thank thee for't, and heaven forbid
     That kings should let their ears hear their faults hid.
     Fit counselor and servant for a prince,
     Who by thy wisdom makes a prince thy servant,
     What wouldst thou have me do?
65   HELICANUS   To bear with patience such griefs
     As you yourself do lay upon yourself.
   PERICLES   Thou speak'st like a physician, Helicanus,
     That ministers a potion unto me
     That thou wouldst tremble to receive thyself.
70   Attend me° then: I went to Antioch,   *Listen to me*
     Where, as thou know'st, against the face of death
     I sought the purchase° of a glorious beauty   *acquisition*
     From whence an issue I might propagate,
     Are arms° to princes, and bring joys to subjects.   *Which are weapons*
75   Her face was to mine eye beyond all wonder,
     The rest—hark in thine ear—as black as incest.
     Which by my knowledge found, the sinful father
     Seemed not to strike but smooth,° but thou know'st this: *smooth over*
     'Tis time to fear when tyrants seem to kiss.
80   Which fear so grew in me, I hither fled—

---

4. Mock name for a flatterer, a soother of egos.
5. *let . . . lading's:* look carefully to find out what vessels are coming and going and what their cargo is.

Under the covering of a careful night
Who seemed my good protector—and, being here,
Bethought me what was past, what might succeed.°   *happen next*
I knew him tyrannous, and tyrants' fears
85   Decrease not but grow faster than the years,
And should he doubt,° as doubt no doubt he doth,   *suspect*
That I should open° to the listening air   *declare*
How many worthy princes' bloods were shed
To keep his bed of blackness unlaid ope,
90   To lop that doubt, he'll fill this land with arms
And make pretense of wrong that I have done him,
When all for mine—if I may call—offense
Must feel war's blow, who° spares not innocence.   *which*
Which love to all of which thyself art one,
Who now reproved'st me for't—
95 HELICANUS   Alas, sir—
PERICLES   Drew sleep out of mine eyes, blood from my cheeks,
Musings into my mind, with thousand doubts
How I might stop this tempest ere it came,
And finding little comfort to relieve them,°   *(his subjects; his doubts)*
100   I thought it princely charity to grieve them.°   *grieve (for) my subjects*
HELICANUS   Well, my lord, since you have given me leave to
    speak,
Freely will I speak. Antiochus you fear,
And justly too, I think, you fear the tyrant
Either by public war or private treason
105   Will take away your life.
Therefore, my lord, go travel for a while,
Till that his rage and anger be forgot, or till
The destinies do cut his thread of life.[6]
Your rule direct° to any. If to me,   *assign*
110   Day serves not light more faithful than I'll be.
PERICLES   I do not doubt thy faith.
But, should he wrong my liberties° in my absence?   *attack my country*
HELICANUS   We'll mingle our bloods together in the earth
From whence we had our being and our birth.
115 PERICLES   Tyre, I now look from thee then, and to Tarsus°   *(St. Paul's birthplace)*
Intend° my travel, where I'll hear from thee,   *Direct*
And by whose letters I'll dispose myself.
The care I had and have of subjects' good
On thee I lay, whose wisdom's strength can bear it.
120   I'll take thy word for faith, not ask thine oath—
Who° shuns not to break one, will sure crack both.   *He who*
But in our orbs° we'll live so round° and safe,   *places / prudently*
That time of both this truth shall ne'er convince:°   *refute*
Thou showed'st a subject's shine,° I a true prince.° *Exeunt.*   *radiance / prince's*

1.3

Enter THALIARD.

THALIARD   So this is Tyre, and this the court. Here must I kill
King Pericles, and if I do it not I am sure to be hanged at
home: 'tis dangerous. Well, I perceive he was a wise fellow
and had good discretion that, being bid to ask what he would

---

6. In Greek mythology, a person died when the   1.3 Location: Scene continues.
three Fates "cut his thread of life."

5 of the king, desired he might know none of his secrets.[1] Now
do I see he had some reason for't, for if a king bid a man be
a villain, he's bound by the indenture° of his oath to be one.   *servant's contract*
Hush, here comes the lords of Tyre.

      [*He stands aside.*] *Enter* HELICANUS, ESCANES,
      with other LORDS.

HELICANUS   You shall not need, my fellow peers of Tyre,
10 Further to question me of your king's departure.
His sealed° commission, left in trust with me,   *(with royal wax)*
Does speak sufficiently: he's gone to travel.
THALIARD [*aside*]   How? The King gone?
HELICANUS   If further yet you will be satisfied
15 Why, as it were, unlicensed of your loves,°   *without your approval*
He would depart, I'll give some light unto you.
Being at Antioch—
THALIARD [*aside*]   What from Antioch?
HELICANUS   Royal Antiochus, on what cause I know not,
Took some displeasure at him—at least he judged so—
20 And, doubting lest° he had erred or sinned,   *And fearing*
To show his sorrow he'd correct° himself.   *he wished to punish*
So puts himself unto the shipman's toil,
With° whom each minute threatens life or death.   *For*
THALIARD [*aside*]   Well, I perceive
25 I shall not be hanged now, although I would.[2]
But since he's gone, the King's ears it must please:
He 'scaped° the land to perish on the seas.   *escaped*
I'll present myself. —Peace to the lords of Tyre.

      [*He gives a letter.*][3]

HELICANUS [*after looking at the letter*][4]   Lord Thaliard from
Antiochus is welcome.
30 THALIARD   From him I come
With message unto princely Pericles,
But since my landing I have understood
Your lord has betook himself to unknown travels.
Now message must return from whence it came.
35 HELICANUS   We have no reason to desire it,
Commended° to our master, not to us.   *Directed*

      [*He returns the letter.*]

Yet ere you shall depart, this we desire:
As friends to Antioch we may feast° in Tyre.   *Exeunt.*   *prepare a feast for you*

1.4

Enter CLEON, *the Governor of Tarsus, with his wife*[,
DIONYZA,] *and others.*

CLEON   My Dionyza, shall we rest us here
And by relating tales of others' griefs
See if 'twill teach us to forget our own?
DIONYZA   That were to blow at fire in hope to quench it.
5 For who digs hills because they do aspire

---

1. According to Plutarch's *Lives* and Barnabe Riche
in *Soldiers Wish to Briton's Welfare* (1604), the poet
Philippides made this request of King Lysimachus of
Thrace.
2. Even if I return home (?); even if that's what I
wanted.

3. Persumably Thaliard's way of getting Pericles
"within my pistol's length" (1.1.169).
4. The stage direction is added to explain how Helicanus knows who Thaliard is.
1.4 Location: Tarsus.

Throws down one mountain to cast up a higher.[1]
O my distressed lord, even such our griefs are.
Here they are but felt and seen with mischief's° eyes, — *the sufferer's*
But, like to groves, being topped° they higher rise. — *pruned*

10 CLEON   O Dionyza,
Who wanteth food and will not say he wants it,
Or can conceal his hunger till he famish?
Let's teach our tongues and sorrows to sound° deep — *proclaim; plumb*
Our woes into the air, our eyes to weep,
15 Till lungs fetch breath that may proclaim them louder,
That if heavens slumber while their° creatures want, — *(heavens')*
They° may awake their° helps to comfort them. — *(creatures) / (heavens')*
I'll then discourse our woes felt several years,
And, wanting° breath to speak, help me with tears. — *when I'm out of*
20 DIONYZA   I'll do my best, sir.
CLEON   This Tarsus o'er which I have the government,
A city on whom plenty held full hand°— — *generously presided*
For riches strewed herself even in her streets—
Whose towers bore heads so high they kissed the clouds,
25 And strangers ne'er beheld but wondered at;° — *without admiring*
Whose men and dames so jetted° and adorned° — *strutted / (themselves)*
Like one another's glass to trim them[2] by;
Their tables were stored full to glad the sight,
And not so much to feed on as delight.
30 All poverty was scorned, and pride so great,
The name of help grew odious to repeat—
DIONYZA   Oh, 'tis too true.
CLEON   But see what heaven can do by this our change:
These mouths who but of late° earth, sea, and air — *just recently*
35 Were all too little to content and please,
Although they° gave their creatures in abundance— — *("earth, sea, and air")*
As houses are defiled for want° of use, — *by lack*
They are now starved for want of exercise.
Those palates who, not yet two summers younger,
40 Must have inventions° to delight the taste, — *Demanded novel foods*
Would now be glad of bread and beg for it.
Those mothers who to nuzzle up° their babes — *raise*
Thought naught too curious° are ready now — *exquisite*
To eat those little darlings whom they loved.
45 So sharp are hunger's teeth that man and wife
Draw lots who first shall die to lengthen life.[3]
Here stands a lord and there a lady weeping;
Here many sink, yet those which see them fall
Have scarce strength left to give them burial.
50 Is not this true?
DIONYZA   Our cheeks and hollow eyes do witness it.
CLEON   Oh, let those cities that of plenty's cup
And her prosperities so largely taste
With their superfluous riots° hear these tears: — *excessive indulgence*
55 The misery of Tarsus may be theirs.

---

1. *For . . . higher*: Digging up hills because "they"
(the hills) "aspire" (rise up) results only in new hills; or,
"they" who "aspire" dig up "hills" (attempt to undermine the eminent)—again, unsuccessfully.

2. Mirror to dress themselves. (Everyone was a model
of fashion.)
3. *lengthen life*: (of the other, through cannibalism).

Enter a LORD.

LORD   Where's the Lord Governor?

CLEON   Here.

Speak out the sorrows which thou bring'st in haste,

For comfort is too far for us to expect.

LORD   We have descried upon our neighboring shore

60   A portly sail° of ships make hitherward.   *stately fleet*

CLEON   I thought as much.

One sorrow never comes but brings an heir

That may succeed as his inheritor.

And so in ours: some neighboring nation,

65   Taking advantage of our misery,

Hath stuffed the hollow vessels with their power°   *soldiers*

To beat us down, the which are down already,

And make a conquest of unhappy men,

Whereas no glory's got to overcome.[4]

70   LORD   That's the least fear,° for by the semblance   *not to be feared*

Of their white flags displayed, they bring us peace

And come to us as favorers, not as foes.

CLEON   Thou speak'st like him's untutored to repeat:[5]

Who makes the fairest show means most deceit.

75   But, bring they° what they will and what they can,   *let them bring*

What need we fear?

Our grave's the lowest,° and we are halfway there.   *lowest we can go*

Go tell their general we attend° him here   *await*

To know for what he comes, and whence he comes,

80   And what he craves.

LORD   I go, my lord.   *[Exit.]*

CLEON   Welcome is peace, if he on peace consist.°   *resolves*

If wars, we are unable to resist.

Enter PERICLES *with Attendants.*

PERICLES   Lord Governor—for so we hear you are—

85   Let not our ships and number of our men

Be like a beacon fired t'amaze° your eyes.   *to terrify*

We have heard your miseries as far as Tyre

And seen the desolation of your streets,

Nor come we to add sorrow to your hearts

90   But to relieve them of their heavy load.

And these our ships, you happily° may think   *which you perhaps*

Are like the Trojan horse was stuffed within

With bloody veins expecting overthrow,[6]

Are stored with corn to make your needy bread,

95   And give them life whom hunger starved half dead.

ALL TARSIANS [*kneeling*]   The gods of Greece protect you,

And we'll pray for you.

PERICLES   Arise, I pray you, rise.

We do not look for reverence but for love

And harborage for ourself, our ships, and men.

100 CLEON   The which when any shall not gratify,

Or pay you with unthankfulness in thought,

Be it our wives, our children, or ourselves,

---

4. Where there's no glory in winning.
5. Like him who hasn't learned (the following lesson) by heart.

6. *was . . . overthrow:* that was laden with Greek soldiers ("bloody veins") who (correctly) expected to sack Troy.

The curse of heaven and men succeed° their evils!   *follow from*
Till when—the which, I hope, shall ne'er be seen—
105   Your grace is welcome to our town and us.
PERICLES   Which welcome we'll accept, feast here a while,
Until our stars that frown lend us a smile.   *Exeunt.*

2.0

Enter GOWER.

GOWER   Here have you seen a mighty king
His child, iwis,° to incest bring;   *certainly*
A better prince° and benign lord   *(Pericles)*
That will prove awful° both in deed and word.   *worthy of respect*
5   Be quiet then, as men should be,
Till he hath passed necessity.[1]
I'll show you those° in troubles reign,   *those who*
Losing a mite, a mountain gain.
The good in conversation,[2]
10   To whom I give my benison,°   *blessing*
Is still at Tarsus, where each man
Thinks all is writ he speken can,[3]
And to remember what he does
Build his statue to make him glorious.
15   But tidings to the contrary°   *news of calamities*
Are brought your eyes; what need speak I?
                    Dumb show.[4]
        Enter at one door PERICLES *talking with* CLEON, *all the*
        train with them. Enter at another door a Gentleman
        with a letter to PERICLES. PERICLES *shows the letter to*
        CLEON. PERICLES *gives the [Gentleman] a reward and*
        knights him:
                Exeunt [with their trains] PERICLES *at one door*
                        and CLEON *at another.*
Good Helicane that stayed at home,
Not to eat honey like a drone
From others' labors, for that he° strive   *but rather to*
20   To killen bad, keep good alive,
And to fulfil his prince' desire,
Sends word of all that haps in Tyre:
How Thaliard came full bent with° sin   *intent on*
And hid intent to murder him,
25   And that in Tarsus was not best
Longer for him to make his rest.[5]
He, doing so, put forth to seas,
Where when men been° there's seldom ease.   *are*
For now the wind begins to blow:
30   Thunder above and deeps below
Makes such unquiet that the ship
Should° house him safe is wrecked and split,   *Which should*
And he, good prince, having all lost,
By waves from coast to coast is tossed.

2.0
1. *necessity:* the suffering that is his lot.
2. The good man (Pericles) in conduct.
3. Archaic (as is often the case in Gower's speeches):

Thinks all Pericles says is holy scripture ("writ").
4. In Renaissance drama, a brief pantomime performance used to advance the plot.
5. It is not clear how Helicanus knows this.

35　All perishen, of man, of pelf,°　　　　　　　　　　　　　　*goods*
　　Ne aught escapen° but himself,　　　　　　　　　*Nothing escaping*
　　Till Fortune, tired with doing bad,
　　Threw him ashore to give him glad.°　　　　　　　　　　*joy*
　　And here he comes. What shall be next
40　Pardon old Gower: this 'longs the text.[6]　　　　[*Exit.*]

2.1

Enter PERICLES *wet.*

PERICLES　Yet cease your ire, you angry stars of heaven!
　　Wind, rain, and thunder, remember earthly man
　　Is but a substance that must yield to you,
　　And I, as fits my nature, do obey you.
5　Alas, the seas hath cast me on the rocks,
　　Washed me from shore to shore, and left me breath°　　　　*life*
　　Nothing° to think on but ensuing death.　　　　　　*With nothing*
　　Let it suffice the greatness of your powers
　　To have bereft a prince of all his fortunes,
10　And, having thrown him from your wat'ry grave,
　　Here to have death in peace is all he'll crave.

Enter three FISHERMEN. [PERICLES *stands aside.*]

FIRST FISHERMAN　What ho, Pelch![1]
SECOND FISHERMAN　Ha, come and bring away the nets.
FIRST FISHERMAN　What, Patch-breech,° I say!　　　　　*(a nickname)*
15　THIRD FISHERMAN　What say you, master?
FIRST FISHERMAN　Look how thou stirr'st now! Come away or
　　I'll fetch thee with a wanion.[2]
THIRD FISHERMAN　Faith, master, I am thinking of the poor
　　men that were cast away before us° even now.　　　*in our sight*
20　FIRST FISHERMAN　Alas, poor souls! It grieved my heart to
　　hear what pitiful cries they made to us to help them, when—
　　welladay!°—we could scarce help ourselves.　　　　　*alas*
THIRD FISHERMAN　Nay, master, said not I as much when I
　　saw the porpoise, how he bounced and tumbled?°　　*(predictive of storms)*
25　they're half fish, half flesh. A plague on them! They ne'er
　　come but I look to be washed.° Master, I marvel how the　　*(by a storm)*
　　fishes live in the sea.
FIRST FISHERMAN　Why, as men do a-land:° the great ones eat　　*on land*
　　up the little ones. I can compare our rich misers to nothing
30　so fitly as to a whale; 'a° plays and tumbles, driving the poor　　*he*
　　fry before him, and at last devours them all at a mouthful.
　　Such whales have I heard on° o'th' land, who never leave　　*of*
　　gaping° till they swallowed the whole parish, church, steeple,　　*close their mouths*
　　bells, and all.
35　PERICLES [*aside*]　A pretty moral.
THIRD FISHERMAN　But, master, if I had been the sexton,° I　　*church bellringer*
　　would have been that day in the belfry.°　　　　　*bell tower*

SECOND FISHERMAN　Why, man?

---

6. *'longs the text:* belongs to the original story (don't
blame me for Pericles' sufferings).
2.1 Location: The seashore at Pentapolis, which was
the coastal area of Cyrenaica, in the northeastern
corner of what is now Libya. This scene locates it in
Greece, however (line 63).

1. Nickname derived from a rustic leather garment.
The nicknames, homely references, and social critiques in this scene have a distinctively English feel.
2. *Look . . . wanion:* Look how quick you are (ironic).
Hurry along, or I'll beat you with a vengeance.

THIRD FISHERMAN Because he should have swallowed me
40 too, and when I had been in his belly, I would have kept
such a jangling of the bells that he should never have left till
he cast° bells, steeple, church, and parish up again. But if   *vomited*
the good King Simonides were of my mind—
PERICLES [*aside*] Simonides?
45 THIRD FISHERMAN —We would purge the land of these drones
that rob the bee of her honey.
PERICLES [*aside*] How from the finny subjects° of the sea³   *citizens*
These fishers tell the infirmities of men
And from their wat'ry empire recollect°   *gather*
50 All that may men approve or men detect!°   *expose*
    [*He comes forward.*]
Peace be at your labor, honest fishermen!
SECOND FISHERMAN "Honest," good fellow—what's that? If it
be a day fits you, search out the calender, and nobody look
after it!⁴
55 PERICLES May° see the sea hath cast upon your coast—   *You may*
SECOND FISHERMAN What a drunken knave was the sea to
cast thee in our way!⁵
PERICLES A man, whom both the waters and the wind
In that vast tennis-court hath made the ball
60 For them to play upon,° entreats you pity him.   *with*
He asks of you that never used to beg.
FIRST FISHERMAN No, friend, cannot you beg? Here's them°   *There are those*
in our country of Greece gets° more with begging than we   *who get*
can do with working.
65 SECOND FISHERMAN Canst thou catch any fishes, then?
PERICLES I never practiced it.
SECOND FISHERMAN Nay, then thou wilt starve, sure, for
here's nothing to be got nowadays unless thou canst fish
for't.°   *get it by deception*
70 PERICLES What I have been, I have forgot to know;
But what I am, want teaches me to think on:
A man thronged up° with cold. My veins are chill,   *overwhelmed*
And have no more of life than may suffice
To give my tongue that heat to ask your help—
75 Which if you shall refuse, when I am dead,
For that° I am a man, pray see me burièd.   *Because*
FIRST FISHERMAN Die, quotha?° Now, gods forbid't, an° I   *says he / if*
have a gown here. Come, put it on, keep thee warm.
    [PERICLES *puts on the First Fisherman's gown.*]
Now, afore me,° a handsome fellow! Come, thou shalt go   *on my word*
80 home, and we'll have flesh for holidays, fish for fasting days
and more°—or puddings° and flapjacks—and thou shalt be   *also other days / sausages*
welcome.
PERICLES I thank you, sir.
SECOND FISHERMAN Hark you, my friend. You said you could
85 not beg?

---

3. Although the Fishermen speak in prose, Pericles
uses verse.
4. *If . . . after it:* Perhaps: If honesty is a day in the
calendar that suits you, you could remove it without
anyone noticing or challenging you for it—honesty

being so rare.
5. Like St. Peter, the Fishermen are literally fishers of
men, who help save Pericles from the sea. Their discussion of whales also evokes the tale of Jonah. The
scene is full of biblical echoes. *cast:* pun on "vomit."

PERICLES I did but crave.

SECOND FISHERMAN But crave? Then I'll turn craver too, and
so I shall 'scape whipping.°   *(for begging)*

PERICLES Why, are your beggars whipped, then?

90   SECOND FISHERMAN Oh, not all, my friend, not all, for if all
your° beggars were whipped, I would wish no better office   *the*
than to be beadle.[6] But, master, I'll go draw up the net.

[*Exeunt* SECOND *and* THIRD FISHERMEN.]

PERICLES [*aside*] How well this honest mirth becomes their
labor!

FIRST FISHERMAN Hark you, sir; do you know where ye are?

95   PERICLES Not well.

FIRST FISHERMAN Why, I'll tell you. This is called Pentapolis,
and our king, the good Simonides.

PERICLES "The good Simonides," do you call him?

FIRST FISHERMAN Ay, sir, and he deserves so to be called for

100   his peaceable reign and good government.

PERICLES He is a happy king, since he gains from his subjects
the name of "good" by his government. How far is his court
distant from this shore?

FIRST FISHERMAN Marry,° sir, half a day's journey. And I'll   *To be sure*

105   tell you, he hath a fair daughter, and tomorrow is her birthday, and there are princes and knights come from all parts
of the world to joust and tourney for her love.

PERICLES Were my fortunes equal to my desires, I could wish
to make one° there.   *be one of the princes*

110   FIRST FISHERMAN O sir, things must be as they may: and
what a man cannot get, he may lawfully deal for with his
wife's soul.[7]

Enter [SECOND *and* THIRD] FISHERMEN, *drawing
up a net.*

SECOND FISHERMAN Help, master, help! Here's a fish hangs
in the net like a poor man's right in the law: 'twill hardly

115   come out.

[*All three* FISHERMEN *haul in the net, which contains
a piece of armor.*]

Ha! Bots on't,° 'tis come at last, and 'tis turned to a rusty   *A pox (plague) on it*
armor.

PERICLES An armor, friends? I pray you, let me see it.

[*aside*] Thanks, Fortune, yet, that after all thy crosses°   *hardships*

120   Thou givest me somewhat to repair myself!
It was mine own, part of my heritage,
Which my dead father did bequeath to me
With this strict charge, even as he left his life:
"Keep it, my Pericles; it hath been a shield

125   Twixt me and death"—and pointed to this brace.°   *arm armor*
"For that° it saved me, keep it. In like necessity,   *Because*
From which the gods protect thee, may't defend thee."
It kept° where I kept, I so dearly loved it,   *remained*
Till the rough seas that spares not any man

6. Minor parish official who administered corporal
punishment.
7. *what . . . soul:* probably ironic: when a man can no
longer "get" (make a living; have children), he can

legitimately do so by persuading his "wife's soul" (her
conscience; also, "his wife's hole") to trade (prostitute) herself (with men who will "get"—beget—children with her).

130 Took it in rage, though, calmed, have given't again.
I thank thee for't—my shipwreck now's no ill,
Since I have here my° father gave in his will.   *what my*
FIRST FISHERMAN   What mean you, sir?
PERICLES [*to* FISHERMEN]   To beg of you, kind friends, this
    coat of worth,
135 For it was sometime target° to a king.   *once a shield*
I know it by this mark. He loved me dearly,
And for his sake I wish the having of it,
And that you'd guide me to your sovereign's court,
Where, with it, I may appear a gentleman,
140 And if that ever my low fortune's better,
I'll pay your bounties;° till then, rest your debtor.   *repay your generosity*
FIRST FISHERMAN   Why, wilt thou tourney for the lady?
PERICLES   I'll show the virtue I have borne in arms.
FIRST FISHERMAN   Why, d'ye take it, and the gods give thee
145 good on't!
SECOND FISHERMAN   Ay, but, hark you, my friend, 'twas we
that made up° this garment through the rough seams of the   *raised; sewed (pun)*
waters. There are certain condolements,[8] certain vails°—I   *tips; leftover cloth*
hope, sir, if you thrive, you'll remember from whence you
150 had them.
PERICLES   Believe't, I will.
By your furtherance I am clothed in steel,
And, spite of all the rapture° of the sea,   *plundering*
This jewel holds his building° on my arm.   *its place*
155 Unto thy° value I will mount myself   *(the jewel's)*
Upon a courser,° whose delightful steps   *a horse*
Shall make the gazer joy to see him tread.
Only, my friend, I yet am unprovided of a pair of bases.[9]
SECOND FISHERMAN   We'll sure provide. Thou shalt have my
160 best gown to make thee a pair, and I'll bring thee to the
court myself.
PERICLES   Then, honor, be but equal to my will!
This day I'll rise, or else add ill to ill.   [*Exeunt.*]

2.2

Enter King SIMONIDES, THAISA, *and* [THREE LORDS,
with] *Attendants.*

SIMONIDES   Are the knights ready to begin the triumph?°   *tournament*
FIRST LORD   They are, my liege,
And stay° your coming to present themselves.   *await*
SIMONIDES   Return° them, we are ready, and our daughter,   *Answer*
5 In honor of whose birth these triumphs are,
Sits here like Beauty's child, whom Nature gat°   *conceived*
For men to see and, seeing, wonder at.   [*Exit* FIRST LORD.]
THAISA   It pleaseth you, my royal father, to express
My commendations great, whose merit's less.
10 SIMONIDES   It's fit it should be so, for princes° are   *rulers*
A model which heaven makes like to itself.
As jewels lose their glory if neglected,

---

8. Blunder for "doles."
9. Skirts for armored knights on horseback.

2.2 Location: Pentapolis, area near the tournament arena, including a reviewing stand.

So princes their renowns if not respected.
'Tis now your honor, daughter, to entertain°   review
15   The labor of each knight in his device.[1]
THAISA   Which, to preserve mine honor, I'll perform.
       [*Enter*] *the* FIRST KNIGHT. [*He*] *passes by* [*and his*
       Squire presents a shield to THAISA].
SIMONIDES   Who is the first that doth prefer° himself?   present
THAISA   A knight of Sparta, my renownèd father,
       And the device he bears upon his shield
20   Is a black Ethiop reaching at the sun:
       The word: *Lux tua vita mihi*.[2]
SIMONIDES   He loves you well, that holds his life of° you.   receives his life from
       The SECOND KNIGHT [*and Squire pass by, as before*].
       Who is the second that presents himself?
THAISA   A prince of Macedon, my royal father,
25   And the device he bears upon his shield
       Is an armed knight that's conquered by a lady:
       The motto thus, in Spanish: *Più per dolcezza che per forza*.[3]
       [*The* THIRD KNIGHT *and Squire pass by*.]
SIMONIDES   And what's the third?
THAISA   The third of Antioch,
       And his device a wreath of chivalry,[4]
30   The word: *Me pompae provexit apex*.[5]
       [*The* FOURTH KNIGHT *and Squire pass by*.]
SIMONIDES   What is the fourth?
THAISA   A burning torch that's turnèd upside down;
       The word: *Qui me alit me extinguit*.[6]
SIMONIDES   Which shows that beauty hath his power and will,
35   Which can as well enflame as it can kill.
       [*The* FIFTH KNIGHT *and Squire pass by*.]
THAISA   The fifth, an hand environèd with clouds,
       Holding out gold that's by the touchstone[7] tried.
       The motto thus: *Sic spectanda fides*.[8]
       [*The* SIXTH KNIGHT (PERICLES), *in rusty armor and*
       without a squire, presents his shield to THAISA *and*
       passes by.]
SIMONIDES   And what's the sixth and last, the which the knight
40   Himself with such a graceful courtesy° delivered?   bow
THAISA   He seems to be a stranger, but his present° is   presented object
       A withered branch that's only green at top,
       The motto: *In hac spe vivo*.°   I live in this hope
SIMONIDES   A pretty moral!
       From the dejected state wherein he is,
45   He hopes by you his fortunes yet may flourish.
FIRST LORD   He had need mean° better than his outward   must intend something
       show
       Can any way speak in his just commend,°   on his behalf

---

1. An emblem in heraldry, consisting of an image and a motto, or "word" (line 21), usually in a foreign language, and displayed on banners, shields, and elsewhere.
2. Your light is my life (Latin).
3. Garbled Italian for: more by gentleness than by force; *in Spanish*: a mishearing or a joke.

4. (Heraldic term): twisted band that joins the crest and the knight's helmet.
5. The summit of glory has led me on (Latin).
6. Who nourishes me extinguishes me (Latin).
7. Black stone used to check the purity of gold and silver; symbol of fidelity.
8. Thus is faith to be examined (Latin).

For by his rusty outside he appears
To have practiced more the whipstock than the lance.[9]
50 SECOND LORD He well may be a stranger,° for he comes   foreigner
To an honored triumph strangely furnishèd.°   bizarrely equipped
THIRD LORD And on set purpose let his armor rust
Until this day—to scour it in the dust.[1]
SIMONIDES Opinion's but a fool that makes us scan
55 The outward habit° for the inward man.   costume
But stay, the knights are coming.
We will withdraw into the gallery.
          [*Exeunt King* SIMONIDES, THAISA, *and* LORDS.]
          [*A banquet table is brought in.*] *Great shouts*
          [*offstage*], *and all cry, "The mean° knight!"*[2]   impoverished

2.3

Enter King [SIMONIDES, THAISA, MARSHALL, LORDS,
Ladies,] *and* KNIGHTS[, *including* PERICLES, *in their
armor,*] *from tilting.*
SIMONIDES Knights, to say you're welcome were superfluous.
To place upon the volume of your deeds,
As in a title page,[1] your worth in arms,
Were more than you expect, or more than's fit,
5 Since every worth in show° commends itself.   in practice
Prepare for mirth, for mirth becomes a feast.
You are princes and my guests.
THAISA [*to* PERICLES] But you, my knight and guest,
To whom this wreath of victory I give,
10 And crown you king of this day's happiness.
          [PERICLES *kneels.* THAISA *crowns him.*]
PERICLES 'Tis more by fortune, lady, than my merit.
SIMONIDES Call it by what you will, the day is yours,
And here, I hope, is none that envies it.
In framing° artists, art hath thus decreed,   making
15 To make some good, but others to exceed,
And you are her labored scholar.[2] [*to* THAISA] Come, queen
      o'th' feast—
For, daughter, so you are—here take your place.
          [THAISA *sits beside King* SIMONIDES.]
      [*to* MARSHALL] Marshall the rest as they deserve their grace.[3]
          [MARSHALL *leads guests to their places.*]
KNIGHTS We are honored much by good Simonides.
20 SIMONIDES Your presence glads our days. Honor we love,
For who hates honor, hates the gods above.
MARSHALL [*to* PERICLES] Sir, yonder is your place.
PERICLES   Some other is more fit.
FIRST KNIGHT Contend not, sir, for we are gentlemen
Have° neither in our hearts nor outward eyes   Who've
25 Envied the great, nor shall the low despise.

---

9. *he appears . . . lance:* he looks more like a manual
laborer (a "whipstock" was the handle of a whip used
to drive workhorses) than a knight.
1. To polish it in the dust (when he is unhorsed).
2. TEXTUAL COMMENT For the staging of the combat,
see Digital Edition TC 4.

2.3 Location: The palace at Pentapolis.
1. Renaissance publishers often advertised the contents on the title page of a book ("volume").
2. Art (creative power) worked hard to make you.
3. Arrange the others according to the honor they
deserve.

PERICLES   You are right courteous knights.

SIMONIDES   Sit, sir, sit.
[*aside*] By Jove I wonder, that is king of thoughts,[4]
These cates resist me, he but thought upon.[5]

THAISA [*aside*]   By Juno, that is queen of marriage,
30   All viands that I eat do seem unsavory,
Wishing him my meat. [*to* SIMONIDES] Sure, he's a gallant
    gentleman.

SIMONIDES   He's but a country gentleman.
He's done no more than other knights have done—
He's broken a staff° or so. So let it pass.   *an opponent's lance*

35 THAISA   To me he seems like diamond to glass.

PERICLES [*aside*]   Yon king's to me like to my father's picture,
Which tells me in that glory once he was:
Had princes sit like stars about his throne,
And he the sun for them to reverence.
40   None that beheld him but, like lesser lights,
Did vail° their crowns to his supremacy;   *lower*
Where now his son's a glowworm in the night,
The which hath fire in darkness, none in light.
Whereby I see that Time's the king of men:
45   He's both their parent and he is their grave,
And gives them what he will, not what they crave.

SIMONIDES   What, are you merry, knights?

KNIGHTS   Who can be other in this royal presence?

SIMONIDES   Here, with a cup that's stored unto the brim,
50   As you do love, fill[6] to your mistress' lips!
We drink this health to you.
            [*He drinks.*]

KNIGHTS   We thank your grace.

SIMONIDES   Yet pause awhile. [*He indicates* PERICLES.] Yon
    knight doth sit too melancholy,
As if the entertainment in our court
Had not a show might countervail° his worth.   *that might equal*
55   Note it not you, Thaisa?

THAISA   What is't to me, my father?

SIMONIDES   Oh, attend, my daughter. Princes in this
Should live like gods above, who freely give
To everyone that come to honor them,
60   And princes not doing so are like to gnats
Which make a sound but, killed, are wondered at.[7]
Therefore, to make his entertain° more sweet,   *entertainment*
Here, say we drink this standing bowl° of wine to him.   *bowl on a pedestal*
            [*He drinks.*]

THAISA   Alas, my father, it befits not me
65   Unto a stranger knight to be so bold.
He may my proffer take for an offense,
Since men take women's gifts for impudence.

---

4. TEXTUAL COMMENT Here, as elsewhere, the line might be an aside or might be addressed to another character. See Digital Edition TC 5.
5. *These . . . upon:* (I'm so taken with him that, merely) thinking of him, I lose my appetite for delicacies.
6. If you are in love, drink up.
7. Which, when dead, appear surprisingly small for all the noise they made alive.

SIMONIDES   How? Do as I bid you, or you'll move° me else.   *anger*
THAISA [*aside*]   Now, by the gods, he could not please me better!
70   SIMONIDES   And further tell him we desire to know
       Of whence he is, his name, and parentage.
              [THAISA *takes the bowl of wine to* PERICLES.]
THAISA   The King my father, sir, has drunk to you—
PERICLES   I thank him—
THAISA   Wishing it so much blood unto your life.
75   PERICLES   I thank both him and you, and pledge° him freely.   *drink to*
              [*He drinks.*]
THAISA   And, further, he desires to know of you
       Of whence you are, your name and parentage.
PERICLES   A gentleman of Tyre, my name Pericles,
       My education been in arts° and arms,   *liberal arts*
80   Who, looking for adventures in the world,
       Was by the rough seas reft° of ships and men,   *bereft*
       And, after shipwreck, driven upon this shore.
              [THAISA *returns to* SIMONIDES.]
THAISA [*to* SIMONIDES]   He thanks your grace; names himself
          Pericles,
       A gentleman of Tyre,
85   Who only by misfortune of the seas,
       Bereft of ships and men, cast on this shore.
SIMONIDES   Now by the gods, I pity his misfortune
       And will awake him from his melancholy.
       —Come, gentlemen, we sit° too long on trifles   *dwell*
90   And waste the time which looks for other revels.
       Even in your armors, as you are addressed,°   *dressed*
       Will well become a soldiers' dance.
       I will not have excuse with saying this:
       "Loud music° is too harsh for ladies' heads,"   *The sound of armor*
95   Since they love men in arms as well as beds.
              [*The* KNIGHTS] *dance.*°   *(without the ladies)*
       So, this was well asked, 'twas so well performed.
       [*to* PERICLES, *indicating* THAISA]   Come, sir, here's a lady
          that wants breathing° too,   *exercise*
       And I have heard you knights of Tyre
       Are excellent in making ladies trip°   *dance; go astray sexually*
100   And that their measures° are as excellent.   *dances; sexual means*
PERICLES   In those that practice them they are, my lord.
SIMONIDES   Oh, that's as much as you would be denied
       Of your fair courtesy.⁸ Unclasp, unclasp!⁹
              [PERICLES *and* THAISA] *dance* [*with the other* KNIGHTS
                 and Ladies.]
       —Thanks, gentlemen, to all. All have done well,
105   [*to* PERICLES] But you the best. —Pages and lights, to
          conduct
       These knights unto their several° lodgings!   *separate*
       [*to* PERICLES] Yours, sir, we have given order be next our own.

8. *that's . . . courtesy:* that's just what your modesty   9. Remove your armor, and dance with the ladies.
about your dancing ability dictates you should say.

PERICLES   I am at your grace's pleasure.
SIMONIDES   Princes, it is too late to talk of love,
110   And that's the mark I know you level° at.   *aim*
         Therefore each one betake him to his rest.
         Tomorrow all for speeding do their best.[1]   [*Exeunt.*]

2.4

Enter HELICANUS *and* ESCANES.
HELICANUS   No, Escanes! Know this of me:
         Antiochus from incest lived not free,
         For which, the most high gods, not minding° longer   *wishing*
         To withhold the vengeance that they had in store
5   Due to this heinous capital offense,
         Even in the height and pride of all his glory,
         When he was seated in a chariot
         Of an inestimable value, and
         His daughter with him, a fire from heaven came
10   And shriveled up their bodies even to loathing—
         For they so stunk
         That all those eyes adored° them ere their fall   *that adored*
         Scorn now their° hands should give them burial.   *that their*
ESCANES   'Twas very strange.
HELICANUS   And yet but justice. For
15   Though this king were great, his greatness was no guard
         To bar heaven's shaft, but sin had his° reward.   *its*
ESCANES   'Tis very true.
         Enter three LORDS. [*They speak apart.*][1]
FIRST LORD   See, not a man in private conference
         Or council has respect° with him but he.°   *influence / (Escanes)*
20   SECOND LORD   It shall no longer grieve° without reproof.   *cause us grief*
     THIRD LORD   And cursed be he that will not second it.
     FIRST LORD   Follow me, then. —Lord Helicane, a word.
HELICANUS   With me? And welcome. Happy day, my lords!
FIRST LORD   Know that our griefs° are risen to the top,   *grievances*
25   And now at length they overflow their banks.
HELICANUS   Your griefs—for what? Wrong not your prince you love.
FIRST LORD   Wrong not yourself, then, noble Helicane.
         But, if the prince do live, let us salute him
         Or know what ground's made happy by his breath.
30   If in the world he live, we'll seek him out;
         If in his grave he rest, we'll find him there
         And be resolved:° he lives to govern us   *know one way or the other*
         Or, dead, gives cause to mourn his funeral
         And leaves us to our free election.
35   SECOND LORD   Whose death's indeed the strongest° in our   *(likelihood)*
             censure.°   *judgment*
         And knowing this: kingdoms without a head,
         Like goodly buildings left without a roof,
         Soon fall to ruin—your noble self,
         That best know how to rule and how to reign,

---

1. Each one do his best to succeed (in wooing the princess).
2.4 Location: Tyre, the Governor's house.

1. TEXTUAL COMMENT For the possible inconsistencies in this scene involving Escanes and the Lords' motives, see Digital Edition TC 6.

40   We thus submit unto: our sovereign!

    ALL LORDS   Live, noble Helicane!

    HELICANUS   For honor's cause, forbear your suffrages!°   *voting (for me)*

    If that you love Prince Pericles, forbear!

    [*aside*] Take I° your wish, I leap into the seas,   *If I accept*

45   Where's° hourly trouble for a minute's ease.   *Where there is*

    —A twelvemonth longer let me entreat you

    To further bear the absence of your king;

    If in which time expired he not return,

    I shall with aged patience bear your yoke.

50   But if I cannot win you to this love,°   *(of Pericles)*

    Go search like nobles, like noble subjects,

    And in your search, spend your adventurous worth,

    Whom° if you find and win unto° return,   *(Pericles) / persuade to*

    You shall like diamonds sit about his crown.

55   FIRST LORD   To wisdom he's a fool that will not yield.

    And since Lord Helicane enjoineth us,

    We with our travels will endeavor.

    HELICANUS   Then you love us, we you, and we'll clasp hands:

    When peers thus knit, a kingdom ever stands.   [*Exeunt.*]

2.5

Enter the King [SIMONIDES] *reading of a letter at one
door; the* KNIGHTS *meet him* [*from another door*].

    FIRST KNIGHT   Good morrow to the good Simonides.

    SIMONIDES   Knights, from my daughter this I let you know:

    That for this twelvemonth she'll not undertake

    A married life.

5   Her reason to herself is only known,

    Which from her by no means can I get.

    SECOND KNIGHT   May we not get access to her, my lord?

    SIMONIDES   Faith, by no means. She hath so strictly tied

    Her to her chamber that 'tis impossible.

10   One twelve moons more she'll wear Diana's livery.¹

    This by the eye of Cynthia² hath she vowed,

    And on her virgin honor will not break it.

    THIRD KNIGHT   Loath to bid farewell, we take our leaves.

                  [*Exeunt* KNIGHTS.]

    SIMONIDES   So, they are well dispatched!

15   Now to my daughter's letter.

    She tells me here she'll wed the stranger knight

    Or never more to view nor° day nor light.   *neither*

    'Tis well, mistress: your choice agrees with mine.

    I like that well. Nay, how absolute she's in't,

20   Not minding whether I dislike or no!

    Well, I do commend her choice

    And will no longer have it be delayed.

    Soft, here he comes. I must dissemble it.

        Enter PERICLES.

    PERICLES   All fortune to the good Simonides.

25   SIMONIDES   To you as much. Sir, I am beholden to you

2.5 Location: The palace at Pentapolis.   2. Another name for Diana, as goddess of the moon.
1. She'll serve Diana, goddess of chastity.

For your sweet music this last night. I do
Protest, my ears were never better fed
With such delightful pleasing harmony.
PERICLES It is your grace's pleasure to commend,
Not my desert.
30 SIMONIDES   Sir, you are music's master.
PERICLES The worst of all her scholars,° my good lord.   *students*
SIMONIDES Let me ask you one thing:
What do you think of my daughter, sir?
PERICLES A most virtuous princess.
35 SIMONIDES And she is fair too, is she not?
PERICLES As a fair day in summer, wondrous fair.
SIMONIDES Sir, my daughter thinks very well of you—
Ay, so well that you must be her master
And she will be your scholar. Therefore look to it.°   *be prepared*
40 PERICLES I am unworthy for° her schoolmaster.   *to be*
SIMONIDES She thinks not so. Peruse this writing else.°   *if you doubt me*
[*He gives* PERICLES *Thaisa's letter.*]
PERICLES [*aside, after reading*] What's here, a letter that she
loves the knight of Tyre?
'Tis the King's subtlety to have my life.
—Oh, seek not to entrap me, gracious lord:
45 A stranger and distressèd gentleman
That never aimed so high to° love your daughter   *as to*
But bent all offices³ to honor her.
SIMONIDES Thou hast bewitched my daughter, and thou art
A villain.
PERICLES By the gods, I have not!
50 Never did thought of mine levy° offense;   *give*
Nor never did my actions yet commence
A deed might° gain her love or your displeasure.   *that might*
SIMONIDES Traitor, thou liest!
PERICLES   Traitor?
SIMONIDES   Ay, traitor.
PERICLES Even in his throat, unless it be the King
55 That calls me traitor, I return the lie.°   *(with my sword)*
SIMONIDES [*aside*] Now, by the gods, I do applaud his courage!
PERICLES My actions are as noble as my thoughts
That never relished of° a base descent.   *gave a hint of*
I came unto your court for honor's cause
60 And not to be a rebel to her state,
And he that otherwise accounts of me,
This sword shall prove he's honor's enemy.
SIMONIDES No? Here comes my daughter; she can witness it.
Enter THAISA.
PERICLES [*to* THAISA] Then, as you are as virtuous as fair,
65 Resolve° your angry father if my tongue   *Inform*
Did ere solicit or my hand subscribe
To any syllable that made love to you.
THAISA Why, sir, say if you had—
Who takes offense at that° would make me glad?   *what*

---

3. *bent all offices:* performed all services.

70 SIMONIDES   Yea, mistress, are you so peremptory?°   *determined*
    (*aside*) I am glad on't with all my heart.
    —I'll tame you; I'll bring you in subjection.
    Will you, not having my consent,
    Bestow your love and your affections,
75   Upon a stranger? (*aside*) —who, for aught I know,
    May be, nor can I think the contrary,
    As great in blood as I myself.
    Therefore, [*to* THAISA] hear you, mistress: either frame°   *mold*
    Your will to mine —[*to* PERICLES] and you, sir, hear you:
80   Either be ruled by me, or I'll make you—
    Man and wife!
    Nay, come, your hands and lips must seal it too.
        [*He joins their hands.* PERICLES *and* THAISA *kiss.*]
    And, being joined, I'll thus your hopes destroy!
        [*He separates them.*]
    And, for further grief [*joining them again*] —God give you joy!
    What, are you both pleased?
85 THAISA   Yes [*to* PERICLES] —if you love me, sir?
PERICLES   Even as my life° my blood that fosters it.   *as my life loves*
SIMONIDES   What, are you both agreed?
THAISA *and* PERICLES   Yes, if't please your majesty.
SIMONIDES   It pleaseth me so well that I will see you wed,
90   And then, with what haste you can, get you to bed.
                                 Exeunt.

3.0

    Enter GOWER.
GOWER   Now sleep y-slackèd hath the rouse:[1]
    No din but snores about the house,
    Made louder by the o'erfed breast°   *stomach*
    Of this most pompous° marriage feast.   *lavish*
5   The cat with eyne° of burning coal   *eyes*
    Now couches fore° the mouse's hole;   *before*
    And crickets sing° at the oven's mouth   *that sing*
    Are the blither for their drouth.[2]
    Hymen° hath brought the bride to bed,   *god of marriage*
10   Where by the loss of maidenhead
    A babe is molded. Be attent,°   *attentive*
    And time that is so briefly spent°   *spent onstage*
    With your fine fancies quaintly eche.°   *skillfully fill out*
    What's dumb in show, I'll plain° with speech.   *clarify*
                    [*Dumb show.*]
    Enter PERICLES *and King* SIMONIDES *at one door with*
    Attendants. A Messenger meets them, kneels, and gives
    PERICLES *a letter.* PERICLES *shows it* SIMONIDES. *The*
    LORDS *kneel to* [PERICLES]. *Then enter* THAISA *with*
    child, with LYCHORIDA, *a nurse. The King shows*
    [THAISA] *the letter. She rejoices. She and* PERICLES
    take leave of her father, and depart [*with* LYCHORIDA.
    Then exeunt SIMONIDES *and his court*].

3.0
1. Sleep has rendered everyone inactive. *rouse:* drinking party.
2. As if happier for being dry.

15   By many a dern° and painful perch°   *wild / patch of land*
      Of Pericles the careful search,
      By the four opposing coigns°   *corners*
      Which the world together joins,
      Is made with all due diligence
20   That horse and sail and high expense
      Can stead° the quest. At last from Tyre,   *sustain in*
      Fame° answering the most strange enquire,°   *Rumor / distant queries*
      To th' court of King Simonides
      Are letters brought, the tenor these:
25   Antiochus and his daughter dead,
      The men of Tyrus on the head
      Of Helicanus would set on
      The crown of Tyre, but he will° none.   *desires*
      The mutiny he there hastes t'appease,
30   Says to 'em, if King Pericles
      Come not home in twice six moons,
      He, obedient to their dooms,°   *judgments*
      Will take the crown. The sum of this
      Brought hither to Pentapolis
35   Y-ravishèd° the regions round,   *Enraptured*
      And every one with claps can° sound,   *started to*
      "Our heir apparent is a king!
      Who dreamt, who thought of such a thing?"
      Brief,° he must hence depart to Tyre.   *In short; quickly*
40   His queen, with child, makes her desire—
      Which who shall cross?—along to go.
      Omit we all their dole and woe.
      Lychorida her nurse she takes.
      And so to sea. Their vessel shakes
45   On Neptunè's billow. Half the flood°   *sea*
      Hath their keel cut, but Fortune's mood
      Varies again: the grizzled° North   *grisly*
      Disgorges such a tempest forth
      That, as a duck for life that dives,
50   So up and down the poor ship drives.
      The lady shrieks and, well-a-near,°   *alas*
      Does fall in travail° with her fear.   *Goes into labor*
      And what ensues in this fell° storm   *cruel*
      Shall for itself itself perform.
55   I nill° relate; action may   *will not*
      Conveniently the rest convey,
      Which might not what by me is told.[3]
      In your imagination hold°   *think*
      This stage the ship, upon whose deck
60   The seas-tossed Pericles appears to speak.   [*Exit.*]

---

3. Which could not easily "convey" what I've related so far.

3.1

[Thunder and lightning.] Enter PERICLES
on shipboard.

PERICLES   Thou god of this great vast,° rebuke these surges   *vast sea*
    Which wash both heaven and hell! And thou that hast
    Upon the winds command, bind them in brass,
    Having called them from the deep. Oh, still°   *quiet*
5   Thy deafening dreadful thunders; gently quench
    Thy nimble sulphurous flashes! Oh! —*[He calls offstage.]*
      How, Lychorida!
    How does my queen? —Thou storm'st venomously;
    Wilt thou spit all thyself? The seaman's whistle
    Is as a whisper in the ears of death,°   *of a dead person*
10   Unheard. —Lychorida! —Lucina,° O   *goddess of childbirth*
    Divinest patroness and midwife gentle
    To those that cry by night, convey thy deity
    Aboard our dancing boat, make swift the pangs
    Of my queen's travails! —Now, Lychorida!
    Enter LYCHORIDA *[carrying a newborn child].*

15 LYCHORIDA   Here is a thing too young for such a place,
    Who if it had conceit° would die, as I   *understanding*
    Am like° to do. Take in your arms this piece   *likely*
    Of your dead queen.
PERICLES   How? How, Lychorida?
LYCHORIDA   Patience, good sir. Do not assist the
    storm.°   *(by ranting and shedding tears)*
20   Here's all that is left living of your queen,
    A little daughter. For the sake of it,
    Be manly, and take comfort.
PERICLES   O you gods!
    Why do you make us love your goodly gifts,
    And snatch them straight away? We here below
25   Recall° not what we give, and therein may   *Demand back*
    Vie honor with you.[1]
LYCHORIDA   Patience, good sir,
    Even for this charge.[2]
PERICLES *[to the child]*   Now, mild may be thy life,
    For a more blusterous birth had never babe;
    Quiet and gentle thy conditions,° for   *circumstances*
30   Thou art the rudeliest welcome to this world
    That ever was prince's child; happy° what follows.   *let be happy*
    Thou hast as chiding° a nativity   *upsetting*
    As fire, air, water, earth, and heaven can make
    To herald thee from the womb.
35   Even at the first, thy loss is more than can
    Thy portage quit, with all thou canst find here.[3]
    Now the good gods throw their best eyes° upon't!   *look favorably*
    Enter [the MASTER *and a* SAILOR].*

3.1 Location: At sea.
1. *therein . . . you:* in this respect may compete with
you in honor.
2. For the sake of this child.

3. *thy . . . here:* Perhaps: your loss of your mother is
more than can be repaid you through your birth,
even along with everything you find in this life.

MASTER   What courage, sir? God save you.

PERICLES   Courage enough. I do not fear the flaw°—   *squall*
40   It hath done to me the worst—yet for the love
Of this poor infant, this fresh new seafarer,
I would it would be quiet.

MASTER [*calls*]   Slack the bow-lines there!
—Thou° wilt not, wilt thou? Blow and split thyself!   *(the storm)*

45   SAILOR   But sea-room!⁴ An° the brine and cloudy billow   *If*
Kiss the moon, I care not!

MASTER [*to* PERICLES]   Sir, your queen must overboard. The
sea works° high, the wind is loud, and will not lie° till the   *surges / lie still*
ship be cleared of the dead.

PERICLES   That's your superstition.

50   MASTER   Pardon us, sir;
With us at sea it hath been still° observed,   *always*
And we are strong in custom. Therefore briefly° yield'er,   *quickly*
For she must overboard straight.

PERICLES   As you think meet.
Most wretched queen!

LYCHORIDA [*reveals Thaisa's body*]   Here she lies, sir.

55   PERICLES   A terrible childbed hast thou had, my dear:
No light, no fire; th'unfriendly elements
Forgot thee utterly. Nor have I time
To give thee hallowed to thy grave, but straight
Must cast thee, scarcely coffined, in the ooze,°   *seabed*
60   Where for° a monument upon thy bones   *in place of*
The e'er-remaining° lamps,⁵ the belching whale,   *ever-burning*
And humming water must o'erwhelm thy corpse,
Lying with simple shells. —O Lychorida,
Bid Nestor bring me spices, ink, and paper,
65   My casket, and my jewels; and bid Nicander
Bring me the satin coffer. Lay the babe
Upon the pillow. Hie° thee, whiles I say   *Hurry*
A priestly farewell to her. Suddenly,° woman!   *Immediately*
                [*Exit* LYCHORIDA.]

SAILOR   Sir, we have a chest beneath the hatches, caulked
70   and bitumed° ready.   *sealed with pitch*

PERICLES   I thank thee. —Mariner, say, what coast is this?

MASTER   We are near Tarsus.

PERICLES   Thither, gentle mariner,
Alter thy course for° Tyre. When canst thou reach it?   *that was for*

MASTER   By break of day, if the wind cease.

75   PERICLES   Oh, make for Tarsus.
There will I visit Cleon, for the babe
Cannot hold out to Tyre. There I'll leave it
At careful nursing. Go thy ways,° good mariner.   *Get to it*
I'll bring the body presently.
                Exeunt [MASTER *and* SAILOR, *followed by* PERICLES].⁶

---

4. As long as we're at sea (safe from the rocks).
5. Either funeral lamps, which, like "a monument" (line 60), will be absent; or the stars as lamps, which, like the "whale" and "water" (lines 61–62), replace the "monument."
6. TEXTUAL COMMENT For the staging of this scene and the handling of Thaisa and the baby, see Digital Edition TC 7.

3.2

Enter Lord CERIMON *with [two* VISITING SERVANTS].[1]

CERIMON Philemon, ho!
Enter PHILEMON.

PHILEMON   Doth my lord call?

CERIMON Get fire and meat for these poor men.°   *the servants or men offstage*
'T has been a turbulent and stormy night.

                              [*Exit* PHILEMON.]

FIRST VISITING SERVANT I have been in many, but such a night
    as this

5   Till now I ne'er endured.

CERIMON [*to him*] Your master will be dead ere you return;
    There's nothing can be ministered to nature
    That can recover him. [*to* SECOND VISITING SERVANT] Give
        this to the 'pothecary,°   *druggist*
    And tell me how it works.

           [*Exeunt* FIRST *and* SECOND VISITING SERVANTS.]
           Enter two GENTLEMEN.

FIRST GENTLEMAN Good morrow.

SECOND GENTLEMAN   Good morrow to your lordship,

10 CERIMON   Gentlemen!
    Why do you stir so early?

FIRST GENTLEMAN   Sir,
    Our lodgings, standing bleak upon° the sea,   *exposed to*
    Shook as° the earth did quake.   *as if*
    The very principals° did seem to rend   *principal rafters*

15 And all to topple. Pure surprise and fear
    Made me to quit the house.

SECOND GENTLEMAN That is the cause we trouble you so early.
    'Tis not our husbandry.°   *good work habits*

CERIMON   Oh, you say well!

FIRST GENTLEMAN But I much marvel that your lordship,
        having

20 Rich tire° about you, should at these early hours   *bed furniture*
    Shake off the golden slumber of repose.
    'Tis most strange
    Nature should be so conversant with pain,[2]
    Being thereto not compelled.

CERIMON   I held it ever,°   *always believed*

25 Virtue and cunning° were endowments greater   *knowledge*
    Than nobleness and riches. Careless heirs
    May the two latter darken and expend,
    But immortality attends the former,
    Making a man a god. 'Tis known I ever°   *always*

30 Have studied physic,° through which secret art,   *medicine*
    By turning o'er authorities,° I have,   *reading learned texts*
    Together with my practice, made familiar
    To me and to my aid° the blest infusions   *benefit*
    That dwells in vegetives,[3] in metals, stones.

35 And I can speak of the disturbances

3.2 Location: Cerimon's house in Ephesus.
1. TEXTUAL COMMENT For the roles of servants in this scene, see Digital Edition TC 8.
2. That your nature should be so accustomed to labor.
3. Beneficial substances in plants.

That Nature works and of her cures, which doth
Give more content in course of true delight
Than to be thirsty after tottering° honor   *unstable*
Or tie my pleasure up in silken bags,°   *(of money)*
To please the fool and Death.[4]

40 SECOND GENTLEMAN   Your honor has
Through Ephesus poured forth your charity,
And hundreds call themselves your creatures[5] who
By you have been restored. And not your knowledge,
Your personal pain,° but even your purse still° open,   *labor / always*
45 Hath built Lord Cerimon such strong renown
As time shall never—
        Enter [PHILEMON *and two* SERVANTS] *with a chest.*

FIRST SERVANT   So, lift there.
CERIMON   What's that?
FIRST SERVANT   Sir, even now
Did the sea toss upon our shore this chest.
'Tis of some wreck.
CERIMON   Set't down. Let's look upon't.
SECOND GENTLEMAN   'Tis like a coffin, sir.
50 CERIMON   Whate'er it be,
'Tis wondrous heavy. [*to* SERVANTS] Wrench it open straight.[6]
       [SERVANTS *get implements.*]
If the sea's stomach be o'ercharged with gold,
'Tis a good constraint of Fortune it belches[7] upon us.
SECOND GENTLEMAN   'Tis so, my lord.
CERIMON   How close° 'tis caulked and bitumed!   *tightly*
55 Did the sea cast it up?
FIRST SERVANT   I never saw so huge a billow, sir,
As tossed it upon shore.
CERIMON   Wrench it open. —Soft!°   *But wait*
It smells most sweetly in my sense!
SECOND GENTLEMAN   A delicate odor!
CERIMON   As ever hit my nostril.
So, up with it.
       [SERVANTS *raise the lid.*]
60   O you most potent gods!
What's here?
A corpse?
SECOND GENTLEMAN   Most strange!
CERIMON   Shrouded in cloth of state,°   *royal fabric*
Balmed and entreasured with full bags of spices.
       [*He finds a paper.*]
A passport° too! Apollo, perfect me   *An identification paper*
65 In the characters.[8]
       [*Reads.*] "Here I give to understand,
         If ere this coffin drives a-land,
         I, King Pericles, have lost
         This queen worth all our mundane cost.°   *earthly wealth*

---

4. To gladden the fool who trusts in wealth, which
death inherits.
5. *call . . . creatures*: owe their lives to you.
6. TEXTUAL COMMENT On the elaborate stage busi-

ness of this scene, see Digital Edition TC 9.
7. It is good that fortune forces the sea to belch.
8. Apollo (patron of both scholars and physicians)
help me read the writing correctly.

70 Who° finds her, give her burying: *Whoever*
She was the daughter of a king.
Besides this treasure for a fee,
The° gods requite his charity."   *May the*
If thou livest, Pericles, thou hast a heart
75 That ever cracks for woe! —This chanced tonight.°   *occurred last night*
SECOND GENTLEMAN   Most likely, sir.
CERIMON   Nay, certainly tonight—
For look how fresh she looks! They were too rough
That threw her in the sea. [*to* SERVANTS] Make a fire within.
Fetch hither all my boxes in my closet.   [*Exeunt* SERVANTS.]
80 Death may usurp on nature many hours,
And yet the fire of life kindle again
The o'er-pressed° spirits. I heard of an Egyptian   *overcome*
That had nine hours lain dead,
Who was by good appliance° recovered.   *medical treatment*
          Enter [SERVANTS] *with* [*boxes,*] *napkins and fire.*
85 Well said, well said; the fire and cloths.
[*to* FIRST GENTLEMAN] The rough° and woeful music that   *harsh; unrefined*
      we have,
Cause it to sound, beseech you.
[*to a* SERVANT] The vial° once more. How thou stirr'st,⁹ thou   *(of medicine)*
      block!
The music there! [*Music sounds.*] I pray you, give her air.
90 Gentlemen, this queen will live. Nature awakes.
A warmth breathes out of her. She hath not been entranced°   *unconscious*
Above five hours. See how she 'gins to blow°   *bloom*
Into life's flower again.
FIRST GENTLEMAN   The heavens, through you,
Increase our wonder, and sets up your fame
Forever.
95 CERIMON   She is alive. Behold,
Her eyelids, cases to those heavenly jewels
Which Pericles hath lost, begin to part
Their fringes of bright gold. The diamonds
Of a most praised water° doth appear.   *luster*
100 [*to* THAISA] To make the world twice rich,¹ live,
And make us weep to hear your fate, fair creature,
Rare° as you seem to be.   *Exquisite*
          She moves.
THAISA   O dear Diana,
Where am I? Where's my lord? What world is this?
SECOND GENTLEMAN   Is not this strange?
FIRST GENTLEMAN   Most rare.
CERIMON   Hush, my gentle neighbors.
105 Lend me your hands. To the next chamber bear her.
Get linen. Now this matter must be looked to,
For her relapse is mortal.° Come, come;   *would be fatal*
And Aesculapius° guide us!   *god of healing*
          They carry [THAISA] *away. Exeunt.*

9. How lively you are (ironic).
1. Once by the precious gold of her eyelids and again by the jewels they conceal.

3.3

Enter PERICLES *at Tarsus with* CLEON, DIONYZA[,
and LYCHORIDA *with the child*].

PERICLES   Most honored Cleon, I must needs be gone.
My twelve months are expired,[1] and Tyrus stands
In a litigious° peace. You and your lady   *conflict-ridden*
Take from my heart all thankfulness. The gods
Make up the rest upon you.[2]

5   CLEON   Your shafts of fortune,
Though they hurt you mortally, yet glance
Full woundingly on us.

DIONYZA   Oh, your sweet queen!
That the strict fates had pleased you had brought[3] her hither
To have blessed mine eyes with her!

PERICLES   We cannot but obey

10   The powers above us. Could° I rage and roar   *Even if*
As doth the sea she lies in, yet the end
Must be as 'tis. My gentle babe Marina,
Whom for° she was born at sea I have named so,   *because*
Here I charge° your charity withal,°   *request; burden / with*

15   Leaving her the infant of your care,
Beseeching you to give her princely training,
That she may be mannered° as she is born.   *brought up*

CLEON   Fear not, my lord, but think
Your grace, that fed my country with your corn,

20   For which the people's prayers still fall upon you,
Must in your child be thought on. If neglection
Should therein make me vile, the common body,°   *the people*
By you relieved, would force me to my duty.
But if to that° my nature need a spur,   *that duty*

25   The gods revenge it upon me and mine
To the end of generation!

PERICLES   I believe you.
Your honor and your goodness teach me to't°   *to do so*
Without your vows. Till she be married, madam,
By bright Diana whom we honor, all

30   Unscissored shall this hair of mine remain,
Though I show ill° in't. So I take my leave.   *look bad*
Good madam, make me blessèd in your care
In bringing up my child.

DIONYZA   I have one myself,
Who shall not be more dear to my respect°   *attention*
Than yours, my lord.

35   PERICLES   Madam, my thanks and prayers.

CLEON   We'll bring your grace e'en to the edge o'th' shore,
Then give you up to the masked Neptune° and   *calm (or treacherous) sea*
The gentlest winds of heaven.

PERICLES   I will embrace your offer.

40   —Come, dearest madam. —Oh, no tears, Lychorida, no tears.
Look to your little mistress, on whose grace°   *favor*
You may depend hereafter. —Come, my lord.   [*Exeunt.*]

3.3 Location: The governor's house in Tarsus.
1. See 3.0.25–33.
2. Give you the rest of what you deserve.

3. *That . . . brought*: I wish it had pleased the "strict
fates" to have allowed you to bring.

3.4

Enter CERIMON *and* THAISA.

CERIMON   Madam, this letter and some certain jewels
 Lay with you in your coffer, which are at your command:
 Know you the character?°   *handwriting*

THAISA   It is my lord's.
 That I was shipped° at sea I well remember,   *on a ship*
5 Even on my groaning° time, but whether there delivered, *birthing*
 By the holy gods I cannot rightly say.
 But since King Pericles, my wedded lord,
 I ne'er shall see again,
 A vestal livery¹ will I take me to
10 And never more have joy.

CERIMON   Madam, if this you purpose° as ye speak,   *intend*
 Diana's temple is not distant far,
 Where you may abide till your date expire.°   *life ends*
 Moreover, if you please, a niece of mine
15 Shall there attend you.

THAISA My recompense is thanks; that's all.
 Yet my good will is great, though the gift small. *Exeunt.*

4.0

Enter GOWER.

GOWER   Imagine Pericles arrived at Tyre,
 Welcomed and settled to his own desire.
 His woeful queen we leave at Ephesus,
 Unto Diana there as votaress.°   *devotee*
5 Now to Marina bend your mind,
 Whom our fast-growing scene must find
 At Tarsus, and by Cleon trained
 In music, letters, who hath gained
 Of education all the grace,
10 Which makes her both the heart and place° *focal point*
 Of general wonder. But, alack,
 That monster envy, oft the wrack°   *ruin*
 Of earnèd praise, Marina's life
 Seeks to take off by treason's knife.
15 And in this kind:° our Cleon hath   *way*
 One daughter and a full-grown wench
 Even ripe for marriage rite. This maid
 Hight° Philoten, and it is said   *Was called*
 For certain in our story, she
20 Would ever° with Marina be.   *always*
 Be't when they weaved the sleided° silk, *divided into filaments*
 With fingers long, small, white as milk,
 Or when she would with sharp needle wound
 The cambric° which she made more sound *fine linen*
25 By hurting it, or when to th' lute
 She sung, and made the night bird° mute *nightingale*
 That still records° with moan, or when *always sings*

3.4 Location: Cerimon's house in Ephesus.
1. Vestal virgin's (metaphorical) uniform of religious chastity.

She would with rich and constant pen,
Vail° to her mistress Dian—still   *Inscribe praises*
30   This Philoten contends in skill
With absolute° Marina. So   *perfect*
With dove of Paphos might the crow
Vie feathers white.[1] Marina gets
All praises, which are paid as debts
35   And not as given.[2] This so darks°   *darkens*
In Philoten all graceful marks
That Cleon's wife with envy rare°   *extreme*
A present murder does prepare
For good Marina, that her daughter
40   Might stand peerless by° this slaughter.   *by means of*
The sooner her vile thoughts to stead,°   *help*
Lychorida, our nurse, is dead,
And cursèd Dionyza hath
The pregnant instrument of wrath
45   Pressed for this blow.[3] The unborn event,°   *outcome*
I do commend to your content.°   *(viewing) pleasure*
Only I carry wingèd Time,
Post° on the lame feet of my rhyme,   *Quickly*
Which never could I so convey,
50   Unless your thoughts went on my way.
Dionyza does appear,
With Leonine, a murderer.   *Exit.*

4.1

Enter DIONYZA *with* LEONINE.

DIONYZA   Thy oath remember—thou hast sworn to do't.
'Tis but a blow which never shall be known.
Thou canst not do a thing in the world so soon°   *quickly*
To yield thee so much profit. Let not conscience,
5   Which is but cold, enflaming thy low° bosom,   *base*
Enflame too nicely;° nor let pity, which   *scrupulously*
Even women have cast off, melt thee, but be
A soldier to thy purpose.
LEONINE   I will do't.
But yet she is a goodly creature.
10   DIONYZA   The fitter then the gods should have her.
Here she comes, weeping for her nurse's death.
Thou art resolved?
LEONINE   I am resolved.

Enter MARINA *with a basket of flowers.*

MARINA   No, I will rob Tellus of her weed°   *earth of its garment*
15   To strew thy green with flowers: the yellows, blues,
The purple violets, and marigolds
Shall as a carpet hang upon thy grave,
While summer days doth last. Ay me, poor maid,
Born in a tempest when my mother died,

4.0
1. *So . . . white:* So might the crow try to be whiter
than the dove. Paphos was a city sacred to Venus.
2. *Marina . . . given:* Marina's gifts compel others to

praise her, willingly or not.
3. Has enlisted a ready means to carry out her anger.
4.1 Location: Tarsus, near the seashore.

20   This world to me is a lasting storm
     Whirring° me from my friends.   *Hurrying*
   DIONYZA   How now, Marina? Why do you keep alone?
     How chance° my daughter is not with you?   *Why is it*
     Do not consume your blood with sorrowing.[1]
25   Have you a nurse of me![2] Lord, how your favor's°   *appearance is*
     Changèd with this unprofitable woe!
     Come, give me your flowers. O'er the sea margin°   *seashore*
     Walk with Leonine. The air is quick° there   *refreshing*
     And it pierces and sharpens the stomach.°   *appetite*
30   Come, Leonine,
     Take her by the arm, walk with her.
   MARINA   No, I pray you.
     I'll not bereave you of your servant.
   DIONYZA   Come, come,
     I love the King your father and yourself
     With more than foreign heart.° We every day   *As if we were kin*
35   Expect him here. When he shall come and find
     Our paragon to all reports thus blasted,[3]
     He will repent the breadth of his great voyage,
     Blame both my lord and me, that we have taken
     No care to your best courses.° Go, I pray you.   *courses of action*
40   Walk and be cheerful once again; reserve°   *preserve*
     That excellent complexion which did steal
     The eyes of young and old. Care not for me—
     I can go home alone.
   MARINA   Well, I will go,
     But yet I have no desire to it.
   DIONYZA   Come, come,
45   I know 'tis good for you. —Walk half an hour,
     Leonine, at the least. Remember what I have said.
   LEONINE   I warrant° you, madam.   *guarantee*
   DIONYZA   I'll leave you, my sweet lady, for a while.
     Pray, walk softly; do not heat your blood.
     What! I must have care of you!
50 MARINA   My thanks, sweet madam.
                                          [*Exit* DIONYZA.]
     Is this wind westerly that blows?
   LEONINE   Southwest.
   MARINA   When I was born the wind was north.
   LEONINE   Was't so?
   MARINA   My father, as nurse says, did never fear,
     But cried, "Good seamen," to the sailors,
55   Galling° his kingly hands hauling° ropes,   *Irritating / pulling*
     And, clasping to the mast, endured a sea
     That almost burst the deck.
   LEONINE   When was this?
   MARINA   When I was born.

---

1. Sighs were thought to consume one's blood.
2. Let me be your nurse.

3. Our universally admired paragon of beauty so blighted.

60	Never was waves nor wind more violent,	
	And from the ladder tackle° washes off	climbing rope; rope-ladder
	A canvas-climber.° "Ha," says one, "wolt out?"[4]	sailor in the rigging
	And with a dropping° industry they skip	dripping-wet
	From stem to stern. The boatswain° whistles, and	senior crew member
65	The master calls, and trebles their confusion—	

LEONINE   Come, say your prayers.

MARINA   What mean you?

LEONINE   If you require a little space for prayer,
   I grant it. Pray, but be not tedious,° for   *drawn out*
   The gods are quick of ear, and I am sworn
   To do my work with haste.

70 MARINA   Why will you kill me?

LEONINE   To satisfy my lady.

MARINA   Why would she have me killed?
   Now, as I can remember, by my troth,°   *faith*
   I never did her hurt in all my life,
   I never spake bad word, nor did ill turn
75 To any living creature: Believe me, la,°   *(exclamation)*
   I never killed a mouse nor hurt a fly.
   I trod upon a worm against my will,
   But I wept for't. How have I offended
   Wherein my death might yield her any profit, or
   My life imply her any danger?

80 LEONINE   My commission
   Is not to reason of the deed, but do't.

MARINA   You will not do't for all the world, I hope.
   You are well favored, and your looks foreshow
   You have a gentle heart. I saw you lately
85 When you caught° hurt in parting two that fought: *got*
   Good sooth,° it showed well in you. Do so now: *Truly*
   Your lady seeks my life; come you between,°   *(Dionyza and me)*
   And save poor me, the weaker.

LEONINE   I am sworn and will dispatch.
      [*He draws his sword.*] *Enter* [*three*] PIRATES.

90 FIRST PIRATE   Hold, villain!
                          [LEONINE *runs off and hides.*]

SECOND PIRATE   A prize,° a prize!   Booty (Marina)

THIRD PIRATE   Half part,° mates, half part. Come, let's have   To be shared
   her aboard suddenly.°   *Exeunt* [*carrying off* MARINA]. quickly
         LEONINE [*comes forward*].

LEONINE   These roguing° thieves serve the great pirate Valdes,[5] law-breaking
95 And they have seized Marina. Let her go.
   There's no hope she will return; I'll swear she's dead
   And thrown into the sea.—But I'll see further:
   Perhaps they will but please themselves upon her,°   will only rape her
   Not carry her aboard. If she remain,
100 Whom they have ravished must by me be slain.   *Exit.*

---

4. So you want to get off ship? (a cruel joke)

5. Probably named after an admiral in the Spanish Armada.

4.2

Enter [PANDER, BAWD *(his wife), and* BOLT].[1]

PANDER Bolt!

BOLT Sir?

PANDER Search the market narrowly.° Mytilene is full of gal-   *carefully*
lants. We lost too much money this mart° by being too   *market time*
5   wenchless.

BAWD We were never so much out of creatures.° We have but   *prostitutes*
poor three,° and they can do no more than they can do, and   *only three*
they with continual action are even as good as rotten.°   *have venereal disease*

PANDER Therefore let's have fresh ones, whate'er we pay for
10   them. If there be not a conscience to be used[2] in every trade,
we shall never prosper.

BAWD Thou say'st true. 'Tis not our bringing up of poor
bastards°—as I think I have brought up some eleven—   *(that enriches us)*

BOLT Ay, to eleven, and brought them down again.[3]—But
15   shall I search the market?

BAWD What else, man? The stuff we have, a strong wind will
blow it to pieces, they are so pitifully sodden.[4]

PANDER Thou sayest true. They're too unwholesome,
o'conscience.° The poor Transylvanian is dead that lay with   *on my conscience*
20   the little baggage.°   *prostitute*

BOLT Ay, she quickly pooped° him; she made him roast meat   *overcame (by disease)*
for worms—but I'll go search the market.   *Exit.*

PANDER Three or four thousand chequins° were as pretty a   *gold coins*
proportion° to live quietly and so give over°—   *sum / retire*

25 BAWD Why "to give over," I pray you? Is it a shame to get°   *earn*
when we are old?

PANDER Oh, our credit comes not in like the commodity, nor
the commodity wages not with the danger.[5] Therefore if in
our youths we could pick up some pretty estate, 'twere not
30   amiss to keep our door hatched.° Besides, the sore terms we   *closed for business*
stand upon with the gods[6] will be strong° with us for giving   *a strong argument*
o'er.

BAWD Come, other sorts offend as well as we.

PANDER As well as we? Ay, and better, too. We offend worse.
35   Neither is our profession any trade. It's no calling°—but   *(religious) vocation*
here comes Bolt.

Enter BOLT *with the* PIRATES *and* MARINA.

BOLT [*to the* PIRATES] Come your ways,° my masters.° You say *Come along / gentlemen*
she's a virgin?

FIRST PIRATE O sir, we doubt it not.

40 BOLT Master, I have gone through° for this piece° you see. If   *bargained / (of flesh)*
you like her, so.° If not, I have lost my earnest.°   *fine / deposit*

BAWD Bolt, has she any qualities?°   *accomplishments*

4.2 Location: Mytilene, on the island of Lesbos;
before a brothel.
1. *Pander:* sexual go-between, after Pandarus in
Chaucer's poem, *Troilus and Criseyde. Bawd:* supplier
of prostitutes. The name "Bolt" may have phallic connotations.
2. We need undiseased prostitutes for both economic and ethical reasons.
3. And prostituted them when they turned eleven.

4. Overboiled in the sweating tub as treatment for
venereal disease.
5. Our reputation doesn't accumulate like our profit,
nor does the profit justify the danger (with extended
economic wordplay: "credit," "commodity," "wages").
6. The Pander's admission here, indicating his
ambivalence, is part of the religious undercurrent of
the scene.

BOLT She has a good face, speaks well, and has excellent
good clothes. There's no farther necessity of qualities can°   *whose absence can*
45   make her be refused.
BAWD What's her price, Bolt?
BOLT I cannot be bated one doit of[7] a thousand pieces.
PANDER [*to the* PIRATES] Well, follow me, my masters; you
shall have your money presently.° —Wife, take her in;   *immediately*
50   instruct her what she has to do, that she may not be raw in
her entertainment.[8]   [*Exeunt* PANDER *and the* PIRATES.]
BAWD Bolt, take you the marks of her—the color of her hair,
complexion, height, her age—with warrant of her virginity,
and cry, "He that will give most shall have her first." Such a
55   maidenhead were no cheap thing if men were as they have
been. Get this done as I command you.
BOLT Performance shall follow.   *Exit.*
MARINA Alack that Leonine was so slack, so slow—
He should have struck, not spoke!—or that° these pirates,   *if only*
60   Not enough barbarous, had but o'erboard thrown me
For to seek my mother!
BAWD Why lament you, pretty one?
MARINA That I am pretty.
BAWD Come, the gods have done their part in you.
65   MARINA I accuse them not.
BAWD You are light° into my hands, where you are like° to   *arrived / likely*
live.
MARINA The more my fault,°   *misfortune*
To scape his hands where I was like to die.
70   BAWD Ay, and you shall live in pleasure.
MARINA No.
BAWD Yes, indeed shall you, and taste gentlemen of all fash-
ions. You shall fare well, you shall have the difference of all
complexions[9]—what? Do you stop your ears?
75   MARINA Are you a woman?
BAWD What would you have me be, an° I be not a woman?   *if*
MARINA An honest° woman or not a woman.   *A chaste*
BAWD Marry, whip the gosling! I think I shall have something
to do° with you. Come, you're a young foolish sapling and   *some trouble*
80   must be bowed as I would have you.
MARINA The gods defend me!
BAWD If it please the gods to defend you by men, then men
must comfort you, men must feed you, men stir you up.
[*Enter* BOLT.]
Bolt's returned. —Now, sir, hast thou cried° her through the   *advertised*
85   market?
BOLT I have cried her almost to° the number of her hairs, I   *down to*
have drawn her picture with my voice.
BAWD And I prithee tell me, how dost thou find the inclina-
tion of the people, especially of the younger sort?

---

7. I cannot get the price reduced a penny (*doit*: small
coin) from.
8. May not be unprepared to entertain customers.

9. The variety of appearances (temperaments; eth-
nicities).

90   BOLT   Faith, they listened to me as they would have harkened
     to their father's testament.° There was a Spaniard's mouth   *will*
     watered, and he went to bed to her very description.

  BAWD   We shall have him here tomorrow with his best ruff° on.   *collar; (sexual?)*

  BOLT   Tonight, tonight! But, mistress, do you know the French
95   knight that cowers i'the hams?[1]

  BAWD   Who, Monsieur Veroles?°   *Mr. Pox*

  BOLT   Ay, he. He offered to cut a caper[2] at the proclama-
     tion, but he made a groan at it and swore he would see her
     tomorrow.

100   BAWD   Well, well, as for him, he brought his disease hither;[3]
     here he does but repair° it. I know he will come in our   *renew*
     shadow, to scatter his crowns in the sun.[4]

  BOLT   Well, if we had of every nation a traveler we should
     lodge them with this sign.[5]

105   BAWD   [*to* MARINA]   Pray you, come hither a while. You have
     fortunes coming upon you.[6] Mark me: you must seem to do
     that fearfully which you commit willlingly, despise profit
     where you have most gain. To weep that you live as ye do°   *(by prostitution)*
     makes pity in your lovers. Seldom but that pity begets you a
110   good opinion, and that opinion a mere° profit.   *clear*

  MARINA   I understand you not.

  BOLT   Oh, take her home,° mistress, take her home. These   *inside; to task*
     blushes of hers must be quenched with some present
     practice.

115   BAWD   Thou sayest true i'faith, so they must, for your° bride   *even a*
     goes to that with shame which is her way to go with
     warrant.[7]

  BOLT   Faith, some do and some do not. But, mistress, if I have
     bargained for the joint°—   *cut of meat*

120   BAWD   Thou mayst cut a morsel off the spit.°   *have a taste yourself*

  BOLT   I may so.

  BAWD   Who should deny it? [*to* MARINA] Come, young one. I
     like the manner of your garments well.

  BOLT   Ay, by my faith, they shall not be changed yet.[8]

125   BAWD   [*gives him money*]   Bolt, spend thou that in the town.
     Report what a sojourner we have. You'll lose nothing by cus-
     tom.[9] When Nature framed this piece,° she meant thee a   *(of work; of flesh)*
     good turn. Therefore, say what a paragon she is, and thou
     hast the harvest out of thine own report.

130   BOLT   I warrant you, mistress. Thunder shall not so awake the
     beds of eels[1] as my giving out her beauty stirs up the lewdly
     inclined. I'll bring home some tonight.   [*Exit.*]

---

1. Who crouches (from venereal disease).
2. He tried to leap up and clap his heels together.
3. Englishmen called syphilis "the French disease." This allusion, as well as the equally anachronistic references to "a Spaniard's mouth" (line 91) and "the French knight" (lines 94–95), is one indication of the contemporary, distinctively English feel of the scene; see also act 2, scene 1.
4. He will come inside our house to spend his French crowns; to lose his hair (on the crown of his head) from syphilis. With a play on "shadow" and "sun."

5. This description would draw them like the painted sign of an inn.
6. You have prosperity (wealthy men) about to come to (have an orgasm on top of) you.
7. Even a bride, who has a legal right to sexual enjoyment, is shy, because, like Marina, she is a virgin.
8. Exchanged or sold (for a prostitute's wardrobe), since they proclaim her virginity and social status.
9. You'll gain in tips if we get more customers.
1. Eels were supposedly roused by thunder.

BAWD [*to* MARINA]   Come your ways, follow me.
MARINA   If fires be hot, knives sharp, or waters deep,
135   Untried I still my virgin knot will keep.[2]
Diana,° aid my purpose!   *goddess of chastity*
BAWD   What have we to do with Diana? Pray you, will you go
with us?   *Exeunt.*

4.3

Enter CLEON *and* DIONYZA.

DIONYZA   Why, are you foolish? Can it be undone?
CLEON   O Dionyza, such a piece of slaughter
The sun and moon ne'er looked upon.
DIONYZA   I think you'll turn a child again.
5   CLEON   Were I chief lord of all this spacious world,
I'd give it to undo the deed. A lady°   *(Marina)*
Much less in blood than virtue, yet a princess
To equal any single crown o'th' earth
I'th' justice of compare!° O villain Leonine!   *In a fair comparison*
10   —Whom thou hast poisoned too!
If thou hadst drunk to him 't had been a kindness
Becoming well thy fact![1] What canst thou say
When noble Pericles shall demand his child?
DIONYZA   That she is dead. Nurses are not the Fates.
15   To foster is not ever° to preserve.   *always*
She died at night—I'll say so; who can cross° it?   *deny*
Unless you play the pious innocent
And for an honest attribute,° cry out,   *reputation*
"She died by foul play."
CLEON   Oh, go to!° Well, well,   *(contemptuous)*
20   Of all the faults beneath the heavens the gods
Do like this worst.
DIONYZA   Be one of those that thinks
The petty wrens of Tarsus will fly hence
And open° this to Pericles. I do shame   *disclose*
To think of what a noble strain° you are,   *bloodline*
And of how coward a spirit.
25   CLEON   To such proceeding
Whoever but° his approbation added,   *only*
Though not his prime° consent, he did not flow   *prior*
From honorable sources.
DIONYZA   Be it so then,
Yet none does know but you how she came dead,
30   Nor none can know, Leonine being gone.
She did distain° my child and stood between   *stain (by comparison)*
Her and her fortunes: none would look on her,
But cast their gazes on Marina's face
Whilst ours was blurted at° and held a malkin°   *scorned / dirty peasant*
35   Not worth the time of day. It pierced me through.
And though you call my course unnatural,
You not your child well loving,[2] yet I find

---

2. *Untried . . . keep:* I will still remain a virgin. Q
reads "Untied," which, with the pun of "knot" and
"not," means not untied—hence, the same thing.
4.3 Location: The governor's house in Tarsus.

1. *If . . . fact:* If you had drunk to his health (from
the same poison), the self-punishment would have fit
the crime.
2. Since you don't love your child very much.

It greets° me as an enterprise of kindness   *strikes*
Performed to your sole daughter.
CLEON   Heavens forgive it!
40 DIONYZA   And as for Pericles, what should he say?
We wept after her hearse, and yet° we mourn.   *still*
Her monument is almost finished, and her epitaphs
In glitt'ring golden characters express
A general praise to her and care in us
At whose expense 'tis done.
45 CLEON   Thou art like the harpy[3]
Which, to betray, dost with thine angel's face
Seize[4] with thine eagle's talons.
DIONYZA   You're like one that superstitiously
Do swear to th' gods that winter kills the flies.[5]
50 But yet I know you'll do as I advise.   [*Exeunt.*]

4.4

[*Enter* GOWER.]
GOWER   Thus time we waste,° and long leagues make short,[1]   *pass quickly*
Sail seas in cockles,° have and wish but for't,[2]   *seashells*
Making to take° our imagination   *Proceeding by*
From bourn° to bourn, region to region.   *border*
5   By you being pardoned, we commit no crime
To use one language in each several clime°   *separate region*
Where our scene seems to live. I do beseech you
To learn of me who stand i'th' gaps° to teach you   *(between scenes)*
The stages of our story. Pericles
10   Is now again thwarting° the wayward seas,   *crossing*
Attended on by many a lord and knight,
To see his daughter, all his life's delight.
Old Helicanus goes along. Behind
Is left to govern, if you bear in mind,
15   Old Escanes, whom Helicanus late°   *recently*
Advanced in Tyre to great and high estate.°   *rank*
Well-sailing ships and bounteous winds have brought
This king to Tarsus—think his pilot thought;[3]
So with his steerage shall your thoughts go on—
20   To fetch his daughter home, who first° is gone.   *already*
Like motes and shadows[4] see them move a while.
Your ears unto your eyes I'll reconcile.
[*Dumb show.*]
Enter PERICLES *at one door with all his train,* CLEON
and DIONYZA *at the other.* CLEON *shows* PERICLES
the tomb, whereat PERICLES *makes lamentation,*
puts on sackcloth,° and in a mighty passion° departs   *mourning clothes / sorrow*
[*with his train. Exeunt* CLEON *and* DIONYZA *separately*].

---

3. Monstrous creature with a woman's face and an
eagle's talons.
4. *Which . . . Seize:* Who deceives with your "angel's
face" and then "Seize[s]."
5. *You're . . . flies:* Perhaps: You're so afraid of the
gods that you'd disclaim responsibility even for petty
things like killing flies.

4.4 Location: Before Marina's tomb in Tarsus.
1. Here, Gower speaks in pentameter couplets.
2. Get something merely by wishing for it.
3. Think that his pilot is swiftly traveling thought.
4. Like specks of dust in a sunbeam and like (theatrical) illusions.

See how belief may suffer by foul show:°   *false appearances*
This borrowed passion stands for true-owed woe,[5]
25   And Pericles, in sorrow all devoured,
With sighs shot through and biggest tears o'ershowered,
Leaves Tarsus and again embarks. He swears
Never to wash his face nor cut his hairs.
He puts on sackcloth, and to sea he bears
30   A tempest which his mortal vessel tears,[6]
And yet he rides it out. Now please you wit°   *know*
The epitaph is° for Marina writ   *that is*
By wicked Dionyza:
> [*He reads the inscription on the tomb.*]
> "The fairest, sweetest, and best lies here,
35   Who withered in her spring of year:°   *early in life*
She was of Tyrus the King's° daughter   *the King of Tyre's*
On whom foul death hath made this slaughter.
Marina was she called, and at her birth
Thetis,[7] being proud, swallowed° some part o'th' earth.   *flooded*
40   Therefore the earth, fearing to be o'erflowed,
Hath Thetis' birth-child on the heavens bestowed,
Wherefore she° does, and swears she'll never stint,   *(Thetis)*
Make raging battery upon shores of flint."°   *rocky shores*
No visor does become black villainy
45   So well as soft and tender flattery.
Let Pericles believe his daughter's dead,
And bear his courses to be orderèd[8]
By Lady Fortune, while our stage must play
His daughter's woe and heavy welladay°   *lamentation*
50   In her unholy service. Patience, then,
And think you now are all in Mytilene.   *Exit.*

4.5

Enter two GENTLEMEN.

FIRST GENTLEMAN   Did you ever hear the like?

SECOND GENTLEMAN   No, nor never shall do in such a place as this, she being once gone.

FIRST GENTLEMAN   But to have divinity preached there—did
5   you ever dream of such a thing?

SECOND GENTLEMAN   No, no. Come, I am for no more bawdy houses. Shall's go hear the vestals sing?[1]

FIRST GENTLEMAN   I'll do anything now that is virtuous, but I am out of the road of rutting° forever.   *Exeunt.*   *fornication*

---

5. Cleon and Dionyza's "woe" is "borrowed," not "true-owed" (owned); perhaps also a self-referential comment on the sorrow simulated by the actor playing Pericles.
6. *he bears . . . tears*: His suffering assaults his body. (Note the internalization of the earlier storms.)
7. A sea nymph here confused with Tethys, wife of Oceanus (in Greek mythology, the ruler of a river that encircled the earth). The image in this passage

is of the ocean (because of Thetis/Tethys) surging happily in response to Marina's birth during the storm of act 3, scene 1, and angrily in response to her death.
8. And allow his fate to be arranged.
4.5 Location: The brothel in Mytilene.
1. Shall we go hear the vestal virgins (religious devotees) sing?

4.6

Enter [PANDER, BAWD, *and* BOLT].

PANDER Well, I had rather than twice the worth of her she
had ne'er come here.

BAWD Fie, fie upon her, she's able to freeze the god Priapus
and undo a whole generation.¹ We must either get her rav-
5   ished or be rid of her. When she should do for clients her
fitment,° and do me the kindness of our profession,² she   *duty*
has° me her quirks, her reasons, her master reasons, her   *gives*
prayers, her knees,° that she would make a puritan of the   *(kneeling to plead)*
devil if he should cheapen° a kiss of her.   *bargain for*

10 BOLT Faith, I must ravish her, or she'll disfurnish us of all
our *cavalleria*° and make our swearers³ priests.   *gentlemen customers*

PANDER Now the pox upon her greensickness,⁴ for me!

BAWD Faith, there's no way to be rid on't but by the way to the
pox.° Here comes the Lord Lysimachus disguised.   *venereal disease*

15 BOLT We should have both lord and loon° if the peevish   *lowborn*
baggage° would but give way to customers.   *worthless woman*

Enter LYSIMACHUS [*masked*].

LYSIMACHUS How now, how° a dozen of virginities?   *how much for*

BAWD Now the gods to-bless your honor!

BOLT I am glad to see your honor in good health.

20 LYSIMACHUS You may so: 'tis the better for you that your
resorters° stand upon sound legs.⁵ How now? Wholesome   *visitors*
iniquity° have you, that a man may deal withal° and defy the   *Healthy whore / with*
surgeon?°   *avoid the doctor*

BAWD We have here one, sir, if she would—but there never
25 came her like in Mytilene.

LYSIMACHUS If she'd do the deeds of darkness, thou wouldst
say.

BAWD Your honor knows what 'tis to say° well enough.   *what I mean*

LYSIMACHUS Well, call forth, call forth.   [*Exit* PANDER.]

30 BOLT For flesh and blood, sir, white and red, you shall see a
rose. And she were a rose indeed, if she had but—⁶

LYSIMACHUS What, prithee?

BOLT O sir, I can be modest.

LYSIMACHUS That dignifies the renown of a bawd, no less
35 than it gives a good report to a number to be chaste.⁷

[*Re-enter* PANDER *with* MARINA.]

BAWD Here comes that which grows to° the stalk: never   *is affixed to*
plucked yet, I can assure you. Is she not a fair creature?

LYSIMACHUS Faith, she would serve after a long voyage at sea.
Well, there's for you. [*He gives the* BAWD *money*.] Leave us.

40 BAWD I beseech your honor, give me leave a word, and I'll
have done presently.°   *be done soon*

4.6 Location: Scene continues.
1. Able to stop the "whole" (hole) work of breeding.
Priapus was the god of procreation, especially of
male virility and lechery.
2. Enable me to profit from her profession of prostitution. "Do me" and "has me" (line 7) are here colloquial expressions of annoyance.
3. Make our customers sincerely worship the gods
they usually invoke blasphemously.

4. Moody stubbornness, supposedly caused by anemia in young women; queasiness from lack of experience.
5. Rather than upon legs bent from venereal disease.
6. If she had but a thorn; if she were sexually experienced (implied pun on "prick").
7. Than it gives many (whores? wives?) a (falsely)
good reputation for chastity.

LYSIMACHUS   I beseech you, do.
          [BAWD *speaks privately with* MARINA.]
BAWD   First, I would have you note, this is an honorable man.
MARINA   I desire to find him so, that I may worthily note him.
45   BAWD   Next, he's the governor of this country and a man
          whom I am bound to.
MARINA   If he govern the country you are bound to him
          indeed, but how honorable he is in that, I know not.
BAWD   Pray you, without any more virginal fencing, will you
50   use him kindly? He will line your apron with gold.
MARINA   What he will do graciously, I will thankfully receive.
LYSIMACHUS   Ha' you done?
BAWD   My lord, she's not paced° yet; you must take some   *trained (like a horse)*
          pains to work her to your manage.[8] —Come, we will leave
55   his honor and her together. —Go thy ways.°   *Come along*
          [*Exeunt* BAWD, PANDER, *and* BOLT.]
LYSIMACHUS   Now, pretty one, how long have you been at this
          trade?
MARINA   What trade, sir?
LYSIMACHUS   Why, I cannot name it but I shall offend.
60   MARINA   I cannot be offended with my trade; please you to
          name it.
LYSIMACHUS   How long have you been of this profession?
MARINA   E'er since I can remember.
LYSIMACHUS   Did you go to't° so young? Were you a gamester°   *copulate / loose woman*
65   at five, or at seven?
MARINA   Earlier, too, sir, if now I be one.
LYSIMACHUS   Why, the house you dwell in proclaims you to be
          a creature of sale.
MARINA   Do you know this house to be a place of such resort,°   *purpose*
70   and will come into't? I hear say you're of honorable parts and
          are the governor of this place.
LYSIMACHUS   Why, hath your principal° made known unto   *employer*
          you who I am?
MARINA   Who is my principal?
75   LYSIMACHUS   Why, your herb-woman, she that sets seeds and
          roots of shame and iniquity.—Oh, you have heard some-
          thing of my power and so stand aloof for more serious woo-
          ing, but I protest to thee, pretty one, my authority shall not
          see thee, or else look friendly upon thee.[9] Come, bring me to
80   some private place. Come, come.
MARINA   If you were born to honor,° show it now.   *high status; virtue*
          If put upon you,[1] make the judgment good
          That thought you worthy of it.
LYSIMACHUS [*aside*]   How's this? How's this? Some more. Be sage.
MARINA   For me
85   That am a maid, though most ungentle Fortune
          Have placed me in this sty, where, since I came,
          Diseases have been sold dearer than physic—[2]
          That the gods

---

8. To bring her under your control (from horsemanship).
9. *my authority . . . upon thee:* Lysimachus won't use
his power to punish prostitution, or he will patronize

her (personally, financially).
1. If you were granted rank not by birth but by merit.
2. Sold at a higher price than medical treatment.

Would set me free from this unhallowed place,
90 Though they did change me to the meanest° bird   *humblest*
That flies i'th' purer air!
LYSIMACHUS   I did not think
Thou couldst have spoke so well, ne'er dreamt thou couldst.
Had I brought hither a corrupted mind,
Thy speech had altered it. Hold, here's gold for thee.
95 Persevere in that clear way thou goest
And the gods strengthen thee.
MARINA   The good gods preserve you!
LYSIMACHUS   For me, be you bethoughten that I came
With no ill intent, for to me the very doors
And windows savor vilely. Fare thee well.
100 Thou art a piece of virtue, and I doubt not
But thy training hath been noble.
Hold, here's more gold for thee.
A curse upon him, die he° like a thief,   *may he die*
That robs thee of thy goodness! If thou dost
105 Hear from me it shall be for thy good.
        [*He opens the door to leave. Enter* BOLT.]
BOLT   I beseech your honor, one piece for me.
LYSIMACHUS   Avaunt,° thou damnèd doorkeeper!   *Begone*
Your house, but for this virgin that doth prop it,
Would sink and overwhelm you. Away!   [*Exit.*]
110 BOLT   How's this? We must take another course with you! If
your peevish chastity, which is not worth a breakfast in
the cheapest country under the cope,° shall undo a whole   *sky*
household, let me be gelded like a spaniel. Come your
ways.
115 MARINA   Whither would you have me?
BOLT   I must have your maidenhead taken off, or the common
hangman shall execute it.³ Come your ways, we'll have no
more gentlemen driven away. Come your ways, I say.
        Enter [BAWD *and* PANDER].
BAWD   How now, what's the matter?
120 BOLT   Worse and worse, mistress; she has here spoken holy
words to the Lord Lysimachus.
BAWD   Oh, abominable!
BOLT   He makes our profession as it were to stink afore the
face of the gods.
125 BAWD   Marry,° hang her up forever.   *(expresses irritation)*
BOLT   The nobleman would have dealt with her like a noble-
man,⁴ and she sent him away as cold as a snowball, saying
his prayers too.
BAWD   Bolt, take her away, use her at thy pleasure. Crack the
130 glass of her virginity, and make the rest malleable.
BOLT   An if° she were a thornier piece of ground than she is,   *Even if*
she shall be plowed.
MARINA   Hark, hark, you gods!

---

3. By cutting off the maidenhead (virginity), as an   4. Would have used her and rewarded her well.
executioner cuts off heads.

BAWD	She conjures°—away with her! Would she had never	*calls on the gods*
135	come within my doors. —Marry, hang you! —She's born to	
	undo us. —Will you not go the way of womenkind? Marry	
	come up, my dish of chastity with rosemary and bays.[5]	

[*Exeunt* BAWD *and* PANDER.]

BOLT	Come, mistress, come your ways with me.	
MARINA	Whither wilt thou have me?	
140 BOLT	To take from you the jewel you hold so dear.	
MARINA	Prithee, tell me one thing first.	
BOLT	Come now, your one thing?	
MARINA	What canst thou wish thine enemy to be?[6]	
BOLT	Why, I could wish him to be° my master, or rather, my	*(as bad as)*
145	mistress.	
MARINA	Neither of these are so bad as thou art,	
	Since they do better thee in their command.[7]	
	Thou hold'st a place for which the painedest° fiend	*most tortured*
	Of hell would not in reputation change.	
150	Thou art the damnèd doorkeeper to every	
	Coistrel° that comes enquiring for his Tib.°	*Base fellow / loose woman*
	To the choleric fisting of every rogue	
	Thy ear is liable;[8] thy food is such	
	As hath been belched on by infected lungs.	
155 BOLT	What would you have me do? Go to the wars, would	
	you—where a man may serve seven years for the loss of° a	*only to lose*
	leg, and have not money enough in the end to buy him a	
	wooden one?	
MARINA	Do anything but this thou dost. Empty	
160	Old receptacles, or common shores,° of filth,	*(where waste was placed)*
	Serve by indenture° to the common hangman—	*as apprentice*
	Any of these ways are yet better than this.	
	For what thou professest, a baboon, could he speak,	
	Would own a name too dear.° —Oh, that the gods	*consider beneath him*
165	Would safely deliver me from this place!	
	—Here, here's gold for thee.	

[*She gives him the money.*]

	If that thy master would gain by me,	
	Proclaim that I can sing, weave, sew, and dance,	
	With other virtues° which I'll keep from boast,	*accomplishments*
170	And will undertake all these to teach.	
	I doubt not but this populous city will	
	Yield many scholars.°	*pupils*
BOLT	But can you teach all this you speak of?	
MARINA	Prove° that I cannot, take me home again	*If you prove*
175	And prostitute me to the basest groom°	*lowest servant*
	That doth frequent your house.	
BOLT	Well, I will see what I can do for thee. If I can place	
	thee, I will.	
MARINA	But amongst honest women.	

---

5. The Bawd chides Marina for thinking herself too exquisite a dish (for making too much of her chastity).
6. What is the worst thing you could wish on your enemy?

7. Since they at least can command you to do what they want.
8. *To . . . liable:* Even the lowest rogue would box your ear if angry.

180 BOLT Faith, my acquaintance lies little amongst them. But
since my master and mistress hath bought you, there's no
going but by their consent; therefore I will make them
acquainted with your purpose, and I doubt not but I shall find
them tractable enough. Come, I'll do for thee what I can.
185 Come your ways.   *Exeunt.*

5.0
Enter GOWER.

GOWER Marina thus the brothel scapes, and chances[1]
Into an honest house, our story says.
She sings like one immortal, and she dances
As goddess-like to her admirèd lays.°   songs
5 Deep clerks she dumbs[2] and with her nee'le° composes   needle
Nature's own shape of bud, bird, branch, or berry,
That even her art sisters° the natural roses;   equals
Her inkle,° silk, twin with the rubied cherry—   linen thread
That° pupils lacks she none of noble race   So that
10 Who pour their bounty on her, and her gain
She gives the cursèd bawd. Here we her place,
And to her father turn our thoughts again.
We left him on the sea; we there him lost,
Where, driven before the winds, he is arrived
15 Here where his daughter dwells, and on this coast
Suppose him now at anchor. The city strived°   endeavored
God Neptune's annual feast to keep, from whence
Lysimachus our Tyrian ship espies—
His° banners sable,° trimmed with rich expense—   Its / black
20 And to him° in his barge with fervor hies.   it
In your supposing° once more put your sight   imagination
Of heavy° Pericles; think this his bark,°   sad / ship
Where what is done in action, more if might,
Shall be discovered.[3] Please you sit and hark.   *Exit.*

5.1
Enter two SAILORS[, *the* FIRST *from Tyre and the*
SECOND *from Mytilene*].

FIRST SAILOR Where is Lord Helicanus? [*to* SECOND SAILOR]
He can resolve° you.   answer
[*Enter* HELICANUS.]
Oh, here he is.
—Sir, there is a barge put off from Mytilene
And in it is Lysimachus, the Governor,
5 Who craves to come aboard. What is your will?
HELICANUS That he have his.   [*Exit* SECOND SAILOR.]
Call up some gentlemen.
FIRST SAILOR Ho, gentlemen, my lord calls!

5.0
1. Unlike Gower's other prologues, which are in tetrameter or, less often, pentameter rhyming couplets, this one rhymes alternate pentameter lines.
2. Her wisdom reduces learned men to silence.

3. *Where . . . discovered:* Where the stage action, which would show more if it could, will reveal what happens.
5.1 Location: Pericles' ship, off Mytilene.

Enter two or three GENTLEMEN.

FIRST GENTLEMAN   Doth your lordship call?

HELICANUS   Gentlemen, there is some of worth°   *some noble visitor*
Would come aboard. I pray, greet him fairly.
                    Enter LYSIMACHUS [*with* SECOND SAILOR *and* LORDS].

10 SECOND SAILOR [*to* LYSIMACHUS]   Sir, this is the man that can
In aught you would resolve° you.   *Answer anything for*

LYSIMACHUS [*to* HELICANUS]   Hail, reverend sir!
The gods preserve you.

HELICANUS   And you, to outlive the age I am
And die as I would do.

LYSIMACHUS   You wish me well.
Being on shore, honoring of Neptune's triumphs,°   *festival*
15 Seeing this goodly vessel ride before us,
I made to it, to know of whence you are.

HELICANUS   First, what is your place?

LYSIMACHUS   I am the governor of this place you lie before.

HELICANUS   Sir, our vessel is of Tyre, in it the King,
20 A man who for this three months hath not spoken
To anyone, nor taken sustenance
But to prorogue° his grief.   *extend*

LYSIMACHUS   Upon what ground is his distemperature?°   *emotional disturbance*

HELICANUS   'Twould be too tedious to repeat,
25 But the main grief springs from the loss
Of a beloved daughter and a wife.

LYSIMACHUS   May we not see him?

HELICANUS   You may,
But bootless° is your sight. He will not speak   *pointless*
To any.

LYSIMACHUS   Yet let me obtain my wish.

HELICANUS   Behold him.
                    [PERICLES *is revealed.*]
30   This was a goodly person,
Till the disaster that one mortal° night   *fatal*
Drove him to this.

LYSIMACHUS   Sir King, all hail! The gods preserve you! Hail,
royal sir!

HELICANUS   It is in vain; he will not speak to you.

35 FIRST LORD   Sir, we have a maid in Mytilene, I durst wager
Would win some words of him.

LYSIMACHUS   'Tis well bethought.
She questionless, with her sweet harmony
And other choice attractions, would allure
And make a batt'ry through his deafened ports,
40 Which now are midway stopped.° She is all happy,°   *half closed / skillful*
And the fairest of all her fellow maids—
[*to* FIRST LORD]   Now upon the leafy shelter that abuts
Against the island's side.   [*Exit* FIRST LORD.]

HELICANUS   Sure, all effectless.
Yet nothing we'll omit
45 That bears recovery's name.° But since your kindness   *That might cure him*
We have stretched thus far, let us beseech you
That for our gold we may provision have,
Wherein we are not destitute for want,
But weary for the staleness.

	LYSIMACHUS	O sir, a courtesy	
50		Which if we should deny, the most just gods	
	For every graft° would send a caterpillar	*cultivated plant*
	And so inflict° our province. Yet once more	*afflict (with famine)*
	Let me entreat to know at large° the cause	*in detail*
	Of your king's sorrow.	
	HELICANUS	Sit, sir; I will	
	Recount it to you—	

[*Re-enter* FIRST LORD *with* MARINA *and another Maid.*]

55 but see, I am prevented.

LYSIMACHUS   Oh, here's the lady that I sent for.
Welcome, fair one. —Is't not a goodly presence?°   *Isn't she attractive*
HELICANUS   She's a gallant° lady.   *fine*
LYSIMACHUS   She's such a one that, were I well assured
60   Came of a gentle kind° and noble stock,   *a gentry family*
I'd wish no better choice, and think me rarely° to wed.   *superbly*
[*to* MARINA]   Fair one, all goodness that consists in bounty
Expect even here, where is a kingly patient.
If that thy prosperous and artificial feat°   *artful skill*
65   Can draw him but to answer thee in aught,
Thy sacred physic° shall receive such pay   *treatment*
As thy desires can wish.
MARINA   Sir, I will use
My utmost skill in his recovery,° provided   *cure*
That none but I and my companion maid
Be suffered° to come near him.   *permitted*
70   LYSIMACHUS   Come, let us leave her,
And the gods make her prosperous.

[*Exeunt all except* MARINA, *the Maid, and* PERICLES.]
The Song.
[MARINA *and the other Maid sing and play to*
PERICLES, *who does not respond. Re-enter*
LYSIMACHUS *and* HELICANUS.]

LYSIMACHUS   Marked° he your music?   *Noticed*
MARINA   No, nor looked on us.
LYSIMACHUS [*to* HELICANUS]   See, she will speak to him.
[LYSIMACHUS, HELICANUS, *and the Maid withdraw.*]
MARINA   Hail, sir! My lord, lend ear!
PERICLES   Hmm? Ha!
[*He pushes her back.*]
75   MARINA   I am a maid, my lord,
That ne'er before invited eyes, but have
Been gazed on like a comet.° She speaks,   *in awe*
My lord, that maybe hath endured a grief
Might° equal yours, if both were justly weighed.   *That might*
80   Though wayward fortune did malign my state,°   *reduce my status*
My derivation was from ancestors
Who stood equivalent with mighty kings.
But time hath rooted out[1] my parentage,
And to the world and awkward casualties°   *adverse events*
85   Bound me in servitude. [*aside*] I will desist.
But there is something glows upon my cheek

---

1. Uprooted me from; obscured; killed.

And whispers in mine ear, "Go not till he speak."
PERICLES My fortunes, parentage—good parentage,
To equal mine—was it not thus? What say you?
90 MARINA I said, my lord, if you did know my parentage,
You would not do me violence.
PERICLES   I do think so.
Pray you, turn your eyes upon me.
You're like something that—What countrywoman?°   *What nationality*
Here, of these shores?
MARINA   No, nor of any shores.
95 Yet I was mortally² brought forth, and am
No other than I appear.
PERICLES [*aside*] I am great° with woe, and shall deliver   *pregnant*
     weeping.
My dearest wife was like this maid, and such a one
My daughter might have been: my queen's square brows,
100 Her stature to an inch, as wand-like straight,
As silver-voiced, her eyes as jewel-like
And cased as richly, in pace° another Juno;   *stride*
Who starves the ears she feeds and makes them hungry
The more she gives them speech. —Where do you live?
105 MARINA Where I am but a stranger.° From the deck   *foreigner*
You may discern the place.
PERICLES   Where were you bred?
And how achieved you these endowments which
You make more rich to owe?°   *by your owning them*
MARINA   If I should tell
My history, it would seem like lies
Disdained in the reporting.°   *as soon as told*
110 PERICLES   Prithee, speak.
Falseness cannot come from thee, for thou lookest
Modest as justice, and thou seemest a palace
For the crowned Truth to dwell in. I will believe thee
And make sense credit thy relation°   *trust your story*
115 To° points that seem impossible, for thou lookest   *Even to*
Like one I loved indeed. What were thy friends?°   *kin*
Didst thou not say when I did push thee back—
Which was when I perceived thee—that thou cam'st
From good descending?
MARINA   So indeed I did.
120 PERICLES Report thy parentage. I think thou said'st
Thou hadst been tossed from wrong to injury,
And that thou thought'st thy griefs might equal mine,
If both were opened.°   *revealed*
MARINA   Some such thing I said,
And said no more but what my thoughts
Did warrant° me was likely.   *assure*
125 PERICLES   Tell thy story.
If thine considered° prove the thousandth part   *yours, when considered,*
Of my endurance,° thou art a man, and I   *suffering*
Have suffered like a girl. Yet thou dost look

---

2. Normally, not supernaturally, despite not being born on "any shores"; perhaps also fatally—to her mother.

Like Patience gazing on kings' graves and smiling
130 Extremity out of act.[3] What were thy friends?
How lost thou them? Thy name, my most kind[4] virgin?
Recount, I do beseech thee. Come, sit by me.

MARINA [*sitting*]   My name is Marina.

PERICLES   Oh, I am mocked,
And thou by some incensèd god sent hither
To make the world to laugh at me.

135 MARINA   Patience, good sir,
Or here I'll cease.

PERICLES   Nay, I'll be patient.
Thou little know'st how thou dost startle me
To call thyself Marina.

MARINA   The name
Was given me by one that had some power:
My father, and a king.

140 PERICLES   How? A king's daughter
And called Marina?

MARINA   You said you would believe me.
But not to be a troubler of your peace,
I will end here.

PERICLES   But are you flesh and blood?
Have you a working pulse, and are no fairy?
145 Motion° as well? Speak on. Where were you born?   (*of life*)
And wherefore called Marina?

MARINA   Called Marina
For I was born at sea.

PERICLES   At sea—what mother?

MARINA   My mother was the daughter of a king,
Who died the minute I was born, as my good nurse
150 Lychorida hath oft delivered weeping.

PERICLES   Oh, stop there a little! [*aside*] This is the rarest
       dream
That e'er dulled sleep did mock sad fools withal!°   *with*
This cannot be my daughter, burièd.
—Well, where were you bred?
155 I'll hear you more, to th' bottom° of your story,   *the end*
And never interrupt you.

MARINA   You scarce believe me; 'twere best I did give o'er.°   *stop*

PERICLES   I will believe you by the syllable
Of what you shall deliver. Yet give me leave:°   (*to ask*)
160 How came you in these parts? Where were you bred?

MARINA   The King my father did in Tarsus leave me,
Till cruel Cleon with his wicked wife
Did seek to murder me and wooed a villain
To attempt it, who having drawn to do't,
165 A crew of pirates came and rescued me,
Brought me to Mytilene. But, good sir, whither
Will you have me? Why do you weep? It may be
You think me an impostor. No, good faith.

---

3. *Yet . . . act:* Yet you resemble a statue of Patience on a royal tomb, facing down the worst extremities with a smile.

4. Sympathetic; related by blood ("kind" also meant "kin").

I am the daughter to King Pericles,
If good King Pericles be.° .... *live*

170 PERICLES   Ho, Helicanus?

[HELICANUS *and* LYSIMACHUS *come forward.*]

HELICANUS   Calls my lord?

PERICLES   Thou art a grave and noble counselor,
     Most wise in general. Tell me, if thou canst,
     What this maid is, or what is like° to be, ... *likely*
     That thus hath made me weep.

175 HELICANUS   I know not,
     But here's the regent, sir, of Mytilene,
     Lysimachus, speaks° nobly of her. .... *who speaks*

LYSIMACHUS   She never
     Would tell her parentage. Being demanded that,
     She would sit still and weep.

180 PERICLES   O Helicanus, strike me, honored sir,
     Give me a gash, put me to present° pain, ... *immediate*
     Lest this great sea of joys rushing upon me
     O'erbear° the shores of my mortality .... *Overflow*
     And drown me with their sweetness. [*to* MARINA] Oh, come
     hither,

185   Thou that begett'st him that did thee beget,[5]
     Thou that wast born at sea, buried at Tarsus,
     And found at sea again. —O Helicanus,
     Down on thy knees, thank the holy gods as loud
     As thunder threatens us! This is Marina.

190   —What was thy mother's name? Tell me but that,
     For truth can never be confirmed enough,
     Though doubts did ever sleep.[6]

MARINA   First, sir, I pray,[7]
     What is your title?

PERICLES   I am Pericles of Tyre.
     But tell me now my drowned queen's name, as in

195   The rest foresaid thou hast been godlike perfect°— .... *have been omniscient*
     The heir of kingdoms, and another life
     To Pericles thy father.

MARINA   Is it no more to be your daughter than
     To say my mother's name was Thaisa?

200   Thaisa was my mother, who did end
     The minute I began.

         [*She kneels. He blesses her.*]

PERICLES   Now blessing on thee. Rise, thou'rt my child.

         [*She rises. He calls to Attendants.*]

     —Give me fresh garments! —Mine own Helicanus,
     She is not dead at Tarsus, as she should have been[8]

205   By savage Cleon. She shall tell thee all
     When thou shalt kneel and justify in knowledge° .... *satisfy yourself that*

---

5. The possible sexual complications here, including incest, can be highlighted in performance by doubling the part of Marina with that of Thaisa or Antiochus's Daughter.
6. Even in the absence of doubts.

7. TEXTUAL COMMENT For problems of lineation and decisions about whether to set certain lines as verse or prose, see Digital Edition TC 10.
8. As she was believed (intended) to be.

She is thy very princess.

[*Attendants enter with robes.* LYSIMACHUS *approaches*
PERICLES.]

Who is this?

HELICANUS   Sir, 'tis the Governor of Mytilene,
Who, hearing of your melancholy state,
Did come to see you.

210   PERICLES [*to* LYSIMACHUS]   I embrace you, sir.
[*to Attendants*] Give me my robes. —I am wild in my
   beholding.[9]
O heavens, bless my girl! —But hark, what music!
—Tell Helicanus, my Marina, tell him
O'er point by point, for yet he seems to doubt,

215   How sure you are my daughter. —But what music?

HELICANUS   My lord, I hear none.

PERICLES   None?
The music of the spheres![1] —List,° my Marina.   Listen

LYSIMACHUS [*aside to the others*]   It is not good to cross him;
   give him way.

PERICLES   Rarest sounds—do ye not hear?

LYSIMACHUS   Music, my lord? I hear.

220   PERICLES   Most heavenly music.
It nips° me unto listening, and thick slumber   compels
Hangs upon mine eyes. Let me rest.
   [*He sleeps.*]

LYSIMACHUS   A pillow for his head. —So, leave him all.
Well, my companion friends, if this but answer to

225   My just belief, I'll well remember° you.   reward; recall
   [*Exeunt, leaving* PERICLES *asleep.*]
   DIANA [*descends*].

DIANA [*to* PERICLES]   My temple stands in Ephesus; hie thee thither
And do upon mine altar sacrifice.
There when my maiden priests are met together,
[

230   ][2] Before the people all
Reveal how thou at sea didst lose thy wife;
To mourn thy crosses° with thy daughter's, call,°   losses / call out loudly
And give them repetition to the life.°   an accurate accounting
Perform my bidding or thou livest in woe.

235   Do't and be happy, by my silver bow.[3]
Awake, and tell thy dream.   [*She ascends.*]

PERICLES [*awakening*]   Celestial Dian, goddess argentine,°   silvery (like the moon)
I will obey thee. —Helicanus!
   [*Enter* HELICANUS, MARINA, *and* LYSIMACHUS.]

HELICANUS   Sir?

PERICLES   My purpose was for Tarsus, there to strike

240   The inhospitable Cleon, but I am
For other service first. Toward Ephesus

---

9. I am too ecstatic to see correctly.
1. PERFORMANCE COMMENT "The music of the
spheres" is a sign of celestial harmony, brought about
by the proper movement of the heavenly bodies
around earth (hence a sign of divine order). For
possible ways of performing this music, see Digital

Edition PC 1.
2. The break in the rhyme scheme of Diana's speech
(no rhyme for "sacrifice") plus the shortness of line
230 suggest that one-and-a-half lines are missing.
3. A crescent moon. Diana was goddess of the moon
and a renowned hunter.

Turn our blown° sails. Eftsoons° I'll tell thee why.   *inflated / Later*
[*to* LYSIMACHUS]   Shall we refresh us, sir, upon your shore,
And give you gold for such provision
As our intents will need?
245   LYSIMACHUS   Sir, with all my heart,
And when you come ashore,
I have another suit.
PERICLES   You shall prevail,
Were it to woo my daughter, for it seems
You have been noble towards her.
LYSIMACHUS   Sir, lend me your arm.
250   PERICLES   Come, my Marina.
                                                            Exeunt.

5.2

[*Enter* GOWER.]
GOWER   Now our sands are almost run.
More a little, and then dumb.°   *silent*
This my last boon give me,
For such kindness must relieve me:
5   That you aptly will suppose°   *readily will imagine*
What pageantry, what feats, what shows,
What minstrelsy and pretty din
The regent° made in Mytilene   *(Lysimachus)*
To greet the king. So he° thrived   *So well (Lysimachus)*
10   That he is promised to be wived
To fair Marina, but in no wise°   *way*
Till he° had done his sacrifice   *(Pericles)*
As Dian bade, whereto being bound,
The interim, pray you all, confound.°   *skip*
15   In feathered° briefness sails are filled   *winged*
And wishes fall out as they're willed.
At Ephesus the temple see
Our king, and all his company.
That he can hither come so soon,
20   Is by your fancy's thankful doom.[1]   [*Exit.*]

5.3

[*Enter the Priestesses of Diana, among them* THAISA,
and Worshippers, including CERIMON. *To them, enter*
PERICLES, MARINA, HELICANUS, LYSIMACHUS, *and*
Attendants.]
PERICLES   Hail, Dian! To perform thy just° command,   *precise*
I here confess myself the King of Tyre
Who, frighted from my country, did
Wed at Pentapolis the fair Thaisa.
5   At sea in childbed died she, but brought forth
A maid° child called Marina who, O goddess,   *girl*
Wears yet thy silver livery.[1] She at Tarsus
Was nursed with° Cleon, who at fourteen years   *by*

5.2
1. Thanks to your imaginations' agreement.

5.3 Location: The temple of Diana in Ephesus.
1. Still wears your uniform (remains a virgin).

He sought to murder, but her better stars

10 Brought her to Mytilene, 'gainst whose shore riding,°   *where we anchored*
Her fortunes brought the maid aboard us, where
By her own most clear remembrance, she
Made known herself my daughter.

THAISA   Voice and favor°—   *appearance*
You are—you are—O royal Pericles!
  [*She faints.*]

15 PERICLES   What means the nun? She dies! Help, gentlemen!
  [CERIMON *and others go to* THAISA.]

CERIMON   Noble sir,
If you have told Diana's altar true,
This is your wife.

PERICLES   Reverend appearer,° no.   *Reverend-looking man*
I threw her overboard with these very arms.

CERIMON   Upon this coast, I warrant you.

20 PERICLES   'Tis most certain.

CERIMON   Look to the lady. Oh, she's but overjoyed.
Early one blustering morn this lady was
Thrown upon this shore. I oped the coffin,
Found there rich jewels, recovered° her, and placed her   *revived*
Here in Diana's temple.

25 PERICLES   May we see them?

CERIMON   Great sir, they shall be brought you to° my house,   *at*
Whither I invite you. Look, Thaisa is
Recoverèd.

THAISA [*rising*]   Oh, let me look!
If he be none of mine, my sanctity

30 Will to my sense bend no licentious ear,
But curb it, spite of seeing.[2] —O my lord,
Are you not Pericles? Like him you spake,
Like him you are. Did you not name a tempest,
A birth, and death?

PERICLES   The voice of dead Thaisa!

35 THAISA   That Thaisa am I, supposèd dead
And drowned.

PERICLES   Immortal Dian!

THAISA   Now I know you better.
When we with tears parted° Pentapolis,   *departed*
The King my father gave you such a ring.

40 PERICLES   This, this! No more, you gods, your present kindness
Makes my past miseries sports.° You shall do well   *trifles (by comparison)*
That° on the touching of her lips I may   *If*
Melt and no more be seen. —Oh, come, be buried
A second time within these arms.
  [PERICLES *and* THAISA *embrace.*]

MARINA [*kneeling to* THAISA]   My heart

45 Leaps to be gone into my mother's bosom.

PERICLES   Look who kneels here—flesh of thy flesh, Thaisa,
Thy burden at the sea, and called Marina,
For she was yielded° there.   *Because she was born*

---

2. *my sanctity . . . seeing:* my religious vows will forbid my sense to feel desire, in spite of what I see.

THAISA [*kissing* MARINA]   Blest, and mine own!

HELICANUS [*kneeling to* THAISA]   Hail, madam, and my queen!

THAISA   I know you not.

50 PERICLES   You have heard me say when I did fly from Tyre,
     I left behind an ancient substitute.
     Can you remember what I called the man?
     I have named him oft.

THAISA   'Twas Helicanus, then.

PERICLES   Still confirmation!

55   Embrace him, dear Thaisa. This is he.
     Now do I long to hear how you were found,
     How possibly preserved, and who to thank,
     Besides the gods, for this great miracle.

THAISA   Lord Cerimon, my lord; this man

60   Through whom the gods have shown their power, that can
     From first to last resolve° you.   *answer everything for*

PERICLES [*to* CERIMON]   Reverend sir,
     The gods can have no mortal officer
     More like a god than you. Will you deliver°   *explain*
     How this dead queen relives?

CERIMON   I will, my lord.

65   Beseech you first, go with me to my house,
     Where shall be shown you all was° found with her,   *that was*
     How she came° placed here in the temple,   *came to be*
     No needful thing omitted.

PERICLES   Pure Dian,
     I bless thee for thy vision,° and will offer   *(in act 5, scene 1)*

70   Night oblations° to thee. —Thaisa,   *offerings*
     This prince, the fair betrothèd of your daughter,
     Shall marry her at Pentapolis.
     [*to* MARINA] And now this ornament°   *this hair that*
     Makes me look dismal will I clip to form,

75   And what this fourteen years no razor touched
     To grace thy marriage day I'll beautify.

THAISA   Lord Cerimon hath letters of good credit,° sir,   *trustworthiness*
     My father's dead.

PERICLES   Heavens make a star of him!
     Yet there, my queen,

80   We'll celebrate their nuptials, and ourselves
     Will in that kingdom spend our following days.
     Our son and daughter shall in Tyrus reign.
     Lord Cerimon, we do our longing stay°   *delay our desire*
     To hear the rest untold. Sir, lead's the way.   [*Exeunt.*]

Epilogue

[*Enter* GOWER.]

GOWER   In Antiochus and his daughter you have heard[1]
     Of monstrous lust the due and just reward;
     In Pericles, his queen, and daughter seen,°   *you have seen*
     Although assailed with fortune fierce and keen,

Epilogue
1. The second of Gower's speeches in pentameter couplets.

5   Virtue preserved from fell° destruction's blast,   *cruel*
      Led on by heaven and crowned with joy at last.
      In Helicanus may you well descry
      A figure of truth, of faith, of loyalty.
      In reverend Cerimon there well appears
10   The worth that learnèd charity aye° wears.   *always*
      For wicked Cleon and his wife, when fame°   *rumor*
      Had spread his cursèd deed to° the honored name   *against*
      Of Pericles, to rage the city turn,°   *turned*
      That° him and his they in his palace burn.   *So that*
15   The gods for murder seemèd so content
      To punish—although not done, but meant.
      So, on your patience evermore attending,
      New joy wait on you. Here our play has ending.   [*Exit.*]

Coriolanus

Hērōs, the Greek word for "hero," originally meant "warrior." By Homer's time, eight centuries before the birth of Christ, the term was already beginning to be applied by extension to other kinds of praiseworthy people, but even today the military connotations of the word remain strong. The Latin word for "virtue" has a similar history, as the ancient historian Plutarch remarks in his biography of Coriolanus, Shakespeare's principal source for his play: "Now in those days valiantness was honored in Rome above all other virtues: which they call *virtūs,* by the name of virtue itself, as including in that general name, all other special virtues besides. So that *virtūs* in the Latin, was as much as valiantness."

Writing *Coriolanus* in 1608, Shakespeare considers the extent to which excellence in battle translates into other forms of meritoriousness. He works in an ageless tradition, still vital in the twenty-first century, of exalting great fighters: the mythically dauntless Hercules and Theseus, the fierce battle chieftains of classical Greek and Roman epic, the indomitable knights of medieval chivalric romance, the superheroes of modern films and comic books. Yet Shakespeare also deviates from that tradition. Caius Martius Coriolanus performs astonishing, almost superhuman, acts of strength and bravery in battle, fighting on behalf of a society that seems to venerate war. His aggressiveness ought to mesh perfectly with the needs of the community. If successful belligerence is the highest, or only, form of excellence, then Coriolanus, the preeminent soldier, is a natural candidate for Rome's top leadership positions.

In fact, however, Coriolanus's career is disastrous. Despite his phenomenal military successes and Rome's esteem for warriors, Coriolanus not only fails to win election as consul (leader) of Rome but barely escapes the death penalty. He is banished from the city and eventually killed while in the employ of Rome's enemies. The connection between "valiantness" and other forms of virtue seems anything but straightforward. Likewise the relationship between the supposedly exemplary individual and the community from which he springs seems profoundly troubled. The "hero" does not operate in a vacuum: if he is to be victorious, someone must be defeated; if he is to be a leader, he must have followers.

Coriolanus is not merely about a heroic individual but about the community from which he springs and how it is to be governed. It is a play, in other words, about politics, and it poses a number of fundamental political questions. What ought to be the relationship between the common people and the elite? Who is entitled to a voice in the running of the state, and on what basis is that voice granted: class status? personal merit? place of residence? Does citizenship, as Coriolanus argues, primarily entail duties such as military service? Or is citizenship, as many of the common people assume, essentially a set of entitlements or privileges? How does the state determine its domestic and military priorities? These are not merely questions for ancient Rome, but recur in any political community. Since the eighteenth century, *Coriolanus* has often been adapted to reflect contemporary politics. In 1930s Germany, the Nazis applauded the play's depiction of a strong military leader; in several famous productions in England during and after World War II, Laurence Olivier likewise associated Coriolanus's militarism and contempt for common people with modern fascism. Yet in postwar East Germany, the Communist playwright Berthold Brecht's adaptation emphasized instead the struggles of the working class against their aristocratic oppressors. In recent years *Coriolanus* has been successfully performed in modern dress, in settings evocative of the Balkans, Afghanistan, or Iraq.

In *Coriolanus*, Shakespeare suggests that his hero brings many of his problems upon his own head. Coriolanus succeeds as a warrior by channeling overpowering anger into feats of extraordinary strength, by refusing to calculate possible harm to himself or to others, and by preferring action to words. In the political domain, by contrast, relative goods are often more important than absolutes, negotiated compromises preferable to flat conquest. The ability to control oneself in the interest of manipulating others is crucial; so, too, is the capacity to predict the effects of one's own and other people's words and actions. Coriolanus's phenomenal forcefulness—such a superb advantage on the battlefield—cripples his effectiveness for other enterprises. His initial lack of political ambitions together with his hopeless awkwardness as a candidate suggest that his military prowess is not merely irrelevant to peacetime employment, but indeed renders him politically incompetent or even dangerous.

Like most of Shakespeare's tragic heroes after Richard II, then, Coriolanus is betrayed not so much by his vices or shortcomings as by what, in different circumstances, would be his best traits. Shakespeare alters his source material in order to make this pattern more distinct. For instance, Shakespeare entirely omits Plutarch's account of the historical Coriolanus's considerable political savvy. Plutarch's Coriolanus had already played several influential political roles before he made his bid for the consulship. He underwent without apparent compunction the traditional rituals required of all seekers after office; the plebeians later repudiated him on the grounds of a long political record that, in Shakespeare, does not exist. After his exile, Plutarch's Coriolanus cleverly exacerbated class strife in Rome by selectively refraining from burning patrician estates as he approached the city with his Volscian army. Shakespeare's relentless but hotheaded character would hardly be capable of such a calculated act.

The effect of Shakespeare's changes is to open up a chasm that does not exist in his sources between military and civic values. The general Cominius, praising Coriolanus in the Senate house, seems superficially to be echoing Plutarch's comment that "*virtūs* in the Latin, was as much as valiantness":

> It is held
> That valor is the chiefest virtue and
> Most dignifies the haver; if it be,
> The man I speak of cannot in the world
> Be singly counterpoised.
>
> (2.2.80–84)

But even in the process of making his argument, Cominius appears, in his evasive passive constructions and his conditional "if," to be partly disowning it.

Coriolanus's tragedy is not, however, merely a matter of personal idiosyncrasy and self-destructiveness; it takes place, as we have seen, in a political context. During Coriolanus's lifetime in the fifth century B.C.E., Rome had already embarked on the expansionist course that would culminate in its domination of Europe, North Africa, and the Middle East 400 years later, in the time of Julius Caesar, Marcus Brutus, and Mark Antony. But in these early years, dreams of world rule were far in the future: Coriolanus's Rome was still battling the nearby Volscians. Roman bellicosity was a cultural tendency, not yet a clear pathway to empire. At home, Rome was struggling to devise a new form of government. In Coriolanus's youth, King Tarquin and his family were expelled from Rome on the grounds that they had been abusing their power (an episode upon which Shakespeare based his narrative poem *The Rape of Lucrece*). The monarchy was replaced by a Senate composed of patricians (aristocrats). For military and civic matters requiring executive authority, the Senate elected "consuls" for short terms. Soon, however, this system proved inadequate, as the large plebeian, or working, class clamored for a say in the city's rule. In the aftermath of the uprising depicted in *Coriolanus* 1.1, the plebeians were granted the right to elect their own representatives, called tribunes.

In its eventual form, therefore, the Roman Republic was a "mixed" form of government that attempted to distribute rather than to concentrate power, as well as to balance the rights and privileges of various constituencies. Inventing republican institutions entailed addressing important questions about the relations between the social classes, questions that were not merely of antiquarian interest to Shakespeare and his contemporaries. *Coriolanus* considers, as we have seen, issues fundamental to any polity, but the question of how power was to be distributed was an especially sensitive one in the early seventeenth century. Most premodern states, including classical republics and Shakespeare's England, consisted of a relatively small, property-owning, politically empowered class and a large subpolitical population that was supposed to submit to the laws but had no voting rights. How small ought to be the privileged group, how large the disempowered group, and how distinct the differences between the two? These were matters of hot debate in Jacobean England. King James I and his son Charles, who liked to associate themselves with the imagery of imperial Rome, were attracted by absolutist models of government in which the monarch exercised virtually unlimited sway. By contrast, their opponents in Parliament often invoked the Roman Republic, which dispersed power over consuls, Senate, and tribunes, as an analogue to the English commonwealth with its monarch, House of Lords, and House of Commons.

Given the contemporary resonances of his story, Shakespeare's extensive alterations of Plutarch's account are fascinating. *Coriolanus* opens with an uprising among Rome's common people. According to Plutarch, the plebeians revolted because the moneyed patricians had promised easier terms on loans if the plebeians would agree to fight the nearby Sabines. After the plebeians acquitted themselves bravely in battle, the patricians reneged on the agreement and sold into slavery those debtors— many of them war veterans—who were bankrupted by high interest rates. Shakespeare's plebeians, by contrast, make only fleeting references to usury. Their main complaint is simple hunger, a familiar grievance to an English audience in 1608. Barely a year before *Coriolanus*'s first performance, food shortages precipitated serious rioting by the rural poor in the Midland counties west of London, near Shakespeare's hometown, Stratford-upon-Avon. The rioters accused the rich of hoarding foodstuffs in hopes of higher prices, and of having created a dearth by replacing the traditional cultivation of cereal grains with lucrative sheep farming. The rich countered that bad weather was to blame.

In updating the motives of his lower-class characters, Shakespeare translates Roman class conflicts into terms more immediate for his contemporaries. But his revision has other consequences, too: it minimizes the plebeians' political sophistication, their military indispensability, and much of the justification for their outrage. The famine might well be a natural rather than a political calamity: there is no hint of any prior betrayed agreement and no suggestion of unrewarded plebeian military service. Unlike Plutarch's plebeians, Shakespeare's are mediocre soldiers or worse: in *Coriolanus*, Shakespeare's Rome fails to appreciate Coriolanus's *virtūs* simply because the society is not, as Plutarch had claimed it to be, fully a warrior culture at all.

In Shakespeare's rendering, valor in battle seems less a "Roman" than a distinctively aristocratic trait, exercised and uniquely cherished by the patrician class. The difficulties Coriolanus experiences in trying to translate that valor into a civilian context reflect a persistent problem in defining the male aristocrat's proper role. Just as the equation of "valiantness" and "virtue" could fail in early republican Rome, it could also be seen to be failing in early modern England. In medieval times, noblemen had been feudally obliged to serve as battle captains over troops of their own vassals; the aristocrat's military function was his raison d'être, although proficiency in war was supposed to carry over into the management of civic affairs. In Shakespeare's time, the aristocrat's function was theoretically unchanged, but altered social circumstances placed it under increasing pressure. Throughout the late sixteenth and early seventeenth centuries, bureaucrats and policy makers like William Cecil, Robert Cecil, and Francis Bacon were sharply at odds with swashbuckling militarists like Walter Ralegh, King James's son Prince Henry, and Shakespeare's erstwhile patron the Earl of Essex. In these conflicts, the bureaucrats almost always had the advantage. Their skill at such tasks as overhauling the taxation system was hardly glamorous but proved indispensable for the newly powerful nation-state. By the early seventeenth century, the notion that the aristocrat rendered his most important service to his king on the battlefield seemed a remnant of a simpler age.

Coriolanus then, like Hotspur in Shakespeare's *1 Henry IV,* seems to embody a conception of aristocratic excellence whose historical moment, for better or worse, has already passed. A sense of the archaic quality of mighty warriors seems almost universal. Homer's epic heroes were already beginning to specialize their functions during the siege of Troy. For Plutarch, writing in the time of the Roman Empire, the original identification of aristocrat and warrior seems to have shattered in the long-ago days of the Roman Republic. Medieval writers locate both the flowering of knightly service and the beginning of its breakdown in the legendary fourth-century Arthurian court. Many Hollywood Westerns look back to a time in the nineteenth century when the older, rougher codes of the Indian fighter or nomadic frontiersman were being displaced by the values of permanent white settlers, including women and professional-caste men. From time immemorial, glorifying warriors has been tied up with nostalgia—not merely for the mighty soldier himself, but for a simpler, "manly" alternative to civilized complexities, an alternative always already lost.

In the tense dramatic milieu of *Coriolanus,* compounded from Shakespeare's own experience and what his sources provided him, the nature of his protagonist's heroism thus seems more intelligible and its failure less surprising. Since the heterogeneous Roman population has difficulty coming to any consensus about what it values, no single individual could possibly exemplify its ideals. Rather, Coriolanus possesses a narrow subset of traits more appealing to some groups (the patricians) than others (the plebeians) and more useful in some situations (war) than in others (peace). Coriolanus's mother, Volumnia, describing her son's education, suggests how his "heroism" has been developed by rigorously selecting for desired traits and just as sternly suppressing others.

> When yet he was but tender-bodied and the only son of my womb, when youth with comeliness plucked all gaze his way, when—for a day of kings' entreaties—a mother should not sell him an hour from her beholding, I—considering how honor would become such a person . . . was pleased to let him seek danger where he was like to find fame. To a cruel war I sent him, from whence he returned, his brows bound with oak. I tell thee, daughter, I sprang not more in joy at first hearing he was a man-child than now in first seeing he had proved himself a man.
>
> (1.3.5–15)

Volumnia's own shrewdness and ferocity seem to belie the "naturalness" of a system that excludes women from politics and combat. Unlike Coriolanus's wife, Virgilia, Volumnia hardly seems content to stay home and do the sewing. But the incongruity between her personality and her prescribed social role does not render her skeptical of that role. Instead, she embraces her gendered destiny with characteristic zeal. In maternity she finds an improbable outlet for her own aggressiveness:

> The breasts of Hecuba
> When she did suckle Hector looked not lovelier
> Than Hector's forehead when it spit forth blood
> At Grecian sword contemning.
>
> (1.3.37–40)

Symbolically equating milk and blood, the lactating mother with her wounded son, Volumnia both identifies vicariously with her war hero and wishes suffering upon him, delighting not merely in his triumphs but in his pain. Virgilia's conventionally feminine recoil from Volumnia's gory fantasies makes their aberrancy clear for the audience. In Volumnia, the discipline required to submit to rules of Roman womanliness seems to have generated a complicated sadomasochistic adaptation. She displaces her own forbidden aggressiveness onto a dream of exaggerated masculinity and then attempts to realize that dream in her son.

Volumnia's ruthless mothering produces a man whose characteristic gesture is violently to resist whatever he perceives to be outside himself. Battle is Coriolanus's model for identity formation, and his ideal self is like an impermeably walled city. Overstated *differences*—between patrician and plebeian, Roman and Volscian, male and female, man and boy—are the principles upon which Coriolanus has established his own sense of identity. Pride, contempt, and anger, like aggression, reinforce and clarify the boundaries of the self, marking it vividly off from those whom one despises or conquers. Coriolanus does not merely happen to be inflexible and narrow-minded; too much tolerance, too much sensitivity, would endanger him to the core. So would introspection, which might reveal an unwelcome complexity within. Coriolanus is hardly a taciturn character, but he is perhaps Shakespeare's most opaque tragic protagonist, for he is not inclined to reflect upon his own motives either in conversation or alone (indeed, he has only a single short soliloquy in the entire play). The great moments of Coriolanus's life are moments of embattled solitude: fighting by himself inside Corioles, standing alone for consul or separated from the Roman people after his exile, reflecting in an unaccompanied moment in Aufidius's hall, isolated in Corioles again at the end of the play, shouting at his old (and new) enemy: "Alone I did it" (5.6.115). He is thrilled by fantasies of absolute independence: "As if a man were author of himself / And knew no other kin" (5.3.36–37). With some justice, the hostile tribunes accuse him of wanting to be the only man left in Rome and of considering himself a god superior to ordinary mortals.

In his defiant self-sufficiency, however, Coriolanus is far needier than he acknowledges. When he allies himself with Aufidius, his former enemy, Aufidius's elated speech of welcome clarifies their shared dilemma.

> I loved the maid I married; never man
> Sighed truer breath. But that I see thee here,
> Thou noble thing, more dances my rapt heart
> Than when I first my wedded mistress saw
> Bestride my threshold. . . .
> . . . .
> . . . Thou hast beat me out
> Twelve several times, and I have nightly since
> Dreamt of encounters twixt thyself and me—
> We have been down together in my sleep,
> Unbuckling helms, fisting each other's throat—
> And waked half dead with nothing.
>
> (4.5.113–25)

The combination of pain and pleasure to which Aufidius bears witness is strikingly reminiscent of Volumnia's maternal feelings, in which aggressiveness toward the beloved seems to loom so large. It is impossible here to distinguish hostility from attraction, competition from dependency, combat from homosexual embrace. The warrior loves his adversary because he needs a manly competitor against whom to establish his own identity. The striving for autonomy depends on the existence of something set off against, beside, or below it.

To distinguish oneself from other people, then, one must rely on them. "Thy valiantness was mine: thou suck'st it from me," Volumnia informs her son (3.2.129).

Coriolanus and the attack on Corioles. Jost Amman, from *Icones Livianae* (1572).

Coriolanus wants to imagine his courage and honor as intrinsically his own, rather than conferred by others. But "our virtues," as Aufidius claims, "lie in th'interpretation of the time" (4.7.49–50). Roman merit, inextricable from social goals and needs, demands an admiring audience. Even while he professes to despise flattery, Coriolanus takes pride in such apparently trivial honorific gestures as the surname that commemorates his victory at Corioles, or the oaken garlands conferred upon him for valor in battle. Insignificant in themselves, such symbols acquire meaning from the way they are regarded by the group. The exiled Coriolanus defiantly insists that "there is a world elsewhere" (3.3.132), but it is impossible for him to retire to a quiet corner of Italy and live out his life in obscurity. He needs to prove himself against an enemy, but now that enemy, Rome, is the place from which his life has drawn its meaning. Threatening to annihilate the community that bore him, he puts himself in a painfully contradictory position.

Thus the superior is always dependent on the inferior, the inside on the outside, the civilized on the barbarian, the patrician on the plebeian, the performer on the audience, the man on the woman and on the boy, even while the "upper" term prides itself on its difference from its subordinate. Just as important, the dependency works in both directions, as the action of *Coriolanus* shows. If Coriolanus depends on the Roman populace in ways he refuses to recognize, so does the populace depend on him. When the tribunes shamelessly manipulate their constituency to orchestrate Coriolanus's exile, they leave the city open to its enemies and come close to bringing destruction upon it.

Since we hear an unusual amount about Coriolanus's boyhood, it is easy to see his conflicted desire for autonomy in terms of his simultaneous flight from and dependence on Volumnia. But that is an oversimplification: Coriolanus is not merely the product of a uniquely bad upbringing. His anxieties about autonomy and dependence, competitiveness and cooperation are shared, in some form, by almost everyone in the play: they are aspects of social and political dilemmas, not merely individual neuroses. Early in the first scene, the First Citizen notes—perhaps envi-

Volumnia entreating Coriolanus. Jost Amman, from *Icones Livianae* (1572).

ously, but also accurately—that the patricians enjoy seeing the lower classes suffer, because that suffering enhances their sense of comparative privilege. Who depends on whom, how far ought that dependency to extend, what forms ought it to take?

These concerns are powerfully evoked in the imagery of *Coriolanus*. It was a cliché already old in Plutarch's time, and still current in Shakespeare's, that human communities were modeled on individual bodies. In the optimistic version of this analogy, the state is a collection of harmoniously interrelated organs, each selflessly performing its own distinctive function in the service of the whole. Interconnectedness is the apparent moral of Menenius's "pretty tale" (1.1.83) of the belly in the opening scene. But even in Menenius's version, the analogy veers toward grotesquerie, the body-state becoming an apparently headless entity equipped with an unnaturally smiling belly. Elsewhere in *Coriolanus,* the body is less a marvel of smooth interaction than a site of disintegration: Coriolanus imagines the plebeians as "fragments" and "voices" (1.1.213, 2.3.118–24); Menenius rebukes a malcontent whom he calls "the great toe of this assembly" (1.1.146). The mutilations of the battlefield begin to seem corporeal equivalents for a profound crisis of the body politic. The shared needs of embodied, vulnerable human beings for food, shelter, and defense provide an obvious material basis for societies. But individual bodies tend to be selfish, unwilling to forgo their own urgent requirements in the interests of a collective good, reluctant to admit their reliance on one another lest that reliance be made a pretext for exploitation. Once again, dependence and autonomy seem simultaneously antithetical and inextricable.

Because the body in *Coriolanus* is so often imagined in negative terms—as starving, wounded, or cut to pieces—attempts to escape corporeal limitation seem understandable, even laudable. In fact, Coriolanus's battlefield heroism seems largely a matter of refusing to acknowledge physical constraints: he is inexhaustible, undaunted by wounds or danger. Late in the play, Menenius describes him as a kind of robot: "When he walks, he moves like an engine, and the ground shrinks before his treading" (5.4.17–18). But within a few lines, Menenius is proven wrong: blood relationships, the ties of the body, prove impossible for Coriolanus to disown. Volumnia, Virgilia, and young Martius come to the Volscian camp to plead for their city and their people; and, in a capitulation that he knows to be virtually suicidal, Coriolanus grasps his mother's hand.

Coriolanus is not only the last of Shakespeare's tragedies but the last of a series of plays about ancient Rome. It seems to look back upon, and anatomize, social and individual pathologies that in *Julius Caesar* and even *Antony and Cleopatra* were merely hinted at: the way "Roman" valor on the battlefield, for instance, becomes both a flight from and a replacement for heterosexuality; the way aggression and repression undergird the psyches of Roman men and women; the way both sexes deform their personalities in order to conform to highly restrictive patterns of masculinity or femininity. While in *Julius Caesar* class tensions serve mainly to exalt the patrician class, here the plebeians' grievances, and their different priorities, are understandable. Coriolanus's inability to comprehend the plebeians is a telling sign of both his personal rigidity and the alienation of rich from poor. *Coriolanus* has seemed to many audiences a relentlessly bleak play, and no wonder. Subjecting both its formidable but unpleasant hero and his society to intense critical scrutiny, *Coriolanus* implies that no political arrangement could possibly satisfy human needs, portrayed here as incorrigibly self-contradictory.

KATHARINE EISAMAN MAUS

SELECTED BIBLIOGRAPHY

Adelman, Janet. "'Anger's My Meat': Feeding, Dependency, and Aggression in *Coriolanus*." *Representing Shakespeare: New Psychoanalytic Essays*. Ed. Murray M. Schwartz and Coppélia Kahn. Baltimore, MD: Johns Hopkins UP, 1980. 129–49. Argues that the play's political and psychological anxieties crystallize around the figure of the mother who does not feed her children.

Barton, Anne. "Livy, Machiavelli, and Shakespeare's *Coriolanus*." *Shakespeare Survey* 38 (1985): 115–29. Looks at the Roman historian Livy and Machiavelli's commentary on Livy as sources of inspiration for *Coriolanus*.

Bloom, Harold, ed. *William Shakespeare's "Coriolanus."* New York: Chelsea House, 1988. Anthology of critical essays.

Cavell, Stanley. "Who Does the Wolf Love?" *Disowning Knowledge in Six Plays by Shakespeare*. Cambridge: Harvard UP, 1987. 143–78. Examines *Coriolanus*'s affinity with sacrificial feasts, especially the Christian ritual of Communion.

Fish, Stanley. "How to Do Things with Austin and Searle: Speech-Act Theory and Literary Criticism." *Is There a Text in This Class?: The Authority of Interpretive Communities*. Cambridge: Harvard UP, 1980. 197–245. Analyzes Coriolanus's problems with speech-acts.

Goldberg, Jonathan. "The Anus in *Coriolanus*." *Historicism, Psychoanalysis, and Early Modern Culture*. Ed. Carla Mazzio and Doug Trevor. New York: Routledge, 2000. 260–71. Assesses the anal imagery and homoeroticism in the play.

Kerrigan, John. "Coriolanus Fidiussed." *Essays in Criticism* 42 (2012): 319–52. Looks at oaths, good faith, and the breaking of promises in *Coriolanus*.

Patterson, Annabel. "Speak, Speak! The Popular Voice and the Jacobean State." *Shakespeare and the Popular Voice*. Cambridge, MA: Blackwood, 1989. Analyzes the connection between *Coriolanus* and disenfranchised groups in Shakespeare's England.

Sanders, Eve Rachel. "The Body of the Actor in *Coriolanus*." *Shakespeare Quarterly* 57 (2006): 382–412. Looks at acting and theatrical display in *Coriolanus*.

Wheeler, David, ed. *"Coriolanus": Critical Essays*. New York: Garland, 1995. An anthology of essays and reviews of theatrical productions.

FILMS

Coriolanus. 1951. Dir. Paul Nickell. USA. 60 min. This Westinghouse Studio One black-and-white abridged television version, interspersed with occasional ads for refrigerators and laundry appliances, is performed in modern dress and strongly marked by the recent traumas of fascism and World War II. Richard Greene is handsome but inexpressive in the role of Coriolanus.

Coriolanus. 1984. Dir. Elijah Moshinsky. UK. 145 min. BBC-TV's spare, gripping production featuring Alan Howard as a tightly wound Coriolanus, Mike Gwilym as a canny Aufidius, and Irene Worth as a terrifying Volumnia.

Coriolanus. 2011. Dir. Ralph Fiennes (who also plays the title role). UK. 123 min. Vanessa Redgrave is Volumnia in this modern-dress version, largely filmed in Serbia and evoking contemporary theaters of war.

TEXTUAL INTRODUCTION

The 1623 Folio (F) is the sole surviving authority for *Coriolanus*. F is probably based on an authorial manuscript that has been annotated for performance, since it contains a number of detailed stage directions, such as those that indicate how an exit or entrance might be performed (e.g., "*Citizens steal away,*" 1.1.241 SD; "*Enter Martius and Aufidius at several doors,*" 1.8.0 SD), or what variety of instruments is required—cornetts, hautboys, trumpets, or drums (see 1.9.65 SD, 1.10.0 SD, 5.6.48 SD). Moreover, no entrances and very few exits are missing. That F's immediate source is likely to be authorial is indicated by certain stage directions containing information that is extraneous to performance (e.g., 1.3.0, where Volumnia and Virgilia are described as "*mother and wife to Martius*"); that exceeds what can readily be shown on the early modern stage (e.g., 1.8.15 SD: "*Martius fights till they be driven in breathless*"); or that acknowledges the illusion of performance, as in 2.2.0 (where officers enter "*to lay cushions, as it were in the Capitol*"). Some of these stage directions anticipate the action they describe; in such cases, in accordance with editorial tradition, *The Norton Shakespeare* moves F's stage directions to their logical location in the text.

F contains act divisions, which have been followed here. Scene divisions have been added, following standard editorial practice by ending a scene when the stage has been emptied, although during the battle scenes of act 1 (particularly during what is in this, and in many editions, designated 1.4) such divisions are not clear-cut.

The punctuation in F sometimes impedes sense, with periods placed in midsentence (e.g., 3.3.66) or no strong punctuation mark where one is obviously needed (e.g., 1.1.153). For the most part, punctuation has been silently modernized; points at which F's punctuation requires radical intervention have been noted in textual variants.

Following the principle of single-text editing, this edition has retained F's designation of characters in stage directions and (where it does not overly hinder the reader) speech prefixes; any changes made are noted in textual variants. Hence, the play's protagonist is known as "*Martius*" until the end of act 1; from act 2 onward—until the moment of his death—he is dubbed "*Coriolanus*" in both speech prefixes and stage directions. Names of individual characters in F's speech prefixes and stage directions are otherwise stable, apart from Lartius, who is variously "*Latius*" and "*Titus*." However, the terms used for different groups of characters are much more fluid. The non-elite of Rome are labeled both "*Citizens*" and "*Plebeians*": the former classification implies political enfranchisement, along with a civic role and civil responsibilities; the latter categorizes the group by their low social status. That F uses *"citizen"* and *"plebeian"* interchangeably is evident from 2.3, where the stage direction at 2.3.146 denotes the entrance of *"plebeians,"* but the speech prefixes that follow allocate the speeches to the *"first,"* *"second,"* and *"Third Citizen"* (2.3.148, 150, 152). Rome's social elite are also known by a variety of terms: senators are a subset of patricians (legally, only patricians could be senators); however, in Shakespeare's Rome we also have lords, nobles, and gentry named in stage directions, speech prefixes, and the dialogue itself. Although historically the "gentry" could equate to the class of *equites* in ancient Rome, "nobles" and "lords" would seem to be synonymous with the patricians, and have been treated as such in the list of the persons of the play, particularly as the sliding nature of F's use of sociopolitical terms is evident from its treatment of the labels *"plebeian"* and *"citizen."* Nonetheless, Aufidius's speech at 4.7.29–30 complicates this pragmatic solution, since at this point he seems to distinguish between "the nobility of Rome" and the "senators and patricians."

By far the greatest editorial problem is lineation. Shakespeare's late style tested the boundaries of the iambic pentameter line, and *Coriolanus*—like other plays at the latter end of his writing career—has lines that run to twelve syllables, have feminine endings, or rely on clipped or syncopated forms, or where the syntax strains against the lineation (e.g., when lines end with a word such as "and" or "but"). There are also a number of short-line exchanges where it is unclear whether verse or prose is intended, and the same characters can slip between prose and verse within the same scene (e.g., the citizens in 1.1, Virgilia and Volumnia in 1.3, Menenius and the Watchmen in 5.2). Some of these problems may arise from the manuscript lying behind *Coriolanus*. If Hand D in the manuscript of *Sir Thomas More* is, as many scholars now believe, that of Shakespeare, then the authorial manuscript may have contributed to the confusion regarding lineation. Like many writers trained in the mid-sixteenth century, the Hand D writer did not automatically capitalize the initial letter in a line of verse; he also tended to cram the ends of overrunning lines into the preceding line in order to save space. The printing process and the need to squeeze the often long lines of *Coriolanus* into two columns in F—particularly problematic where the line includes a speech prefix—may further have exacerbated the lack of clarity of lineation in the manuscript.

Cathy Shrank

PERFORMANCE NOTE

The foremost challenge for companies staging *Coriolanus* may be finding a demigod to play the lead, who conquers one city single-handedly and then brings Rome to its knees. The character is built on several paradoxes: he is Rome's loyal son and its scourge; an experienced soldier and a naïve boy; physically invulnerable and emotionally brittle; a callous anti-hero and a tragic victim. Actors must reconcile these contradictions while creating sympathy for a protagonist commonly considered unsympathetic. Directors often address the problem by shifting the focus of the tragedy from military to political or domestic conflicts. Productions may, for instance, emphasize the cunning and underhandedness of the tribunes, the homoeroticism underlying Coriolanus's rivalry with Aufidius, or the monumentality of Volumnia's personality and the psychological complexity of the relationship between mother and son.

Directors are often interested in *Coriolanus*'s representations of class division, and their productions can argue the contemporary relevance of plebeian complaints by setting the play in such places as occupied Palestine or Wall Street. Whatever a production's politics, it must decide whether Menenius is a shifty politician or a gracious steward; whether the tribunes are humble advocates for the people or self-serving intriguers; whether the citizens are hostile or conciliatory, irrational or fair-minded. Each choice will affect the audience's reception of Coriolanus and his tragic status. In addition, productions must decide whether Volumnia should clash with Virgilia or treat her with indifference; whether Virgilia's silence arises out of natural shyness or a serene confidence in her position and power; and whether Coriolanus understands or even welcomes Aufidius's sexually suggestive images and dreams (see Digital Edition PC 2). Other staging questions include how Coriolanus is to be shut within Corioles' walls (1.3) and whether Coriolanus or Virgilia initiates the kiss in 5.3.

BRETT GAMBOA

The Tragedy of Coriolanus

patricians

1.1

Enter a company of mutinous CITIZENS, *with staves,*
clubs, and other weapons.

FIRST CITIZEN Before we proceed any further, hear me speak.

ALL Speak, speak.

FIRST CITIZEN You are all resolved rather to die than to
famish?

5 ALL Resolved, resolved.

FIRST CITIZEN First, you know Caius Martius is chief enemy
to the people.

1.1 Location: A street in Rome.

ALL   We know't, we know't.

FIRST CITIZEN   Let us kill him, and we'll have corn° at our
10   own price. Is't a verdict?°

ALL   No more talking on't. Let it be done. Away, away!

SECOND CITIZEN   One word, good citizens.

FIRST CITIZEN   We are accounted poor citizens, the patricians
good.° What authority[1] surfeits on would relieve us. If they
15   would yield us but the superfluity° while it were wholesome,°
we might guess they relieved us humanely, but they think we
are too dear.[2] The leanness that afflicts us, the object° of our
misery, is as an inventory to particularize their abundance;[3]
our sufferance° is a gain to them. Let us revenge this with
20   our pikes,° ere we become rakes;[4] for the gods know I speak
this in hunger for bread, not in thirst for revenge.

SECOND CITIZEN   Would you proceed especially against Caius
Martius?

ALL   Against him first: he's a very dog to° the commonalty.[5]

25   SECOND CITIZEN   Consider you what services he has done for
his country?

FIRST CITIZEN   Very well, and could be content to give him
good report for't, but that he pays himself with being proud.

ALL   Nay, but speak not maliciously.

30   FIRST CITIZEN   I say unto you, what he hath done famously,°
he did it to that end.° Though soft-conscienced men can be
content to say it was for his country, he did it to please his
mother and to be partly proud,° which he is, even to the
altitude of his virtue.[6]

35   SECOND CITIZEN   What he cannot help in his nature you
account a vice in him. You must in no way say he is
covetous.

FIRST CITIZEN   If I must not, I need not be barren of accusations. He hath faults, with surplus, to tire in repetition.
        Shouts within.
40   What shouts are these? The other side o'th' city is risen.
Why stay we prating° here? To th' Capitol!

ALL   Come, come!

FIRST CITIZEN   Soft,° who comes here?
        Enter MENENIUS *Agrippa.*

SECOND CITIZEN   Worthy Menenius Agrippa, one that hath
45   always loved the people.

FIRST CITIZEN   He's one honest enough. Would all the rest
were so!

MENENIUS   What work's, my countrymen, in hand? Where go
you
With bats° and clubs? The matter speak, I pray you.

50   SECOND CITIZEN   Our business is not unknown to th' Senate.
They have had inkling this fortnight what we intend to do,
which now we'll show 'em in deeds. They say poor suitors°
have strong[7] breaths; they shall know we have strong arms,
too.

	grain
	Do we agree
	noble; well off
	excess / still edible
	visible fact
	distress
	spears; pitchforks
	persecutor of
	that has won fame
	(to advance his pride)
	partly out of pride
	chattering
	Wait
	cudgels
	petitioners

---

1. The nobility.
2. We cost too much to preserve; we are too rich.
3. To make their prosperity stand out by comparison.
4. Rakes are proverbially thin; playing on "pikes."
5. Common people.
6. That is, his pride is equal to his valor.
7. Strong-smelling, from eating onions, the food of the poor.

55 MENENIUS Why, masters,° my good friends, mine honest   (artisans' title)
      neighbors,
      Will you undo° yourselves?   destroy
SECOND CITIZEN We cannot, sir; we are undone already.
MENENIUS I tell you, friends, most charitable care
      Have the patricians of you. For° your wants,   As for
60   Your suffering in this dearth,° you may as well   famine
      Strike at the heaven with your staves as lift them
      Against the Roman state, whose course will on
      The way it takes, cracking ten thousand curbs[8]
      Of more strong link asunder than can ever
65   Appear in your impediment.[9] For the dearth,
      The gods, not the patricians, make it, and
      Your knees° to them, not arms, must help. Alack,   kneeling (in prayer)
      You are transported by calamity
      Thither where more attends° you, and you slander   awaits
70   The helms° o'th' state, who care for you like fathers,   helmsmen
      When you curse them as enemies.[1]
SECOND CITIZEN Care for us? True indeed! They ne'er cared
      for us yet. Suffer us to famish, and their storehouses crammed
      with grain; make edicts for usury[2] to support usurers; repeal
75   daily any wholesome act established against the rich; and
      provide more piercing° statutes daily to chain up and restrain   severe
      the poor. If the wars eat us not up, they will; and there's all
      the love they bear us.
MENENIUS Either you must
80   Confess yourselves wondrous malicious
      Or be accused of folly. I shall tell you
      A pretty tale. It may be you have heard it,
      But since it serves my purpose, I will venture
      To stale't a little more.°   To make it more familiar
SECOND CITIZEN   Well, I'll hear it, sir.[3]
85   Yet you must not think to fob off our disgrace[4]
      With a tale. But, an't° please you, deliver.   if it
MENENIUS There was a time when all the body's members
      Rebelled against the belly, thus accused it:
      That only like a gulf° it did remain   abyss
90   I'th' midst o'th' body, idle and unactive,
      Still cupboarding the viand,[5] never bearing
      Like° labor with the rest; where th'other instruments°   Equal / organs
      Did see and hear, devise, instruct, walk, feel,
      And, mutually participate,° did minister   participating
95   Unto the appetite and affection° common   desire
      Of the whole body. The belly answered—
SECOND CITIZEN Well, sir, what answer made the belly?
MENENIUS Sir, I shall tell you. With a kind of smile,

---

8. Chain bits used to restrain unruly horses.
9. *than . . . impediment*: than you can ever offer in opposition.
1. PERFORMANCE COMMENT Productions vary in how sympathetically they present the plebian concerns and Menenius's response to them—and more generally, they vary in how much they emphasize the play's class politics. For a fuller discussion, see Digital Edition PC 1.
2. Permitting the lending of money at interest (widely considered immoral, because it enriched wealthy

lenders at the expense of poor borrowers).
3. TEXTUAL COMMENT In *Coriolanus*, upper-class characters typically speak in blank verse and lower-class characters in prose, but the distinction is not always consistently maintained, nor is it always reliably indicated in the Folio text. For the political significance of the Second Citizen's move to blank verse, see Digital Edition TC 1.
4. Dismiss our hardship.
5. Always hoarding the food.

	Which ne'er came from the lungs,° but even thus—	*(organs of laughter)*
100	For, look you, I may make the belly smile	
	As well as speak—it tauntingly replied	
	To th' discontented members, the mutinous parts	
	That envied his receipt;° even so most fitly[6]	*what it received*
	As you malign our senators for that°	*because*
	They are not such as you.	

SECOND CITIZEN   Your belly's answer, what?
The kingly crownèd head, the vigilant eye,
The counselor heart, the arm our soldier,
Our steed the leg, the tongue our trumpeter,
With other muniments° and petty helps   *supports*
In this our fabric,° if that they—   *body*

110 MENENIUS   What then?
Fore me,° this fellow speaks! What then? What then?   *(an oath)*
SECOND CITIZEN   —Should by the cormorant° belly be   *rapacious*
     restrained,
Who is the sink° o'th' body—   *cesspool*
MENENIUS   Well, what then?
SECOND CITIZEN   The former agents, if they did complain,
     What could the belly answer?
115 MENENIUS   I will tell you.
If you'll bestow a small°—of what you have little—   *small amount of*
Patience awhile, you'st° hear the belly's answer.   *you would*
SECOND CITIZEN   You're long about it.
MENENIUS   Note me this, good friend:
Your° most grave belly was deliberate,   *This*
120 Not rash like his accusers, and thus answered:
"True is it, my incorporate° friends," quoth he,   *united in one body*
"That I receive the general food at first
Which you do live upon; and fit it is,
Because I am the storehouse and the shop
125 Of the whole body. But, if you do remember,
I send it through the rivers of your blood
Even to the court, the heart, to th' seat° o'th' brain;   *throne*
And through the cranks and offices[7] of man
The strongest nerves° and small inferior veins   *muscles*
130 From me receive that natural competency°   *sustenance*
Whereby they live. And though that all at once"—
You, my good friends, this says the belly, mark me—
SECOND CITIZEN   Ay, sir, well, well.
MENENIUS   "Though all at once cannot
See what I do deliver out to each,
135 Yet I can make my audit up[8] that all
From me do back receive the flour[9] of all
And leave me but the bran." What say you to't?
SECOND CITIZEN   It was an answer. How apply you this?
MENENIUS   The senators of Rome are this good belly,
140 And you the mutinous members. For examine
Their counsels and their cares, digest[1] things rightly

---

6. In just the way.
7. Through the winding passages and workrooms.
8. Show on my balance sheet.

9. Nourishment (punning on "flower," or choicest part).
1. Interpret (playing on the belly's function).

Touching the weal o'th' common,[2] you shall find
No public benefit which you receive
But it proceeds or comes from them to you
145 And no way from yourselves. What do you think,
You, the great toe of this assembly?
SECOND CITIZEN   I, the great toe? Why the great toe?
MENENIUS   For that being one o'th' lowest, basest, poorest
Of this most wise rebellion, thou goest foremost.
150 Thou rascal, that art worst in blood[3] to run,
Lead'st first to win some vantage.°   benefit
But make you ready your stiff bats and clubs:
Rome and her rats are at the point of battle;
The one side must have bale.°   injury
    Enter Caius MARTIUS.
                              —Hail, noble Martius!
155 MARTIUS   Thanks. —What's the matter, you dissentious° rogues,   rebelling
That, rubbing the poor itch of your opinion,
Make yourselves scabs?
SECOND CITIZEN   We have ever your good word.
MARTIUS   He that will give good words to thee will flatter
Beneath abhorring. What would you have, you curs
160 That like nor° peace nor war? The one affrights you,   neither
The other makes you proud.° He that trusts to you,   rebellious
Where he should find you lions, finds you hares;
Where foxes, geese. You are no surer, no,
Than is the coal of fire upon the ice,
165 Or hailstone in the sun. Your virtue° is   characteristic skill
To make him worthy whose offense subdues him[4]
And curse that justice did it. Who deserves greatness
Deserves° your hate, and your affections° are   Incurs / propensities
A sick man's appetite, who desires most that
170 Which would increase his evil.° He that depends   illness
Upon your favors swims with fins of lead
And hews down oaks with rushes. Hang ye! Trust ye?
With every minute you do change a mind
And call him noble that was now° your hate,   just now
175 Him vile that was your garland.[5] What's the matter,
That in these several° places of the city   various
You cry against the noble Senate, who,
Under the gods, keep you in awe, which else°   who otherwise
Would feed on one another? [*to* MENENIUS] What's their seeking?
180 MENENIUS   For corn at their own rates,° whereof they say   prices
The city is well stored.
MARTIUS   Hang 'em! "They say"?
They'll sit by th' fire and presume to know
What's done i'th' Capitol,[6] who's like to rise,
Who thrives and who declines; side° factions and give out°   side with / announce
185 Conjectural marriages, making parties strong

---

2. Concerning the public good.
3. Most desperate; lowest born. *rascal*: wretch; inferior deer or dog.
4. *To make . . . subdues him*: To extol the man whose

wrongdoing makes him liable to punishment.
5. Hero (traditionally wreathed with laurel or oak leaves).
6. The temple of Jupiter and hub of the Roman state.

And feebling such as stand not in their liking
Below their cobbled° shoes. They say there's grain enough? — *patched*
Would the nobility lay aside their ruth° — *compassion*
And let me use my sword, I'd make a quarry[7]
190 With thousands of these quartered[8] slaves as high
As I could pitch my lance.

MENENIUS   Nay, these are almost thoroughly persuaded,° — *appeased*
For though abundantly they lack discretion,
Yet are they passing° cowardly. But I beseech you, — *exceedingly*
What says the other troop?

195 MARTIUS   They are dissolved, hang 'em.
They said they were an-hungry,° sighed forth proverbs: — *very hungry*
That hunger broke stone walls, that dogs° must eat, — *(even dogs)*
That meat was made for mouths, that the gods sent not
Corn for the rich men only. With these shreds
200 They vented° their complainings, which being answered — *spoke; excreted*
And a petition granted them—a strange one,
To break the heart of generosity° — *the nobility*
And make bold power look pale—they threw their caps
As they would hang them on the horns o'th' moon,
Shouting their emulation.[9]

205 MENENIUS   What is granted them?

MARTIUS   Five tribunes° to defend their vulgar wisdoms, — *representatives*
Of their own choice. One's Junius Brutus,
Sicinius Velutus, and I know not. 'Sdeath,° — *God's death (an oath)*
The rabble should have first unroofed the city
210 Ere so prevailed with me. It will in time
Win upon power° and throw forth greater themes — *Prevail upon authority*
For insurrection's arguing.

MENENIUS   This is strange.

MARTIUS [*to the* CITIZENS]   Go, get you home, you fragments.° — *scraps of uneaten food*
Enter a MESSENGER, *hastily.*

MESSENGER   Where's Caius Martius?

MARTIUS   Here. What's the matter?

215 MESSENGER   The news is, sir, the Volsces are in arms.

MARTIUS   I am glad on't; then we shall ha' means to vent
Our musty superfluity.° — *moldy excess*
Enter SICINIUS *Velutus, Junius* BRUTUS, COMINIUS,
Titus LARTIUS, *with other* SENATORS.
                         See, our best elders.

FIRST SENATOR   Martius, 'tis true that you have lately told us:
The Volsces are in arms.

MARTIUS   They have a leader,
220 Tullus Aufidius, that will put you to't.° — *to the test*
I sin in envying his nobility,
And were I anything but what I am,
I would wish me only he.

COMINIUS   You have fought together?

MARTIUS   Were half to half the world by th'ears[1] and he
225 Upon my party,° I'd revolt to make — *side*

---

7. A pile of animals killed in hunting.
8. Hacked to pieces (a punishment for treason).
9. Rivalry (either to shout loudest or to defy

the nobility).
1. If one-half of the world were fighting the other.

Only my wars with him. He is a lion
That I am proud to hunt.
FIRST SENATOR   Then, worthy Martius,
Attend upon° Cominius to these wars.   *Serve under*
COMINIUS [*to* MARTIUS]   It is your former promise.
MARTIUS   Sir, it is,
230   And I am constant. —Titus Lartius, thou
Shalt see me once more strike at Tullus' face.
What, art thou stiff?² Stand'st out?
LARTIUS   No, Caius Martius,
I'll lean upon one crutch and fight with t'other
Ere stay behind this business.
MENENIUS   O true bred!
235   FIRST SENATOR   Your company to th' Capitol, where I know
Our greatest friends attend us.
LARTIUS [*to* COMINIUS]   Lead you on.
[*to* MARTIUS] Follow Cominius; we must follow you,
Right worthy° your priority.   *Who well deserve*
COMINIUS   Noble Martius.
FIRST SENATOR [*to the* CITIZENS]   Hence to your homes, be gone!
MARTIUS   Nay, let them follow.
240   The Volsces have much corn: take these rats thither
To gnaw their garners.°   CITIZENS *steal away.*   *storehouses*
                    Worshipful mutineers,
Your valor puts well forth.³ [*to the* SENATORS] Pray follow.
                    Exeunt all but SICINIUS *and* BRUTUS.
SICINIUS   Was ever man so proud as is this Martius?
BRUTUS   He has no equal.
245   SICINIUS   When we were chosen tribunes for the people—
BRUTUS   Marked you his lip and eyes?
SICINIUS   Nay, but his taunts.
BRUTUS   Being moved,° he will not spare to gird⁴ the gods.   *angry*
SICINIUS   Bemock the modest moon.
BRUTUS   The present wars devour him! He is grown
Too proud to be so valiant.
250   SICINIUS   Such a nature,
Tickled° with good success, disdains the shadow   *Excited; flattered*
Which he treads on at noon. But I do wonder
His insolence can brook° to be commanded   *endure*
Under Cominius.
BRUTUS   Fame, at the which he aims,
255   In whom already he's well graced, cannot
Better be held nor more attained than by
A place below the first; for what miscarries
Shall be the general's fault, though he perform
To th'utmost of a man, and giddy censure°   *rash opinion*
260   Will then cry out of Martius, "Oh, if he
Had borne the business!"
SICINIUS   Besides, if things go well,
Opinion, that so sticks on° Martius, shall   *clings to*
Of his demerits° rob Cominius.   *Of Cominius's deserts*

---

2. Obstinate (but Lartius understands "stiff with age").

3. Promises well, like a budding plant (ironic).
4. He will not refrain from sneering at.

BRUTUS   Come,
  Half all Cominius' honors are to Martius,
265 Though Martius earned them not; and all his faults
  To Martius shall be honors, though indeed
  In aught he merit not.
SICINIUS   Let's hence and hear
  How the dispatch is made,° and in what fashion,   business is executed
  More than his singularity,⁵ he goes
  Upon this present action.
270 BRUTUS   Let's along.   *Exeunt.*

1.2
Enter Tullus AUFIDIUS *with* SENATORS *of Corioles.*

FIRST SENATOR   So, your opinion is, Aufidius,
  That they of Rome are entered° in our counsels   instructed
  And know how we proceed?
AUFIDIUS   Is it not yours?
  Whatever have been thought on in this state
5 That could be brought to bodily act ere Rome
  Had circumvention?° 'Tis not four days gone   means to circumvent it
  Since I heard thence.° These are the words—I think   from there
  I have the letter here—yes, here it is:
  [*reading*] "They have pressed a power,° but it is not known   conscripted an army
10 Whether for east or west. The dearth is great,
  The people mutinous, and it is rumored
  Cominius, Martius—your old enemy,
  Who is of Rome worse hated than of you—
  And Titus Lartius, a most valiant Roman,
15 These three lead on this preparation
  Whither 'tis bent;° most likely 'tis for you.   Wherever it is bound
  Consider of it."
FIRST SENATOR   Our army's in the field;
  We never yet made doubt but Rome was ready
  To answer us.
AUFIDIUS   Nor did you think it folly
20 To keep your great pretenses° veiled till when   aims
  They needs must show themselves, which in the hatching,
  It seemed, appeared° to Rome. By the discovery   became known
  We shall be shortened in our aim,° which was   have to lower our sights
  To take in° many towns ere, almost, Rome   seize
  Should know we were afoot.
25 SECOND SENATOR   Noble Aufidius,
  Take your commission, hie° you to your bands;°   haste / troops
  Let us alone to guard Corioles.
  If they set down° before's, for the remove°   encamp / to raise the siege
  Bring up your army, but I think you'll find
  They've not prepared for us.
30 AUFIDIUS   Oh, doubt not that;
  I speak from certainties. Nay, more,
  Some parcels° of their power are forth already,   parts
  And only hitherward.° I leave your honors.   marching toward us

---

5. Apart from his idiosyncrasies.   **1.2** Location: Corioles, chief city of the Volscians.

If we and Caius Martius chance to meet,
35 'Tis sworn between us we shall ever strike°   keep fighting
Till one can do no more.
ALL   The gods assist you!
AUFIDIUS And keep your honors safe.
FIRST SENATOR   Farewell.
SECOND SENATOR   Farewell.
ALL Farewell.   *Exeunt all.*

1.3

Enter VOLUMNIA *and* VIRGILIA, *mother and wife to*
MARTIUS. *They set them down on two low stools*
and sew.

VOLUMNIA I pray you, daughter, sing, or express yourself in a
more comfortable sort.° If my son were my husband, I should   cheerful manner
freelier rejoice in that absence wherein he won honor than
in the embracements of his bed where he would show most
5 love. When yet he was but tender-bodied and the only son of
my womb, when youth with comeliness plucked all gaze his
way, when—for a day of kings' entreaties—a mother should
not sell him an hour from her beholding, I—considering
how honor would become such a person,° that it was no bet-   handsome figure
10 ter than picture-like to hang by th' wall, if renown made it
not stir[1]—was pleased to let him seek danger where he was
like to find fame. To a cruel war I sent him, from whence he
returned, his brows bound with oak.[2] I tell thee, daughter, I
sprang not more in joy at first hearing he was a man-child
15 than now in first seeing he had proved himself a man.
VIRGILIA But had he died in the business, madam, how then?
VOLUMNIA Then his good report should have been my son; I
therein would have found issue. Hear me profess sincerely:
had I a dozen sons, each in my love alike, and none less
20 dear than thine and my good Martius, I had rather had
eleven die nobly for their country than one voluptuously
surfeit out of action.[3]
          Enter a GENTLEWOMAN.
GENTLEWOMAN Madam, the Lady Valeria is come to visit you.
VIRGILIA Beseech you give me leave to retire myself.°   to go in
25 VOLUMNIA Indeed you shall not.
Methinks I hear hither your husband's drum;
See him pluck Aufidius down by th' hair;
As children from a bear, the Volsces shunning° him.   fleeing
Methinks I see him stamp thus and call thus,
30 "Come on, you cowards! You were got° in fear,   begotten
Though you were born in Rome!" His bloody brow
With his mailed° hand then wiping, forth he goes,   armored
Like to a harvest-man that's tasked° to mow   ordered
Or° all or lose his hire.°   Either / pay
35 VIRGILIA His bloody brow? O Jupiter, no blood!
VOLUMNIA Away, you fool! It more becomes a man

1.3 Location: Caius Martius's house, in Rome.
1. If desire for fame did not move it to action.
2. A garland of oak leaves (awarded to one who saved

the life of a Roman citizen in battle).
3. Indulge himself to excess away from the
battlefield.

Than gilt° his trophy. The breasts of Hecuba[4]   *gold leaf*
When she did suckle Hector[5] looked not lovelier
Than Hector's forehead when it spit forth blood
40 At Grecian sword contemning.° —Tell Valeria   *expressing contempt*
We are fit° to bid her welcome.   *Exit* GENTLEWOMAN.   *ready*
VIRGILIA   Heavens bless my lord from fell° Aufidius!   *fierce*
VOLUMNIA   He'll beat Aufidius' head below his knee
And tread upon his neck.
          Enter VALERIA *with an Usher and* [*the*] GENTLEWOMAN.
45 VALERIA   My ladies both, good day to you.
VOLUMNIA   Sweet madam.
VIRGILIA   I am glad to see your ladyship.
VALERIA   How do you both? You are manifest housekeepers.[6]
What are you sewing here? A fine spot,° in good faith. [*to*   *embroidered design*
50 VIRGILIA] How does your little son?
VIRGILIA   I thank your ladyship; well, good madam.
VOLUMNIA   He had rather see the swords and hear a drum
than look upon his schoolmaster.
VALERIA   O'my word, the father's son. I'll swear 'tis a very
55 pretty boy. O'my troth, I looked upon him o'Wednesday half
an hour together. He's such a confirmed° countenance. I   *determined*
saw him run after a gilded butterfly, and when he caught it,
he let it go again, and after it again, and over and over° he   *head over heels*
comes, and up again, catched it again. Or whether his fall
60 enraged him, or how 'twas, he did so set° his teeth and tear   *clench*
it. Oh, I warrant, how he mammocked° it!   *shredded*
VOLUMNIA   One on 's ° father's moods.   *of his*
VALERIA   Indeed, la, 'tis a noble child.
VIRGILIA   A crack,° madam.   *lively lad*
65 VALERIA   Come, lay aside your stitchery. I must have you play
the idle housewife° with me this afternoon.   *hussy*
VIRGILIA   No, good madam. I will not out of doors.
VALERIA   Not out of doors?
VOLUMNIA   She shall, she shall.
70 VIRGILIA   Indeed, no, by your patience. I'll not over the
threshold till my lord return from the wars.
VALERIA   Fie, you confine yourself most unreasonably. Come,
you must go visit the good lady that lies in.°   *is confined with child*
VIRGILIA   I will wish her speedy strength and visit her with my
75 prayers, but I cannot go thither.
VOLUMNIA   Why, I pray you?
VIRGILIA   'Tis not to save labor, nor that I want love.°   *lack affection for her*
VALERIA   You would be another Penelope.[7] Yet they say all the
yarn she spun in Ulysses' absence did but fill Ithaca full of
80 moths. Come, I would your cambric° were sensible° as your   *fine white linen/sensitive*
finger, that you might leave pricking it for pity. Come, you
shall go with us.
VIRGILIA   No, good madam, pardon me; indeed I will not
forth.

---

4. Trojan queen, mother of many sons.
5. The greatest Trojan warrior, killed by the Greek
Achilles (see *Troilus and Cressida*).
6. You are clearly being stay-at-homes.

7. In Homer's *Odyssey*, Ulysses' wife, Penelope, pretends during his protracted absence that she cannot
remarry until she finishes her weaving, which she
secretly unravels each night.

85   VALERIA   In truth, la, go with me, and I'll tell you excellent
        news of your husband.
        VIRGILIA   O good madam, there can be none yet.
        VALERIA   Verily, I do not jest with you: there came news from
        him last night.
90   VIRGILIA   Indeed, madam?
        VALERIA   In earnest, it's true. I heard a senator speak it. Thus
        it is: the Volsces have an army forth, against whom Cominius
        the general is gone with one part of our Roman power. Your
        lord and Titus Lartius are set down before their city Corioles;
95   they nothing doubt prevailing[8] and to make it brief wars.
        This is true, on mine honor, and so I pray, go with us.
        VIRGILIA   Give me excuse,° good madam. I will obey you in   *Pardon me*
        everything hereafter.
        VOLUMNIA   Let her alone, lady. As she is now she will but
100   disease° our better mirth.   *trouble*
        VALERIA   In troth, I think she would. [to VIRGILIA] Fare you
        well, then. [to VOLUMNIA] Come, good sweet lady. —Prithee,
        Virgilia, turn thy solemnness out-o'-door, and go along with
        us.
105   VIRGILIA   No, at a word, madam; indeed I must not. I wish
        you much mirth.
        VALERIA   Well, then, farewell.   *Exeunt.*

1.4

Enter MARTIUS, *Titus* LARTIUS, *with* [*a Trumpeter,*]
drum and colors,° with Captains and SOLDIERS [*with*   *drummer and flag bearer*
scaling ladders], *as before the city Corioles;*[1] *to them a*
MESSENGER.

        MARTIUS   Yonder comes news. A wager they have met.
        LARTIUS   My horse to yours, no?
        MARTIUS   'Tis done.
        LARTIUS   Agreed.
        MARTIUS [*to* MESSENGER]   Say, has our general met the enemy?
        MESSENGER   They lie in view, but have not spoke° as yet.   *encountered*
        LARTIUS   So, the good horse is mine.
5   MARTIUS   I'll buy him of you.
        LARTIUS   No, I'll nor° sell nor give him; lend you him I will   *neither*
        For half a hundred years. [*to Trumpeter*] Summon the town.
        MARTIUS [*to* MESSENGER]   How far off lie these armies?
        MESSENGER   Within this mile and half.
10   MARTIUS   Then shall we hear their larum,° and they ours.   *call to arms*
        Now Mars,° I prithee, make us quick in work,   *Roman god of war*
        That we with smoking° swords may march from hence   *steaming (with blood)*
        To help our fielded friends.[2] [*to Trumpeter*] Come, blow thy blast.
                They sound a parley.[3] *Enter two* SENATORS *with others*
                on the walls of Corioles.
        —Tullus Aufidius, is he within your walls?

---

8. They don't at all doubt that they will prevail.
1.4 Location: Before the walls of Corioles.
1. The rear of the stage represented the city walls,
the tiring-house door at the back of the stage the

gate, and the balcony the ramparts.
2. Our comrades in the battlefield.
3. Trumpet call for conference with the enemy.

15 FIRST SENATOR   No, nor a man that fears you less than he:
That's lesser than a little. (*Drum afar off.*) Hark, our drums
Are bringing forth our youth. We'll break our walls
Rather than they shall pound us up;° our gates,   *confine us*
Which yet seem shut, we have but pinned with rushes;°   *hollow reeds*
20 They'll open of themselves. (*Alarum far off.*) Hark you, far off!
There is Aufidius. List what work he makes
Amongst your cloven° army.   *divided; cut to pieces*

MARTIUS   Oh, they are at it!

LARTIUS   Their noise be our instruction. —Ladders ho!
Enter the army of the Volsces.

MARTIUS   They fear us not, but issue forth° their city.   *rush from*
25 Now put your shields before your hearts and fight
With hearts more proof° than shields. —Advance, brave Titus. *impenetrable*
They do disdain us much beyond our thoughts,[4]
Which makes me sweat with wrath. —Come on, my fellows!
He that retires, I'll take him for a Volsce,
30 And he shall feel mine edge.°   [*Exit.*]   *(sword edge)*
Alarum. The Romans are beat back to their trenches.
Enter MARTIUS, *cursing.*

MARTIUS   All the contagion of the south[5] light on you,
You shames of Rome! You herd of— Boils and plagues
Plaster you o'er,[6] that you may be abhorred°   *(by your smell)*
Farther than seen, and one infect another
35 Against the wind a mile!° You souls of geese   *Even a mile upwind*
That bear the shapes of men, how have you run
From slaves that apes would beat! Pluto° and hell!   *god of the underworld*
All hurt behind,[7] backs red, and faces pale
With flight and agued° fear! Mend and charge home,[8]   *shivering*
40 Or, by the fires of heaven,° I'll leave the foe   *the stars*
And make my wars on you. Look to't. Come on.
If you'll stand fast, we'll beat them to their wives,
As they us to our trenches. Follow's!
Another alarum. [*Volsces enter, attacking.*] MARTIUS
[*beats them back and*] *follows them to* [*the*] *gates.*
So, now the gates are ope. Now prove good seconds.°   *supporters*
45 'Tis for the followers fortune widens° them,   *opens*
Not for the fliers. Mark me, and do the like.
[*He*] *enters the gates.*

FIRST SOLDIER   Foolhardiness! Not I.

SECOND SOLDIER   Nor I.
[*The gates close;* MARTIUS] *is shut in.*[9]

FIRST SOLDIER   See,
They have shut him in.
Alarum continues.

ALL   To th' pot,° I warrant him.   *cooking pot*
Enter Titus LARTIUS.

LARTIUS   What is become of Martius?

ALL   Slain, sir, doubtless.

---

4. More than we had imagined.
5. South wind (thought to carry disease).
6. TEXTUAL COMMENT The Folio text is repunctuated by modern editors; for the rationale, see Digital Edition TC 2.
7. An injury taken in flight was a disgrace.

8. Charge to the heart of their defenses.
9. TEXTUAL COMMENT The placement of the Folio stage directions is often imprecise; here modern editors rearrange them to make sense of the action. For a detailed account of this reordering, see Digital Edition TC 3.

50 FIRST SOLDIER Following the fliers at the very heels,
With them he enters, who upon the sudden
Clapped-to° their gates. He is himself alone   *Shut*
To answer° all the city.   *confront*
LARTIUS   O noble fellow,
Who sensibly° outdares his senseless sword   *though having sensation*
55 And, when it bows, stand'st up! —Thou art lost, Martius.
A carbuncle entire,° as big as thou art,   *flawless ruby*
Were not so rich a jewel. Thou wast a soldier
Even to Cato's[1] wish, not fierce and terrible
Only in strokes, but with thy grim looks and
60 The thunder-like percussion of thy sounds
Thou mad'st thine enemies shake as if the world
Were feverous and did tremble.
              Enter MARTIUS, *bleeding, assaulted by the enemy.*
FIRST SOLDIER   Look, sir.
LARTIUS   Oh, 'tis Martius!
Let's fetch him off, or make remain alike.[2]
              They fight and all enter the city. [Exeunt.]

1.5
              Enter certain ROMANS *with spoils.*
FIRST ROMAN This will I carry to Rome.
SECOND ROMAN   And I this.
FIRST ROMAN A murrain° on't; I took this for silver.   *plague*
              Alarum continues still afar off. Enter MARTIUS, *and*
              Titus [LARTIUS] *with a Trumpet[er].*
                          *Exeunt [*ROMANS *with spoils].*
MARTIUS See here these movers[1] that do prize their hours
At a cracked drachma!° Cushions, leaden spoons,   *Greek coin*
5 Irons of a doit,[2] doublets that hangmen would
Bury with those that wore them,[3] these base slaves,
Ere yet the fight be done, pack up. Down with them!
And hark, what noise the general makes. To him!
There is the man of my soul's hate, Aufidius,
10 Piercing our Romans. Then, valiant Titus, take
Convenient numbers to make good° the city,   *secure*
Whilst I, with those that have the spirit, will haste
To help Cominius.
LARTIUS   Worthy sir, thou bleed'st.
Thy exercise hath been too violent
For a second course° of fight.   *bout*
15 MARTIUS   Sir, praise me not:
My work hath yet not warmed me. Fare you well.
The blood I drop is rather physical[4]
Than dangerous to me. To Aufidius thus
I will appear and fight.
LARTIUS   Now the fair goddess Fortune
20 Fall deep in love with thee, and her great charms

---

1. Cato the Censor, Roman general and moralist.
2. Let's rescue him, or share his fate.
1.5 Location: Corioles.
1. Active persons (ironic); plunderers.
2. Worthless swords (a "doit" was a very small coin).
doublets: close-fitting jackets (common male attire in
Jacobean England).
3. That is, even a hangman, whose wage is his victim's clothing, would spurn these garments.
4. Curative (bloodletting was a common medical
practice).

Misguide thy opposers' swords! Bold gentleman,
Prosperity be thy page.°   *Success attend you*
MARTIUS   Thy friend° no less   *(Prosperity)*
Than those she placeth highest. So farewell.   [*Exit.*]
LARTIUS   Thou worthiest Martius!
25   [*to Trumpeter*] Go sound thy trumpet in the market-place.
Call thither all the officers o'th' town,
Where they shall know our mind. Away.   *Exit.*

1.6

Enter COMINIUS, *as it were in retire,*° *with* SOLDIERS.   *controlled, strategic retreat*
COMINIUS   Breathe you,° my friends. Well fought! We are   *Get your breath back*
     come off[1]
Like Romans, neither foolish in our stands
Nor cowardly in retire. Believe me, sirs,
We shall be charged again. Whiles we have struck,°   *we were fighting*
5   By interims and conveying gusts[2] we have heard
The charges of our friends. Ye Roman gods,[3]
Lead their successes as we wish our own,
That both our powers, with smiling fronts° encount'ring,   *faces; front ranks*
May give you° thankful sacrifice!   *(the gods)*
     Enter a MESSENGER.
                      —Thy news?
10 MESSENGER   The citizens of Corioles have issued°   *(from the gates)*
And given to Lartius and to Martius battle.
I saw our party to their trenches driven,
And then I came away.
COMINIUS   Though thou speakest truth,
Methinks thou speak'st not well. How long is't since?
15 MESSENGER   Above an hour, my lord.
COMINIUS   'Tis not a mile; briefly° we heard their drums.   *a short time ago*
How couldst thou in a mile confound° an hour   *waste*
And bring thy news so late?
MESSENGER   Spies of the Volsces
Held me in chase, that I was forced to wheel°   *detour*
20   Three or four miles about, else had I, sir,
Half an hour since brought my report.
     Enter MARTIUS.
COMINIUS   Who's yonder,
That does appear as he were flayed? O gods,
He has the stamp° of Martius, and I have   *form*
Before-time° seen him thus.   *Previously*
MARTIUS   Come I too late?
25 COMINIUS   The shepherd knows not thunder from a tabor°   *small drum*
More than I know the sound of Martius' tongue
From every meaner° man.   *lesser*
MARTIUS   Come I too late?
COMINIUS   Ay, if you come not in the blood of others,
But mantled in your own.

1.6 Location: The battlefield.
1. We have retreated.
2. *By interims . . . gusts:* At intervals, conveyed by the
wind.
3. TEXTUAL COMMENT The Folio text has "The

Roman Gods," a misreading of the "y" that was frequently used to indicate "th" in Shakespeare's time
(and is sometimes used today to convey an old-timey
flavor: "ye olde shoppe"). See Digital Edition TC 4 for
a fuller rationale of the emendation.

MARTIUS	Oh, let me clip° ye	clasp

30   In arms as sound as when I wooed, in heart
As merry as when our nuptial day was done,
And tapers burnt to bedward!
        [*They embrace.*]

COMINIUS   Flower of warriors,
How is't with Titus Lartius?

MARTIUS   As with a man busied about decrees,

35   Condemning some to death, and some to exile,
Ransoming him or pitying, threat'ning th'other;
Holding Corioles in the name of Rome
Even like a fawning greyhound in the leash,

    To let him slip° at will.   *off the leash*

COMINIUS   Where is that slave

40   Which told me they had beat you to your trenches?
Where is he? Call him hither.

MARTIUS   Let him alone:

He did inform° the truth. But for our gentlemen,°   *report / (sarcastic)*
The common file°—a plague! Tribunes for them!—   *sort*
The mouse ne'er shunned the cat as they did budge°   *flinch*
From rascals worse than they.

45   COMINIUS   But how prevailed you?

MARTIUS   Will the time serve to tell? I do not think.
Where is the enemy? Are you lords o'th' field?
If not, why cease you till you are so?

COMINIUS   Martius, we have at disadvantage fought,

50   And did retire to win our purpose.°   *for tactical reasons*

MARTIUS   How lies their battle?° Know you on which side   *army*
They have placed their men of trust?

COMINIUS   As I guess, Martius,
Their bands i'th' vaward° are the Antiates   *front*
Of their best trust, o'er them Aufidius,
Their very heart of hope.

55   MARTIUS   I do beseech you
By all the battles wherein we have fought,
By th' blood we have shed together, by th' vows
We have made to endure° friends, that you directly   *remain*
Set me against Aufidius and his Antiates,

60   And that you not delay the present,° but,   *matter at hand*
Filling the air with swords advanced and darts,
We prove° this very hour.   *try*

COMINIUS   Though I could wish
You were conducted to a gentle bath
And balms applied to you, yet dare I never

65   Deny your asking. Take your choice of those
That best can aid your action.

MARTIUS   Those are they
That most are willing.—If any such be here—
As it were sin to doubt—that love this painting°   *(blood)*
Wherein you see me smeared; if any fear

70   Lesser his person than an ill report;[4]
If any think brave death outweighs bad life

---

4. *Lesser . . . report:* Less for his body than for his reputation.

And that his country's dearer than himself,
Let him alone, or so many so minded,
Wave thus [*waving his sword*] to express his disposition,
75 And follow Martius.
    They all shout and wave their swords, take him up in
    their arms, and cast up their caps.
Oh, me alone! Make you a sword of me?
If these shows be not outward,° which of you   *superficial*
But is four Volsces? None of you but is
Able to bear against the great Aufidius
80 A shield as hard as his. A certain number—
Though thanks to all—must I select from all:
The rest shall bear the business in some other fight
As cause will be obeyed.° Please you to march,   *the situation requires*
And four shall quickly draw out my command,[5]
Which men are best inclined.
85 COMINIUS   March on, my fellows.
Make good this ostentation,° and you shall   *show of enthusiasm*
Divide in all[6] with us.   *Exeunt.*

1.7

Titus LARTIUS, *having set a guard upon Corioles,*
going with drum and trumpet toward COMINIUS *and*
Caius MARTIUS, *enters with a* LIEUTENANT, *other*
SOLDIERS, *and a Scout.*

LARTIUS   So, let the ports° be guarded; keep your duties   *gates*
As I have set them down. If I do send, dispatch
Those centuries[1] to our aid; the rest will serve
For a short holding.° If we lose the field,   *brief occupation*
We cannot keep the town.
5 LIEUTENANT   Fear not our care, sir.
LARTIUS   Hence, and shut your gates upon's.
    [*to the Scout*] Our guider, come: to th' Roman camp conduct us.
                                   Exeunt.

1.8

Alarum, as in battle. Enter MARTIUS *and* AUFIDIUS *at*
several° doors.   *separate*

MARTIUS   I'll fight with none but thee, for I do hate thee
Worse than a promise-breaker.
AUFIDIUS   We hate alike:
Not Afric owns° a serpent I abhor   *Africa doesn't contain*
More than thy fame and envy.° Fix thy foot.   *enviable reputation*
5 MARTIUS   Let the first budger die the other's slave,
And the gods doom him after.
AUFIDIUS   If I fly, Martius,
Holla° me like a hare.   *Shout in pursuit of*
MARTIUS   Within these three hours, Tullus,
Alone I fought in your Corioles' walls,
And made what work I pleased. 'Tis not my blood
10 Wherein thou seest me masked. For thy revenge,
Wrench up thy power to th' highest.

---

5. Select those I will command.   1. Companies of 100 men.
6. Share the honor and winnings.   1.8 Location: The battlefield.
1.7 Location: The gates of Corioles.

AUFIDIUS   Wert thou the Hector
That was the whip of your bragged progeny,[1]
Thou shouldst not scape me here.
          Here they fight, and certain Volsces come in the aid of
          AUFIDIUS.
[*to Volsces*] Officious° and not valiant, you have shamed me   Meddling
15   In your condemnèd seconds.[2]
          MARTIUS *fights till they be driven in breathless.* [*Exeunt.*]

                    1.9

          Flourish.[1] Alarum. A retreat is sounded. Enter at one
          door COMINIUS *with the* ROMANS; *at another door*
          MARTIUS, *with his arm in a scarf.*°   *sling*
COMINIUS   If I should tell thee o'er this thy day's work,
Thout° not believe thy deeds, but I'll report it   *Thou would'st*
Where senators shall mingle tears with smiles,
Where great patricians shall attend and shrug,°   *(with incredulity)*
5   I'th' end admire;° where ladies shall be frighted   *marvel*
And, gladly quaked,° hear more; where the dull° tribunes,   *made to tremble / sullen*
That with the fusty° plebeians hate thine honors,   *moldy; stinking*
Shall say against their hearts,° "We thank the gods   *despite themselves*
Our Rome hath such a soldier."
10   Yet cam'st thou to a morsel of this feast,
   Having fully dined before.[2]
          Enter Titus [LARTIUS], *with his power,*° *from the pursuit.*   *troops*
LARTIUS   O general,
Here is the steed, we the caparison.[3]
Hadst thou beheld—
MARTIUS   Pray now, no more. My mother,
Who has a charter° to extol her blood,°   *right / offspring*
15   When she does praise me grieves me. I have done
As you have done, that's what I can, induced
As you have been, that's for my country.
He that has but effected his good will[4]
Hath overta'en mine act.
COMINIUS   You shall not be
20   The grave of your deserving. Rome must know
The value of her own. 'Twere a concealment
Worse than a theft, no less than a traducement,°   *slander*
To hide your doings, and to silence that
Which to the spire and top of praises vouched°   *declared*
25   Would seem but modest.° Therefore I beseech you—   *inadequate*
In sign° of what you are, not to reward   *As a token*
What you have done—before our army, hear me.
MARTIUS   I have some wounds upon me, and they smart
To hear themselves remembered.
COMINIUS   Should they not,
30   Well might they fester gainst ingratitude

---

1. Romans claimed descent from the Trojans; Hector, the finest Trojan soldier, was the scourge ("whip") of the Greeks.
2. Contemptible assistance.
1.9 Location: The battlefield.
1. Trumpet call for the entry of the victorious Romans. *retreat:* signal to cease pursuit.
2. *Yet . . . before:* either "The feast of description is a morsel compared with the full dinner of your deeds," or "Your final onslaught was a mere morsel in addition to your earlier fighting."
3. That is, here is he who really did the work (Coriolanus, the horse); we are only the horse's trappings ("caparison").
4. Carried out his resolution.

And tent[5] themselves with death. Of all the horses—
Whereof we have ta'en good, and good store[6]—of all
The treasure in this field achieved and city,
We render you the° tenth to be ta'en forth   *one*
35 Before the common distribution,
At your only° choice.   *sole*
MARTIUS   I thank you, general,
But cannot make my heart consent to take
A bribe to pay my sword: I do refuse it
And stand° upon my common part with those   *insist*
40 That have beheld the doing.
    A long flourish. They all cry, "Martius, Martius," cast
    up their caps and lances. COMINIUS *and* [Titus]
    LARTIUS *stand bare.°*   *with hats removed*
May these same instruments, which you profane,
Never sound more. When drums and trumpets shall
I'th' field prove flatterers, let courts and cities be
Made all of false-faced soothing;[7] when steel grows
45 Soft as the parasite's° silk, let him be made   *flatterer's*
An overture for th' wars.[8] No more, I say.
For that I have not washed my nose that bled,
Or foiled some debile° wretch—which, without note,   *feeble*
Here's many else° have done—you shout me forth   *others*
50 In acclamations hyperbolical,°   *In exaggerated praise*
As if I loved my little should be dieted
In praises sauced with lies.[9]
COMINIUS   Too modest are you,
More cruel to your good report than grateful
To us that give° you truly. By your patience,   *describe*
55 If gainst yourself you be incensed, we'll put you,
Like one that means his proper harm,° in manacles,   *harm to himself*
Then reason safely with you. Therefore be it known,
As to us, to all the world, that Caius Martius
Wears this war's garland, in token of the which,
60 My noble steed, known to the camp, I give him,
With all his trim belonging;° and from this time,   *fine trappings*
For what he did before Corioles, call him,
With all th'applause and clamor of the host,
Martius Caius Coriolanus.
65 Bear th'addition° nobly ever!   *title*
    Flourish. Trumpets sound, and drums.
ALL   Martius Caius Coriolanus!
MARTIUS   I will go wash,
And when my face is fair,° you shall perceive   *clean*
Whether I blush or no. Howbeit, I thank you.
I mean to stride° your steed, and at all times   *bestride; ride on*
70 To undercrest° your good addition   *uphold*
To th' fairness° of my power.   *best*
COMINIUS   So, to our tent,
Where, ere we do repose us, we will write

---

5. Heal (a "tent" was a probe that cleansed a wound).
6. We have captured good quality and quantity.
7. Hypocritical compliments.
8. *let . . . wars:* a debated and perhaps corrupt pas-

sage; perhaps "let the parasite call soldiers to war."
9. *As if . . . lies:* As if I enjoyed having my small
achievements bulked up by lying flattery.

To Rome of our success. —You, Titus Lartius,
Must to Corioles back; send us to Rome
75   The best,[1] with whom we may articulate,°   *make terms*
For their own good and ours.
LARTIUS   I shall, my lord.
MARTIUS   The gods begin to mock me. I, that now
Refused most princely gifts, am bound to beg
Of my lord general.
COMINIUS   Take't, 'tis yours: what is't?
80 MARTIUS   I sometime lay here in Corioles
At a poor man's house; he used° me kindly.   *treated*
He cried° to me; I saw him prisoner,   *appealed*
But then Aufidius was within my view,
And wrath o'erwhelmed my pity. I request you
To give my poor host freedom.
85 COMINIUS   Oh, well begged!
Were he the butcher of my son, he should
Be free as is the wind. —Deliver° him, Titus.   *Free*
LARTIUS   Martius, his name?
MARTIUS   By Jupiter, forgot!
I am weary; yea, my memory is tired.
Have we no wine here?
90 COMINIUS   Go we to our tent.
The blood upon your visage dries: 'tis time
It should be looked to. Come.   *Exeunt.*

1.10

A flourish. Cornetts. Enter Tullus AUFIDIUS, *bloody,*
with two or three SOLDIERS.

AUFIDIUS   The town is ta'en.
FIRST SOLDIER   'Twill be delivered back
On good condition.[1]
AUFIDIUS   Condition?
I would I were a Roman, for I cannot,
Being a Volsce, be that I am.° Condition?   *what I am (proud)*
5   What good condition can a treaty find
I'th' part that is at mercy?° Five times, Martius,   *For the conquered side*
I have fought with thee; so often hast thou beat me,
And wouldst do so, I think, should we encounter
As often as we eat. By th'elements,
10 If e'er again I meet him beard to beard,
He's mine, or I am his. Mine emulation°   *rivalry*
Hath not that honor in't it had, for where°   *whereas*
I thought to crush him in an equal force,
True sword to sword, I'll potch° at him some way: *thrust*
Or° wrath or craft may get him.   *Either*
15 FIRST SOLDIER   He's the devil.
AUFIDIUS   Bolder, though not so subtle. My valor's poisoned
With only suff'ring stain° by him; for him   *disgrace*
Shall fly out of itself. Nor sleep nor sanctuary,[2]
Being naked, sick; nor fane,° nor Capitol,   *temple*

---

1. The most noble Volscians.
1.10 Location: Outside Corioles.
1. Terms (Aufidius takes the meaning "state of being").

2. In early modern England, those who sought sanctuary in a church were protected from attack or legal prosecution. *fly out of itself:* deviate from its nature.

20 The prayers of priests, nor times of sacrifice,
   Embarquements° all of fury, shall lift up   *Impediments*
   Their rotten° privilege and custom gainst   *worn-out*
   My hate to Martius. Where I find him, were it
   At home, upon° my brother's guard,° even there   *under / protection*
25 Against the hospitable canon,° would I   *rule of hospitality*
   Wash my fierce hand in 's heart. Go you to th' city;
   Learn how 'tis held, and what they are that must
   Be hostages for Rome.
   FIRST SOLDIER   Will not you go?
   AUFIDIUS   I am attended° at the cypress grove. I pray you— *expected*
30 'Tis south the city mills—bring me word thither
   How the world goes, that to the pace of it[3]
   I may spur on my journey.
   FIRST SOLDIER   I shall, sir.   [*Exeunt.*]

2.1

Enter MENENIUS *with the two tribunes of the people,*
SICINIUS *and* BRUTUS.

MENENIUS   The augurer[1] tells me we shall have news tonight.
BRUTUS   Good or bad?
MENENIUS   Not according to the prayer of the people, for they
   love not Martius.
5 SICINIUS   Nature teaches beasts to know their friends.
MENENIUS   Pray you, who does the wolf love?
SICINIUS   The lamb.
MENENIUS   Ay, to devour him, as the hungry plebeians would
   the noble Martius.
10 BRUTUS   He's a lamb indeed, that baas like a bear.
MENENIUS   He's a bear indeed, that lives like a lamb.[2] You two
   are old men; tell me one thing that I shall ask you.
BOTH   Well, sir?
MENENIUS   In what enormity is Martius poor in that you two
15   have not in abundance?
BRUTUS   He's poor in no one fault but stored° with all.   *well stocked*
SICINIUS   Especially in pride.
BRUTUS   And topping all others in boasting.
MENENIUS   This is strange now. Do you two know how you
20   are censured° here in the city, I mean of us o'th' right-hand   *judged*
   file?[3] Do you?
BOTH   Why? How are we censured?
MENENIUS   Because you talk of pride now—will you not be
   angry?
25 BOTH   Well, well, sir, well.
MENENIUS   Why, 'tis no great matter, for a very little thief of
   occasion will rob you of a great deal of patience.[4] Give your
   dispositions the reins and be angry at your pleasures, at the
   least, if you take it as a pleasure to you in being so. You
30   blame Martius for being proud?

---

3. In accordance with the situation.
2.1 Location: Rome.
1. Religious official who interpreted omens.
2. That is, how can you accuse him of being a bear

when he lives an innocent life?
3. Patrician class (who made up the right-hand "file,"
or line, in battle).
4. The least pretext will make you lose your temper.

BRUTUS　We do it not alone, sir.

MENENIUS　I know you can do very little alone, for your helps
are many, or else your actions would grow wondrous single.° ——— *solitary; trivial*
Your abilities are too infant-like for doing much alone. You
35　talk of pride. Oh, that you could turn your eyes toward the
napes of your necks and make but an interior survey of your
good selves! Oh, that you could!

BOTH　What then, sir?

MENENIUS　Why, then you should discover a brace° of unmer- ——— *pair*
40　iting, proud, violent, testy magistrates—alias fools—as any in
Rome.

SICINIUS　Menenius, you are known well enough, too.

MENENIUS　I am known to be a humorous° patrician, and one ——— *whimsical*
that loves a cup of hot wine with not a drop of allaying
45　Tiber° in't; said to be something imperfect in favoring the ——— *water*
first complaint,[5] hasty and tinder-like upon too trivial motion;° ——— *provocation*
one that converses more with the buttock of the night than
with the forehead of the morning.[6] What I think, I utter,
and spend my malice in my breath. Meeting two such weals-
50　men° as you are—I cannot call you Lycurguses[7]—if the drink ——— *statesmen*
you give me touch my palate adversely, I make a crooked
face at it. I cannot say your worships have delivered the matter well when I find the ass in compound with the major part
of your syllables;[8] and though I must be content to bear with
55　those that say you are reverend grave men, yet they lie
deadly° that tell you have good faces. If you see this in the ——— *extremely*
map of my microcosm,[9] follows it that I am known well
enough too? What harm can your bisson conspectuities° ——— *dim vision*
glean out of this character,[1] if I be known well enough too?

60　BRUTUS　Come, sir, come; we know you well enough.

MENENIUS　You know neither me, yourselves, nor anything.
You are ambitious for poor knaves' caps and legs.[2] You wear
out a good wholesome forenoon in hearing a cause between
an orange-wife and a faucet-seller,[3] and then rejourn° the ——— *adjourn*
65　controversy of threepence to a second day of audience.° ——— *hearing*
When you are hearing a matter between party and party, if
you chance to be pinched with the colic,° you make faces ——— *intestinal gas*
like mummers,[4] set up the bloody flag° against all patience ——— *declare war*
and, in roaring for a chamberpot, dismiss the controversy
70　bleeding,° the more entangled by your hearing. All the peace ——— *unhealed*
you make in their cause is calling both the parties knaves.
You are a pair of strange ones.

BRUTUS　Come, come, you are well understood to be a perfecter giber for the table than a necessary bencher in the
75　Capitol.[5]

---

5. *favoring the first complaint:* accepting the first version of a dispute I hear before considering the other
side.
6. That experiences more late nights than early
mornings.
7. Lycurgus was a famous Spartan lawgiver of the
ninth century B.C.E.
8. *I find the ass . . . syllables:* I find stupidity mixed in
most of what you say.
9. My face (thought to map the "little world" of the

human body).
1. Verbal description.
2. For deferentially doffed caps and bent legs.
3. Between a woman fruit vendor and someone who
sells taps for liquor barrels.
4. Dumb-show actors (who use exaggerated facial
expressions).
5. *perfecter giber . . . Capitol:* better at dinner jests
than at serving in the Senate.

MENENIUS   Our very priests must become mockers if they
shall encounter such ridiculous subjects° as you are. When   *objects; citizens*
you speak best unto the purpose, it is not worth the wagging
of your beards, and your beards deserve not so honorable a
80 grave as to stuff a botcher's° cushion or to be entombed in   *clothes mender's*
an ass's pack-saddle.[6] Yet you must be saying Martius is
proud, who in a cheap estimation° is worth all your prede-   *low estimate*
cessors since Deucalion,[7] though peradventure some of the
best of 'em were hereditary hangmen.[8] Good e'en to your
85 worships; more of your conversation would infect my brain,
being° the herdsmen of the beastly plebeians. I will be bold   *you two being*
to take my leave of you.
        BRUTUS *and* SICINIUS [*stand*] *aside. Enter* VOLUMNIA,
        VIRGILIA, *and* VALERIA.
How now, my as fair as noble ladies—and the moon,[9] were she
earthly, no nobler—whither do you follow your eyes so fast?
90 VOLUMNIA   Honorable Menenius, my boy Martius approaches.
For the love of Juno, let's go.
MENENIUS   Ha! Martius coming home?
VOLUMNIA   Ay, worthy Menenius, and with most prosperous
approbation.[1]
95 MENENIUS [*throwing up his cap*]   Take my cap, Jupiter, and
I thank thee. Hoo! Martius coming home?
VIRGILIA *and* VALERIA   Nay, 'tis true.
VOLUMNIA   Look, here's a letter from him; the state hath
another; his wife another, and I think there's one at home
100 for you.
MENENIUS   I will make my very house reel tonight. A letter for
me?
VIRGILIA   Yes, certain, there's a letter for you: I saw't.
MENENIUS   A letter for me? It gives me an estate° of seven   *endowment; condition*
105 years' health, in which time I will make a lip° at the physi-   *sneer*
cian. The most sovereign° prescription in Galen[2] is but   *effective*
empiricutic° and, to° this preservative, of no better report   *quackish / compared with*
than a horse-drench.[3] Is he not wounded? He was wont° to   *accustomed*
come home wounded!
110 VIRGILIA   Oh, no, no, no.
VOLUMNIA   Oh, he is wounded, I thank the gods for't.
MENENIUS   So do I too, if it be not too much. Brings he° vic-   *Does he bring*
tory in his pocket? The wounds become him.
VOLUMNIA   On 's brows. Menenius, he comes the third time
115 home with the oaken garland.
MENENIUS   Has he disciplined Aufidius soundly?
VOLUMNIA   Titus Lartius writes they fought together, but
Aufidius got off.
MENENIUS   And 'twas time for him too, I'll warrant him that;
120 an° he had stayed by him, I would not have been so 'fidi-   *If*
ussed[4] for all the chests in Corioles and the gold that's in
them. Is the Senate possessed° of this?   *informed*

6. Hair from cut beards was used as stuffing.
7. Deucalion and his wife were sole survivors of a
great flood; their son was the ancestor of the Greeks.
8. A very base occupation.
9. Diana, goddess of chastity.
1. Rich praise; happy success.

2. Ancient medical authority still standard in the
Renaissance (Galen actually lived six centuries after
Coriolanus).
3. Horse medicine.
4. "Aufidiussed," Menenius's coinage for "beaten."

VOLUMNIA   Good ladies, let's go. [*to* MENENIUS] Yes, yes, yes:
the Senate has letters from the general wherein he gives my
125   son the whole name° of the war. He hath in this action out-   credit
done his former deeds doubly.

VALERIA   In troth, there's wondrous things spoke of him.

MENENIUS   Wondrous? Ay, I warrant you, and not without his
true purchasing.°   truly earning it

130   VIRGILIA   The gods grant them true.

VOLUMNIA   True? Pow waw!

MENENIUS   True? I'll be sworn they are true. Where is he
wounded? [*to* BRUTUS *and* SICINIUS] God save your good worships! Martius is coming home. He has more cause to be
135   proud. [*to* VOLUMNIA] Where is he wounded?

VOLUMNIA   I'th' shoulder and i'th' left arm. There will be large
cicatrices° to show the people when he shall stand for his   scars
place.[5] He received in the repulse of Tarquin[6] seven hurts
i'th' body.

140   MENENIUS   One i'th' neck and two i'th' thigh; there's nine
that I know.

VOLUMNIA   He had, before this last expedition, twenty-five
wounds upon him.

MENENIUS   Now it's twenty-seven. Every gash was an enemy's
145   grave.
        A shout and flourish.
        Hark, the trumpets.

VOLUMNIA   These are the ushers of Martius: before him
He carries noise, and behind him he leaves tears.
Death, that dark spirit, in 's nervy° arm doth lie,   muscular
150   Which, being advanced, declines,° and then men die.   being raised, descends
        A sennet.° Trumpets sound. Enter COMINIUS *the general*   ceremonial flourish
        and Titus LARTIUS; *between them* CORIOLANUS,[7]
        crowned with an oaken garland, with Captains and
        SOLDIERS *and a* HERALD.

HERALD   Know, Rome, that all alone Martius did fight
Within Corioles' gates, where he hath won,
With fame, a name to° Martius Caius; these   in addition to
In honor follows "Coriolanus."

155   —Welcome to Rome, renownèd Coriolanus!
        Sound flourish.

ALL   Welcome to Rome, renownèd Coriolanus!

CORIOLANUS   No more of this; it does offend my heart.
Pray now, no more.

COMINIUS   Look, sir, your mother.

CORIOLANUS   Oh!
You have, I know, petitioned all the gods
For my prosperity.°   success
        [*He*] *kneels.*

160   VOLUMNIA   Nay, my good soldier, up.
My gentle Martius, worthy Caius, and

---

5. Will offer himself as a candidate for consul, republican Rome's highest office.
6. Martius's first military experience was in the war against the former King Tarquin.
7. TEXTUAL COMMENT From this point forward the

Folio uses the honorific name "*Coriolanus*" in speech prefixes and stage directions. At 5.6.129, the moment of his death, he once again becomes "*Martius*." See Digital Edition TC 5 for the implications of this name change.

By deed-achieving honor newly named—
What is it?—"Coriolanus" must I call thee?—
But, oh, thy wife!

CORIOLANUS [*to* VIRGILIA]   My gracious silence, hail!
165　Wouldst thou have laughed had I come coffined home,
That weep'st to see me triumph? Ah, my dear,
Such eyes the widows in Corioles wear,
And mothers that lack sons.

MENENIUS　　　　　　　　　Now the gods crown thee!

CORIOLANUS　And live you yet? [*to* VALERIA] O my sweet lady, pardon.
170　VOLUMNIA　I know not where to turn. Oh, welcome home;
　—And welcome, General, and you're welcome all.

MENENIUS　A hundred thousand welcomes! I could weep
And I could laugh; I am light and heavy.° Welcome!   *(of heart)*
A curse begin at very root on 's heart
175　That is not glad to see thee! You are three
That Rome should dote on; yet, by the faith of men,
We have some old crab-trees° here at home that will not   *(gnarled, sour men)*
Be grafted to your relish.° Yet welcome, warriors!   *liking*
We call a nettle but a nettle and
The faults of fools but folly.

180　COMINIUS　　　　　　　　　Ever right.

CORIOLANUS　Menenius, ever, ever.

HERALD　Give way there, and go on!

CORIOLANUS [*to* VOLUMNIA *and* VIRGILIA]   Your hand, and yours!
Ere in our own house I do shade my head,
The good patricians must be visited,
185　From whom I have received not only greetings,
But with them change of honors.°   *a new set of honors*

VOLUMNIA　　　　　　　　　　I have lived
To see inherited° my very wishes   *realized*
And the buildings of my fancy. Only
There's one thing wanting, which I doubt not but
Our Rome will cast upon thee.

190　CORIOLANUS　　　　　　　Know, good mother,
I had rather be their servant in my way
Than sway[8] with them in theirs.

COMINIUS　　　　　　　　On, to the Capitol.

　　　　　Flourish cornetts.
　　　　　Exeunt in state, as before, [*all except*] BRUTUS *and*
　　　　　　　　　SICINIUS*[, who come forward*].

BRUTUS　All tongues speak of him, and the bleared sights°   *dim-sighted people*
Are spectacled to see him. Your prattling nurse
195　Into a rapture° lets her baby cry   *fit*
While she chats him.[9] The kitchen malkin° pins   *wench*
Her richest lockram° 'bout her reechy° neck,   *linen / filthy*
Clamb'ring the walls to eye him. Stalls, bulks,[1] windows
Are smothered up, leads filled, and ridges horsed
200　With variable complexions,[2] all agreeing
In earnestness to see him. Seld-shown flamens°   *Seldom-seen priests*
Do press among the popular° throngs and puff°   *plebeian / pant*

---

8. Rule; prevail; deviate from a straight course.
9. Discusses Coriolanus.
1. Framework projecting from shopfronts ("stalls").

2. *leads . . . complexions:* lead roofs filled and roof-tops bestridden by all types of people.

To win a vulgar station.° Our veiled dames   *a place in the crowd*
Commit the war of white and damask[3] in
205 Their nicely gauded[4] cheeks to th' wanton spoil
Of Phoebus'° burning kisses. Such a pother°   *the sun's / commotion*
As if that whatsoever god who leads him°   *(Coriolanus)*
Were slyly crept into his human powers
And gave him graceful posture.
SICINIUS   On the sudden°   *At once*
I warrant him consul.
210 BRUTUS   Then our office may,
During his power,° go sleep.   *term of authority*
SICINIUS   He cannot temp'rately transport° his honors   *convey*
From where he should begin and end,° but will   *to where he should end*
Lose those he hath won.
BRUTUS   In that there's comfort.
SICINIUS   Doubt not
215 The commoners, for whom we stand, but they
Upon their ancient malice[5] will forget
With the least cause these his new honors, which°   *(which cause)*
That he will give them, make I as little question
As[6] he is proud to do't.
BRUTUS   I heard him swear,
220 Were he to stand for consul, never would he
Appear i'th' marketplace, nor on him put
The napless vesture° of humility,   *threadbare garment*
Nor showing, as the manner is, his wounds
To th' people, beg their stinking breaths.°   *votes*
SICINIUS   'Tis right.
225 BRUTUS   It was his word. Oh, he would miss it° rather   *forgo the consulship*
Than carry° it but by the suit of the gentry to him   *go through with*
And the desire of the nobles.
SICINIUS   I wish no better
Than have him hold that purpose and to put it
In execution.
BRUTUS   'Tis most like he will.
230 SICINIUS   It shall be to him then as our good wills:°   *as our benefit requires*
A sure destruction.
BRUTUS   So it must fall out
To him, or our authority's for an end.
We must suggest° the people in what hatred   *insinuate to*
He still° hath held them; that to 's power he would   *always*
235 Have made them mules, silenced their pleaders,° and   *representatives*
Dispropertied° their freedoms, holding them   *Taken away*
In human action and capacity
Of no more soul nor fitness for the world
Than camels in their war, who have their provand°   *food*
240 Only for bearing burdens, and sore blows
For sinking under them.

---

3. The conflict between white and pink in delicate
skin ("damask" refers to the dark-pink damask rose).
4. Fastidiously made up. TEXTUAL COMMENT
"Gawded" in the Folio is from the verb "gaud," meaning
"to ornament." Although the Norton edition retains
the Folio wording, some editors emend to "guarded."

For the significance of the difference, see Digital Edition TC 6.
5. *Upon . . . malice:* Because of their long-standing
hostility.
6. *make I as . . . as:* I have as little doubt as that.

SICINIUS   This, as you say, suggested
At some time when his soaring insolence
Shall touch° the people—which time shall not want°   *kindle / be lacking*
If he be put upon't, and that's as easy
245   As to set dogs on sheep—will be his fire
To kindle their dry stubble[7] and their blaze
Shall darken him for ever.
           Enter a MESSENGER.
BRUTUS   What's the matter?
MESSENGER   You are sent for to the Capitol. 'Tis thought
That Martius shall be consul. I have seen
250   The dumb men throng to see him, and the blind
To hear him speak. Matrons flung gloves,
Ladies and maids their scarves and handkerchiefs,
Upon him as he passed. The nobles bended
As to Jove's statue, and the commons made
255   A shower and thunder with their caps and shouts.
I never saw the like.
BRUTUS   Let's to the Capitol,
And carry with us ears and eyes for th' time,°   *present occasion*
But hearts for the event.°   *outcome*
SICINIUS   Have with you.°   *Exeunt.*   *Let's go; I'm with you.*

2.2

Enter two OFFICERS *to lay cushions, as it were in the*
Capitol.

FIRST OFFICER   Come, come, they are almost here. How many
stand for consulships?
SECOND OFFICER   Three, they say, but 'tis thought of everyone
Coriolanus will carry it.
5   FIRST OFFICER   That's a brave fellow, but he's vengeance°   *intensely*
proud and loves not the common people.
SECOND OFFICER   Faith, there hath been many great men that
have flattered the people who ne'er loved them, and there be
many that they° have loved they know not wherefore;° so   *(the people) / why*
10   that, if they love they know not why, they hate upon no better
a ground. Therefore, for Coriolanus neither to care whether
they love or hate him manifests the true knowledge he has
in° their disposition, and out of his noble carelessness lets   *of*
them plainly see't.
15   FIRST OFFICER   If he did not care whether he had their love or
no, he waved indifferently[1] twixt doing them neither good
nor harm; but he seeks their hate with greater devotion than
they can render it him and leaves nothing undone that
may fully discover° him their opposite.° Now to seem to   *reveal / adversary*
20   affect° the malice and displeasure of the people is as bad   *desire*
as that which he dislikes, to flatter them for their love.
SECOND OFFICER   He hath deserved worthily of his country,
and his ascent is not by such easy degrees as those who,

---

7. That is, Coriolanus's fiery insolence will kindle   **2.2** Location: The Capitol, Rome.
the dry fuel of the plebeians' resentment.   1. He would waver without caring.

having been supple and courteous to the people, bonneted[2]
25 without any further deed to have them at all into their estimation and report.° But he hath so planted his honors in   *good opinion*
their eyes and his actions in their hearts that for their
tongues to be silent and not confess so much were a kind of
ingrateful injury. To report otherwise were a malice that,
30 giving itself the lie,[3] would pluck reproof and rebuke from
every ear that heard it.
FIRST OFFICER   No more of him; he's a worthy man. Make
way; they are coming.

> *A* sennet. *Enter the* PATRICIANS *and* [SICINIUS *and*
> BRUTUS] *the tribunes of the people, Lictors[4] before
> them;* CORIOLANUS, MENENIUS, COMINIUS *the consul.*
> [*The* SENATORS *sit;*] SICINIUS *and* BRUTUS *take their
> places by themselves;* CORIOLANUS *stands.*

MENENIUS   Having determined of° the Volsces and   *made a decision about*
35 To send for Titus Lartius, it remains
As the main point of this our after-meeting
To gratify° his noble service that   *reward*
Hath thus stood for his country. Therefore please you,
Most reverend and grave elders, to desire
40 The present consul and last° general   *recent*
In our well-found° successes to report   *happily encountered*
A little of that worthy work performed
By Martius Caius Coriolanus, whom
We met here both to thank and to remember
With honors like° himself.   *befitting*
    [CORIOLANUS *sits.*]
45 FIRST SENATOR   Speak, good Cominius.
Leave nothing out for° length, and make us think   *on account of*
Rather our state's defective for requital
Than we to stretch it out.[5] [*to the tribunes*] Masters o'th' people,
We do request your kindest ears and, after,
50 Your loving motion toward° the common body   *persuasion of*
To yield° what passes here.   *agree to*
SICINIUS   We are convented°   *met together*
Upon a pleasing treaty,° and have hearts   *subject for discussion*
Inclinable to honor and advance
The theme of our assembly.
BRUTUS   Which the rather
55 We shall be blessed° to do if he remember   *happy*
A kinder value of the people than
He hath hereto prized them at.
MENENIUS   That's off, that's off.°   *irrelevant*
I would you rather had been silent. Please you
To hear Cominius speak?
BRUTUS   Most willingly,
60 But yet my caution was more pertinent
Than the rebuke you give it.

---

2. Put their bonnets back on (after doffing them as a
gesture of respect).
3. Showing itself to be false.
4. Officers who attended upon magistrates.

5. *Rather our . . . out:* We lack resources for adequate reward, rather than the will to reward him to
the utmost.

MENENIUS   He loves your people,
   But tie him not to be their bedfellow.
   —Worthy Cominius, speak.
           CORIOLANUS *rises and offers° to go away.*   *begins*
              —Nay, keep your place.
FIRST SENATOR   Sit, Coriolanus: never shame to hear
   What you have nobly done.
65 CORIOLANUS   Your honors' pardon,
   I had rather have my wounds to heal again
   Than hear say how I got them.
BRUTUS   Sir, I hope
   My words disbenched° you not?   *unseated*
CORIOLANUS   No, sir. Yet oft,
   When blows have made me stay, I fled from words.
70 You soothed° not, therefore hurt not; but your people,   *flattered*
   I love them as they weigh°—   *deserve*
MENENIUS   Pray now, sit down.
CORIOLANUS   I had rather have one scratch my head i'th' sun
   When the alarum° were struck than idly sit   *battle summons*
   To hear my nothings monstered.[6]   *Exit* CORIOLANUS.
MENENIUS   Masters of the people,
75 Your multiplying spawn° how can he flatter—   *fast-breeding plebeians*
   That's thousand to one good one—when you now see
   He had rather venture all his limbs for honor
   Than one on 's° ears to hear it? —Proceed, Cominius.   *of his*
COMINIUS   I shall lack voice; the deeds of Coriolanus
80 Should not be uttered feebly. It is held
   That valor is the chiefest virtue and
   Most dignifies the haver; if it be,
   The man I speak of cannot in the world
   Be singly counterpoised.° At sixteen years,   *equaled by anyone*
85 When Tarquin made a head for° Rome, he fought   *raised an army against*
   Beyond the mark° of others. Our then dictator,[7]   *reach*
   Whom with all praise I point at, saw him fight
   When with his Amazonian[8] chin he drove
   The bristled lips° before him. He bestrid   *bearded soldiers*
90 An o'erpressed° Roman and i'th' consul's view   *overwhelmed*
   Slew three opposers. Tarquin's self he met
   And struck him on his knee. In that day's feats,
   When he might act the woman in the scene,[9]
   He proved best man i'th' field, and for his meed°   *reward*
95 Was brow-bound with the oak. His pupil age
   Man-entered thus, he waxèd like a sea,
   And in the brunt° of seventeen battles since   *violence*
   He lurched° all swords of the garland. For this last,   *cheated*
   Before and in Corioles, let me say
100 I cannot speak him home.° He stopped the fliers   *praise him enough*
   And by his rare example made the coward
   Turn terror into sport. As weeds before
   A vessel under sail, so men obeyed
   And fell below his stem.° His sword, death's stamp,   *prow*

6. My trivial actions treated as marvels.
7. Roman magistrate with absolute authority, elected during emergencies.

8. Beardless (like a female Amazon warrior).
9. Might be expected to be cowardly (with an allusion to boys acting women's parts in the theater).

105	Where it did mark, it took;[1] from face to foot
	He was a thing of blood whose every motion
	Was timed[2] with dying cries. Alone he entered
	The mortal° gate of th' city, which he painted	*fatal*
	With shunless destiny;[3] aidless came off,
110	And with a sudden reinforcement struck
	Corioles like a planet.[4] Now all's his,
	When by and by the din of war gan° pierce	*began to*
	His ready° sense; then straight his doubled spirit	*alert*
	Requickened° what in flesh was fatigate,°	*Reanimated / exhausted*
115	And to the battle came he, where he did
	Run reeking[5] o'er the lives of men as if
	'Twere perpetual spoil;° and till we called	*slaughter*
	Both field and city ours, he never stood
	To ease his breast with panting.

MENENIUS   Worthy man.

120	FIRST SENATOR He cannot but with measure° fit the honors	*exactly*
	Which we devise him.	

COMINIUS   Our spoils he kicked at°   *spurned*
    And looked upon things precious as° they were   *as if*
    The common muck of the world. He covets less
    Than misery° itself would give, rewards   *poverty*

| 125 | His deeds with doing them, and is content | |
| | To spend the time to° end it. | *merely in order to* |

MENENIUS   He's right noble.
    Let him be called for.

FIRST SENATOR   Call Coriolanus.

FIRST OFFICER   He doth appear.

        Enter CORIOLANUS.

MENENIUS   The Senate, Coriolanus, are well pleased
    To make thee consul.

| 130 | CORIOLANUS   I do owe them still° | *always* |
| | My life and services. | |

MENENIUS   It then remains
    That you do speak to the people.

CORIOLANUS   I do beseech you
    Let me o'erleap that custom, for I cannot
    Put on the gown, stand naked,° and entreat them   *exposed*

| 135 | For my wounds' sake to give their suffrage.° Please you | *vote* |
| | That I may pass this doing. | |

SICINIUS   Sir, the people
    Must have their voices;° neither will they bate°   *votes / forgo*
    One jot of ceremony.

MENENIUS   Put them not to't.°   *Do not defy them*
    Pray you, go fit you° to the custom and   *adapt yourself*

| 140 | Take to you, as your predecessors have, | |
| | Your honor with your form.° | *the custom prescribed you* |

CORIOLANUS   It is a part
    That I shall blush in acting, and might well
    Be taken from the people.

---

1. It made a clear imprint (of death).
2. Rhythmically accompanied.
3. *painted . . . destiny*: covered with the blood of his victims; unable to avoid their fate.
4. Planets were believed to have the power to afflict, or blast, people and places.
5. Steaming (with blood and sweat).

BRUTUS [*to* SICINIUS]   Mark you that?

CORIOLANUS   To brag unto them, "Thus I did, and thus,"
145 Show them th'unaching scars which I should hide,
As if I had received them for the hire
Of their breath° only.   voice

MENENIUS   Do not stand° upon't.   insist
—We recommend° to you, tribunes of the people,   commit
Our purpose° to them, and to our noble consul   proposal
150 Wish we all joy and honor.

SENATORS   To Coriolanus come all joy and honor!
Flourish cornetts, then exeunt [*all except*] SICINIUS
and BRUTUS.

BRUTUS   You see how he intends to use the people.

SICINIUS   May they perceive 's intent! He will require° them   ask from
As if he did contemn° what he requested   scorn that
Should be in them to give.

155 BRUTUS   Come, we'll inform them
Of our proceedings here on th' marketplace;
I know they do attend° us.   [*Exeunt.*]   await

2.3
Enter seven or eight CITIZENS.

FIRST CITIZEN   Once° if he do require our voices, we ought   In short
not to deny him.

SECOND CITIZEN   We may, sir, if we will.

THIRD CITIZEN   We have power in ourselves to do it, but it is a
5   power that we have no power to do,° for if he show us his   no justification to use
wounds and tell us his deeds, we are to put our tongues into
those wounds[1] and speak for them. So if he tell us his noble
deeds, we must also tell him our noble acceptance of them.
Ingratitude is monstrous, and for the multitude to be ingrate-
10   ful were to make a monster of the multitude, of the which
we, being members, should bring ourselves to be monstrous
members.

FIRST CITIZEN   And to make us no better thought of, a little
help will serve;° for once we stood up about the corn, he   it won't take much
15   himself stuck° not to call us the many-headed multitude.   hesitated

THIRD CITIZEN   We have been called so of many, not that our
heads are some brown, some black, some abram,° some   auburn
bald, but that our wits are so diversely colored. And, truly, I
think if all our wits were to issue out of one skull, they would
20   fly east, west, north, south, and their consent of° one direct   agreement to go
way should be at once to all the points o'th' compass.

SECOND CITIZEN   Think you so? Which way do you judge my
wit would fly?

THIRD CITIZEN   Nay, your wit will not so soon out as another
25   man's will: 'tis strongly wedged up in a blockhead. But if it
were at liberty, 'twould sure southward.[2]

SECOND CITIZEN   Why that way?

THIRD CITIZEN   To lose itself in a fog where, being three parts
melted away with rotten° dews, the fourth would return for   unwholesome
30   conscience' sake to help to get thee a wife.

2.3 Location: The marketplace in Rome.   2. The South is associated with plague.
1. That is, let those wounds inspire our voices.

SECOND CITIZEN You are never without your tricks. You may,
you may.°   *(have your joke)*

THIRD CITIZEN Are you all resolved to give your voices? But
that's no matter; the greater part carries it,° I say. If he would   *majority decides*
35 incline to° the people, there was never a worthier man.   *support*

Enter CORIOLANUS *in a gown of humility*[3] [*and a hat*],
with MENENIUS.

Here he comes, and in the gown of humility. Mark his
behavior. We are not to stay all together, but to come by him
where he stands, by ones, by twos, and by threes. He's to
make his requests by particulars,° wherein every one of us   *to individuals*
40 has a single honor in giving him our own voices with our
own tongues. Therefore follow me, and I'll direct you how
you shall go by him.

ALL CITIZENS Content, content.   [*Exeunt* CITIZENS.]

MENENIUS O sir, you are not right. Have you not known
The worthiest men have done't?

45 CORIOLANUS   What must I say?
"I pray, sir?" Plague upon't, I cannot bring
My tongue to such a pace. "Look, sir, my wounds:
I got them in my country's service, when
Some certain of your brethren roared and ran
From th' noise of our own drums."

50 MENENIUS   O me, the gods!
You must not speak of that. You must desire them
To think upon you.

CORIOLANUS   Think upon me? Hang 'em!
I would they would forget me, like the virtues
Which our divines lose by 'em.[4]

MENENIUS   You'll mar all.
55 I'll leave you. Pray you speak to 'em, I pray you,
In wholesome[5] manner.   *Exit.*

CORIOLANUS   Bid them wash their faces
And keep their teeth clean.

Enter three of the CITIZENS.

So, here comes a brace.
—You know the cause, sir, of my standing here.

THIRD CITIZEN We do, sir. Tell us what hath brought you to't.

60 CORIOLANUS Mine own desert.

SECOND CITIZEN Your own desert?

CORIOLANUS Ay, but not mine own desire.

THIRD CITIZEN How not your own desire?

CORIOLANUS No, sir, 'twas never my desire yet to trouble the
65 poor with begging.

THIRD CITIZEN You must think if we give you anything, we
hope to gain by you.

CORIOLANUS Well, then, I pray, your price o'th' consulship?

FIRST CITIZEN The price is to ask it kindly.

70 CORIOLANUS Kindly, sir, I pray let me ha't. I have wounds to
show you, which shall be yours° in private. [*to* SECOND CITI-   *yours to see*
ZEN] Your good voice, sir, what say you?

---

3. Candidates for public office in Rome wore plain
white togas (the word "candidate" derives from Latin
candidus, white).

4. Our priests vainly try to instill in them.
5. Proper (but Coriolanus takes it as "healthy").

SECOND CITIZEN   You shall ha't, worthy sir.

CORIOLANUS   A match,° sir. There's in all two worthy voices   *agreement*
75   begged. I have your alms. Adieu.

THIRD CITIZEN [*to the other* CITIZENS]   But this is something
odd.

SECOND CITIZEN   An° 'twere to give again—but 'tis no matter.   *If*
Exeunt [CITIZENS].
Enter two other CITIZENS.

CORIOLANUS   Pray you now, if it may stand° with the tune of   *accord*
80   your voices that I may be consul, I have here the customary
gown.

FOURTH CITIZEN   You have deserved nobly of your country,
and you have not deserved nobly.

CORIOLANUS   Your enigma?

85   FOURTH CITIZEN   You have been a scourge to her enemies; you
have been a rod to her friends: you have not indeed loved
the common people.

CORIOLANUS   You should account me the more virtuous that
I have not been common° in my love. I will, sir, flatter my   *indiscriminate*
90   sworn brother, the people, to earn a dearer estimation of
them; 'tis° a condition they account gentle.° And since the   *(Flattery) is / noble*
wisdom of their choice is rather to have my hat than my
heart, I will practice the insinuating nod and be off° to them   *take my hat off*
most counterfeitly; that is, sir, I will counterfeit the bewitch-
95   ment° of some popular man° and give it bountiful to the   *charisma / demagogue*
desirers. Therefore beseech you I may be consul.

FIFTH CITIZEN   We hope to find you our friend and therefore
give you our voices heartily.

FOURTH CITIZEN   You have received many wounds for your
100   country.

CORIOLANUS   I will not seal° your knowledge with showing   *confirm*
them. I will make much of your voices and so trouble you no
farther.

BOTH CITIZENS   The gods give you joy, sir, heartily!
[*Exeunt* CITIZENS.]

105   CORIOLANUS   Most sweet voices!
Better it is to die, better to starve,
Than crave the hire which first we do deserve.[6]
Why in this wolvish toge[7] should I stand here
To beg of Hob and Dick[8] that does appear
110   Their needless vouches?°   Custom calls me to't.   *votes*
What custom wills, in all things should we do't,
The dust on antique time would lie unswept
And mountainous error be too highly heaped
For truth to o'erpeer.[9]   Rather than fool it° so,   *act the fool*
115   Let the high office and the honor go
To one that would do thus. I am half through;
The one part suffered, the other will I do.
Enter three CITIZENS *more.*
Here come more voices.

6. Than beg for the wages we have already earned.   humility).
7. F has "woolvish toge"; some editors read "wolvish"   8. Any Tom, Dick, or Harry.
or "wool-less." The "toge" is the toga (gown of   9. To look over the top.

Your voices? For your voices I have fought,
120 Watched° for your voices; for your voices bear   *Gone sleepless*
Of wounds two dozen odd. Battles thrice six
I have seen and heard of. For your voices
Have done many things, some less, some more.
Your voices? Indeed I would be consul.

125 SIXTH CITIZEN   He has done nobly and cannot go without any
honest man's voice.

SEVENTH CITIZEN   Therefore let him be consul. The gods give
him joy and make him good friend to the people!

ALL CITIZENS   Amen, amen. God save thee, noble consul!
                          [*Exeunt* CITIZENS.]

130 CORIOLANUS   Worthy voices.
                  Enter MENENIUS, *with* BRUTUS *and* SICINIUS.

MENENIUS   You have stood your limitation,° and the tribunes   *allotted time*
Endue° you with the people's voice. Remains   *Invest*
That, in th'official marks° invested, you   *insignia*
Anon° do meet the Senate.   *Immediately*

CORIOLANUS   Is this done?

135 SICINIUS   The custom of request° you have discharged: *requesting votes*
The people do admit you and are summoned
To meet anon upon your approbation.[1]

CORIOLANUS   Where? At the Senate-house?

SICINIUS   There, Coriolanus.

CORIOLANUS   May I change these garments?

SICINIUS   You may, sir.

140 CORIOLANUS   That I'll straight do and, knowing myself again,
Repair to th' Senate-house.

MENENIUS   I'll keep you company. [*to the tribunes*] Will you along?

BRUTUS   We stay here for the people.

SICINIUS   Fare you well.
                  Exeunt. CORIOLANUS *and* MENENIUS
He has it now, and by his looks methinks
'Tis warm at 's heart.[2]

145 BRUTUS   With a proud heart he wore
His humble weeds.° Will you dismiss the people?   *garments*
                  Enter the PLEBEIANS.[3]

SICINIUS   How now, my masters, have you chose this man?

FIRST CITIZEN   He has our voices, sir.

BRUTUS   We pray the gods he may deserve your loves.

150 SECOND CITIZEN   Amen, sir. To my poor unworthy notice
He mocked us when he begged our voices.

THIRD CITIZEN   Certainly he flouted us downright.

FIRST CITIZEN   No, 'tis his kind of speech; he did not mock us.

SECOND CITIZEN   Not one amongst us, save yourself, but says

155 He used us scornfully. He should have showed us
His marks of merit: wounds received for 's country.

SICINIUS   Why, so he did, I am sure.

ALL CITIZENS   No, no. No man saw 'em.

THIRD CITIZEN   He said he had wounds which he could show in private
And with his hat, thus waving it in scorn,

---

1. For your ratification as consul.
2. That is, he's well pleased.
3. TEXTUAL COMMENT The Folio has *"Plebeians,"* not

"*Citizens*"; the terms used for the upper and lower
classes in *Coriolanus* are inconsistent. For the connotations of the different terms, see Digital Edition TC 7.

160 "I would be consul," says he: "Agèd custom,
But by your voices, will not so permit me.
Your voices therefore." When we granted that,
Here was, "I thank you for your voices. Thank you,
Your most sweet voices. Now you have left your voices,
165 I have no further° with you." Was not this mockery?   *(to do)*
SICINIUS   Why either were you ignorant° to see't,   *were you either unable*
Or, seeing it, of such childish friendliness
To yield your voices?
BRUTUS   Could you not have told him
As you were lessoned? When he had no power,
170 But was a petty servant to the state,
He was your enemy, ever spake against
Your liberties and the charters that you bear
I'th' body of the weal;° and now, arriving°   *state / reaching*
A place of potency and sway o'th' state,
175 If he should still malignantly remain
Fast foe to th' plebeii,° your voices might   *common people*
Be curses to yourselves. You should have said
That as his worthy deeds did claim no less
Than what he stood for,° so his gracious nature   *the office he sought*
180 Would think upon you for your voices and
Translate° his malice towards you into love,   *Change*
Standing your friendly lord.
SICINIUS   Thus to have said,
As you were fore-advised, had touched° his spirit   *tested*
And tried his inclination; from him plucked
185 Either his gracious promise, which you might—
As cause had called you up—have held him to,
Or else it would have galled his surly nature,
Which easily endures not article,°   *stipulation*
Tying him to aught. So putting him to rage,
190 You should have ta'en th'advantage of his choler°   *wrath*
And passed him unelected.
BRUTUS   Did you perceive
He did solicit you in free contempt
When he did need your loves, and do you think
That his contempt shall not be bruising to you
195 When he hath power to crush? Why, had your bodies
No heart among you? Or had you tongues to cry
Against the rectorship of judgment?°   *rule of common sense*
SICINIUS   Have you
Ere now denied the asker, and now again,
Of him that did not ask but mock, bestow
Your sued-for tongues?
200 THIRD CITIZEN   He's not confirmed. We may
Deny him yet.
SECOND CITIZEN   And will deny him:
I'll have five hundred voices of that sound.
FIRST CITIZEN   I twice five hundred, and their friends to piece° 'em.   *add to*
BRUTUS   Get you hence instantly, and tell those friends
205 They have chose a consul that will from them take
Their liberties, make them of no more voice
Than dogs that are as often beat for barking

As therefore kept to do so.

SICINIUS   Let them assemble,
And on a safer° judgment all revoke   *sounder*
210   Your ignorant election. Enforce° his pride   *Emphasize*
And his old hate unto you. Besides, forget not
With what contempt he wore the humble weed,
How in his suit° he scorned you; but your loves,   *petition; apparel*
Thinking upon his services, took from you
215   Th'apprehension° of his present portance,°   *perception / demeanor*
Which most gibingly,° ungravely, he did fashion   *mockingly*
After the inveterate hate he bears you.

BRUTUS   Lay
A fault on us, your tribunes, that we labored,
No impediment between,[4] but that you must
Cast your election on him.

220   SICINIUS   Say you chose him
More after our commandment than as guided
By your own true affections, and that your minds,
Preoccupied with what you rather must do
Than what you should, made you against the grain
225   To voice him consul. Lay the fault on us.

BRUTUS   Ay, spare us not. Say we read lectures to you
How youngly he began to serve his country,
How long continued, and what stock he springs of,
The noble house o'th' Martians, from whence came
230   That Ancus Martius, Numa's daughter's son,
Who after great Hostilius here was king;
Of the same house Publius and Quintus were,
That our best water brought by conduits hither,
And Censorinus that was so surnamed,[5]
235   And nobly namèd so, twice being censor,[6]
Was his great ancestor.

SICINIUS   One thus descended,
That hath beside well in his person wrought
To be set high in place, we did commend
To your remembrances; but you have found,
240   Scaling° his present bearing with his past,   *Weighing*
That he's your fixèd enemy, and revoke
Your sudden° approbation.   *hasty*

BRUTUS   Say you ne'er had done't—
Harp on that still—but by our putting on,°   *instigation*
And presently, when you have drawn° your number,   *gathered*
Repair to th' Capitol.

245   ALL CITIZENS   We will so: almost all
Repent in their election.   *Exeunt* PLEBEIANS.

BRUTUS   Let them go on:
This mutiny were better put in hazard°   *risked*
Than stay,° past doubt, for greater.   *await*
If, as his nature is, he fall in rage

---

4. *we . . . between:* we refused to allow anything to
stand in the way.
5. TEXTUAL COMMENT A line is missing in F; for a suggestion of what it might be, see Digital Edition TC 8.
6. Roman magistrate who supervised public morals
and drew up the census.

250   With their refusal, both observe and answer
     The vantage of[7] his anger.
SICINIUS   To th' Capitol, come.
     We will be there before the stream o'th' people;
     And this shall seem, as partly 'tis, their own,
     Which we have goaded onward.   *Exeunt.*

3.1

Cornetts. Enter CORIOLANUS, MENENIUS, *all
the gentry,*° COMINIUS, *Titus* LARTIUS, *and other*   *patricians*
SENATORS.

CORIOLANUS   Tullus Aufidius then had made new head?°   *raised a new army*
LARTIUS   He had, my lord, and that it was which caused
     Our swifter composition.[1]
CORIOLANUS   So then the Volsces stand but as at first,
5   Ready when time shall prompt them to make road
     Upon's again.
COMINIUS   They are worn,° Lord Consul, so   *exhausted*
     That we shall hardly in our ages see
     Their banners wave again.
CORIOLANUS   Saw you Aufidius?
LARTIUS   On safeguard° he came to me, and did curse   *Under safe-conduct*
10   Against the Volsces for they had so vilely
     Yielded the town. He is retired to Antium.
CORIOLANUS   Spoke he of me?
LARTIUS   He did, my lord.
CORIOLANUS   How? What?
LARTIUS   How often he had met you sword to sword;
     That of all things upon the earth he hated
15   Your person most; that he would pawn his fortunes
     To hopeless restitution,[2] so he might
     Be called your vanquisher.
CORIOLANUS   At Antium lives he?
LARTIUS   At Antium.
CORIOLANUS   I wish I had a cause to seek him there,
20   To oppose his hatred fully. Welcome home.

Enter SICINIUS *and* BRUTUS.

     Behold, these are the tribunes of the people,
     The tongues o'th' common mouth. I do despise them,
     For they do prank them° in authority   *adorn themselves*
     Against all noble sufferance.[3]
SICINIUS   Pass no further.
CORIOLANUS   Ha? What is that?
25 BRUTUS   It will be dangerous to go on.
     No further.
CORIOLANUS   What makes this change?
MENENIUS   The matter?
COMINIUS   Hath he not passed° the noble and the common?   *been accepted by*
BRUTUS   Cominius, no.
CORIOLANUS   Have I had children's voices?

---

7. *answer the vantage of*: seize the opportunity provided by.
3.1 Location: A street in Rome.
1. Agreement (about returning Corioles to the

Volscians).
2. Without hope of recovery.
3. Beyond what the nobility can endure.

FIRST SENATOR　Tribunes, give way. He shall to th' marketplace.
BRUTUS　The people are incensed against him.
30　SICINIUS　　　　　　　　　　　　　　　Stop,
　　Or all will fall in broil.°　　　　　　　　　　　　　　　　*turmoil*
　　CORIOLANUS　　　　　　　Are these your herd?
　　Must these have voices, that can yield them now
　　And straight° disclaim their tongues? What are your offices?　　*immediately*
　　You being their mouths, why rule you not their teeth?
　　Have you not set them on?
35　MENENIUS　　　　　　　　　　Be calm, be calm.
　　CORIOLANUS　It is a purposed° thing and grows by plot　　*deliberate*
　　To curb the will of the nobility.
　　Suffer't, and live with such as cannot rule
　　Nor ever will be ruled.
　　BRUTUS　　　　　　　　　Call't not a plot.
40　The people cry you mocked them, and of late,
　　When corn was given them gratis, you repined,
　　Scandaled° the suppliants for the people, called them　　*Defamed*
　　Time-pleasers, flatterers, foes to nobleness.
　　CORIOLANUS　Why, this was known before.
　　BRUTUS　　　　　　　　　　　　Not to them all.
　　CORIOLANUS　Have you informed them sithence?°　　*since*
45　BRUTUS　　　　　　　　　　　　How? I inform them?
　　COMINIUS　You are like to do such business.
　　BRUTUS　Not unlike each way to better yours.[4]
　　CORIOLANUS　Why then should I be consul? By yond clouds,
　　Let me deserve so ill as you, and make me
　　Your fellow tribune.
50　SICINIUS　　　　　　　　You show too much of that°　　*(quality)*
　　For which the people stir.° If you will pass　　*are aroused*
　　To where you are bound,[5] you must enquire your way,
　　Which you are out of,° with a gentler spirit,　　*strayed from*
　　Or never be so noble as a consul,
　　Nor yoke with him° for tribune.　　*(Brutus)*
55　MENENIUS　　　　　　　　Let's be calm.
　　COMINIUS　The people are abused, set on. This palt'ring°　　*trifling*
　　Becomes not Rome, nor has Coriolanus
　　Deserved this so dishonored rub,° laid falsely　　*shameful obstruction*
　　I'th' plain way of his merit.
　　CORIOLANUS　　　　　　　Tell me of corn!
60　This was my speech, and I will speak't again—
　　MENENIUS　Not now, not now.
　　FIRST SENATOR　　　　　　Not in this heat, sir, now.
　　CORIOLANUS　Now as I live, I will. My nobler friends,
　　I crave their pardons. For the mutable,
　　Rank-scented meinie,° let them regard me　　*multitude*
65　As I do not flatter and therein behold
　　Themselves. I say again, in soothing them,
　　We nourish gainst our Senate the cockle°　　*weed*
　　Of rebellion, insolence, sedition,

---

4. *Not unlike . . . yours:* Not unlikely in every respect　　5. That is, the marketplace; the consulship.
to do better than you.

Which we ourselves have plowed for, sowed, and scattered,
70   By mingling them with us, the honored number,
Who lack not virtue, no, nor power, but that
Which they have given to beggars.
MENENIUS   Well, no more.
FIRST SENATOR   No more words, we beseech you.
CORIOLANUS   How? No more?
As for my country I have shed my blood,
75   Not fearing outward force, so shall my lungs
Coin words till their decay against those measles°   *skin eruptions*
Which we disdain should tetter° us, yet sought   *infect*
The very way to catch them.
BRUTUS   You speak o'th' people
As if you were a god to punish, not
A man of their infirmity.°   *with the same frailty*
80 SICINIUS   'Twere well
We let the people know't.
MENENIUS   What, what? His choler?
CORIOLANUS   Choler? Were I as patient as the midnight sleep,
By Jove, 'twould be my mind.°   *opinion*
SICINIUS   It is a mind
That shall remain a poison where it is,
Not poison any further.
85 CORIOLANUS   "Shall remain"?
Hear you this Triton[6] of the minnows? Mark you
His absolute "shall"?
COMINIUS   'Twas from the canon.°   *out of order*
CORIOLANUS   "Shall"?
O good but most unwise patricians, why—
You grave but reckless senators—have you thus
90   Given Hydra[7] here to choose an officer
That with his peremptory "shall," being but
The horn and noise° o'th' monster's, wants not spirit   *noisy horn*
To say he'll turn your current° in a ditch   *stream of power*
And make your channel his? If he have power,
95   Then vail° your ignorance; if none, awake°   *bow down / awake from*
Your dangerous lenity.° If you are learned,   *forbearance*
Be not as common fools; if you are not,
Let them have cushions by° you. You are plebeians   *Senate seats beside*
If they be senators; and they are no less
100   When, both your voices blended, the great'st taste
Most palates theirs.[8] They choose their magistrate,
And such a one as he, who puts his "shall,"
His popular° "shall," against a graver bench[9]   *plebeian*
Than ever frowned in Greece. By Jove himself,
105   It makes the consuls base, and my soul aches
To know, when two authorities are up°—   *established*
Neither supreme—how soon confusion°   *chaos*
May enter twixt the gap of both and take°   *overthrow*
The one by th'other.
COMINIUS   Well, on to th' marketplace.

---

6. Neptune's trumpeter, a minor sea god.
7. Mythical many-headed snake, a common figure
for the multitude.

8. *the great'st . . . theirs:* the result tastes more like
(or appeals more to) them than you.
9. A more respected body.

110 CORIOLANUS Whoever gave that counsel to give forth
The corn o'th' storehouse gratis, as 'twas used
Sometime in Greece—
MENENIUS   Well, well, no more of that.
CORIOLANUS Though there the people had more absolute power—
I say they nourished disobedience, fed
The ruin of the state.
115 BRUTUS   Why shall the people give
One that speaks thus their voice?
CORIOLANUS   I'll give my reasons,
More worthier than their voices. They know the corn
Was not our recompense,° resting well assured   a payment from us
They ne'er did service for't: being pressed° to th' war,   conscripted
120 Even when the navel° of the state was touched,°   center / threatened
They would not thread° the gates. This kind of service   go through
Did not deserve corn gratis. Being i'th' war,
Their mutinies and revolts, wherein they showed
Most valor, spoke not° for them. Th'accusation   did not speak well
125 Which they have often made against the Senate,
All cause unborn,° could never be the native°   Without any cause / source
Of our so frank° donation. Well, what then?   liberal
How shall this bosom multiplied¹ digest
The Senate's courtesy? Let deeds express
130 What's like to be their words: "We did request it;
We are the greater poll,° and in true fear   number
They gave us our demands." Thus we debase
The nature of our seats° and make the rabble   senatorial positions
Call our cares "fears," which will in time
135 Break ope the locks o'th' Senate and bring in
The crows to peck the eagles.²
MENENIUS   Come, enough.
BRUTUS Enough, with over-measure.
CORIOLANUS   No, take more!
What may be sworn by, both divine and human,
Seal° what I end withal!° This double worship,³   Authorize / with
140 Where one part does disdain with cause, the other
Insult° without all reason; where gentry, title, wisdom   Behave insolently
Cannot conclude but by the yea and no
Of general ignorance, it must omit°   neglect
Real necessities and give way the while
145 To unstable slightness.° Purpose° so barred, it follows   trifling / Purposefulness
Nothing is done to purpose.° Therefore, beseech you—   any effect
You that will be less fearful than discreet,°   judicious
That love the fundamental part of state
More than you doubt the change on't,⁴ that prefer
150 A noble life before a long, and wish
To jump° a body with a dangerous physic°   risk / medicine
That's sure of death without it—at once pluck out
The multitudinous tongue;⁵ let them not lick

---

1. *bosom multiplied*: multifarious belly (of the many-headed multitude).
2. The eagle not only is associated with courage and nobility but is the symbol of Roman power.
3. Divided magistracy.
4. You fear changing it (by repudiating the tribunes).
5. The tongue of the multitude, as represented by the tribunes.

The sweet which is their poison. Your dishonor
155 Mangles true judgment and bereaves the state
Of that integrity which should become't,
Not having the power to do the good it would
For° th'ill which doth control't.[6]   *Because of*
BRUTUS   He's said enough.
SICINIUS   He's spoken like a traitor and shall answer
As traitors do.
160 CORIOLANUS   Thou wretch, despite° o'erwhelm thee!   *contempt*
What should the people do with these bald° tribunes,   *paltry*
On whom depending, their obedience fails
To th' greater bench?° In a rebellion,   *(of the Senate)*
When what's not meet but what must be was law,[7]
165 Then were they chosen. In a better hour,
Let what is meet be said it must be meet[8]
And throw their power i'th' dust.
BRUTUS   Manifest treason.
SICINIUS   This a consul? No.
BRUTUS   The aediles,° ho!   *tribune's officers*
     Enter an AEDILE.
             Let him be apprehended.
SICINIUS   Go call the people,   [*Exit* AEDILE.]
170 [*to* CORIOLANUS]   in whose name myself
Attach° thee as a traitorous innovator,°   *Arrest / revolutionary*
A foe to th' public weal. Obey, I charge thee,
And follow to thine answer.°   *trial*
     [*He lays hold of* CORIOLANUS.]
CORIOLANUS   Hence, old goat!
ALL PATRICIANS   We'll surety him.°   *ensure his compliance*
COMINIUS [*to* SICINIUS]   Aged sir, hands off.
175 CORIOLANUS   Hence, rotten thing, or I shall shake thy bones
Out of thy garments.
SICINIUS   Help, ye citizens!
     Enter a rabble of PLEBEIANS *with the* AEDILES.
MENENIUS   On both sides more respect.
SICINIUS   Here's he that would
Take from you all your power.
BRUTUS   Seize him, aediles!
ALL CITIZENS   Down with him, down with him!
SECOND SENATOR   Weapons, weapons, weapons!
     They all bustle about CORIOLANUS.
180 ALL [*variously*]   —Tribunes! —Patricians! —Citizens! —What ho!
—Sicinius! —Brutus! —Coriolanus! —Citizens!
—Peace, peace, peace! —Stay, hold, peace!
MENENIUS   What is about to be? I am out of breath.
Confusion's° near; I cannot speak. —You, tribunes   *Chaos is*
185 To th' people! —Coriolanus, patience!
—Speak, good Sicinius.
SICINIUS   Hear me, people. Peace!
ALL CITIZENS   Let's hear our tribune. Peace! Speak, speak, speak!
SICINIUS   You are at point° to lose your liberties: *about*

---

6. Overpower it.
7. *When . . . law:* When necessity rather than propri-

ety prevailed. *meet:* proper.
8. Let what is proper be declared necessary.

Martius would have all from you—Martius,
Whom late you have named for consul.
190 MENENIUS   Fie, fie, fie,
This is the way to kindle, not to quench.
FIRST SENATOR   To unbuild the city and to lay all flat.
SICINIUS   What is the city but the people?
ALL CITIZENS   True, the people are the city.
195 BRUTUS   By the consent of all, we were established
The people's magistrates.
ALL CITIZENS   You so remain.
MENENIUS   And so are like to do.
COMINIUS   That is the way to lay the city flat,
To bring the roof to the foundation
200 And bury all, which yet distinctly ranges[9]
In heaps and piles of ruin.
SICINIUS   This deserves death.
BRUTUS   Or° let us stand to our authority,   *Either*
Or let us lose it. We do here pronounce,
Upon the part o'th' people, in whose power
205 We were elected theirs, Martius is worthy
Of present° death.   *immediate*
SICINIUS   Therefore lay hold of him.
Bear him to th' Rock Tarpeian,[1] and from thence
Into destruction cast him.
BRUTUS   Aediles, seize him.
ALL CITIZENS   Yield, Martius, yield!
MENENIUS   Hear me one word; beseech
You, tribunes, hear me but a word.
210 AEDILES   Peace, peace.
MENENIUS [*to* BRUTUS]   Be that you seem, truly your country's friend,
And temp'rately proceed to what you would
Thus violently redress.
BRUTUS   Sir, those cold ways,
That seem like prudent helps, are very poisonous
215 Where the disease is violent. —Lay hands upon him
And bear him to the Rock.
                CORIOLANUS *draws his sword.*
CORIOLANUS   No, I'll die here.
There's some among you have beheld me fighting;
Come try upon yourselves what you have seen me.
MENENIUS   Down with that sword. —Tribunes, withdraw
awhile.
BRUTUS   Lay hands upon him.
220 MENENIUS   Help Martius, help!
You that be noble, help him, young and old!
ALL CITIZENS   Down with him! Down with him!
                In this mutiny, the tribunes, the AEDILES, *and the*
                people are beat in° [*and*] *exeunt.*   *forced offstage*
MENENIUS [*to* CORIOLANUS]   Go, get you to our house; be
gone, away.
All will be naught else.

---

9. Extends in orderly ranks.
1. The cliff from which murderers and traitors were hurled to their deaths.

SECOND SENATOR	Get you gone.	
CORIOLANUS	Stand fast.	

225 We have as many friends as enemies.

MENENIUS   Shall it be put to that?

FIRST SENATOR   The gods forbid!
—I prithee,° noble friend, home to thy house.   *pray thee (to go)*
Leave us to cure this cause.°   *disease*

MENENIUS   For 'tis a sore upon us
You cannot tent° yourself. Be gone, beseech you.   *treat*

230 COMINIUS   Come, sir, along with us.[2]

CORIOLANUS   I would they were barbarians, as they are,
Though in Rome littered;° not Romans, as they are not,   *born (like animals)*
Though calved i'th' porch o'th' Capitol.

MENENIUS   Be gone!
Put not your worthy° rage into your tongue.   *justifiable*
One time will owe° another.   *occasion will compensate*

235 CORIOLANUS   On fair ground
I could beat forty of them.

MENENIUS   I could myself
Take up a brace o'th' best of them—yea, the two tribunes.

COMINIUS   But now 'tis odds beyond arithmetic,°   *calculation*
And manhood° is called foolery when it stands   *courage*
240 Against a falling fabric.° Will you hence   *building*
Before the tag° return, whose rage doth rend   *rabble*
Like interrupted° waters and o'erbear   *overflowing*
What they are used to bear?[3]

MENENIUS   Pray you, be gone.
I'll try whether my old wit be in request
245 With those that have but little. This must be patched
With cloth of any color.[4]

COMINIUS   Nay, come away.

Exeunt CORIOLANUS *and* COMINIUS [*with other*
PATRICIANS].

A PATRICIAN   This man has marred his fortune.

MENENIUS   His nature is too noble for the world.
He would not flatter Neptune for his trident
250 Or Jove for 's power to thunder. His heart's his mouth:
What his breast forges, that his tongue must vent,
And, being angry, does forget that ever
He heard the name of death.

A noise within.

Here's goodly work.

A PATRICIAN   I would they were abed.

255 MENENIUS   I would they were in Tiber! What the vengeance,
Could he not speak 'em fair?°   *speak to them politely*

Enter BRUTUS *and* SICINIUS *with the rabble* [*of*
CITIZENS] *again.*

SICINIUS   Where is this viper
That would depopulate the city and
Be every man himself?

---

2. TEXTUAL COMMENT The speech prefixes in the
next several lines are confused in F; Digital Edition
TC 9 explains how the editor has sorted them out.
3. *o'erbear . . . bear:* overpower that to which they

ordinarily submit.
4. *patched . . . color:* mended by whatever means
possible.

MENENIUS   You worthy tribunes—
SICINIUS   He shall be thrown down the Tarpeian Rock
260   With rigorous hands. He hath resisted law,
       And therefore law shall scorn° him further trial   *deny*
       Than the severity of the public° power   *commoners'*
       Which he so sets at naught.
FIRST CITIZEN   He shall well know
       The noble tribunes are the people's mouths,
       And we their hands.
ALL CITIZENS   He shall sure on't.
MENENIUS   Sir, sir—
265 SICINIUS   Peace!
MENENIUS   Do not cry havoc⁵ where you should but hunt
       With modest warrant.
SICINIUS   Sir, how com'st that you
       Have holp to make this rescue?⁶
MENENIUS   Hear me speak.
       As I do know the consul's worthiness,
       So can I name his faults.
270 SICINIUS   Consul? What consul?
MENENIUS   The consul Coriolanus.
BRUTUS   He consul?
ALL CITIZENS   No, no, no, no, no!
MENENIUS   If, by the tribunes' leave and yours, good people,
       I may be heard, I would crave a word or two,
275   The which shall turn° you to no further harm   *bring*
       Than so much loss of time.
SICINIUS   Speak briefly, then,
       For we are peremptory to dispatch
       This viperous traitor. To eject him hence
       Were but one danger, and to keep him here
280   Our certain death. Therefore it is decreed
       He dies tonight.
MENENIUS   Now the good gods forbid
       That our renownèd Rome, whose gratitude
       Towards her deservèd° children is enrolled   *deserving*
       In Jove's own book, like an unnatural dam°   *mother*
285   Should now eat up her own!
SICINIUS   He's a disease that must be cut away.
MENENIUS   Oh, he's a limb that has but a disease:
       Mortal to cut it off; to cure it easy.
       What has he done to Rome that's worthy death?
290   Killing our enemies, the blood he hath lost—
       Which I dare vouch is more than that he hath
       By many an ounce—he dropped it for his country;
       And what is left, to lose it by his country
       Were to us all that do't and suffer° it   *allow*
       A brand° to th'end o'th' world.   *stigma*
295 SICINIUS   This is clean cam.°   *completely perverse*
BRUTUS   Merely° awry. When he did love his country,   *Absolutely*
       It honored him.

---

5. "Havoc" was the signal to an army to pillage.
6. Have helped to remove this prisoner from custody ("make rescue" is a legal term).

SICINIUS   The service of the foot,
  Being once gangrened, is not then respected
  For what before it was.
BRUTUS   We'll hear no more.
300 Pursue him to his house and pluck him thence,
  Lest his infection, being of catching nature,
  Spread further.
MENENIUS   One word more, one word!
  This tiger-footed rage, when it shall find
  The harm of unscanned° swiftness, will, too late,   *heedless*
305 Tie leaden pounds° to 's heels. Proceed by process,°   *weights / due process*
  Lest parties°—as he is beloved—break out   *factions*
  And sack great Rome with Romans.
BRUTUS   If it were so—
SICINIUS What do ye talk?
  Have we not had a taste of his obedience?
310 Our aediles smote, ourselves resisted? Come.
MENENIUS Consider this: he has been bred i'th' wars
  Since 'a could draw a sword and is ill-schooled
  In bolted[7] language; meal and bran° together   *flour and husks*
  He throws without distinction. Give me leave,
315 I'll go to him and undertake to bring him
  Where he shall answer by a lawful form,
  In peace, to his utmost peril.[8]
FIRST SENATOR   Noble tribunes,
  It is the humane way. The other course
  Will prove too bloody, and the end of it
  Unknown to the beginning.
320 SICINIUS   Noble Menenius,
  Be you then as the people's officer.
  [*to the* CITIZENS] Masters, lay down your weapons.
BRUTUS   Go not home.
SICINIUS Meet on the marketplace. [*to* MENENIUS] We'll
    attend° you there,   *await*
  Where, if you bring not Martius, we'll proceed
  In our first way.
325 MENENIUS   I'll bring him to you.
  [*to the* SENATORS] Let me desire your company. He must come,
  Or what is worst will follow.
FIRST SENATOR   Pray you, let's to him.   *Exeunt.*

3.2
Enter CORIOLANUS *with* NOBLES.
CORIOLANUS Let them pull all about mine ears, present me
  Death on the wheel or at wild horses' heels,
  Or pile ten hills on the Tarpeian Rock,
  That the precipitation° might down stretch   *steepness*
5 Below the beam of sight, yet will I still
  Be thus to them.
       Enter VOLUMNIA.
A NOBLE   You do the nobler.
CORIOLANUS I muse° my mother   *wonder that*

7. Sifted; that is, carefully considered.   **3.2** Location: Coriolanus's house.
8. Even at peril of his life.

Does not approve me further, who was wont
To call them woolen° vassals, things created °coarsely clad
10   To buy and sell with groats,° to show bare heads °fourpenny pieces
In congregations, to yawn, be still, and wonder
When one but of my ordinance° stood up °rank
To speak of peace or war. [to VOLUMNIA] I talk of you.
Why did you wish me milder? Would you have me
15   False to my nature? Rather say I play
The man I am.
VOLUMNIA   O sir, sir, sir,
I would have had you put your power well on
Before you had worn it out.
CORIOLANUS   Let go.° °Stop
VOLUMNIA   You might have been enough the man you are
20   With striving less to be so. Lesser had been
The taxings° of your dispositions if °challenging
You had not showed them how ye were disposed
Ere they lacked° power to cross you. °Before they lost
CORIOLANUS   Let them hang.
VOLUMNIA   Ay, and burn too.
        Enter MENENIUS *with the* SENATORS.
25   MENENIUS   Come, come, you have been too rough, something
        too rough.
    You must return and mend it.
FIRST SENATOR   There's no remedy,
    Unless, by not so doing, our good city
    Cleave in the midst and perish.
VOLUMNIA   Pray be counseled.
    I have a heart as little apt as yours,
30   But yet a brain that leads my use of anger
    To better vantage.
MENENIUS   Well said, noble woman.
    Before he should thus stoop to th' herd, but that
    The violent fit o'th' time craves it as physic° °medicine
    For the whole state, I would put mine armor on,
    Which I can scarcely bear.
35   CORIOLANUS   What must I do?
MENENIUS   Return to th' tribunes.
CORIOLANUS   Well, what then? What then?
MENENIUS   Repent what you have spoke.
CORIOLANUS   For them? I cannot do it to the gods;
    Must I then do't to them?
VOLUMNIA   You are too absolute,° °inflexible
40   Though therein you can never be too noble,
    But when extremities° speak. I have heard you say °extreme situations
    Honor and policy,° like unsevered friends, °tactical shrewdness
    I'th' war do grow together. Grant that, and tell me
    In peace what each of them by th'other lose
    That they combine not there?
CORIOLANUS   Tush, tush.
45   MENENIUS   A good demand.° °question
VOLUMNIA   If it be honor in your wars to seem
    The same° you are not, which for your best ends °That which
    You adopt your policy, how is it less or worse
    That it° shall hold companionship in peace °(dissimulation)

50	With honor as in war, since that to both	
	It stands in like request?°	*need*
	CORIOLANUS Why force° you this?	*urge*
	VOLUMNIA Because that now it lies you on to speak	
	To th' people, not by your own instruction,°	*conviction*
	Nor by th' matter which your heart prompts you,	
55	But with such words that are but roted° in	*memorized*
	Your tongue, though but bastards and syllables	
	Of no allowance to¹ your bosom's truth.	
	Now, this no more dishonors you at all	
	Than to take in° a town with gentle words,	*capture*
60	Which else would put you to your fortune² and	
	The hazard of much blood.	
	I would dissemble with my nature where	
	My fortunes and my friends at stake required	
	I should do so in honor. I am in this°	*I speak in this for*
65	Your wife, your son, these senators, the nobles;	
	And you will rather show our general° louts	*common*
	How you can frown than spend a fawn° upon 'em	*cringing courtesy*
	For the inheritance° of their loves and safeguard	*acquisition*
	Of what that want° might ruin.	*lack (of their loves)*
	MENENIUS Noble lady!	
70	[*to* CORIOLANUS] Come, go with us. Speak fair.	
	You may salve° so,	*smooth over*
	Not what is dangerous present, but the loss	
	Of what is past.³	
	VOLUMNIA I prithee now, my son,	
	Go to them with this bonnet° in thy hand,	*hat*
	And thus far having stretched it—here be with them,	
75	Thy knee bussing° the stones; for in such business	*kissing*
	Action is eloquence, and the eyes of th'ignorant	
	More learnèd than the ears—waving° thy head,	*repeatedly bowing*
	Which often thus correcting thy stout heart,	
	Now humble⁴ as the ripest mulberry	
80	That will not hold the handling; or say to them	
	Thou art their soldier and, being bred in broils,°	*tumults*
	Hast not the soft way which, thou dost confess,	
	Were fit for thee to use as they to claim°	*for them to expect*
	In asking their good loves, but thou wilt frame	
85	Thyself, forsooth, hereafter theirs so far	
	As thou hast power and person.°	*ability and authority*
	MENENIUS This but done,	
	Even as she speaks, why, their hearts were yours,	
	For they have pardons, being asked, as free	
	As words to little purpose.	
	VOLUMNIA Prithee now,	
90	Go, and be ruled, although I know thou hadst rather	
	Follow thine enemy in a fiery gulf	
	Than flatter him in a bower.°	*arbor*
	Enter COMINIUS.	
	Here is Cominius.	

---

1. *bastards . . . to:* illegitimate words not acknowledged by.
2. *put . . . fortune:* force you to take your chances (in battle).
3. *Not . . . past:* Not only the present danger, but what was lost before.
4. Malleable (or possibly a verb, "let droop").

COMINIUS   I have been i'th' marketplace, and, sir, 'tis fit
  You make strong party,° or defend yourself   *gather strong support*
95   By calmness or by absence. All's in anger.
MENENIUS   Only fair speech.
COMINIUS   I think 'twill serve, if he
  Can thereto frame his spirit.
VOLUMNIA   He must, and will.
  —Prithee now, say you will and go about it.
CORIOLANUS   Must I go show them my unbarbed sconce?°   *unhelmeted head*
    Must I
100   With my base tongue give to my noble heart
  A lie that it must bear? Well, I will do't.
  Yet were there but this single plot° to lose,   *(Coriolanus's body)*
  This mold° of Martius, they to dust should grind it   *form; earth*
  And throw't against the wind. To th' marketplace.
105   You have put me now to such a part which never
  I shall discharge to th' life.°   *perform convincingly*
COMINIUS   Come, come, we'll prompt you.
VOLUMNIA   I prithee now, sweet son, as thou hast said
  My praises made thee first a soldier, so
  To have my praise for this, perform a part
  Thou hast not done before.
110   CORIOLANUS   Well, I must do't.
  Away, my disposition, and possess me
  Some harlot's[5] spirit. My throat of war be turned,
  Which choired° with my drum, into a pipe   *harmonized*
  Small as an eunuch or the virgin voice
115   That babies lull asleep. The smiles of knaves
  Tent° in my cheeks, and schoolboys' tears take up   *Encamp*
  The glasses° of my sight. A beggar's tongue   *windows*
  Make motion through my lips, and my armed knees,
  Who bowed but in my stirrup, bend like his
120   That hath received an alms. I will not do't,
  Lest I surcease° to honor mine own truth   *cease*
  And by my body's action teach my mind
  A most inherent° baseness.   *fixed*
VOLUMNIA   At thy choice, then.
  To beg of thee, it is my more dishonor
125   Than thou of them. Come all to ruin. Let
  Thy mother rather feel° thy pride than fear   *suffer*
  Thy dangerous stoutness,° for I mock at death   *stubbornness*
  With as big heart as thou. Do as thou list.°   *wish*
  Thy valiantness was mine: thou suck'st it from me.
  But owe° thy pride thyself.   *own*
130   CORIOLANUS   Pray be content.
  Mother, I am going to the marketplace.
  Chide me no more. I'll mountebank[6] their loves,
  Cog° their hearts from them, and come home beloved   *Wheedle*
  Of all the trades in Rome. Look, I am going.
135   Commend me to my wife. I'll return consul
  Or never trust to what my tongue can do
  I'th' way of flattery further.

---

5. Vagabond; buffoon; prostitute.
6. Cajole (a mountebank was an itinerant quack who sold his cures from an improvised platform).

VOLUMNIA   Do your will.   *Exit* VOLUMNIA.

COMINIUS   Away! The tribunes do attend you. Arm yourself
 To answer mildly, for they are prepared
140 With accusations, as I hear, more strong
 Than are upon you yet.

CORIOLANUS   The word is "mildly." Pray you, let us go.
 Let them accuse me by invention,° I   *with invented charges*
 Will answer in mine honor.

MENENIUS   Ay, but mildly.

145   CORIOLANUS   Well, mildly be it, then, mildly.   *Exeunt.*

3.3

Enter SICINIUS *and* BRUTUS.

BRUTUS   In this point charge him home,[1] that he affects°   *desires*
 Tyrannical power. If he evade us there,
 Enforce° him with his envy° to the people,   *Urge against / malice*
 And that the spoil got on° the Antiates   *booty taken from*
 Was ne'er distributed.

Enter an AEDILE.

5   —What, will he come?

AEDILE   He's coming.

BRUTUS   How accompanied?

AEDILE   With old Menenius and those senators
 That always favored him.

SICINIUS   Have you a catalog
 Of all the voices° that we have procured,   *votes*
 Set down by th' poll?°   *individually*

10   AEDILE   I have; 'tis ready.

SICINIUS   Have you collected them by tribes?[2]

AEDILE   I have.

SICINIUS   Assemble presently the people hither,
 And when they hear me say, "It shall be so
 I'th' right and strength o'th' commons," be it either
15 For death, for fine, or banishment, then let them,
 If I say "Fine," cry "Fine!", if "Death," cry "Death!",
 Insisting on the old prerogative
 And power i'th' truth o'th' cause.[3]

AEDILE   I shall inform them.

BRUTUS   And when such time they have begun to cry,
20 Let them not cease, but with a din confused
 Enforce the present execution[4]
 Of what we chance to sentence.

AEDILE   Very well.

SICINIUS   Make them be strong and ready for this hint
 When we shall hap° to give't them.   *chance*

BRUTUS   Go about it. [*Exit* AEDILE.]
25 Put him to choler straight.° He hath been used   *anger at once*
 Ever to conquer and to have his worth[5]
 Of contradiction. Being once chafed,° he cannot   *excited*
 Be reined again to temperance; then he speaks

3.3 Location: The marketplace.
1. Press charges against him forcefully.
2. Romans voted by tribes (districts) or by social
class; the former method favored the plebeians.

3. *old prerogative . . . cause:* traditional right to
determine the truth of the case.
4. Insist upon the immediate performance.
5. Enjoy his fill; establish his reputation from.

What's in his heart, and that is there which looks
With us[6] to break his neck.
            Enter CORIOLANUS, MENENIUS, *and* COMINIUS, *with*
            other [SENATORS].

30 SICINIUS   Well, here he comes.
MENENIUS [*to* CORIOLANUS]   Calmly, I do beseech you.
CORIOLANUS   Ay, as an hostler,° that for th' poorest piece°   *stable keeper / coin*
    Will bear the knave by th' volume.[7] —Th'honored gods
    Keep Rome in safety and the chairs of justice
35 Supplied with worthy men; plant love among's;
    Throng our large temples with the shows° of peace   *ceremonies*
    And not our streets with war!
FIRST SENATOR   Amen, amen.
MENENIUS   A noble wish.
            Enter the AEDILE *with the* PLEBEIANS.
SICINIUS   Draw near, ye people.
AEDILE   List to your tribunes. Audience! Peace, I say.
CORIOLANUS   First, hear me speak.
40 BOTH TRIBUNES   Well, say. —Peace, ho!
CORIOLANUS   Shall I be charged no further than this present?°   *at this present time*
    Must all determine° here?   *be determined*
SICINIUS   I do demand
    If you submit you to the people's voices,
    Allow° their officers, and are content   *Acknowledge*
45 To suffer lawful censure for such faults
    As shall be proved upon you.
CORIOLANUS   I am content.
MENENIUS   Lo, citizens, he says he is content.
    The warlike service he has done, consider. Think
    Upon the wounds his body bears, which show
    Like graves i'th' holy churchyard.
50 CORIOLANUS   Scratches with briers,
    Scars to move laughter only.
MENENIUS   Consider further
    That when he speaks not like a citizen,
    You find him like a soldier. Do not take
    His rougher accents for malicious sounds,
55 But, as I say, such as become a soldier
    Rather than envy° you.   *show hatred to*
COMINIUS   Well, well, no more.
CORIOLANUS   What is the matter that, being passed for consul
    With full voice, I am so dishonored that
    The very hour you take it off again?
SICINIUS   Answer to us.
60 CORIOLANUS   Say, then. 'Tis true, I ought so.
SICINIUS   We charge you that you have contrived to take
    From Rome all seasoned° office and to wind°   *time-honored / insinuate*
    Yourself into a power tyrannical,
    For which you are a traitor to the people.
CORIOLANUS   How? "Traitor"?
65 MENENIUS   Nay, temperately. Your promise.

___

6. *looks with us:* promises with our help.
7. Will endure being called knave any number of times.

CORIOLANUS The fires i'th' lowest hell fold in° the people!   *enfold*
　　Call me their traitor, thou injurious° tribune?   *insulting*
　　Within° thine eyes sat twenty thousand deaths,   *If within*
　　In thy hands clutched as many millions, in
70　Thy lying tongue both numbers, I would say,
　　"Thou liest" unto thee with a voice as free
　　As I do pray the gods.
SICINIUS　　　　　　　　Mark you this, people?
ALL CITIZENS　To th' Rock, to th' Rock with him!
SICINIUS　　　　　　　　　　　　　Peace!
　　We need not put new matter to his charge.
75　What you have seen him do and heard him speak—
　　Beating your officers, cursing yourselves,
　　Opposing laws with strokes, and here defying
　　Those whose great power must try him—even this,
　　So criminal and in such capital kind,[8]
　　Deserves th'extremest death.
80　BRUTUS　　　　　　　　　But since he hath
　　Served well for Rome—
　　CORIOLANUS　　　　　What? Do you prate° of service?   *babble*
　　BRUTUS　I talk of that that know it.
　　CORIOLANUS　　　　　　You?
　　MENENIUS　Is this the promise that you made your mother?
　　COMINIUS　Know, I pray you—
　　CORIOLANUS　　　　　　I'll know no further.
85　Let them pronounce the steep Tarpeian death,
　　Vagabond exile, flaying, pent° to linger   *imprisoned*
　　But with a grain a day, I would not buy
　　Their mercy at the price of one fair word,
　　Nor check my courage° for what they can give,   *restrain my spirit*
　　To have't with saying "Good morrow."
90　SICINIUS　　　　　　　　For that° he has,   *Because*
　　As much as in him lies, from time to time
　　Inveighed against the people, seeking means
　　To pluck away their power, as now at last
　　Given hostile strokes, and that not in the presence
95　Of dreaded justice, but on the ministers
　　That doth distribute it, in the name o'th' people
　　And in the power of us the tribunes, we,
　　E'en from this instant, banish him our city,
　　In peril of precipitation
100　From off the Rock Tarpeian, never more
　　To enter our Rome gates. I'th' people's name
　　I say it shall be so.
ALL CITIZENS　　　　It shall be so,
　　It shall be so. Let him away. He's banished,
　　And it shall be so.
105　COMINIUS　Hear me, my masters and my common friends—
　　SICINIUS　He's sentenced; no more hearing.
　　COMINIUS　　　　　　　　　Let me speak.
　　I have been consul and can show for Rome
　　Her enemies' marks upon me. I do love

8. Important; deserving death.

My country's good with a respect more tender,
110 More holy and profound, than mine own life,
My dear wife's estimate,° her womb's increase   *reputation*
And treasure of my loins.° Then if I would   *(that is, children)*
Speak that—
SICINIUS   We know your drift. Speak what?
BRUTUS   There's no more to be said, but he is banished
115 As enemy to the people and his country.
It shall be so.
ALL CITIZENS   It shall be so, it shall be so!
CORIOLANUS   You common cry° of curs, whose breath I hate   *yelping pack*
As reek° o'th' rotten fens,° whose loves I prize   *vapor / swamps*
As the dead carcasses of unburied men
120 That do corrupt my air: I banish you,
And here remain with your uncertainty!
Let every feeble rumor shake your hearts;
Your enemies, with nodding of their plumes,°   *(helmet plumes)*
Fan you into despair! Have the power still
125 To banish your defenders, till at length
Your ignorance—which finds not till it feels,⁹
Making but reservation of° yourselves,   *Seeking only to preserve*
Still your own foes—deliver you as most
Abated° captives to some nation   *Debased*
130 That won you without blows! Despising
For° you the city, thus I turn my back.   *On account of*
There is a world elsewhere.
       Exeunt CORIOLANUS, COMINIUS, *with* [MENENIUS *and*
                  other SENATORS].
AEDILE   The people's enemy is gone, is gone!
ALL CITIZENS   Our enemy is banished! He is gone! Hoo-oo!
      They all shout and throw up their caps.
135 SICINIUS   Go see him out at gates and follow him
As he hath followed you, with all despite.°   *contempt*
Give him deserved vexation. Let a guard
Attend us through the city.
ALL CITIZENS   Come, come, let's see him out at gates, come.
140 The gods preserve our noble tribunes! Come.   *Exeunt.*

4.1

Enter CORIOLANUS, VOLUMNIA, VIRGILIA, MENENIUS,
    COMINIUS, *with the young nobility of Rome.*
CORIOLANUS   Come, leave your tears. A brief farewell. The beast
With many heads butts me away. Nay, mother,
Where is your ancient° courage? You were used   *former*
To say extremities was the trier of spirits;
5 That common chances common men could bear;
That when the sea was calm, all boats alike
Showed mastership in floating; fortune's blows
When most struck home, being gentle wounded craves
A noble cunning.¹ You were used to load me

9. Which does not learn until it suffers.
4.1 Location: Near the city gates of Rome.

1. *being . . . cunning:* to suffer nobly requires a gentleman's skill.

10 With precepts that would make invincible
   The heart that conned° them.   *learned*

VIRGILIA   O heavens! O heavens!

CORIOLANUS   Nay, I prithee, woman—

VOLUMNIA   Now the red pestilence[2] strike all trades in Rome,
   And occupations° perish.   *handicrafts*

CORIOLANUS   What, what, what?

15 I shall be loved when I am lacked. Nay, mother,
   Resume that spirit when you were wont to say,
   If you had been the wife of Hercules,[3]
   Six of his labors you'd have done and saved
   Your husband so much sweat. —Cominius,
20 Droop not. Adieu. —Farewell, my wife, my mother.
   I'll do well yet. —Thou old and true Menenius,
   Thy tears are salter than a younger man's
   And venomous to thine eyes. —My sometime[4] general,
   I have seen thee stern, and thou hast oft beheld
25 Heart-hard'ning spectacles. Tell these sad women
   'Tis fond° to wail inevitable strokes   *as foolish*
   As 'tis to laugh at 'em. —My mother, you wot° well   *know*
   My hazards still° have been your solace, and   *always*
   Believe't not lightly: though I go alone
30 Like to a lonely dragon that his fen
   Makes feared° and talked of more than seen, your son   *fearful*
   Will or° exceed the common° or be caught   *either / usual standard*
   With cautelous° baits and practice.   *deceitful*

VOLUMNIA   My first son,
   Whither will thou go? Take good Cominius
35 With thee a while. Determine on some course
   More than a wild exposure to each chance
   That starts° i'th' way before thee.   *leaps up*

CORIOLANUS   O the gods!

COMINIUS   I'll follow thee a month, devise with thee
   Where thou shalt rest that thou mayst hear of us,
40 And we of thee, so if the time thrust forth
   A cause for thy repeal,° we shall not send   *recall from banishment*
   O'er the vast world to seek a single man
   And lose advantage,° which doth ever cool   *favorable occasion*
   I'th' absence of the needer.

CORIOLANUS   Fare ye well.
45 Thou hast years upon thee, and thou art too full
   Of the wars' surfeits to go rove with one
   That's yet unbruised. Bring me but out at gate.
   —Come, my sweet wife, my dearest mother, and
   My friends of noble touch;° when I am forth,   *proven nobility*
50 Bid me farewell and smile. I pray you, come.
   While I remain above the ground, you shall
   Hear from me still, and never of me aught
   But what is like me formerly.

MENENIUS   That's worthily
   As any ear can hear. Come, let's not weep.
55 If I could shake off but one seven years

---

2. Bubonic plague or typhoid.
3. Mythical hero of great strength who was assigned

twelve near-impossible labors.
4. Former (addressing Cominius).

From these old arms and legs, by the good gods
I'd with thee, every foot.
CORIOLANUS   Give me thy hand. Come. *Exeunt.*

4.2

Enter the two tribunes, SICINIUS *and* BRUTUS, *with the*
AEDILE.

SICINIUS [*to* AEDILE]   Bid them all home. He's gone, and we'll no further.
—The nobility are vexed, whom we see have
Sided in his behalf.
BRUTUS   Now we have shown our power,
Let us seem humbler after it is done
Than when it was a-doing.
5 SICINIUS [*to* AEDILE]   Bid them home.
Say their great enemy is gone, and they
Stand in their ancient strength.
BRUTUS   Dismiss them home.
                                    [*Exit* AEDILE.]
—Here comes his mother.
Enter VOLUMNIA, VIRGILIA, *and* MENENIUS.
SICINIUS   Let's not meet her.
BRUTUS   Why?
SICINIUS   They say she's mad.
10 BRUTUS   They have ta'en note of us. Keep on your way.
VOLUMNIA   Oh, you're well met. Th'hoarded plague o'th' gods
Requite° your love!   Repay
MENENIUS   Peace, peace, be not so loud.
VOLUMNIA   If that I could for weeping, you should hear—
Nay, and you shall hear some. Will you be gone?
15 VIRGILIA   You shall stay too. I would I had the power
To say so to my husband.
SICINIUS [*to* VOLUMNIA]   Are you mankind?[1]
VOLUMNIA   Ay, fool, is that a shame? Note but this, fool,
Was not a man my father? Hadst thou foxship°   slyness
To banish him that struck more blows for Rome
Than thou hast spoken words?
20 SICINIUS   O blessed heavens!
VOLUMNIA   More noble blows than ever thou wise words,
And for Rome's good. I'll tell thee what—yet go.
Nay, but thou shalt stay too. I would my son
Were in Arabia[2] and thy tribe before him,
His good sword in his hand.
SICINIUS   What then?
25 VIRGILIA   What then?
He'd make an end of thy posterity.
VOLUMNIA   Bastards and all!
Good man, the wounds that he does bear for Rome!
MENENIUS   Come, come, peace.
30 SICINIUS   I would he had continued to his country
As he began and not unknit° himself   untied
The noble knot he made.

4.2 Location: Scene continues.
1. Male (thus to speak in public); Volumnia takes the
word to mean "human."

2. That is, in a desert without political institutions
or places to hide.

BRUTUS   I would he had.

VOLUMNIA   "I would he had"! 'Twas you incensed the rabble,
    Cats that can judge as fitly of his worth

35   As I can of those mysteries which heaven
    Will not have earth to know.

BRUTUS [*to* SICINIUS]   Pray, let's go.

VOLUMNIA   Now pray, sir, get you gone.
    You have done a brave deed. Ere you go, hear this:
    As far as doth the Capitol exceed

40   The meanest house in Rome, so far my son—
    This lady's husband here, this, do you see?—
    Whom you have banished, does exceed you all.

BRUTUS   Well, well, we'll leave you.

SICINIUS   Why stay we to be baited
    With one that wants° her wits?   *Exeunt tribunes.*   *lacks*

VOLUMNIA   Take my prayers with you.

45   I would the gods had nothing else to do
    But to confirm my curses. Could I meet 'em
    But once a day, it would unclog° my heart   *unburden*
    Of what lies heavy to't.

MENENIUS   You have told them home,³
    And, by my troth, you have cause. You'll sup° with me?   *dine*

50 VOLUMNIA   Anger's my meat. I sup upon myself
    And so shall starve with feeding. [*to* VIRGILIA] Come, let's go.
    Leave this faint puling and lament as I do,
    In anger, Juno-like.⁴ Come, come, come.
                  Exeunt [VOLUMNIA *and* VIRGILIA].

MENENIUS   Fie, fie, fie.   *Exit.*

4.3

Enter [Nicanor,] a ROMAN, *and [Adrian,] a* VOLSCE.

ROMAN   I know you well, sir, and you know me. Your name,
    I think, is Adrian.

VOLSCE   It is so, sir. Truly, I have forgot you.

ROMAN   I am a Roman, and my services are, as you are, against

5   'em.° Know you me yet?   *(the Romans)*

VOLSCE   Nicanor, no?

ROMAN   The same, sir.

VOLSCE   You had more beard when I last saw you, but your
    favor° is well appeared° by your tongue. What's the news in   *face / attested*

10   Rome? I have a note° from the Volscian state to find you out   *instruction*
    there. You have well saved me a day's journey.

ROMAN   There hath been in Rome strange insurrections: the
    people against the senators, patricians, and nobles.

VOLSCE   Hath been? Is it ended, then? Our state thinks not

15   so. They are in a most warlike preparation and hope to come
    upon them in the heat of their division.

ROMAN   The main blaze of it is past, but a small thing would
    make it flame again, for the nobles receive so to heart the
    banishment of that worthy Coriolanus that they are in a ripe

20   aptness to take all power from the people and to pluck from

---

3. Scolded them thoroughly.
4. Goddess of marriage and childbirth (and frequently infuriated by the infidelities of her husband,
Jupiter, king of the gods).
4.3 Location: A road between Rome and Antium.

them their tribunes forever. This lies glowing,° I can tell   *smoldering*
you, and is almost mature for the violent breaking out.

VOLSCE   Coriolanus banished?

ROMAN   Banished, sir.

25   VOLSCE   You will be welcome with this intelligence, Nicanor.

ROMAN   The day° serves well for them° now. I have heard it   *moment / (the Volscians)*
said the fittest time to corrupt a man's wife is when she's
fallen out with her husband. Your noble Tullus Aufidius will
appear well in these wars, his great opposer Coriolanus

30   being now in no request of° his country.   *unvalued by*

VOLSCE   He cannot choose.° I am most fortunate thus acci-   *He is bound to*
dentally to encounter you. You have ended my business, and
I will merrily accompany you home.

ROMAN   I shall between this and supper tell you most strange

35   things from Rome, all tending to the good of their adversaries. Have you an army ready, say you?

VOLSCE   A most royal one: the centurions and their charges
distinctly billeted, already in th'entertainment,[1] and to be
on foot at an hour's warning.

40   ROMAN   I am joyful to hear of their readiness and am the
man, I think, that shall set them in present° action. So, sir,   *immediate*
heartily well met, and most glad of your company.

VOLSCE   You take my part° from me, sir. I have the most cause   *lines*
to be glad of yours.

45   ROMAN   Well, let us go together.   *Exeunt.*

4.4

Enter CORIOLANUS *in mean apparel, disguised and*
muffled.

CORIOLANUS   A goodly city is this Antium. City,
'Tis I that made thy widows; many an heir
Of these fair edifices fore my wars°   *before my onslaught*
Have I heard groan and drop. Then know me not,

5   Lest that thy wives with spits and boys with stones
In puny battle slay me.
        Enter a CITIZEN.
                    Save° you, sir.   *God save*

CITIZEN   And you.

CORIOLANUS   Direct me, if it be your will,
Where great Aufidius lies. Is he in Antium?

CITIZEN   He is, and feasts the nobles of the state
At his house this night.

10   CORIOLANUS   Which is his house, beseech you?

CITIZEN   This here before you.

CORIOLANUS   Thank you, sir. Farewell.
                         Exit CITIZEN.
O world, thy slippery turns! Friends now fast sworn,
Whose double bosoms seem to wear one heart,
Whose hours, whose bed, whose meal and exercise

15   Are still together, who twin, as 'twere, in love
Unseparable, shall within this hour,

---

1. *their . . . entertainment:* the men under their com-   **4.4** Location: Before Aufidius's house in Antium.
mand already listed unit by unit on the payroll.

On a dissension of a doit,° break out   *trivial quarrel*
To bitterest enmity. So fellest° foes,   *fiercest*
Whose passions and whose plots have broke their sleep
20 To take the one the other,¹ by some chance,
Some trick° not worth an egg, shall grow dear friends   *trifle*
And interjoin their issues.² So with me.
My birthplace hate I, and my love's upon
This enemy town. I'll enter. If he slay me,
25 He does fair justice; if he give me way,°   *allows me to proceed*
I'll do his country service.   *Exit.*

4.5

Music plays. Enter a SERVINGMAN.

FIRST SERVINGMAN   Wine, wine, wine! What service is here?
I think our fellows° are asleep.   [*Exit.*]   *fellow servants*
Enter another SERVINGMAN.

SECOND SERVINGMAN   Where's Cotus? My master calls for
him. Cotus!   *Exit.*
Enter CORIOLANUS.

5 CORIOLANUS   A goodly house. The feast smells well, but I
Appear not like a guest.
Enter the FIRST SERVINGMAN.

FIRST SERVINGMAN   What would you have, friend? Whence are
you? Here's no place for you. Pray go to the door.   *Exit.*

CORIOLANUS   I have deserved no better entertainment
10 In being Coriolanus.
Enter SECOND SERVINGMAN.

SECOND SERVINGMAN   Whence are you, sir? Has the porter his
eyes in his head that he gives entrance to such companions?°   *low persons*
Pray get you out.

CORIOLANUS   Away!

15 SECOND SERVINGMAN   Away? Get you away!

CORIOLANUS   Now thou'rt troublesome.

SECOND SERVINGMAN   Are you so brave?° I'll have you talked   *insolent*
with anon.°   *right away*
Enter THIRD SERVINGMAN; *the* FIRST[*, entering,*] *meets
him.*

THIRD SERVINGMAN   What fellow's this?

20 FIRST SERVINGMAN   A strange one as ever I looked on. I cannot get him out o'th' house. Prithee call my master to him.

THIRD SERVINGMAN   What have you to do° here, fellow? Pray   *are you doing*
you, avoid° the house.   *leave*

CORIOLANUS   Let me but stand. I will not hurt your hearth.

25 THIRD SERVINGMAN   What are you?

CORIOLANUS   A gentleman.

THIRD SERVINGMAN   A marvelous poor one.

CORIOLANUS   True, so I am.

THIRD SERVINGMAN   Pray you, poor gentleman, take up some
30 other station.¹ Here's no place for you. Pray you, avoid. Come.

CORIOLANUS   Follow your function.² Go and batten° on cold   *gorge*
bits.

---

1. *whose plots . . . the other:* whose plots to capture
one another have kept them awake.
2. Unite their causes; marry their children to one
another.

4.5 Location: Inside Aufidius's house.
1. Place to stand (punning on "social rank").
2. Perform your servant's tasks.

[He] *pushes him away from him.*
THIRD SERVINGMAN   What? You will not? —Prithee, tell my
  master what a strange guest he has here.
35 SECOND SERVINGMAN   And I shall.
                                        Exit SECOND SERVINGMAN.
THIRD SERVINGMAN   Where dwell'st thou?
CORIOLANUS   Under the canopy.°   (*of the sky*)
THIRD SERVINGMAN   Under the canopy?
CORIOLANUS   Ay.
40 THIRD SERVINGMAN   Where's that?
CORIOLANUS   I'th' city of kites and crows.°   (*carrion birds*)
THIRD SERVINGMAN   I'th' city of kites and crows? What an ass
  it is. Then thou dwell'st with daws³ too?
CORIOLANUS   No, I serve not thy master.
45 THIRD SERVINGMAN   How, sir? Do you meddle⁴ with my master?
CORIOLANUS   Ay, 'tis an honester service than to meddle with
  thy mistress. Thou prat'st and prat'st. Serve with thy trencher.°   *wooden plate*
  Hence!
            [He] *beats him away.* [*Exit* THIRD SERVINGMAN.]
        Enter AUFIDIUS *with the* [SECOND] SERVINGMAN.
AUFIDIUS   Where is this fellow?
50 SECOND SERVINGMAN   Here, sir. I'd have beaten him like a dog
  but for disturbing the lords within.
        [FIRST *and* SECOND SERVINGMEN *stand aside.*]
AUFIDIUS   Whence com'st thou? What wouldst thou? Thy name?
  Why speak'st not? Speak, man! What's thy name?
CORIOLANUS [*unmuffling his head*]   If, Tullus,
  Not yet thou know'st me and, seeing me, dost not
55 Think me for the man I am, necessity
  Commands me name myself.
AUFIDIUS   What is thy name?
CORIOLANUS   A name unmusical to the Volscians' ears
  And harsh in sound to thine.
AUFIDIUS   Say, what's thy name?
  Thou hast a grim appearance, and thy face
60 Bears a command in't. Though thy tackle's torn,
  Thou show'st° a noble vessel. What's thy name?   *appear to be*
CORIOLANUS   Prepare thy brow to frown. Know'st thou me yet?
AUFIDIUS   I know thee not. Thy name?
CORIOLANUS   My name is Caius Martius, who hath done
65 To thee particularly and to all the Volsces
  Great hurt and mischief; thereto witness may
  My surname, Coriolanus. The painful service,
  The extreme dangers, and the drops of blood
  Shed for my thankless country are requited
70 But with that surname, a good memory°   *reminder*
  And witness of the malice and displeasure
  Which thou shouldst bear me. Only that name remains.
  The cruelty and envy of the people,
  Permitted by our dastard nobles, who
75 Have all forsook me, hath devoured the rest
  And suffered me by th' voice of slaves to be

---

3. Jackdaws (proverbially foolish).
4. Busy yourself; but Coriolanus plays on the sense "have sexual intercourse."

Whooped out of Rome. Now this extremity
Hath brought me to thy hearth, not out of hope—
Mistake me not—to save my life, for if
80   I had feared death, of all the men i'th' world
I would have 'voided thee, but in mere° spite   *utter*
To be full quit of° those my banishers,   *revenged upon; rid of*
Stand I before thee here. Then, if thou hast
A heart of wreak° in thee that wilt revenge   *vengeance*
85   Thine own particular wrongs and stop those maims°   *injuries*
Of shame seen through thy country, speed° thee straight   *hasten*
And make my misery serve thy turn. So use it
That my revengeful services may prove
As benefits to thee, for I will fight
90   Against my cankered° country with the spleen°   *infected / wrath*
Of all the under-fiends.° But if so be   *underworld fiends*
Thou dar'st not this, and that to prove° more fortunes   *try*
Thou'rt tired, then, in a word, I also am
Longer to live most weary, and present
95   My throat to thee and to thy ancient° malice,   *longstanding*
Which not to cut would show thee but a fool,
Since I have ever followed thee with hate,
Drawn tuns° of blood out of thy country's breast,   *huge casks*
And cannot live but to thy shame, unless
It be to do thee service.
100 AUFIDIUS   O Martius, Martius!
Each word thou hast spoke hath weeded from my heart
A root of ancient envy. If Jupiter
Should from yond cloud speak divine things
And say, "'Tis true," I'd not believe them more
105   Than thee, all-noble Martius. Let me twine
Mine arms about that body, where against
My grainèd ash⁵ an hundred times hath broke
And scarred the moon with splinters.
      [*He embraces* CORIOLANUS.]⁶
                    Here I clip°   *embrace*
The anvil⁷ of my sword, and do contest
110   As hotly and as nobly with thy love
As ever in ambitious strength I did
Contend against thy valor. Know thou first,
I loved the maid I married; never man
Sighed truer breath. But that I see thee here,
115   Thou noble thing, more dances my rapt heart
Than when I first my wedded mistress saw
Bestride my threshold. Why, thou Mars, I tell thee,
We have a power on foot,° and I had purpose   *an army in the field*
Once more to hew thy target° from thy brawn°   *shield / arm*
120   Or lose mine arm for't. Thou hast beat me out°   *outright*
Twelve several° times, and I have nightly since   *separate*
Dreamt of encounters twixt thyself and me—
We have been down° together in my sleep,   *(on the ground)*
Unbuckling helms, fisting° each other's throat—   *clutching*

---

5. Close-grained ashwood spear.
6. PERFORMANCE COMMENT In many productions, the relationship between Coriolanus and Aufidius has a homoerotic intensity. See Digital Edition PC 2

for some performance options.
7. Coriolanus's body, on which Aufidius has beaten his sword.

125 And waked half dead with nothing. Worthy Martius,
Had we no other quarrel else to Rome but that
Thou art thence banished, we would muster all°   *enlist everyone*
From twelve to seventy° and, pouring war   *(years old)*
Into the bowels of ungrateful Rome,
130 Like a bold flood o'erbeat. Oh, come, go in,
And take our friendly senators by th' hands
Who now are here, taking their leaves of me,
Who am prepared against your territories,
Though not for Rome itself.
CORIOLANUS   You bless me, gods.
135 AUFIDIUS   Therefore, most absolute° sir, if thou wilt have   *perfect*
The leading of thine own revenges, take
Th'one half of my commission° and set down°—   *force / determine*
As best thou art experienced, since thou know'st
Thy country's strength and weakness—thine own ways:
140 Whether to knock against the gates of Rome,
Or rudely visit° them in parts remote   *afflict*
To fright them ere destroy. But come in,
Let me commend thee first to those that shall
Say yea to thy desires. A thousand welcomes!
145 And more a friend than e'er an enemy;
Yet, Martius, that was much. Your hand. Most welcome!
                    Exeunt [AUFIDIUS *and* CORIOLANUS].
            [*The*] two SERVINGMEN [*come forward*].
FIRST SERVINGMAN   Here's a strange alteration!
SECOND SERVINGMAN   By my hand, I had thought to have
strucken him with a cudgel, and yet my mind gave me° his   *suggested to me that*
150 clothes made a false report of him.
FIRST SERVINGMAN   What an arm he has! He turned me about
with his finger and his thumb as one would set up a top.
SECOND SERVINGMAN   Nay, I knew by his face that there was
something in him. He had, sir, a kind of face, methought—I
155 cannot tell how to term it.
FIRST SERVINGMAN   He had so, looking as it were—would I
were hanged but I thought there was more in him than
I could think.
SECOND SERVINGMAN   So did I, I'll be sworn. He is simply the
160 rarest man i'th' world.
FIRST SERVINGMAN   I think he is, but a greater soldier than
he, you wot one.°   *know of*
SECOND SERVINGMAN   Who, my master?
FIRST SERVINGMAN   Nay, it's no matter for° that.   *no doubt about*
165 SECOND SERVINGMAN   Worth six on him.
FIRST SERVINGMAN   Nay, not so neither, but I take him to be
the greater soldier.
SECOND SERVINGMAN   Faith, look you, one cannot tell how
to say[8] that. For the defense of a town, our general is
170 excellent.
FIRST SERVINGMAN   Ay, and for an assault too.
            Enter the THIRD SERVINGMAN.
THIRD SERVINGMAN   O slaves, I can tell you news! News, you
rascals!

8. There's no basis for saying.

FIRST *and* SECOND SERVINGMEN   What, what, what? Let's
175   partake.
THIRD SERVINGMAN   I would not be a Roman of all nations. I
had as lief° be a condemned man.   *gladly*
FIRST *and* SECOND SERVINGMEN   Wherefore? Wherefore?
THIRD SERVINGMAN   Why, here's he that was wont to thwack
180   our general, Caius Martius.
FIRST SERVINGMAN   Why do you say "thwack our general"?
THIRD SERVINGMAN   I do not say "thwack our general," but he
was always good enough for him.
SECOND SERVINGMAN   Come, we are fellows and friends. He
185   was ever too hard for him; I have heard him say so himself.
FIRST SERVINGMAN   He was too hard for him; directly° to say   *simply*
the truth on't, before Corioles he scotched° him and notched   *scored*
him like a carbonado.[9]
SECOND SERVINGMAN   An° he had been cannibally given, he   *If*
190   might have boiled and eaten him too.
FIRST SERVINGMAN   But more of thy news.
THIRD SERVINGMAN   Why, he is so made on° here within as if   *made so much of*
he were son and heir to Mars, set at upper end o'th' table, no
question asked him by any of the senators but they stand
195   bald° before him. Our general himself makes a mistress   *hatless*
of° him, sanctifies himself with 's hand[1] and turns up the   *woos*
white o'th' eye° to his discourse. But the bottom° of the news   *(in pious devotion)* / *gist*
is our general is cut i'th' middle and but one half of what
he was yesterday, for the other° has half by the entreaty   *(Coriolanus)*
200   and grant of the whole table. He'll go, he says, and sowl° the   *drag*
porter of Rome gates by th'ears. He will mow all down
before him and leave his passage polled.°   *stripped*
SECOND SERVINGMAN   And he's as like to do't as any man I can
imagine.
205   THIRD SERVINGMAN   Do't? He will do't, for look you, sir, he
has as many friends as enemies, which friends, sir, as it were,
durst not—look you, sir—show themselves, as we term it,
his friends whilst he's in directitude.°   *disgraced*
FIRST SERVINGMAN   "Directitude"? What's that?
210   THIRD SERVINGMAN   But when they shall see, sir, his crest up
again and the man in blood,[2] they will out of their burrows,
like conies° after rain, and revel all with him.   *rabbits*
FIRST SERVINGMAN   But when goes this forward?
THIRD SERVINGMAN   Tomorrow, today, presently.° You shall   *at once*
215   have the drum struck up this afternoon. 'Tis, as it were, a
parcel° of their feast, and to be executed ere they wipe their   *part*
lips.
SECOND SERVINGMAN   Why, then, we shall have a stirring°   *busy*
world again. This peace is nothing but to rust iron, increase
220   tailors, and breed ballad-makers.[3]
FIRST SERVINGMAN   Let me have war, say I. It exceeds peace
as far as day does night. It's sprightly walking, audible, and
full of vent.[4] Peace is a very apoplexy, lethargy, mulled,° deaf,   *stupefied*

---

9. Piece of meat for broiling.
1. Treats the touch of his hand as holy.
2. In full vigor (usually refers to hounds).
3. That is, fashionable dress and idle songs flourish

in peacetime while weapons rust.
4. *audible . . . vent:* either loud and full of action, or
quick of hearing and scent (like a hunting dog).

sleepy, insensible, a getter of more bastard children than
225   war's a destroyer of men.
SECOND SERVINGMAN   'Tis so, and as wars in some sort may be
said to be a ravisher, so it cannot be denied but peace is a
great maker of cuckolds.
FIRST SERVINGMAN   Ay, and it makes men hate one another.
230   THIRD SERVINGMAN   Reason: because they then less need one
another. The wars for my money. I hope to see Romans as
cheap as Volscians.
     [*A sound within.*]
They are rising; they are rising.°   *(from dinner)*
FIRST *and* SECOND SERVINGMEN   In, in, in, in!   *Exeunt.*

4.6

Enter the two tribunes, SICINIUS *and* BRUTUS.
SICINIUS   We hear not of him, neither need we fear him.
His remedies are tame:[1] the present peace
And quietness of the people, which before
Were in wild hurry.° Here do we make his friends   *tumult*
5   Blush that the world goes well, who rather had,
Though they themselves did suffer by't, behold
Dissentious numbers pest'ring° streets than see   *obstructing*
Our tradesmen singing in their shops and going
About their functions friendly.
     Enter MENENIUS.
10   BRUTUS   We stood to't° in good time. Is this Menenius?   *acted resolutely*
SICINIUS   'Tis he, 'tis he. Oh, he is grown most kind of late.
—Hail, sir.
MENENIUS   Hail to you both.
SICINIUS   Your Coriolanus is not much missed,
15   But with° his friends. The commonwealth doth stand,   *by*
And so would do were he more angry at it.
MENENIUS   All's well, and might have been much better, if
He could have temporized.
SICINIUS   Where is he, hear you?
MENENIUS   Nay, I hear nothing.
20   His mother and his wife hear nothing from him.
     Enter three or four CITIZENS.
ALL CITIZENS [*to the tribunes*]   The gods preserve you both.
SICINIUS   Good
     e'en,° our neighbors.   *evening*
BRUTUS   Good e'en to you all, good e'en to you all.
FIRST CITIZEN   Ourselves, our wives and children, on our knees
Are bound to pray for you both.
SICINIUS   Live and thrive!
25   BRUTUS   Farewell, kind neighbors.
We wished Coriolanus had loved you as we did.
ALL CITIZENS   Now the gods keep you.
BOTH TRIBUNES   Farewell, farewell.
                         Exeunt CITIZENS.
SICINIUS   This is a happier and more comely time

4.6 Location: A public place in Rome.
1. Those who favor him are unable to act; curing ourselves of him is without violent effects.

Than when these fellows ran about the streets
Crying confusion.
30 BRUTUS   Caius Martius was
A worthy officer i'th' war, but insolent,
O'ercome with pride, ambitious past all thinking,°   *beyond imagination*
Self-loving—
SICINIUS   And affecting one sole throne°   *aspiring to rule alone*
Without assistance.
MENENIUS   I think not so.
35 SICINIUS   We should by this,° to all our lamentation,   *now*
If he had gone forth consul, found it so.
BRUTUS   The gods have well prevented it, and Rome
Sits safe and still without him.

Enter an AEDILE.

AEDILE   Worthy tribunes,
There is a slave, whom we have put in prison,
40 Reports the Volsces with two several powers°   *separate armies*
Are entered in the Roman territories
And with the deepest malice of the war
Destroy what lies before 'em.
MENENIUS   'Tis Aufidius
Who, hearing of our Martius' banishment,
45 Thrusts forth his horns again into the world,
Which were inshelled° when Martius stood for Rome   *(like a snail's)*
And durst not once peep out.
SICINIUS   Come, what talk you of Martius?
BRUTUS   Go see this rumorer whipped. It cannot be
The Volsces dare break° with us.   *(their treaty)*
MENENIUS   Cannot be?
50 We have record that very well it can,
And three examples of the like hath been
Within my age. But reason° with the fellow,   *discuss*
Before you punish him, where he heard this,
Lest you shall chance to whip your information
55 And beat the messenger who bids beware
Of what is to be dreaded.
SICINIUS   Tell not me.
I know this cannot be.
BRUTUS   Not possible.

Enter a MESSENGER.

MESSENGER   The nobles in great earnestness are going
All to the Senate-house. Some news is come in
That turns° their countenances.   *changes*
60 SICINIUS   'Tis this slave.
[*to* AEDILE] Go whip him fore the people's eyes: his raising,°   *incitement*
Nothing but his report.
MESSENGER   Yes, worthy sir,
The slave's report is seconded, and more,
More fearful, is delivered.
SICINIUS   What more fearful?
65 MESSENGER   It is spoke freely out of many mouths—
How probable I do not know—that Martius,
Joined with Aufidius, leads a power gainst Rome
And vows revenge as spacious as between
The young'st and oldest thing.

SICINIUS	This is most likely!°	*(sarcastic)*

70 BRUTUS   Raised only that the weaker sort may wish
   Good Martius home again.

| SICINIUS | The very trick on't.° | *Exactly* |

MENENIUS   This is unlikely. He and Aufidius

| Can no more atone° than violent'st contrariety. | *reconcile* |

Enter [a SECOND] MESSENGER.

SECOND MESSENGER   You are sent for to the Senate.
75   A fearful army, led by Caius Martius,
   Associated with Aufidius, rages
   Upon our territories and have already
   O'erborne their way, consumed with fire, and took
   What lay before them.

Enter COMINIUS.

80 COMINIUS [*to the tribunes*]   Oh, you have made good work!

| MENENIUS | What news? What news? |

COMINIUS You have holp° to ravish your own daughters and	*helped*
To melt the city leads° upon your pates,°	*roof lead / heads*
To see your wives dishonored to° your noses—	*in front of*

MENENIUS   What's the news? What's the news?

| 85 COMINIUS   Your temples burned in their cement,° and | *to their foundations* |
| Your franchises,° whereon you stood,° confined | *freedoms / insisted* |

   Into an auger's bore.[2]
MENENIUS   Pray now, your news.
   [*to the tribunes*]   You have made fair work, I fear me.
   —Pray, your news?
   If Martius should be joined wi'th' Volscians—

| COMINIUS | If? |

90   He is their god. He leads them like a thing
   Made by some other deity than nature,
   That shapes man better, and they follow him

| Against us brats° with no less confidence | *mere children* |

   Than boys pursuing summer butterflies
   Or butchers killing flies.
95 MENENIUS [*to the tribunes*]   You have made good work,

| You and your apron-men,° you that stood so much | *(artisans wore aprons)* |
| Upon the voice of occupation° and | *opinion of tradesmen* |

   The breath of garlic-eaters.

| COMINIUS | He'll shake |

   Your Rome about your ears.

| MENENIUS | As Hercules |

100   Did shake down mellow fruit.[3] You have made fair work!
BRUTUS   But is this true, sir?

| COMINIUS | Ay, and you'll look pale |

Before you find it other.° All the regions	*otherwise*
Do smilingly° revolt, and who resists	*gladly*
Are mocked for valiant° ignorance	*steadfast*
105 And perish constant° fools. Who is't can blame him?	*obstinate*

   Your enemies and his[4] find something in him.
MENENIUS   We are all undone unless
   The noble man have mercy.

---

2. A drill hole (that is, a narrow space).   the Hesperides.
3. Hercules' twelfth labor was to gather the apples of   4. The patricians and the Volscians.

COMINIUS   Who shall ask it?
The tribunes cannot do't for shame; the people
110   Deserve such pity of° him as the wolf   *from*
Does of the shepherds. For his best friends, if they
Should say, "Be good to Rome," they charged° him even   *would direct*
As those should do that had deserved his hate
And therein showed° like enemies.   *would behave*
MENENIUS   'Tis true;
115   If he were putting to my house the brand°   *fire*
That should consume it, I have not the face°   *shamelessness*
To say, "Beseech you, cease." [*to the tribunes*] You have made
fair hands,°   *done well*
You and your crafts. You have crafted fair!
COMINIUS   You have brought
A trembling upon Rome such as was never
120   S'incapable of help.
BOTH TRIBUNES   Say not we brought it.
MENENIUS   How? Was't we? We loved him, but, like beasts
And cowardly nobles, gave way unto your clusters,°   *crowds*
Who did hoot him out o'th' city.
COMINIUS   But I fear
They'll roar° him in again. Tullus Aufidius,   *(in fear)*
125   The second name of men,[5] obeys his points°   *directions*
As if he were his officer. Desperation
Is all the policy, strength, and defense
That Rome can make against them.
              Enter a troop of CITIZENS.
MENENIUS   Here come the clusters.
And is Aufidius with him? You are they
130   That made the air unwholesome when you cast
Your stinking greasy caps in hooting
At Coriolanus' exile. Now he's coming,
And not a hair upon a soldier's head
Which will not prove a whip. As many coxcombs°   *fools*
135   As you threw caps up will he tumble down
And pay you for your voices. 'Tis no matter.
If he could burn us all into one coal,
We have deserved it.
ALL CITIZENS   Faith, we hear fearful news.
FIRST CITIZEN   For mine own part,
140   When I said banish him, I said 'twas pity.
SECOND CITIZEN   And so did I.
THIRD CITIZEN   And so did I, and to say the truth, so did very
many of us. That° we did, we did for the best, and though we   *What*
willingly consented to his banishment, yet it was against our
145   will.
COMINIUS   You're goodly things, you voices.
MENENIUS   You have made good work
You and your cry. —Shall's to the Capitol?
COMINIUS   Oh, ay, what else?
              Exeunt both [COMINIUS *and* MENENIUS].

---

5. The second in reputation only to Coriolanus.

SICINIUS   Go, masters, get you home. Be not dismayed.
150   These are a side° that would be glad to have   *faction*
      This true which they so seem to fear. Go home
      And show no sign of fear.
FIRST CITIZEN   The gods be good to us! Come, masters, let's
      home. I ever said we were i'th' wrong when we banished
155   him.
SECOND CITIZEN   So did we all. But come, let's home.
                                          Exeunt CITIZENS.
BRUTUS   I do not like this news.
SICINIUS   Nor I.
BRUTUS   Let's to the Capitol. Would half my wealth
160   Would buy this for a lie.
SICINIUS   Pray, let's go.   *Exeunt tribunes.*

4.7

Enter AUFIDIUS *with his* LIEUTENANT.
AUFIDIUS   Do they still fly to th' Roman?
LIEUTENANT   I do not know what witchcraft's in him, but
      Your soldiers use him as the grace fore meat,
      Their talk at table, and their thanks at end;
5   And you are darkened° in this action, sir,   *overshadowed*
      Even by your own.°   *(followers)*
AUFIDIUS   I cannot help it now,
      Unless by using means° I lame the foot   *stratagems*
      Of our design. He bears himself more proudlier,
      Even to my person, than I thought he would
10   When first I did embrace him. Yet his nature
      In that's no changeling,° and I must excuse   *waverer*
      What cannot be amended.
LIEUTENANT   Yet I wish, sir—
      I mean for your particular°—you had not   *own sake*
      Joined in commission° with him, but either   *command*
15   Have borne the action of yourself
      Or else to him had left it solely.
AUFIDIUS   I understand thee well, and be thou sure,
      When he shall come to his account,¹ he knows not
      What I can urge against him, although it seems,
20   And so he thinks, and is no less apparent
      To th' vulgar eye, that he bears all things fairly
      And shows good husbandry for the Volscian state,
      Fights dragon-like, and does achieve as soon
      As draw his sword, yet he hath left undone
25   That which shall break his neck or hazard mine
      Whene'er we come to our account.
LIEUTENANT   Sir, I beseech you, think you he'll carry° Rome?   *defeat*
AUFIDIUS   All places yield to him ere he sits down,°   *lays siege*
      And the nobility of Rome are his.
30   The senators and patricians love him too.
      The tribunes are no soldiers, and their people
      Will be as rash in the repeal° as hasty   *recall from exile*
      To expel him thence. I think he'll be to Rome

4.7 Location: The Volscian camp near Rome.   1. That is, with the Volscian state.

As is the osprey to the fish, who takes it
35 By sovereignty of nature.[2] First he was
A noble servant to them, but he could not
Carry his honors even.° Whether 'twas pride,   *equably*
Which out of daily fortune[3] ever taints
The happy° man; whether defect of judgment,   *fortunate*
40 To fail in the disposing of those chances
Which he was lord of; or whether nature,
Not to be other than one thing, not moving
From th' casque° to th' cushion,° but commanding peace   *helmet / Senate seat*
Even with the same austerity and garb°   *stern demeanor*
45 As he controlled the war; but one of these—
As he hath spices° of them all, not all,   *touches*
For I dare so far free him[4]—made him feared,
So hated, and so banished. But he has a merit
To choke it in the utt'rance.[5] So our virtues
50 Lie in th'interpretation of the time,°   *contemporary observers*
And power, unto itself most commendable,
Hath not a tomb so evident as a chair
T'extol what it hath done.[6]
One fire drives out one fire; one nail, one nail;
55 Rights by rights falter, strengths by strengths do fail.
Come, let's away. When, Caius, Rome is thine,
Thou art poor'st of all; then shortly art thou mine.   *Exeunt.*

5.1

Enter MENENIUS, COMINIUS, SICINIUS [*and*] BRUTUS,
the two tribunes, with others.

MENENIUS   No, I'll not go. You hear what he hath said
Which was sometime his general,° who loved him   *(Cominius)*
In a most dear particular.° He called me "Father,"   *affectionate regard*
But what o'that? Go, you that banished him;
5 A mile before his tent fall down and knee°   *crawl*
The way into his mercy. Nay, if he coyed°   *was reluctant*
To hear Cominius speak, I'll keep at home.
COMINIUS   He would not seem° to know me.   *pretended not*
MENENIUS [*to the tribunes*]   Do you hear?
COMINIUS   Yet one time he did call me by my name.
10 I urged our old acquaintance and the drops
That we have bled together. "Coriolanus"
He would not answer to; forbade all names.
He was a kind of nothing, titleless,
Till he had forged himself a name o'th' fire
Of burning Rome.
15 MENENIUS [*to the tribunes*]   Why, so; you have made good work!
A pair of tribunes, that have wrecked° fair Rome   *destroyed*
To make coals cheap. A noble memory!°   *memorial*

---

2. Fish were imagined to surrender to ospreys without a struggle.
3. As a result of repeated successes.
4. For I'm sure he's not guilty of all these vices.
5. *he has . . . utt'rance*: his merit is so great that it overwhelms the recital of his faults; alternatively, his merit is of a kind that impedes attempts to praise it.

6. *Hath not . . . done*: a confusing passage, perhaps meaning, Will fall into certain oblivion unless it receives praise from the public rostrum; alternatively, is clearly ruined by public praise. In the first case, power requires reputation; in the second, reputation threatens power.
5.1 Location: A public place in Rome.

COMINIUS   I minded him how royal 'twas to pardon
　When it was less expected. He replied

20　It was a bare° petition of a state　　　　　　　　　　*worthless; barefaced*
　To one whom they had punished.

MENENIUS　　　　　　　　　　Very well.
　Could he say less?

COMINIUS　　　　　I offered° to awaken his regard　　　　　*tried*
　For 's private friends. His answer to me was
　He could not stay to pick them in° a pile　　　　　　*pick them out from*

25　Of noisome musty chaff. He said 'twas folly
　For one poor grain or two to leave unburnt
　And still to nose° th'offense.　　　　　　　　　　　　*smell*

MENENIUS　　　　　　　　For one poor grain or two?
　I am one of those; his mother, wife, his child,
　And this brave fellow too: we are the grains;

30　[*to the tribunes*] You are the musty chaff, and you are smelt
　Above the moon. We must be burnt for you.

SICINIUS   Nay, pray be patient. If you refuse your aid
　In this so never-needed help, yet do not
　Upbraid 's with our distress. But sure if you

35　Would be your country's pleader, your good tongue,
　More than the instant army we can make,[1]
　Might stop our countryman.

MENENIUS　　　　　　　　No, I'll not meddle.

SICINIUS   Pray you, go to him.

MENENIUS　　　　　　What should I do?

BRUTUS   Only make trial what your love can do

40　For Rome towards Martius.

MENENIUS　　Well, and say that Martius return me
　As Cominius is returned, unheard: what then?
　But as a discontented friend, grief-shot°　　　　　　　*grief-stricken*
　With his unkindness? Say't be so?

SICINIUS　　　　　　　　Yet your good will

45　Must have that thanks from Rome after the measure
　As° you intended well.　　　　　　　　　　　　　　*To the extent that*

MENENIUS　　　　　　I'll undertake't.
　I think he'll hear me. Yet to bite his lip°　　　　　　*(in anger)*
　And hum at good Cominius much unhearts me.
　He was not taken well;[2] he had not dined.

50　The veins unfilled, our blood is cold, and then
　We pout upon the morning, are unapt
　To give or to forgive; but when we have stuffed
　These pipes and these conveyances° of our blood　　*channels*
　With wine and feeding, we have suppler souls

55　Than in our priest-like fasts. Therefore I'll watch him
　Till he be dieted° to my request,　　　　　　　　*made amenable by food*
　And then I'll set upon him.

BRUTUS   You know the very road into his kindness
　And cannot lose your way.

MENENIUS　　　　　Good faith, I'll prove° him,　　　*try*

60　Speed° how it will. I shall ere long have knowledge　*Turn out*
　Of my success.°　　　　　　　　　　*Exit.*　　　*whether I succeed*

---

1. The army we can raise right now.　　　　2. Not tackled at the right time.

COMINIUS He'll never hear him.

SICINIUS Not?

COMINIUS I tell you, he does sit in gold, his eye
Red as 'twould burn Rome, and his injury[3]
The jailer to his pity. I kneeled before him;
65 'Twas very faintly he said, "Rise," dismissed me
Thus with his speechless hand. What he would do
He sent in writing after me; what he would not,
Bound with an oath to yield to his conditions.
So that all hope is vain,
70 Unless his noble mother and his wife
Who, as I hear, mean to solicit him
For mercy to his country. Therefore let's hence,
And with our fair entreaties haste them on. *Exeunt.*

5.2
Enter MENENIUS *to the* WATCH *or Guard.*

FIRST WATCHMAN Stay. Whence are you?

SECOND WATCHMAN Stand, and go back.

MENENIUS You guard like men; 'tis well. But, by your leave,
I am an officer of state and come
To speak with Coriolanus.

FIRST WATCHMAN From whence?

MENENIUS From Rome.

5 FIRST WATCHMAN You may not pass; you must return. Our general
Will no more hear from thence.

SECOND WATCHMAN You'll see your Rome embraced with fire before
You'll speak with Coriolanus.

MENENIUS Good my friends,
If you have heard your general talk of Rome
10 And of his friends there, it is lots to blanks°   the odds are
My name hath touched your ears: it is Menenius.

FIRST WATCHMAN Be it so, go back. The virtue° of your name   power
Is not here passable.[1]

MENENIUS I tell thee, fellow,
Thy general is my lover.° I have been   friend
15 The book° of his good acts whence men have read   recorder
His fame unparalleled happily amplified,
For I have ever verified[2] my friends,
Of whom he's chief, with all the size° that verity   amplitude
Would without lapsing suffer.° Nay, sometimes,   erring allow
20 Like to a bowl upon a subtle° ground,   misleading
I have tumbled past the throw,[3] and in his praise
Have almost stamped the leasing.[4] Therefore, fellow,
I must have leave to pass.

FIRST WATCHMAN Faith, sir, if you had told as many lies in his
25 behalf as you have uttered words in your own, you should
not pass here, no, though it were as virtuous to lie as to live
chastely.[5] Therefore go back.

3. The wrong inflicted on him.
5.2 Location: The Volscian camp near Rome.
1. Current (like a coin); effective (as a password).
2. Testified to the character of.

3. Overshot the mark (from the game of bowls).
4. Authenticated falsehood.
5. Honestly (but playing on "lies with a sexual partner").

MENENIUS Prithee, fellow, remember my name is Menenius,
always factionary on° the party of your general. *adherent to*

30 SECOND WATCHMAN Howsoever you have been his liar, as you
say you have, I am one that, telling true under him, must say
you cannot pass. Therefore go back.

MENENIUS Has he dined, canst thou tell? For I would not
speak with him till after dinner.

35 FIRST WATCHMAN You are a Roman, are you?

MENENIUS I am, as thy general is.

FIRST WATCHMAN Then you should hate Rome, as he does.
Can you, when you have pushed out your gates the very
defender of them and—in a violent popular ignorance—

40 given your enemy your shield, think to front° his revenges *confront*
with the easy⁶ groans of old women, the virginal palms of
your daughters, or with the palsied intercession of such a
decayed dotant° as you seem to be? Can you think to blow *old fool*
out the intended fire your city is ready to flame in with such

45 weak breath as this? No, you are deceived. Therefore back to
Rome and prepare for your execution. You are condemned;
our general has sworn you out of reprieve and pardon.

MENENIUS Sirrah,° if thy captain knew I were here, *(addressed to an inferior)*
He would use me with estimation.° *esteem*

50 FIRST WATCHMAN Come, my captain knows you not.

MENENIUS I mean thy general.

FIRST WATCHMAN My general cares not for you. Back, I say,
go, lest I let forth your half-pint of blood. Back, that's the
utmost of your having.° Back! *the most you'll get*

55 MENENIUS Nay, but fellow, fellow—

Enter CORIOLANUS *with* AUFIDIUS.

CORIOLANUS What's the matter?

MENENIUS Now, you companion,° I'll say an errand° for you. *knave / deliver a message*
You shall know now that I am in estimation; you shall per-
ceive that a jack guardant° cannot office⁷ me from my son *uncouth guard*

60 Coriolanus, guess but my entertainment with him. If thou
stand'st not i'th' state of hanging or of some death more long in
spectatorship and crueller in suffering, behold now presently
and swoon for what's to come upon thee. [*to* CORIOLANUS]
The glorious gods sit in hourly synod° about thy particular *council*

65 prosperity and love thee no worse than thy old father Menenius does. [*Weeping*] O my son, my son! Thou art preparing
fire for us. Look thee, here's water to quench it. I was hardly° *with difficulty*
moved to come to thee, but being assured none but myself
could move thee, I have been blown out of your gates with

70 sighs and conjure thee to pardon Rome and thy petitionary° *suppliant*
countrymen. The good gods assuage thy wrath and turn the
dregs of it upon this varlet here, this, who like a block° hath *blockhead; obstruction*
denied my access to thee.

CORIOLANUS Away!

75 MENENIUS How? Away?

CORIOLANUS Wife, mother, child, I know not. My affairs
Are servanted° to others. Though I owe *subjected*

---

6. Easily obtained; insignificant.　　　　7. Officiously keep.

My revenge properly,[8] my remission° lies   *forgiveness*
In Volscian breasts. That we have been familiar,
80 Ingrate forgetfulness shall poison rather
Than pity note how much.[9] Therefore be gone.
Mine ears against your suits are stronger than
Your gates against my force. Yet, for° I loved thee,   *because*
[*He gives him a letter.*]
Take this along. I writ it for thy sake
85 And would have sent it. Another word, Menenius,
I will not hear thee speak. —This man, Aufidius,
Was my beloved in Rome, yet thou behold'st.
AUFIDIUS You keep a constant temper.
Exeunt [CORIOLANUS *and* AUFIDIUS].
The Guard and MENENIUS *remain.*
FIRST WATCHMAN Now, sir, is your name Menenius?
90 SECOND WATCHMAN 'Tis a spell, you see, of much power. You
know the way home again.
FIRST WATCHMAN Do you hear how we are shent° for keeping   *scolded*
your greatness back?
SECOND WATCHMAN What cause do you think I have to
95 swoon?
MENENIUS I neither care for th' world nor your general. For
such things as you, I can scarce think there's any, you're so
slight. He that hath a will to die by himself° fears it not from   *at his own hand*
another. Let your general do his worst. For you, be that you
100 are, long,[1] and your misery increase with your age. I say to
you, as I was said to, "Away!"   *Exit.*
FIRST WATCHMAN A noble fellow, I warrant him.
SECOND WATCHMAN The worthy fellow is our general.
He's the rock, the oak not to be wind-shaken.
Exeunt WATCH.

5.3

Enter CORIOLANUS *and* AUFIDIUS [*with others*].
CORIOLANUS We will before the walls of Rome tomorrow
Set down our host.° My partner in this action,   *Lay siege with our forces*
You must report to th' Volscian lords how plainly
I have borne this business.
AUFIDIUS   Only their ends
5 You have respected, stopped your ears against
The general suit of Rome, never admitted
A private whisper, no, not with such friends
That thought them sure of you.
CORIOLANUS   This last old man,
Whom with a cracked heart I have sent to Rome,
10 Loved me above the measure of a father,
Nay, godded° me indeed. Their latest refuge°   *deified / last hope*
Was to send him, for whose old love I have—
Though I showed sourly to him—once more offered

8. *owe . . . properly:* possess my own power of
revenge.
9. *That we . . . much:* The memory of our friendship
shall be poisoned by Rome's (alternatively, my own)
ungrateful forgetfulness, rather than compassion be
awakened by my awareness of how intimate we were.
1. *be that you are, long:* remain (as bad) as you are for
a long time.
5.3 Location: Scene continues.

The first conditions, which they did refuse
15 And cannot now accept, to grace him only
That thought he could do more. A very little
I have yielded to. Fresh embassies and suits,
Nor from the state nor private friends, hereafter
Will I lend ear to.
                    Shout within.
                        Ha? What shout is this?
20 Shall I be tempted to infringe my vow
In the same time 'tis made? I will not.
                Enter VIRGILIA, VOLUMNIA, VALERIA, YOUNG MARTIUS,
                with Attendants.
My wife comes foremost, then the honored mould
Wherein this trunk° was framed, and in her hand   *body*
The grandchild to her blood. But out, affection;
25 All bond and privilege of nature break!
Let it be virtuous to be obstinate.
                [VIRGILIA *curtsies.*]
What is that curtsy worth? Or those doves' eyes
Which can make gods forsworn? I melt, and am not
Of stronger earth than others. My mother bows,
30 As if Olympus to a molehill should
In supplication nod, and my young boy
Hath an aspect of intercession,° which   *pleading look*
Great Nature cries, "Deny not!" Let the Volsces
Plow Rome and harrow Italy, I'll never
35 Be such a gosling° to obey instinct, but stand   *(foolish) baby goose*
As if a man were author of himself
And knew no other kin.
VIRGILIA   My lord and husband.
CORIOLANUS   These eyes are not the same I wore in Rome.
VIRGILIA   The sorrow that delivers° us thus changed   *presents*
Makes you think so.
40 CORIOLANUS   Like a dull actor now
I have forgot my part and I am out,°   *at a loss*
Even to a full disgrace. Best of my flesh,
Forgive my tyranny, but do not say
For that, "Forgive our Romans."
                [*They kiss.*][1]
                        Oh, a kiss
45 Long as my exile, sweet as my revenge!
Now, by the jealous queen of heaven,[2] that kiss
I carried from thee, dear, and my true lip
Hath virgined it e'er since. —You gods, I prate,
And the most noble mother of the world
50 Leave unsaluted. Sink, my knee, i'th' earth;
                [*He*] *kneels.*
Of thy deep duty, more impression° show   *indentation; effect*
Than that of common sons.
VOLUMNIA   Oh, stand up blessed,
                [*He rises.*]

---

1. TEXTUAL COMMENT It is not clear from the Folio
SD who initiates the kiss; for the significance of the
ambiguity, see Digital Edition TC 10.

2. Juno, queen of the gods and guardian of
marriage.

Whilst with no softer cushion than the flint
I kneel before thee,
     [*She kneels.*]
          and unproperly°   *against propriety*
55 Show duty as mistaken all this while
Between the child and parent.
CORIOLANUS   What's this?
Your knees to me? To your corrected[3] son?
     [*He raises her to her feet.*]
Then let the pebbles on the hungry beach
Fillip° the stars; then let the mutinous winds   *Strike against*
60 Strike the proud cedars gainst the fiery sun,
Murd'ring[4] impossibility, to make
What cannot be slight work.[5]
VOLUMNIA   Thou art my warrior;
I holp to frame° thee. [*indicating* VALERIA] Do you know this   *helped to make*
  lady?
CORIOLANUS   The noble sister of Publicola,
65 The moon° of Rome, chaste as the icicle   *(emblem of chastity)*
That's curdied° by the frost from purest snow   *crystallized*
And hangs on Dian's[6] temple. Dear Valeria!
VOLUMNIA [*indicating* YOUNG MARTIUS]   This is a poor epitome°   *short version*
  of yours,
Which by th'interpretation of full time[7]
May show like all yourself.
70 CORIOLANUS   The god of soldiers,
With the consent of supreme Jove, inform
Thy thoughts with nobleness, that thou mayst prove
To shame unvulnerable and stick° i'th' wars   *stand firm*
Like a great sea-mark, standing every flaw[8]
And saving those that eye thee.
75 VOLUMNIA [*to* YOUNG MARTIUS]   Your knee, sirrah.
     [YOUNG MARTIUS *kneels.*]
CORIOLANUS   That's my brave boy!
VOLUMNIA   Even he, your wife, this lady, and myself
Are suitors to you.
CORIOLANUS   I beseech you, peace;
Or if you'd ask, remember this before:
80 The thing I have forsworn to grant may never
Be held by you denials.[9] Do not bid me
Dismiss my soldiers or capitulate°   *come to terms*
Again with Rome's mechanics.° Tell me not   *workmen*
Wherein I seem unnatural. Desire not
85 T'allay my rages and revenges with
Your colder reasons.
VOLUMNIA   Oh, no more, no more.
You have said you will not grant us anything,
For we have nothing else to ask but that
Which you deny already. Yet we will ask,

---

3. Rebuked (by Volumnia's irony).
4. Putting an end to the idea of.
5. An easy task of what cannot be.
6. Diana, goddess of the moon and chastity.

7. When time has clarified its full meaning.
8. Like a landmark at sea, withstanding every gust.
9. Be regarded by you as refusals.

90   That, if you fail in our request, the blame
            May hang upon your hardness. Therefore hear us.
     CORIOLANUS   Aufidius and you Volsces, mark, for we'll
            Hear naught from Rome in private.
                    [*He sits.*]
                                        Your request?
       VOLUMNIA   Should we be silent and not speak, our raiment
95   And state of bodies would bewray° what life   *divulge*
            We have led since thy exile. Think with thyself
            How more unfortunate than all living women
            Are we come hither, since that thy sight, which should
            Make our eyes flow with joy, hearts dance with comforts,
100   Constrains them weep and shake with fear and sorrow,
            Making the mother, wife, and child to see
            The son, the husband, and the father tearing
            His country's bowels out; and to poor we
            Thine enmity's most capital.° Thou barr'st us   *fatal*
105   Our prayers to the gods, which is a comfort
            That all but we enjoy. For how can we,
            Alas, how can we for our country pray,
            Whereto we are bound, together with thy victory,
            Whereto we are bound? Alack, or° we must lose   *either*
110   The country, our dear nurse, or else thy person,
            Our comfort in the country. We must find
            An evident° calamity, though we had   *A certain*
            Our wish which side should win. For either thou
            Must as a foreign recreant° be led   *traitor*
115   With manacles through our streets, or else
            Triumphantly tread on thy country's ruin
            And bear the palm for having bravely shed
            Thy wife and children's blood. For myself, son,
            I purpose not to wait on fortune till
120   These wars determine.° If I cannot persuade thee   *conclude*
            Rather to show a noble grace to both parts°   *sides*
            Than seek the end of one, thou shalt no sooner
            March to assault thy country than to tread—
            Trust to't, thou shalt not—on thy mother's womb
            That brought thee to this world.
125   VIRGILIA   Ay, and mine,
            That brought you forth this boy to keep your name
            Living to time.
       YOUNG MARTIUS   'A° shall not tread on me.   *He*
            I'll run away till I am bigger, but then I'll fight.
       CORIOLANUS   Not of a woman's tenderness to be
130   Requires nor child nor woman's face to see.[1]
            I have sat too long.
                    [*He rises.*]
       VOLUMNIA   Nay, go not from us thus.
            If it were so that our request did tend
            To save the Romans, thereby to destroy
            The Volsces whom you serve, you might condemn us
135   As poisonous of your honor. No, our suit

---

1. *Not . . . see:* To avoid having a woman's tenderness, a man must not see a child's or woman's face.

Is that you reconcile them, while the Volsces
May say, "This mercy we have showed," the Romans,
"This we received," and each in either side
Give the all-hail to thee and cry, "Be blessed
140   For making up this peace!" Thou know'st, great son,
The end of war's uncertain, but this certain,
That if thou conquer Rome, the benefit
Which thou shalt thereby reap is such a name
Whose repetition will be dogged with curses,
145   Whose chronicle thus writ:[2] "The man was noble,
But with his last attempt he wiped it out,
Destroyed his country, and his name remains
To th'ensuing age abhorred." Speak to me, son.
Thou hast affected° the fine strains° of honor,   *cherished / qualities*
150   To imitate the graces of the gods,
To tear with thunder the wide cheeks o'th' air,
And yet to charge thy sulfur[3] with a bolt
That should but rive[4] an oak. Why dost not speak?
Think'st thou it honorable for a noble man
155   Still° to remember wrongs? —Daughter, speak you;   *Perpetually*
He cares not for your weeping. —Speak thou, boy;
Perhaps thy childishness will move him more
Than can our reasons. There's no man in the world
More bound to 's mother, yet here he lets me prate
160   Like one i'th' stocks.[5] —Thou hast never in thy life
Showed thy dear mother any courtesy,
When she, poor hen, fond of° no second brood,   *desiring*
Has clucked thee to the wars and safely home,
Loaden with honor. Say my request's unjust
165   And spurn me back, but if it be not so,
Thou art not honest, and the gods will plague thee
That thou restrain'st° from me the duty which   *withhold'st*
To a mother's part belongs. —He turns away.
Down, ladies. Let us shame him with our knees.
170   To his surname Coriolanus 'longs° more pride   *belongs*
Than pity to our prayers.[6] Down! An end;
     [They kneel.]
This is the last. So, we will home to Rome
And die among our neighbors. *[to* CORIOLANUS] Nay, behold's.
This boy, that cannot tell what he would have
175   But kneels and holds up hands for fellowship,
Does reason our petition with more strength
Than thou hast to deny't. —Come, let us go.
     [They rise.]
This fellow had a Volscian to his mother;
His wife is in Corioles, and his child
180   Like him by chance. —Yet give us our dispatch.[7]
I am hushed until our city be afire,
And then I'll speak a little.

---

2. Whose biography will thus be written.
3. To discharge thy thunder (like Jupiter, king of the gods, whose tree was the oak).
4. Tear (destroy a tree, not human beings).
5. *prate . . . stocks*: rail pointlessly like a prisoner

sentenced to public humiliation in the stocks.
6. Volumnia reinterprets the name as a sign of allegiance to Corioles.
7. Dismissal (with wordplay on "deathblow").

[He] holds her by the hand, silent.

CORIOLANUS   O mother, mother!
What have you done?[8] Behold, the heavens do ope,
The gods look down, and this unnatural scene
185 They laugh at. O my mother, mother! O!
You have won a happy victory to Rome;
But for your son—believe it, oh, believe it—
Most dangerously you have with him prevailed,
If not most mortal to him. But let it come.
190 —Aufidius, though I cannot make true° wars,   *(as I vowed)*
I'll frame convenient° peace. Now, good Aufidius,   *suitable*
Were you in my stead, would you have heard
A mother less? Or granted less, Aufidius?
AUFIDIUS   I was moved withal.°   *as well*
CORIOLANUS   I dare be sworn you were,
195 And, sir, it is no little thing to make
Mine eyes to sweat compassion. But, good sir,
What peace you'll make, advise me. For my part,
I'll not to Rome; I'll back with you, and pray you
Stand to° me in this cause. —O mother! Wife!   *by*
200 AUFIDIUS *[aside]*   I am glad thou hast set thy mercy and thy honor
At difference in thee. Out of that I'll work
Myself a former fortune.[9]
CORIOLANUS *[to the ladies]*   Ay, by and by;
But we will drink together, and you shall bear
A better witness back than words, which we,
205 On like conditions, will have counter-sealed.
Come, enter with us. Ladies, you deserve
To have a temple built you. All the swords
In Italy and her confederate arms
Could not have made this peace.   *Exeunt.*

5.4

Enter MENENIUS and SICINIUS.

MENENIUS   See you yond quoin° o'th' Capitol, yond   *corner*
  cornerstone?
SICINIUS   Why, what of that?
MENENIUS   If it be possible for you to displace it with your little
5   finger, there is some hope the ladies of Rome, especially his
  mother, may prevail with him. But I say there is no hope in't.
  Our throats are sentenced and stay upon° execution.   *wait for*
SICINIUS   Is't possible that so short a time can alter the condi-
  tion° of a man?   *character*
10 MENENIUS   There is difference between a grub and a butterfly, yet your butterfly was a grub. This Martius is grown from
  man to dragon. He has wings; he's more than a creeping
  thing.
SICINIUS   He loved his mother dearly.
15 MENENIUS   So did he me, and he no more remembers his
  mother now than° an eight-year-old horse. The tartness of   *than does*
  his face sours ripe grapes. When he walks, he moves like an

8. PERFORMANCE COMMENT The dramatic confrontation between Volumnia and Coriolanus may be
variously staged; see Digital Edition PC 3 for some of

the possibilities.
9. *work . . . fortune:* regain my former preeminence.
5.4 Location: A public place in Rome.

engine,° and the ground shrinks before his treading. He is   *war machine*
able to pierce a corslet° with his eye, talks like a knell, and   *armored shirt*
20 his hum is a battery.° He sits in his state as a thing made for   *bombardment*
Alexander.[1] What he bids be done is finished with his bid-
ding. He wants° nothing of a god but eternity and a heaven   *lacks*
to throne in.

SICINIUS   Yes, mercy, if you report him truly.
25 MENENIUS   I paint him in the character.° Mark what mercy   *as he is*
his mother shall bring from him. There is no more mercy in
him than there is milk in a male tiger. That shall our poor
city find, and all this is 'long° of you.   *on account*

SICINIUS   The gods be good unto us!
30 MENENIUS   No, in such a case the gods will not be good unto
us. When we banished him, we respected not them; and, he
returning to break our necks, they respect not us.

Enter a MESSENGER.

MESSENGER [*to* SICINIUS]   Sir, if you'd save your life, fly to your
house.
The plebeians have got your fellow tribune
35 And hale° him up and down, all swearing if   *drag*
The Roman ladies bring not comfort home,
They'll give him death by inches.°   *little by little*

Enter another MESSENGER.

SICINIUS   What's the news?

SECOND MESSENGER   Good news, good news! The ladies have
prevailed,
The Volscians are dislodged,° and Martius gone.   *broken*
40 A merrier day did never yet greet Rome,
No, not th'expulsion of the Tarquins.

SICINIUS   Friend,
Art thou certain this is true? Is't most certain?

SECOND MESSENGER   As certain as I know the sun is fire.
Where have you lurked that you make doubt of it?
45 Ne'er through an arch so hurried the blown° tide   *swollen*
As the recomforted° through th' gates.   *reinvigorated*

Trumpets, hautboys,° drums beat, all together.   *oboes*
Why, hark you!
The trumpets, sackbuts, psalteries,° and fifes,   *trombones, zithers*
Tabors° and cymbals and the shouting Romans   *Drums*
Make the sun dance.

A shout within.
Hark you!

MENENIUS   This is good news.
50 I will go meet the ladies. This Volumnia
Is worth of consuls, senators, patricians,
A city full; of tribunes such as you,
A sea and land full. You have prayed well today.
This morning for ten thousand of your throats
I'd not have given a doit.°   *small coin*

Sound still with the shouts.
55   Hark how they joy!

SICINIUS [*to* SECOND MESSENGER]   First, the gods bless you for
your tidings; next
Accept my thankfulness.

---

1. Sits on his throne like a statue of Alexander the Great (who actually lived after Coriolanus).

SECOND MESSENGER   Sir, we have all great cause to give great
   thanks.
SICINIUS   They are near the city?
SECOND MESSENGER   Almost at point to enter.
60   SICINIUS   We'll meet them and help the joy.   *Exeunt.*

5.5

Enter two SENATORS, *with [the] ladies [*VOLUMNIA,
   VIRGILIA, *and* VALERIA], *passing over the stage, with
   other* LORDS.
FIRST SENATOR   Behold our patroness, the life of Rome.
   Call all your tribes together, praise the gods,
   And make triumphant fires.° Strew flowers before them,   *(of sacrifice)*
   Unshout the noise that banished Martius;
5   Repeal[1] him with the welcome of his mother.
   Cry, "Welcome, ladies, welcome!"
ALL   Welcome, ladies, welcome!
             A flourish with drums and trumpets. [Exeunt.]

5.6

Enter Tullus AUFIDIUS, *with Attendants.*
AUFIDIUS   Go, tell the lords o'th' city I am here.
   Deliver them this paper. Having read it,
   Bid them repair to th' market-place, where I,
   Even in theirs and in the commons' ears,
5   Will vouch the truth of it. Him I accuse
   The city ports° by this° hath entered and   *gates / this time*
   Intends t'appear before the people, hoping
   To purge himself with words. Dispatch. [*Exeunt Attendants.*]
             Enter three or four CONSPIRATORS *of Aufidius' faction.*
                                Most welcome!
FIRST CONSPIRATOR   How is it with our general?
AUFIDIUS   Even so,
10   As with a man by his own alms empoisoned
   And with his charity slain.
SECOND CONSPIRATOR   Most noble sir,
   If you do hold the same intent wherein
   You wished us parties,° we'll deliver you   *allies*
   Of° your great danger.   *From*
AUFIDIUS   Sir, I cannot tell.
15   We must proceed as we do find the people.
THIRD CONSPIRATOR   The people will remain uncertain whilst
   Twixt you there's difference,° but the fall of either   *disagreement*
   Makes the survivor heir of all.
AUFIDIUS   I know it,
   And my pretext to strike at him admits
20   A good construction.° I raised him, and I pawned   *interpretation*
   Mine honor for his truth, who being so heightened,
   He watered his new plants[1] with dews of flattery,
   Seducing so my friends; and to this end

5.5 Location: Near the city gates of Rome.
1. Recall him from banishment.

5.6 Location: Corioles.
1. Followers (formerly Aufidius's adherents).

He bowed his nature, never known before
25 But to be rough, unswayable, and free.
THIRD CONSPIRATOR   Sir, his stoutness°   *stubbornness*
When he did stand for consul, which he lost
By lack of stooping—
AUFIDIUS   That I would have spoke of.
Being banished for't, he came unto my hearth,
30 Presented to my knife his throat. I took him,
Made him joint-servant° with me, gave him way   *partner*
In all his own desires; nay, let him choose
Out of my files,° his projects to accomplish,   *troops*
My best and freshest men; served his designments°   *plans*
35 In mine own person; holp to reap the fame
Which he did end all his,[2] and took some pride
To do myself this wrong, till at the last
I seemed his follower, not partner, and
He waged° me with his countenance° as if   *paid / appearance*
I had been mercenary.
40 FIRST CONSPIRATOR   So he did, my lord.
The army marveled at it, and in the last,
When he had carried° Rome and that we looked   *was about to vanquish*
For no less spoil than glory—
AUFIDIUS   There was it,
For which my sinews shall be stretched upon him.
45 At a few drops of women's rheum,° which are   *tears*
As cheap as lies, he sold the blood and labor
Of our great action. Therefore shall he die,
And I'll renew me in his fall.
        Drums and trumpets sound, with great shouts of the
        people.
                        But hark!
FIRST CONSPIRATOR   Your native town you entered like a post[3]
50 And had no welcomes home, but he returns
Splitting the air with noise.
SECOND CONSPIRATOR   And patient fools,
Whose children he hath slain, their base throats tear
With giving him glory.
THIRD CONSPIRATOR   Therefore, at your vantage,°   *best opportunity*
Ere he express himself or move the people
55 With what he would say, let him feel your sword,
Which we will second. When he lies along,°   *prostrate*
After your way° his tale pronounced shall bury   *In your version*
His reasons with his body.
AUFIDIUS   Say no more.
Here come the lords.
        Enter the LORDS *of the city.*
ALL LORDS   You are most welcome home.
60 AUFIDIUS   I have not deserved it.
But, worthy lords, have you with heed perused
What I have written to you?
ALL LORDS   We have.

---

2. Which he did conclude was (or did finally make)   3. Messenger (bearing news of Coriolanus).
entirely his own.

FIRST LORD   And grieve to hear't.
What faults he made before the last, I think
Might have found easy fines;° but there to end   *light penalties*
65 Where he was to begin and give away
The benefit of our levies,° answering us   *levied troops*
With our own charge,[4] making a treaty where
There was a yielding, this admits no excuse.
AUFIDIUS   He approaches; you shall hear him.
      Enter CORIOLANUS *marching with drum and colors,*
      the COMMONERS *being with him.*
70 CORIOLANUS   Hail, lords! I am returned your soldier,
No more infected with my country's love
Than when I parted hence, but still subsisting
Under your great command. You are to know
That prosperously[5] I have attempted and
75 With bloody passage led your wars even to
The gates of Rome. Our spoils we have brought home
Doth more than counterpoise a full third part
The charges of the action.[6] We have made peace
With no less honor to the Antiates
80 Than shame to th' Romans; and we here deliver,
Subscribed by th' consuls and patricians,
Together with the seal o'th' Senate, what
We have compounded° on.   *agreed*
AUFIDIUS   Read it not, noble lords,
But tell the traitor in the highest degree
He hath abused your powers.
85 CORIOLANUS   "Traitor"? How now?
AUFIDIUS   Ay, traitor, Martius.
CORIOLANUS   "Martius"?
AUFIDIUS   Ay, Martius, Caius Martius. Dost thou think
I'll grace thee with that robbery, thy stol'n name,
"Coriolanus," in Corioles?
90 —You lords and heads o'th' state, perfidiously
He has betrayed your business and given up
For certain drops of salt° your city Rome—   *(tears)*
I say "your city"—to his wife and mother,
Breaking his oath and resolution like
95 A twist° of rotten silk, never admitting   *thread*
Counsel o'th' war;[7] but at his nurse's tears
He whined and roared away your victory,
That pages[8] blushed at him and men of heart°   *courage*
Looked wond'ring each at others.
CORIOLANUS   Hear'st thou, Mars?
AUFIDIUS   Name not the god, thou boy of tears.
CORIOLANUS   Ha?
100 AUFIDIUS   No more.
CORIOLANUS   Measureless liar, thou hast made my heart

---

4. *answering . . . charge:* rewarding us with our own
costs (of mounting the campaign); answering accusations by saying that he acted on our authority.
5. Successfully; with gain of wealth.
6. *Our spoils . . . action:* The value of our plunder

outweighs by more than a third the costs of the war.
7. *admitting . . . war:* taking any advice about the
war.
8. Youthful servants.

Too great for what contains it. "Boy"? O slave!
—Pardon me, lords, 'tis the first time that ever
I was forced to scold. Your judgments, my grave lords,
105 Must give this cur the lie, and his own notion°— *awareness of the truth*
Who wears my stripes° impressed upon him, that *wounds*
Must bear my beating to his grave—shall join
To thrust° the lie unto him. *turn the accusation of*
FIRST LORD   Peace, both, and hear me speak.
110 CORIOLANUS   Cut me to pieces, Volsces; men and lads,
Stain all your edges° on me. "Boy"! False hound! *sword blades*
If you have writ your annals true, 'tis there
That, like an eagle in a dovecote,° I *pigeon house*
Fluttered your Volscians in Corioles.
Alone I did it. "Boy"!
115 AUFIDIUS   Why, noble lords,
Will you be put in mind of his blind⁹ fortune,
Which was your shame, by this unholy braggart,
Fore your own eyes and ears?
ALL CONSPIRATORS   Let him die for't.
COMMONERS [*variously*]   Tear him to pieces! Do it presently!° *immediately*
120 —He killed my son! —My daughter! —He killed my cousin
Marcus! —He killed my father!
SECOND LORD   Peace, ho! No outrage.° Peace! *violence*
The man is noble, and his fame folds in° *envelops*
This orb o'th' earth. His last offenses to us
125 Shall have judicious hearing. —Stand,° Aufidius, *Hold off*
And trouble not the peace.
CORIOLANUS   Oh, that I had him,
With six Aufidiuses, or more, his tribe,
To use my lawful sword.
AUFIDIUS   Insolent villain.
ALL CONSPIRATORS   Kill, kill, kill, kill, kill him!
    The CONSPIRATORS *draw [their swords] and kill*
    MARTIUS, *who falls;* AUFIDIUS *stands on him.*
LORDS   Hold, hold, hold, hold!
AUFIDIUS   My noble masters, hear me speak.
130 FIRST LORD   O Tullus.
SECOND LORD   Thou hast done a deed whereat valor will weep.
THIRD LORD   Tread not upon him. Masters all, be quiet.
Put up your swords.
AUFIDIUS   My lords, when you shall know—as in this rage
135 Provoked by him you cannot—the great danger
Which this man's life did owe° you, you'll rejoice *hold in store for*
That he is thus cut off. Please it your honors
To call me to your senate, I'll deliver° *show*
Myself your loyal servant or endure
Your heaviest censure.
140 FIRST LORD   Bear from hence his body
And mourn you for him. Let him be regarded
As the most noble corpse that ever herald
Did follow to his urn.

9. Random (fortune was commonly personified as blind).

SECOND LORD His own impatience
Takes from Aufidius a great part of blame.
Let's make the best of it.
145 AUFIDIUS My rage is gone,
And I am struck with sorrow. —Take him up.
Help, three o'th' chiefest soldiers; I'll be one.
Beat thou the drum that it speak mournfully;
Trail your steel pikes. Though in this city he
150 Hath widowed and unchilded many a one,
Which to this hour bewail the injury,
Yet he shall have a noble memory.° Assist.   memorial

Exeunt, bearing the body of MARTIUS,
a dead march sounded.

Cymbeline

Toward the end of *Cymbeline*, one of the chief characters, Posthumus Leonatus, awakens from a dream vision to find a tablet on his chest, left there by Jupiter, king of the gods. In the dream, Jupiter had promised that the tablet would explain Posthumus's future fortunes. But when Posthumus reads the writing on the tablet, it is incomprehensible to him:

> 'Tis still a dream, or else such stuff as madmen
> Tongue . . .
> Or senseless speaking, or a speaking such
> As sense cannot untie.

Yet he concludes: "Be what it is, / The action of my life is like it" (5.4.115–19). By his own estimation, Posthumus's life is a senseless riddle. His immediate circumstances perhaps warrant such a conclusion. When Jupiter appears to him, Posthumus, a Briton crucial to his country's recent defeat of Rome, has subsequently disguised himself as a Roman and been put in a British prison. He deliberately sought his own capture and death because he was overwhelmed by guilt for having ordered the death of his wife, Imogen, the British king's daughter, falsely accused of sexual infidelity. Unbeknownst to him, however, Imogen, not dead but disguised as a Roman boy named Fidele, is likewise among those held captive by the Britons. Posthumus's own name, moreover, is something of a riddle. It literally means "after the death," signifying that Posthumus was born after the death of his father, Leonatus; but it also suggests a more fundamental disordering of expectations in a play in which (1) not only is a son born after his father's death, but other sons are stolen from fathers and wives severed from husbands, and (2) the temporal setting of the play seems simultaneously to be first-century C.E. Britain and seventeenth-century Italy.

Plot complexities abound in *Cymbeline*, leading not only Posthumus but also theatergoers to find it challenging to interpret. An inordinate number of characters assume disguises, have more than one name, don't know who their "real" parents are, or find themselves unable to decipher the complicated events around them. In one of the play's most famous (or infamous) scenes, Imogen, traveling in a page's disguise to find Posthumus, wakes up from a drug-induced sleep to find herself lying beside the body of a headless man dressed in her husband's clothing. The man is really Cloten, Posthumus's rival for Imogen's hand and the wicked son of Imogen's evil stepmother. Seeing the headless body, Imogen breaks into a lament for the man she believes to be her husband. Her grief is genuine and affecting, but it is prompted by a profound misreading of the corpse before her.

The improbabilities and complexities of *Cymbeline*'s plot have given some critics pause, as has the freedom with which times and places are handled. Ostensibly set in Roman Britain at the time of Christ's birth (which, according to early modern chronicles, occurred during the reign of Cymbeline), the play also contains scenes that appear to take place in contemporary Italy. It is in this modern Italy, for example, that Posthumus is tricked into believing that Imogen is sexually unfaithful to him. Reacting to the play's unusual features, the eighteenth-century critic Samuel Johnson complained:

> This play has many just sentiments, some natural dialogues, and some pleasing scenes, but they are obtained at the expense of much incongruity. To remark the folly of the fiction, the absurdity of the conduct, the confusion of the

names, and manners of different times, and the impossibility of the events in any system of life, were to waste criticism upon unresisting imbecility, upon faults too evident for detection, and too gross for aggravation.

This response, however, may say more about Johnson's neoclassical tastes than about the ultimate value of Shakespeare's play. In *Cymbeline,* the complexity of the action seems deliberate rather than inadvertent or unskillful. It creates in the audience both a longing for clarity and control and an anxiety that the play may afford neither. The conclusion of the final act, therefore, comes as a relief when—after a dizzying whirl of events, reversals, revelations, and disguises—peace descends, all identities are revealed, and all riddles are expounded. The sense of wonder produced by this miraculous untangling of complicated events is one of the distinguishing features of Shakespeare's late plays, but *Cymbeline* never quite dispels the sense that the world of the play is fundamentally chaotic and mysterious and the plot's happy ending is a precarious bit of artifice.

This is probably one reason why in the First Folio of 1623 the play appeared as the last of Shakespeare's tragedies and was called *The Tragedy of Cymbeline,* a title retained in this edition in keeping with the emphasis on reproducing as far as possible the features of the text that serves as the basis for *The Norton Shakespeare*'s edition of a given play. In the early modern period, *Cymbeline* might have been classified as a tragedy both because, like *King Lear,* it dramatizes serious historical matter taken from the reign of an early Briton king, and also because of the dark and confusing atmosphere of much of the action and the deaths of Cloten and the Queen in the play's final acts. Modern critics, however, have usually preferred to call the play a tragicomedy or a romance, arguing that, like *The Winter's Tale, Pericles,* and *The Tempest, Cymbeline* does not end with the death of the protagonists but, rather, restores families and transforms suffering to joy. While verging on tragedy, *Cymbeline* does arguably move to a bittersweet conclusion in which shattered families are reconstituted and plot complexities untangled—but at a cost. In all the late plays, mistakes often have tragic consequences: some sons die; years are lost in exile and wandering; women suffer from unjust slander. If, in the end, good fortune returns to the sufferers, it does not cancel their former pain but provides a miraculous contrast to it. It is fitting, therefore, that ambiguity haunts *Cymbeline*'s generic categorization. Whether we call it tragedy, tragicomedy, or romance, the play blends catastrophe with hope in ways that have both confused and delighted audiences.

The date of *Cymbeline* is uncertain, although it is usually given as 1609 or 1610. Scholars differ as to whether it preceded or followed *The Winter's Tale.* We know that it was in performance by 1611 because Simon Forman, a London doctor and astrologer, wrote about seeing it, probably between April 20 and April 30 of that year. It is not clear whether he saw the play at the Globe, the outdoor theater that Shakespeare's company used after 1599, or at Blackfriars, the indoor theater that the company acquired in 1608. The spectacular scenic effects possible in staging this play, such as the descent of Jupiter on the back of an eagle in act 5, suggest that it was designed with the more elaborate technical capacities of the Blackfriars venue in mind. Some critics have tried to date the play by relating it to the investiture of Henry, King James's oldest son, as Prince of Wales in 1610, since a number of key scenes of the play take place in Wales. We have no record of a court performance until 1634, however, when it was played before King Charles, who liked it. Other critics have tried to determine the play's relationship to Beaumont and Fletcher's popular tragicomedy *Philaster,* usually dated 1609, to which *Cymbeline* bears some resemblance, but it is not clear which play influenced the other.

Regardless of its exact date, *Cymbeline* belongs to Shakespeare's late period, and it enabled him to address his long-standing interests in both British and Roman history. The play intertwines three plot lines, the main one involving Imogen, the daughter and apparently the only living heir of Cymbeline, King of Britain, and her thwarted attempts to live with her chosen husband, Posthumus. Angry that Imogen loves a man of lesser social rank than herself and that she has not married Cloten, his second wife's son, Cymbeline banishes Posthumus from Britain. The exiled husband travels to Italy, where he wagers on his wife's chastity with the villain Giacomo, who ultimately makes Posthumus believe that Imogen is unfaithful. Whether the love of Imogen and Posthumus can be restored is one of the key questions of this plot. This wager story draws on two sources: Boccaccio's *Decameron,* a series of prose tales first translated into English in 1620 but available in a French translation in the sixteenth century, and *Frederick of Jennen,* an English translation of a German version of the same story.

A second plot strand deals with Britain's relationship with Rome, especially Rome's demand that Britons pay the tribute pledged to Julius Caesar when he conquered the island. For these events, Shakespeare drew primarily on the brief account of Cymbeline's reign in Raphael Holinshed's *Chronicles of England, Scotland, and Ireland* (2nd ed., 1587). Cymbeline was king when the Roman emperor Augustus Caesar ushered in the famous period of peace known as the Pax Romana. In most of the sources, it was Cymbeline's son Guiderius who refused to pay Rome tribute. Shakespeare modified the story, however, so that Cymbeline, urged on by his Queen and her son, is the one who withholds the tribute and provokes a Roman invasion.

The third plot line has to do with two sons of Cymbeline, stolen from their nursery by a wrongly defamed courtier, Belarius, who raises them in the mountains of Wales. By chance, their sister Imogen, disguised as a boy, stumbles upon their mountain cave on her flight from her father's court in pursuit of Posthumus. Near this cave, Cloten, wearing Posthumus's clothes, is killed by one of these sons; also near this cave, Imogen awakes from her sleep to find herself beside his headless body. For the play to reach its resolution, Cymbeline's sons must be reunited with their father. This reunion occurs, but only after the sons play a decisive role in the final battle against the Roman invaders. Their heroic actions in this battle are modeled on another part of Holinshed, *The History of Scotland,* which recounts the story of a farmer named Hay and his two sons, who routed Danish invaders at the Battle of Luncarty in about 976 C.E.

From these complex and diverse materials, Shakespeare wove a play whose rich allusiveness has invited many kinds of topical interpretations. One line of criticism has focused on *Cymbeline*'s relationship to events and ideas connected to the reign of King James I. James was interested in linking imperial Rome to modern Britain and to his own kingship. He had himself painted crowned with laurel leaves, in the Roman manner, and had coins stamped with his laurel-crowned profile. Like Augustus Caesar, James presented himself as a great peacemaker after Elizabeth's reluctant involvement in wars in Ireland and in defending the Protestant countries of the Continent against Catholic powers. Moreover, just as Augustus ruled over a vast empire, James aspired to unite Scotland and England (along with the already incorporated Wales) into a single entity with one church and one set of laws. His project failed, but he exerted much effort in promoting this union during the first years of his reign. *Cymbeline* uncannily echoes some of James's preoccupations. Sometimes called Shakespeare's last Roman play, *Cymbeline* dramatizes ancient Britain's attempts to come to terms with imperial Rome. Names of Roman gods—particularly Diana, Apollo, and Jupiter—abound (Jupiter alone is mentioned over thirty times); and figures from Roman mythology and history, such as Tarquin, Philomela, and Aeneas, are often evoked. The play's title character, like James, is a British monarch respectful of Rome, even when asserting his independence in the matter of the tribute. The final word of the play, spoken by the King, is "peace." The analogies between the play and the Stuart court, however, have their limits. Cymbeline is also a king duped by his wicked queen and her doltish son—hardly a compliment to James and the royal family if events in the play are seen literally to mirror their circumstances.

Other allusions expand the play's possible range of meanings. For example, Milford Haven, the port in southern Wales where the Romans come ashore for their invasion of England, was also the place where Henry Tudor, Earl of Richmond, landed

James I liked to present himself as heir to Roman greatness. In this 1613 engraving, Crispin van de Passe portrays him crowned with the laurel wreath worn by Roman emperors.

in 1485 to begin his campaign against Richard III. Having defeated Richard, Henry was crowned Henry VII, first of the Tudor kings; Henry's daughter Margaret married James IV of Scotland, grandfather to the James who assumed the English throne in 1603. When the Romans land at Milford Haven in Shakespeare's play, they in effect precipitate a transformation of the kingdom, much as Henry Tudor was to do 1,500 years later. At the time of their arrival, Cymbeline believes his two sons to be dead, and his daughter and Cloten have both fled the court. Britain is without an heir. But through the battle with the Romans, the lost sons of Cymbeline are discovered and the kingdom renewed. So, too, James fancied himself an agent of renewal, a second Henry VII arriving from Scotland to unite the whole island under his rule.

Wales itself is an important symbolic location in this play. Although officially incorporated into England in the 1530s, Wales remained distinct, often stigmatized as rude and uncivilized. (In *1 Henry IV*, it is the home of the dangerous rebel Glyndŵr.) The Welsh language, banned from use in public contexts, was taken to symbolize the barbarity of this borderland region. However, in some narratives Wales was also the place from which sprang the legitimate rulers of England. The mythical King Arthur was given a Welsh origin, and traditionally the eldest son of the British monarch was (and still is) given the title Prince of Wales. In *Cymbeline*, Wales is imagined as a harsh pastoral landscape in which Belarius and the King's sons live in a cave, hunt the food they eat, and have little contact with other human beings. While these sons, Guiderius and Arviragus, frequently complain that they know nothing of the world and its customs and manners, Wales shelters them from the vices of court life. In fact, as is traditional in pastoral literature, the Welsh scenes contain a good deal of anticourt satire. In the play's spatial and symbolic economies, Wales is the place where true British manhood is preserved. *Cymbeline* thus works with material imbued with a new kind of significance under the reign of James.

Yet it may be a mistake to tie the play too closely to the royal family or to particular events that we retrospectively marshall to make sense of its mysteries. The play doesn't just reflect the world around it; it transforms the materials from that world into a powerful and challenging imaginative structure. In the largest sense, *Cymbeline* works to define both Britain and proper British manhood by constructing a complex narrative about national origins. The wager plot, with its story of sexual slander and threatened rape, is central to that narrative, not only because Imogen often seems to stand for Britain itself (she is several times addressed as "Britain," and her name resembles that of Innogen, the wife of Brute, the legendary ancient king of Britain), but also because the realignment of gender relations plays a crucial role in the renewal of Britain and in the play's turn from tragedy to comedy.

Strikingly, this play about Britain's past never mentions the word "England." In the history plays written in the 1590s, the reverse tends to be true: "Britain" is seldom employed, but "England" is invoked with great frequency. There are several reasons for Shakespeare's choice in this later play. He is, of course, deliberately evoking the world of the ancient Britons, the early inhabitants of the island who provide the starting point for his creation of a fictive national past. At the same time, he is to some extent reflecting, and helping to create, the Stuart monarch's sense of the entity over which he ruled. James, after all, was not an "Englander" in the same way Elizabeth had been. He was a Scotsman who spoke with an accent and aspired to bring the entire island into a new political alignment under the name Britannia or Great Britain.

Setting the play during the reign of Cymbeline enabled Shakespeare to imagine a primitive Britain that was also the cosmopolitan heir to the westward movement of empire. The treatment of Rome is particularly interesting in *Cymbeline*. Partly, the Romans are figured as an invading force, threatening the island. Yet the British characters most eager to repel the Romans and to treat them as an enemy are the evil Queen and her evil son. Cymbeline himself, while defending Britain's right to live free and under its own laws, is more disposed to come to terms with his great opponents and invariably treats them with respect. The play is marked by a pervasive tension between Britain's desire to defeat the Romans and to emulate them, to be insular and to be cosmopolitan. This tension is managed in part through the splitting of the Romans into the noble figure of Lucius and the devilish figure of Giacomo, who in his deceit and misogyny resembles the villainous Italians popular on the early modern stage.

When Giacomo comes to Britain to test Imogen's fidelity, he fails in his initial attempt to portray Posthumus as a philanderer upon whom Imogen should seek sexual revenge. He then proceeds more deviously, having himself conveyed in a trunk into her bedroom, from which he emerges in the dead of night to survey her sleeping body and the contents of her room. References to infamous acts of rape frame his incursion. As he steps from the trunk, Giacomo compares himself to Tarquin, the Roman tyrant who raped Lucrece (a story told in Shakespeare's lengthy poem *The Rape of Lucrece*, written in the 1590s). Furthermore, the book that Imogen had been reading when she fell asleep is opened to the story of Tereus, who raped Philomela and cut out her tongue. Although Giacomo does not literally rape Imogen, he violates the privacy of her body with his peering eyes and rapes her honor by lying successfully to Posthumus about her infidelity. At one level, this incident is about the unjust sufferings of a slandered woman. At another level, Imogen is Britain, itself, threatened by a skillful invader. Giacomo penetrates Imogen's bedchamber and later he penetrates and infects the ear of Posthumus with his poisonous slander.

In the play's denouement, the threat of foreign penetration is graphically repelled when Belarius and the sons of Cymbeline come from the Welsh mountains, joined by Posthumus disguised as a British peasant, and take a stand "in a narrow lane," putting

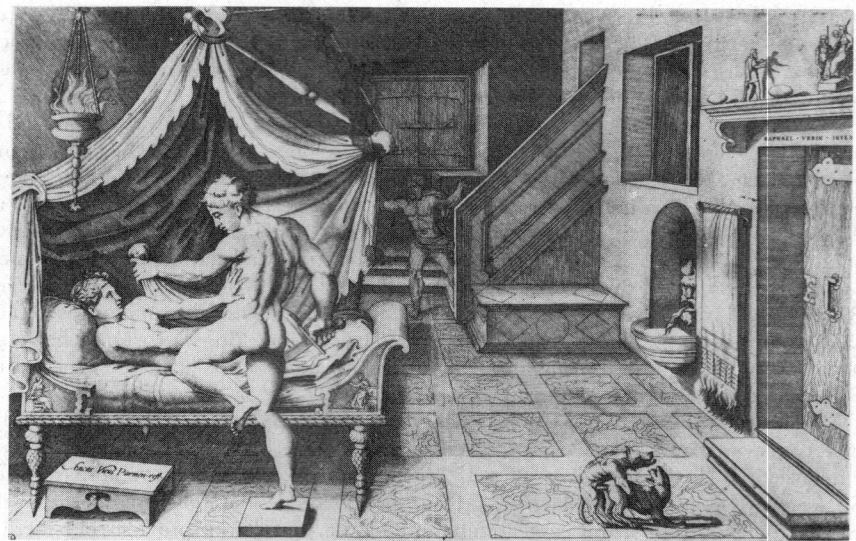

Tarquin's Rape of Lucrece. Sixteenth-century copy of an engraving by Agostino Veneziano.

the Romans to flight and instilling courage in the British. The vulnerable narrow lane is thus barricaded against outsiders by the sons of Cymbeline crying, "Stand, stand!" (5.3.28). The moment has gendered and sexual overtones. A vulnerable and feminized Britain is protected from invasion by the swords of virile young men whose cry, "Stand," means both to hold one's ground and to have an erection. This event proves pivotal, lending itself equally well to aphorism and to Posthumus's mocking rhyme: "Two boys, an old man twice a boy, a lane, / Preserved the Britons, was the Romans' bane" (5.3.57–58). In the play's symbolic economy, the threat of penetration initiated by Giacomo is thus repulsed by Imogen's long-lost brothers, and in the final scene Giacomo kneels to Posthumus, asking his forgiveness—the Italian subdued by the Briton.

Something quite different occurs with Lucius, the Roman military leader, who embodies the laudable virtues of ancient Rome rather than the hideous vices of early modern Italy. Even though the Roman army is defeated, Cymbeline decides to resume paying tribute, and in his final speech the King says: "Let / A Roman and a British ensign wave / Friendly together" (5.5.477–79). This rapprochement of warring powers is ratified by one of the play's several mysterious visions. Before the battle, a Roman soothsayer tells Lucius what the gods had revealed to him:

> I saw Jove's bird, the Roman eagle, winged
> From the spongy south to this part of the west,
> There vanished in the sunbeams; which portends,
> Unless my sins abuse my divination,
> Success to th' Roman host.
>
> (4.2.347–51)

In this play, not even soothsayers have perfect interpretive skills. The outcome of the battle requires some revisions in the exegesis of the vision. After the battle, the soothsayer says:

> For the Roman eagle,
> From south to west on wing soaring aloft,
> Lessened herself, and in the beams o'th' sun
> So vanished; which foreshowed our princely eagle,

> Th'imperial Caesar, should again unite
> His favor with the radiant Cymbeline,
> Which shines here in the west.
>
> (5.5.468–74)

Conquest has been transformed into concord as the Roman eagle and the British sun merge and as Cymbeline celebrates this peace within the temple of Jupiter.

In stressing the final union of Britain and Rome, the play's conclusion makes Britain the heir of Rome's imperial legacy even as Britain proclaims the integrity of its own land, laws, and customs. In the early modern period, the course of empire was thought to move westward. When Troy fell, the Trojan hero Aeneas bore his father on his back from the fires of the burning city and eventually fulfilled his destiny by establishing a new kingdom in Italy in what was to become the center of the Roman Empire. In the soothsayer's vision, the Roman eagle journeys even farther west, renewing itself, as eagles were believed to do, by enduring the burning fires of Britain's sun to purge away old feathers in preparation for the growth of new.

The play's culminating vision of a Britain separate unto itself but also the cosmopolitan heir of an imperial tradition is anticipated in the actions of Imogen and Posthumus. In the final act, both are partly Roman in their dress and sympathies. Posthumus Leonatus comes to Britain in the company of the Italian gentry, but then he dresses as a British peasant and fights with Belarius in the narrow lane before reassuming his Italian garb. Imogen is present at the battle as page to Lucius, the Roman general who had found her weeping over the headless corpse of Cloten. In the final moments of reconciliation, Cymbeline's daughter and her husband stand before the British King in foreign clothes. Imogen, moreover, earlier makes a telling speech about Britain's place in the world when discussing with a trusted servant where she would live after Posthumus has come to believe her unchaste. Her father's court, with Cloten present, she finds unthinkable. She then asks:

> Hath Britain all the sun that shines? Day, night,
> Are they not but in Britain? I'th' world's volume
> Our Britain seems as of it, but not in't:
> In a great pool a swan's nest.
>
> (3.4.136–39)

Imogen nicely captures the play's most complex view of Britain. Eschewing an insular patriotism associated with Cloten and the Queen, she recognizes a vast world beyond the shores of Britain. Punning on the double meaning of "volume" as "expanse" or "book," Imogen suggests Britain's partial separation from a larger entity. Britain is a little part of a bigger expanse, a page detached from a large book, or a swan's nest in a great pool. As the image of the swan's nest suggests, Britain remains the special seat of grace and beauty. But it is also connected to something larger than itself. There are other pages in the volume to which, even if detached, Britain belongs.

The play, then, seems to be negotiating a new vision of the nation suited for the Stuart moment—a vision resulting from the richly suggestive concatenation of discursive traditions that Shakespeare brought together in this play. Reaching back into the chronicle materials of ancient Britain, he provides a genealogy for modern Britain that (1) insists on the integrity and freedom of the island kingdom but (2) presents it as purged—largely through the efforts of the King's "Welsh" sons—of the corruptions of modern court life as embodied in figures such as Giacomo or Cloten, and (3) aligns Britain with the cosmopolitan values of Rome, positioning the island kingdom as the appropriate heir of Roman greatness: both warlike and peace-loving.

The renewed Britain has a fourth striking characteristic, and that is its decidedly masculine coloration. The wager plot makes plain the role of gender in configuring British national identity. Consider first the changing fortunes of Imogen. At the beginning of the play, she is a beloved and important figure in her father's court. Cymbeline's

The eagle, king of birds and emblem of the Roman god Jupiter. According to myth, it could stare at the sun without blinking and fly into the sun in order to burn off its old feathers. From Joachim Camerarius, *Symbolorum et Emblematum* (1605 ed.).

only living heir, the strong-willed and decisive princess chooses Posthumus for her husband even though he has little money and is not of royal birth. By the end of the play, Imogen has been displaced from the succession by her two rediscovered brothers; she has also been ordered killed by her husband, threatened with rape, knocked unconscious by a drug she believes to be medicine, and struck by her husband when, in her page's attire, she steps forward to reveal her identity to him in the last scene. Though cross-dressed for much of the second half of the play, she does not, like Portia in *The Merchant of Venice* and Rosalind in *As You Like It*, use that disguise aggressively to shape her own destiny. Rather, burdened by the knowledge that her husband unjustly and inexplicably desires her death, Imogen grows less powerful and more passive as the play progresses. Her decline can be summarized in the pun on "heir" and "air." Imogen begins as the former and ends as the latter. The mysterious tablet laid on Posthumus's breast contained a riddling prophecy:

> Whenas a lion's whelp shall, to himself unknown, without seeking find, and
> be embraced by a piece of tender air; and when from a stately cedar shall be
> lopped branches which, being dead many years, shall after revive, be jointed
> to the old stock, and freshly grow: then shall Posthumus end his miseries,
> Britain be fortunate and flourish in peace and plenty.   (5.5.434–40)

When the soothsayer finally untangles this riddle, he declares Posthumus Leonatus to be the lion's offspring; Cymbeline the cedar tree; his lost sons the lopped branches; and Imogen the tender air, because "tender air" in Latin translates as *mollis aer*, which (by a stretch of the imagination) derives from *mulier*, Latin for "wife." When Posthumus is embraced by the "tender air" (no longer an "heir"), his miseries will cease. Now less important to the succession, Imogen is finally allowed to live with her chosen husband.

Nineteenth-century critics loved Imogen, idealizing her as a paragon of selfless and long-suffering womanhood. She never, for example, protests her demotion from the position of heir apparent; in fact, she considers finding her brothers worth the loss of the kingdom. To many contemporary critics, however, her role in the play's narrative of nation is a troubling one. Britain renews itself as women are disempowered or disappear. Cymbeline's Queen is an embodiment of hypocritical viciousness (Shakespeare does not even bother to give her a name), and her son, a figure whose father is never mentioned or seen, bears her taint. The play's happy resolution occurs only after all traces of this Queen and her offspring have been erased. When finally united with his children, Cymbeline articulates the fantasy of having himself given birth to all three: "Oh, what am I? / A mother to the birth of three? Ne'er mother / Rejoiced deliverance more" (5.5.367–69). This is the dream of androgenesis, reproduction without union with women.

Much earlier in the play, Posthumus, believing that Imogen has been sexually unfaithful to him, voices a similar wish: "Is there no way for men to be, but women / Must be half-workers?" (2.5.1–2). In one of the most deeply misogynist speeches in the Shakespeare canon, Posthumus then blames all the vices of the world on "The woman's part" (line 20)—on woman herself and on that part of woman lodged in man, the fallen Eve's mark upon the human race. This mistaken projection onto woman of responsibility for evil may partly explain Cymbeline's fantasy of androgenesis and also why, in the last scene, no persons appareled as women are to be seen (Imogen is still dressed as a page). The happy union of Britain and Rome and Wales is overwhelmingly a union of men.

The troubled status of marriage in the play further hints at its difficulties with "the woman's part" in establishing lineage and in forging the nation. Imogen's marriage initially is so slightly regarded by her father and stepmother, who remain intent on her marrying Cloten, that students often ask: is she really married? The answer is yes, but the marriage is never recognized as a proper dynastic union and is quickly further jeopardized by Posthumus's rash wager with Giacomo. The King's first wife is long dead, her role as mother to her male children usurped by Belarius and their nurse and her role as Imogen's mother assumed by Cymbeline's nightmarish second wife. At the end of the play, everyone is relieved when the stepmother abruptly dies, leaving Cymbeline to his happy fantasy of having given birth, alone, to his three children. Heterosexual union is fleeting, disastrous, or vulnerable to slander. By the end of act 5, only Posthumus and Imogen remain married—though in diminished circumstances that put them both firmly out of the line of succession.

To be sure, the play queries its most virulent forms of misogyny by punishing the slanderous Giacomo and highlighting Posthumus's gradual recovery of faith in Imogen. When Posthumus receives a bloody cloth signifying (falsely) that his order to murder Imogen has been fulfilled, he is overcome with remorse and berates husbands like himself for murdering their wives "For wrying but a little" (5.1.5). At this point, Posthumus still believes his wife to have been sexually unfaithful to him, yet he castigates himself for having ordered her punished. His words form a remarkable exception to the more usual patriarchal assumption that female chastity is the primary marker of a woman's value and virtue and that loss of chastity is an unforgivable crime. Critics differ as to how much weight to assign this speech. Posthumus delivers it when he believes Imogen to be dead; and generally it is easier to forgive the dead than the living. By the time he is finally reconciled to the living, breathing woman, Giacomo's lies have been exposed and Posthumus takes to himself a wife whose chastity is not in question.

The play, moreover, clearly punishes the evil Cloten, who had fantasized raping Imogen; and it punishes the misogynous lies of Giacomo, who submits to Posthumus in the final scene. Moreover, Posthumus, having suffered for his lack of faith in Imogen, emerges as the play's one proper husband, though he now assumes the dominant position in his marriage—a position once held by Imogen. Jupiter himself provides the warrant for this reversal. In prison, Posthumus has a dream that not only reconnects him to his familial origins but also provides an image of his own future family. As he sleeps, Posthumus's two warlike brothers and his warlike father appear to him. The father is described as *"leading in his hand an ancient matron (his wife, and mother to Posthumus)"* (stage direction following 5.4.29). After this dream, sent by Jupiter, Posthumus recovers his "true" identity as Imogen's husband and Britain's warrior hero. As he assumes his position in the honored line of Leonati men, the place marked for Imogen is that of Roman/British wife, "led in his hand." *Cymbeline* thus reproves the most virulent forms of misogyny while simultaneously removing women from public power, transforming them into chaste, domesticated wives, and reaffirming the dominance of husbands.

Samuel Johnson was right when he said that *Cymbeline* is a play with many incongruities of time, place, and circumstance. And yet it is not an incoherent play, but rather one that richly interweaves the history of the nation with the stories of the figures who take up their positions within it. What is eerie about *Cymbeline* is that its characters often understand so little about what is happening to them, and yet each appears to play out the part assigned to him or her by some higher power: Jupiter, destiny, time. In this regard, *Cymbeline* is of a piece with Shakespeare's other romances, plays in which a higher power often seems to steer all boats to shore and reunite long-severed families.

But fictions of inevitability can be deceiving. One should remember that the soothsayer had to revise his interpretation of his vision of the eagle and the sun to make his narrative square with events as they actually happened. And to decipher Posthumus's tablet, he could make the prophecy tally with the facts only by means of a tortuous transformation of "tender air" into "wife." This might suggest that in this play, at least, the higher powers determine less than they appear to do; rather, the forms taken by family, nation, and empire are in some measure the result of human efforts, interventions, and narratives. Shakespeare's play is one such narrative. The resolution of its complex plot may invite relieved assent to its culminating vision, but the very artifice of that resolution also reveals its contingency, suggesting that there is nothing either natural or inevitable about the familial and political arrangements that are repeatedly contested and reordered in this tragicomic play.

JEAN E. HOWARD

SELECTED BIBLIOGRAPHY

Berry, Amanda. "desire vomit emptiness: *Cymbeline*'s Marriage Time." *Shakesqueer: A Queer Companion to the Complete Works of Shakespeare*. Ed. Madhavi Menon. Durham, NC: Duke UP, 2011. 89–96. Argues that the play queers heterosexual marriage by underscoring the problematic status and unfulfilled nature of such unions.

Cheney, Patrick. "Venting Rhyme for a Mockery: *Cymbeline* and National Romance," Chapter 8 of *Shakespeare's Literary Authorship*. Cambridge: Cambridge UP, 2008. 234–63. Argues that *Cymbeline* implicitly constructs Shakespeare as Britain's national poet by inserting him into the lineage of other poets whose works are alluded to by the play, by including many references to Shakespeare's earlier works, and by emphasizing the drama's lyricism and embedded songs and poems.

Escobedo, Andrew. "From Britannia to England: *Cymbeline* and the Beginning of Nations." *Shakespeare Quarterly* 59:1 (2008): 60–87. Suggests that the play explores two kinds of nationalism—one based on ancient British origins and embracing heterogeneity, the other drawing on Saxon precedent and stressing English purity.

Jones, Emrys. "Stuart *Cymbeline*." *Essays in Criticism* 11 (1961): 84–99. Takes a historical approach to the play by emphasizing its links to James I's dedication to peace and the role of Milford Haven in Tudor national mythology.

Kahn, Coppélia. "Postscript: *Cymbeline*: Paying Tribute to Rome." *Roman Shakespeare: Warriors, Wounds, and Women.* London: Routledge, 1997. 160–70. Argues that *Cymbeline* shares much with Shakespeare's other Roman plays, including a preoccupation with Roman *virtu* as the root of masculine identity—but an identity constantly made precarious by the woman's part in its formation.

Menon, Madhavi. "Facts: *Cymbeline* and the "Whore" of Historicism." Chapter 2 of *Unhistorical Shakespeare: Queer Theory in Shakespearean Literature and Film.* New York: Palgrave Macmillan, 2008. 51–71. Questions some historical criticism's uncritical embrace of "facts" and argues for a theoretical approach to *Cymbeline* that sees "facts" as fluidly open to retrospective interpretation; uses the play to show how evidence is treacherous and "facts" often lie, as with Giacomo's "proof" of Imogen's infidelity.

Mikalachki, Jodi. "Cymbeline and the Masculine Romance of Roman Britain." *The Legacy of Boadicea: Gender and Nation in Early Modern England.* London: Routledge, 1998. 96–114. From a feminist perspective, explores the respective roles of ancient British savagery and Roman civility in the forging of an all-male national community in *Cymbeline*.

Parker, Patricia. "Romance and Empire: Anachronistic *Cymbeline*." *Unfolded Tales: Essays on Renaissance Romance.* Ed. George M. Logan and Gordon Teskey. Ithaca, NY: Cornell UP, 1989. 189–207. Examines the pervasive allusions to *The Aeneid* in *Cymbeline*, arguing that the play intimates the passing of Rome's imperial greatness westward to Britain.

Warren, Roger. *Cymbeline.* Shakespeare in Performance series. Manchester: Manchester UP, 1989. Focuses on performances of the play, especially on striking stage and television versions from the second half of the twentieth century.

Wayne, Valerie. "The Woman's Parts of *Cymbeline*." *Staged Properties in Early Modern English Drama.* Ed. Jonathan Gil Harris and Natasha Korda. Cambridge: Cambridge UP, 2002. 288–315. Traces the history of three stage properties—manacle, ring, and bloody cloth—as they represent Imogen, and women more generally, in *Cymbeline*.

FILM

Cymbeline. 1982. Dir. Elijah Moshinsky. UK. 175 min. This BBC production boasts such cast luminaries as Richard Johnson (the King), Claire Bloom (the Queen), and Helen Mirren (Imogen), among others.

TEXTUAL INTRODUCTION

Cymbeline was never printed in Shakespeare's lifetime. The only authoritative text is that published in the First Folio of 1623 (F), where the play is included as the last of the tragedies. It was reprinted in the Second Folio of 1632 (F2) with some minor corrections. The relatively heavy punctuation of F, including the frequent use of parentheses, colons, hyphens, and apostrophes, seems to indicate that the text was prepared for publication by a professional scribe, probably Ralph Crane, who also prepared the manuscripts of *The Winter's Tale* and *The Tempest* for publication in F. By early seventeenth-century standards, the text is a good one, requiring little intervention by the editor apart from the correction of a few misprints and obvious minor errors. The lineation is mainly clear and accurate—although, as usual, F does not indicate where a line is divided between two speakers, merely printing such cases as two short lines. Stage directions, especially for the battle scenes in act 5, are relatively full, although they do not include some sound effects such as trumpet flourishes to mark the entrances of royalty, or *"alarums"* and other noises associated with battles. Modern editors routinely add clarification of whether characters are in disguise and whether lines are spoken *"aside."*

Punctuation is a major challenge for the editor of this text. This is not just a question of "translating" the heavy punctuation of the scribe into an acceptable modern format—by substituting dashes for some of the Folio's parentheses, for example—but of attempting to disentangle the complex syntax of very long sentences that can be, by modern standards, ungrammatical or even incoherent. Examples of such speeches are those made by Posthumus at 5.3.14–51 and by Giacomo at 5.5.153–209. Sometimes this style can be attributed to particular characters and situations, but it pervades the whole play. Shorter passages also present problems: the first four speeches made by the First Gentleman in the opening scene of the play contain examples of elliptical structure and frequent self-interruption. We can usually grasp the general meaning, but the actual words and the relations between them give us difficulty.

Another contentious issue is the naming of the characters. This edition reverts to the traditional name of "Imogen" for the heroine. This name is consistently used in the Folio text and in the editorial and critical tradition. The Oxford editors argued that "Imogen" is a misprint for "Innogen." However, their arguments are not entirely compelling. The name "Imogen," which they thought did not occur before the First Folio, can be found both in a fifteenth-century translation of Ralph Higden's *Polychronicon* (Pitcher, "Names in *Cymbeline*," 4) and in the "Second Table" or index to the first volume of the 1586 edition of Holinshed (King, *Constructions of Britain*, 72). In contrast, while the Folio also consistently uses "Iachimo" for the name of the villain, the name is here modernized to Giacomo according to the editorial principle of *The Norton Shakespeare* of using the standard modernizations of foreign names and words.

Finally, the Folio indicates act and scene numbers throughout, but editors disagree about how to divide the fifth act. The usual rule of thumb whereby a new scene begins when the stage is vacated, however briefly, is challenged by the desirability of rendering the battle from 5.2 to 5.4 fluidly as a continuous sequence, and the Folio's elaborate narrative stage directions (at 5.2.0, 5.2.10, 5.2.13, and 5.3.0) are a further complication. Two of these (at 5.2.10 and 5.2.13) prescribe actions that are subsequently described in detail by Posthumus (at 5.3.14–51). An important piece of action is rendered entirely through a stage direction, here given as 5.4.0 SD. In the Folio, this lengthy direction comes at the end of *"Scena Tertia."* It is followed by *"Scena Quarta"* and a new direction for the entrance for Posthumus and his Jailer. The scene changes from the battlefield to a prison—the Jailer tells Posthumus: "You have locks upon you"—although the Folio never directs that the stage be cleared of the large group of people present at the end of 5.3. In this edition, therefore, an *Exeunt* is added at the end of 5.3 and the stage direction moved to 5.4, even though for Posthumus and the Jailer it implies a violation of the "rule of re-entry," whereby characters normally do not exit and re-enter immediately.

Ann Thompson

TEXTUAL BIBLIOGRAPHY

Dessen, Alan C., and Leslie Thomson. *Dictionary of Stage Directions in Early Modern Drama*. Cambridge: Cambridge UP, 1999.

King, Ros. *"Cymbeline": Constructions of Britain*. Aldershot: Ashgate, 2005.

Knight, G. Wilson. *The Crown of Life*. London: Oxford UP, 1947.

Pitcher, John. "Names in *Cymbeline*." *Essays in Criticism* 43 (1993): 1–16.

PERFORMANCE NOTE

Like other late Shakespeare plays, *Cymbeline* abounds with staging challenges. It mingles diverse settings, periods, and genres, and requires actors to portray ghosts, the Roman army, even Jupiter descended from heaven astride an eagle. Its final scene, among Shakespeare's longest and most populated, sustains a sense of climax through twenty-four discrete anagnorises (recognitions or discoveries). Although the play is capable of generating unequaled wonder and delight for audiences, its success nevertheless depends on unusually precise blocking and timing. Trickiest of all, productions must sustain both dramatic momentum and audience interest across the tangle of episodes preceding the climactic series of denouements. In short, *Cymbeline*'s long-absent protagonist, reliance on exposition, and repeated indulgence in lyricism at the expense of plot-advancing action all potentially consort to try the audience's resolve and undermine the god Jupiter's assertion that "the more delayed, [the more] delighted" (5.4.72).

Directors often respond to the play's length (only *Hamlet* is longer), structural unconventionality, and sometimes halting pace by cutting and by tipping the generic balance toward comedy by, for instance, laying exaggerated emphasis on Cloten's role or Imogen's cross-dressing. Some create lavish, fairy tale–inflected productions, seizing on archetypes to simplify the plot and push the play toward melodrama. Others exploit the play's emphasis on dreams to confer visual and tonal coherence on the whole. Still others foreground the plot's challenges to representation and complex characterization as prominent dramaturgical themes, double-casting actors and eliminating costumes, sets, and other conventional tools of representation.

Whatever their approach, directors make critical decisions respecting character and (by extension) genre. Cloten can seem pitiably foolish and inept or irredeemably arrogant and vile; Giacomo can be an attractive mischief-maker or a contemptible would-be rapist. Directors likewise must decide whether the Queen is a Snow White stereotype or a realistic villain; whether Cymbeline's episodes of rage and severely lapsed judgment bespeak insanity, dotage, or mere archetypal duty; and whether Posthumus's pursuit of Imogen's life proceeds from a distraction born of despair or from something profoundly evil within him.

BRETT GAMBOA

The Tragedy of Cymbeline

[THE PERSONS OF THE PLAY

In Cymbeline's Britain:
CYMBELINE, King of Britain
QUEEN, second wife to Cymbeline
IMOGEN, daughter to Cymbeline by his first wife, later disguised as Fidele
POSTHUMUS Leonatus, husband to Imogen
CLOTEN, son to the Queen by a former husband
PISANIO, Posthumus' servant
CORNELIUS, a doctor
FIRST LORD }
SECOND LORD } attending Cloten
LORDS at Cymbeline's court
LADIES at Cymbeline's court
Two GENTLEMEN
Two British CAPTAINS
Two British JAILERS
MESSENGERS
MUSICIANS
Soldiers

In Wales:
BELARIUS, a banished lord, known as Morgan
GUIDERIUS, known as Polydore
ARVIRAGUS, known as Cadwal

In Rome:
PHILARIO, Posthumus' friend in Rome
GIACOMO, an Italian }
FRENCHMAN }
Dutchman } friends of Philario
Spaniard }
Two Roman SENATORS
Roman TRIBUNES

Romans in Britain:
CAIUS LUCIUS, Roman ambassador and general
Roman CAPTAINS
Philharmonus, a SOOTHSAYER
JUPITER
Ghost of SICILIUS Leonatus, father to Posthumus
Ghost of Posthumus' MOTHER, wife to Sicilius
Ghosts of Posthumus' two BROTHERS
Attendants]

1.1

Enter two GENTLEMEN.

FIRST GENTLEMAN   You do not meet a man but frowns. Our bloods
No more obey the heavens than our courtiers
Still seem as does the King.[1]

SECOND GENTLEMAN   But what's the matter?

FIRST GENTLEMAN   His daughter, and the heir of 's° kingdom, whom   *of his*
5   He purposed to° his wife's sole son (a widow   *intended for*
That late° he married) hath referred° herself   *recently / given*
Unto a poor but worthy gentleman. She's wedded,
Her husband banished, she imprisoned. All
Is outward sorrow, though I think the King
Be touched at very heart.

10   SECOND GENTLEMAN   None but the King?

FIRST GENTLEMAN   He° that hath lost her too; so is the Queen,   *(the Queen's son)*
That most desired the match. But not a courtier,
Although they wear their faces to the bent
Of° the King's looks, hath a heart that is not   *In accordance with*
Glad at the thing they scowl at.

15   SECOND GENTLEMAN   And why so?

FIRST GENTLEMAN   He that hath missed the Princess is a thing
Too bad for bad report; and he that hath her—
I mean that married her (alack, good man,
And therefore banished)—is a creature such
20   As to seek through the regions of the earth
For one his like, there would be something failing°   *lacking*
In him that should compare.[2] I do not think
So fair an outward and such stuff° within   *substance; fabric*
Endows a man but he.

SECOND GENTLEMAN   You speak him far.°   *praise him greatly*

25   FIRST GENTLEMAN   I do extend him, sir, within himself,[3]
Crush him together, rather than unfold
His measure duly.[4]

SECOND GENTLEMAN   What's his name and birth?

FIRST GENTLEMAN   I cannot delve him to the root.[5] His father
Was called Sicilius, who did join his honor°   *prowess (as a soldier)*
30   Against the Romans with Cassibelan,
But had his titles by Tenantius,[6] whom
He served with glory and admired success,
So gained the sur-addition, "Leonatus";[7]
And had, besides this gentleman in question,
35   Two other sons who in the wars o'th' time
Died with their swords in hand. For which their father,
Then old and fond of issue,° took such sorrow   *of his offspring*
That he quit being, and his gentle lady,
Big of° this gentleman, our theme, deceased   *Pregnant with*
40   As he was born. The King, he takes the babe

1.1 Location: Cymbeline's court, Britain.
1. *Our . . . King:* Our dispositions ("bloods") are not more subject to planetary influences than our courtiers' moods are determined by the King's. (The planets were believed to affect human actions and emotions.)
2. In any man selected for comparison.
3. I set forth his virtues, sir, within the boundaries of his own merit.
4. *rather . . . duly:* rather than reveal what he is

really worth. The metaphor picks up on the sense of "stuff" as "fabric" in line 23. Fabric can be crushed together and unfolded and accurately measured.
5. I cannot completely account for his lineage.
6. Tenantius was Cymbeline's father and the brother of Cassibelan, who in 3.1.5 is described as Cymbeline's uncle.
7. The additional name "Leonatus" (born of a lion).

To his protection, calls him Posthumus[8] Leonatus,
Breeds him,° and makes him of his bedchamber,[9]   *Brings him up*
Puts to him° all the learnings that his time   *Offers him*
Could make him the receiver of, which he took
45 As we do air, fast as 'twas ministered,
And in 's° spring became a harvest; lived in court—   *in his*
Which rare it is to do—most praised, most loved;
A sample° to the youngest, to the more mature   *An example*
A glass that feated them,[1] and to the graver
50 A child that guided dotards.° To his mistress,   *foolish old men*
For whom he now is banished, her own price
Proclaims how she esteemed him; and his virtue[2]
By her election° may be truly read,   *choice (of him)*
What kind of man he is.
SECOND GENTLEMAN   I honor him
55 Even out° of your report. But pray you tell me,   *Even beyond the limits*
Is she sole child to th' King?
FIRST GENTLEMAN   His only child.
He had two sons—if this be worth your hearing,
Mark it—the eldest of them at three years old,
I'th' swathing° clothes the other, from their nursery   *swaddling*
60 Were stol'n, and to this hour, no guess in knowledge°   *no informed conjecture*
Which way they went.
SECOND GENTLEMAN   How long is this ago?
FIRST GENTLEMAN   Some twenty years.
SECOND GENTLEMAN   That a king's children should be so conveyed,
So slackly guarded, and the search so slow
That could not trace them!
65 FIRST GENTLEMAN   Howso'er 'tis strange,
Or that the negligence may well be laughed at,
Yet is it true, sir.
SECOND GENTLEMAN   I do well believe you.
     Enter the QUEEN, POSTHUMUS, *and* IMOGEN.[3]
We must forbear.° Here comes the gentleman,   *withdraw*
The Queen, and Princess.   *Exeunt [the two* GENTLEMEN.][4]
70 QUEEN   No, be assured you shall not find me, daughter,
After the slander of[5] most stepmothers,
Evil-eyed unto you. You're my prisoner, but
Your jailer shall deliver you the keys
That lock up your restraint. For you, Posthumus,
75 So soon as I can win th'offended King,
I will be known your advocate. Marry,[6] yet
The fire of rage is in him, and 'twere good

8. In Latin, the word means "after death." As applied to a child, it means "one born after his or her father's death."
9. Makes him a personal servant.
1. A mirror that furnished ("feated") them with images of virtue or elegance.
2. *her . . . virtue:* the price she paid (for loving him) demonstrates how much she valued him and his virtue; her own worth ("price") shows the high esteem in which she held him and his virtues.
3. TEXTUAL COMMENT Although some scholars have suggested that the Folio's "Imogen" is a misprint for "Innogen," the name of the wife of the ancient English king Brute in Holinshed's *Chronicles,* this edition reverts to the more familiar "Imogen," since F is consistent in its use of this spelling. See Digital Edition TC 1.
4. F marks *Scena Secunda* (second scene) after the gentlemen exit. Then the Queen, Posthumus, and Imogen enter. There is, however, no change of time or place, and the Queen and the lovers are probably in view at line 68 when the Second Gentleman announces their entrance. Most editors do not indicate a new scene here.
5. In accordance with the slanderous things said about.
6. A mild oath, from the name of the Virgin Mary.

You leaned unto° his sentence with what patience   *You obeyed*
Your wisdom may inform° you.   *instill in*
POSTHUMUS   Please your highness,
I will from hence today.
80 QUEEN   You know the peril.
I'll fetch a turn° about the garden, pitying   *go for a walk*
The pangs of barred affections, though the King
Hath charged you should not speak together.   *Exit.*
IMOGEN   Oh, dissembling courtesy! How fine this tyrant
85 Can tickle° where she wounds! My dearest husband,   *flatter*
I something° fear my father's wrath, but nothing—   *somewhat*
Always reserved my holy duty—what
His rage can do on me.⁷ You must be gone,
And I shall here abide the hourly shot
90 Of angry eyes, not comforted to live
But that there is this jewel in the world
That I may see again.
POSTHUMUS   My queen, my mistress!
O lady, weep no more, lest I give cause
To be suspected of more tenderness
95 Than doth become a man. I will remain
The loyal'st husband that did e'er plight troth.°   *pledge marriage*
My residence in Rome at one Philario's,
Who to my father was a friend, to me
Known but by letter; thither write, my queen,
100 And with mine eyes I'll drink the words you send
Though ink be made of gall.°   *bile; bitter liquid*
    Enter QUEEN.
QUEEN   Be brief, I pray you:
If the King come, I shall incur I know not
How much of his displeasure. [*aside*] Yet I'll move him
To walk this way. I never do him wrong,
105 But he does buy my injuries to be friends,⁸
Pays dear for my offenses.   [*Exit.*]
POSTHUMUS   Should we be taking leave
As long a term° as yet we have to live,   *time*
The loathness° to depart would grow. Adieu.   *unwillingness*
IMOGEN   Nay, stay a little.
110 Were you but riding forth to air yourself
Such parting were too petty. Look here, love:
This diamond was my mother's. Take it, heart,
    [*She gives him a ring.*]
But keep it till you woo another wife,
When Imogen is dead.
POSTHUMUS   How, how? Another?
115 You gentle gods, give me but this I have,
And sear up⁹ my embracements from a next°   *another wife*
With bonds of death!
    [*He puts on the ring.*]

7. *but . . . me:* an ambiguous phrase. My holy duty of obedience to my father excepted (a bond put in jeopardy by Cymbeline's act), I do not at all ("nothing") fear what Cymbeline's rage can do to me. Or: My holy duty to my husband excepted (which Cymbeline could disrupt by interfering with the marriage), I do not at all fear what Cymbeline's rage may do to me.
8. But he does endure the consequences of ("buy") my injuries in order to be friends.
9. And wrap up (in the cerecloth, or waxed linen, used in burial shrouds).

Remain, remain thou here,
While sense° can keep it on; and sweetest, fairest,   *the ability to feel*
As I my poor self did exchange for you
120   To your so infinite loss, so in our trifles°   *love tokens*
I still win of you.[1] For my sake wear this:
It is a manacle of love, I'll place it
Upon this fairest prisoner.
    [*He puts a bracelet on her arm.*]
IMOGEN   O the gods!
When shall we see again?
    Enter CYMBELINE *and* LORDS.
POSTHUMUS   Alack, the King!
125   CYMBELINE Thou basest° thing, avoid hence,° from my sight!   *most lowborn / be off*
If after this command thou fraught° the court   *burden*
With thy unworthiness, thou diest. Away,
Thou'rt poison to my blood.
POSTHUMUS   The gods protect you,
And bless the good remainders of° the court!   *people remaining at*
I am gone.   *Exit.*
130   IMOGEN   There cannot be a pinch° in death   *pain*
More sharp than this is.
CYMBELINE   O disloyal thing
That shouldst repair° my youth, thou heap'st   *restore*
A year's age on me.
IMOGEN   I beseech you, sir,
Harm not yourself with your vexation.
135   I am senseless of° your wrath; a touch° more rare   *unable to feel / an emotion*
Subdues all pangs, all fears.
CYMBELINE   Past grace?° Obedience?   *all sense of duty*
IMOGEN   Past hope and in despair: that way past grace.[2]
CYMBELINE   That mightst have had the sole son of my queen!
IMOGEN   Oh, blest that I might not! I chose an eagle
140   And did avoid a puttock.[3]
CYMBELINE   Thou took'st a beggar, wouldst have made my throne
A seat for baseness.
IMOGEN   No, I rather added
A luster to it.
CYMBELINE   O thou vile one!
IMOGEN   Sir,
It is your fault that I have loved Posthumus:
145   You bred him as my playfellow, and he is
A man worth any woman, overbuys me
Almost the sum he pays.[4]
CYMBELINE   What! Art thou mad?
IMOGEN   Almost, sir. Heaven restore me! Would I were
A neatherd's° daughter, and my Leonatus   *cowherd's*
Our neighbor shepherd's son.
    Enter QUEEN.

---

1. I still am enriched by you. Posthumus suggests that he is unequal in rank and wealth to Imogen. Correspondingly, his love token is of less value than hers.
2. Redemption. Alluding to the Christian belief that those who despair distrust God and are beyond the reach of grace.
3. A kite, or common predatory bird.
4. *overbuys . . . pays:* pays too much for me by almost the amount he gives for me. (Posthumus both gives himself to Imogen in marriage and also pays the price of banishment.) Imogen insists that Posthumus's worth equals her own and that their marriage consequently does not degrade her.

150 CYMBELINE   Thou foolish thing!
   [*to* QUEEN] They were again together; you have done
   Not after° our command. [*to* LORDS] Away with her,   *according to*
   And pen her up.
   QUEEN   Beseech° your patience. —Peace,   *I beseech*
   Dear lady daughter, peace. —Sweet sovereign,
155 Leave us to ourselves, and make yourself some comfort
   Out of your best advice.
   CYMBELINE   Nay, let her languish
   A drop of blood a day⁵ and, being aged,
   Die of this folly.   *Exit* [*with* LORDS].
   QUEEN   Fie, you must give way.
           Enter PISANIO.
   Here is your servant. —How now, sir? What news?
   PISANIO   My lord your son drew° on my master.   *drew a sword*
160 QUEEN   Ha?
   No harm, I trust, is done?
   PISANIO   There might have been,
   But that my master rather played than fought,
   And had no help of anger. They were parted
   By gentlemen at hand.   I am very glad on't.
   QUEEN
165 IMOGEN   Your son's my father's friend; he takes his part
   To draw upon an exile.° O brave sir!   *(Posthumus)*
   I would they were in Afric° both together,   *Africa*
   Myself by with a needle, that I might prick°   *urge on*
   The goer-back.° [*to* PISANIO] Why came you from   *swordsman who retreated*
       your master?
170 PISANIO   On his command. He would not suffer° me   *allow*
   To bring him to the haven; left these notes
   Of what commands I should be subject to,
   When't pleased you to employ me.
   QUEEN   This hath been
   Your faithful servant. I dare lay mine honor
   He will remain so.
175 PISANIO   I humbly thank your highness.
   QUEEN   Pray walk a while.⁶
   IMOGEN [*to* PISANIO]   About some half hour hence, pray you
       speak with me.
   You shall at least go see my lord aboard.
   For this time leave me.   *Exeunt.*

1.2

           Enter CLOTEN *and two* LORDS.
   FIRST LORD   Sir, I would advise you to shift° a shirt;¹ the vio-   *change*
   lence of action hath made you reek° as a sacrifice. Where air   *emit vapors; stink*
   comes out, air comes in; there's none abroad so wholesome
   as that you vent.²

---

5. Referring to the popular belief that one lost a drop
of blood with each sigh.
6. F does not mark a separate exit for the Queen here,
but Imogen appears to be speaking privately to Pisanio, and only Pisanio, in the following three lines.
1.2 Location: Scene continues.
1. PERFORMANCE COMMENT The roles of Cloten and

Posthumus have successfully been doubled in performance, and other characters can be doubled as
well. See Digital Edition PC 1.
2. The First Lord flatters Cloten by saying that the
odorous vapors he is giving off are more healthful
than the outside ("abroad") air that is being exchanged
for them.

5 CLOTEN If my shirt were bloody, then to shift it.° Have I hurt   *then I would change it*
     him?
SECOND LORD [*aside*] No, faith, not so much as his patience.
FIRST LORD Hurt him? His body's a passable° carcass if he be   *pretty good; penetrable*
     not hurt. It is a thoroughfare for steel if it be not hurt.
10 SECOND LORD [*aside*] His steel was in debt: it went o'th' back-
     side the town.[3]
CLOTEN The villain would not stand° me.   *confront; stay still for*
SECOND LORD [*aside*] No, but he fled forward still,° toward   *always*
     your face.
15 FIRST LORD Stand you? You have land enough of your own,
     but he added to your having, gave you some ground.°   *fell back before you*
SECOND LORD [*aside*] As many inches as you have oceans.°   *(i.e., no inches)*
     Puppies!
CLOTEN I would they had not come between us.
20 SECOND LORD [*aside*] So would I, till you had measured how
     long a fool you were upon the ground.
CLOTEN And that she should love this fellow and refuse me!
SECOND LORD [*aside*] If it be a sin to make a true election,[4]
     she is damned.
25 FIRST LORD Sir, as I told you always, her beauty and her brain
     go not together. She's a good sign,° but I have seen small   *She looks good*
     reflection of her wit.
SECOND LORD [*aside*] She shines not upon fools lest the
     reflection should hurt her.
30 CLOTEN Come, I'll to my chamber. Would there had been
     some hurt done.
SECOND LORD [*aside*] I wish not so, unless it had been the fall
     of an ass, which is no great hurt.
CLOTEN You'll go with us?
35 FIRST LORD I'll attend your lordship.
CLOTEN Nay, come, let's go together.
SECOND LORD Well, my lord.   *Exeunt.*

1.3
Enter IMOGEN *and* PISANIO.

IMOGEN I would thou grew'st unto the shores o'th' haven
     And questioned'st every sail. If he should write
     And I not have it, 'twere a paper lost
     As offered mercy is.[1] What was the last
     That he spake to thee?
5 PISANIO   It was his queen, his queen!
IMOGEN Then waved his handkerchief?
PISANIO   And kissed it, madam.
IMOGEN Senseless° linen, happier therein than I!   *Unfeeling*
     And that was all?
PISANIO   No, madam. For so long
     As he could make me with this eye or ear

---

3. Cloten's sword, like a debtor avoiding creditors, kept to the backstreets—that is, avoided the thoroughfare or main street of Posthumus's body (with a possible allusion to anal penetration).
4. A proper choice; with a pun on the Christian doctrine that certain souls are "elected," or predestined for salvation.

1.3 Location: Cymbeline's palace.
1. *'twere . . . is:* the lost letter would be a document written in vain, like an offer of mercy that is not accepted or received (for example, a judge's reprieve that comes too late or God's mercy to an unrepentant sinner).

10 Distinguish him from others, he did keep
The deck, with glove or hat or handkerchief
Still waving, as the fits and stirs of 's mind
Could best express how slow his soul sailed on,
How swift his ship.

IMOGEN   Thou shouldst have made him
15 As little as a crow, or less, ere left
To after-eye him.[2]

PISANIO   Madam, so I did.

IMOGEN   I would have broke mine eyestrings,[3] cracked them, but
To look upon him, till the diminution
Of space had pointed him sharp as my needle;[4]
20 Nay, followed him till he had melted from
The smallness of a gnat to air, and then
Have turned mine eye and wept. But, good Pisanio,
When shall we hear from him?

PISANIO   Be assured, madam,
With his next vantage.°   *his first opportunity*
25 IMOGEN   I did not take my leave of him, but had
Most pretty things to say. Ere I could tell him
How I would think on him at certain hours,
Such thoughts and such; or I could make him swear
The shes° of Italy should not betray   *women*
30 Mine interest° and his honor; or have charged him   *My entitlement (to him)*
At the sixth hour of morn, at noon, at midnight,
T'encounter me with orisons[5]—for then
I am in heaven for him—or ere I could
Give him that parting kiss which I had set
35 Betwixt two charming words,[6] comes in my father,
And, like the tyrannous breathing of the north,°   *north wind*
Shakes all our buds from growing.

Enter a LADY.

LADY   The Queen, madam,
Desires your highness' company.

IMOGEN [*to* PISANIO]   Those things I bid you do, get them
dispatched.
I will attend the Queen.

40 PISANIO   Madam, I shall.   *Exeunt.*

1.4

Enter PHILARIO, GIACOMO,[1] *a* FRENCHMAN,
a Dutchman, and a Spaniard.

GIACOMO   Believe it, sir, I have seen him in Britain. He was
then of a crescent note,° expected to prove so worthy as   *growing reputation*
since he hath been allowed the name of. But I could then
have looked on him without the help of admiration,° though   *wonder*
5 the catalogue of his endowments had been tabled° by his side,   *listed*
and I to peruse him by items.°   *part by part*

---

2. *ere . . . him:* before ceasing to gaze after him.
3. The muscles of the eye, which were supposed to break at death or from overuse.
4. *till . . . needle:* until the distance between us had made him seem as small as the point on my needle.
5. To join me in prayers ("orisons"); to assail me (as an object of devotion) with prayers.

6. Between two words carrying a charm to ward off danger.
1.4 Location: Philario's house, Rome.
1. TEXTUAL COMMENT The character whose name is anglicized in this edition as "Giacomo" is called "Iachimo" in F. See Digital Edition TC 2.

PHILARIO   You speak of him when he was less furnished than now he is with that which makes° him both without and within.   *constitutes*

FRENCHMAN   I have seen him in France. We had very many
10   there could behold the sun with as firm eyes as he.[2]

GIACOMO   This matter of marrying his king's daughter, wherein he must be weighed rather by her value than his own, words him, I doubt not, a great deal from the matter.[3]

FRENCHMAN   And then his banishment—

15   GIACOMO   Ay, and the approbation of those that weep this lamentable divorce under her colors[4] are wonderfully to extend
him,° be it but to fortify her judgment, which else an easy   *exaggerate his worth*
battery° might lay flat for taking a beggar without less qual-   *a slight assault*
ity.° But how comes it he is to sojourn with you? How creeps   *of no rank or merit*
20   acquaintance?[5]

PHILARIO   His father and I were soldiers together, to whom I
have been often bound for no less than my life.

        Enter POSTHUMUS.

Here comes the Briton. Let him be so entertained amongst
you as suits with gentlemen of your knowing° to a stranger° of   *knowledge / foreigner*
25   his quality. I beseech you all, be better known to this gentle-
man, whom I commend to you as a noble friend of mine. How
worthy he is I will leave to appear hereafter rather than story°   *give an account of*
him in his own hearing.

FRENCHMAN   Sir, we have known together° in Orléans.   *been acquainted*

30   POSTHUMUS   Since when I have been debtor to you for courtesies which I will be ever to pay, and yet pay still.

FRENCHMAN   Sir, you o'er-rate my poor kindness; I was glad I did
atone° my countryman and you. It had been pity you should   *reconcile*
have been put together° with so mortal° a purpose as then each   *(in a duel) / deadly*
35   bore, upon importance° of so slight and trivial a nature.   *matters*

POSTHUMUS   By your pardon, sir, I was then a young traveler,
rather shunned to go even° with what I heard than[6] in my   *refused to agree*
every action to be guided by others' experiences: but upon
my mended° judgment—if I offend not to say it is mended—my   *improved*
40   quarrel was not altogether slight.

FRENCHMAN   Faith, yes, to be put to the arbitrement of swords,°   *settlement by duel*
and by such two that would by all likelihood have confounded°   *destroyed*
one the other, or have fallen both.

GIACOMO   Can we with manners ask what was the difference?

45   FRENCHMAN   Safely, I think; 'twas a contention in public, which
may without contradiction suffer° the report. It was much like   *permit*
an argument that fell out last night, where each of us fell in
praise of our country mistresses.[7] This gentleman, at that time
vouching—and upon warrant of bloody affirmation°—his to   *affirming it with blood*
50   be more fair, virtuous, wise, chaste, constant, qualified,° and   *having notable qualities*
less attemptable° than any the rarest of our ladies in France.   *open to seduction*

GIACOMO   That lady is not now living, or this gentleman's
opinion by this° worn out.   *now*

---

2. Alluding to the popular belief that only eagles
could gaze directly on the sun. At 1.1.139, Imogen
described Posthumus as an eagle.
3. *words . . . matter:* causes his reputation, I am sure,
to be amplified beyond what is true.
4. That is, on Imogen's side (with a pun on "colors"

as meaning both "a military banner" and "pretexts").
5. How does he claim a connection to you? Giacomo
implies that Posthumus cunningly insinuated himself into Philario's friendship.
6. Than to appear.
7. The women of our country.

POSTHUMUS   She holds her virtue still, and I my mind.

55   GIACOMO   You must not so far prefer her fore ours of Italy.

POSTHUMUS   Being so far provoked as I was in France, I would abate her nothing,[8] though I profess myself her adorer, not her friend.°   *lover; spouse*

GIACOMO   As fair and as good—a kind of hand in hand com-

60   parison[9]— had been something too fair and too good for any lady in Britain. If she went before° others I have seen as that   *surpassed* diamond of yours outlusters many I have beheld, I could not but believe she excelled many; but I have not seen the most precious diamond that is, nor you the lady.

65   POSTHUMUS   I praised her as I rated° her; so do I my stone.   *valued*

GIACOMO   What do you esteem it at?

POSTHUMUS   More than the world enjoys.°   *possesses*

GIACOMO   Either your unparagoned° mistress is dead, or she's   *matchless* outprized° by a trifle.   *exceeded in value*

70   POSTHUMUS   You are mistaken: the one° may be sold or given,   *(the ring)* or if° there were wealth enough for the purchase, or merit   *if either* for the gift. The other° is not a thing for sale, and only the   *(his mistress)* gift of the gods.

GIACOMO   Which the gods have given you?

75   POSTHUMUS   Which by their graces I will keep.

GIACOMO   You may wear her in title yours,[1] but you know strange fowl light upon neighboring ponds.[2] Your ring[3] may be stol'n too, so your brace of unprizable estimations,[4] the one is but frail and the other casual.[5] A cunning thief or a

80   that-way-accomplished courtier[6] would hazard° the winning   *venture* both of first and last.

POSTHUMUS   Your Italy contains none so accomplished a courtier to convince° the honor of my mistress, if in the   *overcome* holding or loss of that you term her frail. I do nothing

85   doubt you have store° of thieves; notwithstanding, I fear   *an abundance* not° my ring.   *am not worried about*

PHILARIO   Let us leave° here, gentlemen.   *stop the conversation*

POSTHUMUS   Sir, with all my heart. This worthy signor, I thank him, makes no stranger of me; we are familiar at first.

90   GIACOMO   With five times so much conversation I should get ground° of your fair mistress, make her go back,° even to the   *advantage / relent* yielding, had I admittance and opportunity to friend.°   *to assist me*

POSTHUMUS   No, no.

GIACOMO   I dare thereupon pawn the moiety° of my estate to   *one-half*

95   your ring, which in my opinion o'ervalues it something. But I make my wager rather against your confidence than her rep- utation, and to bar your offense[7] herein too, I durst attempt it against any lady in the world.

---

8. I would subtract nothing from my estimation of her.

9. A comparison claiming equality (not superiority).

1. You may claim her as your legal possession (with a pun on "wear" as meaning "enjoy her sexually").

2. *strange . . . ponds:* strangers may come upon your property (with a pun on "pond" as referring to female genitals).

3. Punning on "ring" as another slang term for female genitals.

4. So of the two ("brace of") objects you deem invaluable.

5. And the other subject to accident (referring to the ring).

6. A courtier skilled in that way (in the arts of seduc- tion and theft).

7. To prevent you from feeling personally affronted.

POSTHUMUS You are a great deal abused in too bold a persua-
sion,[8] and I doubt not you sustain° what you're worthy of by   *will receive*
your attempt.
GIACOMO What's that?
POSTHUMUS A repulse; though your attempt, as you call it,
deserve more: a punishment too.
PHILARIO Gentlemen, enough of this. It came in too suddenly;
let it die as it was born, and I pray you be better acquainted.
GIACOMO Would I had put my estate and my neighbor's on
th'approbation° of what I have spoke.   *the proof*
POSTHUMUS What lady would you choose to assail?
GIACOMO Yours, whom in constancy you think stands so safe.
I will lay° you ten thousand ducats to your ring that, commend   *wager*
me to the court where your lady is, with no more advantage
than the opportunity of a second conference, and I will
bring from thence that honor of hers, which you imagine so
reserved.
POSTHUMUS I will wage against your gold, gold to it.° My ring   *gold equal to it*
I hold dear as my finger, 'tis part of it.
GIACOMO You are a friend, and therein the wiser.[9] If you buy
ladies' flesh at a million a dram,[1] you cannot preserve it
from tainting. But I see you have some religion in you, that°   *since*
you fear.
POSTHUMUS This is but a custom in your tongue;[2] you bear a
graver purpose, I hope.
GIACOMO I am the master of my speeches, and would
undergo° what's spoken, I swear.   *undertake*
POSTHUMUS Will you? I shall but lend my diamond till your
return. Let there be covenants° drawn between 's. My mis-   *agreements*
tress exceeds in goodness the hugeness of your unworthy
thinking. I dare you to this match: here's my ring.
PHILARIO I will have it no lay.°   *I will have no wager*
GIACOMO By the gods, it is one. If I bring you no sufficient
testimony that I have enjoyed the dearest bodily part of your
mistress, my ten thousand ducats are yours, so is your diamond too. If I come off and leave her in such honor as you
have trust in, she your jewel, this your jewel, and my gold
are yours—provided I have your commendation for my more
free entertainment.[3]
POSTHUMUS I embrace these conditions; let us have articles
betwixt us. Only thus far you shall answer: if you make your
voyage upon her and give me directly° to understand you   *plainly*
have prevailed, I am no further your enemy; she is not worth
our debate. If she remain unseduced, you not making it
appear otherwise, for your ill opinion, and th'assault you
have made to her chastity, you shall answer me with your
sword.

---

8. A great deal deceived in your too-bold belief.
9. Implying that Posthumus's intimacy with Imogen
("friend" means "lover" or "husband") makes him
wise enough not to risk his ring in a wager on her
chastity or wise enough to know the danger of this
wager.

1. Even if you pay a large amount of money for a very
small amount (a "dram") of female flesh.
2. This is merely a conventional way for you to
speak.
3. Provided I have your introduction (to Imogen) to
ensure a generous reception.

GIACOMO Your hand, a covenant. We will have these things
 set down by lawful counsel, and straight away° for Britain,   *depart at once*
 lest the bargain should catch cold and starve.° I will fetch   *die*
 my gold, and have our two wagers recorded.
150 POSTHUMUS Agreed.   [*Exeunt* POSTHUMUS *and* GIACOMO.]
FRENCHMAN Will this hold, think you?
PHILARIO Signor Giacomo will not from it. Pray, let us follow 'em.   *Exeunt.*

1.5

Enter QUEEN, LADIES, *and* CORNELIUS.
QUEEN Whiles yet the dew's on ground, gather those flowers;
 Make haste. Who has the note° of them?   *list*
LADY   I, madam.
QUEEN Dispatch.°   *Exeunt* LADIES.   *Make haste*
 Now, master doctor, have you brought those drugs?
5 CORNELIUS Pleaseth° your highness, ay. Here they are, madam. *If it please*
  [*He gives her a box.*]
 But I beseech your grace, without offense—
 My conscience bids me ask—wherefore° you have   *why*
 Commanded of me these most poisonous compounds,
 Which are the movers of a languishing death,
 But though slow, deadly.
10 QUEEN   I wonder, doctor,
 Thou ask'st me such a question. Have I not been
 Thy pupil long? Hast thou not learned° me how   *taught*
 To make perfumes, distil, preserve?—yea, so
 That our great King himself doth woo me oft
15 For my confections?° Having thus far proceeded—   *medical compounds*
 Unless thou think'st me devilish—is't not meet°   *fitting*
 That I did amplify my judgment in
 Other conclusions?° I will try° the forces   *experiments / test*
 Of these thy compounds on such creatures as
20 We count not worth the hanging, but none human,
 To try the vigor of them, and apply
 Allayments° to their act,° and by them¹ gather   *Antidotes / operation*
 Their several virtues² and effects.
CORNELIUS   Your highness
 Shall from this practice but make hard your heart.
25 Besides, the seeing these effects will be
 Both noisome° and infectious.   *offensive*
QUEEN   Oh, content thee.
  Enter PISANIO.
 [*aside*] Here comes a flattering rascal; upon him
 Will I first work: he's factor° for his master   *an agent*
 And enemy to my son. —How now, Pisanio?
30 Doctor, your service for this time is ended;
 Take your own way.
CORNELIUS [*aside*]   I do suspect you, madam.
 But you shall do no harm.
QUEEN [*to* PISANIO]   Hark thee, a word.

1.5 Location: Cymbeline's court, Britain.   2. *gather . . . virtues*: determine the compounds'
1. *them*: these experiments.   individual powers.

CORNELIUS [*aside*]   I do not like her. She doth think she has
    Strange ling'ring poisons. I do know her spirit,
35   And will not trust one of her malice with
    A drug of such damned nature. Those she has
    Will stupefy and dull the sense a while,
    Which first, perchance, she'll prove° on cats and dogs,   *test*
    Then afterward up higher; but there is
40   No danger in what show of death it makes
    More than the locking up the spirits a time,[3]
    To be more fresh, reviving. She is fooled
    With a most false effect, and I the truer°   *more loyal*
    So to be false with her.
QUEEN   No further service, doctor,
    Until I send for thee.
45   CORNELIUS   I humbly take my leave.   *Exit.*
QUEEN   Weeps she still, say'st thou? Dost thou think in time
    She will not quench,° and let instructions° enter   *grow cool / good advice*
    Where folly now possesses? Do thou work.
    When thou shalt bring me word she loves my son,
50   I'll tell thee on the instant thou art then
    As great as is thy master—greater, for
    His fortunes all lie speechless, and his name°   *reputation*
    Is at last gasp. Return he cannot, nor
    Continue where he is. To shift his being°   *change his abode*
55   Is to exchange one misery with another,
    And every day that comes comes to decay°   *destroy*
    A day's work in him. What shalt thou expect
    To be depender on a thing that leans,[4]
    Who cannot be new built, nor has no friends
    So much as but to prop him?
             [*She drops the box.* PISANIO *takes it up.*]
60   Thou tak'st up
    Thou know'st not what; but take it for thy labor.
    It is a thing I made, which hath the King
    Five times redeemed from death. I do not know
    What is more cordial.° Nay, I prithee, take it,   *restorative*
65   It is an earnest° of a farther good   *initial payment*
    That I mean to thee. Tell thy mistress how
    The case stands with her; do't as from thyself.
    Think what a chance thou changest on,[5] but think
    Thou hast thy mistress still; to boot,° my son,   *in addition*
70   Who shall take notice of thee. I'll move the King
    To any shape of thy preferment,° such   *any kind of advancement*
    As thou'lt desire; and then myself, I chiefly,
    That set thee on to this desert,° am bound   *action deserving reward*
    To load thy merit richly. Call my women.
    Think on my words.   *Exit* PISANIO.
75   A sly and constant knave,
    Not to be shaked; the agent for his master,

---

3. Other than the temporary suspension of the vital functions.
4. To be dependent on a thing that is about to fall.

5. Consider what opportunity you have to change your service (and become my servant).

And the remembrancer of her° to hold — *he who reminds her*
The handfast° to her lord. I have given him that[6] — *marriage contract*
Which, if he take, shall quite unpeople her
80 Of liegers for her sweet,[7] and which she after,
Except she bend her humor,[8] shall be assured
To taste of too.
   Enter PISANIO *and* LADIES.
     So, so; well done, well done.
The violets, cowslips, and the primroses
Bear to my closet.° Fare thee well, Pisanio. — *private chamber*
Think on my words. *Exeunt* QUEEN *and* LADIES.
85 PISANIO   And shall do.
But when to my good lord I prove untrue,
I'll choke myself—there's all I'll do for you. *Exit.*

1.6

  Enter IMOGEN *alone.*
IMOGEN A father cruel and a stepdame false,
A foolish suitor to a wedded lady
That hath her husband banished.[1] Oh, that husband,
My supreme crown of grief, and those repeated[2]
5 Vexations of it. Had I been thief-stol'n,
As my two brothers, happy;[3] but most miserable
Is the desire that's glorious.[4] Blest be those,
How mean soe'er,[5] that have their honest wills,° — *simple desires*
Which seasons comfort.[6]
  Enter PISANIO *and* GIACOMO.
     Who may this be? Fie!
10 PISANIO Madam, a noble gentleman of Rome
Comes from my lord with letters.
GIACOMO   Change you,° madam? — *Do you turn pale*
The worthy Leonatus is in safety,
And greets your highness dearly.
  [*He gives her the letters.*]
IMOGEN   Thanks, good sir,
You're kindly welcome.
15 GIACOMO [*aside*] All of her that is out of door,° most rich: — *is visible*
If she be furnished with a mind so rare
She is alone th'Arabian bird,[7] and I
Have lost the wager. Boldness, be my friend;
Arm me, audacity, from head to foot,
20 Or, like the Parthian, I shall flying fight[8]—
Rather, directly fly.

6. The box supposedly containing poison.
7. Of ambassadors for her sweetheart.
8. Unless she changes her disposition.
1.6 Location: Scene continues.
1. Who has a banished husband.
2. Those already enumerated. Imogen has already complained of her father, stepmother, and foolish suitor.
3. *happy:* I would have been glad or fortunate.
4. But most wretched is the longing for what is

exalted (in her case, a longing for Posthumus).
5. However low in status.
6. Which adds spice to their comfort.
7. The phoenix, only one of which existed at any given time. This mythical bird consumed itself in fire every five hundred years but then rose from its own ashes.
8. The mounted archers of Parthia were famous for their tactics in warfare, which included shooting arrows behind them as they retreated.

IMOGEN (*reads*)   "He is one of the noblest note,° to whose kind-   *reputation*
nesses I am most infinitely tied. Reflect° upon him accord-   *Bestow attention*
ingly, as you value your trust. Leonatus."

25   So far I read aloud,
But even the very middle of my heart
Is warmed by th' rest and takes it thankfully.
—You are as welcome, worthy sir, as I
Have words to bid you, and shall find it so
In all that I can do.

30   GIACOMO   Thanks, fairest lady.
What, are men mad? Hath nature given them eyes
To see this vaulted arch° and the rich crop°   *the sky / harvest*
Of sea and land, which can distinguish twixt
The fiery orbs above and the twinned° stones   *identical*

35   Upon th'unnumbered beach,[9] and can we not
Partition make with spectacles[1] so precious
Twixt fair and foul?

IMOGEN   What makes your admiration?°   *causes you to wonder*

GIACOMO   It cannot be i'th' eye—for apes and monkeys,
Twixt two such shes,° would chatter this way[2] and   *women*

40   Contemn with mows° the other; nor i'th' judgment—   *Scorn with grimaces*
For idiots in this case of favor° would   *question of preference*
Be wisely definite; nor i'th' appetite—
Sluttery,° to such neat° excellence opposed,   *Sluttishness / elegant*
Should make desire vomit emptiness,

45   Not so allured to feed.[3]

IMOGEN   What is the matter, trow?°   *in truth*

GIACOMO   The cloyed will,°   *sated sexual desire*
That satiate° yet unsatisfied desire, that tub   *glutted*
Both filled and running,° ravening° first the lamb,   *emptying itself / devouring*
Longs after for the garbage.

IMOGEN   What, dear sir,
Thus raps° you? Are you well?   *transports*

50   GIACOMO   Thanks, madam, well.
[*to* PISANIO] Beseech° you, sir,   *I ask*
Desire° my man's abode where I did leave him: *Seek out*
He's strange° and peevish.°   *a foreigner / irritable*

PISANIO   I was going, sir,
To give him welcome.   *Exit.*

55   IMOGEN   Continues well my lord? His health, beseech you?

GIACOMO   Well, madam.

IMOGEN   Is he disposed to mirth? I hope he is.

GIACOMO   Exceeding pleasant; none a stranger° there   *none of the foreigners*
So merry and so gamesome:[4] he is called
The Briton reveler.

60   IMOGEN   When he was here
He did incline to sadness,° and ofttimes   *seriousness*
Not knowing why.

GIACOMO   I never saw him sad.

---

9. Upon the beach whose grains of sand are
uncounted.
1. Make distinction with organs of sight.
2. Would make their preference (for Imogen) clear.

3. *Should . . . feed:* Should destroy sexual desire, not
arouse it (literally, should make desire vomit until it
is empty, not tempt it to eat).
4. Sportive; sexually playful.

There is a Frenchman his companion, one
An eminent monsieur, that it seems much loves
65 A Gallian° girl at home. He furnaces[5]   *French*
The thick sighs from him, whiles the jolly° Briton—   *lively; lustful*
Your lord, I mean—laughs from 's free° lungs, cries "Oh,   *unconstrained*
Can my sides hold, to think that man, who knows
By history, report, or his own proof
70 What woman is, yea, what she cannot choose
But must be, will 's free hours languish° for   *pine away*
Assurèd bondage?"
IMOGEN   Will my lord say so?
GIACOMO   Ay, madam, with his eyes in flood with laughter.
It is a recreation to be by
75 And hear him mock the Frenchman. But heavens know
Some men are much to blame.
IMOGEN   Not he, I hope.
GIACOMO   Not he; but yet heaven's bounty towards him might
Be used more thankfully. In himself 'tis much;
In you, which I account his, beyond all talents.[6]
80 Whilst I am bound to wonder, I am bound
To pity too.
IMOGEN   What do you pity, sir?
GIACOMO   Two creatures heartily.
IMOGEN   Am I one, sir?
You look on me: what wreck° discern you in me   *downfall*
Deserves your pity?
GIACOMO   Lamentable! What,
85 To hide me from the radiant sun, and solace°   *take comfort*
I'th' dungeon by a snuff?°   *candle end*
IMOGEN   I pray you, sir,
Deliver with more openness your answers
To my demands. Why do you pity me?
GIACOMO   That others do—
90 I was about to say enjoy your—but
It is an office° of the gods to venge° it,   *a duty / avenge*
Not mine to speak on't.°   *of it*
IMOGEN   You do seem to know
Something of me, or what concerns me. Pray you,
Since doubting° things go ill often hurts more   *suspecting*
95 Than to be sure they do—for certainties
Either are past remedies or, timely knowing,
The remedy then born[7]—discover° to me   *reveal*
What both you spur and stop.[8]
GIACOMO   Had I this cheek
To bathe my lips upon; this hand whose touch,
100 Whose every touch, would force the feeler's soul
To th'oath of loyalty; this object which
Takes prisoner the wild motion of mine eye,
Fixing it only here: should I, damned then,

---

5. He exhales sighs like a furnace.
6. *In himself . . . talents:* As regards his own qualities, heaven's generosity is considerable. In giving
him you, whom I consider his, heaven's generosity
surpasses all abundance.
7. *or . . . born:* or, they being known about in time,
the remedy is then brought about.
8. What you both urge on and restrain (as one commands a horse).

Slaver with lips as common as the stairs
105　That mount the Capitol;[9] join gripes with hands
Made hard with hourly falsehood—falsehood as
With labor;[1] then by-peeping° in an eye　　　　　　　　　*glancing coyly*
Base and illustrous° as the smoky light　　　　　　　　　*lacking luster*
That's fed with stinking tallow[2]—it were fit
110　That all the plagues of hell should at one time
Encounter° such revolt.°　　　　　　　　　　　　　　*Confront / infidelity*

IMOGEN　　　　　　　　　My lord, I fear,
Has forgot Britain.

GIACOMO　　　　　　　　And himself. Not I
Inclined to this intelligence pronounce
The beggary of his change,[3] but 'tis your graces
115　That from my mutest conscience° to my tongue　　　　*most quiet inner being*
Charms this report out.

IMOGEN　　　　　　　　　Let me hear no more.

GIACOMO　　O dearest soul, your cause doth strike my heart
With pity that doth make me sick. A lady
So fair, and fastened to an empery°　　　　　　　　　　*empire*
120　Would make the great'st king double,° to be partnered　　*twice as great*
With tomboys hired with that self exhibition[4]
Which your own coffers yield; with diseased ventures°　　*prostitutes; vendors*
That play with all infirmities for gold,
Which rottenness can lend nature; such boiled stuff[5]
125　As well might poison poison! Be revenged,
Or she that bore you was no queen, and you
Recoil° from your great stock.　　　　　　　　　　　*Degenerate*

IMOGEN　　　　　　　　　Revenged?
How should I be revenged? If this be true—
As I have such a heart that both mine ears
130　Must not in haste abuse[6]—if it be true,
How should I be revenged?

GIACOMO　　　　　　　　Should he make me
Live like Diana's priest[7] betwixt cold sheets,
Whiles he is vaulting variable ramps[8]
In your despite, upon your purse[9]—revenge it.
135　I dedicate myself to your sweet pleasure,
More noble than that runagate° to your bed,　　　　　　*renegade*
And will continue fast° to your affection,　　　　　　　*constant*
Still close as sure.[1]

IMOGEN　　　　　　　　　What ho, Pisanio!

GIACOMO　　Let me my service tender on your lips—
140　IMOGEN　　Away, I do condemn mine ears that have
So long attended thee. If thou wert honorable

---

9. *Slaver . . . Capitol:* Offer drooling kisses to whores who, like the stairs to the Roman Capitol building, are available to everyone.
1. *join . . . labor:* clasp hands made as hard with hourly lies or sexual infidelities as they might have been made hard with work.
2. Animal fat used for making candles.
3. *Not . . . change:* It is not because I am disposed to give this information that I report the contemptible nature of his change.
4. With whores ("tomboys") hired with that same payment.

5. Such diseased prostitutes. Sweating, usually induced by the steam from boiling water, was a common treatment for syphilis.
6. *a heart . . . abuse:* a heart that my ears must not abuse by too hastily accepting what they hear.
7. That is, live chastely. Diana was the Roman goddess of the hunt known for her chastity and her circle of virgin followers.
8. While he is having sexual intercourse with whores ("ramps") of all kinds.
9. In contempt of you, with your money.
1. Always as secret as I am true.

Thou wouldst have told this tale for virtue, not
For such an end thou seek'st, as base as strange.
Thou wrong'st a gentleman who is as far
145   From thy report as thou from honor, and
Solicits here a lady that disdains
Thee and the devil alike. What ho, Pisanio!
The King my father shall be made acquainted
Of thy assault. If he shall think it fit
150   A saucy stranger in his court to mart°   do business
As in a Romish stew,° and to expound   Roman brothel
His beastly mind to us, he hath a court
He little cares for and a daughter who
He not respects at all. What ho, Pisanio!
155   GIACOMO   O happy Leonatus! I may say
The credit° that thy lady hath of° thee   trust / in
Deserves thy trust, and thy most perfect goodness
Her assured credit.[2] Blessèd live you long,
A lady to the worthiest sir that ever
160   Country called his;° and you his mistress, only   its own
For the most worthiest fit. Give me your pardon;
I have spoke this to know if your affiance°   faith
Were deeply rooted, and shall make your lord
That which he is new o'er;[3] and he is one
165   The truest mannered,[4] such a holy witch°   a charming person
That he enchants societies into° him;   crowds of people to
Half all men's hearts are his.
IMOGEN   You make amends.
GIACOMO   He sits 'mongst men like a descended god;
He hath a kind of honor sets him off
170   More than a mortal seeming.[5] Be not angry,
Most mighty Princess, that I have adventured°   dared
To try° your taking of a false report, which hath   test
Honored with confirmation your great judgment
In the election of a sir so rare,
175   Which° you know cannot err. The love I bear him   Whom
Made me to fan[6] you thus, but the gods made you,
Unlike all others, chaffless.° Pray, your pardon.   without chaff; perfect
IMOGEN   All's well, sir. Take my power i'th' court for yours.
GIACOMO   My humble thanks. I had almost forgot
180   T'entreat your grace but in a small request,
And yet of moment° too, for it concerns   importance
Your lord; myself and other noble friends
Are partners in the business.
IMOGEN   Pray, what is't?
GIACOMO   Some dozen Romans of us, and your lord—
185   The best feather of our wing—have mingled sums
To buy a present for the Emperor,
Which I, the factor for the rest, have done

2. *and . . . credit:* and your most perfect goodness deserves her absolute trust.
3. *and . . . o'er:* and I (by this news of your fidelity) shall make your lord feel afresh what he already is (that is, your lord).
4. *he . . . mannered:* he is above all others the most

perfect in conduct.
5. So that he appears more than mortal.
6. Winnow. When grain was harvested, wheat was winnowed from the chaff; metaphorically, the good was winnowed from the bad.

In France. 'Tis plate⁷ of rare device, and jewels
Of rich and exquisite form; their value's great,

190 And I am something curious,° being strange,   *somewhat anxious*
To have them in safe stowage. May it please you
To take them in protection?

IMOGEN   Willingly,
And pawn mine honor for their safety, since
My lord hath interest° in them. I will keep them   *a stake*
In my bedchamber.

195 GIACOMO   They are in a trunk
Attended by my men. I will make bold
To send them to you, only for this night:
I must aboard tomorrow.

IMOGEN   Oh, no, no!

GIACOMO   Yes, I beseech, or I shall short° my word   *break*

200 By length'ning my return. From Gallia°   *France*
I crossed the seas on purpose and on promise
To see your grace.

IMOGEN   I thank you for your pains;
But not away tomorrow!

GIACOMO   Oh, I must, madam.
Therefore I shall beseech you, if you please

205 To greet your lord with writing, do't tonight.
I have outstood° my time, which is material   *overstayed*
To th' tender° of our present.   *the offering*

IMOGEN   I will write.
Send your trunk to me: it shall safe be kept,
And truly yielded° you. You're very welcome.   *Exeunt.*   *faithfully returned to*

2.1

Enter CLOTEN *and the two* LORDS.

CLOTEN   Was there ever man had such luck? When I kissed
the jack¹ upon an upcast,° to be hit away! I had a hundred   *on a final throw*
pound on't; and then a whoreson jackanapes° must take me   *an idiotic bastard*
up² for swearing, as if I borrowed mine oaths of him and

5 might not spend them at my pleasure.

FIRST LORD   What got he by that? You have broke his pate°   *head*
with your bowl.

SECOND LORD [*aside*]   If his wit had been like him that broke
it, it would have run all out.

10 CLOTEN   When a gentleman is disposed to swear, it is not for
any standers-by to curtail³ his oaths, ha?

SECOND LORD   No, my lord [*aside*] —nor crop the ears of them.

CLOTEN   Whoreson dog! I give him satisfaction? Would he
had been one of my rank.⁴

15 SECOND LORD [*aside*]   To have smelled like a fool.

---

7. Objects, often tableware, either made of precious
metals or covered ("plated") with them.
2.1 Location: Cymbeline's court, Britain.
1. In the game of bowls, the jack is the target ball. To
"kiss the jack" is to roll one's ball so that it touches
the jack.
2. Challenge me; rebuke me.

3. Shorten, as one bobbed the tails (and sometimes
the ears) of certain dogs. This leads the Second Lord
to talk of cropping the ears of oaths in line 12.
4. Social position. Gentlemen were only supposed to
fight ("give satisfaction" to) men of their own rank.
The Second Lord puns on "rank" as meaning "strong
smell."

CLOTEN I am not vexed more at anything in th'earth. A pox on't,[5] I had rather not be so noble as I am! They dare not fight with me because of the Queen my mother. Every jack-slave° hath his belly full of fighting, and I must go up and down like a cock that nobody can match.° *lowborn fellow / equal; fight with*

SECOND LORD [*aside*] You are cock and capon too, an you crow cock with your comb on.[6]

CLOTEN Sayest thou?

SECOND LORD It is not fit your lordship should undertake° every companion° that you give offense to. *take on / fellow*

CLOTEN No, I know that, but it is fit I should commit offense to[7] my inferiors.

SECOND LORD Ay, it is fit for your lordship only.

CLOTEN Why, so I say.

FIRST LORD Did you hear of a stranger that's come to court tonight?

CLOTEN A stranger, and I not know on't?° *of it*

SECOND LORD [*aside*] He's a strange fellow himself, and knows it not.

FIRST LORD There's an Italian come, and 'tis thought, one of Leonatus' friends.

CLOTEN Leonatus? A banished rascal; and he's another, whatsoever he be. Who told you of this stranger?

FIRST LORD One of your lordship's pages.

CLOTEN Is it fit I went to look upon him? Is there no derogation° in't? *loss of dignity*

SECOND LORD You cannot derogate,[8] my lord.

CLOTEN Not easily, I think.

SECOND LORD [*aside*] You are a fool granted;° therefore your issues° being foolish do not derogate. *an acknowledged fool / deeds*

CLOTEN Come, I'll go see this Italian. What I have lost today at bowls I'll win tonight of him. Come, go.

SECOND LORD I'll attend your lordship.
Exeunt [CLOTEN *and* FIRST LORD].

That such a crafty devil as is his mother
Should yield the world this ass! A woman that
Bears all down° with her brain, and this her son *Overcomes everyone*
Cannot take two from twenty, for his heart,° *for the life of him*
And leave eighteen. Alas, poor Princess,
Thou divine Imogen, what thou endur'st,
Betwixt a father by thy stepdame governed,
A mother hourly coining plots, a wooer
More hateful than the foul expulsion is
Of thy dear husband, than that horrid act
Of the divorce he'd make! The heavens hold firm
The walls of thy dear honor, keep unshaked
That temple, thy fair mind, that thou mayst stand
T'enjoy thy banished lord and this great land. *Exit.*

---

5. A mild oath meaning "a plague on it."
6. And a castrated cock too if you brag ("crow") that you are a cock while wearing a fool's cap (coxcomb). There are puns here on "capon" and "cap on," on "cock's comb" and "coxcomb."

7. I should assault, with the perhaps unintended secondary meaning of "to defecate upon."
8. You cannot forfeit your dignity; you have no dignity to lose.

2.2

[*A trunk is brought on.*] *Enter* IMOGEN, *in her bed*
[*reading*], *and a* LADY.[1]

IMOGEN Who's there? My woman Helen?

LADY   Please you, madam.

IMOGEN What hour is it?

LADY   Almost midnight, madam.

IMOGEN I have read three hours then; mine eyes are weak.
Fold down the leaf where I have left. To bed.

5   Take not away the taper; leave it burning,
And if thou canst awake by four o'th' clock,
I prithee call me. Sleep hath seized me wholly.   [*Exit* LADY.]
To your protection I commend me, gods;
From fairies° and the tempters of the night   *evil beings*

10   Guard me, beseech ye.°   *I entreat you*
[*She*] *sleeps.* GIACOMO [*emerges*] *from the trunk.*

GIACOMO   The crickets sing, and man's o'er-labored sense
Repairs itself by rest. Our Tarquin[2] thus
Did softly press the rushes[3] ere he wakened
The chastity he wounded. Cytherea,[4]

15   How bravely° thou becom'st thy bed. Fresh lily,   *splendidly*
And whiter than the sheets! That I might touch,
But kiss, one kiss. Rubies unparagoned,
How dearly they do't.[5] 'Tis her breathing that
Perfumes the chamber thus. The flame o'th' taper

20   Bows toward her, and would underpeep her lids
To see th'enclosèd lights, now canopied
Under these windows,° white and azure laced   *eyelids*
With blue of heaven's own tinct.° But my design[6]—   *hue*
To note the chamber: I will write all down.
[*He starts taking notes.*]

25   Such and such pictures; there the window, such
Th'adornment of her bed; the arras, figures,
Why, such and such; and the contents o'th' story.[7]
Ah, but some natural notes° about her body   *marks*
Above ten thousand meaner movables[8]

30   Would testify t'enrich mine inventory.
O sleep, thou ape° of death, lie dull° upon her,   *mimic / heavy*
And be her sense but as a monument,[9]
Thus in a chapel lying. Come off, come off—
[*He takes the bracelet from her arm.*]

2.2 Location: Imogen's chambers.
1. TEXTUAL COMMENT F's stage direction reads
"*Enter Imogen, in her Bed, and a Lady.*" Imogen
was probably revealed in a bed thrust out from a
curtained space at the back of the stage. Other
properties necessary for the scene, including the
trunk containing Giacomo, would probably have
been carried onstage by the actors. See Digital Edition TC 3.
2. The ancient Roman Sextus Tarquinius, whose
rape of Lucrece (Lucretia) was the subject of a poem
by Shakespeare.
3. Reeds commonly used as a floor covering.
4. A name for Aphrodite, or Venus, the goddess of
beauty and love, who first set foot on the island of
Cytherea after her birth from sea-foam.
5. How dearly do they (her ruby lips) kiss one

another.
6. PERFORMANCE COMMENT The extent to which the
actor playing Giacomo emphasizes the sexual menace of his actions in Imogen's bedroom will affect how
the audience perceives the play's genre. See Digital
Edition PC 2.
7. Possibly the design on the tapestry. In 2.4.67–91,
Giacomo describes in more detail what he saw in
Imogen's bedchamber: a tapestry depicting the story
of Antony and Cleopatra and a chimneypiece carving
of Diana bathing. He could here be referring to the
"figures" and "contents" of either the tapestry or the
chimneypiece.
8. Less important pieces of property, especially furniture or furnishings.
9. And let her senses be like those of an effigy on a
tomb.

As slippery as the Gordian knot was hard.[1]
35   'Tis mine, and this will witness outwardly,
      As strongly as the conscience does within,[2]
      To th' madding° of her lord. On her left breast   *maddening*
      A mole cinque-spotted,° like the crimson drops   *with five spots*
      I'th' bottom of a cowslip. Here's a voucher,°   *piece of evidence*
40   Stronger than ever law could make; this secret
      Will force him think I have picked the lock and ta'en
      The treasure of her honor.[3] No more. To what end?
      Why should I write this down that's riveted,
      Screwed to my memory? She hath been reading late
45   The tale of Tereus;[4] here the leaf's turned down
      Where Philomel gave up. I have enough;
      To th' trunk again, and shut the spring of it.
      Swift, swift, you dragons of the night, that dawning
      May bare the raven's eye.[5] I lodge in fear;
50   Though this a heavenly angel, hell is here.
              Clock strikes.
      One, two, three: time, time.   *Exit [into the trunk].*

2.3

              Enter CLOTEN *and [the two]* LORDS.
FIRST LORD   Your lordship is the most patient man in loss, the
      most coldest° that ever turned up ace.[1]   *least passionate*
CLOTEN   It would make any man cold to lose.
FIRST LORD   But not every man patient after° the noble temper   *according to*
5   of your lordship. You are most hot and furious when you win.
CLOTEN   Winning will put any man into courage. If I could
      get this foolish Imogen I should have gold enough. It's almost
      morning, is't not?
FIRST LORD   Day, my lord.
10   CLOTEN   I would this music would come. I am advised to give
      her music o'mornings; they say it will penetrate.[2]
              Enter MUSICIANS.
      Come on, tune. If you can penetrate her with your fingering,
      so; we'll try with tongue too.[3] If none will do,° let her remain,   *suffice*
      but I'll never give o'er. First, a very excellent good-conceited°   *ingenious*
15   thing; after, a wonderful sweet air, with admirable rich words
      to it, and then let her consider.

---

1. As easy to open as the Gordian knot was difficult to untie. Alluding to the myth of Gordius, King of Phrygia, who tied an impossibly intricate knot and declared that whoever untied it would reign over Asia; with a single thrust of his sword, Alexander the Great cut through it. Giacomo's unclasping of the bracelet has sexual implications. He is metaphorically violating Imogen's chastity and, by stealing Posthumus's love token, is interfering in the marriage bond that links Posthumus and Imogen.
2. As powerfully as does his (Posthumus's) inward consciousness.
3. Giacomo means his knowledge of the mole will make Posthumus believe he has slept with Imogen. To "pick the lock" is a euphemism for "to have sex."
4. In Greek mythology, Tereus, King of Thrace,

raped his wife's sister Philomela and cut out her tongue so she could not reveal what had happened. Philomela later wove the story into a tapestry.
5. May cause the raven to wake. The bird supposedly slept facing east and awakened at dawn.
2.3 Location: A room near Imogen's chambers.
1. *that . . . ace:* who ever threw the lowest score in a game of dice, with a pun on "ass."
2. Affect her emotions; arouse her sexually.
3. If your instrumental music can move her, that's good. We'll try to move her with song as well. These lines also carry an explicitly sexual secondary meaning: If you can insert your fingers inside her, that's good. We'll try oral sex too. It is unclear if Cloten understands the bawdy import of his own words.

Song

MUSICIAN [*sings*]⁴ Hark, hark, the lark at heaven's gate sings,
And Phoebus gins° arise,⁵   *Apollo (sun god) begins*
His steeds to water at those springs
20   On chaliced flowers⁶ that lies,
And winking Mary-buds° begin to ope their   *closed marigold buds*
golden eyes;
With everything that pretty is, my lady
sweet, arise:
Arise, arise!

CLOTEN   So, get you gone. If this penetrate, I will consider°   *value*
25   your music the better; if it do not, it is a vice° in her ears which   *defect*
horsehairs, and calves' guts,⁷ nor the voice of unpaved⁸
eunuch to boot can never amend.   [*Exeunt* MUSICIANS.]
Enter CYMBELINE *and* QUEEN.

SECOND LORD   Here comes the King.

CLOTEN   I am glad I was up so late, for that's the reason I was
30   up so early. He cannot choose but take this service I have
done fatherly. —Good morrow to your majesty, and to my
gracious mother.

CYMBELINE   Attend you here the door of our stern daughter?
Will she not forth?

35   CLOTEN   I have assailed her with musics, but she vouchsafes
no notice.

CYMBELINE   The exile of her minion° is too new;   *darling*
She hath not yet forgot him. Some more time
Must wear the print° of his remembrance out,   *imprint*
And then she's yours.

40   QUEEN [*to* CLOTEN]   You are most bound to th' King,
Who lets go by no vantages° that may   *opportunities*
Prefer° you to his daughter. Frame° yourself   *Recommend / Prepare*
To° orderly solicits,° and be friended   *With / solicitations*
With aptness of the season.⁹ Make denials
45   Increase your services; so seem as if
You were inspired to do those duties which
You tender to her; that you in all obey her,
Save when command to your dismission tends,
And therein you are senseless.¹

CLOTEN   Senseless? Not so.
[*Enter a* MESSENGER.]

50   MESSENGER [*to* CYMBELINE]   So like you,° sir, ambassadors   *If you please*
from Rome;
The one is Caius Lucius.

CYMBELINE   A worthy fellow,
Albeit he comes on angry purpose now;
But that's no fault of his. We must receive him
According to the honor of his sender,

---

4. F does not attribute this song to a particular singer but simply introduces it as "song." It also appears in a seventeenth-century manuscript located in the Bodleian Library at Oxford.
5. These lines also echo Shakespeare's Sonnet 29, lines 10–12: "my state / Like to the lark at break of day arising / From sullen earth, sings hymns at heaven's gate."

6. Flowers with cuplike blossoms.
7. Both were used as strings for musical instruments.
8. Castrated (lacking stones).
9. And be assisted by appropriate timing.
1. *Save . . . senseless:* Except what pertains to your dismissal ("dismission"), which you are incapable of understanding. Cloten, however, takes "senseless" to mean "stupid."

55 And towards himself (his goodness forespent on us[2])
We must extend our notice. Our dear son,
When you have given good morning to your mistress,
Attend the Queen and us; we shall have need
T'employ you towards this Roman. Come, our Queen.

Exeunt [all but CLOTEN].

60 CLOTEN If she be up, I'll speak with her; if not
Let her lie still and dream. By your leave, ho!
[*He knocks.*]
I know her women are about her: what
If I do line° one of their hands? 'Tis gold   *fill (with gold)*
Which buys admittance—oft it doth—yea, and makes
65 Diana's rangers false° themselves, yield up   *gamekeepers turn false*
Their deer to th' stand o'th' stealer;[3] and 'tis gold
Which makes the true man killed and saves the thief,
Nay, sometime hangs both thief and true man. What
Can it not do and undo? I will make
70 One of her women lawyer to° me, for   *advocate for*
I yet not understand the case[4] myself.
—By your leave!
He knocks [again]. Enter a LADY.
LADY Who's there that knocks?
CLOTEN   A gentleman.
LADY   No more?
CLOTEN Yes, and a gentlewoman's son.
LADY   That's more
75 Than some whose tailors are as dear° as yours   *expensive*
Can justly boast of. What's your lordship's pleasure?
CLOTEN Your lady's person. Is she ready?°   *dressed; prepared*
LADY   Ay—
To keep her chamber.
CLOTEN   There is gold for you:
Sell me your good report.
80 LADY How, my good name?° Or to report of you   *reputation*
What I shall think is good?
Enter IMOGEN.
                          The Princess.   [*Exit.*]
CLOTEN Good morrow, fairest sister; your sweet hand.
IMOGEN Good morrow, sir; you lay out too much pains
For purchasing but trouble. The thanks I give,
85 Is telling you that I am poor of thanks
And scarce can spare them.
CLOTEN   Still I swear I love you.
IMOGEN If you but said so, 'twere as deep° with me.   *solemn; binding*
If you swear still,° your recompense is still   *always*
That I regard it not.
CLOTEN   This is no answer.
90 IMOGEN But° that you shall not say I yield being silent,   *Except*
I would not speak. I pray you spare me. Faith,
I shall unfold equal discourtesy[5]

2. *his . . . us:* in view of the virtue he has shown in previous dealings with us.
3. *yield . . . stealer:* surrender their deer to the place where the thief stands to shoot; surrender what is most dear or valuable (their chastity) to the thief's erect penis ("th' stand").

4. *for . . . case:* for I still do not know how to manage the matter (with wordplay on "stand under" as slang for "sexually penetrate" and on "case" as slang for "vagina").
5. I shall display discourtesy equal.

To your best kindness. One of your great knowing°   *knowledge*
Should learn, being taught, forbearance.
95   CLOTEN   To leave you in your madness, 'twere my sin;
I will not.
IMOGEN   Fools cure not mad folks—
CLOTEN   Do you call me fool?
IMOGEN   As I am mad I do.
If you'll be patient, I'll no more be mad;
That cures us both. I am much sorry, sir,
100   You put me to forget a lady's manners
By being so verbal:⁶ and learn now for all
That I, which know my heart, do here pronounce
By th' very truth of it: I care not for you,
And am so near the lack of charity
105   To accuse myself I hate you,⁷ which I had rather
You felt than make't my boast.°   *than I had to say it*
CLOTEN   You sin against
Obedience, which you owe your father. For°   *As for*
The contract you pretend° with that base wretch—   *claim*
One bred of alms and fostered with cold dishes,
110   With scraps o'th' court—it is no contract, none.
And though it be allowed in meaner° parties   *socially inferior*
(Yet who than he more mean?) to knit their souls,
On whom there is no more dependency
But brats and beggary,⁸ in self-figured° knot,   *self-contracted*
115   Yet you are curbed from that enlargement° by   *freedom*
The consequence o'th' crown,⁹ and must not foil°   *defile*
The precious note° of it with a base slave,   *reputation*
A hilding for a livery,¹ a squire's cloth,°   *uniform*
A pantler°—not so eminent.   *pantry servant*
IMOGEN   Profane fellow!
120   Wert thou the son of Jupiter,° and no more   *king of the gods*
But what thou art besides, thou wert too base
To be his° groom. Thou wert dignified enough²   *(Posthumus's)*
Even to the point of envy, if 'twere made
Comparative for your virtues to be styled
125   The under-hangman³ of his kingdom, and hated
For being preferred° so well.   *advanced*
CLOTEN   The south-fog⁴ rot him!
IMOGEN   He never can meet more mischance than come
To be but named of° thee. His meanest garment   *by*
That ever hath but clipped° his body is dearer   *encircled*
130   In my respect than all the hairs above thee,°   *on your head*
Were they all made such men.
                Enter PISANIO.
                How now, Pisanio?

---

6. "Verbal" (talkative; plainspoken) may refer either
to Cloten or to Imogen.
7. *And . . . you:* And I am so near uncharitableness
that I can charge myself with hating you.
8. *On . . . beggary:* Upon whose marriage nothing
depends but worthless children and extreme
poverty.
9. *by . . . crown:* by the importance of the crown; by
the consequences that flow from your inheritance of
the crown.

1. A worthless person fit only to wear the uniform
("livery") of his master's household.
2. You were raised in status sufficiently.
3. *if 'twere . . . under-hangman:* if a comparison were
made between your virtues and those of Posthumus
and you were given the job of assistant hangman; if,
in accordance with your virtues, you were given the
job of assistant hangman.
4. A damp fog brought by the south wind and supposed to breed infections.

CLOTEN His garment? Now the devil—

IMOGEN [*to* PISANIO] To Dorothy my woman hie thee presently.°   *at once*

CLOTEN His garment?

IMOGEN [*to* PISANIO] I am sprited with° a fool,   *am haunted by*

135   Frighted, and angered worse. Go bid my woman

Search for a jewel that too casually

Hath left mine arm; it was thy master's. Shrew me°   *Beshrew me (plague on me)*

If I would lose it for a revenue

Of any king's in Europe! I do think

140   I saw't this morning; confident I am

Last night 'twas on mine arm; I kissed it.

I hope it be not gone to tell my lord

That I kiss aught but he.

PISANIO   'Twill not be lost.

IMOGEN I hope so. Go and search.   [*Exit* PISANIO.]

CLOTEN   You have abused me:

"His meanest garment"?

145 IMOGEN   Ay, I said so, sir.

If you will make't an action,° call witness to't.   *a lawsuit*

CLOTEN I will inform your father.

IMOGEN   Your mother too;

She's my good lady and will conceive,° I hope,°   *think / expect*

But the worst of me. So I leave you, sir,

To th' worst of discontent.   *Exit.*

150 CLOTEN   I'll be revenged.

"His meanest garment"? Well!   *Exit.*

2.4

Enter POSTHUMUS *and* PHILARIO.

POSTHUMUS Fear it not, sir. I would I were so sure

To win the King as I am bold her honor

Will remain hers.

PHILARIO   What means° do you make to him?   *intercessions*

POSTHUMUS Not any; but abide the change of time,

5   Quake in the present winter's state, and wish

That warmer days would come. In these feared° hopes   *timid*

I barely gratify° your love; they failing,   *repay*

I must die much your debtor.

PHILARIO Your very goodness and your company

10   O'erpays all I can do. By this° your king   *By now*

Hath heard of great Augustus. Caius Lucius

Will do 's commission thoroughly. And I think

He'll grant the tribute, send th'arrearages,°   *overdue payments*

Or look upon our Romans, whose remembrance°   *the memory of whom*

Is yet fresh in their grief.[1]

15 POSTHUMUS   I do believe,

Statist° though I am none, nor like to be,   *Statesman*

That this will prove a war, and you shall hear

The legions now in Gallia sooner landed

In our not-fearing Britain than have tidings

20   Of any penny tribute paid. Our countrymen

2.4 Location: Philario's house, Rome.
1. The Britons' grief; the grief inflicted by the Romans.

Are men more ordered° than when Julius Caesar   *better disciplined*
Smiled at their lack of skill but found their courage
Worthy his frowning at. Their discipline,
Now mingled² with their courage, will make known
25 To their approvers° they are people such   *those who test them*
That mend upon the world.³

     Enter GIACOMO.

PHILARIO   See Giacomo.
POSTHUMUS   The swiftest harts° have posted° you by land,   *deer / conveyed*
And winds of° all the corners° kissed your sails   *from / (of the globe)*
To make your vessel nimble.
PHILARIO   Welcome, sir.
30 POSTHUMUS   I hope the briefness of your answer made°   *caused*
The speediness of your return.
GIACOMO   Your lady
Is one of the fairest that I have looked upon.
POSTHUMUS   And therewithal the best, or let her beauty
Look through a casement⁴ to allure false hearts,
And be false with them.
35 GIACOMO   Here are letters for you.
POSTHUMUS   Their tenor good, I trust.
GIACOMO   'Tis very like.

     [POSTHUMUS *reads the letters.*]

PHILARIO   Was Caius Lucius in the Briton court
When you were there?
GIACOMO   He was expected then,
But not° approached.   *had not*
POSTHUMUS   All is well yet.
40 Sparkles this stone as it was wont, or is't not
Too dull for your good wearing?
GIACOMO   If I have lost it
I should have lost the worth of it in gold.
I'll make a journey twice as far t'enjoy
A second night of such sweet shortness which
45 Was mine in Britain—for the ring is won.
POSTHUMUS   The stone's too hard to come by.
GIACOMO   Not a whit,
Your lady being so easy.
POSTHUMUS   Make not, sir,
Your loss your sport. I hope you know that we
Must not continue friends.
GIACOMO   Good sir, we must,
50 If you keep covenant. Had I not brought
The knowledge° of your mistress home, I grant   *A sexual account*
We were to question° farther; but I now   *dispute*
Profess myself the winner of her honor,
Together with your ring, and not the wronger
55 Of her or you, having proceeded but
By both your wills.

---

2. TEXTUAL COMMENT F has "wing-led," which might suggest that the Britons are led with discipline on each flank (each "wing") of the army, or that their courage makes their discipline soar as if it had wings. This edition follows the Second Folio (F2, printed in 1632) in its use of "mingled." See Digital Edition TC 4.
3. *such . . . world:* who improve in the world's estimation.
4. Look out through a window (alluding to the manner in which prostitutes solicited customers).

POSTHUMUS   If you can make't apparent
That you have tasted her in bed, my hand
And ring is yours. If not, the foul opinion
You had of her pure honor gains or loses

60   Your sword or mine,[5] or masterless leaves both°   *both swords*
To who shall find them.
GIACOMO   Sir, my circumstances,°   *detailed evidence*
Being so near the truth as I will make them,
Must first induce you to believe; whose strength
I will confirm with oath, which I doubt not

65   You'll give me leave to spare° when you shall find   *omit*
You need it not.
POSTHUMUS   Proceed.
GIACOMO   First, her bedchamber—
Where I confess I slept not, but profess
Had that was well worth watching°—it was hanged   *staying awake for*
With tapestry of silk and silver; the story

70   Proud Cleopatra when she met her Roman,[6]
And Cydnus[7] swelled above the banks, or for°   *either because of*
The press of boats or pride: a piece of work
So bravely° done, so rich, that it did strive   *splendidly*
In workmanship and value,[8] which I wondered

75   Could be so rarely and exactly wrought,
Since the true life on't was—
POSTHUMUS   This is true;
And this you might have heard of here by me,
Or by some other.
GIACOMO   More particulars
Must justify° my knowledge.   *confirm*
POSTHUMUS   So they must,
Or do your honor injury.

80   GIACOMO   The chimney°   *fireplace*
Is south the chamber, and the chimneypiece[9]
Chaste Dian[1] bathing. Never saw I figures
So likely to report themselves;[2] the cutter
Was as another Nature, dumb; outwent her,
Motion and breath left out.[3]

85   POSTHUMUS   This is a thing
Which you might from relation° likewise reap,   *report*
Being, as it is, much spoke of.
GIACOMO   The roof o'th' chamber
With golden cherubim is fretted.° Her andirons—   *carved*
I had forgot them—were two winking Cupids[4]

---

5. *gains . . . mine:* makes one of us the winner, the other the loser, of his sword in a duel.
6. Alluding to a meeting, described also in Shakespeare's play *Antony and Cleopatra,* between the Egyptian Queen Cleopatra and Mark Antony, one of the Roman triumvirs, who was her lover.
7. A river in Cilicia (now Turkey).
8. *that . . . value:* that craftmanship and monetary worth both competed for preeminence.
9. Ornament above the fireplace.
1. Another reference to the goddess associated in classical mythology with hunting, childbirth, and chastity.
2. So lifelike that they could give an account of themselves.
3. *the cutter . . . out:* the sculptor ("cutter") was like a second nature in creative power. Speechless, the sculpture surpassed nature, apart from its lack of movement and breathing.
4. Two statues of Cupid, the god of love, with eyes shut. Cupid was often depicted as a beautiful boy with wings and a torch and wearing a blindfold to signify the blindness of love.

90 Of silver, each on one foot standing, nicely°   *ingeniously*
  Depending° on their brands.°   *Leaning / torches*
POSTHUMUS   This is her honor!
  Let it be granted you have seen all this—and praise
  Be given to your remembrance—the description
  Of what is in her chamber nothing saves
  The wager you have laid.
95 GIACOMO   Then, if you can
  Be pale,° I beg but leave to air this jewel: see!   *Be unmoved*
    [*He shows the bracelet.*]
  And now 'tis up° again; it must be married   *put away*
  To that your diamond. I'll keep them.
POSTHUMUS   Jove!°   *king of the gods*
  Once more let me behold it. Is it that
  Which I left with her?
100 GIACOMO   Sir, I thank her, that.
  She stripped it from her arm—I see her yet—
  Her pretty action did out-sell° her gift,   *exceed in value*
  And yet enriched it too. She gave it me,
  And said she prized it once.
POSTHUMUS   Maybe she plucked it off
  To send it me.
105 GIACOMO   She writes so to you, doth she?
POSTHUMUS Oh, no, no, no, 'tis true! Here, take this too.
    [*He gives* GIACOMO *his ring.*]
  It is a basilisk⁵ unto mine eye,
  Kills me to look on't. Let there be no honor
  Where there is beauty, truth where semblance,° love *it's merely appearance*
110 Where there's another man. The vows° of women *Let the vows*
  Of no more bondage be to where they are made
  Than they are° to their virtues, which is nothing. *Than women are bound*
  Oh, above measure false!
PHILARIO   Have patience, sir,
  And take your ring again; 'tis not yet won.
115 It may be probable she lost it, or
  Who knows if one° her women, being corrupted,   *one of*
  Hath stol'n it from her?
POSTHUMUS   Very true,
  And so I hope he came by't. Back, my ring!
    [*He takes his ring back.*]
  Render to me some corporal° sign about her   *bodily*
120 More evident° than this, for this was stol'n.   *conclusive*
GIACOMO By Jupiter,⁶ I had it from her arm.
POSTHUMUS Hark you, he swears; by Jupiter he swears.
  'Tis true, nay, keep the ring, 'tis true. I am sure
  She would not lose it. Her attendants are
125 All sworn° and honorable. They induced to steal it? *bound by oaths*
  And by a stranger? No, he hath enjoyed her.
  The cognizance° of her incontinency   *token*
  Is this: she hath bought the name of whore thus dearly.
    [*He gives* GIACOMO *his ring again.*]

---

5. A mythical reptile able to kill with a glance those 6. Another reference to the king of the gods. Only
it gazed upon.   the most solemn vows would be made in his name.

	There, take thy hire,° and all the fiends of hell	*fee*
	Divide themselves between you.	
130	PHILARIO Sir, be patient.	
	This is not strong enough to be believed	
	Of one persuaded° well of.	*thought*
	POSTHUMUS Never talk on't;	
	She hath been colted° by him.	*sexually enjoyed*
	GIACOMO If you seek	
	For further satisfying, under her breast—	
135	Worthy the pressing—lies a mole, right proud	
	Of that most delicate lodging. By my life	
	I kissed it, and it gave me present° hunger	*immediate*
	To feed again, though full. You do remember	
	This stain° upon her?	*mark*
	POSTHUMUS Ay, and it doth confirm	
140	Another stain, as big as hell can hold,	
	Were there no more but it.	
	GIACOMO Will you hear more?	
	POSTHUMUS Spare your arithmetic, never count the turns.°	*sexual acts*
	Once, and a million![7]	
	GIACOMO I'll be sworn.	
	POSTHUMUS No swearing.	
	If you will swear you have not done't, you lie,	
145	And I will kill thee if thou dost deny	
	Thou'st made me cuckold.	
	GIACOMO I'll deny nothing.	
	POSTHUMUS Oh, that I had her here, to tear her limb-meal!°	*limb from limb*
	I will go there and do't i'th' court, before	
	Her father. I'll do something—	*Exit.*
	PHILARIO Quite besides°	*beyond*
150	The government° of patience! You have won.	*control*
	Let's follow him and pervert° the present wrath	*turn aside*
	He hath against himself.	
	GIACOMO With all my heart. *Exeunt.*	

2.5

Enter POSTHUMUS.[1]

	POSTHUMUS Is there no way for men to be,° but women	*to exist*
	Must be half-workers?° We are all bastards,	*be partners*
	And that most venerable man which I	
	Did call my father was I know not where	
5	When I was stamped.[2] Some coiner with his tools[3]	
	Made me a counterfeit; yet my mother seemed	
	The Dian of that time; so doth my wife	
	The nonpareil° of this. Oh, vengeance, vengeance!	*one who has no equal*
	Me of my lawful pleasure[4] she restrained,	
10	And prayed me oft forbearance;[5] did it with	
	A pudency° so rosy the sweet view on't°	*modesty / of it*

---

7. That is, there is no difference between having been unfaithful once and having done it a million times.
2.5 Location: Scene continues.
1. In F, Posthumus's soliloquy is part of 2.4. He is making a reentry, however, after his departure at line 149, and most modern editions mark the soliloquy as a separate scene.
2. Conceived, as coins are stamped with images when they are made.
3. With pun on "tool" as meaning "penis."
4. The sexual pleasure to which marriage entitled him.
5. And often begged me to defer sexual pleasures.

Might well have warmed old Saturn⁶—that I thought her
As chaste as unsunned snow. Oh, all the devils!
This yellow° Giacomo in an hour—was't not?—   *sallow*
15   Or less—at first?° Perchance he spoke not, but   *instantly*
Like a full-acorned boar,⁷ a German one,
Cried "Oh!" and mounted; found no opposition
But what he looked for should oppose⁸ and she
Should from encounter guard. Could I find out
20   The woman's part in me—for there's no motion°   *impulse*
That tends to vice in man but I affirm
It is the woman's part; be it lying, note it,
The woman's; flattering, hers; deceiving, hers;
Lust and rank thoughts, hers, hers; revenges, hers;
25   Ambitions, covetings, change of prides,° disdain,   *varying extravagances*
Nice° longing, slanders, mutability,   *Lustful*
All faults that may be named, nay, that hell knows, why hers
In part, or all, but rather all. For even to vice
They are not constant, but are changing still
30   One vice but of a minute old for one
Not half so old as that. I'll write against them,
Detest them, curse them; yet 'tis greater skill°   *cleverness*
In a true hate, to pray they have their will:°   *desire*
The very devils cannot plague them better.   *Exit.*

3.1

Enter in state CYMBELINE, QUEEN, CLOTEN, *and*
LORDS *at one door, and at another,* CAIUS LUCIUS *and*
Attendants.

CYMBELINE   Now say, what would Augustus Caesar with us?
LUCIUS   When Julius Caesar—whose remembrance yet
Lives in men's eyes, and will to ears and tongues
Be theme and hearing ever—was in this Britain
5   And conquered it, Cassibelan, thine uncle,
Famous in Caesar's praises no whit less
Than in his feats deserving it, for him
And his succession° granted Rome a tribute,   *heirs*
Yearly three thousand pounds, which by thee lately
Is left untendered.°   *unpaid*
10   QUEEN   And, to kill the marvel,¹
Shall be so ever.
CLOTEN   There be many Caesars
Ere such another Julius. Britain's a world
By itself, and we will nothing pay
For wearing our own noses.²
QUEEN   That opportunity
15   Which then they had to take from 's, to resume°   *take back*
We have again. Remember, sir, my liege,°   *sovereign*

---

6. The Roman god of agriculture, usually characterized as cold and melancholy.
7. A boar fed full of acorns (with a pun on "boor" as
meaning "a German or Dutch peasant").
8. *found . . . oppose:* found no opposition except the
body parts he expected to encounter.
3.1 Location: Cymbeline's court, Britain.

1. And, to put a stop to the amazement (which our
nonpayment has caused).
2. Perhaps referring to contemporary theories of
physiognomy that identified specific physical features, such as noses, with racial types. Roman noses
were notoriously prominent.

The kings your ancestors, together with
The natural bravery° of your isle, which stands   *splendor*
As Neptune's park,[3] ribbed and paled in°   *enclosed and fenced in*
20   With oaks unscalable and roaring waters,
With sands that will not bear your enemies' boats
But suck them up to th' top-mast. A kind of conquest
Caesar made here, but made not here his brag
Of "came and saw and overcame."[4] With shame—
25   The first that ever touched him—he was carried
From off our coast, twice beaten; and his shipping,°   *ships*
Poor ignorant baubles,° on our terrible seas   *worthless toys*
Like eggshells moved upon their surges, cracked
As easily 'gainst our rocks. For joy whereof,
30   The famed Cassibelan, who was once at point°—   *ready*
O giglot° Fortune!—to master Caesar's sword,   *fickle; whorish*
Made Lud's Town[5] with rejoicing fires bright
And Britons strut with courage.
CLOTEN   Come, there's no more tribute to be paid. Our king-
35   dom is stronger than it was at that time, and, as I said, there
is no more such Caesars. Other of them may have crooked
noses, but to owe° such straight° arms, none.   *possess / powerful*
CYMBELINE   Son, let your mother end.
CLOTEN   We have yet many among us can gripe° as hard as   *grasp (a sword)*
40   Cassibelan. I do not say I am one, but I have a hand. Why
tribute? Why should we pay tribute? If Caesar can hide the
sun from us with a blanket, or put the moon in his pocket,
we will pay him tribute for light; else, sir, no more tribute,
pray you now.
45   CYMBELINE   You must know,
Till the injurious° Romans did extort   *insulting*
This tribute from us, we were free. Caesar's ambition,
Which swelled so much that it did almost stretch
The sides o'th' world, against all color[6] here
50   Did put the yoke upon 's, which to shake off
Becomes a warlike people, whom we reckon
Ourselves to be. We do say then to Caesar,
Our ancestor was that Mulmutius[7] which
Ordained our laws, whose use the sword of Caesar
55   Hath too much mangled, whose repair and franchise°   *free exercise*
Shall by the power we hold be our good deed,
Though Rome be therefore angry. Mulmutius made our laws,
Who was the first of Britain which did put
His brows within a golden crown and called
Himself a king.
60   LUCIUS   I am sorry, Cymbeline,
That I am to pronounce Augustus Caesar—
Caesar, that hath more kings his servants than

3. As grounds owned by Neptune, Roman god of the
sea.
4. When Julius Caesar, leading an army into Asia,
defeated King Pharnaces and his allies, Plutarch
reports that Caesar wrote three words to his friend
Anitius in Rome: *veni, vidi, vici* ("I came, I saw, I
overcame"). See Plutarch's *Life of Julius Caesar* in his
Lives of the Noble Grecians and Romanes as trans-

lated by Thomas North (1579).
5. London. Contemporary texts such as Holinshed's
Chronicles erroneously asserted that "London" was
derived from "Lud," the name of the mythological
British king who was Cymbeline's grandfather.
6. Without any pretense of justice.
7. According to Holinshed, the first king of Britain.

Thyself domestic officers—thine enemy.
Receive it from me then: war and confusion°   *destruction*
65 In Caesar's name pronounce I 'gainst thee. Look
For fury not to be resisted. Thus defied,
I thank thee for myself.

CYMBELINE   Thou art welcome, Caius.
Thy Caesar knighted me; my youth I spent
Much under him; of him I gathered honor,
70 Which he to seek of me again, perforce,
Behoves me keep at utterance.⁸ I am perfect°   *fully aware*
That the Pannonians and Dalmatians⁹ for
Their liberties are now in arms, a precedent
Which not to read would show the Britons cold;°   *lacking in spirit*
So Caesar shall not find them.
75 LUCIUS   Let proof° speak.   *the result*

CLOTEN His majesty bids you welcome. Make pastime with
us a day or two or longer. If you seek us afterwards in other
terms, you shall find us in our saltwater girdle.¹ If you beat
us out of it, it is yours; if you fall in the adventure, our crows
80 shall fare the better for you, and there's an end.

LUCIUS So, sir.

CYMBELINE I know your master's pleasure, and he mine.
All the remain° is "Welcome."   *Exeunt.* *All that is left to say*

3.2

Enter PISANIO, *reading a letter.*

PISANIO How? Of adultery? Wherefore write you not
What monster's her accuser? Leonatus,
O master, what a strange infection
Is fall'n into thy ear? What false Italian,
5 As poisonous-tongued as handed,¹ hath prevailed
On thy too ready hearing? Disloyal? No.
She's punished for her truth,° and undergoes,   *faithfulness*
More goddess-like than wife-like, such assaults
As would take in° some virtue. O my master,   *overcome*
10 Thy mind to° hers is now as low as were   *compared to*
Thy fortunes. How? That I should murder her,
Upon the love and truth and vows which I
Have made to thy command? I her? Her blood?
If it be so to do good service, never
15 Let me be counted serviceable. How look I,
That I should seem to lack humanity
So much as this fact° comes to? [*He reads.*] "Do't. The letter *action*
That I have sent her, by her own command
Shall give thee opportunity." O damned paper,²
20 Black as the ink that's on thee! Senseless bauble,
Art thou a fedary° for this act and look'st   *an accomplice*
So virgin-like without?° Lo, here she comes.   *on the outside*

---

8. *Which . . . utterance:* His seeking that honor of me again makes it necessary for me to defend ("keep") it to the death.
9. Inhabitants of Hungary and Dalmatia, a region on the Adriatic Sea.
1. In the sea that encircles us (as a girdle does the body).

3.2 Location: Scene continues.
1. Having as many poisons (lies) in his tongue as in his hands. Contemporary texts depicted Italians as infinitely skilled in making and administering poisons.
2. O hellish object (referring to the letter).

Enter IMOGEN.

I am ignorant in° what I am commanded.   *will pretend ignorance of*

IMOGEN   How now, Pisanio?

25 PISANIO   Madam, here is a letter from my lord.

IMOGEN   Who, thy lord that is my lord, Leonatus?

Oh, learned indeed were that astronomer°   *astrologer*

That knew the stars as I his characters;°   *handwriting*

He'd lay the future open. You good gods,

30 Let what is here contained relish° of love,   *taste*

Of my lord's health, of his content—yet not

That we two are asunder; let that grieve him.

Some griefs are med'cinable;° that is one of them,   *beneficial*

For it doth physic love³—of his content

35 All but in that. Good wax,° thy leave. Blest be   *sealing wax*

You bees that make these locks of counsel.° Lovers   *for private matters*

And men in dangerous bonds⁴ pray not alike;

Though forfeiters you cast in prison,⁵ yet

You clasp° young Cupid's tables.° Good news, gods!   *lovingly embrace / tablets*

40 [*She reads.*] "Justice and your father's wrath, should he take

me in his dominion, could not be so cruel to me as° you, O   *but that*

the dearest of creatures, would even renew me° with your   *revive me*

eyes. Take notice that I am in Cambria,° at Milford Haven.⁶   *Wales*

What your own love will out of this advise you, follow. So he

45 wishes you all happiness, that remains loyal to his vow, and

your increasing in love,

Leonatus Posthumus."

Oh, for a horse with wings! Hear'st thou, Pisanio?

He is at Milford Haven. Read, and tell me

50 How far 'tis thither. If one of mean affairs°   *with unimportant business*

May plod it in a week, why may not I

Glide thither in a day? Then, true Pisanio,

Who long'st like me to see thy lord, who long'st—

Oh, let me bate°—but not like me, yet long'st   *moderate my speech*

55 But in a fainter kind; oh, not like me:

For mine's beyond beyond. Say, and speak thick°—   *quickly*

Love's counselor should fill the bores of hearing°   *the ears*

To th' smothering of the sense⁷—how far it is

To this same blessed Milford. And by° th' way   *on*

60 Tell me how Wales was made so happy as

T'inherit such a haven. But first of all,

How we may steal from hence; and for the gap

That we shall make in time from our hence-going

And our return, to excuse; but first, how get hence.

65 Why should excuse be born or ere begot?⁸

We'll talk of that hereafter. Prithee, speak,

---

3. For it nurtures love; for it keeps love in good health.

4. Men bound by agreements imposing penalties (which are sealed with wax). Imogen is contrasting the fear with which men in legal trouble greet sealed documents to the joy with which lovers receive a sealed love letter.

5. Although you cast those who default on agreements in prison (because sealed bonds lead to indictments).

6. A port in southern Wales that became important in later British history when Henry Tudor landed there in 1485. Defeating the army of Richard III, he was crowned Henry VII, bringing to an end the civil strife known as the Wars of the Roses.

7. Until the sense of hearing is overwhelmed.

8. Why should an excuse be born even before it is conceived—that is, be manufactured before it is needed?

How many score of° miles may we well ride   *sets of twenty*
Twixt hour and hour?°   *In an hour*

PISANIO   One score twixt sun and sun,
Madam, 's enough for you, and too much, too.

70 IMOGEN   Why, one that rode to 's execution, man,
Could never go so slow. I have heard of riding wagers
Where horses have been nimbler than the sands
That run i'th' clock's behalf.[9] But this is fool'ry.
Go, bid my woman feign a sickness, say
75 She'll home to her father; and provide me presently°   *at once*
A riding suit no costlier than would fit°   *suit*
A franklin's housewife.[1]

PISANIO   Madam, you're best° consider—   *you'd better*

IMOGEN   I see before° me, man; not here, nor here,   *straight ahead of*
Nor what ensues,[2] but have a fog in them
80 That I cannot look through. Away, I prithee,
Do as I bid thee. There's no more to say:
Accessible is none but Milford way.   *Exeunt.*

3.3

[*A cave is discovered.*[1] *From it*] *enter* BELARIUS,
GUIDERIUS, *and* ARVIRAGUS.

BELARIUS   A goodly day not to keep house° with such   *stay home*
Whose roof's as low as ours. Stoop, boys: this gate
Instructs you how t'adore the heavens, and bows you°   *makes you bow down*
To a morning's holy office.° The gates of monarchs   *a morning prayer*
5   Are arched so high that giants may jet° through   *swagger*
And keep their impious turbans[2] on, without
Good morrow to the sun. Hail thou, fair heaven!
We house i'th' rock, yet use thee not so hardly°   *badly*
As prouder livers° do.   *those living more grandly*

GUIDERIUS   Hail, heaven!

ARVIRAGUS   Hail, heaven!

10 BELARIUS   Now for our mountain sport: up to yond hill.
Your legs are young; I'll tread these flats.° Consider,   *this plain*
When you above perceive me like a crow,
That it is place° which lessens and sets off,°   *position / enhances*
And you may then revolve° what tales I have told you,   *consider*
15 Of courts, of princes, of the tricks in war;
This service is not service, so being done,
But being so allowed.[3] To apprehend thus
Draws us a profit from all things we see,

---

9. *than . . . behalf*: than the sands that run through
the hourglass.
1. The wife of a landowning farmer whose social
status was lower than that of the gentry. Early modern English sumptuary codes prescribed specific fabrics and styles of dress for people of different ranks.
2. *not here . . . ensues*: Neither (what is) on this side,
nor on that, nor what will happen (after Milford
Haven is reached).
3.3 Location: The cave of Belarius, Wales.
1. In his account of a performance of the play in
1611, Simon Forman wrote of "the Cave in the
woods" and of the "woods" where Imogen's supposedly dead body was laid. It is possible that some form

of stage foliage surrounded the entrance to Belarius's
cave.
2. The idea of giants wearing turbans may come
from romances in which giants were often equated
with Saracens, or followers of Islam, who wore turbans and were seen as impious enemies of Christians. See, for example, the Giant Disdain in Edmund
Spenser's *Faerie Queene*, who "on his head a roll
of linnen plight, / Like to the Mores of Malabar"
(6.7.43.5–6).
3. *This service . . . allowed*: That acts of service are
not acts of service simply by being done, but rather by
being acknowledged as such (by superiors).

And often to our comfort shall we find
20 The sharded beetle[4] in a safer hold°   *refuge*
Than is the full-winged eagle. Oh, this life
Is nobler than attending for a check,[5]
Richer than doing nothing for a bribe,
Prouder than rustling in unpaid-for silk;
25 Such gain the cap of him that makes him fine,
Yet keeps his book uncrossed.[6] No life to ours.
GUIDERIUS Out of your proof° you speak. We, poor unfledged,[7] *experience*
Have never winged from view o'th' nest, nor know not
What air's from° home. Haply° this life is best,   *away from / Perhaps*
30 If quiet life be best; sweeter to you
That have a sharper known, well corresponding
With your stiff age; but unto us it is
A cell of ignorance, traveling abed,°   *only while dreaming*
A prison, or a debtor that not dares
To stride a limit.[8]
35 ARVIRAGUS   What should we speak of
When we are old as you? When we shall hear
The rain and wind beat dark December, how,
In this our pinching cave,[9] shall we discourse
The freezing hours away? We have seen nothing.
40 We are beastly:° subtle as the fox for prey,   *like beasts*
Like° warlike as the wolf for what we eat.   *As*
Our valor is to chase what flies; our cage
We make a choir, as doth the prisoned bird,
And sing our bondage freely.
BELARIUS   How you speak!
45 Did you but know the city's usuries,[1]
And felt them knowingly; the art o'th' court,
As hard to leave as keep,° whose top to climb   *dwell in*
Is certain falling, or so slipp'ry that
The fear's as bad as falling; the toil o'th' war,
50 A pain° that only seems to seek out danger   *labor*
I'th' name of fame and honor, which dies i'th' search
And hath as oft a slanderous epitaph
As record of fair act—nay, many times
Doth ill deserve° by doing well; what's worse   *earn ill treatment*
55 Must curtsy at the censure.[2] O boys, this story
The world may read in me: my body's marked
With Roman swords, and my report° was once   *reputation*
First with the best of note.° Cymbeline loved me, *the most renowned*
And, when a soldier was the theme, my name
60 Was not far off. Then was I as a tree
Whose boughs did bend with fruit; but in one night
A storm or robbery—call it what you will—

---

4. The beetle who lives in dung. "Shard" means "patch of dung."
5. Than acting as a servant only to be rebuked.
6. *Such . . . uncrossed:* Such men win the deference (shown by removing "the cap") of the tailor who is the source of their grandeur, yet continue to have their debts standing ("uncrossed") in the tailor's account book.
7. Lacking the feathers necessary for flight (spoken of a young bird).
8. *that . . . limit:* who does not dare to leave a place of sanctuary (for fear of being arrested).
9. Our confining cave; our cave that pinches us with cold.
1. Financial practices whereby money was lent at excessive or illegal rates of interest.
2. Must defer to the person who finds fault.

Shook down my mellow hangings,° nay, my leaves,   *ripe fruit*
And left me bare to weather.
GUIDERIUS   Uncertain favor!
65 BELARIUS   My fault being nothing, as I have told you oft,
But that two villains, whose false oaths prevailed
Before my perfect honor, swore to Cymbeline
I was confederate with the Romans. So
Followed my banishment, and this twenty years
70 This rock and these demesnes° have been my world,   *regions*
Where I have lived at honest freedom, paid
More pious debts to heaven than in all
The fore-end° of my time. But up to th' mountains!   *early days*
This is not hunters' language. He that strikes
75 The venison first shall be the lord o'th' feast,
To him the other two shall minister,
And we will fear no poison which attends°   *is always present*
In place of greater state. I'll meet you in the valleys.
            Exeunt [GUIDERIUS *and* ARVIRAGUS].
How hard it is to hide the sparks of nature!
80 These boys know little they are sons to th' King,
Nor Cymbeline dreams that they are alive.
They think they are mine, and, though trained up thus meanly°   *in a humble style*
I'th' cave wherein they bow, their thoughts do hit
The roofs of palaces, and nature prompts them
85 In simple and low things to prince it° much   *to act like princes*
Beyond the trick° of others. This Polydore,   *custom*
The heir of Cymbeline and Britain, who
The King his father called Guiderius—Jove,
When on my three-foot stool I sit and tell
90 The warlike feats I have done, his spirits fly out
Into my story: say "Thus mine enemy fell,
And thus I set my foot on 's neck," even then
The princely blood flows in his cheek, he sweats,
Strains his young nerves,° and puts himself in posture   *sinews*
95 That acts my words. The younger brother, Cadwal,
Once Arviragus, in as like a figure°   *acting the part as well*
Strikes life into my speech, and shows much more
His own conceiving.°   *imagination*
      [*A hunting horn sounds.*]
               Hark, the game is roused!
O Cymbeline, heaven and my conscience knows[3]
100 Thou didst unjustly banish me, whereon
At three and two years old I stole these babes,
Thinking to bar thee of succession, as
Thou reft'st° me of my lands. Euriphile,   *deprived*
Thou wast their nurse; they took thee for their mother,
105 And every day do honor to her grave.
Myself, Belarius, that am Morgan called,
They take for natural father.
      [*The horn sounds again.*]
              The game is up.°   *Exit.*   *roused*

---

3. Editors have conjectured that lines 99–107 are either a non-Shakespearean addition or a section he added in revision. They stand apart from the rest of the speech, providing a hurried summary of information. Moreover, "the game is roused" (line 98) is repeated in "The game is up" (line 107).

3.4

Enter PISANIO *and* IMOGEN [*in a riding suit*].

IMOGEN   Thou told'st me when we came from horse° the place   *we dismounted*
Was near at hand. Ne'er longed my mother so
To see me first as I have° now. Pisanio, man,   *do*
Where is Posthumus? What is in thy mind
5   That makes thee stare thus? Wherefore breaks that sigh
From th'inward of thee? One but painted thus
Would be interpreted a thing perplexed°   *bewildered*
Beyond self-explication. Put thyself
Into a havior of less fear,[1] ere wildness°   *madness*
10   Vanquish my staider senses. What's the matter?
       [PISANIO *offers her a letter.*]
Why tender'st thou that paper to me with
A look untender? If't be summer news
Smile to't before; if winterly, thou need'st
But keep that count'nance still. My husband's hand?
15   That drug-damned Italy[2] hath out-craftied° him,   *outwitted*
And he's at some hard point.° Speak, man! Thy tongue   *in some crisis*
May take off some extremity° which to read   *reduce the horror*
Would be even mortal° to me.   *fatal*

PISANIO   Please you read,
And you shall find me, wretched man, a thing
20   The most disdained of fortune.

IMOGEN (*reads*)
"Thy mistress, Pisanio, hath played the strumpet in my bed,
the testimonies whereof lies bleeding in me. I speak not out
of weak surmises but from proof as strong as my grief and
as certain as I expect my revenge. That part thou, Pisanio,
25   must act for me, if thy faith be not tainted with the breach
of hers. Let thine own hands take away her life. I shall give
thee opportunity at Milford Haven. She hath my letter for
the purpose, where, if thou fear to strike and to make me
certain it is done, thou art the pander° to her dishonor and   *go-between; procurer*
30   equally to me disloyal."

PISANIO [*aside*]   What shall I need to draw my sword? The paper
Hath cut her throat already. No, 'tis slander,
Whose edge is sharper than the sword, whose tongue
Out-venoms all the worms of Nile,[3] whose breath
35   Rides on the posting° winds and doth belie°   *speeding / deceive*
All corners of the world. Kings, queens, and states,
Maids, matrons, nay, the secrets of the grave
This viperous slander enters. —What cheer, madam?

IMOGEN   False to his bed? What is it to be false?
40   To lie in watch° there and to think on him?   *wakefulness*
To weep twixt clock and clock?° If sleep charge° nature,   *continually / overcome*
To break it with a fearful dream of° him   *a dream fearful for*
And cry myself awake? That's false to 's bed, is it?

3.4 Location: Wales, near Milford Haven.
1. *Put . . . fear:* Adopt a less fearsome manner.
2. *That country* notorious for its poisons.
3. Alluding to the poisonous serpents associated with Egypt's Nile River. Slander was often personified as a woman with snakes issuing from her mouth.

In early modern England, women frequently brought cases in the ecclesiastical courts against those who defamed or slandered them, usually by calling them unchaste. Pisanio rightly assumes that Imogen is the victim of just such slanderous accusations.

PISANIO   Alas, good lady.
45   IMOGEN   I false? Thy conscience witness, Giacomo,
      Thou didst accuse him of incontinency.
      Thou then look'dst like a villain; now, methinks
      Thy favor's° good enough. Some jay° of Italy,   *appearance is / strumpet*
      Whose mother was her painting,⁴ hath betrayed him.
50   Poor I am stale,° a garment out of fashion,   *out of date; not new*
      And for I am richer than to hang by th' walls,
      I must be ripped:⁵ to pieces with me. Oh,
      Men's vows are women's traitors! All good seeming,°   *appearance*
      By thy revolt, O husband, shall be thought
55   Put on for° villainy; not born where't grows,   *Worn to disguise*
      But worn a bait for ladies.
      PISANIO   Good madam, hear me.
      IMOGEN   True honest men being heard like false Aeneas⁶
      Were in his time thought false, and Sinon's⁷ weeping
      Did scandal° many a holy tear, took pity   *discredit*
60   From most true wretchedness. So thou, Posthumus,
      Wilt lay the leaven on all proper men:⁸
      Goodly° and gallant shall be false and perjured   *Admirable*
      From thy great fail.° —Come, fellow, be thou honest;   *failure*
      Do thou thy master's bidding. When thou seest him,
65   A little witness° my obedience. Look: *Briefly attest to*
      I draw the sword myself; take it, and hit
      The innocent mansion of my love, my heart.
      Fear not, 'tis empty of all things but grief.
      Thy master is not there, who was indeed
70   The riches of it. Do his bidding: strike.
      Thou mayst be valiant in a better cause;
      But now thou seem'st a coward.
      PISANIO   Hence, vile instrument,
      Thou shalt not damn my hand.
            [*He puts the sword aside.*]
      IMOGEN   Why, I must die,
      And if I do not by thy hand, thou art
75   No servant of thy master's. Against self-slaughter
      There is a prohibition so divine
      That cravens° my weak hand. Come, here's my heart.   *makes cowardly*
      Something's afore't. Soft,° soft, we'll no defense;   *Gently*
      Obedient as the scabbard. What is here?
            [*She takes letters from her bosom.*]
80   The scriptures° of the loyal Leonatus,   *writing; sacred texts*
      All turned to heresy? Away, away,
      Corrupters of my faith, you shall no more
      Be stomachers⁹ to my heart. Thus may poor fools
      Believe false teachers; though those that are betrayed

4. Whose mother was entirely the product of her cosmetics—that is, who was false.
5. *And . . . ripped:* And because I am too valuable to be discarded (by being hung up and forgotten about), I must be torn apart (so that the material may be reused).
6. Being heard as though they were as false as the hero of Virgil's *Aeneid,* Aeneas, who deserted his love, Dido, the queen of Carthage.

7. Another deceitful character from the *Aeneid.* Sinon betrayed Troy to the Greeks by inducing the Trojans to let into the city a wooden horse in which Greek warriors were concealed.
8. Will corrupt the reputations of all faithful men (as a portion of inferior dough spoils the rest).
9. Ornamented chest coverings worn by women under their bodices.

85 Do feel the treason sharply, yet the traitor
Stands in worse case of woe.
And thou, Posthumus, that didst set up°   *instigate*
My disobedience 'gainst the King my father,
And make me put into contempt the suits
90 Of princely fellows,° shalt hereafter find   *those equal to my rank*
It is no act of common passage, but
A strain of rareness;[1] and I grieve myself
To think, when thou shalt be disedged° by her,   *surfeited*
That now thou tirest on,[2] how thy memory
95 Will then be panged by° me. —Prithee, dispatch;   *pierced by thoughts of*
The lamb entreats the butcher. Where's thy knife?
Thou art too slow to do thy master's bidding
When I desire it too.
PISANIO   O gracious lady,
Since I received command to do this business
I have not slept one wink.
100 IMOGEN   Do't, and to bed, then.
PISANIO   I'll wake mine eyeballs out first.[3]
IMOGEN   Wherefore, then,
Didst undertake it? Why hast thou abused
So many miles with a pretense? This place?
Mine action, and thine own? Our horses' labor,
105 The time inviting thee? The perturbed court
For my being absent, whereunto I never
Purpose° return? Why hast thou gone so far   *Intend*
To be unbent[4] when thou hast ta'en thy stand,°   *shooting position*
Th'elected° deer before thee?   *The chosen*
PISANIO   But to win time
110 To lose so bad employment, in the which
I have considered of a course. Good lady,
Hear me with patience.
IMOGEN   Talk thy tongue weary, speak.
I have heard I am a strumpet, and mine ear,
Therein false struck, can take no greater wound,
Nor tent to bottom that.[5] But speak.
115 PISANIO   Then, madam,
I thought you would not back° again.   *go back (to court)*
IMOGEN   Most like,
Bringing me here to kill me.
PISANIO   Not so, neither.
But if I were as wise as honest, then
My purpose would prove well. It cannot be
120 But that my master is abused.° Some villain,   *deceived*
Ay, and singular° in his art, hath done you both   *unmatched*
This cursèd injury.
IMOGEN   Some Roman courtesan.
PISANIO   No, on my life.
I'll give but notice you are dead, and send him
125 Some bloody sign of it, for 'tis commanded

1. *It . . . rareness:* My choice was no commonplace action but the sign of exceptional qualities.
2. Whom now you feed on (in the manner of a bird of prey).
3. I'll stay awake until my eyes drop out before I'll do it.
4. To be with bow unready.
5. Nor probe ("tent") the depths of that wound.

I should do so. You shall be missed at court,
And that will well confirm it.

IMOGEN   Why, good fellow,
What shall I do the while? Where bide? How live?
Or in my life what comfort, when I am
Dead to my husband?

130 PISANIO   If you'll back° to th' court—   return

IMOGEN   No court, no father, nor no more ado
With that harsh, noble, simple nothing,
That Cloten, whose love-suit hath been to me
As fearful as a siege.

PISANIO   If not at court,
Then not in Britain must you bide.

135 IMOGEN   Where then?
Hath Britain all the sun that shines? Day, night,
Are they not but° in Britain? I'th' world's volume   Do they exist only
Our Britain seems as of it, but not in't:[6]
In a great pool a swan's nest. Prithee, think
There's livers out of Britain.[7]

140 PISANIO   I am most glad
You think of other place. Th'ambassador,
Lucius the Roman, comes to Milford Haven
Tomorrow. Now, if you could wear a mind
Dark° as your fortune is, and but disguise   Secret; dismal

145 That which t'appear itself must not yet be
But by self-danger,[8] you should tread a course
Pretty and full of view;[9] yea, haply° near   perhaps
The residence of Posthumus; so nigh, at least,
That though his actions were not visible, yet

150 Report should render° him hourly to your ear   describe
As truly as he moves.

IMOGEN   Oh, for such means,°   a method of access
Though peril to my modesty, not death on't,°   of it
I would adventure.°   take the risk

PISANIO   Well, then, here's the point:
You must forget to be a woman; change

155 Command[1] into obedience; fear and niceness°—   daintiness
The handmaids of all women, or more truly
Woman it pretty self[2]—into a waggish° courage,   mischievous
Ready in gibes, quick-answered, saucy, and
As quarrelous° as the weasel. Nay, you must   quarrelsome

160 Forget that rarest treasure of your cheek,
Exposing it[3]—but oh, the harder heart![4]
Alack, no remedy—to the greedy touch
Of common-kissing Titan,[5] and forget

---

6. Seems part of the world, yet distinct. The metaphor is of the world as a book in which Britain is a page, but one not bound into the volume.
7. *Prithee . . . Britain:* I pray you, believe that there are people living outside Britain.
8. *and but . . . self-danger:* and simply disguise your appearance, which if it were now to show itself for what it is would put you in danger.
9. Advantageous and with good prospects.
1. The commanding ways of a princess.
2. *or . . . self:* or, more accurately, womanhood itself.

3. In early modern England, English women of the upper classes shielded themselves from the sun and cultivated pale complexions, the "treasure" of their cheeks.
4. The "harder heart" probably refers to Imogen, who must harden her heart even as she tans her skin. It may refer to Posthumus's cruelty to Imogen or to Pisanio's cruelty in forcing these harsh facts upon Imogen.
5. The sun god who shines on ("kisses") everyone alike.

Your laborsome and dainty trims° wherein	*apparel*
You made great Juno° angry.	*queen of the gods*

165 IMOGEN   Nay, be brief.

I see into thy end,° and am almost	*purpose*
A man already.	

PISANIO   First, make yourself but like one.

Forethinking° this, I have already fit°—	*Anticipating / at hand*
'Tis in my cloak-bag—doublet, hat, hose, all	
170	That answer to° them. Would you in their serving,[6]	*go with*
And with what imitation you can borrow	
From youth of such a season,° fore° noble Lucius	*an age / before*
Present yourself, desire his service,° tell him	*to serve him*
Wherein you're happy[7]—which will make him know°	*convince him*
175	If that his head have ear in music—doubtless	
With joy he will embrace you, for he's honorable	
And, doubling that, most holy. Your means° abroad:	*As for your means of support*
You have me, rich, and I will never fail	
Beginning nor supplyment.[8]	

IMOGEN   Thou art all the comfort

180	The gods will diet° me with. Prithee, away.	*feed*
There's more to be considered, but we'll even°	*keep pace with*
All that good time will give us. This attempt	
I am soldier to,° and will abide it with	*committed to*
A prince's courage. Away, I prithee.	

185 PISANIO   Well, madam, we must take a short farewell,

Lest, being missed, I be suspected of	
Your carriage° from the court. My noble mistress,	*removal*
Here is a box—I had it from the Queen—	
What's in't is precious. If you are sick at sea,	
190	Or stomach-qualmed° at land, a dram° of this	*nauseous / tiny portion*
Will drive away distemper. To some shade,	
And fit you to your manhood.[9] May the gods	
Direct you to the best.	

IMOGEN   Amen. I thank thee.   *Exeunt.*

3.5

Enter CYMBELINE, QUEEN, CLOTEN, LUCIUS,
    LORDS[, *and a* MESSENGER].

CYMBELINE   Thus far, and so farewell.

LUCIUS   Thanks, royal sir.

My Emperor hath wrote I must from hence;	
And am right sorry that I must report ye	
My master's enemy.	

CYMBELINE   Our subjects, sir,

5	Will not endure his yoke, and for ourself	
To show less sovereignty than they must needs	
Appear unkinglike.	

LUCIUS   So, sir, I desire of you

A conduct° over land to Milford Haven.	*An escort*
Madam, all joy befall your grace, [*to* CLOTEN] and you.	

---

6. If you would with their help.
7. In which things you are skilled.
8. In providing the initial amount nor in supplementing it.

9. Dress yourself in accordance with your (pretended) manhood.
3.5 Location: Cymbeline's court, Britain.

10 CYMBELINE My lords, you are appointed for that office:°   *duty*
  The due of honor in no point omit.
  So farewell, noble Lucius.
 LUCIUS   Your hand, my lord.
 CLOTEN Receive it friendly, but from this time forth
  I wear it as your enemy.
 LUCIUS   Sir, the event°   *outcome*
15 Is yet to name the winner. Fare you well.
 CYMBELINE Leave not the worthy Lucius, good my lords,
  Till he have crossed the Severn.¹ Happiness.
        Exeunt LUCIUS [*and* LORDS].
 QUEEN He goes hence frowning, but it honors us
  That we have given him cause.
 CLOTEN   'Tis all the better.
20 Your valiant Britons have their wishes in it.
 CYMBELINE Lucius hath wrote already to the Emperor
  How it goes here. It fits° us therefore ripely°   *befits / quickly*
  Our chariots and our horsemen be in readiness.
  The powers° that he already hath in Gallia   *military forces*
25 Will soon be drawn to head,² from whence he moves
  His war for Britain.
 QUEEN   'Tis not sleepy business,
  But must be looked to speedily and strongly.
 CYMBELINE Our expectation that it would be thus
  Hath made us forward.° But, my gentle Queen,   *well prepared*
30 Where is our daughter? She hath not appeared
  Before the Roman, nor to us hath tendered
  The duty of the day. She looks us° like   *seems to us*
  A thing more made of malice than of duty;
  We have noted it. Call her before us, for
  We have been too slight in sufferance.° [*Exit a* MESSENGER.] *mild in our tolerance*
35 QUEEN   Royal sir,
  Since the exile of Posthumus, most retired°   *withdrawn*
  Hath her life been; the cure whereof, my lord,
  'Tis time must do. Beseech your majesty,
  Forbear sharp speeches to her. She's a lady
40 So tender of° rebukes that words are strokes,   *sensitive to*
  And strokes death to her.
     Enter a MESSENGER.
 CYMBELINE   Where is she, sir? How
  Can her contempt be answered?
 MESSENGER   Please you, sir,
  Her chambers are all locked, and there's no answer
  That will be given to th' loud'st of noise we make.
45 QUEEN My lord, when last I went to visit her,
  She prayed me to excuse her keeping close,°   *staying confined*
  Whereto, constrained by her infirmity,
  She should that duty leave unpaid to you
  Which daily she was bound to proffer. This
50 She wished me to make known, but our great court° *court business*
  Made me too blame° in memory.   *too faulty*
 CYMBELINE   Her doors locked?

---

1. River flowing between southern Wales and   2. Be gathered to their full strength.
England.

Not seen of late? Grant heavens that which I fear
Prove false!   *Exit.*

QUEEN   Son, I say, follow the King.
CLOTEN   That man of hers, Pisanio, her old servant,
I have not seen these two days.

55 QUEEN   Go, look after. *Exit* [CLOTEN].
Pisanio, thou that stand'st so for° Posthumus!   *sides so much with*
He hath a drug of mine; I pray his absence
Proceed by° swallowing that, for he believes   *Results from*
It is a thing most precious. But for her,
60 Where is she gone? Haply° despair hath seized her,   *Perhaps*
Or, winged with fervor of her love, she's flown
To her desired Posthumus. Gone she is
To death or to dishonor, and my end
Can make good use of either. She being down,
65 I have the placing of the British crown.
        Enter CLOTEN.
How now, my son?
CLOTEN   'Tis certain she is fled.
Go in and cheer the King. He rages; none
Dare come about him.
QUEEN   All the better. May
This night forestall him of the coming day.³   *Exit.*
70 CLOTEN   I love and hate her. For° she's fair and royal,   *Because*
And that she hath all courtly parts° more exquisite   *features*
Than lady, ladies, woman; from every one
The best she hath, and she, of all compounded,
Outsells° them all. I love her therefore, but   *Exceeds in value*
75 Disdaining me and throwing favors on
The low Posthumus slanders° so her judgment   *discredits*
That what's else° rare is choked; and in that point   *otherwise*
I will conclude to hate her, nay, indeed,
To be revenged upon her. For, when fools
Shall—
        Enter PISANIO.
80 Who is here? What, are you packing,° sirrah?⁴   *scheming*
Come hither. Ah, you precious pander! Villain,
Where is thy lady? In a word, or else
Thou art straightway with the fiends.
PISANIO   O good my lord!
CLOTEN   Where is thy lady? Or, by Jupiter,
85 I will not ask again. Close° villain,   *Secretive*
I'll have this secret from thy heart or rip
Thy heart to find it. Is she with Posthumus,
From whose so many weights° of baseness cannot   *measures*
A dram of worth be drawn?
PISANIO   Alas, my lord,
90 How can she be with him? When was she missed?
He is in Rome.
CLOTEN   Where is she, sir? Come nearer.°   *Be more precise*
No farther halting. Satisfy me home,°   *completely*
What is become of her?

---

3. That is, kill him. *forestall:* deprive.
4. Fellow (a common form of address to a social inferior).

PISANIO   O my all-worthy lord!

CLOTEN   All-worthy villain,

95   Discover° where thy mistress is at once,   *Reveal*
     At the next word. No more of "worthy lord"!
     Speak, or thy silence on the instant is
     Thy condemnation and thy death.

PISANIO   Then, sir,
     This paper is the history of my knowledge
     Touching her flight.
          [*He gives* CLOTEN *a letter.*]

100 CLOTEN   Let's see't. I will pursue her
     Even to Augustus' throne.

PISANIO [*aside*]   Or° this or perish.   *Either*
     She's far enough, and what he learns by this
     May prove his travel,⁵ not her danger.

CLOTEN   Humph!

PISANIO [*aside*]   I'll write to my lord she's dead. O Imogen,

105 Safe mayst thou wander, safe return again!

CLOTEN   Sirrah, is this letter true?

PISANIO   Sir, as I think.

CLOTEN   It is Posthumus' hand; I know't. Sirrah, if thou
     wouldst not be a villain, but do me true service, undergo°   *undertake*
     those employments wherein I should have cause to use thee

110 with a serious industry—that is, what villainy soe'er I bid
     thee do, to perform it directly and truly—I would think thee
     an honest man. Thou shouldst neither want° my means for   *lack*
     thy relief, nor my voice° for thy preferment.°   *support / advancement*

PISANIO   Well, my good lord.

115 CLOTEN   Wilt thou serve me? For since patiently and con-
     stantly thou hast stuck to the bare fortune of that beggar
     Posthumus, thou canst not in the course of gratitude but be
     a diligent follower of mine. Wilt thou serve me?

PISANIO   Sir, I will.

120 CLOTEN   Give me thy hand; here's my purse. Hast any of thy
     late° master's garments in thy possession?   *former*

PISANIO   I have, my lord, at my lodging, the same suit he wore
     when he took leave of my lady and mistress.

CLOTEN   The first service thou dost me, fetch that suit hither.

125 Let it be thy first service, go.

PISANIO   I shall, my lord.   *Exit.*

CLOTEN   Meet thee at Milford Haven! I forgot to ask him one
     thing;⁶ I'll remember't anon. Even there, thou villain Post-
     humus, will I kill thee. I would these garments were come.

130 She said upon a time—the bitterness of it I now belch from
     my heart—that she held the very garment of Posthumus in
     more respect than my noble and natural person, together
     with the adornment of my qualities. With that suit upon my
     back will I ravish her—first kill him, and in her eyes; there

135 shall she see my valor, which will then be a torment to her
     contempt. He on the ground, my speech of insultment°   *contemptuous triumph*
     ended on his dead body, and when my lust hath dined—

---

5. May turn out to be merely a long journey for him.   passed since Imogen set out for Milford Haven (see
6. The "one thing" may be how much time has   Cloten's question at line 143).

which, as I say, to vex her, I will execute in the clothes
that she so praised—to the court I'll knock° her back,   beat
140 foot° her home again. She hath despised me rejoicingly,   kick
and I'll be merry in my revenge.
          Enter PISANIO [*with a suit of clothes*].
     Be those the garments?
PISANIO   Ay, my noble lord.
CLOTEN How long is't since she went to Milford Haven?
PISANIO She can scarce be there yet.
145 CLOTEN Bring this apparel to my chamber; that is the second
thing that I have commanded thee. The third is that thou
wilt be a voluntary mute to° my design. Be but duteous, and be quiet about
true preferment shall tender itself to thee. My revenge is
now at Milford; would I had wings to follow it. Come, and
150 be true.   *Exit.*
PISANIO Thou bidd'st me to my loss:° for true to thee   damnation; ruin
Were to prove false, which I will never be
To him that is most true. To Milford go,
And find not her whom thou pursuest. Flow, flow,
155 You heavenly blessings on her. This fool's speed
Be crossed° with slowness; labor be his meed.° *Exit.* thwarted / reward

3.6

          Enter IMOGEN *alone* [*dressed as a man, before
          the cave*].
IMOGEN   I see a man's life is a tedious one.
I have tired myself, and for two nights together
Have made the ground my bed. I should be sick,
But that my resolution helps me. Milford,
5   When from the mountaintop Pisanio showed thee,
Thou wast within a ken.° O Jove, I think   sight
Foundations[1] fly the wretched—such I mean,
Where they should be relieved.[2] Two beggars told me
I could not miss my way. Will poor folks lie,
10   That have afflictions on them, knowing 'tis
A punishment or trial?[3] Yes; no wonder,
When rich ones scarce tell true. To lapse in fullness°   To do wrong when rich
Is sorer° than to lie for need, and falsehood   worse
Is worse in kings than beggars. My dear lord,
15   Thou art one o'th' false ones. Now I think on thee,
My hunger's gone, but even before° I was   just a moment ago
At point° to sink for° food. But what is this?   Ready / for want of
Here is a path to't. 'Tis some savage hold.°   refuge
I were best not call; I dare not call; yet famine,
20   Ere clean° it o'erthrow nature, makes it valiant.   completely
Plenty and peace breeds cowards; hardness° ever   hardship
Of hardiness is mother. Ho! Who's here?
If anything that's civil, speak! If savage,
Take or lend.[4] Ho! No answer? Then I'll enter.

3.6 Location: Before the cave of Belarius, Wales.
1. Certainties; charitable institutions.
2. *such . . . relieved:* such certainties, I mean, as
should give mental relief to the wretched; such charitable institutions as should give physical relief (food
and rest) to the wretched.
3. *knowing . . . trial:* knowing that poverty is a punishment or a test of one's virtue.
4. Take everything I have, or help me.

25   Best draw my sword, and if mine enemy
    But fear the sword like me, he'll scarcely look on't.
    Such a foe, good heavens!⁵   *Exit [into the cave].*
        Enter BELARIUS, GUIDERIUS, *and* ARVIRAGUS.⁶

BELARIUS   You, Polydore, have proved best woodman° and   *hunter*
    Are master of the feast. Cadwal and I
30   Will play the cook and servant; 'tis our match.°   *bargain*
    The sweat of industry would dry and die
    But for the end it works to. Come, our stomachs
    Will make what's homely° savory. Weariness   *plain*
    Can snore upon the flint when resty° sloth   *lazy*
35   Finds the down pillow hard. Now peace be here,
    Poor house, that keep'st thyself.°   [*Exit into the cave.*]   *goes untended*
GUIDERIUS   I am thoroughly weary.
ARVIRAGUS   I am weak with toil, yet strong in appetite.
GUIDERIUS   There is cold meat i'th' cave; we'll browse° on that   *nibble*
    Whilst what we have killed be cooked.
        [*Enter* BELARIUS *from the cave.*]
BELARIUS   Stay, come not in!
40   But° that it eats our victuals, I should think   *But for the fact*
    Here were a fairy.
GUIDERIUS   What's the matter, sir?
BELARIUS   By Jupiter, an angel—or, if not,
    An earthly paragon.° Behold divineness   *equal*
    No elder than a boy.
        Enter IMOGEN.
IMOGEN   Good masters, harm me not.
45   Before I entered here I called, and thought°   *intended*
    To have begged or bought what I have took. Good troth,
    I have stol'n naught, nor would not, though I had found
    Gold strewed i'th' floor. Here's money for my meat:
    I would have left it on the board so° soon   *as*
50   As I had made my meal, and parted
    With prayers for the provider.
GUIDERIUS   Money, youth?
ARVIRAGUS   All gold and silver rather turn to dirt,
    As 'tis no better reckoned but of° those   *by*
    Who worship dirty gods.
IMOGEN   I see you're angry.
55   Know, if you kill me for my fault, I should
    Have died had I not made it.
BELARIUS   Whither bound?
IMOGEN   To Milford Haven.
BELARIUS   What's your name?
IMOGEN   Fidele,⁷ sir. I have a kinsman who
    Is bound for Italy. He embarked at Milford,
60   To whom being going, almost spent with hunger,
    I am fall'n in° this offense.   *into*
BELARIUS   Prithee, fair youth,
    Think us no churls,° nor measure our good minds   *base fellows*

---

5. May it please heaven I meet such a timid foe.
6. F marks a new scene at this point, but the action is continuous.
7. In French and Italian, the name means "faithful one."

By this rude° place we live in. Well encountered!   *wild*
'Tis almost night; you shall have better cheer°   *provisions*
65 Ere you depart, and thanks to° stay and eat it.   *our gratitude if you*
Boys, bid him welcome.

GUIDERIUS   Were you a woman, youth,
I should woo hard but be° your groom in honesty;   *rather than fail to be*
Ay, bid for you as I'd buy.[8]

ARVIRAGUS   I'll make't my comfort
He is a man; I'll love him as my brother,
70 [*to* IMOGEN] And such a welcome as I'd give to him,
After long absence, such is yours. Most welcome.
Be sprightly,° for you fall 'mongst friends.   *cheerful*

IMOGEN   'Mongst friends,
If brothers.[9] [*aside*] Would it had been so—that they
Had been my father's sons. Then had my price°   *worth*
75 Been less, and so more equal ballasting°   *equal in weight*
To thee, Posthumus.

BELARIUS   He wrings° at some distress.   *twists in pain*

GUIDERIUS   Would I could free't.°   *remove it*

ARVIRAGUS   Or I, whate'er it be,
What° pain it cost, what danger. Gods!   *Whatever*

BELARIUS   Hark, boys.

IMOGEN [*aside*]   Great men
80 That had a court no bigger than this cave,
That did attend° themselves and had the virtue   *wait on*
Which their own conscience sealed° them, laying by°   *assured / disregarding*
That nothing-gift of differing multitudes,[1]
Could not outpeer° these twain. Pardon me, gods,   *surpass*
85 I'd change my sex to be companion with them,
Since Leonatus false—

BELARIUS   It shall be so.
Boys, we'll go dress our hunt.° Fair youth, come in.   *game*
Discourse is heavy, fasting.[2] When we have supped
We'll mannerly demand thee of thy story,
So far as thou wilt speak it.

90 GUIDERIUS   Pray draw near.

ARVIRAGUS   The night to th'owl and morn to th' lark less welcome.

IMOGEN   Thanks, sir.

ARVIRAGUS   I pray draw near.   *Exeunt* [*into the cave*].

3.7

Enter two Roman SENATORS, *and* TRIBUNES.

FIRST SENATOR   This is the tenor of the Emperor's writ:
That since the common men are now in action
'Gainst the Pannonians and Dalmatians,
And that the legions now in Gallia are
5 Full weak° to undertake our wars against   *Too weak*
The fall'n-off° Britons, that we do incite   *rebelling*
The gentry to this business. He creates

---

8. Yes, make an offer for you with every intent to buy
(that is, to marry you).
9. *'Mongst . . . brothers*: Yes, certainly I am among
friends, if you claim me as a brother.

1. That worthless gift offered by a public that cannot
agree on anything.
2. Conversation is difficult when one is without food.
3.7 Location: A public place, Rome.

Lucius proconsul,[1] and to you the tribunes,
For this immediate levy, he commends°   *entrusts*
His absolute commission.° Long live Caesar!   *authority*

TRIBUNE   Is Lucius general of the forces?

SECOND SENATOR   Ay.

TRIBUNE   Remaining now in Gallia?

FIRST SENATOR   With those legions
Which I have spoke of, whereunto your levy
Must be supplyant.° The words of your commission   *auxiliary*
Will tie you to° the numbers and the time   *indicate to you*
Of their dispatch.

TRIBUNE   We will discharge our duty.

Exeunt.

4.1

Enter CLOTEN *alone [in Posthumus' clothes].*

CLOTEN   I am near to th' place where they should meet, if
Pisanio have mapped it truly. How fit° his garments serve me!   *aptly*
Why should his mistress, who was made by him that made
the tailor, not be fit° too? The rather—saving reverence of the   *apt; sexually compatible*
word[1]—for 'tis said a woman's fitness comes by fits;[2] therein I
must play the workman. I dare speak it to myself, for it is not
vainglory for a man and his glass° to confer in his own cham-   *mirror*
ber. I mean the lines of my body are as well drawn as his: no
less young, more strong, not beneath him in fortunes, beyond
him in the advantage of the time,[3] above him in birth, alike
conversant in general services, and more remarkable in single
oppositions;[4] yet this imperceiverant° thing loves him in my   *stupid*
despite.° What mortality[5] is! Posthumus, thy head, which   *to spite me*
now is growing upon thy shoulders, shall within this hour
be off, thy mistress enforced,° thy garments cut to pieces   *raped*
before her face; and all this done, spurn her home to her
father, who may haply be a little angry for my so rough
usage; but my mother, having power of° his testiness, shall   *over*
turn all into my commendations. My horse is tied up safe.
Out, sword, and to a sore purpose! Fortune, put them into
my hand. This is the very description of their meeting-place,
and the fellow dares not deceive me.   *Exit.*

4.2

Enter BELARIUS, GUIDERIUS, ARVIRAGUS, *and* IMOGEN
[dressed as a man] from the cave.

BELARIUS [*to* IMOGEN]   You are not well. Remain here in the cave,
We'll come to you after hunting.

ARVIRAGUS   Brother, stay here.
Are we not brothers?

IMOGEN   So man and man should be,
But clay and clay[1] differs in dignity,°   *social position*

---

1. One who acted as governor or military commander in a Roman province.
4.1 Location: Near the cave of Belarius, Wales.
1. With apologies for my punning.
2. For it is said that a woman's inclination for sexual
intercourse comes intermittently.
3. In the favorable opportunities afforded by the
times.

4. *alike . . . oppositions:* similarly acquainted with
battle tactics, and superior in single combat or duels
(with puns on "service" and "oppositions" as referring
to sexual exploits).
5. Life; humankind.
4.2 Location: Before the cave of Belarius.
1. Yet two humans (alluding to the biblical notion
that humans are formed out of clay).

5   Whose dust[2] is both alike. I am very sick—
GUIDERIUS [*to* BELARIUS *and* ARVIRAGUS] Go you to hunting,
  I'll abide with him.
IMOGEN So sick I am not, yet I am not well;
  But not so citizen a wanton as
  To seem to die ere sick.[3] So please you, leave me.
10 Stick to your journal course:° the breach of custom   *daily routine*
  Is breach of all. I am ill, but your being by me
  Cannot amend me. Society is no comfort
  To one not sociable. I am not very sick,
  Since I can reason of° it. Pray you, trust me here—   *talk about*
15 I'll rob none but myself—and let me die
  Stealing so poorly.[4]
GUIDERIUS   I love thee: I have spoke it;
  How much the quantity,° the weight as much,   *As greatly*
  As I do love my father.
BELARIUS   What? How, how?
ARVIRAGUS If it be sin to say so, sir, I yoke me°   *I share*
20 In my good brother's fault. I know not why
  I love this youth, and I have heard you say
  Love's reason's without reason. The bier[5] at door,
  And a demand who is't shall die, I'd say
  "My father, not this youth."
BELARIUS [*aside*]   O noble strain!°   *inherited character*
25 O worthiness of nature, breed of greatness!
  Cowards father cowards, and base things sire base;
  Nature hath meal and bran,° contempt and grace.   *flour and husks*
  I'm not their father, yet who this should be
  Doth miracle itself, loved before me.[6]
  —'Tis the ninth hour o'th' morn.[7]
30 ARVIRAGUS [*to* IMOGEN]   Brother, farewell.
IMOGEN I wish ye sport.
ARVIRAGUS   You health. —So please you, sir.
IMOGEN [*aside*] These are kind creatures. Gods, what lies I
  have heard!
  Our courtiers say all's savage but at court.
  Experience, O thou disprov'st report.
35 Th'imperious° seas breeds monsters; for the dish,   *imperial*
  Poor tributary rivers as sweet fish.[8]
  I am sick still, heartsick. Pisanio,
  I'll now taste of thy drug.
    [*She swallows the drug. The men speak apart.*]
GUIDERIUS   I could not stir him.
  He said he was gentle,° but unfortunate,   *a gentleman by birth*
40 Dishonestly afflicted, but yet honest.

2. The substance to which all humans return at death.

3. *But . . . sick:* But I am not so city-bred a weakling ("wanton") as to think I am dying even before I am sick.

4. Stealing only from one so poor as myself.

5. The litter, or platform, on which a corpse was carried to the grave.

6. *yet . . . me:* yet who this may be who is loved more than me is a source of great wonder.

7. TEXTUAL COMMENT Guiderius and Arviragus don't hear the first six lines of Belarius's speech, indicated

at line 24 by the phrase "*aside.*" Some editions indicate that at line 4.2.29 he speaks "aloud," but this edition assumes a greater fluidity in stage practice. It was common on the early modern stage for some lines to be heard only by the audience and not by other characters, while succeeding lines would be heard by all. These switch points are determined by context or performers' choices and need not be marked by a stage direction. See Digital Edition TC 5.

8. *for . . . fish:* but when it comes to eating, small tributaries breed fish as sweet as does the sea.

ARVIRAGUS   Thus did he answer me, yet said hereafter
    I might know more.
BELARIUS   To th' field, to th' field!
    —We'll leave you for this time. Go in and rest.
ARVIRAGUS   We'll not be long away.
BELARIUS   Pray be not sick,
    For you must be our housewife.
45 IMOGEN   Well or ill,
    I am bound° to you.   Exit [into the cave].   indebted
BELARIUS   And shalt be ever.
    This youth, howe'er distressed, appears° he hath had   apparently
    Good ancestors.
ARVIRAGUS   How angel-like he sings!
GUIDERIUS   But his neat° cookery! He cut our roots in   dainty
    characters,°   alphabet shapes
50 And sauced our broths as° Juno had been sick   as if
    And he her dieter.°   cook
ARVIRAGUS   Nobly he yokes
    A smiling with a sigh, as if the sigh
    Was that° it was for not being such a smile;   Was what
    The smile mocking the sigh, that° it would fly   because
55 From so divine a temple to commix°   join
    With winds that sailors rail at.
GUIDERIUS   I do note
    That grief and patience rooted in them both,°   (both sighs and smiles)
    Mingle their spurs° together.   roots
ARVIRAGUS   Grow patience,
    And let the stinking elder,[9] grief, untwine
60 His perishing° root with° the increasing vine.   deadly / from
BELARIUS   It is great morning.° Come away! Who's there?   full daylight
         Enter CLOTEN [in Posthumus' clothes].
CLOTEN   I cannot find those runagates;° that villain   runaways; fugitives
    Hath mocked me. I am faint.
BELARIUS   "Those runagates"?
    Means he not us? I partly know him; 'tis
65 Cloten, the son o'th' Queen. I fear some ambush.
    I saw him not these many years, and yet
    I know 'tis he. We are held as outlaws. Hence!
GUIDERIUS   He is but one. You and my brother search
    What companies° are near. Pray you, away.   companions
    Let me alone with him.   [Exeunt BELARIUS and ARVIRAGUS.]
70 CLOTEN   Soft, what are you
    That fly me thus? Some villain mountaineers?°   lowborn mountain people
    I have heard of such. What slave art thou?
GUIDERIUS   A thing
    More slavish did I ne'er than answering
    A slave without a knock.°   without striking him
CLOTEN   Thou art a robber,
75 A lawbreaker, a villain. Yield thee, thief.
GUIDERIUS   To who? To thee? What art thou? Have not I
    An arm as big as thine, a heart as big?
    Thy words, I grant, are bigger, for I wear not

---

9. A tree with strong-smelling leaves and flowers on which Judas, the disciple who betrayed Jesus, is said to
have hanged himself.

My dagger in my mouth.[1] Say what thou art,
Why I should yield to thee?

80   CLOTEN   Thou villain base,
Know'st me not by my clothes?

GUIDERIUS   No, nor thy tailor, rascal,
Who is thy grandfather. He made those clothes,
Which, as it seems, make thee.[2]

CLOTEN   Thou precious varlet,°   *absolute scoundrel*
My tailor made them not.

GUIDERIUS   Hence, then, and thank

85   The man that gave them thee. Thou art some fool;
I am loath to beat thee.

CLOTEN   Thou injurious° thief,   *insulting*
Hear but my name and tremble.

GUIDERIUS   What's thy name?

CLOTEN   Cloten, thou villain.

GUIDERIUS   Cloten, thou double villain, be thy name,

90   I cannot tremble at it. Were it Toad, or Adder, Spider,
'Twould move me sooner.

CLOTEN   To thy further fear,
Nay, to thy mere confusion,° thou shalt know   *absolute destruction*
I am son to th' Queen.

GUIDERIUS   I am sorry for't, not seeming
So worthy as thy birth.

CLOTEN   Art not afeard?

95   GUIDERIUS   Those that I reverence, those I fear: the wise.
At fools I laugh, not fear them.

CLOTEN   Die the death.
When I have slain thee with my proper° hand   *own*
I'll follow those that even now fled hence
And on the gates of Lud's Town° set your heads.[3]   *London*
Yield, rustic mountaineer.   *Fight and exeunt.*

      Enter BELARIUS *and* ARVIRAGUS.

100   BELARIUS   No company's abroad?°   *around*

ARVIRAGUS   None in the world. You did mistake him sure.

BELARIUS   I cannot tell. Long is it since I saw him,
But time hath nothing blurred those lines of favor°   *facial features*
Which then he wore. The snatches° in his voice   *hesitations*

105   And burst° of speaking were as his. I am absolute°   *sudden rush / sure*
'Twas very Cloten.°   *Cloten himself*

ARVIRAGUS   In this place we left them.
I wish my brother make good time with° him,   *is successful with*
You say he is so fell.°   *fierce*

BELARIUS   Being scarce made up,°   *barely full-grown*
I mean to man, he had not apprehension°   *had no consciousness*

110   Of roaring terrors; for defect of judgment
Is oft the cause of fear.[4]

      Enter GUIDERIUS [*with Cloten's head*].
              But see thy brother.

---

1. *for . . . mouth:* for I don't let words substitute for weapons.
2. Alluding to the proverb "The tailor makes the man."
3. The heads of criminals were frequently displayed on poles on London Bridge and other places throughout the city.

4. *for . . . fear:* an obscure passage. It may mean that Cloten's faulty judgment, which led him to know no fear, caused fear in others. A less likely meaning is that while defects in judgment cause fear, Cloten knew no fear because he had absolutely no judgment, being utterly witless.

GUIDERIUS   This Cloten was a fool, an empty purse;
There was no money in't. Not Hercules[5]
Could have knocked out his brains, for he had none.

115 Yet I not doing this,° the fool had borne   *had I not done this*
My head, as I do his.

BELARIUS   What hast thou done?

GUIDERIUS   I am perfect° what: cut off one Cloten's head,   *certain*
Son to the Queen (after his own report)
Who called me traitor, mountaineer, and swore

120 With his own single hand he'd take us in,°   *capture us*
Displace our heads where—thank the gods—they grow,
And set them on Lud's Town.

BELARIUS   We are all undone.

GUIDERIUS   Why, worthy father, what have we to lose
But that° he swore to take, our lives? The law   *what*

125 Protects not us; then why should we be tender
To let[6] an arrogant piece of flesh threat us,
Play judge and executioner all himself,
For° we do fear the law? What company   *Because*
Discover you abroad?[7]

BELARIUS   No single soul

130 Can we set eye on, but in all safe reason
He must have some attendants. Though his humor°   *disposition*
Was nothing but mutation,° ay, and that   *changeableness*
From one bad thing to worse, not° frenzy,   *neither*
Not° absolute madness, could so far have raved°   *Nor / could have made him mad enough*

135 To bring him here alone. Although perhaps
It may be heard at court that such as we
Cave° here, hunt here, are outlaws, and in time   *Live in a cave*
May make some stronger head,° the which he hearing—   *raise a stronger force*
As it is like him—might break out and swear

140 He'd fetch us in, yet is't not probable
To come° alone, either he so undertaking,   *That he would come*
Or they so suffering.[8] Then on good ground we fear,
If we do fear this body hath a tail°   *rear end; followers*
More perilous than the head.

ARVIRAGUS   Let ord'nance°   *destiny*

145 Come as the gods foresay° it; howsoe'er,   *predict*
My brother hath done well.

BELARIUS   I had no mind
To hunt this day. The boy Fidele's sickness
Did make my way long forth.°   *my journey tedious*

GUIDERIUS   With his own sword,
Which he did wave against my throat, I have ta'en

150 His head from him. I'll throw't into the creek
Behind our rock, and let it to the sea
And tell the fishes he's the Queen's son, Cloten.
That's all I reck.°   *Exit.*   *care*

BELARIUS   I fear 'twill be revenged.
Would, Polydore, thou hadst not done't, though valor
Becomes thee well enough.

---

5. Mythical hero of enormous strength.
6. *be tender / To let*: be so meek as to allow.
7. What companions (of Cloten) did you find

hereabouts?
8. *either . . . suffering*: either that he would undertake it or that they would allow it.

155 ARVIRAGUS   Would I had done't,
    So the revenge alone pursued me.° Polydore,   *only pursued me*
    I love thee brotherly, but envy much
    Thou hast robbed me of this deed. I would revenges
    That possible strength might meet would seek us through
    And put us to our answer.[9]
160 BELARIUS   Well, 'tis done.
    We'll hunt no more today, nor seek for danger
    Where there's no profit. I prithee, to our rock.
    You and Fidele play the cooks. I'll stay
    Till hasty Polydore return, and bring him
    To dinner presently.
165 ARVIRAGUS   Poor sick Fidele!
    I'll willingly to him. To gain° his color   *restore*
    I'd let a parish of such Clotens blood[1]
    And praise myself for charity.   *Exit [into the cave].*
BELARIUS   O thou goddess,
    Thou divine Nature, how thyself thou blazon'st[2]
170   In these two princely boys! They are as gentle
    As zephyrs° blowing below the violet,   *breezes from the west*
    Not wagging his sweet head; and yet as rough,°   *violent*
    Their royal blood enchafed,° as the rud'st wind   *inflamed*
    That by the top doth take the mountain pine
175   And make him stoop to th' vale. 'Tis wonder
    That an invisible instinct should frame° them   *shape*
    To royalty unlearned, honor untaught,
    Civility not seen from other,° valor   *not witnessed in others*
    That wildly° grows in them, but yields a crop   *without cultivation*
180   As if it had been sowed. Yet still it's strange
    What Cloten's being here to us portends,
    Or what his death will bring us.
        Enter GUIDERIUS.
GUIDERIUS   Where's my brother?
    I have sent Cloten's clotpoll° down the stream   *blockhead*
    In embassy to his mother. His body's hostage
    For his return.[3]
        Solemn music [plays].
185 BELARIUS   My ingenious° instrument!   *artfully crafted*
    Hark, Polydore, it sounds. But what occasion
    Hath Cadwal now to give it motion? Hark!
GUIDERIUS   Is he at home?
BELARIUS   He went hence even now.
GUIDERIUS   What does he mean? Since death of my dear'st mother
190   It did not speak before. All solemn things
    Should answer° solemn accidents. The matter?   *correspond to*
    Triumphs for nothing and lamenting toys
    Is jollity for apes and grief for boys.[4]
    Is Cadwal mad?

---

9. *I would . . . answer:* I wish that revenges equal to all the power that we might muster would find us out and test our mettle.
1. I'd draw blood from a whole parish full of fools like Cloten.
2. How you proclaim yourself (as in a coat of arms).

3. *His body's . . . return:* I will hold his body hostage until his head returns (which will be never).
4. *Triumphs . . . boys:* Public celebrations for no reason and showing great grief for trivial matters are foolish and unmanly.

Enter ARVIRAGUS *[from the cave] with* IMOGEN
[seeming] dead, bearing her in his arms.

BELARIUS   Look, here he comes,
195   And brings the dire occasion in his arms
Of what we blame him for.

ARVIRAGUS   The bird is dead
That we have made so much on.° I had rather   *of*
Have skipped from sixteen years of age to sixty,
To have turned my leaping time° into a crutch,°   *youth / (old age)*
Than have seen this.

200 GUIDERIUS   O sweetest, fairest lily!
My brother wears thee not the one half so well
As when thou grew'st thyself.

BELARIUS   O melancholy,
Whoever yet could sound thy bottom,° find   *measure your depths*
The ooze, to show what coast thy sluggish crare°   *small ship*
205   Might easiliest harbor in? Thou blessèd thing,
Jove knows what man thou mightst have made; but I,°   *I know*
Thou died'st a most rare boy, of melancholy.
How found you him?

ARVIRAGUS   Stark,° as you see,   *Stiff*
Thus smiling, as° some fly had tickled slumber,   *as if*
210   Not as death's dart being laughed at;[5] his right cheek
Reposing on a cushion.

GUIDERIUS   Where?

ARVIRAGUS   O'th' floor,
His arms thus leagued.° I thought he slept, and put   *linked together*
My clouted brogues° from off my feet, whose rudeness   *hobnailed boots*
Answered° my steps too loud.   *Rendered*

GUIDERIUS   Why, he but sleeps.
215   If he be gone, he'll make his grave a bed.
With female fairies will his tomb be haunted,
And worms will not come to thee.

ARVIRAGUS   With fairest flowers
Whilst summer lasts and I live here, Fidele,
I'll sweeten thy sad grave. Thou shalt not lack
220   The flower that's like thy face, pale primrose, nor
The azured harebell,° like thy veins; no, nor   *blue hyacinth*
The leaf of eglantine,° whom not to slander,   *sweetbriar rose*
Out-sweetened not thy breath. The ruddock would
With charitable bill—O bill sore shaming
225   Those rich-left heirs, that let their fathers lie
Without a monument—bring thee all this,
Yea, and furred moss besides.[6] When flowers are none,
To winter-ground° thy corpse—   *protect for winter*

GUIDERIUS   Prithee have done,
And do not play in wench-like words[7] with that
230   Which is so serious. Let us bury him,
And not protract with admiration° what   *wonder*
Is now due debt. To th' grave.

---

5. Not as if laughing at the approach of death. Death
was often depicted carrying a spear ("dart").
6. *The ruddock . . . besides:* referring to the belief
that the robins ("ruddocks") covered dead bodies
with flowers and moss.

7. Words appropriate to women. In Shakespeare's
plays, speeches about flowers are often delivered by
female characters, perhaps most notably in *Hamlet*
4.4.165–74 and *The Winter's Tale* 4.4.73–134.

ARVIRAGUS   Say, where shall 's° lay him?   *ought we to*

GUIDERIUS   By good Euriphile, our mother.

ARVIRAGUS   Be't so,
And let us, Polydore, though now our voices
235   Have got the mannish crack, sing him to th' ground
As once to our mother; use like note° and words,   *a similar tune*
Save that "Euriphile" must be "Fidele."

GUIDERIUS   Cadwal,
I cannot sing. I'll weep, and word° it with thee;   *speak*
240   For notes of sorrow out of tune are worse
Than priests and fanes° that lie.   *temples*

ARVIRAGUS   We'll speak it then.

BELARIUS   Great griefs, I see, med'cine° the less, for Cloten   *cure*
Is quite forgot. He was a queen's son, boys,
And though he came our enemy, remember
245   He was paid° for that. Though mean° and mighty rotting   *punished / lowborn*
Together have one dust, yet reverence,
That angel of the world,[8] doth make distinction
Of place 'tween high and low. Our foe was princely,
And though you took his life as being our foe,
Yet bury him as a prince.

250   GUIDERIUS   Pray you fetch him hither.
Thersites' body is as good as Ajax'[9]
When neither are alive.

ARVIRAGUS [*to* BELARIUS]   If you'll go fetch him,
We'll say our song the whilst.   [*Exit* BELARIUS.]
                          Brother, begin.

GUIDERIUS   Nay, Cadwal, we must lay his head to th'east;[1]
My father hath a reason for't.

255   ARVIRAGUS   'Tis true.

GUIDERIUS   Come on, then, and remove him.

ARVIRAGUS   So, begin.[2]

          [GUIDERIUS *and* ARVIRAGUS *sing the*] song.

GUIDERIUS   Fear no more the heat o'th' sun,
Nor the furious winter's rages.
Thou thy worldly task hast done,
260   Home art gone and ta'en thy wages.
Golden lads and girls all must,
As° chimney-sweepers, come to dust.   *Like*

ARVIRAGUS   Fear no more the frown o'th' great,
Thou art past the tyrant's stroke.
265   Care no more to clothe and eat,
To thee the reed is as the oak.[3]
The scepter, learning, physic° must   *medical knowledge*
All follow this and come to dust.

---

8. Reverence (respect for someone because of his or her social position) may here be called the "angel of the world" because social hierarchy was thought by some to imitate heavenly hierarchy.
9. Alluding to two Greeks present at the siege of Troy: Thersites, a scurrilous coward, and Ajax, a mighty hero. Both appear in Shakespeare's *Troilus and Cressida*.
1. An allusion to classical or Celtic burial practices. The English Christian custom was to lay the head to the west. This detail reinforces the pagan world of the play.
2. In F, the following duet is introduced as "song." Lines 239–41, in which the brothers say they cannot sing and must speak the words, may have been added because the particular actors who played Arviragus and Guiderius were not good singers.
3. Referring to traditional symbols of weakness and strength, respectively.

GUIDERIUS	Fear no more the lightning flash,	
270 ARVIRAGUS	Nor th'all-dreaded thunder-stone.°	*thunderbolt*
GUIDERIUS	Fear not slander, censure rash.	
ARVIRAGUS	Thou hast finished joy and moan.	
BOTH	All lovers young, all lovers must	
	Consign to thee⁴ and come to dust.	
275 GUIDERIUS	No exorciser° harm thee,	*conjurer of spirits*
ARVIRAGUS	Nor no witchcraft charm thee.	
GUIDERIUS	Ghost unlaid forbear thee.⁵	
ARVIRAGUS	Nothing ill come near thee.	
BOTH	Quiet consummation° have,	*ending*
280	And renownèd be thy grave.	

Enter BELARIUS *with the body of* CLOTEN.

GUIDERIUS We have done our obsequies. Come, lay him down.
BELARIUS Here's a few flowers, but 'bout midnight more;

The herbs that have on them cold dew o'th' night° *of the night*
Are strewings fitt'st for graves. Upon their faces.⁶
285 You were as flowers, now withered; even so
These herblets shall,° which we upon you strew. *shall wither*
Come on, away; apart upon our knees.⁷
The ground that gave them° first has them again. *gave them life*
Their pleasures here are past, so is their pain.

Exeunt [BELARIUS, GUIDERIUS, *and* ARVIRAGUS].

290 IMOGEN (*awakes*) Yes, sir, to Milford Haven. Which is the way?
I thank you. By yond bush? Pray, how far thither?
'Ods pittikins,° can it be six mile yet? *By God's pity (mild oath)*
I have gone° all night. Faith, I'll lie down and sleep. *walked*

[*She sees* CLOTEN's *body.*]

But soft,° no bedfellow! O gods and goddesses! *wait*
295 These flowers are like the pleasures of the world,
This bloody man the care on't.° I hope I dream, *the world's sorrow*
For so° I thought I was a cave-keeper, *For then*
And cook to honest creatures. But 'tis not so.
'Twas but a bolt° of nothing, shot at nothing, *an arrow*
300 Which the brain makes of fumes.⁸ Our very eyes
Are sometimes like our judgments, blind. Good faith,
I tremble still with fear; but if there be
Yet left in heaven as small a drop of pity
As a wren's eye, feared gods, a part of it!
305 The dream's here still: even when I wake it is
Without me as within me; not imagined, felt.
A headless man? The garments of Posthumus?⁹
I know the shape of 's leg; this is his hand,
His foot Mercurial, his Martial¹ thigh,
310 The brawns° of Hercules; but his Jovial² face— *muscles*
Murder in heaven! How? 'Tis gone! Pisanio,

4. Submit to the same terms as you.
5. May spirits who have not been laid to rest leave you alone.
6. TEXTUAL COMMENT Although some editors have suggested that Belarius commands his sons to lay the bodies so that their faces are to the earth, this edition takes Belarius's words to mean that the boys should put the flowers on the front ("faces") of the bodies. See Digital Edition TC 6.
7. Some other place ("apart"), let us pray (be "upon our knees").

8. "Fumes" (vapors) were thought to rise from the stomach and cause dreams and distortions of the imagination.
9. PERFORMANCE COMMENT The overt theatricality of having the Cloten actor play his own dead body (as opposed to using a mannequin) can spur audience engagement. See Digital Edition PC 3.
1. Fashioned for battle, like that of Mars, the god of war. *Mercurial:* Like that of Mercury, the fleet-footed messenger of the gods.
2. Majestic like the face of Jove, king of the gods.

All curses madded Hecuba³ gave the Greeks,
And mine to boot, be darted on thee! Thou,
Conspired° with that irregulous° devil, Cloten,   *Conspiring / lawless*
315   Hath here cut off my lord. To write and read
Be henceforth treacherous. Damned Pisanio
Hath with his forgèd letters—damned Pisanio—
From this most bravest° vessel of the world   *splendid*
Struck the main top!° O Posthumus, alas,   *top mast; (his head)*
320   Where is thy head? Where's that? Ay me, where's that?
Pisanio might have killed thee at the heart
And left thy head on. How should this be? Pisanio?
'Tis he and Cloten: malice and lucre° in them   *greed*
Have laid this woe here. Oh, 'tis pregnant,° pregnant!   *clear*
325   The drug he gave me, which he said was precious
And cordial° to me, have I not found it   *restorative*
Murd'rous to th' senses? That confirms it home:°   *completely*
This is Pisanio's deed, and Cloten. Oh,
Give color to my pale cheek with thy blood,
330   That we the horrider° may seem to those   *more terrifying*
Which chance to find us. O my lord, my lord!
     [*She smears her face with blood and falls on the body.*]
     Enter LUCIUS, CAPTAINS, *and a* SOOTHSAYER.
CAPTAIN   To them,° the legions garrisoned in Gallia   *In addition to them*
After your will⁴ have crossed the sea, attending°   *waiting for*
You here at Milford Haven with your ships:
They are here in readiness.
335 LUCIUS   But what from Rome?
CAPTAIN   The Senate hath stirred up the confiners°   *inhabitants*
And gentlemen of Italy, most willing spirits
That promise noble service, and they come
Under the conduct of bold Giacomo,
Siena's° brother.   *The Duke of Siena's*
340 LUCIUS   When expect you them?
CAPTAIN   With the next benefit o'th' wind.
LUCIUS   This forwardness°   *readiness*
Makes our hopes fair. Command our present numbers
Be mustered; bid the captains look to't.   [*Exit a* CAPTAIN.]
[*to the* SOOTHSAYER]   Now, sir,
What have you dreamed of late of this war's purpose?°   *outcome*
345 SOOTHSAYER   Last night the very gods showed me a vision—
I fast° and prayed for their intelligence°—thus: *fasted / information*
I saw Jove's bird, the Roman eagle, winged
From the spongy° south to this part of the west,   *damp*
There vanished in the sunbeams; which portends,
350   Unless my sins abuse° my divination,   *falsify*
Success to th' Roman host.
LUCIUS   Dream often so,
And never false.° —Soft ho, what trunk is here   *dream falsely*
Without his top? The ruin speaks that sometime°   *once*
It was a worthy building. How, a page?
355   Or° dead or sleeping on him? But dead rather,   *Either*
For nature doth abhor to make his bed

---

3. The queen of Troy, Priam's wife, whose desire for revenge against the Greeks made her insane ("madded").
4. According to your command.

With the defunct, or sleep upon the dead.
Let's see the boy's face.
CAPTAIN   He's alive, my lord.
LUCIUS   He'll then instruct us of this body. Young one,
360   Inform us of thy fortunes, for it seems
They crave to be demanded. Who is this
Thou mak'st thy bloody pillow? Or who was he
That, otherwise than noble nature did,[5]
Hath altered that good picture? What's thy interest
365   In this sad wreck?° How came't? Who is't?   ruin
What art thou?
IMOGEN   I am nothing; or if not,
Nothing to be were better.[6] This was my master,
A very valiant Briton and a good,
That here by mountaineers lies slain. Alas,
370   There is no more such masters. I may wander
From east to occident,° cry out for service,   west
Try many, all good; serve truly, never
Find such another master.
LUCIUS   'Lack,° good youth,   Alas
Thou mov'st no less with thy complaining than
375   Thy master in bleeding. Say his name, good friend.
IMOGEN   Richard du Champ.[7] [aside] If I do lie and do
No harm by it, though the gods hear, I hope
They'll pardon it. —Say you, sir?
LUCIUS   Thy name?
IMOGEN   Fidele, sir.
LUCIUS   Thou dost approve° thyself the very same: show
380   Thy name well fits thy faith,° thy faith thy name.   fidelity
Wilt take thy chance with me? I will not say
Thou shalt be so well mastered, but be sure,
No less beloved. The Roman Emperor's letters,
Sent by a consul to me, should not sooner
385   Than thine own worth prefer° thee. Go with me.   recommend
IMOGEN   I'll follow, sir. But first, an't° please the gods,   if it
I'll hide my master from the flies as deep
As these poor pickaxes° can dig; and when   (her hands)
With wildwood leaves and weeds I ha' strewed his grave
390   And on it said a century of° prayers,   a hundred
Such as I can, twice o'er, I'll weep and sigh,
And leaving so his service, follow you,
So please you entertain° me.   employ
LUCIUS   Ay, good youth,
And rather father thee than master thee. My friends,
395   The boy hath taught us manly duties. Let us
Find out the prettiest daisied plot we can,
And make him with our pikes and partisans[8]
A grave. Come, arm° him. Boy, he is preferred°   lift / recommended

---

5. Who, in a manner different from nature's workings.
6. It were better to be nothing.
7. This French name translates as "Richard of the Field," perhaps an allusion to a well-known London printer named Richard Field, who was born in Stratford-upon-Avon and printed Shakespeare's *Rape of Lucrece* and *Venus and Adonis* in the 1590s.
8. With our spears and our halberds (long-handled weapons with ax-like blades).

By thee to us, and he shall be interred
400   As soldiers can. Be cheerful; wipe thine eyes.
Some falls are means the happier to arise.[9]   *Exeunt.*

4.3

Enter CYMBELINE, LORDS, *and* PISANIO.
CYMBELINE   Again, and bring me word how 'tis with her.
                               [*Exit a* LORD.]

A fever with° the absence of her son,   *on account of*
A madness of which her life's in danger. Heavens,
How deeply you at once do touch° me! Imogen,   *afflict*
5   The great part of my comfort, gone; my Queen
Upon a desperate bed,° and in a time   *Extremely ill in bed*
When fearful wars point at me; her son gone,
So needful for this present!° It strikes me past   *So needed now*
The hope of comfort. [*to* PISANIO] But for thee, fellow,
10   Who needs must know of her departure and
Dost seem so ignorant, we'll enforce it from thee
By a sharp torture.
PISANIO   Sir, my life is yours;
I humbly set it at your will. But for my mistress,
I nothing know° where she remains, why gone,   *know nothing about*
15   Nor when she purposes° return. Beseech° your highness,   *intends to / I beseech*
Hold me° your loyal servant.   *Regard me as*
LORD   Good my liege,
The day that she was missing, he was here.
I dare be bound he's true, and shall perform
All parts of his subjection° loyally. For Cloten,   *duty as a subject*
20   There wants° no diligence in seeking him,   *is lacking*
And will° no doubt be found.   *he will*
CYMBELINE   The time is troublesome.°   *dire*
[*to* PISANIO] We'll slip you° for a season, but our jealousy   *let you go*
Does yet depend.[1]
LORD   So please your majesty,
The Roman legions, all from Gallia drawn,
25   Are landed on your coast with a supply
Of Roman gentlemen by the Senate sent.
CYMBELINE   Now for° the counsel of my son and Queen!   *If only I now had*
I am amazed° with matter.°   *overwhelmed / business*
LORD   Good my liege,
Your preparation can affront no less
30   Than what you hear of.[2] Come more, for more you're ready.
The want° is but to put those powers in motion   *The only thing needed*
That long to move.
CYMBELINE   I thank you. Let's withdraw
And meet the time as it seeks us. We fear not
What can from Italy annoy° us, but   *harm*
35   We grieve at chances° here. Away.   *events*
               Exeunt [CYMBELINE *and* LORDS].
PISANIO   I heard no letter from my master since
I wrote him Imogen was slain. 'Tis strange.

---

9. Some falls are means by which good fortune arises.
4.3 Location: Cymbeline's court, Britain.

1. *but . . . depend:* but our suspicions still hold.
2. *Your . . . of:* Your forces can confront all those you have heard of.

Nor hear I from my mistress, who did promise
To yield me often tidings. Neither know I
40   What is betid° to Cloten, but remain   has happened
Perplexed in all. The heavens still must work.
Wherein I am false, I am honest; not true, to be true.
These present wars shall find I love my country,
Even to the note° o'th' King, or I'll fall in them.   notice
45   All other doubts, by time let them be cleared:
Fortune brings in some boats that are not steered.   *Exit.*

4.4

Enter BELARIUS, GUIDERIUS, *and* ARVIRAGUS.

GUIDERIUS   The noise is round about us.

BELARIUS   Let us from it.

ARVIRAGUS   What pleasure, sir, find we in life to lock it°   shut it off
From action and adventure?

GUIDERIUS   Nay, what hope
Have we in hiding us? This way° the Romans   By this action
5   Must or° for Britons slay us, or receive us   either
For barbarous and unnatural revolts°   rebels
During their use,[1] and slay us after.

BELARIUS   Sons,
We'll higher to the mountains; there secure us.
To the King's party there's no going. Newness
10   Of Cloten's death—we being not known, not mustered
Among the bands°—may drive us to a render°   troops / an account
Where we have lived, and so extort from 's that
Which we have done, whose answer would be death
Drawn on° with torture.   Prolonged

GUIDERIUS   This is, sir, a doubt
15   In such a time nothing becoming you
Nor satisfying us.

ARVIRAGUS   It is not likely
That when they hear the Roman horses neigh,
Behold their quartered fires,[2] have both their eyes
And ears so cloyed importantly[3] as now,
20   That they will waste their time upon our note,°   in observing us
To know from whence we are.

BELARIUS   Oh, I am known
Of° many in the army. Many years,   By
Though Cloten then° but young, you see, not wore° him   was then / have not worn
From my remembrance. And besides, the King
25   Hath not deserved my service nor your loves,
Who find in my exile the want of breeding,
The certainty of this hard life;[4] aye hopeless
To have the courtesy your cradle promised,[5]
But to be still° hot summer's tanlings[6] and   always
The shrinking slaves of winter.

4.4 Location: Before the cave of Belarius, Wales.
1. While they have need of us.
2. Fires set out in each quarter of the Roman encampment, indicating the orderly nature of the Roman forces.
3. So completely taken up with important matters.
4. *Who . . . life:* (You) who experience as a result of

my exile a lack of proper education, the enduring fact of this hard life.
5. *aye . . . promised:* ever without hope to have the cultivated existence your noble birth promised.
6. People exposed to the sun. In England at this time, tanned skin denoted low social status.

30   GUIDERIUS   Than be so,
      Better to cease to be. Pray, sir, to th'army.
      I and my brother are not known; yourself
      So out of thought, and thereto° so o'ergrown,[7]   *in addition*
      Cannot be questioned.
  ARVIRAGUS   By this sun that shines,
35   I'll thither. What thing is't[8] that I never
      Did see man die, scarce ever looked on blood
      But that of coward hares, hot° goats, and venison,   *lecherous*
      Never bestrid a horse save one that had
      A rider like myself, who ne'er wore rowel[9]
40   Nor iron on his heel! I am ashamed
      To look upon the holy sun, to have
      The benefit of his blest beams, remaining
      So long a poor unknown.
  GUIDERIUS   By heavens, I'll go.
      If you will bless me, sir, and give me leave,
45   I'll take the better care;° but if you will not,   *be more careful*
      The hazard therefore due[1] fall on me by
      The hands of Romans.
  ARVIRAGUS   So say I, amen.
  BELARIUS   No reason I, since of your lives you set
      So slight a valuation, should reserve
50   My cracked° one to more care. Have with you,° boys!   *weakened / Come then*
      If in your country° wars you chance to die,   *country's*
      That is my bed too, lads, and there I'll lie.
      Lead, lead! [*aside*] The time seems long; their blood thinks
        scorn°   *disdains itself*
      Till it fly out and show them princes born.   *Exeunt.*

5.1

Enter POSTHUMUS *alone [dressed as a Roman,*
carrying a bloody cloth].

  POSTHUMUS   Yea, bloody cloth, I'll keep thee, for I wished
      Thou shouldst be colored thus. You married ones,
      If each of you should take this course, how many
      Must murder wives much better than themselves
5   For wrying° but a little? O Pisanio,   *erring*
      Every good servant does not all commands;
      No bond but° to do just ones. Gods, if you   *No obligation except*
      Should have ta'en vengeance on my faults, I never
      Had lived to put on this:° so had you saved   *to undertake this deed*
10   The noble Imogen to repent, and struck
      Me, wretch, more worth your vengeance. But alack,
      You snatch some hence for little faults; that's love,
      To have them fall no more.[1] You some permit
      To second° ills with ills, each elder° worse,   *reinforce / later fault*
15   And make them dread it, to the doers' thrift.[2]
      But Imogen is your own; do your best wills,

---

7. So overgrown with hair or beard; so grown in years; so grown out of memory.
8. What a bad state of affairs it is.
9. Small rotating disk at the end of a spur. Wearing spurs was the privilege of gentlemen.
1. May the danger due to me (as a result of my disobedience).

5.1 Location: The Roman camp, Britain.
1. *that's . . . more:* that is a sign of love, to have them no longer sin.
2. And make them fear this escalation of sin, to their own benefit.

And make me blest to obey. I am brought hither
Among th'Italian gentry, and to fight
Against my lady's kingdom. 'Tis enough
20 That, Britain, I have killed thy mistress; peace,
I'll give no wound to thee. Therefore, good heavens,
Hear patiently my purpose: I'll disrobe me
Of these Italian weeds, and suit° myself   *dress*
As does a Briton peasant.
      [*He changes his clothes.*]
                So I'll fight
25 Against the part° I come with; so I'll die   *side*
For thee, O Imogen, even for whom my life
Is every breath a death; and thus unknown,
Pitied° nor hated, to the face of peril   *Neither pitied*
Myself I'll dedicate. Let me make men know
30 More valor in me than my habits° show.   *garments*
Gods, put the strength o'th' Leonati in me.
To shame the guise° o'th' world, I will begin   *customs; dress*
The fashion—less without and more within.   *Exit.*

5.2¹

    Enter LUCIUS, GIACOMO, *and the Roman army at one*
    door and the Briton army at another, Leonatus
    POSTHUMUS *following[, dressed as] a poor soldier. They*
    march over, and go out. Then enter again in skirmish
    GIACOMO *and* POSTHUMUS: *he vanquisheth and*
    disarmeth GIACOMO, *and then leaves him.*

GIACOMO   The heaviness and guilt within my bosom
    Takes off° my manhood. I have belied° a lady,   *Destroys / slandered*
    The princess of this country, and the air on't°   *of it*
    Revengingly enfeebles me; or° could this carl,°   *otherwise / peasant*
5   A very drudge° of nature's, have subdued me   *slave*
    In my profession? Knighthoods and honors borne
    As I wear mine are titles but° of scorn.   *merely*
    If that thy gentry, Britain, go before°   *surpass*
    This lout as he exceeds our lords, the odds
10 Is that we scarce are men and you are gods.   *Exit.*
    The battle continues; the Britons fly, CYMBELINE *is*
    taken. Then enter to his rescue BELARIUS, GUIDERIUS,
    and ARVIRAGUS.
BELARIUS   Stand, stand, we have th'advantage of the ground;
    The lane is guarded. Nothing routs us but
    The villainy of our fears.
GUIDERIUS *and* ARVIRAGUS   Stand, stand, and fight.
    Enter POSTHUMUS [*dressed as a poor soldier*] *and*
    seconds the Britons. They rescue CYMBELINE, *and*
    exeunt. Then enter LUCIUS, GIACOMO, *and* IMOGEN
    [*dressed as a man*].

5.2 Location: A field between the British and Roman
camps, Britain.
1. TEXTUAL COMMENT Editors often disagree over
how and where to divide the sequence of events represented from 5.2 to 5.4 in the present edition. This
edition retains the divisions of the Folio, shifting
only the stage direction at the end of F 5.3 to the
beginning of 5.4 and adding an *Exeunt* to the end of
5.3. See Digital Edition TC 7.

LUCIUS Away, boy, from the troops, and save thyself!
15 For friends kill friends, and the disorder's such
   As° war were hoodwinked.°   *as if / blindfolded*
GIACOMO   'Tis their fresh supplies.
LUCIUS It is a day turned strangely. Or betimes
   Let's reinforce, or fly.[2]   *Exeunt.*

5.3
   Enter POSTHUMUS [*dressed as a poor soldier*], *and a
   Briton* LORD.
LORD Cam'st thou from where they made the stand?
POSTHUMUS   I did,
   Though you, it seems, come from the fliers?
LORD   Ay.
POSTHUMUS No blame be to you, sir, for all was lost,
   But° that the heavens fought. The King himself   *Had it not been*
5 Of his wings destitute,[1] the army broken,
   And but° the backs of Britons seen, all flying   *only*
   Through a strait° lane; the enemy full-hearted,°   *narrow / bold*
   Lolling the tongue with slaught'ring,[2] having work
   More plentiful than tools to do't, struck down
10 Some mortally, some slightly touched,° some falling   *wounded*
   Merely through fear, that the strait pass was dammed°   *clogged*
   With dead men hurt behind,[3] and cowards living
   To die with length'ned shame.[4]
LORD   Where was this lane?
POSTHUMUS Close by the battle, ditched, and walled with turf,
15 Which gave advantage to an ancient soldier,
   An honest one, I warrant, who deserved
   So long a breeding as his white beard came to,[5]
   In doing this for 's country. Athwart° the lane,   *Across*
   He, with two striplings (lads more like° to run   *likely*
20 The country base[6] than to commit such slaughter,
   With faces fit for masks,[7] or rather fairer
   Than those for preservation cased, or shame[8])
   Made good° the passage, cried to those that fled: *Secured*
   "Our Britain's harts° die flying, not our men;   *deer*
25 To darkness fleet° souls that fly backwards. Stand,   *rush*
   Or we are Romans,[9] and will give you that°   *(death)*
   Like beasts which you shun beastly,° and may save   *in cowardly fashion*
   But to look back in frown.[1] Stand, stand!" These three,
   Three thousand confident,[2] in act as many—
30 For three performers are the file,° when all   *entire force*
   The rest do nothing—with this word "Stand, stand!"

2. *Or betimes . . . fly:* Let us either promptly reinforce our troops or flee.
5.3 Location: Scene continues.
1. Deprived of his wings (that is, the troops to either side of the main division of the army).
2. With their tongues hanging out either from the labor of slaughter or from eagerness to commit the slaughter.
3. Hurt on their backs (as they were fleeing).
4. To die later after a life of prolonged shame.
5. *who . . . to:* who deserved to live so long again as his white beard indicated he had already lived.

6. *to run . . . base:* to play a children's game (prisoner's house) that involves running between two bases.
7. Gentlewomen wore masks to protect their complexions from the elements.
8. *fairer . . . shame:* more delicate than those covered with masks for protection ("preservation") or out of modesty.
9. Or we will behave like Romans.
1. *and may . . . frown:* and may prevent only by turning back upon the enemy with threatening face.
2. As confident as if they were three thousand.

Accommodated° by the place, more charming[3]   *Assisted*
With their own nobleness, which could have turned
A distaff to a lance,[4] gilded° pale looks;   *brought color to*
35 Part shame, part spirit renewed,[5] that some, turned coward
But by example[6]—Oh, a sin in war,
Damned in the first beginners[7]—'gan° to look   *began*
The way that they° did and to grin[8] like lions   *(the three)*
Upon the pikes o'th' hunters. Then began
40 A stop° i'th' chaser, a retire; anon°   *halt / soon*
A rout, confusion thick; forthwith they fly
Chickens, the way which they stooped eagles;[9] slaves,
The strides they victors made;[1] and now our cowards,
Like fragments° in hard voyages, became   *scraps of food*
45 The life o'th' need.[2] Having found the back door open
Of the unguarded hearts,[3] heavens, how they wound!
Some slain before,[4] some dying, some their friends
O'erborne° i'th' former wave, ten chased by one,   *Overwhelmed*
Are now each one the slaughterman of twenty.
50 Those that would die or ere° resist are grown   *before they would*
The mortal bugs° o'th' field.   *deadly terrors*
LORD   This was strange chance:
A narrow lane, an old man, and two boys—
POSTHUMUS   Nay, do not wonder at it. You are made
Rather to wonder at the things you hear
55 Than to work° any. Will you rhyme upon't,   *perform*
And vent it[5] for a mock'ry? Here is one:
"Two boys, an old man twice a boy,° a lane,   *in his second childhood*
Preserved the Britons, was the Romans' bane."
LORD   Nay, be not angry, sir.
POSTHUMUS   'Lack,° to what end?   *Alas*
60 Who dares not stand° his foe, I'll be his friend;   *confront*
For if he'll do as he is made° to do,   *inclined*
I know he'll quickly fly my friendship too.
You have put° me into rhyme.   *forced*
LORD   Farewell, you're angry. *Exit.*
POSTHUMUS   Still going?° This is a lord! O noble misery,[6]   *Still running away*
65 To be i'th' field and ask "What news?" of me!
Today how many would have given their honors
To have saved their carcasses; took heel to do't
And yet died too.° I, in mine own woe charmed,[7]   *anyway*
Could not find Death where I did hear him groan,
70 Nor feel him where he struck. Being an ugly monster,
'Tis strange he hides him in fresh cups, soft beds,
Sweet words, or hath more ministers° than we   *other agents*
That draw his knives i'th' war. Well, I will find him;

3. *more charming:* casting a spell on others.
4. *could . . . lance:* that is, could have made women fight. The distaff, an instrument used in spinning wool, was a proverbial symbol of womanhood.
5. Shame inspired some, courage others.
6. Because of the example set by others.
7. In those who first set the example (of cowardly behavior).
8. To bare their teeth.
9. *forthwith . . . eagles:* straightway they (the Romans) fled like chickens along the passage down which they

had just swooped like eagles.
1. *slaves . . . made:* like slaves, they retrace the steps they had made as victors.
2. Vital in the time of crisis.
3. *Having . . . hearts:* Having found unprotected the weak spot of these undefended souls (that is, the Romans).
4. Some that earlier were as good as dead.
5. And circulate ("vent") your rhymes.
6. What noble wretchedness.
7. In my despair preserved, as if by a charm.

[*He resumes his Roman clothes.*]
For being now a favorer to the Briton,[8]
75 No more° a Briton, I have resumed again   *I am no more*
The part° I came in. Fight I will no more,   *role*
But yield me to the veriest hind° that shall   *peasant*
Once touch my shoulder.° Great the slaughter is   *try to arrest me*
Here made by th' Roman; great the answer be°   *great the retaliation*
80 Britons must take. For me, my ransom's death:
On either side I come to spend my breath,
Which neither here I'll keep nor bear° again,   *carry away*
But end it by some means for Imogen.
      Enter two [*Briton*] CAPTAINS, *and Soldiers.*
FIRST CAPTAIN   Great Jupiter be praised, Lucius is taken.
85 'Tis thought the old man and his sons were angels.
SECOND CAPTAIN   There was a fourth man, in a silly habit,°   *rustic garments*
That gave th'affront with them.
FIRST CAPTAIN   So 'tis reported,
But none of 'em can be found. Stand, who's there?
POSTHUMUS   A Roman,
90 Who had not now been drooping here, if seconds°   *supporters*
Had answered him.°   *followed him*
SECOND CAPTAIN   Lay hands on him: a dog!
A leg of Rome shall not return to tell
What crows have pecked them here. He brags his service
As if he were of note:° bring him to th' King.   [*Exeunt.*][9]   *high rank*

5.4

Enter CYMBELINE, BELARIUS, GUIDERIUS, ARVIRAGUS,
PISANIO, *Roman captives*[*, and* JAILERS]. [*Enter*]
the CAPTAINS [*who*] *present* POSTHUMUS [*dressed as
a Roman*] *to* CYMBELINE, *who delivers him over to
a* JAILER.
    [*Exeunt all except*] POSTHUMUS *and* [*two*] JAILERS.
FIRST JAILER   You shall not now be stol'n, you have locks upon you;
So graze as you find pasture.
SECOND JAILER   Ay, or a stomach.
                      [*Exeunt* JAILERS.]
POSTHUMUS   Most welcome bondage, for thou art a way,
I think, to liberty. Yet am I better
5 Than one that's sick o'th' gout, since he had rather
Groan so in perpetuity than be cured
By th' sure physician, death, who is the key
T'unbar these locks. My conscience, thou art fettered
More than my shanks° and wrists. You good gods, give me   *legs*
10 The penitent instrument to pick that bolt,
Then free for ever.[1] Is't enough I am sorry?
So children temporal fathers do appease;
Gods are more full of mercy. Must I repent,
I cannot do it better than in gyves,°   *shackles*

---

8. Since death is now looking kindly upon Britons.
9. TEXTUAL COMMENT F does not mark an exit here,
but this edition adds an *Exeunt* in order to clear the
stage of the large group of people present at the end of
5.3, and to mark the change of scene from the battlefield to a prison. See Digital Edition TC 7.

5.4 Location: A prison.
1. *The . . . ever:* Give me penitence, the instrument
to pick that lock (the lock on his conscience, which is
fettered by guilt). Then (I am) free forever; then free
me (by death).

15	Desired more than constrained.° To satisfy,°	forced (upon me) / atone
	If of my freedom 'tis the main part,[2] take	
	No stricter render° of me than my all.	repayment
	I know you are more clement° than vile men	merciful
	Who of their broken° debtors take a third,	bankrupt
20	A sixth, a tenth, letting them thrive again	
	On their abatement;° that's not my desire.	reduced amount
	For Imogen's dear life take mine, and though	
	'Tis not so dear,° yet 'tis a life; you coined it.	valuable
	'Tween man and man they weigh not every stamp;	
25	Though light, take pieces for the figure's sake,[3]	
	You rather mine, being yours.[4] And so, great powers,	
	If you will take this audit,° take this life,	settle this account
	And cancel these cold bonds.[5] O Imogen,	
	I'll speak to thee in silence.	

> [He sleeps.] Solemn music [plays]. Enter (as in an apparition) SICILIUS Leonatus (father to Posthumus, an old man, attired like a warrior), leading in his hand an ancient matron (his wife, and MOTHER to Posthumus), with music before them. Then, after other music, follow the two young Leonati (BROTHERS to Posthumus), with wounds as they died in the wars. They circle POSTHUMUS round as he lies sleeping.[6]

30	SICILIUS No more, thou thunder-master,[7] show thy spite on	
	mortal flies.°	frail creatures
	With Mars° fall out, with Juno° chide, that° thy adulteries	god of war / Jove's wife / who
	Rates° and revenges.	Berates
	Hath my poor boy done aught but well, whose face I never saw?	
	I died whilst in the womb he stayed, attending nature's law.[8]	
35	Whose father then—as men report, thou orphans' father art—	
	Thou shouldst have been, and shielded him from this earth-	
	vexing smart.[9]	
	MOTHER Lucina° lent not me her aid, but took me in my throes,	goddess of childbirth
	That from me was Posthumus ripped, came crying 'mongst	
	his foes,	
	A thing of pity.	
40	SICILIUS Great nature like his ancestry molded the stuff° so fair	substance
	That he deserved the praise o'th' world as great Sicilius' heir.	
	FIRST BROTHER When once he was mature for man,° in	had matured into manhood
	Britain where was he	
	That could stand up his parallel, or fruitful° object be	life-giving
	In eye of Imogen, that best could deem° his dignity?°	judge / worth

2. If it is the most important element in freeing me from guilt.

3. 'Tween . . . sake: In business dealings between men, they do not weigh every coin ("stamp"). Even though some coins are deficient in weight ("light"), they accept them because of the image (of the King) stamped on them.

4. You should be more inclined to accept my coin (me), since your image is stamped on me. This line refers to the Christian belief that humans are made in the image of God.

5. These old legal agreements; these cruel links with life; these harsh fetters.

6. TEXTUAL COMMENT Before G. Wilson Knight argued for their authenticity in 1947, critics dismissed lines 29 SD–92 SD as un-Shakespearean, in part because of the archaic quality of the ghosts' speeches, which are preserved here in the iambic heptameter in which some of them appear in F. Iambic heptameters are very long poetic lines having fourteen syllables divided into seven poetic feet with the stress falling on the second syllable of each foot. See Digital Edition TC 8.

7. Jupiter, or Jove, the king of the gods, often made himself known to humans through thunder and lightning.

8. Awaiting the decree of nature (for his birth).

9. From this suffering that afflicts all humans.

45	MOTHER With marriage wherefore° was he mocked, to be	*why*
	exiled and thrown	
	From Leonati seat, and cast from her, his dearest one,	
	Sweet Imogen?	
	SICILIUS Why did you suffer Giacomo, slight° thing of Italy,	*worthless*
	To taint his nobler heart and brain with needless jealousy,	
50	And to become the geck° and scorn o'th' other's villainy?	*dupe*
	SECOND BROTHER For this, from stiller seats[1] we came, our	
	parents and us twain,	
	That striking in our country's cause, fell bravely and were slain,	
	Our fealty and Tenantius'° right with honor to maintain.	*(Cymbeline's father)*
	FIRST BROTHER Like hardiment° Posthumus hath to	*Similar bold deeds*
	Cymbeline performed:	
55	Then Jupiter, thou king of gods, why hast thou thus adjourned°	*deferred*
	The graces for his merits due, being all to dolors° turned?	*sorrows*
	SICILIUS Thy crystal window ope,° look out, no longer exercise	*open*
	Upon a valiant race thy harsh and potent injuries.	
	MOTHER Since, Jupiter, our son is good, take off his miseries.	
60	SICILIUS Peep through thy marble mansion, help, or we poor	
	ghosts will cry	
	To th' shining synod° of the rest[2] against thy deity.°	*assembly / godhead*
	BROTHERS Help, Jupiter, or we appeal, and from thy justice fly.	

JUPITER *descends in thunder and lightning, sitting upon an eagle. He throws a thunderbolt. The ghosts fall on their knees.*

	JUPITER No more, you petty spirits of region low,	
	Offend our hearing. Hush! How dare you ghosts	
65	Accuse the thunderer, whose bolt, you know,	
	Sky-planted,° batters all rebelling coasts?	*Rooted in the heavens*
	Poor shadows of Elysium, hence, and rest	
	Upon your never-withering banks of flowers.	
	Be not with mortal accidents° oppressed;	*events*
70	No care of yours it is; you know 'tis ours.	
	Whom best I love, I cross,° to make my gift,	*thwart*
	The more delayed, delighted.° Be content:	*the more pleasing*
	Your low-laid son our godhead will uplift;	
	His comforts thrive, his trials well are spent.°	*ended*
75	Our Jovial star° reigned at his birth, and in	*The planet Jupiter*
	Our temple was he married. Rise, and fade.	
	He shall be lord of Lady Imogen,	
	And happier much by his affliction made.	
	This tablet lay upon his breast, wherein	
80	Our pleasure his full fortune doth confine.[3]	

[*He gives the ghosts a tablet which they lay upon Posthumus' breast.*]

	And so away. No farther with your din
	Express impatience, lest you stir up mine.
	Mount, eagle, to my palace crystalline. [*He*] *ascends.*
	SICILIUS He came in thunder; his celestial breath
85	Was sulfurous to smell.[4] The holy eagle

1. From calmer regions (alluding to the Elysian Fields—in classical mythology the abode of the blessed after death).
2. The rest of the gods.
3. *wherein . . . confine:* wherein it is our pleasure his great fortune precisely to set forth.
4. Sulfur was popularly associated with thunder and lightning. As a constituent of gunpowder, its smell may have been detectable in the theater when gunpowder was used.

Stooped, as to foot us.[5] His ascension is
More sweet than our blest fields. His royal bird
Prunes the immortal wing and claws his beak,
As when his god is pleased.

ALL THE GHOSTS   Thanks, Jupiter.

90 SICILIUS   The marble pavement[6] closes; he is entered
His radiant roof. Away, and, to be blest,
Let us with care perform his great behest. [*The* GHOSTS] *vanish.*

POSTHUMUS [*awaking*]   Sleep, thou hast been a grandsire and begot
A father to me; and thou hast created

95 A mother and two brothers. But oh, scorn,°   *bitter mockery*
Gone! They went hence so soon as they were born,
And so I am awake. Poor wretches that depend
On greatness' favor dream as I have done,
Wake, and find nothing. But, alas, I swerve.°   *go astray*

100 Many dream not to find, neither deserve,
And yet are steeped in favors; so am I,
That have this golden chance and know not why.
What fairies haunt this ground? A book? O rare one,
Be not, as is our fangled world,[7] a garment

105 Nobler than that it covers. Let thy effects
So follow to° be most unlike our courtiers,   *that they*
As good as promise.
(*Reads.*) "Whenas° a lion's whelp shall, to himself unknown,   *When*
without seeking find, and be embraced by a piece of tender

110 air; and when from a stately cedar shall be lopped branches
which, being dead many years, shall after revive, be jointed
to the old stock, and freshly grow; then shall Posthumus end
his miseries, Britain be fortunate and flourish in peace and
plenty."

115 'Tis still a dream, or else such stuff as madmen
Tongue° and brain° not; either both, or nothing,   *Speak / understand*
Or senseless speaking,° or a speaking such   *Either meaningless speech*
As sense° cannot untie. Be what it is,   *reason*
The action of my life is like it, which I'll keep,

120 If but for sympathy.[8]

Enter JAILER.

JAILER   Come, sir, are you ready for death?

POSTHUMUS   Over-roasted rather; ready long ago.

JAILER   Hanging[9] is the word, sir. If you be ready for that, you
are well cooked.

125 POSTHUMUS   So if I prove a good repast to the spectators, the
dish pays the shot.[1]

JAILER   A heavy reckoning for you, sir. But the comfort is, you
shall be called to no more payments, fear no more tavern
bills, which are as often the sadness of parting as the pro-

130 curing of mirth. You come in faint for want of meat, depart
reeling with too much drink; sorry that you have paid too
much, and sorry that you are paid too much;[2] purse and

---

5. Swooped as if to seize us in its talons.
6. Referring to the closing of the trapdoor in the ceiling above the stage, which represents the floor ("pavement") of the heavens.
7. Our world so obsessed with fashions.
8. If only because of the similarity.

9. Death by hanging, with a pun on "hanging" as referring to the practice of hanging up raw meat before cooking.
1. The food pays the reckoning; I am worth what it costs to hang me.
2. Subdued by too much drink.

brain, both empty; the brain the heavier for being too light,° *foolish*
the purse too light, being drawn of heaviness.[3] Oh, of this
135 contradiction you shall now be quit. Oh, the charity of a
penny cord! It sums up thousands in a trice.° You have no *an instant*
true debitor and creditor° but it: of what's past, is, and to come, *account book*
the discharge.° Your neck, sir, is pen, book, and counters;[4] *release from debt*
so the acquittance° follows. *deliverance*

140 POSTHUMUS I am merrier to die than thou art to live.

JAILER Indeed, sir, he that sleeps feels not the toothache; but
a man that were to° sleep your sleep, and a hangman to help *were about to*
him to bed, I think he would change places with his officer;° *(the hangman)*
for look you, sir, you know not which way you shall go.

145 POSTHUMUS Yes, indeed do I, fellow.

JAILER Your death has eyes in 's head then; I have not seen
him so pictured.[5] You must either be directed by some that
take upon them° to know, or take upon yourself that which I *some who profess*
am sure you do not know, or jump° the after-enquiry on your *risk*
150 own peril; and how you shall speed° in your journey's end I *succeed*
think you'll never return to tell one.

POSTHUMUS I tell thee, fellow, there are none want° eyes to *lacking*
direct them the way I am going, but such as wink° and will *shut their eyes*
not use them.

155 JAILER What an infinite mock is this, that a man should have
the best use of eyes to see the way of blindness!° I am sure *the way to death*
hanging's the way of winking.

Enter a MESSENGER.

MESSENGER Knock off his manacles: bring your prisoner to
the King.

160 POSTHUMUS Thou bring'st good news; I am called to be made
free.[6]

JAILER I'll be hanged then.

POSTHUMUS Thou shalt be then freer than a jailer; no bolts
for the dead.[7]

165 JAILER Unless a man would marry a gallows and beget young
gibbets, I never saw one so prone.° Yet, on my conscience, *eager*
there are verier knaves desire to live, for all° he be a Roman; *even though*
and there be some of them, too, that die against their wills;
so should I, if I were one. I would we were all of one mind,
170 and one mind good. Oh, there were desolation° of jailers and *the ruin*
gallowses! I speak against my present profit, but my wish
hath a preferment in't.[8]   *Exeunt.*

5.5

Enter CYMBELINE, BELARIUS, GUIDERIUS, ARVIRAGUS,
PISANIO, *and* LORDS.

CYMBELINE Stand by my side, you whom the gods have made
Preservers of my throne. Woe is my heart

3. Being emptied of the money that makes it heavy.
4. Metal tokens used for making calculations.
5. So depicted (referring to visual representations of death as a skeleton or skull with no eyes).
6. Posthumus means "set free by death." The Jailer thinks he means "set free from prison."
7. Most editions, following F2, have everyone leave the stage here except the Jailer. However, the Jailer himself has been ordered to bring the prisoner to the King, which would mean that he must not be separated from Posthumus.
8. Had a promotion in it (implying that a world without the need for jailers could offer him better employment).
5.5 Location: The camp of Cymbeline, Britain.

That the poor soldier that so richly fought,
Whose rags shamed gilded arms, whose naked breast
5   Stepped before targes of proof,[1] cannot be found.
He shall be happy that can find him, if
Our grace can make him so.

BELARIUS   I never saw
Such noble fury in so poor a thing,
Such precious deeds in one that promised naught
But beggary and poor looks.

10 CYMBELINE   No tidings of him?

PISANIO   He hath been searched° among the dead and living,   sought
But no trace of him.

CYMBELINE   To my grief, I am
The heir of his reward, which I will add
[*to* BELARIUS, GUIDERIUS, *and* ARVIRAGUS] To you, the liver,
heart, and brain of Britain,
15   By whom I grant she lives. 'Tis now the time
To ask of whence you are. Report it.

BELARIUS   Sir,
In Cambria° are we born, and gentlemen.   Wales
Further to boast were neither true nor modest,
Unless I add we are honest.

CYMBELINE   Bow your knees.
        [*They kneel. He knights them.*]
20   Arise, my knights o'th' battle.[2] I create you
Companions to our person, and will fit° you   supply
With dignities becoming your estates.°   (new) rank
        Enter CORNELIUS *and* LADIES.
There's business in these faces. Why so sadly
Greet you our victory? You look like Romans,
And not o'th' court of Britain.

25 CORNELIUS   Hail, great King.
To sour your happiness, I must report
The Queen is dead.

CYMBELINE   Who worse than a physician
Would this report become? But I consider,
By medicine life may be prolonged, yet death
30   Will seize the doctor too. How ended she?

CORNELIUS   With horror, madly dying, like her life,
Which, being cruel to the world, concluded
Most cruel to herself. What she confessed
I will report, so please you. These her women
35   Can trip me° if I err, who with wet cheeks   correct me
Were present when she finished.

CYMBELINE   Prithee, say.

CORNELIUS   First, she confessed she never loved you, only
Affected° greatness got by you, not you;   Desired
Married your royalty, was wife to your place,°   position
Abhorred your person.

40 CYMBELINE   She alone knew this,
And but° she spoke it dying, I would not   except that
Believe her lips in opening it. Proceed.

---

1. *targes of proof:* shields whose strength had been tested.   2. A special group of knights who won their titles for extraordinary bravery on the battlefield.

CORNELIUS Your daughter, whom she bore in hand° to love *she pretended*
With such integrity, she did confess
45 Was as a scorpion to her sight, whose life,
But that her flight prevented it, she had
Ta'en off° by poison. *Ended*
CYMBELINE O most delicate° fiend! *subtle*
Who is't can read a woman? Is there more?
CORNELIUS More, sir, and worse. She did confess she had
50 For you a mortal mineral° which, being took, *a deadly poison*
Should by the minute feed on life and, lingering,
By inches waste you. In which time she purposed
By watching,° weeping, tendance,[3] kissing, to *staying awake*
O'ercome you with her show;° and in time, *performance*
55 When she had fitted you with° her craft, to work *shaped you by*
Her son into th'adoption of the crown;[4]
But failing of her end by his strange absence,
Grew shameless-desperate, opened,° in despite *revealed*
Of heaven and men, her purposes, repented
60 The evils she hatched were not effected; so
Despairing, died.
CYMBELINE Heard you all this, her women?
LADIES We did, so please your highness.
CYMBELINE Mine eyes
Were not in fault, for she was beautiful;
Mine ears that heard her flattery, nor my heart
65 That thought her like her seeming.° It had been vicious° *appearance / wrong*
To have mistrusted her. Yet, O my daughter,
That it was folly in me thou mayst say,
And prove it in thy feeling.[5] Heaven mend all!

Enter LUCIUS, GIACOMO, [*the* SOOTHSAYER,] *and other
Roman prisoners* [*including*] POSTHUMUS *Leonatus*
[*dressed as a Roman, following*] *behind, and* IMOGEN
[*dressed as a man, all guarded by Soldiers*].

Thou com'st not, Caius, now for tribute: that
70 The Britons have razed out,° though with the loss *erased*
Of many a bold one; whose kinsmen have made suit
That their good souls° may be appeased with slaughter *(of the dead Britons)*
Of you their captives, which ourself have granted.
So think of your estate.° *condition*
75 LUCIUS Consider, sir, the chance of war; the day
Was yours by accident. Had it gone with us,
We should not, when the blood was cool, have threatened
Our prisoners with the sword. But since the gods
Will have it thus, that nothing but our lives
80 May be called ransom, let it come. Sufficeth
A Roman with a Roman's heart can suffer—
Augustus lives to think on't[6]—and so much
For my peculiar care.° This one thing only *concern for myself*
I will entreat: my boy, a Briton born,
85 Let him be ransomed. Never master had
A page so kind, so duteous, diligent,

---

3. Showing attention to you.
4. *to work . . . crown:* to work her son into the position of heir to the crown.
5. And find it true by your experience.
6. Augustus lives and can consider what to do.

So tender over his occasions,° true,   *thoughtful of his needs*
So feat,° so nurse-like; let his virtue join   *graceful*
With my request, which I'll make bold your highness
90   Cannot deny. He hath done no Briton harm,
Though he have served a Roman. Save him, sir,
And spare no blood beside.°   *no one else*
CYMBELINE   I have surely seen him;
His favor° is familiar to me. [*to* IMOGEN] Boy,   *face*
Thou hast looked thyself into my grace,[7]
95   And art mine own. I know not why, wherefore,
To say, "Live, boy." Ne'er thank thy master. Live,
And ask of Cymbeline what boon° thou wilt,   *reward*
Fitting my bounty and thy state;° I'll give it,   *rank*
Yea, though thou do demand a prisoner
The noblest ta'en.
100   IMOGEN   I humbly thank your highness.
LUCIUS   I do not bid thee beg my life, good lad,
And yet I know thou wilt.
IMOGEN   No, no; alack,
There's other work in hand. I see a thing[8]
Bitter to me as death. Your life, good master,
Must shuffle° for itself.   *shift*
105   LUCIUS   The boy disdains me;
He leaves me, scorns me. Briefly die their joys
That place them on the truth of girls and boys.[9]
Why stands he so perplexed?
CYMBELINE   What wouldst thou, boy?
I love thee more and more. Think more and more
110   What's best to ask. Know'st him thou look'st on? Speak,
Wilt have him live? Is he thy kin, thy friend?
IMOGEN   He is a Roman, no more kin to me
Than I to your highness, who, being born your vassal,
Am something nearer.
CYMBELINE   Wherefore ey'st him so?
115   IMOGEN   I'll tell you, sir, in private, if you please
To give me hearing.
CYMBELINE   Ay, with all my heart,
And lend my best attention. What's thy name?
IMOGEN   Fidele, sir.
CYMBELINE   Thou'rt my good youth, my page,
I'll be thy master. Walk with me, speak freely.
[CYMBELINE *and* IMOGEN *speak apart.*]
BELARIUS [*aside to* GUIDERIUS *and* ARVIRAGUS]   Is not this boy
revived from death?
120   ARVIRAGUS   One sand° another   *One grain of sand*
Not more resembles that° sweet rosy lad   *than he resembles that*
Who died and was Fidele. What think you?
GUIDERIUS   The same dead thing alive.
BELARIUS   Peace, peace, see further. He eyes us not; forbear.
125   Creatures may be alike. Were't he, I am sure
He would have spoke to us.

---

7. You have by your appearance gained my favor.
8. Referring to the ring that she gave to Posthumus
and that is now on Giacomo's finger.

9. *Briefly . . . boys:* Quickly dies the happiness of
those who depend on the fidelity of girls and boys.

GUIDERIUS	But we see° him dead.	*saw*
BELARIUS	Be silent; let's see further.	
PISANIO [*aside*]	It is my mistress.	

Since she is living, let the time run on
To good or bad.

CYMBELINE [*to* IMOGEN]   Come, stand thou by our side;
130   Make thy demand aloud. [*to* GIACOMO] Sir, step you forth.
  Give answer to this boy, and do it freely,
  Or by our greatness and the grace of it,
  Which is our honor, bitter torture shall
  Winnow° the truth from falsehood. —On, speak to him.   *Separate*

135   IMOGEN   My boon is that this gentleman may render°   *declare*
  Of whom he had this ring.

POSTHUMUS [*aside*]   What's that to him?

CYMBELINE   That diamond upon your finger, say
  How came it yours?

GIACOMO   Thou'lt torture me to leave° unspoken that   *for leaving*
  Which to be spoke would torture thee.

140   CYMBELINE   How? Me?

GIACOMO   I am glad to be constrained to utter that
  Which torments me to conceal. By villainy
  I got this ring; 'twas Leonatus' jewel,
  Whom thou didst banish; and, which more may grieve thee,
145   As it doth me, a nobler sir ne'er lived
  Twixt sky and ground. Wilt thou hear more, my lord?

CYMBELINE   All that belongs to this.

GIACOMO   That paragon, thy daughter,
  For whom my heart drops blood, and my false spirits
  Quail to remember—give me leave, I faint.

150   CYMBELINE   My daughter? What of her? Renew thy strength.
  I had rather thou shouldst live while nature will°   *as long as nature allows*
  Than die ere I hear more. Strive, man, and speak.

GIACOMO   Upon a time—unhappy was the clock[1]
  That struck the hour; it was in Rome—accursed
155   The mansion where; 'twas at a feast—oh, would
  Our viands had been poisoned (or at least
  Those which I heaved to head°); the good Posthumus—   *raised to my mouth*
  What should I say? He was too good to be
  Where ill men were, and was the best of all
160   Amongst the rar'st of good ones—sitting sadly,
  Hearing us praise our loves of Italy
  For beauty that made barren the swelled boast[2]
  Of him that best could speak; for feature, laming
  The shrine of Venus or straight-pight Minerva,[3]
165   Postures beyond brief nature;[4] for condition,°   *character*
  A shop of all the qualities that man
  Loves woman for; besides that hook of wiving,°   *bait for marriage*
  Fairness which strikes the eye—

1. TEXTUAL COMMENT Some editions punctuate the first eight lines of Giacomo's speech with nine dashes, which may suggest that the speech's broken and ungrammatical syntax reflects its speaker's anguish. Such difficult syntax, found elsewhere in the play, may also suggest Shakespeare's experiments with the limits of English grammar. See Digital Edition TC 9.

2. For beauty so great that it rendered hollow even the exaggerated boasts.
3. *for . . . Minerva:* for looks rendering deficient even the body (shrine) of the goddess of love (Venus) or the magisterial goddess of the arts (Minerva). *straight-pight:* uprightly fixed; with erect posture.
4. Forms surpassing those of mere mortals.

CYMBELINE   I stand on fire.
 Come to the matter.
GIACOMO   All too soon I shall,
170 Unless thou wouldst grieve quickly. This Posthumus,
 Most like a noble lord in love, and one
 That had a royal lover, took his hint,
 And not dispraising whom we praised—therein
 He was as calm as virtue—he began
175 His mistress' picture, which by his tongue being made,
 And then a mind put in't, either our brags
 Were cracked° of kitchen trulls, or his description   *uttered in defense*
 Proved us unspeaking sots.°   *fools incapable of speech*
CYMBELINE   Nay, nay, to th' purpose.
GIACOMO Your daughter's chastity—there it begins.
180 He spake of her as° Dian had hot° dreams   *as if / lustful*
 And she alone were cold;° whereat I, wretch,   *chaste*
 Made scruple of° his praise, and wagered with him   *Disputed*
 Pieces of gold, 'gainst this which then he wore
 Upon his honored finger, to attain
185 In suit° the place of 's bed and win this ring   *By urging my suit*
 By hers and mine adultery. He, true knight,
 No lesser of her honor confident
 Than I did truly find her, stakes this ring—
 And would so had it been a carbuncle
190 Of Phoebus' wheel,[5] and might so safely had it
 Been all the worth of 's car.° Away to Britain   *worth the entire chariot*
 Post° I in this design. Well may you, sir,   *Hasten*
 Remember me at court, where I was taught
 Of° your chaste daughter the wide difference   *By*
195 Twixt amorous and villainous. Being thus quenched
 Of hope, not longing,° mine Italian brain   *though not of desire*
 Gan° in your duller Britain[6] operate   *Began*
 Most vilely—for my vantage,° excellent.   *profit*
 And, to be brief, my practice° so prevailed   *deceit*
200 That I returned with simular° proof enough *pretended; specious*
 To make the noble Leonatus mad,
 By wounding his belief in her renown°   *reputation*
 With tokens thus and thus; averring° notes   *confirming*
 Of chamber-hanging, pictures, this her bracelet
205 (Oh, cunning, how I got it!) nay, some marks
 Of secret on her person, that he could not
 But think her bond of chastity quite cracked,
 I having ta'en the forfeit.[7] Whereupon—
 Methinks I see him now—
POSTHUMUS [*coming forward*] Ay, so thou dost,
210 Italian fiend! Ay me, most credulous fool,
 Egregious murderer, thief, anything
 That's due[8] to all the villains past, in being,
 To come! Oh, give me cord, or knife, or poison,
 Some upright justicer!° Thou, King, send out   *judge*

---

5. *had . . . wheel:* even if it had been a precious stone
from the wheel of the sun god's chariot.
6. Alluding to the belief that England's northern climate made its inhabitants sluggish and slow of wit.

7. Believing I had taken what she gave up (her
chastity).
8. *anything / That's due:* any name that's owed.

215 For torturers ingenious: it is I
That all th'abhorred things o'th' earth amend⁹
By being worse than they. I am Posthumus,
That killed thy daughter—villain-like, I lie—
That caused a lesser villain than myself,
220 A sacrilegious thief, to do't. The temple
Of virtue was she; yea, and she herself.° *she was virtue herself*
Spit and throw stones, cast mire upon me, set
The dogs o'th' street to bay me. Every villain
Be called Posthumus Leonatus, and
225 Be villainy less than 'twas.¹ O Imogen!
My queen, my life, my wife, O Imogen,
Imogen, Imogen!
IMOGEN   Peace, my lord, hear, hear—
POSTHUMUS   Shall 's have a play of this? Thou scornful page,
There lie thy part!²
                    [*He strikes her and she falls.*]
PISANIO   O gentlemen, help!
230 Mine and your mistress! O my lord Posthumus,
You ne'er killed Imogen till now. Help, help!
Mine honored lady—
CYMBELINE   Does the world go round?
POSTHUMUS   How comes these staggers³ on me?
PISANIO   Wake, my mistress.
CYMBELINE   If this be so, the gods do mean to strike me
235 To death with mortal° joy.   *death-causing*
PISANIO   How fares my mistress?
IMOGEN   Oh, get thee from my sight!
Thou gav'st me poison. Dangerous fellow, hence!
Breathe not where princes are.
CYMBELINE   The tune of Imogen!
PISANIO   Lady, the gods throw stones of sulfur° on me if   *thunderbolts*
240 That box I gave you was not thought by me
A precious thing; I had it from the Queen.
CYMBELINE   New matter still.
IMOGEN   It poisoned me.
CORNELIUS   O gods!
I left out one thing which the Queen confessed,
Which must approve° thee honest. "If Pisanio   *prove*
245 Have," said she, "given his mistress that confection°   *compound*
Which I gave him for cordial, she is served
As I would serve a rat."
CYMBELINE   What's this, Cornelius?
CORNELIUS   The Queen, sir, very oft importuned me
To temper° poisons for her, still° pretending   *mix / always*
250 The satisfaction of her knowledge only
In killing creatures vile, as cats and dogs
Of no esteem.° I, dreading that her purpose   *value*
Was of more danger, did compound for her
A certain stuff which, being ta'en, would cease

---

9. Who makes all loathsome things seem better.
1. *Every . . . 'twas:* May the word "villainy" be less abhorrent than it was, since "Posthumus Leonatus" has replaced it.

2. Your part (in this play) is to lie there.
3. A disease, usually of horses, that causes an unsteady walk; dizziness.

255   The present power of life, but in short time
       All offices of nature° should again   *All natural faculties*
       Do their due functions. Have you ta'en of it?
IMOGEN   Most like° I did, for I was dead.   *likely*
BELARIUS [*aside to* GUIDERIUS *and* ARVIRAGUS]   My boys,
       There was our error.
GUIDERIUS   This is sure Fidele.
260 IMOGEN   Why did you throw your wedded lady from you?
       Think that you are upon a rock,[4] and now
       Throw me again.
              [*She embraces* POSTHUMUS.]
POSTHUMUS   Hang there like fruit, my soul,
       Till the tree die.
CYMBELINE   How now, my flesh, my child?
       What, mak'st thou me a dullard° in this act?   *sluggish performer*
       Wilt thou not speak to me?
265 IMOGEN   Your blessing, sir.
BELARIUS [*aside to* GUIDERIUS *and* ARVIRAGUS]   Though you
       did love this youth, I blame ye not;
       You had a motive° for't.   *reason*
CYMBELINE   My tears that fall
       Prove holy water on thee! Imogen,
       Thy mother's dead.
IMOGEN   I am sorry for't, my lord.
270 CYMBELINE   Oh, she was naught,° and 'long° of her it was   *worthless / because*
       That we meet here so strangely.° But her son   *like strangers*
       Is gone, we know not how nor where.
PISANIO   My lord,
       Now fear is from me, I'll speak truth. Lord Cloten,
       Upon my lady's missing,° came to me   *absence*
275   With his sword drawn, foamed at the mouth, and swore
       If I discovered° not which way she was gone   *revealed*
       It was my instant death. By accident°   *chance*
       I had a feignèd letter of my master's[5]
       Then in my pocket, which directed him
280   To seek her on the mountains near to Milford,
       Where in a frenzy, in my master's garments,
       Which he enforced from me, away he posts°   *hastens*
       With unchaste purpose and with oath to violate
       My lady's honor. What became of him,
       I further know not.
285 GUIDERIUS   Let me end the story:
       I slew him there.
CYMBELINE   Marry, the gods forfend!
       I would not thy good deeds° should from my lips   *(on the battlefield)*
       Pluck a hard sentence. Prithee, valiant youth,
       Deny't again.°   *Take it back*
GUIDERIUS   I have spoke it, and I did it.
290 CYMBELINE   He was a prince.
GUIDERIUS   A most incivil° one. The wrongs he did me   *barbarous*
       Were nothing prince-like, for he did provoke me

---

4. This is a disputed passage; some editions emend   5. Referring to the letter written by Posthumus to
to "lock," suggesting that Imogen is referring to a   mislead Imogen.
wrestling hold.

With language that would make me spurn the sea
If it could so roar to me. I cut off 's head,
295 And am right glad he is not standing here
To tell this tale of mine.⁶
CYMBELINE   I am sorrow for thee.
By thine own tongue thou art condemned and must
Endure our law. Thou'rt dead.
IMOGEN   That headless man
I thought had been my lord.
CYMBELINE [to Soldiers]   Bind the offender,
And take him from our presence.
300 BELARIUS   Stay, sir King.
This man is better than the man he slew,
As well descended as thyself, and hath
More of thee merited than a band of Clotens
Had ever scar for.⁷ Let his arms alone;
305 They were not born for bondage.
CYMBELINE   Why, old soldier,
Wilt thou undo the worth thou art unpaid for⁸
By tasting of our wrath? How of descent
As good as we?
ARVIRAGUS   In that he spake too far.
CYMBELINE⁹   And thou shalt die for't.
BELARIUS   We will die all three,
310 But I will prove° that two on 's° are as good   *Unless I prove / of us*
As I have given out him. My sons, I must
For mine own part unfold a dangerous speech,
Though haply° well for you.   *perhaps*
ARVIRAGUS   Your danger's ours.
GUIDERIUS   And our good his.
BELARIUS   Have at it, then. By leave,¹
315 Thou hadst, great King, a subject, who
Was called Belarius.
CYMBELINE   What of him?
He is a banished traitor.
BELARIUS   He it is that hath
Assumed° this age. Indeed a banished man;   *Reached*
I know not how a traitor.
CYMBELINE [to Soldiers]   Take him hence.
The whole world shall not save him.
320 BELARIUS   Not too hot.°   *fast*
First pay me for the nursing of thy sons,
And let it° be confiscate all so soon   *(the payment)*
As I have received it.
CYMBELINE   Nursing of my sons?
BELARIUS   I am too blunt and saucy. [He kneels.] Here's my knee.
325 Ere I arise I will prefer° my sons;   *advance*
Then spare not the old father. Mighty sir,

6. To tell a tale of cutting off my head.
7. *than . . . for*: than an army of Clotens ever earned by their battle scars.
8. The merit you are not yet rewarded for.
9. It is unclear to whom—Arviragus or Belarius—Cymbeline speaks the next line. Arviragus has just addressed Cymbeline, and one might expect the King's reply to be directed to him. Belarius, however, made the offending remark about Guiderius being of as good birth as Cloten, and the threat of death probably applies to him.
1. Let's begin, then. With your permission.

These two young gentlemen that call me father
And think they are my sons are none of mine.
They are the issue° of your loins, my liege,   *offspring*
And blood of your begetting.
330 CYMBELINE   How? My issue?
BELARIUS   So sure as you your father's. I, old Morgan,[2]
Am that Belarius whom you sometime° banished.   *once*
Your pleasure was my mere offense,[3] my punishment
Itself, and all my treason; that I suffered
335 Was all the harm I did. These gentle princes,
For such and so they are, these twenty years
Have I trained up; those arts° they have, as I   *accomplishments*
Could put into them. My breeding was, sir,
As your highness knows. Their nurse Euriphile,
340 Whom for the theft I wedded, stole these children
Upon my banishment. I moved° her to't,   *persuaded*
Having received the punishment before
For that which I did then. Beaten° for loyalty   *Having been beaten*
Excited me to treason. Their dear loss,
345 The more of you 'twas felt, the more it shaped°   *suited*
Unto° my end° of stealing them. But, gracious sir,   *With / purpose*
Here are your sons again, and I must lose
Two of the sweet'st companions in the world.
The benediction of these covering heavens
350 Fall on their heads like dew, for they are worthy
To inlay heaven with stars.°   *To become constellations*
CYMBELINE   Thou weep'st and speak'st.
The service that you three have done is more
Unlike° than this thou tell'st. I lost my children;   *Improbable*
If these be they, I know not how to wish
A pair of worthier sons.
355 BELARIUS   Be pleased awhile.
This gentleman, whom I call Polydore,
Most worthy prince, as yours is true Guiderius.
This gentleman, my Cadwal, Arviragus,
Your younger princely son. He, sir, was lapped°   *wrapped*
360 In a most curious° mantle, wrought by th' hand   *delicately fashioned*
Of his queen mother, which for more probation°   *proof*
I can with ease produce.
CYMBELINE   Guiderius had
Upon his neck a mole, a sanguine° star;   *blood-red*
It was a mark of wonder.
BELARIUS   This is he,
365 Who hath upon him still that natural stamp.
It was wise Nature's end in the donation°   *purpose in giving it*
To be his evidence now.
CYMBELINE   Oh, what am I?
A mother to the birth of three? Ne'er mother
Rejoiced deliverance more.[4] Blest pray you be,

---

2. Morgan was the Welsh name Belarius assumed
during the years he spent in Wales.
3. What you pleased (to accuse me of) was my entire
offense.
4. Never did giving birth cause a mother to rejoice
more.

370 That, after this strange starting from your orbs,[5]
You may reign in them now! O Imogen,
Thou hast lost by this a kingdom.

IMOGEN   No, my lord,
I have got two worlds by't. O my gentle brothers,
Have we thus met? Oh, never say hereafter
375 But I am truest speaker. You called me brother
When I was but your sister, I you brothers,
When we were so indeed.

CYMBELINE   Did you e'er meet?

ARVIRAGUS   Ay, my good lord.

GUIDERIUS   And at first meeting loved,
Continued so until we thought he died.

CORNELIUS   By the Queen's dram she swallowed.

380 CYMBELINE   O rare instinct!
When shall I hear all through? This fierce° abridgment   *drastic*
Hath to it circumstantial branches which
Distinction should be rich in.[6] Where? How lived you?
And when came you to serve our Roman captive?
385 How parted with your brothers? How first met them?
Why fled you from the court, and whither? These,
And your three motives° to the battle, with   *the motives of you three*
I know not how much more should be demanded,
And all the other by-dependences,°   *circumstances*
390 From chance° to chance. But nor° the time nor place   *occurrence / neither*
Will serve our long interrogatories.° See,   *lengthy questioning*
Posthumus anchors upon Imogen,
And she, like harmless lightning, throws her eye
On him, her brothers, me, her master, hitting
395 Each object with a joy: the counterchange
Is severally in all.[7] Let's quit this ground,
And smoke° the temple with our sacrifices.   *fill with smoke*
[*to* BELARIUS] Thou art my brother; so we'll hold thee ever.

IMOGEN [*to* BELARIUS]   You are my father too, and did relieve° me   *save*
To see this gracious season.

400 CYMBELINE   All o'erjoyed,
Save these in bonds. Let them be joyful too,
For they shall taste our comfort.

IMOGEN   My good master,
I will yet do you service.

LUCIUS   Happy be you!

CYMBELINE   The forlorn° soldier that so nobly fought,   *wretched*
405 He would have well becomed this place, and graced
The thankings of a king.

POSTHUMUS   I am, sir,
The soldier that did company these three
In poor beseeming.°[8] 'Twas a fitment[8] for   *appearance*
The purpose I then followed. That I was he,
410 Speak, Giacomo: I had you down, and might
Have made you finish.°   *die*

---

5. After this unnatural displacement from your rightful positions. Referring to astrological theories that each heavenly body moved in its proper orb, or circle, around the earth. For a planet to move outside its orb caused disturbances in the heavens.

6. *circumstantial . . . in:* many ramifications that will provide particulars in rich abundance.
7. *the . . . all:* the exchange (of glances) passes from each to each.
8. A suitable disguise.

GIACOMO [*kneels*]   I am down again,
But now my heavy conscience sinks my knee,
As then your force did. Take that life, beseech you,
Which I so often owe;° but your ring first,   °owe so many times over
415 And here the bracelet of the truest princess
That ever swore her faith.
POSTHUMUS   Kneel not to me.
The power that I have on you is to spare you;
The malice towards you to forgive you. Live,
And deal with others better.
CYMBELINE   Nobly doomed!°   °sentenced
420 We'll learn our freeness of a son-in-law:
Pardon's the word to all.
ARVIRAGUS   You holp° us, sir,   °helped
As° you did mean indeed to be our brother;   °As if
Joyed are we that you are.
POSTHUMUS   Your servant, princes. [*to* LUCIUS] Good my lord of
Rome,
425 Call forth your soothsayer. As I slept, methought
Great Jupiter, upon his eagle backed,°   °riding on his eagle
Appeared to me with other spritely shows°   °ghostly apparitions
Of mine own kindred. When I waked, I found
This label° on my bosom, whose containing°   °tablet / contents
430 Is so from sense in hardness that I can
Make no collection of it.[9] Let him° show   °(the soothsayer)
His skill in the construction.°   °interpretation
LUCIUS   Philharmonus!
SOOTHSAYER   Here, my good lord.
LUCIUS   Read, and declare the meaning.
SOOTHSAYER (*reads*)   "Whenas a lion's whelp shall, to himself
435 unknown, without seeking find, and be embraced by a piece
of tender air; and when from a stately cedar shall be lopped
branches which, being dead many years, shall after revive,
be jointed to the old stock, and freshly grow: then shall
Posthumus end his miseries, Britain be fortunate and flour-
440 ish in peace and plenty."
Thou, Leonatus, art the lion's whelp:
The fit and apt construction of thy name,
Being *leo-natus*,° doth import so much.   °lion-born
The piece of tender air, thy virtuous daughter,
445 Which we call *mollis aer*,[1] and *mollis aer*
We term it *mulier*, which *mulier* I divine
Is this most constant wife, who even now
Answering the letter of the oracle,[2]
Unknown to you, unsought, were clipped about°   °embraced
With this most tender air.
450 CYMBELINE   This hath some seeming.
SOOTHSAYER   The lofty cedar, royal Cymbeline,
Personates° thee, and thy lopped branches point   °Stands for
Thy two sons forth, who, by Belarius stol'n,

---

9. **Is . . . it:** Is so difficult to make sense of that I can
draw no conclusion from it.
1. Latin for "gentle air." An ancient (and erroneous)

etymology for *mulier*, Latin for "woman" or "wife."
2. Fulfilling the exact terms of the oracle.

For many years thought dead, are now revived,
455 To the majestic cedar joined, whose issue
Promises Britain peace and plenty.
CYMBELINE   Well,
My peace we will begin; and, Caius Lucius,
Although the victor, we submit to Caesar
And to the Roman empire, promising
460 To pay our wonted tribute, from the which
We were dissuaded by our wicked Queen,
Whom° heavens in justice both on her and hers   *On whom*
Have laid most heavy hand.
SOOTHSAYER   The fingers of the powers above do tune
465 The harmony of this peace. The vision
Which I made known to Lucius ere the stroke
Of this yet scarce-cold battle,³ at this instant
Is full° accomplished. For the Roman eagle,   *entirely*
From south to west on wing soaring aloft,
470 Lessened herself,⁴ and in the beams o'th' sun
So vanished; which foreshowed our princely eagle,
Th'imperial Caesar, should again unite
His favor with the radiant Cymbeline,
Which shines here in the west.
CYMBELINE   Laud we the gods,
475 And let our crookèd° smokes climb to their nostrils   *curling*
From our blest altars. Publish° we this peace   *Proclaim*
To all our subjects. Set we forward.° Let   *Let us go forth*
A Roman and a British ensign° wave   *banner*
Friendly together. So through Lud's Town march,
480 And in the temple of great Jupiter
Our peace we'll ratify, seal it with feasts.
Set on there.° Never was a war did cease,   *March forth*
Ere bloody hands were washed, with such a peace. *Exeunt.*

---

3. *ere . . . battle:* before the action of this battle,   4. Made herself small (by flying into the distance).
which has only just ceased.

The Winter's Tale

Ben Jonson, a playwright and Shakespeare's contemporary, had harsh things to say about plays like *The Winter's Tale*. He claimed that they "make Nature afraid," by which he meant that, eschewing realism, they staged fantastic and improbable events that defied the laws of nature. For example, in *The Winter's Tale,* after a sixteen-year span a lost child is miraculously found, a seemingly dead woman comes alive, and a figure named Time has a speaking part. Jonson himself was a classicist. He wrote plays whose action, usually occurring in one place in the span of one day, aspired to present life in a realistic fashion that spurned the supernatural and the fantastic. But Jonson did not speak for everyone. The romance plays he scorned were wildly popular in the early modern period, and they made for extraordinary theater full of spectacular stage effects, swift reversals of fortune, and fast-paced action. Moreover, rather than make nature afraid, these plays, then and now, invite the audience to ask whether the fantastic and the miraculous may not be as much a part of human experience as sober realism.

Modern editors often group the plays to which Jonson directs his scorn (such as *The Winter's Tale, Pericles, The Tempest,* and *Cymbeline)* together under the label "romances." This is not, however, a category used in the First Folio (1623). There Shakespeare's plays are divided into comedies, tragedies, and histories. *Pericles* is not included in the Folio; *Cymbeline* is placed at the end of the tragedies; *The Tempest* appears as the first of the comedies and *The Winter's Tale* (1610) as the last. These placements are suggestive of the mixed tragicomic nature of these particular dramas. Neither purely comic nor tragic, they exist in a fluid space between. Like Shakespeare's earlier comedies, they usually have mutedly happy endings with some family members reunited and marriages in prospect. But these plays are also marked by deep suffering. They not only depict tyranny, incest, shipwrecks, and the death of children, but they typically give us protagonists whose folly or egotism causes much of the terrible suffering the plays portray. What is distinctive about the romances, however, is how frequently they offer their protagonists second chances—an opportunity to make amends for former wrongdoing or to experience the miracle of forgiveness. Some of the wonder that the endings of these plays evoke stems from the sense that occasionally, for some fortunate characters, the harsh law of punishment and retribution gives way before the healing power of love and generosity.

The title of *The Winter's Tale* signals its affiliations with popular storytelling. In act 2, Mamillius, the King of Sicilia's young son, informs his mother that "A sad tale's best for winter" and offers to tell her one "Of sprites and goblins" (2.1.26–27). The only sprites and goblins in Shakespeare's play turn out to be the internal demons of jealousy and suspicion that erupt in the mind of its protagonist, King Leontes, but *The Winter's Tale* is permeated by sadness, even during its festive conclusion. Trouble starts with King Leontes' sudden certainty that his wife, Hermione, is pregnant not with his own child, but with that of his childhood friend, King Polixenes of Bohemia, a visitor at Leontes' Sicilian court. Warned of Leontes' jealousy, Polixenes flees back to Bohemia, leaving the King to vent his wrath on Hermione. Thrust into prison, Hermione gives birth there to a daughter, Perdita, whom Leontes orders to be abandoned in the countryside far from Sicilia. Even when the oracle of Apollo subsequently declares Hermione innocent, Leontes continues to insist on her guilt. As he does, the death of

In the early modern period, Time was often depicted with wings and an hourglass, both symbolizing how swiftly Time passes, and with a scythe, indicating Time's destructive power. At the beginning of act 4 of *The Winter's Tale*, Time describes himself as having wings and a glass. In this seventeenth-century Dutch painting, a genial Time displays all three: wings, hourglass, and scythe.

Leontes' only son, Mamillius, is announced, and Hermione appears to die of grief. The first three acts of *The Winter's Tale* thus enact a miniature tragedy (not unlike Shakespeare's tragedy of the jealous Othello) in which Leontes' actions result in the loss of wife, daughter, and son. His personal tragedy also affects his kingdom. The oracle proclaims: "the King shall live without an heir if that which is lost be not found" (3.2.132–33). A kingdom without an heir to the throne is a kingdom in danger.

But then something extraordinary happens. The character Time appears onstage, informing the audience that sixteen years have passed and that Perdita, abandoned on the seacoast of Bohemia, has survived. Suddenly, instead of the wintry world of Leontes' Sicilian court, the play bursts with the energies of a Bohemian summer. The Shepherd who rescued Perdita is about to hold a sheepshearing festival, and Florizel, King Polixenes' son, has fallen in love with Perdita. A series of extraordinary events returns the young couple to Leontes' court, where Perdita's true status as his child and heir is revealed. More wonders follow. Taken to see what they believe to be a statue of the long-dead Hermione, the King and his newly recovered daughter witness the seeming miracle of the statue's transformation into flesh and blood.

Shakespeare's chief source for this tale was Robert Greene's popular prose romance *Pandosto: The Triumph of Time*, first published in 1588. Greene provided Shakespeare with the story of a jealous king who loses queen and daughter, though eventually his daughter is restored to him. But the differences between Shakespeare's play and Greene's prose tale are as striking as the similarities. For example, Shakespeare carefully changed the names of most of the characters he borrowed from Greene. In *Pandosto*, the King's lost daughter is Fawnia, but Shakespeare names her Perdita, a word that in Latin means "lost one." In Shakespeare's hands, Perdita's lover ceases to be Dorastus and becomes, instead, Florizel, which suggests the young Prince's connection with the flowers of spring. Greene's protagonist, Pandosto, is transformed into Leontes, evoking the leonine or lionlike nature of his wrath. Shakespeare also reversed the kingdoms ruled by Greene's kings. In *Pandosto*, the protagonist is King of Bohemia and his childhood friend rules Sicilia. In *The Winter's Tale*, the reverse is true, and one reason may be the association of Sicilia with the myth of Proserpina, the beautiful daughter of Ceres abducted by Dis, the god of the underworld, as she was picking flowers. Her mother attempted to free Proserpina, but she was allowed to return to the upper world only six months of each year. During that period, spring and summer visit the earth, but winter reigns when Proserpina returns to Dis's kingdom. Similarly, Perdita's exile from Sicilia soon after her birth brings a wintry sixteen-year period of mourning to Leontes' kingdom before her return heralds the "rebirth" of her mother and the renewal of Leontes and his kingdom.

Shakespeare, however, made much larger changes in Greene's romance. For example, he enhanced the role of Leontes' son, who is barely mentioned by Greene; he added the characters of Paulina, Emilia, Antigonus, Autolycus, Clown, Time, and rustics such as Dorcas and Mopsa (in *Pandosto*, Mopsa was the name of the Old Shepherd's wife; in *The Winter's Tale*, that wife is long dead). The magnificent sheepshearing festival is Shakespeare's invention; nothing like it exists in *Pandosto*. Most important, Greene's romance ends on a tragic note. Although the King and his daughter are finally reunited, Pandosto's wife is never restored to him and, overcome with desire for his grown daughter, he attempts incest and later takes his own life.

Shakespeare thus reverses the trajectory of Greene's grim tale. For despair and suicide, he substitutes redemption and renewal. The play thus feels like a diptych of winter and summer, hinged by the appearance of Time. It is probably a mistake to account for this structure by using only one interpretive lens, for the play's elegant simplicity resonates with many narratives of renewal. Some have read the play in Christian terms, seeing Leontes as a sinner who, after a period of suffering and repentance, receives the gift of God's grace through the return of his daughter and the Christlike resurrection of his wife. The play loosely traces the liturgical calendar, moving from the hospitality associated with Christmas to the Lenten period of deprivation and repentance to the joyous celebration of Easter and the Maying festivals associated with Whitsuntide, which occurs seven weeks after Easter. Other critics have stressed the mythic qualities of the play—its resemblance, for example, to fertility rites in which the coming of spring and sexual fulfillment depend on the sacrifice of a figure, usually an old king, associated with winter. In *The Winter's Tale*, Leontes does not die, but he does mourn for sixteen years; and his servant Antigonus, who takes the babe to Bohemia and there names her Perdita, becomes Leontes' sacrificial substitute. Once he has deposited Perdita, Antigonus is mauled and eaten by a bear, an event preceded by one of the most famous stage directions in any of Shakespeare's plays: *"Exit, pursued by a bear"* (3.3.57). This event has caused scholars to wonder if a *real* bear from the nearby bearbaiting arenas could have been brought onstage at this point to heighten the terror of the scene before the storm passes and attention turns to the rescue of Perdita. As the Shepherd who finds the baby says to his son, who has witnessed the bear dining on Antigonus, "thou mett'st with things dying, I with things newborn" (3.3.103–04). Other critics stress the pattern of generational renewal informing the play as the sins of the father, Leontes, give way to the innocent goodness of Florizel and Perdita. In some productions, the actress playing Hermione also plays Perdita (although a double usually has to be employed in the statue scene when they are onstage together), deepening the sense that it is through their children that parents have a second life. More recently, environmental critics have stressed how contact with the natural world of Bohemia repairs the alienation from natural affection experienced in the sophisticated Sicilian court. Resonating with all these interpretive paradigms, *The Winter's Tale* capaciously embodies collective and ancient nightmares of loss and collective dreams of redemption and renewal.

In modern productions, the symbolic power of the play's diptych structure is often highlighted by contrasts in the costumes and sets used to distinguish Sicilia and Bohemia. Sicilia, for example, is often a snow kingdom, dominated by white clothing and metallic props; Bohemia, by contrast, evokes summer, the stage carpeted in green, the characters at the sheep-shearing festival a riot of variegated colors. When the Bohemian party comes to Sicilia, the winter landscape is literally overwritten with the colorful clothes associated with Whitsuntide.

The play, however, is not simply about the triumph of the young, the rebirth of a world of possibility. *The Winter's Tale*, as befits a tragicomedy, moves from sorrow to joy, but that joy is bittersweet. Whatever the importance of the younger generation to this old tale, the focus stays resolutely on the older generation. It is Leontes who sins and must repent, Leontes whose family is reconstituted. Crucially, that reconstitution is only partial and imperfect. Mamillius, the young son, dies, the ultimate sacrifice to Leontes' tyrannous actions; and in the play's last scene, the "statue" of Hermione has wrinkles, the mark of time on her body. Traduced while a fertile wife and mother, Hermione returns as a woman past childbearing. The ending of Shakespeare's tale induces wonder and joy, but it cannot make an old man young or erase all the consequences of rash deeds. Shakespeare's late plays achieve their rich emotional effects from the deep strains of melancholia that underwrite their measured celebrations of the return of love and hope to a chastened social order.

Nor, despite the archaic quality that permeates these plays, are they simple enactments of timeless patterns and narratives. The precipitating event of the play—the eruption of Leontes' jealousy—is a symptom of the faultlines in a particular patriarchal culture. Often said to be "irrational," this jealousy in actuality has its roots in the cultural practices that in Jacobean England made men the heads of families, lineages, and kingdoms, but at the same time made them crucially dependent on women's reproductive powers to generate legitimate heirs. As *The Winter's Tale* opens, Leontes asks Polixenes to extend his stay in Sicilia. Polixenes refuses, but when Hermione entreats him, he agrees. This event, and the sight of his pregnant wife conversing with his friend and holding him by the hand, triggers in Leontes so deep a suspicion of his wife's fidelity that he plans to have Polixenes killed and doubts the legitimacy of his son as well. In part, what disturbs Leontes is the unknowability of the biological origins of his children. Men theoretically had dominion over their wives, but as Leontes says, "No barricado for a belly" (1.2.203)—that is, no absolute defense of a woman's chastity but her own honor, and that lies in her control, not her husband's.

A deep ambivalence toward women and sexuality, moreover, surfaces earlier in the same scene when, reminiscing about his boyhood friendship with Leontes, Polixenes describes the two of them as twinned lambs who experienced a fall from paradise only when they felt sexual passion and had their first encounters with women. In this conversation, the two men echo a strand of early modern thought that viewed men's friendships with men as more valuable than what were seen as their more dangerous and unpredictable relations with women. Construed as physically imperfect and intellectually inferior to men, women were supposedly ruled by their passions and could in turn evoke dangerous and degrading emotions in men. Yet men were enjoined to marry these irrational creatures to procreate and to continue family lineage. Leontes' rage at Hermione seems to stem in part from his dependence on her to give him legitimate heirs.

Once his jealousy has been triggered, Leontes gives the rein to a deadly rage that finds its chief object in Hermione's pregnant body. This anger is played out in part through Leontes' increasing identification with his young son. In Mamillius, Leontes sees himself as he once was, a young boy not yet wearing either the breeches or the sharp phallic dagger associated with adult manhood (1.2.155–56). It is an image of innocence, but also of vulnerability. The name Mamillius, another of Shakespeare's brilliant inventions, suggests one source of that vulnerability: *mamilla* is the Latin word for the nipple on a breast, a diminutive form of *mamma*, the word for the breast itself. His name thus connects Mamillius to the lactating breast and to the world of women, who in early modern culture presided over childbirth and the early years of children's lives. Infants depended utterly on women, either wet nurses or mothers, to provide their earliest sustenance, breast milk. As was often true of women from the upper class, Hermione does not herself seem to have nursed Mamillius. As Leontes bitterly exclaims: "I am glad you did not nurse him" (2.1.57). Nonetheless, the young boy's name and his appearance in 2.1 with his pregnant mother and her waiting women clearly associate him with the feminine sphere of birth, lactation, and early childhood. In identifying with Mamillius, a boy so young his nurse's milk is scarcely out of him, Leontes seems to feel both the vulnerability of the infant dependent on the lactating body of woman and the vulnerability of the adult husband dependent on the pregnant body and the chastity of his wife for legitimate offspring. As if to deny these dependencies, Leontes banishes Mamillius from his mother's presence and Hermione to prison. Mamillius dies; Leontes appears to lose all that would link him to the future: wife, son, daughter.

The sexual politics of *The Winter's Tale*, though rooted in early modern social structures, remain strikingly relevant to the contemporary moment. How much should men control women and their bodies? How much power and autonomy is it acceptable for women to exercise? These questions are played out in our culture in debates about reproductive rights and glass ceilings, while the prevalence of rape and sexual violence against women suggests that the female body still remains a focal point for some of our culture's deepest and least resolved currents of anger and ambivalence.

The Winter's Tale shows that the end point of Leontes' suspicion and distrust is a profound isolation from all those around him, including his counselors. He becomes a dangerous tyrant whose anger and paranoia torture him and distort his speech. In the first three acts, Leontes' most characteristic action is to turn away from those who love or attempt to help him. He sends his wife to prison; casts out his infant daughter; refuses the good counsel of his courtiers; rages in misogynistic fury at Paulina, who brings Perdita to him from prison; and finally defies the oracle of Apollo. Lacking trust in his wife and in all those around him, Leontes condemns himself to deathlike isolation. As in Shakespeare's other late plays, much of the language of *The Winter's Tale* is difficult and dense. Normal word order is inverted; speeches begin and end in the middle of a line; figurative language is given elliptical expression. During his period of intense jealousy, Leontes' language becomes even more dense and compressed than is typical of the rest of the play. Looking at his son, he exclaims:

> Can thy dam—? May't be?—
> Affection, thy intention stabs the center;
> Thou dost make possible things not so held,
> Communicat'st with dreams—how can this be?—
> With what's unreal thou coactive art,
> And fellow'st nothing. Then 'tis very credent
> Thou mayst cojoin with something, and thou dost,
> And that beyond commission, and I find it,

> And that to the infection of my brains
> And hard'ning of my brows.

(1.2.137–46)

In this difficult passage, Leontes wrestles with the knowledge that his "affection" (the passions of rage, jealousy, and suspicion released in him) wounds him and perhaps leads him to imagine things to be true that are not. On the other hand, his suspicions *may* be justified; he may already be a cuckold. In this horrible state of uncertainty, Leontes' speech verges on incoherence. He interrupts the flow of his own thoughts with questions and ejaculations; his mind darts from boy to mother to his own pain; he realizes he may be wrong, but returns, obsessively, to the coarse and shameful image of his forehead disfigured with the horns of a cuckold.

The inner disorder suggested by this language finds its outward manifestation in Leontes' increasingly tyrannical actions. In the early modern period, the ruler of a kingdom was often compared to the head of a family. Good order in the commonwealth had its foundation in a well-ordered domestic realm. In *The Winter's Tale*, Leontes oversteps his just authority in both domains, refusing to take counsel from his courtiers, defying the gods, and condemning his wife for adultery with no evidence but his own suspicions. Nowhere, however, does he more certainly exceed his patriarchal authority than when he orders Hermione to stand trial before the proper period of her lying-in has passed. In the Renaissance, childbirth was recognized as an event both important and dangerous. Women gave birth surrounded by other women, usually a hired midwife, as well as by neighbors and female family members. The laboring female body, opened to let the child pass into the world, was considered to be in a particularly vulnerable state, needing to be protected from the unhealthful air that might enter the open womb. Consequently, birthing took place in a closed chamber, and after birth had occurred, women lay in their chambers for an extended period, recovering strength and purging their bodies of the blood and other fluids associated with pregnancy. At the end of this period, often lasting a month but sometimes longer, the woman came out of her house and returned to her normal routines. This occasion was marked by a "churching" ceremony, a rite of purification and celebration in which thanks were given for the safe delivery of a child and the woman's body declared cleansed of the impurities of pregnancy and birth.

When Hermione is made to stand trial, the pathos of her dignified defense of herself is heightened by her weakened state. In many productions, she appears on stage unattended, almost unable to stand. Among the wrongs done her, she accuses Leontes of having "with immodest hatred / The childbed privilege denied, which 'longs / To women of all fashion. Lastly, hurried / Here to this place, i'th' open air, before / I have got strength of limit" (3.2.100–104). Leontes' fury against the maternal body extends to denying that body the privileges of the lying-in period and exposing it to the dangers of the open air of a public place. This is domestic tyranny of a hideous sort.

After such cruelty, what recovery? Bohemia seems to be the place of hope in the play, and that feeling is conveyed in part by the vast expansion of character and event in that pastoral locale. After the claustrophobic focus on Leontes, the action unfolds to encompass the tricks of a wily rogue, Autolycus (whose name links him to the Autolycus of classical mythology, a crafty thief and grandfather of Ulysses; Autolycus's own father, Mercury, was the god of thieves); the sports of a sheep-shearing festival; the courtship of Florizel and Perdita; and the intrigues that take many of these players back to Sicilia. The scene depicting the festival at the Shepherd's farm, 4.4, is one of the longest in Shakespeare's canon (820 lines), is entirely his own invention, and is a great feast of languages and events. It includes the singing of ballads, a dance of twelve satyrs, Perdita's lyrical catalog of the flowers appropriate to each stage of life, and the painful moment when Polixenes forbids his son's marriage.

In the early modern period, childbirth was largely the affair of women. In this picture from Jakob Rüff's *De conceptu et generatione hominis* (Concerning the conception and birth of man) (1580), several women attend to a woman in labor while, in the background, two men cast the child's horoscope.

As this last moment shows, although Bohemia is a place of healing, it is not a paradise. In Bohemia, "great creating nature" for a time replaces Apollo as the deity who presides over the action. The fertility of the earth and, by extension, the fertility of woman may here seem to be redeemed from the curse laid upon them by Leontes' suspicion of his wife; and Florizel's staunch commitment to Perdita in the face of mounting obstacles to their love augurs well. But Polixenes just as staunchly opposes their union, threatening to use his patriarchal power in a way that, as with Leontes, would separate him from his son and from the possibility of future lineage. Bohemia also contains the rogue Autolycus, picking the pockets of country bumpkins and hiding his identity by a series of disguises. Further, Bohemian life is marked by enormous disparities of wealth. The Shepherd is rich, in part because of the money he found with Perdita. For the sheep-shearing feast, Perdita can afford ingredients—raisins, rice, and spices, for example—that were exotic luxury goods, foodstuffs in excess of the subsistence diet of bread, beer, and cheese that many people ate. It is also possible that some of the Shepherd's wealth comes from the new profitability of raising sheep. Throughout the sixteenth and seventeenth centuries, land was increasingly enclosed—that is, fenced off for grazing sheep rather than available for communal use in raising food and feeding cattle. These enclosures were popularly blamed for perceived increases in rural poverty

In this late seventeenth-century woodcut from the Pepysian collection of early modern ballads, a peddler carries a huge pack and holds several rabbits, or conies, which suggests that he is also a cony-catcher—that is, a con man (like Autolycus), whose victims were popularly called "conies."

and for the creation of masterless men, poor folk who roamed the countryside without fixed places of residence and who were believed to feign sickness or deformity in order to enforce charity from those they met. Autolycus, pretending to have lost his clothes to a highwayman, is a comic version of such a masterless man, yet his presence in the play, juxtaposed to that of the rich Shepherd, is a reminder of the social tensions and economic stratifications that permeate the landscape with widespread enclosures and other changes in rural life.

Bohemia is also the locale of one of the great set pieces of the play—the debate between Polixenes and Perdita concerning the relative values of art and nature and the relationship between them. Today we find analogs to this debate in the controversy over genetically modified seeds and crops. Does the artifice of genetic modification improve nature in ways beneficial to many, or is it a dangerous distortion of it? The early modern period engaged in similar debates. Given the imperfections of the fallen world and humankind's weaknesses, could art be instrumental in calling into being a better world, or was it merely a temptation to pride or to competition with the divine creator? The refreshing thing about the handling of these issues in *The Winter's Tale* is that the play comes to no abstract resolution concerning them. Rather, it encases the debate between Polixenes and Perdita in multiple ironies, and it complexly connects this debate to the actions of characters who seemingly have no involvement with it. For Perdita, product of the pastoral landscape, art is a bad thing. She wants no grafted or hybrid flowers in her garden. Yet even as she speaks her condemnation of art, Perdita is reluctantly dressed as queen of the sheep-shearing feast, a bit of artifice that reveals a truth she herself cannot know: namely, that she is a queen's daughter. Polixenes, for his part, champions art, declaring that the practice of mixing wild and cultivated plants produces sturdy hybrids and that the art of grafting is itself a gift of nature. Yet when his son wishes to graft himself to a shepherd's daughter, Polixenes finds such a practice abhorrent.

Besides making the obvious point that people don't always act on their stated beliefs, this exchange shows the extreme pressure the play puts on the art-nature dichotomy. In Perdita's case, her "natural" condition as princess is revealed by two kinds of artifice: her dress as queen of the feast and the role Camillo creates for her as Florizel's Libyan princess when he devises a way for the two young lovers to return to Leontes' court. Camillo even goes so far as to provide lines for the two to speak. His goal is ameliorative: to satisfy the desires of the young (as well as his own deep longings to see his homeland again) and to heal the breach between the two disservered kingdoms. The point seems to be not whether in some abstract sense "art" violates "nature," but how artfulness, defined broadly as the representation of the world through painting, statuary, plays, and song, can open new possibilities for imagining what nature is or could be.

This is not an inconsequential point, for in the badly flawed world depicted in *The Winter's Tale* art gradually emerges as one of the resources people can use, either badly or well, to affect the world around them: to correct old mistakes and to forge new realities. Its effects are determined and limited, of course, by the skill and intentions of the artist and by the receptiveness of the audience. Autolycus is a subversive con man who uses disguises and deceptions to fleece money from gulls. By contrast, in the play's second part, Paulina emerges as the chief representative of the ameliorative artist who uses her skills to make better the world around her. Once reviled by Leontes as a witch, Paulina becomes the King's spiritual guide in the last half of the play (her name linking her to the New Testament apostle St. Paul). This strikingly outspoken woman spends sixteen years preparing Leontes to be a fit spectator to the tableau of resurrection and renewal enacted in the last scene. When she had first brought the infant to Leontes from prison, Paulina had seemed to believe in the self-evident nature of truth. Laying the babe at Leontes' feet, she proclaimed that the "good goddess Nature" (2.3.103) had made it an exact copy of the father. Leontes had only to read what nature had written in the face of his child. But jealousy and rage at his wife bleared the King's vision. He would not or could not see himself in the female child he had fathered. So for sixteen years Paulina worked another way, fueling Leontes' remorse and artfully withholding both from him and from the theater audience the knowledge that Hermione lived. When the disguised Princess returns to Sicilia, Leontes gets a second chance. Looking at Perdita, he is finally able to see the unslandered image of his wife in the young girl before him. Having admired Perdita, Leontes says to Paulina, "I thought of her [Hermione] / Even in these looks I made" (5.1.226–27). When he can believe in the potential goodness of women, and specifically in the chastity of the young woman who is the simulacrum of his wife, then Leontes can help to create the reality in which Perdita is truly a princess and his wife a living being rather than the corpse into which his rage and distrust had transformed her.

The statue scene itself is one of the most moving and theatrically effective moments in any of Shakespeare's plays. Like Leontes, the untutored audience does not know that Hermione lives. Consequently, under Paulina's careful guidance, the spectators both onstage and off seem to participate in willing the statue into life. When Hermione descends from her pedestal, the audience can feel itself present at the miraculous resurrection of the dead. In theological terms, this scene touches on controversial matters. Protestants repudiated what they characterized as Catholic idolatry, which involved the veneration of images, including statues of the Virgin Mary. Protestants, by contrast, typically stressed the ear over the eye, words over images, faith over works. In the wake of the Reformation, more radical Protestants went so far as to smash stained-glass windows and the statues of saints that had for many centuries adorned Catholic churches. The final moments of *The Winter's Tale* gesture toward this repudiated world of images and their veneration. While Paulina insists that the audience awaken its faith, she does so in a scene that is visually organized to focus all eyes on a statue that might well evoke memories of prior Catholic practices. Characteristically, Shakespeare seems to have things two ways: drawing on the emotional power of Catholic rituals centered on the image, he simultaneously suggests that there is no statue on the stage at all, only a living woman roused to new vigor by the recovery of a long-lost daughter.

However ambiguous the theological implications of the final scene, it is a striking theatrical climax evoking wonder and awe and allowing the old tale to end happily, or mostly so. A penitent Leontes has been reunited with his wife and daughter, and amity has been restored between him and Polixenes. But such is the maturity of this play that the happy ending is a tempered one. The memory of things that were lost and can never be regained intrudes even on the celebration of the return of Perdita and Hermione. Paulina pointedly recalls her husband, Antigonus, lost in carrying Perdita to Bohemia; Hermione speaks to Perdita of the sixteen long years of their separation; Mamillius is gone forever. Moreover, the highly charged image of the pregnant female body is absent from this final scene. Perdita is not yet a wife; both Paulina and Hermione are probably too old for childbearing. For Perdita and Florizel, perhaps the greatest tests of faith and mutuality lie ahead, when Perdita's transformation from maid into wife and mother will present new occasions for the jealousy and distrust of patriarchal culture to resurface. The point of *The Winter's Tale* hardly seems to be that folly has no consequences or that earthly paradise is possible. Those claims would indeed make nature afraid. Rather, the play celebrates the true miracle of partial restorations, of moments of exquisite joy wrested by work, art, and good fortune from the pains of the imperfect world that men and women have made.

JEAN E. HOWARD

SELECTED BIBLIOGRAPHY

Adelman, Janet. "Masculine Authority and the Maternal Body: The Return to Origins in the Romances." *Suffocating Mothers: Fantasies of Maternal Origin in Shakespeare's Plays, "Hamlet" to "The Tempest."* New York: Routledge, 1992. 193–238. Argues that the romances attempt to redress the loss of the idealized parents enacted in *Hamlet* and that *The Winter's Tale* dramatizes the positive restoration of the sexualized mother in the person of Hermione.

Egan, Robert. "'The Art Itself Is Nature': *The Winter's Tale*." *Drama Within Drama: Shakespeare's Sense of His Art in "King Lear," "The Winter's Tale," and "The Tempest."* New York: Columbia UP, 1975. 56–89. Discusses the role of art in rectifying the disordered world of *The Winter's Tale*.

Frye, Northrop. "The Triumph of Time." *A Natural Perspective: The Development of Shakespearean Comedy and Romance.* New York: Columbia UP, 1965. 72–117. Discusses structures of action and conventions common across Shakespeare's comedies and romances.

Jensen, Phoebe. "Singing Psalms to Hornpipes: Festivity, Iconoclasm and Catholicism in *The Winter's Tale*." *Religion and Revelry in Shakespeare's Festive World.* Cambridge: Cambridge UP, 2008. 194–233. Explores the play's relationship to Catholic and Protestant attitudes toward popular festivity.

Mowat, Barbara A. "Rogues, Shepherds, and the Counterfeit Distressed: Texts and Infracontexts of *The Winter's Tale* 4.3." *Shakespeare Studies* 22 (1994): 58–76. Examines the cultural contexts that help make sense of the figure of Autolycus, rogue and con man, in *The Winter's Tale*.

Newcomb, Lori H. "'If That Which Is Lost Be Not Found': Monumental Bodies, Spectacular Bodies in *The Winter's Tale*." *Ovid and the Renaissance Body.* Ed. Goran V. Stanivukovic. Toronto: U of Toronto P, 2001. Analyzes the tension between the monumental (stasis and constraint) and the spectacular (metamorphosis and performative freedom) both in the text of *The Winter's Tale* and in its material history as book and as theater piece.

O'Connor, Marion. "'Imagine Me, Gentle Spectators': Iconomachy and *The Winter's Tale*." *A Companion to Shakespeare's Works. IV: The Poems, Problem Comedies, Late Plays.* Ed. Richard Dutton and Jean E. Howard. Malden, MA: Blackwell, 2003. 365–88. Discusses the Renaissance theological debate about the value and truth of images as it bears on a number of early modern plays, including *The Winter's Tale*, in which statues are staged. Argues that Shakespeare insists on the collaboration of word and image, eschewing a total embrace of Reformation logocentrism or Catholic image-worship.

Paster, Gail Kern. "Quarreling with the Dug, or 'I Am Glad You Did Not Nurse Him.'" *The Body Embarrassed: Drama and the Disciplines of Shame in Early Modern England.* Ithaca, NY: Cornell UP, 1993. 215–80. Sets *The Winter's Tale* in an

array of Shakespearean texts that anxiously explore early modern cultural practices surrounding reproduction and infant care, especially the practice of
wet-nursing.

Ravelhofer, Barbara. "'Beasts of Recreacion': Henslowe's White Bears." *English Literary Renaissance* 32.2 (2002): 287–323. Explores the possibility that a real bear
was used in performances of *The Winter's Tale* in Shakespeare's time.

Tigner, Amy. "*The Winter's Tale*: Gardens and the Marvels of Transformation."
English Literary Renaissance 36.1 (2006): 114–34. Argues for the centrality of
gardens to *The Winter's Tale* as they represent the body of women and mark the
movement from suspicion to redemption. Discusses the possibility that the final
scene in which Hermione's statue walks occurs in a garden setting.

FILM

The Winter's Tale. 1999. Dir. Robin Lough. UK. 170 min. A dark and moving Royal
Shakespeare Company production with Anthony Sher as a Leontes truly made
mad by jealousy and an impressively dignified Alexandra Gilbreath as Hermione.
Imaginative staging of the bear and riveting statue scene as Hermione very slowly
comes to life.

TEXTUAL INTRODUCTION

The 1623 Folio text contains the only early version of *The Winter's Tale*, where it
appears at the end of the comedies. The play dates probably from 1610, and the first
recorded performance, noted by Simon Forman, took place on May 15, 1611, at the
Globe Theatre. Forman pays attention to Autolycus but has nothing to say about the
extraordinary restoration of Hermione in the last scene. The King's Men performed
the play at court in Whitehall on November 5, 1611, and again at court during the
Christmas season of 1612–13 in a group of plays that led up to the wedding of Princess Elizabeth, King James's only daughter, to Frederick, Elector Palatine of Germany, on February 14, 1613. The play's text includes a satyr dance in 4.4 in the long
sheep-shearing scene, which seems indebted to a dance in Ben Jonson's *Masque of
Oberon*, performed at court on January 1, 1611, in honor of Prince Henry. We cannot
know, however, when or how this dance became part of *The Winter's Tale*.

Scholars generally agree that the scribe Ralph Crane probably created a transcript of the play, as he did for several of the King's Men plays, although we cannot
be certain about what copy went to the printing house. The Folio text bears evidence
of Crane's practice, such as typically indulging in extensive use of parentheses,
hyphens, and apostrophes. Crane also lists all the characters at the beginning of the
scene regardless of when they might appear. For clarity, this edition creates stage
directions that indicate when the characters should enter the action. Beyond an initial stage direction, the printed text of *The Winter's Tale* never offers much more
than simply noting entrances and exits of characters. The notable and famous
exception, unlike anything else in the play, occurs in 3.3, where we find the stage
direction that prompts immediate action from Antigonus: "*Exit, pursued by a bear.*"
This single stage direction has caused consternation, amusement, puzzlement,
much commentary by critics, and many problems for directors.

Curiously, in the Folio text a blank page precedes *The Winter's Tale*, and a blank
page follows it, perhaps suggesting some uncertainty or a late addition of the play
to the collection. Generally, the play lacks serious textual problems, a tribute possibly to Crane and the printer. Act and scene divisions are reliable, and this edition
adheres to them. The text includes "The Names of the Actors" at the conclusion of
the play, making *The Winter's Tale* one of only seven of the Folio texts that include

such a list, and always at the end (four comedies, one history, and two tragedies). This practice contrasts with the usual modern editorial habit of listing the characters first.

David M. Bergeron

PERFORMANCE NOTE

The Winter's Tale takes greater risks with its audience than perhaps any other play by Shakespeare, repeatedly testing the capacities of its actors and the credulity of its audiences. Antigonus's *"Exit, pursued by a bear"* (3.3.57) is only one instance of the play seemingly going out of its way to expose a theater company's limitations. Actors are repeatedly tasked with representing things that are peculiarly resistant to representation, such as the personified abstraction "Time" and the statue of Hermione. In addition, productions must engage with the play's open inquiry into the role of nature and artifice in art, settling whether and how to legitimize Leontes' jealousy, to simulate or stylize the bear, to mask or accentuate Hermione's feigned inanimacy, to emphasize or underplay the fact that the text describes rather than depicts a scene that, by its own admission, was "a sight which was to be seen, cannot be spoken of" (5.2.39–40).

Productions must also address questions of characterization (Does Camillo's mingling of loyalty and treachery signify candor or cunning? Does "Clown" indicate the rustic's job description or his personality? Is Paulina a spiritual healer or a witch?) and genre (How capable of redemption should Leontes appear? Should the ghosts of Mamillius and Antigonus haunt the second half?). And they must decide how to identify and contrast Sicilia and Bohemia. Despite the comparative levity of the action in Bohemia, the love triangle that centers on Clown and the sudden aggression of Polixenes parallel tragic events in Sicilia, and productions sometimes emphasize those parallels by doubling roles or reprising bits of staging.

Brett Gamboa

The Winter's Tale

THE PERSONS OF THE PLAY[1]

LEONTES, King of Sicilia
HERMIONE, Queen to Leontes
MAMILLIUS, young Prince of Sicilia
PERDITA, daughter to Leontes and Hermione
CAMILLO
ANTIGONUS } four lords of Sicilia
CLEOMENES
DION
PAULINA, wife to Antigonus
EMILIA, a lady
JAILER
MARINER
LORDS and GENTLEMEN, LADIES, OFFICERS, and SERVANTS of Leontes' court

POLIXENES, King of Bohemia
FLORIZEL, Prince of Bohemia
SHEPHERD, reputed father of Perdita
CLOWN, his son
MOPSA } shepherdesses
DORCAS
AUTOLYCUS, a rogue
ARCHIDAMUS, a lord of Bohemia
Shepherds and Shepherdesses
Twelve Herdsmen disguised as Satyrs
TIME as Chorus

1.1

Enter CAMILLO *and* ARCHIDAMUS.

ARCHIDAMUS If you shall chance, Camillo, to visit Bohemia on the like occasion whereon my services are now on foot,[2] you shall see, as I have said, great difference betwixt our Bohemia and your Sicilia.

5 CAMILLO I think this coming summer the King of Sicilia means to pay Bohemia the visitation which he justly owes him.

ARCHIDAMUS Wherein our entertainment shall shame us, we will be justified in our loves;[3] for indeed—

CAMILLO Beseech you—

10 ARCHIDAMUS Verily, I speak it in the freedom of my knowledge. We cannot with such magnificence—in so rare—I know not what to say. We will give you sleepy drinks[4] that your

---

1.1 Location: Sicilia. The palace of Leontes.
1. TEXTUAL COMMENT *The Winter's Tale* is one of only seven plays in the Folio that contain a list of characters. As with the other plays, that list is placed at the end of the text. The Folio list overlooks several characters here included, and divides its characters by gender, as this edition does not. See Digital Edition TC 1.

2. *on the like . . . foot:* on an occasion similar to the one in which I am now engaged (that is, as attendant lord to a visiting king).
3. *Wherein . . . lover:* Insofar as our less elaborate hospitality will put us to shame, we will compensate by (the depth of) our love.
4. *sleepy drinks:* drinks to make you drowsy.

senses, unintelligent of our insufficience,[5] may, though they
cannot praise us, as little accuse us.

15 CAMILLO   You pay a great deal too dear for what's given freely.

ARCHIDAMUS   Believe me, I speak as my understanding
instructs me and as mine honesty puts it to utterance.

CAMILLO   Sicilia cannot show himself over-kind to Bohemia.
They were trained together in their childhoods, and there
20 rooted betwixt them then such an affection which cannot
choose but branch[6] now. Since their more mature dignities
and royal necessities made separation of their society,° their   forced them apart
encounters, though not personal, hath been royally attor-
neyed[7] with interchange of gifts, letters, loving embassies,
25 that° they have seemed to be together though absent; shook   so that
hands as over a vast;° and embraced as it were from the ends   wide expanse
of opposed winds.[8] The heavens continue their loves.

ARCHIDAMUS   I think there is not in the world either malice or
matter to alter it. You have an unspeakable° comfort of°   inexpressible / in
30 your young prince Mamillius. It° is a gentleman of the greatest   (He)
promise that ever came into my note.

CAMILLO   I very well agree with you in the hopes of him. It is
a gallant child; one that, indeed, physics the subject,[9] makes
old hearts fresh. They that went on crutches ere he was
35 born desire yet their life° to see him a man.   hope to live long enough

ARCHIDAMUS   Would they else be content to die?

CAMILLO   Yes—if there were no other excuse why they should
desire to live.

ARCHIDAMUS   If the King had no son, they would desire to live
40 on crutches till he had one.   *Exeunt.*

1.2

Enter LEONTES, HERMIONE, MAMILLIUS, POLIXENES,
[*and*] CAMILLO.[1]

POLIXENES   Nine changes of the wat'ry star hath been
The shepherd's note[2] since we[3] have left our throne
Without a burden.° Time as long again   occupant
Would be filled up, my brother, with our thanks,
5 And yet we should for perpetuity
Go hence in debt.[4] And therefore, like a cipher,
Yet standing in rich place,[5] I multiply
With one "We thank you" many thousands more
That go before it.

LEONTES   Stay° your thanks a while,   *Postpone*
And pay them when you part.

10 POLIXENES   Sir, that's tomorrow.

---

5. Unaware of our inadequacy.
6. Flourish and spread (as a tree does when it puts forth branches); divide.
7. Performed by deputies.
8. *from . . . winds:* from opposite ends of the earth. Early modern atlases often showed the four "corners" of the earth as the source of the winds.
9. Restores the health of the King's subjects.
1.2 Location: Scene continues.
1. TEXTUAL COMMENT Though listed in the stage direction in F, Camillo has no part in this scene until line 208, when Leontes says, "What, Camillo there?" Camillo's first entrance may be marked by Leontes'

exclamation, or he may be a silent observer for the first 208 lines. See Digital Edition TC 2.
2. *Nine . . . note:* The Shepherd has observed nine changes of the moon (that is, nine months). The moon is "the wat'ry star" because it governs the tides.
3. Both kings employ the royal "we," speaking of themselves in the plural.
4. *And yet . . . debt:* And even then we would depart forever in your debt.
5. *like . . . place:* like a zero ("cipher"), which is worthless in itself, but valuable when it follows another number.

I am questioned by my fears° of what may chance[6]   *I am afraid*
Or breed upon° our absence, that may blow   *develop because of*
No sneaping winds at home to make us say,
"This is put forth too truly."[7] Besides, I have stayed
To tire your royalty.

15 LEONTES   We are tougher, brother,
Than you can put us to't.[8]

POLIXENES   No longer stay.

LEONTES One sennight° longer.   *week*

POLIXENES   Very sooth,° tomorrow.   *In truth (a mild oath)*

LEONTES We'll part the time° between's, then; and in that   *split the difference*
I'll no gainsaying.°   *allow no contradiction*

POLIXENES   Press me not, beseech you, so.
20 There is no tongue that moves, none, none i'th' world
So soon as yours could win me. So it should now,
Were there necessity in your request, although
'Twere needful I denied it. My affairs
Do even drag me homeward, which to hinder
25 Were in your love a whip to me,[9] my stay
To you a charge and trouble. To save both,
Farewell, our brother.

LEONTES   Tongue-tied our queen? Speak you.

HERMIONE I had thought, sir, to have held my peace until
You had drawn oaths from him not to stay. You, sir,
30 Charge him too coldly. Tell him you are sure
All in Bohemia's well. This satisfaction
The bygone day proclaimed.[1] Say this to him,
He's beat from his best ward.[2]

LEONTES   Well said, Hermione.

HERMIONE To tell° he longs to see his son were strong.   *assert*
35 But let him say so, then, and let him go;
But let him swear so, and he shall not stay:
We'll thwack him hence with distaffs.[3]
[*to* POLIXENES] Yet of your royal presence I'll adventure°   *risk*
The borrow° of a week. When at Bohemia   *loan*
40 You take my lord, I'll give him my commission°   *permission*
To let him there a month behind the gest
Prefixed for 's parting.[4] —Yet, good deed,° Leontes,   *indeed*
I love thee not a jar° o'th' clock behind   *tick*
What lady she her lord.[5] —You'll stay?

POLIXENES   No, madam.

HERMIONE Nay, but you will?

45 POLIXENES   I may not, verily.

HERMIONE Verily?
You put me off with limber° vows. But I,   *weak*

---

6. Happen by chance.
7. *that may . . . too truly:* an obscure passage. Fearing the worst, Polixenes hopes that no biting ("sneaping") winds may blow (that is, no envious forces be active) at home to make him conclude that his worries were justified.
8. Than any test that you put us to.
9. *which to . . . to me:* that is, to hinder me from going home, though lovingly done, would be a punishment ("whip") to me.
1. *This . . . proclaimed:* This good news was announced

yesterday.
2. He's forced to relinquish his strongest position; a fencing metaphor.
3. Wooden sticks, usually about three feet long, which were used in spinning wool. Proverbially, they were female tools and symbols of female authority.
4. *To let . . . parting:* To remain there a month longer than the time ("gest") appointed in advance for his departure.
5. *I love . . . lord:* I love you no less than any noblewoman loves her husband.

Though you would seek t'unsphere the stars[6] with oaths,
Should yet say, "Sir, no going." Verily
50 You shall not go. A lady's "verily" is
As potent as a lord's. Will you go yet?
Force me to keep you as a prisoner,
Not like a guest; so you shall pay your fees
When you depart[7] and save your thanks. How say you?
55 My prisoner? Or my guest? By your dread "verily,"
One of them you shall be.
POLIXENES   Your guest, then, madam;
To be your prisoner should import offending,°   mean I have offended you
Which is for me less easy to commit
Than you to punish.
HERMIONE   Not your jailer, then,
60 But your kind hostess. Come, I'll question you
Of my lord's tricks and yours when you were boys.
You were pretty lordings° then?   young lords
POLIXENES   We were, fair queen,
Two lads that thought there was no more behind°   in the future
But such a day tomorrow as today,
And to be boy eternal.
65 HERMIONE   Was not my lord
The verier wag° o'th' two?   greater mischief-maker
POLIXENES   We were as twinned° lambs that did frisk i'th' sun   identical
And bleat the one at th'other. What we changed°   exchanged
Was innocence for innocence. We knew not
70 The doctrine of ill-doing nor dreamed
That any did. Had we pursued that life,
And our weak spirits ne'er been higher reared
With stronger blood,° we should have answered heaven   With more mature passions
Boldly, "Not guilty," the imposition cleared
Hereditary ours.[8]
75 HERMIONE   By this we gather
You have tripped° since.   sinned
POLIXENES   O my most sacred lady,
Temptations have since then been born to's. For
In those unfledged[9] days was my wife a girl;
Your precious self had then not crossed the eyes
Of my young playfellow.
80 HERMIONE   Grace to boot!°   Heaven help me
Of this make no conclusion,[1] lest you say
Your queen and I are devils. Yet go on.
Th'offenses we have made you do we'll answer°—   answer for
If you first sinned with us, and that with us
85 You did continue fault, and that you slipped not°   did not sin (have sex)
With any but with us.
LEONTES   Is he won° yet?   persuaded
HERMIONE   He'll stay, my lord.

6. To disorder the cosmos; alluding to the idea that
the stars move in fixed orbits around the earth.
7. In early modern England, prisoners were required
to pay fees to jailers both for provisions and upon
their release.
8. Freed even of the charge of original sin. The doctrine of original sin held that everyone at birth was

tainted by sin because the first humans, Adam and
Eve, disobeyed God in the Garden of Eden. Here
original sin is linked to the sexual desires that come
with maturity.
9. Youthful. An unfledged, or young, bird is one as
yet lacking the feathers necessary for flight.
1. Do not follow out this line of reasoning.

LEONTES   At my request he would not.
Hermione, my dearest, thou never spok'st
To better purpose.
HERMIONE   Never?
LEONTES   Never, but once.
90 HERMIONE   What, have I twice said well? When was't before?
I prithee tell me. Cram's° with praise and make's   *Stuff us; overfeed us*
As fat as tame things. One good deed, dying tongueless,
Slaughters a thousand waiting upon that.[2]
Our praises are our wages. You may ride's
95 With one soft kiss a thousand furlongs ere
With spur we heat° an acre.[3] But to th' goal:°   *race over / purpose*
My last good deed was to entreat his stay.
What was my first? It has an elder sister,
Or I mistake you. Oh, would her name were Grace![4]
100 But once before I spoke to th' purpose? When?
Nay, let me have't. I long.
LEONTES   Why, that was when
Three crabbèd° months had soured themselves to death   *bitter*
Ere I could make thee open thy white hand
And clap° thyself my love; then didst thou utter,   *pledge*
"I am yours forever."
105 HERMIONE   'Tis grace indeed.
Why, lo you now, I have spoke to th' purpose twice:
The one for ever earned a royal husband;
Th'other for some while a friend.[5]
            [HERMIONE *and* POLIXENES *stand apart, holding hands.*][6]
LEONTES [*aside*]   Too hot, too hot.
To mingle friendship far is mingling bloods.[7]
110 I have *tremor cordis*[8] on me; my heart dances,
But not for joy, not joy. This entertainment°   *hospitality*
May a free° face put on, derive a liberty   *innocent*
From heartiness, from bounty, fertile bosom,°   *generous affection*
And well become the agent[9]—'t may, I grant—
115 But to be paddling° palms and pinching fingers,[1]   *caressing*
As now they are, and making practiced smiles
As in a looking glass; and then to sigh, as 'twere
The mort o'th' deer[2]—oh, that is entertainment
My bosom likes not, nor my brows.[3] —Mamillius,
Art thou my boy?

2. *One good . . . that:* If one virtuous act goes unre-
marked, then the thousand more that might have
been inspired by it will not come to be.
3. *You may . . . acre:* that is, You'll go much farther
with us if you will treat us kindly (with a pun on
"ride" as meaning "enjoy us sexually").
4. Would that my first good act were virtuous (full of
God's grace). Hermione may be countering Polixenes' earlier suggestion that she first caused Leontes
to sin. With a possible allusion to the Three Graces
(Aglaia, Euphrosyne, and Thalia) of classical mythology. Usually depicted nude and dancing in a circle,
the three women represented the epitome of earthly
beauty and harmony.
5. "Friend" could also mean "lover," a meaning that
Leontes takes up in his next speech.
6. It is not certain when Hermione and Polixenes
join hands, but by line 115 Leontes remarks that they

are "paddling palms and pinching fingers."
7. Uniting in passion; having sexual intercourse.
PERFORMANCE COMMENT Leontes' sudden extreme
jealousy poses challenges for the actor playing the
part. How will he motivate the sudden transformation? See Digital Edition PC 1.
8. A malady marked by an erratic heart rate.
9. And makes the actor of these deeds (Hermione)
appear attractive.
1. Early modern texts often represent hands as erotic
body parts. Moist palms were believed to be signs
of sexual arousal; finger games may suggest sexual
penetration.
2. *to sigh . . . deer:* to sigh as loudly as the horn blast
that proclaims the death of a hunted deer.
3. Alluding to the proverbial notion that a cuckold
sprouted horns from his brow.

MAMILLIUS   Ay, my good lord.

120 LEONTES   I'fecks!°   *In faith (a mild oath)*
Why, that's my bawcock.° What, hast smutched° thy nose?   *fine fellow / dirtied*
They say it is a copy out of mine. Come, captain,
We must be neat—not neat,[4] but cleanly, captain.
And yet the steer, the heifer, and the calf
125 Are all called "neat." —Still virginaling
Upon his palm?[5] —How now, you wanton° calf?   *playful*
Art thou my calf?

MAMILLIUS   Yes, if you will, my lord.

LEONTES   Thou want'st a rough pash° and the shoots°
    that I have   *shaggy head / horns*
To be full° like me. Yet they say we are   *fully grown, fully horned*
130 Almost as like as eggs—women say so,
That will say anything. But were they false
As o'er-dyed blacks,[6] as wind, as waters, false
As dice are to be wished by one that fixes
No bourn° twixt his and mine, yet were it true   *boundary; limit*
135 To say this boy were like me. Come, sir page,
Look on me with your welkin° eye. Sweet villain,   *sky blue*
Most dear'st, my collop.[7] Can thy dam°—? May't be?—   *mother*
Affection, thy intention stabs the center;[8]
Thou dost make possible things not so held,°   *considered impossible*
140 Communicat'st with dreams—how can this be?—
With what's unreal thou coactive art,°   *you collaborate*
And fellow'st° nothing. Then 'tis very credent°   *are companion to / believable*
Thou mayst cojoin with something, and thou dost,
And that beyond commission,° and I find it,   *what is permitted*
145 And that to the infection of my brains
And hard'ning of my brows.°   *(with cuckold's horns)*

    [POLIXENES *and* HERMIONE *step forward.*]

POLIXENES   What means Sicilia?

HERMIONE   He something seems° unsettled.   *seems somewhat*

POLIXENES   How, my lord?

LEONTES   What cheer? How is't with you, best brother?

HERMIONE   You look
As if you held a brow of much distraction.
Are you moved,° my lord?   *angry*

150 LEONTES   No, in good earnest.
How sometimes nature will betray its folly,
Its tenderness, and make itself a pastime°   *source of amusement*
To harder bosoms! Looking on the lines
Of my boy's face, methoughts I did recoil°   *go back*
155 Twenty-three years and saw myself unbreeched,[9]
In my green velvet coat, my dagger muzzled°   *in its sheath; blunted*
Lest it should bite its master and so prove,
As ornaments oft do, too dangerous.

---

4. Punning on "neat" as meaning both "clean" and "cattle with horns."

5. Still caressing his hand as if playing the virginal, a legless keyboard instrument played on the lap; still acting chastely (like a virgin).

6. Referring to textiles dyed black. Such black cloth was made "false" or weakened by the harsh chemicals in the dye. With a possible reference to the dark skin of Africans, who were commonly thought to be licentious and thus sexually "false."

7. That is, my own flesh. (A "collop" is a portion of meat.)

8. *Affection . . . center:* Passion (probably the passion of jealousy), your intensity ("intention") pierces my heart, or to the core of my being.

9. Not yet old enough to wear men's clothing ("breeches"). Before about the age of six, both girls and boys in early modern England wore a dresslike garment. Giving a boy breeches was a sign of his passage out of childhood.

How like, methought, I then was to this kernel,
160   This squash,° this gentleman. —Mine honest friend,   *unripe peapod*
Will you take eggs for money?[1]

MAMILLIUS   No, my lord, I'll fight.

LEONTES   You will? Why, happy man be 's dole.[2] My brother,
Are you so fond of your young prince as we
Do seem to be of ours?

POLIXENES   If at home, sir,
165   He's all my exercise, my mirth, my matter;°   *concern*
Now my sworn friend and then mine enemy;
My parasite, my soldier, statesman, all.
He makes a July's day short as December;
And with his varying childness° cures in me   *youthful ways*
Thoughts that would thick my blood.[3]

LEONTES   So stands this squire
170   Officed with me.[4] We two will walk, my lord,
And leave you to your graver steps. Hermione,
How thou lov'st us show in our brother's welcome.
Let what is dear in Sicily be cheap.
175   Next to thyself and my young rover, he's
Apparent° to my heart.   *Heir apparent*

HERMIONE   If you would seek us,
We are yours i'th' garden. Shall's attend you there?

LEONTES   To your own bents° dispose you. You'll be found,   *inclinations*
Be you beneath the sky. [*aside*] I am angling° now,   *fishing; scheming*
180   Though you perceive me not how I give line.
Go to, go to!
How she holds up the neb, the bill, to him[5]
And arms her° with the boldness of a wife   *herself*
To her allowing° husband.   *approving*

            [*Exeunt* POLIXENES *and* HERMIONE.]
                 Gone already!
185   Inch-thick, knee-deep, o'er head and ears a forked° one.   *horned*
—Go play, boy, play. —Thy mother plays,° and I   *dallies sexually*
Play° too, but so disgraced a part, whose issue[6]   *Play a role*
Will hiss me to my grave. Contempt and clamor
Will be my knell.° —Go play, boy, play. —There have been,   *death bell*
190   Or I am much deceived, cuckolds ere now,
And many a man there is, even at this present,
Now, while I speak this, holds his wife by th'arm,
That little thinks she has been sluiced[7] in's absence,
And his pond[8] fished by his next neighbor, by
195   Sir Smile, his neighbor.[9] Nay, there's comfort in't

---

1. *Will . . . money?*: A proverbial expression meaning "Will you accept a trifle in place of something valuable?"
2. *happy . . . dole*: proverbial for "May you have good luck!"
3. Ideas that would make me melancholy, a physical and emotional malady connected with a supposed excess of "thick blood."
4. *So . . . me*: So this young man performs the same duty for me.
5. *How . . . him*: How she holds up her face, her mouth to him (to be kissed).
6. Outcome, with puns on "issue" as also meaning "offspring" and "the exit an actor makes from a

stage." Leontes' words imply that in playing the part of a cuckold, the result of his role will be disgrace; the illegitimate offspring produced by his wife will bring him disgrace; and his exit from the stage (at death) will be a disgraceful one.
7. Little thinks she has had sexual relations. A sluice was a trough or channel through which water could be directed. To be sluiced was to have water poured down one's "channel," here probably referring to the vagina.
8. Slang term for the sexual organs of his wife.
9. It is possible that "Sir Smile" is a reference to Polixenes.

Whiles other men have gates[1] and those gates opened,
As mine, against their will. Should all despair
That have revolted° wives, the tenth of mankind   *rebellious; unfaithful*
Would hang themselves. Physic° for't there's none.   *Medicine*
200 It is a bawdy planet that will strike
Where 'tis predominant;[2] and 'tis powerful, think it,
From east, west, north, and south; be it concluded,
No barricado for a belly.[3] Know't,
It will let in and out the enemy
205 With bag and baggage.[4] Many thousand on 's°   *of us*
Have the disease and feel't not. —How now, boy?
MAMILLIUS   I am like you, they say.
LEONTES   Why, that's some comfort.
    —What, Camillo there?
CAMILLO [*coming forward*]   Ay, my good lord.
LEONTES   Go play, Mamillius. Thou'rt an honest man.
                              [*Exit* MAMILLIUS.]
210 Camillo, this great sir will yet stay longer.
CAMILLO   You had much ado to make his anchor hold.
When you cast out, it still came home.°   *always failed to hold*
LEONTES   Didst note it?
CAMILLO   He would not stay at your petitions, made
His business more material.°   *important*
LEONTES   Didst perceive it?
215 [*aside*] They're here with me[5] already, whisp'ring, rounding,°   *murmuring*
"Sicilia is a so-forth." 'Tis far gone
When I shall gust° it last. —How came't, Camillo,   *perceive; taste*
That he did stay?
CAMILLO   At the good Queen's entreaty.
LEONTES   "At the Queen's" be't. "Good" should be pertinent,
220 But so° it is, it is not. Was this taken°   *as / perceived*
By any understanding pate° but thine?   *head*
For thy conceit is soaking,° will draw in   *your wit is quick*
More than the common blocks.° Not noted, is't,   *dimwits*
But of° the finer natures, by some severals°   *by / individuals*
225 Of headpiece° extraordinary? Lower messes[6]   *intellect*
Perchance are to this business purblind?° Say.   *blind*
CAMILLO   Business, my lord? I think most understand
Bohemia stays here longer.
LEONTES   Ha?
230 CAMILLO   Stays here longer.
LEONTES   Ay, but why?
CAMILLO   To satisfy your highness and the entreaties
Of our most gracious mistress.
LEONTES   Satisfy?[7]
Th'entreaties of your mistress? Satisfy?
235 Let that suffice. I have trusted thee, Camillo,
With all the nearest things to my heart, as well

---

1. Another slang term for female genitalia. Leontes imagines the vulva as a gateway that ought to be entered only by a husband.
2. Alluding to the notion that planets control human actions and may exercise malign influences ("strike") when they are in certain "predominant" positions.
3. No means of defending a womb.
4. With full military (or sexual) equipment.
5. They know my secret.
6. Those of lower social status at the dining table. A "mess" refers to a group of four people who share meals together.
7. Punning on "satisfy" as meaning both "appease" and "give sexual pleasure to."

My chamber-counsels,° wherein, priestlike, thou   *secret matters*
Hast cleansed my bosom. I from thee departed
Thy penitent reformed. But we have been
240   Deceived in thy integrity, deceived
In that which seems so.

CAMILLO   Be it forbid, my lord.

LEONTES   To bide° upon't: thou art not honest; or   *dwell*
If thou inclin'st that way, thou art a coward,
Which hoxes° honesty behind, restraining   *disables; hamstrings*
245   From course required;[8] or else thou must be counted
A servant grafted in my serious trust,[9]
And therein negligent; or else a fool
That seest a game played home,° the rich stake drawn,°   *in earnest / won*
And tak'st it all for jest.

CAMILLO   My gracious lord,
250   I may be negligent, foolish, and fearful.
In every one of these no man is free,°   *guiltless*
But that his negligence, his folly, fear,
Among the infinite doings of the world,
Sometime puts forth.° In your affairs, my lord,   *reveals itself*
255   If ever I were willful-negligent,
It was my folly; if industriously°   *deliberately*
I played the fool, it was my negligence,
Not weighing well the end. If ever fearful
To do a thing where I the issue° doubted,   *outcome*
260   Whereof the execution did cry out
Against the non-performance,[1] 'twas a fear
Which oft infects the wisest. These, my lord,
Are such allowed infirmities that honesty
Is never free of. But beseech your grace
265   Be plainer with me; let me know my trespass
By its own visage.° If I then deny it,   *face*
'Tis none of mine.

LEONTES   Ha' not you seen, Camillo—
But that's past doubt; you have, or your eye-glass°   *the lens of your eye*
Is thicker than a cuckold's horn—or heard—
270   For, to a vision° so apparent, rumor   *sight*
Cannot be mute—or thought—for cogitation
Resides not in that man that does not think—
My wife is slippery? If thou wilt confess,
Or else be impudently negative,°   *shamelessly deny*
275   To have nor eyes, nor ears, nor thought, then say
My wife's a hobby-horse,[2] deserves a name
As rank° as any flax-wench[3] that puts to°   *indecent / has sexual relations*
Before her troth-plight.° Say't and justify't.   *betrothal*

CAMILLO   I would not be a stander-by to hear
280   My sovereign mistress clouded so without

---

8. *restraining . . . required:* keeping (honesty) from the path it must take (to find out truth).
9. A servant who has grown into my confidence as a cutting is grafted onto a plant.
1. *Whereof . . . non-performance:* Even when the need to do the deed protested against its non-performance.

2. Whore. The image is of a woman who, like a horse, can be mounted. F has "Holy-Horse," an obscure phrase that nearly all modern editors emend to "hobby-horse."
3. A girl or woman, usually of low social status, who worked with flax, a fibrous plant used to make candlewicks, clothing, and linen.

My present° vengeance taken. 'Shrew° my heart,   *immediate / Curse*
You never spoke what did become you less
Than this, which to reiterate° were sin   *repeat*
As deep as that, though true.[4]

LEONTES   Is whispering nothing?
285 Is leaning cheek to cheek? Is meeting noses?
Kissing with inside lip? Stopping the career°   *full gallop*
Of laughter with a sigh—a note° infallible   *sign*
Of breaking honesty?° Horsing foot on foot?[5]   *violating chastity*
Skulking in corners? Wishing clocks more swift?
290 Hours minutes? Noon midnight? And all eyes
Blind with the pin and web° but theirs, theirs only,   *cataract disease*
That would unseen be wicked? Is this nothing?
Why, then, the world and all that's in't is nothing,
The covering sky is nothing, Bohemia nothing,
295 My wife is nothing, nor nothing have these nothings[6]
If this be nothing.

CAMILLO   Good my lord, be cured
Of this diseased opinion, and betimes,°   *quickly*
For 'tis most dangerous.

LEONTES   Say it be, 'tis true.

CAMILLO   No, no, my lord.

LEONTES   It is. You lie, you lie.
300 I say thou liest, Camillo, and I hate thee,
Pronounce thee a gross lout, a mindless slave,
Or else a hovering° temporizer, that   *irresolute*
Canst with thine eyes at once see good and evil,
Inclining to them both. Were my wife's liver
305 Infected as her life,[7] she would not live
The running of one glass.°   *hourglass*

CAMILLO   Who does infect her?

LEONTES   Why he that wears her like her medal,[8] hanging
About his neck—Bohemia—who, if I
Had servants true about me that bare° eyes   *possessed*
310 To see alike mine honor as their profits,
Their own particular thrifts,° they would do that   *personal gain*
Which should undo° more doing.° Ay, and thou   *stop / sexual acts*
His cupbearer[9]—whom I from meaner form°   *lower rank or place*
Have benched and reared to worship,[1] who mayst see
315 Plainly as heaven sees earth and earth sees heaven
How I am galled°—mightst bespice a cup,   *sorely vexed*
To give mine enemy a lasting wink,[2]
Which draft to me were cordial.[3]

---

4. *sin . . . true:* that is, as grave as is the sin that you accuse your wife of, even if it were true (which it is not).
5. Mounting or rubbing one foot on another, a sexually titillating pastime.
6. Alluding to the proverbial notion that nothing can come of nothing. The word "nothing" appears many times in this play.
7. Were Hermione's liver as infected by disease as is her conduct. The liver was believed in Renaissance humoral psychology to be the seat of the passions.

8. As though she were a miniature portrait of herself. Ornate lockets ("medals") containing miniature portraits were popular love tokens among courtiers.
9. In a noble household, a male servant whose responsibilities included serving wine to his master.
1. Given authority and elevated to a dignified position. Referring to his "bench" or place at the dining table as a sign of his high rank.
2. To close my enemy's eyes forever.
3. Which drink would be medicinal to me.

CAMILLO   Sir, my lord,
　I could do this, and that with no rash° potion,   *quick-acting*
320　But with a lingering° dram that should not work   *slow-working*
　Maliciously,° like poison. But I cannot   *Violently*
　Believe this crack° to be in my dread mistress,   *flaw*
　So sovereignly being honorable.
　I have loved thee—
LEONTES   Make that thy question,° and go rot.   *concern*
325　Dost think I am so muddy, so unsettled,
　To appoint° myself in this vexation?   *put*
　Sully the purity and whiteness of my sheets—
　Which to preserve is sleep, which being spotted
　Is goads,° thorns, nettles, tails of wasps—   *sharp sticks*
330　Give scandal to the blood o'th' prince, my son,
　Who I do think is mine and love as mine,
　Without ripe moving° to't? Would I do this?   *good reason*
　Could man so blench?°   *stray (from sense)*
CAMILLO   I must believe you, sir.
　I do, and will fetch off° Bohemia for't—   *kill*
335　Provided that when he's removed your highness
　Will take again your queen as yours at first,
　Even for your son's sake, and thereby for sealing°   *silencing*
　The injury of tongues in courts and kingdoms
　Known and allied to yours.
LEONTES   Thou dost advise me
340　Even so as I mine own course have set down.
　I'll give no blemish to her honor, none.
CAMILLO　My lord, go, then, and with a countenance as clear
　As friendship wears at feasts, keep° with Bohemia   *associate*
　And with your queen. I am his cupbearer.
345　If from me he have wholesome beverage,
　Account me not your servant.
LEONTES   This is all.
　Do't, and thou hast the one half of my heart;
　Do't not, thou splitt'st thine own.
CAMILLO   I'll do't, my lord.
LEONTES　I will seem friendly, as thou hast advised me.
                                                      Exit.

350　CAMILLO　O miserable lady! But for me,
　What case stand I in? I must be the poisoner
　Of good Polixenes, and my ground to do't
　Is the obedience to a master, one
　Who in rebellion with himself will have
355　All that are his so too. To do this deed,
　Promotion follows. If I could find example
　Of thousands that had struck anointed kings
　And flourished after, I'd not do't. But since
　Nor° brass, nor stone, nor parchment bears not one,[4]   *Neither*
360　Let villainy itself forswear't.° I must   *swear not to do it*
　Forsake the court. To do't or no is certain
　To me a break-neck.° Happy° star reign now.   *death / Lucky*

---

4. *since . . . not one*: that is, since no form of historical record shows an example of a man who flourished after killing a king.

Enter POLIXENES.

Here comes Bohemia.

POLIXENES [*aside*]   This is strange. Methinks
My favor here begins to warp. Not speak?
—Good day, Camillo.

365   CAMILLO   Hail, most royal sir.

POLIXENES   What is the news i'th' court?

CAMILLO   None rare,° my lord.   *noteworthy*

POLIXENES   The King hath on him such a countenance
As° he had lost some province and a region   *As if*
Loved as he loves himself. Even now I met him
370   With customary compliment, when he,
Wafting his eyes to th' contrary° and falling   *Shifting his gaze away*
A lip of much contempt,° speeds from me and   *sneering*
So leaves me to consider what is breeding
That changes thus his manners.

CAMILLO   I dare not know, my lord.

375   POLIXENES   How? "Dare not"? Do not? Do you know and dare not?
Be intelligent° to me—'tis thereabouts.[5]   *informative*
For to yourself what you do know you must,°   *(know)*
And cannot say you dare not. Good Camillo,
Your changed complexions are to me a mirror
380   Which shows me mine changed too; for I must be
A party in this alteration,° finding   *(of Leontes' manner)*
Myself thus altered with't.

CAMILLO   There is a sickness
Which puts some of us in distemper, but
I cannot name the disease, and it is caught
Of you that yet are well.

385   POLIXENES   How caught of me?
Make me not sighted like the basilisk.[6]
I have looked on thousands who have sped° the better   *fared*
By my regard, but killed none so. Camillo—
As you are certainly a gentleman, thereto
390   Clerk-like experienced,[7] which no less adorns
Our gentry° than our parents' noble names,   *status as gentlemen*
In whose success we are gentle[8]—I beseech you,
If you know aught which does behoove my knowledge
Thereof to be informed,[9] imprison't not
In ignorant concealment.[1]

395   CAMILLO   I may not answer.

POLIXENES   A sickness caught of me, and yet I well?
I must be answered. Dost thou hear, Camillo—,
I conjure thee, by all the parts° of man   *duties*
Which honor does acknowledge, whereof the least
400   Is not this suit of mine, that thou declare
What incidency° thou dost guess of harm   *event*
Is creeping toward me; how far off, how near,

---

5. That is, I'm more or less right (that you are afraid
to tell me).
6. A mythical serpent whose glance was said to be
fatal.
7. Also having the experience of an educated man.
8. *In whose . . . gentle:* By succession from whom we

are made noble ("gentle").
9. *which . . . informed:* which it is necessary for me
to know.
1. In concealment that keeps me ignorant; in concealment on the pretense that you are ignorant.

Which way to be prevented, if to be;
If not, how best to bear it.
CAMILLO   Sir, I will tell you,
405 Since I am charged in honor and by him
That I think honorable. Therefore mark my counsel,
Which must be e'en as swiftly followed as
I mean to utter it; or both yourself and me
Cry lost, and so good night.°   *good-bye forever*
POLIXENES   On, good Camillo.
410 CAMILLO   I am appointed him° to murder you.   *by him*
POLIXENES   By whom, Camillo?
CAMILLO   By the King.
POLIXENES   For what?
CAMILLO   He thinks—nay, with all confidence he swears,
As he had seen't or been an instrument
To vice° you to't—that you have touched his queen   *force*
Forbiddenly.
415 POLIXENES   Oh, then my best blood turn
To an infected jelly and my name
Be yoked with his° that did betray the best.°   *(Judas's) name / Christ*
Turn then my freshest reputation to
A savor° that may strike the dullest nostril   *foul odor*
420 Where I arrive and my approach be shunned—
Nay, hated too—worse than the greatest infection
That e'er was heard or read.
CAMILLO   Swear his thought over[2]
By each particular star in heaven and
By all their influences,[3] you may as well
425 Forbid the sea for to obey the moon
As or° by oath remove or counsel shake   *either*
The fabric of his folly, whose foundation
Is piled upon his faith and will continue
The standing of his body.°   *As long as he lives*
POLIXENES   How should this grow?°   *come to be*
430 CAMILLO   I know not. But I am sure 'tis safer to
Avoid what's grown than question how 'tis born.
If therefore you dare trust my honesty
That lies enclosèd in this trunk,° which you   *body*
Shall bear along impawned,[4] away tonight!
435 Your followers I will whisper to the business
And will by twos and threes at several posterns°   *city gates*
Clear them o'th' city. For myself, I'll put
My fortunes to your service, which are here
By this discovery° lost. Be not uncertain,   *revelation*
440 For by the honor of my parents, I
Have uttered truth; which if you seek to prove,
I dare not stand by, nor shall you be safer
Than one condemnèd by the King's own mouth,
Thereon his execution sworn.
POLIXENES   I do believe thee.
445 I saw his heart in 's face. Give me thy hand;

2. You may swear that his allegations are false.
3. Substances that, according to contemporary astrological theories, were emitted by stars and
helped to shape human destiny.
4. Shall carry with you as a pledge (of my faith).

Be pilot to me, and thy places° shall ⟶ *your position*
Still neighbor° mine. My ships are ready, and ⟶ *Always be near*
My people did expect my hence departure
Two days ago. This jealousy
450 Is for a precious creature. As she's rare,
Must it be great; and as his person's mighty,
Must it be violent; and as he does conceive
He is dishonored by a man which ever
Professed° to him, why, his revenges must ⟶ *Vowed love*
455 In that be made more bitter. Fear o'ershades me.
Good expedition° be my friend, and comfort ⟶ *speed (in leaving)*
The gracious Queen, part of his theme, but nothing
Of his ill-ta'en suspicion.⁵ Come, Camillo,
I will respect thee as a father if
460 Thou bear'st my life off hence. Let us avoid.° ⟶ *be gone*
CAMILLO   It is in mine authority to command
The keys of all the posterns. Please your highness
To take the urgent hour.° Come, sir, away.   *Exeunt.* ⟶ *seize the moment*

2.1

Enter HERMIONE, MAMILLIUS, [*and*] LADIES.¹
HERMIONE   Take the boy to you; he so troubles me,
'Tis past enduring.
FIRST LADY   Come, my gracious lord,
Shall I be your playfellow?
MAMILLIUS   No, I'll none of you.
5 FIRST LADY   Why, my sweet lord?
MAMILLIUS   You'll kiss me hard and speak to me as if
I were a baby still. [*to* SECOND LADY] I love you better.
SECOND LADY   And why so, my lord?
MAMILLIUS   Not for° because ⟶ *Not*
Your brows° are blacker—yet black brows they say ⟶ *eyebrows*
10 Become° some women best, so° that there be not ⟶ *Suit / provided*
Too much hair there, but in a semicircle
Or a half-moon made with a pen.
SECOND LADY   Who taught° this? ⟶ *taught you*
MAMILLIUS   I learned it out of women's faces. Pray now,
What color are your eyebrows?
SECOND LADY   Blue, my lord.
15 MAMILLIUS   Nay, that's a mock. I have seen a lady's nose
That has been blue,² but not her eyebrows.
FIRST LADY   Hark ye,
The Queen your mother rounds apace;° we shall ⟶ *grows round quickly*
Present our services to a fine new prince

---

5. *and comfort . . . suspicion:* and make easier the situation of the virtuous Queen, who is a part of Leontes' accusation (his proposition, or "theme"), but who is not guilty of his unjustified suspicion.
2.1 Location: Sicilia. The palace of Leontes.
1. TEXTUAL COMMENT Although the Folio text lists all the characters who appear in this scene as entering here, it makes more sense to have Leontes and Antigonus enter later (in this edition, between lines 33 and 34) and interrupt the conversation among Hermione, Mamillius, and the Ladies. See Digital Edition TC 3.
2. It is unclear whether Mamillius is making a joke here or possibly referring to noses made "blue" by the cold.

One of these days, and then you'd wanton° with us,   *play*
 If we would have you.
20 SECOND LADY   She is spread of late
 Into a goodly bulk: good time encounter her!° *good fortune be with her*
 HERMIONE What wisdom stirs amongst you? Come, sir, now
 I am for you again. Pray you sit by us
 And tell's a tale.
 MAMILLIUS   Merry or sad shall't be?
25 HERMIONE As merry as you will.
 MAMILLIUS A sad tale's best for winter. I have one
 Of sprites and goblins.
 HERMIONE   Let's have that, good sir.
 Come on, sit down; come on, and do your best
 To fright me with your sprites. You're powerful at it.
 MAMILLIUS There was a man—
30 HERMIONE   Nay, come, sit down; then on.
 MAMILLIUS Dwelt by a churchyard—I will tell it softly;
 Yond crickets° shall not hear it.   *(the other women)*
 HERMIONE Come on, then, and give't me in mine ear.
   [*Enter* LEONTES, ANTIGONUS, *and* LORDS.]
 LEONTES Was he met there? His train?° Camillo with him? *retinue*
35 LORD Behind the tuft of pines I met them. Never
 Saw I men scour° so on their way. I eyed them *hurry*
 Even to their ships.
 LEONTES   How blest am I
 In my just censure,° in my true opinion!   *judgment*
 Alack, for lesser knowledge!° How accursed *Would I knew less*
40 In being so blest! There may be in the cup
 A spider steeped, and one may drink, depart,
 And yet partake no venom, for his knowledge
 Is not infected.[3] But if one present
 Th'abhorred ingredient to his eye, make known
45 How he hath drunk, he cracks his gorge,° his sides *throat*
 With violent hefts.° I have drunk and seen the spider. *retching*
 Camillo was his help in this, his pander.[4]
 There is a plot against my life, my crown.
 All's true that is mistrusted.° That false villain *suspected*
50 Whom I employed was pre-employed by him.
 He has discovered° my design, and I   *revealed*
 Remain a pinched° thing—yea, a very trick *tormented*
 For them to play at will. How came the posterns
 So easily open?
 LORD   By his great authority,
55 Which often hath no less prevailed than so
 On your command.
 LEONTES   I know't too well.
  [*to* HERMIONE] Give me the boy; I am glad you did not nurse him.[5]
 Though he does bear some signs of me, yet you
 Have too much blood in him.

---

3. Alluding to the belief that a spider consumed with food or drink would be poisonous only if its presence were known to the consumer.
4. A go-between; one who facilitates illicit sexual encounters.
5. Women who breast-fed infants were believed to shape an infant's character by substances transmitted in their milk.

HERMIONE   What is this? Sport?
60 LEONTES   Bear the boy hence; he shall not come about her.
        Away with him, and let her sport herself
        With that she's big with, [*to* HERMIONE] for 'tis Polixenes
        Has made thee swell thus.   [*Exit one with* MAMILLIUS.]
    HERMIONE   But I'd say he had not;
        And I'll be sworn you would believe my saying,
        Howe'er you lean to th' nayward.°   *the contrary*
65 LEONTES   You, my lords,
        Look on her; mark her well. Be but about
        To say she is a goodly lady, and
        The justice of your hearts will thereto add,
        "'Tis pity she's not honest,° honorable."   *chaste*
70   Praise her but for this her without-door° form—   *external*
        Which on my faith deserves high speech—and straight°   *immediately*
        The shrug, the "hum," or "ha," these petty brands°   *expressions; stigmas*
        That calumny° doth use—oh, I am out!°—   *slander / wrong*
        That mercy does, for calumny will sear°   *dry up; wither*
75   Virtue itself[6]—these shrugs, these "hum's" and "ha's,"
        When you have said she's goodly, come between°   *interrupt*
        Ere you can say she's honest. But be't known
        From him that has most cause to grieve it should be,
        She's an adultress.
    HERMIONE   Should a villain say so,
80   The most replenished° villain in the world,   *complete*
        He were as much more° villain. You, my lord,   *by so much more a*
        Do but mistake.
    LEONTES   You have mistook,° my lady,   *erred; improperly taken*
        Polixenes for Leontes. O thou thing
        Which I'll not call a creature of thy place[7]
85   Lest barbarism,° making me the precedent,   *uncivilized rudeness*
        Should a like° language use to all degrees°   *the same / ranks*
        And mannerly distinguishment° leave out   *proper distinction*
        Betwixt the prince and beggar. I have said
        She's an adultress; I have said with whom.
90   More, she's a traitor; and Camillo is
        A federary° with her, and one that knows   *confederate*
        What she should shame to know herself
        But with her most vile principal,° that she's   *partner*
        A bed-swerver,° even as bad as those   *adultress*
95   That vulgars give bold'st titles[8]—ay, and privy
        To this their late° escape.   *recent*
    HERMIONE   No, by my life,
        Privy to none of this. How will this grieve you
        When you shall come to clearer knowledge, that
        You thus have published° me! Gentle my° lord,   *proclaimed / My noble*
100   You scarce can right me thoroughly° then to say   *fully do me justice*
        You did mistake.
    LEONTES   No. If I mistake

---

6. On obscure passage. Leontes seems to mean that
even mercy will use "hum's" and "ha's" to condemn
Hermione because mercy's virtue has been dried up
by calumny's force.

7. To whom I'll not give the title of your (high) social
position.
8. That common people call by the coarsest names.

In those foundations which I build upon,
The center° is not big enough to bear   *earth*
A schoolboy's top. —Away with her to prison.
105　He who shall speak for her is afar-off° guilty,   *indirectly*
But that he speaks.°   *Merely for speaking*
HERMIONE　　　　　　　　There's some ill planet reigns.
I must be patient till the heavens look
With an aspect more favorable.⁹ Good my° lords,   *My good*
I am not prone to weeping as our sex
110　Commonly are, the want° of which vain dew   *lack*
Perchance shall dry your pities. But I have
That honorable grief lodged here which burns
Worse than tears drown. Beseech you all, my lords,
With thoughts so qualified° as your charities   *tempered*
115　Shall best instruct you, measure me; and so
The King's will be performed.
LEONTES　　　　　　　　Shall I be heard?
HERMIONE　Who is't that goes with me? Beseech your highness
My women may be with me, for you see
My plight requires it. —Do not weep, good fools;°   *dear ones*
120　There is no cause. When you shall know your mistress
Has deserved prison, then abound in tears
As I come out. This action I now go on
Is for my better grace.¹ —Adieu, my lord.
I never wished to see you sorry; now
125　I trust I shall. My women, come, you have leave.°   *permission*
LEONTES　　Go, do our bidding. Hence.
　　　　　　　　　　　　　　　[*Exit* HERMIONE *with* LADIES.]
LORD　　Beseech your highness, call the Queen again.
ANTIGONUS　　Be certain what you do, sir, lest your justice
Prove violence, in the which three great ones suffer:
Yourself, your queen, your son.
130　LORD　　　　　　　　　　For her, my lord,
I dare my life lay down, and will do't, sir.
Please you t'accept it that the Queen is spotless
I'th' eyes of heaven, and to you—I mean
In this which you accuse her.
ANTIGONUS　　　　　　　　If it prove
135　She's otherwise, I'll keep my stables where
I lodge my wife;² I'll go in couples with her;³
Than when I feel and see her, no farther trust her.
For every inch of woman in the world—
Ay, every dram° of woman's flesh—is false   *smallest piece*
If she be.
LEONTES　　Hold your peaces.
140　LORD　　　　　　　　Good my lord—
ANTIGONUS　　It is for you we speak, not for ourselves.
You are abused, and by some putter-on°   *instigator*

9. Until the planets are aligned to have a more positive effect (on Hermione's fate).
1. *This action . . . grace:* This trial I am enduring is
for my greater honor (when vindicated); *or* This suffering I am enduring is to refine and purge me, leading to greater virtue. In both cases, an affirmation of
Hermione's confidence and her innocence.

2. *If it prove . . . wife:* an obscure passage. Antigonus
probably means that if Hermione is unchaste, he will
keep his horses in his wife's bedchamber since all
women will have shown themselves no better than
beasts.
3. *go . . . her:* have her tied to me (as hounds were
leashed together for the hunt).

That will be damned for't. Would I knew the villain,
I would land-damn him.[4] Be she honor-flawed,
145   I have three daughters—the eldest is eleven;
The second and the third, nine and some five—
If this prove true, they'll pay for't. By mine honor,
I'll geld 'em all;[5] fourteen they shall not see
To bring false generations.° They are co-heirs,   *illegitimate children*
150   And I had rather glib° myself than they   *castrate*
Should not produce fair issue.°   *legitimate offspring*

LEONTES   Cease, no more.
You smell this business with a sense as cold
As is a dead man's nose. But I do see't and feel't,
As you feel doing thus; and see withal
The instruments that feel.[6]

155   ANTIGONUS   If it be so,
We need no grave to bury honesty;°   *chastity*
There's not a grain of it the face to sweeten°   *to sweeten the face*
Of the whole dungy° earth.   *foul*

LEONTES   What? Lack I credit?

LORD   I had rather you did lack than I, my lord,
160   Upon this ground;° and more it would content me   *In this affair*
To have her honor true than your suspicion,
Be blamed for't how you might.

LEONTES   Why, what need we
Commune with you of this, but rather follow
Our forceful instigation?° Our prerogative   *impulse; motive*
165   Calls not your counsels,[7] but our natural goodness
Imparts this,° which if you—or° stupefied   *this information / either*
Or seeming so in skill°—cannot or will not   *cunningly*
Relish° a truth like us, inform yourselves   *Appreciate*
We need no more of your advice. The matter—
170   The loss, the gain, the ordering on't°—   *of it*
Is all properly ours.

ANTIGONUS   And I wish, my liege,
You had only in your silent judgment tried it,
Without more overture.°   *public disclosure*

LEONTES   How could that be?
Either thou art most ignorant by age,
175   Or thou wert born a fool. Camillo's flight,
Added to their familiarity—
Which was as gross as ever touched conjecture,
That lacked sight only, naught for approbation
But only seeing;[8] all other circumstances
180   Made up to th' deed°—doth push on this proceeding.[9]   *Pointed to the deed*
Yet, for a greater confirmation—
For in an act of this importance 'twere
Most piteous to be wild°—I have dispatched in post,°   *rash / haste*

4. *land-damn*: a term of abuse whose exact meaning
is unclear. It may be a dialect form of "lamback" or
"lambaste," which means "thrash."
5. I'll make them all barren. Literally, I'll cut out
their organs of generation.
6. Leontes here probably does some action (touching
a courtier or rubbing his hands together) that shows
how immediately or directly he feels Hermione's
betrayal and sees as well the fingers ("instruments")

with which he touches things, and with which Hermione and Polixenes touch each other.
7. *Our . . . counsels*: My privileges as King do not
require that I seek your advice.
8. *as gross . . . seeing*: as obvious ("gross") as any suspicion ("conjecture") ever was that only lacked eye-
witnesses ("sight" and "seeing") to confirm its truth.
9. Does urge on this course of action.

To sacred Delphos,[1] to Apollo's temple,
185 Cleomenes and Dion, whom you know
Of stuffed sufficiency.° Now from the oracle   *ample competence*
They will bring all, whose spiritual counsel had,°   *obtained*
Shall stop or spur me. Have I done well?
LORD   Well done, my lord.
190 LEONTES   Though I am satisfied and need no more
Than what I know, yet shall the oracle
Give rest to th' minds of others, such as he
Whose ignorant credulity will not
Come up to th' truth. So have we thought it good
195 From our free° person she should be confined,   *openly accessible*
Lest that the treachery of the two fled hence
Be left her to perform. Come, follow us.
We are to speak in public, for this business
Will raise° us all.   *rouse (to action)*
ANTIGONUS [*aside*]   To laughter, as I take it,
200 If the good truth were known.   *Exeunt.*

2.2

Enter PAULINA, *a Gentleman*[, *and Attendants*].
PAULINA   The keeper of the prison, call to him.
Let him have knowledge who I am.   [*Exit Gentleman.*]
                              Good lady,[1]
No court in Europe is too good for thee.
What dost thou then in prison?
          [*Enter Gentleman with* JAILER.]
                              Now, good sir,
You know me, do you not?
5 JAILER   For a worthy lady,
And one who much I honor.
PAULINA   Pray you, then,
Conduct me to the Queen.
JAILER   I may not, madam.
To the contrary I have express commandment.
PAULINA   Here's ado,°   *Here's such a fuss*
10 To lock up honesty and honor from
Th'access of gentle° visitors. Is't lawful, pray you,   *noble; kind*
To see her women? Any of them? Emilia?
JAILER   So please you, madam,
To put apart these your attendants, I
Shall bring Emilia forth.
15 PAULINA   I pray now call her.
—Withdraw yourselves. [*Exeunt Gentleman and Attendants.*]
JAILER   And, madam,
I must be present at your conference.
PAULINA   Well, be't so, prithee.   [*Exit* JAILER.]
20 Here's such ado to make no stain a stain
As passes coloring.[2]

---

1. Delos, often called Delphos by Renaissance writers, was the island where Apollo, the sun god, was born. It is here conflated with Delphi, the Greek mainland town where the oracle of Apollo could be consulted.
2.2 Location: Sicilia. A prison.

1. *Good lady*: Paulina is addressing Hermione here, even though she has not yet been admitted to her presence.
2. To make from no stain at all a stain that exceeds what the art of dyeing can do; to make of no sin a sin that surpasses all attempts to justify it.

[*Enter* JAILER *and* EMILIA.]
Dear gentlewoman,

How fares our gracious lady?

EMILIA As well as one so great and so forlorn
May hold together. On° her frights and griefs,   *Because of*
25 Which never tender lady hath borne greater,
She is something° before her time delivered.   *somewhat*

PAULINA A boy?

EMILIA   A daughter and a goodly babe,
Lusty° and like° to live. The Queen receives   *Vigorous / likely*
Much comfort in't; says, "My poor prisoner,
I am innocent as you."

30 PAULINA   I dare be sworn.
These dangerous unsafe lunes° i'th' King, beshrew them.   *fits of lunacy*
He must be told on't, and he shall. The office°   *job*
Becomes a woman best. I'll take't upon me.
If I prove honey-mouthed, let my tongue blister[3]
35 And never to my red-looked° anger be   *red-faced*
The trumpet[4] any more. Pray you, Emilia,
Commend° my best obedience to the Queen.   *Send*
If she dares trust me with her little babe,
I'll show't the King, and undertake to be
40 Her advocate to th' loud'st. We do not know
How he may soften at the sight o'th' child.
The silence often of pure innocence
Persuades when speaking fails.

EMILIA   Most worthy madam,
Your honor and your goodness is so evident
45 That your free° undertaking cannot miss   *generous*
A thriving issue;[5] there is no lady living
So meet° for this great errand. Please your ladyship   *suitable*
To visit the next room; I'll presently
Acquaint the Queen of your most noble offer,
50 Who but today hammered of° this design   *mused upon*
But durst not tempt a minister of honor[6]
Lest she should be denied.

PAULINA   Tell her, Emilia,
I'll use that tongue I have. If wit flow from't
As boldness from my bosom, let't not be doubted
I shall do good.

55 EMILIA   Now be you blest for it!
I'll to the Queen. Please you come something° nearer.   *somewhat*

JAILER Madam, if't please the Queen to send the babe,
I know not what° I shall incur to pass it,[7]   *what risk*
Having no warrant.

PAULINA   You need not fear it, sir.
60 This child was prisoner to the womb and is
By law and process of great nature thence
Freed and enfranchised, not a party to

---

3. Alluding to the proverb that deceitfulness causes blisters on the tongue.
4. In early modern warfare, a "trumpet" was a soldier who, bearing a trumpet, went before the red-coated herald who carried messages, often angry ones, to the enemy camp.
5. A successful outcome, with a pun on "issue" as "offspring."
6. But dared not risk asking a person of higher rank.
7. To let it pass (out of the prison).

The anger of the King, nor guilty of—
If any be—the trespass of the Queen.

65 JAILER I do believe it.

PAULINA Do not you fear. Upon mine honor, I
Will stand betwixt you and danger.   *Exeunt.*

2.3

Enter LEONTES.

LEONTES Nor° night nor day, no rest. It is but weakness   *Neither*
To bear the matter thus—mere weakness. If
The cause were not in being°—part o'th' cause,   *alive*
She, th'adultress; for the harlot° King   *lewd*
5   Is quite beyond mine arm, out of the blank°   *target*
And level° of my brain, plot-proof. But she   *aim*
I can hook to me. Say that she were gone,
Given to the fire,[1] a moiety° of my rest   *portion*
Might come to me again. Who's there?
          [*Enter* SERVANT.]

SERVANT   My lord.

LEONTES How does the boy?

10 SERVANT   He took good rest tonight.
'Tis hoped his sickness is discharged.

LEONTES To see his nobleness!
Conceiving° the dishonor of his mother,   .   *Realizing*
He straight° declined, drooped, took it deeply,   *immediately*
15 Fastened and fixed the shame on't° in himself,   *of it*
Threw off his spirit, his appetite, his sleep,
And downright languished. Leave me solely.° Go,   *alone*
See how he fares.   [*Exit* SERVANT.]
              Fie, fie, no thought of him!°   *(Polixenes)*
The very thought of my revenges that way
20 Recoil upon me. In himself too mighty,
And in his parties,° his alliance.° Let him be   *supporters / allies*
Until a time may serve. For present vengeance
Take it on her. Camillo and Polixenes
Laugh at me, make their pastime at my sorrow.
25 They should not laugh if I could reach them, nor
Shall she, within my power.
          Enter PAULINA [*with the baby,* ANTIGONUS, LORDS,
          and SERVANT].

LORD   You must not enter.

PAULINA Nay, rather, good my lords, be second to me.°   *help me*
Fear you his tyrannous passion more, alas,
Than the Queen's life? A gracious innocent soul,
More free° than he is jealous.   *innocent*

30 ANTIGONUS   That's enough.

SERVANT Madam, he hath not slept tonight, commanded
None should come at him.

PAULINA   Not so hot, good sir.
I come to bring him sleep. 'Tis such as you,
That creep like shadows by him and do sigh
35 At each his needless heavings—such as you

2.3 Location: Sicilia. The palace of Leontes.   1. Burned at the stake (for treason against the King).

Nourish the cause of his awaking.° I   *wakefulness*
Do come with words, as medicinal as true,
Honest as either, to purge him of that humor°   *mental disorder*
That presses him from sleep.
LEONTES   What noise there, ho?
40 PAULINA   No noise, my lord, but needful conference
About some gossips² for your highness.
LEONTES   How?
Away with that audacious lady! Antigonus,
I charged thee that she should not come about me.
I knew she would.
ANTIGONUS   I told her so, my lord,
45   On your displeasure's peril° and on mine,   *At the risk of your anger*
She should not visit you.
LEONTES   What, canst not rule her?
PAULINA   From all dishonesty he can. In this,
Unless he take the course that you have done—
Commit° me for committing honor—trust it,   *Imprison*
He shall not rule me.
50 ANTIGONUS   La you now,° you hear.   *Observe this now*
When she will take the rein, I let her run,
But she'll not stumble.
PAULINA [to LEONTES]   Good my liege, I come—
And I beseech you hear me, who professes
Myself your loyal servant, your physician,
55   Your most obedient counselor, yet that dares
Less appear so in comforting° your evils   *condoning*
Than such as most seem yours³—I say I come
From your good queen.
LEONTES   Good queen?
PAULINA   Good queen, my lord, good queen. I say good queen,
60   And would by combat make her good,⁴ so were I
A man, the worst about° you.   *lowest in rank of*
LEONTES   Force her hence.
PAULINA   Let him that makes but trifles of his eyes
First hand° me. On mine own accord I'll off;   *touch*
But first I'll do my errand. The good Queen—
65   For she is good—hath brought you forth a daughter—
Here 'tis—commends it to your blessing.
      [PAULINA *lays down the baby.*]
LEONTES   Out!
A mankind° witch! Hence with her, out o'door—   *manlike*
A most intelligencing bawd.°   *spying go-between*
PAULINA   Not so.
I am as ignorant in that as you
70   In so entitling me,° and no less honest   *In calling me that*
Than you are mad, which is enough, I'll warrant,
As this world goes, to pass for honest.
LEONTES   Traitors!
Will you not push her out? [to ANTIGONUS] Give her the bastard,
Thou dotard; thou art woman-tired,⁵ unroosted

2. Godparents or sponsors at a child's baptism.
3. Than those who (wrongly) seem most loyal.
4. Prove her to be innocent; alluding to the chivalric trials by combat in which knights would establish
innocence or guilt by means of duels.
5. You are pecked at by women; a metaphor from falconry referring to tearing of flesh with the beak.

75   By thy Dame Partlet here.[6] Take up the bastard;
     Take't up, I say; give't to thy crone.°   *old woman*

PAULINA   Forever
     Unvenerable° be thy hands if thou   *Unworthy of respect*
     Tak'st up the Princess by that forcèd baseness[7]
     Which he has put upon't.

LEONTES   He dreads° his wife.   *fears*

80 PAULINA   So I would you did. Then 'twere past all doubt
     You'd call your children yours.

LEONTES   A nest of traitors!

ANTIGONUS   I am none, by this good light.

PAULINA   Nor I, nor any
     But one that's here, and that's himself; for he
     The sacred honor of himself, his queen's,
85   His hopeful son's, his babe's, betrays to slander,
     Whose sting is sharper than the sword's; and will not—
     For as the case now stands, it is a curse
     He cannot be compelled to't—once remove
     The root of his opinion, which is rotten
     As ever oak or stone was sound.

90 LEONTES   A callet°   *scold; harlot*
     Of boundless tongue, who late° hath beat her husband   *recently*
     And now baits° me. This brat is none of mine;   *provokes*
     It is the issue° of Polixenes.   *offspring*
     Hence with it, and together with the dam
     Commit them to the fire!

95 PAULINA   It is yours,
     And might we lay th'old proverb to your charge,°   *apply the proverb to you*
     So like you 'tis the worse. Behold, my lords,
     Although the print° be little, the whole matter   *copy*
     And copy of the father: eye, nose, lip,
100   The trick° of 's frown, his forehead, nay, the valley,[8]   *distinctive character*
     The pretty dimples of his chin and cheek, his smiles,
     The very mold and frame of hand, nail, finger.
     And thou, good goddess Nature, which hast made it
     So like to him that got° it, if thou hast   *begot*
105   The ordering of the mind too, 'mongst all colors
     No yellow[9] in't, lest she suspect, as he does,
     Her children not her husband's.

LEONTES   A gross hag!
     And, [*to* ANTIGONUS] lozel,° thou art worthy to be hanged   *scoundrel*
     That wilt not stay her tongue.

ANTIGONUS   Hang all the husbands
110   That cannot do that feat, you'll leave yourself
     Hardly one subject.

LEONTES   Once more take her hence.

PAULINA   A most unworthy and unnatural lord
     Can do no more.

LEONTES   I'll ha' thee burnt.

PAULINA   I care not.

---

6. *unroosted . . . here:* expelled from your "roost" or "perch," the position of domestic authority assigned to men. "Partlet" is a traditional name for a hen.
7. Under that wrongful name of bastard.

8. Referring to an indentation in the lip or a cleft in the chin.
9. Proverbially, the color of jealousy.

It is an heretic that makes the fire,
115   Not she which burns in't.[1] I'll not call you tyrant;
But this most cruel usage of your queen—
Not able to produce more accusation
Than your own weak-hinged fancy—something savors
Of tyranny and will ignoble make you,
Yea, scandalous to the world.

120 LEONTES   On your allegiance,
Out of the chamber with her! Were I a tyrant,
Where were her life? She durst not call me so,
If she did know me one. Away with her!

PAULINA   —I pray you do not push me; I'll be gone.
125   —Look to your babe, my lord; 'tis yours. Jove° send her   *(king of the gods)*
A better guiding spirit. —What needs these hands?[2]
You that are thus so tender o'er° his follies   *gentle with*
Will never do him good, not one of you.
So, so. Farewell, we are gone.   *Exit.*

130 LEONTES   Thou, traitor, hast set on thy wife to this.
My child? Away with't! Even thou that hast
A heart so tender o'er it, take it hence
And see it instantly consumed with fire.
Even thou and none but thou. Take it up straight.°   *at once*
135   Within this hour bring me word 'tis done,
And by good testimony,° or I'll seize thy life   *with good evidence*
With what thou else call'st thine. If thou refuse,
And wilt encounter with my wrath, say so.
The bastard brains with these my proper° hands   *own*
140   Shall I dash out. Go, take it to the fire,
For thou sett'st on° thy wife.   *instructed; urged on*

ANTIGONUS   I did not, sir.
These lords, my noble fellows, if they please,
Can clear me in't.

LORDS   We can. My royal liege,
He is not guilty of her coming hither.

145 LEONTES   You're liars all.

LORD   Beseech your highness, give us better credit.°   *think us more honorable*
We have always truly served you, and beseech
So to esteem of us. And on our knees we beg,
As recompense of our dear services
150   Past and to come, that you do change this purpose,
Which being so horrible, so bloody, must
Lead on to some foul issue. We all kneel.

LEONTES   I am a feather for each wind that blows.
Shall I live on to see this bastard kneel
155   And call me father? Better burn it now
Than curse it then. But be it; let it live.
It shall not neither. You, sir, come you hither,
You that have been so tenderly officious
With Lady Margery,[3] your midwife there,

---

1. *It is . . . in't:* The heretic is the one who unjustly makes the fire (Leontes), not the woman who burns in it (Paulina or Hermione).
2. *What . . . hands?:* Why is it necessary for you to push me out (spoken to Leontes' attendant lords)?
3. A contemptuous name (like "Dame Partlet") for a disorderly woman. "Margery-prater" is a slang term for "hen."

160 To save this bastard's life—for 'tis a bastard
So sure as this beard's gray. What will you adventure°   *risk*
To save this brat's life?

ANTIGONUS   Anything, my lord,
That my ability may undergo
And nobleness impose—at least thus much:
165 I'll pawn the little blood which I have left[4]
To save the innocent—anything possible.

LEONTES   It shall be possible. Swear by this sword
Thou wilt perform my bidding.

ANTIGONUS   I will, my lord.

LEONTES   Mark and perform it, seest thou? For the fail°   *failure*
170 Of any point in't shall not only be
Death to thyself but to thy lewd-tongued wife,
Whom for this time we pardon. We enjoin thee,
As thou art liegeman° to us, that thou carry   *loyal servant*
This female bastard hence and that thou bear it
175 To some remote and desert place quite out
Of our dominions; and that there thou leave it,
Without more mercy, to it° own protection   *its*
And favor of the climate. As by strange fortune[5]
It came to us, I do in justice charge thee,
180 On thy soul's peril and thy body's torture,
That thou commend it strangely to some place[6]
Where chance may nurse° or end it. Take it up.   *nurture; help*

ANTIGONUS   I swear to do this, though a present death
Had been more merciful. Come on, poor babe;
185 Some powerful spirit instruct the kites° and ravens   *birds of prey*
To be thy nurses. Wolves and bears, they say,
Casting their savageness aside, have done
Like° offices of pity. Sir, be prosperous   *Similar*
In more than this deed does require;[7] and blessing
190 Against° this cruelty fight on thy side,   *To counteract*
Poor thing, condemned to loss.°   *Exit [with the baby].*   *ruin*

LEONTES   No, I'll not rear
Another's issue.
         Enter a SERVANT.

SERVANT   Please your highness, posts°   *messengers*
From those you sent to th'oracle are come
An hour since. Cleomenes and Dion,
195 Being well arrived from Delphos, are both landed,
Hasting to th' court.

LORD   So please you, sir, their speed
Hath been beyond account.°   *without precedent*

LEONTES   Twenty-three days
They have been absent. 'Tis good speed, foretells
The great Apollo suddenly° will have   *at once*
200 The truth of this appear. Prepare you, lords;
Summon a session° that we may arraign   *trial*
Our most disloyal lady. For as she hath

---

4. Aging was thought to reduce the amount of blood in the body.
5. *As ... fortune:* Since by some unusual chance; since by the act of a foreigner (Polixenes).
6. That you take it to some foreign land.
7. To a greater extent or in more ways than this action deserves.

Been publicly accused, so shall she have
A just and open trial. While she lives,
205　My heart will be a burden to me. Leave me
And think upon my bidding.　　　*Exeunt.*

3.1

Enter CLEOMENES *and* DION.

CLEOMENES　The climate's delicate, the air most sweet,
Fertile the isle,[1] the temple much surpassing
The common praise it bears.

DION　　　　　　　　　I shall report,
For most it caught° me, the celestial habits°—　　　*charmed / garments*
5　Methinks I so should term them—and the reverence
Of the grave wearers. Oh, the sacrifice!
How ceremonious, solemn, and unearthly
It was i'th' offering!

CLEOMENES　　　　　　But of all, the burst°　　　*blast (of thunder)*
And the ear-deafening voice o'th' oracle,
10　Kin° to Jove's thunder, so surprised my sense,　　　*Like*
That I was nothing.

DION　　　　　　　　If th'event° o'th' journey　　　*outcome*
Prove as successful to the Queen—oh, be't so!—
As it hath been to us rare, pleasant, speedy,
The time is worth the use on't.[2]

CLEOMENES　　　　　　　Great Apollo
15　Turn all to th' best! These proclamations,
So forcing faults upon Hermione,
I little like.

DION　　　　　The violent carriage° of it　　　*rash handling*
Will clear or end the business. When the oracle,
Thus by Apollo's great divine° sealed up,　　　*priest*
20　Shall the contents discover,° something rare　　　*reveal*
Even then will rush to knowledge. Go. —Fresh horses!
—And gracious be the issue.°　　　*Exeunt.*　　　*result; child*

3.2

Enter LEONTES, LORDS, [*and*] OFFICERS.[1]

LEONTES　This sessions, to our great grief we pronounce,
Even pushes 'gainst our heart; the party tried,
The daughter of a king, our wife, and one
Of us° too much beloved. Let us be cleared　　　*By us*
5　Of being tyrannous, since we so openly
Proceed in justice, which shall have due course
Even to the guilt or the purgation.°　　　*acquittal*
Produce the prisoner.

OFFICER　It is his highness' pleasure that the Queen

3.1 Location: A road in Sicilia.
1. The island of Delphos (Delos), Apollo's birthplace, here conflated with Delphi, where Apollo's oracle was located. See note to 2.1.184.
2. The time will have been well spent.
3.2 Location: Sicilia. A court of justice.

1. Textual Comment F includes all this scene's characters (except Paulina, who has no designated entry) in this opening stage direction; this edition has Paulina and Hermione arrive at line 10, announced by the Officer, and Cleomenes and Dion enter at line 121. See Digital Edition TC 4.

Appear in person here in court.
[*Enter* HERMIONE *as to her trial,* PAULINA, *and* LADIES.]

10   Silence!²

LEONTES   Read the indictment.

OFFICER [*reading*] "Hermione, queen to the worthy Leontes,
    King of Sicilia, thou art here accused and arraigned of high trea-
    son, in committing adultery with Polixenes, King of Bohemia,
15   and conspiring with Camillo to take away the life of our sover-
    eign lord the King, thy royal husband; the pretense° whereof   *purpose*
    being by circumstances partly laid open, thou, Hermione, con-
    trary to the faith and allegiance of a true subject, didst counsel
    and aid them, for their better safety, to fly away by night."

20 HERMIONE   Since what I am to say must be but° that   *only*
    Which contradicts my accusation, and
    The testimony on my part no other
    But what comes from myself, it shall scarce boot° me   *profit*
    To say, "Not guilty." Mine integrity
25   Being counted falsehood, shall, as I express it,
    Be so received. But thus: if powers divine
    Behold our human actions—as they do—
    I doubt not then but innocence shall make
    False accusation blush and tyranny
30   Tremble at patience. You, my lord, best know,
    Who least will seem to do so, my past life
    Hath been as continent, as chaste, as true,
    As I am now unhappy; which° is more   *which unhappiness*
    Than history can pattern,³ though devised
35   And played to take° spectators. For behold me,   *captivate*
    A fellow of the royal bed, which owe°   *who owns*
    A moiety° of the throne, a great king's daughter,   *portion*
    The mother to a hopeful prince, here standing
    To prate and talk for life and honor, fore°   *before*
40   Who please to come and hear. For° life, I prize° it   *As for / value*
    As I weigh° grief, which I would spare.° For honor,   *value / do without*
    'Tis a derivative⁴ from me to mine,°   *(my children)*
    And only that I stand° for. I appeal   *fight*
    To your own conscience, sir, before Polixenes
45   Came to your court, how I was in your grace,
    How merited to be so; since he came,
    With what encounter so uncurrent° I   *conduct so unacceptable*
    Have strained° t'appear thus.° If one jot beyond   *transgressed / (on trial)*
    The bound of honor, or in act or will
50   That way inclining, hardened be the hearts
    Of all that hear me, and my nearest of kin
    Cry "fie" upon my grave.

LEONTES   I ne'er heard yet
    That any of these bolder vices wanted
    Less° impudence to gainsay° what they did   *Were more lacking in / deny*
    Than to perform it first.
55 HERMIONE   That's true enough,
    Though 'tis a saying, sir, not due° to me.   *relevant*

2. TEXTUAL COMMENT In F, the word "Silence" is printed in italics and set as a stage direction. Here it is treated as an imperative and assigned to the Offi-cer who announces the Queen's entrance. See Digi-tal Edition TC 5.
3. Than story or drama can show a precedent for.
4. Something handed on.

LEONTES You will not own it.

HERMIONE   More than mistress of
Which comes to me in name of fault, I must not
At all acknowledge.[5] For Polixenes,
60 With whom I am accused, I do confess
I loved him as in honor he required,°   *was his due*
With such a kind of love as might become
A lady like me; with a love, even such,
So, and no other, as yourself commanded;
65 Which not to have done I think had been in me
Both disobedience and ingratitude
To you and toward your friend, whose love had spoke,
Even since it could speak, from an infant, freely
That it was yours. Now, for conspiracy,
70 I know not how it tastes, though it be dished°   *served*
For me to try how; all I know of it
Is that Camillo was an honest man,
And why he left your court, the gods themselves,
Wotting° no more than I, are ignorant.   *If they know*
75 LEONTES You knew of his departure, as you know
What you have underta'en to do in's absence.

HERMIONE Sir,
You speak a language that I understand not.
My life stands in the level of your dreams,[6]
Which I'll lay down.

80 LEONTES   Your actions are my dreams.
You had a bastard by Polixenes,
And I but° dreamed it. As you were past all shame—   *merely*
Those of your fact° are so—so past all truth,   *(guilty) of your crime*
Which to deny concerns more than avails;[7] for as
85 Thy brat hath been cast out, like to itself,°   *as it should be*
No father owning it—which is indeed
More criminal in thee than it—so thou
Shalt feel our justice, in whose easiest passage
Look for no less than death.[8]

HERMIONE   Sir, spare your threats.
90 The bug° which you would fright me with I seek.   *horrible object*
To me can life be no commodity.°   *profit; comfort*
The crown and comfort of my life, your favor,
I do give° lost, for I do feel it gone   *reckon*
But know not how it went. My second joy°   *(Mamillius)*
95 And first fruits of my body, from his presence
I am barred, like one infectious. My third comfort,
Starred most unluckily,[9] is from my breast,
The innocent milk in it° most innocent mouth,   *its*
Haled° out to murder. Myself on every post[1]   *Dragged*
100 Proclaimed a strumpet; with immodest° hatred   *excessive*

5. *More . . . acknowledge:* I must not answer for ("acknowledge") more than those faults that I actually possess (am "mistress of").
6. *in the . . . dreams:* as the target ("level") of your delusions; a metaphor from archery.
7. *Which . . . avails:* Your denial of the truth costs you more effort than it's worth.

8. *in whose . . . death:* in the mildest course of justice, you can expect death. The implication is that death may well be preceded by torture.
9. Born under most unlucky stars.
1. Alluding to the early modern practice of nailing proclamations to posts in public places.

The childbed privilege[2] denied, which 'longs°   *belongs*
To women of all fashion.° Lastly, hurried   *ranks*
Here to this place, i'th' open air, before
I have got strength of limit.[3] Now, my liege,
105   Tell me what blessings I have here alive,
That I should fear to die? Therefore proceed.
But yet hear this—mistake me not—no life,
I prize it not a straw, but for mine honor,
Which I would free°—if I shall be condemned   *vindicate*
110   Upon surmises, all proofs sleeping else
But° what your jealousies awake, I tell you   *except*
'Tis rigor° and not law. Your honors all,   *severity; tyranny*
I do refer me° to the oracle.   *appeal*
Apollo be my judge.
LORD   This your request
115   Is altogether just. Therefore bring forth,
And in Apollo's name, his oracle.   [*Exeunt* OFFICERS.]
HERMIONE   The Emperor of Russia[4] was my father.
Oh, that he were alive and here beholding
His daughter's trial; that he did but see
120   The flatness° of my misery—yet with eyes   *boundlessness*
Of pity, not revenge.
          [*Enter* OFFICERS *with* CLEOMENES *and* DION.]
OFFICER   You here shall swear upon this sword of justice,
That you, Cleomenes and Dion, have
Been both at Delphos, and from thence have brought
125   This sealed-up oracle, by the hand delivered
Of great Apollo's priest, and that since then
You have not dared to break the holy seal
Nor read the secrets in't.
CLEOMENES *and* DION   All this we swear.
LEONTES   Break up the seals and read.
130   OFFICER [*reads*]   "Hermione is chaste, Polixenes blameless,
Camillo a true subject, Leontes a jealous tyrant, his innocent
babe truly begotten; and the King shall live without an heir
if that which is lost be not found."
LORDS   Now blessèd be the great Apollo.
HERMIONE   Praisèd.
LEONTES   Hast thou read truth?
135   OFFICER   Ay, my lord, even so
As it is here set down.
LEONTES   There is no truth at all i'th' oracle.
The sessions shall proceed. This is mere falsehood.
          [*Enter* SERVANT.]
SERVANT   My lord the King, the King!
LEONTES   What is the business?
140   SERVANT   O sir, I shall be hated to report it.
The Prince your son, with mere conceit° and fear   *thought*

---

2. The right to enjoy a period of bedrest and seclusion after childbirth.
3. Before I have the strength that follows the customary period of confinement. Exposure to air outside the domestic space was considered unsafe for women weakened by childbirth.
4. To early modern theatergoers, Russia would have seemed a distant and exotic place, but the founding of the Muscovy Company in 1553 also showed London merchants' interest in trade with this region.

Of the Queen's speed,° is gone.   *fortune*

LEONTES   How? "Gone"?

SERVANT   Is dead.

LEONTES   Apollo's angry, and the heavens themselves
Do strike at my injustice.

[HERMIONE *swoons*.]

How now there?

145 PAULINA   This news is mortal to the Queen. Look down
And see what death is doing.

LEONTES   Take her hence.
Her heart is but o'ercharged;° she will recover.   *overburdened (by emotion)*
I have too much believed mine own suspicion.
Beseech you, tenderly apply to her
Some remedies for life.

[*Exeunt* PAULINA *and* LADIES *with* HERMIONE.]

150   Apollo, pardon
My great profaneness 'gainst thine oracle.
I'll reconcile me to Polixenes,
New woo my queen, recall the good Camillo,
Whom I proclaim a man of truth, of mercy;
155 For being transported by my jealousies
To bloody thoughts and to revenge, I chose
Camillo for the minister to poison
My friend Polixenes, which had° been done   *would have*
But that the good mind of Camillo tardied°   *delayed*
160 My swift command, though I with death and with
Reward did threaten and encourage him,
Not doing it and being done.[5] He, most humane
And filled with honor, to my kingly guest
Unclasped my practice,° quit his fortunes here,   *Revealed my plot*
165 Which you knew great, and to the hazard
Of all uncertainties himself commended,°   *consigned himself*
No richer than his honor.[6] How he glisters
Through my rust,[7] and how his piety
Does my deeds make the blacker!

[*Enter* PAULINA.]

PAULINA   Woe the while.
170 Oh, cut my lace,[8] lest my heart, cracking it,
Break too.

LORD   What fit is this, good lady?

PAULINA   What studied° torments, tyrant, hast for me?   *expertly devised*
What wheels, racks, fires? What flaying, boiling
In leads or oils?[9] What old or newer torture
175 Must I receive, whose every word deserves
To taste of thy most worst? Thy tyranny,
Together working with thy jealousies—
Fancies too weak for boys, too green and idle°   *immature and foolish*

5. *though . . . done:* that is, though I threatened him
with death if he did not do it and encouraged him
with the promise of reward if he did do it.
6. Possessing no fortune but his honor.
7. How he shines ("glisters") in comparison with my
"rust" (i.e., my evil).
8. Paulina asks that someone cut the fabric that
holds together the tight bodices characteristic of

female dress in this period.
9. A list of early modern forms of torture. The wheel
was a device to which a person was tied and his or her
limbs broken, usually by beating. The rack typically
consisted of a frame with a roller at each end; a person was attached to this frame and his or her limbs
stretched by turning the rollers. To flay was to strip
off someone's skin while he or she was still alive.

For girls of nine—oh, think what they have done,
180 And then run mad indeed, stark mad; for all
Thy bygone fooleries were but spices° of it.   *slight tastes*
That thou betrayed'st Polixenes, 'twas nothing;
That did but show thee of° a fool, inconstant,   *for*
And damnable° ingrateful. Nor was't much   *damnably; cursedly*
185 Thou wouldst have poisoned good Camillo's honor,
To have him kill a king—poor° trespasses,   *minor*
More monstrous standing by;[1] whereof I reckon
The casting forth to crows thy baby daughter
To be or° none or little, though a devil   *either*
190 Would have shed water out of fire ere done't.[2]
Nor is't directly laid to thee the death
Of the young Prince, whose honorable thoughts—
Thoughts high for one so tender°—cleft the heart   *young*
That could conceive a gross° and foolish sire   *stupid*
195 Blemished his gracious dam.° This is not, no,   *mother*
Laid to thy answer.[3] But the last—O lords,
When I have said,° cry woe!—the Queen, the Queen,   *finished speaking*
The sweetest, dearest creature's dead; and vengeance for't
Not dropped down yet.
LORD   The higher powers forbid.
200 PAULINA   I say she's dead. I'll swear't. If word nor oath
Prevail not, go and see. If you can bring
Tincture° or luster in her lip, her eye,   *Color*
Heat outwardly or breath within, I'll serve you
As I would do the gods. But, O thou tyrant,
205 Do not repent these things, for they are heavier
Than all thy woes° can stir.° Therefore betake thee   *grief / remove*
To nothing but despair. A thousand knees,
Ten thousand years together, naked, fasting
Upon a barren mountain and still° winter   *always*
210 In storm perpetual, could not move the gods
To look that way thou wert.°   *in your direction*
LEONTES   Go on, go on.
Thou canst not speak too much. I have deserved
All tongues to talk their bitt'rest.
LORD [*to* PAULINA]   Say no more.
Howe'er the business goes, you have made fault
I'th' boldness of your speech.
215 PAULINA   I am sorry for't.
All faults I make, when I shall come to know them,
I do repent. Alas, I have showed too much
The rashness of a woman. He is touched
To the noble heart. What's gone and what's past help
220 Should be past grief. [*to* LEONTES] Do not receive affliction
At my petition;° I beseech you, rather   *Because of my injunction*
Let me be punished that have minded° you   *reminded*
Of what you should forget. Now, good my liege,
Sir, royal sir, forgive a foolish woman.

---

1. In comparison with more monstrous ones near at
hand.
2. A devil would have shed tears from his fiery eyes

(or from hellfires) before he had done it.
3. *laid to thy answer:* presented as a charge you must
answer.

225　　The love I bore your queen—lo, fool again—
　　　　I'll speak of her no more, nor of your children;
　　　　I'll not remember you of my own lord,
　　　　Who is lost too. Take your patience to you,°　　　　　　　　　*Be patient*
　　　　And I'll say nothing.
　　　LEONTES　　　　　　　Thou didst speak but well
230　　When most the truth, which I receive much better
　　　　Than to be pitied of° thee. Prithee bring me　　　　　　　　　*by*
　　　　To the dead bodies of my queen and son.
　　　　One grave shall be for both. Upon them shall
　　　　The causes of their death appear, unto
235　　Our shame perpetual. Once a day I'll visit
　　　　The chapel where they lie, and tears shed there
　　　　Shall be my recreation.⁴ So long as nature°　　　　　　　　　*my body*
　　　　Will bear up with this exercise, so long
　　　　I daily vow to use it. Come, and lead me
240　　To these sorrows.　　　　　　　　　　　*Exeunt.*

3.3

Enter ANTIGONUS, *a* MARINER, [*with the*] *babe.*¹
ANTIGONUS　Thou art perfect,° then, our ship hath touched upon　　　*certain*
　　　　The deserts of Bohemia?
MARINER　　　　　　　　Ay, my lord, and fear
　　　　We have landed in ill time. The skies look grimly
　　　　And threaten present blusters.° In my conscience°　　　*impending storms / opinion*
5　　　The heavens with that we have in hand are angry
　　　　And frown upon's.
ANTIGONUS　Their sacred wills be done. Go get aboard.
　　　　Look to thy bark.° I'll not be long before　　　　　　　　　*ship*
　　　　I call upon thee.
MARINER　　　　　　Make your best haste, and go not
10　　Too far i'th' land. 'Tis like to be loud° weather.　　　　　　*stormy*
　　　　Besides, this place is famous for the creatures
　　　　Of prey that keep° upon't.　　　　　　　　　　　　　　　　*live*
ANTIGONUS　　　　　　　Go thou away.
　　　　I'll follow instantly.
MARINER　　　　　　　I am glad at heart
　　　　To be so rid o'th' business.　　　　　　　　　*Exit.*
ANTIGONUS　　　　　　　Come, poor babe.
15　　I have heard, but not believed, the spirits o'th' dead
　　　　May walk again. If such thing be, thy mother
　　　　Appeared to me last night, for ne'er was dream
　　　　So like a waking. To me comes a creature,
　　　　Sometimes her head on one side, some another;
20　　I never saw a vessel° of like sorrow　　　　　　　　　*person; receptacle*
　　　　So filled and so becoming.² In pure white robes
　　　　Like very sanctity she did approach

4. My spiritual renewal or re-creation.
3.3 Location: Bohemia. The seacoast. This play, as does Greene's *Pandosto*, credits Bohemia with a coast. Only for two brief periods in the late Middle Ages may Bohemia have controlled a small piece of territory on the Adriatic Sea, but it was otherwise landlocked.
1. TEXTUAL COMMENT The opening stage direction

in the Folio text includes a "babe" (whom Antigonus is obviously carrying), the Shepherd, and Clown, even though the latter two do not appear until after Antigonus's exit, signaled by the striking stage direction: "*Exit, pursued by a bear*" (3.3.57). See Digital Edition TC 6.
2. So filled with sorrow and so beautiful.

My cabin where I lay; thrice bowed before me,
And, gasping to begin some speech, her eyes
25 Became two spouts; the fury spent, anon°   *soon*
Did this break from her: "Good Antigonus,
Since fate, against thy better disposition,
Hath made thy person for the thrower-out
Of my poor babe, according to thine oath,
30 Places remote enough are in Bohemia;
There weep, and leave it crying; and, for° the babe   *because*
Is counted lost for ever, Perdita[3]
I prithee call't. For this ungentle° business   *unkind; ignoble*
Put on thee by my lord, thou ne'er shalt see
35 Thy wife Paulina more." And so with shrieks
She melted into air. Affrighted much,
I did in time collect myself and thought
This was so and no slumber. Dreams are toys,°   *trifles*
Yet for this once—yea, superstitiously—
40 I will be squared° by this. I do believe   *ruled*
Hermione hath suffered death and that
Apollo would, this being indeed the issue°   *child*
Of King Polixenes, it should here be laid,
Either for life or death, upon the earth
45 Of its right father. Blossom, speed° thee well.   *fare*
There lie, and there thy character.[4] There these,[5]
Which may, if fortune please, both breed thee, pretty,
And still rest thine.[6] [*Thunder.*] The storm begins, poor wretch,
That for thy mother's fault art thus exposed
50 To loss and what may follow. Weep I cannot,
But my heart bleeds; and most accursed am I
To be by oath enjoined to this. Farewell!
The day frowns more and more. Thou'rt like to have
A lullaby too rough. I never saw
55 The heavens so dim by day. A savage clamor!
Well may I get aboard. This is the chase.°   *hunt*
I am gone for ever.   *Exit, pursued by a bear.*[7]
    [*Enter* SHEPHERD.]
SHEPHERD   I would there were no age between ten and three-
and-twenty, or that youth would sleep out the rest; for there
60 is nothing in the between but getting wenches with child,
wronging the ancientry,° stealing, fighting. Hark you now: *elderly people*
would any but these boiled brains° of nineteen and two-and-   *lunatics*
twenty hunt this weather? They have scared away two of my
best sheep, which I fear the wolf will sooner find than the
65 master. If anywhere I have them, 'tis by the seaside, browsing
of° ivy. Good luck, an't° be thy will. [*He sees the baby.*] What   *on / if it*
have we here? Mercy on 's, a bairn,° a very pretty bairn. A   *child*
boy or a child,° I wonder? A pretty one, a very pretty one. Sure   *girl*

---

3. Latin for "lost one."
4. The written account of your history and parentage.
5. The gold and jewels with which the Shepherd grows rich and which are later used to identify the Princess. See 5.2.30–36.
6. *Which . . . thine:* Which may, if you are lucky, be sufficient to pay for your upbringing, and still leave

you in possession of a fortune.
7. PERFORMANCE COMMENT One of the most famous stage directions in English drama. Did a real bear come on stage, perhaps from one of the bearbaiting arenas in Shakespeare's London, or a man in a bear costume? For the many staging possibilities, see Digital Edition PC 2.

some scape:[8] though I am not bookish,° yet I can read   *not familiar with books*
70   waiting-gentlewoman in the scape. This has been some
stair-work, some trunk-work, some behind-door-work.[9] They
were warmer that got° this than the poor thing is here. I'll   *begot*
take it up for pity; yet I'll tarry till my son come. He hallooed
but even now. Whoa, ho, hoa!

Enter CLOWN.°   *rustic fellow*

75   CLOWN   Hilloa, loa!

SHEPHERD   What, art so near? If thou'lt see a thing to talk on°   *about*
when thou art dead and rotten, come hither. What ail'st thou,
man?

CLOWN   I have seen two such sights, by sea and by land. But I
80   am not to say it is a sea, for it is now the sky; betwixt the
firmament and it you cannot thrust a bodkin's° point.   *needle's*

SHEPHERD   Why, boy, how is it?

CLOWN   I would you did but see how it chafes, how it rages, how it
takes up the shore—but that's not to the point. Oh, the most
85   piteous cry of the poor souls! Sometimes to see 'em, and not to
see 'em; now the ship boring° the moon with her mainmast,   *piercing*
and anon swallowed with yeast° and froth, as you'd thrust a   *foam*
cork into a hogshead.° And then for the land-service,[1] to see   *cask of liquor*
how the bear tore out his shoulder bone, how he cried to me
90   for help and said his name was Antigonus, a nobleman. But
to make an end of the ship, to see how the sea flapdragoned
it![2] But first, how the poor souls roared, and the sea mocked
them; and how the poor gentleman roared, and the bear
mocked him, both roaring louder than the sea or weather.

95   SHEPHERD   Name of mercy, when was this, boy?

CLOWN   Now, now. I have not winked° since I saw these sights.   *blinked an eye*
The men are not yet cold under water, nor the bear half
dined on the gentleman—he's at it now.

SHEPHERD   Would I had been by to have helped the old man.

100   CLOWN   I would you had been by the ship side to have helped
her; there your charity would have lacked footing.[3]

SHEPHERD   Heavy° matters, heavy matters. But look thee   *Sad*
here, boy. Now bless thyself: thou mett'st with things dying,
I with things newborn. Here's a sight for thee. Look thee, a
105   bearing-cloth[4] for a squire's child. Look thee here: take up,
take up, boy. Open't. So, let's see; it was told me I should be
rich by the fairies. This is some changeling.[5] Open't. What's
within, boy?

CLOWN [*opening the box*]   You're a made° old man. If the sins   *prosperous*
110   of your youth are forgiven you, you're well to live.° Gold, all   *well off; virtuous*
gold![6]

SHEPHERD   This is fairy gold,[7] boy, and 'twill prove so. Up
with't; keep it close.° Home, home the next° way. We are   *secret / nearest*
lucky, boy, and to be so still° requires nothing but secrecy.   *always*
115   Let my sheep go. Come, good boy, the next way home.
CLOWN   Go you the next way with your findings. I'll go see if
the bear be gone from the gentleman, and how much he
hath eaten. They are never curst° but when they are hungry.   *vicious*
If there be any of him left, I'll bury it.
120   SHEPHERD   That's a good deed. If thou mayst discern by that
which is left of him what he is,° fetch me to th' sight of him.   *his identity or rank*
CLOWN   Marry,[8] will I; and you shall help to put him i'th' ground.
SHEPHERD   'Tis a lucky day, boy, and we'll do good deeds
on't.   *Exeunt.*

4.1

Enter TIME,[1] *the Chorus.*

TIME   I, that please some, try° all; both joy and terror   *test*
Of good and bad, that makes and unfolds error,
Now take upon me in the name° of Time   *with the authority*
To use my wings. Impute it not a crime
5   To me or my swift passage that I slide
O'er sixteen years and leave the growth untried°   *development unexamined*
Of that wide gap, since it is in my power
To o'erthrow law, and in one self-born° hour   *selfsame*
To plant and o'erwhelm° custom. Let me pass   *establish and overthrow*
10   The same I am, ere ancient'st order was,
Or what is now received.[2] I witness to
The times that brought them in, so shall I do
To th' freshest things now reigning and make stale
The glistering° of this present, as my tale   *glittering shine*
15   Now seems to it.[3] Your patience this allowing,
I turn my glass,° and give my scene such growing   *hourglass*
As° you had slept between. Leontes leaving—   *As if*
Th'effects of his fond° jealousies so grieving   *foolish*
That he shuts up himself—imagine me,
20   Gentle spectators, that I now may be
In fair Bohemia, and remember well
I mentioned a son o'th' King's, which Florizel
I now name to you; and with speed so pace°   *proceed*
To speak of Perdita, now grown in grace
25   Equal with wond'ring.[4] What of her ensues
I list not° prophesy, but let Time's news   *do not wish to*
Be known when 'tis brought forth: a shepherd's daughter
And what to her adheres,° which follows after,   *pertains*

---

7. Riches left by fairies were unreliable. If not kept
secret, they brought bad luck.
8. A mild oath derived from the name of the Virgin
Mary.
4.1 Location: Bohemia. The seacoast.
1. PERFORMANCE COMMENT In early modern texts,
Time was conventionally represented as an old bald
man with wings, signifying how swiftly time passes.
He often carried an hourglass and a scythe, symbol
of the power of time to destroy life. A common saying
was that Time was the revealer of Truth, or that

Truth was the daughter of Time. Robert Greene's
Pandosto, Shakespeare's chief source for *The Winter's Tale*, was subtitled *The Triumph of Time*. For
ways this figure has been staged, see Digital Edition
PC 3.
2. *Let me . . . received:* Let me remain as I have been
from before the beginnings of civilization even to the
time of present customs.
3. As my tale now seems stale in comparison with
the present.
4. Now grown so gracious as to inspire admiration.

Is th'argument° of Time. Of this allow,   *subject matter*
30 If ever you have spent time worse ere now;
If never, yet that Time himself doth say
He wishes earnestly you never may.   *Exit.*

4.2

Enter POLIXENES *and* CAMILLO.

POLIXENES   I pray thee, good Camillo, be no more importu-
nate.° 'Tis a sickness denying° thee anything, a death to   *ask no longer / to deny*
grant this.

CAMILLO   It is fifteen[1] years since I saw my country. Though
5 I have, for the most part, been aired abroad,° I desire to lay   *breathed foreign air*
my bones there. Besides, the penitent King, my master, hath
sent for me, to whose feeling° sorrows I might be some   *deeply felt*
allay°—or I o'erween° to think so—which is another spur to   *relief / am bold enough*
my departure.

10 POLIXENES   As thou lov'st me, Camillo, wipe not out the rest
of thy services by leaving me now. The need I have of thee
thine own goodness hath made. Better not to have had thee
than thus to want° thee. Thou, having made me businesses[2]   *be without*
which none without thee can sufficiently manage, must
15 either stay to execute them thyself, or take away with thee
the very services thou hast done, which if I have not enough
considered°—as too much I cannot—to be more thankful to   *rewarded*
thee shall be my study, and my profit therein the heaping
friendships.[3] Of that fatal° country Sicilia prithee speak no   *deadly*
20 more, whose very naming punishes me with the remem-
brance of that penitent—as thou call'st him—and reconciled king my brother, whose loss of his most precious queen
and children are even now to be afresh° lamented. Say to   *newly*
me, when sawest thou the Prince Florizel, my son? Kings are
25 no less unhappy, their issue not being gracious,[4] than they
are in losing them when they have approved° their virtues.   *demonstrated*

CAMILLO   Sir, it is three days since I saw the Prince. What his
happier affairs may be are to me unknown, but I have miss-
ingly noted° he is of late much retired from court and is less   *noted by his absence*
30 frequent to° his princely exercises than formerly he hath   *less often engaged in*
appeared.

POLIXENES   I have considered so much, Camillo, and with
some care, so far that I have eyes under my service° which   *spies in my employ*
look upon his removedness,° from whom I have this intelli-   *retirement (from court)*
35 gence: that he is seldom from the house of a most homely°   *simple*
shepherd, a man, they say, that from very nothing, and
beyond the imagination of his neighbors, is grown into an
unspeakable estate.°   *untold wealth*

CAMILLO   I have heard, sir, of such a man, who hath a daugh-
40 ter of most rare note;° the report of her is extended more   *quality*
than can be thought to begin° from such a cottage.   *originate*

POLIXENES   That's likewise part of my intelligence; but, I fear,
the angle° that plucks our son thither. Thou shalt accompany   *fishhook*

4.2 Location: Bohemia. The palace of Polixenes.
1. Although at 4.1.6, Time says that sixteen years
have passed, the Folio reads "fifteene" here. This
apparent error may be due to carelessness on Shakespeare's part or to a misreading of a Roman numeral

by a compositor or scribe.
2. Performed services for me.
3. The accumulation of your kindnesses.
4. Their children not proving virtuous.

us to the place where we will, not appearing what we are,
45 have some question with the shepherd, from whose simplic-
ity I think it not uneasy° to get the cause of my son's resort   *difficult*
thither. Prithee, be my present partner in this business, and
lay aside the thoughts of Sicilia.

CAMILLO   I willingly obey your command.
50 POLIXENES   My best Camillo! We must disguise ourselves.
                                                Exeunt.

4.3

Enter AUTOLYCUS, *singing.*

AUTOLYCUS
    When daffodils begin to peer,
    With heigh, the doxy° over the dale,   *beggar's wench*
    Why, then comes in the sweet° o'the year,   *sweetest part*
    For the red blood reigns in the winter's pale.°   *skin made pale by winter*

5   The white sheet bleaching on the hedge,[1]
    With heigh, the sweet birds—oh, how they sing!—
    Doth set my pugging° tooth on edge,   *thieving*
    For a quart of ale is a dish for a king.

    The lark, that tirra-lirra chants,
10   With heigh, with heigh, the thrush and the jay,
    Are summer songs for me and my aunts[2]
    While we lie tumbling in the hay.

I have served Prince Florizel and in my time wore three-pile,[3]
but now I am out of service.

15 [*Sings.*]   But shall I go mourn for that, my dear?
    The pale moon shines by night,
    And when I wander here and there,
    I then do most go right.

    If tinkers[4] may have leave° to live,   *permission*
20   And bear the sow-skin budget,[5]
    Then my account I well may give,
    And in the stocks avouch it.°   *acknowledge (my crime)*

My traffic° is sheets; when the kite builds, look to lesser lin-   *trade*
en.[6] My father named me Autolycus,[7] who being, as I am,
25 littered under Mercury,[8] was likewise a snapper-up of
unconsidered trifles. With die and drab,° I purchased this   *dice and whores*
caparison,° and my revenue is the silly cheat.[9] Gallows and   *garment*
knock° are too powerful on the highway.[1] Beating and   *beatings*
hanging are terrors to me. For° the life to come, I sleep out   *As for*
30 the thought of it.

4.3 Location: A road in Bohemia.
1. It was common practice in the country to set
clothes out to dry on hedges.
2. Another slang term for women who take beggars
or vagabonds for lovers.
3. A rich velvet cloth with a thick nap or "pile."
4. Menders of metal pots and kettles. The term was
also applied to itinerant beggars and thieves.
5. A pigskin bag in which a tinker carried his tools;
hence, a sign of his trade.
6. The kite, a bird of prey, supposedly stole small
pieces of linen to make its nest. Autolycus steals
larger pieces of linen, probably sheets left to dry on
hedges (4.3.5).
7. In classical mythology, a crafty thief and grandfather of Ulysses.
8. Fathered by Mercury; born when the planet Mercury was ascendant. Mercury, the father of Autolycus, was god of thieves.
9. My income derives from petty swindles.
1. Autolycus fears the penalties meted out to high-
waymen, implying he would rather be a petty thief.

Enter CLOWN.

A prize, a prize.

CLOWN Let me see. Every 'leven wether tods,[2] every tod
yields pound and odd° shilling; fifteen hundred shorn, what   *one*
comes the wool to?

35 AUTOLYCUS [*aside*] If the springe° hold, the cock's[3] mine.   *trap*

CLOWN I cannot do't without counters.[4] Let me see; what am
I to buy for our sheep-shearing feast? Three pound of sugar,
five pound of currants, rice—what will this sister of mine do
with rice? But my father hath made her mistress of the feast,

40 and she lays it on. She hath made me four-and-twenty nosegays for the shearers: three-man songmen[5] all, and very good
ones, but they are most of them means° and basses—but one   *tenors*
puritan amongst them, and he sings psalms to hornpipes.[6] I
must have saffron to color the warden° pies; mace; dates,   *winter pear*

45 none—that's out of my note;° nutmegs, seven; a race° or two   *not on my list / root*
of ginger, but that I may beg; four pound of prunes; and as
many of raisins o'th' sun.°   *sun-dried*

AUTOLYCUS [*groveling on the ground*] Oh, that ever I was born.

CLOWN I'th' name of me.

50 AUTOLYCUS Oh, help me, help me! Pluck but off these rags,
and then death, death!

CLOWN Alack, poor soul; thou hast need of more rags to lay
on thee rather than have these off.

AUTOLYCUS O sir, the loathsomeness of them offend me more

55 than the stripes° I have received, which are mighty ones and   *blows*
millions.

CLOWN Alas, poor man, a million of beating may come to a
great matter.[7]

AUTOLYCUS I am robbed, sir, and beaten; my money and apparel

60 ta'en from me, and these detestable things put upon me.

CLOWN What, by a horseman or a footman?

AUTOLYCUS A footman, sweet sir, a footman.

CLOWN Indeed, he should be a footman, by the garments he
has left with thee. If this be a horseman's coat, it hath seen

65 very hot service. Lend me thy hand; I'll help thee. Come,
lend me thy hand.

AUTOLYCUS O good sir, tenderly. Oh!

CLOWN Alas, poor soul.

AUTOLYCUS O good sir; softly,° good sir. I fear, sir, my shoulder   *gently*

70 blade is out.

CLOWN How now? Canst stand?

AUTOLYCUS [*picking Clown's pocket*] Softly, dear sir; good sir,
softly. You ha' done me a charitable office.°   *service*

CLOWN Dost lack any money? I have a little money for thee.

75 AUTOLYCUS No, good sweet sir, no; I beseech you, sir. I have a
kinsman not past three-quarters of a mile hence unto whom
I was going. I shall there have money, or anything I want.

---

2. Every 11 rams will yield 28 pounds (a "tod") of
wool. Clown and his father could expect to earn a
substantial amount of money (almost 150 pounds) for
their wool.
3. Woodcock, a bird easily caught and hence proverbial for its stupidity.
4. Disks used in calculating sums.
5. Men who sing three-part songs.

6. Shrill-sounding musical instruments often played
at country dances but seldom used to accompany the
singing of psalms. This may be a gentle satire of puritans, who were commonly accused both of being
opposed to festivity and of hypocrisy.
7. A million blows can be a serious affair, with a pun
on "matter" as "pus," caused by an infection from
open wounds.

Offer me no money, I pray you; that kills° my heart.   *touches*

CLOWN   What manner of fellow was he that robbed you?

80   AUTOLYCUS   A fellow, sir, that I have known to go about with
troll-madams.° I knew him once a servant of the Prince. I   *whores*
cannot tell, good sir, for which of his virtues it was, but he
was certainly whipped out of the court.

CLOWN   His vices you would say. There's no virtue whipped
85   out of the court. They cherish it to make it stay there; and
yet it will no more but abide.°   *stay there only briefly*

AUTOLYCUS   Vices I would say, sir. I know this man well; he
hath been since an ape-bearer,[8] then a process-server—a
bailiff[9]—then he compassed a motion° of the Prodigal Son,[1]   *devised a puppet show*
90   and married a tinker's wife within a mile where my land and
living° lies; and, having flown over many knavish professions,   *property*
he settled only in rogue.° Some call him Autolycus.   *on the rogue's profession*

CLOWN   Out upon him! Prig,° for my life, prig. He haunts   *Thief*
wakes,° fairs, and bearbaitings.   *festivals*

95   AUTOLYCUS   Very true, sir. He, sir, he. That's the rogue that
put me into this apparel.

CLOWN   Not a more cowardly rogue in all Bohemia. If you had
but looked big and spit at him, he'd have run.

AUTOLYCUS   I must confess to you, sir, I am no fighter. I am
100   false of heart° that way, and that he knew, I warrant him.   *without courage*

CLOWN   How do you now?

AUTOLYCUS   Sweet sir, much better than I was. I can stand
and walk. I will even take my leave of you, and pace softly
towards my kinsman's.

105   CLOWN   Shall I bring thee° on the way?   *escort you*

AUTOLYCUS   No, good-faced sir, no, sweet sir.

CLOWN   Then fare thee well. I must go buy spices for our
sheep-shearing.   *Exit.*

AUTOLYCUS   Prosper you, sweet sir. Your purse is not hot°   *full*
110   enough to purchase your spice. I'll be with you at your
sheep-shearing, too. If I make not this cheat° bring out°   *deception / lead to*
another and the shearers prove sheep, let me be unrolled[2]
and my name put in the book of virtue.

[*Sings.*]   Jog on, jog on, the footpath way,
115   And merrily hent° the stile[3]-a.   *grab (to leap over)*
A merry heart goes all the day,
Your sad tires in a mile-a.   *Exit.*

4.4

Enter FLORIZEL, [*disguised as Doricles, and*] PERDITA.[1]

FLORIZEL   These your unusual weeds° to each part of you   *garments*
Does give a life—no shepherdess, but Flora°   *goddess of flowers*
Peering in April's front.[2] This your sheep-shearing

---

8. One who carried about a trained monkey.
9. A process-server, or bailiff, is a person who serves
legal summonses that order a person to be brought
into court for litigation.
1. Alluding to the New Testament story in the Gospel of Luke (Luke 15:11–32) of a spendthrift son who
squandered his money and was forgiven by his father.
2. Let my name be taken off the list (of thieves and
vagabonds).
3. Steps by which people pass over a fence or hedge.

4.4 Location: The countryside in Bohemia where
the Shepherd, Clown, and Perdita live.
1. TEXTUAL COMMENT Again, F lists in the initial
stage direction all the major characters who appear
in this very long scene. Florizel and Perdita seem,
however, to have a private conversation before the
Shepherd, Polixenes, and others enter at line 54 and
Autolycus at line 213. See Digital Edition TC 8.
2. Peeping out in early April.

Is as a meeting of the petty gods,
And you the queen on't.°   *of it*

5 PERDITA   Sir, my gracious lord,
To chide at your extremes° it not becomes me—   *extravagances*
Oh, pardon that I name them. Your high self,
The gracious mark o'th' land,[3] you have obscured
With a swain's wearing,° and me, poor lowly maid,   *shepherd's costume*
10 Most goddess-like pranked up.° But that our feasts   *adorned*
In every mess[4] have folly, and the feeders°   *those who eat*
Digest it with a custom,[5] I should blush
To see you so attired; swoon, I think,
To show myself a glass.°   *mirror*
FLORIZEL   I bless the time
15 When my good falcon made her flight across
Thy father's ground.
PERDITA   Now Jove afford you cause!
To me the difference° forges dread; your greatness   *(in rank)*
Hath not been used to fear. Even now I tremble
To think your father by some accident
20 Should pass this way, as you did. Oh, the fates!
How would he look to see his work,° so noble,   *offspring; writings*
Vilely bound up?[6] What would he say? Or how
Should I, in these my borrowed flaunts,° behold   *rich garments*
The sternness of his presence?
FLORIZEL   Apprehend
25 Nothing but jollity. The gods themselves,
Humbling their deities to love, have taken
The shapes of beasts upon them: Jupiter
Became a bull and bellowed; the green Neptune
A ram and bleated; and the fire-robed god,
30 Golden Apollo, a poor humble swain,
As I seem now.[7] Their transformations
Were never for a piece° of beauty rarer,   *person*
Nor in a way so chaste,[8] since my desires
Run not before mine honor, nor my lusts
Burn hotter than my faith.
35 PERDITA   Oh, but sir,
Your resolution cannot hold, when 'tis
Opposed, as it must be, by th' power of the King.
One of these two must be necessities,
Which then will speak that you must change this purpose,
Or I my life.[9]
40 FLORIZEL   Thou dearest Perdita,
With these forced° thoughts I prithee darken not   *unnatural; farfetched*
The mirth o'th' feast—or° I'll be thine, my fair,   *either*
Or not my father's; for I cannot be
Mine own, nor anything to any, if

---

3. The one whose graces make him admired by all.
4. A group of four served at table together; see note
to 1.2.225.
5. *Digest . . . custom:* Tolerate it because they have
grown used to it.
6. Poorly dressed; poorly put between covers (a
bookbinding metaphor).
7. In classical mythology, Jupiter transformed him-

self into a bull and abducted Europa; Neptune took
on the shape of a ram to carry off Theopane; and the
sun god Apollo disguised himself as a shepherd to
court Alcestis.
8. Nor ever conducted with so chaste a purpose.
9. *you . . . life:* either you must change your intent, or
I must change my life (that is, risk death).

45 I be not thine. To this I am most constant,
    Though destiny say no. Be merry, gentle;
    Strangle such thoughts as these with anything
    That you behold the while. Your guests are coming;
    Lift up your countenance as° it were the day   *as if*
50 Of celebration of that nuptial which
    We two have sworn shall come.

PERDITA   O Lady Fortune,
    Stand you auspicious!°   *favorable*

FLORIZEL   See, your guests approach.
    Address° yourself to entertain them sprightly,   *Prepare*
    And let's be red with mirth.

        [*Enter* SHEPHERD, CLOWN, *with* POLIXENES *and*
        CAMILLO *disguised*, MOPSA, DORCAS, *Shepherds and*
        Shepherdesses.][1]

55 SHEPHERD   Fie, daughter! When my old wife lived, upon
    This day she was both pantler,° butler, cook,   *pantry maid*
    Both dame° and servant, welcomed all, served all;   *mistress of the house*
    Would sing her song and dance her turn; now here
    At upper end o'th' table, now i'th' middle;
60 On his° shoulder and his,° her face afire   *one person's / another's*
    With labor, and the thing she took to quench it
    She would to each one sip. You are retired
    As if you were a feasted one° and not   *guest*
    The hostess of the meeting. Pray you bid
65 These unknown friends to 's welcome, for it is
    A way to make us better friends, more known.
    Come, quench your blushes and present yourself
    That which you are, mistress o'th' feast. Come on,
    And bid us welcome to your sheep-shearing,
    As your good flock shall prosper.
70 PERDITA [*to* POLIXENES]   Sir, welcome.
    It is my father's will I should take on me
    The hostess-ship o'th' day. [*to* CAMILLO] You're welcome, sir.
    —Give me those flowers there, Dorcas. —Reverend sirs,
    For you there's rosemary and rue; these keep°   *retain*
75 Seeming° and savor° all the winter long.   *Color / scent*
    Grace and remembrance[2] be to you both,
    And welcome to our shearing.

POLIXENES   Shepherdess,
    A fair one are you. Well you fit our ages
    With flowers of winter.

PERDITA   Sir, the year growing ancient,
80 Not yet on summer's death, nor on the birth
    Of trembling winter, the fairest flowers o'th' season
    Are our carnations and streaked gillyvors,[3]
    Which some call nature's bastards; of that kind
    Our rustic garden's barren, and I care not
    To get slips° of them.   *cuttings*

---

1. PERFORMANCE COMMENT In Bohemia, many characters are introduced, some of whom were probably played by actors who performed different roles in the Sicilian scenes. This practice was known as "doubling." For examples of how it might work, see Digital Edition PC 4.

2. Grace ("repentance") and remembrance are qualities associated with rue and rosemary, respectively.
3. Gillyflowers, or multicolored carnations. Their variations in color were thought to result from cross-breeding with other flowers, which may be why Perdita calls them "nature's bastards."

85 POLIXENES   Wherefore, gentle maiden,
   Do you neglect them?
PERDITA   For I have heard it said
   There is an art[4] which in their piedness° shares   *streaked color*
   With great creating nature.
POLIXENES   Say there be.
   Yet nature is made better by no mean°   *means*
90   But nature makes that mean. So over that art
   Which you say adds to nature is an art
   That nature makes. You see, sweet maid, we marry
   A gentler scion to the wildest stock
   And make conceive a bark of baser kind
95   By bud of nobler race.[5] This is an art
   Which does mend nature—change it, rather—but
   The art itself is nature.
PERDITA   So it is.
POLIXENES   Then make your garden rich in gillyvors,
   And do not call them bastards.
PERDITA   I'll not put
100   The dibble° in earth to set° one slip of them,   *trowel / plant*
   No more than, were I painted,° I would wish   *wearing cosmetics*
   This youth should say 'twere well and only therefore
   Desire to breed by me. Here's flowers for you:
   Hot[6] lavender, mints, savory, marjoram,
105   The marigold that goes to bed wi'th' sun
   And with him rises weeping.[7] These are flowers
   Of middle summer, and I think they are given
   To men of middle age. You're very welcome.
CAMILLO   I should leave grazing, were I of your flock,
   And only live by gazing.
110 PERDITA   Out, alas!
   You'd be so lean that blasts of January
   Would blow you through and through.
   [*to* FLORIZEL]   Now, my fair'st friend,
   I would I had some flowers o'th' spring that might
   Become your time of day— [*to* MOPSA] and yours,
      [*to* DORCAS] and yours,
115   That wear upon your virgin branches yet
   Your maidenheads growing. O Proserpina,[8]
   For the flowers now that, frighted, thou lett'st fall
   From Dis's wagon:° daffodils,   *chariot*
   That come before the swallow dares and take°   *charm*
120   The winds of March with beauty; violets dim,° *with hanging heads*
   But sweeter than the lids of Juno's eyes
   Or Cytherea's breath;[9] pale primroses,

---

4. The art of crossbreeding or grafting.
5. *we marry . . . race:* we marry or graft a mother twig (scion) to a more lowly trunk (stock) so that this lowly tree sends forth new shoots (conceives) by union with the nobler graft (bud). This complicated metaphor implies that high-born and low-born people, as well as plants, can successfully unite.
6. Herbs were divided into "hot" and "cold" varieties based on their supposed temperatures.
7. The marigold, sometimes called "the spouse of the sun," supposedly closed at sunset and opened, filled with dew, in the morning when the sun came up.
8. In Ovid's *Metamorphoses,* Proserpina, the daughter of Ceres, is abducted by Dis, or Pluto, as she gathers flowers and is taken in his chariot ("wagon") to his underworld kingdom. At Ceres' request, Proserpina is allowed to return to earth for six months each year. Her sojourn on earth coincides with spring and summer, her return to the underworld with fall and winter.
9. Juno was queen of the gods; "Cytherea" was another name for Venus, the goddess of love.

That die unmarried ere they can behold
Bright Phoebus° in his strength—a malady   *(the sun god)*
125   Most incident to maids;¹ bold oxlips and
The crown imperial;² lilies of all kinds,
The flower-de-luce³ being one. Oh, these I lack
To make you garlands of and my sweet friend
To strew him o'er and o'er.

FLORIZEL   What, like a corpse?
130   PERDITA   No, like a bank for love to lie and play on.
Not like a corpse—or if, not to be buried,
But quick° and in mine arms. Come, take your flowers.   *living*
Methinks I play as I have seen them do
In Whitsun pastorals.⁴ Sure this robe of mine
Does change my disposition.

135   FLORIZEL   What you do
Still° betters what is done. When you speak, sweet,   *Always*
I'd have you do it ever. When you sing,
I'd have you buy and sell so, so give alms,
Pray so; and for the ordering° your affairs,   *arranging of*
140   To sing them too. When you do dance, I wish you
A wave o'th' sea, that you might ever do
Nothing but that, move still, still so,
And own° no other function. Each your doing,°   *have / Each thing you do*
So singular° in each particular,   *distinctive*
145   Crowns what you are doing in the present deeds,
That all your acts are queens.

PERDITA   O Doricles,⁵
Your praises are too large. But that your youth
And the true blood which peeps fairly through't
Do plainly give you out an unstained shepherd,
150   With wisdom I might fear, my Doricles,
You wooed me the false way.

FLORIZEL   I think you have
As little skill° to fear as I have purpose   *reason*
To put you to't. But come; our dance, I pray.
Your hand, my Perdita. So turtles⁶ pair
That never mean to part.

155   PERDITA [*to* CAMILLO]   I'll swear for 'em.
POLIXENES   This is the prettiest lowborn lass that ever
Ran on the greensward.° Nothing she does or seems   *grassy turf*
But smacks of something greater than herself,
Too noble for this place.

CAMILLO [*to* POLIXENES]   He tells her something
160   That makes her blood look on't.° Good sooth, she is   *makes her blush*
The queen of curds and cream.⁷

CLOWN   Come on, strike up!

1. Alluding to the belief that women who died of a kind of anemia known as green sickness would be transformed into primroses. Green sickness was associated with virgins, and vigorous sexual activity was sometimes advocated as a cure.
2. A lily first imported into England from Turkey in the late sixteenth century.
3. Fleur-de-lis, the national flower of France.
4. English rural festivities traditionally held at Whit-

suntide (Pentecost), the seventh Sunday after Easter. The festivities often included morris dances and Robin Hood plays, and were presided over by a festival king and queen.
5. The name Florizel has assumed.
6. Turtledoves, which proverbially mate for life.
7. Referring perhaps to a cream custard known as "white pot." In some May games, a woman was chosen as queen of white-pot cream.

DORCAS Mopsa must be your mistress. Marry, garlic to mend
 her kissing with.[8]

MOPSA Now in good time.

165 CLOWN Not a word, a word; we stand upon our manners.
 Come, strike up!

  [*Music.*] *Here a dance of Shepherds and Shepherdesses*
  [*including* PERDITA *and* FLORIZEL].

    [*Exeunt Shepherds and Shepherdesses.*]

POLIXENES Pray, good shepherd, what fair swain is this
 Which dances with your daughter?

SHEPHERD They call him Doricles, and boasts himself°   *he boasts*
170 To have a worthy feeding;° but I have it   *good pasture land*
 Upon his own report, and I believe it:
 He looks like sooth.° He says he loves my daughter; *appears to be honest*
 I think so, too; for never gazed the moon
 Upon the water as he'll stand and read,
175 As 'twere, my daughter's eyes. And, to be plain,
 I think there is not half a kiss to choose
 Who loves another° best.   *the other*

POLIXENES   She dances featly.°   *nimbly*

SHEPHERD So she does anything, though I report it
 That° should be silent. If young Doricles   *Who*
180 Do light upon her,° she shall bring him that   *choose*
 Which he not dreams of.

    Enter SERVANT.

SERVANT O master, if you did but hear the peddler at the
 door, you would never dance again after a tabor and pipe.[9]
 No, the bagpipe could not move you. He sings several° tunes *different*
185 faster than you'll tell° money. He utters them as he had *count*
 eaten ballads[1] and all men's ears grew° to his tunes. *listened intently*

CLOWN He could never come better.° He shall come in. I love *at a better time*
 a ballad but even too well, if it be doleful matter merrily set
 down, or a very pleasant thing indeed and sung lamentally.

190 SERVANT He hath songs for man or woman of all sizes. No
 milliner[2] can so fit his customers with gloves. He has the
 prettiest love songs for maids, so without bawdry—which is
 strange—with such delicate burdens° of "dildos" and fadings, *refrains*
 "jump her and thump her."[3] And where some stretch-
195 mouthed° rascal would, as it were, mean mischief and break *obscene*
 a foul gap into the matter,[4] he makes the maid to answer,
 "Whoop, do me no harm, good man"; puts him off, slights
 him, with "Whoop, do me no harm, good man."

POLIXENES This is a brave° fellow.   *fine*

200 CLOWN Believe me, thou talkest of an admirable conceited° *very witty*
 fellow. Has he any unbraided° wares?   *new; not shopworn*

---

8. To make her breath sweet (said ironically).
9. A small drum and fife used for morris dancing.
1. Alluding to the broadside ballads that were sung
and sold by peddlers who traveled throughout the
country.
2. One who sells fashionable articles of clothing
such as hats and gloves.
3. Though the servant claims that the songs are

without bawdiness, the refrains are in fact full of
sexual puns that the servant may not understand.
"Dildos" are artificial penises; "fadings" can mean
"orgasms"; and "jump her and thump her" denotes
sexual relations with a woman.
4. *break . . . matter:* interrupt the song with an indecent insertion.

SERVANT He hath ribbons of all the colors i'th' rainbow; points[5]
more than all the lawyers in Bohemia can learnedly handle,
though they come to him by th' gross; inkles, caddises, cam-
205   brics, lawns.[6] Why, he sings 'em over as they were gods or
goddesses. You would think a smock° were a she-angel, he so   *woman's undergarment*
chants to the sleeve-hand° and the work about the square   *wristband*
on't.[7]
CLOWN Prithee bring him in, and let him approach singing.
210 PERDITA Forewarn him that he use no scurrilous words in 's tunes.
                                        [*Exit* SERVANT.]
CLOWN You have of these° peddlers that have more in them   *There are some*
   than you'd think, sister.
PERDITA Ay, good brother, or go about° to think.   *intend*
         Enter AUTOLYCUS, *singing.*
AUTOLYCUS   Lawn as white as driven snow,
215   Cypress[8] black as e'er was crow,
              Gloves as sweet° as damask roses,   *perfumed*
              Masks for faces and for noses;[9]
              Bugle bracelet,[1] necklace amber,
              Perfume for a lady's chamber:
220   Golden coifs° and stomachers[2]   *caps*
              For my lads to give their dears;
              Pins and poking-sticks of steel,[3]
              What maids lack from head to heel.
              Come buy of me, come; come buy, come buy,
225   Buy, lads, or else your lasses cry. Come buy!
CLOWN If I were not in love with Mopsa, thou shouldst take
   no money of me; but being enthralled as I am, it will also be
   the bondage of certain ribbons and gloves.[4]
MOPSA I was promised them against° the feast, but they come   *in time for*
230   not too late now.
DORCAS He hath promised you more than that, or there be liars.
MOPSA He hath paid° you all he promised you—maybe he   *given; had sex with*
   has paid you more, which will shame you to give him again.[5]
CLOWN Is there no manners left among maids? Will they wear
235   their plackets where they should bear their faces?[6] Is there
   not milking time, when you are going to bed, or kiln-hole° to   *fireplace*
   whistle of these secrets, but you must be tittle-tattling before
   all our guests? 'Tis well they are whispering. Clamor your
   tongues,[7] and not a word more.

---

5. Laces for fastening garments, with a pun on
"points" as meaning "legal arguments."
6. "Inkles" were linen tapes; "caddises" were worsted
tapes used for garters; "cambrics" and "lawns" were
heavy and sheer linens.
7. The stitching about the yoke of the garment.
8. A crepe material imported from Cyprus and used
for mourning clothes.
9. Some English women wore masks to protect their
skin from exposure to the sun. If women's noses were
eaten away by syphilis, masks would also cover this
deformity.
1. A bracelet of shiny black beads.
2. Embroidered bodices for dresses.
3. Metal rods used to iron the ruffs or stiff collars

worn by both men and women. "Poking-stick" was
also slang for "penis."
4. *but being . . . gloves:* because I am the prisoner of
love, certain ribbons and gloves must also be put in
bondage (bound up in a parcel).
5. "More" may mean a pregnancy that will result in
an illegitimate child that Dorcas will give to Clown.
6. *Will . . . faces?:* that is, Will they reveal their most
private affairs in public? (There is a pun on "placket,"
which refers to both an opening in a petticoat and
female genitals.)
7. An obscure phrase. Clown clearly means they are
to be quiet. To "clammer" is a term from bell ringing
that means to make the jangling sound characteristic
of bells before they grow silent.

240   MOPSA   I have done. Come, you promised me a tawdry-lace⁸
          and a pair of sweet gloves.
       CLOWN   Have I not told thee how I was cozened by the way°   *cheated on the road*
          and lost all my money?
       AUTOLYCUS   And indeed, sir, there are cozeners abroad; there-
245   fore it behooves men to be wary.
       CLOWN   Fear not thou, man; thou shalt lose nothing here.
       AUTOLYCUS   I hope so, sir, for I have about me many parcels
          of charge.°   *valuable goods*
       CLOWN   What hast here? Ballads?
250   MOPSA   Pray now, buy some. I love a ballad in print, alife,° for   *on my life*
          then we are sure they are true.
       AUTOLYCUS   Here's one to a very doleful tune, how a usurer's
          wife was brought to bed of twenty money-bags at a burden,°   *in one childbirth*
          and how she longed to eat adders' heads and toads
255   carbonadoed.°   *cut and grilled*
       MOPSA   Is it true, think you?
       AUTOLYCUS   Very true, and but a month old.
       DORCAS   Bless me from marrying a usurer.
       AUTOLYCUS   Here's the midwife's name to't, one Mistress
260   Tale-porter,⁹ and five or six honest° wives that were present.   *truthful; chaste*
          Why should I carry lies abroad?
       MOPSA   Pray you now, buy it.
       CLOWN   Come on, lay it by, and let's first see more ballads.
          We'll buy the other things anon.
265   AUTOLYCUS   Here's another ballad of a fish that appeared
          upon the coast on Wednesday the fourscore° of April, forty   *eightieth day*
          thousand fathom° above water, and sung this ballad against   *measurement of six feet*
          the hard hearts of maids. It was thought she was a woman
          and was turned into a cold fish, for she would not exchange
270   flesh° with one that loved her. The ballad is very pitiful, and   *have sex*
          as true.
       DORCAS   Is it true too, think you?
       AUTOLYCUS   Five justices' hands at it,° and witnesses more   *signatures on it*
          than my pack will hold.
275   CLOWN   Lay it by too. Another.
       AUTOLYCUS   This is a merry ballad, but a very pretty one.
       MOPSA   Let's have some merry ones.
       AUTOLYCUS   Why this is a passing° merry one and goes to the   *very*
          tune of "Two maids wooing a man." There's scarce a maid
280   westward° but she sings it. 'Tis in request, I can tell you.   *in the West*
       MOPSA   We can both sing it; if thou'lt bear a part,¹ thou shalt
          hear. 'Tis in three parts.
       DORCAS   We had the tune on't° a month ago.   *of it*
       AUTOLYCUS   I can bear my part. You must know 'tis my occu-
285   pation.° Have at it with you.   *job*
               Song.
       AUTOLYCUS   Get you hence, for I must go
                       Where it fits not you to know.
       DORCAS   Whither?

---

8. A cheap, brightly colored scarf associated with St.
Audrey's Fair. St. Audrey, founder of Ely Cathedral,
died of a throat tumor that she believed was a punishment for wearing gay neckerchiefs in her youth.

9. The name punningly suggests one who reports
gossip ("tales") as well as one who handles genitalia
(slang meaning of "tail").
1. Sing a part in the song.

	MOPSA	Oh, whither?	
290	DORCAS	Whither?	
	MOPSA	It becomes thy oath full well,	
		Thou to me thy secrets tell.	
	DORCAS	Me, too; let me go thither.	
	MOPSA	Or thou goest to th' grange° or mill.	*farm*
295	DORCAS	If to either thou dost ill.	
	AUTOLYCUS	Neither.	
	DORCAS	What, neither?	
	AUTOLYCUS	Neither.	
	DORCAS	Thou hast sworn my love to be.	
300	MOPSA	Thou hast sworn it more to me.	
		Then whither goest? Say, whither?	

CLOWN We'll have this song out anon by ourselves. My father
and the gentlemen are in sad° talk, and we'll not trouble   *serious*
them. Come, bring away thy pack after me. Wenches, I'll
305 buy for you both. Peddler, let's have the first choice. Follow
me, girls.   [*Exit with* DORCAS *and* MOPSA.]

AUTOLYCUS And you shall pay well for 'em.

Song.   Will you buy any tape,
             Or lace for your cape,
310   My dainty duck, my dear-a?
             Any silk, any thread,
             Any toys° for your head,   *small ornaments*
             Of the new'st and fin'st, fin'st wear-a?
             Come to the peddler,
315   Money's a meddler,
             That doth utter° all men's ware-a.   *Exit.*   *put on sale*
      [*Enter* SERVANT.]

SERVANT Master, there is three carters,° three shepherds,   *drivers of carts*
three neatherds,° three swineherds that have made them-   *keepers of cows*
selves all men of hair.[2] They call themselves saltiers,° and   *jumpers*
320 they have a dance which the wenches say is a gallimaufry of
gambols,° because they are not in't. But they themselves are   *jumble of jumps*
o'th' mind—if it be not too rough for some that know little
but bowling°—it will please plentifully.   *(a more sedate sport)*

SHEPHERD Away! We'll none on't. Here has been too much
325 homely° foolery already. —I know, sir, we weary you.   *rough*

POLIXENES You weary those that° refresh us. Pray let's see   *who*
these four threes° of herdsmen.   *trios*

SERVANT One three of them, by their own report, sir, hath
danced before the King;[3] and not the worst of the three but
330 jumps twelve foot and a half by th' square.°   *exactly*

SHEPHERD Leave your prating. Since these good men are
pleased, let them come in; but quickly now.

SERVANT Why, they stay at door, sir.
      [SERVANT *goes to door. Enter Dancers.*] *Here a dance of*
      twelve satyrs.

                              [*Exeunt Dancers.*]

---

2. Probably they are disguised in animal skins to resemble satyrs—mythical woodland figures, part man, part beast, having the pointed ears, legs, and short horns of a goat.

3. This may be a reference to a court performance of Ben Jonson's *Masque of Oberon,* which included a dance of twelve satyrs. It was performed on January 1, 1611, in honor of Prince Henry.

POLIXENES [*to* SHEPHERD]   O father, you'll know more of that hereafter.
335   [*to* CAMILLO]   Is it not too far gone? 'Tis time to part them.
He's simple and tells much. —How now, fair shepherd?
Your heart is full of something that does take
Your mind from feasting. Sooth, when I was young
And handed love,° as you do, I was wont   *pledged love*
340   To load my she with knacks.° I would have ransacked   *small gifts; trifles*
The peddler's silken treasury and have poured it
To her acceptance.° You have let him go   *For her to choose*
And nothing marted with° him. If your lass   *bought from*
Interpretation should abuse° and call this   *Should misinterpret*
345   Your lack of love or bounty, you were straited°   *hard-pressed*
For a reply, at least if you make a care
Of happy holding her.°   *Of keeping her happy*
FLORIZEL   Old sir, I know
She prizes not such trifles as these are.
The gifts she looks° from me are packed and locked   *expects*
350   Up in my heart, which I have given already
But not delivered. [*to* PERDITA] Oh, hear me breathe my life°   *make vows of eternal love*
Before this ancient sir, who, it should seem,
Hath sometime loved. I take thy hand, this hand
As soft as dove's down and as white as it,
355   Or Ethiopian's tooth, or the fanned snow that's bolted°   *sifted*
By th' northern blasts twice o'er.
POLIXENES   What follows this?
[*to* CAMILLO] How prettily th' young swain seems to wash
The hand was° fair before! [*to* FLORIZEL] I have put you out,°   *that was /*
But to your protestation. Let me hear   *interrupted you*
What you profess.
360   FLORIZEL   Do, and be witness to't.
POLIXENES   And this my neighbor too?
FLORIZEL   And he, and more
Than he, and men, the earth, the heavens, and all.
That were I crowned the most imperial monarch,
Thereof most worthy; were I the fairest youth
365   That ever made eye swerve,° had force and knowledge   *commanded attention*
More than was ever man's, I would not prize them
Without her love; for her, employ them all,
Commend them and condemn them to her service,
Or to their own perdition.[4]
POLIXENES   Fairly offered.
CAMILLO   This shows a sound affection.
370   SHEPHERD   But, my daughter,
Say you the like to him?
PERDITA   I cannot speak
So well, nothing so well; no, nor mean better.
By th' pattern of mine own thoughts I cut out
The purity of his.[5]
SHEPHERD   Take hands, a bargain.
375   And, friends unknown, you shall bear witness to't.

---

4. *Commend . . . perdition:* Either dedicate my attri-   5. *By . . . his:* By my pure thoughts I recognize the
butes to her service or sentence them to destruction.   purity of his.

I give my daughter to him and will make
Her portion° equal his.   *dowry*

FLORIZEL   Oh, that must be
I'th' virtue of your daughter. One° being dead,   *Someone*
I shall have more than you can dream of yet,

380   Enough then for your wonder. But come on,
Contract us fore these witnesses.[6]

SHEPHERD   Come, your hand;
And, daughter, yours.

POLIXENES   Soft,° swain, awhile, beseech you.   *Go slowly*
Have you a father?

FLORIZEL   I have. But what of him?

POLIXENES   Knows he of this?

FLORIZEL   He neither does nor shall.

385   **POLIXENES**   Methinks a father
Is at the nuptial of his son a guest
That best becomes the table. Pray you once more,
Is not your father grown incapable
Of reasonable affairs? Is he not stupid

390   With age and altering rheums?° Can he speak, hear,   *debilitating disease*
Know man from man? Dispute° his own estate?°   *Discuss / condition*
Lies he not bedrid? And again does nothing
But what he did being childish?

FLORIZEL   No, good sir,
He has his health and ampler strength indeed
Than most have of his age.

395   **POLIXENES**   By my white beard,
You offer him, if this be so, a wrong
Something unfilial.° Reason my son[7]   *Somewhat unbecoming a son*
Should choose himself a wife, but as good reason
The father, all whose joy is nothing else

400   But fair posterity, should hold some counsel
In such a business.

FLORIZEL   I yield° all this;   *grant*
But for some other reasons, my grave sir,
Which 'tis not fit you know, I not acquaint
My father of this business.

POLIXENES   Let him know't.

FLORIZEL   He shall not.

POLIXENES   Prithee, let him.

405   **FLORIZEL**   No, he must not.

SHEPHERD   Let him, my son. He shall not need to grieve
At knowing of thy choice.

FLORIZEL   Come, come, he must not.
Mark our contract.

POLIXENES [*removing his disguise*]   Mark your divorce, young sir,
Whom son I dare not call. Thou art too base

410   To be acknowledged. Thou a scepter's heir
That thus affects° a sheephook? —Thou, old traitor,   *desires*
I am sorry that by hanging thee I can

---

6. A pledge of marriage spoken before two witnesses   7. It is reasonable that my son.
was legally binding.

But shorten thy life one week. —And thou, fresh piece
Of excellent witchcraft,[8] who of force° must know   *of necessity*
The royal fool thou cop'st° with—   *deal; have sex*

415 SHEPHERD   Oh, my heart.

POLIXENES   —I'll have thy beauty scratched with briars and made
More homely than thy state. —For thee, fond° boy,   *foolish*
If I may ever know thou dost but sigh
That thou no more shalt see this knack°—as never   *worthless thing*
420 I mean thou shalt—we'll bar thee from succession,
Not hold thee of our blood—no, not our kin—
Far than Deucalion off.[9] Mark thou my words.
Follow us to the court. [*to* SHEPHERD] Thou churl, for this time,
Though full of our displeasure, yet we free thee
425 From the dead° blow of it. [*to* PERDITA] And you, enchantment,   *deadly*
Worthy enough a herdsman—yea, him° too,   *(Florizel)*
That makes himself, but for our honor therein,
Unworthy thee[1]—if ever henceforth thou
These rural latches to his entrance open,
430 Or hoop° his body more with thy embraces,   *encircle*
I will devise a death as cruel for thee
As thou art tender to't.   *Exit.*

PERDITA   Even here undone.
I was not much afeard, for once or twice
I was about to speak and tell him plainly
435 The selfsame sun that shines upon his court
Hides not his visage from our cottage, but
Looks on alike.° [*to* FLORIZEL] Will't please you, sir, be gone?   *both alike*
I told you what would come of this. Beseech you,
Of your own state take care. This dream of mine
440 Being now awake, I'll queen it no inch farther,°   *play the queen no further*
But milk my ewes and weep.

CAMILLO   Why, how now, father?
Speak ere thou diest.

SHEPHERD   I cannot speak nor think,
Nor dare to know that which I know. [*to* FLORIZEL] O sir,
You have undone a man of fourscore-three°   *eighty-three*
445 That thought to fill his grave in quiet, yea,
To die upon the bed my father died,
To lie close by his honest bones. But now
Some hangman must put on my shroud and lay me
Where no priest shovels in dust.[2] [*to* PERDITA] O cursèd wretch,
450 That knew'st this was the Prince and wouldst adventure
To mingle faith° with him. Undone, undone!   *exchange vows*
If I might die within this hour, I have lived
To die when I desire.   *Exit.*

FLORIZEL [*to* PERDITA]   Why look you so upon me?
I am but sorry, not afeard; delayed,

---

8. You beautiful young woman skilled in witchcraft.
9. Less linked in kinship than Deucalion, who according to classical mythology was, along with his wife, the only person to escape a flood sent by Zeus. He thus was the ancestor of humankind and the most distant relation one might have.

1. A difficult passage. Polixenes seems to mean that Florizel, by his actions, has made himself unworthy of even a shepherd's daughter.
2. As a criminal, he would be buried by the hangman without ritual. In regular funeral rites, the priest puts the first shovelful of dirt on the grave.

455 But nothing altered. What I was, I am,
More straining on for plucking back,[3] not following
My leash unwillingly.[4]

CAMILLO   Gracious my lord,
You know your father's temper. At this time
He will allow no speech, which I do guess

460 You do not purpose° to him; and as hardly°   *intend / unwillingly*
Will he endure your sight as yet, I fear;
Then till the fury of his highness settle,
Come not before him.

FLORIZEL   I not purpose it.
I think—Camillo?[5]

CAMILLO   Even he, my lord.

465 PERDITA [*to* FLORIZEL]   How often have I told you 'twould be thus?
How often said my dignity would last
But° till 'twere known?   *Only*

FLORIZEL   It cannot fail but by
The violation of my faith, and then
Let nature crush the sides o'th' earth together

470 And mar the seeds° within. Lift up thy looks.   *sources of life*
From my succession wipe me, father: I
Am heir to my affection.

CAMILLO   Be advised.°   *prudent*

FLORIZEL   I am, and by my fancy.° If my reason   *love*
Will thereto be obedient, I have reason;[6]

475 If not, my senses, better pleased with madness,
Do bid it° welcome.   *(madness)*

CAMILLO   This is desperate, sir.

FLORIZEL   So call it. But it does fulfill my vow:
I needs must think it honesty. Camillo,
Not for Bohemia, nor the pomp that may

480 Be thereat gleaned; for all the sun sees, or
The close° earth wombs,° or the profound seas hides   *secret / holds in her womb*
In unknown fathoms, will I break my oath
To this my fair beloved. Therefore, I pray you,
As you have ever been my father's honored friend,

485 When he shall miss me—as in faith I mean not
To see him any more—cast your good counsels
Upon his passion.° Let myself and fortune   *anger*
Tug° for the time to come. This you may know,   *Contend*
And so deliver:° I am put to sea   *report*

490 With her who here I cannot hold on shore;
And most opportune to her need, I have
A vessel rides fast by,° but not prepared   *anchored nearby*
For this design. What course I mean to hold
Shall nothing benefit your knowledge, nor
Concern me the reporting.[7]

---

3. More eager to go forward because of being pulled back.
4. Not following this course of action unwillingly.
5. Camillo may here have taken off his disguise or been recognized by Florizel even with it on.

6. If my reason will obey love, I will embrace reason.
7. Shall . . . reporting: Would not benefit you to know nor me to report.

495 CAMILLO   O my lord,
     I would your spirit were easier for advice°   *to advise*
     Or stronger for your need.
     FLORIZEL   Hark, Perdita—
     [*to* CAMILLO] I'll hear you by and by.
     CAMILLO [*aside*]   He's irremovable,°   *unyielding*
     Resolved for flight. Now were I happy if
500   His going I could frame to serve my turn,
     Save him from danger, do him love and honor,
     Purchase the sight again of dear Sicilia
     And that unhappy king, my master, whom
     I so much thirst to see.
     FLORIZEL   Now, good Camillo,
505   I am so fraught with curious business° that   *matters requiring care*
     I leave out ceremony.
     CAMILLO   Sir, I think
     You have heard of my poor services, i'th' love
     That I have borne your father?
     FLORIZEL   Very nobly
     Have you deserved. It is my father's music
510   To speak your deeds, not little of his care
     To have them recompensed as thought on.[8]
     CAMILLO   Well, my lord,
     If you may please to think I love the King,
     And through him what's nearest to him, which is
515   Your gracious self, embrace but my direction,°   *simply follow my advice*
     If your more ponderous° and settled project   *weighty*
     May suffer° alteration. On mine honor,   *permit*
     I'll point you where you shall have such receiving
     As shall become your highness, where you may
520   Enjoy your mistress, from the whom I see
     There's no disjunction° to be made but by—   *separation*
     As heavens forfend°—your ruin. Marry her,   *forbid*
     And with my best endeavors in your absence,
     Your discontenting° father strive to qualify°   *discontented / appease*
     And bring him up to liking.°   *to giving approval*
525 FLORIZEL   How, Camillo,
     May this, almost a miracle, be done?—
     That I may call thee something more than man,
     And after that trust to thee.
     CAMILLO   Have you thought on°   *of*
     A place whereto you'll go?
     FLORIZEL   Not any yet.
530   But as th'unthought-on accident is guilty
     To what we wildly do,[9] so we profess
     Ourselves to be the slaves of chance, and flies
     Of every wind that blows.
     CAMILLO   Then list to me.
     This follows, if you will not change your purpose
535   But undergo this flight: make for Sicilia,
     And there present yourself and your fair princess,
     For so I see she must be, fore Leontes;

---

8. *not little . . . thought on:* and no small matter among his affairs to reward your deeds as fully as he values them.

9. But as the unexpected event (Polixenes' discovery of our love) is responsible for our rash behavior now.

She shall be habited° as it becomes   *dressed*
The partner of your bed. Methinks I see
540 Leontes opening his free° arms and weeping   *generous*
His welcomes forth; asks thee there, "Son, forgiveness,"
As 'twere i'th' father's person,[1] kisses the hands
Of your fresh princess; o'er and o'er divides him
Twixt his unkindness and his kindness:[2] th'one
545 He chides° to hell and bids the other grow   *rebukes*
Faster than thought or time.

FLORIZEL   Worthy Camillo,
What color° for my visitation shall I   *pretext*
Hold up before him?

CAMILLO   Sent by the King your father
To greet him and to give him comforts. Sir,
550 The manner of your bearing towards him with
What you, as from your father, shall deliver°—   *say*
Things known betwixt us three—I'll write you down,
The which shall point you forth° at every sitting   *direct you*
What you must say, that he shall not perceive
555 But that you have your father's bosom° there   *trust*
And speak his very heart.

FLORIZEL   I am bound to you.
There is some sap° in this.   *life*

CAMILLO   A course more promising
Than a wild dedication of yourselves
To unpathed waters, undreamed shores, most certain
560 To miseries enough; no hope to help you,
But as you shake off one to take another;
Nothing so certain° as your anchors, who   *(to detain you)*
Do their best office if they can but stay° you   *keep*
Where you'll be loath to be. Besides, you know,
565 Prosperity's the very bond of love,
Whose fresh complexion and whose heart together
Affliction alters.°   *changes for the worse*

PERDITA   One of these is true.
I think affliction may subdue the cheek°   *make one pale*
But not take in° the mind.   *conquer*

CAMILLO   Yea, say you so?
570 There shall not at your father's house these seven years[3]
Be born another such.

FLORIZEL   My good Camillo,
She's as forward of her breeding as
She is i'th' rear our birth.[4]

CAMILLO   I cannot say 'tis pity
She lacks instructions,° for she seems a mistress°   *schooling / teacher*
To most that teach.

575 PERDITA   Your pardon, sir; for this
I'll blush you thanks.

FLORIZEL   My prettiest Perdita!

---

1. *As 'twere . . . person:* As if he were your father (granting you forgiveness), *or,* as if you stood in your father's place (and so could grant Leontes forgiveness for his great sin against Polixenes).
2. *divides . . . kindness:* divides his speech between his past unkindness to your father and the kindness he is eager to perform now.
3. Proverbial expression meaning "for a long time."
4. *She's . . . birth:* that is, She is as superior to her lowly upbringing as she is inferior to our noble birth.

But, oh, the thorns we stand upon! Camillo,
Preserver of my father, now of me,
The medicine of our house, how shall we do?
580 We are not furnished° like Bohemia's son,   *dressed; equipped*
Nor shall appear in Sicilia—
CAMILLO   My lord,
Fear none of this. I think you know my fortunes
Do all lie there. It shall be so my care
To have you royally appointed° as if   *outfitted*
585 The scene you play were mine.° For instance, sir,   *written by me*
That you may know you shall not want—one word.
    [*They speak apart.*]
    Enter AUTOLYCUS.
AUTOLYCUS   Ha, ha, what a fool honesty is, and trust, his
sworn brother, a very simple gentleman! I have sold all my
trumpery; not a counterfeit stone, not a ribbon, glass,
590 pomander,[5] brooch, table-book,° ballad, knife, tape, glove,   *notebook*
shoe-tie, bracelet, horn-ring[6] to keep my pack from fasting.°   *going empty*
They throng who should buy first, as if my trinkets had been
hallowed° and brought a benediction to the buyer, by which   *blessed; made sacred*
means I saw whose purse was best in picture;° and what I   *looked best (to steal)*
595 saw, to my good use I remembered. My clown, who wants
but something° to be a reasonable man, grew so in love with   *lacks only one thing*
the wenches' song that he would not stir his pettitoes° till he   *feet (pigs' toes)*
had both tune and words, which so drew the rest of the herd
to me that all their other senses stuck in ears.° You might   *were devoted to hearing*
600 have pinched a placket, it was senseless;° 'twas nothing to   *felt nothing*
geld a codpiece[7] of a purse. I would have filed keys off that
hung in chains. No hearing, no feeling, but my sir's song,
and admiring the nothing° of it. So that in this time of   *silliness*
lethargy I picked and cut most of their festival purses; and,
605 had not the old man come in with a hubbub against his
daughter and the King's son, and scared my choughs° from   *jackdaws (silly birds)*
the chaff, I had not left a purse alive in the whole army.
    [CAMILLO, FLORIZEL, *and* PERDITA *come forward.*]
CAMILLO   Nay, but my letters by this means being there
So soon as you arrive shall clear that doubt.
610 FLORIZEL   And those that you'll procure from King Leontes—
CAMILLO   Shall satisfy your father.
PERDITA   Happy be you!
All that you speak shows fair.
CAMILLO [*seeing* AUTOLYCUS]   Who have we here?
We'll make an instrument of this, omit
Nothing° may give us aid.   *Nothing that*
615 AUTOLYCUS [*aside*]   If they have overheard me now, why, hanging.
CAMILLO   How now, good fellow? Why shak'st thou so?
Fear not, man. Here's no harm intended to thee.
AUTOLYCUS   I am a poor fellow, sir.
CAMILLO   Why, be so still.° Here's nobody will steal that from   *always*
620 thee. Yet, for the outside of thy poverty,° we must make an   *your ragged clothes*

---

5. A mixture of sweet-smelling substances made into
a ball and carried about for ornament or to prevent
infection.
6. A ring made from horn, which was said to possess

magical qualities.
7. The baglike article of dress attached to the front
of a man's hose and covering his genitals.

exchange. Therefore discase° thee instantly—thou must
think there's a necessity in't—and change garments with
this gentleman. Though the pennyworth° on his side be the
worst, yet hold thee, there's some boot.°   *undress*

                                                                                               bargain
                                                                                      something more

625 AUTOLYCUS   I am a poor fellow, sir. [*aside*] I know ye well
        enough.
       CAMILLO   Nay, prithee dispatch;° the gentleman is half flayed⁸   *hurry*
        already.
       AUTOLYCUS   Are you in earnest,⁹ sir? [*aside*] I smell the trick on't.
630 FLORIZEL   Dispatch, I prithee.
       AUTOLYCUS   Indeed I have had earnest, but I cannot with con-
        science take it.
       CAMILLO   Unbuckle, unbuckle.
                [FLORIZEL *and* AUTOLYCUS *exchange garments.*]
                Fortunate mistress, let my prophecy
635   Come home to ye;¹ you must retire yourself
                Into some covert.° Take your sweetheart's hat   *hiding place*
                And pluck it o'er your brows, muffle your face,
                Dismantle you, and, as you can, disliken°   *disguise*
                The truth of your own seeming,° that you may—   *appearance*
640   For I do fear eyes over°—to shipboard   *spies all about*
                Get undescried.
       PERDITA   I see the play so lies
                That I must bear a part.
       CAMILLO   No remedy.
                Have you done there?
       FLORIZEL   Should I now meet my father,
                He would not call me son.
       CAMILLO   Nay, you shall have no hat.
                —Come, lady, come. —Farewell, my friend.
645 AUTOLYCUS   Adieu, sir.
       FLORIZEL   O Perdita, what have we twain forgot!
                Pray you, a word.
                        [*They talk apart.*]
       CAMILLO [*aside*]   What I do next shall be to tell the King
                Of this escape and whither they are bound;
650   Wherein my hope is I shall so prevail
                To force him after, in whose company
                I shall review Sicilia, for whose sight
                I have a woman's longing.²
       FLORIZEL   Fortune speed us.
                Thus we set on, Camillo, to th' seaside.
655 CAMILLO   The swifter speed, the better.
                        Exeunt [FLORIZEL, PERDITA, *and* CAMILLO].
       AUTOLYCUS   I understand the business; I hear it. To have an
        open ear, a quick eye, and a nimble hand is necessary for a
        cutpurse. A good nose is requisite also to smell out work for
        th'other senses. I see this is the time that the unjust man
660   doth thrive. What an exchange had this been without boot!°   *even without payment*
        What a boot³ is here with this exchange! Sure the gods do

---

8. Half undressed (skinned).
9. Serious, with a pun on "earnest" as meaning both
"sincere" and "an advance payment." See line 631.
1. Let my prophecy (that she be fortunate) be

fulfilled.
2. Women were believed vulnerable to irrational and
very intense cravings.
3. Benefit; shoe.

this year connive at° us, and we may do any thing extempore.°   *indulge / spontaneously*
The Prince himself is about a piece of iniquity, stealing away
from his father with his clog° at his heels. If I thought   *encumbrance (Perdita)*
665   it were a piece of honesty to acquaint the King withal,° I   *with it*
would not do't. I hold it the more knavery to conceal it, and
therein am I constant° to my profession.   *faithful*

          Enter CLOWN *and* SHEPHERD.

Aside, aside! Here is more matter for a hot brain. Every
lane's end, every shop, church, session,° hanging, yields a   *court session*
670   careful man work.

CLOWN   See, see, what a man you are now! There is no other
    way but to tell the King she's a changeling⁴ and none of your
    flesh and blood.

SHEPHERD   Nay, but hear me.

675 CLOWN   Nay, but hear me.

SHEPHERD   Go to,° then.   *Go ahead*

CLOWN   She being none of your flesh and blood, your flesh
    and blood has not offended the King, and so your flesh and
    blood is not to be punished by him. Show those things you
680   found about her, those secret things, all but what she has
    with her. This being done, let the law go whistle, I warrant
    you.

SHEPHERD   I will tell the King all, every word, yea, and his
    son's pranks too, who, I may say, is no honest man, neither
685   to his father nor to me, to go about to make me the King's
    brother-in-law.

CLOWN   Indeed, brother-in-law was the farthest off° you   *most remote relation*
    could have been to him, and then your blood had been the
    dearer by I know how much an ounce.

690 AUTOLYCUS [*aside*]   Very wisely, puppies.

SHEPHERD   Well, let us to the King. There is that in this
    fardel° will make him scratch his beard.   *bundle*

AUTOLYCUS [*aside*]   I know not what impediment this com-
    plaint may be to the flight of my master.°   *(Florizel)*

695 CLOWN   Pray heartily he be at palace.

AUTOLYCUS [*aside*]   Though I am not naturally honest, I am
    so sometimes by chance. Let me pocket up my peddler's
    excrement.°   *hair*

          [*He takes off his false beard and steps forward.*]
How now, rustics, whither are you bound?

700 SHEPHERD   To th' palace, an't° like your worship.   *if it*

AUTOLYCUS   Your affairs there? What? With whom? The
    condition° of that fardel? The place of your dwelling? Your   *nature*
    names? Your ages? Of what having,° breeding,° and anything   *property / upbringing*
    that is fitting to be known, discover.°   *reveal*

705 CLOWN   We are but plain° fellows, sir.   *simple; smooth*

AUTOLYCUS   A lie! You are rough and hairy. Let me have no
    lying; it becomes none but tradesmen, and they often give
    us soldiers the lie;⁵ but we pay them for it with stamped
    coin, not stabbing steel, therefore they do not give us the
710   lie.⁶

4. A child left or abducted by fairies; see note to
3.3.107.
5. They call us soldiers liars; they cheat us soldiers.
6. *we pay . . . the lie:* since soldiers pay with good

currency rather than by stabbing (the appropriate
response to an insult), the tradesmen are prevented
from perpetuating the quarrel.

CLOWN   Your worship had like to have given us one° if you
had not taken yourself with the manner.[7]   *(the lie)*

SHEPHERD   Are you a courtier, an't like you, sir?

AUTOLYCUS   Whether it like me or no, I am a courtier. Seest
715   thou not the air of the court in these enfoldings?° Hath not   *garments*
my gait in it the measure° of the court? Receives not   *stately walk*
thy nose court-odor from me? Reflect I not on thy baseness
court-contempt? Think'st thou for that I insinuate° to   *subtly work*
toze° from thee thy business, I am therefore no courtier?   *tease out*
720   I am courtier cap-à-pie° and one that will either push on   *from head to foot*
or pluck back thy business there. Whereupon I command
thee to open° thy affair.   *reveal*

SHEPHERD   My business, sir, is to the King.

AUTOLYCUS   What advocate hast thou to him?

725   SHEPHERD   I know not, an't like you.

CLOWN   Advocate's the court word for a pheasant.[8] Say you
have none.

SHEPHERD   None, sir. I have no pheasant, cock nor hen.

AUTOLYCUS *[aside]*   How blessed are we that are not simple men!
730   Yet nature might have made me as these are,
Therefore I will not disdain.

CLOWN   This cannot be but° a great courtier.   *anyone but*

SHEPHERD   His garments are rich, but he wears them not
handsomely.

735   CLOWN   He seems to be the more noble in being fantastical.°   *eccentric*
A great man, I'll warrant. I know by the picking on 's teeth.[9]

AUTOLYCUS   The fardel there? What's i'th' fardel? Wherefore
that box?

SHEPHERD   Sir, there lies such secrets in this fardel and
740   box which none must know but the King, and which he
shall know within this hour, if I may come to th' speech of
him.

AUTOLYCUS   Age,° thou hast lost thy labor.   *Old man*

SHEPHERD   Why, sir?

745   AUTOLYCUS   The King is not at the palace; he is gone aboard a
new ship to purge melancholy and air himself. For if thou
beest capable of° things serious, thou must know the King   *can understand*
is full of grief.

SHEPHERD   So 'tis said, sir—about his son that should have
750   married a shepherd's daughter.

AUTOLYCUS   If that shepherd be not in handfast,° let him   *arrested*
fly. The curses he shall have, the tortures he shall feel, will
break the back of man, the heart of monster.

CLOWN   Think you so, sir?

755   AUTOLYCUS   Not he alone shall suffer what wit can make
heavy and vengeance bitter; but those that are germane°   *related*
to him, though removed fifty times, shall all come under the
hangman, which though it be great pity, yet it is necessary.
An old sheep-whistling rogue,[1] a ram-tender, to offer to have

---

7. If you had not stopped yourself in the middle.
8. Clown thinks "advocate" means "bribe" or "gift,"
of which a pheasant would be an example.

9. Ornate toothpicks were considered fashionable
accessories.
1. An old rascal who whistles while he tends sheep.

760 his daughter come into grace!° Some say he shall be stoned,   *favor (at court)*
but that death is too soft for him, say I. Draw our throne
into a sheepcote?° All deaths are too few, the sharpest too   *pen for sheep*
easy.

CLOWN   Has the old man e'er a son, sir, do you hear, an't like
765 you, sir?

AUTOLYCUS   He has a son, who shall be flayed alive, then
'nointed over with honey, set on the head of a wasps' nest,
then stand till he be three-quarters and a dram° dead, then   *a tiny bit*
recovered again with aqua vitae,° or some other hot   *brandy*
770 infusion; then, raw as he is, and in the hottest day prognosti-
cation° proclaims, shall he be set against a brick wall,   *almanac prediction*
the sun looking with a southward eye upon him, where he is
to behold him with flies blown° to death. But what talk   *swollen*
we of these traitorly rascals, whose miseries are to be smiled
775 at, their offenses being so capital? Tell me, for you seem
to be honest plain men, what you have° to the King.   *have to say*
Being something gently considered,[2] I'll bring you where
he is aboard, tender° your persons to his presence, whisper   *deliver*
him in your behalfs; and if it be in man, besides the King, to
780 effect your suits, here is man shall do it.

CLOWN [*aside to* SHEPHERD]   He seems to be of great authority; close° with him, give him gold. And though authority   *make a deal*
be a stubborn bear, yet he is oft led by the nose with gold.
Show the inside of your purse to the outside of his hand,
785 and no more ado. Remember "stoned" and "flayed alive."

SHEPHERD   An't please you, sir, to undertake the business for
us, here is that° gold I have. I'll make it as much more,   *what*
and leave this young man in pawn,° till I bring it you.   *as security*

AUTOLYCUS   After I have done what I promised?

790 SHEPHERD   Ay, sir.

AUTOLYCUS   Well, give me the moiety.° Are you a party in   *half*
this business?

CLOWN   In some sort, sir. But though my case° be a pitiful   *condition; skin*
one, I hope I shall not be flayed out of it.

795 AUTOLYCUS   Oh, that's the case of the shepherd's son. Hang
him, he'll be made an example.

CLOWN [*aside to* SHEPHERD]   Comfort, good comfort. We must
to the King and show our strange sights. He must know 'tis
none of your daughter nor my sister. We are gone else.° —Sir,   *otherwise lost*
800 I will give you as much as this old man does when the
business is performed, and remain, as he says, your pawn
till it be brought you.

AUTOLYCUS   I will trust you. Walk before° toward the   *ahead of me*
seaside; go on the right hand; I will but look upon the
805 hedge[3] and follow you.

CLOWN   We are blessed in this man. As I may say, even
blessed.

SHEPHERD   Let's before, as he bids us. He was provided to do
us good.   [*Exeunt* SHEPHERD *and* CLOWN.]

---

2. *Being . . . considered:* Since I am regarded as a
gentleman (someone of high rank who does not labor
with his hands and so is worthy of the attention of
the King).
3. *look upon the hedge:* slang for "relieve myself."

810 AUTOLYCUS   If I had a mind to be honest, I see Fortune would
       not suffer° me; she drops booties° in my mouth. I am   *permit / prizes*
       courted now with a double occasion:° gold, and a means to   *opportunity*
       do the Prince my master good, which who knows how that
815   may turn back to my advancement? I will bring these two
       moles, these blind ones, aboard him;° if he think it fit   *(his ship)*
       to shore them⁴ again, and that the complaint they have to
       the King concerns him nothing, let him call me rogue for
       being so far officious; for I am proof against° that title and   *impervious to*
       what shame else belongs to't. To him will I present them.
820   There may be matter in it.   *Exit.*

5.1

Enter LEONTES, CLEOMENES, DION, [*and*] PAULINA.

CLEOMENES   Sir, you have done enough and have performed
       A saint-like sorrow. No fault could you make
       Which you have not redeemed, indeed, paid down
       More penitence than done trespass.¹ At the last
5   Do as the heavens have done, forget your evil;
       With them, forgive yourself.
LEONTES   Whilst I remember
       Her and her virtues, I cannot forget
       My blemishes in them,° and so still think of   *in relation to them*
       The wrong I did myself, which was so much
10   That heirless it hath made my kingdom and
       Destroyed the sweet'st companion that e'er man
       Bred his hopes out of. True?
PAULINA   Too true, my lord.
       If one by one you wedded all the world,
       Or from the all that are took something good
15   To make a perfect woman, she you killed
       Would be unparalleled.
LEONTES   I think so. Killed?
       She I killed? I did so, but thou strik'st me
       Sorely to say I did. It is as bitter
       Upon thy tongue as in my thought. Now, good now,°   *if you would*
       Say so but seldom.
20 CLEOMENES   Not at all,° good lady.   *Never (say these things)*
       You might have spoken a thousand things that would
       Have done the time more benefit and graced°   *showed*
       Your kindness better.
PAULINA   You are one of those
       Would have him wed again.
DION   If you would not so,
25   You pity not the state° nor the remembrance   *kingdom*
       Of his most sovereign name,² consider little
       What dangers by his highness' fail of issue°   *lack of offspring*
       May drop upon his kingdom and devour
       Incertain lookers-on.³ What were more holy
30   Than to rejoice the former queen is well?°   *(in heaven)*

---

4. Put them ashore.
5.1 Location: Sicilia. The palace of Leontes.
1. *paid down . . . trespass:* performed more penance
than your sin warranted.

2. *nor . . . name:* nor the perpetuation of his royal
lineage (through a new child).
3. *and . . . lookers-on:* and destroy the confused
bystanders.

What holier, than for royalty's repair,
For present comfort and for future good,
To bless the bed of majesty again
With a sweet fellow to't?

PAULINA   There is none worthy,
35   Respecting° her that's gone. Besides, the gods   *In comparison to*
Will have fulfilled their secret purposes.
For has not the divine Apollo said—
Is't not the tenor of his oracle?—
That King Leontes shall not have an heir
40   Till his lost child be found? Which that it shall
Is all as monstrous° to our human reason   *incredible*
As my Antigonus to break his grave
And come again to me, who, on my life,
Did perish with the infant. 'Tis your counsel
45   My lord should to the heavens be contrary,
Oppose against their wills.
[*to* LEONTES]   Care not for° issue;   *Do not worry about*
The crown will find an heir. Great Alexander
Left his to th' worthiest,[4] so his successor
Was like to be the best.

LEONTES   Good Paulina,
50   Who hast the memory of Hermione
I know in honor—oh, that ever I
Had squared me° to thy counsel! Then even now   *conformed my actions*
I might have looked upon my queen's full eyes,
Have taken treasure from her lips.

PAULINA   And left them
55   More rich for what they yielded.

LEONTES   Thou speak'st truth.
No more such wives, therefore no wife. One worse
And better used° would make her sainted spirit   *treated*
Again possess her° corpse, and on this stage,   *(Hermione's)*
Where we offenders now appear, soul-vexed,°   *with troubled soul*
And begin, "Why° to me?"   *Why offer this insult*

60   PAULINA   Had she such power,
She had just cause.

LEONTES   She had, and would incense me
To murder her I married.

PAULINA   I should so.
Were I the ghost that walked, I'd bid you mark
Her eye and tell me for what dull part in't
65   You chose her. Then I'd shriek that even your ears
Should rift° to hear me; and the words that followed   *split*
Should be, "Remember mine."°   *(my eyes)*

LEONTES   Stars, stars,
And all eyes else° dead coals! Fear thou no wife;   *all other eyes*
I'll have no wife, Paulina.

PAULINA   Will you swear
70   Never to marry but by my free leave?

---

4. Alexander the Great (356–323 B.C.E.), conqueror of Greece, Persia, and Egypt, died before his own son was born and reportedly urged his followers simply to choose the worthiest man as his successor.

LEONTES   Never, Paulina, so be blest my spirit.
PAULINA   Then good my lords, bear witness to his oath.
CLEOMENES   You tempt° him over-much.   *urge*
PAULINA   Unless another,
   As like Hermione as is her picture,
   Affront° his eye.   *Confront*
75 CLEOMENES   Good madam, I have done.[5]
PAULINA   Yet if my lord will marry—if you will, sir,
   No remedy but you will—give me the office
   To choose you a queen. She shall not be so young
   As was your former, but she shall be such
80   As, walked your first queen's ghost,[6] it should take joy
   To see her in your arms.
LEONTES   My true Paulina,
   We shall not marry till thou bidd'st us.
PAULINA   That
   Shall be when your first queen's again in breath.°   *alive*
   Never till then.
      Enter a SERVANT.
85 SERVANT   One that gives out himself° Prince Florizel,   *claims to be*
   Son of Polixenes, with his princess—she
   The fairest I have yet beheld—desires access
   To your high presence.
LEONTES   What° with him? He comes not   *Who comes*
   Like to° his father's greatness. His approach,   *As befits*
90   So out of circumstance° and sudden, tells us   *informal*
   'Tis not a visitation framed,° but forced   *planned*
   By need and accident. What train?°   *retinue*
SERVANT   But few,
   And those but mean.°   *of low rank*
LEONTES   His princess, say you, with him?
SERVANT   Ay, the most peerless piece of earth, I think,
   That e'er the sun shone bright on.
95 PAULINA   O Hermione,
   As every present time doth boast itself
   Above a better, gone, so must thy grave
   Give way to what's seen now.[7] —Sir, you yourself
   Have said and writ so, but your writing now
100 Is colder than that theme. She had not been
   Nor was not to be equaled—thus your verse
   Flowed with her beauty once; 'tis shrewdly° ebbed   *grievously*
   To say you have seen a better.
SERVANT   Pardon, madam.
   The one° I have almost forgot—your pardon—   *(Hermione)*
105 The other, when she has obtained your eye,
   Will have your tongue too. This is a creature,
   Would she begin a sect, might quench the zeal
   Of all professors else,[8] make proselytes°   *converts*

---

5. Many editors emend this line to assign "I have done" to Paulina, rather than Cleomenes. As it stands, the line suggests Cleomenes' exasperation that Paulina will not listen to him. If given to Paulina, the line suggests that she knows she should stop berating the King.
6. *walked . . . ghost:* if Hermione appeared as a ghost.
7. *As every . . . seen now:* As each present time boasts itself to be superior to a time better than itself, but gone from view, so you, in your grave, must be superseded by what is now seen.
8. Of all those who professed other religions.

Of who° she but bid follow.   *Of those who*

PAULINA   How? Not women?

110 SERVANT   Women will love her that she is a woman
More worth° than any man; men, that she is   *worthy*
The rarest of all women.

LEONTES   Go, Cleomenes,
Yourself, assisted with your honored friends,
Bring them to our embracement. Still 'tis strange,
He thus should steal upon us.   *Exit* [CLEOMENES].

115 PAULINA   Had our prince,
Jewel of children, seen this hour, he had paired
Well with this lord; there was not full a month°   *a full month*
Between their births.

LEONTES   Prithee, no more; cease. Thou know'st
He dies to me again when talked of. Sure,
120 When I shall see this gentleman, thy speeches
Will bring me to consider that which may
Unfurnish me of reason.°   *Make me go mad*

Enter FLORIZEL, PERDITA, CLEOMENES, *and others.*
                        They are come.
—Your mother was most true to wedlock, Prince,
For she did print your royal father off,[9]
125 Conceiving you. Were I but twenty-one,
Your father's image is so hit° in you,   *exact*
His very air, that I should call you brother,
As I did him, and speak of something wildly
By us performed before. Most dearly welcome,
130 And your fair princess—goddess! Oh, alas,
I lost a couple that twixt heaven and earth
Might thus have stood begetting wonder as
You, gracious couple, do. And then I lost—
All mine own folly—the society,
135 Amity too, of your brave° father, whom,   *stouthearted*
Though bearing misery, I desire my life
Once more to look on him.[1]

FLORIZEL   By his command
Have I here touched Sicilia and from him
Give you all greetings that a king at friend°   *in friendship*
140 Can send his brother; and but° infirmity,   *were it not that*
Which waits upon worn times,° hath something seized   *accompanies old age*
His wished ability,[2] he had himself
The lands and waters twixt your throne and his
Measured° to look upon you, whom he loves—   *Journeyed across*
145 He bade me say so—more than all the scepters,
And those that bear them, living.

LEONTES   O my brother!
Good gentleman, the wrongs I have done thee stir
Afresh within me, and these thy offices,°   *greetings*
So rarely° kind, are as interpreters   *extraordinarily*
150 Of my behind-hand slackness.[3] Welcome hither,

---

9. *did print . . . off*: made an exact copy of Polixenes, as a printer produces a book.
1. *whom . . . on him*: whom, though I am suffering, I wish to live long enough to look on once more.
2. *hath . . . ability*: has somewhat deprived him of his desired strength.
3. *are . . . slackness*: are reminders of my slowness (in greeting you).

As is the spring to th'earth. And hath he too
Exposed this paragon to th' fearful usage—
At least ungentle—of the dreadful Neptune,°   *(god of the sea)*
To greet a man not worth her pains, much less
Th'adventure° of her person?   *risk*

155 FLORIZEL   Good my lord,
She came from Libya.
LEONTES   Where the warlike Smalus,[4]
That noble honored lord, is feared and loved?
FLORIZEL   Most royal sir, from thence; from him whose daughter
His tears proclaimed his parting with her. Thence,
160 A prosperous south wind friendly, we have crossed
To execute the charge my father gave me
For visiting your highness. My best train
I have from your Sicilian shores dismissed,
Who for Bohemia bend° to signify   *make their way*
165 Not only my success in Libya, sir,
But my arrival and my wife's in safety
Here where we are.
LEONTES   The blessèd gods
Purge all infection from our air whilst you
Do climate° here. You have a holy father,   *reside*
170 A graceful gentleman, against whose person,
So sacred as it is, I have done sin,
For which the heavens, taking angry note,
Have left me issueless; and your father's blessed,
As he from heaven merits it, with you,
175 Worthy his goodness. What might I have been,
Might I a son and daughter now have looked on,
Such goodly things as you?
Enter a LORD.
LORD   Most noble sir,
That which I shall report will bear no credit
Were not the proof so nigh. Please you, great sir,
180 Bohemia greets you from himself by me;
Desires you to attach° his son, who has,   *arrest*
His dignity and duty[5] both cast off,
Fled from his father, from his hopes, and with
A shepherd's daughter.
LEONTES   Where's Bohemia? Speak.
185 LORD   Here in your city; I now came from him.
I speak amazedly,° and it becomes°   *confusedly / befits*
My marvel° and my message. To your court   *astonishment*
Whiles he was hast'ning—in the chase, it seems,
Of this fair couple—meets he on the way
190 The father of this seeming° lady and   *apparent; false*
Her brother, having both their country quitted
With this young prince.
FLORIZEL   Camillo has betrayed me,
Whose honor and whose honesty till now
Endured all weathers.

---

4. *Smalus:* an obscure allusion; the name may be a
misprint for "Synalus," a soldier from Carthage mentioned by Plutarch.
5. His royal status and his duty to his father.

LORD   Lay't so to his charge.°   *Accuse him directly*
He's with the King your father.

195 LEONTES   Who, Camillo?
LORD   Camillo, sir. I spake with him, who now
Has these poor men in question. Never saw I
Wretches so quake: they kneel, they kiss the earth,
Forswear° themselves as often as they speak.   *Perjure*
200 Bohemia stops his ears and threatens them
With divers deaths in death.°   *With diverse tortures*

PERDITA   O my poor father!
The heaven sets spies upon us, will not have
Our contract celebrated.

LEONTES   You are married?
FLORIZEL   We are not, sir, nor are we like to be.
205 The stars, I see, will kiss the valleys first;
The odds for high and low's alike.[6]

LEONTES   My lord,
Is this the daughter of a king?

FLORIZEL   She is,
When once she is my wife.

LEONTES   That "once," I see, by your good father's speed
210 Will come on very slowly. I am sorry,
Most sorry, you have broken from his liking,
Where you were tied in duty; and as sorry
Your choice is not so rich in worth° as beauty,   *rank*
That you might well enjoy her.

FLORIZEL   —Dear, look up.
215 Though Fortune, visible an enemy,
Should chase us with my father, power no jot
Hath she to change our loves.[7] —Beseech you, sir,
Remember since you owed no more to time
Than I do now.° With thought of such affections,   *when you were my age*
220 Step forth mine advocate; at your request
My father will grant precious things as trifles.

LEONTES   Would he do so, I'd beg your precious mistress,
Which he counts but a trifle.

PAULINA   Sir, my liege,
Your eye hath too much youth in't. Not a month
225 Fore your queen died, she was more worth such gazes
Than what you look on now.

LEONTES   I thought of her
Even in these looks I made. —But your petition
Is yet unanswered. I will to your father.
Your honor not o'erthrown by your desires,[8]
230 I am friend to them and you. Upon which errand
I now go toward him; therefore follow me,
And mark what way I make. Come, good my lord.

                                         Exeunt.

---

6. *The odds . . . alike:* that is, Chance treats those of
high and low rank identically.
7. *power . . . our loves:* even if Lady Fortune were to
make herself apparent as our enemy and join my

father in pursuit, she would remain powerless to
change our love.
8. *Your honor . . . desires:* So long as you have not
allowed passion to destroy your virtue.

5.2

Enter AUTOLYCUS *and a* GENTLEMAN.

AUTOLYCUS Beseech you, sir, were you present at this
relation?°   *when this was told*

FIRST GENTLEMAN I was by at the opening of the fardel, heard
the old shepherd deliver the manner how he found it; where-
5 upon, after a little amazedness, we were all commanded out
of the chamber. Only this: methought I heard the shepherd
say he found the child.

AUTOLYCUS I would most gladly know the issue° of it.   *outcome*

FIRST GENTLEMAN I make a broken delivery° of the business,   *confused report*
10 but the changes I perceived in the King and Camillo were
very notes of admiration.[1] They seemed almost, with staring
on one another, to tear the cases° of their eyes. There   *burst the sockets*
was speech in their dumbness, language in their very ges-
ture. They looked as° they had heard of a world ransomed   *as if*
15 or one destroyed. A notable passion of wonder appeared in
them, but the wisest beholder that knew no more but seeing
could not say if th'importance were joy or sorrow. But in the
extremity of the one,° it must needs be.   *of the one or the other*

Enter another GENTLEMAN.

Here comes a gentleman that happily° knows more. The   *perhaps*
20 news, Rogero?

SECOND GENTLEMAN Nothing but bonfires. The oracle is ful-
filled; the King's daughter is found. Such a deal° of wonder   *great quantity*
is broken out within this hour that ballad-makers cannot be
able to express it.

Enter another GENTLEMAN.

25 Here comes the Lady Paulina's steward. He can deliver you
more. How goes it now, sir? This news which is called true is
so like an old tale that the verity of it is in strong suspicion.
Has the King found his heir?

THIRD GENTLEMAN Most true, if ever truth were pregnant by
30 circumstance.° That which you hear you'll swear you see,   *proven by evidence*
there is such unity in the proofs. The mantle of Queen
Hermione's; her jewel about the neck of it; the letters of
Antigonus found with it, which they know to be his charac-
ter;° the majesty of the creature in resemblance of the   *handwriting*
35 mother; the affection of° nobleness, which nature shows   *instinct toward*
above her breeding;[2] and many other evidences, proclaim
her with all certainty to be the King's daughter. Did you see
the meeting of the two kings?

SECOND GENTLEMAN No.

40 THIRD GENTLEMAN Then have you lost a sight which was to
be seen, cannot be spoken of. There might you have beheld
one joy crown another, so and in such manner that it
seemed sorrow wept to take leave of them, for their joy
waded in tears. There was casting up of eyes, holding up
45 of hands, with countenance° of such distraction[3] that   *face*
they were to be known by garment, not by favor.° Our   *features*

5.2 Location: Scene continues.
1. Were the very marks of wonder.
2. *which . . . breeding:* which naturally shows in her

in excess of her upbringing.
3. So altered by emotion.

King being ready to leap out of himself for joy of his found
daughter, as if that joy were now become a loss, cries, "Oh,
thy mother, thy mother!"; then asks Bohemia forgiveness,
50 then embraces his son-in-law, then again worries he° his   *he agitates*
daughter with clipping° her. Now he thanks the old   *embracing*
shepherd, which stands by like a weather-bitten conduit
of⁴ many kings' reigns. I never heard of such another
encounter, which lames report to follow it⁵ and undoes°   *defies*
55 description to do° it.   *express*

SECOND GENTLEMAN   What, pray you, became of Antigonus
that carried hence the child?

THIRD GENTLEMAN   Like an old tale still, which will have mat-
ter to rehearse° though credit° be asleep and not an ear open: *relate / belief*
60 he was torn to pieces with a bear. This avouches° the   *vows*
shepherd's son, who has not only his innocence,° which   *simplemindedness*
seems much to justify him, but a handkerchief and rings
of his° that Paulina knows.   *(of Antigonus)*

FIRST GENTLEMAN   What became of his bark° and his followers?   *ship*

65 THIRD GENTLEMAN   Wrecked the same instant of their master's death, and in the view of the shepherd; so that all the
instruments which aided to expose the child were even then
lost when it was found. But, oh, the noble combat that twixt
joy and sorrow was fought in Paulina: she had one eye
70 declined for the loss of her husband, another elevated that
the oracle was fulfilled. She lifted the Princess from the
earth, and so locks her in embracing as if she would pin her
to her heart, that she might no more be in danger of losing.°   *of being lost*

FIRST GENTLEMAN   The dignity of this act was worth the audi
75 ence of kings and princes, for by such was it acted.

THIRD GENTLEMAN   One of the prettiest touches of all, and
that which angled for mine eyes—caught the water° though   *(my tears)*
not the fish—was when at the relation of the Queen's death,
with the manner how she came to't bravely confessed
80 and lamented by the King, how attentiveness° wounded   *intent listening*
his daughter till from one sign of dolor° to another she   *grief*
did, with an "Alas," I would fain say bleed tears; for I am
sure my heart wept blood. Who was most marble° there   *unfeeling*
changed color. Some swooned, all sorrowed. If all the
85 world could have seen't, the woe had been universal.

FIRST GENTLEMAN   Are they returned to the court?

THIRD GENTLEMAN   No. The Princess hearing of her mother's
statue, which is in the keeping of Paulina, a piece many
years in doing and now newly performed° by that rare   *completed*
90 Italian master, Giulio Romano,⁶ who, had he himself eternity and could put breath into his work, would beguile°   *cheat*
nature of her custom,° so perfectly he is her ape.° He so   *business / imitator*
near to Hermione hath done Hermione that they say one
would speak to her and stand in hope of answer. Thither

---

4. *weather-bitten . . . of*: battered waterspout from.
5. Which makes any account of it seem deficient.
6. An Italian painter, a follower of Raphael, who

died in 1546 and may have contributed to a well-
known series of erotic drawings, *I modi*, illustrating
sexual positions, or "postures."

95   with all greediness of affection are they gone, and there
      they intend to sup.

SECOND GENTLEMAN   I thought she had some great matter
      there in hand, for she hath privately twice or thrice a day
      ever since the death of Hermione visited that removed°   distant; hidden
100   house. Shall we thither and with our company piece° the   join
      rejoicing?

FIRST GENTLEMAN   Who would be thence that has the benefit
      of access? Every wink of an eye some new grace will be
      born. Our absence makes us unthrifty to our knowledge.[7]
105   Let's along.   *Exeunt* [GENTLEMEN].

AUTOLYCUS   Now, had I not the dash° of my former life in me,   stain; touch
      would preferment° drop on my head. I brought the old   royal favor
      man and his son aboard the° Prince, told him I heard   aboard the ship of the
      them talk of a fardel, and I know not what. But he at that
110   time over-fond of the shepherd's daughter—so he then took
      her to be—who began to be much seasick and himself little
      better, extremity of weather continuing, this mystery
      remained undiscovered. But 'tis all one to me, for had I been
      the finder-out of this secret, it would not have relished°   appeared well
115   among my other discredits.

      Enter SHEPHERD *and* CLOWN.

      Here come those I have done good to against my will, and
      already appearing in the blossoms of their fortune.

SHEPHERD   Come, boy. I am past more children, but thy sons
      and daughters will be all gentlemen born.

120 CLOWN [*to* AUTOLYCUS]   You are well met, sir. You denied to
      fight with me this other° day because I was no gentleman   the other
      born. See you these clothes? Say you see them not and think
      me still no gentleman born. You were best say these robes
      are not gentlemen born. Give me the lie,[8] do, and try whether
125   I am not now a gentleman born.

AUTOLYCUS   I know you are now, sir, a gentleman born.

CLOWN   Ay, and have been so any time these four hours.

SHEPHERD   And so have I, boy.

CLOWN   So you have; but I was a gentleman born before my
130   father, for the King's son took me by the hand and called me
      brother; and then the two kings called my father brother;
      and then the Prince my brother and the Princess my sister
      called my father, father. And so we wept, and there was the
      first gentleman-like tears that ever we shed.

135 SHEPHERD   We may live, son, to shed many more.

CLOWN   Ay, or else 'twere hard luck, being in so preposterous
      estate[9] as we are.

AUTOLYCUS   I humbly beseech you, sir, to pardon me all the
      faults I have committed to your worship, and to give me your
140   good report to the Prince my master.

---

7. Makes us squander an opportunity to add to our knowledge.
8. Insult me (so that I must respond like a gentleman, perhaps by offering to duel).
9. Clown probably means "prosperous," but "prepos-terous" is a nice blunder because preposterous means (1) contrary to nature or (2) putting last what should be first. By becoming gentlemen, the shepherds have inverted the social order and put "real" gentlemen behind "false" ones.

SHEPHERD   Prithee, son, do, for we must be gentle° now we
　 are gentlemen.   *act nobly*
CLOWN   Thou wilt amend thy life?
AUTOLYCUS   Ay, an it like your good worship.
145 CLOWN   Give me thy hand. I will swear to the Prince thou art
　 as honest a true fellow as any is in Bohemia.
SHEPHERD   You may say it, but not swear it.
CLOWN   Not swear it now I am a gentleman? Let boors° and
　 franklins° say it; I'll swear it.   *peasants*
                                                                                          small farmers
150 SHEPHERD   How if it be false, son?
CLOWN   If it be ne'er so false,° a true gentleman may swear it   *Even if it is false*
　 in the behalf of his friend. And I'll swear to the Prince thou
　 art a tall fellow of thy hands° and that thou wilt not   *brave man of action*
　 be drunk. But I know thou art no tall fellow of thy hands
155 and that thou wilt be drunk, but I'll swear it, and I would
　 thou wouldst be a tall fellow of thy hands.
AUTOLYCUS   I will prove so, sir, to my power.°   *as well as I can*
CLOWN   Ay, by any means prove a tall fellow. If I do not wonder
　 how thou dar'st venture to be drunk, not being a tall fellow,
160 trust me not. Hark, the kings and princes, our kindred, are
　 going to see the Queen's picture.° Come, follow us. We'll   *likeness*
　 be thy good masters.   *Exeunt.*

<h3 style="text-align:center">5.3</h3>

Enter LEONTES, POLIXENES, FLORIZEL, PERDITA, CAMILLO,
　 PAULINA, HERMIONE (*like a statue*), LORDS, *etc.*[1]
LEONTES   O grave and good Paulina, the great comfort
　 That I have had of thee!
PAULINA   What,° sovereign sir,   *Whatever*
　 I did not well, I meant well. All my services
　 You have paid home;° but that you have vouchsafed°   *fully rewarded / vowed*
5　 With your crowned brother and these your contracted
　 Heirs of your kingdoms my poor house to visit,
　 It is a surplus° of your grace which never   *additional sign*
　 My life may last to answer.
LEONTES   O Paulina,
　 We honor you with trouble,[2] but we came
10　 To see the statue of our queen. Your gallery
　 Have we passed through, not without much content
　 In many singularities;° but we saw not   *In seeing many rarities*
　 That which my daughter came to look upon,
　 The statue of her mother.
PAULINA   As she lived peerless,
15　 So her dead likeness I do well believe
　 Excels whatever yet you looked upon,
　 Or hand of man hath done; therefore I keep it
　 Lonely,° apart. But here it is. Prepare   *Alone*
　 To see the life as lively mocked° as ever   *realistically imitated*

5.3 Location: Sicilia. Paulina's house.
1. TEXTUAL COMMENT Hermione needs to enter here
since the text gives her no other way to enter this
scene, but the scene must be performed in a way that
maintains for theatergoers the illusion that she is a
statue. See Digital Edition TC 9.
2. *We honor you with trouble:* The honor we pay to
you demands effort from you.

20   Still° sleep mocked death. Behold, and say 'tis well.   *Quiet*
        [PAULINA *reveals* HERMIONE, *standing like a statue.*][3]
    I like your silence; it the more shows off
    Your wonder. But yet speak; first you, my liege,
    Comes it not something° near?   *somewhat*
    LEONTES   Her natural posture.
    —Chide me, dear stone, that I may say indeed
25   Thou art Hermione; or, rather, thou art she
    In thy not chiding, for she was as tender
    As infancy and grace. —But yet, Paulina,
    Hermione was not so much wrinkled, nothing°   *not at all*
    So aged as this seems.
    POLIXENES   Oh, not by much.
30   PAULINA   So much the more our carver's excellence,
    Which lets go by some sixteen years and makes her
    As° she lived now.   *As if*
    LEONTES   As now she might have done,
    So much to my good comfort as it is
    Now piercing to my soul. Oh, thus she stood,
35   Even with such life of majesty—warm life,
    As now it coldly stands—when first I wooed her.
    I am ashamed. Does not the stone rebuke me
    For being more stone° than it? O royal piece,°   *hard / work of art*
    There's magic in thy majesty, which has
40   My evils conjured° to remembrance, and   *summoned*
    From thy admiring° daughter took the spirits,   *wondering*
    Standing like stone with thee.
    PERDITA   And give me leave,
    And do not say 'tis superstition that
    I kneel and then implore her blessing.[4] Lady,
45   Dear Queen, that ended when I but began,
    Give me that hand of yours to kiss.
    PAULINA   Oh, patience!
    The statue is but newly fixed;° the color's   *painted*
    Not dry.
    CAMILLO   My lord, your sorrow was too sore° laid on,   *painfully*
50   Which sixteen winters cannot blow away,
    So many summers dry.° Scarce any joy   *dry up*
    Did ever so long live; no sorrow
    But killed itself much sooner.
    POLIXENES [*to* LEONTES]   Dear my brother,
    Let him that was the cause of this have power
55   To take off so much grief from you as he
    Will piece up in himself.[5]
    PAULINA   Indeed, my lord,
    If I had thought the sight of my poor image
    Would thus have wrought you°—for the stone is mine—   *made you distraught*
    I'd not have showed it.
    LEONTES   Do not draw the curtain.

---

3. PERFORMANCE COMMENT The challenge for the actor playing Hermione is how to imitate a statue convincingly and for a considerable period of stage time. See Digital Edition PC 5.

4. A possible reference to the Catholic practice of kneeling before images of the Virgin Mary.
5. Will make a part of himself.

60 PAULINA   No longer shall you gaze on't, lest your fancy
    May think anon it moves.
  LEONTES   Let be, let be.
    Would I were dead but that methinks already⁶—
    What was he that did make it? See, my lord,
    Would you not deem it breathed and that those veins
    Did verily bear blood?
65 POLIXENES   Masterly done.
    The very life seems warm upon her lip.
  LEONTES   The fixure of her eye has motion in't,⁷
    As° we are mocked with art.   *In such a way that*
  PAULINA   I'll draw the curtain.
    My lord's almost so far transported that
    He'll think anon it lives.
70 LEONTES   O sweet Paulina,
    Make me to think so twenty years together.
    No settled senses° of the world can match   *calm state of mind*
    The pleasure of that madness. Let 't alone.
  PAULINA   I am sorry, sir, I have thus far stirred you; but
    I could afflict you farther.
75 LEONTES   Do, Paulina.
    For this affliction has a taste as sweet
    As any cordial° comfort. Still methinks   *restorative*
    There is an air comes from her.° What fine chisel   *she seems to breathe*
    Could ever yet cut breath? Let no man mock me,
    For I will kiss her.
80 PAULINA   Good my lord, forbear.
    The ruddiness upon her lip is wet.
    You'll mar it if you kiss it, stain your own
    With oily painting.° Shall I draw the curtain?   *paint*
  LEONTES   No, not these twenty years.
  PERDITA   So long could I
    Stand by, a looker-on.
85 PAULINA   Either forbear,
    Quit presently° the chapel, or resolve you   *immediately*
    For more amazement. If you can behold it,
    I'll make the statue move indeed, descend,
    And take you by the hand. But then you'll think—
90 Which I protest against—I am assisted
    By wicked powers.
  LEONTES   What you can make her do,
    I am content to look on; what to speak,
    I am content to hear; for 'tis as easy
    To make her speak as move.
  PAULINA   It is required
95 You do awake your faith. Then all stand still.
    On! Those that think it is unlawful° business   *unauthorized; illegal*
    I am about, let them depart.

---

6. *Would . . . already:* May I die if I do not think it already moves.
7. Textual Comment Most editors emend to "fixture." This edition keeps the Folio's "fixure," mean-ing "fixed position," which seems to have been an intentional choice on Shakespeare's part. See Digital Edition TC 10.

LEONTES   Proceed.
No foot shall stir.
PAULINA   Music; awake her; strike!°   *strike up!*
    [*Music.*]
    [*to* HERMIONE] 'Tis time. Descend. Be stone no more. Approach.
100   Strike all that look upon with marvel. Come,
    I'll fill your grave up. Stir. Nay, come away.
    Bequeath to death your numbness, for from him°   *(death)*
    Dear life redeems you. [*to* LEONTES] You perceive she stirs.
    Start not. Her actions shall be holy as
105   You hear my spell is lawful. Do not shun her
    Until you see her die again, for then
    You kill her double.[8] Nay, present your hand.
    When she was young, you wooed her; now, in age
    Is she become the suitor?
LEONTES   Oh, she's warm!
110   If this be magic, let it be an art
    Lawful as eating.
POLIXENES   She embraces him.
CAMILLO   She hangs about his neck.
    If she pertain to life,° let her speak too.   *be truly alive*
POLIXENES   Ay, and make it manifest where she has lived,
    Or how stolen from the dead.
115   PAULINA   That she is living,
    Were it but told you, should be hooted at
    Like an old tale. But it appears she lives,
    Though yet she speak not. Mark a little while.
    [*to* PERDITA] Please you to interpose, fair madam. Kneel
120   And pray your mother's blessing. [*to* HERMIONE] Turn, good lady:
    Our Perdita is found.
HERMIONE   You gods, look down,
    And from your sacred vials pour your graces
    Upon my daughter's head. Tell me, mine own,
    Where hast thou been preserved? Where lived? How found
125   Thy father's court? For thou shalt hear that I,
    Knowing by Paulina that the oracle
    Gave hope thou wast in being,° have preserved   *alive*
    Myself to see the issue.°   *outcome; child*
PAULINA   There's time enough for that,
    Lest they desire upon this push to trouble
130   Your joys with like relation.[9] —Go together,
    You precious winners all. Your exultation
    Partake° to every one. I, an old turtle,[1]   *Spread your happiness*
    Will wing me to some withered bough, and there
    My mate, that's never to be found again,
    Lament till I am lost.°   *dead*
135   LEONTES   Oh, peace, Paulina!
    Thou shouldst a husband take by my consent,
    As I by thine a wife. This is a match,

---

8. *You kill her double*: that is, If you were to shun her
in this new life, you would kill her again.
9. Lest they (bystanders?) desire at this crucial

moment to trouble your happiness with similar
stories.
1. Turtledove, a symbol of faithful love.

And made between's by vows. Thou hast found mine,
But how is to be questioned, for I saw her,
140   As I thought, dead, and have in vain said many
A prayer upon her grave. I'll not seek far—
For him, I partly know his mind—to find thee
An honorable husband. Come, Camillo,
And take her by the hand, whose worth and honesty
145   Is richly noted, and here justified°   *testified to*
By us, a pair of kings. Let's from this place.
[*to* HERMIONE] What? Look upon my brother. Both your pardons,
That e'er I put between your holy looks
My ill suspicion. This° your son-in-law,   *This is*
150   And son unto the King, whom heavens directing
Is troth-plight° to your daughter. —Good Paulina,   *betrothed*
Lead us from hence where we may leisurely
Each one demand and answer to his part
Performed in this wide gap of time since first
155   We were dissevered. Hastily lead away.   *Exeunt.*

The Tempest

The Tempest opens on a remote island of exile where Duke Prospero, deposed from power and thrust out of Milan by his wicked brother, has found shelter with his only daughter, Miranda. For the story that then unfolds, Shakespeare does not seem to have relied, as he often did, on a single dominant source, but rather to have drawn on motifs he had explored throughout his career. The play's preoccupation with loss and recovery and its air of wonder link *The Tempest* most closely to a succession of plays written toward the end of Shakespeare's professional life that modern editors generally call "romances" (*Pericles, The Winter's Tale, Cymbeline*), but it resonates as well with issues that long haunted his imagination: the painful necessity for a father to let his daughter go; the treacherous betrayal of a legitimate ruler; the murderous hatred of one brother for another; the perilous passage from civilized society to the wilderness and the dream of a return; the plight of a young woman, torn from her place in the social hierarchy; the dream of manipulating others by means of art; the threat of a radical loss of identity; the relationship between nature and nurture; the harnessing of magical powers. *The Tempest* is a kind of echo chamber of Shakespeare's lifelong preoccupations.

Though it is printed first among the plays in the First Folio (1623), *The Tempest* is probably one of the last that Shakespeare wrote. It can be dated fairly precisely: it uses material that was not available until late 1610, and there is a record of a performance before the king on Hallowmas Night, 1611. Since Shakespeare retired soon after to Stratford, *The Tempest* has seemed to many to be his valedictory to the theater. In this view, Prospero's strangely anxious and moving Epilogue—"Now my charms are all o'erthrown, / And what strength I have's mine own"—is the expression of the playwright's own professional leave-taking.

There are reasons to be skeptical: after finishing *The Tempest*, Shakespeare collaborated on at least two other plays, *Henry VIII* and *The Two Noble Kinsmen,* and it is risky to identify the author too closely with any of his characters, let alone an exiled, embittered, morally ambiguous wizard bent on recovering his lost dukedom. The wizard is in significant ways less like a playwright than an experimental scientist, one who creates and manipulates artificial situations in nature in order to observe the results.

Yet the echo-chamber effect is striking, and when Prospero and others speak of his powerful "art," it is difficult not to associate the skill of the great magician with the skill of the great playwright. Near the end of the play, the association is made explicit when Prospero uses his magic powers to produce what he terms "some vanity of mine art" (4.1.41), a betrothal masque performed by spirits whom he calls forth "to enact / My present fancies" (4.1.121–22). The masque, typically a lavish courtly performance with music and dancing, may have seemed particularly appropriate on the occasion of another early performance: *The Tempest* was one of fourteen plays provided as part of the elaborate festivities in honor of the betrothal and marriage of King James's daughter Elizabeth to Frederick, who as elector palatine ruled a territory in Germany. As Prospero's gift of the beautiful spectacle displays his magnificence and authority, so *The Tempest* and the other plays commanded by the king for his daughter's wedding would have enhanced his own prestige.

The Tempest opens with a spectacular storm that is indifferent to the ruler's authority: "What cares these roarers for the name of king?" (1.1.15–16), shouts the exasperated Boatswain at the aristocrats who are standing in his way. The Boatswain's outburst

Magical storm. From Olaus Magnus, *Historia de Gentibus Septentrionalibus* (1555 ed.).

seems unanswerable: like the implacable thunder in *King Lear,* the tempest marks the point at which exalted titles are revealed to be absurd pretensions, substanceless in the face of the elemental forces of nature and the desperate struggle for survival. But we soon learn that this tempest is not in fact natural and that it emphatically does hear and respond to human power, a power that is terrifying but, at least by its own account, benign: "The direful spectacle of the wreck," Prospero tells his daughter, "I have with such provision in mine art / So safely ordered" (1.2.26, 28–29) that no one on board has been harmed.

Shakespeare's contemporaries were fascinated by the figure of the magus, the great magician who by dint of deep learning, ascetic discipline, and patient skill could command the secret forces of the natural and supernatural world. Distinct from the village witch and "cunning man," figures engaged in local acts of healing and malice, and distinct, too, from alchemical experimenters bent on turning base metal into gold, the magus, cloaked in a robe covered with mysterious symbols, pronounced his occult charms, called forth spirits, and ranged in his imagination through the heavens and the earth, conjoining contemplative wisdom with action in the world. But there was a shiver of fear mingled with the popular admiration: when the person in Shakespeare's time most widely identified as a magus, the wizard John Dee, was away from his house, his library, one of the greatest private collections of books in England, was vandalized and plundered.

Book, costume, powerful language, the ability to enact the fancies of the brain: these are key elements of both magic and theater. "I have bedimmed / The noontide sun," Prospero declares (5.1.41–42), beginning an enumeration of extraordinary accomplishments that culminates with the revelation that "[g]raves at my command / Have waked their sleepers, oped, and let 'em forth / By my so potent art" (5.1.48–50). For the playwright who conjured up the ghosts of Caesar and old Hamlet, the claim does not seem extravagant, but for a magician it amounts to an extremely dangerous confession. Necromancy—communing with the spirits of the dead—was the very essence of black magic, the hated practice from which Prospero is careful to distance himself throughout the play. Before his exile, the island had been the realm of the "damned witch Sycorax," who was banished there "[f]or mischiefs manifold and sorceries terrible" (1.2.263–64). The legitimacy of Prospero's power, including power over his slave Caliban, Sycorax's son, depends on his claims to moral authority, but for one disturbing moment it is difficult to see the difference between "foul witch" and princely magician. Small wonder that as soon as he has disclosed that he has trafficked with the dead, Prospero declares that he abjures his "rough magic" (5.1.50).

Prospero does not give an explicit reason for this abjuration, but it appears to be a key stage in the complex process that has led, before the time of the play, to his overthrow and will lead, after the play's events are over, to his return to power. This process in its entirety requires years to unfold, but the play depicts only a small, though crucially important, fragment of it. Together with his early *Comedy of Errors, The Tempest* is unusual among Shakespeare's plays in observing what literary critics of the age called the unities of time and place; unlike *Antony and Cleopatra*, for example, which ranges over a huge territory, or *The Winter's Tale*, which covers a huge span of time, the actions of *The Tempest* all take place in a single locale—the island—during the course of a single day. In a long scene of exposition just after the spectacular opening storm, Prospero tells Miranda that he is at a critical moment; everything depends on his seizing the opportunity that fortune has granted him. The whole play, then, is the spectacle of his timing—timing that might be cynically termed political opportunism or theatrical cunning but that Prospero himself associates with the working out of "Providence divine" (1.2.159). The opportunity he seizes has its tangled roots in what he calls "the dark backward and abysm of time" (1.2.50). Many years before, when he was Duke of Milan, Prospero's preoccupation with "secret studies" gave his ambitious and unscrupulous brother Antonio the opportunity to topple him from power. Now those same studies, perfected during his long exile, have enabled Prospero to cause Antonio and his shipmates, sailing back to Italy from Tunis, to be shipwrecked on his island, where they have fallen unwittingly under his control. His magic makes it possible not only to wrest back his dukedom but to avenge himself for the terrible wrong that his brother and his brother's principal ally, Alonso, the King of Naples, have done him: "They now are in my power" (3.3.91). Audiences in Shakespeare's time would have had an all too clear image of how horrendous the vengeance of enraged princes usually was. That Prospero restrains himself from the full exercise of his power to harm his enemies, that he breaks his magic staff and drowns his book, is his highest moral achievement, a triumphant display of self-mastery: "The rarer action is / In virtue than in vengeance" (5.1.27–28).

All of those who are shipwrecked on the island undergo the same shock of terror and unexpected survival, but their experiences, as they cross the yellow sands and make their way toward the interior of the island, differ markedly. The least affected are the mariners, including the feisty Boatswain; after their exhausting labors in the storm, they have sunk into a strange, uneasy sleep, only to be awakened in time to sail the miraculously restored ship back to Italy. The others are put through more complex trials; exposed to varying degrees of anxiety, temptation, grief, fear, and penitence, they are in effect subjects in a psychological experiment carefully conducted by Prospero, who attempts to instill in them moral self-control and work-discipline. The most generously treated is Ferdinand, the only son of the King of Naples, whom Prospero, in what is essentially a carefully planned dynastic alliance, has secretly chosen to be his son-in-law. As Ferdinand bewails what he assumes is his father's death by drowning, he hears strange, haunting music, including the remarkable song of death and metamorphosis, "Full fathom five thy father lies" (1.2.395). Ferdinand is the only one of the shipwrecked company, until the play's final scene, to encounter Prospero directly; the magician makes the experience menacing, humiliating, and frustrating, but this is the modest, salutary price the young man must pay to win the hand of the beautiful Miranda, who seems to him a goddess and who, for her part, has fallen in love with him at first sight.

Prospero directs the experience of the rest as well, but not in person; instead, they principally encounter his diligent servant, Ariel. Ariel is not human, although at a crucial moment he is able to imagine what he would feel "were I human" (5.1.20). He is, as the cast of characters describes him, an "airy spirit," capable of moving at

The conjurer. Engraving by Theodore de Bry after a drawing by John White. From Thomas Hariot, *A Brief and True Report of the New Found Land of Virginia* (1590).

immense speed, altering the weather, and producing vivid illusions. We learn that Ariel possesses an inherent moral "delicacy," a delicacy that in the past (that is, before the time depicted in the play) has brought him pain. For, as Prospero reminds him, he had been Sycorax's servant and was, for refusing "[t]o act her earthy and abhorred commands" (1.2.273), imprisoned by the witch for many years in a cloven pine. Prospero freed him from confinement and now demands in return a fixed term of service, which Ariel provides with a mixture of brilliant alacrity and grumbling. Prospero responds in turn with mingled affection and anger, alternating warm praises and dire threats. Although Prospero's "art," through which he commands Ariel and the lesser spirits, seems to foresee and control everything, this control is purchased through constant discipline.

And, for all his godlike powers, there are limits to what Prospero can do. He can make the loathed Antonio and the others know something of the bitterness of loss and isolation; he can produce in them irresistible drowsiness and startled awakenings; he can command Ariel to lay before them a splendid banquet and then make it suddenly vanish; he can drive them to desperation and madness. But in the case of his own brother and Alonso's similarly wicked brother Sebastian, Prospero cannot reshape their inner lives and effect a moral transformation. The most he can do with these deeply cynical men is to limit through continual vigilance any further harm they might do and to take back what is rightfully his. When, with an obvious effort, Prospero declares that he forgives his brother's "rankest fault" (5.1.132), Antonio is conspicuously silent.

But the higher moral purpose of Prospero's art is not all a failure. With Alonso, the project of provoking repentance by generating intense grief and fear succeeds admirably: Alonso not only gives up his power over the dukedom of Milan but begs Prospero's pardon for the wrong he committed in conspiring to overthrow him. (Both rulers, Alonso and Prospero, can look forward to a unification of their states in the next generation, through the marriage of Ferdinand and Miranda.) Moreover, Prospero's carefully contrived scenarios succeed in confirming the decency, loyalty, and goodness of Alonso's counselor, Gonzalo, who had years before provided the exiled Duke and his daughter with the means necessary for their survival.

It is Gonzalo's goodness that at the end of the play enables him to grasp the dynastic providence in the bewildering tangle of events—"Was Milan thrust from Milan that his issue / Should become kings of Naples?" (5.1.205–6)—and that earlier inspires him to sense the miraculous nature of their survival. Indifferent to the contemptuous mockery of Antonio and Sebastian, Gonzalo responds to shipwreck on the strange island by speculating on how he would govern it were he responsible for its "plantation":

> I'th' commonwealth I would by contraries
> Execute all things. For no kind of traffic
> Would I admit; no name of magistrate;
> Letters should not be known; riches, poverty,
> And use of service, none; contract, succession,
> Bourn, bound of land, tilth, vineyard, none;
> No use of metal, corn, or wine, or oil;
> No occupation, all men idle, all . . .
> (2.1.142–49)

Shakespeare adapted Gonzalo's utopian speculations from a passage in "Of Cannibals" (1580), a remarkably free-spirited essay by the French humanist Michel de Montaigne. The Brazilian Indians, Montaigne admiringly writes (in John Florio's 1603 translation), have "no kind of traffic, no knowledge of letters, no intelligence of numbers, no name of magistrate nor of politic superiority, no use of service, of riches or of poverty, no contracts, no successions . . . no occupation but idle, no respect of kindred but common, no apparel but natural, no manuring of lands, no use of wine, corn, or metal." For Montaigne, the European adventurers and colonists, confident in their cultural superiority, are the real barbarians, while the American natives, with their cannibalism and free love, live in accordance with nature.

The issues raised by Montaigne, and more generally by New World voyages, may have been particularly interesting to The Tempest's early audiences as news reached London of the extraordinary adventures of the Virginia Company's colony at Jamestown. Shakespeare seems to have read a detailed account of these adventures in a letter written by the colony's secretary, William Strachey; although the letter was not printed until 1625, it was evidently circulating in manuscript in 1610. In 1609, a fleet carrying more than four hundred persons that had been sent out to reinforce the colony was struck by a hurricane near the Virginia coast. Two of the vessels reached their destination, but the third, the ship carrying the governor, Sir Thomas Gates, ran aground on an uninhabited island in the Bermudas. Remarkably enough, all of the passengers and crew survived; but their tribulations were not over. By forcing everyone to labor side by side in order to survive, the violence of the storm had weakened the governor's authority, and both the natural abundance and the isolation of the island where they were shipwrecked weakened it further. Gates ordered the company to build new ships in order to sail to Jamestown, but his command met with ominous grumblings and threats of mutiny. According to Strachey's letter, the main troublemaker directly challenged Gates's authority: "therefore let the Governour (said he) kiss, etc." In response, Gates had the troublemaker shot to death. New ships were built, and in an impressive feat of navigation the entire company reached Jamestown. The group found the settlement deeply demoralized: illness was rampant, food was scarce, and relations with the neighboring Indians, once amicable, had completely broken down. Only harsh military discipline kept the English colony from falling apart.

With the possible exception of some phrases from Strachey's description of the storm and a few scattered details, The Tempest does not directly use any of this vivid narrative. Prospero's island is evidently in the Mediterranean, and its immediate

America. Engraving by Theodor Galle after a drawing by Jan van der Straet (ca. 1580).

contemporary reference points are stories of dynastic intrigue, captivity, enslavement, and redemption associated with the perilous waters off the coast of North Africa. The New World is only mentioned as a far-off place, "the still-vexed Bermudas" (1.2.229), where the swift Ariel flies to fetch dew. Yet Shakespeare's play seems constantly to echo precisely the issues raised by the Bermuda shipwreck and its aftermath. What does it take to survive? How do men of different classes and moral character react during a state of emergency? What is the proper relation between theoretical understanding and practical experience or between knowledge and power? Is obedience to authority willing or forced? How can those in power protect themselves from the conspiracies of malcontents? Is it possible to detect a providential design in what looks at first like a succession of accidents? If there are natives to contend with, how should colonists establish friendly and profitable relations with them? What is to be done if relations turn sour? How can those who rule prevent an alliance between hostile natives and the poorer colonists, often disgruntled and themselves exploited? And—Montaigne's more radical questions—what is the justification of one person's rule over another? Who is the civilized man, and who is the barbarian?

The unregenerate nastiness of Antonio and Sebastian, conjoined with the goodness of Gonzalo, might seem indirectly to endorse Montaigne's critique of the Europeans and his praise of the cannibals, were it not for the disturbing presence in *The Tempest* of the character whose name is almost an anagram for "cannibal," Caliban. Caliban, whose god Setebos is mentioned in accounts of Magellan's voyages as a Patagonian deity, is anything but a noble savage. Shakespeare does not shrink from the darkest European fantasies about the Wild Man. Indeed, he exaggerates them: Caliban is deformed, lecherous, evil-smelling, treacherous, naive, drunken, lazy, rebellious, violent, and devil-worshipping. According to Prospero, he is not even human: "A devil, a born devil, on whose nature / Nurture can never stick" (4.1.188–89). When he first came to the island, Prospero recalls, he treated Caliban "with humane care" (1.2.346), lodging him in his own cell until the savage tried to rape Miranda. The arrival of the other Europeans brings out still worse qualities. Encountering the basest of the company, Alonso's jester, Trinculo, and drunken butler, Stefano, Caliban falls at their feet in brutish worship and then devises a conspiracy to murder Prospero in his sleep. Were the conspiracy to succeed, Caliban would get neither the girl for whom he lusts nor the freedom for which he shouts—he would become "King" Stefano's "foot-licker" (4.1.218)—but he would satisfy the enormous hatred he feels for Prospero.

Prospero's power, Caliban reasons, derives from his superior knowledge. "Remember / First to possess his books," he urges the louts, "for without them / He's but a sot as I am. . . . Burn but his books" (3.2.85–89). The strategy is a canny one, in recognizing an underlying link between literacy and authority, but the problem is not only that Stefano and Trinculo are hopeless fools but also that Prospero, like all Renaissance princes, has a diligent spy network: the invisible Ariel overhears the conspirators and warns his master of the approaching danger. Prospero's sudden recollection of the warning leads him to break off the betrothal masque with one of the most famous speeches in all of Shakespeare, "Our revels now are ended" (4.1.148ff). This brooding meditation on the theatrical insubstantiality of the entire world and the dreamlike nature of human existence has seemed to many readers and audiences the pinnacle of the play's visionary wisdom. But it does not subsume in its rich cadences the other voices in *The Tempest*; specifically, it does not silence the surprising power of Caliban's voice.

That voice has been amplified in the centuries that followed the first performances of *The Tempest*, as European colonialism saw its grand political, moral, and economic claims disputed and, after violent struggles, dismantled. During these struggles, many anticolonial writers and critics rewrote Shakespeare's play, casting Prospero as a smugly racist, sexist oppressor, Ariel as a native coopted and corrupted by his colonial master, and Caliban as a victimized hero. "Prospero invaded the islands," declared the Cuban writer Roberto Fernández Retamar, "killed our ancestors, enslaved Caliban, and taught him his language to make himself understood. What else can Caliban do but use that same language—today he has no other—to curse him, to wish that the 'red plague' would fall on him?"

Shakespeare, who wrote when the colonialist project was still in its early stages, could not have anticipated this afterlife, and some scholars have argued that the relevance to *The Tempest* of the New World voyages has been greatly exaggerated. But, as the Barbadian writer George Lamming puts it, "Caliban keeps answering back." Caliban enters the play cursing, grumbling, and, above all, disputing Prospero's authority: "This island's mine by Sycorax my mother, / Which thou tak'st from me" (1.2.331–32). By the close, his attempt to kill Prospero foiled and his body racked with cramps and bruises, Caliban declares that he will "be wise hereafter / And seek for grace" (5.1.296–97). Yet it is not his mumbled reformation but his vehement protests that leave an indelible mark on *The Tempest*. The play may depict Caliban, in Prospero's ugly term, as "filth," but it gives him a remarkable, unforgettable eloquence, the eloquence of bare life. To Miranda's taunting reminder that she taught him to speak, Caliban retorts, "You taught me language, and my profit on't / Is I know how to curse" (1.2.362–63). It is not only in cursing, however, that Caliban is gifted: in richly sensuous poetry, he speaks of the island's natural resources and of his dreams. Caliban can be beaten into submission, but the master cannot eradicate his slave's desires, his pleasures, and his inconsolable pain. And across the vast gulf that divides the triumphant prince and the defeated savage, there is a momentary, enigmatic glimpse of a hidden bond: "This thing of darkness," Prospero says of Caliban, "I / Acknowledge mine" (5.1.278–79). The words need only be a claim of ownership, but they seem to hint at a deeper, more disturbing link between father and monster, legitimate ruler and savage, judge and criminal. Perhaps the link is only an illusion, a trick of the imagination on a strange island, but as Prospero leaves the island, it is he who begs for pardon.

STEPHEN GREENBLATT

SELECTED BIBLIOGRAPHY

Callaghan, Dympna. "Irish Memories in *The Tempest*." *Shakespeare without Women: Representing Gender and Race on the Renaissance Stage*. London: Routledge, 2000. 97–138. Using the play's Irish echoes, considers how selective colonial recollection suppresses the cultural memory of the colonized.

Cartelli, Thomas. "Prospero in Africa: *The Tempest* as Colonialist Text and Pretext." *Repositioning Shakespeare: National Formations, Postcolonial Appropriations*. London: Routledge, 1999. 87–104. Argues that *The Tempest* can be made to operate both for and against the interests of modern Western ideology.

Greenblatt, Stephen. "Martial Law in the Land of Cockaigne." *Shakespearean Negotiations: The Circulation of Social Energy in Renaissance England*. Berkeley: U of California P, 1988. 129–63. Explores how the play apparently celebrates the restoration of patriarchal order yet also ironically scrutinizes the political manipulation of anxiety.

Hulme, Peter, and William H. Sherman, eds. *"The Tempest" and Its Travels*. Philadelphia: U of Pennsylvania P, 2000. Offers a range of critical and creative materials, situating the play amid the local and global contexts of its time and beyond.

Lupton, Julia. "Creature Caliban." *Shakespeare Quarterly* 51 (2000): 1–23. Asserts that at once Adamic and monstrous, Caliban is the embodiment of pure creaturely sentience.

Mowat, Barbara A. "Prospero's Book." *Shakespeare Quarterly* 52 (2001): 1–33. Posits that Prospero's particular magic book is likely to have been what Shakespeare's contemporaries called a "grimoire," a manual for the summoning of spirits.

Neill, Michael. "'Noises, / Sounds, and Sweet Airs': The Burden of Shakespeare's *Tempest*." *Shakespeare Quarterly* 59.1 (Spring 2008): 36–59. Argues that, uniquely among the plays of its time, *The Tempest* is equipped with its own elaborate sound track, one in which violent, chaotic, and discordant noise is set against harmony.

Orgel, Stephen. *The Illusion of Power: Political Theater in the English Renaissance*. Berkeley: U of California P, 1975. Compares public and court theater practice, highlighting the masque's role in the allegorized expression of sovereign power.

Spiller, Elizabeth. "Shakespeare and the Making of Early Modern Science: Resituating Prospero's Art." *South Central Review* 26 (2009): 24–41. Discusses how *The Tempest* enables us to understand the role that art, poetry, and drama had on the early modern development of science.

Wilson, Richard. "Voyage to Tunis: New History and the Old World of *The Tempest*." *Secret Shakespeare: Studies in Theatre, Religion, and Resistance*. Manchester: Manchester UP, 2004. 206–29. Asserts that Shakespeare's contemporaries would have understood *The Tempest* as a play about enslavement and redemption.

FILMS

Forbidden Planet. 1956. Dir. Fred M. Wilcox. USA. 98 min. A science fiction cult classic in which Ariel is a robot and Caliban a monster of the id.

The Tempest. 1960. Dir. George Schaefer. USA. 76 min. A made-for-TV, one-camera film of a solid though short stage rendition, with Richard Burton standing out as Caliban.

The Tempest. 1979. Dir. Derek Jarman. UK. 95 min. Part Gothic, part punk; renders Juno's masque as a Broadway musical number.

Tempest. 1982. Dir. Paul Mazursky. USA. 140 min. A disenchanted New York architect escapes to a Greek island to reexamine his life.

Prospero's Books. 1991. Dir. Peter Greenaway. UK. 129 min. Surreal and baroque; focuses on the imagined contents of Prospero's library. John Gielgud stars.

TEXTUAL INTRODUCTION

The Tempest was first printed in the First Folio of 1623 (F), where it appears as the opening play in the volume. This is the only surviving text with any claim to authority, and it seems to have been prepared with care: it is the basis of *The Norton Shakespeare* edition.

The text was evidently printed from copy supplied by Ralph Crane, the professional scribe who was responsible for the preparation of at least four other plays in the First Folio. We probably owe to Crane a number of the conspicuous features of the text, including the systematic divisions into acts and scenes, the detailed stage directions, and the list of characters at the end of the play. Crane may also have been responsible for the relatively heavy punctuation: surviving transcripts in his hand show a strong preference for colons, hyphens, and parentheses, and the frequency of each of these marks in *The Tempest* is roughly double that found in the Folio's non-Crane texts. Crane's habits may have been very different from those of Shakespeare, or indeed from the three or four printers who set the text and imposed their own conventions and quirks; but the 1623 printing is all we have to work with, and we have tried to make that text as accessible as possible to readers without sacrificing the Folio's stylistic cues and effects.

There are some confusions in the Folio's distinctions between verse and prose and, occasionally, in its line divisions: the layout of the songs is particularly muddled, and editors have tended to follow mid-seventeenth-century manuscripts for the structure of repeats and refrains. The modernization of spelling has, in places, forced us to choose between separate senses that Shakespeare might well have wanted to keep in play: for instance, when Ariel tells Prospero that his affections toward the courtiers would become tender "were I human" (5.1.20), the Folio spelling supports both "humane" and "human." And even though there are very few obvious errors in need of correction, there are some famous cruxes that require the intervention of editors: Does Ferdinand refer to "[s]o rare a wondered father and a wise" or ". . . a wife" (4.1.123)? Do his female acquaintances in 3.1.46 "put it to the foil" or the "soil"? When, where, and how does Juno descend at the beginning of the masque in 4.1? And what are the "scamels" that Caliban promises to fetch for Stefano and Trinculo (in 2.2.163, the only known use of this word in English)?

Full discussions of some of these problems can be found in the Textual Comments, and we also encourage readers to examine the original printings for themselves: comparing even a short passage in the Folio with the text in this or other modernized editions will immediately reveal how many choices editors make without their readers' knowledge. Modern eyes and ears will be especially struck by the different rhythms produced in the original syntax and may find that the play's many compound words convey a sense of compression or exoticism that is very much in keeping with the style and setting of the plot.

WILLIAM H. SHERMAN

PERFORMANCE NOTE

The Tempest is conspicuously lacking in dramatic action. Very little happens in the play, and what does happen seems entirely at the discretion of Prospero, the agency of his counterparts effectively nullified by his magic. Directors therefore must engage audiences without legitimate conflict or dramatic uncertainty—a challenge amplified both by a protagonist who spends much of the play threatening his friends and by an adherence to the unity of time that blunts potential developmental arcs for the supporting cast. Directors typically respond to these challenges in two ways: by approaching the play as a kind of masque and appealing to audiences through a collection of striking visual and auditory effects; or, more commonly, by creating conflicts between characters based on subtextual cues and political topicality. Though Prospero can be portrayed as a benign scholar or disturbed magus, directors today frequently present him as a colonialist oppressor. Making Caliban a long-suffering hero, Ariel an unwilling captive, and Miranda the daughter to a domineering father, productions highlight Prospero's deficiencies and cloud the play's resolution.

Other productions locate the central conflict within Prospero, emphasizing his anxieties about authority, or his reluctance to forgive his enemies and relinquish power. Still others generate drama through contrasts between Prospero's love for Miranda and hate for Caliban; by suggesting that Ariel and Caliban represent contrasting aspects of Prospero's psyche; or by hinting that his affection for either, or even for Miranda, is attended by sexual frustration. Whatever the approach, directors and actors must determine whether Prospero will seem mild or severe; whether Caliban displays childlike innocence or mature hostility; whether Miranda is a pliable princess or a rebellious teen; and whether Ariel is male or female, ethereal or earthy, eager or reluctant to serve. Directors must also decide on the sources and manifestations of Prospero's Art, and on a degree of realism for spectacular effects (e.g., the shipwreck, the vanishing banquet, Juno's descent). Other considerations in performance include Caliban's deformity and costume; producing the near-constant soundscape called for in stage directions (e.g., thunder, solemn music and songs); managing the difficult drunken comedy of Stefano and Trinculo; and deciding on Sebastian and Antonio's ultimate state of reconciliation or estrangement.

BRETT GAMBOA

The Tempest

THE PERSONS OF THE PLAY

PROSPERO, the right Duke of Milan
MIRANDA, daughter to Prospero
ANTONIO, his brother, the usurping Duke of Milan

ALONSO, King of Naples
SEBASTIAN, his brother
FERDINAND, son to Alonso

GONZALO, an honest old councillor
ADRIAN and FRANCISCO, lords

ARIEL, an airy spirit
CALIBAN, a savage and deformed slave

TRINCULO, a jester
STEFANO, a drunken butler

MASTER of a ship
BOATSWAIN
MARINERS

SPIRITS *appearing as*
IRIS
CERES
JUNO
Nymphs
Reapers

THE SCENE: *An uninhabited island.*[1]

1.1

A tempestuous noise of thunder and lightning heard.
Enter a ship['s] MASTER *and a* BOATSWAIN.[2]

MASTER   Boatswain!
BOATSWAIN   Here, Master. What cheer?
MASTER   Good,[3] speak to th' mariners. Fall to't yarely,° or we   promptly
   run ourselves aground. Bestir, bestir!   *Exit.*
   Enter MARINERS.

---

1. TEXTUAL COMMENT *The Tempest* is unusual among the plays gathered in the First Folio in having a specific setting. For more on the significance of the play's location, see Digital Edition TC 1.
1.1 Location: A ship at sea.

2. The Boatswain probably enters after the shipmaster calls him; the latter is perhaps on the upper stage.
3. Acknowledging the Boatswain's presence; or perhaps short for "good man."

5   BOATSWAIN   Heigh, my hearts!° Cheerly, cheerly, my hearts!   *hearties*
Yare, yare! Take in the topsail.[4] Tend° to th' Master's whistle.   *Attend*
[*to the storm*] Blow till thou burst thy wind, if room enough![5]
      Enter ALONSO, SEBASTIAN, ANTONIO, FERDINAND,
      GONZALO, *and others.*
  ALONSO   Good Boatswain, have care. Where's the Master? [*to
the MARINERS] Play the men!°   *Act like men*
10   BOATSWAIN   I pray now, keep below.
  ANTONIO   Where is the Master, Boatswain?
  BOATSWAIN   Do you not hear him? You mar our labor. Keep
your cabins: you do assist the storm!
  GONZALO   Nay, good,° be patient.   *good man*
15   BOATSWAIN   When the sea is. Hence! What cares these roarers for the name of king?[6] To cabin! Silence! Trouble us not.
  GONZALO   Good, yet remember whom thou hast aboard.
  BOATSWAIN   None that I more love than myself. You are a councillor:[7] if you can command these elements to silence and
20   work the peace of the present,[8] we will not hand° a rope more.   *handle*
Use your authority! If you cannot, give thanks you have lived
so long, and make yourself ready in your cabin for the mischance of the hour, if it so hap.° [*to the* MARINERS] Cheerly,   *happen*
good hearts! [*to* GONZALO] Out of our way, I say!
      Exit [BOATSWAIN *with* MARINERS].
25   GONZALO   I have great comfort from this fellow. Methinks he
hath no drowning mark[9] upon him; his complexion is perfect
gallows.[1] Stand fast, good Fate, to his hanging; make the
rope of his destiny our cable,[2] for our own doth little advantage.° If he be not born to be hanged, our case is miserable.   *good*
      Exeunt [GONZALO, ALONSO, SEBASTIAN,
      ANTONIO, *and* FERDINAND].
    Enter BOATSWAIN.
30   BOATSWAIN   Down with the topmast![3] Yare! Lower, lower! Bring
her to try with main-course.[4] (*A cry within.*) A plague upon
this howling! They are louder than the weather or our office.[5]
    Enter SEBASTIAN, ANTONIO, *and* GONZALO.
Yet again? What do you here? Shall we give o'er° and drown?   *up*
Have you a mind to sink?
35   SEBASTIAN   A pox o' your throat, you bawling, blasphemous,
incharitable dog!
  BOATSWAIN   Work you, then.
  ANTONIO   Hang, cur! Hang, you whoreson insolent noise-maker!
We are less afraid to be drowned than thou art.
40   GONZALO   I'll warrant him from drowning,[6] though° the ship   *even if*
were no stronger than a nutshell and as leaky as an unstanched°   *a freely menstruating*
wench.

---

4. To reduce the surface area of the sail and thereby
lessen the force of the wind pushing the ship toward
the island.
5. Blow as hard as you like, as long as we have room
between the ship and the rocks.
6. "Roarers," referring here to the waves, was also a
term for riotous people.
7. Member of the King's council; also an adviser or
persuader.
8. Of the present circumstances.
9. Birthmark whose position was held to portend
death by drowning. "He that was born to be hanged

will never be drowned" was proverbial.
1. His physiognomy, or appearance, shows that he
will certainly be hanged.
2. Anchor cable (an anchor is actually useless in a
storm).
3. To reduce the top weight of the ship and make it
more stable.
4. Bring the ship close to the wind, sailing only with
the mainsail.
5. Duties (in shouting orders).
6. I'll guarantee him against drowning.

BOATSWAIN   Lay her a-hold, a-hold! Set her two courses!⁷ Off
    to sea again! Lay her off!
       Enter MARINERS, *wet.*
45 MARINERS   All lost! To prayers, to prayers! All lost!
                         [*Exeunt* MARINERS.]

BOATSWAIN   What, must our mouths be cold?⁸
GONZALO   The King and Prince at prayers! Let's assist them,
    for our case is as theirs.
SEBASTIAN   I'm out of patience.
50 ANTONIO   We are merely° cheated of our lives by drunkards.   *utterly*
    This wide-chopped° rascal—would thou mightst lie drown-   *large-mouthed*
    ing the washing of ten tides!⁹
GONZALO   He'll be hanged yet, though every drop of water
    swear against it and gape at widest to glut° him.   *its widest to swallow*
     *A confused noise within.*¹
55 MARINERS [*within*]   Mercy on us! We split, we split! Farewell, my
    wife and children! Farewell, brother! We split, we split, we split!
                      [*Exit* BOATSWAIN.]

ANTONIO   Let's all sink wi'th' King.
SEBASTIAN   Let's take leave of him.   *Exit* [*with* ANTONIO].
GONZALO   Now would I give a thousand furlongs of sea for an
60 acre of barren ground: long heath, brown furze,² anything.
    The wills above be done, but I would fain die a dry death.
                          Exit.

1.2

    Enter PROSPERO *and* MIRANDA.
MIRANDA¹   If by your art,² my dearest father, you have
    Put the wild waters in this roar, allay them.
    The sky, it seems, would pour down stinking pitch
    But that the sea, mounting to th' welkin's° cheek,   *sky's*
5 Dashes the fire out. Oh, I have suffered
    With those that I saw suffer: a brave° vessel—   *splendid*
    Who had, no doubt, some noble creature in her—
    Dashed all to pieces! Oh, the cry did knock
    Against my very heart! Poor souls, they perished.
10 Had I been any god of power, I would
    Have sunk the sea within the earth or ere°   *before*
    It should the good ship so have swallowed and
    The fraughting souls³ within her.
PROSPERO⁴   Be collected.
    No more amazement.° Tell your piteous° heart   *consternation / pitying*
    There's no harm done.
MIRANDA   Oh, woe the day!

---

7. Set the foresail in addition to the mainsail.
8. To be cold in the mouth—to be dead—was proverbial; may also suggest that the mariners warm their
mouths with liquor (line 50).
9. Pirates were hanged on the shore at low-water mark
and left there for the ebbing and flowing of three tides.
1. PERFORMANCE COMMENT How a production stages
the capsizing of Alonso's vessel can powerfully affect
the play's emotional undercurrents. A highly realistic
storm might seem to confirm that the mariners have
been lost at sea, heightening the sense of loss running
through the play, while a more abstract or symbolic
approach could emphasize Prospero's control. For
more, see Digital Edition PC 1.
2. Heather and gorse—both shrubs that grow in poor

soil.
1.2 Location: The rest of the play is set in various
parts of Prospero's island.
1. "Miranda" in Latin means "admirable" or "wondering." Miranda uses the formal "you," contrasting with
Prospero's more familiar "thou."
2. Skill; magic; learning; science. TEXTUAL COM-
MENT In the Folio, Miranda speaks of "Art" with a
capital "A." For information on early modern practices of capitalization, and the special significance of
"art" for *The Tempest*, see Digital Edition TC 2.
3. Souls constituting the freight; perhaps also suggesting "burdened."
4. "Prospero" in Italian and Spanish means "fortunate" or "prosperous."

15   PROSPERO   No harm.
      I have done nothing but in care of thee—
      Of thee, my dear one, thee, my daughter—who
      Art ignorant of what thou art, naught knowing
      Of whence I am, nor that I am more better°   *higher in rank*
20   Than Prospero, master of a full poor cell⁵
      And thy no greater father.
    MIRANDA   More to know
      Did never meddle with° my thoughts.   *intrude upon*
    PROSPERO   'Tis time
      I should inform thee farther. Lend thy hand
      And pluck my magic garment from me.—
            [*She helps him remove the cloak, and he puts it aside.*]
                             —So,
25   Lie there, my art. —Wipe thou thine eyes; have comfort.
      The direful spectacle of the wreck, which touched
      The very virtue of compassion in thee,
      I have with such provision° in mine art   *foresight*
      So safely ordered that there is no soul—
30   No, not so much perdition° as an hair   *loss*
      Betid° to any creature in the vessel   *Happened*
      Which° thou heard'st cry, which thou saw'st sink. Sit down, *Whom*
      For thou must now know farther.
    MIRANDA   You have often
      Begun to tell me what I am, but stopped
35   And left me to a bootless inquisition,°   *profitless inquiry*
      Concluding, "Stay: not yet."
    PROSPERO   The hour's now come;
      The very minute bids thee ope° thine ear.   *open*
      Obey, and be attentive. Canst thou remember
      A time before we came unto this cell?
40   I do not think thou canst, for then thou wast not
      Out° three years old.   *Fully*
    MIRANDA   Certainly, sir, I can.
    PROSPERO   By what? By any other house or person?
      Of anything the image tell me that
      Hath kept with thy remembrance.
    MIRANDA   'Tis far off,
45   And rather like a dream than an assurance°   *a certainty*
      That my remembrance warrants.° Had I not   *guarantees is true*
      Four or five women once that tended me?
    PROSPERO   Thou hadst, and more, Miranda. But how is it
      That this lives in thy mind? What seest thou else
50   In the dark backward° and abysm of time?   *past*
      If thou rememb'rest aught° ere thou cam'st here,   *anything*
      How thou cam'st here thou mayst.
    MIRANDA   But that I do not.
    PROSPERO   Twelve year since, Miranda, twelve year since,
      Thy father was the Duke of Milan⁶ and
      A prince of power.
55   MIRANDA   Sir, are not you my father?
    PROSPERO   Thy mother was a piece° of virtue,° and *perfect example / chastity*
      She said thou wast my daughter, and thy father

---

5. Suggesting a hermit's or a poor man's dwelling.   6. Pronounced with stress on the first syllable.
full: very.

Was Duke of Milan, and his only heir
And princess no worse issued.°   *no less nobly born*

MIRANDA   O the heavens!

60   What foul play had we that we came from thence?
Or blessèd° was't we did?   *providential*

PROSPERO   Both, both, my girl.
By foul play, as thou say'st, were we heaved thence,
But blessedly holp° hither.   *helped*

MIRANDA   Oh, my heart bleeds
To think o'th' teen° that I have turned you to,   *sorrow; trouble*

65   Which is from° my remembrance! Please you, farther.   *out of*

PROSPERO   My brother and thy uncle, called Antonio—
I pray thee mark me, that a brother should
Be so perfidious!—he whom next° thyself   *after*
Of all the world I loved, and to him put

70   The manage° of my state, as at that time   *control*
Through all the signories° it was the first   *lordships*
And Prospero the prime° duke, being so reputed   *foremost*
In dignity, and for the liberal arts[7]
Without a parallel. Those being all my study,

75   The government I cast upon my brother
And to my state grew stranger, being transported[8]
And rapt in secret studies. Thy false uncle—
Dost thou attend me?

MIRANDA   Sir, most heedfully.

PROSPERO   Being once perfected how to grant suits,[9]

80   How to deny them, who t'advance, and who
To trash for overtopping,[1] new created
The creatures° that were mine, I say, or changed 'em,   *dependents*
Or else new formed 'em;[2] having both the key°   *control*
Of officer and office, set all hearts i'th' state

85   To what tune pleased his ear, that° now he was   *so that*
The ivy which had hid my princely trunk
And sucked my verdure° out on't. Thou attend'st not.   *vitality; power*

MIRANDA   O good sir, I do.

PROSPERO   I pray thee, mark me.
I, thus neglecting worldly ends, all dedicated

90   To closeness° and the bettering of my mind   *seclusion*
With that which, but° by being so retired,   *merely*
O'er-prized all popular rate,[3] in my false brother
Awaked an evil nature; and my trust,
Like a good parent,[4] did beget of him

95   A falsehood in its contrary° as great   *inverse qualities*
As my trust was, which had indeed no limit,
A confidence sans° bound. He being thus lorded   *without*
Not only with what my revenue yielded,
But what my power might else exact, like one

100   Who, having into truth by telling of it,

---

7. As opposed to the "mechanical arts," the "liberal arts" encompassed the trivium (grammar, logic, and rhetoric) and the quadrivium (arithmetic, geometry, music, and astronomy).
8. Enraptured, with suggestions of "conveyed to another place." *grew stranger:* grew alienated from; became a foreigner to.
9. Having mastered the handling of formal requests.

1. For rising too high. *trash:* restrain, hold back (as by a leash).
2. *changed . . .'em:* changed the duties and allegiance of existing officials, or created new ones.
3. Became too precious for the people to value or understand.
4. From the colloquial "Good parents breed bad children."

Made such a sinner of his memory
To credit his own lie,[5] he did believe
He was indeed the duke, out o'th'° substitution   *as a consequence of the*
And executing° th'outward face° of royalty   *portraying / image*
105   With all prerogative. Hence his ambition growing—
Dost thou hear?

MIRANDA   Your tale, sir, would cure deafness.

PROSPERO   To have no screen between this part he played
And him he played it for, he needs will be
Absolute Milan.[6] Me,° poor man, my library   *As for me*
110   Was dukedom large enough. Of temporal royalties°   *rule*
He thinks me now incapable; confederates,°   *(he) plots*
So dry° he was for sway,° wi'th' King of Naples   *thirsty / power*
To give him annual tribute, do him homage,
Subject his coronet to his crown,[7] and bend
115   The dukedom yet unbowed—alas, poor Milan!—
To most ignoble stooping.[8]

MIRANDA   O the heavens!

PROSPERO   Mark his condition° and th'event;° then tell me   *treaty / outcome*
If this might be a brother.

MIRANDA   I should sin
To think but° nobly of my grandmother.   *anything but*
Good wombs have borne bad sons.[9]

120   PROSPERO   Now the condition.
This King of Naples, being an enemy
To me inveterate, hearkens my brother's suit;
Which was that he, in lieu o'th' premises[1]
Of homage and I know not how much tribute,
125   Should presently extirpate me and mine
Out of the dukedom and confer fair Milan,
With all the honors, on my brother. Whereon,
A treacherous army levied, one midnight
Fated to th' purpose did Antonio open
130   The gates of Milan, and i'th' dead of darkness,
The ministers° for th' purpose hurried thence   *agents*
Me and thy crying self.

MIRANDA   Alack, for pity!
I, not remembering how I cried out then,
Will cry it o'er again; it is a hint°   *an occasion*
That wrings mine eyes to't.

135   PROSPERO   Hear a little further,
And then I'll bring thee to the present business
Which now's upon's, without the which this story
Were most impertinent.°   *irrelevant*

MIRANDA   Wherefore did they not
That hour destroy us?

PROSPERO   Well demanded, wench:[2]
140   My tale provokes that question. Dear, they durst not,
So dear the love my people bore me, nor set

---

5. *like one . . . lie:* like someone who comes to believe
his own repeatedly stated lie. *To:* So as to.
6. *To have . . . Milan:* He wanted to be the Duke of
Milan in actual fact, rather than merely exercising
power as the Duke's proxy. *screen:* partition, barrier.
7. Subject Antonio's coronet to Alonso's crown. *coronet:* a lesser crown indicating the wearer's inferiority
to the sovereign.

8. *and bend . . . stooping:* by making Milan, previously free, a tributary subject of Naples.
9. Antonio's character need not imply that his mother
was a bad parent (see line 94).
1. In return for the conditions agreed upon.
2. A young woman; also, term of endearment to wife,
daughter, or sweetheart.

A mark so bloody on the business, but
With colors fairer painted their foul ends.
In few,° they hurried us aboard a bark,°   *short / ship*
145 Bore us some leagues to sea, where they prepared
A rotten carcass of a butt,[3] not rigged,
Nor tackle, sail, nor mast—the very rats
Instinctively have quit it. There they hoist us
To cry to th' sea that roared to us; to sigh
150 To th' winds, whose pity, sighing back again,
Did us but loving wrong.[4]

MIRANDA   Alack, what trouble
Was I then to you!

PROSPERO   Oh, a cherubin
Thou wast that did preserve me. Thou didst smile,
Infusèd with a fortitude from heaven,
155 When I have decked° the sea with drops° full salt,   *covered; adorned / tears*
Under my burden groaned,[5] which° raised in me   *(Miranda's smile)*
An undergoing stomach° to bear up   *A courage*
Against what should ensue.

MIRANDA   How came we ashore?

PROSPERO   By Providence divine.
160 Some food we had and some fresh water that
A noble Neapolitan, Gonzalo,
Out of his charity—who being then appointed
Master of this design—did give us, with
Rich garments, linens, stuffs, and necessaries,
165 Which since have steaded° much. So, of his gentleness,[6]   *been useful*
Knowing I loved my books, he furnished me
From mine own library with volumes that
I prize above my dukedom.

MIRANDA   Would I might
But ever see that man.

PROSPERO   Now I arise.[7]
170 Sit still,° and hear the last of our sea-sorrow.   *Continue to sit*
Here in this island we arrived, and here
Have I, thy schoolmaster, made thee more profit°   *profit more*
Than other princes[8] can, that have more time
For vainer hours, and tutors not so careful.°   *caring*
175 MIRANDA   Heavens thank you for't. And now I pray you, sir,
For still 'tis beating in my mind, your reason
For raising this sea-storm?

PROSPERO   Know thus far forth:
By accident most strange, bountiful Fortune,
Now my dear lady,[9] hath mine enemies
180 Brought to this shore; and by my prescience
I find my zenith[1] doth depend upon
A most auspicious star,[2] whose influence

---

3. Cask or tub: here, deprecatory for "boat."
4. The winds, responding sympathetically to our
sighs, only blew us farther out to sea.
5. The secondary sense provides an image of giving
birth.
6. Nobility; kindness.
7. Referring to the action of standing; or to Prospero's rising fortunes (as in lines 179–84). The former
might visually reinforce the latter, especially if Pros-

pero also resumes his magical powers by putting on
his cloak.
8. *princes:* a generic plural for "princes and princesses."
9. Traditional characterization of Fortune as a woman
changeable in her affections.
1. Highest point, as of a star in the sky.
2. Referring to the belief that celestial bodies had
astrological influence on people and events.

<table>
<tr><td></td><td>If now I court not but omit,° my fortunes</td><td>disregard</td></tr>
<tr><td></td><td>Will ever after droop. Here cease more questions.</td><td></td></tr>
<tr><td>185</td><td>Thou art inclined to sleep. 'Tis a good dullness,°</td><td>drowsiness</td></tr>
<tr><td></td><td>And give it way. I know thou canst not choose.</td><td></td></tr>
</table>

[MIRANDA *sleeps*.]

[*to* ARIEL] Come away,° servant, come! I am ready now.   *Come here*
Approach, my Ariel.[3] Come!

    Enter ARIEL.

ARIEL   All hail, great master; grave sir, hail! I come
190   To answer thy best pleasure, be't to fly,
    To swim, to dive into the fire, to ride
    On the curled clouds. To thy strong bidding task
    Ariel and all his quality.°   *cohorts; faculties*
PROSPERO   Hast thou, spirit,
    Performed to point° the tempest that I bade thee?   *in detail*
195 ARIEL   To every article.
    I boarded the King's ship. Now on the beak,°   *prow*
    Now in the waist,° the deck,° in every cabin,   *midship / poop*
    I flamed amazement.[4] Sometimes I'd divide
    And burn in many places;[5] on the topmast,
200   The yards, and bowsprit would I flame distinctly,
    Then meet and join. Jove's lightning, the precursors
    O'th' dreadful thunderclaps, more momentary
    And sight-outrunning° were not. The fire and cracks   *quicker than the eye*
    Of sulfurous[6] roaring the most mighty Neptune
205   Seem to besiege and make his bold waves tremble,
    Yea, his dread trident shake.
PROSPERO   My brave spirit!
    Who was so firm, so constant, that this coil°   *turmoil*
    Would not infect his reason?
ARIEL   Not a soul
    But felt a fever of the mad° and played   *such as madmen feel*
210   Some tricks of desperation. All but mariners
    Plunged in the foaming brine and quit the vessel,
    Then all afire with me; the King's son Ferdinand,
    With hair upstaring°—then like reeds, not hair—   *standing on end*
    Was the first man that leapt, cried, "Hell is empty,
    And all the devils are here!"
215 PROSPERO   Why, that's my spirit.
    But was not this nigh shore?
ARIEL   Close by, my master.
PROSPERO   But are they, Ariel, safe?
ARIEL   Not a hair perished.
    On their sustaining[7] garments not a blemish,
    But fresher than before; and, as thou bad'st° me,   *commanded*
220   In troops° I have dispersed them 'bout the isle.   *groups*
    The King's son have I landed by himself,
    Whom I left cooling of° the air with sighs   *cooling*
    In an odd angle° of the isle, and sitting,   *corner*
    His arms in this sad knot.[8]

---

3. Ariel's name, along with sounding like "airy," also means in Hebrew "lion of God." The name appears as that of a magical spirit in various occult texts.
4. I appeared as flames, causing terror.
5. The phosphorescent effect of St. Elmo's fire, caused in a thunderstorm by the charge of static electricity

that builds up particularly around metal projections.
6. Sulfur was popularly associated with thunder and lightning.
7. Buoying up, and thus suggesting "life-giving."
8. Folded sadly, like this (folded arms implied sorrow).

PROSPERO   Of the King's ship,
225   The mariners, say how thou hast disposed,
     And all the rest o'th' fleet.

ARIEL   Safely in harbor
     Is the King's ship; in the deep nook where once
     Thou called'st me up at midnight to fetch dew
     From the still-vexed° Bermudas, there she's hid;   *ever-stormy*
230   The mariners all under hatches stowed,
     Who, with° a charm joined to° their suffered labor,   *by virtue of / with*
     I have left asleep; and for the rest o'th' fleet,
     Which I dispersed, they all have met again
     And are upon the Mediterranean float,°   *billow; sea*
235   Bound sadly home for Naples,
     Supposing that they saw the King's ship wrecked
     And his great person perish.

PROSPERO   Ariel, thy charge
     Exactly is performed; but there's more work.
     What is the time o'th' day?

ARIEL   Past the mid-season.°   *noon*
240 PROSPERO   At least two glasses.° The time twixt six and now   *hourglasses*
     Must by us both be spent most preciously.

ARIEL   Is there more toil? Since thou dost give me pains,°   *tasks*
     Let me remember° thee what thou hast promised,   *remind*
     Which is not yet performed me.

PROSPERO   How now? Moody?
     What is't thou canst demand?

245 ARIEL   My liberty.

PROSPERO   Before the time be out? No more.

ARIEL   I prithee,
     Remember I have done thee worthy service,
     Told thee no lies, made no mistakings, served
     Without or° grudge or grumblings. Thou did promise   *either*
     To bate° me a full year.   *remit; excuse*
250 PROSPERO   Dost thou forget
     From what a torment I did free thee?

ARIEL   No.

PROSPERO   Thou dost, and think'st it much to tread the ooze
     Of the salt deep,
     To run upon the sharp wind of the north,
255   To do me business in the veins⁹ o'th' earth
     When it is baked° with frost.   *dried and hardened*

ARIEL   I do not, sir.

• PROSPERO   Thou liest, malignant thing!¹ Hast thou forgot
     The foul witch Sycorax, who with age and envy
     Was grown into a hoop?° Hast thou forgot her?   *bent over with age*

ARIEL   No, sir.
260 PROSPERO   Thou hast. Where was she born? Speak. Tell me.

ARIEL   Sir, in Algiers.

PROSPERO   Oh, was she so? I must
     Once in a month recount what thou hast been,

---

9. Mineral veins or subterranean rivers.
1. PERFORMANCE COMMENT Prospero's threats to Ariel can disturb audiences by making the play's protagonist seem bullying and tyrannical. Some performances intensify the outbursts to affirm a despotic conception of the magician, while others moderate his anger, explaining his threats as needful attempts to maintain order. For more on how casting choices and other decisions affect the power dynamics between Prospero and Ariel, see Digital Edition PC 2.

Which thou forgett'st. This damned witch Sycorax,
For mischiefs manifold and sorceries terrible
265 To enter human hearing, from Algiers,
Thou know'st, was banished. For one thing she did
They would not take her life.[2] Is not this true?
ARIEL Ay, sir.
PROSPERO This blue-eyed[3] hag was hither brought with child
270 And here was left by th' sailors. Thou, my slave,
As thou report'st thyself, was then her servant;
And for° thou wast a spirit too delicate   *because*
To act her earthy[4] and abhorred commands,
Refusing her grand hests,° she did confine thee,   *commands*
275 By help of her more potent ministers,°   *agents; slaves*
And in her most unmitigable rage,
Into a cloven pine; within which rift
Imprisoned thou didst painfully remain
A dozen years, within which space she died
280 And left thee there, where thou didst vent thy groans
As fast as millwheels strike.° Then was this island—   *hit the water*
Save for the son that she did litter° here,   *give birth to*
A freckled whelp, hag-born—not honored with
A human shape.
ARIEL   Yes, Caliban her son.
285 PROSPERO Dull thing, I say so:[5] he, that Caliban
Whom now I keep in service. Thou best know'st
What torment I did find thee in: thy groans
Did make wolves howl, and penetrate° the breasts   *arouse sympathy in*
Of ever-angry bears. It was a torment
290 To lay upon the damned, which Sycorax
Could not again undo. It was mine art,
When I arrived and heard thee, that made gape
The pine and let thee out.
ARIEL   I thank thee, master.
PROSPERO If thou more murmur'st, I will rend an oak
295 And peg thee in his° knotty entrails till   *its*
Thou hast howled away twelve winters.
ARIEL   Pardon, master.
I will be correspondent° to command   *compliant*
And do my spriting gently.°   *graciously*
PROSPERO   Do so, and after two days
I will discharge thee.[6]
ARIEL   That's my noble master!
300 What shall I do? Say what, what shall I do?
PROSPERO Go make thyself like a nymph o'th' sea. Be subject
To no sight but thine and mine, invisible
To every eyeball else.[7] Go, take this shape°   *appearance; disguise*
And hither come in't. Go! Hence with diligence.

Exit [ARIEL].

---

2. *For . . . life:* Only because she got pregnant. Capital sentences were commuted for pregnant women; ordinarily, condemned witches were either hanged or burned at the stake.
3. TEXTUAL COMMENT The description of Sycorax as "blew ey'd" has puzzled many readers, and editors have proposed a variety of emendations and interpretations. For more on this issue, see Digital Edition TC 3.

4. Difficult for Ariel, whose element is air; also, grossly material, coarse.
5. You dullard, that's just what I said.
6. Prospero reduces this to within two days at lines 419–20 and actually releases Ariel in about four hours' time.
7. *Be . . . else:* Ariel may wear a conventional costume, indicating his invisibility to other characters onstage.

305 [*to* MIRANDA] Awake, dear heart, awake! Thou hast slept well.
　　Awake.

MIRANDA　　The strangeness of your story put
　　Heaviness° in me.　　　　　　　　　　　　　　　　　　　　　　*Sleepiness*

PROSPERO　　　　　　Shake it off. Come on;
　　We'll visit Caliban, my slave, who never
　　Yields us kind answer.

MIRANDA　　　　　　　　'Tis a villain, sir,
　　I do not love to look on.

310 PROSPERO　　　　　　　　But, as 'tis,
　　We cannot miss° him. He does make our fire,　　　　　*avoid; do without*
　　Fetch in our wood, and serves in offices°　　　　　　*capacities; duties*
　　That profit us. What ho! Slave! Caliban!
　　Thou earth, thou: speak!

CALIBAN (*within*)　　　　　There's wood enough within.

315 PROSPERO　　Come forth, I say! There's other business for thee.
　　Come, thou tortoise! When?
　　　　　Enter ARIEL *like a water nymph.*
　　—Fine apparition! My quaint[8] Ariel,
　　Hark in thine ear.
　　[*He whispers.*]

ARIEL　　　　　　My lord, it shall be done.　　　　　*Exit.*

PROSPERO　　Thou poisonous slave, got° by the devil[9] himself　　*begot*
320　　Upon thy wicked dam,° come forth!　　　　　*harmful, foul mother*
　　　　　Enter CALIBAN.[1]

CALIBAN　　As wicked dew as e'er my mother brushed[2]
　　With raven's feather from unwholesome fen°　　　　　　　　*bog*
　　Drop on you both! A southwest[3] blow on ye
　　And blister you all o'er!

325 PROSPERO　　For this, be sure, tonight thou shalt have cramps,
　　Side-stitches that shall pen thy breath up; urchins[4]
　　Shall forth at vast of° night that they may work　　*during the boundless*
　　All exercise on thee;[5] thou shalt be pinched
　　As thick as honeycomb,[6] each pinch more stinging
　　Than bees that made 'em.°　　　　　　　　　　　　*(honeycomb cells)*

330 CALIBAN　　　　　　　I must eat my dinner.
　　This island's mine by Sycorax my mother,
　　Which thou tak'st from me. When thou cam'st first
　　Thou strok'st me and made much of me; wouldst give me
　　Water with berries in't, and teach me how
335　　To name the bigger light and how the less[7]
　　That burn by day and night. And then I loved thee
　　And showed thee all the qualities o'th' isle:
　　The fresh springs, brine-pits, barren place and fertile.
　　Cursèd be I that did so! All the charms°　　　　　　　　*spells*

---

8. The term could simultaneously mean "ingenious," "curious in appearance," and "elegant."
9. Not merely an insult, but also an allusion to Caliban's birth from the devil (incubus) and witch.
1. PERFORMANCE COMMENT Caliban's costume and conduct in this first entrance often reveal whether a production has chosen to portray him as monstrous, or human, or both. Such choices help to determine whether the audience is moved more by Prospero's suffering or by Caliban's. For more on the complexities of the role, see Digital Edition PC 3.
2. Brushed up, collected. Dew was a common ingre-dient of magical potions.
3. A southerly wind was considered plague-bearing.
4. Hedgehogs; but here indicates spirits disguised as hedgehogs.
5. *that . . . thee:* in order that they may perform their habitual activity.
6. *thou . . . honeycomb:* The pinch marks will be as closely packed as, and of similar texture to, the cells of a honeycomb.
7. Recalls Genesis 1:16: "God then made two great lights: the greater light to rule the day, and the less light to rule the night."

340 Of Sycorax—toads, beetles, bats—light on you!
For I am all the subjects that you have,
Which first was mine own king; and here you sty me°   *pen me up*
In this hard rock whiles you do keep from me
The rest o'th' island.

PROSPERO   Thou most lying slave,
345 Whom stripes° may move, not kindness. I have used° thee,   *lashes / treated*
Filth as thou art, with humane care, and lodged thee
In mine own cell till thou didst seek to violate
The honor of my child.

CALIBAN   Oh ho, oh ho! Would't had been done!
Thou didst prevent me; I had peopled else
This isle with Calibans.

350 MIRANDA[8]   Abhorrèd slave,
Which any print° of goodness wilt not take,   *impression*
Being capable of° all ill. I pitied thee,   *susceptible to*
Took pains to make thee speak, taught thee each hour
One thing or other. When thou didst not, savage,
355 Know thine own meaning but wouldst gabble like
A thing most brutish, I endowed thy purposes
With words that made them known. But thy vile race,°   *hereditary nature*
Though thou didst learn, had that in't which good natures
Could not abide to be with; therefore wast thou
360 Deservedly confined into this rock,
Who hadst deserved more than a prison.

•CALIBAN   You taught me language, and my profit on't
Is I know how to curse. The red plague rid you[9]
For learning me your language!

PROSPERO   Hag-seed,° hence!   *Offspring of a hag*
365 Fetch us in fuel; and be quick, thou'rt best,
To answer other business.° Shrugg'st thou, malice?   *perform other tasks*
If thou neglect'st or dost unwillingly
What I command, I'll rack thee with old[1] cramps,
Fill all thy bones with aches,[2] make thee roar,
That beasts shall tremble at thy din.

370 CALIBAN   No, pray thee.
[*aside*] I must obey. His art is of such power
It would control my dam's god Setebos[3]
And make a vassal of him.

PROSPERO   So, slave, hence.   *Exit* CALIBAN.
          Enter FERDINAND, *and* ARIEL, *invisible, playing*
          and singing.[4]

•ARIEL [*sings*]   Come unto these yellow sands,
375   And then take hands.
          Curtsied when you have, and kissed,
          The wild waves whist.[5]
          Foot it featly° here and there,   *Dance nimbly*

8. TEXTUAL COMMENT For roughly two and a half
centuries, editors reassigned this speech to Prospero,
finding it inappropriate for Miranda. For more, see
Digital Edition TC 4.
9. The plague that gives red sores destroy, kill you.
1. As of aged people; long-accustomed.
2. As a noun, this was probably pronounced "aitches."
3. A name found in travel narratives as a god of the
Patagonians.
4. This probably does not imply that Ferdinand enters
first, even though such a staging is possible if Ferdinand is bewildered as to where this music is coming
from. Ariel is invisible to all but Prospero and the audience. He is probably still dressed as a water nymph.
5. Become hushed and attentive.

	And sweet sprites bear°	*spirits sing*
380	The burden.[6]	

SPIRITS [*within, sing the*] (*burden dispersedly*)   Hark, hark! Bow-wow!
    The watch-dogs bark: bow-wow!

ARIEL   Hark, hark. I hear
    The strain of strutting Chanticleer

385   Cry cock-a-diddle-dow.

FERDINAND   Where should this music be? I'th' air or th'earth?

It sounds no more; and sure it waits° upon   *attends*
Some god o'th' island. Sitting on a bank,
Weeping again the King my father's wreck,

390 This music crept by me upon the waters,
Allaying both their fury and my passion°   *grief*
With its sweet air.° Thence I have followed it,   *melody*
Or it hath drawn me rather; but 'tis gone.
No, it begins again.

395 ARIEL [*sings*]   Full fathom five thy father lies;
    Of his bones are coral made;
    Those are pearls that were his eyes;
    Nothing of him that doth fade,
    But doth suffer a sea-change

400   Into something rich and strange.
    Sea-nymphs hourly ring his knell.

SPIRITS [*within, sing the*] (*burden*)   Ding dong.

ARIEL   Hark, now I hear them.

SPIRITS [*within*]   Ding dong, bell.

FERDINAND   The ditty does remember[7] my drowned father.

405 This is no mortal° business, nor no sound   *human*
That the earth owes.° I hear it now above me.   *owns*

PROSPERO [*to* MIRANDA]   The fringèd curtains of thine eye
    advance°   *raise*
And say what thou seest yond.

MIRANDA   What is't? A spirit?
    Lord, how it looks about. Believe me, sir,

410 It carries a brave° form. But 'tis a spirit.   *splendid; gallant*

PROSPERO   No, wench, it eats and sleeps and hath such senses
As we have—such. This gallant° which thou seest   *fine gentleman*
Was in the wreck; and but° he's something° stained   *except that / somewhat*
With grief—that's beauty's canker[8]—thou mightst call him

415 A goodly person. He hath lost his fellows
And strays about to find 'em.

MIRANDA   I might call him
    A thing divine, for nothing natural
    I ever saw so noble.

PROSPERO [*aside*][9]   It° goes on, I see,   (*My plan*)
    As my soul prompts it. [*to* ARIEL] Spirit, fine spirit, I'll free thee
    Within two days for this.

---

6. TEXTUAL COMMENT "Burden" is a technical term from Renaissance music meaning "refrain" or "under-song," but its other associations may lend extra significance to Ariel's use of the word in this song. For more, see Digital Edition TC 5.
7. Commemorate. *ditty:* the words of the song.
8. Cankerworm; caterpillar ("beauty" being seen as a flower); spreading sore.

9. Prospero's asides here and at lines 437, 449, and 492 may be either private utterances or addressed to Ariel. If the former, Ariel may nevertheless hear them; Prospero speaks to Ariel after all these instances. Their import may well be purposefully enigmatic.

420 FERDINAND   Most sure, the goddess
      On whom these airs attend![1] Vouchsafe° my prayer   *Grant*
      May know if you remain° upon this island,   *dwell*
      And that you will some good instruction give
      How I may bear me° here. My prime request,   *conduct myself*
425   Which I do last pronounce, is—O you wonder![2]—
      If you be maid[3] or no?
      MIRANDA   No wonder, sir,
      But certainly a maid.
      FERDINAND   My language? Heavens!
      I am the best[4] of them that speak this speech,
      Were I but where 'tis spoken.
      PROSPERO   How? The best?
430   What wert thou if the King of Naples heard thee?
      FERDINAND   A single[5] thing, as I am now, that wonders
      To hear thee speak of Naples. He does hear me,[6]
      And that he does I weep. Myself am Naples,°   *King of Naples*
      Who with mine eyes, never since at ebb,° beheld   *ceasing to flow*
      The King my father wrecked.
435   MIRANDA   Alack, for mercy!
      FERDINAND   Yes, faith, and all his lords, the Duke of Milan
      And his brave son[7] being twain.
      PROSPERO [*aside*]   The Duke of Milan
      And his more braver daughter could control[8] thee
      If now 'twere fit to do't. At the first sight
440   They have changed eyes.[9] [*to* ARIEL] Delicate° Ariel,   *Graceful; artful*
      I'll set thee free for this! [*to* FERDINAND] A word, good sir.
      I fear you have done yourself some wrong.[1] A word.
      MIRANDA   Why speaks my father so ungently?° This   *discourteously*
      Is the third man that e'er I saw, the first
445   That e'er I sighed for. Pity move my father
      To be inclined my way.
      FERDINAND   Oh, if a virgin,
      And your affection not gone forth,[2] I'll make you
      The Queen of Naples.
      PROSPERO   Soft, sir! One word more.
      [*aside*] They are both in either's powers. But this swift business
450   I must uneasy° make, lest too light[3] winning   *difficult*
      Make the prize light. [*to* FERDINAND] One word more! I charge
         thee
      That thou attend me. Thou dost here usurp
      The name thou ow'st° not, and hast put thyself   *own*
      Upon this island as a spy to win it
      From me, the lord on't.°   *of it*

---

1. *Most . . . attend:* Probably spoken aside, but possibly an invocation. *Most sure the goddess:* Echoes Aeneas's reaction to seeing Venus after his shipwreck, "o dea certe" (*Aeneid* I.328). *airs:* Ariel's melodies.
2. Miracle, punning on the meaning of Miranda's name.
3. Unmarried virgin; made (human).
4. Highest in rank, assuming he has succeeded his father.
5. Weak and helpless; solitary; one and the same.
6. "He" and "me" both refer to Ferdinand. Presuming his father to be dead, Ferdinand takes himself to

be the new King of Naples (and as such, he hears himself speaking). Alternatively, Ferdinand thinks his father's spirit hears him.
7. The only instance in which Antonio is mentioned as having a son.
8. Challenge; take to task; exercise power over.
9. Exchanged loving glances; fallen in love at first sight.
1. Euphemistic for "told a lie about yourself."
2. Given over to someone else.
3. Easy; playing on the meanings of "little valued" and also "promiscuous" in line 451.

455 FERDINAND   No, as I am a man.

MIRANDA   There's nothing ill can dwell in such a temple.[4]
     If the ill spirit have so fair a house,
     Good things will strive to dwell with't.

PROSPERO [*to* FERDINAND]   Follow me.
     [*to* MIRANDA] Speak not you for him: he's a traitor. [*to*
         FERDINAND] Come!

460   I'll manacle thy neck and feet together.
     Sea-water shalt thou drink; thy food shall be
     The fresh-brook mussels,[5] withered roots, and husks
     Wherein the acorn cradled. Follow!

FERDINAND   No.
     I will resist such entertainment° till   *treatment*
     Mine enemy has more power.

         He draws [his sword], and is charmed from moving.

465 MIRANDA   O dear father,
     Make not too rash a trial of him, for
     He's gentle and not fearful.[6]

PROSPERO   What, I say,
     My foot° my tutor? [*to* FERDINAND] Put thy sword up, traitor,   *inferior*
     Who mak'st a show but dar'st not strike, thy conscience
470   Is so possessed with guilt. Come from thy ward,°   *defensive stance*
     For I can here disarm thee with this stick°   *magician's wand*
     And make thy weapon drop.

MIRANDA   Beseech you, father—

PROSPERO   Hence! Hang not on my garments.

MIRANDA   Sir, have pity.
     I'll be his surety.

PROSPERO   Silence! One word more
475   Shall make me chide thee, if not hate thee. What,
     An advocate for an imposter? Hush!
     Thou think'st there is no more such shapes° as he,   *forms; men*
     Having seen but him and Caliban. Foolish wench,
     To° th' most of men this is a Caliban,   *Compared to*
     And they to him are angels.

480 MIRANDA   My affections
     Are then most humble. I have no ambition
     To see a goodlier man.

PROSPERO [*to* FERDINAND]   Come on, obey.
     Thy nerves° are in their infancy again,   *sinews*
     And have no vigor in them.

FERDINAND   So they are.
485   My spirits,° as in a dream, are all bound up.   *mental powers*
     My father's loss, the weakness which I feel,
     The wreck of all my friends, nor this man's threats
     To whom I am subdued, are but light to me,
     Might I but through my prison once a day
490   Behold this maid. All corners else o'th' earth
     Let liberty make use of; space enough
     Have I in such a prison.

---

4. A common metaphor for the body; also, a conventional Renaissance notion that moral qualities were physically manifest.

5. Freshwater mussels are inedible.
6. He's noble and, therefore, not cowardly. Alternatively, not fearsome.

PROSPERO [*aside*] It works. [*to* FERDINAND] Come on!
[*to* ARIEL] Thou hast done well, fine Ariel. [*to* FERDINAND]
Follow me.
[*to* ARIEL] Hark what thou else shalt do me.

MIRANDA [*to* FERDINAND] Be of comfort;
495 My father's of a better nature, sir,
Than he appears by speech. This is unwonted°   *unusual*
Which now came from him.

PROSPERO [*to* ARIEL] Thou shalt be as free
As mountain winds; but then° exactly do   *until then*
All points of my command.

ARIEL To th' syllable.

500 PROSPERO [*to* FERDINAND] Come, follow. [*to* MIRANDA] Speak not
for him.   *Exeunt.*

2.1

Enter ALONSO, SEBASTIAN, ANTONIO, GONZALO,
ADRIAN, *and* FRANCISCO.

GONZALO Beseech you, sir, be merry. You have cause—
So have we all—of joy; for our escape
Is much beyond our loss. Our hint° of woe   *occasion*
Is common: every day some sailor's wife,
5 The masters of some merchant, and the merchant[1]
Have just° our theme of woe. But for the miracle—   *exactly*
I mean our preservation—few in millions
Can speak like us. Then wisely, good sir, weigh
Our sorrow with° our comfort.   *against*

ALONSO Prithee, peace.[2]

10 SEBASTIAN [*to* ANTONIO] He receives comfort like cold porridge.°   *broth*

ANTONIO [*to* SEBASTIAN] The visitor[3] will not give him o'er so.°   *leave him alone*

SEBASTIAN Look, he's winding up the watch of his wit; by and
by it will strike.

GONZALO [*to* ALONSO] Sir—

15 SEBASTIAN One. Tell.°   *Keep count*

GONZALO When every grief is entertained° that's offered, comes   *harbored*
to th'entertainer[4]—

SEBASTIAN A dollar.[5]

GONZALO Dolor° comes to him, indeed. You have spoken truer   *Sorrow*
20 than you purposed.

SEBASTIAN You have taken it wiselier than I meant you should.

GONZALO [*to* ALONSO] Therefore, my lord—

ANTONIO Fie, what a spendthrift is he of his tongue!

ALONSO I prithee, spare.°   *spare your words*

25 GONZALO Well, I have done. But yet—

SEBASTIAN He will be talking.

ANTONIO Which of he or Adrian, for a good wager, first
begins to crow?[6]

SEBASTIAN The old cock.

2.1
1. The chief officers of some merchant ship and its
owner.
2. Sebastian takes this as "pease," as in "pease
porridge."

3. Antonio compares Gonzalo with one who visits
and comforts the sick and distressed.
4. There comes to the person who accepts that grief.
5. *dollar:* English name for the German thaler.
6. Which of the two will first begin to speak ("crow")?

30	ANTONIO The cockerel.[7]
	SEBASTIAN Done. The wager?
	ANTONIO A laughter.[8]
	SEBASTIAN A match.
	ADRIAN Though this island seem to be desert°—
35	ANTONIO Ha, ha, ha!
	SEBASTIAN So, you're paid.[9]
	ADRIAN Uninhabitable and almost inaccessible—
	SEBASTIAN Yet—
	ADRIAN Yet—
40	ANTONIO He could not miss't.

ADRIAN It must needs be of subtle, tender, and delicate[1] temperance.° *climate*

ANTONIO Temperance was a delicate wench.[2]

SEBASTIAN Ay, and a subtle, as he most learnedly delivered.[3]

45 ADRIAN The air breathes upon us here most sweetly.

SEBASTIAN As if it had lungs, and rotten ones.

ANTONIO Or as 'twere perfumed by a fen.° *bog*

GONZALO Here is everything advantageous to life.

ANTONIO True, save° means to live. *except*

50 SEBASTIAN Of that there's none, or little.

GONZALO How lush and lusty° the grass looks! How green! *tender and luxuriant*

ANTONIO The ground indeed is tawny.

SEBASTIAN With an eye[4] of green in't.

ANTONIO He misses not much.

55 SEBASTIAN No, he doth but mistake the truth totally.

GONZALO But the rarity[5] of it is, which is indeed almost beyond credit—

SEBASTIAN As many vouched° rarities are. *alleged; accepted*

GONZALO That our garments being, as they were, drenched in the sea, hold notwithstanding their freshness and gloss, being rather new-dyed than stained with salt water.

ANTONIO If but one of his pockets[6] could speak, would it not say he lies?

SEBASTIAN Ay, or very falsely pocket up his report.[7]

65 GONZALO Methinks our garments are now as fresh as when we put them on first in Africa, at the marriage of the King's fair daughter Claribel to the King of Tunis.

SEBASTIAN 'Twas a sweet marriage, and we prosper well in our return.

70 ADRIAN Tunis was never graced before with such a paragon to° their queen. *for*

GONZALO Not since widow Dido's[8] time.

ANTONIO Widow?[9] A pox o' that! How came that "widow" in? Widow Dido!

---

7. "The young cock crows as the old hears" was proverbial. "Old cock" refers to Gonzalo and "cockerel" to Adrian.

8. From the proverb "He laughs that wins."

9. Antonio's laugh is his prize.

1. Exquisite, but in Antonio's usage (line 43), "given to pleasure." *subtle:* fine, but in Sebastian's usage (line 44), "sexually expert" or "crafty."

2. Antonio takes "Temperance" to be the name of a girl.

3. "Learnedly delivered" was a popular phrase among puritans who wanted to appear pious.

4. A tinge. In Antonio's reply, an "eye of green" refers to Gonzalo's optimistic capacity to see green.

5. Exceptional quality; but in Sebastian's usage (line 58), "uncommon thing."

6. Seen as the garments' "mouth"; also implying that Gonzalo's pockets are stained.

7. The evidence of stained pockets would confute Gonzalo's words and reputation for honesty. *pocket up:* suppress, or keep silent; also, receive unprotestingly.

8. Queen of ancient Carthage, whose tragic love affair with Aeneas is related in Virgil's *Aeneid.*

9. Antonio picks on this designation for a woman abandoned by her lover as being either irrelevant or conspicuously prudish. Dido, however, was in fact a widow when she met Aeneas.

75 SEBASTIAN   What if he had said "widower Aeneas" too? Good
Lord, how you take° it!   *fuss about*
ADRIAN   "Widow Dido," said you? You make me study of° that: *examine*
she was of Carthage, not of Tunis.
GONZALO   This Tunis, sir, was Carthage.[1]
80 ADRIAN   Carthage?
GONZALO   I assure you, Carthage.
ANTONIO   His word is more than the miraculous harp.[2]
SEBASTIAN   He hath raised the wall, and houses too.
ANTONIO   What impossible matter will he make easy next?
85 SEBASTIAN   I think he will carry this island home in his pocket
and give it his son for an apple.
ANTONIO   And sowing the kernels° of it in the sea, bring forth   *seeds*
more islands.
GONZALO   Ay.[3]
90 ANTONIO   Why, in good time.
GONZALO [*to* ALONSO]   Sir, we were talking, that our garments
seem now as fresh as when we were at Tunis at the marriage
of your daughter, who is now queen.
ANTONIO   And the rarest that e'er came there.
95 SEBASTIAN   Bate,[4] I beseech you, widow Dido.
ANTONIO   Oh, widow Dido? Ay, widow Dido.
GONZALO   Is not, sir, my doublet as fresh as the first day I
wore it? I mean, in a sort.[5]
ANTONIO   That "sort" was well fished for.
100 GONZALO   When I wore it at your daughter's marriage.
ALONSO   You cram these words into mine ears against
The stomach of my sense.[6] Would I had never
Married my daughter there; for coming thence
My son is lost, and, in my rate,° she too,   *consideration*
105 Who is so far from Italy removed
I ne'er again shall see her. O thou mine heir
Of Naples and of Milan, what strange fish
Hath made his meal on thee?
FRANCISCO   Sir, he may live.
I saw him beat the surges under him
110 And ride upon their backs. He trod the water
Whose enmity he flung aside, and breasted
The surge, most swol'n, that met him. His bold head
'Bove the contentious waves he kept, and oared
Himself with his good arms in lusty° stroke   *vigorous*
115 To th' shore, that o'er his wave-worn basis bowed,[7]
As° stooping to relieve him. I not° doubt   *As if / do not*
He came alive to land.
ALONSO   No, no, he's gone.
SEBASTIAN   Sir, you may thank yourself for this great loss,
That would not bless our Europe with your daughter,
120 But rather loose° her to an African,   *lose; release*

1. The city of Tunis was actually built ten miles from
the site of Carthage.
2. Referring to Amphion's harp, to the music of which
the walls (but not the houses) of Thebes arose.
3. Affirming his belief that Tunis was Carthage;
Antonio mocks the length of time this took.
4. Except (as a verb); don't mention.

5. Comparatively speaking; Antonio plays on "drawing
lots."
6. *You . . . sense:* The image is of one being force-fed
words against the appetite ("stomach") for hearing
them.
7. *that . . . bowed:* that extended out and drooped over
the foot of the cliff, which had been eroded by waves.

Where she, at least, is banished from your eye,
Who° hath cause to set the grief on't.   *(Claribel)*
ALONSO   Prithee, peace.
SEBASTIAN   You were kneeled to and importuned otherwise[8]
By all of us; and the fair soul herself
125   Weighed, between loathness and obedience, at
Which end o'th' beam should bow.[9] We have lost your son,
I fear, forever. Milan and Naples have
More widows in them of this business' making
Than we bring men to comfort them. The fault's
Your own.
130   ALONSO   So is the dearest o'th' loss.[1]
GONZALO   My lord Sebastian,
The truth you speak doth lack some gentleness,
And time° to speak it in. You rub the sore[2]   *(appropriate time)*
When you should bring the plaster.
SEBASTIAN   Very well.
135   ANTONIO   And most chirurgeonly.°   *surgeonlike*
GONZALO [*to* ALONSO]   It is foul weather in us all, good sir,
When you are cloudy.
SEBASTIAN   Foul weather?
ANTONIO   Very foul.
GONZALO   Had I plantation[3] of this isle, my lord—
ANTONIO   He'd sow't with nettle-seed.
SEBASTIAN   Or docks, or mallows.[4]
140   GONZALO   And were the king on't, what would I do?
SEBASTIAN   Scape being drunk for want of wine.
GONZALO   I'th' commonwealth I would by contraries
Execute all things.[5] For no kind of traffic°   *commerce*
Would I admit; no name of magistrate;
145   Letters° should not be known; riches, poverty,   *Writing; erudition*
And use of service,° none; contract, succession,[6]   *servants*
Bourn,° bound of land, tilth,° vineyard, none;   *Boundary / tillage*
No use of metal, corn,° or wine, or oil;   *grain*
No occupation, all men idle, all;
150   And women too, but innocent and pure;[7]
No sovereignty—
SEBASTIAN   Yet he would be king on't.
ANTONIO   The latter end of his commonwealth forgets the
beginning.
GONZALO   —All things in common° nature should produce   *for communal use*
155   Without sweat or endeavor. Treason, felony,
Sword, pike, knife, gun, or need of any engine°   *weapon*
Would I not have; but nature should bring forth
Of it own kind, all foison,° all abundance,   *plenty*
To feed my innocent people.

8. *otherwise:* to act differently.
9. *Weighed . . . bow:* Weighed loathness to marry against obedience to her father to find out which end of the scales' beam would sink.
1. That is, the most grievous, or costliest, part of the loss is also my own.
2. "To rub the sore" was proverbial. *plaster* (line 134): a soothing remedy.
3. Had I responsibility for colonization of the island; but also interpreted as "planting" by Antonio and Sebastian.

4. Cited as wild plants prone to grow on uncultivated land; but dock is a traditional soother of nettle stings, and mallow roots were used to make soothing ointment.
5. *I would . . . things:* I would advance the opposite to what would be usual. This speech is based on a passage in John Florio's translation of Montaigne's essay "Of Cannibals."
6. Inheritance of property.
7. Idleness proverbially begets lust.

160 SEBASTIAN No marrying[8] 'mong his subjects?

ANTONIO None, man, all idle: whores and knaves.

GONZALO I would with such perfection govern, sir,
  T'excel the golden age.[9]

SEBASTIAN   Save° his majesty!   *God save*

ANTONIO Long live Gonzalo!

165 GONZALO And do you mark me, sir?

ALONSO Prithee, no more. Thou dost talk nothing to me.

GONZALO I do well believe your highness, and did it to minis-
  ter occasion[1] to these gentlemen, who are of such sensible°   *sensitive*
  and nimble lungs that they always use° to laugh at nothing.   *are accustomed*

170 ANTONIO 'Twas you we laughed at.

GONZALO Who in this kind of merry fooling am nothing to
  you. So you may continue, and laugh at nothing still.

ANTONIO What a blow was there given!

SEBASTIAN An it had not fallen flatlong.[2]

175 GONZALO You are gentlemen of brave mettle;[3] you would lift
  the moon out of her sphere if she would continue in it five
  weeks without changing.[4]

          Enter ARIEL [*invisible,*] *playing solemn music.*

SEBASTIAN We would so, and then go a-bat-fowling.[5]

ANTONIO Nay, good my lord, be not angry.

180 GONZALO No, I warrant you, I will not adventure my discretion
  so weakly.[6] Will you laugh me asleep, for I am very heavy?°   *tired; serious*

ANTONIO Go sleep, and hear us.

          [*All sleep, except* ALONSO, SEBASTIAN, *and* ANTONIO.]

ALONSO What, all so soon asleep? I wish mine eyes
  Would, with themselves, shut up my thoughts. I find
  They are inclined to do so.

185 SEBASTIAN   Please you, sir,
  Do not omit° the heavy offer° of it.   *neglect / opportunity*
  It seldom visits sorrow; when it doth,
  It is a comforter.

ANTONIO   We two, my lord,
  Will guard your person while you take your rest,
  And watch your safety.

190 ALONSO   Thank you. Wondrous heavy.

          [ALONSO *sleeps. Exit* ARIEL.]

SEBASTIAN What a strange drowsiness possesses them!

ANTONIO It is the quality o'th' climate.

SEBASTIAN   Why
  Doth it not then our eyelids sink? I find
  Not myself disposed to sleep.

195 ANTONIO Nor I: my spirits are nimble.
  They fell together all as by consent;°   *consensus*
  They dropped, as by a thunderstroke. What might,
  Worthy Sebastian, oh, what might—? No more.

---

8. Seen as irrelevant to sexually innocent people;
also a form of contract (line 146).
9. In classical mythology, the earliest of the ages—a
time without strife, labor, or injustice, when abundant food grew without cultivation.
1. *minister occasion*: afford opportunity.
2. If it had not fallen on the flat, harmless side of the
sword.

3. Courage; punning on "metal," as of a sword blade.
4. *you would . . . changing*: You would even steal the
moon, if she were to stand still in her orbit ("sphere").
5. Trapping birds by using light to attract them and
bats to strike them down; may also mean swindling
and victimizing the simple.
6. I will not put my sound judgment at risk so
foolishly.

And yet methinks I see it in thy face
200 What thou shouldst be. Th'occasion speaks° thee, and   *opportunity speaks to*
My strong imagination sees a crown
Dropping upon thy head.
SEBASTIAN   What? Art thou waking?°   *awake*
ANTONIO   Do you not hear me speak?
SEBASTIAN   I do, and surely
It is a sleepy language, and thou speak'st
205 Out of thy sleep. What is it thou didst say?
This is a strange repose, to be asleep
With eyes wide open; standing, speaking, moving,
And yet so fast asleep.
ANTONIO   Noble Sebastian,
Thou lett'st thy fortune sleep—die rather; wink'st°   *shut your eyes*
Whiles thou art waking.
210 SEBASTIAN   Thou dost snore distinctly;°   *meaningfully*
There's meaning in thy snores.
ANTONIO   I am more serious than my custom. You
Must be so too, if heed° me; which to do   *if you heed*
Trebles thee o'er.
SEBASTIAN   Well, I am standing water.[7]
ANTONIO   I'll teach you how to flow.
215 SEBASTIAN   Do so. To ebb
Hereditary sloth[8] instructs me.
ANTONIO   Oh!
If you but knew how you the purpose cherish
Whiles thus you mock it;[9] how in stripping it
You more invest° it. Ebbing° men, indeed,   *clothe / Declining*
220 Most often do so near the bottom run
By their own fear or sloth.
SEBASTIAN   Prithee, say on.
The setting° of thine eye and cheek proclaim   *fixed look*
A matter° from thee; and a birth, indeed,   *Something important*
Which throes[1] thee much to yield.
ANTONIO   Thus, sir:
225 [*indicating* GONZALO] Although this lord of weak
     remembrance,° this,   *memory*
Who shall be of as little memory°   *as little remembered*
When he is earthed,° hath here almost persuaded—   *buried*
For he's a spirit of persuasion, only
Professes[2] to persuade—the King his son's alive,
230 'Tis as impossible that he's undrowned
As he that sleeps here swims.
SEBASTIAN   I have no hope
That he's undrowned.
ANTONIO   Oh, out of that no hope
What great hope have you! No hope that way° is   *(that he's not drowned)*
Another way so high a hope that even
235 Ambition cannot pierce a wink° beyond,   *catch a glimpse*

---

7. Between tides, and thus open to suggestion; also, associated with being slothful. *Trebles thee o'er:* Makes you three times as great.
8. Inherited laziness, or the slowness to attain prosperity arising from being born a younger brother.
9. *If . . . it:* If you only understood that your mockery reveals how great your aspirations really are; also, the hereditary position you mock is actually to your advantage. *cherish:* hold dear; cultivate.
1. Which puts in agony, as in childbirth.
2. *only / Professes:* his sole vocation is.

But doubt discovery there.[3] Will you grant with me
That Ferdinand is drowned?

SEBASTIAN   He's gone.

ANTONIO   Then tell me,
Who's the next heir of Naples?

SEBASTIAN   Claribel.

ANTONIO   She that is Queen of Tunis; she that dwells
240 Ten leagues beyond man's life;° she that from Naples   *lifetime journey*
Can have no note,° unless the sun were post°—   *information / messenger*
The man i'th' moon's too slow—till newborn chins
Be rough and razorable; she that from° whom   *returning from*
We all were sea-swallowed, though some cast again,[4]
245 And by that destiny to perform an act
Whereof what's past is prologue, what to come
In yours and my discharge.°   *performance*

SEBASTIAN   What stuff is this? How say you?
'Tis true my brother's daughter's Queen of Tunis;
So is she heir of Naples, twixt which regions
There is some space.

250 ANTONIO   A space whose ev'ry cubit°   *about 18 to 22 inches*
Seems to cry out, "How shall that Claribel
Measure us° back to Naples? Keep° in Tunis,   *(the cubits) / Stay*
And let Sebastian wake."° Say this were death   *(to his opportunity)*
That now hath seized them: why, they were no worse
255 Than now they are. There be that° can rule Naples   *those that*
As well as he that sleeps; lords that can prate
As amply and unnecessarily
As this Gonzalo; I myself could make
A chough of as deep chat.[5] Oh, that you bore
260 The mind that I do! What a sleep were this
For your advancement! Do you understand me?

SEBASTIAN   Methinks I do.

ANTONIO   And how does your content
Tender° your own good fortune?   *Regard; care for*

SEBASTIAN   I remember
You did supplant your brother Prospero.

ANTONIO   True:
265 And look how well my garments sit upon me,
Much feater° than before. My brother's servants   *more trimly*
Were then my fellows; now they are my men.

SEBASTIAN   But for your conscience?

ANTONIO   Ay, sir, where lies that? If 'twere a kibe,[6]
270 'Twould put me to° my slipper; but I feel not   *make me wear*
This deity in my bosom. Twenty consciences
That stand twixt me and Milan, candied[7] be they,
And melt ere they molest. Here lies your brother,
No better than the earth he lies upon
275 If he were that which now he's like—that's dead—
Whom I with this obedient steel,° three inches of it,   *sword*
Can lay to bed forever; whiles you, doing thus,

---

3. Doubt that there is anything to achieve beyond
the high hope of the crown.
4. Regurgitated, cast ashore; also, possibly, theatrical role-playing.

5. *I . . . chat:* I could train a jackdaw (known for imi-
tating speech) to speak as profoundly.
6. Chilblain; sore on the heel.
7. Turned to sugar; crystallized in sugar.

To the perpetual wink for aye° might put   *sleep forever*
This ancient morsel, this Sir Prudence, who
280   Should not upbraid our course. For all the rest,
They'll take suggestion° as a cat laps milk;   *prompting to evil*
They'll tell the clock° to any business that   *chime; agree*
We say befits the hour.

SEBASTIAN   Thy case, dear friend,
Shall be my precedent. As thou gott'st Milan,
285   I'll come by Naples. Draw thy sword: one stroke
Shall free thee from the tribute which thou payest,
And I the King shall love thee.

ANTONIO   Draw together;
And when I rear my hand, do you the like
To fall it on Gonzalo.

SEBASTIAN   Oh, but one word.

Enter ARIEL, [*invisible,*] *with music and song.*

290   ARIEL   My master through his art foresees the danger
That you his friend are in, and sends me forth—
For else° his project dies—to keep them[8] living.   *otherwise*

         [*He*] *sings in Gonzalo's ear.*
         While you here do snoring lie,
         Open-eyed conspiracy
295   His time° doth take.   *opportunity*
         If of life you keep a care,
         Shake off slumber and beware.
         Awake, awake!

ANTONIO   Then let us both be sudden.

    [ANTONIO *and* SEBASTIAN *draw their swords.*]

300   GONZALO [*waking*]   Now, good angels preserve the King.

    [*He wakes* ALONSO.]

ALONSO   Why, how now? Ho! Awake! Why are you° drawn?   *your weapons*
Wherefore this ghastly° looking?   *fearful*

GONZALO   What's the matter?

SEBASTIAN   Whiles we stood here securing° your repose,   *guarding*
Even now we heard a hollow burst of bellowing,
305   Like bulls, or rather lions. Did't not wake you?
It struck mine ear most terribly.

ALONSO   I heard nothing.

ANTONIO   Oh, 'twas a din to fright a monster's ear,
To make an earthquake: sure it was the roar
Of a whole herd of lions.

ALONSO   Heard you this, Gonzalo?

310   GONZALO   Upon mine honor, sir, I heard a humming,
And that a strange one too, which did awake me.
I shaked you, sir, and cried.° As mine eyes opened,   *called out*
I saw their weapons drawn. There was a noise,
That's verily.° 'Tis best we stand upon our guard,   *the truth*
315   Or that we quit this place. Let's draw our weapons.

ALONSO   Lead off this ground, and let's make further search
For my poor son.

GONZALO   Heavens keep him from these beasts,
For he is sure i'th' island.

---

8. Gonzalo and Alonso.

ALONSO   Lead away.
ARIEL[9]   Prospero my lord shall know what I have done.
320   So, King, go safely on to seek thy son.   *Exeunt.*

2.2

Enter CALIBAN *with a burden of wood.*
CALIBAN   All the infections that the sun sucks up
From bogs, fens, flats,° on Prosper fall, and make him   *marshes*
By inchmeal° a disease!   *inch by inch*
      A noise of thunder heard.[1]
                        His spirits hear me,
And yet I needs must curse. But they'll nor pinch,
5   Fright me with urchin-shows,[2] pitch me i'th' mire,
Nor lead me like a firebrand in the dark
Out of my way, unless he bid 'em. But
For every trifle are they set upon me;
Sometime like apes that mow° and chatter at me   *grimace*
10   And after bite me; then like hedgehogs, which
Lie tumbling in my barefoot way and mount
Their pricks at my footfall; sometime am I
All wound with° adders, who with cloven tongues   *entwined by*
Do hiss me into madness.
      Enter TRINCULO.[3]
                  Lo, now, lo!
15   Here comes a spirit of his, and to torment me
For bringing wood in slowly. I'll fall flat.
Perchance he will not mind° me.   *notice*
TRINCULO   Here's neither bush nor scrub to bear off° any   *ward off*
weather at all, and another storm brewing: I hear it sing i'th'
20   wind. Yond same black cloud, yond huge one, looks like a
foul bombard[4] that would shed his liquor. If it should thunder as it did before, I know not where to hide my head. Yond
same cloud cannot choose but fall by pailfuls. [*He sees* CALI-
BAN.] What have we here? A man or a fish? Dead or alive? A
25   fish: he smells like a fish; a very ancient and fishlike smell; a
kind of not-of-the-newest poor-john.[5] A strange fish. Were I
in England now, as once I was, and had but this fish painted,[6]
not a holiday fool there but would give a piece of silver. There
would this monster make a man;[7] any strange beast there
30   makes a man. When they will not give a doit° to relieve a   *small coin*
lame beggar, they will lay out ten to see a dead Indian.[8] Legged
like a man, and his fins like arms. Warm, o'my troth! I do now
let loose my opinion, hold it no longer: this is no fish, but an
islander that hath lately suffered by a thunderbolt. [*Thun-*
35   *der.*] Alas, the storm is come again. My best way is to creep
under his gaberdine; there is no other shelter hereabout.
Misery acquaints a man with strange bedfellows. I will here
shroud° till the dregs[9] of the storm be past.   *take cover*

---

9. Ariel's following lines are spoken as the other characters depart; he probably exits in another direction.
2.2
1. Caliban takes this as a response to his curse; in F,
the direction comes before Caliban speaks.
2. With the sight of hedgehoglike spirits.
3. Trinculo is probably dressed in traditional fool's
motley (many-colored garment).
4. Large leather drinking vessel; stone-throwing

military engine.
5. Dried hake, a poor person's staple.
6. On a sign to attract spectators.
7. Make a fortune for a man; become a man.
8. An allusion to exhibitions of American Indians in
London.
9. Last drinks, as from the bottom of a "bombard" of
wine.

[*He crawls under Caliban's cloak.*]
Enter STEFANO *singing.*

STEFANO   I shall no more to sea, to sea,
40   Here shall I die ashore.
This is a very scurvy tune to sing at a man's funeral. Well,
here's my comfort.

[*He*] *drinks* [*and*] *sings.*

        The master, the swabber, the boatswain and I,
        The gunner and his mate,
45   Loved Moll, Meg, and Marian, and Margery,
        But none of us cared for Kate.
        For she had a tongue with a tang,°   *sting*
        Would cry to a sailor, "Go hang!"
        She loved not the savor of tar nor of pitch,
50   Yet a tailor might scratch her where'er she did itch.[1]
        Then to sea, boys, and let her go hang!
This is a scurvy tune, too; but here's my comfort.

[*He*] *drinks.*

CALIBAN   Do not torment me! Oh!
STEFANO   What's the matter?° Have we devils here? Do you   *What's going on?*
55 put tricks upon 's with savages and men of Ind?° Ha? I have   *India*
    not scaped drowning to be afeared now of your four legs; for
    it hath been said, "As proper a man as ever went on four
    legs[2] cannot make him give ground"; and it shall be said so   *at the*
    again, while Stefano breathes at'° nostrils.
60 CALIBAN   The spirit torments me! Oh!
STEFANO   This is some monster of the isle with four legs who
    hath got, as I take it, an ague.° Where the devil should he   *a fit of fever*
    learn our language? I will give him some relief if it be but for
    that. If I can recover° him and keep him tame and get to   *cure*
65 Naples with him, he's a present for any emperor that ever
    trod on neat's leather.°   *cowhide; shoes*
CALIBAN   Do not torment me, prithee! I'll bring my wood
    home faster.
STEFANO   He's in his fit now, and does not talk after° the wis-   *in the manner of*
70 est. He shall taste of my bottle. If he have never drunk wine
    afore, it will go near to° remove his fit. If I can recover him   *almost*
    and keep him tame, I will not take too much for him.[3] He
    shall pay for him that hath° him, and that soundly.   *gets*
CALIBAN   Thou dost me yet but little hurt; thou wilt anon, I
75 know it by thy trembling. Now Prosper works upon thee.
STEFANO   Come on your ways.° Open your mouth: here is that   *Come on*
    which will give language to you, cat.[4] Open your mouth: this
    will shake° your shaking, I can tell you, and that soundly.   *dislodge*
    [CALIBAN *drinks.*] You cannot tell who's your friend. Open
80 your chaps again.
TRINCULO   I should know that voice. It should be—but he is
    drowned, and these are devils. Oh, defend me!
STEFANO   Four legs and two voices: a most delicate° monster!   *exquisitely made*
    His forward voice now is to speak well of his friend; his
85 backward voice is to utter foul speeches and to detract. If all

---

1. Implying sexual desire and gratification. Tailors were often mocked for supposed lack of virility.
2. Comically varying "on two legs" (upright); also suggesting "on crutches."
3. No sum can be too high for him.
4. "Ale will make a cat speak" was proverbial.

the wine in my bottle will recover him,[5] I will help his ague. Come. [CALIBAN *drinks*.] Amen.° I will pour some in thy other mouth.

TRINCULO   Stefano!

90   STEFANO   Doth thy other mouth call me? Mercy, mercy! This is a devil and no monster. I will leave him; I have no long spoon.[6]

TRINCULO   Stefano? If thou beest Stefano, touch me and speak to me, for I am Trinculo—be not afeard—thy good friend
95   Trinculo.

STEFANO   If thou beest Trinculo, come forth: I'll pull thee by the lesser legs. If any be Trinculo's legs, these are they. [*He pulls him out.*] Thou art very° Trinculo indeed! How cam'st thou to be the siege° of this mooncalf?[7] Can he vent° Trinculos?

100 TRINCULO   I took him to be killed with a thunderstroke. But art thou not drowned, Stefano? I hope now thou art not drowned. Is the storm overblown? I hid me under the dead mooncalf's gaberdine, for fear of the storm. And art thou living, Stefano? O Stefano, two Neapolitans scaped!

105 STEFANO   Prithee, do not turn me about, my stomach is not constant.

CALIBAN [*aside*]   These be fine things, an if° they be not sprites. That's a brave° god, and bears celestial liquor. I will kneel to him.

110 STEFANO   How didst thou scape? How cam'st thou hither? Swear by this bottle how thou cam'st hither. I escaped upon a butt of sack[8] which the sailors heaved o'erboard, by this bottle, which I made of the bark of a tree, with mine own hands, since I was cast ashore.

115 CALIBAN   I'll swear upon that bottle to be thy true subject, for the liquor is not earthly.

STEFANO   Here. Swear then how thou escaped'st.

TRINCULO   Swum ashore, man, like a duck. I can swim like a duck, I'll be sworn.

120 STEFANO [*giving TRINCULO the bottle*]   Here, kiss the Book.[9] Though thou canst swim like a duck, thou art made like a goose.[1]

TRINCULO   O Stefano, hast any more of this?

STEFANO   The whole butt, man. My cellar is in a rock by the
125 seaside, where my wine is hid. [*to CALIBAN*] How now, mooncalf, how does thine ague?

CALIBAN   Hast thou not dropped from heaven?

STEFANO   Out o'th' moon I do assure thee. I was the man i'th' moon, when time was.°

130 CALIBAN   I have seen thee in her, and I do adore thee. My mistress° showed me thee, and thy dog, and thy bush.[2]

STEFANO [*giving the bottle to CALIBAN*]   Come, swear to that: kiss the Book. I will furnish it anon with new contents. Swear.

Enough

actual excrement / defecate

an if =if an excellent; a fine

once upon a time

(Miranda)

---

5. If it takes all the wine in my bottle to cure him.
6. From the proverbial "He should have a long spoon that sups with the devil."
7. Deformed creature; miscarriage, owing to the supposed detrimental influence of the moon.
8. Cask of Spanish or Canary wine.
9. Confirming an oath by kissing the Bible; or the

proverbial "Kiss the cup" ("Drink").
1. Probably alluding to Trinculo's outstretched neck with the bottle as a beak; also, a byword for giddiness and unsteadiness on the feet.
2. A dog and a thornbush were traditional attributes of the man in the moon; cf. *A Midsummer Night's Dream* 5.1.247–49.

135 TRINCULO   By this good light,° this is a very shallow monster.   *sun*
I afeared of him? A very weak monster. The man i'th' moon?
A most poor credulous monster. Well drawn,° monster, in   *drunk*
good sooth.

CALIBAN   I'll show thee every fertile inch o'th' island, and I
140 will kiss thy foot. I prithee, be my god.

TRINCULO   By this light, a most perfidious and drunken monster! When 's god's asleep he'll rob his bottle.

CALIBAN   I'll kiss thy foot. I'll swear myself thy subject.

STEFANO   Come on, then: down and swear.

145 TRINCULO   I shall laugh myself to death at this puppy-headed
monster. A most scurvy monster. I could find in my heart to
beat him—

STEFANO [*to* CALIBAN]   Come, kiss.

TRINCULO   —but that the poor monster's in drink.° An abomi-   *drunk*
150 nable monster.

CALIBAN   I'll show thee the best springs; I'll pluck thee berries;
I'll fish for thee, and get thee wood enough.
A plague upon the tyrant that I serve!
I'll bear him no more sticks but follow thee,
155 Thou wondrous man.

TRINCULO   A most ridiculous monster, to make a wonder of a
poor drunkard.

CALIBAN   I prithee, let me bring thee where crabs° grow;   *crab apples*
And I with my long nails will dig thee pig-nuts,°   *edible tubers*
160 Show thee a jay's nest, and instruct thee how
To snare the nimble marmoset. I'll bring thee
To clust'ring filberts, and sometimes I'll get thee
Young scamels³ from the rock. Wilt thou go with me?

STEFANO   I prithee now lead the way without any more talking.
165 Trinculo, the King and all our company else being drowned,
we will inherit here. [*to* CALIBAN] Here, bear my bottle.
—Fellow Trinculo, we'll fill him° by and by again.   *it*

CALIBAN (*sings drunkenly*)⁴   Farewell, master; farewell, farewell.

TRINCULO   A howling monster, a drunken monster.

170 CALIBAN [*continuing to sing*]   No more dams I'll make for° fish,   *to trap*
                  Nor fetch in firing°   *firewood*
                  At requiring,
                  Nor scrape trencher, nor wash dish,
                  'Ban, 'Ban, Ca-Caliban
175   Has a new master: get a new man.⁵
Freedom, high-day;° high-day, freedom; freedom, high-day,   *holiday*
freedom!

STEFANO   O brave° monster, lead the way!   *Exeunt.*   *excellent; fine*

---

3. TEXTUAL COMMENT Shakespeare may have invented
this exotic word, which appears nowhere else in the
English language, but it seems more likely that "scamel"
was the result of an error in transmission. For a survey
of the many emendations editors have proposed, see

Digital Edition TC 6.
4. This stage direction may be misplaced and may
actually refer to the following song, "No more dams."
5. Addressed to the old master, Prospero.

3.1

Enter FERDINAND, *bearing a log.*

FERDINAND There be some sports are painful, and their labor
Delight in them sets off.[1] Some kinds of baseness
Are nobly undergone, and most poor matters
Point to rich ends. This my mean° task   *lowly*
5 Would be as heavy to me as odious, but°   *except that*
The mistress which I serve quickens° what's dead   *enlivens*
And makes my labors pleasures. Oh, she is
Ten times more gentle than her father's crabbed,
And he's composed of harshness. I must remove
10 Some thousands of these logs and pile them up,
Upon a sore° injunction. My sweet mistress   *harsh*
Weeps when she sees me work and says such baseness
Had never like executor. I forget;
But these sweet thoughts do even refresh my labors,
Most busil'est,[2] when I do it.°   *(labor)*

Enter MIRANDA, *and* PROSPERO [*unseen*].

15 MIRANDA   Alas now, pray you,
Work not so hard. I would the lightning had
Burnt up those logs that you are enjoined to pile.
Pray set it down and rest you. When this burns
'Twill weep[3] for having wearied you. My father
20 Is hard at study. Pray now, rest yourself.
He's safe° for these three hours.   *We are safe from him*
FERDINAND   O most dear mistress,
The sun will set before I shall discharge
What I must strive to do.
MIRANDA   If you'll sit down
I'll bear your logs the while. Pray give me that:
I'll carry it to the pile.
25 FERDINAND   No, precious creature,
I had rather crack my sinews, break my back,
Than you should such dishonor undergo
While I sit lazy by.
MIRANDA   It would become me
As well as it does you; and I should do it
30 With much more ease, for my goodwill is to it,
And yours it is against.
PROSPERO [*aside*]   Poor worm, thou art infected:[4]
This visitation[5] shows it.
MIRANDA   You look wearily.
FERDINAND No, noble mistress, 'tis fresh morning with me
When you are by at night. I do beseech you,
35 Chiefly that I may set it in my prayers,
What is your name?
MIRANDA   Miranda. —O my father,
I have broke your hest° to say so!   *disobeyed your command*

3.1
1. *their . . . off:* the greater effort invested amounts to
more pleasure; the labor of painful activities ("sports")
is offset by whatever delight we take in them.
2. Most busily (giving a double superlative).
3. By exuding drops of resin.

4. Afflicted with lovesickness. *worm:* an expression
of tenderness; but a worm was often thought to carry
disease.
5. Suggesting a pastoral or charitable visit to the
sick; or may indicate a visit by the plague—here,
lovesickness.

FERDINAND   Admired[6] Miranda!
  Indeed the top of admiration, worth
  What's dearest to the world. Full many a lady

40   I have eyed with best regard, and many a time
  Th' harmony of their tongues hath into bondage
  Brought my too diligent° ear. For several virtues   *attentive*
  Have I liked several° women; never any   *various*
  With so full soul but some defect in her

45   Did quarrel with the noblest grace she owed°   *owned*
  And put it to the foil.[7] But you, O you,
  So perfect and so peerless, are created
  Of every creature's best.

MIRANDA   I do not know
  One of my sex; no woman's face remember

50   Save, from my glass,° mine own. Nor have I seen   *mirror*
  More that I may call men than you, good friend,
  And my dear father. How features are abroad[8]
  I am skilless° of; but by my modesty,°   *ignorant / virginity*
  The jewel in my dower,° I would not wish   *dowry*

55   Any companion in the world but you,
  Nor can imagination form a shape
  Besides° yourself to like of. But I prattle   *Other than*
  Something° too wildly, and my father's precepts   *Somewhat*
  I therein do forget.

FERDINAND   I am in my condition°   *rank*

60   A prince, Miranda; I do think a king—
  I would° not so!—and would no more endure   *wish it were*
  This wooden slavery[9] than to suffer
  The flesh fly[1] blow my mouth. Hear my soul speak:
  The very instant that I saw you did

65   My heart fly to your service, there resides
  To make me slave to it, and for your sake
  Am I this patient log-man.

MIRANDA   Do you love me?

FERDINAND   O heaven, O earth, bear witness to this sound,
  And crown what I profess with kind event°   *favorable outcome*

70   If I speak true! If hollowly,° invert   *falsely*
  What best is boded° me to mischief!° I,   *foretold to / misfortune*
  Beyond all limit of what° else i'th' world,   *whatsoever*
  Do love, prize, honor you.

MIRANDA   I am a fool
  To weep at what I am glad of.

PROSPERO [*aside*]   Fair encounter

75   Of two most rare affections. Heavens rain grace
  On that which breeds between 'em.

FERDINAND   Wherefore weep you?

MIRANDA   At mine unworthiness, that dare not offer
  What I desire to give, and much less take
  What I shall die to want.[2] But this is trifling,

6. Playing on the meaning of Miranda's name.
7. Foiled it, or made it ineffectual; challenged it, as in a fencing match (compare "quarrel" in line 45).
8. What people look like elsewhere.
9. The log as a symbol of Prospero's oppression.

1. Species of fly that deposits its eggs ("blows") in dead flesh.
2. At . . . *want*: Miranda is not at liberty to bestow her virginity or to obtain the consummation that she desires and lacks.

80 And all the more it seeks to hide itself
The bigger bulk it shows.³ Hence, bashful cunning,°   *artful shyness*
And prompt me, plain and holy innocence!
I am your wife if you'll marry me;
If not, I'll die your maid.° To be your fellow°   *virgin; servant / equal*
85 You may deny me, but I'll be your servant
Whether you will or no.

FERDINAND   My mistress,° dearest,   *sweetheart*
And I thus humble ever.

MIRANDA   My husband, then?

FERDINAND   Ay, with a heart as willing°   *desirous*
As bondage e'er of freedom. Here's my hand.⁴

90 MIRANDA   And mine, with my heart in't. And now farewell
Till half an hour hence.

FERDINAND   A thousand thousand!°   *(farewells)*

Exeunt [FERDINAND *and* MIRANDA, *separately*].

PROSPERO   So glad of this as they I cannot be,
Who are surprised withal;° but my rejoicing   *overwhelmed by all*
At nothing can be more. I'll to my book,°   *book of magic*
95 For yet ere suppertime must I perform
Much business appertaining.   *Exit.*

3.2

Enter CALIBAN, STEFANO, *and* TRINCULO.

STEFANO   Tell not me. When the butt is out we will drink water,
not a drop before. Therefore bear up and board 'em.¹ —Servant
monster, drink to me!

TRINCULO   "Servant monster"? The folly° of this island! They   *absurdity*
5 say there's but five upon this isle. We are three of them; if
th'other two be brained° like us, the state totters.   *have brains*

STEFANO   Drink, servant monster, when I bid thee. Thy eyes
are almost set° in thy head.   *fixed by drunkenness*

TRINCULO   Where should they be set° else? He were a brave   *placed*
10 monster indeed if they were set in his tail.

STEFANO   My man-monster hath drowned his tongue in sack.
For my part, the sea cannot drown me. I swam, ere I could
recover the shore, five and thirty leagues,° off and on.² By this   *about 100 miles*
light, thou shalt be my lieutenant, monster, or my standard.³

15 TRINCULO   Your lieutenant, if you list;° he's no standard.   *wish*

STEFANO   We'll not run, Monsieur Monster.

TRINCULO   Nor go° neither, but you'll lie⁴ like dogs and yet say   *walk*
nothing neither.

STEFANO   Mooncalf, speak once in thy life, if thou beest a good
20 mooncalf.

CALIBAN   How does thy honor? Let me lick thy shoe.
I'll not serve him; he is not valiant.

---

3. *all . . . shows:* an image of secret pregnancy.
4. *I am your wife* (line 83) . . . *hand:* Such an exchange
could actually have constituted a marriage ceremony.
In Shakespeare's time, weddings did not need to be
witnessed and performed in a church to be valid
(compare 4.1.14–19).
3.2

1. Force a way aboard, continuing the terminology of
naval warfare; take onboard (drink). *bear up:* sail to
the attack.
2. Tacking away from and toward the shore.
3. Standard-bearer; but in Trinculo's reply, "one who
can stand up."
4. Lie (down); tell lies; excrete.

TRINCULO Thou liest, most ignorant monster; I am in case°   *prepared*
to jostle a constable. Why, thou debauched fish thou, was
25 there ever man a coward that hath drunk so much sack as I
do today? Wilt thou tell a monstrous lie, being but half a fish
and half a monster?

CALIBAN Lo, how he mocks me. Wilt thou let him, my lord?

TRINCULO "Lord," quoth he? That a monster should be such a
30 natural!⁵

CALIBAN Lo, lo again! Bite him to death, I prithee.

STEFANO Trinculo, keep a good tongue in your head. If you
prove a mutineer, the next tree!° The poor monster's my sub-   *(for a gallows)*
ject, and he shall not suffer indignity.

35 CALIBAN I thank my noble lord. Wilt thou be pleased
To hearken once again to the suit I made to thee?

STEFANO Marry, will I. Kneel and repeat it. I will stand, and
so shall Trinculo.

       Enter ARIEL *invisible.*

CALIBAN As I told thee before, I am subject to a tyrant,
40 A sorcerer, that by his cunning hath
Cheated me of the island.

ARIEL   Thou liest.

CALIBAN [*to* TRINCULO] Thou liest, thou jesting monkey, thou!
I would my valiant master would destroy thee.
I do not lie.

45 STEFANO Trinculo, if you trouble him any more in 's tale, by
this hand, I will supplant° some of your teeth.   *uproot*

TRINCULO Why, I said nothing.

STEFANO Mum, then, and no more. —Proceed.

CALIBAN I say by sorcery he got this isle;
50 From me he got it. If thy greatness will
Revenge it on him—for I know thou dar'st,
But this thing⁶ dare not—

STEFANO That's most certain.

CALIBAN Thou shalt be lord of it, and I'll serve thee.

55 STEFANO How now shall this be compassed?° Canst thou bring   *accomplished*
me to the party?°   *person concerned*

CALIBAN Yea, yea, my lord. I'll yield him thee asleep,
Where thou mayst knock a nail into his head.⁷

ARIEL Thou liest; thou canst not.

60 CALIBAN What a pied ninny's° this! Thou scurvy patch!°   *fool in motley / jester; idiot*
I do beseech thy greatness give him blows
And take his bottle from him. When that's gone,
He shall drink naught but brine, for I'll not show him
Where the quick freshes° are.   *fast-flowing springs*

65 STEFANO Trinculo, run into no further danger. Interrupt the
monster one word further and, by this hand, I'll turn my
mercy out o'doors and make a stockfish of thee.⁸

TRINCULO Why, what did I? I did nothing. I'll go farther off.

STEFANO Didst thou not say he lied?

70 ARIEL Thou liest.

---

5. An idiot, punning on the idea that monsters were
unnatural.
6. Trinculo; or perhaps Caliban himself.
7. As Jael murdered sleeping Sisera in Judges 4:21

and 5:26.
8. Proverbial allusion to the beating of dried fish
before cooking it.

STEFANO Do I so?

    [*He beats* TRINCULO.]

Take thou that! As you like this, give me the lie° another time.   *call me a liar*

TRINCULO I did not give the lie! Out o'your wits, and hearing

    too? A pox o'your bottle. This can sack and drinking do. A

75   murrain° on your monster, and the devil take your fingers!   *plague*

CALIBAN Ha, ha, ha!

STEFANO Now forward with your tale. —Prithee stand fur-

    ther off.

CALIBAN Beat him enough. After a little time I'll beat him too.

80 STEFANO Stand farther. —Come, proceed.

CALIBAN Why, as I told thee, 'tis a custom with him

    I'th' afternoon to sleep. There° thou mayst brain him,   *Then*

    Having first seized his books; or with a log

    Batter his skull, or paunch° him with a stake,   *disembowel*

85   Or cut his weasand° with thy knife. Remember   *windpipe*

    First to possess his books, for without them

    He's but a sot° as I am, nor hath not   *stupid fool*

    One spirit to command—they all do hate him

    As rootedly as I. Burn but his books.

90   He has brave utensils,[9] for so he calls them,

    Which, when he has a house, he'll deck withal.

    And that most deeply to consider is

    The beauty of his daughter. He himself

    Calls her a nonpareil.° I never saw a woman   *one without equal*

95   But only Sycorax my dam and she;

    But she as far surpasseth Sycorax

    As great'st does least.

STEFANO   Is it so brave° a lass?   *excellent; fine*

CALIBAN Ay, lord. She will become thy bed, I warrant,

    And bring thee forth brave brood.

100 STEFANO Monster, I will kill this man. His daughter and I will

    be king and queen—save° our graces—and Trinculo and thy-   *God save*

    self shall be viceroys. Dost thou like the plot, Trinculo?

TRINCULO Excellent.

STEFANO Give me thy hand. I am sorry I beat thee. But while

105   thou liv'st, keep a good tongue in thy head.

CALIBAN Within this half hour will he be asleep.

    Wilt thou destroy him then?

STEFANO   Ay, on mine honor.

ARIEL [*aside*] This will I tell my master.

CALIBAN Thou mak'st me merry. I am full of pleasure;

110   Let us be jocund. Will you troll° the catch°   *sing / round; song*

    You taught me but whilere?°   *a short time ago*

STEFANO At thy request, monster, I will do reason, any reason.°   *anything reasonable*

    Come on, Trinculo, let us sing.

    (*Sings.*)[1]   Flout 'em, and scout 'em

115   And scout° 'em, and flout 'em.   *mock*

                Thought is free.

CALIBAN That's not the tune.

---

9. Perhaps confusing implements for magic and household goods.
1. The stage direction suggests that the others cannot
manage the catch and remain in bewildered silence.
But Trinculo, and perhaps Caliban, may attempt to
join in.

ARIEL *plays the tune on a tabor and pipe.*[2]

STEFANO What is this same?

TRINCULO This is the tune of our catch, played by the picture
120 of Nobody.[3]

STEFANO If thou beest a man, show thyself in thy likeness. If
thou beest a devil, take't as thou list.°   wish

TRINCULO Oh, forgive me my sins!

STEFANO He that dies pays all debts.[4] I defy thee! Mercy
125 upon us![5]

CALIBAN Art thou afeard?

STEFANO No, monster, not I.

CALIBAN Be not afeard: the isle is full of noises,
Sounds and sweet airs° that give delight and hurt not.   tunes
130 Sometimes a thousand twangling instruments
Will hum about mine ears; and sometimes voices,
That, if I then had waked after long sleep,
Will make me sleep again; and then, in dreaming,
The clouds methought would open and show riches
135 Ready to drop upon me, that when I waked
I cried to dream again.

STEFANO This will prove a brave kingdom to me, where I shall
have my music for nothing.[6]

CALIBAN When Prospero is destroyed.

140 STEFANO That shall be by and by:° I remember the story.   very soon

[*Exit* ARIEL *playing music.*]

TRINCULO The sound is going away; let's follow it, and after do
our work.

STEFANO Lead, monster, we'll follow. I would I could see this
taborer: he lays it on.[7]

145 TRINCULO [*to* CALIBAN] Wilt come? I'll follow Stefano.

Exeunt.

3.3

Enter ALONSO, SEBASTIAN, ANTONIO, GONZALO,
ADRIAN, *and* FRANCISCO.

GONZALO By'r lakin,[1] I can go no further, sir.
My old bones aches. Here's a maze trod indeed
Through forthrights and meanders.° By your patience,   direct and winding paths
I needs must rest me.

ALONSO   Old lord, I cannot blame thee,
5 Who am myself attached° with weariness   seized
To th' dulling of my spirits. Sit down and rest.
Even° here I will put off my hope, and keep it   Exactly
No longer for° my flatterer: he is drowned   as
Whom thus we stray to find, and the sea mocks
10 Our frustrate° search on land. Well, let him go.   vain

---

2. The tabor was a small drum slung on the left-hand
side of the body; the tabor pipe was a long narrow
pipe played with the left hand. The combination was
associated with rustic dances and merrymaking.
3. "Nobody" was a character in a comedy who was
depicted on the title page of the printed text. Large
breeches up to his neck made him appear to have no
trunk.
4. Varying the proverbial "Death pays all debts."

5. Stefano's defiance comically collapses.
6. James I spent large sums on court music, but not
typically of the popular kind Ariel now plays.
7. He sets himself to his music vigorously. Stefano
deserts Caliban in order to follow the music. Trinculo and Caliban in turn follow Stefano (line 145).
3.3
1. Ladykin: a colloquial form of reference to the Virgin Mary.

ANTONIO [*aside to* SEBASTIAN]   I am right glad that he's so out
    of hope.
  Do not, for° one repulse, forgo the purpose   *on account of*
  That you resolved t'effect.
SEBASTIAN [*aside to* ANTONIO]   The next advantage
  Will we take throughly.°   *thoroughly*
ANTONIO [*aside to* SEBASTIAN]   Let it be tonight;
15 For now they are oppressed with travail,° they   *journey; effort*
  Will not nor cannot use such vigilance
  As when they are fresh.
SEBASTIAN [*aside to* ANTONIO]   I say tonight: no more.
      Solemn and strange music. [*Enter*] PROSPERO *on the*
      top,[2] *invisible.*
ALONSO   What harmony is this? My good friends, hark!
20 GONZALO   Marvelous sweet music.
      Enter several strange shapes, bringing a banquet; and
      dance about it with gentle actions of salutations, and
      inviting the King etc. to eat, they depart.
ALONSO   Give us kind keepers,° heavens! What were these?   *guardian angels*
SEBASTIAN   A living drollery.[3] Now I will believe
  That there are unicorns; that in Arabia
  There is one tree, the phoenix' throne, one phoenix[4]
  At this hour reigning there.
25 ANTONIO   I'll believe both;
  And what does else want credit,° come to me,   *lack belief*
  And I'll be sworn 'tis true. Travelers ne'er did lie,[5]
  Though fools at home condemn 'em.
GONZALO   If in Naples
  I should report this now, would they believe me?
30 If I should say I saw such islanders—
  For certes° these are people of the island—   *certainly*
  Who, though they are of monstrous shape, yet note
  Their manners are more gentle, kind, than of
  Our human generation you shall find
  Many, nay, almost any.
35 PROSPERO [*aside*]   Honest lord,
  Thou hast said well; for some of you there present
  Are worse than devils.
ALONSO   I cannot too much muse°   *marvel at*
  Such shapes, such gesture, and such sound, expressing—
  Although they want the use of tongue°—a kind   *language*
  Of excellent dumb discourse.
40 PROSPERO [*aside*]   Praise in departing.[6]
FRANCISCO   They vanished strangely.
SEBASTIAN   No matter, since
  They have left their viands° behind; for we have stomachs.°   *food / good appetites*
  Wilt please you taste of what is here?
ALONSO   Not I.
GONZALO   Faith, sir, you need not fear. When we were boys,

---

2. A small acting area above the upper stage.
3. A puppet show with live actors.
4. The unicorn and phoenix, a bird, were two mythological creatures that sometimes figured in travelers'

tales. Only one phoenix was said to exist in the world
at any one time.
5. Proverbially, "A traveler may lie with authority."
6. Reserve your praise until the end of the event.

45	Who would believe that there were mountaineers,°	mountain dwellers
	Dewlapped like bulls, whose throats had hanging at 'em	
	Wallets° of flesh? Or that there were such men	Pouches
	Whose heads stood in their breasts? Which now we find	
	Each putter-out of five for one[7] will bring us	
	Good warrant of.	
50	ALONSO I will stand to and feed;°	begin eating
	Although my last, no matter, since I feel	
	The best is past. Brother, my lord the duke,	
	Stand to and do as we.	

> [ALONSO, SEBASTIAN, *and* ANTONIO *approach the
> table.*] *Thunder and lightning.*
> *Enter* ARIEL, *like a harpy;*[8] *claps his wings upon
> the table, and with a quaint device*° *the banquet
> vanishes.*[9]   an ingenious mechanism

	ARIEL You are three men of sin, whom destiny—	
55	That hath to° instrument this lower world	as its
	And what is in't—the never-surfeited sea	
	Hath caused to belch up you, and on this island,	
	Where man doth not inhabit—you 'mongst men	
	Being most unfit to live. I have made you mad;	
60	And even with suchlike valor[1] men hang and drown	
	Their proper selves.°	Themselves

> [ALONSO, SEBASTIAN, *and* ANTONIO *draw their
> swords.*][2]
>   You fools, I and my fellows

	Are ministers of fate. The elements	
	Of whom your swords are tempered[3] may as well	
	Wound the loud winds, or with bemocked-at stabs	
65	Kill the still-closing[4] waters, as diminish	
	One dowl° that's in my plume.° My fellow ministers	featherlet / plumage
	Are like° invulnerable. If you could hurt,	similarly
	Your swords are now too massy° for your strengths	heavy
	And will not be uplifted. But remember—	
70	For that's my business to you—that you three	
	From Milan did supplant good Prospero;	
	Exposed unto the sea, which hath requit it,	
	Him and his innocent child; for which foul deed	
	The powers, delaying not forgetting,[5] have	
75	Incensed the seas and shores—yea, all the creatures[6]—	
	Against your peace. Thee of thy son, Alonso,	
	They have bereft; and do pronounce by me	

7. A traveler could profit from a voyage by laying down a sum with a broker before departing and undertaking to bring back evidence of having reached his destination; if successful, he was repaid fivefold.
8. A mythological monster with a vulture's wings and claws and a woman's face. Aeneas and his companions encountered these harpies, who stole their meals and threatened to punish them with slow starvation. *Thunder and lightning:* both spectacular and functional for disguising the mechanics of the "quaint device."
9. The simplest effective staging is by means of a rotating tabletop with the vessels of the banquet fixed to its surface. Leg-to-leg planks supporting the tabletop or a hanging cloth would conceal the vanished banquet. The harpy's wings would hide the mechanics from the audience, and clapping them would provide a visual distraction.

1. *suchlike valor:* fearlessness that comes from madness.
2. Ariel perhaps ascends beyond their reach here. Aeneas's companions, like Alonso here, similarly attempted to kill the harpies with swords.
3. Compounded and hardened. Metal was sometimes thought of as being compounded of earth and fire, here contrasted with winds and waters.
4. Self-healing, since they close immediately once parted.
5. Related to the proverb "God stays long but strikes at last."
6. Compare Genesis 1:21: "Then God created . . . everything living and moving."

Ling'ring perdition[7]—worse than any death
Can be at once—shall step by step attend
80 You and your ways; whose[8] wraths to guard you from,
Which here in this most desolate[9] isle else falls
Upon your heads, is nothing° but heart's sorrow   *there is no alternative*
And a clear life° ensuing.   *a life innocent of sin*

He vanishes[1] in thunder; then, to soft music, enter
the shapes again, and dance with mocks and mows,°   *grimaces*
and [then exeunt], carrying out the table.

PROSPERO [*aside*]   Bravely the figure of this harpy hast thou
85 Performed, my Ariel; a grace it had, devouring.[2]
Of my instruction hast thou nothing bated°   *omitted*
In what thou hadst to say. So with good life[3]
And observation strange[4] my meaner ministers°   *lesser spirits*
Their several kinds° have done.° My high charms work,   *various roles / performed*
90 And these mine enemies are all knit up
In their distractions. They now are in my power;
And in these fits I leave them, while I visit
Young Ferdinand, whom they suppose is drowned,
And his and mine loved darling.   [*Exit.*]
95 GONZALO   I'th' name of something holy, sir, why stand you
In this strange stare?
ALONSO   Oh, it is monstrous, monstrous!
Methought the billows spoke and told me of it,
The winds did sing it to me, and the thunder,
That deep and dreadful organ pipe, pronounced
100 The name of Prosper. It did bass my trespass.[5]
Therefore° my son i'th' ooze is bedded, and   *For that*
I'll seek him deeper than e'er plummet sounded,
And with him there lie mudded.   [*Exit.*]
SEBASTIAN   But one fiend at a time,
I'll fight their legions o'er!°   *from beginning to end*
ANTONIO   I'll be thy second.
                    Exeunt [SEBASTIAN *and* ANTONIO].
105 GONZALO   All three of them are desperate:° their great guilt,   *in despair; reckless*
Like poison given to work° a great time after,   *take effect*
Now gins to bite the spirits. I do beseech you
That are of suppler joints, follow them swiftly,
And hinder them from what this ecstasy°   *madness*
May now provoke them to.
110 ADRIAN   Follow, I pray you.   *Exeunt.*

4.1

Enter PROSPERO, FERDINAND, *and* MIRANDA.
PROSPERO [*to* FERDINAND]   If I have too austerely punished you,
Your compensation makes amends, for I

---

7. Slow starvation; hell on earth of spiritual suffering. The phrase is first the object of "pronounce" and
then the subject of "shall . . . attend."
8. Refers to "the powers" in line 74.
9. Joyless, wretched; barren, deserted.
1. Ariel is raised out of sight into the canopy.
2. In clapping his wings, Ariel has created the illu-

sion of having devoured the banquet.
3. Convincingly; with vitality. *So:* In the same way.
4. Remarkable attention to the requirements of their
parts, or instructions.
5. The thunder proclaimed my sin ("trespass") in a
bass voice, or with a bass background; perhaps, wordplay on the "utter baseness" of trespass.

Have given you here a third[1] of mine own life—
Or that for which I live—who° once again   *whom*
5   I tender° to thy hand. All thy vexations   *offer*
Were but my trials of thy love, and thou
Hast strangely° stood the test. Here, afore heaven,   *wonderfully*
I ratify this my rich gift. O Ferdinand,
Do not smile at me that I boast her off,°   *sing her praises*
10   For thou shalt find she will outstrip all praise
And make it halt° behind her.   *limp*
FERDINAND   I do believe it against an oracle.[2]
PROSPERO   Then, as my guest, and thine own acquisition
Worthily purchased,° take my daughter. But   *Gained by effort*
15   If thou dost break her virgin-knot° before   *hymen*
All sanctimonious° ceremonies may   *holy*
With full and holy rite be ministered,
No sweet aspersion° shall the heavens let fall   *shower of grace*
To make this contract grow; but barren hate,
20   Sour-eyed disdain, and discord shall bestrew
The union of your bed with weeds[3] so loathly
That you shall hate it both. Therefore take heed,
As Hymen's[4] lamps shall light you.
FERDINAND   As I hope
For quiet days, fair issue,° and long life,   *children*
25   With such love as 'tis now, the murkiest den,°   *cave*
The most opportune place, the strong'st suggestion°   *temptation*
Our worser genius can,[5] shall never melt
Mine honor into lust, to take away
The edge° of that day's celebration   *unblunted desire*
30   When I shall think or° Phoebus' steeds are foundered,[6]   *either*
Or night kept chained below.
PROSPERO   Fairly spoke.
Sit then and talk with her: she is thine own.
—What,° Ariel! My industrious servant, Ariel!   *Now then*
          Enter ARIEL.
ARIEL   What would my potent master? Here I am.
35   PROSPERO   Thou and thy meaner° fellows your last service   *lesser*
Did worthily perform, and I must use you
In such another trick. Go bring the rabble[7]
O'er whom I give thee pow'r here to this place.
Incite them to quick motion, for I must
40   Bestow upon the eyes of this young couple
Some vanity[8] of mine art. It is my promise,
And they expect it from me.
ARIEL   Presently?°   *At once*
PROSPERO   Ay, with a twink.[9]

4.1
1. Miranda. The usual poetic conceit was a half; commentators variously conjecture the other third to be his dukedom, his books, or his late wife.
2. *I . . . oracle:* I would believe it even if an oracle said otherwise.
3. Weeds in place of the flowers traditionally strewn on the marriage bed; wordplay on both "marriage bed" and "seed-bed."
4. Classical god of marriage.

5. Is capable of. *worser genius:* evil spirit corresponding to a guardian angel.
6. Collapsed and made lame. *Phoebus' steeds:* the mythological horses that drew the chariot of the sun. Ferdinand anticipates that on his wedding day he will, in his impatience, think that the night will never come.
7. Troupe of lesser spirits. *trick:* theatrical device, or clever artifice.
8. Trifle; conceit; illusion; display.
9. In the twinkling of an eye.

ARIEL   Before you can say "come" and "go,"
45   And breathe twice and cry "so, so,"
Each one tripping on his toe,
Will be here with mop and mow.[1]
Do you love me, master? No?
PROSPERO   Dearly, my delicate Ariel. Do not approach
Till thou dost hear me call.
50 ARIEL   Well; I conceive.°   *Exit.*   understand
PROSPERO [*to* FERDINAND]   Look thou be true;[2] do not give
dalliance
Too much the rein.[3] The strongest oaths are straw
To th' fire i'th' blood. Be more abstemious,
Or else good night your vow.
FERDINAND   I warrant you, sir,
55   The white cold virgin snow upon my heart
Abates the ardor of my liver.[4]
PROSPERO   Well.
—Now come, my Ariel: bring a corollary°   surplus
Rather than want° a spirit. Appear, and pertly.°   lack / briskly
          Soft music.
No tongue, all eyes! Be silent!
          Enter IRIS.[5]
60 IRIS   Ceres, most bounteous lady, thy rich leas[6]
Of wheat, rye, barley, vetches,[7] oats, and peas;
Thy turfy mountains where live nibbling sheep,
And flat meads° thatched with stover,[8] them to keep;   meadows
Thy banks with pionèd and twillèd[9] brims,
65   Which spongy° April at thy hest betrims[1]   wet
To make cold nymphs chaste crowns; and thy broom-groves,[2]
Whose shadow the dismissèd bachelor° loves,   rejected suitor
Being lass-lorn; thy poll-clipped vineyard,[3]
And thy sea-marge,° sterile and rocky-hard,   seashore
70   Where thou thyself dost air°—the queen o'th' sky,[4]   take fresh air
Whose wat'ry arch° and messenger am I,   rainbow
Bids thee leave these, and with her sovereign grace,
Here on this grass-plot,[5] in this very place
To come and sport. Her peacocks fly amain.[6]
75   Approach, rich Ceres, her to entertain.
          Enter CERES.[7]
CERES   Hail, many-colored messenger, that ne'er

1. With derisive and grimacing gestures.
2. Take care that you remain faithful to your promise. Prospero may have caught the lovers just indulging in dalliance.
3. To "give the rein" is to make a horse gallop.
4. *The . . . liver:* Virgin snow lies on his heart because he has remained chaste, never having given in to his ardent liver. The liver was held to be the seat of passion.
5. Goddess of the rainbow and messenger of Juno; her apparel is in the colors of the rainbow, and she wears "saffron wings" (line 78).
6. Arable land. Ceres was the Roman goddess of agriculture and generative nature.
7. Pealike plants grown for fodder.
8. Hay for winter fodder.
9. Reinforced with channels ("pioned") and with entwined branches ("twilled") to prevent riverbank

erosion.
1. Adorns with flowers; recalls the colloquial "April showers bring forth May flowers."
2. Thickets of gorse, yellow-flowered shrubs. *cold:* chaste.
3. Vineyard with vines embracing, twined around, their supporting poles; pruned vineyard. "Vineyard" was pronounced as three syllables. *lass-lorn:* abandoned by the girl he wooed. *poll-clipped:* pruned short.
4. Juno, queen of the heavens and goddess of women, held to protect marriages and preside over childbirth.
5. Compare "this short-grassed green" (line 83) and "this green land" (line 130): a green carpet on the acting area is indicated.
6. In haste. Peacocks, sacred to Juno, drew her chariot.
7. Her part is probably played by Ariel (see line 167).

Dost disobey the wife of Jupiter;° | (Juno)
Who with thy saffron wings upon my flowers
Diffusest honey-drops, refreshing showers,
80 And with each end of thy blue bow dost crown
My bosky[8] acres and my unshrubbed down,
Rich scarf[9] to my proud earth. Why hath thy queen
Summoned me hither to this short-grassed green?

IRIS   A contract of true love to celebrate
85 And some donation freely to estate° | bestow
On the blessed lovers.

CERES   Tell me, heavenly bow,° | rainbow
If Venus or her son,[1] as° thou dost know, | as far as
Do now attend the Queen? Since they did plot
The means that dusky Dis[2] my daughter got,
90 Her and her blind boy's scandaled° company | scandalous; notorious
I have forsworn.

IRIS   Of her society
Be not afraid. I met her deity
Cutting the clouds towards Paphos,[3] and her son
Dove-drawn[4] with her. Here thought they to have done
95 Some wanton charm upon[5] this man and maid,
Whose vows are that no bed-right[6] shall be paid
Till Hymen's torch be lighted;[7] but in vain.
Mars's hot minion° is returned again; | lover; Venus
Her waspish-headed[8] son has broke his arrows,
100 Swears he will shoot no more but play with sparrows,[9]
And be a boy right out.° | an ordinary boy

JUNO *descends.*[1]

CERES   Highest queen of state,
Great Juno comes; I know her by her gait.° | majestic bearing

JUNO   How does my bounteous sister? Go with me
To bless this twain that they may prosperous be
105 And honored in their issue.

[JUNO *and* CERES] *sing.*[2]

Honor, riches, marriage-blessing,
Long continuance and increasing,
Hourly joys be still° upon you, | always
Juno sings her blessings on you.

110 CERES   Earth's increase and foison° plenty, | abundance
Barns and garners° never empty, | granaries
Vines with clust'ring bunches growing,
Plants with goodly burden bowing;
Spring come to you at the farthest,

---

8. Covered with bushes and thickets.
9. Ornamental and hung across the body rather than around the neck.
1. Cupid, proverbially blind.
2. King of the underworld in classical mythology. Venus and her son Cupid made him fall in love with Ceres' daughter Proserpine, whom he abducted (Ovid, *Metamorphoses* 5.395ff).
3. City in Cyprus: associated with Venus.
4. Doves were sacred to Venus and drew her chariot.
5. *done . . . upon:* cast a lustful spell upon.
6. Right to consummate the marriage; also, suggesting a rite, as in line 17.
7. Until the wedding ceremony is performed.

8. Peevish, irritable, and with arrows like the wasp's sting.
9. Sparrows were associated with Venus because they were proverbially lustful.
1. TEXTUAL COMMENT Although most editors place "JUNO *descends*" at the point where Juno enters and speaks, in the Folio this stage direction appears around line 74. For possible explanations of the Folio's placement, and their implications for the way the scene is staged, see Digital Edition TC 7.
2. Ceres and Juno might be raised together in the flight apparatus and sing suspended above the stage. They would then vanish (line 138 stage direction) by being raised into the heavens.

115   In the very end of harvest.[3]
                    Scarcity and want shall shun you,
                    Ceres' blessing so is on you.
     FERDINAND   This is a most majestic vision, and
          Harmonious charmingly.[4] May I be bold°   *Would I be right*
          To think these spirits?
120 PROSPERO   Spirits, which by mine art
          I have from their confines[5] called to enact
          My present fancies.
     FERDINAND   Let me live here ever!
          So rare a wondered° father and a wise[6]   *endowed with wonders*
          Makes this place paradise.
                    JUNO *and* CERES *whisper, and send* IRIS *on*
                    employment.
     PROSPERO   Sweet° now, silence.   *Softly*
125   Juno and Ceres whisper seriously.
          There's something else to do. Hush and be mute,
          Or else our spell is marred.
     IRIS   You nymphs called naiads of the wind'ring[7] brooks,
          With your sedged crowns° and ever-harmless looks,   *garlands of reeds*
130   Leave your crisp channels, and on this green land
          Answer your summons; Juno does command.
          Come, temperate nymphs, and help to celebrate
          A contract of true love. Be not too late.
                    Enter certain Nymphs.
          —You sunburned sicklemen° of August weary,   *harvesters*
135   Come hither from the furrow and be merry;
          Make holiday; your rye-straw hats put on,
          And these fresh nymphs encounter every one
          In country footing.
                    Enter certain Reapers, properly habited.[8] They
                    join with the Nymphs in a graceful dance, towards
                    the end whereof PROSPERO *starts suddenly and speaks,*
                    after which, to a strange, hollow, and confused noise,
                    they heavily vanish.[9]
     PROSPERO   I had forgot that foul conspiracy
140   Of the beast Caliban and his confederates
          Against my life. The minute of their plot
          Is almost come. [*to the Spirits*] Well done. Avoid;° no more!   *Begone*
     FERDINAND   This is strange: your father's in some passion
          That works° him strongly.   *agitates*
     MIRANDA   Never till this day
145   Saw I him touched with anger so distempered.°   *troubled; distracted*
     PROSPERO   You do look, my son, in a movèd sort,°   *disturbed manner*
          As if you were dismayed. Be cheerful, sir.

---

3. Let spring return immediately after harvest, without any intervening winter. (In Greek mythology, winter was originally caused by Ceres abandoning the earth in search of Proserpine.)
4. Delightfully; magically; harmoniously.
5. Regions of dwelling. The word is accented on the second syllable.
6. TEXTUAL COMMENT Since the eighteenth century, some editors have changed "wise" to "wife," an emen-
dation backed by disputed typographical evidence but with implications for the play's representation of women. For more on the long and vexed editorial history of this short word, see Digital Edition TC 8.
7. Perhaps a conflation of "wandering" and "winding." The naiads were mythical river nymphs.
8. Either appropriately or finely dressed.
9. Sorrowfully depart (probably not implying a trick of staging).

Our revels[1] now are ended. These our actors,
As I foretold you,° were all spirits and   *told you before*
150 Are melted into air, into thin air;
And like the baseless fabric[2] of this vision,
The cloud-capped towers, the gorgeous palaces,
The solemn temples, the great globe[3] itself,
Yea, all which it inherit,[4] shall dissolve,
155 And, like this insubstantial pageant faded,
Leave not a rack° behind. We are such stuff   *wisp of cloud*
As dreams are made on,° and our little life   *of*
Is rounded[5] with a sleep. Sir, I am vexed.
Bear with my weakness: my old brain is troubled.
160 Be not disturbed with my infirmity.
If you be pleased, retire into my cell
And there repose. A turn or two I'll walk
To still my beating mind.
FERDINAND *and* MIRANDA   We wish your peace.   *Exeunt.*
PROSPERO   Come with a thought.[6] I thank thee, Ariel. Come.
          Enter ARIEL.
ARIEL   Thy thoughts I cleave to. What's thy pleasure?
165 PROSPERO   Spirit,
We must prepare to meet with Caliban.
ARIEL   Ay, my commander. When I presented[7] Ceres
I thought to have told thee of it, but I feared
Lest I might anger thee.
170 PROSPERO   Say again, where didst thou leave these varlets?°   *ruffians*
ARIEL   I told you, sir, they were red hot with drinking;
So full of valor that they smote the air
For breathing in their faces, beat the ground
For kissing of their feet; yet always bending°   *aiming*
175 Towards their project. Then I beat my tabor,°   *side drum*
At which like unbacked° colts they pricked their ears,   *never-ridden*
Advanced° their eyelids, lifted up their noses   *Opened*
As° they smelt music. So I charmed their ears   *As if*
That calf-like they my lowing° followed through   *mooing*
180 Toothed briars, sharp furzes, pricking gorse,° and thorns,   *prickly shrubs*
Which entered their frail shins. At last I left them
I'th' filthy-mantled[8] pool beyond your cell,
There dancing up to th' chins, that° the foul lake   *so that*
O'erstunk[9] their feet.
PROSPERO   This was well done, my bird.°   *chick; dear*
185 Thy shape invisible retain thou still.
The trumpery° in my house, go bring it hither   *cheap goods*
For stale° to catch these thieves.   *decoy; bait*
ARIEL   I go, I go.   *Exit.*
PROSPERO   A devil, a born devil, on whose nature
Nurture can never stick; on whom my pains,
190 Humanely taken, all, all lost, quite lost;

---

1. Entertainment, in both festive and theatrical senses.
2. An edifice or substance without foundations; insubstantial, alluding to buildings in masque scenery.
3. World; also, with a passing allusion to the Globe theater.
4. All who come into possession of it.
5. Rounded off; surrounded; or, possibly, crowned.
6. Come as fast as thought, a colloquial simile.
7. Acted; produced the masque of; introduced while playing Iris.
8. Covered with filthy scum.
9. Made smelly; smelled worse than.

And, as with age his body uglier grows,
So his mind cankers.° I will plague them all,   *festers*
Even to roaring.
        Enter ARIEL, *laden with glistering apparel, etc.*
            —Come, hang them on this line.[1]
     Enter CALIBAN, STEFANO, *and* TRINCULO, *all wet.*
CALIBAN   Pray you tread softly, that the blind mole may not
195   Hear a foot fall. We now are near his cell.
STEFANO   Monster, your fairy, which you say is a harmless
    fairy, has done little better than played the jack° with us.   *knave; will-o'-the-wisp*
TRINCULO   Monster, I do smell° all horse-piss, at which my nose   *smell of*
    is in great indignation.
200   STEFANO   So is mine. Do you hear, monster? If I should take a
    displeasure against you, look you—
TRINCULO   Thou wert but a lost monster.
CALIBAN   Good my lord, give me thy favor still.
    Be patient, for the prize I'll bring thee to
205   Shall hoodwink[2] this mischance. Therefore speak softly;
    All's hushed as midnight yet.
TRINCULO   Ay, but to lose our bottles in the pool!
STEFANO   There is not only disgrace and dishonor in that,
    monster, but an infinite loss.
210   TRINCULO   That's more to me than my wetting. Yet this is your
    harmless fairy, monster.
STEFANO   I will fetch off[3] my bottle, though I be o'er ears° for   *drowned*
    my labor.
CALIBAN   Prithee, my king, be quiet. Seest thou here:
215   This is the mouth o'th' cell. No noise, and enter.
    Do that good mischief which may make this island
    Thine own forever, and I, thy Caliban,
    For aye° thy foot-licker.   *ever*
STEFANO   Give me thy hand. I do begin to have bloody thoughts.
220   TRINCULO   O King Stefano, O peer! O worthy Stefano, look
    what a wardrobe here is for thee.[4]
CALIBAN   Let it alone, thou fool. It is but trash.
TRINCULO   Oh ho, monster! We know what belongs to a frip-
    pery.° O King Stefano!   *old-clothes shop*
225   STEFANO   Put off that gown, Trinculo: by this hand, I'll have
    that gown.
TRINCULO   Thy grace shall have it.
CALIBAN   The dropsy[5] drown this fool! What do you mean
    To dote thus on such luggage?° Let't alone   *encumbrances*
230   And do the murder first. If he awake,
    From toe to crown he'll fill our skins with pinches,
    Make us° strange stuff.   *Turn us into*
STEFANO   Be you quiet, monster. Mistress line, is not this my
    jerkin?° Now is the jerkin under the line.[6] Now, jerkin, you   *leather jacket*

---

1. Variant of lind, the lime tree or linden, probably indicating stage property tree.
2. Blind with a hood, as was done to pacify a hawk—hence, make harmless; also, put out of sight.
3. Recover; rescue; drink off.
4. Recalling "King Stephen was and a worthy peer, / His breeches cost him but a crown," a popular ballad about King Stephen, sung in part in *Othello* 2.3.77ff.

5. A disease characterized by the accumulation of fluid in connective tissue.
6. Below the lime tree; south of the equator; below the waist. Also, a possible allusion to the proverb "Thou hast stricken the ball under the line," meaning "You have cheated." Stefano has taken the jerkin from the lime tree.

235   are like to lose your hair and prove a bald jerkin.[7]

TRINCULO   Do, do! We steal by line and level,[8] an't like° your *if it please*
    grace.

STEFANO   I thank thee for that jest. Here's a garment for't. Wit
    shall not go unrewarded while I am king of this country.

240   "Steal by line and level" is an excellent pass of pate.[9] There's
    another garment for't.

TRINCULO   Monster, come, put some lime upon your fingers[1]
    and away with the rest.

CALIBAN   I will have none on't. We shall lose our time

245   And all be turned to barnacles,[2] or to apes
    With foreheads villainous° low.   *wretchedly*

STEFANO   Monster, lay to° your fingers. Help to bear this away,   *apply*
    where my hogshead of wine is, or I'll turn you out of my
    kingdom. Go to, carry this.

250 TRINCULO   And this.

STEFANO   Ay, and this.

        A noise of hunters heard. Enter diverse° SPIRITS *in*   *various*
        shape of dogs and hounds, hunting them about,
        PROSPERO *and* ARIEL *setting them on.*

PROSPERO   Hey, Mountain, hey!

ARIEL   Silver! There it goes, Silver!

PROSPERO   Fury, Fury! There, Tyrant, there! Hark, hark!
        [CALIBAN, STEFANO, *and* TRINCULO *are chased off by*
        SPIRITS.]

255   [*to* ARIEL] Go, charge my goblins that they grind their joints
    With dry convulsions, shorten up their sinews
    With agèd cramps, and more pinch-spotted[3] make them
    Than pard or cat o'mountain.[4]

ARIEL   Hark, they roar!

PROSPERO   Let them be hunted soundly.° At this hour   *thoroughly*

260   Lies at my mercy all mine enemies.
    Shortly shall all my labors end, and thou
    Shalt have the air at freedom. For a little,
    Follow and do me service.   *Exeunt.*

5.1

Enter PROSPERO *in his magic robes, and* ARIEL.

PROSPERO   Now does my project gather to a head:[1]
    My charms crack not, my spirits obey, and time
    Goes upright with his carriage.[2] How's the day?

ARIEL   On the sixth hour; at which time, my lord,
    You said our work should cease.

---

7. Baldness caused either through tropical disease or by sailors who customarily shaved the heads of passengers when they crossed the line of the equator for the first time. "Under the [waist]line" (line 234) could also be an allusion to baldness from syphilis.
8. An idiomatic expression for "properly, by the rules"—literally, "by plumb line and carpenter's level"; also, punning on "lime." *Do, do*: an expression of approval.
9. Thrust of wit (fencing term).
1. Be "lime-fingered," sticky-fingered (alluding to birdlime, a gluey substance used to catch birds).

2. Barnacle geese, also known as "tree geese" and supposed to begin life as barnacle shells.
3. Spotted with bruises from pinches. *agèd cramps:* the convulsions of old age.
4. Both terms are synonymous with "leopard"; the second is from Jeremiah 13:23: "May a man of Ind change his skin, and the cat of the mountain her spots?" (Bishops' Bible).
5.1
1. Draw to its fulfillment. "Project" suggests an alchemical projection or "experiment."
2. Because his carriage, or burden, is now light.

5 PROSPERO   I did say so
      When first I raised the tempest. Say, my spirit,
      How fares the King and 's° followers?   *and his*
   ARIEL   .   Confined together
      In the same fashion as you gave in charge,
      Just as you left them; all prisoners, sir,
10   In the line-grove which weather-fends³ your cell:
      They cannot budge till your release.° The King,   *you release them*
      His brother, and yours abide all three distracted,°   *out of their wits*
      And the remainder mourning over them,
      Brimful of sorrow and dismay; but chiefly
15   Him that you termed, sir, the good old Lord Gonzalo:
      His tears runs down his beard like winter's drops
      From eaves of reeds.° Your charm so strongly works 'em   *thatched roofs*
      That if you now beheld them, your affections°   *feelings*
      Would become tender.
   PROSPERO   Dost thou think so, spirit?
   ARIEL   Mine would, sir, were I human.
20 PROSPERO   And mine shall.
      Hast thou, which art but air, a touch,° a feeling   *sense*
      Of their afflictions, and shall not myself—
      One of their kind, that relish all as sharply
      Passion as they⁴—be kindlier⁵ moved than thou art?
25   Though with their high° wrongs I am struck to th' quick,   *great*
      Yet with my nobler reason 'gainst my fury
      Do I take part.° The rarer action is   *side*
      In virtue than in vengeance. They being penitent,
      The sole drift of my purpose doth extend
30   Not a frown further. Go, release them, Ariel.
      My charms I'll break, their senses I'll restore,
      And they shall be themselves.
   ARIEL   I'll fetch them, sir.   *Exit.*
      [PROSPERO *makes a circle on the stage.*]⁶
   PROSPERO⁷   Ye elves of hills, brooks, standing lakes, and groves,
      And ye that on the sands with printless foot
35   Do chase the ebbing Neptune, and do fly him
      When he comes back; you demi-puppets⁸ that
      By moonshine do the green sour ringlets⁹ make,
      Whereof the ewe not bites; and you, whose pastime
      Is to make midnight°-mushrooms, that rejoice   *springing up overnight*
40   To hear the solemn curfew;¹ by whose aid—
      Weak masters² though ye be—I have bedimmed
      The noontide sun, called forth the mutinous winds,
      And twixt the green sea and the azured vault°   *the sky*
      Set roaring war; to the dread rattling thunder

3. Which protects from the weather.
4. *that . . . they:* who feel as much strong emotion as they do.
5. More tenderly; more naturally.
6. The original text does not indicate when the circle is drawn. Other possibilities are at the beginning of the scene or before the entry at line 57.
7. Prospero's speech closely follows Ovid's *Metamorphoses* 7.265–77, in Arthur Golding's translation (1567); the speaker in Ovid is the sorceress Medea,

who uses her witchcraft to vengeful ends.
8. Puppets; elves; quasi puppets.
9. Fairy rings: distinctive circles of grass supposed to be caused by dancing fairies but actually caused by mushrooms.
1. The bell rung at nightfall, indicating the time when spirits are abroad.
2. Ineffectual when acting independently; without supernatural power; subordinate spirits.

45   Have I given fire, and rifted° Jove's stout oak   *split*
       With his own bolt;° the strong-based promontory   *lightning bolt*
       Have I made shake, and by the spurs° plucked up   *roots*
       The pine and cedar. Graves at my command
       Have waked their sleepers, oped, and let 'em forth
50   By my so potent art. But this rough³ magic
       I here abjure; and when I have required°   *summoned*
       Some heavenly music—which even now I do—
       To work mine end upon their senses that°   *the senses of whom*
       This airy⁴ charm is for, I'll break my staff,
55   Bury it certain° fathoms in the earth,   *several*
       And deeper than did ever plummet sound
       I'll drown my book.

              Solemn music.
              Here enters ARIEL *before; then* ALONSO *with a frantic*
              gesture, attended by GONZALO; SEBASTIAN *and* ANTONIO
              in like manner, attended by ADRIAN *and* FRANCISCO.
              They all enter the circle which PROSPERO *had made,*
              and there stand charmed; which PROSPERO *observing,*
              *speaks.*⁵
       A solemn air° and° the best comforter   *song / which is*
       To an unsettled fancy° cure thy brains,   *imagination*
60   Now useless, boiled within thy skull. There stand,
       For you are spell-stopped.
       Holy Gonzalo, honorable man,
       Mine eyes, e'en sociable° to the show° of thine,   *sympathetic / appearance*
       Fall fellowly drops. [*aside*] The charm dissolves apace
65   And, as the morning steals upon the night,
       Melting the darkness, so their rising senses
       Begin to chase the ignorant fumes⁶ that mantle°   *envelop*
       Their clearer° reason. —O good Gonzalo,   *growing clearer*
       My true preserver and a loyal sir°   *gentleman*
70   To him thou follow'st, I will pay° thy graces   *requite*
       Home° both in word and deed. Most cruelly   *Fully*
       Didst thou, Alonso, use me and my daughter.
       Thy brother was a furtherer° in the act: *an accomplice*
       Thou art pinched° for't now, Sebastian. Flesh and blood, *tortured; afflicted*
75   You, brother mine, that entertained ambition,
       Expelled remorse and nature,⁷ whom° with Sebastian—   *who*
       Whose inward pinches therefore are most strong—
       Would here have killed your king, I do forgive thee,
       Unnatural though thou art. [*aside*] Their understanding
80   Begins to swell,° and the approaching tide   *(as does a tide)*
       Will shortly fill the reasonable shore
       That now lies foul and muddy. Not° one of them   *There is not*
       That yet looks on me or would know me. —Ariel,
       Fetch me the hat and rapier⁸ in my cell.
                     [ARIEL *exits and returns.*]
85   I will discase° me and myself present   *undress*

---

3. Violent; discordant; crudely approximate.
4. Wrought by spirits of the air.
5. Prospero remains invisible and inaudible to Alonso and his party until he greets Alonso at line 106.

6. Fogs of ignorance; the image is of the sun ("rising senses") dissipating morning mist.
7. Pity and brotherly affection.
8. Elements of normal aristocratic dress.

As I was sometime Milan.[9] Quickly, spirit!
Thou shalt ere long be free.

ARIEL sings and helps to attire him.

ARIEL   Where the bee sucks, there suck I;
       In a cowslip's bell I lie;
90   There I couch when owls do cry;
       On the bat's back I do fly
       After summer merrily.
       Merrily, merrily shall I live now,
       Under the blossom that hangs on the bough.

95 PROSPERO   Why, that's my dainty Ariel! I shall miss
Thee, but yet thou shalt have freedom.—So, so, so.[1]
To the King's ship, invisible as thou art;
There shalt thou find the mariners asleep
Under the hatches. The Master and the Boatswain
100 Being awake, enforce them to this place,
And presently,° I prithee.   *immediately*

ARIEL   I drink the air before me and return
Or ere° your pulse twice beat.   *Exit.*   *Before*

GONZALO   All torment, trouble, wonder, and amazement°   *bewilderment*
105 Inhabits here. Some heavenly power guide us
Out of this fearful° country!   *fearsome*

PROSPERO   Behold, sir King,
The wrongèd Duke of Milan, Prospero.
For more assurance that a living prince
Does now speak to thee, I embrace thy body
110 And to thee and thy company I bid
A hearty welcome.

ALONSO   Whe'er° thou beest he or no,   *Whether*
Or some enchanted trifle[2] to abuse° me—   *delude; maltreat*
As late I have been—I not know. Thy pulse
Beats as of flesh and blood; and since I saw thee,
115 Th'affliction of my mind amends, with which,
I fear, a madness held me. This must crave°—   *requires, as explanation*
An if this be at all[3]—a most strange story.
Thy dukedom[4] I resign and do entreat
Thou pardon me my wrongs. But how should Prospero
Be living, and be here?

120 PROSPERO [*to* GONZALO]   First, noble friend,
Let me embrace thine age,° whose honor cannot   *old body*
Be measured or confined.

GONZALO   Whether this be
Or be not, I'll not swear.

PROSPERO   You do yet taste
Some subtleties[5] o'th' isle, that will not let you
125 Believe things certain. Welcome, my friends all.
[*aside to* SEBASTIAN *and* ANTONIO] But you, my brace° of   *pair*
    lords, were I so minded

---

9. Formerly, when Duke of Milan.
1. Prospero arranges his attire approvingly.
2. With a suggestion of the old sense of "trifle" as "deception."
3. If this is really happening.

4. Alonso's rights of homage and tribute from it.
5. *You . . . subtleties:* You still experience some of the illusions. "Subtleties" were also sweet confections shaped like castles, temples, beasts, allegorical figures, and the like, and arranged like a pageant.

I here could pluck his highness' frown upon you
And justify° you traitors. At this time   *prove*
I will tell no tales.
SEBASTIAN [*to* ANTONIO]   The devil speaks in him!
PROSPERO   No.

130   [*to* ANTONIO] For you, most wicked sir, whom to call brother
Would even infect my mouth, I do forgive
Thy rankest fault—all of them—and require
My dukedom of thee, which perforce° I know   *necessarily*
Thou must restore.
ALONSO   If thou beest Prospero,

135   Give us particulars of thy preservation;
How thou hast met us here, whom three hours since
Were wrecked upon this shore, where I have lost—
How sharp the point of this remembrance is—
My dear son Ferdinand.
PROSPERO   I am woe° for't, sir.   *I grieve*

140   ALONSO   Irreparable is the loss, and patience
Says it is past her cure.
PROSPERO   I rather think
You have not sought her help, of° whose soft grace°   *by / mercy*
For the like loss I have her sovereign aid
And rest myself content.
ALONSO   You the like loss?

145   PROSPERO   As great to me as late;° and supportable   *recent*
To make the dear loss[6] have I means much weaker
Than you may call to comfort you, for I
Have lost my daughter.[7]
ALONSO   A daughter?
O heavens, that they were living both in Naples,

150   The King and Queen there! That they were, I wish
Myself were mudded in that oozy bed
Where my son lies. When did you lose your daughter?
PROSPERO   In this last tempest. I perceive these lords
At this encounter do so much admire°   *wonder*

155   That they devour their reason[8] and scarce think
Their eyes do offices of truth,° their words   *function accurately*
Are natural breath. But, howsoe'er you have
Been jostled from your senses, know for certain
That I am Prospero, and that very duke

160   Which was thrust forth of Milan, who most strangely
Upon this shore where you were wrecked, was landed
To be the lord on't. No more yet of this,
For 'tis a chronicle of day by day,
Not a relation for a breakfast, nor

165   Befitting this first meeting. Welcome, sir;
This cell's my court. Here have I few attendants
And subjects none abroad.[9] Pray you look in.
My dukedom since you have given me again,

---

6. *supportable . . . loss:* in order to make the heartfelt loss bearable.
7. Prospero apparently means that Alonso still has a child, his daughter Claribel, to comfort him.
8. "Reason" has the additional sense of "discourse"; hence, the phrase is an extension of "swallow their words."
9. Elsewhere about the island; beyond the cell.

I will requite you with as good a thing;
170 At least bring forth a wonder to content ye
As much as me my dukedom.

> *Here* PROSPERO *discovers*[1] FERDINAND *and* MIRANDA
> *playing at chess.*

MIRANDA Sweet lord, you play me false.°   trick me
FERDINAND   No, my dearest love,
I would not for the world.
MIRANDA Yes, for a score of kingdoms you should wrangle,
And I would call it fair play.[2]
175 ALONSO   If this prove
A vision of the island, one dear son
Shall I twice lose.
SEBASTIAN   A most high miracle!
FERDINAND Though the seas threaten, they are merciful:
I have cursed them without cause.
          [FERDINAND *kneels.*]
ALONSO   Now all the blessings
180 Of a glad father compass thee about!°   surround you
Arise, and say how thou cam'st here.
MIRANDA   Oh, wonder!
How many goodly creatures are there here!
How beauteous mankind is! Oh, brave new world
That has such people in't!
PROSPERO   'Tis new to thee.
185 ALONSO [*to* FERDINAND] What is this maid with whom
          thou wast at play?
Your eld'st° acquaintance cannot be three hours.   longest
Is she the goddess that hath severed us
And brought us thus together?
FERDINAND   Sir, she is mortal;
But by immortal Providence she's mine.
190 I chose her when I could not ask my father
For his advice, nor thought I had one. She
Is daughter to this famous Duke of Milan—
Of whom so often I have heard renown
But never saw before—of whom I have
195 Received a second life; and second father
This lady makes him to me.
ALONSO   I am hers.[3]
But oh, how oddly will it sound that I
Must ask my child° forgiveness!   (Miranda)
PROSPERO   There, sir, stop.
Let us not burden our remembrances with
A heaviness° that's gone.   sorrow
200 GONZALO   I have inly wept,
Or should have spoke ere this. Look down, you gods,
And on this couple drop a blessèd crown.
For it is you that have chalked forth° the way   marked out
Which brought us hither.

---

1. Reveals by drawing back a curtain hanging in front
of the discovery space.
2. *for . . . play:* you could quarrel for twenty kingdoms,
and I would still call it fair play.
3. I will be her second father: Alonso's assent to the
betrothal.

ALONSO   I say "Amen," Gonzalo.

205 GONZALO Was Milan° thrust from Milan that his issue   *the Duke of Milan*
  Should become kings of Naples? Oh, rejoice
  Beyond a common joy and set it down
  With gold on lasting pillars:[4] in one voyage
  Did Claribel her husband find at Tunis,
210 And Ferdinand her brother found a wife
  Where he himself was lost; Prospero his dukedom
  In a poor isle; and all of us ourselves
  When no man was his own.[5]

ALONSO [*to* FERDINAND *and* MIRANDA] Give me your hands.
215 Let grief and sorrow still° embrace his heart   *always*
  That° doth not wish you joy.   *Who*

GONZALO   Be it so. Amen.

  Enter ARIEL, *with the* MASTER *and* BOATSWAIN
  amazedly following.

  Oh, look, sir, look, sir: here is more of us.
  I prophesied if a gallows were on land
  This fellow could not drown. [*to* BOATSWAIN] Now,
   blasphemy,°   *blasphemer*
220 That swear'st grace o'erboard, not an oath on shore?
  Hast thou no mouth by land? What is the news?

BOATSWAIN The best news is that we have safely found
  Our king and company; the next, our ship,
  Which but three glasses° since we gave out° split, *hourglasses / declared*
225 Is tight and yare[6] and bravely rigged as when
  We first put out to sea.

ARIEL [*to* PROSPERO] Sir, all this service
  Have I done since I went.

PROSPERO [*to* ARIEL] My tricksy° spirit!   *capricious; neat*
230 ALONSO These are not natural events; they strengthen° *increase*
  From strange to stranger. Say, how came you hither?

BOATSWAIN If I did think, sir, I were well awake,
  I'd strive to tell you. We were dead of° sleep   *with*
  And—how we know not—all clapped° under hatches, *shut up*
235 Where but even now with strange and several° noises *various*
  Of roaring, shrieking, howling, jingling chains,
  And more diversity of sounds, all horrible,
  We were awaked; straightway at liberty,
  Where we, in all our trim, freshly beheld
240 Our royal, good, and gallant ship, our Master
  Cap'ring to eye° her. On° a trice, so please you, *Dancing to see / In*
  Even in a dream were we divided from them
  And were brought moping° hither.   *dazed*

ARIEL [*to* PROSPERO]   Was't well done?
PROSPERO [*to* ARIEL] Bravely, my diligence. Thou shalt be free.
245 ALONSO This is as strange a maze as e'er men trod,
  And there is in this business more than nature
  Was ever conduct° of. Some oracle   *conductor*
  Must rectify our knowledge.

PROSPERO   Sir, my liege,

---

4. Suggesting, perhaps, the triumphal arches commissioned to celebrate notable occasions.

5. When we all had lost our senses.
6. Is sound and ready to sail.

Do not infest° your mind with beating on[7]   *trouble*
250   The strangeness of this business. At picked leisure,
Which shall be shortly, single° I'll resolve you—   *in private*
Which to you shall seem probable°—of every   *plausible*
These happened accidents.° Till when, be cheerful   *occurrences*
And think of each thing well. [*to* ARIEL] Come hither, spirit.
255   Set Caliban and his companions free:
Untie the spell.   [*Exit* ARIEL.]
[*to* ALONSO]   How fares my gracious sir?
There are yet missing of your company
Some few odd lads that you remember not.
          Enter ARIEL, *driving in* CALIBAN, STEFANO, *and*
          TRINCULO *in their stolen apparel.*
STEFANO   Every man shift for all the rest, and let no man take
260   care for himself;[8] for all is but fortune. *Coraggio*, bully mon-
ster,[9] *coraggio!*
TRINCULO   If these° be true spies which I wear in my head,   *these eyes*
here's a goodly sight!
CALIBAN   O Setebos, these be brave spirits indeed!
265   How fine° my master is! I am afraid   *splendidly dressed*
He will chastise me.
SEBASTIAN   Ha, ha! What things are these, my lord Antonio?
Will money buy 'em?
ANTONIO   Very like.° One of them   *likely*
Is a plain° fish, and no doubt marketable.   *mere*
270   PROSPERO   Mark but the badges[1] of these men, my lords;
Then say if they° be true. This misshapen knave,   *(the men); (the badges)*
His mother was a witch, and one so strong
That could control the moon, make flows and ebbs,
And deal in her command without her power.[2]
275   These three have robbed me, and this demi-devil[3]—
For he's a bastard one—had plotted with them
To take my life. Two of these fellows you
Must know and own;[4] this thing of darkness I
Acknowledge mine.
CALIBAN   I shall be pinched to death.
280   ALONSO   Is not this Stefano, my drunken butler?
SEBASTIAN   He is drunk now. Where had he wine?
ALONSO   And Trinculo is reeling-ripe.° Where should they   *drunk*
Find this grand liquor that hath gilded[5] 'em?
How cam'st thou in this pickle?[6]
285   TRINCULO   I have been in such a pickle since I saw you last that I
fear me will never out of my bones: I shall not fear flyblowing.[7]
SEBASTIAN   Why, how now, Stefano?
STEFANO   Oh, touch me not! I am not Stefano, but a cramp.
PROSPERO   You'd be king o'the isle, sirrah?

---

7. With repeatedly worrying about.
8. Stefano drunkenly confuses the saying "Every man for himself."
9. Gallant monster. *Coraggio:* "Take courage" (Italian).
1. Livery. Servants often wore their master's emblem, but Prospero probably refers to the stolen apparel.
2. And wield her (the moon's) power without her authority, or beyond the reach of her might.
3. Being the offspring of Sycorax and the devil.

4. And acknowledge to be yours.
5. Probably alluding to the alchemical elixir ("liquor") known as *aurum potabile* (drinkable gold); hence, "gilded" (flushed).
6. Sorry plight; Trinculo takes up the literal sense of "preserving liquid," recalling both his drunkenness and his drenching in the lake.
7. Not fear being infested with flies, since he has been "pickled" (preserved).

290 STEFANO   I should have been a sore° one then.   *an inept; severe; pained*
ALONSO [*indicating* CALIBAN]   This is a strange thing as e'er
      I looked on.
PROSPERO   He is as disproportioned in his manners[8]
      As in his shape. Go, sirrah, to my cell;
      Take with you your companions. As you look
295   To have my pardon, trim° it handsomely.   *tidy; decorate*
CALIBAN   Ay, that I will; and I'll be wise hereafter
      And seek for grace. What a thrice-double ass
      Was I to take this drunkard for a god
      And worship this dull fool!
PROSPERO   Go to, away.
300 ALONSO   Hence, and bestow your luggage where you found it.
SEBASTIAN   Or stole it rather.
              [*Exeunt* CALIBAN, STEFANO, *and* TRINCULO.]
PROSPERO   Sir, I invite your highness and your train
      To my poor cell, where you shall take your rest
      For this one night; which—part of it°—I'll waste°   *part of which / spend*
305   With such discourse as, I not doubt, shall make it
      Go quick away: the story of my life
      And the particular accidents° gone by   *events*
      Since I came to this isle. And in the morn
      I'll bring you to your ship, and so to Naples,
310   Where I have hope to see the nuptial
      Of these our dear-belovèd solemnized,
      And thence retire me to my Milan, where
      Every third thought shall be my grave.
ALONSO   I long
      To hear the story of your life, which must
315   Take° the ear strangely.   *Captivate*
PROSPERO   I'll deliver° all,   *relate*
      And promise you calm seas, auspicious gales,
      And sail so expeditious that shall° catch   *it will*
      Your royal fleet far off. —My Ariel, chick,
      That is thy charge. Then to the elements
320   Be free, and fare thou well. —Please you draw near.[9]
                  Exeunt all [except PROSPERO].[1]

Epilogue
          Spoken by PROSPERO.
      Now my charms are all o'erthrown,
      And what strength I have's mine own,
      Which is most faint. Now 'tis true
      I must be here confined by you,
5   Or sent to Naples. Let me not,
      Since I have my dukedom got
      And pardoned the deceiver, dwell
      In this bare island° by your spell,   *(the stage)*

8. Behavior; moral character.
9. PERFORMANCE COMMENT Though most productions of *The Tempest* end happily, many questions remain unresolved. Are Antonio and Prospero truly reconciled, or do they remain suspicious of each other? What is Prospero's attitude toward abjuring his magical powers and leaving the island? Is Caliban left behind, content to be his own king, or is he miserable at the prospect of abandonment? Directors often explore such questions to suggest how the drama will continue when the play is done. For more, see Digital Edition PC 4.
1. The general exeunt is through Prospero's cell; Ariel departs in another direction.

But release me from my bands°   *fetters*
10 With the help of your good hands.°   *(applause)*
Gentle breath° of yours my sails   *Favorable comment*
Must fill or else my project fails,
Which was to please. Now I want°   *lack*
Spirits to enforce, art to enchant;
15 And my ending[1] is despair,
Unless I be relieved by prayer,
Which pierces so that it assaults
Mercy itself and frees all faults.
As you from crimes would pardoned be,
20 Let your indulgence[2] set me free.   [*Exit.*]

Epilogue
1. Punning on the sense "death."   2. Approval; appeasement; remission for sin.

Cardenio

Many readers have interpreted the end of *The Tempest* (1610–11), when the magician Prospero breaks his magic staff and drowns his book, as Shakespeare's own farewell to the theater. But in fact in the years that followed he collaborated on at least three plays with John Fletcher, the playwright Shakespeare seems to have chosen to succeed him as the principal dramatist of his company, the King's Men. One of these collaborations, *Henry VIII*, was included in the First Folio of 1623; another, *The Two Noble Kinsmen*, appeared in quarto in 1624. A third play left only a shadowy trace of its existence: two documents from the King's Treasurer's accounts for May and June 1613 record payments to John Heminges, then leader of the King's Men, for the presentation at court of a play called *Cardenna* or *Cardenno*. Heminges did not include this play in the First Folio he helped to edit, but many years later, on September 9, 1653, the London publisher Humphrey Moseley entered in the Stationers' Register a batch of plays including "The History of Cardenio, by Mr Fletcher and Shakespeare." For whatever reason, this play was either not printed at all or has been lost. *Cardenio,* then, is a ghost that has haunted those who long to read anything to which Shakespeare set his hand.

It is possible at least to conjure up the likely subject of the missing play. Cardenio is a character in Part One of Cervantes' *Don Quixote.* Cervantes' masterpiece, first published in Spanish in 1605, was translated into English remarkably quickly by the Dublin-born Catholic Thomas Shelton and, after some delay, was printed in London in 1612. Fletcher and Shakespeare must have read this translation almost immediately and set to work. Surprisingly, to Cervantes' modern readers, they evidently did not choose to dramatize the mad knight and his squire, but instead seized upon the story of a young man, Cardenio, whose false friend attempts to steal away the woman he loves.

Cardenio and Luscinda grow up together and fall in love. Before they can secure their fathers' consent to their marriage, Cardenio is compelled to leave home to serve in the court of a powerful nobleman with whose son, Don Fernando, he becomes close friends. Don Fernando, who has seduced the humbly born Dorotea with promises of marriage, now regrets his promise and, to escape Dorotea, goes home with Cardenio. There the irresponsible nobleman promptly falls in love with Luscinda. Having sent his friend Cardenio away on a pretext, Fernando asks Luscinda's parents for their daughter's hand, and, despite her protests, her parents, who are delighted by the socially advantageous match, agree. Luscinda desperately writes to Cardenio, who rushes home, arriving only in time to witness the marriage ceremony from behind a curtain. When he sees his beloved give her hand to the treacherous Fernando, Cardenio rushes away in despair. What he does not see then is that at the decisive moment, Luscinda swoons. A note is discovered in her bodice, declaring her intention to stab herself, whereupon Fernando storms off in a rage. Luscinda flees to a convent.

Unaware of these developments, Cardenio turns his back on civilization and, like Lear on the heath, wanders as a lunatic in the Sierra Morena. Meanwhile, learning that Fernando's marriage to Luscinda had been voided, the seduced and abandoned Dorotea decides (like Julia in *Two Gentlemen of Verona*) to go in search of him. Like Julia and any number of other Shakespearean heroines, she dresses herself as a boy, but the expedient does not in Dorotea's case provide safety. Fighting off an attempted rape, she pushes her assailant off a cliff. Then she too flees to the Sierra Morena.

Six months pass. Fernando discovers Luscinda in the convent and abducts her. Cardenio and Dorotea meet in the mountains; Cardenio's hopes (and his sanity) revive when Dorotea tells him that in her note Luscinda had declared that she could not marry Fernando since she was already pledged to Cardenio. They arrive with others at an inn, where a priest discovers a story among the innkeeper's possessions and proceeds to read it to the company. The story involves the newlywed Anselmo, who asks his best friend, Lothario, to attempt to seduce his wife in order to test her virtue. The wife and the friend fall in love and deceive the husband, and the love tangle ends for all in despair and death. In the wake of this storytelling interlude, Fernando and the abducted Luscinda arrive by chance at the same inn. When Dorotea reproaches Fernando for his treatment of her, he is ashamed and agrees to marry her, allowing Cardenio to have Luscinda. There is general rejoicing.

This characteristic Renaissance tragicomedy of male friendship and sexual betrayal was the kind of story that had gripped Shakespeare's imagination throughout his career, from the early *Two Gentlemen of Verona* to the late *Two Noble Kinsmen*. If this was the story that Shakespeare and Fletcher plucked from *Don Quixote*, it is not one that was immediately ripe for the plucking. The English playwrights had to disentangle it from the complex mesh in which Cervantes had interwoven it with the adventures of his chivalry-obsessed knight. The *Cardenio* plot only emerges in fits and starts, in the interstices of Quixote's encounters after he has arrived in the Sierra Morena and has decided to go mad for the love of Dulcinea. Nothing is delivered in straightforward narrative sequence, and the two English collaborators must have laughed or groaned as they tried to tease a coherent narrative out of Cervantes' deliberately mad tangle. The only hard evidence from the period that they succeeded in doing so is the title of the lost play: not *Don Quixote* but *Cardenio*.

No more information about this play survives from the seventeenth century, but in 1728 the talented but unreliable playwright, entrepreneur, and editor Lewis Theobald published a play based on the story of Cardenio called *Double Falsehood, or The Distrest Lovers,* which he claimed to have "revised and adapted" from one "written originally by W. Shakespeare." Theobald's play had been successfully produced at Drury Lane on December 13, 1727, and was repeatedly performed thereafter.

Theobald claimed to own several manuscripts of an original play by Shakespeare, and remarked that some of his contemporaries thought the style was Fletcher's, not Shakespeare's. When he himself came to edit Shakespeare's plays he did not include either *Double Falsehood* or the play on which he claimed to have based it; he simply edited the plays of the First Folio, not adding either *Pericles* or *The Two Noble Kinsmen*, though he believed they were partly by Shakespeare. And what of the documents Theobald claims to have found that led back to whatever it was that Shakespeare and Fletcher had written? In 1770 a newspaper stated that "the original manuscript" was "treasured up in the Museum of Covent Garden Playhouse"; fire destroyed the theater, including its library, in 1808.

STEPHEN GREENBLATT

Henry the Eighth

Henry VIII (1613) is the Shakespearean play that brought down the house. During a performance on June 29, 1613, when it "had beene acted not passing 2 or 3 times before," "certain Chambers" (small cannons) were shot off. The thatch of the Globe Theater ignited, and the building burned down. Contemporary accounts disagree about whether the accident occurred early in the play, when King Henry participates in "a Masque at the Cardinal Wolsey's house" and the stage direction reads "*Chambers discharged*" (1.4.49), or, more improbably, when it "was almost ended." Apparently, there was only one injury—to a man who "was scalded with the fire by adventuring in to save a child which otherwise had been burnt." Another version claims that the injured man "had his breeches set on fire, that would perhaps have broyled him, if he had not by the benefit of a provident wit put it out with bottle Ale." (See the Henry Wotton letter, page 3272.)

Henry VIII does indeed show "a provident wit" and "save a child," though not as the two commentators suggest. In dramatizing important events and historical figures of Henry's reign, the play reveals that a divine providence watches over England, ensuring the birth of the future Queen Elizabeth. It achieves this effect by mixing dramatic genres: the national history play and the tragicomic romance. The text is a collaborative effort of Shakespeare and John Fletcher, with Shakespeare apparently composing most of the first half and Fletcher almost all of the second—hence, a slight majority of the entire work. It draws on narratives of recent English history—primarily Raphael Holinshed's *Chronicles of England, Scotland, and Ireland* (1587 ed.), Shakespeare's main source for his earlier English history plays as well. In drawing on these sources, the playwrights returned to a genre that Shakespeare had dominated during its heyday in the 1590s. By contrast, tragicomic romance, influenced by late Renaissance elite Italian theater, was very much in vogue in 1613, thanks to recent works by Shakespeare, Francis Beaumont, and Fletcher.

The Shakespearean history play focuses primarily on dynastic instabilities and civil conflicts of the late fourteenth and fifteenth centuries, and especially on the national implications of struggles among aristocratic factions. Shakespearean romance characteristically deploys a fictional plot in which long suffering and separation are transcended through the virtuous daughter, who redeems her father, and through magical interventions that produce providential outcomes. By initially calling the play *All Is True* (though *The Famous History of the Life of King Henry the Eighth* became the title no later than 1623), Shakespeare and Fletcher may have intended a contrast with *The Winter's Tale* (1610), whose title suggests a fictitious, unrealistic plot. Thus, *Henry VIII*, like romance, emphasizes providential patterns, but, like the English history play, of true events. The implication that past antagonisms are justified by present felicity may sound like servile flattery. Yet *Henry VIII* also challenges this celebratory interpretation: the play's interest lies in the tension between these two tendencies.

The plot combines close reliance on the sources with chronological compression and rearrangement. Its principal structural unit, first alluded to in the Prologue (lines 25–30), is *de casibus* tragedy, which recounts the fall of illustrious figures and resembles the morality play's allegorical focus on virtue and vice. The wheel of fortune is the dominant, cyclical image: what goes up must come down. Providential romance, however, is linear and unidirectional. Moreover, it ends in triumph rather than disaster. *Henry VIII* reconciles these apparently incompatible movements by making multiple local *de casibus* tragedies serve an overarching providential purpose that emerges only at the very end. Much of the play accordingly seems unrelated to a transcendently ordered pattern. It does not even concern the ups and downs of monarchs and their rivals, as in Shakespeare's earlier histories. Instead, we witness the successive falls of people close to Henry VIII—Buckingham, Queen Catharine, and Wolsey—and the near fall of Thomas Cranmer, Archbishop of Canterbury. Each is momentarily prominent before passing from the scene. These downfalls, like other events in the play, are rendered through stirring speeches and pageantry that recall the contemporary court theatrical form known as the "masque" (see 1.4). For centuries this emphasis on spectacle made the work a success on the stage; more recently, it has left its mark on film depictions of Henry's reign, even those not based on *Henry VIII*.

Initially, the repetitive *de casibus* structure doesn't seem to be going anywhere. Yet the linguistic patterning suggests a larger purpose. Beginning with the Prologue's invocation of tears and pity (lines 5–6), the play emphasizes suffering, life's burdens, acquiescence in defeat, forgiveness of one's foes, patience, religious serenity, and an understanding of the fall from power as a natural occurrence. Wolsey's undoing strikingly transforms conflict into reconciliation. Surrey correctly blames Wolsey for the execution of Buckingham, Surrey's father-in-law. Taunting the Cardinal at the moment of the churchman's ruin, he is rebuked:

> CHAMBERLAIN   O my lord,
> Press not a falling man too far. 'Tis virtue.
> His faults lie open to the laws; let them,
> Not you, correct him. My heart weeps to see him
> So little of his great self.
> SURREY   I forgive him.
>   (3.2.332–36)

Once the lords have left, Wolsey, in a departure from Holinshed, repents. Discovering his religious vocation only after his secular career collapses, the Cardinal experiences a moral shift that aligns him with his victims, Buckingham and Catharine. Asked how he feels, Wolsey replies:

>   Why, well.
> Never so truly happy, my good Cromwell:
> I know myself now, and I feel within me
> A peace above all earthly dignities,
> A still and quiet conscience.
>   (3.2.376–80)

Thus, like Buckingham's and Catharine's precipitous descents, but also like Adam and Eve's, Wolsey's fall is a fortunate one.

The Cardinal considers his former responsibilities "a burden / Too heavy for a man that hopes for heaven" (3.2.384–85). But not too heavy for a woman: the burden is delivered at the end of the play when Queen Anne gives birth to the future Queen Elizabeth. The critic Northrop Frye noted in the play "an invisible but omnipotent and ruthless providence who is ready to tear the whole social and religious structure of England to pieces in order to get Queen Elizabeth born." Buckingham has a serious claim to the crown, so he must be removed. Catharine's defect is that she is not the queen who will bear Elizabeth. Wolsey, who favors a diplomatically useful French alliance for Henry and hence opposes the King's marriage to Anne, unwittingly brings them together at a party he hosts (1.4). The individual tragedies are thus politically fortunate as well. Elizabeth's birth promises not only her own reign but also that of her successor, King James I, England's sovereign at the time of *Henry VIII*'s first performance. Archbishop Cranmer's concluding prophecy makes the link explicit:

> when
> The bird of wonder dies, the maiden phoenix,
> Her ashes new create another heir
> As great in admiration as herself. . . .
>   (5.4.39–42)

And the overt thematic statement is reinforced by the verbal and visual echo between "Her" and "heir," between Elizabeth and James.

This connection also retrospectively lays to rest Henry's persistent desire for a male heir. That absent royal son earlier justifies Henry's divorce of Catharine. "[M]ethought / I stood not in the smile of heaven," the King says:

> I weighed the danger which my realms stood in
> By this my issue's fail, and that gave to me
> Many a groaning throe.
>   (2.4.183–96)

Henry assumes the burden himself, experiencing "many a groaning throe" as if he could deliver the son that Catharine cannot. When Anne takes on the burden, Henry reveals his ongoing anxiety:

> KING   Is the Queen delivered?
> Say, "Ay, and of a boy."
> OLD LADY   Ay, ay, my liege,
> And of a lovely boy. The God of heaven
> Both now and ever bless her: 'tis a girl
> Promises boys hereafter.
>   (5.1.162–66)

The Old Lady's flattery reveals the truth: Elizabeth *is* "a girl / Promises boys hereafter." In having James succeed her, she fulfills the function of women in this patriarchal fantasy, delivering to Henry what Anne could not—a male heir. Catharine and Anne are also measured by this yardstick—and found wanting, overtly or covertly. *Henry VIII* differs from Shakespeare's English history plays of the 1590s in being unconcerned with war, domestic or foreign. Instead, its overarching issue is procreation. As a result, women are more prominent here than in any of the other history plays. Elizabeth, unlike her mother, succeeds, even though she never had any children. But this lack also enables her to absorb the virtues of the dying Catharine, who asks to be strewn "over / With maiden flowers" (4.2.168–69) and who thus anticipates "the maiden phoenix."

Although the providential logic that leads Elizabeth and then James to the throne often works against human intentions, Henry takes an increasingly active role in securing the destined end. The crucial moment is Cranmer's trial. Just before it begins, the stage direction reads *"Enter the King . . . at a window above"* (5.2.18). There, seeing but unseen, he is quasi-divine, as he himself suggests in angrily observing the council's humiliation of Cranmer: "Is this the honor they do one another? / 'Tis well there's one above 'em yet" (5.2.25–26). The "one above 'em" can be either God or the King, a distinction the scene blurs. Henry's intervention later in the scene to protect Cranmer preserves the man who went on to establish the doctrinal basis of the English Reformation. As suggested by Cranmer's prophetic promise about Elizabeth's reign—"God shall be truly known" (5.4.36)—this religious outcome is also part of the providential pattern: the playwrights' reorganization of chronology enables the birth of Elizabeth to coincide with the birth of English Protestantism. Yet except in Cranmer's conflict with the Catholic Gardiner, who accuses him of being "a sectary" and Cromwell of being "a favorer / Of this new sect" (5.2.104, 114–15), and in Wolsey's dismissive description of Anne as "a spleeny Lutheran" (3.2.99), little is made of the central event of Henry's reign: the break with Rome. The characters are judged not by their religion but by their integrity. Accordingly, the outstanding figures are an English Protestant, Cranmer, and a Spanish Catholic, Catharine. The notion of conscience, far more prominent here than in Holinshed's *Chronicles* and used by Protestants against the papacy to repudiate blind adherence to any human doctrinal authority, is deployed by the playwrights to judge Catholics and Protestants alike. This impartiality may be more Shakespeare's work than Fletcher's; in any case, the result is the characteristic national reconciliation of Shakespeare's history plays.

National reconciliation also transcends class antagonism, an issue largely absent from the sources. Like the other lords, Buckingham resents the usurpation of the nobility's traditional power by the proud "beggar" Wolsey, a "butcher's cur" (1.1.122, 120): the Cardinal's father was supposedly a butcher. Despite these humble origins, Wolsey adopts the aristocratic outlook of the position he has risen to. He opposes Henry's marriage to Anne, who is from the gentry rather than the nobility and who had been one of Catharine's ladies-in-waiting: "A knight's daughter / To be her mistress' mistress? The Queen's queen?" (3.2.94–95). But the play also posits a harmony between upper class and lower that can be disturbed only by self-serving intermediaries. Buckingham is betrayed to Wolsey by his surveyor, whom he fired for oppressing his tenants. Catharine gets Henry to repeal a tax levied by Wolsey that is so onerous it drives the poor to rebellion. Interclass unity is affirmed in the popular excitement about the baby Elizabeth, which the play refracts through the lower-class

---

Now, to let matters of State sleep, I will entertain you at the present with what hath happened this week at the banks side. The Kings Players had a new Play, called *All is true*, representing some principall pieces of the raign of *Henry* 8. which was set forth with many extraordinary circumstances of Pomp and Majesty, even to the matting of the stage; the Knights of the Order, with their Georges and Garter, the Guards with their embroidered Coats, and the like: sufficient in truth within a while to make greatness very familiar, if not ridiculous. Now, King *Henry* making a Masque at the Cardinal *Wolsey's* house, and certain Chambers being shot off at his entry, some of the paper, or other stuff wherewith one of them was stopped, did light on the thatch, where being thought at first but an idle smoak, and their eyes more attentive to the show, it kindled inwardly, and ran round like a train, consuming within less then an hour the whole house to the very grounds.

This was the fatal period of that vertuous fabrique, wherein yet nothing did perish, but wood and straw, and a few forsaken cloaks; only one man had his breeches set on fire, that would perhaps have broyled him, if he had not by the benefit of a provident wit put it out with bottle Ale. The rest when we meet: till when, I protest every minute is the siege of Troy. Gods dear blessings till then and ever be with you.

Your poor Uncle and faithful servant.

HENRY WOTTON.

One of several accounts of the burning of the Globe Theater. From a letter of July 2, 1613, in *Letters of Sir Henry Wotton to Sir Edmund Bacon* (1661).

Cardinal Wolsey is forced to "render up the great seal" to Norfolk and Suffolk (3.2.229). From George Cavendish, *The Life and Death of Cardinal Wolsey* (1557).

prose of the exasperated Porter (5.3). Similarly, at Anne's earlier coronation, one of the gentlemen, who act as a chorus absent from the sources, remarks,

> The citizens,
> I am sure, have shown at full their royal minds—
> As, let 'em have their rights, they are ever forward—
>   (4.1.7–9)

And Cranmer renders hereditary class hierarchy a thing of the past. "[T]hose about" Elizabeth "[f]rom her shall read the perfect ways of honor, / And by those claim their greatness, not by blood" (5.4.36–38).

Yet this patterning is countered in at least two ways. The first is stylistic. The play begins with this exchange:

> BUCKINGHAM   Good morrow and well met. How have ye done
>   Since last we saw in France?
> NORFOLK   I thank your grace,
>   Healthful, and ever since a fresh admirer
>   Of what I saw there.
> BUCKINGHAM   An untimely ague
>   Stayed me a prisoner in my chamber when
>   Those suns of glory, those two lights of men,
>   Met in the vale of Andres.
>   (1.1.1–7)

Like Shakespeare's early English history plays—especially *3 Henry VI* (1591–92), *Richard III* (1592), and *King John* (1595)—*Henry VIII* consists almost entirely of blank verse. These opening lines are no exception. But the similarity is deceptive. In the early plays, the verse tends to be end-stopped: the individual line consists of a complete phrase, clause, or sentence. Moreover, the ten-syllable norm of iambic pentameter is routinely respected. And speeches usually begin at the beginning of a line and end at the end—of the same line or another. None of this is true of *Henry VIII*, as the passage above demonstrates. Most of the lines employ enjambment: the sense runs over from one line to the next; syntax and versification are disconnected. Further, the third and fourth lines each have an extra, eleventh syllable, thus producing what is traditionally called a feminine ending (appropriately prominent in Cranmer's praise of Elizabeth). Finally, the speeches begin or end in the middle of a line. This kind of blank verse, characteristic of both Fletcher's and Shakespeare's sections of the work (and of Shakespeare's last plays more generally) cuts against *Henry VIII*'s ceremonial dimension, introducing instead an informal, conversational, naturalistic, almost prosy feel.

Second, as recent productions have emphasized, the play offers a critical account of Henry's reign. In particular, *Henry VIII* implicitly suggests the costs of the Elizabethan Protestant succession. Even though only Buckingham is executed, *Henry VIII* makes that execution resonate. "Divorce" refers not only to Henry's legal repudiation of Catharine: condemned to death, Buckingham speaks of "the long divorce of steel [that] falls on me" (2.1.76). The innocent and virtuous Catharine is given a strength of character, impressiveness, and spiritual coronation absent both from Holinshed's portrayal and from her successor, Anne. Yet Henry's "princely commendations" to the dying Catharine are "like a pardon after execution" (4.2.118, 121). As Catharine is succeeded by Anne, so Wolsey is replaced by Sir Thomas More, Cromwell, and Cranmer (3.2.393–459). All four of these successors were later executed, as the audience knew. Wolsey hopes that More will "do justice / For truth's sake and his conscience" (3.2.396–97)—principles that later cost the Catholic More his life. Anne actually predicts her own fate in lamenting Catharine's mistreatment:

> Much better
> She ne'er had known pomp; though't be temporal,
> Yet if that quarrel and fortune do divorce
> It from the bearer, 'tis a sufferance panging
> As soul and body's severing.
>
> (2.3.12–16)

Wolsey advises Cromwell:

> Be just, and fear not.
> Let all the ends thou aim'st at be thy country's,
> Thy God's, and truth's. Then if thou fall'st, O Cromwell,
> Thou fall'st a blessèd martyr.
>
> (3.2.446–49)

Gardiner's anti-Protestant attacks on Cranmer and Cromwell foreshadow his later success in sending both men to their deaths. Even the Porter's admonishment of noisy "rascals" (5.3.2) prior to Elizabeth's christening evokes execution: "Belong to th' gallows, and be hanged" (5.3.5).

Ambivalence extends as well to the centrally providential characters. Men extol the "[b]eauty and honor" of that "angel" Anne Boleyn (2.3.76, 4.1.44). Skepticism about her "honor" is instead voiced by a woman. When Anne denies any desire for political advancement, the Old Lady calls this position "hypocrisy," ridicules Anne's pliant "conscience," and finds her claim "strange" (2.3.26, 32, 36). Yet Anne does become queen, without an explanation of her supposed change of heart but with a suggestive pun on "quean" (whore) characteristic of their sexualized exchange and of Anne's earlier banter (1.4.45–48). The scene with the Old Lady, apparently invented by Shakespeare, thus sullies Anne before she becomes a ceremonial figure reduced to bearing a royal child. Moreover, Elizabeth's conception before Henry and Anne's marriage may be alluded to in the "[g]reat-bellied women" at Anne's coronation and the "fry of fornication" at Elizabeth's christening (4.1.76, 5.3.33).

Although Henry himself is repeatedly praised by his victims (2.1.86–94, 3.2.380–92, 4.2.160–64), his increasing attention to government raises questions about his earlier behavior. The play's Henry, more troubling than Holinshed's, seems detached, culpably unaware or dishonestly disavowing knowledge of foreign affairs, taxation, and treason. The self-destructive zigzags in foreign policy—alliance with France, alliance with

Spain, attempted alliance with France—are Wolsey's, not his: the buck stops elsewhere. Moreover, his interventions are not reassuring. His charges against Wolsey ignore major issues to focus on personal, peripheral concerns. Even his protection of Cranmer is necessary only because Henry allows his biased council to proceed in the first place. Indeed, the play suggests that the law serves the man with power, whether Wolsey or the King.

Explicit skepticism about Henry is produced by his divorce. He is "afflicted" by a "wounded conscience," by "conscience, conscience," by "my conscience" (2.2.61, 73, 141; 2.4.167, 179, 200). But earlier, at Wolsey's banquet, he is attracted to Anne Boleyn: "The fairest hand I ever touched! O Beauty, / Till now I never knew thee" (1.4.75–76). This meeting is the play's invention. A disabused view follows:

Henry VIII, age fifty-two, in the posthumous portrait engraved by Cornelis Metsys in 1548. Gardiner's unsuccessful attack on Cranmer probably occurred around this time.

CHAMBERLAIN It
seems the marriage with his brother's wife
    Has crept too near his conscience.
SUFFOLK   No, his conscience
    Has crept too near another lady.

                                        (2.2.15–17)

Even apologists for Henry's behavior suspect his motives. Overwhelmed by the sight of Anne, the Second Gentleman remarks, "I cannot blame his conscience" (4.1.47). Does such criticism undermine the providential pattern or render the transcendence of such obstacles all the more miraculous? Like many Shakespearean plays, *Henry VIII* opposes means and ends, showing and telling, dramatized plot and asserted conclusion, pity and jubilation. Is there a larger shape to human destiny, or is there nothing more than the unrelated events and random (in)justice that are surely part of the experience of the play?

The critique of Henry may also have targeted James. At the very least, there are suggestive parallels between the two reigns. The satire on French fashion (1.3) ridicules behavior at James's court in which the King participated. Like Henry, James neglected affairs of state, to the dismay of his subjects. His divine-right view of monarchy at times resulted in subordination of law to royal desire. His court was riven by factionalism—not least the conflict between the Queen and the male royal favorite, whose shoulder James tended to lean on, just as Henry does on Wolsey's (1.2.0 SD). The surprising sympathy for the Catholic Catharine may nod toward James's Queen Anne, suspected of secret Catholicism. Cranmer's praise of Elizabeth also compliments James's daughter Elizabeth, who married in February 1613 and who, like Queen Elizabeth, was compared to the phoenix. By contrast, following the death of many of the courtiers with whom James came to power, the death in late 1612 of the popular Henry Stuart, James's oldest son and heir to the throne, might have cast a shadow on a celebratory account of recent English royal history, while tilting the presentation from male to female royal lineage. More generally, these parallels are accentuated by the repetition of names: King Henry and James's son Henry, Queen Elizabeth and James's daughter Elizabeth, Queen Anne (Boleyn) and James's Queen Anne.

Yet a crucial contemporary parallel lies elsewhere. In urging punishment of Cranmer's Protestantism, Gardiner recounts the dangers of laxity:

> Commotions, uproars, with a general taint
> Of the whole state, as of late days our neighbors,
> The upper Germany, can dearly witness. . . .
>
> (5.2.62–64)

The reference is to the Peasants' War in Germany (1524–26), in which the aristocracy massacred perhaps a hundred thousand peasants. At home, the court fears "loud rebellion" and the unruly "rabble" (1.2.29, 5.3.64): the Midland grain riots were as recent as 1607. The rowdies at Elizabeth's christening, men and women alike, are "[y]our faithful friends o'th' suburbs" (5.3.65), the location of outdoor theaters such as the Globe. The Porter remarks, "These are the youths that thunder at a playhouse and fight for bitten apples, that no audience but the Tribulation of Tower Hill or the Limbs of Limehouse, their dear brothers, are able to endure" (5.3.54–57). The comparison is between the disorderly apprentices who come to the theater and the rough crowds who attend public executions or frequent the dockyards. A christening recalls an execution; an ostensibly orthodox play in a suburban theater emphasizes the criminal character of suburb and audience alike. Such popular revelry can be considered a complement to royal extravagance, a challenge to monarchical authority, or both.

Thus, the interaction between *Henry VIII* and its audience may undermine orthodoxy. Something of the sort was perhaps felt in earlier centuries, when performances of the play at times ended with Anne's coronation or Catharine's vision, thus eliminating both Cranmer's trial and Elizabeth's birth. But in the full play, interaction with the audience is self-reflexive. While realistically dramatizating events, the play simultaneously indicates that it is merely a play by calling attention to the venue of performance—the "suburbs," the "playhouse," the "audience." Yet this self-referentiality is the very opposite of aesthetic detachment: it reinforces the parallels between Henry's and James's courts. Furthermore, the Globe, the playhouse referred to in this scene, is not the only commercial theater that acquires resonance in *Henry VIII*. By 1613, Shakespeare's acting company, the King's Men, divided its time—in the summer working at the Globe; in the winter at Blackfriars, an elite indoor theater in London itself rather than the suburbs. When Henry decides upon a trial to determine whether his marriage to Catharine should be annulled, he specifies the location:

> The most convenient place that I can think of
> For such receipt of learning is Blackfriars. . . .
>
> (2.2.136–37)

Consequently, the audience of the play sits in judgment exactly where the decision was rendered almost a century earlier. And when Henry expropriates Wolsey's residence at York Place, he renames it Whitehall (4.1.94–99), the site, in James's reign, of the court masques that *Henry VIII* emulates.

By placing Blackfriars' affluent audience in a position to evaluate the conduct of a king, did *Henry VIII* undermine aristocratic and royal authority? Perhaps less than when the play was performed in the outdoor theater. According to Sir Henry Wotton, a spectator the day the Globe burned down, the work presented "some principall pieces of the raign of *Henry* 8 which was set forth with many extraordinary circumstances of Pomp and Majesty . . . sufficient in truth within a while to make greatness very familiar, if not ridiculous." Rather than provoking awe, the play's pageantry reduced the mystique of monarchy, turning the popular audience into moral arbiters of royal power. James's favorite, the Duke of Buckingham, may have felt as much when, in 1628, he commissioned a performance of *Henry VIII*, only to walk out after his predecessor's beheading. In 1649, a Parliament driven by popular pressure emulated the play by staging an execution of its own. This time, however, the victim was James I's own son: the man on the scaffold was the King.

WALTER COHEN

SELECTED BIBLIOGRAPHY

Aaron, Melissa D. *Global Economics: A History of the Theater Business, the Chamberlain's/King's Men, and Their Plays, 1599–1642.* Newark: U of Delaware P, 2005. 107–16. Connects the play to the court masque and other royal pageantry, linking theatrical spaces to political ones.

Anderson, Judith H. *Biographical Truth: The Representation of Historical Persons in Tudor-Stuart Writing.* New Haven, CT: Yale UP, 1984. 124–54. Explores the problem of truth and fiction in the play, with particular attention to source material; argues for ambiguity in the portrayal of Henry and especially Wolsey.

Carney, Jo Eldridge. "Queenship in Shakespeare's *Henry VIII*: The Issue of Issue." *Political Rhetoric, Power, and Renaissance Women.* Ed. Carole Levin and Patricia A. Sullivan. Albany: State U of New York P, 1995. 189–202. Argues that the play turns on the three queens—Catharine, Anne, and Elizabeth—but as potential bearers of male heirs.

Cobb, Christopher J. *The Staging of Romance in Late Shakespeare: Text and Theatrical Technique.* Newark: U of Delaware P, 2007. 224–32. Describes *Henry VIII* as more tragic than other Shakespearean romances, since virtue is recognized but unrewarded in the political world; argues that the play's individual spectacles are theatrically engaging but not linked together into a dramatic whole.

Dillon, Janette. *Shakespeare and the Staging of English History.* Oxford: Oxford UP, 2012. Examines the power of the "state," or throne, whether occupied by the king or not, as an ambivalent symbol of royal authority, surveillance, or neglect.

Frye, Susan. "Queens and the Structure of History in *Henry VIII*." *A Companion to Shakespeare's Works.* Vol. 4: *Poems, Problem Comedies, Late Plays.* Ed. Richard Dutton and Jean E. Howard. Malden, MA: Blackwell, 2003. 427–44. Identifies parallels between the courts of Henry VIII and James I, centered on queens struggling with a succession of male favorites.

Healy, Thomas. "History and Judgement in *Henry VIII*." *Shakespeare's Late Plays: New Readings.* Ed. Jennifer Richards and James Knowles. Edinburgh: Edinburgh UP, 1999. 158–75. Argues that the play is structured to encourage the audience to respond with judgment rather than emotion to the conflicting possible interpretations of history.

Hodgdon, Barbara. *The End Crowns All: Closure and Contradiction in Shakespeare's History.* Princeton, NJ: Princeton UP, 1991. 212–34. Focuses on women, especially Elizabeth, uniting masquelike and anti-masquelike (or carnivalesque) elements, with attention to performance history—notably, the elimination of the last act in earlier centuries.

McMullan, Gordon, ed. *King Henry VIII (All Is True).* Arden. London: Bloomsbury, 2000. An outstanding scholarly edition with a book-length critical introduction.

Shirley, Frances A., ed. *"King John" and "Henry VIII": Critical Essays.* New York: Garland, 1988. Offers twelve essays on the play from nineteenth- and twentieth-century theatrical and literary criticism.

FILMS

Henry VIII. 1979. Dir. Kevin Billington. 166 min. UK. Highly praised BBC-TV production that minimizes the pomp and ceremony typically found in plays or films on Henry and his age in favor of the contrast between public political life and inwardness and morality, with a particular focus on Catharine (Claire Bloom).

The following films are based on the life of Henry VIII, not on Shakespeare's and Fletcher's play.

The Private Life of Henry VIII. 1933. Dir. Alexander Korda. UK. 97 min. Starring Charles Laughton.
A Man for All Seasons. 1966. Dir. Fred Zinnemann. UK. 120 min. Based on Robert Bolt's play about Sir Thomas More's religious conflict over Henry's decision to divorce Catherine and wed Anne Boleyn. With Paul Scofield as More.
Anne of the Thousand Days. 1969. Dir. Charles Jarrott. UK. 145 min. Explores Anne Boleyn's rise and fall. With Genevieve Bujold as Anne and Richard Burton as Henry.

TEXTUAL INTRODUCTION

There is only one source for the text of *Henry VIII*, that of the First Folio of 1623. With the title *The Famous History of the Life of King Henry the Eighth*, the play concludes the series of English histories that the Folio orders according to the chronology of the reigns depicted. It seems, though, from a contemporary eyewitness account of the burning down of the Globe Theater during a June 1613 performance of the play, that when originally performed it was called *All Is True*—something of an ambiguous title, to say the least, and one that tends to underline the gap between this play and the next-most-recent history, *Henry V*, which had first been performed nearly a decade and a half earlier. The First Folio may group *Henry VIII* with the other "history" plays, but the play arguably has a lot more in common with Shakespeare's early Jacobean output than with his Elizabethan histories.

    Henry VIII originates—as do so many of Shakespeare's plays—in multiple prior narratives, the most important one being Holinshed's *Chronicles of England, Scotland, and Ireland*, in almost every case the primary source for Shakespeare's English history plays. *Henry VIII* also draws on a chronicle that postdates Shakespeare's earlier history plays, John Speed's 1610 *Theatre of the Empire of Great Britain*, though its influence appears only in the scenes of the play usually attributed to John Fletcher, with whom Shakespeare appears to have collaborated on three plays—the missing *Cardenio*, *Henry VIII*, and *The Two Noble Kinsmen*—in the last eighteen months or so of his writing life. There is no mention of Fletcher in the First Folio, just as there is no mention, say, of Thomas Middleton's share in *Timon of Athens*; but collaboration was the norm in theatrical writing of this period—something like two-thirds of early modern English plays seem to have been collaboratively written—and it is now widely acknowledged that *Henry VIII* was jointly written by Shakespeare and Fletcher, with the latter in due course becoming Shakespeare's successor as "house playwright" for the King's Men.

    How do we know, in the absence of external evidence (an attribution in print or in the Stationers' Register, say), who wrote a given play? When this question was first asked about *Henry VIII* in the mid-nineteenth century, the answer was intuition—notably, that of the poet Tennyson, who felt that he could "hear" the "voice" of Fletcher in certain scenes. Subsequent, more technical analysis—manual and digital counts of linguistic features considered characteristic of each playwright—

broadly confirms Tennyson's intuition (see, e.g., Hope 1994; see also Vickers 2002, pp. 44–136, for a summary of attributional methods, and pp. 333–432 for analysis of the authorship of *Henry VIII*); such methods will no doubt be refined over the next while as enhanced digital techniques for the assessment of texts are developed. Despite the continuing reluctance of some scholars to acknowledge Shakespearean collaboration, it is clear that Shakespeare, though he wrote the majority of his plays without a collaborator, also in certain circumstances worked with fellow playwrights; *Henry VIII* is one of the products of such joint effort.

How did Shakespeare and Fletcher's rough draft come to appear as a printed text ten years after it was first performed? It seems to have been quite meticulously copied by one anonymous scribe; the scribal copy was set into type by two compositors, B and I, and then proofread with care. Throughout the writing and printing processes, there were inevitably many opportunities for amendments, unintentional misreadings, omissions, or misprints, yet the Folio text of *Henry VIII* is of good quality: clear act and scene divisions, duly marked entrances and exits, only unimportant variations in the forms of speech prefixes, carefully detailed stage directions, and relatively few errors. For an analysis of the typesetting and printing of the play, see McMullan's introduction (2000, pp. 155–58). The remarkably numerous and substantial stage directions of the original text have been lightly adapted in places so as to clarify the likely action for readers, for example, to point to a change of addressee (see, e.g., 1.2.177 SD, when the King answers Catharine and then turns to the Surveyor) or to indicate an aside (Catharine's personal comment, while in conversation with Wolsey and Campeius, revealing her lucidity, 3.1.66—see Digital Edition TC 1). Some unusually short lines have been reshaped into pentameters (see 1.3.63 and Digital Edition TC 3); some have not, depending on local circumstances. The substantial stage direction providing the order of the coronation has been rearranged as a list for the sake of clarity (see 4.1.36 SD). Some speech prefixes have been harmonized, as in the case of the character Griffith: the present edition assumes that the *"gentleman usher"* (2.4) and the *"gentleman"* (3.1) are the same character as Griffith (see Digital Edition TC 7). Finally, in the first scene of act 2 and again of act 4, lines of dialogue between two (or three) anonymous gentlemen that lack speech prefixes have been respectively distributed to *"First Gentleman,"* *"Second Gentleman,"* and *"Third Gentleman."*

PASCALE DROUET

TEXTUAL BIBLIOGRAPHY

Hope, Jonathan. *The Authorship of Shakespeare Plays: A Socio-linguistic Study.* Cambridge: Cambridge UP, 1994.
Vickers, Brian. *Shakespeare, Co-Author: A Historical Study of Five Collaborative Plays.* Oxford: Oxford UP, 2002.

PERFORMANCE NOTE

The relative scarcity of *Henry VIII* productions likely owes something to the piece's emphasis on pageantry over plot. The prominent spectacles of Catharine's trial, Anne's coronation, and Elizabeth's savior-like nativity stand out amid a profusion of set speeches, dances, and masques, and the resultant demand for supernumeraries can stretch theater companies to extremes (Henry Beerbohm-Tree famously deployed 142 actors in his production). Yet companies face even greater staging challenges, such as finding unity in a conspicuously episodic narrative and negotiating the play's lack of a clear, prominent leading role. Some productions address these challenges by stressing the parallelism of the downfalls (and subsequent redemptive experiences) of Buckingham, Catharine, and Wolsey, potentially extending the cycle by hinting that Anne's fall, too, is coming. Others reshape the play as a star vehicle for Catharine or Wolsey. Still others address the disjunction of episodes by amplifying Henry's role, either portraying him as the bluff gourmandizer and skirt-chaser with which most audiences are acquainted, or granting him psychological complexity that the play does not, as if he were oppressed not only by the lack of an heir but also by presentiments of the bloody acts his future will bring.

Productions must also determine whether to share the optimism of Cranmer's prophecy or to allude bleakly to the fates awaiting Cromwell, More, and Anne Boleyn. Regardless of the desired tone, though, each must decide whether Buckingham is an actual traitor or a sacrificial lamb for Wolsey; whether Anne is flirtatious or innocent; whether Catharine is patient in her suffering or defiant; and whether Wolsey's final retreat to spirituality is sincere or an attempt to deceive God himself. Henry, moreover, might appear reluctant to move against Catharine and the supposed traitors, or he can enjoy their falls from grace. Other considerations in performance include the staging of Catharine's dream vision; managing the rhythms of abundant lines with feminine endings (especially in Buckingham's and Catharine's speeches); the treatment of foreign Catholics in the court; and the assignation of the Prologue and Epilogue.

Brett Gamboa

HENRY VIII

The Famous History of the Life of King Henry the Eighth

[THE PERSONS OF THE PLAY

In order of appearance:

PROLOGUE
Duke of NORFOLK
Duke of BUCKINGHAM
Lord ABERGAVENNY, son-in-law to the Duke of Buckingham
Cardinal WOLSEY
SECRETARY to Cardinal Wolsey
BRANDON
SERGEANT-at-Arms
KING Henry the Eighth
Sir Thomas LOVELL
CATHARINE of Aragon, Queen of England, later Princess Dowager
Duke of SUFFOLK, High Steward
SURVEYOR to the Duke of Buckingham
Lord CHAMBERLAIN
Lord SANDYS
ANNE Boleyn, maid of honor to Catharine, later Queen of England
Sir Henry GUILDFORD
SERVANT in Wolsey's household
FIRST GENTLEMAN
SECOND GENTLEMAN
Sir Nicholas VAUX
Cardinal CAMPEIUS, papal legate
GARDINER, secretary to the King, later Bishop of Winchester
OLD LADY, companion to Anne Boleyn
SCRIBE to the court
Archbishop of Canterbury
Bishop of LINCOLN
Bishop of Ely
Bishop of Rochester
Bishop of St. Asaph
GRIFFITH, Gentleman Usher to Catharine
CRIER to the court
WOMAN, attendant on Catharine, a singer
Earl of SURREY, son-in-law to the Duke of Buckingham
Thomas CROMWELL, secretary to Cardinal Wolsey, later Secretary to the Privy
Council
Sir Thomas More, Lord CHANCELLOR
Lord Mayor of London
GARTER King-at-Arms
Marquess of Dorset
Marchioness Dorset, godmother to the baby Elizabeth

Barons of the Cinque Ports
Bishop of London
Duchess of Norfolk
THIRD GENTLEMAN
PATIENCE, attendant on Catharine
Six Spirits in Catharine's vision
MESSENGER of Catharine's household at Kimbolton
Lord CAPUTIUS, ambassador from the Holy Roman Emperor
PAGE to Gardiner
Sir Anthony DENNY
Thomas CRANMER, Archbishop of Canterbury
KEEPER of the Council Chamber door
Doctor BUTTS, physician to the King
PORTER
Porter's MAN
ONE of the crowd
EPILOGUE
Musicians, Secretaries, Guards, Masquers, Vergers, Scribes, Gentlemen, Priests,
Gentleman Usher, Noblemen, Attendants to Queen Catharine, Judges, Choris-
ters, Ladies, Grooms, Aldermen, Tipstaves, Halberds, Common People]

Prologue

[*Enter*] PROLOGUE.

PROLOGUE   I come no more to make you laugh. Things now
    That bear a weighty and a serious brow,
    Sad, high and working,° full of state° and woe,   *full of pathos / grandeur*
    Such noble scenes as draw the eye to flow,
5   We now present. Those that can pity here
    May—if they think it well—let fall a tear:
    The subject will deserve it. Such as give
    Their money out of hope they may believe
    May here find truth too. Those that come to see
10   Only a show or two and so agree
    The play may pass, if they be still and willing
    I'll undertake may see away their shilling
    Richly in two short hours.[1] Only they
    That come to hear a merry, bawdy play,
15   A noise of targets,° or to see a fellow   *shields*
    In a long motley coat guarded[2] with yellow,
    Will be deceived. For, gentle hearers, know
    To rank our chosen truth with such a show
    As fool and fight is, beside forfeiting
20   Our own brains and the opinion that we bring
    To make that only true we now intend,[3]
    Will leave us never an understanding[4] friend.
    Therefore, for goodness' sake, and as you are known

Prologue

1. *Those . . . hours:* If those who come only for a
spectacle ("show") and approve the play on those
terms are quiet and willing, I promise they'll get their
shilling's worth (the price of more expensive, genteel
seating) in two hours (plays ran two to three hours).
2. Ornamented on its border. The fool's "motley," or
patchwork, coat may refer to other plays about Henry's
life, including Samuel Rowley's *When You See Me,
You Know Me* (1605), which featured Henry's fool,

Will Summers, and was reprinted and perhaps
revived in 1613.
3. *beside . . . intend:* in addition to acting foolishly
(or wasting our mental labor) and our intention of
(or our reputation for) presenting an entirely truthful
play.
4. Punning reference to the lower-class groundlings,
who are literally "understanding" in the sense of
"standing under" the raised stage.

The first and happiest hearers° of the town,   *finest audience*
25 Be sad° as we would make ye. Think ye see   *grave*
The very persons of our noble story
As they were living; think you see them great°   *of high rank*
And followed with the general throng and sweat
Of thousand friends; then, in a moment, see
30 How soon this mightiness meets misery;
And if you can be merry then, I'll say
A man may weep upon his wedding day.   [*Exit.*]

1.1

Enter the Duke of NORFOLK *at one door. At the other,*
the Duke of BUCKINGHAM *and the Lord* ABERGAVENNY.

BUCKINGHAM Good morrow and well met. How have ye done
 Since last we saw° in France?   *met*
NORFOLK   I thank your grace,
 Healthful, and ever since a fresh° admirer   *an eager*
 Of what I saw there.[1]
BUCKINGHAM   An untimely ague
5 Stayed me a prisoner in my chamber[2] when
 Those suns of glory, those two lights of men,
 Met in the vale of Andres.
NORFOLK   Twixt Guînes and Ardres[3]
 I was then present, saw them salute on horseback,
 Beheld them when they lighted,° how they clung   *got off*
10 In their embracement as° they grew together—   *as if*
 Which had they,° what four throned ones could have weighed[4] *if they had*
 Such a compounded one?
BUCKINGHAM   All the whole time
 I was my chamber's prisoner.
NORFOLK   Then you lost
 The view of earthly glory. Men might say
15 Till this time pomp was single, but now married
 To one above itself.[5] Each following day
 Became the next day's master, till the last
 Made former wonders its.[6] Today the French,
 All clinquant,° all in gold, like heathen gods,   *glittering*
20 Shone down° the English; and tomorrow they   *outshone*
 Made Britain India.[7] Every man that stood
 Showed like a mine. Their dwarfish pages were
 As cherubim, all gilt.[8] The *mesdames,*° too,   *ladies*
 Not used to toil, did almost sweat to bear
25 The pride° upon them, that° their very labor *fancy adornment / so that*
 Was to them as a painting.[9] Now this masque
 Was cried° incomparable; and th'ensuing night   *called*

1.1. Location: The court at London.
1. The reference is to the rendezvous of Henry VIII and Francis I of France near Calais in June 1520, at the Field of the Cloth of Gold, named for the sumptuous displays by the two kings.
2. Actually, Buckingham (but not Norfolk) was present, if reluctantly (because of the expense), at the Field of the Cloth of Gold. The fictional "ague," or fever, allows the dramatist to show Buckingham responding to Norfolk's detailed description.
3. Guînes belonged to England, Ardres to France.
4. Been as heavy as.

5. *Till . . . itself:* The pomp of each king now joins ("marries") that of the other, making a greater pomp than either one alone could display.
6. *Each . . . its:* Each day learned wonders from the previous one, making the last day the most wonderful of all. *master:* standard.
7. *they . . . India:* the English made Britain look as (fabulously) rich as India or the West Indies.
8. Gold-plated statues of cherubim, often found in churches.
9. Made them rosy, as if with makeup.

Made it a fool and beggar. The two kings,
Equal in luster, were now best, now worst,
30 As presence did present them:[1] him in eye,
Still him in praise,[2] and being present both,
'Twas said they saw but one, and no discerner
Durst wag his tongue in censure.[3] When these suns—
For so they phrase 'em—by their heralds challenged
35 The noble spirits to arms, they did perform
Beyond thought's compass, that former fabulous story
Being now seen possible enough, got credit,
That *Bevis* was believed.[4]

BUCKINGHAM   Oh, you go far!°   *go too far*
NORFOLK   As I belong to worship° and affect   *the aristocracy*
40 In honor, honesty,[5] the tract of everything
Would by a good discourser lose some life
Which action's self was tongue to.[6] All was royal:
To the disposing° of it naught rebelled;   *arrangement*
Order gave each thing view; the office did
Distinctly his full function.[7]
45 BUCKINGHAM   Who did guide—
I mean, who set the body and the limbs
Of this great sport° together, as you guess?   *show*
NORFOLK   One, certes, that promises no element[8]
In such a business.
BUCKINGHAM   I pray you who, my lord?
50 NORFOLK   All this was ordered by the good discretion
Of the right reverend Cardinal of York.°   *(Wolsey)*
BUCKINGHAM   The devil speed° him: no man's pie is freed   *ruin*
From his ambitious finger! What had he
To do in these fierce° vanities? I wonder   *excessive; military*
55 That such a keech[9] can, with his very bulk,
Take up the rays o'th' beneficial sun°   *(Henry)*
And keep it from the earth.
NORFOLK   Surely, sir,
There's in him stuff that puts° him to these ends.   *spurs*
For being not propped by ancestry, whose grace
60 Chalks successors their way,[1] nor called upon
For high feats done to th' crown, neither allied
To eminent assistants,° but spider-like,   *ministers of state*
Out of his self-drawing° web, 'a° gives us note   *spun from himself / he*
The force of his own merit makes his way—
65 A gift that heaven gives for him, which buys
A place next to the King.
ABERGAVENNY   I cannot tell
What heaven hath given him; let some graver eye

1. According to who was present.
2. *him . . . praise:* to the king on display at the time always went all the acclaim.
3. *no . . . censure:* no one watching dared say one outshone the other.
4. *they did . . . believed:* their performance was such that stories formerly deemed mere fables, now looking possible, gained plausibility. Even *Sir Bevis of Hampton* (Southampton), a popular medieval romance, was believed.
5. *and . . . honesty:* and honorably love truth.

6. *the tract . . . to:* the events surpass their telling.
7. *Order . . . function:* Careful organization made everything appropriately visible (or arranged according to rank). Each responsible person properly fulfilled his role.
8. One, without doubt, who seems out of place.
9. A hunk of fat from a slaughtered animal. Wolsey was said to be a butcher's son.
1. *ancestry . . . way:* noble ancestors, whose honorable qualities mark the way for future generations.

Pierce into that. But I can see his pride
Peep through each part of him. Whence has he that?°   *(such pride)*
70 If not from hell, the devil is a niggard°   *cheapskate*
Or has given all before,° and he° begins   *already / (Wolsey)*
A new hell in himself.

BUCKINGHAM   Why the devil,
Upon this French going out,° took he upon him,   *journey*
Without the privity° o'th' King, t'appoint   *private sanction*
75 Who should attend on him? He makes up the file°   *roll*
Of all the gentry, for the most part such
To whom as great a charge as little honor
He meant to lay upon;[2] and his own letter,
The honorable Board of Council out,
Must fetch him in he papers.[3]

80 ABERGAVENNY   I do know
Kinsmen of mine, three at the least, that have
By this so sickened° their estates that never   *wasted*
They shall abound as formerly.

BUCKINGHAM   Oh, many
Have broke their backs with laying manors on 'em[4]
85 For this great journey. What did this vanity
But minister communication of
A most poor issue?[5]

NORFOLK   Grievingly, I think
The peace between the French and us not values°   *does not merit*
The cost that did conclude it.

BUCKINGHAM   Every man,
90 After the hideous storm that followed, was
A thing inspired and, not consulting,° broke   *without conferring*
Into a general° prophecy: that this tempest,   *collective*
Dashing the garment of this peace, aboded°   *foreshadowed*
The sudden breach on't.°   *of it*

NORFOLK   Which is budded out,°   *has occurred*
95 For France hath flawed° the league and hath attached°   *betrayed / seized*
Our merchants' goods at Bordeaux.

ABERGAVENNY   Is it therefore°   *on this account*
Th'ambassador is silenced?[6]

NORFOLK   Marry is't.°   *Of course it is*

ABERGAVENNY   A proper title of a° peace, and purchased   *A fine thing to call*
At a superfluous rate.°   *too high a cost*

BUCKINGHAM   Why, all this business
Our reverend cardinal carried.°   *oversaw*

100 NORFOLK   Like it° your grace,   *May it please*
The state takes notice of the private difference°   *dispute*
Betwixt you and the Cardinal. I advise you—
And take it from a heart that wishes towards you
Honor and plenteous safety—that you read°   *assess*

2. *To whom . . . upon:* (Wolsey gave) places of little honor to the noblemen on whom he laid the greatest expense for the display.
3. *and . . . papers:* and with the Privy Council [the King's top advisors] ignored ("out"), his own summons ("letter") forces every person whom he lists ("papers") to comply.
4. *many . . . 'em:* many have sold off their estates— and thus bankrupted themselves—to pay for a costly wardrobe; with a pun on "manners."
5. *What . . . issue:* What did such wasteful expense do but bankrupt their own children ("poor issue"); or encourage talk for a trivial outcome ("poor issue")?
6. The French ambassador in England was forced by the English to remain in his home.

105 The Cardinal's malice and his potency
Together; to consider further that
What his high hatred would effect wants° not   *lacks*
A minister° in his power. You know his nature,   *An agent*
That he's revengeful, and I know his sword
110 Hath a sharp edge: it's long, and't may be said
It reaches far, and where 'twill not extend,
Thither he darts it. Bosom up° my counsel;   *Keep secret; take to heart*
You'll find it wholesome. Lo, where comes that rock
That I advise your shunning.

Enter Cardinal WOLSEY, *the purse[7] borne before him,*
certain of the Guard, and two SECRETARIES *with*
papers. The Cardinal, in his passage, fixeth his eye on
BUCKINGHAM, *and* BUCKINGHAM *on him, both full of*
disdain.

115 WOLSEY   The Duke of Buckingham's surveyor?° Ha?   *overseer of an estate*
Where's his examination?°   *testimony*
SECRETARY   Here, so please you.
WOLSEY   Is he in person ready?
SECRETARY   Ay, please your grace.
WOLSEY   Well, we shall then know more, and Buckingham
Shall lessen this big° look.   *proud*

Exeunt Cardinal WOLSEY *and his train.*

120 BUCKINGHAM   This butcher's cur is venom-mouthed, and I
Have not the power to muzzle him. Therefore best
Not wake him in his slumber. A beggar's book°   *learning*
Outworths a noble's blood.°   *inherited privilege*
NORFOLK   What, are you chafed?°   *heated to a rage*
Ask God for temp'rance: that's th'appliance only°   *the only medicine*
Which your disease requires.
125 BUCKINGHAM   I read in's looks
Matter against me, and his eye reviled
Me as his abject° object. At this instant,   *discarded; socially base*
He bores° me with some trick. He's gone to th' King.   *pierces; defrauds*
I'll follow and outstare him.
NORFOLK   Stay, my lord,
130 And let your reason with your choler° question°   *anger / dispute*
What 'tis you go about. To climb steep hills
Requires slow pace at first; anger is like
A full hot° horse who, being allowed his way,   *feisty*
Self-mettle° tires him. Not a man in England   *His own disposition*
135 Can advise me like you: be to yourself
As you would to your friend.[8]
BUCKINGHAM   I'll to the King
And, from a mouth of honor,[9] quite cry down
This Ipswich° fellow's insolence, or proclaim   *(Wolsey's lowly hometown)*
There's difference in no persons.°   *Rank no longer matters*
NORFOLK   Be advised:°   *Be careful*
140 Heat not a furnace for your foe so hot
That it do singe yourself. We may outrun,
By violent swiftness, that which we run at°   *toward*

---

7. A special bag that held the "great seal," part of the
Lord Chancellor's insignia of office.
8. *be . . . friend:* don't do anything you wouldn't

advise a friend to do.
9. An aristocratic, virtuous mouth.

And lose by overrunning. Know you not
The fire that mounts° the liquor till't run over,   swells (by boiling)
145 In seeming to augment it, wastes it? Be advised:
I say again there is no English soul
More stronger to direct you than yourself,
If with the sap of reason you would quench
Or but allay° the fire of passion.   abate

BUCKINGHAM   Sir,
150 I am thankful to you, and I'll go along
By your prescription. But this top-proud° fellow—   proudest of all
Whom from the flow of gall I name not, but
From sincere motions¹—by intelligence°   covert information
And proofs as clear as founts° in July when   springs
155 We see each grain of gravel, I do know
To be corrupt and treasonous.

NORFOLK   Say not "treasonous."

BUCKINGHAM   To th' King I'll say't, and make my vouch° as strong   case
As shore of rock. Attend.° This holy fox,   Pay attention
Or wolf, or both—for he is equal° rav'nous   as
160 As he is subtle, and as prone to mischief
As able to perform't, his mind and place°   high position
Infecting one another, yea, reciprocally—
Only to show his pomp, as well in France
As here at home, suggests° the King our master   tempts
165 To this last° costly treaty, th'interview°   latest / the meeting
That swallowed so much treasure and, like a glass,
Did break i'th' rinsing.

NORFOLK   Faith, and so it did.

BUCKINGHAM   Pray give me favor,° sir. This cunning Cardinal   let me continue
The articles o'th' combination° drew   terms of the treaty
170 As himself pleased. And they were ratified
As he cried, "Thus let be," to as much end°   effect
As give a crutch to th' dead. But our Count-Cardinal²
Has done this, and 'tis well; for worthy Wolsey—
Who cannot err—he did it. Now this follows—
175 Which, as I take it, is a kind of puppy
To th'old dam° treason—Charles the Emperor,³   bitch; mother
Under pretense to see the Queen his aunt°—   (Catharine)
For 'twas indeed his color,° but he came   alibi
To whisper° Wolsey—here makes visitation: meet covertly with
180 His fears were that the interview betwixt
England and France might, through their amity,
Breed him some prejudice, for from this league
Peeped harms that menaced him. Privily° he   Clandestinely
Deals with our Cardinal, and as I trow°—   believe
185 Which I do well, for I am sure the Emperor
Paid ere he promised, whereby his suit was granted
Ere it was asked—but when the way was made
And paved with gold, the Emperor thus desired
That he° would please to alter the King's course   (Wolsey)
190 And break the foresaid peace. Let the King know,

---

1. *Whom . . . motions*: Whom I name not from a ran-
corous impulse but from pure motives.
2. Church leader assuming secular, aristocratic rank

(compare "King-Cardinal," 2.2.18).
3. Charles V, Holy Roman Emperor and King of
Spain.

As soon he shall by me, that thus the Cardinal
Does buy and sell his° honor as he° pleases,   *(Henry's) / (Wolsey)*
And for his own advantage.

NORFOLK   I am sorry
To hear this of him and could wish he were
Something mistaken° in't.   *Partly misrepresented*

195 BUCKINGHAM   No, not a syllable:
I do pronounce him in that very shape
He shall appear in proof.°   *in practice*

  Enter BRANDON, *a* SERGEANT-*at-Arms before him, and*
  two or three of the Guard.

BRANDON   Your office, Sergeant: execute it.

SERGEANT   Sir,
My lord the Duke of Buckingham, and Earl
200 Of Hereford, Stafford and Northampton, I
Arrest thee of high treason in the name
Of our most sovereign king.

BUCKINGHAM [*to* NORFOLK]   Lo° you, my lord,   *Look*
The net has fall'n upon me: I shall perish
Under device and practice.°   *trickery and schemes*

BRANDON   I am sorry
205 To see you ta'en from liberty to look on°   *concerning*
The business present. 'Tis his highness' pleasure
You shall to th' Tower.

BUCKINGHAM   It will help me nothing
To plead mine innocence, for that dye is on me
Which makes my whit'st° part black. The will of heav'n   *whitest*
210 Be done in this and all things. I obey.
O my lord Abergavenny, fare you well.

BRANDON   Nay, he must bear you company.
[*to* ABERGAVENNY]   The King
Is pleased you shall to th' Tower till you know
How he determines further.

ABERGAVENNY   As the Duke said,
215 The will of heaven be done, and the King's pleasure
By me obeyed.

BRANDON   Here is a warrant from
The King t'attach° Lord Montague and the bodies   *to seize*
Of the Duke's confessor, John de la Court,
One Gilbert Park, his chancellor—

BUCKINGHAM   So, so;
220 These are the limbs o'th' plot.° No more, I hope.   *plotters*

BRANDON   A monk o'th' Chartreux°—   *Carthusian order*

BUCKINGHAM   Oh, Nicholas Hopkins?

BRANDON   He.

BUCKINGHAM   My surveyor is false: the o'er-great Cardinal
Hath showed him gold. My life is spanned° already;   *marked out*
I am the shadow of poor Buckingham,
225 Whose figure even this instant cloud puts on
By darkening my clear sun.[4] [*to* NORFOLK] My lord, farewell.

          Exeunt.

---

4. A cloud (Wolsey; the accusation) overshadows my former glory and comes between me and my king ("sun"
may refer to either Buckingham or Henry).

1.2

Cornetts. Enter KING *Henry, leaning on the Cardinal*
[Wolsey]'s shoulder, the nobles and Sir Thomas
LOVELL. *The Cardinal places himself under the King's*
feet° on his right side. [His SECRETARY *attends him.]*   *below the throne*

KING   My life itself, and the best heart° of it,   *essential core*
   Thanks you for this great care. I stood i'th' level°   *line of fire*
   Of a full-charged confederacy,° and give thanks   *loaded conspiracy*
   To you that choked it. Let be called before us
5   That gentleman of Buckingham's:° in person   *(the surveyor)*
   I'll hear him his confessions justify,°   *verify*
   And, point by point, the treasons of his master
   He shall again relate.
       A noise within crying, "Room for the Queen!" [who is
       to be] ushered by the Duke of NORFOLK. *Enter Queen*
       *[*CATHARINE*],* NORFOLK *and [the Duke of]* SUFFOLK.
       She kneels; [the] KING *riseth from his state,° takes her*   *throne*
       up, [and] kisses [her].

CATHARINE   Nay, we must longer kneel: I am a suitor.
KING   Arise and take place by us.
       He placeth her by him.
10   Half your suit
   Never name to us: you have half our power;
   The other moiety° ere you ask is given.   *half*
   Repeat your will,° and take it.   *State your wish*
CATHARINE   Thank your majesty.
   That you would love yourself, and in that love
15   Not unconsidered leave your honor, nor
   The dignity of your office, is the point
   Of my petition.
KING   Lady mine, proceed.
CATHARINE   I am solicited°—not by a few,   *apprised*
   And those of true condition°—that your subjects   *loyal character*
20   Are in great grievance. There have been commissions
   Sent down among 'em¹ which hath flawed° the heart   *broken*
   Of all their loyalties. —Wherein, although,
   My good lord Cardinal, they vent reproaches
   Most bitterly on you as putter-on
25   Of these exactions,° yet the King our master—   *taxes*
   Whose honor heaven shield from soil°—even he escapes not   *blemish*
   Language unmannerly, yea, such which breaks
   The sides² of loyalty and almost appears
   In loud rebellion.
NORFOLK   Not "almost appears";
30   It doth appear. For, upon these taxations,
   The clothiers all, not able to maintain
   The many to them 'longing,° have put off°   *they employ / let go*
   The spinsters, carders, fullers,³ weavers, who,
   Unfit for other life, compelled by hunger
35   And lack of other means, in desperate manner

1.2 Location: A council chamber at court.
1. *There . . . 'em:* They have received writs authorizing the collection of taxes.
2. *which . . . sides:* which oversteps the limits.

3. All involved in wool production: "spinsters" spun the wool; "carders" combed through, extracting impurities; and "fullers" beat the wool to thicken and cleanse it.

Daring th'event to th' teeth,[4] are all in uproar—
And danger serves among them.
KING   Taxation?
Wherein? And what taxation? My lord Cardinal,
You that are blamed for it alike with us,
Know you of this taxation?
40 WOLSEY   Please you, sir,
I know but of a single° part in aught°   (his own) / anything
Pertains to th' state, and front but in that file
Where others tell steps with me.[5]
CATHARINE   No, my lord?
You know no more than others? But you frame
45 Things that are known alike, which are not wholesome
To those which would not know them, and yet must
Perforce be their acquaintance.[6] These exactions—
Whereof my sovereign would have note°—they are   knowledge
Most pestilent to th' hearing, and to bear 'em
50 The back is sacrifice to° th' load. They say   broken by
They are devised by you, or else you suffer
Too hard an exclamation.°   accusation
KING   Still "exaction"!
The nature of it? In what kind, let's know,
Is this exaction?
CATHARINE   I am much too venturous
55 In tempting of your patience, but am boldened
Under your promised pardon. The subjects' grief°   grievance
Comes through commissions which compels from each
The sixth part of his substance° to be levied   wealth
Without delay. And the pretense for this
60 Is named your wars in France. This makes bold mouths;
Tongues spit their duties out, and cold hearts freeze
Allegiance in them. Their curses now
Live where their prayers did, and it's come to pass
This tractable obedience is a slave
65 To each incensèd will.[7] I would your highness
Would give it quick consideration, for
There is no primer baseness.°   more pressing evil
KING   By my life,
This is against our pleasure.
WOLSEY   And for me,
I have no further gone in this than by
70 A single voice,[8] and that not passed me but°   I gave only
By learned approbation° of the judges.° If I am   approval / Privy Council
Traduced° by ignorant tongues—which neither know   Slandered
My faculties° nor person, yet will be   outlook
The chronicles of my doing°—let me say   report my deeds
75 'Tis but the fate of place° and the rough brake°   rank / thicket
That virtue must go through. We must not stint°   halt
Our necessary actions in the fear

4. Refusing adamantly to comply with the result.
5. front . . . me: I walk at the front of a line only of those who have power equal to my own (though, literally, who march in step behind me). Wolsey is denying that he is unilaterally responsible.
6. But . . . acquaintance: But you originate measures

that all know, that harm even those who would rather not accept them yet must.
7. This . . . will: Each subject's formerly compliant obedience is dominated by his or her anger.
8. I . . . voice: I have cast only my single vote; I have concurred with a unanimous vote.

To cope° malicious censurers, which ever, *Of facing*
As rav'nous fishes, do a vessel follow
80 That is new-trimmed,° but benefit no further *newly rigged*
Than vainly longing. What we oft do best,
By sick interpreters, or weak ones, is
Not ours, or not allowed;[9] what° worst, as oft, *what we do*
Hitting a grosser quality,° is cried up *Appealing to the base*
85 For our best act. If we shall stand still
In fear our motion° will be mocked or carped at, *proposal; action*
We should take root here where we sit,
Or sit state-statues only.[1]
KING   Things done well
And with a care exempt themselves from fear;
90 Things done without example° in their issue° *precedent / effects*
Are to be feared. Have you a precedent
Of this commission? I believe not any.
We must not rend our subjects from our laws
And stick them in our will.° Sixth part of each? *use them at our whim*
95 A trembling contribution! Why, we take
From every tree, lop,° bark, and part o'th' timber, *branches*
And though we leave it with a root, thus hacked
The air will drink the sap. To every county
Where this is questioned° send our letters with *challenged*
100 Free pardon to each man that has denied° *refused*
The force of this commission. Pray look to't:
I put it to your care.
WOLSEY [*apart to his* SECRETARY] A word with you.
Let there be letters writ to every shire
Of the King's grace° and pardon. The grieved commons *mercy*
105 Hardly° conceive of me; let it be noised° *Severely / rumored*
That through our intercession this revokement
And pardon comes. I shall anon advise you
Further in the proceeding.   *Exit* SECRETARY.
        Enter SURVEYOR.
CATHARINE I am sorry that the Duke of Buckingham
Is run in° your displeasure. *Has provoked*
110 KING   It grieves many.
The gentleman is learned and a most rare speaker,
To nature none more bound,[2] his training such
That he may furnish and instruct great teachers
And never seek for aid out of° himself. Yet see, *outside of*
115 When these so noble benefits shall prove
Not well disposed,° the mind growing once corrupt, *employed*
They turn to vicious forms, ten times more ugly
Than ever they were fair. This man so complete,° *accomplished*
Who was enrolled 'mongst wonders—and when we,
120 Almost with ravished° listening, could not find *spellbound*
His hour of speech a minute[3]—he, my lady,
Hath into monstrous habits° put the graces *shapes; behavior; clothes*

9. *What . . . allowed:* Those who are envious ("sick") or of dubious faith ("weak," presumably alluding to early Protestants) never attribute to us or approve in us what we do best.
1. Or become nothing but decorative statues of leaders.
2. No man has been given greater gifts by nature.
3. *could . . . minute:* though an hour had passed, it seemed only a minute had gone by (owing to his gifted speaking).

That once were his and is become as black
As if besmeared in hell. Sit by us; you shall hear—
125 This was his gentleman in trust°—of him   *trusted assistant*
Things to strike honor sad. —Bid him recount
The fore-recited practices,° whereof   *schemes*
We cannot feel too little, hear too much.

WOLSEY Stand forth and, with bold spirit, relate what you,
130 Most like a careful subject, have collected°   *gathered as evidence*
Out of° the Duke of Buckingham.   *By observing*

KING   Speak freely.

SURVEYOR First, it was usual with him—every day
It would infect his speech—that if the King
Should without issue die, he'll carry it so°   *arrange so as*
135 To make the scepter his. These very words
I've heard him utter to his son-in-law,
Lord Abergavenny, to whom by oath he menaced
Revenge upon the Cardinal.

WOLSEY   Please your highness note
His dangerous conception in this point,
140 Not friended by his wish to your high person.[4]
His will is most malignant, and it stretches
Beyond you to your friends.

CATHARINE   My learned lord Cardinal,
Deliver all with charity.

KING   Speak on.
How grounded he his title to the crown
145 Upon our fail?° To this point hast thou heard him   *childlessness; death*
At any time speak aught?

SURVEYOR   He was brought to this
By a vain prophecy of Nicholas Hopkins.

KING What was that Hopkins?

SURVEYOR   Sir, a Chartreux friar,
His confessor, who fed him every minute
With words of sovereignty.

150 KING   How know'st thou this?

SURVEYOR Not long before your highness sped to France,
The Duke, being at the Rose[5] within the parish
Saint Laurence Pountney, did of me demand
What was the speech° among the Londoners   *gossip*
155 Concerning the French journey. I replied
Men feared the French would prove perfidious,
To the King's danger. Presently,° the Duke   *At once*
Said 'twas the fear indeed, and that he doubted°   *suspected*
'Twould prove the verity of certain words
160 Spoke by a holy monk, "that oft," says he,
"Hath sent to me, wishing me to permit
John de la Court, my chaplain, a choice hour°   *a suitable time*
To hear from him a matter of some moment;
Whom after, under the commission's° seal,   *confession's*
165 He solemnly had sworn that what he spoke
My chaplain, to no creature living but
To me, should utter with demure° confidence,   *grave*

---

4. Since he has not been granted ("friended by") his
wish that the King die without an heir.

5. Manor owned by Buckingham just outside
London.

This pausingly ensued: 'Neither the King, nor 's heirs—
Tell you the Duke—shall prosper. Bid him strive
170   To purchase the love o'th' commonalty.° The Duke   *common people*
Shall govern England.'"
CATHARINE   If I know you well,
You were the Duke's surveyor, and lost your office
On the complaint o'th' tenants. Take good heed
You charge not in your spleen° a noble person   *spite*
175   And spoil° your nobler soul. I say, take heed;   *ruin*
Yes, heartily beseech you.
KING   Let him on.°   *continue*
[*to the* SURVEYOR][6] Go forward.
SURVEYOR   On my soul, I'll speak but truth!
I told my lord the Duke by th' devil's illusions
The monk might be deceived, and that 'twas dangerous
180   For him to ruminate on this so far until
It forged him some design—which, being believed,
It was much like to do.[7] He answered, "Tush,
It can do me no damage," adding further
That, had the King in his last sickness failed,°   *died*
185   The Cardinal's and Sir Thomas Lovell's heads
Should have gone off.
KING   Ha? What, so rank?° Ah, ha!   *rotten*
There's mischief in this man! Canst thou say further?
SURVEYOR   I can, my liege.[8]
KING   Proceed.
SURVEYOR   Being at Greenwich,[9]
After your highness had reproved the Duke
About Sir William Bulmer—
190   KING   I remember
Of such a time: being my sworn servant,
The Duke retained him his.° But on: what hence?   *for his own*
SURVEYOR   "If," quoth he, "I for this had been committed"—
As to the Tower, I thought—"I would have played
195   The part my father[1] meant to act upon
Th'usurper Richard who, being at Salisbury,
Made suit to come in 's presence; which, if granted—
As he made semblance of his duty°—would   *seemed to kneel*
Have put his knife into him."
KING   A giant traitor!
200   WOLSEY   Now, madam, may° his highness live in freedom   *can*
And this man out of prison?
CATHARINE   God mend all.
KING   —There's something more would out of thee: what
    say'st?

---

6. TEXTUAL COMMENT The stage direction added
here indicates a midspeech change in the person
addressed. See Digital Edition TC 1 for more on this
practice.
7. *until . . . do:* until the Duke's ruminations made
him imagine ("forged him") some scheme that, if he
believed in it (and hence in the Monk's prophecy), he
would probably do (come up with a plan or carry it
out).
8. TEXTUAL COMMENT The three speeches in line 188

appear as separate lines in the Folio (F). Here, they
are presented as part of a single pentameter line. For
this typographical reaarangement here and elsewhere, see Digital Edition TC 2.
9. TEXTUAL COMMENT Lines 188–92 are set as prose
in F, though probably intended to be in verse, as presented here. For more on this passage and similar
ones, see Digital Edition TC 3.
1. The Duke of Buckingham during Richard III's
reign.

SURVEYOR   After "the Duke his father," with "the knife,"
    He stretched him,° and with one hand on his dagger,   *stood up straight*
205 Another spread on's breast, mounting° his eyes,   *raising up*
    He did discharge a horrible oath, whose tenor
    Was, were he evil used,° he would outgo   *poorly treated*
    His father by as much as a performance°   *true performance*
    Does an irresolute purpose.
KING   There's his period:°   *ultimate goal*
210 To sheathe his knife in us. He is attached.°   *arrested*
    Call him to present° trial. If he may   *immediate*
    Find mercy in the law, 'tis his; if none,
    Let him not seek't of us. By day and night,
    He's traitor to th' height.°   *Exeunt.*   *to the greatest degree*

1.3

Enter Lord CHAMBERLAIN *and Lord* SANDYS.

CHAMBERLAIN   Is't possible the spells of France should juggle°   *enchant*
    Men into such strange mysteries?°   *outlandish conduct*
SANDYS   New customs,
    Though they be never so ridiculous—
    Nay, let 'em be unmanly°—yet are followed.   *effeminate*
5 CHAMBERLAIN   As far as I see, all the good our English
    Have got by the late voyage° is but merely   *(to France)*
    A fit or two o'th' face.° But they are shrewd ones,   *Odd expressions*
    For when they hold 'em° you would swear directly   *maintain these looks*
    Their very noses had been counsellors
10 To Pépin or Clotharius, they keep state so.[1]
SANDYS   They have all new legs,° and lame ones: one would take it,   *new walks and bows*
    That never see 'em pace° before, the spavin   *saw them walk*
    Or springhalt reigned among 'em.[2]
CHAMBERLAIN   Death,° my lord,   *By God's death*
    Their clothes are after such a pagan cut to't
    That sure they've worn out Christendom.[3]

Enter Sir Thomas LOVELL.

15   How now?
    What news, Sir Thomas Lovell?
LOVELL   Faith, my lord,
    I hear of none but the new proclamation
    That's clapped upon the Court Gate.
CHAMBERLAIN   What is't for?
LOVELL   The reformation of our traveled gallants
20 That fill the court with quarrels, talk, and tailors.
CHAMBERLAIN   I'm glad 'tis there. Now I would pray our *messieurs*
    To think an English courtier may be wise
    And never see the Louvre.°   *French king's palace*
LOVELL   They must either—
    For so run the conditions—leave those remnants
25 Of fool and feather° that they got in France   *folly and adornment*

1.3 Location: The court.
1. *To . . . so:* To sixth- and seventh-century kings of France, their noses ("they") have such dignified (but convoluted) postures.
2. *the spavin . . . 'em:* they seem to be lame. *spavin:* swelling in horses' legs. *springhalt:* spasms in horses' legs.
3. *Their . . . Christendom:* They have run out of the fashions of Christendom and have moved on to pagan habits. This mockery reflects contemporary anxieties about "unmanly" (line 4) imported Continental fashions. *are after:* have.

With all their honorable points of ignorance[4]
Pertaining thereunto—as fights and fireworks,°   *dueling and whoring*
Abusing better men than they can be
Out of a foreign wisdom—renouncing clean
30   The faith they have in tennis and tall stockings,
Short blistered breeches, and those types of travel[5]—
And understand° again like honest men,   *reason (or walk) correctly*
Or pack° to their old playfellows. There, I take it,   *return*
They may, *cum privilegio, oui* away
35   The lag end of their lewdness[6] and be laughed at.
SANDYS   'Tis time to give 'em physic,° their diseases   *medicine*
Are grown so catching.
CHAMBERLAIN   What a loss our ladies
Will have of these trim vanities![7]
CHAMBERLAIN   Ay, marry,°   *indeed*
There will be woe indeed, lords. The sly whoresons
40   Have got a speeding° trick to lay down° ladies: *an effectual / seduce*
A French song and a fiddle has no fellow.[8]
SANDYS   The devil fiddle 'em! I am glad they are going,
For sure there's no converting of 'em.° Now   *(in fashion; in religion)*
An honest country lord as I am, beaten
45   A long time out of play,° may bring his plainsong°   *love; music / unadorned tune*
And have an hour of hearing—and, by'r Lady,
Held current° music too.   *modern; stylish*
CHAMBERLAIN   Well said, Lord Sandys.
Your colt's tooth is not cast yet?[9]
SANDYS   No, my lord,
Nor shall not while I have a stump.°   *(of a tooth; penis)*
CHAMBERLAIN   Sir Thomas,
Whither were you a-going?
50   LOVELL   To the Cardinal's.
Your lordship is a guest too.
CHAMBERLAIN   Oh, 'tis true.
This night he makes° a supper, and a great one,   *gives*
To many lords and ladies. There will be
The beauty of this kingdom, I'll assure you.
55   LOVELL   That churchman bears a bounteous mind indeed,
A hand as fruitful° as the land that feeds us: *benevolent*
His dews fall everywhere.
CHAMBERLAIN   No doubt he's noble—
He had a black mouth that said other of him.[1]
SANDYS   He may, my lord; 'has wherewithal.° In him,   *he can afford to*

4. With all the unimportant things that, in their ignorance, they consider honorable.
5. *Abusing . . . travel:* They must stop "abusing" their betters out of a misplaced faith in French "wisdom" and start "renouncing" French habits like "tennis," "tall stockings," puffed upper leggings, and such marks of travel (which were affected by Henry VIII in the play and James I at the time of its performance, as well as by James's courtiers).
6. *They . . . lewdness:* They may, with immunity ("*cum privilegio*"), indulge their remaining silliness (or evil, or sexual misconduct) by copying the French—where "*cum privilegio*" is an "in" joke: these are the first words in a printer's statement of the exclusive right to

publish. *oui:* yes.
7. Well-dressed fops; mindless styles.
8. *a fiddle has no fellow:* a musical instrument (or sex) has no equal.
9. Proverbial: you haven't abandoned your youthful lasciviousness ("colt's tooth") yet?
1. Anyone who denies this generosity must have an evil mouth. But since the praise is ironic, the courtiers are here doing precisely what they pretend to criticize: "dews" (pun on "dues," taxes, line 57); clergymen as "examples" (line 62) of extravagance, not piety ("doctrine," line 60); Wolsey as a "great" example (line 63), in the sense of girth.

60   Sparing° would show a worse sin than ill doctrine.°   *Stinginess / heresy*
    Men of his way° should be most liberal: *profession*
    They are set here for examples.
    CHAMBERLAIN   True, they are so,
    But few now give so great ones.° My barge stays;°   *examples / waits*
    Your lordship shall along.° —Come, good Sir Thomas,   *join me*
65   We shall be late else, which I would not be,
    For I was spoke to,° with Sir Henry Guildford,   *invited*
    This night to be comptrollers.°   *stewards*
    SANDYS   I am your lordship's.
                          Exeunt.

1.4

Hautboys.[1] *A small table under a [cloth of] state*[2] *for the Cardinal; a longer table for the guests. Then enter* ANNE *Boleyn and diverse other Ladies and Gentlemen, as guests, at one door. At another door enter Sir Henry* GUILDFORD.

  GUILDFORD   Ladies, a general welcome from his grace
  Salutes ye all. This night he dedicates
  To fair content and you. None here, he hopes,
  In all this noble bevy,° has brought with her   *company*
5   One care abroad:° he would have all as merry   *out of her house*
  As, first, good company, good wine, good welcome
  Can make good people.
        Enter Lord CHAMBERLAIN, *Lord* SANDYS, *and [Sir Thomas]* LOVELL.
                —O my lord, you're tardy.
  The very thought of this fair company
  Clapped wings to me.
  CHAMBERLAIN   You are young, Sir Harry Guildford.
10   SANDYS   Sir Thomas Lovell, had the Cardinal
  But half my lay° thoughts in him, some of these   *secular*
  Should find a running banquet[3] ere they rested
  I think would better please 'em. By my life,
  They are a sweet society of fair ones.
15   LOVELL   Oh, that your lordship were but now confessor
  To one or two of these—
  SANDYS   I would I were:
  They should find easy penance.
  LOVELL   Faith, how easy?
  SANDYS   As easy as a down bed would afford it.
  CHAMBERLAIN   Sweet ladies, will it please you sit? —Sir Harry,
20   Place you° that side, I'll take the charge of this.   *Arrange seating on*
  His grace is entering. —Nay, you must not freeze:
  Two women placed together makes cold weather.
  My lord Sandys, you are one will keep 'em waking;°   *spirited*
  Pray, sit between these ladies.
  SANDYS   By my faith,
25   And thank your lordship. —By your leave, sweet ladies—

1.4 Location: Westminster, a hall in York Place.
1. An early reeded wind instrument, ancestor of the oboe.

2. A canopy over an official chair of royal government.
3. Light refreshments; furtive, stolen pleasures.

If I chance to talk a little wild, forgive me:
I had it from my father.

ANNE   Was he mad, sir?

SANDYS   Oh, very mad, exceeding mad—in love, too—
But he would bite° none: just as I do now,   *(sign of madness)*
He would kiss you twenty with a breath.[4]

30 CHAMBERLAIN   Well said,° my lord.   *done*
So, now you're fairly seated, gentlemen,
The penance lies on you if these fair ladies
Pass away frowning.

SANDYS   For my little cure,°   *duty; (of souls)*
Let me alone.

        Hautboys. Enter Cardinal WOLSEY *and takes his state.*

35 WOLSEY   You're welcome, my fair guests. That noble lady
Or gentleman that is not freely merry
Is not my friend. [*He drinks.*][5] This to confirm my welcome
And to you all: good health!

SANDYS   Your grace is noble.
Let me have such a bowl may° hold my thanks   *as may*
And save me so much talking.

40 WOLSEY   My lord Sandys,
I am beholden to you. Cheer° your neighbors!   *Amuse*
—Ladies, you are not merry. —Gentlemen,
Whose fault is this?

SANDYS   The red wine first must rise
In their fair cheeks, my lord; then we shall have 'em
Talk us to silence.

45 ANNE   You are a merry gamester,°   *fellow; gambler*
My lord Sandys.

SANDYS   Yes, if I make my play.[6]
Here's to your ladyship! And pledge it,° madam,   *drink to it*
For 'tis to such a thing—

ANNE   You cannot show me!°   *(sexual)*

SANDYS   I told your grace they would talk anon.

      Drum and trumpet. Chambers discharged.[7]

WOLSEY   What's that?

CHAMBERLAIN   Look out there, some of ye.

50 WOLSEY   What warlike voice
And to what end is this? —Nay, ladies, fear not:
By all the laws of war you're privileged.°   *safe (because female)*

       Enter a SERVANT.

CHAMBERLAIN   How now, what is't?

SERVANT   A noble troop of strangers,
For so they seem. They've left their barge and landed,
55 And hither make, as° great ambassadors   *come, like*
From foreign princes.

WOLSEY   Good Lord Chamberlain,
Go, give 'em welcome—you can speak the French tongue—

---

4. He would kiss you twenty times with a single
breath.
5. TEXTUAL COMMENT This stage direction, which
specifies the action of a character, is not in F. On the
rationale for adding it to a Folio text that is unusually
rich in stage directions, see Digital Edition TC 4.

6. If I win my hand (at cards or love).
7. Small cannon fired. The firing of this cannon in
a June 29, 1613, performance of the play probably
caused the fire that destroyed the Globe Theater. See
the Introduction.

And pray receive 'em nobly and conduct 'em
Into our presence, where this heaven of beauty
60 Shall shine at full upon them. —Some attend him.

                          [*Exit* CHAMBERLAIN, *attended.*][8]
        All rise, and tables removed.
You have now a broken banquet, but we'll mend it.
A good digestion to you all! And, once more,
I shower a welcome on ye: welcome all!

        Hautboys. Enter KING *and others as Masquers,*[9]
        habited° *like shepherds, ushered by the Lord*   dressed
        CHAMBERLAIN. *They pass directly before Cardinal*
        WOLSEY *and gracefully salute him.*
A noble company. —What are their pleasures?

65 CHAMBERLAIN Because they speak no English, thus they prayed
To tell your grace that, having heard by fame°   rumor
Of this so noble and so fair assembly
This night to meet here, they could do no less,
Out of the great respect they bear to beauty,
70 But leave their flocks and, under your fair conduct,°   *if you'll allow them*
Crave leave° to view these ladies and entreat   *permission*
An hour of revels[1] with 'em.
WOLSEY   Say, Lord Chamberlain,
They have done my poor house grace, for which I pay 'em
A thousand thanks and pray 'em take their pleasures.

        [*The Masquers*] *choose Ladies.* [*The*] KING [*chooses*]
        ANNE *Boleyn.*
75 KING The fairest hand I ever touched! O Beauty,
Till now I never knew thee.
        Music. [*They*] *dance.*
WOLSEY My lord.
CHAMBERLAIN   Your grace?
WOLSEY   Pray tell 'em thus much from me:
There should be one amongst 'em by his person
More worthy this place° than myself, to whom—   *chair of state*
80 If I but knew him—with my love and duty
I would surrender it.
CHAMBERLAIN   I will, my lord.
        [*He*] *whisper*[*s with the Masquers*].
WOLSEY What say they?
CHAMBERLAIN   Such a one, they all confess,
There is indeed, which they would have your grace
Find out, and he will take it.°   (*the place of honor*)
WOLSEY   Let me see, then—
        [*He takes a close look at them.*]
85 By all your good leaves, gentlemen, here I'll make
My royal choice.
KING   Ye have found him, Cardinal.
        [*The* KING *unmasks.*]
You hold a fair assembly; you do well, lord.

---

8. TEXTUAL COMMENT This stage direction, which
indicates that a character leaves the stage, is also not
in F. It is inserted here because it is close to a logical
necessity. See Digital Edition TC 5.
9. Actors with masks on in anything from a dance

(probably the meaning here) to a complete play.
1. Entertainment; perhaps, more specifically, the
dancing with the audience of the actors in a court
masque.

You are a churchman or—I'll tell you, Cardinal—
I should judge now unhappily.[2]

WOLSEY   I am glad
Your grace is grown so pleasant.°   *merry*

90 KING   —My lord Chamberlain,
Prithee come hither. What fair lady's that?

CHAMBERLAIN   An't° please your grace, Sir Thomas Boleyn's   *If it*
    daughter,
The Viscount Rochford, one of her highness' women.

KING   By heaven, she is a dainty one. [*to* ANNE] Sweetheart,

95 I were unmannerly to take you out°   *(to dance)*
And not to kiss you. —A health,° gentlemen!   *toast*
    [*He drinks.*]
Let it go round!°   *Everyone drink in turn!*

WOLSEY   Sir Thomas Lovell, is the banquet ready
I'th' privy° chamber?   *private*

LOVELL   Yes, my lord.

WOLSEY   Your grace,

100 I fear, with dancing is a little heated.

KING   I fear too much.

WOLSEY   There's fresher air, my lord,
In the next chamber.

KING   —Lead in your ladies, everyone. —Sweet partner,
I must not yet forsake you. —Let's be merry,

105 Good my lord Cardinal: I have half a dozen healths
To drink to these fair ladies, and a measure°   *majestic dance*
To lead 'em once again. And then let's dream
Who's best in favor.[3] Let the music knock it!°   *strike it up*

             Exeunt with trumpets.

2.1

Enter two GENTLEMEN *at several*° *doors.*   *separate*

FIRST GENTLEMAN[1]   Whither away so fast?

SECOND GENTLEMAN   Oh, God save ye.
Ev'n to the Hall° to hear what shall become   *Westminster Hall*
Of the great Duke of Buckingham.

FIRST GENTLEMAN   I'll save you
That labor, sir. All's now done but the ceremony
Of bringing back the prisoner.

5 SECOND GENTLEMAN   Were you there?

FIRST GENTLEMAN   Yes, indeed was I.

SECOND GENTLEMAN   Pray speak what has happened.

FIRST GENTLEMAN   You may guess quickly what.

SECOND GENTLEMAN   Is he found guilty?

FIRST GENTLEMAN   Yes, truly is he, and condemned upon't.

SECOND GENTLEMAN   I am sorry for't.

FIRST GENTLEMAN   So are a number more.

10 SECOND GENTLEMAN   But pray, how passed it?°   *how did the trial go?*

---

2. I would unfavorably judge such ostentatiousness (especially the beautiful young women, whom a clergyman, required to be celibate, was in principle supposed to be uninterested in).
3. Who's most popular with the ladies; who's best looking, male or female.
2.1 Location: A street in Westminster.

1. TEXTUAL COMMENT The speech prefixes are missing from the dialogue of the two gentlemen—perhaps an indication that they are meant to function like a chorus or a relatively undifferentiated set of onlookers. For this point and related issues, see Digital Edition TC 6.

FIRST GENTLEMAN I'll tell you in a little.° The great Duke   *concisely*
Came to the bar, where to his accusations
He pleaded still not guilty and alleged°   *offered up*
Many sharp reasons to defeat the law.°   *the crown's case*
15   The King's attorney, on the contrary,
Urged on the examinations,° proofs,° confessions   *depositions / statements*
Of diverse witnesses, which the Duke desired
To him brought *viva voce*° to his face;   *in person*
At which appeared against him his surveyor,
20   Sir Gilbert Park his chancellor, and John Court,
Confessor to him, with that devil monk,
Hopkins, that made this mischief.
SECOND GENTLEMAN   That was he
That fed him with his prophecies.
FIRST GENTLEMAN   The same.
All these accused him strongly, which he fain°   *which charges he gladly*
25   Would have flung from him, but indeed he could not;
And so his peers, upon this evidence,
Have found him guilty of high treason. Much
He spoke, and learnedly, for life, but all
Was either pitied in him or forgotten.[2]
30   SECOND GENTLEMAN   After all this, how did he bear himself?
FIRST GENTLEMAN   When he was brought again to th' bar to hear
His knell rung out, his judgment,° he was stirred   *sentence*
With such an agony he sweat extremely,
And something spoke in choler,° ill and hasty.   *anger*
35   But he fell to° himself again, and sweetly   *got control of*
In all the rest showed a most noble patience.
SECOND GENTLEMAN   I do not think he fears death.
FIRST GENTLEMAN   Sure he does not;
He never was so womanish.° The cause   *(as to fear death)*
He may a little grieve at.
SECOND GENTLEMAN   Certainly
The Cardinal is the end° of this.   *source*
40   FIRST GENTLEMAN   'Tis likely,
By all conjectures: first Kildare's attainder,
Then deputy of Ireland,[3] who, removed,
Earl Surrey was sent thither, and in haste too,
Lest he should help his father.°   *father-in-law (Buckingham)*
SECOND GENTLEMAN   That trick of state
Was a deep envious° one.   *deeply spiteful*
45   FIRST GENTLEMAN   At his return
No doubt he will requite it. This is noted,
And generally:° whoever the King favors,   *by all*
The Card'nal instantly will find employment—
And far enough from court, too.
SECOND GENTLEMAN   All the commons°   *common people*
50   Hate him perniciously° and, o'my conscience,   *want him dead*
Wish him ten fathom deep. This Duke as much
They love and dote on; call him "Bounteous Buckingham,

2. *all . . . forgotten:* (Buckingham's defense) either
was fruitless or brought only pity.
3. Thomas Fitzgerald, Earl of Kildare, Lord Lieutenant of Ireland, lost his estates and position
("attainder"—dishonor) and was sentenced to death
by Wolsey.

The mirror° of all courtesy"[4]—   *exemplar*

Enter BUCKINGHAM *from his arraignment, Tipstaves*
before him, the ax with the edge toward him, Halberds
on each side, accompanied with Sir Thomas LOVELL,
Sir Nicholas VAUX, *[Lord]* SANDYS,[5] *[Attendants,] and*
common people.

FIRST GENTLEMAN   Stay there, sir,
And see the noble ruined man you speak of.

SECOND GENTLEMAN   Let's stand close° and behold him.   *near; sympathetically*

55 BUCKINGHAM   All good people,
You that thus far have come to pity me,
Hear what I say, and then go home and lose° me.   *forget*
I have this day received a traitor's judgment,°   *sentence*
And by that name must die; yet heaven bear witness,
60 And if I have a conscience, let it sink° me   *destroy*
Even as the ax falls, if I be not faithful.
The law I bear no malice for my death—
'T has done upon the premises° but justice—   *evidence*
But those that sought it I could wish more° Christians.   *truer*
65 Be what they will, I heartily forgive 'em.
Yet let 'em look° they glory not in mischief,   *beware*
Nor build their evils on the graves of great men,[6]
For then my guiltless blood must cry against 'em.
For further life in this world I ne'er hope,
70 Nor will I sue, although the King have mercies
More than I dare make faults.° You few that loved me   *commit misdeeds*
And dare be bold to weep for Buckingham—
His noble friends and fellows, whom to leave
Is only bitter to him, only dying[7]—
75 Go with me like good angels to my end
And, as the long divorce° of steel falls on me,   *(of body and soul)*
Make of your prayers one sweet sacrifice°   *offering*
And lift my soul to heaven. [*to the Tipstaves*] Lead on, i'God's name.

LOVELL   I do beseech your grace, for charity,
80 If ever any malice in your heart
Were hid against me, now to forgive me frankly.

BUCKINGHAM   Sir Thomas Lovell, I as free forgive you
As I would be forgiven: I forgive all.
There cannot be those numberless offenses
85 'Gainst me that I cannot take° peace with; no black envy°   *make / spite*
Shall make my grave. Commend me to his grace,
And if he speak of Buckingham, pray tell him
You met him half in heaven. My vows and prayers
Yet are the King's and, till my soul forsake,°   *depart (my body)*
90 Shall cry for blessings on him. May he live
Longer than I have time to tell° his years;   *count*
Ever beloved and loving may his rule be;

---

4. Polished manners, but also courtliness more
generally.
5. *Tipstaves:* court-appointed arresting officers who
carried tipstaves, staffs tipped with metal. *Halberds:*
guards who carried halberds, long-handled weapons
with both spear tips and battle-ax blades. "Sir William Sandys" is called "Lord Sandys" in the stage
directions at the beginning of 1.3 and at 1.4.7. The
discrepancy occurs because the play violates chronology here: Henry and Anne actually met years after
Buckingham's trial, and Sandys became a baron in
the interim.
6. Nor advance their evil designs through plotting
the downfall of noblemen.
7. *His . . . dying:* Leaving his friends is the only bitter
part of Buckingham's sentence, the only death.

And when old Time° shall lead him to his end,   *old age*
Goodness and he fill up one monument.°   *share one tomb*
95   LOVELL   To th' water side I must conduct your grace;
Then give my charge up to Sir Nicholas Vaux,
Who undertakes° you to your end.   *leads*
VAUX [*to Attendants*]   Prepare there:
The Duke is coming. See the barge be ready,
And fit it with such furniture° as suits   *trappings*
The greatness of his person.
100   BUCKINGHAM   Nay, Sir Nicholas,
Let it alone: my state[8] now will but mock me.
When I came hither, I was Lord High Constable
And Duke of Buckingham; now, poor Edward Bohun.[9]
Yet I am richer than my base accusers,
105   That never knew what truth meant. I now seal it,°   *show my loyalty ("truth")*
And with that blood will make 'em one day groan for't.
My noble father, Henry of Buckingham,
Who first raised head° against usurping Richard,   *an army*
Flying for succor to his servant Banister,
110   Being distressed, was by that wretch betrayed,
And without trial fell. God's peace be with him.
Henry the Seventh succeeding, truly pitying
My father's loss, like a most royal prince,
Restored me to my honors, and out of ruins
115   Made my name once more noble. Now his son,
Henry the Eighth, life, honor, name, and all
That made me happy, at one stroke has taken
For ever from the world. I had my trial,
And must needs say a noble one, which makes me
120   A little happier than my wretched father.
Yet thus far we are one in fortunes: both
Fell by our servants, by those men we loved most—
A most unnatural and faithless service.
Heaven has an end° in all. —Yet, you that hear me,   *a purpose*
125   This from a dying man receive as certain:
Where you are liberal of your loves and counsels,
Be sure you be not loose;° for those you make friends   *unrestrained*
And give your hearts to, when they once perceive
The least rub° in your fortunes, fall away   *obstacle*
130   Like water from ye, never found again
But where they mean to sink° ye. All good people,   *destroy*
Pray for me. I must now forsake ye. The last hour
Of my long weary life is come upon me.
Farewell, and when you would say something that is sad,
135   Speak how I fell. I have done, and God forgive me.
                    Exeunt Duke [of BUCKINGHAM] *and train.*
FIRST GENTLEMAN   Oh, this is full of pity, sir. It calls,
I fear, too many curses on their heads
That were the authors.
SECOND GENTLEMAN   If the Duke be guiltless,
'Tis full of woe. Yet I can give you inkling°   *forewarning*

8. Status; "furniture" (line 99).
9. Actually, Edward Stafford; Shakespeare copies Holinshed's mistake.

140 Of an ensuing evil, if it fall,°   *should occur*
Greater than this.
FIRST GENTLEMAN   Good angels, keep it from us.
What may it be? You do not doubt my faith,[1] sir?
SECOND GENTLEMAN   This secret is so weighty 'twill require
A strong faith to conceal it.
FIRST GENTLEMAN   Let me have it—
I do not talk much.
145 SECOND GENTLEMAN   I am confident;°   *I trust you*
You shall, sir. Did you not of late days hear
A buzzing° of a separation   *gossip*
Between the King and Catharine?
FIRST GENTLEMAN   Yes, but it held not.°   *did not persist*
For when the King once heard it, out of anger
150 He sent command to the Lord Mayor straight
To stop the rumor and allay° those tongues   *suppress*
That durst disperse it.
SECOND GENTLEMAN   But that slander, sir,
Is found a truth now, for it grows again
Fresher than e'er it was, and held° for certain   *is believed*
155 The King will venture at it. Either the Cardinal
Or some about him near° have, out of malice   *his confidants*
To the good Queen, possessed him with a scruple°   *doubt*
That will undo her. To confirm this, too,
Cardinal Campeius[2] is arrived, and lately,
As all think, for this business.
160 FIRST GENTLEMAN   'Tis the Cardinal—
And merely to revenge him on the Emperor[3]
For not bestowing on him, at his asking,
The archbishopric of Toledo this is purposed.
SECOND GENTLEMAN   I think you have hit the mark.° But is't   *guessed correctly*
not cruel
165 That she should feel the smart° of this? The Cardinal   *pain*
Will have his will, and she must fall.
FIRST GENTLEMAN   'Tis woeful.
We are too open° here to argue this;   *exposed*
Let's think in private more.   *Exeunt.*

2.2

Enter Lord CHAMBERLAIN, *reading this letter.*

CHAMBERLAIN "My lord, the horses your lordship sent for,
with all the care I had I saw well chosen, ridden, and furnished.° They were young and handsome and of the best   *trained and equipped*
breed in the North. When they were ready to set out for
5 London, a man of my lord Cardinal's, by commission and
main power,[1] took 'em from me, with this reason: his master
would be served before a subject, if not before the King,
which stopped our mouths, sir."

---

1. "Faith" (here and in line 144) picks up the religious language of "curses" (line 137) and "angels"
(line 141), while suggesting fidelity, loyalty, trustworthiness, and, as line 145 suggests, discretion.
2. Henry had to get a special dispensation from the
pope before marrying Catharine, because her previous husband was Prince Arthur, Henry's brother,
who died a year after the marriage took place. Wolsey

had Cardinal Laurence Campeius (Lorenzo Campeg-
gio) come to London as a papal legate in 1528 to
reopen debate about the marriage and to aid his plot
to have it annulled.
3. Charles V, Holy Roman Emperor and King of
Spain, was Catharine's nephew.
2.2 Location: The court at London.
1. By warrant and superior strength.

I fear he will indeed. Well, let him have them;
10   He will have all, I think.
       Enter to the Lord CHAMBERLAIN *the Dukes of* NORFOLK
       and SUFFOLK.
NORFOLK   Well met, my lord Chamberlain.
CHAMBERLAIN   Good day to both your graces.
SUFFOLK   How is the King employed?
CHAMBERLAIN   I left him private,°   *alone*
       Full of sad° thoughts and troubles.   *grave*
NORFOLK   What's the cause?
15   CHAMBERLAIN   It seems the marriage with his brother's wife
       Has crept too near his conscience.
SUFFOLK   No, his conscience
       Has crept too near another lady.
NORFOLK   'Tis so.
       This is the Cardinal's doing. The King-Cardinal,
       That blind priest, like the eldest son of fortune,
20   Turns what he list.² The King will know him° one day.   *(for what he is)*
SUFFOLK   Pray God he do. He'll never know himself else.
NORFOLK   How holily he° works in all his business,   *(Wolsey)*
       And with what zeal! For now he has cracked the league
       Between us and the Emperor, the Queen's great nephew.³
25   He dives into the King's soul and there scatters
       Dangers, doubts, wringing° of the conscience,   *affliction*
       Fears, and despairs—and all these for his marriage.
       And out of all these, to restore the King,
       He counsels a divorce, a loss of her
30   That like a jewel has hung twenty years
       About his neck yet never lost her luster;
       Of her that loves him with that excellence
       That angels love good men with; even of her
       That, when the greatest stroke° of fortune falls,   *severest blow*
35   Will bless the King⁴—and is not this course° pious?°   *(of action) / (ironic)*
CHAMBERLAIN   Heaven keep me from such counsel! 'Tis
       most true:
       These news are everywhere; every tongue speaks 'em,
       And every true heart weeps for't. All that dare
       Look into these affairs see this main end:°   *ultimate aim*
40   The French king's sister.⁵ Heaven will one day open
       The King's eyes, that so long have slept, upon
       This bold bad man.
SUFFOLK   And free us from his slavery.
NORFOLK   We had need pray,
       And heartily, for our deliverance,
45   Or this imperious man will work us all
       From princes into pages. All men's honors
       Lie like one lump° before him, to be fashioned   *(of clay)*
       Into what pitch° he please.   *stature*
SUFFOLK   For me, my lords,

2. *The King-Cardinal . . . list:* Like Fortune, his mother, Wolsey blindly turns the wheel of fortune as he likes ("list").
3. Wolsey has now broken the alliance between Henry and Charles V to get additional revenge on Charles: see 2.1.160–63. Previously (1.1.176–93), to gain favor with Charles, he engineered the breaking of the treaty with France sealed at the Field of the Cloth of Gold.
4. Prophetic: Catharine does later "bless the King" who has repudiated her (4.2.163–64).
5. Henry's marriage to the Duchess of Alençon will reunite the English and French kings, thus still further injuring Charles V. See 3.2.85–86.

I love him not, nor fear him: there's my creed.
50 As I am made without him, so I'll stand,[6]
If the King please. His curses and his blessings
Touch me alike: they're breath I° not believe in.   *I do*
I knew him and I know him; so I leave him
To him that made him proud, the Pope.
NORFOLK   Let's in,
55 And with some other business put the King
From these sad thoughts that work too much upon him.
—My lord, you'll bear us company?
CHAMBERLAIN   Excuse me;
The King has sent me otherwhere. Besides,
You'll find a most unfit time to disturb him.
Health to your lordships.
60 NORFOLK   Thanks, my good lord Chamberlain.
Exit Lord CHAMBERLAIN, *and the* KING *draws the*
curtain[7] *and sits reading pensively.*
SUFFOLK   How sad he looks! Sure he is much afflicted.°   *distressed*
KING   Who's there? Ha?
NORFOLK   Pray God he be not angry.
KING   Who's there I say? How dare you thrust yourselves
Into my private meditations?
65 Who am I? Ha?
NORFOLK   A gracious King that pardons all offenses
Malice ne'er meant. Our breach of duty this way°   *in this respect*
Is business of estate,° in which we come   *state*
To know your royal pleasure.
KING   Ye are too bold.
70 Go to! I'll make ye know your times of business.
Is this an hour for temporal affairs? Ha?
Enter WOLSEY *and* CAMPEIUS *with a commission.*
Who's there? My good lord Cardinal? O my Wolsey,
The quiet° of my wounded conscience,   *ease*
Thou art a cure° fit for a King. [*to* CAMPEIUS] You're welcome,   *balm; curate (priest)*
75 Most learned reverend sir, into our kingdom;
Use us and it. [*to* WOLSEY] My good lord, have great care
I be not found a talker.[8]
WOLSEY   Sir, you cannot;
I would your grace would give us but an hour
Of private conference.
KING [*to* NORFOLK *and* SUFFOLK]   We are busy. Go.
NORFOLK [*aside to* SUFFOLK]   This priest has no pride in him!°   *(more irony)*
80 SUFFOLK [*aside to* NORFOLK]   Not to speak of.
I would not be so sick, though, for his place.[9]
But this cannot continue.
NORFOLK [*aside to* SUFFOLK]   If it do,
I'll venture one have-at-him.°   *thrust (in fencing)*
SUFFOLK [*aside to* NORFOLK]   I another.
Exeunt NORFOLK *and* SUFFOLK.

---

6. Since not Wolsey but the King granted my nobility of rank, I'll remain firm in my position.
7. Almost certainly drawn by an attendant. The King's chamber is upstage in the discovery space, a curtained-off, possibly recessed area at the back of the stage.
8. have . . . talker: make sure my offer of hospitality counts for more than mere words.
9. I would not want to be afflicted with such pride, even for his exalted position.

WOLSEY Your grace has given a precedent° of wisdom *model*
85 Above all princes in committing freely
Your scruple to the voice of Christendom.[1]
Who can be angry now? What envy reach you?
The Spaniard,° tied by blood and favor to her, *(Charles V)*
Must now confess, if they have any goodness,
90 The trial just and noble. All the clerks°— *clerics*
I mean the learned ones in Christian kingdoms—
Have their free voices.° Rome, the nurse of judgment, *May vote freely*
Invited by your noble self, hath sent
One general tongue° unto us: this good man, *representative voice*
95 This just and learned priest, Card'nal Campeius,
Whom once more I present unto your highness.
KING And once more in mine arms I bid him welcome,
And thank the holy conclave° for their loves: *College of Cardinals*
They have sent me such a man I would have wished for.
100 CAMPEIUS Your grace must needs deserve all strangers'° loves, *foreigners'*
You are so noble. To your highness' hand
I tender my commission, by whose virtue,
The court of Rome commanding, you, my lord
Cardinal of York, are joined with me, their servant,
105 In the unpartial° judging of this business. *impartial*
KING Two equal° men. The Queen shall be acquainted° *fair / apprised*
Forthwith for what you come. —Where's Gardiner?
WOLSEY I know your majesty has always loved her
So dear in heart not to deny her that° *that which*
110 A woman of less place° might ask by law: *rank*
Scholars allowed freely to argue for her.
KING Ay, and the best she shall have, and my favor
To him that does best—God forbid else. Cardinal,
Prithee call Gardiner to me, my new secretary.[2]
115 I find him a fit fellow.
            Enter GARDINER.
WOLSEY Give me your hand. Much joy and favor to you;
You are the King's now.
GARDINER [*aside to* WOLSEY] But to be commanded
For ever by your grace, whose hand has raised me.
KING Come hither, Gardiner.
    [*The* KING] *walks and whispers* [*with* GARDINER].
120 CAMPEIUS My lord of York, was not one Doctor Pace[3]
In this man's place before him?
WOLSEY   Yes, he was.
CAMPEIUS Was he not held a learnèd man?
WOLSEY   Yes, surely.
CAMPEIUS Believe me, there's an ill opinion spread, then,
Even of yourself, Lord Cardinal.
WOLSEY   How? Of me?
125 CAMPEIUS They will not stick° to say you envied him, *scruple*
And fearing he would rise—he was so virtuous—

---

1. *voice of Christendom:* the papal legate Campeius and the representatives of the great European universities who have come to England to hear the case.
2. Stephen Gardiner, former secretary to Wolsey, became Henry's secretary in July 1529 through Wolsey's recommendation, and Bishop of Winchester in

1531.
3. Richard Pace, the King's former secretary, was now sent frequently abroad by Wolsey on diplomatic business, apparently as punishment for becoming too close to the King.

Kept him a foreign man still,° which so grieved him   *always abroad*
That he ran mad and died.

WOLSEY   Heaven's peace be with him—
That's Christian care enough. For living murmurers°   *malcontents*
130 There's places of rebuke. He was a fool,
For he would needs be° virtuous. [*He indicates* GARDINER.]   *insisted on being*
    That good fellow,
If I command him, follows my appointment;°   *orders*
I will have none so near[4] else. Learn this, brother:
We live not to be griped° by meaner persons.   *grasped; brought down*
135 KING [*to* GARDINER]   Deliver this with modesty° to th' Queen.   *Announce this mildly*
                                Exit GARDINER.
The most convenient place that I can think of
For such receipt of learning[5] is Blackfriars:
There ye shall meet about this weighty business.
—My Wolsey, see it furnished.° O my lord,   *fitted out properly*
140 Would it not grieve an able° man to leave   *a (sexually) vigorous*
So sweet a bedfellow? But conscience, conscience—
Oh, 'tis a tender place,° and I must leave her.   *Exeunt.*   *(conscience); (sexual)*

2.3

Enter ANNE *Boleyn and an* OLD LADY.

ANNE   Not for that, neither! Here's the pang that pinches:°   *pain that torments*
His highness having lived so long with her and she
So good a lady that no tongue could ever
Pronounce dishonor of her—by my life,
5 She never knew harm-doing—oh, now, after
So many courses of the sun° enthroned,   *years*
Still° growing in a majesty and pomp, the which   *Ever*
To leave a thousandfold more bitter than
'Tis sweet at first t'acquire[1]—after this process,
10 To give her the avaunt!° It is a pity   *boot*
Would move a monster.

OLD LADY   Hearts of most hard temper°   *constitution*
Melt and lament for her.

ANNE   Oh, God's will! Much better
She ne'er had known pomp; though 't be temporal,°   *only of this world*
Yet if that quarrel° and fortune do divorce   *(with Henry)*
15 It from the bearer, 'tis a sufferance panging°   *as painful*
As soul and body's severing.

OLD LADY   Alas, poor lady,
She's a stranger° now again.   *foreigner*

ANNE   So much the more
Must pity drop upon her. Verily,
I swear, 'tis better to be lowly born
20 And range with humble livers in content
Than to be perked up in a glist'ring grief[2]
And wear a golden sorrow.

---

4. I want no one else on such intimate terms with the King.
5. For hearing such scholarly disputation, or such scholars.
2.3 Location: The Queen's apartments at court.
1. *the which . . . t'acquire:* it is far more unpleasant to lose "majesty and pomp" than it is pleasurable to get it in the first place.
2. *'tis . . . grief:* it's better to be born poor and to occupy a lowly rank happily than to be unhappy despite one's riches (literally, to be dressed up in a glittering sadness).

OLD LADY	Our content	
Is our best having.°		*possession*
ANNE	By my troth° and maidenhead,°	*faith / virginity*
I would not be a queen.		
OLD LADY	Beshrew me,° I would,	*Devil take me*

25 And venture maidenhead for't; and so would you
For all this spice° of your hypocrisy.   *sample*
You, that have so fair parts° of woman on you,   *qualities; beauty*
Have, too, a woman's heart which ever yet
Affected° eminence, wealth, sovereignty;   *Craved*
30 Which, to say sooth,° are blessings; and which gifts—   *truth*
Saving your mincing°—the capacity   *Despite your affectation*
Of your soft cheverel conscience would receive,
If you might please to stretch it.[3]

ANNE   Nay, good troth.[4]
OLD LADY   Yes, troth and troth. You would not be a queen?
35 ANNE   No, not for all the riches under heaven.
OLD LADY   'Tis strange. A threepence bowed would hire me,
Old as I am, to queen it.[5] But I pray you,
What think you of a duchess? Have you limbs
To bear that load of title?
ANNE   No, in truth.
40 OLD LADY   Then you are weakly made. Pluck off[6] a little:
I would not be a young count in your way
For more than blushing comes to.[7] If your back
Cannot vouchsafe this burden,[8] 'tis too weak
Ever to get a boy.
ANNE   How you do talk!
45 I swear again I would not be a queen
For all the world.
OLD LADY   In faith, for little England
You'd venture an emballing.[9] I myself
Would for Caernarfonshire,[1] although there longed°   *belonged*
No more to th' crown but that.
                Enter Lord CHAMBERLAIN.
                          —Lo, who comes here?
50 CHAMBERLAIN   Good morrow, ladies. What were't worth to know
The secret of your conference?°   *conversation*
ANNE   My good lord,
Not your demand; it values not your asking.[2]
Our mistress' sorrows we were pitying.
CHAMBERLAIN   It was a gentle business, and becoming
55 The action of good women. There is hope

3. Your roomy and elastic conscience, if you choose to stretch it, would obtain the crown and its accompanying benefits. The implication is that Anne can gain power sexually ("capacity," "soft," "receive"). *cheverel:* kid leather (hence, pliant).
4. Faith (exclamatory); perhaps a pun on "trot," a demeaning term for an old woman.
5. *A threepence . . . it:* A bent ("bowed") and hence worthless coin would convince me to be a queen. Sexual puns ("queen"—"quean," or whore; "bowed"—bawd) continue through the scene.
6. Come lower in rank; undress.
7. *I . . . to:* Perhaps: If you persist in this "way" (path; being unable to bear the load of being duchess; condition of virginity), a "count" (an earl, the rank below duke) will get no more from you than blushes. Alternatively: if you come upon a "count," you won't be so modest. Also: I would give up being a young virginal cunt ("count") like you with no more than a blush.
8. Cannot bear these honors. "Burden," like "bear" (line 39), suggests both intercourse and childbearing.
9. *for . . . emballing:* for England you'd accept investiture with the royal emblem of ball and scepter (you'd get laid).
1. A particularly poor Welsh county.
2. (It is) not something you should be inquiring about; it does not merit "your asking."

All will be well.

ANNE   Now, I pray God, amen.

CHAMBERLAIN   You bear a gentle mind, and heav'nly blessings
　　Follow such creatures. That you may, fair lady,
　　Perceive I speak sincerely, and high note's
60　Ta'en of your many virtues, the King's majesty
　　Commends his good opinion of you,° and   *Sends his compliments*
　　Does purpose° honor to you no less flowing°   *intend / copious*
　　Than Marchioness of Pembroke; to which title
　　A thousand pound a year annual support
　　Out of his grace he adds.

65　ANNE   I do not know
　　What kind of my obedience I should tender:
　　More than my all is nothing. Nor my prayers
　　Are not° words duly hallowed, nor my wishes   *no more than*
　　More worth than empty vanities; yet prayers and wishes
70　Are all I can return. Beseech your lordship,
　　Vouchsafe° to speak my thanks and my obedience,   *Condescend*
　　As from a blushing handmaid, to his highness,
　　Whose health and royalty I pray for.

CHAMBERLAIN   Lady,
　　I shall not fail t'approve° the fair conceit°   *endorse / opinion*
75　The King hath of you. [*aside*] I have perused her well.
　　Beauty and honor in her are so mingled
　　That they have caught the King, and who knows yet
　　But from this lady may proceed a gem
　　To lighten[3] all this isle. [*to* ANNE] I'll to the King
　　And say I spoke with you.

80　ANNE   My honored lord.
　　　　　　　　　　　　　　Exit Lord CHAMBERLAIN.

OLD LADY   Why, this it is! See, see!
　　I have been begging sixteen years in court—
　　Am yet a courtier beggarly,° nor could   *still begging*
　　Come pat betwixt too early and too late
85　For any suit of pounds[4]—and you—O fate!—
　　A very fresh fish here—fie, fie, fie upon
　　This compelled° fortune!—have your mouth filled up   *forced upon you*
　　Before you open it.

ANNE   This is strange to me.

OLD LADY   How tastes it? Is it bitter? Forty pence, no.[5]
90　There was a lady once—'tis an old story—
　　That would not be a queen, that would she not,
　　For all the mud in Egypt.[6] Have you heard it?

ANNE   Come, you are pleasant.°   *merry; joking*

OLD LADY   With your theme I could
　　O'ermount° the lark. The Marchioness of Pembroke?   *fly (or sing) higher than*
95　A thousand pounds a year, for pure° respect?   *mere*
　　No other obligation? By my life,
　　That promises more thousands: honor's train

3. To bring light to (alluding to Elizabeth), with religious connotations. Gems were believed to emit light.
4. *nor . . . pounds:* nor could I arrive at just the right moment to succeed in any petition for money.

5. I'll bet a small sum (conventionally, 40 pence) that it isn't; "forty pence" says "no."
6. For all the wealth (in this case, the fertile land, or "mud") of Egypt.

Is longer than his foreskirt.[7] By this time
I know your back will bear a duchess. Say,
Are you not stronger than you were?

100 ANNE   Good lady,
Make yourself mirth with your particular fancy°   *private fantasies*
And leave me out on't.° Would I had no being   *of it*
If this salute° my blood a jot; it faints me°   *agitates / I faint*
To think what follows.[8]

105 The Queen is comfortless and we forgetful
In our long absence. Pray do not deliver
What here you've heard to her.

OLD LADY   What do you think me?
                                                          Exeunt.

2.4

Trumpets, sennet,° and cornetts.   *fanfare*
Enter two Vergers[1] with short silver wands; next them
two SCRIBES *in the habit of doctors;[2] after them the*
[Arch]bishop of Canterbury alone; after him the
Bishops of LINCOLN, *Ely, Rochester, and St Asaph;*
next them, with some small distance, follows a
Gentleman bearing the purse with the great seal and a
cardinal's hat; then two Priests bearing each a silver
cross; then a Gentleman Usher, bare-headed,
accompanied with a SERGEANT-*at-Arms, bearing a*
silver mace;° then two Gentlemen bearing two great   *ceremonial staff*
silver pillars; after them, side by side, the two
*Cardinals [*WOLSEY *and* CAMPEIUS*]; two Noblemen*
with the sword and mace. The KING *takes place under*
the cloth of state. The two Cardinals sit under him as
*judges. The Queen [*CATHARINE, *attended by*
GRIFFITH,*][3] takes place some distance from the* KING.
The Bishops place themselves on each side the court in
manner of a consistory;° below them, the SCRIBES *[and*   *church court*
a CRIER*]. The Lords sit next the Bishops. The rest of the*
Attendants stand in convenient order about the stage.

WOLSEY   Whilst our commission from Rome is read,
   Let silence be commanded.

KING   What's the need?
   It hath already publicly been read,
   And on all sides th'authority allowed.°   *accepted*
   You may then spare that time.

5 WOLSEY   Be't so. Proceed.

SCRIBE   Say, "Henry, King of England, come into the court."

CRIER   Henry, King of England, come into the court!

KING   Here.

SCRIBE   Say, "Catharine, Queen of England, come into the court."

---

7. *That . . . foreskirt:* Future rewards will exceed
present ones, just as a noblewoman's dress is longer
in back than in front.
8. "What follows," ultimately, is Anne's execution at
Henry's order in 1536, on the charge of adultery.
2.4 Location: A hall in Blackfriars.
1. Officials who carry the verge (a staff symbolizing

the authority of office) before a bishop or other
dignitary.
2. Furred black gowns and flat caps of doctors of law.
3. TEXTUAL COMMENT F calls this character "*Gent.
Vsh.*," only at the start of 4.2 explaining that Catharine's
gentleman usher is named Griffith. That name is
accordingly used throughout. See Digital Edition TC 7.

10 CRIER   Catharine, Queen of England, come into the court!
          *The Queen [*CATHARINE*] makes no answer, rises out of*
          her chair, goes about the court, comes to the KING,
          and kneels at his feet, then speaks.

    CATHARINE   Sir, I desire you do me right and justice,
          And to bestow your pity on me, for
          I am a most poor woman, and a stranger°   foreigner
          Born out of your dominions, having here
15   No judge indifferent,° nor no more assurance   impartial
          Of equal° friendship and proceeding.° Alas, sir,   just / legal order
          In what have I offended you? What cause
          Hath my behavior given to your displeasure
          That thus you should proceed to put me off°   abandon me
20   And take your good grace° from me? Heaven witness   goodwill; yourself
          I have been to you a true and humble wife,
          At all times to your will conformable,
          Ever in fear to kindle your dislike—
          Yea, subject to your countenance, glad or sorry
25   As I saw it inclined. When was the hour
          I ever contradicted your desire?
          Or made it not mine too? Or which of your friends
          Have I not strove to love, although I knew
          He were mine enemy? What friend of mine
30   That had to him derived° your anger did I   incurred
          Continue in my liking? Nay, gave notice
          He was from thence discharged? Sir, call to mind
          That I have been your wife in this obedience
          Upward of twenty years, and have been blessed
35   With many children by you.[4] If in the course
          And process of this time you can report—
          And prove it, too—against mine honor aught,°   anything
          My bond to wedlock, or my love and duty
          Against° your sacred person, in God's name   Toward
40   Turn me away, and let the foul'st contempt
          Shut door upon me, and so give me up
          To the sharp'st kind of justice. Please you, sir,
          The King, your father, was reputed for
          A prince most prudent, of an excellent
45   And unmatched wit° and judgment. Ferdinand,   wisdom
          My father, King of Spain, was reckoned one
          The wisest[5] prince that there had reigned by many
          A year before. It is not to be questioned
          That they had gathered a wise council to them
50   Of every realm that did debate this business,
          Who deemed our marriage lawful. Wherefore I humbly
          Beseech you, sir, to spare me till I may
          Be by my friends in Spain advised, whose counsel
          I will implore. If not, i'th' name of God,
          Your pleasure be fulfilled.
55 WOLSEY   You have here, lady,
          And of your choice,° these reverend fathers, men   picked by you

4. Catharine bore five of Henry's children. All but   5. *was . . . wisest:* was judged the very wisest.
one, later Queen Mary, died at birth or in infancy.

Of singular integrity and learning,
Yea, the elect o'th' land, who are assembled
To plead your cause. It shall be therefore bootless°   *pointless*
60 That longer you desire° the court, as well   *beg (for a delay)*
For your own quiet° as to rectify   *peace of mind*
What is unsettled in the King.
CAMPEIUS   His grace
Hath spoken well and justly. Therefore, madam,
It's fit this royal session do proceed
65 And that, without delay, their arguments
Be now produced and heard.
CATHARINE   Lord Cardinal,
To you I speak.
WOLSEY   Your pleasure, madam.
CATHARINE   Sir,
I am about to weep; but, thinking that
We are a queen—or long have dreamed so—certain°   *without doubt*
70 The daughter of a king, my drops of tears
I'll turn to sparks of fire.
WOLSEY   Be patient yet.
CATHARINE   I will, when you are humble; nay, before,
Or God will punish me. I do believe,
Induced° by potent circumstances,° that   *Convinced / information*
75 You are mine enemy and make my challenge°   *legal objection that*
You shall not be my judge. For it is you
Have blown this coal betwixt my lord and me,
Which God's dew quench. Therefore, I say again,
I utterly abhor,° yea, from my soul   *loathe; reject*
80 Refuse you for my judge, whom yet once more
I hold my most malicious foe and think not
At all a friend to truth.[6]
WOLSEY   I do profess°   *declare*
You speak not like yourself, who ever yet°   *always*
Have stood to° charity, and displayed th'effects   *upheld*
85 Of disposition gentle and of wisdom,
O'er-topping woman's power. Madam, you do me wrong:
I have no spleen° against you, nor injustice   *malevolence*
For you or any. How far I have proceeded,
Or how far further shall, is warranted
90 By a commission from the Consistory,°   *College of Cardinals*
Yea, the whole Consistory of Rome. You charge me
That I have "blown this coal": I do deny it.
The King is present. If it be known to him
That I gainsay my deed,° how may he wound,   *deny what took place*
95 And worthily,° my falsehood—yea, as much   *justly*
As you have done my truth. If he know
That I am free of your report, he knows
I am not of your wrong.[7] Therefore in him
It lies to cure° me, and the cure is to   *absolve*
100 Remove these thoughts from you, the which before

---

6. TEXTUAL COMMENT Catharine's lines here, probably composed by Shakespeare, differ stylistically
from a later speech of hers, probably composed by
Fletcher. See Digital Edition TC 8.

7. *If . . . wrong:* If he agrees that I am innocent
("free") of your accusation, then he knows that I have
done you no wrong, and that I have no part in the
wrong you do me by thus accusing me.

His highness shall speak in,° I do beseech   *about*
You, gracious madam, to unthink your speaking,
And to say so no more.
CATHARINE   My lord, my lord,
I am a simple woman, much too weak
105 T'oppose your cunning. You're meek and humble-mouthed;
You sign your place and calling, in full seeming,
With meekness and humility,[8] but your heart
Is crammed with arrogancy, spleen and pride.
You have, by fortune and his highness' favors,
110 Gone slightly° o'er low steps, and now are mounted   *effortlessly*
Where powers are your retainers and your words,
Domestics to you, serve your will as't please
Yourself pronounce their office.[9] I must tell you,
You tender more° your person's honor than   *have more regard for*
115 Your high profession spiritual, that again
I do refuse you for my judge, and here,
Before you all, appeal unto the Pope,
To bring my whole cause fore his holiness,
And to be judged by him.
She curtsies to the KING *and offers to depart.*
CAMPEIUS   The Queen is obstinate,
120 Stubborn° to justice, apt to accuse it, and   *Impervious*
Disdainful to be tried by't. 'Tis not well.
She's going away.
KING   Call her again.
CRIER Catharine, Queen of England, come into the court!
GRIFFITH Madam, you are called back.
125 CATHARINE What° need you note it? Pray you keep your   *Why*
      way.°   *keep going*
When you are called, return. Now the Lord help—
They vex me past my patience. Pray you, pass on.
I will not tarry; no, nor ever more
Upon this business my appearance make
In any of their courts.
Exeunt Queen [CATHARINE] *and her Attendants.*
130 KING   Go thy ways, Kate,
That man i'th' world who shall report he has
A better wife, let him in naught be trusted
For speaking false in that. Thou art alone—
If thy rare qualities, sweet gentleness,
135 Thy meekness saint-like, wife-like government,°   *restraint*
Obeying in commanding,[1] and thy parts°   *qualities*
Sovereign and pious else,° could speak thee out°—   *besides / describe you*
The queen of earthly queens. She's noble born,
And like her true nobility she has
Carried° herself towards me.   *Conducted*
140 WOLSEY   Most gracious sir,
In humblest manner I require° your highness   *entreat*
That it shall please you to declare in hearing

8. *You . . . humility:* You mark your office and role
with great outward display of meekness and humility.
9. *and now . . . office:* and now have attained a place
where men of authority ("powers") serve you (also:
you have political authority; you have power over

nature), and your words are like attendants ("domestics"), which transform into deeds anything you pronounce as your will.
1. Acting like an obedient wife even as you rule like
a queen.

Of all these ears—for where I am robbed and bound,
There must I be unloosed, although not there
145 At once and fully satisfied°—whether ever I   *given recompense*
Did broach this business to your highness, or
Laid any scruple in your way which might
Induce you to the question on't,° or ever   *of it*
Have to you, but with thanks to God for such
150 A royal lady, spake one the least° word that might   *the very least*
Be to the prejudice of her present state
Or touch° of her good person?   *censure*
KING   My lord Cardinal,
I do excuse you;° yea, upon mine honor,   *forgive you fully*
I free you from't. You are not° to be taught   *do not require*
155 That you have many enemies that know not
Why they are so but, like to village curs,
Bark when their fellows do. By some of these
The Queen is put in anger. You're excused.
But will you be more justified?° You ever   *vindicated*
160 Have wished the sleeping of this business; never desired
It to be stirred, but oft have hindered, oft,
The passages° made toward it. —On my honor,   *proceedings*
I speak my good lord Card'nal to this point,
And thus far clear him.[2] Now, what moved me to't?°   *convinced me of it*
165 I will be bold with time and your attention:
Then mark th'inducement.° Thus it came—give heed to't.   *what influenced me*
My conscience first received a tenderness,°   *sensitivity*
Scruple, and prick on° certain speeches uttered   *from*
By th' Bishop of Bayonne, then French ambassador,
170 Who had been hither sent on the debating
A marriage 'twixt the Duke of Orléans[3] and
Our daughter Mary. I'th' progress of this business,
Ere a determinate resolution,° he—   *decisive settlement*
I mean the Bishop—did require a respite
175 Wherein he might the King his lord advertise°   *make aware*
Whether our daughter were legitimate
Respecting this our marriage with the dowager,
Sometimes° our brother's wife. This respite shook   *Formerly*
The bosom of my conscience, entered me—
180 Yea, with a spitting° power—and made to tremble   *piercing*
The region of my breast, which forced such way
That many mazed considerings did throng
And pressed in with this caution.[4] First, methought
I stood not in the smile of heaven, who had
185 Commanded nature that my lady's womb,
If it conceived a male child by me, should
Do no more offices of life to't than
The grave does to th' dead: for her male issue
Or° died where they were made or shortly after   *Either*
190 This world had aired them.° Hence I took a thought   *given life to; shown*
This was a judgment on me, that my kingdom—
Well worthy the best heir[5] o'th' world—should not

---

2. *I speak . . . him:* Here the King speaks to the court as a whole, announcing that up to this point he exonerates the Cardinal of any wrongdoing.
3. Second son of King Francis I of France, he later became Henry II of France.
4. *many . . . caution:* many confused thoughts crowded in at this warning.
5. Pun on "aired" (line 190).

Be gladded° in't by me. Then follows that   *made joyful*
I weighed the danger which my realms stood in
195   By this my issue's fail,° and that gave to me   *lack; death*
Many a groaning throe.° Thus hulling in[6]   *pang (of pregnancy)*
The wild sea of my conscience, I did steer
Toward this remedy whereupon we are
Now present here together: that's to say,
200   I meant to rectify my conscience, which
I then did feel full sick—and yet° not well—   *still*
By all the reverend fathers of the land
And doctors learned. —First, I began in private
With you, my lord of Lincoln.[7] You remember
205   How under my oppression I did reek°   *sweat*
When I first moved° you?   *appealed to*

LINCOLN   Very well, my liege.

KING   I have spoke long. Be pleased yourself to say
How far you satisfied me.

LINCOLN   So please your highness,
The question did at first so stagger me,
210   Bearing a state of mighty moment° in't   *so weighty, urgent a matter*
And consequence of dread,° that I committed   *dire consequences*
The daring'st counsel which I had to doubt,[8]
And did entreat your highness to this course
Which you are running here.

KING   —I then moved you,
215   My lord of Canterbury, and got your leave
To make this present summons. Unsolicited
I left no reverend person in this court,
But by particular consent proceeded
Under your hands and seals.[9] Therefore go on,
220   For no dislike i'th' world against the person
Of the good Queen, but the sharp thorny points
Of my alleged reasons,° drives this forward.   *reasons advanced by me*
Prove but our marriage lawful, by my life
And kingly dignity, we are contented
225   To wear our mortal state to come, with her—
Catharine, our Queen—before the primest° creature   *most perfect*
That's paragoned o'th'° world.   *considered a model by the*

CAMPEIUS   So please your highness,
The Queen being absent, 'tis a needful fitness°   *only appropriate*
That we adjourn this court till further° day.   *a later*
230   Meanwhile must be an earnest motion°   *plea*
Made to the Queen to call back her appeal
She intends unto his holiness.

KING [*aside*]   I may perceive
These cardinals trifle with me. I abhor
This dilatory sloth and tricks of Rome.
235   —My learn'd and well-belovèd servant, Cranmer,[1]

---

6. Floating aimlessly, like a ship adrift in the current that is not making use of its sails.
7. The Bishop of Lincoln, according to Holinshed, was the King's confessor.
8. *I committed . . . doubt:* I distrusted even the boldest advice I myself could offer.
9. With your written agreement.

1. The King here addresses the absent Thomas Cranmer, who is traveling on the Continent collecting opinions on the status of Henry and Catharine's marriage. See 3.2.400–401 for mention of his return and his elevation to the position of Archbishop of Canterbury.

Prithee return. With thy approach, I know
My comfort comes along. —Break up the court!
I say, set on.°   *Exeunt in manner as they entered.*   *proceed*

3.1

Enter Queen [CATHARINE] *and her* WOMEN, *as at work.*
CATHARINE   Take thy lute, wench. My soul grows sad with troubles.
Sing, and disperse 'em if thou canst. Leave° working.   *Cease*

                       Song.
WOMAN [*sings*]   Orpheus,[1] with his lute, made trees
          And the mountaintops that freeze
          Bow themselves when he did sing.
          To his music, plants and flowers
          Ever sprung, as° sun and showers   *as if*
          There had made a lasting spring.
          Everything that heard him play,
          Even the billows of the sea,
          Hung their heads and then lay by.°   *were still*
          In sweet music is such art
          Killing care and grief of heart
          Fall asleep or, hearing, die.[2]
         Enter GRIFFITH.
CATHARINE   How now?
GRIFFITH   An't please your grace, the two great cardinals
Wait in the presence.°   *reception chamber*
CATHARINE   Would they speak with me?
GRIFFITH   They willed me say so, madam.
CATHARINE   Pray their graces
To come near.   [*Exit* GRIFFITH.]
          What can be their business
With me, a poor weak woman, fall'n from favor?
I do not like their coming, now I think on't.
They should be good men, their affairs as righteous—
But all hoods make not monks.[3]
        Enter the two Cardinals, WOLSEY *and* CAMPEIUS.
WOLSEY   Peace to your highness.
CATHARINE   Your graces find me here part of a housewife—
I would be all,[4] against° the worst may happen.   *in case*
What are your pleasures with me, reverend lords?
WOLSEY   May it please you, noble madam, to withdraw
Into your private chamber? We shall give you
The full cause of our coming.
CATHARINE   Speak it here.
There's nothing I have done yet, o'my conscience,
Deserves a corner.° Would all other women   *subterfuge*
Could speak this with as free° a soul as I do.   *innocent*
My lords, I care not—so much I am happy°   *favored*
Above a number°—if my actions   *many*

3.1 Location: The Queen's apartments at court.
1. In Greek mythology, he was famous for the power of his music.
2. "Music" is so soothing that, upon "hearing" it, "care and grief" either "Fall asleep" or "die."

3. Proverbial: religious trappings do not ensure piety.
4. I would like to be not just partly but completely a housewife.

35 Were tried by ev'ry tongue—ev'ry eye saw 'em,	
Envy and base opinion° set against 'em—	*Spite and base gossip*
I know my life so even.° If your business	*uniformly virtuous*
Seek me out, and that way I am wife in,[5]	
Out with it boldly: truth loves open dealing.	
40 WOLSEY *Tanta est erga te mentis integritas, regina serenissima*[6]—	
CATHARINE O good my lord, no Latin.	
I am not such a truant° since my coming°	*so idle / (to England)*
As not to know the language I have lived in.	
A strange° tongue makes my cause more strange, suspicious.	*foreign*
45 Pray speak in English. Here are some will thank you,	
If you speak truth, for their poor mistress' sake—	
Believe me, she has had much wrong. Lord Cardinal,	
The willing'st° sin I ever yet committed	*most premeditated*
May be absolved in English.	
WOLSEY Noble lady,	
50 I am sorry my integrity should breed—	
And service to his majesty and you—	
So deep suspicion where all faith° was meant.	*loyalty*
We come not by the way° of accusation	*for the sake*
To taint that honor every good tongue blesses,	
55 Nor to betray you any way° to sorrow—	*by any means*
You have too much, good lady—but to know	
How you stand minded° in the weighty difference	*Your deliberation*
Between the King and you, and to deliver,°	*recount*
Like free° and honest men, our just opinions	*unprejudiced*
And comforts to your cause.	
60 CAMPEIUS Most honored madam,	
My lord of York, out of his noble nature,	
Zeal, and obedience he still bore° your grace,	*has always borne*
Forgetting—like a good man—your late censure	
Both of his truth and him—which was° too far—	*went*
65 Offers, as I do, in a sign of peace,	
His service and his counsel.	
CATHARINE [*aside*] To betray me.	
—My lords, I thank you both for your goodwills;	
Ye speak like honest men—pray God ye prove so.	
But how to make ye suddenly° an answer	*without deliberation*
70 In such a point of weight, so near° mine honor—	*bound up with*
More near my life, I fear—with my weak wit,°	*comprehension*
And to such men of gravity and learning?	
In truth, I know not. I was set° at work	*sitting*
Among my maids, full little—God knows—looking	
75 Either for such men or such business.	
For her sake that I have been[7]—for I feel	
The last fit° of my greatness—good your graces,	*spell*
Let me have time and counsel for my cause.	
Alas, I am a woman friendless, hopeless.	
80 WOLSEY Madam, you wrong the King's love with these fears.	
Your hopes and friends are infinite.	

5. *If . . . in:* If your business concerns me and my behavior as wife.
6. So great is the integrity of (my) mind toward you, most serene Queen (Latin).
7. For the sake of the woman—the Queen—I once was.

CATHARINE   In England
But little for my profit.° Can you think, lords,   *of little use to me*
That any Englishman dare give me counsel?
Or be a known friend 'gainst his highness' pleasure—
85   Though he be grown so desperate° to be honest—   *rash enough*
And live a subject?° Nay, forsooth:° my friends,   *survive in England / truly*
They that must weigh out° my afflictions,   *offset*
They that my trust must grow to, live not here;
They are—as all my other comforts—far hence
In mine own country, lords.
90 CAMPEIUS   I would your grace
Would leave your griefs and take my counsel.
CATHARINE   How, sir?
CAMPEIUS   Put your main cause into the King's protection.
He's loving and most gracious. 'Twill be much
Both for your honor better and your cause,
95   For if the trial of the law o'ertake ye,
You'll part away° disgraced.   *leave*
WOLSEY   He tells you rightly.
CATHARINE   Ye tell me what ye wish for both:° my ruin.   *both wish for*
Is this your Christian counsel? Out upon ye!
Heaven is above all yet; there sits a judge
That no king can corrupt.
100 CAMPEIUS   Your rage mistakes° us.   *misrepresents*
CATHARINE   The more shame for ye. Holy men I thought ye,
Upon my soul, two reverend cardinal virtues;[8]
But cardinal sins and hollow hearts I fear ye.
Mend° 'em for shame, my lords. Is this your comfort?   *Reform*
105   The cordial° that ye bring a wretched lady,   *restoring medicine*
A woman lost° among ye, laughed at, scorned?   *ruined*
I will not wish ye half my miseries,
I have more charity. But say I warned ye:
Take heed, for heaven's sake, take heed, lest at once°   *all at once*
110   The burden of my sorrows fall upon ye.
WOLSEY   Madam, this is a mere distraction.°   *utter madness; evasion*
You turn the good we offer into envy.°   *malevolence*
CATHARINE   Ye turn me into nothing. Woe upon ye,
And all such false professors!° Would you have me—   *(of religion)*
115   If you have any justice, any pity,
If ye be anything but churchmen's habits°—   *vestments*
Put my sick cause into his hands that hates me?
Alas, he's banished me his bed already;
His love too, long ago. I am old, my lords,
120   And all the fellowship I hold now with him
Is only my obedience. What can happen
To me above° this wretchedness? All your studies   *beyond*
Make me a curse like this.[9]
CAMPEIUS   Your fears are worse.°   *(than reality)*
CATHARINE   Have I lived thus long—let me speak° myself,   *represent*

8. The cardinal virtues (justice, temperance, prudence, and fortitude, with a play on their rank), which, along with the three theological virtues (faith, hope, and charity), constitute the seven virtues. These oppose the seven deadly ("cardinal," punning on "carnal") sins referred to in the next line.
9. *All . . . this:* All your endeavors (and inquiries) bring me only these miseries.

125 Since virtue finds no friends—a wife, a true one—
A woman, I dare say without vainglory,°   *conceit*
Never yet branded with suspicion—
Have I with all my full affections
Still° met the King, loved him next° heav'n, obeyed him,   *Always / next to*
130 Been, out of fondness, superstitious° to him,   *overly devoted*
Almost forgot my prayers to content him—
And am I thus rewarded? 'Tis not well, lords.
Bring me a constant woman to her husband,
One that ne'er dreamed a joy beyond his pleasure,
135 And to that woman, when she has done most,
Yet will I add an° honor: a great patience.   *another*

WOLSEY   Madam, you wander from° the good we aim at.   *misinterpret*

CATHARINE   My lord, I dare not make myself so guilty
To give up willingly that noble title
140 Your master wed me to. Nothing but death
Shall e'er divorce my dignities.

WOLSEY   Pray hear me.

CATHARINE   Would I had never trod this English earth
Or felt the flatteries that grow upon it!
Ye have angels' faces, but heaven knows your hearts.
145 What will become of me now, wretched lady?
I am the most unhappy woman living.
[*to her* WOMEN] Alas, poor wenches, where are now your fortunes?
Shipwrecked upon a kingdom where no pity,
No friends, no hope, no kindred weep for me,
150 Almost no grave allowed me? Like the lily
That once was mistress of the field and flourished,
I'll hang my head and perish.

WOLSEY   If your grace
Could but be brought to know our ends° are honest,   *intentions*
You'd feel more comfort. Why should we, good lady—
155 Upon what cause—wrong you? Alas, our places,°   *official duties*
The way of our profession, is against it;
We are to cure such sorrows, not to sow 'em.
For goodness' sake, consider what you do,
How you may hurt yourself, ay, utterly
160 Grow from the King's acquaintance by this carriage.°   *behavior*
The hearts of princes kiss obedience,
So much they love it, but to stubborn spirits
They swell and grow as terrible as storms.
I know you have a gentle, noble temper,°   *temperament*
165 A soul as even° as a calm. Pray think us   *unwavering*
Those we profess: peacemakers, friends, and servants.

CAMPEIUS   Madam, you'll find it so. You wrong your virtues
With these weak women's fears. A noble spirit,
As yours was put into° you, ever casts   *given to*
170 Such doubts as false coin from it. The King loves you;
Beware you lose it not. For° us, if you please   *As for*
To trust us in your business, we are ready
To use our utmost studies in your service.

CATHARINE   Do what ye will, my lords, and pray forgive me
175 If I have used° myself unmannerly.   *behaved*
You know I am a woman lacking wit°   *understanding*

To make a seemly answer to such persons.
Pray do my service° to his majesty.   *give my respects*
He has my heart yet, and shall have my prayers
180   While I shall have my life. Come, reverend fathers,
Bestow your counsels on me. She now begs
That° little thought when she set footing here°   *Who / (in England)*
She should have bought her dignities so dear.   *Exeunt.*

3.2

Enter the Duke of NORFOLK, *Duke of* SUFFOLK,
Lord SURREY, *and Lord* CHAMBERLAIN.

NORFOLK   If you will now unite in your complaints
And force them with a constancy,° the Cardinal   *persevere in them*
Cannot stand under them. If you omit°   *neglect*
The offer of this time,° I cannot promise   *This opportunity*
5   But that you shall sustain more new disgraces
With these you bear already.
SURREY   I am joyful
To meet the least occasion that may give me
Remembrance of my father-in-law, the Duke,°   *(of Buckingham)*
To be revenged on him.°   *(Wolsey)*
SUFFOLK   Which of the peers
10   Have uncontemned gone° by him, or at least   *not been disdained*
Strangely neglected?° When did he regard   *Snubbed as a stranger*
The stamp of nobleness in any person
Out of° himself?   *Aside from*
CHAMBERLAIN   My lords, you speak your pleasures.
What he deserves of you and me, I know;
15   What we can do to him—though now the time
Gives way to° us—I much fear. If you cannot   *Favors*
Bar his access to th' King, never attempt
Anything on° him, for he hath a witchcraft   *against*
Over the King in 's tongue.
NORFOLK   Oh, fear him not.
20   His spell in that is out:° the King hath found   *past*
Matter against him that for ever mars
The honey of his language. No, he's settled—
Not to come off—in his displeasure.[1]
SURREY   Sir,
I should be glad to hear such news as this
Once every hour.
25   NORFOLK   Believe it, this is true.
In the divorce, his contrary proceedings°   *double-dealing*
Are all unfolded,° wherein he appears   *exposed*
As I would wish mine enemy.
SURREY   How came
His practices° to light?   *schemes*
SUFFOLK   Most strangely.
SURREY   Oh, how? How?
30   SUFFOLK   The Cardinal's letters to the Pope miscarried°   *went astray; got diverted*
And came to th'eye o'th' King, wherein was read
How that the Cardinal did entreat his holiness

3.2 Location: The court.
1. No, Wolsey is stuck, with no way out, in Henry's

displeasure. Or: No, Henry is firm, with no possibility of changing, in his displeasure toward Wolsey.

To stay° the judgment o'th' divorce—for, if   *delay*
It did take place, "I do," quoth he, "perceive
35   My King is tangled in affection, to
A creature° of the Queen's, Lady Anne Boleyn."   *servant*
SURREY   Has the King this?
SUFFOLK   Believe it.
SURREY   Will this work?
CHAMBERLAIN   The King in this perceives him how he coasts°   *sails indirectly*
And hedges° his own way. But in this point   *moves secretly*
40   All his tricks founder, and he brings his physic°   *medicine*
After his patient's death: the King already
Hath married the fair lady.
SURREY   Would he had!
SUFFOLK   May you be happy in your wish, my lord,
For I profess you have it.
SURREY   Now all my joy
Trace the conjunction.°   *Follow the union*
SUFFOLK   My amen to't.
45   NORFOLK   All men's.
SUFFOLK   There's order given for her coronation.
Marry, this is yet but young,° and may be left   *recent*
To some ears unrecounted.[2] But, my lords,
She is a gallant° creature, and complete°   *an excellent / perfect*
50   In mind and feature. I persuade me° from her   *am sure*
Will fall some blessing to this land, which shall
In it be memorized.[3]
SURREY   But will the King
Digest° this letter of the Cardinal's?   *Tolerate*
The Lord forbid!
NORFOLK   Marry, amen.
SUFFOLK   No, no.
55   There be more wasps that buzz about his nose
Will make this sting the sooner. Cardinal Campeius
Is stol'n away to Rome, hath ta'en no leave,
Has left the cause o'th' King unhandled,° and   *unsettled*
Is posted° as the agent of our cardinal   *Has rushed*
60   To second all his plot. I do assure you
The King cried "Ha!"[4] at this.
CHAMBERLAIN   Now God incense him,
And let him cry "Ha!" louder.
NORFOLK   But, my lord,
When returns Cranmer?
SUFFOLK   He is returned in his opinions, which
65   Have satisfied the King for his divorce,
Together with all famous colleges,
Almost, in Christendom.[5] Shortly, I believe,
His second marriage shall be published,° and   *announced publicly*
Her coronation. Catharine no more
70   Shall be called "Queen," but "Princess Dowager"

2. May not be common knowledge; shouldn't be told to everyone.
3. Be made memorable (alluding to Elizabeth).
4. Henry's characteristic expression of impatience and part of his legend in the Renaissance. See, for instance, 1.2.186 and 2.2.62, 65.
5. *He . . . Christendom:* Cranmer has sent ahead the opinions concerning the King's marriage that he collected on the Continent, and the results have satisfied both the King and most learned clerics.

And "widow to Prince Arthur."

NORFOLK   This same Cranmer's
A worthy fellow, and hath ta'en much pain°   *great pains*
In the King's business.

SUFFOLK   He has, and we shall see him
For it an archbishop.

NORFOLK   So I hear.

SUFFOLK   'Tis so.

       Enter [Cardinal] WOLSEY *and* CROMWELL.

The Cardinal!

75 NORFOLK   Observe, observe: he's moody.

       [They stand apart.]

WOLSEY   The packet,° Cromwell, gave't you the King?   *parcel of letters*

CROMWELL   To his own hand, in 's bedchamber.

WOLSEY   Looked he
O'th' inside of the paper?°   *wrapper*

CROMWELL   Presently°   *Immediately*
He did unseal them, and the first he viewed

80 He did it with a serious mind; a heed°   *concerned look*
Was in his countenance. You he bade
Attend him here this morning.

WOLSEY   Is he ready
To come abroad?

CROMWELL   I think by this° he is.   *by this time*

WOLSEY   Leave me a while.   *Exit* CROMWELL.

85 —It shall be to the Duchess of Alençon,
The French king's sister: he shall marry her.
Anne Boleyn? No, I'll no Anne Boleyns for him;
There's more in't than fair visage. Boleyn?
No, we'll no Boleyns. Speedily I wish

90 To hear from Rome. The Marchioness of Pembroke?[6]

NORFOLK   He's discontented.

SUFFOLK   Maybe he hears the King
Does whet his anger to° him.   *against*

SURREY   Sharp enough,
Lord, for thy justice.

WOLSEY   The late° Queen's gentlewoman? A knight's daughter   *former*

95 To be her mistress' mistress? The Queen's queen?
This candle burns not clear;° 'tis I must snuff it,   *bright*
Then out it goes. What though I know her virtuous
And well deserving? Yet I know her for
A spleeny Lutheran[7] and not wholesome° to   *beneficial*

100 Our cause, that she should lie i'th' bosom of
Our hard-ruled° King. Again, there is sprung up   *hard-to-advise*
An heretic, an arch-one, Cranmer, one°   *one who*
Hath crawled into the favor of the King
And is his oracle.[8]

NORFOLK   He is vexed at something.

       Enter KING, *reading of a schedule*°[*, and* LOVELL].   *scroll*

105 SURREY   I would 'twere something that would fret the string,

---

6. Anne Boleyn's new title, invoked with contempt, anger, disbelief.
7. A passionately spirited Lutheran—that is, an early Protestant, possibly with the implication that Anne is moved by the inner workings of the spirit, rather than by church dogma. Cardinal Wolsey, as a pillar of institutional Catholicism, may have objected to Henry's marriage to Anne for religious reasons, as well as on the grounds of social hierarchy that he outlines in this speech.
8. *is his oracle:* is considered by Henry to be divinely inspired.

The master-cord on 's heart.[9]

SUFFOLK   The King, the King!

KING [*aside*]   What piles of wealth hath he accumulated
To his own portion!° And what expense by th'hour   *share*
Seems to flow from him! How i'th' name of thrift
110   Does he rake this together? —Now, my lords,
Saw you the Cardinal?

NORFOLK   My lord, we have
Stood here observing him. Some strange commotion°   *rebellion*
Is in his brain. He bites his lip, and starts,
Stops on a sudden, looks upon the ground,
115   Then lays his finger on his temple, straight°   *immediately*
Springs out into fast gait, then stops again,
Strikes his breast hard, and anon he casts
His eye against the moon. In most strange postures
We have seen him set himself.

KING   It may well be
120   There is a mutiny in 's mind. This morning,
Papers of state he sent me to peruse
As I required, and wot° you what I found   *know*
There—on my conscience put unwittingly?
Forsooth, an inventory thus importing°   *delineating*
125   The several parcels of his plate,[1] his treasure,
Rich stuffs and ornaments of household, which
I find at such proud rate° that it outspeaks   *high value*
Possession of a subject.[2]

NORFOLK   It's heaven's will.
Some spirit put this paper in the packet,
To bless your eye withal.°   *with*

130   KING   If we did think
His contemplation were above the earth
And fixed on spiritual object, he should still
Dwell in his musings; but I am afraid
His thinkings are below the moon,° not worth   *mundane*
His serious considering.

KING *takes his seat.* [*He*] *whispers* [*with*] LOVELL, *who
goes to the Cardinal.*

135   WOLSEY   Heaven forgive me.
[*to the* KING] Ever God bless your highness.

KING   Good my lord,
You are full of heavenly stuff,[3] and bear the inventory
Of your best graces in your mind, the which
You were now running o'er. You have scarce time
140   To steal from spiritual leisure a brief span
To keep your earthly audit. Sure, in that
I deem you an ill husband, and am glad
To have you therein my companion.[4]

9. *would . . . heart*: would eat through ("fret") the
heartstrings (tying Henry to Wolsey), with a pun on
"cord," Latin for heart (singular *cor*, plural *corda*) and
a musical allusion: "fret" (fingering bar), "string," and
"cord" (chord).
1. *plate*: gold and silver functional household equipment that also stored and displayed wealth.
2. *at . . . subject*: it inventories more wealth than is
fit for a subject.
3. Godly qualities, but Henry's ironic language
("stuff," "steal," "audit") refers to both worldly and

spiritual matters.
4. Henry ironically jokes that both he and Wolsey
are "ill husbands": Wolsey because he cannot manage ("husband") his household resources (ostensibly,
he is otherworldly, but really he is a greedy spendthrift) and because he now opposes Henry's remarriage; and perhaps Henry because he has literally
been a poor husband to Catharine. He may also
mean that he has husbanded his resources badly in
trusting them to Wolsey.

WOLSEY   Sir,
    For holy offices I have a time; a time
145   To think upon the part of business which
    I bear i'th' state; and nature does require
    Her times of preservation which, perforce,
    I, her frail son, amongst my brethren mortal,
    Must give my tendance to.[5]

KING   You have said well.
150 WOLSEY And ever may your highness yoke together,
    As I will lend you cause, my doing well
    With my well saying.

KING   'Tis well said again;
    And 'tis a kind of good deed to say well,
    And yet words are no deeds. My father loved you:
155   He said he did, and with his deed did crown°   *make good*
    His word upon you. Since I had my office,
    I have kept you next° my heart, have not alone   *nearest to*
    Employed you where high profits might come home,
    But pared my present havings° to bestow   *given up possessions*
    My bounties upon you.
160 WOLSEY *[aside]*   What should this mean?
SURREY *[aside]* The Lord increase this business!

KING   Have I not made you
    The prime° man of the state? I pray you tell me   *principal*
    If what I now pronounce you have found true
    And, if you may confess it, say withal°   *furthermore*
165   If you are bound to us or no. What say you?
WOLSEY My sovereign, I confess your royal graces,°   *favors*
    Showered on me daily, have been more than could
    My studied purposes requite, which[6] went
    Beyond all man's endeavors. My endeavors
170   Have ever come too short of my desires,°   *aspirations*
    Yet filed° with my abilities. Mine own ends° *matched / aims*
    Have been mine so that° evermore they pointed *only insofar as*
    To th' good of your most sacred person and
    The profit of the state. For your great graces
175   Heaped upon me—poor undeserver—I
    Can nothing render but allegiant° thanks,   *loyal*
    My prayers to heaven for you, my loyalty
    Which ever has and ever shall be growing
    Till death, that winter, kill it.

KING   Fairly answered.
180   A loyal and obedient subject is
    Therein illustrated. The honor of it
    Does pay the act of it, as i'th' contrary
    The foulness is the punishment.[7] I presume
    That as my hand has opened° bounty to you,   *freely offered*
185   My heart dropped love, my power rained honor more
    On you than any, so your hand and heart,

---

5. *Sir . . . tendance to:* I divide my time among religious duties, affairs of state, and humanly unavoidable personal needs/pleasures.
6. *could / My . . . requite, which:* my conscious efforts could repay, "which" efforts. Possibly, "which" refers instead, or in addition, to "royal graces" (line 166), in which case the contrast is not just between Wolsey's "endeavors" and "desires" (lines 169–70)

but also, less boastfully and more flatteringly, between Henry's magnificent "graces" and Wolsey's comparatively inadequate "endeavors."
7. *The honor . . . punishment:* The reward for loyalty and obedience is the honor they bring. Similarly, disloyalty and corruption are their own punishment, causing the subject dishonor.

Your brain, and every function of your power
Should, notwithstanding that° your bond of duty,°   *despite / (to Rome)*
As 'twere in love's particular,° be more   *peculiar intimacy*
To me, your friend, than any.°   *than to any other*
190   WOLSEY   I do profess
That for your highness' good I ever labored
More than mine own that am, have° and will be.[8]   *have been*
Though all the world should crack° their duty to you   *forswear*
And throw it from their soul, though perils did
195   Abound, as thick as thought could make 'em, and
Appear in forms more horrid, yet my duty,
As doth a rock against the chiding° flood,   *roaring*
Should the approach of this wild river break°   *check*
And stand unshaken yours.
    KING   'Tis nobly spoken.
200   —Take notice, lords, he has a loyal breast,
For you have seen him open't. [*He gives papers to* WOLSEY.]
    Read o'er this
And, after, this—and then to breakfast with
What appetite you have.
        Exit KING, *frowning upon the Cardinal. The nobles*
           throng after him, smiling and whispering.
    WOLSEY   What should this mean?
What sudden anger's this? How have I reaped° it?   *acquired*
205   He parted frowning from me, as if ruin
Leaped from his eyes. So looks the chafèd° lion   *angry*
Upon the daring huntsman that has galled° him,   *wounded*
Then makes him nothing.° I must read this paper—   *slaughters the hunter*
I fear the story of his anger.
    [*He reads the paper.*]
           'Tis so,
210   This paper has undone° me; 'tis th'account   *ruined*
Of all that world° of wealth I have drawn together   *vast quantity*
For mine own ends—indeed, to gain the popedom
And fee° my friends in Rome. Oh, negligence   *pay off*
Fit for a fool to fall by! What cross° devil   *perverse*
215   Made me put this main° secret in the packet   *most important*
I sent the King? Is there no way to cure this,
No new device to beat this from his brains?
I know 'twill stir him strongly. Yet I know
A way, if it take right,° in spite of fortune   *if it succeed*
220   Will bring me off° again. What's this? "To th' Pope"?   *save me*
[*He reads the letter.*] The letter, as I live, with all the business
I writ to 's holiness! Nay, then, farewell:
I have touched the highest point of all my greatness,
And from that full meridian° of my glory   *a star's highest point*
225   I haste now to my setting. I shall fall
Like a bright exhalation° in the evening,   *shooting star*
And no man see me more.
        Enter to WOLSEY *the Dukes of* NORFOLK *and* SUFFOLK,
        the Earl of SURREY, *and the Lord* CHAMBERLAIN.
    NORFOLK   Hear the King's pleasure, Cardinal, who commands you
To render up the great seal presently°   *immediately*

---

8. *More than . . . will be:* "More than" for my "own" good today, previously, or in the future.

230 Into our hands, and to confine yourself
    To Esher House, my lord of Winchester's,
    Till you hear further from his highness.
WOLSEY   Stay!
    Where's your commission,° lords? Words cannot carry   *written warrant*
    Authority so weighty.
SUFFOLK   Who dare cross° 'em,   *challenge*
235 Bearing the King's will from his mouth expressly?
WOLSEY   Till I find more than will or words to do it—
    I mean your malice—know, officious lords,
    I dare and must deny it. Now I feel
    Of what coarse metal° ye are molded: envy!⁹   *(also) mettle*
240 How eagerly ye follow my disgraces,
    As if it fed ye, and how sleek° and wanton°   *slimy / impetuous*
    Ye appear in everything may bring my ruin!
    Follow your envious courses, men of malice;
    You have Christian warrant for 'em, and no doubt
245 In time will find their fit rewards.° That seal   *(ironic)*
    You ask with such a violence,° the King,   *vehemence*
    Mine and your master, with his own hand gave me,
    Bade me enjoy it, with the place° and honors,   *position*
    During my life; and, to confirm his goodness,
250 Tied it by letters patents.° Now, who'll take it?   *open letters*
SURREY   The King that gave it.
WOLSEY   It must be himself, then.
SURREY   Thou art a proud traitor, priest.
WOLSEY   Proud lord, thou liest!
    Within these forty hours Surrey durst better
    Have burnt that tongue than said so.
SURREY   Thy ambition,
255 Thou scarlet sin,¹ robbed this bewailing land
    Of noble Buckingham, my father-in-law.
    The heads of all thy brother cardinals—
    With thee and all thy best parts° bound together—   *attributes*
    Weighed° not a hair of his. Plague of° your policy!°   *Equaled / on / scheming*
260 You sent me deputy for Ireland,
    Far from his succor, from the King, from all
    That might have mercy on the fault thou gav'st him,°   *charged him with*
    Whilst your great goodness, out of holy pity,
    Absolved him with an ax.
WOLSEY   This, and all else
265 This talking lord can lay upon my credit,°   *good reputation*
    I answer is most false. The Duke by law
    Found his deserts. How innocent I was
    From° any private malice in his end,   *Of*
    His noble jury and foul cause can witness.
270 If I loved many words, lord, I should tell you
    You have as little honesty as honor,
    That° in the way of loyalty and truth   *I who*
    Toward the King, my ever royal master,
    Dare mate° a sounder man than Surrey can be,   *rival*
    And all that love his follies.

9. Malice; jealousy.   280. *scarlet sin:* egregious sin in the Bible; see Isaiah
1. *scarlet:* referring to the Cardinal's robes; see line   1:18.

275 SURREY   By my soul,
Your long coat, priest, protects you; thou shouldst feel
My sword i'th' lifeblood of thee else. My lords,
Can ye endure to hear this arrogance?
And from this fellow?° If we live thus tamely,   *(contemptuous)*
280 To be thus jaded° by a piece of scarlet,   *cowed*
Farewell, nobility: let his grace go forward
And dare us with his cap, like larks.[2]
WOLSEY   All goodness
Is poison to thy stomach.
SURREY   Yes, that "goodness"
Of gleaning° all the land's wealth into one,   *bringing together*
285 Into your own hands, Card'nal, by extortion;
The "goodness" of your intercepted packets
You writ to th' Pope against the King; your "goodness"—
Since you provoke me—shall be most notorious.
—My lord of Norfolk, as you are truly noble,
290 As you respect the common good, the state
Of our despised nobility, our issues°—   *sons*
Who, if he° live, will scarce be gentlemen—   *(Wolsey)*
Produce the grand sum of his sins, the articles°   *charges against him*
Collected from his life. —I'll startle you
295 Worse than the sacring-bell when the brown wench
Lay kissing in your arms,[3] Lord Cardinal.
WOLSEY   How much, methinks, I could despise this man,
But that I am bound in charity against it.
NORFOLK   Those articles, my lord, are in the King's hand;°   *possession*
But thus° much: they are foul ones.   *I'll tell you this*
300 WOLSEY   So much fairer
And spotless shall mine innocence arise
When the King knows my truth.°   *loyalty*
SURREY   This cannot save you.
I thank my memory I yet remember
Some of these articles, and out they shall.
305 Now, if you can blush and cry "Guilty," Cardinal,
You'll show a little honesty.
WOLSEY   Speak on, sir,
I dare your worst objections.° If I blush,   *accusations*
It is to see a nobleman want° manners.   *lack*
SURREY   I had rather want those than my head. Have at you!°   *(a challenge)*
310 First, that without the King's assent or knowledge
You wrought to be a legate,[4] by which power
You maimed the jurisdiction of all bishops.
NORFOLK   Then, that in all you writ to Rome, or else
To foreign princes, *"ego et rex meus"*[5]
315 Was still° inscribed, in which you brought the King   *always*
To be your servant.
SUFFOLK   Then, that without the knowledge

---

2. And befuddle us with his scarlet cap, as larks are
caught by dazzling them with scarlet cloth.
3. *I'll . . . arms:* The small "sacring-bell" was rung at
Mass when the priest elevated the consecrated Host.
Surrey imagines Wolsey surprised with a country girl
("brown" because tanned or dirty from working, or
perhaps ugly or promiscuous) when he should have

been at Mass.
4. You schemed to be a papal representative.
5. "I and my king." Norfolk accuses Wolsey of putting
himself before the King and of making the King his
dependent. Technically, however, the Latin word
order is correct and means "my king and I," thus making it less offensive.

Either of King or Council, when you went
Ambassador to the Emperor° you made bold   *Charles V*
To carry into Flanders the great seal.

320 SURREY *Item:*° you sent a large commission°   *Next / delegation*
To Gregory de Cassado to conclude,
Without the King's will or the state's allowance,°   *consent*
A league between his highness and Ferrara.

SUFFOLK That, out of mere° ambition, you have caused   *pure*
325 Your holy hat to be stamped on the King's coin.[6]

SURREY Then, that you have sent innumerable substance°—   *untold riches*
By what means got, I leave to your own conscience—
To furnish° Rome and to prepare the ways   *supply; bribe*
You have for dignities[7], to the mere undoing°   *complete destruction*
330 Of all the kingdom. Many more there are,
Which since they are of you, and odious,
I will not taint my mouth with.

CHAMBERLAIN   O my lord,
Press° not a falling man too far. 'Tis virtue.°   *Oppress / (not to)*
His faults lie open to° the laws; let them,   *exposed before*
335 Not you, correct him. My heart weeps to see him
So little of his great self.

SURREY   I forgive him.

SUFFOLK Lord Cardinal, the King's further pleasure is,
Because all those things you have done of late
By your power legative within this kingdom,
340 Fall into th' compass of a *praemunire*,[8]
That therefore such a writ be sued° against you,   *served*
To forfeit all your goods, lands, tenements,
Castles, and whatsoever, and to be
Out of the King's protection. This is my charge.

345 NORFOLK And so we'll leave you to your meditations
How to live better. For your stubborn answer
About the giving back the great seal to us,
The King shall know it and, no doubt, shall thank you.
So fare you well, my little good lord Cardinal.

Exeunt all but WOLSEY.

350 WOLSEY So, farewell to the little good you bear me.
Farewell? A long farewell to all my greatness.
This is the state of man. Today he puts forth
The tender leaves of hopes; tomorrow blossoms
And bears his blushing° honors thick upon him;   *resplendent*
355 The third day comes a frost, a killing frost—
And when he thinks, good easy° man, full surely   *trusting*
His greatness is a-ripening—nips his root,
And then he falls, as I do. I have ventured,
Like little wanton boys that swim on bladders,[9]
360 This many summers in a sea of glory,
But far beyond my depth. My high-blown pride

---

6. Allowed to produce half groats and half pennies with his insignia in his home diocese of York, Wolsey had his cardinal's hat stamped on a groat, thereby usurping the King's monopoly on coins of larger denominations.
7. To become pope.
8. Having made himself a representative of the pope, Wolsey is subject to punishment because he has bro-
ken the law of *praemunire*—that is, he has appealed to an outside (here, papal) court when the offense fell under the jurisdiction of English courts. Wolsey is thus charged with elevating the pope's authority over his sovereign's.
9. Like frolicsome little boys who stay afloat (only by) using inflated membranes from an animal's body.

At length broke under me and now has left me,
Weary and old with service, to the mercy
Of a rude stream° that must for ever hide me.   *turbulent current*
365   Vain pomp and glory of this world, I hate ye!
I feel my heart new opened. Oh, how wretched
Is that poor man that hangs on princes' favors!
There is betwixt that smile we would aspire to,
That sweet aspect of princes, and their ruin[1]
370   More pangs and fears than wars or women have;
And when he falls, he falls like Lucifer,°   *(from heaven to hell)*
Never to hope again.
          Enter CROMWELL, *standing amazed.*
                 Why, how now, Cromwell?
CROMWELL   I have no power to speak, sir.
WOLSEY   What, amazed
At my misfortunes? Can thy spirit wonder
375   A great man should decline?° Nay, an° you weep   *fall from power / if*
I am fall'n indeed.
CROMWELL   How does your grace?
WOLSEY   Why, well.
Never so truly happy, my good Cromwell:
I know myself now, and I feel within me
A peace above all earthly dignities,
380   A still and quiet conscience. The King has cured me—
I humbly thank his grace—and from these shoulders,
These ruined pillars,[2] out of pity, taken
A load would sink a navy: too much honor.
Oh, 'tis a burden, Cromwell, 'tis a burden
385   Too heavy for a man that hopes for heaven.
CROMWELL   I am glad your grace has made that right use of it.
WOLSEY   I hope I have. I am able now, methinks,
Out of a fortitude of soul I feel,
To endure more miseries and greater far
390   Than my weak-hearted enemies dare offer.
What news abroad?
CROMWELL   The heaviest and the worst
Is your displeasure° with the King.   *disgrace*
WOLSEY   God bless him.
CROMWELL   The next is that Sir Thomas More is chosen
Lord Chancellor in your place.
WOLSEY   That's somewhat sudden.
395   But he's a learnèd man. May he continue
Long in his highness' favor, and do justice
For truth's sake and his conscience, that his bones,
When he has run his course and sleeps in blessings,
May have a tomb of orphans' tears wept on him.[3]
What more?
400   CROMWELL   That Cranmer is returned° with welcome,   *(from the Continent)*
Installed Lord Archbishop of Canterbury.[4]

---

1. *their ruin:* the destruction they cause.
2. Perhaps the pillars carried during Wolsey's triumphal entrance in 2.4.
3. The Lord Chancellor's duties included guardianship of all children under age twenty-one, particu-
larly orphans. Henry had More beheaded in 1535 for his Catholicism; hence, there is irony and perhaps pathos in Wolsey's good wishes.
4. In 1533; Cranmer was beheaded by Henry's oldest daughter, Queen Mary, in 1556 for his Protestantism.

WOLSEY   That's news indeed!

CROMWELL   Last, that the Lady Anne,
  Whom the King hath in secrecy long married,
  This day was viewed in open as his queen,
405 Going to chapel, and the voice° is now   *gossip*
  Only about her coronation.

WOLSEY   There was the weight that pulled me down.
      O Cromwell,
  The King has gone beyond° me. All my glories   *overreached*
  In° that one woman I have lost for ever.   *Due to*
410 No sun shall ever usher forth mine honors,
  Or gild again the noble troops° that waited   *retainers*
  Upon my smiles. Go, get thee from me, Cromwell,
  I am a poor fall'n man, unworthy now
  To be thy lord and master. Seek the King—
415 That sun I pray may never set. I have told him
  What and how true thou art: he will advance thee.
  Some little memory of me will stir him—
  I know his noble nature—not to let
  Thy hopeful° service perish too. Good Cromwell,   *potentially valuable*
420 Neglect him not. Make use° now, and provide   *Seize your chance*
  For thine own future safety.

CROMWELL   O my lord,
  Must I then leave you? Must I needs forgo°   *renounce*
  So good, so noble, and so true a master?
  Bear witness, all that have not hearts of iron,
425 With what a sorrow Cromwell leaves his lord.
  The King shall have my service, but my prayers
  For ever and for ever shall be yours.

WOLSEY   Cromwell, I did not think to shed a tear
  In all my miseries, but thou hast forced me,
430 Out of thy honest truth, to play the woman.°   *to weep*
  Let's dry our eyes, and thus far hear me, Cromwell,
  And when I am forgotten, as I shall be,
  And sleep in dull cold marble where no mention
  Of me more must be heard of, say I taught thee;
435 Say Wolsey, that once trod the ways of glory
  And sounded° all the depths and shoals of honor,   *fathomed*
  Found thee a way, out of his wreck,° to rise in—   *shipwreck*
  A sure and safe one, though thy master missed it.
  Mark but my fall and that that ruined me.
440 Cromwell, I charge thee, fling away ambition;[5]
  By that sin fell the angels. How can man, then,
  The image of his maker, hope to win° by it?   *profit*
  Love thyself last, cherish those hearts that hate thee;
  Corruption wins not more than honesty.
445 Still° in thy right hand carry gentle peace   *Ever*
  To silence envious tongues. Be just, and fear not.
  Let all the ends thou aim'st at be thy country's,
  Thy God's, and truth's. Then if thou fall'st, O Cromwell,
  Thou fall'st a blessèd martyr.[6]

---

5. Cromwell did not take Wolsey's advice; Henry had   6. As Cromwell was sometimes thought to be in
him beheaded in 1540 for treason and heresy after an   Shakespeare's time.
even more rapid rise and fall than Wolsey's.

450 Serve the King. And prithee lead me in;
There take an inventory of all I have
To the last penny: 'tis the King's. My robe
And my integrity to heaven is all
I dare now call mine own. O Cromwell, Cromwell,
455 Had I but served my God with half the zeal
I served my King, he would not in mine age
Have left me naked° to mine enemies.   *utterly exposed*

CROMWELL   Good sir, have patience.

WOLSEY   So I have. Farewell
The hopes of court; my hopes in heaven do dwell. *Exeunt.*

4.1

Enter two GENTLEMEN, *meeting one another.*

FIRST GENTLEMAN   You're well met once again.[1]

SECOND GENTLEMAN   So are you.

FIRST GENTLEMAN   You come to take your stand here and behold
The Lady Anne pass from her coronation.

SECOND GENTLEMAN   'Tis all my° business. At our last encounter,   *my only*
5   The Duke of Buckingham came from his trial.

FIRST GENTLEMAN   'Tis very true. But that time offered sorrow,
This, general joy.

SECOND GENTLEMAN   'Tis well. The citizens,
I am sure, have shown at full their royal minds°—   *allegiance; nobility*
As, let 'em have their rights, they are ever forward[2]—
10   In celebration of this day with shows,
Pageants, and sights of honor.

FIRST GENTLEMAN   Never greater,
Nor, I'll assure you, better taken,° sir.   *received*

SECOND GENTLEMAN   May I be bold to ask what that contains,
That paper in your hand?

FIRST GENTLEMAN   Yes, 'tis the list
15   Of those that claim their offices this day
By custom of the coronation.
The Duke of Suffolk is the first, and claims
To be High Steward; next, the Duke of Norfolk,
He to be Earl Marshal. You may read the rest.
20   SECOND GENTLEMAN   I thank you, sir. Had I not known those customs,
I should have been beholden to your paper.
But I beseech you, what's become of Catharine,
The Princess Dowager? How goes her business?

FIRST GENTLEMAN   That I can tell you, too. The Archbishop
25   Of Canterbury, accompanied with other
Learnèd and reverend fathers of his order,
Held a late° court at Dunstable, six miles off   *Recently held a*
From Ampthill, where the Princess lay;° to which   *resided*
She was often cited° by them, but appeared not.   *summoned*
30   And, to be short, for not appearance and
The King's late scruple, by the main assent°   *consensus*
Of all these learnèd men, she was divorced
And the late marriage made of none effect;°   *null*

4.1 Location: A street in Westminster.   2. As, to give them their due, they are always eager
1. See 2.1.1, note 1   to demonstrate.

Since which she was removed to Kimbolton,
Where she remains now sick.

35 SECOND GENTLEMAN   Alas, good lady.
     [*Trumpets.*]
The trumpets sound. Stand close:° the Queen is coming.   aside

The order of the coronation.

1 A lively flourish of trumpets.
2 Then two Judges.
3 Lord CHANCELLOR, *with purse and mace before him.*
4 Choristers° singing. Music.   choir members
5 Mayor of London, bearing the mace. Then GARTER,°   herald; royal emcee
in his coat of arms, and on his head he wears a gilt
copper crown.
6 Marquess Dorset, bearing a scepter of gold; on his
head, a demi-coronal° of gold. With him, the Earl of   small crown
SURREY, *bearing the rod of silver with the dove,*
crowned with an earl's coronet. Collars of esses.[3]
7 Duke of SUFFOLK, *in his robe of estate, his coronet*
on his head, bearing a long white wand, as High
Steward. With him, the Duke of NORFOLK, *with the*
rod of marshalship, a coronet on his head. Collars of
esses.
8 A Canopy, borne by four of the Cinque Ports;[4] *under*
it, the Queen [ANNE] *in her robe, in her hair, richly*
adorned with pearl, crowned. On each side her, the
Bishop of London and [GARDINER, *Bishop of*]
Winchester.
9 The old Duchess of Norfolk, in a coronal of gold
wrought with flowers, bearing the Queen's train.
10 Certain Ladies or Countesses, with plain circlets of
gold without flowers.
    Exeunt, first passing over the stage in order and state,
           and then a great flourish of trumpets.

SECOND GENTLEMAN A royal train,° believe me. These I know.   procession
Who's that that bears the scepter?
FIRST GENTLEMAN   Marquess Dorset,
And that the Earl of Surrey, with the rod.
40 SECOND GENTLEMAN A bold brave gentleman. That should be
The Duke of Suffolk.
FIRST GENTLEMAN   'Tis the same: High Steward.
SECOND GENTLEMAN And that my lord of Norfolk?
FIRST GENTLEMAN   Yes.
SECOND GENTLEMAN [*seeing* ANNE]   Heaven bless thee!
Thou hast the sweetest face I ever looked on.
Sir, as I have a soul, she is an angel.
45 Our King has all the Indies[5] in his arms,
And more, and richer, when he strains° that lady.   embraces
I cannot blame his conscience.

---

3. Heavy gold chains made of S-shaped links worn around the neck by men of high office.
4. By traditional prerogative, the barons of the Cinque Ports (literally, five ports: Hastings, Sandwich, Dover, Romney, and Hythe on the southeast-ern coast of England) carried a canopy over the sovereign at state occasions.
5. The East and West Indies were considered sources of great wealth. See 1.1.21.

FIRST GENTLEMAN   They that bear
The cloth of honor over her are four barons
Of the Cinque Ports.
50 SECOND GENTLEMAN   Those men are happy, and so are all°   *all who*
are near her.
I take it she that carries up the train
Is that old noble lady, Duchess of Norfolk?
FIRST GENTLEMAN   It is, and all the rest are countesses.
SECOND GENTLEMAN   Their coronets say so. These are stars
indeed—
FIRST GENTLEMAN   And sometimes falling ones.°   *meteors; (sexual)*
55 SECOND GENTLEMAN   No more of that.

Enter a THIRD GENTLEMAN.

FIRST GENTLEMAN   God save you, sir. Where have you been
broiling?°   *overheating*
THIRD GENTLEMAN   Among the crowd i'th' Abbey, where
a finger
Could not be wedged in more.[6] I am stifled
With the mere rankness° of their joy.   *exuberance; odor*
SECOND GENTLEMAN   You saw
The ceremony?
THIRD GENTLEMAN   That I did.
60 FIRST GENTLEMAN   How was it?
THIRD GENTLEMAN   Well worth the seeing.
SECOND GENTLEMAN   Good sir, speak° it to us.   *describe*
THIRD GENTLEMAN   As well as I am able. The rich stream
Of lords and ladies, having brought the Queen
To a prepared place in the choir,° fell off°   *company / drew back*
65 A distance from her, while her grace sat down
To rest a while, some half an hour or so,
In a rich chair of state, opposing° freely   *displaying*
The beauty of her person to the people—
Believe me, sir, she is the goodliest° woman   *fairest*
70 That ever lay by man—which, when the people
Had the full view of, such a noise arose
As the shrouds° make at sea in a stiff tempest,   *ship's rigging*
As loud and to as many tunes. Hats, cloaks—
Doublets,° I think—flew up, and had their faces   *Short jackets*
75 Been loose, this day they had been lost. Such joy
I never saw before! Great-bellied women
That had not half a week to go, like rams°   *battering rams*
In the old time of war, would shake the press°   *crowd*
And make 'em reel before 'em. No man living
80 Could say, "This is my wife" there, all were woven
So strangely in one piece.
SECOND GENTLEMAN   But what followed?
THIRD GENTLEMAN   At length her grace rose, and with modest paces
Came to the altar, where she kneeled and, saint-like,
Cast her fair eyes to heaven and prayed devoutly;
85 Then rose again and bowed her to the people,
When by the Archbishop of Canterbury

---

6. The undertones here ("a finger . . . wedged in")
and in a subsequent speech of the Third Gentleman
("Great-bellied women," line 76; "No man living /
Could say, 'This is my wife,'" lines 79–80) suggest
the sexual energy somehow connected with, and
unleashed by, Anne.

She had all the royal makings° of a Queen,   *essential trappings*
As holy oil, Edward Confessor's crown,
The rod, and bird of peace, and all such emblems
90 Laid nobly on her. Which performed, the choir,
With all the choicest music° of the kingdom,   *musicians*
Together sung *Te Deum*.[7] So she parted,°   *departed*
And with the same full state° paced back again   *ceremony*
To York Place, where the feast is held.
FIRST GENTLEMAN   Sir,
95 You must no more call it "York Place"—that's past,
For since the Cardinal fell, that title's lost;
'Tis now the King's, and called Whitehall.[8]
THIRD GENTLEMAN   I know it,
But 'tis so lately altered that the old name
Is fresh about me.
SECOND GENTLEMAN What two reverend bishops
100 Were those that went on each side of the Queen?
THIRD GENTLEMAN Stokesley and Gardiner, the one of
    Winchester,
Newly preferred° from the King's secretary;   *promoted*
The other, London.[9]
SECOND GENTLEMAN He of Winchester
Is held no great good lover of the Archbishop's,
The virtuous Cranmer.
105 THIRD GENTLEMAN   All the land knows that.
However, yet there is no great breach. When it comes,
Cranmer will find a friend will not° shrink from him.   *who will not*
SECOND GENTLEMAN Who may that be, I pray you?
THIRD GENTLEMAN   Thomas Cromwell,
A man in much esteem with th' King, and truly
110 A worthy friend. The King has made him
Master o'th' Jewel House,[1]
And one already of the Privy Council.
SECOND GENTLEMAN He will deserve more.
THIRD GENTLEMAN   Yes, without all doubt.
Come, gentlemen, ye shall go my way,
115 Which is to th' court, and there ye shall be my guests;
Something° I can command. As I walk thither,   *Some influence*
I'll tell ye more.
FIRST *and* SECOND GENTLEMEN You may command us, sir.
                             Exeunt.

4.2

Enter CATHARINE *Dowager, sick, led between*
GRIFFITH, *her Gentleman Usher, and* PATIENCE,
her Woman.
GRIFFITH How does your grace?
CATHARINE   O Griffith, sick to death.
My legs like loaden° branches bow to th'earth,   *heavily laden*

---

7. A hymn of praise and thanksgiving beginning *"Te Deum laudamus,"* "We praise thee, O Lord."
8. By the time *Henry VIII* was first performed, Whitehall was the site of court masques similar to the ones staged in the play.
9. John Stokesley was Bishop of London; already sec-retary to the King, Gardiner also became Bishop of Winchester following Wolsey's demise.
1. Officer in charge of the Crown Jewels, which are housed in the Tower of London.
4.2 Location: Catharine's apartments in Kimbolton.

Willing to leave their burden. Reach a chair.
[GRIFFITH *brings her a chair. She sits.*]
So now, methinks, I feel a little ease.

5 Didst thou not tell me, Griffith, as thou led'st me,
That the great child of honor,° Cardinal Wolsey,   *(ironic)*
Was dead?

GRIFFITH   Yes, madam, but I think your grace,
Out of the pain you suffered, gave no ear to't.

CATHARINE   Prithee, good Griffith, tell me how he died.

10 If well, he stepped before me happily°   *aptly*
For my example.

GRIFFITH   Well, the voice° goes, madam.   *talk*
For after the stout Earl Northumberland
Arrested him at York and brought him forward,
As a man sorely tainted,° to his answer,°   *disgraced / hearing*

15 He fell sick suddenly and grew so ill
He could not sit his mule.

CATHARINE   Alas, poor man.

GRIFFITH   At last, with easy roads,° he came to Leicester,   *stages of a journey*
Lodged in the abbey, where the reverend abbot,
With all his convent,° honorably received him;   *monastery*

20 To whom he gave these words: "O father abbot,
An old man, broken with the storms of state,
Is come to lay his weary bones among ye.
Give him a little earth,° for charity."   *resting place*
So went to bed, where eagerly his sickness

25 Pursued him still; and, three nights after this,
About the hour of eight—which he himself
Foretold should be his last—full of repentance,
Continual meditations, tears, and sorrows,
He gave his honors to the world again,

30 His blessèd part° to heaven, and slept in peace.   *soul*

CATHARINE   So may he rest; his faults lie gently on him.
Yet thus far, Griffith, give me leave to speak° him,   *describe*
And yet with charity. He was a man
Of an unbounded stomach,° ever ranking   *ambition*

35 Himself with princes; one that by suggestion°   *underhanded dealing*
Tied° all the kingdom. Simony¹ was fair play.   *Shackled*
His own opinion was his law. I'th' presence°   *King's chamber*
He would say untruths, and be ever double°   *duplicitious*
Both in his words and meaning. He was never—

40 But where he meant to ruin—pitiful.°   *merciful*
His promises were as he then was, mighty;
But his performance, as he is now, nothing.
Of his own body he was ill,° and gave   *sexually immoral*
The clergy ill example.

GRIFFITH   Noble madam,

45 Men's evil manners live in brass; their virtues
We write in water.² May it please your highness
To hear me speak his good now?

CATHARINE   Yes, good Griffith,
I were malicious else.

---

1. Trading, for money or favors, in ecclesiastical offices.
2. *Men's . . . water:* Evil deeds are long remembered; good ones soon forgotten (proverbial).

GRIFFITH   This cardinal,
Though from an humble stock, undoubtedly
50   Was fashioned to much honor. From his cradle
He was a scholar, and a ripe and good one,
Exceeding° wise, fair-spoken and persuading,°   *Exceedingly / persuasive*
Lofty and sour to them that loved him not,
But to those men that sought him,° sweet as summer.   *befriended him*
55   And though he were unsatisfied° in getting°—   *insatiable / (riches)*
Which was a sin—yet in bestowing, madam,
He was most princely: ever witness for him
Those twins of learning that he raised° in you,   *set up*
Ipswich and Oxford³—one of which fell with him,
60   Unwilling to outlive the good that did° it;   *created*
The other, though unfinished, yet so famous,
So excellent in art,° and still so rising,   *scholarship*
That Christendom shall ever speak his virtue.
His overthrow heaped happiness upon him,
65   For then, and not till then, he felt° himself,   *recognized*
And found the blessèdness of being little.°   *humble*
And to add greater honors to his age
Than man could give him, he died fearing God.
CATHARINE   After my death I wish no other herald,
70   No other speaker of my living actions
To keep mine honor from corruption,
But such an honest chronicler as Griffith.
Whom I most hated living,° thou hast made me,   *while alive*
With thy religious truth and modesty,°   *equanimity*
75   Now in his ashes honor. Peace be with him.
—Patience, be near me still, and set me lower;
I have not long to trouble thee. —Good Griffith,
Cause the musicians play me that sad note°   *melody*
I named my knell, whilst I sit meditating
80   On that celestial harmony I go to.⁴
            Sad and solemn music.
GRIFFITH   She is asleep. Good wench, let's sit down quiet
For fear we wake her. Softly, gentle Patience.

                        The Vision.

Enter, solemnly tripping° one after another, six   *moving nimbly*
personages, clad in white robes, wearing on their heads
garlands of bays, and golden vizards on their faces,⁵
branches of bays or palm in their hands. They first
congé° unto her, then dance; and at certain changes,°   *dance movements*
the first two hold a spare garland over her head, at
which the other four make reverend curtsies. Then the
two that held the garland deliver the same to the other
next two, who observe the same order in their changes,
and holding the garland over her head. Which done,
they deliver the same garland to the last two, who
likewise observe the same order. At which, as it were by
inspiration, she makes in her sleep signs of rejoicing,

---

3. Wolsey founded colleges at Ipswich and Oxford; the latter survives as Christ Church.
4. After death, the soul supposedly could hear the music of the spheres (the heavenly bodies) as they revolved around the earth.
5. White to signify purity; bay leaves ("bays") to indicate triumph or joy; golden masks ("vizards") perhaps to suggest they are spirits.

and holdeth up her hands to heaven. And so in their
dancing vanish, carrying the garland with them.
The music continues.

CATHARINE Spirits of peace, where are ye? Are ye all gone,
And leave me here in wretchedness behind ye?

GRIFFITH Madam, we are here.

85 CATHARINE   It is not you I call for.
Saw ye none enter since I slept?

GRIFFITH   None, madam.

CATHARINE No? Saw you not, even now, a blessèd troop
Invite me to a banquet, whose bright faces
Cast thousand beams upon me, like the sun?

90 They promised me eternal happiness
And brought me garlands, Griffith, which I feel
I am not worthy yet to wear. I shall, assuredly.

GRIFFITH I am most joyful, madam, such good dreams
Possess your fancy.°   *Fill your imagination*

CATHARINE   Bid the music° leave.   *musicians*
They are harsh and heavy° to me.   *tiresome*
Music ceases.

95 PATIENCE [*aside to* GRIFFITH]   Do you note
How much her grace is altered on the sudden?
How long her face is drawn? How pale she looks,
And of an earthy cold. Mark her eyes.

GRIFFITH She is going, wench. Pray, pray.

PATIENCE   Heaven comfort her!
Enter a MESSENGER.

MESSENGER An't like° your grace—   *If it please*

100 CATHARINE   You are a saucy fellow.
Deserve we no more reverence?

GRIFFITH [*to the* MESSENGER]   You are to blame,
Knowing she will not lose her wonted° greatness,   *forgo her usual*
To use so rude behavior. Go to, kneel.

MESSENGER [*kneeling*] I humbly do entreat your highness'
pardon;

105 My haste made me unmannerly. There is staying°   *waiting*
A gentleman sent from the King to see you.

CATHARINE Admit him entrance, Griffith. But this fellow
Let me ne'er see again.   *Exit* MESSENGER.
Enter Lord CAPUTIUS.

                   —If my sight fail not,
You should be lord ambassador from the Emperor,°   *(Charles V)*

110 My royal nephew, and your name Caputius.

CAPUTIUS Madam, the same. Your servant.

CATHARINE   O my lord,
The times and titles now are altered strangely
With me since first you knew me. But I pray you,
What is your pleasure with me?

CAPUTIUS   Noble lady,

115 First mine own service to your grace; the next,
The King's request that I would visit you,
Who grieves much for your weakness, and by me
Sends you his princely commendations°   *compliments*
And heartily entreats you take good comfort.

120 CATHARINE O my good lord, that comfort comes too late:
'Tis like a pardon after execution.

That gentle physic,° given in time, had cured me;   *medicine*
But now I am past all comforts here but prayers.
How does his highness?

CAPUTIUS   Madam, in good health.

125 CATHARINE So may he ever do, and ever flourish,
When I shall dwell with worms and my poor name
Banished the kingdom. —Patience, is that letter
I caused you write yet sent away?

PATIENCE   No, madam.

CATHARINE Sir, I most humbly pray you to deliver
This to my lord the King—

130 CAPUTIUS   Most willing,° madam.   *willingly*

CATHARINE   —In which I have commended to his goodness
The model° of our chaste loves, his young daughter[6]—   *image*
The dews of heaven fall thick in blessings on her!—
Beseeching him to give her virtuous breeding°—   *raise her virtuously*
135 She is young and of a noble modest nature;
I hope she will deserve well—and a little
To love her for her mother's sake, that loved him
Heaven knows how dearly. My next poor petition
Is that his noble grace would have some pity
140 Upon my wretched women, that so long
Have followed both my fortunes° faithfully;   *(good and bad)*
Of which there is not one, I dare avow—
And now I should not lie[7]—but will deserve,
For virtue and true beauty of the soul,
145 For honesty° and decent carriage,°   *chastity / conduct*
A right good husband—let him be a noble—
And sure those men are happy that shall have 'em.
The last is for my men—they are the poorest,
But poverty could never draw 'em from me—
150 That they may have their wages duly paid 'em,
And something over to remember me by.
If heaven had pleased to have given me longer life
And able° means, we had not parted thus.   *sufficient*
These are the whole contents; and, good my lord,
155 By that you love the dearest in this world,
As you wish Christian peace to souls departed,
Stand these poor people's friend and urge the King
To do me this last rite.°   *(also) right*

CAPUTIUS   By heaven, I will,
Or let me lose the fashion of a man.°   *forfeit my humanity*

160 CATHARINE I thank you, honest lord. Remember me
In all humility unto his highness.
Say his long trouble now is passing
Out of this world. Tell him in death I blessed him,
For so I will. Mine eyes grow dim. Farewell,
165 My lord. —Griffith, farewell. —Nay, Patience,
You must not leave me yet. I must to bed:
Call in more women. When I am dead, good wench,
Let me be used° with honor. Strew me over   *treated*

---

6. Mary was Catharine and Henry's only child who
survived infancy (see 2.4.35 and note). She was
queen for five years (1553–58) before Elizabeth, her
half-sister.

7. Now, on the point of death, I would not (ought not
to) lie. It was generally thought that people spoke
truth on their deathbeds.

With maiden° flowers, that all the world may know °(signifying chastity)
170 I was a chaste wife to my grave. Embalm me,
Then lay me forth.° Although unqueened, yet like °prepare me for burial
A queen and daughter to a king inter me.
I can° no more. *Exeunt leading* CATHARINE. °can say or do

5.1

Enter GARDINER, *Bishop of Winchester, a* PAGE *with a torch before him, met by Sir Thomas* LOVELL.

GARDINER   It's one o'clock, boy, is't not?
PAGE   It hath struck.
GARDINER   These should be hours for necessities,
   Not for delights; times to repair° our nature   °restore
   With comforting repose, and not for us
5   To waste these times. —Good hour of night, Sir Thomas.
   Whither so late?
LOVELL   Came you from the King, my lord?
GARDINER   I did, Sir Thomas, and left him at primero°   °(a card game)
   With the Duke of Suffolk.
LOVELL   I must to him, too,
   Before he go to bed. I'll take my leave.
10 GARDINER   Not yet, Sir Thomas Lovell. What's the matter?
   It seems you are in haste. An if there be
   No great offense° belongs to't, give your friend   °inappropriateness
   Some touch° of your late business. Affairs that walk,   °hint
   As they say spirits do, at midnight, have
15   In them a wilder nature than the business
   That seeks dispatch° by day.   °to be done
LOVELL   My lord, I love you,
   And durst commend° a secret to your ear   °entrust
   Much weightier than this work.° The Queen's in labor—   °my affairs
   They say in great extremity—and feared°   °it is feared that
   She'll with the labor end.
20 GARDINER   The fruit she goes with
   I pray for heartily, that it may find
   Good time° and live. But for the stock,° Sir Thomas,   °Fortune / trunk (Anne)
   I wish it grubbed up° now.   °rooted out
LOVELL   Methinks I could
   Cry the amen,° and yet my conscience says   °Agree
25   She's a good creature and, sweet lady, does
   Deserve our better wishes.
GARDINER   But sir, sir,
   Hear me, Sir Thomas. You're a gentleman
   Of mine own way;¹ I know you wise, religious.
   And let me tell you, it will ne'er be well—
30   'Twill not, Sir Thomas Lovell, take't of me—
   Till Cranmer, Cromwell—her two hands—and she
   Sleep in their graves.
LOVELL   Now, sir, you speak of two
   The most remarked° i'th' kingdom. As for Cromwell,   °regarded
   Beside that of the Jewel House, is made Master
35   O'th' Rolls² and the King's secretary. Further, sir,

5.1 Location: London, a gallery at court.
1. Of my religious persuasion (Catholicism, as opposed to Anne's Lutheranism).

2. Officer in charge of documents from the Court of Chancery and various records made under the Great Seal.

Stands in the gap and trade° of more preferments,　　　　　　　　*open road*
With which the time will load him. Th'Archbishop
Is the King's hand and tongue, and who dare speak
One syllable against him?
GARDINER　　　　　　　　　　　Yes, yes, Sir Thomas,
40　There are that dare, and I myself have ventured
To speak my mind of him. And indeed this day,
Sir—I may tell it you, I think—I have
Incensed° the lords o'th' Council, that he is—　　　　　　　　*Angered*
For so I know he is, they know he is—
45　A most arch-heretic, a pestilence
That does infect the land; with which they, moved,°　　　　　　　*angered*
Have broken with° the King, who hath so far　　　　　　　　*revealed to*
Given ear to our complaint, of his great grace
And princely care foreseeing those fell mischiefs
50　Our reasons laid before him, hath° commanded　　　　　　　*that he has*
Tomorrow morning to the Council board
He be convented.° He's a rank° weed, Sir Thomas,　　　*summoned / rotten*
And we must root him out. From your affairs
I hinder you too long. Good night, Sir Thomas.
　　　　　　　　　　　Exeunt GARDINER *and* PAGE.
55　LOVELL　Many good nights, my lord. I rest° your servant.　　　*remain*
　　　　　　　Enter KING *and* SUFFOLK.
KING　Charles, I will play no more tonight:
My mind's not on't; you are too hard° for me.　　　　　　　*skillful*
SUFFOLK　Sir, I did never win of you before.
KING　But little, Charles,
60　Nor shall not when my fancy's° on my play.　　　　　　　*attention is*
Now, Lovell, from the Queen what is the news?
LOVELL　I could not personally deliver to her
What you commanded me, but by her woman
I sent your message, who returned her thanks
65　In the great'st humbleness, and desired your highness
Most heartily to pray for her.
KING　　　　　　　　　　　What say'st thou? Ha?
To pray for her? What, is she crying out?
LOVELL　So said her woman, and that her suff'rance° made　　　*suffering*
Almost each pang a death.
KING　　　　　　　　　　Alas, good lady.
70　SUFFOLK　God safely quit° her of her burden, and　　　　　　*release*
With gentle travail,° to the gladding° of　　　*labor / making joyful*
Your highness with an heir.
KING　　　　　　　　　　'Tis midnight, Charles.
Prithee to bed, and in thy prayers remember
Th'estate° of my poor queen. Leave me alone,　　　　　　*condition*
75　For I must think of that which company
Would not be friendly to.³
SUFFOLK　　　　　　　　　I wish your highness
A quiet night, and my good mistress will°　　　　　　　*I will*
Remember in my prayers.
KING　　　　　　　　　Charles, good night.　*Exit* SUFFOLK.
　　　　　Enter Sir Anthony DENNY.
Well, sir, what follows?

---

3. *which . . . to:* which requires privacy.

80 DENNY Sir, I have brought my lord the Archbishop,
As you commanded me.
KING   Ha? Canterbury?
DENNY Ay, my good lord.
KING   'Tis true. Where is he, Denny?
DENNY He attends your highness' pleasure.
KING   Bring him to us.
                                    [*Exit* DENNY.]

LOVELL [*aside*] This is about that which the Bishop° spake.   (Gardiner)
85   I am happily° come hither.   fortunately
                 Enter CRANMER *and* DENNY.
KING Avoid° the gallery!   Quit
                 LOVELL *seems to stay.*
                           Ha? I have said. Begone!
What?   *Exeunt* LOVELL *and* DENNY.   Why
CRANMER [*aside*] I am fearful. Wherefore° frowns he thus?   countenance
'Tis his aspect° of terror. All's not well.
KING How now, my lord? You do desire to know
Wherefore I sent for you.
90 CRANMER [*kneeling*]   It is my duty
T'attend your highness' pleasure.
KING   Pray you, arise,
My good and gracious lord of Canterbury.
Come, you and I must walk a turn together;
I have news to tell you. Come, come, give me your hand.
                 [CRANMER *rises.*]
95   Ah, my good lord, I grieve at what I speak
And am right sorry to repeat what follows.
I have, and most unwillingly, of late
Heard many grievous°—I do say, my lord,   serious
Grievous—complaints of you which, being considered,
100 Have moved us and our Council that you shall
This morning come before us, where I know
You cannot with such freedom purge° yourself   with ease clear
But that, till further trial in those charges
Which will require your answer, you must take
105 Your patience to you[4] and be well contented
To make your house our Tower. You a brother of us,°   a fellow councillor
It fits we thus proceed, or else no witness
Would come against you.
CRANMER [*kneeling again*] I humbly thank your highness,
And am right glad to catch this good occasion
110 Most throughly to be winnowed, where my chaff
And corn shall fly asunder.[5] For I know
There's none stands under° more calumnious tongues   is subject to
Than I myself, poor man.
KING   Stand up, good Canterbury.
Thy truth and thy integrity is rooted
115 In us, thy friend. Give me thy hand, stand up.
Prithee, let's walk. [CRANMER *rises.*]
                           Now, by my halidom,°   by our Lady
What manner of man are you? My lord, I looked°   predicted

4. *must . . . you:* must be patient.
5. *And am . . . asunder:* And I am glad to have the
occasion thoroughly to see the bad ("chaff") separated from the good ("corn," or wheat) in my character. See Matthew 3:12 and Luke 3:17.

You would have given me your petition that
I should have ta'en some pains to bring together
120 Yourself and your accusers and to have heard you
Without endurance° further.   imprisonment
CRANMER   Most dread liege,
The good° I stand on is my truth and honesty.   virtue
If they shall fail, I with mine enemies
Will triumph o'er my person, which I weigh not
125 Being of those virtues vacant.⁶ I fear nothing°   not at all
What can be said against me.
KING   Know you not
How your state stands i'th' world, with the whole world?
Your enemies are many, and not small;° their practices   insignificant
Must bear the same proportion, and not ever
130 The justice and the truth o'th' question carries
The due o'th' verdict with it.⁷ At what ease°   How easily
Might corrupt minds procure knaves as corrupt
To swear against you? Such things have been done.
You are potently° opposed, and with a malice   powerfully
135 Of as great size. Ween you of° better luck—   Do you anticipate
I mean in perjured witness°—than your master,°   evidence / (Christ)
Whose minister you are, whiles here He lived
Upon this naughty° earth? Go to, go to: wicked
You take a precipice for no leap of danger,
And woo your own destruction.
140 CRANMER   God and your majesty
Protect mine innocence, or I fall into
The trap is° laid for me.   that is
KING   Be of good cheer:
They shall no more prevail than we give way to.°   let them
Keep comfort to you, and this morning see
145 You do appear before them. If they shall chance,
In charging you with matters, to commit° you,   imprison
The best persuasions to the contrary
Fail not to use, and with what vehemency
Th'occasion shall instruct you. If entreaties
150 Will render you no remedy, this ring
Deliver them, and your appeal to us
There make before them. [aside] Look, the good man weeps.
He's honest, on mine honor. God's blest mother,
I swear he is true-hearted, and a soul
155 None better in my kingdom. —Get you gone,
And do as I have bid you.   Exit CRANMER.
                      He has strangled
His language in his tears.
          Enter OLD LADY.
LOVELL [within]   Come back! What mean you?
OLD LADY I'll not come back. The tidings that I bring
Will make my boldness manners.° [to the KING] Now, good   into manners
          angels
160 Fly o'er thy royal head and shade thy person
Under their blessèd wings.

6. If . . . vacant: If I lack truth and honesty, I will   7. their . . . it: their schemes are equally numerous
agree with my enemies in condemning myself, whom   and powerful, and justice and truth do not always
I do not value in the absence of truth and honesty.   prevail.

KING   Now, by thy looks
I guess thy message. Is the Queen delivered?
Say, "Ay, and of a boy."
OLD LADY   Ay, ay, my liege,
And of a lovely boy. The God of heaven
165   Both now and ever bless her: 'tis a girl°   *(Anne; Elizabeth)*
Promises boys hereafter. Sir, your queen
Desires your visitation and° to be   *and for you*
Acquainted with this stranger. 'Tis as like you
As cherry is to cherry.
KING   Lovell!
LOVELL   Sir?
170   KING   Give her an hundred marks.° I'll to the Queen. *Exit* KING.   *roughly 65 pounds*
OLD LADY   An hundred marks? By this light, I'll ha' more!
An ordinary groom is for° such payment.   *deserves*
I will have more or scold it out of him.
Said I for this the girl was like to him? I'll
175   Have more, or else unsay't; and now, while 'tis hot,
I'll put it to the issue.   *Exeunt.*

5.2

Enter CRANMER, *Archbishop of Canterbury.*

CRANMER   I hope I am not too late, and yet the gentleman
That was sent to me from the Council prayed me
To make great haste. All fast?° What means this? —Ho?   *The doors closed?*
Who waits there?
          Enter KEEPER.
            Sure you know me?
KEEPER   Yes, my lord,
But yet I cannot help you.
5   CRANMER   Why?
KEEPER   Your grace must wait till you be called for.
          Enter Doctor BUTTS.
CRANMER   So.
BUTTS [*aside*]   This is a piece of malice. I am glad
I came this way so happily.° The King   *fortunately*
Shall understand it presently.°   *Exit* BUTTS.   *immediately*
CRANMER   'Tis Butts,
10   The King's physician. As he passed along
How earnestly he cast his eyes upon me.
Pray heaven he sound° not my disgrace. For certain,   *fathom; publicize*
This is of purpose laid° by some that hate me—   *carried out*
God turn their hearts; I never sought their malice—
15   To quench° mine honor. They would shame to make me   *destroy*
Wait else at door,[1] a fellow councillor
'Mong boys, grooms, and lackeys. But their pleasures
Must be fulfilled, and I attend° with patience.   *wait*
       Enter the KING *and* BUTTS *at a window above.*
BUTTS   I'll show your grace the strangest sight—
KING   What's that, Butts?
20   BUTTS   —I think your highness saw this many a day.
KING   Body o'me, where is it?
BUTTS   There, my lord:

5.2 Location: Anteroom and council chamber at court.

1. *They . . . door:* Otherwise they would be too ashamed to make me wait at the door.

The high promotion° of his grace of Canterbury,   *(ironic)*
Who holds his state² at door 'mongst pursuivants,°   *servants*
Pages, and footboys.
KING   Ha? 'Tis he indeed.
25   Is this the honor they do one another?
'Tis well there's one above 'em³ yet. I had thought
They had parted° so much honesty among 'em,   *shared*
At least good manners, as not thus to suffer
A man of his place,° and so near° our favor,   *rank / much in*
30   To dance attendance on their lordships' pleasures—
And at the door, too, like a post with packets.°   *courier with letters*
By holy Mary, Butts, there's knavery!
Let 'em alone, and draw the curtain close:
We shall hear more anon.

    A council table brought in with chairs and stools and
    placed under the state. Enter Lord CHANCELLOR,
    places himself at the upper end of the table, on the
    left hand, a seat being left void above him, as° for
    Canterbury's seat. Duke of SUFFOLK, *Duke of* NORFOLK,
    SURREY, *Lord* CHAMBERLAIN, GARDINER *seat themselves*
    in order on each side; CROMWELL *at lower end, as°*   *as if*
    secretary.

35   CHANCELLOR   Speak to the business, master secretary.
    Why are we met in council?
CROMWELL   Please your honors,
    The chief cause concerns his grace of Canterbury.
GARDINER   Has he had° knowledge of it?   *been given*
CROMWELL   Yes.
NORFOLK   Who waits there?
KEEPER   Without,° my noble lords?   *Outside*
GARDINER   Yes.
KEEPER   My lord Archbishop,
40   And has done half an hour to know your pleasures.
CHANCELLOR   Let him come in.
KEEPER   Your grace may enter now.
    CRANMER *approaches the council table.*
CHANCELLOR   My good lord Archbishop, I'm very sorry
    To sit here at this present° and behold   *moment*
    That chair stand empty. But we all are men
45   In our own natures frail, and capable°   *prone to failings*
    Of our flesh; few are angels. Out of which frailty
    And want° of wisdom, you, that best should teach us,   *lack*
    Have misdemeaned yourself,° and not a little,   *behaved badly*
    Toward the King first, then his laws, in filling
50   The whole realm by your teaching and your chaplains'—
    For so we are informed—with new opinions,
    Diverse and dangerous, which are heresies
    And, not reformed, may prove pernicious.°   *lethal*
GARDINER   Which reformation must be sudden too,
55   My noble lords, for those that tame wild horses
    Pace 'em not in their hands to make 'em gentle,⁴
    But stop their mouths with stubborn bits and spur 'em

2. Ironic: occupies a location befitting his rank;
unironic: waits with dignity.
3. Both God and King, here implicitly linked.

4. Do not put them through their paces with only a
hand for restraint.

Till they obey the *manège*.° If we suffer,°   *training / allow*
Out of our easiness° and childish pity   *leniency*
60   To one man's honor, this contagious sickness,
Farewell, all physic!° And what follows then?   *remedies*
Commotions, uproars, with a general taint
Of the whole state, as of late days our neighbors,
The upper Germany, can dearly witness,[5]
65   Yet freshly pitied in our memories.
CRANMER   My good lords, hitherto, in all the progress
Both of my life and office, I have labored,
And with no little study,° that my teaching   *effort*
And the strong course of my authority
70   Might go one way, and safely, and the end
Was ever to do well. Nor is there living—
I speak it with a single° heart, my lords—   *pure*
A man that more detests, more stirs against,°   *actively resists*
Both in his private conscience and his place,°   *office*
75   Defacers° of a public peace than I do.   *Destroyers*
Pray heaven the King may never find a heart
With less allegiance in it! Men that make
Envy and crooked malice nourishment
Dare bite the best. I do beseech your lordships
80   That, in this case of justice, my accusers,
Be what they will,° may stand forth face to face   *Whoever they are*
And freely urge against° me.   *openly accuse*
SUFFOLK   Nay, my lord,
That cannot be: you are a councillor,
And by that virtue° no man dare accuse you.   *by virtue of that*
85   GARDINER   My lord, because we have business of more moment,°   *import*
We will be short° with you. 'Tis his highness' pleasure   *brief*
And our consent, for better trial of you,
From hence you be committed to the Tower,
Where, being but a private man again,
90   You shall know many dare accuse you boldly—
More than, I fear, you are provided for.°   *ready for*
CRANMER   Ah, my good lord of Winchester, I thank you;
You are always my good friend. If your will pass,°   *is approved*
I shall both find your lordship judge and juror,[6]
95   You are so merciful. I see your end:°   *aim*
'Tis my undoing. Love and meekness, lord,
Become a churchman better than ambition.
Win straying souls with modesty again;
Cast none away. That I shall clear myself,
100   Lay all the weight ye can upon my patience,
I make as little doubt as you do conscience[7]
In doing daily wrongs. I could say more,
But reverence to your calling makes me modest.°   *temperate*
GARDINER   My lord, my lord, you are a sectary:°   *Protestant*
105   That's the plain truth. Your painted gloss discovers,
To men that understand you, words and weakness.[8]

---

5. Alluding to Protestant sects in Germany who fomented uprisings in urban centers in the 1520s and 1530s (the Peasants' War, 1524–26, and perhaps the rebellion of the Münster Anabaptists in 1535)—uprisings that led to fierce reprisals and, in the first case, mass killing of the German peasantry.

6. Gardiner would both try (as "judge") and pass judgment (as "juror")—to Cranmer, an injustice.
7. I doubt no more than you act ethically.
8. *Your . . . weakness:* Your false exterior (or, perhaps, your specious language) exposes, to men who can see through you, empty words and human frailty.

CROMWELL   My lord of Winchester, you're a little,
By your good favor,° too sharp. Men so noble,   *If you'll excuse me*
However faulty, yet should find° respect   *be offered*
110   For what they have been. 'Tis a cruelty
To load° a falling man.   *burden further*
GARDINER   Good master secretary,
I cry your honor mercy:[9] you may worst°   *least justifiably*
Of all this table say so.
CROMWELL   Why, my lord?
GARDINER   Do not I know you for a favorer
Of this new sect? Ye are not sound.°   *loyal; orthodox*
115   CROMWELL   Not sound?
GARDINER   Not sound, I say.
CROMWELL   Would you were half so honest!
Men's prayers then would seek you, not their fears.
GARDINER   I shall remember this bold language.
CROMWELL   Do.
Remember your bold life, too.
CHAMBERLAIN   This is too much!
Forbear, for shame, my lords.
GARDINER   I have done.
120   CROMWELL   And I.
CHAMBERLAIN   Then thus for you, my lord, it stands agreed,
I take it, by all voices,° that forthwith   *votes*
You be conveyed to th' Tower a prisoner,
There to remain till the King's further pleasure
125   Be known unto us. Are you all agreed, lords?
ALL   We are.
CRANMER   Is there no other way of mercy,
But I must needs to° th' Tower, my lords?   *must go to*
GARDINER   What other
Would you expect? You are strangely° troublesome.   *extraordinarily*
Let some o'th' guard be ready there.
                    Enter the Guard.
CRANMER   For me?
Must I go like a traitor thither?
130   GARDINER   Receive° him,   *Take*
And see him safe i'th' Tower.
CRANMER   Stay, good my lords,
I have a little yet to say. Look there, my lords:
By virtue of that ring, I take my cause
Out of the gripes° of cruel men and give it   *clutches*
135   To a most noble judge, the King my master.
CHAMBERLAIN   This is the King's ring.
SURREY   'Tis no counterfeit.
SUFFOLK   'Tis the right ring, by heav'n! I told ye all,
When we first put this dangerous stone a-rolling,
'Twould fall upon ourselves.
NORFOLK   Do you think, my lords,
140   The King will suffer but the little finger
Of this man to be vexed?
CHAMBERLAIN   'Tis now too certain.
How much more is his life in value with him?°   *esteemed by the King*
Would I were fairly out on't.°   *out of it (the plot)*

_____
9. I beg your pardon.

CROMWELL   My mind gave me,°   *I suspected*
　In seeking tales and informations
145　Against this man, whose honesty the devil
　And his disciples only envy at,°   *covet; despise*
　Ye blew the fire that burns ye. Now have at ye!°   *be on guard*
　　　　Enter KING, *frowning on them. [He] takes his seat.*
　GARDINER   Dread sovereign, how much are we bound to heaven
　In daily thanks, that gave us such a prince,
150　Not only good and wise, but most religious;
　One that, in all obedience, makes the church
　The chief aim of his honor and, to strengthen
　That holy duty, out of dear respect,°   *sincere piety*
155　His royal self in judgment comes to hear
　The cause betwixt her° and this great offender.   *(the church)*
　KING   You were ever good at sudden commendations,°   *off-the-cuff flattery*
　Bishop of Winchester. But know I come not
　To hear such flattery now; and, in my presence,
　They are too thin and bare to hide offenses.
160　To me you cannot reach. You play the spaniel,
　And think with wagging of your tongue to win me;
　But whatsoe'er thou tak'st me for, I'm sure
　Thou hast a cruel nature and a bloody.
　[*to* CRANMER] Good man, sit down. Now, let me see the proudest,
165　He° that dares most, but wag his finger at thee.   *The man*
　By all that's holy, he had better starve°   *die*
　Than but once think his place becomes thee not.
　SURREY   May it please your grace—
　KING   No, sir, it does not please me.
　I had thought I had had men of some understanding
170　And wisdom of° my council, but I find none.   *in*
　—Was it discretion, lords, to let this man,
　This good man—few of you deserve that title—
　This honest man, wait like a lousy footboy
　At chamber door? And one as great as you are?
175　Why, what a shame° was this! Did my commission   *shameful act*
　Bid ye so far forget yourselves? I gave ye
　Power as he was a councillor to try him,
　Not as a groom. There's some of ye, I see,
　More out of malice than integrity,
180　Would try him to the utmost, had ye mean,°   *the means*
　Which ye shall never have while I live.
　CHANCELLOR   Thus far,
　My most dread sovereign, may it like° your grace   *please*
　To let my tongue excuse all. What was purposed°   *intended*
　Concerning his imprisonment was rather—
185　If there be faith in men—meant for his trial
　And fair purgation° to the world than malice,   *acquittal of suspicion*
　I'm sure, in me.
　KING   Well, well, my lords, respect him,
　Take him, and use him well; he's worthy of it.
　I will say thus much for him: if a prince
190　May be beholden to a subject, I
　Am, for his love and service, so to him.
　Make me no more ado, but all embrace him;
　Be friends, for shame, my lords. —My lord of Canterbury,
　I have a suit which you must not deny me,

195   That is, a fair young maid that yet wants baptism;
You must be godfather and answer for her.
  CRANMER   The greatest monarch now alive may glory
In such an honor. How may I deserve it,
That am a poor and humble subject to you?

200   KING   Come, come, my lord, you'd spare your spoons![1] You
shall have two noble partners with you: the old Duchess of
Norfolk and Lady Marquess Dorset. Will these please you?
—Once more, my lord of Winchester, I charge you
Embrace and love this man.

  GARDINER   With a true heart
And brother-love I do it.

205   CRANMER   And let heaven
Witness how dear I hold this confirmation.
  KING   Good man, those joyful tears show thy true heart.
The common voice,° I see, is verified   *opinion*
Of thee, which says thus: "Do my lord of Canterbury

210   A shrewd turn,° and he's your friend for ever."   *An act of malice*
—Come, lords, we trifle time away. I long
To have this young one made a Christian.
As I have made ye one, lords, one remain;
So I grow stronger, you more honor gain.   *Exeunt.*

5.3

    Noise and tumult within.°   *offstage*
    Enter PORTER *and his* MAN.

  PORTER *[to those within]*   You'll leave° your noise anon, ye   *stop*
rascals! Do you take the court for Paris Garden?[1] Ye rude
slaves, leave your gaping!°   *yelling*
  ONE *[within]*   Good master Porter, I belong to th' larder.°   *serve in the pantry*

5   PORTER   Belong to th' gallows, and be hanged, ye rogue! Is
this a place to roar in? —Fetch me a dozen crab-tree staves,
and strong ones; these are but switches to 'em. —I'll scratch
your heads! You must be seeing christenings? Do you look
for ale and cakes here, you rude rascals?

10   MAN   Pray, sir, be patient. 'Tis as much impossible,
Unless we sweep 'em from the door with cannons,
To scatter 'em as 'tis to make 'em sleep
On May Day morning[2]—which will never be.
We may as well push against Paul's° as stir 'em.   *St. Paul's Cathedral*

15   PORTER   How got they in, and be hanged?°   *(a curse or expletive)*
  MAN   Alas, I know not. How gets the tide in?
As much as one sound cudgel° of four foot—   *club*
You see the poor remainder°—could distribute,   *what's left of it*
I made no spare,° sir.   *spared no one*
  PORTER   You did nothing, sir.

20   MAN   I am not Samson, nor Sir Guy, nor Colbrand,[3]
To mow 'em down before me; but if I spared any

---

1. The King teases Cranmer that he hesitates only because he wants to spare himself the expense of christening spoons—the customary gift from a godparent to a child.
5.3 Location: The palace yard.
1. A park for bear- and bullbaiting in Southwark, a London suburb, where the Globe also stood.

2. On May Day, revelers rose before dawn for festivities to greet spring.
3. Figures of legendary physical powers. In the Bible, Samson is renowned for his strength; in the romance tradition, Sir Guy of Warwick, who killed the Danish giant Colebrand, was also known for his prowess.

That had a head to hit, either young or old,
He or she, cuckold or cuckold-maker,
Let me ne'er hope to see a chine° again—   *cut of beef*
25 And that I would not for a cow,° God save her!   *for anything*

ONE [*within*] Do you hear, master Porter?

PORTER I shall be with you presently, good master puppy! —
Keep the door close, sirrah!

MAN What would you have me do?

30 PORTER What should you do, but knock 'em down by th' dozens? Is this Moorfields[4] to muster in? Or have we some
strange Indian with the great tool come to court,[5] the women
so besiege us? Bless me, what a fry of fornication[6] is at door!
On my Christian conscience, this one christening will beget a
35 thousand: here will be father, godfather, and all together.

MAN The spoons° will be the bigger, sir. There is a fellow   *(for christening)*
somewhat near the door, he should be a brazier° by his face,   *brass worker*
for, o'my conscience, twenty of the dog-days° now reign in 's   *hottest summer days*
nose. All that stand about him are under the line;[7] they need
40 no other penance. That fire-drake° did I hit three times on   *fiery dragon*
the head, and three times was his nose discharged against
me. He stands there like a mortar-piece, to blow us.[8] There
was a haberdasher's wife of small wit near him that railed
upon me till her pinked porringer[9] fell off her head for kin-
45 dling such a combustion° in the state. I missed the meteor°   *tumult / brazier*
once and hit that woman, who cried out "Clubs!",[1] when I
might see from far some forty truncheoners° draw to her suc-   *men with cudgels*
cor, which were the hope o'th' Strand,[2] where she was quar-
tered.° They fell on;° I made good my place; at length, they   *lived / attacked*
50 came to th' broom staff to° me; I defied 'em still, when suddenly   *right next to*
a file of boys behind 'em, loose shot,[3] delivered such a shower of
pebbles that I was fain° to draw mine honor in and let 'em win   *obliged*
the work.° The devil was amongst 'em, I think, surely.   *fort*

PORTER These are the youths° that thunder at a playhouse   *apprentices*
55 and fight for bitten apples, that no audience but the Tribula-
tion of Tower Hill or the Limbs of Limehouse,[4] their dear
brothers, are able to endure. I have some of 'em *in limbo
patrum*,[5] and there they are like to dance these three days,
besides the running banquet of two beadles that is to come.[6]

Enter Lord CHAMBERLAIN.

60 CHAMBERLAIN Mercy o'me, what a multitude are here!
They grow still, too. From all parts they are coming,
As if we kept a fair here! Where are these porters,
These lazy knaves? —You've made a fine hand,° fellows: *nice work (ironic)*

4. Parkland outside London's walls where citizen militias may have trained.
5. Native Americans brought to England and exhibited at court excited popular fascination—here, about their genitalia.
6. A crowd of would-be fornicators or bastards.
7. All those near him seem to be standing at the equator, his face is so red.
8. Like a cannon, ready to blow us up; ready to blow his nose at us.
9. A perforated small cap.
1. London apprentices would shout this when about to begin or end a street fight.
2. A fashionable shopping and residential part of London.

3. Marksmen (here, throwers) unattached to a company.
4. The tough crowds at the Tower for executions; or farther east in Limehouse, a rough part of London near the docks.
5. In prison (literally, limbo of the fathers). Jewish patriarchs, because they predated Christ, at death were thought not to go to Christian heaven but to limbo, near hell, where they remained until Judgment Day. With echoes of "Limbs of Limehouse" (line 56).
6. *dance . . . come:* festively celebrate ("dance") with dessert ("running banquet"); public whipping of prisoners (like a "running banquet," or dessert) after imprisonment (the main course) by minor law-enforcement officials ("beadles").

There's a trim° rabble let in! Are all these   *an elegant (ironic)*
65   Your faithful friends o'th' suburbs?[7] We shall have
Great store of room, no doubt, left for the ladies,
When they pass back from the christening!

PORTER   An't° please your honor,   *If it*
We are but men, and what so many may do,
Not being torn a-pieces, we have done.
An army cannot rule 'em!°   *keep them in order*
70 CHAMBERLAIN   As I live,
If the King blame me for't, I'll lay ye all
By th' heels,° and suddenly, and on your heads   *In the stocks*
Clap round° fines for neglect. You're lazy knaves,   *large*
And here ye lie baiting of bombards° when   *you lie drinking*
75   Ye should do service. Hark! The trumpets sound:
They're come already from the christening.
Go break among the press° and find a way out   *crowd*
To let the troop pass fairly,° or I'll find   *fittingly*
A Marshalsea shall hold ye play[8] these two months.
PORTER   Make way there for the Princess!
80 MAN   You, great fellow,[9]
Stand close up,° or I'll make your head ache!   *Move aside*
PORTER   You i'th' chamblet,° get up o'th' rail!   *rough cloth*
I'll peck you o'er the pales else.[1]   *Exeunt.*

5.4

*Enter Trumpets, sounding; then two Aldermen, Lord
Mayor,* GARTER, CRANMER, *Duke of* NORFOLK *with his
Marshal's staff, Duke of* SUFFOLK, *two Noblemen
bearing great standing bowls for the christening gifts;
then four Noblemen bearing a canopy, under which
the Duchess of Norfolk, godmother, bearing the child
richly habited in a mantle, etc., train borne by a
Lady; then follows the Marchioness Dorset, the other
godmother, and Ladies. The troop pass once about the
stage, and* GARTER *speaks.*

GARTER   Heaven, from thy endless goodness, send prosperous
life, long, and ever happy, to the high and mighty Princess
of England, Elizabeth.[1]
    Flourish. Enter KING *and Guard.*
CRANMER [*kneeling*]   And to your royal grace and the good
    Queen.
5   My noble partners° and myself thus pray: *fellow godparents*
All comfort, joy, in this most gracious lady,
Heaven ever laid up to make parents happy,
May hourly fall upon ye.
KING   Thank you, good lord Archbishop.
What is her name?
CRANMER   Elizabeth.
KING   Stand up, lord.

7. From the suburbs, areas outside London's city
walls, and beyond the city's legal jurisdiction; hence,
considered lawless.
8. *I'll . . . play:* I'll shut you in the Marshalsea, a
prison in Southwark.
9. Addressed to someone either onstage or in the
audience.
1. *get . . . else:* get off the rail (the railing running

around the edge of the stage), or I'll throw you off.
5.4 Location: The court.
1. This formulaic speech is similar to one given at the
1613 wedding of King James I's daughter Elizabeth to
Prince Frederick, the Elector Palatine. This scene
connects the christening celebration of one Princess
Elizabeth, in the play, to the wedding celebration of
another, at the time of the play's first production.

[CRANMER *rises.*]

10 [*to the child*] With this kiss, take my blessing. God protect thee,
Into whose hand I give thy life.

CRANMER   Amen.

KING   My noble gossips,° you've been too prodigal.°   *godparents / generous*
I thank ye heartily; so shall this lady,
When she has so much English.

CRANMER   Let me speak, sir,
15 For heaven now bids me; and the words I utter
Let none think flattery, for they'll find 'em truth.
This royal infant—heaven still° move about her—   *always*
Though in her cradle, yet now promises
Upon this land a thousand thousand blessings,
20 Which time shall bring to ripeness. She shall be—
But few now living can behold that goodness—
A pattern to all princes living with her
And all that shall succeed. Saba[2] was never
More covetous° of wisdom and fair virtue   *desirous*
25 Than this pure soul shall be. All princely graces
That mould up° such a mighty piece° as this is,   *produce / masterpiece*
With all the virtues that attend the good,
Shall still be doubled on her. Truth shall nurse her;
Holy and heavenly thoughts still counsel her.
30 She shall be loved and feared. Her own° shall bless her;   *own people*
Her foes shake like a field of beaten° corn,   *windswept*
And hang their heads with sorrow. Good grows with her.
In her days, every man shall eat in safety
Under his own vine what he plants, and sing
35 The merry songs of peace to all his neighbors.
God shall be truly known,° and those about her   *(via Protestantism)*
From her shall read° the perfect ways of honor,   *learn*
And by those claim their greatness, not by blood.
Nor shall this peace sleep with her, but as when
40 The bird of wonder dies, the maiden phoenix,[3]
Her ashes new create another heir
As great in admiration° as herself,   *deserving of wonder*
So shall she leave her blessedness to one°—   *(James I)*
When heaven shall call her from this cloud of darkness°—   *earthly state*
45 Who from the sacred ashes of her honor
Shall star-like rise, as great in fame as she was,
And so stand fixed. Peace, plenty, love, truth, terror,
That were the servants to this chosen infant,
Shall then be his, and like a vine grow to him.
50 Wherever the bright sun of heaven shall shine,
His honor and the greatness of his name
Shall be, and make new nations.[4] He shall flourish
And, like a mountain cedar, reach his branches
To all the plains about him. Our children's children
Shall see this and bless heaven.

2. The Queen of Sheba (Saba) visited Solomon in Jerusalem in order to benefit from his wisdom and thus became a model for wise (but presumably deferential) women. See 1 Kings 10:1–10.
3. A mythical Arabian bird, the only one of its kind, which, when it dies after a long life, regenerates itself from its own ashes. James I inherits the spirit of the phoenix, Queen Elizabeth—a spirit now, perhaps, being passed on to his daughter, Princess Elizabeth.
4. See Genesis 17:4: "A father of many nations have I made thee." The passage was frequently invoked in relation to Princess Elizabeth's marriage. The play here also compliments James on the "new nation" he has established in America, appropriately named Virginia after the "virgin" Queen Elizabeth (line 60).

55 KING   Thou speakest wonders.
  CRANMER   She shall be, to the happiness of England,
      An agèd princess; many days shall see her,
      And yet no day without a deed° to crown it.   *an accomplishment*
      Would I had known no more. But she must die,
60   She must, the saints must have her; yet a virgin,
      A most unspotted lily, shall she pass
      To th' ground, and all the world shall mourn her.
  KING   O Lord Archbishop,
      Thou hast made me now a man: never before
65   This happy child did I get° anything.   *beget; achieve*
      This oracle of comfort has so pleased me
      That when I am in heaven I shall desire
      To see what this child does, and praise my maker.
      —I thank ye all. To you, my good lord Mayor,
70   And you, good brethren, I am much beholden:
      I have received much honor by your presence,
      And ye shall find me thankful. Lead the way, lords;
      Ye must all see the Queen, and she must thank ye—
      She will be sick° else. This day, no man think   *unhappy*
75   'Has° business at his house, for all shall stay:°   *He has / stop work*
      This little one shall make it holiday.   *Exeunt.*

Epilogue
[*Enter* EPILOGUE.]
  EPILOGUE   'Tis ten to one this play can never please
      All that are here. Some come to take their ease
      And sleep an act or two—but those, we fear,
      We've frighted with our trumpets, so 'tis clear
5   They'll say 'tis naught.° Others to hear the city   *worth nothing*
      Abused extremely and to cry, "That's witty!"[1]—
      Which we have not done, neither—that° I fear   *such that*
      All the expected good° we're like to hear   *anticipated praise*
      For this play at this time is only in
10   The merciful construction of° good women,   *interpretation by*
      For such a one[2] we showed 'em. If they smile
      And say 'twill do, I know within a while
      All the best men are ours—for 'tis ill hap°   *luck*
      If they hold° when their ladies bid 'em clap.   [*Exit.*]   *refrain*

Epilogue
1. "The city," both London and its citizens, was satirized in "city comedies" at the private theaters (as opposed to public playhouses like the Globe, whose leading dramatist here retaliates).
2. Probably Catharine, possibly Elizabeth, conceivably Anne.

The Two Noble Kinsmen

When Prospero proclaims near the end of *The Tempest* (1611), "But this rough magic / I here abjure" (5.1.50–51), audiences often think they are hearing Shakespeare's farewell to the theater. But the final passage Shakespeare wrote for the stage probably comes at the conclusion of *The Two Noble Kinsmen* (1613–14). Theseus, Duke of Athens, the play's highest-ranking character, attempts to grasp the paradoxical twists of fate he has witnessed:

> Never Fortune
> Did play a subtler game. The conquered triumphs;
> The victor has the loss. Yet in the passage
> The gods have been most equal. . . .
> . . . .
> . . . Let us be thankful
> For that which is, and with you [the gods] leave dispute
> That are above our question.
> (5.4.112–15, 134–36)

It is tempting to interpret Theseus's resigned disillusionment as Shakespeare's last word on things. The play's message is not easy to determine, however. Theseus's confidence in divine justice ("The gods have been most equal") underestimates the grimness that accompanies the pathos of the play. Chivalric military and sexual norms lend nobility to the action, but also generate the misery to which Theseus attempts to respond.

The problem of the work's tone is related to the question of authorship. Shakespeare wrote *The Two Noble Kinsmen* with John Fletcher (1579–1625), a younger contemporary who succeeded him as the leading dramatist of Shakespeare's acting company, the King's Men. Several of Shakespeare's very early and very late plays may have involved collaboration. In his final years, he worked with Fletcher on the lost *Cardenio* (1612–13; probably based on an episode from Part 1 of Cervantes' *Don Quixote*, 1605; translated 1612), on *Henry VIII* (1613), and on *The Two Noble Kinsmen*. For this last play, Shakespeare probably wrote most of the first and last acts plus a little more, while his colleague composed the rest. This division suggests that Shakespeare was the senior partner. The two dramatists differ in style, presentation, and outlook. The rhetorically knotty, ritualistic, near-tragic grandeur in Shakespeare's share contrasts with the syntactically simpler, dynamic, near-absurd deflation in Fletcher's. The play as a whole is, therefore, essentially neither Shakespearean nor Fletcherian. A product of collaboration, it is marked by both unity and dissonance.

The Two Noble Kinsmen is transitional between the more popular theater of Shakespeare's time and the more elite drama of Fletcher's. Typical in many ways of Shakespeare's last phase, it may be compared to other tragicomic romances written separately by Shakespeare and Fletcher in the preceding six or seven years. Among Shakespeare's leading works in this genre—*Pericles, The Winter's Tale, Cymbeline,* and *The Tempest*—one finds parallels to *The Two Noble Kinsmen*'s medieval source, pseudo-historical classical setting, spectacle and ceremony, innocence in the midst of corruption, striving for self-mastery, and transcendence of self-interest. Further similarities include insistence on death as a price of the survivors' happiness, successful supplication to the gods for aid, and consequent sense of a metaphysical presence that orders events in a manner beyond human control. Although limited to dry land, the work replicates even the trademark maritime imagery of Shakespearean romance, with its focus on peril: the dying Arcite "such a vessel 'tis that floats but for / The surge that next approaches" (5.4.83–84).

Yet *The Two Noble Kinsmen* feels different from other Shakespearean plays of the time. As the Prologue explains, "Chaucer—of all admired—the story gives" (line 13). The main plot is taken—with greater freedom by Shakespeare than by Fletcher—from *The Knight's Tale,* which immediately follows the General Prologue in *The Canterbury Tales* (late fourteenth century). Its subject is the mortal rivalry between Palamon and Arcite (two syllables, accented on the first), the two cousins referred to in the title, for the hand of Emilia. But the play's atypicality stems only partly from its resulting chivalric ethos and acts of courtesy, both emphasized more than in Chaucer. *The Two Noble Kinsmen* is set apart by the unusually somber resolution to its impossible dilemmas. Despite Theseus's assertions, the gods' behavior does not restore confidence in a benevolent Providence. Mars, whose intercession Arcite requests, and Venus, to whom Palamon prays, emblematize the chaos of human affairs. The play is also structurally distinctive. Shakespearean romance reveals the passage from suffering to serenity, the redemption of the older generation by the younger (and particularly by the virtuous daughter). But Shakespeare and Fletcher's play ignores the restorative workings of time. All relationships occur within a single generation, the young woman (Emilia) incites violence rather than reconciliation, and the work begins with a marriage and funeral—only to end the same way. This lack of movement may be connected to the play's well-defined five-act structure, a consequence of performance at the Blackfriars, an elite indoor theater that Shakespeare's company began using late in his career.

For these reasons, *The Two Noble Kinsmen* is sometimes viewed as an anti-romance. As such, it bears comparison both to Shakespeare's other collaborations with Fletcher and to several of Shakespeare's earlier plays, which are echoed particularly in Fletcher's scenes. Palamon and Arcite's initial resignation in prison recalls *Richard II;* their conflict over Emilia, *The Two Gentlemen of Verona;* Emilia's comparison of pictures, *Hamlet.* When Arcite asks for a sign before his decisive battle with Palamon, he correctly takes Mars's thunder as a promise of victory. But this reassurance is as duplicitous as the guarantee that "none of woman born / Shall harm Macbeth" (*Macbeth* 4.1.79–80), with the important difference that Macbeth is a mass murderer, whereas Arcite merely desires a woman his cousin saw first. The divine poetic justice often thought to be operating, however deviously, in *Macbeth* seems like a dirty trick in *The Two Noble Kinsmen.*

The subplot, mainly the work of Fletcher, dramatizes the unrequited love of the Jailer's Daughter for Palamon and has no known source. It borrows the morris dance before Theseus and Hippolyta in 3.5 not from Shakespeare but from a masque (an aristocratic theatrical event emphasizing song, dance, and spectacle) that Francis Beaumont composed for court performance in February 1613. (The morris dance itself is a rural folk form often performed on May Day by dancers in outlandish costumes who employ stock characters to partly mime traditional stories.) And the pastoral scenes of the second and third acts owe a more general debt to contemporary aristocratic dramatic forms. Otherwise, the Shakespearean legacy is pronounced. The Daughter's fall into madness when ignored by Palamon is modeled on Ophelia's in *Hamlet,* complete with attempted suicide. Her "Willow Song" (4.1.79–80) was earlier sung by Desdemona in *Othello.* The Doctor who prescribes her cure previously ministered to King Lear and, more unsuccessfully, to Lady Macbeth. When the Daughter joins the people whom "ruder tongues distinguish 'villager'" (3.5.107) in the morris dance, the allusion is to another play indebted to *The Knight's Tale:* in *A Midsummer Night's Dream,* "rude mechanicals" (artisans, 3.2.9) also perform before Theseus and Hippolyta at their wedding, and mismatched, frustrated lovers wander through the forest.

But *The Two Noble Kinsmen* is *A Midsummer Night's Dream* with a difference. *The Winter's Tale* might be understood as the tragic jealousy of *Othello* lightened by the pastoral experience of a romantic comedy, *As You Like It*. In *The Two Noble Kinsmen*, the comic tone of *A Midsummer Night's Dream* is darkened by the intervening experience of *Troilus and Cressida*, which also draws on Chaucer for a chivalric sensuality leading to violence and an indifference to the desires of the idealized woman. Indeed, Theseus's final words, quoted earlier, may recall Gloucester's metaphysical despair in *King Lear*:

> As flies to wanton boys are we to th' gods:
> They kill us for their sport.
>> (Folio, 4.1.38–39)

A geographical, legendary legacy underlies this outlook. Although almost all of the play is set in and around Athens, the darker influence of Thebes is immediately felt. In the opening episode, greatly expanded from the source, three widowed queens beg Theseus to aid them against Thebes, thus introducing the military dimension of chivalric conduct. Theseus yields to Hippolyta's and Emilia's entreaties to defer his own pleasure (marriage to Hippolyta) to help dowagers in distress. His intervention pits him against Palamon and Arcite, who fight for their home city despite hating its ruler. This sequence implicitly invokes Thebes's history of intrafamilial violence: Cadmus sows the soil with serpent's teeth, from which armed men grow; these men slaughter each other and, with Cadmus, the survivors found Thebes. Later, Oedipus unwittingly murders his father. As the play opens, his two sons have killed each other in a battle for the throne that has also widowed the three queens.

The two cousins, imprisoned following Theseus's victory over Thebes, repeat this history. When Theseus catches them fighting over Emilia, he orders their deaths, only to reverse course at Hippolyta's and Emilia's request. He orders a chivalric combat in which each cousin is aided by three knights and all members of the losing side are to be executed. This plan unnecessarily increases the expected death toll, beyond what is found in Chaucer. It is thwarted by Arcite's accidental death, a death hard to see as providential but undeniably less brutal than Theseus's strategy. Earlier, Palamon laments "Mars's so scorned altar" and yearns for war "[t]o get the soldier work, that peace might purge / For her repletion" (1.2.20, 23–24). Arcite echoes this notion of war as a virtuous means of purging the excesses of peace in a prayer to Mars, who

> heal'st with blood
> The earth when it is sick, and cur'st the world
> O'th' pleurisy of people.
>> (5.1.64–66)

Yet *The Two Noble Kinsmen* finds in war and chivalric combat less a cure for society than a loss of life.

A compulsive sexuality bears considerable blame for the resulting havoc. As Theseus says, "being sensually subdued, / We lose our human title" (1.1.232–33). Arcite and especially Palamon are willing to kill and die over a woman whom they know only by appearance, and that only from afar. Arcite seems partly motivated by competitive emulation, by a desire to spite Palamon. He tells his cousin that when he sees Emilia, he will "pitch between her arms to anger thee" (2.2.220). The kinsmen claim Emilia while in prison for life and without her knowing they exist, much less expressing interest in them. Her feelings don't matter. From this perspective, chivalric combat seems an appropriate mechanism for determining which cousin deserves her. Their stance is validated through the intervention of Theseus. Emilia doesn't have the choice of rejecting them both. When asked to choose, she is unable to decide between "[t]wo such young handsome men" (4.2.3). She, too, looks only to looks.

Palamon's prayer to Venus reveals a simultaneous approval and denigration of sexuality:

> I knew a man
> Of eighty winters—this I told them—who
> A lass of fourteen brided. 'Twas thy power
> To put life into dust: the agèd cramp
> Had screwed his square foot round;
> The gout had knit his fingers into knots;
> Torturing convulsions from his globy eyes
> Had almost drawn their spheres, that what was life
> In him seemed torture. This anatomy
> Had by his young fair fere [mate] a boy, and I
> Believed it was his, for she swore it was—
> And who would not believe her?
>
> (5.1.107–18)

The power of love is exalted through repellent description. The reference to the "boy" anticipates imagery of sexuality and reproduction at the conclusion— "consummation," "miscarry," "conceives," "deliver" (5.3.94, 101, 137, 138)—that is associated with loss. The account ends with an apparently rhetorical but actually open question that undermines both Venus's sovereignty and female chastity. The very celebration of love thus raises anxieties about women's fidelity.

Heterosexual desire is rendered even more unappealing by representation of what it destroys. This positive alternative is same-sex attachment, whether understood as Renaissance ideal male friendship, girlish intimacy, or homoerotic attraction. In *Much Ado About Nothing,* a romantic comedy, rejection of heterosexual bonding is an immature foible to be overcome. Here, the movement from same-sex innocence to heterosexual experience is figured primarily as loss—comically in the Prologue, with its comparison of "[n]ew plays and maidenheads" (line 1), more grimly thereafter. Although temperamentally no military Amazon, Emilia prefers virginity and the company of females to marriage. She tells Theseus that if he does not grant her petition, she will not "be so hardy / Ever to take a husband" (1.1.204–05). In her sexual joking with her Woman, she says that "Men are mad things" (2.2.126) and praises the rose above all other flowers because "It is the very emblem of a maid" (2.2.137). Even after coming to admire the cousins, she still prays to Diana either that the more loving and deserving win her or that she be allowed to continue a virgin "in thy band" (5.1.162). When Theseus tells her, "[I]f you can love, end this difference" by choosing one of the kinsmen, she evasively replies, "I cannot, sir; they are both too excellent" (3.6.278, 287).

This stance is explained by Emilia's recollection of her intimacy with Flavina, who died when each was eleven. Her account of two girls who "[l]oved for [simply because] we did" (1.3.61) culminates in this exchange:

The beginning of *The Knight's Tale*, from *The Workes of Our Ancient and Learned English Poet, Geffrey Chaucer* (1602 edition).

The imprisoned Palamon and Arcite gazing at Emilia in the garden below. From a French translation of about 1455 of Giovanni Boccaccio's *Teseida* (the source of Chaucer's *Knight's Tale*), by René of Anjou.

> EMILIA ... the true love tween maid and maid may be
> More than in sex individual.
> HIPPOLYTA   You're out of breath,
> And this high-speeded pace is but to say
> That you shall never, like the maid Flavina,
> Love any that's called man.
> EMILIA   I am sure I shall not.
> (1.3.81–85)

Female friendship thus stands against the monarch's commitment to enforced marriage. The play never repudiates this position.

Palamon and Arcite do so, however, choosing to kill and die—and hence to ruin their most precious possession, their love for each other—out of desire for Emilia. This resolution of the Renaissance debate over the claims of love and friendship has a paradoxical effect. The collapse of the cousins' attachment, which is not stressed in Chaucer, only highlights its value. Though they regret that life imprisonment precludes marriage and family, their thoughts quickly turn to each other. Arcite recommends "the enjoying of our griefs together" (2.2.60) and misogynistically notes the danger of freedom, which "might—like women— / Woo us to wander from" "the ways of honor" (lines 75–76, 73). "Were we at liberty, / A wife might part us lawfully," but in prison "[w]e are one another's wife, ever begetting / New births of love" (lines 88–89, 80–81).

But Palamon's first sight of Emilia undermines their resolution, though in surprising fashion. Talking to her Woman about the narcissus flower, Emilia reflects upon the myth of Narcissus, who fell in love with his own reflection in a pool and died pining for it: "That was a fair boy, certain, but a fool / To love himself. Were there not maids enough?" (2.2.120–21). The connection between Palamon and Narcissus is made explicit when Emilia remarks that Palamon shows

> not a smile.
> Yet these that we count errors may become him:
> Narcissus was a sad boy, but a heavenly.
> (4.2.30–32)

Palamon's suggested autoeroticism and preference for males over females is antici-pated in Emilia's homosexual description of Arcite:

> Just such another wanton Ganymede
> Set Jove afire with, and enforced the god
> Snatch up the goodly boy and set him by him. . . .
> (4.2.15–17)

Similarly, as the cousins prepare to battle each other, Arcite admiringly remarks, "Defy me in these fair terms, and you show / More than a mistress to me" (3.6.25–26). And when Arcite is released from prison, Palamon imagines what would happen if the roles were reversed:

> Were I at liberty, I would do things
> Of such a virtuous greatness that this lady,
> This blushing virgin, should take manhood to her
> And seek to ravish me.
> (2.2.259–62)

Even the thought of the woman he loves becomes a fantasy of homosexual rape.

If the play offers a balance between same-sex and other-sex bonding, it is in Theseus, whose friendship with Pirithous coexists with his impending marriage to Hippolyta. As noted earlier, however, Theseus's conduct is open to question. It is also suggested that marriage to Hippolyta will never measure up to friendship with Pirithous. Most important, the catastrophic experience of Emilia and the kinsmen outweighs Theseus's success with potentially antagonistic emotional and sexual attach-ments. Nonetheless, Theseus may be an idealized image of King James I, who com-bined marriage with homosexual behavior. In this interpretation, Arcite's death corresponds to that of James's oldest son, Prince Henry, in the fall of 1612. The con-cluding, bittersweet union of Emilia with Palamon parallels the marriage soon after of James's daughter Elizabeth with the Elector Palatine. The probable 1619–20 and 1625–26 revivals, as well as the First Quarto in 1634, may also have resonated with royal life. Yet evidence for the play's direct connection to the court is uncertain. Its members might not have been flattered by the comparisons. Such issues could not matter to subsequent audiences, however. Except for an adaptation in the late 1660s, *The Two Noble Kinsmen* probably remained unstaged until 1928. Since then, effective performances have tended to eschew realism for ritual. But a 1979 production provided an interesting alternative by employing an all-male cast to emphasize the work's homo-erotic motifs.

Beginning with the late seventeenth-century adaptation, however, the most suc-cessful feature of the staging has been the Jailer's Daughter, who, though isolated and powerless, often emerges as the central figure. This prominence is consistent with the unusual number and importance of female roles in the work. The Daughter's mid-play soliloquies (2.4, 2.6, 3.2, 3.4), three of them probably—the fourth perhaps—by Fletcher, are marked by exclamations, questions, and a consequent intimacy with the audience denied the other characters. The Daughter's special stage position thus helps win sympathy for her. In Shakespeare, this position is characteristically reserved for a lower-class male character, a clown or fool, with whom the groundlings might identify. Here, Shakespeare's interest in folk culture meshes with Fletcher's fascination with strong women.

The Daughter is at the heart of a subplot that interacts with, and reflects on, the main action. Following the morris dancers' frank sexual talk in 2.3, she delivers her first soliloquy and frees Palamon from prison, hoping he will satisfy her sexual desire for him. Though the genders are reversed, the situation is the same in the main plot: the person in love knows little of the beloved, who is largely oblivious of the lover.

A joust celebrating the marriage of Henry IV of England to Joan of Navarre. From the Beauchamp Pageant (1485–90).

Her illness is cured amorally. On the Doctor's advice, and over the objections of her father (the Jailer), the Wooer pretends to be Palamon and has intercourse with her. Tricked into losing a virginity she was not trying to preserve, "she's well restored / And to be married shortly" (5.4.27–28) to the man who actually is right for her (earlier, he foils her attempted suicide). This outcome makes sense in light of Renaissance medicine, which believed hysteria was caused by a wandering womb that intercourse returned to its proper place. One might conclude, however, that all women really need is sex and that any man will do.

The Daughter thinks she is marrying one man only to end up with another. Similarly, as Emilia settles into her fate, fate forces her to resettle her affections. Neither woman is given a choice—which is just as well, since neither is capable of making distinctions. The generic names in the subplot—Daughter, Jailer, Wooer, Doctor, Brother, Friends—highlight a lack of individuality while pointing toward a similar absence in the main plot. The critical effort to discriminate between Palamon and Arcite inadvertently reaffirms what it seeks to deny: that it takes an effort to tell the cousins apart.

Even the Daughter's madness is much less destructive and arguably no more deviant than Palamon and Arcite's behavior. Yet the two noble kinsmen are taken seriously in a way she is not. Because she is a lower-class woman, she cannot expect her feelings to be reciprocated, even though she does more for Palamon than either cousin does for Emilia. It is unclear whether the play aims to call attention to this double standard. Her service to Palamon saves his life, however. Palamon meets the Jailer on his way to the executioner's block, acknowledges his gratitude to "[y]our gentle daughter" (5.4.24), and *gives the* JAILER *a purse* (5.4.32 SD) as part of the dowry for her marriage. His generosity infects the other knights slated to die with him:

> FIRST KNIGHT   Nay, let's be offerers all.
> SECOND KNIGHT   Is it a maid?
> PALAMON   Verily, I think so—
>   (5.4.32–33)

Ironically, "[t]*hey give their purses*" (5.4.35 SD) on a doubly false assumption—that they are doomed and that they are contributing to a virgin's dowry. But in another sense, the Daughter is bought off. Palamon speaks with greater accuracy than he knows in saying she is "more to me deserving / Than I can 'quite [requite] or speak of" (5.4.34–35).

Long before this, the Daughter's sequence of soliloquies has come to an end. In the second half of the play, having moved from one form of folly to another, she appears only in dialogue scenes and hence loses her unique contact with the audience. Yet even here, her vigor produces an immediacy that blends with the pathos of her predicament. She shares this pathos with the characters in the main plot, who watch uncomprehendingly as their ideals fail them when it matters most.

WALTER COHEN

SELECTED BIBLIOGRAPHY

Bruster, Douglas. "The Jailer's Daughter and the Politics of Madwomen's Language." *Shakespeare Quarterly* 46 (1995): 277–300. Sees the Daughter as powerless and isolated but nonetheless central to the play, her unique language marked by class and gender, her madness constituting a form of resistance; more generally, her depiction is understood as the intersection of Shakespeare's interest in the folk and Fletcher's in strong women characters, and also as indicative of a transition to a less popular drama.

Clark, Sandra. "*The Two Noble Kinsmen*: Shakespeare's Final Phase: *The Two Noble Kinsmen* in Its Context." *Late Shakespeare: 1608–1613.* Ed. Andrew J. Power and Rory Loughnane. Cambridge: Cambridge UP, 2013. 124–38. Compares *Two Noble Kinsmen* to Shakespeare's other collaborations with Fletcher and to earlier Shakespeare plays, emphasizing the play's bleakness.

Crawforth, Hannah. "'Bride-habited, but maiden-hearted': Language and Gender in *The Two Noble Kinsmen.*" *Women Making Shakespeare: Text, Reception, Performance.* Ed. Gordon McMullan, Lena Cowen Orlin, and Virginia Mason Vaughan. London: Bloomsbury, 2014. 25–34. Argues that the play's dualities of sameness and difference are embodied in its language through hyphenated coinages juxtaposing Latin and Germanic words, and the co-presence of contemporary and archaic meanings.

Gossett, Suzanne. "*The Two Noble Kinsmen* and *Henry VIII*: The Last Last Plays." *The Cambridge Companion to Shakespeare's Last Plays.* Ed. Catherine M. S. Alexander. Cambridge: Cambridge UP, 2009. 185–202. Reviews issues of authorship, collaboration, and publication and performance history, with emphasis on the darkness of tone.

Herman, Peter C. "'Is This Winning?': Prince Henry's Death and the Problem of Chivalry in *The Two Noble Kinsmen.*" *South Atlantic Review* 62 (1997): 1–31. Discusses the death of King James's son and heir as a blow to chivalry, generating in the play a skepticism about its martial and erotic implications.

Masten, Jeffrey. *Textual Intercourse: Collaboration, Authorship, and Sexualities in Renaissance Drama.* Cambridge: Cambridge UP, 1997. 49–60. Emphasizes the homoerotic dimensions of the play, with parallels between the titular kinsmen and the two collaborative playwrights.

Potter, Lois, ed. *The Two Noble Kinsmen.* 3d ed. Walton-on-Thames, Surrey: Thomas Nelson, 1997. Outstanding scholarly edition with a lengthy critical introduction.

Sanders, Julie. "Mixed Messages: The Aesthetics of *The Two Noble Kinsmen.*" *A Companion to Shakespeare's Works.* Ed. Richard Dutton and Jean Howard. Vol. 4: *The Poems, Problem Comedies, Late Plays.* Malden, MA: Blackwell, 2003. 445–61. Examines the play's innovative exploitation of five-act structure, partly to dramatize relations between court and country, and its more general relationship to elite theatrical and political events of the time.

Sprang, Felix C. H. "'Never Fortune did play a subtler game': The Creation of 'Medieval' Narratives in *Pericles* and *The Two Noble Kinsmen.*" *European Journal of English Studies* 15 (2011): 115–28. Ties the play's conscious medievalism to the thematic emphasis on fate and formal turn to tragicomedy, seen, paradoxically, as a self-referentially modern genre.

Teramura, Misha. "The Anxiety of Auctoritas: Chaucer and *The Two Noble Kinsmen.*" *Shakespeare Quarterly* 63 (2012): 544–76. Sees Chaucer's prestige as undermined from within by the play's challenge to heterosexuality; his relationship to the two playwrights is mirrored in the relationship of the older dramatist (Shakespeare) to the younger (Fletcher).

TEXTUAL INTRODUCTION

The Two Noble Kinsmen, cowritten by William Shakespeare and John Fletcher in 1613–14, was not included in Shakespeare's First Folio (1623), but was printed in quarto in 1634. This is the only plausible base text, significantly predating the play's subsequent appearance in the Beaumont and Fletcher (Second) Folio (1679), its only other seventeenth-century printing. The 1634 Quarto (Q) was produced by the printer Thomas Cotes, who was also responsible for Shakespeare's Second Folio (1632), and it seems likely that the Quarto was partially designed to complement this publication. Cotes would also see a quarto of *Pericles* through his press in 1635; both volumes seem to have sold well, judging by the number of surviving copies. The practices of the Quarto's two compositors may cast light on important decisions in the printing of the Second Folio, a subject as yet little explored by critics.

Two key textual issues have dominated bibliographical scholarship on this play. The first is the collaborative nature of the text, which is reflected in certain internal inconsistencies, particularly regarding the use of verse and prose, which Shakespeare and Fletcher appear to treat quite differently (see Digital Edition TC 5). Scholars have tended to attribute to Shakespeare scenes 1.1–5, 3.1–2, 5.1, 5.3–5, and probably 2.1 and 4.3, while Fletcher is usually thought to have written 2.2–6, 3.3–6, 4.1–2, and 5.2. The handover from one playwright to another seems to explain certain peculiarities of the Quarto, such as the doubling of some entrances and exits (see Digital Edition TC 4). Scholars continue to apply stylometrics and computational analysis to the problem of how best to attribute authorship of its various scenes, and results vary around a reasonably clear core; what is beyond doubt, however, is that the play offers particularly interesting insight into the collaborative processes that characterize the latter phase of Shakespeare's career.

The second important textual consideration is the fact that Q contains nine marginal stage directions of a kind unseen elsewhere in early modern drama, and which afford an unprecedented glimpse into what went on backstage during a performance of one of Shakespeare's plays (see Digital Edition TC 3). In this edition, they have been assimilated into standard stage direction format. They stop after the end of the third act, when, we must imagine, the compositors learned they were not supposed to be setting these directions in this way and began incorporating them into the text. Some of these later directions name specific actors from the company of the King's Men ("*Curtis*," presumably Curtis Greville, at 4.2.70, and "*T. Tucke*," thought to be Thomas Tuckfield, at the start of 5.3). This supports the idea that the compositors worked from an annotated promptbook prepared by Edward Knight, bookkeeper to the company, for a revival of *The Two Noble Kinsmen* in 1625–26. Oddities in the formatting of these directions can largely be explained as attempts on the compositors' part to mimic the presentation of this hypothesized scribal copy. As such, the Quarto offers an unusual amount of information regarding early modern printing-house practice. For this reason, along with its implications for our understanding of life in the playhouses of Shakespeare's London and of the collaborative nature of his last plays, the text rewards detailed study.

HANNAH CRAWFORTH

PERFORMANCE NOTE

The Two Noble Kinsmen—which is rarely staged—often inspires directors to adopt open artifice as a staging principle. Stylized acting, storybook sets, and elaborate presentations of ritual, pageantry, and divine intercession respond to the play's many elements of chivalric romance (courtly speeches, idealized heroes, abundant ceremony). Prioritizing unity of action over psychological depth, such staging also has the value of preempting objections to the play's thinly drawn characters while deepening the impact of comparatively realistic scenes, especially those featuring the Jailer's Daughter. Nevertheless the play is unusually malleable in production, capable of accommodating representations defined by sentimentality on the one hand, and emotional truth on the other. It is not uncommon for the protagonists to be distinguished by different styles of acting within the same production, Arcite typically playing the earthy foil to Palamon's starry-eyed dreamer. Depending on the production's approach, Palamon and Arcite can be perfect opposites or nearly indistinguishable from one another, and either kinsman can seem more deserving of the audience's sympathy or condemnation.

Much like Palamon and Arcite, Emilia and the Jailer's Daughter can complement or counteract each other. Some productions contrast Emilia's celibacy and inhibition with the unbridled sexuality of the Jailer's Daughter; others underscore the commonality whereby each, against her liking, marries a replacement for her intended. Some focus on the Daughter's misery at losing Palamon to one who had refused him; others show the women joyfully embracing their matches, unaware of the complications this presents to the generic outcome. Productions must clarify Emilia's initial reluctance to marry (whether because of commitment to chastity, same-sex desire, feminist rejection of patriarchy) and decide whether she marries eagerly or grudgingly. They must also decide whether the Daughter's sexual desire reflects experience or naïveté, and whether her marriage cures madness or feeds it. Other considerations include determining whether Arcite pursues Emilia out of sincere affection or competitive rivalry; whether the daughter's mad wanderings are scary or sweet; whether Theseus and Hippolyta's relationship is idealized or reflective of her subjugation; and whether to exploit the parallels among several robust homosocial—potentially homoerotic—relationships (Theseus/Perithous, Emilia/Flavina, Palamon/Arcite).

BRETT GAMBOA

The Two Noble Kinsmen

[THE PERSONS OF THE PLAY

PROLOGUE

Hymen
BOY

THESEUS
HIPPOLYTA
EMILIA
PIRITHOUS
Artesius, officer
HERALD

Three QUEENS

PALAMON
ARCITE
VALERIUS
KNIGHTS, three seconding Palamon and three Arcite

JAILER
JAILER'S DAUGHTER
WOOER to Jailer's Daughter
JAILER'S BROTHER
Two FRIENDS to Jailer
Emilia's WOMAN
DOCTOR

Gerald, a SCHOOLMASTER
BAVIAN
NELL
Timothy, a TABORER
Four COUNTRYMEN
Four Countrywomen

GENTLEMEN
MESSENGERS
SERVANTS
Women, Nymphs, Attendants, Dancers, Executioner, Guard

EPILOGUE]

Prologue

Flourish.° [Enter PROLOGUE.] — *Trumpet call*

PROLOGUE New plays and maidenheads are near akin:
Much followed° both, for both much money gi'en, — *pursued*
If they stand sound and well.[1] And a good play—
Whose modest scenes blush on his marriage day
5 And shake to lose his honor[2]—is like her
That after holy tie° and first night's stir — *marriage*
Yet still is modesty, and still retains
More of the maid to sight than husband's pains.[3]
We pray our play may be so.° For I am sure — *(modest)*
10 It has a noble breeder° and a pure, — *begetter*
A learnèd, and a poet never went° — *lived*
More famous yet twixt Po and silver Trent.[4]
Chaucer—of° all admired—the story gives; — *by*
There,° constant to eternity,° it lives. — *In his words / immortal*
15 If we let fall° the nobleness of this,° — *demean / (the poem)*
And the first sound this child° hear be a hiss, — *play*
How will it shake the bones of that good man,° — *(Chaucer)*
And make him cry from under ground: "Oh, fan
From me the witless chaff of such a writer
20 That blasts my bays and my famed works makes lighter
Than Robin Hood!"[5] This is the fear we bring;
For to say truth, it were an endless° thing — *never-ending; pointless*
And too ambitious to aspire to him,° — *(Chaucer)*
Weak as we are, and almost breathless swim
25 In this deep water. Do but you hold out
Your helping hands, and we shall tack about
And something do to save us:[6] you shall hear
Scenes, though below his art, may° yet appear — *that may*
Worth two hours' travail.[7] To his bones, sweet sleep;
30 Content° to you. If this play do not keep — *Contentment*
A little dull time from us,[8] we perceive
Our losses fall so thick we must needs leave.[9]

Flourish. [Exit.]

Prologue

1. *stand sound and well:* sexual wordplay about virility and lack of venereal disease.
2. *Whose ... honor:* Whose previously unwatched scenes are "modest" and shy (they "blush") on opening night and "shake" with fear at the thought of being viewed (losing their virginity).
3. *still ... pains:* still looks more like a virgin ("maid") than like a married woman who has experienced her husband's sexual exertions.
4. *a poet ... Trent:* there has never been a more famous poet from Italy to England. The Po is a river in Italy, the Trent an English waterway.
5. *That ... Hood:* Who disgraces my fame as a poet (garlands of bay or laurel were awarded to great poets, hence the name "poet laureate") and makes my renowned creations seem more trivial than a popular tale or ballad (such as that of Robin Hood).

6. *Do but ... us:* Help us by applauding, and we will turn like a sailboat in the breeze produced by your clapping hands, thereby saving our reputation.
7. *two hours' travail:* the actors' labor ("travail") for two hours in performing the play (standard length was two to three hours); also, since Q reads "travel," the audience will take part in a two-hour imaginative journey while watching the play. "Travail" continues the metaphor of childbirth and rearing begun in line 10, which itself develops from the image of the loss of virginity on the marriage night.
8. *keep ... us:* keep us amused.
9. Our losses will be so great that we will need to quit the theater. The "losses" refer to the decline in reputation from a poorly received play, and perhaps also to the burning of the Globe Theater on June 29, 1613, during a performance of *Henry VIII.*

1.1

Enter Hymen,° with a torch burning; a BOY *in a white robe*   god of marriage
before,° singing and strewing flowers; after Hymen, a Nymph,   ahead (of Hymen)
encompassed in her tresses, bearing a wheaten garland.[1] *Then*
THESEUS, *between two other Nymphs with wheaten chaplets°*   wreaths
on their heads. Then HIPPOLYTA,[2] *the bride, led by* PIRITHOUS,
and another [Nymph], holding a garland over her head, her
tresses likewise hanging. After her, EMILIA, *holding up her*
train[; Artesius, and Attendants].

	The Song. *Music.*
BOY [*sings*]	Roses, their sharp spines being gone,
	Not royal in their smells alone,
	But in their hue.

		Maiden pinks,° of odor faint,	low flowering plants
5		Daisies, smell-less, yet most quaint,°	fine
		And sweet thyme° true.	(with pun on "time")

		Primrose, firstborn child of Ver,°	Spring
		Merry springtime's harbinger,
10		With harebells dim.°	dark hyacinths
		Oxlips,° in their cradles growing,	Flowering herbs
		Marigolds, on deathbeds blowing,°	flowering on graves
		Lark's-heels trim.°	Fine larkspur

| | [*He] strews flowers.* |

		All dear Nature's children sweet
		Lie fore bride and bridegroom's feet
15		Blessing their sense.°	Gratifying their senses
		Not an angle of the air,°	noisy, ravenous bird
		Bird melodious, or bird fair,
		Is absent hence.

		The crow, the sland'rous cuckoo,[3] nor
20		The boding° raven, nor chough hoar,[4]	ominous
		Nor chatt'ring pie,°	magpie
		May on our bridehouse° perch or sing,	wedding venue
		Or with them any discord bring,
		But from it fly.

Enter three QUEENS *in black, with veils stained,° with*   dyed black
imperial crowns. The FIRST QUEEN *falls down at the*
foot of THESEUS; *the* SECOND *falls down at the foot of*
Hippolyta; the THIRD *before* EMILIA.

25	FIRST QUEEN [*to* THESEUS] For pity's sake and true gentility's,
	Hear and respect° me. attend to
	SECOND QUEEN [*to* HIPPOLYTA] For your mother's sake
	And as you wish your womb may thrive with fair ones,
	Hear and respect me.
	THIRD QUEEN [*to* EMILIA] Now for the love of him whom Jove
	hath marked° singled out for
30	The honor of your bed and for the sake

1.1 Location: Athens, near the temple where Hippolyta and Theseus are to be married.
1. The young woman's hair hangs loose, indicating
virginity; her garland signifies fertility.
2. According to legend, Hippolyta was queen of the
Amazons before Theseus conquered her race of
women warriors and brought her to Thebes as his
captive and bride.
3. Because it yelled out "cuckold" (husband of an
adulterous wife), impugning faithful wives.
4. A jackdaw—a small, rare, gray-headed ("hoar"),
red-beaked, cliff-dwelling member of the crow family.

Of clear° virginity, be advocate   *unspotted*
For us and our distresses. This good deed
Shall raze you out o'th' book of trespasses
All you are set down there.[5]

THESEUS [*to* FIRST QUEEN]   Sad lady, rise.
HIPPOLYTA [*to* SECOND QUEEN]   Stand up.

35 **EMILIA** [*to* THIRD QUEEN]   No knees to me.
What woman I may stead° that is distressed   *assist*
Does bind me to her.
     [SECOND *and* THIRD QUEENS *rise.*]

THESEUS   What's your request? [*to* FIRST QUEEN] Deliver° you   *Speak*
    for all.

FIRST QUEEN   We are three queens, whose sovereigns fell before
40 The wrath of cruel Creon;[6] who° endured   *(the sovereigns)*
The beaks of ravens, talons of the kites,°   *birds of prey*
And pecks of crows in the foul fields° of Thebes.   *battlefields*
He will not suffer us to burn their bones,
To urn their ashes, nor to take th'offense
45 Of mortal loathsomeness from the blessed eye
Of holy Phoebus,° but infects the winds   *the sun*
With stench of our slain lords. O pity, Duke,
Thou purger of the earth;[7] draw thy feared sword
That does good turns to th' world; give us the bones
50 Of our dead kings, that we may chapel° them;   *entomb (in a chapel)*
And of° thy boundless goodness take some note   *in*
That for our crownèd heads we have no roof,
Save this° which is the lion's, and the bear's,   *(the sky)*
And vault° to every thing.   *ceiling*

THESEUS [*to* FIRST QUEEN]   Pray you kneel not;
55 I was transported with° your speech and suffered   *moved by*
Your knees to wrong themselves.° I have heard the fortunes   *(by kneeling)*
Of your dead lords, which gives me such lamenting
As wakes my vengeance and revenge for 'em.
King Capaneus was your lord; the day
60 That he should° marry you, at such a season   *was about to*
As now it is with me, I met your groom.
By Mars's altar, you were that time fair!
Not Juno's mantle fairer than your tresses,
Nor in more bounty spread her;[8] your wheaten° wreath   *wedding (see 5.1.160)*
65 Was then nor° threshed nor blasted;° Fortune at you   *neither / withered*
Dimpled her cheek with smiles. Hercules our kinsman—
Then weaker than° your eyes—laid by his club;   *overwhelmed by*
He tumbled down upon his Nemean hide
And swore his sinews thawed.[9] O grief and time,
70 Fearful° consumers, you will all devour!   *Terrifying*

---

5. *Shall . . . there:* Will expunge your sins from the divine ledger.
6. Brother to Jocasta and, hence, both brother-in-law and uncle to Oedipus. Creon succeeded Oedipus's son Eteocles as king of Thebes following the siege known as the "Seven Against Thebes," in which both Eteocles and all the attackers, led by Eteocles' brother Polynices, were killed. Creon refused to bury any of the seven, including the husbands of the three Queens.
7. Like his cousin Hercules (see 1.1.66, 3.6.175), Theseus was known for ridding the world of monsters and evildoers.
8. Nor is Juno (goddess of marriage) more luxuriantly wrapped in her mantle than you were in your hanging tresses.
9. *He . . . thawed:* He (Hercules) flopped down on the hide of the Nemean lion (which he wore after killing it as one of his twelve labors) and swore his muscles were turned to liquid by your beauty. Most powerful of Greek mythological heroes, performer of "twelve strong labors" set for him by his cousin (3.6.175), Hercules was typically portrayed armed with a club.

FIRST QUEEN   Oh, I hope some god,
Some god has put his mercy in your manhood,
Whereto he'll infuse power and press you forth,
Our undertaker.°   *champion*

THESEUS   Oh, no knees, none, widow;
75   Unto the helmeted Bellona° use them,   *Roman goddess of war*
And pray for me, your soldier.
          [FIRST QUEEN *rises*.]
Troubled I am.
          [*He*] *turns away.*

SECOND QUEEN [*kneeling*]   Honored Hippolyta,
Most dreaded Amazonian, that hast slain
The scythe-tusked boar;[1] that with thy arm, as strong
80   As it is white, wast near to° make the male   *almost managed to*
To thy sex captive, but that this thy lord—
Born to uphold creation in that honor
First nature styled it in[2]—shrunk thee into
The bound thou wast o'er-flowing,[3] at once subduing
85   Thy force and thy affection. Soldieress,
That equally canst poise° sternness with pity,   *balance*
Whom now I know hast much more power on° him   *over*
Than ever he had on thee, who ow'st° his strength   *owns*
And his love too, who is a servant for
90   The tenor of thy speech;[4] dear glass of° ladies, *mirror for*
Bid him that we, whom flaming war doth scorch,
Under the shadow of his sword may cool us;
Require him he° advance it o'er our heads.   *Ask him to*
Speak't in a woman's key, like such a woman
95   As any of us three. Weep ere you fail.
Lend us a knee,[5]
But touch the ground for us no longer time
Than a dove's motion when the head's plucked off.
Tell him, if he i'th' blood-sized° field lay swollen,   *blood-soaked*
100   Showing the sun his teeth, grinning at the moon,
What you would do.

HIPPOLYTA [*to* SECOND QUEEN]   Poor lady, say no more.
I had as lief trace[6] this good action with you
As that° whereto I am going, and never yet   *(marriage)*
Went I so willing way. My lord is taken°   *affected*
105   Heart-deep with your distress. Let him consider:
I'll speak anon.°   *soon*
          [SECOND QUEEN *rises*.]

THIRD QUEEN [*kneeling to* EMILIA]   Oh, my petition was
Set down in ice,[7] which by hot grief uncandied°   *thawed*
Melts into drops; so sorrow wanting form
Is pressed with deeper matter.[8]

---

1. *Honored . . . boar:* Hippolyta is here confused with Atalanta, another Amazon, who participated with Meleager in the hunt for the Calydonian boar. See note to 3.5.14.
2. *Born . . . in:* Born to sustain the natural order of creation—the order of man over woman.
3. *shrunk . . . o'er-flowing:* returned you to the limits of your sex, which you had previously exceeded.
4. *who is . . . speech:* who (Theseus, not Hippolyta, who is referred to by the previous "Whom" and

"who"), like a good lover, obeys your every spoken desire.
5. *Speak't . . . knee:* Don't speak like an Amazon. Use tears to avoid defeat. Join us in kneeling.
6. I would as willingly follow through.
7. *my . . . ice:* my former speech was cold and formal.
8. *so . . . matter:* so sorrow, lacking a way to express itself, is made yet more oppressive by its inarticulateness; or, perhaps, receives the stamp of "deeper" impulses.

EMILIA   Pray stand up;
 Your grief is written in your cheek.

110 THIRD QUEEN [*rising*]   Oh, woe,   *In my eye*
 You cannot read it there. There,° through my tears,
 Like wrinkled pebbles in a glassy stream
 You may behold 'em.° Lady, lady, alack!   *(my sorrows)*
 He that will all the treasure know o'th' earth
115 Must know° the center too; he that will fish   *dig deep throughout*
 For my least minnow, let him lead° his line   *weight with lead*
 To catch one at my heart. Oh, pardon me;
 Extremity, that sharpens sundry wits,
 Makes me a fool.[9]
 EMILIA   Pray you say nothing, pray you:
120 Who cannot feel nor see the rain, being in't,
 Knows neither wet nor dry. If that you were
 The ground-piece of some painter,[1] I would buy you
 T'instruct me 'gainst° a capital° grief, indeed *To prepare me for / deadly*
 Such heart-pierced° demonstration. But, alas,   *heartrending*
125 Being a natural sister of our sex[2]
 Your sorrow beats so ardently° upon me   *burningly*
 That it shall make a counter-reflect 'gainst[3]
 My brother's° heart and warm it to some pity, *brother-in-law's*
 Though it were made of stone. Pray have good comfort.
130 THESEUS Forward to th' temple;° leave not out a jot *(for the wedding)*
 O'th' sacred ceremony.
 FIRST QUEEN   Oh, this celebration
 Will longer last and be more costly than
 Your suppliants' war!° Remember that your fame *requested war*
 Knolls° in the ear o'th' world: what you do quickly *Tolls like a bell*
135 Is not done rashly; your first thought is more
 Than others' labored meditance,° your premeditating *careful meditation*
 More than their actions. But, O Jove, your actions,
 Soon as they move, as ospreys do the fish,[4]
 Subdue before they touch. Think, dear Duke, think
 What beds our slain kings have!
140 SECOND QUEEN   What griefs our beds,
 That our dear lords have none.
 THIRD QUEEN   None fit for th' dead.
 Those that with cords, knives, drams' precipitance,° *poisons' suddenness*
 Weary of this world's light, have to themselves
 Been death's most horrid agents, human grace° *mercy*
 Affords them dust and shadow—
145 FIRST QUEEN   But our lords
 Lie blist'ring fore the visitating° sun,   *inspecting*
 And were good kings, when living.
 THESEUS It is true. And I will give you comfort,
 To give° your dead lords graves;   *By giving*
150 The which to do must make some work with Creon—

---

9. *Extremity . . . fool:* Extreme suffering, which makes some minds more clear, has made me speak inappropriately.
1. *If . . . painter:* If you were merely the subject (model; preliminary sketch?) of a painting.
2. Since you are actually a live woman (rather than a representation of a grieving wife).
3. That, like a mirror, I'll reflect your (sunlike) sorrow back toward.
4. According to popular legend, ospreys had the power to compel fish to rise to the surface and turn over, making themselves available for capture.

FIRST QUEEN   And that work presents itself to th' doing.[5]
Now 'twill take form; the heats are gone tomorrow.[6]
Then, bootless° toil must recompense itself°   *fruitless / itself only*
With its own sweat. Now he's secure,°   *unaware of danger*
155   Nor dreams we stand before your puissance,°   *power*
Rinsing° our holy begging in our eyes   *(by crying)*
To make petition clear.°   *pure; manifest*
SECOND QUEEN   Now you may take him,
Drunk with his victory.
THIRD QUEEN   And his army full
Of bread and sloth.
THESEUS   Artesius—that best knowest
160   How to draw out,° fit to this enterprise,   *select*
The prim'st° for this proceeding, and the number   *best soldiers*
To carry° such a business—forth° and levy   *conduct; win / go forth*
Our worthiest instruments, whilst we dispatch
This grand act of our life, this daring deed
Of fate[7] in wedlock.
165   FIRST QUEEN [*to* SECOND *and* THIRD QUEENS]   Dowagers,° take° hands.   *Widows / join*
Let us be widows to our woes; delay
Commends us to a famishing hope.[8]
ALL QUEENS   Farewell.
SECOND QUEEN   We come unseasonably,° but when could grief   *at a bad time*
Cull forth,° as unpanged° judgment can, fitt'st time   *Choose/ untormented*
For best solicitation?
170   THESEUS   Why, good ladies,
This is a service, whereto I am going,
Greater than any war; it more imports me°   *means more to me*
Than all the actions that I have foregone°   *done to date*
Or futurely can cope.°   *(with in battle)*
FIRST QUEEN   The more proclaiming°   *Clearly showing that*
175   Our suit shall be neglected when her arms,
Able to lock Jove from a synod,[9] shall
By warranting° moonlight corslet thee;[1] oh, when   *authorizing*
Her twining cherries° shall their sweetness fall°   *parting lips / let fall*
Upon thy taste-full° lips, what wilt thou think   *savoring*
180   Of rotten kings or blubbered° queens? What care   *tear-soaked*
For what thou feel'st not, what thou feel'st being able
To make Mars spurn his drum?° Oh, if thou couch   *(battle signal)*
But one night with her, every hour in't will
Take hostage of thee° for a hundred,° and   *Commit you / (more)*
185   Thou shalt remember nothing more than what
That banquet bids° thee to.   *appetizer invites*
HIPPOLYTA   Though much unlike
You should be so transported, as much sorry
I should be such a suitor;[2] yet I think
Did I not by th'abstaining of my joy—

---

5. And that work needs to be done as soon as possible.
6. While the plan, like molten metal, is still hot, it
can be transformed into something—once it grows
cold, it can no longer be shaped.
7. *this daring deed / Of fate:* this act (marriage) that
challenges fate.
8. *Let . . . hope:* Let us mourn our misfortunes as we
mourned our husbands (or, let us, widow-like, part
from our woes), since by delaying the battle until his

marriage is completed, Theseus consigns us to failure.
9. Able to keep Jupiter from a meeting of the gods.
1. Encircle you like a "corslet," close-fitting defensive armor. Theseus has traded arms (armor) for
arms (embraces).
2. *Though . . . suitor:* Although it's highly unlikely
you'd be so carried away by desire, and I'm just as
sorry to inspire that and also request you to postpone
the wedding.

190 Which breeds a deeper longing—cure their surfeit°   *excess of grief*
That craves a present medicine,° I should pluck   *an immediate relief*
All ladies' scandal° on me. [*She kneels.*] Therefore, sir,   *reproach*
As I shall here make trial of my prayers—
Either presuming them to have some force,
195 Or sentencing for aye their vigor dumb[3]—
Prorogue° this business we are going about and hang   *Delay*
Your shield afore your heart, about that neck   *fight first (with care)*
Which is my fee,° and which I freely lend   *property*
To do these poor queens service.

ALL QUEENS [*to* EMILIA]   Oh, help now;
Our cause cries for your knee.

200 EMILIA [*kneeling to* THESEUS]   If you grant not
My sister her petition—in that force,°   *with that energy*
With that celerity° and nature which   *speed*
She makes it in—from henceforth I'll not dare
To ask you anything, nor be so hardy°   *bold*
Ever to take a husband.

205 THESEUS   Pray, stand up.
I am entreating of myself to do
That which you kneel to have me.° [*They rise.*] —Pirithous,   *have me do*
Lead on the bride; get you° and pray the gods   *go*
For success and return; omit not anything
210 In the pretended° celebration. —Queens,   *planned*
Follow your soldier.° [*to Artesius*] As before, hence, you,   *Theseus*
And at the banks of Aulis[4] meet us with
The forces you can raise, where we shall find
The moiety of a number, for a business
More bigger-looked.[5]   [*Exit Artesius.*]
215 [*to* HIPPOLYTA]   Since that our theme is haste,
I stamp this kiss upon thy current lip;
Sweet, keep it as my token.[6] Set you forward,
For I will see you gone.
      [*Procession moves toward the temple.*]
—Farewell, my beauteous sister. —Pirithous,
Keep the feast full;° bate° not an hour on't.°   *fully / reduce / of it*
220 PIRITHOUS   Sir,
I'll follow you at heels; the feast's solemnity°   *ceremonial splendor*
Shall want° till your return.   *be lacking*
THESEUS   Cousin,° I charge you,   *Friend*
Budge not from Athens. We shall be returning
Ere you can end this feast; of which, I pray you,
225 Make no abatement.° —Once more, farewell all.   *reduction*
      [*Exeunt all except* THESEUS *and* QUEENS.]
FIRST QUEEN   Thus dost thou still make good the tongue o'th' world.[7]
SECOND QUEEN   And earn'st a deity equal with Mars—
THIRD QUEEN   If not above him, for

---

3. Or forever "sentencing" my prayers to silence, than which they are no more effectual.
4. Port where the Greek troops assembled before sailing for Troy.
5. *where . . . looked:* where we shall find part of an army already assembled for a larger campaign than this one (and for more dangerous "business" than marriage, line 196).

6. *I . . . token:* puns on coining and engraving. *stamp:* press (a kiss); make a coin by impressing an image on metal. *current:* flowing away (like a stream); red (current); genuine, not counterfeit. *token:* memento (often of love); metal stamped and used as a coin.
7. In this way, you (Theseus) prove true everything the world says of you.

Thou, being but mortal, makest affections bend
230   To godlike honors;[8] they themselves, some say,
Groan under such a mast'ry.[9]

THESEUS   As we are men,
Thus should we do; being sensually subdued,°   *overcome by appetites*
We lose our human title.° Good cheer, ladies;   *claim to humanity*
Now turn we toward your comforts.   *Flourish. Exeunt.*

1.2

Enter PALAMON *and* ARCITE.

ARCITE   Dear Palamon, dearer in love than blood°   *a blood relation*
And our prime cousin,° yet unhardened in   *nearest kin*
The crimes of nature[1] let us leave the city
Thebes—and the temptings° in't—before we further   *temptations*
5   Sully our gloss of° youth.   *Tarnish our pristine*
And here to keep in abstinence we shame
As in incontinence;[2] for not to swim
I'th' aid o'th' current° were almost to sink—   *With the flow*
At least to frustrate striving[3]—and to follow
10   The common stream 'twould bring us to an eddy
Where we should turn° or drown; if labor through,   *spin endlessly*
Our gain but life and weakness.[4]

PALAMON   Your advice
Is cried up with example.[5] What strange ruins,°   *ruined men*
Since first we went to school, may we perceive
15   Walking in Thebes! Scars and bare weeds°   *tattered clothes*
The gain o'th' martialist,° who did propound   *soldier*
To his bold ends[6] honor and golden ingots—
Which, though he won, he had not[7]—and, now, flirted°   *(is) mocked*
By peace for whom he fought; who then shall offer
20   To Mars's so scorned altar? I do bleed
When such I meet and wish great Juno[8] would
Resume her ancient° fit of jealousy   *former*
To get the soldier work, that peace might purge
For her repletion[9] and retain° anew   *take into service*
25   Her° charitable heart, now hard and harsher   *(Juno's); (peace's)*
Than strife or war could be.

ARCITE   Are you not out?°   *off the point*
Meet you no ruin but the soldier in
The cranks and turns° of Thebes? You did begin   *winding streets*
As if you met decays of many kinds.
30   Perceive you none that do arouse your pity
But th'unconsidered° soldier?   *neglected*

PALAMON   Yes, I pity

---

8. *makest . . . honors:* subordinate your human passions to godlike deeds.
9. *they . . . mast'ry:* the gods themselves complain of such self-restraint; suffer because their passions master them.
1.2 Location: Thebes.
1. *unhardened . . . nature:* inexperienced in the natural vices of man.
2. *here . . . incontinence:* we incur as much shame here (in a corrupt city) by remaining innocent as we would elsewhere by debauching ourselves.
3. And at least renders our exertions (on behalf of goodness) pointless.

4. *if . . . weakness:* if we were to pass through such a whirlpool ("eddy"), we would gain only our lives in a weakened state.
5. Is borne out by numerous examples.
6. *propound . . . ends:* propose as recompense for his courage.
7. Which, though victorious in battle, he didn't receive.
8. Juno, whose jealousy led to the Trojan War, also hated Thebes.
9. *purge / For her repletion:* take medicine to alleviate her (peace's) overeating (the indulgent life of peacetime).

Decays where'er I find them, but such most
That, sweating in an honorable toil,
Are paid with ice° to cool 'em.   *treated coldly*

ARCITE   'Tis not this
35 I did begin to speak of; this° is virtue   *soldiers' merit*
Of no respect in Thebes. I spake of Thebes—
How dangerous, if we will keep our honors,
It is for our residing—where every evil
Hath a good color;° where ev'ry seeming good's *appearance*
40 A certain evil; where not to be e'en jump
As they are here were to be strangers and,
Such things to be, mere monsters.[1]

PALAMON   'Tis in our power—
Unless we fear that apes can tutor's°—to *that we're mere mimics*
Be masters of our manners. What need I
45 Affect another's gait, which is not catching° *infectious; attractive*
Where there is faith,[2] or to be fond° upon *to dote*
Another's way of speech, when by mine own
I may be reasonably conceived,° saved too, *understood*
Speaking it° truly? Why am I bound° *If I speak / (financially)*
                 noble
50 By any generous° bond to follow him *Who heeds / at least*
Follows° his tailor, haply° so long until *(for unpaid bills)*
The followed make pursuit?° Or let me know
Why mine own barber is unblessed, with him
My poor chin too, for° 'tis not scissored just *since*
55 To such a favorite's glass?° What canon° is there *image / law; cannon*
That does command my rapier from my hip
To dangle't in my hand, or to go tiptoe
Before the street be foul?[3] Either I am
The fore-horse in the team or I am none
60 That draw i'th' sequent trace.[4] These poor slight sores
Need not a plantain;[5] that which rips my bosom
Almost to th' heart's—

ARCITE   Our uncle Creon—
PALAMON   He—
A most unbounded° tyrant—whose successes *unrestrained*
Makes heaven unfeared and villainy assured° *assured that*
65 Beyond its power there's nothing, almost puts
Faith in a fever,[6] and deifies alone
Voluble chance;° who only attributes *Variable fortune*
The faculties of other instruments
To his own nerves and act;[7] commands men service,
70 And what they win in't, boot° and glory; one *booty; gain*
That fears not to do harm; good, dares not.° Let *dares not to do good*
The blood of mine that's sib° to him be sucked *related*
From me with leeches;° let them break° and fall *medically purified / burst*
Off me with that° corruption.   *(Creon's)*

---

1. *where . . . monsters:* where failure to conform exactly ("jump") makes you a foreigner and perfect conformity makes you a monster.
2. Self-reliance. Palamon's speech echoes familiar criticisms of the contrived, "effeminate" manners of courtiers and men of fashion, here contrasted with implicit religious norms ("faith"; "saved," line 48; "canon," line 55).
3. *go . . . foul:* tiptoe on a clean street (like a cowardly soldier).
4. *Either . . . trace:* I will not pull behind the lead ("fore-") horse (follow fashion).
5. Herb used for treating wounds.
6. *puts . . . fever:* undermines religion.
7. *attributes . . . act:* takes credit for others' successes.

ARCITE   Clear-spirited° cousin,   *Noble-spirited*
75   Let's leave his court, that we may nothing share
        Of his loud° infamy. For our milk   *well-known*
        Will relish of the pasture,[8] and we must
        Be vile or disobedient—not his kinsmen
        In blood, unless in quality.[9]
PALAMON   Nothing truer.
80   I think the echoes of his shames have deafed
        The ear of heav'nly justice. Widows' cries
        Descend again into their throats and have not
        Due audience of° the gods.   *Proper notice from*
                Enter VALERIUS.
                                            Valerius—
VALERIUS   The King calls for you; yet be leaden-footed°   *go slowly*
85   Till his great rage be off him. Phoebus, when
        He broke his whipstock and exclaimed against
        The horses of the sun,[1] but° whispered to°   *merely / compared to*
        The loudness of his fury.
PALAMON   Small winds shake him.
        But what's the matter?
90 VALERIUS   Theseus—who, where he threats, appalls—hath sent
        Deadly defiance to him° and pronounces   *(Creon)*
        Ruin to Thebes, who° is at hand to seal   *(Theseus)*
        The promise of his wrath.[2]
ARCITE   Let him approach.
        But that we fear the gods in him,° he brings not   *justness of his cause*
95   A jot of terror to us. Yet what man
        Thirds his own worth—the case is each of ours—
        When that his action's dregged with mind assured
        'Tis bad he goes about?[3]
PALAMON   Leave that unreasoned.°   *Forget that*
        Our services stand now for Thebes, not Creon;
100   Yet° to be neutral to him were dishonor,   *Still*
        Rebellious° to oppose. Therefore we must   *Treasonable*
        With him stand to the mercy of° our fate,   *submit to*
        Who hath bounded our last minute.[4]
ARCITE   So we must.
        [*to* VALERIUS] Is't said this war's afoot, or it shall be
        On fail of° some condition?   *If Thebes rejects*
105 VALERIUS   'Tis in motion.
        The intelligence of state° came in the instant   *official announcement*
        With the defier.°   *herald of Theseus*
PALAMON   Let's to the King—who, were he
        A quarter carrier of that honor which
        His enemy come in, the blood we venture
110   Should be as for our health,[5] which were not spent,°   *wasted*
        Rather laid out for purchase.° But, alas,   *invested for profit*

---

8. Like cows whose milk absorbs the taste of whatever they eat.
9. *not . . . quality:* we ought not to act like his kinsmen unless we're willing to act like him; we're not his
kinsmen unless we act like him.
1. After his son Phaëthon died driving the horses of
the sun, Phoebus (the sun) vented his grief at the
horses—hence the broken whip handle ("whipstock").

2. *seal . . . wrath:* turn anger to action.
3. *Yet . . . about:* Yet any man reduces his worth by
two-thirds—as we do—when he knows the action he
undertakes is unworthy.
4. *Who . . . minute:* Which has determined when we
die.
5. *the blood . . . health:* our loss of blood in combat
would be equivalent to a therapeutic bloodletting.

Our hands advanced before° our hearts, what will   *beyond*
The fall o'th' stroke do damage?[6]
ARCITE   Let th'event,°   *the outcome*
That never-erring arbitrator, tell us
115 When we know all ourselves[7]—and let us follow
The becking° of our chance.   *Exeunt.*   *calling*

1.3

Enter PIRITHOUS, HIPPOLYTA, [*and*] EMILIA.

PIRITHOUS   No further.
HIPPOLYTA   Sir, farewell. Repeat my wishes
To our great lord, of whose success I dare not
Make any timorous question—yet I wish him
Excess and overflow of power, an't might be°   *if possible*
5   To dure° ill-dealing fortune. Speed to him;   *endure*
Store[1] never hurts good governors.
PIRITHOUS   Though I know
His ocean needs not my poor drops, yet they
Must yield their tribute there. [*to* EMILIA] My precious maid,
Those best affections° that the heavens infuse   *inclinations*
10   In their best-tempered pieces° keep enthroned   *greatest creations*
In your dear heart.
EMILIA   Thanks, sir. Remember me
To our all-royal brother, for whose speed°   *success*
The great Bellona I'll solicit; and,
Since in our terrene state° petitions are not   *earthly condition*
15   Without gifts understood, I'll offer to her
What I shall be advised she likes. Our hearts
Are in his army, in his tent.
HIPPOLYTA   In 's bosom.
We have been soldiers,° and we cannot weep   *(as Amazons)*
When our friends don their helms,° or put to sea,   *helmets*
20   Or tell of babes broached° on the lance, or women   *speared*
That have sod° their infants in—and after ate them— *boiled*
The brine they wept at killing 'em.[2] Then, if
You stay to see of us such spinsters, we
Should hold you here for ever.[3]
PIRITHOUS   Peace be to you
25   As I pursue this war, which° shall be then   *(peace)*
Beyond further requiring.°   *Exit* PIRITHOUS.   *In no need of prayer*
EMILIA   How his longing
Follows his friend! Since his depart,° his sports,   *Theseus's departure*
Though craving° seriousness and skill, passed slightly *requiring*
His careless execution,[4] where nor° gain   *neither*
30   Made him regard or loss consider, but
Playing one business in his hand, another
Directing in his head, his mind nurse equal
To these so-diff'ring twins.[5] Have you observed him
Since our great lord departed?

---

6. *what . . . damage:* what harm will "the fall o'th' stroke" do?
7. *tell . . . ourselves:* speak for itself.
1.3 Location: The outskirts of Athens.
1. Abundant resources (here, good men like Pirithous).
2. Miriam killed, cooked, and ate her son during the Roman siege of Jerusalem, adding her own tears for sauce.
3. *Then . . . for ever:* if you wait long enough for us to turn into spinners (housewives), you'll wait forever.
4. *passed . . . execution:* were pursued carelessly.
5. *his . . . twins:* his attention divided equally between sports and Theseus.

HIPPOLYTA　　　　　　　　　　　With much labor°—　　　　　　　　*diligence*
35　And I did love him for't. They two have cabined°　　　*shared quarters*
　　In many as dangerous as poor a corner,
　　Peril and want contending;[6] they have skiffed°　　　*sailed across*
　　Torrents whose roaring tyranny and power
　　I'th' least of these° was dreadful; and they have　　　*At the weakest point*
40　Sought out together where Death's self was lodged;[7]
　　Yet fate hath brought them off. Their knot of love
　　Tied, weaved, entangled, with so true, so long,
　　And with a finger of so deep a cunning,°　　　　　　　*skill*
　　May be outworn,° never undone. I think　　　*worn out (in death)*
45　Theseus cannot be umpire to himself,
　　Cleaving his conscience into twain and doing
　　Each side like° justice, which[8] he loves best.　　　　*equal*

EMILIA　　　　　　　　　　　　　　Doubtless
　　There is a best, and reason has no manners
　　To say it is not you. I was acquainted
50　Once with a time when I enjoyed a playfellow;
　　You were at wars when she the grave enriched,
　　Who made too proud the bed,° took leave o'th' moon[9]—　　*grave*
　　Which then looked pale at parting—when our count°　　　*age*
　　Was each eleven.

HIPPOLYTA　　　　　　　　'Twas Flavina.

EMILIA　　　　　　　　　　　　　Yes.
55　You talk of Pirithous' and Theseus' love;
　　Theirs has more ground,° is more maturely seasoned,　　*a stronger base*
　　More buckled° with strong judgment, and their needs　　*joined together*
　　The one of th'other may be said to water
　　Their intertangled roots of love; but I
60　And she I sigh and spoke of were things innocent,
　　Loved for° we did, and like the elements[1]　　　　　*simply because*
　　That know not what, nor why, yet do effect°　　　　　*create*
　　Rare issues° by their operance, our souls　　　　　*Amazing results*
　　Did so to one another. What she liked
65　Was then of° me approved; what not, condemned—　　　*by*
　　No more arraignment.° The flower that I would pluck　　*inquiry*
　　And put between my breasts—oh, then but beginning
　　To swell about the blossom—she would long°　　　　　*desire*
　　Till she had such another and commit it
70　To the like innocent cradle where, phoenix-like,
　　They died in perfume.[2] On my head no toy°　　　　　*trifle*
　　But was her pattern;° her affections—pretty,　　　　*model*
　　Though happily her careless wear—I followed
　　For my most serious decking.[3] Had mine ear
75　Stolen some new air° or at adventure° hummed one　　*tune / by chance*
　　From musical coinage,° why, it was a note　　　　　*improvisation*
　　Whereon her spirits would sojourn—rather, dwell on—

---

6. Contending for which was the greater hardship.
7. *where . . . lodged*: the underworld, to rescue Proserpina, Roman fertility goddess abducted to the underworld by the god of the infernal region.
8. Pirithous or Hippolyta; or, Pirithous or Theseus.
9. Died. Diana (the moon goddess), who watched over virgins and Amazons; hence Emilia's (equivocal) patron.

1. Air, fire, earth, and water—constituents of all matter.
2. The phoenix died by being burned on aromatic wood, only to be reborn from its own ashes.
3. *her affections . . . decking*: whatever she wore—appealing, even though perhaps put on without thought—I'd imitate for my most serious clothing choices.

And sing it in her slumbers. This rehearsal—
Which, fury-innocent wots well, comes in
80 Like old emportment's bastard[4]—has this end:
That the true love tween maid and maid may be
More than in sex individual.[5]

HIPPOLYTA   You're out of breath,
And this high-speeded pace is but to say
That you shall never, like the maid Flavina,[6]
Love any that's called man.

85 EMILIA   I am sure I shall not.

HIPPOLYTA   Now alack, weak sister,
I must no more believe thee in this point—
Though in't I know thou dost believe thyself—
Than I will trust a sickly appetite
90 That loathes even as it longs. But sure, my sister,
If I were ripe for your persuasion,° you   *open to your views*
Have said enough to shake me from the arm
Of the all-noble Theseus, for whose fortunes
I will now in and kneel with great assurance
95 That we, more than his Pirithous, possess
The high throne in his heart.

EMILIA   I am not
Against your faith, yet I continue mine.   *Exeunt.*
Two hearses ready with PALAMON *and* ARCITE.
The three QUEENS, THESEUS, *and his lords ready.*[7]

1.4

Cornetts. A battle struck within; then a retreat.
Flourish.[1] *Then enter* THESEUS, *[as] victor[, followed*
by HERALD *and Attendants with two hearses,*° *bearing*   *biers*
ARCITE *and* PALAMON]. *The three* QUEENS *meet him*
and fall on their faces before him.

FIRST QUEEN   To thee no star be dark.°   *unfavorable*

SECOND QUEEN   Both heaven and earth
Friend thee forever.

THIRD QUEEN   All the good that may
Be wished upon thy head, I cry "Amen" to't.

THESEUS   Th'impartial gods, who from the mounted° heavens   *high*
5 View us, their mortal herd, behold who err
And, in their time, chastise. Go and find out
The bones of your dead lords and honor them
With treble ceremony; rather than a gap
Should be in their dear° rites,° we would supply't.   *valued / (also "rights")*
10 But those we will depute, which shall invest°   *clothe*
You in your dignities, and even° each thing   *rectify*
Our haste does leave imperfect. So adieu,

---

4. TEXTUAL COMMENT *This . . . bastard:* This narrative, which, as innocent passionate love well knows,
is an illegitimate descendant (poor likeness) of my
former passion (or, the former significance of the relationship). For the enigmatic phrase "fury-innocent,"
see Digital Edition TC 1.
5. *sex individual:* the different genders, male and
female.

6. TEXTUAL COMMENT For inconsistent use of names
here and elsewhere, see Digital Edition TC 2.
7. TEXTUAL COMMENT For the distinctiveness of this
stage direction and others in the play, which refer to
events offstage, see Digital Edition TC 3.
1.4 Location: The outskirts of Thebes.
1. Small horns sound offstage, signaling the start of
battle, a retreat, and then a triumphal entrance.

And heaven's good eyes look on you.   *Exeunt* QUEENS.
[*He notices the hearses.*]   What are those?

HERALD   Men of great quality,° as may be judged   rank
15   By their appointment.° Some of Thebes have told's°   battle gear / told us
They are sisters' children, nephews to the King.

THESEUS   By th' helm of Mars, I saw them in the war,
Like to a pair of lions, smeared with prey,
Make lanes in troops aghast. I fixed my note°   attention
20   Constantly on them, for they were a mark°   striking sight
Worth a god's view. What prisoner was't that told me
When I inquired their names?

HERALD   Wi' leave, they're called
Arcite and Palamon—

THESEUS   'Tis right; those, those.
They are not dead?

25   HERALD   Nor in a state of life. Had they been taken
When their last hurts were given, 'twas possible
They might have been recovered;° yet they breathe   healed
And have the name of men.

THESEUS   Then like men use 'em.
The very lees of such, millions of rates,
30   Exceed the wine of others.[2] All our surgeons
Convent° in their behoof;° our richest balms,   Assemble / behalf
Rather than niggard,° waste; their lives concern us   use stingily
Much more than Thebes is worth. Rather than have 'em
Freed of this plight and in their morning° state,   former (healthy)
35   Sound and at liberty, I would 'em dead;
But forty-thousandfold we had rather have 'em
Prisoners to us than death. Bear 'em speedily
From our kind air—to them unkind[3]—and minister
What man to man may do, for our sake—more,°   even more
40   Since I have known frights, fury, friends' behests,
Love's provocations, zeal, a mistress' task,
Desire of liberty, a fever, madness,
Hath set a mark which nature could not reach to
Without some imposition, sickness in will
45   O'er-wrestling strength in reason.[4] For our love
And great Apollo's° mercy, all our best   god of healing
Their best skill tender. Lead into the city,
Where, having bound things scattered,° we will post°   reimposed order / hurry
To Athens fore° our army.   *Flourish. Exeunt.*   prior to

1.5

Music. Enter the QUEENS *with the [Attendants
bearing] hearses of their knights, in a funeral
solemnity, etc.*

QUEENS [*sing*]   Urns and odors bring away;
Vapors, sighs darken the day;
Our dole° more deadly looks than dying.   mourning; fate

---

2. *The very . . . others:* The dregs of such men far
exceed the best that others can offer.
3. Fresh air was thought dangerous to wounds.
4. *Since . . . reason:* Since compelling incentives can

impel men to perform beyond their normal abilities,
whereas otherwise weak will triumphs over strong
reason. *mark:* target. *imposition:* powerful pressure.
1.5 Location: Scene continues.

	Balms and gums¹ and heavy cheers,°	*sad countenances*
5	Sacred vials filled with tears,	
	And clamors through the wild air flying.	

Come, all sad and solemn shows
That are quick-eyed pleasure's foes;
We convent naught else but woes.
10 We convent, etc.

THIRD QUEEN   This funeral path brings° to your household's grave: *leads*
Joy seize on you again; peace sleep with him.
SECOND QUEEN   And this to yours.
FIRST QUEEN   Yours this way. Heavens lend
A thousand differing ways to one sure end.°   *death*
15 THIRD QUEEN   This world's a city full of straying streets,
And death's the marketplace where each one meets.
                                        Exeunt severally.°   *separately*

2.1

Enter JAILER *and* WOOER.

JAILER   I may depart with° little while I live; something I may   *may spare*
cast° to you, not much. Alas, the prison I keep, though it be   *give (as a dowry)*
for great ones, yet they seldom come; before one salmon,
you shall take a number of minnows. I am given out to be bet-
5 ter lined° than it can appear to me report° is a true speaker. I   *said to be richer / rumor*
would I were really that° I am delivered° to be. Marry,¹ what   *what / reported*
I have—be it what it will—I will assure upon° my daughter   *bequeath to*
at the day of my death.
WOOER   Sir, I demand no more than your own offer, and I will
10 estate° your daughter in what I have promised—   *settle*
JAILER   Well, we will talk more of this when the solemnity² is
passed. But have you a full promise of° her?   *from*
        Enter [JAILER'S] DAUGHTER[, *carrying rushes*].°   *(as floor coverings)*
When that shall be seen, I tender my consent.
WOOER   I have, sir. Here she comes.
15 JAILER [*to* JAILER'S DAUGHTER]   Your friend and I have chanced
to name you here, upon the old business. But no more of
that now; so soon as the court hurry is over, we will have an
end of it. I'th' meantime, look tenderly° to the two prisoners.   *carefully*
I can tell you they are princes.
20 JAILER'S DAUGHTER   These strewings° are for their chamber.   *rushes*
'Tis pity they are in prison, and 'twere pity they should be
out. I do think they have patience to make any adversity
ashamed; the prison itself is proud of 'em, and they have all
the world in their chamber.³
25 JAILER   They are famed° to be a pair of absolute° men.   *reputed / perfect*
JAILER'S DAUGHTER   By my troth, I think fame but stammers°   *underrates*
'em; they stand a grise° above the reach of report.°   *step / their reputation*
JAILER   I heard them reported in the battle to be the only doers.°   *supreme achievers*

---

1. Aromatic substances used in mourning rituals.
2.1 Location: The palace garden in Athens, perhaps with the second, or higher, gallery above representing the window of the cell where Palamon and Arcite are being held.

1. To be sure (originally, by the Virgin Mary).
2. Theseus and Hippolyta's wedding.
3. They have everything they need in their prison cell, because they have each other. See 2.2.61–62.

JAILER'S DAUGHTER Nay, most likely, for they are noble
30   suff'rers.[4] I marvel how they would have looked, had they been
victors, that with such a constant nobility enforce a freedom
out of bondage, making misery their mirth and affliction a
toy° to jest at.   *trifle*
JAILER Do they so?
35 JAILER'S DAUGHTER It seems to me they have no more sense of
their captivity than I of ruling Athens. They eat well, look
merrily, discourse of many things, but nothing of their own
restraint° and disasters. Yet sometime a divided° sigh, mar-   *captivity / partial*
tyred° as 'twere i'th' deliverance, will break from one of   *suppressed*
40   them—when the other presently° gives it so sweet a rebuke   *immediately*
that I could wish myself a sigh to be so chid,° or at least a   *chided*
sigher to be comforted.
WOOER I never saw 'em.
JAILER The Duke himself came privately in the night, and so
45   did they;[5] what the reason of it is, I know not.
    Enter PALAMON *and* ARCITE, *above.*
[*He points at* PALAMON *and* ARCITE.] Look, yonder they are;
that's Arcite looks out.
JAILER'S DAUGHTER No, sir, no, that's Palamon. Arcite is the
lower° of the twain; [*pointing at* ARCITE] you may perceive a   *shorter*
50   part of him.
JAILER Go to,° leave your pointing; they would not make us   *Come now*
their object.[6] Out of their sight!
JAILER'S DAUGHTER It is a holiday to look on them. Lord, the
difference of° men!   *between*
            Exeunt [JAILER, WOOER, *and* JAILER'S DAUGHTER.
                PALAMON *and* ARCITE *remain*].[7]

2.2

PALAMON How do you, noble cousin?
ARCITE   How do you, sir?
PALAMON Why, strong enough to laugh at misery
And bear the chance° of war yet; we are prisoners,   *uncertainties*
I fear, forever, cousin.
ARCITE   I believe it,
5   And to that destiny have patiently
Laid up my hour to come.°   *Consigned my future*
PALAMON   O cousin Arcite,
Where is Thebes now?[1] Where is our noble country?
Where are our friends and kindreds? Never more
Must we behold those comforts, never see
10   The hardy youths strive for° the games of honor—   *in*
Hung with the painted favors° of their ladies,   *love tokens*
Like tall ships under sail—then start amongst 'em

---

4. For they endure nobly what others do to them. To
do and to suffer are antithetical.
5. Theseus brought them secretly at night.
6. They would not be so rude as to point at us; they
don't want to look at us.
7. TEXTUAL COMMENT For the exits and nonexits
here, as well as for the probable staging of the next
scene on an upper stage and the possibility of Fletcher

taking over from Shakespeare here, see Digital Edition TC 4.
2.2 Location: The prison in Athens, upper stage; as
in 2.1, the garden is located on the main stage.
1. The kinsmen's view of Thebes in 1.2 is very different, perhaps because Shakespeare probably wrote
the earlier scene and Fletcher this one, or perhaps
because of their changed circumstances.

And, as an east° wind, leave 'em all behind us (deadly)
Like lazy clouds, whilst Palamon and Arcite,
15 Even in the wagging of a wanton leg,[2]
Outstripped the people's praises, won the garlands,
Ere they have time to wish 'em ours. Oh, never
Shall we two exercise, like twins of honor,
Our arms again, and feel our fiery horses
20 Like proud seas under us; our good swords now— Better swords
Better° the red-eyed god of war ne'er wore— Torn from
Ravished° our sides, like age must run to rust Juno; Minerva (Athena)
And deck the temples of those gods° that hate us;
These hands shall never draw 'em out like lightning annihilate
To blast° whole armies more.
25 ARCITE   No, Palamon,
Those hopes are prisoners with us. Here we are,
And here the graces of our youths must wither
Like a too-timely° spring; here age must find us Like buds in a premature
And—which is heaviest,° Palamon—unmarried. what is saddest
30 The sweet embraces of a loving wife,
Loaden with kisses, armed with thousand cupids,
Shall never clasp our necks. No issue° know us; children
No figures° of ourselves shall we e'er see images
To glad our age, and like young eagles teach 'em
35 Boldly to gaze against bright arms[3] and say,
"Remember what your fathers were, and conquer!"
The fair-eyed maids shall weep our banishments,
And in their songs curse ever-blinded Fortune
Till she for shame see what a wrong she has done
40 To youth and nature. This is all our world;
We shall know nothing here but one another,
Hear nothing but the clock that tells° our woes. enumerates
The vine shall grow, but we shall never see it;
Summer shall come and with her all delights,
45 But dead-cold winter must inhabit here still.
PALAMON 'Tis too true, Arcite. To our Theban hounds
That shook the agèd forest with their echoes
No more now must we halloo; no more shake
Our pointed javelins whilst the angry swine° the wild boar
50 Flies like a Parthian[4] quiver from our rages,
Struck with our well-steeled darts. All valiant uses°— activities
The food and nourishment of noble minds—
In us two here shall perish; we shall die—
Which is the curse of honor—lastly,° at last
Children of grief and ignorance.° Sad and unknown
55 ARCITE   Yet, cousin,
Even from the bottom of these miseries,
From all that Fortune can inflict upon us,
I see two comforts rising, two mere° blessings, pure
If the gods please: to hold here a brave patience,
60 And the enjoying of our griefs together.

2. *Even . . . leg:* Effortlessly; rapidly; playfully.
3. Eagles supposedly could gaze at the sun without being blinded.
4. During the era of ancient Rome's supremacy, the

Parthians were renowned archers, famous for shooting behind them at their enemies as they pretended to flee.

Whilst Palamon is with me, let me perish
If I think this our prison.

PALAMON   Certainly,
'Tis a main° goodness, cousin, that our fortunes   great
Were twined together. 'Tis most true, two souls
65 Put in two noble bodies, let 'em suffer
The gall of hazard,° so° they grow together   bitterest luck / if
Will never sink;° they must not, say° they could.   succumb / even if
A willing man dies sleeping,[5] and all's done.

ARCITE   Shall we make worthy uses of this place
That all men hate so much?

70 PALAMON   How, gentle cousin?

ARCITE   Let's think this prison holy sanctuary,
To keep us from corruption of worse men.
We are young and yet desire the ways of honor
That liberty and common conversation,°   worldly acquaintances
75 The poison of pure spirits, might—like women—
Woo us to wander from. What worthy blessing
Can be,° but our imaginations   Can there be
May make it ours? And here being thus together,
We are an endless mine° to one another;   resource
80 We are one another's wife, ever begetting
New births of love; we are father, friends, acquaintance;
We are in one another families;
I am your heir and you are mine. This place
Is our inheritance; no hard oppressor
85 Dare take this from us; here, with a little patience,
We shall live long and loving. No surfeits° seek us;   diseases from excess
The hand of war hurts none here, nor the seas
Swallow their youth. Were we at liberty,
A wife might part us lawfully, or business;
90 Quarrels consume us; envy of ill men
Crave our acquaintance.[6] I might sicken, cousin,
Where you should never know it, and so perish
Without your noble hand to close mine eyes,
Or prayers to the gods. A thousand chances,
Were we from hence, would sever us.

95 PALAMON   You have made me—
I thank you, cousin Arcite—almost wanton°   frolicsome
With my captivity. What a misery
It is to live abroad° and everywhere!   out of captivity
'Tis like a beast, methinks. I find the court here,
100 I am sure, a more content;° and all those pleasures   greater happiness
That woo the wills of men to vanity
I see through now, and am sufficient°   in a position
To tell the world 'tis but a gaudy shadow
That old Time, as he passes by, takes with him.
105 What had we been, old° in the court of Creon,   grown old
Where sin is justice, lust and ignorance
The virtues of the great ones? Cousin Arcite,
Had not the loving gods found this place for us,

---

5. A man resigned to his fate dies in peace, as if
merely falling asleep.

6. *envy . . . acquaintance*: we might emulate the malice (or, our envy) of evil men.

We had died as they do—ill° old men, unwept—   *wicked*
110 And had° their epitaphs, the people's curses.   *had for*
Shall I say more?

ARCITE   I would hear you still.
PALAMON   Ye shall.
Is there record of any two that loved
Better than we do, Arcite?

ARCITE   Sure there cannot.
PALAMON   I do not think it possible our friendship
Should ever leave us.

115 ARCITE   Till our deaths it cannot,
      Enter EMILIA *and her* WOMAN [*below*°].   *(in the garden)*
And after death our spirits shall be led
To those that love eternally.° Speak on, sir.   *(in Elysium)*

EMILIA [*to her* WOMAN]   This garden has a world of pleasures in't.
What flower is this?

WOMAN   'Tis called "narcissus," madam.
120 EMILIA   That was a fair boy, certain, but a fool
To love himself.[7] Were there not maids enough?

ARCITE [*to* PALAMON]   Pray, forward.°   *go on speaking*
PALAMON   Yes.

EMILIA [*to her* WOMAN]   Or were they all hard-hearted?
WOMAN   They could not be to one so fair.

EMILIA   Thou wouldst not.
WOMAN   I think I should not, madam.

EMILIA   That's a good wench.
But take heed to your kindness, though.

125 WOMAN   Why, madam?
EMILIA   Men are mad things.

ARCITE [*to* PALAMON]   Will ye go forward, cousin?
EMILIA [*to her* WOMAN]   Canst not thou work° such flowers in   *embroider*
silk, wench?

WOMAN   Yes.
EMILIA   I'll have a gown full of 'em, and of these.
This is a pretty color; will't not do
Rarely° upon a skirt, wench?   *Beautifully*
                                                            Very nicely
130 WOMAN   Dainty,° madam.   *Very nicely*
ARCITE   —Cousin, cousin! How do you, sir? Why, Palamon!
PALAMON   Never till now I was in prison, Arcite.
ARCITE   Why, what's the matter, man?
PALAMON [*gesturing to* EMILIA]   Behold and wonder!
By heaven, she is a goddess.

ARCITE   Ha!
PALAMON   Do reverence.
She is a goddess, Arcite.

135 EMILIA [*to her* WOMAN]   Of all flowers,
Methinks a rose is best.

WOMAN   Why, gentle madam?
EMILIA   It is the very emblem of a maid.
For, when the west wind courts her gently,
How modestly she blows° and paints the sun[8]   *blooms*

---

7. Narcissus fell in love with his own reflection in a
pool and drowned trying to embrace it. After his
death, he was turned into a flower.

8. Tints the sunlight pink; the inside of a rose looks
like an image of the sun.

140 With her chaste blushes! When the north° comes near her—   *north wind*
Rude and impatient—then, like chastity,
She locks her beauties in her bud again
And leaves him to base briars.°   *thorns*

WOMAN   Yet, good madam,
Sometimes her modesty will blow° so far   *open*
145 She falls for't.° A maid—   *because of it*
If she have any honor—would be loath
To take example by her.

EMILIA   Thou art wanton.
ARCITE [*to* PALAMON]   She is wondrous fair.
PALAMON   She is all the beauty extant.
EMILIA [*to her* WOMAN]   The sun grows high; let's walk in.
     Keep these flowers;
150 We'll see how near art can come near their colors.
I am wondrous merry-hearted; I could laugh now.

WOMAN   I could lie down, I am sure.[9]

EMILIA   And take one° with you?   *(a rose); (a lover)*

WOMAN   That's as we[1] bargain, madam—

EMILIA   Well, agree,° then.   *let's bargain*
     Exeunt EMILIA *and* WOMAN.

PALAMON   What think you of this beauty?

ARCITE   'Tis a rare one.

PALAMON   Is't but a rare one?

155 ARCITE   Yes, a matchless beauty.

PALAMON   Might not a man well lose himself and love her?

ARCITE   I cannot tell what you have done; I have,
Beshrew mine eyes° for't. Now I feel my shackles.   *Curse me (an oath)*

PALAMON   You love her, then?

ARCITE   Who would not?

PALAMON   And desire her?

ARCITE   Before my liberty.

160 PALAMON   I saw her first.

ARCITE   That's nothing—

PALAMON   But it shall be.

ARCITE   I saw her too.

PALAMON   Yes, but you must not love her.

ARCITE   I will not, as you do, to worship her
As she is heavenly and a blessèd goddess;
165 I love her as a woman, to enjoy her.
So both may love.

PALAMON   You shall not love at all.

ARCITE   Not love at all? Who shall deny me?

PALAMON   I that first saw her; I that took possession
First with mine eye of all those beauties
170 In her revealed to mankind. If thou[2] lov'st her,
Or entertain'st a hope to blast my wishes,
Thou art a traitor, Arcite, and a fellow
False as thy title to° her. Friendship, blood,   *claim to possess*
And all the ties between us I disclaim,

---

9. "Laugh and lie down" was an Elizabethan card game; sexual allusion.
1. The Woman and her lover; or, the Woman and Emilia—with different implications.
2. The contemptuous "thou" replaces the more polite "you." Arcite follows suit at line 217.

If thou once think upon her.

175 ARCITE   Yes, I love her,
And if the lives of all my name lay° on it,   *my family depended*
    I must do so; I love her with my soul.
    If that will lose ye, farewell, Palamon.
    I say again I love, and, in loving her, maintain³
180   I am as worthy and as free° a lover   *noble*
    And have as just a title to her beauty
    As any Palamon or any living
    That is a man's son.

PALAMON   Have I called thee friend?

ARCITE   Yes, and have found me so; why are you moved° thus?   *incensed*
185   Let me deal coldly° with you. Am not I   *dispassionately*
    Part of your blood, part of your soul? You have told me
    That I was Palamon and you were Arcite.

PALAMON   Yes.

ARCITE   Am not I liable to those affections,°   *passions*
190   Those joys, griefs, angers, fears my friend shall suffer?

PALAMON   Ye may be.

ARCITE   Why, then, would you deal so cunningly,°   *trickily*
    So strangely,° so unlike a noble kinsman   *unlike a friend*
    To love alone? Speak truly: do you think me
    Unworthy of her sight?°   *to gaze at her*
195 PALAMON   No, but unjust
    If thou pursue that sight.

ARCITE   Because another
    First sees the enemy, shall I stand still,
    And let mine honor down, and never charge?

PALAMON   Yes, if he be but one.°   *is alone*

ARCITE   But say that one
    Had rather combat me?

200 PALAMON   Let that one say so,
    And use thy freedom. Else, if thou pursuest her,
    Be as that cursèd man that hates his country,
    A branded villain.

ARCITE   You are mad.

PALAMON   I must be,
    Till thou art worthy, Arcite—it concerns me;
205   And in this madness, if I hazard° thee   *endanger*
    And take thy life, I deal but truly.°   *fairly*

ARCITE   Fie, sir!
    You play the child extremely. I will love her,
    I must, I ought to do so, and I dare;
    And all this justly.

PALAMON   Oh, that now, that now
210   Thy false self and thy friend had but this fortune:
    To be one hour at liberty and grasp
    Our good swords in our hands! I would quickly teach thee
    What 'twere to filch affection from another;
    Thou art baser in it than a cutpurse.°   *thief*

---

3. TEXTUAL COMMENT For attribution of scenes to Fletcher based on his more frequent use of hypermetric lines like this one, see Digital Edition TC 5.

215 Put but thy head out of this window more,
And—as I have a soul—I'll nail thy life to't.°   *to the window frame*
ARCITE Thou dar'st not, fool; thou canst not; thou art feeble.
Put my head out? I'll throw my body out
And leap° the garden when I see her next   *jump down to*
220 And pitch° between her arms to anger thee.   *hurl myself*
         Enter [JAILER].
PALAMON No more—the keeper's coming. I shall live
To knock thy brains out with my shackles.
ARCITE   Do—
JAILER By your leave, gentlemen.
PALAMON   Now, honest keeper—
JAILER Lord Arcite, you must presently° to th' Duke;   *immediately*
The cause I know not yet.
225 ARCITE   I am ready, keeper.
JAILER Prince Palamon, I must awhile bereave you
Of your fair cousin's company.
                                    Exeunt ARCITE *and* [JAILER].
PALAMON   And me too,
Even when you please, of life. Why is he sent for?
It may be he shall marry her; he's goodly,°   *handsome*
230 And like enough the Duke hath taken notice
Both of his blood° and body. But his falsehood!   *noble family*
Why should a friend be treacherous? If that
Get him a wife so noble and so fair,
Let honest men ne'er love again. Once more
235 I would but see this fair one. Blessèd garden,
And fruit and flowers more blessèd that still° blossom   *perpetually*
As her bright eyes shine on ye! Would I were—
For all the fortune of my life hereafter—[4]
Yon little tree, yon blooming apricot!
240 How I would spread and fling my wanton arms
In at her window! I would bring her fruit
Fit for the gods to feed on; youth and pleasure
Still as° she tasted should be doubled on her;   *Whenever*
And, if she be not heavenly, I would make her
245 So near the gods in nature they should fear her,
And then I am sure she would love me.
         Enter [JAILER].
                                  How now, keeper?
Where's Arcite?
JAILER   Banished. Prince Pirithous
Obtained his liberty;[5] but never more,
Upon his oath and life, must he set foot
Upon this kingdom.
250 PALAMON   He's a blessèd man.
He shall see Thebes again, and call to arms
The bold young men that, when he bids 'em charge,
Fall on like fire. Arcite shall have a fortune,°   *chance*
If he dare make himself a worthy lover,
255 Yet in the field to strike a battle for her;

---

4. *For . . . hereafter*: And this is the only piece of
good fortune I'd ever hope for.

5. The motives behind Pirithous's intercession are
not explained.

And if he lose her then, he's a cold coward.
How bravely may he bear himself to win her,
If he be noble Arcite—thousand ways!
Were I at liberty, I would do things
260   Of such a virtuous greatness that this lady,
This blushing virgin, should take manhood to her
And seek to ravish me.

JAILER   My lord, for you
I have this charge° to—   *order*

PALAMON   To discharge my life.

JAILER   No, but from this place to remove your lordship;
The windows are too open.

265   PALAMON   Devils take 'em
That are so envious° to me. Prithee, kill me—   *spiteful*

JAILER   And hang for't afterward?

PALAMON   By this good light,
Had I a sword I would kill thee.

JAILER   Why, my lord?

PALAMON   Thou bring'st such pelting° scurvy news continually,   *paltry*
270   Thou art not worthy life. I will not go.

JAILER   Indeed you must, my lord.

PALAMON   May I° see the garden?   *Will I be able to*

JAILER   No.

PALAMON   Then I am resolved—I will not go.

JAILER   I must constrain you, then; and—for° you are dangerous—   *because*
I'll clap more irons on you.

PALAMON   Do, good keeper!
275   I'll shake 'em so ye shall not sleep;
I'll make ye a new morris.[6] Must I go?

JAILER   There is no remedy.

PALAMON   Farewell, kind window;
May rude wind never hurt thee. —O my lady,
If ever thou hast felt what sorrow was,
280   Dream how I suffer. —Come; now bury me.[7]
                    Exeunt PALAMON *and* [JAILER].

2.3

                    Enter ARCITE.

ARCITE   Banished the kingdom? 'Tis a benefit,
A mercy I must thank 'em for; but banished
The free enjoying of that face I die for—
Oh, 'twas a studied° punishment, a death   *deliberate*
5   Beyond imagination, such a vengeance
That, were I old and wicked, all my sins
Could never pluck upon me. Palamon,
Thou hast the start° now; thou shalt stay and see   *advantage*
Her bright eyes break° each morning 'gainst thy window   *(like dawn)*
10   And let in life into thee; thou shalt feed
Upon the sweetness of a noble beauty
That nature ne'er exceeded nor ne'er shall.
Good gods! What happiness has Palamon!

6. Morris dancers wore bells on their clothes.   will be banished from Emilia.
7. Palamon's new cell will be like a grave because he   2.3 Location: The countryside outside Athens.

Twenty to one, he'll come to speak to her
15 And, if she be as gentle as she's fair,
I know she's his; he has a tongue will tame
Tempests and make the wild rocks wanton.° Come what can   *full of joy*
    come—
The worst is death—I will not leave the kingdom.
I know mine own° is but a heap of ruins,   *(Thebes)*
20 And no redress there. If I go, he has her.
I am resolved another shape° shall make me,   *a disguise*
Or end my fortunes. Either way I am happy:
I'll see her and be near her, or no more.°   *or die*
    Enter four COUNTRYMEN, *and one with a garland*
    before them. [ARCITE *stands aside.*]

FIRST COUNTRYMAN My masters, I'll be there, that's certain.
SECOND COUNTRYMAN And I'll be there.
25 THIRD COUNTRYMAN   And I.
FOURTH COUNTRYMAN Why, then, have with ye,° boys. 'Tis   *I'll come too*
    but a chiding.[1]
Let the plow play° today; I'll tickle't out   *be idle*
Of the jades' tails tomorrow.[2]
FIRST COUNTRYMAN   I am sure
To have my wife as jealous as a turkey[3]—
30 But that's all one. I'll go through—let her mumble.°   *grumble*
SECOND COUNTRYMAN Clap her aboard tomorrow night, and
    stow her,[4]
And all's made up again.
THIRD COUNTRYMAN   Ay, do but put
A fescue° in her fist, and you shall see her   *teacher's pointer; penis*
Take a new lesson out° and be a good wench.   *Learn a new lesson*
35 Do we all hold against the Maying?[5]
FOURTH COUNTRYMAN Hold? What should ail us?°   *prevent us*
THIRD COUNTRYMAN Arcas will be there.
SECOND COUNTRYMAN   And Sennois,
And Rycas—and three better lads ne'er danced
Under green tree—and ye know what wenches, ha?
40 But will the dainty dominie,° the schoolmaster,   *fussy teacher*
Keep touch,° do you think? For he does all,[6] ye know.   *Keep his word*
THIRD COUNTRYMAN He'll eat a hornbook[7] ere he fail. Go
    to—the matter's too far driven° between him and the tan-   *affair's gone too far*
    ner's daughter to let slip now; and she must° see the Duke,   *really wants to*
45 and she must dance too.
FOURTH COUNTRYMAN Shall we be lusty?°   *lively*
SECOND COUNTRYMAN All the boys in Athens blow wind i'th'
    breech on's.[8] [*He dances.*] And here I'll be, and there I'll be,
    for our town, and here again, and there again. Ha, boys, hey
50 for the weavers![9]

1. The worst punishment I'll get (for not working) is
a scolding.
2. *I'll . . . tomorrow:* I'll whip extra work out of the
horses ("jades"—also women, hence sexual)
tomorrow.
3. Thought to be jealously territorial.
4. Sexual metaphor: board her (like a ship) and fill
up her cargo hold.
5. Are we still going to participate in the May Day
celebrations (of fertility and the coming of spring)?
6. For he arranges everything.
7. A primer or tablet, protected by a translucent plate
of horn, inscribed with the alphabet.
8. Will race to try—and fail—to keep up with us;
will fart.
9. Hooray for the weavers (the profession to which
the speaker apparently belongs).

FIRST COUNTRYMAN   This° must be done i'th' woods.   *(the Maying)*
FOURTH COUNTRYMAN   Oh, pardon me.°   *really?*
SECOND COUNTRYMAN   By any° means. Our thing of learning°   *all / Our teacher*
55 says so; where he himself will edify the Duke most parlously°   *impressively (ironic)*
in our behalfs. He's excellent i'th' woods; bring him to th'
plains, his learning makes no cry.°   *is ignored*
THIRD COUNTRYMAN   We'll see the sports; then every man
to's tackle.° And, sweet companions, let's rehearse—by any   *morris-dancing gear*
means—before the ladies see us, and do sweetly—and God
60 knows what may come on't.
FOURTH COUNTRYMAN   Content; the sports once ended, we'll
perform. Away, boys—and hold!°   *keep this promise*
        [ARCITE *steps forward.*]
ARCITE   By your leaves, honest friends; pray you—whither go you?
FOURTH COUNTRYMAN   Whither? Why, what a° question's that!   *what sort of a*
65 ARCITE   Yes, 'tis a question to me that know not.
THIRD COUNTRYMAN   To the games, my friend.
SECOND COUNTRYMAN [*to* ARCITE]   Where were you bred, you
know it not?
ARCITE   Not far, sir. Are there such games today?
70 FIRST COUNTRYMAN   Yes, marry, are there, and such as you
never saw. The Duke himself will be in person there.
ARCITE   What pastimes are they?
SECOND COUNTRYMAN   Wrestling and running. [*aside to the others*]
'Tis a pretty fellow.
75 THIRD COUNTRYMAN [*to* ARCITE]   Thou wilt not go along?
ARCITE   Not yet, sir.
FOURTH COUNTRYMAN   Well, sir—take your own time. Come,
boys—
FIRST COUNTRYMAN [*aside to the others*]   My mind misgives
80 me. This fellow has a vengeance trick o'th' hip[1]—mark how
his body's made for't.
SECOND COUNTRYMAN [*aside*]   I'll be hanged, though, if he dare
venture. Hang him, plum porridge![2] He wrestle? He roast
eggs![3] Come, let's be gone, lads.
                        Exeunt four [COUNTRYMEN].
85 ARCITE   This is an offered° opportunity   *unsought*
I durst not° wish for. Well I could have wrestled[4]—   *would not have dared*
The best men called it excellent—and run
Swifter than wind upon a field of corn,°   *wheat*
Curling the wealthy° ears, never° flew. I'll venture   *abundant / ever*
90 And in some poor disguise be there; who knows
Whether my brows may not be girt with garlands,
And happiness prefer° me to a place   *good fortune promote*
Where I may ever dwell in sight of her?   *Exit* ARCITE.

2.4

Enter JAILER'S DAUGHTER, *alone.*

JAILER'S DAUGHTER   Why should I love this gentleman? 'Tis odds°   *Chances are*
He never will affect° me. I am base,   *love*

---

1. *My . . . hip:* I fear that this man may be a skillful
wrestler.
2. Contemptuous, suggesting that Arcite is out of
shape. Plum porridge was a heavy dessert of stewed
dried fruits eaten at Christmas.
3. He'd be a better cook than wrestler (?); he probably can't cook an egg (?).
4. I knew how to wrestle.
2.4 Location: The prison in Athens.

My father the mean° keeper of his prison,   *lowly*
And he a prince. To marry him is hopeless;
5 To be his whore[1] is witless. Out upon't!° *(expressing abhorrence)*
What pushes° are we wenches driven to   *extremities*
When fifteen° once has found us? First I saw him; *(the age)*
I, seeing, thought he was a goodly man;
He has as much to please a woman in him,
10 If he please to bestow it so, as ever
These eyes yet looked on. Next I pitied him—
And so would any young wench, o' my conscience,
That ever dreamed, or vowed her maidenhead° *virginity*
To a young handsome man. Then I loved him—
15 Extremely loved him, infinitely loved him!
And yet he had a cousin, fair as he, too;
But in my heart was Palamon and there,
Lord, what a coil he keeps!° To hear him *turmoil he makes*
Sing in an evening, what a heaven it is!
20 And yet his songs are sad ones. Fairer spoken
Was never gentleman. When I come in
To bring him water in a morning, first
He bows his noble body, then salutes° me thus: *greets*
"Fair gentle maid, good morrow; may thy goodness
25 Get thee a happy husband." Once he kissed me:
I loved my lips the better ten days after—
Would he would do so every day! He grieves much—
And me as much to see his misery.
What should I do to make him know I love him?
30 For I would fain° enjoy him.° Say I ventured *eagerly / (sexually)*
To set him free—what says the law then? Thus much
For law or kindred! I will do it—
And this night, or tomorrow, he shall love me. *Exit.*

2.5

Enter THESEUS, HIPPOLYTA, PIRITHOUS, EMILIA,
ARCITE [*disguised as a countryman*] *with a garland,*
[*and Attendants*]. *A short flourish of cornetts and*
shouts within.[1]

THESEUS You have done worthily; I have not seen,
Since Hercules, a man of tougher sinews.° *muscles*
Whate'er you are, you run the best, and wrestle,° *wrestle the best*
That these times can allow.°   *show*
ARCITE   I am proud to please you.
THESEUS What country bred you?
5 ARCITE   This—but far off, prince.
THESEUS Are you a gentleman?
ARCITE   My father said so,
And to those gentle uses gave me life.[2]
THESEUS Are you his heir?
ARCITE   His youngest, sir.
THESEUS   Your father

---

1. To engage in premarital sex, not prostitution.
2.5 Location: Athens, near the site of the athletic games.
1. TEXTUAL COMMENT For the misnumbering of this—and other—scenes, and the relationship of these errors to the Jailer's Daughter's soliloquies, see Digital Edition TC 6.
2. And raised me for those genteel pursuits.

Sure is a happy sire, then.³ What proves you?°   *(a gentleman)*
10   ARCITE   A little of all noble qualities.°   *accomplishments*
  I could have kept° a hawk, and well have hallooed   *I knew how to keep*
  To a deep° cry of dogs; I dare not praise   *loud*
  My feat in horsemanship—yet they that knew me
  Would say it was my best piece;° last, and greatest,   *attribute*
  I would° be thought a soldier.   *used to*
15   THESEUS   You are perfect.°   *perfectly well-rounded*
  PIRITHOUS   Upon my soul, a proper° man.   *handsome*
  EMILIA   He is so.
  PIRITHOUS [*to* HIPPOLYTA]   How do you like him, lady?
  HIPPOLYTA   I admire° him.   *am amazed at*
  I have not seen so young a man so noble—
  If he say true—of his sort.°   *rank*
  EMILIA   Believe°   *Be sure*
20   His mother was a wondrous handsome woman—
  His face, methinks, goes that way.°   *demonstrates that*
  HIPPOLYTA   But his body
  And fiery mind illustrate° a brave father.   *indicate; copy*
  PIRITHOUS   Mark how his virtue,° like a hidden sun,   *excellence*
  Breaks through his baser garments.
  HIPPOLYTA   He's well got,° sure.   *well-born*
  THESEUS [*to* ARCITE]   What made you seek this place, sir?
25   ARCITE   Noble Theseus,
  To purchase name° and do my ablest service   *get a reputation*
  To such a well-found° wonder as thy worth—   *well-deserved*
  For only in thy court, of all the world,
  Dwells fair-eyed honor.
  PIRITHOUS   All his words are worthy.
30   THESEUS   Sir, we are much indebted to your travel,°   *journey; effort*
  Nor shall you lose your wish. —Pirithous,
  Dispose of° this fair gentleman.   *Place*
  PIRITHOUS   Thanks, Theseus.
  [*to* ARCITE] Whate'er you are, you're mine, and I shall give you
  To a most noble service—to this lady,
35   This bright young virgin [*gesturing to* EMILIA]; pray observe°   *respect*
   her goodness.
  You have honored her fair birthday with your virtues,
  And, as your due, you're hers—kiss her fair hand, sir.
  ARCITE   Sir, you're a noble giver. [*to* EMILIA] Dearest beauty,
  Thus let me seal my vowed faith. [*He kisses her hand.*] When
   your servant—
40   Your most unworthy creature—but offends you,
  Command him die; he shall.
  EMILIA [*to* ARCITE]   That were too cruel.
  If you deserve well, sir, I shall soon see't.
  You're mine, and somewhat better than your rank° I'll use you.   *position*
  PIRITHOUS [*to* ARCITE]   I'll see you furnished,° and because you   *equipped*
   say
45   You are a horseman, I must needs entreat you
  This afternoon to ride—but 'tis a rough one.°   *(horse)*
  ARCITE   I like him better, prince: I shall not then

---

3. Since even his younger (and presumably lesser) son is so accomplished.

Freeze in my saddle.

THESEUS [*to* HIPPOLYTA]   Sweet, you must be ready—
And you, Emilia, and [*to* PIRITHOUS] you, friend, and all—
50 Tomorrow, by the sun,° to do observance°   *by sunrise / honor*
To flow'ry May in Dian's wood. [*to* ARCITE] Wait well, sir,
Upon your mistress. —Emily, I hope
He shall not go afoot.

EMILIA   That were a shame, sir,
While I have horses. [*to* ARCITE] Take your choice, and what
55 You want° at any time, let me but know it.   *lack*
If you serve faithfully, I dare assure you
You'll find a loving mistress.

ARCITE   If I do not,
Let me find that° my father ever hated;   *that which*
Disgrace and blows.

THESEUS   Go, lead the way; you have won it.[4]
60 It shall be so: you shall receive all dues
Fit for the honor you have won—'twere wrong else.
[*aside to* EMILIA] Sister, beshrew my heart, you have a servant
That—if I were a woman—would be master.
But you are wise—

EMILIA   I hope too wise for that, sir.

Flourish. Exeunt.

2.6

Enter JAILER'S DAUGHTER, *alone.*

JAILER'S DAUGHTER   Let all the dukes and all the devils roar;
He is at liberty! I have ventured° for him,   *taken a risk*
And out I have brought him. To a little wood
A mile hence I have sent him—where a cedar
5 Higher than all the rest spreads like a plane°   *plane tree*
Fast° by a brook—and there he shall keep close°   *Close / shall hide*
Till I provide him files and food, for yet
His iron bracelets° are not off. O Love,°   *shackles / Cupid*
What a stouthearted child thou art! My father
10 Durst better have endured cold iron than done it.[1]
I love him beyond love and beyond reason,
Or wit,° or safety. I have made him know it;   *sense*
I care not; I am desperate. If the law
Find me and then condemn me for't, some wenches,
15 Some honest-hearted maids, will sing my dirge,
And tell to memory my death was noble,
Dying almost a martyr. That way he takes,
I purpose, is my way too. Sure he cannot
Be so unmanly as to leave me here;
20 If he do, maids will not so easily
Trust men again. And yet he has not thanked me
For what I have done; no, not so much as kissed me,
And that, methinks, is not so well; nor scarcely
Could I persuade him to become a free man,

---

4. Won the honor of leading the procession.
2.6 Location: Near the prison in Athens.
1. *My . . . it:* My father would sooner have been run

through (or decapitated, or chained up) than have
freed a prisoner.

25 He made such scruples of the wrong he did
To me and to my father. Yet I hope,
When he considers more, this love of mine
Will take more root within him. Let him do
What he will with me, so he use me kindly,[2]
30 For use me° so he shall—or I'll proclaim him,   *(sexually)*
And to his face, no man.° I'll presently   *(sexually)*
Provide him necessaries and pack my clothes up,
And where there is a path of ground I'll venture,
So he° be with me; by him like a shadow   *As long as he'll*
35 I'll ever dwell. Within this hour the hubbub
Will be all o'er the prison; I am then
Kissing the man they look for. Farewell, father—
Get° many more such prisoners, and such daughters,   *Catch; beget*
And shortly you may keep yourself.[3] Now to him!   [*Exit.*]

3.1

Cornetts in sundry° places; noise and hallooing as   *various (offstage)*
people a-Maying.[1]
Enter ARCITE, *alone.*

ARCITE   The Duke has lost Hippolyta; each took°   *went to*
A several laund.° This is a solemn rite   *A different clearing*
They owe bloomed May, and the Athenians pay° it   *observe*
To th' heart of° ceremony. O Queen Emilia,   *With the utmost*
5 Fresher than May, sweeter
Than her gold buttons° on the boughs, or all   *buds*
Th'enameled knacks° o'th' mead° or garden; yea,   *flowers / meadow*
We challenge too the bank of any nymph
That makes the stream seem flowers.[2] Thou—O jewel
10 O'th' wood, o'th' world—hast likewise blessed a place°   *path through the woods*
With thy sole° presence. In thy rumination   *mere; solo*
That I, poor man, might eftsoons come between
And chop on some cold thought![3] Thrice blessèd chance
To drop on° such a mistress; expectation   *run into*
15 Most guiltless on't.° Tell me, O Lady Fortune—   *unexpectedly*
Next, after Emily, my sovereign—how far
I may be proud. She takes strong note of me,
Hath made me near her, and this beauteous morn—
The prim'st° of all the year—presents me with   *best*
20 A brace° of horses; two such steeds might well   *pair*
Be by a pair of kings backed,° in a field   *ridden*
That their crowns' titles tried.[4] Alas, alas,
Poor cousin Palamon, poor prisoner, thou
So little dream'st upon my fortune that
25 Thou think'st thyself the happier thing, to be
So near Emilia; me thou deem'st at Thebes,

---

2. Provided that he treat me gently; naturally; nobly, in a manner befitting a man of his kind.
3. You yourself may use the jail, since everyone else will either have escaped or been freed.
3.1 Location: All of act 3 takes place in a forest near Athens.
1. May Day celebrations included feasts, hunting, music, entertainments (such as the morris dance of 3.5.140), and dancing around the maypole. See note to 2.3.35.

2. *We . . . flowers:* Emilia surpasses in beauty even a nymph's flowered riverbank, whose reflection makes the river itself seem covered with flowers.
3. *That . . . thought:* Would that I, "poor man," might suddenly come upon you and seize some chaste thought.
4. *in . . . tried:* on a battlefield where they were fighting for each other's kingdoms.

And therein wretched, although free. But if
Thou knew'st my mistress breathed on me, and that
I eared her language,° lived in her eye—O coz,   *listened to her*
What passion would enclose° thee!   *rage would possess*
  Enter PALAMON *as out of a bush, with his shackles.*
  [*He*] *bends*° *his fist at* ARCITE.   *shakes*

30 PALAMON   Traitor kinsman,
Thou shouldst perceive my passion if these signs
Of prisonment[5] were off me and this hand
But owner of a sword! By all oaths in one,
I—and the justice of my love—would make thee
35 A confessed traitor. O thou most perfidious
That ever gently looked,° the void'st of honor   *seemed gentlemanly*
That e'er bore gentle token,° falsest cousin   *wore noble emblems*
That ever blood made kin: call'st thou her thine?
I'll prove it in my shackles—with these hands,
40 Void of appointment°—that thou liest and art   *Devoid of weapons*
A very thief in love, a chaffy° lord   *worthless*
Not worth the name of villain. Had I a sword,
And these house-clogs° away—   *fetters*
ARCITE   Dear cousin Palamon—
PALAMON Cozener° Arcite, give me language such *Cheater (punning)*
As thou hast showed me feat.[6]
45 ARCITE   Not finding in
The circuit of my breast any gross stuff
To form me like your blazon holds me to
This gentleness of answer;[7] 'tis your passion
That thus mistakes, the which, to you being enemy,
50 Cannot to me be kind.[8] Honor and honesty
I cherish and depend on, howsoe'er
You skip° them in me—and with them, fair coz,   *ignore*
I'll maintain my proceedings. Pray be pleased
To show in generous° terms your griefs,° since that *genteel / grievances*
55 Your question's° with your equal, who professes *dispute is*
To clear his own way[9] with the mind and sword
Of a true gentleman—
PALAMON   That thou durst,° Arcite! *You wouldn't dare*
ARCITE My coz, my coz, you have been well advertised° *informed*
How much I dare; you've seen me use my sword
60 Against th'advice° of fear. Sure, of° another   *the warning / by*
You would not hear me doubted, but your silence
Should break out, though i'th' sanctuary![1]
PALAMON   Sir,
I have seen you move in such a place° which well *battle; tournament*
Might justify your manhood; you were called
65 A good knight and a bold. But the whole week's not fair

5. *signs / Of prisonment:* shackles.
6. *give . . . feat:* use words that accord better with your (perfidious) actions.
7. *Not . . . answer:* Since I find nothing in me that fits your description of me, I answer gently. *blazon:* (description of a) coat of arms.
8. *'tis . . . kind:* your anger ("passion") is your enemy (distorts your judgment) and thus to me cannot be

kind (because you are my kinsman—"kind" also means "kin"—and friend, and hence we share all enemies).
9. To justify; to make his own way.
1. *your . . . sanctuary:* you would speak to defend me even if you were hiding in a safe place (or in a church).

If any day it rain. Their valiant temper°   *attitude*
Men lose when they incline to treachery,
And then they fight like compelled bears—would fly
Were they not tied.²

ARCITE   Kinsman, you might as well
70   Speak this and act it in your glass° as to   *mirror*
His ear which now disdains you.

PALAMON   Come up to me;
Quit° me of these cold gyves;° give me a sword—   *Free / chains*
Though it be rusty—and the charity
Of one meal lend me. Come before me then,
75   A good sword in thy hand, and do but say
That Emily is thine—I will forgive
The trespass° thou hast done me, yea, my life   *wrong*
If then thou carry't,° and brave souls in shades°   *beat me / Hades*
That have died manly, which will seek of me
80   Some news from earth, they shall get none but this:
That thou art brave and noble.

ARCITE   Be content;
Again betake you to° your hawthorn house.   *go back into*
With counsel of the night³ I will be here
With wholesome viands;° these impediments°   *food / shackles*
85   Will I file off; you shall have garments, and
Perfumes to kill the smell o'th' prison. After,
When you shall stretch yourself and say but, "Arcite,
I am in plight,"° there shall be at your choice   *I am ready*
Both sword and armor.

PALAMON   O you heavens, dares any
90   So noble bear a guilty business?° None,   *act shamefully*
But only Arcite; therefore none but Arcite
In this kind is so bold.

ARCITE   Sweet Palamon—

PALAMON   I do embrace you and your offer; for
Your offer do't I only, sir; your person
95   Without hypocrisy I may not wish
More than my sword's edge on't—⁴
               Wind° horns off.° Cornetts.   *Sound / (offstage)*

ARCITE   You hear the horns;
Enter your musit,° lest this match between's   *gap in a thicket*
Be crossed ere met.° Give me your hand. Farewell!   *prevented before begun*
I'll bring you every needful thing. I pray you
Take comfort and be strong.

100 PALAMON   Pray hold your promise,
And do the deed with a bent brow.° Most certain   *stern countenance*
You love me not; be rough with me, and pour
This oil° out of your language. By this air,   *smoothness; flattery*
I could for each word give a cuff, my stomach°   *anger*
Not reconciled by reason—
105 ARCITE   Plainly spoken.
Yet pardon me hard language. When I spur

---

2. In bearbaiting competitions (a popular pastime
with connections to the theater), bears were tied to a
stake.
3. With darkness to assist (and hide) me.
4. *for . . . on't:* I embrace you (physically) and your

offer (metaphorically) only because of the nobility of
that offer; as for your "person" (your body) itself: I
want to run my sword through it. Claiming to want to
do anything else would be hypocritical.

My horse, I chide him not; content and anger
In me have but one face.°   *the same expression*
      Wind horns.
                     Hark, sir, they call
The scattered to the banquet; you must guess
I have an office° there.   *assigned duty*

110 PALAMON   Sir, your attendance
Cannot please heaven, and I know your office
Unjustly is achieved.°   *Was earned unfairly*

ARCITE   'Tis a good title.°   *It was won justly*
I am persuaded this question—sick between's—
By bleeding must be cured.[5] I am a suitor°   *I beg*
115 That to your sword you will bequeath this plea°   *lawsuit*
And talk of it no more.

PALAMON   But this one word:
You are going now to gaze upon my mistress—
For note you, mine she is—

ARCITE   Nay, then—

PALAMON   Nay, pray you—
You talk of feeding me to breed me strength;°   *strengthen me*
120 You are going now to look upon a sun
That strengthens what it looks on—there
You have a vantage° o'er me. But enjoy't till   *advantage*
I may enforce my remedy. Farewell.   *Exeunt.*

3.2

     Enter JAILER'S DAUGHTER, *alone.*

JAILER'S DAUGHTER   He has mistook the brake° I meant, is gone   *thicket*
After[1] his fancy. 'Tis now well-nigh morning;
No matter—would it were perpetual night
And darkness lord o'th' world. —Hark, 'tis a wolf!
5 In me hath grief slain fear and, but for one thing,
I care for nothing—and that's Palamon.
I reck° not if the wolves would jaw° me, so°   *care / gnaw / if*
He had this file. What if I hallooed for him?
I cannot halloo. If I whooped, what then?
10 If he not answered I should call a wolf
And do him but that service.[2] I have heard
Strange howls this livelong night; why, may't not be
They have made prey of him? He has no weapons;
He cannot run—the jangling of his gyves
15 Might call fell° things to listen, who have in them   *fiercely fatal*
A sense to know a man unarmed and can
Smell where resistance is. I'll set it down°   *record it as fact*
He's torn to pieces; they howled many together,
And then they feed on him. So much for that!
20 Be bold to ring the bell,° how stand I then?   *ring his death knell*
All's chared° when he is gone. No, no, I lie—   *My work is all done*
My father's to be hanged for his escape;
Myself to beg,° if I prized life so much   *I'd be reduced to beggary*
As to deny my act—but that I would not,

---

5. *I am . . . cured:* I am convinced that the dispute
between us (here, imagined as a sick person) can
only be settled (cured) by a bloodletting.

3.2 Location: Scene continues.
1. *is gone / After:* is led by (only).
2. I would at least serve him by calling a wolf to
attack him or herself (ironic).

25 Should I try death by dozens.³ I am moped;°   *dazed*
Food took I none these two days;
Sipped some water. I have not closed mine eyes,
Save when my lids scoured off their brine.⁴ Alas,
Dissolve, my life! Let not my sense unsettle,°   *reason come unhinged*
30 Lest I should drown, or stab, or hang myself.
O state of nature,° fail together° in me,   *life / entirely; all at once*
Since thy best props° are warped. So, which way now?   *supports*
The best way is the next° way to a grave;   *nearest*
Each errant step beside⁵ is torment. Lo,
35 The moon is down, the crickets chirp, the screech owl
Calls in the dawn; all offices are done
Save what I fail in.⁶ But the point is this:
An end,° and that is all.   *Exit.*   *A death*

3.3

Enter ARCITE *with meat, wine, and files.*

ARCITE   I should be near the place. Ho! Cousin Palamon!
    Enter PALAMON.
PALAMON   Arcite?
ARCITE   The same. I have brought you food and files.
    Come forth and fear not; here's no Theseus.
PALAMON   Nor none so honest, Arcite.
ARCITE   That's no matter;
5 We'll argue that hereafter. Come, take courage;
You shall not die thus beastly.° Here, sir, drink—   *like an animal*
I know you are faint—then I'll talk further with you.
PALAMON   Arcite, thou mightst now poison me.
ARCITE   I might.
But I must° fear you first. Sit down and, good now,°   *should need to / please*
10 No more of these vain parleys;° let us not,   *pointless comments*
Having our ancient¹ reputation with us,
Make talk for² fools and cowards. *[He raises his glass.]* To your health—
          Do.°   *You drink first*
PALAMON
ARCITE   Pray, sit down, then, and let me entreat you,
By all the honesty and honor in you,
15 No mention of this woman; 'twill disturb us.
We shall have time enough.
PALAMON   Well, sir, I'll pledge you.°   *drink your health in reply*
    [He drinks.]
ARCITE   Drink a good hearty draught; it breeds good blood,° man!   *makes you strong*
Do not you feel it thaw you?
PALAMON   Stay—I'll tell you
After a draught or two more.
ARCITE   Spare it not;
The Duke has more, coz. Eat now.
PALAMON   Yes.
    [He eats.]

---

3. Even if I had to die dozens of times (ways).
4. Except when I blinked to clear my eyes of tears.
5. Each step that wanders from the direct path to the grave.
6. all . . . in: all tasks are done, except the one I've failed to complete (either giving the file to Palamon

or killing herself).
3.3 Location: Scene continues.
1. Of long standing; former (now reestablished through escape).
2. Talk as though we were; make ourselves the talk of.

20	ARCITE	I am glad

ARCITE   I am glad
   You have so good a stomach.°   *an appetite; an anger*
PALAMON   I am gladder
   I have so good meat° to't.   *(to feed my anger)*
ARCITE   Is't not mad° lodging   *strange; maddening*
   Here in the wild woods,³ cousin?
PALAMON   Yes, for them
   That have wild° consciences.   *uncivilized*
ARCITE   How tastes your victuals?
   Your hunger needs no sauce, I see.
25 PALAMON   Not much.
   But if it did, yours is too tart,⁴ sweet cousin.
   [*He lifts a piece of meat.*] What is this?
ARCITE   Venison.
PALAMON   'Tis a lusty° meat.   *hearty*
   Give me more wine. Here, Arcite, to the wenches
   We have known in our days! The Lord Steward's daughter—
   Do you remember her?
30 ARCITE   After you,⁵ coz.
PALAMON   She loved a black-haired man—
ARCITE   She did so. Well, sir?
PALAMON   And I have heard some call him Arcite. And—
ARCITE   Out with't, faith.
PALAMON   She met him in an arbor.
   What did she there, coz? Play o'th' virginals?⁶
35 ARCITE   Something° she did, sir.   *To some extent*
PALAMON   Made her groan° a month for't—or two, or three,   *(in pregnancy)*
   or ten.
ARCITE   The Marshal's sister
   Had her share too, as I remember, cousin,
   Else there be tales° abroad. You'll pledge her?   *false rumors*
PALAMON   Yes.
40 ARCITE   A pretty brown° wench 'tis. There was a time   *brunette*
   When young men went a-hunting, and a wood,
   And a broad beech—and thereby hangs a tale. [*He sighs.*]
   Heigh-ho!
PALAMON   For Emily, upon my life! Fool,
   Away with this strained mirth. I say again—
45   That sigh was breathed for Emily! Base cousin,
   Dar'st thou break⁷ first?
ARCITE   You are wide.°   *wide of the mark*
PALAMON   By heaven and earth, there's nothing in thee honest.
ARCITE   Then I'll leave you; you are a beast° now.   *behaving savagely*
PALAMON   As thou mak'st me, traitor.
50 ARCITE   There's all things needful: files, and shirts, and
    perfumes.
   I'll come again some two hours hence and bring
   That that shall quiet° all—   *silence*
PALAMON   A sword and armor.
ARCITE   Fear° me not. You are now too foul;° farewell.   *Doubt / beastly*
   Get off your trinkets;° you shall want naught.   *shackles*

---

3. *woods*: Pun on "wode" (mad).
4. Your insolence ("sauce," line 25) is too bitter ("tart").
5. Finish your toast first, before I propose mine.
6. Small keyboard instrument; (sexual).
7. Break our agreement (not to refer to Emilia).

PALAMON   Sirrah°—   *(an insult)*

ARCITE   I'll hear no more.   *Exit.*

55   PALAMON   If he keep touch,° he dies for't.

                                             Exit.   *keeps his promise*

3.4

Enter JAILER'S DAUGHTER.

JAILER'S DAUGHTER   I am very cold, and all the stars are out, too—
    The little stars and all, that look like aglets.°   *shiny ornaments*
    The sun has seen my folly. Palamon!
    Alas, no—he's in heaven. Where am I now?
5   Yonder's the sea, and there's a ship—how't tumbles!
    And there's a rock lies watching under water;
    Now, now, it° beats upon it; now, now, now!   *(the ship)*
    There's a leak sprung, a sound° one; how they cry!   *large*
    Run[1] her before the wind, you'll lose all else;
10   Up with a course° or two, and tack° about, boys!   *lower sail / turn*
    Good night, good night; you're gone. I am very hungry.
    Would I could find a fine frog—he would tell me
    News from all parts o'th' world; then would I make
    A carrack° of a cockleshell and sail   *cargo ship*
15   By east and northeast to the king of pygmies,
    For he tells fortunes rarely.° Now, my father   *wonderfully*
    Twenty to one is trussed up in a trice°   *to be hanged quickly*
    Tomorrow morning; I'll say never a word.
    (*Sings.*) For I'll cut my green coat a foot above my knee,
20   And I'll clip my yellow locks an inch below mine eye.
          Hey nonny, nonny, nonny.
          He's buy° me a white cut,[2] forth for to ride,   *He shall buy*
          And I'll go seek him through the world that is so wide.
          Hey nonny, nonny, nonny.
25   Oh, for a prick now, like a nightingale to put my breast
    Against.[3] I shall sleep like a top° else.   *Exit.*   *soundly*

3.5

Enter [*Gerald*] *a* SCHOOLMASTER, *four* COUNTRYMEN,
[BAVIAN,][1] [NELL, *and four other Countrywomen,*]
  with a TABORER.°   *Player of a small drum*

SCHOOLMASTER   Fie, fie, what tediosity and disinsanity[2] is
  here among ye! Have my rudiments° been labored so long   *lessons; rehearsals*
  with ye, milked unto ye, and—by a figure°—even the very   *figure of speech*
  plum broth and marrow[3] of my understanding laid upon ye,
5   and do you still cry "Where?" and "How?" and "Wherefore?"
  You most coarse-frieze capacities, ye jean judgments[4]—have
  I said, "Thus let be," and "There let be," and "Then let be,"

3.4 Location: Scene continues.
1. TEXTUAL COMMENT For the emendation to "Run" here and what it suggests about the printing of the play, see Digital Edition TC 7.
2. Horse (called a "cut" because it was a gelding or had a cropped tail).
3. *Oh . . . Against:* Nightingales supposedly pricked themselves to stay awake at night. "Prick" also carries a sexual meaning; compare the sexual punning here with that in Ophelia's "mad" speeches in *Hamlet.*

3.5 Location: Scene continues.
1. *Bavian:* a countryman dressed as a baboon for the morris dance, a rural folk dance of north English origin, performed in costume. The dancer who took the part of the fool always dressed as an ape or a baboon.
2. What tedium and insanity (pedantic).
3. "Plum broth" (hearty stew of dried fruits and suet) and "marrow" both suggest essence or fortifying sustenance.
4. *You . . . judgments:* You people of rudimentary intellects. "Frieze" and "jean" were coarse fabrics worn by laborers.

and no man understand me? *Proh deum! Medius fidius!*[5] Ye
are all dunces. For why? Here stand I; here the Duke comes;

10 there are you close° in the thicket; the Duke appears; I meet   °hidden
him, and unto him I utter learned things and many figures;
he hears, and nods, and hums,° and then cries "Rare!" and I   °murmurs approval
go forward.° At length, I fling my cap up—mark there! Then   °continue
do you, as once did Meleager and the boar,[6] break comely

15 out° before him; like true lovers,[7] cast yourselves in a body   °appear decorously
decently;[8] and sweetly, by a figure, trace° and turn, boys.   °follow the steps

FIRST COUNTRYMAN   And sweetly we will do it, Master Gerald.
SECOND COUNTRYMAN   Draw up the company. Where's the
taborer?
      [TABORER *steps forward.*]

20 THIRD COUNTRYMAN   Why, Timothy!
TABORER   Here, my mad boys, have at ye!°   °go ahead; I'm ready
SCHOOLMASTER   But, I say, where's their women?
      [NELL *and other Countrywomen step forward.*]
FOURTH COUNTRYMAN   Here's Friz and Maudlin.

25 SECOND COUNTRYMAN   And little Luce with the white legs,
and bouncing° Barbary.   °robust
FIRST COUNTRYMAN   And freckled Nell, that never failed her
master.°   °(with sexual overtone)
SCHOOLMASTER   Where be your ribbons,[9] maids? Swim° with   °Dance gracefully
your bodies,
And carry it° sweetly and deliverly,°   °move / nimbly

30 And now and then a favor° and a frisk.°   °kiss; bow / leap
NELL   Let us alone,° sir.   °Leave it to us
SCHOOLMASTER   Where's the rest o'th' music?°   °musicians
THIRD COUNTRYMAN   Dispersed° as you commanded.   °Placed here and there
SCHOOLMASTER   Couple,° then,   °Pair up
And see what's wanting.° [*They assemble for the dance.*]   °who's missing
Where's the Bavian?
      [BAVIAN *steps forward.*]
—My friend, carry your tail without offense°   °sexual offense

35 Or scandal to the ladies, and be sure
You tumble with audacity and manhood,°   °bravery
And when you bark,[1] do it with judgment.
BAVIAN   Yes, sir.

40 SCHOOLMASTER   *Quo usque tandem!*[2] Here is a woman wanting.
FOURTH COUNTRYMAN   We may go whistle; all the fat's i'th' fire.[3]
SCHOOLMASTER   We have, as learnèd authors utter, washed a
tile;°   °worked in vain
We have been *fatuus,*° and labored vainly.   °foolish (Latin)
SECOND COUNTRYMAN   This is that scornful piece,° that scurvy   °person
hilding°   °worthless woman
That gave her promise faithfully she would be here—

---

5. O God, heaven help me (mangled Latin).
6. Meleager was a Greek warrior who killed the great
Calydonian boar and brought its head to the Amazon
warrior Atalanta.
7. Like loving subjects of Theseus; in couples, as lovers do.
8. Position yourselves appropriately for the dance.
9. Morris dancers carried ribbons or streamers as props.

1. Baboons were considered half man, half dog.
2. How much longer (must I wait)? (Latin, as
throughout the scene.) Expression of impatience that
opens the ancient Roman writer Cicero's first oration
against Catiline, but here indicates the Schoolmaster's pomposity.
3. We may as well give up, since all our work has
produced nothing. Both phrases were proverbial,
although the second has a different meaning today.

Cicely, the sempster's° daughter.   *seamstress's*

45 The next gloves that I give her shall be dogskin!°   *cheap leather*

Nay, an° she fail me once—you can tell, Arcas,°   *if / one of the countrymen*

She swore by wine and bread she would not break.°   *(her solemn oath)*

SCHOOLMASTER   An eel and woman—

A learnèd poet says—unless by th' tail

50 And with thy teeth thou hold, will either° fail.   *both*

In manners this was false position.[4]

FIRST COUNTRYMAN   A fire ill take her;° does she flinch now?   *A pox infect her*

THIRD COUNTRYMAN   What shall we determine,° sir?   *decide to do*

SCHOOLMASTER   Nothing—our business is become a nullity,

55 Yea, and a woeful and a piteous nullity.

FOURTH COUNTRYMAN   Now when the credit of our town lay
on it,

Now to be frampold, now to piss o'th' nettle![5]

Go thy ways—I'll remember thee; I'll fit thee°—   *get even with you*

     Enter JAILER'S DAUGHTER.

JAILER'S DAUGHTER [*sings*]   The George Alow[6] came from the South,

60   From the coast of Barbary-a;

And there he met with brave gallants of war,°   *warships*

By one, by two, by three-a.

"Well hailed, well hailed, you jolly gallants,

And whither now are you bound-a?

65 Oh, let me have your company

Till I come to the sound-a."

There was three fools fell out about an owlet—

[*Sings.*] The one he said it was an owl,

The other he said nay,

70 The third he said it was a hawk,

And her bells were cut away.[7]

THIRD COUNTRYMAN   There's a dainty° madwoman, master—   *fine*

comes i'th' nick°—as mad as a March hare. If we can get her   *(of time)*

dance, we are made again.° I warrant her, she'll do the rarest   *all will be well*

75 gambols.°   *finest capers*

FIRST COUNTRYMAN   A madwoman? We are made, boys!

SCHOOLMASTER   And are you mad, good woman?

JAILER'S DAUGHTER   I would be sorry else. Give me your
hand.

SCHOOLMASTER   Why?

JAILER'S DAUGHTER   I can tell your fortune.

80 You are a fool. Tell ten. —I have posed him.[8] Buzz!°   *Silence*

—Friend, you must eat no white bread; if you do,

Your teeth will bleed extremely.[9] Shall we dance, ho?

I know you, you're a tinker.° Sirrah tinker,   *mender of kettles*

---

4. A false (pro)position is a logical fallacy. The Schoolmaster compares Cicely's flawed manners to faulty logic.

5. Now to be temperamental, to lose her temper.

6. Probably taken from "The George Alow and the Sweepstake," a ballad published in 1611. The George Alow was a ship.

7. Hawks used for falconry wore bells in order to make them easier to catch.

8. *Tell . . . him:* Count to ten (a common test for insanity or idiocy)—I have stumped ("posed") him. The Jailer's Daughter tests the Schoolmaster for idiocy and fails him.

9. *Your . . . extremely:* Perhaps drawing on the popular belief that a woman's pregnancy causes the man's toothache.

Stop no more holes° but what you should. *(sexual)*

85 SCHOOLMASTER *Dii boni!*° A tinker, damsel? *Good gods*

JAILER'S DAUGHTER Or a conjurer.° Raise me a devil° now, *magician / (sexual)*
and let him play *Chi passa* o'th' bells and bones.[1]

SCHOOLMASTER Go, take her and fluently persuade her to a
peace.° *Et opus exegi, quod nec Jovis ira, nec ignis.*[2] Strike *to do what we want*

90 up! And lead her in.

[TABORER *plays.*]

SECOND COUNTRYMAN Come, lass, let's trip it.° *let's dance*

JAILER'S DAUGHTER I'll lead— [*She dances.*]

THIRD COUNTRYMAN Do, do!

SCHOOLMASTER Persuasively, and cunningly.° Away, boys! *skillfully*

95 (*Wind horns.*) I hear the horns. Give me some
meditation°—and mark° your cue. *time to think / don't forget*

Exeunt all but SCHOOLMASTER.

Pallas,° inspire me. *goddess of wisdom*

Enter THESEUS, PIRITHOUS, HIPPOLYTA, EMILIA,
ARCITE, *and train.*

THESEUS This way the stag took.

SCHOOLMASTER Stay, and edify.° *be edified*

THESEUS What have we here?

100 PIRITHOUS Some country sport, upon my life, sir.

THESEUS [*to* SCHOOLMASTER] Well, sir, go forward, we will
"edify."

Chair and stools [brought] out.

Ladies, sit down; we'll stay it.° *stay to watch*

[THESEUS, HIPPOLYTA *and* EMILIA *sit.*]

SCHOOLMASTER Thou doughty Duke, all hail! All hail, sweet
ladies!

THESEUS This is a cold° beginning— *(punning on "hail")*

105 SCHOOLMASTER If you but favor,[3] our country pastime made is.
We are a few of those collected here
That ruder tongues distinguish° "villager." *call*
And—to say verity, and not to fable—
We are a merry rout, or else a rabble,

110 Or company, or—by a figure°—chorus, *figure of speech*
That fore thy dignity will dance a morris.
And I that am the rectifier° of all, *director; connector*
By title *pedagogus*°—that let fall *teacher*
The birch upon the breeches of the small ones,

115 And humble with a ferula° the tall ones— *cane (to whip students)*
Do here present this machine or this frame.[4]
And dainty Duke—whose doughty dismal° fame *awe-inspiring*
From Dis to Daedalus,[5] from post to pillar,
Is blown abroad—help me, thy poor well-willer,° *well-wisher*

---

1. *Chi passa* (Italian: who passes) were the first words of a common dance tune. Bones were used as percussion instruments, along with bells.
2. "And I have created a work that neither Jove's anger nor fire [can destroy]." Slightly misquoted from Ovid's *Metamorphoses* 15.871.
3. Approve. Compare Quince's speech to Theseus in *A Midsummer Night's Dream* 5.1.126–50.

4. Both "machine" and "frame" mean "structure" or "production."
5. Dis was god of the underworld; Daedalus was creator of the Cretan labyrinth and inventor of wings for human flight. Theseus triumphed over both the underworld and the labyrinth. Daedalus is invoked for the sake of alliteration and, because of his association with flight and hence the heavens, for contrast to Dis.

120	And with thy twinkling eyes, look right and straight	
	Upon this mighty "Moor" of mickle° weight.	*much*
	"Is" now comes in[6]—which, being glued together,	
	Makes "Morris," and the cause that we came hither:	
	The body of our sport, of no small study.[7]	
125	I first appear—though rude, and raw, and muddy—	
	To speak before thy noble grace this tenor,[8]	
	At whose great feet I offer up my penner;°	*pen case*
	The next,° the Lord of May and Lady bright;	*next to appear*
	The Chambermaid and Servingman, by night	
130	That seek out silent hanging;[9] then mine Host,	
	And his fat Spouse, that welcomes to their cost	
	The gallèd° traveler and with a beck'ning	*saddle-sore*
	Informs the tapster° to inflame the reck'ning;°	*bartender / overcharge*
	Then the beest-eating Clown,[1] and next the fool,	
135	The Bavian with long tail and eke long tool,°	*penis*
	Cum multis aliis° that make a dance.	*With many others (Latin)*
	Say "Ay," and all shall presently° advance.	*at once*
	THESEUS Ay, ay, by any means, dear *Domine*.°	*Teacher*
	PIRITHOUS Produce.°	*Lead them out*
140	SCHOOLMASTER *Intrate filii!*[2] Come forth and foot it.	
	[SCHOOLMASTER *knocks. Enter the dance.*]	
	Music; dance.	
	[*Sings.*] Ladies, if we have been merry	
	And have pleased thee with a derry,	
	And a derry and a down,°	*(song refrain words)*
	Say the Schoolmaster's no clown.	
145	Duke, if we have pleased thee too,	
	And have done as good boys should do,	
	Give us but a tree or twain	
	For a maypole, and again	
	Ere another year run out,	
150	We'll make thee laugh and all this rout.°	*company*
	THESEUS Take twenty,° *Domine*. [*to* HIPPOLYTA] How does my	*(trees)*
	sweetheart?	
	HIPPOLYTA Never so pleased, sir.	
	EMILIA 'Twas an excellent dance,	
	And for a preface° I never heard a better.	*as for the prologue*
	THESEUS —Schoolmaster, I thank you. —One° see 'em all	*Someone*
	rewarded.	
155	PIRITHOUS And here's something to paint your pole withal.	
	[*He gives* SCHOOLMASTER *money*.]	
	THESEUS Now to our sports again.	
	SCHOOLMASTER [*sings*] May the stag thou hunt'st stand long,°	*give a good chase*
	And thy dogs be swift and strong;	

---

6. The Schoolmaster displays the word "morris" from two placards, possibly held by the dancers. In Q the word is split into two syllables, "Morr" (here emended to "Moor") and "Is," perhaps an old spelling of "Ice." They may have been spelled out, or perhaps pictograms were used, with the first placard depicting a Moor and the second the allegorical figure Winter.
7. The main part in our entertainment, carefully prepared.

8. Argument; tenner (ten-syllable line).
9. Curtain behind which they can make love.
1. Clown or country shepherd (see line 144) who likes "beest," the thick milk produced by a cow for the first few days after calving.
2. Come in, my sons (children). The masculine *filii* is especially appropriate, since the women's parts were played by boy actors.

160 May they kill him without lets,°   *obstacles*
And the ladies eat his dowsets.°   *testicles (a delicacy)*
Wind horns.   [*Exeunt* THESEUS *and party.*]
—Come, we are all made.
Dii deaeque omnes;° ye have danced rarely, wenches.   *Gods and goddesses all*
                              Exeunt.

3.6

Enter PALAMON *from the bush.*

PALAMON   About this hour my cousin gave his faith°   *word*
To visit me again, and with him bring
Two swords and two good armors;° if he fail,   *suits of armor*
He's neither man nor soldier. When he left me
5 I did not think a week could have restored
My lost strength to me, I was grown so low
And crestfall'n with my wants. I thank thee, Arcite:
Thou art yet a fair foe; and I feel myself,
With this refreshing, able once again
10 To outdure° danger. To delay it longer   *endure; outlast*
Would make the world think—when it comes to hearing°—   *when word gets out*
That I lay fatting like a swine to fight,
And not a soldier.[1] Therefore this blessed morning
Shall be the last, and that sword he refuses,°   *(in choosing first)*
15 If it but hold,° I kill him with; 'tis justice.   *Unless it breaks*
So, love and fortune for me!

           Enter ARCITE *with armors and swords.*
                     —Oh, good morrow.
ARCITE   Good morrow, noble kinsman.
PALAMON   I have put you
To too much pains, sir.
ARCITE   That too much, fair cousin,
Is but a debt to honor, and my duty.
20 PALAMON   Would you were so in all, sir; I could wish ye
As kind a kinsman as you force me find
A beneficial foe, that my embraces
Might thank ye, not my blows.
ARCITE   I shall think either,
Well done, a noble recompense.
PALAMON   Then I shall quit° you.   *repay*
25 ARCITE   Defy me in these fair terms, and you show°   *show yourself to be*
More than a mistress to me. No more anger,
As you love anything that's honorable!
We were not bred to talk, man. When we are armed
And both upon our guards, then let our fury,
30 Like meeting of two tides, fly strongly from us,
And then to whom the birthright° of this beauty   *rightful possession*
Truly pertains°—without upbraidings, scorns,   *belongs*
Despisings of our persons, and such poutings
Fitter for girls and schoolboys—will be seen,
35 And quickly, yours or mine. Will't please you arm, sir?

3.6 Location: Scene continues.
1. *fatting . . . soldier:* being fattened like a swine for the slaughter, rather than preparing myself like a warrior
for the fight.

Or, if you feel yourself not fitting° yet   *ready*
And furnished with your old strength, I'll stay,° cousin,   *wait*
And every day discourse you into health,
As I am spared.° Your person I am friends with,   *In my spare time*
40 And I could wish I had not said I loved her,
Though I had died.[2] But loving such a lady,
And justifying° my love, I must not fly from't.   *affirming*
PALAMON Arcite, thou art so brave an enemy
That no man but thy cousin's fit to kill thee.
45 I am well and lusty.° Choose your arms.   *eager to do battle*
ARCITE   Choose you, sir.
PALAMON Wilt thou exceed in all,[3] or dost thou do it
To make me spare thee?
ARCITE   If you think so, cousin,
You are deceived—for, as I am a soldier,
I will not spare you.
PALAMON   That's well said.
ARCITE   You'll find it.°   *find it so*
50 PALAMON Then, as I am an honest man, and love
With all the justice of affection,[4]
I'll pay thee soundly.° [*He chooses his armor.*] This I'll take.   *punish you properly*
ARCITE [*taking the other set of armor*]   That's mine then.
I'll arm you first.
PALAMON   Do. [ARCITE *helps him into his armor.*]
Pray thee tell me, cousin,
Where gott'st thou this good armor?
ARCITE   'Tis the Duke's—
55 And, to say true, I stole it. Do I pinch you?
PALAMON No.
ARCITE   Is't not too heavy?
PALAMON   I have worn a lighter,
But I shall make it serve.
ARCITE   I'll buckle't close.°   *tightly*
PALAMON By any means.
ARCITE   You care not for a grand guard?[5]
PALAMON No, no—we'll use no horses. I perceive
You would fain be at that fight.°   *rather fight mounted*
60 ARCITE   I am indifferent.
PALAMON Faith, so am I. Good cousin, thrust the buckle
Through far enough.
ARCITE   I warrant you.°   *Trust me*
PALAMON   My casque,° now.   *helmet*
ARCITE Will you fight bare-armed?
PALAMON   We shall be the nimbler.
ARCITE But use your gauntlets, though; those are o'th' least.°   *too small*
Prithee take mine, good cousin.
65 PALAMON   Thank you, Arcite.
How do I look? Am I fall'n much away?°   *much thinner*
ARCITE Faith, very little; love has used you kindly.
PALAMON I'll warrant thee—I'll strike home.

2. Although it would have killed me to keep silent.
3. Will you always outdo me in courtesy (as here, by
letting me choose my arms first)?

4. Palamon's love of Emilia is just; Palamon will deal
justly (honorably) with Arcite because he loves him.
5. Chestplate for fighting on horseback.

ARCITE   Do, and spare not;
  I'll give you cause, sweet cousin.
PALAMON   Now to you, sir.
    [*He helps* ARCITE *into his armor.*]
70 Methinks this armor's very like that, Arcite,
    Thou wor'st that day the three kings fell—but lighter.
ARCITE   That was a very good one. And that day,
    I well remember, you outdid me, cousin;
    I never saw such valor. When you charged
75 Upon the left wing of the enemy,
    I spurred hard to come up,° and under me   keep up with you
    I had a right good horse—
PALAMON   You had indeed—
    A bright bay, I remember.
ARCITE   Yes, but all
    Was vainly labored in me; you outwent me,
80 Nor could my wishes reach you.[6] Yet a little
    I did by imitation.
PALAMON   More by virtue;°   valor
    You are modest, cousin.
ARCITE   When I saw you charge first,
    Methought I heard a dreadful clap of thunder
    Break from the troop.
PALAMON   But still before that flew
85 The lightning of your valor. [ARCITE *starts to move away.*]
      Stay a little,
    Is not this piece too strait?°   tight
ARCITE   No, no, 'tis well.
PALAMON   I would have nothing hurt thee but my sword;
    A bruise would be dishonor.
ARCITE   Now I am perfect.°   ready
PALAMON   Stand off,° then.   Step back
ARCITE   Take my sword; I hold° it better. consider
90 PALAMON   I thank ye, no; keep it, your life lies° on it.[7]   depends
    Here's one—if it but hold,° I ask no more   holds together
    For all my hopes: my cause and honor guard me.
ARCITE   And me my love.
      They bow several ways,[8] *then advance and stand.*
                Is there aught else to say?
PALAMON   This only, and no more: thou art mine aunt's son,
95 And that blood we desire to shed is mutual—
    In me, thine, and in thee, mine. My sword
    Is in my hand, and if thou kill'st me,
    The gods and I forgive thee. If there be
    A place prepared for those that sleep in honor,
100 I wish his weary soul that falls may win it.
    Fight bravely, cousin; give me thy noble hand.
ARCITE   Here, Palamon. This hand shall never more
    Come near thee with such friendship.
PALAMON   I commend thee.°   (to God)

---

6. My wishes to keep up with you were not answered.
7. TEXTUAL COMMENT For the effect of decisions about punctuation on the characterization of Palamon and consequent stage action, see Digital Edition TC 8.
8. They make ceremonial bows in various directions, as if they were jousting in a tournament.

ARCITE If I fall, curse me and say I was a coward,
105 For none but such dare die in these just trials.°   *(disagreeing with Palamon)*
    Once more, farewell, my cousin.
PALAMON   Farewell, Arcite.
    [They] fight. Horns within; they stand.
ARCITE Lo, cousin, lo; our folly has undone us!
PALAMON   Why?
ARCITE This is the Duke, a-hunting as I told you;
    If we be found, we are wretched. Oh, retire,
110 For honor's sake; and safely, presently,
    Into your bush again. Sir, we shall find
    Too many° hours to die in; gentle cousin,   *More than enough*
    If you be seen, you perish instantly
    For breaking prison, and I—if you reveal me—
115 For my contempt.[9] Then all the world will scorn us
    And say we had a noble difference,
    But base disposers of it.°   *settled it ignobly*
PALAMON   No, no, cousin,
    I will no more be hidden, nor put off
    This great adventure° to a second trial.   *undertaking*
120 I know your cunning, and I know your cause;°   *motive (for delay)*
    He that faints° now, shame take him! Put thyself   *is fainthearted*
    Upon thy present guard°—   *At once on guard*
ARCITE   You are not mad?
PALAMON —Or° I will make th'advantage of this hour   *Either I'm mad or*
    Mine own, and what to come shall threaten me
125 I fear less than my fortune.° Know, weak cousin,   *(in this fight)*
    I love Emilia, and in that I'll bury
    Thee and all crosses else.°   *all other obstacles*
ARCITE   Then come what can come,
    Thou shalt know, Palamon, I dare as well
    Die as discourse or sleep. Only this fears° me: *frightens*
130 The law will have the honor of our ends.[1]
    Have at thy life!
PALAMON   Look to thine own° well, Arcite.   *(own life)*
    [They] fight again. Horns.
    Enter THESEUS, HIPPOLYTA, EMILIA, PIRITHOUS, *and*
    train.
THESEUS What ignorant and mad malicious° traitors   *evil-minded*
    Are you, that, 'gainst the tenor° of my laws   *purport*
    Are making battle, thus like knights appointed,°   *armed*
135 Without my leave and officers of arms?[2]
    By Castor,[3] both shall die!
PALAMON   Hold° thy word, Theseus.   *Keep*
    We are certainly both traitors, both despisers°   *disobedient*
    Of thee and of thy goodness. I am Palamon,
    That cannot love thee, he that broke thy prison—
140 Think well what that deserves—and this is Arcite:
    A bolder traitor never trod thy ground;
    A falser ne'er seemed friend. This is the man

9. For my disobedience to Theseus's order that I be   2. Overseers of chivalric combat.
banished.   3. Common Roman oath. Castor and Pollux, twins,
1. We will die by execution rather than combat.   were sons of Jupiter.

Was begged° and banished; this is he condemns thee | petitioned for
And what thou dar'st do; and in this disguise,
145 Against thy own edict, follows thy sister,° | sister-in-law
That fortunate bright° star, the fair Emilia— | luck-bringing
Whose servant,° if there be a right in seeing | courtly lover
And first bequeathing of the soul to, justly
I am—and, which is more, dares think her his.
150 This treachery, like a most trusty lover,
I called him now to answer. If thou beest
As thou art spoken°—great and virtuous, | reported to be
The true decider of all injuries—
Say, "Fight again," and thou shalt see me, Theseus,
155 Do such a justice thou thyself wilt envy.
Then take my life; I'll woo thee to't.° | urge; persuade

PIRITHOUS   O heaven,
What more than man is this!

THESEUS   I have sworn—

ARCITE   We seek not
Thy breath of mercy, Theseus. 'Tis to me
A thing as soon to die as thee to say it,
160 And no more moved. Where this man calls me traitor,
Let me say thus much: if in love be treason
In service of so excellent a beauty
As I love most and in that faith will perish,
As I have brought my life here to confirm it,
165 As I have served her truest, worthiest,
As I dare kill this cousin that denies it,
So let me be most traitor, and ye please me.
For° scorning thy edict, Duke, [*indicating* EMILIA] ask that lady | As for
Why she is fair, and why her eyes command me
170 Stay here to love her; and if she say "traitor,"
I am a villain fit to lie unburied.

PALAMON   Thou shalt have pity of° us both, O Theseus, | on
If unto neither thou show mercy. Stop,
As thou art just, thy noble ear against us;
175 As thou art valiant—for thy cousin's° soul, | (Hercules')
Whose twelve strong labors crown his memory—
Let's° die together at one instant, Duke. | Allow us
Only a little let him fall before me,
That I may tell my soul he shall not have her.
180 **THESEUS**   I grant your wish, for, to say true, your cousin
Has ten times more offended, for I gave him
More mercy than you found, sir, your offenses
Being no more than his. None here speak for 'em,
For, ere the sun set, both shall sleep forever.
185 **HIPPOLYTA**   Alas, the pity! —Now or never, sister,
Speak not° to be denied. That face of yours | Speak so as not
Will bear the curses else° of after ages | otherwise
For these lost cousins.

EMILIA   In my face, dear sister,
I find no anger to 'em, nor no ruin;
190 The misadventure of their own eyes kill° 'em. | kills
Yet that° I will be woman and have pity, | to show that
My knees shall grow to th' ground but° I'll get mercy. | unless
Help me, dear sister, in a deed so virtuous

The powers of all women will be with us.
    [EMILIA *and* HIPPOLYTA *kneel.*]
—Most royal brother—

195 HIPPOLYTA   Sir, by our tie of marriage—
EMILIA By your own spotless honor—
HIPPOLYTA   By that faith,
  That fair hand, and that honest heart you gave me—
EMILIA By that you would have pity in another;[4]
  By your own virtues infinite—
HIPPOLYTA   By valor;
200 By all the chaste° nights I have ever pleased you—   *faithful only to you*
THESEUS These are strange conjurings.°   *incantations*
PIRITHOUS   Nay, then I'll in too.
  [*He kneels.*] By all our friendship, sir; by all our dangers;
  By all you love most—wars and [*indicating* HIPPOLYTA] this
    sweet lady—
EMILIA By that° you would have trembled to deny   *(chivalric aid)*
  A blushing maid—
205 HIPPOLYTA   By your own eyes; by strength,
  In which you swore I went beyond° all women,   *I excelled*
  Almost all men, and yet I yielded, Theseus—
PIRITHOUS To crown all this, by your most noble soul,
  Which cannot want° due mercy, I beg first.   *lack*
HIPPOLYTA Next hear my prayers.
210 EMILIA   Last let me entreat, sir.
PIRITHOUS For mercy.
HIPPOLYTA   Mercy.
EMILIA   Mercy on these princes.
THESEUS Ye make my faith reel.[5]
    [EMILIA, HIPPOLYTA, *and* PIRITHOUS *rise.*]
                   Say I felt
  Compassion to 'em both, how would you place° it?   *have me bestow*
EMILIA Upon their lives—but with their banishments.
215 THESEUS You are a right° woman, sister; you have pity,   *typical*
  But want the understanding where to use it.
  If you desire their lives, invent a way
  Safer than banishment. Can these two live,
  And have the agony of love about 'em,
220 And not kill one another? Every day
  They'd fight about you; hourly bring your honor
  In public question with their swords.[6] Be wise, then,
  And here forget 'em. It concerns your credit°   *reputation*
  And my oath equally; I have said they die—
225 Better they fall by th' law than one another.
  Bow not my honor.[7]
EMILIA   O my noble brother,
  That oath was rashly° made, and in your anger;   *impulsively*
  Your reason will not hold° it. If such vows   *sustain*
  Stand for express will,° all the world must perish. *steadfast resolve*
230 Besides, I have another oath 'gainst yours,

---

4. By whatever you would expect someone else to pity.
5. You make my constancy to my own oath (to kill the kinsmen) waver.
6. *They'd . . . swords:* They'd fight publicly over you, thus compromising your honor.
7. Don't force me to lower my standards of honor.

Of more authority, I am sure more love,
Not made in passion, neither, but good heed.°   *thoughtfulness*
THESEUS   What is it, sister?
PIRITHOUS   Urge it home, brave lady.
EMILIA   That you would ne'er deny me anything
235   Fit for my modest suit, and your free granting—
I tie you to your word now. If ye fail in't,
Think how you maim your honor—
For now° I am set a-begging, sir, I am deaf   *now that*
To all but your compassion—how their lives
240   Might breed the ruin of my name, opinion.°   *my reputation*
Shall anything that loves me perish for° me?   *because of*
That were a cruel wisdom. Do men prune
The straight young boughs that blush with thousand
    blossoms
Because they may be° rotten? O Duke Theseus,   *become*
245   The goodly mothers that have groaned for these°   *(in childbirth)*
And all the longing maids that ever loved,
If your vow stand,° shall curse me and my beauty,   *holds*
And in their funeral songs for these two cousins
Despise my cruelty and cry woe worth° me,   *befall*
250   Till I am nothing but the scorn of women.
For heaven's sake, save their lives and banish 'em.
THESEUS   On what conditions?
EMILIA   Swear 'em° never more   *Have them swear*
To make me their contention, or to know me,°   *think of me*
To tread upon thy dukedom, and to be—
255   Wherever they shall travel—ever strangers
To one another.
PALAMON   I'll be cut a-pieces
Before I take this oath. Forget I love her?
O all ye gods, despise me then! Thy banishment
I not mislike, so we may fairly carry
260   Our swords and cause along; else never trifle,
But take our lives, Duke. I must love, and will,
And for that love must, and dare, kill this cousin
On any piece° the earth has.   *spot of ground*
THESEUS   Will you, Arcite,
Take these conditions?
PALAMON   He's a villain, then.
265 PIRITHOUS   These are men—
ARCITE   No, never, Duke! 'Tis worse to me than begging
To take° my life so basely. Though I think   *save*
I never shall enjoy her, yet I'll preserve
The honor of affection and die for her,
270   Make death a devil.°   *Even horribly*
THESEUS   What may be done? For now I feel compassion.
PIRITHOUS   Let it not fail° again, sir.   *diminish*
THESEUS   Say, Emilia,
If one of them were dead, as one must, are you
Content to take th'other to your husband?
275   They cannot both enjoy you. They are princes
As goodly as your own eyes and as noble
As ever fame yet spoke of; look upon 'em,
And, if you can love, end this difference—

I give consent. Are you content too, princes?
PALAMON *and* ARCITE   With all our souls.
280 THESEUS   He that she refuses
Must die, then.
PALAMON *and* ARCITE   Any death thou canst invent, Duke.
PALAMON   If I fall from that mouth,° I fall with favor,   *(because of her decision)*
And lovers yet unborn shall bless my ashes.
285 ARCITE   If she refuse me, yet my grave will wed me
And soldiers sing my epitaph.
THESEUS [*to* EMILIA]   Make choice, then.
EMILIA   I cannot, sir; they are both too excellent;
For° me, a hair shall never fall of° these men.   *On account of / from*
HIPPOLYTA   What will become of 'em?
THESEUS   Thus I ordain it,
290 And by mine honor once again it stands,
Or both shall die. You shall both to your country,
And each within this month, accompanied
With three fair knights, appear again in this place,
In which I'll plant° a pyramid; and whether,°   *fix / whichever*
295 Before us that are here, can force his cousin,
By fair and knightly strength, to touch the pillar,
He shall enjoy her; the other lose his head,
And all his friends. Nor shall he grudge to fall,[8]
Nor think he dies with interest in° this lady.   *a rightful claim to*
Will this content ye?
300 PALAMON   Yes. Here, cousin Arcite,
I am friends again till that hour.
ARCITE   I embrace ye.
THESEUS   Are you content, sister?
EMILIA   Yes, I must, sir,
Else both miscarry.°   *perish*
THESEUS [*to* PALAMON *and* ARCITE]   Come, shake hands again,
then,
And take heed—as you are gentlemen—this quarrel
305 Sleep till the hour prefixed, and hold your course.°   *keep your resolve*
PALAMON   We dare not fail thee, Theseus.
THESEUS   Come, I'll give ye
Now usage like to princes and to friends.
When ye return, who wins, I'll settle here;°   *set up in Athens*
Who loses, yet I'll weep upon his bier.   *Exeunt.*

4.1
Enter JAILER *and* FIRST FRIEND.
JAILER   Heard you no more? Was nothing said of me
Concerning the escape of Palamon?
Good sir, remember!
FIRST FRIEND   Nothing that I heard,
For I came home before the business
5 Was fully ended. Yet I might perceive,
Ere I departed, a great likelihood
Of both their pardons. For Hippolyta

---

8. And all his friends will die with him; nor should   **4.1** Location: The prison in Athens.
he consider his execution unjust.

And fair-eyed Emily, upon their knees,
Begged with such handsome pity that the Duke
10   Methought stood staggering° whether he should follow   *wavering as to*
His rash oath or the sweet compassion
Of those two ladies; and, to second them,
That truly noble prince, Pirithous—
Half his own heart[1]—set in too, that° I hope   *so that*
15   All shall be well. Neither heard I one question
Of your name, or his scape.

        Enter SECOND FRIEND.

JAILER   Pray heaven it hold° so—   *continue*
SECOND FRIEND   Be of good comfort, man; I bring you news,
Good news!
JAILER   They are welcome.
SECOND FRIEND   Palamon has cleared you,
And got your pardon, and discovered° how,   *exposed*
20   And by whose means, he escaped—which was your daughter's—
Whose pardon is procured too, and the prisoner,
Not to be held ungrateful to her goodness,
Has given a sum of money to her marriage—
A large one, I'll assure you.
JAILER   Ye are a good man
And ever bring good news.
25   FIRST FRIEND   How was it ended?
SECOND FRIEND   Why, as it should be. They that ne'er begged
But they prevailed° had their suits fairly granted: *Without prevailing*
The prisoners have their lives.
FIRST FRIEND   I knew 'twould be so.
SECOND FRIEND   But there be new conditions, which you'll hear of
At better time.
JAILER   I hope they are good—
30   SECOND FRIEND   They are honorable;
How good they'll prove, I know not.

        Enter WOOER.

FIRST FRIEND   'Twill be known.
WOOER [*to* JAILER]   Alas, sir, where's your daughter?
JAILER   Why do you ask?
WOOER   O sir, when did you see her?
SECOND FRIEND [*aside*]   How he looks!
JAILER   This morning.
WOOER   Was she well? Was she in health?
Sir, when did she sleep?
35   FIRST FRIEND [*aside*]   These are strange questions.
JAILER   I do not think she was very well, for now
You make me mind° her. But this very day   *remind me of*
I asked her questions, and she answered me
So far from what she was,° so childishly,   *her usual manner*
40   So sillily, as if she were a fool,
An innocent, and I was very angry.
But what of her, sir?
WOOER   Nothing but my pity.[2]
But you must know it, and as good by me
As by another that less loves her—

---

1. Hippolyta is (has) the other half.   2. My pity for you and her makes me speak.

JAILER   Well, sir?
FIRST FRIEND   Not right?°   *in her right mind*
SECOND FRIEND   Not well?
45   WOOER   No, sir, not well.
      'Tis too true—she is mad.
FIRST FRIEND   It cannot be.
WOOER   Believe—you'll find it so.
JAILER   I half suspected
      What you told me. The gods comfort her!
      Either this was her love to Palamon,
50   Or fear of my miscarrying[3] on his scape,
      Or both—
WOOER   'Tis likely.
JAILER   But why all this haste, sir?
WOOER   I'll tell you quickly. As I late was angling°   *fishing*
      In the great lake that lies behind the palace,
      From the far shore, thickset with reeds and sedges,
55   As patiently I was attending sport,°   *awaiting a fish*
      I heard a voice—a shrill one—and, attentive,
      I gave my ear—when I might well perceive
      'Twas one that sung and, by the smallness° of it,   *high pitch*
      A boy or woman. I then left my angle°   *fishing rod*
60   To his own skill,° came near, but yet perceived not   *To fish by itself*
      Who made the sound, the rushes and the reeds
      Had so encompassed it.° I laid me down   *overgrown the place*
      And listened to the words she sung—for then,
      Through a small glade cut by the fishermen,
      I saw it was your daughter.
65   JAILER   Pray, go on, sir.
WOOER   She sung much, but no sense; only I heard her
      Repeat this often: "Palamon is gone,
      Is gone to th' wood to gather mulberries—
      I'll find him out tomorrow."
FIRST FRIEND   Pretty soul!
70   WOOER   "His shackles will betray him; he'll be taken,
      And what shall I do then? I'll bring a bevy,°   *company*
      A hundred black-eyed maids that love as I do—
      With chaplets° on their heads of daffadillies,   *wreaths*
      With cherry lips, and cheeks of damask roses—
75   And all we'll dance an antic° fore the Duke   *a grotesque dance*
      And beg his pardon."[4] [*to the* JAILER] Then she talked of you, sir—
      That you must lose your head tomorrow morning,
      And she must gather flowers to bury you,
      And see the house made handsome.° Then she sung   *neat*
80   Nothing but "Willow, willow, willow"[5] and, between,
      Ever was "Palamon, fair Palamon"
      And "Palamon was a tall° young man." The place   *valiant*
      Was knee-deep° where she sat; her careless tresses   *(in rushes)*
      A wreath of bullrush rounded;° about her stuck   *encircled*
85   Thousand freshwater flowers of several° colors,   *various*
      That° methought she appeared like the fair nymph   *Such that*

---

3. My being punished because of.
4. Beg Duke Theseus to pardon Palamon.

5. Refrain of a popular song, also sung by Desdemona in *Othello* 4.3.

That feeds the lake with waters, or as Iris[6]
Newly dropped down from heaven. Rings she made
Of rushes that grew by,[7] and to 'em spoke
90 The prettiest posies:[8] "Thus our true love's tied,"
"This you may lose, not me," and many a one.
And then she wept, and sung again, and sighed,
And with the same breath smiled and kissed her hand.
SECOND FRIEND   Alas, what pity it is!
WOOER   I made in to° her;   *approached*
95 She saw me and straight sought the flood.° I saved her   *at once jumped in*
And set her safe to land, when presently
She slipped away and to the city made
With such a cry and swiftness that, believe me,
She left me far behind her. Three or four
100 I saw from far off cross° her—[*to the* JAILER] one of 'em   *intercept*
I knew to be your brother—where she stayed°   *stopped*
And fell, scarce to be got away. I left them with her
And hither came to tell you.

Enter JAILER'S BROTHER, JAILER'S DAUGHTER, *and
others.*

                        Here they are.
JAILER'S DAUGHTER [*sings*] May you never more enjoy the
   light,° etc.   *(unknown song)*
   —Is not this a fine song?
105 JAILER'S BROTHER   Oh, a very fine one.
JAILER'S DAUGHTER   I can sing twenty more.
JAILER'S BROTHER   I think you can.
JAILER'S DAUGHTER   Yes, truly can I—I can sing "The Broom"
   And "Bonny Robin."[9] Are not you a tailor?
JAILER'S BROTHER   Yes.
JAILER'S DAUGHTER   Where's my wedding gown?
JAILER'S BROTHER   I'll bring it tomorrow.
110 JAILER'S DAUGHTER   Do, very rarely;° I must be abroad else°   *early / or I'll be out*
   To call the maids and pay the minstrels—
   For I must lose my maidenhead by cocklight;°   *before dawn*
   'Twill never thrive else.[1]
   [*Sings.*] O fair, O sweet, etc.[2]
JAILER'S BROTHER [*aside to* JAILER] You must e'en take it patiently.
115 JAILER   'Tis true,
JAILER'S DAUGHTER [*to* JAILER *and others*] Good e'en,° good   *(evening)*
   men. Pray, did you ever hear
   Of one young Palamon?
JAILER   Yes, wench, we know him.
JAILER'S DAUGHTER   Is't not a fine young gentleman?
JAILER   'Tis, love.
JAILER'S BROTHER [*aside to* JAILER] By no mean cross her—
   she is then distempered

---

6. Goddess of the rainbow and Juno's messenger.
7. *Rings . . . by:* sometimes used as wedding rings in
rural (or mock) wedding ceremonies.
8. Mottoes and aphorisms, sometimes engraved on
the inside of rings.
9. "The Broom" and "Bonny Robin" were popular

songs (Ophelia sings a line of the latter in *Hamlet*
4.5). "Robin" could mean "penis."
1. Otherwise things (or possibly the marriage) won't
prosper for me.
2. A song adapted from the seventh of Sir Philip
Sidney's *Certain Sonnets* (1598).

Far worse than now she shows.³

120 FIRST FRIEND [*to* JAILER'S DAUGHTER]   Yes, he's a fine man.

JAILER'S DAUGHTER   Oh, is he so? You have a sister?

FIRST FRIEND   Yes.

JAILER'S DAUGHTER   But she shall never have him—tell her so—

For° a trick that I know. You'd best look to her—   *Because of*

For if she see him once she's gone, she's done

125 And undone⁴ in an hour. All the young maids

Of our town are in love with him, but I laugh at 'em

And let 'em all alone. Is't not a wise course?

FIRST FRIEND   Yes.

JAILER'S DAUGHTER   There is at least two hundred now with

    child by him;

There must be four!° Yet I keep close⁵ for all this,   *four hundred*

130 Close as a cockle.° And all these° must be boys—   *clam / (the offspring)*

He has the trick on't°—and at ten years old   *of producing boys*

They must be all gelt for musicians,⁶

And sing the wars of Theseus.

SECOND FRIEND [*aside*]   This is strange.

JAILER'S BROTHER [*aside*]   As ever you heard—but say nothing.

FIRST FRIEND [*aside*]   No.

135 JAILER'S DAUGHTER   They come from all parts of the dukedom

    to him.

I'll warrant ye, he had not so few last night

As twenty to dispatch; he'll tickle't up°   *do the (sexual) job*

In two hours, if his hand be in.°   *if he's in good shape*

JAILER   She's lost

Past all cure.

JAILER'S BROTHER   Heaven forbid, man.

140 JAILER'S DAUGHTER [*to* JAILER]   Come hither; you are a wise man.

FIRST FRIEND [*aside to* SECOND FRIEND]   Does she know him?°   *recognize her father*

SECOND FRIEND [*to* FIRST FRIEND]   No, would she did.

JAILER'S DAUGHTER [*to* JAILER]   You are master of a ship?

JAILER   Yes.

JAILER'S DAUGHTER   Where's your compass?

JAILER   Here.

JAILER'S DAUGHTER   Set it to th' north.

And now direct your course to th' wood, where Palamon

145 Lies longing for me. For the tackling,°   *rigging*

Let me alone.° Come, weigh,° my hearts, cheerily!   *I'll do it / lift anchor*

ALL   Ugh, ugh, ugh!⁷

'Tis up!° The wind's fair! Top the bowline!⁸   *(the anchor)*

Out with the mainsail! —Where's your whistle, master?

150 JAILER'S BROTHER   Let's get her in.°   *inside (an aside)*

JAILER   Up to the top,° boy.   *top of the mast*

JAILER'S BROTHER   Where's the pilot?

FIRST FRIEND   Here—

JAILER'S DAUGHTER   What kenn'st thou?°   *What do you see*

---

3. *By . . . shows:* Don't contradict her in any way, or
she'll become far more deranged than she is now.
4. *She's done / And undone:* she will fall in love with
him and lose her virginity.
5. Keep my mouth (and thighs) closed.
6. They must all be castrated so that their voices do

not deepen and they can become singers (of higher
parts). Castrati, castrated male singers, became popular in sixteenth-century Italy.
7. Grunts of exertion; possibly the sound of the wind
in the sails.
8. *Top the bowline:* Tighten the sail-steadying rope.

SECOND FRIEND   A fair wood.

JAILER'S DAUGHTER   Bear for° it, master.   *Steer toward*
  Tack about!
[*Sings.*] When Cynthia° with her borrowed light, etc.[9]   *the moon*

                              Exeunt.

4.2

Enter EMILIA *alone, with two pictures.*°   *(of Palamon and Arcite)*

EMILIA   Yet I may bind those wounds up that must open
  And bleed to death for my sake else;° I'll choose   *otherwise*
  And end their strife. Two such young handsome men
  Shall never fall for° me; their weeping mothers,   *die because of*
5 Following the dead cold ashes of their sons,
  Shall never curse my cruelty. [*She looks at one picture.*]
    Good heaven,
  What a sweet face has Arcite! If wise Nature—
  With all her best endowments, all those beauties
  She sows into the births of noble bodies—
10 Were here a mortal woman, and had in her
  The coy° denials of young maids, yet doubtless   *modest*
  She would run mad for this man. What an eye,
  Of what a fiery sparkle and quick° sweetness,   *lively*
  Has this young prince! Here° Love himself sits smiling—   *In his eye*
15 Just such another wanton Ganymede
  Set Jove afire with, and enforced the god
  Snatch up the goodly boy and set him by him,
  A shining constellation.[1] What a brow,
  Of what a spacious majesty, he carries,
20 Arched like the great-eyed Juno's but far sweeter,
  Smoother than Pelops' shoulder!° Fame and honor   *(made of ivory)*
  Methinks from hence,° as from a promontory   *his brow*
  Pointed° in heaven, should clap their wings and sing   *Reaching its peak*
  To all the underworld° the loves and fights   *lower world, of humanity*
25 Of gods and such men near 'em.° [*She looks at the other*   *men most like gods*
    picture.] Palamon
  Is but his foil;[2] to him a mere dull shadow;
  He's swarth and meager;° of an eye as heavy°   *dark and thin / sad*
  As if he had lost his mother; a still temper°—   *lethargic disposition*
  No stirring in him, no alacrity;
30 Of all this° sprightly sharpness, not a smile.°   *(Arcite's) / trace*
  Yet these° that we count errors may become him: *these qualities*
  Narcissus was a sad° boy, but a heavenly.°   *serious / beautiful*
  Oh, who can find the bent of woman's fancy?[3]
  I am a fool; my reason is lost in me;
35 I have no choice[4]—and I have lied so lewdly°   *wickedly*
  That women ought to beat me. On my knees
  I ask thy pardon, Palamon: thou art alone°   *uniquely*

---

9. Line from an unknown song.
4.2 Location: Theseus's palace in Athens.
1. With "Just such another [smile], wanton Gany- mede / Set Jove afire." Ganymede was a beautiful youth whom Jupiter became enamored of and carried off to be his cupbearer on Mt. Olympus. In the end, Ganymede was transformed into the constellation Aquarius.
2. Piece of thin, reflective metal in which a jewel was set, enhancing the jewel's brilliance (setting it off by contrast).
3. Who can discern which way a woman's affections will tend?
4. I am incapable of choosing.

And only beautiful, and these the eyes,
These the bright lamps of beauty, that command
40 And threaten love—and what young maid dare cross° 'em?   oppose
What a bold gravity, and yet inviting,
Has this brown manly face! O Love, this only,
From this hour, is complexion!⁵ [*She puts down Arcite's
  picture.*] —Lie there, Arcite;
45 Thou art a changeling to him, a mere gypsy,⁶
[*She turns back to Palamon's picture.*] And this the noble
  body.—I am sotted,°   made stupid
Utterly lost. My virgin's faith⁷ has fled me.
For if my brother but even now had asked me
Whether I loved, I had run mad for Arcite;
Now, if my sister, more for Palamon.
50 Stand both together.° Now, come ask me, brother;   (comparing portraits)
Alas, I know not. Ask me now, sweet sister;
I may go look.° What a mere child is Fancy,   seek further
That having two fair gauds° of equal sweetness   toys
Cannot distinguish,° but must cry for both.   choose
          Enter GENTLEMAN.
EMILIA How now, sir?
55 GENTLEMAN   From the noble Duke your brother,
    Madam, I bring you news: the knights are come.
EMILIA To end the quarrel?
GENTLEMAN   Yes.
EMILIA   Would I might end first!
  —What sins have I committed, chaste Diana,⁸
That my unspotted youth must now be soiled°   defiled
60 With blood of princes, and my chastity
Be made the altar where the lives of lovers—
Two greater and two better never yet
Made mothers joy—must be the sacrifice
To my unhappy beauty?
          Enter THESEUS, HIPPOLYTA, PIRITHOUS, *and*
          Attendants.
THESEUS   Bring 'em in
65 Quickly, by any means; I long to see 'em.
  [*to* EMILIA] Your two contending lovers are returned,
And with them their fair knights. Now, my fair sister,
You must love one of them.
EMILIA   I had rather both,
So° neither for my sake should fall untimely.°   So that / prematurely
THESEUS —Who saw 'em?
PIRITHOUS   I, awhile.
70 GENTLEMAN   And I.
          Enter MESSENGER.
THESEUS
  —From whence come you, sir?

---

5. *this only . . . complexion:* the only "complexion"
I'll appreciate from now on is a dark one.
6. A changeling was an ugly or deformed child left by
fairies in exchange for one they stole. Gypsies were
also thought to steal children; otherwise the meaning is unclear, since the word generally referred to a
swarthy person and Palamon has the dark complexion. Perhaps if a dark complexion is "fair," Arcite's
fair skin will be considered the "gypsy" one.
7. My prior oath (1.3.85) to remain a virgin.
8. Virgin goddess of the moon and of the Amazons.
See 1.3.52 and note.

MESSENGER   From the knights.
THESEUS   Pray, speak,
    You that have seen them, what they are.
MESSENGER   I will, sir,
    And truly what I think. Six braver spirits
    Than these they have brought—if we judge by the outside—
75   I never saw nor read of.[9] He that stands
    In the first place with Arcite, by his seeming°   *appearance*
    Should be a stout° man, by his face a prince—   *brave*
    His very looks so say° him. His complexion,   *declare*
    Nearer a brown than black, stern, and yet noble—
80   Which shows him hardy, fearless, proud° of dangers.   *scornful*
    The circles of his eyes show fire within him,
    And as a heated° lion, so he looks.   *an angry*
    His hair hangs long behind him, black and shining,
    Like ravens' wings. His shoulders, broad and strong,
85   Armed long and round,[1] and on his thigh a sword,
    Hung by a curious baldric, when he frowns,
    To seal his will with.[2] Better,° o'my conscience,   *A better sword*
    Was never soldier's friend.
THESEUS   Thou hast well described him—
PIRITHOUS   Yet a great deal short,
90   Methinks, of him that's first with Palamon.
THESEUS   Pray, speak° him, friend.   *describe*
PIRITHOUS   I guess he is a prince too,
    And, if it may be, greater; for his show°   *appearance*
    Has all the ornament of honor in't.
    He's somewhat bigger than the knight he° spoke of,   *(the messenger)*
95   But of a face far sweeter. His complexion
    Is as a ripe grape, ruddy. He has felt
    Without doubt what he fights for,° and so apter   *(love)*
    To make this cause his own. In 's face appears
    All the fair hopes of° what he undertakes,   *confidence about*
100   And when he's angry, then a settled° valor—   *steady*
    Not tainted with extremes—runs through his body
    And guides his arm to brave things. Fear he cannot;
    He shows no such soft temper. His head's yellow,
    Hard-haired,[3] and curled, thick-twined like ivy tods,°   *bushy branches of ivy*
105   Not to undo with° thunder. In his face   *Not to be destroyed by*
    The livery of the warlike maid[4] appears,
    Pure red and white, for yet no beard has blessed him;
    And in his rolling° eyes sits Victory,   *passionate*
    As if she ever° meant to court his valor.   *(Victory) always*
110   His nose stands high, a character° of honor.   *distinguishing mark*
    His red lips, after fights, are fit for ladies.
EMILIA [*aside*]   Must these men die too?
PIRITHOUS   When he speaks, his tongue

---

9. *nor read of:* possibly a joke on the playwright's part; the following descriptions closely follow Chaucer's *Knight's Tale* 2129–78.
1. With long, well-muscled arms.
2. *Hung . . . with:* Hung from an artfully crafted ("curious") sword belt ("baldric"), which he uses to carry out his will when he is angry.

3. Perhaps influenced by Thomas Speght's 1602 edition of Chaucer's *Knight's Tale,* where King Emetrius's hair "was of yron" (was made of iron) instead of "yronne" (curled).
4. *The . . . maid:* His allegiance to Bellona, goddess of war (or possibly to Athena, also associated with warlike powers).

Sounds like a trumpet. All his lineaments°   *body parts*
Are as a man would wish 'em—strong and clean;°   *perfectly shaped*
115 He wears a well-steeled° ax, the staff° of gold;   *well-honed / handle*
His age some five-and-twenty.
MESSENGER   There's another—
A little man, but of a tough soul, seeming
As great° as any; fairer promises   *noble*
In such a body yet I never looked on.
PIRITHOUS   Oh, he that's freckle-faced?
120 MESSENGER   The same, my lord.
Are they° not sweet ones?   *(the freckles)*
PIRITHOUS   Yes, they are well.
MESSENGER   Methinks,
Being so few and well disposed,° they show   *arranged*
Great and fine art in nature. He's white-haired°—   *blond*
Not wanton white,° but such a manly color   *effeminately fair*
125 Next to an auburn; tough and nimble set,°   *lithe*
Which shows an active soul. His arms are brawny,
Lined with strong sinews; to the shoulder piece
Gently they swell—like women new-conceived°—   *starting pregnancy*
Which speaks him prone to labor, never fainting
130 Under the weight of arms; stout-hearted, still°—   *when motionless*
But when he stirs, a tiger. He's gray-eyed,[5]
Which yields compassion where he conquers; sharp
To spy advantages, and where he finds 'em,
He's swift to make 'em his. He does no wrongs,
135 Nor takes none.° He's round-faced, and when he smiles,   *tolerates any*
He shows° a lover; when he frowns, a soldier.   *looks like*
About his head he wears the winner's oak[6]
And in it stuck the favor of his lady.
His age, some six-and-thirty. In his hand
140 He bears a charging-staff,° embossed with silver.   *lance*
THESEUS   Are they all thus?
PIRITHOUS   They are all the sons of honor.
THESEUS   Now as I have a soul I long to see 'em.
  [*to* HIPPOLYTA] Lady, you shall see men fight now.
HIPPOLYTA   I wish it,
But not the cause, my lord. They would show
145 Bravely about the titles of two kingdoms;[7]
'Tis pity love should be so tyrannous.
  —O my soft-hearted sister, what think you?
Weep not till they weep blood, wench: it must be.
THESEUS   You have steeled 'em° with your beauty.   *made them determined*
  [*to* PIRITHOUS]   Honored friend,
150 To you I give the field;° pray, order it   *charge of the combat*
Fitting° the persons that must use it.   *So it is fit for*
PIRITHOUS   Yes, sir.
THESEUS   Come, I'll go visit 'em. I cannot stay:°   *wait*
Their fame° has fired me so. —Till they appear,   *This account of them*
Good friend, be royal.°   *treat them royally*

---

5. With eyes of blue or blue-gray. Eyes of this color supposedly implied compassion.
6. Valiant soldiers received a wreath of oak leaves, particularly if they saved their friends in battle.
7. *They . . . kingdoms:* It would be more appropriate if they were fighting for each other's kingdoms.

PIRITHOUS   There shall want° no bravery.°   *lack / splendor*
155 EMILIA   Poor wench,° go weep; for whosoever wins   *(addressing herself)*
     Loses a noble cousin for thy sins.   *Exeunt.*

4.3

Enter JAILER, WOOER, [*and*] DOCTOR.[1]

DOCTOR Her distraction is more at some time of the moon than
     at other some,° is it not?   *at others*
JAILER She is continually in a harmless distemper;° sleeps   *state of confusion*
     little; altogether without appetite, save often drinking;
5   dreaming of another world and a better; and what broken
     piece of matter soe'er she's about, the name Palamon lards
     it,[2] that she farces° every business withal,° fits it to every   *stuffs / with it*
     question.
          Enter JAILER'S DAUGHTER.
     Look where she comes; you shall perceive her behavior.
10 JAILER'S DAUGHTER I have forgot it quite. The burden on't°   *refrain of the song*
     was "Down-a, down-a," and penned by no worse man than
     Geraldo, Emilia's schoolmaster. He's as fantastical,° too, as   *fanciful*
     ever he may go upon's legs°—for in the next world will Dido   *as any man*
     see Palamon, and then will she be out of love with Aeneas.[3]
15 DOCTOR What stuff's here? Poor soul—
    JAILER E'en thus all day long.
    JAILER'S DAUGHTER Now for this charm that I told you of: you
     must bring a piece of silver on the tip of your tongue, or no
     ferry;[4] then if it be your chance to come where the blessed
20   spirits are—there's a sight now! We maids that have our livers
     perished,[5] cracked to pieces with love, we shall come there
     and do nothing all day long but pick flowers with Proser-
     pine.[6] Then will I make Palamon a nosegay;° then let him   *flower bouquet*
     mark° me; then—   *notice*
25 DOCTOR How prettily she's amiss! Note her a little further.
    JAILER'S DAUGHTER Faith, I'll tell you, sometime we go to
     barley-break[7]—we of the blessed. Alas, 'tis a sore life they
     have i'th' other place°—such burning, frying, boiling, hissing,   *(hell)*
     howling, chattering, cursing—oh, they have shrewd mea-
30   sure,° take heed! If one be mad, or hang or drown themselves,   *harsh retribution*
     thither they go—Jupiter bless us!—and there shall we be put
     in a cauldron of lead and usurers' grease[8] amongst a whole
     million of cutpurses, and there boil like a gammon° of bacon   *side*
     that will never be enough.°   *cooked enough*
35 DOCTOR How her brain coins!°   *invents*

4.3 Location: The prison.
1. TEXTUAL COMMENT For the problem of whether
this scene should be in prose or verse, see Digital
Edition TC 9.
2. Whatever disjointed piece of business she tries
to do (or discuss), Palamon's name is inserted into it
(like a piece of fat into lean meat in order to make it
cook better).
3. Presumably the Schoolmaster has written a song
about Dido and her lover, Aeneas, who abandons her
in Virgil's *Aeneid.* The Jailer's Daughter imagines a
new ending in which Dido falls in love with Palamon
rather than Aeneas in the afterworld.
4. Charon demanded payment for ferrying dead
souls across the river Styx to the underworld. Hence

the custom of placing a coin on the tongues of the
dead.
5. Shrivel up from unrequited love. The liver was
supposed to be the seat of the passions.
6. One day while she was picking flowers, Proserpine was spotted by Pluto, who carried her off to the
underworld to be his queen. Her mother, Demeter,
got Zeus to allow her to spend six months on earth
each year.
7. A game played with male-female couples: one couple assigned to a place in the field called "hell"
attempted to entrap the other couples.
8. The traditional punishment for avarice was boiling
in oil (here, imagined as the sweat, "grease," given off
by usurers).

JAILER'S DAUGHTER   Lords and courtiers that have got maids
with child—they are in this place; they shall stand in fire up
to the navel and in ice up to th' heart, and there th'offending
part burns and the deceiving part freezes—in truth a very
40 grievous punishment, as one would think, for such a trifle.
Believe me, one would marry a leprous witch to be rid on't,
I'll assure you.

DOCTOR   How she continues this fancy! 'Tis not an engraft
madness but a most thick and profound melancholy.[9]

45 JAILER'S DAUGHTER   To hear there a proud° lady and a proud   *an aristocratic*
city wife° howl together! I were a beast an° I'd call it good   *merchant's wife / if*
sport. One cries, "Oh, this smoke!"; another, "This fire!"
One cries, "Oh, that ever I did it behind the arras!"° and   *wall hanging*
then howls; th'other curses a suing fellow and her garden
50 house.[1]
(*Sings.*) I will be true, my stars, my fate°—   *(unknown song)*
                    Exit JAILER'S DAUGHTER.

JAILER   What think you of her, sir?

DOCTOR   I think she has a perturbed mind, which I cannot
minister to.

55 JAILER   Alas, what then?

DOCTOR   Understand you she ever affected° any man ere she   *loved*
beheld Palamon?

JAILER   I was once, sir, in great hope she had fixed her liking
on this gentleman [*gesturing to* WOOER], my friend.

60 WOOER   I did think so too, and would account I had a great
penn'orth° on't to give half my state that both she and I at *bargain*
this present stood unfeignedly on the same terms.[2]

DOCTOR   That intemp'rate surfeit of her eye hath distempered
the other senses;[3] they may return and settle again to exe-
65 cute their preordained faculties, but they are now in a most
extravagant vagary.° This you must do: confine her to a place *errant wandering*
where the light may rather seem to steal in than be permit-
ted; take upon you [*gesturing to* WOOER]—young sir, her
friend—the name of Palamon; say you come to eat with her
70 and to commune of love. This will catch her attention, for
this her mind beats upon;° other objects that are inserted   *is obsessed with*
tween her mind and eye become the pranks and friskins° of   *tricks and frolics (tools)*
her madness. Sing to her such green songs[4] of love as she
says Palamon hath sung in prison. Come to her stuck in° as   *decorated with*
75 sweet flowers as the season is mistress of, and thereto make
an addition of some other compounded odors° which are   *blended perfumes*
grateful° to the sense. All this shall become° Palamon, for   *pleasant / befit*
Palamon can sing, and Palamon is sweet and ev'ry good
thing. Desire to eat with her, crave her, drink to her, and, still
80 among,[5] intermingle your petition of grace and acceptance
into her favor. Learn what maids have been her companions

---

9. It is not a rooted ("an engraft") madness, but a
deep depression (what today might be called love
sickness).
1. *a suing . . . garden house:* a persuasive wooer who
lured the lamenting woman into a house in a garden,
a site notorious for amorous trysts.
2. *to give . . . same terms:* if I could give half my prop-

erty so that she and I were as we were before her
madness.
3. Her excessive gazing at Palamon has thrown her
other senses off.
4. Songs typical of youth.
5. Among these pastimes.

and play-feres,° and let them repair to her with "Palamon" in   playmates
their mouths and appear with tokens, as if they suggested°   interceded
for him. It is a falsehood° she is in, which is with falsehoods   delusion
85 to be combated. This may bring° her to eat, to sleep, and   induce
reduce what's now out of square° in her into their former   disordered
law and regiment.° I have seen it approved⁶—how many   rule
times I know not—but to make the number more I have
great hope in this. I will between the passages° of this proj-   stages
90 ect come in with my appliance.⁷ Let us put it in execution
and hasten the success,° which, doubt not, will bring forth   outcome
comfort.   *Exeunt.*

5.1

Flourish. Enter THESEUS, PIRITHOUS, HIPPOLYTA,
[*and*] *Attendants.*
THESEUS   Now let 'em enter, and before the gods
  Tender their holy prayers. Let the temples
  Burn bright with sacred fires and the altars
  In hallowed clouds commend° their swelling incense   deliver
5   To those above us. Let no due° be wanting—   proper ritual
  They have a noble work in hand will° honor   that will
  The very powers that love 'em.
        Flourish of cornetts. Enter PALAMON *and* ARCITE *and*
        their KNIGHTS.
PIRITHOUS   Sir, they enter.
THESEUS   You valiant and strong-hearted enemies,
  You royal german° foes, that this day come   closely related
10 To blow that nearness° out that flames between ye: close kinship
  Lay by your anger for an hour and, dove-like,
  Before the holy altars of your helpers,
  The all-feared gods, bow down your stubborn bodies.
  Your ire° is more than mortal; so° your help be,   anger / so may
15 And—as the gods regard° ye—fight with justice.   are watching
  I'll leave you to your prayers, and betwixt ye
  I part my wishes.°   divide my hopes
PIRITHOUS   Honor crown the worthiest.
        Exeunt THESEUS *and his train* [*and* PIRITHOUS].
PALAMON   The glass° is running now that cannot finish   hourglass
  Till one of us expire. Think you but thus:
20 That were there aught in me which strove to show°   to expose itself as
  Mine enemy in this business, were't one eye
  Against another, arm oppressed by arm,
  I would destroy th'offender, coz—I would,
  Though parcel° of myself. Then from this gather   it were a piece
  How I should tender° you.   treat
25 ARCITE   I am in labor
  To push your name, your ancient love, our kindred°   kinship
  Out of my memory, and i'th' selfsame place

---

6. I have seen this type of treatment successfully
carried out.
7. My final mode of treatment (see 5.2).
5.1 Location: The forest. A single altar is probably
visible upstage, perhaps on the inner stage, for this
scene (at least from line 34) and the next two. Here,
it is dedicated to Mars. Q treats these first three
scenes as a single one. This makes sense if there are
three altars onstage, rather than, as assumed here,
only one, which successively represents three different altars, presumably in different locations.

To seat something I would confound.° So hoist we   *destroy*
The sails that must these vessels port, even where°   *bring to port, wherever*
The heavenly limiter° pleases.   *(of life)*

30 PALAMON   You speak well.
Before I turn,° let me embrace thee, cousin—
    [*They embrace.*]   *turn away*
This I shall never do again.
ARCITE   One farewell.
PALAMON   Why, let it be so. Farewell, coz.

       Exeunt PALAMON *and his* KNIGHTS.

ARCITE   Farewell, sir.
—Knights, kinsmen, lovers—yea, my sacrifices[1]—
35 True worshippers of Mars, whose spirit in you
Expels the seeds of fear and th'apprehension
Which still is farther off it[2]—go with me
Before the god of our profession.° There   *god we worship*
Require° of him the hearts of lions and   *Request*
40 The breath° of tigers; yea, the fierceness too;   *endurance*
Yea, the speed also—to go on,° I mean—   *go forward*
Else° wish we to be snails. You know my prize   *Otherwise (in retreat)*
Must be dragged out of blood; force and great feat
Must put my garland on, where she sticks
45 The queen of flowers.[3] Our intercession, then,
Must be to him° that makes the camp a cistern   *(Mars)*
Brimmed with the blood of men. Give me your aid,
And bend your spirits toward him.

    They [*prostrate themselves before the altar and then*]
    kneel [*to address Mars*].

Thou mighty one, that with thy power hast turned
50 Green Neptune° into purple,[4] whose approach   *god of the sea*
Comets prewarn,° whose havoc in vast field   *forecast*
Unearthèd° skulls proclaim, whose breath blows down   *As yet unburied*
The teeming Ceres' foison,[5] who dost pluck°   *pull down*
With hand armipotent[6] from forth blue clouds
55 The masoned° turrets, that both mak'st and break'st   *stone*
The stony girths° of cities; me thy pupil,   *walls*
Youngest follower of thy drum, instruct this day
With military skill, that to thy laud°   *praise*
I may advance my streamer° and by thee   *banner*
60 Be styled° the lord o'th' day; give me, great Mars,   *named*
Some token of thy pleasure.

    Here they fall on their faces as formerly, and there is
    heard clanging of armor, with a short thunder, as the
    burst of a battle, whereupon they all rise and bow to
    the altar.

O great corrector of enormous° times,   *disordered*
Shaker of o'er-rank° states; thou grand decider   *overripe*

---

1. The three knights may literally become human sacrifices from Arcite to Mars if Arcite loses the battle.
2. *th'apprehension . . . it*: the anticipation of a daunting situation, which always is more distant from fear itself.
3. *Must put . . . flowers*: Will win for my head (where Emilia already resides) the victor's laurels, of which she, as the most beautiful of flowers, is part.
4. Red with blood.
5. *whose breath . . . foison*: whose breath (wind) destroys the plenty of the fields produced by Ceres, goddess of agriculture.
6. *armipotent*: powerful in arms. TEXTUAL COMMENT For Shakespeare's use of archaic Chaucerian language, see Digital Edition TC 10.

Of dusty and old titles, that heal'st with blood° *through bloodletting*
65 The earth when it is sick, and cur'st the world
O'th' pleurisy° of people: I do take *excess*
Thy signs auspiciously, and in thy name
To my design march boldly. —Let us go.

Exeunt [ARCITE *and his* KNIGHTS].
Enter PALAMON *and his* KNIGHTS, *with the former observance.°* *same rituals as Arcite*

PALAMON   Our stars must glister° with new fire or be *fortunes must glisten*
70 Today extinct.° Our argument is love, *extinguished*
Which, if the goddess of it grant, she gives
Victory too. Then blend your spirits with mine,
You whose free nobleness° do make my cause *generous nobility*
Your personal hazard; to the goddess Venus
75 Commend° we our proceeding and implore *Commit*
Her power unto our party.

Here they kneel as formerly [*to address Venus*].
Hail, sovereign queen of secrets,[7] who hast power
To call the fiercest tyrant from his rage
And weep unto a girl;[8] that hast the might,
80 Even with an eye-glance, to choke° Mars' drum *silence*
And turn th'alarm° to whispers; that canst make *call to arms*
A cripple flourish with° his crutch and cure him *brandish*
Before Apollo;[9] that mayst force the king
To be his subject's vassal and induce
85 Stale gravity° to dance! The polled° bachelor— *old men / bald*
Whose youth, like wanton boys through bonfires,
Have skipped° thy flame—at seventy thou canst catch, *Has escaped*
And make him, to the scorn° of his hoarse throat, *(by listeners)*
Abuse young lays of love.[1] What godlike power
90 Hast thou not power upon? To Phoebus° thou *the sun*
Add'st flames hotter than his; the heavenly fires
Did scorch his mortal son,[2] thine him; the huntress,
All moist and cold, some say, began to throw
Her bow away and sigh.[3] Take to thy grace
95 Me, thy vowed soldier—who do bear thy yoke
As 'twere a wreath of roses, yet is° heavier *though the yoke is*
Than lead itself, stings more than nettles.
I have never been foul-mouthed against thy law;
Ne'er revealed secret, for I knew none—would not,
100 Had I kenned° all that were. I never practiced *known*
Upon[4] man's wife, nor would the libels° read *(against love)*
Of liberal° wits. I never at great feasts *licentious*
Sought to betray° a beauty, but have blushed *expose the affairs of*
At simpering sirs that did. I have been harsh
105 To large confessors[5] and have hotly asked them
If they had mothers; I had one—a woman—

---

7. As the speech later indicates, beginning at line 99, secrecy and discretion were essential components of the chivalric love code.
8. Make him weep for a girl (or, weep so much that he becomes like a girl).
9. Even more quickly than Apollo, the god of medicine.

1. Botch young lovers' love songs.
2. See note to 1.2.85–87.
3. *the huntress . . . sigh:* Diana, notwithstanding her vow of chastity, fell in love with the shepherd Endymion. *cold:* chaste.
4. *practiced / Upon:* wooed.
5. To those who boast of their love conquests.

And women 'twere they wronged. I knew a man
Of eighty winters—this I told them—who
A lass of fourteen brided.° 'Twas thy° power   *wedded / Venus's*
110   To put life into dust: the agèd cramp°   *cramp of old age*
Had screwed° his square foot round;   *twisted*
The gout had knit his fingers into knots;
Torturing convulsions from his globy eyes°   *swollen sockets*
Had almost drawn their spheres,° that° what was life   *eyeballs / so that*
115   In him seemed torture. This anatomy°   *skeleton*
Had by his young fair fere° a boy, and I   *mate*
Believed it was his, for she swore it was—
And who would not believe her? Brief,° I am,   *In short*
To those that prate and have done,[6] no companion;
120   To those that boast and have not,° a defier;   *have done nothing*
To those that would and cannot, a rejoicer.
Yea, him I do not love that tells close offices°   *secret matters*
The foulest way, nor names concealments[7] in
The boldest language. Such a one I am,
125   And vow that lover never yet made sigh
Truer than I. O, then, most soft sweet goddess,
Give me the victory of this question,° which   *conflict*
Is true love's merit,° and bless me with a sign   *just deserts*
Of thy great pleasure.
     Here music is heard; doves° are seen to flutter. They   *(sacred to Venus)*
     fall again upon their faces, then [rise to] their knees.
130   O thou that from eleven to ninety reign'st
In mortal bosoms, whose chase° is this world   *hunting ground*
And we in herds thy game, I give thee thanks
For this fair token which, being laid unto°   *added to*
Mine innocent true heart, arms in assurance
135   My body to this business. [*to his* KNIGHTS] Let us rise
And bow before the goddess.
     They bow.
                Time comes on.°   *It's time (for combat)*
         Exeunt [PALAMON *and his* KNIGHTS].
     Still° music of recorders. Enter EMILIA *in white, her hair*   *Soft*
     about her shoulders, [wearing] a wheaten wreath, [with]
     one [Woman] in white holding up her train, her hair stuck
     with flowers, [and] one [Woman] before her carrying a
     silver hind,[8] in which is conveyed incense and sweet odors,
     which being set up on the altar, her maids standing aloof,
     she sets fire to it. Then they curtsey and kneel.
EMILIA   O sacred, shadowy, cold, and constant queen;[9]
Abandoner of revels; mute, contemplative,
Sweet, solitary, white, as chaste and pure
140   As wind-fanned° snow; who to thy female knights   *wind-blown*
Allow'st no more blood° than will make a blush,   *sexual desire*
Which is their order's robe: I here thy priest
Am humbled fore thine altar. Oh, vouchsafe,
With that thy rare green eye, which never yet

---

6. To those who talk of deeds they have actually done.
7. Nor exposes what should remain hidden.
8. Female deer associated with virginity and hence linked to Diana.
9. *shadowy*: as goddess of the moon, Diana was associated with the night. See 1.3.52, 4.2.58, and 5.1.92–94, notes to these lines.

145 Beheld thing maculate,° look on thy virgin;   *tainted*
And, sacred silver mistress, lend thine ear—
Which ne'er heard scurrile° term, into whose port°   *scurrilous / opening*
Ne'er entered wanton° sound—to my petition,   *lewd*
Seasoned with holy fear.° This is my last   *pious awe*
150 Of vestal office.[1] I am bride-habited,°   *dressed as a bride*
But maiden-hearted; a husband I have 'pointed,°   *have been assigned*
But do not know him. Out of two, I should
Choose one and pray for his success, but I
Am guiltless of election.[2] Of mine eyes,
155 Were I to lose one, they are equal precious;
I could doom neither—that which perished should
Go to't unsentenced.[3] Therefore, most modest queen,
He of the two pretenders° that best loves me   *suitors*
And has the truest title in't,° let him   *claim to me*
160 Take off my wheaten garland,° or else grant   *Deflower me (see 1.1.64)*
The file and quality I hold I may
Continue in thy band.[4]
　　　Here the hind vanishes under the altar, and in the
　　　place ascends a rose tree, having one rose° up on it.   *(symbol of virginity)*
See what our general of ebbs and flows[5]
165 Out from the bowels of her holy altar
With sacred act advances: but one rose!
If well inspired,[6] this battle shall confound°   *destroy*
Both these brave knights and I, a virgin flower,
Must grow alone, unplucked.
　　　Here is heard a sudden twang of instruments, the rose
　　　falls from the tree[, and the tree descends].
The flower is fall'n; the tree descends. O mistress,
170 Thou here dischargest me. I shall be gathered[7]—
I think so—but I know not thine own will:
Unclasp thy mystery!° [*to her Women*] I hope she's pleased;   *Reveal your meaning*
Her signs were gracious.　　　　*They curtsey and exeunt.*

5.2

　　　Enter DOCTOR, JAILER, *and* WOOER *in [the] habit of°*   *dressed as*
　　　Palamon.
DOCTOR　Has this advice I told you done any good upon her?
WOOER　Oh, very much! The maids that kept her company
Have half persuaded her that I am Palamon.
Within this half-hour she came smiling to me,
5 And asked me what I would eat and when I would kiss her.
I told her "Presently!"° and kissed her twice.   *at once*
DOCTOR　'Twas well done; twenty times had been far better,
For there° the cure lies mainly.   *(in kissing)*
WOOER　　　　　　　　　Then she told me

1. *my . . . office:* my last duty as your virginal
devotee.
2. Am not guilty of having made a choice (and hence
of having betrayed my vows).
3. *of mine . . . unsentenced:* In "my eyes" the two
noble kinsmen "are equal precious," and hence it is
impossible for me to condemn either. Or, I couldn't
prefer to "lose one" of my eyes over the other, since
"they are equal precious"; I feel the same way about

the two men as I do about my eyes.
4. *grant . . . band:* grant that I may continue to hold
the rank and condition (of virginity) as one of your
devotees.
5. Our ruler of the moon and, hence, of tides.
6. If this is a true omen.
7. I shall be married; I shall lose my virginity.
5.2 Location: The prison.

She would watch° with me tonight, for well she knew   *stay up*
What hour my fit° would take me.   *urgent inclination*

10 DOCTOR   Let her do so—
And when your fit comes, fit her home,[1]
And presently.
WOOER   She would have me sing.
DOCTOR   You did so?
WOOER   No.
DOCTOR   'Twas very ill done then;
You should observe° her ev'ry way.   *accommodate*
WOOER   Alas,

15 I have no voice, sir, to confirm° her that way.   *persuade*
DOCTOR   That's all one,° if ye make a noise.   *That doesn't matter*
If she entreat° again, do anything—   *beg*
Lie with her if she ask you.
JAILER   Whoa there, Doctor!
DOCTOR   Yes, in the way of cure.
JAILER   But first, by your leave,
I'th' way of honesty.°   *(after marriage)*
20 DOCTOR   That's but a niceness.°   *an excessive scruple*
Ne'er cast your child away for honesty;[2]
Cure her first this way; then if she will° be honest,°   *wants to / chaste*
She has the path° before her.   *(of marriage)*
JAILER   Thank ye, Doctor.
DOCTOR   Pray bring her in and let's see how she is.
25 JAILER   I will, and tell her her Palamon stays° for her.   *waits*
But, Doctor, methinks you are i'th' wrong still.   *Exit* JAILER.
DOCTOR   Go, go!
You fathers are fine fools: her honesty?
An we should give her physic till we find that[3]—
30 WOOER   Why, do you think she is not honest, sir?
DOCTOR   How old is she?
WOOER   She's eighteen.
DOCTOR   She may be,
But that's all one; 'tis nothing to our purpose.°   *it makes no difference*
Whate'er her father says, if you perceive
Her mood inclining that way that I spoke of,
35 *Videlicet*,° the way of flesh—you have me?   *Namely*
WOOER   Yes, very well, sir.
DOCTOR   Please her appetite,
And do it home;° it cures her, *ipso facto*,[4]   *completely*
The melancholy humor° that infects her.   *mood (medical)*
WOOER   I am of your mind, Doctor.
        Enter JAILER [*and*] JAILER'S DAUGHTER, *mad*.
40 DOCTOR   You'll find it so. She comes; pray, humor her.
JAILER [*to* JAILER'S DAUGHTER]   Come, your love Palamon stays
    for you, child,
And has done this long hour, to visit you.
JAILER'S DAUGHTER   I thank him for his gentle patience;

1. Fully serve her needs (have sex with her).
2. A paradox: don't lose your daughter (to her madness) in order to keep her (chaste).
3. If we were to treat her until we could be sure of her virginity (the obvious continuation of the unfinished thought being, we'd be treating her forever).
4. By the very act (*ipso facto*) of having sex, she'll be cured. The Doctor assumes, correctly in the event, that the Daughter suffers from hysteria, thought to be caused by a wandering womb and cured by intercourse.

He's a kind gentleman, and I am much bound° to him.   *obliged*
Did you ne'er see the horse he gave me?

45 JAILER   Yes.

JAILER'S DAUGHTER   How do you like him?

JAILER   He's a very fair° one.   *beautiful*

JAILER'S DAUGHTER   You never saw him dance?

JAILER   No.

JAILER'S DAUGHTER   I have, often.
He dances very finely, very comely—
And for a jig, come cut and long tail to him,[5]
He turns ye like a top.

50 JAILER   That's fine indeed.

JAILER'S DAUGHTER   He'll dance the morris twenty mile an hour,
And that will founder the best hobbyhorse[6]—
If I have any skill°—in all the parish;   *judgment*
And gallops to the tune of "Light o' Love."[7]
What think you of this horse?

55 JAILER   Having these virtues,
I think he might be brought° to play at tennis.   *taught*

JAILER'S DAUGHTER   Alas, that's nothing.

JAILER   Can he write and read too?

JAILER'S DAUGHTER   A very fair hand, and casts himself th'accounts[8]
Of all his hay and provender—that ostler
60 Must rise betimes that cozens° him. You know   *get up early to cheat*
The chestnut mare the Duke has?

JAILER   Very well.

JAILER'S DAUGHTER   She is horribly in love with him, poor beast!
But he is like his master—coy° and scornful.   *aloof*

JAILER   What dowry has she?

JAILER'S DAUGHTER   Some two hundred bottles°   *bales of hay*
65 And twenty strike° of oats; but he'll ne'er have her.   *bushels*
He lisps in 's neighing, able to entice a miller's mare.[9]
He'll be the death of her.

DOCTOR   What stuff she utters!

JAILER [to JAILER'S DAUGHTER]   Make curtsey—here your love comes.

WOOER [approaching JAILER'S DAUGHTER]   Pretty soul,
How do ye? [She curtsies.] That's a fine maid; there's a curtsey!

70 JAILER'S DAUGHTER   Yours to command i'th' way of honesty.
—How far is't now to th'end o'th' world, my masters?

DOCTOR   Why, a day's journey, wench.

JAILER'S DAUGHTER   Will you go with me?

WOOER   What shall we do there, wench?

JAILER'S DAUGHTER   Why, play at stool-ball;[1]
What is there else to do?

WOOER   I am content
If we shall keep our wedding° there.   *As long as we marry*

---

5. *He . . . him:* He dances finely no matter what horse he is compared with. *cut:* a horse with a docked tail (see note to 3.4.22). There is sexual wordplay throughout this scene.
6. That will lame ("founder") the best morris dancer. *hobbyhorse:* one extremely agile morris dancer was dressed as a horse and imitated its movements.
7. Popular ballad, also referred to in *Much Ado About Nothing* 3.4.39 and *The Two Gentlemen of*
Verona 1.2.83. The title means "inconstant in love."
8. He has beautiful penmanship and reckons his own expenses.
9. *He . . . mare:* He's such a smooth talker he could seduce even a miller's mare—a workhorse renowned for its steadfast, circular plodding and, hence, least likely to be distracted.
1. A game, somewhat like cricket, played with ball and bat by women or by men and women together.

75 JAILER'S DAUGHTER 'Tis true—
    For there, I will assure you, we shall find
    Some blind priest for the purpose that will venture
    To marry us; for here they are nice° and foolish.   *too scrupulous*
    Besides, my father must be hanged tomorrow,
80 And that would be a blot i'th' business.
    Are not you Palamon?
WOOER   Do not you know me?
JAILER'S DAUGHTER Yes, but you care not for me; I have nothing
    But this poor petticoat and two coarse smocks.°   *undergarments*
WOOER That's all one—I will have you.
JAILER'S DAUGHTER   Will you surely?
WOOER Yes, by this fair hand, will I.
    [*He takes her hand.*]
85 JAILER'S DAUGHTER   We'll to bed, then.
WOOER E'en when you will.°   *Whenever you like*
    [*He kisses her.*]
JAILER'S DAUGHTER [*She rubs off the kiss.*] O sir, you would fain
    be nibbling!
WOOER Why do you rub my kiss off?
JAILER'S DAUGHTER   'Tis a sweet one,
    And will perfume me finely against° the wedding.   *in preparation for*
    [*She gestures to the* DOCTOR.] Is not this your cousin, Arcite?
DOCTOR   Yes, sweetheart,
90 And I am glad my cousin Palamon
    Has made so fair a choice.
JAILER'S DAUGHTER   Do you think he'll have me?
DOCTOR Yes, without doubt.
JAILER'S DAUGHTER [*to* JAILER] Do you think so too?
JAILER   Yes.
JAILER'S DAUGHTER We shall have many children.
    [*to* DOCTOR]   Lord, how you're grown!
    My Palamon, I hope, will grow too,² finely,
95 Now he's at liberty. Alas, poor chicken,
    He was kept down with hard meat° and ill lodging—   *coarse food*
    But I'll kiss him up again.
        Enter a MESSENGER.
MESSENGER What do you here? You'll lose the noblest sight
    That e'er was seen!
JAILER   Are they i'th' field?
MESSENGER   They are.
    You bear a charge° there too.   *have a duty*
100 JAILER   I'll away straight;
    [*to* DOCTOR] I must e'en leave you here.
DOCTOR   Nay, we'll go with you—
    I will not lose the sight.
JAILER [*gesturing to* JAILER'S DAUGHTER] How did you like her?
DOCTOR I'll warrant you, within these three or four days
    I'll make her right again. [*to* WOOER] You must not from her,
    But still preserve° her in this way.   *keep treating*
105 WOOER   I will.
DOCTOR Let's get her in.

2. Get fat; have an erection.

WOOER [*to* JAILER'S DAUGHTER]   Come, sweet—we'll go to dinner,
  And then we'll play at cards.
JAILER'S DAUGHTER   And shall we kiss too?
WOOER   A hundred times.
JAILER'S DAUGHTER   And twenty?
WOOER   Ay, and twenty.
DAUGHTER   And then we'll sleep together.
DOCTOR [*aside to* WOOER]   Take her offer.
WOOER [*to* JAILER'S DAUGHTER]   Yes, marry, will we.
110 JAILER'S DAUGHTER   But you shall not hurt me.
WOOER   I will not, sweet.
JAILER'S DAUGHTER   If you do, love, I'll cry.   *Exeunt.*

5.3

Flourish. Enter THESEUS, HIPPOLYTA, EMILIA,
  PIRITHOUS, *and some Attendants.*
EMILIA [*hanging back, aside to* PIRITHOUS]   I'll no step further.
PIRITHOUS   Will you lose this sight?
EMILIA   I had rather see a wren hawk at° a fly   attack in midair
  Than this decision. Ev'ry blow that falls
  Threats a brave life; each stroke laments
5 The place whereon it falls and sounds more like
  A bell° than blade. I will stay here: death knell
  It is enough my hearing shall be punished
  With what shall happen, gainst the which there is
  No deafing, but to hear, not taint mine eye[1]
  With dread sights it may shun.
10 PIRITHOUS [*calling ahead to* THESEUS]   Sir, my good lord,
  Your sister will no further.
THESEUS   Oh, she must.
  She shall see deeds of honor in their kind,°   true nature
  Which sometime show well penciled.° Nature now   even when just drawn
  Shall make and act° the story, the belief   invent and perform
15 Both sealed with eye and ear.[2] —You must be present:
  You are the victor's meed,° the prize and garland,   reward
  To crown the question's title.[3]
EMILIA   Pardon me,
  If I were there, I'd wink°—   keep my eyes closed
THESEUS   You must be there:
  This trial is, as 'twere, i'th' night, and you
  The only star to shine.
20 EMILIA   I am extinct.°   extinguished
  There is but envy° in that light which shows   malice
  The one the other.[4] Darkness—which ever was
  The dam° of horror, who does stand accursed   mother
  Of many mortal millions—may even now,
25 By casting her black mantle over both
  That° neither could find other, get herself   So that

5.3 Location: The forest, near the tournament field.
1. *there . . . eye:* there is no way to block out the noise
in order not to hear, but I will not upset my sight
("taint mine eye").
2. *the belief . . . ear:* the story will be rendered credi-

ble by all that is seen and heard.
3. To crown the rightful victor in the dispute.
4. *shows . . . other:* reveals Palamon to Arcite, and
vice versa.

Some part of a good name, and many a murder
Set off whereto° she's guilty.   *Atone for of which*

HIPPOLYTA   You must go.

EMILIA   In faith, I will not.

THESEUS   Why, the knights must kindle

30   Their valor at your eye. Know of this war
You are the treasure, and must needs be by°   *nearby*
To give the service pay.°   *reward the winner*

EMILIA   Sir, pardon me—
The title of a kingdom may be tried
Out of itself.°   *Outside the kingdom*

THESEUS   Well, well, then—at your pleasure.

35   Those that remain with you could wish their office
To any of their enemies.

HIPPOLYTA   Farewell, sister.
I am like to know your husband fore yourself
By some small start of time. He whom the gods
Do of the two know° best, I pray them he   *know to be*
40   Be made your lot.

Exeunt [all except EMILIA].

EMILIA *[comparing the kinsmen's portraits]*   Arcite is gently
visaged,° yet his eye   *has a gentle expression*
Is like an engine bent[5] or a sharp weapon
In a soft sheath; mercy and manly courage
Are bedfellows in his visage. Palamon
45   Has a most menacing aspect; his brow
Is graved° and seems to bury what it frowns on—   *furrowed*
Yet sometime 'tis not so, but alters to°   *according to*
The quality° of his thoughts. Long time his eye   *nature*
Will dwell upon his object. Melancholy
50   Becomes° him nobly. So does Arcite's mirth,   *Suits*
But Palamon's sadness is a kind of mirth,
So mingled as if mirth did make him sad
And sadness merry. Those darker humors° that   *moods*
Stick misbecomingly° on others, on him   *Seem misplaced*
55   Live in fair dwelling.[6]

Cornetts. Trumpets sound as to a charge.

Hark how yon spurs to spirit° do incite   *bravery*
The princes to their proof!° Arcite may win me—   *to prove themselves*
And yet may Palamon wound Arcite to
The spoiling of his figure.° Oh, what pity   *(so as to disfigure him)*
60   Enough for such a chance?[7] If I were by,
I might do hurt, for they would glance their eyes
Toward my seat, and in that motion might
Omit a ward or forfeit an offense
Which craved that very time.[8] It is much better
65   I am not there. Oh, better never born
Than minister to such harm!

Cornetts. A great cry and noise within crying,
"A Palamon!"[9]

5. Is like a weapon, such as a bow, ready to be
released.
6. *on him . . . dwelling:* suit him well.
7. Would be sufficient for such a (sad) turn of events.

8. *might . . . time:* might miss the perfect moment for
a defensive parry or an offensive move.
9. War cry supporting Palamon.

Enter SERVANT.

What is the chance?°   *Who won*

SERVANT The cry's "A Palamon!"

EMILIA Then he has won. 'Twas ever likely—
He looked all grace and success, and he is

70 Doubtless the prim'st° of men. I prithee, run   *most perfect*
And tell me how it goes.

Shout, and cornetts; crying, "A Palamon!"

SERVANT   Still "Palamon!"

EMILIA Run and inquire.   [*Exit* SERVANT.]
[*to Arcite's portrait*]   Poor servant,° thou hast lost.   *lover (Arcite)*
Upon my right side still I° wore thy picture,   *I always*
Palamon's on the left; why so, I know not—

75 I had no end° in't—else chance would have it so.   *purpose*
On the sinister side the heart lies: Palamon
Had the best boding chance.[1]

Another cry and shout within, and cornetts.

This burst of clamor
Is sure th'end o'th' combat.

Enter SERVANT.

SERVANT They said that Palamon had Arcite's body

80 Within an inch o'th' pyramid, that the cry
Was general "A Palamon!" But anon
Th'assistants° made a brave redemption,° and   *knights / rescue*
The two bold titlers° at this instant are   *fighters for the title*
Hand-to-hand at it.

EMILIA   Were they° metamorphosed   *I wish they were*

85 Both into one! Oh, why? There were no woman
Worth so composed a man.[2] Their single share,
Their nobleness peculiar to them, gives
The prejudice of disparity—value's shortness—
To any lady breathing.[3]

Cornetts. Cry within: "Arcite! Arcite!"

More exulting?
"Palamon" still?

90 SERVANT   Nay, now the sound is "Arcite!"

EMILIA I prithee, lay attention to the cry;
Set both thine ears to th' business.

Cornetts. A great shout and cry: "Arcite! Victory!"

SERVANT   The cry is
"Arcite!" and "Victory!" Hark! "Arcite! Victory!"
The combat's consummation° is proclaimed   *conclusion*
By the wind instruments.

95 EMILIA   Half-sights saw°   *Mere glimpses showed*
That Arcite was no babe. God's lid,° his richness   *By God's eyelid*
And costliness of spirit looked through him; it could
No more be hid in him than fire in flax,°   *straw*
Than humble banks can go to law with° waters   *can battle*

100 That drift° winds force to raging. I did think   *driving*

---

1. *On . . . chance:* The location of Palamon's picture—on Emilia's left ("sinister") side, where her
heart is—portended victory, since the contest is
about love.
2. *There . . . man:* No woman could be worthy of this

composite man made up of both Palamon and Arcite.
3. *Their single . . . breathing:* No woman could have
as much nobility as either one of them. *their single
share:* each one's value.

Good Palamon would miscarry—yet I knew not
Why I did think so. Our reasons are not prophets
When oft our fancies are. They are coming off.°   *leaving the field*
Alas, poor Palamon!
      Cornetts. Enter THESEUS, HIPPOLYTA, PIRITHOUS,
      ARCITE *as victor, and Attendants.*
105 THESEUS Lo, where our sister is in expectation,
Yet quaking and unsettled. —Fairest Emily,
The gods by their divine arbitrament°   *arbitration*
Have given you this knight [*indicating* ARCITE]—he is a
    good one
As ever struck at head. Give me your hands:
110 [*joining their hands*] Receive you her, you him; be plighted
    with
A love that grows as you decay.
ARCITE   Emily,
To buy you I have lost what's dearest to me,
Save what is bought°—and yet I purchase cheaply,   *(Emilia)*
As I do rate your value.
THESEUS   O loved sister,
115 He speaks now of as brave a knight as e'er
Did spur a noble steed. Surely the gods
Would have him die a bachelor, lest his race
Should show i'th' world too godlike. His behavior
So charmed me that methought Alcides° was   *Hercules*
120 To him a sow of lead.[4] If I could praise
Each part of him to th'all I have spoke,[5] your Arcite
Did° not lose by't. For he that was thus good   *Would*
Encountered yet his better. I have heard
Two emulous Philomels[6] beat the ear o'th' night
125 With their contentious throats—now one the higher,
Anon the other, then again the first,
And by and by out-breasted—that the sense[7]
Could not be judge between 'em. So it fared
Good space° between these kinsmen, till heavens did   *For a good while*
130 Make hardly° one the winner. [*to* ARCITE] Wear the garland   *Barely make*
With joy that you have won. —For the subdued,°   *losers*
Give them our present° justice, since I know   *immediate*
Their lives but pinch° 'em. Let it here be done.   *torment*
The scene's not for our seeing; go we hence,
135 Right joyful, with some sorrow. [*to* ARCITE] Arm° your prize;   *Give your arm to*
I know you will not lose her. —Hippolyta,
I see one eye of yours conceives a tear,
The which it will deliver.
      Flourish.
EMILIA   Is this winning?
O all you heavenly powers, where is your mercy?
140 But that your wills have said it must be so—
And charge me live to comfort this unfriended,°   *deprived of his friend*

---

4. *To . . . lead:* Compared to him, like an ingot.
5. *to . . . spoke:* in the same way I have praised Palamon as a whole.
6. Two rival nightingales. In Greek mythology, Philomela was raped by her sister's husband, who cut out her tongue so she couldn't accuse him. By weaving the story into cloth, she nonetheless informed her sister, who fed her husband their son. The gods turned the sister into a nightingale and Philomela into a swallow.
7. *And . . . sense:* And in turn outsung, so that the sense of hearing.

This miserable prince, that cuts away
A life more worthy from him than all women—
I should and would die too.

HIPPOLYTA   Infinite pity,
145   That four such eyes should be so fixed on one°   *one woman*
That two must needs be blind for't.⁸

THESEUS   So it is.   *Exeunt.*

5.4

Enter PALAMON *and his* KNIGHTS, *pinioned,* JAILER,
Executioner, and Guard [bringing in a block].

PALAMON   There's many a man alive that hath outlived
The love o'th' people; yea, i'th' selfsame state
Stands many a father with his child—some comfort
We have by so considering. We expire,
5   And not without men's pity; to live still,
Have their good wishes.¹ We prevent°   *avoid*
The loathsome misery of age, beguile°   *cheat*
The gout and rheum° that in lag° hours attend°   *coughing / final / wait*
For gray approachers.° We come toward the gods   *(to death)*
10   Young and unwappered,° not halting under° crimes   *untired / weighed down by*
Many and stale°—that sure shall please the gods   *of long duration*
Sooner than such,° to give us nectar with 'em,   *(sinful old men)*
For we are more clear° spirits. [*to his* KNIGHTS] My dear   *innocent*
    kinsmen,
Whose lives for this poor comfort are laid down,
You have sold 'em° too, too cheap.   *(your lives)*

15 FIRST KNIGHT   What ending could be
Of more content? O'er us the victors have
Fortune, whose title° is as momentary   *claim*
As to us death is certain. A grain of honor
They not o'er-weigh us.²

SECOND KNIGHT   Let us bid farewell,
20   And with our patience anger tottering° Fortune,   *unstable*
Who at her certain'st reels.³

THIRD KNIGHT   Come, who begins?

PALAMON   E'en he that led you to this banquet shall
Taste to you all.⁴ [*to* JAILER] Aha, my friend, my friend,
Your gentle daughter gave me freedom once;
25   You'll see't done° now for ever. Pray, how does she?   *see me set free*
I heard she was not well; her kind of ill°   *illness*
Gave me some sorrow.

JAILER   Sir, she's well restored,
And to be married shortly.

PALAMON   By my short life,
I am most glad on't. 'Tis the latest° thing   *last*

---

8. That two eyes must be blinded (in death); that two
men could be so blind as to fight to the death for one
woman.
5.4 Location: Scene continues.
1. *We expire . . . wishes:* Even though we are to die,
we have men's good wishes that we might go on
living.

2. *A grain . . . us:* They have no more honor than we
do.
3. Who, when she seems most certain, suddenly
changes direction.
4. Taste (death) first, like the servant at a state banquet who was required to taste the food before the
king and guests to make sure it wasn't poisoned.

30 I shall be glad of—prithee, tell her so.
Commend me to her, and to piece her portion°   *increase her dowry*
Tender her this.
    [*He gives the* JAILER *a purse.*]
FIRST KNIGHT   Nay, let's be offerers all.
SECOND KNIGHT   Is it a maid?°   *virgin*
PALAMON
                        Verily, I think so—
A right good creature, more to me° deserving   *from me*
Than I can 'quite° or speak of.   *requite*
35 ALL KNIGHTS   Commend us to her.
    They give their purses.
JAILER   The gods requite you all and make her thankful.
PALAMON   Adieu—and let my life be now as short
As my leave-taking.
    [*He*] *lies on the block.*
FIRST KNIGHT   Lead, courageous cousin.
FIRST *and* SECOND KNIGHTS   We'll follow cheerfully—
    A great noise within, crying, "Run! Save! Hold!"
    Enter in haste a MESSENGER.
40 MESSENGER   Hold, hold! Oh, hold, hold, hold!
    Enter PIRITHOUS *in haste.*
PIRITHOUS   Hold, ho! It is a cursèd haste you made
If you have done° so quickly. —Noble Palamon,   *finished*
The gods will show their glory in a life
That thou art yet to lead.
PALAMON   Can that be,
45 When Venus, I have said, is false? How do things fare?
PIRITHOUS   Arise, great sir, and give the tidings ear
That are most rarely sweet and bitter.
PALAMON [*rising from the block*]   What
Hath waked us from our dream?
PIRITHOUS   List,° then. Your cousin,   *Listen*
Mounted upon a steed that Emily
50 Did first bestow on him, a black one, owing°   *owning*
Not a hair-worth of white—which some will say
Weakens his price, and many will not buy
His goodness with this note,[5] which superstition
Here finds allowance°—on this horse is Arcite   *gains support*
55 Trotting the stones of Athens, which the calkins
Did rather tell than trample,[6] for the horse
Would make his length° a mile if't pleased his rider   *length of stride*
To put pride in him.° As he thus went counting   *let him show his spirit*
The flinty pavement, dancing as 'twere to th' music
60 His own hoofs made—for, as they say, from iron
Came music's origin[7]—what envious flint,°   *cobblestone*
Cold as old Saturn[8] and, like him, possessed
With fire malevolent, darted a spark,

---

5. *Weakens . . . note:* Makes him less valuable, because dark horses were considered vicious or ill-omened, and "many will not buy" such a horse, despite his good qualities, because of this feature.
6. *which . . . trample:* the horse's gait was so long and light that its feet seemed more to count ("tell") the cobbles one by one than to trample them. *calkins:* turned-down edges of a horseshoe.

7. Pythagoras is supposed to have discovered music when walking through a blacksmith's forge.
8. According to Chaucer's *Knight's Tale*, Saturn, father of Jupiter, was responsible for the reversal of fortune described here, because he had promised Venus that Palamon would win Emilia. Shakespeare and Fletcher limit Saturn's responsibility to a simile.

Or what fierce sulfur else to this end made,[9]
65 I comment not. The hot horse, hot as fire,
Took toy° at this and fell to what disorder   *a capricious dislike*
His power could give his will, bounds, comes on end,°   *bucks and rears*
Forgets school-doing°—being therein trained   *school training*
And of kind *manège*.° Pig-like he whines   *well disciplined*
70 At the sharp rowel,° which he frets at rather   *spur*
Than any jot obeys, seeks all foul means
Of boist'rous and rough jadery° to disseat   *behavior like a nag*
His lord, that kept it bravely.° When naught served— *who kept his seat well*
When neither curb° would crack, girth break, nor diff'ring° *jaw restraint/ / various*
plunges
75 Disroot his rider whence he grew,° but that   *was fixed*
He kept him tween his legs—on his hind hoofs,
On end he stands,
That Arcite's legs, being higher than his head,
Seemed with strange art to hang. His victor's wreath
80 Even then fell off his head, and presently
Backward the jade comes o'er, and his full poise°   *weight*
Becomes the rider's load. Yet is he living,
But such a vessel 'tis that floats but for
The surge that next approaches.[1] He much desires
85 To have some speech with you.
      Enter THESEUS, HIPPOLYTA, EMILIA, [*and*] ARCITE, *in a*
      chair [*carried by Attendants*].
                                 Lo, he appears.
PALAMON   Oh, miserable end of our alliance!
The gods are mighty. Arcite, if thy heart—
Thy worthy, manly heart—be yet unbroken,
Give me thy last words. I am Palamon,
One that yet loves thee dying.
90 ARCITE   Take Emilia,
And with her all the world's joy. Reach° thy hand—   *Give me*
Farewell. I have told° my last hour. I was false,   *counted*
Yet never treacherous.[2] Forgive me, cousin.
One kiss from fair Emilia. [EMILIA *kisses him.*] 'Tis done.
Take her. I die. [*He dies.*]
95 PALAMON   Thy brave soul seek Elysium!
EMILIA   I'll close thine eyes, prince; blessed souls be with thee.
Thou art a right good man, and while I live,
This day I give to tears.
PALAMON   And I to honor.
THESEUS   In this place first you fought; e'en very here
100 I sundered you.° Acknowledge to the gods   *separated your fight*
Our thanks that you are living.
His part is played and, though it were too short,
He did it well. Your day is lengthened, and
The blissful dew of heaven does arrose° you.   *sprinkle*
105 The powerful Venus well hath graced her altar
And given you your love. Our master Mars

---

9. Or some spark of hellfire made for this purpose.
1. *But such . . . approaches:* But he can live only until
the next onslaught (like a boat that can stay afloat
only until the next wave hits).

2. *I was . . . treacherous:* I was "false" to our friendship (because Palamon did see Emilia first) but
"never treacherous" in vying for Emilia's love.

Hast vouched° his oracle and to Arcite gave *made good on*
The grace of the contention.° So the deities *victory in the battle*
Have showed due justice.
    [*to the Attendants, indicating Arcite's corpse*]
               Bear this hence.

PALAMON   O cousin,

110 That we should things desire which do cost us
The loss of our desire! That naught could buy
Dear love but loss of dear love!
    [*Arcite's corpse is carried out.*]
THESEUS   Never Fortune
Did play a subtler game. The conquered triumphs;
The victor has the loss. Yet in the passage° *proceedings*

115 The gods have been most equal.° —Palamon, *impartial*
Your kinsman hath confessed the right o'th' lady° *the right to Emilia*
Did lie in you,° for you first saw her and *Was yours*
Even then proclaimed your fancy. He restored her
As your stolen jewel and desired your spirit

120 To send him hence forgiven. The gods my justice
Take from my hand, and they themselves become
The executioners.° Lead your lady off, *executors of justice*
And call your lovers from the stage of death,° *friends from the scaffold*
Whom I adopt my friends. A day or two

125 Let us look sadly and give grace unto
The funeral of Arcite, in whose end° *after which*
The visages of bridegrooms we'll put on
And smile with Palamon—for whom an hour,
But one hour since, I was as dearly sorry

130 As glad of Arcite, and am now as glad
As for him sorry. O you heavenly charmers,° *gods who enchant us*
What things you make of us! For what we lack,
We laugh;° for what we have, are sorry, still *enjoy contemplating*
Are children in some kind. Let us be thankful

135 For that which is, and with you leave dispute
That are above our question.³ Let's go off,
And bear us like° the time.   *Flourish. Exeunt.* *act in accordance with*

Epilogue

[*Enter* EPILOGUE.]
EPILOGUE   I would now ask ye how ye like the play,
But, as it is with schoolboys, cannot say;° *speak*
I am cruel fearful.° Pray yet stay awhile¹ *horribly afraid*
And let me look upon ye. No man smile?

5 Then it goes hard, I see. He that has
Loved a young handsome wench, then, show his face—
'Tis strange if none be here—and if he will,
Against his conscience° let him hiss and kill *actual feelings*
Our market.° 'Tis in vain, I see, to stay° ye; *Our prospects / prevent*

10 Have at the worst can come,° then! Now, what say ye? *Do your worst*
And yet mistake me not. I am not bold;
We have no such cause.° If the tale we have told, *reason to invite criticism*

---

3. *with . . . question:* cease to dispute with you, who
are beyond our questioning.

Epilogue
1. Don't hiss or applaud yet.

For 'tis no other, any way content° ye—   please
For to that honest purpose it was meant ye°—   intended for you
15 We have our end,° and ye shall have ere long,   achieved our aim
I dare say, many a better, to prolong
Your old loves to us.° We and all our might°   (the actors) / all we can do
Rest at your service. Gentlemen, good night! *Flourish.* [*Exit.*]

APPENDICES

APPENDICES

Attributed Poems

None of the attributed poems is incontrovertibly by Shakespeare, though the case is much better for some than for others. (See the Textual Introduction.) "A song, 'Shall I die?'"—probably not by Shakespeare—is noteworthy mainly as a virtuoso display of rhyming: there are usually eight pairs of rhyme words in each eight-line stanza, with the rhymes occurring as often as every three syllables and on occasion every two syllables ("Being set, lips met," line 31). Several of the other poems are, like the last part of "The Phoenix and Turtle," elegies—compositions in memory of the dead, though sometimes written while the subject was still alive. The first of the two epitaphs on the usurer John Combe reveals a conventional hostility to usury. The second, however, deploys the complex, sometimes positive, metaphorical relationship between usury and breeding characteristic of the early sonnets. Combe

> did gather [wealth from usury]
> To make the poor his issue [heirs]; he, their father,
> . . . [made] record of his tilth and seeds.
>
> (lines 3–5)

Urging marriage and a family, Sonnet 3 speaks of "the tillage of thy husbandry" (line 6). And Sonnet 6 argues:

> That use is not forbidden usury
> Which happies those that pay the willing loan:
> That's for thyself to breed another thee,
> Or ten times happier, be it ten for one.
>
> (lines 5–8)

Thus, in the sonnets, the language of usury helps clarify paternity, whereas in the second epitaph the language of paternity helps clarify usury. In both, however, the two terms are mutually illuminating. The last line quoted from Sonnet 6 is also reminiscent of the opening of the first epitaph: "Ten in the hundred here lies engraved; / A hundred to ten his soul is ne'er saved." Both refer to the highest legal interest rate—ten in a hundred, or 10 percent. But where the sonnet converts the allusion into a positive image, the elegy reverses the interest rate to denote the long odds against the usurer's salvation.

Similarly, "Verses on the Stanley Tomb at Tong" closely parallels the language of some of Shakespeare's sonnets concerned with the destructive power of time. The "register" and the "sky-aspiring pyramids" (East end 3, West end 2) also appear in Sonnet 123 ("pyramids built up," "registers," lines 2, 9). Closer still is the connection to Sonnet 55: "Not marble nor the gilded monuments / Of princes shall outlive this powerful rhyme" (lines 1–2). Stanley's "fame is more perpetual than these stones" (East 4); "Not monumental stone preserves our fame" (West 1). Stanley's "memory," however, "[s]hall outlive marble and defacers' hands" as well as "time's consumption" (West 3, 4, 5), just as "memory" need not worry that "war shall statues overturn" and is not dependent on "unswept stone besmeared with sluttish time" in Sonnet 55 (lines 8, 5, 4). Although the guarantee of immortality seems to rest on Stanley's life rather than the "powerful rhyme" of the sonnet (line 2), the end is the same: Stanley "is not dead; he doth but sleep" (East 2), while in the sonnet, "'[g]ainst death and all oblivious enmity / Shall you pace forth" (lines 9–10). Ultimately, poetic fame in the sonnet lasts only "till the judgment that yourself arise" (on Judgment Day, line 13); analogously, "Stanley for whom this stands shall stand in heaven" (West 6). The pun on the name in this concluding line ("Stanley/stands/stand") is similar to the sign of the author's hand left in "Upon a Pair of Gloves that Master Sent to his Mistress," where "[t]he will is all" recalls Shakespeare's emphatic references to his first name in Sonnets 135 and 136.

"Upon a Pair of Gloves" seems to reveal the poet intruding himself into a composition ostensibly from Alexander Aspinall to his (future?) wife; the "Epitaph on Himself" is strikingly impersonal. The lack of specificity may in this case be a poetic signature, however. By 1616, perhaps only Shakespeare could have written about Shakespeare without reference to his theatrical or literary career. This modesty coincides with an open threat: "cursed be he that moves my bones" (line 4). The apparently conventional warning was designed to forestall the very real danger of his body being dug up to make room for fresh corpses; in this case, it proved successful.

WALTER COHEN

SELECTED BIBLIOGRAPHY

Kerrigan, John. "Shakespeare, Elegy, and Epitaph 1557–1640." *The Oxford Handbook of Shakespeare's Poetry.* Ed. Jonathan F. S. Post. Oxford: Oxford UP, 2013. 225–44. Links "The Phoenix and Turtle" to the elegies attributed to Shakespeare, to the volume in which the poem appeared, to the period's competition—in poetry and in stone—in constructing memorials, and to the relationship between Catholic Wales and Protestant England.
Schoenfeldt, Michael. *The Cambridge Introduction to Shakespeare's Poetry.* Cambridge: Cambridge UP, 2010. 135–43. Focuses on the "fantasies of Shakespearean authorship" in the attributed poems.

TEXTUAL INTRODUCTION

The present edition prints nine poems attributed to William Shakespeare in the seventeenth century. None of them can be confirmed as written by the author. Nonetheless, scholars have made compelling cases for the funeral verse (Poems 3, 4, 5, 6, 7, 9), with circumstantial evidence supporting attribution for the epitaph on Elias James (Poem 5), that on the Stanley tomb at Tong (Poem 3), and especially the second of the two poems on John Combe (Poem 7).

James was a brewer whose establishment was located near Shakespeare's accommodation in Puddle Dock Hill, London, and Combe was a noted usurer in Stratford-upon-Avon, while Shakespeare himself is known to have had links with the Stanley family. It is also not impossible that he wrote the epitaph upon himself (Poem 9); it has become hard to think about this wry poem as being written by someone other than the Bard. Of course, Shakespeare was a friend and rival of Ben Jonson, even if the capping of verses here (Poem 4) feels apocryphal. The gift poem to Alexander Aspinall (Poem 2), a schoolmaster in Stratford, is a smaller matter, however charming, while the verse on James I (Poem 8)—by the leading playwright of the King's Men—feels appropriately weighty. The longest of the poems, "A Song, 'Shall I Die?'" (Poem 1), is now believed by few to have been written by Shakespeare.

The texts for the nine attributed poems come from a variety of sources: manuscripts, books, engravings, funeral monuments themselves. "A Song, 'Shall I die?'" exists in two manuscripts: one at Yale University and one in the Bodleian Library (dating to the 1630s). Since only the latter attributes the poem to Shakespeare, it is used here as control text; its readings also tend to be preferred, although, as the list of variants indicates, in a few cases recent editors have found the Yale version preferable. Consensus continues to build denying Shakespeare's authorship.

Only one contemporary attribution exists for "Upon a Pair of Gloves"—in a manuscript miscellany compiled around 1629 by Sir Francis Fane and now in the Shakespeare Birth Place Trust Records Office, Stratford. This manuscript also includes an inscription of "Epitaph on Himself" and a version of the first epitaph on Combe. Aspinall was married to Anne Shaw, the widow of Ralph Shaw; the Shaws were neighbors of the Shakespeares, and in 1616 their son July (or Julianus) was a witness of Shakespeare's will. It was conventional to write a poem and include it with the gift of a pair of gloves, and the poem is so slight that it does not secure authorship one way or another, even though critics have been attracted to the word "will" in line 2 as a personal signature.

The text for the "Verses on the Stanley Tomb at Tong" come directly from the inscription at St. Bartholomew Church, so there are no textual variants. The tomb, as well as its inscription, is undated. A manuscript dating to the 1630s is the first to assign authorship to Shakespeare, although Milton in his 1630 memorial poem to Shakespeare (first published in the 1632 Folio) shows evidence that he understood the poem to be by Shakespeare. The link between Shakespeare and the Stanley family—especially Ferdinando Stanley, Lord Strange, patron of Lord Strange's Men—has been reasonably well established. Of all the nine poems, this one feels the most like William Shakespeare. It includes several verbal echoes of such freestanding poems as the sonnets and *The Rape of Lucrece*.

"On Ben Jonson" comes from a manuscript in the Bodleian Library compiled by Nicholas Burghe, perhaps in the mid-seventeenth century.

"An Epitaph on Elias James" is first printed by John Stow in his 1633 *Survey of London*, where it was unattributed. Originally, however, it appeared in the church of St. Andrews by the Wardrobe, London, at the lower end of the south aisle, but the church was destroyed by the Great Fire in 1666. A manuscript version in the Bodleian Library attributes the epitaph to Shakespeare, the same manuscript that attributes to him "A Song, 'Shall I die?'" James worked close to the Blackfriars Theatre; the church where he is buried is opposite to the Blackfriars Gate-House, which Shakespeare owned. Scholars are uncertain whether Shakespeare wrote the epitaph.

The two epitaphs on John Combe are not created equal. Shakespeare almost certainly knew the Stratford moneylender, who died on July 10, 1614: in 1602, Combe and his uncle sold Old Stratford land to Shakespeare; and in his will of 1616 the author left Combe's brother Thomas his sword. The epitaph on the tomb in Holy Trinity Church has disappeared, but in 1673 Robert Dobyns transcribed it in a manuscript preserved at the Folger Library. Despite the connection with Combe, scholars do not think Shakespeare wrote "An Extemporary Epitaph on John Combe, a Noted Usurer." The case is stronger for "Another Epitaph on John Combe," which is attributed to Shakespeare in a manuscript in the Bodleian Library.

"Upon the King" has a complicated transmission history that is still being tracked, but the four-line verse appears beneath a picture of James I in the 1616 edition of his own *Works*, from which the text for the present edition comes. The poem was attributed to Shakespeare in two manuscripts, now in the Folger Library, dating to ca. 1633–34 and ca. 1650, respectively, perhaps simply because he was the leading writer for the King's Men. While the dating of the poem is widely disputed, it may have been written around 1611, making Shakespeare's authorship possible.

Shakespeare's "Epitaph on Himself" comes from the inscription on his grave in Holy Trinity Church, Stratford.

PATRICK CHENEY

Attributed Poems

1
A song, "Shall I die?"[1]

[1]

Shall I die? Shall I fly
Lovers' baits and deceits, sorrow breeding?
Shall I tend?° Shall I send?   *wait passively*
Shall I shew,° and not rue my proceeding?°   *appear / (as in a lawsuit)*
5   In all duty her beauty
Binds me her servant forever.
    If she scorn, I mourn,
I retire to despair, joining° never.   *(sexually; militarily)*

[2]

    Yet I must vent my lust
10 And explain inward pain by my love breeding.[2]
    If she smiles, she exiles
All my moan; if she frown, all my hope's deceiving.
    Suspicious doubt,° oh, keep out,   *fear (of rejection)*
For thou art my tormentor.
15   Fly away, pack away;
I will love, for hope bids me venture.

[3]

    'Twere abuse to accuse
My fair love, ere I prove° her affection.   *test*
    Therefore, try! Her reply
20 Gives thee joy or annoy or affliction.[3]
    Yet howe'er, I will bear
Her pleasure with patience, for beauty
    Sure will not seem to blot
Her deserts; wronging him doth her duty.[4]

[4]

25   In a dream it did seem
(But alas, dreams do pass as do shadows)
    I did walk, I did talk
With my love, with my dove, through fair meadows.
    Still° we passed till at last   *Continually*
30 We sat to repose us for pleasure.
    Being set, lips met,
Arms twined, and did bind my heart's treasure.

1
1. TEXTUAL COMMENT For differences between the two manuscript versions of this poem (lines 4, 8, 10, 15, 54), see Digital Edition TC 1.
2. Yet I must give expression to my lust by explaining (in poetry) the pain caused by my love.

3. "Affliction" may also suggest a sexually transmitted disease.
4. *for beauty . . . duty*: for true beauty will not allow her reputation to appear tarnished; wronging him serves her well.

[5]

Gentle wind sport did find
Wantonly° to make fly her gold tresses.   *Capriciously*
35 As they shook, I did look,
But her fair° did impair all my senses.   *beauty*
As amazed, I gazed
On more than a mortal complexion.
You that love can prove[5]
40 Such force in beauty's inflection.°   *bending*

[6]

Next° her hair, forehead fair,   *Next to*
Smooth and high; next doth lie, without wrinkle,
Her fair brows;° under those,   *forehead*
Star-like eyes win love's prize when they twinkle.
45 In her cheeks who° seeks   *whoever*
Shall find there displayed beauty's banner.°   *(a blush)*
Oh, admiring desiring
Breeds, as I look still upon her.

[7]

Thin lips red, fancy's[6] fed
50 With all sweets when he meets, and is granted
There to trade,[7] and is made
Happy, sure, to endure still undaunted.
Pretty chin doth win
Of all that's called commendations;[8]
55 Fairest neck, no speck.
All her parts merit high admirations.

[8]

Pretty bare, past compare,
Parts, those plots which besots still asunder.[9]
It is meet naught but sweet
60 Should come near that so rare 'tis a wonder.[1]
No mishap, no scape°   *transgression*
Inferior to nature's perfection.
No blot, no spot:
She's beauty's queen in election.

[9]

65 Whilst I dreamt, I exempt
From all care, seemed to share pleasure's plenty.
But awake, care take,
For I find to my mind pleasures scanty.
Therefore I will try
70 To compass° my heart's chief contenting.   *accomplish*
To delay, some say,
In such a case causeth repenting.

---

5. You who are in love are able to test.
6. Affection is; imagination is.
7. *granted / There to trade:* allowed to kiss there.
8. Wins praise from all people.
9. *Pretty . . . asunder:* Incomparably pretty "bare" skin and breasts (exposed above a low neckline), those nipples ("plots") that, always separated, (always) cause infatuation.
1. It is proper that nothing but good should come near that which is so wonderfully valuable.

2
Upon a Pair of Gloves That Master Sent to His Mistress

The gift is small,
The will is all:[1]
Alexander Aspinall[2]

3
Verses on the Stanley Tomb at Tong

[East end]
Ask who lies here, but do not weep.
He is not dead; he doth but sleep.
This stony register° is for his bones;   record
His fame is more perpetual than these stones,
5   And his own goodness, with himself being gone,
Shall live when earthly monument is none.

[West end]
Not monumental stone preserves our fame,
Nor sky-aspiring pyramids our name.
The memory of him for whom this stands
Shall outlive marble and defacers' hands.
5   When all to time's consumption shall be given,
Stanley for whom this stands shall stand in heaven.

4
On Ben Jonson[1]

Master Ben Jonson and Master William Shakespeare, being
merry at a tavern, Master Jonson having begun this for his
epitaph:
          Here lies Ben Jonson
5   That was once one,°   alive
he gives it to Master Shakespeare to make up who presently
writes:
          Who while he lived was a slow thing,[2]
          And now, being dead, is no thing.

5
An Epitaph on Elias James

When God was pleased, the world unwilling yet,[1]
Elias James to nature paid his debt,
And here reposeth. As he lived, he died,
The saying strongly in him verified:
5   "Such life, such death."° Then, a known truth to tell,   One dies as one lives
He lived a godly life, and died as well.

2
1. With a characteristic pun on the poet's name: the
goodwill behind the gift is all-encompassing; it's the
thought that counts.
2. Stratford schoolmaster from 1582 to 1624.
4

1. One of the best known of Shakespeare's fellow
playwrights (1572–1637).
2. Jonson was a notoriously slow writer.
5
1. Though the world was still unwilling.

6
An Extemporary Epitaph on John Combe, a Noted Usurer

Ten in the hundred[1] here lies engraved;
A hundred to ten° his soul is ne'er saved.
    If anyone ask who lies in this tomb,
    "O ho!" quoth the devil, "'tis my John-a-Combe."

(odds)

7
Another Epitaph on John Combe

Howe'er he livèd judge not,
John Combe shall never be forgot
While poor hath memory, for he did gather[1]
To make the poor his issue;° he, their father,
5   As record of his tilth and seeds[2]
Did crown° him in his latter deeds.

offspring; heirs

honor; praise

8
Upon the King

Crowns have their compass,° length of days their date,°
Triumphs their tombs, felicity her fate:
Of more than earth, can earth make none partaker,[1]
But knowledge makes the King most like his maker.

boundaries / limit

9
Epitaph on Himself

Good friend, for Jesus' sake forbear
To dig the dust enclosèd here.
Blessed be the man that spares these stones,
And cursed be he that moves my bones.

6
1. *Ten . . . hundred*: a slang term for "usurer," suggesting one who lends money at 10 percent interest.
7
1. Accumulate wealth (through usury).

2. Tillage and planting (offspring).
8
1. No earthly power (not even a king) has power over the afterlife.

Early Modern Map Culture

In the early modern period, maps were often considered rare and precious objects, and seeing a map could be an important and life-changing event. This was so for Richard Hakluyt, whose book *The Principal Navigations, Voyages, Traffics and Discoveries of the English Nation* (1598–1600) was the first major collection of narratives describing England's overseas trading ventures. Hakluyt tells how, as a boy still at school in London, he visited his uncle's law chambers and saw a book of cosmography lying open there. Perceiving his nephew's interest in the maps, the uncle turned to a modern map and "pointed with his wand to all the knowen Seas, Gulfs, Bayes, Straights, Capes, Rivers, Empires, Kingdomes, Dukedomes, and Territories of ech part, with declaration also of their speciall commodities and particular wants, which by the benefit of traffike, and entercourse of merchants, are plentifully supplied. From the Mappe he brought me to the Bible, and turning to the 107 Psalme, directed mee to the 23 and 24 verses, where I read, that they which go downe to the sea in ships, and occupy [work] by the great waters, they see the works of the Lord, and his woonders in the deepe." This event, Hakluyt records, made so deep an impression on him that he vowed he would devote his life to the study of this kind of knowledge. *The Principal Navigations* was the result, a book that mixes a concern with the profit to be made from trade and from geographical knowledge with praise for the Christian god who made the "great waters" and, in Hakluyt's view, looked with special favor on the English merchants and sailors who voyaged over them.

In the early modern period, access to maps was far less easy than it is today. Before the advent of printing in the late fifteenth century, maps were drawn and decorated by hand. Because they were rare and expensive, these medieval maps were for the most part owned by the wealthy and the powerful. Sometimes adorned with pictures of fabulous sea monsters and exotic creatures, maps often revealed the Christian worldview of those who composed them. Jerusalem appeared squarely in the middle of many maps (called T and O maps), with Asia, Africa, and Europe, representing the rest of the known world, arranged symmetrically around the Holy City. Because they had not yet been discovered by Europeans, North and South America were not depicted.

Mapping practices changed markedly during the late fifteenth and sixteenth centuries both because of the advent of print and also because European nations such as Portugal and Spain began sending ships on long sea voyages to open new trade routes to the East and, eventually, to the Americas. During this period, monarchs competed to have the best cartographers supply them with accurate maps of their realms and especially of lands in Africa, Asia, or the Americas, where they hoped to trade or plant settlements. Such knowledge was precious and jealously guarded. The value of such maps and the secrecy that surrounded them are indicated by a story in Hakluyt's *Principal Navigations*. An English ship had captured a Portuguese vessel in the Azores, and a map was discovered among the ship's valuable cargo, which included spices, silks, carpets, porcelain, and other exotic commercial objects. The map was "inclosed in a case of sweete Cedar wood, and lapped up almost an hundred fold in fine calicut-cloth, as though it had been some incomparable jewell." The value of the map and an explanation for the careful way in which it was packed lay in the particular information it afforded the English about Portuguese trading routes. More than beautiful objects, maps like this one were crucial to the international race to find safe sea routes to the most profitable trading centers in the East.

In the sixteenth century, books of maps began to be printed, making them more affordable for ordinary people, though some of these books, published as big folio volumes, remained too dear for any but wealthy patrons to buy. Yet maps were increasingly a part of daily life, and printing made many of them more accessible. Playgoers in Shakespeare's audiences must have understood in general the value and uses of maps, for they appear as props in a number of his plays. Most famously, at the beginning of *King Lear*, the old king has a map brought onstage showing the extent of his kingdom. He then points on the map to the three separate parts into which he intends to divide his realm to share among his daughters. The map, often unfurled with a flourish on a table or held up for view by members of Lear's retinue, signals the crucial relationship of the land to the monarch. He is his domains, and the map signifies his possession of them. To divide the kingdom, in essence to tear apart the map, would have been judged foolish and destructive by early modern political theorists. Similarly, in *1 Henry IV*, when rebels against the sitting monarch, Henry IV, plot to overthrow him, they bring a map onstage in order to decide what part of the kingdom will be given to each rebel leader. Their proposed dismemberment of the realm signifies the danger they pose. Treasonously, they would rend in pieces the body of the commonwealth.

Maps, of course, had other uses besides signifying royal domains. In some instances, they were used pragmatically to help people find their way from one place to another. A very common kind of map, a portolan chart, depicted in minute detail the coastline of a particular body of water. Used by sailors, these maps frequently were made by people native to the region they described. Many world or regional maps, because they were beautifully decorated and embellished with vivid colors, were used for decorative purposes. John Dee, a learned adviser to Queen Elizabeth and a great book collector, wrote that some people used maps "to beautifie their Halls, Parlers, Chambers, Galeries, Studies, or Libraries." He also spoke of more scholarly uses for these objects. They could, for example, be useful aids in the study of history or geography, enabling people to locate "thinges past, as battels fought, earthquakes, heavenly fyringes, and such occurents in histories mentioned." Today we make similar use of maps, like those included in this volume, when, in reading Shakespeare's plays, we resort to a map to find out where the Battle of Agincourt took place or where Othello sailed when he left Venice for Cyprus.

The print edition of *The Norton Shakespeare* includes five maps; the Digital Edition seven. Four of these maps, found in both editions, are modern ones drawn specifically to show the location of places important to Shakespeare's plays. They depict the British Isles and western France, London, and the Mediterranean world, in addition to a map of England showing the typical routes the Chamberlain's Men followed when they went on tour outside of London. The print and digital editions also both contain a period map of the Christian Holy Lands at the eastern tip of the Mediterranean Sea. This map was included in what was known as the Bishops' Bible, first printed in London in 1568. Put together under the leadership of the Archbishop of Canterbury, Matthew Parker, working with a committee of Anglican bishops, the 1568 edition featured beautiful typography and illustrations. The text continued to undergo revisions, and twenty editions of it were published between 1568 and 1602.

This last map shows places mentioned in the first four Gospels (Matthew, Mark, Luke, and John), which collectively tell of the life and deeds of Jesus. It indicates, for example, the location of Bethlehem, where he was born; Nazareth, where he spent his youth; and Cana of Galilee, where he turned water into wine at a marriage. It suggests that, to the English reader, this particular territory was overwritten by and completely intertwined with Christian history. Yet in the Mediterranean Sea, on the left of the map, several large ships are visible, reminders of another fact about this region: it was a vigorous trading arena where European Christian merchants did business with local merchants—Christian, Jew, and Muslim—and with traders bringing luxury goods by overland routes from the East. A number of Shakespeare's plays are set in this complex eastern Mediterranean region where several religious traditions laid claim to territory and many commercial powers competed for preeminence. *Pericles*, for example, has a hero who is the ruler of Tyre, a city on the upper right side of the map. In the course of his wanderings, Pericles visits many cities along the eastern coasts of the Mediterranean. The conclusion of the play, in which the hero is reunited both with his long-lost daughter and with the wife he believes dead, has seemed to many critics to share in a sense of Christian miracle, despite its ostensibly pagan setting. *The Comedy of Errors* and parts of *Othello* and of *Antony and Cleopatra* are also set in the Eastern Mediterranean. One of Shakespeare's earliest plays, *The Comedy of Errors*, is an urban comedy in which the protagonists are merchants deeply involved in commercial transactions. It is also the first play in which Shakespeare mentions the Americas, which he does in an extended joke in which he compares parts of a serving woman's body to the countries on a map including Ireland, France, and the Americas. In *Othello*, the eastern Mediterranean island of Cyprus is represented as a tense Christian outpost defending Venetian interests against the Muslim Turks. In *Antony and Cleopatra*, Egypt figures as the site of Eastern luxury and also of imperial conquest, an extension of the Roman Empire. Clearly, this region was to Shakespeare and his audiences one of the most complex and highly charged areas of the world: a site of religious, commercial, and imperial significance.

Two other maps occur only in the Digital Edition, where their colors and their details can be appreciated. The first is a map of London that appeared in a 1574 edition of a famous German atlas, *Civitates Orbis Terrarum* (*Cities of the World*), compiled by George Braun with engravings by Franz Hogenberg. This remarkable atlas includes maps and information on cities throughout Europe, Asia, and North Africa; the first of its six volumes appeared in 1572, the last in 1617. Being included in the volume indicated a city's status as a recognized metropolitan center. In a charming touch, Braun added to his city maps pictures of figures in local dress. At the bottom of the map of London, for example, there are four figures who appear to represent the city's prosperous citizens. In the center, a man in a long robe holds the hand of a soberly dressed matron. On either side of them are younger and more ornately dressed figures. The young man sports a long sword and a short cloak, the woman a dress with elaborate skirts. In the atlas, the map is colored, and the clothes of the two young people echo one another in shades of green and red.

At the time the map was made, London was a rapidly expanding metropolis. In 1550, it contained about 55,000 people; by 1600, it would contain nearly 200,000. The map shows the densely populated old walled city north of the Thames River, in the middle of which was Eastcheap, the commercial district where, in Shakespeare's plays about the reign of Henry IV, Falstaff holds court in a tavern. The map also shows that by 1570 London was spreading westward beyond the wall toward Westminster Palace. This medieval structure, which appears on the extreme left side of the map, was where English monarchs resided when in London and where, at the end of *2 Henry IV*, the king dies in the fabled Jerusalem Chamber of the Westminster complex. On the far right of the map, one can see the Tower of London, where Edward IV's young sons were imprisoned by Richard III, an event depicted in Shakespeare's *The Tragedy of King Richard the Third*. The map also indicates the centrality of the Thames to London's commercial life. It shows the river full of boats; some of those on the east side of London Bridge are large oceangoing vessels with several masts. South of the river, where many of the most famous London theaters, including Shakespeare's Globe, were to be constructed in the 1590s, there are relatively few buildings. By 1600, this would change, as Southwark, as it was known, came to be an increasingly busy entertainment, residential, and commercial district.

The final map, of Great Britain and Ireland, comes from a 1612 edition of John Speed's *The Theatre of the Empire of Great Britain*, an innovative atlas containing individual maps of counties and towns in England and Wales, as well as larger maps that include Scotland and Ireland. Speed was by trade a tailor who increasingly devoted his time to the study of history and cartography. Befriended by the antiquarian scholar William Camden, he eventually won patronage from Sir Fulke Greville, who gave him a pension that allowed him to devote himself full-time to his scholarly endeavors. *The Theatre* was one product of this newfound freedom. The map included here, one of his most ambitious, shows the entire British Isles, nominated by Speed as "The Kingdome of Great Britaine and Ireland," though at this time Ireland was far from under the control of the English crown and Scotland was still an independent kingdom. James I, a Scot by birth, had unsuccessfully tried to forge a formal union between England and Scotland. This problem of the relationship of the parts of the British Isles to one another, and England's assertion of power over the others, is treated in *Henry V*, in which officers from Wales, Ireland, and Scotland are sharply delineated yet all depicted as loyal subjects of the English king.

One striking aspect of Speed's map is the balance it strikes between the two capital cities, London on the left, prominently featuring the Thames and London Bridge, and Edinburgh on the right. This would have pleased James, whose interest in his native country Shakespeare played to in his writing of *Macbeth*, which is based on material from Scottish history. Speed's map acknowledges the claims of the monarch to the territory it depicts. In the upper left corner, the British lion and the Scottish unicorn support a roundel topped with a crown. When James became king of England in 1603, he created this merged symbol of Scottish-English unity. The motto of the Royal Order of the Garter, *"Honi soit qui mal y pense"* (Shamed be he who thinks ill of it), is inscribed around the circumference. In the bottom left corner of the map, another locus of authority is established. Two cherubs, one holding a compass, the other a globe, sit beneath a banner on which is inscribed "Performed by John Speed." If the territory is the monarch's, the craft that depicts it belongs to the tailor turned cartographer.

Today, maps are readily available from shops or on the Internet, but in early modern England they were rare and valuable objects that could generate great excitement in those who owned or beheld them. Along with other precious items, maps were sometimes put on display in libraries and sitting rooms, but they had functions beyond the ornamental. They helped to explain and order the world, indicating who claimed certain domains, showing where the familiar stories of the Bible or of English history occurred, helping merchants find their way to distant markets. As John Dee, the early modern map enthusiast concluded, "Some, for one purpose: and some, for an other, liketh, loveth, getteth, and useth, Mappes, Chartes, and Geographicall Globes."

JEAN E. HOWARD

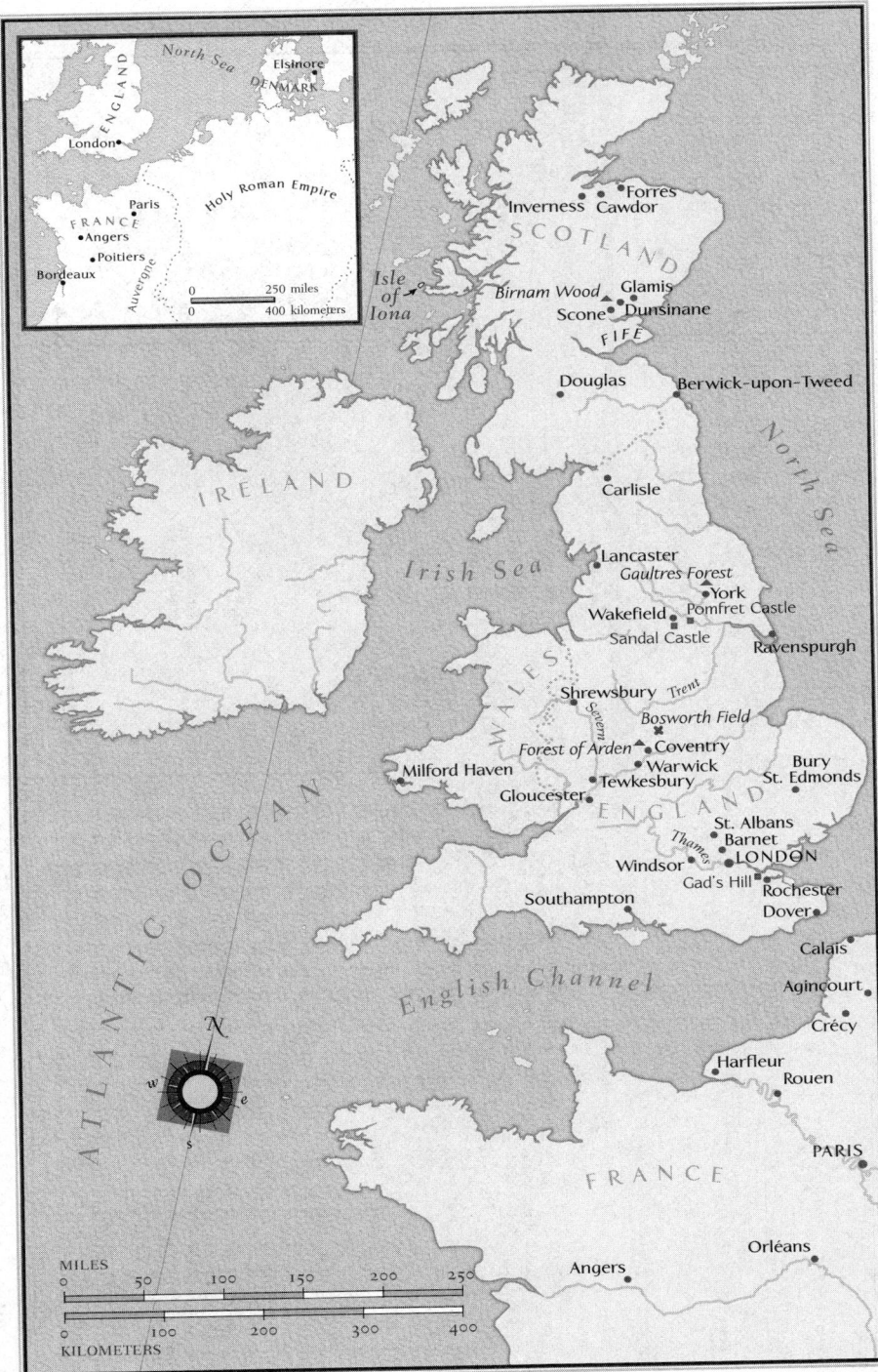

Ireland, Scotland, Wales, England, and Western France: Places Important to Shakespeare's Plays

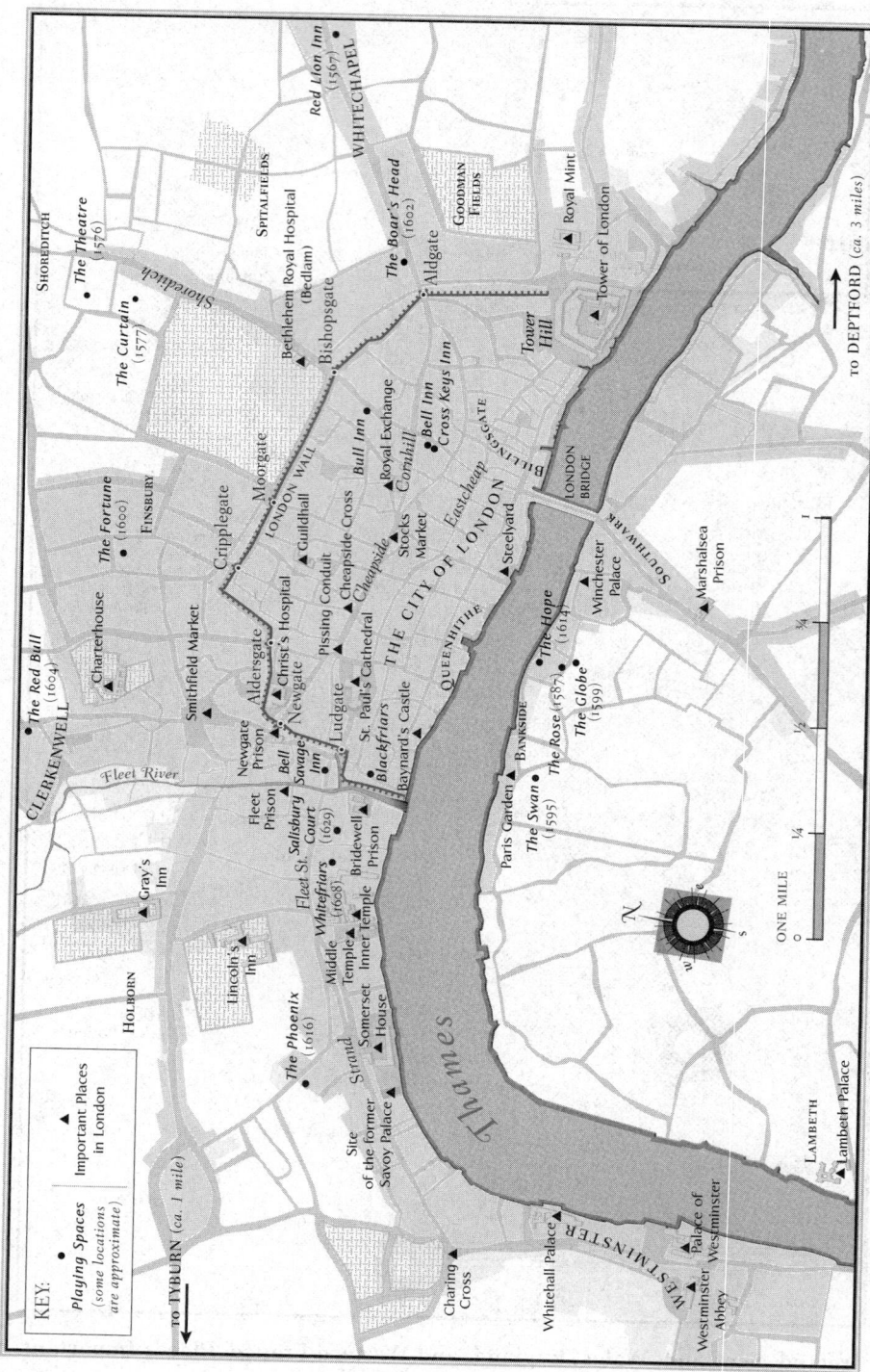

London: Places Important to Shakespeare's Plays and London Playgoing

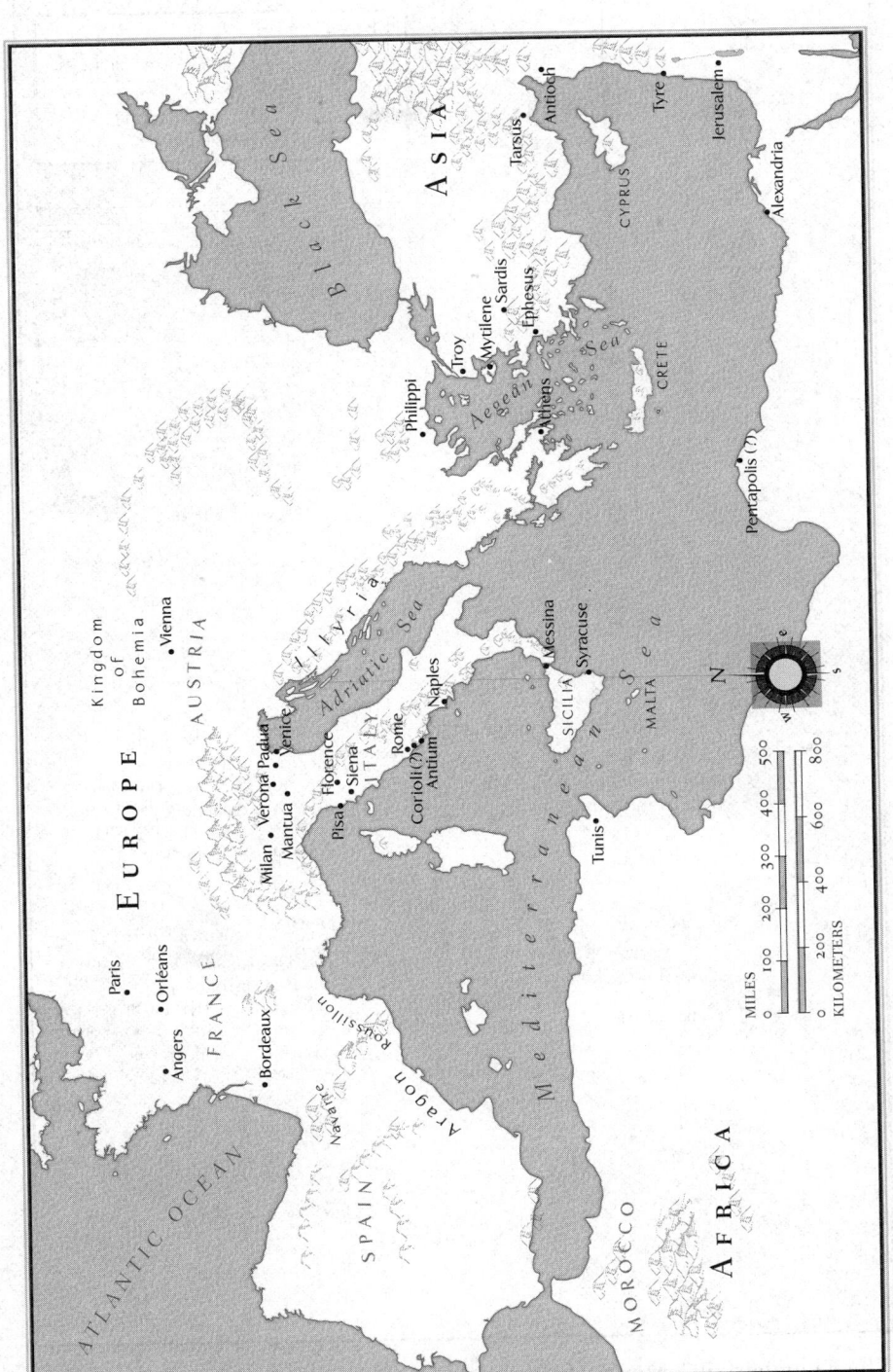

The Mediterranean World: Places Important to Shakespeare's Plays

The Chamberlain's Men and King's Men on Tour (adapted from a map first published by Sally-Beth MacLean in "Tour Routes: 'Provincial Wanderings' or 'Traditional Circuits'?" *Medieval and Renaissance Drama in England* 6 [1992]: 1–14).

Map of the Holy Land, from the Bishops' Bible, printed in London, 1568

Documents

This selection of documents illustrates three pivotal moments: Shakespeare's first recorded appearance on the London literary scene, an appreciation by one of his most enthusiastic early critics, and the canonization of his dramatic works in the First Folio, the single most important Shakespearean document that survives today. A much more extensive selection of documents can be found in the Digital Edition of *The Norton Shakespeare*, providing a broad range of contemporary testimony about Shakespeare's character, his art, and the social and institutional conditions under which it was produced. The first digital section, "Shakespeare and His Works," includes records of Shakespeare's life and career, evidence of his reputation in the literary community, and a variety of reactions to his plays and poems. The second section, "The Theater Scene," takes a wider view of Shakespeare's professional world with playhouse documents that offer a behind-the-scenes glimpse of companies acquiring scripts and properties, actors rehearsing their parts, and new theaters being constructed, while government documents show dramatic patronage, regulation, and censorship in action.

MISHA TERAMURA

Robert Greene on Shakespeare (1592)

[Robert Greene (1558–1592), a prolific author of plays, romances, and pamphlets, attacked Shakespeare in his *Greenes, Groats-worth of witte, bought with a million of Repentance*. Greene had studied at Cambridge, and his "M.A." was prominently displayed on his title pages. Shakespeare's lack of a university education is clearly one motive for the professional resentment expressed in the following excerpt. Another is probably that Greene was poor and very ill and felt forsaken while writing the *Groats-worth of witte*; the preface refers to it as his "swan-like song," and the narrative is framed as the repentance of a dying man. (Some scholars have held that the posthumously published work contains fabrications by a publisher attempting to capitalize on Greene's name.) The three colleagues Greene addresses are likely to be Christopher Marlowe, Thomas Nashe, and George Peele. The text is modernized from the first edition of *Greenes, Groats-worth of witte* (London, 1592).]

> *To those gentlemen, his quondam acquaintance,*
> *that spend their wits in making plays, R.G.*
> *wisheth a better exercise, and wisdom*
> *to prevent his extremities.*[1] . . .

Base-minded men, all three of you, if by my misery you be not warned, for unto none of you (like me) sought those burs to cleave—those puppets[2] (I mean) that spake from our mouths, those antics garnished in our colors. Is it not strange that I, to whom they all have been beholding—is it not like that you, to whom they all have been beholding, shall (were ye in that case as I am now) be both at once of

---

1. Adversity.
2. Actors.

them forsaken? Yes, trust them not: for there is an upstart crow, beautified with our feathers, that with his *tiger's heart wrapped in a player's hide*[3] supposes he is as well able to bombast out a blank verse as the best of you, and, being an absolute *Johannes factotum*,[4] is in his own conceit the only Shake-scene in a country. Oh, that I might entreat your rare wits to be employed in more profitable courses, and let those apes imitate your past excellence and nevermore acquaint them with your admired inventions! I know the best husband of you all will never prove an usurer,[5] and the kindest of them all will never prove a kind nurse. Yet, whilst you may, seek you better masters, for it is pity men of such rare wits should be subject to the pleasure of such rude grooms.

Francis Meres on Shakespeare (1598)

[Francis Meres (1565–1647) was educated at Cambridge and was active in London literary circles in 1597–98, after which he became a rector and schoolmaster in the country. The descriptions of Shakespeare are taken from a section on poetry in *Palladis Tamia. Wits Treasury*, a work largely consisting of translated classical quotations and *exempla*. Unlike the main body of the work, the subsections on poetry, painting, and music include comparisons of English artists to figures of antiquity. Meres goes on after the extract below to list Shakespeare among the best English writers of lyric, tragedy, comedy, and love poetry. The text is modernized from the first edition of *Palladis Tamia* (London, 1598).]

As the Greek tongue is made famous and eloquent by Homer, Hesiod, Euripides, Aeschylus, Sophocles, Pindarus, Phocylides, and Aristophanes, and the Latin tongue by Virgil, Ovid, Horace, Silius Italicus, Lucanus, Lucretius, Ausonius, and Claudianus, so the English tongue is mightily enriched and gorgeously invested in rare ornaments and resplendent habiliments[1] by Sir Philip Sidney, Spenser, Daniel, Drayton, Warner, Shakespeare, Marlowe, and Chapman. . . .

As the soul of Euphorbus was thought to live in Pythagoras, so the sweet witty soul of Ovid lives in mellifluous and honey-tongued Shakespeare. Witness his *Venus and Adonis*, his *Lucrece*, his sugared sonnets among his private friends, etc.

As Plautus and Seneca are accounted the best for comedy and tragedy among the Latins, so Shakespeare among the English is the most excellent in both kinds for the stage. For comedy, witness his *Gentlemen of Verona*, his *Errors*, his *Love Labor's Lost*, his *Love Labor's Won*,[2] his *Midsummer's Night Dream*, and his *Merchant of Venice*; for tragedy, his *Richard the 2*, *Richard the 3*, *Henry the 4*, *King John*, *Titus Andronicus*, and his *Romeo and Juliet*.

As Epius Stolo said that the Muses would speak with Plautus' tongue if they would speak Latin, so I say that the Muses would speak with Shakespeare's fine-filed phrase if they would speak English.

---

3. A parody of *Richard Duke of York* (3 *Henry VI*) 1.4.138: "O tiger's heart wrapped in a woman's hide!" This obvious allusion and the following pun on Shakespeare's name make it certain that Shakespeare is the "crow" described here.
4. Jack-of-all-trades. *conceit*: imagination.
5. Even the thriftiest among you will never commit usury.
1. Sumptuous clothing.
2. Either the play has not survived, or it is now known by a different name. However, this title is recorded elsewhere, in a bookseller's jottings of 1603, where it again appears following *Love's Labor's Lost*.

Front Matter from the First Folio
of Shakespeare's Plays (1623)

After Shakespeare's death in 1616, his friends and colleagues John Heminges and Henry Condell organized this first publication of his collected (thirty-six) plays. Eighteen of the plays had not appeared in print before, and for these the First Folio is the sole surviving source. Only *Pericles, The Two Noble Kinsmen, Sir Thomas More,* and *Edward III* are not included in the volume. Reproduced below in reduced facsimile are the title page (which includes Droeshout's famous portrait of Shakespeare), Heminges and Condell's prefatory address "To the great Variety of Readers," the book's table of contents, and the first page of text from *The Tempest.* Following the facsimile images is a commendatory poem by Shakespeare's great contemporary Ben Jonson (1572–1637), which was also published in the First Folio's front matter.

Mr. WILLIAM

SHAKESPEARES

COMEDIES,
HISTORIES, &
TRAGEDIES.

Published according to the True Originall Copies.

Martin Droeshout sculpsit London.

LONDON
Printed by Isaac Iaggard, and Ed. Blount. 1623.

To the great Variety of Readers.

Rom the moſt able,to him that can but ſpell: There you are number'd.We had rather you were weighd. Eſpecially, when the fate of all Bookes depends vpon your capacities : and not of your heads alone, but of your purſes. Well ! It is now publique, & you wil ſtand for your priuiledges wee know : to read, and cenſure. Do ſo,but buy it firſt. That doth beſt commend a Booke, the Stationer ſaies. Then,how odde ſoeuer your braines be, or your wiſedomes, make your licence the ſame,and ſpare not. Iudge your ſixe-pen'orth, your ſhillings worth, your fiue ſhillings worth at a time, or higher, ſo you riſe to the iuſt rates, and welcome. But, what euer you do, Buy. Cenſure will not driue a Trade, or make the lacke go. And though you be a Magiſtrate of wit, and ſit on the Stage at *Black-Friers*, or the *Cock-pit*, to arraigne Playes dailie, know, theſe Playes haue had their triall alreadie, and ſtood out all Appeales ; and do now come forth quitted rather by a Decree of Court, then any purchas'd Letters of commendation.

It had bene a thing, we confeſſe, worthie to haue bene wiſhed,that the Author himſelfe had liu'd to haue ſet forth, and ouerſeen his owne writings ; But ſince it hath bin ordain'd otherwiſe,and he by death departed from that right,we pray you do not envie his Friends,the office of their care, and paine, to haue collected & publiſh'd them; and ſo to haue publiſh'd them, as where (before) you were abuſ'd with diuerſe ſtolne, and ſurreptitious copies, maimed,and deformed by the frauds and ſtealthes of iniurious impoſtors, that expoſ'd them : euen thoſe, are now offer'd to your view cur'd, and perfect of their limbes; and all the reſt, abſolute in their numbers, as he conceiued thē.Who,as he was a happie imitator of Nature,was a moſt gentle expreſſer of it.His mind and hand went together: And what he thought, he vttered with that eaſineſſe, that wee haue ſcarſe receiued from him a blot in his papers. But it is not our prouince,who onely gather his works, and giue them you, to praiſe him. It is yours that reade him. And there we hope,to your diuers capacities, you will finde enough, both to draw, and hold you : for his wit can no more lie hid, then it could be loſt. Reade him, therefore ; and againe, and againe : And if then you doe not like him, ſurely you are in ſome manifeſt danger, not to vnderſtand him. And ſo we leaue you to other of his Friends, whom if you need,can bee your guides : if you neede them not, you can leade your ſelues,and others. And ſuch Readers we wiſh him.

A 3
Iohn Heminge.
Henrie Condell.

Line 8. *Stationer:* bookseller.

Line 13. *lacke:* machine.

Lines 13–14. *And though . . . dailie:* addressed in particular to men of fashion who occupied seats onstage so they could be seen while watching the play.

Lines 15–17. *these Playes . . . commendation:* The legal puns that began with "Magistrate of wit" (fashionable playgoer) in line 13 continue here. The "purchas'd Letters of commendation" refer to escaping the conse-

quences of a crime by means of bribery or other undue influence; Shakespeare's plays, by contrast, have been acquitted after a proper and rigorous trial (approved by theater audiences and not insinuated into the public favor by some outside influence).

Line 27. *absolute in their numbers:* correct in their versification. *thē:* them.

Line 28. *a happie:* an apt; a successful.

A CATALOGVE

of the feuerall Comedies, Histories, and Tragedies contained in this Volume.

Troilus and Cressida, despite its absence from the "Catalogue," was in fact printed in the First Folio. Due to negotiations over printing rights, it was included only at the last minute and placed between the histories and tragedies.

THE
TEMPEST.

Actus primus, Scena prima.

A tempestuous noise of Thunder and Lightning heard: Enter a Ship-master, and a Botesmaine.

Master.

BOte-swaine.

Botes. Heere Master: What cheere?

Mast. Good: Speake to th'Mariners: fall too't, yarely, or we run our selues a ground, bestirre, bestirre.   *Exit.*

Enter Mariners.

Botes. Heigh my hearts, cheerely, cheerely my harts: yare, yare: Take in the toppe-sale: Tend to th'Masters whistle: Blow till thou burst thy winde, if roome enough.

Enter Alonso, Sebastian, Anthonio, Ferdinando, Gonzalo, and others.

Alon. Good Boteswaine haue care: where's the Master? Play the men.

Botes. I pray now keepe below.

Anth. Where is the Master, Boson?

Botes. Do you not heare him? you marre our labour, Keepe your Cabines: you do assist the storme.

Gonz. Nay, good be patient.

Botes. When the Sea is: hence, what cares these roarers for the name of King? to Cabine; silence: trouble vs not.

Gon. Good, yet remember whom thou hast aboord.

Botes. None that I more loue then my selfe. You are a Counsellor, if you can command these Elements to silence, and worke the peace of the present, wee will not hand a rope more, vse your authoritie: If you cannot, giue thankes you haue liu'd so long, and make your selfe readie in your Cabine for the mischance of the houre, if it so hap. Cheerely good hearts: out of our way I say.   *Exit.*

Gon. I haue great comfort from this fellow:methinks he hath no drowning marke vpon him, his complexion is perfect Gallowes: stand fast good Fate to his hanging, make the rope of his destiny our cable, for our owne doth little aduantage: If he be not borne to bee hang'd, our case is miserable.   *Exit.*

Enter Boteswaine.

Botes. Downe with the top-Mast: yare, lower, lower, bring her to Try with Maine-course. A plague——

A cry within. *Enter Sebastian, Anthonio & Gonzalo.*

vpon this howling: they are lowder then the weather, or our office: yet againe? What do you heere? Shal we giue ore and drowne, haue you a minde to sinke?

Sebas. A poxe o'your throat, you bawling, blasphemous incharitable Dog.

Botes. Worke you then.

Anth. Hang cur, hang, you whoreson insolent Noysemaker, we are lesse afraid to be drownde, then thou art.

Gonz. I'le warrant him for drowning, though the Ship were no stronger then a Nutt-shell, and as leaky as an vnstanched wench.

Botes. Lay her a hold, a hold, set her two courses off to Sea againe, lay her off.

Enter Mariners wet.

Mari. All lost, to prayers, to prayers, all lost.

Botes. What must our mouths be cold?

Gonz. The King, and Prince, at prayers, let's assist them, for our case is as theirs.

Sebas. I'am out of patience.

An. We are meerly cheated of our liues by drunkards, This wide-chopt-rascall, would thou mightst lye drowning the washing of ten Tides.

Gonz. Hee'l be hang'd yet,
Though euery drop of water sweare against it,
And gape at widst to glut him.   *A confused noyse within.*
Mercy on vs.
We split, we split, Farewell my wife, and children,
Farewell brother: we split, we split, we split.

Anth. Let's all sinke with' King

Seb. Let's take leaue of him.   *Exit.*

Gonz. Now would I giue a thousand furlongs of Sea, for an Acre of barren ground: Long heath, Browne firrs, any thing; the wills aboue be done, but I would faine dye a dry death.   *Exit.*

Scena Secunda.

Enter Prospero and Miranda.

Mira. If by your Art (my deerest father) you haue
Put the wild waters in this Rore; alay them:
The skye it seemes would powre down stinking pitch,
But that the Sea, mounting to th' welkins cheeke,
Dashes the fire out. Oh! I haue suffered
With those that I saw suffer: A braue vessell

A   (Who

To the memory of my beloved,
The AUTHOR
MR. WILLIAM SHAKESPEARE:
AND
what he hath left us.*

To draw no envy, Shakespeare, on thy name,
  Am I thus ample to° thy book and fame,   *copious in praising*
While I confess thy writings to be such
  As neither man nor muse can praise too much:
5 'Tis true, and all men's suffrage.° But these ways   *agreement*
  Were not the paths I meant° unto thy praise,   *(to take)*
For seeliest[1] ignorance on these may light,
  Which, when it sounds, at best, but° echoes right;   *merely*
Or blind affection, which doth ne'er advance
10   The truth, but gropes, and urgeth all by chance;
Or crafty malice might pretend this praise,
  And think° to ruin, where it seemed to raise.   *intend*
These are as° some infamous bawd or whore   *as though*
  Should praise a matron: what could hurt her more?
15 But thou art proof against° them, and indeed   *impervious to*
  Above th' ill fortune of them, or the need.
I therefore will begin. Soul of the age!
  The applause, delight, the wonder of our stage!
My Shakespeare, rise! I will not lodge thee by
20   Chaucer or Spenser, or bid Beaumont lie
A little further to make thee a room;[2]
  Thou art a monument without a tomb
And art alive still while thy book doth live,
  And we have wits to read and praise to give.
25 That I not mix thee so, my brain excuses,
  I mean with great but disproportioned° muses.   *not comparable*
For if I thought my judgment were of years°   *mature*
  I should commit° thee surely with thy peers,   *compare*
And tell how far thou didst our Lyly outshine,
30   Or sporting Kyd, or Marlowe's mighty line.[3]
And though thou hadst small Latin and less Greek,[4]
  From thence to honor thee I would not seek°   *lack*

* By Ben Jonson.
1. Silliest; blindest (falcons' eyelids were "seeled," or stitched shut, while they were being tamed).
2. Geoffrey Chaucer, Edmund Spenser, and Francis Beaumont were all buried near each other in Westminster Abbey (known today as the "Poets' Corner"), while Shakespeare was buried in Stratford-upon-Avon. An earlier elegy for Shakespeare had begun: "Renownèd Spenser, lie a thought more nigh / To learned Chaucer, and, rare Beaumont, lie / A little nearer Spenser to make room / For Shakespeare . . ."
3. John Lyly, Thomas Kyd, and Christopher Marlowe were all celebrated Elizabethan playwrights. *sporting:* gamesome; frolicking (like a young goat, or "kid").
4. The underrating of Shakespeare's Latin was likely influenced by Jonson's pride in his own impressive classical learning.

For names, but call forth thund'ring Aeschylus,
   Euripides, and Sophocles to us,
35 Pacuvius, Accius, him of Cordova dead,[5]
   To life again, to hear thy buskin tread
And shake a stage; or, when thy socks were on,[6]
   Leave thee alone for the comparison
Of all that insolent Greece or haughty Rome
40   Sent forth, or since did from their ashes come.
Triumph, my Britain; thou hast one to show
   To whom all scenes° of Europe homage owe.   *stages*
He was not of an age, but for all time!
   And all the Muses still were in their prime
45 When like Apollo° he came forth to warm   *god of poetry*
   Our ears, or like a Mercury° to charm!   *god of eloquence*
Nature herself was proud of his designs,
   And joyed to wear the dressing of his lines,
Which were so richly spun and woven so fit
50   As, since, she will vouchsafe° no other wit.   *grant*
The merry Greek, tart Aristophanes,
   Neat Terence, witty Plautus[7] now not please,
But antiquated and deserted lie,
   As they were not of Nature's family.
55 Yet must I not give Nature all; thy art,
   My gentle Shakespeare, must enjoy a part.
For though the poet's matter° nature be,   *raw material*
   His art doth give the fashion.° And that he°   *form / that he=he*
Who casts° to write a living line must sweat   *intends*
60   (Such as thine are) and strike the second heat
Upon the Muses' anvil, turn the same,
   And himself with it, that he thinks to frame,
Or for the laurel he may gain a scorn;[8]
   For a good poet's made as well as born,
65 And such wert thou. Look how the father's face
   Lives in his issue;° even so, the race   *offspring*
Of Shakespeare's mind and manners brightly shines
   In his well-turnèd and true-filèd° lines,   *truly polished*
In each of which he seems to shake a lance,[9]
70   As brandished at the eyes of ignorance.
Sweet swan of Avon, what a sight it were
   To see thee in our waters yet appear,
And make those flights upon the banks of Thames
   That so did take° Eliza and our James![1]   *transport*
75 But stay; I see thee in the hemisphere
   Advanced and made a constellation there.[2]

5. While the Latin tragedians Marcus Pacuvius and Lucius Accius were known to Jonson only by reputation, Seneca the Younger ("him of Cordova") was a major influence on Renaissance revenge tragedies.
6. The boots ("buskins") and shoes ("socks") worn by classical actors were symbolic of tragedy and comedy, respectively.
7. Aristophanes was a Greek writer of satirical comedies; Terence and Plautus were Roman comic dramatists.
8. Or else, instead of the laurel (the symbol of poetic accomplishment), he may gain derision.
9. Punning on Shakespeare's name.
1. Queen Elizabeth and King James.
2. It was a commonplace in classical literature that those who lived glorious lives became constellations after death.

Shine forth, thou star of poets, and with rage
  Or influence,³ chide or cheer the drooping° stage,   *dejected*
Which, since thy flight from hence, hath mourned like night,
80 And despairs day, but for thy volume's light.

BEN: JONSON.

---

3. Stars and planets were thought to affect human affairs. "Rage" suggests poetic inspiration.

Timeline

Dates for plays by Shakespeare and others are conjectural dates of composition, based on current understanding of the evidence. Works of poetry and prose are listed by date of publication.

TEXT	CONTEXT
	1558 Queen Mary I, a Roman Catholic, dies; her sister, Elizabeth, raised Protestant, is proclaimed queen.
	1559 Church of England is reestablished under the authority of the sovereign with the passage of the Act of Uniformity and the Act of Supremacy.
1562 *The Tragedy of Gorboduc*, by Thomas Norton and Thomas Sackville; the first English play in blank verse.	**1563** The Church of England adopts the Thirty-nine Articles of Religion, detailing its points of doctrine and clarifying its differences both from Roman Catholicism and from more radical forms of Protestantism.
	1564 William Shakespeare is born in Stratford to John and Mary Arden Shakespeare; he is christened a few days later, on April 26.
	1565 John Shakespeare is made an alderman of Stratford.
	1567 Mary Queen of Scots is imprisoned on suspicion of the murder of her husband, Lord Darnley. Their infant son, Charles James, is crowned James VI of Scotland. John Brayne builds the first English professional theater in the garden of a farmhouse called the Red Lion on the outskirts of London.
	1568 John Shakespeare is elected Bailiff of Stratford, the town's highest office. Performances in Stratford by the Queen's Players and the Earl of Worcester's men.
	1572 An act is passed that severely punishes vagrants and wanderers, including actors not affiliated with a patron. Performances in Stratford by the Earl of Leicester's men.

TEXT	CONTEXT
	1574 The Earl of Warwick's and Earl of Worcester's men perform in Stratford.
	1576 James Burbage, father of Richard, later the leading actor in Shakespeare's company, builds The Theatre in Shoreditch, a suburb of London.
1577 First edition of Holinshed's *Chronicles*.	**1577** The Curtain Theater opens in Shoreditch.
	1577–80 Sir Francis Drake circumnavigates the globe.
	1578 Mary Shakespeare pawns her lands, suggesting that the family is in financial distress. Lord Strange's Men and Lord Essex's Men perform at Stratford.
1579 Sir Thomas North's English translation of Plutarch's *Lives*.	**1580** A Jesuit mission is established in England with the aim of reconverting the nation to Roman Catholicism. Francis Drake returns from circumnavigation of globe.
	1582 Shakespeare marries Anne Hathaway.
	1583 The birth of Shakespeare's older daughter, Susanna.
	1584 Sir Walter Ralegh establishes the first English colony in the New World at Roanoke Island in modern North Carolina; the colony fails.
	1585 The birth of Shakespeare's twin son and daughter, Hamnet and Judith. John Shakespeare is fined for not going to church.
	1586 Sir Philip Sidney dies from battle wounds.
1587 Thomas Kyd, *The Spanish Tragedy;* Christopher Marlowe, *Tamburlaine*.	**1587** Mary Queen of Scots is executed for treason against Elizabeth I. Francis Drake, leading a daring raid at Cádiz, destroys many Spanish naval vessels and materiel. John Shakespeare loses his position as an alderman. Philip Henslowe builds the Rose theater at Bank-side, on the Thames.
	1588 The Spanish Armada attempts an invasion of England but is defeated.

TEXT	CONTEXT
1589 Robert Greene, *Friar Bacon and Friar Bungay*. Thomas Kyd(?), *Hamlet* (not extant; perhaps a source for Shakespeare's *Hamlet*). Christopher Marlowe, *The Jew of Malta*. Anonymous, *The True Chronicle History of King Leir, and His Three Daughters*.	**1589** Shakespeare is possibly affiliated with Strange's men, Pembroke's men, or both between this time and 1594.
1590 Edmund Spenser, *The Faerie Queene* (1st edition, Books 1–3). Sir Philip Sidney, *Arcadia*.	**1590** James VI of Scotland marries Anne of Denmark. James believes that witches raised a magical storm in an attempt to sink the ship carrying him home with his bride. Witch trials in Scotland.
1591–92 *Two Gentlemen of Verona*. *2 and 3 Henry VI*. *The Taming of the Shrew*. *1 Henry VI*.	**1592** The theatrical entrepreneur and financial manager of the Admiral's Men, Philip Henslowe, begins a diary—an important source for theater historians—recording his business transactions; continued until 1604.
1592–93 *Titus Andronicus*. *Richard III*. *Edward III*. *Venus and Adonis*.	From June 1592 to June 1594, London theaters are frequently shut down because of the plague; acting companies tour the provinces.
1594 *The Rape of Lucrece*. *The Comedy of Errors*.	**1594** Roderigo Lopez, a Christian physician of Portuguese Jewish descent, is executed on slight evidence for having plotted to poison Elizabeth I. The birth of James VI's first son, Henry.
1594–96 *Love's Labor's Lost*. *Richard II*. *Romeo and Juliet*. *A Midsummer Night's Dream*. *King John*.	**1595** Shakespeare lives in St. Helen's Parish, Bishopsgate, London. Shakespeare apparently becomes a sharer in (provides capital for) the newly formed Lord Chamberlain's Men. The Swan Theater is built in Bankside. Hugh O'Neill, Earl of Tyrone, rebels against English rule in Ireland. Walter Ralegh explores Guiana, on the north coast of South America.
1596 Edmund Spenser, *The Faerie Queene* (2nd edition, with Books 4–6). **1596–97** *1 Henry IV*. *The Merchant of Venice*.	**1596** John Shakespeare is granted a coat of arms; hence the title of "gentleman." William Shakespeare's son Hamnet dies. James Burbage buys a medieval hall in the former Blackfriars monastery and transforms it into an indoor theater.
	1597 The landlord refuses to renew the lease on the land under The Theatre in Shoreditch.

TEXT	CONTEXT
1598 *2 Henry IV.* *Much Ado About Nothing.* George Chapman begins to publish his translation of Homer. Ben Jonson, *Every Man in His Humor,* which lists Shakespeare as one of the actors.	**1598** Unable to renew the lease, the Chamberlain's Men move from The Theatre to the nearby Curtain Theater. The Edict of Nantes ends the French civil wars, granting toleration to Protestants. Materials from the demolished Theatre in Shoreditch are transported across the Thames to be used in building the Globe Theater, which opens in the following year.
1599 *The Merry Wives of Windsor.* *Henry V.* *As You Like It.* *Julius Caesar.* *The Passionate Pilgrim,* attributed entirely to Shakespeare. Michael Drayton and several collaborators, who object to Shakespeare's depiction of Oldcastle-Falstaff in the *Henry IV* plays, write *The First Part of the True and Honorable History of the Life of Sir John Oldcastle, the Good Lord Cobham.*	**1599** The Queen's favorite, Robert Devereux, Earl of Essex, leads an expedition to Ireland in March, but returning home without royal permission in September, is rebuked by the Queen and imprisoned. Satires and other offensive books are prohibited by ecclesiastical order. Extant copies are gathered and burned. Two notorious satirists, Thomas Nashe and Gabriel Harvey, are forbidden to publish.
1600–1601 *Hamlet.* *Twelfth Night.*	**1600** The Earl of Essex is suspended from some of his offices and confined to house arrest. The birth of James VI's second son, Charles. The founding of the East India Company. Edward Alleyn and Philip Henslowe build the Fortune Theater for the Lord Admiral's Men.
1601 "The Phoenix and Turtle" published in Robert Chester's *Love's Martyr.* In the "War of the Theaters," Ben Jonson, John Marston, and Thomas Dekker write a series of satiric plays mocking one another.	**1601** The Earl of Essex leads a rebellion against the principal adviser to Elizabeth I and possibly against the Queen herself. The previous afternoon, hoping to enlist support, some of the rebels pay for a performance of *Richard II.* Implicated in the uprising, which is quickly quelled, Shakespeare's patron, the Earl of Southampton, is imprisoned. The Earl of Essex is convicted of treason and beheaded, along with several of his chief supporters. Shakespeare's father dies.
1601–02 *Troilus and Cressida.*	**1602** Shakespeare makes substantial real-estate purchases in Stratford. The opening of the Bodleian Library in Oxford.

TEXT	CONTEXT
1601–03 *Othello.*	
1603 John Florio's translation of Montaigne's *Essays.* Ben Jonson, *Sejanus,* which lists Shakespeare as one of the actors.	**1603** Queen Elizabeth dies; she is succeeded by her cousin, James VI of Scotland (now James I of England).
1603–04 *Sir Thomas More* (revised version).	
	Plague closes the London theaters from mid-1603 to April 1604. Hugh O'Neill surrenders in Ireland.
1604 *Measure for Measure.*	**1604** The conclusion of a peace with Spain makes travel across the Atlantic safer, encouraging plans for English colonies in the Americas.
1605 *The History of King Lear.*	**1605** The discovery of the Gunpowder Plot by some radical Catholics to blow up the Houses of Parliament during its opening ceremonies, when the royal family, Lords, and Commons are assembled in one place. The Red Bull Theater built.
1606–07 *Timon of Athens. All's Well That Ends Well. Macbeth. Antony and Cleopatra.* Middleton(?), *The Revenger's Tragedy.*	**1606** The London and Plymouth Companies receive charters to colonize Virginia. Parliament passes "An Act to Restrain Abuses of Players," prohibiting oaths or blasphemy onstage.
1607–08 *Pericles.*	**1607** An English colony is established in Jamestown, Virginia. Shakespeare's daughter Susanna marries John Hall. Shakespeare's brother Edmund (described as a player) dies.
1608 *Coriolanus.*	
1609 *Shakespeare's Sonnets.*	
1610 *Cymbeline.* Ben Jonson, *The Alchemist.*	**1610** Henry is made Prince of Wales. Shakespeare probably returns to Stratford and settles there. The King's Men begin using Blackfriars Theater as a second, indoor venue.

TEXT	CONTEXT
1611 *The Winter's Tale.* *The Tempest.* Francis Beaumont and John Fletcher, *A King and No King.* Publication of the Authorized (King James) Bible.	**1611** Plantation of Ulster in Ireland, a colony of English and Scottish Protestants settled on land confiscated from Irish rebels.
1612–13 *Cardenio*, with John Fletcher (not extant). *Henry VIII*, with John Fletcher. John Webster, *The White Devil.*	**1612** Prince Henry dies.
1613–14 *The Two Noble Kinsmen,* with John Fletcher.	**1613** Princess Elizabeth marries Frederick V, Elector Palatine. The Globe Theater burns down during a performance of *Henry VIII.*
1614 Ben Jonson, *Bartholomew Fair.* John Webster, *The Duchess of Malfi.*	**1614** Philip Henslowe and Jacob Meade build the Hope Theater, used both for play performances and as a bearbaiting arena. The Globe Theater reopens.
1616 Ben Jonson publishes his *Works*, including the first collection of plays by a commercial English dramatist.	**1616** William Harvey describes the circulation of the blood. Shakespeare's daughter Judith marries. Shakespeare dies on April 23.
1623 Members of the King's Men publish the First Folio of Shakespeare's plays.	

Glossary

STAGE TERMS

"above"   The gallery on the upper level of the stage's back wall (see *frons scenae*). In open-air theaters, such as the Globe, this space may have included the lords' rooms. The central section of the gallery was sometimes used by the players for short scenes. Indoor theaters such as Blackfriars featured a curtained alcove for musicians above the stage.

"aloft"   See *"above."*

amphitheater   An open-air theater, such as the Globe.

arras   See *curtain.*

cellarage   See *trap.*

chorus   In the works of Shakespeare and other Elizabethan playwrights, a single individual (not, as in Greek tragedy, a group) who speaks before the play (and sometimes before each act or, in *Pericles*, at other times), describing events not shown on stage as well as commenting on the action witnessed by the audience.

curtain   Curtains, or arras (hanging tapestries), probably covered a part of the stage's back wall (see *frons scenae*), thus concealing the discovery space, and may also have been draped around the edge of the stage to conceal the open area underneath.

discovery space   A central opening or alcove concealed behind a curtain in the center of the stage's back wall (see *frons scenae*). The curtain could be drawn aside to "discover" tableaux such as Portia's caskets, the body of Polonius, or the statue of Hermione. Shakespeare appears to have used this stage device only sparingly.

doubling   The common practice of having one actor play multiple roles, so that a play with a large cast of characters might be performed by a relatively small company.

dumb shows   Mimed scenes performed before a play or as part of the play itself, summarizing or foreshadowing the plot. Dumb shows were popular in early Elizabethan drama; although they already seemed old-fashioned in Shakespeare's time, they were employed by writers up to the 1640s.

epilogue   A brief speech or poem addressed to the audience by an actor after the play. In some cases, as in *2 Henry IV*, the epilogue could be combined with, or could merge into, the jig.

frons scenae   The wall at the back of the stage, behind which lay the players' tiring house. The *frons scenae* of the Globe featured two doors flanking the central discovery space, with a gallery "above."

gallery   Covered seating area surrounding the open yard of the public amphitheater. There were three levels of galleries at the Globe; admission to these seats cost an extra penny (in addition to the basic admission fee of one penny to the yard), and seating in the higher galleries another penny yet.

gatherers Persons employed by the playing company to take money at the entrances to the theater.

groundlings Audience members who paid the minimum price of admission (one penny) to stand in the yard of the open-air theaters; also referred to as "understanders." "Groundling" is an unusual word, possibly coined by Shakespeare; it is unclear whether it was in common usage at the time.

heavens The canopied roof over the stage in the open-air theaters, protecting the players and their costumes from rain. The "heavens" may have been brightly decorated with sun, moon, and stars, and perhaps the signs of the zodiac.

jig A song-and-dance performance by the clown and other members of the company at the conclusion of a play. These performances were frequently bawdy and were officially banned in 1612.

lords' rooms Partitioned sections of the gallery above the stage, or just to the left and right of the stage, where the most prestigious and expensive seats in the public playhouses were located. These rooms did not provide the best view of the action on the stage below. They were designed to make their privileged occupants conspicuous to the rest of the audience.

open-air theaters Unroofed public playhouses in the suburbs of London, such as The Theatre, the Rose, and the Globe.

part The character played by an actor. In Shakespeare's theater, actors were given a roll of paper called a "part" containing all of the speeches and all of the cues belonging to their character. The term "role," synonymous with "part," is derived from such rolls of paper.

patrons Important nobles and members of the royal family under whose protection the theatrical companies of London operated; players not in the service of patrons were punishable as vagabonds. The companies were referred to as their patrons' "Men" or "Servants." Thus the company to which Shakespeare belonged for most of his career was first known as the Lord Chamberlain's Servants, then became the King's Men in 1603, when James I became their patron.

pillars The "heavens" were supported by two tall painted pillars or posts near the front of the stage. These occasionally played a role in stage action, allowing a character to "hide" while remaining in full view of the audience.

pit The area in front of the stage in indoor theaters such as Blackfriars; unlike an open-air playhouse's yard, the pit was designed for a seated audience.

posts See *pillars.*

proscenium The arch that divides the stage, scenery, and backstage area from the auditorium in many theaters built in and after the eighteenth century. It also separates actors and audiences, potentially creating the so-called fourth wall. The stages on which Shakespeare's plays were first performed had no proscenium.

repertory The stock of plays a company had ready for performance at a given time. Companies generally performed a different play each day, often more than a dozen plays in a month and more than thirty in the course of the season.

role See *part.*

sharers Senior actors holding shares in a joint-stock theatrical company; they paid for costumes, hired hands, and new plays, and they shared profits and losses equally. Shakespeare was not only a longtime "sharer" of the Lord Chamberlain's Men but, from 1599, a "housekeeper," the holder of a one-eighth share in the Globe playhouse.

tiring house The players' dressing (attiring) room, a structure located at the back of the stage and connected to the stage by two or more doors in the *frons scenae*.

trap A trapdoor near the front of the stage that allowed access to the cellarage beneath and was frequently associated with hell's mouth. Another trapdoor in the heavens opened for the descent of gods to the stage below.

"within" The tiring house, from which offstage sound effects such as shouts, drums, and trumpets were produced.

yard The central space in open-air theaters such as the Globe, into which the stage projected and in which audience members stood. Admission to the yard in the public theaters cost a penny, the cheapest admission available.

TEXTUAL TERMS

aside See *stage direction.*

autograph Text written in the author's own hand. With the possible exception of a few pages of the collaborative play *Sir Thomas More,* no dramatic works or poems written in Shakespeare's hand are known to survive.

"bad quartos" A polemical term for a group of Shakespeare quartos that are different from and often demonstrably inferior to other versions of the plays in question as they are found in later quartos or in the First Folio. Some of these texts are very short; others include notable distortions of language. Explanations for the "bad quartos" (or, more neutrally, "short quartos") include the possibility that they were Shakespeare's early drafts, abbreviated scripts prepared for performance under circumstances such as touring, or "memorial reconstructions."

base text The early text upon which a modern edition is based, also known as a "control text."

canonical Of an author, the writings generally accepted as authentic. In the case of Shakespeare's dramatic works, only two plays that are not among the thirty-six plays contained in the First Folio, *Pericles* and *The Two Noble Kinsmen,* have won widespread acceptance into the Shakespearean canon, but recent scholarship suggests that he wrote parts of a number of others, including *Edward III* and *Sir Thomas More.*

casting off The practice of dividing up a manuscript to anticipate the number of pages needed to contain it in print. Errors in casting off sometimes led compositors to crowd lines, abbreviate spellings, and print verse as prose. If on the contrary a compositor found he had too much space remaining, he might leave spaces around stage directions, add ornaments, or break prose up into short "verse" lines.

catchword A word printed below the text at the bottom of a page, matching the first word on the following page. The catchword enabled the printer to keep the pages in their proper sequence. Where the catchword fails to match the word at the top of the next page, there is reason to suspect that something has been lost or misplaced.

collaboration The practice of two or more writers working together to create a play (or other literature). More than half of the plays in Shakespeare's period were collaborative. Shakespeare collaborated with John Fletcher on *Henry VIII*, *The Two Noble Kinsmen*, and the missing *Cardenio*; with George Wilkins on *Pericles*; and with Thomas Middleton on *Timon of Athens*. Shakespeare plays that probably have sections composed by others include *Titus Andronicus*, *1 Henry VI*, and *Macbeth*; in turn, Shakespeare seems to have contributed a section to *Sir Thomas More*.

compositor A person employed in a print shop to set type. To speed the printing process, most of Shakespeare's plays were set by more than one compositor. Compositors were expected to adjust spelling and provide punctuation and can often be identified by their different habits and preferences (e.g., *been/beene* or *O/Oh* and speech prefixes such as *Que./Queene*). They invariably introduced errors into the texts—for instance, by selecting the wrong letter from the type case or by setting the correct letter upside down.

conflation A version of a play created by combining readings from more than one substantive text. Since the early eighteenth century, for example, most versions of *King Lear* and of several other plays by Shakespeare have been conflations of quarto and First Folio texts.

deus ex machina Literally, "god from a machine," the term can refer to any plot device introduced to resolve a seemingly insurmountable problem.

dramatis personae (or The Persons of the Play) A list of the characters that appear in the play. In the First Folio such lists, called "The Names of the Actors," were printed at the end of some but not all of the plays. In 1709 the editor Nicholas Rowe first provided lists of dramatis personae for all of Shakespeare's dramatic works.

emendation A correction made in a text by an editor where he or she believes on the basis of evidence and/or inference that it has been corrupted in transmission and needs to be altered for coherence or sense.

exeunt / exit See *stage direction*.

fair copy A transcript of the "foul papers" made either by a scribe or by the playwright.

folio A bookmaking format in which each large sheet of paper is folded once, making two leaves (a leaf is part of a folded sheet of paper with a page on each side). This format produced large volumes, generally handsome and expensive. The First Folio of Shakespeare's plays was printed in 1623.

forme A body of type secured in a chase, or wooden frame, ready for printing. The forme would be placed into the press and inked and a sheet of paper lowered onto it for imprinting.

foul papers A term for a playwright's working draft of a play, which is presumed to have contained "false starts," blotted-out passages, ghost characters, and revisions. To judge by apparent errors in the printed texts, several of Shakespeare's plays appear to have been printed from foul papers rather than fair copy; however, no clearcut instance of his foul papers survives, though certain pages in the manuscript of *Sir Thomas More* may represent this stage of the writing process.

ghost characters Characters named in a stage direction who have no lines during the ensuing action. They may represent a "false start" as the author composed the play, and may not have actually appeared onstage in performance.

licensing By an order of 1581, new plays could not be performed until they had received a license from the Master of the Revels. A separate license, granted by the Court of High Commission, was required for publication, though in practice plays were often printed without license. From 1610, the Master of the Revels had the authority to license plays for publication as well as for performance.

manent / manet See *stage direction.*

massed entry The grouping of all characters who will appear at any point in a scene into a single opening direction. Playwrights such as Ben Jonson preferred this style because of its conformity with classical practice, and it was followed by certain scribes. Modern editors write entry directions to show the point in the scene at which each character enters.

memorial reconstruction The theory that some texts may have been reconstructed from memory by one or more actors, either because a promptbook had been destroyed or because it was not available—for example, while touring. It has been proposed that memorial reconstruction might explain the existence of "bad" or inferior quartos of some of Shakespeare's plays, though this is no longer universally accepted.

octavo A bookmaking format in which each large sheet of paper is folded three times, making eight leaves (sixteen pages front and back). Only one of Shakespeare's plays, *3 Henry VI* (1595), was published in octavo format.

playbook See *promptbook.*

press variants Minor textual variations among pages in books of the same edition, resulting from corrections made in the course of printing or from damaged or slipped type.

promptbook A manuscript of a play (either foul papers or fair copy) annotated and adapted for performance by the theatrical company. The promptbook incorporated stage directions, notes on properties and special effects, and revisions, sometimes including those required by the Master of the Revels. Promptbooks may be identifiable by the replacement of characters' names with actors' names.

quarto A bookmaking format in which each large sheet of paper is folded twice, making four leaves (eight pages front and back). Quarto volumes were smaller and less expensive than books printed in the folio format.

recto Literally, the right-hand page; in a quarto volume, each signature consisted of four leaves each of which had a recto and a verso; the pages were then numbered 1r[ecto], 1v[erso], 2r, 2v, 3r, 3v, 4r, 4v.

scribal copy A transcript of a play produced by a professional scribe (or "scrivener"). Scribes tended to employ their own preferred spellings, abbreviations, and punctuation and could be responsible for introducing a variety of errors.

signature A section of an early book consisting of one group of folded pages (e.g., in a quarto, four leaves or eight pages). Early modern printers indicated each signature by a letter (e.g., A) to assist them in keeping track of the parts of the book to bind together.

single-text editing Editing a work by staying as close as possible to a single early authoritative base text, emending only where necessary for sense and without either conflating by incorporating words or passages from other cognate texts or by reconstructing passages from source materials or other forms of inference.

speech prefix (SP) The indication of the identity of the speaker of the following line or lines. Early editions of Shakespeare's plays often use different prefixes at different points to designate the same person. On occasion, the name of the actor who was to play the role appears in place of the name of the character.

stage direction (SD) The part of the text that is not spoken by any character but that indicates actions to be performed onstage. Stage directions in the earliest editions of Shakespeare's plays are sparse; some necessary directions, most notably exits, are missing, and others may appear earlier or later than the plot requires. Directions for action (e.g., "Pray you, undo this button") may be implied in the dialogue but are not necessarily followed in a given production. By convention, the most basic stage directions were written in Latin. "Exit" indicates the departure of a single actor from the stage, "exeunt" the departure of more than one. "Manet" indicates that a single actor remains onstage, "manent" that more than one remains. Lines accompanied by the stage direction "aside" are spoken so as not to be heard by the others onstage. This stage direction appeared in some early editions of Shakespeare plays, but other means were also used to indicate such speech (such as placing the words within parentheses), and sometimes no indication was provided.

Stationers' Register The account books of the Company of Stationers (the guild of printers, publishers, and booksellers that controlled the London book trade), recording the fees paid by publishers to secure their rights to certain texts, as well as the transfer of these rights between publishers. The Stationers' Register thus provides a valuable if incomplete record of publication in England.

substantive text The text of an edition based upon access to a manuscript, as opposed to a derivative text based only on an earlier edition.

typecase The compartmentalized box in which movable type (metal letters, punctuation, etc.) was stored; capital, or "upper-case," letters were traditionally stored at the top of the typecase, "lower-case" letters at the bottom. Compositors drew individual type from the typecase for placing into a "compositor's stick" that held one line of type; from there the type would be transferred to a chase and secured to create a forme. Mistakes in sorting used type back into the typecase may account for some textual errors.

variorum editions Comprehensive editions of a work or works in which the various views of previous editors and commentators are compiled.

verso See *recto*

Essential Reference Books

Bate, Jonathan, and Russell Jackson, eds. *Shakespeare: An Illustrated Stage History.* New York: Oxford UP, 1996.

Bullough, Geoffrey, ed. *Narrative and Dramatic Sources of Shakespeare.* 8 vols. New York: Columbia UP, 1957–75.

Chambers, E. K. *The Elizabethan Stage.* 4 vols. Oxford: Clarendon, 1923.

———. *William Shakespeare: A Study of Facts and Problems.* 2 vols. Oxford: Clarendon, 1930.

Crystal, David. *Pronouncing Shakespeare: The Globe Experiment.* Cambridge: Cambridge UP, 2005.

Dent, R. W. *Shakespeare's Proverbial Language: An Index.* Berkeley: U of California P, 1981.

Dessen, Alan C., and Leslie Thomson. *A Dictionary of Stage Directions in English Drama, 1580–1642.* New York: Cambridge UP, 1999.

Dobson, E. J. *English Pronunciation, 1500–1700.* 2nd ed. 2 vols. Oxford: Clarendon, 1968.

Dobson, Michael, and Stanley Wells, eds. *The Oxford Companion to Shakespeare.* Oxford: Oxford UP, 2001.

Duffin, Ross W. *Shakespeare's Songbook.* New York: Norton, 2004.

Foakes, R. A. *Illustrations of the English Stage, 1580–1642.* Stanford: Stanford UP, 1985.

Greenblatt, Stephen, and Peter G. Platt, eds. *Shakespeare's Montaigne: The Florio Translation of the Essays, a Selection.* New York: New York Review Books, 2014.

Greg, W. W., ed. *Dramatic Documents from the Elizabethan Playhouses: Stage Plots: Actors' Parts: Prompt Books.* 2 vols. Oxford: Clarendon, 1931.

Gurr, Andrew. *Playgoing in Shakespeare's London.* 3rd ed. New York: Cambridge UP, 2004.

———. *The Shakespearean Stage, 1574–1642.* 4th ed. New York: Cambridge UP, 2009.

Henslowe, Philip. *Henslowe's Diary.* Ed. R. A. Foakes. 2nd ed. New York: Cambridge UP, 2002.

Hosley, Richard, ed. *Shakespeare's Holinshed: An Edition of Holinshed's Chronicles, 1587.* New York: Putnam, 1968.

Murphy, Andrew. *Shakespeare in Print: A History and Chronology of Shakespeare Publishing.* New York: Cambridge UP, 2003.

Oxford Dictionary of National Biography. Oxford: Oxford UP, 2004. www.oxforddnb.com/

Oxford English Dictionary. Oxford: Clarendon, 1989. www.oed.com/

Partridge, A. C. *Orthography in Shakespeare and Elizabethan Drama.* London: E. Arnold, 1964.

Partridge, Eric. *Shakespeare's Bawdy: A Literary and Psychological Essay and a Comprehensive Glossary.* 3rd ed. New York: Routledge, 2001.

Schoenbaum, Samuel. *William Shakespeare: A Documentary Life.* New York: Oxford UP, 1975.

Spevack, Marvin. *A Complete and Systematic Concordance to the Works of Shakespeare.* 9 vols. Hildesheim: George Olms, 1968–80.

Stern, Tiffany. *Documents of Performance in Early Modern England.* Cambridge: Cambridge UP, 2009

Tilley, Morris Palmer. *A Dictionary of the Proverbs in England in the Sixteenth and Seventeenth Centuries*. Ann Arbor: U of Michigan P, 1950.

Wells, Stanley. *A Dictionary of Shakespeare*. 2nd ed. New York: Oxford UP, 2005.

———. *Re-Editing Shakespeare for the Modern Reader*. New York: Oxford UP, 1984.

Wickham, Glynne. *Early English Stages, 1300 to 1660*. 4 vols. New York: Routledge, 2002.

Williams, Gordon. *A Dictionary of Sexual Language and Imagery in Shakespearean and Stuart Literature*. 3 vols. London: Athlone, 1994.

For a much fuller bibliography, including critical and historical works bearing on the study of Shakespeare, see the Digital Edition of *The Norton Shakespeare*.

ILLUSTRATION ACKNOWLEDGMENTS

Index of Poems:
Titles and First Lines

THE HOUSE OF LANCASTER

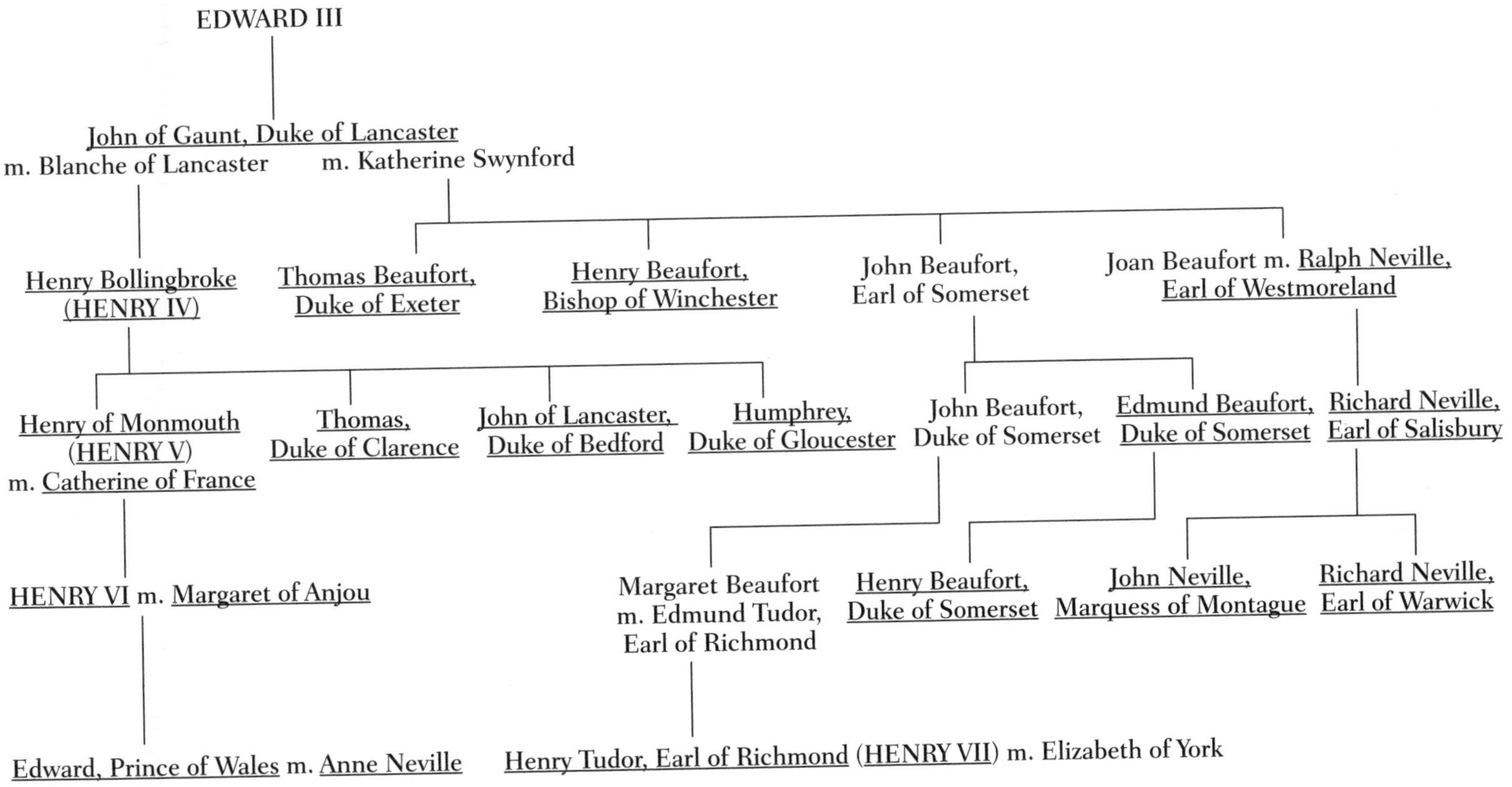

EDWARD III

John of Gaunt, Duke of Lancaster   m. Katherine Swynford
m. Blanche of Lancaster

Henry Bollingbroke (HENRY IV)

Thomas Beaufort, Duke of Exeter

Henry Beaufort, Bishop of Winchester

John Beaufort, Earl of Somerset

Joan Beaufort m. Ralph Neville, Earl of Westmoreland

Henry of Monmouth (HENRY V)
m. Catherine of France

Thomas, Duke of Clarence

John of Lancaster, Duke of Bedford

Humphrey, Duke of Gloucester

John Beaufort, Duke of Somerset

Edmund Beaufort, Duke of Somerset

Richard Neville, Earl of Salisbury

HENRY VI m. Margaret of Anjou

Margaret Beaufort m. Edmund Tudor, Earl of Richmond

Henry Beaufort, Duke of Somerset

John Neville, Marquess of Montague

Richard Neville, Earl of Warwick

Edward, Prince of Wales m. Anne Neville

Henry Tudor, Earl of Richmond (HENRY VII) m. Elizabeth of York

The House of York

EDWARD III

Edmund of Langley, Duke of York

Edward, Duke of Aumerle

Richard, Duke of Gloucester
(RICHARD III) m. <u>Anne Neville</u>

Lionel, Duke of Clarence

Anne Mortimer m. <u>Richard, Earl of Cambridge</u>

<u>Richard Plantagenet, Duke of York</u> m. <u>Cicely Neville</u>

<u>George, Duke of Clarence</u>
m. Isabella Neville

Philippa m. Edmund Mortimer

<u>Edmund Mortimer, Earl of March</u>

<u>Edmund, Earl of Rutland</u>

Elizabeth m. <u>HENRY VII</u>

<u>Edward, Earl of March (EDWARD IV)</u>
m. <u>Elizabeth Woodville</u>

<u>Richard, Duke of York</u>

<u>Edward, Prince of Wales
(EDWARD V)</u>